OXFORD COMMENTARIES ON INTERNATIONAL LAW

General Editors: *Professor Philip Alston*, Professor of International Law
at New York University, and *Professor Vaughan Lowe QC*, Essex Court Chambers,
London and Emeritus Fellow of All Souls College, Oxford.

The European Convention
on Human Rights

The European Convention on Human Rights

A Commentary

by

WILLIAM A. SCHABAS OC MRIA

UNIVERSITY PRESS

OXFORD
UNIVERSITY PRESS

Great Clarendon Street, Oxford, OX2 6DP,
United Kingdom

Oxford University Press is a department of the University of Oxford.
It furthers the University's objective of excellence in research, scholarship,
and education by publishing worldwide. Oxford is a registered trade mark of
Oxford University Press in the UK and in certain other countries

Published in the United States of America by Oxford University Press
198 Madison Avenue, New York, NY 10016, United States of America

British Library Cataloguing in Publication Data
Data available

Library of Congress Control Number: 2015937610

ISBN 978-0-19-959406-1

Printed and bound by
CPI Group (UK) Ltd, Croydon, CR0 4YY

To Peter and Charles

Preface

My first visit to Strasbourg was in 1993 when I accompanied a team of law students from the Université du Québec à Montréal to participate in a French-language moot court held before a simulated European Court of Human Rights. The following year, the student team from my university actually won the competition. I was able to share with them a two-week *stage* at the European Commission on Human Rights later that year, sworn to silence because of the secrecy of the proceedings.

There was great concern then about the future of the Convention institutions. Indeed, it seemed then as if the European Court was confronting a profound crisis. The case load was increasingly burdensome, several new countries had recently joined the system as the Council of Europe expanded eastward, and there appeared to be a degree of tension between the two Convention organs that we were able to see in action, the Commission and the Court. This sense of uncertainty did not diminish in the years that followed. Modifications were made to the system in an effort to adjust. But the amendments had barely entered into force before talk began about a new phase of changes. Yet the Court's survival, and its success, cannot be doubted. In modern human rights, it is one of the great stories of success. Moreover, it has contributed hugely to the creation and maintenance of a zone of peace within a continent that, over the decades and indeed centuries that preceded its establishment, had seen the most destructive wars in human history.

The seeds of the European Convention on Human Rights were sown by the Universal Declaration of Human Rights, adopted by the United Nations General Assembly on 10 December 1948. Several of the personalities involved in that process went on to play an important role in the drafting of the Convention. Of course, only some of the rights in the Universal Declaration were transposed to the Convention. Those that were incorporated, be it in the Convention itself or the Protocols adopted subsequently, were then applied and interpreted by the European Commission and the European Court as well as, but to a lesser extent, by national courts where the Convention was applicable. In this way, albeit indirectly, the case law under the European Convention on Human Rights also constitutes judicial interpretation of the provisions of the Universal Declaration of Human Rights. Thereby, an important contribution is made to the elaboration of the general law of human rights, valid throughout the world, even in the absence of treaty obligations and a monitoring system. That is an enormous contribution. Not only has the Convention helped mould and protect European public order, it is responsible for important components of the global *ius commune* that ensures human rights and dignity for all.

Without any doubt, there is more academic literature on the European Convention on Human Rights than on any other treaty or system of modern human rights law. At the institutional level, the European Court of Human Rights, as well as the European Commission of Human Rights, before it closed its doors in 1998, have generated more case law than any other comparable bodies. It would take many volumes and thousands of pages to attempt to cover this material in anything resembling an exhaustive fashion. Of course, that is not the purpose of an article-by-article commentary. Rather, such an endeavour aims to provide a relatively succinct guideline to the treaty as a whole, with

links and cross-references as well as indications for further reading in both the jurisprudence and the secondary literature. The case law is up to date as of 31 December 2014.

The idea for this project belongs to John Louth of Oxford University Press. The
research and writing took somewhat longer than was expected, partly because the
enormity of the venture was underestimated and partly because there were distractions
along the way. I am grateful to John for asking me to undertake this challenge, and for his
constant support and encouragement. The institutional support of the School of Law at
Middlesex University is greatly appreciated. Special thanks are due to Catherine Funnell,
the law librarian, for her invaluable assistance. I am also grateful to Zhao Xin, a student of
mine at Sciences Po, who assisted me with some research. The most important support,
however, was from Penelope, who insisted upon the book's importance. She encouraged
me at every step of the way, not to mention her precious help in the final stages of
proofreading.

William Schabas
London and Paris
January 2015

Contents

Table of Cases   xiv
Table of Legislation   xcvii
List of Abbreviations   cxxii

PART ONE: INTRODUCTION

Adoption of the Convention   3
Adding new rights to the Convention   11
Amending the Convention and reforming its machinery   26
Interpretation of the Convention   33

PART TWO: CONVENTION FOR THE PROTECTION OF HUMAN
           RIGHTS AND FUNDAMENTAL FREEDOMS

Preamble   53
Article 1. Obligation to respect human rights   84

SECTION I. RIGHTS AND FREEDOMS

Article 2. Right to life   117
Article 3. Prohibition of torture   164
Article 4. Prohibition of slavery and forced labour   201
Article 5. Right to liberty and security   219
Article 6. Right to a fair trial   264
Article 7. No punishment without law   328
Article 8. Right to respect for private and family life   358
Article 9. Freedom of thought, conscience and religion   412
Article 10. Freedom of expression   444
Article 11. Freedom of assembly and association   483
Article 12. Right to marry   528
Article 13. Right to an effective remedy   546
Article 14. Prohibition of discrimination   555
Article 15. Derogation in time of emergency   587
Article 16. Restrictions on political activity of aliens   606
Article 17. Prohibition of abuse of rights   611
Article 18. Limitation on use of restrictions on rights   623

SECTION II. EUROPEAN COURT OF HUMAN RIGHTS

Article 19. Establishment of the Court   631
Article 20. Number of judges   643
Article 21. Criteria for office   647
Article 22. Election of judges   658
Article 23. Terms of office and dismissal   668
Article 24. Registry and rapporteurs   675
Article 25. Plenary Court   678
Article 26. Single-judge formation, Committees, Chambers, and
             Grand Chamber   686
Article 27. Competence of single judges   696
Article 28. Competence of Committees   699
Article 29. Decisions by Chambers on admissibility and merits   705
Article 30. Relinquishment of jurisdiction to the Grand Chamber   709
Article 31. Powers of the Grand Chamber   713
Article 32. Jurisdiction of the Court   715
Article 33. Inter-State cases   723
Article 34. Individual applications   731
Article 35. Admissibility criteria   753
Article 36. Third-party intervention   788
Article 37. Striking out applications   796
Article 38. Examination of the case   803
Article 39. Friendly settlements   816
Article 40. Public hearings and access to documents   825
Article 41. Just satisfaction   830
Article 42. Judgments of Chambers   841
Article 43. Referral to the Grand Chamber   843
Article 44. Final judgments   849
Article 45. Reasons for judgments and decisions   857
Article 46. Binding force and execution of judgments   861
Article 47. Advisory opinions   874
Article 48. Advisory jurisdiction of the Court   884
Article 49. Reasons for advisory opinions   887
Article 50. Expenditure on the Court   889
Article 51. Privileges and immunities of judges   891

SECTION III. MISCELLANEOUS PROVISIONS

Article 52. Inquiries by the Secretary General   897
Article 53. Safeguard for existing human rights   902
Article 54. Powers of the Committee of Ministers   905
Article 55. Exclusion of other means of dispute settlement   907
Article 56. Territorial application   916

Article 57. Reservations 930
Article 58. Denunciation 941
Article 59. Signature and ratification 944

PART THREE: PROTOCOL NO. 1 TO THE CONVENTION
FOR THE PROTECTION OF HUMAN RIGHTS
AND FUNDAMENTAL FREEDOMS

Preamble 955
Article 1. Protection of property 958
Article 2. Right to education 986
Article 3. Right to free elections 1011
Article 4. Territorial application 1033
Article 5. Relationship to the Convention 1037
Article 6. Signature and ratification 1039

PART FOUR: PROTOCOL NO. 4 TO THE CONVENTION FOR
THE PROTECTION OF HUMAN RIGHTS AND
FUNDAMENTAL FREEDOMS, SECURING CERTAIN
RIGHTS AND FREEDOMS OTHER THAN THOSE
ALREADY INCLUDED IN THE CONVENTION
AND IN THE FIRST PROTOCOL THERETO

Preamble 1045
Article 1. Prohibition of imprisonment for debt 1048
Article 2. Freedom of movement 1052
Article 3. Prohibition of expulsion of nationals 1067
Article 4. Prohibition of collective expulsion of aliens 1075
Article 5. Territorial application 1081
Article 6. Relationship to the Convention 1085
Article 7. Signature and ratification 1087

PART FIVE: PROTOCOL NO. 6 TO THE CONVENTION FOR
THE PROTECTION OF HUMAN RIGHTS AND
FUNDAMENTAL FREEDOMS, CONCERNING
THE ABOLITION OF THE DEATH PENALTY

Preamble 1091
Article 1. Abolition of the death penalty 1098
Article 2. Death penalty in time of war 1103
Article 3. Prohibition of derogations 1110
Article 4. Prohibition of reservations 1111

Article 5. Territorial application 1113
Article 6. Relationship to the Convention 1115
Article 7. Signature and ratification 1117
Article 8. Entry into force 1120
Article 9. Depositary functions 1121

PART SIX: PROTOCOL NO. 7 TO THE CONVENTION
           FOR THE PROTECTION OF HUMAN RIGHTS
           AND FUNDAMENTAL FREEDOMS

Preamble 1125
Article 1. Procedural safeguards relating to expulsion of aliens 1126
Article 2. Right of appeal in criminal matters 1134
Article 3. Compensation for wrongful conviction 1142
Article 4. Right not to be tried or punished twice 1147
Article 5. Equality between spouses 1157
Article 6. Territorial application 1160
Article 7. Relationship to the Convention 1164
Article 8. Signature and ratification 1166
Article 9. Entry into force 1168
Article 10. Depositary functions 1170

PART SEVEN: PROTOCOL NO. 12 TO THE CONVENTION
             FOR THE PROTECTION OF HUMAN RIGHTS
             AND FUNDAMENTAL FREEDOMS

Preamble 1173
Article 1. General prohibition of discrimination 1177
Article 2. Territorial application 1189
Article 3. Relationship to the Convention 1191
Article 4. Signature and ratification 1192
Article 5. Entry into force 1193
Article 6. Depositary functions 1194

PART EIGHT: PROTOCOL NO. 13 TO THE CONVENTION FOR
             THE PROTECTION OF HUMAN RIGHTS AND
             FUNDAMENTAL FREEDOMS, CONCERNING
             THE ABOLITION OF THE DEATH PENALTY
             IN ALL CIRCUMSTANCES

Preamble 1197
Article 1. Abolition of the death penalty 1201
Article 2. Prohibition of derogations 1203

Article 3. Prohibition of reservations 1204
Article 4. Territorial application 1205
Article 5. Relationship to the Convention 1207
Article 6. Signature and ratification 1208
Article 7. Entry into force 1209
Article 8. Depositary functions 1210

PART NINE: PROTOCOL NO. 16 TO THE CONVENTION
FOR THE PROTECTION OF HUMAN RIGHTS
AND FUNDAMENTAL FREEDOMS

Preamble 1213
Article 1. Requests for an advisory opinion 1215
Article 2. Acceptance of requests 1219
Article 3. Participation in proceedings 1222
Article 4. Content and issuance of advisory opinions 1224
Article 5. Non-binding nature of advisory opinions 1225
Article 6. Relationship to the Convention 1227
Article 7. Signature and ratification 1228
Article 8. Entry into force 1229
Article 9. Reservations 1230
Article 10. Designation of courts or tribunals 1231
Article 11. Depositary functions 1232

Index 1233

Table of Cases

EUROPEAN COURT OF HUMAN RIGHTS

A. v Croatia, no. 55164/08, 14 October 2010 . . . . .369, 773
A. v Norway, no. 28070/06, 9 April 2009 385
A. v. United Kingdom, 23 September 1998, *Reports of Judgments and Decisions* 1998-VI 189, 191
A. v. United Kingdom, no. 35373/97, ECHR 2002-X 81, 286–7
A.A. v. United Kingdom, no. 8000/08, 20 September 2011 . . . . .367, 396, 405
A. and Others v Bulgaria, no. 51776/08, 29 November 2011 . . . . .227, 241
A. and Others v. United Kingdom [GC], no. 3455/05, ECHR 2009 . . . . 76–7, 83, 168, 171,
180–1, 184, 186–8, 226, 231–2, 234, 243, 254–7, 288, 310, 551,
592, 595–7, 600, 780, 815, 836, 838
A.B. v. Poland (dec.), no. 33878/96, 18 October 2001 275
A.B. v. Poland (dec.), no. 33878/96, 13 March 2003 1072
A, B, and C v Ireland [GC], no. 25579/05, ECHR 2010 . . . . .81, 92, 124–5, 171, 372, 373,
388, 707, 769, 773
Abbasov v Azerbaijan, no. 24271/05, 17 January 2008 869
Abdu v Bulgaria, no. 26827/08, 11 March 2014 . . . . .191–2, 197–8
Abdulaziz, Cabales and Balkandali v United Kingdom, 28 May 1985, Series A no. 94 . . . . 181, 194,
196, 243, 367, 390, 395, 398, 563, 565, 574, 576,
1174, 1178, 1183
Abdülsamet Yaman v Turkey, no. 32446/96, 2 November 2004 . . . . .128, 603
Abdurashidova v Russia, no. 32968/05, 8 April 2010 137
Abdurrahman Orak v Turkey, no. 31889/96, 14 February 2002 134
Abu-Salem v Portugal (dec.), no. 26844/04, 9 May 2006 146
Acampora v Italy (dec.), no. 2072/08, 8 January 2013 1144
Achour v France [GC], no. 67335/01, ECHR 2006-IV 280, 336, 338, 340,
342, 345, 350, 354

Achour v France [GC], no. 67335/01, Concurring Opinion of Judge Zupančić,
ECHR 2006-IV (extracts) 334
Açış v Turkey, no. 7050/05, 1 February 2011 170
A.D. and O.D. v United Kingdom, no. 28680/06, 16 March 2010 392–3
Ada Rossi and Others v Italy (dec.), nos 55185/08, 55483/05, 55516/08, 56010/08,
56278/08, 58420/08, and 58424/08, 16 December 2008 743
Adalı v Turkey, no. 38187/97, 31 March 2005 . . . . .491, 495
Adamczuk v Poland (revision), no. 30523/07, 15 June 2010 853
Adamkiewicz v Poland, no. 54729/00, 2 March 2010 319
Adams v United Kingdom (dec.), no. 70601/11, 12 November 2013 1145
Adamson v United Kingdom (dec.), no. 42293/98, 26 January 1999 . . . . .346, 384
Adamsons v Latvia, no. 3669/03, 24 June 2008 . . . . .1026, 1029
Adolf v Austria, 26 March 1982, Series A no. 49 277
Adrian Mihai Ionescu v Romania (dec.), no. 36659/04, 1 June 2010 .782–4
A.D.T. v United Kingdom, no. 35765/97, ECHR 2000-IX 381, 406–7
Advisory opinion on certain legal questions concerning the lists of candidates submitted
with a view to the election of judges to the European Court of Human Rights [GC],
12 February 2008 . . . . 653, 661, 666, 877, 879, 882, 885
Advisory opinion on certain legal questions concerning the lists of candidates submitted
with a view to the election of judges to the European Court of Human Rights (no. 2)
[GC], 22 January 2010 . . . . 651, 660, 662–3, 672, 877, 879–80, 882, 885
A.E. v Poland, no. 14480/04, 31 March 2009 1061
A.E.L. v Poland (dec.), no. 59435/10, 10 December 2013 828

Aerts v Belgium, 30 July 1998, *Reports of Judgments and Decisions* 1998-V 41, 174, 184, 232, 275

AGOSI v United Kingdom, 24 October 1986, Series A no. 108 . . . . 282, 974, 979

Agrotexim and Others v Greece, 24 October 1995, Series A no. 330-A 92, 736

A.H. v United Kingdom, no. 3868/68, Collection 34, p. 10. 369

A.H. Khan v United Kingdom, no. 6222/10, 20 December 2011. . . . . .367, 397

Ahmed v Austria, 17 December 1996, *Reports of Judgments and Decisions* 1996-VI 194

Ahmed v Romania, no. 34621/03, 13 July 2010 1130

Ahmed and Others v United Kingdom, 2 September 1998, *Reports of Judgments and*
   Decisions 1998-VI 465, 522, 790, 1018, 1030

Ahmed Ali v Netherlands (dec.), no. 26494, 24 January 2012 . . . . .793, 795

Ahmet Arslan and Others v Turkey, no. 41135/98, 23 February 2010 . . . . .431, 437

Ahmet Özkan and Others v Turkey, no. 21689/93, 6 April 2004 . . . . .153, 812

Ahmet Sadık v Greece, 15 November 1996, *Reports of Judgments and Decisions* 1996-V 769

Ahmet Yıldırım v Turkey, no. 3111/10, ECHR 2012 . . . . 452, 455, 456, 462, 466

Ahmet Yıldırım v Turkey, no. 3111/10, Concurring Opinion of Judge Pinto de Albuquerque,
   ECHR 2012 455

Air Canada v United Kingdom, 5 May 1995, Series A no. 316-A 282, 974

Airey v Ireland, 9 October 1979, Series A no. 32 . . . . 273, 285, 368, 388, 764, 900

Ajayi and Others v United Kingdom (dec.), no. 27663/95, 22 June 1999 . . . . .396, 398

Akay v Turkey (dec.), no. 34501/97, 19 February 2002 . . . . .301–2, 640

Akdaş v Turkey, no. 41056/04, 16 February 2010 . . . . .464, 472

Akdeniz v Turkey, no. 25165/94, 31 May 2005 721

Akdeniz and Others v Turkey, no. 23954/94, 31 May 2000 811

Akdivar and Others v Turkey, 16 September 1996, *Reports of Judgments and*
   Decisions 1996-IV 627, 765–6

Akdivar and Others v Turkey (Article 50), 1 April 1998, *Reports of Judgments and*
   Decisions 1998-II 839

Akgöl and Göl v Turkey, nos 28495/06 and 28156/06, 17 May 2011 . . . . .280, 476, 499

Akhmadov and Others v Russia, no. 21586/02, 14 November 2008 137

Akhmadova and Sadulayeva v Russia, no. 40464/02, 10 May 2007 811

Akhmatov v Russia, nos 38828/10, 2543/11, 2650/11, 2685/11, 7409/11, 14321/11,
   and 26277/11, 16 January 2014 811

Akkum and Others v Turkey, no. 21894/93, ECHR 2005-II (extracts) 170, 813

Akman v Turkey (striking out), no. 37453/97, ECHR 2001-VI 797

Akpınar and Altun v Turkey, no. 56760/00, 27 February 2007 151

Aksoy v Turkey, 18 December 1996, *Reports of Judgments and Decisions* 1996-VI. 44, 83, 168,
   179–80, 175, 226, 247–8, 598, 600, 747, 764–6, 768, 809

Aksu v Turkey [GC], nos 4149/04 and 41029/04, ECHR 2012 . . . . 368–9, 375, 379–80, 742, 848

Aktaş v Turkey, no. 24351/94, ECHR 2003-V (extracts) 570

A.L. v Germany, no. 72758/01, 28 April 2005 304

Al-Adsani v United Kingdom, no. 35763/97, ECHR 2001-XI 37–9, 43–4, 65, 100, 179, 286

Al-Adsani v United Kingdom, no. 35763/97, Concurring Opinion of Judge Pellonpää
   Joined by Judge Sir Nicholas Bratza, ECHR 2001-XI 179

Al-Dulimi and Montana Management Inc. v Switzerland, no. 5809/08,
   26 November 2013 . . . . .88, 92, 95, 712

Al-Dulimi and Montana Management Inc. v Switzerland, no. 5809/08, Dissenting
   Opinion of Judge Lorenzen Joined by Judges Raimondi and Jočiené, 26 November 2013 36

Al-Dulimi and Montana Management Inc. v Switzerland, no. 5809/08, Partly Dissenting
   Opinion of Judge Sajó, 26 November 2013 44

Al Fayed v France (dec.), no. 38501/02, 27 September 2007 132

Al Husin v Bosnia and Herzegovina, no. 3727/08, 7 February 2012 . . . . .239, 243

Al-Jedda v United Kingdom [GC], no. 27021/08, ECHR 2011 235

Al-Khawaja and Tahery v United Kingdom [GC], nos 26766/05 and 22228/06,
   ECHR 2011 312–3

Al-Nashif v Bulgaria, no. 50963/99, 20 June 2002. 257, 403, 435, 780

Al Nashiri v Poland, no. 28761/11, 24 July 2014 . . . . .35, 42, 89, 96, 123, 145, 191,
                            684, 810, 814, 827–8, 837, 900, 1099, 1101, 1115, 1128, 1199
Al-Saadoon and Mufdhi v United Kingdom (dec.), no. 61498/08, 30 June 2009. 102
Al-Saadoon and Mufdhi v United Kingdom, no. 61498/08,
    ECHR 2010 (extracts). 17, 37, 47, 73, 94, 144, 190, 282, 747, 749–50, 923, 1092,
                                                              1099, 1101, 1115, 1128, 1199
Al Shari v France (dec.), no. 57/03, 5 July 2005 . . . . .145, 1100
Al-Skeini and Others v United Kingdom [GC], no. 55721/07,
    ECHR 2011. . . . . 92, 101–5, 153, 793, 924, 926
Al-Skeini and Others v United Kingdom, no. 55721/07, Concurring Opinion of Judge
    Bonello, ECHR 2011 . . . . .62, 92, 136
Alatulkkila and Others v Finland, no. 33538/96, 28 July 2005. . . . . .573, 979
Alaverdyan v Armenia (dec.), no. 4523/04, 24 August 2010. 272
Albekov and Others v Russia, no. 68216/01, 9 October 2008. 148
Albert and Le Compte v Belgium, 10 February 1983, Series A no. 58. . . . . .181, 283
Aleksandr Makarov v Russia, no. 15217/07, 12 March 2009 253
Aleksandr Novikov v Russia, no. 7087/04, 11 July 2013 240
Aleksandr Zaichenko v Russia, no. 39660/02, 18 February 2010 280
Aleksanyan v Russia, no. 46468, 22 December 2008 . . . . .252, 781, 869
Aleksentseva and 28 Others v Russia (dec.), no. 75025/01, 23 March 2006. 801
Alekseyev v Russia, nos 4916/07, 25924/08, and 14599/09, 21 October 2010 . . . 494–5, 500, 518, 535
Alexandridis v Greece, no. 19516/06, 21 February 2008 428
Ali v United Kingdom, no. 40385/06, 11 January 2011. 998
Alida Maria Fränklin-Beentjes and CEFLU-Luz da Floresta v Netherlands (dec.),
    no. 28167/07, 6 May 2014 431
Aliev v Georgia, no. 522/04, 13 January 2009. 745
Aliev v Ukraine, no. 41220/98, 29 April 2003. . . . . .372, 389
Alikaj and Others v Italy, no. 47357/08, 29 March 2011. 151
Alimuçaj v Albania, no. 20134/05, 7 February 2012 339
Alınak v Turkey, no. 40287/98, 29 March 2005 464
Ališić and Others v Bosnia and Herzegovina, Serbia, Slovenia and the former Yugoslav
    Republic of Macedonia [GC], no. 60642/08, 16 July 2014 . . . . .42, 968
Ališić and Others v Bosnia and Herzegovina, Serbia, Slovenia and the former Yugoslav
    Republic of Macedonia [GC], no. 60642/08, Partly Dissenting Opinion of Judge Nußburger,
    Joined by Judge Popović, 16 July 2014. 78
Alkaya v Turkey, no. 42811/06, 9 October 2012. 399
Allan v United Kingdom, no. 48539/99, ECHR 2002-IX 319–20
Allan Jacobsson v Sweden (no. 2), 19 February 1998, *Reports of Judgments and Decisions*
    1998-I 289, 979
Allen v United Kingdom [GC], no. 25424/09, 12 July 2013 . . . . 305–6, 1143, 1145–6, 1165
Allenet de Ribemont v France, 10 February 1995, Series A no. 308 . . . . .298, 302–3
Allenet de Ribemont v France (interpretation), 7 August 1996, *Reports of Judgments and Decisions*
    1996-III 852
Almeida Garrett, Mascarenhas Falcáo and Others v Portugal, nos 29813/96 and 30229/96,
    ECHR 2000-I. 109
Altinay v Turkey, no. 37222/04, 9 July 2013 . . . . .996–7, 1005
Altinay v Turkey, no. 37222/04, Partly Dissenting Opinion of Judges Vučinić and Pinto de
    Albuquerque, 9 July 2013 1005
Altınok v Turkey, no. 31610/08, 29 November 2011 255
Altuğ Taner Akçam v Turkey, no. 27520/07, 25 October 2011 . . . . .279, 452, 471, 743
Amann v Switzerland [GC], no. 27798/95, ECHR 2000-II .382, 403, 470
Amat-G Ltd and Mebaghishvili v Georgia, no. 2507/03, ECHR 2005-VIII. 736
Ambruosi v Italy, no. 31227/96, 19 October 2000 . . . . .967, 971
Amirov v Russia, no. 51857/13, 27 November 2014 . . . . .748, 750
A.M.M. v Romania, no. 2151/10, 14 February 2012. . . . . .376, 388

Amrollahi v Denmark (dec.), no. 56811/00, 28 June 2001 1149
Amrollahi v Denmark, no. 56811/00, 11 July 2002 395
Amuur v France, 25 June 1996, *Reports of Judgments and Decisions*
    1996-III 71, 227, 234, 243, 744, 798
Anakomba Yula v Belgium, no. 45413/07, 10 March 2009 . . . . .285, 322
Anam v United Kingdom (dec.), no. 21783/08, 7 June 2011 . . . . .367, 397
Ananyev v Russia, no. 20292/04, 30 July 2009 77
Ananyev and Others v Russia, nos 42525/07, & 60800/08, 10 January 2012 . . . . .552, 764–5
Anatoliy Rudenko v Ukraine, no. 50264/08, 17 April 2014 242
Anayo v Germany, no. 20578/07, 21 December 2010 391
Anchugov and Gladkov v Russia, nos 11157/04 and 15162/05, 4 July 2013 . . . . .35, 1021, 1028
Anderle v Czech Republic, no. 6268/08, 17 February 2011 563
Andrášik and Others v Slovakia (dec.), nos 57984/00, 60226/00, 60237/00, 60242/00,
    60679/00, 60680/00, and 68563/01, ECHR 2002-IX 770
Andrejeva v Latvia [GC], no. 55707/00, ECHR 2009 . . . . 33, 81, 90, 92–3, 265, 286, 288,
                                     562, 566, 764, 781, 836–7, 839, 868, 970–2
Andrejeva v Latvia [GC], no. 55707/00, Partly Dissenting Opinion of Judge Ziemele,
    ECHR 2009 . . . . 36, 38
Andreou v Turkey, no. 45653/99, 27 October 2009 151
Andric v Sweden (dec.), no. 45917/99, 23 February 1999 1077
Andronicou and Constantinou v Cyprus, 9 October 1997, *Reports of Judgments and
    Decisions* 1997-VI 147, 149, 152
Angelova and Iliev v Bulgaria, no. 55523/00, 26 July 2007 160
Anghel v Romania, no. 28183/03, 4 October 2007 300
Anguelova v Bulgaria, no. 38361/97, ECHR 2002-IV 123, 133–4, 230, 552
Anguelova v Bulgaria, no. 38361/97, Partial Dissenting Opinion of Judge Bonello,
    ECHR 2002-IV 159
Anheuser-Busch Inc. v Portugal [GC] no. 73049/01, ECHR 2007-I 480, 971, 979
Anibal Vieira & Filhos LDA and Maria Rosa Ferreira da Costa LDA v Portugal (dec.),
    nos 980/12 and 18385/12, 13 November 2012 781
Anık and Others v Turkey, no. 63758/00, 5 June 2007 151
Animal Defenders International v United Kingdom [GC], no. 48876/08, ECHR 2013
    (extracts) 452
Animal Defenders International v United Kingdom [GC], no. 48876/08, Joint Dissenting
    Opinion of Judges Ziemele, Sajó, Kalaydjieva, Vučinić and De Gaetano,
    ECHR 2013 (extracts) 454
Ankarcrona v Sweden (dec.), no. 35178/97, 27 June 2000 741
Ankerl v Switzerland, 23 October 1996, *Reports of Judgments and Decisions* 1996-V 764
Anna Todorova v Bulgaria, no. 23302/03, 24 May 2011 137
Annen II v Germany (dec.), nos 2373/07 and 2396/07, 30 March 2010 475
Annoni di Gussola and Others v France, nos 31819/96 and 33293/96, ECHR 2000-XI 286
Annunziata v Italy (dec.), no. 24423/03, 7 July 2009 778
Antayev and Others v Russia, no. 37966/07, 3 July 2014 197–8
Anthony Aquilina v Malta, no. 3851/12, 11 December 2014 . . . . .974, 980
Antonenkov and Others v Ukraine, no. 14183/02, 22 November 2005 1058
A.P., M.P., and T.P. v Switzerland, 29 August 1997, *Reports of Judgments and Decisions* 1997-V 280
Aparicio Benito v Spain (dec.), no. 36150/03, 4 May 2004 1127
APIS a.s. v Slovakia (dec.), no. 39794/98, 13 January 2002 275
Appietto v France (dec.), no. 56927/00, 26 February 2002 . . . . 698, 702, 708, 849
Appleby and Others v United Kingdom, no. 44306/98, ECHR 2003-VI 453, 492
A.Q. v Italy (dec.), no. 44994/98, 14 March 2002 1051
Aquilina v Malta [GC], no. 25642/94, ECHR 1999-III 247–9, 767
Aquilina and Others v Malta, no. 28040/08, 14 June 2011 . . . . 458, 468–9, 472, 475
Aras v Turkey (no. 2), no. 15065/07, 18 November 2014 310
Arat v Turkey, no. 10309/03, 10 November 2009 744

Aresti Charalambous v Cyprus, no. 43151/04, 19 July 2007 541–2
Armando Grasso v Italy (revision), no. 48411/99, 29 April 2003 853
Armonienė v Lithuania, no. 36919/02, 25 November 2008 461
Arnolin and Others v France, nos 20127/03, 31795/03, 35937/03, 2185/04, 4208/04,
    12654/04, 15466/04, 15612/04, 27549/04, 27552/04, 27554/04, 27560/04, 27566/04,
    27572/04, 27586/04, 27588/04, 27593/04, 27599/04, 27602/04, 27605/04, 27611/04,
    27615/04, 27632/04, 34409/04 and 12176/05, 9 January 2007 38
Arras and Others v Italy, no. 17972/07, 14 February 2012 981
Artemi and Gregory v Cyprus, Austria, Belgium, Czech Republic, Denmark, Estonia, Finland,
    France, Germany, Hungary, Ireland, Italy, Latvia, Lithuania, Luxembourg, Malta,
    Netherlands, Poland, Portugal, Slovakia, Slovenia, and Sweden (dec.), no. 35524/06,
    30 November 2010 694
Artemov v Russia, no. 4945/03, 3 April 2014 77
Artico v Italy, 13 May 1980, Series A no. 37 . . . . 27, 33, 307–8, 311
Artner v Austria, 28 August 1992, Series A no. 242-A 313
Artun and Güvener v Turkey, no. 75510/01, 26 June 2007 . . . . .476, 478
Arutyunyan v Russia, no. 48977/09, 10 January 2012 . . . . 169, 171–2, 180, 184, 186
Artyomov v Russia, no. 14146/02, 27 May 2010 . . . . .288, 290
Arvanitaki-Roboti and Others v Greece [GC], no. 27278/03, 15 February 2008 . . . . .836, 838
Asadbeyli and Others v Azerbaijan, nos 3653/05, 14729/05, 20908/05, 26242/05, 36083/05,
    and 16519/06, 11 December 2012 . . . . 286, 312, 739, 1151, 1152, 1154
Asadov and Others v Azerbaijan (striking out), no. 138/03, 26 October 2006 800
Asch v Austria, 26 April 1991, Series A no, 203 312
Ashendon and Jones v United Kingdom (revision), nos 35730/07 and 4285/08,
    15 December 2011 304
Ashingdane v United Kingdom, 28 May 1985, Series A no. 93 . . . . 226, 242, 286, 624, 1056
Ashingdane v United Kingdom, 28 May 1985, Concurring Opinion of Judge Lagergren,
    Series A no. 93 69
Ashlarba v Georgia, no. 45554/08 15 July 2014 341
Ashot Harutyunyan v Armenia, no. 34334/04, 15 June 2010 185
Ashughyan v Armenia, no. 33268/03, 17 July 2008 . . . . .309, 1137
Ashworth and Others v United Kingdom (dec.), no. 39561/98, 20 January 2004 387
Asito v Moldova (no. 2), no. 39818/06, 13 March 2012 72
Aslakhanova and Others v Russia, nos 2944/06, 8300/07, 50184/07, 332/08, and 42509/10,
    18 December 2012 . . . . 136–7, 739, 807, 811
Asproftas v Turkey, no. 16079/90, 27 May 2010 355
Assanidze v Georgia [GC], no. 71503/01, ECHR 2004-II 92, 229, 234, 868, 1058
Assenov and Others v Bulgaria, 28 October 1998, *Reports of Judgments and Decisions*
    1998-VIII 44, 134–5, 168, 179, 191, 247, 249, 552, 592
Associated Society of Locomotive Engineers and Fireman (ASLEF) v United Kingdom,
    no. 11002/05, 27 February 2007 . . . . .502, 506, 514
Association '21 December 1989' and Others v Romania, nos 33810/07 and 18817/08,
    24 May 2011 . . . . .77, 128, 138, 400
Association Ekin v France (dec.), no. 39288/98, 18 January 2000 744
Association Ekin v France, no. 39288/98, ECHR 2001-VIII 466
Association for European Integration and Human Rights and Ekimdzhiev v Bulgaria,
    no. 62540/00, 28 June 2007 . . . . .403, 744
Association Les Témoins de Jéhovah v France, no. 8916/05, 30 June 2011 425
Association of Citizens Radko and Paunkovski v 'former Yugoslav Republic of Macedonia',
    no. 74651/01, ECHR 2009 (extracts) 490–1, 495, 510–1, 513, 618
Association Rhino and Others v Switzerland, no. 48848/07, 11 October 2011 . . . . . 501, 513, 517, 521
Association SOS Attentats and de Boery v France [GC] (dec.), no. 76642/01, 2006-XIV 799
Associazione Nazionale Reduci Dalla prigionia dall'Internamento e dalla Guerra di
    Liberazione and 275 Others v Germany (dec.), no. 45563/04, 4 September 2007 202
Atik v Germany (dec.), no. 67500/01, 13 May 2004 766

Atiman v Turkey, no. 62279/09, 30 September 2104 130
Attard v Malta (dec.), no. 46750/99, 28 September 2000. 258
Austin and Others v United Kingdom [GC], nos 39692/09, 40713/09, and 41008/09,
    ECHR 2012 . . . . 47, 74, 78, 227, 1038
Autronic AG v Switzerland, 22 May 1990, Series A no. 178 455
A.V. [Velikova] v Bulgaria (dec.), no. 41488/98, 18 May 1999. 738, 742
Avotiņš v Latvia, no. 17502/07, 25 February 2014 783
Avşar v Turkey, no. 25657/94, ECHR 2001-VII 123, 147, 569, 807
A.W. and F.W. v Finland, no. 26570/95, 25 January 2001 324
A.W. Khan v United Kingdom, no. 47486/06, 12 January 2010 397–8
Axel Springer AG v Germany [GC] no. 39954/08, 7 February 2012. . . . . 451, 458, 460,
                                                                        462, 469, 472, 580
Axel Springer AG v Germany (dec.), no. 44585/10, 13 March 2012 480
Axen v Germany, 8 December 1983, Series A no. 72 . . . . .289, 291
Ay v Turkey, no. 30951/96, 22 March 2005 191
Ay Ali v Italy, no. 24691/04, 14 December 2006. 1135
Aydan v Turkey, no. 16281/10, 12 March 2013 151
Aydin v Germany, no. 16637/07, 27 January 2011 272
Aydın v Turkey, 25 September 1997, *Reports of Judgments and Decisions* 1997-VI 176, 180, 790
Aytaş and Others v Turkey, no. 6758/05, 8 December 2009 516
Ayuntamiento de Mula v Spain, (dec.), no. 55346/00, 1 February 2001 . . . . .90, 737
Azienda Agicola Silverfunghi S.a.s. and Others v Italy, nos 48357/07, 52677/07, 52687/07,
    and 52701/07, 24 June 2014. 981
Azinas v Cyprus [GC], no. 56679/00, ECHR 2004-III 764–5, 769, 785, 845
Aziyevy v Russia, no. 7626/01, 20 March 2008 811
B. v Austria, 28 March 1990, Series A no. 175 235
B. v Belgium, no. 4320/11, 10 July 2012 392
B. v France, 25 March 1992, Series A no. 232-C 367, 380
B. v Republic of Moldova, no. 61382/09, 16 July 2013 192
B. v United Kingdom, 8 July 1987, Series A no. 21 827
B. and L. v United Kingdom, no. 36536/02, 13 September 2005 . . . . 82, 533–4, 539, 543
Baars v Netherlands, no. 44320/98, 28 October 2003 304
Babar Ahmad and Others v United Kingdom, nos 24027/07, 11949/08, 36742/08, 66911/09,
    and 67354/09, 10 April 2012. 195
Babenko v Ukraine (dec.), no. 43476/98, 4 May 1999. 1025
Bachmaier v Austria (dec.), no. 77413/01, 2 September 2004. 1153
Bachowski v Poland (dec.), no. 32463/06, 2 November 2010. 1144
Backlund v Finland, no. 36498/05, 6 July 2010 391
Bacuzzi v Italy (dec.), no. 43817/04, 24 May 2011 542
Bączkowski and Others v Poland, no. 1543/06, 3 May 2007 . . . . 490, 494, 496, 510, 514, 525
Bader and Kanbor v Sweden, no. 13284/04, ECHR 2005-XI .141, 1100
Bagheri and Maliki v Netherlands (dec.), no. 30164/06, 15 May 2007 780
Bah v United Kingdom, no. 56328/07, ECHR 2011 574
Bahçeci v Turkey, no. 33340/03, 16 June 2009. 455
Baillard v France (dec.), no. 6032/04, 25 September 2008 780
Baisan and Liga Apararii Drepturilor Omului din Romania v Romania (dec.), no. 28973/95,
    30 October 1995. 518
Bajrami v Albania (revision), no. 35853/04, 18 December 2007 853
Bakan v Turkey, no. 50939/99, 12 June 2007 129–30
Bălăşoiu v Romania (dec.), no. 37424/97, 2 September 2003 111
Baláž v Slovakia (dec.), no. 60243/00, 16 September 2003. 981
Balçik and Others v Turkey, no. 25/02, 29 November 2007 . . . . .497, 516
Baldi v Italy (striking out), no. 32584/96, 11 December 2003 798
Balenović v Croatia (dec.), no. 28369/07, 30 September 2010 822–3
Baltaji v Bulgaria, no. 12919/04, 12 July 2011 1130

Banković and Others v Belgium and Others (dec.), no. 52207/99, ECHR 2001-XII 54, 87, 92–3, 95, 97, 102–4, 1045

Bannikov v Latvia, no. 19279/03, 11 June 2013 783

Baran v Turkey, no. 48988/99, 10 November 2004. 455

Barankevich v Russia (dec.), no. 10519/03, 20 October 2005. 772

Barankevich v Russia, no. 10519/03, 26 July 2007 . . . . 431, 491, 493–5

Baranowski v Poland, no. 28358/95, ECHR 2000-III 230–1, 256

Barberà, Messegué and Jabardo v Spain, 6 December 1988, Series
   A no. 146. . . . . 110, 271, 287, 298, 300

Barbu Anghelescu v Romania, no. 46430/99, 5 October 2004 . . . . .193, 807

Barišič v Slovenia, no. 32600/05, 18 October 2012 855

Bartik v Russia, no. 55565/00, ECHR 2006-XV 55, 378, 1011, 1058, 1062

Barraco v France, no. 32684/05, 5 March 2009. . . . . .495, 498–9, 516

Basileo and Others v Italy (dec.), no. 11303/02, 23 August 2011 780

Basque Nationalist Party—Iparralde Regional Organisation v France, no. 71251/01,
   ECHR 2007-II 41

Bastone v Italy (dec.), no. 59638/00, ECHR 2005-II. 398

Batı and Others v Turkey, nos 33097/96 and 57834/00, ECHR 2004-IV (extracts). 179

Baucher v France, no. 53640/00, 24 July 2007 1135

Baudinière and Vauzelle v France, nos 25708/03 and 25719/03,
   6 December 2007 973

Baumann v Austria (revision), no. 76809/01, 9 June 2005 . . . . .853, 855

Baumann v France, no. 33592/96, ECHR 2001-V (extracts) 769, 1056, 1058, 1061

Bayatyan v Armenia, no. 23459/03, 27 October 2009 848

Bayatyan v Armenia, no. 23459/03, Concurring Opinion of Judge Fura,
   27 October 2009. 712

Bayatyan v Armenia [GC], no. 23459/03, ECHR 2011 . . . . .40, 47–8, 216, 420–1, 427, 433–4, 436, 471, 512, 848

Baybaşın v Netherlands, no. 13600/02, 6 July 2006. 69

Baybora and Others v Cyprus (dec.), no. 77116/01, 22 October 2002 770

Bayer v Germany, no. 8453/04, 16 July 2009 283

Bayram and Yıldırım v Turkey (dec.), no. 38587/97, ECHR 2002-III 773

Baytar v Turkey, no. 45440/04, 14 October 2014. 314

Bazorkina v Russia, no. 69481/01, 27 July 2006 . . . . 123, 170, 748, 808, 811, 813

Becciev v Moldova, no. 9190/03, 4 October 2005 . . . . .240, 251–2

Beer and Regan v Germany [GC], no. 28934/95, 18 February 1999. 287

Beganović v Croatia, no. 46423/06, 25 June 2009 . . . . .126, 192, 197

Begheluri and Others v Georgia, no. 28490/02, 7 October 2014 .196–7

Behrami and Behrami v France and Saramati v France, Germany and
   Norway (dec.) [GC], nos 71412/01 and 78166/01, 2 May 2007 . . . . .54, 67, 106, 694

Beiere v Latvia, no. 30954/05, 29 November 2011 236

Beker v Turkey, no. 27866/03, 24 March 2009. . . . . .123, 134

Bekir-Ousta and Others v Greece, no. 35151/05, 11 October 2007 500

Bekirski v Bulgaria, no. 71420/01, 2 September 2010 813

Bekos and Koutropoulos v Greece, no. 15250/02, ECHR 2005-XIII (extracts) 41

Belaousof and Others v Greece, no. 66296/01, 27 May 2004. 770

Belashev v Russia, no. 28617/03, 4 December 008 290

Belchev v Bulgaria, no. 39270/98, 8 April 2004. 250

Beldjoudi v France, 26 March 1992, Series A no. 234-A 395

Belevitskiy v Russia, no. 72967/01, 1 March 2007. . . . . .233, 250

Belilos v Switzerland, 29 April 1988, Series A no. 132 . . . . .35, 42, 294, 325, 933–4, 93–8, 111

Belilos v Switzerland, 29 April 1988, Concurring Opinion of Judge de Meyer,
   Series A no. 132 933

Bellerin Lagares v Spain (dec.), no. 31548/02, 4 November 2003 297

Bellet v France, 4 December 1995, Series A no. 333-B. 285

Belziuk v Poland, 25 March 1998, *Reports of Judgments and Decisions* 1998-II 316
Bendenoun v France, 24 February 1994, Series A no. 284 . . . . .277–8, 284
Benet Praha, Spol S.R.O. v Czech Republic (dec.), no. 38354/06, 28 September 2010. . . . . . . .770, 772
Benham v United Kingdom, 10 June 1996, *Reports of Judgments and Decisions*
   1996-III 230, 236, 277
Benjamin and Wilson v United Kingdom, no. 28212/95, 26 September 2002. 255
Bensaid v United Kingdom, no. 44599/98, ECHR 2000-I. 172, 380
Benthem v Netherlands, 23 October 1985, Series A no. 97 272
Benzer and Others v Turkey, no. 23502/06, 12 November 2013 . . . . .130, 157, 813
Berdji v France (striking out), no. 74184/01, 7 March 2006. 798
Berezovskiy v Ukraine (dec.), no. 70908/01, 15 June 2004. 572
Beraru v Romania, no. 40107/04, 18 March 2014. 309
Bergauer and Others v Czech Republic (dec.), no. 17120/04, 13 December 2005 109
Bergmann v Estonia, no. 38241/04, 29 May 2008. 247
Berić and Others v Bosnia and Herzegovina (dec.), nos 36357/04, 36360/04, 38346/04,
   41705/04, 45190/04, 45578/04, 45579/04, 45580/04, 91/05, 97/05, 100/05,
   101/05, 1121/05, 1123/05, 1125/05, 1129/05, 1132/05, 1133/05, 1169/05,
   1172/05, 1175/05, 1177/05, 1180/05, 1185/05, 20793/05 and 25496/05,
   16 October 2007. . . . . .42, 107
Berisha and Haljiti v former Yugoslav Republic of Macedonia (dec.), no. 18670/03,
   16 June 2005 1077
Berladir and Others v Russia, no. 34202/06, 10 July 2012. . . . . .491, 497–8, 517
Berliński v Poland, nos 27715/95 and 30209/96, 20 June 2002 307
Bessenyei v Hungary, no. 37509/06, 21 October 2008 . . . . .1061, 1064
Bevacqua and S. v Bulgaria, no. 71127/01, 12 June 2008. 370
Beyazgül v Turkey, no. 27849/03, 22 September 2009 151
Beyeler v Italy [GC], no. 33202/96, ECHR 2000-I. 627, 967, 973, 975–7
Beyeler v Italy (just satisfaction) [GC], no. 33202/96, 28 May 2002 839
Bezicheri v Italy, 25 October 1989, Series A no. 164 257
Bezrukovy v Russia, no. 34616/02, 10 May 2012 72
Biblical Centre of the Chuvash Republic v Russia, no. 33203/08, 12 June 2014 517
Biç and Others v Turkey, no. 55955/00, 2 February 2006 73
Biçici v Turkey, no. 30357/05, 27 May 2010 191
Bigaeva v Greece, no. 26713/05, 28 May 2009 . . . . 374, 407, 568, 581
Bigaeva v Greece, no. 26713/05, Partly Dissenting Opinion of Judges Vajić,
   Malinverni, and Nicolaou, 28 May 2009 374
Bijelić v Montenegro and Serbia, no. 11890/05, 28 April 2009. . . . . 93, 720, 869, 905–6, 951
Bilen v Turkey, no. 34482/97, 21 February 2006 . . . . .598, 600, 603
Bimer S.A. v Moldova, no. 15084/03, 10 July 2007 . . . . .971, 973
Bingöl v Turkey, no. 36141/04, 22 June 2010 454
Biriuk v Lithuania, no. 23373/03, 25 November 2008. 383
Birk-Levy v France (dec.), no. 39416/06, 21 September 2010. .456, 579
Birol v Turkey, no. 44104/98, 1 March 2005 477
Bitiyeva and Others v Russia, no. 36156/04, 23 April 2009 171
Bitsinas v Greece (striking out), no. 33076/02) 15 November 2005 798
Bittó and Others v Slovakia, no. 30255/09, 28 January 2014. 980
Bizzotto v Greece, 15 November 1996, *Reports of Judgments and Decisions* 1996-V. 791
Björk Eiðsdóttir v Iceland, no. 46443/09, 10 July 2012 . . . . .454, 478
Blackstock v United Kingdom, no. 59512/00, 21 June 2005 258
Bladet Tromsø and Stensaas v Norway [GC], no. 21980/93, ECHR 1999-III 458, 468–9
Blagojević v Netherlands (dec.), no. 49032/07, 9 June 2009. 98–9
Blečić v Croatia, no. 59532/00, 29 July 2004 . . . . .36, 793
Blečić v Croatia [GC], no. 59532/00, 8 March 2006 785
Blečić v Croatia [GC], no. 59532/00, ECHR 2006-III. 43, 93, 107, 109–10, 721, 770, 785, 848
Block v Hungary, no. 56282/09, 25 January 2011. 308–9

Blokhin v Russia, no. 47152/06, 14 November 2013. 319
'Blondje' v Netherlands (dec.), no. 7245/09, 15 September 2009 774
Błońska v Poland (dec.), no. 26330/12, 1 April 2014. 130
Blumberg v Germany (dec.), no. 14618/03, 18 March 2008 .421, 427
Blumberga v Latvia, no. 70930/01, 14 October 2008. 968
Boca v Belgium, no. 50615/99, ECHR 2002-IX 275
Bock v Germany, 29 March 1989, Series A no. 15. 541
Bogdel v Lithuania, no. 41248/06, 26 November 2013 . . . . .72, 977
Bogumil v Portugal, no. 35228/03, 7 October 2008 311
Boicenco v Moldova, no. 41088/05, 11 July 2006. 193, 252, 258, 747–8
Bok v Netherlands, no. 45482/06, 18 January 2011. 304
Bolat v Russia, no. 14139/03, ECHR 2006-XI (extracts) 1059, 1127, 1129–30
Boldea v Romania, no. 19997/02, 15 February 2007 297
Bollan and Others v United Kingdom (dec.), no. 42117/98, 4 May 2000 228
Bolovan v Romania (revision), no. 64541/01, 20 September 2011 853
Bölükbaş and Others v Turkey (dec.), no. 37793/97, 12 October 1999. 771
Bone v France (dec.), no. 69869/01, 1 March 2005. 132
Bopayeva and Others v Russia, no. 40799/06, 7 November 2013 .134, 811
Bordovskiy v Russia, no. 49491/99, 8 February 2005. 245
Borgers v Belgium, 30 October 1991, Series A no. 214-B. 288
Borghi v Italy (dec.), no. 54767/00, 20 June 2001. 1021
Boris Popov v Russia, no. 23284/04, 28 October 2010 261
Borodin v Russia, no. 41867/04, 6 November 2012. 189
Bortesi and Others v Italy (revision), no. 71399/01, 8 December 2009 853
Bortesi and Others v Italy (revision), no. 71399/01, Partially Dissenting Opinion
    of Judges Zagrebelsky and Sajó, 8 December 2009 853
Borysiewicz v Poland, no. 71146/01, 1 July 2008 387
Boškoski v 'former Yougoslav Republic of Macedonia' (dec.), no. 11676/04, ECHR
    2004-VI. 1020–2
Boso v Italy (dec.), no. 50490/99, ECHR 2002-VII. 124, 534, 543
Bosphorus Hava Yollari Turizm ve Ticaret Anonim Şirketi v Ireland [GC],
    no. 45036/98, ECHR 2005-VI 37, 94–5, 97, 106, 948
Bosphorus Hava Yollari Turizm ve Ticaret Anonim Şirketi v Ireland [GC],
    no. 45036/98, Joint Concurring Opinion of Judges Rozakis, Tulkens, Traja,
    Botoucharova, Zagrebelsky, and Garlicki, ECHR 2005-VI. 65
Botmeh and Alami v United Kingdom, no. 15187/03, 7 June 2007 288
Botta v Italy, 24 February 1998, *Reports of Judgments and Decisions* 1998-I 368, 380
Bottazzi v Italy [GC], no. 34884/97, ECHR 1999-V. 77
Bouamar v Belgium, 29 February 1988, Series A no. 129. . . . . 232, 241, 255, 260, 584
Bouchacourt v France, no. 5335/06, 17 December 2009 815
Bouchelkia v France, 29 January 1997, *Reports of Judgments and Decisions* 1997-I. 397, 405
Bouglame v Belgium (dec.), no. 16147/08, 2 March 2010 744
Boujlifa v France, 21 October 1997, *Reports of Judgments and Decisions* 1997-VI 194, 395, 397, 405
Boulois v Luxembourg [GC], no. 37575/04, ECHR 2012 . . . . 183, 272–3, 275
Boultif v Switzerland, no. 54273/00, ECHR 2001-IX 395–7, 405
Boumediène and Others v Bosnia and Herzegovina (dec.), nos 38703/06, 40123/06,
    43301/06, 43302/06, 2131/07, and 2141/07, 18 November 2008. 1100
Bousarra v France, no. 25672/07, 23 September 2010 . . . . .397, 405
Bowman v United Kingdom, 19 February 1998, *Reports of Judgments and Decisions* 1998-I. 743
Boyle and Rice v United Kingdom, 27 April 1988, Series A no. 31. 551
Bozano v France, 18 December 1986, Series A no. 111 . . . . 228–30, 232, 244, 627, 721, 791
Bozgan v Romania, no. 35097/02, 11 October 2007 . . . . .500, 520
Brand v Netherlands, no. 49902/99, 11 May 2004 242
Brânduşe v Romania, no. 6586/03, 7 April 2009. . . . . .181, 184, 388
Branko Tomašići and Others v Croatia, no. 46598/06, 15 January 2009. 129

Brannigan and McBride v United Kingdom, 26 May 1993, Series A
no. 258-B 83, 596, 600–2, 791
Brannigan and McBride v United Kingdom, 26 May 1993, Concurring Opinion of
Judge Martens, Series A no. 258-B 794
Bratyakin v Russia (dec.), no. 72776/01, 9 March 2006 1154
Braun v Poland, no. 30162/10, 4 November 2014 458
Brecknell v United Kingdom, no. 32457/04, 27 November 2007 134
Brega v Moldova, no. 52100/08, 20 April 2010 227
Brega and Others v Moldova, no. 61485/08, 24 January 2012 . . . . 227, 239
Brike v Latvia (dec.), no. 47135/99, 29 June 2000 1030
Brincat v Italy, 26 November 1992, Series A no. 249-A 249, 791
British-American Tobacco Company Ltd v Netherlands, 20 November 1995,
Series A no. 331 791
Brogan and Others v United Kingdom, 29 November 1988, Series
A no. 145-B 46, 71, 238, 246–8, 254, 256, 597, 600
Broka v Latvia, no. 70926/01, 28 June 2007 77
Bronda v Italy, 9 June 1998, *Reports of Judgments and Decisions* 1998-IV 389
Broniowski v Poland [GC], no. 31443/96, ECHR 2004-V 869, 968, 970, 976–7
Broniowski v Poland [GC] (dec.), no. 31443/96, ECHR 2002-X 107, 109
Broniowski v Poland (friendly settlement) [GC], no. 31443/96, ECHR 2005-IX 77, 822
Brosset-Triboulet and Others v France [GC], no. 34078/02, 29 March 2010 . . . . 969–70, 975
Brosset-Triboulet and Others v France [GC], no. 34078/02, Concurring Opinion of Judge
Casadevell, 29 March 2010 969
Brosset-Triboulet and Others v France [GC], no. 34078/02, Joint Dissenting Opinion
of Judges Bratza, Vajić, David Thòr Bjöorgvinsson, and Kalaydjleva, 29 March 2010 967
Brozicek v Italy, 19 December 1989, Series A no. 167 . . . . 769, 809
Brudnicka and Others v Poland, no. 54723/00, ECHR 2005-II 294
Brumărescu v Romania [GC], no. 28342/95, ECHR 1999-VII 72, 744, 975
Brunet-Lecomte and Lyon Mag v France, no. 17265/05, 6 May 2010 469
Brusco v Italy (dec.), no. 69789/01, ECHR 2001-IX 766, 769
Bubbins v United Kingdom, no. 50196/99, ECHR 2005-II (extracts) 149–50, 152
Bucha v Slovakia, no. 43259/07, 20 September 2011 212
Buckley v United Kingdom, 25 September 1996, *Reports of Judgments and Decisions*
1996-IV 81, 400
Buffalo S.R.L. en liquidation v Italy, no. 38746/97, 3 July 2003 980–1
Bugajny and Others v Poland (revision), no. 22531/05, 15 December 2009 854
Bukta and Others v Hungary, no. 25691/04, ECHR 2007-III 497, 499, 516
Buldan v Turkey, no. 28298/95, 20 April 2004 135
Bulski v Poland (dec.), nos 46254/99 and 31888/02, 9 May 2006 1001
Bulut v Austria, 22 February 1996, *Reports of Judgments and Decisions* 1996-II 323, 791
Bulut and Yavuz v Turkey (dec.), no. 73065/01, 28 May 2002 772–3
Burden v United Kingdom [GC], no. 13378/05, 29 April 2008 737
Burden v United Kingdom [GC], no. 13378/05, ECHR 2008 . . . . 533, 737, 738, 743, 765, 981–2
Burden v United Kingdom [GC], no. 13378/05, Dissenting Opinion of Judge Zupančić,
ECHR 2008 574
Burdov v Russia, no. 59498/00, ECHR 2002-III 293, 744, 971
Burdov v Russia (no. 2), no. 33509/04, ECHR 2009 . . . . 77, 744, 869
Burg v France (dec.), no. 34763/02, ECHR 2003-II 297, 857
Burghartz v Switzerland, 22 February 1994, Series A no. 280-B 375574, 576, 1158, 1165, 1178
Buscarini and Others v San Marino [GC], no. 24645/94, ECHR 1999-I 420
Butkevičius v Lithuania, no. 48297/99, ECHR 2002-II 303
Buzescu v Romania, no. 61302/00, 24 May 2005 . . . . 297, 971
Bykov v Russia [GC], no. 4378/02, 10 March 2009 . . . . 250, 252–3, 287, 319–20, 401, 403
Bykov v Russia [GC], no. 4378/02, Concurring Opinion of Judge Cabral Barretto,
10 March 2009 320–1

Bykov v Russia [GC], no. 4378/02, Partly Dissenting Opinion of Judge Spielmann,
Joined by Judges Rozakis, Tulkens, Casadevall, and Mijović, 10 March 2009 320
Byrzykowski v Poland, no. 11562/05, 27 June 2006 . . . . .131, 134, 138
Cable and Others v United Kingdom [GC], nos 24436/94, 24582/94, 24583/94, 24584/94,
24895/94, 25937/94, 25939/94, 25940/94, 25941/94, 26271/95, 26525/95, 27341/95,
27342/95, 27346/95, 27357/95, 27389/95, 27409/95, 27760/95, 27762/95, 27772/95,
28009/95, 28790/95, 30236/96, 30239/96, 30276/96, 30277/96, 30460/96, 30461/96,
30462/96, 31399/96, 31400/96, 31434/96, 31899/96, 32024/96, and 32944/96,
Partly Dissenting Opinion of Judge Zupančić, 18 February 1999 835
Căcescu v Romania (dec.), no. 10762/04, 2 October 2012. 77
Çağdaş Şahin v Turkey, no. 28137/02, 11 April 2006 258
Çakıcı v Turkey [GC], no. 23657/94, ECHR 1999-IV 123, 135, 171, 627, 739–40, 809, 811
Caleffi v Italy, 24 May 1991, Series A no. 206-B. 790
Calmanovici v Romania, no. 42250/02, 1 July 2008 233
Calogero Diana v Italy, 15 November 1996, *Reports of Judgments and Decisions* 1996-V 401
Calvelli and Ciglio v Italy [GC], no. 32967/96, ECHR 2002-I. 128, 131–2, 134, 138
Camberrow MM5 AD v Bulgaria (dec.), no. 50357/99, 1 April 2004 736
Camilleri v Malta, no. 42931/10, 22 January 2013 . . . . .336, 338–40
Camp and Bourimi v Netherlands, no. 28369/95 ECHR 2000-X. 574
Campbell v United Kingdom, 25 March 1992, Series A no. 233. 401
Campbell and Cosans v United Kingdom, 25 February 1982, Series A no. 48 . . . . 421, 996,
998, 1000–1
Campbell and Cosans v United Kingdom, 25 February 1982, Partly Dissenting
Opinion of Judge Sir Vincent Evans, Series A no. 48. . . . . .1002, 1004, 1007
Campbell and Fell v United Kingdom, 28 June 1984, Series A no. 80. . . . . . 278–9, 282, 294, 621, 625
Campos Dâmaso v Portugal, no. 17107/05, 24 April 2008. 460
Can v Austria, 30 September 1985, Series A no. 96 784
Canea Catholic Church v Greece, 16 December 1997, *Reports of Judgments and
Decisions* 1998-VIII 1178
Cankoçak v Turkey, nos 25182/94 and 26956/95, 20 February 2001 108
Cantoni v France, 15 November 1996, *Reports of Judgments and Decisions* 1996-V 336, 338, 341
Capeau v Belgium, no. 42914/98, ECHR 2005-I 306
Capeau v Belgium (dec.), no. 42914/98, 6 April 2004 304
Capital Bank AD v Bulgaria, no. 49429/99, 24 November 2005 . . . . .368, 973
Capital Bank AD v Bulgaria, no. 49429/99, ECHR 2005-XII (extracts) 368, 971, 973
Capital Bank AD v Bulgaria (dec.), no. 49429/99, 9 September 2004. 736
Capuano v Italy, 25 June 1987, Series A no. 119. 790
Carabulea v Romania, no. 45661/99, 13 July 2010 123
Carbonara and Ventura v Italy, no. 24638/94, ECHR 2000-VI 368
Cardot v France, 19 March 1991, Series A no. 200 . . . . .766, 768
Carmuirea Spirituala a Musulmanilor din Republica Moldova v Moldova (dec.),
no. 12282/02, 14 June 2005 518
Carolla v Italy (revision), no. 51127/99, 28 November 2002 853
Carson and Others v United Kingdom, no. 42184/05, 4 November 2008. 575
Carson and Others v United Kingdom [GC], no. 42184/05, ECHR 2010 . . . . .572–3, 765
Carson and Others v United Kingdom [GC], no. 42184/05, Joint Dissenting Opinion of
Judges Tulkens, Vajić, Spielmann, Jaeger, Jočienė, and López Guerra, ECHR 2010. 573
C.A.S. and C.S. v Romania, no. 26692/05, 20 March 2012. . . . . .279**
Case 'relating to certain aspects of the laws on the use of languages in education in Belgium'
(preliminary objections), 9 February 1967, Series A no. 5. 88
Case 'relating to certain aspects of the laws on the use of languages in education in Belgium'
(merits), 23 July 1968, Series A no. 6. . . . . 34, 46, 74–6, 80, 159, 551, 562–3,
565–6, 579, 709, 957, 996–7, 999, 1174, 1178, 1182–3
Castells v Spain, 23 April 1992, Series A no. 236. . . . . .474, 769
Castillo Algar v Spain, 28 October 1998, *Reports of Judgments and Decisions* 1998-VIII. 296

Castravet v Moldova, no. 23393/05, 13 March 2007 250
Çatal v Turkey, no. 26808/08, 17 April 2012 255
Catan and Others v Republic of Moldova and Russia (dec.), nos 43370/04, 8252/05,
    18454/06, 15 June 2010 712
Catan and Others v Republic of Moldova and Russia [GC], nos 43370/04, 8252/05,
    18454/06, Partly Dissenting Opinion of Judge Kovler, ECHR 2012 (extracts) 1000
Catan and Others v Republic of Moldova and Russia [GC], nos 43370/04, 8252/05,
    18454/06, ECHR 2012 (extracts). 37, 65, 99, 103, 712, 996–7, 999–1000
C.B. v Romania (revision), no. 21207/03, 19 July 2011. 853
C.C. v Spain, no. 1425/06, 6 October 2009 383
CDI Holding Aktiengesellschaft and Others v Slovakia (dec.), no. 37398/97,
    18 October 2001. 736
Cebotari v Moldova, no. 35615/06, 13 November 2007 626
Çelik v Turkey (dec.), no. 52991/99, 23 September 2004 771
Çelik (Bozkurt) v Turkey, no. 34388/05, 12 April 2011. 304
Çelikkaya v Turkey, no. 34026/03, 1 June 2010 259
Celniku v Greece, no. 21449/04, 5 July 2007 . . . . .159, 776, 778
Cemalettin Canlı v Turkey, no. 22427/04, 18 November 2008 383
Cennet Ayhan and Mehmet Salih Ayhan v Turkey, no. 41964/98, 27 June 2006 765
Centre for Legal Resources on behalf of Valentin Câmpeanu v Romania [GC], no. 47848/08,
    17 July 2014. . . . . .739, 794–5
Centro Europa 7 S.R.L. and di Stefano v Italy [GC], no. 38433/09,
    ECHR 2012. . . . . 453, 466–7, 470, 973
Cernecki v Austria (dec.), no. 31061/96, 11 July 2000. 1158
Cernescu and Manolache v Romania (revision), no. 28607/04, 30 November 2010 853–4
Cerva Osorio de Moscoso and Others v Spain (dec.), nos 41127/98, 41503/98, 41717/98,
    and 45726/99, 28 October 1999 375
Çetin and Others v Turkey, nos 40153/98 and 40160/98, ECHR 2003-III (extracts) 455
Çetinkaya v Turkey, no. 75569/01, 27 June 2006 455
Ceyhan Demir and Others v Turkey, no. 34491/97, 13 January 2005 135
Ceylan v Turkey [GC], no. 23556/94, ECHR 1999-IV 475
C.G. and Others v Bulgaria, no. 1365/07, 24 April 2008 1130–1
C.G.P. v Netherlands (dec.), no. 29835/96, 15 January 1997. 309
Cha'are Shalom Ve Tsedek v France [GC], no. 27417/95, ECHR 2000-VII 427, 431, 563
Chabauty v France [GC], no. 57412/08, 4 October 2012 973
Chagos Islanders v United Kingdom (dec.), no. 35622/04, 11 December 2012 . . . . .97, 104, 923
Chahal v United Kingdom, 15 November 1996, *Reports of Judgments and Decisions*
    1996-V. 64, 94, 168, 195, 233–4, 243, 254, 257, 395, 794, 1128
Chalkley v United Kingdom (dec.), no. 63831/00, 26 September 2002. 772
Chapman v United Kingdom [GC], no. 27238/95, ECHR 2001-I 38, 40, 47, 379, 399, 582, 1004
Chappell v United Kingdom, 30 March 1989, Series A no 152-A 399
Chassagnou and Others v France [GC], nos 25088/94, 28331/95, and 28443/95,
    ECHR 1999-III 491, 502, 514, 524, 570, 573, 583, 811, 973, 1178
Chassagnou and Others v France [GC], nos 25088/94, 28331/95, and 28443/95,
    Dissenting Opinion of Judge Costa, ECHR 1999-III. 972
Chau v France (dec.), no. 39144/02, 14 June 2005 542
Chaudet v France, no. 49037/06, 29 October 2009. 274
Chauvy and Others v France, no. 64915/01, ECHR 2004-VI 385, 472, 480
Chbihi Loudoudi and Others v Belgium, no. 52265/10, 16 December 2014. 394
Cheilas v Greece (dec.), no. 9693/03, 12 May 2005. 770
Chelu v Romania, no. 40274/04, 12 January 2010 399
Cheminade v France (dec.), no. 31599/96, 19 January 1999 971
Chentiev and Ibragimov v Slovakia (dec.), nos 21022/08 and 51946/08,
    14 September 2010 . . . . .146, 1100
Chepelev v Russia, no. 58077/00, 26 July 2007. 1158

Chernitsyn v Russia, no. 5964/02, 6 April 2006 781
Chevrol v France, no. 49636/99, ECHR 2003-III 273
Chiragov v Armenia [GC] (dec.), no. 13216/05, 14 December 2011. .... 36, 89
Chorherr v Austria, 25 August 1993, Series A no. 266-B 262, 936–7
Chraidi v Germany, no. 65655/01, ECHR 2006-XII 251
Christian Democratic People's Party v Moldova, no. 28793/02, ECHR 2006-II 490–1, 496,
521, 1020
Christine Goodwin v United Kingdom [GC], no. 28957/95, ECHR 2002-VI............ 33, 39, 48,
370, 375, 380, 534, 536, 543, 837
Chumakov v Russia, no. 41794/04, 24 April 2012. 231
Church of Jesus Christ of Latter-Day Saints v United Kingdom, no. 7552/09,
4 March 2014. ....429, 550, 563
Church of Scientology Moscow v Russia, no. 18147/02, 5 April 2007............. 420–1, 425, 429,
491, 499–501, 511, 524
Church of Scientology of St. Petersburg and Others v Russia, no. 47191/06,
2 October 2014 429
Ciechońska v Poland, no. 19776/04, 14 June 2011. 132
C.I.G.L. and Cofferati v Italy, no. 46967/07, 24 February 2009...................... 769
Çiloğlu and Others v Turkey, no. 73333/01, 6 March 2007. ....41, 148, 497
Cioban v Romania (dec.), no. 18295/08, 11 March 2014. ....127, 137
Cipriani v Italy (dec.), no. 22142/07, 30 March 2010 1100
Cisse v France, no. 51346/99, ECHR 2002-III 495, 513
Ciubotaru v Moldova, no. 27138/04, 27 April 2010 .... 368, 375, 379, 404
Ciulla v Italy, 22 February 1989, Series A no. 148........................239, 258
Claes and Others v Belgium, nos 46825/99, 47132/99, 47502/99, 49010/99,
49104/99, 49195/99, and 49716/99, 2 June 2005 869
Clift v United Kingdom, no. 7205/07, 13 July 2010 .... 259, 564, 572–5, 583
Clinique Mozart SARL v France (dec.), no. 46098/99, 1 July 2003. 775
Clooth v Belgium, 12 December 1991, Series A no. 225 252
C.M. v France (dec.), no. 28078/95, ECHR 2001-VII. 974
C.N. v United Kingdom, no. 4239/08, 13 November 2012...................206–7, 210
C.N. and V. v France, no. 67724/09, 11 October 2012..................... 201, 207–9, 212, 279
Cobzaru v Romania, no. 48254/99, 26 July 2007 .... 41, 551, 553, 571
Coëme and Others v Belgium, nos 32492/96, 32547/96, 32548/96, 33209/96,
and 33210/96, ECHR 2000-VII 321, 334, 336, 338, 356
Colaço Mestre and SIC–Sociedade Independente de Comunicação, S.A. v Portugal,
nos 11182/03 and 11319/03, 26 April 2007. ....377, 462
Colibaba v Moldova, no. 29089/06, 23 October 2007. 747
Collette and Michael Hemsworth v United Kingdom, no. 58559/09, 16 July 2013 135
Colombani and Others v France, no. 51279/99, ECHR 2002-V. 458, 478
Colon v Netherlands (dec.), no. 49458/06, 15 May 2012. 386
Colozza v Italy, 12 February 1985, Series A no. 89 ....308, 316–7
Comak v Turkey (dec.), no. 225/02, 4 October 2005 323
Comingersoll S.A. v Portugal [GC], no. 35382/97, ECHR 2000-IV. 838
Communist Party of Turkey and Others v Turkey, 30 January 1998, *Reports of
Judgments and Decisions* 1998-I. 491
Cone v Romania, no. 35935/02, 24 June 2008 773
Čonka v Belgium, no. 51564/99, ECHR 2002-I 232, 243, 245–6, 1077–8
Čonka and Others, la Ligue des droits de l'homme v Belgium (dec.), no. 51564/99,
13 March 2001. 741
Connolly v United Kingdom (dec.), no. 27245/95, 26 June 1996. 308
Connors v United Kingdom, no. 66746/01, 27 May 2004. ....582, 1004
Constantin Florea v Romania, no. 21534/05, 19 June 2012. 304
Constantinescu v Romania, no. 28871/95, ECHR 2000-VIII. 744
Cooke v Austria, no. 25878/94, 8 February 2000 747

Cooperatieve Producentenorganisatie van de Nederlandse Kokkelvisserij U.A. v
   Netherlands (dec.), no. 13645/05, ECHR 2009 . . . . .97, 948
Cooperativa Agricola Slobozia-Hanesei v Moldova, no. 39745/02, 3 April 2007 90
Copland v United Kingdom, no. 62617/00, ECHR 2007-I 387
Cordova v Italy (no. 1), no. 40877/98, ECHR 2003-I 286–7
Cordova v Italy (no. 2), no. 45649/99, ECHR 2003-I (extracts) 286–7
Correia de Matos v Portugal (dec.), no. 48188/99, 15 November 2001, ECHR 2001-XII 281
Corsacov v Moldova, no. 18944/02, 4 April 2006 551
Coscodar v Romania (dec.), no. 36020/06, 9 March 2010 775
Ćosić v Croatia, no. 28261/06, 15 January 2009 . . . . .81, 400
Cossey v United Kingdom, 27 September 1990, Series A no. 184 . . . . 380, 533, 536, 575
Costa and Pavan v Italy, no. 54270/10, 28 August 2012 373
Costello-Roberts v United Kingdom, 25 March 1993, Series A no. 247-C 171, 189, 370
Cotleţ v Romania, no. 38565/97, 3 June 2003 . . . . .401, 747
C.R. v United Kingdom, 22 November 1995, Series A no. 335-C 330, 335
Craxi v Italy (no. 1), no. 34896/97, 5 December 2002 313
Craxi III v Italy (dec.), no. 63226/00, 14 June 2001 295
Creangă v Romania [GC], no. 29226/03, 23 February 2012 . . . . 123, 226–7, 231–2, 810
Croissant v Germany, 25 September 1992, Series A no. 237-B 311
Cruz Varas and Others v Sweden, 20 March 1991, Series A no. 201 . . . . .95, 685, 749
Csepyová v Slovakia (dec.), no. 67199/01, 14 May 2002 1135
Csiki v Romania, no. 11273/05, 5 July 2011 293
Csoszánszki v Sweden (dec.), no. 22318/02, 27 June 2006 348
Cudak v Lithuania [GC], no. 15869/02, ECHR 2010 . . . . 39, 41, 100, 274, 285
Cumhuriyetçi Eğitim Ve Kültür Merkezi Vakfı v Turkey, no. 32093/10,
   2 December 2014 . . . . .429, 440, 563
Cumpănă and Mazăre v Romania [GC], no. 33348/96, ECHR 2004-XI 455, 475–6, 845
Cuscani v United Kingdom, no. 32771/96, 24 September 2002 314
Custers and Others v Denmark, nos 11843/03, 11847/03, and 11849/03,
   3 May 2007 . . . . .334, 336, 338
Cyprus v Turkey [GC], no. 25781/94, ECHR 2001-IV 99, 102–3, 105, 131, 196, 400,
                                                    564, 695, 725, 728, 808–9, 811, 834, 973, 999
Cyprus v Turkey (just satisfaction) [GC], no. 25781/94, 12 May 2014 . . . . 42, 726, 834, 838, 867
Cyprus v Turkey (just satisfaction) [GC], no. 25781/94, Concurring Opinion of Judge
   Pinto de Albuquerque, Joined by Judge Vučinić, 12 May 2014 . . . . .68, 726, 839, 867
Cyprus v Turkey (just satisfaction) [GC], no. 25781/94, Partly Concurring and Partly
   Dissenting Opinion of Judge Casadevall, 12 May 2014 . . . . .726, 834
Cyprus v Turkey (just satisfaction) [GC], no. 25781/94, Partly Concurring Opinion
   of Judges Tulkens, Vajić, Raimondi, and Bianku, Joined by Judge Karakaş,
   12 May 2014 . . . . .867, 872
Cyprus v Turkey (just satisfaction) [GC], no. 25781/94, ECHR 2001-IV 867
Czekalla v Portugal, no. 38830/97, ECHR 2002-VIII 311
D. v Ireland (dec.), no. 26499/02, 28 June 2006 769
D. v United Kingdom, 2 May 1997, *Reports of Judgments and Decisions* 1997-III 172
Da Luz Domingues Ferriera v Belgium (dec.), no. 50049/99, 6 July 2006 1149
Dacosta Silva v Spain, no. 69966/01, ECHR 2006-XIII .227, 261, 935–6
Dadouch v Malta, no. 38816/07, 20 July 2010 . . . . .366–7, 376
Dahlab v Switzerland (dec.), no. 42393/98, ECHR 2001-V 426, 437
Daktaras v Lithuania, no. 42095/98, ECHR 2000-X 303
Dalban v Romania [GC], no. 28114/95, ECHR 1999-VI .740, 744, 798
Dalia v France, 19 February 1998, *Reports of Judgments and Decisions* 1998-I 765–6
Dallos v Hungary, no, 29082/95, 1 March 2001 310
Damayev v Russia, no. 36150/04, 29 May 2012 171
Damian-Burueana and Damian v Romania, no. 6773/02, 26 May 2009 258
Damir Sibgatullin v Russia, no. 1413/05, 24 April 2012 813–4

Damir Sibgatullin v Russia (revision), no. 1413/05, 28 May 2014. 853–4
Damjanac v Croatia, no. 52943/10, 24 October 2013 . . . . 35, 94
Dammann v Switzerland, no. 77551/01, 25 April 2006. 452
D'Ammassa and Frezza v Italy (revision), no. 44513/98, 9 January 2003. 853
Danderyds Kommun v Sweden (dec.), no. 52559199, 7 June 2001 .90, 737
Danev v Bulgaria, no. 9411/05, 2 September 2010 259
Davydov v Estonia (dec.), no. 16387/03, 31 May 2005 1077
Davydov and Others v Ukraine, nos 17674/02 and 39081/02, 1 July 2010. . . . . .809, 812–4
D.D. v France (striking out), no. 3/02, 8 November 2005 798
D.D. v Lithuania, no. 13469/06, 14 February 2012. 228
De Cubber v Belgium, 26 October 1984, Series A no. 86. 296
De Bruin v Netherlands (dec.), no. 9765/09, 17 September 2013. . . . . .272–3, 279
De Diego Nafría v Spain, no. 46833/99, 14 March 2002, no. 4063/04, 19 February 2009 465
De Geouffre de la Pradelle v France, 16 December 1992, Series A no. 253-B. 551
De Haes and Gijsels v Belgium, 24 February 1997, *Reports of Judgments and Decisions*
   1997-I 456, 458
De Jong, Baljet, and Van den Brink v Netherlands, 22 May 1984, Series A no. 77 247–9
De Jorio v Italy, no. 73936/01, 3 June 2004. 287
De Luca v Italy (revision), no. 43870/04, 8 July 2014 854
De Moor v Belgium, 23 June 1994, Series A no. 292-A. 273
De Pace v Italy, no. 22728/03, 17 July 2008. 778
De Souza Ribeiro v France, no. 22689/07, 30 June 2011. 741
De Souza Ribeiro v France [GC], no. 22689/07, ECHR 2012 76
De Wilde, Ooms and Versyp v Belgium, 18 June 1971, Series A no. 12 . . . . 27, 80, 141, 226–8,
                                                         235, 243, 255–6, 706, 719–20, 767
De Wilde, Ooms and Versyp v Belgium (article 50), 10 March 1972, Separate Opinion
   of Judge Mosler, Series A no. 14. 42
Debelianovi v Bulgaria, no. 61951/00, 29 March 2007 976
Decision on the competence of the Court to Give an Advisory Opinion [GC]
   ECHR 2004-VI 876, 879–80, 882, 884
Dedovskiy and Others v Russia, no. 7178/03, ECHR 2008 (extracts) 169, 175, 177–8, 189
Deés v Hungary, no. 2345/06, 9 November 2010. 388
Del Giudice v Italy (dec.), no. 42351/98, 6 July 1999 302
Del Latte v Netherlands, no. 44760/98, 9 November 2004 304
Del Río Prada v Spain, no. 42750/09, 10 July 2012. . . . . .338–40, 346, 349
Del Río Prada v Spain [GC], no. 42750/09, 21 October 2013 . . . . .334, 339, 346, 348
Del Río Prada v Spain [GC], no. 42750/09, Concurring Opinion of Judge Nicolaov,
   21 October 2013. 339
Del Río Prada v Spain [GC], no. 42750/09, Joint Partly Dissenting Opinion of
   Judges Mahoney and Vehabović, 21 October 2013 348
Delbos and Others v France (dec.), no. 60819/00, ECHR 2004-IX 339
Delcourt v Belgium, 17 January 1970, Series A no. 11. . . . . .288, 294
Demades v Turkey (just satisfaction), no. 16219/90, 22 April 2008 108
Demicoli v Malta, 27 August 1991, Series A no. 210. . . . . .278, 283
Demir and Baykara v Turkey [GC], no. 34503/97, ECHR 2008 . . . . .39–41, 54–5, 65, 179,
                                                         493, 505–9, 522–4, 1045
Demir and Others v Turkey, 23 September 1998, *Reports of Judgments and Decisions*
   1998-VI 600
Demir and Others v Turkey, 23 September 1998, Concurring Opinion of Judge
   De Meyer, *Reports of Judgments and Decisions* 1998-VI. 600
Demiroğlu and Others v Turkey (dec.), no. 56125/10, 4 June 2013. . . . . .641, 769
Demopoulos and Others v Turkey (dec.) [GC], nos 46113/99, 3843/02, 13751/02, 13466/03,
   10200/04, 14163/04, 19993/04, and 21819/04, ECHR 2010. . . . . 76, 769, 779, 791, 859
Demuth v Switzerland, no. 38743/97, ECHR 2002-IX 466–7
Denisov v Russia (dec.), no. 33408/03, 6 May 2004 770–1

Denisova and Moiseyeva v Russia, no. 16903/03, 1 April 2010. 976
Denizci and Others v Cyprus, nos 25316–25321/94, and 27207/95, ECHR 2001-V. 1059, 1072
Denmark v Turkey (dec.), no. 34382/97, 8 June 1999. 727–8
Denmark v Turkey (friendly settlement), no. 34382/97, ECHR 2000-IV 726, 820
Dennis and Others v United Kingdom (dec.), no. 76573/01, 2 July 2002. . . . . .770, 772
Depa v Poland, no. 62324/00, 12 December 2006 255
Depalle v France [GC], no. 34044/02, ECHR 2010 971
Deperrois v France (dec.), no. 48203/99, 22 June 2000 1138
Dereci v Turkey, no. 77845/01, 24 May 2005 251
Des Fours Walderode v Czech Republic (dec.), no. 40057/98, ECHR 2004-V 697, 702, 708, 849
Deumeland v Germany, 29 May 1986, Series A no. 100 63
Deweer v Belgium, 27 February 1980, Series A no. 35. . . . . 277, 286, 293, 298, 307–8
D.G. v Ireland, no. 39474/98, ECHR 2002-III 240
D.H. and Others v Czech Republic [GC], no. 57325/00, ECHR 2007-IV 40–1, 564, 566,
568–70, 572, 575, 578, 582, 714, 764, 793,
848, 1004
Di Giorgio and Others v Italy (dec.), no. 35808/03, 29 September 2009. 770
Di Giovine v Portugal (dec.), no. 39912/98, 31 August 1999. 641
Di Mauro v Italy [GC], no. 34256/96, ECHR 1999-V 77
Di Salvo v Italy (dec.), no. 16098/05, 11 January 2007 781
Di Sarno and Others v Italy, no. 30765/08, 10 January 2012. 388
Diacenco v Romania, no. 124/04, 7 February 2012. 304–5
Diallo v Sweden (dec.), no. 13205/07, 5 January 2010. 314–5
Diamante and Pelliccioni v San Marino, no. 32250/08, 27 September 2011 . . . . .1056, 1060–4
Dickson v United Kingdom, no. 44362/04, ECHR 2007-V. 183, 275, 368, 372, 389, 534,
539–540, 848
Dickson v United Kingdom [GC], no. 44362/04, Concurring Opinion of Judge Bratza,
ECHR 2007-V 692
Dicle for the Democracy Party (DEP) v Turkey, no. 25141/94, 10 December 2002 520
Diennet v France, 26 September 1995, Series A no. 325-A. 289–90, 295
Dikme v Turkey, no. 20869/92, ECHR 2000-VIII 27, 175, 179, 246
Dimcho Dimov v Bulgaria, no. 57123/08, 16 December 2014. 748
Dimitras and Others v Greece, nos 42837/06, 3237/07, 3269/07, 35793/07, and 6099/08,
3 June 2010 428
Dimov and Others v Bulgaria, no. 30086/05, 6 November 2012 152
Dinç v Turkey (dec.), no. 4243798, 22 November 2001 775
Dink v Turkey, nos 2668/07, 6102/08, 30079/08, 7072/09, and 7124/09,
14 September 2010 . . . . .453, 471, 707
Dirdizov v Russia, no. 41461/10, 27 November 2012 552
Direkçi and Direkçi v Turkey (dec.), no. 47826/99, 3 October 2006 73
D.J. v Croatia, no. 42418/10, 24 July 2012. 855
D.J. and A.-K.R. v Romania (dec.), no. 34175/05, 20 October 2009 745
Djavit An v Turkey, no. 20652/92, ECHR 2003-III .491–2, 494–7, 510
Djelani Sufi Hassan Guduud and Others v Netherlands and Greece (dec.), no. 28631/09,
20 September 2011 795
Djokaba Lambi Longa v Netherlands (dec.), no. 33917/12, 9 October 2012. . . . . 94, 98–9, 394, 640
Djundiks v Latvia, no. 14920/05, 15 April 2014 242
Dmitrijevs v Latvia, no. 49037/09, 16 December 2014 174
D.M.T. and D.K.I. v Bulgaria, no. 29476/06, 24 July 2012. . . . . .293, 308, 374–5
D.N. v Switzerland [GC], no. 27154/95, ECHR 2001-III 255
Dobbertin v France, 25 February 1993, Series A no. 256-D 791
Dobriyeva and Others v Russia, no. 18407/10, 19 December 2013. 134
Dodov v Bulgaria, no. 59548/00, 17 January 2008 . . . . .131, 138
Dogru v France, no. 27058/05, 4 December 2008. 423
Doinov v Bulgaria (dec.), no. 68358/01 3 November 2005 355

Domalewski v Poland (dec.), no. 34610/97, ECHR 1999-V 971
Dombo Beheer B.V. v Netherlands, 27 October 1993, Series A no. 274 287–8
Donaldson v United Kingdom (dec.), no. 56975/09, 25 January 2011 . . . . .472, 475, 480
Doorson v Netherlands, 26 March 1996, *Reports of Judgments and Decisions* 1996-II 288, 313
Dorca v Romania (dec.), no. 59651/13, 15 April 2014 1158
Đorđevic v Croatia, no. 41526/10, ECHR 2012 . . . . .76, 172, 192, 563
Döring v Germany (dec.), no. 37595/97, 9 November 1999 . . . . .971, 976
Doronin v Ukraine, no. 16505/02, 19 February 2009 231
Dörr v Germany (dec.), no. 2894/08, 22 January 2013 236
Döry v Sweden, no. 28394/95, 12 November 2002 289
Döşemealtı Belediyesi v Turkey (dec.), no. 50108/06, 23 March 2010 . . . . .90, 737
Douglas-Williams v United Kingdom (dec.), no. 56413/00, 8 January 2002 135
Dougoz v Greece, no. 40907/98, ECHR 2001-II 184
Douiyeb v Netherlands [GC] no. 31464/96, 4 August 1999 . . . . .231, 254
Doyle v United Kingdom (dec.), no. 30158/06, 6 February 2007 1027
D.P. and J.C. v United Kingdom, no. 38719/97, 10 October 2002 370
Dragostea Copiilor–Petrovschi–Nagornii v Moldova, no. 25575/08, 13 September 2011 72
Draon v France [GC], no. 1513/03, 6 October 2005 971
Dragotoniu and Militaru-Pidhorni v Romania, nos 77193/01 and 77196/01,
    24 May 2007 . . . . .335, 339, 341
Drassich v Italy, no. 25575/04, 11 December 2007 308
Drijfhout v Netherlands (dec.), no. 51721/09, 22 February 2011 780
Dritsas v Italy (dec.), no. 2344/02, 1 February 2011 1077
Driza v Albania, no. 33771/02, ECHR 2007-V (extracts) 72
Drozd and Janousek v France and Spain, 26 June 1992, Series A no. 240 . . . . . . .95–6, 101, 103, 235,
                                                                                        282, 1099
Dubjakova v Slovakia (dec.), no. 67299/01, 19 October 2004 744
Dudgeon v United Kingdom, 22 October 1981, Series A no. 45 . . . . .38, 182, 279, 380–1,
                                                                            406–7, 438, 513, 524, 743, 1064
Dudgeon v United Kingdom, 22 October 1981, Dissenting Opinion of Judge Matscher,
    Series A no. 45 781
Duinhof and Duijf v Netherlands, 22 May 1984, Series A no. 79 249
Dumitru Popescu v Romania (no. 2), no. 71525/01, 26 April 2007 400
Dunn and Others v United Kingdom (dec.), no. 566/10, 13 May 2014 1026
Dupuis and Others v France, no. 1914/02, ECHR 2007-VII 460
Đurđević v Croatia, no. 52442/09, ECHR 2011 (extracts) 169, 189, 193, 370
Duringer and Grunge v France (dec.), nos 61164/00 and 18589/02, ECHR 2003-II 780
Durmaz and Others v Turkey (dec.), nos 46506/99, 46569/99, 46570/99, and 46939/99,
    4 September 2001 999
Duško Ivanovski v former Yugoslav Republic of Macedonia, no. 10718/05, 24 April 2014 288
Duveau v France (striking out), no. 77403/01, 26 April 2005 798
Dzhabrailov v Russia, nos 8620/99, 11674/09, 16488/09, 21133/09, 36354/09,
    47770/09, 54728/09, 25511/10, and 3279/10, 27 February 2014 136
Dzhaksybergenov v Ukraine, no. 12343/10, 10 February 2011 1064
E. v Ireland (friendly settlement), no. 42734/09, 1 October 2013 820
E. v Norway, 29 August 1990, Series A no. 181-A 46, 256–7
E. and Others v United Kingdom, no. 33218/96, 26 November 2002 191
E.B. v France [GC], no. 43546/02, 22 January 2008 . . . . .389, 394, 562, 584
Eberhard and M. v Slovenia, no. 8673/05, and 9733/05, 1 December 2009 764
Eckle v Germany, 15 July 1982, Series A no. 51 . . . . .292–3, 744
Editions Périscope v France, 26 March 1992, Series A no. 234-B 272
Editions Plon v France, no. 58148/00, ECHR 2004-IV 461, 476
Editorial Board of Pavoye Delo and Shtekel v Ukraine, no. 33014/05, ECHR 2011
    (extracts) 453, 455, 462, 470, 477
Edwards v Malta, no. 17647/04, 24 October 2006 979–80

Edwards v United Kingdom (dec.), no. 46477/99, 7 June 2001 ....770, 772
Edwards v United Kingdom, 16 December 1992, Series A no. 247-B 310, 807
Edwards and Lewis v United Kingdom [GC], nos 39647/98 and 40461/98, ECHR 2004-X 310
Eerikäinen and Others v Finland, no. 3514/02, 10 February 2009 ....458, 460, 469
Efstratiou v Greece, 18 December 1996, *Reports of Judgments and Decisions* 1996-VI 1004
E.G. v Poland and 175 Other Bug River Applications (dec.), no. 50425/99,
    23 September 2008... 641
Egeland and Hanseid v Norway, no. 34438/04, 16 April 2009.................377–8, 461
Eğitim ve Bilim Emekçileri Sendikası v Turkey, no. 20641/05, 25 September 2012........455–6, 499
E.H.I and Others v Austria, 23 April 1987, Series A no. 117 323
Ehrmann and SCI VHI v France (dec.), no. 2777/10, 7 June 2011...............472, 1150
Einhorn v France (dec.), no. 71555/01, ECHR 2001-XI 146, 195, 316, 1100
Eisenstecken v Austria, no. 29477/95, ECHR 2000-X 323, 935–6
E.K. v Turkey, no. 28496/95, 7 February 2002...................... 336
Ekbatani v Sweden, 26 May 1988, Series A no. 134.................317, 1135
Ekşi and Ocak v Turkey, no. 44920/04, 23 February 2010 516
E.L., R.L. and J.O.-L. v Switzerland, 29 August 1997, *Reports of Judgments and Decisions*
    1997-V... 280
El Majjaoui and Stichting Touba Moskee v Netherlands (striking out) [GC], no. 25525/03,
    20 December 2007 ....798, 801
El Majjaoui and Stichting Touba Moskee v Netherlands (striking out) [GC], no. 25525/03,
    Joint Dissenting Opinion of Judges Zupančič, Zagrebelsky, and Myjer,
    20 December 2004 434
El Masri v 'former Yugoslav Republic of Macedonia' [GC], no. 39630/09,
    13 December 2012 ....137–8, 771
El Masri v 'former Yugoslav Republic of Macedonia' [GC], no. 39630/09,
    ECHR 2012............................78, 96, 137–8, 552, 771, 807, 810–1, 837, 901
El Masri v 'former Yugoslav Republic of Macedonia' [GC], no. 39630/09, Joint concurring
    Opinion of Judges Tulkens, Speilmann, Sicilianos, and Keller, ECHR 2012 139
El Morsli v France (dec.), no. 15585/06, 4 March 2008...................... 439
Elci and Others v Turkey, nos 23145 and 25091/94, 13 November 2003................. 238
Elia S.r.l. v Italy, no. 37710/97, ECHR 2001-IX.............................. 974
Elli Poluhas Dödsbo v Sweden, no. 61564/00, ECHR 2006-I 367, 382
Elsholz v Germany [GC], no. 25735/94, ECHR 2000-VIII......................392, 838
E.M.B. v Romania (dec.), no. 4488/03, 28 September 2010.................... 1059
E.M.B. v Romania, no. 4488/03, 13 November 2012 1057
Emonet and Others v Switzerland, no. 39051/03, 13 December 2007 38
Enea v Italy [GC], no. 74912/01, ECHR 2009 .... 169, 171–2, 184, 186, 272, 275, 283,
                                                                   285, 398, 404
Enerji Yapı-Yol Sen v Turkey, no. 68959/01, 21 April 2009.......................508, 522
Engel and Others v Netherlands, 8 June 1976, Series A no. 22.........71, 80, 226–7, 234, 237,
                                                      277–9, 282, 472, 573, 1056–7, 1138–9, 1151–2
Engel and Others v Netherlands (Article 50), 23 November 1976, Series A no. 22............... 235
Englert v Germany, 25 August 1987, Series A no. 123-B 299, 304, 306
Enhorn v Sweden, no. 56529/00, ECHR 2005-I..........................232–3, 241
Enukidze and Girgvliani v Georgia, no. 25091/07, 26 April 2011....................747, 813–4
Eon v France, no. 26118/10, 14 March 2013 784
Epistatu v Romania, no. 29343/10, 24 September 2013........................... 999
Epözdemir v Turkey (dec.), no. 57039/00, 31 January 2002 766
Epple v Germany, no. 77909/01, 24 March 2005 236–7
Er and Others v Turkey, no. 23016/04, 31 July 2012 137
Erçep v Turkey, no. 43965/04, 22 November 2011...................436, 471, 512
Erdagöz v Turkey, 22 October 1997, *Reports of Judgments and Decisions* 1997-VI.............. 238
Erdoğan and Fırat v Turkey (revision), nos 15121/03 and 15127/03, 20 July 2010 853
Erdoğan and Others v Turkey, no. 19807/92, 25 April 2006 ....129, 151

Eremia v Republic of Moldova, no. 3564/11, 28 May 2013 198
Eren and Others v Turkey (dec.), no. 42428/98, 4 July 2002 773
Ergi v Yurkey, 28 July 1998, *Reports of Judgments and Decisions* 1998-IV 134, 147, 153, 747
Ergin v Turkey (no. 6), no. 47533/99, ECHR 2006-VI (extracts) 43
Erikson v Italy (dec.), no. 37900/97, 26 October 1999 131
Eriksson v Sweden, 22 June 1989, Series A no. 156 . . . . .391–2, 1000
Erkalo v Netherlands, 2 September 1998, *Reports of Judgments and Decisions* 1998-VI 230–1, 234
Erkner and Hofauer v Austria, 23 April 1987, Series A no. 117 974
Erkol v Turkey, no. 50172/06, 19 April 2011 304
Ernst and Others v Belgium, no. 33400/96, 15 July 2003 892
Ertan and Others v Turkey (dec.), no. 57898/00, 21 March 2006 518
E.S. v Sweden, no. 5786/08, 21 June 2012 . . . . 82, 368, 370, 377, 764
Escoubet v Belgium [GC], no. 26780/95, ECHR 1999-VII 283
Esmukhambetov and Others v Russia, no. 23445/03, 29 March 2011 . . . . .156, 158, 170
Estamirov and Others v Russia, no. 60272/00, 12 October 2006 137
Eugenia Lazăr v Romania, no. 32146/05, 16 February 2010 131
Eurofinacom v France (dec.), no. 58753/00, ECHR 2004-VII (extracts) 339
Éva Molár v Hungary, no. 10346/05, 7 October 2008 . . . . .497–8, 516
Evaldsson and Others v Sweden (dec.), no. 75252/01, 28 March 2006 . . . . .38, 776
Evans v United Kingdom [GC], no. 6339/05, ECHR 2007-I 82, 124, 368, 372, 374, 389, 848
Eweida and Others v United Kingdom, no. 48420/10, ECHR 2013 (extracts) 82, 420, 422,
    427, 431, 439, 569, 574, 584
Eweida and Others v United Kingdom, no. 48420/10, Joint Partly Dissenting Opinion of Judges
    Bratza and Davíd Thór Björgvinsson, ECHR 2013 (extracts) 434
Eweida and Others v United Kingdom, no. 48420/10, Joint Partly Dissenting Opinion of
    Judges Vučinić and De Gaetano, ECHR 2013 (extracts) 420, 424
Ezeh and Connors v United Kingdom [GC], nos 39665/98 and 40086/98,
    ECHR 2003-X 275, 277–9, 283, 1152
Ezelin v France, 26 April 1991, Series A no. 202 . . . . .457, 491, 509
F. v Switzerland, 18 December 1987, Series A no. 128 . . . . .533–4, 541–2
F. Santos, Lda. and Fachadas v Portugal (dec.), no. 49020/99, ECHR 2000-X 741
Fáber v Hungary, no. 40721/08, 24 July 2012 455
Fabris v France (just satisfaction – striking out) [GC], no. 16574/08, 28 June 2013 822
Fabris v France [GC], no. 16574/08, ECHR 2013 (extracts) 574, 968, 970
Fabris v France [GC], no. 16574/08, Concurring Opinion of Judge Pinto de
    Albuquerque, ECHR 2013 (extracts) 50, 65, 89
Fadeyeva v Russia, no. 55723/00, ECHR 2005-IV 388, 812
Fägerskiöld v Sweden (dec.), no. 37664/04, 26 February 2008 387
Fairfield v United Kingdom (dec.), no. 24790/04, ECHR 2005-VI 738, 739
Fakiridou and Schina v Greece, no. 6789/06, 14 November 2008 837
Falcão dos Santos v Portugal, no. 50002/08, 3 July 2012 311
Falk v Netherlands (dec.), no. 66273/01, 19 October 2004 300
Falkner v Austria (dec.), no. 6072/02, 30 September 2004 1149
Falkovych v Ukraine (dec.), no. 64200/00, 29 June 2004 262
Falter Zeitschriften GmbH v Austria (no. 2), no. 3084/07, 18 September 2012 460
Family H. v United Kingdom, no. 10233/83, 6 March 1984 1002
Farbtuhs v Latvia, no. 4672/02, 2 December 2004 186
Farhad Aliyev v Azerbaijan, no. 37138/06, 9 November 2010 227
Fatullayev v Azerbaijan, no. 40984/07, 22 April 2010 . . . . 452, 458, 474, 480, 619
Fayed v United Kingdom, 21 September 1994, Series A no. 294-B 273
Fazilet Partisi and Kutan v Turkey (striking out), no. 1444/02, 27 April 2006 800
Fazliyski v Bulgaria, no. 40908/05, 16 April 2013 290
F.C.B. v Italy, 28 August 1991, Series A no. 208-B 307, 316
Federación Nacionalista Canaria v Spain (dec.), no. 56618/00, 7 June 2001 . . . . .1021, 1023
Fédération chrétienne des témoins de Jéhovah de France v France (dec.), no. 53430/99,
    6 November 2011 742–3

Fedorchenko and Lozenko v Ukraine, no. 387/03, 20 September 2012 159–60
Fedorov and Fedorova v Russia, no. 31008/02, 13 October 2005 1058
Fedorova and Others v Latvia (dec.), no. 69405/01, 9 October 2003 1072
Fedotov v Russia, no. 5140/02, 25 October 2005 258
Fedotova v Russia, no. 73225/01, 13 April 2006 747–8
Fehér and Dolnik v Slovakia (dec.), nos 14927/12 and 30415/12, 21 May 2013 . . . . .379, 1192
Feldbrugge v Netherlands, 29 May 1986, Series A no. 99. 274
Feldek v Slovakia, no. 29032/95, ECHR 2001-VIII. 477, 793
Féret v Belgium, no. 15615/07, 16 July 2009 . . . . .479, 618
Féret v Belgium, no. 15615/07, Opinion dissidente du Juge Andràs Sajó laquelle declarant
    se rallier les Juges Vladimiro Zagrebelsky et Nona Tsotsoria, 16 July 2009 618
Fernández Martínez v Spain, no. 56030/07, 15 May 2012 . . . . .368, 374–5, 430
Fernández Martínez v Spain [GC], no. 56030/07, 12 June 2014 374
Fernie v United Kingdom (dec.), no. 14881/04, 5 January 2006. 771–2
Ferrantelli and Santangelo v Italy, 7 August 1996, *Reports of Judgments and Decisions*
    1996-III 295–6
Ferrazzini v Italy [GC], no. 44759/98, ECHR 2001-VII 274, 276
Fey v Austria, 24 February 1993, Series A no. 255. . . . . .295, 791
FEYA, MPP and Others v Ukraine, no. 27617/06 and 126 other applications,
    21 February 2013 702
F.G. v Sweden, no. 43611/11, 16 January 2014 127
F.H. v Sweden, no. 32621/06, 20 January 2009 146
Fidan v Turkey (dec.), no. 24209/94, 29 February 2000 742
Financial Times Ltd and Others v United Kingdom, no. 821/03, 15 December 2009 459
Finger v Bulgaria, no. 37346/05, 10 May 2011 784
Findlay v United Kingdom, 25 February 1997, *Reports of Judgments and Decisions* 1997-I. . . .289, 293–4
Finogenov and Others v Russia, nos 18299/03 and 27311/03, ECHR 2011
    (extracts). 78, 130, 135, 147–8
Firth and Others v United Kingdom, nos 7784/09, 47806/09, 47812/09, 47818/09, 47829/09,
    49001/09, 49007/09, 49018/09, 49033/09, and 49036/09, Dissenting Opinion of
    Judge Wojtyczek, 12 August 2014 . . . . .66, 68–70
Fischer v Austria, 26 April 1995, Series A no. 312 . . . . .323, 935
Fischer v Austria, 26 April 1995, Separate Opinion of Judge Martens, Series A no. 312 323
Fitzmartin and Others v United Kingdom (dec.), no. 34953/97, 21 January 2003 745
Fjodorova and Others v Latvia (dec.), no. 69405/01, 6 April 2006 745
Flinkkilä and Others v Finland, no. 25576/04, 6 April 2010 378
Floriou v Romania (dec.), no. 15303/10, 12 March 2013. 214
Flux v Moldova (no. 2) no. 31001/03, 3 July 2007 295
Fogarty v United Kingdom [GC], no. 37112/97, ECHR 2001-XI (extracts) 39, 100, 286–7
Foka v Turkey, no. 28940/90, 24 June 2008. . . . . .227, 238
Földes and Földesné Hajlik v Hungary, no. 41463/02, ECHR 2006-XII. 1061, 1064
Foley v United Kingdom, no. 39197/98, 22 October 2002 293
Folgerø and Others v Norway (dec.), 15472/02, 14 February 2006. . . . . .774, 776
Folgerø and Others v Norway [GC], no. 15472/02, ECHR 2007-III 33, 380, 433, 1000, 1002–3
Fonyódi v Hungary (revision), no. 30799/04, 7 April 2009 853
Former King of Greece and Others v Greece [GC], no. 25701/94, ECHR 2000-XII 972
Forte v Italy, no. 77986/01, 10 November 2005 1060
Foti and Others v Italy, 10 December 1982, Series A no. 56 109
Foucher v France, 18 March 1997, *Reports of Judgments and Decisions* 1997-II. 309
Fox, Campbell and Hartley v United Kingdom, 30 August 1990, Series A no. 182 . . . . .238, 245–6
Francesco Sessa v Italy, no. 28790/08, ECHR 2012 (extracts). 426, 432, 437
Francesco Sessa v Italy, no. 28790/08, Joint Dissenting Opinion of Judges Tulkens, Popović
    and Keller, ECHR 2012 (extracts) 440, 569
Franz Fischer v Austria no. 37950/97, 29 May 2001 1153
Franz Hofstädter v Austria (dec.), no. 25407/94, 12 September 2000 772

Frasik v Poland, no. 22933/02, ECHR 2010 (extracts). 257, 533–4, 538–40
Frăsilă and Ciocîrlan v Romania, no. 25329/03, 10 May 2012 454
Fredin v Sweden (no. 2), 23 February 1994, Series A no. 283-A. 289
Freedom and Democracy Party (ÖZDEP) v Turkey [GC], no. 23885/94, ECHR
   1999-VIII. 491, 521, 620
Frerot v France, no. 70204/01, 12 June 2007 401
Fressoz and Roire v France [GC], no. 29183/95, ECHR 1999-I. 469, 764, 769
Fretté v France, no. 36515/97, ECHR 2002-I. 394
Frodl v Austria, no. 20201/04, 8 April 2010 . . . . .1023, 1028
Frydlender v France [GC], no. 30979/96, ECHR 2000-VII 292
Fuentes Bobo v Spain, no. 39293/98, 27 February 2000 . . . . .368, 453, 477
Funke v France, 25 February 1993, Series A no. 256-A 301, 386
Furdik v Slovakia (dec.), no. 42994/05, 2 December 2008. . . . . .132, 137
Fușcă v Romania, no. 34630/07, 13 July 2010 391
G. v Germany, no. 65210/99, 7 June 2012. . . . . .592, 828
G. v United Kingdom (dec.), no. 37334/08, 30 August 2011. . . . . .279, 300
Gäfgen v Germany [GC], no. 22978/05, ECHR 2010. . . . . 168, 180, 194, 744, 848
Gäfgen v Germany [GC], no. 22978/05, Joint Partly Concurring Opinion of Judges Tulkens,
   Ziemele, and Bianku, ECHR 2010. 78
Gagiu v Romania, no. 63258/00, 24 February 2009 . . . . .133, 401, 748
Gagliano Giorgi v Italy, no. 23563/07, ECHR 2012 (extracts) 783
Gajić v Germany (dec.), no. 31446/02, 28 August 2007 107
Galev and Others v Bulgaria (dec.), no. 18324/04, 29 December 2009 388
Galić v Netherlands (dec.), no. 22617/07, 9 June 2009 . . . . .98–9, 106, 705
Gallo v Italy (dec.), no. 24406/03, 7 July 2009 778
Galstyan v Armenia, no. 26986/03, 15 November 2007. . . . . 235, 308–9, 491–2, 495–6, 498,
                                                           512, 514, 771–2, 1135, 1137–8, 1140, 1151
Ganea v Moldova, no. 2474/06, 17 May 2011 258
Gani v Spain, no. 61800/08, 19 February 2013. 312–3
Garabayev v Russia, no. 38411/02, 7 June 2007 230
Garaudy v France (dec.), no. 65831/01, ECHR 2003-IX 480, 615, 617, 619
Garcia Alva v Germany, no. 23541/94, 13 February 2001 255
Garcia Mateos v Spain, no. 38285/09, 19 February 2013. 322
García Ruiz v Spain [GC], no. 30544/96, ECHR 1999-I. 78, 640
Gardean and S.C. Grup qs SA v Romania (revision), no. 25787/04, 30 April 2013 854
Gardel v France, no. 16428/05, ECHR 2009 . . . . .348, 384
Garretta v France (dec.) no. 2529/04, 4 March 2008 1153
Garycki v Poland, no. 14348/02, 6 February 2007. . . . . .251, 302
Gasiņš v Latvia, no. 69458/01, 19 April 2011 245
Gąsior v Poland, no. 34472/07, 21 February 2012. 476
Gąsior v Poland, no. 34472/07, Dissenting Opinion of Judge David Thór Björgvinsson,
   21 February 2012 455
Gaskin v United Kingdom, 7 July 1989, Series A no. 160 .376, 457
Gasparini v Italy and Belgium (dec.), no. 10750/03, 12 May 2009 95
Gasparyan v Armenia (no. 2), no. 22571/05, 16 June 2009 1137
Gasus Dosier- und Fördertechnik GmbH v Netherlands, 23 February 1995, Series
   A no. 306-B 791, 970, 974
Gatt v Malta, no. 28221/08, ECHR 2010. 236–7
Gauthier v France (dec.), no. 61178/00, 24 June 2003. 1153
Gautrin and Others v France, 20 May 1998, *Reports of Judgments and Decisions*
   1998-III 295
Gawęda v Poland, no. 26229/95, ECHR 2002-II 458
Gaygusuz v Austria, 16 September 1996, *Reports of Judgments and Decisions*
   1996-IV 567, 574, 581, 1178
G.B. v Switzerland, no. 27426/95, 30 November 2000 257

G.C.P. v Romania, no. 20899/03, 20 December 2011 . . . . .281, 298, 302–3

Gebremedhin [Gaberamadhien] v France, no. 25389/05, ECHR 2007-II 234, 243–4, 741

Geerings v Netherlands, no. 30810/03, 1 March 2007 304

Gelfmann v France, no. 25875/03, 14 December 2004 . . . . .174, 185

Gençel v Turkey, no. 53431, 23 October 2003 869

Genovese v Italy (dec.), no. 24407/03, 10 November 2009 778

Gentilhomme and Others v France, nos 48205/99, 48207/99, and 48209/99,
14 May 2002 . . . . .92, 101

Georgel and Georgeta Stoicescu v Romania, no. 9718/03, 26 July 2011 370

Georgia v Russia (I) [GC], no. 13255/07, 3 July 2004 . . . . .641, 728, 809–12, 814, 829, 1077–9

Georgia v Russia (I) [GC], no. 13255/07, Partly Dissenting Opinion of Judge López
Guerra, Joined by Judges Bratza and Kalaydjieva, 3 July 2004 254

Georgia v Russia (I) [GC], no. 13255/07, Partly Dissenting Opinion of Judge Tsotsoria,
3 July 2014 . . . . .44, 626–7

Georgia v Russia (I) (dec.), no. 13255/07, 30 June 2009 . . . . .707, 727–9

Georgia v Russia (II) (dec.), no. 38263/08, 13 December 2011 . . . . .707, 727–8, 914

Georgiadis v Greece, 29 May 1997, *Reports of Judgments and Decisions* 1997-III 273

Georgian Labour Party v Georgia, no. 9103/04, 8 July 2008 1020

Georgian Labour Party v Georgia (dec.), no. 9103/04, 22 May 2007 . . . . .738, 741, 781

Georgiev v Bulgaria, no. 47823/99, 15 December 2005 173

Georgieva v Bulgaria, no. 16085/02, 3 July 2008 253

Georgiou v Greece (dec.), no. 45138/98, 13 January 2000 . . . . .999, 1143

Geppa v Russia, no. 8532/06, 3 February 2011 . . . . .134, 136

Gerger v Turkey [GC], no. 24919/94, 8 July 1999 . . . . .259, 323, 490

Gestra v Italy (dec.), no. 21072/92, 16 January 1995 1149

Getiren v Turkey, no. 10301/03, 22 July 2008 740

Gheorghe v Romania (dec.), no. 19215/04, 22 September 2005 131

Ghigo v Malta, no. 31122/05, 26 September 2006 980

Ghulami v France (dec.), no. 45302/05, 7 April 2009 1077

Giacomelli v Italy, no. 59909/00, ECHR 2006-XII 388

Gillan and Quinton v United Kingdom, no. 4158/05, ECHR 2010 (extracts) 226–7, 370, 386

Gillberg v Sweden [GC], no. 41723/06, 3 April 2012 . . . . .369–70, 381, 385, 456–7, 714, 764

Gillow v United Kingdom, 24 November 1986, Series A no. 109 . . . . 104, 399, 925, 927, 1036

Giniewski v France, no. 64016/00, ECHR 2006-I 480

Gitonas and Others v Greece, 1 July 1997, *Reports of Judgments and Decisions*
1997-IV 1030

Giulia Manzoni v Italy, 1 July 1997, *Reports of Judgments and Decisions* 1997-IV 234

Giuliani and Gaggio v Italy, no. 23458/02, 24 March 2011 . . . . 122, 129, 131, 147, 807, 810

Giuliani and Gaggio v Italy [GC], no. 23458/02, ECHR 2011 (extracts) 152, 848

Giuliani and Gaggio v Italy [GC], no. 23458/02, Joint Partly Dissenting Opinion of
Judges Rozakis, Tulkens, Zupančič, Gyulumyan, Ziemele, Kalaydjieva, and Karakaş,
ECHR 2011 152

Giuran v Romania, no. 24360/04, ECHR 2011 (extracts) 72, 784

Giza v Poland (dec.), no. 1997/11, 23 November 2012 355

G.J. v Luxembourg, no. 21156/93, 26 October 2000 736

G.K. v Poland, no. 38816/97, 20 January 2004 230

G.K. v Poland (dec.), no. 36714/09, 16 November 2010 281

Gladysheva v Russia, no. 7097/10, 6 December 2011 400

Glas Nadezhda EOOD and Anatoliy Elenkov v Bulgaria, no. 14134/02, 11 October 2007 741

Glasenapp v Germany, 28 August 1986, Series A no. 104 . . . . .13, 19, 64, 721

Glass v United Kingdom, no. 61827/00, ECHR 2004-II 40, 371

Glender v Sweden (dec.), no. 28070/03, 6 September 2005 1143

Glor v Switzerland, no. 13444/04, ECHR 2009 . . . . 215, 369, 380, 565, 567, 569, 583

Gluhaković v Croatia, no. 21188/09, 12 April 2011 . . . . .391, 393

Glykantzi v Greece, no. 40150/09, 30 October 2012 640

G.M.B. and K.M. v Switzerland (dec.), no. 36797/97, 27 September 2001 565
G.N. and Others v Italy, no. 43134/05, 1 December 2009. . . . . .126, 160
Gnahoré v France, no. 40031/98, ECHR 2000-IX. 285
Gochev v Bulgaria, no. 34383/03, 26 November 2009. 1062–4
Göç v Turkey [GC], no. 36590/97, ECHR 2002-V. 289, 714, 845
Goddi v Italy, 9 April 1984, Series A no. 76 . . . . .308, 790
Godelli v Italy, no. 33783/09, 25 September 2012. 376
Göktan v France, no. 33402/96, ECHR 2002-V 1153
Goktepe v Belgium, no. 50372/99, 2 June 2005 297
Golder v United Kingdom, 21 February 1975, Series A no. 18 . . . . .35–6, 41, 54–5, 71, 80, 89,
 284 620–1, 625, 955, 1045–6
Golder v United Kingdom, 21 February 1975, Separate Opinion of Judge Sir G. Fitzmaurice,
 Series A no. 18 48
Golder v United Kingdom, 21 February 1975, Separate Opinion of Judge Zekia,
 Series A no. 18 620
Golubeva v Russia, no. 1062/03, 17 December 2009. .78, 135, 152
Gömi and Others v Turkey, no. 35962/97, 21 December 2006 . . . . .135, 153, 193
Gongadze v Ukraine, no. 34056/02, ECHR 2005-XI. 137, 170
Goodwin v United Kingdom, 27 March 1996, *Reports of Judgments and Decisions*
 1996-II. 458–9, 469
Gorbulya v Russia, no. 31535/09, 6 March 2014. 186
Gorelov v Russia, no. 49072/11, 9 January 2014. 126
Görgülü v Germany, no. 74969/01, 26 February 2004 392
Gorodnitchev v Russia, no. 52058/99, 24 May 2007 185
Gorou v Greece (no. 2), no. 12686/03, 20 March 2009. 272–3
Gorovenky and Bugara v Ukraine, nos 36146/05 and 42418/05, 12 January 2012. 130
Gorraiz Lizarraga and Others v Spain, no. 62543/00, ECHR 2004-III 288, 738, 979
Górski v Poland, no. 28904/02, 4 October 2005 250
Gorzelik and Others v Poland [GC], no. 44158/98, ECHR 2004-I. 55, 490, 491, 500,
 503, 510, 514–5, 518–9, 582
Goţia v Romania (dec.), no. 24315/06, 5 October 2010. 394
Gough v United Kingdom, no. 49327/11, 24 October 2014 .377, 455
Gourepka v Ukraine, no. 61406/00, 6 September 2005 1138
Grabchuk v Ukraine, no. 8599/02, 21 September 2006 304
Gradinger v Austria, 23 October 1995, Series A no. 328-C. 262, 936–7, 1146, 1153, 1156
Grămadă v Romania, no. 14974/09, 11 February 2014 815
Grande Oriente d'Italia di Palazzo Giustiniani v Italy, no. 35972/97, ECHR
 2001-VIII. 501, 512, 517, 523, 742
Grande Oriente d'Italia di Palazzo Giustiniani v Italy (dec.), no. 35972/97,
 21 October 1999. 741
Grande Oriente d'Italia di Palazzo Giustiniani v Italy (no. 2), no. 26740/02,
 31 May 2007 . . . . .512, 524–5
Grande Stevens and Others v Italy, nos 18640/10, 18647/10, 18663/10,
 18668/10, and 18698/10, 4 March 2014 . . . . 277, 780, 783–4, 937
Grant v United Kingdom, no. 32570/03, ECHR 2006-VII 380
Gratzinger and Gratzingerova v Czech Republic (dec.) [GC], no. 39794/98,
 ECHR 2002-VII. 779, 970
Grauslys v Lithuania, no. 36743/97, 10 October 2000. 935
Grava v Italy, no. 43522/98, 10 July 2003 349
Grava v Italy (dec.), no. 43522/98, 5 December 2002 281
Grayson and Barnham v United Kingdom, no. 19955/05, 23 September 2008 299
Graziani-Weiss v Austria, no. 31950/06, 18 October 2011. . . . . .211–2, 217
Grecu v Romania, no. 75101/01, 30 November 2006 1139
Gribenko v Latvia (dec.), no. 76878/01, 15 May 2003. 1072
Grinenko v Ukraine, no. 33627/06, 15 November 2012 230

Groppera Radio AG and Others v Switzerland, 28 March 1990, Series A no. 173 . . . . . 340–1, 467, 741
Gruber v Germany (dec.), no. 45198/04, 20 November 2007 565
Grzelak v Poland, no. 7710/02, 15 June 2010 . . . . 423, 428, 580, 815
Guerra and Others v Italy, 19 February 1998, *Reports of Judgments and Decisions*
    1998-I 388, 456, 714, 746, 775, 815
Guillot v France, 24 October 1996, *Reports of Judgments and Decisions* 1996-V 367, 376
Guiso-Gallisay v Italy (just satisfaction) [GC], no. 58858/00, 22 December
    2009. . . . . 43, 837–8, 848, 868
Guja v Moldova [GC], no. 14277/04, ECHR 2008 . . . . .464–5, 473, 475
Gül v Switzerland, 19 February 1996, *Reports of Judgments and Decisions* 1996-I 791
Gül v Turkey, no. 22676/93, 14 December 2000 . . . . .150, 193
Gülbahar and Others v Turkey, no. 5264/03, 21 October 2008 191
Gülbahar Özer and Others v Turkey (revision), no. 44125/06, 10 June 2014 853
Güleç v Turkey, 27 July 1998, *Reports of Judgments and Decisions* 1998-IV 135, 153
Gülen v Turkey, no. 28226/02, 14 October 2008 150
Güler and Uğur v Turkey, nos 31706/10 and 33088/10, 2 December 2014 436
Guliyev v Azerbaijan (dec.), no. 35584/02, 27 May 2004. 1022
Gülmez v Turkey, no. 16330/02, 20 May 2008. 272
Günaydin v Turkey (dec.), no. 27526/95, 25 April 2002 767
Gündüz v Turkey, no. 35071/97, ECHR 2003-XI 54
Güneri and Others v Turkey, nos 42853/98, 43609/98, and 44291/98, 12 July 2005 497
Güngör v Germany (dec.), no. 31540/96, 17 May 2001 315
Gurepka v Ukraine, no. 61406/00, 6 September 2005 . . . . .771, 1137–8
Gurepka v Ukraine (no. 2), no. 38789/04, 8 April 2010 . . . . 1135, 1137, 1139
Gurguchiani v Spain, no. 16012/06, 15 December 2009 . . . . .346–7, 349
Gurguenidze v Georgia, no. 71678/01, 17 October 2006 . . . . .368, 378
Gürtekin and Others v Cyprus, nos 60441/13, 68206/13, and 68667/13, 11 March 2014 128
Gusinskiy v Russia, no. 70276/01, ECHR 2004-IV. 624–6
Gustafsson v Sweden, 25 April 1996, *Reports of Judgments and Decisions* 1996-II 493–4, 502
Gustafsson v Sweden, 25 April 1996, Dissenting Opinion of Judge Martens,
    Joined by Judge Matscher, *Reports of Judgments and Decisions* 1996-II 71
Gustafsson v Sweden (revision – merits), 30 July 1998, *Reports of Judgments and*
    Decisions 1998-V. 853
Gutfreund v France, no. 45681/99, ECHR 2003-VII 282
Gutiérrez Dorado and Dorado Ortiz v Spain (dec.), no. 30141/09, 27 March 2012. 773
Güveç v Turkey, no. 70337/01, ECHR 2009 (extracts) 251
Güzel Erdagöz v Turkey, no. 37483/02, 21 October 2008 376
Guzzardi v Italy, 6 November 1980, Series A no. 39 . . . . .226–7, 235, 237, 239, 241,
                                         243, 746, 836, 1056–7
Gypsy Council and Others v United Kingdom (dec.), no. 66336/01, 14 May 2002. 741
H. v Belgium, 30 November 1987, Series A no. 127-B 290, 294
H. v Finland, no. 37359/09, 13 November 2012. 534
H. v Netherlands (dec.), no. 37833/10, 18 October 2011 . . . . .94, 394
H. v United Kingdom, 8 July 1987, Series A no. 120 827
H. v United Kingdom (friendly settlement), no. 22241/08, 18 September 2012 823
Haarvig v Norway (dec.), no. 11187/05, 11 December 2007 1151
Haas v Switzerland, no. 31322/07, ECHR 2011 . . . . .132–3, 369, 382
Hachette Filipacchi Associés (ICI PARIS) v France, no. 12268/03,
    23 July 2009. . . . . 368, 377–8, 461–2
Hachette Filipacchi Presse Automobile and Dupuy v France, no. 13353/05,
    5 March 2009. . . . . .481, 574
Hadjianastassiou v Greece, 16 December 1992, Series A no. 252 465
Hadrabová and Hadrabová v Czech Republic (dec.), nos 42165/02 & 466/03,
    25 September 2007. . . . . .781, 823
Hadri-Vionnet v Switzerland, no. 55525/00, 14 February 2008 . . . . .369, 382

Hajibeyli v Azerbaijan, no. 16528/05, 10 July 2008 1058–9

Håkansson and Sturesson v Sweden, 21 February 1990, Series A no. 171-A 271, 289–90, 976

Hakizimana v Sweden (dec.), no. 37913/05, 27 March 2008 . . . . .145, 1100

Hakobyan and Others v Azerbaijan, no. 34320/04, 10 April 2012 . . . . .309, 1137

Halford v United Kingdom, 25 June 1997, *Reports of Judgments and Decisions* 1997-III 374, 387

Halis Akın v Turkey, no. 30304/02, 13 January 2009 151

Halit Çelebi v Turkey, no. 54182/00, 2 May 2006 . . . . .78, 151

Halit Dinç and Others v Turkey, no. 32597/96, 19 September 2006 151

Hämäläinen v Finland [GC], no. 37359/09, 16 July 2014 . . . . .534–5, 544

Hamer v Belgium, no. 21861/03, ECHR 2007-V (extracts) 281

Hamer v France, 7 August 1996, *Reports of Judgments and Decisions* 1996-III 791

Hammern v Norway, no. 30287/96, 11 February 2003 . . . . .304, 306

Handyside v United Kingdom, 7 December 1976, Series A no. 24 . . . . .75–6, 80, 451, 458, 490,
521, 580, 765, 979

Hanzelkovi v Czech Republic, no. 43643/10, 11 December 2014 367

Haralambidis and Others v Greece, no. 36706/97, 29 March 2001 771

Haran v Turkey (striking out), no. 25754/94, 26 March 2002 799

Hardy v Ireland (dec.), no. 23456/94, 29 June 1994 299

Harkins and Edwards v United Kingdom, nos 9146/07 and 32650/07,
17 January 2012 . . . . .44, 146, 187

Harkmann v Estonia, no. 2192/03, 11 July 2006 258

Harrach v Czech Republic (dec.), no. 77532/01, 18 May 2004 . . . . .697, 702, 708, 849

Harrison McKee v Hungary, no. 22840/07, 3 June 2014 286

Harroudj v France, no. 43631/09, 4 October 2012 . . . . .38, 389, 394

Hartung v Germany (dec.), no. 10231/07, 3 November 2009 399

Harutyunyan v Armenia, no. 36549/03, ECHR 2007-III 109

Hasan and Chaush v Bulgaria [GC], no. 30985/96, ECHR 2000-XI 368, 403, 429–30,
436, 469, 492, 510, 765

Hasan and Eylem Zengin v Turkey, no. 1448/04, ECHR 2007-XI 1002–3

Hasdemir v Turley, no. 44027/09, 22 May 2012 702

Haser v Switzerland (dec.), no. 33050/96, 27 April 2000 1136–7

Hashman and Harrup v United Kingdom [GC], no. 25594/94, ECHR 1999-VIII 455

Hassan v United Kingdom, no. 29750/09, 16 September 2014 . . . . .36–7, 39, 43, 154–5,
235, 596, 641, 924, 926

Hassan v United Kingdom, no. 29750/09, Partly Dissenting Opinion of Judge Spano,
Joined by Judges Nicolaou, Bianku, and Kalaydjieva, 16 September 2014 . . . . .89, 154

Hatton and Others v United Kingdom [GC], no. 36022/97, ECHR 2003-VIII 91, 387, 493

Hauschildt v Denmark, 24 May 1989, Series A no. 154 295

Hauser v Austria, no. 26808/95, 16 January 1996 1138

Hauser-Sporn v Austria, no. 37301/03, 7 December 2006 . . . . .1136, 1138, 1153

Haxhia v Albania, no. 29861/03, 8 October 2013 . . . . .310, 320, 857

Haxhishabani v Luxembourg, no. 52131/07, 20 January 2011 299

H.C.W. Schilder v Netherlands, no. 2158/12, 16 October 2012 91

Heaney and McGuinness v Ireland, no. 34720/97, ECHR 2000-XII 287, 301, 319

Heglas v Czech Republic, no. 5935/02, 1 March 2007 320

Heinisch v Germany, no. 28274/08, ECHR 2011 (extracts) 465, 469, 475

Hellborg v Sweden, no. 47473/99, 28 February 2006 293

Helle v Finland, 19 December 1997, *Reports of Judgments and Decisions* 1997-VIII 297, 324, 857

Helmers v Sweden, 29 October 1991, Series A no. 212-A 791

Henaf v France, no. 65436/01, ECHR 2003-XI 184

Henryk Urban and Ryszard Urban v Poland, no. 23614/08, 30 November 2010 . . . . .77, 295

Hentrich v France, 22 September 1994, Series A no. 296-A 976

Hentrich v France (interpretation), 3 July 1997, *Reports of Judgments and Decisions* 1997-IV 852

Hermi v Italy [GC], no. 18114/02, ECHR 2006-XII 271, 308–9, 314–5

Hermida Paz v Spain (dec.), no. 4160/02, 28 January 2003 641

Herri Batasuna and Batasuna v Spain, nos 25803/04, and 25817/04, ECHR 2009 . . . . 491–2, 514,
519–21, 712
Herrmann v Germany [GC], no. 9300/07, 26 June 2012. . . . . .47, 973
Herrmann v Germany [GC], no. 9300/07, Partly Concurring and Partly Dissenting Opinion
of Judge Pinto de Albuquerque, 26 June 2012. 424
Hertel v Switzerland, 25 August 1998, *Reports of Judgments and Decisions* 1998-VI. 475
Hertel v Switzerland (dec.), no. 3440/99, ECHR 2002-I 869
Hilal v United Kingdom, no. 45276/99, ECHR 2001-II 195
Hilbe v Liechtenstein (dec.), no. 31981/96, ECHR 1999-VI .1021, 1027
Hilda Hafsteinsdóttir v Iceland, no. 40905/98, 8 June 2004. . . . . 147, 151, 233, 242
Hirschhorn v Romania, no. 29294/02, 26 July 2007 972
Hiro Balani v Spain, 9 December 1994, Series A no. 303-B 297, 857
Hirsi Jamaa and Others v Italy [GC], no. 27765/09, ECHR 2012 . . .47, 88–9, 102, 812, 1077–9, 1083
Hirsi Jamaa and Others v Italy [GC], no. 27765/09, Concurring Opinion of Judge Pinto de
Albuquerque, ECHR 2012 . . . . 44, 55
Hirst v United Kingdom (no. 2) [GC], no. 74025/01, ECHR 2005-IX 71, 275, 793, 848,
1012, 1019, 1023–6, 1028
Hirst v United Kingdom (no. 2) [GC], no. 74025/01, Dissenting Opinion of Judge Costa,
ECHR 2005-IX 929
Hizb ut-Tahrir and Others v Germany (dec.), no. 31098/08, 12 June 2012 . . . . .617, 619
H.L. v United Kingdom, no. 45508/99, ECHR 2004-IX. .226–8, 242
H.L.R. v France, 29 April 1997, *Reports of Judgments and Decisions* 1997-III 195
H.M. v Switzerland, no. 39187/98, ECHR 2002-I 227
H.N. and Others v Sweden (dec.), no. 50043/09, 24 January 2012 195
Hode and Abdi v United Kingdom, no. 22341/09, 6 November 2012 575
Hoffmann v Austria, 23 June 1993, Series A no. 255-C. 579, 1178
Hokkanen v Finland, 23 September 1994, Series A no. 299-A 392
Holub v Czech Republic (dec.), no. 24880/05, 14 December 2010 785
Hood v United Kingdom [GC], no. 27267/95, ECHR 1999-I. 249
Holy Monasteries v Greece, 9 December 1994, Series A no. 301-A. 737, 967, 977
Holy Synod of the Bulgarian Orthodox Church (Metropolitan Inokentiy) and Others v
Bulgaria, nos 412/03 and 35677/04, 22 January 2009. 518
Hoogendijk v Netherlands (dec.), no. 58461/00, 6 January 2005 . . . . .566, 568, 572
Hopia v Finland (dec.), no. 30632/96, 25 November 1999 324
Horciag v Romania (dec.), no. 70982/01, 15 March 2005 . . . . .1149, 1153
Hornsby v Greece, 19 March 1997, *Reports of Judgments and Decisions* 1997-II 71, 276, 293, 791
Horoz v Turkey, no. 1639/03, 31 March 2009 132
Horvath v Belgium (dec.), no. 6224/07, 24 January 2012 314
Horváth and Kiss v Hungary, no. 11146/11, 29 January 2013 . . . . .578, 1004
Hovanesian v Bulgaria, no. 31814/03, 21 December 2010 .280, 315
Hristova v Bulgaria, no. 60859/00, 7 December 2006 253
Hristozov and Others v Bulgaria, nos 47039/11 and 358/12,
13 November 2012 . . . . 131, 181, 191, 368, 371
Hrvatski Liječnički sindikat v Croatia, no. 36701/09, Concurring Opinion of Judge Pinto
de Albuquerque, 27 November 2014 . . . . .508, 510
Huber v Switzerland, 23 October 1990, Series A no. 188. 249
Hubner v Austria (dec.), no. 34311/96, 31 August 1999 1136
Hugh Jordan v United Kingdom, no. 24746/94, 4 May 2001 . . . . .135, 566
Hugh Jordan v United Kingdom, no. 24746/94, ECHR 2001-III (extracts) 130–1, 135,
147, 566, 572, 793
Hülsmann v Germany (dec.), no. 33375/03, 18 March 2008. 391
Humen v Poland [GC], no. 26614/95, 15 October 1999. 109
Hummatov v Azerbaijan (dec.), nos 9852/03 and 13413/04, 29 November 2007 350
Huohvanainen v Finland, no. 57389/00, 13 March 2007. . . . . .130, 152
Husain v Italy (dec.), no. 18913/03, 24 February 2005 . . . . .281, 315

Husayn (Abu Zubaydah) v Poland, no. 7511/13, 24 July 2014. . . . . .35, 96, 550, 552, 684, 793, 806–7, 809–11, 814, 827–8, 837, 900

Hüseyin Turan v Turkey, no. 11529/02, 4 March 2008. 283

Huseynov v Azerbaijan (friendly settlement), no. 36666/11, 22 October 2013. 823

Hutchison Reid v United Kingdom, no. 50272/99, ECHR 2003-IV. 241–2, 256

Hutten-Czapska v Poland, no. 35014/97, 22 February 2005 . . . . .792, 974

Hutten-Czapska v Poland [GC], no. 35014/97, ECHR 2006-VII. 109, 974, 979

Hutten-Czapska v Poland [GC], no. 35014/97, Partly Concurring, Partly Dissenting
 Opinion of Judge Zupančić, ECHR 2006-VII. 77

Hutten-Czapska v Poland (friendly settlement) [GC], no. 35014/97, 28 April 2008. 77

Hüttner v Germany (dec.), no. 23130/04, 19 June 2006 780

Huvig v France, 24 April 1990, Series A no. 176-B 403

Hyde Park and Others v Moldova (no. 4), no. 18491/07, 7 April 2009. . . . . .736, 969

Hyde Park and Others v Modlova (nos 5 and 6), nos 6991/08 and 15084/08,
 14 September 2010. . . . . 490, 498, 516, 736, 741–2, 969

I. v Sweden, no. 61204/09, 5 September 2013 . . . . .105, 788, 792

I. v United Kingdom [GC], no. 25680/94, 11 July 2002. . . . . .534, 536–7, 794

I.A. v France, 23 September 1998, *Reports of Judgments and Decisions* 1998-VII. 252

I.I. v Bulgaria (dec.), no. 44082/98, 25 March 2004 281

I.I. v Bulgaria, no. 44082/98, 9 June 2005 227

Iambor v Romania, (no. 1), no. 64536/01, 24 June 2008. 747

Iatridis v Greece [GC], no. 31107/96, ECHR 1999-II. 71, 368, 764, 767, 967, 976

Iatridis v Greece (just satisfaction) [GC], no. 31107/96, ECHR 1999-II 839

Iavarazzo v Italy (dec.), no. 50498/99, 4 December 2001. 317

Ichin and Others v Ukraine, nos 28189/04 and 28192/04, 21 December 2010. 240–1

İçyer v Turkey, (dec.), no. 18888/02, ECHR 2006-I 770

Idalov v Russia [GC], no. 5826/03, 22 May 2012. . . . . .250–1, 253, 255–6

Iglesias Gil and A.U.I. v Spain, no. 56673/00, ECHR 2003-V 391

Iglin v Ukraine, no. 39908/05, 12 January 2012 . . . . .309, 311

Ignaccolo-Zenide v Romania, no. 31679/96, ECHR 2000-I. 391–3

Ignatov v Bulgaria, no. 50/02, 2 July 2009 1062–3

Ignatov v Russia, no. 27193/02, 24 May 2007 1058

Igor Shevchenko v Ukraine, no. 22737/04, 12 January 2012 125

Ilaşcu and Others v Moldova and Russia [GC], no. 48787/99, ECHR 2004-VII 43, 70, 89,
 90, 92, 95–6, 99, 101, 103, 110, 177, 180, 186, 190, 229, 235, 810, 812

Ilaşcu and Others v Moldova and Russia (dec.) [GC], no. 48787/99, 4 July 2001 . . . . . 798, 933, 937–8

İletmiş v Turkey, no. 29871/96, ECHR 2005-XII. 378

Ilgar Mammadov v Azerbaijan, no. 15172/13, 22 May 2014 624–7

Ilhan v Turkey [GC], no. 22277/93, ECHR 2000-VII. 73, 125, 177, 185, 764, 785

Ilić v Croatia (dec.), no. 42389/98, 19 September 2000. 973

Ilijkov v Bulgaria, no. 33977/96, 26 July 2001 . . . . .251–2, 256

Iliya Stefanov v Bulgaria, no. 65755/01, 22 May 2008. . . . . .237, 744

Illiu and Others v Belgium (dec.), no. 14301/08, 19 May 2009 776–8

I.M. v France, no. 9152/09, 2 February 2012 . . . . .76, 741

Imakayeva v Russia, no. 7615/02, ECHR 2006-XIII (extracts) 193, 739, 807, 811–2

Imbrioscia v Switzerland, 24 November 1993, Series A no. 275 . . . . 280, 287, 307, 311, 791

Indelicato v Italy, no. 31143/96, 18 October 2001 . . . . .168, 193

Independent News and Media and Independent Newspapers Ireland Limited v Ireland (dec.),
 no. 55120/00, 19 June 2003 769

Inderbiyeva v Russia, no. 56765/08, 27 March 2012 171

Informationsverein Lentia and Others v Austria, 24 November 1993, Series A no. 276 467

Inze v Austria, 28 October 1987, Series A no. 126. . . . . 524, 567, 574, 583, 1178

Iordachi and Others v Moldova, no. 25198/02, 10 February 2009 .401, 744

Iorgov v Bulgaria (no. 2), no. 36295/02, 2 September 2010. 256

Iosséliani v Georgia (dec.), no. 64803/01, 6 September 2005 110

Iosub Caras v Romania, no. 7198/04, 27 July 2006. 1158
Ipek v Turkey, no. 25760/94, ECHR 2004-II (extracts). 809
İpek and Others v Turkey, nos 17019/02 and 30070/02, 3 February 2009 248
IPSD and Others v Turkey, no. 35832/97, 25 October 2005. . . . . .500, 520
Ireland v United Kingdom, 18 January 1978, Series A no. 25. . . . . 73, 80, 83–4, 88, 90,
105, 123, 169, 171, 175, 177, 180–1, 235, 238, 260,
551, 597, 599, 621, 640, 721–2, 725–9, 735, 803, 809–12, 834, 854
Ireland v United Kingdom, 18 January 1978, Separate Opinion of Judge Sir Gerald
Fitzmaurice, Series A no. 25. 172
Irfan Temel and Others v Turkey, no. 36458/02, 3 March 2009 998
Isaak and Others v Turkey (dec.), no. 44587/98, 28 September 2006. . . . . .101, 104, 149
Isaković Vidović v Serbia, no. 41694/07, 1 July 2014. 370
Isaksen v Norway (dec.), no. 13596/02, 2 October 2003 1154
Isayeva v Russia, no. 57950/00, 24 February 2005. . . . . .148, 154–7
Isayeva and Others V Russia, nos 59947/00, 57948/00, and 57949/00,
24 February 2005 . . . . .149, 156–7
Iskandarov v Russia, no. 17185/05, 23 September 2010. 227
Islamic Republic of Iran Shipping Lines v Turkey, no. 40998/98, ECHR 2007-V 737
Ismaili v Germany (dec.), no. 58128/00, 15 March 2001. .145, 1100
Ismailova v Russia, no. 37614/02, 29 November 2007. 580
Ismoilov and Others v Russia, no. 2947/06, 24 April 2008. . . . . .146, 1100
Issa and Others v Turkey, no. 31821/96, 16 November 2004. .101–2
Istituto Nazionale Case Srl v Italy (striking out), no 41479/78, 6 November 203. 798
Işyar v Bulgaria, no. 391/03, 20 November 2008. 315
Iulian Popescu v Romania, no. 24999/04, 4 June 2013 748
Ivanov v Ukraine, no. 15007/02, 7 December 2006. . . . . .1059, 1061
Ivanova v Bulgaria, no. 52435/99, 12 April 2007. . . . . 41, 420, 426, 431, 433, 440
Ivanţoc and Others v Moldova and Russia, no. 23687/05, 15 November 2011 712
İzmir Savaşa Karşıtları Derneği and Others v Turkey, no. 46257/99, 2 March 2006. . . . . .502, 513
J.A. v France, no. 45310/11, 27 May 2014. 206
J.A. Pye (Oxford) Ltd v United Kingdom, no. 44302/02, 15 November 2005. 975
J.A. Pye (Oxford) Ltd and J.A. Pye (Oxford) Land Ltd v United Kingdom [GC],
no. 44302/02, ECHR 2007-III 969, 974
J.A. Pye (Oxford) Ltd and J.A. Pye (Oxford) Land Ltd v United Kingdom [GC],
no. 44302/02, Joint Dissenting Opinion of Judges Rozakis, Bratza, Tsata-Nikolovska,
Gylumyan, and Šikuta, ECHR 2007-III 974
J.A. Pye (Oxford) Ltd and J.A. Pye (Oxford) Land Ltd v United Kingdom [GC], no. 44302/02,
Dissenting Opinion of Judge Loucaides, Joined by Judge Kovler, ECHR 2007-III. 974
Jablonski v Poland, no. 33492/96, 21 December 2000. 257
Jaffredou v France (dec.), no. 39843/98, 15 December 1998 275
Jakóbski v Poland, no. 18429/06, 7 December 2010 . . . . 421–2, 429, 431, 435, 440
Jalloh v Germany [GC], no. 54810/00, ECHR 2006-IX 172, 181, 183, 186, 319–21
Jaloud v Netherlands, no. 47708/08, 20 November 2014. . . . . .42, 102
James and Others v United Kingdom, 21 February 1986, Series A no. 98 . . . . 42, 90, 273,
552, 567, 573, 583, 967, 975, 978
Jamil v France, 8 June 1995, Series A no. 317-B 346–7
Janković v Croatia (dec.), no. 43440/98, ECHR 2000-X 971
Janosevic v Sweden, no. 34619/97, ECHR 2002-VII. 279, 299
Janowiec and Others v Russia, nos 55508/07 and 29520/09, 16 April 2012 . . . . .740, 792
Janowiec and Others v Russia, nos 55508/07 and 29520/09, Joint Partly Dissenting
Opinion of Judges Spielmann, Villiger and Nußburger, 16 April 2012 134
Janowiec and Others v Russia [GC], nos 55508/07 and 29520/09, Concurring Opinion of
Judge Dedov, 21 October 2013 45
Janowiec and Others v Russia [GC], nos 55508/07 and 29520/09, Concurring Opinion of
Judge Gyulumyan, 21 October 2013 111

Janowiec and Others v Russia [GC], nos 55508/07 and 29520/09, Joint Partly Dissenting
    Opinion of Judges Ziemele, De Gaetano, Laffranque, and Keller, 21 October 2013. . . . . . . .111, 139
Janowiec and Others v Russia [GC], nos 55508/07 and 29520/09, ECHR 2013 . . . . 35, 59, 89,
                        112, 134, 170, 739–40, 792, 812, 814, 827–8, 845, 848, 950
Janowski v Poland [GC], no. 25716/94, ECHR 1999-I 468, 476
Jantner v Slovakia, no. 39050/97, 4 March 2003 970
Janyr v Czech Reoublic, no. 42937/08, 31 October 2013. 311
Jaremowicz v Poland, no. 24023/03, 5 January 2010 . . . . .533, 538
Jashi v Georgia, no. 10799/06, 9 December 2008 801
Jasinskis v Latvia, no. 45744/08, 21 December 2010 . . . . .134, 767
Jasińska v Poland, no. 28326/05, 1 June 2010. 133
Jasper v United Kingdom [GC], no. 27052/95, ECHR 2000-II 288, 310
J.B. v Switzerland, no. 31827/96, ECHR 2001-III. 319
Jėčius v Lithuania, no. 34578/97, ECHR 2000-IX. 230–2, 235, 238, 261, 935
Jehovah's Witnesses of Moscow v Russia, no. 302/02, 10 June 2010. . . . . 369, 371, 375, 426,
                        429–31, 438, 499, 501, 511, 517
Jeličić v Bosnia and Herzegovina (dec.), no. 41183/02, 15 November 2005. . . . . .767–8, 777
Jeličić v Bosnia and Herzegovina, no. 41183/02, ECHR 2006-XII 793
Jendrowiak v Germany, no. 30060/04, 14 April 2011 592
Jensen and Rasmussen v Denmark (dec.), no. 52620/99, 20 March 2003 744
Jeronovičs v Latvia (dec.), no. 547/02, 10 February 2009. 1143
Jerry Olajide Sarumi v United Kingdom (dec.), no. 43279/98, 26 January 1999 398
Jersild v Denmark, 23 September 1994, Series A no. 298 . . . . 54, 457–8, 477, 688, 710, 790
J.F. v France (dec.), no. 39616/98, 20 April 1999 . . . . .94, 276
Jian v Romania (dec.), no. 46640/99, 30 March 2004 780
Jimnez Alonso and Jimenez Merino v Spain (dec.), no. 52288/99, 25 May 2000 1003
J.L. and Others v United Kingdom (just satisfaction), nos 29522/95, 30056/96,
    and 30574/96, 25 September 2001 839
Johansen v Norway, 7 August 1996, *Reports of Judgments and Decisions* 1996-III 394
John Murray v United Kingdom, 8 February 1996, *Reports of Judgments and Decisions*
    1996-I 319, 791
Johnston and Others v Ireland, 18 December 1986, Series A no. 112 . . . . .36, 49, 54–5, 64, 351,
                        432, 538, 540–1, 743, 791, 1045
Johnston and Others v Ireland, 18 December 1986, Separate Opinion, Partly Dissenting
    and Partly Concurring, of Judge de Meyer, Series A no. 112 .541, 544
Jokitaipale and Others v Finland, no. 43349/05, 6 April 2010 378
Jokšas v Lithuania, no. 25330/07, 12 November 2013. . . . . .288, 584
Jones v United Kingdom (dec.), no. 30900/02, 9 September 2003 316–7
Jones v United Kingdom (dec.), no. 42639/04, 13 September 2005 432
Jones and Others v United Kingdom, nos 34356/06 and 40528/06, 14 January 2014 . . . . . . 37, 42, 44,
                        100, 179, 285–6, 712
Jones and Others v United Kingdom, nos 34356/06 and 40528/06, Concurring Opinion of
    Judge Bianku, 14 January 2014 712
Jorgić v Germany, no. 74613/01, ECHR 2007-III. 44, 342, 344, 354
Josef v Belgium, no. 70055/10, Dissenting Opinion of Judge Power-Forde, 27 February 2014 191
Jovanović v Croatia (dec.), no. 59109/00, ECHR 2002-III. 108
J.S. and A.S. v Poland, no. 40732/98, 24 May 2005 273
Jussila v Finland [GC], no. 73053/01, ECHR 2006-XIV 277–8, 289–90, 1151–2
K. v Germany, no. 61827/09, 7 June 2012 592
K. and T. v Finland [GC], no. 25702/94, ECHR 2001-VII. .389, 393, 845
K.A. and A.D. v Belgium, no. 42758/98 and 45558/99, 17 February 2005. . . . . .337–8, 340–1
K.A.B. v Sweden, no. 886/11, 5 September 2013 127
K.-H.W. v Germany [GC], no. 37201/97, ECHR 2001-II (extracts) 342, 355–6
K.-H.W. v Germany [GC], no. 37201/97, Concurring Opinion of Judge Sir Nicolas Bratza,
    Joined by Judge Vajić, ECHR 2001-II (extracts) 343

K. and T. v Finland [GC], no. 25702/94, ECHR 2001-VII 714, 764, 785

Kaboulov v Ukraine, no. 41015/04, 19 November 2009 . . . . 96, 127, 146, 245, 1100, 1128

Kadem v Malta, no. 55263/00, 9 January 2003 257

Kadikis v Latvia (dec.), no. 47634/99, 29 June 2000 108

Kadiķis v Latvia (no. 2), no. 62393/00, 4 May 2006 41

Kadirova and Others v Russia, no. 5432/07, 27 March 2012 811

Kadiÿis v Latvia (no. 2) (dec.), no. 62393/00, 25 September 2003 771

Kafkaris v Cyprus (dec.), no. 9644/09, 21 June 2011 256

Kafkaris v Cyprus [GC], no. 21906/04, ECHR 2008 . . . . .38, 171, 187, 236, 335, 337, 339,
345, 347–9, 845

Kaftailova v Latvia (striking out) [GC], no. 59643/00, 7 December 2007 745

Kahraman v Turkey, no. 42104/92, 26 April 2007 311

Kakabadze and Others v Georgia, no. 1484/07, 2 October 2012 1137

Kakoulli v Turkey, no. 38595/97, 22 November 2005 . . . . .131, 151

Kalaç v Turkey, 1 July 1997, *Reports of Judgments and Decisions* 1997-IV 427, 431

Kalashnikov v Russia, no. 47095/99, ECHR 2002-VI 41, 181, 184, 250, 253, 261

Kalashnikov v Russia, no. 47095/99, Separate Concurring Opinion of Judge Kovler,
ECHR 2002-VI 261

Kalashnikov v Russia (dec.), no. 47095/99, ECHR 2001-XI .372, 389

Kalendar v Turkey, no. 4314/02, 15 December 2009 132

Kallis and Androulla Panayi v Turkey, no. 45388/99, 27 October 2009 . . . . .130, 150

Kalogeropoulou and Others v Greece and Germany (dec.), no. 59021/00,
ECHR 2002-X 44, 100, 286

Kamasinski v Austria, 19 December 1989, Series A no. 168 . . . . 81, 308, 311, 314–5, 317

Kamburov v Bulgaria (no. 2), no. 31001/02, 23 April 2009, .1138–9

Kampanis v Greece, 13 July 1995, Series A no. 318-B 255

Kanayev v Russia, no. 43726/02, 27 July 2006 274

Kandzhov v Bulgaria, no. 68294/01, 6 November 2008 . . . . .239, 248

Kane v Cyprus (dec.), no. 33655/06, 13 September 2011 . . . . .94, 245, 394

Kangasniemi v Finland (dec.), no. 43828/98, 1 June 1999 324

Kanlibaş v Turkey, no. 32444/96, 8 December 2005 154

Käns and Others v Latvia (dec.), no. 57823/00, 9 December 2003 771

Kaperzyński v Poland, no. 43206/07, 3 April 2012 . . . . .458–9, 469, 476

Kaplan v Austria, no. 45983/99, 18 January 2007 1158

Karácsony and Others v Hungary, no. 42461/13, 16 September 2014 476

Karademirci and Others v Turkey, nos 37096/97 and 37101/97, ECHR 2005-I 453, 471, 492

Karakó v Hungary, no. 39311/05, 28 April 2009 385

Karaman v Germany, no. 17103/10, 17 February 2014 . . . . .298, 301

Karandia v Bulgaria, no. 69180/01, 7 October 2010 151

Karapetyan v Armenia, no. 22387/05, 27 October 2009 1137

Karassev and family v Finland (dec.), no. 31414/96, ECHR 1999-II 379, 1072

Karataş v Turkey [GC], no. 23168/94, ECHR 1999-IV 451, 455, 463–4, 472

Karchen and Others v France (dec.), no. 5722/04, 4 March 2008 126

Karhuvaara and Iltalehti v Finland, no. 53678/00, ECHR 2004-X 378

Karimov v Azerbaijan, no. 12535/06, 25 September 2014 .1019, 1023–5

Karkın v Turkey, no. 43928/98, 23 September 2003 455

Karlheinz Schmidt v Germany, 18 July 1994, Series A no. 291-B 213, 216–7, 574, 1178

Karmo v Bulgaria (dec.), 76965/01, 9 February 2006 249

Karner v Austria, no. 40016/98, ECHR 2003-IX. 407, 574, 584, 726, 738, 740, 794, 800

Karoussiotis v Portugal, no. 23205/08, ECHR 2011 (extracts) 778

Karpacheva and Karpachev v Russia, no. 34861/04, 27 January 2011 1060

Karpenko v Russia, no. 5605/04, 13 March 2012 271

Karrer v Romania, no. 16965/10, 21 February 2012 392–3

Karsai v Hungary, no. 5380/07, 1 December 2009 480

Kart v Turkey [GC], no. 8917/05, ECHR 2009 (extracts) 81, 285–7, 291, 307

Kasa v Turkey, no. 45902/99, 20 May 2008 150
Kasap and Others v Turkey, no. 8656/10, 14 January 2014 136
Kasumaj v Greece (dec.), no. 6974/05, 5 July 2007 107
Kasymakhunov v Russia, no. 296041/12, 14 November 2013 .749, 751
Kasymakhunov and Saybatalov v Russia, nos 26261/05 and 26377/06,
    14 March 2013 . . . . 438, 616–7, 619
Katić and Katić v Serbia, no. 13920/04, 7 July 2009 801
Katritsch v France, no. 22575/08, 4 November 2010 314–5
Kats and Others v Ukraine, no. 29971/04, 18 December 2008 133
Kaushal and Others v Bulgaria, no. 1537/08, 2 September 2010 1130
Kavak v Turkey (dec.), no. 34719/04 and 37472/05, 19 May 2009 784
Kawogo v United Kingdom (dec.), no. 56921/09, 3 September 2013 210
Kaya v Romania, no. 33970/05, 12 October 2006 . . . . 1130, 1132
Kaya v Turkey, 19 February 1998, *Reports of Judgments and Decisions* 1998-I 135, 550, 552
Keegan v Ireland, 26 May 1994, Series A no. 290 . . . . .368, 376, 390, 406, 438, 513, 1063
Keenan v United Kingdom, no. 27229/95, ECHR 2001-III 132–3, 172, 174, 184, 742
Kefalas and Others v Greece, 8 June 1995, Series A no. 318-A 108
Kehayov v Bulgaria, no. 41035/98, 18 January 2005 173
Keles v Germany, no. 32231/02, 27 October 2005 395
Keller v Russia, no. 26824/04, 17 October 2013 133
Kelly and Others v United Kingdom, no. 30054/96, 4 May 2001 139
Kemaloğlu and Kemaloğlu v Turkey, no. 19986/06, 10 April 2012 132
Kemevuaku v Netherlands (dec.), no. 65938/09, 1 June 2010 772
Kemmache v France (no. 3), 24 November 1994, Series A no. 296-C 779
Kenedi v Hungary, no. 31475/05, 26 May 2009 469
Kennedy v United Kingdom, no. 26839/05, 18 May 2010 400–1
Kępka v Poland (dec.) nos 31439/96 and 35123/97, ECHR 2000-IX 274
Kerechashvili v Georgia (dec.), no. 5667/02, 2 May 2006 780
Kerimova v Azerbaijan, no. 20799/06, 30 September 2010 1029
Kerimova and Others v Russia, nos 17170/04, 20792/04, 22448/04, 23360/04, 5681/05,
    and 5684/05, 3 May 2011 148
Kerr v United Kingdom (dec.), no. 40451/98, 7 December 1999 245–6
Keskin and Others v Turkey (dec.), no. 36091/97, 7 September 1999 771
Kesyan v Russia, no. 36496/02, 19 October 2006 968
K.H. and Others v Slovakia, no. 32881/04, ECHR 2009 (extracts) 374, 383, 855
Khachatryan and Others v Armenia, no. 23978/06, 27 November 2012 238–9
Khadzhialiyev and Others v Russia, no. 3013/04, 6 November 2008 . . . . .135, 170
Khalitova v Russia, no. 39166/04, 5 March 2009 155
Khamzayev and Others v Russia, no. 1503/02, 3 May 2011 .148, 155–7
Khan v United Kingdom, no. 35394/97, ECHR 2000-V 320
Khan v United Kingdom, no. 35394/97, Partly Concurring, Partly Dissenting Opinion of
    Judge Loucaides, ECHR 2000-V 320
Khan v United Kingdom (dec.), no. 11987/11, 28 January 2014 . . . . .95, 101
Kharchenko v Ukraine, no. 40107/02, 10 February 2011 . . . . .239, 262
Kharin v Russia, no. 37345/03, 3 February 2011 242
Khashiyev and Akayeva v Russia, nos 57942/00 and 57945/00, 24 February 2005 . . . . .137, 552
Khashuyeva v Russia, no. 25553/07, 19 July 2011 171
Khatchadourian v Belgium (dec.), no. 22738/08, 12 January 2010 315
Khatsiyeva and Others v Russia, no. 5108/02, 17 January 2008 . . . . .147, 158
Khaydarov v Russia, no. 21055/09, 20 May 2010 302
Khelili v Switzerland, no. 16188/07, 18 October 2011 . . . . .382, 384
Khlyustov v Russia, no. 28975/05, 11 July 2013 1062–3
Khodorkovskiy v Russia, no. 5829/04, 31 May 2011 . . . . 185, 230, 237, 625
Khodorkovskiy and Lebedev v Russia, nos 11082/06 and 13772/05, 25 July 2013 . . . . .77, 626, 967
Kholodov and Kholodova v Russia (dec.), no. 30651/05, 14 September 2006 111

Khudoyorov v Russia, no. 6847/02, ECHR 2005-X (extracts) 230, 233–4, 252–3
Khutsayev and Others v Russia, no. 16622/05, 27 May 2010 811
Khuzhin and Others v Russia, no. 13470/02, 23 October 2008 303
K.-H.W. v Germany [GC], no. 37201/97, ECHR 2001-II (extracts) 68, 71, 119
Kiiskinen v Finland (dec.), no. 26323/95, ECHR 1999-V 769
Kiliç v Turkey, no. 22492/93, ECHR 2000-III 552
Kimlya and Others v Russia, nos 76836/01 and 32782/03, ECHR 2009 .... 425, 429–30
King v United Kingdom, no. 13881/02, 8 April 2003 299
King v United Kingdom (dec.), no. 6234/06, 6 March 2007 259
Kingsley v United Kingdom [GC], no. 35605/97, ECHR 2002-IV 837–8
Kirakosyan v Armenia, no. 31237/03, 2 December 2008 1137
Kiselyov v Ukraine, no. 42953/04, 13 June 2013 702
Kişmir v Turkey, no. 27306/95, 31 May 2005 813
Kjartan Ásmundsson v Iceland, no. 60669/00, ECHR 2004-IX 971
Kjeldsen, Busk, Madsen, and Pedersen v Denmark, 7 December 1976, Series A no. 23 .... 45, 68,
                                                                             572, 986, 995–6, 1000–2
Klass v Germany, 22 September 1993, Series A no. 269 ....169, 807
Klass and Others v Germany, 6 September 1978, Series A no. 28 .... 27, 49, 68, 71, 386,
                                                                             401, 735, 738, 744, 1126
Kleyn and Aleksandrovich v Russia, no. 40657/04, 3 May 2012 ....123, 134
Kleyn and Others v Netherlands [GC], nos 39343/98, 39651/98, 43147/98, and 46664/99,
    ECHR 2003-VI 765–6
Klip and Krüger v Netherlands (dec.), no. 33257/96, 3 December 1997 540
Klishyn v Ukraine, no. 30671/04, 23 February 2012 ....233, 258
Klouvi v France, no. 30754/03, 30 June 2011 299
Klyakhin v Russia, no. 46082/99, 30 November 2004 109
Knaags and Khachik v United Kingdom (dec.), no. 46559/06 and 22921/06, 30 August 2011 73
Knebl v Czech Republic, no. 20157/05, 28 October 2010 255
Knecht v Romania, no. 10048/10, 2 October 2012 372
Koç and Tosun v Turkey (dec.), no. 23852/04, 13 November 2008 771
Koch v Germany, no. 497/09, 19 July 2012 ....382, 388
Koendjbiharie v Netherlands, 25 October 1990, Series A no. 185-B 257
Kök v Turkey, no. 1855/02, 19 October 2006 ....273, 997
Kokkinakis v Greece, 25 May 1993, Series A no. 260-A 334, 336, 338, 420–1, 426–7, 431, 438
Kokkinakis v Greece, 25 May 1993, Dissenting Opinion of Judge Valtikos, Series A
    no. 260-A 431
Kokkinakis v Greece, 25 May 1993, Partly Concurring Opinion of Judge Pettiti, Series A
    no. 260-A 427
Kokkinakis v Greece, 25 May 1993, Partly Dissenting Opinion of Judge Martens, Series A
    no. 260-A 426–7
Koku v Turkey, no. 27305/95, 31 May 2005 ....742, 813
Kolb and Others v Austria, nos 35021/97 and 45774/99, 17 April 2003 323
Kolevi v Bulgaria, no. 1108/02, 5 November 2009 ....135, 193
Kolk and Kislyiy v Estonia (dec.), nos 23052/04 and 24018/04, ECHR 2006-I 345, 354
Kolompar v Belgium, 24 September 1992, Series A no. 235-C 254, 257, 815
Kolyadenko and Others v Russia, nos 17423/05, 20534/05, 20678/05, 23263/05, 24283/05,
    and 35673/05, 28 February 2012 131
Komatinović v Serbia (dec.), no. 75381/10, 29 January 2013 780
Komyakov v Russia (dec.), no. 7100/02, 8 January 2009 744
Konečný v Czech Republic, nos 47269/99, 64656/01, and 65002/01, 26 October 2004 950
Koniarska v United Kingdom (dec.), no. 33670/96, 12 October 2000 240
König v Germany, 28 June 1978, Series A no. 27 ....274, 276, 293
Kononov v Latvia, no. 36376/04, 24 July 2008 ....352, 354, 791
Kononov v Latvia, no. 36376/04, Joint Dissenting Opinion of Judges Fura-Strandström,
    David Thór Björgvinsson, and Ziemele, 24 July 2008 ....352, 355

Kononov v Latvia [GC], no. 36376/04, ECHR 2010. . . . . .55, 71, 334, 338, 342–3,
                                345, 352–3, 354, 791
Kononov v Latvia [GC], no. 36376/04, Joint Concurring Opinion of Judges Rozakis,
  Tulkens, Spielmann, and Jebens, ECHR 2010 343
Konrad v Germany (dec.), no. 35504/03, ECHR 2006-XIII. 1002
Konstantin Markin v Russia, no. 30078/06, 7 October 2010 576
Konstantin Markin v Russia [GC], no. 30078/06, Partly Concurring, Partly Dissenting
  Opinion of Judge Pinto de Albuquerque, ECHR 2012 (extracts) 63
Kontrová v Slovakia, no. 7510/04, 31 May 2007. 129
Kopczynski v Poland (dec.), no. 28863/95,1 July 1998 1135
Köpke v Germany (dec.), no. 420/07, 5 October 2010 377
Kopecký v Slovakia [GC], no. 44912/98, ECHR 2004-IX 107, 969–71
Kopylov v Russia, no. 3933/04, 29 July 2010 744
Korbely v Hungary [GC], no. 9174/02, ECHR 2008 . . . . .43, 342, 345
Koretskyy and Others v Ukraine, no. 40269/02, 3 April 2008 . . . . .499, 501, 514
Korizno v Latvia (dec.), no. 68163/01, 28 Septemeber 2006. 110
Kornakovs v Latvia, no. 61005/00, 15 June 2006 747
Korneykova v Ukraine, no. 39884/05, 19 January 2012. . . . . .238, 258
Korolev v Russia (dec.), no. 25551/05, ECHR 2010 . . . . .79, 782–4
Koroniotis v Germany (striking out), no. 66046/01, 21 April 2005. 800
Kortesis v Greece, no. 60593/10, 12 June 2012. 245
Kosiek v Germany, 28 August 1986, Series A no. 105 . . . . .13, 19, 64, 721
Koslova and Smirnova v Latvia (dec.), no. 57381/00, 23 October 2001 . . . . .936–7, 984
Kosteski v 'former Yugoslav Republic of Macedonia', no. 55170/00, 13 April 2006 431
Koşti and Others v Turkey, no. 74321/01. 3 May 2007. 251
Kostovski v Netherlands, 20 November 1989, Series A no. 166 312–3
Kotov v Russia [GC], no. 54522/00, 3 April 2012. 971
Koua Poirrez v France, no. 40892/98, ECHR 2003-X 574, 581, 793
Koumoutsea and Others v Greece (dec.), no. 56625/00, 13 December 2011 782
Kovach v Ukraine, no. 39424/02, ECHR 2008 1026
Kovačić and Others v Slovenia [GC], nos 44574/98, 45133/98, and 48316/99,
  3 October 2008 845
Kovačić and Others v Slovenia (striking out) [GC], nos 44574/98, 45133/98, and 48316/99,
  3 October 2008 846
Kozacıoğlu v Turkey [GC], no. 2334/03, 19 February 2009. . . . . 767, 837, 967, 972, 975–7
Kozhayev v Russia, no. 60045/10, 5 June 2012. 144
Krajisnik v United Kingdom (dec.), no. 6017/11, 23 October 2012 . . . . .99, 260
Krasnov and Skuratov v Russia, nos 17864/04 and 21396/04, 19 July 2007 1026
Krastanov v Bulgaria, no. 50222/99, 30 September 2004 . . . . .178, 194
Krčmář and Others v Czech Republic (dec.), no. 69190/01, 30 March 2004. 866
Krejčić v Czech Republic, nos 39298/04 and 8723/05, 26 March 2009 249
Kress v France [GC], no. 39594/98 ECHR 2001-VI 48, 275
Krivobokov v Ukraine (dec.), no. 38707/04, 19 February 2013 1021
Krivonogova v Russia (dec.), no. 74694/01, 1 April 2004. 968
Krivova v Ukraine, no. 25732/05, 9 November 2010. .125, 127
Krombach v France, no. 29731/96, ECHR 2001-II. 307, 316–7, 792, 1136–7
Krone Verlag GmbH & Co KG v Austria (no. 3), no. 39069/97, ECHR 2003-XII 455
Kroon and Others v Netherlands, 27 October 1994, Series A no. 297-C. 389
Kruez v Poland, no. 28249/95, ECHR 2001-VI 286
Krumpholz v Austria, no. 13201/05, 18 March 2010. .299–301
Krušković v Croatia, no. 46185/08, 21 June 2011. .376, 389
Kruslin v France, 24 April 1990, Series A no. 176-A 339
K.U. v Finland, no. 2872/02, ECHR 2008. 279, 369, 387, 463
Kučera v Slovakia, no. 48666/99, 17 July 2007 255
Kucherenko v Ukraine, no. 27347/02, 15 December 2005. 239

Kudeshkina v Russia, no. 29492/05, 26 February 2009 464
Kudła v Poland [GC], no. 30210/96, ECHR 2000-XI 75, 169, 171, 173–4, 180–1,
184, 250, 550–1, 765
Kuliś and Różycki v Poland, no. 27209/03, 6 October 2009 458
Kurić and Others v Slovenia [GC], no. 26828/06, ECHR 2012 (extracts) 109, 379, 404–5,
407, 566, 581, 744–5, 870
Kurić and Others v Slovenia [GC], no. 26828/06, Partly Concurring, Partly Dissenting
Opinion of Judge Vučinić, ECHR 2012 (extracts). 379
Kurier Zeitungsverlag und Druckerei GmbH v Austria, no. 3401/07, 17 January 2012 460
Kurt v Turkey, 25 May 1998, *Reports of Judgments and Decisions* 1998-III. 230, 256, 552,
739, 747–8, 790, 809
Kusnetsova v Russia (dec.), no. 67579/01, 19 January 2006. 774
Kuvikas v Lithuania, no. 21837/02, 27 June 2006. . . . . .303, 312
Kuznetsov v Russia, no. 10877/04, 23 October 2008. 772
Kuznetsov and Others v Russia, no. 184/02, 11 January 2007 . . . . .425, 431, 436
Kvashko v Ukraine, no. 40939/05, 26 September 2013 258
Kwakye-Nti and Dufie v Netherlands (dec.), no. 31519/96, 7 November 2000 . . . . .367, 397
Kwiek v Poland, no. 51895/99, 30 May 2006. 401
Kyprianou v Cyprus, no. 73797/01, 27 January 2004 278
Kyprianou v Cyprus [GC], no. 73797/01, ECHR 2005-XIII 294–6, 283, 455, 474–5
Kyprianou v Cyprus [GC], no. 73797/01, Concurring Opinion of Judges Sir Nicolas Bratza
and Pellonpää, ECHR 2005-XIII 296
Kyprianou v Cyprus [GC], no. 73797/01, Partly Dissenting Opinion of Judge Costa,
ECHR 2005-XIII 692, 844
L. v Lithuania, no. 27527/03, ECHR 2007-IV 173, 381
L. v Netherlands, no. 45582/99, ECHR 2004-IV 390–1
L. and V. v Austria, nos 39392/98 and 39829/98, ECHR 2003-I. 584
La Ligue des Musulmans de Suisse v Switzerland (dec.), no. 66274/09, 28 June 2011 . . . . .738, 742
Laaksonen v Finland, no. 70216/01, 12 April 2007. 324
Labita v Italy [GC], no. 26772/95, ECHR 2000-IV. 169, 180, 193, 234,
239, 592, 1018, 1023–4, 1029, 1058, 1061
Labzov v Russia (dec.), no. 62208/00, 28 February 2002 . . . . .261, 934
Lăcătuş and Others v Romania, no. 12694/04, 13 November 2012 . . . . 196, 292–3, 297, 322
Ladent v Poland, no. 11036/03, 18 March 2008 . . . . .226, 230, 247
Ladygin v Russia (dec.), no. 35365/05, 30 August 2011. 782
Lagardère v France, no. 18851/07, 12 April 2012 304
Lagerblom v Sweden, no. 26891/95, 14 January 2003 310–1
Lakićević and Others v Montenegro and Serbia, nos 27458/06, 37205/06, 37207/06,
and 33604/07, 13 December 2011. 951
Lala v Netherlands, 22 September 1994, Series A no. 297-A. .307, 317
Lalmahomed v Netherlands, no. 26036/08, 22 February 2011 1135
Lalmahomed v Netherlands, no. 26036/08, Concurring Opinion of Judge Ziemele,
22 February 2011 40
Lamanna v Austria, no. 28923/95, 10 July 2001 . . . . .291, 299
Lambert v France, 24 August 1998, *Reports of Judgments and Decisions* 1998-V 386
Langborger v Sweden, 22 June 1989, Series A no. 155. 400
Larissis and Others v Greece, 24 February 1998, *Reports of Judgments and Decisions* 1998-I 427, 431
Larkos v Cyprus [GC], no. 29515/95, ECHR 1999-I 574, 583, 1178
Lars and Astrid Fägerskiöld v Sweden (dec.), no. 37664/04, 26 February 2008 979
Lashin v Russia, no. 33117/02, 22 January 2013. 534
Laska and Lika v Albania, nos 12315/04 and 17605/04, 20 April 2010. 89
Laskey, Jaggard, and Brown v United Kingdom, 19 February 1997, *Reports of Judgments and
Decisions* 1997-I 381, 385
Laskey, Jaggard, and Brown v United Kingdom, 19 February 1997, Concurring Opinion of
Judge Pettiti, *Reports of Judgments and Decisions* 1997-I 381

László Magyar v Hungary, no. 73593/10, 20 May 2014. 187
Laukkanen and Manninen v Finland (dec.), no. 50230/99, 3 February 2004. 324
Lauko v Slovakia, 2 September 1998, *Reports of Judgments and Decisions* 1998-VI 278, 347
Lauruc v Romania, no. 34236/03, 23 April 2013. 233
Lautsi and Others v Italy [GC], no. 30814/06, ECHR 2011 (extracts) 421, 433, 440, 848, 1001–3
Lautsi and Others v Italy [GC], no. 30814/06, Concurring Opinion of Judge Bonello,
   ECHR 2011 (extracts). 464
Lavents v Latvia, no. 58442/00, 28 November 2002 227
Lavida and Others v Greece, no. 7973/10, 30 May 2013. 1004–5
Lavrechov v Czech Republic, no. 57404/08, ECHR 2013 976
Lawless v Ireland (no. 1), 14 November 1960, Series A no. 1 . . . . 10, 579, 720, 826
Lawless v Ireland (no. 1), Dissenting Opinion of Mr G Maridakis, 14 November 1960,
   Series A no. 1 684
Lawless v Ireland (no. 3), 1 July 1961, Series A no. 3. . . . . .34, 45, 235, 238, 595, 599, 603, 616
L.C.B. v United Kingdom, 9 June 1998, *Reports of Judgments and Decisions* 1998-III 122, 126
Le Compte, Van Leuven and De Meyere v Belgium, 23 June 1981, Series A no. 43. . . . . 272, 274,
                                                                                       290, 294
Le Petit v United Kingdom (dec.), no. 35574/97, 5 December 2000 350
Le Syndicat de copropriétaires du 20 bd de la Mer à Dinard v France (dec.), no. 47339/99,
   22 May 2003 . . . . 697, 702, 708, 849
Leander v Sweden, 26 March 1987, Series A no. 116. . . . . 382, 403, 457, 552
Lebedev v Russia, no. 4493/04, 25 October 2007 . . . . .249, 764, 786
Lederer v Germany (dec.), no. 6213/03, 22 May 2006. 971
Lee v United Kingdom [GC], no. 25289/94, 18 January 2001. 1000
Leela Förderkreis e.V. v Germany, no. 58911/00, 6 November 2008 . . . . 421–2, 425–6, 437
Leela Förderkreis e.V. v Germany, no. 58911/00, 6 November 2008, Partly Dissenting
   Opinion of Judge Lazarova Trajakovska 425
Leempoel & S.A. ED. Ciné Revue v Belgium, no. 64772/01, 9 November 2006. . . . . . . .377, 461, 903
Léger v France (striking out) [GC]. No. 19324/02, 30 March 2009 784
Lehideux and Isorni v France, 23 September 1998, *Reports of Judgments and Decisions*
   1998-VII 451, 479–80, 615, 617–9
Lehideux and Isorni v France, 23 September 1998, Joint Dissenting Opinion of Judges
   Foighel, Loizou and Sir John Freeland, *Reports of Judgments and Decisions* 1998-VII. 615
Lelièvre v Belgium, no. 11287/03, 8 November 2007 253
Lenev v Bulgaria, no. 41452/07, 4 December 2012. 281
Lenskaya v Russia, no. 28730/03, 29 January 2009 72
Leon and Agnieszka Kania v Poland, no. 12605/03, 21 July 2009. 387
Lepojić v Serbia, no. 13909/05, 6 November 2007 109
Leray and Others v France (dec.), no. 44617/98, 16 January 2008 132
Leroy v France, no. 36109/03, 2 October 2008. . . . . .455, 616–7
Lesnina Veletrgovina d.o.o. v former Yugoslav Republic of Macedonia (dec.), no. 37619/04,
   2 March 2010. 822
Letellier v France, 26 June 1991, Series A no. 207. 252
Leterme v France, 29 April 1998, *Reports of Judgments and Decisions* 1998-III 869
Leutscher v Netherlands, 26 March 1996, *Reports of Judgments and Decisions* 1996-II. 304
Levages Prestations Services v France, 23 October 1996, *Reports of Judgments and Decisions*
   1996-V. 286
Leyla Şahin v Turkey, no. 44774/98, 29 June 2004. . . . . .38, 575
Leyla Şahin v Turkey [GC], no. 44774/98, ECHR 2005-XI. 55, 403, 413, 420–1,
                                         426–7, 431, 435, 437, 469, 510, 575, 848, 995–7, 1063
Leyla Şahin v Turkey [GC], no. 44774/98, Dissenting Opinion of Judge Tulkens,
   ECHR 2005-XI 421
L.H. v Latvia, no. 52019/07, 29 April 2014 640
Libert v Belgium (dec.), no. 44734/98, 8 July 2004. 275
Liberty and Others v United Kingdom, no. 58243/00, 1 July 2008 744

Liepājnieks v Latvia (dec.), no. 37586/06, 2 November 2010 . . . . .937, 984
Lietzow v Germany, no. 24479/94, ECHR 2001-I 255
Likvidējamā pls Selga and Vasiļevska v Latvia (dec.), nos 17126/02 and 24991/02,
    1 October 2013 968
Lindheim and Others v Norway, nos 13221/08 and 2139/10, 12 June 2012 979–80
Lindon, Otchakovsky-Laurens, and July v France, nos 21279/02 and 36448/02, ECHR
    2007-IV 451, 463–4, 468, 470, 473, 475–7, 580
Lindon, Otchakovsky-Laurens, and July v France, nos 21279/02 and 36448/02,
    Concurring Opinion of Judge Loucaides, ECHR 2007-IV 461
Lingens v Austria, 8 July 1986, Series A no. 103 . . . . 451, 458, 468, 474, 478, 790
Linkov v Czech Republic, no. 10504/03, 7 December 2006 . . . . .352, 503, 515
Lithgow and Others v United Kingdom, 8 July 1986, Series A no. 102 . . . . 36, 42, 45, 54,
                                                                              524, 564, 976–8, 1045
Litovchenko v Russia (dec.), no. 69580/01, 18 April 2002 108
Liu v Russia, no. 42086/05, 6 December 2007 230
Lloyd and Others v United Kingdom, nos 29798/96, 30395/96, 34327/96, 34341/96,
    35445/97, 36267/97, 36367/97, 37551/97, 37706/97, 38261/97, 39378/98, 41590/98,
    41593/98, 42040/98, 42097/98, 45420/99, 45844/99, 46326/99, 47144/99, 53062/99,
    53111/99, 54969/00, 54973/00, 54997/00, 55046/00, 55068/00, 55071/00, 56109/00,
    56231/00, 56232/00, 56233/00, 56429/00, 56441/00, 2460/03, 2482/03, 2483/03,
    2484/03, and 2490/03, 1 March 2005 230
Loewenguth v France (dec.), no. 53183/99, ECHR 2000-VI 1136, 1138
Loizidou v Turkey (Article 50), 29 July 1998, *Reports of Judgments and Decisions* 1998-IV 73
Loizidou v Turkey (merits), 18 December 1996, *Reports of Judgments and Decisions*
    1996-VI 95, 103–4, 154, 973
Loizidou v Turkey (preliminary objections), 23 March 1995, Series A no. 310 . . . . 37, 65, 73,
                             95, 99, 102–3, 105, 109, 640, 735, 788, 791, 925, 933, 937, 939, 1086
Lolova-Karadzhova v Bulgaria, no. 17835/07, 27 March 2012 237
Lopes Gomes da Silva v Portugal, no. 37698/97, ECHR 2000-X 478
López Ostra v Spain, 9 December 1994, Series A no. 303-C 172, 388
Lordos and Others v Turkey (just satisfaction), no. 15973/90, 10 January 2012 . . . . .712, 846
Lorenzetti v Italy, no. 32075/09, 10 April 2012 304
Lorsé and Others v Netherlands (dec.), no. 52750/99, 28 August 2001 275
Losonci Rose and Rose v Switzerland, no. 664/06, 9 November 2010 407
Lotter and Lotter v Bulgaria (dec.), no. 39015/97, 6 February 2003 435
Loyen and Others v France, no. 55926/00, 29 April 2003 740
Luberti v Italy, 23 February 1984, Series A no. 75 242
Lucà v Italy, no. 33354/96, ECHR 2001-I 312–3
Lucà v Italy, no. 33354/96, Partly Concurring Opinion of Judge Zupančić, ECHR 2001-II 835–6
Lucas v United Kingdom (dec.), no. 39013/02, 18 March 2003 496
Luchaninova v Ukraine, no. 16347/02, 9 June 2011 . . . . 289, 309–11, 1140
Lucky Dev v Sweden, no. 7356/10, 27 November 2014 1150
Lucoch v Poland, no. 37469/05, 15 January 2008 309
Luedicke, Belkacem, and Koç v Germany, 28 November 1978, Series A no. 29 . . . . .46, 315
Luka v Romania, no. 34197/02, 21 July 2009 294
Luli and Others v Albania, nos 64480/09, 64482/09, 12874/10, 56935/10, 3129/12,
    and 31355/09, 1 April 2014 77
Luluyev and Others v Russia, no. 69480/01, ECHR 2006-XIII (extracts) 170, 811
Lundkvist v Sweden (dec.), no. 48518/99, ECHR 2003-XI 304
Luordo v Italy, no. 32190/96, ECHR 2003-IX 1060–1, 1064
Luordo v Italy (dec.), no. 32190/96, 23 May 2002 1050
Lupsa v Romania, no. 10337/04, 8 June 2006 1130
Lutsenko v Ukraine, no. 6492/11, 3 July 2012 . . . . .230, 625–6
Lutz v Germany, 25 August 1987, Series A no. 123 . . . . .277, 283, 304
Lyanova and Aliyeva v Russia, nos 12713/02 and 28440/03, 2 October 2008 126

Lykourezos v Greece, no. 33554/03, ECHR 2006-VIII 1030
Lyons and Others v United Kingdom (dec.), no. 15227/03, ECHR 2003-IX............. 866
M. v Germany, no. 19359/04, ECHR 2009 .... 188, 235–6, 239, 346, 348–9
M. v Switzerland, no. 41199/06, 26 April 2011.. 378
M. and Others v Italy and Bulgaria, no. 40020/03, 31 July 2012 ....105, 191, 207–9
M. and V. v Romania, no. 29032/04, 27 September 2011 ....370, 391–2
M.A. v Cyprus, no. 41872/10, 23 July 2013....................................741, 1077
M.A. v Switzerland, no. 52589/13, 18 November 2014 189
Maaouia v France [GC], no. 39652/98, ECHR 2000-X.....................74, 275, 282, 957
McCann v United Kingdom, no. 19009/04, 13 May 2008........................... 399
McCann and Others v United Kingdom, 27 September 1995, Series A no. 324......... 117, 122–3,
                                                            130, 134–5, 147, 152, 158, 738
McElhinney v Ireland, [GC], no. 31253/96, ECHR 2001-XI...................39, 100, 273, 286
McFarlane v Ireland [GC], no. 31333/06, 10 September 2010................. 277, 292–3, 765–6
McGinley and Egan v United Kingdom, 9 June 1998, *Reports of Judgments and Decisions*
    1998-III.. 790
McGinley and Egan v United Kingdom (revision), nos 21825/93 and 23414/94,
    ECHR 2000-I...849, 853–4
McGlinchey and Others v United Kingdom, no. 50390/99, ECHR 2003-V 133, 174
McHugo v Switzerland (dec.), no. 55705/00, 12 May 2005........................... 304
Maciariello v Italy, 27 February 1992, Series A no. 230-A 541
McIlvanny v United Kingdom (dec.), no. 6239/06, 6 March 2007...................... 259
McKay v United Kingdom [GC], no. 543/03, ECHR 2006-X 226, 229, 231, 248–50, 252
McKeown v United Kingdom, no. 6684/05, 11 January 2011 310
McKerr v United Kingdom, no. 28883/95, ECHR 2001-III 131, 136, 793
McKerr v United Kingdom (dec.), no. 28883/95, 4 April 2000 807
McLean and Cole v United Kingdom (dec.), nos 12626/13 and 2522/12, 11 June 2013 1026
McShane v United Kingdom, no. 43290/98, 28 May 2002 ....568, 747–8
McVicar v United Kingdom, no. 46311/99, ECHR 2002-III..........................468–9
Maestri v Italy [GC], no. 39748/98, ECHR 2004-I....................... 403, 436, 469, 510–1
Magee v United Kingdom, no. 28135/95, ECHR 2000-VI 573
Maggio and Others v Italy, nos 46286/09, 52851/08, 53727/08, 54486/08, and
    56001/08, 31 May 2011 981
Magnago and Südtiroler Volkspartei v Italy (dec.), no. 25035/94, 15 April 1996............. 1030
Mahdid and Harrar v Austria (dec.), no. 74762/01, 8 December 2005 227
Mahmut Kaya v Turkey, no. 22535/93, ECHR 2000-III.................... 135, 151, 206, 550
Maiorano and Others v Italy, no. 28634/06, 15 December 2009 ....129, 188
Maire v Portugal, no. 48206/99, ECHR 2003-VII...............................38, 40, 392
Makaratzis v Greece [GC], no. 50385/99, ECHR 2004-XI 125–6, 129–31, 151
Makbule Kaymaz and Others v Turkey, no. 651/10, 25 February 2014 151
Makedonski v Bulgaria, no. 36036/04, 20 January 2011 1064
Makhmudov v Russia, no. 35082/04, 26 July 2007.....................491, 494, 496, 812
Maksymenko and Gerasymenko v Ukraine, no. 49317/07, 16 May 2013 977
Maktouf and Damjanović v Bosnia and Herzegovina [GC], nos 2312/08 and 34179/08,
    ECHR 2013 (extracts).....................99, 294–5, 352, 355, 564, 573, 1106, 1182
Maktouf and Damjanović v Bosnia and Herzegovina [GC], nos 2312/08 and 34179/08,
    Concurring Opinion of Judge Pinto de Albuquerque, Joined by Judge Vučinić, ECHR
    2013 (extracts) 334–5, 353–4
Malarde v France (dec.), no. 46813/99, 5 September 2000............................ 1021
Malhous v Czech Republic (dec.) [GC], no. 33071/96, ECHR 2000-XII 109, 740, 800, 970
Malige v France, 23 September 1998, *Reports of Judgments and Decisions* 1998-VII..........283, 1151
Mallah v France, no. 29681/08, 10 November 2011 389
Malone v United Kingdom, 2 August 1984, Series A no. 82............. 368, 386–7, 401, 403, 790
Malsagova and Others v Russia (dec.), no. 27244/03, 6 March 2008 ....774, 776–8
Mamatkulov and Abdurasulovic v Turkey, nos 46827/99 and 46951/99, 6 February 2003.....731, 749

Mamatkulov and Askarov v Turkey [GC], nos 46827/99 and 46951/99, ECHR 2005-I 49, 54,
    70, 73, 194–5, 282, 685, 735, 746, 749–50, 1045
Mamedova v Russia, no. 7064/05, 1 June 2006. 257
Mamère v France, no. 12697/03, ECHR 2006-XIII. 475
Manasson v Sweden (dec.), no. 41265/98, 8 April 2003. 1153
Mancini v Italy, no. 44955/98, ECHR 2001-IX 227
Mandil v France (dec.), no. 67037/09, 13 December 2011. 822–3
Mangouras v Spain [GC], no. 12050/04, ECHR 2010. 253
Manoilescu and Dobrescu v Romania and Russia (dec.), no. 60861/00, ECHR 2005-VI 100, 285–6
Mansur v Turkey, 8 June 1995, Series A no 319-B 253
Mansur Yalçin and Others v Turkey, no. 21163/11, 16 September 2014 1003
Mansuroğlu v Turkey, no. 43443/98, 26 February 2008 . . . . .151, 811
Mantovanelli v France, 18 March 1997, *Reports of Judgments and Decisions* 1997-II 288
Manushaqe Puto and Others v Albania, nos 604/07, 43628/07, 46684/07, and 34770/09,
    31 July 2012. . . . . .77, 869–70, 970
Margareta and Roger Andersson v Sweden, 25 February 1992, Series A no. 226-A. 338
Maravić Markeš v Craotia, no. 70923/11, 9 January 2014 . . . . .288, 783
Marckx v Belgium, 13 June 1979, Series A no. 31 . . . . 39, 389, 391, 534, 538, 583, 743,
    866, 969, 973, 1178
Marguš v Croatia, no. 4455/10, 13 November 2012 . . . . 128, 295, 317, 1150, 1155
Marguš v Croatia [GC], no. 4455/10, 27 May 2014 . . . . .39, 43, 67, 128–9, 179,
    295–6, 848, 1038, 1155
Marguš v Croatia [GC], no. 4455/10, Joint Concurring Opinion of Judges Šikuta,
    Wojtyczek, and Vehabović, 27 May 2014. 89
Maria Atanasiu and Others v Romania, nos 30767/05 and 33800/06,
    12 October 2010. . . . . .696, 870, 970
Mariani v France, no. 43640/98, 31 March 2005 . . . . .317, 1137
Marie-Louise Loyen and Bruneel v France, no. 55929/00, 5 July 2005 800
Marina Alekseyeva v Russia, no. 22490/05, 19 December 2013 133–4
Markass Car Hire Ltd v Cyprus (dec.), no. 51591/99, 23 October 2001 275
Marshall v United Kingdom (dec.), no. 41571/98, 10 July 2001. 600
Martin v Estonia, no. 35985/09, 30 May 2013 319
Martinie v France [GC], no. 58675/00, ECHR 2006-VI 94, 289, 290
Martins Silva v Portugal, no. 12959/10, 28 May 2014. 782
Marturana v Italy, no. 63154/00, 4 March 2008 230–1
Martynov v Ukraine, no. 36202/03, 14 December 2006 903
Masaev v Moldova, no. 6303/05, 12 May 2009. 420
Maširević v Serbia, no. 30671, 11 February 2014. 286
Maskhadova and Others v Russia, no. 18071/05, 6 June 2013 135
Maslov v Austria [GC], no. 1638/03, ECHR 2008 . . . . .397, 405
Maslova and Nalbandov v Russia, no. 839/02, 24 January 2008 . . . . .176, 178, 813
Mason and Van Zon v Netherlands, 28 September 1995, Series A no. 327-A 273
Massey v United Kingdom, no. 14399/02, 16 November 2004 293
Mastromatteo v Italy [GC], no. 37703/97, ECHR 2002-VIII. 129, 134, 137, 188
Mata Estevez v Spain (dec.), no. 56501/00, ECHR 2001-VI 390
Mateescu v Romania, no. 1944/10, 14 January 2014. . . . . .712, 846
Matencio v France, no. 58749/00, 15 January 2004. . . . . .174, 186
Mathieu-Mohin and Clerfayt v Belgium, 2 March 1987, Series A no. 113. . . . . 68, 1018–21, 1024
Matijašević v Serbia, no. 23037/04, ECHR 2006-X. 302
Matko v Slovenia, no. 43393/98, 2 November 2006 78
Matos e Silva Ltd, and Others v Portugal, 16 September 1996, *Reports of Judgments and
    Decisions* 1996-IV 972
Matrot S.A. and Others v France (dec.), no. 43798/98, 3 February 2000 736
Matthews v United Kingdom [GC], no. 24833/94, ECHR 1999-I. 97, 927, 1020–1, 1023
Matúz v Hungary, no. 73571/10, 21 October 2014. 465

Matveyev v Russia, no. 26601/02, 3 July 2008 . . . . .110, 1144
Matveyev and Matveyeva v Russia (dec.), no. 26601/02, 14 December 2004. 1146
Matyar v Turkey, no. 23423/94, 21 February 801 801
Matyjek v Poland (dec.), no. 38184/03, ECHR 2007-V. 284, 309
Matytsina v Russia, no. 58428/10, 27 March 2014 288
Matznetter v Austria, 10 November 1969, Series A no. 10 252
Matznetter v Austria, 10 November 1969, Concurring Opinion of Judge G. Balladore Pallieri,
    Series A no. 10 239
Matznetter v Austria, 10 November 1969, Dissenting Opinion of Judge M. Zekia, Series A
    no. 10. 239
Mayaeva v Russia, no. 37287/09, 18 September 2014 137
Mayali v France, no. 69116/01, 14 June 2005. 313
Mayzit v Russia, no. 63378/00, 20 January 2005. 308
Mazurek v France, no. 34406/97, ECHR 2000-II 574, 583
M.B. v Switzerland, no. 28256/95, 30 November 2000 257
M.C. v Bulgaria, no. 39272/98, ECHR 2003-XII 182, 191–2, 279, 369–70, 576
M.C. v Bulgaria, no. 39272/98, Concurring Opinion of Judge Tulkens, ECHR 2003-XII 192
M.C. v Finland (dec.), no. 28460/95, 25 January 2001 324
M.D. and Others v Malta, no. 64791/10, 17 July 2012. 393–4
Medenica v Switzerland, no. 20491/92, ECHR 2001-VI 316–7
Medova v Russia, no. 25385/04, 15 January 2009. . . . . .129, 229
Medvedyev and Others v France [GC], no. 3394/03, ECHR 2010. . . . . 102, 226–7, 229, 231, 848
Megadat.com SRL v Moldova, no. 21151/04, ECHR 2008. . . . . .971, 977
Mehemi v France (no. 2), no. 53470, ECHR 2003-IV. 869
Mehmet Emin Yüksel v Turkey, no. 40154/98, 20 July 2004. 135
Mehmet Nuri Özen v Turkey, no. 37619/05, 2 February 2010 401
Mehmet Salih and Abdülsamet Çakmak v Turkey, no. 45630/99, 29 April 2004. 400
Mehmet Ümit Erdem v Turkey, no. 42234/02, 17 July 2008. 191
Melnik v Ukraine, no. 72286/01, 28 March 2006 780
Melnychenko v Ukraine, no. 17707/02, ECHR 2004-X. 35, 947, 1029, 1030
Melnychuk v Ukraine (dec.), no. 28743/03, ECHR 2005-IX 78, 460, 971
Melnyk v Ukraine, no. 23436/03, 28 March 2006. 286
Meltex Ltd v Armenia (dec.), no. 37780/02, 27 May 2008. 108
Meltex Ltd and Movseyan v Armenia, no. 32283/04, 17 June 2008 736
Members of the Gldani Congregation of Jehovah's Witnesses and Others v Georgia,
    no. 71156/01, 3 May 2007 . . . . .181, 421–2, 425
Menesheva v Russia, no. 59261/00, ECHR 2006-III 176, 178, 230, 551, 1151
Mennitto v Italy [GC], no. 33804/96, ECHR 2000-X. 272
Menson v United Kingdom (dec.), no. 47916/99, 6 May 2003 159
Menteş and Others v Turkey (Article 50), 24 July 1998, *Reports of Judgments and Decisions*
    1998-IV 627
Mentzen v Latvia (dec.), no. 71074/01, 7 December 2004. 375–6
Mentzen alias Mencena v Latvia (dec.), no. 71041/01, 7 December 2004 779
Merger and Cros v France (dec.), no. 68864/01, 11 March 2004 766
Merschdorf v Romania (dec.), no. 31918/08, 21 May 2013 .1180, 1182–3
Meriakri v Moldova (striking out), no. 53487/99, 1 March 2005 799
Messina v Italy (no. 2) (dec.), no. 25498/94, ECHR 1999-V 174, 186, 398
Metin Turan v Turkey, no. 20868/02, 14 November 2006 514
Metropolitan Church of Bessarabia and Others v Moldova, no. 45701/99, ECHR
    2001-XII 420–1, 425, 427, 429–30, 440, 499
Mezhidov v Russia, no. 67326/01, 25 September 2008 155
Mežnarić v Croatia, no. 71615/01, 15 July 2005 296
MGN Limited v United Kingdom, no. 39401/04, 18 January 2011 . . . . .368, 458, 461
M.H. and A.S. v United Kingdom (dec.), nos 38267/07 and 14293/07, 16 December 2008 799
Miah v United Kingdom (dec.), no. 53080/07, 27 April 2010 397

Miailhe v France (no. 1), 25 February 1993, Series A no. 256-C. 767
Miailhe v France (no. 2), 26 September 1996, *Reports of Judgments and Decisions* 1996-IV 287
Miażdżyk v Poland, no. 23592/07, 24 January 2012 1061
Micallef v Malta, no. 17056/06, 15 January 2008 . . . . .74, 296
Micallef v Malta [GC], no. 17056/06, ECHR 2009. . . . . .33, 266, 272–3, 275, 295–6,
737–8, 740, 764, 767, 800, 838
Micallef v Malta [GC], no. 17056/06, Joint Concurring Opinion of Judges Rozakis,
Tulkens, and Kalaydyieva, ECHR 2009 276
Micallef v Malta [GC], no. 17056/06, Joint Dissenting Opinion of Judge Costa, Jungwiert,
Kovler, and Fura, ECHR 2009. . . . . .276, 781
Mieg de Boofzheim v France (dec.), no. 52938/99, 2 December 2002 284
Mignon v Belgium (dec.), no. 20022/09 5 June 2012 355
Mijailović v Serbia (dec.), no. 14366/08, 5 February 2013 1183
Mikayil Mammadov v Azerbaijan, no. 4762/05, 17 December 2009. 132
Mikheyev v Russia, no. 77617/01, 26 January 2006. . . . . .135, 178, 193
Mikheyeva v Latvia (dec.), no. 50029/99, 12 September 2002 745
Mikolajová v Slovakia, no. 4479/03, 18 January 2011 385
Mikolenko v Estonia (dec.), no. 16944/03, 5 January 2006 777–8
Mikolenko v Estonia (dec.), no. 10664/05, 8 January 2008 1078
Mikulić v Croatia, no. 53176/99, ECHR 2002-I. 376
Mileva and Others v Bulgaria, nos 43449/02 and 21475/04, 25 November 2010 387–8
Millan I Tornes v Andorra (friendly settlement), no. 35052/97, ECHR 1999-IV. 820
Miller v Sweden, no. 55853/00, 8 February 2005 289
Miller and Others v United Kingdom, nos 45825/99, 45826/99, and 45827/99,
26 October 2004. 296
Milošević v Netherlands (dec.), no. 77631/01, 19March 2002 766
Minelli v Switzerland, 25 March 1983, Series A no. 62 .299, 303–4, 306
Minelli v Switzerland (dec.), no. 14991/02, 14 June 2005 378
Minjat v Switzerland, no. 38223/97, 28 October 2003 233–4
Mir Isfahani v Netherlands (dec.), no. 31252/03, 31 January 2008. 189
Miroļubovs and Others v Latvia, no. 798/05, 15 September 2009. . . . . 430, 780–1, 822–3
Mirosław Garlicki v Poland, no. 36921/07, 14 June 2011. 185
Miszczyński v Poland (dec.), no. 23672/07, 8 February 2011. 780
Misick v United Kingdom (dec.), no. 10781/10, 16 October 2012. . . . . .47, 375, 1031
Mitap and Müftüoğlu v Turkey, 25 March 1996, *Reports of Judgments and Decisions* 1996-II 108
Mitchell v United Kingdom (dec.), no. 40447/98, 24 November 1998. 398
Mitchell and Holloway v United Kingdom, no. 44808/98, 17 December 2002 293
Miulescu v Romania, no. 35493/06, 9 April 2013. 1050
Mižigárová v Slovakia, no. 74832/01, 14 December 2010 133
Mizzi v Malta, no. 26111/02, ECHR 2006-I (extracts) 322, 391
Mjelde v Norway (dec.), no. 11143/04, 1 February 2007. 1152
Mkrtchyan v Armenia, no. 6562/03, 11 January 2007. . . . . .496, 510, 779
M.M. v Netherlands (dec.), no. 39339/98, 21 May 2002. 279
M.M. v United Kingdom, no. 24029/07, 13 November 2012. . . . . .382, 384, 815
Mocanu and Others v Romania, nos 10865/09, 45886/07, and 32431/08, Concurring
Opinion of Judge Pinto d'Albuquerque, Joined by Judge Vučinić, 17 September 2014 179
Modinos v Cyprus, 22 April 1993, Series A no. 259 . . . . .38, 182, 279, 381
Mogoş v Romania, no. 20420/02, 13 October 2005 227
Mohammad Hassan v Netherlands and Italy (dec.), no. 40524/10, 27 August 2013. 828
Moiseyev v Russia, no. 62936/00, 9 October 2008 398
Mokrani v France, no. 52206/99, 15 July 2003. 397
Moldovan v Romania (no. 2), nos 41138/98 and 64320/01, ECHR 2005-VII (extracts) 111, 196,
321–2
Moldovan and Others and Rostaş and Others v Romania (dec.), nos 41138/98 and 64320/01,
13 March 2001. 111

Mółka v Poland (dec.), no. 56550/00, ECHR 2006-IV 370, 375

Monedero Angora v Spain (dec.), no. 41138/05, 7 October 2008. 282

Monnat v Switzerland, no. 73604/01, ECHR 2006-X 451, 474, 738

Monnell and Morris v United Kingdom, 2 March 1987, Series A no. 115. . . . . .236, 790

Monory v Romania and Hungary, no. 71099/01, 5 April 2005 391

Montcornet de Caumont v France (dec.), no. 59290/00, 13 May 2003. 281

Montcornet de Caumont v France (dec.), no. 59290/00, ECHR 2003-VII 275

Montera v Italy (dec.), no. 64713/01, 9 July 2002. 284

Mooren v Germany [GC], no. 11364/03, 9 July 2009 . . . . .230–34, 254–7, 764–7, 785–6, 845

Mooren v Germany [GC], no. 11364/03, Joint Partially Dissenting Opinion of Judges
    Rozakis, Tulkens, Casadevall, Gyulumyan, Hayiyev, Spielmann, Berro-Lefévre, and
    Bianku, 9 July 2009 . . . . .231, 233

Moreira Barbosa v Portugal (dec.), no. 65681/01, 29 April 2004 767

Moreno Gómez v Spain, no. 4143/02, ECHR 2004-X. 387, 399

Morsink v Netherlands, no. 48865/99, 11 May 2004 242

Moscow Branch of the Salvation Army in Russia, no. 72881/01, ECHR 2006-XI . . . 492, 501, 511, 524

Mosendz v Ukraine, no. 52013/08, 17 January 2013. . . . . .123, 132, 134

Moser v Austria, no. 12643/02, 21 September 2006 291

Moskal v Poland, no. 10373/05, 15 September 2009. . . . . .972, 977

Mosley v United Kingdom, no. 48009/08, 10 May 2011 . . . . 82, 367–9, 385, 455, 458, 461–2

Mosteanu and Others v Romania, no. 33176/96, 26 November 2002. 972

Mouisel v France, no. 67263/01, ECHR 2002-IX 133, 171, 174, 184–6

Moullet v France (dec.), no. 27521/04, 13 September 2007. .278, 283, 304

Moustaquim v Belgium, 18 February 1991, Series A no. 193. . . . . .389, 395

Mouvement raëlien suisse v Switzerland, no. 16354/06, 13 January 2011 452

Mouvement raëlien suisse v Switzerland [GC], no. 16354/06, ECHR 2012 (extracts). 452, 474

Mouvement raëlien suisse v Switzerland [GC], no. 16354/06, Concurring Opinion of Judge
    Bratza, ECHR 2012 (extracts) 91

Mouvement raëlien suisse v Switzerland [GC], no. 16354/06, Dissenting Opinion of
    Judge Pinto de Albuquerque, ECHR 2012 (extracts) 91, 462

Mouvement raëlien suisse v Switzerland [GC], no. 16354/06, Joint Dissenting Opinion of
    Judges Tulkens, Sajó, Lazarova Trajkovska, Bianku, Power-Force, Vučinić, and Yudkivska,
    ECHR 2012 (extracts). 44, 463

Moyo Alvarez v Spain (dec.), no. 44677/98, 23 November 1999 771

M.P. and Others v Bulgaria, no. 22457/08, 15 November 2011. 369

Mrkić v Croatia (dec.), no. 7118/03, 8 June 2006 110

Mróz v Poland (striking out), no. 35192/97, 9 December 2003 798

Mrozowski v Poland, no. 9258/04, 12 May 2009 172

M.S. v United Kingdom, no. 24527/08, Declaration of Judge Kalaydjieva, 3 May 2012. 855

M.S.S. v Belgium and Greece [GC], no. 30696/09, ECHR 2011 . . . . 75–6, 551, 707, 792–5, 812

M.S.S. v Belgium and Greece [GC], no. 30696/09, Partly Dissenting Opinion of Judge Bratza,
    ECHR 2011. 795

Mubilanzila Mayeka and Kaniki Mitunga v Belgium, no. 13178/03, ECHR 2006-XI 168, 170, 240

Mudric v Republic of Moldova, no. 74839/10, 16 July 2013 192

Mulaj and Sallahi v Austria (dec.), no. 48886/99, 27 June 2002. 304

Müller v Austria, no. 12555/03, 5 October 2006. . . . . .299, 1138

Müller v Czech Republic (dec.), no. 48058/09, 6 September 2011 348–9

Müller v Switzerland, no. 41202/98, 5 November 2002. . . . . .451, 464

Müller and Others v Switzerland, 24 May 1988, Series A no. 133. . . . . 39, 455, 463, 472

Mulosmani v Albania, no. 29864/03, 8 October 2013 . . . . .277, 308

Muñoz Díaz v Spain, no. 49151/07, ECHR 2009 . . . . .533, 544

Murat Vural v Turkey, no. 9540/07, 21 October 2014 . . . . .455, 476, 1029

Murphy v Ireland, no. 44179/98, ECHR 2003-IX. 451, 458

Murray v Netherlands, no. 10511/10, 10 December 2013 182

Murray v United Kingdom [GC], 28 October 1994, Series A no. 300-A 234, 238, 245–6,
319, 688, 710

Mürsal Eren v Turkey, no. 60856/00, ECHR 2006-II 997

Musa and Others v United Kingdom (striking out), no. 8276/07, 26 June 2012 800

Musayev and Others v Russia, nos 57941/00, 58699/00, and 60403/00, 26 July 2007 . . . . 147, 170

Musiał v Poland [GC], no. 24557/94, ECHR 1999-II 257

Müslim v Turkey, no. 53566/99, 26 April 2005 195

Mustafa and Armağan Akın v Turkey, no. 4694/03, 6 April 2010. 389

Musuc v Moldova, no. 42440/06, 6 November 2007 . . . . .250, 253

Mutlag v Germany, no. 40601/05, 25 March 2010 395

Mutlu v Turkey, no. 8006/02, 10 October 2006 . . . . .400, 740

Mykhaylenky and Others v Ukraine, nos 35091/02, 35196/02, 35201/02, 35204/02, 35945/02,
35949/02, 35953/02, 36800/02, 38296/02, and 42814/02, ECHR 2004-XII. 90

N. v Finland, no. 38885/02, 26 July 2005 195

N. v United Kingdom, no. 26565/05, ECHR 2008 191

N. and Others v United Kingdom (dec.), no. 16458/12, 15 April 2014 194–5

N.A. v United Kingdom, no. 25904/07, 17 July 2008 . . . . .194–5, 812

Nachova and Others v Bulgaria, nos 43577/98 and 43579/98, 26 February 2004 159

Nachova and Others v Bulgaria [GC], nos 43577/98 and 43579/98, ECHR 2005-VII 123,
129–31, 150–1, 159, 553, 564, 570, 578, 810

Nada v Switzerland [GC], no. 10593/08, ECHR 2012 . . . . .37, 73, 92, 94, 106, 369,
371, 738, 744, 793–4, 1056, 1058

Nagla v Latvia, no. 73469/10, 16 July 2013 459

Nagula v Estonia (dec.), no. 39203/02, 25 October 2005 1072

Najafli v Azerbaijan, no. 2594/07, 2 October 2012 . . . . .458, 461

Nakhmanovich v Russia, no. 55669/00, 2 March 2006 233

Nakov v former Yugoslav Republic of Macedonia (dec.), no. 68286/01, 24 October 2003 143

Nalbantski v Bulgaria, no. 30943/04, 10 February 2011 .1058, 1061–3

Namat Aliyev v Azerbaijan, no. 18705/06, 8 April 2010 . . . . 1020, 1025–6, 1029

Napijalo v Croatia, no. 66485/01, 13 November 2003 . . . . .378, 1058, 1061

Narcisio v Netherlands (dec.), no. 47810/99, 27 January 2005 173

Nart v Turkey, no. 20817/04, 6 May 2008 251

Nasrulloyev v Russia, no. 656/06, 11 October 2007 . . . . .231–2, 243

Năstase-Silivestru v Romania, no. 74785/01, 4 October 2007 248

Natetilić v Croatia (dec.), 4 May 2000 354

National & Provincial Building Society, Leeds Permanent Building Society and Yorkshire
Building Society v United Kingdom, 23 October 1997, *Reports of Judgments and Decisions*
1997-VII 81, 335, 564, 567–8, 981, 1184

National Union of Belgian Police v Belgium, 27 October 1975, Series A no. 19 . . . . 46, 505–6,
523–4, 563, 565

National Union of Belgian Police v Belgium, 27 October 1975, Joint Separate Opinion of
Judges Wiarda, Ganshof van der Meersch, and Bindschedler-Robert, Series A no. 19 524

National Union of Belgian Police v Belgium, 27 October 1975, Separate Opinion of Sir Gerald
Fitzmaurice, Series A no. 19 . . . . .41, 523

National Union of Rail, Maritime, and Transport Workers v United Kingdom, no. 31045/10,
8 April 2014 . . . . .508, 778

National Union of Rail, Maritime, and Transport Workers v United Kingdom, no. 31045/10,
Concurring Opinion of Judge Wojtyczek, 8 April 2014 903

Natsvlishvili and Togonidze v Georgia, no. 9043/05, 29 April 2014 . . . . .271, 302, 1140

Naumenko v Ukraine, no. 42023/98, 10 February 2004 . . . . .171, 185

Naumoski v former Yugoslav Republic of Macedonia (revision), no. 25248/05,
5 December 2013 853

Naumov v Albania (dec.), no. 10513/03, 3 December 2002 1072

Navalnyy and Yashin v Russia, no. 76204/11, 4 December 2014 . . . . .173, 627

Navarra v France, 23 November 1993, Series A no. 273-B 255–6

Naviede v United Kingdom (dec.), no. 38072/97, 7 September 1999 309
Naydyon v Ukraine, no. 16474/03, 14 October 2010 748
Nazarenko v Ukraine, no. 39483/98, 29 April 2003. 41
N.C. v Italy [GC] no. 24952/94, ECHR 2002-X 258, 764, 786
Necdet Bulut v Turkey, no. 77092/01, 20 November 2007 172
Nechiporuk and Yonkalo, v Ukraine, no. 42310/04, 21 April 2011 . . . . .258, 640
Nedzela v France, no. 73695/01, 27 July 2006 1135
Nee v Ireland (dec.), no. 52787/99, 30 January 2003. 772
Negrepontis-Giannisis v Greece, no. 56759/08, 3 May 2011 . . . . 375, 394, 407, 389, 391
Negyeliczky v Hungary (dec.), no. 42622/14, 14 October 2014 1158
Neigel v France, 17 March 1997, *Reports of Judgments and Decisions* 1997-II 272
Neij and Sunde Kolmisoppi v Sweden (dec.), no. 40397/12, 19 February 2013 . . . . .455, 480
Nejdet Şahin and Perihan Şahin v Turkey [GC], no. 13279/05, 20 October 2011 271
Nekvedavicius v Germany (dec.), no. 46165/99, 19 June 2003. 391
Nemtsov v Russia, no. 1774/11, 31 July 2014. 551–2
Nerva and Others v United Kingdom, no. 42295/98, ECHR 2002-VIII. 970
Nespala v Czech Republic (dec.), no. 68198/10, 24 September 2013 212
Něšťák v Slovakia, no. 65559/01, 27 February 2007 . . . . .233, 303
Neulinger and Shuruk v Switzerland [GC], no. 41615/07, ECHR 2010 . . . . .55, 393
Neumeister v Austria, 27 June 1968, Series A no. 8. . . . . 250–1, 253, 275, 288
Nevmerzhitsky v Ukraine, no. 54825/00, ECHR 2005-II (extracts) 132, 262
News Verlags GmbH & Co KG v Austria, no. 31457/96, ECHR 2000-I 460
N.F. v Italy, no. 37119/97, ECHR 2001-IX 491–2, 510–1
Nicola v Turkey (revision), no. 18404/91, 26 October 2010 854
Nicoleta Gheorghe v Romania, no. 23470/05, 3 April 2012. .299, 784
Nicolova and Vandova v Bulgaria, no. 20688/04, 17 December 2013. 290
Niculescu v Romania, no. 25333/03, 25 June 2013. 308
Niedbała v Poland, no. 27915/95, 4 July 2000 249
Niedźwiedź v Poland (dec.), no. 1345/06, 11 March 2008. 1021
Nielsen v Denmark, 28 November 1988, Series A no. 144. 227
Niemietz v Germany, 16 December 1992, Series A no. 251-B 374, 386, 399
Nikitin v Russia, no. 50178/99, ECHR 2004-VIII 1149–50, 1154
Nikolova v Bulgaria [GC], no. 31195/96, ECHR 1999-II 249, 254–5, 836
Nikolova v Bulgaria (no. 2), no. 40896/98, 30 September 2004 227
Nikowitz and Verlagsgruppe News GmbH v Austria, no. 5266/03, 22 February 2007 . . . . .377, 462
Nikula v Finland, no. 31611/96, ECHR 2002-II. 455
Nilsen and Johnsen v Norway [GC], no. 23118/93, ECHR 1999-VIII 468
Nilsson v Sweden, no. 11811/05, 26 February 2008 973
Nilsson v Sweden (dec.), no. 73661/01, 13 December 2005. . . . . .1151, 1153
Nitecki v Poland (dec.), no. 65653/01, 21 March 2002 . . . . .131, 371
Nivette v France (dec.), no. 44190/98, ECHR 2001-VII .146, 195, 1100
N.K.M. v Hungary, no. 66529/11, 14 May 2013 979
Nolan and K. v Russia, no. 2512/04, 12 February 2009. . . . .425, 434, 436–7, 440, 812, 814, 1127–30
Nold v Germany, no. 27250/02, 29 June 2006 780
Nölkenbockhoff v Germany, 25 August 1987, Series A no. 123 . . . . .299, 304, 306
Nordisk Film & TV A/S v Denmark (dec.), no. 40485/02, ECHR 2005-XII 459
Normann v Denmark (dec.), no. 44704/98 14 June 2001 744
Norris v Ireland, 26 October 1988, Series A no. 142 . . . . .38, 182, 279, 340, 381, 738, 742–3
Norwood v United Kingdom (dec.), no. 23131/03, 16 November 2004, *Reports of Judgments*
    and Decisions 2004-VII (extracts) 617, 619
Nosov v Russia (dec.), no. 30877/02, 20 October 2005 . . . . .736, 741
Novotka v Slovakia (dec.), no. 47244/99, 4 November 2003 .234, 236
Nowak v Ukraine, no. 60846/10, 31 March 2011. . . . . .245, 1128
Nowicka v Poland, no. 30218/96, 3 December 2002. 236
Nowicky v Austria, no. 34983/02, 24 February 2005. 293

Nunez v Norway, no. 55597/09, 28 June 2011 . . . . 366, 368, 395–6, 398

Nunez v Norway, no. 55597/09, Joint Dissenting Opinion of Judges Mojović and
  De Gaetano, 28 June 2011 398

Nurettin Aldemir and Others v Turkey, nos 32124/02, 32126/02, 32129/02, 32132/02,
  32133/02, 32137/02, and 32138/02, 18 December 2007 498

Nurmagomedov v Russia, no. 30138/02, 7 June 2007 748

Nuutinen v Finland, no. 32842/96, ECHR 2000-VIII. 391

Nuutinen v Finland, no. 32842/96, Dissenting Opinion of Judge Zupančić, Joined by Judges
  Panţiru and Türmen, ECHR 2000-VIII 849

Nykänen v Finland, no. 11828/11, 20 May 2014 1150

Nylund v Finland (dec.), no. 27110/95, ECHR 1999-VI. 391, 538

O. v Norway, no. 29327/95, ECHR 2003-II. 304

O. v United Kingdom, 8 July 1987, Series A no. 120 . . . . .791, 827

OAO Neftyanaya Kompaniya Yukos v Russia, no. 14902/04, 20 September 2011 776

Oates v Poland (dec.), no. 35036/97, 11 May 2000. 625

Obasa v United Kingdom, no. 50034/99, 16 January 2003 292

Oberschlick v Austria (no. 2), 1 July 1997, *Reports of Judgments and Decisions* 1997-IV 476

Observer and Guardian v United Kingdom, 26 November 1991, Series A no. 216. . . . . .452, 456

Öcalan v Turkey, no. 46221/99, 12 March 2003. . . . . .141, 144, 1199

Öcalan v Turkey (interim measures), no. 46221/99, 30 November 1999. 1096

Öcalan v Turkey (dec.), no. 46221/99, 14 December 2000 246

Öcalan v Turkey [GC], no. 46221/99, ECHR 2005-IV. 101, 144, 185–6, 190, 244, 246,
  627, 768, 848, 866, 869, 1115, 1199

Öcalan v Turkey [GC], no. 46221/99, Partly Concurring, Partly Dissenting Opinion of
  Judge Garlicki, ECHR 2005-IV. 36, 144

Öcalan v Turkey (no. 2), nos 24069/03, 197/04, 6201/06, and 10464/07,
  18 March 2014. . . . . .187, 350

Occhetto v Italy (dec.), no. 14507/07, 12 November 2013. . . . . .641, 1021, 1029

Ocone v Italy (dec.), no. 48889/99, 19 February 2004. 640

Odièvre v France [GC], no. 42326/98, ECHR 2003-III. 367, 369, 376, 785

O'Donoghue and Others v United Kingdom, no. 34848/07, ECHR 2010 (extracts) . . . 533–4, 540, 544

Oferta Plus SRL v Moldova, no. 14385/04, 19 December 2006 747–8

Ognyanova and Choban v Bulgaria, no. 46317/99, 23 February 2006. 553

Oğur v Turkey [GC], no. 21594/93, ECHR 1999-III 135

O.H. v Germany, no. 4646/08, 24 November 2011 . . . . .242, 592

O'Halloran and Francis v United Kingdom [GC], nos 15809/02 and 25624/02, ECHR
  2007-III. 277, 319

O'Halloran and Francis v United Kingdom [GC], nos 15809/02 and 25624/02, Dissenting
  Opinion of Judge Myjer, ECHR 2007-III. 781

O'Hara v United Kingdom, no. 37555/97, ECHR 2001-X 232, 239

O'Keefe v Ireland [GC], no. 35810/09, Joint Partly Dissenting Opinion of Judges Zupančić,
  Gyulumyan, Kalaydjieva, De Gaetano, and Wojtyczek, 28 January 2014 78

Okpisz v Germany, no. 59140/00, 25 October 2005. 564

Okyay and Others v Turkey, no. 36220/97, ECHR 2005-VII 903

O.L. v Finland (dec.), no. 61110/00, 5 July 2005 304

Olaechea Cahuas v Spain, no. 24668/03, ECHR 2006-X. 751

Olbertz v Germany (dec.), no. 37592/97, 25 May 1999. 971

Olczak v Poland, no. 30417/96, 7 November 2002 . . . . .741, 971

Oleksandr Volkov v Ukraine, no. 21722/11, 9 January 2013 794

Oleksy v Poland (dec.), no. 1379/06, 16 May 2009. . . . . .281, 744

Oliveira v Switzerland, 30 July 1998, *Reports of Judgments and Decisions* 1998-V 1153

Olivier Gaillard v France (dec.), no. 47337/99, 11 July 2000 772

Olivieira v Netherlands, no. 33129/96, ECHR 2002-IV. 1059

Öllinger v Austria, no. 76900/01, ECHR 2006-IX. 492, 494

Ölmez v Turkey (dec.), no. 39464/98, 1 February 2005. 771

Ölmez v Turkey (dec.), no. 39464/98, 5 July 2005 771
Ölmez and Others v Turkey, no. 22746/03, 9 November 2010 151
Ölmez v Turkey (dec.), no. 39464/98, 5 July 2005 . . . . 697, 702, 708, 771, 849
O'Loughlin and Others v United Kingdom (dec.), no. 23274/04, 25 August 2005 . . . . .770, 772
Olsson v Sweden (no. 1), 24 March 1988, Series A no. 130 391–2
Olsson v Sweden (no. 2), 27 November 1992, Series A no. 250 392
Oluić v Croatia, no. 61260/08, 20 May 2010 387
Olujić v Croatia, no. 22330/05, 5 February 2009 . . . . .274, 289
Olymbiou v Turkey, no. 16091/90, 27 October 2009 355
Omojudi v United Kingdom, no. 1820/08, 24 November 2009 405
Öneryıldız v Turkey, no. 48939/99, 18 June 2002 38
Öneryıldız v Turkey [GC], no. 48939/99, ECHR 2004-XII 38, 40–1, 127, 131, 971
Ongun v Turkey (dec.), no. 15737/02, 10 October 2006 1153
Onoufriou v Cyprus, no. 24407/04, 7 January 2010 186
Onur v United Kingdom, no. 27319/07, 17 February 2009 398
Open Door and Dublin Well Woman v Ireland, 29 October 1992, Series A no. 246-A 742–3
Opinion of the European Court of Human Rights on Draft Protocol No. 12 to the European
    Convention on Human Rights, 6 December 1999 . . . . 565, 1180, 1182
Opinion of the Court on Draft Protocol No. 15 to the European Convention on Human Rights,
    6 February 2013 . . . . 75, 79, 650, 680, 711
Opinion of the European Court of Human Rights on Draft Protocol No. 16 to the European
    Convention on Human Rights extending its competence to give advisory opinions on the
    interpretation of the Convention, 6 May 2013 . . . . 680, 887, 1217, 1220, 1225
Opuz v Turkey, no. 33401/02, ECHR 2009 . . . . 37, 126, 127, 129, 160, 192, 198, 279,
                                              572, 575, 576, 742
Oral and Atabay v Turkey, no. 39686/02, 23 June 2009 248–9
Oran v Turkey, nos 28881/07 and 37920/07, 15 April 2014 . . . . 1023, 1026–7
Orban and Others v France, no. 20985/05, 15 January 2005 619
Orhan v Turkey, no. 25656/94, ECHR 2002 . . . . .123, 171, 193, 552, 627, 751, 813, 839
Orr v Norway, no. 31283/04, 15 May 2008 304–5
Oršuš and Others v Croatia, no. 15766/03, Joint Partly Dissenting Opinion of Judges
    Jungwiert, Vajić, Kovler, Gyulumyan, Jaeger, Myjer, Berro-Lefevre, and Vučinić,
    17 July 2008 574
Oršuš and Others v Croatia [GC], no. 15766/03, ECHR 2010 . . . . . . 40, 570, 575, 578, 848, 1004–5
Orujov v Azerbaijan, no. 4508/06, 26 July 2011 1025
Osman v Denmark, no. 38058/09, 14 June 2011 397
Osman v United Kingdom, 28 October 1998, *Reports of Judgments and Decisions*
    1998-VIII 126, 129, 274, 370, 454
Osmanoğlu v Turkey, no. 48804/99, 24 January 2008 170
Osmanov and Yuseinov v Bulgaria (dec.), nos 54178/00 and 59901/00, 23 September
    2004 . . . . .281, 744
Ostendorf v Germany, no. 15598/08, 7 March 2013 237
Ostendorf v Germany, no. 15598/08, Concurring Opinion of Judges Lemmens and
    Jäderblom, 7 March 2013 237
Österreichischer Rundfunk v Austria (dec.), no. 57597/00, 25 May 2004 455
Österreichischer Rundfunk v Austria, no. 35841/02, 7 December 2006 737
Ostrovar v Moldova, no. 35207/03, 13 September 2005 401
Osypenko v Ukraine, no. 4634/04, 9 November 2010 . . . . .227, 237
Otegi Mondragon v Spain, no. 2034/07, ECHR 2011 . . . . .456, 474–8
Othman (Abu Qatada) v United Kingdom, no. 8139/09, ECHR 2012 (extracts) 96, 282, 1128
Otto v Germany (dec.), no. 21425/06, 10 November 2009 772
Otto-Preminger-Institut v Austria, 20 September 1994, Series A no. 295-A 426, 472–3, 742
Ould Dah v France (dec.), no. 13113/03, ECHR 2009 . . . . 44, 128, 164, 179,
                                     280, 335–6, 342, 344, 354, 616–7
Ouranio Toxo and Others v Greece, no. 74989/01, ECHR 2005-X (extracts) 491, 494, 499, 503

Oya Ataman v Turkey, no. 74552/01, ECHR 2006-XIII 148, 484, 497–8, 514, 516
Özcan v Turkey (dec.), no. 12822, 21 November 2006 314
Özer v Turkey, nos 35721/04 and 3832/05, 5 May 2009 455
Özgür Gündem v Turkey, no. 23144/93, ECHR 2000-III 453
Özgürlük ve Dayanışma Partisi (ÖDP) v Turkey, no. 7819/03, 10 May 2012 . . . . 1018, 1022
Özgürlük ve Dayanışma Partisi (ÖDP) v Turkey, no. 7819/03, Partly Dissenting
  Opinion of Judges Tulkens and Sajó, 10 May 2012 1022
Öztürk v Germany, 21 February 1984, Series A no. 73 . . . . 277, 315, 346, 1151
P. and S. v Poland, no. 57375/08, 30 October 2012 . . . . 82, 124, 240, 366, 373, 383, 404–5, 431
Pachla v Poland (dec.), no. 8812/02, 8 November 2005 769
Padovani v Italy, 26 February 1993, Series A no. 257-B 294
Paeffgen GmbH v Germany (dec.), nos 25379/04, 21688/05, 21722/05, and 21770/05,
  18 September 2007 971
Pailot v France, 22 April 1998, *Reports of Judgments and Decisions* 1998-II 869
Pakdemirli v Turkey, no. 35839/97, 22 February 2005 . . . . 476, 478
Paksas v Lithuania [GC], no. 34932/04, ECHR 2011 (extracts) 274, 284, 616–7,
                                                                                          619, 1021, 1023–4
Paladi v Moldova [GC], no. 39806/05, 10 March 2009 . . . . 73, 184–5, 735, 746–7, 749–51, 808
Palaoro v Austria, 23 October 1995, Series A no. 329-B 262, 1151
Palau-Martinez v France, no. 64927/01, ECHR 2003-XII 579
Palazzolo v Italy (dec.), no. 32328/09, 24 September 2013 271
Palić v Bosnia and Herzegovina, no. 4704/04, 15 February 2011 . . . . 36, 110
Palomo Sánchez and Others v Spain [GC], nos 28955/06, 28957/06, 28959/06, and
  28964/06, ECHR 2011 . . . . 43, 81, 451, 453, 464, 473, 476–7, 492, 580
Palomo Sánchez and Others v Spain [GC], nos 28955/06, 28957/06, 28959/06, and
  28964/06, Joint Dissenting Opinion of Judges Tulkens, David Thór Björgvinsson, Jočiené,
  Popović, and Vučinić, ECHR 2011 . . . . 465, 477
Panaitescu v Romania, no. 30909/06, 10 April 2012 131
Pančenko v Latvia (dec.), no. 40772/98, 28 October 1999 745
Panchenko v Russia, no. 45100/98, 8 February 2005 . . . . 251–2, 257
Pankiewicz v Poland, no. 34151/04, 12 February 2008 242
Pannullo and Forte v France, no. 37794/97, ECHR 2001-X 382
Panou v Greece, no. 44058/05, 8 January 2009 1136
Panovits v Cyprus, no. 4268/04, 11 December 2008 319
Pantea v Romania, no. 33343/96, ECHR 2003-VI (extracts) 233, 247, 249, 258
Panteleyenko v Ukraine, no. 11901/02, 29 June 2006 304
Papachelas v Greece [GC], no. 31423/96, ECHR 1999-II 771
Papamichalopoulos and Others v Greece, 24 June 1993, Series A no. 260-B 109
Papamichalopoulos and Others v Greece (Article 50), 31 October 1995, Series A no. 330-B 868
Papon v France (no. 1) (dec.), no. 64666/01, ECHR 2001-VI 174, 186
Papon v France (no. 2) (dec.), no. 54210/00, ECHR 2001-XII 297, 354
Papon v France, no. 54210/00, ECHR 2002-VII 1137
Paradis v Germany (dec.), no. 4065/04, 4 September 2007 236
Paraskeva Todorova v Bulgaria, no. 37193/07, 25 March 2010 322
Pardo v France (revision – admissibility), 10 July 1996, *Reports of Judgments and Decisions*
  1996-III 853
Parry v United Kingdom (dec.), no. 42971/05, ECHR 2006-XV 534, 536, 537
Parti nationaliste basque – Organisation régionale d'Iparralde v France, no. 71251/01, ECHR
  2007-II 484, 505, 513, 793, 807
Parti nationaliste basque – Organisation régionale d'Iparralde v France, no. 71251/01,
  Dissenting Opinion of Judge Rozakis, ECHR 2007-II 505
Partidul Comunistilor (Nepeceristi) and Ungureanu v Romania, no. 46626/99, ECHR
  2005-I (extracts) 491, 500, 503, 505, 515, 516, 520–1
Paşa and Erkan Erol v Turkey, no. 51358/99, 12 December 2006 131
Paskhalidis and Others v Greece, 19 March 1997, *Reports of Judgments and Decisions* 1997-II 791

Patera v Czech Republic (dec.), no. 25326/03, 10 January 2006.............................776–7
Patyi v Hungary, no. 35127/08, 17 January 2012 ....492, 498, 514
Patyi and Others v Hungary, no. 5529/05, 7 October 2008.........................496, 742
Pauger v Austria, 28 May 1997, *Reports of Judgments and Decisions* 1997-III 323
Paul and Audrey Edwards v United Kingdom, no. 46477/99, ECHR 2002-II............. 126, 129,
133–6, 193, 742, 772
Pavel Ivanov v Russia (dec.), no. 35222/04, 20 February 2007.......................617, 619
Pavlenko v Russia, no. 42371/02, 1 April 2010... 311
Pavlinović and Tonić v Croatia (dec.), nos 17124/05 and 17126/05, 3 September 2009......... 979
P.B. and J.S. v Austria, no. 18984/02, 22 July 2010 390
Peck v United Kingdom, no. 44647/98, ECHR 2003-I....................380, 383, 387
Pedersen and Baadsgaard v Denmark [GC], no. 49017/99, ECHR 2004-XI 82, 457–8, 475
Peers v Greece, no. 28524/95, ECHR 2001-III............................173, 181, 747
Pejic v Croatia (dec.), no. 66894/01, 19 December 2002...................................... 771
Peker v Turkey, no. 53014/99, 23 October 2003 321
Pélissier and Sassi v France [GC], no. 25444/94, ECHR 1999-II 292–3, 308–9
Pelladoah v Netherlands, 22 September 1994, Series A no. 297-B........................... 317
Pellegrin v France [GC], no. 28541/95, ECHR 1999-VIII.....................274, 523
Peñafiel Salgado v Spain (dec.), no. 65964/01, 16 April 2002..........................94, 282
Penart v Estonia (dec.), no. 14685/04, 24 January 2006..................................... 345
Pentiacova and Others v Moldova (dec.), no. 14462/03, ECHR 2005-I 131, 371
Peraldi v France (dec.), no. 2096/05, 7 April 2009.......................................777–8
Perdigão v Portugal [GC], no. 24768/06, 16 November 2010 981
Pereira Henriques and Others v Luxembourg (dec.), no. 60255/00, 26 August 2003 131
Perez v France [GC], no. 47287/99, ECHR 2004-I.. 297
Pérez de Rada Cavanilles v Spain, 28 October 1998, *Reports of Judgments and Decisions*
1998-VIII.. 781
Perinçek v Switzerland, no. 27510/08, 17 December 2013.......................44, 280, 480
Perişan and Others v Turkey, no. 12336/03, 20 May 2010 ....135, 153, 184, 707
Perk and Others v Turkey, no. 50739/99, 28 March 2006................................... 152
Perna v Italy [GC], no. 48898/99, ECHR 2003-V.......................82, 475, 714, 785, 845
Perry v Latvia, no. 30273/03, 8 November 2007.. 434
Perry v Latvia (dec.), no. 30273/03, 18 January 2007 771
Pescador Valero v Spain, no. 62435/00, ECHR 2003-VII 296
Pessino v France, no. 40403/02, 10 October 2006... 339
Pesti and Frondl v Austria (dec.), nos 27618/95 and 27619/95, ECHR 2000-I
(extracts)...1135–6, 1138
PETA Deutschland v Germany, no. 43481/09, 8 November 2012......................475, 479
PETA Deutschland v Germany, no. 43481/09, Concurring Opinion of Judge Zupančič,
Joined by Judge Spielmann, 8 November 2012 479
Petimat Ismailova and Others v Russia, nos 25088/11, 44277/11, 44284/11, 44313/11,
48134/11, 49486/11, 52076/11, 52182/11, 55055/11, 56574/11, 64266/11, and
66831/11, 18 September 2014.. 137
Petra v Romania, 23 September 1998, *Reports of Judgments and Decisions* 1998-VII 747
Petrakidov v Turkey, no. 16081/90, 27 May 2010... 355
Petrenco v Moldova, no. 20928/05, 30 March 2010 378
Petrov v Bulgaria, no. 15197/02, 22 May 2008.. 401
Petrov v Bulgaria, no. 19202/03, 24 April 2012... 126
Petrovic v Austria, 27 March 1998, *Reports of Judgments and Decisions* 1998-II.......... 524, 563–4,
567, 574, 576
Petukhova v Russia, no. 28796/07, 2 May 2013 ....236, 242
Pétur Thór Sigurðsson v Iceland, no. 39731/98, Concurring Opinion of Judge Zupančić,
ECHR 2003-IV 835
Pfarrmeier v Austria, 23 October 1995, Series A no. 329-C 262
Pfeifer v Austria, no. 12556/03, ECHR 2007-XII 385, 472

P.G. and J.H. v United Kingdom, no. 44787/98, ECHR 2001-IX 320, 383, 386
P.G. and J.H. v United Kingdom, no. 44787/98, Partly Dissenting Opinion of Judge
  Tulkens, ECHR 2001-IX. 320
Pham Hoang v France, 25 September 1992, Series A no. 243. . . . . .299, 790
Philis v Greece (no. 1), 27 August 1991, Series A no. 209 714
Phillips v United Kingdom, no. 41087/98, ECHR 2001-VII 281, 293, 299
Phull v France (dec.), no. 35753/03, 11 January 2005 . . . . .431, 439, 1059
Pichkur v Ukraine, no. 10441/06, 7 November 2013. 982
Pichon and Sajous v France (dec.), no. 49853/99, *Reports of Judgments and Decisions* 2001-X . . .428, 432
Pichugin v Russia, no. 38623/03, 23 October 2012. 239
Pierre-Bloch v France, 21 October 1997, *Reports of Judgments and Decisions* 1997-VI 274, 284
Piermont v France, 27 April 1995, Series A no. 314. . . . . 608–9, 791, 926–7, 1083
Piermont v France, 27 April 1995, Joint Partly Dissenting Opinion of Judges Ryssdal, Matscher,
  Sir John Freeland and Jungwiert, Series A no. 314. . . . . .309, 927
Piersack v Belgium, 1 October 1982, Series A no. 53. 294
Piersack v Belgium (Article 50), 26 October 1984, Series A no. 85 868
Piippo v Sweden, no. 70518/01, 21 March 2006. 973
Pine Valley Developments Ltd and Others v Ireland, 27 November 1991, Series A no. 222 815
Pini and Others v Romania, nos 78028/01 and 78030/01, ECHR 2004-V 38, 390, 394,
                                                                                          793, 1060
Piotr Baranowski v Poland, no. 39742/05, 2 October 2007 250
Piruzyan v Armenia, no. 33376/07, ECHR 2012 (extracts) 185, 252, 253
Pisano v Italy (striking out) [GC], no. 36732/97, 24 October 2002 . . . . 785, 797–8, 801, 846
Pitsayeva and Others v Russia, nos 53036/08, 61785/08, 8594/09, 24708/09, 30327/09,
  36965/09, 61258/09, 63608/09, 67322/09, 4334/10, 4345/10, 11873/10, 25515/10,
  30592/10, 32797/10, 33944/10, 36141/10, 52446/10, 62244/10, and 66420/10,
  9 January 2014 136
P.K. v Finland (dec.), no. 37442/97, 9 July 2002 324
Pla and Puncernau v Andorra, no. 69498/01, ECHR 2004-VIII. 394, 968
Platform 'Ärzte für das Leben' v Austria, 21 June 1988, Series A no. 139 . . . . .493, 497, 741
Plechanow v Poland, no. 22279/04, 7 July 2009 971
Plechkov v Russia, no. 1660/03, 16 September 2014. 339
Pleşca v Romania, no. 2158/08, 18 June 2013. 815
P.M. v United Kingdom (dec.), no. 6638/03, 24 August 2004. .770, 772
Põder and Others v Estonia (dec.), no. 67723/01, 26 April 2005 . . . . .935, 984
Podkolzina v Latvia, no. 46726/99, ECHR 2002-II 1023–4
Poghosyan and Baghdasaryan v Armenia, no. 22999/06, ECHR 2012. 1146
Poiss v Austria, 23 April 1987, Series A no. 117. 974
Poitrimol v France, 23 November 1993, Series A no. 277-A. 271, 307, 317
Polanco Torres and Movilla Polanco v Spain, no. 34147/06, 21 September 2010. . . . . .385, 472
Polednová v Czech Republic (dec.), no. 2615/10, 21 June 2011. . . . . 128, 337, 342, 354, 640
Poleshchuk v Russia, no. 60776/00, 7 October 2004. 812
Poltoratskiy v Ukraine, no. 38812/97, ECHR 2003-VI 190
Ponomaryovi v Bulgaria, no. 5335/05, ECHR 2011 . . . . .38, 997, 1006
Ponsetti and Chesnel v France (dec.), nos 36855/97 and 41731/98, ECHR 1999-VI. 1153
Popa v Romania (dec.), no. 4233/09, 18 June 2013. 376
Popov v France, nos 39472/07 and 39474/07, 19 January 2012. . . . . 389, 391–2, 404
Popov v France, nos 39472/07 and 39474/07, Partly Dissenting Opinion of Judge Power-Forde,
  19 January 2012 193
Popov v Moldova, no. 74153/01, 18 January 2005 . . . . .781, 823
Popov v Russia, no. 26853/04, 13 July 2006. 869
Porter v United Kingdom (dec.), no. 15814/02, 8 April 2003. 427
Poslu and Others v Turkey, nos 6162/04, 6297/04, 6304/04, 6305/04, 6149/04, 9724/04, and
  9733/04, 8 June 2010. 772
Post v Netherlands (dec.), no. 21727/08, 20 January 2009. 745

Powell and Powell v United Kingdom (dec.), no. 45305/99, ECHR 2000-V 131, 138, 383
Powell and Rayner v United Kingdom, 21 February 1990, Series A no.172 . . . . .746, 775, 815
Pozhyvotko v Ukraine, no. 42752/08, 17 October 2013 134
Poznanski and Others v Germany (dec.), no. 25101/05, 3 July 2007 780
Prager and Oberschlicke v Austria, 26 April 1995, Series A no. 313 . . . . .458, 460, 477
Pramstaller v Austria, 23 October 1995, Series A no. 329-A 262
Preda and Others v Romania, nos 9584/02, 33514/02, 38052/02, 25821/03, 29652/03, 3736/03,
    17750/03, and 28688/04, 29 April 2014 697
Predescu v Romania, no. 21447/03, 2 December 2008 780
Prencipe v Monaco, no. 43376/06, 16 July 2009 . . . . .252, 769
Prescher v Bulgaria, no. 6767/04, 7 June 2011 1061
Pressos Compania Naviera S.A. and Others v Belgium, 20 November 1995, Series A
    no. 332 . . . . .765, 972
Pretto and Others v Italy, 8 December 1983, Series A no. 71 291
Pretty v United Kingdom, no. 2346/02, ECHR 2002-III .67, 127–8, 168, 172,
    180–1, 190–1, 366, 369–71, 382, 406, 432
Preussische Treuhand GmbH & Co Kg a.A. v Poland (dec.), 7 October 2008 109
Previti v Italy (dec.), no. 1845/08, 12 February 2013 356
Price v United Kingdom, no. 33394/96, ECHR 2001-VII 171, 174, 180–1
Price and Lowe v United Kingdom, nos 43185/98 and 43186/98, 29 July 2003 293
Priebke v Italy (dec.), no. 48799/99, 5 April 2001 . . . . .186, 302
Prince Hans-Adam II of Liechtenstein v Germany [GC], no. 42527/98, ECHR
    2001-VIII 38, 97, 265, 969–70
Professional Trades Union for Prison, Correctional, and Secure Psychiatric Workers and
    Others v United Kingdom (dec.), no. 59253/11, 21 May 2013 778
Prokopovich v Russia, no. 58255/00, ECHR 2004-XI 399, 764
Proshkin v Russia, no. 28869/03, 7 February 2012 231
Protopapa v Turkey, no. 16084/90, 24 February 2009 . . . . .308, 315
Province of Bari, Sorrentino and Messeni Nemagna v Italy (dec.), no. 41877/98, 22 March
    2001 . . . . .90, 737
Prystavska v Ukraine, no. 21287/02, 17 December 2002 769
Przemyk v Poland, no. 22426/11, 17 September 2013 36
Puig Panella v Spain, no. 1483/02, 25 April 2006 304
Pullar v United Kingdom, 10 June 1996, *Reports of Judgments and Decisions* 1996-III 296
Pūpēdis v Latvia (dec.), no. 53631/00, 15 February 2001 936
Pursiheimo v Finland (dec.), no. 57795/00, 25 November 2003 289
Putintseva v Russia, no. 33498/04, 10 May 2012 151
Putistin v Ukraine, no. 16882/03, 21 November 2013 77
Putz v Austria, 22 February 1996, *Reports of Judgments and Decisions* 1996-I 283
Py v France, no. 66289/01, ECHR 2005-I (extracts) 793, 926–7
Pyrantiené v Lithuania, no. 45092/07, 12 November 2013 976–7
Quaranta v Switzerland, 24 May 1991, Series A no. 205 791
Quark Fishing Ltd v United Kingdom (dec.), no. 15305/06, ECHR 2006-XIV 104, 923
Quinn v France, 22 March 1995, Series A no. 311 234
R. v United Kingdom, 8 July 1987, Series A no. 121 827
R. and F. v United Kingdom (dec.), no. 35748/05, 28 November 2006 . . . . .534, 536–7
R. and H. v United Kingdom, no. 35348/06, 31 May 2011 393
Rache and Ozon v Romania, no. 21468/03, 31 March 2009 297
Radio ABC v Austria, 20 October 1997, *Reports of Judgments and Decisions* 1997-VI 467
Radio France and Others v France, no. 53984/00, ECHR 2004-II 299–300, 339, 458, 476
Radio France and Others v France (dec.), no. 53984/00, 23 September 2003 . . . . .90, 92, 736–7
Răducu v Romania, no. 70787/01, 21 April 2009 133
Raf v Spain (dec.), no. 53652/00, 21 November 2000 275
Rahbar-Pagard v Bulgaria, nos 45466/99 and 29903/02, 6 April 2006 255
Rai and Evans v United Kingdom (dec.), nos 26258/07 and 26255/07, 17 November 2009 . . . .497, 516

Railean v Moldova, no. 23401/04, 5 January 2010 . . . . .127, 132

Raimondo v Italy, 22 February 1994, Series A no. 281-A 281, 740, 1058, 1061

Rainys and Gasparavicius v Lithuania, nos 70665/01 and 74345/01, 7 April 2005 574

Rajkowska v Poland (dec.), no. 37393/02, 27 November 2007 132

Rakevich v Russia, no. 58973/00, 28 October 2003 . . . . .242, 254

Ramaer and Van Willigen v Netherlands (dec.), no. 34880/12, 23 October 2012 1183

Ramazanova and Others v Azerbaijan, no. 44363/02, 1 February 2007 . . . . .500, 511

Ramirez Sanchez v France [GC], no. 59450/00, ECHR 2006-IX 168, 172, 184, 186, 592, 848

Ramishvili and Kokhreidze v Georgia, no. 1704/06, 27 January 2009 185–6

Ramishvili and Kokhreidze v Georgia (dec.), no. 1704/06, 27 June 2007 625

Ramsahai and Others v Netherlands, no. 52391/99, 10 November 2005 150

Ramsahai and Others v Netherlands [GC], no. 52391/99, ECHR 2007-II 150

Rando v Italy, no. 38498/97, 15 February 2000 869

Rangelov v Germany, no. 5123/07, 22 March 2012 . . . . .260, 574

Raninen v Finland, 16 December 1997, *Reports of Judgments and Decisions* 1997-VIII 185, 370

Rantsev v Cyprus and Russia, no. 25965/04, ECHR 2010 (extracts) 38, 63, 65, 129,
201, 206–7, 209–10, 226–7, 229, 279, 792

Rasmussen v Denmark, 28 November 1984, Series A no. 87 . . . . 273, 376, 391, 524,
565, 567, 1182, 1184

Ravnsborg v Sweden, 23 March 1994, Series A no. 283-B 277, 283

Raza v Bulgaria, no. 31465/08, 11 February 2010 290–1

Redfearn v United Kingdom, no. 47335/06, 6 November 2012 . . . . 494, 503, 522, 524

Rees v United Kingdom, 17 October 1986, Series A no. 106 . . . . 367, 380, 454, 533–6, 542

Reeves v Norway (dec.), no. 4248/02, 8 July 2004 304

Refah Partisi (the Welfare Party) and Others v Turkey, nos 41340/98, 41362/98, 41343/98,
and 41344/98, 31 July 2001 . . . . .519, 618

Refah Partisi (the Welfare Party) and Others v Turkey (dec.), nos 41340/98, 41362/98,
41343/98, and 41344/98, 3 October 2000 284

Refah Partisi (the Welfare Party) and Others v Turkey [GC], nos 41340/98, 41362/98,
41343/98, and 41344/98, ECHR 2003-II 438, 503–5, 512, 515, 520–1, 616, 618, 627

Registe v Netherlands (dec.), no. 28620/99, 23 March 2010 1101

Řehák v Czech Republic (dec.), no. 67208/01, 18 May 2004 780

Rehbock v Slovenia, no. 29462/95, ECHR 2000-XII 172, 256–7

Reinboth and Others v Finland, no. 30865/08, 25 January 2011 476

Reinprecht v Austria, no. 67175/01, ECHR 2005-XII 255

Rejeva v Latvia [GC], no. 55707/00, ECHR 2009 . . . . 564, 570, 574, 581

Reklos and Davourlis v Greece, no. 1234/05, 15 January 2009 377–8

Rekvényi v Hungary [GC], no. 25390/94, ECHR 1999-III 445, 469, 510, 522–3

Rekvényi v Hungary [GC], no. 25390/94, Partly Dissenting Opinion of Judge Fischbach,
ECHR 1999-III 522

Religionsgemeinschaft der Zeugen Jehovas and Others v Austria, no. 40825/98,
31 July 2008 . . . . 425, 429–30, 437, 441, 566

Remli v France, 23 April 1996, *Reports of Judgments and Decisions* 1996-II 765

Remuszko v Poland, no. 1562/10, 16 July 2013 454

Republican Party of Russia v Russia, no. 12976/07, 12 April 2011 . . . . . . 499, 504–5, 511–3, 518, 521

Ressegatti v Switzerland, no. 17671/02, 13 July 2006 740

Riad and Idiab v Belgium, nos 29787/03 and 29810/03, 24 January 2008 . . . . .227, 767

Ribitsch v Austria, 4 December 1995, Series A no. 336 810

Rieme v Sweden, 22 April 1992, Series A no. 226-B 791

Riener v Bulgaria, no. 46343/99, 23 May 2006 . . . . .1061, 1064

Riepan v Austria, no. 35115/97, ECHR 2000-XII 289

Riera Blume and Others v Spain, no. 37680/97, ECHR 1999-VII 229

Rigolio v Italy (dec.), no. 20148/09, 13 May 2014 1138

Rinck v France (dec.), no. 18774/09, 19 October 2010 782–3

Ringeisen v Austria, 16 July 1971, Series A no. 13 . . . . 141, 274, 295, 323, 746, 767

Ringeisen v Austria, 16 July 1971, Separate Opinion of Judge Verdross, Series A no. 13. . . . . .35, 42, 45
Ringeisen v Austria (Article 50), 22 June 1972, Series A no. 15 841
Ringeisen v Austria (interpretation), 23 June 1973, Series A no. 16. .841, 852
Ringvold v Norway, no. 34964/97, ECHR 2003-II 278, 304
Rivière v France, no. 33834/03, 11 July 2006 . . . . .174, 184
R.K. and A.K. v United Kingdom, no. 38000/05, 30 September 2008 392–3
R.L. and M.-J.D. v France, no. 44568/98, 19 May 2004 242
R.M.D. v Switzerland, 26 September 1997, *Reports of Judgments and Decisions* 1997-VI 256–7
Robathin v Austria, no. 30457/06, 3 July 2012 386
Roche v United Kingdom [GC], no. 32555/96, ECHR 2005-X 273, 276
Rodrigues da Silva and Hoogkamer v Netherlands, no. 50435/99, ECHR 2006. 398
Roemen and Schmit v Luxembourg, no. 51772/99, ECHR 2003-IV 459
Rohde v Denmark, no. 6933/01, 21 July 2005 186
Rokhlina v Russia, no. 54071/00, 7 April 2005 252
Roldan Texeira and Others v Italy (dec.), no. 40655/98, 26 October 2000 1062
Rolf Gustafson v Sweden, 1 July 1997, *Reports of Judgments and Decisions* 1997-IV 272
Romańczyke v France, no. 7618/05, 18 November 2010 276
Romankevic v Lithuania, no. 25747/10, 2 December 2014 977
Romero Martin v Spain (dec.), no. 32045/03, 12 June 2006 295
Romet v Netherlands, no. 7094/06, 14 February 2012. 378
Rooney v Ireland, no. 32614/10, 31 October 2013 702
Roşca v Moldova, no. 6267/02, 22 March 2005 72
Rosengren v Romania, no. 70786/01, 24 April 2008 1059
Rosengren v Romania (dec.), no. 70786/01, 4 May 2006. 1071
Rosenquist v Sweden (dec.), no. 33402/96, ECHR 2002-V 1151
Rosenzweig and Bonded Warehouses Ltd v Poland, no. 51728/99, 28 July 2005. . . . . .971, 973
Rotaru v Romania [GC], no. 28341/95, ECHR 2000-V 382–3, 386, 403, 469, 510
Rousk v Sweden, no. 27183/04, 25 July 2013. 981
Rowe and Davis v United Kingdom [GC], no. 28901/95, ECHR 2000-II 310
Różański v Poland, no. 55339/00, 18 May 2006 391
R.R. v Italy, no. 42191/02, 9 June 2005 1135
R.R. v Italy (dec.), no. 42191/02, 2 December 2004 1051
R.R. v Poland, no. 27617/04, ECHR 2011 (extracts). 373, 431
R.R. and Others v Hungary, no. 19400/11, 4 December 2012. 125
Rrapo v Albania, no. 58555/10, 25 September 2012 . . . . .73, 146
R.Sz. v Hungary, no. 41838/11, 2 July 2013. 979
R.T. v Switzerland (dec.), no. 31982/96, 30 May 2000 1153
RTBF v Belgium, no. 50084/06, ECHR 2011 (extracts) 452
Ruano Morcuende v Spain (dec.), no. 75287/01, 6 September 2005. 387
Rudakov v Russia, no. 43239/04, 28 October 2010. 189
Ruiz Torija v Spain, 9 December 1994, Series A no. 303-A 297
Ruiz-Mateos v Spain, 23 June 1993, Series A no. 262 274
Rujak v Croatia (dec.), no. 57942/10, 2 October 2012 456
Rumor v Italy, no. 72964/10, 27 May 2014 198
Rumyana Ivanova v Bulgaria, no. 36207/03, 14 February 2008 476
Rupa v Romania (dec.), no. 37971/02, 23 February 2010 775
Rushiti v Austria, no. 28389/95, 21 March 2000. . . . . .299, 304–6
Russian Conservative Party of Entrepreneurs and Others v Russia, nos 55066/00 and
    55638/00, 11 January 2007 . . . . .41, 1026
R.W. and T.G.-W. v Austria (dec.), no. 36222/97) 22 November 2001 1158
Ryabov v Russia, no. 3896/04, 31 January 2008 747–8
Ryabykh v Russia, no. 52854, ECHR 2003-IX 72
Rywin v Poland (Application nos 6091/06, 4047/07, and 4070/070 (pending) 793
S. v Germany, no. 3300/10, 28 June 2012 . . . . .236, 242

S. and Marper v United Kingdom [GC], nos 30562/04 and 30566/04,
    4 December 2008 . . . . 369, 379, 382, 384–5, 837
Saadi v Italy [GC], no. 37201/06, ECHR 2008. . . . . .54, 168, 194–6, 792, 812,
                                                                            837, 1045, 1100, 1128
Saadi v United Kingdom, no. 13229/03, 11 July 2006. 245
Saadi v United Kingdom [GC], no. 13229/03, ECHR 2008 . . . . 37, 40, 47, 65, 231–4, 243–5
Sabanchiyeva and Others v Russia, no. 38450/05, ECHR 2013 (extracts) 739
Šabanović v Montenegro and Serbia, no. 5995/06, 31 May 2011 951
Sabeh El Leil v France [GC], no. 34869/05, 29 June 2011. . . . . .100, 286–7
Sabou and Pircalab v Romania, no. 46572/99, 28 September 2004. 393–4
Saccocia v Austria (dec.), no. 69917/01, 5 July 2007 349
Saccomanno and Others v Italy, no. 11583/08, 13 March 2012. . . . . .621, 625
Sadak v Turkey, nos 251421/94 and 27099/95, 8 April 2004. 775
Sadak and Others v Turkey (no. 1), nos 29900/96, 29901/96, 29902/96, and 29903/96,
    ECHR 2001-VIII 313, 775
Sadak and Others v Turkey (no. 2), nos 25144/94, 26149/95 to 26154/95, 27100/95,
    and 27101/95, ECHR 2002-IV 492, 775, 1018, 1024
Sadegül Özdemir v Turkey, no. 61441/00, 2 August 2005. 247
Sadet v Romania (dec.), no. 36416/02, 20 September 2007 1071
Saghinadze and Others v Georgia, no. 18768/05, 27 May 2010 . . . . .255, 969, 971
Şahin v Germany [GC], no. 30943/96, 11 October 2001. 574
Şahin v Germany, no. 30943/96, ECHR 2003-VIII. 563
Şahin v Turkey, no. 44774/98, 29 June 2004 575
Şahmo v Turkey (dec.), no. 37415/97, 1 April 2003 771
Sailer v Austria (dec.), no. 38237/97, 6 June 2002. 1153
Sakik and Others v Turkey, 26 November 1997, *Reports of Judgments and Decisions*
    1997-VII 258, 603
Sakkopoulos v Greece, no. 61828/00, 15 January 2004 . . . . .174, 185–6
Salabiaku v France, 7 October 1988, Series A no. 141-A 279, 299
Salah v Netherlands, no. 8196/02, ECHR 2006-IX (extracts) 69
Salah Sheekh v Netherlands, no. 1948/04, 11 January 2007 194
Salakhov and Islyamova v Ukraine, no. 28005/08, 14 March 2013 . . . . .170, 751
Salayev v Azerbaijan, no. 40900/05, 9 November 2010 227
Salduz v Turkey [GC], no. 36391/02, ECHR 2008. . . . . 33, 280, 301, 310
Saleck Bardi v Spain, no. 66167/09, 24 May 2011. 388
Salem v Portugal (dec.), no. 26844/04, 9 May 2006 . . . . .195, 1100
Salgueiro sa Silva Mouta v Portugal, no. 33290/96, ECHR 1999-IX. 584, 1178, 1184
Salleras Llinares v Spain (dec.), no. 52226/99, 12 October 2000. 1021
Salman v Turkey [GC], no. 21986/93, ECHR 2000-VII 123, 133, 169, 570, 811
Salov v Ukraine (dec.), no. 65518/01, 27 April 2004. . . . . .247, 262
Salvatore v Italy (dec.), no. 42285/98, 7 May 2002 398
Şaman v Turkey, no. 35292/05, 5 April 2011 . . . . .280, 314
Sâmbata Bihor Greco-Catholic Parish v Romania, no. 48107/99, 12 January 2010 322
Sambiyev and Pokayeva v Russia, no. 38693/04, 22 January 2009 171
Samoilă and Cionca v Romania, no. 33065/03, 4 March 2008. 303
Sambor v Poland, no. 15579/05, 1 February 2011. 172
Sampani and Others v Greece, no. 59608/09, 11 December 2012 1005
Sampanis and Others v Greece, no. 32526/05, 5 June 2008. . . . . 40, 578, 1004–5
Samsonnikov v Estonia, no. 52178/10, 3 July 2012. . . . . .366–7, 396
Samüt Karabulut v Turkey, no. 16999/04, 27 January 2009. 497
Samy v Netherlands (friendly settlement), no. 36499/97, 18 June 2002 851
Sanchez Cardenas v Norway, no. 12148/03, 4 October 2007 385
Sanchez-Reisse v Switzerland, 21 October 1986, Series A no. 107. . . . . .255, 257
Sancho Cruz and 14 other 'Agrarian Reform' cases v Portugal, nos 8851/07, 8854/07,
    8856/07, 8865/07, 10142/07, 10144/07, 24622/07, 32733/07, 32744/07, 41645/07,
    19150/08, 22885/08, 22887/08, 26612/08, and 202/09, 18 January 2011. 783
Sanders v France (dec.), no. 31401/96, 16 October 1996. 540

Sandra Janković v Croatia, no. 38478/05, 5 March 2009 . . . . .279, 370
Şandru v Romania, no. 3382/05, 15 October 2013 313
Şandru and Others v Romania, no. 22465/03, 8 December 2009 138
Sanles Sanles v Spain (dec.), no. 48335/09, ECHR 2000-XI. 73, 738
Sanocki v Poland, no. 28949/03, 17 July 2007 476
Sanoma Uitgevers B.V. v Netherlands [GC], no. 38224/03, 14 September 2010 . . . . 403, 435,
                                                     459, 469–70, 510, 845, 1063
Sanoma Uitgevers B.V. v Netherlands [GC], no. 38224/03, Concurring Opinion of Judge
    Myjer, 14 September 2010. 692
Saoudi v Spain (dec.), no. 22871/06, 18 September 2006. 1100
Sapan v Turkey, no. 44102/04, 8 June 2010. . . . . .377, 462
Saramati v France, Germany, and Norway [GC] (dec.), no. 78166/01, 2 May 2007. 694
Sarban v Moldova, no. 3456/05, 4 October 2005 . . . . .185, 250
Sardinas Albo v Italy (dec.), no. 56271/00, ECHR 2004-I 275, 314, 766
Sardón Alvira v Spain, no. 46090/10, 24 September 2013 287
Sarigiannis v Italy, no. 14569/05, 5 April 2011 236–8
Sarkizov and Others v Bulgaria, nos 37981/06, 38022/06, 39122/06, and 44278/06,
    17 April 2012 1064
SARL du Parc d'Activités de Blotzheim v France, no. 72377/01, 11 July 2006 . . . . .738, 742
Şarli v Turkey, no. 24490/94, 22 May 2001 748
Sarria v Poland (dec.), no. 45618/09, 18 December 2012. 1149
S.A.S. v France [GC], no. 43835/11, 1 July 2014 . . . . .89, 173, 376–7, 402, 404–5,
                                         437, 439, 471, 512, 743, 780–1, 793–4, 1063
S.A.S. v France [GC], no. 43835/11, Joint Partly Dissenting Opinion of Judges Nußburger
    and Jäderblom, 1 July 2014 404–5
Sasita Israilova and Others v Russia, no. 35079/04, 28 October 2010 828
Saunders v United Kingdom, 17 December 1996, *Reports of Judgments and Decisions*
    1996-VI. 300–1, 319
Savda v Turkey, no. 42730/05, 12 June 2012 434
Savez crkava 'Riječ života' and Others v Croatia, no. 7798/08, 9 December 2010 . . . . 563, 1180,
                                                  1182, 1186, 1191
Savgın v Turkey, no. 13304/03, 2 February 2010 455
Savino and Others v Italy, nos 17214/05, 20329/05, and 42113/04, 28 April 2009. 274
Savinskiy v Ukraine (dec.), no. 6965/02, 31 May 2005 1154
Savitskyy v Ukraine, no. 38773/05, 26 July 2012 193
Savriddin Dzhurayev v Russia, no. 71386/10 ECHR 2013 (extracts). 89, 749
Sawoniuk v United Kingdom (dec.), no. 63716/00, ECHR 2001-VI 182–3, 186
S.B.C. v United Kingdom, no. 39360/98, 19 June 2001 253
S.C. v United Kingdom, no. 60958/00, ECHR 2004-IV 318
S.C. v United Kingdom, no. 60958/00, Dissenting Opinion of Judge Pellonpää, Joined by
    Judge Sir Nicolas Bratza, ECHR 2004-IV. 318
SCEA Ferme de Fresnoy v France (dec.), no. 61093/00, ECHR 2005-XIII 976
Schädler-Eberle v Liechtenstein, no. 56422/09, 18 July 2013 . . . . .323, 934–6
Schalk and Kopf v Austria, no. 30141/04, ECHR 2010 . . . . .390, 535–7, 584
Schalk and Kopf v Austria, no. 30141/04, Concurring Opinion of Judge Malinverni,
    Joined by Judge Kovler, ECHR 2010 537
Schenk v Switzerland, 12 July 1988, Series A no. 140 . . . . .320, 640
Schenk v Switzerland, 12 July 1988, Joint Dissenting Opinion of Judges Pettiti, Spielmann,
    De Meyer, and Carrillo Salcedo, Series A no. 140 320
Scheper v Netherlands, (dec.), no. 39209/02, 5 April 2005. 312
Scherer v Switzerland, 25 March 1994, Series A no. 287 740
Schiesser v Switzerland, 4 December 1979, Series A no. 34. . . . . .238, 248–9
Schmautzer v Austria, 23 October 1995, Series A no. 328-A. 262, 283, 933
Schmidt and Dahlström v Sweden, 6 February 1976, Series A no. 21 . . . . .506, 508
Schneider v Germany, no. 17080/07, 15 September 2011 390–2

Schneider v Luxembourg, no. 2113/04, 10 July 2007 973
Schober v Austria (dec.), no. 34891/97, 9 November 1999 1072
Schöps v Germany, no. 25116/94, ECHR 2001-I 255
Schouten and Meldrum v Netherlands, 9 December 1994, Series A no. 304 274
Schuitemaker v Netherlands (dec.), no. 15906/08, 4 May 2010 212
Schuler-Zgraggen v Switzerland, 24 June 1993, Series A no. 263 . . . . 289–90, 323, 574, 576
Schüth v Germany, no. 1620/03, ECHR 2010 . . . . .375, 429
Schutte v Austria, no. 18015/03, 26 July 2007 1153
Schwabe and M.G. v Germany, nos 8080/08 and 8577/08, ECHR 2011 (extracts) 82, 237–8,
                                                                    491–2, 495–6, 516, 518
Schwizgebel v Switzerland, no. 25762/07, ECHR 2010 (extracts) .573, 584
Sciacca v Italy, no. 50774/99, ECHR 2005-I 378
Scopelliti v Italy, 23 November 1993, Series A no. 278 293
Scoppola v Italy (no. 2) (dec.), no. 10249/03, 8 September 2005 712
Scoppola v Italy (no. 2) [GC], no. 10249/03, 17 September 2009 . . . . 33, 39, 47–9, 271,
                334–6, 338–40, 346, 349–51, 707, 712, 714, 746,
                764–6, 768–9, 775, 785, 815, 849, 868–70, 904
Scoppola v Italy (no. 2) [GC], no. 10249/03, Partly Dissenting Opinion of Judge Nicolaou,
    Joined by Judges Bratza, Lorenzen, Jočiené, Villiger, and Sajó, 17 September 2009 351
Scoppola v Italy (no. 3) [GC], no 126/05, 22 May 2012 . . . . 71, 848, 1012, 1018, 1023, 1028
Scordino v Italy (no. 1) [GC], no. 36813/97, ECHR 2006-V 77, 291, 335, 744, 976–7
Scott v Spain, 18 December 1996, *Reports of Judgments and Decisions* 1996-VI 791
Scozzari and Giunta v Italy [GC], nos 39221/98 and 41963/98, ECHR 2000-VIII 738, 868
Šečić v Croatia, no. 40116/02, 31 May 2007. . . . . .159, 197
Seckerson v United Kingdom and Time Newspapers Limited v United Kingdom (dec.),
    nos 32844/10 and 33510/10, 24 January 2012. 461
Section de commune d'Antilly v France (dec.), no. 42129/98, 23 November 1999 . . . . .90, 737
Segame SA v France, no. 4837/06, ECHR 2012 (extracts) 297
Segerstedt-Wiberg and Others v Sweden, no. 62332/00, ECHR 2006-VII 383
Segi and Gestoras Pro-Amnistia and Others v Austria, Belgium, Denmark, Finland, France,
    Germany, Greece, Ireland, Italy, Luxembourg, Netherlands, Portugal, Spain, Sweden
    and United Kingdom (dec.), nos 6422/02 and 9916/02, ECHR 2002-V 743
Seguin v France (dec.), no. 42400/98 207
Sejdić and Finci v Bosnia and Herzegovina [GC], nos 27996/06 and 34836/06,
    ECHR 2009. . . . . 90, 93, 159, 562–7, 574, 577–8, 738,
                743, 779, 871, 949, 1020–1, 1031, 1180–3
Sejdić and Finci v Bosnia and Herzegovina [GC], nos 27996/06 and 34836/06, Dissenting
    Opinion of Judge Bonello, ECHR 2009 67
Sejdovic v Italy [GC], no. 56581/00, ECHR 2006-II 271, 282, 308, 314, 316–7, 764–5, 786, 792
Sejdovic and Sulejmanovic v Italy (dec.), no. 57575/00, 14 March 2002. 1128
Sekanina v Austria, 25 August 1993, Series A no. 266-A 299, 303–6
Selçuk v Turkey, no. 21768/02, 10 January 2006 251–2
Selim v Cyprus (friendly settlement), no. 47293/99, 16 July 2002 820
Selmouni v France [GC], no. 25803/94, ECHR 1999-V 44, 168, 175–6, 179, 592, 764, 768, 838
Senator Lines GmbH v Austria, Belgium, Denmark, Finland, France, Germany, Greece,
    Ireland, Italy, Luxembourg, Netherlands, Portugal, Spain, Sweden, and United Kingdom
    (dec.) [GC], no. 56672/00, ECHR 2004-IV. 743
Sentges v Netherlands (dec.), no. 27677/02, 8 July 2003 371
Sergey Kuznetsov v Russia, no. 10877/04, 23 October 2008 . . . . .495, 497, 509
Sergey Shevchenko v Ukraine, no. 32478/02, 4 April 2006 132
Sergey Zolotukhin v Russia [GC], no. 14939/03, ECHR 2009. . . . . 33, 47–9, 745, 764,
                                                    799, 849, 1149–53
Serif v Greece, no. 38178/97, ECHR 1999-IX 421, 430
Şerife Yiğit v Turkey [GC] no. 3976/05, 2 November 2010. . . . . .533, 538, 815
Serves v France (dec.), no. 38642/97, 4 May 2000. 775

Seyidzade v Azerbaijan, no. 37700/05, 3 December 2009 1029
Seyidzade v Azerbaijan, no. 37700/05, Concurring Opinion of Judge Malinverni, Joined
    by Judges Vajić and Kovler, 3 December 2009 1029
S.H. v Netherlands (dec.), no. 47607/07, 5 March 2013 828
S.H. v United Kingdom, no. 19956/06, 15 June 2010. 196
S.H. and Others v Austria [GC], no. 57813/00, ECHR 2011. . . . . 40, 372, 848
Shabani v Switzerland, no. 29044/06, 5 November 2009 . . . . .247, 253
Shackell v United Kingdom (dec.), no. 45851/99, 27 April 2000 533
Shakhgiriyeva and Others v Russia, no. 27251/03, 8 January 2009 814
Shamayev and Others v Georgia and Russia (dec.), no. 36378/02, 16 September 2002. 774
Shamayev and Others v Georgia and Russia, no. 36378/02, ECHR 2005-III. 73–4, 76,
                                       146, 245–6, 721, 747, 774, 829, 1115
Shamsa v Poland, nos 45355/99 and 45357/99, 27 November 2003. 227
Shanaghan v United Kingdom, no. 37715/97, 4 May 2001 793
Sharifi and Others v Italy and Greece, no. 16643/09, 21 October 2014 1079–80
Sharomov v Russia, no. 8927/02, 15 January 2009 744
Shaw v Hungary, no. 6457/09, 26 July 2011. . . . . .391, 393
Shchebetov v Russia, no. 21731/02, 10 April 2012 123
Shchiborshch and Kuzmina v Russia, no. 5269/08, 16 January 2014. . . . . .134, 147
Sheabashov v Latvia (dec.), no. 50065/99, 22 May 1999 398
Shefer v Russia (dec.), no. 45175/04, 13 March 2012 . . . . .782, 784
Sheffield and Horsham v United Kingdom, 30 July 1998, *Reports of Judgments and Decisions*
    1998-V. 380, 536, 575, 794
Sheffield and Horsham v United Kingdom, 30 July 1998, Dissenting Opinion of Judge Van
    Dijk, *Reports of Judgments and Decisions* 1998-V 66
Shestakov v Russia (dec.), no. 48757/99, 18 June 2002 968
Shestjorkin v Estonia (dec.), no. 49450/99, 15 June 2000 .935–6, 984
Shevanova v Latvia (striking out) [GC], no. 58822/00, 7 December 2007. . . . . .745, 798
S.H.H. v United Kingdom, no. 60367/10, 29 January 2013 195
Shimovolos v Russia, no. 30194/09, 21 June 2011 . . . . 227, 234, 370, 383, 404
Shindler v United Kingdom, no. 19840/09, 7 May 2013. 1027
Shingara Mann Singh v France (dec.), no. 24479/07, 13 November 2008. 439
Shmushkovych v Ukraine, no. 3276/10, 14 November 2013 290
Shokkarov and Others v Russia, no. 41009/04, 3 May 2011. 829
Shopov v Bulgaria, no.11373/04, 2 September 2010 371
Shtukaturov v Russia, no. 44009/05, ECHR 2008. . . . . .228, 748
Shukhardin v Russia, no. 65734/01, 28 June 2007 231
Shvydka v Ukraine, no. 17888/12, 30 October 2014. . . . . 456, 475, 1135–6
Sidabras and Džiautas v Lithuania, nos 55480/00 and 59330/00, ECHR 2004-VIII 374, 385, 574
Sidabras and Džiautas v Lithuania (dec.), nos 55480/00 and 59330/00, 1 July 2003 284
Sidiropoulos and Others v Greece, 10 July 1998, *Reports of Judgments and Decisions*
    1998-IV 440, 499–500, 512, 516
Siebenhaar v Germany, no. 18136/02, 3 February 2011. 429
Sigurður A. Sigurjónsson v Iceland, 30 June 1993, Series A no. 264 . . . . .38, 502
Sigurður A. Sigurjónsson v Iceland, 30 June 1993, Dissenting Opinion of Judge Thór Vilhjálmsson,
    Series A no. 264 64
Sijakova v 'former Yugoslav Republic of Macedonia' (dec.), no. 67914/01, 6 March 2003 534
Šikić v Croatia, no. 9143/08, 15 July 2010. 304
Sılay v Turkey, no. 8681/02, 5 April 2007 . . . . .492, 1024
Siliadin v France, no. 73316/01, ECHR 2005-VII. 38, 201, 203, 206–9, 211–2, 279
Silickienė v Lithuania, no. 20496/02, 10 April 2012 280
Šilih v Slovenia [GC], no. 71463/01, 9 April 2009 . . . . .36, 107–8, 110–1, 122, 134,
                                  137–8, 721, 770, 845, 848, 950
Silver and Others v United Kingdom, 25 March 1983, Series A no. 61. . . . . .90, 401–2
Šimšić v Bosnia and Herzegovina (dec.), no. 51552/10, 10 April 2012 . . . . .342, 564, 1182–4

Sinan Işık v Turkey, no. 21924/05, ECHR 2010. 428
Sindicatul 'Păstorul cel Bun' v Romania, no. 2330/09, 31 January 2012 . . . . 484, 506, 514, 516
Sindicatul 'Păstorul cel Bun' v Romania, no. 2330/09, Joint Dissenting Opinion of Judges
 Ziemele and Tsotsoria, 31 January 2012 499
Sindicatul 'Păstorul cel Bun' v Romania [GC], no. 2330/09, Concurring Opinion of Judge
 Wojtyczek, ECHR 2013 (extracts) 78
Singh v United Kingdom, 21 February 1996, *Reports of Judgments and Decisions* 1996-I 255
Sipavičius v Lithuania, no. 49093/99, 21 February 2002 310
Şişman and Others v Turkey, no. 1305/05, 27 September 2011 514
Sisojeva and Others v Latvia (striking out) [GC], no. 60654/00, ECHR 2007-I. 271, 745,
 763, 798, 801
Sitaropoulos and Giakoumopoulos v Greece [GC], no. 42202/07, ECHR 2012 . . . . .1018, 1027
Siveri and Chiellini v Italy (dec.), no. 13148/04, 3 June 2008. 524–5
Sizarev v Ukraine, no. 17116/04, 17 January 2013 238
Skałka v Poland, no. 43425/98, 27 May 2003. 475
Skiba v Poland (dec.), 10 10659/03, 7 July 2009. . . . . 490–2, 495, 497–8, 516
Skorobogatykh v Russia (dec.), no. 37966/02, 8 June 2006 272
Skugar and Others v Russia (dec.), no. 40010/04, 3 December 2009 . . . . .421–2, 428, 431
S.L. v Austria (dec.), no. 45330/99, 22 November 2001 743
S.L. v Austria, no. 45330/99, ECHR 2003-I. 279
Slimani v France, no. 57671/00, ECHR 2004-IX 41, 134
Slivenko v Latvia (dec.) [GC], no. 48321/99, ECHR 2002-II. 721, 969, 971, 1072
Slivenko v Latvia [GC], no. 48321/99, ECHR 2003-X 367, 397–8, 933–4, 937
Smirnova v Russia, nos 46133/99 and 48183/99, ECHR 2003-IX (extracts) 252, 378
Smirnova and Smirnova v Russia (dec.), nos 46133/99 and 48183/99, 3 October 2002 . . . . . .776, 1150
Smith and Grady v United Kingdom, nos 33985/96 and 33986/96, ECHR 1999-VI 173, 198,
 381, 406–7, 438, 513, 574–5, 584, 1064
Smith and Grady v United Kingdom (just satisfaction), nos 33985/96 and 33986/96,
 ECHR 2000-IX 838
Smoleanu v Romania, no. 30324/96, 3 December 2002. 109
S.N. v Sweden, no. 34209/96, ECHR 2002-V 288, 312–3
Šneersone and Kampanella v Italy, no. 14737/09, 12 July 2011 392–3
Soare and Others v Romania, no. 24329/02, 22 February 2011 237
Socialist Party and Others v Turkey, 25 May 1998, *Reports of Judgments and Decisions*
 1998-III 499, 520–1, 627
Sociedad Anónima del Ucieza v Spain, no. 38963/08, 4 November 2014 977
Société Colas Est and Others v France, no. 37971/97, ECHR 2002-III. 337, 386, 399
Société de conception de presse et d'édition and Ponson v France, no. 26935/05,
 5 March 2009. . . . . .455, 481, 574
Société Faugyr Finance S.A. v Luxembourg (dec.), no. 38788/97, 23 March 2000 . . . . .92, 736
Société Prisma Presse v France (dec.), nos 66910/01 and 71612/01, 1 July 2003 461
Söderman v Sweden [GC], no. 5786/08, 12 November 2013. . . . . .38, 368–9
Soering v United Kingdom, 7 July 1989, Series A no. 161 . . . . 37–9, 49, 68, 70,
 73, 88, 95–6, 141–3, 145, 169, 190, 244, 282,
 395, 434, 788, 790–1, 794, 1092, 1115, 1128
Soering v United Kingdom, 7 July 1989, Concurring Opinion of Judge de Meyer, Series A
 no. 161. . . . . .143, 1099
Sofianopoulos and Others v Greece (dec.), nos 988/02, 1997/02, and 1977/02,
 12 December 2002 428
Sofri and Others v Italy (dec.), no. 37235/97, ECHR 2003-VIII 765
Sohby v United Kingdom (dec.), no. 34108/07, 18 June 2013. 271
Solmaz v Turkey, no. 27561/02, 16 January 2007. 250
Soldatenko v Ukraine, no. 2440/07, 23 October 2008. 243
Solomon v Netherlands (dec.), no. 44328/98, 5 September 2000 396
Solomou and Others v Turkey, no. 36832/97, 24 June 2008 . . . . 123, 150–1, 153

Solovey and Zozulya v Ukraine, nos 40774/02 and 4048/03, 27 November 2008 231
Solovyev v Russia, no. 2708/02, 24 May 2007. 231
Soltysyak v Russia, no. 4663/05, 10 February 2011 . . . . .1058, 1062
Sommerfeld v Germany [GC], no. 31871/96, ECHR 2003-VIII 392, 574
Somogyi v Italy, no. 67972/01, ECHR 2004-IV 316
Sørensen and Rasmussen v Denmark [GC], nos 52562/99 and 52620/99, ECHR
    2006-I 38–9, 64, 91, 493, 502, 506–8
Sørensen and Rasmussen v Denmark [GC], nos 52562/99 and 52620/99, Dissenting
    Opinion of Judge Lorenzen, ECHR 2006-I. 64, 507
Sørensen and Rasmussen v Denmark [GC], nos 52562/99 and 52620/99, Partly Dissenting
    Opinion of Judges Rozakis, Bratza, and Vajić, ECHR 2006-I. 508
Sorguç v Turkey, no. 17089/03, 23 June 2009 855
Sovtransavto Holding v Ukraine, no. 48553/99, ECHR 2002-VII 968, 971
Söyler v Turkey, no. 29411/07, 17 September 2013 . . . . .1023, 1028–9
Soysal v Turkey, no. 50091/99, 3 May 2007. 245
S.P. v Belgium (dec.), no. 12572/08, 14 June 2011 244
Sporer v Austria, no. 35637/03, 3 February 2011 408
Sporrong and Lönnroth v Sweden, 23 September 1982, Series A no. 52 . . . . 272, 274,
                                                                                    622, 967, 972–5, 979
S.R. v Netherlands (dec.), no. 13837/07, 18 September 2012. 241
S.R. v Sweden (dec.), no. 62806/00, 23 April 2002 145
Srpska pravoslavna Opština na Rijeci v Croatia (dec.), no. 38312/02, 18 May 2006. 979
Staatkundig Gereformeerde Parij v Netherlands (dec.), no. 58369/10, 10 July 2012. . . . . 68, 405,
                                                                                    490, 576
Stafford v United Kingdom [GC], no. 46295/99, ECHR 2002-IV 48, 233, 236, 295, 567
Stagno v Belgium, no. 1062/07, 7 July 2009. 286
Stallinger and Kuso v Austria, 23 April 1997, *Reports of Judgments and Decisions* 1997-II 323, 935
Stamose v Bulgaria, no. 29713/05, ECHR 2012 1062
Stamoulakatos v Greece (dec.), no. 42155/98, 9 November 1999 1144
Stamoulakatos v Greece (no. 1), 26 October 1993, Series A no. 271 108
Stanchev v Bulgaria, no. 8682/02, 1 October 2009 1139
Stanculescu v Romania and Chitac v Romania (dec.), nos 2555/09 and 42204/09, 3 July 2012 355
Standard Verlags GmbH v Austria, no. 13071/03, 2 November 2006. 458
Standard Verlags GmbH v Austria (no. 2), no. 21277/05, 4 June 2009. . . . . .377–8, 478
Stanev v Bulgaria [GC], no.36760/06, ECHR 2012. . . . . 171, 182, 184, 226–8, 241
Stanford v United Kingdom, 23 February 1994, Series A no. 282-A 310
Stankov and the United Macedonian Organisation Ilinden v Bulgaria, nos 29221/95 and
    29225/95, ECHR 2001-IX 430, 490, 494–5, 497, 512, 518
Stašaitis v Lithuania, no. 47679/99, 21 March 2002 233
Statileo v Croatia, no. 12027/10, 10 July 2014 . . . . .740, 980
Stec and Others v United Kingdom (dec.) [GC], nos 65731/01 and 65900/01,
    ECHR 2005-X 38, 47, 562, 801, 859, 972, 982
Stec and Others v United Kingdom [GC], nos 65731/01 and 65900/01,
    ECHR 2006-VI 81, 562, 564, 566–8, 574, 971, 982, 1038
Stec and Others v United Kingdom [GC], nos 65731/01 and 65900/01, Concurring
    Opinion of Judge Borrego Borrego, ECHR 2006-VI 958
Steck-Risch v Liechtenstein (dec.), no. 63151/00, ECHR 2004-II. 323, 936–7
Steel and Morris v United Kingdom, no. 68416/01, ECHR 2005-II. 285, 474–5
Steel and Others v United Kingdom, 23 September 1998, *Reports of Judgments and
    Decisions* 1998-VII. 231, 236, 258, 496
Stefan Iliev v Bulgaria, no. 53121/99, 10 May 2007 173
Stefan Iliev v Bulgaria, no. 53121, Joint Partly Dissenting Opinion of Judges Lorenzen,
    Jungwierr, and Maruste, 10 May 2007 173
Stefanescu v Roumaine (dec.), no. 11774/04, 12 April 2011. 783
Steindel v Germany (dec.), no. 29878/07, 14 September 2010 212

Stempfer v Austria, no. 18294/03, 26 July 2007 1137
Stephens v Malta (no. 1), no. 11956/07, 21 April 2009 ....97, 255
Stephens v Malta (no. 2), no. 33740/06, 21 April 2009 ....247, 249
Stepuleac v Moldova, no. 8207/06, 6 November 2007 238
Steur v Netherlands, no. 39657/98, ECHR 2003-XI 455
Stichting Mothers of Srebrenica and Others v Netherlands (dec.), no. 65542/12, ECHR
   2013 (extracts) 35, 44, 273, 287, 948
Štitić v Croatia, no. 29660/03, 8 November 2007 ....282, 1152
Stocké v Germany, 19 March 1991, Series A no. 199. 809
Stögmüller v Austria, 10 November 1969, Series A no. 9 251
Stoichkov v Bulgaria, no. 9808/02, 24 March 2005 ....96, 235, 282, 316
Stokić v Serbia (dec.), no. 54689/12, 12 February 2013 744
Stolder v Italy, no. 24418/03, 1 December 2009 778
Stoll v Switzerland [GC], no. 69698/01, ECHR 2007-V 46, 279, 468, 473, 475
Storbråten v Norway (dec.), no. 12277/04. 1151
Storck v Germany, no. 6160/03, ECHR 2005-V 227–9, 371, 697, 702, 708, 849
Storck v Germany (dec.), no. 6160/03, 26 October 2004 .... 697, 702, 708, 849
Stoyanovi v Bulgaria, no. 42980/04, 9 November 2010 132
Stran Greek Refineries and Stratis Andreadis v Greece, 9 December 1994, Series A
   no. 301-B. 276, 335, 971
Streletz, Kessler, and Krenz v Germany [GC], nos 34044/96, 35532/97, and 44801/98,
   ECHR 2001-II 40, 68, 71, 88, 119, 128, 151, 640, 1052
Streletz, Kessler, and Krenz v Germany [GC], nos 34044/96, 35532/97, and 44801/98,
   Concurring Opinion of Judge Zupančić, ECHR 2001-II 334, 337, 339, 342, 354–5
Stretch v United Kingdom, no. 44277/98, 24 June 2003 970
Stubbings and Others v United Kingdom, 22 October 1996, *Reports of Judgments and
   Decisions* 1996-IV 286, 974
Stübing v Germany, no. 43547/08, 12 April 2012. ....82, 380–1
Stukus and Others v Poland, no. 12534/03, 1 April 2008 738
Stummer v Austria [GC], no. 37452/02, ECHR 2011 .... 201, 206, 211, 213–4, 275
Stummer v Austria [GC], no. 37452/02, Partly Dissenting Opinion of Judge Tulkens,
   ECHR 2011 66
Sud Fondi srl and Others v Italy, no. 75909/01, 20 January 2009. 340
Sufi and Elmi v United Kingdom, nos 8319/07 and 11449/07, 28 June 2011 ......189, 812
Süheyla Aydın v Turkey, no. 25660/94, 24 May 2005. ....134, 552, 813
Sukhovetskyy v Ukraine, no. 13716/02, ECHR 2006-VI. 1026
Sükran Aydın and Others v Turkey, nos 49197/06, 23196/07, 50242/08, 60912/08,
   and 14871/09, 22 January 2013. 279
Suküt v Turkey (dec.), no. 59773/00, 11 September 2007 282
Sulaoja v Estonia, no. 55939/00 15 February 2005 251–2
Sulejmanovic and Sultanovic v Italy (dec.), no. 57574/00, 14 March 2002 1128
Suleymanov v Russia, no. 32501/11, 22 January 2013. 193
Sultan Karabulut v Turkey, no. 45784/99, 19 September 2006 ....135, 147
Sultani v France, no. 45223/05, ECHR 2007-IV (extracts). 195, 1077, 1128
Sunday Times v United Kingdom (no. 1), 26 April 1979,
   Series A no. 30 .... 336–7, 402–3, 469, 474, 510
Sunday Times v United Kingdom (no. 2), 26 November 1991, Series A no. 217. ......82, 452
Suominen v Finland, (dec.), no. 37801/97, 26 February 2002 324
Supreme Holy Council of the Muslim Community v Bulgaria, no. 39023/97,
   16 December 2004 ....430–1, 437
Sürek and Özdemir v Turkey [GC], no. 23927/94 and 24277/94,
   8 July 1999. 627
Surugiu v Romania, no. 48995/99, 20 April 2004 400
Suso Musa v Malta, no. 42337/12, 23 July 2013. 254
Sutter v Switzerland, 22 February 1984, Series A no. 74. ....291, 621

Table of Cases

Svenska Flygföretagens Riksförbund and Skyways Express AB v Sweden (dec.), no. 32535/02,
12 December 2006 273
Svinarenko and Slyadnev v Russia [GC], nos 32541/08 and 43441/08, 17 July 2014 . . . . . . .43, 67, 185
Svipsta v Latvia, no. 66820/01, ECHR 2006-III (extracts) 255, 839
Svyato-Mykhaylivska Parafiya v Ukraine, no. 77703/01, 14 June 2007 . . . . .429–30, 436
S.W. v United Kingdom, 22 November 1995, Series A no. 335-B 335, 337, 339, 1181
Swedish Engine Drivers' Union v Sweden, 6 February 1976, Series A no. 20 . . . . . 90, 505–6, 509, 524
Sylla v Netherlands, no. 14683/03, 6 July 2006 69
Szabó v Sweden (dec.), no. 28578/03, 27 June 2006 . . . . .281, 348
Szél and Others v Hungary, no. 44357/13, 16 September 2014 476
Szima v Hungary, no. 29723/11, 9 October 2012 . . . . 465, 469, 472, 492
Szott-Medyńska v Poland (dec.), no. 47414/99, 9 October 2003 769
Szücs v Austria, 24 November 1997, *Reports of Judgments and Decisions* 1997-VII 323
Szuluk v United Kingdom, no. 36936/05, ECHR 2009 . . . . 82, 401, 406, 438, 517
T. v Italy, 12 October 1992, Series A no. 245-C 316
T. v United Kingdom [GC], no. 24724/94, 16 December 1999 . . . . 182–3, 233, 318
T.A. v Turkey, no. 26307/95, 9 April 2002 799
Tabaï v France (dec.), no. 73805/01, 17 February 2004 . . . . .308, 314
Tadevosyan v Armenia, no. 41698/04, 2 December 2008 1137
Tahsin Acar v Turkey [GC], no. 26307/95, ECHR 2004-III 78, 627, 739, 846
Tahsin Acar v Turkey (preliminary issue) [GC], no. 26307/95, ECHR 2003-VI 799, 823
Tahsin Acar v Turkey (preliminary issue) [GC], no. 26307/95, Concurring Opinion of Judge
Ress, ECHR 2003-VI 799
Tahsin Acar v Turkey (preliminary issue) [GC], no. 26307/95, Joint Concurring Opinion of
Sir Nicolas Bratza, Tulkens, and Vajić, ECHR 2003-VI 799
Taïs v France, no. 39922/03, 1 June 2006 133
Takush v Greece, no. 2853/09, 17 January 2012 . . . . 1127, 1130, 1132
Taliadorou and Stylianou v Cyprus, nos 39627/05 and 39631/05, 16 October 2008 . . . . .304, 306
Tammer v Estonia, no. 41205/98, ECHR 2001-I 82
Tamminen and Tammelin v Finland (dec.), no. 33003/96, 28 September 1999 324
Tamosius v United Kingdom (dec.), no. 62002/00, ECHR 2002-VIII 386
Tănase v Moldova [GC], no. 7/08, ECHR 2010 . . . . 94, 505, 1023, 1030
Tanda-Muzinga v France, no. 2260/10, 10 July 2014 797–8
Tangiyeva v Russia, no. 57935/00, 29 November 2007 171
Taniş and Others v Turkey, no. 65899/01, ECHR 2005-VIII 123, 171, 812–3
Tanlı v Turkey, no. 26129/95, ECHR 2001-III 134, 171
Tanrıkulu v Turkey [GC], no. 23763/94, ECHR 1999-IV 135, 193, 748, 751
Tanrıkulu and Others v Turkey (dec.), no. 40150/98, 6 November 2001 742
Tarakhel v Switzerland [GC], no. 29217/12, 4 November 2014 . . . . .97, 194
Taran v Ukraine, no. 31898/06, 17 October 2013 238–9
Tarantino and Others v Italy, nos 25851/09, 29284/09, and 64090/09, ECHR 2013
(extracts) 996–8
Tarantino and Others v Italy, nos 25851/09, 29284/09, and 64090/09, Partly Dissenting
Opinion of Judge Pinto de Albuquerque, ECHR 2013 (extracts) 89, 997–8, 1005
Tarbuk v Croatia, no. 31360/10, 11 December 2012 1145
Tase v Romania, no. 29761/02, 10 June 2008 . . . . .233, 250, 253
Taşkın and Others v Turkey, no. 46117/99, ECHR 2004-X 388
Taşkın and Others v Turkey, no. 49517/99, 4 December 2003 40
Tătar v Romania, no. 67021/01, 27 January 2009 388
Tătar and Fáber v Hungary, nos 26005/08 and 26160/08, 12 June 2012 . . . . 455, 471, 492, 494
Tatishvili v Russia, no. 1509/02, ECHR 2007-I 1057, 1059
Tavlı v Turkey, no. 11449/02, 9 November 2006 368
Taxquet v Belgium, no. 926/05, 13 January 2009 857
Taxquet v Belgium [GC], no. 926/05, ECHR 2010 . . . . 297–8, 793–4, 857
Taysumov and Others v Russia, no. 21810/03, 14 May 2009 155
Tchitchinadze v Georgia, no. 18156/05, 27 May 2010 72

Tebieti Mühafize Cemiyyeti and Israfilov v Azerbaijan, no. 37083/03,
   ECHR 2009 . . . . 500–1, 510, 517–8
Teixeira de Castro v Portugal, 9 June 1998, *Reports of Judgments and Decisions* 1998-IV 320
Tele 1 Privatfernsehgesellscahft mbH v Austria, no. 32240/96, 21 September 2000 467
Telegraaf Media Nederland Landelijke Media B.V. and Others v Netherlands, no. 39315/06,
   22 November 2012 459
Telfner v Austria, no. 33501/96, 20 March 2001 298–9
Tendam v Spain, no. 25720/05, 13 July 2010 304
Tepeli and Others v Turkey (dec.), no. 31876/96, 11 September 2001 282
Teret v Belgium (striking out), no. 49497/99, 15 November 2002 798
Ternovskis v Latvia, no. 33637/02, 29 April 2014 288
Ternovszky v Hungary, no. 67545/09, 14 December 2010 372
Tess v Latvia (dec.), no. 34854/02, 3 December 2002 352
Thaler v Austria (dec.), no. 58141/00, 15 September 2003 766
Themeli v Albania, no. 63756/09, 15 January 2013 702
Thlimmenos v Greece [GC], no. 34369/97, ECHR 2000-IV 215, 374, 566, 568
Thoma v Luxembourg, no. 38432/97, ECHR 2001-III 477
Thomasi v Finland (dec.), no. 28339/95, 19 March 2002 324
Thomann v Switzerland, 10 June 1996, *Reports of Judgments and Decisions* 1996-III 295
Thorgeir Thorgeirson v Iceland, 25 June 1992, Series A no. 239 .458, 474
TH-tekniika Oy:n Konkurssipesä v Finland (dec.), no. 35897/97, 28 September 1999 324
Thynne, Wilson, and Gunnell v United Kingdom, 25 October 1990, Series A no. 190-A 256
Tiemann v France and Germany (dec.), nos 47457/99 and 47458/99, ECHR 2000-IV 393
Tigran Ayrapetyan v Russia, no. 75472/01, 10 September 2010 813
Timciuc v Romania (dec.), no. 28999/03, 1 October 2010 462
Times Newspapers Ltd v United Kingdom (nos 1 and 2), nos 3002/03 and 23676/03,
   ECHR 2009 . . . . .458, 462
Timishev v Russia, nos 55762/00 and 55974/00, ECHR 2005-XII 564, 570, 575,
                                                                     577–8, 811, 995–7, 1059, 1065
Timishev v Russia (dec.), nos 55762/00 and 55974/00, 30 March 2004 1058
Timurtaş v Turkey, no. 23531/94, ECHR 2000-VI 123, 813
Tinnelly & Sons Ltd and Others and McElduff and Others v United Kingdom,
   10 July 1998, *Reports of Judgments and Decisions* 1998-IV 257, 790
Tiron v Romania, no. 17689/03, 7 April 2009 252
Titarenko v Ukraine, no. 31720/02, 20 September 2012 185
T.K. v Finland (dec.), no. 29347/95, 13 September 2001 324
Tkachevy v Russia, no. 35430/05, 14 February 2012 74
T.M. and C.M. v Republic of Moldova, no. 26608/11, 28 January 2014 . . . . .170, 192, 198
Toimi v Sweden (friendly settlement), no. 55164/00, 22 March 2005 851
Tolstoy Miloslavsky v United Kingdom, 13 July 1995, Series A no. 316-B 403, 469, 510
Tomasi v France, 27 August 1992, Series A no. 241-A 247
Tonkevi v Bulgaria (dec.), no. 21302/13, 30 September 2014 150
Tønsbergs Blad A.S. and Haukom v Norway, no. 510/04, ECHR 2007-III 469
Torri v Italy, 1 July 1997, *Reports of Judgments and Decisions* 1997-IV 276
Toshev v Bulgaria, no. 56308/00, 10 August 2006 253
Toteva v Bulgaria, no. 42027/98, 19 May 2004 . . . . .170, 740
Toth v Austria, 12 December 1991, Series A no. 224 . . . . .247, 255
Toth v Croatia (dec.), no. 49635/10, 6 November 2012 1151–2
Tourkiki Enosi Xanthis and Others v Greece, no. 26698/05, 27 march 2008 738
T.P. and K.M. v United Kingdom [GC], no. 28945/95, ECHR 2001-V (extracts) 392, 793
Trabelsi v Belgium, no. 140/10, 4 September 2014 . . . . 187, 749–50,
                                                                                    837, 1149
Trade Union of the Police in the Slovak Republic and Others v Slovakia, no. 11828/08,
   25 September 2012 . . . . 492, 500, 514, 522
Tre Traktörer AB v Sweden, 7 July 1989, Series A no. 159 . . . . 274, 971, 973, 976
Tremblay v France, no. 37194/02, 11 September 2007 38

Trévalec v Belgium, no. 30812/07, 14 June 2011 . . . . .125, 149
Trofimchuk v Ukraine (dec.), no. 4241/03, 31 May 2005 780
Trosin v Ukraine, no. 39758/05, 23 February 2012. 398
Trubnikov v Russia, no. 49790/99, 5 July 2005 . . . . .132, 813
Trzepałko v Poland (dec.), no. 25124/09, 13 September 2011 131
T.S. and D.S. v United Kingdom (dec.), no. 61540/09, 19 January 2010 393
Tsalkitzis v Greece, no. 11801/04, 16 November 2006 285–6
Tsechoyev v Russia, no. 39358/05, 15 March 2011. . . . . .123, 829
Tsfayo v United Kingdom, no. 60860/00, 14 November 2006. 855
Tsonev v Bulgaria, no. 45963/99, 13 April 2006 500
Tsonyo Tsonev v Bulgaria (no. 2), no. 2376/03, 14 January 2010 309
Tsygoniy v Ukraine, no. 19213/04, 24 November 2011. 239
Tüm Haber Sen and Çınar v Turkey, no. 28602/95, ECHR 2006-II 38, 506, 509, 515, 522
Tumilovich v Russia (dec.), no. 47033/99, 2 June 1999. 771
Tuncer Güneş v Turkey, no. 26268/08, 3 September 2013 407
Turán v Hungary, no. 33068/05, 6 July 2010. 374
Turgut and Others v Turkey (just satisfaction), no. 1411/03, 13 October 2009. 837
Tushaj v Albania, no. 13620/10, 15 January 2013. 702
Tutmaz and Others v Turkey, no. 51053/99, 23 October 2003 321
T.W. v Malta [GC], no. 25644/94, 29 April 1999. 247
Twomey, Cameron and Guthrie v United Kingdom (dec.), nos 67318/09 and 22226/12,
    28 May 2013 280
Tymoshenko v Ukraine, no. 49872/11, 30 April 2013. . . . . .230–1, 626
Tymoshenko v Ukraine, no. 49872/11, Concurring Opinion of Judges Jungwiert,
    Nußberger, and Potocki, 30 April 2013 626–7
Tyrer v United Kingdom, 25 April 1978, Series A no. 26. . . .33, 48, 67, 70, 172, 182, 186, 189, 926–8
Tysiąc v Poland, no. 5410/03 ECHR 2007-I. 367, 369, 371, 373, 388, 407
Tzekov v Bulgaria, no. 45500/99, 23 February 2006 151
Üçak and Kargili and Others v Turkey (dec.), nos 75527/01 and 11837/02, 28 March 2006 773
Udayeva and Yusupova v Russia, no. 36542/05, 21 December 2010. 171
Uj v Hungary, no. 23954/10, 19 July 2011. . . . . .456, 473
Ukraine v Russia (I) (interim measures), no. 20958/14, not yet reported 729
Ukraine v Russia (II) (interim measures), no. 43800/14, not yet reported 729
Ülke v Turkey, no. 39437/98, 24 January 2006. 215
Ulyanov v Ukraine (dec.), no. 16472/04, 5 October 2010 273
Umayeva v Russia, no. 1200/03, 4 December 2008 155
Umlauft v Austria, 23 October 1995, Series A no. 328-B. 262, 933
Unabhängige Initiative Informationsvielfalt v Austria, no. 28525/95, ECHR 2002-I 455
Ünal Tekeli v Turkey, no. 29865/96, ECHR 2004-X (extracts) 407, 524, 567, 574, 576
Unédic v France, no. 20153/04, 18 December 2008 . . . . .92, 336, 736
Üner v Netherlands [GC], no. 46410/99, ECHR 2006-XII .194, 396–7
UNISON v United Kingdom (dec.), no. 53574/99, ECHR 2002-I 508
United Christian Broadcasters Ltd v United Kingdom (dec.), no. 44802/98, 7 December 2000 467
United Communist Party of Turkey and Others v Turkey, 30 January 1998, *Reports of
    Judgments and Decisions* 1998-I. 68, 70, 74, 76, 95, 490, 499,
                                                            501, 503, 512, 516, 519–21, 615–6, 618, 1011
United Macedonian Organisation Ilinden and Others v Bulgaria, no. 59491/00,
    19 January 2006 500
United Macedonian Organisation Ilinden – PIRIN and Others v Bulgaria, no. 59489/00,
    20 October 2005. 521
Unterpertinger v Austria, 24 November 1986, Series A no. 110 312
Ursu v Romania, no. 21949/04, 4 June 2013 2050
Usta and Others v Turkey, no. 57084/00, 21 February 2008 150
Ustün v Turkey, no. 37685/02, 10 May 2007. 744
Utsayeva and Others v Russia, no. 29133/03, 29 May 2008. 811

Uttley v United Kingdom (dec.), no. 36946/03, 29 November 2005 347
Uzun v Germany, no. 35623/05, ECHR 2010 (extracts) 383, 387
V. v Finland, no. 40412/98, 24 April 2007 324
V. v United Kingdom [GC], no. 24888/94, ECHR 1999-IX 171, 182–3, 318
Vacher v France, 17 December 1996, *Reports of Judgments and Decisions* 1996-VI 286
Vachev v Bulgaria, no. 42987/98, ECHR 2004-VIII (extracts) 258
Vachkovi v Bulgaria, no. 2747/02, 8 July 2010 152
Vagapova and Zubirayev v Russia, no. 21080/05, 26 February 2009 126
Vaillant v France, no. 30609/04, 18 December 2008 295
Vajnai v Hungary, no. 33629/06, 8 July 2008 470
Vajnai v Hungary, no. 33629/06, ECHR 2008 . . . . .279, 619
Valašinas v Lithuania, no. 44558/98, ECHR 2001-VIII 180–1
Valenzuela Contreras v Spain, 30 July 1998, *Reports of Judgments and Decisions* 1998-V 403
Valico S.r.l. v Italy (dec.), no. 70074/01, ECHR 2006-III 279, 347, 979
Valiuliene v Lithuania, no. 33234/07, 26 March 2013 192
Vallianatos and Others v Greece [GC], no. 29381/09 and 32684/09, ECHR 2013 . . . . 390, 408,
                                                                         574, 736–7, 742, 765
Vallianatos and Others v Greece [GC], no. 29381/09 and 32684/09, Joint Concurring
    Opinion of Judges Casadevall, Ziemele, Jočiené, and Sicilianos, ECHR 2013 408
Vallianatos and Others v Greece [GC], no. 29381/09 and 32684/09, Partly Dissenting
    Opinion of Judge Pinto de Albuquerque, ECHR 2013 744
Valsamis v Greece and Efstratiou v Greece, 18 December 1996, *Reports of Judgments and
    Decisions* 1996-VI 432, 1001–2
Van Anraat v Netherlands (dec.), no. 65389/09, 6 July 2010 . . . . .339, 352
Van de Hurk v Netherlands, 19 April 1994, Series A no. 288 . . . . .297, 857
Van der Heijden v Netherlands [GC], no. 42857/05, 3 April 2012 . . . . 389, 459, 538, 544
Van der Leer v Netherlands, 21 February 1990, Series A no. 170-A 245
Van der Mussele v Belgium, 23 November 1983, Series A no. 70 . . . . .210–3, 217, 971
Van der Tang v Spain, 13 July 1995, Series A no. 321 . . . . .736, 791
Van der Velden v Netherlands (dec.), no. 29514/05, ECHR 2006-XV 346
Van Droogenbroeck v Belgium, 24 June 1982, Series A no. 50 . . . . 214, 235–6, 254, 273
Van Houten v Netherlands (striking out), no. 25149/03, ECHR 2005-IX 784
Van Geyseghem v Belgium [GC], no. 26103/95, ECHR 1999-I 307, 317
Van Marle and Others v Netherlands, 26 June 1986, Series A no. 101 971
Van Mechelen and Others v Netherlands, 23 April 1997, *Reports of Judgments and Decisions*
    1997-III 288
Van Oosterwijck v Belgium, 6 November 1980, Series A no. 40 768
Van Raalte v Netherlands, 21 February 1997, *Reports of Judgments and Decisions*
    1997-I 567, 574–5, 1178
Vaney v France, no. 53946/00, 30 November 2004 766
Vanjak v Croatia, no. 29889/04, 14 January 2010 305
Varbanov v Bulgaria, no. 31365/96, ECHR 2000-X 241, 256, 780
Varela Geis v Spain, no. 61005/09, 5 March 2013 617
Varga v Romania, no. 73957/01, 1 April 2008 248
Varnava and Others v Turkey, nos 16064/90, 16065/90, 16066/90, 16068/90, 16069/90,
    16070/90, 16071/90, 16072/90, and 16073/90, 10 January 2008 .155, 791
Varnava and Others v Turkey [GC], nos 16064/90, 16065/90, 16066/90, 16068/90, 16069/90,
    16070/90, 16071/90, 16072/90, and 16073/90, ECHR 2009 . . . . .33, 36, 43, 78, 107–8,
                                                110, 126, 134, 137, 155, 170, 193, 229, 738–40,
                                                765, 770–4, 791, 811, 837–9, 871, 950
Varnava and Others v Turkey [GC], nos 16064/90, 16065/90, 16066/90, 16068/90, 16069/90,
    16070/90, 16071/90, 16072/90, and 16073/90, Concurring Opinion of Judge Ziemele,
    ECHR 2009 . . . . .740, 773
Varnava and Others v Turkey [GC], nos 16064/90, 16065/90, 16066/90, 16068/90, 16069/90,
    16070/90, 16071/90, 16072/90, and 16073/90, Concurring Opinion of Judge Spielmann,
    Joined by Judges Ziemele and Kaladjieva, ECHR 2009 870

Varnava and Others v Turkey [GC], nos 16064/90, 16065/90, 16066/90, 16068/90, 16069/90,
 16070/90, 16071/90, 16072/90, and 16073/90, Concurring Opinion of Judge Villiger,
 ECHR 2009 773
Varnienė v Lithuania, no. 42916/04, 12 November 2013. 72
Vasileva v Denmark, no. 52792/99, 25 September 2003 236–7
Vassilios Stavropoulos v Greece, no. 35522/04, 27 September 2007 304
Västberga Taxi Aktiebolag and Vulic v Sweden, no. 36985/97, 23 July 2002. 299
Vatan v Russia, no. 47978/99, 7 October 2004 742
V.C. v Slovakia, no. 18968/07, ECHR 2011 (extracts). 38, 184, 191, 372, 388, 534
V.D. v Romania, no. 7078/02, 16 February 2010 313
Veeber v Estonia (no. 1), no. 37571/97, 7 November 2002 108
Veeber v Estonia (no. 2), no. 45771/99, 21 January 2003 336
Vejdeland v Sweden, no. 1813/07, 7 February 2012 . . . . .479, 584
Velikova v Bulgaria, no. 41488/98, ECHR 2000-VI 745, 786
Velinov v former Yugoslav Republic of Macedonia, no. 16880/08, 19 September 2013 . . . . . .236, 258
Velkhiyev and Others v Russia, no. 34085/06, 5 July 2011 . . . . .171, 811
Vellutini and Michel v France, no. 32820/09, 6 October 2011. . . . . .464, 476
Velyo Velev v Bulgaria, no. 16032/07, 27 May 2014. 998
Verein gegen Tierfabriken Schweiz (VgT) v Switzerland (no. 2) [GC], no. 32772/02,
 ECHR 2009 . . . . 35, 89, 451–4, 474, 580, 766, 774, 837, 866, 868–9, 871
Vereinigung Bildender Künstler v Austria, no. 68354/01, 25 January 2007 . . . . .455, 472
Vereinigung demokratischer Soldaten Österreichs and Gubi v Austria, 19 December 1994,
 Series A no. 302 . . . . 406, 438, 465, 472, 513, 1064
Veriter v France, no. 31508/07, 14 October 2010 766
Verlagsgruppe News GMBH v Austria (dec.), no. 62763/00, 16 January 2003 275
Verlagsgruppe News GmbH v Austria (no. 2), no. 10520/02, 14 December 2006 455
Vermeire v Belgium, 29 November 1991, Series A no. 214-C. 583
Vernillo v France, 20 February 1991, Series A no. 198. 791
Vesterby v Estonia, no. 34476/97, 1 July 1998 984
V.F. v France (dec.), no. 7196/10, 29 November 2011 206
VgT Verein gegen Tierfabriken v Switzerland, no. 24699/94, ECHR 2001-VI 467
Victor-Emmanuel De Savoie v Italy (dec.), no. 53360/99, 13 September 2001 . . . . .933, 1072–3
Victor-Emmanuel De Savoie v Italy (striking out), no. 53360/99, 24 April 2003 . . . . .934, 1073
Vidaković v Serbia (dec.), no. 16231/07, 24 May 2011 744
Vides Aizsardzibas Klubs v Latvia, no. 57829/00, 27 May 2004 478
Vidgen v Netherlands, no. 29353/06, 10 July 2012. 313
Vijayanathan and Pusparajah v France, nos 17550/90 and 17825/91, 27 August 1992. 743
Vilho Eskelinen and Others v Finland [GC], no. 63235/00, ECHR 2007-II 39, 47, 273–4,
 293, 374, 849, 969, 971
Villa v Italy, no. 19675/06, 20 April 2010. 1057
Vilnes and Others v Norway, nos 52806/09 and 22703/10, 5 December 2013 . . . . .126, 131
Vilvarajah and Others v United Kingdom, 30 October 1991, Series A no. 215 . . . 64, 94–5, 194–5, 395
Vinnik and Others v Ukraine, no. 13977/05 and 45 other applications, 7 November 2013 702
Vinter and Others v United Kingdom [GC], nos 66069/09, 130/10, and 3896/10, Concurring
 Opinion of Judge Power-Forde, 9 July 2013. 187
Vinter and Others v United Kingdom [GC], nos 66069/09, 130/10, and 3896/10,
 ECHR 2013 (extracts). 44, 81, 182–3, 187, 350, 870
Viorel Burzo v Romania, nos 75109/01 and 12639/02, 30 June 2009. 248
Virabyan v Armenia, no. 40094/05, 2 October 2012 302–3
Vitzthum v Austria, no. 8140/04, 26 July 2007. 1137
V.K. v Croatia, no. 38380/08, 27 November 2012 . . . . .539, 541
Vlad and Others v Romania, nos 40756/06, 41508/07, and 50806/07,
 16 November 2013. . . . . .292, 784
Vo v France [GC] no. 53924/00, ECHR 2004-VIII .40, 81, 92, 94, 124–5,
 128, 131, 137–8, 286, 373

Voggenreiter v Germany (dec.), no. 47169/99, 28 November 2002 766
Vogt v Germany, 26 September 1995, Series A no. 323 . . . . 82, 374, 464–5, 523, 611
Voica v France, no. 60995/09, 10 January 2013 297
Von Hannover v Germany, no. 59320/00, ECHR 2004-VI 377–8, 461, 478
Von Hannover v Germany (no. 2) [GC], nos 40660/08 and 60641/08,
    ECHR 2012 . . . . 368, 370, 378, 461
Von Maltzan and Others v Germany (dec.) [GC], nos 71916/01, 71917/01, and 10260/02,
    ECHR 2005-V 109, 969–70, 779
Vona v Hungary, no. 35943/10, 9 July 2013 618
Vontas and Others v Greece, no. 43588/06, 5 February 2009 71
Vörður Ólafsson v Iceland, no. 20161/06, ECHR 2010 . . . . 38, 491, 502, 505, 508
Voskuil v Netherlands, no. 64752/01, 22 November 2007 . . . . 231, 459
V.P. v Russia, no. 61362/12, 23 October 2014 392
Vučkovići and Others v Serbia, no. 17153/11, 28 August 2012 76
Vulakh and Others v Russia, no. 33468/03, 10 January 2012 304
Vyerentsov v Ukraine, no. 20372/11, 11 April 2013 308–9
W. v United Kingdom, 8 July 1987, Series A no. 121 827
Wagner and J.M.W.L. v Luxembourg, no. 76240/01, 28 June 2007 . . . . 38, 394
Wainwright v United Kingdom, no. 12350/04, ECHR 2006-X 173, 181
Waite v United Kingdom, no. 53236/99, 10 December 2002 258
Waite and Kennedy v Germany [GC], no. 26083/94, ECHR 1999-I 97, 106, 285, 287
Walker v United Kingdom (dec.), no. 34979/97 ECHR 2000-I 770
Wałkuska v Poland (dec.), no. 6817/04, 29 April 2008 388
Wasmuth v Germany, no. 12884/03, 17 February 2011 428
Wassink v Netherlands, 27 September 1990, Series A no. 185-A 258–9
Weber v Switzerland, 22 May 1990, Series A no. 177 . . . . 278, 283, 324, 936
Weber and Saravia v Germany (dec.), no. 54934/00, ECHR 2006-XI 400, 404, 744
Weeks v United Kingdom, 2 March 1987, Series A no. 114 . . . . 235–6, 254–5
Weh v Austria, no. 38544/97, 8 April 2004 300–1
Weh v Austria, no. 38544/97, Joint Dissenting Opinion of Judges Lorenzen, Levits, and
    Hajiyev, 8 April 2004 301
Weh and Weh v Austria (dec.), no. 38544/97, 4 July 2002 1136
Weinsztal v Poland, no. 43748/98, 30 May 2006 252
Weissman and Others v Romania, no. 63945/00, ECHR 2006-VII (extracts) 286
Weixelbraun v Austria, no. 33730/96, 20 December 2001 . . . . 304, 306
Welch v United Kingdom, 9 February 1995, Series A no. 307-A 346
Welke and Białek v Poland, no. 15924/05, 1 March 2011 290
Wemhoff v Germany, 27 June 1968, Series A no. 7 . . . . 34, 46, 66, 236, 250
Wemhoff v Germany, 27 June 1968, Individual Opinion of Judge Terje Wold, Series A no. 7 46
Wendenburg and Others v Germany (dec.), no. 71630/01, 6 February 2003 971
Werner v Austria, 24 November 1997, *Reports of Judgments and Decisions* 1997-VII 291, 323
Wettstein v Switzerland, no. 33958/96, ECHR 2000-XII 295–6
White v Sweden, no. 42435/02, 19 September 2006 377
Wiater v Poland (dec.), no. 42290/08, 15 May 2012 131
Wierciszewska v Poland, no. 41431/98, 25 November 2003 292
Wieser v Austria, no. 2293/03, 22 February 2007 181
Wieser and Bicos Beteiligungen GmbH v Austria, no. 74336/01, ECHR 2007-IV 386
Willcox and Hurford v United Kingdom (dec.), nos 43759/10 and 43771/12,
    ECHR 2013 . . . . 96, 299, 349
Wille v Liechtenstein [GC], no. 28396/95, ECHR 1999-VII 90
Williams v United Kingdom (dec.), no. 32567/06, 17 February 2009 770–2
Williamson v United Kingdom, no. 27008/95, 17 May 1995 577
Willis v United Kingdom, no. 36042/97, ECHR 2002-IV 564, 574
Wilson, National Union of Journalists and Others v United Kingdom, nos 30668/96,
    30671/96, and 30678/96, ECHR 2002-V 492–4, 506, 508

Wingrove v United Kingdom, 25 November 1996, *Reports of Judgments and Decisions*
1996-V..473–4
Winterwerp v Netherlands, 24 October 1979, Series A no. 33 ..... 226, 232, 234, 239, 241, 255, 788
Wiot v France (dec.), no. 43722/98, 15 March 2001................................... 275
Wirtschafts-Trend Zeitschriften-Verlags GmbH v Austria, no. 58547/00, 27 October 2005....... 476
Wirtschafts-Trend Zeitschriften-Verlagsgesellschaft m.b.H. v Austria (no. 3), nos 66298/01
and 15653/02, 13 December 2005.. 378
Witczak v Poland (striking out), no. 47404/99, 6 May 2003 798
Withey v United Kingdom (dec.), no. 59493/00, 26 August 2003 307
Witkowski v Poland (dec.), no. 53804/00, 3 February 2003............................ 744
Witold Litwa v Poland, no. 26629/95, ECHR 2000-III.............. 36, 54, 233–4, 241–2, 1045
Witzsch v Germany (dec.), no. 7485/03, 13 December 2005 ....617, 619
Wizerkaniuk v Poland, no. 18990/05, 5 July 2011.........................279, 469, 474
Włoch v Poland, no. 27785/95, ECHR 2000-XI............................238, 255
Włoch v Poland (dec.), no. 27785/95, 30 March 2000 302
Włoch v Poland (no. 2), no. 33475/08, 10 May 2011 258–9
Wojtas-Kaleta v Poland, no. 20436/02, 16 July 2009............................... 45
Wołek, Kasprów, and Łęski v Poland (dec.), no 20953/06, 21 October 2008 469
Women on Waves and Others v Portugal, no. 31276/05, 3 February 2009................91, 451
Worm v Austria, 29 August 1997, *Reports of Judgments and Decisions* 1997-V 474, 770–1
Wortmann v Germany (dec.), no. 70929/01, 18 November 2003............... 698, 702, 708, 849
W.P. and Others v Poland (dec.), no. 42264/98, ECHR 2004-VII (extracts)..........519, 617, 619
X. v Austria (dec.), no. 7720/76, 8 May 1978 349
X. v Finland, no. 34806/04, ECHR 2012 (extracts).............................. 371
X. v France, 31 March 1992, Series A no. 234-C................................. 274
X. v Latvia, no. 27853/09, 13 December 2011 392
X. v United Kingdom, 5 November 1981, Series A no. 46.................... 141, 235, 245, 255
X. and Others v Austria [GC], no. 19010/07, ECHR 2013 ....408, 574
X. and Others v Austria [GC], no. 19010/07, Joint Partly Dissenting Opinion of Judges
Casadevall, Ziemele, Kovler, Jočienė, Šikuta, De Gaetano, and Sicilianos, ECHR 2013 ......48, 408
X. and Y. v Netherlands, 26 March 1985, Series A no. 91 .... 279, 368–70, 1187
X., Y., and Z. v United Kingdom, 22 April 1997, *Reports of Judgments and Decisions* 1997-II 380
Xenides-Arestis v Turkey, no, 46347/99, 22 December 2005 77
Xuereb v Malta (dec.), no. 52492/99, 15 June 2000 1021
Y. v Norway, no. 56568/00, ECHR 2003-II (extracts)...........................278, 304–5
Yağcı and Sargın v Turkey, 8 June 1995, Series A no. 319-A 107, 250, 252
Yağmurdereli v Turkey (dec.), no. 29590/96, 13 February 2001.......................777–8
Yakovenko v Ukraine, no. 15825/06, 25 October 2007 740
Yandiyev and Others v Russia, nos 34541/06, 43811/06, and 1578/07, 10 October 2013 136
Yang Chun Jin alias Yang Xiaolin v Hungary (striking out), no. 58073/00, 8 March 2001........ 745
Yankov v Bulgaria, no. 39084/97, ECHR 2003-XII (extracts)......................... 376
Yaremenko v Ukraine, no. 32092/02, 12 June 2008 310
Yaşa v Turkey, 2 September 1998, *Reports of Judgments and Decisions* 1998-VI 73, 134, 738–9, 742
Yaşa v Turkey, no. 46412/99, 24 January 2006.................................. 553
Yasin Ateş v Turkey, no. 30949/96, 31 May 2005................................171, 813
Yassar Hussain v United Kingdom, no. 8866/04, ECHR 2006-III 304
Yazar and Others v Turkey, nos 22723/93, 22724/93, and 22725/93, ECHR 2002-II........... 520
Y.C. v United Kingdom, no. 4547/10, 13 March 2012 392–3
Yeloyev v Ukraine, no. 17283/02, 6 November 2008...............................231, 239
Yetişen and Others v Turkey (dec.), no. 21099/06, 10 July 2012 137
Y.F. v Turkey, no. 24209/94, ECHR 2003-IX 371
Yiğitoğan v Turkey, no. 72174/10, 3 June 2014 310
Yildirim v Austria (dec.), no. 34308/96, 19 October 1999 391
Yilmaz v Germany, no. 52853/99, 17 April 2003 395
Yoh-Ekale Mwanje v Belgium, no. 10486/10, 20 December 2011 243–4

Yonghong v Portugal (dec.), no. 50887/99, ECHR 1999-IX. 104, 922, 1114

Yordanova and Others v Bulgaria, no. 25446/06, 24 April 2012. . . . . 81, 399–400, 405, 407

Yotova v Bulgaria, no. 43606/04, 23 October 2012 160

Young, James and Webster v United Kingdom, 13 August 1981, Series A no. 44. . . . . 64, 90,
491–3, 502, 505, 507, 514, 788

Young, James and Webster v United Kingdom, 13 August 1981, Concurring Opinion of
Judges Ganshof van der Meersch, Bindschedler-Robert, Liesch, Gölcüklü, Matscher,
Pinheiro Farinha, and Pettiti, Series A no. 44 507

Young, James and Webster v United Kingdom, 13 August 1981, Dissenting Opinion of
Judge Sørensen, Joined by Judges Thór Vilhjálmsson and Lagergren, Series A no. 44. . . . . . . .64, 507

Yousef v Netherlands, no. 33711/96. 392

Yumak and Sadak v Turkey [GC], no. 10226/03, ECHR 2008 1025

Yuriy Nikolayevich Ivanov v Ukraine, no. 40450/04, 15 October 2009. 846

Yüksel Erdoğan and Others v Turkey, no. 57049/00, 15 February 2007 . . . . .136, 149

Yurttas v Turkey, nos 25143/94 and 27098/95, 27 May 2004 775

Z. v Finland, 25 February 1997, *Reports of Judgments and Decisions* 1997-I 383

Ž. v Latvia, no. 14755/03, 24 January 2008 313

Z. v Poland, no. 46132/08, November 2012. 131

Z. and Others v United Kingdom [GC], no. 29392/95, ECHR 2001-V 76, 91, 191,
273–4, 369, 551, 793, 827

Zabiyeva and Others v Russia, no. 35052/04, 17 September 2009 123

Zagaria v Italy (dec.), no. 24408/03, 3 June 2008 777–8

Zaicevs v Latvia, no. 65022/01, 31 July 2007 . . . . .283, 839, 1138–9

Zana v Turkey, 25 November 1997, *Reports of Judgments and Decisions* 1997-VII 109, 475

Zanguropol v Romania (striking out), no. 29959/96, 8 April 2003 798

Zaoui v Switzerland (dec.), no. 41615/98, 18 January 2001 . . . . .427, 432

Zaprianov v Bulgaria (dec.), no. 41171/98, 6 March 2003 350

Zarb Adami v Malta (dec.), no. 17209/02, 24 May 2005. 766

Zarb Adami v Malta, no. 17209/02, ECHR 2006-VIII 213, 216–7, 524, 565–8, 572, 574

Zarmayev v Belgium (dec.), no. 35/10, 27 February 2014 . . . . .282, 1128

Zaunegger v Germany, no. 22028/04, 3 December 2009 408

Ždanoka v Latvia [GC], no. 58278/00, ECHR 2006-IV 68, 70, 452, 492, 621,
625, 1018–9, 1024–5, 1029

Ždanoka v Latvia [GC], no. 58278/00, Dissenting Opinion of Judge Rozakis, ECHR 2006-I 492

Ždanoka v Latvia [GC], no. 58278/00, Dissenting Opinion of Judge Zupančić, ECHR 2006-I 574

Ždanoka v Latvia [GC], no. 58278/00, Partly Dissenting Opinion of Judges Spielmann and
Jaeger, ECHR 2006-I 492, 502

Ždanoka v Latvia [GC], no. 58278/00, Partly Dissenting Opinion of Judge Wildhaber,
ECHR 2006-I. 492

Zehentner v Austria, no. 20082/02, 16 July 2009 736

Zhechev v Bulgaria, no. 57045, 21 June 2007. . . . . 491, 499–500, 504, 512, 515

Zhelyazkov v Bulgaria, no. 11332/04, 9 October 2012. . . . . .214, 1139

Zielinski and Pradal and Gonzalez and Others v France [GC], nos 24846/94 and 34165/96,
ECHR 1999-VII. 335

Ziętal v Poland, no. 64972/01, 12 May 2009 738

Zigarella v Italy (dec.), no. 48154/99, 3 October 2002. . . . . .1149, 1151

Ziliberberg v Moldova, no. 61821/00, 1 February 2005. . . . . .516, 1151

Ziliberberg v Moldova (dec.), no. 61821/00, 4 May 2004 496–7

Zima v Hungary, no. 29723/11, 9 October 2012 464

Znamenskaya v Russia, no. 77785/01, 2 June 2005. . . . . .375, 390–1

Zollmann v United Kingdom (dec.), no. 62902/00, 27 November 2003, ECHR 2003-XII 307

Zolotas v Greece (no. 2), no. 66610/09, ECHR 2013 (extracts) .968, 974–5

Zontul v Greece, no. 12294/07, 17 January 2012 43

Zornić v Bosnia and Herzegovina, no. 3681/06, 15 July 2014 . . . . .1031, 1182

Zornić v Bosnia and Herzegovina, no. 3681/06, Partly Dissenting Opinion of Judge
Wojtyczek, 15 July 2014 70
Z.Y. v Turkey (dec.), no. 27532/95, 19 June 2001 771

EUROPEAN COMMISSION OF HUMAN RIGHTS

3 East African Asians (British protected persons) v United Kingdom, nos 4715/70, 4783/71,
and 4827/71, Commission decision of 6 March 1978, DR 13, p. 17 228
15 Foreign Students v United Kingdom, no. 7671/76 and Fourteen other applications,
Commission decision of 19 May 1977 . . . . .997, 999
36 East African Asians (Citizens of the United Kingdom and Colonies) v United Kingdom,
no. 4626/70 and 35 others, Commission decision of 6 March 1978, DR 13, p. 5 228
A. v Switzerland, no. 10640/83, Commission decision of 9 May 1984, DR 38, p. 219 . . . . .215, 434
A.B. v Switzerland, no. 20872/92, Commission decision of 22 February 1995, DR 80-B, p. 66 281
Acmanne and Others v Belgium, no. 10435/83, Commission decision of 10 December 1984,
DR 40, p. 251 371
Adesina v France, no. 16964/90, Commission decision of 29 May 1991 775
Adesina v France, no. 31398/96, Commission decision of 13 September 1996. 775
Agee v United Kingdom, no. 7729/76, Commission decision of 17 December 1976, DR 7,
p. 164. . . . . .1127, 1131
Agrotexim Hellos S.A., Biotex S.A., Hymifix Hellas S.A., Kykladiki S.A., Mepex S.A., and
Texema S.A. v Greece, no. 14807/89, Commission decision of 12 February 1991, (1992)
35 YB 39, DR 71, p. 148 773
Aires v Portugal, no. 21775/93, Commission decision of 25 May 1995, DR 81, p. 48 981
Airey v Ireland, no. 6289/73, Commission decision of 7 July 1977 236
Aksoy v Turkey, no. 21987/93, Commission report of 23 October 1995. 809
Aldrian v Austria, no. 10532/83, Commission decision of 15 December 1987, DR 54, p. 19 281
Aldrian v Austria, no. 16266/90, Commission decision of 7 May 1990, DR 65, p. 337 281
Alibaks and Others v Netherlands, no. 14209/88, Commission decision of 16 December 1988,
DR 59, p. 274 1077
Alla Raidl v Austria, no. 25342/94, Commission decision of 4 September 1995, (1995)
38 YB 132, DR 82-A, p. 134. . . . . .275, 1099
Altieri v France, no. 28140/95, Commission decision of 15 May 1996 . . . . .1136, 1138
Andorfer Tonwerke v Austria, no. 7987/77, Commission decision of 19 December 1978,
(1980) 23 YB 190, DR 18, p. 31 640
Andreas and Pareskevoula Andronicou and Yiolanda Constantinou v Cyprus, no. 25052/94,
Commission report of 23 May 1996. 117
Andreas and Pareskevoula Andronicou and Yiolanda Constantinou v Cyprus, no. 25052/94,
Commission decision of 5 July 1995, (1995) 38 YB 120, DR 82, p. 102 738
Andrei Karlov Lukanov v Bulgaria, no. 21915/93, Commission decision of 12 January 1995,
(1995) 38 YB 55, DR 80-B, p. 108 777
Angela and Rodney Price v United Kingdom, no. 12402/85, Commission decision of
9 March 1988, DR 55, p. 224 389
Arrondelle v United Kingdom, no. 7889/77, Commission decision of 15 July 1980, (1980)
23 YB 166, DR 19, p. 186 387
Arrowsmith v United Kingdom, no. 7050/75, Commission report of 12 October 1978,
DR 19, p. 5 431
Arthur Hilton v United Kingdom, no. 5613/72, Commission decision of 6 March 1978 809
Asensio Serqueda v Spain, no. 23151/94, Commission decision of 9 May 1994, DR 77-B,
p. 122. 1030
Asociación de Aviadores de la República and Others v Spain, no. 10733/84, Commission
decision of 11 March 1985, DR 41, p. 211. 281
Association 'Regele Mhai' v Romania, no. 26916/95, Commission decision of
4 September 1995 1072
Association X. v Austria, no. 473/59, Commission decision of 29 August 1959 (1958–59)
2 YB 400 983

Association X. v United Kingdom, no. 7154/75, Commission decision of 12 July 1978,
  DR 14, p. 31 140
Austria v Italy, no. 788/60, Commission decision of 11 January 1961, (1961) 4 YB 116,
  p. 148. .... 9, 43, 54, 73–4, 89, 108, 725–6, 767–8, 834
Austria v Italy, no. 788/60, Commission report of 31 March 1963, (1963) 6 YB 740 9
Aylor-Davis v France, no. 22742/93, Commission decision of 20 January 1994, DR 76,
  p. 164. .... 146, 195, 1099
B. v France, no. 13706/88, Commission decision of 9 December 1988 1099
B. and Others v Netherlands, no. 14457/88, Commission decision of 16 December 1988 1077
Bader v Austria, no. 26633/95, Commission decision of 15 March 1996. 1021
Baggs v United Kingdom, no. 9310/81, Commission decision of 16 October 1985,
  DR 44, p. 13 387
Baragiola v Switzerland, no. 17265/90, Commission decision of 21 October 1993, (1993)
  36 YB 90, DR 75, p. 76 302
Barajas v France, no. 26241/95, Commission decision of 12 April 1996 1050
Baskauskaite v Lithuania, no. 41090/98, Commission decision of 21 October 1998. .... 375, 1021
Bejaoui v Greece, no. 23916/94, Commission decision of 6 April 1995. 246
Belilos v Switzerland, no. 10328/83, Commission report of 7 May 1986. 325
Berns and Ewert v Luxembourg, no. 13251/87, Commission decision of 6 March 1991,
  (1991) 34 YB 65, DR 68, p. 147 302
Bertrand Russel [sic] Peace Foundation v United Kingdom, no. 7597/76, Commission
  decision of 2 May 1978, DR 14, p. 117 105
B.H., M.W., H.P., and G.K. v Austria, no. 12774/87, Commission decision of 12 October 1989,
  DR 62, p. 216 479
Bitte v France, no.28645/95, Commission decision of 15 May 1996. 1050
Bolignari v Italy, no. 37175/97, Commission decision of 22 April 1998 542
Booth-Clibborn and Others v United Kingdom, no. 11391/85, Commission decision of
  5 July 1985, DR 43, p. 236. 1021
Bozano v France, no. 9990/82, Commission decision of 15 May 1984, (1984) 27 YB 118,
  DR 39 .... 254, 259, 625
Brüggemann and Scheuten v Federal Republic of Germany, no. 6959/75, Commission
  report of 12 July 1977, DR 10, p. 100 .... 125, 369, 373
Buckley v United Kingdom, no. 20348/92, Commission report of 11 January 1995 399
Bui van Thanh and Others v United Kingdom, no. 16137/90, Commission decision of
  12 March 1990, (1990) 33 YB 59, DR 65-A, p. 330. .... 104, 922, 928
Burghartz and Schnyder Burghartz v Switzerland, no. 16213/90, Commission decision of
  19 February 1992 .... 1157, 1159
C. v United Kingdom, no. 10358/83, Commission decision of 15 December 1983, DR 37,
  p. 142. .... 422, 431
Çakici v Turkey, no. 23657/94, Commission report of 12 March 1998. .... 627, 809
Calcerrada Fornieles et Cabeza Mato v Spain, no. 17512/90, Commission decision of
  6 July 1992, (1992) 35 YB 63, DR 73, p. 214 776–7
Can v Austria, no. 9300/81, Commission report of 12 July 1984, DR 35, p. 523 .... 46, 308
Capoccia v Italy, no. 16479/90, Commission decision of 13 October 1993 452
Cereceda Martin v Spain, no. 16358/90, Commission decision of 12 October 1992, DR 73,
  p. 120. 776–7
Chammas v Switzerland, no. 35438/97, Commission decision of 30 May 1997. 766
Chappex v Switzerland, no. 20338/92, Commission decision of 12 October 1994. 775
Christakis v Cyprus, no. 34399/97, Commission decision of 21 May 1997 1051
Christians against Racism and Fascism v United Kingdom, Commission decision of
  16 July 1980, (1981) 24 YB 178, DR 21, p. 138 .... 494–5, 736, 741, 969
Chrysostomos and Others v Turkey, nos 15299/89, 15300/89, and 15318/89, Commission
  decision of 4 March 1991, (1991) 34 YB 35, DR 68, p. 216 73
Church of X. v United Kingdom, no. 3798/68, Commission decision of 17 December 1968,
  (1969) 12 YB 306, Collection 29, p. 70 421

Clerfayt, Legros and Alii v Belgium, no. 10650/83, Commission decision of 17 May 1985,
   DR 42, p. 218 . . . . .456, 579, 1021
Commune de Rothenthurm v Switzerland, no. 13252/87, Commission decision of
   14 December 1988, 59 DR 251. . . . . .90, 737
Confédération française démocratique du travail v European Communities, no. 8030/77,
   Commission decision of 10 July 1978, (1978) 21 YB 530, DR 13, p. 231 97
Confédération française démocratique du travail v European Communities, alternatively:
   their Member States a) jointly and b) severally, no. 8030/77, Commission decision of
   10 July 1978, (1978) 21 YB 530, DR 13, p. 231 105
Conscientious objectors v Denmark, no. 7565/76, Commission decision of 7 March 1977,
   DR 9, p. 117 . . . . .215, 433
Consejo General de Colejos Ociciales de Economista de España v Spain, nos 26114/95
   and 26455/95, Commission decision of 28 June 1995, DR 82-B, p. 150 . . . . .90, 737
Costello-Roberts v United Kingdom, Commission report of 8 October 1991, Dissenting
   Opinion of Mrs Thune, Joined by Mr Geus, Dissenting Opinion of Mr Loukaides 170
Council of Civil Service Unions and Others v United Kingdom, no. 11603/85, Commission
   decision of 20 December 1987, DR 50, p. 228. . . . . .523, 776–7
Crociani, Palmiotti, Tanassi, and Lefebvre d'Ovidio v Italy, nos 8603/79, 8722/79, 8723/79,
   and 8729/79, Commission decision of 18 December 1980, (1981) 24 YB 222, DR 22,
   p. 192. . . . . .291, 323
Cumber v United Kingdom, no. 28779/95, Commission decision of 27 November 1996 258
C.W. v Finland, no. 17230/90, Commission decision of 9 October 1991 777
Cyprus v Turkey, nos 6780/74 and 6950/75, Commission report of 10 July 1976. . . . . .602–3, 808
Cyprus v Turkey, nos 6780/74 and 6950/75, Dissenting Opinion of Mr G. Sperduti,
   Joined by Mr S. Trechsel, Commission report of 10 July 1976. 603
Cyprus v Turkey, nos 6780/74 and 6950/75, Separate Opinion of Mr F. Ermacora, Commission
   report of 10 July 1976. 594
Cyprus v Turkey, nos 6780/74 and 6950/75, Commission decision of 26 May 1975, (1975)
   18 YB 84, DR 2, p. 125 . . . . .727, 926
Cyprus v Turkey, no. 8007/77, Commission decision of 10 July 1978, (1978) 21 YB 101,
   DR 13, p. 85 . . . . .73, 89, 727
Cyprus v Turkey, no. 25781/94, Commission report of 4 June 1999 . . . . .725–7, 808
Cyprus v Turkey, no. 25781/94, Commission decision of 28 June 1996, (1996) 39 YB 130,
   DR 86, p. 104 . . . . .727–8, 914
De Becker v Belgium, no. 214/56, Commission decision of 9 June 1958 (1958–59)
   2 YB 214 . . . . .10, 353
De Francesco v Italy, no. 13741/88, Commission decision of 12 March 1990. 534
De Geillustreerde v Netherlands, Commission decision of 6 July 1976, DR 8, p. 13 467
De Luca v Italy, no. 13823/88, Commission decision of 12 March 1990 534
de Lukats v Sweden, no, 12920/87, Commission decision of 13 December 1988. 105
Delcourt v Belgium, no. 2689/65, Commission decision of 7 February 1967, (1967)
   10 YB 238 246
Delcourt v Belgium, no. 2689/65, Commission decision of 6 April 1967, (1967) 10 YB 282 246
Delcourt v Belgium, no. 2689/65, Commission report of 1 October 1968. 246
Denmark, Norway, and Sweden v Greece, no. 4448/70, Commission decision of 26 May 1970,
   (1970) 13 YB 108. 943
Denmark, Norway, and Sweden v Greece, no. 4448/70, Commission decision of 16 July 1970,
   (1970) 13 YB 122, Collection 34, p. 70 . . . . .726, 728, 943
Denmark, Norway, and Sweden v Greece, no. 4448/70, Report of the Commission on the
   Present State of the Proceedings, 5 October 1970 943
Denmark, Norway, and Sweden v Greece, no. 4448/70, Commission Report of
   4 October 1976 . . . . .797, 943
Denmark, Norway, Sweden and the Netherlands v Greece, nos 3321/67, 3322/67, 3323/67,
   and 3344/67, Commission decision of 24 January 1968, (1968) 11 YB 690, Collection
   25, p. 92. . . . . .80, 604, 727–9

Denmark, Norway, Sweden and the Netherlands v Greece, nos 3321/67, 3322/67, 3323/67, and 3344/67, Commission report of 5 November 1969, (1969) 12 YB 'The Greek Case' 1 . . . . 174, 177, 181, 595, 598–9, 603, 726–7, 943

Deweer v Belgium, no. 6903/75, Commission report of 5 October 1978 307

D.G. and D.W. Linday v United Kingdom, no. 11089/84, Commission decision of 11 November 1986, (1986) 29 YB 102, DR 49, p. 181. . . . . .538, 544

D.I. v Germany, no. 26551/95, Commission decision of 29 June 1996. 479

Di Lazzaro v Italy, no 31924/96, Commission decision of 10 July 1997, DR 90-B, p. 134. . . . . .94, 543

Dobberstein v Germany, no. 25045/94, Commission decision of 12 April 1996 105

Donnelly and Others v United Kingdom, nos 5577–5583/72, Commission decision of 15 December 1975, (1976) 19 YB 84, DR 4, p. 4. 809

Draper v United Kingdom, no. 8186/78, Commission decision of 1 May 1979, DR 24, p. 72. 539

D.S. v United Kingdom, no. 14067/88, Commission decision of 6 July 1989 640

Dubos v France, no. 31104/96, Commission decision of 14 January 1998 278

Dufay v European Communities, no. 13539/88, Commission decision of 19 January 1989 97

Dujardin and Others v France, no. 16734/90, Commission decision of 2 September 1991, (1991) 34 YB 119, DR 72, p. 236 128

Durini and Others v Italy, no. 19217/91, Commission decision of 12 January 1994, DR 76-B, p. 76. 105

Dyrwold v Sweden, no. 12259/86, Commission decision of 7 September 1990 741

E. v Sweden, no. 11453/85, Commission decision of 7 July 1986. 640

East African Asians v United Kingdom, nos 4403/70–4419/70, 4422/70, 4423/70, 4434/70, 4443/70, 4476/70–4478/70, 4486/70, 4501/70, and 4526/70–4530/70, Commission report of 14 December 1973, DR 78-A, p. 5. . . . . 66, 181, 196, 563

Eggs v Switzerland, no. 7341/76, Commission decision of 4 March 1978, (1977) 20 YB 412. 1152

Eğinlioğlu v Turkey, no. 31312/96, Comission decision of 21 October 1998 . . . . .281, 744

E.L.H. and P.B.H. v United Kingdom, nos 32094/96 and 32568/96, Commission decision of 22 October 1997, DR 91-A, p. 61 . . . . .372, 389

Elias v Estonia, no. 41456/98, Commission decision of 21 October 1998 984

E.M. v Norway, no. 20087/92, Commission decision of 26 October 1995, DR 83-B, p. 5 1137

Ergi v Turkey, no. 23818/94, Commission report of 20 May 1997. 118

E.S. v Federal Republic of Germany, no. 262/57, Commission decision of 28 August 1957 . . . . .89, 105

Family H. v United Kingdom, no. 10233/83, Commission decision of 6 March 1983 1001

Farmakopoulos v Belgium, no. 11683/85, Commission decision of 8 February 1990, (1990) 33 YB 38, DR 64, p. 52 275

Federation of French Medical Trade Unions and the National Federation of Nurses v France, no. 10983/84, Commission decision of 12 May 1986 774

Ferretti v Italy, no. 25083/94, Commission decision of 26 February 1997. 981

F.H. jr. v Austria, no. 1452/62, Commission decision of 18 December 1963, (1963) 6 YB 268 983

Fifty-five inhabitants of Louvain and Environs v Belgium, no. 1994/63, Commission decision of 5 March 1964, (1964) 7 YB 252 767–8

Firestone Tire and Rubber Co., Firestone Tyre and Rubber Co. Ltd and the International Synthetic Rubber Co. v United Kingdom, no. 5460/72, Commission decision of 2 April 1973, Collection 43, p. 99 857

Four companies v Austria, no. 7427/76, Commission decision of 27 September 1976, DR 7, p. 148 . . . . .206, 217

France, Norway, Denmark, Sweden, and Netherlands v Turkey, nos 9940–9944/82, Commission decision of 6 December 1983, (1983) 26 YB COMM.EUR.JURIS. 1, DR 35, p. 143 . . . . .604, 726–9

France, Norway, Denmark, Sweden, and Netherlands v Turkey, nos 9940–9944/82, Commission report of 7 December 1985, DR 35, p. 143. 809

Freda v Italy, no. 8916/80, Commission decision of 7 October 1980, (1981) 24 YB 354. 236

Friedl v Austria, no. 15225/89, Commission report of 19 May 1994. 369

Fritz Neumeister v Austria, no. 1936/63, Commission decision of 6 July 1964, (1964)
 7 YB 224, Collection 14, p. 38 288
Fryske nationale partij v Netherlands, no. 11100/84, Commission decision of 12 December 1985,
 DR 45, p. 240 . . . . .456, 579
G. v Austria, no. 1451/62, Commission decision of 23 July 1963 213
G. v Germany, no. 13079/87, Commission decision of 6 March 1989, DR 60, p. 256 495
G. and E. v Norway, nos 9278/81 and 9415/81, Commission decision of 3 October 1983,
 DR 35, p. 30 . . . . .379, 581
G. Vearncombe, W. Herbst, L. Clemens, and E. Spielhagen v United Kingdom and the Federal
 Republic of Germany, no. 12816/87, Commission decision of 18 January 1989, (1989)
 32 YB 74, DR 59, p. 186 387
G.A. v Sweden, no. 12671/87, Commission decision of 13 March 1989 387
Gisela, Mayer, Hans-Christoph Weidlich, and Bernd-Joachim Fullbrecht, Ortwin A. Hasen
 Kamp, Hartwig Golf, Werner Klaussner v Germany, nos 18890/91, 19048/91, 19342/92,
 and 19549/92, Commission decision of 4 March 1996, (1996) 39 YB 86, DR 85, p. 5 970
Government of Denmark v Government of Greece; Denmark, Norway, Sweden, and the
 Netherlands v Greece, nos 3321/67, 3322/67, 3323/67, and 3344/67, Commission
 decision of 24 January 1968, (1968) 11 YB 690, Collection 25, pp. 92 641
Graeme v United Kingdom, no. 13887/88, 5 February 1990, DR 64, p. 158 1000
Grandrath v Federal Republic of Germany, no. 2299/64, Commission report of 12 December
 1966, (1967) 10 YB 630 . . . . .215, 433
Greece v United Kingdom, no. 176/56, Commission decision of 2 June 1956, (1958–59)
 2 YB 182 . . . . 9, 80, 105, 140, 725, 728, 766
Greece v United Kingdom, no. 176/56, Commission report of 26 September 1958 . . . . .188, 808
Greece v United Kingdom, no. 299/57, Commission decision of 12 October 1957,
 (1958–59) 2 YB 186 . . . . .9, 140, 725
Gudmundsson v Iceland, no. 511/59, Commission decision of 20 December 1960, (1960)
 3 YB 394 978
Guenat v Switzerland, no. 24722/94, Commission decision of 10 April 1995, DR 81-A,
 p. 130. 234
H. v Netherlands, no. 9914/82, Commission decision of 4 July 1983, DR 33, p. 246 1028
H. v United Kingdom and Ireland, no. 9833/82, Commission decision of 7 March 1985,
 DR 42, p. 53 738
Habsburg-Lothringen v Austria, no. 15344/89, Commission decision of 14 December 1989,
 (1989) 32 YB 116, DR 64-B, p. 211 . . . . .1022, 1073
Hagmann-Hüsler v Switzerland, no. 8042/77, Commission decision of 15 December 1977,
 DR 12, p. 202 544
Håkansson and Sturesson v Sweden, no. 11855/85, Commission decision of 15 July 1987,
 DR 53, p. 190 975
Hamer v United Kingdom, no. 7114/75, Commission decision of 13 October 1977, (1978)
 21 YB 302, DR 24, p. 5 . . . . .534, 538–9
Handyside v United Kingdom, no. 5493/72, Commission report of 30 September 1979 . . . . . .975, 978
Hannak v Austria, no. 17208/90, Commission decision of 13 October 1993 1058
Haseldine v United Kingdom, no. 18957/91, Commission decision of 13 May 1992, (1992)
 35 YB 47 473
Hauser v Austria, no. 26808/95, Commission decision of 16 January 1996, DR 84,
 p. 164. . . . . .1136, 1138
Heinz v the Contracting States party to the European Patent Convention insofar as they
 are High Contracting Parties to the European Convention on Human Rights, i.e. Austria,
 Belgium, Denmark, France, Germany, Greece, Ireland, Italy, Liechtenstein, Luxembourg,
 Netherlands, Norway, Portugal, Spain, Sweden, Switzerland, and the United Kingdom,
 no. 21090/92, Commission decision of 15 October 1992, (1994) 37 YB 38, DR 76-A,
 p. 125. 106
Henning Becker v Denmark, no. 7011/75, Commission decision of 3 October 1975, (1976)
 19 YB 416, DR 4, p. 215 1077

Herbecq and the Association «Ligue des droits de l'homme» v Belgium, nos 32200/96
   and 32201/96, Commission decision of 14 January 1998, (1998) 41 YB 60, DR
   92-B, p. 92 387
Hess v United Kingdom, no. 6231/73, Commission decision of 28 May 1975, (1975) 18
   YB 147, DR 2, p. 72 98
Hogben v United Kingdom, no. 11653/85, Commission decision of 3 March 1986, DR
   46, p. 231 347
Honsik v Austria, no. 25062/94, Commission decision of 18 October 1995, DR 83-A, p. 77 479
Hosein v United Kingdom, no. 26293/95, Commission decision of 28 February 1996 . . . . .347, 349
Huber v Switzerland, no. 12794/87, Commission decision of 9 July 1988, DR 57, p. 259 766
Hunter v France, no. 22247/93, Commission decision of 22 February 1995 1050
Hurtado v Switzerland, no. 17549/90, Commission report of 8 July 1993 . . . . .174, 181, 184
I. v Norway, no. 1468/62, Commission decision of 17 December 1963 80
Ibbotson v United Kingdom, no. 40146/98, Commission decision of 21 October 1998 346
Illich Sanchez Ramirez v France, no. 28780/95, Commission decision of 24 June 1996,
   DR 86, p. 155 101
Inhabitants of Leeuw-Saint-Pierre v Belgium, no. 2333/64, Commission decision of
   16 December 1968, (1968) 11 YB 228, Collection 28, p. 1 . . . . .456, 579
Ireland v United Kingdom, nos 5310/71 and 5451/72, Commission decision of
   1 October 1972, (1972) 15 YB 80 . . . . .727–9, 766
Iversen v Norway, no. 1468/62, Commission decision of 17 December 1962, (1963)
   6 YB 278 . . . . .212, 216
I.Z. v Greece, no. 18997/91, Commission decision of 28 February 1994, DR 76-B, p. 65 1025
J. Glimmerveen and J. Hagenbeek v Netherlands, nos 8348/78 and 8406/78 (joined),
   Commission decision of 11 October 1979, (1980) 23 YB 366, DR 18, p. 187 . . . . .479, 619
Jamal-Aldin v Switzerland, no. 19959/92, Commission decision of 23 May 1996 766
Jamil v France, no. 15917/89, Commission decision of 10 March 1994 1050
Jespers v Belgium, no. 8403/78, Commission decision of 15 October 1980, DR 22, p. 116 310
J.-M.B. v France, no. 26198/95, Commission decision of 15 May 1996 1050
Johansen v Norway, no. 10600/83, Commission decision of 14 October 1985, DR 44,
   p. 155 . . . . .215, 237
J.P., K.R., and G.H. v Austria, nos 15135/89, 15136/89, and 15137/89, Commission
   decision of 5 September 1989, DR 62, p. 319 301
J.U. v France, no. 20978/92, Commission decision of 21 October 1993 1152
K. v Belgium, no. 10819/84, Commission decision of 5 July 1984, DR 38, p. 230 245–6
Kamma v Netherlands, no. 4774/71, Commission report of 14 July 1974, (1975) 18
   YB 301, DR 1, p. 4 625
Kapas v United Kingdom, no. 12822/87, Commission decision of 9 December 1987,
   DR 54, p. 201 105
Kara v United Kingdom, no. 36528/97, Commission decision of 22 October 1998 376
Karaduman v Turkey, no. 16278/90, Commission decision of 3 May 1993, (1993) 36
   YB 66, DR 74, p. 93 437
Kaya v Turkey, no. 22729/93, Commission report of 24 October 1996 118
Keenan v United Kingdom, no. 27229/95, Commission decision of 22 May 1998 772
Kelly v United Kingdom, no. 10626/83, Commission decision of 7 May 1985 770
Khan v United Kingdom, no. 11579/85, Commission decision of 7 July 1986, DR 48, p. 253 438
Kirkwood v United Kingdom, no. 10479/83, Commission decision of 12 March 1984,
   DR 37, p. 158 190
Kjeldsen, Busk Madsen and Pedersen v Denmark, nos 5095/71, 50920/72, and 5926/72,
   Commission report of 21 March 1975 . . . . .934, 1008
Knudsen v Norway, no. 11045/84, Commission decision of 8 March 1985, (1985) 28
   YB 129, DR 42, p. 247 426
Konttinen v Finland, no. 24949/94, Commission decision of 3 December 1996, (1997)
   40 YB 94, DR 87-A, p. 68 . . . . .426, 432
Kurt v Turkey, no. 24276/94, Commission report of 5 December 1996 809

Ladislav and Aurel Brežny v Slovakia, no. 23131/93, Commission decision of 4 March 1996,
(1996) 39 YB 96, DR 85, p. 65 970
Lawless v Ireland, no. 332/57, Commission decision of 30 August 1958, (1958–59)
2 YB 308 . . . . .10, 767
Lawless v Ireland, no. 332/57, Commission report of 19 December 1959 . . . . .34, 80, 602, 767
Le Compte v Belgium, no. 6878/75, Commission decision of 6 October 1976, (1977)
20 YB 254, DR 6, p. 76 766
Lehto v Finland, no. 31043/96, Commission decision of 4 March 1998 640
Lena and Anna Angelini v Sweden, no. 10491/83, Commission decision of 3 December 1986,
(1986) 29 YB 113 1008
Lindsay v United Kingdom, no. 8364/78, Commission decision of 8 March 1979, (1979)
22 YB 344, DR 15, p. 247 1025
Luksch v Germany, no. 35385/97, Commission decision of 21 May 1997, DR 89-B, p. 175 1027
Lupander v Finland, no. 28941/95, Commission decision of 3 December 1997 640
M. v Federal Republic of Germany, no. 10307/83, Commission decision of 6 March 1984,
(1984) 27 YB 161, DR 37, p. 113 . . . . .1058, 1061
M. v United Kingdom, no. 13284/87, Commission decision of 15 October 1987 781
McCann, Farrell, and Savage v United Kingdom, no. 18984/91, Commission decision of
3 September 1993 738
McFeeley and Others v United Kingdom, no. 8317/78, Commission decision of 15 May 1980,
(1980) 23 YB 256, DR 20, p. 44 . . . . .376, 781
McGinley and Egan v United Kingdom, nos 21825/93 and 23414/95, Commission
decision of 28 November 1995 543
McVeigh and Others v United Kingdom, nos 8022/77, 8025/77, and 8027/77, Commission
report of 18 March 1981 . . . . .234, 236–7
Malige v France, no. 26135/95, Commission decision of 5 March 1996 781
Marais v France, no. 31159/96, Commission decision of 24 June 1996, DR 86, p. 184 479
Marangos v Cyprus, no. 31106/96, Commission decision of 20 May 1997 1062
Marcel Fournier v France, no. 11406/85, Commission decision of 10 March 1988, (1988)
31 YB 45, DR 55, p. 130 1021
Martinus Godefridus Aarts v Netherlands, no. 14056/88, Commission decision of 28 May 1991,
DR 70, p. 208 771
Mattelin v France, no. 22238/93, Commission decision of 9 April 1996 1050
Matthews v United Kingdom, no. 24833/94, Commission report of 29 October 1997, Concurring
Opinion of Mr E. Busuttil and Concurring Opinion of Mr L. Loucaides 927
Melchers and Co. v Germany, no. 13258/87, Commission decision of 9 February 1990, (1990)
33 YB 46, DR 64, p. 138 . . . . .94–5, 97, 106
Murphy v United Kingdom, no. 4681/70, Commission decision of 3 and 4 October 1972,
DR 43, p. 1 337
Musa v Austria, no. 40477/98, Commission decision of 10 September 1998 981
N. v Sweden, no. 10410/83, Commission decision of 11 October 1984, DR 40, p. 203 . . . . . .215, 434
Naddaf v Federal Republic of Germany, no. 11604/85, Commission decision of
10 October 1986, DR 50, p. 259 132
Näss v Sweden, no. 18066/91, Commission decision of 6 April 1994, DR 77, p. 37 1138
Nationaldemokratische Partei Deutschlands Bezirksverband München-Oberbayern v Germany,
Commission decision of 29 November 1995, DR 84, p. 149 479
Natoli v Italy, no. 26161/95, Commission decision of 18 May 1998 999
Nielsen v Denmark, no. 343/57, Commission decision of 2 September 1959, (1958–59)
YB 412 . . . . .721, 765
Nielsen v Denmark, no. 19028/91, Commission decision of 9 September 1992, (1992)
35 YB 72, DR 73, p. 239 . . . . .1136, 1138
Ninin v France, no. 27373/95, Commission decision of 15 May 1996 1050
Noël Narvii Tauira and 18 Others v France, no. 28204/95, Commission decision of
4 December 1995, (1995) 38 YB 155, DR 83, p. 112 743
Nordblad v Sweden, no. 19076/91, Commission decision of 13 October 1993 1062

N.W. v Luxembourg, no. 19715/92, Commission decision of 8 December 1992. . . . . .1136, 1138

Öhlinger v Austria, no. 21444/93, Commission report of 14 January 1997 740

Oudrhiri v France, no. 19554/92, Commission decision of 31 March 1993. 1071

Öz v Germany, no. 32168/96, Commission decision of 3 December 1996 434

P. v France, no. 11691/85, Commission decision of 10 October 1986 1152

P. v France, no. 12514/86, Commission decision of 12 December 1988 355

P. and R.H. and L.L. v Austria, no. 15776/89, Commission decision of 5 December 1989,
    DR 64, p. 264 275

Patrick Holland v Ireland, no. 24827/94, Commission decision of 14 April 1998, (1998)
    41 YB 90, DR 93, p. 15 . . . . .769, 1028

Pauger v Austria, no. 24872/94, Commission decision of 9 January 1995, DR 80-A,
    p. 170. . . . . .774, 777

Peltonen v Finland, no. 19583/92, Commission decision of 20 February 1995, DR 80-A,
    p. 38 . . . . .1058, 1062

Philis v Greece, no. 28970/95, Commission decision of 17 October 1996. 781

Piermont v France, nos 15773/89 and 15774/89, Commission report of 20 January 1994 . . . . .606, 609

Piermont v France, nos 15773/89 and 15774/89, Commission report of 20 January 1994,
    Concurring Opinion of Mr L. Loucaides, Joined by Mr M. Pellonpää and Opinion
    partiellement dissidente de M.H. Dandelius á laquelle se rallient MM. E Busuttil,
    G. Jörundsson, Mme J. Liddy, et M.B. Marxer 608

Piermont v France, nos 15773/89 and 15774/89, Commission report of 20 January 1994,
    Opinion concordante de M.C.A. Nørgaard et de Mme G.H, Thune. 609

Pierre Marais v France, no. 31159/96, Commission decision of 24 June 1996, DR 86, p. 184 615

Pietrzyk v Poland, no. 28346/95, Commission decision of 26 February 1997 1051

Planka v Austria, no. 25852/94, Commission decision of 15 May 1996 297

Polacco and Garofalo v Italy, no. 23450/94, Commission decision of 15 September 1997, (1998)
    41 YB 42, DR 90-B, p. 5. . . . . .38, 1024, 1027

Purcell and Others v Ireland, no. 15404/89, Commission decision of 16 April 1991, (1991)
    34 YB 90 617

Putz v Austria, no. 18892/91, Commission decision of 3 December 1993, DR 76-A, p. 51 1140

R. v Belgium, no. 15957/90, Commission decision of 30 March 1992, DR 72, p. 195 297

R. v Federal Republic of Germany, no. 1854/63, Commission decision of 28 September 1964. 213

Raimondo v Italy, no. 12954/87, Commission decision of 6 December 1991 1050

Rassemblement jurassien and Unité jurassienne v Switzerland, no. 8191/78, Commission
    decision of 10 October 1979, DR 17 . . . . .495, 497

Rayner v United Kingdom, no. 9310/81, Commission decision of 16 July 1986, DR 47, p. 5 387

Rees v United Kingdom, no. 9532/81, Commission decision of 15 March 1983, DR 36, p. 78 575

Reitmayr v Austria, no. 23866/94, Commission decision of 28 June 1995. 212

Rékási v Hungary, no. 31506/96, Commission decision of 25 November 1996 . . . . .324, 937

RENFE v Spain, no. 35216/97, Commission decision of 8 September 1997, DR 90-B,
    p. 179. . . . . .90, 737

Retimag SA v Federal Republic of Germany, no. 712/60, Commission decision of
    16 December 1961, (1961) 4 YB 384. 767–8

Reyntjens v Belgium, no. 16810/90, Commission decision of 9 September 1992, DR 73,
    p. 136. . . . . .236, 238

Ringeisen v Austria, no. 2614/65, Commission decision of 18 July 1968, (1968) 11 YB 268 767

Ringeisen v Austria, no. 2614/65, Commission report of 19 March 1970 80

Rommelfanger v Federal Republic of Germany, no. 12242/86, Commission decision of
    6 September 1989, (1989) 32 YB 57, DR 62, p. 151 368

Rune Andersson v Sweden, no. 12781/87, Commission decision of 13 December 1998,
    DR 59, p. 171 497

S. v Federal Republic of Germany, no. 9686/82, Commission decision of 4 October 1984,
    DR 39, p. 90 216

S. v France, no. 13728/88, Commission decision of 17 May 1990, DR 65, p. 250 388

Salonen v Finland, no. 27868/95, Commission decision of 2 July 1997 432

Samo Pahor v Italy, no. 19927/92, Commission decision of 29 June 1994 . . . . .456, 579
Sanders v France, no. 31401/96, Commission decision of 16 October 1996, DR 87-B,
    p. 160. 540
Saussier v France, no. 35884/97, Commission decision of 20 May 1998 1136
Schmidt v Austria, no. 10670/83, Commission decision of 9 July 1985, DR 44, p. 195. 1061
S.D.P. v Italy, no. 27962/95, Commission decision of 16 April 1996 541
Seven individuals v Sweden, no. 8811/79, Commission decision of 13 May 1982, DR 29,
    p. 104. 189
Silvius Magnago and Südtiroler Volkspartei v Italy, no. 25035/94, Commission decision of
    15 April 1996, (1996) 39 YB 117, DR 85-A, p. 112. 1023
Simon Herold v Austria, no. 4340/69, Commission report of 19 December 1972 809
Şimşek v Turkey, no. 28010/95, Commission report of 1 March 1999 603
Singh and Uppal v United Kingdom, no. 8244/78, Commission decision of 2 May 1979,
    DR 17, p. 149 1131
Soering v United Kingdom, no. 14038/88, Commission report of 19 January 1989. 190
Soering v United Kingdom, no. 14038/88, Commission report of 19 January 1989, Dissenting
    Opinion of Mr H. Danelius, joined by Mr G. Jörundsson and Mr H. Vandenberghe 142
Soering v United Kingdom, no. 14038/88, Commission report of 19 January 1989, Dissenting
    Opinion of Mr J.A. Frowein 141
Soering v United Kingdom, no. 14038/88, Commission report of 19 January 1989, Dissenting
    Opinion of Mr S. Trechsel. 142
Sorabjee v United Kingdom, no. 23938/94, Commission decision of 23 October 1995 999
Sporrong and Lönnroth v Sweden, nos 7151/75 and 7152/75, Commission report of
    8 October 1980 . . . . .621, 624
Stalas v Estonia, no. 40108/98, Commission decision of 21 October 1998 984
Stamoulakatos v Greece, no. 27567/95, Commission decision of 9 April 1997. 780
Stedman v United Kingdom, no. 29107/95, Commission decision of 9 April 1997, DR 89-A,
    p. 104. 432
Stewart v United Kingdom, no. 10044/82, Commission decision of 10 July 1984, (1984)
    27 YB 129, DR 39, p. 162 . . . . 117, 122, 139, 148, 153
Stocké v Federal Republic of Germany, no. 11755/85, Commission report of 12 October 1989 244
Strohal v Austria, no. 20871/92, Commission decision of 7 April 1994. 456
Sulak v Turkey, no. 24515/94, Commission decision of 17 January 1996, DR 84-A, p. 98 998
Swami Omkarananda and the Divine Light Zentrum v Switzerland, no. 8118/77, Commission
    decision of 19 March 1981, DR 25, p. 105. 434
T. v Switzerland, no. 18079/91, Commission decision of 4 December 1991, DR 72, p. 263 766
Tahiri v Sweden, no. 25129/94, Commission decision of 11 January 1995 1077
Temeltasch v Switzerland, no. 9116/80, Commission report of 5 May 1982, DR 31,
    p. 147. . . . . 933, 935–6, 938
Tête v France, no. 11123/84, Commission decision of 9 December 1987, DR 54, p. 52 1023
Timke v Germany, no. 27311/95, Commission decision of 11 September 1995 1020
Tora Tolmos v Spain, no. 23816/94, Commission decision of 17 May 1995, DR 81, p. 82 301
Touvier v France, no. 29420/95, Commission decision of 13 January 1997, DR 88-B,
    p. 161. . . . . .352, 354
Trouche v France, no. 19867/92, Commission decision of 1 September 1993 388
Twenty-one Detained Persons v Federal Republic of Germany, nos 3134/67, 3172/67,
    3188–3206/67, Commission decision of 6 April 1968, Collection 27, p. 97 214
Tyrer v United Kingdom, no. 5856/72, Commission decision of 9 March 1976 800
Tyrer v United Kingdom, no. 5856/72, Commission report of 14 December 1976 . . . . . .784, 800, 927
V. v Austria, no. 2066/63, Commission decision of 17 December 1965 213
Vakili Rad v France, no. 31222/96, Commission decision of 10 September 1997 314
Van Buitenen v Netherlands, no. 11775/85, Commission decision of 2 March 1987 563
Van Droogenbroeck v Belgium, Commission report of 9 July 1980, Series B no. 44 207
Varna and Others v Turkey, nos 16064/90, 16065/90, 16066/90, 16068/90, 16069/90,
    16070/90, 16071/90, 16072/90, and 16073/90, Commission decision of 14 April 1998. . . .775, 777

Vijayanathan and Pusparajah v France, nos 17550/90 and 17825/91, Commission decision of
 4 June 1991, DR 70, p. 309 73
Voulfovitch and Oulianova v Sweden, no. 19373/92, Commission decision of
 13 January 1993 1129
W. v United Kingdom, no. 11095/84, Commission report of 7 March 1989, Partially
 Dissenting Opinion of Mr Schermers 533, 537
W., X., Y., and Z. v Belgium, nos 6745/76 and 6746/76, Commission decision of 30 May 1975,
 (1975) 18 YB 237, DR 2, p. 111 . . . . .1019, 1021
W., X., Y., and Z., v United Kingdom, nos 3435/67, 3436/67, 3437/67, and 3438/67,
 Commission decision of 19 July 1968, (1968) 11 YB 562, Collection 28, p. 109 . . . . .213, 215
Wakefield v United Kingdom, no. 5817/89, Commission decision of 1 October 1990, DR 66,
 p. 251. 390
Whiteside v United Kingdom, no. 20357/92, Commission decision of 7 March 1994, DR 76,
 p. 80 766
Wiggins v United Kingdom, no. 7456/76, Commission decision of 8 February 1978, DR 13,
 p. 40 927
William Grice v United Kingdom, no. 22564/93, Commission decision of 14 April 1994 126
W.M. v Denmark, no. 17392/90, Commission decision of 14 October 1993 102
W.M. v Germany, no. 35638/97, Commission decision of 2 July 1997. 132
Wójcik v Poland, no. 26757/95, Commission decision of 7 July 1997, DR 90, p. 24. 767
Wolfgram v Federal Republic of Germany, no. 11257/84, Commission decision of
 6 October 1986, DR 49, p. 213. 738
X. v Austria, no. 833/60, Commission decision of 20 December 1960, (1960) 3 YB 428,
 p. 440. 213
X. v Austria, no. 1140/61, Commission decision of 19 December 1961, Collection 8, p. 57. 640
X. v Austria, no. 1747/62, Commission decision of 13 December 1963, Collection 13, p. 42. 288
X. v Austria, no. 5575/72, Commission decision of 8 July 1975, DR 1, p. 44 281
X. v Austria, no. 5591/72, Commission decision of 2 April 1973, Collection 43, p. 161 . . . . . .215, 433
X. v Austria, no. 6185/73, Commission decision of 29 May 1975, DR 2, p. 68. 315
X. v Austria, no. 7008/75, Commission decision of 12 July 1976, DR 6, p. 120 1030
X. v Austria, no. 8180/78, Commission decision of 10 May 1979, DR 20, p. 2. 983
X. v Austria, no. 8278/78, Commission decision of 13 December 1979, DR 18, p. 154. . .234, 236, 371
X. v Austria, no. 9295/81, Commission decision of 6 October 1982, DR 30, p. 227 303
X. v Austria and Federal Republic of Germany, no. 3479/68, Commission decision of
 14 December 1968 781
X. v Austria and Yugoslavia, no. 2143/64, Commission decision of 30 June 1964, (1964)
 7 YB 314, Collection 14, p. 15 105
X. v Belgium, no. 458/59, Commission decision of 29 March 1960, (1960) 3 YB 222. 640
X. v Belgium, no. 1038/61, Commission decision of 18 September 1961, (1961) 4 YB 338. 1019
X. v Belgium, no. 1065/61, Commission decision of 30 May 1961, (1961) 4 YB 260 925
X. v Belgium, no. 2758/66, Commission decision of 21 May 1969, (1969) 12 YB 174, Collection
 30, p. 11. 139
X. v Belgium and Netherlands, no. 6482/74, Commission decision of 10 July 1975, DR 7,
 p. 76 543
X. v Federal Republic of Germany, no. 235/56, Commission decision of 10 June 1958, (1958–59)
 2 YB 256 97
X. v Federal Republic of Germany, no. 892/60, (1961) 4 YB 240, Collection 6, p. 17 539
X. v Federal Republic of Germany, no. 1322/62, Commission decision of 14 December 1963,
 Collection 13, p. 55. 235
X. v Federal Republic of Germany, no. 1611/62, Commission decision of 25 September 1965,
 (1965) 8 YB 158. 102
X. v Federal Republic of Germany, no. 1628/62 Commission decision of 12 December 1963,
 Collection 12, p. 61. 80
X. v Federal Republic of Germany, no. 1870/63, Commission decision of 16 December 1965,
 (1965) 8 YB 218. 978

X. v Federal Republic of Germany, no. 2413/65, Commission decision of 16 December 1966,
Collection 23, p. 1 . . . . .80, 213

X. v Federal Republic of Germany, no. 2606/65, Commission decision of 1 April 1968 775

X. v Federal Republic of Germany, no. 2699/65, Commission decision of 1 April 1968, (1968)
11 YB 366, Collection 26, p. 33. 80

X. v Federal Republic of Germany, no. 2728/66, Commission decision of 6 October 1967,
(1967) 10 YB 336, Collection 25, pp. 38–41 1019–20

X. v Federal Republic of Germany, no. 3745/68, Commission decision of 15 December 1969,
Collection 31, p. 107. 1072

X. v Federal Republic of Germany, no. 4653/73, Commission decision of 1 April 1974, (1974)
17 YB 148, Collection 46, p. 22. 212

X. v Federal Republic of Germany, no. 5025/71, Commission decision of 18 December 1971,
(1971) 14 YB 692. 1051

X. v Federal Republic of Germany, no. 6742/74, Commission decision of 10 July 1975, DR 3,
p. 98 94

X. v Federal Republic of Germany, no. 6859/74, Commission decision of 10 December 1975 236

X. v Federal Republic of Germany, no. 7705/76, Commission decision of 5 July 1977, DR 9,
p. 196. . . . . .215, 433

X. v Federal Republic of Germany, no. 7900/77, Commission decision of 6 March 1978,
DR 13, p. 70 350–1

X. v Federal Republic of Germany, no. 8098/77, Commission decision of 13 December 1978,
DR 16, p. 111 245

X. v Federal Republic of Germany, no. 8410/78, Commission decision of 13 December 1979,
(1980) 23 YB 386. 212

X. v Federal Republic of Germany, no. 8741/79, Commission decision of 10 March 1981,
DR 24, p. 137 . . . . .382, 432

X. v Federal Republic of Germany, no. 9235/81, Commission decision of 16 July 1982, DR 29,
p. 194. 479

X. v Iceland, no. 6825/74, Commission decision of 18 May 1976, (1976) 19 YB 342, DR 5,
p. 86 369

X. v Ireland, no. 361/58, Commission decision of 1 September 1958 774

X. v Netherlands, no. 6573/74, Commission decision of 19 December 1974, DR 1, p. 87. 1028

X. v Netherlands, no. 7230/75, Commission decision of 4 October 1976, DR 7, p. 109 . . . . .94, 924

X. v Netherlands, no. 8239/78, Commission decision of 4 December 1978, DR 16, p. 184. 371

X. v Netherlands, no. 15216/89, Commission decision of 16 January 1991. 1099

X. v Norway, no. 867/60, Commission decision of 29 May 1961, Collection 6, p. 34 124

X. v Switzerland, no. 8500/79, Commission decision of 14 December 1979, DR 18 . . . . .240, 244

X. v Switzerland, no. 8778/79, Commission decision of 8 July 1980, (1980) 23 YB 404 1152

X. v United Kingdom, no. 5155/71, Commission decision of 12 July 1976, DR 6, p. 13. 1021

X. v United Kingdom, no. 5962/72, Commission decision of 13 March 1975, DR 2, p. 50. . . .997, 999

X. v United Kingdom, no. 6956/75, Commission decision of 10 December 1976, DR 8,
p. 103. 105

X. v United Kingdom, no. 7140/75, DR 7, p. 95 1025

X. v United Kingdom, no. 7547/76, Commission decision of 15 December 1977 102

X. v United Kingdom, no. 7730/76, Commission decision of 28 February 1979, DR 5, p. 137 . . . 1027

X. v United Kingdom, no. 7902/77, Commission decision of 18 May 1977, DR 9, p. 224 1131

X. v United Kingdom, no. 7992/77, Commission decision of 12 July 1978, DR 14, p. 234. 439

X. v United Kingdom, no. 8083/77, Commission decision of 13 March 1980, DR 19,
p. 223. . . . . .281, 744

X. v United Kingdom, no. 8416/79, Commission decision of 13 May 1980, DR 19, p. 244 124

X. v United Kingdom, no. 8873/80, Commission decision of 13 May 1982, DR 99, p. 99 925

X. and Association Y. v Italy, no. 8987/80, Commission decision of 6 May 1981, DR 24,
p. 192. 1027

X. and the German Association of Z. v Federal Republic of Germany, no. 1167/61, Commission
decision of 16 December 1963, Collection 12, p. 70 80

X. and Y. v Switzerland, nos 7289/75 and 7349/76, Commission decision of 14 July 1977,
(1977) 20 YB 372, DR 9, p. 57 101
X. and Y. v United Kingdom, no. 7229/75, Commission decision of 15 December 1977,
DR 12, p. 32 543
X., Y., and Z. v United Kingdom, no. 9285/81, Commission decision of 6 July 1982, DR 29,
p. 205. 1131
Y. v Netherlands, no. 16531/90, Commission decision of 16 January 1991, (1991) 34 YB 31,
DR 68, p. 299 1099
Yanasik v Turkey, no. 14524/89, Commission decision of 6 January 1993, DR 74, p. 14 997–8
Yaşa v Turkey, no. 22495/93, Commission report of 8 April 1997 118
Y.M. v France, no. 24948/94, Commission decision of 28 June 1995. 1143
Zarouali v Belgium, no. 20664/92, Commission decision of 29 June 1994, DR 78-B, p. 97. 297
Zénon Bernard and Others v Luxembourg, no. 17187/90, Commission decision of
8 September 1993, (1993) 36 YB 83, DR 75, p. 57 1000
Ziegler v Switzerland, no. 19890/92, Commission decision of 3 May 1993, (1993) 36 YB 73,
DR 74, p. 234 640

EUROPEAN COURT OF JUSTICE

Berlusconi and Others, Cases C-387/02, C-391/02 and C-403/02, 3 May 2005 350
Denilauler/Couchet Frères, Case C-125/79, 21 May 1980 272
Hoechst AG v Commission, [1989] ECR 2839 399
J. Nold v Commission, Case 4/73, [1974] 2 C.M.L.R. 354 948
Netherlands v European Parliament and Council, Case C-377/98, [2001] ECR I-7079 66
Opinion no. 2/94, [1996] ECR I-1759. 948

INTER-AMERICAN COURT OF HUMAN RIGHTS

Advisory Opinion OC-20/09 of September 29, 2009, requested by the Republic of Argentina,
Article 55 of the American Convention on Human Rights, Series A no. 20 693–4
Case of Barrios Altos v Peru, Reparations and Costs, Judgment of November 30, 2001, Series C
no. 87. 43
Case of Blake v Guatemala, Preliminary Objections, Judgment of 2 July 1996, Series C no. 27. 43
Case of Cantoral Benavides v Peru, Merits, Judgment of August 18, 2000, Series C no. 69. 43
Case of Durand and Ugarte v Peru, Merits, Judgment of August 16, 2000, Series C no. 68 43
Case of Gelman v Uruguay, Merits and Reparations, Judgment of February 24, 2011, Series C
no. 221. 43
Case of Gomes Lund et al ('Guerrilha do Araguaia') v Brazil, Preliminary Objections, Merits,
Reparations, and Costs, Judgment of November 24, 2010, Series C no. 219 . . . . .43, 139
Case of Heliodoro-Portugal v Panama, Preliminary Objections, Merits, Reparations and Costs,
Judgment of August 12, 2008, Series C no. 186 139
Case of the Massacres of El Mozote and Nearby Places v El Salvador, Interpretation of the
Judgment on Merits, Reparations and Costs, Judgment of August 19, 2013, Series C no, 264 43
Compulsory Membership in an Association Prescribed by Law for the Practice of Journalism
(Arts 13 and 29 American Convention on Human Rights), Advisory Opinion OC-5/85 of
November 13, 1985, Series A no. 5 . . . . .43, 464–5

INTERNATIONAL ARBITRAL AWARDS

Ambatielos Claim (Greece, United Kingdom of Great Britain and Northern Ireland), (1956)
12 RIAA 83 768
Cairo case (France v Mexico), (1929) 5 RIAA 516. 43
Finnish Ships case (Finland v United Kingdom), (1934) 3 RIAA 1479 768
Texaco Overseas Petroleum Company and California Asiatic Oil Company v Libya, (1977)
104 *Journal de droit international* 350 . . . . .43, 350, 837

INTERNATIONAL COURT OF JUSTICE

Accordance with International Law of the Unilateral Declaration of Independence in Respect
of Kosovo, Advisory Opinion, I.C.J. Reports 2010, p. 403. 42

Ahmadou Sadio Diallo (Republic of Guinea v Democratic Republic of the Congo),
    Compensation, Judgment, I.C.J. Reports 2012, p. 324 . . . . .105, 725
Ahmadou Sadio Diallo (Republic of Guinea v Democratic Republic of the Congo), Merits,
    Judgment, I.C.J. Reports 2010, p. 639 731
Application for Review of Judgment No. 158 of the United Nations Administrative Tribunal,
    Advisory Opinion, I.C.J. Reports 1973, p. 172 878
Application of the Convention on the Prevention and Punishment of the Crime of Genocide
    (Bosnia and Herzegovina v Serbia and Montenegro), Judgment, I.C.J. Reports 2007, p. 43 42
Application of the Convention on the Prevention and Punishment of the Crime of Genocide,
    Provisional Measures, Order of 13 September 1993, I.C.J. Reports 1993, p. 325, Separate
    Opinion of Judge Lauterpacht 694
Application of the International Convention on the Elimination of All Forms of Racial
    Discrimination (Georgia v Russian Federation), Provisional Measures, Order of
    15 October 2008, I.C.J. Reports 2008, p. 353 914
Application of the International Convention on the Elimination of All Forms of Racial
    Discrimination (Georgia v Russian Federation) (Preliminary Objections), Judgment, I.C.J.
    Reports 2011, p. 70. 914
Armed Activities on the Territory of the Congo (Democratic Republic of the Congo v Uganda),
    Judgment, I.C.J. Reports 2005, p. 168 43
Armed Activities on the Territory of the Congo (New Application: 2002) (Democratic Republic
    of the Congo v Rwanda), Jurisdiction and Admissibility, Judgment, I.C.J. Reports 2006,
    p. 6, Separate Opinion of Judge ad hoc Dugard. 179
Avena and Other Mexican Nationals (Mexico v United States of America), Judgment, I.C.J.
    Reports 2004, p. 12. 105
Barcelona Traction, Light and Power Company Limited, Judgment, I.C.J. Reports 1970,
    p. 3 . . . . .736, 741, 767
Certain Expenses of the United Nations (Article 17, paragraph 2 of the Charter), Advisory
    Opinion, I.C.J. Reports 1962, p. 155. 878
Certain Phosphate Lands in Nauru (Nauru v Australia), Preliminary Objections, Judgment,
    I.C.J. Reports 1992, p. 240 42
Competence of the General Assembly for the Admission of a State to the United Nations,
    Advisory Opinion, I.C.J. Reports 1950, pp. 6–7 878
Conditions of Admission of a State to Membership in the United Nations (Article 4 of
    the Charter), Advisory Opinion, I.C.J. Reports 1947–1948, pp. 61–2 878
Corfu Channel Case, Judgment of 9 April 1949, I.C.J. Reports 1949, p. 4 . . . . .352, 908
Dispute regarding Navigational and Related Rights (Costa Rica v Nicaragua), Judgment,
    I.C.J. Reports 2009, p. 237 35
Effect of awards of compensation made by the U.N. Administrative Tribunal, Advisory Opinion
    of 13 July 1954, I.C.J. Reports 1954, p. 47 849
Elettronica Sicula S.P.A. (ELSI), Judgment, I.C.J. Reports 1989, p. 15 767
Gabčíkovo-Nagymaros Project (Hungary/Slovakia), Judgment, I.C.J. Reports 1997, p. 7 834
Interhandel Case (Switzerland v United States), Judgment of 21 March 1959, I.C.J. Reports 1959,
    p. 6 767
Interpretation of Peace Treaties, Advisory Opinion, I.C.J. Reports 1950, p. 65 877
Jurisdictional Immunities of the State (Germany v Italy), Counter-Claim, Order of
    6 July 2010, I.C.J. Reports 2010, p. 310, Dissenting Opinion of Judge Cançado Trindade 179
Jurisdictional Immunities of the State (Germany v Italy: Greece intervening), Judgment,
    I.C.J. Reports 2012, p. 99 . . . . 42, 44
Jurisdictional Immunities of the State (Germany v Italy: Greece intervening), Judgment,
    I.C.J. Reports 2012, p. 99, Dissenting Opinion of Judge Cançado Trindade. 179
Kasikili/Sedudu Island (Botswana v Namibia), Judgment, I.C.J. Reports 1999 (II), p. 1059 35
LaGrand (Germany v United States of America), Judgment, I.C.J. Reports 2001, p. 466 . . . . . . .46, 749
Legal Consequences of the Construction of a Wall in the Occupied Palestinian Territory,
    Advisory Opinion, I.C.J. Reports 2004, p. 136 . . . . .42–3, 154, 877

Legality of the Threat or Use of Nuclear Weapons, Advisory Opinion, I.C.J. Reports 1996,
  p. 226. . . . . 43, 117, 154, 877–8, 887
Maritime Dispute (Peru v Chile), Judgment, 27 January 2014 35
Military and Paramilitary Activities in and against Nicaragua (Nicaragua v United States of
  America), Merits, Judgment, I.C.J. Reports 1986, p. 14. 43
Nottebohm case (second phase), Judgment of 6 April 1955, I.C.J. Reports 1955,p. 4. 43
Questions relating to the Obligations to Prosecute or Extradite (Belgium v Senegal),
  Judgment, I.C.J. Reports 2012, p. 422 . . . . .164, 179
Reservations to the Convention on Genocide, Advisory Opinion, I.C.J. Reports 1951, p. 15 352
Sovereignty over Pulau Ligitan and Pulau Sipaden (Indonesia/Malaysia), Judgment, I.C.J.
  Reports 2002, pp. 645–6. 35
Western Sahara, Advisory Opinion, I.C.J. Reports 1975, p. 18. 878

INTERNATIONAL CRIMINAL COURT

Prosecutor v Bemba and Others (ICC-01105–01113 OA 2), Judgment on Appeal of
  Mr Aimé Kilolo Musamba against the decision of Pre-Trial Chamber II of 14 March 2014,
  11 July 2014. 240
Prosecutor v Katanga (ICC-01/04–01/07), Décision relative à la mise en œuvre de la
  norme 55 du Règlement de la Cour et prononçant la disjonction des charges portées contre
  les accuses, 21 November 2012 310
Prosecutor v Katanga (ICC-01/04–01/07), Dissenting Opinion of Judge Christine Van Den
  Wyngaert, 21 November 2012. 310

INTERNATIONAL CRIMINAL TRIBUNAL FOR RWANDA

Prosecutor v Akayesu (ICTR-96-4-T), Judgment, 2 September 1998 43
Prosecutor v Musema (ICTR-96-13-T), Judgment and Sentence, 27 January 2000 43
Prosecutor v Rutaganda (ICTR-96-3-A), Dissenting Opinion of J. Pocar, 26 May 2003. 1134

INTERNATIONAL CRIMINAL TRIBUNAL FOR THE
FORMER YUGOSLAVIA

Prosecutor v Delalić et al (IT-96-21-T), Judgment, 16 November 1998 179
Prosecutor v Furundžija (IT-95-17/1-T), Judgment, 10 December 198. . . . . .43, 179–80
Prosecutor v Gotovina et al. (IT-06-90-T), Judgment, 15 April 2011 158
Prosecutor v Gotovina et al (IT-06-90-A), Judgment, 16 November 2012. 158
Prosecutor v Kordić et al (IT-95-14/2-T), Judgment, 26 February 2001 353
Prosecutor v Kunarac et al (IT-96-23/1-A), Judgment, 12 June 2002 43
Prosecutor v Milošević (IT-02/54-AR73.7), Decision on Interlocutory Appeal of the Trial
  Chamber's Decision on the Assignment of Defence Counsel, 1 November 2004 311
Prosecutor v Milošević (IT-02/54-T), Reasons for Decision on Assignment of Defence
  Counsel, 22 September 2004 311
Prosecutor v Šešelj (IT-03-67-T), Decision on Defence Motion for Disqualification of Judge
  Frederik Harhoff and Report to Vice President, 28 August 2013 668
Prosecutor v Strugar (IT-01-43-T), 31 January 2005 158
Prosecutor v Tadić (IT-94-1-AR72), Decision on the Defence Motion for Interlocutory
  Appeal on Jurisdiction, 2 October 1995 . . . . .595, 715
Prosecutor v Tadić (IT-94-1-A-AR77), Appeal Judgment on Allegations of Contempt
  Against Prior Counsel, Milan Vujin, 27 February 2001 1134

INTERNATIONAL MILITARY TRIBUNAL

France et al. v Goering et al. (1948) 22 IMT 411 . . . . 136, 202, 329, 344, 602

IRAN–UNITED STATES CLAIMS TRIBUNAL

Amoco International Finance Corporation (Amoco International Finance Corporation v Iran),
  Interlocutory Award of 14 July 1987, Iran–United States Claims Tribunal Reports (1987-II) 43

PERMANENT COURT OF INTERNATIONAL JUSTICE

Access to German Minority Schools in Upper Silesia, Series A/B No. 40 . . . . .379, 631
Advisory Opinion of 31 July 1930 on the Greco-Bulgarian Community, Series B No. 17. 379
Consistency of Certain Danzig Legislative Decrees with the Constitution of the Free City,
    Series A/B No. 65 . . . . .329, 631
Exchange of Greek and Turkish Populations, Series B No. 10. 1067
Factory at Chorzów (Germany v Poland), Series A no. 17. 43
Factory at Chorzów (Jurisdiction), Judgment No. 8, Series A No. 9 834
German Settlers in Poland, Series B No. 6. 379
Interpretation of Judgments Nos 7 and 8 (Chorzów Factory), Series A No. 13, Dissenting
    Opinion of M. Anzilotti. 849
Mavrommatis Palestine Concessions, Series A No. 2 . . . . .43, 725, 731
Minority Schools in Albania, Series A/B No. 64. . . . . .379, 731, 999
Panevezys-Saldutiskls Railway, Series A/B, No. 76 43
Panevezys-Saldutiskls Railway, Series A/B, No. 75 768
Phosphates in Morocco (Preliminary Objections), Series A/B No. 74 43
Rights of Minorities in Upper Silesia (Minority Schools), Series A No. 15 . . . . .379, 731, 999

UNITED NATIONS HUMAN RIGHTS COMMITTEE

A.P. v Italy, no. 204/1986, UN Doc. CCPR/C/OP/2, p. 67 1149
Chongwe v Zambia, no. 821/1998, UN Doc. CCPR/C/79/D/821/1998 229
de Guerrero v Columbia, no. 45/1979, UN Doc. CCPR/OP/1, p. 112. 117
Delgado Páez v Namibia, no. 195/1985, UN Doc. CCPR/C/39/D/195/1985. 229
Delia Saldias de Lopez v Uruguay, no. 52/1979, UN Doc. CCPR/C/OP 1, p. 88 616
Dias v Angola, no. 711/1996, UN Doc. CCPR/C/68/D/711/1996. 229
Gunaratna v Sri Lanka, no. 1432/2005, UN Doc. CCPR/C/95/D/1432/2005 229
Jayawardena v Sri Lanka, no. 916/2000, UN Doc. CCPR/C/675/D/916/2000 229
Judge v Canada, no. 829/1998, UN Doc. CCPR/C/78/D/829/1998 145
Koller v Austria, no. 989/2001, UN Doc. CCPR/C/78/D/989/2001 777
Länsman et al v Finland, no. 511/1992, UN Doc. CCPR/C/52/D/511/1992 83
Lilian Celiberli de Casariego v Uruguay, no. 56/1979, UN Doc. CCPR/C/OP/1, p. 92. 616
Loth v Germany, no. 1754/2008, UN Doc. CCPR/C/98/D/1754/2008. 777
Mahabir v Austria, no. 944/2000, UN Doc. CCPR/C/82/D/944/2000. 777
Mikhail Pustovoit v Ukraine, no. 1405/2005, UN Doc. CCPR/C/110/D/1405/2005 43
Peterson v Germany, no. 1115/2002, UN Doc. CCPR/C/80/D/1114/2002 777

SPECIAL COURT FOR SIERRA LEONE

Prosecutor v Norman (SCSL-04-14-AR72(E)), Decision on Preliminary Motion based on Lack
    of Jurisdiction (Child Recruitment), 31 May 2004 353
Prosecutor v Taylor (SCSL-03-01-A), Separate Opinion of Justice George Gelaga King on
    Decision on Charles Ghankay Taylor's Motion for Partial Voluntary Withdrawal or
    Disqualification of Appeal Chamber Judges, 13 September 2012 668

SPECIAL TRIBUNAL FOR LEBANON

Unnamed defendant (STL-11/01/I), Interlocutory Decision on the Applicable Law: Terrorism,
    Conspiracy, Homicide, Perpetration, Cumulative Charging, 16 February 2011, Appeals
    Chamber 328

NATIONAL CASES

Bosnia and Herzegovina

Damjanović v Federation of Bosnia and Herzegovina, Human Rights Chamber CH/96/30,
    5 September 1997. 1105–6
Damjanović v Federation of Bosnia and Herzegovina, Human Rights Chamber CH/96/30,
    5 September 1997, Concurring Opinion of Viktor Masenko-Mavi and Rona Aybay 1105

Canada

Bouzari v Islamic Republic of Iran, (2004) 71 OR (3d) 675 44
Crookes v Newton, [2011] 3 SCR 269 44
Halpern v Canada (Attorney General), (2003) 85 OR (3d) 161 (CA) 535
Hashemi v Islamic Republic of Iran and Others, (2012) QCCA 1449 44
Kindler v Canada, [1991] 2 SCR 779 1093
Malette v Shulman, (1990) 72 OR 417 (CA) (Ontario Court of Appeal) 371
Public Service Employee Relations Act (Alberta), Re, [1987] 1 SCR 313 38
United States v Burns, [2001] SCR 283 . . . . .44, 1093

France

Fidan, (1987) II *Rec. Dalloz-Sirey* 3 OS (Conseil d'État) 1099
Gacem, (1988) I *Semaine juridique* IV-86, (Conseil d'État), 14 December 1987 1099
Grosz v Germany, No. 04-475040, 3 January 2006 44

Germany

BverfGE 12, 45 – Kriegsdienstverweigerung I, 20 December 1960 424
Empire v Dithmar and Boldt (Hospital Ship 'Llandovery Castle'), Imperial High Court, (1922)
    16 AJIL 708 341
Life Imprisonment case (Iebenslange Freiheitsstrafe), 21 June 1977, 45 BverfGE 187 44

Netherlands

Short v Netherlands, Supreme Court of the Netherlands, 30 March 1990, (1990) 76 *Rechtspraak*
    van de Week 358, (1990) 29 *International Legal Materials* 1378 1100

South Africa

Makwanyane and Mchunu v The State [1995] ZACC 3 . . . . .38, 1093
Minister of Home Affairs v Fourie (2005) and Lesbian and Gay Equality Project and Eighteen
    Others v Minister of Home Affairs, (2006) 3 BCLR 355 (CC) 535
Niemand v The State, [2001] ZACC 11 44
S. v Dodo, [2001] ZACC 16 44

Spain

Judgment 235/2007, Spanish Constitutional Court., 7 November 2007 44

United Kingdom

In re Von Makensen and Maelzer (Ardeatine Caves Massacre Case) (1949) 8 LRTWC 1,
    13 ILR 258 (British Military Court, Rome) 59
R. v Bow Street Metropolitan Stipendiary and Others, ex parte Pinochet Ugarte (no. 3), [2000]
    1 AC 147 44
Zoernsch v Waldock, [1964] 1 WLR 675, [1964] 2 All ER 256 892

United States

Ex parte Yerger, 75 US (8 Wall.) 85, 95 (1869) 220
Fosmire v Nicoleau, 75 NY2d 218, 551 NE2d 77, 551 NYS2d 876 (1990) 371
Jones v Cunningham, 371 US 236 (1963) 220
Lawrence v Texas, 539 US 558 (2003) 38, 381
Marrero v Warden of Louisberg Penitentiary, (1974) 417 US 653 347
Near v Minnesota, 283 US 697 (1931) 452
Palko v State of Connecticut, 302 US 319 (1937) 423
Princz v Germany, 26 F.3d 1166 (1994) 44
Sampson v Germany, 250 F.3d 1145 (2001) 44
Siderman de Blake v Argentina, 965 F. 2d 699 (1992) 44
Smith v Libya, 101 F.3d 239 (1997) 44

United States v Altstötter et al., (Justice case), (1948) 3 TWC 954 (US Military
　　Tribunal 136, 1095
United States v Krupp et al., (1950) 9 TWC 1327 (US Military Tribunal) 202

Zimbabwe

Catholic Commission for Justice and Peace in Zimbabwe v Attorney-General et al., [1993]
　　14 HRLJ 323 1093

Table of Legislation

EUROPEAN CONVENTION ON HUMAN RIGHTS AND RELATED INSTRUMENTS

European Convention on Human Rights

European Convention for the Protection of Human Rights and Fundamental Freedoms, ETS 5

Preamble 11, 36, 47–8, 53–4, 56–60, 62, 64, 68–73, 75, 247, 285, 503, 556, 640, 938, 955–7, 1011, 1024, 1031, 1045–6, 1214

Preamble, recital 1 59–60

Preamble, recital 2 . . . . 59, 62

Preamble, recital 3 65

Preamble, recital 4 . . . . 60, 66–8

Preamble, recital 5 . . . . 59, 62, 69–71, 73–4, 335, 956–7, 1046

Preamble, recital 6 . . . . . . 58, 73, 78, 551, 784

Section I 87–8, 94, 107, 747, 881

Art 1 . . . . . . 54, 74–5, 84, 86–8, 90–5, 97–9, 101–5, 101, 124, 191, 194, 367, 519, 606, 720, 778, 918, 923, 933, 950, 1083, 1187, 1201

Art 2 . . . . 11, 14–6, 37, 47, 59, 61, 67, 85–6, 88, 91–2, 110–1, 117–9, 121–9, 131–45, 147–8, 153, 155–6, 159–60, 165, 171, 186, 188, 190–1, 205–6, 336, 395, 434, 552, 570, 577–9, 592, 601, 625, 707, 728, 734, 738, 740, 742, 773, 792, 815, 848, 867, 933, 995, 1092, 1101, 1105–7, 1115, 1128, 1198–9, 1207

Art 2(1) 17, 37, 49, 122, 127, 129, 139–44, 190, 235, 1091–3, 1094, 1099, 1107, 1116, 1118, 1198–1200, 1207, 1216

Art 2(2) 122–3, 126–7, 129, 146–50, 152, 156–7, 1207

Art 2(2)(a) 147–50, 153, 156, 161

Art 2(2)(b) 147, 150, 156

Art 2(2)(c) 147, 149, 152–3

Art 3 . . . . .15–6, 37, 47, 59, 62, 66–7, 96, 98, 101, 110, 118, 138, 140, 142–4, 157, 164–5, 167–78, 180–98, 206, 238, 318, 320, 350, 370–2, 376, 395, 423, 434, 461, 552–3, 563–4, 570, 576–8, 584, 592, 707, 734, 739–40, 773, 792, 801, 815, 831, 845, 867, 914, 926–7, 933, 995, 1094, 1101, 1106, 1115, 1126, 1128, 1178, 1199

Art 4 . . . . .63, 169, 213–5, 217, 433, 734, 933, 1175

Art 4(1) 202, 205, 592, 995

Art 4(2) 202, 206, 210–2, 216–7

Art 4(3) 206, 210–3

Art 4(3)(a) 213–4

Art 4(3)(b) 214–6, 218, 433–4

Art 4(3)(c) 216

Art 4(3)(d) 211, 216–7

Art 5 . . . . 36–7, 92, 96, 124, 127, 154, 201, 205–11, 213, 220–1, 226–34, 234–6, 239, 244–5, 249–50, 258–62, 275, 323, 336, 423, 588, 599, 617, 621, 625–6, 641, 867, 1049, 1075, 1142

Art 5(1) 226–9, 231–4, 236, 240, 243–4, 246–7, 254–6, 262, 621, 624, 1049–50, 1056–7

Art 5(1)(a)–(f) 234

Art 5(1)(a) 141, 235–6, 250, 1216

Art 5(1)(b) 141, 233, 235–7, 242, 1216

Art 5(1)(c) 45, 234, 238–9, 243, 245–50, 255, 262, 626–7

Art 5(1)(d) 233, 240–1, 584

Art 5(1)(e) 233–4, 241–3, 255

Art 5(1)(f) 233, 243–4

Art 5(2) 226, 245–6, 248

Art 5(3) 46, 226, 238, 245–50, 252–3, 255–6, 261–3, 597, 600, 935

Art 5(4) 141, 226, 235, 245–6, 248, 254–7, 259, 261–2, 1049, 1216

Art 5(5) 10, 226, 257–8, 306, 899, 1143

Art 6 . . . . 36, 74, 92, 100, 110, 124, 144, 186, 235, 249, 266, 270–76, 278–81, 283–4, 287, 289, 297–8, 300, 307, 312, 316, 319–24, 335–6, 395, 409, 429, 460, 473, 541–2, 547, 617, 621, 648, 731, 740, 809, 815, 826, 857, 869–70, 957, 1075, 1107, 1131, 1135, 1137–8, 1151, 1158, 1175

Art 6(1) 41, 69, 72, 100, 140, 235, 249, 254, 265–6, 270, 272–6, 278, 281–91, 293–5, 297–8, 301, 307–8, 312, 318,

Table of Legislation

324–5, 345, 460, 523, 551, 554,
584, 620–1, 782, 825–6, 936,
1136–7, 1216
Art 6(2) 265–6, 271, 276, 298–303,
305–7, 319, 325, 1142–3, 1145, 1164–5
Art 6(3) 235, 265–6, 271, 276,
287, 307, 310, 1138
Art 6(3)(a) 307–9, 314, 317
Art 6(3)(b) 46, 308–9
Art 6(3)(c) 309, 311, 316–7, 324
Art 6(3)(d) 312–3, 316, 325
Art 6(3)(e) 46, 314–6, 324, 936, 1216
Art 7 . . . . .49, 140, 169, 186, 265, 285, 328,
330, 334–44, 347, 349–53, 355–6, 592–3,
734, 870, 904, 995, 1107, 1151
Art 7(1) 49, 335–6, 338, 342–9,
351, 354–5, 767
Art 7(2) 41, 352–6, 719
Arts 8–11 . . . . 124, 533, 996, 1019,
1023, 1025
Art 8 . . . . 39, 47, 80, 92, 125–7,
171–3, 189, 318, 320, 322,
324, 336, 359, 366–95, 397–400,
402, 404, 407–9, 420, 430,
435, 437, 439–40, 451–2,
461–3, 467–8, 471–2, 490,
503, 509, 534, 540–2, 563,
579, 584, 617, 620, 625, 741,
747, 815, 899, 914, 988,
1000–1, 1126, 1128, 1157–8,
1165, 1178, 1187
Art 8(1) 306, 359, 365, 367, 377,
401–2, 405, 435, 468, 1060
Art 8(2) 82, 147, 285, 359, 365–7,
371, 384, 398, 400–6, 420, 437,
469, 471, 512, 534, 612, 623,
1055, 1063, 1186
Art 9 . . . . 189, 215–6, 336, 367,
375–6, 414, 419–23, 425–36,
439–41, 451–2, 467–8, 471–2,
490–2, 499, 502–3, 509, 523,
540, 562, 569, 577, 579–80,
617, 620, 625, 867, 899, 1001
Art 9(1) 402, 419–21, 424–5,
427, 429, 431, 433, 435–6, 457, 468
Art 9(2) 82, 147, 285, 401–2, 404,
419–20, 422, 424, 427, 429,
435–8, 469, 471, 512–3, 612,
618, 623, 1055, 1062–3
Art 10 . . . . 80, 92, 336, 367, 376,
380, 384, 420, 435, 437, 440,
445, 450–59, 461–4, 466–7,
469, 471, 474–7, 480–1, 490–2,
499, 502–3, 509, 523, 580, 608–9, 615,
617–8, 619–20, 625, 741, 899,
903, 1001, 1018

Art 10(1) 39, 302, 402, 435, 445,
450–1, 457, 463, 466, 468,
472, 481, 618, 623, 1186
Art 10(2) 82, 147, 285, 336, 401, 404,
420, 437, 445–6, 450–1,
453–4, 467–9, 471–3, 512,
608–9, 612, 617–8, 620, 915,
975, 1055, 1062–3
Art 11 . . . . 23, 92, 152, 336, 367,
375, 420, 429, 435, 437, 440,
451–2, 464, 467–8, 471–2, 484,
490–4, 498–503, 505–10, 513–6,
519–25, 503, 523, 580, 608–9,
617, 620, 625, 742, 899, 1018
Art 11(1) 402, 435, 464, 468, 490–1,
495, 497, 505–6, 508, 522–3
Art 11(2) 82, 147, 285, 401, 404, 420,
437, 469, 471, 490, 495, 509,
511–3, 519, 521–3, 608, 612,
618, 623, 1055, 1062–3
Art 12 . . . .64, 375, 388–9, 529, 532–45, 741,
1157
Art 13 . . . . .75, 124, 138, 140, 254, 547,
550–4, 571, 608, 616, 620, 731,
741, 765, 784, 867, 1075, 1126–7,
1135, 1142
Art 14 . . . . .12, 19, 21–2, 46, 63, 88, 91,
159–60, 196–8, 217, 259–60,
321–4, 355–6, 379, 407–9, 440–1,
479–80, 523–5, 532, 543–4, 552–3,
556, 561–77, 579–81, 583–4, 608,
620, 624, 655, 914, 968, 981–2,
1004–6, 1031, 1065, 1132, 1174–5,
1177–85, 1191
Art 14(1) 556
Arts 15–18 88
Art 15 . . . . .77, 82, 235, 155, 335, 457,
587–8, 591–4, 596, 598, 600–4,
621, 625, 1104, 1110, 1155, 1203
Art 15(1) 247, 420, 587, 591, 594,
598, 600, 767, 1105–6
Art 15(2) 153, 206, 591–3, 598,
601, 1051, 1107, 1110
Art 15(3) 591, 602–3
Art 16 . . . . 560, 583, 606, 608–10, 625, 1191
Art 17 . . . . . . .33, 336, 457, 479, 519, 611–2,
614–22, 620, 671, 701, 993
Art 18 . . . . 88, 623–7
Art 19 . . . . 74, 631, 639–41, 743, 839
Art 20 . . . . 644, 646
Art 20(2) 762
Art 21 . . . . . 583, 649–54, 656, 661, 665, 672
Art 21(1) 648–9, 651, 662, 664
Art 21(2) 648–51
Art 21(3) 656
Art 22 . . . . . 651, 660–2, 664–5, 672, 879–80

Art 23. . . . . .650, 660, 669–72
Art 23(1) 671
Art 23(2) 650, 654–5, 668, 671
Art 23(3) 668, 671
Art 23(4) 668, 681
Art 23(6) 654
Art 24. 675, 677
Art 24(1) 684
Art 24(2) 675–6, 690
Art 25. . . . . 620, 639, 678, 680, 691
Art 25(a). 27, 681
Art 25(b) 683
Art 25(c). 683
Art 25(d) 684
Art 25(f) 680
Art 26. . . . . .688–9, 691, 1220
Art 26(1) 683
Art 26(2) 689
Art 26(3) 690, 698
Art 26(4) 656, 661, 689, 692,
694, 701, 1221
Art 26(5) 684
Art 27. . . . . . 690, 697, 699, 701–2, 761, 814
Art 27(1) 763
Art 27(2) 694, 851
Art 28. . . . 689, 700, 706, 759, 761, 805, 859
Art 28(1) 763
Art 28(1)(b) 703, 791
Art 28(2) 701, 851
Art 28(3) 701, 703
Art 29. . . . . 703, 706–7, 759, 763, 805
Art 29(1) 445, 712
Art 30. . . . . 92, 691, 709–11, 844, 847
Art 31. . . . . .92, 713, 763
Art 31(b) 714, 865
Art 31(c). 883
Art 32. . . . . 92–3, 719–21, 778,
876, 906, 1191
Art 32(1) 28, 719, 721
Art 32(2) 719, 721, 885
Art 33. . . . . 108, 706, 713, 725–9,
738, 762, 788, 797, 880–1, 915, 1220
Art 34. . . . . .92, 401, 700, 706, 713, 721,
726, 735–8, 741–2, 745–8,
750–1, 754, 759, 762–3, 785,
797, 805, 812–3, 880, 922, 969,
1220, 1225
Art 34 *in fine* 746, 881
Art 35. . . . . 92, 551, 698, 727, 754,
759–60, 762, 764, 772, 785–6, 911,
914, 1026
Art 35(1) 75–6, 727, 745, 759, 762–5,
767–70, 785, 1216
Art 35(2)–(4) 759
Art 35(2) 727, 762, 768, 785, 885
Art 35(2)(a) 773

Art 35(2)(b) 768, 774, 776–8, 842, 879
Art 35(3) 705, 727, 760, 762, 785, 823
Art 35(3)(a) 778–80, 854
Art 35(3)(b) 698, 760, 762, 781–2,
784–5, 800, 1216
Art 35(4) 727, 760, 764, 785, 845
Art 36. . . . . .143, 769, 790–1
Art 36(1) 105, 788, 790–2, 1222
Art 36(2) 790–1, 807, 1222
Art 36(3) 790, 794, 1222
Art 37. . . . . 796–7, 802, 822–3, 846
Art 37(1) 740, 761, 784, 798, 822, 1101
Art 37(1) *in fine* 800, 845
Art 37(1)(a) 797–8, 800
Art 37(1)(b) 797–8
Art 37(1)(c) 796–7, 799–800, 823
Art 37(2) 799, 801
Art 38. . . . . .169, 641, 721, 748, 803–5,
812–4, 819, 853
Art 38(1) 819
Art 38(2) 685
Art 39. . . . . . 797, 800, 805, 819, 821–2, 846
Art 39(1) 784, 821
Art 39(2) 781, 822
Art 39(3) 649, 821
Art 39(4) 797, 822
Art 40. 685, 826
Art 40(1) 826
Art 40(2) 685
Art 41. . . . . .726, 738, 831, 833–4, 836, 838,
848, 867
Art 42. . . . . .841–2, 852, 859
Art 43. . . . . .111, 691–2, 709–1, 713,
843–4, 846–7, 851, 858, 1219–20
Art 43(1) 845
Art 43(2) 844–5, 1216
Art 43(3) 845–6
Art 44. . . . . .841, 849–51, 859
Art 44(1) 850
Art 44(2) 841, 851
Art 44(2)(c) 846
Art 44(3) 841
Art 45. . . . . .846, 857–8, 887
Art 45(1) 841, 858
Art 46. . . . . .77, 93, 639, 696, 719, 830,
842, 864, 866, 870, 905, 951, 1225
Art 46(1) 720, 864–6, 1225
Art 46(2) 798, 867, 871, 887
Art 46(3) 852, 865, 872
Art 46(4) 691–2, 713, 865–6, 872
Art 46(5) 865, 872
Arts 47–49 876
Art 47. . . . . .27, 691–2, 713, 859, 874–8,
884–5, 1219
Art 47(1) 879–80, 885
Art 47(2) 880–2, 885

Art 47(3) 827, 876
Art 48. 884–5
Art 49. 887
Art 50. 889–90
Art 51. 892–3
Art 52. . . . . .881, 897–900
Art 53. . . . . .902–4, 1191
Art 54. . . . . .720, 905–6
Art 55. . . . . . . 89, 723, 758, 866, 907, 912–5
Art 56. . . . . 62, 97, 100, 104, 917,
      921–8, 937–8, 943, 1017, 1033–6,
      1082, 1113–4, 1161–2, 1206, 1216
Art 56(1) 921–2, 1162
Art 56(2) 922
Art 56(3) 921–2, 926–7, 1162
Art 56(4) 922–3, 927–8, 1162, 1190
Art 57. . . . . 94, 262, 323–5, 931, 933–8, 984,
      1006, 1008, 1065, 1073, 1111, 1119,
      1146, 1156, 1204, 1207, 1230
Art 57(1) 933–5
Art 57(2) 323, 936
Art 58. . . . . .942–3, 1038, 1227
Art 58(1) 942–3
Art 58(2) 942
Art 58(3) 942–3
Art 58(4) 942–3
Art 59. . . . . .59, 946, 1039–41, 1087–8,
      1116–7, 1166
Art 59(1) 946–7, 950
Art 59(2) 106, 946, 948
Art 59(3) 108, 786, 949
Art 59(4) 108, 949
Art 59(5) 950

**Original text (1950) of the European
Convention on Human Rights**

European Convention for the Protection of
  Human Rights and Fundamental
  Freedoms, ETS 5. . . . . 670, 671–2, 697, 706,
      713, 723–4, 726, 762, 796, 803,
      817, 825, 841, 843, 851, 875, 902,
      928, 990, 1174, 1185
Section I. 875, 956
Art 19. 634–9
Art 20. 645
Art 20(3) 700
Art 22. 675
Art 22(1) 670
Art 23. 648–9
Art 24. . . . . .724, 727, 881, 939
Art 25. . . . . 49, 675, 734–5, 1085–6
Art 25(1) 881
Art 26. 759, 881
Art 27. . . . . .706, 759, 881
Art 27(1)(a) 759
Art 27(2) 759

Art 27(3) 759
Art 28. . . . . .803–4, 816, 819
Art 28(1) 805, 819
Art 28(1)(a) 804
Art 28(b) 818
Art 28(2) 819
Art 29. . . . . .700, 760, 785
Art 31. 632
Art 32. . . . . .632–3, 879, 882
Art 33. . . . . 685, 826
Art 36. 684
Art 38. . . . . 644, 820
Art 39. . . . . 648, 651, 659–60, 820, 879
Art 39(2) 649
Art 39(3) 648–9, 651
Art 40. . . . . .656, 669–70
Art 40(3) 670
Art 40(4) 670
Art 40(5) 670
Art 40(6) 670
Art 40(7) 649, 651, 656
Art 41. . . . . 679, 681
Art 42. 889
Art 43. . . . . .688, 694, 843
Art 45. 718–20
Art 46. . . . . .725, 735, 1085–6
Art 46(2) 821–2
Art 47. 720
Art 48. . . . . .718, 725, 878
Art 48(b) 788–91
Art 49. . . . . .706, 718–21, 884
Art 50. 833
Art 51. 858
Art 52. 841, 850
Art 53. . . . . .720, 864, 1164
Art 54. . . . . 633, 864
Art 55. . . . . .679, 684, 876
Art 57. . . . . 881, 898
Art 58. 889
Art 59. . . . . 89, 891
Art 60. 903
Art 61. 905
Art 62. . . . . .911, 913, 942
Art 63 . . .562, 922–3, 925–6, 933, 1034–6, 1161
Art 63(1) 1034–5
Art 63(3) 927
Art 64. . . . . . . 945–6, 984, 1006, 1008, 1111

**Provisions of the European Convention on
Human Rights resulting from Protocol No 5
(in force 1971) that have since been repealed**

Art 40(1) 670
Art 40(2) 670
Art 40(5) 670
Art 40(6) 670

Provisions of the European Convention on Human Rights resulting from Protocol No 8 (in force 1990) that have since been repealed

Art 30 796
Art 30(1) 797
Art 30(2) 797
Art 30(3) 797

Provisions of the European Convention on Human Rights resulting from Protocol No 11 (in force 1998) that have since been repealed or renumbered

Art 22 680
Art 23 680
Art 23(1) 680
Art 23(2) 654–5, 671
Art 23(3) 671
Art 23(4) 671
Art 23(5) 671
Art 23(6) 671
Art 23(7) 671
Art 24 671
Art 25 675
Art 26 680
Art 26(1) 680
Art 27 . . . . 675, 688
Art 38(1) 805
Art 38(1)(a) 805, 813
Art 38(2) 805

Protocols to the European Convention on Human Rights

Protocol No. 1 to the Convention for the Protection of Human Rights and Fundamental Freedoms, ETS 9 . . . . .6, 11–2, 18, 23, 45, 63, 73, 205, 592, 720, 899, 906, 923, 925, 934, 951, 955–7, 966, 970, 978, 983–4, 986, 988, 995, 997, 999, 1006–7, 1017, 1031, 1036, 1038, 1040–1, 1046, 1093, 1114, 1117, 1120, 1161, 1168, 1227, 1229
Preamble 956–7, 1046, 1173
Preamble, recital 1 956
Preamble, recital 2 956
Preamble, recital 3 956
Art 1 . . . . . . .41, 45, 63, 400, 402, 435, 468, 480, 622, 720, 731, 741, 767, 867, 906, 937, 939, 958, 960, 965, 967–79, 981–4, 1035, 1037
Art 1, para 1 . . . . .967, 974, 979–80
Art 1, para 2 . . . . .967, 974, 979–81
Art 2 . . . . .419, 421, 431, 433, 569, 579, 582, 934, 957, 986, 988, 994–1009, 1035, 1037

Art 3 . . . . .47, 68, 375, 492, 499, 608, 617, 741, 1012, 1018–29, 1032, 1035–7, 1181
Art 4 . . . . . 1008, 1031, 1035–6, 1082, 1161
Art 5 . . . . .955, 957, 1037–8, 1116
Art 6 .1040–1, 1087
Protocol No. 2 to the Convention for the Protection of Human Rights and Fundamental Freedoms, conferring upon the European Court of Human Rights competence to give advisory opinions, ETS 44 . . . . 14, 26–7, 31, 875–80, 882, 884, 887
Arts 1–4 876
Art 1 875–6
Art 1(3) 876
Art 2 . . . . .875–6, 884, 1058–9
Art 2(1) 1138
Art 3 . . . . 859, 875
Art 3(1) 883
Art 3(2)–(4) 887
Art 3(2) 876
Art 3(4) 876
Art 4 . . . . 679, 876
Protocol No. 3 to the Convention for the Protection of Human Rights and Fundamental Freedoms, amending Articles 29, 30 and 34 of the Convention, ETS 45 . . . . 14, 26–7
Protocol No. 4 to the Convention for the Protection of Human Rights and Fundamental Freedoms, securing certain rights and freedoms other than those already included in the Convention and in the first Protocol thereto, ETS 46 . . . . .14, 18–20, 22, 45, 73, 205, 402, 496, 581, 592, 720, 906, 922, 951, 1046, 1052, 1063, 1065, 1068, 1073–4, 1078, 1083–5, 1087–8, 1093, 1114, 1117, 1120, 1125, 1127, 1162, 1164, 1168, 1174, 1227
Preamble 1046
Arts 1–4 1085
Art 1 . . . 169, 591, 621, 1046, 1048, 1050–1
Art 2 . . . . . .92, 226, 378, 745, 1052, 1056–9, 1061, 1065, 1068, 1072–4, 1083, 1128
Art 2(1) 1057, 1060–3
Art 2(2) 1060–3, 1066
Art 2(3) 402, 435, 468, 625, 1056, 1061–3, 1066
Art 2(4) 1056, 1062–3
Art 3 . . . . . 169, 1047, 1057, 1060, 1068–75, 1079, 1083, 1144, 1150
Art 3(1) 1070, 1073, 1127
Art 3(2) 933, 1068, 1070–1

Art 4 . . . . . 608, 1047, 1068, 1070, 1075–80,
          1083, 1127, 1130, 1153–4
Art 5 . . . . .1083, 1161
Art 5(3) 1083
Art 5(4) 1057, 1083
Art 5(5) 1082
Art 6 . . . . 1045, 1065, 1085, 1086
Art 6(1) 1116
Art 6(2) 1086
Art 7 1087–8
Protocol No. 5 to the Convention for
    the Protection of Human Rights
    and Fundamental Freedoms, amending
    Articles 22 and 40 of the Convention,
    ETS 55. . . . . 26–7, 670
Protocol No. 6 to the Convention for the
    Protection of Human Rights and
    Fundamental Freedoms concerning the
    Abolition of the Death Penalty,
    ETS 114. . . . . . . 14, 16–7, 49, 140, 143, 190,
          720, 906, 950–1, 1091–101,
          1104–10, 1112, 1114–21, 1162,
          1168, 1197–201, 1207, 1227–8, 1232
    Preamble. 1094, 1198, 1200
    Preamble, recital 1. 1198
    Preamble, recital 2. . . . . . . .1094, 1097, 1198
    Art 1 . . . . .169, 1093, 1098–101, 1103,
          1108, 1128, 1201
    Art 2 . . . 17, 594, 601, 1098, 1103–10, 1112,
          1198, 1207
    Art 3 . . . . .592, 1110–1, 1203
    Art 4 .1111, 1204
    Art 5 . . . . 1112, 1114, 1162, 1205
    Art 6 . . . . .1115–6, 1207
    Art 7 . . . . 1116–8, 1166, 1192, 1208
    Art 8 .1120, 1209
    Art 9 . . . . 1121, 1170, 1194, 1210, 1232
Protocol No. 7 to the Convention for the
    Protection of Human Rights and
    Fundamental Freedoms,
    ETS 117. . . . . 18–9, 64, 73, 265, 286,
          541, 720, 906, 922, 951, 1125, 1127,
          1132, 1135, 1139–41, 1146, 1149,
          1156, 1161–4, 1166–9, 1227–8, 1232
    Preamble. 1125
    Arts 1–5 1165
    Art 1 . . . . 608, 1076, 1079,
          1126–32, 1161
    Art 1(1) 1131–2
    Art 1(1)(a) 1131
    Art 1(1)(b) 1131
    Art 1(1)(c) 1131
    Art 1(2) 625, 1132
    Arts 2–4 . . . . .1140–1, 1146, 1155–6
    Art 2 . . . . .92, 1135–41, 1216
    Art 2(1) 1134, 1136–41, 1162

Art 2(2) 402, 435, 468, 1139–40
Art 3 . . . . 110, 306, 1142–6, 1164–5
Art 4 . . 169, 745, 1110, 1144, 1148, 1150–1,
          1153
Art 4(1) 1150–1
Art 4(2) 1150, 1154
Art 4(3) 592, 1110, 1155
Art 5 . . . . 529, 541, 1157–9, 1165
Art 6 . . . . .1140, 1161–2
Art 6(1) 1162
Art 6(3) 1162
Art 6(4) 1161–2, 1189
Art 6(5) 1162
Art 6(6) 1161–2
Art 7 1164
Art 7(1) 1164
Art 7(2) 1164
Art 8 .1166, 1193
Art 9 1168
Art 10. 1170
Protocol No. 8 of the Convention for
    the Protection of Human Rights
    and Fundamental Freedoms,
    ETS 118. . . . . . . 27, 648, 688, 700, 799–800
    Art 1 700
    Art 6 796
    Art 9 . . . . 649, 679
    Art 11. 688
Protocol No. 9 of the Convention
    for the Protection of Human Rights
    and Fundamental Freedoms,
    ETS 140. . . . . .27–8, 699, 735
    Art 5(2) 844
    Art 7 1229
Protocol No. 10 to the Convention for
    the Protection of Human Rights
    and Fundamental Freedoms,
    ETS 146. 28, 876
    Art 1 882
Protocol No. 11 to the Convention for the
    Protection of Human Rights and
    Fundamental Freedoms, restructuring
    the control machinery established
    thereby, ETS 155 . . . . 27–30, 87, 108,
          367, 639, 644, 646, 649–51, 656,
          660, 663, 670–2, 675, 678, 680–2,
          684, 688, 690, 692, 694, 699–701,
          706–7, 710, 713, 719–20, 723–4,
          726, 735, 779, 785, 790–1, 797,
          804, 819–20, 825–6, 833, 841,
          843–4, 846–7, 850–2, 858, 864,
          866, 876–7, 882, 884, 887, 889,
          891–2, 898, 902, 912, 917, 921–2,
          928, 933, 937, 942, 949, 969, 1035,
          1057, 1085, 1111, 1130 1164
    Art 1 . . . . .654, 700, 706, 759

Art 2(2) 87, 58, 122, 168, 205, 226,
           270, 334, 366, 419, 450, 490, 533,
           550, 562, 591, 608, 614, 624,
           889, 892, 898, 903, 905, 912,
           922, 933, 942
Art 2(4)(a) 946
Art 2(5)(a) . . . 1046, 1050, 1056, 1071, 1077,
           1086-7
Art 2(5)(c) 1086
Art 2(6)(a) 1094, 1098, 1104, 1110-1,
           1114-5, 1117, 1120-1
Art 2(7)(a) 1125, 1127, 1135, 1142,
           1148, 1157, 1161, 1164, 1166
Art 4(a). 956, 967, 995, 1018, 1035,
           1038, 1040
Art 4(b) 1035
Art 5 1082-3
Art 7(a). 1170
Art 7(b) 1161
Protocol No. 12 to the Convention for
the Protection of Human Rights
and Fundamental Freedoms,
ETS 177. . . . . 13, 19, 21-2, 24-5, 556,
     564, 573, 655, 720, 906, 938, 951, 1174-6,
     1180-4, 1186-7, 1190-3, 1227-9, 1232
Preamble. 1173-4, 1179
Preamble, recital 1. . . . . .1174, 1181
Preamble, recital 2. 1174
Preamble, recital 3. 1175
Art 1 . . . . .63, 169, 564, 1174, 1176,
           1179-83, 1185-7, 1191
Art 1(1) 564, 1180, 1182-5
Art 1(2) 1179-80, 1185-6
Art 2 1190-1
Art 2(1) 1189
Art 2(2) 1189
Art 2(3) 1189
Art 2(4) 1189
Art 2(5) 1189
Art 3 .1187, 1191
Art 4 1192
Art 5 1193
Art 6 1194
Protocol No. 13 to the Convention for
the Protection of Human Rights and
Fundamental Freedoms, concerning
the abolition of the death penalty
in all circumstances, ETS 187 17,
           140, 144, 190, 720, 906, 938, 951,
           1092, 1094, 1097-8, 1101, 1103,
           1106, 1110-1, 1198-200, 1203,
           1206-9, 1227, 1229
Preamble. 1198-200
Preamble, recital 1. 1198
Preamble, recital 2. 1199
Preamble, recital 3. . . . . .1103, 1199

Preamble, recital 4. 1200
Art 1 . . . . 169, 1098-101, 1128, 1201, 1207
Art 2 . . . . .592, 1201, 1203
Art 3 1204
Art 4 1205-6
Art 4(3) 1205
Art 5 . . . . .1203-4, 1207
Art 6 1208
Art 7 1209
Art 8 1210
Protocol No. 14 to the Convention for
the Protection of Human Rights and
Fundamental Freedoms amending
the control system of the Convention,
ETS 194. . . . . 30, 74-5, 77, 645, 655,
           660, 670-1, 675, 680, 689-91,
           694, 696, 698-703, 707, 719-20,
           762, 782, 785-6, 793, 805, 819,
           821, 864-5, 872, 906, 948-9, 951
Preamble. 697
Art 8 . . . . .697, 701, 703
Art 9 706
Art 10. 714
Art 11. 719
Art 12. 760
Art 13. 790
Art 17. 946
Art 20(2) 698, 782
Protocol No. 14*bis* to the Convention
for the Protection of Human Rights
and Fundamental Freedoms,
ETS 204. 30, 689
Protocol No. 15 amending the Convention
for the Protection of Human Rights
and Fundamental Freedoms,
ETS 213. . . . . 31-2, 54, 75, 78, 551,
           650, 671-2, 712, 762, 955, 1045
Art 1 . . . . 53, 58
Art 2 . . . . .647, 650, 668
Art 3 709-10
Art 4 . . . . .753, 762, 770
Art 5 . . . . 753, 762
Art 8 655
Art 8(3) 762
Art 8(4) 762
Protocol No. 16 to the Convention for
the Protection of Human Rights and
Fundamental Freedoms, ETS 214. 26,
           32, 875, 877, 924, 1213, 1215-6,
           1219-20, 1222-5, 1227-31
Preamble. 1213
Preamble, recital 1. 1213
Preamble, recital 4. 1213
Arts 1-5 1227
Art 1 924
Art 1(1) 1213, 1215, 1219, 1231

Art 1(2) .1216, 1219
Art 1(3) .1217, 1219
Art 2(1) 1219
Art 2(2) 1220
Art 2(3) 1220–1
Art 3 1222–4
Art 4 1223
Art 4(3) 1224
Art 4(4) 1224
Art 5 . . . . .866, 877, 1225
Art 6 .1227, 1230
Art 7 1228
Art 8 1229
Art 9 1230
Art 10. .1215–6, 1231
Art 11. 1232
Art 11(d) 1232

**Provisions of the Protocols to the European
Convention on Human Rights that have since
been repealed**

Protocol No. 4 to the Convention for the
   Protection of Human Rights and
   Fundamental Freedoms, securing
   certain rights and freedoms other than
   those already included in the Convention
   and in the first Protocol thereto, ETS 46
   Art 6(2) 1086
Protocol No. 7 to the Convention for the
   Protection of Human Rights and
   Fundamental Freedoms, ETS 117
   Art 7(2) 1164

Rules of Court

Rules of Court of the European Court of
   Human Rights, 18 September 1959 679,
                  684, 841, 844, 851
   r 1(b) 679
   r 7(2) 679
   r 16 679
   r 17 679
   r 18 825
   r 21(4) 679
   r 25(2) 679
   r 38 789
   r 38(1) 788–9
   r 47(3) 819
   r 48 .679, 709, 844
   r 52 . . . . 825, 851
   r 53 852
   r 54(1) 854
   r 54(4) 852
   r 76 684
Rules of Court of the European Court of
   Human Rights, as amended on
   24 October 1961
   r 52 851

Rules of Court of the European Court of
   Human Rights, 23–25 October 1962
   r 56(2) 825
Rules of Court of the European Court of
   Human Rights, 27 August 1974
   r 47(2) 819
Rules of Court of the European Court of
   Human Rights, 24 November 1982,
   amended 26 January 1989 789
   r 11 675
   r 12 675
   r 18 825
   r 37(2) 790
   r 50 . . . . 709, 844
   r 51 . . . . 709, 844
   r 56 851
Rules of Court of the European Court of
   Human Rights 'A', 1 February 1994
   r 49(2) 819
   r 49(3) 821
   r 51 . . . . .688, 710, 713
   r 58 854
Rules of Court of the European Court of
   Human Rights, amended 17 June and
   8 July 2002
   r 44(3) 821
Rules of Court of the European Court of
   Human Rights 682, 684–5, 690, 692,
            710, 712, 762, 797–8, 803,
            805, 808, 849, 865, 1223
   r 1(d) 683
   r 1(t) 639
   r 2 . . . . 671, 674
   r 3 656
   r 4 656
   r 5 . . . . 673, 681
   r 6 671
   r 7 . . . . 672, 681
   r 8(1) 681, 683
   r 8(2) 683
   r 8(3) 681
   r 8(4) 681
   r 8(5) 681
   r 9(1) 682
   r 9(2) 682
   r 9(3) 682
   r 9A(1)(a) 683
   r 9A(1)(b) 683
   r 9A(2) 683
   r 9A(3) 683
   r 9A(4) 683
   r 9A(5) 684
   r 9A(6) 684
   r 10 682
   r 11 682
   r 12 683
   r 13 694

r 14 681
r 15(1) 676–7
r 15(2) 677, 681, 695
r 15(3) 677, 695
r 15(4) 677
r 16 677
r 17 676
r 17(2) 676
r 17(3) 677
r 17(4) 676
r 18 683
r 18(1) 676
r 18A 677
r 18A(1) 690
r 19 641
r 20(1) 681
r 20(2) 681
r 23(1) 859
r 23(2) 859
r 23A 681
r 24(1) 691
r 24(2)(a) 691
r 24(2)(b) 691
r 24(2)(d) 692
r 24(2)(f) 692
r 24(2)(g) 692
r 24(5)(a) 846
r 24(5)(b) 846
r 24(5)(c) 846
r 24(4) 671
r 24(5)(a) 692
r 24(5)(b) 692
r 24(5)(c) 692
r 25 683
r 25(2) 683
r 26(1) 691
r 26(1)(a) 691
r 26(3) 671
r 27(1) 690
r 27(2) 690
r 27(3) 690
r 27A 690, 711
r 27A(1) 690
r 27A(2) 690
r 27A(3) 690
r 27A(4) 690
r 29 . . . . 690, 694
r 30(1) 694
r 33 827–8
r 33(1) 822
r 33(2) 828–9
r 34(2) 746
r 38(1) 788
r 38(2) 781
r 39 749–50
r 39(1) 749
r 43(1) 797

r 43(2) 797
r 43(3) 798, 821
r 43(4) 802
r 44(1)(a) 792
r 44(2) 794
r 44(3) 802
r 44(3)(b) 792
r 44(5) 799
r 44A 812
r 44B 813
r 45 801
r 45(1) 745
r 45(2) 745
r 45(3) 745
r 46 729
r 46(d) 763
r 47 746
r 47(1)(f) 763
r 47(1)(h) 748
r 47(3) 746
r 47(3.1)(b) 763
r 47(3.1)(c) 763
r 47(4) 773
r 47(6) 745, 780
rr 48–50 677
r 48 . . . . 729, 746
r 48(1) 763
r 49(1) 690, 763
r 51(1) 763, 806
r 51(3) 763, 806
r 51(4) 763, 806
r 51(5) 763, 806
r 52A(1) 698, 763, 805, 828
r 52A(2) 698
r 52A(3) 763
r 53(1) 702, 805
r 53(2) 806
r 53(3) 703, 763
r 53(4) 701
r 53(5) 702, 828
r 53(6) 763
r 54 690
r 54(1) 805
r 54(2)(a) 806
r 54(2)(b) 806
r 54(2)(c) 806
r 54(5) 806
r 54A 821
r 54A(1) 707
r 54A(2) 707
r 55 764
r 58(1) 806
r 58(2) 806
r 59(1) 806
r 59(3) 806
r 60 836
r 60(2) 838

r 61(1) 870
r 61(2)(b) 870
r 61(3) 870
r 61(4) 870
r 62 827
r 62(1) 821
r 62(3) 822
r 62A(1)(a) 823
r 62A(1)(b) 823
r 62A(1)(c) 823
r 62A(2) 823
r 62A(3) 823
r 63 806
r 63(1) 826
r 63(2) 826
r 63(3) 826
r 64 806
r 64(2) 806
r 65 806
r 70 806
r 72 710
r 72(3) 712
r 72(4) 712
r 73(1) 846
r 73(2) 846
r 74 859
r 75 . . . . 822, 838
r 75(1) 836
r 75(2) 836
r 75(3) 837
r 76(1) 855
r 76(2) 855
r 77 855
r 78 855
r 79 851–2
r 80(1) 852, 854
r 80(3) 852
r 81 . . . . 853, 855
rr 82–86 882
r 84(2) 882
r 86 882
r 87 884
r 87(2) 885
r 92 872
r 93 872
rr 94–99 872
r 96 872
r 100 748
r 101 748
Annex 807
Annex, r A 1(1) 807
Annex, r A 1(2) 792, 807
Annex, r A 1(3) 807–8
Annex, r A 1(4) 807
Annex, r A 1(5) 808
Annex, r A 2(1) 808

Annex, r A 2(2) 808
Annex, r A 3 808
Annex, r A 5(4) 808
Annex, r A 6 810
Annex, r A 7 810
Annex, r A 8 810

Miscellaneous resolutions and decisions of the European Court of Human Rights

Resolution of the Court, 29 September
   1970, (1970) 13 YB 43 672
Decision of European Court of Human
   Rights on immunities of judges,
   29 November 2011, Press release, ECHR
   265 (2011), 29 November 2011 893

Practice Directions

Practice Direction, Institution of Proceedings
   (Individual applications under article 34
   of the Convention), 1 November 2003,
   amended 22 September 2008 and
   24 June 2009 745
Practice Direction, Just Satisfaction
   Claims, 28 March 2007 . . . . .836–7, 839
Practice Direction, Requests for Anonymity
   (Rules 33 and 47 of the Rules of
   Court), 14 January 2010 746
Practice Direction, Requests for Interim
   Measures (Rule 39 of the Rules of
   Court), 5 March 2003, amended
   16 October 2009 and 7 July 2011 749
Practice Direction, Secured Electronic
   Filing, 22 Septmber 2008 806
Practice Direction, Written Pleadings,
   10 December 2007 806

Rules of the European Commission of Human Rights

Rules of the Commission 684

TREATIES AND CONVENTIONS

Additional Protocol to the Convention
   on the Transfer of Sentenced
   Persons, ETS 167 348
Additional Protocol I to the 1949 Geneva
   Conventions and relating to the
   Protection of Victims of International
   Armed Conflicts, (1979) 1125
   UNTS 3 . . . . 39, 155, 602, 1104, 1106
   Art 57(2)(a)(ii) 158
Additional Protocol II to the 1949
   Geneva Conventions and relating
   to the Protection of Victims
   of Non-international Armed
   Conflicts, (1979) 1125
   UNTS 609 . . . . 39, 155, 602, 1106

Additional Protocol III to the 1949 Geneva
  Conventions and relating to the Adoption
  of an Additional Distinctive
  Emblem 39, 155, 1106
African Charter on Human and People's
  Rights, (1981) 1520 UNTS 217
  Preamble, recital 3 60
  Art 11 495
  Art 50 767
  Art 56(5) 767
Agreement among the States Parties to
  the North Atlantic Treaty and
  the Other States Participating in
  the Partnership for Peace regarding
  the Status of Their Forces, Additional
  Protocol 1100
  Art 1 1100
Agreement between the Governments of the
  States of the Benelux Economic Union,
  the Federal Republic of Germany and
  the French Republic on the gradual
  abolition of checks at their common
  borders (Schengen Agreement),
  OJ *L 239* 1053
Agreement between the Parties to the
  1949 North Atlantic Treaty regarding
  the Status of Their Forces, (1951)
  199 UNTS 67 . . . . 98, 1100
American Convention on Human Rights,
  (1978) 1144 UNTS 123 . . . . .39, 141,
                      350, 693, 1197, 1201
  Preamble, recital 4 60
  Art 4 . . . . .15, 124, 140
  Art 4(3) 1197
  Art 13(2) 452
  Art 14 459
  Art 23(2) 1026
  Art 27 587
  Art 27(1) 594
  Art 27(2) 592
  Art 46 767
  Art 64 874
  Art 75 930
Arab Charter on Human Rights
  Art 15 335
Charter of Fundamental Rights of the
  European Union, 2010 OJ C 83/02 39,
          165, 202, 220, 282, 334, 536, 573,
                      583, 606, 609, 623, 1097
  Art 1 66
  Art 2 . . . . 119, 1093
  Art 4 165
  Art 5 202
  Art 5(1) 202
  Art 5(2) 202
  Art 7 359

Art 8 383
Art 9 . . . . 529, 537
Art 10 414
Art 10(2) 414, 433
Art 11(1) 445
Art 12 484
Art 14 988
Art 14(1) 988
Art 14(3) 988
Art 15(2) 1071
Art 17 960
Art 19 1075
Art 19(2) 165, 1093
Art 21 . . . . 556, 1184
Art 28 508
Art 45 . . . . 1053, 1071
Art 47 . . . . .265–6, 272, 547
Art 47(2) 266
Art 47(3) 266
Art 49 330
Art 49(1) 330, 350
Art 49(2) 330
Art 49(3) 183, 330
Art 50 1148
Art 52(3) 39
Art 54 612
Ch V 1012
Charter of the International Military
  Tribunal, (1951) 82 UNTS 279,
  annex 343
  Art 6(c) 202
  Art 8 341
Charter of the United Nations,
  (1945) 1 UNTS XVI 3, 54, 555–7,
                            575, 602
  Preamble 69, 555, 576, 1177
  Art 1 1177
  Art 1(3) 69, 555
  Art 33 913
  Art 96(1) 874
  Art 96(2) 874, 878
  Ch VII 106–7
Convention against Torture and Other
  Cruel, Inhuman, or Degrading Treatment
  or Punishment, (1987) 1465
  UNTS 85 . . . . .39, 164, 169, 176
  Art 1 . . . . .176–7, 902
  Art 3 1128
  Art 4(1) 279
  Art 15 321
Convention Concerning the Exchange
  of Greek and Turkish Populations,
  (1923) 32 LNTS 76 1067
Convention on Access to Information,
  Public Participation in Decision
  Making and Access to Justice in

Environmental Matters (Aarhus
   Convention), (2001) 2161
   UNTS 447 . . . . 24, 40
Convention on Civil Liability for
   Damage resulting from Activities
   Dangerous to the Environment,
   ETS 150. . . . . 38, 40
Convention on Consent to Marriage,
   Minimum Age for Marriage and
   Registration of Marriages, (1964)
   521 UNTS 232. 528
Convention on Human Rights and
   Fundamental Freedoms of the
   Commonwealth of Independent
   States 876, 879, 882, 885
Convention on Nationality of Married
   Women, (1958) 309 UNTS 65 528
   Art 8 930
Convention on the Applicability of Statutory
   Limitations to War Crimes and Crimes
   against Humanity, (1970)
   754 UNTS 73 39
Convention on the Elimination of All Forms
   of Discrimination against Women,
   (1980) 1249 UNTS 13 . . . . . . .192, 556, 1186
   Art 4(1) 567, 1175
   Art 10. 987
   Art 23. 902
   Art 28. 930
Convention on the Establishment of
   Maternal Decent of Natural Children 39
Convention on the Political Rights
   of Women, (1954) 193 UNTS 135 528
   Art VII. 930
Convention on the Prevention and
   Punishment of the Crime of
   Genocide, (1951) 78
   UNTS 277 . . . . . . 1, 39, 118, 914, 924, 1067
   Art 5 279
   Art 13. 924
Convention on the Protection of the
   Environment through Criminal
   Law, ETS 172. 40
Convention on the Recognition of
   Qualifications concerning Higher
   Education in the European
   Region, ETS 165. . . . . 38, 55
Convention on the Rights of Persons with
   Disabilities, UN Doc. A/RES/61/106,
   Annex I 556, 583
   Preamble, recital (b). 59
   Art 5(4) 1175
   Art 48. 941
Convention on the Rights of the Child, (1990)
   1577 UNTS 3 . . . . . . .38, 318, 392, 394, 556
   Art 10(2) 1060

Art 20. 394
Art 21. 394
Arts 28–29 987
Art 28. 996–7
Art 29(1) 996
Art 29(2) 996
Art 37(c). 251, 1060
Art 40(3)(a) 318
Art 51. 930
Convention on the Transfer of
   Sentenced Persons, ETS 112 348
Convention Relating to the Status
   of Refugees, (1951) 189
   UNTS 137 . . . . .55, 76,
                                        395, 947, 1053
   Art 32. 1126
   Art 33. 1126–7
   Art 42(1) 930
Council of Europe Convention on Action
   against Trafficking of Human
   Beings, ETS 197 . . . . .38, 203, 209
   Preamble. 203
   Art 4(a). 209
Council of Europe Convention on the
   Prevention of Terrorism, ETS 196 38
Covenant of the League of Nations,
   [1919] UKTS 4
   Art 14. 874
European Agreement relating to Persons
   Participating in Proceedings of
   the European Court of Human
   Rights, ETS 161 747
European Charter for Regional and
   Minority Languages, ETS 148 . . . . 581, 1024
European Convention for the Peaceful
   Settlement of Disputes, ETS 23
   Art 28(2) 912
European Convention for the Prevention
   of Torture and Inhuman or Degrading
   Treatment or Punishment,
   ETS 126. . . . . 165, 174
   Art 17(2) 912
European Convention on Establishment,
   ETS 19. . . . . .1071, 1129
   Art 3 . . . . .1076, 1126
   Art 33. 1076
European Convention on Extradition,
   ETS 24. 1149
European Convention on Nationality,
   ETS 166
   Art 4(a). 378
European Convention on Social and
   Medical Assistance, ETS 14 1129
   Art 11. 1129
European Convention on State Immunity,
   (1972) 1495 UNTS 182 39

European Convention on the International
  Validity of Criminal Judgments,
  ETS 70. . . . . .1143, 1149
European Convention on the Legal Status
  of Children Born out of Wedlock,
  ETS 85. . . . . 39, 55
European Convention on the Transfer of
  Proceedings in Criminal Matters,
  ETS 73. 1149
European Social Charter,
  ETS 35. . . . . .38, 484, 506
  Preamble. 556, 1106
  Art 2(5) 432
  Art 5 484
  Art 6 484
  Art 16. 529
  Art 19(8) 1126
  Art 30. 1106
  Art 30(1) 587
  App, Art 30 594
European Social Charter (revised),
  ETS 163. . . . . 23, 484, 499, 588, 898
  Art 5 . . . . 515, 522
  App, Art F(1) 587, 594
Extradition Treaty between the Government
  of the United Kingdom of Great
  Britain and Northern Ireland and
  the Government of the United States
  of America, (1977) 1049 UNTS 167
  Art IV. 145
Fifth Protocol to the General Agreement
  on Privileges and Immunities of
  the Council of Europe, ETS 137 892
Fourth Protocol to the General Agreement
  on Privileges and Immunities of
  the Council of Europe, ETS 36 892
Framework Convention for the
  Protection of National Minorities,
  ETS 157. . . . . .38, 55, 581, 1024
  Preamble. 491, 582
  Art 4(2) 1176
  Art 4(3) 1174
General Agreement on Privileges and
  Immunities of the Council of Europe, ETS 2
  Art 18. 892
General Framework Agreement for Peace
  in Bosnia and Herzegovian
  (Dayton Agreement), (1995) 35
  ILM 75 . . . . .99, 565, 768, 1105
Geneva Convention (I) for the Amelioration
  of the Condition of the Wounded and
  Sick in Armed Forces in the Field,
  (1950) 75 UNTS 31 . . . . .39, 155,
                                164, 601, 1106
  Art 3 1106

Geneva Convention (II) for the Amelioration
  of the Condition of Wounded, Sick
  and Shipwrecked Members of Armed
  Forces at Sea, (1950) 75
  UNTS 85 . . . . 39, 155, 164, 601, 1106
  Art 3 1106
Geneva Convention (III) Relative to
  Treatment of Prisoners of War,
  (1950) 75 UNTS 135 . . . . 37, 39, 155,
                                164, 601, 641, 1106
  Art 3 1106
Geneva Convention (IV) Relative to the
  Protection of Civilian Persons in
  Time of War, (1950) 75
  UNTS 287 . . . . 37, 39, 155, 164,
                                601, 641, 1106
  Art 3 1106
  Art 68. 1106
Geneva General Act for the Pacific
  Settlement of Disputes, (1928)
  93 *LNTS* 343
  Art 31(2) 758
  Art 32. 835
Treaty on Arbitration and Conciliation
  between the Swiss Confederation and
  the German Reich, (1921) 12 LNTS 271
  Art 10. 835
Hague Convention on the Civil Aspects
  of International Child Abduction,
  (1983) 1343 UNTS 98 . . . . 55, 392
Hague Convention on the Peaceful
  Settlement of International
  Disputes 1899. 647
Hague Convention Respecting the
  Law and Customs of War on
  Land 1899, 32 Stat. 1803, TS 403
  Preamble. 158, 424
Hague Convention Respecting the Law and
  Customs of War on Land (and Annex
  Regulations Concerning the Law and
  Customs of War on Land) 1907,
  36 Stat. 2277 55
  Preamble. 158, 424
  Regulations 602
  Art 42. 102
ILO Convention No. 29 concerning Forced
  or Compulsory Labour 1930, (1946)
  39 UNTS 55 . . . . 202, 210–2, 214–6
  Art 1 210
  Art 2 211
  Art 2(1) 211
  Art 2(2) 216
  Art 2(2)(a) 214
  Art 2(2)(b) 216
  Art 2(2)(c) 213

Art 2(2)(e) 216
ILO Convention No. 87 on Freedom of
  Association and Protection of the
  Right to Organise, (1950)
  68 UNTS 17 ....484, 515, 522
  Art 3 508
  Art 8 508
  Art 10........................... 508
ILO Convention No. 98 concerning
  the Application of the Principles of
  the Right to Organise and to Bargain
  Collectively, (1951) 96 *UNTS* 258 522
ILO Convention No. 102 (Minimum
  Standards) Convention, (1952)
  210 UNTS 131................... 982
ILO Convention No. 105 concerning
  the Abolition of Forced Labour,
  (1959) 320 UNTS 291 211
ILO Convention No. 151 concerning
  Protection of the Right to Organise
  and Procedures for Determining
  Conditions of Employment in the
  Public Service, (1981) 1218
  UNTS 87........................ 55
ILO Convention No. 169 concerning Indigenous
  and Tribal Peoples in Independent
  Countries, (1991) 1650 UNTS 383
  Art 14(1) 959
Inter-American Convention on the
  Prevention, Punishment, and
  Eradication of Violence against
  Women 192, 576
International Convention for the
  Protection of All Persons from Enforced
  Disappearance, UN Doc.
  A/RES/61/177, annex 136
  Preamble, recital 3................. 59
  Art 2 137
  Art 16.......................... 1128
International Convention on the Elimination
  of All Forms of Racial Discrimination,
  (1966) 660 UNTS 195 413,
                              555, 914, 1186
  Art 1 577
  Art 1(4) 567, 1175
  Art 2(2) 1176
  Art 4(1) 193
  Art 5(2) 1060
  Art 5(e)(v)....................... 987
  Art 6 193
  Art 12(2) 693
  Art 20.......................... 930
International Convention on the Protection
  of the Rights of All Migrant Workers
  and Members of Their Families,
  (2003) 2220 UNTS 3 1060

International Covenant on Civil and
  Political Rights, (1976) 999
  UNTS 171 ....6, 12, 18–9, 22,
                61, 83, 140–1, 164, 204, 210,
                228, 291, 330, 369, 435, 546,
                556, 588, 593, 595, 600–1,
                609, 614, 616, 631, 912–3, 941,
                1046, 1053, 1055, 1060, 1069–70,
                1125–6, 1134, 1147–8, 1155, 1157, 1201
  Preamble........................ 412
  Preamble, recital 4................. 59
  Art 2 1012
  Art 2(1) 19, 84, 609, 1179
  Art 2(3) 546
  Art 3 1185
  Art 4 600–1
  Art 4(1) 600
  Art 4(2) 1051
  Art 4(3) 603
  Art 5 587
  Art 5(1) 594, 611
  Art 5(2) 592, 902
  Art 6 .... 118–9, 140–1, 1092, 1197
  Art 6(2) 140, 145
  Art 6(6) 1197
  Art 7 164
  Art 9 ....228–9, 593
  Art 9(2) 244
  Art 9(3) 250
  Art 10(2)(b) 251
  Art 11............. 593, 1046, 1048, 1051
  Art 12.....................1053, 1056
  Art 12(3) 1055
  Art 13...............1068, 1126, 1131
  Art 13(2) 1126
  Art 14.............265, 267, 1135, 1142
  Art 14(3)(d) 316
  Art 14(3)(g) 301
  Art 14(5) 1134
  Art 14(6) 1142, 1145
  Art 14(7) 1147, 1149
  Art 15......................330–1, 353
  Art 15(1) 343, 350
  Art 15(2) 356
  Art 17........................... 402
  Art 18........................... 423
  Art 19........................... 609
  Art 19(2) 39, 463
  Art 19(3) 468
  Art 20(2) 478
  Art 21....................... 509, 609
  Art 22....................... 522, 609
  Art 22(2) 509
  Art 22(3) 509
  Art 23.......................... 529
  Art 23(4) 529

Art 25. . . . . .13, 19, 1012, 1019
Art 26. . . . . .19, 21, 1179–80
Art 27. . . . . .13, 19, 22, 581, 593
Art 41. 913, 1155
Art 41(1)(c) 767
Art 42(2) 693
Art 44. 912
International Covenant on Economic,
  Social and Cultural Rights, (1976)
  993 UNTS 3 . . . . 6, 18, 61
Preamble. 412
Preamble, recital 4. 59
Art 8(1)(a) 510
Art 8(1)(c) 510
Art 8(1)(d) 508
Art 13. 997
Art 14. 987
Art 14(1) 987
Art 14(3) 987
Art 14(4) 987
Art 15. 987
North Atlantic Treaty, (1949) 34
  UNTS 243 1100
Optional Protocol to the Convention on
  the Rights of the Child on the Sale
  of Children, Child Prostitution, and
  Child Pornography, (2002) 2171
  UNTS 227
Art 15. 941
Optional Protocol to the Convention on
  the Rights of the Child on the
  Involvement of Children in Armed
  Conflict, (2002) 2173 UNTS 222
Art 11. 941
Optional Protocol to the International
  Covenant on Civil and Political Rights,
  (1976) 999 UNTS 171 . . . . 18, 61, 777
Art 2 767
Art 5(2)(b) 767
Optional Protocol to the International
  Covenant on Economic, Social and
  Cultural Rights, UN Doc. A/63/435 61
Oviedo Convention on Human Rights
  and Biomedicine, ETS 164 39–40
Potsdam Protocol, 1 August 1945
Art XII 1067
Protocol Relating to the Status of Refugees,
  (1967) 606 UNTS 267 . . . . 395, 1053
Art VII 930
Protocol to Prevent, Suppress and Punish
  Trafficking in Persons, especially
  Women and Children, supplementing
  the United Nations Convention
  against Transnational Organised Crime
  ('the Palermo Protocol'),
  UN Doc. A/RES/55/25, Annex II 209

Art 3 210
Protocol to the African Charter on Human
  and Peoples' Rights on the Establishment
  of an African Court on Human and
  Peoples' Rights, OAU Doc.
  OAU/LEG/EXP/AFCHPR/PROT (III)
Art 22. 693
Protocol to the American Convention on
  Human Rights to Abolish the Death
  Penalty, OASTS No. 73 . . . . .1093, 1200
Art 2(1) 1104
Protocol to the European Convention on
  Establishment, ETS 19
Section II 1129
Rome Statute of the International Criminal
  Court, (2002) 2187 UNTS 90 602,
                              723, 1134, 1148
Preamble. 424
Art 3 . . . . 99, 641
Art 7(1)(d) 1071
Art 8 . . . . 345, 602
Art 8(1)(i). 136
Art 8(2)(ii) 136
Art 8*bis*. 602
Art 17. . . . . 705, 767
Art 24(2) 350
Art 33. 341–2
Art 55(1)(c) 315
Art 66. 300
Art 66(3) 123
Art 69(1) 428
Art 120. 930, 1111
Second Optional Protocol to the International
  Covenant on Civil and Political Rights
  Aimed at the Abolition of the Death
  Penalty, (1991) 1642
  UNTS 414 . . . . 1093, 1097, 1103,
                              1106–8, 1200
Preamble. 1094
Art 2 930
Art 2(1) 1104
Sixth Protocol to the General Agreement
  on Privileges and Immunities of
  the Council of Europe, ETS 162 892–3
Preamble. 892
Arts 1–2 892
Art 1 892
Art 4 .680, 892–3
Art 5 892
Slavery Convention 1926, (1927)
  60 LNTS 253 202
Preamble. 211
Art 1(1) 207
Statute of the Council of Europe,
  ETS 1. . . . . .3, 54, 65, 71, 556, 905
Preamble. 71, 1011

Art 1 . . . . 65, 69
Art 1(b) 3
Art 3 . . . . .65, 71, 906, 946
Art 5(a). 946
Art 7 . . . . 906, 943
Art 8 . . . . 866, 906
Art 10. 905
Art 13. 906
Art 16. 672
Art 38. 897
Art 40. 891
Ch II 946
Statute of the International Court of
    Justice. 42, 632, 635, 637, 651,
                                724, 878, 891
Art 2 . . . . 648, 651
Art 4(1) 658
Art 8 658
Art 18(1) 672
Art 22(1) 641
Art 31. 693
Art 36. . . . . .637, 716, 910–1
Art 38. . . . . 40, 44, 716, 719–20, 849
Art 38(1) 38
Art 38(1)(c) 41, 352
Art 57. 857
Art 61(1) 852
Art 65(1) 877–8
Statute of the Permanent Court of
    International Justice, (1921)
    6 *LNTS* 379
Art 2 647
Arts 65–68 874
Statute of the Special Court for Sierra
    Leone, (2002) 2178 UNTS 145, annex
Art 9 1148
Treaty between the Principal Allied and
    Associated Powers and Czechoslovakia,
    [1919] TS 20
Art 1 118
Treaty between the Principal Allied and
    Associated Powers and Roumania,
    (1921) 5 LNTS 336
Art 1 118
Treaty establishing the European Economic
    Community, (1958) 298 UNTS 11
Art 48. 1126
Treaty of Amsterdam, amending the
    Treaty on European Union, the
    Treaties establishing the European
    Communities and Certain Related
    Acts, 97/C 340/01. . . . . .1092, 1185
Treaty of Establishment, (1960) 382
    UNTS 160 924
Treaty of Lisbon amending the Treaty on
    European Union and The Treaty

Establishing the European Community,
    OJ 2007/C 306/01
Art 6(2) 948
Treaty of Peace between the Principal Allied
    and Associated Powers and the
    Serb-Croat-Slovene State, [1919] TS 17
Art 2 118
Treaty of Peace between the United States
    of America, the British Empire, France,
    Italy, and Japan and Poland,
    [1919] TS 8 118
Art 2 413
Arts 10–11 413
Treaty of Saint-Germain-en-Laye, [1919]
    TS 11
Art 63. 118
Treaty of Utrecht 1713
Art XIV 413
Treaty of Peace between the Allied and
    Associated Powers and Germany
    (Treaty of Versailles), [1919]
    UKTS 4 328
Art 93. 413
Treaty on European Union (Maastricht
    Treaty), OJ 92/C 191/01. . . . . . . .1021, 1185
Art F(2) 1092
Treaty on the Functioning of the European
    Union, C326/47
Art 344. 949
Vienna Convention on Succession of
    States in respect of State Property,
    Archives and Debts, UN Doc.
    A/CONF.117/14 42
Vienna Convention on Succession of
    States in respect of Treaties,
    (1996) 1946 UNTS 3 42
Vienna Convention on the Law of Treaties,
    (1980) 1155 UNTS 331 . . . . 34–5, 37,
                46, 54, 180, 924, 934, 938, 955,
                1045, 1113, 1117, 1168, 1170
Preamble. 88
Preamble, recital 3. 866
Art 1(b) 1118
Art 2 . . . . .54, 89, 955, 1045
Art 2(1)(b) 948
Art 2(1)(d) 35, 933
Art 3(c). 88
Art 11. 947–8
Art 12. 947
Art 14. 947
Art 15(c). 88
Art 18. . . . . 35, 947
Art 19. . . . . 786, 1111
Art 19(b) 930
Art 20. 939
Art 20(2) 88

Art 26. . . . . .35, 89, 814, 866, 900
Art 27. 35
Art 28. . . . . .35, 107, 786
Art 29. . . . . 922, 925, 937, 1033,
         1082, 1113–4, 1161
Art 30. 36
Arts 31–33 35
Art 31. . . . . . . 34–6, 45, 54, 933, 955, 1045
Art 31(1) 36
Art 31(1)(c) 38
Art 31(2) 36
Art 31(3) 36
Art 31(3)(a) 36
Art 31(3)(b) 36–7
Art 31(3)(c) 37, 40, 46, 154, 642, 719
Art 32. . . . . 35, 45
Art 33. . . . . 35, 45–6
Art 39. 36
Art 53. . . . . 42, 593
Art 64. 42
Arts 77–80 1121
Art 77. . . . . 950, 1121

COUNCIL OF EUROPE DOCUMENTS
High level meetings

Vienna Declaration (of the Heads of State
 and Government of the member States
 of the Council of Europe),
 9 October 1993 . . . . .633, 645, 1023
Interlaken Declaration of the High
 Level Conference of the Council of
 Europe on the Future of the European
 Court of Human Rights,
 19 February 2010 664
 para 8(a). 652
Final Declaration of the High Level
 Conference on the Future of the
 Court, İzmir, 26–27 April 2011. 750
 para 2(e). 847
Brighton Declaration, High Level
 Conference on the Future of the
 European Court of Human Rights,
 20 April 2012. . . . . 79, 650
 para 12(b). 58, 79
 para 22. 651
 para 24. 650
 para 25(f) 650

Committee of Ministers

Decision of the Committee of Ministers,
 Recognition of service as a judge of
 the European Court of Human
 Rights, DD(2013)1321 and
 DD(2014)302. 673
Declaration Regarding Intolerance – a Threat
 to Democracy, Decl-14.05.81E, 14 May 1981
 para IV.ii 20
Declaration of the Committee of Ministers
 on human rights and the rule of law
 in the Information Society,
 CM(2005)56 final. 462
Guidelines on the Selection of Candidates
 for the Post of Judge at the European
 Court of Human Rights,
 CM(2012)40 addendum
 para 20. 651
 para 23. 652
 para 25. 654
 para 27. 652
Model Final Clauses 1962 . . . .1113, 1117, 1168
Model Final Clauses 1980 . . . . 1113–4, 1117–8,
     1121, 1161–2, 1168, 1189, 1192–4,
      1205, 1208–10, 1228–9, 1232
Recommendation Rec(74)26 on the right of
 reply–Position of the individual in
 relation to the press 460
Recommendation R(85)2 on legal
 protection against sex
 discrimination. 576, 1176
Recommendation R(97)20 on
 'Hate Speech' 479
Recommendation R(2000)2 on the
 re-examination or reopening of certain
 cases at domestic level following
 judgments of the European Court of
 Human Rights 868
Recommendation R(2000)7 on the right
 of journalists not to disclose their
 sources of information
 App, principle 1 459
Recommendation Rec(2000)15 concerning
 the security of residence of
 long-term migrants 395
Recommendation Rec(2001)10 on the
 European Code of Police Ethics 522
Recommendation Rec(2003)4 of
 8 April 2003 on common rules
 against corruption in the funding
 of political parties and electoral
 campaigns. 505
Recommendation Rec(2003)13 on
 the provision of information
 through the media in relation
 to criminal proceedings
 App 460
Recommendation Rec(2004)6 on the
 improvement of domestic remedies. 292
Recommendation Rec(2004)16 on the
 right of reply in the new
 media environment 460
Recommendation Rec(2006)2 on the
 European Prison Rules. 251, 998
 para 28. 998
 App 251

Recommendation CM/Rec(2007)11 on
  promoting freedom of expression
  and information in the new information
  and communications environment 462
Recommendation CM/Rec(2007)14 on
  the legal status of non-governmental
  organisations in Europe
  para 44. 501
Recommendation CM/Rec(2007)16 on
  measures to promote the public service
  value of the Internet 462
Recommendation CM/Rec(2008)6 on
  measures to promote the respect for
  freedom of expression and information
  with regard to Internet filters 462
Recommendation CM/Rec(2010)3 on
  effective remedies for excessive
  length of proceedings. 292
  paras 10–1 292
Recommendation CM/Rec(2012)3 on the
  protection of human rights with
  regard to search engines 462
Resolution (52)1, Protocol to the Convention
  for the Protection of Human Rights and
  Fundamental Freedoms 967
Resolution (59)12, Human Rights
  (Application No. 176/56) 9
Resolution (59)32, Human Rights
  (Application No. 299/57) 9
Resolution (60)6, European Convention
  on Human Rights - Second
  Protocol - Recommendation 234 13,1085
Resolution (60)20, Extension of the
  compentence of the European
  Court - Recommendation 232 26
Resolution (70)17, UN Covenant on Civil
  and Political Rights and the European
  Convention on Human Rights: Procedure
  for dealing with inter-state
  complaints 913
  Preamble. 913
Resolution (74)2, The Greek Case (Denmark,
  Norway, Sweden, the Netherlands v
  Greece). 943
Resolution (78)37 on equality of spouses
  in civil law 576
Resolution (99)50 on the Council of
  Europe Commissioner for Human
  Rights 794
Resolution (2002)59 concerning the
  practice in respect of friendly
  settlements 816
Resolution (2004)50 on the status and
  conditions of service of judges of the
  European Court of Human
  Rights, 15 December 2004 673

Resolution (2007)7 inviting the Republic
  of Montenegro to become a member
  of the Council of Europe 720, 906, 951
Resolution (2009)5 on the status and
  conditions of service of judges of the
  European Court of Human Rights
  and of the Commissioner for
  Human Rights, 23 September
  2009. 673
  para 2. 892
  para 5. 673
  para 10. 673
Resolution (2010)25 on member States' duty
  to respect and protect the right of individual
  application to the Court. 747
Resolution (2010)26 on the establishment
  of an Advisory Panel of Experts on
  Candidates for the Election of Judge
  to the European Court of Human
  Rights. 664
Resolution (2013)4 amending Resolution
  CM/Res(2009)5 on the status and
  conditions of service of judges of the
  European Court of Human Rights
  and of the Commissioner for
  Human Rights 673
Rules for the supervision of the execution of
  judgments and the terms of
  friendly settlements
  r 6 871
  r 6(2)(b) 868

**Parliamentary Assembly (formerly
Consultative Assembly)**

Opinion No. 190 (1995), Application by Ukraine
  for membership of the Council of Europe
  para 12.1 . . . . .1088, 1067
Opinion No. 193 (1996), Application by
  Russia for membership of the
  Council of Europe
  para 10.1 . . . . .1088, 1167
Opinion No. 195 (1996), Application by
  Croatia for membership of the
  Council of Europe
  para 9.2 .1088, 1167
Opinion No. 216 (2000) on Draft Protocol
  No. 12 to the European Convention
  on Human Rights 21, 24, 1185
  para 16. 1181
  para 25. 1174
  para 29. 1181
Opinion No. 233 (2002) on the Draft
  Protocol to the European Convention
  on Human Rights concerning the
  Abolition of the Death Penalty
  in All Circumstances

para 5 144
para 6 1207
Opinion No. 251 (2004) on Draft Protocol
No. 14 to the Convention on
the Protection of Human Rights and
Fundamental Freedoms amending the
control system of the Convention
para 7 645
paras 11–12 760
para 10 . . . . 689, 701
para 11 760
para 14.i 649
para 14.ii 660
para 14.iv 689, 701
Opinion No. 261 (2007), Accession of the
Republic of Montenegro to the
Council of Europe
para 10 951
Opinion No. 285 (2013) on Draft Protocol
No. 16 to the Convention for the
Protection of Human Rights and
Fundamental Freedoms,
28 June 2013 1213–4
Order No. 519 664
Recommendation No. 38 to the
Committee of Ministers adopted
8 September 1949 on the conclusion
of the debates, Doc. AS(1), 108 56,
85, 120, 166, 204, 221, 266, 331,
362, 415, 446, 485, 531, 559, 613,
636, 669, 700, 755, 908, 1013
Art 11 . . . . 724, 732
Art 12 758
Art 13 803
Art 15 817
Recommendation 232 (1960) on the
extension of the competence of the
European Court of Human Rights
as regards the interpretation of the
Convention on Human Rights,
22 January 1960 . . . . 26, 875
Recommendation 234 (1960), Draft for a
Second Protocol to the Convention
for the Protection of Human Rights and
Fundamental Freedoms 12, 13, 19,
1046, 1049, 1054, 1069, 1075, 1087
Recommendation 285 (1961) on the rights
of minorities 13, 22, 581
Recommendation 316 (1962) on accession
to the Convention of States that are not
members of the Council of Europe 947
Recommendation 583 (1970) on suppression
of and guaranteeing against
unjustifiable discrimination 20
Recommendation 683 (1972) on action to
be taken on the conclusions of the

Parliamentary Conference on human
rights (Vienna, 18–20 October 1972) 28
para A(4) 20
Recommendation 791 (1976) on the
protection of human rights in Europe
Art 12.c.i 18
Art 12.c.iv 25
Recommendation 799 (1977) on the
political rights and positions of
aliens 609
Recommendation 838 (1978) on widening
the scope of the European Convention
on Human Rights
para. 13 23
Recommendation 951 (1982) on voting
rights of national of Council of Europe
member States 1027
Recommendation 1087 (1988) on the
improvement of the procedures of
the European Convention on Human
Rights
para 10 29
Recommendation 1116 (1989) on
AIDS and human rights
para 8.A 21
Recommendation 1134 (1990) on the
rights of minorities 22
Recommendation 1177(1992) on the
rights of minorities 22
Recommendation 1194 (1992) on the reform
of the control mechanism of the
European Convention on Human
Rights 29
Recommendation 1201 (1993) on an
additional protocol on the rights of
national minorities to the European
Convention on Human Rights 22, 581
Recommendation 1223 (1993) on
reservations made by member States
to the Council of Europe
Convention 931
Recommendation 1229 (1994) on equality
of rights between men and women
para 8.i 24
Recommendation 1246 (1994) on the
abolition of capital punishment 16
Recommendation 1255 (1995) on the
protection of rights of national
minorities 22
Recommendation 1269 (1995) on
achieving real progress in women's
rights as from 1995
para 6.1 24
Recommendation 1302 (1996) on the
abolition of the death penalty in
Europe 16

Recommendation 1354 (1998),
Future of the European Social Charter
para 18 23
para 23.2 23
Recommendation 1429 (1999), National
procedures for nominating candidates
for election to the European Court of
Human Rights 653
para 5 .653, 661, 665
para 6.i 662
para 6.ii 654
para 6.v 662
Recommendation 1431 (1999), Future action
to be taken by the Council of Europe
in the field of environment protection
para 8 23
Recommendation 1492 (2001), Rights of
national minorities. 22
Recommendation 1504 (2001) on
Non-expulsion of long-term
immigrants 395
Recommendation 1516 (2001) on the
financing of political parties 484
Recommendation 1519 (2001) on the
coexistence of the Convention on
Human Rights and Fundamental
Freedoms of the Commonwealth of
Independent States and the European
Convention on Human Rights 876
Recommendation 1592 (2003), Towards full
social inclusion of people with
disabilities 583
Recommendation 1614 (2003), Environment
and human rights
para 10.i 24
Recommendation 1640 (2004), 3rd Annual
Report on the Activities of the Council
of Europe Commissioner for Human
Rights (1 January – 31 December
2002) 790
Recommendation 1649 (2004), Candidates
for the European Court of Human
Rights. 661, 665, 671, 673
para 19(i) 662
para 19(ii) 654
para 19(iii) 665
para 19(iv) 653
para 19(v) 662
para 19(vi) 694
Recommendation 1663 (2004): Domestic
slavery: servitude, au pairs and
'mail-order brides' 202–3
Recommendation 1671 (2004), Ratification
of protocols and withdrawal of
reservations and derogations made in
respect of the European Convention
on Human Rights

para 2 931
para 7 931
para 9 931
Recommendation 1798 (2007) on Respect for the
principle of gender equality in civil law
para 7 24
Recommendation 1875 (2009),
Reconsideration on substantive
grounds of previously ratified credentials
of the Ukrainian delegation
(Rule 9 of the Assembly's Rules of
Procedure) 877
Recommendation 1885 (2009), Drafting
an additional protocol to the European
Convention on Human Rights
concerning the right to a
healthy environment 24
para 10.1 24
para 11.2.b 24
Recommendation 1994 (2012), an
additional protocol to the European
Convention on Human Rights on
minorities 22
para 3 23
Resolution 337 (1967) on the rights of
conscientious objection 433
Resolution 428 (1970) containing a
declaration on mass communication
media and human rights 369
Resolution 683 (1972) on action to be taken
on the conclusions of the Parliamentary
Conference on Human Rights
(Vienna, 18-20 October 1971) 18
Resolution 1044 (1994) on the abolition
of capital punishment 16, 1118
Resolution 1200 (1999), Election of judges
to the European Court of Human Rights
para 3 663
App I 654, 662
Resolution 1271 (2002), Combating terrorism
and respect for human rights
para 9 588
Resolution 1366 (2004), Candidates for the
European Court of Human Rights
para 3 653–4
para 3(b) 651
para 3(ii) 665
para 4 663
para 4(vi) 665
Resolution 1426 (2005), Candidates for the
European Court of Human Rights
para 4 665
para 5 665
Resolution 1432 (2005), Procedure for
elections held by the Parliamentary
Assembly other than those of its President
and Vice-Presidents 662

App 662
App, para 1. 662
App, para 2. 663
App, para 3. 662
Resolution 1627 (2008), Candidates
  for the European Court of Human
  Rights. 666
Resolution 1646 (2009), Nomination of
  candidates and election of judges to
  the European Court of Human
  Rights. 662
  para 2. 661
  para 4. 654
  para 4.4 653
  para 4.5 694
  App 653, 662
Resolution 1713 (2010), Minority
  protection in Europe: best practices
  and deficiencies in implementation
  of common standards. 581
Resolution 1860 (2012), Advancing women's
  rights worldwide
  para 10.7 24
Resolution 1863 (2012), Enforced
  population transfer as a human
  rights violation 1067
Resolution 1866 (2012), an additional
  protocol to the European
  Convention on Human Rights
  on national minorities
  para 3. 21
  para 6. 22

**Steering Committee on Human
Rights (CDDH)**

Opinion of the CDDH on Recommendation
  1883 (2009), *The challenges posed by
  climate change*, DH-DEV(2010)03
  App III, para 3 24
Drafting an additional protocol to the
  European Convention on Human Rights
  concerning the right to a healthy
  environment, DH-DEV(2010)03
  App III, para 3 24
Opinion on the CDDH report on the
  Advisory Panel, 15 April 2014
  para 5. 664

**Venice Commission (European Commission
for Democracy through Law)**

Code of Good Practice in Electoral Matters,
  CDL-AD (2002) 23 rev.
  para 1.1.d.iii 1029
  para 1.1.d.iv 1028
Guidelines and Report on the Financing of
  Political Parties, 9-10 March 2001 505

Commissioner for Human Rights

Opinion of the Commissioner for Human
  Rights, Mr Alvaro Gil-Robles, on
  certain aspects of the United Kingdom
  2001 derogation from Article 5 par.1
  of the European Convention on
  Human Rights, CommDH(2007)7
  para 5. 593
  para 33. 597

**European Commission against Racism and
Intolerance**

General Policy Recommendation No. 7. 577

UNITED NATIONS DOCUMENTS
General Assembly

Affirmation of the Principles of International
  Law Recognised by the Nürnberg Charter,
  GA Res. 95 (I) 343
Basic Principles on the Independence of
  the Judiciary, UN Doc. A/RES/40/32
  and UN Doc. A/RES/40/46. 294
  Principle 1 294
Crime of Genocide, GA Res. 96 (I)
  OP1. 343
Declaration on the Elimination of All
  Forms of Intolerance and of
  Discrimination Based on Religion or
  Belief, UN Doc. A/RES/36/55. 413
  Art 1 414
  Art 1(3) 414
  Art 6 414
Declaration on the Protection of All Persons
  from Being Subjected to Torture and
  Other Cruel, Inhuman or Degrading
  Treatment or Punishment 1975,
  GA Res. 3452 (XXX)
  para 1. 175
  para 1(1). 175, 177
  para 2. 175
Declaration on the Rights of Indigenous
  Peoples, UN Doc. A/RES/61/295
  Annex, art 11(2) 959
  Annex, art 31(1) 959
Definition of Aggression, GA Res. 3314
  (XXIX),
  Annex. 602
Draft Convention on Freedom of
  Information, GA Res. 313 (IV), ... 447
Permanent Sovereignty over Natural
  Resources, GA Res. 1803 (XVII),
  para 4. 978
Permanent Sovereignty over Natural
  Resources, GA Res. 3171 (XXVIII),
  para 3. 978

Preparation of a Draft Declaration
and a Draft Convention on the
Elimination of All Forms of Religious
Intolerance, GA Res. 1781 (XVII), ... 413
Protection of All Persons from Being
Subjected to Torture and Other
Cruel, Inhuman or Degrading Treatment
or Punishment, GA Res. 3452
(XXX), ... 164
Question of South-West Africa, GA
Res. 227 (III), ... 447
Right of peoples to peace, UN Doc.
A/RES/39/11 67
Standard Minimum Rules for the
Administration of Juvenile Justice
('The Beijing Rules'), UN Doc.
A/RES/33/40 318
Universal Declaration of Human Rights,
GA Res. 217 A (III), ... 1–7, 11, 22,
45, 47–8, 56–7, 59–66, 70,
73, 94, 119, 164–5, 167, 180, 209,
265, 328, 330–3, 358–9, 361–4,
369, 412–3, 416, 418, 445, 448,
450, 466, 484, 487, 489, 528,
530–2, 535, 540, 555–8,
575–6, 580–1, 588, 590, 607,
609, 623, 631, 916–7, 920–1,
956, 958, 960, 986–7, 995–6,
1046, 1048, 1055, 1060, 1068,
1079, 1125, 1147, 1155 1157,
1178, 1184
Preamble. 60, 69, 71, 412, 535
Preamble, recital 1. . . . . 60, 66
Preamble, recital 7. 69
Art 1 . . . . 124, 1177
Art 2 . . . . . . .61, 119, 555, 557–8, 562, 572,
580, 582, 916, 1177
Art 2(1) 1184
Art 2(2) 62
Art 3 . . . . .62, 118–21, 165–6, 220–1,
223–5, 228, 547, 987
Art 4 202–4
Art 5 . . . . 119–20, 164–8, 180, 221, 547
Art 6 . . . . .13, 379, 740, 1175
Art 7 . . 478, 546, 555, 1174, 1177, 1179–80
Art 8 . . . . . 119–20, 165–6, 221, 223, 546–9
Art 9 . . . . . 220–4, 266, 331, 716, 830, 1069
Art 10. . . . 221–3, 265–7, 331, 716, 825, 830
Art 10(1) 265
Art 11. . . . . 221–3, 265–6, 331, 716, 830
Art 11(1) 265, 267, 298
Art 11(2) 265, 328, 331–2, 343, 355
Art 12. . . . . 358, 359–63, 367, 384, 386
Art 13. 1053
Art 13(2) 1047, 1068
Art 14(1) 63, 395, 1053

Art 15. . . . . .378, 1069, 1072
Art 15(1) 581
Art 16. . . . . . . 528–32, 535, 540, 555, 1157
Art 16(1) 64, 541, 987
Art 16(2) 987
Art 16(3) 388, 987
Art 17. . . . . .4, 957–8, 960
Art 18. . . . . .413, 415–6, 426
Art 19. . . . . 444, 446–7, 451, 466
Art 20. . . . . .483, 485, 487
Art 20(1) 483, 485
Art 20(2) 64, 483, 485, 507
Art 21. . . . . .606, 957, 1012
Art 21(2) 13, 64
Art 21(3) 19
Arts 22–27 63
Art 23(2) 555
Art 23(4) 484–5, 487–9, 505
Art 24. 432
Art 25(2) 124
Art 26. . . . . .957, 986, 995, 997
Art 26(1) 996
Art 26(2) 987
Art 26(3) 4, 988
Art 27(1) 464
Art 27(2) 959
Art 29. . . . . .414, 445, 485
Art 29(2) 359, 402, 435, 445,
468, 509, 589, 612, 623
Art 30. 611–3

Security Council

Statute of the International Criminal
Tribunal for Rwanda, UN Doc.
S/RES/955 (1994), annex
Art 9 1148
Statute of the International Criminal
Tribunal for the former Yugoslavia,
UN Doc. S/RES/837 (1993), annex
Art 10. 1148

Human Rights Council

Promotion of the right to peace,
UN Doc. A/HRC/RES/23/16 67

International Law Commission

Draft articles on Jurisdictional Immunities
of States and Their Property,
UN Doc. A/46/10, at para. 28 41
Draft Articles on State Responsibility
for Internationally Wrongful Acts,
UN Doc. A/56/10; UN Doc.
A/RES/56/83, annex 89, 101
Art 13. 107
Art 14. 109
Art 35. . . . . 837, 868

Commission on Human Rights

Commission on Human Rights
Updated Set of Principles for the
Protection and Promotion of Human
Rights Through Action to Combat
Impunity, UN Doc. E/CN.4/RES/2005/81
para 2 139
para 3 139

Human Rights Committee

General Comment No. 6, The right to
life, UN Doc. CCPR/C/21/Add.1 117
General Comment No. 22, The right to
freedom of thought, conscience and
religion, UN Doc. HRI/GEN/1/Rev.1,
p. 35 423
General Comment No. 23, The rights of
minorities, UN Doc. CCPR/C/21/
Rev.1/Add.6
para 10 593
General Comment No. 24, Issues relating to
reservations made upon ratification or
accession to the Covenant or the Optional
Protocols thereto, or in relation to
declarations under article 41 of the Covenant,
UN Doc. CCPR/C/21/ Rev.1/Add.6
para 10 420
General Comment No. 26, Continuity of
Obligations, UN Doc. CCPR/C/21/
Rev.1/Add.8, Rev.1
para 3 941
General Comment No. 29, States of
emergency (art. 4), UN Doc.
CCPR/C/21/Rev.1/Add.11 599
para 2 . . . . 595, 601
para 4 599
para 5 599
para 11 593
General Comment No. 32, Art 14: Right
to equality before courts and tribunals
and to a fair trial, UN Doc.
CCPR/C/GC/32 298

Committee on the Elimination of All
Forms of Racial Discrimination

Committee for the Elimination of Racial
Discrimination General Recommendation
No. 32, the meaning and scope of
special measures in the International
Convention on the Elimination of Racial
Discrimination, UN Doc. CERD/C/GC/32
para 14 566

International Court of Justice

Rules of Court of the International Court of Justice
r 79(1) 705

Documents adopted by United Nations conferences

Basic Principles on the Use of Force and
Firearms by Law Enforcement Officials,
UN Doc. A/CONF.144/28/Rev.1,
p. 112 130
para 5 130
para 7 130
para 9 130
para 23 131
para 24 131
Standard Minimum Rules for the Treatment
of Prisoners, UN doc. A/CONF/611,
annex I 175

ORGANISATION FOR SECURITY AND COOPEERATION IN EUROPE DOCUMENTS

Document of the Meeting of the Conference
on the Human Dimension,
29 June 1990 1023

EUROPEAN UNION DOCUMENTS

Employment Equality Directive 2000/78/EC . . . 583
Racial Equality Directive 2000/43/EC
Art 2 568

NATIONAL LEGISLATION

Andorra

Constitution
Art 42 604

Austria

Penal Code 1153
s. 188 473
Road Traffic Act 1153
State Treaty of 15th May 1955 for the
Restoration of an Independent and
Democratic Austria 937
Pt IV 983
Pt V 983

Azerbaijan

Code of Administrative Offences 1154
Criminal Code 1154
Non-governmental Organisation Act 510

Belgium

Constitution
Art 25 903

Bosnia and Herzegovina

Constitution 67, 1107

Bulgaria

Constitution
Art 22(1) 984

Denmark

Administration of Justice Act 1140

Estonia

Property Reform (Principles) Act. 984

France

Act of 9 August 1849. 604
Act of 3 April 1878
    Section I. 604
Act No. 55-385 of 3 April 1955
    Section I. 604
Act No. 72-553 of 10 July 1972. 481
Code Civil. 390
Code of Criminal procedure
    ss 359 et seq.. 1146
Constitution
    Art 16. . . . . 604, 1118
Déclaration des droits de l'homme et du
    citoyen 444
    Art 7 220
Déclaration des droits de l'homme et du
    citoyen 1789. . . . . 328, 958
    Art 17. 958
Déclaration des droits de l'homme et du
    citoyen 1793
    Art 16. 958
Loi Verdeille 1964. 973
Penal Code 1095, 1137

Germany

Basic Law 1949 611
Control Council Law No. 10
    Art II(1)(c) 202

Greece

Education Acts 934, 1006

Ireland

Constitution 540, 603
Emergency Powers Act 1976 598
Offences Against the State (Amendment)
    Act 1940. 598

Italy

Constitution 921
    Art 3(2) 1073

Liberia

Constitution
    Art 1, s 7 1147

Liechtenstein

Criminal Code 1852
    Art 2(g) 161
    para 129 408
    para 130 408

Macedonia

Constitution 511
    Art 45. 1008

Malta

Act 1 of 1987, An act to regulate the
    limitations on the political
    activities of aliens. 609
Constitution
    s 41(2)(a)(ii) 609
Criminal Code. 160
    s 737 160
    s. 738. 160

Moldova

Declaration of Independence 1991 1030

Monaco

Constitution 554, 585
    Art 2 441

Norway

Royal Decree of 30 November 1956. 441

Philippines

Constitution
    Art 3, s. 1(20). 1147

Portugal

Constitution 525
    Art 38(6) 481
    Art 43. 1008
    Art 75. 1008
    Art 82. . . . . 939, 983
    Art 276. 218

Romania

Law No. 18/1991 1182

Russia

Religions Act 1997. 501

Soviet Union

Constitution 1936. 580

Spain

Constitution 525
    Art 33. 984
    Art 55. . . . . 604, 622
    Art 116. . . . . 604, 622

Switzerland

Constitution
    Art 70. 1132

Turkey

Constitution 939
Criminal Code
    Art 301. 470–1

Law on Associations 471
Loi No 430, 3 March 1924 1008
Loi No 6366 1008
Penal Code
    Art 125 1096

Ukraine

Code of Criminal Procedure 262
    Art 43 325
    Art 43 325
    Art 142 325
    Art 263 325
    Art 303 325
Criminal Code 1109
    Art 25 1109
Law of 22 February 2000 'On the Introduction
    of Amendments to the Criminal,
    Criminal Procedure and Correctional
    Labour Codes of Ukraine' 1109
Law 'On the ratification of Protocol No. 6
    to the Convention for the Protection
    of Human Rights and Fundamental
    Freedoms concerning the abolition
    of the death penalty, of 1983' 1109

United Kingdom

Act for Regulating the Privie Councell
    and for taking away the Court
    commonly called the Star Chamber,
    1640, 16 Car. c.10
    s 1 220
Age of Legal Capacity (Scotland)
    Act 1991 (c.50) 240
Bill of Rights 1688 444
Death Penalty Act 1965 1095
Education Acts 1006
Magna Carta, 1225, 9 Hen. 3, c. 30
    Art 39 220
Terrorism Act 2000 597

United States

Constitution 444
    Art I, s. 9 220
    Art 4 385
    First Amendment 444,
                                      452, 483
    Fourth Amendment 358
    Fifth Amendment 1147

List of Abbreviations

AJIL	*American Journal of International Law*
DR	Decisions and Reports [of the European Commission on Human Rights]
EHRLR	*European Human Rights Law Review*
EJIL	*European Journal of International Law*
ETS	European Treaty Series
Frowein/Peukert, *MenschenRechtsKonvention*	Jochen Abr. Frowein and Wolfgang Peukert, *Europäische MenschenRechtsKonvention, EMRK-Kommentar*, 3rd edn, Kehl am Rhein, Germany: N.P. Engel, 2009
Grabenwarter, *European Convention*	Christoph Grabenwarter, *European Convention on Human Rights, Commentary*, Munich/Oxford/Baden-Baden: C.H. Beck/Hart/Nomos, 2014
Harris et al., *Law of the European Convention*	David Harris, Michael O'Boyle, Ed Bates, and Carla Buckley, *Law of the European Convention on Human Rights*, 2nd edn, Oxford: Oxford University Press, 2009
HRLJ	*Human Rights Law Journal*
HRLR	*Human Rights Law Review*
ICLQ	*International and Comparative Law Quarterly*
ILR	International Law Reports
IMT	Trial of the Major War Criminals before the International Military Tribunal, Nuremberg, 14 November 1945–1 October 1946
LNTS	League of Nations Treaty Series
LRTWC	Law Reports of the Trials of the War Criminals
Macdonald, *The European System*	Ronald St J. Macdonald, F. Matscher, and H. Petzold, eds, *The European System for the Protection of Human* Rights, Dordrecht: Martinus Nijhoff, 1993
Mahoney et al., *Mélanges Ryssdal*	Paul Mahoney, Franz Matscher, Herbert Petzold, and Luzius Wildhaber, eds, *Protection des droits de l'homme: La perspective européenne. Mélanges à la mémoire de Rolf Ryssdal*, Cologne/Berlin/Bonn/Munich: Carl Heymanns, 2000
OASTS	Organisation of American States Treaty Series
Ovey/White, *Jacobs and White, European Convention*	Claire Ovey and Robin White, *Jacobs and White, The European Convention on Human Rights*, 3rd edn, Oxford: Oxford University Press, 2002
Pettiti et al., *La Convention européenne*	Louis-Edmond Pettiti, Emmanuel Decaux, and Pierrre-Henri Imbert, eds, *La Convention européenne des droits de l'homme, Commentaire article par article*, 2nd edn, Paris: Economica, 1999
RTDH	*Revue trimestrielle des droits de l'homme*
SCR	Supreme Court Reports (Canada)

TP	Collected Edition of the '*Travaux préparatoires*' of the European Convention on Human Rights
TS	Treaty Series
TWC	Trials of War Criminals before the Nurenberg Military Tribunals
UNTS	United Nations Treaty Series
van Dijk et al., *Theory and Practice*	Pieter van Dijk, Fried van Hoof, Arjen van Rijn, and Leo Zwaak, eds, *Theory and Practice of the European Convention on Human Rights*, 4th edn, Antwerp and Oxford: Intersentia, 2006
YB	Yearbook of the European Convention on Human Rights
ZACC	Constitutional Court of South Africa

PART ONE

INTRODUCTION

The European Convention on Human Rights was the first comprehensive treaty for the protection of human rights to emerge from the post-Second-World-War law-making process. The honour of being the first post-war human rights treaty might actually be accorded to the Convention on the Prevention and Punishment of the Crime of Genocide, adopted by the United Nations General Assembly on 9 December 1948.[1] But the Genocide Convention addresses a single manifestation of human rights violation and it is in many ways more akin to an international criminal law treaty, in that its main features are the definition of a crime and the identification of related obligations concerning its punishment. Adopted on 5 November 1950, the European Convention—its full name, rarely used today, does not even contain the adjective 'European': 'Convention for the Protection of Human Rights and Fundamental Freedoms'—provides a list and definitions of several core human rights. It is far from comprehensive, its drafters having taken a very deliberate decision to exclude so-called economic and social rights. The Convention's focus is largely on rights derived from national constitutions inspired by the ideas of Enlightenment.

The most significant normative influence on the drafters of the Convention was the Universal Declaration of Human Rights, a resolution of the United Nations General Assembly adopted on 10 December 1948.[2] Prominent Europeans participated in the preparation of the Universal Declaration, first and foremost the French jurist René Cassin. Later, Cassin served as a judge and as President of the European Court of Human Rights. It was on Cassin's insistence that the name of the Declaration was changed from 'international' to 'universal' in the final stages of the General Assembly's work in 1948.[3] The adoption of the Universal Declaration was in one sense premature because the initial intent of the United Nations had been to prepare a package of instruments, one of them a manifesto or declaration and the other a treaty or covenant, together with mechanisms for implementation of human rights. Collectively, these are referred to as the International Bill of Rights.[4] Although the work on these projects went on simultaneously, sometimes within

---

[1] Convention on the Prevention and Punishment of the Crime of Genocide, (1951) 78 UNTS 277.

[2] Universal Declaration of Human Rights, GA Res. 217 A (III), UN Doc. A/810.

[3] UN Doc. A/C.3/339; *Official Records of the General Assembly*, Third Session, 1948, pp. 742, 759–60, 786. Credit for the first use of the term 'universal declaration of human rights' belongs, however, to a member of the Commission on the Status of Women, Evdokia Uralova of the Byelorussian Soviet Socialist Republic: UN Doc. E/CN.6/SR.36/Corr.1, p. 1.

[4] Report of the Preparatory Commission of the United Nations, UN Doc. PC/20, para. 16(a); Report of the Committee on the Organisation of the Economic and Social Council, UN Doc. E/20, Resolution (Commission on Human Rights). For the Economic and Social Council, see UN Doc. E/27, para. 2(a). For the Nuclear Commission on Human Rights, see UN Doc. E/38, p. 6, para. 1.

distinct working groups of the Commission on Human Rights,[5] by mid-1948 it had become clear that the Universal Declaration was nearing completion while the other instruments required more work and consultation. The General Assembly chose to forge on with adoption of the Universal Declaration, insisting that the United Nations Commission on Human Rights pursue its work on the other components of the Universal Bill of Rights. In 1949, the Commission on Human Rights made considerable headway on a draft covenant on human rights. That text, together with the International Declaration adopted the previous December, provided the European negotiators with model provisions on which their own convention was to be based.

[5] Report of the Fifth Session of the Commission on Human Rights to the Economic and Social Council, UN Doc. E/1371(Supp.), annex.

Adoption of the Convention

The origins of the European Convention on Human Rights and of a Court with the jurisdiction to adjudicate complaints filed by individuals against their own governments date to the Congress of Europe convened in The Hague in May 1948 by the International Committee of Movements for European Unity. The Congress issued a 'Message to Europeans' that included the following:

2. We desire a Charter of Human Rights guaranteeing liberty of thought, assembly and expression as well as the right to form a political opposition;
3. We desire a Court of Justice with adequate sanctions for the implementation of this Charter...

The Congress also adopted a resolution expressing its conviction that a European Assembly 'should make proposals for the establishment of a Court of Justice with adequate sanctions for the implementation of this Charter [of Human Rights], and to this end any citizen of the associated countries shall have redress before the Court, at any time and with the least possible delay, of any violation of his rights as formulated in the Charter'.[1] The International Council of the European Movement met in Brussels in February 1949, adopting recommendations on human rights that also included proposals on the European Court.[2]

The Council of Europe was founded on 5 May 1949 by the Treaty of London. The Statute of the Council of Europe was signed in London on that day by ten states: Belgium, Denmark, France, Ireland, Italy, Luxembourg, the Netherlands, Norway, Sweden, and the United Kingdom. Much like the Charter of the United Nations, although the Statute of the Council of Europe leaves no doubt about a commitment to human rights, it does not offer any real insight into the substance of the subject. There had been an unsuccessful proposal to integrate a declaration of human rights within the Statute of the Council of Europe.[3] The Preparatory Commission for the Council of Europe met in Paris from 11 May to 13 July 1949. One of its tasks was the adoption of a draft agenda for the Council's Consultative Assembly. The initial proposal contained an item labelled '[m]aintenance and further realisation of human rights a fundamental freedoms'.[4] It was agreed that this item should be included 'out of consideration for a particular provision in Article I(b) of the Statute'. The Commission's Report noted that although most countries represented 'have subscribed to the Universal Declaration of Human Rights' it was useful to keep the

---

[1] Ed Bates, *The Evolution of the European Convention on Human Rights*, Oxford: Oxford University Press, 2010, at p. 49.

[2] Recommendations adopted at the meeting of the International Council of the European Movement held at Brussels in February 1949, INF/2/F, p. 3. This is reproduced in CDH (67) 5, at pp. 2–3, with the indication that the original English version no longer exists.

[3] Elisabeth Steiner, 'Some Reflections on the Process Which Led to the Preparation of the European Convention on Human Rights (ECHR)', in Dean Spielmann, Marialena Tsirli, and Panayotis Voyatzis, eds, *La Convention européenne des droits de l'homme, un instrument vivant, Mélanges en l'honneur de Christos L. Rozakis*, Brussels: Bruylant, 2011, pp. 597–623, at p. 617.

[4] 18th meeting [of the Preparatory Commission for the Council of Europe]—5 July 1949, I *TP* 2.

point on the agenda because 'two of the member States of the Council do not yet belong
to the United Nations'.[5]

Consultative Assembly, 1949

Meeting in August of that year, the Consultative Assembly of the Council considered the
drafting of a convention on human rights. At the time, the Consultative Assembly was
described as a 'unique' organ, 'something between the two extremes of an interparlia-
mentary union and a federal parliament'.[6] Its delegates represented much of the political
spectrum that prevailed in post-war western Europe, although there is no evidence of
participation from the communist parties that were relatively strong in countries like
France and Italy. The contrast is striking with the debates about the codification of
human rights within the United Nations, where there were sharp disagreements between
political blocs aligned with the capitalist 'West', the Soviet Union, and the still nascent
'third world'.

The Consultative Assembly based its work upon a draft prepared by the Legal
Committee of the International Council of the European Movement that had been
presented to the Committee of Ministers in July 1949. The draft provided a list of
fundamental rights, derived from the Universal Declaration of Human Rights, but
contemplated their detailed definition in a supplementary instrument that was to be
negotiated, a process that was expected to be 'difficult and protracted'. Petitions concerning alleged breaches of the convention were to be implemented by a 'European Human
Rights Commission' and a 'European Court of Human Rights'.[7]

During late August and early September 1949, the Committee on Legal and Administrative Questions of the Consultative Assembly debated the draft text under the
leadership of its Rapporteur, Pierre-Henri Teitgen. He presented the Committee's report
to the plenary Assembly, where the text was again debated. On 8 September, the
Consultative Assembly adopted a resolution calling upon the Committee of Ministers
to adopt a human rights convention and to create a commission and court for its
implementation. It also adopted a draft convention that was relatively succinct and that
was largely derived from provisions of the Universal Declaration of Human Rights. The
draft convention did not include economic, social, and cultural rights, to the disappointment of several of the more left-wing members of the Assembly. There was an unresolved
debate about whether to include the right to property and the right of parents to
determine the education of their children, set out in articles 17 and 26(3), respectively,
of the Universal Declaration of Human Rights.[8]

---

[5] 25th meeting [of the Preparatory Commission for the Council of Europe]—13 July 1949, I *TP* 6.

[6] A.H. Robertson, 'The Council of Europe, 1949–1953-I', (1954) 7 *ICLQ* 235, at p. 235.

[7] Convention for the collective protection of individual rights and democratic liberties by the States,
Members of the Council of Europe, and for the establishment of a European Court of Human Rights to
ensure observance of the Convention, Doc. INF/5/E/R, I *TP* 296–303. See Ed Bates, *The Evolution of the
European Convention on Human Rights*, Oxford: Oxford University Press, 2010, at pp. 51–8.

[8] Ed Bates, *The Evolution of the European Convention on Human Rights*, Oxford: Oxford University Press,
2010, at pp. 58–74.

Committee of Experts

The Committee of Ministers of the Council of Europe met in November 1949 and decided to convene a Committee of Experts for the purposes of advancing the work on the draft, 'paying due attention to the progress which had been achieved in this matter by the competent organs of the United Nations'.[9] This did not sit well with the Consultative Assembly, whose Standing Committee adopted a resolution objecting to the approach taken by the Committee of Ministers. The Standing Committee said that 'it would be regrettable if this Committee [of Experts] was to be given a mandate to undertake the study of the question *ab initio*; the more so since the Assembly's draft was in fact based on work done by the United Nations'.[10]

Nevertheless, the Committee of Experts met in February and March 1950. In fact, there were few 'experts' in international human rights law at the time, at least in the sense that we now understand this notion. Virtually all of the names of the participants are unrecognizable to scholars and jurists working in the field of human rights today. By and large, they were functionaries within foreign ministries, politicians, and academics, perhaps with some knowledge of public international law in a general sense.[11] The few important Europeans whose names are familiar because of their participation in the debates during the 1940s surrounding the adoption of the Universal Declaration of Human Rights and their authorship of serious doctrinal studies—Hersch Lauterpacht, René Cassin, Charles de Visscher—were apparently not called upon by their governments to assist in drafting the Convention. Another distinguishing feature is the total absence of women from the Committee of Experts. Indeed, there is no evidence in the *travaux préparatoires* of any significant involvement of women in the drafting of the European Convention. By contrast, one of the very important features of the drafting of the Universal Declaration of Human Rights was the participation of women. The United Nations Commission on Human Rights was chaired by a woman, Eleanor Roosevelt, and her name is best known, but many other women—Hansa Mehta, Bodil Begtrup, Jessie Street, Minerva Bernardino, to name only a few—participated actively in its drafting through their membership in various United Nations bodies, including the Commission on Human Rights, the Commission on the Status of Women, and the General Assembly.

The Committee of Experts set up by the Committee of Ministers could not agree on the approach to be followed. The difficulty was not about whether to follow the initiatives already taken in the United Nations but rather about which initiative to follow. The United Nations International Bill of Rights consisted of two distinct instruments: a manifesto or declaration, already adopted as the Universal Declaration of Human Rights, and a convention or covenant, still very much in draft stage. There were two main schools of thought within the Committee of Experts. The first was supportive of the text adopted the previous year by the Consultative Assembly. The provisions setting out fundamental rights were based upon those of the Universal Declaration of Human Rights. The second

---

[9] Letter addressed on 18 November 1949 by the Secretary General to the Ministers for Foreign Affairs of the Member States, Ref. D 26/2/49, II *TP* 302–5.

[10] Letter addressed by Mr Paul Henri Spaak, President of the Consultative Assembly to Mr Gustave Rasmussen, Chairman of the Committee of Ministers, 10 November 1949, Doc. AS/CP/PV (1) 2/5, A 514, II *TP* 298–301.

[11] For the list, see List of experts who attended the first meeting [of the Committee of Experts], Doc. A 814, III *TP* 178–80.

school, of which the United Kingdom was the most prominent member, took the view that 'the fundamental rights to be safeguarded, and, even more important, the limitations of these rights, should be defined in as detailed a manner as possible'.[12] Its reference was the much more detailed draft treaty or covenant then being considered by the United Nations Commission on Human Rights. France and the Netherlands felt that if the United Kingdom's approach were to be followed, the work on drafting the European convention ought to be suspended until the United Nations had concluded its work,[13] a view that thankfully was not accepted because the United Nations texts were only adopted in 1966. The Committee of Experts agreed that it was impossible to reconcile the two approaches 'since the systems on which these two drafts were based were essentially different'.[14] Therefore, it submitted both drafts to the Committee of Ministers, inviting it to take a decision on the model to be followed. The text based on the Universal Declaration of Human Rights, and described as 'Enumeration of Human Rights', was labelled Alternative A. The text that was derived from the British draft, characterized as 'Definition of Human Rights', was labelled Alternative B. In fact, each of the two Alternatives had two variants. Alternatives A and B were premised on a system with both a Commission and a Court, while for Alternatives A/2 and B/2 there was a Commission but no Court.

Regardless of the approach to be taken, it is clear that those who drafted the European Convention devoted little interest to the content of the fundamental rights. With some exceptions, they were generally content to rely upon the conclusions reached within the United Nations Commission on Human Rights and the General Assembly as to the substance of the rights and their formulation. There was an important debate with the Consultative Assembly about whether to include economic and social rights. But when it came to the definitions of the rights, something on which the United Nations organs had laboured intensively, there was almost no debate during the drafting of the European Convention. The most controversial rights were the three that were left out of the Convention itself, although they were incorporated in Protocol No. 1, adopted the following year. The debates about defining those three rights consumed more time and energy than all of the substantive rights in the Convention itself taken together.

The real focus of the attention of the Committee of Experts was on the mechanisms for implementation of the Convention. The initial idea, advanced by the Congress of Europe at its meeting in The Hague in 1948, was for a human rights court. The idea had been actually been mooted within the United Nations as part of the early discussions about the International Bill of Rights. Just as it proved difficult to secure any consensus in New York, the proposal for a fully fledged court was also controversial in Europe. In order to answer critics who said the court would be overwhelmed by frivolous claims and abused for political aims, the suggestion emerged that a human rights commission also be

---

[12] Report to the Committee of Ministers Submitted by the Committee of Experts Instructed to Draw Up a Draft Convention of Collective Guarantee of Human Rights and WP 1 (5) 15, A 924/WP 1 (5) 15, A 924, IV *TP* 2–55, at p. 8. See Geoffrey Marston, 'The United Kingdom's Part in the Preparation of the European Convention on Human Rights, 1950', (1993) 42 *ICLQ* 796.

[13] Report to the Committee of Ministers Submitted by the Committee of Experts Instructed to Draw Up a Draft Convention of Collective Guarantee of Human Rights and Fundamental Freedoms, Doc. CM/WP 1 (5) 15, A 924, IV *TP* 2–55, at p. 12. Also Amendments to the Report of the Committee, Doc. CN/WP 1 (50) 6, A 907, III *TP* 304; Amendments proposed by the French expert, Doc. CM/WP 1 (50) 8, A 909, III *TP* 304–7.

[14] Report to the Committee of Ministers Submitted by the Committee of Experts Instructed to Draw Up a Draft Convention of Collective Guarantee of Human Rights and Fundamental Freedoms, Doc. CM/WP 1 (5) 15, A 924, IV *TP* 2–55, at p. 16.

established. The idea of a commission proved to be less controversial than a court. The Committee of Ministers suggested two alternative systems, one with a court and one without. The package was complex: a European Commission of Human Rights with authority to deal with the admissibility of petitions, fact-finding, the encouragement of friendly settlement, and jurisdiction to provide an opinion on whether there was a violation of the substantive provisions of the Convention; a Court empowered to make final, binding judgments on cases referred to it by the Commission or by a State Party; and the Committee of Ministers, also entitled to provide a final and binding decision with respect to cases that could not be or were not referred to the Court.

Conference of Senior Officials

The Committee of Experts submitted its report and the two drafts to the Committee of Ministers. The latter decided to convene a Conference of Senior Officials whose mandate would be to finalize a draft proposal. When the Conference of Senior Officials met in June 1950, it was fairly evenly divided between partisans of the two alternative approaches, with France, Ireland, Italy, and Turkey favouring the 'enumeration' approach based on the Universal Declaration of Human Rights and Greece, Norway, the Netherlands, and the United Kingdom championing much more detailed provisions containing definitions.[15] It was also split on the desirability of establishing a Court, although the majority was opposed to the idea.[16] The two ideas were somewhat linked because both Belgium and Luxembourg said that if a Court were created they would prefer enumeration, whereas if it were not they favoured definition.[17] The Conference agreed to set up a drafting committee whose task was 'to improve alternative B by including certain provisions from alternative A' and to incorporate any new amendments that had already been adopted.[18] In substance, the Conference opted for the much more detailed approach to definition of rights favoured by the British. The result was 'submitted to the Committee of Ministers as a compromise suggestion, supported by the majority of the Conference'.[19] The compromise was subsequently endorsed by the Committee on Legal and Administrative Questions of the Consultative Assembly at its meeting held later in June 1950.[20]

[15] Draft report to the Committee of Ministers, Doc. CM/WP 4 (50) 16, A 1426, IV *TP* 204–17, at p. 210; Text of the report submitted by the Conference to the Committee of Ministers, Doc. CM/WP 4 (50) 19, CM/WP 4 (50) 16 rev., A 1431, IV *TP* 242–73, at p. 248. Also, e.g., Minutes of the morning sitting [of 9 June 1950 of the Conference of Senior Officials], Doc. CM/WP 4 (50) 3, IV *TP* 110–19, at p. 112; Minutes of the morning sitting [of 10 June 1950 of the Conference of Senior Officials] (unreferenced document], IV *TP* 132–41, at p. 132.
[16] Minutes of the morning sitting [of 10 June 1950 of the Converence of Senior Officials] (unreferenced document), IV *TP* 132–41, at p. 132.
[17] Draft report to the Committee of Ministers, Doc. CM/WP 4 (50) 16, A 1426, IV *TP* 204–17. See also, e.g., Minutes of the morning sitting [of 12 June 1950] (unreferenced document, IV *TP* 164–71, at p. 168; Minutes of the afternoon sitting [of 12 June 1950] (unreferenced document), IV *TP* 170–81.
[18] Minutes of the afternoon sitting [of 12 June 1950] (unreferenced document), IV *TP* 170–81, at p. 176. See the discussion of the general approach of the Committee with respect to enumeration and definition: Text of the report submitted by the Conference to the Committee of Ministers, Doc. CM/WP 4 (50) 19, CM/WP 4 (50) 16 rev., A 1431, IV *TP* 242–73, at p. 258.
[19] Text of the report submitted by the Conference to the Committee of Ministers, Doc. CM/WP 4 (50) 19, CM/WP 4 (50) 16 rev., A 1431, IV *TP* 242–73, at p. 248.
[20] Minutes of the meeting [of 23 June 1950 of the Committee on Legal and Administrative Questions of the Consultative Assembly], Doc. AS/JA (2) PV I, A 1840, V *TP* 2–11, at p. 8; Draft of a letter to the Chairman of the Committee of Ministers, Doc. AS/JA (2) 2, A 1579, V *TP* 10–15, at pp. 10–12.

Final stages

The Committee of Ministers met in early August to finalize the draft Convention. Agreement had already been reached on the definition of the substantive rights with the exception of property, education, and free elections. The heart of the debate concerned the means of enforcement. Strong opposition remained to the creation of the Court as well as to the existence of a right of individual petition. The Committee of Ministers found a compromise by means of two distinct optional clauses. The first recognized a right of individual petition to the European Commission on Human Rights, but only if the State Party to the Convention had accepted this by means of a separate declaration. The second acknowledged the jurisdiction of the European Court of Human Rights, provided, once again, that this had been agreed to by the State Party through a declaration.

The draft adopted by the Committee of Ministers was then transmitted to the Consultative Assembly for its renewed consideration. The Consultative Assembly recommended that the draft be amended so as to include recognition of the right to property, the rights of parents to determine the education of their children, and the right to free elections. It did not reconsider the decisions of the Committee of Ministers to adopt the 'definition' approach rather than the 'enumeration' approach that the Assembly had favoured a year earlier. Speaking to the point, Pierre-Henri Teitgen lamented the decision, noting that '[t]he definitions put forward by the British might well be very dangerous, indeed, if they were to be taken as restrictive, for it is extremely difficult to list all the possibilities contained in a single freedom and all those excluded therefrom'.[21] In an attempt to correct the problem, Teitgen proposed an additional article for the Convention, declaring that it be interpreted in light of 'general principles of law recognised by civilised nations'.[22] The Assembly's Committee on Legal and Administrative Questions did not take up his idea.[23] In the Consultative Assembly, David Maxwell Fyfe urged adoption of the Convention as 'a beacon to our friends who are now in the darkness of totalitarianism' and as 'a passport for the return of their countries into our midst'.[24] There was also much dismay among the members of the Consultative Assembly with the decision to relegate the right of individual petition to an optional clause.

Adoption and entry into force

The Committee of Ministers proceeded with the adoption of the text but without most of the changes proposed by the Consultative Assembly. These were referred to a committee of experts for consideration, the suggestion being that they should be incorporated subsequently in a protocol. On 4 November 1950, the Convention was signed by all but two of the Member States of the Council of Europe in the Barberini Palace in Rome.

---

[21] Report of the Sitting [of 16 August 1950], V *TP* 272–351, at pp. 282–4.

[22] Ibid., p. 286; Original Draft, 16 August 1950, Doc. AS/JA (2) 6, A 2207, VI *TP* 6–11, at p. 8; Revised Text, 17 August 1950, Doc. AS/JA (2) 6 rev., A 2238, VI *TP* 10–15, at p. 12.

[23] First Report [of the Committee on Legal and Administrative Questions], Doc. AS/JA (2) 15, A 2298, VI *TP* 46–52, at p. 50; Second Report [of the Committee on Legal and Administrative Questions], Doc. AS/JA (2) rev., A 2493, VI *TP* 52–8, at p. 56; Text of the Report [of the Committee on Legal and Administrative Questions], Doc. AS (2) 93, VI *TP* 58–72, at p. 62.

[24] Report of the Sitting [of the Consultative Assembly, 25 August 1950, morning], VI *TP* 74–143, at p. 82.

According to the memoirs of David Maxwell Fyfe, Paul-Henri Spaak notified him of the signing ceremony in the following terms: 'It is not a very good Convention, but it is a lovely Palace.' Inevitably, some were disappointed with the political compromises that led to omissions in the Convention. Maxwell Fyfe was more positive than Spaak, believing that 'we had succeeded in doing what the United Nations had failed to do, namely to create an enforceable convention guaranteeing democratic rights'.[25] Later that month, Greece and Sweden also signed the Convention. The first ratification, by the United Kingdom, was submitted on 8 March 1951. On 3 September 1953, Luxembourg became the tenth State to ratify the Convention, bringing with it the entry into force of treaty.

With the Convention in force, the Committee of Ministers elected the initial members of the European Commission of Human Rights in May 1954. The Commission held its first session in July 1954. At the time, it had no individual applications to consider because the 1950 text of the Convention required a separate declaration by States for the individual petition mechanism. However, no such declaration was required for inter-State complaints. On 7 May 1956, the first such application was filed. It was submitted by Greece against the United Kingdom concerning the application of the Convention in Cyprus.[26] The Commission issued a report on the first of the applications in 1958. It was critical of British conduct in Cyprus but did not actually conclude that there had been violations of the Convention. The Committee of Ministers decided to take no further action when Greece and the United Kingdom indicated that agreement had been reached on the independence of Cyprus.[27] Greece had also filed a second application against the United Kingdom about Cyprus.[28] The Commission's report was not finished at the time of the independence agreement. The Committee of Ministers treated it in the same way as the first application. A report on the second application was not completed because Greece settled the case with the United Kingdom.[29] The third inter-State application was filed by Austria against Italy, in 1960, with regard to the rights of German-speaking residents in the Süd Tirol/Alto Adige. The Commission did not conclude that the Convention had been violated.[30]

The right of individual application came into force on 5 July 1955. Almost immediately, individual applications began to be lodged at the headquarters of the Council of Europe in Strasbourg, although at a rate that seems paltry by comparison with the present day. Between the entry into force of the procedure and the end of 1957, 343 individual applications were filed with the Commission, an average of about 31 per month.[31] In 1958 and 1959, 329 applications were registered, a slight quickening of the pace.[32] The vast majority of these early applications were declared inadmissible on such grounds as failure to exhaust domestic remedies and lack of temporal jurisdiction. By 1958, the

---

[25] David Maxwell Fyfe, *Political Adventure, The Memoirs of the Earl of Kilmuir*, London: Weidenfeld and Nicolson, 1964, pp. 183–4.
[26] *Greece v. the United Kingdom*, no. 176/56, Commission decision of 2 June 1956, (1958–59) 2 YB 182. Also (1955–56–57) 1 YB 128–30; (1958–59) 2 YB 174–81.
[27] Resolution (59) 12, 20 April 1959.
[28] *Greece v. the United Kingdom*, no. 299/57, Commission decision of 12 October 1957, (1958–59) 2 YB 186. Also (1955–56–57) 1 YB 128–30; (1958–59) 2 YB 174–81.
[29] Resolution (59) 32, 14 December 1959.
[30] *Austria v. Italy*, no. 788/60, Commission decision of 11 January 1961, (1961) 4 YB 116; *Austria v. Italy*, no. 788/60, Commission report of 31 March 1963, (1963) 6 YB 740.
[31] (1955–56–57) 1 YB 132.
[32] (1958–59) 2 YB 202.

Commission had begun to rule that certain applications were admissible.[33] In 1960, the Commission referred cases to the European Court of Human Rights, which had only just become operational. The Court issued its first judgment, dismissing the respondent State's objections to admissibility in *Lawless v. Ireland* and deciding to proceed to examine the case on the merits.[34]

---

[33] *De Becker v. Belgium*, no. 214/56, Commission decision of 9 June 1958, (1958–59) 2 YB 214; *Lawless v. Ireland*, no. 332/57, Commission decision of 30 August 1958, (1958–59) 2 YB 308.

[34] *Lawless v. Ireland (no. 1)*, 14 November 1960, Series A no. 1.

Adding new rights to the Convention

Those who drafted the European Convention, in 1949 and 1950, never intended it to be an exhaustive codification of fundamental rights. This can be seen in the final recital of the Preamble to the Convention, which speaks of the inclusion of 'certain of the rights stated in the Universal Declaration'. Since the adoption of the Convention, the catalogue of substantive rights that it sets out has been supplemented by six Protocols. Some of the Protocols add new rights, reflecting developments outside the Council of Europe whereby certain norms were deemed to be part of the core entitlement of fundamental freedoms. Two of them reflect changing views within the Council of Europe and also more broadly about the compatibility of capital punishment, whose exercise was reserved as an exception to the right to life in article 2 of the Convention, with international law, human dignity, and the prohibition of ill treatment. At various times, the Council of Europe has also considered the adoption of protocols to the Convention dealing with the rights of national minorities, the rights of persons deprived of their freedom,[1] protection of the environment, and the inclusion of a fundamental right to equality between men and women.[2] Perhaps it will return to these ideas with future initiatives.

The six protocols that set out new rights within the Convention system are additional in nature in that they require ratification by States that are already party to the Convention. They do not amend the Convention as such. They have entered into force after acceptance by a relatively limited number of States Parties. Even Protocol No. 1 has not been ratified by all of the States Parties to the Convention. The consequence is a rather complex legal situation whereby the Convention itself and Protocol No. 1 applies to all States, subject to the occasional reservation, but the amending protocols apply in a somewhat piecemeal fashion. Fewer than half of the States Parties to the Convention have ratified all of the additional protocols.

Protocol No. 1: Property, education, elections

The first of the additional instruments was adopted in March 1952, very shortly after the Convention itself. It is technically known as the 'Protocol' because there were no others at the time. It was ordinarily referred to as the 'First Protocol' until the 1990s and since then as 'Protocol No. 1'. Three rights were added to the Convention system by Protocol No. 1: the right to property, the rights of parents with respect to the education of their children, and the right to free elections. All of them were inspired by provisions in the Universal Declaration of Human Rights.

When the Convention was adopted in November 1950, the Consultative Assembly had expressed considerable outrage at the absence in the Convention of provisions concerning the right to property, to education, and to democratic elections. However, despite the proposals included in the draft Convention that the Assembly endorsed in August 1950,

---

[1] (1993) 36 YB 447; (1994) 37 YB 506; (1995) 38 YB 969; (1996) 39 YB 594.
[2] (1994) 37 YB 505; (1995) 38 YB 969, 971; (1996) 39 YB 594, 598.

the Committee of Ministers did not include these rights in the final version. Complaining that the original draft convention prepared by the Assembly had been 'curiously emasculated' by the expert bodies in 1950,[3] Pierre-Henri Teitgen blamed the British for the omissions, charging that within the Committee of Ministers 'the will of the majority yields when confronted with one individual veto'.[4]

The Committee of Experts designated by the Committee of Ministers completed a preliminary report on the proposed Protocol in February 1951. It was then instructed by the Committee of Ministers to prepare a draft protocol. The matter returned to the Committee of Experts and further reports were submitted in April 1951 and June 1951. In July 1951, the Ministers' Advisers adopted the draft protocol prepared by the Committee of Experts and referred it to the Consultative Assembly for an opinion. The Consultative Assembly considered the subject at its December 1951 meeting, proposing some changes to the draft that were in turn accepted by the Committee of Ministers. In March 1952, the fifteen Member States of the Council of Europe signed the Protocol. It entered into force on 18 May 1953 with the tenth ratification, that of Turkey.

Protocol No. 4: Mainly movement and migration

As early as 1958, inspired by the work of the United Nations Congress on the Prevention of Crime and the Treatment of Offenders, the Consultative Assembly began work on a second protocol to the Convention by which new rights would be added.[5] Several rights were considered, all of them appearing in the current draft of the United Nations International Covenant on Civil and Political Rights: freedom from imprisonment on the ground of inability to fulfil a contractual obligation; freedom of movement; freedom to choose one's residence; freedom to emigrate; prohibition of arbitrary exile; the right to enter one's own country; prohibition of arbitrary expulsion; the right to recognition everywhere as a person before the law; right of access on general terms of equality to public services in one's country; equality before the law (as opposed to equality in the exercise of rights and freedoms enshrined in the Convention, something assured by article 14); the right of minorities to their own cultural life.[6]

In January 1960, the Consultative Assembly formally adopted its proposal for a 'second protocol'.[7] It had dropped several of the rights from its initial ambitious proposal. It removed the right of equal access to the public service.[8] The Court has since observed that

---

[3] Reports of the Consultative Assembly, 2nd Session, Part III, 22nd sitting, pp. 674–5, VII *TP* 90–121, at p. 92.

[4] Ibid., p. 96. See also Ed Bates, *The Evolution of the European Convention on Human Rights*, Oxford: Oxford University Press, 2010, at pp. 6–10.

[5] Report submitted, on behalf of Sub-Committee No. 10 (Penal Reform) by Mr Hale, Rapporteur, 20 August 1958.

[6] Preliminary Report by M. Lannung, Rapporteur, 21 August 1958, Doc. AS/Jur XII (10) 1; Minutes of the meeting [of the Legal Committee, Consultative Assembly], held on 9 and 10 June 1958, Doc. AS/Jur (10) PV 2 Revised; Minutes of the meeting [of the Legal Committee, Sub-Committee No. 12 (Human Rights), Consultative Assembly], held on Tuesday 16 September, 1958, Doc. AS/Jur XII (10) PV 1.

[7] Recommendation 234 (1960), 22 January 1960.

[8] See Preparatory Work on the Draft Second Protocol to the Convention on Human Rights. Appended to Recommendation 234 (1960) of the Consultative Assembly. XII. Omission from the draft of a clause regarding 'access on general terms of equality to public service in his country'. Memorandum by the Directorate of Human Rights, DX/Exp (20) 21, 4 November 1960.

the drafting history of the Protocol shows 'unequivocally' that the Member States of the Council of Europe did not wish to recognize a right of access to public service similar to that of article 21(2) of the Universal Declaration of Human Rights and article 25 of the International Covenant on Civil and Political Rights.[9] A text recognizing the rights of minorities to enjoy their culture was also eliminated from the draft adopted by the Consultative Assembly in 1960.[10] The rapporteur, Hermod Lannung, said the draft was 'not of much help' and he reminded delegates that 'the proposal had been made that the matter be dealt with in a separate international instrument'.[11]

The Assembly recommended that a Committee of Experts be convened by the Committee of Ministers in order to develop the text and produce a definitive version. The Committee of Ministers agreed to set up a Committee of Governmental Experts with instructions to study problems relating to the European Convention on Human Rights.[12] Chaired by an Italian expert, Ugo Caldarera, sessions of the Committee of Experts were held from late 1960 to early 1963. The list of rights in the Protocol was further reduced. Equality before the law had been included in the 1960 draft of the Consultative Assembly. Adopted 'tentatively' by the Committee of Experts at its first meeting,[13] it was later dropped from the draft text, only to reappear decades later in Protocol No. 12. The Committee of Experts also rejected the idea of a provision on the right to recognition as a person under the law, modelled on article 6 of the Universal Declaration of Human Rights.[14]

In the meantime, the Consultative Assembly returned to the subject of minority rights a year later with a recommendation that the Protocol contain a provision based on the following text: 'Persons belonging to a national minority shall not be denied the right, in community with the other members of their group, and as far as compatible with public order, to enjoy their own culture, to use their own language, to establish their own schools and receive teaching in the language of their choice or to profess and practise their own religion.'[15] The initiative was obviously inspired by the adoption of article 27 of the draft International Covenant on Civil and Political Rights by the relevant United Nations organs, although it actually went further, adding the right of minorities 'to establish their own schools and receive teaching in the language of their choice'. The Committee of Experts did not agree, excluding minority rights from the text.

---

[9] *Glasenapp v. Germany*, 28 August 1986, § 48, Series A no. 104; *Kosiek v. Germany*, 28 August 1986, § 34, Series A no. 105.

[10] See Preparatory Work on the Draft Second Protocol to the Convention on Human Rights. Appended to Recommendation 234 (1960) of the Consultative Assembly. XIII. Omission from the draft of a clause regarding 'the right of minorities to enjoy their own culture'. Memorandum by the Directorate of Human Rights, DX/Exp (20) 23 and Appendix I to V, 4 November 1960.

[11] Doc. AS/Jur XII (11) PV 1, 25 August 1959, p. 6.

[12] Resolution (60) 6, 22 March 1960.

[13] Doc. DH/Exp (60) 27, 10 February 1961, para. 6(5).

[14] Memorandum by the Human Rights Directorate on the proceedings of the Committee's first meeting, 7–11 November 1960, DX/Exp (60) 27, 10 February 1961, paras 58–60.

[15] Recommendation 285, 28 April 1961. See A.H. Robertson, 'The United Nations International Covenant on Civil and Political Rights and the European Convention on Human Rights', (1968–69) 32 *British Yearbook of International Law* 21, at p. 33; H. Lannung, 'The Rights of Minorities', in *Mélanges offerts à Polys Modinos— Problèmes des droits de l'homme et de l'unification européenne*, Paris: Pedone, 1968, pp. 181–95; C. Hillgruber and M. Jestaedt, *The European Convention on Human Rights and the Protection of National Minorities*, Cologne: Verlag Wissenschaft und Politik, 1994.

The Committee of Experts presented its final text to the Committee of Ministers in early 1963. As the work on the 'second protocol' had advanced, two other Protocols dealing with legal and procedural matters were conceived and adopted.[16] Consequently, what had been proposed as the 'second protocol' in 1960 was eventually adopted as Protocol No. 4.[17] An Explanatory Report prepared by the Committee of Experts accompanied it. The Explanatory Report compared the draft of the Consultative Assembly with that proposed by the Committee of Experts, providing additional comments on the provisions and reflecting some individual comments. The Explanatory Report does not offer any guidance as to its own legal significance. Subsequently, explanatory reports to Protocols to the Convention contain the following caveat: 'The text of the explanatory report prepared by the Steering Committee for Human Rights and submitted to the Committee of Ministers of the Council of Europe does not constitute an instrument providing an authoritative interpretation of the text of the Protocol, although it might be of such a nature as to facilitate the understanding of the provisions contained therein.'

Protocol No. 4 was adopted by the Committee of Ministers and opened for signature and ratification on 16 September 1963. It entered into force on 2 May 1968 as a consequence of the fifth ratification.

Protocol No. 6 and Protocol No. 13: The death penalty

Two additional Protocols to the European Convention concern capital punishment. The first of them, Protocol No. 6, was adopted in 1983. Although article 2 of the European Convention recognized capital punishment as an exception to the right to life, subsequent human rights treaties in the United Nations and Inter-American systems adopted in the 1960s not only imposed several limitations on the use of the death penalty, but also contemplated the abolition of the practice. Legislation and judicial practice within Council of Europe Member States also evolved rapidly on the subject, making the reference in article 2 increasingly anachronistic.

Within the Council of Europe, the subject of capital punishment first appeared on the agenda of the newly created European Committee on Crime Problems in 1957.[18] In 1962, the Committee created a special sub-committee on the death penalty and named French jurist Marc Ancel as rapporteur, with the mandate to prepare a study on capital punishment in Europe.[19] The European Committee also asked the Centre français de droit comparé to conduct an inquiry on the subject, creating a scientific commission for this purpose. It was understood that the investigation would concern only common law crimes and exclude political and military crimes. Ancel's report concerned the status of capital punishment in the Member States of the Council of Europe, as well as Finland, Monaco, Portugal, San Marino, and Spain. Ancel's study noted that because of political

---

[16] Protocol No. 2 to the Convention for the Protection of Human Rights and Fundamental Freedoms, conferring upon the European Court of Human Rights competence to give advisory opinions, ETS 44; Protocol No. 3 to the Convention for the Protection of Human Rights and Fundamental Freedoms, amending Articles 29, 30, and 34 of the Convention, ETS 45.

[17] The drafting of Protocol No. 4 is reviewed in the Explanatory Report on Protocol No. 4, issued by the Committee of Ministers.

[18] 'Les activités du Comité européen pour les problèmes criminels du Conseil de l'Europe', (1961) 16 *Revue de science criminelle et de droit pénal comparé* n.s. 646, at pp. 646–7.

[19] Marc Ancel, *The Death Penalty in European Countries*, Strasbourg: Council of Europe, 1962.

developments in Europe earlier in the century some abolitionist countries had revived the death penalty, but that it would be an error to consider this as a renunciation of their commitment to abolition.[20] In 1966, the Committee of Ministers decided to discontinue any further study of the consequences of the abolition of the death penalty.[21]

Interest in the death penalty revived in 1973, when the Consultative Assembly of the Council of Europe sent a draft resolution[22] on the abolition of capital punishment to the Legal Affairs Committee.[23] In June 1978, at a meeting of the European Ministers of Justice, the issue of capital punishment was addressed based upon a report presented by Christian Broda, the Austrian Minister of Justice and a well-known abolitionist. The meeting recommended: '. . . that the Committee of Ministers of the Council of Europe refer questions concerning the death penalty to the appropriate Council of Europe bodies for study as part of the Council's work programme, especially in the light of the Austrian memorandum and the exchange of views at the present conference'.[24] Pursuant to this resolution, the issue was then taken up by the European Committee on Crime Problems and by the Steering Committee on Human Rights, which sent a questionnaire on the subject to governments of the Member States.

The European Committee on Crime Problems issued an opinion that noted the widespread abolition of the death penalty *de jure* and recommended that new norms be adopted with a view to abolition. The Steering Committee on Human Rights also prepared an opinion stating that the time had come for the Council of Europe to consider either aligning article 2 of the Convention with the more recent article 4 of the American Convention on Human Rights or simply abolishing the death penalty.

In May 1980, spurred by an announcement the previous year from the Austrian and West German Ministers of Justice, the Conference of European Ministers of Justice noted that article 2 of the European Convention 'does not adequately reflect the situation actually attained in regard to the death penalty in Europe'. It recommended that the Committee of Ministers study the possibility of establishing new norms in Europe that would contemplate abolition of the death penalty. The meeting suggested two solutions: amendment of article 2 of the European Convention, along the lines of similar 'amending' protocols, or adoption of an optional protocol requiring a certain number of ratifications before it would come into force. A 1980 report by the Legal Affairs Committee of the Parliamentary Assembly said that the death penalty was 'inconsistent with the new trends in criminology and criminal law' and that furthermore it was also contrary to human rights law,[25] notably the right to be protected from inhuman and degrading treatment or punishment, as provided by article 3 of the European Convention. The report noted: 'Legally speaking, however, the European Convention on Human Rights does not preclude capital punishment. Article 2 even allows it *expressis verbis*.'[26] The report

---

[20] Ibid., p. 1.
[21] Erik Harremoes, 'L'activité du Comité européen pour les problèmes criminels du Conseil de l'Europe 1966–1974', (1975) 30 *Revue de science criminelle et de droit pénal comparé* 327.
[22] Motion for a resolution on the abolition of capital punishment, Doc. 3297.
[23] Council of Europe, Consultative Assembly, Debates, 18 May 1973, p. 246.
[24] Report of the Legal Affairs Committee, Doc. 4509, Appendix III.
[25] Ibid., para. 23, p. 12.
[26] Ibid., para. 25, p. 13.

concluded that article 2 of the European Convention on Human Rights should be amended in order to abolish capital punishment.[27]

In September 1981, the Committee of Ministers mandated the Steering Committee on Human Rights to prepare a draft protocol concerning abolition of the death penalty 'in time of peace'.[28] At a meeting of Deputies in September 1982, the Steering Committee's draft additional protocol to the Convention was discussed and approved, formally adopting the text of the protocol in December 1982. Protocol No. 6 was opened for signature the following year and entered into force in 1985. The ink on Protocol No. 6 was hardly dry before efforts began to take abolition a decisive step further so as to prohibit capital punishment at all times and in all circumstances.

In 1994, the Parliamentary Assembly of the Council of Europe adopted a resolution calling upon Member States that had not yet done so to ratify Protocol No. 6. The resolution praised Greece, which in 1993 had abolished the death penalty for crimes committed in wartime as well as in peacetime. It stated: 'In view of the irrefutable arguments against the imposition of capital punishment, it calls on the parliaments of all Member States of the Council of Europe, and of all states whose legislative assemblies enjoy special guest status at the Assembly, which retain capital punishment for crimes committed in peacetime and/or in wartime, to strike it from their statute books completely.' It urged all heads of State and all parliaments in whose countries death sentences are passed to grant clemency to the convicted.[29]

On the same date, the Parliamentary Assembly also adopted a recommendation that deplored the fact that the death penalty was still provided by law in eleven Council of Europe Member States and seven States whose legislative assemblies had special status with respect to the organization.[30] The Assembly expressed shock that 59 people were legally put to death in Europe in 1993, and that at least 575 prisoners were known to be awaiting their execution. The Assembly said that application of the death penalty 'may well be compared with torture and be seen as inhuman and degrading punishment within the meaning of Article 3 of the European Convention on Human Rights'. The Recommendation urged the Committee of Ministers to draft an additional protocol to the European Convention on Human Rights, abolishing the death penalty both in peace- and wartime, and obliging the parties not to re-introduce it under any circumstances. The recommendation also proposed establishing a control mechanism that would oblige States where the death penalty was still provided by law to set up a commission with a view to abolishing capital punishment.

The Parliamentary Assembly's 1994 recommendation that a new protocol be adopted, abolishing the death penalty in wartime, was greeted favourably by the Council of Europe's Steering Committee for Human Rights. However, the Committee of Ministers, in its decision of 16 January 1996, considered that the political priority was moratoria on executions, to be consolidated by complete abolition of the death penalty.[31] The idea of a new protocol lingered until the Ministerial Conference, held in Rome on 3–4

---

[27] Ibid., para. 5, p. 22.

[28] Explanatory Report on Protocol No. 6.

[29] Resolution 1044 (1994) on the abolition of capital punishment, 4 October 1994, para. 6.i.

[30] Recommendation 1246 (1994) on the abolition of capital punishment, 4 October 1994.

[31] This point was soon taken up by the Parliamentary Assembly in Recommendation 1302 (1996) on the abolition of the death penalty in Europe, 28 June 1996.

November 2000, to commemorate the fiftieth anniversary of the adoption of the European Convention on Human Rights. A resolution adopted at that meeting invited the Committee of Ministers 'to consider the feasibility of a new additional protocol to the Convention which would exclude the possibility of maintaining the death penalty in respect of acts committed in time of war or of imminent threat of war'.[32]

Sweden took the initiative to prepare the text of a draft Protocol No. 13 whose legal effect would be to neutralize the wartime exception set out in article 2 of Protocol No. 6. Sweden's proposal was presented to the 7 December 2000 meeting of Ministers' Deputies and, a month later, that body instructed the Steering Committee for Human Rights 'to study the Swedish proposal for a new protocol to the Convention . . . and submit its views on the feasibility of a new protocol on this matter'. Using the Swedish proposal as a basis, the Committee asked its Committee of Experts for the Development of Human Rights to finalize a draft protocol and an explanatory report.

The Committee of Experts for the Development of Human Rights addressed this mandate at its June 2001 meeting. There was little disagreement about the substantive and procedural provisions of the Swedish proposal, which essentially replicate Protocol No. 6 except that article 2, which allows for capital punishment in time of war and imminent threat of war, has been eliminated. An informal survey at the meeting indicated that twenty-six of the thirty-five States that were represented were in immediate compliance with the proposed protocol. Of the nine that were not, seven experts indicated that the legal position in their countries might be reconsidered in the foreseeable future. One of the experts objected that the Protocol might impose different rules for Parties to conflict, particularly if one of the combatant parties was not a member of the Council of Europe.[33] The initial Swedish draft did not provide a descriptive title for the Protocol. It was added by the Committee of Experts in order 'to emphasise that abolition was complete, total and absolute'. Initially, the Committee opted to refer to 'complete abolition', but later returned to the suggestion that the title speak of 'abolition of the death penalty in all circumstances'.[34]

The Committee of Experts for the Development of Human Rights transmitted the draft protocol and explanatory report to the Committee of Ministers on 8 November 2001. The Ministers' Deputies adopted the text of the Protocol and the Explanatory Report on 21 February 2002. It was opened for signature in Vilnius 3 May 2002.

The 2010 ruling of the European Court of Human Rights in *Al Saddoon and Mufti* holding the reference to capital punishment in article 2(1) of the European Convention to be no longer valid brings with it the conclusion that Protocol No. 13 (and Protocol No. 6) no longer serve any useful purpose.[35] If the death penalty is not recognized as an exception or restriction on the right to life in article 2(1), there is no need for a protocol. Two States, Russia and Azerbaijan, have not yet even signed Protocol No. 13. But if they are bound to protect the right to life pursuant to article 2(1), signature or ratification of the Protocol will not really change anything in their legal position.

---

[32] Paragraph 14(ii) of Resolution IIB.
[33] Steering Committee for Human Rights, 27th meeting, 22 June 2001, DH-DEV (2001) 3, para. 7.
[34] Ibid., para. 12.
[35] *Al-Saadoon and Mufdhi v. the United Kingdom*, no. 61498/08, ECHR 2010 (extracts).

Protocol No. 7: Concordance with the Covenant

Both the Convention and Protocol No. 4—but not Protocol No. 1—had been drafted with an eye to the current drafts of the international human rights covenant of the United Nations system. The International Covenant on Civil and Political Rights was adopted by the United Nations General Assembly in December 1966.[36] The following year, the Committee of Ministers decided to consider 'problems [that] might arise from the coexistence of the European Convention on Human Rights and the United Nations Covenants'.[37] In 1969, the Committee of Experts reported back to the Committee of Ministers on various differences between the Convention and the Covenant.[38] In 1972, the Parliamentary Assembly of the Council of Europe, formerly known as the Consultative Assembly, considered the further development of the Convention system. Recommending the extension of the rights protected, the Assembly recalled that the objectives of the Council of Europe consisted of 'not only the maintenance but also the further realisation of human rights and fundamental freedoms'. It noted 'the work already done for the maintenance of human rights, thanks to the establishment and day-to-day functioning of the European Convention on Human Rights and its Protocols', adding that 'the growth of Europe can be soundly based only if it is founded on respect for the human being and if it endeavours to provide an increasingly wide guarantee of his fundamental rights'.[39]

The International Covenant on Civil and Political Rights entered into force in 1976 with thirty-five States parties, several of them members of the Council of Europe.[40] That year, the Parliamentary Assembly recommended that the Committee of Ministers endeavour to insert as many as possible of the substantive provisions of the Covenant on Civil and Political Rights in the Convention.[41] The same year, a sub-committee of the Committee of Experts on Human Rights began consideration of extending the rights in the Convention, using the earlier report as a basis. In preparing what was to become Protocol No. 7, 'the committee of experts kept in mind in particular the need to include in the Convention only such rights as could be stated in sufficiently specific terms to be guaranteed within the framework of the system of control instituted by the Convention'.[42] Moreover, '[i]t was understood that participation of member States in this Protocol would in no way affect the interpretation or application of provisions containing obligations, among themselves, or between them and other States, under any other international instrument'.[43]

The Steering Committee for Human Rights finalized the draft text and transmitted it to the Committee of Ministers. Protocol No. 7 was adopted at the 374th meeting of the

---

[36] International Covenant on Economic, Social and Cultural Rights, International Covenant on Civil and Political Rights and Optional Protocol to the International Covenant on Civil and Political Rights, GA Res. 2200A (XXI), annex.

[37] Explanatory Report on Protocol No. 7, para. 2. On this subject, see Polys Modinos, 'Coexistence de la Convention européenne des Droits de l'Homme et le Pacte des Droits civils et politiques des Nations Unies', (1968) 1 *Revue des droits de l'homme* 41.

[38] Doc. H (70) 7.

[39] Resolution 683 (1972).

[40] International Covenant on Civil and Political Rights, (1976) 999 UNTS 171.

[41] Recommendation 791 (1976) on the protection of human rights in Europe, art. 12.c.i.

[42] Explanatory Report on Protocol No. 7, para. 3.

[43] Ibid., para. 4.

Ministers' Deputies. It was opened for signature on 22 November 1984, accompanied by an Explanatory Report. Protocol No. 7 only partially fulfilled the recommendation of the Parliamentary Assembly and did not achieve genuine concordance with the International Covenant on Civil and Political Rights. For example, there is no recognition of the right of peoples to self determination, of the protection of minorities, or of the prohibition of hate propaganda and propaganda for war. Early drafts of Protocol No. 7 recognized a right of access to the public service similar to what appears in article 25 of the Covenant (and article 21(3) of the Universal Declaration of Human Rights), something that has been noted by the Court.[44]

Nevertheless, with the adoption of Protocol Nos 4 and 7, many of the differences between the protection of human rights ensured by the European Convention and by the International Covenant on Civil and Political Rights were removed. Nevertheless, two significant norms remained to be incorporated in the Convention: recognition of an autonomous right to equality and non-discrimination comparable to that of article 26 of the Covenant and recognition of the rights of minorities as set out in in article 27 of the Covenant. The first of these was addressed with the adoption of Protocol No. 12. The second remains an active issue but with no resolution in sight.[45]

Protocol No. 12: Non-discrimination

Unlike the Covenant, the original version of the European Convention contained only a limited equality rights provision. Article 14 is clearly an accessory right and its provisions only apply when another substantive right set out in the Convention is engaged. In 1958, the Consultative Assembly of the Council of Europe began to consider adding a general prohibition of discrimination to the Convention system by means of an additional protocol. The rapporteur of the Legal Committee prepared a list of suggested rights that included 'equality before the law' as set out in the draft of what became article 26 of the International Covenant on Civil and Political Rights. He contrasted this with 'equality in the exercise of rights and freedoms guaranteed by the Convention', which was already covered by article 14 of the Convention and which had a counterpart in draft article 2(1) of the International Covenant.[46] The Consultative Assembly proposed two alternative provisions on the subject of equality before the law. The second of these contained a stand-alone prohibition of discrimination: 'No one shall be subjected by the State to any discrimination based on any ground such as sex, race, colour, language, religion, political or other opinion, national or social origin, belonging to a national minority, property, birth or other status.'[47] The rapporteur warned, however, that:

[44] *Glasenapp v. Germany*, 28 August 1986, § 48, Series A no. 104; *Kosiek v. Germany*, 28 August 1986, § 34, Series A no. 105.
[45] See An additional protocol to the European Convention on Human Rights on national minorities, Doc. 12879.
[46] Preliminary Report by M. Lannung, Rapporteur, AS/Jur XII (10) 1, 21 August 1958.
[47] Recommendation 234 (1960), Draft for a Second Protocol to the Convention for the Protection of Human Rights and Fundamental Freedoms; Preparatory Work on the Draft Second Protocol to the Convention on Human Rights, Appended to Recommendation 234 (1960) of the Consultative Assembly. VII. Article 6—Equality before the law—Memorandum presented by the Directorate of Human Rights, DH/Exp (60) 16 and Appendix I, 28 October 1960.

a general non-discrimination clause is liable to cause insoluble problems, for instance, in regard to the treatment of foreigners; it might also cover private or social relations which are not within the province of the law. Such a provision might put all member countries under the obligation to write into their legislation effective guarantees against discrimination in every field of activity, including such private matters as the employment of workers in private enterprises, the lease of dwellings, the limitation by private associations of trade unions of their membership to certain categories of people, and so on. I, for my part, could not subscribe to a clause containing so vague, unlimited and imprecise a commitment—nor, I am sure, could the member States.[48]

His views were endorsed by Marc-André Eissen, who spoke on behalf of Polys Modinos, the Council of Europe's Director of Human Rights.[49] The Assembly draft was subsequently considered by a Committee of Experts. It decided to exclude the equality provision from the draft of Protocol No. 4. The Committee of Experts noted that 'for various historical and sociological reasons the notion of equality before the law varied from country to country'. It concluded that '[i]n these circumstances, it was not thought possible to recognise the very general principle of equality before the law in a multilateral Protocol to the Convention on Human Rights'.[50]

In 1970, the Parliamentary Assembly instructed the Committee of Experts on Human Rights to draft an additional protocol to 'secure the equal treatment of persons in the enforcement of the law and prohibit discrimination' with respect to voting rights in national and local elections, employment, particularly in public or publicly financed bodies, equitable allocation of public housing and access to the public service.[51] The Committee of Ministers reacted negatively, concluding that 'it is not desirable or expedient to prepare such a protocol'. The Parliamentary Assembly returned to the point in 1972, with a Recommendation that the Committee of Minsters instruct the Committee of Experts to study the question of preparing a new protocol that would 'secure as an enforceable right the right of an individual not to be unfairly discriminated against on religious, political, racial or other grounds in respect of access to employment and allocation of housing' and also 'secure the equal treatment of persons in the enforcement of the law'.[52]

In 1981, the Committee of Ministers issued a declaration on intolerance in which it decided to implement 'a programme of activities including, in particular, the study of legal instruments applicable in the matter with a view to their reinforcement where appropriate'.[53] This was an implied reference to the idea of a protocol to the Convention concerning equality and the prohibition of discrimination. The Steering Committee for Human Rights was pessimistic about the chances that the proposal could succeed.[54]

---

[48] Report on the Second Protocol to the Convention on Human Rights, M. Lannung, Rapporteur, Doc. 1057, 17 November 1959. Also Doc. AS/Jur XII (11) 1, 6 June 1959, p. 7.

[49] Doc. AS/Jur XII (11) PV 1, 25 August 1959, pp. 5–6.

[50] Memorandum of the Human Rights Directorate on the Committee's third meeting, 2 to 11 October 1961, DH/Exp (61) 35 Final, 17 October 1961, para. 60.

[51] Recommendation 583 (1970). Suppression of and guaranteeing against unjustifiable discrimination, para. 8.

[52] Recommentation 683 (1972) on action to be taken on the conclusions of the Parliamentary Conference on Human Rights (Vienna, 18–20 October 1972), para. A(4).

[53] Declaration Regarding Intolerance—a Threat to Democracy, Committee of Ministers, 14 May 1981, para. IV.ii.

[54] Michael Head, 'The Genesis of Protocol No. 12', in *Non-Discrimination, A Human Right—Seminar to Mark the Entry into Force of Protocol No. 12*, Strasbourg: Council of Europe Publishing, 2006, pp. 35–45, at p. 38.

Discussion about a new protocol resumed with a Recommendation of the Parliamentary Assembly, in 1989, that the Committee of Ministers 'instruct the Steering Committee for Human Rights to give priority to reinforcing the non-discrimination clause in Article 14 of the European Convention on Human Rights, either by adding health to the prohibited grounds of discrimination or by drawing up a general clause on equality of treatment before the law'.[55] Work by the Steering Committee for Equality between Women and Men and the European Commission against Racism and Intolerance led the Committee of Ministers to begin work on an additional protocol.[56] Concerns were largely addressed to issues of gender equality and those of racial discrimination and xenophobia.

In 1998, the Committee of Ministers mandated the Steering Committee for Human Rights to draft an additional protocol 'broadening in a general fashion the field of application of Article 14, and containing a non-exhaustive list of discrimination grounds'.[57] It finalized a draft protocol following consultation with the European Court of Human Rights and the Parliamentary Assembly. The latter was not at all happy with the draft prepared by the Steering Committee, criticizing its neglect of the right to equality as distinct from the prohibition of discrimination.[58] Its complaints were ignored, however, and the Committee adopted the text of Protocol No. 12 on 26 June 2000 and opened it for signature on 4 November 2000, the fiftieth anniversary of the adoption of the European Convention on Human Rights. Protocol No. 12 entered into force on 1 April 2005. In a sense, its impact has been slight. There are only a handful of decisions of the Court that consider the provisions of Protocol No. 12. This might seem a surprising result considering the very dynamic role that article 26 of the International Covenant on Civil and Political Rights has had in the jurisprudence of the United Nations Human Rights Committee. According to Martin Scheinin, 'insufficient attention has been given to the fact that all member States of the Council of Europe already are parties to a very similar substantive human rights provision, the freestanding right to equality and non-discrimination enshrined in Article 26 of the ICCPR, and that almost all member States also have accepted the right of individual complaint in relation to the said provision'.[59] Alas, Protocol No. 12 has only been ratified by a minority of States Parties to the European Convention. The Parliamentary Assembly has said that it 'deplores the limited number of ratifications of Protocol No. 12'.[60]

Unfinished business: minorities, economic, social, and cultural rights, the environment, etc.

Periodically, the proposal that an additional protocol be drafted to include the rights of persons belonging to national minorities returns to the agenda. Early drafts of the

---

[55] Recommendation 1116 (1989) on AIDS and human rights, para. 8.A.

[56] Explanatory Report on Protocol No. 12, para. 5.

[57] Ibid., para. 10.

[58] Opinion of the Assembly on draft Protocol No. 12 to the European Convention on Human Rights, Report, Committee on Legal Affairs and Human Rights, Doc. 8614.

[59] Martin Scheinin, 'Experiences of the Application of Article 26 of the International Covenant on Civil and Political Rights', in *Non-Discrimination, A Human Right—Seminar to Mark the Entry into Force of Protocol No. 12*, Strasbourg: Council of Europe Publishing, 2006, pp. 10–22, at p. 10.

[60] An additional protocol to the European Convention on Human Rights on national minorities, Resolution 1866 (2012), para. 3.

Universal Declaration of Human Rights contained provisions on the rights of minorities but they received insufficient support and were ultimately excluded from the final text. Proponents of the importance of the subject renewed the campaign during the drafting of the International Covenant on Civil and Political Rights, where they met with more success. Article 27 of the Covenant declares: 'In those States in which ethnic, religious or linguistic minorities exist, persons belonging to such minorities shall not be denied the right, in community with the other members of their group, to enjoy their own culture, to profess and practise their own religion, or to use their own language.'[61] Inclusion of minority rights within the European Convention was proposed as early as 1949 by Hermod Lannung of Denmark.[62] Efforts were renewed a decade later, when Protocol No. 4 was being negotiated,[63] and again in the 1990s, when the subject returned to prominence within international human rights.[64] In 1995, members of the Committee of Ministers 'renewed their support for continuation of work on the drawing-up of an additional protocol to the European Convention on Human Rights in the cultural field, containing provisions guaranteeing individual rights, particularly for persons belonging to national minorities'.[65]

As recently as 2012, the Parliamentary Assembly called for the preparation of a protocol to the Convention dealing with the rights of persons belonging to national minorities.[66] It suggested that such a protocol might include the right of every person to express freely his or her belonging to a national minority, political rights (such as freedom of association, the creation of political parties, participation in elections, representation in public bodies), at both national and regional level, cultural rights, including the right to cultural autonomy to preserve national identity, the right to take decisions on different forms of autonomy, and the right to freely use a minority language in private and public life.[67] But as with previous initiatives, the Assembly met with stubborn resistance in the Committee of Ministers. Its Steering Committee on Human Rights replied to the latest proposal by referring to several instruments whereby the rights of members of minority groups are protected, including article 14 of the Convention and Protocol No. 12. The Committee said that the present legal framework had led it to conclude that 'a new normative work in this field is not necessary'. It noted 'the absence of consensus on the very notion of "national minority"', adding that 'any effort to draft an instrument would inevitably come up against this major difficulty'. Finally, it expressed 'its opinion that it is not appropriate

---

[61] International Covenant on Civil and Political Rights, (1976) 999 UNTS 171.

[62] Report of the Sitting [of the Consultative Assembly, 19 August 1949], I *TP* 38–154, at p. 54.

[63] Recommendation 285 (1961) on the rights of national minorities.

[64] Recommendation 1134 (1990) on the rights of minorities; Recommendation 1177 (1992) on the rights of minorities; Recommendation 1201 (1993) on an additional protocol on the rights of national minorities to the European Convention on Human Rights; Recommendation 1492 (2001), Rights of national minorities.

[65] Joint interim reply to Recommendation 1134 (1990) on the rights of minorities; Recommendation 1177 (1992) on the rights of minorities; Recommendation 1201 (1993) on an additional protocol on the rights of national minorities to the European Convention on Human Rights; and Recommendation 1255 (1995) on the protection of the rights of national minorities (adopted by the Committee of Ministers on 24 May 1995 at the 538th meeting of the Ministers' Deputies), Doc. 7316.

[66] An additional protocol to the European Convention on Human Rights on national minorities, Recommendation 1994 (2012). See also the Report to the Committee on Legal Affairs and Human Rights by György Frunda, Doc. 12879.

[67] An additional protocol to the European Convention on Human Rights on national minorities, Resolution 1866 (2012), para. 6.

to accompany the ECHR with protocols setting out a range of rights applicable to specific groups of people'.[68]

As early as 1978, the Parliamentary Assembly had proposed adding economic, social, and cultural rights to the European Convention. Specifically, it felt that the following rights were suitable for consideration: the right freely to choose or to accept a paid activity; the right of access to free employment services, vocational guidance and vocational training; the right to an adequate standard of living in the event of involuntary unemployment; the right to be affiliated to a social security scheme.[69] The rapporteur of the Legal Affairs Committee cautioned against adding a right to education. Given that it is already partially included in Protocol No. 1, he was concerned that such a measure might run the risk of lowering the level of protection if States did not ratify the new instrument. For the same reason, he did not consider trade union rights should be added, given their protection by article 11 of the Convention.

The idea was revived in 1998 by the Parliamentary Assembly with a request that 'the possibility of transferring individual rights from the Social Charter to the European Convention on Human Rights' be examined 'in order to create the basis for stricter legal observance'.[70] It asked the Committee of Ministers to consider the 'possible introduction of a procedure for the lodging of a complaint by either an individual and/or a government by further studying whether this could be best achieved in this new framework or by integrating some fundamental social rights into the system of the European Convention on Human Rights'.[71] The following year, the rapporteur of the Social, Health and Family Affairs Committee of the Parliamentary Assembly wrote that '[a] protocol to the European Convention on Human Rights would make it possible to remedy deficiencies and would constitute an instrument for strengthening social cohesion, in particular with a view to putting an end to inequalities and safeguarding the interests of the most vulnerable sectors of society. The elaboration of such a protocol is, for the Council of Europe, the challenge of the next millennium.[72]

A protocol concerning recognition of the right to a healthy environment in the European Convention on Human Rights has also received attention in the Parliamentary Assembly. In 1999, the Parliamentary Assembly referred to 'changing living conditions and growing recognition of the importance of environmental issues', stating that 'the Convention could include the right to a healthy and viable environment as a basic human right'.[73] In 2009, it recommended that the Committee of Ministers draw up an additional protocol to the European Convention on Human Rights 'recognising the right to a

[68] Recommendation 1994 (2012) on an additional protocol to the European Convention on Human Rights on national minorities, para. 3.

[69] Recommendation 838 (1978) on widening the scope of the European Convention on Human Rights, para. 13. See generally H. Berchtold, 'Council of European Activities in the Field of Economic, Social and Cultural Rights', in F. Matscher, ed., *The Implementation of Economic and Social Rights*, Kehl, Germany: N.P. Engel, 1991, pp. 355–70.

[70] Recommendation 1354 (1998), Future of the European Social Charter, para. 18.

[71] Ibid., para. 23.2.

[72] Report, Social, Health and Family Affairs Committee, Doc. 8357. Also Opinion, Committee on Legal Affairs and Human Rights, Doc. 8433.

[73] Recommendation 1431 (1999), Future action to be taken by the Council of Europe in the field of environment protection, para 8.

healthy and viable environment'.[74] It recommended that the feasibility of drafting an amendment or an additional protocol concerning the right of individuals to a healthy and viable environment be examined.[75] The Assembly returned to the matter in 2003, calling for an additional protocol 'concerning the recognition of individual procedural rights intended to enhance environmental protection, as set out in the Aarhus Convention'.[76] The Steering Committee on Human Rights did not support the idea of an additional protocol, although it noted that the Convention system 'indirectly contributes to the protection of the environment through existing Convention rights', something it said was confirmed in the case law of the European Court of Human Rights.[77] When the Parliamentary Assembly again raised the issue in 2009,[78] it met with the same objections from the Committee of Ministers.[79]

Two other unsuccessful proposals for new protocols were considered during the 1990s. In 1994, the Assembly proposed that the Committee of Ministers 'establish the principle of equality of rights between women and men as a fundamental human right in an additional protocol to the Convention for the Protection of Human Rights and Fundamental Freedoms'.[80] When Protocol No. 12 was being drafted, the Consultative Assembly unsuccessfully proposed that it include the following: 'Men and women are equal before the law.'[81] In 2007, the Parliamentary Assembly reiterated its request for a new protocol to the European Convention on Human Rights to be drawn up enshrining gender equality as a human right. It stated that it was 'convinced that only a new protocol to the European Convention on Human Rights enshrining gender equality as a human right can ensure that remaining discrimination against women in civil law, both in the domestic legislation of Council of Europe member states and in private international law, is finally eliminated'.[82] Again, in 2012, the Assembly called upon the Committee of Ministers to 'consider including the principle of gender equality in the system of the European Convention on Human Rights (ETS No. 5), through the elaboration of a new protocol'.[83]

The other proposal concerned the rights of persons deprived of their freedom.[84] Work on the project by the Steering Committee on Human Rights was underway as

---

[74] Recommendation 1885 (2009), Drafting an additional protocol to the European Convention on Human Rights concerning the right to a healthy environment, para. 10.1.

[75] Ibid., para. 11.2.b.

[76] Recommendation 1614 (2003), Environment and human rights, para 10.i. The 'Aarhus Convention' is a reference to the United Nations Convention on Access to Information, Public Participation in Decision Making and Access to Justice in Environmental Matters, (2001) 2161 UNTS 447.

[77] CDDH (2003) 026, Annex VI.

[78] Recommendation 1885 (2009), Drafting an additional protocol to the European Convention on Human Rights concerning the right to a healthy environment.

[79] Reply adopted by the Committee of Ministers on 8 July 2009 at the 1063rd meeting of the Ministers' Deputies, CM/AS(2009)Rec1862 final, para. 9. Also Opinion of the CDDH on Recommendation 1883 (2009), The challenges posed by climate change, and Recommendation 1885 (2009) Drafting an additional protocol to the European Convention on Human Rights concerning the right to a healthy environment, DH-DEV(2010)03, Appendix III, para. 3.

[80] Recommendation 1229 (1994) on equality of rights between men and women, para, 8.i. Also Recommendation 1269 (1995) on achieving real progress in women's rights as from 1995, para. 6.i.

[81] Opinion of the Assembly on draft Protocol No. 12 to the European Convention on Human Rights, Report, Committee on Legal Affairs and Human Rights, Doc. 8614.

[82] Recommendation 1798 (2007) on Respect for the principle of gender equality in civil law, para. 7.

[83] Resolution 1860 (2012), Advancing women's rights worldwide, para. 10.7.

[84] (1993) 36 YB 447; (1994) 37 YB 506; (1995) 38 YB 969; (1996) 39 YB 594.

early as 1992.[85] In 1996, the Steering Committee on Human Rights prepared a draft—it was to be Protocol No. 12—to the European Commission and the European Court of Human Rights for opinions. Subsequently, the Committee of Ministers said that the work of the Steering Committee 'has proved to be difficult' and that '[i]t appears necessary to take a fresh look at the question of how a protocol to the Convention could make a meaningful contribution to the protection of the rights of persons deprived of their liberty'.[86]

There have been other suggestions for additional protocols but they have not had any significant momentum or generated serious developmental work. For example, in 1977, the Parliamentary Assembly recommended that the Committee of Ministers instruct the Committee of Experts on Human Rights to study the feasibility of adding a protocol to the European Convention 'to guarantee the independence of legal assistance'.[87] Some-times, proposals take the form of unsuccessful motions within the Parliamentary Assembly, such as the 2013 suggestion of a protocol for 'protection of whistle-blowers who disclose governmental action violating international law and fundamental rights'.[88]

[85] Communication on the Activities of the Committee of Ministers, CM(92)182, Doc. 6672.
[86] Reply from the Committee of Ministers, Doc. 7918.
[87] Recommendation 791 (1976) on the protection of human rights in Europe, art. 12.c.iv.
[88] Motion for a Recommendation, Doc. 13278.

Amending the Convention and reforming its machinery

Beginning with Protocol Nos 2 and 3 to the Convention, which were opened for signature and ratification on 6 May 1963, eleven Protocols have been adopted that modify or add to the provisions governing administration, procedure, and implementation. All but one of them, Protocol No. 16, is an amending protocol, requiring unanimous consent for entry into force. Protocol No. 16, which is not yet in force, enables the highest courts and tribunals of a State Party to submit a request for an advisory opinion to the Grand Chamber of the European Court. Unlike the other modifications to the implementation provisions, it would appear that such an advisory opinion procedure is able to operate without difficulty even if it is not accepted or desired by all States Parties to the Convention.

Protocol Nos 2, 3, and 5: Advisory opinions, procedural adjustments

Protocol No. 2 conferred upon the European Court the competence to deliver advisory opinions.[1] The original proposal first appeared in January 1960 in a Recommendation of the Consultative Assembly.[2] The Committee of Ministers reacted by asking the Committee of Experts to examine the desirability of such a modification of the Convention.[3] The Committee of Experts reached a favourable conclusion and proceeded, upon further instruction of the Committee of Ministers, to prepare a draft protocol.[4] It considered a request from the European Commission on Human Rights to give it the authority to request an advisory opinion but a majority of the Committee did not consider this to be an appropriate measure.[5] Protocol No. 3 introduced several changes to the Convention concerning the functioning of the European Commission on Human Rights.[6] It abolished the 'Sub-Commissions' that had been part of the original conception in the 1950 text of the Convention, and made minor changes to facilitate expeditious treatment of unfounded applications by the Commission.[7] Protocol No. 5, adopted in 1966, was the result of proposals from the Court and the Commission intended to ensure an even rotation of terms of the members of the two bodies.[8] As amending protocols, entry into force of Protocol Nos 2, 3, and 5 required unanimity of all States Parties to the European Convention. They entered into force in the 1970s. From that point on, their substantive

---

[1] Protocol No. 2 to the Convention for the Protection of Human Rights and Fundamental Freedoms, conferring upon the European Court of Human Rights competence to give advisory opinions, ETS 44.

[2] Recommendation 232 on the extension of the competence of the European Court of Human Rights as regards the interpretation of the Convention on Human Rights, 22 January 1960.

[3] Committee of Ministers, Resolution (60) 20 of 15 September, 1960.

[4] Explanatory Report on Protocol No. 2, paras 3–6.

[5] Ibid., paras 7, 10.

[6] Protocol No. 3 to the Convention for the Protection of Human Rights and Fundamental Freedoms amending Articles 29, 30, and 34 of the Convention, ETS 45.

[7] Explanatory Report on Protocol No. 3.

[8] Protocol No. 5 to the Convention for the Protection of Human Rights and Fundamental Freedoms, amending Articles 22 and 40 of the Convention, ETS 55.

provisions were deemed to be part of the Convention and ratification of the three Protocols was required of all new States Parties to the Convention. The relevant provisions of Protocol No. 2 were incorporated into the Convention as article 47, the result of Protocol No. 11. Those of Protocol Nos 3 and 5 became irrelevant with the abolition of the Commission, also a consequence of Protocol No. 11.

Protocol Nos 8, 9, and 10: Adjusting to the growing caseload

There were no further changes to the Convention mechanisms until the mid-1980s. Then, over the space of about a decade, very major reforms were undertaken by means of a series of Protocols that transformed the enforcement of human rights under the European Convention. Unlike the earlier Protocols, these were not efforts to fine-tune the provisions of the original Convention. Rather, they were prompted by the success of the system and the challenges posed by its growing caseload. The first such initiative, Protocol No. 8, was opened for signature on 19 March 1985.[9] The major change effected by Protocol No. 8 was the authorization it gave the Commission to set up Chambers capable of exercising all the powers previously enjoyed by the plenary Commission. Provision was made so that the member of the Commission elected from the respondent State would sit *ex officio* in the relevant Chamber, a rule similar to what already existed for the Court. The Explanatory Report noted that '[t]he importance of ensuring that this member can participate in the examination of the petition lies in the fact that in most cases he will be the member who is most familiar with the legal system of the State concerned. The practice to date has indeed shown the usefulness of enabling a member of the Commission to sit when a case concerning his country is examined.'[10] The reform also allowed restricted committees of the Commission to filter individual petitions that were manifestly inadmissible. A number of other reforms resulted from the Protocol. Seemingly important at the time, this was all quite ephemeral because more important amendments were yet to come. The only reform from Protocol No. 8 that still endures whose roots can be traced to this initiative is the provision for two Vice-presidents of the Court now found in article 25(a).

Protocol No. 9, which was adopted on 6 November 1990 and entered into force on 1 October 1994, allowed individual applicants a direct right of access to the European Court of Human Rights.[11] Until that point, the European Commission of Human Rights was the gatekeeper to the Court, where it acted on behalf of the applicant. The Plenary Court described the Commission's role as one of 'sifting'.[12] As the Explanatory Report noted, '[t]he idea of empowering individuals to seize the European Court of Human Rights is not a new one. It was mentioned as early as May 1948, at the Congress of Europe, and appeared in the draft European Convention on Human Rights drawn up by the European Movement in July 1949.'[13] Rejected at the time, the idea was revived by a

---

[9] Protocol No. 8 to the Convention for the Protection of Human Rights and Fundamental Freedoms, ETS 118.

[10] Explanatory Report on Protocol No. 8, para. 8.

[11] Protocol No. 9 to the Convention for the Protection of Human Rights and Fundamental Freedoms, ETS 140.

[12] *De Wilde, Ooms and Versyp v. Belgium*, 18 June 1971, § 51, Series A no. 12. Also *Klass and Others v. Germany*, 6 September 1978, § 32, Series A no. 28; *Artico v. Italy*, 13 May 1980, § 27, Series A no. 37; *Dikme v. Turkey*, no. 20869/92, § 47, ECHR 2000-VIII.

[13] Explanatory Report on Protocol No. 9, para. 1.

Parliamentary Assembly Recommendation in 1972.[14] Consulted by the Committee of Experts, both the Court and the Commission called for direct access by individuals to the Court.[15] But in 1978, the Steering Committee for Human Rights, which was the successor body of the Committee of Experts on Human Rights, did not think a majority of States Parties was ready for such a change.[16] The idea continued to gain momentum, and in 1990 the Committee of Ministers adopted a draft protocol providing for direct access to the Court.[17]

The Explanatory Report on Protocol No. 9 presented this as an idea whose time had come. It noted that individual access to the Strasbourg organs was already recognized, although only to the European Commission, and that all States Parties to the Convention had not only accepted the right of petition to the Commission but also the compulsory jurisdiction of the Court. It said that enabling the individual to seize the Court directly instead of depending upon the initiative of the Commission 'merely completes the existing structure'. It added that a system 'whereby the individual is granted rights but not given the possibility to exploit fully the control machinery provided for enforcing them, could today be regarded as inconsistent with the spirit of the Convention, not to mention compatibility with domestic-law procedures in States Parties'.[18] It even signalled incompatibilities with the norms enshrined in the Convention: a denial of 'equality of arms', of the right to access to a tribunal and of participation in proceedings.[19]

Protocol No. 10, adopted in 1992, reduced the majority required for a finding of a violation of the Convention by the Committee of Ministers from two-thirds, as set out in the 1950 version of article 32(1) of the Convention, to a simple majority.[20] The Protocol never entered into force. It was overtaken by Protocol No. 11, which did away altogether with the determination of a violation of the Convention by the Committee of Ministers.

Protocol Nos 11, 14, 14*bis*, and 15: Consolidating the institutions, further reforms

The idea of merging the Commission and the Court had been considered since the early 1980s.[21] The growing success of the Convention organs coupled with the expansion of the Council of Europe resulting from the end of the Cold War brought greater urgency to the reform initiatives. The caseload of both the Commission and the Court appeared to be growing almost exponentially. In 1988, the Parliamentary Assembly adopted a Recommendation stating it was 'convinced that it is particularly important to consider the possibility of replacing the Commission and Court by a single court with full-time judges

---

[14] Recommendation 683 (1972) on action to be taken on the conclusions of the Parliamentary Conference on Human Rights (Vienna, 18–20 October 1972).

[15] Explanatory Report on Protocol No. 9, para. 4.

[16] Ibid., para. 6.

[17] Ibid., para. 11.

[18] Ibid., para. 12.

[19] Ibid.

[20] Protocol No. 10 to the Convention for the Protection of Human Rights and Fundamental Freedoms, ETS 146.

[21] Explanatory Report on Protocol No. 11, paras 10–14. See, e.g., O. Jacot-Guillarmod, ed., *La fusion de la Commission et de la Cour européennes des droits de l'homme*, Engel: Strasbourg, 1987.

resident in Strasbourg, while weighing carefully the arguments for and against'.[22] The Steering Committee for Human Rights considered a report on the idea prepared by the Committee of Experts for the improvement of procedures for the protection of human rights. It instructed the Committee of Experts to draw up the detailed structure of such a single court.[23] The following year, the Committee of Ministers said that the idea of merging the two bodies 'albeit controversial, is still being examined'.[24] In 1990, Sweden and the Netherlands separately advanced proposals by which decisions of the Commission would be binding, as if it was a court of first instance rather than a preliminary chamber of the Court. The idea was considered by the Steering Committee for Human Rights.[25] However, this approach did not meet with consensus.[26]

In November 1991, the Ministers of Foreign Affairs of the Council of Europe decided to give priority to the reform of the Convention control mechanisms. The following year, the Parliamentary Assembly adopted a Recommendation supporting the creation of a single Court as a full-time body, a measure entailing the disappearance of the Commission. It insisted upon the urgency of the reform in light of the recent expansion of the membership of the Council of Europe to seventeen States, the expectation that this number 'will continue to rise in the next few years and that a considerable increase in the number of applications submitted to the Commission and to the Court is thus to be expected'.[27] Following a special meeting of the Ministers' Deputies on 28 May 1993, the Committee of Ministers decided to replace the existing system with a Court able to work in committees and Chambers with an effective mechanism to filter applications and to enable friendly settlements. It gave the Steering Committee on Human Rights terms of reference in this sense and instructed it to prepare a draft amending protocol.[28]

Protocol No. 11 was finalized and opened for signature and ratification on 11 May 1994.[29] That year, the Commission and the Court moved into their new premises, a spectacular building designed by architect Richard Rogers that featured two saucer-like appendages, each containing a chamber. One was designated for the Commission, the

---

[22] Recommendation 1087 (1988) on the improvement of the procedures of the European Convention on Human Rights, para. 10.

[23] (1988) 31 YB 260.

[24] Interim reply by the Committee of Ministers [to Recommendation 1087 of the Parliamentary Assembly], (1989) 32 YB 261, para. 4.

[25] (1990) 33 YB 301.

[26] Explanatory Report on Protocol No. 11, paras 15–16.

[27] Recommendation 1194 (1992) on the reform of the control mechanism of the European Convention on Human Rights.

[28] Supplementary reply from the Committee of Ministers [to Recommendation 1194 (1992) of the Parliamentary Assembly], (1992) 36 YB 373–374.

[29] On Protocol No. 11, see R. Abraham, 'La réforme du mécanisme de contrôle de la Convention européenne des droits de l'homme: le Protocole no 11 à la Convention', [1994] *Annuaire français du droit international* 625; Rudolf Bernhardt, 'Reform of the Control Machinery under the European Convention on Human Rights', 91995) 89 *AJIL* 145; P. Boillat, 'Aperçu des négociations du Protocole no. 11', (1999) 9 *Revue Suisse de droit international et de droit européen* 5; Andrew Drzemczewski, 'A Major Overhaul of the European Convention Control Mechanism: Protocol No. 11', [1997] *Collected Courses of the Academy of European Law* 125; Olivier Jacot-Guillarmod, 'Protocol No. 11 to the European Convention on Human Rights: A Response to Some Recent Criticisms', (1995) 38A YB 172; Yvonne Klerk, 'Protocol No. 11 to the European Convention for Human Rights: A Drastic Revision of the Supervisory Mechanism under the ECHR', (1996) 14 *Netherlands Quarterly of Human Rights* 35; Paul Tavernier, 'Rupture ou continuité? Le protocole no 11 et les problèmes de compétence ratione temporis de la nouvelle Cour', in Mahoney et al., *Mélanges Ryssdal*, pp. 1391–402; Friedrich Vogel, 'The Role of the Parliamentary Assembly of the Council of Europe in Bringing Protocol No. 11 into Being', in Mahoney et al., *Mélanges Ryssdal*, pp. 21–4.

other for the Court. This symbolized the vision of the Convention organs as set out in the 1950 text. Alas, in the course of construction the Council of Europe decided to abolish the Commission! Under Protocol No. 11, whereas judges in the 'former' European Court of Human Rights had served part-time, generally for one week per month, the 'new' Court consisted of full-time judges based in Strasbourg. It was established in 1998 following the entry into force of Protocol No. 11.[30]

It was immediately apparent that the difficulties of the continually increasing caseload and the consequent unacceptable delays had not been solved by the disappearance of the Commission and the establishment of a full-time Court.[31] Work on yet another amending protocol culminated in the adoption of Protocol No. 14, on 13 May 2004.[32] The focus of Protocol No. 14 was on the filtering and subsequent processing of applications. Its changes to the operation of the Court included authorizing a single judge and a three-judge committee to deal with routine applications, as well as various other means enabling repetitive applications reflecting structural problems to be dealt with expeditiously.

Protocol No. 14 did not enter into force until 1 June 2010. Every State Party but Russia had ratified the Protocol by mid-2006.[33] The Duma ultimately agreed to ratification once an assurance had been given that a Russian judge would always sit in cases concerning the country.[34] In the meantime, frustrated by Russian obstruction, the Council of Europe adopted Protocol No. 14*bis*, a measure allowing for provisional application of certain provisions of Protocol No. 14 by those States that agreed until the main instrument could enter into force.[35] Protocol No. 14*bis*, which entered into force with three ratifications, actually applied for less than a year, from 1 October 2009 until 1 June 2010. The Explanatory Report noted that the delayed entry into force of Protocol 14 had made the situation confronting the Court 'deteriorate yet further in the face of an ever-accelerating influx of new applications and a constantly growing backlog of

---

[30] Protocol No. 11 to the Convention for the Protection of Human Rights and Fundamental Freedoms, restructuring the control machinery established thereby, ETS 155.

[31] Explanatory Report on Protocol No. 14, para. 20.

[32] Protocol No. 14 to the Convention for the Protection of Human Rights and Fundamental Freedoms, amending the control system of the Convention, ETS 194. See Explanatory Report on Protocol No. 14, paras 29–33; M.-A. Beernaert, 'Protocol 14 and New Strasbourg Procedures: Towards Greater Efficiency? And at What Price?', [2004] *EHRLR* 544; L. Caflisch, 'The Reform of the European Court of Human Rights: Protocol No. 14 and Beyond', (2006) 6 *HRLR* 403; Lucius Caflisch and Martina Keller, 'Le Protocole additionnel no 14 à la Convention européenne des droits de l'homme', in Lucius Caflisch, Johan Callewaert, Roderick Liddell, Paul Mahoney, and Mark Villiger, eds, *Liber Amicorum Luzius Wildhaber*, Kehl, Germany: N.P. Engel, 2007, pp. 91–114; Martin Eaton and Jeroen Schokkenbroek, 'Reforming the Human Rights Protection System Established by the European Convention on Human Rights/A New Protocol No. 14 to the Convention and Other Measures to Guarantee the Long-term Effectiveness of the Convention System', (2005) 26 *Human Rights Law Journal* 1; Steven Greer, 'Protocol 14 and the Future of the European Court of Human Rights', [2005] *Public Law* 83; Christina G. Hioureas, 'Behind the Scenes of Protocol No. 14: Politics in Reforming the European Court of Human Rights', (2006) 24 *Berkeley Journal of International Law* 718; Laurence R. Helfer, 'Redesigning the European Court of Human Rights: Embeddedness as a Deep Structural Principle of the European Human Rights Regime', (2008) 19 *EJIL* 125; Philip Leach, 'Access to the European Court of Human Rights—From a Legal Entitlement to a Lottery?', (2006) 27 *HRLJ* 24.

[33] Some of Russia's objections can be seen in the lengthy declaration that it formulated upon signature of Protocol No. 14: (2006) 49 YB 11. The statement was renewed upon ratification: (2010) 53 YB 28.

[34] On Russia and Protocol No. 14, see Bill Bowring, 'Russia and Human Rights: Incompatible Opposites', (2009) 1 *Göttingen Journal of International Law* 257; Bill Bowring, 'Russian Federation, Protocol No. 14 (and 14*bis*), and the Battle for the Soul of the ECHR', (2010) 2 *Göttingen Journal of International Law* 589.

[35] For the relevant declarations, see (2009) 52 YB 12–15.

cases'. It said that this 'unsustainable situation represents a grave threat to the effectiveness of the Court as the centre-piece of the European human rights protection system'.[36]

Protocol No. 15 followed a series of high-level meetings on the future and operation of the Court, beginning with the Interlaken conference, in February 2010, and the İzmir conference, in April 2011. The final such gathering was held in Brighton, in April 2012. It resulted in a Declaration containing a number of proposals for changes to the Convention. In short order, Protocol No. 15 was prepared in order to deal with some of these. It implements the unusual, perhaps unprecedented, change to the Preamble of the Convention with the addition of a new recital. It also addresses the retirement age of judges of the Court, in practice making it possible for them to serve until the age of 75, rather than 70. The Protocol also contains measures concerning procedure and admissibility, including a reduction to four months of the delay given applicants in making their initial submission to the Court following the exhaustion of the domestic remedies. The draft protocol and the draft explanatory report were prepared by the Steering Committee on Human Rights, then submitted to the Court itself and the Parliamentary Assembly for comments before final adoption by the Committee of Ministers on 24 June 2013.[37] Protocol No. 15 is not yet in force.

Protocol No. 16: Judicial dialogue

When Protocol No. 2 was being negotiated, in the early 1960s, the Court itself proposed the addition of two provisions, one to give the Court competence to deliver a 'prejudicial ruling' by which it would interpret a provision at the request of other courts or tribunals, the other to issue an advisory opinion at the request of a government arising from draft legislation.[38] These ideas were not pursued at the time. Frustrated with both the narrow scope of Protocol No. 2 and the fact that it was not in fact being implemented, the Court issued an opinion expressing its bewilderment at the failure of the Committee of Ministers to allow it to issue advisory opinions in response to requests from States for the interpretation of the Convention.[39] In 1978, the Steering Committee on Human Rights proposed that the enlargement of the jurisdiction of the Court with a view to allowing advisory opinions at the request of States be examined. However, after reviewing the situation it decided against recommending any modification to Protocol No. 2.[40]

The Group of Wise Persons in a 2005 report to the Committee of Ministers revived the idea. Its conclusion was that:

it would be useful to introduce a system under which the national courts could apply to the Court for advisory opinions on legal questions relating to interpretation of the Convention and the protocols thereto, in order to foster dialogue between courts and enhance the Court's 'constitutional' role. Requests for an opinion, which would be submitted only by constitutional courts or

---

[36] Explanatory Report on Protocol No. 14*bis*, para. 1.

[37] Protocol No. 15 amending the Convention for the Protection of Human Rights and Fundamental Freedoms, ETS 213.

[38] Explanatory Report on Protocol No. 2, 'Further commentary relating to the draft prepared in October, 1962', para. 1.

[39] Andrew Drzemczewski, 'Protocol No. 2, Article 1-4', in Pettiti et al., *La Convention européenne*, pp. 1028–36, at p. 1031.

[40] Ibid., pp. 1032–4.

courts of last instance, would always be optional and the opinions given by the Court would not be binding.[41]

Protocol No. 16, adopted on 10 October 2013, allows the highest courts and tribunals of a State Party to request the European Court of Human Rights to give advisory opinions on questions of principle relating to the interpretation or application of the Convention or the Protocols.[42] Like Protocol No. 15, the origins of Protocol No. 16 can be traced to the Declaration of the Brighton High-level Conference on the Future of the Court of April 2012. The Conference noted:

that the interaction between the Court and national authorities could be strengthened by the introduction into the Convention of a further power of the Court, which States Parties could optionally accept, to deliver advisory opinions upon request on the interpretation of the Convention in the context of a specific case at domestic level, without prejudice to the non-binding character of the opinions for the other States Parties; invites the Committee of Ministers to draft the text of an optional protocol to the Convention with this effect by the end of 2013; and further invites the Committee of Ministers thereafter to decide whether to adopt it.[43]

The Committee of Ministers prepared a draft that met with the approval of the Parliamentary Assembly and of the Court prior to its adoption. Protocol No. 16 is not yet in force.

---

[41] Report of the Group of Wise Persons to the Committee of Ministers, CM(2006)203, 15 November 2006.

[42] Protocol No. 16 to the Convention for the Protection of Human Rights and Fundamental Freedoms, ETS 214.

[43] High Level Conference on the Future of the European Court of Human Rights, Brighton Declaration, 20 April 2012, para. 12.d.

Interpretation of the Convention

In a formulation that appears in many judgments, the Court insists that 'the Convention must be interpreted and applied in a manner which renders its rights practical and effective, not theoretical and illusory'.[1] A variety of interpretative approaches can be taken to the European Convention on Human Rights.[2] Scholars of legal hermeneutics have often suggested that rules and maxims of interpretation are in reality arguments that judges use to justify a result that they already favour. The process of interpretation is not so much an objective exercise in establishing meaning as a rationalization for views that may be the result of policy orientations and personal prejudices. This is not the place to discuss the nature of legal interpretation. But bearing in mind the uncertainties in the process, the subject will be presented in an essentially descriptive fashion, setting out the various approaches that have been adopted in the case law.

At the time of the adoption of the European Convention on Human Rights, an existing body of international law had been developed in the jurisprudence of international courts and tribunals, and notably the Permanent Court of International Justice that operated from the early 1920s until it was replaced by the International Court of Justice at the time of the establishment of the United Nations. The International Court of Justice had only issued a few decisions when the European Convention on Human Rights was adopted. The principles of interpretation developed for the interpretation of treaties by the existing international courts as well as by arbitration tribunals were presumably understood by the drafters, who would have assumed that these would be applied to the European Convention. The Convention itself speaks to rules or principles of interpretation in only one place. Article 17 declares that '[n]othing in this Convention may be interpreted as implying for any State, group or person any right to engage in any activity or perform any act aimed at the destruction of any of the rights and freedoms set forth herein or at their limitation to a greater extent than is provided for in the Convention'.

---

[1] E.g., *Sergey Zolotukhin v. Russia* [GC], no. 14939/03, § 80, ECHR 2009; *Tyrer v. the United Kingdom*, 25 April 1978, § 31, Series A no. 26; *Christine Goodwin v. the United Kingdom* [GC], no. 28957/95, § 75, ECHR 2002-VI; *Andrejeva v. Latvia* [GC], no. 55707/00, § 98, ECHR 2009; *Artico v. Italy*, 13 May 1980, § 33, Series A no. 37; *Varnava and Others v. Turkey* [GC], nos 16064/90, 16065/90, 16066/90, 16068/90, 16069/90, 16070/90, 16071/90, 16072/90, and 16073/90, § 160, ECHR 2009; *Folgerø and Others v. Norway* [GC], no. 15472/02, § 100, ECHR 2007-III; *Salduz v. Turkey* [GC], no. 36391/02, § 51, ECHR 2008; *Scoppola v. Italy (no. 2)* [GC], no. 10249/03, § 104, 17 September 2009; *Micallef v. Malta* [GC], no. 17056/06, § 81, ECHR 2009.

[2] On interpretation of the Convention, see M.E. Villiger, 'Articles 31 and 32 of the Vienna Convention on the Law of Treaties in the Case Law of the European Court of Human Rights', in Roland Bröhmer, Christian Collins, Christine Langenfeld et al., eds, *Internationale Gemeinschaft und Meschenrechte*, Cologne: Carl Heymanns, 2005, pp. 330–52; Laurence Burgorgue-Larsen, 'Interpreting the European Convention: What Can the African Human Rights System Learn from the Case Law of the European Court of Human Rights on the Interpretation of the European Convention?', (2012) 5 *Inter-American and European Human Rights Journal* 90; Olivier Jacot-Guillarmod, 'Règles, méthodes et principes d'interprétation dans la jurisprudence de la Cour européenne des droits de l'homme', in Pettiti et al., *La Convention européenne*, pp. 41–63; François Ost, 'Originalité des méthodes d'interprétation de la Cour européenne des droits de l'homme', in Mireille Delmas-Marty, ed., *Raisonner la raison d'État (vers une Europe des droits de l'homme)*, Paris: Presses universitaires de France, 1989, pp. 405–63; F. Matscher, 'Methods of Interpretation of the Convention', in Macdonald, *The European System*, pp. 63–82.

Early case law of the Court and the Commission referred to a variety of interpretative principles. For example, in *Lawless v. Ireland* members of the Commission made reference to the preliminary work or *travaux préparatoires* as a guide to interpretation,[3] 'literal, historical interpretation',[4] and 'strict interpretation'.[5] In its judgment in the case, the Court rejected the use of the preparatory work given that the test of the Convention seemed clear and unambiguous, 'having regard to a generally recognised principle regarding the interpretation of international treaties'.[6] In *Wemhoff v. Germany*, it considered the rules applicable to interpretation of bilingual treaties as well as purposive interpretation or teleology.[7] In the *Belgian Linguistic case*, the Court rejected an interpretation likely to lead to an absurd result.[8] In none of these early cases were their references to international jurisprudence as authority for the principles of interpretation. It cannot be said that at this stage in their development, the Convention organs had a coherent theory of interpretation of the Convention.

Vienna Convention on the Law of Treaties

The rules of treaty interpretation applied by international courts and tribunals were codified in the Vienna Convention on the Law of Treaties, adopted in 1969 following an intense period of debate and negotiation within the United Nations International Law Commission.[9] Three familiar articles of the Vienna Convention specifically address the interpretation of treaties:

Article 31. General rule of interpretation

1. A treaty shall be interpreted in good faith in accordance with the ordinary meaning to be given to the terms of the treaty in their context and in the light of its object and purpose.
2. The context for the purpose of the interpretation of a treaty shall comprise, in addition to the text, including its preamble and annexes:
    (a) any agreement relating to the treaty which was made between all the parties in connexion with the conclusion of the treaty;
    (b) any instrument which was made by one or more parties in connexion with the conclusion of the treaty and accepted by the other parties as an instrument related to the treaty.
3. There shall be taken into account, together with the context:
    (a) any subsequent agreement between the parties regarding the interpretation of the treaty or the application of its provisions;
    (b) any subsequent practice in the application of the treaty which establishes the agreement of the parties regarding its interpretation;
    (c) any relevant rules of international law applicable in the relations between the parties.
4. A special meaning shall be given to a term if it is established that the parties so intended.

---

[3] *Lawless v. Ireland*, no. 332/57, Commission report of 19 December 1959, Opinion of M. Eustathiades.
[4] Ibid., Opinion of M. Dominedo.
[5] Ibid.
[6] *Lawless v. Ireland (no. 3)*, 1 July 1961, p. 24, § 14, Series A no. 3.
[7] *Wemhoff v. Germany*, 27 June 1968, p. 19, § 8, Series A no. 7.
[8] *Case 'relating to certain aspects of the laws on the use of languages in education in Belgium'* (merits), 23 July 1968, p. 32, § 11, Series A no. 6.
[9] Vienna Convention on the Law of Treaties, (1980) 1155 UNTS 331.

Article 32. Supplementary means of interpretation

Recourse may be had to supplementary means of interpretation, including the preparatory work of the treaty and the circumstances of its conclusion, in order to confirm the meaning resulting from the application of article 31, or to determine the meaning when the interpretation according to article 31:

(a) leaves the meaning ambiguous or obscure; or

(b) leads to a result which is manifestly absurd or unreasonable.

Article 33. Interpretation of treaties authenticated in two or more languages

1. When a treaty has been authenticated in two or more languages, the text is equally authoritative in each language, unless the treaty provides or the parties agree that, in case of divergence, a particular text shall prevail.
2. A version of the treaty in a language other than one of those in which the text was authenticated shall be considered an authentic text only if the treaty so provides or the parties so agree.
3. The terms of the treaty are presumed to have the same meaning in each authentic text.
4. Except where a particular text prevails in accordance with paragraph 1, when a comparison of the authentic texts discloses a difference of meaning which the application of articles 31 and 32 does not remove, the meaning which best reconciles the texts, having regard to the object and purpose of the treaty, shall be adopted.

Since the adoption of the Convention in 1969, the European Court and European Commission of Human Rights have relied upon the provisions in the Convention dealing with treaty interpretation. Indeed, the Court began citing the Vienna Convention even before it had entered into force. In the 1975 judgment in *Golder v. the United Kingdom*, noting its agreement with submissions by both of the parties, the Court said that 'Articles 31 to 33 enunciate in essence generally accepted principles of international law to which the Court has already referred on occasion'.[10] The European Court is not alone in applying the Vienna Convention principles to a treaty adopted prior to 1969, or to the entry into force of the Convention. For example, this practice has also been followed by the International Court of Justice.[11] The European Court has explained that although the Vienna Convention postdates the European Convention, 'the Court must have regard to its provisions in so far as they codify pre-existing international law'.[12] In addition to articles 31 to 33, the Court has occasionally invoked other provisions of the Vienna Convention.[13]

---

[10] *Golder v. the United Kingdom*, 21 February 1975, § 29, Series A no. 18. See the Separate Opinion of Judge Zekia: 'There appears to be a virtual consensus of opinion that Articles 31, 32 and 33 of the Vienna Convention on the Law of Treaties, although with no retroactive effect, contain the guiding principles of interpretation of a treaty.' Also *Ringeisen v. Austria*, 16 July 1971, Separate Opinion of Judge Verdross, Series A no. 13.

[11] *Maritime Dispute (Peru v. Chile)*, Judgment, 27 January 2014, para. 57; *Dispute regarding Navigational and Related Rights (Costa Rica v. Nicaragua)*, Judgment, I.C.J. Reports 2009, p. 237, para. 47; *Sovereignty over Pulau Ligitan and Pulau Sipadan (Indonesia/Malaysia)*, Judgment, I.C.J. Reports 2002, pp. 645–6, paras 37–38; *Kasikili/Sedudu Island (Botswana/Namibia)*, Judgment, I.C.J. Reports 1999 (II), p. 1059, para. 18.

[12] *Stichting Mothers of Srebrenica and Others v. the Netherlands* (dec.), no. 65542/12, § 144, ECHR 2013 (extracts).

[13] Article 2(1)(d): *Belilos v. Switzerland*, 29 April 1988, § 42, Series A no. 132. Article 18: *Melnychenko v. Ukraine*, no. 17707/02, § 49, ECHR 2004-X. Article 26: *Janowiec and Others v. Russia* [GC], nos 55508/07 and 29520/09, § 211, ECHR 2013; *Al Nashiri v. Poland*, no. 28761/11, § 366, 24 July 2014; *Husayn (Abu Zubaydah) v. Poland*, no. 7511/13, § 358, 24 July 2014; *Verein gegen Tierfabriken Schweiz (VgT) v. Switzerland (no. 2)* [GC], no. 32772/02, § 87, ECHR 2009. Article 27: *Al Nashiri v. Poland*, no. 28761/11, § 366, 24 July 2014; *Damjanac v. Croatia*, no. 52943/10, § 101, 24 October 2013; *Anchugov and Gladkov v. Russia*, nos 11157/04 and 15162/05, § 128, 4 July 2013. Article 28 in *Šilih v. Slovenia* [GC], no. 71463/01, § 128, 9 April 2009; *Blečić v. Croatia*, no. 59532/00, §§ 90–91, 29 July 2004; *Palić v. Bosnia and Herzegovina*, no. 4704/04, §

The 'general rule' or 'basis of interpretation' is set out in the four paragraphs of article 31 of the Vienna Convention. The core of the rule is in paragraph 1,[14] although it cannot be dissociated from the subsequent paragraphs. Judge Ziemele has described it as 'the backbone for the interpretation of the Convention' and as 'one single rule of interpretation with several parts'.[15] Referring to article 31 in *Golder*, the Court said 'the process of interpretation of a treaty is a unity, a single combined operation; this rule, closely integrated, places on the same footing the various elements enumerated in the four paragraphs of the Article'.[16] Paragraph 2 has been described as 'the internal context' and paragraph 3 as 'the external context'. Paragraph 4 provides the 'reintegration of the intention of the parties'.[17]

In *Golder*, in resisting the incorporation of the rule of law as being within the object and purpose of the Convention the government referred to the preambular proviso that the Convention only codifies 'certain of the rights stated in the Universal Declaration'. The Court disagreed, affirming the 'profound belief in the rule of law' of the drafters, adding that it was 'natural and in conformity with the principle of good faith (Article 31 para. 1 of the Vienna Convention) to bear in mind this widely proclaimed consideration' in the interpretation of article 6 of the Convention.[18]

The Preamble to the European Convention has often been cited by the Court, sometimes with reference to article 31(2) of the Vienna Convention, which says it forms part of the 'context'. The Court has said that the preamble of a treaty is 'an integral part of the context'.[19]

Referring to article 31(3)(a) and (b), George Ress has described treaties as being 'set on wheels' by the processes of subsequent agreement and subsequent practice.[20] The first sub-paragraph of article 31(3), which deals with a 'subsequent agreement' between the States Parties, has attracted no significant attention from the European Court. In one judgment, without citing article 31(3)(a) the Court simply noted that '[t]here has been no subsequent agreement between the High Contracting Parties as to the interpretation of Article 5 in situations of international armed conflict'.[21] There is more case law with respect to 'subsequent practice', something governed by article 31(3)(b).

46, 15 February 2011; *Chiragov v. Armenia* [GC] (dec.), no. 13216/05, § 93, 14 December 2011; *Varnava and Others v. Turkey* [GC], nos 16064/90, 16065/90, 16066/90, 16068/90, 16069/90, 16070/90, 16071/90, 16072/90, and 16073/90, § 130, ECHR 2009; *Przemyk v. Poland*, no. 22426/11, § 46, 17 September 2013. Article 30: *Al-Dulimi and Montana Management Inc. v. Switzerland*, no. 5809/08, Dissenting Opinion of Judge Lorenzen Joined by Judges Raimondi and Jočienė, 26 November 2013. Article 39: *Öcalan v. Turkey* [GC], no. 46221/99, Partly Concurring, Partly Dissenting Opinion of Judge Garlicki, § 4, ECHR 2005-IV.

[14] *Johnston and Others v. Ireland*, 18 December 1986, § 51, Series A no. 112; *Lithgow and Others v. the United Kingdom*, 8 July 1986, § 114, Series A no. 102; *Witold Litwa v. Poland*, no. 26629/95, §§ 57–59, ECHR 2000-III.

[15] *Andrejeva v. Latvia* [GC], no. 55707/00, Partly Dissenting Opinion of Judge Ziemele, § 19, ECHR 2009.

[16] *Golder v. the United Kingdom*, 21 February 1975, § 30, Series A no. 18.

[17] Jean-Marc Sorel and Valérie Boré Eveno, 'Article 31', in Olivier Corten and Pierre Klein, eds, *The Vienna Convention on the Law of Treaties, A Commentary*, Vol. I, Oxford: Oxford University Press, 2011, pp. 804–37.

[18] *Golder v. the United Kingdom*, 21 February 1975, § 34, Series A no. 18.

[19] Ibid.

[20] Georg Ress, 'Verfassungsrechtliche Auswirkungen der Fortentwicklung völkerrechtlicher Verträge', in Walther Fürst, Roman Herzog, and Dieter Umbach, eds, *Festschrift für Wolfgang Zeidler*, Vol. 2, Berlin: Walther de Gruyter, 1987, pp. 1775–97, at p. 1779.

[21] *Hassan v. the United Kingdom*, no. 29750/09, § 101, 16 September 2014.

The Court has generally invoked 'subsequent practice' of States Parties to the Convention without referring to the Vienna Convention provision. Dealing with provisions that have since been abrogated governing declarations recognizing the competence of the Commission and the Court, and concluding that these could not be accompanied by restrictions on territorial scope, the Court said: 'Since the entry into force of the Convention until the present day, almost all of the thirty parties to the Convention, apart from the respondent Government, have accepted the competence of the Commission and Court to examine complaints without restrictions *ratione loci* or *ratione materiae*.'[22] It noted 'evidence of a practice denoting practically universal agreement amongst Contracting Parties'.[23] In *Soering*, the Court acknowledged that '[s]ubsequent practice in national penal policy, in the form of a generalised abolition of capital punishment, could be taken as establishing the agreement of the Contracting States to abrogate the exception provided for under Article 2 § 1 (art. 2-1) and hence to remove a textual limit on the scope for evolutive interpretation of Article 3'.[24] Two decades later, the Court referred to 'consistent State practice in observing the moratorium on capital punishment' as evidence 'that Article 2 has been amended so as to prohibit the death penalty in all circumstances'.[25] Finally, in *Hassan v. the United Kingdom*, it cited explicitly article 31(3)(b) in support of the view that 'a consistent practice on the part of the High Contracting Parties, subsequent to their ratification of the Convention, could be taken as establishing their agreement not only as regards interpretation but even to modify the text of the Convention'. In this respect, the Court noted a practice of States Parties of not derogating from obligations under article 5 of the European Convention in order to detain persons on the basis of the Third and Fourth Geneva Conventions during international armed conflicts.[26]

Article 31(3)(c) provides that relevant rules of international law applicable in the relations between the parties are germane to the context of the treaty. Indeed, the Convention 'cannot be interpreted in a vacuum'.[27] The Court has indicated that it has regard to the international law background as 'a set of rules and principles that are accepted by the vast majority of States' because 'the common international or domestic law standards of European States reflect a reality that the Court cannot disregard when it is called upon to clarify the scope of a Convention provision that more conventional means of interpretation have not enabled it to establish with a sufficient degree of certainty'.[28]

The Court has an 'obligation to take account of the relevant rules and principles of international law and to interpret the Convention so far as possible in harmony with other rules of international law of which it forms part'.[29] Such relevant rules of international law

[22] *Loizidou v. Turkey* (preliminary objections), 23 March 1995, § 79, Series A no. 310.
[23] Ibid., § 80.
[24] *Soering v. the United Kingdom*, 7 July 1989, § 103, Series A no. 161.
[25] *Al-Saadoon and Mufdhi v. the United Kingdom*, no. 61498/08, § 120, ECHR 2010.
[26] *Hassan v. the United Kingdom*, no. 29750/09, § 101, 16 September 2014.
[27] *Al-Adsani v. the United Kingdom* [GC], no. 35763/97, § 55, ECHR 2001-XI; *Bosphorus Hava Yolları Turizm ve Ticaret Anonim Şirketi v. Ireland* [GC], no. 45036/98, § 150, ECHR 2005-VI; *Saadi v. the United Kingdom* [GC], no. 13229/03, § 62, ECHR 2008; *Nada v. Switzerland* [GC], no. 10593/08, § 169, ECHR 2012.
[28] *Opuz v. Turkey*, no. 33401/02, §184, ECHR 2009.
[29] *Jones and Others v. the United Kingdom*, nos 34356/06 and 40528/06, § 195, 14 January 2014; *Al-Saadoon and Mufdhi v. the United Kingdom*, no. 61498/08, § 126, ECHR 2010 (extracts); *Catan and Others v. the Republic of Moldova and Russia* [GC], nos 43370/04, 8252/05, and 18454/06, § 136, ECHR 2012 (extracts).

come from several sources of which the three most important are identified in article 38(1) of the Statute of the International Court of Justice: treaties, customary law, and general principles. There are many examples of international treaties being considered as part of the context for the purposes of interpreting the scope of provisions of the Convention.[30] Human rights treaties such as the Convention on the Rights of the Child,[31] the Framework Convention for the Protection of National Minorities,[32] and the European Social Charter[33] are especially important here. The Court has cited many Council of Europe treaties on such matters as trafficking in human beings,[34] life imprisonment,[35] higher education,[36] and environmental protection.[37] This sort of reference to international law is very similar to what is increasingly the practice of national courts around the world, especially those dealing with human rights and constitutional matters. They refer to international law, including the European Convention on Human Rights,[38] as being relevant and persuasive[39] rather than as a binding source in the interpretation of their own domestic legal provisions.

With respect to the first of the international sources, treaties and conventions, although strictly speaking article 31(1)(c) is limited to treaties and other norms that are in force between the parties, the Court also considers international law more generally. Occasionally, the Court has insisted upon the fact that a State be bound by a particular treaty,[40] but

---

[30] *Prince Hans-Adam II of Liechtenstein v. Germany* [GC], no. 42527/98, §§ 54–59, ECHR 2001-VIII; *Al-Adsani v. the United Kingdom* [GC], no. 35763/97, § 57, ECHR 2001-XI; *Andrejeva v. Latvia* [GC], no. 55707/00, Partly Dissenting Opinion of Judge Ziemele, § 20, ECHR 2009.

[31] *Harroudj v. France*, no. 43631/09, § 42, 4 October 2012; *Wagner and J.M.W.L. v. Luxembourg*, no. 76240/01, § 120, 28 June 2007; *Pini and Others v. Romania*, nos 78028/01 and 78030/01, §§ 139 and 144, ECHR 2004-V; *Emonet and Others v. Switzerland*, no. 39051/03, §§ 65–66, 13 December 2007; *Maire v. Portugal*, no. 48206/99, § 72, ECHR 2003-VII; *Siliadin v. France*, no. 73316/01, §§ 85–87, ECHR 2005-VII; *Ponomaryovi v. Bulgaria*, no. 5335/05, § 57, ECHR 2011; *Söderman v. Sweden* [GC], no. 5786/08, § 82, 12 November 2013.

[32] ETS 157, cited in *Polacco and Garofalo v. Italy*, no. 23450/94, Commission decision of 15 September 1997, (1998) 41 YB 42, DR 90-B, p. 5; *Chapman v. the United Kingdom* [GC], no. 27238/95, §§ 93, 94, 98, 127, ECHR 2001-I.

[33] ETS 35, cited in *Vörður Ólafsson v. Iceland*, no. 20161/06, §§ 22, 53, ECHR 2010; *Arnolin and Others v. France*, nos 20127/03, 31795/03, 35937/03, 2185/04, 4208/04, 12654/04, 15466/04, 15612/04, 27549/04, 27552/04, 27554/04, 27560/04, 27566/04, 27572/04, 27586/04, 27588/04, 27593/04, 27599/04, 27602/04, 27605/04, 27611/04, 27615/04, 27632/04, 34409/04, and 12176/05, § 75, 9 January 2007; *Evaldsson and Others v. Sweden* (dec.), no. 75252/01, 28 March 2006; *Tüm Haber Sen and Çinar v. Turkey*, no. 28602/95, §§ 12, 24, 39, ECHR 2006-II; *Stec and Others v. The United Kingdom* (dec.) [GC], nos 65731/01 and 65900/01, §§ 25, 34, 52, ECHR 2005-X; *Sigurður A. Sigurjónsson v. Iceland*, 30 June 1993, §35, Series A no. 264; *Sørensen and Rasmussen v. Denmark* [GC], nos 52562/99 and 52620/99, §§ 72–75, ECHR 2006-I.

[34] Council of Europe Convention on Action in Trafficking in Human Beings, ETS 197, cited in *Rantsev v. Cyprus and Russia*, no. 25965/04, §§160–174, 281–289, 296, 307, ECHR 2010 (extracts); *Tremblay v. France*, 48 697 015 801 no. 37194/02, § 25, 11 September 2007; *Siliadin v. France* no. 73316/01, § 111, ECHR 2005-VII.

[35] Council of Europe Convention on the Prevention of Terrorism, ETS 196, cited in *Kafkaris v. Cyprus* [GC], no. 21906/04, §§ 68, 101, ECHR 2008.

[36] Council of Europe Convention on the Recognition of Qualifications concerning Higher Education in the European Region, ETS 165, cited in *Leyla Şahin v. Turkey*, no. 44774/98, § 136, 29 June 2004.

[37] Council of Europe Convention on Civil Liability for Damage resulting from Activities Dangerous to the Environment, ETS 150, cited in *Öneryıldız v. Turkey*, no. 48939/99, § 59, 18 June 2002.

[38] See, e.g., *Lawrence v. Texas*, 539 US 558 (2003), at pp. 573, 576 (citing *Dudgeon v. The United Kingdom*, 22 October 1981, Series A no. 45; *Norris v. Ireland*, 26 October 1988, Series A no. 142; *Modinos v. Cyprus*, 22 April 1993, Series A no. 259); *S v. Makwanyane and Another*, [1995] ZACC 3, paras 68, 81 (citing *Soering v. the United Kingdom*, 7 July 1989, Series A no. 161).

[39] *Re Public Service Employee Relations Act (Alberta)*, [1987] 1 SCR 313, at p. 348.

[40] *V.C. v. Slovakia*, no. 18968/07, § 117, ECHR 2011 (extracts).

this is the exception, and as a general rule in referring to international treaties for interpretative purposes the Court 'has never distinguished between sources of law according to whether or not they have been signed or ratified by the respondent State'.[41] The European Union Charter of Fundamental Rights, adopted in 2000 and offering a fresher, more modern formulation than the sometimes archaic provisions of the European Convention, is especially influential, although it cannot be ratified by the significant minority of Council of Europe Member States that are not also part of the Union.[42] Article 52(3) of the Charter specifies: 'In so far as this Charter contains rights which correspond to rights guaranteed by the Convention for the Protection of Human Rights and Fundamental Freedoms, the meaning and scope of those rights shall be the same as those laid down by the said Convention. This provision shall not prevent Union law providing more extensive protection.' The Court has also invoked the American Convention on Human Rights, unlikely ever to apply directly to more than a few European states.[43] In a case dealing with freedom of expression, the Court noted the reference in article 19(2) of the International Covenant on Civil and Political Rights to information and ideas 'in the form of art' to support its conclusion that artistic expression was also included in article 10(1) of the Convention, despite the silence of the provision on this matter.[44] It has also relied upon the Convention on the Non-applicability of Statutory Limitations to War Crimes and Crimes against Humanity,[45] the Convention on the Prevention and Punishment of the Crime of Genocide,[46] and the Convention against Torture and Other Cruel, Inhuman, or Degrading Treatment or Punishment.[47]

The reference to international treaties goes beyond the sphere of human rights instruments. In recent years, the Court has made important references to international humanitarian law instruments, including the Geneva Conventions and their additional protocols.[48] In *Marckx v. Belgium*, article 8 of the Convention was interpreted with regard to the Convention on the Establishment of Maternal Descent of Natural Children, which Belgium had signed but not ratified, and the European Convention on the Legal Status of Children Born out of Wedlock,[49] which Belgium had not even signed.[50] Other examples include the European Convention on State Immunity,[51] the Oviedo Convention on

---

[41] *Demir and Baykara v. Turkey* [GC], no. 34503/97, § 78, ECHR 2008.

[42] See, e.g., *Demir and Baykara v. Turkey* [GC], no. 34503/97, § 105, ECHR 2008; *Scoppola v. Italy (no. 2)* [GC], no. 10249/03, § 105, 17 September 2009; *Christine Goodwin v. the United Kingdom* [GC], no. 28957/95, § 100, ECHR 2002-VI, *Vilho Eskelinen and Others v. Finland* [GC], no. 63235/00, § 60, ECHR 2007-II; *Sørensen and Rasmussen v. Denmark* [GC], nos 52562/99 and 52620/99, § 74, ECHR 2006-I.

[43] *Scoppola v. Italy (no. 2)* [GC], no. 10249/03, § 105, 17 September 2009; *Soering v. the United Kingdom*, 7 July 1989, §§ 88, 105, Series A no. 161.

[44] *Müller and Others v. Switzerland*, 24 May 1988, § 27, Series A no. 133.

[45] (1970) 754 UNTS 73, cited in *Marguš v. Croatia*, no. 4455/10 [GC], § 133, 27 May 2014.

[46] (1951) 78 UNTS 277, cited in *Marguš v. Croatia*, no. 4455/10 [GC], § 132, 27 May 2014.

[47] (1987) 1465 UNTS 85, cited in *Marguš v. Croatia*, no. 4455/10 [GC], § 132, 27 May 2014.

[48] *Marguš v. Croatia*, no. 4455/10 [GC], §§ 131–132, 27 May 2014; *Hassan v. The United Kingdom*, no. 29750/09, § 106, 16 September 2014.

[49] ETS 85.

[50] *Marckx v. Belgium*, 13 June 1979, §§ 20, 41, Series A no. 31.

[51] (1972) 1495 UNTS 182, cited in *Cudak v. Lithuania* [GC], no. 15869/02, § 56, ECHR 2010; *McElhinney v. Ireland* [GC], no. 31253/96, § 36, ECHR 2001-XI; *Al-Adsani v. the United Kingdom* [GC], no. 35763/97, § 55, ECHR 2001-XI; *Fogarty v. the United Kingdom* [GC], no. 37112/97, § 35, ECHR 2001-XI.

Human Rights and Biomedicine,[52] the Convention on Civil Liability for Damage resulting from Activities Dangerous to the Environment,[53] the Convention on the Protection of the Environment through Criminal Law,[54] and the Convention on Access to Information, Public Participation in Decision-making and Access to Justice in Environmental Matters.[55]

The Court has said that it 'in defining the meaning of terms and notions in the text of the Convention, can and must take into account elements of international law other than the Convention, the interpretation of such elements by competent organs, and the practice of European States reflecting their common values', noting that the 'consensus emerging from specialised international instruments may constitute a relevant consideration for the Court when it interprets the provisions of the Convention in specific cases'.[56] In particular, it has said that the Convention is to be applied in accordance with principles relating to the international protection of human rights.[57] Rather than associate such reliance upon international law generally upon the reference in article 31(3)(c) of the Vienna Convention, the Court has explained that 'the common international or domestic law standards of European States reflect a reality that the Court cannot disregard when it is called upon to clarify the scope of a Convention provision that more conventional means of interpretation have not enabled it to establish with a sufficient degree of certainty'.[58] That is because in considering the object and purposes of provisions of the Convention, it may turn to the 'international law background to the legal question before it', which is 'made up of a set of rules and principles that are accepted by the vast majority of States'.[59] One example of such an 'emerging international consensus amongst the Member States of the Council of Europe' is the 'special needs of minorities and an obligation to protect their security, identity and lifestyle, not only for the purpose of safeguarding the interests of the minorities themselves but to preserve a cultural diversity of value to the whole community'.[60]

References in the case law of the Court to the second source listed in article 38 of the Statute of the International Court of Justice are rare. Customary and conventional law have a symbiotic relationship, and treaties often provide evidence to be considered in assessing the existence of customary legal rules at the universal or regional level.[61] Accordingly, '[w]here the customary rule turns out to be different from the Convention provision, at least in its original form and intent, that rule may indeed affect the

---

[52] ETS 164, cited in *S.H. and Others v. Austria* [GC], no. 57813/00, § 107, ECHR 2011; *Vo v. France* [GC], no. 53924/00, § 84, ECHR 2004-VIII; *Glass v. the United Kingdom*, no. 61827/00, § 75, ECHR 2004-II.

[53] ETS 150, cited in *Öneryıldız v. Turkey* [GC], no. 48939/99, § 59, ECHR 2004-XII.

[54] ETS 172, cited in *Öneryıldız v. Turkey* [GC], no. 48939/99, § 59, ECHR 2004-XII.

[55] (2001) 2161 UNTS 447, cited in *Taşkın and Others v. Turkey*, no. 49517/99, §§ 99 and 119, 4 December 2003.

[56] *Bayatyan v. Armenia* [GC], no. 23459/03, § 102, ECHR 2011; *Demir and Baykara v. Turkey* [GC], no. 34503/97, § 85, 12 November 2008.

[57] *Streletz, Kessler, and Krenz v. Germany* [GC], nos 34044/96, 35532/97, and 44801/98, § 90, ECHR 2001-II; *Maire v. Portugal*, no. 48206/99, § 72, ECHR 2003-VII.

[58] *Demir and Baykara v. Turkey* [GC], no. 34503/97, § 76, 12 November 2008.

[59] Ibid., § 76. Also *Saadi v. the United Kingdom* [GC], no. 13229/03, § 63, ECHR 2008.

[60] *D.H. and Others v. the Czech Republic* [GC], no. 57325/00, § 181, ECHR 2007-IV. Also *Oršuš and Others v. Croatia* [GC], no. 15766/03, § 148, ECHR 2010; *Chapman v. The United Kingdom* [GC], no. 27238/95, § 96, ECHR 2001-I; *Sampanis and Others v. Greece*, no. 32526/05, § 73, 5 June 2008.

[61] *Lalmahomed v. the Netherlands*, no. 26036/08, Concurring Opinion of Judge Ziemele, 22 February 2011.

subsequent reading of the Convention provision'.[62] Without suggesting that they are evidence of customary international law as such, the Court will often cite 'intrinsically non-binding instruments of Council of Europe organs, in particular recommendations and resolutions of the Committee of Ministers and the Parliamentary Assembly',[63] and the materials generated by the European Commission for Democracy through Law or 'Venice Commission'[64] and the European Commission against Racism and Intolerance,[65] and of the reports of the European Committee for the Prevention of Torture and Inhuman or Degrading Treatment or Punishment.[66] In a case dealing with immunities, it said that a provision of the International Law Commission's draft articles on immunities adopted in 1991 applied to the respondent State 'under customary law', with the consequence that it must be taken into consideration in assessing the right of access to a court.[67]

The European Court of Human Rights has confirmed that 'general principles of law recognised by civilised nations', the expression used in article 38(1)(c) of the Statute of the International Court of Justice, are among the relevant rules applicable to interpretation of the European Convention.[68] For example, '[t]he principle whereby a civil claim must be capable of being submitted to a judge ranks as one of the universally "recognised" fundamental principles of law; the same is true of the principle of international law which forbids the denial of justice. Article 6 para. 1 (art. 6-1) must be read in the light of these principles.'[69] For Judge Fitzmaurice, '[g]eneral principles of law, it may be said, can, where relevant, properly be applied in the interpretation and application of a treaty provision, provided that the terms of that provision do not clearly exclude them'.[70] The Convention itself refers to 'the general principles of law recognised by civilised nations' in article 7(2) and to the 'the general principles of international law' in article 1 of Protocol No. 1.

The European Court of Human Rights has also referred to 'general international law', an expression that seems a convenient way of combining the two non-conventional

---

[62] Ibid.

[63] *Demir and Baykara v. Turkey* [GC], no. 34503/97, § 74, ECHR 2008; *Öneryıldız v. Turkey* [GC], no. 48939/99, §§ 59, 71, 90, and 93, ECHR 2004-XII.

[64] *Demir and Baykara v. Turkey* [GC], no. 34503/97, § 75, ECHR 2008; *Russian Conservative Party of Entrepreneurs and Others v. Russia*, nos 55066/00 and 55638/00, §§ 70–73, 11 January 2007; *Basque Nationalist Party—Iparralde Regional Organisation v. France*, no. 71251/01, §§ 45–52, ECHR 2007-II; *Çiloğlu and Others v. Turkey*, no. 73333/01, § 17, 6 March 2007.

[65] *Demir and Baykara v. Turkey* [GC], no. 34503/97; § 75, ECHR 2008; *Bekos and Koutropoulos v. Greece*, no. 15250/02, §§ 33–36, ECHR 2005-XIII (extracts); *Ivanova v. Bulgaria*, no. 52435/99, §§ 65–66, 12 April 2007; *Cobzaru v. Romania*, no. 48254/99, §§ 49–50, 26 July 2007; *D.H. and Others v. the Czech Republic* [GC], no. 57325/00, §§ 59–65, 184, 192, 200, and 205, ECHR 2007-IV.

[66] *Demir and Baykara v. Turkey* [GC], no. 34503/97, § 75, ECHR 2008; *Aerts v. Belgium*, 30 July 1998, § 42, *Reports of Judgments and Decisions* 1998-V; *Slimani v. France*, no. 57671/00, §§ 22 et seq., ECHR 2004-IX; *Nazarenko v. Ukraine*, no. 39483/98, §§ 94–102, 29 April 2003; *Kalashnikov v. Russia*, no. 47095/99, § 97, ECHR 2002-VI; *Kadiķis v. Latvia (no. 2)*, no. 62393/00, § 52, 4 May 2006.

[67] *Cudak v. Lithuania* [GC], no. 15869/02, § 67, ECHR 2010.

[68] See Gérard Cohen-Jonathan, 'Le rôle des principes généraux dans l'interprétation et l'application de la Convention européenne des droits de l'homme', in G. Flécheux, ed., *Mélanges en hommage à Louis*, Brussels: Bruylant, 1998, pp. 165–96.

[69] *Golder v. the United Kingdom*, 21 February 1975, § 35, Series A no. 18; *Demir and Baykara v. Turkey* [GC], no. 34503/97, § 71, ECHR 2008.

[70] *National Union of Belgian Police v. Belgium*, 27 October 1975, Separate Opinion of Sir Gerald Fitzmaurice, Series A no. 19.

sources of international law listed in the classic enumeration, namely customary law and general principles,[71] although it must also include *jus cogens*.[72] Josef Kunz defined 'general international law' as consisting of 'norms binding all members of the international community'.[73] The expression 'general international law' is used in the provisions of the Vienna Convention on the Law of Treaties dealing with peremptory norm[74] and appears in judgments of the International Court of Justice.[75] The expression has been used since the earliest cases before the Court.[76] In an inter-State case involving a dispute about whether the applicant had acted with appropriate diligence, the Grand Chamber said 'general international law does, in principle, recognise the obligation of the applicant Government in an inter-State dispute to act without undue delay in order to uphold legal certainty and not to cause disproportionate harm to the legitimate interests of the respondent State'.[77] It cited as authority a judgment of the International Court of Justice.[78] In another case, the Court referred to 'rules of general international law reflected in the 1978 Vienna Convention on Succession of States in respect of Treaties and, to a certain extent, in the 1983 Vienna Convention on Succession of States in respect of State Property, Archives and Debts', a treaty not yet in force.[79] It has spoken of principles governing State responsibility for an internationally wrongful act under 'general international law'[80] and of the rules of general international law applicable to reservations to treaties.[81]

The Statute of the International Court of Justice also mentions two subsidiary sources of international law, case law and scholarly writing. The Court has made abundant use of such materials in its interpretation of the Convention. It has described the judgments of the International Court of Justice as being 'authoritative as regards the content of customary international law'.[82] It has even gone somewhat further, holding that it 'must

---

[71] Note the use by the Plenary Court of the term 'general international law' under the rubric 'General principles of international law': *James and Others v. the United Kingdom*, 21 February 1986, § 60, Series A no. 98; *Lithgow and Others v. the United Kingdom*, 8 July 1986, § 113, Series A no. 102.

[72] See Grigory Tunkin, 'Is General International Law Customary Law Only?', (1993) 4 *EJIL* 534.

[73] Josef Kunz, 'General International Law and the Law of International Organizations', (1953) 47 *AJIL* 456, at p. 456.

[74] Vienna Convention on the Law of Treaties, (1980) 1155 UNTS 331, arts 53, 64.

[75] For example, *Legal Consequences of the Construction of a Wall in the Occupied Palestinian Territory*, Advisory Opinion, I.C.J. Reports 2004, p. 136, para. 150; *Accordance with International Law of the Unilateral Declaration of Independence in Respect of Kosovo*, Advisory Opinion, I.C.J. Reports 2010, p. 403, paras 78–84; *Application of the Convention on the Prevention and Punishment of the Crime of Genocide (Bosnia and Herzegovina v. Serbia and Montenegro)*, Judgment, I.C.J. Reports 2007, p. 43, para. 149.

[76] For example, *Ringeisen v. Austria*, 16 July 1971, Separate Opinion of Judge Verdross, Series A no. 13; *De Wilde, Ooms and Versyp v. Belgium* (Article 50), 10 March 1972, Separate Opinion of Judge Mosler, § 3, Series A no. 14.

[77] *Cyprus v. Turkey* (just satisfaction) [GC], no. 25781/94, 12 May 2014.

[78] *Certain Phosphate Lands in Nauru (Nauru v. Australia), Preliminary Objections*, Judgment, I.C.J. Reports 1992, p. 240.

[79] *Ališić and Others v. Bosnia and Herzegovina, Croatia, Serbia, Slovenia and the former Yugoslavia Republic of Macedonia* [GC], no. 60642/08, § 59, 16 July 2014. Also ibid., Partly Dissenting Opinion of Judge Nußburger, Joined by Judge Popović.

[80] *Jaloud v. The Netherlands*, no. 47708/08, § 154, 20 November 2014; *Al Nashiri v. Poland*, no. 28761/11, § 457, 24 July 2014.

[81] *Belilos v. Switzerland*, 29 April 1988, § 47, Series A no. 132.

[82] *Jones and Others v. the United Kingdom*, nos 34356/06 and 40528/06, § 198, 14 January 2014, citing *Jurisdictional Immunities of the State (Germany v. Italy: Greece intervening)*, Judgment, I.C.J. Reports 2012, p. 99. See also *Berić and Others v. Bosnia and Herzegovina* (dec.), nos. 36357/04, 36360/04, 38346/04, 41705/04, 45190/04, 45578/04, 45579/04, 45580/04, 91/05, 97/05, 100/05, 101/05, 1121/05, 1123/05, 1125/05,

endeavour to interpret and apply the Convention in a manner which is consistent with the framework under international law delineated by the International Court of Justice'.[83] The Court has also cited decisions of the Permanent Court of International Justice,[84] international arbitration tribunals,[85] and the United Nations *ad hoc* criminal tribunals,[86] of regional tribunals such as the Inter-American Court of Human Rights,[87] of treaty bodies such as the United Nations Human Rights Committee,[88] and of national courts

1129/05, 1132/05, 1133/05, 1169/05, 1172/05, 1175/05, 1177/05, 1180/05, 1185/05, 20793/05, and 25496/05, § 7, 16 October 2007, citing *Military and Paramilitary Activities in and against Nicaragua (Nicaragua v. United States of America)*. Merits, Judgment, I.C.J. Reports 1986, p. 14; *Austria v. Italy*, no. 788/60, Commission decision of 11 January 1961, (1961) 4 YB 116, at p. 148, citing *Nottebohm case (second phase)*, Judgment I.C.J. Reports 1955, p. 4; *Hassan v. the United Kingdom* [GC], no. 29750/09, §§ 77 and 35–37, 16 September 2014, citing *Legality of the Threat or Use of Nuclear Weapons*, Advisory Opinion, I.C. J. Reports 1996, p. 226; *Legal Consequences of the Construction of a Wall in the Occupied Palestinian Territory*, Advisory Opinion, I.C.J. Reports 2004, p. 136; *Armed Activities on the Territory of the Congo (Democratic Republic of the Congo v. Uganda)*, Judgment, I.C.J. Reports 2005, p. 168.

[83] *Hassan v. the United Kingdom* [GC], no. 29750/09, §§ 77, 102, 16 September 2014.

[84] *Blečić v. Croatia* [GC], no. 59532/00, § 46, ECHR 2006-III, citing *Phosphates in Morocco (Preliminary Objections)*, PCIJ, Series A/B, no. 74, pp. 10–30. Also *Austria v. Italy*, no. 788/60, Commission decision of 11 January 1961, (1961) 4 YB 116, citing the *Panevezys-Saldutiskls Railway*, Series A/B no. 76, p. 19 and *Mavrommatis Palestine Concessions*, Series A no. 2, p 35; *Guiso-Gallisay v. Italy* (just satisfaction) [GC], no. 58858/00, §§ 49, 51, 22 December 2009, citing *Factory at Chorzów (Germany v. Poland)*, PCIJ, Series A no. 17.

[85] *Ilaşcu and Others v. Moldova and Russia* [GC], no. 48787/99, § 319, ECHR 2004-VII, citing *The Cairo case (France v. Mexico)*, (1929) 5 RIAA 516; *Guiso-Gallisay v. Italy* (just satisfaction) [GC], no. 58858/00, § 12, 22 December 2009, citing *Texaco Overseas Petroleum Company and California Asiatic Oil Company v. Libya*, (1977) 104 *Journal de droit international* 350; *Guiso-Gallisay v. Italy* (just satisfaction) [GC], no. 58858/00, § 50, 22 December 2009, citing *Amoco International Finance Corporation (Amoco International Finance Corporation v. Iran)*, Interlocutory Award of 14 July 1987, Iran–United States Claims Tribunal Reports (1987-II), para. 192.

[86] *Al-Adsani v. the United Kingdom* [GC], no. 35763/97, § 60, ECHR 2001-XI, citing *Prosecutor v. Furundžija* (IT-95-17/1-T), Judgment of 10 December 1998; *Zontul v. Greece*, no. 12294/07, §§ 61–64, 91, 17 January 2012, citing *Kunarac et al.* (IT-96-23/1-A), Judgment, 12 June 2002, *Prosecutor v. Akayesu* (ICTR-96-4-T), Judgment of 2 September 1998, *Prosecutor v. Furundžija* (IT-95-17/1-T), Judgment of 10 December 1998, and *Prosecutor v. Musema* (ICTR-96-13-T), Judgment and Sentence of 27 January 2000; *Korbely v. Hungary* [GC], no. 9174/02, § 87, ECHR 2008, citing *Prosecutor v. Akayesu* (ICTR-96-4-T), Judgment of 2 September 1998.

[87] *Marguš v. Croatia* [GC], no. 4455/10, § 138, 27 May 2014, citing I/A Court H.R., *Case of Barrios Altos v. Peru. Reparations and Costs*, Judgment of 30 November 2001, Series C no. 87, I/A Court H.R., *Case of Gomes Lund et al. ('Guerrilha do Araguaia') v. Brazil, Preliminary Objections, Merits, Reparations, and Costs*, Judgment of 24 November 2010, Series C no. 219, I/A Court H.R., *Case Gelman v. Uruguay. Merits and Reparations*. Judgment of 24 February 2011, Series C no. 221, and I/A Court H.R., *Case of the Massacres of El Mozote and Nearby Places v. El Salvador, Interpretation of the Judgment on Merits, Reparations and Costs*, Judgment of 19 August 2013, Series C no. 264; *Varnava and Others v. Turkey* [GC], nos 16064/90, 16065/90, 16066/90, 16068/90, 16069/90, 16070/90, 16071/90, 16072/90, and 16073/90, §§ 93–97, 147, ECHR 2009, citing I/A Court H.R., *Case of Blake v. Guatemala, Preliminary Objections*, Judgment of 2 July 1996, Series C no. 27; *Palomo Sánchez and Others v. Spain* [GC], nos 28955/06, 28957/06, 28959/06, and 28964/06, § 56, ECHR 2011, citing I/A Court H.R., *Compulsory Membership in an Association Prescribed by Law for the Practice of Journalism (Arts 13 and 29 American Convention on Human Rights)*, Advisory Opinion OC-5/85 of 13 November 1985, Series A no. 5; *Ergin v. Turkey (no. 6)*, no. 47533/99, § 25, 45, ECHR 2006-VI (extracts), citing I/A Court H.R., *Case of Cantoral Benavides v. Peru*, Merits, Judgment of 18 August 2000, Series C no. 69 and I/A Court H.R., *Case of Durand and Ugarte v. Peru*, Merits, Judgment of 16 August 2000, Series C no. 68.

[88] *Svinarenko and Slyadnev v. Russia* [GC], nos 32541/08 and 43441/08, §§ 70, 132, 17 July 2014, citing *Mikhail Pustovoit v. Ukraine*, no. 1405/2005, UN Doc. CCPR/C/110/D/1405/2005.

from within Europe (Germany,[89] the United Kingdom,[90] France,[91] Spain[92]) and abroad (Canada,[93] the United States[94] and South Africa[95]).

Although it is the classic statement of the sources of international law, article 38 of the Statute of the International Court of Justice does not provide an exhaustive list. One important source of law that is not explicitly included is *jus cogens* or peremptory norms. On several occasions the Court has described the prohibition of torture as a peremptory norm or *jus cogens*.[96] It has also recognized the prohibition of genocide as a *jus cogens* norm.[97] It has followed the International Court of Justice in holding that the *jus cogens* status of a norm does not override the immunity from suit that a State enjoys before the courts of another State.[98] In individual opinions, several judges of the Court have ventured opinions about the scope of *jus cogens*. The statements are almost never supported with any authority in defence of the position taken. In a separate opinion, one judge said that '[p]rohibition of discrimination has crystallised into a *jus cogens* norm'.[99] Another said that the prohibition against the use of force, the right to self-determination, the prohibition of genocide, and certain fundamental human rights were 'established peremptory norms' norms, but that enjoyment of possessions, economic freedom, or access to a court or tribunal, particularly in civil proceedings, were not.[100] Yet another described the prohibition of *refoulement* of refugees in this manner.[101]

---

[89] *Vinter and Others v. the United Kingdom* [GC], nos 66069/09, 130/10, and 3896/10, § 69, ECHR 2013 (extracts), citing *Life Imprisonment case (lebenslange Freiheitsstrafe)*, 21 June 1977, 45 BVerfGE 187.

[90] *Al-Adsani v. the United Kingdom* [GC], no. 35763/97, § 60, ECHR 2001-XI, citing *R. v. Bow Street Metropolitan Stipendiary and Others, ex parte Pinochet Ugarte (no. 3)*, [2000] 1 AC 147.

[91] *Jones and Others v. the United Kingdom*, nos 34356/06 and 40528/06, § 197, 14 January 2014, citing *Grosz v. Germany* (No. 04-475040, 3 January 2006).

[92] *Perinçek v. Switzerland*, no. 27510/08, §§ 34–38, 121, 17 December 2013, citing Spanish Constitutional Court, Judgment 235/2007, 7 November 2007.

[93] *Jones and Others v. the United Kingdom*, nos 34356/06 and 40528/06, § 197, 14 January 2014, citing *Bouzari v. Islamic Republic of Iran*, (2004) 71 OR (3d) 675 and *Hashemi v. Islamic Republic of Iran and Others*, (2012) QCCA 1449; *Harkins and Edwards v. the United Kingdom*, nos 9146/07 and 32650/07, § 44, 17 January 2012, citing *United States v. Burns*, [2001] SCR 283; *Mouvement raëlien suisse v. Switzerland* [GC], no. 16354/06, Joint Dissenting Opinion of Judges Tulkens, Sajó, Lazarova Trajkovska, Bianku, Power-Force, Vučinić, and Yudkivska, ECHR 2012 (extracts), citing *Crookes v. Newton*, [2011] 3 SCR 269.

[94] *Jones and Others v. the United Kingdom*, nos 34356/06 and 40528/06, § 197, 14 January 2014, citing *Siderman de Blake v. Argentina*, 965 F.2d 699 (1992), *Princz v. Germany*, 26 F.3d 1166 (1994), *Smith v. Libya*, 101 F.3d 239 (1997), and *Sampson v. Germany*, 250 F.3d 1145 (2001).

[95] *Vinter and Others v. the United Kingdom* [GC], nos 66069/09, 130/10 and 3896/10, §§ 63–64, ECHR 2013 (extracts), citing *S. v. Dodo*, [2001] ZACC 16 and *Niemand v. The State*, [2001] ZACC 11.

[96] *Ould Dah v. France* (dec.), no. 13113/03, ECHR 2009; *Al-Adsani v. the United Kingdom*, 21 November 2001, § 60, *Reports of Judgments and Decisions* 2001-XI. *Aksoy v. Turkey*, 18 December 1996, § 62, *Reports of Judgments and Decisions* 1996-VI; *Assenov and Others v. Bulgaria*, 28 October 1998, § 93, *Reports of Judgments and Decisions* 1998-VIII; *Selmouni v. France* [GC], no. 25803/94, § 95, ECHR 1999-V.

[97] *Jorgic v. Germany*, no. 74613/01, § 68, ECHR 2007-III; *Stichting Mothers of Srebrenica and Others v. the Netherlands* (dec.), no. 65542/12, § 157, ECHR 2013 (extracts).

[98] *Stichting Mothers of Srebrenica and Others v. the Netherlands* (dec.), no. 65542/12, § 158, 11 June 2013, following *Jurisdictional Immunities of the State (Germany v. Italy: Greece intervening)*, Judgment, I.C.J. Reports 2012, p. 99, paras 81–97. See also *Kalogeropoulou and Others v. Greece and Germany* (dec.), no. 59021/00, ECHR 2002-X.

[99] *Georgia v. Russia (I)* [GC], no. 13255/07, Partly Dissenting Opinion of Judge Tsotsoria, 3 July 2014.

[100] *Al-Dulimi and Montana Management Inc. v. Switzerland*, no. 5809/08, Partly Dissenting Opinion of Judge Sajó, 26 November 2013.

[101] *Hirsi Jamaa and Others v. Italy* [GC], no. 27765/09, Concurring Opinion of Judge Pinto de Albuquerque, ECHR 2012.

Judge Dedov has spoken of 'a breach of a *jus cogens* rule such as the prohibition of war crimes'.[102] In a very early decision of the Court, Judge Verdross said that the rule of exhaustion of domestic remedies did not form part of the *jus cogens* rule.[103]

Article 32 of the Vienna Convention on the Law of Treaties invites resort 'to supplementary means of interpretation, including the preparatory work of the treaty and the circumstances of its conclusion'. It may either confirm the meaning reached in applying article 31, or provide its own guidance as to the meaning when article 31 leaves the meaning ambiguous or obscure or leads to a result that is manifestly absurd or unreasonable. The preparatory work or *travaux préparatoires* of the European Convention are rather sparse, especially with respect to the definitions of fundamental rights and issues related to their interpretation and application. There can be no comparison with, for example, the drafting record of the Universal Declaration of Human Rights, where records of meetings that took place over many months and hundreds of proposed amendments may be consulted. In the 1970s and 1980s, the Council of Europe published a collection of materials covering the drafting of the Convention itself and Protocol No. 1. Records of the drafting of some of the subsequent Protocols have been issued in internal Court documents.[104] Beginning with Protocol No. 4, the Committee of Ministers has issued an 'explanatory report' in which there are some references to debates about the formulation of certain provisions.

Despite the limited material available, the Convention organs have often cited the *travaux préparatoires*, generally without specifying whether this is to confirm the interpretation resulting from article 31 or to provide guidance where article 31 does not deliver an acceptable result. For example, in the interpretation of the reference to general principles of international law in article 1 of Protocol No. 1 the Court has referred in detail to the debates as well as to the resolution of the Committee of Ministers approving the final text.[105] Sometimes, the Court has used the *travaux préparatoires* in order to confirm the interpretation resulting from a literal reading of the provision in question.[106] In any early case, the Court refused to consider the *travaux* of article 5(1)(c) 'having regard to a generally recognised principle regarding the interpretation of international treaties, resort to the preparatory work', finding that the Convention text was 'clear in itself'.[107]

The European Convention is authenticated in both English and French. Consequently, the principles of article 33 of the Vienna Convention on the Law of Treaties are relevant to its interpretation. Even before the Vienna Convention on the Law of Treaties had been adopted, the Court acknowledged that 'confronted with two versions of

---

[102] *Janowiec and Others v. Russia* [GC], nos 55508/07 and 29520/09, Concurring Opinion of Judge Dedov, 21 October 2013.

[103] *Ringeisen v. Austria*, 16 July 1971, Separate Opinion of Judge Verdross, Series A no. 13.

[104] Travaux Préparatoires *Relating to Protocol No. 2 to the Convention for the Protection of Human Rights and Fundamental Freedoms, conferring upon the European Court of Human Rights competence to give advisory opinions*, Strasbourg: Council of Europe, 1966; *Collected Edition of the* 'Travaux Préparatoires' *of Protocol No. 3 to the Convention amending Articles 29, 30 and 34 of the Convention*, Strasbourg: Council of Europe, 1970; *Collected Edition of the* 'Travaux Préparatoires' *of Protocol No. 4 to the Convention, securing certain rights and freedoms other than those already included in the Convention and in the first Protocol thereto*, Strasbourg: Council of Europe, 1976; *Collected Edition of the* 'Travaux Préparatoires' *of Protocol No. 5 to the Convention amending Articles 22 and 40*, Strasbourg: Council of Europe, 1975.

[105] *Lithgow and Others v. the United Kingdom*, 8 July 1986, § 117, Series A no. 102.

[106] *Kjeldsen, Busk Madsen and Pedersen v. Denmark*, 7 December 1976, § 50, Series A no. 23.

[107] *Lawless v. Ireland (no. 3)*, 1 July 1961, p. 24, § 14, Series A no. 3.

a treaty which are equally authentic but not exactly the same, the Court must, following established international law precedents, interpret them in a way that will reconcile them as far as possible'.[108] In subsequent judgments where discrepancies in the two texts were at issue, the Court referred to the principle set out in article 33 of the Vienna Convention.[109] In a recent case, it affirmed that article 33 'reflects international customary law'.[110]

In *Wemhoff*, the Court noted that the English version of article 5(3) could support two interpretations, one of them a narrow approach by which an unacceptable delay in criminal proceedings concerned the pre-trial period only, and the French version, where the word *jugée* was employed, left no doubt that the right to a speedy trial continued until the completion of the proceedings.[111] Similarly, the Court compared the rather limited scope of the notion of 'promptness' in the English text of article 5(3) with the immediacy of the French equivalent, *aussitôt*, concluding that the French term 'confirms that the degree of flexibility attaching to the notion of "promptness" is limited'.[112] In a case decided before the adoption of the Vienna Convention, the Court compared the French and English versions of article 14, but without referring to any established principle or rule of interpretation. It noted the 'very general wording' of the French text (*sans distinction aucune*), which does not seem to prohibit every difference of treatment, and said it must be read in light of the 'more restrictive text' of the English version ('without discrimination'). It said that the French version alone might lead to 'absurd results'.[113] Addressing the meaning of *gratuitement*/'free' in article 6(3)(e), which concerns the right to a funded interpreter in criminal trials, the Court concluded that the two terms were equivalent. Although it made reference to the relevant provisions of the Vienna Convention, this was not really an application of article 33 because there was no difference in meaning in the two authoritative texts.[114] The right to 'adequate time' for preparation of the defence, in article 6(3)(b), is made stronger and more imperative with the word *nécessaires* in the French version, as the European Commission of Human Rights observed.[115]

Respect for precedent

The implied mention of case law in the reference to 'rules of international law' in article 31(3)(c) of the Vienna Convention on the Law of Treaties is not generally taken to suggest a rule of binding precedent or *stare decisis*. Nevertheless, the 'normal course' is to follow precedent.[116] Certainly, the judgments of the Court are replete with citations to its

[108] *Wemhoff v. Germany*, 27 June 1968, p. 19, § 8, Series A no. 7. Also *Wemhoff v. Germany*, 27 June 1968, Individual Opinion of Judge Terje Wold, Series A no. 7.

[109] *Brogan and Others v. the United Kingdom*, 29 November 1988, § 59, Series A no. 145-B.

[110] *Stoll v. Switzerland* [GC], no. 69698/01, § 59, ECHR 2007-V, citing *LaGrand (Germany v. United States of America)*, Judgment, I.C.J. Reports 2001, p. 466, para. 101.

[111] *Wemhoff v. Germany*, 27 June 1968, p. 19, §§ 7–8, Series A no. 7.

[112] *Brogan and Others v. the United Kingdom*, 29 November 1988, § 59, Series A no. 145-B. Also *E. v. Norway*, 29 August 1990, § 64, Series A no. 181-A.

[113] *Case 'relating to certain aspects of the laws on the use of languages in education in Belgium'* (merits), 23 July 1968, p. 31, § 10, Series A no. 6. See also *National Union of Belgian Police v. Belgium*, 27 October 1975, § 46, Series A no. 19.

[114] *Luedicke, Belkacem and Koç v. Germany*, 28 November 1978, § 40, Series A no. 29.

[115] *Can v. Austria*, no. 9300/81, Commission report of 12 July 1984, § 53, DR 35, p. 523.

[116] Luziuz Wildhaber, 'Precedent in the European Court of Human Rights', in Mahoney et al., *Mélanges Ryssdal*, pp. 1529–46, at p. 1538. Also A. Mowbray, 'An Examination of the European Court of Human Rights' Approach to Overruling its Previous Case Law' (2009) 9 *HRLR* 179.

earlier case law and that of the European Commission. Indeed, most judgments contain a section dealing with the general principles the Court will apply regarding a provision that is usually copied, often word for word, from earlier rulings. Obedience to precedent has been held out as dictated by 'the interests of legal certainty, foreseeability and equality before the law'.[117] However, 'the Court is not formally bound to follow any of its previous judgments',[118] and on occasion it is prepared to depart from precedent. It has noted that 'a failure by the Court to maintain a dynamic and evolutive approach would risk rendering it a bar to reform or improvement'.[119]

Read as a whole, promote harmony

Sometimes, the Court has insisted that 'the Convention must be read as a whole, and interpreted in such a way as to promote internal consistency and harmony between its various provisions'.[120] In *Misick*, the United Kingdom had withdrawn the application of article 3 of Protocol No. 1 to the Turks and Caicos Islands. The applicant, who had been an elected official in the territory, could not invoke that provision, so he based his claim on article 8. Finding the case inadmissible, the Court said 'that Article 8 should not, in principle, be interpreted in such a way as to incorporate the requirements of Article 3 of Protocol No. 1 in respect of territories to which the latter Article does not apply'.[121]

Nevertheless, in the case of articles 2 and 3, for many years the Court has wrestled with the tension between the two provisions, given the apparent acknowledgement of capital punishment in article 2 yet the prohibition of inhuman and degrading punishment in article 3. Eventually, the Court resolved the contradiction by considering the reference to the death penalty in article 2 to be inoperative, in light of evolving practice within the Council of Europe. Even then, it did not go so far as to hold that the death penalty was inhuman and degrading punishment, but rather condemned it as 'ill-treatment'.[122]

Dynamic and evolutive interpretation

The European Convention is largely derived from the Universal Declaration of Human Rights, as the Preamble to the Convention confirms. The Declaration was itself intended as a 'common standard of achievement'. Its drafters recognized that they were setting out a

---

[117] *Sergey Zolotukhin v. Russia* [GC], no. 14939/03, § 80, ECHR 2009; *Vilho Eskelinen and Others v. Finland* [GC], no. 63235/00, § 56, ECHR 2007-II; *Scoppola v. Italy (no. 2)* [GC], no. 10249/03, § 104, 17 September 2009; *Chapman v. the United Kingdom* [GC], no. 27238/95, § 70, ECHR 2001-I; *Bayatyan v. Armenia* [GC], no. 23459/03, § 98, ECHR 2011.

[118] *Herrmann v. Germany* [GC], no. 9300/07, § 78, 26 June 2012; *Scoppola v. Italy (no. 2)* [GC], no. 10249/03, § 104, 17 September 2009.

[119] *Sergey Zolotukhin v. Russia* [GC], no. 14939/03, § 80, ECHR 2009; *Vilho Eskelinen and Others v. Finland* [GC], no. 63235/00, § 56, ECHR 2007-II.

[120] *Misick v. the United Kingdom* (dec.), no. 10781/10, § 23, 16 October 2012. Also *Stec and Others v. the United Kingdom* (dec.) [GC], nos 65731/01 and 65900/01, § 48, ECHR 2005-X; *Austin and Others v. the United Kingdom* [GC], nos 39692/09, 40713/09, and 41008/09, § 54, ECHR 2012; *Saadi v. the United Kingdom* [GC], no. 13229/03, § 62, ECHR 2008; *Hirsi Jamaa and Others v. Italy* [GC], no. 27765/09, § 171, ECHR 2012.

[121] *Misick v. the United Kingdom* (dec.), no. 10781/10, § 23, 16 October 2012. Also *Stec and Others v. the United Kingdom* (dec.) [GC], nos 65731/01 and 65900/01, § 48, ECHR 2005-X; *Austin and Others v. the United Kingdom* [GC], nos 39692/09, 40713/09, and 41008/09, § 54, ECHR 2012.

[122] *Al-Saadoon and Mufdhi v. the United Kingdom*, no. 61498/08, § 120, ECHR 2010 (extracts).

programme for the development of rights rather than a rigid and definitive codification. Those who wrote the European Convention acknowledged, in the Preamble, that they were taking the 'first steps for the collective enforcement of certain of the rights stated in the Universal Declaration'. This initial understanding was of a dynamic body of law capable of adjusting itself to a changing environment. Therefore, and because it is 'first and foremost a system for the protection of human rights',[123] the Convention must be interpreted in a manner that bears in mind changing conditions and an emerging consensus as to the appropriate standards. It is 'a living instrument which must be interpreted in the light of present-day conditions and of the ideas prevailing in democratic States today'.[124]

The approach to interpretation is often described as 'dynamic and evolutive'. The term 'evolutive' can be found in the Oxford English Dictionary, although it is not in very common use; the Court seems to have imported it from the French *évolutive*. In one sense, such a dynamic and evolutive approach is not interpretation at all. It amounts to judicial law making, albeit an authority that finds its justification in an interpretation of the Convention. It is not dissimilar from what is allowed and even expected in constitutional interpretation within domestic systems. It is recognized that a measure of judicial initiative is mandated by the nature of constitutional documents that have often been drafted long ago and that are difficult to alter. Nevertheless, the boldness of allowing an international court to adjust the scope of an international agreement reached by a large number of sovereign states, without their explicit consent and without allowing them the possibility of reservation to such changes, cannot be gainsaid.

It is a quite unprecedented development in international law, and one to which there was some initial resistance. Judge Fitzmaurice objected, noting that the Convention and other human rights treaties had made 'heavy inroads on some of the most cherished preserves of governments in the sphere of their domestic jurisdiction or *domaine réservé*'. He said this 'could justify even a somewhat restrictive interpretation of the Convention but, without going as far as that, they must be said, unquestionably, not only to justify, but positively to demand, a cautious and conservative interpretation, particularly as regards any provisions the meaning of which may be uncertain, and where extensive constructions might have the effect of imposing upon the contracting States obligations they had not really meant to assume, or would not have understood themselves to be assuming'.[125] In a recent decision, several judges cautioned against too much judicial activism. Noting that that 'the point of the evolutive interpretation, as conceived by the Court, is to accompany and even channel change' they said 'it is not to anticipate change, still less to try to impose it'.[126]

[123] *Stafford v. the United Kingdom* [GC], no. 46295/99, § 68, ECHR 2002-IV; *Scoppola v. Italy (no. 2)* [GC], no. 10249/03, § 104, 17 September 2009.
[124] *Tyrer v. the United Kingdom*, 25 April 1978, § 31, Series A no. 26; *Kress v. France* [GC], no. 39594/98, § 70, ECHR 2001-VI; *Christine Goodwin v. the United Kingdom* [GC], no. 28957/95, § 75, ECHR 2002-VI; *Bayatyan v. Armenia* [GC], no. 23459/03, § 102, ECHR 2011; *Sergey Zolotukhin v. Russia* [GC], no. 14939/03, § 80, ECHR 2009.
[125] *Golder v. the United Kingdom*, 21 February 1975, Separate Opinion of Judge Sir Gerald Fitzmaurice, §§ 38–39, Series A no. 18.
[126] *X and Others v. Austria* [GC], no. 19010/07, Joint Partly Dissenting Opinion of Judges Casadevall, Ziemele, Kovler, Jočienė, Šikuta, De Gaetano, and Sicilianos, ECHR 2013.

To the claim that evolutive or dynamic interpretation is required by the nature of the European Convention, it can be answered that amendment mechanisms exist. The proof can be seen in the seventeen Protocols to the Convention that have been adopted over the years. In 1989, the Court rejected the proposal that it should deem out-dated and inoperative the reference to capital punishment in article 2(1) of the Convention. It noted the adoption of Protocol No. 6 to the Convention, explaining that 'as a subsequent written agreement [it] shows that the intention of the Contracting Parties as recently as 1983 was to adopt the normal method of amendment of the text in order to introduce a new obligation to abolish capital punishment in time of peace and, what is more, to do so by an optional instrument allowing each State to choose the moment when to undertake such an engagement'.[127]

But where there is no protocol to obstruct such judicial innovation, judges of the Court are capable of great creativity. In *Scopolla*, for example, they agreed that despite the silence of article 7(1) on a right of a person to benefit from a favourable change in an applicable penalty by comparison with what was in force when the offence was committed, 'a consensus has gradually emerged in Europe and internationally around the view that application of a criminal law providing for a more lenient penalty, even one enacted after the commission of the offence, has become a fundamental principle of criminal law'.[128] Dissenting judges objected that this amounted to re-writing article 7 and that it 'oversteps the limits'.[129] They invoked an injunction from a ruling in the mid-1980s that 'the Court cannot, by means of an evolutive interpretation, derive from these instruments a right that was not included therein at the outset'.[130] But that is most certainly what it does. If decades ago judges might have been concerned that such judicial activism would discourage ratification or promote denunciation of the Convention, history has shown this not to be the case.

Principle of effectiveness

The provisions of an international treaty such as the Convention must be construed in the light of their object and purpose and also in accordance with the principle of effectiveness.[131] Hersch Lauterpacht explained that the principle of effectiveness, which he also described as 'liberal interpretation', was the opposite of strict interpretation of treaty obligations.[132]

In *Klass*, the Court invoked 'the effectiveness (*l'effet utile*) of the Convention' when interpreting former article 25, now repealed, governing access to the European Commission of Human Rights.[133] Sometimes it is invoked as a general principle underpinning the

---

[127] *Soering v. the United Kingdom*, 7 July 1989, § 103, Series A no. 161.

[128] *Scoppola v. Italy (no. 2)* [GC], no. 10249/03, § 106, 17 September 2009.

[129] Ibid., Partly Dissenting Opinion of Judge Nicolaou, Joined by Judges Bratza, Lorenzen, Jočiené, Villiger, and Sajó, 17 September 2009.

[130] *Johnston and Others v. Ireland*, 18 December 1986, § 53, Series A no. 112.

[131] *Sergey Zolotukhin v. Russia* [GC], no. 14939/03, § 80, ECHR 2009; *Mamatkulov and Askarov v. Turkey* [GC], nos 46827/99 and 46951/99, § 123, ECHR 2005-I.

[132] Hersch Lauterpacht, 'Restrictive Interpretation and the Principle of Effectiveness in the Interpretation of Treaties', (1940) 26 *British Yearbook of International Law* 48, at pp. 67–8.

[133] *Klass and Others v. Germany*, 6 September 1978, § 34, Series A no. 28. See Jochen A. Frowein, 'L'effet utile dans la jurisprudence de la Commission européenne des droits de l'homme entre 1970 et 1985', in *Liberté, justice, tolérance. Mélanges en homage au doyen Gérard Cohen Jonathan*, Brussels: Bruylant, 2004, pp. 855–64.

Convention, rather than as a canon of interpretation: 'To ensure that human rights do not become a mere mirage, the most protective interpretation of the Convention's rights and freedoms is required: to guarantee real, not virtual, independence of the judicial power and an *effet utile*, not apparent, of the rights and freedoms of the Convention, it is indispensable that the Court be vested with the implied power to oversee the execution of its judgments, and, if need be, to contradict a decision of the Committee of Ministers in this regard.'[134]

---

[134] *Fabris v. France* [GC], no. 16574/08, Concurring Opinion of Judge Pinto de Albuquerque, ECHR 2013 (extracts).

PART TWO

CONVENTION FOR THE PROTECTION OF HUMAN RIGHTS AND FUNDAMENTAL FREEDOMS

Preamble/Préambule

The governments signatory hereto, being members of the Council of Europe,

Considering the Universal Declaration of Human Rights proclaimed by the General Assembly of the United Nations on 10th December 1948;

Considering that this Declaration aims at securing the universal and effective recognition and observance of the Rights therein declared;

Considering that the aim of the Council of Europe is the achievement of greater unity between its members and that one of the methods by which that aim is to be pursued is the maintenance and further realisation of human rights and fundamental freedoms;

Reaffirming their profound belief in those fundamental freedoms which are the foundation of justice and peace in the world and are best maintained on the one hand by an effective political democracy and on the other by a common understanding and observance of the human rights upon which they depend;

Being resolved, as the governments of European countries which are like-minded and have a common heritage of political traditions, ideals, freedom and the rule of law, to take the first steps for the collective enforcement of certain of the rights stated in the Universal Declaration,

Affirming that the High Contracting Parties, in accordance with the principle of subsidiarity, have the primary responsibility to secure the rights and freedoms defined in this Convention and the Protocols thereto, and that in doing so they enjoy a margin of appreciation, subject to the supervisory jurisdiction of the European Court of Human Rights established by this Convention,[1]

Have agreed as follows:

Les Gouvernements signataires, membres du Conseil de l'Europe,

Considérant la Déclaration universelle des droits de l'homme, proclamée par l'Assemblée générale des Nations Unies le 10 décembre 1948;

Considérant que cette déclaration tend à assurer la reconnaissance et l'application universelles et effectives des droits qui y sont énoncés;

Considérant que le but du Conseil de l'Europe est de réaliser une union plus étroite entre ses membres, et que l'un des moyens d'atteindre ce but est la sauvegarde et le développement des droits de l'homme et des libertés fondamentales;

Réaffirmant leur profond attachement à ces libertés fondamentales qui constituent les assises mêmes de la justice et de la paix dans le monde et dont le maintien repose essentiellement sur un régime politique véritablement démocratique, d'une part, et, d'autre part, sur une conception commune et un commun respect des droits de l'homme dont ils se réclament;

Résolus, en tant que gouvernements d'Etats européens animés d'un même esprit et possédant un patrimoine commun d'idéal et de traditions politiques, de respect de la liberté et de prééminence du droit, à prendre les premières mesures propres à assurer la garantie collective de certains des droits énoncés dans la Déclaration universelle,

Affirmant qu'il incombe au premier chef aux Hautes Parties contractantes, conformément au principe de subsidiarité, de garantir le respect des droits et libertés définis dans la présente Convention et ses protocoles, et que, ce faisant, elles jouissent d'une marge d'appréciation, sous le contrôle de la Cour européenne des Droits de l'Homme instituée par la présente Convention,

Sont convenus de ce qui suit:

---

[1] This paragraph, added pursuant to article 1 of Protocol No. 15 amending the Convention for the Protection of Human Rights and Fundamental Freedoms, ETS 213, is not yet in force.

Introductory comments

One of the earliest decisions of the European Commission of Human Rights reviewed the Preamble of the Convention and concluded:

> [I]t clearly appears from these pronouncements that the purpose of the High Contracting parties in concluding the Convention was not to concede to each other reciprocal rights and obligations in pursuance of their individual national interests but to realise the aims and ideals of the Council of Europe, as expressed in its Statute, and to establish a common public order of the free democracies of Europe with the object of safeguarding their common heritage of political traditions, ideals, freedom and the rule of law...'[2]

The Commission promised that the Preamble would inspire the case law of the Convention organs. Actually, the Preamble of the European Convention on Human Rights has been referred to only sporadically in the case law of the Commission and the Court, and by academic commentators. Many works of analysis of the Convention begin abruptly with article 1, as if the Preamble did not exist at all. The Court's website enables users to search the case law according to the provision of the Convention, but reference to the Preamble does not seem to be contemplated.

Yet the preamble is an important component of treaties, often consuming considerable energy when the instrument is being drafted. It provides an opportunity to add texture and nuance, to place the treaty within its historical context, and to offer guides for interpreters in the future. For that reason, there is an explicit reference to the preamble in the 'General rule of interpretation' set out in article 31 of the Vienna Convention on the Law of Treaties: 'The context for the purpose of the interpretation of a treaty shall comprise, in addition to the text, including its preamble...'[3] Although the Vienna Convention was drafted many years after the European Convention, and it is not binding upon all States Parties, the European Court has nevertheless made reference to its provisions on interpretation on many occasions.[4] Indeed, noting the provision in the Vienna Convention, it has described the Preamble as being 'generally very useful for the determination of the "object" and "purpose" of the instrument to be construed'.[5]

What better indication of the importance of the Convention's Preamble is there than its amendment with the addition of a paragraph in accordance with Protocol No. 15? It is an exceedingly unusual development for the preamble of a treaty to be amended in this manner. That the Committee of Ministers deemed it useful and important to modify the Preamble attests to its significance within the general law of the Convention.

The European Court has referred to the preambles of other treaties as bases for their interpretation, including the Charter of the United Nations,[6] the Statute of the Council

---

[2] *Austria v. Italy*, no. 788/60, Commission decision of 11 January 1961, (1961) 4 YB 116, at p. 138.

[3] Vienna Convention on the Law of Treaties, (1980) 1155 UNTS 331, art. 2.

[4] *Golder v. the United Kingdom*, 21 February 1975, § 29, Series A no. 18; *Johnston and Others v. Ireland*, 18 December 1986, §§ 51 et seq., Series A no. 112; *Lithgow and Others v. the United Kingdom*, 8 July 1986, §§ 114 and 117, Series A no. 102; *Witold Litwa v. Poland*, no. 26629/95, §§ 57–59, ECHR 2000-III; *Banković and Others v. Belgium and Others* (dec.) [GC], no. 52207/99, §§ 16–17, ECHR 2001-XII; *Mamatkulov and Askarov v. Turkey* [GC], nos 46827/99 and 46951/99, ECHR 2005-I; *Saadi v. Italy* [GC], no. 37201/06, § 61, ECHR 2008; *Demir and Baykara v. Turkey* [GC], no. 34503/97, § 65, ECHR 2008.

[5] *Golder v. the United Kingdom*, 21 February 1975, § 34, Series A no. 18.

[6] (1945) 1 UNTS XVI, cited in *Jersild v. Denmark*, 23 September 1994, § 21, Series A no. 298; *Gündüz v. Turkey*, no. 35071/97, § 21, ECHR 2003-XI; *Behrami and Behrami v. France and Saramati v. France, Germany and Norway* (dec.) [GC], nos 71412/01 and 78166/01, §§ 20–21, 148, 2 May 2007.

of Europe,[7] the Convention relating to the Status of Refugees,[8] the Hague Convention on the Civil Aspects of International Child Abduction,[9] ILO Convention No. 151 concerning Protection of the Right to Organise and Procedures for Determining Conditions of Employment in the Public Service,[10] the Hague Convention (IV) respecting the Laws and Customs of War on Land 1907,[11] the European Convention on the Legal Status of Children born out of Wedlock,[12] the Council of Europe Framework Convention for the Protection of National Minorities[13] and the Convention on the Recognition of Qualifications concerning Higher Education in the European Region.[14]

Jann Kleffner has pointed out that nothing in the law of treaties suggests that provisions of the preamble have an inferior legal force to other provisions or no legal force whatsoever.[15] According to Charles Rousseau, '[o]n a parfois considéré le préambule des traités comme doué d'une force obligatoire inférieure à celle du dispositif. Mais c'est là une opinion isolée'.[16]

Drafting of the provision

The initial draft of the European Convention on Human Rights was prepared by the International Juridical Section of the European Movement, chaired by Pierre-Henri Teitgen, with David Maxwell Fyfe and Fernand Dehousse as rapporteurs. Both Maxwell Fyfe and Dehousse had been involved in the drafting of the Universal Declaration of Human Rights the previous year. The text they proposed for the European Convention began with a four-paragraph preamble.

The States Parties to this Convention, members of the Council of Europe, wishing:
To preserve the moral values and democratic principles which are their common heritage,
To assure the rule of law and to guarantee human rights and fundamental freedoms in accordance with Article 3 of the Statute of the Council of Europe,
To ensure by progressive measures the universal application of the Declaration of Human Rights adopted by the United Nations,
Have agreed as follows:[17]

[7] ETS 1, cited in *Golder v. the United Kingdom*, 21 February 1975, § 34, Series A no. 18; *Bartik v. Russia*, no. 55565/00, § 50, ECHR 2006-XV.

[8] (1954) 189 UNTS 137, cited in *Hirsi Jamaa and Others v. Italy* [GC], no. 27765/09, Concurring Opinion of Judge Pinto de Albuquerque, ECHR 2012.

[9] (1982) 1343 UNTS 98, cited in *Neulinger and Shuruk v. Switzerland* [GC], no. 41615/07, § 104, ECHR 2010.

[10] (1981) 1218 UNTS 87, cited in *Demir and Baykara v. Turkey* [GC], no. 34503/97, § 44, ECHR 2008.

[11] 6 Stat. 2277, 1 Bevans 631, 205 Consol. T.S. 277, 3 Martens Nouveau Recueil (ser. 3) 461, cited in *Kononov v. Latvia* [GC], no. 36376/04, §§ 85–86, ECHR 2010.

[12] ETS 85, cited in *Johnston and Others v. Ireland*, 18 December 1986, § 74, Series A no. 112.

[13] ETS 157, cited in *Gorzelik and Others v. Poland* [GC], no. 44158/98, §§ 68, 93, ECHR 2004-I.

[14] ETS 165, cited in *Leyla Şahin v. Turkey* [GC], no. 44774/98, § 67, ECHR 2005-XI.

[15] Jann K. Kleffner, 'Auto-referrals and the Complementary Nature of the ICC', in Carsten Stahn and Goran Sluiter, *The Emerging Practice of the International Criminal Court*, Leiden: Brill, 2009, pp. 41–53, at p. 45, fn. 18.

[16] Charles Rousseau, *Droit International Public, I, Introductions et Sources*, Paris: Sirey, 1970, at p. 87.

[17] Convention for the Collective Protection of Individual Rights and Democratic Liberties by the States, Members of the Council of Europe, and for the Establishment of a European Court of Human Rights to Ensure Observance of the Convention, Doc. INF/5/E/R, I *TP* 296–303, at p. 296.

The draft formed the basis of discussions at the first session of the Consultative Assembly, in 1949, but there was no consideration of the proposed preamble. The Recommendation to the Committee of Ministers adopted by the Assembly did not contain a preamble.[18]

The idea of a preamble seems to have been revived during the second session of the Consultative Assembly, in 1950, by Lord Layton, one of the British members of the Committee on Legal and Administrative Questions. Referring to the debate about inclusion or exclusion of certain rights from the Convention itself, Lord Layton suggested that there be a preamble 'in which it would be pointed out that all the Member States accepted the Universal Declaration of Human Rights'. In the proposed preamble of the Convention,

> the distinction, important in the eyes of many members, could be drawn between human rights in general and those particular rights which should be safeguarded internationally. The Preamble could also specify that the aim of the Convention was to ensure a common responsibility which covered human rights as far as possible, and would point out clearly that what had been done was only a beginning and that later on this Convention should be extended to cover a wider field.[19]

The drafting of the Convention's Preamble began with a proposal from Mr Mitchison of the United Kingdom, submitted mid-way through the second session of the Parliamentary Assembly, which was held in August 1950:

> Insert in the draft a preamble worded as follows:
> 'Whereas the Members of the General Assembly of the United Nations have proclaimed the Universal Declaration of Human Rights approved by the General Assembly on 10 December 1948;
> And whereas that Declaration was proclaimed to the end, among others, that every organ of society should by progressive measures, national and international, strive to secure the universal and effective recognition and observance of the rights therein declared, both among the peoples of Member States themselves and among the peoples of territories under their jurisdiction;
> And whereas the High Contracting Parties are the Governments of European countries, like-minded and having a common heritage of political traditions, ideals, freedom and the rule of law, and accordingly are in a position to take a first step towards the collective enforcement of certain of the Rights stated in the Universal Declaration and to restate them in a form suitable for that purpose;
> And whereas the aim of the Council of Europe is the achievement of greater unity between its Members, who are the High Contracting Parties, and one of the methods by which that aim is to be pursued is by agreement and common action in legal and administrative matters and in the maintenance and further realisation of human rights and fundamental freedoms;
> Now therefore the High Contracting Parties, reaffirming their profound belief in those fundamental freedoms which are the foundation of justice and peace in the world and are best maintained on the one hand by an effective political democracy and on the other by a common understanding and observance of the Human Rights upon which they depend,
> Declare and agree as follows:'[20]

---

[18] Recommendation No. 38 to the Committee of Ministers adopted 8 September 1949 on the conclusion of the debates, Doc. AS (1) 108, II *TP* 274–83.

[19] Minutes of the morning meeting [of 24 June 1950, of the Committee on Legal and Administrative Questions of the Consultative Assembly], Doc. AS/JA (2) PV 2, A 1841, V *TP* 14–21, at p. 16.

[20] Motion proposed by Mr Mitchison, Doc. AS/JA (2) 14, A 2355, AS/JA (2) PV 7, VI *TP* 28–31.

The text was adopted without change by the Drafting Sub-Committee, which 'strongly urge[d] the Committee of Ministers to complete or modify the text' by its addition.[21]

The Committee on Legal and Administrative Questions said it was 'unanimously felt that a preamble in suitable terms would be a fitting beginning to the Convention...'[22] When the rapporteur of the Committee, David Maxwell Fyfe, presented the report to the Consultative Assembly on 25 August 1950, he explained in some detail the additions and amendments that were being proposed, with the exception of the Preamble, about which he was silent.[23] Indeed, during the general debate on the Committee's report, which focused upon the right to property and to education, there was not the slightest mention of the Preamble. The President of the Assembly proposed a vote on the report, but was interrupted on a point of order by Mr Mitchison of the United Kingdom, who drew attention to the Preamble.[24] Mitchison said that he hoped it would not be stymied by a question of procedure, noting that 'the Preamble is wholly non-contentious, and that it would be fitting to the dignity of the instrument and the dignity of this Assembly that something of the sort should be stated in the proposed Convention'.[25] Without further comment on the substance, the Preamble was adopted.[26]

A significantly revised version appeared in the draft prepared by the Secretariat; it bears no date, but presumably was issued in September or October 1950:

The Governments signatory hereto, being Members of the Council of Europe,

Considering that the General Assembly of the United Nations has adopted and proclaimed the Universal Declaration of Human Rights 10th December 1948;

Considering that this Universal Declaration was proclaimed to the end, among others, of securing the universal and effective recognition and observance of the Rights therein declared;

Considering that it is for them, as the Governments of European countries which are like-minded and have a common heritage of political traditions, ideals, freedom and the rule of law, to take the first steps for the collective enforcement of certain of the Rights stated in the Universal Declaration;

Considering that the aim of the Council of Europe is the achievement of greater unity between its Members and one of the methods by which that aim is to be pursued is in the maintenance and further realisation of human rights and fundamental freedoms;

Re-affirming their profound belief in those Fundamental Freedoms which are the foundation of justice and peace in the world and are best maintained on the one hand by an effective political

---

[21] Report of the Committee on Legal and Administrative Questions to the Consultative Assembly (24 August 1950), Doc. AS (2) 93, VI *TP* 61–73, at p. 66. Also Draft Recommendation submitted to the Consultative Assembly, 23 August 1950, Doc. AS/JA (2) 20, A 2491, VI *TP* 42–47, at p. 44.

[22] Second Report [of the Committee on Legal and Administrative Questions], Doc. AS/JA (2) rev., A 2493, VI *TP* 52–58, at p. 54; Report of the Committee on Legal and Administrative Questions to the Consultative Assembly (24 August 1950), Doc. AS (2) 93, VI *TP* 61–73, at pp. 60, 66–8.

[23] Report of the Sitting [of the Consultative Assembly, 25 August 1950, morning], VI *TP* 74–143, at pp. 74–84.

[24] Report of the Sitting [of the Consultative Assembly, 25 August 1950, afternoon], VI *TP* 144–91, at p. 184.

[25] Ibid.

[26] Ibid., pp. 186–7. The English version says that it was adopted by ninety-one votes with one abstention, whereas the French says ninety-one to one, with one abstention. An explanatory note prepared by the Secretariat-General subsequent to the session of the Assembly clarifies the ambiguity and confirms the French version: Explanatory Note by the Secretariat General, 9 September 1950, Doc. CM (50) 57, A 2781, VI *TP* 230–9, at pp. 232–3.

democracy and on the other by a common understanding and observance of the Human Rights upon which they depend;

Have agreed as follows:[27]

In a subsequent exchange of notes between officials in the Secretariat, a question was raised about the formulation in the final phrase: 'Have agreed as follows:'. H.T. Adam explained: 'There cannot, of course, be any question of deleting the Preamble to which the Assembly attaches some importance.'[28] The Secretariat proposed that the Preamble begin with the phrase 'The Governments signatory hereto, being Members of the Council of Europe' but without listing the governments by name. This would 'make it possible for certain Governments, if they wish, to sign the Convention as original signatories, even though they are unable to sign on the date of formal signature in Rome...'[29]

The Committee of Legal Experts, in light of the recommendations of the Secretariat, made final changes during the Sixth Session of the Committee of Ministers in Rome on 2–3 November 1950.[30] A resolution of the Committee of Ministers noted the adoption of the text of the Convention 'adding to it a Preamble in conformity with the proposals of the Assembly'.[31] Several weeks later, when an angry Consultative Assembly protested the omission of many of its proposals in the final version of the Convention, Mitchison recalled that 'there was one little thing which went through, I believe, without a dissentient voice—just a small preamble'. He added: 'What importance is there in preambles? Only that in this case it did in its terms treat this Convention as a first step. We said so; the Committee of Ministers accepted it.'[32]

The heading 'Preamble' was added pursuant to Protocol No. 11.[33]

The sixth recital of the Preamble, introducing the concepts of subsidiarity and margin of appreciation, is the result of Protocol No. 15.[34] The origin of this unusual initiative is the Brighton Declaration, adopted in April 2012 by the High Level Conference on the Future of the European Court of Human Rights: 'The Conference therefore... Concludes that, for reasons of transparency and accessibility, a reference to the principle of subsidiarity and the doctrine of the margin of appreciation as developed in the Court's case law should be included in the Preamble to the Convention and invites the Committee of Ministers to adopt the necessary amending instrument by the end of 2013, while recalling the States Parties' commitment to give full effect to their obligation to secure the rights and freedoms defined in the Convention.'[35]

---

[27] Draft Preamble and Draft Signature Clause, Doc. A 2518, VI *TP* 272–4.

[28] Letter No. SG/P/44 Sent on 14 October 1950 by Mr Adam (Member of the Secretariat) to Mr Struycken (Political Director), VI *TP* 280–5, at p. 280.

[29] Drafting Changes Proposed by the Secretariat-General, Doc. A 2520, no date, VI *TP* 274–9, at pp. 274–6.

[30] Report of the Committee [of Legal Experts], Doc. CM/Adj (50) 3, A 2530, VII *TP* 8; Doc. CM/Adj (50) 3 revised, A 2531, VII *TP* 10.

[31] Minutes of the fourth meeting [of the Committee of Ministers] held in the afternoon of 5 November 1950, Doc. AS/CP (2) PV 6, A 3058, VII *TP* 84–9, at p. 86.

[32] Sitting of the Consultative Assembly on 18 November 1950 (afternoon), Rep. 1950, V, pp. 1308–12, VII *TP* 106–8.

[33] Protocol No. 11 to the Convention for the Protection of Human Rights and Fundamental Freedoms, restructuring the control machinery established thereby, ETS 155, art. 2(2).

[34] Protocol No. 15 amending the Convention for the Protection of Human Rights and Fundamental Freedoms, ETS 213, art. 1.

[35] High Level Conference on the Future of the European Court of Human Rights, Brighton Declaration, 20 April 2012, para. 12(b). Also Explanatory Report on Protocol No. 15, para. 7.

Analysis and interpretation

'The governments signatory hereto...'

The Preamble begins with the words the 'governments signatory hereto'. In fact, signature is only a preliminary act to the acceptance of the obligations in the Convention, which involves ratification or accession in accordance with article 59. The Preamble reads as if it is a declaration by the twelve founding members of the Council of Europe. They were the States that negotiated the text of the Convention. This may be confirmed by the signature clause at the very end of the Convention: 'Done at Rome this 4th day of November 1950, in English and French, both texts being equally authentic, in a single copy which shall remain deposited in the archives of the Council of Europe. The Secretary General shall transmit certified copies to each of the signatories.'

The signing ceremony took place on 4 November 1950 at the Barberini Palace in Rome. It sits at one end of the Via Rasella, the site of a famous ambush of Nazi soldiers by young partisans that provoked a notorious reprisal, now memorialized at the Fosse Ardeatine on the outskirts of the city.[36] The French Foreign Minister Robert Schuman had told the Committee of Ministers that he 'was anxious that the Convention should be signed in Rome, the historic city which had been the cradle of Europe [sic] civilisation, particularly as the United Nations Declaration on Human Rights had been proclaimed in Paris in 1948'.[37] The date of signature itself—technically, the date when the instrument became open for signature—is given no particular legal significance in the Convention itself. The Convention did not in fact enter into force for three more years, after obtaining the requisite number of ratifications. Nevertheless, the date of 4 November 1950 was fixed by the Grand Chamber as the effective date for the beginning of the legal order established by the Convention. The Grand Chamber said this was when the Convention 'began its existence as an international human rights treaty'.[38] The Court did this in order to establish a jurisdictional boundary, denying the admissibility of claims relating to the procedural obligation under articles 2 and 3 of the Convention to the extent that the substantive violation of fundamental rights took place prior to 4 November 1950.

The Universal Declaration of Human Rights (recitals 1, 2, and 5)

The Universal Declaration of Human Rights is referred to three times in the Preamble of the Convention, in recitals 1, 2, and 5. The European Convention is the first human rights treaty to invoke the Universal Declaration in its Preamble, beginning a practice that became very common in modern human rights law.[39] For example, such references also appear in treaties of the universal system adopted under the aegis of the United Nations, notably the two Covenants on human rights,[40] as well as in regional instruments like the

---

[36] *In re Von Mackensen and Maelzer (Ardeatine Caves Massacre Case)*, (1949) 8 LRTWC 1, 13 ILR 258 (British Military Court, Rome).
[37] Report of the Meeting [of the Committee of Ministers, 3 November 1950], VII *TP* 24–34, at p. 30.
[38] *Janowiec and Others v. Russia* [GC], nos 55508/07 and 29520/09, § 151, 21 October 2013.
[39] Convention on the Rights of Persons with Disabilities, UN Doc. A/RES/61/106, Annex I, preamble, recital (b); International Convention for the Protection of All Persons from Enforced Disappearance, UN Doc. A/RES/61/177, annex, preamble, recital 3.
[40] International Covenant on Civil and Political Rights, (1976) 999 UNTS 171, preamble, recital 4; International Covenant on Economic, Social and Cultural Rights, (1976) 993 UNTS 3, preamble, recital 4.

American Convention on Human Rights[41] and the African Charter on Human and Peoples' Rights.[42] The Universal Declaration of Human Rights is not, however, mentioned in the preambles of the Protocols to the European Convention.

Most of the preambular references in human rights treaties are nothing more than perfunctory acknowledgements of the ancestry of international human rights norms. The references in the Preamble of the European Convention cannot be dismissed in the same way. They convey significant nuances of meaning that may impact upon the interpretation of the Convention as a whole. Of the provisions in the European Convention that concern the content of human rights, the majority can trace their lineage to the Universal Declaration of Human Rights. The Convention's Preamble stands out as an exception in this respect. Although making three references to the Declaration, the Preamble of the Convention echoes that of the Universal Declaration in only a limited manner. In particular, the reference to 'the foundation of justice and peace in the world' in recital 4 is inspired by the text of recital 1 of the Preamble of the Declaration. The Preamble of the Convention is considerably shorter than that of the Declaration (175 words, compared with 320 words). One way to understand this is that the Convention was meant to incorporate by reference the ideas in the Declaration. Yet the Convention's specifically European focus, which is not so subtly communicated in the Preamble, might also be taken as a message that rights were perhaps not understood in the same way everywhere in the world, or even within Europe itself.

The first recital is comparable to what appears more generally in human rights treaties. It simply acknowledges the Declaration as having been 'proclaimed' by the General Assembly of the United Nations on 10 December 1948. After its own lengthy Preamble, the Declaration states:

The General Assembly,
    Proclaims this Universal Declaration of Human Rights as a common standard of achievement for all peoples and all nations, to the end that every individual and every organ of society, keeping this Declaration constantly in mind, shall strive by teaching and education to promote respect for these rights and freedoms and by progressive measures, national and international, to secure their universal and effective recognition and observance, both among the peoples of Member States themselves and among the peoples of territories under their jurisdiction.

The Universal Declaration of Human Rights was adopted by the United Nations General Assembly on 10 December 1948. That year its meetings were held in Paris, the first and only time a full regular session of the General Assembly took place outside of New York. Most of the States that were to establish the Council of Europe the following May were present and active in the debate on the text of the Universal Declaration as full members of the United Nations. Two of the ten founding members of the Council of Europe, Ireland and Italy, were not involved in drafting the Universal Declaration and only joined the United Nations in 1955. The pre-eminent European in the discussions was the French jurist, René Cassin. Two decades later, when he was serving as president of the European Court of Human Rights, Cassin received the Nobel Peace Prize in recognition of his contribution to the adoption of the Universal Declaration of Human Rights.

---

[41] American Convention on Human Rights, (1979) 1144 UNTS 123, preamble, recital 4.
[42] African Charter on Human and People's Rights, (1986) 1520 UNTS 217, preamble, recital 3.

The Universal Declaration was intended to be one part of a larger *ensemble* of instruments known collectively as the International Bill of Rights. The Bill was to contain a manifesto or declaration, but also a fully fledged treaty (or covenant) and provision for means of enforcement. In 1948, the General Assembly found itself divided on whether to proceed with this project in a piecemeal fashion, given that the draft Universal Declaration was in more or less final form, whereas the other two components of the International Bill of Rights had yet to find an adequate degree of consensus. Over some resistance, and at the urging of individuals like Cassin, the Assembly agreed to adopt the Universal Declaration with a view to returning, the following year, to the draft covenant and the means of enforcement. There was concern that the postponement would become permanent. A belief that the United Nations would be unable to complete the International Bill of Rights may have compelled some States to push for adoption of the European Convention. In fact, the United Nations General Assembly took nearly two decades more on the project. In 1966, it adopted the International Covenant on Civil and Political Rights and the International Covenant on Economic, Social, and Cultural Rights, together with an Optional Protocol providing for individual petitions concerning civil and political rights. These instruments entered into force a decade later. An Optional Protocol authorizing individual petitions concerning economic, social, and cultural rights only entered into force in 2013.[43]

To a great extent, the drafting of the European Convention took place in the wake of the Universal Declaration of Human Rights. The Consultative Assembly of the Council of Europe responsible for the first working draft of the Convention, in September 1949, satisfied itself with a summary text that referred to the relevant provisions of the Universal Declaration. In the report of the Committee on Legal and Administrative Questions to the Consultative Assembly, on 5 September 1949, *rapporteur* Pierre-Henri Teitgen said that:

> ...the Committee considered that it was preferable (as much from a desire to co-ordinate the activity of the Council of Europe with that of the United Nations, as by reason of the moral authority and technical value of the document in question) to make use, as far as possible, of the definitions set out in the 'Universal Declaration of Human Rights' approved by the General Assembly of the United Nations. It thus based itself, as far as possible, on this document.[44]

Speaking to the Assembly, Teitgen added that the Committee also sought 'to avoid making a distinction between European and world order'.[45]

Later, it was felt preferable that the formulations of rights and not only the titles or headings found in the Declaration should be incorporated within the text of the European Convention. The final version of the Convention manifests the influence of the Universal Declaration in many provisions, yet there is no single article that merely reproduces the corresponding text of the Declaration. In some cases, such as the right to life (art. 2), the Declaration provides a succinct statement ('everyone shall have the right to life...', whereas the Convention offers a detailed codification and an enumeration of exceptions.

---

[43] Optional Protocol to the International Covenant on Economic, Social and Cultural Rights, UN Doc. Doc. A/63/435.

[44] Report presented by Mr P.H. Teitgen, 5 September 1949, Doc. A 290, I *TP* 192–213, at p. 194. See also Report [of the Committee on Legal and Administrative Questions], 5 September 1949, Doc. AS (1) 77, I *TP* 216–39, at p. 218.

[45] Report of the Sitting [of the Consultative Assembly, 7 September 1949], I *TP* 258–95, at p. 268.

In others, such as the prohibition of torture and ill treatment (art. 3), the two texts are virtually identical as drafted and probably equivalent in terms of their legal content.

The second recital of the Preamble states that the Declaration 'aims at securing the universal and effective recognition and observance of the Rights therein declared'. The words are taken almost literally from the introductory paragraph of the Declaration. The bulk of the introductory paragraph of the Declaration is addressed to its legal and political significance ('a common standard of achievement for all peoples and all nations'), to those for whom the Declaration is destined ('every individual and every organ of society') and to the means of implementation ('by teaching and education to promote respect for these rights and freedoms and by progressive measures'). By its very nature, these notions did not really apply to the European Convention. It was a binding treaty, addressed to States, with its own legal enforcement mechanisms.

In a concurring opinion, Judge Bonello of the European Court of Human Rights described these words as the Convention's 'agenda heralded in its preamble'. Arguing for an extensive approach to territorial jurisdiction of the Convention, he said that '"Universal" hardly suggests an observance parcelled off by territory on the checkerboard of geography'.[46] His words echo those of Léopold Senghor, the Senegalese poet and political leader who participated in the drafting of the Convention on behalf of France. Senghor objected to article 56 whereby the Convention did not automatically extend to subject territories and colonies of the European States. Senghor noted that the Universal Declaration of Human Rights asserted explicitly, in article 2(2), that 'no distinction shall be made on the basis on [sic] the political, jurisdictional or international status of the country or territory to which a person belongs, whether it be independent, trust, non-self-governing or under any other limitation of sovereignty'. In excluding this principle, the Council of Europe would 'transform the European Declaration of Human Rights into the Declaration of European Human Rights', he said.[47]

The fifth recital sets out the intention of the 'likeminded' governments of European countries 'to take the first steps for the collective enforcement of certain of the Rights stated in the Universal Declaration' (*les premières mesures propres à assurer la garantie collective de certains des droits énoncés dans la Déclaration universelle*). The Convention was understood to represent an initial effort at rendering the Declaration enforceable. Although the Universal Declaration was an inspiring and hortatory document, it did not contemplate any international measures for enforcement. During the preparatory work in the Council of Europe the significance of establishing mechanisms for collective enforcement of the Universal Declaration was highlighted. For example, the Belgian Henri Rolin explained that in adopting the European Convention, the Council of Europe would 'have substituted a clearly categorical text for the Declaration of Human Rights of the United Nations Organisation, of which, all too often, the Governments feel justified in emphasising the so-called purely moral scope, neither juridical nor mandatory'.[48]

The final paragraph of the Preamble also highlights the fact that the implementation of the Universal Declaration of Human Rights is not meant to be comprehensive. The

---

[46] *Al-Skeini and Others v. the United Kingdom* [GC], no. 55721/07, Concurring Opinion of Judge Bonello, § 9, ECHR 2011.

[47] Report of the Sitting [of the Consultative Assembly, 25 August 1950, afternoon], VI *TP* 144–91, at p. 174.

[48] Report of the Sitting [of the Consultative Assembly, 25 August 1950, morning], VI *TP* 74–143, at pp. 130–2.

Convention incorporates 'certain' rights included in the Declaration and thereby excludes many others, being 'selective in the protection it affords'.[49] During the drafting of the European Convention, the point was often made that the document was not intended to reproduce all of the rights in the Universal Declaration. There was very much the sense that the Convention represented an initial effort in a difficult and innovative area. It should be minimalist in scope so as to ensure adoption. Sometimes, the drafters were urged to drop one or another right from the list because it was suggested that the right was not important enough.

The most significant omission is the entire category of economic, social, and cultural rights. These had been set out in articles 22 to 27 of the Universal Declaration of Human Rights, although there was no formal heading or rubric distinguishing them from the other rights. After much debate, the Consultative Assembly of the Council of Europe agreed to postpone consideration of economic, social, and cultural rights as a category. In two areas where the boundary between civil and political rights and economic, social, and cultural rights is difficult to define, the drafters of the European Convention continued to consider the inclusion: the right to property and the right of parents to determine the education of their children. These were recognized in Protocol No. 1, agreed to shortly after the Convention itself was adopted. Issues at the core of economic, social, and cultural rights such as the right to medical care, to housing, and to appropriate working conditions have to a large extent remained outside the scope of the Convention and its Protocols. They arise, although somewhat indirectly, in cases dealing with the right to property under article 1 of Protocol No. 1, and the right to equality under article 14 of the Convention and article 1 of Protocol No. 12.[50] Of course, they are addressed in other instruments of the Council of Europe. Discussing the 'flawed argument' that 'the founding fathers intended to recognise in the Convention only civil and political rights', Judge Pinto de Albuquerque said that this 'ignore[d] the purpose of the Convention as a treaty which envisages the "development" of human rights in the light of the Universal Declaration on [sic] Human Rights, where economic and social rights are foreseen'.[51]

Differences between the European Convention and the Universal Declaration have given rise to judicial comment. For example, the European Court has explained that the absence of an express reference to human trafficking in article 4 is unsurprising given that the Convention was inspired by the Universal Declaration of Human Rights, which itself makes no reference to the term.[52] The Court has also noted that although article 14(1) of the Universal Declaration of Human Rights recognizes the right of everyone 'to seek and

---

[49] *Deumeland v. Germany*, 29 May 1986, § 24, Series A no. 100.

[50] Jean-Paul Costa, 'La Cour Européenne des Droits de l'Homme et la Protection des Droits Sociaux', (2010) 21 *RTDH* 212; Eberhard Eichenhofer, 'Der sozialrechtliche Gehalt der EMRK-Menschenrechte', in Hohmann-Dennhardt, Masuch, and Villiger, *Festschrift für Renate Jaeger, Grundrechte und Solidarität, Durchsetzung und Verfahren*, 2011, pp. 628–35; M. Pellonpää, 'Economic, Social and Cultural Rights', in Macdonald, *The European System*, pp. 859–66; Frédéric Sudre, 'La protection des Droits Sociaux par la Cour Européenne des Droits de l'Homme: Un Exercise de "Jurisprudence Fiction"?', (2003) 55 *RTDH* 770.

[51] *Konstantin Markin v. Russia* [GC], no. 30078/06, Partly Concurring, Partly Dissenting Opinion of Judge Pinto de Albuquerque, ECHR 2012 (extracts). See also A. Berenstein, 'Economic and Social Rights: Their Inclusion in the European Convention on Human Rights, Problems of Formulation and Interpretation', (1981) 2 *HRLJ* 257.

[52] *Rantsev v. Cyprus and Russia*, no. 25965/04, § 272, ECHR 2010 (extracts).

enjoy in other countries asylum from persecution', there is no reflection of this provision in the European Convention.[53]

The drafters of the European Convention clearly decided not to include a provision based on article 20(2) of the Universal Declaration to the effect that 'no one may be compelled to belong to an association'. The Conference of Senior Officials deliberately excluded this in order to shelter the closed shop system that then prevailed in several Council of Europe member States.[54] This passage has generated much debate and no consensus among members of the Court.[55] Judge Thór Vilhjálmsson explained that the issue was of 'particular significance' because of the preambular reference to the Universal Declaration, and the idea that the aim of the Convention was to take 'the first steps for the collective enforcement of certain of the rights stated in the Universal Declaration'. He said that the *travaux préparatoires* of the Convention showed a reluctance to include the negative freedom of association at that time and that '[n]one of the ten protocols has changed that situation'.[56]

Article 12 of the Convention, dealing with the right to marry, provides a similar example. When it was being drafted, the rapporteur of the Committee on Legal and Administrative Questions of the Consultative Assembly explained that article 16(1) of the Universal Declaration had been incorporated in the draft but not the subsequent paragraphs 'concerning equal rights after marriage, since we only guarantee the right to marry'.[57] As the Court has held, 'the travaux préparatoires disclose no intention to include in Article 12 (art. 12) any guarantee of a right to have the ties of marriage dissolved by divorce'.[58] The Court has described the omission of the right to divorce from article 12 as 'deliberate'.[59]

The Universal Declaration also provides, in article 21(2), for the right of everyone to equal access to public service. There is nothing equivalent in the European Convention or the Protocols. Noting that the matter had been considered during the drafting of Protocol No. 7, the Court said this was not a chance omission, adding that 'as the Preamble to the Convention states, they are designed to ensure the collective enforcement of "certain" of the rights stated in the Universal Declaration'.[60]

It is commonly said that the Universal Declaration of Human Rights is 'non-binding', in contrast with the subsequent treaties like the European Convention, where its significance is acknowledged in the Preamble. This rather trite formulation does not do justice to the role the Universal Declaration of Human Rights has played and continues to play in

---

[53] *Vilvarajah and Others v. the United Kingdom*, 30 October 1991, § 102, Series A no. 215; *Chahal v. the United Kingdom*, 15 November 1996, § 73, *Reports of Judgments and Decisions* 1996-V.

[54] Text of the report submitted by the Conference to the Committee of Ministers, Doc. CM/WP 4 (50) 19, CM/WP 4 (50) 16 rev., A 1431, IV *TP* 242–57, at p. 262. See *Sørensen and Rasmussen v. Denmark* [GC], nos 52562/99 and 52620/99, Dissenting Opinion of Judge Lorenzen, § 2, ECHR 2006-I.

[55] *Young, James and Webster v. the United Kingdom*, 13 August 1981, § 51, Series A no. 44; *Young, James and Webster v. the United Kingdom*, 13 August 1981, Dissenting Opinion of Judge Sørensen, Joined by Judges Thór Vilhjálmsson and Lagergren, § 2, Series A no. 44; *Sørensen and Rasmussen v. Denmark* [GC], nos 52562/99 and 52620/99, § 33, ECHR 2006-I; *Sørensen and Rasmussen v. Denmark* [GC], nos 52562/99 and 52620/99, Dissenting Opinion of Judge Lorenzen, § 2, ECHR 2006-I.

[56] *Sigurður A. Sigurjónsson v. Iceland*, 30 June 1993, Dissenting Opinion of Judge Thór Vilhjálmsson, Series A no. 264.

[57] *Johnston and Others v. Ireland*, 18 December 1986, § 52, Series A no. 112.

[58] Ibid.

[59] Ibid., § 53.

[60] *Glasenapp v. Germany*, 28 August 1986, § 48, Series A no. 104; *Kosiek v. Germany*, 28 August 1986, § 34, Series A no. 105.

defining the international law of human rights. There can be no doubt that, unlike many of the human rights treaties, the Universal Declaration contains no enforcement mechanisms. Yet it has established the nomenclature of human rights, framed the debate and set the priorities for an increasingly elaborate system of law of which it can be said to be the touchstone. The enduring significance of the Universal Declaration is confirmed by its inclusion as one of the bases of the Universal Periodic Review, today among the primary monitoring activities of the United Nations Human Rights Council.[61]

In its interpretation of the provisions of the European Convention, the European Court of Human Rights takes into account 'any relevant rules and principles of international law applicable in relations between the Contracting Parties' with a view that 'the Convention should so far as possible be interpreted in harmony with other rules of international law of which it forms part'.[62] In this context, it has made reference to the Universal Declaration of Human Rights.[63] This suggests that the Declaration is more than a 'non-binding' statement of moral principles. Rather, it is a source of 'relevant rules and principles of international law' and part of the general international law framework to which the Convention belongs.

The aim of the Council of Europe (recital 3)

Recital 3 of the Preamble makes an association between 'the aim of the Council of Europe', which is described as 'the achievement of greater unity between its members', and the 'maintenance and further realisation of human rights and fundamental freedoms'. The latter is said to be one of the methods of achieving the aim. The paragraph echoes the language in the Statute of the Council of Europe. Article 1 of that instrument declares: 'The aim of the Council is to achieve a greater unity between its Members, for the purpose of safeguarding and realising the ideals and principles which are their common heritage.' Article 3 states: 'Every Member of the Council of Europe must accept the principles of the rule of law and of the enjoyment by all persons within its jurisdiction of human rights and fundamental freedoms . . .'. Compliance with this provision is a condition of membership, and serious breach is a ground for suspension.

It has been suggested that recital 3 of the Preamble, with its reference to 'achievement of greater unity between its members' underscores the *erga omnes* character of the Convention.[64] In *Loizidou*, the Court considered that a restrictive interpretation of the optional clauses recognizing the jurisdiction of the Commission and the Court that were then still in force might 'run counter to the aim, as expressed in the Preamble to the Convention, to achieve greater unity in the maintenance and further realisation of human rights'.[65] For Judge Wojtyczek, the 'further realisation of human rights and fundamental

---

[61] Institution-building of the United Nations Human Rights Council, UN Doc. A/HRC/RES/5/1, annex, para. 1(b).

[62] *Al-Adsani v. the United Kingdom* [GC], no. 35763/97, § 55, ECHR 2001-XI; *Demir and Baykara v. Turkey* [GC], no. 34503/97, § 67, ECHR 2008; *Saadi v. The United Kingdom* [GC], no. 13229/03, § 62, ECHR 2008; *Rantsev v. Cyprus and Russia*, no. 25965/04, §§ 273–274, ECHR 2010 (extracts).

[63] *Catan and Others v. the Republic of Moldova and Russia* [GC], nos 43370/04, 8252/05 and 18454/06, § 138, ECHR 2012 (extracts).

[64] *Fabris v. France* [GC], no. 16574/08, Concurring Opinion of Judge Pinto de Albuquerque, ECHR 2013 (extracts).

[65] *Loizidou v. Turkey* (preliminary objections), 23 March 1995, § 77, Series A no. 310. Cited in *Bosphorus Hava Yolları Turizm ve Ticaret Anonim Şirketi v. Ireland* [GC], no. 45036/98, Joint Concurring Opinion of Judges Rozakis, Tulkens, Traja, Botoucharova, Zagrebelsky, and Garlicki, ECHR 2005-VI.

freedoms ... it implies that the actors of this task are the national governments. It refers to only one instrument for this purpose, namely the conclusion of treaties.'.[66] He described this 'further realisation' as 'a tool for the achievement of greater unity between the member States of the Council of Europe'.[67]

Referring to the expression 'maintenance and further realisation', Judge Tulkens cited the *Wemhoff* case as authority for the notion that as a 'law-making treaty' the Convention mandates 'the interpretation that is most appropriate in order to realise the aim and achieve the object of the treaty, not that which would restrict to the greatest possible degree the obligations undertaken by the Parties'.[68] She wrote: '"Maintenance" requires the Court to ensure in particular that the rights and freedoms set out in the Convention continue to be effective in changing circumstances. "Further realisation" allows for a degree of innovation and creativity, which may extend the scope of the Convention guarantees.'[69]

Justice and peace (recital 4)

In recital 4 of the Preamble, the signatory States '[r]eaffirm[...] their profound belief in those fundamental freedoms which are the foundation of justice and peace in the world'. The phrase is obviously inspired by recital 1 of the Preamble to the Universal Declaration of Human Rights: 'Whereas recognition of the inherent dignity and of the equal and inalienable rights of all members of the human family is the foundation of freedom, justice and peace in the world.'[70] The *travaux préparatoires* do not indicate why other important concepts, such as human dignity and freedom were not repeated in the Convention and to attempt some explanation is probably a hazardous exercise. Perhaps it was merely an effort at concision. According to Jean-Paul Costa, one explanation could be that 'the Convention is a more practical, pragmatic, and mechanism-oriented text than that of the Declaration'.[71] The importance of human dignity within the overall vision of human rights has been enhanced by its recognition in article 1 of the European Union Charter of Fundamental Rights: 'Human dignity is inviolable. It must be respected and protected.'[72] The absence of a reference to 'dignity' in the European Convention has not prevented the Convention organs from invoking the concept, notably with respect to article 3.[73] The

---

[66] *Firth and Others v. the United Kingdom*, nos 7784/09, 47806/09, 47812/09, 47818/09, 47829/09, 49001/09, 49007/09, 49018/09, 49033/09, and 49036/09, Dissenting Opinion of Judge Wojtyczek, 12 August 2014.
[67] Ibid.
[68] *Stummer v. Austria* [GC], no. 37452/02, Partly Dissenting Opinion of Judge Tulkens, § 3, ECHR 2011, citing *Wemhoff v. Germany*, 27 June 1968, p. 23, § 8, Series A no. 7.
[69] Ibid.
[70] See the reference to recital 1 of the Preamble in *Sheffield and Horsham v. the United Kingdom*, 30 July 1998, Dissenting Opinion of Judge Van Dijk, *Reports of Judgments and Decisions* 1998-V.
[71] Jean-Paul Costa, 'Human Dignity in the Jurisprudence of the European Court of Human Rights', in Christopher McCrudden, ed., *Understanding Human Dignity*, Oxford: Oxford University Press, 2013, pp. 393–403, at p. 394.
[72] The right to dignity has been recognized by the European Court of Justice: Case C-377/98 *Netherlands v. European Parliament and Council* [2001] ECR I-7079, at 70–7. See Christopher McCrudden, 'Human Dignity and Judicial Interpretation of Human Rights', (2008) 19 *EJIL* 655.
[73] *East African Asians v. the United Kingdom*, nos 4403/70-4419/70, 4422/70, 4423/70, 4434/70, 4443/70, 4476/70-4478/70, 4486/70, 4501/70, and 4526/70-4530/70, Commission report of 14 December 1973, § 207, DR 78-A, p. 5 ('The Commission recalls in this connection that, as generally recognised, a special importance should be attached to discrimination based on race; that publicly to single out a group of persons for differential treatment on the basis of race might, in certain circumstances, constitute a special form of affront to human dignity; that differential treatment of a group of persons on the basis of race might therefore be capable

Court has said that '[t]he very essence of the Convention is respect for human dignity and human freedom'.[74]

Recital 4 contains the Convention's only reference to 'peace'. Although there has been much activity aimed at recognizing a 'right to peace', either as a human right or a 'peoples' right',[75] in human rights instruments the issue is generally consigned to preambular allusions. There is no quarrel with the proposition that the promotion and protection of human rights require peace. Where difficulties arise is in determining when and under what conditions the interests of promoting peace may to some extent override individual rights. For example, in the name of resolving violent armed conflicts, amnesty and similar measures may be granted. However, this plainly conflicts with the right of victims to justice, recognized in the procedural obligations associated with articles 2 and 3 of the European Convention. Such issues have only very infrequently confronted the European Court of Human Rights.[76] Referring to the preambular reference, a Chamber of the Court accepted that 'ensuring respect for human rights represents an important contribution to achieving international peace', but went on to affirm the 'unique' and 'primary responsibility' of the United Nations Security Council in this area.[77]

In *Sejdić and Finci*, the Grand Chamber considered provisions of the Constitution of Bosnia and Herzegovina that had, in effect, been part of a peace agreement ending the armed conflict of the early 1990s. A contested component of the settlement was a discriminatory provision that prevented persons of certain ethnicities from being elected as the head of State. When the Grand Chamber concluded that this was a violation of the Convention, dissenting Judge Bonello warned that the Court had 'not found a hazard of civil war, the avoidance of carnage or the safeguard of territorial cohesion to have sufficient social value to justify some limitation on the rights of the two applicants'. He concluded: 'I cannot endorse a Court that sows ideals and harvests massacre.'[78] In its consideration of the permissibility of amnesty as an exception to the general principle of accountability for serious violations of human rights, the Grand Chamber acknowledged this might be legitimate if accompanied by measures of reparation or reconciliation but stopped short of recognizing the role amnesty may play in achieving a peaceful resolution of violent conflict.[79]

---

of constituting degrading treatment when differential treatment on some other ground would raise no such question.'); *Tyrer v. the United Kingdom*, 25 April 1978, § 33, Series A no. 26: ('Thus, although the applicant did not suffer any severe or long-lasting physical effects, his punishment—whereby he was treated as an object in the power of the authorities—constituted an assault on precisely that which it is one of the main purposes of Article 3 (art. 3) to protect, namely a person's dignity and physical integrity.')

[74] *Svinarenko and Slyadnev v. Russia* [GC], nos 32541/08 and 43441/08, § 118, 17 July 2014; *Pretty v. the United Kingdom*, no. 2346/02, § 65, ECHR 2002-III.

[75] Right of peoples to peace, UN Doc. A/RES/39/11; Promotion of the right to peace, UN Doc. A/HRC/RES/23/16. See Karel Vasek, 'Le droit de l'homme à la paix', in G. Flécheux, ed., *Mélanges en hommage à Louis Edmond Pettiti*, Brussels: Bruylant, 1998, pp. 751–60; William A. Schabas, 'The Human Right To Peace', in Asbjørn Eide, Jakob Th. Möller, and Inete Ziemele, eds, *Making Peoples Heard, Essays on Human Rights in Honour of Gudmundur Alfredsson*, Leiden/Boston: Martinus Nijhoff, 2011, pp. 43–57.

[76] On this subject generally, see James A. Sweeney, *The European Court of Human Rights in the Post-Cold War Era*, London/New York: Routledge, 2013.

[77] *Behrami and Behrami v. France and Saramati v. France, Germany and Norway* (dec.) [GC], nos. 71412/01 and 78166/01, § 148, 2 May 2007.

[78] *Sejdić and Finci v. Bosnia and Herzegovina* [GC], nos 27996/06 and 34836/06, Dissenting Opinion of Judge Bonello, ECHR 2009.

[79] *Marguš v. Croatia* [GC], no. 4455/10, § 139, 27 May 2014.

'[T]the most important contribution to peace in Europe in the history of the European Court of Human Rights', is how Judge Pinto de Albuquerque spoke of the just satisfaction judgment in the *Cyprus v. Turkey* inter-State case.[80] Describing the award of €90 million as punitive damages, he said: '[a]fter all, there is punishment for unjust war and its tragic consequences in Europe'.[81]

Effective political democracy (recital 4)

According to recital 4 of the Preamble, fundamental freedoms 'are best maintained on the one hand by an effective political democracy'. The association between the protection of human rights and political democracy is underscored by several provisions of the Convention and the Protocols, notably those dealing with freedom of expression, freedom of association and peaceful assembly, and electoral rights. The notion of 'democratic society' also appears in many clauses of the Convention and the Protocols as a concept guiding the determination of restrictions or limitations on fundamental rights. Referring to recital 4 of the Preamble, the Court has said that '[s]ince it enshrines a characteristic principle of democracy, Article 3 of Protocol No. 1 (P1-3) is accordingly of prime importance in the Convention system'.[82]

As the Grand Chamber has explained, '[d]emocracy constitutes a fundamental element of the "European public order". That is apparent, first, from the Preamble to the Convention, which establishes a very clear connection between the Convention and democracy.'[83] As the Court has often explained, the Convention was designed to maintain and promote the ideals and values of a democratic society. For this reason, 'democracy is the only political model contemplated by the Convention and, accordingly, the only one compatible with it'.[84] The Convention was designed to maintain and promote the ideals and values of a democratic society.[85] But there have actually only been a few references in the Court's jurisprudence to this portion of the Preamble.[86] In a dissenting opinion, Judge Wojtyczek said that this preambular provision expressed the idea that '[d]emocracy and rights are thus not seen to collide but rather to be in a symbiotic relationship with each other. The wording used may be understood, especially when read in conjunction with Article 3 of Protocol No. 1, as justifying a presumption in favour of broad powers of national legislatures.'[87]

---

[80] *Cyprus v. Turkey* (just satisfaction) [GC], no. 25781/94, Concurring Opinion of Judge Pinto de Albuquerque, Joined by Judge Vučinić, § 1, 12 May 2014.

[81] Ibid., § 24.

[82] *Mathieu-Mohin and Clerfayt v. Belgium*, 2 March 1987, § 47, Series A no. 113.

[83] *Ždanoka v. Latvia* [GC], no. 58278/00, § 98, ECHR 2006-IV.

[84] Ibid.

[85] *United Communist Party of Turkey and Others v. Turkey*, 30 January 1998, § 48, *Reports of Judgments and Decisions* 1998-I; *Kjeldsen, Busk Madsen and Pedersen v. Denmark*, 7 December 1976, § 53, Series A no. 23; *Soering v. the United Kingdom*, 7 July 1989, § 87, Series A no. 161.

[86] *Staatkundig Gereformeerde Parij v. the Netherlands* (dec.), no. 58369/10, § 69, 10 July 2012; *Streletz, Kessler, and Krenz v. Germany* [GC], nos 34044/96, 35532/97 and 44801/98, § 83, ECHR 2001-II; *K.-H. W. v. Germany* [GC], no. 37201/97, § 86, ECHR 2001-II (extracts); *Klass and Others v. Germany*, 6 September 1978, § 59, Series A no. 28.

[87] *Firth and Others v. the United Kingdom*, nos 7784/09, 47806/09, 47812/09, 47818/09, 47829/09, 49001/09, 49007/09, 49018/09, 49033/09, and 49036/09, Dissenting Opinion of Judge Wojtyczek, 12 August 2014.

Common understanding and observance of human rights (recital 4)

In addition to 'effective political democracy', recital 5 of the Preamble indicates that fundamental freedoms are also 'best maintained' by 'a common understanding and observance of the human rights upon which they depend'. The nomenclature is of interest, because 'human rights' and 'fundamental freedoms' are often used synonymously. For example, article 1(3) of the Charter of the United Nations refers to 'encouraging respect for human rights and for fundamental freedoms'. The expression is used in the same way in recital 7 of the Preamble of the Universal Declaration of Human Rights. The United Nations instruments may have added the notion of 'freedoms' to 'rights' in homage to President Roosevelt, who first advanced the idea of the 'four freedoms' in his January 1941 address to the American Congress. What is intriguing about recital 5 of the Preamble of the European Convention is its suggestion that 'fundamental freedoms' depend upon 'human rights', thereby suggesting that they are not exactly synonymous, but rather bound in some symbiotic relationship.

In a case concerning article 6(1), Judge Lagergren argued for what he called an 'autonomous' interpretation of the Convention, meaning an approach to terms that is independent of what is given to them in different national legal orders. He warned of the danger that human rights be interpreted differently from State to State, arguing instead for 'a uniform interpretation, resulting, in the words of the Preamble to the Convention, in "a common understanding and observance of the human rights" protected'.[88] Judge Wojtyczek referred to the phrase, noting that '[t]he Convention should therefore be construed in a way which reflects the common understanding of human rights among the High Contracting Parties. The Court should try to avoid imposing an interpretation which goes against that common understanding.'[89]

Common heritage (recital 5)

Recital 5 notes that the governments of Europe are both 'like-minded' and that they 'have a common heritage of political traditions, ideals, freedom and the rule of law'. The term 'common heritage' is an allusion to article 1 of the Statute of the Council of Europe: 'The aim of the Council is to achieve a greater unity between its Members, for the purpose of safeguarding and realising the ideals and principles which are their common heritage.' Taken as a whole, recital 5 has been described as 'the most significant passage' of the Preamble.[90] The context of adoption might have prompted the drafters to make some reference to the Second World War, but there is nothing of the kind in the Preamble. There is a striking contrast with the Preamble of the Charter of the United Nations, which speaks of 'the scourge of war, which twice in our lifetime has brought untold sorrow to mankind'. However, there is no explicit reference to the Second World War in the Preamble of the Universal Declaration of Human Rights. Indeed, the impression delivered by paragraph 5 of the Preamble is one of political harmony within Europe,

---

[88] *Ashingdane v. the United Kingdom*, 28 May 1985, Concurring Opinion of Judge Lagergren, Series A no. 93.

[89] *Firth and Others v. the United Kingdom*, nos 7784/09, 47806/09, 47812/09, 47818/09, 47829/09, 49001/09, 49007/09, 49018/09, 49033/09, and 49036/09, Dissenting Opinion of Judge Wojtyczek, § 2, 12 August 2014.

[90] *Salah v. the Netherlands*, no. 8196/02, § 68, ECHR 2006-IX (extracts); *Sylla v. the Netherlands*, no. 14683/03, § 70, 6 July 2006; *Baybaşın v. The Netherlands*, no. 13600/02, § 70, 6 July 2006.

which was, of course, very far from the case in the recent past as well as the time when the Convention was being adopted. The imprecise reference to 'like-minded' cleverly avoids indicating that there were many states in Europe that were not in fact of the same mind on major issues of rights, freedoms, and social policies. The reference to a 'common heritage' in the Preamble also serves as a reminder that despite the claim that the Convention was promoting the universal values of the United Nations Universal Declaration, it may also have been reinforcing a view of cultural relativism.

According to the Grand Chamber, '[t]his common heritage consists in the underlying values of the Convention'.[91] The first embodiment of the common heritage is often found in national constitutions.[92] The Grand Chamber has said that '[i]t would hardly be compatible with the "common heritage of political traditions, ideals, freedom and the rule of law" to which the Preamble refers, were a Contracting State knowingly to surrender a person to another State where there were substantial grounds for believing that he would be in danger of being subjected to torture or inhuman or degrading treatment or punishment'.[93]

In *Tyrer v. The United Kingdom*, the Court rejected an argument based upon the claim that the local population of the Isle of Man was not outraged by corporal punishment. The Court found it noteworthy that 'in the great majority of the member States of the Council of Europe, judicial corporal punishment is not, it appears, used and, indeed, in some of them, has never existed in modern times'. It went on to note that '[t]he Isle of Man not only enjoys long-established and highly-developed political, social and cultural traditions but is an up-to-date society. Historically, geographically and culturally, the Island has always been included in the European family of nations and must be regarded as sharing fully that "common heritage of political traditions, ideals, freedom and the rule of law" to which the Preamble to the Convention refers.'[94]

In a partly dissenting opinion, Judge Wojtyczek noted the role of recital 5 in interpretation of the Convention, stating: 'The same idea may also be expressed in slightly different words: the interpretation of the Convention should take into due account the common European constitutional heritage. The paradigm of European constitutionalism is an inescapable point of reference for interpretation of the Convention.'[95] In another opinion, he said that '[t]he common European constitutional heritage co-determines the meaning and the scope of the Convention rights'.[96]

[91] *Ždanoka v. Latvia* [GC], no. 58278/00, § 98, ECHR 2006-IV; *Soering v. the United Kingdom*, 7 July 1989, § 88, Series A no. 161; *United Communist Party of Turkey and Others v. Turkey*, 30 January 1998, § 28, *Reports of Judgments and Decisions* 1998-I.

[92] *United Communist Party of Turkey and Others v. Turkey*, 30 January 1998, § 28, *Reports of Judgments and Decisions* 1998-I.

[93] *Mamatkulov and Askarov v. Turkey* [GC], nos 46827/99 and 46951/99, § 68, ECHR 2005-I. Also *Soering v. the United Kingdom*, 7 July 1989, § 88, Series A no. 161; *Ilaşcu and Others v. Moldova and Russia* [GC], no. 48787/99, § 317, ECHR 2004-VII.

[94] *Tyrer v. the United Kingdom*, 25 April 1978, § 38, Series A no. 26.

[95] *Zornić v. Bosnia and Herzegovina*, no. 3681/06, Partly Dissenting Opinion of Judge Wojtyczek, 15 July 2014.

[96] *Firth and Others v. the United Kingdom*, nos 7784/09, 47806/09, 47812/09, 47818/09, 47829/09, 49001/09, 49007/09, 49018/09, 49033/09, and 49036/09, Dissenting Opinion of Judge Wojtyczek, § 2, 12 August 2014.

Rule of law (recital 5)

The allusion to a 'common heritage' in recital 5 of the Preamble concludes with a reference to the rule of law. It may be the most important concept within the entire Preamble. The words echo a provision in the Preamble of the Universal Declaration of Human Rights: 'Whereas it is essential, if man is not to be compelled to have recourse, as a last resort, to rebellion against tyranny and oppression, that human rights should be protected by the rule of law...' The Statute of the Council of Europe also refers to the rule of law, first, in the Preamble, and second, in article 3 with the requirement that 'every Member of the Council of Europe must accept the principle of the rule of law...'[97] It is described as being one of the three pillars of the Council of Europe.[98]

In the French versions of both the Statute of the Council of Europe and the European Convention on Human Rights, 'rule of law' is translated as *prééminence du droit* and not as *état de droit*. Nevertheless, the term *état de droit* is occasionally used in French versions of judgments of the Court as the equivalent of 'rule of law'.[99]

The rule of law has been described as 'one of the fundamental principles of a democratic society'. Mentioned by name only in the Preamble, it is described as being 'inherent in all the Articles of the Convention',[100] one of the 'cornerstones of the Convention',[101] an 'essential protection of the individual',[102] and a concept from which the entire Convention draws its inspiration.[103] As it was understood at the time the Convention was drafted, and probably until the 1990s, the concept of rule of law meant that the government was accountable to the courts. As one judgment put it, 'an interference by the executive authorities with an individual's rights should be subject to an effective control which should normally be assured by the judiciary, at least in the last resort, judicial control offering the best guarantees of independence, impartiality and a proper procedure'.[104] It entails a duty on the part of the State or other public authority to comply with judicial orders or decisions against it.[105]

In *Golder*, the United Kingdom argued that the drafters engaged in a 'selective process', choosing to adopt only 'certain of the Rights stated in the Universal Declaration'.[106] The Court concluded:

The 'selective' nature of the Convention cannot be put in question. It may also be accepted, as the Government have submitted, that the Preamble does not include the rule of law in the object and

---

[97] See *Golder v. the United Kingdom*, 21 February 1975, § 34, Series A no. 18.

[98] Report on the Rule of Law Adopted by the Venice Commission at its 86th Plenary Session (Venice, 25–26 March 2011), CDL-AD(2011)003rev.

[99] E.g., *Scoppola v. Italy (no. 3)* [GC], no. 126/05, §§ 82, 90, 92, 22 May 2012; *Kononov v. Latvia* [GC], no. 36376/04, § 241, ECHR 2010; *Hirst v. the United Kingdom (no. 2)* [GC], no. 74025/01, § 74, ECHR 2005-IX.

[100] *Vontas and Others v. Greece*, no. 43588/06, § 34, 5 February 2009; *Iatridis v. Greece* [GC], no. 31107/96, § 58, ECHR 1999-II; *Amuur v. France*, 25 June 1996, § 50, *Reports of Judgments and Decisions* 1996-III.

[101] *Streletz, Kessler, and Krenz v. Germany* [GC], nos 34044/96, 35532/97, and 44801/98, § 82, ECHR 2001-II. Also *K.-H.W. v. Germany* [GC], no. 37201/97, § 84, ECHR 2001-II (extracts).

[102] *Gustafsson v. Sweden*, 25 April 1996, Dissenting Opinion of Judge Martens, Joined by Judge Matscher, § 11, *Reports of Judgments and Decisions* 1996-II.

[103] *Brogan and Others v. the United Kingdom*, 29 November 1988, § 58, Series A no. 145-B; *Engel and Others v. the Netherlands*, 8 June 1976, § 69, Series A no. 22.

[104] *Klass and Others v. Germany*, 6 September 1978, § 56, Series A no. 28.

[105] *Iatridis v. Greece* [GC], no. 31107/96, § 58, ECHR 1999-II; *Hornsby v. Greece*, 19 March 1997, § 41, *Reports of Judgments and Decisions* 1997-II.

[106] *Golder v. the United Kingdom*, 21 February 1975, § 34, Series A no. 18.

purpose of the Convention, but points to it as being one of the features of the common spiritual heritage of the member States of the Council of Europe. The Court however considers, like the Commission, that it would be a mistake to see in this reference a merely 'more or less rhetorical reference', devoid of relevance for those interpreting the Convention. One reason why the signatory Governments decided to 'take the first steps for the collective enforcement of certain of the Rights stated in the Universal Declaration' was their profound belief in the rule of law.[107]

A central aspect of the rule of law is the right to a fair hearing before a tribunal, guaranteed by article 6(1) of the Convention and a principle to be interpreted in the light of the Preamble. According to the Court, '[o]ne of the fundamental aspects of the rule of law is the principle of legal certainty, which requires, inter alia, that where the courts have finally determined an issue, their ruling should not be called into question'.[108]

A report of the Venice Commission of the Council of Europe has endorsed a succinct statement of the rule of law by British judge Tom Bingham: '[A]ll persons and authorities within the state, whether public or private, should be bound by and entitled to the benefit of laws publicly made, taking effect (generally) in the future and publicly administered in the courts.'[109] The Commission has said it should be expanded with the following eight 'ingredients': accessibility of the law (that it be intelligible, clear, and predictable); questions of legal right should be normally decided by law and not discretion; there should be equality before the law; power must be exercised lawfully, fairly, and reasonably; human rights must be protected; means must be provided to resolve disputes without undue cost or delay; trials must be fair; the State must comply with its obligations in international law as well as in national law.[110] Judgments of the Court have said that 'the role played by limitation periods is of major importance when interpreted in the light of the Preamble to the Convention, which, in its relevant part, declares the rule of law to be part of the common heritage of the Contracting States'.[111]

Recently the notion of 'rule of law' has come to be associated with a much broader notion of assistance in the development of functioning justice systems. According to the United Nations Secretary General, the concept 'refers to a principle of governance in which all persons, institutions and entities, public and private, including the State itself, are accountable to laws that are publicly promulgated, equally enforced and independently adjudicated, and which are consistent with international human rights norms and standards. It requires, as well, measures to ensure adherence to the principles of supremacy of law, equality before the law, accountability to the law, fairness in the application of the law, separation of powers, participation in decision-making, legal certainty, avoidance of arbitrariness and procedural and legal transparency.'[112]

---

[107] Ibid., § 34.

[108] *Brumărescu v. Romania* [GC], no. 28342/95, § 61, ECHR 1999-VII; *Ryabykh v. Russia*, no. 52854/99, §§ 51–56, ECHR 2003-IX; *Roşca v. Moldova*, no. 6267/02, § 24, 22 March 2005; *Driza v. Albania*, no. 33771/02, § 63, ECHR 2007-V (extracts); *Lenskaya v. Russia*, no. 28730/03, § 30, 29 January 2009; *Tchitchinadze v. Georgia*, no. 18156/05, § 53, 27 May 2010; *Asito v. Moldova (no. 2)*, no. 39818/06, § 22, 13 March 2012; *Varnienė v. Lithuania*, no. 42916/04, § 37, 12 November 2013; *Giuran v. Romania*, no. 24360/04, § 28, ECHR 2011 (extracts); *Bezrukovy v. Russia*, no. 34616/02, § 32, 10 May 2012; *Dragostea Copiilor—Petrovschi—Nagornii v. Moldova*, no. 25575/08, § 25, 13 September 2011.

[109] Tom Bingham, *The Rule of* Law, London: Allen Lane, 2010, p. 8.

[110] Report on the Rule of Law Adopted by the Venice Commission at its 86th Plenary Session (Venice, 25–26 March 2011), CDL-AD(2011)003rev, para. 37.

[111] *Bogdel v. Lithuania*, no. 41248/06, § 80, 26 November 2013.

[112] The Rule of Law and Transitional Justice in Conflict and Post-conflict Societies, Report of the Secretary General, Doc. S/2004/616, para. 6.

Collective enforcement (recital 5)

The Convention system considers that the rights and freedoms it protects are subject to 'collective enforcement', as stated in recital 5 of the Preamble: '. . . to take the first steps for the collective enforcement of certain of the rights stated in the Universal Declaration . . .' This is the only reference in the Preamble to the Convention as a system of enforcement of human rights rather than merely as a standard-setting instrument. Its importance is underscored by the reprisal of these words in the much more succinct preambles to Protocol Nos 1, 4, and 7 of the Convention. Referring to recital 5 and the reference to 'collective enforcement', the European Commission of Human Rights observed 'that the purpose of the High Contracting parties in concluding the Convention was not to concede to each other reciprocal rights and obligations in pursuance of their individual national interests but to realise the aims and ideals of the Council of Europe, as expressed in its Statute, and to establish a common public order of the free democracies of Europe with the object of safeguarding their common heritage of political traditions, ideals, freedom and the rule of law'.[113] The Commission went on to refer to the 'objective character' of the obligations imposed by the Convention, noting that this appeared in the machinery provided for the observance of such obligations 'founded upon the concept of a collective guarantee by the High Contracting Parties of the rights and freedoms set forth in the Convention'.[114]

The Court has spoken of 'the Convention's special character as a treaty for the collective enforcement of human rights and fundamental freedoms'.[115] Thus, it is said that '[u]nlike international treaties of the classic kind, the Convention comprises more than mere reciprocal engagements between Contracting States. It creates, over and above a network of mutual, bilateral undertakings, objective obligations which, in the words of the Preamble benefit from a "collective enforcement".'[116] The reference to collective enforcement in the Preamble has also been linked to the requirement that the Convention 'be interpreted and applied so as to make its safeguards practical and effective'.[117] The mechanisms for collective enforcement 'serve the public order of Europe'.[118]

The insistence on collective enforcement must be considered alongside the principle of subsidiarity, explicitly mentioned in recital 6 of the Preamble, whereby the primary

[113] *Austria v. Italy*, no. 788/60, Commission decision of 11 January 1961, (1961) 4 YB 116, at p. 138.

[114] Ibid., p. 140. See also *Chrysostomos and Others v. Turkey*, nos 15299/89, 15300/89, and 15318/89, Commission decision of 4 March 1991, § 20, (1991) 34 YB 35, DR 68, p. 216.

[115] *Nada v. Switzerland* [GC], no. 10593/08, § 198, ECHR 2012; *Ireland v. the United Kingdom*, 18 January 1978, § 239, Series A no. 25; *Al-Saadoon and Mufdhi v. the United Kingdom*, no. 61498/08, § 127, ECHR 2010 (extracts); *Mamatkulov and Askarov v. Turkey* [GC] (nos 46827/99 and 46951/99), § 100, ECHR 2005-I; *Rrapo v. Albania*, no. 58555/10, § 127, 25 September 2012; *Soering v. the United Kingdom*, 7 July 1989, § 87, Series A no. 161; *Loizidou v. Turkey (Article 50)*, 29 July 1998, § 48, *Reports of Judgments and Decisions* 1998-IV. Also *Vijayanathan and Pusparajah v. France*, nos 17550/90 and 17825/91, Commission decision of 4 June 1991, DR 70, p. 309.

[116] *Ireland v. the United Kingdom*, 18 January 1978, § 239, Series A no. 25. Also *Loizidou v. Turkey* (preliminary objections), 23 March 1995, § 70, Series A no. 310; *Mamatkulov and Askarov v. Turkey* [GC] (nos 46827/99 and 46951/99), § 100, ECHR 2005-I; *Paladi v. Moldova* [GC], no. 39806/05, § 84, 10 March 2009; *Knaags and Khachik v. the United Kingdom* (dec.), nos 46559/06 and 22921/06, § 199, 30 August 2011.

[117] *Biç and Others v. Turkey*, no. 55955/00, § 18, 2 February 2006; *Shamayev and Others v. Georgia and Russia*, no. 36378/02, § 302, ECHR 2005-III; *Direkçi and Direkçi v. Turkey* (dec.), no. 47826/99, 3 October 2006; *Sanles Sanles v. Spain* (dec.), no. 48335/99, ECHR 2000-XI; *İlhan v. Turkey* [GC], no. 22277/93, § 51, ECHR 2000-VII; *Yaşa v. Turkey*, 2 September 1998, § 64, *Reports of Judgments and Decisions* 1998-VI.

[118] *Cyprus v. Turkey*, no. 8007/77, Commission decision of 10 July 1978, § 11, (1978) 21 YB 101, DR 13, p. 85.

responsibility for the enforcement of human rights lies with the individual States Parties themselves.[119] The issue was highlighted in one of the early decisions of the Court, where reference was made to the 'subsidiary nature of the international machinery of collective enforcement established by the Convention'.[120] Even earlier, the Commission had addressed the tension between the collective enforcement and subsidiarity in the context of the rule on exhaustion of domestic remedies: the mere fact that the system of international protection in the Convention is founded upon the concept of a collective guarantee of the rights and freedoms contained in the Convention does not in any way weaken the force of the principle on which the domestic remedies rule is founded or the considerations which led to its introduction'.[121] Occasionally, the case law has attempted to address the relationship. For example, one Chamber has noted that '[t]hrough its system of collective enforcement of the rights it establishes, the Convention reinforces, in accordance with the principle of subsidiarity, the protection afforded at national level'.[122] Another has insisted that 'the international machinery of collective enforcement established by the Convention is subsidiary to the national systems safeguarding human rights'.[123]

The reference to 'collective enforcement' in recital 5 of the Preamble has been used by the Grand Chamber to support the position that article 6 of the Convention does not apply to measures of expulsion.[124]

Principle of subsidiarity (recital 6)

According to the principle of subsidiarity, the primary responsibility for the enforcement of the European Convention lies with States. Only when they fail to do so does the machinery of the Convention, in particular the Court, intervene in the process.[125] It also contains within it a notion of deference to national justice systems with respect to their determinations of both fact and law. Subsidiary has been described as 'the very basis of the Convention', its basis within the texts being a combined reading of articles 1 and 19.[126] According to the Explanatory Report on Protocol No. 14,

Under Article 1 of the Convention, it is with the High Contracting Parties that the obligation lies 'to secure to everyone within their jurisdiction the rights and freedoms' guaranteed by the Convention, whereas the role of the Court, under Article 19, is 'to ensure the observance of the engagements

---

[119] Herbert Petzold, 'The Convention and the Principle of Subsidiarity', in Macdonald, *The European System*, pp. 41–62; Jonas Christoffersen, *Fair Balance: Proportionality, Subsidiarity and Primacy in the European Convention on Human Rights*, Leiden/Boston: Martinus Nijhoff, 2009.

[120] *Case 'relating to certain aspects of the laws on the use of languages in education in Belgium'* (merits), 23 July 1968, p. 32, § 10, Series A no. 6.

[121] *Austria v. Italy*, no. 788/60, Commission decision of 11 January 1961, (1961) 4 YB 116, at p. 140.

[122] *Shamayev and Others v. Georgia and Russia*, no. 36378/02, § 500, ECHR 2005-III; *United Communist Party of Turkey and Others v. Turkey*, 30 January 1998, § 28, *Reports of Judgments and Decisions* 1998-I.

[123] *Tkachevy v. Russia*, no. 35430/05, § 35, 14 February 2012. Also *Micallef v. Malta*, no. 17056/06, § 44, 15 January 2008.

[124] *Maaouia v. France* [GC], no. 39652/98, § 36, ECHR 2000-X.

[125] Jonas Christoffersen, *Fair Balance: Proportionality, Subsidiarity and Primacy in the European Convention on Human Rights*, Leiden: Brill/Nijhoff, 2009; P. Mahoney, 'Universality versus Subsidiarity', [1997] *EHRLR* 364.

[126] *Austin and Others v. the United Kingdom* [GC], nos 39692/09, 40713/09, and 41008/09, § 61, ECHR 2012.

undertaken by the High Contracting Parties in the Convention'. In other words, securing rights and freedoms is primarily the responsibility of the Parties; the Court's role is subsidiary.[127]

Subsidiarity is also manifested in article 13, the provision ensuring availability at the national level of a remedy to enforce the substance of the Convention rights and freedoms in whatever form they may happen to be secured in the domestic legal order.[128] For decades, the principle of subsidiarity has been acknowledged in decisions of the Court.[129] It was formally recognized by a recital in the Preamble, added as part of the amendments resulting from Protocol No. 15. The Explanatory Report states that the intention was 'to enhance the transparency and accessibility' of this characteristic of the Convention system.[130] The preambular reference was a compromise with the more extreme suggestion, advanced by the United Kingdom, to incorporate the concept within an operative provision of the Convention.[131] In an opinion on the text issued at the request of the Committee of Ministers, the Court welcomed the insertion of the reference to subsidiarity in the Preamble. 'The wording used in this respect, and in the explanatory report, reflects the Court's pronouncements on the principle', it said.[132] The Parliamentary Assembly also presented an opinion on the amendment. The Rapporteur of the Committee on Legal Affairs and Human Rights said the addition 'can only be welcomed'. He continued:

The States Parties to the Convention are obliged to secure to everyone within their jurisdiction the rights and freedoms defined in the Convention, and to provide an effective remedy before a national authority for everyone whose rights and freedoms are violated. The Court authoritatively interprets the Convention. It also acts as a safeguard for individuals whose rights and freedoms are not secured at the national level. The Convention places primary responsibility on States Parties to secure fundamental rights and freedoms to everyone within their jurisdiction (Article 1) and to provide effective remedies for allegations of violations (Article 13), and the Court should be seized only 'after all domestic remedies are exhausted' (Article 35, paragraph 1). Subsidiarity and, to a certain extent, the related doctrine of a 'margin of appreciation', as developed by the Court, require that the Strasbourg Court plays a complementary role to domestic court decisions and legislation: States have the duty to integrate Convention standards, as interpreted by the Court, within their own legal systems. In other words, the principle of subsidiarity has two aspects: one procedural, requiring individuals to go through all the relevant procedures at national level before seizing the Court, and the other substantive, based on the assumption that States are, in principle, better placed to assess the necessity and proportionality of specific measures that may interfere with certain rights. That said, a State can and often does guarantee a higher level of protection, and the Court obviously accords certain latitude to the domestic authorities to strike their own balance regarding Convention rights, guided by the relevant European case-law. But the Court has the final say on the interpretation of the Convention in all cases brought before it.[133]

---

[127] Explanatory Report on Protocol No. 14, para. 12.

[128] *M.S.S. v. Belgium and Greece* [GC], no. 30696/09, § 288, ECHR 2011; *Kudła v. Poland* [GC], no. 30210/96, § 152, ECHR 2000-XI.

[129] *Case 'relating to certain aspects of the laws on the use of languages in education in Belgium'* (merits), 23 July 1968, p. 35, § 10, Series A no. 6; *Handyside v. the United Kingdom*, 7 December 1976, § 48, Series A no. 24.

[130] Explanatory Report on Protocol No. 15, para. 7.

[131] Klaus Lörcher, 'The Future of the European Court of Human Rights in the Light of the Brighton Declaration', in Filip Dorssemont, Klaus Lörcher, and Isabelle Schömann, eds, *The European Convention on Human Rights and the Employment Relation*, Oxford/Portland, OR: Hart, 2013, pp. 93–104, at pp. 96–8.

[132] Opinion of the Court on Draft Protocol No. 15 to the European Convention on Human Rights, 6 February 2013, para. 5.

[133] Draft Protocol No. 15 amending the Convention for the Protection of Human Rights and Fundamental Freedoms, Report, Committee on Legal Affairs and Human Rights, Doc. 13154, para. 8 (internal references omitted).

The principle of subsidiarity applies in at least three different contexts. First, it defines the relationship between the law of the Convention and internal law, in the sense that it is primarily the duty of internal law to ensure that rights are respected.[134] Of course, in many countries the Convention will be incorporated directly into internal law.[135] But this is not a requirement of the Convention. Where there is no direct incorporation, the burden falls first upon the internal legal order to protect fundamental rights. According to the Court, the Convention reinforces, in accordance with the principle of subsidiarity, the protection afforded at national level, but never limits it'.[136]

Secondly, the principle of subsidiarity defines the relationship between the system of enforcement established by the Convention, and in particular the European Court of Human Rights, and the mechanisms of internal law. As early as the *Belgian Linguistic case*, the Court indicated that it should not 'assume the role of the competent national authorities, for it would thereby lose sight of the subsidiary nature of the international machinery of collective enforcement established by the Convention'.[137] The Court has declared that '[i]t is fundamental to the machinery of protection established by the Convention that the national systems themselves provide redress for breaches of its provisions, with the Court exercising a supervisory role subject to the principle of subsidiarity'.[138]

In terms of the enforcement machinery, the principle is reflected above all in article 35 (1) of the Convention in the requirement that domestic remedies be exhausted before recourse may be had to the European Court. The rationale for exhaustion of domestic remedies is 'the subsidiary nature of the Convention instruments, that is to say, the principle that the national authorities must be first given the opportunity to remedy the violation complained of'.[139] Given that the rule of exhaustion is limited by the availability of adequate or effective remedies within the national system, 'the principle of subsidiarity [is] not absolute'.[140]

According to the principle of subsidiarity, in immigration cases the 'sole concern' of the Court is 'to examine the effectiveness of the domestic procedures and ensure that they respect human rights'.[141] In cases involving asylum seekers, the Court has said that its task is not to examine how States honour their obligations under the Refugee Convention, but rather to determine that effective guarantees exist against arbitrary *refoulement*.[142]

---

[134] Explanatory Report on Protocol No. 14, para. 15; *Handyside v. the United Kingdom*, 7 December 1976, § 48, Series A no. 24.

[135] See J. Polakiewicz, 'The Status of the Convention in National Law', in Robert Blackburn and Jörg Polakiewicz, eds, *Fundamental Rights in Europe, The European Convention on Human Rights and its Member States, 1950–2000*, Oxford: Oxford University Press, 2001, pp. 31–50; Ed Bates, *The Evolution of the European Convention on Human Rights*, Oxford: Oxford University Press, 2010, at pp. 158–63.

[136] *United Communist Party of Turkey and Others v. Turkey*, 30 January 1998, § 28, *Reports of Judgments and Decisions* 1998-I; *Shamayev and Others v. Georgia and Russia*, no. 36378/02, § 500, ECHR 2005-III.

[137] *Case 'relating to certain aspects of the laws on the use of languages in education in Belgium'* (merits), 23 July 1968, p. 35, § 10, Series A no. 6.

[138] *A. and Others v. the United Kingdom* [GC], no. 3455/05, § 174, ECHR 2009; *Z. and Others v. the United Kingdom*, no. 29392/95, § 103, ECHR 2001-V.

[139] *Đorđević v. Croatia*, no. 41526/10, § 110, ECHR 2012. Also *Demopoulos and Others v. Turkey* (dec.) [GC], nos 46113/99, 3843/0213751/02, 13466/03, 10200/04, 14163/04, 19993/04, 21819/04, § 101, ECHR 2010.

[140] *Vučković and Others v. Serbia*, no. 17153/11, § 63, 28 August 2012.

[141] *De Souza Ribeiro v. France* [GC], no. 22689/07, § 84, ECHR 2012.

[142] *M.S.S. v. Belgium and Greece* [GC], no. 30696/09, § 286, ECHR 2011; *I.M. v. France*, no. 9152/09, § 127, 2 February 2012.

Under the principle of subsidiarity, a State is free to choose the means by which it implements a decision of the Court, subject to monitoring by the Committee of Ministers.[143] Effective implementation of judgments, pursuant to article 46 of the Convention, helps to alleviate a burden upon the Court that may result from an avalanche of similar cases if a State does not properly comply with a judgment.[144] The pilot judgment procedure, by which emblematic cases provide States with guidelines facilitating remediation of structural problems, has been described as the implementation of the principle of subsidiarity.[145]

It may seem a paradox, but just as the European Convention exists to ensure that the national legal order respects human rights, at the same time the European Court manifests considerable deference towards domestic courts and their determinations. This is particularly true when constitutional courts are involved, given that they apply principles similar, if not identical in nature, to those enshrined in the Convention, and often rely upon the case law of the European Court itself.[146] As one judge explained, the Court does not have, 'with the usual paraphernalia of constitutional law, an interest in meddling in what national legislation should or should not do. Subsidiarity is a healthy collateral effect of the simple fact that an international judicial body does not know how to, and thus does not want to, enter into the details of national legislative happenings.'[147] More generally, 'the principle of subsidiarity dictates that the Court will not overrule interpretations of the domestic law given by the domestic courts, except in specific circumstances ... The Court retains only residual control in this sphere.'[148] This approach applies even when the national courts rule against the government, for example in deciding that legislation is not sheltered by derogation pursuant to article 15. Where the highest courts concluded that derogation by the United Kingdom was inconsistent with article 15 because the measures taken to deal with a public emergency were not strictly required by the exigencies of the situation, the European Court of Human Rights said 'it would be justified in reaching a contrary conclusion only if satisfied that the national court had misinterpreted or misapplied Article 15 or the Court's jurisprudence under that Article or reached a conclusion which was manifestly unreasonable'.[149]

It is often said that the Court does not operate as a fourth-instance court, reviewing matters concerning sentences imposed and damages awarded, in the absence of evidence that there is arbitrariness.[150] Nor is it a first-instance court, assessing issues of fact, whose

---

[143] *Association '21 December 1989' and Others v. Romania*, nos 33810/07 and 18817/08, § 126, 24 May 2011; *Broniowski v. Poland* (friendly settlement) [GC], no. 31443/96, § 34, ECHR 2005-IX.

[144] *Luli and Others v. Albania*, nos 64480/09, 64482/09, 12874/10, 56935/10, 3129/12, and 31355/09, § 116, 1 April 2014; *Scordino v. Italy (no. 1)* [GC], no. 36813/97, § 233, ECHR 2006; *Xenides-Arestis v. Turkey*, no. 46347/99, §§ 39, 40, 22 December 2005; *Bottazzi v. Italy* [GC], no. 34884/97, § 22, ECHR 1999-V; *Di Mauro v. Italy* [GC], no. 34256/96, § 23, ECHR 1999-V. Also Explanatory Report on Protocol No. 14, para. 16.

[145] *Ananyev v. Russia*, no. 20292/04, § 182, 30 July 2009; *Hutten-Czapska v. Poland* (friendly settlement) [GC], no. 35014/97, § 34, 28 April 2008; *Burdov v. Russia (no. 2)*, no. 33509/04, § 127, ECHR 2009; *Manushaqe Puto and Others v. Albania*, nos 604/07, 43628/07, 46684/07, and 34770/09, § 104, 31 July 2012.

[146] *Henryk Urban and Ryszard Urban v. Poland*, no. 23614/08, § 51, 30 November 2010.

[147] *Hutten-Czapska v. Poland* [GC], no. 35014/97, Partly Concurring, Partly Dissenting Opinion of Judge Zupančič, ECHR 2006-VIII.

[148] *Khodorkovskiy and Lebedev v. Russia*, nos 11082/06 and 13772/05, § 841, 25 July 2013.

[149] *A. and Others v. the United Kingdom* [GC], no. 3455/05, § 174, ECHR 2009.

[150] *Artemov v. Russia*, no. 4945/03, § 115, 3 April 2014; *Putistin v. Ukraine*, no. 16882/03, § 43, 21 November 2013; *Căcescu v. Romania* (dec.), no. 10762/04, § 32, 2 October 2012; *Broka v. Latvia*, no. 70926/

investigation and assessment is 'to be resolved in so far as possible at the domestic level'.[151] Although 'the Court is not bound by the findings of domestic courts and remains free to make its own appreciation in the light of all the material before it, in normal circumstances it requires cogent elements to lead it to depart from the findings of fact reached by the domestic courts'.[152] For example, '[w]here the circumstances of a particular case so require, especially where the death of a victim is arguably attributable to the use of lethal force by State agents, the Court may entertain a fresh assessment of evidence.[153]

Thirdly, the principle of subsidiary governs not only the relationship between the national legal order and the Convention system but also the application of law within a given State. It has been said by some judges that '[t]he notion of a democratic society encompasses the idea of subsidiarity'. Accordingly, 'a democratic society may flourish only in a State that respects the principle of subsidiarity and allows the different social actors to self-regulate their activities'.[154] Along the same lines, a judge has insisted that the 'democratic ideal' requires that 'the principle of State subsidiarity should not be overlooked'.[155] In another context, some judges have invoked the notion of subsidiarity with respect to criminal law, arguing that 'use of the weapon of punishment is acceptable only if there are no other means of protecting the values or interests at stake'.[156]

Margin of appreciation (recital 6)

Like the principle of subsidiarity, with which it is closely related,[157] the 'margin of appreciation' is a concept that is well entrenched in the case law of the Court. Pursuant to Protocol No. 15, an explicit recognition of the doctrine is now contained in recital 6 of the Preamble. According to the Explanatory Report on Protocol No. 15,

The jurisprudence of the Court makes clear that the States Parties enjoy a margin of appreciation in how they apply and implement the Convention, depending on the circumstances of the case and the rights and freedoms engaged. This reflects that the Convention system is subsidiary to the safeguarding of human rights at national level and that national authorities are in principle better placed than an international court to evaluate local needs and conditions. The margin of appreciation goes hand in hand with supervision under the Convention system. In this respect, the role of

01, §§ 25–26, 28 June 2007; *Melnychuk v. Ukraine* (dec.), no. 28743/03, ECHR 2005-IX; *García Ruiz v. Spain* [GC], no. 30544/96, § 28, ECHR 1999-I.

[151] *El Masri v. 'the former Yugoslav Republic of Macedonia'* [GC], no. 39630/09, § 141, ECHR 2012. Also *Varnava and Others v. Turkey* [GC], nos 16064/90, 16065/90, 16066/90, 16068/90, 16069/90, 16070/90, 16071/90, 16072/90, and 16073/90, § 164, ECHR 2009; *Tahsin Acar v. Turkey* [GC], no 26307/95, § 213, ECHR 2004-III; *Halit Çelebi v. Turkey*, no. 54182/00, § 40, 2 May 2006.

[152] *Austin and Others v. the United Kingdom* [GC], nos 39692/09, 40713/09, and 41008/09, § 61, ECHR 2012.

[153] *Finogenov and Others v. Russia*, nos 18299/03 and 27311/03, § 237, ECHR 2011 (extracts). Also *Golubeva v. Russia*, no. 1062/03, § 95, 17 December 2009; *Matko v. Slovenia*, no. 43393/98, § 100, 2 November 2006.

[154] *O'Keeffe v. Ireland* [GC], no. 35810/09, Joint Partly Dissenting Opinion of Judges Zupančić, Gyulumyan, Kalaydjieva, De Gaetano, and Wojtyczek, § 7, 19, 28 January 2014.

[155] *Sindicatul 'Păstorul cel Bun' v. Romania* [GC], no. 2330/09, Concurring Opinion of Judge Wojtyczek, § 2, ECHR 2013 (extracts).

[156] *Gäfgen v. Germany* [GC], no. 22978/05, Joint Partly Concurring Opinion of Judges Tulkens, Ziemele, and Bianku, § 5, ECHR 2010.

[157] *Ališić and Others v. Bosnia and Herzegovina, Croatia, Serbia, Slovenia, and the former Yugoslavia Republic of Macedonia* [GC], no. 60642/08, Partly Dissenting Opinion of Judge Nußburger, Joined by Judge Popović, 16 July 2014.

the Court is to review whether decisions taken by national authorities are compatible with the Convention, having due regard to the State's margin of appreciation.[158]

The Court was not entirely content with the formulation of the margin of appreciation in the draft text. In light of the Court's opinion, the Steering Committee on Human Rights took its views into account and decided to 'clarify' in the Explanatory Report that its intention was 'to be consistent with the doctrine of the margin of appreciation as developed by the Court in its case-law'. However, it also chose not to amend the text as drafted.[159] The Court responded, in an opinion on the draft issued at the request of the Committee of Ministers, that '[t]he intended meaning can therefore be said to be in line with the relevant terms of the Brighton Declaration'.[160] It referred to paragraph 12b of the Brighton Declaration calling for the addition to the Preamble, 'for reasons of transparency and accessibility [of] a reference to the principle of subsidiarity and the doctrine of the margin of appreciation as developed in the Court's case law'. The Court affirmed that 'there clearly was no common intention of the High Contracting Parties to alter either the substance of the Convention or its system of international, collective enforcement'. The Court said it would have preferred 'a more developed text', but it acknowledged that the result represented a compromise among States. 'In any event, both the explanation given and the context in which the text was drafted are themselves legally significant, as illustrated by the Court's references to the Explanatory Report to Protocol No. 14 and to the Interlaken Action Plan in *Korolev v. Russia* (dec.), no. 25551/05, ECHR 2010', the Court said. 'Moreover, the report of the relevant meeting of the CDDH—an extract of which the Committee of Ministers appended to its request for the present opinion—forms part of the *travaux préparatoires* of the Protocol and thus is relevant to its interpretation.'[161]

Speaking of the addition of a reference to the margin of appreciation, the Rapporteur of the Committee on Legal Affairs and Human Rights of the Parliamentary Assembly said that '[n]eedless to add, no "margin of appreciation" exists with respect to the Convention's non-derogable rights in matters of life and death, torture or slavery'. Consequently, he wrote, it is important to bear in mind, as indicated in both the Explanatory Report and the opinion of the Court, 'the clear intention of the drafters of the text to make express reference to "the doctrine of the margin of appreciation as developed by the Court in its case-law"'.[162]

Much attention has been accorded to the margin of appreciation doctrine in the academic literature.[163] The European Commission of Human Rights developed the

---

[158] Explanatory Report on Protocol No. 15, para. 9.

[159] Report, 76th meeting, Strasbourg, 27–30 November 2012, CDDH(2012)R76, para. 9.

[160] Opinion of the Court on Draft Protocol No. 15 to the European Convention on Human Rights, 6 February 2013, para. 4.

[161] Ibid.

[162] Draft Protocol No. 15 amending the Convention for the Protection of Human Rights and Fundamental Freedoms, Report, Committee on Legal Affairs and Human Rights, Doc. 13154, para. 8 (internal references omitted).

[163] Y. Arai-Takahashi, *The Margin of Appreciation Doctrine and the Principle of Proportionality in the Jurisprudence of the ECHR*, Antwerp/Oxford/New York: Intersentia, 2002; E. Benvenisti, 'Margin of Appreciation, Consensus, and Universal Standards', (1998) 31 *NYU Journal of International Law & Politics* 843; J.A. Brauch, 'The Margin of Appreciation and the Jurisprudence of the European Court of Human Rights: Threat to the Rule of Law', (2004) 11 *Columbia Journal of European Law* 113; E. Brems, 'The Margin of Appreciation Doctrine in the Case-Law of the European Court of Human Rights', (1996) 56 *Zeitschrift für Auslandisches Offentliches Recht und Volkrecht* 240; Johan Callewaert, 'Is there a Margin of Appreciation in the Application of Articles 2, 3 and 4 of the Convention?', (1998) 19 *HRLJ* 6; Johan Callewaert, 'Quel avenir pour

doctrine of margin of appreciation in its very early case law, essentially with regard to the determination of states of emergency,[164] and the application of articles 8 and 10.[165] It also employed the term 'margin of discretion', seemingly as a synonym for margin of appreciation.[166] The Court took note of the Commission's doctrine of the margin of appreciation[167] but did not endorse or adopt it immediately. It initially spoke of the 'power of appreciation'[168] reserved to States, before finally introducing the sanctified phrase 'margin of appreciation' into its judicial jargon in the mid-1970s.[169]

la marge d'appréciation?', in Mahoney et al., *Mélanges Ryssdal*, pp. 147–66; Steven Greer, 'The Interpretation of the European Convention of Human Rights: Universal Principle or Margin of Appreciation?', (2010) 3 *UCL Law Review* 1; Michael R. Hutchinson, 'The Margin of Appreciation Doctrine in the European Court of Human Rights', (1998) 48 *ICLQ* 638; Elias Kastanas, *Unité et diversité: notion autonomes et marge d'appréciation dans la jurisprudence de la Cour europénne de droits de l'homme*, Brussels: Bruylant, 1999; Jan Kratochvíl, 'The Inflation of the Margin of Appreciation by the European Court of Human Rights', (2011) 29 *Netherlands Quarterly of Human Rights* 324; N. Lavender, 'The Problem of the Margin of Appreciation', [1997] *EHRLR* 380; Rew Legg, *The Margin of Appreciation in International Human Rights Law: Deference and Proportionality*, Oxford: Oxford University Press, 2012; G. Letsas, 'Two Concepts of the Margin of Appreciation', (2006) 26 *Oxford Journal of Legal Studies* 705; Ronald St J. Macdonald, 'The Margin of Appreciation in the Jurisprudence of the European Court of Human Rights', in *International Law at the Time of its Codification, Essays in Honour of Judge Roberto Ago*, Milan: Giuffrè, 1987, pp. 187–208; Ronald St J. Macdonald, 'The Margin of Appreciation', in Macdonald, *The European System*, pp. 83–124; Michael O'Boyle, 'The Margin of Appreciation and Derogation under Article 15: Ritual Incantation or Principle?', (1998) 19 *HRLJ* 23; Thomas A. O'Donnell, 'The Margin of Appreciation Doctrine: Standards in the Jurisprudence of the European Court of Human Rights', (1982) 4 *Human Rights Quarterly* 474; Clare Ovey, 'The Margin of Appreciation and Article 8 of the Convention', (1998) 19 *HRLJ* 10; Soren Prebensen, 'The Margin of Appreciation and Articles 9, 10 and 11 of the Convention', (1998) 19 *HRLJ* 13; Ignacio de la Rasilla del Mortal, 'The Increasingly Marginal Appreciation of the Margin of Appreciation Doctrine', (2006) 7 *German Law Journal* 611; Annette Rupp-Swienty, *Die Doktrin von der Margin of Appreciation in der Rechtsprechung des Europäischen Gerichtshofs für Menschenrechte*, Munich: VVF-Verlag, 1999; Rosario Sapienza, 'Sul Margine d'Apprezzamento Statate nel Sistema della Convenzione Europea dei Diritti del Uomo', (1991) 74 *Rivista di Diritto Internazionale* 571; Jeroen Schokkenbroeck, 'The Basis, Nature and Application of the Margin-of-Appreciation Doctrine in the Case-law of the European Court of Human Rights', (1998) 19 *HRLJ* 30; Yuval Shany, 'Toward a General Margin of Appreciation Doctrine in International Law?', (2005) 16 *EJIL* 907; D. Spielmann, 'En jouant sur les marges. La Cour européenne des droits de l'homme et la théorie de la marge d'appréciation nationale: abandon ou subsidiarité du contrôle européen?', (2010) 13 *Actes de la Section des Sciences Morales et Politiques* 203; J.A. Sweeney, 'Margins of Appreciation: Cultural Relativity and the European Court of Human Rights in the Post-Cold War Era', (2005) 54 *ICLQ* 459; Yves Winisdoerffer, 'Margin of Appreciation and Article 1 of Protocol Nr.1', (1998) 19 *HRLJ* 18; Howard Yourow, *The Margin of Appreciation Doctrine in the Dynamics of European Human Rights Jurisprudence*, Dordrecht: Martinus Nijhoff, 1996.

164 *Greece v. the United Kingdom*, no. 176/56, Commission decision of 2 June 1956, (1958–59) 2 YB 182; *Lawless v. Ireland*, no. 332/57, Commission report of 19 December 1959, pp. 85, 101, 119, 124, 137, 158; *I. v. Norway*, no. 1468/62, Commission decision of 17 December 1963; *Denmark, Norway, Sweden, and the Netherlands v. Greece*, nos 3321/67, 3322/67, 3323/67, and 3344/67, Commission decision of 24 January 1968, (1968) 11 YB 690, Collection 25, p. 92.

165 *X. v. Federal Republic of Germany*, no. 1628/62, Commission decision of 12 December 1963, Collection 12, p. 61; *X. v. Federal Republic of Germany*, no. 2413/65, Commission decision of 16 December 1966, Collection 23, p. 1; *X. v. Federal Republic of Germany*, no. 2699/65, Commission decision of 1 April 1968, (1968) 11 YB 366, Collection 26, p. 33; *X. and the German Association of Z. v. Federal Republic of Germany*, no. 1167/61, Commission decision of 16 December 1963, Collection 12, p. 70.

166 *Lawless v. Ireland*, no. 332/57, Commission report of 19 December 1959, pp. 91, 93; *Ringeisen v. Austria*, no. 2614/65, Commission report of 19 March 1970, p. 51.

167 *Case 'relating to certain aspects of the laws on the use of languages in education in Belgium'* (merits), 23 July 1968, p. 25, § 3, Series A no. 6.

168 *De Wilde, Ooms, and Versyp v. Belgium*, 18 June 1971, § 93, Series A no. 12; *Golder v. the United Kingdom*, 21 February 1975, § 45, Series A no. 18.

169 *Engel and Others v. the Netherlands*, 8 June 1976, §§ 59, 72, 100, Series A no. 22; *Handyside v. the United Kingdom*, 7 December 1976, §§ 49, 54, 57, Series A no. 24; *Ireland v. the United Kingdom*, 18 January 1978, § 207, Series A no. 25.

The 'margin' of appreciation varies considerably, depending upon the nature of the right in question and the context in which it is being invoked. In determining the margin of appreciation, the Court normally distinguishes between infringements that are attributable to the State and those resulting from the acts of other individuals, whose rights must also be considering in striking the right balance.[170]

Generally, a wide margin of appreciation is attributed with respect to general measures of economic or social strategy'.[171] States are considered to be better placed than international judges to assess the best interests of the public with respect to economic and social issues. Consequently, the Court will generally respect the legislative policy choices unless they are 'manifestly without reasonable foundation'.[172] When housing issues relate to social policy, especially in an urban or rural planning context, '[i]n so far as the exercise of discretion involving a multitude of local factors is inherent in the choice and implementation of planning policies, the national authorities in principle enjoy a wide margin of appreciation'.[173] But 'where the right at stake is crucial to the individual's effective enjoyment of intimate or key rights', the margin of appreciation is not as broad.[174] In a case dealing with pension schemes, the Court said that 'the precise timing and means of putting right the inequality were not so manifestly unreasonable as to exceed the wide margin of appreciation allowed it in such a field'.[175]

Similarly, the European Court acknowledges that 'issues relating to just and proportionate punishment are the subject of rational debate and civilised disagreement',[176] granting States a margin of appreciation in setting the appropriate length of sentence. The margin of appreciation has been invoked to justify considerable latitude with respect to parliamentary immunities[177] and rules of criminal justice concerning presence of the accused at trial.[178]

When very sensitive political, moral, and ethical issues are involved, and on which there is nothing resembling a degree of European consensus, such as when the right to life begins, the Court will relegate the matter to the margin of appreciation.[179] In *A, B and C*, the Grand Chamber held that there was 'a consensus amongst a substantial majority of the Contracting States of the Council of Europe towards allowing abortion on broader grounds than accorded under Irish law', but said this could not displace Ireland's margin of appreciation on the subject.[180] But in a Polish case, the Court said 'the fact that the

---

[170] *Palomo Sánchez and Others v. Spain* [GC], nos 28955/06, 28957/06, 28959/06, and 28964/06, § 54, ECHR 2011.

[171] *National & Provincial Building Society, Leeds Permanent Building Society and Yorkshire Building Society v. the United Kingdom*, 23 October 1997, § 80, *Reports of Judgments and Decisions* 1997-VII; *Stec and Others v. the United Kingdom* [GC], nos 65731/01 and 65900/01, § 52, ECHR 2006-VI; *Andrejeva v. Latvia* [GC], no. 55707/00, § 83, ECHR 2009.

[172] *National & Provincial Building Society, Leeds Permanent Building Society and Yorkshire Building Society v. the United Kingdom*, 23 October 1997, § 80, *Reports of Judgments and Decisions* 1997-VII; *Stec and Others v. the United Kingdom* [GC], nos 65731/01 and 65900/01, § 52, ECHR 2006-VI; *Andrejeva v. Latvia* [GC], no. 55707/00, § 83, ECHR 2009.

[173] *Buckley v. the United Kingdom*, 25 September 1996, § 75 *in fine*, *Reports of Judgments and Decisions* 1996-IV; *Ćosić v. Croatia*, no. 28261/06, § 18, 15 January 2009.

[174] *Yordanova and Others v. Bulgaria*, no. 25446/06, § 120, 24 April 2012.

[175] *Stec and Others v. the United Kingdom* [GC], nos 65731/01 and 65900/01, § 66, ECHR 2006-VI.

[176] *Vinter and Others v. the United Kingdom* [GC], nos 66069/09, 130/10, and 3896/10, § 105, ECHR 2013 (extracts).

[177] *Kart v. Turkey* [GC], no. 8917/05, § 82, ECHR 2009 (extracts); *A. v. the United Kingdom*, no. 35373/97, § 88, ECHR 2002-X.

[178] *Kamasinski v. Austria*, 19 December 1989, § 106, Series A no. 168.

[179] *Vo v. France* [GC], no. 53924/00, § 82, EC-VIII HR 2004-VIII.

[180] *A, B, and C v. Ireland* [GC], no. 25579/05, § 235, ECHR 2010.

issue of the availability of legal abortion in Poland is a subject of heated debate does not confer on the State a margin of appreciation so wide as to absolve the medical staff from their uncontested professional obligations regarding medical secrecy'.[181]

The State's margin of appreciation is more restrained when 'a particularly important facet of an individual's existence or identity is at stake'. This is also the case when intimate aspects of private life are involved.[182] Nevertheless, 'domestic authorities enjoy a wide margin of appreciation in determining how to confront incestuous relationships between consenting adults, notwithstanding the fact that this decision concerns an intimate aspect of an individual's private life'.[183] According to the Court, 'a broad consensus transpires that sexual relationships between siblings are neither accepted by the legal order nor by society as a whole'.[184] In a case concerning refusal by a local registry official to validate same-sex civil partnerships, the Court said that it 'generally allows the national authorities a wide margin of appreciation when it comes to striking a balance between competing Convention rights', particularly when the policy at issue was 'aimed to secure the rights of others which are also protected under the Convention'.[185] On the other hand, 'given the sensitive moral choices concerned and the importance to be attached to the protection of children and the fostering of secure family environments, this Court must not rush to substitute its own judgment in place of the authorities who are best placed to assess and respond to the needs of society'.[186]

The margin of appreciation is almost invariably considered when the Court is considering restrictions on rights, notably in light of paragraph 2 of articles 8, 9, 10, and 11 of the Convention. The adjective 'necessary' is often taken to imply a 'pressing social need'. According to the Court, '[b]ecause of their direct, continuous contact with the realities of the country, a State's courts are in a better position than an international court to determine how, at a given time, the right balance can be struck' in evaluating such pressing social needs.[187] But the margin of appreciation 'goes hand in hand with European supervision'.[188] Although the national authorities make the initial assessment of necessity, 'the final evaluation as to whether the reasons cited for the interference are relevant and sufficient remains subject to review by the Court for conformity with the requirements of the Convention'.[189]

The margin of appreciation is also important when rights are restricted or in the case of derogation, in accordance with article 15 of the Convention. The Court may be quite deferential towards assessments by a government as to what constitutes a threat to 'the life

---

[181] *P. and S. v. Poland*, no. 57375/08, § 133, 30 October 2012.

[182] *E.S. v. Sweden*, no. 5786/08, § 58, 21 June 2012; *Evans v. the United Kingdom* [GC], no. 6339/05, § 77, ECHR 2007-I; *Mosley v. the United Kingdom*, no. 48009/08, § 109, 10 May 2011.

[183] *Stübing v. Germany*, no. 43547/08, § 61, 12 April 2012.

[184] Ibid.

[185] *Eweida and Others v. the United Kingdom*, no. 48420/10, § 106, ECHR 2013 (extracts).

[186] *B. and L. v. the United Kingdom*, no. 36536/02, § 36, 13 September 2005.

[187] *Tammer v. Estonia*, no.41205/98, § 60, ECHR 2001-I; *Pedersen and Baadsgaard v. Denmark* [GC], no. 49017/99, § 68, ECHR 2004-XI.

[188] *The Sunday Times v. the United Kingdom (no. 2)*, 26 November 1991, §§ 50–51, Series A no. 217; *Vogt v. Germany*, 26 September 1995, § 52, Series A no. 323; *Perna v. Italy* [GC], no. 48898/99, § 39, ECHR 2003-V; *Schwabe and M.G. v. Germany*, nos 8080/08 and 8577/08, § 113, ECHR 2011 (extracts).

[189] *Szuluk v. the United Kingdom*, no. 36936/05, § 45, ECHR 2009.

of [its] nation', granting States a wide margin.[190] The Court's role is to determine whether States have gone beyond the 'extent strictly required by the exigencies' of the crisis. In supervising such measures, 'the Court must give appropriate weight to such relevant factors as the nature of the rights affected by the derogation and the circumstances leading to, and the duration of, the emergency situation'.[191]

An indication of the controversial nature of the margin of appreciation doctrine can be seen in the refusal of any endorsement by the United Nations Human Rights Committee in its interpretation of essentially similar provisions in the International Covenant on Civil and Political Rights. When Finland referred to the margin of appreciation noting its adoption by the European Court of Human Rights in many cases,[192] the argument was dismissed,[193] a position confirmed subsequently in a General Comment of the Committee.[194]

Further reading

Theo Van Boven, 'Préambule', in Pettiti et al., *La Convention européenne*, pp. 125–34.
Frowein/Peukert, *MenschenRechtsKonvention*, pp. 10–14.
Javier García Roca, 'The Preamble, the Convention's Hermeneutic Context: A Constitutional Instrument of European Public Order', in Javier García Roca and Pablo Santolaya, eds, *Europe of Rights: A Compendium on the European Convention of Human Rights*, Leiden/Boston: Martinus Nijhoff, 2012, pp. 1–26.

---

[190] *A. and Others v. the United Kingdom* [GC], no. 3455/05, § 173, ECHR 2009; *Ireland v. the United Kingdom*, 18 January 1978, § 207, Series A no. 25; *Brannigan and McBride v. the United Kingdom*, 26 May 1993, § 43, Series A no. 258-B.

[191] *A. and Others v. the United Kingdom* [GC], no. 3455/05, § 173, ECHR 2009; *Ireland v. the United Kingdom*, 18 January 1978, § 207, Series A no. 25; *Brannigan and McBride v. the United Kingdom*, 26 May 1993, § 43, Series A no. 258; *Aksoy v. Turkey*, 18 December 1996, § 68, *Reports of Judgments and Decisions* 1996-VI.

[192] *Länsman et al. v. Finland*, no. 511/1992, UN Doc. CCPR/C/52/D/511/1992, para. 7.3

[193] Ibid., para. 9.4.

[194] General comment No. 34, Article 19: Freedoms of opinion and expression, para. 36.

Article 1. Obligation to respect human rights/Obligation de respecter les droits de l'homme

The High Contracting Parties shall secure to everyone within their jurisdiction the rights and freedoms defined in Section I of this Convention.	Les Hautes Parties contractantes reconnaissent à toute personne relevant de leur juridiction les droits et libertés définis au titre I de la présente Convention.

Introductory comments

Article 1 'demarcates the scope of the Convention *ratione personae, materiae* and *loci*'.[1] Comparable, although slightly different, clauses can be found in other international human rights treaties. For example, the International Covenant on Civil and Political Rights specifies that a State Party 'undertakes to respect and to ensure to all individuals within its territory and subject to its jurisdiction the rights recognised in the present Covenant, without distinction of any kind, such as race, colour, sex, language, religion, political or other opinion, national or social origin, property, birth or other status'.[2]

Drafting of the provision

The initial draft European Convention on Human Rights was prepared by the International Juridical Section of the European Movement, chaired by Pierre-Henri Teitgen, with David Maxwell Fyfe and Fernand Dehousse as rapporteurs. Both Maxwell Fyfe and Dehousse had been involved in the drafting of the Universal Declaration of Human Rights the previous year. The text began: 'Art. I. Every State a party to this Convention shall guarantee to all persons within its territory the following rights: . . .'[3] The European Movement text formed the basis of the discussions that took place in the Consultative Assembly, initially in its Committee on Legal and Administrative Questions. The Committee adopted the following text: 'In this Convention, the Member States shall undertake to ensure to all persons residing within their territories . . .'[4] It had considered but rejected using the term 'domiciled' rather than 'residing', and agreed not to limit the word 'territories' with 'metropolitan'.[5] Its report noted that with respect to extension of the rights 'not only to all persons residing within its metropolitan territory, but also to all persons residing within its overseas territories or in its colonial possessions, the majority of

---

[1] *Ireland v. the United Kingdom*, 18 January 1978, § 238, Series A no. 25.

[2] International Covenant on Civil and Political Rights, (1976) 999 UNTS 171, art. 2(1).

[3] Convention for the Collective Protection of Individual Rights and Democratic Liberties by the States, Members of the Council of Europe, and for the Establishment of a European Court of Human Rights to Ensure Observance of the Convention, Doc. INF/5/E/R, I *TP* 296–303, at p. 296.

[4] Report [of the Committee on Legal and Administrative Questions], 5 September 1949, Doc. AS (1) 77, I *TP* 216–39, at p. 228.

[5] Proposals by Mr P.H. Teitgen, Rapporteur, 29 August 1949, Doc. A 116, I *TP* 166–8; Minutes of the Sitting [of the Committee for Legal and Administrative Affairs of the Consultative Assembly, 29 August 1949], Doc. A 142, I *TP* 170–3; Minutes of the Sitting [of the Committee for Legal and Administrative Affairs of the Consultative Assembly, 31 August 1949], Doc. A 199, I *TP* 182–3.

the Committee replied in the affirmative'. It noted that 'reservations were made on this point by some members of the Committee, who were not able to appreciate exactly the difficulties which this solution might raise'.[6] The plenary Consultative Assembly endorsed the proposed text and adopted it without amendment.[7]

Weeks earlier, the United Nations Commission on Human Rights had agreed upon a similar provision as part of the draft International Covenant on Human Rights: 'Each State party hereto hereby undertakes to ensure to all individuals within its jurisdiction the rights defined in this Covenant. Where not already provided by legislative or other measures, each State undertakes, in accordance with its constitutional processes and in accordance with the provisions of this Covenant, to adopt within a reasonable time such legislative or other measures to give effect to the rights defined in this Covenant.'[8] Commenting on the differences between the United Nations draft Covenant and the Consultative Assembly draft Convention, the Secretariat of the Council of Europe noted that the former guaranteed rights to 'persons within the State's jurisdiction' whereas the latter referred to 'all persons residing within their territories'.[9]

In the Committee of Experts, meeting in February 1950, the United Kingdom tabled the following amendment: 'Each State party hereto undertakes to ensure to all individuals within its jurisdiction the rights defined in this Convention. Every deposit of an instrument of accession shall be accompanied by a solemn declaration made by the Government of the State concerned with full and complete effect as given by the law of that State of the provisions of the Convention.'[10] The Italian expert proposed replacing the words 'residing within' in the draft of the Consultative Assembly with the words 'living in'.[11] Considering the proposed amendments, a Sub-Committee of the Committee of Experts noted that 'the aim of this amendment is to widen as far as possible the categories of persons who are to benefit by the guarantee contained in the Convention'. It suggested, then, that the wording adopted by the United Nations Commission on Human Rights would be preferable. The Sub-commission acknowledged that some rights 'cannot be guaranteed to aliens without any restrictions'.[12]

The Committee of Experts adopted the following provision: 'The High Contracting Parties undertake to accord to any person within their jurisdiction the rights set out in Article 2 of this Convention, subject to the conditions given below.'[13] In its report to the Committee of Ministers, the Committee noted 'the ambiguity which might arise by the

[6] Report presented by Mr P.H. Teitgen, 5 September 1949, Doc. A 290, I *TP* 192–213, at p. 202; Report [of the Committee on Legal and Administrative Questions], 5 September 1949, Doc. AS (1) 77, I *TP* 216–39, at p. 224.

[7] Recommendation No. 38 to the Committee of Ministers adopted 8 September 1949 on the conclusion of the debates, Doc. AS (1) 108, II *TP* 274–83, at p. 276.

[8] Report of the Fifth Session of the Commission on Human Rights to the Economic and Social Council, UN Doc. E/1371(Supp.), annex.

[9] Preparatory Report by the Secretariat-General concerning a Preliminary Draft Convention to Provide a Collective Guarantee of Human Rights, Doc. B 22, III *TP* 2–37, at p. 26.

[10] Amendments to articles 4 and 7 of the Recommendation of the Consultative Assembly proposed by the expert of the United Kingdom, Doc. A 782, III *TP* 188–91.

[11] Amendments to the Recommendation of the Consultative Assembly proposed by the expert of Italy, Doc. A 786, III *TP* 194.

[12] First part of the Report of the Sub-Committee Instructed to Make a Preliminary Study of the Amendments Proposed by the Members of the Committee, Doc. A 796, III *TP* 200–5, at p. 200.

[13] Preliminary Draft Convention for the Maintenance and Further Realisation of Human Rights and Fundamental Freedoms, 15 February 1950, Doc. A 833, III *TP* 236–46, at p. 236.

word "guarantee," since the aim of the Convention was not to set up an international guarantee to be undertaken by the signature States themselves', adding that the Committee had decided the word should be replaced with 'accord'.[14] It noted that the term 'all persons residing within the territories of the signatory States' in the Constituent Assembly draft 'might be considered too restrictive'. The Committee 'felt that there were good grounds for extending the benefits of the Convention to all persons in the territories of the signatory States, even those who could not be considered as residing there in the legal sense of the word. This word, moreover, has not the same meaning in all national laws.' The Committee therefore adopted the words 'within their jurisdiction', just as the United Nations Commission on Human Rights had done.[15]

The Committee of Experts met again in March, adopting two alternative models of the Convention, the first (Alternatives A and A/2) based on simple enumeration and the second (Alternatives B and B/2) upon precise definition of fundamental rights. Although there was no reason for the general clause on the obligation of States parties to differ in the two versions, there were separate proposals:

Alternatives A and A/2.
Art. 1. The High Contracting Parties undertake to accord to every person within their jurisdiction the rights set out in Art. 2 of this Convention, subject to the conditions given below.[16]

Alternatives B and B/2.
Art. 1(1). The High Contracting Parties undertake to accord to all individuals within their jurisdiction the rights defined in Section I of this Convention.[17]

The accompanying Explanatory Report said that article 1 of Alternatives A and A/2 replaced article 1 of the Consultative Assembly proposal 'which, in reality, was not part of the Convention but expressed the tenor of the Recommendation which the Assembly submitted to the Committee of Ministers'. The report noted the 'ambiguity' that might arise from the use of the word 'guarantee', noting that the aim of the Convention was not to set up an international guarantee to be undertaken by States but rather the safeguarding of rights by the establishment of European bodies. For this reason, the term 'accord' was preferred. The Committee of Experts explained that it had decided not to employ the word 'residing' because '[i]t was felt that there were good grounds for extending the benefits of the Convention to all persons in the territories of the signatory States, even those who could not be considered as residing there in the legal sense'.[18]

Although the approaches in the two alternatives were quite different, the two texts of article 1 were not, and they do not appear to have attracted any attention during the general debate in the Conference of Senior Officials that took place in June 1950.[19] The

---

[14] Preliminary draft of the Report to the Committee of Ministers, 24 February 1950, Doc. CM/WP 1 (50), A 847, III *TP* 246–79, at p. 260.

[15] Ibid.

[16] Appendix to the Report of the Committee of Experts on Human Rights: Draft Convention of Protection of Human Rights and Fundamental Freedoms, 16 March 1950, Doc. C/WP 1 (50) 15 appendix, CM/WP 1 (50) 14 revised, A 925, IV *TP* 50–79, at p. 52.

[17] Ibid., p. 56.

[18] Report to the Committee of Ministers Submitted by the Committee of Experts Instructed to Draw Up a Draft Convention of Collective Guarantee of Human Rights and Fundamental Freedoms, Doc. CM/WP 1 (5) 15, A 924, IV *TP* 2–55, at pp. 20, 30.

[19] See: New draft alternatives B and B/2, Doc. CM/WP 4 (50) 9, A 1372, IV *TP* 182–91, at p. 182, for a minor drafting change to article 1 in Alternative B that made it more like the text in Alternative A.

Conference decided unanimously that the Convention should not include a solemn declaration to the effect that domestic legislation gave full effect to the provisions of the Convention.[20] Its report added that 'in the absence of any provision to the contrary, every signatory State is presumed to give full effect to the provisions of the Convention from the moment the State has given its adherence'.[21] The Conference settled on a formulation that blended the two alternative texts: 'The High Contracting Parties undertake to secure to all individuals within their jurisdiction the rights and freedoms defined in Section 1 of this Convention.'[22] The words 'and freedoms' had been added after 'rights'.

In a letter to the Committee of Ministers, the chairman of the Constituent Assembly's Committee on Legal and Administrative Questions made the following observation:

[I]n order to avoid any misunderstanding as to the legal scope of the Convention, it would be desirable the words 'undertake to secure' be replaced by the words 'hereby secure' in respect of the attitude of the High Contracting Parties towards the rights and freedoms enumerated in Section II of the Convention; for the former phrasing appears to imply for each of them a separate action apart from the simple acceptance of the Convention.[23]

The Sub-Committee on Human Rights of the Committee of Ministers met in August 1950. It replaced the words 'undertake to secure' with 'shall secure',[24] on a proposal from the United Kingdom.[25] There was no further discussion of article 1, aside from a decision of the Committee of Ministers in November 1950 to change the words 'all persons' to 'everyone' for reasons of consistency with other provisions in the Convention.[26]

The Grand Chamber considered the *travaux préparatoires* of article 1 in *Banković*.[27] It said that they 'constitute a clear indication of the intended meaning of Article 1 of the Convention which cannot be ignored' and 'clear confirmatory evidence of the ordinary meaning of Article 1'.[28]

The heading 'Obligation to respect human rights' was added according to the provisions of Protocol No. 11.[29]

---

[20] Draft report to the Committee of Ministers, Doc. CM/WP 4 (50) 16, A 1426, IV *TP* 204–16, at p. 216; Text of the report submitted by the Conference to the Committee of Ministers, Doc. CM/WP 4 (50) 19, CM/WP 4 (50) 16 rev., A 1431, IV *TP* 242–57, at p. 256.

[21] Draft report to the Committee of Ministers, Doc. CM/WP 4 (50) 16, A 1426, IV *TP* 204–216, at p. 216.

[22] Draft Convention annexed to the Report, Doc. CM/WP 4 (50) 19 annex, CM/WP 4 (50) rev., A 1452, IV *TP* 274–95, at p. 274.

[23] Letter of 24 June 1950 from Sir David Maxwell Fyfe, Chairman of the Committee on Legal and Administrative Questions, to the Chairman of the Committee of Ministers, Ref. D 280/3/50, Doc. CM (50) 29, V *TP* 32–41, at p. 34.

[24] Text of amended articles after deliberation at the sitting of 4 August 1950, Doc. CM 1 (50) 9, V *TP* 74–6, at p. 74; Draft Convention adopted by the Sub-Committee, Doc. CM 1 (50) 52, A 1884, V *TP* 76–99, at p. 76; Letter dated 7 August 1950 sent by Mr MacBride, Chairman of the Committee of Ministers, to M. Spaak, President of the Consultative Assembly, Doc. No. 11, pp. 600–619, V *TP* 144–71, at p. 146.

[25] Amendments proposed by the United Kingdom Delegation, Doc. CM 1 (50) 6, A 1867, V *TP* 66–70, at p. 66.

[26] Drafting changes proposed by the Secretariat-General, Doc. A 2520, no date, VI *TP* 274–9, at p. 278.

[27] The drafting history of article 1 is briefly discussed in *Banković and Others v. Belgium and Others* (dec.) [GC], no. 52207/99, §§ 19–21, ECHR 2001-XII.

[28] *Banković and Others v. Belgium and Others* (dec.) [GC], no. 52207/99, § 65, ECHR 2001-XII.

[29] Protocol No. 11 to the Convention for the Protection of Human Rights and Fundamental Freedoms, restructuring the control machinery established thereby, ETS 155, art. 2(2).

Analysis and interpretation

Article 1 is 'one of the many Articles that attest the binding character of the Convention'.[30] Nevertheless, it is a 'framework provision that cannot be breached on its own'.[31] It is drafted 'by reference to the provisions contained in Section I and thus comes into operation only when taken in conjunction with them; a violation of Article 1 (art. 1) follows automatically from, but adds nothing to, a breach of those provisions'.[32] In *Soering v. The United Kingdom*, the Plenary Court explained the significance of article 1:

Article 1 ... sets a limit, notably territorial, on the reach of the Convention. In particular, the engagement undertaken by a Contracting State is confined to 'securing' ('reconnaître' in the French text) the listed rights and freedoms to persons within its own 'jurisdiction'. Further, the Convention does not govern the actions of States not Parties to it, nor does it purport to be a means of requiring the Contracting States to impose Convention standards on other States.[33]

Article 1 applies to Section I of the Convention. One of three Sections in the Convention, Section I consists of articles 2 to 18. It contains the substantive rights, set out in articles 2 to 14, but also the special provisions dealing with derogation, political activity of aliens, abuse of rights, and limitations on use of restrictions contained in articles 15 to 18. Each of the Protocols contains an article entitled 'Relationship to the Convention', where it is stated that the substantive provisions 'shall be regarded as additional Articles to the Convention and all the provisions of the Convention shall apply accordingly'. As a result, there is no doubt about the application of article 1 to the Protocols.

In the *Belgian Linguistic case*, the respondent State submitted that there was an inherent limitation on the scope of the Convention imposed by the 'reserved domain'. It created 'an inherent limit to the exercise of the Court's jurisdiction, this limit being so evident that it depends neither on an explicit clause of the Convention nor on a reservation'.[34] Relying upon article 1, the Plenary Court said that although the Convention relates to matters normally falling within the domestic legal order of the Contracting States, it is an international instrument whose main purpose is to lay down certain international standards to be observed by the Contracting States in their relations with persons under their jurisdiction.[35]

'The High Contracting Parties...'

The European Convention uses the term 'High Contracting Parties' to refer to the States that have ratified or acceded to it. Today, this is somewhat archaic usage. Modern treaties tend to refer to 'States Parties' or 'Parties'.[36] These terms are sometimes employed in place

[30] *Ireland v. the United Kingdom*, 18 January 1978, § 238, Series A no. 25.
[31] *Streletz, Kessler, and Krenz v. Germany* [GC], nos 34044/96, 35532/97, and 44801/98, § 112, ECHR 2001-II.
[32] *Ireland v. the United Kingdom*, 18 January 1978, § 238, Series A no. 25.
[33] *Soering v. the United Kingdom*, 7 July 1989, § 86, Series A no. 161. Cited in *Banković and Others v. Belgium and Others* (dec.) [GC], no. 52207/99, § 66, ECHR 2001-XII; *Hirsi Jamaa and Others v. Italy* [GC], no. 27765/09, § 70, ECHR 2012; *Al-Dulimi and Montana Management Inc. v. Switzerland*, no. 5809/08, § 88, 26 November 2013.
[34] *Case 'relating to certain aspects of the laws on the use of languages in education in Belgium'* (Preliminary objection), 9 February 1967, p. 10, § 1, Series A no. 5.
[35] Ibid., p. 13.
[36] See, e.g., Vienna Convention on the Law of Treaties, (1980) 1155 UNTS 331, preamble, arts 3(c), 15(c), 20(2), etc.

of 'High Contracting Parties' in the judgments and individual opinions of the European Court of Human Rights.[37] Article 2 of the Vienna Convention on the Law of Treaties indicates a distinction: 'Contracting Party' designates 'a State which has consented to be bound by the treaty, whether or not the treaty has entered into force', whereas 'State Party' refers to 'a State which has consented to be bound by the treaty and for which the treaty is in force'. According to an isolated pronouncement of the European Commission of Human Rights, 'il découle d'autre part de l'article [59] de la Convention que seuls les pays membres du Conseil de l'Europe ayant dûment signé et ratifié la Convention possèdent la qualité de Parties Contractantes'.[38]

In a traditional treaty-law context, each of the 'High Contracting Parties' assumes obligations with respect to the other States that are party to the Convention. The States Parties are subject to the principle *pacta sunt servanda*: 'Every treaty in force is binding upon the parties to it and must be performed by them in good faith.'[39] General rules governing the responsibility of States are set out in the Draft articles on Responsibility of States for Internationally Wrongful Acts, adopted by the United Nations International Law Commission in 2001.[40] They are applicable to the European Convention,[41] bearing in mind the restriction on alternate means of dispute resolution provided in article 55 of the Convention.

The contractual arrangements between the States that are party to the Convention are not really reciprocal in the sense that they are concerned with a bilateral relationship. Rather, States Parties have stipulated obligations or duties with respect to 'everyone within their jurisdiction'. As the European Commission of Human Rights stated in one of its earliest decisions, in an inter-State application,

... the obligations undertaken by the High Contracting Parties in the European Convention are essentially of an objective character being designed rather to protect the fundamental rights of individual human beings from infringements by any of the High Contracting Parties than to create subjective and reciprocal rights for the High Contracting Parties themselves.[42]

The Convention creates 'special obligations' that are owed by a State 'towards persons within its jurisdiction, not to other High Contracting Parties'.[43]

---

[37] *S.A.S. v. France* [GC], no. 43835/11, § 129, 1 July 2014; *Al Nashiri v. Poland*, no. 28761/11, §241, 24 July 2014; *Hirsi Jamaa and Others v. Italy* [GC], no. 27765/09, § 177, ECHR 2012. Many judges refer to 'States Parties' in in their individual opinions. See, e.g., *Marguš v. Croatia* [GC], no. 4455/10, Joint Concurring Opinion of Judges Šikuta, Wojtyczek, and Vehabović, § 2, 27 May 2014; *Fabris v. France* [GC], no. 16574/08, Concurring Opinion of Judge Pinto de Albuquerque, ECHR 2013 (extracts); *Tarantino and Others v. Italy*, nos 25851/09, 29284/09, and 64090/09, Partly Dissenting Opinion of Judge Pinto de Albuquerque, ECHR 2013 (extracts); *Hassan v. the United Kingdom* [GC], no. 29750/09, Partly Dissenting Opinion of Judge Spano joined by Judges Nicolaou, Bianku, and Kalaydjieva, § 13, 16 September 2014.

[38] *E.S. v. Federal Republic of Germany*, no. 262/57, Commission decision of 28 August 1957, p. 2.

[39] Vienna Convention on the Law of Treaties, (1980) 1155 UNTS 331, art. 26. See *Janowiec and Others v. Russia* [GC], nos 55508/07 and 29520/09, § 211, 21 October 2013; *Verein gegen Tierfabriken Schweiz (VgT) v. Switzerland (no. 2)* [GC], no. 32772/02, § 87, ECHR 2009; *Golder v. The United Kingdom*, 21 February 1975, § 34, Series A no. 18.

[40] Draft articles on Responsibility of States for Internationally Wrongful Acts, UN Doc. A/56/10.

[41] *Ilaşcu and Others v. Moldova and Russia* [GC], no. 48787/99, §§ 319–320, ECHR 2004-VII; *Chiragov and Others v. Armenia* (dec.) [GC], no. 13216/05, 14 December 2011; *Savriddin Dzhurayev v. Russia*, no. 71386/10, § 248, ECHR 2013 (extracts); *Verein gegen Tierfabriken Schweiz (VgT) v. Switzerland (no. 2)* [GC], no. 32772/02, § 86, ECHR 2009; *Laska and Lika v. Albania*, nos 12315/04 and 17605/04, § 75, 20 April 2010.

[42] *Austria v. Italy*, no. 788/60, Commission decision of 11 January 1961, (1961) 4 YB 116, at p. 140.

[43] *Cyprus v. Turkey*, no. 8007/77, Commission decision of 10 July 1978, § 11, (1978) 21 YB 101, DR 13, p. 85.

The responsibility of the State applies to all of its organs, 'whether they belong to the legislature, the executive or the judiciary'.[44] It is required to ensure that its legislation is consistent with the Convention. Even the constitution must be compatible with the Convention.[45] The State is also responsible for the conduct of its administrative authorities, as well as various bodies associated with the State including, in some cases, State-owned companies[46] and decentralized authorities that exercise public functions, regardless of their degree of autonomy.[47] Such bodies include various municipal and territorial institutions,[48] as well as professional corporations that exercise 'des fonctions officielles... attribuées par la Constitution et par la loi'[49] and national railway companies under state control in a monopolistic situation.[50] The State may also be responsible for acts of private individuals that violate Convention rights where there is evidence that the authorities connived or acquiesced.[51]

The obligation also extends beyond conduct of the State itself and its organs to the extent that there is also a duty to ensure that third parties do not infringe the rights of individuals. This is one aspect of the positive obligation associated with the duties of the State party.

'...shall secure...', negative and positive obligations

Referring to the *travaux préparatoires*, the Plenary Court noted that '[b]y substituting the words "shall secure" for the words "undertake to secure" in the text of Article 1, the drafters of the Convention also intended to make it clear that the rights and freedoms set out in Section I would be directly secured to anyone within the jurisdiction of the Contracting States'.[52] Nevertheless, article 1 does not require States to incorporate the Convention directly into national law and thereby make it directly applicable before domestic courts. In some 'dualist' countries, international law does not have such a direct effect. There, States Parties are required to ensure that Convention rights are enforceable, although they need not do this by incorporating the text into the domestic legal system. The Court has confirmed that the Convention does not prescribe 'any given manner for ensuring within their internal law the effective implementation of any of the provisions of the Convention'.[53]

---

[44] *Andrejeva v. Latvia* [GC], no. 55707/00, § 56, ECHR 2009; *Young, James, and Webster v. The United Kingdom*, 13 August 1981, § 49, Series A no. 44; *Wille v. Liechtenstein* [GC], no. 28396/95, § 46, ECHR 1999-VII.

[45] *Sejdić and Finci v. Bosnia and Herzegovina* [GC], nos 27996/06 and 34836/06, § 56, ECHR 2009.

[46] *Mykhaylenky and Others v. Ukraine*, nos 35091/02, 35196/02, 35201/02, 35204/02, 35945/02, 35949/02, 35953/02, 36800/02, 38296/02, and 42814/02, §§ 43–45, ECHR 2004-XII; *Cooperativa Agricola Slobozia-Hanesei v. Moldova*, no. 39745/02, § 19, 3 April 2007.

[47] *Radio France and Others v. France* (dec.), no. 53984/00, § 26, 23 September 2009.

[48] *Commune de Rothenthurm v. Switzerland*, no. 13252/87, Commission decision of 14 December 1988, 59 DR 251; *Section de commune d'Antilly v. France* (dec.), no. 42129/98, 23 November 1999; *The Province of Bari, Sorrentino, and Messeni Nemagna v. Italy* (dec.), no. 41877/98, 22 March 2001; *Ayuntamiento de Mula v. Spain* (dec.), no. 55346/00, 1 February 2001; *Danderyds Kommun v. Sweden* (dec.) no. 52559199, 7 June 2001; *Döşemealtı Belediyesi v. Turkey* (dec.), no. 50108/06, 23 March 2010.

[49] *Consejo General de Colejos Ociciales de Economista de España v. Spain*, nos 26114/95 and 26455/95, Commission decision of 28 June 1995.

[50] *RENFE v. Spain*, no. 35216/97, Commission decision of 8 September 1997.

[51] *Ilaşcu and Others v. Moldova and Russia* [GC], no. 48787/99, § 318, ECHR 2004-VII.

[52] *Ireland v. the United Kingdom*, 18 January 1978, § 239, Series A no. 25.

[53] *Swedish Engine Drivers' Union v. Sweden*, 6 February 1976, § 50, Series A no. 20. Also *Silver and Others v. the United Kingdom*, 25 March 1983, § 113, Series A no. 61; *James and Others v. the United Kingdom*, 21 February 1986, § 84, Series A no. 98.

The obligation to respect human rights has both negative and positive dimensions. In a negative sense, States are under an obligation not to violate articles 2 to 14, as well as the substantive provisions of the Protocols to the extent these have been ratified. But they must also ensure respect for the Convention and the Protocols through, for example, establishing a legal framework for the protection of these rights and enforcing measures to ensure its observance. This is what is meant by the positive dimension. With respect to the right to life defined in article 2, States are under a duty not only to refrain from taking the lives of those subject to their jurisdiction but also to ensure that lives are protected, through the enforcement of criminal justice, punishment of murder and attempted murder, appropriate measures of inquiry and investigation when there is loss of life under questionable circumstances, and minimum standards of medical care. Similarly, article 1 applies in cases of ill-treatment falling under article 3 to the extent that 'States must take measures designed to ensure that individuals within their jurisdiction are not subjected to ill-treatment administered not only by State agents but also by private individuals.'[54]

According to the Court, 'by virtue of Article 1 of the Convention, each Contracting Party "shall secure to everyone within [its] jurisdiction the rights and freedoms defined in . . . [the] Convention". The discharge of this general duty may entail positive obligations inherent in ensuring the effective exercise of the rights guaranteed by the Convention.'[55] In the context of freedom of religion, the Court has invoked 'the States' positive obligation under Article 1 of the Convention to secure to everyone within its jurisdiction the rights and freedoms defined therein' in holding that '[i]n democratic societies, in which several religions and beliefs coexist within one and the same population, it may be necessary to place restrictions on the freedom to manifest one's religion or belief in order to reconcile the interests of the various groups and to ensure that everyone's beliefs are respected'.[56]

Although the distinction between positive and negative obligations is often quite clear, sometimes the Court refuses to determine the nature of the duty.[57] It notes that whether the basis of its analysis is a positive duty to take measures to secure the rights of the individual or a negative duty upon a public authority not to interfere, 'the applicable principles are broadly similar. In both contexts regard must be had to the fair balance that has to be struck between the competing interests of the individual and of the community as a whole.'[58] However, in some cases, there is considerable debate about whether or not to characterize the alleged infringement as being related to a negative or a positive obligation.[59] If the obligation is positive rather than negative, the margin of appreciation granted to the State may be larger.[60]

'... to everyone ...'

The rights enshrined in the Convention must be secured to 'everyone'. In a concurring opinion, Judge Bonello highlighted the importance of rights being secured to 'everyone',

[54] *Z and Others v. the United Kingdom* [GC], no. 29392/95, § 73, ECHR 2001-V.
[55] *Sørensen and Rasmussen v. Denmark* [GC], nos 52562/99 and 52620/99, § 57, ECHR 2006-I.
[56] *H.C.W. Schilder v. the Netherlands* (dec.), no. 2158/12, § 21, 16 October 2012.
[57] *Hatton and Others v. the United Kingdom* [GC], no. 36022/97, § 119, ECHR 2003-VIII.
[58] Ibid., § 93.
[59] *Mouvement raëlien suisse v. Switzerland* [GC], no. 16354/06, Concurring Opinion of Judge Bratza, §§ 3–4, ECHR 2012 (extracts); ibid., Dissenting Opinion of Judge Pinto de Albuqeruque.
[60] *Women On Waves and Others v. Portugal*, no. 31276/05, § 40, 3 February 2009.

noting that the universality it establishes was 'the cornerstone of the Convention'.[61] The word 'everyone' also appears in articles 2, 5, 6, 8, 9, 10, and 11 of the Convention, and in a few provisions of the Protocols.[62] Sometimes the Convention formulates a right in a negative sense: 'No one shall be subjected to torture or to inhuman or degrading treatment or punishment.' The word 'everyone' in article 1 should be read in conjunction with article 34, where a right of petition to the Court is recognized to 'any person, non-governmental organisation or group of individuals'. It applies to corporate bodies or moral persons, which are viewed as non-governmental organizations for the purposes of article 34.[63] For some rights, however, the context makes it clear that only physical persons are contemplated. Article 34 concerns admissibility criteria. However, it would make no sense that article 34 could have a broader scope than article 1.

No decision of the Court has clarified whether the unborn child is subsumed within the term 'everyone'. The issue is particularly sensitive given variation in practice within European States on the issue of abortion. The current position is that 'the issue of when the right to life begins comes within the margin of appreciation which the Court generally considers that States should enjoy in this sphere'.[64] According to the Grand Chamber, Europe lacks a 'consensus on the scientific and legal definition of the beginning of life'.[65] The Court has spoken of 'the impossibility of finding a uniform European conception of morals including on the question of when life begins'.[66]

'...within their jurisdiction...'

The obligation imposed by article 1 upon States is to secure rights 'within their jurisdiction'. The term 'jurisdiction' in article 1 is 'a threshold criterion', a condition necessary for a Contracting State to be held liable for acts and omissions under the Convention.[67] It reflects the concept of jurisdiction of public international law,[68] and is 'closely linked to that of the international responsibility of the State concerned'.[69] The notion of jurisdiction in article 1 applies to States. The enforcement of the Convention will be ensured, first and foremost, by the national Courts.

The term jurisdiction also appears in articles 30, 31, and 32, and in the title of article 35 of the Convention, where the context indicates it refers to the jurisdiction of the European

---

[61] *Al-Skeini and Others v. the United Kingdom* [GC], no. 55721/07, Concurring Opinion of Judge Bonello, § 9, ECHR 2011.

[62] Protocol No. 4 to the Convention for the Protection of Human Rights and Fundamental Freedoms, securing certain rights and freedoms other than those already included in the Convention and in the first Protocol thereto, ETS 46, art. 2; Protocol No. 7 to the Convention for the Protection of Human Rights and Fundamental Freedoms, ETS 117, art. 2.

[63] *Agrotexim and Others v. Greece*, 24 October 1995, § 66, Series A no. 330-A; *Société Faugyr Finance S.A. v. Luxembourg* (dec.), no. 38788/97, 23 March 2000; *Unédic v. France*, no. 20153/04, §§ 48–59, 18 December 2008; *Radio France and Others v. France* (dec.), no. 53984/00, § 26, 23 September 2003.

[64] *Vo v. France* [GC], no. 53924/00, § 82, ECHR 2004-VIII.

[65] Ibid.

[66] *A, B, and C v. Ireland* [GC], no. 25579/05, § 222, ECHR 2010.

[67] *Ilaşcu and Others v. Moldova and Russia* [GC], no. 48787/99, § 311, ECHR 2004-VII; *Al-Skeini and Others v. the United Kingdom* [GC], no. 55721/07, § 130, ECHR 2011.

[68] *Nada v. Switzerland* [GC], no. 10593/08, § 119, ECHR 2012; *Assanidze v. Georgia*, no. 71503/01, § 137, ECHR 2004-II; *Gentilhomme and Others v. France*, nos 48205/99, 48207/99, and 48209/99, § 20, 14 May 2002; *Banković and Others v. Belgium and Others* (dec.) [GC], no. 52207/99, §§ 59–61, ECHR 2001-XII; *Al-Dulimi and Montana Management Inc. v. Switzerland*, no. 5809/08, § 89, 26 November 2013.

[69] *Andrejeva v. Latvia* [GC], no. 55707/00, § 56, ECHR 2009; *Ilaşcu and Others v. Moldova and Russia* [GC], no. 48787/99, § 312, ECHR 2004-VII.

Court of Human Rights rather than to the jurisdiction of the Convention. Article 32 is entitled 'Jurisdiction of the Court'. It states that the Court's jurisdiction 'shall extend to all matters concerning the interpretation and application of the Convention and the Protocols thereto...' This is a different sense from that of article 1, however. Article 1 concerns the territorial (*ratione loci*), temporal (*ratione temporis*), personal (*ratione personae*), and subject-matter (*ratione materiae*) jurisdiction. Taken in that sense, the scope of the obligations under the Convention is identical to the jurisdiction of the European Court.

The Court acts where it has jurisdiction and where a case is admissible. These notions of jurisdiction and admissibility are similar but not identical. In particular, the Court should be satisfied that it has jurisdiction whether or not this matter is raised by the parties to a dispute.[70] Indeed, a State may be estopped from raising an argument about jurisdiction and yet the Court will in any case be required to consider it *proprio motu*. The failure of a party to proceedings to contest admissibility does not entitle the Court to proceed if it is without jurisdiction. This is because 'the scope of the Court's jurisdiction is determined by the Convention itself... and not by the parties' submissions in a particular case'.[71] Otherwise, 'where a respondent State waived its right to plead or omitted to plead incompatibility, the Court would have to rule on the merits of a complaint against that State concerning a right not guaranteed by the Convention or on a Convention right not yet binding on it, for example by virtue of a valid reservation clause (incompatibility *ratione materiae*) or because it has not yet ratified an additional Protocol (incompatibility *ratione personae*)'.[72] The notion of jurisdiction under article 1 of the Convention is not to be confused with whether or not an applicant to the Court may be considered a 'victim' of a violation. The two are 'separate and distinct admissibility conditions'.[73]

A violation of human rights may be attributable to more than one State and possibly to factors that are in part outside the jurisdiction as defined in article 1. But 'the fact that the factual or legal situation complained of by the applicant is partly attributable to another State is not in itself decisive for the determination of the respondent State's "jurisdiction"'.[74]

Although infrequent, there are cases where States parties to the Convention have broken up. Problems may arise concerning the attribution of responsibility where the alleged violation took place prior to the breakup but where the claim is being made after. The Court has taken the view that 'given the practical requirements of Article 46 of the Convention, as well as the principle that fundamental rights protected by international human rights treaties should indeed belong to individuals living in the territory of the State party concerned, notwithstanding its subsequent dissolution or succession', the Convention should apply without interruption.[75]

---

[70] *Sejdić and Finci v. Bosnia and Herzegovina* [GC], nos 27996/06 and 34836/06, § 27, ECHR 2009.
[71] *Blečić v. Croatia* [GC], no. 59532/00, § 67, ECHR 2006-III.
[72] Ibid.
[73] *Andrejeva v. Latvia* [GC], no. 55707/00, § 56, ECHR 2009; *Banković and Others v. Belgium and Others* (dec.) [GC], no. 52207/99, ECHR 2001-XII.
[74] *Andrejeva v. Latvia* [GC], no. 55707/00, § 56, ECHR 2009.
[75] *Bijelić v. Montenegro and Serbia*, no. 11890/05, § 69, 28 April 2009.

Ratione materiae

The subject-matter or *ratione materiae* jurisdiction of the Court consists of the substantive provisions found in Section I of the Convention, as well as in the relevant provisions of the Protocols. Although raised as a preliminary issue concerning jurisdiction,[76] most debates about jurisdiction *ratione materiae* take place during the debate on the merits because they concern what is covered and what is not covered by the substantive provisions of the Convention.[77] The issue also presents itself with respect to the admissibility issue of exhaustion of domestic remedies because the applicant is required to have raised the substantive issue during domestic litigation prior to submitting a claim to the Court.[78]

There are, to be sure, fundamental rights and freedoms that do not fall within the scope of the European Convention on Human Rights. This is implied in the Preamble, where it is stated that the Convention is intended 'to take the first steps for the collective enforcement of certain of the rights stated in the Universal Declaration'. For example, the Convention does not apply to the right to self-determination,[79] the right to political asylum,[80] or the right of foreign nationals to enter and reside within a State Party.[81] These rights are not provided for in the Convention or its Protocols, although they may exist pursuant to other international human rights instruments or by virtue of customary international law. When European States present their reports to the United Nations Human Rights Council as part of the Universal Periodic Review process, they are expected to account for their observance both of treaties to which they are a party and also of the Universal Declaration of Human Rights.[82] However, the European Court of Human Rights is without any jurisdiction to rule upon violations of treaties other than the European Convention and its Protocols.[83]

The scope *ratione materiae* of the Convention may also be limited where a State has made a reservation. The issue is discussed in this Commentary in the chapter on article 57 of the Convention in Section 2.III.

States parties are responsible, pursuant to article 1, for acts and omissions of their own organs regardless of whether this is a consequence of domestic law or a result of an attempt at compliance with an international legal obligation imposed by treaty or by customary law.[84]

---

[76] For example, *Martinie v. France* [GC], no. 58675/00, §§ 24–30, ECHR 2006-VI.

[77] *Tănase v. Moldova* [GC], no. 7/08, §§ 131–133, ECHR 2010; *Damjanac v. Croatia*, no. 52943/10, § 62, 24 October 2013.

[78] See, e.g., *Vo v. France* [GC], no. 53924/00, §§ 44–45, ECHR 2004-VIII.

[79] *X v. Federal Republic of Germany*, no. 6742/74, Commission decision of 10 July 1975, DR 3, p. 98; *X v. the Netherlands*, no. 7230/75, § 2, Commission decision of 4 October 1976, DR 7, p. 109.

[80] *Djokaba Lambi Longa v. the Netherlands* (dec.), no. 33917/12, § 81, 9 October 2012; *Vilvarajah and Others v. the United Kingdom*, 30 October 1991, § 102, Series A no. 215; *Chahal v. The United Kingdom*, 15 November 1996, § 73, *Reports of Judgments and Decisions* 1996-V.

[81] *Peñafiel Salgado v. Spain* (dec.), no. 65964/01, 16 April 2002; *Djokaba Lambi Longa v. the Netherlands* (dec.), no. 33917/12, § 81, 9 October 2012; *Kane v. Cyprus* (dec.), no. 33655/06, 13 September 2011; *H. v. the Netherlands* (dec.), no. 37833/10, 18 October 2011.

[82] Institution-building of the United Nations Human Rights Council, UN Doc. A/HRC/RES/5/1, Annex, para. 1(b).

[83] *J.F. v. France* (dec.), no. 39616/98, 20 April 1999. For the Commission, see *Di Lazzaro v. Italy* no. 31924/96, Commission decision of 10 July 1997, DR 90-B, p. 134: *Melchers and Co. v. Germany*, no. 13258/87, Commission decision of 9 February 1990, (1990) 33 YB 46, DR 64, p. 138.

[84] *Al-Saadoon and Mufdhi v. the United Kingdom*, no. 61498/08, § 128, ECHR 2010; *Nada v. Switzerland* [GC], no. 10593/08, § 75, ECHR 2012; *Bosphorus Hava Yolları Turizm ve Ticaret Anonim Şirketi v. Ireland* [GC], no. 45036/98, § 175, ECHR 2005-VI.

According to the Court, 'Article 1 makes no distinction as to the type of rule or measure concerned and does not exclude any part of a Contracting Party's "jurisdiction" from scrutiny under the Convention.'[85] Nevertheless, when State action is taken in order to comply with legal obligations imposed by an international organization such as the European Union, the Court will show a degree of deference or tolerance, to the extent that there is a presumption that the relevant organization protects the fundamental rights in both a substantive and procedural sense in a manner considered at least equivalent or comparable to that of the European Convention regime.[86] This presumption is rebuttable if the protection of Convention rights is 'manifestly deficient',[87] however, in light of the Convention's role as a 'constitutional instrument of European public order' in the field of human rights.[88]

Ratione loci

The State's jurisdiction as this is meant by article 1 of the Convention is 'primarily territorial'.[89] There exists a presumption that jurisdiction is normally exercised throughout the territory of a State Party.[90] However, in principle the Convention 'does not require the Contracting Parties to impose its standards on third States or territories'.[91] There are exceptions in two respects. Some acts that take place on the territory of a State Party are not attributable to it, for example when these are associated with international organizations, or when the perpetrator benefits from a form of immunity under international law. Then, even a positive obligation to prevent the violation cannot be imposed upon the State. Some acts that take place outside the territory of a State Party are attributable to it, principally in circumstances where a State agent exercises authority and control outside its territory, for example when it acts on the high seas, or when the State has effective control over an area, for example in a situation of military occupation.

Extradition, expulsion, and refoulement

Extraterritoriality may also arise when an act performed within the State Party has effects outside the territory. This is the case in extradition or expulsion cases, where the actual violation or threatened violation of the Convention occurs as a consequence of the conduct of a State Party but actually takes place within the third State.[92] The responsibility of the State Party may be engaged 'on account of acts which have sufficiently

---

[85] *Al-Dulimi and Montana Management Inc. v. Switzerland*, no. 5809/08, § 111, 26 November 2013. Also *Bosphorus Hava Yolları Turizm ve Ticaret Anonim Şirketi v. Ireland* [GC], no. 45036/98, § 153, ECHR 2005-VI; *United Communist Party of Turkey and Others v. Turkey*, 30 January 1998, § 29, *Reports of Judgments and Decisions* 1998-I.

[86] *Melchers and Co. v. Germany*, no. 13258/87, Commission decision of 9 February 1990, (1990) 33 YB 46, DR 64, p. 138.

[87] *Bosphorus Hava Yolları Turizm ve Ticaret Anonim Şirketi v. Ireland* [GC], no. 45036/98, § 156, ECHR 2005-VI; *Gasparini v. Italy and Belgium* (dec.), no. 10750/03, 12 May 2009.

[88] *Loizidou v. Turkey* (Preliminary objections), 23 March 1995, § 75, Series A no. 310.

[89] *Banković and Others v. Belgium and Others* (dec.) [GC], no. 52207/99, § 59, ECHR 2001-XII; *Khan v. the United Kingdom* (dec.), no. 11987/11, § 25, 28 January 2014.

[90] *Ilaşcu and Others v. Moldova and Russia* [GC], no. 48787/99, § 312, ECHR 2004-VII.

[91] *Drozd and Janousek v. France and Spain*, 26 June 1992, § 110, Series A no. 240.

[92] *Soering v. the United Kingdom*, 7 July 1989, § 91, Series A no. 161; *Cruz Varas and Others v. Sweden*, 20 March 1991, §§ 69–70, Series A no. 201; *Vilvarajah and Others v. the United Kingdom*, 30 October 1991, § 103, Series A no. 215; *Loizidou v. Turkey* (Preliminary objections), 23 March 1995, § 62, Series A no. 310; *Loizidou v. Turkey* (merits), 18 December 1996, § 52, *Reports of Judgments and Decisions* 1996-VI.

proximate repercussions on rights guaranteed by the Convention, even if those repercussions occur outside its jurisdiction'.[93] The Court has explained:

While the establishment of the sending State's responsibility inevitably involves an assessment of conditions in the destination country against the standards set out in the Convention, there is no question of adjudicating on or establishing the responsibility of the destination country, whether under general international law, under the Convention or otherwise. In so far as any liability under the Convention is or may be incurred, it is liability incurred by the sending Contracting State by reason of its having taken action which has as a direct consequence the exposure of an individual to proscribed ill-treatment or other violations of the Convention.[94]

The application of the Convention in situations where an individual who may be expelled or transferred to a third State runs a real risk of a violation of the right to life or the prohibition of ill-treatment or torture is well established.[95] If the sending State knew, or ought to have known at the relevant time, that the person being removed would be subject to 'extraordinary rendition', by which is meant 'an extra-judicial transfer of persons from one jurisdiction or State to another, for the purposes of detention and interrogation outside the normal legal system, where there was a real risk of torture or cruel, inhuman or degrading treatment', the Court has said that a possible violation of article 3 'is particularly strong and must be considered intrinsic in the transfer'.[96] Article 5 of the Convention may be violated if an individual has been removed where there is a real risk of arbitrary detention.[97] That risk is also inherent in cases of 'extraordinary rendition'.[98] Concerns about extraterritorial violations of the Convention may also arise, but only 'exceptionally', where there might be a flagrant denial of a fair trial in the third State.[99] However, the European Court will refuse to conduct any general oversight of judicial proceedings in a third State out of concerns that such a review 'would also thwart the current trend towards strengthening international cooperation in the administration of justice'.[100]

However, the Court has refused to recognize extraterritorial jurisdiction based on a notion of effects analogous to what exists in criminal law in relation to conspiracy or complicity. Thus, the fact that a decision may have been taken within a State Party whose effects constitute a violation of the Convention does not suffice to give the Court

---

[93] *Ilaşcu and Others v. Moldova and Russia* [GC], no. 48787/99, § 317, ECHR 2004-VII; *Soering v. the United Kingdom*, 7 July 1989, §§ 88–91, Series A no. 161.

[94] *Al Nashiri v. Poland*, no. 28761/11, § 457, 24 July 2014; *Husayn (Abu Zubaydah) v. Poland*, no. 7511/13, § 454, 24 July 2014.

[95] *Al Nashiri v. Poland*, no. 28761/11, § 453, 24 July 2014; *Husayn (Abu Zubaydah) v. Poland*, no. 7511/13, § 450, 24 July 2014; *Soering v. the United Kingdom*, 7 July 1989, §§ 90–91 and 113; Series A no. 161; *El Masri v. 'the former Yugoslav Republic of Macedonia'* [GC], no. 39630/09, §§ 218–221, ECHR 2012.

[96] *Al Nashiri v. Poland*, no. 28761/11, § 454, 24 July 2014; *Husayn (Abu Zubaydah) v. Poland*, no. 7511/13, § 451, 24 July 2014; *El Masri v. 'The former Yugoslav Republic of Macedonia'* [GC], no. 39630/09, § 212, ECHR 2012.

[97] *El Masri v. 'the former Yugoslav Republic of Macedonia'* [GC], no. 39630/09, § 239, ECHR 2012; *Othman (Abu Qatada) v. the United Kingdom*, no. 8139/09, § 233, ECHR 2012 (extracts).

[98] *Al Nashiri v. Poland*, no. 28761/11, § 455, 24 July 2014; *Husayn (Abu Zubaydah) v. Poland*, no. 7511/13, § 452, 24 July 2014.

[99] *Soering v. the United Kingdom*, 7 July 1989, § 113, Series A no. 161. See also *Willcox and Hurford v. the United Kingdom* (dec.), nos 43759/10 and 43771/12, §§ 96–98, ECHR 2013; *Stoichkov v. Bulgaria*, no. 9808/02, § 51, 24 March 2005; *Othman (Abu Qatada) v. the United Kingdom*, no. 8139/09, § 259, 17 January 2012; *Kaboulov v. Ukraine*, no. 41015/04, § 99, 19 November 2009; *Al Nashiri v. Poland*, no. 28761/11, § 456, 24 July 2014.

[100] *Drozd and Janousek v. France and Spain*, 26 June 1992, § 110, Series A no. 240.

jurisdiction over an overseas territory of the State Party if the latter has not made the declarations contemplated by article 56 of the Convention. The fact that the ultimate decision-making authority of politicians or officials lies within a State Party is 'not a sufficient ground on which to base competence under the Convention for an area otherwise outside the Convention space'.[101] For example, in *Banković*, the fact that decisions about the aerial attacks on Belgrade, which was then outside 'the Convention space', were taken within European States, did not bring the NATO bombing within the competence of the Court.[102]

Extradition may also involve responsibility under the Convention in cases where a State launches an extradition proceeding that results in violations of the Convention within the third State. A State Party that sets in motion a request for detention in a third State pending extradition assumes responsibility to ensure that the arrest warrant and the related materials are consistent with its own law. If it fails to do so, the blame cannot be placed on the third State, even if is a State Party to the Convention. The third State is entitled to presume the validity of the extradition request. Accordingly, an unlawful detention in Spain premised on irregular documents issued in the requesting State, Malta, was attributed to Malta, notwithstanding the fact that the actual detention took place in Spain.[103]

Activities of international organizations

Although not explicitly mentioned in article 1, a State Party is not required to ensure observance of the European Convention by certain international or intergovernmental organizations that may operate on its territory.[104] In the *Bosphorus* case, the European Court said that the Convention did not 'prohibit Contracting Parties from transferring sovereign power to an international (including a supranational) organisation in order to pursue cooperation in certain fields of activity'.[105] Moreover, the international body to which authority is transferred 'is not itself held responsible under the Convention for proceedings before, or decisions of, its organs as long as it is not a Contracting Party'.[106] By way of exception to this principle, however, if the international agreement reserves to a State the right to intervene in some form despite its multilateral obligations, then it may still be held responsible for its conduct.[107]

---

[101] *Chagos Islanders v. the United Kingdom* (dec.), no. 35622/04, § 65, 11 December 2012.

[102] *Banković and Others v. Belgium and Others* (dec.) [GC], no. 52207/99, ECHR 2001-XII.

[103] *Stephens v. Malta (no. 1)*, no. 11956/07, § 52, 21 April 2009.

[104] *Waite and Kennedy v. Germany* [GC], no. 26083/94, § 67, ECHR 1999-I; *Prince Hans-Adam II of Liechtenstein v. Germany* [GC], no. 42527/98, § 48, ECHR 2001-VIII; *X v. Federal Republic of Germany*, no. 235/56 Commission decision of 10 June 1958, (1958–59) 2 YB 256, at p. 298.

[105] *Bosphorus Hava Yolları Turizm ve Ticaret Anonim Şirketi v. Ireland* [GC], no. 45036/98, §§ 152–156, ECHR 2005-VI; *Cooperatieve Producentenorganisatie van de Nederlandse Kokkelvisserij U.A. v. the Netherlands* (dec.), no. 13645/05, ECHR 2009; *Melchers and Co. v. Germany*, no. 13258/87, Commission decision of 9 February 1990, (1990) 33 YB 46, DR 64, p. 138; *Matthews v. the United Kingdom* [GC], no. 24833/94, § 32, ECHR 1999-I.

[106] *Bosphorus Hava Yolları Turizm ve Ticaret Anonim Şirketi v. Ireland* [GC], no. 45036/98, §§ 152–156, ECHR 2005-VI; *Confédération française démocratique du travail v. European Communities*, no. 8030/77, Commission decision of 10 July 1978, (1978) 21 YB 530, DR 13, p. 231; *Dufay v. European Communities*, no. 13539/88, Commission decision of 19 January 1989; *Melchers and Co. v. Germany*, no. 13258/87, Commission decision of 9 February 1990, (1990) 33 YB 46, DR 64, p. 138; *Matthews v. the United Kingdom* [GC], no. 24833/94, § 32, ECHR 1999-I.

[107] *Tarakhel v. Switzerland* [GC], no. 29217/12, § 90, 4 November 2014.

Several international criminal tribunals are located in Europe, almost exclusively in The Hague in The Netherlands. The proceedings before these tribunals raise many issues, notably concerning detention and procedural fairness, which are relevant to provisions of the European Convention. Indeed, the tribunals often refer to the case law of the European Court of Human Rights when they address such issues. The institutions include the International Criminal Court and several bodies established by the United Nations, notably the International Criminal Tribunal for the former Yugoslavia, its residual 'Mechanism', and the Special Tribunal for Lebanon. At various times, the Special Court for Sierra Leone and the International Criminal Tribunal for Rwanda have also had activities in The Hague.[108] In addition, many European States have undertaken to detain persons convicted by these tribunals. Several individuals are currently serving sentences within the penitentiaries of States Parties to the European Convention for lengthy terms that might be deemed contrary to article 3 were they imposed pursuant to judgments of domestic tribunals.

Much earlier in time, the detention facility of the International Military Tribunal was located within a State Party. The operations of Spandau Prison, where the last remaining Nazi prisoner convicted by the Tribunal was detained, were located on the territory of Germany. However, the European Commission of Human Rights held that the Convention did not apply, dismissing an application by the wife of Nazi leader Rudolf Hess.[109] More recently, the European Court of Human Rights has ruled that it is without jurisdiction to consider applications that concern the activity of the International Criminal Tribunal for the former Yugoslavia. It has said that 'it is not axiomatic that a criminal trial must engage the responsibility under public international law of the State on whose territory it is held'.[110] Similarly, it has stated that the fact someone is detained on the territory of a State Party by an international criminal tribunal 'does not of itself suffice to bring questions touching on the lawfulness of his detention within the "jurisdiction" of the Netherlands as that expression is to be understood for the purposes of Article 1 of the Convention'.[111]

The Court has discussed situations where trials are held on the territory of a State but under the auspices of a foreign justice system, giving as examples the implementation of the NATO Status of Forces Agreement in various European states, as well as the trial before a Scottish court of persons accused of terrorism that actually took place within the Netherlands pursuant to a complex international agreement. Speaking of the International Criminal Tribunal for the former Yugoslavia, it said that it could not find that 'the sole fact that the [International Criminal Tribunal for the former Yugoslavia] has its seat and premises in The Hague sufficient ground to attribute the matters complained of to the Kingdom of the Netherlands. In arriving at that conclusion the Court has had regard to the particular context in which the question arises before it. The Court stresses that the present case involves an international tribunal established by the Security Council

---

[108] For discussion of the relationship, see Carsten Stahn and Larissa van den Herik, '"Fragmentation", Diversification and "3D" Legal Pluralism: International Criminal Law as the Jack-in-the-Box?', in Larissa van den Herik and Carsten Stahn, eds, *The Diversification and Fragmentation of International Criminal Law*, Leiden/Boston: Martinus Nijhoff, 2012, pp. 21–89, at pp. 47–55.

[109] *Hess v. the United Kingdom*, no. 6231/73, Commission decision of 28 May 1975, (1975) 18 YB 147, DR 2, p. 72.

[110] *Galić v. the Netherlands* (dec.), no. 22617/07, § 44, 9 June 2009; *Blagojević v. the Netherlands* (dec.), no. 49032/07, § 44, 9 June 2009.

[111] *Djokaba Lambi Longa v. the Netherlands* (dec.), no. 33917/12, § 73, 9 October 2012.

of the United Nations, an international organisation founded on the principle of respect for fundamental human rights, and that moreover the basic legal provisions governing that tribunal's organisation and procedure are purposely designed to provide those indicted before it with all appropriate guarantees.'[112] With regard to the International Criminal Court, which has its seat in The Hague pursuant to article 3 of the Rome Statute, '[t]he Convention does not impose on a State that has agreed to host an international criminal tribunal on its territory the burden of reviewing the lawfulness of deprivation of liberty under arrangements lawfully entered into between that tribunal and States not party to it'.[113] But in a case concerning service of a prison sentence pursuant to a conviction by the International Criminal Tribunal for the former Yugoslavia, the Court did not object on a jurisdictional basis. It declared the application, which charged discriminatory treatment in parole eligibility, inadmissible on substantive grounds.[114]

In Bosnia and Herzegovina, the war crimes chambers of the State Courts set up under the authority of the Dayton Agreement and in pursuit of the completion strategy of the International Criminal Tribunal for the former Yugoslavia have been subject to charges that they did not operate in a manner consistent with the European Convention. The European Court of Human Rights avoided deciding whether Bosnia and Herzegovina was responsible for the court, which was 'an initiative of international institutions', by ruling a challenge ill-founded on other grounds.[115]

Territory not controlled by the State

The presumption of responsibility for acts committed on its territory may be limited in cases where a State cannot exercise authority over part of its territory. This may be the result of military occupation by another State that effectively controls the territory in question,[116] or a consequence of acts of war or rebellion, or the acts of a foreign State supporting the installation of a separatist entity within the State Party. Although the State may not be able to fulfil all of its obligations, positive duties remain, requiring it to take all appropriate measures within its power in order to secure Convention rights in accordance with article 1.[117] Referring to the Moldavian Republic of Transdniestria region, a pro-Russian secessionist pseudo-State, the Court has said that although Moldova lacked any effective control over the acts of the Moldavian Republic of Transdniestria, 'the fact that the region is recognised under public international law as part of Moldova's territory gives rise to an obligation, under Article 1 of the Convention, to use all legal and diplomatic means available to it to continue to guarantee the enjoyment of the rights and freedoms defined in the Convention to those living there'.[118]

---

[112] *Galić v. the Netherlands* (dec.), no. 22617/07, § 46, 9 June 2009; *Blagojević v. the Netherlands* (dec.), no. 49032/07, § 46, 9 June 2009.

[113] *Djokaba Lambi Longa v. the Netherlands* (dec.), no. 33917/12, § 80, 9 October 2012.

[114] *Krajišnik v. the United Kingdom* (dec.), no. 6017/11, 23 October 2012.

[115] *Maktouf and Damjanović v. Bosnia and Herzegovina* [GC], nos 2312/08 and 34179/08, § 48, ECHR 2013 (extracts). See Antonio Cassese, 'The Impact of the European Convention on Human Rights on the International Criminal Tribunal for the former Yugoslavia', in Mahoney et al., *Mélanges Ryssdal*, pp. 213–36.

[116] *Loizidou v. Turkey* (Preliminary objections), 23 March 1995, Series A no. 310; *Cyprus v. Turkey* [GC], no. 25781/94, §§ 76–80, ECHR 2001-IV.

[117] *Ilaşcu and Others v. Moldova and Russia* [GC], no. 48787/99, § 313, ECHR 2004-VII.

[118] *Catan and Others v. the Republic of Moldova and Russia* [GC], nos 43370/04, 8252/05, and 18454/06, § 110, ECHR 2012 (extracts). Also *Ilaşcu and Others v. Moldova and Russia* [GC], no. 48787/99, § 333, ECHR 2004-VII.

Territory over which the State exercises responsibility for international relations

Article 56 of the Convention authorizes States Parties to declare that the Convention applies to a territory for which it exercises responsibility in the field of international relations. The expression is a euphemism for what has often been called the 'colonial clause'. It is discussed in detail in the chapter on article 56.

Immunity

In accordance with general international law, States recognize a range of immunities to foreign diplomats, heads of State, and functionaries of international organizations. Although responsible in a general sense for ensuring compliance by individuals within their jurisdiction, such positive obligations are reduced or eliminated where immunities are granted.[119] Thus, while in principle a State is required to investigate violations of the right to life committed on its territory, this would not be possible in practice if a foreign embassy were involved. The European Court has explained that 'sovereign immunity is a concept of international law, developed out of the principle *par in parem non habet imperium*, by virtue of which one State shall not be subject to the jurisdiction of another State'. It has said that '[t]he grant of sovereign immunity to a State in civil proceedings pursues the legitimate aim of complying with international law to promote comity and good relations between States through the respect of another State's sovereignty'.[120]

The Court approaches such questions not as a matter of jurisdiction but rather within the framework of restrictions or limitations. Typically, immunity raises problems with article 6 by preventing lawsuits. According to the Court, 'measures taken by a State which reflect generally recognised rules of public international law on State immunity cannot in principle be regarded as imposing a disproportionate restriction on the right of access to a court as embodied in Article 6 § 1'.[121]

Extraterritorial jurisdiction

Exceptionally, a State Party may incur liability under article 1 of the Convention for acts that it actually perpetrates outside its territory. This 'was not foreseen—indeed, might well have been met with astonishment—when the Convention was drafted'.[122] It may well be that the extraterritorial activity of a given State is conducted with the consent, invitation, or acquiescence of the State that is actually sovereign. Even then, in cases where 'in accordance with custom, treaty or other agreement, authorities of the Contracting State carry out executive or judicial functions on the territory of another State, the

---

[119] *McElhinney v. Ireland* [GC], no. 31253/96, § 38, ECHR 2001-XI; *Al-Adsani v. the United Kingdom* [GC], no. 35763/97, § 56, ECHR 2001-XI; *Fogarty v. the United Kingdom* [GC], no. 37112/97, § 38, ECHR 2001-XI.

[120] *Jones and Others v. the United Kingdom*, nos 34356/06 and 40528/06, § 188, 14 January 2014; *Fogarty v. the United Kingdom* [GC], no. 37112/97, § 34, ECHR 2001-XI; *McElhinney v. Ireland* [GC], no. 31253/96, § 35, ECHR 2001-XI; *Al-Adsani v. the United Kingdom* [GC], no. 35763/97, § 54, ECHR 2001-XI; *Al-Adsani v. the United Kingdom* [GC], no. 35763/97, § 54, ECHR 2001-XI; *Kalogeropoulou and Others v. Greece and Germany* (dec.), no. 59021/00, ECHR 2002-X; *Cudak v. Lithuania* [GC], no. 15869/02, § 60, ECHR 2010; *Sabeh El Leil v. France* [GC], no. 34869/05, § 52, 29 June 2011.

[121] *Jones and Others v. the United Kingdom*, nos 34356/06 and 40528/06, § 189, 14 January 2014; *Al-Adsani v. the United Kingdom* [GC], no. 35763/97, §§ 52–56, ECHR 2001- XI; *Fogarty v. the United Kingdom* [GC], no. 37112/97, § 36, ECHR 2001-XI; *McElhinney v. Ireland* [GC], no. 31253/96, § 37, 21 November 2001; *Manoilescu and Dobrescu v. Romania and Russia* (dec.), no. 60861/00, § 80, ECHR 2005-VI.

[122] Ed Bates, *The Evolution of the European Convention on Human Rights*, Oxford: Oxford University Press, 2010, at p. 111.

Contracting State may be responsible for breaches of the Convention thereby incurred, as long as the acts in question are attributable to it rather than to the territorial State'.[123]

As a general rule, the Convention does not apply to acts or threats in a third State if an individual has left a State Party voluntarily. Indeed, in addressing issues of extraterritorial application 'there is no principled reason to distinguish between, on the one hand, someone who was in the jurisdiction of a Contracting State but voluntarily left that jurisdiction and, on the other, someone who was never in the jurisdiction of that State'.[124] As a result, immigration authorities within a Convention State need not consider a threat of torture or violation of the right to life if the individual in question is abroad, in a third State, something that would imply 'an unlimited obligation on Contracting States to allow entry to an individual who might be at real risk of ill-treatment contrary to Article 3, regardless of where in the world that individual might find himself'.[125]

State agent authority and control

A State Party may be liable for a violation of the Convention rights and freedoms of persons that occurs outside the territory where the perpetrators are under its authority and control.[126] In such situations, accountability 'stems from the fact that Article 1 of the Convention cannot be interpreted so as to allow a State party to perpetrate violations of the Convention on the territory of another State, which it could not perpetrate on its own territory'.[127] It does not matter whether or not the State's agents are acting outside their authority, or even unlawfully. On this point, the Court has referred to the International Law Commission Articles on State Responsibility, whereby 'a State's authorities are strictly liable for the conduct of their subordinates; they are under a duty to impose their will and cannot shelter behind their inability to ensure that it is respected'.[128]

Use of force by agents of the State operating outside its territory may engage the responsibility of a State Party to the Convention. The Court has said that 'whenever the State through its agents exercises control and authority over an individual, and thus jurisdiction, the State is under an obligation under Article 1 to secure to that individual the rights and freedoms under Section 1 of the Convention that are relevant to the situation of that individual'.[129] According to the Court, '[w]hat is decisive in such cases is the exercise of physical power and control over the person in question'.[130] For example, when Turkish agents were given custody over Abdulah Öcalan by Kenyan authorities, 'the applicant was effectively under Turkish authority and therefore within the "jurisdiction" of that State for the purposes of Article 1 of the Convention, even though in this instance Turkey exercised its authority outside its territory'.[131] In *Issa and Others*, Turkish soldiers had taken individuals into custody and then murdered them; although all of the relevant events took place in Northern Iraq, this was held to be an exercise of

[123] *Drozd and Janousek v. France and Spain*, 26 June 1992, Series A no. 240; *Gentilhomme, Schaff-Benhadji and Zerouki v. France*, nos 48205/99, 48207/99, and 48209/99, 14 May 2002; *X and Y v. Switzerland*, nos 7289/75 and 7349/76, Commission decision of 14 July 1977, (1977) 20 YB 372, DR 9, p. 57.
[124] *Khan v. the United Kingdom* (dec.), no. 11987/11, § 26, 28 January 2014.
[125] Ibid.
[126] *Illich Sanchez Ramirez v. France*, no. 28780/95, Commission decision of 24 June 1996, DR 86, p. 155.
[127] *Isaak and Others v. Turkey* (dec.), no. 44587/98, 28 September 2006.
[128] *Ilaşcu and Others v. Moldova and Russia* [GC], no. 48787/99, § 319, ECHR 2004-VII.
[129] *Al-Skeini and Others v. the United Kingdom* [GC], no. 55721/07, § 138, ECHR 2011.
[130] Ibid., § 137.
[131] *Öcalan v. Turkey* [GC], no. 46221/99, § 91, ECHR 2005-IV.

jurisdiction subject to article 1 by Turkey.[132] Iraqi nationals detained in military prisons within Iraq that were controlled by British forces were also protected by the European Convention.[133]

In an Italian case, the Court acknowledged the application of the Convention when the alleged violation took place on board military ships flying the Italian flag.[134] It said that Italy could not avoid jurisdiction under the Convention by describing the events as rescue operations conducted on the high seas.[135] This is really no more than application of the general rule that States normally exercise territorial jurisdiction over ships and aircraft flying their flag.[136] Under international law, vessels sailing on the high seas are subject to the exclusive jurisdiction of the flag State.[137] Customary international law recognizes the validity of the exercise of universal jurisdiction on board such vessels, both ships and aircraft.[138]

But even when the events took place in international waters on a ship flagged in Cambodia, the Court found that French drug enforcement officials were exercising jurisdiction within the meaning of article 1 of the Convention. In that case, a French frigate named the *Lieutenant de vaisseau Le Hénaff* had boarded the *Winner*, taking control of the vessel, detaining the crew, and sailing it to France. The Court held that France had 'exercised full and exclusive control over the *Winner* and its crew, at least *de facto*, from the time of its interception, in a continuous and uninterrupted manner until they were tried in France', putting the alleged victims under French jurisdiction for the purposes of Article 1 of the Convention.[139]

Extraterritorial exercise of jurisdiction by a State undertaken by diplomatic or consular agents is recognized by customary international law.[140]

Effective control over an area

The Convention may also apply extraterritorially when a State Party exercises effective control over an area outside its national territory. This will generally occur as a consequence of military occupation. This is a question of fact, and 'the status of "occupying power" within the meaning of Article 42 of the Hague Regulations, or lack of it, is not per se determinative'.[141] In such cases, the obligation under article 1 of the Convention derives from the fact of such control, whether it be exercised directly, through the Contracting State's own armed forces, or through a subordinate local administration.[142]

---

[132] *Issa and Others v. Turkey*, no. 31821/96, 16 November 2004.
[133] *Al-Saadoon and Mufdhi v. the United Kingdom* (dec.), no. 61498/08, §§ 86–89, 30 June 2009.
[134] *Hirsi Jamaa and Others v. Italy* [GC], no. 27765/09, §§ 76, 78, ECHR 2012.
[135] Ibid., § 79.
[136] Doris König, 'Flag of Ships', in Rüdiger Wolfrum, *The Max Planck Encyclopedia of Public International Law*, Vol. IV, Oxford: Oxford University Press, 2012, pp. 98–116.
[137] *Hirsi Jamaa and Others v. Italy* [GC], no. 27765/09, § 77, ECHR 2012.
[138] *Banković and Others v. Belgium and Others* (dec.) [GC], no. 52207/99, § 73, ECHR 2001-XII.
[139] *Medvedyev and Others v. France* [GC], no. 3394/03, § 87, ECHR 2010.
[140] *Banković and Others v. Belgium and Others* (dec.) [GC], no. 52207/99, § 73, ECHR 2001-XII; *X v. Federal Republic of Germany*, no. 1611/62, Commission decision of 25 September 1965, (1965) 8 YB 158, at p. 169; *X v. the United Kingdom*, no. 7547/76, Commission decision of 15 December 1977; *WM v. Denmark*, no. 17392/90, Commission decision of 14 October 1993); *Al-Skeini and Others v. the United Kingdom* [GC], no. 55721/07, § 134, ECHR 2011.
[141] *Jaloud v. the Netherlands* [GC], no. 47708/08, § 142, 20 November 2014.
[142] *Al-Skeini and Others v. the United Kingdom* [GC], no. 55721/07, § 138, ECHR 2011; *Loizidou v. Turkey* (Preliminary objections), 23 March 1995, § 62, Series A no. 310; *Cyprus v. Turkey* [GC], no. 25781/94, § 76, ECHR 2001-IV; *Banković and Others v. Belgium and Others* (dec.) [GC], no. 52207/99, § 70, ECHR 2001-XII;

It is not necessary to establish whether the State actually exercises detailed control over the policies and actions of the authorities in the occupied area.[143] The responsibility extends beyond the acts of the State's own soldiers or officials to the local administration that may have survived and that continues to operate with the support or tolerance of the military occupier.[144] With effective control by military occupation goes an 'obligation to secure, in such an area, the rights and freedoms set out in the Convention.'[145] In other words, the State Party must ensure both the positive and negative dimensions of rights. Obligations upon the occupying power to protect fundamental rights also exist pursuant to the laws of armed conflict.[146]

Whether or not a State exercises effective control over an area outside its own national territory is a question of fact.[147] Relevant factors in assessing whether the State Party exercises effective control will include the strength of the military presence, as well as the extent to which the military, economic, and political support for the local subordinate administration provides it with influence and control over the region.[148] Effective control may be combined with 'decisive influence'.[149] There is no need to determine whether the State Party exercises detailed control over the policies and acts of the local administration because its existence and survival as a consequence of the military occupation is sufficient to engage the jurisdiction of the occupying State.[150] The State's responsibility under the Convention covers the territory of the State, subject to exceptions for the activities of international organizations and certain immunities under international law. It also extends to territory effectively controlled by the State, such as territory under military occupation.[151]

The Court has declined to recognize the application of article 1 to all acts of armed conflict that take place outside the territory. In a case concerning bombing of Serbia by NATO forces, it held that the Convention did not apply when 'an instantaneous extra-territorial act is at issue, since the wording of Article 1 does not accommodate such an approach to "jurisdiction"'.[152] But in a case involving a demonstration that took place in

Ilaşcu and Others v. Moldova and Russia [GC], no. 48787/99, §§ 314–316, ECHR 2004-VII; *Loizidou v. Turkey* (merits), 18 December 1996, § 52, *Reports of Judgments and Decisions* 1996-VI.

[143] *Ilaşcu and Others v. Moldova and Russia* [GC], no. 48787/99, § 315, ECHR 2004-VII.
[144] Ibid., § 316; *Cyprus v. Turkey* [GC], no. 25781/94, § 77, ECHR 2001-IV.
[145] *Catan and Others v. the Republic of Moldova and Russia* [GC], nos 43370/04, 8252/05, and 18454/06, § 106, ECHR 2012 (extracts); *Loizidou v. Turkey* (Preliminary objections), 23 March 1995, § 62, Series A no. 310; *Cyprus v. Turkey* [GC], no. 25781/94, § 76, ECHR 2001-IV; *Banković and Others v. Belgium and Others* (dec.) [GC], no. 52207/99, § 70, ECHR 2001-XII; *Ilaşcu and Others v. Moldova and Russia* [GC], no. 48787/99, §§ 314–316, ECHR 2004-VII; *Loizidou v. Turkey* (merits), 18 December 1996, § 52, *Reports of Judgments and Decisions* 1996-VI; *Al-Skeini and Others v. the United Kingdom* [GC], no. 55721/07, § 138, ECHR 2011.
[146] Jean-Marie Henckaerts and Louise Doswald-Beck, *Customary International Humanitarian Law, Volume I: Rules*, Cambridge: Cambridge University Press, 2005, pp. 296–491.
[147] *Catan and Others v. the Republic of Moldova and Russia* [GC], nos 43370/04, 8252/05, and 18454/06, § 119, ECHR 2012 (extracts).
[148] *Al-Skeini and Others v. the United Kingdom* [GC], no. 55721/07, § 140, ECHR 2011; *Ilaşcu and Others v. Moldova and Russia* [GC], no. 48787/99, § 387, ECHR 2004-VII; *Loizidou v. Turkey* (merits), 18 December 1996, §§ 16, 56, *Reports of Judgments and Decisions* 1996-VI.
[149] *Catan and Others v. the Republic of Moldova and Russia* [GC], nos 43370/04, 8252/05, and 18454/06, §§ 121–122, ECHR 2012 (extracts).
[150] *Al-Skeini and Others v. the United Kingdom* [GC], no. 55721/07, § 139, ECHR 2011; *Cyprus v. Turkey* [GC], no. 25781/94, §§ 76–77 ECHR 2001-IV.
[151] *Cyprus v. Turkey* [GC], no. 25781/94, §§ 75–81, ECHR 2001-IV; *Drozd and Janousek v. France and Spain*, 26 June 1992, §§ 84–90, Series A no. 240.
[152] *Banković and Others v. Belgium and Others* (dec.) [GC], no. 52207/99, § 75, ECHR 2001-XII.

the United Nations buffer zone located between the territory of Cyprus controlled by the government and the territory occupied by Turkey, the Court considered that Turkey could be deemed to have a sufficient degree of 'effective control' when its police beat to death a Greek-Cypriot demonstrator within the buffer zone.[153]

The Court has made an important distinction respecting extraterritorial control by a State Party. This is related to the idea of the 'legal space' (or *espace juridique*) of the Convention.[154] In such cases, 'the occupying State should in principle be held account-able under the Convention for breaches of human rights within the occupied territory, because to hold otherwise would be to deprive the population of that territory of the rights and freedoms hitherto enjoyed and would result in a "vacuum" of protection within the "Convention legal space"'.[155]

The extension of jurisdiction to territory over which a State exercises 'effective control' is difficult to reconcile with article 56 of the Convention. Drafted at a time when many States in Western Europe still had extensive colonial empires, article 56 enabled them to extend the benefit of the Convention to what were euphemistically described as 'territories for whose international relations they were responsible'. Put otherwise, it meant that the Convention did not automatically and as of right apply to the non-metropolitan territor-ies of a State Party. Although the empires are greatly diminished, several States Parties continue to control territories that are far from the European continent. It does not make much sense for them to issue a declaration under article 56 if the benefit of the Convention has already been extended to the territory in question because of the extraterritorial 'effective control' notion that results from the interpretation of article 1.

In *Al-Skeini v. the United Kingdom*, the Grand Chamber insisted that the 'effective control' principle of jurisdiction did not replace the system of declarations provided for by article 56 of the Convention.[156] In another case, dealing with the displaced Chagos islanders, a Chamber wrote: 'Anachronistic as colonial remnants may be, the meaning of Article 56 is plain on its face and it cannot be ignored merely because of a perceived need to right an injustice. Article 56 remains a provision of the Convention which is in force and cannot be abrogated at will by the Court in order to reach a purportedly desirable result.'[157] In another case directed against the United Kingdom, the Court held that the existence of effective control over a territory did not provide a basis of jurisdiction replacing the system of declarations contemplated by article 56.[158] The situation that results is quite paradoxical. States with dependent territories, like the United Kingdom, are only responsible under the Convention with respect to those territories if they have made a declaration under article 56. But if they occupy a territory militarily they are automatically responsible under the Convention.

---

[153] *Isaak and Others v. Turkey* (dec.), no. 44587/98, 28 September 2006.

[154] Ralph Wilde, 'The "Legal Space" or "Espace Juridique" of the European Convention on Human Rights: Is it Relevant to Extraterritorial State Action?', [2005] *EHRLR* 115.

[155] *Al-Skeini and Others v. the United Kingdom* [GC], no. 55721/07, § 141, ECHR 2011. Also *Loizidou v. Turkey* (merits), 18 December 1996, § 78, *Reports of Judgments and Decisions* 1996-VI; *Banković and Others v. Belgium and Others* (dec.) [GC], no. 52207/99, § 80, ECHR 2001-XII.

[156] *Al-Skeini and Others v. the United Kingdom* [GC], no. 55721/07, § 140, ECHR 2011. Also *Chagos Islanders v. the United Kingdom* (dec.), no. 35622/04, § 71, 11 December 2012.

[157] *Chagos Islanders v. the United Kingdom* (dec.), no. 35622/04, § 74, 11 December 2012.

[158] *Quark Fishing Ltd v. the United Kingdom* (dec.), no. 15305/06, ECHR 2006-XIV. Also *Gillow v. the United Kingdom*, 24 November 1986, § 62, Series A no. 109; *Bui van Thanh and Others v. the United Kingdom*, no. 16137/90, Commission decision of 12 March 1990, (1990) 33 YB 59, DR 65-A, p. 330; *Yonghong v. Portugal* (dec.), no. 50887/99, ECHR 1999-IX.

Diplomatic protection

Diplomatic protection, by which a State attempts to promote and enforce the rights of its nationals with respect to the conduct of another State, is a significant aspect of the application of international human rights law.[159] Within the States Parties to the Convention, this extraterritorial dimension of the protection of human rights may manifest itself, albeit very occasionally, in inter-State applications[160] and in the right of a State Party to intervene when one of its nationals is an applicant against another State Party, in accordance with article 36(1) of the Convention.[161] The Convention organs have declined to recognize that the Convention offers any right of a citizen of a State Party to the exercise of diplomatic protection on his or her behalf.[162]

Ratione personae

The obligations set out in article 1 are only imposed upon 'High Contracting Parties'. As an instrument of European public order,[163] the Convention 'does not govern the actions of States not Parties to it, nor does it purport to be a means of requiring the Contracting States to impose Convention standards on other States'.[164] It does not apply to third States,[165] although the latter's conduct in the area of human rights may present itself indirectly in cases of extradition or expulsion, a matter discussed earlier in this chapter.

The Convention obligations are not imposed upon individuals,[166] although the State may be held responsible in the sense of a positive obligation for the conduct of individuals. Issues of jurisdiction *ratione personae* generally arise in the case of positive obligations because they concern whether or not responsibility can be attributed to the State Party for the acts of others. In the case of obligations upon the State for its own acts and legislation, and that of organs and institutions within the State structure, there can be no serious objection to the jurisdiction *ratione personae*.

Nor do the obligations under the Convention apply to international organizations, even if the organizations are themselves composed of States Parties to the Convention.[167]

---

[159] E.g., *Ahmadou Sadio Diallo (Republic of Guinea v. Democratic Republic of the Congo)*, Compensation, Judgment, I.C.J. Reports 2012, p. 324; *Avena and Other Mexican Nationals (Mexico v. United States of America)*, Judgment, I.C.J. Reports 2004, p. 12.

[160] E.g., *Greece v. the United Kingdom*, no. 176/56, Commission decision of 2 June 1956, (1958-59) 2 YB 182; *Ireland v. the United Kingdom*, 18 January 1978, Series A no. 25; *Cyprus v. Turkey* [GC], no. 25781/94, ECHR 2001-IV.

[161] *I v. Sweden*, no. 61204/09, § 42, 5 September 2013.

[162] *M. and Others v. Italy and Bulgaria*, no. 40020/03, § 127, 31 July 2012; *Bertrand Russel* [sic] *Peace Foundation v. the United Kingdom*, no. 7597/76, Commission decision of 2 May 1978, DR 14, p. 117; *Kapas v. the United Kingdom*, no. 12822/87, Commission decision of 9 December 1987, DR 54, p. 201; *de Lukats v. Sweden*, no. 12920/87, Commission decision of 13 December 1988; *Dobberstein v. Germany*, no. 25045/94, Commission decision of 12 April 1996.

[163] *Loizidou v. Turkey* (Preliminary objections), 23 March 1995, § 75, Series A no. 310.

[164] *Al-Skeini and Others v. the United Kingdom* [GC], no. 55721/07, § 141, ECHR 2011.

[165] *E.S. v. Federal Republic of Germany*, no. 262/57, Commission decision of 28 August 1957, p. 2; *X. v. Austria and Yugoslavia*, no. 2143/64, Commission decision of 30 June 1964, (1964) 7 YB 314, Collection 14, p. 15.

[166] *X. v. the United Kingdom*, no. 6956/75, Commission decision of 10 December 1976, DR 8, p. 103; *Durini and Others v. Italy*, no. 19217/91, Commission decision of 12 January 1994, DR 76-B, p. 76.

[167] *Confédération française démocratique du travail v. the European Communities, alternatively: their Members States* [Belgium, Denmark, France, Ireland, Italy, Luxembourg, the Federal Republic of Germany, the Netherlands, the United Kingdom] *a) jointly and b) severally*, no. 8030/77, Commission decision of 10 July 1978, § 3, DR 13, p. 231; *Heinz v. the Contracting States party to the European Patent Convention insofar as they are High Contracting Parties to the European Convention on Human Rights, i.e. Austria, Belgium, Denmark,*

Nevertheless, there is a kind of reduced or 'light' positive obligation on States when they delegate or assign responsibilities to an international organization in the sense that they must ensure a certain level of compliance with the Convention. This is because 'absolving Contracting States completely from their Convention responsibility in the areas covered by such a transfer would be incompatible with the purpose and object of the Convention; the guarantees of the Convention could be limited or excluded at will, thereby depriving it of its peremptory character and undermining the practical and effective nature of its safeguards'.[168]

In the past, the Convention organs have refused to consider European Union bodies as falling within the jurisdiction *ratione personae*,[169] something that will obviously change with the accession of the European Union to the Convention in accordance with article 59(2). As for the United Nations, it is 'an intergovernmental international organisation with a legal personality separate from that of its member states and is not itself a Contracting Party'.[170] The Court has operated a distinction between the activities of the United Nations and those of its subordinate bodies, such as the United Nations Mission in Kosovo and the International Criminal Tribunal for the former Yugoslavia, and acts carried out by States Parties but pursuant to obligations imposed by the United Nations Security Council. In the latter case, there can be no objection *ratione personae* to jurisdiction under the Convention.[171]

Where peacekeeping activities of European States in Kosovo were concerned, pursuant to a Security Council mandate, the Court considered that this was less a question of exercise of extraterritorial control and more one of the participation within a joint force; consequently, the debate was primarily one of *ratione personae*.[172] The Chamber noted that a central issue was the relationship between the European Convention and the United Nations acting under Chapter VII of its Charter. It said such peacekeeping operations were fundamental to the mission of the United Nations and that acts and omissions of States Parties to the European Convention that were 'covered by' Security Council Resolutions were outside the jurisdiction of the Convention. It said the reasoning also applied to voluntary acts of States Parties, for example the vote of a permanent member of the Security Council and a contribution of troops to a security mission.

France, Germany, Greece, Ireland, Italy, Liechtenstein, Luxembourg, Netherlands, Norway, Portugal, Spain, Sweden, Switzerland, and the United Kingdom, no. 21090/92, Commission decision of 15 October 1992, (1994) 37 YB 38, DR 76-A, p. 125.

[168] *Bosphorus Hava Yolları Turizm ve Ticaret Anonim Şirketi v. Ireland* [GC], no. 45036/98, § 153, ECHR 2005-VI; *Waite and Kennedy v. Germany* [GC], no. 26083/94, § 67, ECHR 1999-I; *Melchers and Co. v. Germany*, no. 13258/87, Commission decision of 9 February 1990, (1990) 33 YB 46, DR 64, p. 138.

[169] *Melchers and Co. v. Germany*, no. 13258/87, Commission decision of 9 February 1990, (1990) 33 YB 46, DR 64, p. 138.

[170] *Galić v. the Netherlands* (dec.), no. 22617/07, § 36, 9 June 2009; *Behrami and Behrami v. France and Saramati v. France, Germany and Norway* (dec.) [GC], nos 71412/01 and 78166/01, § 144, 2 May 2007.

[171] *Nada v. Switzerland* [GC], no. 10593/08, §§ 120–123, ECHR 2012.

[172] *Behrami and Behrami v. France and Saramati v. France, Germany and Norway* (dec.) [GC], nos 71412/01 and 78166/01, §§ 71–72, 2 May 2007. See Pierre Klein, 'Responsabilité pour les faits commis dans le cadre d'opérations de paix et étendue du pouvoir de contrôle de la Cour européenne des droits de l'homme: quelques considérations critiques sur l'arrêt Behrami et Saramati', (2007) 53 *Annuaire français de droit international* 43; K.M. Larsen, 'Attribution of Conduct in Peace Operations: The "Ultimate Authority and Control" Test', (2008) 19 *EJIL* 509 at pp. 521–2; M. Milanović and T. Papić, 'As Bad as It Gets: The European Court of Human Rights Behrami and Saramati Decision and General International Law', (2009) 58 *ICLQ* 267; P. Palchetti, 'Azioni di forze istituite o autorizzate dalle Nazioni Unite davanti alla Corte europea dei diritti dell'uomo: i casi Behrami e Saramati', (2007) 90 *Rivista di Diritto Internazionale* 681; A. Sari, 'Jurisdiction and International Responsibility in Peace Support Operations: The Behrami and Saramati Cases', (2008) 8 *HRLR* 151.

Although such acts may not have flowed from membership in the United Nations, they 'remained crucial to the effective fulfilment' of a Chapter VII initiative and thereby the 'imperative peace and security aim' of the organization.[173] The Chamber noted that nine of the twelve original signatories to the Convention had been founding members of the United Nations and that the great majority of States Parties to the Convention had joined the United Nations prior to signing the Convention. Aside from this general attachment to the United Nations, the Chamber also noted the imperative nature of the 'principle [sic] aim' of the United Nations, the maintenance of international peace, and security.[174] In a subsequent decision, a Chamber of the Court held it was without jurisdiction *ratione materiae* with regard to decisions of the High Representative, who was mandated by the Security Council to act as the interim administrator of Bosnia and Herzegovina. The Chamber said that the Security Council retained 'effective overall control' over the High Representative and that as a consequence his decisions could not be attributed to Bosnia and Herzegovina, a State Party to the European Convention.[175] The High Representative 'was exercising lawfully delegated [United Nations Security Council] Chapter VII powers, so that the impugned action was, in principle, "attributable" to the UN'.[176]

Ratione temporis

From the moment that it enters into force for any given State, the European Convention applies immediately. There is an obligation upon the State Party to 'secure to everyone' the rights and freedoms set out in Section I of the Convention. Beginning with this 'critical date', all of the State's acts and omissions 'not only must conform to the Convention but are also undoubtedly subject to review by the Convention institutions'.[177] The corollary to this is rooted in the presumption that international treaties do not operate retroactively unless a different intention appears from the treaty or is otherwise established. Consequently, the treaty provisions 'do not bind a party in relation to any act or fact which took place or any situation which ceased to exist before the date of the entry into force of the treaty with respect to that party'.[178] According to the Court, 'the Convention imposes no specific obligation on the Contracting States to provide redress for wrongs or damage caused prior to that date'.[179] The Grand Chamber has stated that this principle is 'beyond dispute'.[180]

---

[173]   *Behrami and Behrami v. France and Saramati v. France, Germany and Norway* (dec.) [GC], nos 71412/01 and 78166/01, § 149, 2 May 2007.

[174]   Ibid., §§ 147–148.

[175]   *Berić and Others v. Bosnia and Herzegovina* (dec.), nos 36357/04, 36360/04, 38346/04, 41705/04, 45190/04, 45578/04, 45579/04, 45580/04, 91/05, 97/05, 100/05, 101/05, 1121/05, 1123/05, 1125/05, 1129/05, 1132/05, 1133/05, 1169/05, 1172/05, 1175/05, 1177/05, 1180/05, 1185/05, 20793/05, and 25496/05, § 27, 16 October 2007. See also *Kasumaj v. Greece* (dec.), no. 6974/05, 5 July 2007; *Gajić v. Germany* (dec.), no. 31446/02, 28 August 2007.

[176]   *Berić and Others v. Bosnia and Herzegovina* (dec.), nos 36357/04, 36360/04, 38346/04, 41705/04, 45190/04, 45578/04, 45579/04, 45580/04, 91/05, 97/05, 100/05, 101/05, 1121/05, 1123/05, 1125/05, 1129/05, 1132/05, 1133/05, 1169/05, 1172/05, 1175/05, 1177/05, 1180/05, 1185/05, 20793/05, and 25496/05, § 28, 16 October 2007.

[177]   *Yağcı and Sargın v. Turkey*, 8 June 1995, § 41, Series A no. 319-A; *Broniowski v. Poland* [GC] (dec.), no. 31443/96, §§ 74 et seq., ECHR 2002-X.

[178]   Vienna Convention on the Law of Treaties, (1980) 1155 UNTS 331, art. 28. Also Draft articles on Responsibility of States for Internationally Wrongful Acts, UN Doc. A/56/10, art. 13.

[179]   *Kopecký v. Slovakia* [GC], no. 44912/98, § 38, ECHR 2004-IX.

[180]   *Varnava and Others v. Turkey* [GC], nos 16064/90, 16065/90, 16066/90, 16068/90, 16069/90, 16070/90, 16071/90, 16072/90, and 16073/90, § 130, ECHR 2009; *Blečić v. Croatia* [GC], no. 59532/00, § 70, ECHR 2006-III; *Šilih v. Slovenia* [GC], no. 71463/01, § 140, 9 April 2009.

There is a special application of this in the case of inter-State applications submitted pursuant to article 33. The applicant State may invoke a violation by another State that occurred prior to entry into force of the Convention for the applicant State. That the respondent State was undoubtedly bound to respect the Convention at the relevant time is undisputed. Whether or not the Convention also applied to the applicant State is not relevant because it is said to be acting not in its own interest but rather in the enforcement of the 'public order of Europe'. The European Commission also rejected the charge that applying the Convention in this way might appear unfair, answering that the applicant State was also vulnerable to such applications with respect to the period subsequent to its acceptance of the Convention. '[I]f the High Contracting Parties had wished to make the right to file a complaint under article [33] subject to a condition of reciprocity in regard to the element of time, it was open to them to insert an express condition to that effect in Article [33], but they did not do so', opined the Commission.[181]

In principle, the 'critical date' is that of entry into force of the Convention or the Protocols for the State Party concerned.[182] The Convention entered into force on 3 September 1953 following the deposit of the tenth ratification by a Member State of the Council of Europe, as provided for by article 59(3) of the Convention. For States that have ratified or acceded to the Convention subsequent to that date, the Convention enters into force on the date of deposit of its instrument of ratification or accession with the Secretary General of the Council of Europe, pursuant to article 59(4). For the Protocols, the rules concerning entry into force are similar, although there are some minor variations.

Prior to 1998 and the entry into force of Protocol No. 11, there was a distinction between application of the Convention itself and the jurisdiction of the European Commission and the European Court to examine applications. It was possible for the Convention to be applicable, yet for the Convention organs to be without jurisdiction because the relevant declarations had not been made. Some States made declarations accepting the competence of the Commission and the Court but subject to temporal limitations.[183]

The temporal scope of the Convention is determined with regard to the facts that are responsible for the alleged interference with fundamental rights and freedoms. In order to bring a case before the European Court, the victim must first attempt to remedy the situation in domestic proceedings. However, the failure of such domestic remedies to redress the situation does not alter the 'critical date' for the establishment of temporal jurisdiction. This remains the date of the interference as such.[184]

In the exercise of a remedy for an interference with a fundamental right, violations of the right to a fair trial may take place. The procedural violation is the 'critical date' for the

---

[181] *Austria v. Italy*, no. 788/60, Commission decision of 11 January 1961, (1961) 4 YB 116, at p. 140.

[182] *Šilih v. Slovenia* [GC], no. 71463/01, § 164, 9 April 2009.

[183] For example, *Stamoulakatos v. Greece (no. 1)*, 26 October 1993, § 32, Series A no. 271; *Mitap and Müftüoğlu v. Turkey*, 25 March 1996, §§ 26–28, *Reports of Judgments and Decisions* 1996-II; *Varnava and Others v. Turkey* [GC], nos 16064/90, 16065/90, 16066/90, 16068/90, 16069/90, 16070/90, 16071/90, 16072/90, and 16073/90, § 133, ECHR 2009; *Cankoçak v. Turkey*, nos 25182/94 and 26956/95, § 26, 20 February 2001; *Demades v. Turkey* (just satisfaction), no. 16219/90, § 21, 22 April 2008.

[184] *Kefalas and Others v. Greece*, 8 June 1995, § 45, Series A no. 318-A; *Kadikis v. Latvia* (dec.), no. 47634/99, 29 June 2000; *Veeber v. Estonia (no. 1)*, no. 37571/97, § 55, 7 November 2002; *Jovanović v. Croatia* (dec.), no. 59109/00, ECHR 2002-III; *Litovchenko v. Russia* (dec.), no. 69580/01, 18 April 2002; *Meltex Ltd v. Armenia* (dec.), no. 37780/02, 27 May 2008.

purposes of the Convention.[185] In some cases, the alleged interference with fundamental rights may well be the final judgment of a national court. Then, the 'critical date' for determining the application of the Convention is that of the judgment, that is, the date that the issue becomes *res judicata*.[186] If there is a subsequent decision by a Court that allows the impugned judgment to subsist, it will not have the consequence of changing the 'critical date'.[187] Temporal jurisdiction issues arise with respect to the right to a speedy trial where the lengthy proceedings began before the 'critical date' but continued after.[188]

The rule against retroactivity does not prevent consideration of facts that arose before the entry into force of the Convention for the State in question, in particular where these have created a continuing situation of violation of the Convention[189] or where they are necessary for the understanding of facts that are subsequent to the entry into force.[190] A continuing violation may take place in cases concerning the right to property, for example where there is on-going unlawful occupation,[191] denial of access to property,[192] and failure to pay compensation in cases of nationalization.[193] However, the mere deprivation of property is an 'instantaneous act' that does not create a situation of continuous interference with the right.[194] This exception applies to expropriation measures connected with post-Second-World-War regulation of ownership relations.[195] What has been called 'erasure', a situation in which an individual becomes effectively stateless, has been treated as a continuing interference with private or family life, even if the 'erasure' itself occurred before the 'critical date'.[196]

The 'continuing' procedural obligation exists where there is a situation of disappearance that occurred before the 'critical date'. According to the Grand Chamber:

A disappearance is a distinct phenomenon, characterised by an on-going situation of uncertainty and unaccountability in which there is a lack of information or even a deliberate concealment and obfuscation of what has occurred. This situation is very often drawn out over time, prolonging the torment of the victim's relatives. It cannot therefore be said that a disappearance is, simply, an 'instantaneous' act or event; the additional distinctive element of subsequent failure to account for the whereabouts and fate of the missing person gives rise to a continuing situation. Thus, the procedural obligation will, potentially, persist as long as the fate of the person is unaccounted for;

---

[185] *Harutyunyan v. Armenia*, no. 36549/03, § 50, ECHR 2007-III; *Zana v. Turkey*, 25 November 1997, § 42, *Reports of Judgments and Decisions* 1997-VII.

[186] *Lepojić v. Serbia*, no. 13909/05, § 45, 6 November 2007.

[187] *Blečić v. Croatia* [GC], no. 59532/00, § 85, ECHR 2006-III.

[188] *Humen v. Poland* [GC], no. 26614/95, §§ 58–59, 15 October 1999; *Foti and Others v. Italy*, 10 December 1982, § 53, Series A no. 56. On pre-trial detention, see *Klyakhin v. Russia*, no. 46082/99, §§ 58–59, 30 November 2004.

[189] See Draft articles on Responsibility of States for Internationally Wrongful Acts, UN Doc. A/56/10, art. 14.

[190] *Hutten-Czapska v. Poland* [GC], no. 35014/97, §§ 147–153, ECHR 2006-VIII; *Broniowski v. Poland* [GC] (dec.), no. 31443/96, §§ 74 et seq., ECHR 2002-X.

[191] *Papamichalopoulos and Others v. Greece*, 24 June 1993, § 40, Series A no. 260-B;

[192] *Loizidou v. Turkey* (Preliminary objections), 23 March 1995, §§ 46–47, Series A no. 310.

[193] *Almeida Garrett, Mascarenhas Falcão and Others v. Portugal*, nos 29813/96 and 30229/96, § 43, ECHR 2000-I.

[194] *Blečić v. Croatia* [GC], no. 59532/00, § 86, ECHR 2006-III.

[195] *Preussische Treuhand GmbH & Co. Kg a. A. v. Poland* (dec.), § 57, 7 October 2008; *Malhous v. the Czech Republic* [GC] (dec.) no. 33071/96, ECHR 2000-XII; *Smoleanu v. Romania*, no. 30324/96, § 46, 3 December 2002; *Bergauer and Others v. the Czech Republic* (dec.), no. 17120/04, 13 December 2005; *Von Maltzan and Others v. Germany* [GC] (dec.), nos 71916/01, 71917/01, and 10260/02, § 74, ECHR 2005-V.

[196] *Kurić and Others v. Slovenia* [GC], no. 26828/06, § 339, ECHR 2012 (extracts).

the on-going failure to provide the requisite investigation will be regarded as a continuing violation. This is so, even where death may, eventually, be presumed.[197]

Imposition of a death sentence prior to the 'critical date', to the extent that it has not been set aside, constitutes a continuous violation.[198]

Exceptionally, the Court may take into account facts that took place prior to the 'critical date' in considering the procedural obligation associated with certain fundamental rights, notably those in articles 2 and 3 of the Convention. For example, where a substantive violation of the right to life has taken place prior to the 'critical date', the Convention may nevertheless apply to the duty of the State Party to conduct an investigation and to ensure that measures of accountability exist. In disappearance cases, even if the body has been found, '[t]his only casts light on one aspect of the fate of the missing person and the obligation to account for the disappearance and death, as well as to identify and prosecute any perpetrator of unlawful acts in that connection, will generally remain'.[199] In an article 6 case dealing with criminal proceedings that had started prior to the critical date but that continued after it, the Court considered the proceedings as a whole in assessing the issue of fairness. The Court was evaluating safeguards at an early stage in the criminal proceedings so as to assess whether they made up for problems at the trial stage.[200]

In *Blečić v. Croatia*, the Grand Chamber held that where the interference with a right took place prior to the 'critical date' and where a refusal to remedy this occurred subsequently, 'to retain the date of the latter act in determining the Court's temporal jurisdiction would result in the Convention being binding for that State in relation to a fact that had taken place before the Convention came into force in respect of that State. However, this would be contrary to the general rule of non-retroactivity of treaties.'[201] The Grand Chamber explained that 'affording a remedy usually presupposes a finding that the interference was unlawful under the law in force when the interference occurred (*tempus regit actum*). Therefore, any attempt to remedy, on the basis of the Convention, an interference that had ended before the Convention came into force would necessarily lead to its retroactive application.'[202]

Where a procedural right is recognized explicitly, as in article 5(5), it does not fall under the Convention if the infringement on liberty took place before the 'critical date'.[203] But the right to compensation for wrongful conviction, enshrined article 3 of Protocol No. 7, exists as long as the judgment quashing the conviction is after the 'critical date'.[204] If the exercise of the remedy has already begun prior to the 'critical date' and where it continues after, the Court has considered that there is some room for application of the Convention.

---

[197] *Varnava and Others v. Turkey* [GC], nos 16064/90, 16065/90, 16066/90, 16068/90, 16069/90, 16070/90, 16071/90, 16072/90, and 16073/90, § 148, ECHR 2009.

[198] *Ilaşcu and Others v. Moldova and Russia* [GC], no. 48787/99, §§ 407–408, ECHR 2004-VII.

[199] *Palić v. Bosnia and Herzegovina*, no. 4704/04, § 46, 15 February 2011.

[200] *Šilih v. Slovenia* [GC], no. 71463/01, § 143, 9 April 2009; *Barberà, Messegué, and Jabardo v. Spain*, 6 December 1988, §§ 60, 61, and 84, Series A no. 146.

[201] *Blečić v. Croatia* [GC], no. 59532/00, § 79, ECHR 2006-III. Also *Mrkić v. Croatia* (dec.), no. 7118/03, 8 June 2006.

[202] *Blečić v. Croatia* [GC], no. 59532/00, § 80, ECHR 2006-III.

[203] *Korizno v. Latvia* (dec.), no. 68163/01, 28 September 2006; *Iosséliani v. Georgia* (dec.), no. 64803/01, 6 September 2005.

[204] *Matveyev v. Russia*, no. 26601/02, § 38, 3 July 2008.

Following divergences in the case law of the Chambers,[205] in 2009 in *Šilih v. Slovenia* the Grand Chamber confronted the temporal jurisdiction issue with respect to the procedural obligation in a case dealing with medical malpractice. It opted for the more generous approach by which there was a procedural obligation pursuant to article 2 of the Convention, even if the actual killing took place prior to the entry into force of the Convention for the respondent State. By fifteen votes to two, the Grand Chamber held that 'the procedural obligation to carry out an effective investigation under Article 2 has evolved into a separate and autonomous duty' that constitutes 'a detachable obligation arising out of Article 2 capable of binding the State even when the death took place before the critical date'.[206] Nevertheless, the Court said that 'having regard to the principle of legal certainty' this extension of the temporal jurisdiction of the Court was 'not open-ended'.[207] The Grand Chamber explained the limitations it was placing on the procedural obligation:

162. First, it is clear that, where the death occurred before the critical date, only procedural acts and/or omissions occurring after that date can fall within the Court's temporal jurisdiction.

163. Second, there must exist a genuine connection between the death and the entry into force of the Convention in respect of the respondent State for the procedural obligations imposed by Article 2 to come into effect. Thus a significant proportion of the procedural steps required by this provision—which include not only an effective investigation into the death of the person concerned but also the institution of appropriate proceedings for the purpose of determining the cause of the death and holding those responsible to account—will have been or ought to have been carried out after the critical date. However, the Court would not exclude that in certain circumstances the connection could also be based on the need to ensure that the guarantees and the underlying values of the Convention are protected in a real and effective manner.[208]

In this way, the Grand Chamber established an exception within an exception. The Court could only exercise jurisdiction with respect to a violation of the procedural obligation contained in article 2 if a 'significant proportion of the procedural steps' had been undertaken after the 'critical date'. However, this requirement could be waived if 'certain circumstances' required the Court 'to ensure that the guarantees and the underlying values of the Convention are protected in a real and effective manner'. This 'underlying values' exception has sometimes been called the 'humanitarian clause'.[209]

The scope of the 'humanitarian clause' was subsequently constrained by the Grand Chamber in *Janowiec v. Russia* in accordance with article 43 of the Convention. According to the Grand Chamber, the Court could not consider the 'underlying values' exception if the loss of life had taken place prior to 4 November 1950. It held that

---

[205] *Moldovan and Others and Rostaş and Others v. Romania* (dec.), nos 41138/98 and 64320/01, 13 March 2001. Followed by *Moldovan and Others v. Romania (no. 2)*, nos 41138/98 and 64320/01, § 102, ECHR 2005-VII (extracts); *Kholodov and Kholodova v. Russia* (dec.), no. 30651/05, 14 September 2006; *Bălăşoiu v. Romania* (dec.), no. 37424/97, 2 September 2003.

[206] *Šilih v. Slovenia* [GC], no. 71463/01, § 159, 9 April 2009. See E. Bjorge, 'Right for the Wrong Reasons: *Šilih v. Slovenia* and Jurisdiction *Ratione Temporis* in the European Court of Human Rights', (2013) 84 *British Yearbook of International Law* 115.

[207] *Šilih v. Slovenia* [GC], no. 71463/01, § 161, 9 April 2009.

[208] Ibid., §§ 162–163 (interior reference omitted).

[209] For example, *Janowiec and Others v. Russia* [GC], nos 55508/07 and 29520/09, Concurring Opinion of Judge Gyulumyan, 21 October 2013; *Janowiec and Others v. Russia* [GC], nos 55508/07 and 29520/09, Joint Partly Dissenting Opinion of Judges Ziemele, De Gaetano, Laffranque, and Keller, §§ 7, 31, 21 October 2013.

'a Contracting Party cannot be held responsible under the Convention for not investigating even the most serious crimes under international law if they predated the Convention'.[210]

Further reading

J. Altiparmak, 'Banković: An Obstacle to the Application of the European Covnention on Human Rights', (2004) 9 *Journal of Conflict and Security Law* 213.

Natasha Bakirci, *'Al-Skeini and Others v. the United Kingdom* (No. 55721/07)—Grand Chamber Judgment of 7 July 2011', (2012) 1 *Cyprus Human Rights Law Review* 88.

Antoine Buyse, 'A Legal Minefield—The Territorial Scope of the European Convention', (2008) 1 *Inter-American and European Human Rights Journal* 269.

Juan Antonio Carrillo-Salcedo, 'Article 1', in Pettiti et al., *La Convention européenne*, pp. 134–41.

Gérard Cohen-Jonathan, 'La territorialisation de la juridiction de la Cour européenne des droits de l'homme', (2002) 13 *RTDH* 1069.

Gérard Cohen-Jonathan, 'Quelques observations sur les notions de "juridiction" et d'injonction', [2005] *RTDH* 772.

Jean-Paul Costa, 'Qui relève de la juridiction de quell(s) état(s) au sens de l'article 1er de la Convention européenne des droits de l'homme?', in *Libertés, justice, tolerance; Mélanges en homage au Doyen Gérard Cohen-Jonathan*, Brussels: Bruylant, 2004, pp. 483–500.

Karen da Costa, *The Extraterritorial Application of Selected Human Rights Treaties*, Leiden/Boston: Martinus Nijhoff, 2013.

A. Cowen, 'A New Watershed? Reevaluating Banković in Light of Al-Skeini', (2012) 1 *Cambridge Journal of International and Comparative Law* 213.

E. Decaux, 'De l'imprévisibilité de la jurisprudence européenne en matière de droit humanitaire', [2011] *RTDH* 343.

E. Decaux, 'Le territoire des droits de l'homme', in *Liber Amicorum Marc-André Eissen*, Brussels: Bruylant, 1995, pp. 65–78.

Frowein/Peukert, *MenschenRechtsKonvention*, pp. 14–27.

M. Gondek, 'Extraterritorial Application of the European Convention on Human Rights: Territorial Focus in the Age of Globalisation?', (2005) 52 *Netherlands International Law Review* 349.

Grabenwarter, *European Convention*, pp. 1–11.

Matthew Happold, *'Bankovic v. Belgium* and the Territorial Scope of the European Convention on Human Rights', (2003) 3 *HRLR* 77.

Harris et al., *Law of the European Convention*, pp. 37–68.

Corina Heri, 'Enforce Disappearance and the European Court of Human Rights' *ratione temporis* Jurisdiction: A Discussion of Temporal Elements in *Janowiec and Others v. Russia*', (2014) 12 *Journal of International Criminal Justice* 751.

Matthias Klatt, 'Positive Obligations under the European Convention on Human Rights', (2011) 71 *ZaöRV* 691.

Rick Lawson, 'Life After *Bankovic*: On the Extraterritorial Application of the European Convention on Human Rights', in Fons Coomans and Menno Kamminga, eds, *Extraterritorial Application of Human Rights Treaties*, Antwerp: Intersentia, 2004, pp. 83–92.

L. Lijnzaad, 'Trouble in Tiraspol, Some Reflections on the *Ilascu* Case and the Territorial Scope of the European Convention on Human Rights', (2002) 15 *Hague Yearbook of International Law* 23.

---

[210] *Janowiec and Others v. Russia* [GC], nos 55508/07 and 29520/09, §§ 151, 21 October 2013. See Corina Heri, 'Enforce Disappearance and the European Court of Human Rights' *ratione temporis* Jurisdiction: A Discussion of Temporal Elements in *Janowiec and Others v. Russia*', (2014) 12 *Journal of International Criminal Justice* 751.

L. Loucaides, 'Determining the Extra-territorial Effect of the European Convention: Facts, Jurisprudence and the *Banković* Case', [2006] *European Human Rights Law Review* 391.

Marko Milanovic, 'From Compromise to Principle: Clarifying the Concept of State Jurisdiction in Human Rights Treaties', (2008) 8 *HRLJ* 411.

Marko Milanovic, 'Al-Skeini and Al-Jedda in Strasbourg', (2012) 23 *European Journal of International Law* 121.

Alastair Mowbray, *The Development of Positive Obligations under the European Convention on Human Rights by the European Court of Human Rights*, Oxford: Hart, 2004.

M. O'Boyle, 'The European Convention on Human Rights and Extraterritorial Jurisdiction', in Fons Coomans and Menno Kamminga, eds, *Extraterritorial Application of Human Rights Treaties*, Antwerp: Intersentia, 2004, pp. 128–45.

Alexander Orekashvili, 'Restrictive Interpretation of Human Rights Treaties in the Recent Jurisprudence of the European Court of Human Rights', (2003) 14 *European Journal of International Law* 529.

Ovey/White, *Jacobs and White, European Convention*, pp. 42–57.

M.P. Pedersen, 'Territorial Jurisdiction in Article 1 of the European Convention on Human Rights', (2004) 73 *Nordic Journal of International Law*.

G. Ress, 'State Responsibility for Extraterritorial Human Rights Violations. The Case of Bankovic', (2003) 6 *Zeitschrift für Europarechtliche Studien* 73.

Christos L. Rozakis, 'The Contribution of the European Court of Human Rights to the Development of the Law on State Immunity', in Lucius Caflisch, Johan Callewaert, Roderick Liddell, Paul Mahoney, and Mark Villiger, eds, *Liber Amicorum Luzius Wildhaber*, Kehl, Germany: N.P. Engel, 2007, pp. 387–402.

Christos L. Rozakis, 'How Far Can We Go? Recent Developments of Strasbourg Case-Law on the Concept of Jurisdiction', in Lucius Caflisch, R. Bermejo Garcia, J. Diez-Hochleitner, and C. Gutiérrez, eds, *Il derecho internactional: normas, hechos y valores. Liber Amicorum José Antonio Pastor ridruejo*, Madrid: Universidad Complutense, 2005, pp. 209–27.

William Schabas, 'Do the "Underlying Values" of the European Convention on Human Rights Begin in 1950?', (2013) 33 *Polish Yearbook of International Law* 247.

Carsten Stahn and Larissa van den Herik, '"Fragmentation", Diversification and "3D" Legal Pluralism: International Criminal Law as the Jack-in-the-Box?', in Larissa van den Herik and Carsten Stahn, eds, *The Diversification and Fragmentation of International Criminal Law*, Leiden/Boston: Martinus Nijhoff, 2012, pp. 21–89.

Paul Tavernier, 'La Cour européenne des droits de l'Homme et la mer', in *La mer et son droit: Mélanges offerts à Laurent Lucchini et Jean-Pierre Quéneudec*, Paris: Pedone, 2003, pp. 575–89.

Nina Vajić, 'Before . . . and After: *Ratione Temporis* Jurisdiction of the (New) European Court of Human Rights and the Blečić case', in Lucius Caflisch, Johan Callewaert, Roderick Liddell, Paul Mahoney, and Mark Villiger, eds, *Liber Amicorum Luzius Wildhaber*, Kehl, Germany: N.P. Engel, 2007, pp. 483–506.

Ralph Wilde, 'The "Legal Space" or "Espace Juridique" of the European Convention on Human Rights: Is it Relevant to Extraterritorial State Action?', [2005] *EHRLR* 115.

Dimitrris Xenos, *The Positive Obligations of the State under the European Convention of Human Rights*, Abingdon, UK: Routledge, 2012.

Inete Ziemele, 'International Courts and *Ultra Vires* Acts', in Lucius Caflisch, Johan Callewaert, Roderick Liddell, Paul Mahoney, and Mark Villiger, eds, *Liber Amicorum Luzius Wildhaber*, Kehl, Germany: N.P. Engel, 2007, pp. 537–56.

Leo Zwaak, 'Right to Life (Article 2)', in Van Dijk et al., *Theory and Practice*, pp. 351–403.

SECTION I

RIGHTS AND FREEDOMS

Article 2. Right to life/Droit à la vie

1. Everyone's right to life shall be protected by law. No one shall be deprived of his life intentionally save in the execution of a sentence of a court following his conviction of a crime for which this penalty is provided by law.

2. Deprivation of life shall not be regarded as inflicted in contravention of this article when it results from the use of force which is no more than absolutely necessary:

(a) in defence of any person from unlawful violence;

(b) in order to effect a lawful arrest or to prevent the escape of a person lawfully detained;

(c) in action lawfully taken for the purpose of quelling a riot or insurrection.

1. Le droit de toute personne à la vie est protégé par la loi. La mort ne peut être infligée à quiconque intentionnellement, sauf en exécution d'une sentence capitale prononcée par un tribunal au cas où le délit est puni de cette peine par la loi.

2. La mort n'est pas considérée comme infligée en violation de cet article dans les cas où elle résulterait d'un recours à la force rendu absolument nécessaire:

a) pour assurer la défense de toute personne contre la violence illégale;

b) pour effectuer une arrestation régulière ou pour empêcher l'évasion d'une personne régulièrement détenue;

c) pour réprimer, conformément à la loi, une émeute ou une insurrection.

Introductory comments

The 'right to life' has been described as 'the supreme right',[1] 'one of the most important rights',[2] and as 'one of the rights which constitute the irreducible core of human rights'.[3] Basic as it appears, it is at the same time intangible in scope and vexingly difficult to define with precision. Its content is continuously evolving, in step with the hegemony of ever more progressive attitudes to capital punishment, nuclear arms, abortion, and euthanasia, to mention only a few of the many issues that have figured in the interpretation and application of article 2 of the European Convention. The case law is almost entirely of recent vintage. The European Court of Human Rights did not issue a decision on the merits with respect to article 2 of the Convention until 1995.[4] At the time, the European Commission of Human Rights, which by then had been in operation for four decades, had yet to make a finding of a violation of article 2. In 1996, the Commission held that the right to life had been violated in a case involving the use of lethal force by the authorities.[5]

---

[1] General Comment 6(16), UN Doc. CCPR/C/21/Add.1, also published as UN Doc. A/37/40, Annex V, UN Doc. CCPR/3/Add.1, at pp. 382–3. See also *de Guerrero v. Columbia* (No. 45/1979), UN Doc. CCPR/OP/1, p. 112, at p. 117.

[2] *Stewart v. the United Kingdom*, no. 10044/82, Commission decision of 10 July 1984, (1984) 27 YB 129, DR 39, p. 162.

[3] *Legality of the Threat or Use of Nuclear Weapons*, Advisory Opinion, I.C.J. Reports 1996, p. 226, Dissenting Opinion of Judge Weeramantry, at p. 506.

[4] *McCann and Others v. the United Kingdom*, 27 September 1995, Series A no. 324.

[5] *Andreas and Pareskevoula Andronicou and Yiolanda Constantinou v. Cyprus*, no. 25052/94, § 190, Commission report of 23 May 1996.

In its final years, the Commission concluded that the right to life had been violated in a string of Turkish cases.[6]

The right to life, enshrined in article 2, is often linked with the prohibition of torture and inhuman or degrading treatment or punishment, set out in article 3. The two provisions confront some of the most dire threats to bodily integrity. The relationship is not without its mysteries, however. Article 3 is often presented as an absolute prohibition. It is so fundamental that it brooks no exceptions. By contrast, a mere reading of article 2 indicates the central role that exceptions play in our understanding of the right to life. The State cannot torture but it can kill, in a myriad of ways, including law enforcement, military action, and the death penalty. It cannot permit others to torture, yet it can permit deprivations of the right to life by others, in the course of self-defence, or negligent acts and even, perhaps, in the exercise of mercy.

Although it was recognized in national constitutions as early as the eighteenth century, the first formulations of the right to life in international law appear in some of the post-First-World-War treaties. For example, the treaty that revived the State of Poland out of the remnants of the Russian, Prussian, and Austrian empires began, in article 2, with the following: 'Poland undertakes to assure full and complete protection of life and liberty to all inhabitants of Poland without distinction of birth, nationality, language, race or religion.'[7] The direct ancestor of article 2 is, of course, article 3 of the Universal Declaration of Human Rights: 'Everyone has the right to life, liberty and security of person.' Article 6 of the International Covenant on Civil and Political Rights develops more detailed norms on certain aspects of the right to life:

1. Every human being has the inherent right to life. This right shall be protected by law. No one shall be arbitrarily deprived of his life.
2. In countries which have not abolished the death penalty, sentence of death may be imposed only for the most serious crimes in accordance with the law in force at the time of the commission of the crime and not contrary to the provisions of the present Covenant and to the Convention on the Prevention and Punishment of the Crime of Genocide. This penalty can only be carried out pursuant to a final judgment rendered by a competent court.
3. When deprivation of life constitutes the crime of genocide, it is understood that nothing in this article shall authorize any State Party to the present Covenant to derogate in any way from any obligation assumed under the provisions of the Convention on the Prevention and Punishment of the Crime of Genocide.
4. Anyone sentenced to death shall have the right to seek pardon or commutation of the sentence. Amnesty, pardon or commutation of the sentence of death may be granted in all cases.
5. Sentence of death shall not be imposed for crimes committed by persons below eighteen years of age and shall not be carried out on pregnant women.
6. Nothing in this article shall be invoked to delay or to prevent the abolition of capital punishment by any State Party to the present Covenant.

---

[6] E.g., *Kaya v. Turkey*, no. 22729/93, Commission report of 24 October 1996; *Yaşa v. Turkey*, no. 22495/93, Commission report of 8 April 1997; *Ergi v. Turkey*, no. 23818/94, Commission report of 20 May 1997.

[7] Treaty of Peace between the United States of America, the British Empire, France, Italy and Japan, and Poland, [1919] TS 8. Also Treaty of Saint-Germain-en-Laye, [1919] TS 11, art. 63; Treaty of Peace between the Principal Allied and Associated Powers and the Serb-Croat-Slovene State, [1919] TS 17, art. 2; Treaty between the Principal Allied and Associated Powers and Roumania, (1921) 5 LNTS 336, art. 1; Treaty between the Principal Allied and Associated Powers and Czechoslovakia, [1919] TS 20, art. 1.

The Grand Chamber of the European Court of Human Rights has noted that 'the pre-eminence of the right to life' has been constantly reaffirmed in relevant conventions and instruments, citing in this respect article 3 of the Universal Declaration of Human Rights, as well as article 6 of the International Covenant on Civil and Political Rights.[8] The convergence of these instruments on the subject is 'significant' as it 'indicates that the right to life is an inalienable attribute of human beings and forms the supreme value in the hierarchy of human rights'.[9]

The European Charter of Fundamental Rights proclaims the right to life in the following terms:

Article 2. Right to life
1. Everyone has the right to life.
2. No one shall be condemned to the death penalty, or executed.

The provision is meant to have the same meaning and scope as article 2 of the European Convention.[10]

Drafting of the provision

The initial draft European Convention on Human Rights was prepared by the International Juridical Section of the European Movement, chaired by Pierre-Henri Teitgen, with David Maxwell Fyfe and Fernand Dehousse as rapporteurs. Both Maxwell Fyfe and Dehousse had been involved in the adoption of the Universal Declaration of Human Rights by the United Nations the previous year. But contrary to what might have been expected, this first draft of the European Convention did not closely follow the right to life provision in the Universal Declaration ('Everyone has the right to life, liberty and security of person'). The enumeration of rights in the draft began: 'Every State a party to this Convention shall guarantee to all persons within its territory the following rights: a) Security of life and limb.'[11]

Asked to prepare a text for discussion in the Committee on Legal and Administrative Questions at the first session of the Consultative Assembly, held from 22 August to 5 September 1949, Teitgen proposed the following: 'Security of person, in accordance with Articles 3, 5 and 8 of the Universal Declaration of Human Rights adopted by the United Nations General Assembly.'[12] At its sitting of 29 August 1949, the Committee on Legal and Administrative Questions accepted inclusion of 'the safety of the person, as laid down

---

[8] *Streletz, Kessler and Krenz v. Germany* [GC], nos 34044/96, 35532/97, and 44801/98, §§ 92–93, ECHR 2001-II; *K.-H.W. v. Germany* [GC], no. 37201/97, §§ 94–95, ECHR 2001-II (extracts).

[9] *Streletz, Kessler and Krenz v. Germany* [GC], nos 34044/96, 35532/97, and 44801/98, § 94, ECHR 2001-II; *K.-H.W. v. Germany* [GC], no. 37201/97, § 96, ECHR 2001-II (extracts).

[10] Explanation relating to the Charter of Fundamental Rights, Official Journal of the European Union, C 303/33, 14 December 2007.

[11] Convention for the Collective Protection of Individual Rights and Democratic Liberties by the States, Members of the Council of Europe, and for the establishment of a European Court of Human Rights to ensure observance of the Convention, Doc. INF/5/E/R, I *TP* 296–303, at p. 296, art. I(a). On the drafting history of the right to life provision of the European Convention, see Bertrand G. Ramcharan, 'The Drafting History of Article 2 of the European Convention on Human Rights', in Bertrand G. Ramcharan, ed., *The Right to Life in International Law*, Dordrecht/Boston/Lancaster: Martinus Nijhoff, 1985, pp. 57–61; Jacques Velu and Rusen Ergec, *La Convention européenne des droits de l'homme*, Brussels: Bruylant, 1990, pp. 169–71; Alphonse Spielman, 'La Convention européenne des droits de l'homme et la peine de mort', in *Présence du droit public et les droits de l'homme, Mélanges offerts à Jacques Vélu*, Brussels: Bruylant, 1992, pp. 1503–27.

[12] Proposals by Mr P.H. Teitgen, Rapporteur, 29 August 1949, Doc. A 116, I *TP* 166–8.

in Articles 3, 5 and 8 of the Universal Declaration on [sic] Human Rights'.[13] The word 'safety' was an awkward translation of the French *sûreté* and was changed to 'security', the term used in article 3 of the Universal Declaration of Human Rights, in the final report adopted by the Committee: 'Security of person, in accordance with Articles 3, 5 and 8 of the United Nations Declaration'.[14] The Consultative Assembly adopted the text proposed by the Committee.[15]

At the first meeting of the Committee of Experts, the United Kingdom tabled a more elaborate text containing an autonomous right to life provision and making specific provision for use of the death penalty:

1. No one shall be deprived of his life intentionally save in the execution of the sentence of the court following his conviction of a crime for which his penalty is defined by law.
2. Deprivation of life shall not be regarded as intentional when it results from the use of force, which is no more than absolutely necessary
   a) in defence of any person from unlawful violence;
   b) in order to effect a lawful arrest or to prevent an escape from lawful custody,
   c) any action lawfully taken for the purpose of quelling a riot or insurrection or for prohibiting entry to clearly defined places to which access is forbidden on grounds of national security.[16]

The provision was almost identical to a proposal for the right to life provision of the draft covenant that had been submitted by the United Kingdom to the United Nations Commission on Human Rights.[17] But at the conclusion of its first session, the Committee of Experts adopted a text derived from article 3 of the Universal Declaration of Human Rights: 'Everyone has the right to life, liberty and security of person.'[18] At the second session of the Committee of Experts, in March 1950, the United Kingdom representative submitted a slightly different proposal, with minor changes that were entirely stylistic:

1. No one shall be deprived of his life intentionally save in the execution of a sentence of a court following his conviction of a crime for which this penalty is defined by law.
2. Deprivation of life shall not be regarded as intentional when it results from the use of force which is no more than absolutely necessary
   a) in defence of any person from unlawful violence;
   b) in order to effect lawful arrest or to prevent an escape from lawful custody,
   c) in action lawfully taken for the purpose of quelling a riot or insurrection or for prohibiting entry to a clearly defined place to which access is forbidden on grounds of national security.[19]

---

[13] Minutes of the Sitting [of the Committee for Legal and Administrative Affairs of the Consultative Assembly, 29 August 1949], Doc. A 142, I *TP* 170–3, at p. 172.

[14] Report presented by Mr P.H. Teitgen, 5 September 1949, Doc. A 290, I *TP* 192–213, at p. 206. See also Report [of the Committee on Legal and Administrative Questions], 5 September 1949, Doc. AS (1) 77, I *TP* 216–39, at p. 228.

[15] Recommendation No. 38 to the Committee of Ministers adopted 8 September 1949 on the conclusion of the debates, Doc. AS (1) 108, II *TP* 274–83, at p. 276.

[16] Amendment to Article 2 of the Recommendation of the Consultative Assembly proposed by the expert of the United Kingdom, Doc. A 779, III *TP* 186.

[17] UN Doc. E/CN.4/188; UN Doc. E/CN.4/204; UN Doc. E/CN.4/353/Add.2; UN Doc. E/CN.4/365, at p. 23. The text is reproduced in III *TP* 158.

[18] Preliminary Draft Convention for the Maintenance and Further Realisation of Human Rights and Fundamental Freedoms, 15 February 1950, Doc. A 833, III *TP* 236–46, at p. 236. Also Draft text of the first section of a draft Convention based on the work of the Consultative Assembly, Doc. A 809, III *TP* 220–31, at p. 222.

[19] Amendments to Articles 1, 2, 4, 5, 6, 8, and 9 of the Committee's preliminary draft proposal by the expert of the United Kingdom, Doc. CM/WP 1 (50) 2, A 915, III *TP* 280–9, at p. 282.

The Committee of Experts concluded its work with the submission to the Committee of Ministers of two different drafts. The first, 'Alternatives A and A/2', consisted of the laconic text adopted by the Committee of Experts at the first session.[20] The second, labelled 'Alternatives B and B/2', contained the text that had been proposed by the United Kingdom.[21]

The Conference of Senior Officials that convened in June 1950 assigned a Drafting Committee to attempt to reconcile the competing versions. It prepared a new formulation of the right to life with a first paragraph that was inspired by the text of article 3 of the Universal Declaration of Human Rights, followed by a slightly modified version of the British proposal in the Committee of Experts. In particular, the reference at the very end of the British text to the prohibition of entry on grounds of national security was removed:

1. Everyone's right to life shall be protected by law.
2. No one shall be deprived of his life intentionally, save in the execution of a sentence of a court following his conviction of a crime for which this penalty is provided by law.
3. Deprivation of life shall not be regarded as a contravention of the preceding paragraph when it results from the use of force which is no more than absolutely necessary:
   a) in defence of any person from unlawful violence;
   b) in order to effect lawful arrest or to prevent an escape from lawful custody;
   c) in action lawfully taken for the purpose of quelling a riot or insurrection.[22]

The Conference adopted it without change.[23]

The draft text of article 2 was modified slightly by a Sub-Committee of the Committee of Ministers at its fifth session, in early August 1950. The text in the first paragraph was combined with the second paragraph. The words 'as a contravention of the preceding paragraph' in paragraph 3 were changed to 'in contravention of this Article'. With these changes accepted, the Committee of Ministers adopted the revised text of article 2.[24]

There were no further modifications of the text, and the version confirmed at the fifth session of the Committee of Ministers is the definitive one. During the August 1950 session of the Consultative Assembly, Giovanni Persico of Italy described the right-to-life provision as 'the basic Article of the Convention'. He said '[t]hat is as it should be', but went on to insist that 'something else needed to be added'. He proposed that the right-to-life provision be followed by a distinct article setting out the following: 'Genocide, whether committed in time of peace or war, is a crime under International Law, the perpetrators of which must be charged and punished in accordance with the Convention

[20] Report to the Committee of Ministers Submitted by the Committee of Experts Instructed to Draw Up a Draft Convention of Collective Guarantee of Human Rights and Fundamental Freedoms, Doc. CM/WP 1 (5) 15, A 924, IV *TP* 2–55, at p. 52. See also Preliminary Draft Convention, Doc. CM/WP 1 (50) 14, A 932, III *TP* 312–35, at p. 320.

[21] Report to the Committee of Ministers Submitted by the Committee of Experts Instructed to Draw Up a Draft Convention of Collective Guarantee of Human Rights and Fundamental Freedoms, Doc. CM/WP 1 (5) 15, A 924, IV *TP* 2–55, at p. 58. See also Preliminary Draft Convention, Doc. CM/WP 1 (50) 14, A 932, III *TP* 312–35, at pp. 312–14.

[22] New draft alternatives B and B/2, Doc. CM/WP 4 (50) 9, A 1372, IV *TP* 182–91, at pp. 182–4.

[23] Draft Convention appended to the draft report, Doc. CM/WP 4 (50) 16, appendix, A 1445, IV *TP* 218–40, at p. 218; Draft Convention annexed to the report, Doc. CM/WP 4 (50) 19 annex, CM/WP 4 (50) 16 rev., A 1452, IV *TP* 274–95, at p. 274.

[24] Draft Convention adopted by the Sub-Committee, Doc. CM 1 (50) 52, A 1884, V *TP* 76–99, at p. 76; Draft Convention adopted by the Committee of Ministers, 7 August 1950, Doc. A 1937, V *TP* 120–45, at pp. 120–2.

approved by UNO on 9 December 1948.'[25] Persico later withdrew the amendment on the condition that reference was made to it in the report.[26] In effect, the report refers to the motion, noting that 'every speaker expressed his abhorrence of the crime' of genocide but that 'the Committee thought that at present that subject could be more suitably dealt with by a motion in the Assembly'.[27]

The heading of article 2 ('Right to life/Droit à la vie') was added pursuant to the provisions of Protocol No. 11.[28]

Analysis and interpretation

Article 2 has been described by the Court as one of 'the most fundamental provisions in the Convention', a text that 'enshrine[s] the basic values of the democratic societies making up the Council of Europe'.[29] It is to be interpreted and applied 'so as to make its safeguards practical and effective'.[30] The Court must be 'especially vigilant' in right-to-life cases.[31] The Grand Chamber has spoken of 'the principle of strict proportionality inherent in Article 2'.[32]

The first paragraph of article 2 sets out the general principle of the protection of the right to life: 'Everyone's right to life shall be protected by law.' It also specifies, in the second sentence, that intentional deprivation of life is not permitted 'save in the execution of a sentence of a court following his conviction of a crime for which this penalty is provided by law'. Thus, paragraph 1 of article 2 has both positive and negative dimensions. Not only must the State refrain from 'intentionally' depriving a person of life, it must also 'take appropriate steps to safeguard the lives of those within its jurisdiction'.[33] This 'flows from the wording and structure of Article 2'.[34] Paragraph 1 addresses substantive violations of the right to life when persons are killed or when loss of life is threatened. It also has a procedural dimension, requiring the State to conduct investigations into killings and, where appropriate, to proceed with criminal justice and other measures to deal with those responsible. Paragraph 1 contemplates the death penalty as the sole exception to the principles that it sets out.

Paragraph 2 lists three additional exceptions to the first sentence of article 2(1). These three enumerated exceptions are not primarily concerned with permissible intentional killing but rather with the use of force that is necessary for legitimate ends but that may have deprivation of life as an unintended outcome.[35] Use of lethal force within

---

[25] Proposed by Mr Persico, Doc. AS/JA (2) 2, A 2134, VI *TP* 2–3. Also Report of the sitting [of the Consultative Assembly, 14 August 1950], V *TP* 216–71, at p. 258.

[26] Minutes of the sitting [of the Consultative Assembly, 23 August 1950], VI *TP* 36–59.

[27] Ibid., p. 64.

[28] Protocol No. 11 to the Convention for the Protection of Human Rights and Fundamental Freedoms, restructuring the control machinery established thereby, ETS 155, art. 2(2).

[29] *Šilih v. Slovenia* [GC], no. 71463/01, § 147, 9 April 2009.

[30] *McCann and Others v. the United Kingdom*, 27 September 1995, § 146, Series A no. 324.

[31] *Giuliani and Gaggio* v. *Italy*, no. 23458/02, § 182, 24 March 2011.

[32] Ibid., § 209.

[33] *L.C.B. v. the United Kingdom*, 9 June 1998, § 36, *Reports of Judgments and Decisions* 1998-III.

[34] *Stewart v. the United Kingdom*, no. 10044/82, Commission decision of 10 July 1984, § 15, (1984) 27 YB 129, DR 39, p. 162.

[35] *Giuliani and Gaggio v. Italy*, no. 23458/02, § 175, 24 March 2011.

the context of paragraph 2 must be no more than is 'absolutely necessary' to achieve the purpose.[36]

The applicable standard of proof under article 2 is 'beyond reasonable doubt'.[37] This formulation is familiar to jurists, especially from common law systems, and it has been incorporated into the Rome Statute of the International Criminal Court.[38] But when the European Court refers to 'beyond reasonable doubt', it is not borrowing the notion from national legal systems. The Court rules on the responsibility of States under the Convention and on criminal guilt or civil liability.[39] Evidence that meets the reasonable doubt standard may 'follow from the coexistence of sufficiently strong, clear and concordant inferences or of similar unrebutted presumptions of fact. In this context, the conduct of the parties when evidence is being obtained has to be taken into account.'[40] Some right-to-life cases do not 'lend themselves to a rigorous application of the principle whereby a person who alleges something must prove that allegation'.[41] Thus, the burden of proof will shift depending upon the circumstances. According to the Court, 'where the events in issue lie wholly or in large part within the exclusive knowledge of the authorities, as in the case of persons under their control in detention, strong presumptions of fact will arise in respect of injuries and death occurring during that detention. The burden of proof may be regarded as resting on the authorities to provide a satisfactory and convincing explanation.'[42] If the authorities do not provide full access to information in their control, the Court may draw inferences from the government's conduct.[43] Presumptions are of special importance with respect to article 2 in forced disappearance cases.[44] When an individual is taken into custody by the authorities, the failure to provide 'a plausible explanation as to a detainee's fate, in the absence of a body' may, depending upon the circumstances of the case, support the presumption of death.[45] The period of time in detention is relevant, although not decisive. Certainly, 'the more time goes by without any news of the detained person, the greater the likelihood that he or she has died'.[46]

[36] *McCann and Others v. the United Kingdom*, 27 September 1995, § 148, Series A no. 324; *Solomou and Others v. Turkey*, no. 36832/97, § 64, 24 June 2008.

[37] *Ireland v. the United Kingdom*, 18 January 1978, § 161, Series A no. 25; *Orhan v. Turkey*, no. 25656/94, § 264, ECHR 2002; *Avşar v. Turkey*, no. 25657/94, § 282, ECHR 2001-VII; *Kleyn and Aleksandrovich v. Russia*, no. 40657/04, § 49, 3 May 2012.

[38] Rome Statute of the International Criminal Court, (2002) 2187 UNTS 90, art. 66(3).

[39] *Al Nashiri v. Poland*, no. 28761/11, § 394, 24 July 2014; *Nachova and Others v. Bulgaria* [GC], nos 43577/98 and 43579/98, § 147, ECHR 2005-VII; *Creangă v. Romania* [GC], no. 29226/03, § 88, 23 February 2012.

[40] *Tsechoyev v. Russia*, no. 39358/05, § 128, 15 March 2011; *Tanış and Others v. Turkey*, no. 65899/01, § 160, ECHR 2005-VIII.

[41] *Bazorkina v. Russia*, no. 69481/01, § 170, 27 July 2006.

[42] *Shchebetov v. Russia*, no. 21731/02, § 44, 10 April 2012; *Çakıcı v. Turkey* [GC], no. 23657/94, § 85, ECHR 1999-IV; *Salman v. Turkey* [GC], no. 21986/93, § 100, ECHR 2000-VII; *Anguelova v. Bulgaria*, no. 38361/97, §§ 109–11, ECHR 2002-IV; *Carabulea v. Romania*, no. 45661/99, § 109, 13 July 2010; *Beker v. Turkey*, no. 27866/03, §§ 41–42, 24 March 2009; *Mosendz v. Ukraine*, no. 52013/08, §§ 96–114, 17 January 2013.

[43] *Zabiyeva and Others v. Russia*, no. 35052/04, § 87, 17 September 2009.

[44] See Helen Keller and Corina Heri, 'Enforced Disappearance and the European Court of Human Rights', (2014) 12 *Journal of International Criminal Justice* 735.

[45] *Timurtaş v. Turkey*, no. 23531/94, § 82, ECHR 2000-VI.

[46] Ibid., § 83.

'Everyone': Beneficiaries of the right to life

Article 2 begins with the word 'Everyone's' (*toute personne*). The word is used in several other provisions of the Convention affirming fundamental rights. The principal reference here is article 1, which secures the rights in the Convention to 'everyone', but the term is also used in articles 5, 6, 8–11, and 13. It has particular salience with respect to the right to life because of the debate about whether it extends to the unborn child. The Universal Declaration of Human Rights hints at an exclusion of the unborn in the opening words of article 1: 'All human beings are born...' But article 25(2) of the Declaration might be taken to imply the opposite in its reference to the protection of 'motherhood'. By contrast with the European Convention, article 4 of the American Convention on Human Rights protects life 'in general, from the moment of conception', as the European Court of Human Rights has observed.[47]

According to the Court, it is 'neither desirable nor possible to answer the question of whether the unborn was a person for the purposes of Article 2 of the Convention'.[48] In a very early decision, the European Commission of Human Rights suggested that the right to life of the foetus might be protected by article 2 'in certain circumstances... notwithstanding that there is in the Contracting States a considerable divergence of views on whether or to what extent Article 2 protects the unborn life'.[49] Later, it declined to take a firm view on whether article 2 applied to the unborn child, although it said that both the general usage of the term 'everyone' in the Convention and the context of article 2 'tend to support the view that it does not include the unborn'.[50] It excluded an interpretation of article 2 by which it provided the foetus with an 'absolute' right to life.[51] The European Commission considered that even if the foetus was protected by article 2, this could not outweigh the right to life of the mother, which was also entitled to protection,[52] a position confirmed by the Court.[53] The Grand Chamber has held that stored embryos not yet implanted in the uterus cannot benefit from the protection of article 2.[54]

The current position is that 'the issue of when the right to life begins comes within the margin of appreciation which the Court generally considers that States should enjoy in this sphere'.[55] This also 'translates into a margin of appreciation for that State as to how it balances the conflicting rights of the mother'.[56] However, it would be misleading to suggest that the Court is neutral or indifferent on the issue of abortion. While acknowledging the lack of a 'common approach regarding the beginning of life', the Court has acknowledged that 'there is indeed a consensus amongst a substantial majority of the Contracting States of the Council of Europe towards allowing abortion and that most Contracting Parties have in their legislation resolved the conflicting rights of the foetus and the mother in favour of greater access to abortion'.[57] Indeed, in abortion cases the

[47] *Vo v. France* [GC], no. 53924/00, § 75, ECHR 2004-VIII.
[48] *A, B, and C v. Ireland* [GC], no. 25579/05, § 222, ECHR 2010.
[49] *X v. Norway*, no. 867/60, Commission decision of 29 May 1961, Collection 6, p. 34.
[50] *X v. the United Kingdom*, no. 8416/79, § 9, Commission decision of 13 May 1980, DR 19, p. 244.
[51] Ibid., § 18.
[52] Ibid., §§ 19–20.
[53] *Boso v. Italy* (dec.), no. 50490/99, ECHR 2002-VII.
[54] *Evans v. the United Kingdom* [GC], no. 6339/05, § 56, ECHR 2007-I.
[55] *Vo v. France* [GC], no. 53924/00, § 82, ECHR 2004-VIII.
[56] *A, B, and C v. Ireland* [GC], no. 25579/05, § 237, ECHR 2010.
[57] *P. and S. v. Poland*, no. 57375/08, § 97, 30 October 2012.

mother's right to life may also be threatened to the extent that she may be denied appropriate access to measures in order to terminate a pregnancy. This was raised in an Irish case, but the Court considered that the right-to-life issue could not be sustained because it was possible for the woman to travel abroad and obtain an abortion.[58] The Court's approach with respect to article 2 has enabled it to deal with the issue of abortion within the context of the right of a pregnant woman to private life enshrined in article 8.[59] In a French case, the Grand Chamber gave two reasons for invoking the margin of appreciation. First, the issue of protecting the unborn child has not been resolved within the majority of Contracting States, in particular in France, and secondly, Europe lacks a 'consensus on the scientific and legal definition of the beginning of life'.[60] In an Irish case, the Court spoke of 'the impossibility of finding a uniform European conception of morals including on the question of when life begins'.[61]

Article 2 may apply even if there has not been loss of life, but where 'the circumstances of the case and the nature of inflicted injuries indicate that the applicant's life was in serious danger'.[62] The reasoning seems to be that the text of article 2 covers not only intentional killing but also situations where force may result in unintended deprivation of life.[63] Where potentially lethal force is used, article 2 is engaged even if the victim does not die. This seems to open up the provision uncontrollably, but the Court has said that only in exceptional circumstances can physical ill-treatment by State agents not resulting in death disclose a violation of article 2.[64] According to the Court, 'the degree and type of force used and the intention or aim behind the use of force may, among other factors, be relevant in assessing whether in a particular case the State agents' actions in inflicting injury short of death are such as to bring the facts within the scope of the safeguard afforded by Article 2'.[65] Resort to force is deemed to be potentially lethal when public officials use firearms that are directed at an individual who is wounded, and the fact that they did not intend to kill the victim is irrelevant.[66]

But article 2 has been applied in cases where the victim did not die even when the force was not attributable to State agents. For example, the Court held article 2 applicable when, following a traffic accident, an applicant was in a coma for several years, then became severely disabled and completely lost personal autonomy.[67] The Court also found there had been a violation of article 2 when a woman and her children were withdrawn from a witness protection programme, making them vulnerable to life-threatening reprisal attacks by organized crime.[68] Article 2 was engaged as a result of life-threatening injuries to minor children who entered premises housing an electronic transformer and who

[58] *A, B, and C v. Ireland* [GC], no. 25579/05, § 159, ECHR 2010.
[59] *Brüggemann and Scheuten v. Federal Republic of Germany*, no. 6959/75, Commission report of 12 July 1977, DR 10, p. 100.
[60] *Vo v. France* [GC], no. 53924/00, § 82, ECHR 2004-VIII.
[61] *A, B, and C v. Ireland* [GC], no. 25579/05, § 222, ECHR 2010.
[62] *Krivova v. Ukraine*, no. 25732/05, § 45, 9 November 2010.
[63] *Makaratzis v. Greece* [GC], no. 50385/99, § 49, ECHR 2004-XI. Also *Ilhan v. Turkey* [GC], no. 22277/93, § 75, ECHR 2000-VII.
[64] *Makaratzis v. Greece*, [GC], no. 50385/99, § 49, ECHR 2004-XI.
[65] Ibid., § 51.
[66] *Trévalec v. Belgium*, no. 30812/07, §§ 58–59, 14 June 2011.
[67] *Igor Shevchenko v. Ukraine*, no. 22737/04, § 43, 12 January 2012.
[68] *R.R. and Others v. Hungary*, no. 19400/11, § 32, 4 December 2012.

were electrocuted.[69] It also applied to a prisoner who contracted HIV/AIDS while in detention[70] and to a prisoner with AIDS who argued that denial of compassionate release had shortened his life,[71] and where persons who had received blood transfusions were contaminated.[72] However, where inadequate regulation of deep-sea diving created risks to health that were not life-threatening, the Court preferred to consider the matter under article 8 and not article 2.[73]

A presumption of death may arise in the case of missing persons. The Court has said that such a presumption is 'not automatic and is only reached on examination of the circumstances of the case, in which the lapse of time since the person was seen alive or heard from is a relevant element'.[74] Generally, the presumption has applied when governments claim that a person is still alive or that there is insufficient evidence of official involvement in the disappearance.[75] The procedural obligation associated with article 2, discussed below, is of particular relevance in such cases. It will continue even when death is proven or presumed because the obligation 'to account for the disappearance and death, and to identify and prosecute any perpetrator of unlawful acts in that connection, will generally remain'.[76]

'Protected by law': Positive obligations

The obligation of the State with respect to the right to life has both negative and positive dimensions. In a negative sense, the State must refrain from deprivation of life of the individual except in the case of the death penalty, as well as the other exceptions set out in paragraph 2 of article 2 and the exceptions that are implicit. The positive obligations result from the requirement that the right to life be 'protected by law'. But the manner in which article 2 has been interpreted indicates that the obligation is far more extensive. In effect, not only must the State 'protect by law' the right to life, it must also pursue policy measures aimed at its respect and fulfilment.

States must take 'appropriate steps to safeguard the lives of those within their jurisdiction'.[77] This involves a 'primary duty' to put in place an 'appropriate legal and administrative framework to deter the commission of offences against the person, backed up by law enforcement machinery for the prevention, suppression and punishment of breaches of such provisions'.[78] Several features of the positive obligation to protect the right to life

---

[69] *Petrov v. Bulgaria*, no. 19202/03, § 64, 24 April 2012.

[70] *Gorelov v. Russia*, no. 49072/11, §§ 50–51, 9 January 2014.

[71] *William Grice v. the United Kingdom*, no. 22564/93, Commission decision of 14 April 1994.

[72] *Karchen and Others v. France* (dec.), no. 5722/04, 4 March 2008; *G.N. and Others v. Italy*, no. 43134/05, §§ 62–72, 1 December 2009.

[73] *Vilnes and Others v. Norway*, nos 52806/09 and 22703/10, § 234, 5 December 2013.

[74] *Varnava and Others v. Turkey* [GC], nos 16064/90, 16065/90, 16066/90, 16068/90, 16069/90, 16070/90, 16071/90, 16072/90, and 16073/90, § 143, ECHR 2009; *Vagapova and Zubirayev v. Russia*, no. 21080/05, §§ 85–86, 26 February 2009.

[75] *Varnava and Others v. Turkey* [GC], nos 16064/90, 16065/90, 16066/90, 16068/90, 16069/90, 16070/90, 16071/90, 16072/90, and 16073/90, § 143, ECHR 2009; *Lyanova and Aliyeva v. Russia*, nos 12713/02 and 28440/03, §§ 94–95, 2 October 2008.

[76] *Varnava and Others v. Turkey* [GC], nos 16064/90, 16065/90, 16066/90, 16068/90, 16069/90, 16070/90, 16071/90, 16072/90, and 16073/90, § 145, ECHR 2009.

[77] *L.C.B. v. the United Kingdom*, 9 June 1998, § 36, *Judgments and Decisions* 1998-III; *Opuz v. Turkey*, no. 33401/02, § 25, ECHR 2009; *Osman v. the United Kingdom*, 28 October 1998, § 115, ECHR 1998-VIII; *Paul and Audrey Edwards v. the United Kingdom*, no. 46477/99, § 71, ECHR 2002-II.

[78] *Makaratzis v. Greece* [GC], no. 50385/99, § 57, ECHR 2004-XI. See also *Beganović v. Croatia*, no. 46423/06, §§ 85–86, 25 June 2009.

have been considered in the case law of the Convention organs. They are discussed in some detail below. The list is not exhaustive and potentially covers any activity, whether public or not, where life is at stake.[79] For example, it could be extended deep into the realm of economic and social rights. However, the Court has stated that article 2 is 'unconcerned with issues to do with the quality of living or what a person chooses to do with his or her life. To the extent that these aspects are recognised as so fundamental to the human condition that they require protection from state interference, they may be reflected in the rights guaranteed by other articles of the Convention, or in other international Human Rights instruments.'[80] According to the Court, '[w]ithout in any way negating the principle of sanctity of life protected under the Convention, the Court considers that it is under Article 8 that notions of the quality of life take on significance'.

It is well established that a State may not extradite, deport, or otherwise expel someone to another State where there is a real risk of a violation of the right to life.[81] Until recently, the Court had resisted affirming that the death penalty itself would constitute such a violation, given the reference to capital punishment in article 2(1) of the Convention. The position has now changed, a matter discussed later in this chapter.

Criminal justice

Much of article 2 of the Convention, but especially the second paragraph, deals with the protection against violent death, be it at the hands of State agents such as police and prison officials or private individuals. Criminal law provides the framework through the prohibition of various forms of homicide. The effective enforcement of such legal norms is at the heart of positive obligations of the State to ensure that article 2 is respected. According to the Court, 'the first sentence of Article 2 of the Convention requires States, in particular, to put in place a legislative and administrative framework designed to provide effective deterrence against threats to the right to life in the context of any activity, whether public or not, in which the right to life may be at stake'.[82] An effective judicial system 'may, and under certain circumstances must, include recourse to the criminal law'.[83] The European Court will assess the scope of positive obligations with respect to law enforcement '[b]earing in mind the difficulties in policing modern societies, the unpredictability of human conduct and the operational choices which must be made in terms of priorities and resources'. The Convention does not impose 'an impossible or disproportionate burden on the authorities'. According to the Court:

For a positive obligation to arise, it must be established that the authorities knew or ought to have known at the time of the existence of a real and immediate risk to the life of an identified individual from the criminal acts of a third party and that they failed to take measures within the scope of their powers which, judged reasonably, might have been expected to avoid that risk. Another relevant consideration is the need to ensure that the police exercise their powers to control and prevent crime in a manner which fully respects the due process and other guarantees which legitimately place

---

[79] *Öneryıldız v. Turkey* [GC], no. 48939/99, § 71, ECHR 2004-XII.

[80] *Pretty v. the United Kingdom*, no. 2346/02, § 39, ECHR 2002-III.

[81] *Kaboulov v. Ukraine*, no. 41015/04, § 99, 19 November 2009; *F.G. v. Sweden*, no. 43611/11, § 36, 16 January 2014; *K.A.B. v. Sweden*, no. 886/11, § 73, 5 September 2013.

[82] *Öneryıldız v. Turkey* [GC], no. 48939/99, §§ 89–90, ECHR 2004-XII; *Krivova v. Ukraine*, no. 25732/05, § 44, 9 November 2010.

[83] *Railean v. Moldova*, no. 23401/04, § 27, 5 January 2010; *Cioban v. Romania* (dec.), no. 18295/08, 11 March 2014.

restraints on the scope of their action to investigate crime and bring offenders to justice, including the guarantees contained in Articles 5 and 8 of the Convention.[84]

The Court has said that 'in the normal course of events, a criminal trial, with an adversarial procedure before an independent and impartial judge, must be regarded as furnishing the strongest safeguards of an effective procedure for the finding of facts and the attribution of criminal responsibility'.[85]

Obviously, all States Parties prohibit homicide within their domestic criminal law. Exceptions, in the form of justifications and excuses, such as self-defence and duress, do not pose any particular problem here, although in principle they constitute exceptions to the prosecution of homicide. A criminal justice system may provide for various forms and modalities of homicide, such as involuntary homicide or manslaughter, without running afoul of article 2.[86] Indeed, it may extend to negligent forms of killing, such as medical malpractice.[87] But it would appear that the requirement that killing be dealt with by criminal law only applies to intentional homicide.[88] There is authority for the view that criminal law need not punish homicide that results from omission, a matter on which criminal justice policy varies considerably within Europe. For example, some European States prosecute the crime of failing to assist a person whose life is in danger, while others consider that there is no obligation in such circumstances. This is relevant to the euthanasia debate, where the case law of the Strasbourg organs is not clear.[89]

Limitations on the prosecution of homicide may also result from other features of criminal law, such as pardon, amnesty, and statutory limitation. The Commission held that amnesty for killing was not inconsistent with article 2 'unless it can be seen to form part of a general practice aimed at the systematic presentation of prosecution of the perpetrators of such crimes'.[90] The position has evolved, however, reflecting a 'growing tendency in international law' associated with a 'unanimously recognised obligation of States to prosecute and punish grave breaches of fundamental human rights'.[91] The Court has said that it 'considers that an amnesty is generally incompatible with the duty incumbent on the States to investigate'.[92] Similar reasoning applies to statutory limitations, where the Court considers 'it is of the utmost importance that criminal proceedings and sentencing are not time-barred'.[93] Moreover, 'it is legitimate for a State governed by the rule of law to bring criminal proceedings against persons who have committed crimes under a former regime'.[94] At the same time, it has recognized the possible conflict between the duty to prosecute criminals and 'a country's determination to promote

---

[84] *Opuz v. Turkey*, no. 33401/02, § 129, ECHR 2009.

[85] *Gürtekin and Others v. Cyprus*, nos 60441/13, 68206/13, and 68667/13, § 20, 11 March 2014.

[86] Harris et al., *Law of the European Convention*, p. 38.

[87] *Calvelli and Ciglio v. Italy* [GC], no. 32967/96, § 49, ECHR 2002-I.

[88] *Vo v. France* [GC], no. 53924/00, § 90, ECHR 2004-VIII.

[89] *Pretty v. the United Kingdom*, no. 2346/02, ECHR 2002-III.

[90] *Dujardin and Others v. France*, no. 16734/90, Commission decision of 2 September 1991, (1991) 34 YB 119, DR 72, p. 236.

[91] *Marguš v. Croatia* [GC], no. 4455/10, § 139, 27 May 2014.

[92] *Ould Dah v. France* (dec.), no. 13113/03, ECHR 2009. Also *Association '21 December 1989' and Others v. Romania*, nos 33810/07 and 18817/08, § 106, 24 May 2011; *Abdülsamet Yaman v. Turkey*, no. 32446/96, § 55, 2 November 2004.

[93] *Marguš v. Croatia*, no. 4455/10, § 72, 13 November 2012. The position seems to be different when civil claims are concerned: *Vo v. France* [GC], no. 53924/00, § 92, ECHR 2004-VIII.

[94] *Polednová v. Czech Republic* (dec.), no. 2615/10, 21 June 2011; *Streletz, Kessler, and Krenz v. Germany* [GC], nos 34044/96, 35532/97, and 44801/98, § 81, ECHR 2001-II.

reconciliation in society',[95] refusing to rule out the possibility of a general amnesty 'where there are some particular circumstances, such as a reconciliation process and/or a form of compensation to the victim'.[96]

In addition to prosecution, which necessarily arises after the violation of the right to life, the State also has a positive obligation to take 'preventive operational measures to protect an individual whose life is at risk from the criminal acts of another individual'.[97] It must be established that 'the authorities knew or ought to have known at the time of the existence of a real and immediate risk to the life of an identified individual from the criminal acts of a third party and that they failed to take measures within the scope of their powers which, judged reasonably, might have been expected to avoid that risk'.[98] In a case involving domestic violence, the Court considered that the fact the victim had complained that the perpetrator was invading her privacy and wandering around her property with guns and knives, that he had a shotgun and had made violent threats, and that the authorities refused to put the individual in detention was a violation of article 2.[99] The Court has made a distinction between cases that concern personal protection of individuals[100] and those involving the obligation to afford general protection to society.[101]

Use of firearms

Many issues concerning the use of firearms by State officials are addressed under the specific headings of article 2(2). The Court has examined the broader issue within the framework of article 2(1). Thus, the primary duty on the State to secure the right to life necessitates 'an appropriate legal and administrative framework defining the limited circumstances in which law enforcement officials may use force and firearms, in the light of the relevant international standards'.[102] Any recourse to firearms must also be dependent 'on a careful assessment of the situation'.[103] National legislation regulating police operations 'must secure a system of adequate and effective safeguards against arbitrariness and abuse of force and even against avoidable accident'.[104]

For example, a legal framework allowing police to fire upon a fugitive member of the armed forces who did not comply with a warning to surrender and firing of a warning shot was not consisting with article 2(1).[105] Similarly, antiquated legislation authorizing the police to use firearms without consequences in a broad range of circumstances was not

---

[95] *Ould Dah v. France* (dec.), no. 13113/03, ECHR 2009.

[96] *Marguš v. Croatia* [GC], no. 4455/10, § 139, 27 May 2014.

[97] *Opuz v. Turkey*, no. 33401/02, § 128, ECHR 2009. Also *Osman v. the United Kingdom*, 28 October 1998, § 115, *Reports of Judgments and Decisions* 1998-VIII, cited in *Kontrová v. Slovakia*, no. 7510/04, § 49, 31 May 2007; *Mastromatteo v. Italy* [GC], no. 37703/97, § 67 *in fine*, ECHR 2002-VIII; *Branko Tomaši and Others v. Croatia*, no. 46598/06, § 50, 15 January 2009.

[98] *Opuz v. Turkey*, no. 33401/02, §§ 26–27, ECHR 2009; *Osman v. the United Kingdom*, 28 October 1998, § 116, *Reports of Judgments and Decisions* 1998-VIII; *Paul and Audrey Edwards v. the United Kingdom*, no. 46477/99, § 55, ECHR 2002-II; *Medova v. Russia*, no. 25385/04, § 96, 15 January 2009; *Rantsev v. Cyprus and Russia*, no. 25965/04, § 222, ECHR 2010 (extracts).

[99] *Opuz v. Turkey*, no. 33401/02, §§ 28–30, ECHR 2009. Also *Kontrová v. Slovakia*, no. 7510/04, § 53, 31 May 2007.

[100] *Mastromatteo v. Italy* [GC], no. 37703/97, § 69, ECHR 2002-VIII.

[101] *Maiorano and Others v. Italy*, no. 28634/06, § 107, 15 December 2009; *Giuliani and Gaggio v. Italy*, no. 23458/02, § 247, 24 March 2011.

[102] *Giuliani and Gaggio v. Italy*, no. 23458/02, § 209, 24 March 2011; *Makaratzis v. Greece* [GC], no. 50385/99, §§ 57–59, ECHR 2004-XI; *Bakan v. Turkey*, no. 50939/99, § 49, 12 June 2007.

[103] *Giuliani and Gaggio v. Italy*, no. 23458/02, § 209, 24 March 2011.

[104] Ibid.; *Makaratzis v. Greece* [GC], no. 50385/99, § 59, ECHR2004-XI.

[105] *Nachova and Others v. Bulgaria* [GC], nos 43577/98 and 43579/98, §§ 99–102, ECHR 2005-VII.

deemed acceptable.[106] The Court did not object when regulations provided an exhaustive list of situations when firearms could be used, specifying that they were to be a last resort and to be preceded by warning shots, before shots were fired at the legs or indiscriminately.[107] Warning shots must be fired 'whenever possible'.[108]

For guidance in this area, States should consider the United Nations Basic Principles on the Use of Force and Firearms by Law Enforcement Officials.[109] These principles were adopted by the Eighth United Nations Congress on the Prevention of Crime and the Treatment of Offenders. The Grand Chamber has referred to 'the primary duty on the State to secure the right to life by putting in place an appropriate legal and administrative framework defining the limited circumstances in which law enforcement officials may use force and firearms, in the light of the relevant international standards', referring specifically to paragraph 9 of the Basic Principles:

Law enforcement officials shall not use firearms against persons except in self-defence or defence of others against the imminent threat of death or serious injury, to prevent the perpetration of a particularly serious crime involving grave threat to life, to arrest a person presenting such a danger and resisting their authority, or to prevent his or her escape, and only when less extreme means are insufficient to achieve these objectives. In any event, intentional lethal use of firearms may only be made when strictly unavoidable in order to protect life.[110]

The Grand Chamber has also invoked paragraph 5, requiring law enforcement officials to 'act in proportion to the seriousness of the offence and the legitimate objective to be achieved', paragraph 7, stating that 'Governments shall ensure that arbitrary or abusive use of force and firearms by law enforcement officials is punished as a criminal offence under their law.' The Court has also drawn attention to provisions of the Basic Principles encouraging States to develop 'a range of means as broad as possible and equip law enforcement officials with various types of weapons and ammunition that would allow for a differentiated use of force and firearms. These should include the development of non-lethal incapacitating weapons for use in appropriate situations, with a view to increasingly restraining the application of means capable of causing death or injury to persons.' Furthermore, 'the development and deployment of non-lethal incapacitating weapons should be carefully evaluated in order to minimize the risk of endangering uninvolved persons, and the use of such weapons should be carefully controlled'. With reference to the Basic Principles, the Court has said that '[w]henever the lawful use of force and firearms is unavoidable, law-enforcement officials must, in particular, "ensure that assistance and medical aid are rendered to any injured or affected persons at the earliest possible moment", and ensure that arbitrary or abusive use of force and firearms by law-enforcement officials is punished as a criminal offence under their law'.[111] It has insisted that '[t]he Basic Principles also stipulate that "exceptional circumstances such as internal

---

[106] *Erdoğan and Others v. Turkey*, no. 19807/92, §§ 77–78, 25 April 2006.
[107] *Bakan v. Turkey*, no. 50939/99, § 51, 12 June 2007.
[108] *Kallis and Androulla Panayi v. Turkey*, no. 45388/99, § 62, 27 October 2009.
[109] UN Doc. A/CONF.144/28/Rev.1, p. 112. See *Atiman v. Turkey*, no. 62279/09, §§ 23, 30, September 2014; *Błońska v. Poland* (dec.), no. 26330/12, § 55, 1 April 2014; *Benzer and Others v. Turkey*, no. 23502/06, § 90, 12 November 2013; *Gorovenky and Bugara v. Ukraine*, nos 36146/05 and 42418/05, § 22, 12 January 2012; *Makaratzis v. Greece* [GC], no. 50385/99, § 30, ECHR 2004-XI; *Hugh Jordan v. the United Kingdom*, no. 24746/94, § 88, ECHR 2001-III (extracts); *McCann and Others v. the United Kingdom*, 27 September 1995, § 139, Series A no. 324; *Huohvanainen v. Finland*, no. 57389/00, § 75, 13 March 2007.
[110] *Nachova and Others v. Bulgaria* [GC], nos 43577/98 and 43579/98, § 72, ECHR 2005-VII.
[111] *Finogenov and Others v. Russia*, nos 18299/03 and 27311/03, § 163, ECHR 2011 (extracts).

political instability or any other public emergency may not be invoked to justify any departure from these basic principles".[112] With respect to a duty to investigate, reference has been made to paragraph 23, requiring that victims or their family should have access to an independent process, 'including a judicial process', and paragraph 24: 'Governments and law enforcement agencies shall ensure that superior officers are held responsible if they know, or should have known, that law enforcement officials under their command are resorting, or have resorted, to the unlawful use of force and firearms, and they did not take all measures in their power to prevent, suppress or report such use.'[113]

Public health and safety

Positive obligations also apply in the sphere of public health and safety. The Court has recognized that 'acts and omissions of the authorities in the field of health care policy may in certain circumstances engage their responsibility under the positive limb of Article 2'.[114] States are required 'to make regulations compelling hospitals, whether private or public, to adopt appropriate measures for the protection of patients' lives'.[115] However, if a State has provided for high professional standards among health professionals, matters such as error of judgment or negligent co-ordination among health professionals in the treatment of a particular patient are not sufficient to engage the positive obligations under article 2 of the Convention to protect life.[116]

Where the State has undertaken to make health care available to the population in general, a violation of article 2 may arise if a person's life is put at risk when this is denied.[117] The State may even be required to provide appropriate drugs for treatment of life-threatening illness.[118] However, the Court has refused to extend the scope of article 2 so as to require that the State provide access to unauthorized medicinal products for the terminally ill.[119]

In the area of public safety where building sites[120] or dangerous industrial activities pose a threat to life they must be regulated by the State.[121] The State must ensure safety

[112] Ibid.

[113] *Nachova and Others v. Bulgaria* [GC], nos 43577/98 and 43579/98, §§ 73–74, ECHR 2005-VII. Also *Giuliani and Gaggio* v. *Italy*, no. 23458/02, § 154, 24 March 2011; *Makaratzis v. Greece* [GC], no. 50385/99, §§ 30–32, ECHR 2004-XI; *Kakoulli v. Turkey*, no. 38595/97, § 114, 22 November 2005; *McKerr v. the United Kingdom*, no. 28883/95, §§ 92–97, ECHR 2001-III; *Hugh Jordan v. the United Kingdom*, no. 24746/94, §§ 87–89, ECHR 2001-III (extracts).

[114] *Powell and Powell v. the United Kingdom* (dec.), no. 45305/99, ECHR 2000-V; *Nitecki v. Poland* (dec.), no. 65653/01, 21 March 2002; *Trzepałko v. Poland* (dec.), no. 25124/09, § 23, 13 September 2011; *Wiater v. Poland* (dec.), no. 42290/08, 15 May 2012.

[115] *Vo v. France* [GC], no. 53924/00, § 89, ECHR 2004-VIII; *Calvelli and Ciglio v. Italy* [GC], no. 32967/96, § 49, ECHR 2002-I; *Erikson v. Italy* (dec.), no. 37900/97, 26 October 1999; *Dodov v. Bulgaria*, no. 59548/00, §§ 70, 79–83, and 87, 17 January 2008; *Byrzykowski v. Poland*, no. 11562/05, §§ 104 and 106, 27 June 2006. See, however, *Z. v. Poland*, no. 46132/08, § 76, November 2012.

[116] *Powell and Powell v. the United Kingdom* (dec.), no. 45305/99, 4 May 2000; *Eugenia Lazăr v. Romania*, no. 32146/05, § 68, 16 February 2010.

[117] *Cyprus v. Turkey* [GC], no. 25781/94, § 219, ECHR 2001-IV; *Wiater v. Poland* (dec.), no. 42290/08, § 35, 15 May 2012; *Pentiacova and Others v. Moldova* (dec.), no. 14462/03, ECHR 2005-I; *Gheorghe v. Romania* (dec.), no. 19215/04, 22 September 2005.

[118] *Panaitescu v. Romania*, no. 30909/06, § 37, 10 April 2012.

[119] *Hristozov and Others v. Bulgaria*, nos 47039/11 and 358/12, § 108, 13 November 2012.

[120] *Pereira Henriques and Others v. Luxembourg* (dec.), no. 60255/00, 26 August 2003.

[121] *Öneryildiz v. Turkey* [GC], no. 48939/99, § 71, ECHR 2004-XII; *Kolyadenko and Others v. Russia*, nos 17423/05, 20534/05, 20678/05, 23263/05, 24283/05, and 35673/05, § 158, 28 February 2012; *Paşa and Erkan Erol v. Turkey*, no. 51358/99, § 21, 12 December 2006; *Vilnes and Others v. Norway*, nos 52806/09 and 22703/10, § 220, 5 December 2013.

on the roads[122] and on board ships within its jurisdiction.[123] The right to life may be engaged where a school system does not ensure that young children may return home in dangerous weather conditions.[124] More generally, the State must regulate the protection of public safety in public spaces and ensure the regulatory framework functions effectively.[125] The State must also guarantee that emergency services are available.[126]

A distinction is made when the State organizes or authorizes activities that are inherently dangerous, such as intense military training. In such cases, 'it must ensure through a system of rules and through sufficient control that the risk is reduced to a reasonable minimum. If nevertheless damage arises, it will only amount to a breach of the State's positive obligations if it was due to insufficient regulations or insufficient control, but not if the damage was caused through the negligent conduct of an individual or the concatenation of unfortunate events.'[127]

Suicide and euthanasia

The positive obligation to protect the right to life extends to regulating risks to which individuals submit themselves voluntarily,[128] including self-harm.[129] Article 2 'obliges the national authorities to prevent an individual from taking his or her own life if the decision has not been taken freely and with full understanding of what is involved'.[130] In cases dealing with hunger strikes of prisoners, the Convention organs have declined to blame the State for a violation of article 2 provided that there has been no abuse in its management of the situation.[131]

The European Commission dismissed a case where the applicant claimed she would be induced to commit suicide if her husband was forced to serve a prison sentence.[132] Similarly, it concluded there was no issue under article 2 of the Convention in a case where an internally displaced person confronted with eviction from a temporary residence took her own life. The Court said that 'reasonably speaking, self-immolation as a protest tactic does not constitute predictable or reasonable conduct in the context of eviction from an illegally occupied dwelling, even in a situation involving such a particularly vulnerable sector of the population as refugees and internally displaced persons'.[133]

---

[122] *Rajkowska v. Poland* (dec.), no. 37393/02, 27 November 2007; *Al Fayed v. France* (dec.), no. 38501/02, §§ 73–78, 27 September 2007; *Railean v. Moldova*, no. 23401/04, § 30, 5 January 2010.

[123] *Leray and Others v. France* (dec.), no. 44617/98, 16 January 2008.

[124] *Kemaloğlu and Kemaloğlu v. Turkey*, no. 19986/06, § 41, 10 April 2012.

[125] *Calvelli and Ciglio v. Italy* [GC], no. 32967/96, § 49, ECHR 2002-I; *Ciechorśka v. Poland*, no. 19776/04, § 70, 14 June 2011.

[126] *Furdik v. Slovakia* (dec.), no. 42994/05, 2 December 2008.

[127] *Stoyanovi v. Bulgaria*, no. 42980/04, § 61, 9 November 2010; *Kalender v. Turkey*, no. 4314/02, §§ 43–47, 15 December 2009.

[128] *Haas v. Switzerland*, no. 31322/07, § 54, ECHR 2011; *Bone v. France* (dec.), no. 69869/01, 1 March 2005.

[129] *Sergey Shevchenko v. Ukraine*, no. 32478/02, § 56, 4 April 2006; *Keenan v. the United Kingdom*, no. 27229/95, § 90, ECHR 2001-III; *Trubnikov v. Russia*, no. 49790/99, § 89, 5 July 2005; *Mosendz v. Ukraine*, no. 52013/08, § 80, 17 January 2013.

[130] *Haas v. Switzerland*, no. 31322/07, § 54, ECHR 2011.

[131] *Horoz v. Turkey*, no. 1639/03, § 30, 31 March 2009; *W.M. v. Germany*, no. 35638/97, Commission decision of 2 July 1997; *Naddaf v. Federal Republic of Germany*, no. 11604/85, Commission decision of 10 October 1986, DR 50, p. 259. For principles governing hunger strikes of detainees, including force feeding, see *Nevmerzhitsky v. Ukraine*, no. 54825/00, §§ 63–69, ECHR 2005-II (extracts).

[132] *Naddaf v. Federal Republic of Germany*, no. 11604/85, Commission decision of 10 October 1986, DR 50, p. 259.

[133] *Mikayil Mammadov v. Azerbaijan*, no. 4762/05, §§ 111, 115, 17 December 2009.

However, in a situation where an individual threatens to take his or her own life in plain view of State agents and, moreover, where this threat is an emotional reaction directly induced by the State agents' actions or demands, the latter should treat this threat with the utmost seriousness as constituting an imminent risk to that individual's life, regardless of how unexpected that threat might have been. In the Court's opinion, in such a situation as in the present case, if the State agents become aware of such a threat a sufficient time in advance, a positive obligation arises under Article 2 requiring them to prevent this threat from materialising, by any means which are reasonable and feasible in the circumstances.[134]

Once they become aware of such a threat, State agents are required to take action, such as attempting to calm the situation and even physically preventing someone from taking his or her life. Other measures include provision of first aid and ensuring emergency medical services.

In an application directed against Switzerland, the Court warned about underestimating 'the risks of abuse inherent in a system that facilitates access to assisted suicide'.[135] It endorsed the view of the Federal Tribunal, itself interpreting article 2 of the Convention, whereby the right to life requires States 'to establish a procedure capable of ensuring that a decision to end one's life does indeed correspond to the free wish of the individual concerned'. The Court said that a medical prescription following a full psychiatric examination would fulfil this requirement.[136]

Detainees

As a general rule, 'persons in custody are in a vulnerable position and . . . the authorities are under a duty to protect them'.[137] There is a positive obligation to protect a detainee if the authorities 'knew or ought to have known at the time of the existence of a real and immediate risk to the life of an identified individual by a third party or himself and that they failed to take measures within the scope of their powers which, judged reasonably, might have been expected to avoid that risk'.[138] But even if it cannot be established that the authorities knew or should have known of such a risk, certain precautions must be taken by police officers and prison officials in order to protect the health and well-being of a person who has been detained.[139]

The obligation to protect life with respect to persons who are detained implies the provision of medical care required to prevent fatality with an appropriate degree of due diligence.[140] When persons die in detention as a result of a health problem, 'the State must offer an explanation as to the cause of death and the treatment administered to the

[134] Ibid., § 115.
[135] *Haas v. Switzerland*, no. 31322/07, § 58, ECHR 2011.
[136] Ibid.
[137] *Salman v. Turkey* [GC], no. 21986/93, § 99, ECHR 2000-VII; *Marina Alekseyeva v. Russia*, no. 22490/05, § 120, 19 December 2013; *Kats and Others v. Ukraine*, no. 29971/04, § 104, 18 December 2008; *Jasińska v. Poland*, no. 28326/05, §§ 60–62, 1 June 2010; *Mouisel v. France*, no. 67263/01, § 40, ECHR 2002-IX; *McGlinchey and Others v. the United Kingdom*, no. 50390/99, § 46, ECHR 2003-V.
[138] *Keller v. Russia*, no. 26824/04, § 82, 17 October 2013; *Keenan v. the United Kingdom*, no. 27229/95, § 90, ECHR 2001-III; *Paul and Audrey Edwards v. the United Kingdom*, no. 46477/99, § 55, ECHR 2002-II.
[139] *Mižigárová v. Slovakia*, no. 74832/01, § 89, 14 December 2010; *Keller v. Russia*, no. 26824/04, § 82, 17 October 2013.
[140] *Gagiu v. Romania*, no. 63258/00, § 57, 24 February 2009; *Taïs v. France*, no. 39922/03, § 98, 1 June 2006; *Anguelova v. Bulgaria*, no. 38361/97, § 130, ECHR 2002-IV; *Răducu v. Romania*, no. 70787/01, § 56, 21 April 2009.

person concerned prior to his or her death'.[141] The State may also be responsible for failing to provide adequate emergency medical care to detainees.[142] Similar principles apply in the case of involuntary hospitalization[143] as well as to members of the armed forces, particularly when they are conscripts.[144]

The procedural obligation

The case law of the European Court speaks of a 'procedural obligation' that is comprised within article 2.[145] At the core of the procedural obligation is the need to hold accountable those who are responsible for the deprivation of life. Thus, it is first and foremost a requirement of the criminal justice system of the State in question. But the procedural obligation also goes beyond criminal prosecution. Depending upon the circumstances and the nature of the violation it may require other forms of inquiry. The procedural obligation 'is not an obligation of result but of means only'.[146]

The procedural obligation under article 2 has been held to be 'separate and autonomous' from the substantive obligation and is independent of the issue of a substantive breach of article 2.[147] Even if the State is not responsible for the death itself, it will still have an obligation to inquire into the circumstances, cause, and responsibility for the deprivation of life to the extent that it takes place 'under suspicious circumstances, leaving room for allegations to be made of the intentional taking of life'.[148] Applicants before the Court have made claims solely on the basis of the procedural obligation without reference to the substantive violation.[149] Moreover, it is possible for the Court to consider the procedural obligation even when it has no jurisdiction *ratione temporis* over the substantive issue.[150]

[141] *Geppa v. Russia*, no. 8532/06, § 69, 3 February 2011. Also *Anguelova v. Bulgaria*, no. 38361/97, § 110, ECHR 2002-IV; *Jasinskis v. Latvia*, no. 45744/08, § 67, 21 December 2010; *Slimani v. France*, no. 57671/00, § 27, ECHR 2004-IX (extracts); *Kleyn and Aleksandrovich v. Russia*, no. 40657/04, § 44, 3 May 2012; *Tanlı v. Turkey*, no. 26129/95, § 147, ECHR 2001-III (extracts).
[142] *Anguelova v. Bulgaria*, no. 38361/97, §§ 130–131, ECHR 2002-IV; *Abdurrahman Orak v. Turkey*, no. 31889/96, § 78–80, 14 February 2002.
[143] *Shchiborshch and Kuzmina v. Russia*, no. 5269/08, § 241, 16 January 2014.
[144] *Marina Alekseyeva v. Russia*, no. 22490/05, § 121, 19 December 2013; *Beker v. Turkey*, no. 27866/03, §§ 41–42, 24 March 2009; *Mosendz v. Ukraine*, no. 52013/08, § 98, 17 January 2013.
[145] *Šilih v. Slovenia* [GC], no. 71463/01, § 153, 9 April 2009; *McCann and Others v. the United Kingdom*, 27 September 1995, §§ 157–164, Series A no. 324; *Ergi v. Turkey*, 28 July 1998, § 82, *Reports of Judgments and Decisions* 1998-IV; *Mastromatteo v. Italy* [GC], no. 37703/97, § 89, ECHR 2002-VIII; *Assenov and Others v. Bulgaria*, 28 October 1998, §§ 101–106, *Reports of Judgments and Decisions* 1998-VIII.
[146] *Šilih v. Slovenia* [GC], no. 71463/01, § 193, 9 April 2009; *Paul and Audrey Edwards v. the United Kingdom*, no. 46477/99, § 71, ECHR 2002-II; *Bopayeva and Others v. Russia*, no. 40799/06, § 81, 7 November 2013; *Pozhyvotko v. Ukraine*, no. 42752/08, § 39, 17 October 2013.
[147] *Šilih v. Slovenia* [GC], no. 71463/01, § 159, 9 April 2009.
[148] *Pozhyvotko v. Ukraine*, no. 42752/08, § 38, 17 October 2013; *Dobriyeva and Others v. Russia*, no. 18407/10, § 70, 19 December 2013; *Šilih v. Slovenia* [GC], no. 71463/01, § 156, 9 April 2009; *Yaşa v. Turkey*, 2 September 1998, § 100, *Reports of Judgments and Decisions* 1998-VI; *Ergi v. Turkey*, 28 July 1998, § 82, *Reports of Judgments and Decisions* 1998-IV; *Süheyla Aydın v. Turkey*, no. 25660/94, § 171, 24 May 2005.
[149] *Šilih v. Slovenia* [GC], no. 71463/01, § 158, 9 April 2009; *Calvelli and Ciglio v. Italy* [GC], no. 32967/96, §§ 41–57, ECHR 2002-I; *Byrzykowski v. Poland*, no. 11562/05, §§ 86 and 94–118, 27 June 2006; *Brecknell v. the United Kingdom*, no. 32457/04, § 53, 27 November 2007.
[150] *Šilih v. Slovenia* [GC], no. 71463/01, § 159, 9 April 2009; *Varnava and Others v. Turkey* [GC], nos 16064/90, 16065/90, 16066/90, 16068/90, 16069/90, 16070/90, 16071/90, 16072/90, and 16073/90, § 149, ECHR 2009; *Janowiec and Others v. Russia*, nos 55508/07 and 29520/09, Joint Partly Dissenting Opinion of Judges Spielmann, Villiger, and Nußburger, 16 April 2012; *Janowiec and Others v. Russia* [GC], nos 55508/07 and 29520/09, § 141, ECHR 2013.

When use of lethal force results in death, article 2 read in conjunction with article 1 requires that there be 'some form of effective official investigation'.[151] The purpose is securing effective implementation of domestic legislation protecting the right to life and ensuring accountability for those responsible. Such an interpretation of article 2 is justified 'not only because any allegations of such an offence normally give rise to criminal liability, but also because often, in practice, the true circumstances of the death are, or may be, largely confined within the knowledge of State officials or authorities'.[152] This investigation must be thorough[153] and independent,[154] accessible to the family of the victim,[155] carried out promptly,[156] capable of leading to a determination as to whether the use of force was justified, and allowing appropriate public scrutiny of the investigation or its results.[157] The inquiry must be 'effective', although that does not mean it will confirm the applicant's version of the events. But it should be capable of establishing the facts and leading to the identification and punishment of those responsible.[158] The form the investigation takes may vary depending upon the circumstances and cannot be codified in a simplified list.[159] The authorities must always make a serious attempt to find out what happened and should not rely on hasty or ill-founded conclusions to close their investigation or as the basis of their decisions. They must take all reasonable steps available to them to secure the evidence concerning the incident, including, inter alia, eyewitness testimony, forensic evidence, and so on.[160] The relatives of the victims must have access to the materials and conclusions of the investigation,[161] although the

[151] *McCann and Others v. The United Kingdom*, 27 September 1995, § 161, Series A no. 324; *Çakıcı v. Turkey* [GC], no. 23657/94, § 86, ECHR 1999-IV; *Kaya v. Turkey*, 19 February 1998, § 86, *Reports of Judgments and Decisions* 1998-I; *Gömi and Others v. Turkey*, no. 35962/97, §§ 62, 63, 21 December 2006; *Ceyhan Demir and Others v. Turkey*, no. 34491/97, §§ 106–107, 13 January 2005; *Perişan and Others v. Turkey*, no. 12336/03, § 102, 20 May 2010; *Oğur v. Turkey* [GC], no. 21594/93, § 88, ECHR 1999-III; *Kolevi v. Bulgaria*, no. 1108/02, § 191, 5 November 2009.
[152] *Maskhadova and Others v. Russia*, no. 18071/05, § 163, 6 June 2013.
[153] *Assenov and Others v. Bulgaria*, 28 October 1998, §§ 103 ff., *Reports of Judgments and Decisions* 1998-VIII.
[154] *Oğur v. Turkey* [GC], no. 21594/93, §§ 91–92, ECHR 1999-III. See also *Mehmet Emin Yüksel v. Turkey*, no. 40154/98, § 37, 20 July 2004; *Güleç v. Turkey*, 27 July 1998, §§ 80–82, *Reports of Judgments and Decisions* 1998-IV.
[155] But see *Golubeva v. Russia*, no. 1062/03, § 91, 17 December 2009, where exclusion of the next-of-kin was not considered to be decisive.
[156] *Collette and Michael Hemsworth v. the United Kingdom*, no. 58559/09, §§ 69–74, 16 July 2013.
[157] *Hugh Jordan v. the United Kingdom*, no. 24746/94, §§ 105–109, ECHR 2001-III (extracts); *Douglas-Williams v. the United Kingdom* (dec.), no. 56413/00, 8 January 2002; *Sultan Karabulut v. Turkey*, no. 45784/99, §§ 73–74, 19 September 2006.
[158] *Finogenov and Others v. Russia*, nos 18299/03 and 27311/03, § 269, ECHR 2011 (extracts); *Mahmut Kaya v. Turkey*, no. 22535/93, § 124, ECHR 2000-III. See also *Paul and Audrey Edwards v. the United Kingdom*, no. 46477/99, § 71, ECHR 2002-II.
[159] *Sultan Karabulut v. Turkey*, no. 45784/99, § 71, 19 September 2006; *Tanrıkulu v. Turkey* [GC], no. 23763/94, §§ 101–110, ECHR 1999-IV; *Kaya v. Turkey*, 19 February 1998, §§ 89–91, *Reports of Judgments and Decisions* 1998-I; *Güleç v. Turkey*, 27 July 1998, §§ 79–81, *Reports of Judgments and Decisions* 1998-IV; *Buldan v. Turkey*, no. 28298/95, § 83, 20 April 2004.
[160] *Finogenov and Others v. Russia*, nos 18299/03 and 27311/03, § 271, ECHR 2011 (extracts); *Mikheyev v. Russia*, no. 77617/01, §§ 107 ff., 26 January 2006; *Assenov and Others v. Bulgaria*, 28 October 1998, §§ 102 ff., *Reports of Judgments and Decisions* 1998-VIII.
[161] *Oğur v. Turkey* [GC], no. 21594/93, § 92, ECHR 1999-III; *Khadzhialiyev and Others v. Russia*, no. 3013/04, § 106, 6 November 2008.

requirement of an inquiry cannot be left to their initiative.[162] The authorities must act with dispatch even if the next of kin of the victim does not.[163]

In the case of a death in custody, article 2 requires

an independent and impartial official investigation that satisfies certain minimum standards as to effectiveness. Accordingly, the competent authorities must act with exemplary diligence and promptness and must, of their own motion, initiate investigations capable of, firstly, ascertaining the circumstances in which the incident took place and any shortcomings in the operation of the regulatory system and, secondly, identifying the State officials or authorities involved.[164]

Although recourse to criminal justice will often be necessary in order to fulfil the procedural obligation, it will not suffice in some situations where effective criminal investigation is fundamentally flawed or to all intents and purposes ineffective because of a systemic problem.[165] The aim of criminal prosecution should be to show that killing will not be tolerated. Where judges in a case involving negligent homicide by law enforcement officials made a finding of guilt but suspended the proceedings, thereby minimizing the significance of the killing, the European Court held that article 2 had been breached. It said that the criminal justice system 'proved to be far from rigorous and had little deterrent effect capable of ensuring the effective prevention of unlawful acts, such as those complained of by the applicants'.[166]

Enforced disappearance is an important human rights violation that often results in a breach of the right to life, where it generally takes the form of an extra-judicial execution. In a particular form known as *Nacht und Nebel*, an expression that Hitler borrowed from Richard Wagner's opera *Das Rheingold*, persons characterized as terrorists or saboteurs were either executed immediately or secretly transferred to Germany without being allowed to communicate with family and friends.[167] More recently, enforced disappearance was defined as a specific act of crime against humanity in the Rome Statute of the International Criminal Court.[168] It is described in the International Convention for the Protection of All Persons from Enforced Disappearance as 'the arrest, detention, abduction or any other form of deprivation of liberty committed by agents of the State or by persons or groups of persons acting with the authorisation, support or acquiescence of the State, followed by a refusal to acknowledge the deprivation of liberty or by concealment of the fate or whereabouts of the disappeared person, which place such a person outside the

[162] *Al-Skeini and Others v. the United Kingdom* [GC], no. 55721/07, § 165, ECHR 2011; *McKerr v. the United Kingdom*, no. 28883/95, § 111, ECHR 2001-III; *Yüksel Erdoğan and Others v. Turkey*, no. 57049/00, § 73, 15 February 2007.
[163] *Paul and Audrey Edwards v. the United Kingdom*, no. 46477/99, § 69, ECHR 2002-II.
[164] *Geppa v. Russia*, no. 8532/06, § 72, 3 February 2011.
[165] *Yandiyev and Others v. Russia*, nos 34541/06, 43811/06, and 1578/07, § 132, 10 October 2013; *Dzhabrailov and Others v. Russia*, nos 8620/09, 11674/09, 16488/09, 21133/09, 36354/09, 47770/09, 54728/09, 25511/10, and 32791/10, § 320, 27 February 2014; *Pitsayeva and Others v. Russia*, nos 53036/08, 61785/08, 8594/09, 24708/09, 30327/09, 36965/09, 61258/09, 63608/09, 67322/09, 4334/10, 4345/10, 11873/10, 25515/10, 30592/10, 32797/10, 33944/10, 36141/10, 52446/10, 62244/10, and 66420/10, § 471, 9 January 2014; *Aslakhanova and Others v. Russia*, nos 2944/06, 8300/07, 50184/07, 332/08, and 42509/10, §§ 123–125, 18 December 2012.
[166] *Kasap and Others v. Turkey*, no. 8656/10, §§ 60–61, 14 January 2014.
[167] *France et al. v. Goering et al.*, (1948) 22 IMT 411, at p. 510. Also *United States v. Alstötter et al.* (Justice case), (1951) 3 TWC 954 (US Military Tribunal), at pp. 1031–62.
[168] Rome Statute of the International Criminal Court, (2002) 2187 UNTS 90, art. 8(1)(i), (2)(ii).

protection of the law'.[169] The Court has referred to this formulation as the international law definition of the phenomenon.[170] According to the Court, disappearance is 'characterised by an on-going situation of uncertainty and unaccountability in which there is a lack of information or even a deliberate concealment and obfuscation of what has occurred'.[171]

Before the European Court enforced disappearance cases have been dealt with under the procedural obligation comprised within article 2 to the extent that the right to life is at stake. The State authorities are required to act rapidly and decisively in responding to the disappearance precisely in order to reduce the risk to the life of the missing person.[172] Disappearance is often protracted, 'prolonging the torment of the victim's relatives', raising issues under article 3 as well as article 2 of the Convention. It is a continuing violation that persists as long as the fate of the person is not accounted for, even when death is presumed.[173] An onus is placed upon the next of kin by the Court in disappearance cases. They 'cannot wait indefinitely before coming to Strasbourg' and 'must make proof of a certain amount of diligence and initiative and introduce their complaints without undue delay'.[174]

Where killing is intentional, a civil action for redress cannot, in the absence of other remedies, be considered adequate.[175] The European Court considers that a civil court is unable to pursue an independent investigation or to make meaningful findings about the identity of perpetrators or the attribution of responsibility without the benefit of a criminal investigation.[176] However, if killing is not intentional a criminal law remedy is not necessarily required.[177] For example, in the case of motor vehicle accidents 'caused by pure negligence without aggravating circumstances, the Court may be satisfied if the legal system affords victims a remedy in the civil courts enabling any liability of the parties concerned to be established and any appropriate civil redress, such as an order for damages, to be obtained'.[178] This does not rule out criminal prosecution, which may be based upon a theory of negligence, but it means that the 'the procedural obligation imposed by Article 2 to set up an effective judicial system does not necessarily require the provision of a criminal-law remedy in every case'.[179]

---

[169] International Convention for the Protection of All Persons from Enforced Disappearance, UN Doc. A/61/488, art. 2.

[170] *El Masri v. 'the former Yugoslav Republic of Macedonia'* [GC], no. 39630/09, § 240, ECHR 2012.

[171] *Aslakhanova and Others v. Russia*, nos 2944/06, 8300/07, 50184/07, 332/08, and 42509/10, § 122, 18 December 2012.

[172] *Mayaeva v. Russia*, no. 37287/09, §§ 104–106, 18 September 2014; *Gongadze v. Ukraine*, no. 34056/02, § 170, ECHR 2005-XI.

[173] *Varnava and Others v. Turkey* [GC], nos 16064/90, 16065/90, 16066/90, 16068/90, 16069/90, 16070/90, 16071/90, 16072/90, and 16073/90, § 148, ECHR 2009.

[174] Ibid., § 161; *Petimat Ismailova and Others v. Russia*, nos 25088/11, 44277/11, 44284/11, 44313/11, 48134/11, 49486/11, 52076/11, 52182/11, 55055/11, 56574/11, 64266/11, and 66831/11, §§ 332–334, 18 September 2014; *Er and Others v. Turkey*, no. 23016/04, §§ 55–58, 31 July 2012; *Yetişen and Others v. Turkey* (dec.), no. 21099/06, 10 July 2012.

[175] *Khashiyev and Akayeva v. Russia*, nos 57942/00 and 57945/00, §§ 119–121, 24 February 2005; *Estamirov and Others v. Russia*, no. 60272/00, § 77, 12 October 2006; *Abdurashidova v. Russia*, no. 32968/05, § 56, 8 April 2010.

[176] *Akhmadov and Others v. Russia*, no. 21586/02, § 83, 14 November 2008.

[177] *Vo v. France* [GC], no. 53924/00, § 90, ECHR 2004-VII.

[178] *Cioban v. Romania* (dec.), no. 18295/08, § 25, 11 March 2014; *Furdik v. Slovakia* (dec.), no 42994/05, 2 December 2008; *Anna Todorova, v. Bulgaria*, no. 23302/03, §§ 79–80, 24 May 2011.

[179] *Šilih v. Slovenia* [GC], no. 71463/01, § 194, 9 April 2009; *Mastromatteo v. Italy* [GC], no. 37703/97, § 90, ECHR 2002-VIII.

A common problem with respect to non-intentional killing is raised in medical negligence cases. There must be an 'effective judicial system for establishing both the cause of death of an individual under the care and responsibility of health professionals and any responsibility on the part of the latter'.[180] This applies, for example, in the case of determining the cause of death of patients in the care of the medical profession.[181] The inquiry must be undertaken with celerity, if for no other reason than that '[k]nowledge of the facts and of possible errors committed in the course of medical care are essential to enable the institutions concerned and medical staff to remedy the potential deficiencies and prevent similar errors. The prompt examination of such cases is therefore important for the safety of users of all health services.'[182]

One dimension of the procedural obligation is the right of victims, their families, and heirs to know the truth about circumstances associated with a violation of the right to life, especially when this is related to a large-scale or massive violation of fundamental rights.[183] The Court has stressed the importance of this 'in the event of widespread use of lethal force against the civilian population during anti-Government demonstrations preceding the transition from a totalitarian regime to a more democratic system'.[184] Although the issue arises in the context of individual rights, there is some authority for the significance of a broader collective or social dimension to this right to know the truth. In one decision, the Court framed the importance of an investigation into events in light not only of the rights of the individual applicants but 'in view also of the importance to Romanian society of knowing the truth about the events of December 1989'.[185] In *El Masri*, where 'extraordinary renditions' were involved, the Grand Chamber underscored 'the great importance of the present case not only for the applicant and his family, but also for other victims of similar crimes and the general public, who had the right to know what had happened'.[186] In a concurring opinion in that case, several judges noted that the right to truth was implied within the Convention, in particular within the procedural obligation of articles 2 and 3, although they argued that it was best approached from the perspective of article 13. They wrote:

In practice, the search for the truth is the objective purpose of the obligation to carry out an investigation and the raison d'être of the related quality requirements (transparency, diligence, independence, access, disclosure of results and scrutiny). For society in general, the desire to ascertain the truth plays a part in strengthening confidence in public institutions and hence the rule of law. For those concerned—the victims' families and close friends—establishing the true facts and securing an acknowledgment of serious breaches of human rights and humanitarian law constitute forms of redress that are just as important as compensation, and sometimes even more

---

[180] *Šilih v. Slovenia* [GC], no. 71463/01, § 155, 9 April 2009; *Calvelli and Ciglio v. Italy* [GC], no. 32967/96, § 49, ECHR 2002-I; *Powell and Powell v. the United Kingdom* (dec.), no. 45305/99, ECHR 2000-V; *Dodov v. Bulgaria*, no. 59548/00, § 83, 17 January 2008; *Byrzykowski v. Poland*, no. 11562/05, §§ 104–118, 27 June 2006.

[181] *Vo v. France* [GC], no. 53924/00, § 89, ECHR 2004-VIII. Also *Powell and Powell v. the United Kingdom* (dec.), no. 45305/99, ECHR 2000-V; *Calvelli and Ciglio v. Italy* [GC], no. 32967/96, § 49, ECHR 2002-I.

[182] *Šilih v. Slovenia* [GC], no. 71463/01, § 196, 9 April 2009; *Byrzykowski v. Poland*, no. 11562/05, § 117, 27 June 2006.

[183] *Association '21 December 1989' and Others v. Romania*, nos 33810/07 and 18817/08, § 106, 24 May 2011.

[184] Ibid.

[185] Ibid., § 130. Also *Şandru and Others v. Romania*, no. 22465/03, § 79, 8 December 2009.

[186] *El Masri v. 'the former Yugoslav Republic of Macedonia'* [GC], no. 39630/09, § 191, ECHR 2012.

so. Ultimately, the wall of silence and the cloak of secrecy prevent these people from making any sense of what they have experienced and are the greatest obstacles to their recovery.[187]

Another decision, referring to the killings by soldiers during the conflict in Northern Ireland, insisted upon the importance of a 'reasoned decision available to reassure a concerned public that the rule of law had been respected'.[188] In other words, the procedural obligation may be informed by a right to know the historical truth.

In the case dealing with the procedural obligation to disclose about the Katyn massacre that took place in the Soviet Union in 1940, it was argued that one factor justifying extension of the temporal jurisdiction of the Court, on an exceptional basis, was the importance of truth seeking in order to enable nations to learn from their history and to take measures to prevent future atrocities.[189] Reliance was placed upon the Updated Set of Principles for the Protection and Promotion of Human Rights Through Action to Combat Impunity issued by the United Nations Commission on Human Rights in 2005,[190] the International Committee of the Red Cross rules of customary international law[191] and the case law of the Inter-American Court of Human Rights.[192] However, the Grand Chamber distinguished the procedural obligation of individual victims comprised in article 2 from 'other types of inquiries that may be carried out for other purposes, such as establishing a historical truth'.[193] Four dissenting judges said that in addition to the rights of the individual victims, 'it is equally clear that the obligation to investigate and prosecute those responsible for grave human rights and serious humanitarian law violations serves fundamental public interests by allowing a nation to learn from its history and by combating impunity'.[194]

'Intentionally'

The drafting history of the Convention suggests that article 2 was only meant to cover intentional killing.[195] In proceedings before the European Commission, the United Kingdom took the position that negligent or accidental killing was not contemplated by article 2.[196] The Commission adopted the view that the first sentence of article 2(1) was broader than the second, in that it required States not only to refrain from intentional

---

[187] Ibid., Joint Concurring Opinion of Judges Tulkens, Speilmann, Sicilianos, and Keller, § 6.

[188] *Kelly and Others v. the United Kingdom*, no. 30054/96, § 118, 4 May 2001.

[189] *Janowiec and Others v. Russia* [GC], nos 55508/07 and 29520/09, §§ 124, 126, ECHR 2013.

[190] UN Doc. E/CN.4/RES/2005/81, paras 2 and 3.

[191] Jean-Marie Henckaerts and Louise Doswald-Beck, eds, *Customary International Humanitarian Law*, Vol. I, Cambridge: Cambridge University Press, 2005, Rule 117.

[192] I/A Court H.R., *Case of Heliodoro-Portugal v. Panama*, Preliminary objections, Merits, Reparations, and Costs. Judgment of 12 August 2008, Series C no. 186; I/A Court H.R., *Case of Gomes Lund et al. ('Guerrilha do Araguaia') v. Brazil*, Preliminary objections, Merits, Reparations, and Costs, Judgment of 24 November 2010. Series C no. 219.

[193] *Janowiec and Others v. Russia* [GC], nos 55508/07 and 29520/09, § 143, ECHR 2013. However, see ibid., Joint Partly Dissenting Opinion of Judges Ziemele, De Gaetano, Laffranque, and Keller, §§ 8 and 9, 21 October 2013.

[194] Ibid., Joint Partly Dissenting Opinion of Judges Ziemele, De Gaetano, Laffranque, and Keller, § 24, 21 October 2013.

[195] *X. v. Belgium*, no. 2758/66, Commission decision of 21 May 1969, (1969) 12 YB 174, Collection 30, p. 11.

[196] *Stewart v. the United Kingdom*, no. 10044/82, Commission decision of 10 July 1984, § 13, (1984) 27 YB 129, DR 39, p. 162.

deprivation of life but also to take steps to safeguard life.[197] The issue is no longer in serious dispute.

The death penalty

The death penalty is presented as an exception to the right to life in article 2(1) of the Convention. Capital punishment was certainly consistent with the practice of European States at the time the Convention was adopted. Some had long abandoned the death penalty, only to bring it back for post-Second-World-War prosecutions of Nazis and their collaborators. Very soon after the Convention entered into force, a strong trend towards abolition began to emerge. In 1953, a United Kingdom Royal Commission on capital punishment declined to recommend abolition,[198] although only a few more executions actually took place before the practice was abandoned. Brian Simpson has explained that executions conducted in Cyprus by the United Kingdom in 1956 were 'the trigger' that led Greece to file the first inter-State case at the Commission.[199] The application by Greece was lodged on 7 May 1956, the date when clemency was refused to two Cypriot independence fighters, Michael Karaolis and Andreas Demetriou. However, the reports of the Commission do not indicate that Greece ever raised the issue of capital punishment or questioned the United Kingdom's compliance with article 2 of the Convention.[200] Ireland's last execution took place in 1954. But France continued to execute people until the late 1970s and only removed the death penalty from its laws in 1981. In Belgium, death sentences were still being pronounced in the early 1990s, although no executions have taken place there since 1950. Latvia hosted the last execution in a Council of Europe Member State, in 1997. Today, the death penalty no longer exists within the territory of the Council of Europe. The reference to capital punishment in article 2(1) of the Convention is, for all practical purposes, repealed. Protocol Nos 6 and 13 to the Convention entrench the abolitionist commitment of the Council of Europe. The case law of the Strasbourg organs concerning article 2 and the death penalty is almost entirely confined to extraterritorial imposition of capital punishment, essentially extradition and expulsion cases.

The counterparts of article 2(1) in subsequent human rights treaties, notably article 6 of the International Covenant on Civil and Political Rights and article 4 of the American Convention on Human Rights, impose several restrictions on the exercise of capital punishment, including the requirement that it only be imposed for the 'most serious crimes' and that it not be imposed on juvenile offenders or pregnant women. In a comparative study of the European Convention and the International Covenant on Civil and Political Rights, a Committee of Experts on Human Rights appointed by the Council of Europe implied that article 2 of the Convention provides essentially the same protections in death penalty cases as article 6 of the Covenant, but this is obviously not the case.[201]

---

[197] *Association X. v. the United Kingdom*, no. 7154/75, Commission decision of 12 July 1978, DR 14, p. 31.
[198] *Royal Commission on Capital Punishment, 1949–1953, Report*, Cmd 8932, London: Her Majesty's Stationery Office, 1953.
[199] A.W. Brian Simpson, *Human Rights and the End of Empire, Britain and the Genesis of the European Convention*, Oxford: Oxford University Press, 2001, p. 919.
[200] *Greece v. the United Kingdom*, no. 176/56, Commission decision of 2 June 1956, (1958–59) 2 YB 182; *Greece v. the United Kingdom*, no. 299/57, Commission decision of 12 October 1957, (1958–59) 2 YB 186.
[201] 'Corresponding provisions [to article 6(2) of the *Covenant*] appear in different places of the European Convention (in particular in Article 3, 6(1), 7 and 13) so that the adoption of the Covenant text should not, in

Comparing the two instruments, a senior lawyer in the Council of Europe described the death penalty provisions in article 6 of the Covenant as 'distinctly more progressive' than those in article 2 of the Convention.[202] In 1979, when the issue of amending article 2 of the Convention arose so as to bring it into step with the more advanced norms of the American Convention on Human Rights, the Steering Committee on Human Rights of the Council of Europe was concerned that such an amendment might imply acceptance of the death penalty at a time when there was a general trend towards abolition.[203]

Two explicit limitations to the death penalty appear in article 2: the sentence must be pronounced by a 'court' and it must be 'provided for by law'. The word 'court' appears elsewhere in the Convention, in article 5(1)(a), 5(1)(b), 5(4). It has been interpreted as implying a body independent of the executive branch of government and offering the guarantees of a judicial procedure.[204] In *Öcalan*, the Court said that it 'follows from the requirement in Article 2 § 1 that the deprivation of life be pursuant to the "execution of a sentence of a court", that the "court" which imposes the penalty be an independent and impartial tribunal within the meaning of the Court's case-law and that the most rigorous standards of fairness are observed in the criminal proceedings both at first instance and on appeal'.[205] The term 'provided by law' imposes an obligation on any State that wishes to impose the death penalty to ensure that this is in fact authorized by law that is both foreseeable and accessible.[206]

The International Covenant on Civil and Political Rights and the American Convention on Human Rights, both adopted during the 1960s, reflect evolving international standards in the area. They include several limitations upon resort to capital punishment that do not appear in the text of article 2(1) of the European Convention. In particular, the death penalty can only be imposed for the 'most serious crimes', the relevant fair trial provisions must be honoured, and certain categories of individuals—namely pregnant women, juveniles, and the elderly—cannot be executed. Whether these might be implicit limitations to article 2(1) has never really been tested by the Convention organs. In *Soering v. the United Kingdom*, the Court noted that article 2(1) permitted the death penalty 'under certain conditions'.[207] When the case was examined by the European Commission, several members penned dissenting opinions in which they indicated that there were indeed such limitations. Jochen Frowein said that article 2 only authorized the death penalty for the 'most serious crimes', echoing the rule contained in the Covenant and the American Convention.[208] Three other members of the Commission agreed that although the death penalty was expressly permitted by article 2 and could not therefore 'in general'

---

this respect, impose any additional obligations on the States bound by the European Convention', according to Doc. H(70)7, para. 91. See also Marc-André Eissen, 'European Convention on Human Rights and the United Nations Covenant on Civil and Political Rights: Problems of Coexistence', (1972) 22 *Buffalo Law Review* 18.

[202] A.H. Robertson, 'The United Nations International Covenant on Civil and Political Rights and the European Convention on Human Rights', (1968–69) 32 *British Yearbook of International Law* 21, at p. 31.

[203] 'Opinion of the Steering Committee on Human Rights', 12–16 November 1979.

[204] *De Wilde, Ooms and Versyp v. Belgium*, 18 June 1971, § 78, Series A no. 12; *Ringeisen v. Austria*, 16 July 1971, § 36, Series A no. 13; *X v. the United Kingdom*, 5 November 1981, § 39, Series A no. 46.

[205] *Öcalan v. Turkey*, no. 46221/99, § 203, 12 March 2003. Also *Bader and Kanbor v. Sweden*, no. 13284/04, § 42, ECHR-2005.

[206] *Öcalan v. Turkey*, no. 46221/99, § 203, 12 March 2003.

[207] *Soering v. the United Kingdom*, 7 July 1989, § 101, Series A no. 161.

[208] *Soering v. the United Kingdom*, no. 14038/88, Commission report of 19 January 1989, Dissenting Opinion of Mr J.A. Frowein.

be regarded as in conflict with article 3, this did not exclude 'special circumstances justifying a different conclusion. Such circumstances may relate to the nature of the crime (e.g. a trivial offence under the laws of the Convention States) or the personal circumstances of the offender (e.g. his young age or his poor state of health) or indeed to the manner of execution'.[209]

The Soering case

Death penalty issues have general involved consideration of article 3 as well as article 2(1) of the Convention. In an early case, the European Commission held 'that notwithstanding the terms of article 2§1, it cannot be excluded that the circumstances surrounding the protection of one of the other rights contained in the Convention might give rise to an issue under article 3'.[210] The case concerned the 'death row phenomenon' in California, a subject that returned some years later in one of the most emblematic cases, *Soering v. the United Kingdom*. Threatened with extradition from the United Kingdom to the United States, where there was the possibility of imposition of capital punishment, Soering contended that prolonged incarceration prior to execution and conditions of detention on death row would breach article 3 of the Convention. By six votes to five, the European Commission of Human Rights rejected the application. The Commission noted that article 2 'expressly permits the imposition of the death penalty' and that as a result 'extradition of a person to a country where he risks the death penalty cannot, in itself, raise an issue either under Article 2 or Article 3 of the Convention'.[211] The Commission conceded that 'notwithstanding the terms of Article 2 para. 1, it cannot be excluded that the circumstances surrounding the protection of one of the other rights contained in the Convention might give rise to an issue under Article 3'.[212] One of the dissenting members, Stefan Trechsel, wrote:

It may seem surprising that the Convention prohibits inhuman and degrading treatment but permits capital punishment which could be regarded as a clear example of such treatment. This paradox is to be explained by the historic context of the drafting of the Convention. Today, however, Article 2 para. 1, inasmuch as it accepts capital punishment, must be regarded as reflecting an attitude to the death penalty which has since undergone substantial change and is now outdated...its growing rejection leads one to conclude that aggravating circumstances, i.e. suffering beyond that necessarily inherent in execution, injustice or an element of disproportionality brings capital punishment into the realm of inhuman treatment prohibited by Article 3.[213]

In this initial discussion of capital punishment by the Commission, the dissenting members considered that to the extent that the implied limitations of article 2(1) were not complied with, there was a violation of article 3. This linkage between articles 2 and 3 when the death penalty is concerned persists throughout the subsequent case law.

   The European Court's landmark ruling held that the planned extradition of Soering to the United States was a violation of article 3 because of the prolonged detention that was likely prior to execution, coupled with the harsh conditions of detention and the young

---

[209] Ibid., Dissenting Opinion of Mr H. Danelius, joined by Mr G. Jörundsson and Mr H. Vandenberghe.
[210] *Kirkwood v. the United Kingdom*, no. 10479/83, Commission decision of 12 March 1984, DR 37, p. 158.
[211] *Soering v. the United Kingdom*, 7 July 1989, §§ 100, 102, Series A no. 161.
[212] Ibid., § 103.
[213] *Soering v. the United Kingdom*, no. 14038/88, Commission report of 19 January 1989, Dissenting Opinion of Mr S. Trechsel.

age of the applicant. The Court noted that in light of the wording of article 2(1), neither Soering nor the two Government parties[214] had taken the position that the death penalty per se violated article 3 of the *Convention*. However, the intervener Amnesty International argued that evolving standards of interpretation of the Convention meant that the death penalty should now be considered to breach article 3. The Court observed, in this respect, that '[d]*e facto* the death penalty no longer exists in time of peace in the contracting States of the Convention. In the few Contracting States which retain the death penalty in law for some peacetime offenses, death sentences, if ever imposed, are nowadays not carried out.'[215] The Court rejected the argument that the interpretation of the Convention could be extended in this way, so that article 3, in effect, rendered inoperative a portion of article 2(1). According to the Court, article 3 'cannot have been intended by the drafters of the Convention to include a general prohibition of the death penalty since that would nullify the clear wording of Article 2§1'.[216] The Court acknowledged that subsequent practice could support the argument that the reference to the death penalty was no longer operative. Nevertheless, the adoption of Protocol No. 6 to the Convention in 1983 'as a subsequent written agreement, shows that the intention of the Contracting Parties as recently as 1983 was to adopt the normal method of amendment of the text in order to introduce a new obligation to abolish capital punishment in time of peace and, what is more, to do so by an optional instrument allowing each State to choose the moment when to undertake such an engagement'.[217]

The suggestion that the Convention's recognition of the death penalty as an exception to the right to life is now obsolete and incompatible with the legal conscience and practice of contemporary Europe was advanced by a single judge of the Court, Judge De Meyer, in a concurring opinion. Judge De Meyer said extradition of Soering would breach article 2 of the Convention. Because article 2(1) permits imposition of the death penalty only where this 'is provided by law' and because the death penalty was not 'provided by law' in the United Kingdom, the fact that it is allowed in Virginia is irrelevant, he wrote. 'When a person's right to life is involved, no requested State can be entitled to allow a requesting State to do what the requested State is not itself allowed to do.'[218]

Towards abolition as such

The issue of capital punishment returned to the Court a decade later in *Öcalan v. Turkey*. Although Öcalan was sentenced to death, Turkey had abolished capital punishment and, by the time the case was heard in Strasbourg, commuted the sentence to one of life imprisonment.[219] The Chamber agreed that there was no threat that capital punishment would actually be imposed,[220] but nevertheless considered the matter because a death sentence had been pronounced against the applicant. The Court elected to consider the matter from the standpoint of article 3 'against the background of Article 2'. It reviewed the position taken by the Court in *Soering*, but said 'the legal position as regards the death

---

[214] Because Soering was a German national, Germany intervened in the proceedings pursuant to article 36 of the Convention.

[215] *Soering v. the United Kingdom*, 7 July 1989, § 102, Series A no. 161.

[216] Ibid., § 103.

[217] Ibid.

[218] Ibid., Concurring Opinion of Judge de Meyer, Series A no. 161.

[219] *Öcalan v. Turkey*, no. 46221/99, § 47, 12 March 2003.

[220] Ibid., § 186.

penalty has undergone a considerable evolution' since then.[221] The Chamber took note of a recent pronouncement of the Parliamentary Assembly of the Council of Europe:

The second sentence of Article 2 of the European Convention on Human Rights still provides for the death penalty. It has long been in the interest of the Assembly to delete this sentence, thus matching theory with reality. This interest is strengthened by the fact that more modern national constitutional documents and international treaties no longer include such provisions.[222]

The Chamber said that 'it cannot now be excluded, in the light of the developments that have taken place in this area, that the States have agreed through their practice to modify the second sentence in Article 2 § 1 in so far as it permits capital punishment in peacetime'.[223] Moreover, 'it can also be argued that the implementation of the death penalty can be regarded as inhuman and degrading treatment contrary to Article 3'.[224] But the Chamber said it was not necessary to reach 'any firm conclusion' because in any event the conviction had been the result of an unfair trial and could be addressed by article 6. The Grand Chamber essentially endorsed the conclusions of the Chamber. It put more emphasis on the role of Protocol No. 13, returning to the view expressed by the Plenary Court in *Soering* by which the States Parties have elected to follow 'the traditional method of amendment of the text of the Convention'.[225] Judge Garlicki wrote an individual opinion contesting the majority's 'replication of the *Soering* approach' and disputing whether the 'doctrine of pre-emption' meant the Court was prevented from stating the 'obvious truth' that the death penalty had been abolished within Europe.[226]

In *Al Saddoon and Mufthi v. The United Kingdom*, involving the transfer of two prisoners to the Iraqi authorities by British occupying forces, the Court revisited the issue. The Chamber noted that there had been an evolution in the position since *Öcalan*, with further ratifications of Protocol No. 13. This, together with consistent State practice in observing the moratorium on capital punishment, was 'strongly indicative that Article 2 has been amended so as to prohibit the death penalty in all circumstances'.[227] The Chamber said that '[a]gainst this background, the Court does not consider that the wording of the second sentence of Article 2 § 1 continues to act as a bar to its interpreting the words "inhuman or degrading treatment or punishment" in Article 3 as including the death penalty'.[228] Having concluded that the reference to capital punishment had in effect been deleted from the second sentence of article 2(1), the Court concluded that the applicants had suffered a violation of article 3. The Court said that the applicants had been 'subjected to a well-founded fear of execution' that caused them 'intense psychological suffering',[229] and that this constituted inhuman treatment.[230]

[221] Ibid., § 195.
[222] Opinion No. 233 (2002) on the Draft Protocol to the European Convention on Human Rights concerning the abolition of the death penalty in all circumstances, para. 5.
[223] *Öcalan v. Turkey*, no. 46221/99, § 198, 12 March 2003.
[224] Ibid., § 198.
[225] *Öcalan v. Turkey* [GC], no. 46221/99, §§ 164–165, ECHR 2005-IV.
[226] Ibid., Partly Concurring, Partly Dissenting Opinion of Judge Garlicki.
[227] *Al-Saadoon and Mufdhi v. the United Kingdom*, no. 61498/08, § 120, ECHR 2010 (extracts). Also *Kozhayev v. Russia*, no. 60045/10, § 81, 5 June 2012.
[228] *Al-Saadoon and Mufdhi v. the United Kingdom*, no. 61498/08, § 120, ECHR 2010 (extracts).
[229] Ibid., § 136.
[230] Ibid., § 144.

The most advanced statement on the subject is found in one of the cases dealing with CIA detention centres in Poland. In *Al Nashiri v. Poland*, the Court said the fact that 'imposition and use of the death penalty negates fundamental human rights has been recognised by the member States of the Council of Europe'. It described judicial executions as 'the deliberate and premeditated destruction of a human being by the State authorities', adding that the extinction of human life involves physical pain regardless of the method of execution. Furthermore, 'the foreknowledge of death at the hands of the State must inevitably give rise to intense psychological suffering'.[231]

Throughout its jurisprudence, from *Soering* to *Al Nashiri*, the Court has focused its consideration of capital punishment not on imposition of the penalty itself but on the psychological suffering imposed upon persons sentenced to death. Its approach contrasts with that taken by the Human Rights Committee. Because the International Covenant on Civil and Political Rights is universal and not regional in scope, the Committee cannot conclude that there is a consensus on abolition on a global scale comparable to what obtains within the Council of Europe. Instead, it had parsed the words of article 6(2) of the Covenant so that States Parties cannot invoke them where the death penalty has already been abolished.[232] The result is similar to that of the European Court, in that the reference to the death penalty in the right-to-life provision is deemed to be inoperative. However, the Human Rights Committee remains within the frame of the right to life rather than following the European Court and shifting the discussion to the issue of inhuman treatment.

Refoulement

Before the European Court of Human Rights, the issue of capital punishment now only arises with respect to the threat of transfer of an individual from a European State to one of the declining number of countries in the world where capital punishment still exists. In *Al Nashiri v. Poland*, of 24 July 2014, the European Court confirmed that 'Article 2 of the Convention prohibits the extradition or deportation of an individual to another State where substantial grounds have been shown for believing that he or she would face a real risk of being subjected to the death penalty there.'[233] In most death penalty cases before the Convention organs, diplomatic assurances that capital punishment would not take place or an assessment of the likelihood that it would be imposed[234] have been important issues. In *Soering*, although the United Kingdom was entitled to request diplomatic assurances under the extradition treaty,[235] its decision not to seek them provoked the litigation. After the Court's decision, the United States promptly provided diplomatic assurances that were deemed acceptable by the Committee of Ministers.[236] In several

---

[231] *Al Nashiri v. Poland*, no. 28761/11, § 577, 24 July 2014.

[232] *Judge v. Canada*, no. 829/1998 UN Doc. CCPR/C/78/D/829/1998.

[233] *Al Nashiri v. Poland*, no. 28761/11, § 577, 24 July 2014. Also *S.R. v. Sweden* (dec.), no. 62806/00, 23 April 2002; *Ismaili v. Germany* (dec.), no. 58128/00, 15 March 2001.

[234] *Ismaili v. Germany* (dec.), no. 58128/00, 15 March 2001; *Al-Shari and Others v. Italy* (dec.), no. 57/03, § 2, 5 July 2005; *Hakizimana v. Sweden* (dec.), no. 37913/05, 27 March 2008.

[235] *Extradition Treaty between the Government of the United Kingdom of Great Britain and Northern Ireland and the Government of the United States of America*, (1977) 1049 UNTS 167, art. IV.

[236] Council of Europe, *Information Sheet No. 26*, Strasbourg, 1990, p. 116. Soering was subsequently extradited, tried, and sentenced to life imprisonment. See Richard B. Lillich, 'The *Soering* Case', (1991) 85 *AJIL* 128.

subsequent cases, applicants have contested the sufficiency of diplomatic assurances.[237] A recent Albanian case provides an example of the nature of such assurances, in the form of a diplomatic note from the government of the United States: '. . . the Government of the United States hereby assures the Government of Albania that should Mr Rrapo be extradited to stand trial on the charges for which his extradition has been granted, the death penalty will not be sought or imposed against Almir Rrapo upon his extradition to the United States'.[238] The Court harshly criticized the lower courts in Albania for their apparent willingness to allow Rrapo's extradition without assurances that the death penalty would be imposed in the United States.[239] Eventually, however, the assurances were obtained. The Court said there was nothing to cast doubt on their validity, adding that there were no reported examples of the United States failing to respect similar assurances. The long-term interest of the United States in honouring its extradition commitments 'alone would be sufficient to give rise to a presumption of good faith against any risk of a breach of those assurances', it said.[240] Similarly, in a case involving extradition to the Russian Federation, a Chamber considered assurances from the authorities that the death penalty would not be imposed to be acceptable. It referred to several factors that enhanced the credibility of the assurances, including a judgment of the Constitutional Court declaring the death penalty unconstitutional and the fact of Russia's membership in the Council of Europe.[241]

The death penalty issue may also arise in expulsion cases, where there is no extradition request and where the question of diplomatic assurances on capital punishment under the relevant treaty does not therefore arise. An applicant must demonstrate a real risk that such *refoulement* will result in criminal prosecution and the prospect that capital punishment be imposed if guilt is established.[242] For example, the European Court has concluded that there is no real risk of execution in Kazakhstan, given the country's moratorium on the death penalty and systematic commutation of death sentences despite the fact that capital punishment still exists within the legal framework of the country.[243]

Permitted use of lethal force (art. 2(2))

Paragraph 2 of article 2 authorizes the use of lethal force under three circumstances: defence of any person from unlawful violence; effecting a lawful arrest or preventing the escape of a person lawfully detained; or action to quell a riot or insurrection. The exceptions listed in article 2(2) appear to be exhaustive. The possibility that there exist non-enumerated exceptions cannot, however, be excluded. In one case, where the Court considered a military attack on civilians in a conflict zone, it said it would leave unresolved 'whether a State could be justified under Article 2 § 2 of the Convention in using lethal

---

[237] *Aylor-Davis v. France*, no. 22742/93, Commission decision of 20 January 1994, DR 76, p. 164; *Nivette v. France* (dec.), no. 44190/98, ECHR 2001-VII; *Einhorn v. France* (dec.), no. 71555/01, ECHR 2001-XI; *Abu Salem v. Portugal* (dec.), no. 26844/04, 9 May 2006; *Shamayev and Others v. Georgia and Russia*, no. 36378/02, §§ 343–345, ECHR 2005-III.

[238] *Rrapo v. Albania*, no. 58555/10, § 19, 25 September 2012.

[239] Ibid., § 70.

[240] Ibid., § 73. Also *Harkins and Edwards v. the United Kingdom*, nos 9146/07 and 32650/07, §§ 86, 91, 17 January 2012.

[241] *Chentiev and Ibragimov v. Slovakia* (dec.), nos 21022/08 and 51946/08, 14 September 2010.

[242] *F.H. v. Sweden*, no. 32621/06, §§ 98–99, 20 January 2009.

[243] *Kaboulov v. Ukraine*, no. 41015/04, §§ 101–103, 19 November 2009; *Ismoilov and Others v. Russia*, no. 2947/06, § 119, 24 April 2008.

force against civilians for mere failure to comply with official safety instructions in an area of an armed conflict'.[244] The application of article 2 in armed conflict is discussed below under the heading 'Armed conflict'.

Of the three listed exceptions to the right to life in article 2, paragraphs b and c seem largely confined to a law enforcement context, whereas paragraph a confirms the justifiable taking of life in defence of any person. The introductory paragraph or *chapeau* indicates that the exceptions are only permitted when they result 'from the use of force which is no more than absolutely necessary'. The words 'absolutely necessary' dictate that 'a stricter and more compelling test of necessity must be employed than that normally applicable when determining whether State action is "necessary in a democratic society" under paragraphs 2 of Articles 8 to 11 of the Convention'.[245] Use of force must be 'strictly proportionate to the achievement of the aims set out in sub-paragraphs 2 (a), (b) and (c) of Article 2'.[246] In addition, any deprivations of life must be subjected 'to the most careful scrutiny', bearing in mind 'all the surrounding circumstances, including such matters as the planning and control of the actions under examination'.[247] Law enforcement operations must be 'planned and controlled so as to minimise to the greatest extent possible recourse to lethal force or incidental loss of life'.[248]

Article 2 authorizes the use of potentially lethal force in law enforcement, but it does not grant the authorities *carte blanche*. Their action must not be 'unregulated and arbitrary'. Not only must it be authorized under national law, it must also be sufficiently regulated with a system of 'adequate and effective safeguards against arbitrariness and abuse of force'.[249] The Court has noted the difficulty in separating a State's negative obligations from its positive obligations when lethal force is employed in policing.[250] The use of force may be justifiable when based upon a mistaken but 'honest belief which is perceived, for good reasons, to be valid at the time'.[251] Anything more demanding would impose an unrealistic burden on the State and on law enforcement authorities.[252]

Because the use of lethal force is only authorized in order to pursue one of the purposes listed in the three sub-paragraphs of article 2(2), there will inevitably be disputes about whether this was the genuine intent of the authorities. In *Finogenov et al.*, which concerned a huge hostage taking in a Moscow theatre by Chechen militants, the applicants, who were the innocent hostages, contended that the authorities were

---

[244] *Khatsiyeva and Others v. Russia*, no. 5108/02, § 140, 17 January 2008.

[245] *Giuliani and Gaggio v. Italy*, no. 23458/02, § 176, 24 March 2011; *Shchiborshch and Kuzmina v. Russia*, no. 5269/08, § 205, 16 January 2014.

[246] *Giuliani and Gaggio v. Italy*, no. 23458/02, § 176, 24 March 2011; *Sultan Karabulut v. Turkey*, no. 45784/99, § 50, 19 September 2006.

[247] *Giuliani and Gaggio v.* Italy, no. 23458/02, § 176, 24 March 2011. Also *McCann and Others v. the United Kingdom*, 27 September 1995, §§ 149–150, Series A no. 324; *Andronicou and Constantinou v. Cyprus*, 9 October 1997, § 171, *Reports of Judgments and Decisions* 1997-VI; *Avşar v. Turkey*, no. 25657/94, § 391, ECHR 2001-VII; *Musayev and Others v. Russia*, nos 57941/00, 58699/00, and 60403/00, § 142, 26 July 2007.

[248] *McCann and Others v. the United Kingdom*, 27 September 1995, § 194, Series A no. 324; *Ergı v. Turkey*, 28 July 1998, § 79, *Reports of Judgments and Decisions* 1998-IV; *Andronicou and Constantinou v. Cyprus*, 9 October 1997, §§ 171, 181, 186, 192, and 193, *Reports of Judgments and Decisions* 1997-VI; *Hugh Jordan v. the United Kingdom*, no. 24796/94, §§ 102–104, ECHR 2001-III.

[249] *Finogenov and Others v. Russia*, nos 18299/03 and 27311/03, § 207, ECHR 2011 (extracts); *Hilda Hafsteinsdóttir v. Iceland*, no. 40905/98, § 56, 8 June 2004.

[250] *Finogenov and Others v. Russia*, nos 18299/03 and 27311/03, § 208, ECHR 2011.

[251] *Giuliani and Gaggio v. Italy*, no. 23458/02, § 178, 24 March 2011.

[252] *McCann and Others v. the United Kingdom*, 27 September 1995, § 200, Series A no. 324; *Andronicou and Constantinou v. Cyprus*, 9 October 1997, § 192, *Reports of Judgments and Decisions* 1997-VI.

unconcerned with their welfare and were principally concerned with eliminating those responsible for the crisis. In that case, the Court said there was insufficient evidence of bad faith, and that it would presume that the authorities were pursuing all three of the legitimate aims listed in article 2(2), adding that defence of any person from unlawful violence was predominant.[253] It wrote:

> In sum, the situation appeared very alarming. Heavily armed separatists dedicated to their cause had taken hostages and put forward unrealistic demands. The first days of negotiations did not bring any visible success; in addition, the humanitarian situation (the hostages' physical and psychological condition) had been worsening and made the hostages even more vulnerable. The Court concludes that there existed a real, serious and immediate risk of mass human losses and that the authorities had every reason to believe that a forced intervention was the 'lesser evil' in the circumstances. Therefore, the authorities' decision to end the negotiations and storm the building did not in the circumstances run counter to Article 2 of the Convention.[254]

One of the important proportionality issues concerns the means of lethal force. Usually, this will involve some form of firearm, although the Strasbourg organs have considered cases involving the use of rubber bullets,[255] gas,[256] fragmentation bombs,[257] and even pepper spray.[258] The Court has held that article 2 of the Convention also imposes a positive duty on the State to locate and deactivate mines, to mark and seal off mined areas so as to prevent anyone from freely entering them, and to provide comprehensive warnings concerning mines laid in the vicinity of non-combatants.[259] According to the Court, 'the massive use of indiscriminate weapons . . . cannot be considered compatible with the standard of care prerequisite to an operation involving use of lethal force by State agents'.[260] The Court has noted approvingly a judgment of the German Constitutional Court finding that a law authorizing the use of force to shoot down a hijacked aircraft believed intended for a terrorist attack was incompatible with protection of the right to life.[261]

Defence from unlawful violence (art. 2(2)(a))

The words 'defence from unlawful violence' evoke the defence of self-defence in criminal law. It is defined with slight variations in the national criminal legislation of European States. Generally, legal systems consider the use of reasonable force by an individual to protect himself or herself, others for whom he or she is responsible, and his or her property. Article 2(2)(a) of the Convention is much narrower than the general rule because it deals only with lethal force, where the test of reasonableness will be stringent. Lethal force in self-defence will only be justified if a serious threat of death or serious

---

[253] *Finogenov and Others v. Russia*, nos 18299/03 and 27311/03, §§ 216, 218, ECHR 2011 (extracts).

[254] Ibid.

[255] *Stewart v. the United Kingdom*, no. 10044/82, Commission decision of 10 July 1984, §§ 28–30, (1984) 27 YB 129, DR 39, p. 162.

[256] *Finogenov and Others v. Russia*, nos 18299/03 and 27311/03, §§ 231–236, ECHR 2011 (extracts).

[257] *Khamzayev and Others v. Russia*, no. 1503/02, § 185, 3 May 2011; *Kerimova and Others v. Russia*, nos 17170/04, 20792/04, 22448/04, 23360/04, 5681/05, and 5684/05, § 253, 3 May 2011.

[258] *Oya Ataman v. Turkey*, no. 74552/01, §§ 20–27, ECHR 2006-XIII; *Çiloğlu and Others v. Turkey*, no. 73333/01, §§ 26–29, 6 March 2007.

[259] *Albekov and Others v. Russia*, no. 68216/01, § 90, 9 October 2008.

[260] *Isayeva v. Russia*, no. 57950/00, § 191, 24 February 2005; *Khamzayev and Others v. Russia*, no. 1503/02, § 189, 3 May 2011; *Kerimova and Others v. Russia*, nos 17170/04, 20792/04, 22448/04, 23360/04, 5681/05, and 5684/05, § 257, 3 May 2011.

[261] *Finogenov and Others v. Russia*, nos 18299/03 and 27311/03, § 231, ECHR 2011 (extracts).

injury is perceived. This conclusion results from the terms 'absolutely necessary' in the introductory words of article 2(2).

Although paragraph 2(2) is generally considered to deal with unintended killing, there may be cases when self-defence from life-threatening violence involves deliberate taking of human life, or certainly a degree of recklessness as to whether death will result. In a case involving police attempts to subdue an armed man who aimed a firearm at one of them and was then shot by a marksman, the Court said that 'the use of lethal force in the circumstances of this case, albeit highly regrettable, was not disproportionate and did not exceed what was absolutely necessary to avert what was honestly perceived by Officer B to be a real and immediate risk to his life and the lives of his colleagues'.[262] In another case involving a hostage taking, the Court disagreed with the European Commission, concluding that when two armed police used lethal force they had an honest belief that it was necessary to kill the victim in order to save the lives of both the hostage and of themselves.[263] But when an isolated protester was set upon by a hostile mob with sticks and other weapons, the Court said that at the moment of the attack he 'seemed unarmed and was not attacking anyone. In any event, once he was lying on the ground, he was not posing a danger to others.'[264]

In *Isayeva, Yusupova et al.*, Russia invoked article 2(2)(a) with respect to conduct of its armed forces, claiming they were acting in self-defence: 'the use of air power was justified by the heavy fire opened by members of illegal armed formations, which constituted a threat not only to the pilots, but also to the civilians who were in the vicinity. The pilots had to act in order to stop these illegal actions.'[265] The Court did not explore the interpretation of article 2(2)(a), assuming that it was applicable but subject to a test of proportionality that Russia failed. It said: 'The Court is also prepared to accept that if the planes were attacked by illegal armed groups, that could have justified use of lethal force, thus falling within paragraph 2 of Article 2.'[266] It referred to the 'attack' on Russian forces but the account, which is confused and about which the Court had serious doubts as to the credibility, is more like a rather classic military engagement than an exercise of self-defence. Russia seemed to adopt a very broad view, by which self-defence covers any action to protect society from violence. This seems an extravagant interpretation. Surely Russia was entitled to use force to deal with the Chechen uprising, but the applicable provision is article 2(2)(c) rather than 2(2)(a).

In a Turkish case, where three suspected terrorists were killed by police in an Istanbul café, the Court noted that the use of force 'was the direct result of the unlawful violence emanating from the deceased suspects'. The police had told civilians to leave the café and gave 'the necessary warnings' before going upstairs. The victims fired the first shot. The Court considered 'that when the police officers entered the café and were confronted with the shootings coming from the suspects, they believed that it was necessary to continue firing until the suspects stopped firing back'.[267] The Court said that the killings could be

[262] *Bubbins v. the United Kingdom*, no. 50196/99, §§ 140, 152, ECHR 2005-II (extracts). Also *Trévalec v. Belgium*, no. 30812/07, § 76, 14 June 2011.
[263] *Andronicou and Constantinou v. Cyprus*, 9 October 1997, § 129, *Reports of Judgments and Decisions* 1997-VI.
[264] *Isaak v. Turkey*, no. 44587/98, § 115, 24 June 2008.
[265] *Isayeva and Others v. Russia*, nos 57947/00, 57948/00, and 57949/00, § 160, 24 February 2005.
[266] Ibid., § 178.
[267] *Yüksel Erdoğan and Others v. Turkey*, no. 57049/00, § 98, 15 February 2007.

considered to have occurred 'in defence of any person from unlawful violence' and 'in order to effect a lawful arrest'.[268] It considered it unnecessary 'to speculate on the question of the possibility to use non-lethal methods by the security forces in order to arrest the deceased'.[269] This was, therefore, a situation of an attempt to arrest and not a case of defence from unlawful violence. The Court should not have confused the two.

Rejecting the justification of defence from unlawful violence in a case where a Cypriot demonstrator was shot to death when he crossed into Turkish-occupied Cyprus and climbed a flagpole, the Court noted that the victim 'was unarmed and had not attacked anyone; he was climbing a pole and smoking a cigarette, two actions which were not compatible with violent action against other individuals'.[270] Similarly, when an unarmed Greek Cypriot soldier was shot dead after breaching the ceasefire line and entering the buffer zone in order to fraternize with Turkish soldiers, the Court held that the victim's behaviour did not pose a threat sufficient to justify the use of lethal force.[271]

In a case where police were trying to apprehend an individual who then drew a pistol in a threatening manner, the Court felt that the terms of article 2(2) were fulfilled and rejected the application.[272] When making an arrest, the police opened fire possibly in response to a door bolt being drawn back, thinking that they were about to come under fire. The Court said that firing fifty to fifty-five shots at the door, resulting in the death of the suspect who was behind the door, was not justified by any reasonable belief of the officers that their lives were at risk from the occupants of the flat.[273] Moreover, 'opening fire with automatic weapons on an unseen target in a residential block inhabited by innocent civilians, women and children was as the Commission found, grossly disproportionate'.[274] But when a suspect took the first shot at two police officers who were attempting to arrest her, the Court accepted that they had acted in self-defence and were therefore justified under article 2(2)(a).[275] The Court 'cannot substitute its own assessment of the situation for that of an officer who was required to react in the heat of the moment to avert an honestly perceived danger to his life'.[276]

Lawful arrest or prevention of escape (art. 2(2)(b))

The wording of subparagraph (b) of article 2(2) might suggest that lethal force may be used even when there is no danger posed by the victim, in contrast with subparagraph (a) where, at least implicitly, the concept of self-defence implies that there is a serious threat justifying the use of lethal force. But the Court does not tolerate the use of lethal force where the victim does not pose a threat. In the leading case, *Nachova v. Bulgaria*, the Grand Chamber said that the legitimate aim of carrying out a lawful arrest could only justify a risk of death in circumstances of absolute necessity. It said that 'in principle there

[268] Ibid., § 95. Similarly, *Usta and Others v. Turkey*, no. 57084/00, § 58, 21 February 2008.
[269] *Yüksel Erdoğan and Others v. Turkey*, no. 57049/00, § 99, 15 February 2007.
[270] *Solomou and Others v. Turkey*, no. 36832/97, § 75, 24 June 2008.
[271] *Kallis and Androulla Panayi v. Turkey*, no. 45388/99, § 63, 27 October 2009.
[272] *Ramsahai and Others v. the Netherlands* [GC], no. 52391/99, §§ 288–289, ECHR 2007-II; *Ramsahai and Others v. the Netherlands*, no. 52391/99, §§ 356–371, 10 November 2005.
[273] *Gül v. Turkey*, no. 22676/93, § 82, 14 December 2000.
[274] Ibid.
[275] *Gülen v. Turkey*, no. 28226/02, § 38, 14 October 2008. Also *Kasa v. Turkey*, no. 45902/99, §§ 86–88, 20 May 2008.
[276] *Tonkevi v. Bulgaria* (dec.), no. 21302/13, § 33, 30 September 2014; *Bubbins v. the United Kingdom*, no. 50196/99, § 139, ECHR 2005-II (extracts).

can be no such necessity where it is known that the person to be arrested poses no threat to life or limb and is not suspected of having committed a violent offence, even if a failure to use lethal force may result in the opportunity to arrest the fugitive being lost'.[277] When firearms are to be used by law enforcement authorities, warning shots should be fired first.[278]

In some states, the relevant regulatory framework allows the use of lethal force when effecting an arrest regardless of the offence, a situation the Court has condemned as 'deficient'.[279] Law enforcement authorities must not 'be left in a vacuum' about the extent to which they may use lethal force, in particular with firearms.[280] Policing operations require proper regulation and adequate and effective safeguards against arbitrariness and abuse of force, including unavoidable accident.[281] Turkish legislation authorizing the use of lethal force within security zones, in particular border regions, where the victim does not obey an order to stop, without any requirement of proportionality in the use of firearms, has been deemed not to provide the requisite degree of protection of the right to life.[282] At the same time, it must be recognized that police must often react quickly, and without prior preparation, to difficult situations.[283]

The suggestion in judgments that the use of lethal force could be justified where the victim is suspected of having committed a 'violent offence' seems excessive, although the Court has not actually adjudicated a matter on this point. Even persons suspected of perpetrating violence offences will often pose no serious threat. The distinction between violent and non-violent offences only confuses matters. A person fleeing arrest for a serious non-violent offence may well be dangerous. The test should be whether there is an immediate threat of grave violence justifying lethal force.

In practice, in modern societies even a person fleeing arrest or escaping from detention is unlikely to get very far. Where a Cypriot demonstrator in Turkish-occupied Cyprus was shot to death after climbing a flagpole, the Court dismissed the defence of lawful arrest or prevention of escape, observing that 'it is obvious that he could hardly have escaped from the control of the security forces and that the authorities could have awaited his descent from the flagpole before arresting him'.[284] But even had it been possible for him to escape, could it be acceptable to kill a demonstrator under such circumstances?

---

[277] *Nachova and Others v. Bulgaria* [GC], nos 43577/98 and 43579/98, § 95, ECHR 2005-VII. Also *Putintseva v. Russia*, no. 33498/04, §§ 68–71, 10 May 2012; *Streletz, Kessler, and Krenz v. Germany* [GC], nos 34044/96, 35532/97, and 44801/98, §§ 87, 96, and 97, ECHR 2001-II; *Kakoulli v. Turkey*, no. 38595/97, § 108, 22 November 2005; *Alikaj and Others v. Italy*, no. 47357/08, §§ 72–73, 29 March 2011.

[278] *Makbule Kaymaz and Others v. Turkey*, no. 651/10, § 99, 25 February 2014; *Aydan v. Turkey*, no. 16281/10, § 66, 12 March 2013; *Andreou v. Turkey*, no. 45653/99, § 54, 27 October 2009.

[279] *Nachova and Others v. Bulgaria* [GC], nos 43577/98 and 43579/98, § 100, ECHR 2005-VII. Also *Tzekov v. Bulgaria*, no. 45500/99, §§ 28, 29, and 54, 23 February 2006; *Karandja v. Bulgaria*, no. 69180/01, §§ 56–57, 7 October 2010; *Putintseva v. Russia*, no. 33498/04, §§ 64–67, 10 May 2012.

[280] *Mansuroğlu v. Turkey*, no. 43443/98, § 73, 26 February 2008; *Anık and Others v. Turkey*, no. 63758/00, § 54, 5 June 2007; *Erdoğan and Others v. Turkey*, no. 19807/92, § 68, 25 April 2006; *Makaratzis v. Greece* [GC], no. 50385/99, § 59, ECHR 2004-XI.

[281] *Makaratzis v. Greece* [GC], no. 50385/99, § 58, ECHR 2004-XI; *Hilda Hafsteinsdóttir v. Iceland*, no. 40905/98, § 56, 8 June 2004; *Akpınar and Altun v. Turkey*, no. 56760/00, § 50, 27 February 2007; *Halit Dinç and Others v. Turkey*, no. 32597/96, § 56, 19 September 2006.

[282] *Ölmez and Others v. Turkey*, no. 22746/03, §§ 69–72, 9 November 2010; *Halis Akın v. Turkey*, no. 30304/02, §§ 29–33, 13 January 2009; *Beyazgül v. Turkey*, no. 27849/03, § 55, 22 September 2009.

[283] *Makaratzis v. Greece* [GC], no. 50385/99, § 69, ECHR 2004-XI; *Mahmut Kaya v. Turkey*, no. 22535/93, § 86, ECHR 2000-III; *Halit Çelebi v. Turkey*, no. 54182/00, § 48, 2 May 2006.

[284] *Solomou and Others v. Turkey*, no. 36832/97, § 75, 24 June 2008.

The Court has dealt with many cases in which the authorities attempted to apprehend individuals who were armed and dangerous.[285] Obviously, a perceived immediate threat to innocent lives lends urgency to the use of force.[286] Nevertheless, the use of lethal force must not only be necessary under the circumstances but it must also be used in such a way as to minimize the risk of death. This will be examined by considering the behaviour of the law-enforcement officials in the circumstances of the use of force, but also the planning and control of the operation. In a Bulgarian case, an armed criminal had fled into a residential building from which he had no means of escape. The Court said it was 'struck by the fact that the police do not appear to have had, or to have attempted to employ, any strategy aimed at minimising to the greatest extent possible recourse to lethal force'. There was no evidence of urgency or danger warranting recourse to armed force in order to effect the arrest. The Court said it was not convinced:

> that it was impossible for the police, for example, to attempt to warn Mr Vachkov of their intentions, or negotiate with him to put down his weapon, if he was armed, and surrender, or otherwise prevent recourse to lethal force, including a suicide attempt by him. Instead, apparently without considering any other possible course of action, the SATS officers entered into the building and engaged in gunplay.[287]

In other cases, the Court has reached the conclusion that the siege of premises where an armed and dangerous person was located needed to be broken in order to effect an arrest and was therefore justified under the circumstances.[288]

Quelling riot or insurrection (art. 2(2)(c))

The final category enumerated in article 2(2) of the Convention where lethal force is permissible is 'action lawfully taken for the purpose of quelling a riot or insurrection'. There is a degree of tension between article 2(2)(c) and the right of freedom of peaceful assembly in article 11. On the one hand, the Court has stated that 'where demonstrators do not engage in acts of violence, it is important for the public authorities to show a certain degree of tolerance towards peaceful gatherings if the freedom of assembly guaranteed by Article 11 of the Convention is not to be deprived of all substance'.[289] But '[i]n the case of mass demonstrations, which are becoming more and more frequent in a globalised world, the obligation to protect the right to life safeguarded by the Convention necessarily takes on another dimension'.[290]

The European Commission noted that the legal definition of 'riot' was a matter on which there could be divergences in national practice. It said that, like other concepts in the Convention, it was an 'autonomous' concept to be defined and interpreted by the

---

[285] For a lengthy list of these cases, see *Dimov and Others v. Bulgaria*, no. 30086/05, § 69, 6 November 2012.

[286] *McCann and Others v. the United Kingdom*, 27 September 1995, § 200, Series A no. 324; *Andronicou and Constantinou v. Cyprus*, 9 October 1997, § 185, *Reports of Judgments and Decisions* 1997-VI; *Perk and Others v. Turkey*, no. 50739/99, §§ 63–68, 28 March 2006.

[287] *Vachkovi v. Bulgaria*, no. 2747/02, § 75, 8 July 2010. Also *Golubeva v. Russia*, no. 1062/03, § 106, 17 December 2009.

[288] *Huohvanainen v. Finland*, no. 57389/00, §§ 99–108, 13 March 2007; *Bubbins v. the United Kingdom*, no. 50196/99, §§ 141–51, ECHR 2005-II (extracts).

[289] *Giuliani and Gaggio v. Italy* [GC], no. 23458/02, § 251, ECHR 2011 (extracts).

[290] Ibid., Joint Partly Dissenting Opinion of Judges Rozakis, Tulkens, Zupančič, Gyulumyan, Ziemele, Kalaydjieva, and Karakaş, § 2.

Commission and the Court.[291] It declined to provide an exhaustive definition of the term, but said that 'an assembly of 150 persons throwing missiles at a patrol of soldiers to the point that they risked serious injury must be considered, by any standard, to constitute a riot'.[292] Determination of the boundary between 'une désobéissance' and 'une insurrection, nécessitant ainsi l'intervention des forces de l'ordre'[293] or 'la tentative de soulèvement',[294] permitting application of article 2(2)(c) is a rather subjective determination that has resisted precise clarification in the case law. Context may contribute to the assessment. The Court has shown a considerable degree of deference when this involves a prison environment, given 'le potentiel de violence qui existe dans un établissement pénitentiaire' and 'le fait qu'une désobéissance des détenus puisse dégénérer rapidement en une mutinerie'.[295]

The Court considered the applicability of 'riot or insurrection' as a justification for killing a Greek Cypriot demonstrator who crossed the border into Turkish-occupied Cyprus and was killed while climbing a flagpole. It noted that it was unclear whether the demonstration was in fact relatively peaceful and under United Nations control, and seemed to accept that 'the demonstrators had sticks and iron bars and were seen throwing stones at the Turkish forces. This led to a situation of tension and to a risk of potentially more violent developments.'[296] Without firmly concluding that this was a riot or insurrection, the Court held there was a violation of article 2 because 'a potential illegal or violent action from a group of persons cannot, as such, justify the immediate shooting and killing of one or more other individuals who are not themselves posing a threat'.[297]

One factor that the Court may consider in assessing the necessity of resort to lethal force will be the number of injuries sustained by law enforcement officials.[298] In this respect, the facts may also lend themselves to the application of article 2(2)(a), although there must be precise evidence, rather than generalities, about the violent nature of the confrontation.[299]

Armed conflict

Article 2 makes no reference to the protection of the right to life during armed conflict. That the Convention might apply during wartime was clearly contemplated by the drafters, because article 15(2) refers to the possibility of derogation from article 2 with respect to 'lawful acts of war'. The Court has not left any doubt about the fact that it considers the obligations imposed by the European Convention, including the procedural obligation of article 2, to apply during armed conflict.[300] In a series of decisions, the

---

[291] *Stewart v. the United Kingdom*, no. 10044/82, § 24, Commission decision of 10 July 1984, (1984) 27 YB 129, DR 39, p. 162.
[292] Ibid.
[293] *Gömi and Others v. Turkey*, no. 35962/97, § 57, 21 December 2006.
[294] *Perişan and Others v. Turkey*, no. 12336/03, § 78, 20 May 2010.
[295] *Gömi and Others v. Turkey*, no. 35962/97, § 57, 21 December 2006.
[296] *Solomou and Others v. Turkey*, no. 36832/97, §§ 76–77, 24 June 2008.
[297] Ibid., § 77.
[298] *Gömi and Others v. Turkey*, no. 35962/97, § 52, 21 December 2006.
[299] *Perişan and Others v. Turkey*, no. 12336/03, § 77, 20 May 2010.
[300] *Al-Skeini and Others v. the United Kingdom* [GC], no. 55721/07, § 164, ECHR 2011; *Güleç v. Turkey*, 27 July 1998, § 81, *Reports of Judgments and Decisions* 1998-IV; *Ergi v. Turkey*, 28 July 1998, §§ 79 and 82, *Reports of Judgments and Decisions* 1998-IV; *Ahmet Özkan and Others v. Turkey*, no. 21689/93, §§ 85–90,

International Court of Justice has made it clear that human rights law cannot simply be displaced by war. In particular, it has acknowledged the application of the human right to life in time of war but with the caveat that the law of armed conflict operates as a *lex specialis*.[301]

Application of the law of armed conflict

The law of armed conflict, also described as international humanitarian law, is a distinct body of law whose origins are different from those of international human rights law. Nevertheless, it has many affinities with the international law of human rights, particularly when the treatment of victims of armed conflict, including people under military occupation, are concerned. The two bodies of law may overlap in certain areas. As a general rule, the humanitarian dimension of the law of armed conflict means that it leads to solutions that are similar to, if not identical with, those of human rights law. In some areas, the two bodies of law do not resolve issues in the same way. In *Hassan v. The United Kingdom*, the European Court acknowledged the difficulty in reconciling the principles dealing with arbitrary detention set out in article 5 with the general permissibility under the law of armed conflict of the internment of civilians. It concluded that the latter should be viewed as compatible with article 5, despite the fact that armed conflict is not dealt with explicitly in the text of the provision.[302]

In *Hassan*, the European Court said it considered that 'even in situations of international armed conflict, the safeguards under the Convention continue to apply, albeit interpreted against the background of the provisions of international humanitarian law'.[303] Previously, the Court had justified its rare references to the law of armed conflict not by a *lex specialis* principle but rather on the basis of article 31(3)(c) of the Vienna Convention on the Law of Treaties, which authorizes consideration of 'any relevant rules of international law applicable in the relations between the parties' for the purposes of interpretation.[304] The *Hassan* decision went somewhat further in that it relied not only on the Vienna Convention provision but also on the case law of the International Court of Justice, where the rationale is about reconciling two bodies of law that are not entirely compatible rather than using one body of law as an aid to interpretation of another.[305]

Whether the consequences of the *Hassan* ruling will extend to other rights set out in the European Convention remains to be seen. In right-to-life cases, the European Court of Human Rights had been chary of invoking international humanitarian law in its interpretation and application of the European Convention, although invited to do this by both applicants[306] and intervening non-governmental organizations.[307] Exceptionally,

---

309–320, and 326–330, 6 April 2004; *Isayeva v. Russia*, no. 57950/00, §§ 180 and 210, 24 February 2005; *Kanlibaş v. Turkey*, no. 32444/96, §§ 39–51, 8 December 2005.

[301] *Legality of the Threat or Use of Nuclear Weapons*, Advisory Opinion, I.C.J. Reports 1996, p. 226, §§ 25–26; *Legal Consequences of the Construction of a Wall in the Occupied Palestinian Territory*, Advisory Opinion, I.C.J. Reports 2004, p. 136, § 106.

[302] *Hassan v. the United Kingdom* [GC], no. 29750/09, §§ 77, 102, 16 September 2014.

[303] Ibid., § 104.

[304] *Loizidou v. Turkey* (merits), 18 December 1996, § 43, *Reports of Judgments and Decisions* 1996-VI.

[305] For a view that is critical of attempts to reconcile international human rights law and international humanitarian law, see *Hassan v. the United Kingdom* [GC], no. 29750/09, Partly Dissenting Opinion of Judge Spano Joined by Judges Nicolaou, Bianky, and Kalaydjieva, 16 September 2014.

[306] *Isayeva v. Russia*, no. 57950/00, § 157, 24 February 2005.

[307] Ibid., §§ 162–164.

the Court has made reference to the law of armed conflict in the context of article 2 with respect to the treatment of prisoners of war:

Article 2 must be interpreted in so far as possible in light of the general principles of international law, including the rules of international humanitarian law which play an indispensable and universally-accepted role in mitigating the savagery and inhumanity of armed conflict... The Court therefore concurs with the reasoning of the Chamber in holding that in a zone of inter-national conflict Contracting States are under obligation to protect the lives of those not, or no longer, engaged in hostilities. This would also extend to the provision of medical assistance to the wounded; where combatants have died, or succumbed to wounds, the need for accountability would necessitate proper disposal of remains and require the authorities to collect and provide information about the identity and fate of those concerned, or permit bodies such as the ICRC to do so.[308]

Of particular interest are the rules concerning the use of lethal force by the military and the consequent loss of life of civilians who do not participate actively in hostilities, a phenomenon that commonly goes under the name of 'collateral damage'. Although it does not use this term, familiar in the context of the law of armed conflict, it has acknowledged that military action may have, 'as a regrettable but unavoidable conse-quence, human casualties'.[309] The right to life is also germane to killing of combatants, whether they are organized opposition forces or civilians who participate directly in the conflict. Although the law of armed conflict and the case law of international criminal tribunals dealing with war crimes provide rather detailed answers to these issues, the Court has found the framework of the European Convention entirely adequate to address them without any need to apply other norms or defer to a *lex specialis*.

   In some cases involving essentially military activities, such as artillery attacks where there were civilian casualties, Russia bluntly denied any responsibility. Consequently, as it offered no justification such as military necessity that might excuse such 'collateral damage', the Court summarily concluded that there was a violation of article 2.[310] But in others it has admitted that it used lethal force as part of military activity directed at insurgents. The Court noted that Russia had not declared martial law or a state of emergency, and that no derogation had been formulated in accordance with article 15 of the European Convention.[311] As a result, the situation was to be judged 'against a normal legal background'.[312] The expression 'normal legal background' indicates that the Court examines the use of lethal force in military engagements using the same criteria as it would in peacetime law enforcement. This should not mean that as a factual matter there is an absence of armed conflict, however, although in one case the Court made the

---

[308] *Varnava and Others v. Turkey* [GC], nos 16064/90, 16065/90, 16066/90, 16068/90, 16069/90, 16070/90, 16071/90, 16072/90, and 16073/90, § 185, ECHR 2009 (the paragraph contains a reference to the four Geneva Conventions and the three Additional Protocols, which has been omitted here). Also *Varnava and Others v. Turkey*, nos 16064/90, 16065/90, 16066/90, 16068/90, 16069/90, 16070/90, 16071/90, 16072/90, and 16073/90, § 130, 10 January 2008.

[309] *Khamzayev and Others v. Russia*, no. 1503/02, § 178, 3 May 2011.

[310] *Taysumov and Others v. Russia*, no. 21810/03, §§ 94–95, 14 May 2009. Also *Mezhidov v. Russia*, no. 67326/01, §§ 60–62, 25 September 2008; *Umayeva v. Russia*, no. 1200/03, §§ 82–83, 4 December 2008; *Khalitova v. Russia*, no. 39166/04, § 58, 5 March 2009.

[311] The lack of derogation may no longer be considered relevant in light of the Grand Chamber's remarks in *Hassan*: *Hassan v. the United Kingdom* [GC], no. 29750/09, § 103, 16 September 2014.

[312] *Isayeva v. Russia*, no. 57950/00, § 191, 24 February 2005; *Khamzayev and Others v. Russia*, no. 1503/02, § 187, 3 May 2011.

confused observation that an aerial attack in Chechnya took place 'outside wartime'.[313] The Court has not had to address the scope of the term 'lawful acts of war', something that might be required had Russia effectively derogated from article 2.

Legitimate aim and proportionality

Before examining the proportionality of the use of lethal force, the Court must first determine whether it is in pursuit of a legitimate aim contemplated by article 2(2) of the Convention. Where Russian planes bombed a village killing several inhabitants, the Court said the justifications provided by paragraphs (a) and (b) of article 2(2) did not apply because of a lack of 'reliable evidence that any unlawful violence was threatened or likely, or that the lethal force was used in an attempt to effect a lawful arrest of any person'. It added that 'even assuming that the use of lethal force in the present case can be said to have pursued any of the aforementioned aims, the Court does not consider that the Government properly accounted for the use of that force resulting in the deaths of the five residents'.[314] It described the attack as 'indiscriminate bombing'.[315] In others, however, the Court has accepted that the use of lethal force by the military may have been necessary. In a case involving aerial attacks on a residential neighbourhood in a fortified village, the State relied upon article 2(2)(a), invoking 'the need to eliminate a danger to the local population emanating from illegal fighters' occupying the town at the time. So-called 'pinpoint aerial strikes' were used to enable Russian forces to retake the town. Russia argued that air power was necessary, citing the concern that a land operation 'would have led to considerable losses among federal servicemen'.[316] The Court admitted that this argument was 'not without foundation'.[317] In another, bombs were dropped on a civilian convoy at the border between Chechnya and Ingushetia. Russian authorities had issued a press statement denying civilian damage, claiming that a column of trucks with fighters and ammunition had provoked the encounter by firing upon a government aircraft.[318] The Court stated that it was 'prepared to accept that if the planes were attacked by illegal armed groups, that could have justified use of lethal force, thus falling within paragraph 2 of Article 2'.[319]

More generally, the justification for the use of lethal force must be to pursue a lawful purpose. In the Chechen jurisprudence, the Court has accepted that Russia was entitled to repress a secessionist movement. Thus, its findings were essentially confined to the norms applicable to the conduct of the armed forces, the *jus in bello*. The argument that killing of non-combatants in a conflict conducted in violation of international law, that is, contrary to *jus ad bellum*, would be per se contrary to the European Convention, regardless of issues of necessity and proportionality, remains to be considered by the Court. One of the consequences of the *lex specialis* approach of the International Court of Justice is to confine the examination of the applicable law during armed conflict to the *jus in bello*, as this is the frame within which the law of armed conflict sits. Yet article 2 of the European Convention necessarily requires that the use of lethal force be pursuant to legitimate

---

[313] Ibid., § 200.
[314] *Esmukhambetov and Others v. Russia*, no. 23445/03, § 141, 29 March 2011.
[315] Ibid., §§ 148, 150.
[316] *Khamzayev and Others v. Russia*, no. 1503/02, § 177, 3 May 2011.
[317] Ibid., § 179.
[318] *Isayeva and Others v. Russia*, nos 57947/00, 57948/00, and 57949/00, § 32, 24 February 2005.
[319] Ibid., § 178.

purpose. Killing that results from resort to illegal war and acts of aggression could never meet this standard and would be *prima facie* a violation of the human right to life.

Even if the use of lethal force is deemed to be justifiable for legitimate military purposes, the Court must still assess the proportionality of the actual measures. This inquiry generally focuses on targeting and on choice of weapons. In one case, Russia attempted to justify the use of force where a bomb dropped by a Russian plane exploded near the minivan of the applicant and her relatives as they were fleeing the village of Katyr-Yurt through what they had perceived as a safe exit from heavy fighting. The Court said:

the State's responsibility was not confined to circumstances where there was significant evidence that misdirected fire from agents of the state has killed a civilian. It may also be engaged where they fail to take all feasible precautions in the choice of means and methods of a security operation mounted against an opposing group with a view to avoiding and, in any event, minimising, incidental loss of civilian life.[320]

In a case involving aerial attacks on a residential neighbourhood in a fortified village, the Court said it was 'not convinced, having regard to the materials at its disposal, that the necessary degree of care was exercised in preparing the operation of 19 October 1999 in such a way as to avoid or minimise, to the greatest extent possible, the risk of a loss of life, both for the persons at whom the measures were directed and for civilians'.[321] Another judgment condemned the use of aviation bombs in a populated area without prior evacuation of the civilians as being 'impossible to reconcile with the degree of caution expected'.[322] In the border convoy case, the Court said that 'even assuming that the military were pursuing a legitimate aim in launching 12 S-24 non-guided air-to-ground missiles on 29 October 1999, the Court does not accept that the operation near the village of Shaami-Yurt was planned and executed with the requisite care for the lives of the civilian population'.[323]

In one case, the Court found that Turkish warplanes had bombed Kurdish villages. Turkey had denied the acts and therefore had not invoked any of the grounds set out in article 2(2) in defence. The Court said that in any case, 'indiscriminate aerial bombardment of civilians and their villages cannot be acceptable in a democratic society . . . and cannot be reconcilable with any of the grounds regulating the use of force which are set out in Article 2 § 2 of the Convention or, indeed, with the customary rules of international humanitarian law or any of the international treaties regulating the use of force in armed conflicts'.[324] In this respect, the Court referred to common article 3 to the Geneva Conventions, which sets minimum standards applicable to non-international armed conflict.[325] The reference was not particularly precise because common article 3 governs protected persons rather than the conduct of hostilities, which was the core of the issue in the Kurdish village case.

These issues are also very familiar within the context of the law of armed conflict. At the International Criminal Tribunal for the former Yugoslavia, for example, the minimization of civilian casualties has been addressed in the context of artillery attacks on cities and

[320] *Isayeva v. Russia*, no. 57950/00, § 176, 24 February 2005.
[321] *Khamzayev and Others v. Russia*, no. 1503/02, § 180, 3 May 2011.
[322] *Isayeva v. Russia*, no. 57950/00, § 191, 24 February 2005.
[323] *Isayeva and Others v. Russia*, nos 57947/00, 57948/00, and 57949/00, § 199, 24 February 2005.
[324] *Benzer and Others v. Turkey*, no. 23502/06, § 184, 12 November 2013.
[325] Ibid., § 89.

towns where the legal framework is the law of armed conflict rather than the law of human rights.[326] United Nations fact-finding commissions have made similar assessments using the law of armed conflict, but combined with human rights law. Investigating Israeli shelling of Palestinian settlements in Gaza in 2009, the Commission established by the Human Rights Council concluded that there had been a violation of the right to life and a violation of the obligation in the law of armed conflict, set out in article 57(2)(a)(ii) of the first Optional Protocol to the Geneva Conventions, because of a failure to '[t]ake all feasible precautions in the choice of means and methods of attack with a view to avoiding, and in any event to minimising, incidental loss of civilian life'.[327]

Within the law of armed conflict there is some debate, however, about whether those participating in combat can be targets of lethal force even if this is not strictly necessary to achieve the military objective.[328] The International Committee of the Red Cross has taken the view that even combatants benefit from a right to life to the extent that 'the kind and degree of force which is permissible against persons not entitled to protection against direct attack must not exceed what is actually necessary to accomplish a legitimate military purpose in the prevailing circumstances'.[329] This position finds support in the work of Jean Pictet, who wrote: 'If we can put a soldier out of action by capturing him, we should not wound him; if we can obtain the same result by wounding him, we must not kill him. If there are two means to achieve the same military advantage, we must choose the one which causes the lesser evil.'[330] Along similar lines, Hersch Lauterpacht wrote that the law on conduct of hostilities 'must be shaped—so far as it can be shaped at all—by reference not to existing law but to more compelling considerations of humanity, of the survival of civilisation, and of the sanctity of the individual human being'.[331] Such conclusions flow inexorably from the earliest codifications of the law of armed conflict, the 1868 Declaration of St Petersburg and the 1899 Martens Clause.[332] Thus, when combatants as well as non-combatants who participated actively in hostilities are concerned, it is also possible for the two legal systems to find common ground. Even combatants, even 'terrorists', benefit from the right to life, and cannot be deprived of it unless this is absolutely necessary.[333]

---

[326] See, e.g., *Prosecutor v. Gotovina et al.* (IT-06-90-T), Judgment, 15 April 2011; *Prosecutor v. Gotovina et al.* (IT-06-90-A), Judgment, 16 November 2012; *Prosecutor v. Strugar* (IT-01-42-T), 31 January 2005.

[327] Report of the United Nations Fact-finding Mission on the Gaza Conflict, UN Doc. A/HRC/12/48, paras 691–703. Also Report of the Secretary General's Panel of Experts on Accountability in Sri Lanka, 31 March 2011, paras 193–205.

[328] Jennifer Daskal, 'The Geography of the Battlefield: A Framework for Detention and Targeting Outside the "Hot" Conflict Zone', (2013) 161 *University of Pennsylvania Law Review*; W. Hays Parks, 'Part IX of the ICRC "Direct Participation in Hostilities" Study: No Mandate, No Expertise, and Legally Incorrect', (2010) 42 *New York University Journal of International Law and Politics* 769.

[329] International Committee of the Red Cross, 'Interpretive Guidance on the Notion of Direct Participation in Hostilities under International Humanitarian Law', (2008) 90 *International Review of the Red Cross* 991, at pp. 1040–4.

[330] Jean Pictet, *Development and Principles of International Humanitarian Law*, Dordrecht: Martinus Nijhoff, 1985, pp. 75 ff.

[331] Hersch Lauterpacht, 'The Problem of the Revision of the Law of War', (1952) 29 *British Yearbook of International Law* 360, at p. 379.

[332] See Nils Melzer, 'Keeping the Balance between Military Necessity and Humanity: A Response to Four Critiques of the ICRC's Interpretive Guidance on the Notion of Direct Participation in Hostilities', (2010) 42 *International Law and Politics* 831; Ryan Goodman, 'The Power to Kill or Capture Enemy Combatants', (2013) 24 *EJIL* 819.

[333] *McCann and Others v. the United Kingdom*, 27 September 1995, § 146, Series A no. 324; *Esmukhambetov and Others v. Russia*, no. 23445/03, § 146, 29 March 2011; *Khatsiyeva and Others v. Russia*, no. 5108/02, § 138, 17 January 2008.

Discrimination

The provision prohibiting discrimination, article 14, does not have an independent existence because it applies only to 'the enjoyment of the rights and freedoms' safeguarded by other provisions of Convention law. Nevertheless, it is autonomous to the extent that it does not require that there be a breach of one of the other substantive provisions. Article 14 is applicable when 'the facts at issue fall "within the ambit" of one or more of the latter'.[334] It can hardly be doubted that there are many manifestations of life-threatening violence perpetrated in Europe where the motivation may be discrimination or hatred directed against one of the groups listed in article 14. Most, if not all, of this will involve acts perpetrated by individuals. In such cases, the State's responsibility may be engaged under the procedural wing of article 2. The Court has rejected the argument formulated by a respondent State that article 14 could only be invoked in the case of violence attributable directly to the State where discriminatory motives may have been involved.[335]

There do not appear to have been any findings that the substantive obligation contained in article 2 have been violated in conjunction with article 14. In a dissenting opinion, Judge Bonello said he found it 'particularly disturbing that the Court, in over fifty years of pertinacious judicial scrutiny, has not, to date, found one single instance of violation of the right to life . . . induced by the race, colour or place of origin of the victim'. He lamented the impression given by the jurisprudence of the Convention organs of Europe as 'an exemplary haven of ethnic fraternity, in which peoples of the most diverse origin coalesce without distress, prejudice or recrimination. The present case energises that delusion.'[336] The Court seems to require proof beyond a reasonable doubt of racist motivation,[337] making this extraordinarily difficult to establish in practice.

Where there are suspicions of a racist dimension to lethal attacks on individuals, the State authorities are required to investigate the presence of such prohibited or aggravating motives. According to the Court,

States have a general obligation under Article 2 of the Convention to conduct an effective investigation in cases of deprivation of life. That obligation must be discharged without discrimination, as required by Article 14 of the Convention . . . [W]here there is suspicion that racial attitudes induced a violent act it is particularly important that the official investigation is pursued with vigour and impartiality, having regard to the need to reassert continuously society's condemnation of racism and ethnic hatred and to maintain the confidence of minorities in the ability of the authorities to protect them from the threat of racist violence. Compliance with the State's positive obligations under Article 2 of the Convention requires that the domestic legal system must demonstrate its capacity to enforce criminal law against those who unlawfully took the life of another, irrespective of the victim's racial or ethnic origin.[338]

---

[334] *Sejdić and Finci v. Bosnia and Herzegovina* [GC], nos 27996/06 and 34836/06, § 39, ECHR 2009; *Case 'relating to certain aspects of the laws on the use of languages in education in Belgium'* (merits), 23 July 1968, p. 30, § 9, Series A no. 6.

[335] *Fedorchenko and Lozenko v. Ukraine*, no. 387/03, §§ 61–64, 20 September 2012. Also *Menson v. the United Kingdom* (dec.), no. 47916/99, 6 May 2003.

[336] *Anguelova v. Bulgaria*, no. 38361/97, Partly Dissenting Opinion of Judge Bonello, § 2, ECHR 2002-IV.

[337] See, e.g., *Celniku v. Greece*, no. 21449/04, § 81, 5 July 2007.

[338] *Nachova and Others v. Bulgaria*, nos 43577/98 and 43579/98, §§ 156–159, 26 February 2004; *Nachova and Others v. Bulgaria* [GC], nos 43577/98 and 43579/98, §§ 160–161, ECHR 2005-VII; *Šečić v. Croatia*, no. 40116/02, §§ 66–70, 31 May 2007.

The Court has acknowledged that it may often be difficult in practice to establish racist motives. According to the Court, '[l]'absence de distinction dans la façon dont des situations qui sont essentiellement différentes sont gérées peut constituer un traitement injustifié inconciliable avec l'article 14 de la Convention'.[339] Where there was no question about the racism behind murderous attacks, the Court held that the State had breached article 14 by failing to charge racially motivated offences.[340] In a Bulgarian case, the government had argued that the investigators did not have sufficient indications of racist motivation but the Court pointed to a number of factors that showed the contrary. It concluded that in the course of an investigation that took thirteen years, the failure of the Bulgarian authorities to investigate the possibility of racist motivation constituted a violation of article 14 in conjunction with article 2.[341] In a case involving Roma victims in Ukraine, the Court considered that suspicions of racist motivation were justified by the widespread discrimination and violence against Roma in Ukraine as explained in reports of the European Centre on Racism and Intolerance. Consequently, the Court said 'it cannot be excluded that the decision to burn the houses of the alleged drug traffickers had been additionally nourished by ethnic hatred and thus it necessitated verification'.[342]

A similar approach was taken by the Court in a case involving violence against women. It noted that 'the general and discriminatory judicial passivity in Turkey [to domestic violence against women] created a climate that was conducive to domestic violence' and contributed to the murder of a woman by her husband, The Court said this was a violation of article 14 taken in conjunction with articles 2.[343]

In Italy, the government provided a compensation scheme for persons who had been contaminated with the human immunodeficiency virus by blood transfusions. The Court noted that it was not required by the Convention to do this but once it had done so it was necessary to implement the programme without discrimination. However, while available to haemophiliacs, it was not offered to persons with thalassemia. The Court concluded that this was a violation of article 14 in conjunction with article 2, in that the applicants were victims of discrimination based upon genetic features.[344]

Reservations

At the time of signature, on 12 December 1966, and ratification, on 23 January 1967, Malta made a reservation regarding 'the principle of lawful defence', stating that it was to apply in Malta to defence of property to the extent required by provisions of its Criminal Code. The reservation was accompanied by the texts of sections 737 and 738 of the Criminal Code, where it is stated that '[c]ases of actual necessity of lawful defence' include: 'where the homicide or bodily harm is committed in the act of repelling, during the night-time, the scaling or breaking of enclosures, walls, or the entrance doors of any house or inhabited apartment, or of the appurtenances thereof having a direct or an indirect communication with such house or apartment' and 'where the homicide or

---

[339] *Yotova v. Bulgaria*, no. 43606/04, § 104, 23 October 2012.
[340] *Angelova and Iliev v. Bulgaria*, no. 55523/00, § 116, 26 July 2007.
[341] *Yotova v. Bulgaria*, no. 43606/04, §§ 109–111, 23 October 2012.
[342] *Fedorchenko and Lozenko v. Ukraine*, no. 387/03, § 68, 20 September 2012.
[343] *Opuz v. Turkey*, no. 33401/02, § 202, ECHR 2009.
[344] *G.N. and Others v. Italy*, no. 43134/05, §§ 131–134, 1 December 2009.

bodily harm is committed in the act of defence against any person committing theft or plunder, with violence, or attempting to commit such theft or plunder'.[345]

Upon ratification in 1982, Liechtenstein made a reservation to article 2(2)(a) stating that the principle of self-defence 'shall in the Principality of Liechtenstein also apply to the defence of property and freedom in accordance with the principles at present embodied in Article 2, paragraph (g) of the Liechtenstein Criminal Code of 27 May 1852'. The reservation was withdrawn in 1991.[346]

Further reading

William Abresch, 'A Human Rights Law of Internal Armed Conflict: The European Court of Human Rights in Chechnya', (2005) 16 *European Journal of International Law* 741.

Çali Başak, 'The Logics of Supranational Human Rights Litigation, Official Acknowledgement, and Human Rights Reform: The Southeast Turkey Cases Before the European Court of Human Rights, 1996–2006', (2010) 35 *Law and Social Inquiry* 311.

L. Bieules Binzarun, 'Compétence ratione temporis', in P. Dourneau-Josette and E. Lambert-Abdelgawad, eds, *Quel filtrage des requêtes par la Cour européenne des droits de l'homme?*, Strasbourg: Editions du Conseil de l'Europe, 2011, pp. 255–92.

Carla Buckley, 'The European Convention on Human Rights and the Right to Life in Turkey', (2001) 1 *HRLR* 35.

Johan Callewaert, 'Is there a Margin of Appreciation in the Application of Articles 2, 3 and 4 of the Convention?', (1998) 19 *HRLJ* 6.

Andrew Clapham, 'Symbiosis in International Human Rights Law: The Öcalan Case and the Evolving Law on the Death Sentence', (2003) 1 *Journal of International Criminal Justice* 475.

Jean-Paul Costa and Michael O'Boyle, 'The European Court of Human Rights and International Humanitarian Law', in Dean Spielmann, Marialena Tsirli, and Panayotis Voyatzis, eds, *La Convention européenne des droits de l'homme, un instrument vivant, Mélanges en l'honneur de Christos L. Rozakis*, Brussels: Bruylant, 2011, pp. 107–31.

Emmanuel Decaux, 'La problématique des disparitions forcées à la lumière des articles 2 et 3 ECHR', in C.-A. Chassin, ed., *La portée de l'article 3 de la Convention européenne des droits de l'homme*, Brussels: Bruylant, 2006, pp. 157–78.

Frowein/Peukert, *MenschenRechtsKonvention*, pp. 28–41.

G. Gaggioli and R. Kolb, 'A Right to Life in Armed Conflicts? The Contribution of the European Court of Human Rights', [2007] *Israel Yearbook of International Law* 115.

Andrea Gioia, 'The Role of the European Convention of Human Rights in Monitoring Compliance with Humanitarian Law in Armed Conflict', in Orna Ben-Naftali, ed., *International Humanitarian Law and International Human Rights Law*, Oxford: Oxford University Press, 2011, pp. 201–49.

Feyyaz Gölcüklü, 'Le droit à la vie dans la jurisprudence de la Court européenne des des droits de l'homme', in G. Flécheux, ed., *Mélanges en hommage à Louis Edmond Pettiti*, Brussels: Bruylant, 1998, pp. 415–36.

Grabenwarter, *European Convention*, pp. 12–30.

Gilbert Guillaume, 'Article 2', in Pettiti et al., *La Convention européenne*, pp. 143–54.

Erik Harremoes, 'The Council of Europe and its Efforts to Promote the Abolition of the Death Penalty', (1986) 12–13 *Crime Prevention and Criminal Justice Newsletter* 62.

Harris et al., *Law of the European Convention*, pp. 37–68.

---

[345] (1966) 9 YB 24–27.
[346] (1991) 34 YB 5.

Helen Keller and Olga Chernishova, 'Disappearance Cases Before the European Court of Human Rights and the UN Human Rights Committee: Convergences and Divergences', (2012) 32 *HRLJ* 237.

Rosalyn Higgins, 'Extradition, the Right to Life, and the Prohibition against Cruel and Inhuman Punishment and Treatment: Similarities and Differences in the ECHR and the ICCPR', in Mahoney et al., *Mélanges Ryssdal*, pp. 605–16.

Stefan Kirchner, 'The Personal Scope of the Right to Life Under Article 2(1) of the European Convention on Human Rights After the Judgment in *A, B and C v. Ireland*', (2012) 13 *German Law Journal* 783.

Kirill Koroteev, 'Legal Remedies for Human Rights Violations in the Armed Conflict in Chechnya: The Approach of the European Court of Human Rights in Context', (2010) 1 *International Humanitarian Legal Studies* 275.

Julia Lapitskaya, 'ECHR, Russia, and Chechnya: Two Is Not Company and Three Is Definitely a Crowd', (2011) 43 *New York University Journal of International Law and Policy* 479.

Philip Leach, 'The Chechen Conflict: Analysing the Oversight of the European Court of Human Rights, (2008) 6 *EHRLR* 732.

Michel Levinet, ed., *Le droit au respect de la vie au sens de la Convention européenne des droits de l'homme*, Brussels: Bruylant, 2010.

Torkel Opsahl, 'The Right to Life', in Macdonald, *The European System*, pp. 207–23.

Ovey/White, *Jacobs and White, European Convention*, pp. 42–57; Bertrand G. Ramcharan, 'The Drafting History of Article 2 of the European Convention on Human Rights', in Bertrand G. Ramcharan, ed., *The Right to Life in International Law*, Dordrecht/Boston/Lancaster: Martinus Nijhoff Publishers, 1985, pp. 57–61.

Caroline Ravaud and Stefan Trechsel, 'The Death Penalty and the Case Law of the Institutions of the European Convention on Human Rights', in *The Death Penalty: Abolition in Europe*, Strasbourg: Council of Europe Publishing, 1999, pp. 79–90.

A. Reidy, 'The Approach of the European Commission and Court of Human Rights to International Humanitarian Law', (1998) 324 *International Review of the Red Cross* 513.

J. Remmelink, 'The Legal Position on Euthanasia in the Netherlands in Light of Article 2 of the ECHR', in Mahoney et al., *Mélanges Ryssdal*, pp. 1157–72.

Diarmuid Rossa Phelan, 'Right to Life of the Unborn v Promotion of Trade in Services: The European Court of Justice and the Normative Shaping of the European Union', (1992) 55 *Modern Law Review* 670.

Marco Sassòli, 'La Cour européenne des droits de l'homme et les conflits armés', in S. Breitenmoser, Bernhard Ehrenzeller, Marco Sassòli, Walter Stoffel, and Beatrice Wagner Pfeifer, eds, *Droits de l'homme, démocratie et État de droit, Liber amicorum Luzius Wildhaber*, Zurich: Dike, 2007, pp. 709–31.

L. Sermet, 'Le droit à la vie, valeur fondamentale des sociétés démocratiques, et le réalisme jurisprudentiel (Aspects récents de la jurisprudence de la Cour européenne des droits de l'homme)', [1999] *Revue française de droit administratif* 988.

Alphonse Spielman, 'La Convention européenne des droits de l'homme et la peine de mort', in *Présence du droit public et les droits de l'homme, Mélanges offerts à Jacques Vélu*, Brussels: Bruylant, 1992, pp. 1503–27.

Paolo De Stefani, 'La sentenza della Corte europea dei diritti umani per l'omicidio Giuliani: prima condanna per violazione del diretto alla vita pronunciata contro l'Italia', (2009) 4:2 *Pace diritti umani* 147.

F. Sudre, 'Les incertitudes du juge européen face au droit à la vie', in *Mélanges C. Mouly*, Paris: Litec, 1998, pp. 375–81.

H. Surrel, 'L'extension audacieuse de la compétence ratione temporis de la Cour européenne des droits de l'homme en matière de protection des droits procéduraux garantis par les articles 2 et 3 de la Convention', [2012] *RTDH* 271.

Paul Tavernier, 'Le recours à la force par la police', in Christian Tomuschat, Evelyne Lagrange, and Stefan Oeter, eds, *The Right to Life*, Leiden/Boston: Martinus Nijhoff, 2010, pp. 41–64.

H. Tigroudja 'La Cour européenne des droits de l'Homme face au conflit en Tchétchénie', [2006] *RTDH* 111.

Françoise Tulkens, 'Le droit à la vie et le champ des obligations des États dans la jurisprudence récente de la Court européenne des droits de l'Homme', in *Libertés. Justice. Tolérance. Mélanges en hommage au Doyen Gérard Cohen-Jonathan*, Brussels: Bruylant, 2004, pp. 1606–26.

Jon Yorke, 'The Right to Life and Abolition of the Death Penalty in the Council of Europe', (2009) 34 *European Law Review* 205.

Jon Yorke, 'Inhuman and Degrading Punishment and Abolition of the Death Penalty in the Council of Europe', (2010) 16 *European Public Law* 77.

Leo Zwaak, 'Right to Life (Article 2)', in Van Dijk et al., *Theory and Practice*, pp. 351–403.

Article 3. Prohibition of torture/Interdiction de la torture

No one shall be subjected to torture or to inhuman or degrading treatment or punishment.

Nul ne peut être soumis à la torture ni à des peines ou traitements inhumains ou dégradants.

Introductory comments

The prohibition of torture, and of inhuman or degrading treatment or punishment, is frequently cited as one of the most absolute and sacred of fundamental human rights. As the Court has noted, 'the prohibition of torture occupies a prominent place in all international instruments on the protection of human rights'.[1] In the Convention, the prohibition is formulated concisely in fifteen words, by far the shortest normative provision in the entire instrument. Furthermore, it is given a privileged position as the second right on the list, immediately following the right to life, with which it is often associated. It is true that there is no formal hierarchy in the list of fundamental rights. But it cannot be gainsaid that attention is directed to the special significance of a right when it is placed close to the beginning of the Convention.

The International Court of Justice has described the prohibition of torture as part of customary international law, adding that it has become a peremptory norm (*jus cogens*). The Court explained:

> That prohibition is grounded in a widespread international practice and on the *opinio juris* of States. It appears in numerous international instruments of universal application (in particular the Universal Declaration of Human Rights of 1948, the 1949 Geneva Conventions for the protection of war victims; the International Covenant on Civil and Political Rights of 1966; General Assembly resolution 3452/30 of 9 December 1975 on the Protection of All Persons from Being Subjected to Torture and Other Cruel, Inhuman or Degrading Treatment or Punishment), and it has been introduced into the domestic law of almost all States; finally, acts of torture are regularly denounced within national and international fora.[2]

Article 3 of the Convention closely resembles article 5 of the Universal Declaration of Human Rights, from which it is derived. The only difference is omission of the word 'cruel' in article 3 of the European Convention, an apparently inadvertent change and a difference to which probably no legal consequences should be attached. The first sentence of the corresponding provision in the International Covenant on Civil and Political Rights is identical to that of the Universal Declaration. However, a second sentence is added to the text of the Covenant: 'In particular, no one shall be subjected without his free consent to medical or scientific experimentation.'[3] A specialized treaty, the Convention Against Torture and Other Cruel, Inhuman or Degrading Treatment or Punishment, completes the United Nations system of human rights instruments.[4]

---

[1] *Ould Dah v. France* (dec.), no. 13113/03, ECHR 2009.

[2] *Questions relating to the Obligation to Prosecute or Extradite (Belgium v. Senegal)*, Judgment, I.C.J. Reports 2012, p. 422, para. 99.

[3] International Covenant on Civil and Political Rights, (1976) 999 UNTS 171, art. 7.

[4] (1987) 1465 UNTS 85.

The European Charter of Fundamental Rights proclaims the prohibition of torture in terms that are identical to the text of article 3 of the Convention except that the title of article 4 of the Charter is 'Prohibition of torture and inhuman or degrading treatment or punishment'. The provision is meant to have the same meaning and scope as article 2 of the European Convention.[5] Article 19(2) of the European Charter also proclaims a principle of *non-refoulement*: 'No one may be removed, expelled or extradited to a State where there is a serious risk that he or she would be subjected to the death penalty, torture or other inhuman or degrading treatment or punishment.' It is also meant to have the same meaning and scope as article 3 of the European Convention, 'as interpreted by the European Court of Human Rights'.[6]

The extraordinary attention devoted to the issue of torture in the field of human rights has resulted in specialized instruments with bodies for their monitoring and implementation. Within the Council of Europe, the European Convention for the Prevention of Torture and Inhuman or Degrading Treatment or Punishment provides for the establishment of the Committee for the Prevention of Torture. It has the authority to make unannounced visits to 'places of detention' within all Member States of the Council of Europe.

Drafting of the provision

The initial draft European Convention on Human Rights, prepared by the International Juridical Section of the European Movement, did not closely follow the Universal Declaration, with its autonomous provision on torture and cruel, inhuman or degrading treatment or punishment. The enumeration of rights in the draft began: 'Every State a party to this Convention shall guarantee to all persons within its territory the following rights: a) Security of life and limb.'[7] This seems surprising, given that two of the rapporteurs responsible for drafting the text, David Maxwell Fyfe and Fernand Dehousse, had been involved in the adoption of the Universal Declaration of Human Rights at the United Nations the previous year.

Asked to prepare a text for discussion in the Committee on Legal and Administrative Questions at the first session of the Consultative Assembly, held from 22 August to 5 September 1949, Pierre-Henri Teitgen proposed the following: 'Security of person, in accordance with Articles 3, 5 and 8 of the Universal Declaration of Human Rights adopted by the United Nations General Assembly.'[8] At its sitting of 29 August 1949 the Committee on Legal and Administrative Questions accepted inclusion of 'the safety of the person, as laid down in Articles 3, 5 and 8 of the Universal Declaration on [sic] Human Rights'.[9] The word 'safety' was evidently an awkward translation of the French *sûreté* and was changed to security—the term used in article 3 of the Universal Declaration of Human Rights—in the final report adopted by the Committee: 'Security of person, in

---

[5] Explanation relating to the Charter of Fundamental Rights, Official Journal of the European Union, C 303/33, 14 December 2007.

[6] Ibid.

[7] Convention for the Collective Protection of Individual Rights and Democratic Liberties by the States, Members of the Council of Europe, and for the establishment of a European Court of Human Rights to ensure observance of the Convention, Doc. INF/5/E/R, I *TP* 296–303, at p. 296, art. I(a).

[8] Proposals by Mr P.H. Teitgen, Rapporteur, 29 August 1949, Doc. A 116, I *TP* 166–8.

[9] Minutes of the Sitting [of the Committee for Legal and Administrative Affairs of the Consultative Assembly, 29 August 1949], Doc. A 142, I *TP* 170–3.

accordance with Articles 3, 5 and 8 of the United Nations Declaration'.[10] Yet, despite the references to article 5 of the Declaration, the word 'torture' was not even mentioned.

In presenting his draft report to the Commission on Legal and Administrative Questions to the first Session of the Consultative Assembly, Teitgen said that 'in recommending a collective guarantee not only of freedom to express convictions, but also of thought, conscience, religion and opinion, the Committee wished to protect all nationals of any member State, not only from breaches of obligation for so-called reasons of State, but also from those abominable methods of police enquiry or judicial process which rob the suspected or accused person of control of his intellectual faculties and of conscience'.[11] In the debate on the report of the Commission on Legal and Administrative Questions in the Consultative Assembly, Seymour Cocks, of the British Labour Party, proposed:

In particular no person shall be subjected to any form of mutilation or sterilisation, nor to any form of torture or beating. Nor shall he be forced to take drugs nor shall they be administered to him without his knowledge and consent. Nor shall he be subjected to imprisonment with such an excess of light, darkness, noise or silence as to cause mental suffering.'[12]

This was withdrawn by the proposer and replaced with:

The Consultative Assembly takes this opportunity of declaring that all forms of physical torture, whether inflicted by the police, military authorities, members of private organisations or any other persons are inconsistent with civilised society, are offences against heaven and humanity and must be prohibited.

They declare that this prohibition must be absolute and that torture cannot be permitted by any purpose whatsoever, neither by extracting evidence for saving life nor even for the safety of the State.

They believe that it would be better even for Society to perish than for it to permit this relic of barbarism to remain.[13]

Explaining his proposal in the Consultative Assembly, Cocks said the object was to give greater emphasis to the condemnation of torture. He described how as a child he had been taught that torture belonged to ancient civilizations but that it had been 'done away with hundreds of years ago, that the world had become civilised'. But '[t]he most terrible event in my lifetime in this century has been that torture and violence have returned—returned fortified by many discoveries of modern science—and that in many countries people are even becoming accustomed to it'.[14] After explanations that the matter was already adequately addressed, through the reference to article 5 of the Universal Declaration of Human Rights, Cocks agreed to withdraw his proposal.[15]

The Consultative Assembly adopted the text proposed by the Committee.[16] But a report prepared by the Secretariat-General following the adoption of the Consultative

[10] Report presented by Mr P.H. Teitgen, 5 September 1949, Doc. A 290, I *TP* 192–213, at p. 206. See also Report [of the Committee on Legal and Administrative Questions], 5 September 1949, Doc. AS (1) 77, I *TP* 216–39, at p. 228.

[11] Report presented by Mr P.H. Teitgen, 5 September 1949, Doc. A 290, I *TP* 192–213, at pp. 198–200.

[12] Amendment proposed by Mr Cocks, Doc. No. 90, p. 235, I *TP* 252.

[13] Amendment proposed by Mr Cocks, Doc. No. 91, p. 236, I *TP* 252–4.

[14] Official Report of the Sitting [of the Consultative Assembly, 8 September 1949], II *TP* 14–274, at p. 38.

[15] Ibid., pp. 46, 238–46. See the brief discussion of the debate in Preparatory Report by the Secretariat-General concerning a Preliminary Draft Convention to Provide a Collective Guarantee of Human Rights, Doc. B 22, III *TP* 2–37, at p. 28.

[16] Recommendation No. 38 to the Committee of Ministers adopted 8 September 1949 on the conclusion of the debates, Doc. AS (1) 108, II *TP* 274–83, at p. 276.

Assembly text compared the latter with the draft International Covenant being considered by the United Nations Commission on Human Rights and noted that the explicit prohibition of torture was '[e]xcluded from the European system' and would instead be the subject of a solemn declaration to be adopted by the Assembly.[17] If this was a genuine omission, the matter was soon addressed in proposed amendments from the United Kingdom. It submitted a text identical to article 5 of the Universal Declaration of Human Rights: 'No one shall be subjected to torture or to cruel, inhuman or degrading treatment or punishment.' Accompanying the proposal was a second sentence, taken from the draft International Covenant considered by the United Nations Commission on Human Rights in mid-1949: 'No one shall be subjected to any form of physical mutilation or medical or scientific experimentation against his will.'[18]

At the conclusion of its first session, in February 1950, the Committee of Experts adopted the following provision: 'No one shall be subjected to torture or to cruel, inhuman or degrading treatment or punishment.'[19] The report of the Committee explains that instead of enumerating rights by reference to the relevant provision in the Universal Declaration, as had been done by the Consultative Assembly, it was better to incorporate the text verbatim. Accordingly, the Committee 'scrupulously adhered to the text of the Universal Declaration'.[20] The text it adopted is, of course, identical to article 5 of the Universal Declaration of Human Rights. At the second session of the Committee of Experts, in March 1950, the United Kingdom representative submitted an amendment that removed the adjectives 'cruel' and 'degrading': 'No one shall be subjected to torture or to inhuman treatment or punishment.'[21]

The Committee of Experts submitted two different drafts to the Committee of Ministers. The first, 'Alternatives A and A/2', consisted of the text adopted by the Committee of Experts at its first session and that was taken verbatim from article 5 of the Universal Declaration of Human Rights.[22] The second, labelled 'Alternatives B and B/2', contained the most recent text proposed by the United Kingdom.[23]

The Conference of Senior Officials that convened in June 1950 assigned a Drafting Committee to attempt to reconcile the competing versions. It prepared a new formulation of the prohibition of torture and ill-treatment that corresponds to the final version of article 3 of the European Convention.[24] The published *travaux préparatoires* do not

[17] Preparatory Report by the Secretariat-General concerning a Preliminary Draft Convention to Provide a Collective Guarantee of Human Rights, Doc. B 22, III *TP* 2–36, at p. 28.

[18] Amendments to Article 2 of the Recommendation of the Consultative Assembly proposed by the Expert of the United Kingdom, Doc. A 798, III *TP* 204–7, at p. 206.

[19] Preliminary Draft Convention for the Maintenance and Further Realisation of Human Rights and Fundamental Freedoms, 15 February 1950, Doc. A 833, III *TP* 236–46, at p. 236. Also Draft text of the first section of a draft Convention based on the work of the Consultative Assembly, Doc. A 809, III *TP* 220–31, at p. 222.

[20] Preliminary Draft of the Report to the Committee of Ministers, 24 February 1950, Doc. CM/WP 1 (50) 1, A 847, III *TP* 246–79, at pp. 260–2.

[21] Amendments to Articles 1, 2, 4, 5, 6, 8, and 9 of the Committee's Preliminary Draft Proposal by the Expert of the United Kingdom, Doc. CM/WP 1 (50) 2, A 915, III *TP* 280–9, at p. 280.

[22] Report to the Committee of Ministers Submitted by the Committee of Experts Instructed to Draw Up a Draft Convention of Collective Guarantee of Human Rights and Fundamental Freedoms, Doc. CM/WP 1 (5) 15, A 924, IV *TP* 2–55, at p. 52. See also Preliminary Draft Convention, Doc. CM/WP 1 (50) 14, A 932, III *TP* 312–35, at p. 320.

[23] Report to the Committee of Ministers Submitted by the Committee of Experts Instructed to Draw Up a Draft Convention of Collective Guarantee of Human Rights and Fundamental Freedoms, Doc. CM/WP 1 (5) 15, A 924, IV *TP* 2–55, p. 58. See also Preliminary Draft Convention, Doc. CM/WP 1 (50) 14, A 932, III *TP* 312–35, at pp. 312–14.

[24] New draft alternatives B and B/2, Doc. CM/WP 4 (50) 9, A 1372, IV *TP* 182–91, at p. 184.

indicate whether any distinction in substance was intended by comparison with article 5 of the Universal Declaration of Human Rights, in particular the absence of the word 'cruel' in the European Convention. Usually, the British preference was for the more detailed and precise text. It would have made sense for the British and their allies to agree to the more detailed formulation of article 5 of the Universal Declaration. The Drafting Committee text became the definitive one in the draft adopted by the Conference of Senior Officials[25] and was confirmed by the Committee of Ministers at its fifth session in August 1950.[26]

The heading 'Prohibition of torture' was added pursuant to the provisions of Protocol No. 11.[27]

Analysis and interpretation

Article 3 of the European Convention on Human Rights 'enshrines one of the most fundamental values of democratic societies'.[28] The prohibition of torture and inhuman or degrading treatment or punishment is set out in 'absolute terms', making 'no provision for exceptions'.[29] Indeed, 'even in the most difficult of circumstances, such as the fight against organised terrorism and crime, the Convention prohibits in absolute terms torture or inhuman or degrading treatment or punishment'.[30] As an absolute prohibition, it applies regardless of the conduct of the victim[31] or the nature of any offence that has allegedly been committed.[32] The European Court has rejected the suggestion that it should apply article 3 more flexibly, in particular in cases involving expulsion or *refoulement*, simply because the alleged victim is associated with terrorist activities.[33]

In this respect, the Court has noted the comparison between article 3 and most of the other substantive clauses of the Convention and the Protocols, where exceptions and derogation are allowed.[34] It is perhaps not surprising that the prohibition of torture and ill-treatment might be more absolute than the right to marry or to property or the

---

[25] Draft Convention appended to the Draft Report, Doc. CM/WP 4 (50) 16, appendix, A 1445, IV *TP* 218–40, at p. 218; Draft Convention annexed to the Report, Doc. CM/WP 4 (50) 19 annex, CM/WP 4 (50) 16 rev., A 1452, IV *TP* 274–95, at p. 274.

[26] Draft Convention adopted by the Sub-Committee, Doc. CM 1 (50) 52, A 1884, V *TP* 76–99, at p. 76; Draft Convention adopted by the Committee of Ministers, 7 August 1950, Doc. A 1937, V *TP* 120–45, at p. 122.

[27] Protocol No. 11 to the Convention for the Protection of Human Rights and Fundamental Freedoms, restructuring the control machinery established thereby, ETS 155, art. 2(2).

[28] *A. and Others v. the United Kingdom* [GC], no. 3455/05, § 126, ECHR 2009; *Ramirez Sanchez v. France* [GC], no. 59450/00, §§ 115–16, ECHR 2006-IX; *Assenov and Others v. Bulgaria*, 28 October 1998, § 93, *Reports of Judgments and Decisions* 1998-VIII; *Selmouni v. France* [GC], no. 25803/94, § 95, ECHR 1999-V.

[29] *Mubilanzila Mayeka and Kaniki Mitunga v. Belgium*, no. 13178/03, § 48, ECHR 2006-XI.

[30] *Aksoy v. Turkey*, 18 December 1996, § 62, *Reports of Judgments and Decisions* 1996-VI.

[31] *Chahal v. the United Kingdom*, 15 November 1996, § 79, Reports of Judgments and Decisions 1996-V; *Saadi v. Italy* [GC], no. 37201/06, § 127, ECHR 2008.

[32] *Indelicato v. Italy*, no. 31143/96, § 30, 18 October 2001; *Ramirez Sanchez v. France* [GC], no. 59450/00, §§ 115–116, ECHR 2006-IX.

[33] *Saadi v. Italy* [GC], no. 37201/06, § 140, ECHR 2008.

[34] *A. and Others v. the United Kingdom* [GC], no. 3455/05, § 126, ECHR 2009; *Ramirez Sanchez v. France* [GC], no. 59450/00, §§ 115–116, ECHR 2006-IX; *Pretty v. The United Kingdom*, no. 2346/02, § 49, ECHR 2002-III; *Chahal v. the United Kingdom*, 15 November 1996, § 79, *Reports of Judgments and Decisions* 1996-V; *Selmouni v. France* [GC], no. 25803/94, § 95, ECHR 1999-V; *Gäfgen v. Germany* [GC], no. 22978/05, § 69, ECHR 2010.

prohibition of imprisonment for debt, for example. But this observation also holds true for the right to life, for which there are both exceptions or limitations and the possibility of derogation. One of the enigmas of human rights law is the apparent absolute prohibition of torture and inhuman or degrading treatment or punishment set alongside the acceptance of limitations on the right to life, including capital punishment and killing in armed conflict.

Under the European Convention, there is no particular consequence to the distinction between torture and inhuman or degrading treatment or punishment. In either case, there is a violation of article 3 of the Convention. This contrasts, for example, with the United Nations Convention against Torture and Other Cruel, Inhuman or Degrading Treatment or Punishment, where certain obligations apply only in the case of torture and not with respect to other cruel, inhuman, or degrading treatment or punishment. One of the differences between torture and inhuman or degrading treatment or punishment that is often signalled concerns the severity of the measure. Apparently, all torture will also be inhuman or degrading treatment or punishment, but not all inhuman or degrading treatment or punishment will be torture. In a sense, therefore, torture is the *lex specialis*.

Allegations of torture or ill-treatment frequently raise challenging evidentiary issues. The Court requires 'appropriate evidence'[35] that satisfies a standard of proof 'beyond reasonable doubt'.[36] Such proof 'may follow from the coexistence of sufficiently strong, clear and concordant inferences or of similar unrebutted presumptions of fact'.[37]

The victim

Article 3 begins with the words 'No one', a formulation that is favoured when the Convention sets out a prohibition. The same expression is also used in articles 4 and 7 and in Protocol No. 4 (arts 1 and 3), No. 6 (art. 1), No. 7 (art. 4), No. 12 (art. 1, and No. 13 (art. 1). Personal characteristics play a role in determining whether or not an individual may be considered a victim of torture or ill-treatment.

The Court has said that it will consider various factors including sex, age, and state of health of the victim in its assessment.[38] There are several examples in the case law of age being considered relevant in this respect. In *Soering v. the United Kingdom*, for example, the plenary Court concluded that there was a real risk of ill-treatment taking into consideration the applicant's age and mental state. Soering was nineteen at the time of the offence for which he faced the death penalty, although he was nearly twenty-four when the Court issued its judgment declaring that extradition to the United States to stand trial would raise a real risk of inhuman or degrading treatment.[39] In assessing the seriousness of injuries sustained in police custody by an older person, the Court considered that they fell within the scope of article 3 in light of 'the applicant's advanced

---

[35] *Arutyunyan v. Russia*, no. 48977/09, § 68, 10 January 2012; *Enea v. Italy* [GC], no. 74912/01, § 55, ECHR 2009; *Klaas v. Germany*, 22 September 1993, § 30, Series A no. 269.

[36] *Kudła v. Poland* [GC], no. 30210/96, §§ 98–99, ECHR 2000-XI.

[37] *Đurđević v. Croatia*, no. 52442/09, § 79, ECHR 2011 (extracts); *Salman v. Turkey* [GC], no. 21986/93, § 100, ECHR 2000-VII; *Dedovskiy and Others v. Russia*, no. 7178/03, § 74, ECHR 2008 (extracts); *Ireland v. the United Kingdom*, 18 January 1978, § 161 *in fine*, Series A no. 25; *Labita v. Italy* [GC], no. 26772/95, § 121, ECHR 2000-IV. For a general discussion of evidence, see the chapter in this Commentary on article 38 of the Convention.

[38] *Ireland v. the United Kingdom*, 18 January 1978, § 162, Series A no. 25.

[39] *Soering v. the United Kingdom*, 7 July 1989, §§ 108–109, Series A no. 161.

age—67 years at the relevant time'.[40] The two-month detention by Belgian authorities of a five-year-old child in an immigration centre where similar incarceration of adults would not raise any particular difficulties 'demonstrated a lack of humanity to such a degree that it amounted to inhuman treatment'.[41] The 'tender age' of an eight-year-old girl, who was a victim of physical violence by her father, and who also witnessed her mother being abused, was significant in a finding that article 3 applied.[42] But in a case involving corporal punishment of a seven-year-old in a boarding school, only two dissenters within the European Commission attached significance to the young age of the applicant.[43]

Family members of victims of serious human rights violations may themselves be victims of a violation of article 3. In order to conclude that there has been a separate violation of article 3 with respect to relatives, the Grand Chamber has insisted upon special factors 'giving their suffering a dimension and character distinct from the emotional distress inevitably stemming' from the initial violation.[44] These include the proximity of the family tie, the circumstances of the relationship, the extent the family member witnessed the events in question and involvement in the attempts to obtain information about the fate of the victims of the primary violation.[45] There have been findings of a separate violation of article 3 with respect to close family members who have directly witnessed the suffering or death of their relatives that was in itself a violation of the Convention.[46] Examples include a mother who witnessed the slow death in detention of her son and was unable to help him,[47] applicants who saw the killing of family members and neighbours,[48] and parents who were unable to bury the dismembered and decapitated bodies of their children in a proper manner[49] or who were presented with a mutilated corpse.[50] The detention of a five-year-old caused 'deep distress and anxiety' to the mother, resulting in a violation of article 3.[51]

The issue of collateral consequences for family members is especially relevant in the case of forced disappearances as the act itself is often followed by a long period of uncertainty, ending in some cases with the discovery of the body and confirmation of death. According to the Grand Chamber, '[t]he essence of the issue under Article 3 in this type of case lies not so much in a serious violation of the missing person's human rights but rather in the authorities' dismissive reactions and attitudes in respect of that situation when it was brought to their attention'.[52] In that sense, there is a close relationship to the procedural

---

[40] *Toteva v. Bulgaria*, no. 42027/98, § 52, 19 May 2004.

[41] *Mubilanzila Mayeka and Kaniki Mitunga v. Belgium*, no. 13178/03, § 58, ECHR 2006-XI.

[42] *T.M. and C.M. v. Moldova*, no. 26608/11, § 41, 28 January 2014.

[43] *Costello-Roberts v. the United Kingdom*, no. 13134/87, Commission report of 8 October 1991, Dissenting opinion of Mrs Thune joined by Mr Geus, Dissenting Opinion of Mr Loukaides.

[44] *Janowiec and Others v. Russia* [GC], nos 55508/07 and 29520/09, § 177, ECHR 2013.

[45] Ibid.

[46] Ibid., § 181.

[47] *Salakhov and Islyamova v. Ukraine*, no. 28005/08, § 204, 14 March 2013.

[48] *Esmukhambetov and Others v. Russia*, no. 23445/03, § 190, 29 March 2011; *Musayev and Others v. Russia*, nos 57941/00, 58699/00, and 60403/00, § 169, 26 July 2007.

[49] *Khadzhialiyev and Others v. Russia*, no. 3013/04, § 121, 6 November 2008.

[50] *Akkum and Others v. Turkey*, no. 21894/93, §§ 258–259, ECHR 2005-II (extracts).

[51] *Mubilanzila Mayeka and Kaniki Mitunga v. Belgium*, no. 13178/03, § 62, ECHR 2006-XI.

[52] *Janowiec and Others v. Russia* [GC], nos 55508/07 and 29520/09, § 178, ECHR 2013; *Açış v. Turkey*, no. 7050/05, §§ 36 and 51–54, 1 February 2011; *Varnava and Others v. Turkey* [GC], nos 16064/90, 16065/90, 16066/90, 16068/90, 16069/90, 16070/90, 16071/90, 16072/90, and 16073/90, § 200, ECHR 2009; *Osmanoğlu v. Turkey*, no. 48804/99, § 96, 24 January 2008; *Luluyev and Others v. Russia*, no.69480/01, § 114, ECHR 2006-XIII (extracts); *Bazorkina v. Russia*, no. 69481/01, § 139, 27 July 2006; *Gongadze v.*

obligation. In effect, certain breaches of the procedural obligation thereby amount to substantive acts of ill-treatment or torture that are distinct from those acts that were the basis of the procedural obligation. The Court has generally refused to consider that article 3 has been breached in this manner in cases where the disappearance is for a relatively short period,[53] when there has been a finding that both the substantive and procedural aspects of article 2 have been violated,[54] and in cases of killing by the authorities given that there is no uncertainty about the fate of the victim.[55] Dismissing a claim submitted by relatives of the victim of the Katyn massacre, which took place in 1940, the Grand Chamber held that given the long lapse of time since the killings and material that came to light over the years, it was no longer accurate to speak of uncertainty about the fate of the victims, at least with respect to the period since Russia's ratification of the European Convention. Consequently, 'it cannot be held that the applicants' suffering reached a dimension and character distinct from the emotional distress which may be regarded as inevitably caused to relatives of victims of a serious human rights violation'.[56]

Threshold of application of article 3

In establishing the threshold for the application of article 3, the case law of the Court speaks of 'ill-treatment' attaining a 'minimum level of severity [that] involves actual bodily injury or intense physical or mental suffering'.[57] The assessment of the minimum level is 'relative' and depends on the circumstances, bearing in mind such factors as the duration of the treatment, its physical and mental effects and, in some cases, the sex, age, and state of health of the victim.[58] In circumstances where treatment does not reach the level required for application of article 3, it may nevertheless engage issues relating to article 8 of the Convention.

Clearly, not all punishment is contemplated by article 3; it must necessarily be 'inhuman or degrading'. In order for a punishment or treatment associated with it to be 'inhuman' or 'degrading', or to amount to torture, the suffering or humiliation involved must go beyond that which is inevitably connected with a given form of

---

Ukraine, no. 34056/02, § 184, ECHR 2005-XI; *Tanış and Others v. Turkey*, no. 65899/01, § 219, ECHR 2005–VIII; *Orhan v. Turkey*, no. 25656/94, § 358, ECHR 2002; *Çakıcı v. Turkey* [GC], no. 23657/94, § 98, ECHR 1999-IV.

[53] *Janowiec and Others v. Russia* [GC], nos 55508/07 and 29520/09, § 179, 21 October 2013; *Tanlı v. Turkey*, no. 26129/95, § 159, ECHR 2001-III; *Bitiyeva and Others v. Russia*, no. 36156/04, § 106, 23 April 2009.

[54] *Janowiec and Others v. Russia* [GC], nos 55508/07 and 29520/09, § 179, 21 October 2013; *Velkhiyev and Others v. Russia*, no. 34085/06, §137, 5 July 2011; *Sambiyev and Pokayeva v. Russia*, no. 38693/04, §§ 74–75, 22 January 2009; *Tangiyeva. Russia*, no. 57935/00, § 104, 29 November 2007.

[55] *Janowiec and Others v. Russia* [GC], nos 55508/07 and 29520/09, § 180, 21 October 2013 *Damayev v. Russia*, no. 36150/04, § 97, 29 May 2012; *Yasin Ateş v. Turkey*, no. 30949/96, § 135, 31 May 2005; *Udayeva and Yusupova v. Russia*, no.36542/05, § 82, 21 December 2010; *Khashuyeva v. Russia*, no. 25553/07, § 154, 19 July 2011; *Inderbiyeva v. Russia*, no. 56765/08, § 110, 27 March 2012.

[56] *Janowiec and Others v. Russia* [GC], nos 55508/07 and 29520/09, § 188, 21 October 2013.

[57] *Ireland v. the United Kingdom*, 18 January 1978, § 167, Series A no. 25; *V. v. The United Kingdom* [GC], no. 24888/94, § 71, ECHR 1999-IX; *Costello-Roberts v. The United Kingdom*, 25 March 1993, § 30, Series A no. 247-C.

[58] *Arutyunyan v. Russia*, no. 48977/09, § 68, 10 January 2012; *A, B and C v. Ireland* [GC], no. 25579/05, § 164, ECHR 2010; *Stanev v. Bulgaria* [GC], no. 36760/06, § 202, ECHR 2012; *Kudła v. Poland* [GC], no. 30210/96, § 91, ECHR 2000-XI; *Price v. the United Kingdom*, no. 33394/96, § 24, ECHR 2001-VII; *A. and Others v. the United Kingdom* [GC], no. 3455/05, § 127, ECHR 2009; *Kafkaris v. Cyprus* [GC], no. 21906/04, § 95, ECHR 2008; *Costello-Roberts v. the United Kingdom*, 25 March 1993, § 30, Series A no. 247-C; *Enea v. Italy* [GC], no. 74912/01, § 55, ECHR 2009; *Price v. the United Kingdom*, no. 33394/96, § 24, ECHR 2001-VII; *Mouisel v. France*, no. 67263/01, § 37, ECHR 2002-IX; *Naumenko v. Ukraine*, no. 42023/98, § 108, 10 February 2004.

legitimate treatment or punishment.[59] As for torture, because the Convention organs have tended to treat it as an extreme or aggravating form of ill-treatment, comprised within the concept of 'inhuman or degrading treatment or punishment', there can be no notion of insignificant or minor torture.

Examples of the severity of bodily harm inflicted by State agents that the Court has considered to reach the required degree of severity include an injury to a person's leg which caused necrosis and subsequently led to the leg being amputated, a gunshot wound to a person's knee, a double fracture of the jaw and facial contusions or an injury to a person's face that required stitches, with three of the person's teeth being knocked out.[60] Suffering that results from illness, be it physical or mental, may also fall under article 3 where it is or risks being exacerbated by treatment for which the authorities are responsible.[61] For example, an AIDS sufferer was threatened with removal from the United Kingdom to St Kitts, where there was no appropriate treatment available, either medical or palliative. He would have faced a risk of dying under the 'most distressing circumstances', a situation aggravated by the State Party and therefore a treatment contemplated by article 3.[62] Bullying and harassment of a mentally disabled man by local children, including spitting, verbal abuse, and the infliction of cigarette burns, where a racist dimension was present, amounted to a breach of article 3.[63] However, extending the notion of 'treatment' to the refusal of the prosecuting authority to make an undertaking not to take proceedings against the husband of a terminally ill patient if he were to assist her in taking her own life 'places a new and extended construction on the concept of treatment [that] goes beyond the ordinary meaning of the word'.[64] In his separate opinion in the *Ireland v. the United Kingdom* case, Judge Fitzmaurice warned of the temptation to lower the threshold, explaining that 'the Convention contains no prohibition covering intermediate forms of maltreatment'.[65]

Often the Court has considered that ill-treatment does not reach the threshold of article 3 but has held that there was a violation of article 8 of the Convention. For example, it declined to conclude there had been a violation of article 3 in an application from the victim of environmental damage caused by the location of a waste processing plant that was responsible for health problems. Agreeing with the claim under article 8, the Court appeared to accept that the 'well-being' of the victims had been affected adversely 'without, however, seriously endangering their health'.[66] Where two members of the armed forces were discharged because they were homosexual, the Court concluded that article 8 had been violated but declined to apply article 3. Saying it accepted that the anti-homosexual

[59] *Tyrer v. the United Kingdom*, 25 April 1978, Series A no. 26, § 30; *Ramirez Sanchez v. France* [GC], no. 59450/00, §§ 118–119, ECHR 2006-IX; *Jalloh v. Germany* [GC], no. 54810/00, § 68, ECHR 2006-IX; *Arutyunyan v. Russia*, no. 48977/09, § 69, 10 January 2012; *Enea v. Italy* [GC], no. 74912/01, § 56, ECHR 2009.

[60] *Sambor v. Poland*, no. 15579/05, § 36, 1 February 2011; *Necdet Bulut v. Turkey*, no. 77092/01, § 24, 20 November 2007; *Rehbock v. Slovenia*, no. 29462/95, §§ 76–77, ECHR 2000-XII; *Mrozowski v. Poland*, no. 9258/04, § 28, 12 May 2009.

[61] *D. v. the United Kingdom*, 2 May 1997, *Reports of Judgments and Decisions* 1997-III; *Keenan v. the United Kingdom*, no. 27229/95, ECHR 2001-III; *Bensaid v. the United Kingdom*, no. 44599/98, ECHR 2000-I.

[62] *D. v. the United Kingdom*, 2 May 1997, *Reports of Judgments and Decisions* 1997–III

[63] *Đorđević v. Croatia*, no. 41526/10, § 96, ECHR 2012.

[64] *Pretty v. the United Kingdom*, no. 2346/02, § 54, ECHR 2002-III.

[65] *Ireland v. the United Kingdom*, 18 January 1978, Separate Opinion of Judge Sir Gerald Fitzmaurice, § 15, Series A no. 25.

[66] *López Ostra v. Spain*, 9 December 1994, §§ 58–60, Series A no. 303-C.

policy as well as the resulting investigation and discharge 'were undoubtedly distressing and humiliating for each of the applicants', nevertheless the Court did not consider, 'having regard to all the circumstances of the case, that the treatment reached the minimum level of severity which would bring it within the scope of Article 3 of the Convention'.[67]

Even in a case of police brutality directed at a seventy-two-year-old victim, the Court said that 'the injuries suffered by the applicant were restricted to the area of his hands and that the degree of bruising established during the medical examination of 20 December 1996 was not particularly excessive or severe in nature'.[68] Consequently, there was no breach of article 3, although three of the seven judges in the Chamber dissented, noting that '[t]he Court has constantly held in its case-law that in respect of a person deprived of his liberty recourse to physical force which has not been made strictly necessary by his own conduct diminishes human dignity and is in principle an infringement of the right set forth in Article 3'.[69] In a case involving difficulty in obtaining gender reassignment surgery, the Court said the situation, 'whilst revealing the applicant's understandable distress and frustration, does not indicate circumstances of such an intense degree, involving the exceptional, life-threatening conditions'. As a result, it opted to treat the complaint under article 8 rather than article 3.[70] It reached the same conclusion where the applicant was threatened with a criminal sanction for wearing a full-face veil or *burqa*.[71]

Many problems in defining the threshold arise in the context of detention and imprisonment, where an element of ill-treatment is almost inherent in the circumstances.[72] The Court declined finding a violation of article 3 in a case where a detainee was being transferred from the Netherlands to a prison in Curaçao that had been condemned by the European Committee for the Prevention of Torture. The Court said this did not automatically mean there was a breach of article 3, noting that the complaint was confined to allegations of a lack of access to running water and sanitary facilities, insufficient furniture, and the state of the telephones.[73] Requiring inmates to use an unenclosed toilet when they share a cell constitutes degrading treatment.[74] Detention conditions in Russian police stations, where applicants have no food, drink, or toilet access, have frequently been held to violate article 3.[75] In a strip search of visitors to a prison, one of whom was severely disabled, the Court held that 'there was a regrettable lack of courtesy [but] there was no verbal abuse by the prison officers and, importantly, there was no touching'. Consequently, although the treatment 'undoubtedly caused the applicants distress', it did not reach the article 3 threshold. The Court found there was a violation of article 8, nevertheless.[76] Complete sensory isolation coupled with total social isolation can destroy the personality, amounting to inhuman treatment that cannot be justified by the requirements of security or any other reason. But prohibition of contacts with other prisoners for security, disciplinary, or protective reasons does not in itself

---

[67] *Smith and Grady v. the United Kingdom*, nos 33985/96 and 33986/96, § 122, ECHR 1999-VI.

[68] *Stefan Iliev v. Bulgaria*, no. 53121/99, § 44, 10 May 2007.

[69] Ibid., Joint Partly Dissenting Opinion of Judges Lorenzen, Jungwiert, and Maruste.

[70] *L. v. Lithuania*, no. 27527/03, § 47, ECHR 2007-IV.

[71] *S.A.S. v. France* [GC], no. 43835/11, §§ 69–71, 1 July 2014.

[72] *Kudła v. Poland* [GC], no. 30210/96, § 93, ECHR 2000-XI.

[73] *Narcisio v. the Netherlands* (dec.), no. 47810/99, 27 January 2005.

[74] *Georgiev v. Bulgaria*, no. 47823/99, § 62, 15 December 2005; *Peers v. Greece*, no. 28524/95, § 75, ECHR 2001-III; *Kehayov v. Bulgaria*, no. 41035/98, § 71, 18 January 2005.

[75] *Navalnyy and Yashin v. Russia*, no. 76204/11, §§ 111–112, 4 December 2014.

[76] *Wainwright v. the United Kingdom*, no. 12350/04, §§ 46–49, ECHR 2006-X.

constitute a violation of article 3.[77] The Court rejected a claim based on article 3 in the case of a prisoner who had served ten years of a fifteen-year sentence after initially been sentenced to death and who was transferred, without any lawful basis, to a more severe detention regime than the one to which he was entitled. The Court acknowledged that although '[t]he fact that the applicant was aware that his transfer was not lawful and that his complaint did not stop the execution of the decision to transfer him would certainly have generated psychological distress going beyond that which is inextricably linked to imprisonment as such', the eighteen-day duration of the measures was not sufficient to constitute a breach of article 3.[78]

There is no general obligation resulting from article 3 requiring the release of a prisoner on health grounds or transfer to a hospital, even where the illness is particularly difficult to treat.[79] Nevertheless, the authorities have an obligation to provide a detained person with adequate medical care.[80] In particular, where detainees suffer from mental illness, it is necessary to take into account their vulnerability as well as their incapacity, in some cases, to complain about their circumstances.[81] A detainee who was found to be suffering from mental illness and who was transferred to a psychiatric ward of the prison hospital complained of inhuman treatment. The Court insisted that despite an inevitable degree of suffering, it could not state that detention on remand in and of itself raised an issue under article 3, nor could the provision 'be interpreted as laying down a general obligation to release a detainee on health grounds or to place him in a civil hospital to enable him to obtain a particular kind of medical treatment'.[82] The Court has also considered cases involving serious illness,[83] disability,[84] the elderly,[85] and withdrawal from drug addiction[86] in this context.

Distinguishing torture from inhuman or degrading treatment or punishment

Torture is not defined in either the European Convention on Human Rights or the specialized instrument adopted by the Council of Europe on the subject, the European Convention for the Prevention of Torture and Inhuman or Degrading Treatment or Punishment. The case law of the Court has generally approached torture as an aggravated form of ill-treatment. However, from the earliest decisions of the Commission, the case law has also insisted upon a deliberate and purposive dimension of torture, aimed at obtaining of information or confession or the infliction of punishment.[87]

---

[77] *Messina v. Italy (no. 2)* (dec.), no. 25498/94, ECHR 1999-V.
[78] *Dmitrijevs v. Latvia*, no. 49037/09, §§ 43–45, 16 December 2014.
[79] *Mouisel v. France*, no. 67263/01, § 40, ECHR 2002-IX.
[80] *Hurtado v. Switzerland*, no. 17549/90, §§ 78–81, Commission report of 8 July 1993.
[81] *Rivière v. France*, no. 33834/03, § 63, 11 July 2006; *Aerts v. Belgium*, 30 July 1998, § 66, *Reports of Judgments and Decisions* 1998-V; *Keenan v. the United Kingdom*, no. 27229/95, § 111, ECHR 2001-III.
[82] *Kudła v. Poland* [GC], no. 30210/96, § 93, ECHR 2000-XI.
[83] *Gelfmann v. France*, no. 25875/03, 14 December 2004; *Matencio v. France*, no. 58749/00, 15 January 2004; *Sakkopoulos v. Greece*, no. 61828/00, 15 January 2004; *Mouisel v. France*, no. 67263/01, ECHR 2002-IX.
[84] *Price v. the United Kingdom*, no. 33394/96, ECHR 2001-VII.
[85] *Papon v. France (no. 1)* (dec.), no. 64666/01, ECHR 2001-VI.
[86] *McGlinchey and Others v. the United Kingdom*, no. 50390/99, ECHR 2003-V.
[87] *Denmark, Norway, Sweden, and the Netherlands v. Greece*, nos 3321/67, 3322/67, 3323/67, 3344/67, Commission report of 5 November 1969, (1969) 12 YB 'The Greek Case' 1.

In the seminal case on the subject, the inter-State application filed by Ireland against the United Kingdom, the Court said 'this distinction derives principally from a difference in the intensity of the suffering inflicted'.[88] The Court supported its interpretation with reference to the Declaration on the Protection of All Persons from Being Subjected to Torture and Other Cruel, Inhuman or Degrading Treatment or Punishment adopted by the United Nations General Assembly in 1975, which stated: 'Torture constitutes an aggravated and deliberate form of cruel, inhuman or degrading treatment or punishment.'[89]

The context is important here, because in the *Ireland v. the United Kingdom* case the Court did not refer to the entire definition in the 1975 Declaration. Paragraph 1 of the Declaration centres the analysis on the purpose of the ill-treatment rather than its severity:

For the purpose of this Declaration, torture means any act by which severe pain or suffering, whether physical or mental, is intentionally inflicted by or at the instigation of a public official on a person for such purposes as obtaining from him or a third person information or confession, punishing him for an act he has committed or is suspected of having committed, or intimidating him or other persons. It does not include pain or suffering arising only from, inherent in or incidental to, lawful sanctions to the extent consistent with the Standard Minimum Rules for the Treatment of Prisoners.

The isolated reference to paragraph 2 of the 1975 Declaration was used by the Court to justify its conclusion, in the subsequent sentence of its judgment, that the so-called five techniques used by the British on detainees in Northern Ireland 'did not occasion suffering of the particular intensity and cruelty implied by the word torture as so understood'.[90] In the *Ireland v. the United Kingdom* case, the Court said that:

whilst there exists on the one hand violence which is to be condemned both on moral grounds and also in most cases under the domestic law of the Contracting States but which does not fall within Article 3 (art. 3) of the Convention, it appears on the other hand that it was the intention that the Convention, with its distinction between 'torture' and 'inhuman or degrading treatment, should by the first of these terms attach a special stigma to deliberate inhuman treatment causing very serious and cruel suffering.[91]

It has returned again and again to this formulation.[92]

Subsequent decisions of the European Court have attempted to trace the parameters of torture by using severity as the central criterion. In *Aksoy v. Turkey*, the Court found that the applicant had been subjected to 'Palestinian hanging' whereby he was stripped naked with his arms tied together behind his back and then suspended by his arms. Medical evidence showed this led to a paralysis for a period of time. It said 'this treatment was of such a serious and cruel nature that it can only be described as torture'.[93] Another involved a Turkish detainee who was raped by an unnamed prison official, something 'considered to be an especially grave and abhorrent form of ill-treatment given the ease

---

[88] *Ireland v. the United Kingdom,* 18 January 1978, § 167, Series A no. 25.
[89] GA Res. 3452 (XXX), art. 1(1), cited in *Ireland v. the United Kingdom,* 18 January 1978, § 167, Series A no. 25.
[90] *Ireland v. the United Kingdom,* 18 January 1978, § 167, Series A no. 25.
[91] Ibid.
[92] For example, *Selmouni v. France* [GC], no. 25803/94, § 96, ECHR 1999-V; *Dikme v. Turkey,* no. 20869/92, § 93, ECHR 2000-VIII; *Dedovskiy and Others v. Russia,* no. 7178/03, § 84, ECHR 2008 (extracts).
[93] *Aksoy v. Turkey,* 18 December 1996, § 64, *Reports of Judgments and Decisions* 1996-VI.

with which the offender can exploit the vulnerability and weakened resistance of his victim'. She was also subjected to various other 'particularly terrifying and humiliating experiences' as well as being 'paraded naked in humiliating circumstances thus adding to her overall sense of vulnerability and on one occasion she was pummelled with high-pressure water while being spun around in a tyre'.[94] The Court concluded that 'the accumulation of acts of physical and mental violence inflicted on the applicant and the especially cruel act of rape to which she was subjected amounted to torture'.[95]

Then, with reference to the 'living instrument' doctrine of interpretation, the Court's position began to evolve. In *Selmouni v. France*, the Grand Chamber said that 'certain acts which were classified in the past as "inhuman and degrading treatment" as opposed to "torture" could be classified differently in future'.[96] This was warranted because 'the increasingly high standard being required in the area of the protection of human rights and fundamental liberties correspondingly and inevitably requires greater firmness in assessing breaches of the fundamental values of democratic societies'.[97] Selmouni was brutally interrogated by French law enforcement officers, who suspected his involvement in drug traffic. The Court said that '[w]hatever a person's state of health, it can be presumed that such intensity of blows will cause substantial pain'. It continued its description of the ill-treatment:

> The Court also notes that the applicant was dragged along by his hair; that he was made to run along a corridor with police officers positioned on either side to trip him up; that he was made to kneel down in front of a young woman to whom someone said 'Look, you're going to hear somebody sing'; that one police officer then showed him his penis, saying 'Here, suck this', before urinating over him; and that he was threatened with a blowlamp and then a syringe ... Besides the violent nature of the above acts, the Court is bound to observe that they would be heinous and humiliating for anyone, irrespective of their condition.[98]

The Grand Chamber said it was 'satisfied that the physical and mental violence, considered as a whole, committed against the applicant's person caused "severe" pain and suffering and was particularly serious and cruel'.[99] The Court put the word 'severe' in inverted commas in order to make it clear that it was referring to this term as it appears in article 1 of the United Nations Convention against Torture. It said it considered that this notion of severity was similar to the 'minimum severity' required for the application of article 3 of the European Convention, something that is necessarily, 'in the nature of things, relative'. The Grand Chamber said this 'depends on all the circumstances of the case, such as the duration of the treatment, its physical or mental effects and, in some cases, the sex, age and state of health of the victim, etc.'.[100] But that is the extent of the Grand Chamber's methodological and analytical clarity in its attempt to broaden the definition of torture.

A year later, the Grand Chamber acknowledged that '[i]n addition to the severity of the treatment, there is a purposive element', citing in support the United Nations

---

[94] *Aydın v. Turkey*, 25 September 1997, §§ 83–84, *Reports of Judgments and Decisions* 1997-VI.

[95] Ibid., § 86. Rape has also been described as torture in *Maslova and Nalbandov v. Russia*, no. 839/02, §§ 101, 104–106, 24 January 2008; *Menesheva v. Russia*, no. 59261/00, § 14, ECHR 2006-III.

[96] *Selmouni v. France* [GC], no. 25803/94, § 101, ECHR 1999-V.

[97] Ibid.

[98] Ibid., §§ 103–104.

[99] Ibid., § 105.

[100] Ibid., § 100.

Convention.[101] Article 1 of the Convention Against Torture, adopted in 1984, develops the approach taken in article 1(1) of the 1975 Declaration, which of course also includes the purposive element that the European Court had ignored in the *Ireland v. the United Kingdom* case:

For the purposes of this Convention, torture means any act by which severe pain or suffering, whether physical or mental, is intentionally inflicted on a person for such purposes as obtaining from him or a third person information or a confession, punishing him for an act he or a third person has committed or is suspected of having committed, or intimidating or coercing him or a third person, or for any reason based on discrimination of any kind, when such pain or suffering is inflicted by or at the instigation of or with the consent or acquiescence of a public official or other person acting in an official capacity. It does not include pain or suffering arising only from, inherent in or incidental to lawful sanctions.

Principally, the 1984 Convention adds the reference to 'any reason based on discrimination of any kind' and, more importantly, requires that torture be 'inflicted by or at the instigation of or with the consent or acquiescence of a public official or other person acting in an official capacity'. According to the United Nations Special Rapporteur on Torture, commenting on the interpretation of the 1984 Convention, the decisive criteria for distinguishing torture from cruel, inhuman, and degrading treatment 'may best be understood to be the purpose of the conduct and the powerlessness of the victim, rather than the intensity of the pain or suffering inflicted'.[102] Although presented as an innovation in the case law of the Court, the observation that torture amounts to 'inhuman treatment, which has a purpose, such as the obtaining of information or confession, or the infliction of punishment', can actually be found in an early decision of the European Commission of Human Rights.[103]

On the sliding scale between torture and inhuman or degrading treatment the relative proportions may have evolved as the Court has become less demanding in making a finding of torture. To determine whether a form of ill-treatment should be qualified as torture, the Court says it must consider the 'distinction, embodied in Article 3, between this notion and that of inhuman or degrading treatment. It appears that it was the intention that the Convention should, by means of this distinction, attach a special stigma to deliberate inhuman treatment causing very serious and cruel suffering.'[104] Findings that torture has been committed are rather rare. To some, this may suggest that the definition applied by the Court is still too strict. But it might also lead to the conclusion that the phenomenon has been largely eradicated, at least within Europe itself. Today, most torture cases concern acts perpetrated outside the continent, but where European States may be complicit.

Recent cases where the Court has concluded that torture was perpetrated have, with some exceptions,[105] tended to refer to both the severity and the purpose of the ill-treatment. In a Russian case involving a man who was wrongfully charged with a serious

[101] *Ilhan v. Turkey* [GC], no. 22277/93, § 85, ECHR 2000-VII.
[102] Report of the Special Rapporteur on torture and other cruel, inhuman, or degrading treatment of punishment, UN Doc. E/CN.4/2006/6, para 39.
[103] *Denmark, Norway, Sweden, and the Netherlands v. Greece*, nos 3321/67, 3322/67, 3323/67, 3344/67, Commission report of 5 November 1969, (1969) 12 YB 'The Greek Case' 1.
[104] *Dedovskiy and Others v. Russia*, no. 7178/03, § 84, ECHR 2008 (extracts).
[105] *Ilaşcu and Others v. Moldova and Russia* [GC], no. 48787/99, §§ 440, 447, ECHR 2004-VII.

criminal offence, the Court accepted evidence that he had been seriously ill-treated by State agents who had the intention of extracting a confession or information. The ill-treatment was so severe that the applicant attempted suicide, resulting in a general and permanent physical disability. The Court held that torture had taken place in view of the 'severity and the purpose of the ill-treatment'.[106] A suspect in a murder investigation in Nizhniy Novgorod was raped by one of her interrogators, in addition to a range of ill-treatment including beatings, suffocation, and electrocution:

The Court observes that according to its settled case-law a rape of a detainee by an official of the State must be considered to be an especially grave and abhorrent form of ill-treatment given the ease with which the offender can exploit the vulnerability and weakened resistance of his victim. Furthermore, rape leaves deep psychological scars on the victims which do not respond to the passage of time as quickly as other forms of physical and mental violence. The victim also experiences the acute physical pain of forced penetration, which leaves her feeling debased and violated both physically and emotionally. In view of the above, the Court is satisfied that the accumulation of the acts of physical violence inflicted on the first applicant... and the especially cruel acts of repeated rape to which she was subjected... amounted to torture in breach of Article 3 of the Convention.[107]

In another case, where a schoolteacher had been beaten and brutalized by police, causing serious physical pain and suffering with lasting consequences to health, the Court said 'it does not appear that the pain and suffering were inflicted on the applicant intentionally for the purpose of, for instance, making him confess to a crime or breaking his physical and moral resistance' and held the State responsible for inhuman treatment, but not torture.[108]

With respect to various forms of abuse directed at prisoners by a special unit of correctional officers in a Russian penal colony, the Court made a finding of torture:

As noted above, the use of rubber truncheons against the applicants was retaliatory in nature. It was not, and could not be, conducive to facilitating execution of the tasks the officers were set to achieve. The gratuitous violence, to which the officers deliberately resorted, was intended to arouse in the applicants feelings of fear and humiliation and to break their physical or moral resistance. The purpose of that treatment was to debase the applicants and drive them into submission. In addition, the truncheon blows must have caused them intense mental and physical suffering, even though they did not apparently result in any long-term damage to health. In these circumstances, the Court finds that the applicants were subjected to treatment which can be described as torture.[109]

In another Russian application, police who were investigating a murder questioned a young woman. One of the officers 'started strangling her with his hands and several other policemen started beating her. For about two hours they administered kicks and blows to her legs, threw her across the room, beat her with a baton and hit her head against the walls. While beating her they accused her of telling lies, insulted her and threatened her with rape and violence against her family.'[110] The Court held that 'taken as a whole and having regard to its purpose and severity, the ill-treatment in issue amounted to torture'.[111]

---

[106] *Mikheyev v. Russia*, no. 77617/01, § 135, 26 January 2006.
[107] *Maslova and Nalbandov v. Russia*, no. 839/02, §§ 104–106, 24 January 2008.
[108] *Krastanov v. Bulgaria*, no. 50222/99, § 53, 30 September 2004.
[109] *Dedovskiy and Others v. Russia*, no. 7178/03, § 85, ECHR 2008 (extracts).
[110] *Menesheva v. Russia*, no. 59261/00, § 14, ECHR 2006-III.
[111] Ibid., § 62.

With regard to treatment of several Turkish political activists who were held for questioning by the Istanbul police, the Court said that 'taken as a whole and having regard to their purpose and duration, the acts of violence to which the applicants were subjected were particularly serious and cruel and capable of causing "severe" pain and suffering'.[112]

Torture as *jus cogens*

On several occasions the Court has described the prohibition of torture as a peremptory norm, or *jus cogens*.[113] Such statements seem to be made to emphasize the importance of the prohibition but it does not appear that there are any legal consequences to the determination, at least within the scheme of the Convention. Indeed, some judges have expressed caution about an extensive application of the concept, warning that although 'giving absolute priority to the prohibition of torture may at first sight seem very "progressive", a more careful consideration tends to confirm that such a step would also run the risk of proving a sort of "Pyrrhic victory"'.[114]

In recent years, the International Court of Justice has referred to *jus cogens* norms but in a fairly summary manner, perhaps confirming the difficulty that the judges have in reaching any consensus on a more detailed discussion of the subject.[115] A more elaborate discussion of the subject can be found in some of the individual opinions, notably those of *ad hoc* Judge Dugard[116] and Judge Cançado Trindade.[117] The most authoritative pronouncement on the subject of torture and *jus cogens* is the ruling of a Trial Chamber of the International Criminal Tribunal for the former Yugoslavia, in *Furundžija*: '[T]he prohibition on torture is a peremptory norm or jus cogens. This prohibition is so extensive that States are even barred by international law from expelling, returning or extraditing a person to another State where there are substantial grounds for believing that the person would be in danger of being subjected to torture.'[118]

---

[112] *Bati and Others v. Turkey*, nos 33097/96 and 57834/00, §123, ECHR 2004-IV (extracts). Also *Dikme v. Turkey*, no. 20869/92, § 96, ECHR 2000-VIII.

[113] *Ould Dah v. France* (dec.), no. 13113/03, ECHR 2009; *Al-Adsani v. the United Kingdom*, 21 November 2001, § 60, ECHR 2001-XI; *Aksoy v. Turkey*, 18 December 1996, § 62, *Reports of Judgments and Decisions* 1996-VI; *Assenov and Others v. Bulgaria*, 28 October 1998, § 93, *Reports of Judgments and Decisions* 1998-VIII; *Selmouni v. France* [GC], no. 25803/94, § 95, ECHR 1999-V.

[114] *Al-Adsani v. the United Kingdom* [GC], no. 35763/97, Concurring Opinion of Judge Pellonpää Joined by Judge Sir Nicholas Bratza, ECHR 2001-XI.

[115] *Questions relating to the Obligation to Prosecute or Extradite (Belgium v. Senegal)*, Judgment, I.C.J. Reports 2012, p. 422, para. 99.

[116] *Armed Activities on the Territory of the Congo (New Application: 2002) (Democratic Republic of the Congo v. Rwanda), Jurisdiction and Admissibility*, Judgment, I.C.J. Reports 2006, p. 6, Separate Opinion of Judge *ad hoc* Dugard, para. 8.

[117] *Jurisdictional Immunities of the State (Germany v. Italy: Greece intervening)*, Judgment, I.C.J. Reports 2012, p. 99, Dissenting Opinion of Judge Cançado Trindade, paras 117–20; *Jurisdictional Immunities of the State (Germany v. Italy), Counter-Claim, Order of 6 July 2010*, I.C.J. Reports 2010, p. 310, Dissenting Opinion of Judge Cançado Trindade, paras 124–153.

[118] *Prosecutor v. Furundžija* (IT-95-17/1-T), Judgment, 10 December 1998, paras 144 and 153–157, cited in *Jones and Others v. the United Kingdom*, nos 34356/06 and 40528/06, § 69, 14 January 2014; *Marguš v. Croatia* [GC], no. 4455/10, § 55, 27 May 2014; *Demir and Baykara v. Turkey* [GC], no. 34503/97, § 73, ECHR 2008; *Al-Adsani v. the United Kingdom* [GC], no. 35763/97, §§ 30, 60–61, ECHR 2001-XI; *Mocanu and Others v. Romania*, nos 10865/09, 45886/07 and 32431/08, Concurring Opinion of Judge Pinto d'Albuquerque, Joined by Judge Vučinić, § 7, 17 September 2014. Also *Prosecutor v. Delalić et al.* (IT-96-21-T), Judgment, 16 November 1998, para. 225. See Erika de Wet, 'The Prohibition of Torture as an International Norm of jus cogens and Its Implications for National and Customary Law', (2004) 15 *EJIL* 97.

The pronouncement in *Furundžija* considerably expands the consequences of a finding of *jus cogens* from what is proposed in the Vienna Convention on the Law of Treaties. But even *Furundžija* is confined to the statement that the prohibition of 'torture' is a *jus cogens* norm, without reference to whether the same applies to cruel, inhuman, or degrading treatment or punishment. Perhaps some of the judicial formulations have used the term 'torture' as a short form and actually intended to include 'cruel, inhuman or degrading treatment or punishment'. Yet of the numerous references in case law to torture as a peremptory norm, there are none that even imply that this also pertains to the broader notion of ill-treatment. It seems reasonable to conclude that the concept of *jus cogens* does not apply to matters such as corporal punishment in schools, which fall within the broader rubric of ill-treatment.

'Inhuman or degrading'

Article 3 protects the individual against treatment or punishment that is 'inhuman or degrading'. The European Convention does not employ the adjective 'cruel' that is used in equivalent provisions in other international human rights instruments, including article 5 of the Universal Declaration of Human Rights. The reasons for the choice made by the drafters of the European Convention are obscure. It seems imprudent to attach any significance to the distinction between the European Convention formulation ('inhuman and degrading') and that of the other international instruments derived from the Universal Declaration of Human Rights ('cruel, inhuman and degrading'). It is certainly of interest to reflect on the extent to which the notion of cruelty plays a role in the interpretation of article 3 of the Convention. The term has often been used when the Court has found that the violation of article 3 should be described as torture.[119] This might suggest that cruel treatment, as it is understood by the United Nations instruments, should be deemed torture under the European Convention.

Treatment has been held by the Court to be 'inhuman' because it was premeditated or was applied for hours at a stretch and caused either actual bodily injury or intense physical and mental suffering.[120] When torture is threatened but not imposed, as a means of obtaining information, the Grand Chamber has described such a method of interrogation as 'inhuman treatment'.[121] The Court described as 'inhuman treatment' the detention conditions of a prisoner who was seriously disabled and quite ill and who was kept in a regular prison where he was forced to climb four flights of stairs in order to obtain regular haemodialysis treatments.[122]

In assessing the application of the term 'degrading', the Court will consider whether the object of the impugned treatment or punishment was to humiliate and debase the person concerned.[123] Nevertheless, the absence of any such purpose or intention does not

---

[119] For example, *Aksoy v. Turkey*, 18 December 1996, § 64, *Reports of Judgments and Decisions* 1996-VI; *Aydın v. Turkey*, 25 September 1997, § 86, *Reports of Judgments and Decisions* 1997-VI; *Ilaşcu and Others v. Moldova and Russia* [GC], no. 48787/99, §§ 426, 440, 447, ECHR 2004-VII. And see *Ireland v. the United Kingdom*, 18 January 1978, § 167, Series A no. 25, where the absence of 'cruelty' was noted.

[120] *Labita v. Italy* [GC], no. 26772/95, § 120, ECHR 2000-IV; *A. and Others v. the United Kingdom* [GC], no. 3455/05, § 127, ECHR 2009; *Kudła v. Poland* [GC], no. 30210/96, § 92, ECHR 2000-XI.

[121] *Gäfgen v. Germany* [GC], no. 22978/05, § 70, ECHR 2010.

[122] *Arutyunyan v. Russia*, no. 48977/09, § 81, 10 January 2012.

[123] *Pretty v. the United Kingdom*, no. 2346/02, § 52, ECHR 2002-III; *Price v. the United Kingdom*, no. 33394/96, §§ 24–30, ECHR 2001-VII; *Valašinas v. Lithuania*, no. 44558/98, § 117, ECHR 2001-VIII.

conclusively rule out a finding of a violation of article 3.[124] Treatment or punishment is also degrading if it shows a lack of respect for or diminishes the human dignity of the victim.[125] Treatment or punishment may be deemed degrading if it 'arouses feelings of fear, anguish or inferiority capable of breaking an individual's moral and physical resistance'[126] or drives persons 'to act against their will or conscience'.[127] The Court considers the consequences and whether such treatment affects adversely the personality of the applicant.[128] Where treatment does not denote 'any contempt or lack of respect for the personality of the applicants' it may not be deemed 'degrading'.[129]

Sometimes both adjectives, 'inhuman' and 'degrading', will apply. In *The Greek case*, the European Commission said that 'all torture must be inhuman and degrading treatment, and inhuman treatment is also degrading'.[130] The so-called 'five techniques' of interrogation employed by the British in Northern Ireland were deemed to be both inhuman and degrading.[131] The severe beating of Jehovah's Witnesses at the instigation of an Orthodox priest was deemed 'inhuman treatment'.[132] In the case of some others, who were also beaten at the time but without details being provided, the Court found it 'impossible to assess whether the latter reached the level required to be classified as inhuman within the meaning of Article 3 of the Convention'.[133] This was also deemed 'degrading treatment', given that 'the attackers' aim was to humiliate and publicly debase the applicants in such a way as to arouse a feeling of terror and inferiority, so that, morally broken by this physical and verbal abuse, they would act against their wills and conscience and desist from holding religious meetings in line with their faith, considered unacceptable by Father Basil and his supporters'.[134]

Finding that treatment is incompatible with article 3, the Court does not always specify whether this is because it is inhuman or because it is degrading. In a case concerning prison conditions in Romania, it noted the prolonged detention of the applicant in a cell of small proportions with very limited opportunity for exercise, saying that this was a violation of article 3, but without further detail.[135]

---

[124] *Brânduşe v. Romania*, no. 6586/03, § 50, 7 April 2009; *Peers v. Greece*, no. 28524/95, §§ 67, 68, and 74, ECHR 2001-III; *Kalashnikov v. Russia*, no. 47095/99, § 95, ECHR 2002-VI.

[125] *East African Asians v. the United Kingdom*, nos 4403/70-4419/70, 4422/70, 4423/70, 4434/70, 4443/70, 4476/70-4478/70, 4486/70, 4501/70, and 4526/70-4530/70, Commission report of 14 December 1973, § 208, DR 78-A, p. 5.

[126] *Pretty v. the United Kingdom*, no. 2346/02, § 52, ECHR 2002-III; *Price v. The United Kingdom*, no. 33394/96, §§ 24–30, ECHR 2001-VII; *Valašinas v. Lithuania*, no. 44558/98, § 117, ECHR 2001-VIII; *A. and Others v. the United Kingdom* [GC], no. 3455/05, § 127, ECHR 2009; *Kudła v. Poland* [GC], no. 30210/96, § 92, ECHR 2000-XI; *Hurtado v. Switzerland*, no. 17549/90, Commission report of 8 July 1993, §§ 78–81; *Wieser v. Austria*, no. 2293/03, § 36, 22 February 2007.

[127] *Jalloh v. Germany* [GC], no. 54810/00, § 68, ECHR 2006-IX.

[128] *Hristozov and Others v. Bulgaria*, nos 47039/11 and 358/12, § 110, 13 November 2012; *Wainwright v. the United Kingdom*, no. 12350/04, § 41, ECHR 2006-X.

[129] *Abdulaziz, Cabales, and Balkandali v. the United Kingdom*, 28 May 1985, § 91, Series A no. 94; *Albert and Le Compte v. Belgium*, 10 February 1983, § 22, Series A no. 58.

[130] *Denmark, Norway, Sweden, and the Netherlands v. Greece*, nos 3321/67, 3322/67, 3323/67, 3344/67, Commission report of 5 November 1969, (1969) 12 YB 'The Greek Case' 1.

[131] *Ireland v. the United Kingdom*, 18 January 1978, § 168, Series A no. 25.

[132] *Members of the Gldani Congregation of Jehovah's Witnesses and Others v. Georgia*, no. 71156/01, § 102, 3 May 2007.

[133] Ibid., § 104.

[134] Ibid., § 105 (references omitted).

[135] *Brânduşe v. Romania*, no. 6586/03, §§ 46–50, 7 April 2009.

'Treatment or punishment'

Frequently treatment and punishment go together, especially in the many cases that the Convention organs have considered dealing with prison conditions. However, although detainees are often being punished, pursuant to a criminal conviction, there are other forms of detention or deprivation of liberty that are not associated with punishment. As the Court has explained, 'the prohibition of ill-treatment in Article 3 applies equally to all forms of deprivation of liberty, and in particular makes no distinction according to the purpose of the measure in issue; it is immaterial whether the measure entails detention ordered in the context of criminal proceedings or admission to an institution with the aim of protecting the life or health of the person concerned'.[136] Of course, issues concerning both treatment and punishment may also arise where the alleged victim is not being detained at all. In the early case of *Tyrer v. the United Kingdom*, the Court said it would be 'absurd to hold that judicial punishment generally, by reason of its usual and perhaps almost inevitable element of humiliation, is "degrading" within the meaning of Article 3'.[137] Precisely for this reason, the adjectives 'inhuman' and 'degrading' imply that some further feature is required before punishment falls foul of article 3.

Although much of the European Convention on Human Rights deals with criminal justice, it is mainly concerned with matters of procedure, as well as issues of law enforcement such as arrest and detention. The Convention actually treads very gingerly when it addresses the substance of crime and punishment that lies at the core of criminal justice. For example, it generally limits its intrusion into the definitions of crimes when they have some discriminatory aspect or violate the right to private life.[138] Similarly, the European Court acknowledges that 'issues relating to just and proportionate punishment are the subject of rational debate and civilised disagreement',[139] granting States a fairly generous margin of appreciation in setting the appropriate length of sentence. As the Grand Chamber has explained, '[i]t is not the European Court's role to decide what is the appropriate term of detention applicable to a particular offence or to pronounce on the appropriate length of detention or other sentence which should be served by a person after conviction by a competent court'.[140]

The ancient and often misunderstood maxim of *lex talionis*—'eye for eye, tooth for tooth'—is an early affirmation of the principle of proportionality in the punishment of crime. While it may be fair and also desirable, from a criminological perspective, that all sentences be proportionate, it might be going too far to suggest that this is a requirement imposed by article 3 of the Convention. The European Convention intervenes only when a sentence or punishment is 'grossly disproportionate'.[141] The Court has explained that it

---

[136] *Stanev v. Bulgaria* [GC], no. 36760/06, § 206, ECHR 2012.

[137] *Tyrer v. the United Kingdom*, 25 April 1978, § 30, Series A no. 26.

[138] *M.C. v. Bulgaria*, no. 39272/98, ECHR 2003-XII; *Dudgeon v. the United Kingdom*, 22 October 1981, Series A no. 45; *Norris v. Ireland*, 26 October 1988, Series A no. 142; *Modinos v. Cyprus*, 22 April 1993, Series A no. 259.

[139] *Vinter and Others v. the United Kingdom* [GC], nos 66069/09, 130/10, and 3896/10, § 105, ECHR 2013 (extracts); *Murray v. the Netherlands*, no. 10511/10, § 50, 10 December 2013.

[140] *T. v. the United Kingdom* [GC], no. 24724/94, § 117, 16 December 1999; *V. v. the United Kingdom* [GC], no. 24888/94, § 118, ECHR 1999-IX; *Sawoniuk v. the United Kingdom* (dec.), no. 63716/00, ECHR 2001-VI.

[141] *Vinter and Others v. the United Kingdom* [GC], nos 66069/09, 130/10, and 3896/10, § 102, ECHR 2013 (extracts).

is not its role 'to decide what is the appropriate term of detention applicable to a particular offence or to pronounce on the appropriate length of detention or other sentence which should be served by a person after conviction by a competent court'.[142]

According to the Court, '[i]t is axiomatic that a prisoner cannot be detained unless there are legitimate penological grounds for that detention'.[143] It has noted the four classic grounds invoked by justice systems around the world as a justification for detention as criminal punishment: punishment, deterrence, public protection, and rehabilitation.[144] For the Grand Chamber, 'the emphasis in European penal policy is now on the rehabilitative aim of imprisonment'.[145] Explaining that the balance between the justifications is not static and may shift during the sentence, especially a lengthy one, '[i]t is only by carrying out a review of the justification for continued detention at an appropriate point in the sentence that these factors or shifts can be properly evaluated'.[146] Nevertheless, '[a] State's choice of a specific criminal justice system, including sentence review and release arrangements, is in principle outside the scope of the supervision the Court carries out at the European level'.[147] It is not for the Court to decide upon the appropriate term of detention applicable to a particular offence or to pronounce on the appropriate length of detention or other sentence that should be served by a person after conviction by a competent court.[148] The European Union Charter of Fundamental Rights appears to take a slightly more interventionist position on this issue, stating that '[t]he severity of penalties must not be disproportionate to the criminal offence'.[149]

Ill-treatment may arise as a result of medical treatment, in particular if it is administered to detained persons against their will. According to the Grand Chamber, a measure that is of therapeutic necessity from the point of view of established principles of medicine cannot in principle be regarded as inhuman and degrading. Medical necessity must be demonstrated convincingly, and appropriate guarantees for the decision complied with.[150] But even when medical treatment appears to be voluntary, issues under article 3 may arise. The Court has held that there was a violation of article 3 in the sterilization of an unemployed Roma woman with very limited education following childbirth. The judgment explains:

[A]fter she had been in labour for several hours and was in pain, the medical personnel of Prešov Hospital had asked her whether she wanted to have more children. The applicant responded in the affirmative but was told by the medical personnel that if she had one more child, either she or the baby would die. The applicant started to cry and as she was convinced that her next pregnancy would be fatal, she told the medical personnel 'Do what you want to do'. She was then asked to sign

---

[142] *T. v. the United Kingdom* [GC], no. 24724/94, § 117, 16 December 1999; *V. v. the United Kingdom* [GC], no. 24888/94, § 118, ECHR 1999-IX; *Sawoniuk v. the United Kingdom* (dec.), no. 63716/00, ECHR 2001-VI.

[143] *Vinter and Others v. the United Kingdom* [GC], nos 66069/09, 130/10, and 3896/10, § 111, ECHR 2013 (extracts).

[144] Ibid., § 111.

[145] Ibid., § 115; *Dickson v. the United Kingdom* [GC], no. 44362/04, § 75, ECHR 2007-V; *Boulois v. Luxembourg* [GC], no. 37575/04, § 83, ECHR 2012.

[146] *Vinter and Others v. the United Kingdom* [GC], nos 66069/09, 130/10, and 3896/10, § 111, 9 July 2013.

[147] Ibid., § 104.

[148] *T. v. The United Kingdom* [GC], no. 24724/94, § 117, 16 December 1999; *V. v. the United Kingdom* [GC], no. 24888/94, § 118, ECHR 1999-IX; *Sawoniuk v. the United Kingdom* (dec.), no. 63716/00, ECHR 2001-VI.

[149] Charter of Fundamental Rights of the European Union, 2010 OJ C 83/02, art. 49(3).

[150] *Jalloh v. Germany* [GC], no. 54810/00, § 69, ECHR 2006-IX.

the delivery record under the note indicating that she had requested sterilisation. The applicant did not understand the term sterilisation and she signed the form out of fear that there would otherwise be fatal consequences. As she was in the last stage of labour, her recognition and cognitive abilities were influenced by labour and pain.[151]

The Court noted that though there was no indication that medical personnel acted with an intent of ill-treatment, there was nevertheless 'gross disregard to her right to autonomy and choice as a patient'.[152]

Detention

Conditions of detention obviously raise issues with respect to inhuman or degrading treatment or punishment. Measures depriving a person of his or her liberty may often involve a breach of article 3. The State must ensure that prisoners are detained 'in conditions that are compatible with respect for their human dignity, that the manner and method of the execution of the measure do not subject them to distress or hardship of an intensity exceeding the unavoidable level of suffering inherent in detention and that, given the practical demands of imprisonment, their health and well-being are adequately secured'.[153] Prisoners must be held in conditions compatible with respect for human dignity and in such a way that the manner and method of detention does not impose distress or hardship 'of an intensity exceeding the unavoidable level of suffering inherent in detention and that, given the practical demands of imprisonment, [the detainee's] health and well-being are adequately secured by, among other things, providing him with the requisite medical assistance'.[154] Measures taken with respect to prisoners must also be necessary to attain a legitimate aim.[155] For example, the Court has examined whether extreme measures of restraint such as handcuffing or shackling of such prisoners is warranted by security concerns.[156] When persons are deprived of their liberty, use of physical force against them where this is not justified by their conduct in principle amounts to a violation of article 3.[157] In assessing whether conditions of detention are compatible with article 3, 'account has to be taken of the cumulative effects of those conditions, as well as the specific allegations made by the applicant'.[158]

---

[151] *V.C. v. Slovakia*, no. 18968/07, § 15, ECHR 2011 (extracts).

[152] Ibid., § 119.

[153] *Ramirez Sanchez v. France* [GC], no. 59450/00, § 119, ECHR 2006-IX; *Kalashnikov v. Russia*, no. 47095/99, § 95, ECHR 2002-VI.

[154] *Stanev v. Bulgaria* [GC], no. 36760/06, § 204, ECHR 2012; *Arutyunyan v. Russia*, no. 48977/09, § 70, 10 January 2012; *Rivière v. France*, no. 33834/03, § 62, 11 July 2006; *Enea v. Italy* [GC], no. 74912/01, § 57, ECHR 2009; *Kudła v. Poland* [GC], no. 30210/96, § 94, ECHR 2000-XI; *Paladi v. Moldova* [GC], no. 39806/05, § 85, 10 March 2009; *A. and Others v. the United Kingdom* [GC], no. 3455/05, § 128, ECHR 2009; *Brânduşe v. Romania*, no. 6586/03, § 47, 7 April 2009; *Mouisel v. France*, no. 67263/01, § 40, ECHR 2002-IX; *Aerts v. Belgium*, 30 July 1998, § 66, *Reports of Judgments and Decisions* 1998-V; *Keenan v. the United Kingdom*, no. 27229/95, § 111, ECHR 2001-III); *Kudła v. Poland* [GC], no. 30210/96, § 94, ECHR 2000-XI; *Rivière v. France*, no. 33834/03, § 62, 11 July 2006; *Hurtado v. Switzerland*, no. 17549/90, Commission report of 8 July 1993, § 79.

[155] *Ramirez Sanchez v. France* [GC], no. 59450/00, § 119, ECHR 2006-IX; *Kalashnikov v. Russia*, no. 47095/99, § 95, ECHR 2002-VI.

[156] *Arutyunyan v. Russia*, no. 48977/09, § 72, 10 January 2012; *Henaf v. France*, no. 65436/01, §§ 49 et seq., ECHR 2003-XI.

[157] *Perişan and Others v. Turkey*, no. 12336/03, § 92, 20 May 2010.

[158] *A. and Others v. the United Kingdom* [GC], no. 3455/05, § 128, ECHR 2009; *Ramirez Sanchez v. France* [GC], no. 59450/00, §§ 118–119, ECHR 2006-IX; *Dougoz v. Greece*, no. 40907/98, § 46, ECHR 2001-II.

Prisoners may be restrained using handcuffs and similar techniques, particularly at the time of arrest and during appearances in the courtroom. Such measures do not normally raise an issue under article 3 'where they have been imposed in connection with lawful arrest or detention and do not entail the use of force, or public exposure, exceeding what is reasonably considered necessary in the circumstances'.[159] Factors to be considered are whether there is reason to think the prisoner might resist arrest or abscond, cause injury or damage, or suppress evidence.[160] As for the employment of metal cages in the courtroom, in some cases the Court has found its 'excessive' use to amount to degrading treatment.[161] It has described such a measure as 'stringent' and 'humiliating'.[162] In addition to the factors mentioned above, the presence of the public and media coverage of the proceedings may also be relevant.[163] After noting that the practice was commonplace in Russia, the Grand Chamber observed that:

the applicants must have had objectively justified fears that their exposure in a cage during hearings in their case would convey to their judges, who were to take decisions on the issues concerning their criminal liability and liberty, a negative image of them as being dangerous to the point of requiring such an extreme physical restraint, thus undermining the presumption of innocence. This must have caused them anxiety and distress, given the seriousness of what was at stake for them in the proceedings in question.[164]

The Grand Chamber concluded that 'holding a person in a metal cage during a trial constitutes in itself—having regard to its objectively degrading nature which is incompatible with the standards of civilised behaviour that are the hallmark of a democratic society—an affront to human dignity in breach of Article 3'.[165]

Where inmates require medical treatment and assistance, this must be provided at an appropriate level, failing which there is a violation of article 3.[166] Various factors have been deemed relevant in assessing whether article 3 is engaged, including the medical condition of the prisoner, the adequacy of medical assistance and care in detention, the advisability of maintaining the detention considering the prisoner's health,[167] the dynamics of the medical condition, the possibility of conditional release if health deteriorated, and the prisoner's own attitude[168] and potential dangerousness.[169] If an illness or condition is difficult to treat in prison, article 3 does not impose a general obligation to release detainees or place them in a civil hospital, but there is nonetheless a duty to protect

---

[159] *Svinarenko and Slyadnev v. Russia* [GC], nos 32541/08 and 43441/08, § 117, 17 July 2014.

[160] *Raninen v. Finland*, 16 December 1997, § 56, *Reports of Judgments and Decisions* 1997-VIII; *Öcalan v. Turkey* [GC], no. 46221/99, § 182, ECHR 2005-IV; *Gorodnitchev v. Russia*, no. 52058/99, §§ 101, 102, 105 and 108, 24 May 2007; *Mirosław Garlicki v. Poland*, no. 36921/07, §§ 73–75, 14 June 2011.

[161] For an example where it declined to find a violation, see *Titarenko v. Ukraine*, no. 31720/02, §§ 58–64, 20 September 2012.

[162] *Ramishvili and Kokhreidze v. Georgia*, no. 1704/06, § 102, 27 January 2009; *Ashot Harutyunyan v. Armenia*, no. 34334/04, §§ 128–129, 15 June 2010; *Piruzyan v. Armenia*, no. 33376/07, §§ 73–74, ECHR 2012 (extracts).

[163] *Sarban v. Moldova*, no. 3456/05, § 89, 4 October 2005; *Khodorkovskiy v. Russia*, no. 5829/04, § 125, 31 May 2011.

[164] *Svinarenko and Slyadnev v. Russia* [GC], nos 32541/08 and 43441/08, § 133, 17 July 2014.

[165] Ibid., § 138.

[166] *Paladi v. Moldova* [GC], no. 39806/05, § 72, 10 March 2009; *İlhan v. Turkey* [GC], no. 22277/93, § 87, ECHR 2000-VII; *Naumenko v. Ukraine*, no. 42023/98, § 112, 10 February 2004.

[167] *Mouisel v. France*, no. 67263/01, §§ 40–42, ECHR 2002-IX.

[168] *Gelfmann v. France*, no. 25875/03, 14 December 2004.

[169] *Sakkopoulos v. Greece*, no. 61828/00, § 44, 15 January 2004.

their physical well-being. This may require, in some circumstances, remedies in the form of humanitarian measures.[170] The Court has declined to exclude the possibility that remedies be taken that may involve conditional release where a prisoner is seriously ill or disabled,[171] sometimes combined with old age.[172] Vulnerable detainees suffer from particular stress and uncertainty that may affect their physical and mental health and well-being.[173]

Solitary confinement is one of the most serious measures that can be imposed in a prison or penitentiary.[174] Although removal from association with others is not desirable, the Court considers that 'the prohibition of contacts with other prisoners for security, disciplinary or protective reasons does not in itself amount to inhuman treatment or punishment'.[175] Nevertheless, 'complete sensory isolation, coupled with total social isolation can destroy the personality and constitutes a form of inhuman treatment which cannot be justified by the requirements of security or any other reason'.[176] The Court will take into account a range of factors, including the absolute or partial nature of the isolation of the prisoner, the conditions of detention while in solitary confinement, and the length of the measures in assessing whether or not there has been a breach of article 3.[177] Indeed, '[i]n view of the gravity of the measure, the domestic authorities are under an obligation to assess all relevant factors in an inmate's case before placing him in solitary confinement'.[178]

Extreme punishments

Unlike 'treatment', which may be meted out or imposed in the absence of any real legal framework, 'punishment' is in principle ordained by national legislation and is to be imposed after conviction for a crime. Thus, as a preliminary, articles 6 and 7 of the Convention must be observed. There is somewhat of a tautology in the Convention to the extent that article 3 is deemed to be inapplicable to suffering or humiliation that is inherent in any particular form of legitimate punishment imposed by law.[179] Indeed, this is underscored by the reference in article 2 of the Convention to the most extreme punishment of all, the death penalty. As a very general rule the Convention organs have

---

[170] *Enea v. Italy* [GC], no. 74912/01, § 58, ECHR 2009; *Matencio v. France*, no. 58749/00, § 76, 15 January 2004; *Sakkopoulos v. Greece*, no. 61828/00, § 38, 15 January 2004; *Mouisel v. France*, no. 67263/01, § 40, ECHR 2002-IX.

[171] *Arutyunyan v. Russia*, no. 48977/09, § 71, 10 January 2012.

[172] *Farbtuhs v. Latvia*, no. 4672/02, 2 December 2004; *Papon v. France (no. 1)* (dec.), no. 64666/01, ECHR 2001-VI; *Sawoniuk v. the United Kingdom* (dec.), no. 63716/00, ECHR 2001-VI; *Priebke v. Italy* (dec.), no. 48799/99, 5 April 2001; *Enea v. Italy* [GC], no. 74912/01, § 59, ECHR 2009.

[173] *A. and Others v. the United Kingdom* [GC], no. 3455/05, § 130, ECHR 2009.

[174] *Gorbulya v. Russia*, no. 31535/09, § 75, 6 March 2014.

[175] *Messina v. Italy (no. 2)* (dec.), no. 25498/94, ECHR 1999-V; *Öcalan v. Turkey* [GC], no. 46221/99, § 191, ECHR 2005-IV; *Ilaşcu and Others v. Moldova and Russia* [GC], no. 48787/99, § 432, ECHR 2004-VII.

[176] *Messina v. Italy (no. 2)* (dec.), no. 25498/94, ECHR 1999-V; *Öcalan v. Turkey* [GC], no. 46221/99, § 191, ECHR 2005-IV; *Ilaşcu and Others v. Moldova and Russia* [GC], no. 48787/99, § 432, ECHR 2004-VII.

[177] *Ramirez Sanchez v. France* [GC], no. 59450/00, §§ 126–150, ECHR 2006-IX; *Rohde v. Denmark*, no. 6933/01, § 93, 21 July 2005.

[178] *Gorbulya v. Russia*, no. 31535/09, § 75, 6 March 2014; *Ramishvili and Kokhreidze v. Georgia*, no. 1704/06, § 83, 27 January 2009; *Onoufriou v. Cyprus*, no. 24407/04, § 71, 7 January 2010.

[179] *Tyrer v. the United Kingdom*, 25 April 1978, Series A no. 26, § 30; *Ramirez Sanchez v. France* [GC], no. 59450/00, §§ 118–119, ECHR 2006-IX; *Jalloh v. Germany* [GC], no. 54810/00, § 68, ECHR 2006-IX; *Arutyunyan v. Russia*, no. 48977/09, § 69, 10 January 2012; *Enea v. Italy* [GC], no. 74912/01, § 56, ECHR 2009.

refused to sit in judgment with respect to sentencing policy in States Parties, as discussed above. However, exceptionally they have intervened with respect to so-called extreme punishments: life imprisonment, corporal punishment, and capital punishment.

Life imprisonment

Although in some European States it is not possible to sentence a person to life imprisonment, the majority still retain this option. In several jurisdictions, the likelihood that such a sentence will actually be served in full is relatively remote. Often, a sentence of life imprisonment may be imposed on adult offenders for especially serious crimes such as murder.[180] In a few States, it remains possible to impose an 'irreducible' life sentence by which there is no realistic prospect of release. Citing a celebrated judgment of the German Constitutional Court dealing with extreme sentences, the Grand Chamber has noted that detention with no possibility of release is contrary to human dignity.[181] The rationale for its position was eloquently stated by Judge Power-Forde in her concurring opinion:

Those who commit the most abhorrent and egregious of acts and who inflict untold suffering upon others, nevertheless retain their fundamental humanity and carry within themselves the capacity to change. Long and deserved though their prison sentences may be, they retain the right to hope that, someday, they may have atoned for the wrongs which they have committed. They ought not to be deprived entirely of such hope. To deny them the experience of hope would be to deny a fundamental aspect of their humanity and, to do that, would be degrading.[182]

Determining when a sentence is truly 'irreducible' is not always straightforward, however, and in a pre-*Vinter* decision that is probably no longer good law the Court did not find a violation in the case of extradition of two fugitives to the United States who were facing a sentence of 'life without parole'.[183] On a number of occasions, the Court has held that '[t]he imposition of an irreducible life sentence on an adult, without any prospect of release, may raise an issue under Article 3'. However, 'where national law affords the possibility of review of a life sentence with a view to its commutation, remission, termination or the conditional release of the prisoner, this will be sufficient'.[184] A life sentence does not become irreducible by the mere fact that in practice it may be served in full.[185] In *Vinter v. The United Kingdom*, the Grand Chamber said that there is no issue under article 3 if a prisoner sentenced to life is refused release because he or she is deemed to pose a danger to society. The reason for this, according to the Grand Chamber, is that States have a duty under the Convention to protect the public from violent crime. '[T]he Convention does not prohibit States from subjecting a person convicted of a serious crime

[180] *Kafkaris v. Cyprus* [GC], no. 21906/04, § 97, ECHR 2008.
[181] *Vinter and Others v. the United Kingdom* [GC], nos 66069/09, 130/10, and 3896/10, § 113, ECHR 2013 (extracts). Followed in *Öcalan v. Turkey (No. 2)*, nos 24069/03, 197/04, 6201/06, and 10464/07, § 197, 18 March 2014; *László Magyar v. Hungary*, no. 73593/10, § 58, 20 May 2014.
[182] *Vinter and Others v. the United Kingdom* [GC], nos 66069/09, 130/10, and 3896/10, Concurring Opinion of Judge Power-Forde.
[183] *Harkins and Edwards v. the United Kingdom*, nos 9146/07 and 32650/07, §§ 140–142, 17 January 2012.
[184] *A. and Others v. the United Kingdom* [GC], no. 3455/05, § 128, ECHR 2009; *Kafkaris v. Cyprus* [GC], no. 21906/04, §§ 97–98, ECHR 2008; *Vinter and Others v. the United Kingdom* [GC], nos 66069/09, 130/10, and 3896/10, § 107, ECHR 2013 (extracts); *Trabelsi v. Belgium*, no. 140/10, § 115, 4 September 2014.
[185] *Vinter and Others v. the United Kingdom* [GC], nos 66069/09, 130/10, and 3896/10, § 108, 9 July 2013.

to an indeterminate sentence allowing for the offender's continued detention where necessary for the protection of the public', it has said.[186]

Preventive detention, whereby an individual is held in prison because of a risk of recidivism, raises similar issues to those of life imprisonment. Nevertheless, because remedies exist to bring it to an end, indefinite detention is not necessarily comparable to a sentence of life imprisonment.[187] As the sentence is by nature indefinite in duration, persons subject to such regimes are 'in particular need of psychological care and support'.[188] This is a necessary feature of a 'genuine attempt to reduce the risk that they will reoffend, thus serving the purpose of crime prevention and making their release possible'.[189]

Corporal punishment

As a form of punishment prescribed by law for criminal offences, corporal punishment had no doubt virtually disappeared within the Member States of the Council of Europe even before the Convention was adopted. Vestiges of the practice remained within the United Kingdom and its subject territories; indeed, much of the very limited practice of judicial corporal punishment today can be found in former British colonies. The imposition of punishment by whipping for juveniles in 1955 by the British government in Cyprus under emergency powers was almost immediately challenged in the inter-State application filed by Greece before the European Commission of Human Rights. The Commission received evidence that 118 persons had been sentenced to be whipped, including 13 who were under 14 years of age.[190] The United Kingdom insisted that corporal punishment was not in itself contrary to article 3, arguing that 'all doubt on this point was removed by *Article 2 of the Convention* which recognised the right of the Contracting Parties to impose the death penalty. In view of this it could hardly be maintained that less extreme forms of corporal punishment than the penalty of violent death were in themselves contrary to Article 3.'[191] The Sub-Commission of the European Commission proposed the repeal of the corporal punishment measures as a means of obtaining a friendly settlement. The Governor of Cyprus complied later the same day.[192] Although the friendly settlement did not materialize, the abolition of whipping remained in force. In its report to the Committee of Ministers, the European Commission said it was necessary to reach a legal conclusion on the compatibility of whipping with article 3 of the Convention. However, it said 'the trend of opinion today among the peoples of the Council of Europe is not sympathetic to corporal punishment as a penal sanction for young persons' and 'venture[d] to mark its satisfaction at the fact that this measure was revoked'.[193]

One of the first article 3 cases to come before the Court concerned the administration of corporal punishment within the juvenile justice system of the Isle of Man, which is

---

[186] Ibid. Also *Mastromatteo v. Italy* [GC], no. 37703/97, § 72, ECHR 2002-VIII; *Maiorano and Others v. Italy*, no. 28634/06, § 108, 15 December 2009.

[187] *A. and Others v. the United Kingdom* [GC], no. 3455/05, § 131, ECHR 2009.

[188] *M. v. Germany*, no. 19359/04, § 129, ECHR 2009.

[189] Ibid.

[190] *Greece v. the United Kingdom*, no. 176/56, Commission report of 26 September 1958, §§ 163–165.

[191] Ibid., § 175 (emphasis in the original).

[192] Ibid., § 200.

[193] Ibid., § 203.

subject to the Convention as a self-governing dependency of the United Kingdom. Holding that there had been a violation of article 3, the Court said:

The very nature of judicial corporal punishment is that it involves one human being inflicting physical violence on another human being. Furthermore, it is institutionalised violence that is in the present case violence permitted by the law, ordered by the judicial authorities of the State and carried out by the police authorities of the State . . . Thus, although the applicant did not suffer any severe or long-lasting physical effects, his punishment—whereby he was treated as an object in the power of the authorities—constituted an assault on precisely that which it is one of the main purposes of Article 3 (art. 3) to protect, namely a person's dignity and physical integrity.[194]

Judicial corporal punishment appears to have virtually disappeared from the territory of the Council of Europe. There has been some evidence of its imposition in a disciplinary or reprisal context within Russian prisons.[195] Issues may nevertheless arise in cases of *refoulement* to one of the remaining States on the planet where it is still practiced.[196]

Corporal punishment has remained present within national legislation as a form of justification or excuse that may be raised, under precise circumstances, by parents or schoolteachers charged with assault for imposition of disciplinary corporal punishment. Article 3 also applies to school discipline in relations among pupils.[197] In a case involving discipline of a seven-year-old by 'slippering' ('three "whacks" on the bottom through his shorts with a rubber-soled gym shoe'), the Court considered that the level of ill-treatment was far less than that in the *Tyrer* case and concluded that there was no violation of article 3.[198] However, in the case of a nine-year-old who was beaten by his stepfather with a garden cane applied with considerable force on more than one occasion, leaving bruises on various parts of the body, the government itself conceded that article 3 had been violated. The perpetrator had been acquitted of assault after invoking 'reasonable chastisement', a defence that is available to parents and others who are *in loco parentis* under English law. Finding that article 3 had been violated, the Court noted that 'the Government have accepted that this law currently fails to provide adequate protection to children and should be amended'.[199] In an Issue Paper published in 2009, the Council of Europe Commissioner of Human Rights noted that the execution of the judgment in that case was still being supervised, given that the United Kingdom had amended its legislation but had not removed the defence of 'reasonable chastisement'.[200] In litigation under articles 8 and 9, the Convention organs have held that legislation prohibiting all corporal punishment of children, even by parents, does not breach the right to family life or freedom of religion.[201]

[194] *Tyrer v. the United Kingdom*, 25 April 1978, § 33, Series A no. 26.

[195] *Borodin v. Russia*, no. 41867/04, § 108, 6 November 2012; *Rudakov v. Russia*, no. 43239/04, § 53, 28 October 2010; *Dedovskiy and Others v. Russia*, no. 7178/03, § 83, ECHR 2008 (extracts).

[196] *M.A. v. Switzerland*, no. 52589/13, § 36, 18 November 2014; *Sufi and Elmi v. the United Kingdom*, nos 8319/07 and 11449/07, § 276, 28 June 2011; *Mir Isfahani v. the Netherlands* (dec.), no. 31252/03, 31 January 2008.

[197] *Đurđević v. Croatia*, no. 52442/09, § 104, ECHR 2011 (extracts).

[198] *Costello-Roberts v. the United Kingdom*, 25 March 1993, § 28, Series A no. 247-C.

[199] *A. v. The United Kingdom*, 23 September 1998, §§ 19–24, *Reports of Judgments and Decisions* 1998-VI .

[200] Commissioner on Human Rights, Children and corporal punishment: 'the right not to be hit, also a children's right', Strasbourg: Council of Europe, 2009, p. 9.

[201] *Seven individuals v. Sweden*, no. 8811/79, Commission decision of 13 May 1982, DR 29, p. 104.

Capital punishment

The issue of capital punishment highlights the intriguing relationship between articles 2 and 3 of the Convention. The two provisions have always been closely related in the case law of the Court as they are both components of the basic values respected by democratic societies.[202] When the death penalty is concerned, there is an obvious tension—the European Commission spoke of a 'certain disharmony'[203]—because article 2(1) of the Convention authorizes the State to impose such a sanction yet article 3 prohibits any punishment that is inhuman or degrading. Until very recently, both the Commission and the Court took the view that the death penalty cannot not per se be viewed as contrary to article 3.[204] According to the Court, article 3 'evidently cannot have been intended by the drafters of the Convention to include a general prohibition of the death penalty since that would nullify the clear wording of Article 2 § 1'.[205] The Court acknowledged that subsequent State practice could indicate an agreement that capital punishment was no longer permitted by the Convention. It referred to the adoption of Protocol No. 6, noting this was the 'normal method of amendment' of the Convention. Protocol No. 6 was an 'optional instrument allowing each State to choose the moment when to undertake such an engagement'. Consequently, article 3 'cannot be interpreted as generally prohibiting the death penalty'.[206]

That conclusion did not exclude the possibility of violations associated with execution, such as the intolerably long period of detention prior to execution in some jurisdictions. In one of its most significant and influential judgments, the Court ruled that the 'death row phenomenon' constituted a breach of article 3 because of the suffering and anguish of the condemned person while awaiting execution. Under the circumstances, the expected delay between conviction and execution was eight years, although there were other aggravating factors such as the relatively young age of the applicant.[207]

Eventually, in 2010, the Court concluded that developments within the Council of Europe entitled it to disregard the terms of article 2(1) to the extent that they authorized the use of the death penalty. The case concerned applicants who were handed over by occupying British forces to Iraqi authorities. If convicted, they could face the death penalty. The Court resisted finding that there was a violation of the right to life set out in article 2 and instead shifted the analysis to article 3. It said that 'the applicants' well-founded fear of being executed by the Iraqi authorities during the period May 2006 to July 2009 must have given rise to a significant degree of mental suffering and that to subject them to such suffering constituted inhuman treatment within the meaning of Article 3 of the Convention'.[208] In effect, it returned to the spirit of its death row phenomenon jurisprudence by condemning the mental anguish associated with

---

[202] *Pretty v. the United Kingdom*, no. 2346/02, § 54, ECHR 2002-III.

[203] *Kirkwood v. the United Kingdom*, no. 10479/83, Commission decision of 12 March 1984, DR 37, p. 158.

[204] *Soering v. the United Kingdom*, no. 14038/88, Commission report of 19 January 1989; *Soering v. the United Kingdom*, 7 July 1989, §§ 101–104, Series A no. 161; *Öcalan v. Turkey* [GC], no. 46221/99, § 162, ECHR 2005-IV.

[205] *Soering v. the United Kingdom*, 7 July 1989, § 103, Series A no. 161.

[206] Ibid. Also, with respect to Protocol No. 13, *Öcalan v. Turkey* [GC], no. 46221/99, § 165, ECHR 2005-IV.

[207] *Soering v. the United Kingdom*, 7 July 1989, § 104, Series A no. 161. Also *Poltoratskiy v. Ukraine*, no. 38812/97, § 133, ECHR 2003-VI; *Ilaşcu and Others v. Moldova and Russia* [GC], no. 48787/99, § 429, ECHR 2004-VII.

[208] *Al-Saadoon and Mufdhi v. the United Kingdom*, no. 61498/08, § 137, ECHR 2010 (extracts).

imposition of a death sentence rather than declaring it to be inhuman or degrading regardless of the degree of pre-execution suffering experienced by the victim. The same understanding emerges from the Court's most recent pronouncement, in *Al Nashiri v. Poland*, condemning resort to capital punishment because 'the foreknowledge of death at the hands of the State must inevitably give rise to intense psychological suffering'.[209]

Positive obligations

Article 3 has mainly been applied where the risk to the individual of a violation emanates from intentional acts inflicted by State agents or public authorities.[210] It therefore imposes 'a primarily negative obligation' on the State to refrain from inflicting serious harm.[211] Nevertheless, there is a positive dimension to the right requiring the State to take action to prevent torture and inhuman or degrading treatment being inflicted by persons not acting on behalf of the State.[212] The positive obligations are also associated with article 1 of the Convention. An important part of the positive obligations consists of what has been called the 'procedural obligation', a concept that also exists with respect to article 2 of the Convention.

Positive obligations requiring the State to provide protection against inhuman or degrading treatment have been recognized in a broad range of cases, such as corporal punishment of a child by a stepfather,[213] and the protection of children severely abused and neglected by their parents.[214] Positive obligations may also arise where the consequences of a naturally occurring illness may be exacerbated by treatment stemming from measures for which the authorities can be held responsible, although the threshold may be high because the harm results from the illness rather than the acts or omissions of the authorities.[215]

As with article 2 of the Convention, the Court has developed a 'procedural obligation' contained within article 3, assisted by article 1, by which the State is required to investigate and prosecute cases of torture and inhuman or degrading treatment or punishment.[216] This aspect of article 3 applies not only when there is an allegation of ill-treatment by the police or other agents of the State, but also when the acts themselves cannot be imputed to the State at all.[217] The authorities must investigate allegations of ill-treatment when they are 'arguable' and 'raise a reasonable suspicion'.[218]

---

[209] *Al Nashiri v. Poland*, no. 28761/11, § 577, 24 July 2014.

[210] *Pretty v. the United Kingdom*, no. 2346/02, § 50, ECHR 2002-III.

[211] Ibid.; *Hristozov and Others v. Bulgaria*, nos 47039/11 and 358/12, § 111, 13 November 2012.

[212] *A. v. the United Kingdom*, 23 September 1998, § 22, *Reports of Judgments and Decisions* 1998-VI; *Z and Others v. the United Kingdom* [GC], no. 29392/95, §§ 73–75, ECHR 2001-V; *E. and Others v. the United Kingdom*, no. 33218/96, 26 November 2002; *Abdu v. Bulgaria*, no. 26827/08, § 40, 11 March 2014.

[213] *A. v. the United Kingdom*, 23 September 1998, *Reports of Judgments and Decisions* 1998-VI.

[214] *Z and Others v. the United Kingdom* [GC], no. 29392/95, ECHR 2001-V.

[215] *N. v. the United Kingdom* [GC], no. 26565/05, §§ 29, 43, ECHR 2008. See, however, *Josef v. Belgium*, no. 70055/10, Dissenting Opinion of Judge Power-Forde, 27 February 2014.

[216] *V.C. v. Slovakia*, no. 18968/07, § 123, ECHR 2011 (extracts); *Assenov and Others v. Bulgaria*, 28 October 1998, § 102, *Reports of Judgments and Decisions* 1998-VIII; *Biçici v. Turkey*, no. 30357/05, § 39, 27 May 2010.

[217] *M.C. v. Bulgaria*, no. 39272/98, § 151, ECHR 2003-XII; *Ay v. Turkey*, no. 30951/96, § 59, 22 March 2005; *Gülbahar and Others v. Turkey*, no. 5264/03, § 72, 21 October 2008.

[218] *M. and Others v. Italy and Bulgaria*, no. 40020/03, § 100, 31 July 2012; *Ay v. Turkey*, no. 30951/96, §§ 59–60, 22 March 2005; *Mehmet Ümit Erdem v. Turkey*, no. 42234/02, § 26, 17 July 2008.

An effective criminal justice system that addresses physical attacks on the bodily integrity of citizens is one important manifestation of the positive obligations associated with article 3. Of course, it is an obligation of means, and the State cannot be held responsible simply because inhuman or degrading treatment is inflicted by one individual on another or, if it is, that criminal proceedings necessarily lead to a particular sanction. For there to be a violation of the Convention, 'it must in the view of the Court be shown that the domestic legal system, and in particular the criminal law applicable in the circumstances of the case, fails to provide practical and effective protection of the rights guaranteed by Article 3'.[219] The Court has insisted that 'the obligation on the State to bring to justice perpetrators of acts contrary to Article 3 of the Convention serves mainly to ensure that acts of ill-treatment do not remain ignored by the relevant authorities and to provide effective protection against acts of ill-treatment'.[220] But the Court has also suggested that the purpose of criminal prosecution is specific deterrence of the offender and, thereby, protection of the victim against violence.[221] Criminal justice may not necessarily be the appropriate remedy.[222] Moreover, it may be unavailable because the perpetrators of the acts are not subject to prosecution, for example because of their young age.[223]

All states will have measures in place within their criminal justice systems to deal with various forms of assault, including sexual assault. Where the provisions of the criminal justice legislation or prosecutorial policy applied by the authorities reflect outdated stereotypes that contribute to impunity, there may be a breach of article 3. For example, in a Bulgarian case the Court held that the insistence upon evidence of physical resistance by the victim of a sexual assault was incompatible with the prohibitions enshrined in article 3.[224] Domestic violence raises special issues with respect to the procedural obligation comprised within article 3.[225] The Court has explained that it is 'a general problem which concerns all member States and which does not always surface since it often takes place within personal relationships or closed circuits and it is not only women who are affected'.[226] In applying the Convention, the Court will bear in mind specialized international instruments applicable to the problem, including the Convention on the Elimination of All Forms of Discrimination against Women and the Inter-American Convention on the Prevention, Punishment, and Eradication of Violence against Women.[227]

Where there are suspicions that racist attitudes may be involved in violent attacks, the authorities also must address this aspect in their investigation.[228] The Court has noted that making special provision for violent crimes that are racially motivated is consistent

---

[219] *Beganović v. Croatia*, no. 46423/06, § 71, 25 June 2009.
[220] Ibid., § 79.
[221] Ibid., §§ 85–87.
[222] *M.C. v. Bulgaria*, no. 39272/98, Concurring Opinion of Judge Tulkens, § 2, ECHR 2003-XII.
[223] *Đorđević v. Croatia*, no. 41526/10, §§ 142–150, ECHR 2012.
[224] *M.C. v. Bulgaria*, no. 39272/98, §§ 169–187, ECHR 2003-XII.
[225] See, for example, *T.M. and C.M. v. the Republic of Moldova*, no. 26608/11, § 46, 28 January 2014; *Mudric v. the Republic of Moldova*, no. 74839/10, §§ 44–55, 16 July 2013; *B. v. the Republic of Moldova*, no. 61382/09, §§ 47–61, 16 July 2013; *Valiulienė v. Lithuania*, no. 33234/07, §§ 73–86, 26 March 2013.
[226] *Opuz v. Turkey*, no. 33401/02, § 132, ECHR 2009. See Tarik Abdel-Monem, '*Opuz v. Turkey*: Europe's Landmark Judgment on Violence against Women', (2009) 17:1 *Human Rights Brief* 29.
[227] *Opuz v. Turkey*, no. 33401/02, § 164, ECHR 2009.
[228] *Abdu v. Bulgaria*, no. 26827/08, § 44, 11 March 2014.

with obligations under international law, including the International Convention on the Elimination of All Forms of Racial Discrimination.[229]

An official investigation required by article 3 must be capable of leading to the identification of those responsible. Otherwise, the Court has held, 'the general legal prohibition of torture and inhuman and degrading treatment and punishment would, despite its fundamental importance, be ineffective in practice and it would be possible in some cases for agents of the State to abuse the rights of those within their control with virtual impunity'.[230] A thorough investigation requires that all reasonable steps be taken to secure eyewitness and forensic evidence,[231] that it be expeditious,[232] and that it be conducted by persons who have sufficient independence.[233] It is an obligation of means and not of result; the failure to reach a conclusive result does not mean that the procedural obligation has not been respected.[234] The procedural obligation will arise when there is a failure to conduct an inquiry into injuries suffered by inmates at the hands of the security forces following a prison riot.[235] Often, when the State is not ostensibly involved, there may be a strong suspicion that its failure to intervene or to investigate and prosecute amounts to tolerance and even collusion in illegal acts.

The State's procedural obligation was first developed within international human rights law by the Inter-American Court of Human Rights in cases dealing with enforced disappearance. The relatives of missing persons are themselves potential victims of the violation of article 3 to the extent that they are 'kept in ignorance of the fate of their loved ones and suffer the anguish of uncertainty'. This form of secondary victimization might also arise where parents are helpless onlookers while their children are treated in a degrading and inhumane manner.[236] According to the European Court, in disappearance cases the 'essence of the violation is not that there has been a serious human rights violation concerning the missing person; it lies in the authorities' reactions and attitudes to the situation when it has been brought to their attention'.[237] The violation may occur not only in circumstances where the State itself is responsible for the disappearance, but also where it is the act of third parties and 'where the failure of the authorities to respond to the quest for information by the relatives or the obstacles placed in their way, leaving them to bear the brunt of the efforts to uncover any facts, may be regarded as disclosing a

---

[229] Ibid., referring to articles 4(1) and 6 of the International Convention on the Elimination of All Forms of Racial Discrimination, (1966) 660 UNTS 195.

[230] *Labita v. Italy* [GC], no. 26772/95, § 83, ECHR 2000-IV; *Boicenco v. Moldova*, no. 41088/05, § 120, 11 July 2006; *Đurđević v. Croatia*, no. 52442/09, §§ 83–85, ECHR 2011 (extracts); *Suleymanov v. Russia*, no. 32501/11, § 129, 22 January 2013.

[231] *Tanrıkulu v. Turkey* [GC], no. 23763/94, ECHR 1999-IV, § 104 et seq. and *Gül v. Turkey*, no. 22676/93, § 89, 14 December 2000; *Savitskyy v. Ukraine*, no. 38773/05, § 99, 26 July 2012; *Suleymanov v. Russia*, no. 32501/11, § 137, 22 January 2013.

[232] *Suleymanov v. Russia*, no. 32501/11, § 138, 22 January 2013; *Mikheyev v. Russia*, no. 77617/01, § 113, 26 January 2006; *Indelicato v. Italy*, no. 31143/96, § 37, 18 October 2001.

[233] *Đurđević v. Croatia*, no. 52442/09, § 85, ECHR 2011 (extracts); *Barbu Anghelescu v. Romania*, no. 46430/99, § 66, 5 October 2004; *Kolevi v. Bulgaria*, no. 1108/02, § 193, 5 November 2009.

[234] *Paul and Audrey Edwards v. the United Kingdom*, no. 46477/99, § 71, ECHR 2002-II.

[235] *Gömi and Others v. Turkey*, no. 35962/97, § 80, 21 December 2006.

[236] *Popov v. France*, nos 39472/07 and 39474/07, Partly Dissenting Opinion of Judge Power-Forde, 19 January 2012.

[237] *Varnava and Others v. Turkey* [GC], nos 16064/90, 16065/90, 16066/90, 16068/90, 16069/90, 16070/90, 16071/90, 16072/90, and 16073/90, § 200, ECHR 2009; *Orhan v. Turkey*, no. 25656/94, § 358, ECHR 2002; *Imakayeva v. Russia*, no. 7615/02, § 164, ECHR 2006-XIII (extracts).

flagrant, continuous and callous disregard of an obligation to account for the whereabouts and fate of a missing person'.[238]

The procedural obligation is related to the need to deter violations of the Convention. Robust prosecution through criminal law may be required, particularly in cases of wilful ill-treatment by State agents. The Court has held that '[i]f the authorities could confine their reaction to incidents of intentional police ill-treatment to the mere payment of compensation, while remaining passive in the prosecution of those responsible, it would be possible in some cases for agents of the State to abuse the rights of those within their control with virtual impunity and the general legal prohibition of torture and inhuman and degrading treatment and punishment, despite its fundamental importance, would be ineffective in practice'.[239] The Court 'must retain its supervisory function and intervene in cases of manifest disproportion between the gravity of the act and the punishment imposed'.[240] This is because 'punishment, which is manifestly disproportionate to a breach of one of the core rights of the Convention, does not have the necessary deterrent effect in order to prevent further violations of the prohibition of ill-treatment in future difficult situations'.[241]

Extraterritorial application

The expulsion or *refoulement* of persons from States Parties often raise issues with respect to article 3 of the Convention. This is a special application of the general principles governing extraterritorial application of the Convention, discussed in this Commentary in the chapter on article 1. The Court has framed its discussion by noting that States are entitled, as a matter of international law and subject to their treaty obligations, to control the entry, residence, and expulsion of aliens.[242] Nor is there any right to political asylum under the Convention.[243] Where 'substantial grounds have been shown for believing that the person concerned, if deported, faces a real risk of being subjected to treatment contrary to Article 3', the Convention requires that the victim not be removed to the country in question.[244] In a case involving the transfer of asylum seekers from Switzerland to Italy pursuant to the Dublin Agreement, the Grand Chamber concluded that 'were the applicants to be returned to Italy without the Swiss authorities having first obtained individual guarantees from the Italian authorities that the applicants would be taken charge of in a manner adapted to the age of the children and that the family would be kept together, there would be a violation of Article 3 of the Convention'.[245] The Court will assess the conditions in the receiving country in light of the standards imposed by article 3.[246]

---

[238] *Varnava and Others v. Turkey* [GC], nos 16064/90, 16065/90, 16066/90, 16068/90, 16069/90, 16070/90, 16071/90, 16072/90, and 16073/90, § 200, ECHR 2009

[239] *Krastanov v. Bulgaria*, no. 50222/99, § 60, 30 September 2004.

[240] *Gäfgen v. Germany* [GC], no. 22978/05, § 123, ECHR 2010.

[241] *Krastanov v. Bulgaria*, no. 50222/99, § 60, 30 September 2004.

[242] *Üner v. the Netherlands* [GC], no. 46410/99, § 54, ECHR 2006-XII; *Abdulaziz, Cabales and Balkandali v. the United Kingdom*, 28 May 1985, § 67, Series A no. 94; *N.A. v. the United Kingdom*, no. 25904/07, § 109, 17 July 2008; *Boujlifa v. France*, 21 October 1997, § 42, *Reports of Judgments and Decisions* 1997-VI.

[243] *N. and Others v. the United Kingdom* (dec.), no. 16458/12, § 110, 15 April 2014; *Salah Sheekh v. the Netherlands*, no. 1948/04, § 135, 11 January 2007; *Vilvarajah and Others v. the United Kingdom*, 30 October 1991, § 102, Series A no. 215; *Ahmed v. Austria*, 17 December 1996, § 38, *Reports of Judgments and Decisions* 1996-VI.

[244] *Saadi v. Italy* [GC], no. 37201/06, § 125, ECHR 2008.

[245] *Tarakhel v. Switzerland* [GC], no. 29217/12, § 122, 4 November 2014.

[246] *Mamatkulov and Askarov v. Turkey* [GC], nos 46827/99 and 46951/99, § 67, ECHR 2005-I.

In *refoulement* cases, the European Court has generally avoided pronouncing itself on the distinction between torture and ill-treatment.[247] Its explanation is that 'in the extra-territorial context, a prospective assessment is required [and] it is not always possible to determine whether the ill-treatment which may ensue in the receiving State will be sufficiently severe as to qualify as torture'.[248]

Assessment of the risk depends upon all of the circumstances.[249] It must be rigorous, a heavy burden being placed upon the applicant to demonstrate the real risk of ill-treatment to adduce 'substantial grounds'.[250] At the same time, because of the special circumstances in which asylum seekers may find themselves, the Court has said they must frequently be given 'the benefit of the doubt when it comes to assessing the credibility of their statements and the documents submitted in support thereof'.[251] On the other hand, when there is information that 'gives strong reasons to question the veracity of an asylum seeker's submissions, the individual must provide a satisfactory explanation for the alleged discrepancies'.[252]

If the risk emanates from non-State actors, the receiving State must ensure appropriate protection to protect the potential victim.[253] The assessment of risk focuses on the foreseeable consequences of removal, in light of the general situation in the receiving State as well as the person circumstances of the applicant.[254] However, a general situation of violence in the receiving State does not normally lead to the conclusion that there is a real risk of a violation of article 3.[255] Although the Court has not excluded the possibility that a general situation of violence in a country of destination will be of a sufficient level of intensity, 'the Court would adopt such an approach only in the most extreme cases of general violence, where there was a real risk of ill-treatment simply by virtue of an individual being exposed to such violence on return'.[256]

In response to allegations that expulsion will entail a violation of article 3, respondent States have sometimes proffered 'diplomatic assurances'. These are undertakings made by the receiving State about treatment to be received if the person is transferred. In death penalty cases, for example, it has been common for such diplomatic undertakings to be provided. These have generally been regarded by the Convention organs to be satisfactory.[257] The death penalty will be governed by legal provisions making it relatively straightforward to assess the binding nature of any assurances. The situation is quite different when assurances

---

[247] *Chahal v. the United Kingdom*, 15 November 1996, § 79, *Reports of Judgments and Decisions* 1996-V; *Mamatkulov and Askarov v. Turkey* [GC], nos 46827/99 and 46951/99, § 67, ECHR 2005-I; *Saadi v. Italy* [GC], no. 37201/06, § 125, ECHR 2008.

[248] *Babar Ahmad and Others v. the United Kingdom*, nos 24027/07, 11949/08, 36742/08, 66911/09, and 67354/09, § 170, 10 April 2012.

[249] *Hilal v. the United Kingdom*, no. 45276/99, § 60, ECHR 2001-II.

[250] *Chahal v. the United Kingdom*, 15 November 1996, § 96, *Reports of Judgments and Decisions* 1996-V; *Saadi v. Italy* [GC], no. 37201/06, § 128, 28 February 2008; *N. v. Finland*, no. 38885/02, § 167, 26 July 2005.

[251] *N. and Others v. the United Kingdom* (dec.), no. 16458/12, §§ 112, 122–126, 15 April 2014.

[252] *H.N. and Others v. Sweden* (dec.), no. 50043/09, 24 January 2012; *S.H.H. v. the United Kingdom*, no. 60367/10, § 71, 29 January 2013.

[253] *H.L.R. v. France*, 29 April 1997, § 40, *Reports of Judgments and Decisions* 1997-III.

[254] *Vilvarajah and Others v. the United Kingdom*, 30 October 1991, § 108, Series A no. 215.

[255] *Sultani v. France*, no. 45223/05, § 67, ECHR 2007-IV (extracts); *Müslim v. Turkey*, no. 53566/99, § 70, 26 April 2005; *H.L.R. v. France*, 29 April 1997, § 41, *Reports of Judgments and Decisions* 1997-III.

[256] *N.A. v. the United Kingdom*, no. 25904/07, § 115, 17 July 2008.

[257] *Aylor-Davis v. France*, no. 22742/93, Commission decision of 20 January 1994, DR 76, p. 164; *Nivette v. France* (dec.), no. 44190/98, ECHR 2001-VII; *Einhorn v. France* (dec.), no. 71555/01, ECHR 2001-XI; *Salem v. Portugal* (dec.), no. 26844/04, 9 May 2006.

involve torture, an act that is in principle prohibited by law in the receiving State. In *Saadi v. Italy*, the respondent State Party invoked assurances it had been given by Tunisia. They had been requested in the most civil and obtuse language, given the diplomatic challenge involved in asking a State to guarantee that it will not commit an international crime. The response given to Italy, that its authorities judged to be satisfactory, read as follows: 'The Minister of Foreign Affairs hereby confirms that the Tunisian laws in force guarantee and protect the rights of prisoners in Tunisia and secure to them the right to a fair trial. The Minister would point out that Tunisia has voluntarily acceded to the relevant international treaties and conventions.'[258] The Court was not impressed with such assurances but it added that even if they were satisfactory this would not be sufficient given the requirement that it make its own assessment. It did not rule out the significance of diplomatic assurances in such cases, but said '[t]he weight to be given to assurances from the receiving State depends, in each case, on the circumstances prevailing at the material time'.[259]

Discrimination

Both the Court and the Commission have taken the view that discrimination may in and of itself constitute inhumane treatment in breach of article 3 of the Convention where it attains a sufficient level of severity.[260] Referring approvingly to an early case of the Commission, the Court has said, 'with respect to an allegation of racial discrimination, that a special importance should be attached to discrimination based on race and that publicly to single out a group of persons for differential treatment on the basis of race might, in certain circumstances, constitute a special affront to human dignity'.[261] The presence of racial discrimination may also be deemed an aggravating factor to be considered in assessing whether ill-treatment meets the threshold of seriousness required for the application of article 3.[262]

Article 14 of the Convention provides the basis for a distinct assessment of the role of prohibited discrimination in violations of article 3. Article 14 is complementary to the other substantive provisions of the Convention and the Protocols. It has no independent existence, applying only with respect to other protected rights and freedoms. The Court found that article 14 had been breached in conjunction with article 3 in a case involving persecution of Jehovah's Witnesses in Georgia. Although much of the conduct was imputable to another religious organization, the Court recognized that several acts involved the direct participation of police and other authorities. Victims were subjected to religious insults when lodging complaints with the police and, more generally, 'there was a systematic practice on the part of the Georgian authorities of tolerating religious violence against Jehovah's Witnesses'.[263] The Court said the applicants had made a *prima*

---

[258] *Saadi v. Italy* [GC], no. 37201/06, § 55, ECHR 2008.

[259] Ibid., § 148.

[260] *Lăcătuş and Others v. Romania*, no. 12694/04, § 89, 13 November 2012; *Cyprus v. Turkey* [GC], no. 25781/94, § 311, ECHR 2001-IV; *Abdulaziz, Cabales and Balkandali v. the United Kingdom*, 28 May 1985, §§ 90–92, Series A no. 94; *East African Asians v. the United Kingdom*, nos 4403/70-4419/70, 4422/70, 4423/70, 4434/70, 4443/70, 4476/70-4478/70, 4486/70, 4501/70, and 4526/70-4530/70, Commission report of 14 December 1973, § 208, DR 78-A, p. 5.

[261] *Cyprus v. Turkey* [GC], no. 25781/94, § 306, ECHR 2001-IV.

[262] *Moldovan v. Romania (no. 2)*, nos 41138/98 and 64320/01, § 111, ECHR 2005-VII (extracts); *S.H. v. the United Kingdom*, no. 19956/06, § 70, 15 June 2010.

[263] *Begheluri and Others v. Georgia*, no. 28490/02, § 144, 7 October 2014.

facie case that religious hatred had played a principal role in the way they had been treated by the State authorities, and that the State had failed to provide any satisfactory explanation or response.[264] The Court concluded first that 'the various forms of violence directed against the applicants either by State agents or private individuals were instigated by a bigoted attitude towards the community of Jehovah's Witnesses and, secondly, that the very same discriminatory state of mind was at the core of the relevant public authorities' failure to investigate the incidents of religiously motivated violence in an effective manner, which confirmed that the authorities at least tolerated that violence'.[265]

Racism was also found to have played a role in the ill-treatment of Chechens by Russian law enforcement authorities during residential searches. The applicants reported on various forms of physical brutality associated with abusive remarks about their ethnicity. The Court insisted that 'where evidence comes to light of racist verbal abuse being uttered by law-enforcement agents in the context of the alleged ill-treatment of detained persons from an ethnic or other minority, a thorough examination of all the facts should be undertaken in order to discover any possible racial motives'.[266] Observing that the applications had made a *prima facie* case of racially based ill-treatment and that the Government had offered no satisfactory explanation, the Court concluded that the conduct of the authorities 'constituted discrimination based on ethnicity, which is a form of racial discrimination'.[267] This was held to be a violation of article 14 taken together with both the substantive and procedural aspects of article 3.

Several cases have involved violence directed against vulnerable groups based upon race, religion, or other grounds where the complicity of the State was not alleged but where it was accused of failing to fulfil adequately its 'procedural obligation'. Even when complaints are investigated by the authorities, the Convention requires that if there is a discriminatory dimension this must feature as part of the inquiry. The combined effect of articles 3 and 14 requires that appropriate attention be directed to the role of racism and other prohibited forms of discrimination, because '[t]raiter la violence et les brutalités à motivation raciste sur un pied d'égalité avec les affaires sans connotation raciste équivaudrait à fermer les yeux sur la nature spécifique d'actes particulièrement destructeurs des droits fondamentaux'.[268] In effect, 'an obligation to unmask a possible discriminatory motive behind violent incidents is implied in the responsibilities under Article 14 of the Convention'.[269] The reason for this is that '[r]acial violence is a particular affront to human dignity and, in view of its dangerous consequences, requires special vigilance and a vigorous reaction from the authorities. It is for this reason that the authorities must use all available means to combat racism and racist violence, thereby reinforcing democracy's vision of a society in which diversity is not perceived as a threat but as a source of its enrichment.'[270]

In a case involving a violent attack by two Bulgarians on two Sudanese, in their report to the authorities the victims had insisted on having heard racist remarks at the time of the

---

[264] Ibid., §§ 176–177.

[265] Ibid., § 179.

[266] *Antayev and Others v. Russia*, no. 37966/07, § 126, 3 July 2014.

[267] Ibid., §§ 127–128.

[268] *Abdu v. Bulgaria*, no. 26827/08, § 44, 11 March 2014; *Šečić v. Croatia*, no. 40116/02, §§ 66–67, 31 May 2007; *Beganoviić v. Croatia*, no. 46423/06, §§ 93–94, 25 June 2009.

[269] *Begheluri and Others v. Georgia*, no. 28490/02, § 173, 7 October 2014.

[270] *Antayev and Others v. Russia*, no. 37966/07, § 120, 3 July 2014.

assault. Moreover, the two perpetrators were identified in the police file as being skinheads known for their extremist ideology. There was a failure to pursue the thesis that racist motives were responsible.[271] The Court said there was a violation of the procedural aspect of article 3 taken on its own and in combination with article 14 of the Convention.[272] In such cases, the Court has spoken of 'the interplay of the two provisions', explaining that such matters may be examined under one or the other provision or under both, something to be decided in each case on its facts and depending on the nature of the allegations.[273]

Gender discrimination, especially in the context of domestic violence, has resulted in similar case law with respect to the procedural obligation contained within article 3. In a case involving violence against women, where 'the general and discriminatory judicial passivity in Turkey [to domestic violence against women] created a climate that was conducive to domestic violence' and contributed to violence within the family, the Court said this was a violation of article 14 taken in conjunction with article 3.[274] In cases from Moldova, the Court has cited a number of factors that it said amounted to condoning of domestic violence and therefore discriminatory treatment based upon gender.[275]

Where homosexuals were discharged from the armed forces, the Court said that it 'would not exclude that treatment which is grounded upon a predisposed bias on the part of a heterosexual majority against a homosexual minority of the nature described above could, in principle, fall within the scope of Article 3'.[276]

Reservations

There have been no reservations or declarations with regard to article 3 of the European Convention.

Further reading

M. Addo and N. Grief, 'Is There a Policy Behind the Decisions and Judgments Relating to Article 3 of the European Convention on Human Rights?', (1995) 20 *European Law Review* 178.

M. Addo and N. Grief, 'Does Article 3 of The European Convention on Human Rights Enshrine Absolute Rights?', (1998) 9 *European Journal of International Law* 510.

J.-F. Akandji-Kombé, 'L'obligation positive d'enquête sur le terrain de l'article 3 ECHR', in C.-A. Chassin, ed., *La portée de l'article 3 de la Convention européenne des droits de l'homme*, Brussels: Bruylant, 2006, pp. 123–40.

Stephan Ast, 'The Gafgen Judgment of the European Court of Human Rights: On the Consequences of the Threat of Torture for Criminal Proceedings', (2010) 11 *German Law Journal* 1393.

Natasha Bakirci, '*Al-Skeini and Others v. the United Kingdom* (No. 55721/07)—Grand Chamber Judgment of 7 July 2011', (2012) 1 *Cyprus Human Rights Law Review* 88.

D. Bonner, '*Ireland v. the United Kingdom*', (1978) 27 *ICLQ* 897.

---

[271] *Abdu v. Bulgaria*, no. 26827/08, §§ 49–50, 11 March 2014.

[272] Ibid., § 53.

[273] *Antayev and Others v. Russia*, no. 37966/07, § 122, 3 July 2014.

[274] *Opuz v. Turkey*, no. 33401/02, § 202, ECHR 2009. See, however, *Rumor v. Italy*, no. 72964/10, §§ 63–77, 27 May 2014.

[275] *Eremia v. the Republic of Moldova*, no. 3564/11, §§ 85–90; 28 May 2013; *T.M. and C.M. v. the Republic of Moldova*, no. 26608/11, §§ 62–64, 28 January 2014.

[276] *Smith and Grady v. the United Kingdom*, nos 33985/96 and 33986/96, § 121, ECHR 1999-VI.

Antoine Buyse, '*Gäfgen v. Germany* (Eur. Ct. H.R), Introductory Note', (2010) 49 *International Legal Materials* 1597.

Johan Callewaert, 'L'article 3 de la Convention européenne: une norme relativement absolue ou absolument relative?', in *Liber Amicorum Marc-André Eissen*, Brussels: Bruylant, 1995, pp. 13–38.

Antonio Cassese, 'Prohibition of Torture and Inhuman or Degrading Treatment or Punishment', in Macdonald, *The European System*, pp. 225–62.

Theodora Christodoulidou, 'Case Analysis—Life Imprisonment as Inhuman and Degrading Treatment: *Kafkaris v. Cyprus* before the European Court of Human Rights', (2008) 5 *EHRLR* 656.

Theodora Christodoulidou, '*Kafkaris v. Cyprus* (No. 9644/09)—Grand Chamber Judgment of 21 June 2010', (2012) 1 *Cyprus Human Rights Law Review* 111.

Anthony Cullen, 'Defining Torture in International Law: A Critique of the Concept Employed by the European Court of Human Rights', (2003–2004), 34 *California Western International Law Journal* 29.

Hans Danelius, 'Protection against Torture in Europe and the World', in Macdonald, *The European System*, pp. 263–75.

Emmanuel Decaux, 'La problématique des disparitions forcées à la lumière des articles 2 et 3 ECHR', in C.-A. Chassin, ed., *La portée de l'article 3 de la Convention européenne des droits de l'homme*, Brussels: Bruylant, 2006, pp. 157–78.

Haritini Dipla, 'The Contribution of the European Court of Human Rights to the Absolute Ban of Torture. The Practice of Diplomatic Assurances', in Dean Spielmann, Marialena Tsirli, and Panayotis Voyatzis, eds, *La Convention européenne des droits de l'homme, un instrument vivant, Mélanges en l'honneur de Christos L. Rozakis*, Brussels: Bruylant, 2011, pp. 155–80.

Michelle Farrell, *The Prohibition of Torture in Exceptional Circumstances*, Cambridge: Cambridge University Press, 2013.

Frowein/Peukert, *MenschenRechtsKonvention*, pp. 42–58.

W. Ganshof van der Meersch, 'L'extradition et la Convention européenne des droits de l'homme. L'affaire Soering', (1990) *RTDH* 5.

David L. Gappa, 'European Court of Human Rights—Extradition—Inhuman or Degrading Treatment or Punishment, Soering Case, 161 Eur.Ct.H.R. (Ser. A) 1989)', (1990) 20 *Georgia J. Int'l Comp. L.* 463.

Grabenwarter, *European Convention*, pp. 31–52.

Ela Grdinic, 'Application of the Elements of Torture and Other Forms of Ill-treatment, as Defined by the European Court and Commission of Human Rights, to the Incidents of Domestic Violence', (1999–2000) 23 *Hastings International & Comparative Law Review* 217.

Harris et al., *Law of the European Convention*, pp. 69–112.

Helen Keller and Olga Chernishova, 'Disappearance Cases before the European Court of Human Rights and the UN Human Rights Committee: Convergences and Divergences', (2012) 32 *HRLJ* 237.

Henri Labayle, 'Droits de l'homme, traitement inhumain et peine capitale: Réflexions sur l'édification d'un ordre public européen en matière d'extradition par la Cour européenne des droits de l'homme', (1990) 64 *Semaine juridique* 3452.

Richard B. Lillich, 'The *Soering* case', (1991) 85 *AJIL* 128.

Patricia Mallia, 'European Court of Human Rights: *M.S.S. v. Belgium & Greece*, Introductory Note', (2011) 50 *International Legal Materials* 364.

Susan Marks, 'Yes, Virginia, Extradition May Breach the European Convention on Human Rights', (1990) 49 *Cambridge Law Journal* 194.

Natasa Mavronicola and Francesco Messineo, 'Relatively Absolute? The Undermining of Article 3 ECHR in *Ahmad v. UK*', (2013) 76 *Modern Law Review* 589.

Michael O'Boyle, 'Torture and Emergency Powers under the European Convention on Human Rights: *Ireland v. The United Kingdom*', (1977) 71 *AJIL* 674.

Michael O'Boyle, 'Extradition and Expulsion under the European Convention on Human Rights, Reflections on the *Soering* Case', in James O'Reilly, ed., *Human Rights and Constitutional Law, Essays in Honour of Brian Walsh*, Dublin: The Round Hall Press, 1992, p. 93.

Ovey/White, *Jacobs and White, European Convention*, pp. 58–89.

L.E. Pettiti, 'Arrêt Soering c./Grande-Bretagne du 8 juillet 1989', [1989] *Revue de science criminelle et de droit pénal comparé* 786.

Alka Pradhan, 'European Court of Human Rights: *Al-Jedda v. the United Kingdom* & *Al-Skeini and Others v. the United Kingdom*', (2011) 50 *International Legal Materials* 947.

J. Quigley and J. Shank, 'Death Row as a Violation of Human Rights: Is it Illegal to Extradite to Virginia?', (1989) 30 *Virginia International Law Journal* 251.

Heiko Sauer and Mirja Trilsch, '*Gäfgen v. Germany*: European Court of Human Rights Grand Chamber Judgment on Prohibiting Torture in Situations where Other Lives may be at Stake, and the Admissibility of Evidence Secured under Threat of Torture', (2011) 105 *AJIL* 313.

Ann Sherlock, 'Extradition, Death Row and the Convention', (1990) 15 *European Law Review* 87.

Martha Spurrier, '*Gäfgen v. Germany*: Fruit of the Poisonous Tree', [2010] *EHRLR* 513.

Stijn Smet, 'The "Absolute" Prohibition of Torture and Inhuman or Degrading Treatment in Article 3 ECHR: Truly a Question of Scope Only?', in Eva Brems and Janneke Gerards, eds, *Shaping Rights in the ECHR*, Cambridge: Cambridge University Press, 2013, pp. 273–93.

Frédéric Sudre, 'Extradition et peine de mort—arrêt Soering de la Cour européenne des droits de l'homme du 7 juillet 1989', [1990] *Revue générale de droit international public* 103.

Frédéric Sudre, 'Article 3', in Pettiti et al., *La Convention européenne*, pp. 154–75.

Ben Vermeulen, 'Freedom from Torture and Other Inhuman or Degrading Treatment or Punishment (Article 3)', in Van Dijk et al., *Theory and Practice*, pp. 405–41.

Colin Warbrick, 'Coherence and the European Court of Human Rights: The Adjudicative Background to the *Soering* case', (1989–90) 11 *Michigan Journal of International Law* 107.

H. Wattendorff and E. du Perron, 'Human Rights v. Extradition: The *Soering* case', (1990) 11 *Michigan Journal of International Law* 845.

Wubbo Wierenga and Sabrina Wirtz, 'Case of Gafgen versus Germany', (2009) 16 *Maastricht Journal of European & Comparative Law* 365.

Christine van den Wyngaert, 'Applying the European Convention on Human Rights to Extradition: Opening Pandora's Box?', (1990) 39 *ICLQ* 757.

Article 4. Prohibition of slavery and forced labour/Interdiction de l'esclavage et du travail forcé

1. No one shall be held in slavery or servitude.

2. No one shall be required to perform forced or compulsory labour.

3. For the purpose of this article the term 'forced or compulsory labour' shall not include:

(a) any work required to be done in the ordinary course of detention imposed according to the provisions of Article 5 of this Convention or during conditional release from such detention;

(b) any service of a military character or, in case of conscientious objectors in countries where they are recognised, service exacted instead of compulsory military service;

(c) any service exacted in case of an emergency or calamity threatening the life or well-being of the community;

(d) any work or service which forms part of normal civic obligations.

1. Nul ne peut être tenu en esclavage ni en servitude.

2. Nul ne peut être astreint à accomplir un travail forcé ou obligatoire.

3. N'est pas considéré comme « travail forcé ou obligatoire » au sens du présent article:

a) tout travail requis normalement d'une personne soumise à la détention dans les conditions prévues par l'article 5 de la présente Convention, ou durant sa mise en liberté conditionnelle;

b) tout service de caractère militaire ou, dans le cas d'objecteurs de conscience dans les pays où l'objection de conscience est reconnue comme légitime, à un autre service à la place du service militaire obligatoire;

c) tout service requis dans le cas de crises ou de calamités qui menacent la vie ou le bien-être de la communauté;

d) tout travail ou service formant partie des obligations civiques normales.

Introductory comments

The Court has said that article 4 enshrines 'one of the fundamental values of democratic societies'.[1] Slavery has been practised since antiquity and was often enshrined within the national legal order. Hugo Grotius wrote favourably about the phenomenon.[2] He was attacked by Jean-Jacques Rousseau, who explained: 'Dire qu'un homme se donne gratuitement, c'est dire une chose absurde et inconcevable; un tel acte est illégitime et nul, par cels eule que celui qui le fait n'est pas dans son bon sens. Dire la même-chose de tout un peuple, c'est supposer un peuple de foux: la folie ne fait pas droit.'[3]

The slave trade was prohibited by the British Parliament only in 1807, although the practice persisted in most of the Empire until 1833. France abolished slavery and the slave trade at the time of the Revolution. It was subsequently restored, and only definitively

---

[1] *Stummer v. Austria* [GC], no. 37452/02, § 116, ECHR 2011. Also *Siliadin v. France,* no. 73316/01, §§ 82, 112, ECHR 2005-VII; *Rantsev v. Cyprus and Russia,* no. 25965/04, § 283, ECHR 2010 (extracts); *C.N. and V. v. France,* no. 67724/09, § 68, 11 October 2012.

[2] See, e.g., Hugo Grotius, *On the Law of War and Peace*, Oxford: Clarendon Press, 1925, pp. 255–8.

[3] Jean-Jacques Rousseau, *Du contrat social*, in *Œuvres complètes*, Vol. III, Paris: Gallimard, 1964, pp. 347–469, at p. 356.

ended in 1848. Russia continued the related practice of serfdom until 1861. Slavery was abolished a few years later in the United States of America.

Slavery returned to Europe during the 1940s, practised by the Nazi regime during the Second World War. The International Military Tribunal said that the Nazi government planned 'to exploit the inhabitants of the occupied countries for slave labour on the very greatest scale', considering that slave labour was 'an integral part of the war economy'. According to the judgment, '[w]hole populations were deported to Germany for the purposes of slave labour upon defence works, armament production and similar tasks connected with the war effort'.[4] An estimated 5 million people were moved by force to Germany to work as slaves in this way.[5] Leading Nazis were condemned for the crime against humanity of enslavement in accordance with article 6(c) of the Charter of the International Military Tribunal and article II(1)(c) of Control Council Law No. 10.[6]

International law first addressed the matter comprehensively in the 1926 Slavery Convention.[7] It was followed by the International Labour Organisation Forced Labour Convention, adopted in 1930.[8] Article 4 of the Universal Declaration of Human Rights states: 'No one shall be held in slavery or servitude; slavery and the slave trade shall be prohibited in all their forms.'

The European Charter of Fundamental Rights declares:

1. No one shall be held in slavery or servitude.
2. No one shall be required to perform forced or compulsory labour.
3. Trafficking in human beings is prohibited.

The first two paragraphs of article 5 of the Charter are identical to the first two paragraphs of article 4 of the Convention and are meant to have the same meaning and scope.[9]

The barbaric phenomenon of chattel slavery is probably relegated to history, although there continue to be reports that it persists in Mauritania.[10] The legacy of the African slave trade manifests itself in on-going claims, including litigation before various national courts, for forms of reparation and compensation. Within the present-day human rights movement, the prohibition mainly concerns what are called contemporary forms of slavery. These include debt bondage, human trafficking, domestic slavery, forced prostitution, and similar practices.[11] According to a Recommendation by the Parliamentary Assembly of the Council of Europe, adopted in 2004:

1. The Parliamentary Assembly is dismayed that slavery continues to exist in Europe in the twenty-first century. Although, officially, slavery was abolished over 150 years ago, thousands of people

---

[4] *France et al. v. Goering et al.*, (1948) 22 IMT 411, at p. 470.

[5] See, e.g., *Associazione Nazionale Reduci Dalla Prigionia dall'Internamento e dalla Guerra di Liberazione and 275 Others v. Germany* (dec.), no. 45563/04, 4 September 2007.

[6] *United States v. Krupp et al.*, (1950) 9 TWC 1327 (US Military Tribunal), at pp. 1396–1435.

[7] Slavery Convention, (1927) 60 LNTS 253.

[8] International Labour Organisation Convention No. 29 concerning Forced or Compulsory Labour, (1946) 39 UNTS 55.

[9] Explanation relating to the Charter of Fundamental Rights, Official Journal of the European Union, C 303/33, 14 December 2007.

[10] In its report to the Human Rights Council within the framework of the Universal Periodic Review mechanism (UN Doc. A/HRC/WG.6/9/MRT/1, paras 141–3), Mauritania discussed its campaign of 'eradication of the consequences of slavery' involving 'furthering the emancipation of populations affected by the consequences of slavery'.

[11] For an estimate of the scope of contemporary slavery in Europe, see Monti Narayan Datta and Kevin Bales, 'Slavery in Europe: Part 1, Estimating the Dark Figure', (2013) 35 *Human Rights Quarterly* 817.

are still held as slaves in Europe, treated as objects, humiliated and abused. Modern slaves, like their counterparts of old, are forced to work (through mental or physical threat) with no or little financial reward. They are physically constrained or have other limits placed on their freedom of movement and are treated in a degrading and inhumane manner.

2. Today's slaves are predominantly female and usually work in private households, starting out as migrant domestic workers, au pairs or 'mail-order brides'. Most have come voluntarily, seeking to improve their situation or escaping poverty and hardship, but some have been deceived by their employers, agencies or other intermediaries, have been debt-bonded and even trafficked. Once working (or married to a 'consumer husband'), however, they are vulnerable and isolated. This creates ample opportunity for abusive employers or husbands to force them into domestic slavery.[12]

The Council of Europe Convention on Action against Trafficking in Human Beings was adopted in 2005 and entered into force in 2008. It enjoys near-universal acceptance by Council of Europe States. The Convention's Preamble states that 'trafficking in human beings may result in slavery for victims'.[13]

Drafting of the provision

The initial draft European Convention on Human Rights, adopted by the International Council of the European Movement in 1949, contained the following: 'Every State a party to this Convention shall guarantee to all persons within its territory the following rights: ... c) Freedom from slavery and servitude and from compulsory labour of a discriminatory kind.'[14] At the first session of the Consultative Assembly, Pierre-Henri Teitgen called for adoption of a convention that would recognize 'freedom from slavery and servitude'.[15] Asked to prepare a text for discussion in the Committee on Legal and Administrative Questions, Teitgen proposed the following: 'Exemption from slavery and servitude, as laid down in Article 4 of the United Nations Declaration.'[16] At its sitting of 29 August 1949, the Committee on Legal and Administrative Questions accepted inclusion of '[e]xemption from any slavery or servitude as laid down in Article 4 of the Declaration of the United Nations.'[17] The word 'any' was changed to 'all' in the English language version of the draft report adopted by the Committee[18] and then omitted altogether in the final report submitted to the Consultative Assembly: 'Exemption from

---

[12] Domestic slavery: servitude, au pairs and 'mail-order brides', Recommendation 1663 (2004), cited in *Siliadin v. France*, no. 73316/01, §§ 49, 88, ECHR 2005-VII.

[13] Council of Europe Convention on Action against Trafficking in Human Beings, ETS 197.

[14] Convention for the Collective Protection of Individual Rights and Democratic Liberties by the States, Members of the Council of Europe, and for the establishment of a European Court of Human Rights to ensure observance of the Convention, Doc. INF/5/E/R, I *TP* 296–303, at p. 296, art. I(c).

[15] Report of the Sitting [of the Consultative Assembly, 19 August 1949], I *TP* 38–154, at p. 46. See also remarks by Cingolani (Italy), ibid., I *TP* 34, Jaquet (France), ibid., I *TP* 53, and McEntee (Ireland), ibid., I *TP* 55.

[16] Proposals by Mr P.H. Teitgen, Rapporteur, 29 August 1949, Doc. A 116, I *TP* 166–8. Also Report presented by Mr P.H. Teitgen, 5 September 1949, Doc. A 290, I *TP* 192–213, at p. 206. See also Report [of the Committee on Legal and Administrative Questions], 5 September 1949, Doc. AS (1) 77, I *TP* 216–39, at p. 228.

[17] Minutes of the Sitting [of the Committee for Legal and Administrative Affairs of the Consultative Assembly, 29 August 1949], Doc. A 142, I *TP* 170–3, at p. 172.

[18] Report presented by Mr P.H. Teitgen, 5 September 1949, Doc. A 290, I *TP* 192–213, at p. 206.

slavery or servitude, in accordance with Article 4 of the United Nations Declaration.'[19] The text proposed by the Committee was adopted without debate by the Consultative Assembly.[20]

In the Committee of Experts, the United Kingdom proposed a somewhat more detailed text that was based on the current draft of the corresponding provision in the United Nations Covenant:

1) No one shall be held in slavery; slavery and the slave trade shall be prohibited in all their forms.
2) No one shall be held in servitude.
3) No one shall be required to perform forced or compulsory labour except pursuant to a sentence to such punishment for a crime by a competent court.[21]

At the second session of the Committee of Experts, in March 1950, the United Kingdom representative submitted a more elaborate proposal:

1) No one shall be held in slavery or servitude.
2) No one shall be required to perform forced or compulsory labour.
3) For the purpose of this article, the term 'forced or compulsory labour' shall not include:
   a) any work required to be done in the ordinary course of detention imposed by the lawful order of a court;
   b) any service of a military character or service in the case of conscientious objectors exacted in virtue of compulsory military service laws;
   c) any service exacted in case of an emergency or calamity threatening the life or well-being of the community;
   d) any work or service which forms part of normal civil obligations.[22]

The Committee of Experts concluded its work with the submission to the Committee of Ministers of two different drafts. The first, 'Alternatives A and A/2', consisted of the text adopted by the Committee of Experts at its first session, taken verbatim from article 4 of the Universal Declaration of Human Rights.[23] The second, labelled 'Alternatives B and B/2', contained the text that had been proposed by the United Kingdom, with two minor alterations.[24]

The Conference of Senior Officials that convened in June 1950 assigned a Drafting Committee to attempt to reconcile the competing versions. It prepared a new formulation of the prohibition of slavery and servitude based largely on the British proposal, with a few

---

[19] Report [of the Committee on Legal and Administrative Questions], 5 September 1949, Doc. AS (1) 77, I *TP* 216–39, at p. 228.

[20] Recommendation No. 38 to the Committee of Ministers adopted 8 September 1949 on the conclusion of the debates, Doc. AS (1) 108, II *TP* 274–83, at p. 276.

[21] Amendments to Article 2 of the Recommendation of the Consultative Assembly proposed by the Expert of the United Kingdom, Doc. A 798, III *TP* 204–7, at p. 206.

[22] Amendments to Articles 1, 2, 4, 5, 6, 8, and 9 of the Committee's preliminary draft proposal by the Expert of the United Kingdom, Doc. CM/WP 1 (50) 2, A 915, III *TP* 280–9, at p. 282.

[23] Report to the Committee of Ministers submitted by the Committee of Experts Instructed to Draw Up a Draft Convention of Collective Guarantee of Human Rights and Fundamental Freedoms, Doc. CM/WP 1 (5) 15, A 924, IV *TP* 2–55, at p. 52. See also Preliminary Draft Convention, Doc. CM/WP 1 (50) 14, A 932, III *TP* 312–35, at p. 320.

[24] Report to the Committee of Ministers submitted by the Committee of Experts Instructed to Draw Up a Draft Convention of Collective Guarantee of Human Rights and Fundamental Freedoms, Doc. CM/WP 1 (5) 15, A 924, IV *TP* 2–55, at p. 58. See also Preliminary Draft Convention, Doc. CM/WP 1 (50) 14, A 932, III *TP* 312–35, at pp. 312–14. The minor changes were: in paragraph 3(a), 'the lawful order of a court' was changed to 'by a lawful order'; in para. 3(b), 'exacted in virtue of compulsory military service laws' was changed to ', service exacted instead of compulsory military service'.

very minor stylistic changes, as well as one of substance: the suggestion that the issue of conscientious objection only arose in countries where it was recognized.

1) No one shall be held in slavery or servitude.
2) No one shall be required to perform forced or compulsory labour.
3) For the purposes of this article, the term 'forced or compulsory labour' shall not include:
   a) any work required to be done in the ordinary course of detention imposed by a lawful order of a court;
   b) any service of a military character or, in case of conscientious objectors in countries where they are recognised, service exacted instead of compulsory military service laws;
   c) any service exacted in case of an emergency or calamity threatening the life or well-being of the community;
   d) any work or service which forms part of normal civil obligations.[25]

The Drafting Committee undertook one further change with the replacement, in paragraph 3(a), of the words 'by a lawful order of a court' with 'according to the provisions of article 5 hereof'.[26] Article 5 was the draft provision concerning arbitrary detention, just as it is in the final version of the Convention.

At the fifth session of the Committee of Ministers, in early August 1950, the Netherlands proposed a series of amendments, including the following comment: 'It is assumed that article 4 does not apply to labour imposed upon a prisoner in case of conditional release.'[27] The Committee of Ministers modified paragraph 3(a) of article 4, replacing the words 'by a lawful order of a court' with 'according to the provisions of Article 5 of this Convention or during conditional release from such detention'.[28] With this change accepted, the Committee of Ministers adopted the revised text of article 2. There were no further modifications and the version confirmed at the fifth session of the Committee of Ministers is the definitive one.

The heading 'Prohibition of Slavery and Forced Labour' was added pursuant to the provisions of Protocol No. 11.[29]

Analysis and interpretation

Article 4 consists of three paragraphs, the third of which has four sub-paragraphs.

Paragraph 1 states the general principle: 'No one shall be held in slavery or servitude.' The text is identical to the first phrase in article 4 of the Universal Declaration of Human Rights, although the latter provision is completed with the words 'slavery and the slave trade shall be prohibited in all their forms'. As has been noted by the Court, '[u]nlike most of the substantive clauses of the Convention and of Protocols Nos. 1 and 4, Article 4 makes no provision for exceptions and no derogation from it is permissible under Article

---

[25] New draft alternatives B and B/2, Doc. CM/WP 4 (50) 9, A 1372, IV *TP* 182–91, at p. 184.

[26] Draft Convention annexed to the Report, Doc. CM/WP 4 (50) 19 annex, CM/WP 4 (50) 16 rev., A 1452, IV *TP* 274–95, at p. 278.

[27] Amendments proposed by the Netherlands Delegation, Doc. CM 1 (50) 5, A 1866, V *TP* 64–5.

[28] Draft Convention adopted by the Sub-Committee, Doc. CM 1 (50) 52, A 1884, V *TP* 76–99, at p. 76; Draft Convention adopted by the Committee of Ministers, 7 August 1950, Doc. A 1937, V *TP* 120–45, at p. 122. Article 5 of the draft, to which the Committee of Ministers was referring, is substantially the same provision as article 5 of the European Convention.

[29] Protocol No. 11 to the Convention for the Protection of Human Rights and Fundamental Freedoms, restructuring the control machinery established thereby, ETS 155, art. 2(2).

15 § 2 even in the event of a public emergency threatening the life of the nation'.[30] Paragraph 2 addresses the distinct phenomenon of forced or compulsory labour: 'No one shall be required to perform forced or compulsory labour.' It is completed by paragraph 3, whose very detailed provisions explain in a negative sense the scope of the notion of forced or compulsory labour.

Perhaps more than any other provision of the Convention, article 4 is essentially about positive, rather than negative, obligations. The nature and scope of this obligation is very similar to what the Court has held with respect to articles 2 and 3, [31] and for the same reasons. But in the case of slavery and servitude, much more than that of killing and torture, in modern times the perpetrator will not be the State, but rather individuals. There are several components to the positive obligation.

There is an obligation on the State to take operational measures to protect victims, or potential victims, of treatment in breach of article 4.[32] It arises where 'State authorities were aware, or ought to have been aware that an identified individual had been, or was at real and immediate risk of being subjected to such treatment.' In such cases, the State must then take appropriate measures within its powers to address the situation of the victim.[33] The judgments include a standard paragraph, identical to one used in cases involving the positive obligations of articles 2 and 3: 'Bearing in mind the difficulties involved in policing modern societies and the operational choices which must be made in terms of priorities and resources, the obligation to take operational measures must, however, be interpreted in a way which does not impose an impossible or disproportionate burden on the authorities.'[34] It has not been decided whether article 4 can be applied to corporate bodies as well as natural persons.[35]

As with articles 2 and 3, there is a procedural obligation associated with article 4. Where there is a 'credible suspicion'[36] that rights under article 4 have been violated, the State must ensure that there is a prompt, effective and independent investigation, regardless of whether there is a complaint from the victim or next-of-kin. Generally, the 'credible suspicion' will result from a complaint by the victim. In the absence of a complaint, the Court may be inclined to relieve the State of a finding that it was in breach of its obligations.[37] The investigation must be capable of leading to identification and punishment of those who are responsible, although this is an obligation of means rather than of result. The victim or the next-of-kin must be involved in the procedure to the extent necessary to safeguard their legitimate interests.[38]

In order to complete the procedural dimension of the obligation, States must penalize and prosecute any act that is aimed at maintaining a person in a situation of slavery,

---

[30] *Siliadin v. France*, no. 73316/01, § 112, ECHR 2005-VII; *Stummer v. Austria* [GC], no. 37452/02, § 116, ECHR 2011; *Rantsev v. Cyprus and Russia*, no. 25965/04, § 283, ECHR 2010 (extracts); *C.N. v. the United Kingdom*, no. 4239/08, § 65, 13 November 2012.

[31] *Siliadin v. France*, no. 73316/01, § 89, ECHR 2005–VII.

[32] *Rantsev v. Cyprus and Russia*, no. 25965/04, § 286, ECHR 2010 (extracts); *Mahmut Kaya v. Turkey*, no. 22535/93, § 115, ECHR 2000-III; *C.N. v. the United Kingdom*, no. 4239/08, § 67, 13 November 2012.

[33] *C.N. v. the United Kingdom*, no. 4239/08, § 67, 13 November 2012; *J.A. v. France*, no. 45310/11, § 37, 27 May 2014.

[34] *C.N. v. the United Kingdom*, no. 4239/08, § 68, ECHR 2010; *Rantsev v. Cyprus and Russia*, no. 25965/04, § 287, ECHR 2010 (extracts).

[35] *Four companies v. Austria*, no. 7427/76, Commission decision of 27 September 1976, DR 7, p. 148.

[36] *Rantsev v. Cyprus and Russia*, no. 25965/04, § 286, ECHR 2010 (extracts).

[37] *V.F. v. France* (dec.), no. 7196/10, 29 November 2011.

[38] *C.N. v. the United Kingdom*, no. 4239/08, § 69, 13 November 2012.

servitude, or forced or compulsory labour.[39] This requires the existence of an effective legislative and administrative framework.[40] Other consequences of the obligation include the adoption of adequate measures to regulate businesses that are typically used to front or cover for human trafficking. Immigration rules must address issues of encouragement, facilitation, or tolerance of trafficking.[41] Officials in the system must receive appropriate training about the phenomenon.[42] For example, in Cyprus, the Council of Europe Commissioner for Human Rights had noted in a 2004 report that the lack of an immigration policy and related shortcomings 'encouraged the trafficking of women to Cyprus'.[43] The Cypriot regime of 'artiste visas' was being exploited as a vehicle to traffic for purposes of prostitution.[44] Even the government had admitted that the number of young women migrating to Cyprus as nightclub performers was well out of proportion to the country's population.[45]

Violations of article 4 will frequently have a transnational dimension. As the Court noted in *Rantsev*, when trafficking takes place there may be offences in the State of origin, the State of transit, and the State of destination, and relevant evidence and witnesses may be located in several jurisdictions. It insisted that in cross-border trafficking cases the Convention imposes an obligation 'to cooperate effectively with the relevant authorities of other States concerned in the investigation of events which occurred outside their territories'.[46]

Slavery and servitude (art. 4(1))

Slavery is defined in the 1926 Slavery Convention as 'the status or condition of a person over whom any or all of the powers attaching to the right of ownership are exercised'.[47] This definition is widely considered to be authoritative, and has been endorsed by the Court for the purposes of the application of article 4.[48] The Court described this as the 'classic' meaning of slavery as it was practised for centuries. Servitude is distinguished from slavery in that it does not involve the notion of ownership. It consists of an obligation to provide services that is imposed by coercion.[49] The European Commission on Human Rights described servitude as a 'particularly serious form of denial of freedom'.[50] It said that 'in addition to the obligation to perform certain services for others ... the obligation for the "serf" to live on another person's property and the impossibility of altering his condition'.[51] For the Court,

[39] *Siliadin v. France*, no. 73316/01, §§ 89 and 112, ECHR 2005-VII; *C.N. and V. v. France*, no. 67724/09, § 105, 11 October 2012; *C.N. v. the United Kingdom*, no. 4239/08, § 66, 13 November 2012.
[40] *Rantsev v. Cyprus and Russia*, no. 25965/04, § 285, ECHR 2010 (extracts).
[41] Ibid.
[42] Ibid., § 287.
[43] Cited in *Rantsev v. Cyprus and Russia*, no. 25965/04, §§ 91–94 (extracts).
[44] Ibid., §§ 290–293 (extracts).
[45] Ibid., § 94.
[46] Ibid., § 289.
[47] Slavery Convention, (1927) 60 LNTS 253, art. 1(1).
[48] *Siliadin v. France*, no. 73316/01, § 122, ECHR 2005-VII; *Rantsev v. Cyprus and Russia*, no. 25965/04, § 276, ECHR 2010 (extracts); *M. and Others v. Italy and Bulgaria*, no. 40020/03, § 146, 31 July 2012.
[49] Ibid., § 124; *C.N. and V. v. France*, no. 67724/09, § 89, 11 October 2012; *Seguin v. France* (dec.), no. 42400/98, 7 March 2000; *Rantsev v. Cyprus and Russia*, no. 25965/04, § 276, ECHR 2010 (extracts).
[50] *Van Droogenbroeck v. Belgium*, Commission's report of 9 July 1980, §§ 78–80, Series B no. 44.
[51] Ibid.

la servitude constitue une qualification spéciale du travail forcé ou obligatoire ou, en d'autres termes, un travail forcé ou obligatoire «aggravé». En l'occurrence, l'élément fondamental qui distingue la servitude du travail forcé ou obligatoire, au sens de l'article 4 de la Convention, consiste dans le sentiment des victimes que leur condition est immuable et que la situation n'est pas susceptible d'évoluer. A cet égard, il suffit que ce sentiment repose sur des éléments objectifs suscités ou entretenus par les auteurs des agissements.[52]

Abolished in Europe over the course of the eighteenth and nineteenth centuries, slavery is not a genuine problem likely to be litigated before the Court, and there have been no findings of violation of this part of article 4. In *Siliadin v. France*, the Court considered the application of the concept of slavery to the circumstances of a young African woman who worked as a domestic servant every day for many years without any real rest or leisure. 'Although the applicant was, in the instant case, clearly deprived of her personal autonomy, the evidence does not suggest that she was held in slavery in the proper sense, in other words that Mr and Mrs B. exercised a genuine right of legal ownership over her, thus reducing her to the status of an "object"', said the judgment.[53] Given the young age when she was sent to work, the harsh conditions of her work, the fact a promise she would be educated was not honoured, and her identity papers confiscated, the Court considered the circumstances to amount to servitude within the scope of article 4.[54]

The Court also considered the application of the term 'slavery' to the case of a Roma girl who was allegedly sold to criminals in Italy, although she had been through a form of marriage. It said there was not sufficient evidence to support the claim of slavery. Even assuming that a sum of money changed hands at the time of the 'marriage', the Court said 'such a monetary contribution cannot be considered to amount to a price attached to the transfer of ownership, which would bring into play the concept of slavery'. The Court said 'marriage has deep-rooted social and cultural connotations which may differ largely from one society to another', and the transfer of money on such an occasion 'can reasonably be accepted as representing a gift from one family to another, a tradition common to many different cultures in today's society'.[55]

The Court recognized a situation of servitude in a case concerning two sisters from Burundi who had been sent to Paris to live with relatives when they were still minor children. There, they were subject to various forms of abuse, and were housed in deplorable conditions, and this led to criminal proceedings. One of the sisters was kept in the home, where she performed a range of domestic work and was denied public education, while the other attended school. The Court distinguished between the two situations. The woman who remained at home believed her status in France depended upon residing with the family, and that she could not leave without jeopardizing her right to remain in the country. Because she was not educated, she had no hope of working outside the home. She did not have any day of rest, no leisure or recreation, and no possibility of developing contacts outside the house whom she could then call upon for help. 'Ainsi, la Cour considère que la première requérante avait le sentiment que sa condition, à savoir le fait d'effectuer un travail forcé ou obligatoire au domicile des époux

---

[52] *C.N. and V. v. France*, no. 67724/09, § 91, 11 October 2012.
[53] *Siliadin v. France*, no. 73316/01, § 122, ECHR 2005-VII.
[54] Ibid., § 129.
[55] *M. and Others v. Italy and Bulgaria*, no. 40020/03, § 161, 31 July 2012.

M., ne pouvait pas évoluer et que cette condition était immuable, d'autant plus qu'elle a duré quatre années', the Court wrote, concluding that this was a situation of servitude.[56] On the other hand, the other sister was less isolated, attending school, where she had good results, and where the opportunity to continue life outside the home of the relatives was more plausible. As a result, she was not deemed to be in servitude.[57]

Human trafficking

The term 'trafficking' does not appear in the European Convention, although it is used in several of the more modern international legal instruments, notably the 2000 Protocol to Prevent, Suppress and Punish Trafficking in Persons, especially Women and Children ('the Palermo Protocol') and the 2005 Council of Europe Convention on Action against Trafficking in Human Beings. The Court has explained that the absence of an express reference to trafficking is unsurprising given that the Convention was inspired by the Universal Declaration of Human Rights, which itself makes no reference to the term.[58] According to the Court, trafficking in human beings as a global phenomenon has increased significantly. Its growth in Europe was 'facilitated in part by the collapse of former Communist blocs'.[59] In *Rantsev*, the Chamber noted that another Chamber of the Court had already addressed trafficking under the rubric of servitude, in *Siliadin*, but it said: 'In light of the proliferation of both trafficking itself and of measures taken to combat it, the Court considers it appropriate in the present case to examine the extent to which trafficking itself may be considered to run counter to the spirit and purpose of Article 4 of the Convention such as to fall within the scope of the guarantees offered by that Article without the need to assess which of the three types of proscribed conduct are engaged by the particular treatment in the case in question.'[60] Another Chamber has taken note of the two approaches, but without adopting a firm position.[61] Examining the same issue, a Chamber considered that the situation it was examining was closer to that of *Siliadin* than *Rantsev*, and preferred to remain within the enumerated categories of article 4, that is, forced labour and servitude.[62]

The Council of Europe Convention provides a definition of trafficking that demonstrates its close relationship to the subject matter of article 4 of the European Convention on Human Rights:

Trafficking in human beings shall mean the recruitment, transportation, transfer, harbouring or receipt of persons, by means of the threat or use of force or other forms of coercion, of abduction, of fraud, of deception, of the abuse of power or of a position of vulnerability or of the giving or receiving of payments or benefits to achieve the consent of a person having control over another person, for the purpose of exploitation. Exploitation shall include, at a minimum, the exploitation of the prostitution of others or other forms of sexual exploitation, forced labour or services, slavery or practices similar to slavery, servitude or the removal of organs.[63]

---

[56] *C.N. and V. v. France*, no. 67724/09, § 92, 11 October 2012.
[57] Ibid., § 93.
[58] *Rantsev v. Cyprus and Russia*, no. 25965/04, § 272, ECHR 2010 (extracts).
[59] Ibid., § 278.
[60] Ibid., § 279.
[61] *M. and Others v. Italy and Bulgaria*, no. 40020/03, § 150, 31 July 2012.
[62] *C.N. and V. v. France*, no. 67724/09, § 88, 11 October 2012.
[63] Council of Europe Convention on Action against Trafficking in Human Beings, ETS 197, art. 4(a).

A similar definition is found in article 3 of the Palermo Protocol.[64] Both have been endorsed by the Court as describing activity that falls within article 4 of the Convention.[65]

In *Rantsev,* the Court said it considered that trafficking 'by its very nature and aim of exploitation, is based on the exercise of powers attaching to the right of ownership. It treats human beings as commodities to be bought and sold and put to forced labour, often for little or no payment, usually in the sex industry but also elsewhere.'[66] It said trafficking implied 'close surveillance of victims, whose movements are often circumscribed', and 'the use of violence and threats against victims, who live and work under poor conditions'.[67]

Domestic servitude

Domestic servitude has been addressed as a distinct violation of article 4. Indeed, the Court has been critical of national legislation that focuses on domestic servitude solely from the standpoint of trafficking, resulting in distortions in investigations and leading to the conclusion that there is an inadequate legal framework capable of fulfilling the positive obligations imposed by article 4. According to the Court,

domestic servitude is a specific offence, distinct from trafficking and exploitation, which involves a complex set of dynamics, involving both overt and more subtle forms of coercion, to force compliance. A thorough investigation into complaints of such conduct therefore requires an understanding of the many subtle ways an individual can fall under the control of another.[68]

A specific offence of 'domestic servitude' is required as well as a distinct treatment of the phenomenon by the authorities.[69]

Forced or compulsory labour (art. 4(2))

Paragraphs 2 and 3 are concerned with 'forced or compulsory labour'. The *travaux préparatoires* do not provide any assistance in interpreting this concept. However, the Court has said that it was 'evident' that the drafters of the European Convention, like those of the early version of the International Covenant on Civil and Political Rights, relied 'to a large extent'[70] upon International Labour Organisation Convention No. 29 concerning Forced or Compulsory Labour, which was adopted in 1930 and entered into force in 1932. The Convention has been widely ratified by members of the Council of Europe and arguably is generally accepted, at least as far as the definitions are concerned. Pursuant to Convention No. 29, States undertake to 'suppress the use of forced or compulsory labour in all its forms within the shortest possible period' with a view to 'complete suppression' of the phenomenon.[71]

The main objective of Convention No. 29 was preventing the exploitation of labour in colonies. The Convention did not coin the expression 'forced or compulsory labour',

---

[64] Protocol to Prevent, Suppress and Punish Trafficking in Persons, Especially Women and Children, supplementing the United Nations Convention against Transnational Organised Crime, UN Doc. A/RES/55/25, Annex II.

[65] *Rantsev v. Cyprus and Russia,* no. 25965/04, § 282, ECHR 2010 (extracts).

[66] Ibid., § 281.

[67] Ibid.

[68] *C.N. v. the United Kingdom,* no. 4239/08, § 80, 13 November 2012.

[69] Ibid. See also *Kawogo v. the United Kingdom* (dec.), no. 56921/09, 3 September 2013.

[70] *Van der Mussele v. Belgium,* 23 November 1983, § 32, Series A no. 70.

[71] International Labour Organisation Convention No. 29 concerning Forced or Compulsory Labour, (1946) 39 UNTS 55, art. 1.

which had already appeared in the Preamble of the 1926 Slavery Convention: 'The High Contracting Parties recognise that recourse to compulsory or forced labour may have grave consequences and undertake, each in respect of the territories placed under its sovereignty, jurisdiction, protection, suzerainty or tutelage, to take all necessary measures to prevent compulsory or forced labour from developing into conditions analogous to slavery.' The 1930 Convention was subsequently complemented, in 1957, by the adoption of Convention No. 105 concerning the Abolition of Forced Labour.[72] According to the Court, there is a 'striking similarity, which is not accidental' between article 2 of Convention No. 29 and article 4(3) of the European Convention on Human Rights.[73] Article 2(1) of Convention No. 29 states that 'forced or compulsory labour' shall mean 'all work or service which is exacted from any person under the menace of any penalty and for which the said person has not offered himself voluntarily'. The Court said it provides a 'starting-point for interpretation of article 4', although 'sight should not be lost of that Convention's special features or of the fact that it is a living instrument to be read "in the light of the notions currently prevailing in democratic States"'.[74]

Article 4(2) speaks of 'labour' (*travail*), whereas Convention No. 29 refers to 'all work or service' (*tout travail ou service*), terms that are reprised with slight modification in article 4(3)(d) of the European Convention ('any work or service', *tout travail ou service*). Responding to the argument that 'labour' was confined to manual labour, the Court noted these variations in terminology, pointing as well to the very name of the International Labour Organisation (*Organisation Internationale du Travail*) in concluding that 'labour' within the meaning of article 4(2) was not limited to the field of manual labour.[75]

The term 'forced' suggests physical or mental constraint, something the Court noted was absent in a case involving a lawyer who was required to work without remuneration as part of a legal aid scheme.[76] It also held that the term 'compulsion' could not refer to any form of legal compulsion or obligation. It gave as an example work carried out pursuant to a freely negotiated contract; it would not be deemed the result of compulsion solely because one part would be subject to sanctions for failure to honour the agreement. Therefore, in order to conclude that there is 'forced or compulsory labour', there must be a degree of physical or mental constraint, as well as some overriding of the victim's will.[77]

Referring to the definition in Convention No. 29, the Court has insisted that the notion of compulsory labour means that it must be 'exacted . . . under the menace of any penalty' and performed against the will of the person concerned, which is to say work for which the person 'has not offered himself voluntarily'.[78] In the case of the legal aid requirement for lawyers, the Court has considered that the possibility of being excluded from the practice of law for failure to fulfil a requirement of unpaid labour is indeed a form of 'penalty'.[79] It reached a similar conclusion with respect to a practising lawyer who

---

[72] (1959) 320 UNTS 291.
[73] *Van der Mussele v. Belgium*, 23 November 1983, § 32, Series A no. 70; *Siliadin v. France*, no. 73316/01, § 116, ECHR 2005-VII; *Stummer v. Austria* [GC], no. 37452/02, §§ 117–118, ECHR 2011.
[74] *Van der Mussele v. Belgium*, 23 November 1983, § 32, Series A no. 70; *Graziani-Weiss v. Austria*, no. 31950/06, § 36, 18 October 2011.
[75] *Van der Mussele v. Belgium*, 23 November 1983, § 33, Series A no. 70.
[76] Ibid., § 34.
[77] Ibid.; *Siliadin v. France*, no. 73316/01, § 117, ECHR 2005-VII.
[78] *Van der Mussele v. Belgium*, 23 November 1983, § 34, Series A no. 70.
[79] Ibid., § 35.

was obliged to serve as a legal guardian.[80] In a case involving a domestic labourer, the Court considered the penalty to be the threat of expulsion from the country.[81] The Court declined to find a 'penalty' in a similar case of domestic labour, but said the victim was 'in an equivalent situation in terms of the perceived seriousness of the threat'. She was an adolescent girl living unlawfully in a foreign country in fear of arrest. Her oppressors 'nurtured that fear' through suggestions that they would regularize her status.[82]

The second requirement drawn from Convention No. 29 is that the victim 'has not offered himself voluntarily'. Prior consent will generally be determined by considering all of the circumstances in order to assess whether it was in fact implied. Sometimes the terrible working conditions will make it obvious that there could be no genuine consent.[83] In the cases involving unpaid work by lawyers, the Court has noted that when an individual joins a professional body the existence of such duties is known to them, providing an element of prior consent, but it has said this is not sufficient to overcome the charge of compulsory labour.[84] Early case law of the European Commission took the position that in addition to being performed by the person against his or her will, it had to be 'unjust', 'oppressive', 'an unavoidable hardship', 'needlessly distressing', or 'somewhat harassing',[85] but the Court has not followed this approach.[86] For the Court, the issue is whether such requirements are so disproportionate that they could not have been accepted implicitly, bearing in mind the advantages attributed to professionals, including an effective monopoly over certain services, and the relatively insignificant amount of work required.[87] For much the same reason applications by other professionals, including notaries[88] and physicians, have been rejected.[89] A beneficiary of social assistance objected when she was required to take up employment deemed 'generally accepted' or else lose her entitlement to benefits. Declaring the application inadmissible, the Court said that 'a condition to the effect that a person must make demonstrable efforts in order to obtain and take up generally accepted employment cannot be considered unreasonable'.[90]

'Delimitations' on forced or compulsory labour (art. 4(3))

Article 4(3) has been said not to 'limit' the exercise of the right set out in article 4(2) but rather to 'delimit' the content of the right. According to the Court, 'it forms a whole' with article 4(2), indicating what is not included within the term 'forced or

---

[80] *Graziani-Weiss v. Austria*, no. 31950/06, § 39, 18 October 2011. Also *Nespala v. Czech Republic* (dec.), no. 68198/10, 24 September 2013.

[81] *C.N. and V. v. France*, no. 67724/09, § 78, 11 October 2012.

[82] *Siliadin v. France*, no. 73316/01, § 118, ECHR 2005-VII.

[83] Ibid., § 119.

[84] *Van der Mussele v. Belgium*, 23 November 1983, § 36, Series A no. 70; *Graziani-Weiss v. Austria*, no. 31950/06, § 40, 18 October 2011; *Bucha v. Slovakia*, no. 43259/07, 20 September 2011, §§ 43–45.

[85] *X v. Federal Republic of Germany*, no. 4653/73, Commission decision of 1 April 1974, (1974) 17 YB 148, Collection 46, p. 22, at p. 32; *Iversen v. Norway*, no. 1468/62, Commission decision of 17 December 1962, (1963) 6 YB 278, at pp. 327–9.

[86] *Van der Mussele v. Belgium*, 23 November 1983, § 37, Series A no. 70.

[87] Ibid.; *Graziani-Weiss v. Austria*, no. 31950/06, § 41, 18 October 2011.

[88] *X v. Federal Republic of Germany*, no. 8410/78, Commission decision of 13 December 1979, (1980) 23 YB 386.

[89] *Steindel v. Germany* (dec.), no. 29878/07, 14 September 2010; *Reitmayr v. Austria*, no. 23866/94, Commission decision of 28 June 1995.

[90] *Schuitemaker v. the Netherlands* (dec.), no. 15906/08, 4 May 2010.

compulsory labour'.[91] The four sub-paragraphs of article 4(3) are diverse, but they are all 'grounded on the governing ideas of the general interest, social solidarity and what is in the normal or ordinary course of affairs'.[92] For the European Commission on Human Rights, although 'forced or compulsory labour' will overlap with 'servitude', these two terms 'cannot be treated as equivalent'. Consequently, even a phenomenon contemplated by one of the sub-paragraphs of article 4(3) can, at least in principle, be addressed within the framework of the prohibition on slavery and servitude.[93]

Work associated with detention (art. 4(3)(a))

Work that is required in the ordinary course of detention is not deemed to be 'forced or compulsory labour'. The rather verbose exception reads as follows: 'any work required to be done in the ordinary course of detention imposed according to the provisions of Article 5 of this Convention or during conditional release from such detention'. This delimitation is derived from article 2(2)(c) of International Labour Organisation Convention No. 29, where an even more elaborate formulation is employed: 'any work or service exacted from any person as a consequence of a conviction in a court of law, provided that the said work or service is carried out under the supervision and control of a public authority and that the said person is not hired to or placed at the disposal of private individuals, companies or associations'. It may be that the intent of the provision in Convention No. 29 was to address sentences where labour was imposed as part of a custodial sentence. An early decision by the European Commission of Human Rights rejected the suggestion that article 4(3)(a) be interpreted as if it incorporated the terms of article 2(2)(c) of Convention No. 29.

In an early case heard by the European Commission of Human Rights, several German prisoners argued they were not being adequately remunerated for their work and that no social security contributions were being made on their behalf. They submitted that the work was performed for private businesses that had made their own contractual arrangements with the prison authorities. At the outset, the Commission noted that article 4 made no reference to remuneration of prisoners; for this reason, several applications by prisoners claiming higher payment for their work or the right to social security coverage had been declared inadmissible.[94] The Commission referred to the *travaux préparatoires* of the Convention, noting that article 4 was derived from the draft Covenant on Human Rights then before the United Nations Commission on Human Rights. The reason it contained a provision concerning work done in the ordinary course of detention was to provide a 'safeguard against arbitrary decision by authorities with regard to the work which might be required'.[95] There was no evidence, said the Commission, that the

[91] *Van der Mussele v. Belgium*, 23 November 1983, § 38, Series A no. 70; *Karlheinz Schmidt v. Germany*, 18 July 1994, § 22, Series A no. 291-B; *Zarb Adami v. Malta*, no. 17209/02, § 44, ECHR 2006-VIII; *Stummer v. Austria* [GC], no. 37452/02, § 120, ECHR 2011.
[92] *Van der Mussele v. Belgium*, 23 November 1983, § 38, Series A no. 70. See also *Karlheinz Schmidt v. Germany*, 18 July 1994, § 22, Series A no. 291-B; *Zarb Adami v. Malta*, no. 17209/02, § 44, ECHR 2006-VIII; *Stummer v. Austria* [GC], no. 37452/02, § 120, ECHR 2011.
[93] *W, X, Y, and Z v. the United Kingdom*, nos 3435/67, 3436/67, 3437/67, and 3438/67, Commission decision of 19 July 1968, (1968) 11 YB 562, Collection 28, p. 109.
[94] *X v. Austria*, no. 833/60, Commission decision of 20 December 1960, (1960) 3 YB 428, at p. 440; *R. v. Federal Republic of Germany*, no. 1854/63, Commission decision of 28 September 1964; *V. v. Austria*, no. 2066/63, Commission decision of 17 December 1965; *X v. Federal Republic of Germany*, no. 2413/65, Commission decision of 16 December 1966, Collection 23, p. 1; *G. v. Austria*, no. 1451/62, Commission decision of 23 July 1963.
[95] UN Doc. E/CN.4/SR.142 and 143.

term 'ordinary' was in any way related to employment involving private businesses. The Commission referred to a United Nations study of prison labour indicating the involvement of private business interests in a number of States, including several in the Council of Europe.[96] The Commission noted the 1930 International Labour Organisation Convention's pejorative reference to prisoners being 'hired to or placed at the disposal of private individuals, companies or associations', but said that the draft Covenant provision on which article 4 of the European Convention was based omitted these terms. Although nothing in the *travaux préparatoires* helped to explain the omission, the Commission took the view that this must have been due to an awareness that there was widespread involvement of private enterprise in prison labour.[97]

When a recidivist prisoner claimed that he was forced to work because his early release was conditional on having some savings from work done in prison, the Court agreed that this was not far away from an obligation in the strict sense of the term.[98] Applying article 4(3)(a), the Court noted 'the work which Mr. Van Droogenbroeck was asked to do did not go beyond what is "ordinary" in this context since it was calculated to assist him in reintegrating himself into society and had as its legal basis provisions which find an equivalent in certain other member States of the Council of Europe'.[99]

In a more recent case, the Grand Chamber considered the complaint of an Austrian prisoner whose prison work was not subject to contributions for old-age pension. The applicant submitted that the early decision of the European Commission dealing with the German prisoners should no longer be followed, and that the Court should recognize that prison labour without entitlement to old-age pension was no longer 'ordinary'. The Grand Chamber noted an 'evolving trend' within Europe to enable prisoners to benefit from social security systems, but added that 'while an absolute majority of Council of Europe member States provide prisoners with some kind of social security, only a small majority affiliate prisoners to their old-age pension system'.[100] Rejecting the application, it said there was not sufficient consensus within the Member States of the Council of Europe on the matter.[101]

The fact that prison labour may not be remunerated does not mean it is not covered by the exception set out in paragraph 4(a).[102]

Military service (art. 4(3)(b))

Article 4(3)(b) excludes 'any service of a military character or, in case of conscientious objectors in countries where they are recognised, service exacted instead of compulsory military service' from the ambit of forced or compulsory labour. The 1930 Convention on Forced Labour of the International Labour Organisation formulates this delimitation without reference to conscientious objection: 'any work or service exacted in virtue of compulsory military service laws for work of a purely military character'.[103] At the time

---

[96] *Prison Labour*, United Nations, 1955, ST/SOA/SO/5, Sales No.: 1955.LV.7.

[97] *Twenty-one Detained Persons v. Federal Republic of Germany*, nos 3134/67, 3172/67, 3188–3206/67, Commission decision of 6 April 1968, Collection 27, p. 97.

[98] *Van Droogenbroeck v. Belgium*, 24 June 1982, § 59, Series A no. 50.

[99] Ibid.

[100] *Stummer v. Austria* [GC], no. 37452/02, § 105, ECHR 2011.

[101] Ibid., §§ 132–134.

[102] Ibid., § 122; *Zhelyazkov v. Bulgaria*, no. 11332/04, § 36, 9 October 2012; *Floriou v. Romania* (dec.), no. 15303/10, § 33, 12 March 2013.

[103] International Labour Organisation Convention No. 29 concerning Forced or Compulsory Labour, (1930) 39 UNTS 55, art. 2(2)(a).

the European Convention was adopted, compulsory military service was fairly general among the founding members of the Council of Europe. It has now largely been done away with, although the practice persists in some countries in Central and Eastern Europe, as well as Cyprus and Switzerland. The European Court has taken note of this trend, citing the replacement of conscript armies with professional ones in Spain (2002), Portugal (2004), Hungary and the Czech Republic (2005), Slovakia and Bosnia and Herzegovina (2006), Romania, Italy, and Latvia (2007).[104]

Issues concerning article 4 and military service do not only arise as a result of conscription, however. In 1968, the European Commission examined the application of four British soldiers who had been recruited as adolescents, some of them as young as fifteen, within the United Kingdom and its colonies. The Commission referred to the *travaux préparatoires*, noting the influence of the 1930 International Labour Organisation Convention, where the words 'any work or service exacted in virtue of compulsory military service laws' were employed. It observed that in the early draft of the United Nations Covenant, which formed a model for article 4 of the Convention, those words were replaced with 'any service of a military character', although without any explanation for this change being provided in the documentation. The Commission said that 'it is safe to assume that in admitting the word "compulsory" it was intended also to cover the obligation to continue a service entered into on a voluntary basis'.[105]

With respect to conscientious objection, the European Commission on Human Rights noted that the Convention does not require States to make alternative civilian service available. However, if States make civilian service a requirement as a substitute for military service, the Commission said it was clear that this could not be regarded as forced or compulsory labour.[106] The Commission also linked the reference to conscientious objection in article 4(3)(b) to article 9 of the Convention, where some have invoked freedom of thought, conscience, and religion in order to resist both military and alternative service on religious grounds.[107] It concluded that by using the words 'in countries where they are recognised', the Convention left States with the choice as to whether conscientious objection should be allowed and, if so, to permit alternative service.[108] The question only came before the Court in 2011. The Court had explicitly reserved the question of the relationship between article 4(3)(b) and article 9 on two earlier occasions.[109] Rejecting the Commission's approach, the Grand Chamber cited a comment in the *travaux préparatoires*:

In sub-paragraph [(b)], the clause relating to conscientious objectors was intended to indicate that any national service required of them by law would not fall within the scope of forced or compulsory labour. As the concept of conscientious objection was not recognised in many countries, the phrase 'in countries where conscientious objection is recognised' was inserted.

[104] *Glor v. Switzerland*, no. 13444/04, § 86, 30 April 2009.
[105] *W, X, Y, and Z v. the United Kingdom*, nos 3435/67, 3436/67, 3437/67, and 3438/67, Commission decision of 19 July 1968, (1968) 11 YB 562, Collection 28, p. 109.
[106] *Johansen v. Norway*, no. 10600/83, Commission decision of 14 October 1985, DR 44, p. 155.
[107] *Grandrath v. Federal Republic of Germany*, no. 2299/64, Commission report of 12 December 1966, (1967) 10 YB 630; *X v. Austria*, no. 5591/72, Commission decision of 2 April 1973, Collection 43, p. 161.
[108] *X v. Federal Republic of Germany*, no. 7705/76, Commission decision of 5 July 1977, DR 9, p. 196; *Conscientious objectors v. Denmark*, no. 7565/76, Commission decision of 7 March 1977, DR 9, p. 117; *A. v. Switzerland*, no. 10640/83, Commission decision of 9 May 1984, DR 38, p. 219; *N. v. Sweden*, no. 10410/83, Commission decision of 11 October 1984, DR 40, p. 203.
[109] *Thlimmenos v. Greece* [GC], no. 34369/97, §§ 43 and 53, ECHR 2000-IV; *Ülke v. Turkey*, no. 39437/98, §§ 53–54 and 63–64, 24 January 2006.

According to the Grand Chamber, this confirmed that the sole purpose of article 4(3)(b) was to clarify the scope of article 4(2). 'In itself it neither recognises nor excludes a right to conscientious objection and should therefore not have a delimiting effect on the rights guaranteed by Article 9', it said.[110]

Emergency service (art. 4(3)(c))

Any service exacted in case of an emergency or calamity threatening the life or well-being of the community is excluded from the scope of forced or compulsory labour by article 4(3)(c). The corresponding provision in the 1930 International Labour Organisation Convention reads: 'any work or service exacted in cases of emergency, that is to say, in the event of war or of a calamity or threatened calamity, such as fire, flood, famine, earthquake, violent epidemic or epizootic diseases, invasion by animal, insect or vegetable pests, and in general any circumstance that would endanger the existence or the well-being of the whole or part of the population'.

This provision has only been interpreted in a few cases before the European Commission, and apparently never by the Court. In one, the Commission deemed that a requirement of work in a public dental service in northern Norway was covered by the provision.[111] In another, a Hamburg lawyer objected to the requirement that he assist in the gassing of foxholes as a measure to protect against rabies. The Commission said that even if the obligation could be considered compulsory labour, 'which is doubtful', the requirement that a hunting tenant participate in measures to control epidemics would be justified under article 4(3)(c) or (d).[112]

Normal civil obligations (art. 4(3)(d))

Any work or service that forms part of normal civic obligations is excluded from the scope of forced or compulsory labour in accordance with article 4(3)(d). There are two paragraphs in article 2(2) of the 1930 International Labour Organisation Convention that appear to be at the origin of the provision: 'any work or service which forms part of the normal civic obligations of the citizens of a fully self-governing country';[113] and 'minor communal services of a kind which, being performed by the members of the community in the direct interest of the said community, can therefore be considered as normal civic obligations incumbent upon the members of the community, provided that the members of the community or their direct representatives shall have the right to be consulted in regard to the need for such services'.[114] Jury service[115] and service in a fire brigade, or alternatively a payment in lieu of service,[116] have been recognized by the Court as examples of such normal civic obligations.[117]

---

[110] *Bayatyan v. Armenia* [GC], no. 23459/03, § 100, ECHR 2011.

[111] *Iversen v. Norway*, no. 1468/62, Commission decision of 17 December 1962, (1963) 6 YB 278, at pp. 327–9.

[112] *S. v. Federal Republic of Germany*, no. 9686/82, Commission decision of 4 October 1984, DR 39, p. 90.

[113] Convention concerning Forced or Compulsory Labour, (1946) 39 UNTS 55, art. 2(2)(b).

[114] Ibid., art. 2(2)(e).

[115] *Zarb Adami v. Malta*, no. 17209/02, § 47, ECHR 2006-VIII.

[116] *Karlheinz Schmidt v. Germany*, 18 July 1994, § 23, Series A no. 291-B.

[117] *Zarb Adami v. Malta*, no. 17209/02, § 47, ECHR 2006-VIII.

Discrimination

Article 14 of the Convention provides the basis for a distinct assessment of the role of prohibited discrimination with respect to slavery and servitude. Article 14 is complementary to the other substantive provisions of the Convention and the Protocols. It has no independent existence, applying only with respect to other protected rights and freedoms, including article 4. A violation of article 4 is not necessary for article 14 to be engaged, but the claim of discrimination must bear upon the rights that are protected by article 4. The Court has considered whether special obligations imposed upon practising lawyers without remuneration, including the provision of legal aid and service as a guardian, could be deemed discriminatory. After concluding that the duty to act as a guardian was not forced or compulsory labour in accordance with article 4(2), the Court considered whether limiting the duty to notaries and lawyers was discriminatory, in breach of article 14 of the Convention. It accepted that this amounted to a difference in treatment between practising lawyers and other persons who would have studied law and possibly even received professional legal training but who were not practicing as lawyers. Noting various functions entrusted to lawyers on an exclusive basis, the Court said this was enough for it to conclude that the two groups were not in relevantly similar situations.[118] It reached the same conclusion in a case concerning legal aid.[119]

Several companies in Austria claimed to be victims of discrimination with respect to article 4(2) because of an obligation imposed upon them to calculate and withhold certain taxes and other social security contributions from salaries and wages of their employees. Declaring the application manifestly ill-founded, the Commission said that there was no differentiation in any way between groups of persons that could be considered comparable.[120]

In a case concerning the obligation of jury duty, the applicant demonstrated that this was imposed upon men in a disproportionate manner. The respondent State argued that this could be explained by several factors, including the selection of jurors from the sector of the population active in the economy and professional life and the availability of exemptions from jury service for those caring for a family. Also, 'for cultural reasons', the State claimed that defence lawyers might tend to challenge female jurors and thereby exclude them from service. The Court was not impressed, and said it had not been shown that the difference in treatment 'pursued a legitimate aim and that there was a reasonable relationship of proportionality between the means employed and the aim sought to be realised'. As a result, Malta was found to be in breach of article 14 taken in conjunction with article 4(3)(d).[121]

There was a similar manifestation of gender discrimination in the requirement of service in the fire brigade, or alternatively to make a financial contribution, imposed by the Land of Baden-Württemberg. This was compulsory for men but not women, resulting in a violation of article 14 in conjunction with article 14(3)(d).[122]

---

[118] *Graziani-Weiss v. Austria,* no. 31950/06, §§ 58–66, 18 October 2011.
[119] *Van der Mussele v. Belgium,* 23 November 1983, §§ 42–46, Series A no. 70.
[120] *Four companies v. Austria,* no. 7427/76, 27 September 1976.
[121] *Zarb Adami v. Malta,* no. 17209/02, §§ 81–83, ECHR 2006-VIII.
[122] *Karlheinz Schmidt v. Germany,* 18 July 1994, § 23, Series A no. 291-B.

Reservations

Portugal formulated the following reservation: 'Article 4(3)(b) of the Convention will be applied subject to Article 276 of the Constitution of the Portuguese Republic, which provides for compulsory civic service.'[123] It was withdrawn in 1987.[124]

Moldova made a reservation 'with a view to retaining the possibility of enforcing criminal sentences in the form of non-custodial forced labour'. The reservation specified that it would be valid for one year.[125]

Further reading

J. Allain, 'The Definition of Slavery in International Law', (2009) 59 *Howard Law Journal* 239.

J. Allain, '*Rantsev v. Cyprus and Russia*: The European Court of Human Rights and Trafficking as Slavery', (2010) 3 *HRLR* 546.

H. Askola, *Legal Responses to Trafficking in Women for Sexual Exploitation in the European Union*, Oxford: Hart Publishing, 2007.

H. Cullen, '*Siliadin v. France*: Positive Obligations under Article 4 of the European Convention on Human Rights', (2006) 6 *HRLR* 585.

S. Farrior, 'Human Trafficking Violates Anti-Slavery Provision: Introductory Note to *Rantsev v. Cyprus and Russia*', (2010) 49 *International Legal Materials* 415.

Frowein/Peukert, *MenschenRechtsKonvention*, pp. 59–69.

Grabenwarter, *European Convention*, pp. 53–60.

Harris et al., *Law of the European Convention*, pp. 113–20.

Giorgio Malinverni, 'Article 4', in Pettiti et al., *La Convention européenne*, pp. 177–88.

Virginia Mantouvalou, 'The Prohibition of Slavery, Serbitude and Forced and Compulsory Labour under Article 4 ECHR', in Filip Dorssemont, Klaus Lörcher and Isabelle Schömann, eds, *The European Convention on Human Rights and the Employment Relation*, Oxford and Portland, OR: Hart, 2013, pp. 143–58.

N. McGeehan, 'Misunderstood and Neglected: The Marginalization of Slavery in International Law', (2011) 16 *International Journal of Human Rights* 1.

A. Nicholson, 'Reflections on *Siliadin v. France*: slavery and legal definition', (2010) 14 *International Journal of Human Rights* 705.

Ovey/White, *Jacobs and White, European Convention*, pp. 90–101.

R. Pati, 'States' Positive Obligations with Respect to Human Trafficking: The European Court of Human Rights Breaks New Ground in *Rantsev v. Cyprus and Russia*', (2011) 29 *Boston University International Law Journal* 79.

Vladislava Stoyanova, 'Dancing on the Borders of Article 4: Human Trafficking and the European Court of Human Rights in the *Rantsev* Case', (2012) 30 *Netherlands Quarterly of Human Rights* 163.

Leo Zwaak, 'Freedom from Salvery, Servitude and Forced or Compulsory Labour (Article 4)', in Van Dijk et al., *Theory and Practice*, pp. 443–53.

---

[123] (1978) 21 YB 14–15.
[124] (1987) 30 YB 4–5.
[125] (1997) 40 YB 36.

Article 5. Right to liberty and security/Droit à la liberté et à la sûreté

1. Everyone has the right to liberty and security of person. No one shall be deprived of his liberty save in the following cases and in accordance with a procedure prescribed by law:

(a) the lawful detention of a person after conviction by a competent court;

(b) the lawful arrest or detention of a person for non-compliance with the lawful order of a court or in order to secure the fulfilment of any obligation prescribed by law;

(c) the lawful arrest or detention of a person effected for the purpose of bringing him before the competent legal authority on reasonable suspicion of having committed an offence or when it is reasonably considered necessary to prevent his committing an offence or fleeing after having done so;

(d) the detention of a minor by lawful order for the purpose of educational supervision or his lawful detention for the purpose of bringing him before the competent legal authority;

(e) the lawful detention of persons for the prevention of the spreading of infectious diseases, of persons of unsound mind, alcoholics or drug addicts or vagrants;

(f) the lawful arrest or detention of a person to prevent his effecting an unauthorised entry into the country or of a person against whom action is being taken with a view to deportation or extradition.

2. Everyone who is arrested shall be informed promptly, in a language which he understands, of the reasons for his arrest and of any charge against him.

3. Everyone arrested or detained in accordance with the provisions of paragraph 1.c of this article shall be brought promptly before a judge or other officer authorised by law to exercise judicial power and shall be entitled to trial within a reasonable time or to release

1. Toute personne a droit à la liberté et à la sûreté. Nul ne peut être privé de sa liberté, sauf dans les cas suivants et selon les voies légales:

a) s'il est détenu régulièrement après condamnation par un tribunal compétent;

b) s'il a fait l'objet d'une arrestation ou d'une détention régulière pour insoumission à une ordonnance rendue, conformément à la loi, par un tribunal ou en vue de garantir l'exécution d'une obligation prescrite par la loi;

c) s'il a été arrêté et détenu en vue d'être conduit devant l'autorité judiciaire compétente, lorsqu'il y a des raisons plausibles de soupçonner qu'il a commis une infraction ou qu'il y a des motifs raisonnables de croire à la nécessité de l'empêcher de commettre une infraction ou de s'enfuir après l'accomplissement de celle-ci;

d) s'il s'agit de la détention régulière d'un mineur, décidée pour son éducation surveillée ou de sa détention régulière, afin de le traduire devant l'autorité compétente;

e) s'il s'agit de la détention régulière d'une personne susceptible de propager une maladie contagieuse, d'un aliéné, d'un alcoolique, d'un toxicomane ou d'un vagabond;

f) s'il s'agit de l'arrestation ou de la détention régulières d'une personne pour l'empêcher de pénétrer irrégulièrement dans le territoire, ou contre laquelle une procédure d'expulsion ou d'extradition est en cours.

2. Toute personne arrêtée doit être informée, dans le plus court délai et dans une langue qu'elle comprend, des raisons de son arrestation et de toute accusation portée contre elle.

3. Toute personne arrêtée ou détenue, dans les conditions prévues au paragraphe 1.c du présent article, doit être aussitôt traduite devant un juge ou un autre magistrat habilité par la loi à exercer des fonctions judiciaires et a le droit d'être jugée dans un délai raisonnable, ou

pending trial. Release may be conditioned by guarantees to appear for trial.

libérée pendant la procédure. La mise en liberté peut être subordonnée à une garantie assurant la comparution de l'intéressé à l'audience.

4. Everyone who is deprived of his liberty by arrest or detention shall be entitled to take proceedings by which the lawfulness of his detention shall be decided speedily by a court and his release ordered if the detention is not lawful.

4. Toute personne privée de sa liberté par arrestation ou détention a le droit d'introduire un recours devant un tribunal, afin qu'il statue à bref délai sur la légalité de sa détention et ordonne sa libération si la détention est illégale.

5. Everyone who has been the victim of arrest or detention in contravention of the provisions of this article shall have an enforceable right to compensation.

5. Toute personne victime d'une arrestation ou d'une détention dans des conditions contraires aux dispositions de cet article a droit à réparation.

Introductory comments

The right to liberty and security of the person is essentially concerned with arbitrary detention. In positive law, protection against arbitrary detention can be traced back at least as far as the edict of *de homine libero exhibendo* in the Digest of Justinian. Its most celebrated early formulation is in clause 39 of the Magna Carta: 'No free man shall be seized or imprisoned, or stripped of his rights or possessions, or outlawed or exiled, or deprived of his standing in any other way, nor will we proceed with force against him, or send others to do so, except by the lawful judgement of his equals or by the law of the land.'[1] Protection against arbitrary detention was ensured through the 'great writ'[2] of *habeas corpus*,[3] a procedural mechanism enshrined in statute law at the time of the English revolution.[4] Its importance was confirmed by article 7 of the French *Déclaration des droits de l'homme et du citoyen* ('Nul homme ne peut être accusé, arrêté ni détenu que dans les cas déterminés par la loi, et selon les formes qu'elle a prescrites') and in the Constitution of the United States ('[t]he Privilege of the Writ of Habeas Corpus shall not be suspended, unless when in Cases of Rebellion or Invasion the public Safety may require it'[5]).

Article 5 of the European Convention is derived from two of the most laconic provisions of the Universal Declaration of Human Rights, article 3 ('Everyone has the right to life, liberty and security of person') and article 9 ('No one shall be subjected to arbitrary arrest, detention or exile.') Translated into treaty norms in article 5 of the European Convention, these succinct and straightforward principles drawn from the Universal Declaration required 371 words for their expression.

The provisions in article 5 are both extremely detailed and also, in part, somewhat embarrassingly archaic, with their references to 'persons of unsound mind' and 'vagrants'. By contrast, the succinct texts of the Universal Declaration of Human Rights remain fresh and contemporary. The Charter of Fundamental Rights returns to a simple formulation, reproducing the first sentence of article 5 of the Convention: 'Everyone has the right to

---

[1] Magna Carta, 1225, 9 Hen. 3, *c.* 30, art. 39.
[2] *Ex Parte Yerger*, 75 US (8 Wall.) 85, 95 (1869).
[3] Paul Halliday, *Habeas Corpus: From England to Empire*, Cambridge, MA: Belknap Press, 2010, p. 41.
[4] An Act for the Regulating the Privie Councell and for taking away the Court commonly called the Star Chamber, 1640, 16 Car., *c.* 10, § 1.
[5] Constitution of the United States, art. I, s. 9. Also *Jones v. Cunningham*, 371 US 236, 237 (1963).

liberty and security of person.' It is meant to have the same meaning and scope as article 5 of the European Convention.[6]

Drafting of the provision

The initial draft European Convention on Human Rights prepared by the International Juridical Section of the European Movement recognized '[f]reedom from arbitrary arrest, detention and exile'.[7] At the first session of the Consultative Assembly, Pierre-Henri Teitgen called for adoption of a convention that would include 'freedom from arbitrary arrest'.[8] Asked to prepare a draft text for discussion in the Committee on Legal and Administrative Questions at the first session of the Consultative Assembly, Teitgen proposed the following: 'Security of person, in accordance with Articles 3, 5 and 8 of the Universal Declaration of Human Rights, approved by the General Assembly of the United Nations' and 'Immunity from all arbitrary arrest, detention and exile, in accordance with Articles 9, 10 and 11 of the United Nations Declaration'.[9] There was no disagreement on the text dealing with security of person. With respect to the provision on arbitrary arrest, an amendment to replace 'arrest, detention or arbitrary exile' with 'arbitrary arrest, sentence, detention or exile' was defeated, as was a proposal from Giovanni Persico of Italy to insert 'or other measures or sentences' after 'arbitrary exile', both by twelve votes to three with two abstentions. The Legal Committee accepted an amendment to replace 'or arbitrary exile' by 'exile or other arbitrary measures'.[10] The two provisions were adopted by the plenary Consultative Assembly for transmission to the Committee of Ministers.[11]

The Committee of Ministers decided to refer the Consultative Assembly draft to a Committee of Experts. The Committee of Experts, which convened in February and March 1950, was instructed to pay 'due attention' to the draft Covenant that had been adopted by the United Nations Commission of Human Rights in June 1949.[12] Indeed, the United Nations Commission on Human Rights had considered a detailed provision on arbitrary arrest and detention in its work on the draft Covenant on human rights:

1. No one shall be subjected to arbitrary arrest or detention.
2. No one shall be deprived of his liberty except on such grounds and in accordance with such procedure as established by law.
3. Any one who is arrested shall be informed promptly of the reasons for his arrest and of any charges against him.

[6] Explanation relating to the Charter of Fundamental Rights, Official Journal of the European Union, C 303/33, 14 December 2007.

[7] Convention for the Collective Protection of Individual Rights and Democratic Liberties by the States, Members of the Council of Europe, and for the establishment of a European Court of Human Rights to ensure observance of the Convention, Doc. INF/5/E/R, I *TP* 296–303, at p. 296, art. I(b).

[8] Report of the Sitting [of the Consultative Assembly, 19 August 1949], I *TP* 38–154, at p. 46.

[9] Proposals by Mr P.H. Teitgen, Rapporteur, 29 August 1949, Doc. A 116, I *TP* 166–8.

[10] Minutes of the Sitting [of the Committee for Legal and Administrative Affairs of the Consultative Assembly, 29 August 1949], Doc. A 142, I *TP* 170–3.

[11] Recommendation No. 38 to the Committee of Ministers adopted 8 September 1949 on the conclusion of the debates, Doc. AS (1) 108, II *TP* 274–83, at p. 276.

[12] Letter addressed on 18 November 1949 by the Secretary General to the Ministers for Foreign Affairs of the Member States, Ref. D 26/2/49, II *TP* 302–5.

4. Any one arrested or detained on the charge of having committed a crime or of preparing to commit a crime shall be brought promptly before a judge or other officer authorised by law to exercise judicial power and shall be entitled to trial within a reasonable time or to release. Pending trial, release may be conditioned by guarantees to appear for trial.
5. Every one who is deprived of his liberty by arrest or detention shall be entitled to take proceedings by which the lawfulness of his detention shall be decided speedily by a court and his release ordered if the detention is not lawful.
6. Every person who has been the victim of unlawful arrest or deprivation of liberty shall have an enforceable right to compensation.[13]

A competing version had been proposed in the Commission on Human Rights by Australia, Denmark, France, Lebanon, and the United Kingdom as 'a more satisfactory basis for further consideration':

1. No person shall be deprived of his liberty save by legal procedure in the case of:
   (a) the lawful detention of a person after a conviction or as a security measure involving deprivation of liberty;
   (b) the lawful arrest and detention of a person for non-compliance with the lawful order or injunction of a court;
   (c) the arrest of a person effected for the purpose of bringing him before the competent legal authority on a reasonable suspicion of having committed an offence or which is reasonably considered to be necessary to prevent his committing a crime or fleeing after having done so;
   (d) the lawful detention of persons of unsound mind or of minors, by lawful order, the purpose of educational surveillance;
   (e) the lawful arrest or detention of a person to prevent his effecting an unauthorised entry into the country or of a person against whom deportation or extradition proceedings are pending.

The texts of paragraphs 3 to 5 of the initial draft were to be added. The five States expressed their belief that 'it is possible thus to define all the limitations of these rights which contracting States can reasonably require, in a form that is both brief and comprehensive'.[14]

A document prepared by the Secretariat-General of the Council of Europe for the Committee of Experts commented upon the draft provision in the Covenant, noting that it contained 'details, regulations and limitations concerning the right of the State to encroach on individual freedom which are not to be found in Articles 9, 10 and 11 of the Universal Declaration to which paragraph 3 of Article 2 of the European Resolution refers. In any case, the Assembly had not taken into consideration the case of so-called administrative internment.'[15] It also noted that 'the American system guaranteeing "the due process of law" for the taking of life and liberty was rejected owing to its non-existence in other States', that 'enumeration of exceptions was rejected', and that 'an American amendment adding the word "arbitrarily" was rejected pending a further study by the Commission'.[16]

At the first Committee of Experts session in February 1950, Sweden proposed adding the following the text: 'This provision should not exclude the right to take necessary measures to fight vagrancy and alcoholism or to ensure respect of obligations to pay a

---

[13] Report of the Fifth Session of the Commission on Human Rights to the Economic and Social Council, UN Doc. E/1371(Supp.), p. 19.

[14] Ibid., pp. 31–3.

[15] Preparatory Report by the Secretariat-General concerning a Preliminary Draft Convention to Provide a Collective Guarantee of Human Rights, Doc. B 22, III *TP* 2–37, at p. 28.

[16] Ibid.

family upkeep allowance.'[17] The United Kingdom also proposed an amendment with reference to article 9 of the draft United Nations Covenant and its mention of 'arbitrary arrest'. The United Kingdom said the word 'arbitrary' was 'vague and its force undefined'. It proposed a text largely based on the five-State draft of the corresponding provision in the Covenant being considered by the Commission on Human Rights:

No one shall be deprived of his liberty save by legal procedure in the case of:
a) The lawful detention of a person after conviction by a competent court or as a security measure;
b) The lawful arrest and detention of a person for non-compliance with the lawful order of a court;
c) The arrest of a person effected for the purpose of bringing him before the competent legal authority on suspicion of having committed an offence or which is reasonable considered to be necessary to prevent his committing a crime or fleeing after having done so;
d) The lawful detention of persons of unsound mind or of minors by lawful order for the purpose of educational surveillance;
e) The lawful arrest and detention of a person to prevent his effecting an unauthorised entry into the country or of a person against whom deportation or extradition proceedings are pending.[18]

The text of paragraphs 3 to 5 of the initial United Nations draft were to be added without change.

The representative of Luxembourg commented on the terms 'exile and other measures'.

No doubt the reference to Articles 10 and 11 of the United Nations Declaration gives an idea of the meaning of the expression 'and other measures.' However, the text might give rise to uncertainties. In using the expression 'and other measures' after the word 'exile,' it is possible to take into consideration the expulsion measures which certain States take by administrative action against undesirable aliens. Since these measures are taken by administrative and not legal action, they might be interpreted as meaning that they are arbitrary measures (cf. Articles 8 and 10 of the United Nations Declaration). It is therefore suggested that it should be indicated that the word 'exile' refers only to the victims of an expulsion measure taken by the State of which they are nationals.[19]

It was agreed to acknowledge in the report the difficulty indicated but there was no agreement to amend the provision.[20]

The first session of the Committee of Experts agreed upon provisions that reproduced word for word articles 3 and 9 of the Universal Declaration. Sweden's proposal was withdrawn on the condition that the issues it raised were to be mentioned in the report. As a result, the following comment was included:

The Swedish representative further requested that it be put on record that the text of Article 6 covered, in particular, the right of signatory States to take the necessary measures for combating vagrancy and drunkenness or to ensure respect of obligations to pay alimony costs; the Committee had no doubt that this could be agreed to since such restrictions were justified by the requirements of public morality and order.[21]

---

[17] Amendments to Article 2, para. 3, 5, and 6 of the Recommendation of the Consultative Assembly proposed by the Swedish expert, Doc. A 777, III *TP* 184.
[18] Amendment to Article 2, para. 3 of the Recommendation of the Consultative Assembly proposed by the Expert of the United Kingdom, Doc. A 790, III *TP* 186.
[19] Amendments to Article 2, para. 3 of the Recommendation of the Consultative Assembly proposed by the Expert of Luxembourg, Doc. A 784, III *TP* 192–5.
[20] Continuation of the Report of the Sub-Committee Instructed to Make a Preliminary Study of the Amendments Proposed by the Members of the Committee, Doc. A 802, III *TP* 206–13, at p. 208.
[21] Preliminary draft of the Report to the Committee of Ministers, 24 February 1950, Doc. CM/WP 1 (50) 1, A 847, III *TP* 246–79, at p. 266.

At the second session of the Committee of Experts, the British presented a revised draft:

1. No one shall be deprived of his liberty save in the following cases and in accordance with a procedure prescribed by law:
   a) The lawful detention of a person after conviction by a competent court;
   b) The lawful arrest and detention of a person for noncompliance with the lawful order of a court;
   c) The arrest and detention of a person effected for the purpose of bringing him before the competent legal authority on reasonable suspicion of having committed an offence or which is reasonable considered to be necessary to prevent his committing a crime or fleeing after having done so;
   d) The lawful detention of a person of unsound mind or of a minor by lawful order for the purpose of educational supervision;
   e) The lawful arrest and detention of a person to prevent his effecting an unauthorised entry into the country or of a person against whom deportation or extradition proceedings are pending.[22]
2. Any one who is arrested shall be informed promptly of the reasons for his arrest and of any charges against him.
3. Any one arrested or detained on the charge of having committed a crime or to prevent his committing a crime shall be brought promptly before a judge or other officer authorised by law to exercise judicial power and shall be entitled to trial within a reasonable time or to release pending trial. Release may be conditioned by guarantees to appear for trial.
4. Every one who is deprived of his liberty by arrest or detention shall be entitled to take proceedings by which the lawfulness of his detention shall be decided speedily by a court and his release ordered if the detention is not lawful.
5. Everyone who has been the victim of unlawful arrest or deprivation of liberty shall have an enforceable right to compensation.[23]

A drafting committee modified paragraph 1(b) by the addition of the phrase 'or in order to secure the fulfilment of any obligation prescribed by law'. Paragraph 1(d) was divided into two distinct provisions:

(d) the lawful detention of minors by lawful order for the purpose of educational supervision;
(e) the lawful detention of persons for prevention of the spreading of infectious diseases, of persons of unsound mind, alcoholic or drug addicts or vagrants.

Paragraph 2 was changed by the drafting committee as follows: 'Anyone who is arrested shall be informed promptly, in a language he understands, of the reasons for his arrest and of any charges against him.'[24] The right to compensation in case of unlawful arrest or deprivation of liberty had been removed.

The Committee of Experts submitted two alternative provisions to the Committee of Ministers, one corresponding to articles 3 and 9 of the Universal Declaration of Human Rights, the other the British draft with some very minor drafting changes.[25]

---

[22] Amendment to Article 2, para. 3 of the Recommendation of the Consultative Assembly proposed by the Expert of the United Kingdom, Doc. A 790, III *TP* 186.

[23] Amendments to Articles 1, 2, 4, 5, 6, 8, and 9 of the Committee's Preliminary Draft Proposal by the Expert of the United Kingdom, Doc. CM/WP 1 (50) 2, A 915, III *TP* 280–9, at pp. 282–5.

[24] Amendments to the British draft proposed by the Drafting Committee composed of Sir Oscar Dowson, MM le Quesne, Dons Moeller, and Salén, Doc. CM/WP 1 (50) 10, p. 3, A 919, III *TP* 288–95, at p. 288.

[25] Appendix to the Report of the Committee of Experts on Human Rights: Draft Convention of Protection of Human Rights and Fundamental Freedoms, 16 March 1950, Doc. CM/WP 1 (50) 15 appendix, CM/WP 1 (50) 14 revised, A 925, IV *TP* 50–79, at pp. 52, 58–60.

A commentary accompanying the drafts explained the removal of the provision dealing with an enforceable right to compensation. It said that the majority of members considered that the text might be held to impose an obligation to ensure payment of damages, for example as a result of a civil action, and that this was an 'undesirable requirement'. The United Kingdom delegate registered his disagreement with the omission.[26]

The Conference of Senior Officials that met in June 1950 combined the two proposals of the Committee of Experts by placing a text based upon article 3 of the Universal Declaration at the beginning of the provision ('Everyone has the right to liberty and security of person') and then continuing with the longer text derived from the British proposal. In paragraph 3, after the words 'committed a crime', the words 'in accordance with the provisions of para. 1(c)' were added. Finally, the controversial paragraph concerning compensation returned as paragraph 5: 'Anyone who has been victim of unlawful arrest or deprivation of liberty shall have an enforceable right to compensation.'[27] Comments were attached to the draft:

Article 5, para. 1)c) and 3.

The Conference considered it useful to point out that where authorised arrest or detention is effected on reasonable suspicion of preventing the commission of a crime, it should not lead to the introduction of a regime of a Police State. It may, however, be necessary in certain circumstances to arrest an individual in order to prevent his committing a crime, even if the facts which show his intention to commit the crime do not of themselves constitute a penal offence. In order to avoid any possible abuses of the right thus conferred on public authorities, Article 13, para. 2 will have to be applied strictly.[28]

A comment also explained the inclusion of the provision dealing with compensation. Reservations were expressed by the Italian and Danish delegates on this issue.[29]

In the Committee of Ministers, the United Kingdom made the following observation:

Article 5(1)(d), as at present drafted, does not provide for the possibility of detaining minors for the purpose of bringing them before the court for the making of a 'lawful order'. Many children brought before the courts have committed no offence at all and the purpose of their detention is to secure their removal from harmful surroundings, so that they are not covered by article 5(1)(c). At the same time, the circumstances of the case usually demand that the child should be removed from harmful surroundings before he can be brought before the court. H.M. Government therefore wish Article 5(1)(d) to be expanded to read: 'The lawful detention of minors by lawful order for the purpose of educational supervision, or their lawful detention for the purpose of brining them before the competent legal authorities.'[30]

This proposal met with agreement in the Sub-Committee on Human Rights and was incorporated in the final draft.

---

[26] Report to the Committee of Ministers submitted by the Committee of Experts Instructed to Draw Up a Draft Convention of Collective Guarantee of Human Rights and Fundamental Freedoms, Doc. CM/WP 1 (5) 15, A 924, IV *TP* 2–55, at p. 32.

[27] Draft Convention annexed to the Report [of the Conference of Senior Officials], Doc. CM/WP 4 (50) 19 annex, CM/WP 4 (50) 16 rev., A 1452, IV *TP* 274–95, at pp. 274–6.

[28] Text of the Report submitted by the Conference [of Senior Officials] to the Committee of Ministers, Doc. CM/WP 4 (50) 19, CM/WP 4 (50) 16 rev., A 1431, IV *TP* 242–73, at p. 260. Article 13(3) of the draft corresponds to article 18 of the final version of the Convention.

[29] Ibid.

[30] Amendments proposed by the United Kingdom Delegation, Doc. CM 1 (50) 6, A 1867, V *TP* 66–70, at p. 66.

The final text of article 5 was agreed to by the Committee of Ministers at its meeting on 7 August 1950.[31] Minor technical adjustments to the text were made by a Committee of Legal Experts on 3 November 1950.[32]

The heading 'Right to liberty and security' was added by Protocol No. 11.[33]

Analysis and interpretation

Article 5 of the Convention guarantees the right to liberty and security, which is of primary importance in a 'democratic society' within the meaning of the Convention.[34] It enshrines a fundamental human right, namely 'the protection of the individual against arbitrary interference by the State with his or her right to liberty'.[35] The guarantees in article 5 apply to 'everyone'.[36]

The first paragraph of article 5 sets out the general principle, followed by an exhaustive enumeration of exceptions, that is, of permissible deprivation of liberty. Paragraphs 2, 3, and 4 are mainly procedural in nature, in that they specify the requirements in terms of arrest and detention and the modalities for verification and contestation of their lawfulness. Paragraph 5 provides a right to compensation in the event that article 5 has been violated.

Physical liberty and scope of application

The right to liberty as proclaimed in article 5 is concerned with physical liberty. Its purpose is to protect against any arbitrary deprivation of that liberty in its classic sense of imprisonment. It is not concerned with 'mere restrictions' on freedom of movement, a right that is addressed by article 2 of Protocol No. 4 to the Convention.[37] Nevertheless, the difference between restrictions on movement serious enough to fall under article 5(1) rather than article 2 of Protocol No. 4 is one of degree or intensity, not of nature or substance.[38] Classifying them is 'no easy task in that some borderline cases are a matter of pure opinion'.[39] For example, persons stopped by police for a search lasting less than 30 minutes were nevertheless deprived of their liberty. They would have been liable to arrest, detention, and criminal charge had they refused. 'This element of coercion is indicative of

---

[31] Draft Convention adopted by the Sub-Committee, Doc. CM 1 (50) 52, A 1884, V *TP* 76–99, at p. 78.

[32] Report of the Committee of Legal Experts, 2–3 November 1950, Doc. CM/Adj. (50) 3 Rev., A 2531, VII *TP* 10–13.

[33] Protocol No. 11 to the Convention for the Protection of Human Rights and Fundamental Freedoms, restructuring the control machinery established thereby, ETS 155, art. 2(2).

[34] *De Wilde, Ooms, and Versyp v. Belgium*, 18 June 1971, § 65, Series A no. 12; *Winterwerp v. the Netherlands*, 24 October 1979, § 37, Series A no. 33; *Medvedyev and Others v. France* [GC], no. 3394/03, § 76, ECHR 2010; *Ladent v. Poland*, no. 11036/03, § 45, 18 March 2008.

[35] *A. and Others v. the United Kingdom* [GC], no. 3455/05, § 162, ECHR 2009; *Aksoy v. Turkey*, 18 December 1996, § 76, *Reports of Judgments and Decisions* 1996-VI; *McKay v. the United Kingdom* [GC], no. 543/03, § 30, ECHR 2006-X.

[36] *A. and Others v. the United Kingdom* [GC], no. 3455/05, § 162, ECHR 2009.

[37] *Engel and Others v. the Netherlands*, 8 June 1976, § 58, Series A no. 22; *Creangă v. Romania* [GC], no. 29226/03, § 92, 23 February 2012; *Gillan and Quinton v. the United Kingdom*, no. 4158/05, § 56, ECHR 2010 (extracts).

[38] *Guzzardi v. Italy*, 6 November 1980, § 93, Series A no. 39; *Rantsev v. Cyprus and Russia*, no. 25965/04, § 314, ECHR 2010 (extracts); *Stanev v. Bulgaria* [GC], no. 36760/06, § 115, ECHR 2012.

[39] *Guzzardi v. Italy*, 6 November 1980, § 93, Series A no. 39; *Ashingdane v. the United Kingdom*, 28 May 1985, § 41, Series A no. 93; *H.L. v. the United Kingdom*, no. 45508/99, § 89, ECHR 2004-IX; *Gillan and Quinton v. the United Kingdom*, no. 4158/05, § 56, ECHR 2010 (extracts).

a deprivation of liberty within the meaning of Article 5 § 1', said the Court.[40] In making the determination, 'the starting point must be his concrete situation and account must be taken of a whole range of criteria such as the type, duration, effects and manner of implementation of the measure in question'.[41] The European Court of Human Rights is not bound by the legal characterization given to the situation by the domestic authorities and makes its own autonomous assessment of the matter.[42]

Deprivation of liberty, within the meaning of article 5(1), has both an objective and a subjective dimension. It is objective to the extent the person is confined for a length of time that is not negligible. It is subjective in that the person has not consented to such confinement.[43]

In assessing the objective factors, account will be taken of the existence of a possibility of leaving the restricted area, the degree of supervision and control over the person, his or her isolation, and the availability of social contacts.[44] If the facts indicate a deprivation of liberty, the relatively short duration of detention does not affect the conclusion.[45] For example, police powers to stop and search indicate a deprivation of liberty despite the short duration of the measure.

Aside from formal arrest and detention within a criminal law setting, article 5 has been applied to the placement of persons in institutions for psychiatric care and social services,[46] international zones in airports,[47] interrogation in police stations,[48] house arrest,[49] confinement in an 'open prison',[50] and crowd control efforts.[51] On the other

---

[40] *Gillan and Quinton v. the United Kingdom*, no. 4158/05, § 57, ECHR 2010 (extracts); *Foka v. Turkey*, no. 28940/09, §§ 74–79, 24 June 2008.

[41] *Engel and Others v. the Netherlands*, 8 June 1976, §§ 58–59, Series A no. 22; *Gillan and Quinton v. the United Kingdom*, no. 4158/05, § 56, ECHR 2010 (extracts); *Guzzardi v. Italy*, 6 November 1980, § 92, Series A no. 39; *Medvedyev and Others v. France* [GC], no. 3394/03, § 73, ECHR 2010; *Creangă v. Romania* [GC], no. 29226/03, § 91, 23 February 2012; *Austin and Others v. the United Kingdom* [GC], nos 39692/09, 40713/09, and 41008/09, § 59, ECHR 2012.

[42] *H.L. v. the United Kingdom*, no. 45508/99, § 90, ECHR 2004-IX; *H.M. v. Switzerland*, no. 39187/98, §§ 30, 48, ECHR 2002-I; *Creangă v. Romania* [GC], no. 29226/03, § 92, 23 February 2012.

[43] *Storck v. Germany*, no. 61603/00, § 74, ECHR 2005-V; *Stanev v. Bulgaria* [GC], no. 36760/06, § 117, ECHR 2012.

[44] *Guzzardi v. Italy*, 6 November 1980, § 95, Series A no. 39; *H.M. v. Switzerland*, no. 39187/98, § 45, ECHR 2002-I; *H.L. v. the United Kingdom*, no. 45508/99, § 91, ECHR 2004-IX; *Storck v. Germany*, no. 61603/00, § 73, ECHR 2005-V.

[45] *Rantsev v. Cyprus and Russia*, no. 25965/04, § 317, ECHR 2010 (extracts); *Iskandarov v. Russia*, no. 17185/05, § 140, 23 September 2010.

[46] *De Wilde, Ooms, and Versyp v. Belgium*, 18 June 1971, Series A no. 12; *Nielsen v. Denmark*, 28 November 1988, Series A no. 144; *H.M. v. Switzerland*, no. 39187/98, 48, ECHR 2002-I; *H.L. v. the United Kingdom*, no. 45508/99, ECHR 2004-IX; *Storck v. Germany*, no. 61603/00, ECHR 2005-V; *A. and Others v. Bulgaria*, no. 51776/08, 29 November 2011.

[47] *Amuur v. France*, 25 June 1996, *Reports of Judgments and Decisions* 1996-III; *Shamsa v. Poland*, nos 45355/99 and 45357/99, 27 November 2003; *Mogoş v. Romania*, no. 20420/02, 13 October 2005; *Mahdid and Harrar v. Austria* (dec.), no. 74762/01, 8 December 2005; *Riad and Idiab v. Belgium*, nos 29787/03 and 29810/03, 24 January 2008.

[48] *I.I. v. Bulgaria*, no. 44082/98, 9 June 2005; *Osypenko v. Ukraine*, no. 4634/04, 9 November 2010; *Salayev v. Azerbaijan*, no. 40900/05, 9 November 2010; *Farhad Aliyev v. Azerbaijan*, no. 37138/06, 9 November 2010; *Creangă v. Romania* [GC], no. 29226/03, 23 February 2012.

[49] *Mancini v. Italy*, no. 44955/98, ECHR 2001-IX; *Lavents v. Latvia*, no. 58442/00, 28 November 2002; *Nikolova v. Bulgaria (no. 2)*, no. 40896/98, 30 September 2004; *Dacosta Silva v. Spain*, no. 69966/01, ECHR 2006-XIII.

[50] *Foka v. Turkey*, no. 28940/95, § 78, 24 June 2008; *Gillan and Quinton v. the United Kingdom*, no. 4158/05, § 57, ECHR 2010 (extracts); *Shimovolos v. Russia*, no. 30194/09, § 50, 21 June 2011; *Brega and Others v. Moldova*, no. 61485/08, § 43, 24 January 2012; *Brega v. Moldova*, no. 52100/08, § 43, 20 April 2010.

[51] *Austin and Others v. the United Kingdom* [GC], nos 39692/09, 40713/09, and 41008/09, ECHR 2012.

hand, disciplinary measures taken within a prison that affect conditions of detention do not fall within the scope of article 5(1). A decision by prison authorities to confine an inmate to her cell 'was part of the normal operation of the prison' and was 'concerned rather with restriction of movement not with liberty'.[52]

As for the subjective aspect, the Court has not attached too much importance to this. In one case, it held that 'the right to liberty is too important in a democratic society for a person to lose the benefit of Convention protection for the single reason that he may have given himself up to be taken into detention'.[53] That a person lacks legal capacity does not necessarily mean that he or she cannot understand and consent to the situation.[54]

Security of person and positive obligations

Using words taken from article 3 of the Universal Declaration of Human Rights, article 5 protects the 'liberty and security of person' of the individual. The case law of the Convention organs has focused almost exclusively on 'liberty' and no distinct or autonomous meaning has been given to 'security of person'. In a very early case, the Commission noted that just because 'liberty' and 'security' were closely connected did not mean that 'the term "security" is otiose'.

In the Commission's view, the protection of 'security' is in this context concerned with arbitrary interference, by a public authority, with an individual's personal 'liberty'. Or, in other words, any decision taken within the sphere of Article 5 must, in order to safeguard the individual's right to 'security of person', conform to the procedural as well as the substantive requirements laid down by an already existing law. This interpretation is confirmed both by the text of Article 5 and by the preparatory work of the Convention, which show that the protection against arbitrary arrest and detention was one of the principal considerations of the drafters of this treaty.[55]

In a case involving a disguised extradition from France to Switzerland, the Court said: 'What is at stake here is not only the "right to liberty" but also the "right to security of person".'[56] It concluded that there was a breach both of the right to liberty and of the right to security of person, but without attempting to explain or discuss the distinction.[57]

Interpreting the equivalent provision in the International Covenant on Civil and Political Rights, where the wording is identical to that of article 5 of the European Convention, the Human Rights Committee has stated that '[a]lthough in the Covenant the only reference to the right to security of person is to be found in article 9, there is no evidence that it was intended to narrow the concept of the right to security only to situations of formal deprivation of liberty'. It has used the concept in order to develop the obligation of States to protect horizontal violations, by non-State actors, explaining that

---

[52] *Bollan and Others v. the United Kingdom* (dec.), no. 42117/98, 4 May 2000.

[53] *H.L. v. the United Kingdom*, no. 45508/99, § 90, ECHR 2004-IX. Also *De Wilde, Ooms, and Versyp v. Belgium*, 18 June 1971, §§ 64–65, Series A no. 12; *Stanev v. Bulgaria* [GC], no. 36760/06, § 119, ECHR 2012; *Storck v. Germany*, no. 61603/00, § 75, ECHR 2005-V.

[54] *Shtukaturov v. Russia*, no. 44009/05, §§ 107–109, ECHR 2008; *Stanev v. Bulgaria* [GC], no. 36760/06, § 130, ECHR 2012; *D.D. v. Lithuania*, no. 13469/06, § 150, 14 February 2012.

[55] *36 East African Asians (Citizens of the United Kingdom and Colonies) v. the United Kingdom*, no. 4626/70 and 35 others, Commission decision of 6 March 1978, DR 13, p. 5; *3 East African Asians (British protected persons) v. the United Kingdom*, nos 4715/70, 4783/71, and 4827/71, Commission decision of 6 March 1978, DR 13, p. 17.

[56] *Bozano v. France*, 18 December 1986, § 54, Series A no. 111.

[57] Ibid., § 60.

'[a]n interpretation of article 9 which would allow a State party to ignore threats to the personal security of non-detained persons within its jurisdiction would render totally ineffective the guarantees of the Covenant'.[58] The Committee has applied the right to security of person in cases involving death threats, harassment, and various forms of intimidation.[59]

The European Court of Human Rights has addressed the acts of private individuals involving deprivation of liberty, for example in human trafficking cases, but without invoking the notion of 'security of person'.[60] Article 5 imposes upon the State a positive obligation 'to take measures providing effective protection of vulnerable persons, including reasonable steps to prevent a deprivation of liberty of which the authorities have or ought to have knowledge'.[61]

The positive obligation is also engaged in disappearance cases. When the Court considered several applications involving Greek Cypriots who had last been seen during the Turkish invasion of the island in 1974, 'in circumstances falling within the control of the Turkish or Turkish Cypriot forces', it concluded: 'While there is no evidence that any of the missing persons were still in detention in the period under the Court's consideration, it remains incumbent on the Turkish Government to show that they have since carried out an effective investigation into the arguable claim that the two missing men had been taken into custody and not seen subsequently.' The Court said that the failure to conduct the requisite investigation constituted 'a continuing violation of article 5'.[62]

'Lawfulness'

The notion of 'lawfulness' is fundamental to article 5. The introductory portion of article 5(1) sets out the condition that any deprivation of liberty be 'in accordance with a procedure prescribed by law'. Each of the sub-paragraphs of article 5(1) employs the word 'lawful'. When it uses the words 'lawful' and 'lawfulness', the Convention is referring essentially to national law. It sets out an obligation to conform to the substantive and procedural rules of national law.[63] Unacknowledged detention of an individual, without some detailed records of such matters as the date, time, and location of detention, the name of the detainee, the reasons for the detention, and the name of the person effecting it 'must be seen as incompatible with the requirement of lawfulness and with the

[58] *Delgado Páez v. Namibia*, no. 195/1985, UN Doc. CCPR/C/39/D/195/1985, para. 5.5. See also Manfred Nowak, *UN Covenant on Civil and Political Rights, CCPR Commentary*, 2nd rev. edn, Kehl, Germany: N.P. Engel, 2005, pp. 210–40.

[59] *Gunaratna v. Sri Lanka*, no. 1432/2005, UN Doc. CCPR/C/95/D/1432/2005, para. 8.4; *Chongwe v. Zambia*, no. 821/1998, UN Doc. CCPR/C/79/D/821/1998, para. 5.4; *Dias v. Angola*, no. 711/1996, UN Doc. CCPR/C/68/D/711/1996, para. 8.3; *Jayawardena v. Sri Lanka*, no. 916/2000, UN Doc. CCPR/C/675/D/916/2000, para. 7.2.

[60] *Rantsev v. Cyprus and Russia*, no. 25965/04, §§ 319–321, ECHR 2010 (extracts).

[61] *Storck v. Germany*, no. 61603/00, § 102, ECHR 2005-V. Also *Riera Blume and Others v. Spain*, no. 37680/97, § 35, ECHR 1999-VII; *Medova v. Russia*, no. 25385/04, §§ 123–124, 15 January 2009.

[62] *Varnava and Others v. Turkey* [GC], nos 16064/90, 16065/90, 16066/90, 16068/90, 16069/90, 16070/90, 16071/90, 16072/90, and 16073/90, § 208, ECHR 2000.

[63] *Medvedyev and Others v. France* [GC], no. 3394/03, § 79, ECHR 2010; *Bolzano v. France*, 18 December 1986, § 54, Series A no. 111; *Ilaşcu and Others v. Moldova and Russia* [GC], no. 48787/99, § 461, ECHR 2004-VII; *Assanidze v. Georgia* [GC], no. 71503/01, § 171, ECHR 2004-II; *McKay v. the United Kingdom* [GC], no. 543/03, § 30, ECHR 2006-X.

very purpose of Article 5 of the Convention'.[64] Various violations of national law have been held to constitute unlawful detention and violations of the right to liberty. For example, where the authorities had not applied to extend a detention order within the time limit authorized by law the Court held that there was a breach of article 5.[65] Nevertheless, not every flaw in a detention order will be fatal and lead to a violation. Unless it constitutes a 'gross and obvious irregularity', a defect in a detention order may be remedied by appellate courts without the implication that the initial detention was contrary to article 5.[66]

There will be deference to the national authorities in the interpretation and application of their own law. However, because failure to comply with national law constitutes a breach of the Convention, the Court is entitled to review whether the national law has been respected.[67] In addition, in assessing the lawfulness of deprivation of liberty, 'the Court is not confined to the declared, ostensible purposes of the arrest or detention in question, but also looks at the real intent and purposes behind it'.[68]

The starting point for determination of 'lawfulness' is the existence of a court order. Sometimes, a court order of detention will be found to be unlawful by a superior court, in accordance with national law, but this does not mean that it is necessarily invalid.[69] The national courts may recognize that there have been flaws in domestic proceedings without the detention itself being contrary to article 5.[70] Nevertheless, where there is a 'gross and obvious irregularity' the detention will be contrary to article 5.[71] In making its autonomous determination, the Court 'will have regard to all the circumstances of the case, including, in particular, the assessment made by the domestic courts. It observes that according to the findings of the German courts, the order in question did not suffer from a serious and obvious defect which rendered it null and void.'[72] Similarly, failure to officially notify a detention order was not a 'gross or obvious irregularity where the

---

[64] *Anguelova v. Bulgaria*, no. 38361/97, § 154, ECHR 2002-IV. See also *Kurt v. Turkey*, 25 May 1998, § 125, *Reports of Judgments and Decisions* 1998-III; *Menesheva v. Russia*, no. 59261/00, § 87, ECHR 2006-III; *Grinenko v. Ukraine*, no. 33627/06, § 74, 15 November 2012.

[65] *G.K. v. Poland*, no. 38816/97, § 76, 20 January 2004.

[66] *Mooren v. Germany* [GC], no. 11364/03, §§ 74–76, 9 July 2009; *Liu v. Russia*, no. 42086/05, § 81, 6 December 2007; *Garabayev v. Russia*, no. 38411/02, § 89, 7 June 2007; *Marturana v. Italy*, no. 63154/00, § 79, 4 March 2008.

[67] *Mooren v. Germany* [GC], no. 11364/03, § 73, 9 July 2009; *Benham v. the United Kingdom*, 10 June 1996, § 41, *Reports of Judgments and Decisions* 1996-III; *Baranowski v. Poland*, no. 28358/95, § 50, ECHR 2000-III; *Ječius v. Lithuania*, no. 34578/97, § 68, ECHR 2000-IX; *Ladent v. Poland*, no. 11036/03, § 47, 18 March 2008.

[68] *Tymoshenko v. Ukraine*, no. 49872/11, § 263, 30 April 2013; *Lutsenko v. Ukraine*, no. 6492/11, § 65, 3 July 2012; *Khodorkovskiy v. Russia*, no. 5829/04, § 142, 31 May 2011.

[69] *Bozano v. France*, 18 December 1986, § 55, Series A no. 111.

[70] *Erkalo v. the Netherlands*, 2 September 1998, §§ 55–56, *Reports of Judgments and Decisions* 1998-VI; *Ječius v. Lithuania*, no. 34578/97, § 68, ECHR 2000-IX; *Benham v. the United Kingdom*, 10 June 1996, §§ 42–47, *Reports of Judgments and Decisions* 1996-III.

[71] *Khudoyorov v. Russia*, no. 6847/02, § 129, ECHR 2005-X (extracts); *Lloyd and Others v. the United Kingdom*, nos 29798/96, 30395/96, 34327/96, 34341/96, 35445/97, 36267/97, 36367/97, 37551/97, 37706/97, 38261/97, 39378/98, 41590/98, 41593/98, 42040/98, 42097/98, 45420/99, 45844/99, 46326/99, 47144/99, 53062/99, 53111/99, 54969/00, 54973/00, 54997/00, 55046/00, 55068/00, 55071/00, 56109/00, 56231/00, 56232/00, 56233/00, 56429/00, 56441/00, 2460/03, 2482/03, 2483/03, 2484/03, and 2490/03, §§ 108–116, 1 March 2005.

[72] *Mooren v. Germany* [GC], no. 11364/03, § 86, 9 July 2009.

authorities genuinely believed that the order had been notified'.[73] The Court has excused 'mere clerical error' in an arrest warrant or detention order that was later corrected by a judicial authority.[74] But according to a compelling dissenting opinion, the fact that a defect is procedural or formal rather than substantive 'does not make the defect any less serious. The Court's case law makes no distinction between substantive and procedural rules of domestic law: both have to be complied with to ensure the lawfulness and legality of the detention.'[75] An order of indefinite detention is incompatible with the 'lawfulness' requirement of article 5.[76]

It is not sufficient for the State to comply with national law in order for it to respect article 5: 'Article 5 § 1 requires in addition that any deprivation of liberty should be in keeping with the purpose of protecting the individual from arbitrariness.'[77] This requires an assessment whether the domestic law itself is consistent with the Convention, 'including the general principles expressed or implied therein, notably the principle of legal certainty'.[78] Where deprivation of liberty is concerned, it is particularly important that the general principle of legal certainty be satisfied.[79] Legal certainty means that the law governing conditions for deprivation of liberty be accessible, clearly defined, and that its application be foreseeable.[80]

In Poland, a domestic practice of keeping a person in detention under a bill of indictment had no specific basis in either legislation or case law. As the government conceded, this 'stemmed from the fact that Polish criminal legislation at the material time lacked clear rules governing the situation of a detainee in court proceedings, after the expiry of the term of his detention fixed in the last detention order made at the investigation stage'. It was a short step for the Court to conclude that the absence of any precise provisions governing prolongation of detention at the investigation stage could not satisfy the requirement of foreseeability.[81] Moreover, the practice that developed in order to address the lacuna in the statute by which a person could be detained 'for an unlimited and unpredictable time and without his detention being based on a

---

[73] *Marturana v. Italy*, no. 63154/00, § 79, 4 March 2008. However, see *Voskuil v. the Netherlands*, no. 64752/01, § 83, 22 November 2007.

[74] *Douiyeb v. the Netherlands* [GC], no. 31464/96, §§ 51–52, 4 August 1999; *Proshkin v. Russia*, no. 28869/03, § 72, 7 February 2012.

[75] *Mooren v. Germany* [GC], no. 11364/03, Joint Partly Dissenting Opinion of Judges Rozakis, Tulkens, Casadevall, Gyulumyan, Hayiyev, Spielmann, Berro-Lefèvre, and Bianku, § 4, 9 July 2009; *McKay v. the United Kingdom*, [GC], no. 543/03, ECHR 2006-X.

[76] *Tymoshenko v. Ukraine*, no. 49872/11, § 267, 30 April 2013; *Chumakov v. Russia*, no. 41794/04, § 130, 24 April 2012; *Yeloyev v. Ukraine*, no. 17283/02, §§ 52–55, 6 November 2008; *Solovey and Zozulya v. Ukraine*, nos 40774/02 and 4048/03, § 59, 27 November 2008; *Solovyev v. Russia*, no. 2708/02, §§ 95–100, 24 May 2007; *Shukhardin v. Russia*, no. 65734/01, §§ 65–70, 28 June 2007; *Doronin v. Ukraine*, no. 16505/02, § 59, 19 February 2009.

[77] *A. and Others v. the United Kingdom* [GC], no. 3455/05, § 164, ECHR 2009; *Mooren v. Germany* [GC], no. 11364/03, § 72, 9 July 2009; *Erkalo v. the Netherlands*, 2 September 1998, § 52, *Reports of Judgments and Decisions* 1998-VI; *Steel and Others v. the United Kingdom*, 23 September 1998, § 54, *Reports of Judgments and Decisions* 1998-VII; *Saadi v. the United Kingdom* [GC], no. 13229/03, § 67, ECHR 2008.

[78] *Mooren v. Germany* [GC], no. 11364/03, § 73, 9 July 2009; *Baranowski v. Poland*, no. 28358/95, §§ 51–52, ECHR 2000-III; *Ječius v. Lithuania*, no. 34578/97, § 56, ECHR 2000-IX; *Nasrulloyev v. Russia*, no. 656/06, § 71, 11 October 2007.

[79] *Mooren v. Germany* [GC], no. 11364/03, § 76, 9 July 2009; *Baranowski v. Poland*, no. 28358/95, §§ 51–52, ECHR 2000-III; *Ječius v. Lithuania*, no. 34578/97, § 125, ECHR 2000-IX.

[80] *Creangă v. Romania* [GC], no. 29226/03, § 120, 23 February 2012; *Medvedyev and Others v. France* [GC], no. 3394/03, § 80, ECHR 2010.

[81] *Baranowski v. Poland*, no. 28358/95, §§ 54–55, ECHR 2000-III.

concrete legal provision or on any judicial decision' was itself contrary to the principle of legal certainty.[82]

Problems of legal certainty often manifest themselves when the authorities themselves cannot agree upon how legal provisions are to be interpreted and applied. Russian authorities and courts provided inconsistent and mutually exclusive interpretations of legal regulations governing detention for the purpose of extradition. The European Court of Human Rights said that Russian laws were 'neither precise nor foreseeable in their application and fell short of the "quality of law" standard required under the Convention'.[83] Similarly, Lithuanian authorities provided three different interpretations of national legislation, leading the Court to observe that the measures were 'vague enough to cause confusion even amongst the competent State authorities'.[84]

Complexity in national law does not mean there is no certainty. What may appear to be an inscrutable text can nevertheless provide foreseeable guidance to a detained person, 'if necessary with the advice of counsel'.[85] The Court has said that 'in general, the principle of legal certainty may be compromised if domestic courts introduce exceptions in their case law which run counter to the wording of the applicable statutory provisions'. However, it has said that legal certainty is not threatened in every case, particularly where there is well-established precedent.[86]

Arbitrariness

Protecting the individual from arbitrariness is said to be the underlying purpose of article 5 of the Convention. No detention that is arbitrary can be compatible with article 5.[87] The notion of 'arbitrariness' in this context extends beyond the lack of conformity with national law. As a consequence, a deprivation of liberty that is lawful under domestic law can still be arbitrary and thus contrary to the Convention.[88]

Detention will be deemed 'arbitrary' where there is an element of bad faith or deception by the authorities, even if national law has been observed in a technical sense.[89] Also, the order of detention and its execution or implementation must genuinely conform to the purposes of the restrictions set out in the sub-paragraphs of article 5(1).[90] There must also be a relationship between the ground justifying detention and the place and conditions of detention.[91] The necessity of the detention is a factor in assessing arbitrariness. Even if

[82] Ibid., § 56.
[83] *Nasrulloyev v. Russia*, no. 656/06, § 77, 11 October 2007.
[84] *Ječius v. Lithuania*, no. 34578/97, § 59, ECHR 2000-IX.
[85] *Mooren v. Germany* [GC], no. 11364/03, § 91, 9 July 2009.
[86] Ibid., § 93.
[87] *A. and Others v. the United Kingdom* [GC], no. 3455/05, § 164, ECHR 2009; *Saadi v. the United Kingdom* [GC], no. 13229/03, § 67, ECHR 2008.
[88] *Mooren v. Germany* [GC], no. 11364/03, § 77, 9 July 2009; *Saadi v. the United Kingdom* [GC], no. 13229/03, §§ 67–68, ECHR 2008; *Creangă v. Romania* [GC], no. 29226/03, § 84, 23 February 2012; *A. and Others v. the United Kingdom* [GC], no. 3455/05, § 164, ECHR 2009.
[89] *Saadi v. the United Kingdom* [GC], no. 13229/03, § 69, ECHR 2008; *Bozano v. France*, 18 December 1986, Series A no. 111; *Čonka v. Belgium*, no. 51564/99, ECHR 2002-I.
[90] *Saadi v. the United Kingdom* [GC], no. 13229/03, § 69, ECHR 2008; *Winterwerp v. the Netherlands*, 24 October 1979, § 39, Series A no. 33; *Bouamar v. Belgium*, 29 February 1988, § 50, Series A no. 129; *O'Hara v. The United Kingdom*, no. 37555/97, § 34, ECHR 2001-X.
[91] *Saadi v. the United Kingdom* [GC], no. 13229/03, § 69, ECHR 2008; *Bouamar v. Belgium*, 29 February 1988, § 50, Series A no. 129; *Aerts v. Belgium*, 30 July 1998, § 46, *Reports of Judgments and Decisions* 1998-V; *Enhorn v. Sweden*, no. 56529/00, § 42, ECHR 2005-I.

national law is respected, meeting the test of 'lawfulness', deprivation of liberty must also be necessary in the circumstances.[92] In assessing arbitrariness, the absence[93] or extreme brevity[94] of reasoning in a detention order is an important consideration. In several cases involving denial of interim release on grounds of 'public order', the Court has found there to be a violation of article 5(1) because of a lack of any reasons for the decision.[95] However, the Court did not find a violation of article 5 where the domestic courts quashed a detention order because it was not reasoned, yet considered there were grounds for detention.[96]

The assessment of arbitrariness varies depending on the rationale for the deprivation of liberty.[97] With respect to detention pursuant to a criminal conviction in accordance with sub-paragraph (a), the decision to impose a sentence of detention and the length of that sentence are matters for the national authorities and not for the Court, absent evidence of bad faith.[98] In the case of detention for non-compliance with a court order (sub-para. 5(1)(b)), detention of a minor (sub-para. 5(1)(d)) and detention on medical grounds (sub-para. 5(1)(e)), the notion of arbitrariness dictates an assessment whether detention was necessary in order to achieve the stated aim, and whether the result could have been achieved using less severe measures.[99] According to the Court, 'detention of an individual is such a serious measure that it is only justified where other, less severe measures have been considered and found to be insufficient to safeguard the individual or public interest which might require that the person concerned be detained'.[100]

In immigration and deportation cases (sub-para. 5(1)(f)), the Grand Chamber has said that it is unnecessary for the State to demonstrate that detention be reasonably considered necessary, for example to prevent the commission of an offence or flight.[101] All that is required is that 'action is being taken with a view to deportation' and it is 'immaterial . . . whether the underlying decision to expel can be justified under national or Convention law'.[102] Nevertheless, detention for such a purpose can only be justifiable as long as

---

[92] *Něsták v. Slovakia*, no. 65559/01, § 74, 27 February 2007; *Klishyn v. Ukraine*, no. 30671/04, § 89, 23 February 2012.

[93] *Stašaitis v. Lithuania*, no. 47679/99, § 67, 21 March 2002; *Nakhmanovich v. Russia*, no. 55669/00, § 70, 2 March 2006; *Belevitskiy v. Russia*, no. 72967/01, § 91, 1 March 2007; *Mooren v. Germa Reports of Judgments and Decisions* 1998ny [GC], no. 11364/03, § 79, 9 July 2009; *Mooren v. Germany* [GC], no. 11364/03, Joint Partly Dissenting Opinion of Judges Rozakis, Tulkens, Casadevall, Gyulumyan, Hayiyev, Spielmann, Berro-Lefèvre, and Bianku, § 3, 9 July 2009.

[94] *Khudoyorov v. Russia*, no. 6847/02, § 157, ECHR 2005-X (extracts); *Mooren v. Germany* [GC], no. 11364/03, § 79, 9 July 2009. In particular, see *Mooren v. Germany* [GC], no. 11364/03, Joint Partly Dissenting Opinion of Judges Rozakis, Tulkens, Casadevall, Gyulumyan, Hayiyev, Spielmann, Berro-Lefèvre, and Bianku, § 5, 9 July 2009.

[95] *Lauruc v. Romania*, no. 34236/03, § 62, 23 April 2013; *Pantea v. Romania*, no. 33343/96, §§ 222–223, ECHR 2003-VI (extracts); *Tase v. Romania*, no. 29761/02, § 29, 10 June 2008; *Calmanovici v. Romania*, no. 42250/02, § 66, 1 July 2008.

[96] *Minjat v. Switzerland*, no. 38223/97, §§ 43–47, 28 October 2003.

[97] *Saadi v. the United Kingdom* [GC], no. 13229/03, § 68, ECHR 2008; *Mooren v. Germany* [GC], no. 11364/03, § 77, 9 July 2009.

[98] *T. v. the United Kingdom* [GC], no. 24724/94, § 103, 16 December 1999; *Stafford v. the United Kingdom* [GC], no. 46295/99, § 64, ECHR 2002-IV.

[99] *Saadi v. the United Kingdom* [GC], no. 13229/03, § 70, ECHR 2008.

[100] *Witold Litwa v. Poland*, no. 26629/95, § 78, ECHR 2000-III; *Hilda Hafsteinsdóttir v. Iceland*, no. 40905/98, § 51, 8 June 2004; *Enhorn v. Sweden*, no. 56529/00, § 44, ECHR 2005-I.

[101] *Saadi v. the United Kingdom* [GC], no. 13229/03, § 73, ECHR 2008.

[102] *Chahal v. the United Kingdom*, 15 November 1996, § 112, *Reports of Judgments and Decisions* 1996-V.

deportation proceedings are in progress. If they are not or are no longer being pursued with due diligence, detention will no longer be compatible with article 5.[103]

With respect to appearance before a court of someone who has been arrested (sub-paragraph 5(1)(c)) or detained on medical grounds (sub-paragraph 5(1)(e)), the speed with which the national courts replace a detention order that has expired or that has been found to be defective is also relevant in assessing arbitrariness.[104] Although it is 'inconceivable' that a person should remain detained if there is a court order for release,[105] it is recognized that some delay in implementing a decision is understandable and even inevitable, although this must be kept to a minimum.[106]

Grounds for detention (art. 5(1))

After stating the principle that everyone has the right to liberty and security of person, article 5(1) states that deprivation of liberty may be allowed 'in accordance with a procedure prescribed by law' in six situations, set out in sub-paragraphs (a) to (f). The list of permissible grounds is an exhaustive one,[107] and 'no deprivation of liberty will be lawful unless it falls within one of those grounds'.[108] The list of permissible grounds is to be interpreted restrictively.[109] Even detention of very short duration falls within the scope of article 5(1).[110] The categories are not mutually exclusive. There is no reason why more than one may not apply to the same situation at any given time. The purpose and character of the detention may change with the passage of time so that one ground ceases to be relevant but another takes its place.[111]

Suggestions that article 5(1) permits a balance to be struck between the right to liberty of the individual and the interest of the State in protecting its population, for example from terrorist threats, have been rejected as inconsistent with the codification of limitations on the right to freedom in the provision: 'If detention does not fit within the confines of the paragraphs as interpreted by the Court, it cannot be made to fit by an appeal to the need to balance the interests of the State against those of the detainee.'[112]

---

[103] *Chahal v. the United Kingdom*, 15 November 1996, § 112, *Reports of Judgments and Decisions* 1996-V; *Gebremedhin [Gaberamadhien] v. France*, no. 25389/05, § 74, ECHR 2007-II.

[104] *Mooren v. Germany* [GC], no. 11364/03, § 80, 9 July 2009; *Minjat v. Switzerland*, no. 38223/97, §§ 46, 48, 28 October 2003; *Khudoyorov v. Russia*, no. 6847/02, §§ 136–137, ECHR 2005-X (extracts); *Quinn v. France*, 22 March 1995, §§ 39–43, Series A no. 311; *Winterwerp v. the Netherlands*, 24 October 1979, § 49, Series A no. 33; *Erkalo v. the Netherlands*, 2 September 1998, §§ 57–60, *Reports of Judgments and Decisions* 1998-VI.

[105] *Assanidze v. Georgia* [GC], no. 71503/01, § 173, ECHR 2004-II.

[106] *Giulia Manzoni v. Italy*, 1 July 1997, § 25, *Reports of Judgments and Decisions* 1997-IV.

[107] *Labita v. Italy* [GC], no. 26772/95, § 170, ECHR 2000-IV; *Quinn v. France*, 22 March 1995, § 42, Series A no. 311.

[108] *A. and Others v. the United Kingdom* [GC], no. 3455/05, § 163, ECHR 2009; *Saadi v. the United Kingdom* [GC], no. 13229/03, § 43, ECHR 2008.

[109] *Engel and Others v. the Netherlands*, 8 June 1976, § 58, Series A no. 22; *Amuur v. France*, 25 June 1996, § 42, *Reports of Judgments and Decisions* 1996-III; *A. and Others v. the United Kingdom* [GC], no. 3455/05, § 171, ECHR 2009.

[110] *Murray v. the United Kingdom* [GC], 28 October 1994, §§ 49 ff, Series A no. 300-A; *Novotka v. Slovakia* (dec.), no. 47244/99, 4 November 2003; *Shimovolos v. Russia*, no. 30194/09, §§ 49–50, 21 June 2011; *Witold Litwa v. Poland*, no. 26629/95, § 46, ECHR 2000-III; *X v. Austria*, no. 8278/78, Commission decision of 13 December 1979, DR 18, p. 154; *Guenat v. Switzerland*, no. 24722/94, Commission decision of 10 April 1995, DR 81-A, p. 130.

[111] *McVeigh and Others v. the United Kingdom*, nos 8022/77, 8025/77, and 8027/77, Commission report of 18 March 1981, § 163.

[112] *A. and Others v. the United Kingdom* [GC], no. 3455/05, § 171, ECHR 2009.

Internment and preventive detention without charge are incompatible with the fundamental right to liberty.[113] States may only resort to these practices, in peacetime, if they derogate from article 5 in accordance with article 15.[114] According to the Grand Chamber, these practices can only be compatible with article 5 'in cases of international armed conflict, where the taking of prisoners of war and the detention of civilians who pose a threat to security are accepted features of international humanitarian law'.[115]

Post-conviction detention (art. 5(1)(a))

Post-conviction detention is obviously not a violation of article 5. Article 5(1)(a) applies to a 'conviction by a competent court' that results in deprivation of liberty. It does not matter that the conviction is pronounced in a disciplinary rather than a genuinely criminal matter.[116] In a case where compulsory residence was ordered not for a specific offence but because of a 'propensity to crime', the Court held that this did not fit within the terms of article 5(1)(a). It said that for there to be a 'conviction', there must be an offence. Anything else would not be compatible with 'the principle of narrow interpretation to be observed in this area . . . nor with the fact that that word implies a finding of guilt'.[117]

Article 5(1)(a) does not prevent States from enforcing detention orders imposed by foreign courts,[118] without them being required to verify that the trial proceedings respected all of the requirements of article 6, as this could 'thwart the current trend towards strengthening international cooperation in the administration of justice'.[119] However, detention resulting from a conviction by a foreign court that constituted a 'flagrant denial of justice' cannot be compatible with article 5(1)(a).[120]

The 'court' contemplated by article 5(1)(a) 'does not necessarily have to be a court of law of the classic kind integrated within the standard judicial machinery of the country'.[121] The Convention uses the word 'court' (in French, *tribunal*) in several provisions[122] in order to 'denote bodies which exhibit not only common fundamental features, of which the most important is independence of the executive and of the parties to the case . . . but also the guarantees of judicial procedure'.[123] The 'court' should have the competence to order release should the detention be unlawful.[124]

---

[113] Ibid., § 172; *Ireland v. the United Kingdom*, 18 January 1978, §§ 194–196 and 212–213, Series A no. 25.

[114] *Lawless v. Ireland (no. 3)*, 1 July 1961, §§ 13 and 14, Series A no. 3; *Ireland v. the United Kingdom*, 18 January 1978, § 196, Series A no. 25; *Guzzardi v. Italy*, 6 November 1980, § 102, Series A no. 39; *Ječius v. Lithuania*, no. 34578/97, §§ 47–52, ECHR 2000-IX; *Al-Jedda v. the United Kingdom* [GC], no. 27021/08, § 100, ECHR 2011; *Hassan v. the United Kingdom* [GC], no. 29750/09, § 97, 16 September 2014.

[115] *Hassan v. the United Kingdom* [GC], no. 29750/09, § 104, 16 September 2014.

[116] *Engel and Others v. the Netherlands* (Article 50), 23 November 1976, § 68, Series A no. 22; *Galstyan v. Armenia*, no. 26986/03, § 46, 15 November 2007.

[117] *Guzzardi v. Italy*, 6 November 1980, § 100, Series A no. 39. Also *M. v. Germany*, no. 19359/04, § 87, ECHR 2009; *Van Droogenbroeck v. Belgium*, 24 June 1982, § 35, Series A no. 50; *B. v. Austria*, 28 March 1990, § 38, Series A no. 175.

[118] *X v. Federal Republic of Germany*, no. 1322/62, Commission decision of 14 December 1963, Collection 13, p. 55.

[119] *Drozd and Janousek v. France and Spain*, 26 June 1992, § 110, Series A no. 240.

[120] Ibid.; *Stoichkov v. Bulgaria*, no. 9808/02, § 51, 24 March 2005; *Ilaşcu and Others v. Moldova and Russia* [GC], no. 48787/99, § 461, ECHR 2004-VII.

[121] *X v. the United Kingdom*, 5 November 1981, § 53, Series A no. 46.

[122] Articles 2(1), 5(1)(a), 5(1)(b), 5(4), 6(1), 6(3).

[123] *De Wilde, Ooms, and Versyp v. Belgium*, 18 June 1971, § 78, Series A no. 12.

[124] *Weeks v. the United Kingdom*, 2 March 1987, § 61, Series A no. 114.

Detention contemplated by article 5(1)(a) must take place 'after conviction'. Not only does it follow the conviction in a chronological sense but it must also be a consequence of the conviction.[125] It applies from the moment of conviction at trial, even if the trial judgment is under appeal, given that the guilt of the person has already been determined.[126] Although appellate proceedings may subsequently determine that detention is unlawful, this will not necessarily have as a consequence a determination that the deprivation of liberty is contrary to article 5.[127] Nevertheless, as time passes, in the course of detention the causal link with the conviction itself may become increasingly remote from the objectives of the legislature or the court, and may thereby become unreasonable and arbitrary.[128]

Non-compliance with a court order or legal obligation (art. 5(1)(b))

The second sub-paragraph of article 5(1) applies to detention resulting from a court order or from a legal obligation. Examples in the case law of the first limb of sub-paragraph (b), namely, detention pursuant to a court order, include failure to obey an order to pay a fine,[129] refusal to submit to a psychiatric examination[130] or to take a blood test,[131] failure to respect residence restrictions,[132] failure to return children to the custodial parent,[133] failure to agree to make an undertaking not to breach the peace ('binding over order'),[134] breach of bail conditions,[135] and confinement in a psychiatric hospital.[136] In such cases, the individual must have had an opportunity to comply with the court order but have failed to do so, or defied it.[137] Necessarily, the individual cannot be detained if he or she has not been informed of the order.[138]

The second limb of article 5(1)(b) concerns failure to submit to a legal obligation. Examples include a refusal to provide identification when requested,[139] to submit to a security check at an international border,[140] to leave an area when so ordered by police,[141]

---

[125] *Van Droogenbroeck v. Belgium*, 24 June 1982, § 35, Series A no. 50; *Weeks v. the United Kingdom*, 2 March 1987, § 42, Series A no. 114; *M. v. Germany*, no. 19359/04, §§ 87–88, ECHR 2009; *Kafkaris v. Cyprus* [GC], no. 21906/04, § 117, ECHR 2008; *Stafford v. the United Kingdom* [GC], no. 46295/99, § 64, ECHR 2002-IV; *Monnell and Morris v. the United Kingdom*, 2 March 1987, § 40, Series A no. 115; *S. v. Germany*, no. 3300/10, § 90, 28 June 2012; *Dörr v. Germany* (dec.), no. 2894/08, 22 January 2013.

[126] *Wemhoff v. Germany*, 27 June 1968, § 9, Series A no. 7.

[127] *Benham v. the United Kingdom*, 10 June 1996, § 42, *Reports of Judgments and Decisions* 1996-III.

[128] *Van Droogenbroeck v. Belgium*, 24 June 1982, § 40, Series A no. 50; *Weeks v. the United Kingdom*, 2 March 1987, § 49, Series A no. 114; *M. v. Germany*, no. 19359/04, § 88, ECHR 2009.

[129] *Airey v. Ireland*, no. 6289/73, Commission decision of 7 July 1977; *Velinov v. the former Yugoslav Republic of Macedonia*, no. 16880/08, §§ 48–57, 19 September 2013.

[130] *Petukhova v. Russia*, no. 28796/07, §§ 46–64, 2 May 2013; *Nowicka v. Poland*, no. 30218/96, § 62, 3 December 2002; *X v. Federal Republic of Germany*, no. 6859/74, Commission decision of 10 December 1975.

[131] *X. v. Austria*, no. 8278/78, Commission decision of 13 December 1979.

[132] *Freda v. Italy*, no. 8916/80, Commission decision of 7 October 1980, (1981) 24 YB 354.

[133] *Paradis v. Germany* (dec.), no. 4065/04, 4 September 2007.

[134] *Steel and Others v. the United Kingdom*, 23 September 1998, *Reports of Judgments and Decisions* 1998-VII.

[135] *Gatt v. Malta*, no. 28221/08, ECHR 2010.

[136] *Beiere v. Latvia*, no. 30954/05, 29 November 2011.

[137] Ibid., § 49; *Petukhova v. Russia*, no. 28796/07, § 58, 2 May 2013.

[138] *Beiere v. Latvia*, no. 30954/05, § 50, 29 November 2011.

[139] *Vasileva v. Denmark*, no. 52792/99, 25 September 2003; *Novotka v. Slovakia* (dec.), no. 47244/99, 4 November 2003; *Sarigiannis v. Italy*, no. 14569/05, § 44, 5 April 2011; *Reyntjens v. Belgium*, no. 16810/90, Commission decision of 9 September 1992, DR 73, p. 136.

[140] *McVeigh and Others v. the United Kingdom*, nos 8022/77, 8025/77, and 8027/77, Commission report of 18 March 1981.

[141] *Epple v. Germany*, no. 77909/01, § 36, 24 March 2005.

questioning at a police station,[142] and to appear at a court hearing.[143] The obligation must be 'specific and concrete'.[144] The Convention organs have consistently rejected a broad interpretation by which article 5(1)(b) is invoked to justify internment or administrative detention for the purpose of compelling a person to comply with general obligations arising from the law.[145] The State cannot rely upon a vague duty not to commit a criminal offence in the imminent future. However, an order to keep the peace will be valid if specific measures have been prescribed and these have not been observed[146] or if the individual is required to make clear and positive steps that indicate the obligation will not be complied with,[147] provided that 'the place and time of the imminent commission of the offence and its potential victim(s) have been sufficiently specified'.[148]

The arrest and detention must be truly necessary for the purpose of fulfilment of the obligation. In assessing a justification for deprivation of liberty, a fair balance has to be struck between the significance in a democratic society of securing the fulfilment of the obligation in issue and the importance of the right to liberty. Relevant factors are the nature and the purpose of the obligation, the detained person, the specific circumstances that led to his or her detention, and the length of the detention.[149] For example, if a witness fails to appear for questioning without a good reason, he or she may be detained in order to be brought before the investigator or the court. Nevertheless, 'the decision-making process in such matters, where the person's liberty is at stake, should not be overly formalistic, and should take into account all relevant circumstances of the case. Thus, the same reason (a business trip, an illness, a family event, etc.) may be a valid excuse in one context and not in another.'[150]

The detention will only be acceptable if it 'cannot be fulfilled by milder means'.[151] Detention is permitted only in order to 'secure the fulfilment' of the obligation. It must not be punitive in nature.[152] The obligation itself must be compatible with the Convention.[153] Once the obligation is fulfilled the justification for detention ceases to exist.[154]

[142] *Iliya Stefanov v. Bulgaria*, no. 65755/01, § 75, 22 May 2008; *Osypenko v. Ukraine*, no. 4634/04, §§ 56–64, 9 November 2010.
[143] *Lolova-Karadzhova v. Bulgaria*, no. 17835/07, §§ 31–32, 27 March 2012.
[144] *Engel and Others v. the Netherlands*, 8 June 1976, § 69, Series A no. 22; *Guzzardi v. Italy*, 6 November 1980, § 101, Series A no. 39.
[145] *McVeigh and Others v. the United Kingdom*, nos 8022/77, 8025/77, and 8027/77, Commission report of 18 March 1981, § 171; *Engel and Others v. the Netherlands*, 8 June 1976, § 69, Series A no. 22.
[146] *Ostendorf v. Germany*, no. 15598/08, § 69, 7 March 2013; *Schwabe and M.G. v. Germany*, nos 8080/08 and 8577/08, § 82, ECHR 2011 (extracts).
[147] *Ostendorf v. Germany*, no. 15598/08, § 94, 7 March 2013.
[148] Ibid., § 93. But see *Ostendorf v. Germany*, no. 15598/08, Concurring Opinion of Judges Lemmens and Jäderblom, 7 March 2013.
[149] *Vasileva v. Denmark*, no. 52792/99, §§ 37–38, 25 September 2003; *Epple v. Germany*, no. 77909/01, § 37, 24 March 2005.
[150] *Khodorkovskiy v. Russia*, no. 5829/04, § 137, 31 May 2011.
[151] Ibid., § 136.
[152] *Johansen v. Norway*, no. 10600/83, Commission decision of 14 October 1985, DR 44, p. 155; *Ostendorf v. Germany*, no. 15598/08, § 97, 7 March 2013; *Vasileva v. Denmark*, no. 52792/99, § 36, 25 September 2003; *Gatt v. Malta*, no. 28221/08, § 46, ECHR 2010; *Soare and Others v. Romania*, no. 24329/02, § 236, 22 February 2011.
[153] *McVeigh and Others v. the United Kingdom*, nos 8022/77, 8025/77, and 8027/77, Commission report of 18 March 1981, § 176; *Ostendorf v. Germany*, no. 15598/08, § 72, 7 March 2013.
[154] *Osypenko v. Ukraine*, no. 4634/04, § 57, 9 November 2010; *Vasileva v. Denmark*, no. 52792/99, § 36, 25 September 2003; *Sarigiannis v. Italy*, no. 14569/05, § 43, 5 April 2011; *Lolova-Karadzhova v. Bulgaria*, no. 17835/07, § 29, 27 March 2012.

In assessing the proportionality of the detention, account will be taken of the length of time the person is held.[155]

Detention for criminal prosecution (art. 5(1)(c))

Sub-paragraph (c) of article 5(1) governs detention for the purpose of bringing a person before a competent legal authority who is suspected of having committed an offence. Necessarily, it is only applicable in criminal proceedings.[156] Article 5(1)(c) has a 'close affinity' with article 3 in terms of the relevant principles.[157] Three distinct grounds are set out for detention under this paragraph: where there is reasonable suspicion that an offence has been committed; when it is reasonably considered necessary to prevent the person committing an offence; when it is reasonably considered necessary to prevent the person fleeing after having committed an offence. Thus, 'the expression "effected for purpose of bringing him before the competent legal authority" qualifies every category of cases of arrest or detention referred to in that sub-paragraph'.[158]

The term 'competent legal authority', described in one judgment as being 'rather vague' and in 'abbreviated form',[159] has the same meaning as 'judge or other officer authorised by law to exercise judicial power' in article 5(3).[160] To constitute a 'competent legal authority', the institution must have the power to order release.[161]

Having a 'reasonable suspicion' means that there must be 'facts or information which would satisfy an objective observer that the person concerned may have committed the offence'.[162] The meaning of 'reasonable' will depend upon all the circumstances.[163] This is not a particularly high threshold and is certainly not comparable to what is necessary to warrant a conviction or even to bring a charge, issues that arise at subsequent stages in the criminal investigation and trial process.[164] Accordingly, there is no violation of article 5(1)(c) simply because after the arrest and detention the authorities do not then press charges. There may be many explanations for a failure to proceed, including unavailability or likely inadmissibility of evidence, or the need to protect the lives of others.[165] Nevertheless, article 5(1)(c) will be breached if there is a failure by the authorities to make a genuine inquiry into the basic facts of the case in order to verity if a complaint is well founded.[166] There can be no 'reasonable suspicion' if the acts attributed to the

---

[155] *Reyntjens v. Belgium*, no. 16810/90, Commission decision of 9 September 1992, DR 73, p. 136; *Sarigiannis v. Italy*, no. 14569/05, § 46, 5 April 2011; *Foka v. Turkey*, no. 28940/95, § 75, 24 June 2008.

[156] *Ječius v. Lithuania*, no. 34578/97, § 50, ECHR 2000-IX; *Schwabe and M.G. v. Germany*, nos. 8080/08 and 8577/08, § 72, ECHR 2011 (extracts); *Włoch v. Poland*, no. 27785/95, § 108, ECHR 2000-XI; *Khachatryan and Others v. Armenia*, no. 23978/06, § 136, 27 November 2012.

[157] *Taran v. Ukraine*, no. 31898/06, § 70, 17 October 2013; *Korneykova v. Ukraine*, no. 39884/05, § 38, 19 January 2012; *Sizarev v. Ukraine*, no. 17116/04, §§161-4, 17 January 2013.

[158] *Lawless v. Ireland (no. 3)*, 1 July 1961, p. 3, § 14, Series A no. 3.

[159] *Schiesser v. Switzerland*, 4 December 1979, § 29, Series A no. 34.

[160] *Ireland v. the United Kingdom*, 18 January 1978, § 199, Series A no. 25.

[161] Ibid.

[162] *Fox, Campbell, and Hartley v. the United Kingdom*, 30 August 1990, § 32, Series A no. 182.

[163] Ibid.

[164] *Murray v. the United Kingdom*, 28 October 1994, § 55, Series A no. 300-A; *Erdagöz v. Turkey*, 22 October 1997, § 51, *Reports of Judgments and Decisions* 1997-VI.

[165] *Brogan and Others v. the United Kingdom*, 29 November 1988, § 53, Series A no. 145-B.

[166] *Stepuleac v. Moldova*, no. 8207/06, § 73, 6 November 2007; *Elci and Others v. Turkey*, nos 23145/93 and 25091/94, § 674, 13 November 2003.

detained person were not an offence at the time of their commission.[167] The production of evidence with the possibility of it being examined and challenged by the detained person is an important safeguard against arbitrary arrest.[168] In a case where detention of demonstrators was justified on the grounds that they had insulted police officers and resisted arrest, but where a video of the events showed this to be a false accusation, the Court said there could be no 'reasonable suspicion' and that consequently the detention was not 'lawful'.[169]

In justifying the reasonableness of arrest and detention, the State may confront particular difficulties in terrorism and organized crime cases, where confidential information cannot be disclosed. However, 'the exigencies of dealing with terrorist crime cannot justify stretching the notion of "reasonableness" to the point where the safeguard secured by Article 5 § 1 (c) is impaired'.[170] In an organized crime case, uncorroborated hearsay evidence from an anonymous informant did not meet the 'reasonable suspicion' requirement.[171]

The term 'offence' has the same meaning as 'criminal offence' in article 6. It must be 'specific and concrete'.[172] Although article 5(1)(c) authorizes arrest and detention to prevent commission of an offence, this phrase cannot be taken to allow a policy of general prevention directed against an individual or a category of individuals who, like mafiosi, present a danger on account of their continuing propensity to crime.[173] Such an interpretation is confirmed by the use of the word 'offence' (in French, *celle-ci*) in the singular[174] as well as by the general purpose of article 5, which is to ensure that no person is dispossessed of liberty in an arbitrary fashion.[175] A practice in Ukraine of holding defendants in custody solely because a bill of indictment has been submitted to the trial court, with the consequence that they may be deprived of liberty indefinitely without any judicial authorization, has been deemed to lack certainty and violate the norm against arbitrariness.[176]

Detention pursuant to article 5(1)(c) involves a proportionality requirement.[177] The Court may consider whether detention in custody is strictly necessary or whether presence at trial can be ensured using less stringent measures sufficient for such a purpose.[178] In assessing the risk of flight should the person be released pending trial, the Court considers the relevance of a broad range of factors, including a person's character, morals, home,

---

[167] *Khachatryan and Others v. Armenia*, no. 23978/06, §§ 136, 138, 27 November 2012; *Kandzhov v. Bulgaria*, no. 68294/01, § 136, 6 November 2008.

[168] *Pichugin v. Russia*, no. 38623/03, § 126, 23 October 2012.

[169] *Brega and Others v. Modova*, no. 61485/08, § 42, 24 January 2012.

[170] *O'Hara v. the United Kingdom*, no. 37555/97, § 35, ECHR 2001-X.

[171] *Labita v. Italy* [GC], no. 26772/95, § 156 et seq., ECHR 2000-IV.

[172] *Ciulla v. Italy*, 22 February 1989, § 40, Series A no. 148.

[173] *Guzzardi v. Italy*, 6 November 1980, § 102, Series A no. 39; *Al Husin v. Bosnia and Herzegovina*, no. 3727/08, § 65, 7 February 2012.

[174] *Matznetter v. Austria*, 10 November 1969, Concurring Opinion of Judge G. Balladore Pallieri, Series A no. 10; Ibid., Dissenting Opinion of Judge M. Zekia.

[175] *Winterwerp v. the Netherlands*, 24 October 1979, § 37, Series A no. 33; *Guzzardi v. Italy*, 6 November 1980, § 102, Series A no. 39; *M. v. Germany*, no. 19359/04, § 89, ECHR 2009.

[176] *Taran v. Ukraine*, no. 31898/06, § 67, 17 October 2013; *Kharchenko v. Ukraine*, no. 40107/02, § 71, 10 February 2011; *Tsygoniy v. Ukraine*, no. 19213/04, § 60, 24 November 2011; *Kucherenko v. Ukraine*, no. 27347/02, §§ 35–38, 15 December 2005; *Yeloyev v. Ukraine*, no. 17283/02, § 50, 6 November 2008.

[177] *Ladent v. Poland*, no. 11036/03, § 55, 18 March 2008.

[178] *Ambruszkiewicz v. Poland*, no. 38797/03, §§ 29–32, 4 May 2006.

occupation, assets, and family ties, as well as the expected length of the sentence and the weight of evidence.[179]

Minors (art. 5(1)(d))

The fourth category of permissible deprivation of liberty concerns minors. They may be detained on two grounds: for the purpose of educational supervision; or for the purpose of bringing the minor before the competent legal authority. Paragraph (d) has been described as 'a specific, but not exhaustive, example of circumstances in which minors might be detained'.[180] Obviously, minors may also be detained pursuant to the other sub-paragraphs of article 5(1).[181] The term 'minor' has been held to encompass persons under the age of eighteen.[182] The European Commission, in a 1979 decision, considered that an adolescent of sixteen was a 'minor' for the purposes of article 5(1), noting that none of the States Parties to the Convention had an age of majority lower than eighteen.[183] But this is no longer the case since 1991, when Scotland set the age of majority at sixteen.[184]

Detention for the purpose of 'educational supervision' may be given a very broad reading, in effect providing the state with justification for compulsory attendance at school, which obviously amounts to a deprivation of liberty. Indeed, human rights law requires States to ensure compulsory education at the primary level. The words 'educational supervision' should not be 'equated rigidly with notions of classroom teaching. Such supervision must embrace many aspects of the exercise, by the authority, of parental rights for the benefit and protection of the person concerned.'[185]

Sub-paragraph (d) applies to all minors and not only persons below the official school leaving age. The fact that an individual can no longer be required to attend ordinary school does not prevent a detention order being made to the extent that it is 'for the purpose of educational supervision'.[186] Where an adolescent was detained in order to prevent her from obtaining an abortion, the Court held that article 5(1)(d) could not apply because 'by no stretch of the imagination can the detention be considered to have been ordered for educational supervision'.[187] Nor did the Court consider detention in a penal facility where educational activities were entirely voluntary and optional as being 'for the purpose of educational supervision'.[188]

The Court has considered that a juvenile holding facility, where adolescents were temporarily detained for various reasons including criminal prosecution, did not amount

---

[179] *Aleksandr Novikov v. Russia*, no. 7087/04, § 46, 11 July 2013; *Becciev v. Moldova*, no. 9190/03, § 58, 4 October 2005. The relevant case law of the European Court has been considered in decisions of the International Criminal Court. See, for example, *Prosecutor v. Bemba and Others* (ICC-Oll05-01l13 OA 2), Judgment on the appeal of Mr Aimé Kilolo Musamba against the decision of Pre-Trial Chamber II of 14 March 2014 entitled 'Décision on the "Demande de mise en liberté provisoire de Maître Aimé Kilolo Musamba"', 11 July 2014, para. 111.

[180] *Mubilanzila Mayeka and Kaniki Mitunga v. Belgium*, no. 13178/03, § 100, ECHR 2006-XI.

[181] For an example where this was considered, see *Ichin and Others v. Ukraine*, nos 28189/04 and 28192/04, § 37, 21 December 2010.

[182] *Koniarska v. the United Kingdom* (dec.), no. 33670/96, 12 October 2000.

[183] *X v. Switzerland*, no. 8500/79, Commission decision of 14 December 1979, DR 18, p. 244.

[184] Age of Legal Capacity (Scotland) Act 1991 (*c.*50).

[185] *Ichin and Others v. Ukraine*, nos 28189/04 and 28192/04, § 39, 21 December 2010; *D.G. v. Ireland*, no. 39474/98, § 80, ECHR 2002-III.

[186] *Koniarska v. the United Kingdom* (dec.), no. 33670/96, 12 October 2000; *D.G. v. Ireland*, no. 39474/98, § 76, ECHR 2002-III.

[187] *P. and S. v. Poland*, no. 57375/08, § 148, 30 October 2012.

[188] *D.G. v. Ireland*, no. 39474/98, § 81, ECHR 2002-III.

to 'educational supervision' and that therefore sub-paragraph (d) was inapplicable.[189] But the words 'for the purpose of' indicate that confinement of a juvenile in a remand prison does not necessarily breach sub-paragraph (d), even if it is not specifically directed at 'educational supervision' to the extent that it is a means of ensuring that the minor is placed under 'educational supervision'. In other words, sub-paragraph (d) 'does not preclude an interim custody measure being used as a preliminary to a regime of supervised education, without itself involving any supervised education'. However, any such imprisonment 'must be speedily followed by actual application of such a regime in a setting (open or closed) designed and with sufficient resources for the purpose'.[190]

Under the second limb of sub-paragraph (d), detention of a minor may be authorized in order to bring him or her before the competent legal authority.

Medical or social reasons (art. 5(1)(e))

Medical and social reasons may justify the restriction on liberty of individuals, including their detention. Article 5(1)(e) enables detention in a general sense with respect to medical or social reasons. It provides an enumeration of several categories of persons: those spreading infectious diseases, persons of unsound mind, alcoholics, drug addicts, and vagrants. There is an assumption implied in the provision that such persons may be deprived of their liberty either in order to be given medical treatment or because of considerations dictated by social policy, or on both medical and social grounds.[191] According to the Court, the Convention allows such individuals, 'all of whom are socially maladjusted', to be deprived of their liberty both because 'they have to be considered as occasionally dangerous for public safety but also [because] their own interests may necessitate their detention'.[192]

The first ground for detention listed in the sub-paragraph is prevention of the spreading of infectious diseases. In determining the lawfulness of such detention, there are two main criteria: spreading of the disease must be dangerous to public health or safety; and measures less severe than detention must have been considered and been found to be insufficient to safeguard the public interest.[193]

'Persons of unsound mind' is the second category for which detention is authorized under article 5(1)(e) of the Convention. In the application of this provision, the Court applies what are sometimes called 'Winterwerp criteria', after the case in which they were set out: the person must reliably be shown to be of unsound mind; the mental disorder must be of a kind or degree warranting confinement without consent; and the continued validity of detention depends upon the persistence of the disorder.[194] Although the term 'person of unsound mind' evades precise definition, it cannot be used to permit detention of someone simply because his or her views or behaviour deviate from

---

[189] *Ichin and Others v. Ukraine*, nos 28189/04 and 28192/04, § 39, 21 December 2010.
[190] *Bouamar v. Belgium*, 29 February 1988, § 50, Series A no. 129; *A. and Others v. Bulgaria*, no. 51776/08, § 69, 29 November 2011.
[191] *Enhorn v. Sweden*, no. 56529/00, § 43, ECHR 2005-I.
[192] *Guzzardi v. Italy*, 6 November 1980, § 98, Series A no. 39. Also: *Witold Litwa v. Poland*, no. 26629/95, § 60, ECHR 2000-III.
[193] *Enhorn v. Sweden*, no. 56529/00, § 44, ECHR 2005-I.
[194] *Winterwerp v. the Netherlands*, 24 October 1979, § 39, Series A no. 33; *Varbanov v. Bulgaria*, no. 31365/96, § 45, ECHR 2000-X; *Hutchison Reid v. the United Kingdom*, no. 50272/99, § 48, ECHR 2003-IV; *Stanev v. Bulgaria* [GC], no. 36760/06, § 145, ECHR 2012; *S.R. v. the Netherlands* (dec.), no. 13837/07, § 29, 18 September 2012.

established norms.[195] National authorities are given a margin of discretion in deciding whether a person is 'of unsound mind'.[196] Nevertheless, if it is to show deference to the national authorities, 'the Court must be satisfied that they have assessed and scrutinised the pertinent issues thoroughly. These principles are fully applicable to situations of deprivation of liberty, given the fundamental importance of this right in a democratic society.'[197] Detention pursuant to sub-paragraph (e) should not be confused with detention for the purpose of a psychiatric examination, which is governed by sub-paragraph (b).[198]

Detention of a person by reason of 'unsound mind' may be necessary not only to provide clinical treatment in order to address the condition but also to provide control and supervision, and in order to prevent the individual from causing harm.[199] In making the assessment, the relevant point in time for the purposes of article 5(1)(e) is the date when the measure depriving the person of liberty is adopted.[200] Evaluating whether the medical evidence indicates recovery may take some time,[201] but continued deprivation of liberty for purely administrative reasons is not justified.[202] Detention of persons of unsound mind on the basis of article 5(1)(e) must take place in a hospital, clinic, or other suitable institution properly authorized for this purpose.[203] It is permitted on a temporary basis to detain a person in an institution not specifically designed for persons of 'unsound mind', providing the waiting period for transfer to an appropriate facility is not excessive.[204]

The Court has considered that an 'alcoholic' need not be someone in a clinical state of alcoholism.[205] The provision has been viewed broadly as permitting detention in order to prevent alcohol abuse and to prevent dangerous conduct by persons following the consumption of drink.[206] On this point, the Court noted that when the Convention was being drafted, the Committee of Experts 'had no doubt that this could be agreed "since such restrictions were justified by the requirements of public morality and order"'.[207] According to the Court, not only may the harmful use of alcohol represent a danger to society, 'a person who is in a state of intoxication may pose a danger to himself and others, regardless of whether or not he is addicted to alcohol'.[208] Where conduct and behaviour poses a threat to public order or to the individual concerned, article 5(1)(e) permits detention in order to protect both the public and the person who is abusing alcohol.[209] Nevertheless, the Convention does not allow the detention of a person solely because of high alcohol intake.[210]

---

[195] *Rakevich v. Russia*, no. 58973/00, § 26, 28 October 2003.
[196] *H.L. v. the United Kingdom*, no. 45508/99, § 98, ECHR 2004-IX.
[197] *Anatoliy Rudenko v. Ukraine*, no. 50264/08, § 101, 17 April 2014.
[198] *Petukhova v. Russia*, no. 28796/07, § 49, 2 May 2013.
[199] *Hutchison Reid v. the United Kingdom*, no. 50272/99, § 52, ECHR 2003-IV.
[200] *O.H. v. Germany*, no. 4646/08, § 78, 24 November 2011.
[201] *Luberti v. Italy*, 23 February 1984, § 28, Series A no. 75.
[202] *R.L. and M.-J.D. v. France*, no. 44568/98, § 129, 19 May 2004.
[203] *Ashingdane v. the United Kingdom*, 28 May 1985, § 44, Series A no. 93; *O.H. v. Germany*, no. 4646/08, § 79, 24 November 2011.
[204] *Pankiewicz v. Poland*, no. 34151/04, §§ 44–45, 12 February 2008; *Morsink v. the Netherlands*, no. 48865/99, §§ 67–69, 11 May 2004; *Brand v. the Netherlands*, no. 49902/99, §§ 64–66, 11 May 2004.
[205] *Witold Litwa v. Poland*, no. 26629/95, § 61, ECHR 2000-III.
[206] *Kharin v. Russia*, no. 37345/03, § 34, 3 February 2011; *S. v. Germany*, no. 3300/10, § 83, 28 June 2012.
[207] *Witold Litwa v. Poland*, no. 26629/95, § 51, ECHR 2000-III.
[208] Ibid.
[209] *Hilda Hafsteinsdóttir v. Iceland*, no. 40905/98, § 42, 8 June 2004; *Djundiks v. Latvia*, no. 14920/05, § 87, 15 April 2014.
[210] *Witold Litwa v. Poland*, no. 26629/95, §§ 61–62, ECHR 2000-III.

The final category contemplated by article 5(1)(e) is 'vagrants'. This is a rather archaic provision, reflecting views that still prevailed in some parts of Western Europe in the late 1940s but that are almost certainly obsolete today. In an early case, the Court adopted three criteria derived from Belgian law: persons who have no fixed abode, no means of subsistence, and no regular trade or profession.[211] In one of the few cases dealing with this concept, the Court ruled that Italy could not invoke 'vagrancy' in a case where it had imposed compulsory residence on an island for someone suspected of being a *mafioso*. The agent for Italy had described the applicant as 'a vagrant in the wide sense of the term' (*vagabondo nel senso largo dell'espressione*) and 'a monied vagrant' (*vagabondo ricco*), but the Court insisted that the exceptions allowed by article 5(1) required a narrow interpretation and held that there had been a violation of the Convention.[212]

Detention to prevent entry or for expulsion and deportation (art. 5(1)(f))

Sub-paragraph (f) of article 5(1) permits States to arrest and detain persons in order to prevent unauthorized entry into the country and for the purposes of deportation or extradition. There is no doubt that the Convention allows States to control the liberty of aliens in an immigration context. States Parties to the Convention have an 'undeniable sovereign right to control aliens' entry into and residence in their territory'.[213] This necessarily implies that States may detain would-be immigrants who have applied for permission to enter, whether by way of asylum or not.[214]

Unlike other sub-paragraphs of article 5(1), and notably article 5(1)(c), there is no requirement in article 5(1)(f) that detention be justified by protection of crime or public safety, or out of concern for the individual being detained. It does not demand that detention be considered reasonably necessary, for example to prevent the individual from committing an offence or fleeing.[215] All the provision requires is that detention be directed at preventing unauthorized entry or at removal from the country. It is therefore immaterial whether the underlying decision to expel can be justified under national or Convention law.[216] But where proceedings are not underway to expel or extradite a person, the exception of 5(1)(f) does not apply. Detention must be carried out in good faith, it must be closely connected to the purpose of preventing unauthorized entry, deportation, or extradition, the place and conditions of detention should be appropriate, and the length of the detention should not exceed that reasonably required for the purpose being pursued.[217] Deprivation of liberty in view of deportation or extradition can only be justified as long as proceedings are underway. If they are not conducted with due diligence, a violation of article 5(1)(f) may arise.[218]

---

[211] *De Wilde, Ooms, and Versyp v. Belgium*, 18 June 1971, § 68, Series A no. 12.

[212] *Guzzardi v. Italy*, 6 November 1980, § 98, Series A no. 39.

[213] *Amuur v. France*, 25 June 1996, § 41, *Reports of Judgments and Decisions* 1996-III; *Abdulaziz, Cabales and Balkandali v. the United Kingdom*, 28 May 1985, §§ 67–68, Series A no. 94.

[214] *Saadi v. the United Kingdom* [GC], no. 13229/03, § 64, ECHR 2008.

[215] *Al Husin v. Bosnia and Herzegovina*, no. 3727/08, § 61, 7 February 2012.

[216] *Chahal v. the United Kingdom*, 15 November 1996, § 112, *Reports of Judgments and Decisions* 1996-V; *Čonka v. Belgium*, no. 51564/99, § 38, ECHR 2002-I; *Nasrulloyev v. Russia*, no. 656/06, § 69, 11 October 2007; *Soldatenko v. Ukraine*, no. 2440/07, § 109, 23 October 2008.

[217] *Saadi v. the United Kingdom* [GC], no. 13229/03, § 74, ECHR 2008; *Yoh-Ekale Mwanje v. Belgium*, no. 10486/10, §§ 117–119, 20 December 2011; *Gebremedhin [Gaberamadhien] v. France*, no. 25389/05, § 74, ECHR 2007-II.

[218] *A. and Others v. the United Kingdom* [GC], no. 3455/05, § 164, ECHR 2009; *Chahal v. the United Kingdom*, 15 November 1996, § 113, *Reports of Judgments and Decisions* 1996-V.

The Court has spoken of the two 'limbs' of article 5(1)(f), the first concerning prevention of unauthorized entry, and the second governing removal of persons already on the territory. The principle that detention should not be arbitrary applies to detention under the first limb of article 5(1)(f) in the same manner as it applies to detention under the second limb.[219] When the first limb of article 5(1)(f) is concerned, in determining the place and conditions of detention the State must bear in mind 'that the measure is applicable not to those who have committed criminal offences but to aliens who, often fearing for their lives, have fled from their own country'.[220] Detention under the second limb of article 5(1)(f) may be justified by enquiries from the competent authorities, even if a formal request or an order of extradition has not been issued. Such enquiries may be considered 'actions' taken for the purpose of removal.[221]

The Convention does not prescribe the circumstances for which extradition may be granted or the procedure to be followed. It does not prevent international judicial cooperation between States, and notably extradition for the purposes of bringing fugitive suspects to justice, provided that there is no interference with specific rights recognized by the Convention.[222] In exceptional circumstances, problems may arise, for example where deportation amounts to a disguised form of extradition designed to circumvent a domestic court ruling denying extradition.[223]

In expulsion cases, the Court sometimes requests a stay pending its determination of the merits, given the potential for irreversible harm. Such provisional measures requests are not relevant to the issue of the legality of detention under article 5(1).[224] The fact that the Court's interim measures request blocks the expulsion does not make the detention itself irregular, provided that the authorities continue to seek expulsion and the detention itself is not unreasonably prolonged.[225]

Information on reasons for arrest (art. 5(2))

A person who is arrested must be informed promptly, in a language that he or she understands, of the reasons for arrest and of any charges that have been made. Article 9(2) of the International Covenant on Civil and Political Rights formulates the norm slightly differently: 'Anyone who is arrested shall be informed, at the time of arrest, of the reasons for his arrest and shall be promptly informed of any charges against him.' The right to be informed is an 'elementary safeguard' that constitutes 'an integral part of the scheme of protection afforded by Article 5'. The arrested person 'must be told, in simple, non-technical language that he can understand, the essential legal and factual grounds for

---

[219] *Saadi v. the United Kingdom* [GC], no. 13229/03, § 73, ECHR 2008.

[220] Ibid., § 74.

[221] *X. v. Switzerland*, no. 9012/80, Commission decision of 9 December 1980, (1981) 24 YB 360, DR 24, p. 205.

[222] *Öcalan v. Turkey* [GC], no. 46221/99, § 86, ECHR 2005-IV; *Soering v. the United Kingdom*, 7 July 1989, § 87, Series A no. 161.

[223] *Stocké v. Federal Republic of Germany*, no. 11755/85, Commission report of 12 October 1989, § 189; *Bozano v. France*, 18 December 1986, § 59, Series A no. 111.

[224] *Gebremedhin [Gaberamadhien] v. France*, no. 25389/05, § 74, ECHR 2007-II.

[225] *S.P. v. Belgium* (dec.), no. 12572/08, 14 June 2011; *Yoh-Ekale Mwanje v. Belgium*, no. 10486/10, § 120, 20 December 2011.

his arrest, so as to be able, if he sees fit, to apply to a court to challenge its lawfulness in accordance with paragraph 4'.[226]

Use of the terms 'arrested' and 'charge' in article 5(2) implies that the text belongs to a criminal law context. It might be argued that the scope of article 5(2) is confined to situations of detention contemplated by article 5(1)(c). However, unlike article 5(3), which explicitly applies to article 5(1)(c), article 5(2) has no such formal limitation. The Court has held that article 5(2) should be interpreted 'autonomously' so as to extend the notion of 'arrest' beyond the realm of criminal law. Applying a purposive approach, the Court said that in using the words 'any charge', 'the intention of the drafters was not to lay down a condition for its applicability, but to indicate an eventuality of which it takes account'.[227] It did not in fact refer to the *travaux préparatoires* for evidence of the drafters' intent and instead turned to the text of article 5 itself in order to support its interpretation. The Court noted that article 5(4) was not confined to criminal law situations, and that one of the objectives of article 5(2) was to enable a detained person to exercise the right to challenge detention in accordance with article 5(4).[228] Article 5(2) has been applied in cases of detention for medical reasons,[229] extradition,[230] expulsion,[231] and conditional release from prison.[232]

The information, as article 5(2) makes abundantly clear, must be provided to the individual or to his or her representative.[233] Whether the content and promptness of the information conveyed are sufficient is to be assessed in each case according to its special features.[234] The information need not be related in its entirety by the arresting officer at the very moment of the arrest.[235] Nor is a complete list of the charges against the arrested person required by article 5(2).[236] But 'a bare indication of the legal basis for an arrest cannot, taken on its own, be sufficient'.[237] There is no requirement that the reasons be in writing or in any special form.[238] This is especially true in the case of arrest for purposes of extradition, where the reasons may be even more summary than in the case of arrest for criminal prosecution.[239] This is because a challenge to extradition does not involve

---

[226] *Fox, Campbell and Hartley v. the United Kingdom,* 30 August 1990, § 40, Series A no. 182; *Shamayev and Others v. Georgia and Russia,* no. 36378/02, § 413, ECHR 2005-III.

[227] *Van der Leer v. the Netherlands,* 21 February 1990, § 27, Series A no. 170-A.

[228] Ibid., § 28.

[229] *X v. the United Kingdom,* 5 November 1981, Series A no. 46.

[230] *Shamayev and Others v. Georgia and Russia,* no. 36378/02, ECHR 2005-III.

[231] *Čonka v. Belgium,* no. 51564/99, ECHR 2002-I; *Saadi v. the United Kingdom* [GC], no. 13229/03, ECHR 2008.

[232] *X v. the United Kingdom,* 5 November 1981, Series A no. 46.

[233] *Saadi v. the United Kingdom,* no. 13229/03, § 53, 11 July 2006; *Saadi v. the United Kingdom* [GC], no. 13229/03, §§ 84–85, ECHR 2008.

[234] *Čonka v. Belgium,* no. 51564/99, § 50, ECHR 2002-I.

[235] *Fox, Campbell and Hartley v. the United Kingdom,* 30 August 1990, § 40, Series A no. 182; *Murray v. the United Kingdom,* 28 October 1994, § 72, Series A no. 300-A.

[236] *Bordovskiy v. Russia,* no. 49491/99, § 56, 8 February 2005; *Soysal v. Turkey,* no. 50091/99, § 68, 3 May 2007; *Nowak v. Ukraine,* no. 60846/10, § 63, 31 March 2011; *Gasiņš v. Latvia,* no. 69458/01, § 53, 19 April 2011.

[237] *Kerr v. the United Kingdom* (dec.), no. 40451/98, 7 December 1999; *Murray v. the United Kingdom,* 28 October 1994, § 76, Series A no. 300-A; *Kortesis v. Greece,* no. 60593/10, §§ 61–62, 12 June 2012.

[238] *Kane v. Cyprus* (dec.), no. 33655/06, 13 September 2011; *X. v. Federal Republic of Germany,* no. 8098/77, Commission decision of 13 December 1978, DR 16, p. 111.

[239] *Kaboulov v. Ukraine,* no. 41015/04, § 144, 19 November 2009; *Bordovskiy v. Russia,* no. 49491/99, § 76, 8 February 2005; *K. v. Belgium,* no. 10819/84, Commission decision of 5 July 1984, DR 38, p. 230.

contestation of the charges as such.[240] But whatever the nature of the proceedings, the arrested person must receive information sufficient to enable recourse pursuant to article 5(4).[241]

Reasons for arrest may be provided or become apparent in the course of interrogation or questioning following the arrest.[242] An arrested person cannot claim not to have understood the reasons for arrest when this is apparent from the circumstances.[243] In the *Abdullah Öcalan* case, the Court said that because of the notoriety of the proceedings against him coupled with the illegal nature under Turkish law of the organisation in question, 'the applicant must or should already have been aware at that juncture that he was being arrested for his activities as the leader of a banned organisation, the PKK'.[244] If the warrant of arrest is written in a language that the accused does not understand, the requirements of article 5(2) are complied with if the person is subsequently interrogated and informed of the reasons for arrest in a language that is understood.[245] If the authorities use translators for this purpose, they must make sure that requests for translation are formulated with meticulousness and precision.[246]

As with the content of the information, the promptness of its delivery is also assessed in each case according to its special features.[247] The information must be provided 'promptly' (in French, *dans le plus court délai*).[248] The term 'promptly' is also used in article 5(3), where the Court has distinguished it from the 'the less strict requirement' of 'reasonable time' (*délai raisonnable*) as well as that of 'speedily' (*à bref délai*) with respect to a challenge to detention pursuant to article 5(4).[249] The temporal requirements are met if the arrested person is informed of the reasons within 'a few hours'.[250]

Prompt appearance before judicial authorities (art. 5(3))

Article 5(3) requires that persons arrested or detained in accordance with article 5(1)(c) must be brought promptly before a judge or other officer authorized by law to exercise judicial power. Thus, this requirement applies to those for whom the arrest and detention are associated with prosecution within the criminal justice system and not to the other categories of detention set out in the subparagraphs of article 5(1). The provision entitles persons arrested or detained on suspicion of having committed a criminal offence to a

---

[240] *Bejaoui v. Greece*, no. 23916/94, Commission decision of 6 April 1995; *K. v. Belgium*, no. 10819/84, Commission decision of 5 July 1984, DR 38, p. 230.

[241] *Shamayev and Others v. Georgia and Russia*, no. 36378/02, § 427, ECHR 2005-III.

[242] *Fox, Campbell and Hartley v. the United Kingdom*, 30 August 1990, § 41, Series A no. 182; *Kerr v. the United Kingdom* (dec.), no. 40451/98, 7 December 1999; *Murray v. the United Kingdom*, 28 October 1994, § 77, Series A no. 300-A.

[243] *Dikme v. Turkey*, no. 20869/92, § 54, ECHR 2000-VIII.

[244] *Öcalan v. Turkey* (dec.), no. 46221/99, 14 December 2000.

[245] *Delcourt v. Belgium*, no. 2689/65, Commission decision of 7 February 1967, (1967) 10 YB 238; *Delcourt v. Belgium*, no. 2689/65, Commission decision of 6 April 1967, (1967) 10 YB 282; *Delcourt v. Belgium*, no. 2689/65, Commission report of 1 October 1968, p. 9.

[246] *Shamayev and Others v. Georgia and Russia*, no. 36378/02, § 425, ECHR 2005-III.

[247] *Čonka v. Belgium*, no. 51564/99, § 50, ECHR 2002-I.

[248] *Fox, Campbell and Hartley v. the United Kingdom*, 30 August 1990, § 40, Series A no. 182.

[249] *Brogan and Others v. the United Kingdom*, 29 November 1988, § 59, Series A no. 145-B.

[250] *Fox, Campbell and Hartley v. the United Kingdom*, 30 August 1990, § 42, Series A no. 182; *Kerr v. the United Kingdom* (dec.), no. 40451/98, 7 December 1999.

guarantee against any arbitrary or unjustified deprivation of liberty.[251] Article 5(3) imposes two conditions: prompt access to a judicial authority and consideration by the judicial authority of the merits of the detention. Article 5(1)(c) and article 5(3) are closely associated. The Court has noted that article 5(3) 'forms a whole with paragraph 1 (c)'.[252] But article 5(3) is neither a 'constituent element' of article 5(1)(c) nor a *lex specialis*. It enshrines a specific right applicable to cases that fall under article 5(1)(c), namely to be brought promptly before a judge.[253]

Access to a court in order to supervise deprivation of liberty by the State is an essential feature of the guarantee set out in article 5(3).[254] By requiring judicial control or supervision of any detention by the authorities, article 5(3) affirms the centrality of the rule of law. Reference here is made to the Preamble of the Convention, where there is express reference to the rule of law as 'one of the fundamental principles of a democratic society' from which 'the whole Convention draws its inspiration'.[255] The Court has associated the procedural requirement set out in article 5(3) with the non-derogability of the prohibition of ill-treatment.[256] Article 5(3) does not allow any exceptions to the requirement of prompt appearance before a judicial authority,[257] although derogation from the provision in accordance with article 15(1) of the Convention cannot be ruled out. The right of an accused in detention to have the case examined with particular expedition 'must not unduly hinder the efforts of the judicial authorities to carry out their tasks with proper care'.[258]

The structure of article 5(3) relates to two separate and distinct matters: 'the early stages following an arrest when an individual is taken into the power of the authorities and the period pending eventual trial before a criminal court during which the suspect may be detained or released with or without conditions'.[259] The two limbs of article 5(3) confer distinct rights and are not linked either logically or temporally.[260] The right to appear before a judicial authority has been referred to in the case law as 'the opening part of article 5(3)'.[261] The Court has explained that this judicial control 'serves to provide effective safeguards against the risk of ill-treatment, which is at its greatest in this early stage of detention, and against the abuse of powers bestowed on law enforcement officers or other authorities for what should be narrowly restricted purposes and exercisable strictly in accordance with prescribed procedures'.[262]

---

[251] *Aquilina v. Malta* [GC], no. 25642/94, § 47, ECHR 1999-III; *Assenov and Others v. Bulgaria*, 28 October 1998, § 146, *Reports of Judgments and Decisions* 1998-VIII.

[252] *Aquilina v. Malta* [GC], no. 25642/94, § 47, ECHR 1999-III.

[253] *De Jong, Baljet and Van den Brink v. the Netherlands*, 22 May 1984, §§ 44, 51, Series A no. 77; *Salov v. Ukraine* (dec.), no. 65518/01, 27 April 2004.

[254] *Brogan and Others v. the United Kingdom*, 29 November 1988, § 58, Series A no. 145-B; *Aksoy v. Turkey*, 18 December 1996, § 76, *Reports of Judgments and Decisions* 1996-VI; *Pantea v. Romania*, no. 33343/96, § 236, ECHR 2003-VI (extracts).

[255] *Brogan and Others v. the United Kingdom*, 29 November 1988, § 58, Series A no. 145–B

[256] *Aksoy v. Turkey*, 18 December 1996, § 76, *Reports of Judgments and Decisions* 1996-VI.

[257] *Bergmann v. Estonia*, no. 38241/04, § 45, 29 May 2008.

[258] *Tomasi v. France*, 27 August 1992, § 102, Series A no. 241-A; *Toth v. Austria*, 12 December 1991, § 77, Series A no. 224; *Shabani v. Switzerland*, no. 29044/06, § 65, 5 November 2009; *Sadegül Özdemir v. Turkey*, no. 61441/00, § 44, 2 August 2005.

[259] *Stephens v. Malta (no. 2)*, no. 33740/06, § 52, 21 April 2009.

[260] *T.W. v. Malta* [GC], no. 25644/94, § 49, 29 April 1999.

[261] *Stephens v. Malta (no. 2)*, no. 33740/06, § 52, 21 April 2009.

[262] *Ladent v. Poland*, no. 11036/03, § 75, 18 March 2008.

Judicial control upon arrest or detention must be automatic.[263] It does not depend upon a demand by the person who is arrested and detained.[264] In this respect, it is distinct from the right to challenge detention recognized in article 5(4), whose exercise depends upon the initiative of the person detained or of someone acting on his or her behalf.[265] The automatic nature of the review assured by article 5(3) 'is necessary to fulfil the purpose of the paragraph, as a person subjected to ill-treatment might be incapable of lodging an application asking for a judge to review their detention'.[266] This may also be relevant 'for other vulnerable categories of arrested persons, such as the mentally weak or those who do not speak the language of the judicial officer'.[267]

The review of detention must be 'prompt'. Prompt judicial review of detention is an important safeguard against ill-treatment of the individual who has been taken into custody.[268] The strict time constraint imposed by article 5(3) provides 'little flexibility in interpretation, otherwise there would be a serious weakening of a procedural guarantee to the detriment of the individual and the risk of impairing the very essence of the right protected by this provision'.[269] There are two references to celerity in article 5(3). The Court has noted the distinction between the term 'promptly' (in French, *aussitôt*) in article 5(3) and 'the less strict requirement' of 'reasonable time' (*délai raisonnable*) in terms of being brought to trial, as well as that of 'speedily' (*à bref délai*) with respect to a challenge to detention pursuant to article 5(4).[270] The term 'promptly' (*dans le plus court délai*) also appears in article 5(2). According to the Court, '[t]he use in the French text of the word "aussitôt", with its constraining connotation of immediacy, confirms that the degree of flexibility attaching to the notion of "promptness" is limited, even if the attendant circumstances can never be ignored for the purposes of the assessment under paragraph 3'.[271] In the case law of the Convention organs, a period of four days in detention without appearance before a judge appears to be the maximum that can be tolerated under article 5(3).[272] But periods of less than four days may also be considered unacceptable if the State cannot demonstrate special difficulties or exceptional circumstances that explain why the individual could not appear before judicial authorities any sooner.[273]

The expression 'judge or other officer authorised by law to exercise judicial power' (in French, *un juge ou un autre magistrat habilité par la loi à exercer des fonctions judiciaires*) has been held to have the same meaning as 'competent legal authority' in article 5(1)(c).[274] The term 'judicial power' is broad enough to encompass officials in public prosecution departments as well as sitting judges.[275] It has been noted that the term *magistrat* in the

[263] *De Jong, Baljet and Van den Brink v. the Netherlands*, 22 May 1984, § 51, Series A no. 77.
[264] *Aquilina v. Malta* [GC], no. 25642/94, § 49, ECHR 1999-III; *Viorel Burzo v. Romania*, nos 75109/01 and 12639/02, § 107, 30 June 2009.
[265] *Varga v. Romania*, no. 73957/01, § 52, 1 April 2008.
[266] *McKay v. the United Kingdom* [GC], no. 543/03, § 34, ECHR 2006-X.
[267] *Aquilina v. Malta* [GC], no. 25642/94, § 49, ECHR 1999-III.
[268] *Aksoy v. Turkey*, 18 December 1996, § 76, *Reports of Judgments and Decisions* 1996-VI.
[269] *McKay v. the United Kingdom* [GC], no. 543/03, § 33, ECHR 2006-X.
[270] *Brogan and Others v. the United Kingdom*, 29 November 1988, § 59, Series A no. 145-B.
[271] Ibid.
[272] Ibid., § 62; *Oral and Atabay v. Turkey*, no. 39686/02, § 43, 23 June 2009; *McKay v. the United Kingdom* [GC], no. 543/03, § 47, ECHR 2006-X; *Năstase-Silivestru v. Romania*, no. 74785/01, § 32, 4 October 2007
[273] *İpek and Others v. Turkey*, nos 17019/02 and 30070/02, §§ 36–37, 3 February 2009; *Kandzhov v. Bulgaria*, no. 68294/01, § 66, 6 November 2008.
[274] *Schiesser v. Switzerland*, 4 December 1979, § 29, Series A no. 34.
[275] Ibid.

French version and 'even more "officer" in English manifestly have a wider meaning than "juge" and "judge"'.[276] The Court has noted that many European States recognize such authority to *les magistrats du parquet* who are associated with the office of the public prosecutor as well as full-fledged *juges du siège*.[277] What is important is that the officer be independent and impartial.[278] The officer must have the power to order release.[279] In determining whether the officer meets the requirements of article 5(3), the Court has stressed the importance of 'formal, visible requirements stated in the "law"' as opposed to standard practices.[280] The 'judge or other officer' must be independent of the executive and the parties in the same manner as a tribunal within the meaning of article 6(1) of the Convention.[281]

Use of the word 'brought' indicates that the 'officer' is required by article 5(3) to conduct a hearing before taking the appropriate decision.[282] The Court has explained that the procedural requirements of article 5 are 'more flexible' than those of article 6. This is because detention proceedings 'require special expedition'. Consequently, 'Article 5 does not contain any explicit mention of a right to legal assistance' and 'as a rule, the judge may decide not to wait until a detainee avails himself of legal assistance, and the authorities are not obliged to provide him with free legal aid in the context of the detention proceedings'.[283] This does not mean that a judge is entitled to exclude counsel from the article 5(3) proceeding if the detained person already has retained counsel.[284]

The officer or judge is required to consider the merits of the detention.[285] The review itself must be able to examine the issue of 'lawfulness' and whether there is a reasonable suspicion that the arrested or detained person committed an offence (that is, whether it falls within the terms of article 5(1)(c)).[286] It must also consider whether the detention itself is justifiable.[287]

The Court has said it is both 'good practice' and 'highly desirable in order to minimise delay' that the judicial officer conducting the automatic review prescribed by article 5(3) is

---

[276] Ibid.

[277] Ibid.

[278] *Schiesser v. Switzerland*, 4 December 1979, § 31, Series A no. 34; *Huber v. Switzerland*, 23 October 1990, § 43, Series A no. 188; *Brincat v. Italy*, 26 November 1992, §§ 20–21, Series A no. 249-A; *Hood v. the United Kingdom* [GC], no. 27267/95, § 57, ECHR 1999-I; *Nikolova v. Bulgaria* [GC], no. 31195/96, § 49, ECHR 1999-II; *Pantea v. Romania*, no. 33343/96, § 236, ECHR 2003-VI (extracts).

[279] *Assenov and Others v. Bulgaria*, 28 October 1998, § 146, *Reports of Judgments and Decisions* 1998-VIII; *Nikolova v. Bulgaria* [GC], no. 31195/96, § 49, ECHR 1999-II; *Niedbała v. Poland*, no. 27915/95, § 49, 4 July 2000; *McKay v. the United Kingdom* [GC], no. 543/03, § 40, ECHR 2006-X.

[280] *Duinhof and Duijf v. the Netherlands*, 22 May 1984, § 34, Series A no. 79; *De Jong, Baljet and Van den Brink v. the Netherlands*, 22 May 1984, § 48, Series A no. 77; *Hood v. the United Kingdom* [GC], no. 27267/95, § 60, ECHR 1999-I.

[281] *McKay v. the United Kingdom* [GC], no. 543/03, § 35, ECHR 2006-X.

[282] *Nikolova v. Bulgaria* [GC], no. 31195/96, § 49, ECHR 1999-II; *Schiesser v. Switzerland*, 4 December 1979, § 31, Series A no. 34; *De Jong, Baljet, and Van den Brink v. The Netherlands*, 22 May 1984, § 51, Series A no. 77.

[283] *Lebedev v. Russia*, no. 4493/04, § 84, 25 October 2007.

[284] Ibid., § 91.

[285] *Schiesser v. Switzerland*, 4 December 1979, § 31, Series A no. 34; *Pantea v. Romania*, no. 33343/96, § 231, ECHR 2003-VI (extracts); *Aquilina v. Malta* [GC], no. 25642/94, § 47, ECHR 1999-III; *Krejčíř v. the Czech Republic*, nos 39298/04 and 8723/05, § 89, 26 March 2009.

[286] *McKay v. the United Kingdom* [GC], no. 543/03, § 40, ECHR 2006-X; *Oral and Atabay v. Turkey*, no. 39686/02, § 41, 23 June 2009.

[287] *Aquilina v. Malta* [GC], no. 25642/94, § 52, ECHR 1999-III; *Stephens v. Malta (no. 2)*, no. 33740/06, § 58, 21 April 2009.

also empowered to consider release on bail. This is not a requirement of the Convention, however. There can be two separate procedures conducted by different judicial officers providing that the requirement of promptness is respected.[288]

Trial within reasonable time or release pending trial (art. 5(3))

The second limb of article 5(3) requires that a person arrested and detained pursuant to article 5(1)(c), that is, for the purpose of criminal proceedings, be entitled to trial within a reasonable time or to release pending trial. The text might be read to suggest that the authorities are free to choose between speedy trial or release, but article 5(3) has not been interpreted so as to allow such an option.[289] The person accused can only be detained pending trial if the State can demonstrate that there are 'relevant and sufficient' reasons for this.[290] Even the shortest period of detention requires convincing justification.[291]

In making the determination under article 5(3), the relevant time period begins when the person is taken into custody and ends with a decision on the merits of the charge, even if this is only at first instance.[292] Article 5(3) ceases to apply once a person has been convicted. Then, the individual can no longer be regarded as being detained 'for the purpose of bringing him before the competent legal authority on reasonable suspicion of having committed an offence'. Once he or she is convicted at trial, the person falls under the scope of article 5(1)(a), where deprivation of liberty 'after conviction by a competent court' is authorized.[293]

The settled case law of the Court establishes a presumption under Article 5 in favour of release.[294] This flows from the presumption of innocence and applies until conviction. The equivalent provision in the International Covenant on Civil and Political Rights, article 9(3), is more explicit in this respect, stating that '[i]t shall not be the general rule that persons awaiting trial shall be detained in custody'. According to the Court, 'the purpose of the provision under consideration is essentially to require his provisional release once his continuing detention ceases to be reasonable'.[295] For this reason, '[c]ontinued detention therefore can be justified in a given case only if there are specific indications of a genuine requirement of public interest which, notwithstanding the presumption of innocence, outweighs the rule of respect for individual liberty laid down in Article 5 of the Convention'.[296]

[288] *McKay v. the United Kingdom* [GC], no. 543/03, § 47, ECHR 2006-X.

[289] *Neumeister v. Austria*, 27 June 1968, p. 33, § 4, Series A no. 8; *Idalov v. Russia* [GC], no. 5826/03, § 140, 22 May 2012; *Tase v. Romania*, no. 29761/02, § 40, 10 June 2008; *Belchev v. Bulgaria*, no. 39270/98, § 82, 8 April 2004.

[290] *Musuc v. Moldova*, no. 42440/06, § 40, 6 November 2007; *Yağcı and Sargın v. Turkey*, 8 June 1995, § 52, Series A no. 319-A.

[291] *Tase v. Romania*, no. 29761/02, § 40, 10 June 2008; *Sarban v. Moldova*, no. 3456/05, §§ 95 and 97, 4 October 2005; *Castravet v. Moldova*, no. 23393/05, §§ 32–33, 13 March 2007; *Musuc v. Moldova*, no. 42440/ 06, § 41, 6 November 2007; *Belchev v. Bulgaria*, no. 39270/98, § 82, 8 April 2004.

[292] *Wemhoff v. Germany*, 27 June 1968, p. 19, § 9, Series A no. 7; *Solmaz v. Turkey*, no. 27561/02, §§ 23–24, 16 January 2007; *Kalashnikov v. Russia*, no. 47095/99, § 110, ECHR 2002-VI.

[293] *Belevitskiy v. Russia*, no. 72967/01, § 99, 1 March 2007; *Piotr Baranowski v. Poland*, no. 39742/05, § 45, 2 October 2007; *Górski v. Poland*, no. 28904/02, § 41, 4 October 2005.

[294] *Bykov v. Russia* [GC], no. 4378/02, § 61, 10 March 2009.

[295] *Neumeister v. Austria*, 27 June 1968, p. 33, § 4, Series A no. 8; *Bykov v. Russia* [GC], no. 4378/02, § 61, 10 March 2009.

[296] *Bykov v. Russia* [GC], no. 4378/02, § 62, 10 March 2009; *Kudła v. Poland* [GC], no. 30210/96, §§ 110 et seq., ECHR 2000-XI.

Pre-trial detention of minors is to be used only as a last resort. Where deemed strictly necessary, it should be as short as possible. Detained minors are to be kept separate from adults.[297] In this respect, the International Covenant on Civil and Political Rights provides an explicit guarantee, something lacking in the European Convention.[298] The Convention on the Rights of the Child is similar in scope.[299] The Court has also referred to relevant principles in the European Prison Rules.[300]

The case law recognizes four grounds to refuse bail or interim release. The first is the risk that the accused will fail to appear for trial. The possibility that the accused person would abscond if released pending trial must be assessed in light of a number of relevant factors. The gravity of the possible sentence in the event of conviction cannot be the sole criterion in making such a determination.[301] The existence and persistence of 'serious indications of guilt' is certainly a relevant factor to be considered.[302] Although 'the state of evidence' may provide serious indications of guilt, it alone cannot justify lengthy pre-trial detention.[303]

Matters to be taken into account include the person's character, morals, home, occupation, assets, family ties, and various links with the country in which he is being prosecuted.[304] In one case, the Court observed that the judicial orders authorizing detention on remand 'were based on a brief standard formula that the detention was justified, namely that the applicant had been previously convicted, did not have a place of residence, a job nor a family and that he could commit new offences, and abscond'.[305] The Court held that the mere absence of a fixed residence is insufficient to conclude the existence of a real risk of non-appearance. 'Nor can it be concluded from the lack of a job or a family that a person is inclined to commit new offences', it said, adding that there were doubts that the reasons for detention, 'as reflected in the perfunctorily reasoned court orders, retained their sufficiency for the whole period of the pre-trial detention'.[306] The Court has reasoned that 'the danger of flight necessarily decreases as the time spent in detention passes by for the probability that the length of detention on remand will be deducted from the period of imprisonment which the person concerned may expect if convicted, is likely to make the prospect seem less awesome to him and reduce his temptation to flee'.[307]

The other grounds for denying interim release concern the possibility that if allowed to be at liberty the accused person might take action to prejudice the administration of

---

[297] *Nart v. Turkey*, no. 20817/04, § 31, 6 May 2008; *Güveç v. Turkey*, no. 70337/01, § 109, ECHR 2009 (extracts); *Selçuk v. Turkey*, no. 21768/02, § 35, 10 January 2006; *Koşti and Others v. Turkey*, no. 74321/01, § 30, 3 May 2007.

[298] International Covenant on Civil and Political Rights, (1976) 999 UNTS 171, art. 10(2)(b).

[299] Convention on the Rights of the Child, (1990) 1577 UNTS 3, art. 37(c).

[300] *Nart v. Turkey*, no. 20817/04, §§ 17–22, 6 May 2008. See Recommendation Rec(2006)2 of the Committee of Ministers to member states on the European Prison Rules, Appendix,

[301] *Panchenko v. Russia*, no. 45100/98, § 106, 8 February 2005; *Idalov v. Russia* [GC], no. 5826/03, § 145, 22 May 2012; *Garycki v. Poland*, no. 14348/02, § 47, 6 February 2007; *Chraidi v. Germany*, no. 65655/01, § 40, ECHR 2006-XII; *Ilijkov v. Bulgaria*, no. 33977/96, §§ 80–81, 26 July 2001. But see *Neumeister v. Austria*, 27 June 1968, p. 35, § 10, Series A no. 8.

[302] *Stögmüller v. Austria*, 10 November 1969, p. 40, § 4, Series A no. 9.

[303] *Dereci v. Turkey*, no. 77845/01, § 38, 24 May 2005.

[304] *Neumeister v. Austria*, 27 June 1968, p. 35, § 10, Series A no. 8; *Becciev v. Moldova*, no. 9190/03, § 58, 4 October 2005.

[305] *Sulaoja v. Estonia*, no. 55939/00, § 64, 15 February 2005.

[306] Ibid.

[307] *Neumeister v. Austria*, 27 June 1968, p. 35, § 10, Series A no. 8.

justice, commit further offences, or cause public disorder.[308] The danger that the detained person will hinder the proper conduct of the proceedings if released must be supported by factual evidence.[309] Any justification of detention based upon the requirements of the investigation will diminish with the passage of time.[310] If the possibility that further offences will be committed is relied upon, this must be plausible in light of the circumstances of the case and the history and personality of the suspect and not purely automatic.[311] Previous convictions may indicate a risk that further offences will be perpetrated.[312] Lack of a job or family does not suggest a propensity to re-offend.[313] Preservation of public order may be taken into account in exceptional circumstances, but only where it can be shown that release of the accused would actually pose a threat.[314]

Although reasonable suspicion that the detained person has committed an offence is 'a condition *sine qua non* for the lawfulness of the continued detention' at the preliminary stages, with the passage of time it is no longer sufficient. The Court must then establish if the other grounds given by the judicial authorities of the State continue to justify the deprivation of liberty. In justifying detention, the national judicial authorities must examine all of the relevant facts, setting them out in their decisions on the applications for release.[315] The Court will rely essentially on the reasons given by such decisions in determining whether article 5(3) has been respected.[316] If circumstances that could have warranted a person's detention may have existed but were not mentioned in the domestic decisions, 'it is not the Court's task to establish them and to take the place of the national authorities which ruled on the applicant's detention'.[317]

Arguments for and against release must not be 'general and abstract'.[318] They must contain references to the specific facts and the applicant's personal circumstances justifying detention.[319] Even if such grounds are deemed to be 'relevant' and 'sufficient', the Court must nevertheless also be satisfied that the national authorities have displayed 'special diligence' in conducting the proceedings.'[320] The burden of proof cannot be reversed so as to require the detained person to show reasons justifying release.[321]

---

[308] *Tiron v. Romania*, no. 17689/03, § 37, 7 April 2009; *Smirnova v. Russia*, nos. 46133/99 and 48183/99, § 59, ECHR 2003-IX (extracts); *Piruzyan v. Armenia*, no. 33376/07, § 94, ECHR 2012 (extracts).
[309] *Becciev v. Moldova*, no. 9190/03, § 59, 4 October 2005.
[310] *Clooth v. Belgium*, 12 December 1991, § 44, Series A no. 225.
[311] Ibid., § 40.
[312] *Selçuk v. Turkey*, no. 21768/02, § 34, 10 January 2006; *Matznetter v. Austria*, 10 November 1969, p. 29, § 9, Series A no. 10.
[313] *Sulaoja v. Estonia*, no. 55939/00, § 64, 15 February 2005.
[314] *Letellier v. France*, 26 June 1991, § 51, Series A no. 207; *I.A. v. France*, 23 September 1998, § 104, *Reports of Judgments and Decisions* 1998-VII; *Prencipe v. Monaco*, no. 43376/06, § 79, 16 July 2009; *Tiron v. Romania*, no. 17689/03, §§ 41–42, 7 April 2009.
[315] *Aleksanyan v. Russia*, no. 46468/06, § 179, 22 December 2008.
[316] *Bykov v. Russia* [GC], no. 4378/02, § 63, 10 March 2009; *Weinsztal v. Poland*, no. 43748/98, § 50, 30 May 2006; *McKay v. the United Kingdom* [GC], no. 543/03, § 43, ECHR 2006-X.
[317] *Bykov v. Russia* [GC], no. 4378/02, § 66, 10 March 2009; *Panchenko v. Russia*, no. 45100/98, §§ 99 and 105, 8 February 2005; *Ilijkov v. Bulgaria*, no. 33977/96, § 86, 26 July 2001.
[318] *Clooth v. Belgium*, 12 December 1991, § 44, Series A no. 225; *Boicenco v. Moldova*, no. 41088/05, § 142, 11 July 2006; *Khudoyorov v. Russia*, no. 6847/02, § 175, ECHR 2005-X (extracts).
[319] *Panchenko v. Russia*, no. 45100/98, § 107, 8 February 2005; *Aleksanyan v. Russia*, no. 46468/06, § 179, 22 December 2008.
[320] *Bykov v. Russia* [GC], no. 4378/02, § 64, 10 March 2009; *Letellier v. France*, 26 June 1991, § 35, Series A no. 207; *Yağcı and Sargın v. Turkey*, 8 June 1995, § 50, Series A no. 319-A.
[321] *Aleksanyan v. Russia*, no. 46468/06, § 179, 22 December 2008; *Rokhlina v. Russia*, no. 54071/00, § 67, 7 April 2005; *Ilijkov v. Bulgaria*, no. 33977/96, § 85, 26 July 2001.

In a Russian case, where detention prior to and during trial lasted more than twenty months, the national courts refused an application for release at least ten times, noting in each decision the gravity of the charges and the likelihood of flight, as well as concerns about obstructing the course of justice and of exerting pressure on witnesses. But the European Court explained that 'the judicial decisions did not go any further than listing these grounds, omitting to substantiate them with relevant and sufficient reasons. The Court also notes that with the passing of time the courts' reasoning did not evolve to reflect the developing situation and to verify whether these grounds remained valid at the advanced stage of the proceedings.' Also, at a certain point the decisions extending detention no longer established any time limits, implying that detention would continue until the end of the trial.[322] Any '[q]uasi-automatic prolongation of detention' contravenes article 5(3).[323]

Guarantees to appear for trial (art. 5(3))

The final sentence in paragraph 3 specifies that release may be conditioned upon guarantees to appear for trial. In deciding whether to release or detain an individual, the authorities must consider alternative methods of ensuring appearance at trial.[324] Typically, such a guarantee involves a deposit of money or a bond. Such bail may be imposed only as long as the reasons justifying detention continue.[325] To the extent that a justification for bail remains valid, the amount required is to be 'assessed principally in relation to the person concerned, his assets . . . in other words to the degree of confidence that is possible that the prospect of loss of security in the event of his non-appearance at a trial will act as a sufficient deterrent to dispel any wish on his part to abscond'.[326] Because the purpose is not to ensure reparation for loss, but rather to compel the appearance of the accused, the amount is to be established principally 'by reference to [the accused], his assets and his relationship with the persons who are to provide the security, in other words to the degree of confidence that is possible that the prospect of loss of the security or of action against the guarantors in case of his non-appearance at the trial will act as a sufficient deterrent to dispel any wish on his part to abscond'.[327] The amount that is set must be justified in the decision where bail is set.[328] Any automatic refusal of bail established by law where there is no judicial control is a violation of article 5(3).[329]

Habeas corpus (art. 5(4))

Habeas corpus—the 'great writ'—was present at the birth of human rights litigation. In England, where early codification of human rights provided the models for revolutionary

[322] *Bykov v. Russia* [GC], no. 4378/02, § 65, 10 March 2009.

[323] *Tase v. Romania,* no. 29761/02, § 40, 10 June 2008; *Mansur v. Turkey,* 8 June 1995, § 55, Series A no. 319-B; *Kalashnikov v. Russia,* no. 47095/99, §§ 116–118, ECHR 2002-VI.

[324] *Idalov v. Russia* [GC], no. 5826/03, § 140, 22 May 2012; *Khudoyorov v. Russia,* no. 6847/02, § 184, ECHR 2005-X (extracts); *Lelièvre v. Belgium,* no. 11287/03, § 97, 8 November 2007; *Shabani v. Switzerland,* no. 29044/06, § 62, 5 November 2009.

[325] *Musuc v. Moldova,* no. 42440/06, § 42, 6 November 2007; *Aleksandr Makarov v. Russia,* no. 15217/07, § 139, 12 March 2009.

[326] *Neumeister v. Austria,* 27 June 1968, p. 40, § 14, Series A no. 8.

[327] *Mangouras v. Spain* [GC], no. 12050/04, § 78, ECHR 2010; *Hristova v. Bulgaria,* no. 60859/00, § 111, 7 December 2006; *Toshev v. Bulgaria,* no. 56308/00, §§ 69–73, 10 August 2006.

[328] *Georgieva v. Bulgaria,* no. 16085/02, §§ 15, 30–31, 3 July 2008.

[329] *Piruzyan v. Armenia,* no. 33376/07, § 105, ECHR 2012 (extracts); *S.B.C. v. the United Kingdom,* no. 39360/98, §§ 23–24, 19 June 2001.

texts in France and the United States during the late eighteenth century, *habeas corpus* had already been enshrined for centuries as a fundamental entitlement of the citizen. It was central to the rule of law in its affirmation of an entitlement to have detention reviewed by the courts.

It is the only distinct remedy provision set out in the European Convention. As such, '[a]rticle 5 § 4 provides a *lex specialis* in relation to the more general requirements of Article 13'.[330] It gives a detained person a distinct right to seek judicial review of their detention.[331] Article 5(4) is not adjectival in that it does not depend upon a preliminary finding of a violation of article 5(1) of the Convention. These paragraphs are separate and autonomous. The right to review of detention may be violated even if the detention itself is lawful.[332]

The term 'lawfulness', which is related to the word 'lawful' used in all of the sub-paragraphs of article 5(1), refers to both the procedural and the substantive conditions. This means that 'the "lawfulness" of an "arrest or detention" has to be determined in the light not only of domestic law but also of the text of the Convention, the general principles embodied therein and the aim of the restrictions permitted' by article 5(1).[333] Therefore, the review must be substantive as well as procedural. The person concerned must be able to obtain a review not only of the domestic procedural requirements, in order to ensure that the law has been observed in a more technical sense, but also of the grounds for the detention, including 'the reasonableness of the suspicion grounding the arrest and the legitimacy of the purpose pursued by the arrest and the ensuing detention'.[334] The judicial review is not 'of such breadth as to empower the court, on all aspects of the case including questions of pure expediency, to substitute its own discretion for that of the decision-making authority'.[335] But it must be 'wide enough to bear on those conditions which are essential for the lawful detention of a person according to Article 5 § 1'.[336] The court contemplated by article 5(4) must be able to assess whether there is sufficient evidence to give rise to a reasonable suspicion that the detained person has committed an offence. The existence of such evidence is essential for the detention to be considered 'lawful'.[337]

The procedural fairness requirements under article 5(4) are flexible in that there is no 'uniform, unvarying standard to be applied irrespective of the context, facts and circumstances'.[338] According to the Grand Chamber, it is not always necessary that the procedure required by article 5(4) 'be attended by the same guarantees as those required under Article 6 § 1 of the Convention for criminal or civil litigation', but they must have

---

[330] *A. and Others v. the United Kingdom* [GC], no. 3455/05, § 202, ECHR 2009; *Chahal v. the United Kingdom*, 15 November 1996, § 126, *Reports of Judgments and Decisions* 1996-V; *Bozano v. France*, no. 9990/82, Commission decision of 15 May 1984; *Georgia v. Russia (No. 1)* [GC], no. 31255/07, Partly Dissenting Opinion of Judge López Guerra, Joined by Judges Bratza and Kalaydjieva, 3 July 2014.

[331] *Mooren v. Germany* [GC], no. 11364/03, § 106, 9 July 2009; *Rakevich v. Russia*, no. 58973/00, § 43, 28 October 2003.

[332] *Douiyeb v. the Netherlands* [GC], no. 31464/96, § 57, 4 August 1999; *Kolompar v. Belgium*, 24 September 1992, § 45, Series A no. 235-C.

[333] *Van Droogenbroeck v. Belgium*, 24 June 1982, § 48, Series A no. 50; *Weeks v. the United Kingdom*, 2 March 1987, § 57, Series A no. 114.

[334] *Brogan and Others v. the United Kingdom*, 29 November 1988, § 65, Series A no. 145-B.

[335] *Suso Musa v. Malta*, no. 42337/12, § 50, 23 July 2013.

[336] Ibid.

[337] *Nikolova v. Bulgaria* [GC], no. 31195/96, § 58, ECHR 1999-II.

[338] *A. and Others v. the United Kingdom* [GC], no. 3455/05, § 203, ECHR 2009.

'a judicial character and provide guarantees appropriate to the kind of deprivation of liberty in question'.[339] The proceedings must be adversarial and 'equality of arms' must be ensured between the parties.[340] If the State allows for appeal or review of the article 5(4) determination, the system must in principle accord to the detainee the same guarantees on appeal as at first instance.[341] The judicial review must be conducted by a 'court', although this does not necessarily need to be a classic court within the regular judicial system of a country.[342] This requires appropriate procedural guarantees and a satisfactory level of independence and impartiality with respect to the authorities.[343] The court must also have the power to address thoroughly the illegality of the detention. Therefore, it must have the authority to order release. If it can only make a recommendation, the body does not amount to a 'court' within the meaning of article 5(4).[344]

There are differences in formulation between paragraphs 3 and 4 of article 5 that have led to suggestions that a hearing is not required in the latter case. Paragraph 3 speaks of the 'right to be brought before a judge or other officer', whereas paragraph 4 recognizes a 'right to take proceedings'. The Court has not insisted upon the need for a hearing before the judicial authority in all situations contemplated by article 5(1). Nevertheless, a hearing must take place when sub-paragraphs 5(1)(c) and 5(1)(e) are engaged. It is sufficient if the person concerned is present for the proceedings at first instance; it is not also necessary for the person to be present at an appeal hearing.[345] This is because '[t]he opportunity for a detainee to be heard either in person or through some form of representation features among the fundamental guarantees of procedure applied in matters of deprivation of liberty'.[346] Article 5(4) does not require that a detained person be heard every time he or she lodges an appeal against a decision extending detention. However, it should be possible to exercise the right to be heard at regular intervals.[347]

---

[339] *Idalov v. Russia* [GC], no. 5826/03, § 161, 22 May 2012; *A. and Others v. the United Kingdom* [GC], no. 3455/05, § 203, ECHR 20093. Also *Reinprecht v. Austria*, no. 67175/01, § 31, ECHR 2005-XII; *Winterwerp v. the Netherlands*, 24 October 1979, § 57, Series A no. 33; *Bouamar v. Belgium*, 29 February 1988, §§ 57, 60, Series A no. 129; *Włoch v. Poland*, no. 27785/95, § 125, ECHR 2000-XI.

[340] *A. and Others v. the United Kingdom* [GC], no. 3455/05, § 204, ECHR 2009; *Reinprecht v. Austria*, no. 67175/01, § 31, ECHR 2005-XII; *Mooren v. Germany* [GC], no. 11364/03, § 124, 9 July 2009; *Schöps v. Germany*, no. 25116/94, § 44, ECHR 2001-I; *Lietzow v. Germany*, no. 24479/94, § 44, ECHR 2001-I; *Garcia Alva v. Germany*, no. 23541/94, § 39, 13 February 2001; *Svipsta v. Latvia*, no. 66820/01, § 129, ECHR 2006-III (extracts).

[341] *Kučera v. Slovakia*, no. 48666/99, § 107, 17 July 2007; *Navarra v. France*, 23 November 1993, § 28, Series A no. 273-B; *Toth v. Austria*, 12 December 1991, § 84, Series A no. 224.

[342] *Weeks v. the United Kingdom*, 2 March 1987, § 61, Series A no. 114; *De Wilde, Ooms, and Versyp v. Belgium*, 18 June 1971, §§ 76, 86, Series A no. 12; *X v. the United Kingdom*, 5 November 1981, § 53, Series A no. 46.

[343] *Stephens v. Malta (no. 1)*, no. 11956/07, § 95, 21 April 2009.

[344] *Benjamin and Wilson v. the United Kingdom*, no. 28212/95, §§ 33–34, 26 September 2002; *Singh v. the United Kingdom*, 21 February 1996, §66, *Reports of Judgments and Decisions* 1996-I; *D.N. v. Switzerland* [GC], no. 27154/95, § 39, ECHR 2001-III.

[345] *Nikolova v. Bulgaria* [GC], no. 31195/96, § 58, ECHR 1999-II; *Idalov v. Russia* [GC], no. 5826/03, § 161, 22 May 2012; *A. and Others v. the United Kingdom* [GC], no. 3455/05, § 204, ECHR 2009; *Çatal v. Turkey*, no. 26808/08, § 34, 17 April 2012; *Rahbar-Pagard v. Bulgaria*, nos 45466/99 and 29903/02, § 67, 6 April 2006; *Depa v. Poland*, no. 62324/00, §§ 48–49, 12 December 2006; *Saghinadze and Others v. Georgia*, no. 18768/05, § 150, 27 May 2010.

[346] *Idalov v. Russia* [GC], no. 5826/03, § 161, 22 May 2012. Also *Kampanis v. Greece*, 13 July 1995, § 47, Series A no. 318-B; *De Wilde, Ooms, and Versyp v. Belgium*, 18 June 1971, § 76, Series A no. 12; *Winterwerp v. the Netherlands*, 24 October 1979, § 60, Series A no. 33; *Sanchez-Reisse v. Switzerland*, 21 October 1986, § 51, Series A no. 107.

[347] *Altınok v. Turkey*, no. 31610/08, § 54, 29 November 2011; *Knebl v. the Czech Republic*, no. 20157/05, § 85, 28 October 2010; *Çatal v. Turkey*, no. 26808/08, § 33, 17 April 2012.

If a person is deprived of liberty as a result of conviction for an offence, the judgment imposing a sentence of detention constitutes the judicial determination required by article 5(4). This rule even applies to mandatory life sentences that are 'purely punitive in nature because of the gravity of the offence'.[348] No separate review of legality of detention is required.[349] Nevertheless, in the case of lengthy sentences of imprisonment, 'where the grounds justifying the person's deprivation of liberty are susceptible to change with the passage of time',[350] there may be a justification in periodic review, bringing article 5(4) into play. In the case of discretionary life sentences imposed in the United Kingdom, the Court held that prisoners were entitled to test the legality of their detention 'at reasonable intervals'.[351] One reason is that 'factors of mental instability and dangerousness are susceptible to change over the passage of time and new issues of lawfulness may thus arise in the course of detention'.[352] However, article 5(4) cannot be taken to provide a right to release on parole.[353]

The requirement of judicial review does not extend to providing an appeal from a decision at first instance, nor does it necessitate a review of all aspects of the case so that the discretion of the original decision-maker can be substituted with that of the reviewing body.[354] The appeal respecting detention need not address every issue raised by the applicant, but it must provide for consideration of concrete facts capable of putting in doubt the conditions that are essential for the 'lawfulness' of the detention.[355] The notion of 'lawfulness' in paragraph 4 is the same as in paragraph 1 of article 5. Thus, the review is undertaken not only in light of requirements of domestic law, 'but also of the Convention, the general principles embodied therein and the aim of the restrictions permitted by Article 5 § 1'.[356]

The challenge to detention contemplated by article 5(4) must 'be decided speedily'.[357] The word 'speedily' (in French, *à bref délai*) indicates a lesser degree of urgency than 'promptly' (*aussitôt*), the term used in article 5(3) in the context of appearance before a court upon arrest or detention.[358] Whether the right to a speedy decision has been respected must be determined in the light of the circumstances of each case.[359] When more than one level of jurisdiction is involved in the proceedings, an overall assessment of the time taken is necessary.[360] The Court will begin its consideration of the celerity with the initial challenge to detention, which is often at the administrative level, and not when

---

[348] *Iorgov v. Bulgaria (no. 2)*, no. 36295/02, §§ 73–77, 2 September 2010.

[349] *De Wilde, Ooms, and Versyp v. Belgium*, 18 June 1971, § 76, Series A no. 12.

[350] *Kafkaris v. Cyprus* (dec.), no. 9644/09, § 58, 21 June 2011. Also *Kurt v. Turkey*, 25 May 1998, § 123, *Reports of Judgments and Decisions* 1998-III; *Varbanov v. Bulgaria*, no. 31365/96, § 58, ECHR 2000-X.

[351] *Thynne, Wilson, and Gunnell v. the United Kingdom*, 25 October 1990, § 76, Series A no. 190-A.

[352] Ibid.

[353] *Kafkaris v. Cyprus* (dec.), no. 9644/09, § 58, 21 June 2011.

[354] *A. and Others v. the United Kingdom* [GC], no. 3455/05, § 202, ECHR 2009; *E. v. Norway*, 29 August 1990, § 50, Series A no. 181.

[355] *Ilijkov v. Bulgaria*, no. 33977/96, § 94, 26 July 2001.

[356] *A. and Others v. the United Kingdom* [GC], no. 3455/05, § 202, ECHR 2009.

[357] *Baranowski v. Poland*, no. 28358/95, § 68, ECHR 2000-III; *Idalov v. Russia* [GC], no. 5826/03, § 154, 22 May 2012; *R.M.D. v. Switzerland*, 26 September 1997, § 42, *Reports of Judgments and Decisions* 1997-VI.

[358] *E. v. Norway*, 29 August 1990, § 64, Series A no. 181-A; *Brogan and Others v. the United Kingdom*, 29 November 1988, § 59, Series A no. 145-B.

[359] *Rehbock v. Slovenia*, no. 29462/95, § 84, ECHR 2000-XII.

[360] *Mooren v. Germany* [GC], no. 11364/03, § 106, 9 July 2009; *Navarra v. France*, 23 November 1993, § 28, Series A no. 273-B; *Hutchison Reid v. the United Kingdom*, no. 50272/99, § 78, ECHR 2003-IV.

formal legal proceedings are taken.[361] The relevant time concludes with the final determination of legality of detention, including the appeal if this is possible.[362] This cannot be determined in the abstract[363] but depends upon the circumstances of each case.[364] Relevant circumstances include 'the complexity of the proceedings, their conduct by the domestic authorities and by the applicant and what was at stake for the latter'.[365] Much of the analysis is similar to that undertaken with respect to the requirement of a speedy trial, with both types of proceedings taking into account the diligence of the authorities and any contributing factors attributable to the applicant or victim.[366] But in the case of article 5(4), the requirements are more stringent ('strict standards').[367] The urgency of remedies to challenge detention is underscored by the European Court's reluctance to accept excuses such as a judicial recess or excessive workload.[368] Any prolonged period of time before a decision is taken will attract scrutiny.[369] The European Court of Human Rights has considered a time period of seventeen days for the review of detention to be excessive.[370] It held that twenty-six days for the appeal of a decision was too long.[371]

By its very nature, detention may require periodic review, because an application for release that fails at one point may have more merit with the passage of time. Periodic review of detention on remand may be more frequent than in other situations,[372] given that the detained person benefits from the presumption of innocence.[373]

Detention cases sometimes raise issues of national security. The State authorities may not fully disclose to the individual concerned the information that is available to the decision-maker.[374] The European Court has suggested that the unfairness in such a situation may be addressed through the use of special advocates.[375]

Compensation (art. 5(5))

Article 5(5) recognizes an 'enforceable right to compensation' with respect to '[e]veryone who has been the victim of arrest or detention in contravention of the provisions' of

[361] *Sanchez-Reisse v. Switzerland*, 21 October 1986, § 54, Series A no. 107.
[362] Ibid.; *E. v. Norway*, 29 August 1990, § 64, Series A no. 181-A.
[363] *R.M.D. v. Switzerland*, 26 September 1997, § 42, *Reports of Judgments and Decisions* 1997-VI.
[364] *Rehbock v. Slovenia*, no. 29462/95, § 84, ECHR 2000-XII.
[365] *Mooren v. Germany* [GC], no. 11364/03, § 106, 9 July 2009; *G.B. v. Switzerland*, no. 27426/95, §§ 34–49, 30 November 2000; *M.B. v. Switzerland*, no. 28256/95, §§ 38–43, 30 November 2000.
[366] *Mooren v. Germany* [GC], no. 11364/03, § 106, 9 July 2009; *Kolompar v. Belgium*, 24 September 1992, § 42, Series A no. 235-C; *Rehbock v. Slovenia*, no. 29462/95, § 84, ECHR 2000-XII; *G.B. v. Switzerland*, no. 27426/95, § 33, 30 November 2000; *M.B. v. Switzerland*, no. 28256/95, § 37, 30 November 2000.
[367] *G.B. v. Switzerland*, no. 27426/95, §§ 34–39, 30 November 2000; *M.B. v. Switzerland*, no. 28256/95, §§ 38–43, 30 November 2000; *Panchenko v. Russia*, no. 45100/98, § 117, 8 February 2005.
[368] *E. v. Norway*, 29 August 1990, § 66, Series A no. 181-A; *Bezicheri v. Italy*, 25 October 1989, § 25, Series A no. 164.
[369] *Musiał v. Poland* [GC], no. 24557/94, § 44, ECHR 1999-II; *Koendjbiharie v. the Netherlands*, 25 October 1990, § 29, Series A no. 185-B.
[370] *Kadem v. Malta*, no. 55263/00, §§ 44–45, 9 January 2003.
[371] *Mamedova v. Russia*, no. 7064/05, § 96, 1 June 2006.
[372] *Bezicheri v. Italy*, 25 October 1989, § 21, Series A no. 164.
[373] *Jablonski v. Poland*, no. 33492/96, §§ 91–93, 21 December 2000; *Frasik v. Poland*, no. 22933/02, § 63, ECHR 2010 (extracts).
[374] *Chahal v. the United Kingdom*, 15 November 1996, §§ 130–131, *Reports of Judgments and Decisions* 1996-V.
[375] *A. and Others v. the United Kingdom* [GC], no. 3455/05, § 209, ECHR 2009; *Tinnelly & Sons Ltd and Others and McElduff and Others v. the United Kingdom*, 10 July 1998, § 78, *Reports of Judgments and Decisions* 1998-IV; *Al-Nashif v. Bulgaria*, no. 50963/99, §§ 93–97, 137, 20 June 2002.

article 5. Consequently, article 5(5) presupposes a violation of one of the other provisions of article 5, 'either by a domestic authority or by the Convention institutions'.[376] Effective enjoyment of the right to compensation must be ensured with a sufficient degree of certainty.[377] Article 5(5) does not depend upon a finding by a domestic court that one of the paragraphs of article 5 has been breached.[378]

The Court found that Italian law allowing for compensation—whether the person had been judged to have been unlawfully detained or whether he or she had been acquitted—complied with the requirements of article 5(5).[379] Ukrainian law allowing for compensation only in the case of an ultimate acquittal of a detained person or termination of the criminal proceedings on exonerative grounds was judged by the Court to violate article 5(5).[380] Requiring someone whose claim for compensation had been ignored to reopen proceedings was deemed inconsistent with the provision.[381]

States are free to make compensation dependent upon a demonstration by the victim that damage has resulted from the breach of article 5.[382] The Court has said that in the context of article 5(5), 'the status of "victim" may exist even where there is no damage, but there can be no question of "compensation" where there is no pecuniary or non-pecuniary damage to compensate'.[383] Article 5(5) is respected even if there is no specific remedy, but where an ordinary action in damages against the authorities is possible.[384] Nevertheless, the possibility of reparation through an ordinary damage suit must be realistic.[385] Romania's failure to produce any evidence that such a remedy had been effective led the Court to conclude that article 5(5) had been breached.[386]

The right to compensation does not mean that an applicant is entitled to any particular amount,[387] although it cannot be a trivial or derisory amount[388] or an amount substantially less than awards in similar situations.[389] States may make such an award dependent

[376] *N.C. v. Italy* [GC], no. 24952/94, § 49, ECHR 2002-X; *Pantea v. Romania*, no. 33343/96, § 262, ECHR 2003-VI (extracts); *Vachev v. Bulgaria*, no. 42987/98, § 78, ECHR 2004-VIII (extracts).

[377] *N.C. v. Italy* [GC], no. 24952/94, § 52, ECHR 2002-X; *Sakık and Others v. Turkey*, 26 November 1997, § 60, *Reports of Judgments and Decisions* 1997-VII; *Ciulla v. Italy*, 22 February 1989, § 44, Series A no. 148.

[378] *Blackstock v. the United Kingdom*, no. 59512/00, § 51, 21 June 2005; *Waite v. The United Kingdom*, no. 53236/99, § 73, 10 December 2002. *Harkmann v. Estonia*, no. 2192/03, § 50, 11 July 2006.

[379] *N.C. v. Italy* [GC], no. 24952/94, § 57, ECHR 2002-X.

[380] *Kvashko v. Ukraine*, no. 40939/05, §§ 76–78, 26 September 2013; *Klishyn v. Ukraine*, no. 30671/04, §§ 97–98, 23 February 2012; *Nechiporuk and Yonkalo v. Ukraine*, no. 42310/04, §§ 229–234, 21 April 2011; *Korneykova v. Ukraine*, no. 39884/05, §§ 80–82, 19 January 2012.

[381] *Velinov v. the former Yugoslav Republic of Macedonia*, no. 16880/08, §§ 73–74, 19 September 2013.

[382] *Włoch v. Poland (no. 2)*, no. 33475/08, § 32, 10 May 2011; *Wassink v. the Netherlands*, 27 September 1990, § 38, Series A no. 185-A.

[383] *Wassink v. the Netherlands*, 27 September 1990, § 38, Series A no. 185-A.

[384] *Steel and Others v. the United Kingdom*, 23 September 1998, §83, *Reports of Judgments and Decisions* 1998-VII.

[385] *Fedotov v. Russia*, no. 5140/02, §§ 84–87, 25 October 2005.

[386] *Pantea v. Romania*, no. 33343/96, § 269, ECHR 2003-VI (extracts).

[387] *Damian-Burueana and Damian v. Romania*, no. 6773/02, § 89, 26 May 2009; *Çağdaş Şahin v. Turkey*, no. 28137/02, § 34, 11 April 2006.

[388] *Cumber v. the United Kingdom*, no. 28779/95, Commission decision of 27 November 1996; *Attard v. Malta* (dec.), no. 46750/99, 28 September 2000.

[389] *Ganea v. Moldova*, no. 2474/06, § 30, 17 May 2011; *Boicenco v. Moldova*, no. 41088/05, § 43, 11 July 2006.

upon demonstration of actual damage.[390] However, the Court has warned that an excessively formalist approach may have the consequence of denying compensation in a large number of cases.[391] Although the right to compensation may be broader than that of a financial nature, it does not extend to a right to secure termination of a deprivation of liberty, as this is governed by article 5(4).[392]

Discrimination

As with other provisions of the Convention, issues concerning arrest and detention may involve differential treatment and discrimination in violation of article 14 of the Convention. There have been many general allegations of discrimination in matters governed by article 5, although most have been determined by the Court to be unsubstantiated and have been dismissed at the admissibility stage. Certain principles emerge, mainly from cases involving conditional release or parole following imposition of a prison sentence. Recalling that article 5 does not guarantee a right to automatic parole of persons convicted of an offence,[393] there is nevertheless no doubt that if procedures governing release operate in a discriminatory fashion, article 14 is engaged in conjunction with article 5.[394]

Noting that determinations of parole eligibility were essentially a 'risk assessment exercise', the Court said it could see no justification for a policy of treating prisoners serving determinate terms of less than 15 years, those serving indeterminate terms, and those serving life terms any differently. As a result, all three categories were in an 'analogous position' and thereby governed by article 14.[395] British legislation requiring that prisoners serving indeterminate terms exceeding fifteen years obtain the approval of the Secretary of State, something not required for the other categories, was differential treatment lacking any objective justification and therefore contrary to article 14.[396]

Turkish legislation dealing with treasonous and 'anti-Turkish' conduct did not allow for parole eligibility until three-quarters of the sentence had been served, in contrast with the general rule applicable to ordinary crimes of eligibility after serving one-half the sentence. The Court said that the purpose of the legislation was to treat those convicted of such offences 'less favourably with regard to automatic parole', but deduced from that fact 'that the distinction is made not between different groups of people, but between different types of offence, according to the legislature's view of their gravity'. Therefore, it was not discrimination within the meaning of article 14.[397]

In a German case, social therapy treatments for the purposes of preparing inmates for release were denied to foreign prisoners who were awaiting expulsion upon completion of their prison sentences. The available therapists were considered to be not in a position to prepare prisoners for social integration in countries where they were not familiar with the

---

[390] *Włoch v. Poland (no. 2)*, no. 33475/08, § 32, 10 May 2011; *Wassink v. the Netherlands*, 27 September 1990, § 38, Series A no. 185-A.

[391] *Danev v. Bulgaria*, no. 9411/05, § 34, 2 September 2010.

[392] *Bozana v. France*, no. 9990/82, Commission decision of 15 May 1984, DR 39, p. 119.

[393] *Gerger v. Turkey* [GC], no. 24919/94, § 69, 8 July 1999; *Çelikkaya v. Turkey*, no. 34026/03, § 60, 1 June 2010.

[394] *Gerger v. Turkey* [GC], no. 24919/94, § 69, 8 July 1999; *Çelikkaya v. Turkey*, no. 34026/03, § 63, 1 June 2010; *Clift v. the United Kingdom*, no. 7205/07, § 42, 13 July 2010.

[395] *Clift v. the United Kingdom*, no. 7205/07, §§ 67–68, 13 July 2010.

[396] Ibid., § 78. See, however *King v. the United Kingdom* (dec.), no. 6234/06, 6 March 2007; *McIlvanny v. the United Kingdom* (dec.), no. 6239/06, 6 March 2007.

[397] *Gerger v. Turkey* [GC], no. 24919/94, § 69, 8 July 1999.

living conditions.[398] As a result, 'the applicant was treated differently compared to prisoners in a relevantly similar situation on grounds of his national origin in relation to the order for the execution of his preventive detention. He was denied a chance to fulfil essential preconditions for the domestic courts to conclude that the execution of the preventive detention order against him could be suspended and probation be granted.'[399]

A prisoner detained in a British prison but pursuant to conviction and sentence imposed by the International Criminal Tribunal for the former Yugoslavia challenged the parole eligibility regulations applicable to his situation, which were different from those of other prisoners in the prison. Several countries in Europe and elsewhere have agreements with the International Criminal Tribunal by which they take responsibility for service of sentences within their national prisons. The Tribunal itself has no prison of its own for this purpose, although it retains authority over parole eligibility. The European Court of Human Rights said it was satisfied that there was a difference in treatment and that it related to 'other status' within the terms of article 14, namely that the applicant was a prisoner convicted by the International Criminal Tribunal, but it rejected the complaint because he was not in an 'analogous situation to those convicted by British courts'.[400]

It is not discrimination to provide a different detention regime for adults than for children. Admittedly, the treatment of the two categories is different, but there is an objective and reasonable justification in the protective rather than punitive nature of juvenile detention.[401]

In the *Ireland v. the United Kingdom* inter-State case, the Court noted that extrajudicial powers of detention were only employed initially against persons suspected of IRA terrorism, although subsequently they were used, 'but to a far lesser extent', against so-called Loyalists associated with the Protestant majority.[402] The Court felt this could be explained by 'profound differences between Loyalist and Republican terrorism', the scale of those attributable to the former being 'minute' compared with those of the latter.[403] Subsequently, there was a 'spectacular increase' in Loyalist terrorism, although the British did not react immediately by imposing similar measures to those they had used against the Republican terrorists. The British had denied that there was any difference in treatment, but the Court made the argument for them, holding that the aim of eliminating 'the most formidable organisation first of all' could be regarded as legitimate and not disproportionate.[404]

Reservations

Article 5 has been subject to many reservations. The majority of these have concerned the military discipline regime in force in certain countries, including Armenia,[405] Azerbaijan,[406]

---

[398] *Rangelov v. Germany*, no. 5123/07, § 93, 22 March 2012.
[399] Ibid., § 99.
[400] *Krajisnik v. the United Kingdom* (dec.), no. 6017/11, § 71, 23 October 2012.
[401] *Bouamar v. Belgium*, 29 February 1988, § 66, Series A no. 129.
[402] *Ireland v. the United Kingdom*, 18 January 1978, § 225, Series A no. 25.
[403] Ibid., §§ 226–228.
[404] Ibid., § 230.
[405] (2002) 45 YB 16.
[406] Ibid., pp. 16–17.

Czech Republic,[407] France,[408] Lithuania,[409] Moldova,[410] Portugal,[411] Romania,[412] and Slovakia.[413] Russia's reservation[414] concerning military discipline refers only to paragraphs 3 and 4 of article 5, while Ukraine's reservation[415] refers only to paragraph 3. Spain made a reservation concerning military discipline at the time of reservation.[416] Then, some years later Spain informed the Council of Europe that the relevant legislation had been amended so as to reduce the duration of deprivation of liberty that can be applied without judicial intervention and increase the guarantees of persons during the preliminary investigation. Nevertheless, Spain also confirmed that it maintained its reservation to article 5. The revised reservation was formally deposited as an updated reservation on 23 May 2007. The Court has held Spain's reservation to be inapplicable to the disciplinary regime for the Civil Guard.[417]

Switzerland formulated a reservation to article 5 stating that it 'shall not affect the operation of the cantonal legislation authorising the detention of certain categories of persons by decision of an administrative authority or cantonal provisions governing the procedure for placing a child or ward in an institution in accordance with federal legislation on paternal authority or guardianship'.[418] It was subsequently withdrawn.[419]

Some States with criminal procedure systems that allow detention of suspects upon a determination by the prosecutor, without any judicial intervention, have formulated reservations. Lithuania made a temporary reservation to article 5(3) of the Convention, intended to remain in effect for one year, concerning detention of persons suspected of committing crimes pursuant to a decision of the prosecutor.[420] Considering the validity of the reservation, the Court noted its 'linguistic flaws' but said it was sufficiently clear and precise.[421] The Russian Federation formulated a reservation to paragraphs 3 and 4 of article 5 with respect to procedure for the arrest and detention of persons suspected of committing a criminal offence.[422] It has been held to be compatible with the Convention[423] but has also been subject to a restrictive interpretation.[424] Ukraine made a similar reservation, declaring it to be of temporary effect, from 11 September 1997 until 28 June 2001.[425]

---

[407] As Czechoslovakia: (1992) 35 YB 4. Confirmed by Czech Republic: (1993) 36 YB 6–7.
[408] (1974) 17 YB 4–5.
[409] (1995) 37 YB 17.
[410] (1997) 40 YB 36.
[411] (1978) 21 YB 12–17.
[412] (1994) 37 YB 16.
[413] As Czechoslovakia: (1992) 35 YB 4.
[414] (1998) 41 YB 10.
[415] (1997) 40 YB 44. Amended: (2000) 43 YB 15.
[416] (1979) 22 YB 22–25.
[417] *Dacosta Silva v. Spain*, no. 69966/01, § 38, ECHR 2006-XIII.
[418] (1974) 17 YB 6–7.
[419] (1982) 25 YB EUR.CONV.RES./DECL. 1.
[420] (1995) 38 YB 16–17. Withdrawn: (1996) 39 YB 21.
[421] *Ječius v. Lithuania*, no. 34578/97, § 81, ECHR 2000-IX.
[422] *Boris Popov v. Russia*, no. 23284/04, § 44, 28 October 2010.
[423] *Labzov v. Russia* (dec.), no. 62208/00, 28 February 2002; *Boris Popov v. Russia*, no. 23284/04, § 72, 28 October 2010.
[424] *Kalashnikov v. Russia*, no. 47095/99, §§ 105–108, ECHR 2002-VI. But see *Kalashnikov v. Russia*, no. 47095/99, Separate Concurring Opinion of Judge Kovler, § 1, ECHR 2002-VI.
[425] (1997) 40 YB 44.

In proceedings before the European Court of Human Rights concerning its reservation to paragraphs 3 and 4 of article 5, the government of Ukraine explained that the purpose was to preserve the procedure governing arrest and detention on remand at the time of ratification. Pursuant to the existing procedure, arrest and detention was authorized by a public prosecutor. According to the government, it 'clearly intended to exclude arrest authorised by a judicial officer in the course of a pre-trial investigation from the scope of their obligations under Article 5 of the Convention and to preserve this situation until the amendments to the Code of Criminal Procedure had been introduced'.[426] Eventually, the legislation was changed so that arrest and detention decisions can now only be made by a court. The European Court has ruled that the reservation was validly formulated, in accordance with article 57,[427] but has refused to accept Ukraine's contention that the reservation applies not only to article 5(1) but also to article 5(3). It has noted the distinction with the other Ukrainian reservation, concerning procedure before the military justice system, where express reference is made to article 5(3). Consequently, the Court has held that no reservation has been made to article 5(3) concerning judicial review of detention, aside from the reservation concerning the military justice system.[428]

Andorra made a reservation to article 5, stating that it applied without prejudice to a provision of its constitution: 'Police custody shall take no longer then the time needed to carry out the enquiries in relation to the clarification of the case, and in all cases the detained shall be brought before the judge within 48 hours.'

Austria ratified the Convention with a reservation to article 5 concerning deprivation of liberty prescribed by legislation concerning administrative procedure.[429] It has been upheld in several decisions of the Convention organs.[430]

Serbia and Montenegro made a reservation to paragraphs 1(c) and 3 concerning its legislation whereby detention is mandatory if a person is under reasonable suspicion regarding an offence subject to imprisonment for forty years.[431] Serbia and Montenegro also made a reservation to article 5 declaring that it was subject to its legislation governing minor offences, although the statement did not make it clear what the precise problem was. The declaration stated that the reservation would be withdrawn as soon as the legislation was amended.[432] In 2011, Serbia withdrew the reservation to article 5.[433]

Andorra made a reservation with respect to legislation specifying that '[p]olice cusody shall take no longer than the time needed to carry out enquiries in relation to the clarification of the case, and in all cases the detainee shall be brought before the judge within 48 hours'.[434]

---

[426] *Salov v. Ukraine* (dec.), no. 65518/01, 27 April 2004.

[427] *Falkovych v. Ukraine* (dec.), no. 64200/00, 29 June 2004.

[428] *Salov v. Ukraine* (dec.), no. 65518/01, 27 April 2004; *Falkovych v. Ukraine* (dec.), no. 64200/00, 29 June 2004; *Nevmerzhitsky v. Ukraine*, no. 54825/00, §§ 112–114, ECHR 2005-II (extracts); *Kharchenko v. Ukraine*, no. 40107/02, § 67, 10 February 2011.

[429] (1958-59) 2 YB 88–91.

[430] *Chorherr v. Austria*, 25 August 1993, § 21, Series A no. 266-B; *Schmautzer v. Austria*, 23 October 1995, § 31, Series A no. 328-A; *Umlauft v. Austria*, 23 October 1995, § 34, Series A no. 328-B; *Gradinger v. Austria*, 23 October 1995, § 39, Series A no. 328-C; *Pramstaller v. Austria*, 23 October 1995, § 36, Series A no. 329-A; *Palaoro v. Austria*, 23 October 1995, § 38, Series A no. 329-B; *Pfarrmeier v. Austria*, 23 October 1995, § 35, Series A no. 329-C.

[431] (2004) 48 YB 21.

[432] (2004) 48 YB 22; (2006) 49 YB 8.

[433] (2011) 54 YB 8–9.

[434] (1996) 39 YB 19.

Moldova made a reservation to article 5(3) 'with a view to extending the validity of an arrest warrant issued by the public prosecutor'. The reservation specified that it would be valid for six months.[435]

Further reading

Edwin Bleichrodt, 'Right to Liberty and Security of Person (Article 5)', in Van Dijk et al., *Theory and Practice*, pp. 455–509.

Frowein/Peukert, *MenschenRechtsKonvention*, pp. 70–139.

C.A. Gearty, 'The European Court of Human Rights and the Protection of Civil Liberties: An Overview', (1993) 52 *Cambridge Law Journal* 89.

Regis de Gouttes, 'Article 5§2', in Pettiti et al., *La Convention européenne*, pp. 203–1.

Grabenwarter, *European Convention*, pp. 61–97.

Harris et al., *Law of the European Convention*, pp. 121–200.

Renée Koering-Joulin, 'Article 5§4', in Pettiti et al., *La Convention européenne*, pp. 229–38.

Jan de Meyer, 'Article 5§1', in Pettiti et al., *La Convention européenne*, pp. 189–201.

Egbert Myjer, 'The Plain Meaning of the Word "Promptly"', in Mahoney et al., *Mélanges Ryssdal*, pp. 975–92.

Ovey/White, *Jacobs and White, European Convention*, pp. 102–38.

Michèle Picard and Patrick Titiun, 'Article 5§3', in Pettiti et al., *La Convention européenne*, pp. 211–27.

---

[435] (1997) 40 YB 36.

Article 6. Right to a fair trial/Droit à un procès équitable

1. In the determination of his civil rights and obligations or of any criminal charge against him, everyone is entitled to a fair and public hearing within a reasonable time by an independent and impartial tribunal established by law. Judgment shall be pronounced publicly but the press and public may be excluded from all or part of the trial in the interests of morals, public order or national security in a democratic society, where the interests of juveniles or the protection of the private life of the parties so require, or to the extent strictly necessary in the opinion of the court in special circumstances where publicity would prejudice the interests of justice.

2. Everyone charged with a criminal offence shall be presumed innocent until proved guilty according to law.

3. Everyone charged with a criminal offence has the following minimum rights:

(a) to be informed promptly, in a language which he understands and in detail, of the nature and cause of the accusation against him;

(b) to have adequate time and facilities for the preparation of his defence;

(c) to defend himself in person or through legal assistance of his own choosing or, if he has not sufficient means to pay for legal assistance, to be given it free when the interests of justice so require;

(d) to examine or have examined witnesses against him and to obtain the attendance and examination of witnesses on his behalf under the same conditions as witnesses against him;

(e) to have the free assistance of an interpreter if he cannot understand or speak the language used in court.

1. Toute personne a droit à ce que sa cause soit entendue équitablement, publiquement et dans un délai raisonnable, par un tribunal indépendant et impartial, établi par la loi, qui décidera, soit des contestations sur ses droits et obligations de caractère civil, soit du bien-fondé de toute accusation en matière pénale dirigée contre elle. Le jugement doit être rendu publiquement, mais l'accès de la salle d'audience peut être interdit à la presse et au public pendant la totalité ou une partie du procès dans l'intérêt de la moralité, de l'ordre public ou de la sécurité nationale dans une société démocratique, lorsque les intérêts des mineurs ou la protection de la vie privée des parties au procès l'exigent, ou dans la mesure jugée strictement nécessaire par le tribunal, lorsque dans des circonstances spéciales la publicité serait de nature à porter atteinte aux intérêts de la justice.

2. Toute personne accusée d'une infraction est présumée innocente jusqu'à ce que sa culpabilité ait été légalement établie.

3. Tout accusé a droit notamment à:

(a) être informé, dans le plus court délai, dans une langue qu'il comprend et d'une manière détaillée, de la nature et de la cause de l'accusation portée contre lui;

(b) disposer du temps et des facilités nécessaires à la préparation de sa défense;

(c) se défendre lui-même ou avoir l'assistance d'un défenseur de son choix et, s'il n'a pas les moyens de rémunérer un défenseur, pouvoir être assisté gratuitement par un avocat d'office, lorsque les intérêts de la justice l'exigent;

(d) interroger ou faire interroger les témoins à charge et obtenir la convocation et l'interrogation des témoins à décharge dans les mêmes conditions que les témoins à charge;

(e) se faire assister gratuitement d'un interprète, s'il ne comprend pas ou ne parle pas la langue employée à l'audience.

Introductory comments

The right to a fair trial is important in and of itself. But it is also quite central to the enforcement and vindication of the other fundamental rights. The 'rule of law', which is set out in the Preamble to the Convention and which is central to its vision, cannot exist if there is no fair trial. The European Court has often spoken of 'the prominent place held in a democratic society by the right to a fair trial'.[1]

The Universal Declaration of Human Rights provides for the right to a fair trial in two provisions, articles 10 and 11:

Article 10
Everyone is entitled in full equality to a fair and public hearing by an independent and impartial tribunal, in the determination of his rights and obligations and of any criminal charge against him.

Article 11
(1) Everyone charged with a penal offence has the right to be presumed innocent until proved guilty according to law in a public trial at which he has had all the guarantees necessary for his defence.
(2) No one shall be held guilty of any penal offence on account of any act or omission which did not constitute a penal offence, under national or international law, at the time when it was committed. Nor shall a heavier penalty be imposed than the one that was applicable at the time the penal offence was committed.

The Universal Declaration of Human Rights recognizes the difference between civil or administrative ('rights and obligations') and criminal trials, something that corresponds to a distinction familiar to most if not all legal systems. Article 10 applies to both categories, whereas article 11 is only applicable to a person charged with a 'penal offence'. The distinction between civil or administrative proceedings and the criminal trial is maintained in the European Convention on Human Rights but with some modification in the presentation. Paragraphs 1 of articles 10 and 11 become the two first paragraphs of article 6, while paragraph 2 of article 11 becomes a distinct provision, article 7. Moreover, in the third paragraph of article 6 of the Convention a new concept is introduced of somewhat detailed minimum guarantees applicable in a criminal trial.

This detailed codification of minimum guarantees in a criminal trial was further developed in article 14 of the International Covenant on Civil and Political Rights, where additional rights to those in the European Convention on Human Rights were set out. In turn, the Council of Europe incorporated most of these additional rights by means of Protocol No. 7 to the European Convention.

Article 47 of the Charter of Fundamental Rights of the European Union guarantees the right to a fair trial in the following terms:

Article 47. Right to an effective remedy and to a fair trial
Everyone whose rights and freedoms guaranteed by the law of the Union are violated has the right to an effective remedy before a tribunal in compliance with the conditions laid down in this Article.

Everyone is entitled to a fair and public hearing within a reasonable time by an independent and impartial tribunal previously established by law. Everyone shall have the possibility of being advised, defended and represented.

---

[1] *Andrejeva v. Latvia* [GC], no. 55707/00, § 98, ECHR 2009; *Prince Hans-Adam II of Liechtenstein v. Germany* [GC], no. 42527/98, § 45, ECHR 2001-VIII.

Legal aid shall be made available to those who lack sufficient resources in so far as such aid is necessary to ensure effective access to justice.

The second and third paragraphs of article 47 of the European Charter correspond to article 6(1) of the Convention, but the limitation to the determination of civil rights and obligations or criminal charges does not apply as regards Union law and its implementation,[2] as has been noted by the Grand Chamber.[3] Article 47 is meant to have the same meaning and scope as paragraphs 2 and 3 of article 6 of the European Convention.[4]

Drafting of the provision

The initial draft European Convention on Human Rights prepared by the International Juridical Section of the European Movement did not contain a provision that in any way resembles the fair trial guarantees set out in article 6.[5] This seems surprising given the recognition of fair trial guarantees in articles 10 and 11 of the Universal Declaration of Human Rights and the fact that the subject had been part of the debate about human rights since January 1946, when Cuba submitted a proposed draft declaration to the United Nations Economic and Social Council.[6] There was a reference by a Belgian delegate, M. Fayat, during the first Plenary Sitting of the Consultative Assembly of the Council of Europe, on 19 August 1949, to 'the necessity of having a magistrature independent of parliamentary majorities and of the executive power'. Fayat said that the convention 'must take into account not only the substance of these freedoms, but also the political and legal safeguards by which these freedoms must be protected'.[7] One of the Irish delegates, Sean MacEntee, said that the first twelve articles of the Universal Declaration of Human Rights should be accepted 'without reservation', thereby implying the fair trial guarantees of articles 10 and 11.[8]

The final proposal of the Consultative Assembly did not incorporate a fair trial provision. The issue of fair trial appears to have been dealt with entirely as an adjectival matter and in the context of the jurisdiction of the European Court. If rights were denied as a result of an unfair trial, the European Court would then be entitled to review the decision of the national courts. The Draft Recommendation of the Consultative Assembly to the Committee of Ministers contained the following: 'Freedom from arbitrary arrest, detention and other measures in accordance with Articles 9, 10 and 11 of the United Nations Declaration'.[9]

---

[2] Explanation relating to the Charter of Fundamental Rights, Official Journal of the European Union, C 303/34, 14 December 2007.

[3] *Micallef v. Malta* [GC], no. 17056/06, § 32, ECHR 2009.

[4] Explanation relating to the Charter of Fundamental Rights, Official Journal of the European Union, C 303/34, 14 December 2007.

[5] Convention for the Collective Protection of Individual Rights and Democratic Liberties by the States, Members of the Council of Europe, and for the establishment of a European Court of Human Rights to ensure observance of the Convention, Doc. INF/5/E/R, I *TP* 296–303.

[6] Draft Declaration on Human Rights, UN Doc. E/HR/1, p. 3.

[7] Report of the Sitting [of the Consultative Assembly, 19 August 1949], I *TP* 38–154, at p. 88.

[8] Ibid., p. 142.

[9] Recommendation No. 38 to the Committee of Ministers adopted 8 September 1949 on the conclusion of the debates, Doc. AS (1) 108, II *TP* 274–83, at p. 276.

The Committee of Ministers agreed that the draft of the Consultative Assembly should be studied by a Committee of Experts. The Committee of Experts met in February and March of 1950. It had been told by the Committee of Ministers that it was to pay 'due attention' to the draft Covenant adopted by the United Nations Commission on Human Rights in June 1949.[10] Unlike the Consultative Assembly text, the United Nations draft included a detailed provision dealing with fair trial guarantees:

1. In the determination of any criminal charge against him, or of his rights and obligations in a suit of law, everyone is entitled to a fair and public hearing, by an independent and impartial tribunal established by law. Judgment shall be pronounced publicly but the press and public may be excluded from all or part of the trial in the interest of morals, public order or national security or where the interest of juveniles or incapacitated persons so require.
2. Everyone charged with a penal offence has the right to be presumed innocent until proved guilty according to law. In the determination of any criminal charge against him, everyone is entitled to the following minimum guarantees in full equality:
   (a) to be informed promptly of the nature and cause of the accusation against him;
   (b) to defend himself in person or through legal assistance which shall include the right to legal assistance of his own choosing, or, if he does not have such, to be informed of his right and, if unobtainable by him, to have legal assistance assigned;
   (c) to examine, or have examined, the witnesses against him and to obtain compulsory attendance of witnesses in his behalf;
   (d) to have the free assistance of an interpreter if he cannot understand or speak the language used in court.
3. Everyone who has undergone punishment as a result of an erroneous conviction of crime shall have an enforceable right to compensation. This right shall accrue to the heirs of a person executed by virtue of an erroneous sentence.[11]

This is the direct ancestor of article 14 of the International Covenant on Civil and Political Rights.

The Committee of Experts developed two rather different drafts of the Convention. The first, subsequently labelled 'Alternatives A and A/2', was derived from the Consultative Assembly text. However, rather than simply make a reference to articles 10 and 11(1) of the Universal Declaration of Human Rights, the Committee of Experts draft repeated them in full.[12] The second draft ('Alternatives B and B/2') was based upon a United Kingdom proposal containing a fair trial text modelled on the provision in the draft United Nations Covenant. There were two significant differences with the United Nations draft. The final paragraph concerning compensation for miscarriage of justice was deleted and the sub-paragraph dealing with legal aid was modified, to read as follows: 'to defend himself in person or through legal assistance of his own choosing and, if he has not sufficient means to pay for such assistance, to be given it free when the interests of justice so require'.[13] The United Kingdom proposal was then refined by the drafting committee:

---

[10] Letter addressed on 18 November 1949 by the Secretary General to the Ministers for Foreign Affairs of the Member States, Ref. D 26/2/49, II *TP* 302–5.

[11] Report of the Fifth Session of the Commission on Human Rights to the Economic and Social Council, UN Doc. E/1371(Supp.), p. 20.

[12] Draft text of the first section of a draft Convention based on the work of the Consultative Assembly, Doc. A 809, III *TP* 220–31, at pp. 222–5; Preliminary Draft Convention for the Maintenance and Further Realisation of Human Rights and Fundamental Freedoms, 15 February 1950, Doc. A 833, III *TP* 236–46, at pp. 236–9.

[13] Amendments to Articles 1, 2, 4, 5, 6, 8, and 9 of the Committee's Preliminary Draft Proposal by the Expert of the United Kingdom, Doc. CM/WP 1 (50) 2, A 915, III *TP* 280–9, at p. 284.

1. In the determination of any criminal charge against him or of his rights and obligations in a suit of law, everyone is entitled to a fair and public hearing, by an independent and impartial tribunal established by law. Judgment shall be pronounced publicly but the press or public may be excluded from all or part of the trial to the extent strictly necessary in the opinion of the court, in the interest of morals, public order or national security, or where, in the special circumstances of the case, publicity would prejudice the interests of justice.
2. Everyone charged with a penal offence has the right to be presumed innocent until proved guilty according to law.
3. In the determination of any criminal charge against him, everyone is entitled:
   (a) to be informed promptly, in a language he understands, of the nature and cause of the accusation against him;
   (b) to have adequate time and facilities for the preparation of his defence;
   (c) to defend himself in person or through legal assistance of his own choosing and, if he has not sufficient means to pay for such assistance, to be given it free when the interests of justice so require;
   (d) to examine or have examined the witnesses against him and to obtain compulsory attendance of witnesses on his behalf;
   (e) to have free assistance of an interpreter if he cannot understand or speak the language used in court.[14]

The plenary Committee added the words 'and within a reasonable time' to paragraph 1 of the British text following the phrase 'established by law'.[15] The British draft was accompanied by the following comments:

The word 'special' in the last sentence of [paragraph 1] is intended to underline the fact that such circumstances are an exception to the normal rule stated in the first sentence of the paragraph. It is not intended to bear the additional meaning that such circumstances should be of any particular degree of infrequency.
   It was further agreed that the phrase 'the interests of justice' included cases in which the interests of one or the two parties or a third party would be manifestly prejudiced by publicity.[16]

The two competing versions were transmitted to the Committee of Ministers. It decided that they should be further examined by a Conference of Senior Officials.

The Conference of Senior Officials, meeting in June 1950, adopted the British draft with a few minor additions and changes. The words 'in a democratic society' were added at the end of the first sentence of paragraph 1. In paragraph 2, 'penal offence' was changed to 'criminal offence'. The words 'to the following minimum guarantees' were added at the end of the introductory phrase in paragraph 3. Paragraph 3(d) was changed to read: 'to obtain the attendance and examination of witnesses on his own behalf under the same conditions as witnesses against him'.[17] The report of the Conference contained some comments on the provision. The Italian delegate 'considered that the drafting of this

---

[14] Amendments to the British draft proposed by the Drafting Committee composed of Sir Oscar Dowson, MM le Quesne, Dons Moeller, and Salén, Doc. CM/WP 1 (50) 10, p. 3, A 919, III *TP* 288–295, at pp. 288–91.
[15] Appendix to the Report of the Committee of Experts on Human Rights: Draft Convention of Protection of Human Rights and Fundamental Freedoms, 16 March 1950, Doc. C/WP 1 (50) 15 appendix, CM/WP 1 (50) 14 revised, A 925, IV *TP* 50–79, at p. 60.
[16] Report to the Committee of Ministers submitted by the Committee of Experts Instructed to Draw Up a Draft Convention of Collective Guarantee of Human Rights and Fundamental Freedoms, Doc. CM/WP 1 (5) 15, A 924, IV *TP* 2–55, at p. 32.
[17] Draft Convention annexed to the Report [of the Conference of Senior Officials], Doc. CM/WP 4 (50) 19 annex, CM/WP 4 (50) 16 rev., A 1452, IV *TP* 274–95, at pp. 276–8.

paragraph did not bring out the fact that courts dealing with penal cases should be constituted prior to the commission of the offence'. The report said that '[o]ther delegates considered that it might be possible to admit exceptions to this rule'. The French and Italian delegates thought that the paragraph concerning legal aid discriminated between those who could pay for defence counsel and those who could not because the former had 'the right, in any case, to have legal assistance of their own choosing, while the others are only entitled to the service of a defence counsel when the interests of justice so require'. They said the rule was contrary to the principle of non-discrimination enshrined in the draft. Finally, the report said that the purpose of revised paragraph 3(d) was 'to put the accused on a footing of equality with the public prosecutor, as regards the hearing of witnesses. It is obviously not a question of giving the accused the right to summon witnesses without any restriction.'[18]

In the Committee of Ministers, the United Kingdom proposed some amendments. With respect to the public nature of hearings, it said:

The present text of this Article leaves to the discretion of the court the exclusion of the press or public in a number of cases where, under English law, exclusion is enjoined by statute. Nor does it make provision for the cases in which the public may, under English law, be excluded from the hearing and determination by a court of summary jurisdiction of domestic proceedings, as well as cases concerning juveniles.

H.M. Government therefore propose that the second sentence of this paragraph be amended to read: 'The press and public may be excluded from all or part of a trial in the interests of morals, public order or national security in a democratic society, or where the interests of juveniles or the parties to proceedings concerning their domestic relationships so require, or to the extent strictly necessary in the opinion of the court in special circumstances where publicity would prejudice the interests of justice; but the judgment shall be pronounced publicly except where the interests of juveniles or of the parties to proceedings concerning their domestic relationships otherwise require.'[19]

The final sentence of paragraph 1 was amended following deliberations at the sitting of 4 August 1950: 'Judgment shall be pronounced publicly but the press and public may be excluded from all or part of a trial in the interests of morals, public order or national security in a democratic society, or where the interests of juveniles or the parties to proceedings concerning their domestic relationships so require, or to the extent strictly necessary in the opinion of the court in special circumstances where publicity would prejudice the interests of justice.'[20] It was changed slightly in the final version, the words 'in a democratic society, or where' being replaced by 'in a democratic society where'.[21] Paragraph 6(3)(a) was also amended at the 4 August 1950 session with the replacement of the word 'cause' by 'details'.[22] This too was changed in the final version so that the text read: 'to be informed promptly, in a language which he understands and in detail of the

[18] Text of the Report submitted by the Conference [of Senior Officials] to the Committee of Ministers, Doc. CM/WP 4 (50) 19, CM/WP 4 (50) 16 rev., A 1431, IV *TP* 242–73, at p. 260.

[19] Amendments proposed by the United Kingdom Delegation, Doc. CM 1 (50) 6, A 1867, V *TP* 66–70, at p. 66.

[20] Text of amended articles after deliberation at the sitting of 4 August 1950, Doc. CM 1 (50) 9, V *TP* 74–6, at p. 74.

[21] Draft Convention adopted by the Sub-Committee, Doc. CM 1 (50) 52, A 1884, V *TP* 76–99, at pp. 78–80.

[22] Text of amended articles after deliberation at the sitting of 4 August 1950, Doc. CM 1 (50) 9, V *TP* 74–6, at p. 74.

nature and cause of the accusation against him'.[23] Paragraph 6(3)(d) was amended as follows: 'to examine or have examined witnesses against him and to obtain the attendance and examination of witnesses on his behalf under the same conditions as witnesses against him'. In paragraph 6(3)(d), the word 'the' was added before 'free assistance'.[24]

The Consultative Assembly accepted the draft without comment. However, in the context of discussing the role of the Court, Pierre-Henri Teitgen complained that the Committee of Ministers had altered the intent of the Assembly with respect to review of national judicial decisions. He said that the Consultative Assembly had not intended to guarantee Europeans protection against the judicial errors of their own courts: 'We simply desired to secure for them freedom of defence, and procedural safeguards, because those safeguards are the very expression of individual liberty and of individual rights.'[25]

The Committee of Legal Experts, meeting on 3 November 1950, made several amendments to the text.[26] The draft of paragraph 1 had begun with the words 'In the determination of any criminal charge against him or of his rights and obligations in a suit of law...' The order was reversed, putting rights and obligations ahead of criminal charges, adding the word 'civil' before 'rights and obligations' and removing the words 'suit at law': 'In the determination of his civil rights and obligations or of any criminal charge against him...' The final sentence was amended, replacing the words 'or the parties to proceedings' with 'or the protection of the private life of the parties'. Paragraph 3, which began with the words 'In the determination of any criminal charge against him...' was changed to 'Everyone charged with a criminal offence...' In paragraph (c), the conjunction 'and' following 'choosing' was replaced with 'or'. Two small changes were also made to the French text of the Convention. The penultimate draft of the final sentence of paragraph 1 read: 'Le jugement doit être rendu publiquement, mais l'accès de la salle d'audience peut être interdit à la presse et au public, pendant la totalité ou une partie du procès dans l'intérêt de la moralité, de l'ordre public ou de la sécurité nationale dans une société démocratique, lorsque les intérêts des mineurs ou de la vie privée des parties au procès l'exigent, ou dans la mesure jugée strictement nécessaire par la Cour, lorsque dans des circonstances spéciales la publicité serait de nature à porter atteinte aux intérêts de la justice.' The words 'la protection' were added immediately before 'de la vie privée' and the words 'la Cour' replaced with 'le tribunal'.

The title of article 6, 'Right to a fair trial', was added by Protocol No. 11.[27]

Analysis and interpretation

Article 6 consists of three paragraphs, the first of which sets out a series of general principles applicable to the two basic categories of trials in modern justice systems, those that are civil and administrative ('rights and obligations') and those that are criminal in nature. Paragraph 1 enshrines the right to a 'fair and public hearing within a reasonable

---

[23] Draft Convention adopted by the Sub-Committee, Doc. CM 1 (50) 52, A 1884, V *TP* 76–99, at pp. 78–80.

[24] Ibid.

[25] Report of the Sitting [of the Consultative Assembly, 16 August 1950], VI *TP* 270–351, at p. 300.

[26] Report of the Committee of Legal Experts, 2–3 November 1950, Doc. CM/Adj. (50) 3 Rev., A 2531, VII *TP* 10–13.

[27] Protocol No. 11 to the Convention for the Protection of Human Rights and Fundamental Freedoms, restructuring the control machinery established thereby, ETS 155, art. 2(2).

time by an independent and impartial tribunal established by law'. The second and third paragraphs of article 6 only apply to criminal trials. Paragraph 2 recognizes the presumption of innocence. Paragraph 3 provides a list of minimum guarantees that apply to the criminal trial.

Article 6 is confined to the fairness of the proceedings. The European Court does not sit in review of the decisions of national tribunals, correcting errors of law or fact that may be present in their rulings. This is sometimes described as the 'fourth instance doctrine'.[28] The Court has insisted that it is the role of the domestic courts 'to interpret and apply the relevant rules of procedural or substantive law. The domestic courts are best placed to assess the credibility of witnesses and the relevance of evidence to the issues in the case. It is also for the domestic courts to exclude evidence which is considered to be irrelevant.'[29] The Court will only question the assessments by domestic authorities if there is evidence of arbitrariness.[30]

Fair trial rights set out in article 6 may be waived either expressly or tacitly. But to be effective for Convention purposes, any such waiver must 'be established in an unequivocal manner and be attended by minimum safeguards' commensurate with the importance or article 6.[31] Usually, an individual will waive the benefit of certain rights in exchange for some perceived tactical advantage. According to the Grand Chamber, the person charged with a criminal offence should be able 'to expect the state to act in good faith and take due account of the procedural choices made by the defence, using the possibilities made available by law'. Any unilateral reduction in the advantages in exchange for which the individual has waived rights 'is contrary to the principle of legal certainty and the protection of the legitimate trust of persons engaged in judicial proceedings' and cannot be regarded as fair.[32] An example of a waiver that has become increasingly common in some European States is so-called 'plea bargaining', by which an accused person agrees to an abbreviated procedure and to an admission of guilt in exchange for a reduction in the charges or some commitment to a mitigated sentence. The Court has said that plea bargaining is not in principle incompatible with article 6.[33]

The right to a fair trial applies to the determination of 'civil rights and obligations' and 'any criminal charge'. The general principles set out in paragraph 1 are applicable to both categories. Criminal proceedings require more specific guarantees, such as the presumption of innocence (art. 6(2)) and the very precise matters addressed in paragraph 3. But the presence of special rules listed in paragraph 3 does not suggest in any way that the principles they reflect are not applicable to paragraph 1 as well. Frequently, when criminal trials are concerned, the Convention organs examine paragraphs 1 and 3 of article 6 together.

---

[28] *Nejdet Şahin and Perihan Şahin v. Turkey* [GC], no. 13279/05, § 88, 20 October 2011; *Sohby v. the United Kingdom* (dec.), no. 34108/07, § 37, 18 June 2013; *Palazzolo v. Italy* (dec.), no. 32328/09, § 86, 24 September 2013.

[29] *Karpenko v. Russia*, no. 5605/04, § 80, 13 March 2012; *Barberà, Messegué and Jabardo v. Spain*, 6 December 1988, § 68, Series A no. 146.

[30] *Sisojeva and Others v. Latvia* (striking out) [GC], no. 60654/00, § 89, ECHR 2007-I.

[31] *Scoppola v. Italy (no. 2)* [GC], no. 10249/03, § 135, 17 September 2009; *Poitrimol v. France*, 23 November 1993, § 31, Series A no. 277-A; *Hermi v. Italy* [GC], no. 18114/02, § 73, ECHR 2006-XII. No important public interest can be infringed: *Håkansson and Sturesson v. Sweden*, 21 February 1990, § 66, Series A no. 171-A; *Sejdovic v. Italy* [GC], no. 56581/00, § 86, ECHR 2006-II.

[32] *Scoppola v. Italy (no. 2)* [GC], no. 10249/03, § 135, 17 September 2009.

[33] *Natsvlishvili and Togonidze v. Georgia*, no. 9043/05, §§ 91–92, 29 April 2014.

The fair trial provision in the Charter of Fundamental Rights of the European Union is broader than article 6. Article 47 of the Charter does not confine the right to a fair trial to disputes relating to 'civil rights and obligations' or to 'any criminal charge', and does not refer to a 'determination', as the Grand Chamber observed in *Micallef v. Malta*.[34] The Grand Chamber was considering the somewhat restrictive approach taken by the European Court to the scope of article 6, in particular the general exclusion of interim or preliminary proceedings. It noted that even before the adoption of the European Charter, the European Court of Justice had considered that fair trial standards applied to provisional measures granted *ex parte*, that is, in the absence of the defendant.[35]

Determination of civil rights and obligations

The so-called 'civil limb' of article 6 governs the 'determination of civil rights and obligations'. This requires that there be a dispute (in French, *contestation*) over a 'civil right' that is arguably recognized by domestic law, regardless of whether it is also protected by the European Convention.[36] There is a difference in the English and French versions of the Convention. The English text speaks of 'determination of his rights and obligations', whereas the French uses the expression *'des contestations sur ses droits et obligations'*. It has been held that '[c]onformity with the spirit of the Convention' requires that the text 'should not be construed too technically and that it should be given a substantive rather than a formal meaning'.[37] Article 6 will not be applicable in a judicial procedure that is by its very nature unilateral, without opposing parties, such as certain modifications in civil status.[38]

Furthermore, the dispute must be 'genuine and serious'.[39] There is a presumption that a claim that has been submitted to a tribunal meets this criterion. There must be 'clear indications' to justify a conclusion that a claim is frivolous, vexatious, or lacking in foundation.[40] It may relate either to the actual existence of a right or to its scope and the manner of its exercise.[41] The result of the proceedings 'must be directly decisive for the right in question, mere tenuous connections or remote consequences not being sufficient to bring Article 6 § 1 into play'.[42] Accordingly, if the Court considers that the proceedings undertaken by an applicant do not provide a remedy capable of addressing his or her contentions on the merits, it will conclude that the domestic proceedings

---

[34] *Micallef v. Malta* [GC], no. 17056/06, § 32, ECHR 2009.

[35] Ibid., citing *Denilauler/Couchet Frères*, ECJ, Case C 125/79, 21 May 1980.

[36] *Enea v. Italy* [GC], no. 74912/01, § 103, ECHR 2009; *Editions Périscope v. France*, 26 March 1992, § 35, Series A no. 234-B.

[37] *Le Compte, Van Leuven and De Meyere v. Belgium*, 23 June 1981, § 45, Series A no. 43; *Gorou v. Greece (no. 2)* [GC], no. 12686/03, § 27, 20 March 2009.

[38] *Alaverdyan v. Armenia* (dec.), no. 4523/04, § 34, 24 August 2010.

[39] *Enea v. Italy* [GC], no. 74912/01, § 99, ECHR 2009; *Sporrong and Lönnroth v. Sweden*, 23 September 1982, § 81, Series A no. 52.

[40] *Skorobogatykh v. Russia* (dec.), no. 37966/02, 8 June 2006; *Benthem v. the Netherlands*, 23 October 1985, § 32, Series A no. 97; *Rolf Gustafson v. Sweden*, 1 July 1997, § 38, *Reports of Judgments and Decisions* 1997-IV.

[41] *Boulois v. Luxembourg* [GC], no. 37575/04, § 90, ECHR 2012; *Micallef v. Malta* [GC], no. 17056/06, § 74, ECHR 2009; *Mennitto v. Italy* [GC], no. 33804/96, § 23, ECHR 2000-X; *Gülmez v. Turkey*, no. 16330/02, § 28, 20 May 2008.

[42] *Le Compte, Van Leuven and De Meyere v. Belgium*, 23 June 1981, § 47, Series A no. 43; *Neigel v. France*, 17 March 1997, § 38, *Reports of Judgments and Decisions* 1997-II; *Micallef v. Malta* [GC], no. 17056/06, § 74, 15 October 2009; *Boulois v. Luxembourg* [GC], no. 37575/04, § 90, ECHR 2012; *De Bruin v. the Netherlands* (dec.), no. 9765/09, 17 September 2013.

cannot result in a determination of the alleged civil rights and obligations. Consequently, the application under the Convention will be deemed incompatible *ratione materiae* with article 6.[43]

No particular substantive content is contemplated by the concept of civil rights and obligations. The Court cannot create through article 6(1) a substantive right that has no foundation in national law.[44] The distinction between substantive and procedural matters, 'fine as it may be in a particular case', nevertheless 'remains determinative of the applicability and, as appropriate, the scope of the guarantees of Article 6 of the Convention'.[45] The guarantees enshrined in article 6 extend only to rights that can be said, 'at least on arguable grounds', to be recognized by domestic law.[46] Thus, the starting point for the application of 'rights and obligations' is the domestic law as interpreted by the courts.[47] Other criteria that the Court may consider will include 'recognition of the alleged right in similar circumstances by the domestic courts or the fact that the latter examined the merits of the applicant's request'.[48] But '[t]he character of the legislation which governs how the matter is to be determined (civil, commercial, administrative law, and so on) and that of the authority which is invested with jurisdiction in the matter (ordinary court, administrative body, and so forth) are therefore of little consequence'.[49] Nevertheless, the concept of 'civil rights and obligations' is autonomous in the sense that it has its own meaning under the Convention, regardless of how the term may be understood in domestic legislation.[50] Otherwise, States would be able to circumvent article 6 by labelling rights as being matters of public or administrative law rather than civil law. It is necessary to 'look beyond the appearances and the language used and concentrate on the realities of the situation'.[51]

Obviously, article 6 will apply to private law disputes concerning tort or civil responsibility and contractual matters. Family law issues such as an action contesting paternity[52] and judicial separation[53] also fall under article 6. Article 6 applies to conditions for admission to an occupation or a profession[54] as well as to disciplinary matters within

---

[43] *Ulyanov v. Ukraine* (dec.), no. 16472/04, 5 October 2010; *Svenska Flygföretagens Riksförbund and Skyways Express AB v. Sweden* (dec.), no. 32535/02, 12 December 2006.

[44] *Boulois v. Luxembourg* [GC], no. 37575/04, § 91, ECHR 2012; *Fayed v. the United Kingdom*, 21 September 1994, § 65, Series A no. 294-B; *Roche v. the United Kingdom* [GC], no. 32555/96, § 119, ECHR 2005-X; *Z and Others v. the United Kingdom* [GC], no. 29392/95, § 87, ECHR 2001-V; *Stichting Mothers of Srebrenica and Others v. the Netherlands* (dec.), no. 65542/12, § 168, ECHR 2013 (extracts); *De Bruin v. the Netherlands* (dec.), no. 9765/09, 17 September 2013.

[45] *Roche v. the United Kingdom* [GC], no. 32555/96, § 119, ECHR 2005-X.

[46] Ibid., § 117; *James and Others v. the United Kingdom*, 21 February 1986, § 81, Series A no. 98; *McElhinney v. Ireland* [GC], no. 31253/96, § 23, ECHR 2001-XI (extracts).

[47] *Masson and Van Zon v. the Netherlands*, 28 September 1995, § 49, Series A no. 327-A; *Roche v. the United Kingdom* [GC], no. 32555/96, § 120, ECHR 2005-X.

[48] *Vilho Eskelinen and Others v. Finland* [GC], no. 63235/00, § 41, ECHR 2007-II; *Boulois v. Luxembourg* [GC], no. 37575/04, § 91, ECHR 2012.

[49] *Micallef v. Malta* [GC], no. 17056/06, § 74, ECHR 2009; *J.S. and A.S. v. Poland*, no. 40732/98, § 46, 24 May 2005.

[50] *Georgiadis v. Greece*, 29 May 1997, § 34, *Reports of Judgments and Decisions* 1997-III.

[51] *Van Droogenbroeck v. Belgium*, 24 June 1982, § 38, Series A no. 50; *Roche v. the United Kingdom* [GC], no. 32555/96, § 120, ECHR 2005-X; *Boulois v. Luxembourg* [GC], no. 37575/04, § 93, ECHR 2012; *Gorou v. Greece (no. 2)* [GC], no. 12686/03, §§ 27, 29, 20 March 2009.

[52] *Rasmussen v. Denmark*, 28 November 1984, § 32, Series A no. 87.

[53] *Airey v. Ireland*, 9 October 1979, § 21, Series A no. 32.

[54] *De Moor v. Belgium*, 23 June 1994, Series A no. 292-A; *Chevrol v. France*, no. 49636/99, ECHR 2003-III; *Kök v. Turkey*, no. 1855/02, 19 October 2006.

the profession where the right to practice is at stake.[55] Closer to the boundary between civil law and administrative or public law, the Court has held that article 6(1) applies to lawsuits for negligence against the police,[56] the local authorities,[57] and the State.[58] Article 6(1) may also be invoked in constitutional proceedings to the extent that they have a decisive bearing on a dispute concerning a civil right.[59]

Where issues that are governed by public law are decisive in determining private rights and obligations, they fall within article 6(1). Examples included planning permission,[60] permission to sell land,[61] authorization to operate a private clinic,[62] compensation for work-related illness,[63] and a licence to serve alcoholic beverages.[64] Article 6(1) also applies to issues concerning social rights such as proceedings relating to social security benefits and contributions.[65]

With respect to government employees, the Convention organs initially considered them to be outside the ambit of article 6(1) altogether. Eventually, this exclusion was softened by the application of a 'functional criterion' whereby police officials and similar functionaries were excluded from article 6 because of their role within the exercise of State power.[66] However, the Court found this to be an imperfect approach and shifted its view in favour of deciding that this could lead to anomalies. It refined its approach, creating a presumption favouring application of article 6. The Grand Chamber said that 'it is primarily for the Contracting States, in particular the competent national legislature, not the Court, to identify expressly those areas of public service involving the exercise of the discretionary powers intrinsic to State sovereignty where the interests of the individual must give way'.[67] If an applicant has access to a court under national law, then article 6(1) will apply. The Court has recognized the applicability of the Convention to employment-related disputes of embassy staff,[68] parliamentary officials,[69] and even judges.[70]

However, tax assessments fall outside the scope of article 6(1),[71] as do disputes about the results of elections.[72] Extradition proceedings are excluded from the notion of rights

---

[55] *Le Compte, Van Leuven and De Meyere v. Belgium*, 23 June 1981, Series A no. 43.

[56] *Osman v. the United Kingdom*, 28 October 1998, *Reports of Judgments and Decisions* 1998-VIII.

[57] *Z and Others v. the United Kingdom* [GC], no. 29392/95, ECHR 2001-V.

[58] *X v. France*, 31 March 1992, Series A no. 234-C.

[59] *Ruiz-Mateos v. Spain*, 23 June 1993, Series A no. 262. But see *Paksas v. Lithuania* [GC], no. 34932/04, ECHR 2011 (extracts).

[60] *Sporrong and Lönnroth v. Sweden*, 23 September 1982, § 79, Series A no. 52.

[61] *Ringeisen v. Austria*, 16 July 1971, § 94, Series A no. 13.

[62] *König v. Germany*, 28 June 1978, §§ 94–95ß, Series A no. 27.

[63] *Chaudet v. France*, no. 49037/06, § 60, 29 October 2009.

[64] *Tre Traktörer AB v. Sweden*, 7 July 1989, § 43, Series A no. 159.

[65] *Feldbrugge v. the Netherlands*, 29 May 1986, Series A no. 99; *Schouten and Meldrum v. the Netherlands*, 9 December 1994, Series A no. 304.

[66] *Pellegrin v. France* [GC], no. 28541/95, §§ 64–71, ECHR 1999-VIII; *Kępka v. Poland* (dec.), nos 31439/96 and 35123/97, ECHR 2000-IX; *Kanayev v. Russia*, no. 43726/02, § 18, 27 July 2006.

[67] *Vilho Eskelinen and Others v. Finland* [GC], no. 63235/00, § 61, ECHR 2007-II.

[68] *Cudak v. Lithuania* [GC], no. 15869/02, ECHR 2010.

[69] *Savino and Others v. Italy*, nos 17214/05, 20329/05, and 42113/04, 28 April 2009.

[70] *Olujić v. Croatia*, no. 22330/05, 5 February 2009.

[71] *Ferrazzini v. Italy* [GC], no. 44759/98, ECHR 2001-VII.

[72] *Pierre-Bloch v. France*, 21 October 1997, *Reports of Judgments and Decisions* 1997-VI.

and obligations.[73] Similarly, decisions about the entry, the right to remain, and deportation of aliens do not fall under article 6(1).[74]

Prisoners are not excluded from the scope of article 6 for the reason that 'justice cannot stop at the prison gate'.[75] The case law of the Convention organs confirms that 'prisoners in general continue to enjoy all the fundamental rights and freedoms guaranteed under the Convention save for the right to liberty, where lawfully imposed detention expressly falls within the scope of Article 5 of the Convention'.[76] However, issues concerning the detention regime itself do not generally fall under the 'rights and obligations' branch of article 6.[77]

Preliminary proceedings, such as the grant of an interim measure like an injunction, were traditionally excluded from the scope of article 6 because they were not considered to determine civil rights and obligations.[78] Typically, such measures are granted following summary proceedings, sometimes even in the absence of one of the parties, and are designed to preserve rights until the merits of a dispute can be resolved rather than address the merits themselves, or even prejudice their eventual determination. The Court's reticence to extend the protections of article 6 to such proceedings can be seen in applications concerning delays, where the Convention organs generally make the determination of the relevant time period from the start of the case on the merits and not from the request for preliminary measures.[79] The Court made exceptions in cases where the preliminary or interim proceedings appeared to be decisive to the civil rights at issue.[80] In 2009, in *Micallef v. Malta*, the Grand Chamber recognized that such a view was inconsistent with the practice of European States and that there was widespread consensus at the national level on the application of article 6 to interim proceedings.[81] The Grand Chamber pointed to problems of backlogs in 'overburdened justice systems leading to excessively long proceedings', where a ruling on an interim injunction may in reality amount to a ruling on the merits, with long-lasting or permanent effect.[82] Consequently,

---

[73] *Raf v. Spain* (dec.), no. 53652/00, 21 November 2000; *A.B. v. Poland* (dec.), no. 33878/96, 18 October 2001; *Farmakopoulos v. Belgium*, no. 11683/85, Commission decision of 8 February 1990, (1990) 33 YB 38, DR 64, p. 52; *P. and R.H. and L.L. v. Austria*, no. 15776/89, Commission decision of 5 December 1989, DR 64, p. 264; *Alla Raidl v. Austria*, no. 25342/94, Commission decision of 4 September 1995, (1995) 38 YB 132, DR 82-A, p. 134.

[74] *Maaouia v. France* [GC], no. 39652/98, §§ 33–41, ECHR 2000-X; *Sardinas Albo v. Italy* (dec.), no. 56271/00, ECHR 2004-I.

[75] *Enea v. Italy* [GC], no. 74912/01, § 105, ECHR 2009; *Ezeh and Connors v. the United Kingdom* [GC], nos 39665/98 and 40086/98, § 83, ECHR 2003-X.

[76] *Boulois v. Luxembourg* [GC], no. 37575/04, § 82, ECHR 2012. Also *Hirst v. the United Kingdom (no. 2)* [GC], no. 74025/01, §§ 69–70, ECHR 2005-IX; *Dickson v. the United Kingdom* [GC], no. 44362/04, § 67, ECHR 2007-V; *Stummer v. Austria* [GC], no. 37452/02, § 99, ECHR 2011.

[77] *Neumeister v. Austria*, 27 June 1968, pp. 27–8, §§ 22–23, Series A no. 8; *Lorsé and Others v. the Netherlands* (dec.), no. 52750/99, 28 August 2001; *Montcornet de Caumont v. France* (dec.), no. 59290/00, ECHR 2003-VII; *Boulois v. Luxembourg* [GC], no. 37575/04, § 87, ECHR 2012.

[78] *Micallef v. Malta* [GC], no. 17056/06, §§ 75, 79, ECHR 2009; *Wiot v. France* (dec.), no. 43722/98, 15 March 2001; *APIS a.s. v. Slovakia* (dec.), no. 39794/98, 13 January 2002; *Verlagsgruppe News GMBH v Austria* (dec.), no. 62763/00, 16 January 2003; *Libert v. Belgium* (dec.), no. 44734/98, 8 July 2004.

[79] *Micallef v. Malta* [GC], no. 17056/06, § 75, ECHR 2009; *Jaffredou v. France* (dec.), no. 39843/98, 15 December 1998, and *Kress v. France* [GC], no. 39594/98, § 90, ECHR 2001-VI.

[80] *Micallef v. Malta* [GC], no. 17056/06, § 75, ECHR 2009; *Aerts v. Belgium*, 30 July 1998, *Reports of Judgments and Decisions* 1998-V; *Boca v. Belgium*, no. 50615/99, ECHR 2002-IX; *Markass Car Hire Ltd v. Cyprus* (dec.), no. 51591/99, 23 October 2001.

[81] *Micallef v. Malta* [GC], no. 17056/06, §§ 31, 78, ECHR 2009.

[82] Ibid., § 79.

'the Court no longer finds it justified to automatically characterise injunction proceedings as not determinative of civil rights or obligations'.[83]

Explaining its new approach to article 6 within the context of interim proceedings, the Grand Chamber said there were two elements. First, 'the right at stake in both the main and the injunction proceedings should be "civil" within the autonomous meaning of that notion under Article 6 of the Convention'.[84] Second, 'the nature of the interim measure, its object and purpose as well as its effects on the right in question should be scrutinised. Whenever an interim measure can be considered effectively to determine the civil right or obligation at stake, notwithstanding the length of time it is in force, Article 6 will be applicable.'[85] The Grand Chamber conceded that there would be exceptional cases where the effectiveness of a measure sought would depend upon speedy determination and that compliance with article 6 might not be entirely possible. In such cases, the State would be required to demonstrate that specific procedural safeguards could not be respected without unduly prejudicing the attainment of the objectives sought by the interim measure in question.[86]

Article 6(1) continues to apply through to the enforcement stage. For example, in legal systems where liability is determined initially in criminal proceedings but where the amount of damages is set subsequently, article 6(1) remains relevant.[87] Execution of a judgment is deemed to be part of the trial itself and therefore is governed by article 6(1).[88] However, proceedings to reopen a case have been excluded from the ambit of article 6(1) by the Convention organs to the extent that they are not concerned with determining the rights or obligations of an individual but rather assessing whether there is admissible new evidence or some similar ground. But once a decision is taken to permit the proceedings to be reopened, the ensuing determination on the merits certainly falls within the scope of article 6(1).[89]

Determination of a criminal charge

Article 6(1) also applies to the 'determination of . . . a criminal charge' (in French, *du bien-fondé de toute accusation en matière pénale dirigée contre elle*). Paragraphs 2 and 3 of article 6 also apply to persons charged with a criminal offence. The criminal limb of paragraph 1 of article 6 is engaged by 'any criminal charge'. Paragraphs 2 and 3 of article 6 apply to a person 'charged with a criminal offence'. Sometimes it is easy to determine that a person is subject to a criminal charge, in that formal criminal charges will have been laid against the individual in question. The criminal charge has been defined as 'the official notification given to an individual by the competent authority of an allegation that he has committed a

---

[83] Ibid., § 80. But see *Micallef v. Malta* [GC], no. 17056/06, Joint Dissenting Opinion of Judges Costa, Jungwiert, Kovler, and Fura, § 4, ECHR 2009.

[84] *Micallef v. Malta* [GC], no. 17056/06, § 84, ECHR 2009; *Stran Greek Refineries and Stratis Andreadis v. Greece*, 9 December 1994, § 39, Series A no. 301-B; *König v. Germany*, 28 June 1978, §§ 89–90, Series A no. 27; *Ferrazzini v. Italy* [GC], no. 44759/98, §§ 24–31, ECHR 2001-VII; *Roche v. the United Kingdom* [GC], no. 32555/96, § 119, ECHR 2005-X. Note, however, the dissenting judgment on this point: *Micallef v. Malta* [GC], no. 17056/06, Joint Concurring Opinion of Judges Rozakis, Tulkens, and Kalaydyieva, ECHR 2009.

[85] *Micallef v. Malta* [GC], no. 17056/06, § 85, ECHR 2009.

[86] Ibid., § 86.

[87] *Torri v. Italy*, 1 July 1997, § 19, *Reports of Judgments and Decisions* 1997-IV.

[88] *Romańczyk v. France*, no. 7618/05, § 53, 18 November 2010; *Hornsby v. Greece*, 19 March 1997, § 40, *Reports of Judgments and Decisions* 1997-II.

[89] *J.F. v. France* (dec.), no. 39616/98, 20 April 1999.

criminal offence'. This definition also corresponds to the test whether the suspect's situation has been 'substantially affected'.[90]

The Engel *criteria*

Three criteria, originally set out in *Engel and Others v. the Netherlands*,[91] have been used to assess whether the criminal limb of article 6 applies: the classification of the offence in domestic law, the nature of the offence, and the severity of the penalty that is at risk. Because the concept of 'criminal charge' has an autonomous meaning under the Convention regardless of how it is defined or characterized in national law,[92] the first of these criteria is the least important. It is 'no more than a starting point'.[93] The same cannot be said of the second and third criteria.[94] The second and third criteria are alternative and not cumulative,[95] although they may collectively lead to the conclusion that the applicant has been charged with a criminal offence when one of them alone does not provide a convincing answer.[96] Application of the *Engel* criteria has led to 'a gradual broadening of the criminal head to cases not strictly belonging to the traditional categories of the criminal law, for example administrative penalties'.[97] While acknowledging that 'a certain gravity attaches' to criminal proceedings, which involve the imposition of punitive and deterrent sanctions, 'it is self-evident that there are criminal cases which do not carry any significant degree of stigma'.[98]

Several factors are considered in evaluating whether to describe the nature of the offence—the second of the *Engel* criteria—as criminal: the legal rule should be of a generally binding character and not directed against a specific group;[99] the proceedings should be instituted by a public body with statutory powers of enforcement;[100] the prohibition should be commensurate with a deterrent and punitive purpose;[101] imposition of a penalty should be dependent upon a finding of guilt;[102] and the classification of similar matters in the law of other Council of Europe Member States.[103] The consequence of a criminal record upon conviction is of significance but it is not decisive because this is dependent upon the classification of the offence in domestic law.[104] The relative

---

[90] *McFarlane v. Ireland* [GC], no. 31333/06, § 143, 10 September 2010; *Mulosmani v. Albania*, no. 29864/03, § 38, 8 October 2013.

[91] *Engel and Others v. the Netherlands*, 8 June 1976, § 82, Series A no. 22. Affirmed: *Grande Stevens and Others v. Italy*, nos 18640/10, 18647/10, 18663/10, 18668/10, and 18698/10, § 94, 4 March 2014; *Ezeh and Connors v. the United Kingdom* [GC] nos 39665/98 and 40086/98, § 82, ECHR 2003-X.

[92] *O'Halloran and Francis v. the United Kingdom* [GC], nos 15809/02 and 25624/02, § 35, ECHR 2007-III; *Deweer v. Belgium*, 27 February 1980, § 42, Series A no. 35; *Adolf v. Austria*, 26 March 1982, § 30, Series A no. 49.

[93] *Engel and Others v. the Netherlands*, 8 June 1976, § 82, Series A no. 22.

[94] *Jussila v. Finland* [GC], no. 73053/01, § 38, ECHR 2006-XIV.

[95] *Lutz v. Germany*, 25 August 1987, § 55, Series A no. 123.

[96] *Bendenoun v. France*, 24 February 1994, § 47, Series A no. 284.

[97] *Jussila v. Finland* [GC], no. 73053/01, § 43, ECHR 2006-XIV.

[98] Ibid.

[99] *Bendenoun v. France*, 24 February 1994, § 47, Series A no. 284.

[100] *Benham v. the United Kingdom*, 10 June 1996, § 56, *Reports of Judgments and Decisions* 1996-III.

[101] *Jussila v. Finland* [GC], no. 73053/01, § 38, ECHR 2006-XIV; *Öztürk v. Germany*, 21 February 1984, § 53, Series A no. 73.

[102] *Benham v. the United Kingdom*, 10 June 1996, § 56, *Reports of Judgments and Decisions* 1996-III.

[103] *Öztürk v. Germany*, 21 February 1984, § 53, Series A no. 73.

[104] *Ravnsborg v. Sweden*, 23 March 1994, § 38, Series A no. 283-B.

lack of seriousness of a sanction 'cannot deprive an offence of its inherently criminal character'.[105]

The third *Engel* criterion is the maximum penalty to which the individual is exposed.[106] The actual penalty imposed is also of relevance,[107] but it does not diminish the importance of what was initially at stake.[108] Detention ('strict arrest') of two days as part of military discipline was held to be of too short a duration to indicate a criminal offence.[109] On the other hand, committal to a disciplinary unit for a period of several months meets the criminal law standard.[110] A five-day sentence of detention is sufficiently criminal for article 6(1) to apply.[111] A fine of 500 Swiss francs, with the possibility that it be converted into a term of imprisonment if not paid, was considered to cross the threshold into criminal law.[112] When the second *Engel* criterion is clearly present, the relatively low amount of an administrative fine does not suffice to exclude the matter from the scope of article 6(1).[113] As with the nature of the 'crime' itself, the label given to the sanction by national law may disguise the reality of the punishment. Where deprivation of liberty may be imposed, there is a presumption that the related charges are criminal within the meaning of article 6. It can only be rebutted, 'entirely exceptionally', if the deprivation of liberty is not deemed to be 'appreciably detrimental' in light of the nature, duration, or manner of execution.[114]

Domestic legal systems generally distinguish between criminal or penal offences and disciplinary offences.[115] Treating a matter as a disciplinary issue has advantages for the individual, who generally receives a milder sanction and, moreover, does not have a criminal record imposed. While States have the right to distinguish between criminal and disciplinary law, and there is a presumption that an offence classified as disciplinary under national law is not to be deemed criminal in nature, the Court 'has reserved the power to satisfy itself that the line drawn between these does not prejudice the object and purpose of Article 6'.[116] The first of the *Engel* criteria makes it clear that the classification given to an offence by a State is without prejudice to the Court's autonomous assessment. Genuine disciplinary sanctions fall outside the second of the *Engel* criteria because they are not intended to apply generally. Rather, they are 'designed to ensure that the members of particular groups comply with the specific rules governing their conduct'.[117] The fact that a disciplinary violation may also be a criminal offence, however, does not suffice to make the disciplinary proceedings criminal in nature.[118] Nor is there any problem in principle

---

[105] *Lauko v. Slovakia*, 2 September 1998, § 58, *Reports of Judgments and Decisions* 1998-VI.

[106] *Campbell and Fell v. the United Kingdom*, 28 June 1984, § 72, Series A no. 80; *Demicoli v. Malta*, 27 August 1991, § 34, Series A no. 210.

[107] *Campbell and Fell v. the United Kingdom*, 28 June 1984, § 73, Series A no. 80; *Bendenoun v. France*, 24 February 1994, § 47, Series A no. 284.

[108] *Engel and Others v. the Netherlands*, 8 June 1976, § 85, Series A no. 22.

[109] Ibid.

[110] Ibid.

[111] *Kyprianou v. Cyprus*, no. 73797/01, § 31, 27 January 2004.

[112] *Weber v. Switzerland*, 22 May 1990, § 34, Series A no. 177.

[113] *Jussila v. Finland* [GC], no. 73053/01, § 38, ECHR 2006-XIV.

[114] *Ezeh and Connors v. the United Kingdom* [GC], nos 39665/98 and 40086/98, § 126, ECHR 2003-X.

[115] *Engel and Others v. the Netherlands*, 8 June 1976, § 80, Series A no. 22.

[116] *Weber v. Switzerland*, 22 May 1990, § 30, Series A no. 177.

[117] Ibid., § 33.

[118] *Moullet v. France* (dec.), no. 27521/04, 13 September 2007; *Y. v. Norway*, no. 56568/00, §§ 41–43, ECHR 2003-II (extracts); *Ringvold v. Norway*, no. 34964/97, § 38, ECHR 2003-II; *Dubos v. France*, no. 31104/96, Commission decision of 14 January 1998.

with conduct being the subject of both criminal and disciplinary proceedings.[119] The Court must only 'satisfy itself that the disciplinary does not improperly encroach upon the criminal'.[120]

Substantive criminal law

Although in its application to criminal law article 6 is not exclusively confined to procedural issues, States have a very broad discretion in the identification and definition of crimes. The scope of criminal law will certainly not be the same in each national system, with choices being made by national legislators about what should and should not fall within the scope of criminal justice. According to the Court, '[t]he Convention leaves the States free to designate as a criminal offence an act or omission not constituting the normal exercise of one of the rights that it protects'.[121] It does not 'dictate the content of domestic criminal law, including whether or not a blameworthy state of mind should be one of the elements of the offence or whether there should be any particular defence available to the accused'.[122] States may, 'in principle and under certain conditions, penalise a simple or objective fact as such, irrespective of whether it results from criminal intent or from negligence'.[123]

States may indeed be required to criminalize certain acts either as a result of the Convention[124] or by virtue of other international obligations,[125] but this is not a matter that arises under article 6. Decisions of the Court have recognized an obligation flowing from provisions of the Convention to define certain acts as criminal: rape;[126] forced labour;[127] willful attack on personal integrity;[128] human trafficking;[129] disclosure of certain types of information;[130] and certain offences against children.[131] At the same time, the Court has condemned the criminalization of certain acts as discriminatory or excessive: homosexual activity;[132] and acts related to the exercise of freedom of expression[133] and

---

[119] *Campbell and Fell v. the United Kingdom*, 28 June 1984, § 71, Series A no. 80.

[120] *Ezeh and Connors v. the United Kingdom* [GC], nos 39665/98 and 40086/98, § 100, ECHR 2003.

[121] *Engel and Others v. the Netherlands*, 8 June 1976, § 81, Series A no. 22; *Salabiaku v. France*, 7 October 1988, § 27, Series A no. 141-A; *M.M. v. the Netherlands* (dec.), no. 39339/98, 21 May 2002; *De Bruin v. the Netherlands* (dec.), no. 9765/09, 17 September 2013.

[122] *G. v. the United Kingdom* (dec.), no. 37334/08, § 27, 30 August 2011.

[123] *Janosevic v. Sweden*, no. 34619/97, § 100, ECHR 2002-VII. Also *Salabiaku v. France*, 7 October 1988, § 27, Series A no. 141-A; *Valico S.r.l. v. Italy* (dec.), no. 70074/01, ECHR 2006-III.

[124] *M.C. v. Bulgaria*, no. 39272/98, § 153, ECHR 2003-XII; *Siliadin v. France*, no. 73316/01, § 112, ECHR 2005-VII; *Opuz v. Turkey*, no. 33401/02, ECHR 2009.

[125] For example, Convention against Torture and Other Cruel, Inhuman or Degrading Treatment or Punishment, (1987) 1465 UNTS 85, art. 4(1); Convention on the Prevention and Punishment of the Crime of Genocide, (1951) 78 UNTS 277, art. 5.

[126] *X and Y v. the Netherlands*, 26 March 1985, § 27, Series A no. 91; *M.C. v. Bulgaria*, no. 39272/98, §§ 50, 166, ECHR 2003-XII.

[127] *Siliadin v. France*, no. 73316/01, § 112, ECHR 2005-VII; *C.N. and V. v. France*, no. 67724/09, §§ 105–108, 11 October 2012.

[128] *Sandra Jankovic v. Croatia*, no. 38478/05, § 36, 5 March 2009.

[129] *Rantsev v. Cyprus and Russia*, no. 25965/04, §§ 284, 288, ECHR 2010.

[130] *Stoll v. Switzerland* [GC], no. 69698/01, § 155, ECHR 2007-V.

[131] *K.U. v. Finland*, no. 2872/02, § 46, ECHR 2008; *C.A.S. and C.S. v. Romania*, no. 26692/05, 20 March 2012.

[132] *Dudgeon v. the United Kingdom*, 22 October 1981, § 60, Series A no. 45; *Norris v. Ireland*, 26 October 1988, § 46, Series A no. 142; *Modinos v. Cyprus*, 22 April 1993, § 24, Series A no. 259; *S.L. v. Austria*, no. 45330/99, § 44, ECHR 2003-I.

[133] *Vajnai v. Hungary*, no. 33629/06, § 54–56, ECHR 2008; *Altug Taner Akçam v. Turkey*, no. 27520/07, §§ 93–95, 25 October 2011; *Wizerkaniuk v. Poland*, no. 18990/05, §§ 82–83, 86, 5 July 2011; *Sükran Aydin*

peaceful assembly.[134] All forms of collective guilt, whereby individuals are punished not for their acts or omissions but for their association with others, raise difficulties with the presumption of innocence. Noting that 'it is a fundamental rule of criminal law that criminal liability does not survive the person who has committed the criminal act', the Court has held that '[i]nheritance of the guilt of the dead is not compatible with the standards of criminal justice in a society governed by the rule of law'.[135]

Criminal procedure varies considerably throughout Europe. The Court has insisted that 'the High Contracting Parties [are free] to determine their own criminal policy, which is not in principle a matter for it to comment on' and that 'a State's choice of a particular criminal justice system is in principle outside the scope of the supervision it carries out at European level, provided that the system chosen does not contravene the principles set forth in the Convention'.[136] It is not the Court's job to standardize the criminal justice systems that prevail throughout the continent.[137] Nevertheless, there can be no doubt that the decisions and reports of the Commission and the judgments of the Court dealing with article 6 have influenced the evolution of criminal procedure and substantive criminal law across the continent. The common denominator is larger today than it was six decades ago. The Convention and its organs are at least partially responsible for this.

Procedural stages

One consequence of a broad and purposive approach to the notion of 'charged' is that article 6 is applicable to the preliminary investigation stage of criminal prosecution. Although the primary objective of the provision is ensuring that the trial proceedings are fair, it 'may be relevant before a case is sent for trial if and so far as the fairness of the trial is likely to be seriously prejudiced by an initial failure to comply with its provisions'.[138] Difficulties may arise during the period prior to the issuance of formal charges when in practice the individual is already suspected of the crime. For example, a person stopped at a road check who is questioned without being told of suspicions against him or her or that any statement could be used was 'substantially affected', although not formally accused of a criminal offence.[139] The Court has held that although a person has 'not yet been charged with an offence, the preliminary acts of investigation carried out by the authorities together with their attempt to impose an order on the applicant not to leave the city formed part of the judicial investigation initiated against him and made him a

---

and Others v. Turkey, nos 49197/06, 23196/07, 50242/08, 60912/08, and 14871/09, § 55, 22 January 2013; Perinçek v. Switzerland, no. 27510/08, §§ 129–130, 17 December 2013.

[134] Akgöl and Göl v. Turkey, nos 28495/06 and 28156/06, § 43, 17 May 2011.

[135] A.P., M.P., and T.P. v. Switzerland, 29 August 1997, § 48, Reports of Judgments and Decisions 1997-V; E.L., R.L. and J.O.-L. v. Switzerland, 29 August 1997, § 53, Reports of Judgments and Decisions 1997-V. Also Silickienė v. Lithuania, no. 20496/02, § 51, 10 April 2012, where the Court said '[i]mposing criminal sanctions on the living in respect of acts apparently committed by the deceased person calls for its careful scrutiny'.

[136] Achour v. France [GC], no. 67335/01, §§ 44, 51, ECHR 2006-IV; Ould Dah v. France (dec.), no. 13113/03, ECHR 2009.

[137] Twomey, Cameron and Guthrie v. the United Kingdom (dec.), nos 67318/09 and 22226/12, § 30, 28 May 2013.

[138] Şaman v. Turkey, no. 35292/05, § 30, 5 April 2011. Also Salduz v. Turkey [GC], no. 36391/02, § 50, ECHR 2008; Imbrioscia v. Switzerland, 24 November 1993, § 36, Series A no. 275; Hovanesian v. Bulgaria, no. 31814/03, § 30, 21 December 2010.

[139] Aleksandr Zaichenko v. Russia, no. 39660/02, § 43, 18 February 2010.

person "charged with a criminal offence"'.[140] A 'substantive' rather than a 'formalist' understanding of the notions of 'charge' and 'charged' must prevail in order to respect the importance of fairness in the criminal trial process. This 'impels the Court to look behind appearances and examine the realities of the procedure in question in order to determine whether there has been a "charge" within the meaning of Article 6'.[141]

In principle, if criminal trial proceedings result in an acquittal or if the prosecution is discontinued, the individual who was once charged with an offence cannot claim to have been a victim of a violation of article 6.[142] There is an exception to this principle in subsequent proceedings to the extent that the presumption of innocence has been infringed upon. Nevertheless, there is much authority for the exclusion of proceedings relating to execution of a sentence from the scope of article 6(1),[143] including service of a committal warrant.[144]

Because article 6(1) applies throughout the proceedings, it includes the sentencing phase even where this is a distinct procedural step.[145] This may extend to various consequences of a criminal law determination, such as demolition of a house constructed without planning permission.[146] However, measures concerning execution or enforcement of a sentence including application for amnesty have generally been excluded from the scope of article 6(1).[147] The criminal limb of article 6(1) does not apply to parole proceedings[148] and to those involving transfer of prisoners from one country to another.[149]

Within the realm of criminal procedure, there are many incidental or related proceedings that do not qualify as 'determination... of a criminal charge'. Certain police measures undertaken for the prevention of crime or disorder are, by their nature, related to criminal justice, but they do not involve criminal charges and have generally been excluded from the scope of article 6(1). For example, Italian legislation provided for the adoption of preventive measures in respect of 'persons presenting a danger for security and public morality'. The applicant, who was suspected of participating in organized crime, challenged the special police supervision to which he was subject. Declaring inadmissible the application based upon article 6(1), the Court held that 'special supervision is not comparable to a criminal sanction because it is designed to prevent the commission of offence'.[150] In the absence of criminal proceedings as such, forfeiture measures are not

---

[140] *G.C.P. v. Romania*, no. 20899/03, § 41, 20 December 2011.

[141] Ibid., § 38.

[142] *Lenev v. Bulgaria*, no. 41452/07, § 158, 4 December 2012; *X v. Austria*, no. 5575/72, Commission decision of 8 July 1975, DR 1, p. 44; *X v. the United Kingdom*, no. 8083/77, Commission decision of 13 March 1980, DR 19, p. 223; *Eğinlioğlu v. Turkey*, no. 31312/96, Commission decision of 21 October 1998; *Correia de Matos v. Portugal* (dec.), no. 48188/99, 15 November 2001, ECHR 2001-XII; *Osmanov and Yuseinov v. Bulgaria* (dec.), no. 59901/00, 4 September 2003; *I.I. v. Bulgaria* (dec.), no. 44082/98, 25 March 2004; *Oleksy v. Poland* (dec.), no. 1379/06, 16 June 2009; *G.Ł. v. Poland* (dec.), no. 36714/09, 16 November 2010.

[143] *Grava v. Italy* (dec.), no. 43522/98, 5 December 2002; *Aldrian v. Austria*, no. 16266/90, Commission decision of 7 May 1990, DR 65, p. 337; *A.B. v. Switzerland*, no. 20872/92, Commission decision of 22 February 1995, DR 80-B, p. 66.

[144] *Husain v. Italy* (dec.), no. 18913/03, 24 February 2005.

[145] *Phillips v. the United Kingdom*, no. 41087/98, § 39, ECHR 2001-VII.

[146] *Hamer v. Belgium*, no. 21861/03, § 60, ECHR 2007-V (extracts).

[147] *A.B. v. Switzerland*, no. 20872/92, Commission decision of 22 February 1995, DR 80-B, p. 66; *Asociación de Aviadores de la República and Others v. Spain*, no. 10733/84, Commission decision of 11 March 1985, DR 41, p. 211; *Montcornet de Caumont v. France* (dec.), no. 59290/00, 13 May 2003.

[148] *Aldrian v. Austria*, no. 10532/83, Commission decision of 15 December 1987, DR 54, p. 19.

[149] *Szabó v. Sweden* (dec.), no. 28578/03, 27 June 2006.

[150] *Raimondo v. Italy*, 22 February 1994, § 43, Series A no. 281-A.

considered to fall within the 'determination of a criminal charge'.[151] Although not unrelated to the determination of a criminal trial, legal aid applications with respect to obtaining defence counsel do not normally touch upon the legal or factual merits of the charge and are therefore excluded from the scope of the criminal limb of article 6(1).[152]

Expulsion, deportation, and extradition matters are not generally contemplated by the criminal limb of article 6(1), even if they may often involve matters that are ancillary to criminal prosecution.[153] Nevertheless, article 6(1) may apply extraterritorially to the extent that expulsion, *refoulement*, or deportation may result in a real risk that the individual would be subject to a 'flagrant denial of justice' in the receiving country.[154] The notion is synonymous with a trial that is 'manifestly contrary to the provisions of Article 6 or the principles embodied therein'.[155]

Disciplinary offences

Military discipline was the subject of the leading case in this area, *Engel and Others v. The Netherlands*. Because of the relatively minor nature of the sanctions imposed, the European Court concluded that two of the applicants fell outside the criminal sphere. Three of them, however, were exposed to 'serious punishments involving deprivation of liberty', leading the Court to conclude that article 6(1) applied.[156] The criminal limb of article 6(1) does not apply to discharge from the armed forces.[157]

Prison discipline matters often cross the threshold from simple disciplinary matters into the realm of criminal law. In an early judgment, the Court said it was 'well aware that in the prison context there are practical reasons and reasons of policy for establishing a special disciplinary regime, for example security considerations and the interests of public order, the need to deal with misconduct by inmates as expeditiously as possible, the availability of tailor-made sanctions which may not be at the disposal of the ordinary courts and the desire of the prison authorities to retain ultimate responsibility for discipline within their establishments'.[158] The classic distinction in terms of sanctions by which deprivation of liberty is in principle sufficient to engage the criminal law classification does not necessarily apply to the prison environment, because liberty has already been deprived. A Chamber of the Court has held that a disciplinary sanction of one week in solitary confinement 'did not in any way extend the applicant's prison term' and was therefore 'not of such nature and severity that the matter would thereby have been brought within the "criminal" sphere'.[159] When the United Kingdom argued that loss of entitlement to

---

[151] *AGOSI v. the United Kingdom*, 24 October 1986, §§ 65–66, Series A no. 108; *Air Canada v. the United Kingdom*, 5 May 1995, § 54, Series A no. 316-A.

[152] *Gutfreund v. France*, no. 45681/99, §§ 31–37, ECHR 2003-VII.

[153] *Maaouia v. France* [GC], no. 39652/98, § 39, ECHR 2000-X; *Peñafiel Salgado v. Spain* (dec.), no. 65964/01, 16 April 2002; *Monedero Angora v. Spain* (dec.), no. 41138/05, 7 October 2008.

[154] *Othman (Abu Qatada) v. the United Kingdom*, no. 8139/09, § 258, ECHR 2012 (extracts); *Zarmayev v. Belgium* (dec.), no. 35/10, 27 February 2014; *Soering v. the United Kingdom*, 7 July 1989, § 113, Series A no. 161; *Mamatkulov and Askarov v. Turkey* [GC], nos 46827/99 and 46951/99, §§ 90–91, ECHR 2005-I; *Al-Saadoon and Mufdhi v. the United Kingdom*, no. 61498/08, § 149, ECHR 2010 (extracts).

[155] *Sejdovic v. Italy* [GC], no. 56581/00, § 84, ECHR 2006-II; *Stoichkov v. Bulgaria*, no. 9808/02, § 56, 24 March 2005; *Drozd and Janousek v. France and Spain*, 26 June 1992, § 110, Series A no. 240.

[156] *Engel and Others v. the Netherlands*, 8 June 1976, § 85, Series A no. 22.

[157] *Tepeli and Others v. Turkey* (dec.), no. 31876/96, 11 September 2001; *Suküt v. Turkey* (dec.), no. 59773/00, 11 September 2007.

[158] *Campbell and Fell v. the United Kingdom*, 28 June 1984, § 69, Series A no. 80.

[159] *Štitić v. Croatia*, no. 29660/03, § 56, 8 November 2007.

remission of sentence as a sanction for disciplinary offences was not really a 'punishment' in a criminal sense, the Grand Chamber said that the 'reality' of the system was that 'prisoners were detained in prison beyond the date on which they would otherwise have been released, as a consequence of separate disciplinary proceedings which were legally unconnected to the original conviction and sentence'.[160] Matters relating to administration of the prison system, such as placement in a high-supervision unit, do not fall under the criminal limb of article 6(1), although they may be addressed under the civil limb.[161]

The case law of the Convention organs has placed the discipline of professional bodies under the civil limb of article 6(1).[162] With respect to legal professionals, the Court has considered that issues concerning the misconduct during judicial proceedings are excluded from the criminal limb of article 6(1), 'noting that courts may need to respond to such conduct even if it is neither necessary nor practicable to bring a criminal charge against the person concerned'.[163] However, because of the nature and severity of the penalty, contempt of court proceedings may constitute an exception to this general rule.[164] To the extent that they may apply not only to legal professionals but also to the public at large, they fall under the criminal law limb of article 6(1) by virtue of the second Engel criterion.[165] A similar approach has been taken to sanctions imposed for contempt of Parliament, where significance was attached to the fact that the applicant was a private individual and not only an elected member of the legislature.[166] A sanctions regime imposed upon public employees involved in corrupt practices leading, in extreme cases, to 'compulsory retirement', was considered to fall outside the criminal limb of article 6.[167] The criminal limb of article 6 is not applicable in proceedings regarding dismissal of a bailiff for a range of misdemeanours.[168]

Regulatory offences

Another important distinction that is usually made in domestic legal systems is between administrative or regulatory offences and truly criminal offences. With respect to road traffic offences, the European Court of Human Rights has considered article 6(1) to be applicable to the extent infractions are punishable by fines or driving restrictions, including penalty points.[169] However, precautionary measures such as immediate withdrawal of a driving licence and suspension from driving for a short period of time do not quality as criminal offences.[170] The Court has applied article 6(1) to violations of social security legislation, even when relatively modest fines are involved.[171] In a case involving

---

[160] *Ezeh and Connors v. the United Kingdom* [GC], nos 39665/98 and 40086/98, § 123, ECHR 2003-X.
[161] *Enea v. Italy* [GC], no. 74912/01, §§ 97–98, ECHR 2009.
[162] *Albert and Le Compte v. Belgium*, 10 February 1983, § 30, Series A no. 58.
[163] *Ravnsborg v. Sweden*, 23 March 1994, § 34, Series A no. 283-B; *Putz v. Austria*, 22 February 1996, § 34, *Reports of Judgments and Decisions* 1996-I.
[164] *Kyprianou v. Cyprus* [GC], no. 73797/01, §§ 61–64, ECHR 2005-XIII; *Zaicevs v. Latvia*, no. 65022/01, § 33–34, 31 July 2007.
[165] *Weber v. Switzerland*, 22 May 1990, § 33, Series A no. 177.
[166] *Demicoli v. Malta*, 27 August 1991, § 33, Series A no. 210.
[167] *Moullet v. France* (dec.), no. 27521/0413 September 2007.
[168] *Bayer v. Germany*, no. 8453/04, § 37, 16 July 2009.
[169] *Lutz v. Germany*, 25 August 1987, §§ 56–57, Series A no. 123; *Schmautzer v. Austria*, 23 October 1995, § 28, Series A no. 328-A; *Malige v. France*, 23 September 1998, §§ 31–40, *Reports of Judgments and Decisions* 1998-VII.
[170] *Escoubet v. Belgium* [GC], no. 26780/95, §§ 28–36, ECHR 1999-VII.
[171] *Hüseyin Turan v. Turkey*, no. 11529/02, §§ 18–21, 4 March 2008.

administrative imposition of tax penalties that were very substantial where the taxpayer was not in good faith, the Court noted in features of the scheme 'the predominance of those which have a criminal connotation. None of them is decisive on its own, but taken together and cumulatively they made the "charge" in issue a "criminal" one within the meaning of Article 6 para. 1 (art. 6-1), which was therefore applicable.'[172]

Regulation of the democratic process often involves sanctions or penalties in various forms, raising difficulties in the application of article 6(1). Sanctions imposed as part of the regulation of democratic elections have been excluded from the criminal limb of article 6(1). For example, disqualification from standing for office where a candidate exceeded limits on election spending was not considered to be criminal in nature.[173] Proceedings before the Constitutional Court to challenge the dissolution of a political party involved 'par excellence, ... droit de nature politique', so that article 6(1) could not be invoked.[174] Similarly, criminal law did not apply to impeachment proceedings directed at a country's president.[175] The Court has noted a close connection between lustration proceedings, by which individuals are excluded from various forms of political and other activities as part of the process of 'dismantling the heritage of former communist totalitarian systems', and the criminal law sphere.[176] But in a Lithuanian case, it noted that '[t]he purpose of the penalties was thus to prevent former employees of a foreign secret service from employment in public institutions and other spheres of activity vital to the national security of the State', placing the complaint outside of the criminal limb of article 6(1).[177] The activities of commissions of inquiry set up to investigate corruption within elected bodies do not normally involve criminal sanctions. In an Italian case, the Court noted that the commission in question 'se bornait à examiner le phénomène mafieux dans le but de l'étudier et de vérifier tant l'exécution des lois existantes, tant la nécessité de procéder à des modifications législatives. Dans ce type de questions d'intérêt général et véritablement public, rien n'indique que les travaux de la commission parlementaire aient constitué une quelconque forme déguisée de procédure pénale.'[178]

Access to a court

Article 6 does not provide an explicit guarantee of a right of access to a court. This right results from a creative interpretation of the provision by the Court in the leading case of *Golder v. the United Kingdom*. In that decision, the Court noted that article 6(1) 'does not state a right of access to the courts or tribunals in express terms'; rather, it enunciates distinct rights that 'stem from the same basic idea and which, taken together, make up a single right not specifically defined in the narrower sense of the term'.[179] The Court said it was 'inconceivable' that article 6(1) could offer a detailed description of procedural guarantees, yet that it 'should not first protect that which alone makes it in fact possible

[172] *Bendenoun v. France*, 24 February 1994, § 47, Series A no. 284. See also *Mieg de Boofzheim v. France* (dec.), no. 52938/99, 2 December 2002.

[173] *Pierre-Bloch v. France*, 21 October 1997, §§ 53–60, *Reports of Judgments and Decisions* 1997-VI.

[174] *Refah Partisi (le Parti de Prospérité), Necmettin Erbakan, Sevket Kazan and Ahmet Tekdal v. Turkey* (dec.), nos 41340/98, 41342/98–41344/98, 3 October 2000.

[175] *Paksas v. Lithuania* [GC], no. 34932/04, §§ 66–67, ECHR 2011 (extracts).

[176] *Matyjek v. Poland* (dec.), no. 38184/03, ECHR 2007-V.

[177] *Sidabras and Džiautas v. Lithuania* (dec.), nos 55480§00 and 59330§00, 1 July 2003.

[178] *Montera v. Italy* (dec.), no. 64713/01, 9 July 2002.

[179] *Golder v. the United Kingdom*, 21 February 1975, § 28, Series A no. 18.

to benefit from such guarantees, that is, access to a court. The fair, public and expeditious characteristics of judicial proceedings are of no value at all if there are no judicial proceedings.'[180] It described the right as 'inherent', explaining that this was not 'an extensive interpretation forcing new obligations on the Contracting States: it is based on the very terms of the first sentence of Article 6 § 1 read in its context and having regard to the object and purpose of the Convention, a law-making treaty'.[181]

The right of access must be effective. Consequently, it may be necessary for the State to ensure that litigants are provided with legal assistance. The right to legal aid in civil proceedings was recognized by the Court on this basis, although it accepted that there are also circumstances where it would be sufficient for an individual to appear before a tribunal without professional legal assistance.[182] Legal aid must be provided by the State only 'when such assistance proves indispensable for an effective access to court either because legal representation is rendered compulsory or by reason of the complexity of the procedure or of the case'.[183] Availability of legal assistance is relevant to another feature of the right to a fair trial, namely the concept of 'equality of arms', something discussed in more detail below.[184]

Legal certainty has been identified as one component of this right of access to a court. According to the Court, '[t]he right of access to a court is impaired when the rules cease to serve the aims of legal certainty and the proper administration of justice and form a sort of barrier preventing the litigant from having his or her case determined on the merits by the competent court'.[185] The principle of legal certainty is also part of the rule of law, referred to in the Preamble of the Convention, and the principle of legality, set out in article 7. Moreover, it forms part of the requirement that any restriction on fundamental rights be 'in accordance with the law' (art. 8(2)) or 'prescribed by law' (arts. 9(2), 10(2) and 11(2)).

This right of access is not absolute. The right of access to a court may be subject to limitations because the right itself 'by its very nature calls for regulation by the State'.[186] The Court 'must be satisfied that the limitations applied do not restrict or reduce the access left to the individual in such a way or to such an extent that the very essence of the right is impaired. Furthermore, a limitation will not be compatible with Article 6 § 1 if it does not pursue a legitimate aim and if there is not a reasonable relationship of proportionality between the means employed and the aim sought to be achieved.'[187] An example of a permissible limitation on the right of access is provided by court costs. However, these must bear in mind the specific circumstances of the case, including the resources of the

---

[180] Ibid., § 35.

[181] Ibid., § 36; *Enea v. Italy* [GC], no. 74912/01, § 104, ECHR 2009.

[182] *Airey v. Ireland*, 9 October 1979, § 26, Series A no. 32.

[183] *Gnahoré v. France*, no. 40031/98, § 38, ECHR 2000-IX.

[184] *Steel and Morris v. the United Kingdom*, no. 68416/01, § 72, ECHR 2005-II.

[185] *Kart v. Turkey* [GC], no. 8917/05, § 79, ECHR 2009 (extracts); *Tsalkitzis v. Greece*, no. 11801/04, § 44, 16 November 2006.

[186] *Jones and Others v. the United Kingdom*, nos 34356/06 and 40528/06, § 186, 14 January 2014; *Kart v. Turkey* [GC], no. 8917/05, § 79, ECHR 2009 (extracts).

[187] *Jones and Others v. the United Kingdom*, nos 34356/06 and 40528/06, § 186, 14 January 2014; *Waite and Kennedy v. Germany* [GC], no. 26083/94, § 59, ECHR 1999-I; *Kart v. Turkey* [GC], no. 8917/05, § 79, ECHR 2009 (extracts); *Manoilescu and Dobrescu v. Romania and Russia* (dec.), no. 60861/00, §§ 66 and 68, ECHR 2005-VI; *Cudak v. Lithuania* [GC], no. 15869/02, §§ 54–55, ECHR 2010; *Anakomba Yula v. Belgium*, no. 45413/07, § 31, 10 March 2009; *Bellet v. France*, 4 December 1995, § 31, Series A no 333-B.

litigant and the phase of the procedure.[188] Others include the decision not to prosecute and the discontinuance of proceedings,[189] restrictions on abusive litigants,[190] statutory limitation periods,[191] time limits for appeals,[192] and mandatory legal representation.[193]

There is no requirement of a right to appeal in article 6(1). Protocol No. 7 added this with respect to criminal trials. However, if courts of appeal do exist and are applicable to any given litigation, they must comply with the requirements of article 6(1) in guaranteeing an effective right of access to the courts.[194] In assessing whether there has been a violation of article 6, the Court will take into account whether it was possible for the violation to be corrected on appeal.[195]

The right of access to a tribunal may be restricted by immunities that protect one of the parties, generally the defendant or respondent. Ordinarily, these take two forms: the immunity of foreign states and intergovernmental bodies derived from international law and, in certain countries, the immunity of parliamentarians resulting from national legal provisions. As a general principle, the Court has said that 'it would not be consistent with the rule of law in a democratic society if a State could remove from the jurisdiction of the courts a whole range of civil claims or confer immunities from civil liability on large groups or categories of persons'.[196] From the point of view of its compatibility with the Convention, 'the broader an immunity, the more compelling must be its justification'.[197]

Sovereign immunity protects a State from being sued in the courts of another country, where the rights of litigants to access to a tribunal find themselves limited accordingly. This has its source in public international law, including customary international law. On this matter, the judgments of the International Court of Justice are authoritative. In the context of article 6, recognition of sovereign immunity pursues a legitimate aim of 'complying with international law to promote comity and good relations between States through the respect of another State's sovereignty'.[198] The Court has held the 'measures

---

[188] *Weissman and Others v. Romania*, no. 63945/00, § 37, ECHR 2006-VII (extracts); *Kreuz v. Poland*, no 28249/95, § 60, ECHR 2001-VI; *Harrison McKee v. Hungary*, no. 22840/07, §§ 24–27, 3 June 2014.

[189] *Deweer v. Belgium*, 27 February 1980, § 49, Series A no. 35.

[190] *Ashingdane v. the United Kingdom*, 28 May 1985, § 58, Series A no. 93.

[191] *Stubbings and Others v. the United Kingdom*, 22 October 1996, § 51, *Reports of Judgments and Decisions* 1996-IV; *Vo v. France* [GC], no. 53924/00, § 92, ECHR 2004-VIII; *Stagno v. Belgium*, no. 1062/07, § 25, 7 July 2009.

[192] *Melnyk v. Ukraine*, no. 23436/03, § 23, 28 March 2006.

[193] *Maširević v. Serbia*, no. 30671, § 47, 11 February 2014; *Vacher v. France*, 17 December 1996, §§ 24, 28, *Reports of Judgments and Decisions* 1996-VI.

[194] *Andrejeva v. Latvia* [GC], no. 55707/00, § 97, ECHR 2009; *Levages Prestations Services v. France*, 23 October 1996, § 44, *Reports of Judgments and Decisions* 1996-V; *Annoni di Gussola and Others v. France*, nos 31819/96 and 33293/96, § 54, ECHR 2000-XI.

[195] *Asadbeyli and Others v. Azerbaijan*, nos 3653/05, 14729/05, 20908/05, 26242/05, 36083/05, and 16519/06, § 137, 11 December 2012.

[196] *A. v. The United Kingdom*, no. 35373/97, § 63, ECHR 2002-X; *Cordova v. Italy (no. 1)*, no. 40877/98, § 58, ECHR 2003-I; *Cordova v. Italy (no. 2)*, no. 45649/99, § 59, ECHR 2003-I (extracts); *Tsalkitzis v. Greece*, no. 11801/04, § 46, 16 November 2006; *Kart v. Turkey* [GC], no. 8917/05, § 65, ECHR 2009 (extracts).

[197] *Kart v. Turkey* [GC], no. 8917/05, § 83, ECHR 2009 (extracts); *A. v. the United Kingdom*, no. 35373/97, § 78, ECHR 2002-X.

[198] *Jones and Others v. the United Kingdom*, nos 34356/06 and 40528/06, § 186, 14 January 2014; *Al-Adsani v. the United Kingdom* [GC], no. 35763/97, §§ 55–56, ECHR 2001-XI; *Fogarty v. the United Kingdom* [GC], no. 37112/97, § 34, ECHR 2001-XI (extracts); *Kalogeropoulou and Others v. Greece and Germany* (dec.), no. 59021/00, ECHR 2002-X; *Manoilescu and Dobrescu v. Romania and Russia* (dec.), no. 60861/00, ECHR 2005-VI; *McElhinney v. Ireland* [GC], no. 31253/96, § 35, ECHR 2001-XI (extracts); *Sabeh El Leil v. France* [GC], no. 34869/05, § 52, 29 June 2011.

taken by a State which reflect generally recognised rules of public international law on State immunity cannot in principle be regarded as imposing a disproportionate restriction on the right of access to a court as embodied in Article 6 § 1'.[199] Similar considerations apply to intergovernmental organizations.[200]

Parliamentary immunity is a long-standing practice by which States shelter elected officials from lawsuits for the purpose of protecting freedom of expression within the legislature and maintaining the separation of powers so that the courts do not interfere inappropriately with the activities of democratic representatives.[201] The Court recognizes a wide margin of appreciation in this area of parliamentary law.[202] However, the scrutiny will be stricter where there is no clear connection between the parliamentary activity and the immunity accorded, as in the case of a personal quarrel.[203]

Fair and public hearing (art. 6(1))

Regardless of whether the trial concerns criminal or civil matters, it must be 'fair'. According to the text of article 6(1), this consists of two components: a hearing must take place 'within a reasonable time'; and it must be held before 'an independent and impartial tribunal established by law'. Case law has added a number of other principles: equality of arms; the right to be present at the hearing; protection against self-incrimination; and protection from pre-trial publicity. There is also a concept of cumulative violation, by which several irregularities result in overall unfairness, even if taken individually they are not enough to constitute a breach of a fair trial.[204] The fairness of proceedings is considered in light of the proceedings as a whole.[205]

Special components of fairness in criminal proceedings are addressed in article 6(3). Article 6(1) provides a broad guarantee of fairness that is of general application. Of course, despite the *lex specialis* of article 6(3), '[t]he general requirements of fairness contained in Article 6 apply to all criminal proceedings, irrespective of the type of offence at issue.[206] Nevertheless, because the features of article 6(3) are not included in article 6(1), States have greater latitude when their courts are dealing with civil rights and obligations than when criminal matters are concerned.[207]

---

[199] *Jones and Others v. the United Kingdom*, nos 34356/06 and 40528/06, § 189, 14 January 2014; *Fogarty v. the United Kingdom* [GC], no. 37112/97, §§ 35–36, ECHR 2001-XI (extracts); *Sabeh El Leil v. France* [GC], no. 34869/05, §§ 48–49, 29 June 2011.

[200] *Waite and Kennedy v. Germany* [GC], no. 26083/94, § 72, ECHR 1999-I; *Beer and Regan v. Germany* [GC], no. 28934/95, § 58, 18 February 1999; *Stichting Mothers of Srebrenica and Others v. the Netherlands* (dec.), no. 65542/12, § 164, ECHR 2013 (extracts).

[201] *Kart v. Turkey* [GC], no. 8917/05, § 81, ECHR 2009 (extracts); *A. v. the United Kingdom*, no. 35373/97, §§ 75–78, ECHR 2002-X; *Cordova v. Italy (no. 1)*, no. 40877/98, § 55, ECHR 2003-I; *Cordova v. Italy (no. 2)*, no. 45649/99, § 56, ECHR 2003-I (extracts); *De Jorio v. Italy*, no. 73936/01, § 49, 3 June 2004. See also Venice Commission Report on the Regime of Parliamentary Immunity, CDL-INF (96) 7, 4 June 1996.

[202] *Kart v. Turkey* [GC], no. 8917/05, §§ 82–83, ECHR 2009; *A. v. the United Kingdom*, no. 35373/97, § 88, ECHR 2002-X.

[203] *Kart v. Turkey* [GC], no. 8917/05, § 83, ECHR 2009.

[204] *Barberà, Messegué and Jabardo v. Spain*, 6 December 1988, § 89, Series A no. 146.

[205] *Miailhe v. France (no. 2)*, 26 September 1996, § 32, *Reports of Judgments and Decisions* 1996-IV; *Imbrioscia v. Switzerland*, 24 November 1993, § 38, Series A no. 275.

[206] *Bykov v. Russia* [GC], no. 4378/02, § 93, 10 March 2009; *Heaney and McGuinness v. Ireland*, no. 34720/97, §§ 57–58, ECHR 2000-XII.

[207] *Sardón Alvira v. Spain*, no. 46090/10, § 50, 24 September 2013; *Dombo Beheer B.V. v. the Netherlands*, 27 October 1993, § 32, Series A no. 274.

The principle of 'equality of arms' is a component of the right to a fair hearing. It first appeared in very early decisions of the European Commission of Human Rights[208] before being endorsed in the case law of the Court.[209] It requires that 'as regards litigation involving opposing private interests, "equality of arms" implies that each party must be afforded a reasonable opportunity to present his case—including his evidence—under conditions that do not place him at a substantial disadvantage vis-à-vis his opponent'.[210] For example, the Court held that the Belgian criminal justice system, whereby submissions at the appellate level were made by the *avocat général* who then participated in the deliberations of the court in the absence of the other party, who had no opportunity to reply, was in breach of this principle.[211] In cases involving civil proceedings and detainees, the Court has accepted that transporting a party from a prison to a civil tribunal may be troublesome. It has concluded that allowing a party to be represented rather than appear in person does not breach the principle of equality of arms and that article 6(1) does not guarantee a right to be present at civil proceedings.[212]

There is a close relationship between the notion of 'equality of arms' and the desirability of adversarial proceedings. The Court has frequently spoken of the 'right to adversarial proceedings'.[213] For example, the principle of equality of arms is compromised when one of the parties is not given access to the entire court record,[214] or when the court does not serve evidence from one party upon the other.[215] Similarly, the inability of a defendant to challenge expert evidence submitted by the public prosecutor contravenes the principle of equality of arms.[216] Nevertheless, restrictions on adversarial procedure may be allowed when strictly necessary 'in the light of a strong countervailing public interest, such as national security, the need to keep secret certain police methods of investigation or the protection of the fundamental rights of another person'.[217]

Public hearing and public pronouncement of judgment

Article 6(1) imposes the requirement that in the determination of civil rights and obligations or of any criminal charge, there must be 'a hearing'. A full and proper hearing means that 'an applicant has an entitlement to have his case "heard", with the

[208] *X v. Austria*, no. 1747/62, Commission decision of 13 December 1963, Collection 13, p. 42; *Fritz Neumeister v. Austria*, no. 1936/63, Commission decision of 6 July 1964, (1964) 7 YB 224, Collection 14, p. 38.

[209] *Neumeister v. Austria*, 27 June 1968, p. 39, § 22, Series A no. 8.

[210] *Dombo Beheer B.V. v. the Netherlands*, 27 October 1993, § 33, Series A no. 274. Also *Andrejeva v. Latvia* [GC], no. 55707/00, § 96, ECHR 2009; *Gorraiz Lizarraga and Others v. Spain*, no. 62543/00, § 56, ECHR 2004-III.

[211] *Borgers v. Belgium*, 30 October 1991, §§ 26–27, Series A no. 214-B, reversing *Delcourt v. Belgium*, 17 January 1970, Series A no. 11.

[212] *Artyomov v. Russia*, no. 14146/02, §§ 201–202, 27 May 2010.

[213] *Mantovanelli v. France*, 18 March 1997, § 33, *Reports of Judgments and Decisions* 1997-II; *Jokšas v. Lithuania*, no. 25330/07, § 55, 12 November 2013.

[214] *Ternovskis v. Latvia*, no. 33637/02, § 72, 29 April 2014.

[215] *Maravić Markeš v. Croatia*, no. 70923/11, §§ 52–54, 9 January 2014.

[216] *Duško Ivanovski v. the Former Yugoslav Republic of Macedonia*, no. 10718/05, § 60, 24 April 2014; *Matytsina v. Russia*, no. 58428/10, § 207, 27 March 2014.

[217] *A. and Others v. the United Kingdom* [GC], no. 3455/05, § 205, ECHR 2009; *Doorson v. the Netherlands*, 26 March 1996, § 70, *Reports of Judgments and Decisions* 1996-II; *Van Mechelen and Others v. the Netherlands*, 23 April 1997, § 58, *Reports of Judgments and Decisions* 1997-III; *Jasper v. the United Kingdom* [GC], no. 27052/95, §§ 51–53, ECHR 2000-II; *S.N. v. Sweden*, no. 34209/96, § 47, ECHR 2002-V; *Botmeh and Alami v. the United Kingdom*, no. 15187/03, 7 June 2007, § 37.

opportunity, inter alia, to give evidence in his own defence, hear the evidence against him, and examine and cross-examine the witnesses'.[218] The *raison d'être* for the public nature of the hearing, the Grand Chamber has explained, is its protection of litigants against the administration of justice without public scrutiny. This is 'one of the means whereby confidence in the courts, superior and inferior, can be maintained. By rendering the administration of justice visible, publicity contributes to the achievement of the aim of Article 6 § 1, namely a fair trial, the guarantee of which is one of the fundamental principles of any democratic society, within the meaning of the Convention.'[219] The public hearing has been described as a 'fundamental principle'.[220]

Despite the literal terms of article 6(1), the Court has said that this obligation is not an absolute one and that a 'hearing' may be dispensed with. There may be circumstances where the procedure is entirely written and where the parties do not have an opportunity to have any direct contact with the members of the tribunal concerned, without this being deemed a violation of article 6(1). In particular, a hearing may not be required where issues of credibility or contested facts do not arise, and where a fair assessment may reasonably be made based upon written submissions and other materials.[221] The principle of a hearing is said to be particularly important in the criminal trial context, 'where generally there must be at first instance a tribunal which fully meets the requirements of Article 6',[222] although even in criminal matters, 'the nature of the issues to be dealt with before the tribunal or court may not require an oral hearing'.[223] National authorities may take into account factors such as efficiency and economy in determining that holding hearings on a systematic basis may pose an obstacle to the requirement of a determination within a reasonable time, as required by article 6(1).[224] Early cases before the Convention organs emphasized the exceptional nature of dispensing with a hearing,[225] but the Court has since explained that the relevant circumstances capable of justifying this are the nature of the issues to be decided and not the frequency of such situations. Thus, the denial of a hearing is not confined only to 'rare cases'.[226]

Article 6(1) requires that the hearing be 'public'. This means that it must be genuinely accessible. Infringements on the public nature of a hearing occur when it is held in a venue where there is restricted access, where persons other than those participating in the hearing are not allowed to be present, and where there is an absence of information available to the public about the date and place of the hearing.[227] A litigant may waive the

---

[218] *Jussila v. Finland* [GC], no. 73053/01, § 40, ECHR 2006-XIV.

[219] *Martinie v. France* [GC], no. 58675/00, § 39, ECHR 2006-VI; *Axen v. Germany*, 8 December 1983, § 25, Series A no. 72; *Olujić v. Croatia*, no. 22330/05, § 70, 5 February 2009; *Diennet v. France*, 26 September 1995, § 33, Series A no. 325-A.

[220] *Riepan v. Austria*, no. 35115/97, § 27, ECHR 2000-XII; *Luchaninova v. Ukraine*, no. 16347/02, § 55, 9 June 2011.

[221] *Döry v. Sweden*, no. 28394/95, § 37, 12 November 2002; *Pursiheimo v. Finland* (dec.), no. 57795/00, 25 November 2003; *Göç v. Turkey* [GC], no. 36590/97, § 47, ECHR 2002-V.

[222] *Jussila v. Finland* [GC], no. 73053/01, § 40, ECHR 2006-XIV; *Findlay v. the United Kingdom*, 25 February 1997, § 79, *Reports of Judgments and Decisions* 1997-I.

[223] *Jussila v. Finland* [GC], no. 73053/01, § 43, ECHR 2006-XIV.

[224] Ibid., § 42; *Schuler-Zgraggen v. Switzerland*, 24 June 1993, § 58, Series A no. 263.

[225] *Håkansson and Sturesson v. Sweden*, 21 February 1990, § 64, Series A no. 171-A; *Fredin v. Sweden (no. 2)*, 23 February 1994, §§ 21–22, Series A no. 283-A; *Allan Jacobsson v. Sweden (no. 2)*, 19 February 1998, § 46, *Reports of Judgments and Decisions* 1998-I.

[226] *Miller v. Sweden*, no. 55853/00, § 29, 8 February 2005.

[227] *Luchaninova v. Ukraine*, no. 16347/02, § 56, 9 June 2011.

right to a public hearing[228] as long as it is done in an unequivocal manner and does not run counter to an important public interest.[229] However, absent wholly exceptional circumstances, as a minimum, litigants must have the opportunity to request a public hearing. Where the public hearing is not mandatory, however, the tribunal may deny such an application and proceed in private.[230]

The second sentence of article 6(1) states that 'the press and public may be excluded from all or part of the trial in the interests of morals, public order or national security in a democratic society, where the interests of juveniles or the protection of the private life of the parties so require, or to the extent strictly necessary in the opinion of the court in special circumstances where publicity would prejudice the interests of justice'. The application of these provisions should be 'strictly required by the circumstances'.[231] For example, while disciplinary hearings to disqualify practicing physicians may require confidentiality in order to protect the privacy of patients, a systematic practice of holding such proceedings *in camera*, even when patient-related information is not at issue, is inconsistent with article 6(1).[232] The presence of classified information in the case file resulting from national security concerns does not automatically warrant exclusion of the public. This must be assessed on a case-by-case basis rather than automatically, 'weighing the principle that court hearings should be held in public against the need to protect public order and national security'.[233] Courts must consider alternative measures with the intent to minimize the exclusion of the public and the press, such as restricting access to certain documents or holding only some sessions *in camera*.[234]

Article 6(1) provides specifically for public pronouncement of the judgment. It is an additional right, however, one that is 'free-standing',[235] and is not to be taken as a substitute for holding the hearing in public. Announcement of the judgment in public does not correct a proceeding from which the public was excluded.[236] According to the Court, '[t]he publicity of judicial decisions aims to ensure scrutiny of the judiciary by the public and constitutes a basic safeguard against arbitrariness'.[237]

The requirement of public pronouncement of the judgment 'must be assessed in the light of the special features of the proceedings in question, having regard to their entirety, and by reference to the object and purpose of Article 6 § 1'.[238] In reality, the Court has shown considerable flexibility in the application of this right. In several early cases, it noted that in many Member States there was a practice of not reading a judgment aloud but of depositing the judgment in a registry accessible to the public. 'The authors of the

[228] *Jussila v. Finland* [GC], no. 73053/01, § 40, ECHR 2006-XIV; *Schuler-Zgraggen v. Switzerland*, 24 June 1993, § 58, Series A no. 263; *Le Compte, Van Leuven and De Meyere v. Belgium*, 23 June 1981, § 59, Series A no. 43; *H. v. Belgium*, 30 November 1987, § 54, Series A no. 127.
[229] *Håkansson and Sturesson v. Sweden*, 21 February 1990, § 66, Series A no. 171-A.
[230] *Martinie v. France* [GC], no. 58675/00, § 42, ECHR 2006-VI.
[231] *Diennet v. France*, 26 September 1995, § 34, Series A no. 325-A; *Belashev v. Russia*, no. 28617/03, § 83, 4 December 2008.
[232] *Diennet v. France*, 26 September 1995, § 34, Series A no. 325-A.
[233] *Nicolova and Vandova v. Bulgaria*, no. 20688/04, § 74, 17 December 2013; *Belashev v. Russia*, no. 28617/03, § 83, 4 December 2008; *Welke and Białek v. Poland*, no. 15924/05, § 77, 1 March 2011.
[234] *Nicolova and Vandova v. Bulgaria*, no. 20688/04, § 75, 17 December 2013; *Belashev v. Russia*, no. 28617/03, § 84, 4 December 2008.
[235] *Fazliyski v. Bulgaria*, no. 40908/05, § 65, 16 April 2013.
[236] *Artyomov v. Russia*, no. 14146/02, § 109, 27 May 2010.
[237] *Raza v. Bulgaria*, no. 31465/08, § 53, 11 February 2010.
[238] *Shmushkovych v. Ukraine*, no. 3276/10, § 54, 14 November 2013.

Convention cannot have overlooked that fact, even if concern to take it into account is not so easily identifiable in their working documents as in the travaux préparatoires of the 1966 Covenant', wrote the Plenary Court, saying that it did not 'feel bound to adopt a literal interpretation'.[239]

The European Court declined to find a violation in a case where the tribunal of first instance held a public hearing yet did not pronounce a judgment in public; however, the appellate court delivered its judgment, which included a summary of the impugned decision, in public.[240] On the other hand, the provision was breached in a case concerning compensation for detention where hearings of two levels of jurisdiction were held *in camera* and where the judgments of both tribunals were not delivered publicly and were not otherwise accessible.[241] In another case where the hearing itself was not public, merely allowing access to the case file by those who could establish a legal interest was not consistent with article 6(1).[242] Concealment of an entire decision from public scrutiny because the matter concerned national security was held to be unwarranted: 'Indeed, even in indisputable national security cases, such as those relating to terrorist activities, the authorities of countries which have already suffered and are currently at risk of terrorist attacks have chosen to keep secret only those parts of their decisions whose disclosure would compromise national security or the safety of others ... thus illustrating that there exist techniques which can accommodate legitimate security concerns without fully negating fundamental procedural guarantees such as the publicity of judicial decisions.'[243]

Reservations to the Convention with respect to the right to a public hearing are discussed below under the heading 'Reservations'.

Reasonable time

The right to a trial within a reasonable time applies to both civil and criminal proceedings. In criminal trials, the issue of delay may also be governed by article 5(3), to the extent that the individual is detained. The rationale for the principle, in criminal proceedings, 'is based on the need to ensure that accused persons do not have to remain too long in a state of uncertainty as to the outcome of the criminal accusations against them'.[244] Furthermore, 'the vicissitudes of criminal proceedings that remain pending for too long generally also harm the reputation of the alleged offender'.[245] The Court has explained that 'the reason it has been led to rule on so many length-of-proceedings cases is because certain Contracting Parties have for years failed to comply with the "reasonable time" requirement under Article 6 § 1 and have not provided a domestic remedy for this type of complaint'.[246]

The Committee of Ministers has declared that excessive length of proceedings 'is by far the most common issue raised in applications to the Court and that it thereby represents

[239] *Pretto and Others v. Italy*, 8 December 1983, § 26, Series A no. 71; *Axen v. Germany*, 8 December 1983, § 31, Series A no. 72; *Sutter v. Switzerland*, 22 February 1984, § 33, Series A no. 74. See also *Crociani, Palmiotti, Tanassi, and Lefebvre d'Ovidio v. Italy*, nos 8603/79, 8722/79, 8723/79, and 8729/79, Commission decision of 18 December 1980, § 56, (1981) 24 YB 222, DR 22, p. 192.

[240] *Lamanna v. Austria*, no. 28923/95, §§ 33–34, 10 July 2001.

[241] *Werner v. Austria*, 24 November 1997, §§ 56–60, *Reports of Judgments and Decisions* 1997-VII.

[242] *Moser v. Austria*, no. 12643/02, § 103, 21 September 2006.

[243] *Raza v. Bulgaria*, no. 31465/08, § 53, 11 February 2010.

[244] *Kart v. Turkey* [GC], no. 8917/05, § 68, ECHR 2009 (extracts).

[245] Ibid., § 70.

[246] *Scordino v. Italy (no. 1)* [GC], no. 36813/97, § 174, ECHR 2006-V.

an immediate threat to the effectiveness of the Court and hence the human rights protection system based upon the Convention'.[247] It has called upon Member States to ensure that mechanisms and remedies exist to deal with the problem, that reasonable amounts of compensation be awarded in the case of breaches of the rule, and that there is 'a strong but rebuttable presumption that excessively long proceedings will occasion non-pecuniary damage'.[248] It has also urged States to consider forms of non-monetary redress such as a reduction of sanctions or discontinuance of proceedings, and that such measures be retroactive in appropriate circumstances.[249]

To borrow the words of John Selden, 'reasonable time' is a roguish thing, and rather like the Chancellor's foot it may be long, or short, or indeterminate, depending upon many factors. In attempting to set guidelines for application of the principle of trial within a reasonable time, the case law does little more than proclaim that this is to be assessed 'in the light of the particular circumstances of the case . . . in particular the complexity of the case, the applicant's conduct and the conduct of the competent authorities'.[250] Although the subject seems to resist mathematical analysis, two commentators have suggested what they describe as a 3–5–7 schematic for criminal proceedings: less than three years and the Court is unlikely to find an infringement, more than seven and it will usually consider there is a violation. The threshold between reasonable and unreasonable is around five years, 'where the different criteria interact in a difficult puzzle and where predicting an outcome seems the most hazardous'.[251]

With respect to the conduct of the authorities, unjustified delays and periods of inactivity during the investigation are relevant.[252] The Court considers that although it is not in a position to examine the juridical quality of domestic justice systems, where there is repeated remittal of cases for re-examination because of errors committed by lower courts within the same set of proceedings, this indicates 'a serious deficiency in the judicial system' imputable to the State in the determination of reasonable time.[253] In the case of litigation between private parties, the State cannot be considered responsible for delays in the same way as if it were itself a party to proceedings, as in criminal and administrative matters. Nevertheless, each State is required 'to equip itself with legal instruments which are adequate and sufficient to ensure the fulfilment of positive obligations imposed upon the State'.[254] Delays by judges in delivering their decisions are imputable to the State and are taken into account in the calculation of 'reasonable time'.[255] Execution of the final judgment is considered to be an integral part of the 'trial' for the purposes of assessing the

---

[247] Recommendation CM/Rec(2010)3 of the Committee of Ministers to Member States on effective remedies for excessive length of proceedings. See also Recommendation Rec(2004)6 of the Committee of Ministers to Member States on the improvement of domestic remedies.

[248] Recommendation CM/Rec(2010)3 of the Committee of Ministers to Member States on effective remedies for excessive length of proceedings, para. 9.

[249] CM/Rec(2010)3, paras 10–11.

[250] *Pélissier and Sassi v. France* [GC], no. 25444/94, § 67, ECHR 1999-II; *Frydlender v. France* [GC], no. 30979/96, § 43, ECHR 2000-VII; *McFarlane v. Ireland* [GC], no. 31333/06, § 121, 10 September 2010.

[251] Marc Henzelin and Héloïse Rordorf, 'When Does the Length of Criminal Proceedings Become Unreasonable According to the European Court of Human Rights?', (2014) 5 *New Journal of European Criminal Law* 78, at p. 96.

[252] *Pélissier and Sassi v. France* [GC], no. 25444/94, § 72, ECHR 1999-II.

[253] *Wierciszewska v. Poland*, no. 41431/98, § 46, 25 November 2003; *Vlad and Others v. Romania*, nos 40756/06, 41508/07, and 50806/07, § 133, 16 November 2013.

[254] *Lăcătuş and Others v. Romania*, no. 12694/04, § 118, 13 November 2012.

[255] *McFarlane v. Ireland* [GC], no. 31333/06, § 121, 10 September 2010; *Eckle v. Germany*, 15 July 1982, § 84, Series A no. 51; *Obasa v. the United Kingdom*, no. 50034/99, § 34, 16 January 2003.

criterion of reasonable time,[256] although there may be circumstances justifying delay in some cases.[257]

In criminal matters, the 'reasonable time' determination begins from the moment the person is 'charged' with a criminal offence. This is 'the official notification given to an individual by the competent authority of an allegation that he has committed a criminal offence', a definition that also corresponds to the test whether 'the situation of the [suspect] has been substantially affected'.[258] Police and prosecution activity prior to that date may also be relevant to the extent that they impact upon the overall fairness of the trial.[259] In examining the complexity of the case, consideration will be given to such factors as the number of defendants.[260] Economic crimes are often relatively complicated,[261] although this is hardly a presumption. If the accused has used sophisticated legal structures that impede the work of investigators, the Court will take this into account.[262] There is a 'particular obligation of expedition on the State' when criminal proceedings begin a significant period of time after the impugned events.[263] Even where the accused is entitled to apply for an expedited hearing date and fails to do so, this does not exempt the State from its responsibility for holding the trial within a reasonable time.[264] In criminal trials, the 'reasonable time' continues until the proceedings when sentence is fixed.[265]

In non-criminal matters, the starting point for determination of the 'reasonable time' may begin even before issuance of the writ commencing proceedings in the court to which the dispute is submitted, for example in cases where proceedings cannot be initiated until some preliminary procedural step has been taken such as applying for an administrative decision.[266] In legal systems where a plaintiff may join criminal proceedings as a *partie civile*, the period taken into consideration for the length of proceedings with respect to that person starts on the date he or she joins the criminal proceedings.[267] Although the parties to civil proceedings may have the primary responsibility for ensuring that proceedings take place within a reasonable time by means of procedural tools to prevent one party delaying things, 'the domestic courts retain an obligation to ensure compliance with the guarantees of Article 6 § 1 of the Convention'.[268]

---

[256] *Lăcătuş and Others v. Romania*, no. 12694/04, § 117, 13 November 2012; *Hornsby v. Greece*, 19 March 1997, § 40, *Reports of Judgments and Decisions* 1997-II.

[257] *Burdov v. Russia*, no. 59498/00, § 35, ECHR 2002-III.

[258] *Deweer v. Belgium*, 27 February 1980, § 46, Series A no. 35; *Eckle v. Germany*, 15 July 1982, § 73, Series A no. 51.

[259] *McFarlane v. Ireland* [GC], no. 31333/06, § 144, 10 September 2010.

[260] *Pélissier and Sassi v. France* [GC], no. 25444/94, § 71, ECHR 1999-II.

[261] *D.M.T. and D.K.I. v. Bulgaria*, no. 29476/06, § 94, 24 July 2012.

[262] *Pélissier and Sassi v. France* [GC], no. 25444/94, § 71, ECHR 1999-II.

[263] *McFarlane v. Ireland* [GC], no. 31333/06, § 151, 10 September 2010; *Massey v. the United Kingdom*, no. 14399/02, § 27, 16 November 2004.

[264] *Mitchell and Holloway v. the United Kingdom*, no. 44808/98, §§ 55–56, 17 December 2002.

[265] *Findlay v. the United Kingdom*, 25 February 1997, § 69, *Reports of Judgments and Decisions* 1997-I; *Phillips v. the United Kingdom*, no. 41087/98, § 39, ECHR 2001-VII.

[266] *Vilho Eskelinen and Others v. Finland* [GC], no. 63235/00, §§ 65–66, ECHR 2007-II; *König v. Germany*, 28 June 1978, § 98, Series A no. 27; *Hellborg v. Sweden*, no. 47473/99, § 59, 28 February 2006; *Nowicky v. Austria*, no. 34983/02, § 47, 24 February 2005.

[267] *Lăcătuş and Others v. Romania*, no. 12694/04, § 107, 13 November 2012; *Csiki v. Romania*, no. 11273/05, § 91, 5 July 2011.

[268] *Scopelliti v. Italy*, 23 November 1993, § 25, Series A no. 278; *Foley v. the United Kingdom*, no. 39197/98, § 40, 22 October 2002; *Price and Lowe v. the United Kingdom*, nos. 43185/98 and 43186/98, § 23, 29 July 2003.

Independent and impartial tribunal established by law

A fair trial must be conducted before an 'independent and impartial tribunal established by law'. As the Grand Chamber has explained, 'it is of fundamental importance in a democratic society that the courts inspire confidence in the public and above all, as far as criminal proceedings are concerned, in the accused'.[269] Consequently, '[t]o that end Article 6 requires a tribunal falling within its scope to be impartial'.[270] According to the Plenary Court, 'a "tribunal" is characterised in the substantive sense of the term by its judicial function, that is to say determining matters within its competence on the basis of rules of law and after proceedings conducted in a prescribed manner'.[271] In addition, it must satisfy 'a series of further requirements—independence, in particular of the executive; impartiality; duration of its members' terms of office; guarantees afforded by its procedure—several of which appear in the text' of article 6(1).[272]

Although the case law focuses on the issue of impartiality, article 6(1) also requires that the tribunal be independent. Independence of a tribunal points to a separation of powers, something that is fundamental to the rule of law. Specific features of the judicial framework may be relevant to independence, such as adequate remuneration for judges, protection against dismissal, and terms of sufficient length. Useful reference in this respect can be made to the Basic Principles on the Independence of the Judiciary, adopted by the Seventh United Nations Congress on the Prevention of Crime and the Treatment of Offenders in 1985 and subsequently endorsed by the United Nations General Assembly.[273] Principle 1 affirms: 'The independence of the judiciary shall be guaranteed by the State and enshrined in the Constitution or the law of the country. It is the duty of all governmental and other institutions to respect and observe the independence of the judiciary.' But from the standpoint of individual rights, the independence of the judiciary is a means to an end, namely, the impartiality of the judge charged with the case.

In particular, a court or tribunal must be independent of the executive and of the parties to the case. The European Court will look at such factors as the manner of appointment of the members of the adjudicative body, the duration of their term of office, the existence of guarantees against outside pressures, and the appearance of independence.[274] Security of tenure, sometimes called 'irremovability' or 'inamovability', should 'in general be considered as a corollary of their independence', although the absence of such protection in law is not decisive if the principle is recognized in fact and associated with other necessary guarantees.[275] In a very recent decision, the Grand Chamber explained that the notion of the separation of powers between the political organs of government and the judiciary has

---

[269] *Kyprianou v. Cyprus* [GC], no. 73797/01, § 118, ECHR 2005-XIII. Also *Padovani v. Italy*, 26 February 1993, § 27, Series A no. 257-B.

[270] *Kyprianou v. Cyprus* [GC], no. 73797/01, § 118, ECHR 2005-XIII.

[271] *H. v. Belgium*, 30 November 1987, § 50, Series A no. 127-B.

[272] *Belilos v. Switzerland*, 29 April 1988, § 64, Series A no. 132.

[273] UN Doc. A/RES/40/32 and UN Doc. A/RES/40/146.

[274] *Maktouf and Damjanović v. Bosnia and Herzegovina* [GC], nos 2312/08 and 34179/08, § 49, ECHR 2013 (extracts); *Delcourt v. Belgium*, 17 January 1970, § 31, Series A no. 11; *Le Compte, Van Leuven and De Meyere v. Belgium*, 23 June 1981, § 55, Series A no. 43; *Piersack v. Belgium*, 1 October 1982, § 27, Series A no. 53; *Campbell and Fell v. the United Kingdom*, 28 June 1984, § 78, Series A no. 80; *Brudnicka and Others v. Poland*, no. 54723/00, § 38, ECHR 2005-II; *Findlay v. the United Kingdom*, 25 February 1997, § 73, *Reports of Judgments and Decisions* 1997-I; *Luka v. Romania*, no. 34197/02, § 37, 21 July 2009.

[275] *Campbell and Fell v. the United Kingdom*, 28 June 1984, § 80, Series A no. 80; *Maktouf and Damjanović v. Bosnia and Herzegovina* [GC], nos 2312/08 and 34179/08, § 49, ECHR 2013 (extracts).

assumed growing importance in the Court's case law.[276] Nevertheless, 'appointment of judges by the executive or the legislature is permissible, provided that appointees are free from influence or pressure when carrying out their adjudicatory role'.[277]

Assessing the independence of the war crimes chambers in Bosnia and Herzegovina, the European Court noted that the presence of international judges was intended to reassure those concerned about independence of the judiciary. This could not really be in doubt. The Court considered such factors as the mode of appointment (by the High Representative designed by the Organisation for Security and Cooperation in Europe, upon the recommendation of 'the highest judicial figures in Bosnia and Herzegovina'), the taking of a solemn oath, the fact that they were drawn from professional judges in their countries of origin, and the term of office ('admittedly . . . rather short').[278] In a Polish case, the European Court considered that the independence of an assessor in a criminal court was not satisfactorily assured, 'the reason being that she could have been removed by the Minister of Justice at any time during her term of office and that there were no adequate guarantees protecting her against the arbitrary exercise of that power by the Minister'.[279]

Impartiality 'normally denotes the absence of prejudice or bias'.[280] In determining whether a tribunal is impartial within the meaning of article 6(1), two tests are applied, the first described as 'subjective' and the second as 'objective'. The subjective test involves determining whether the personal convictions of a particular judge in a particular case are relevant. If issues in this respect are raised, an assessment must then be made as to whether the judge provided sufficient guarantees, including the composition of the tribunal, to remove any legitimate doubt concerning a lack of impartiality.[281] Although the Court generally focuses on the subjective test, 'there is no watertight division between subjective and objective impartiality since the conduct of a judge may not only prompt objectively held misgivings as to impartiality from the point of view of the external observer (objective test) but may also go to the issue of his or her personal conviction (subjective test)'.[282] The mere fact that a judge has participated in previous cases involving the same issues or offences does not justify concerns about impartiality.[283] A judge who has conducted *in absentia* proceedings is not subsequently barred from sitting in the same case when the accused person appears.[284] Suspicions of a lack of impartiality do not arise when the same

[276] *Maktouf and Damjanović v. Bosnia and Herzegovina* [GC], nos 2312/08 and 34179/08, § 49, ECHR 2013 (extracts), citing *Stafford v. the United Kingdom* [GC], no. 46295/99, § 78, ECHR 2002-IV. Also *Henryk Urban and Ryszard Urban v. Poland*, no. 23614/08, § 46, 30 November 2010.

[277] *Maktouf and Damjanović v. Bosnia and Herzegovina* [GC], nos 2312/08 and 34179/08, § 49, 18 July 2013. Also *Flux v. Moldova (no. 2)*, no. 31001/03, § 27, 3 July 2007.

[278] *Maktouf and Damjanović v. Bosnia and Herzegovina* [GC], nos 2312/08 and 34179/08, § 51, 18 July 2013.

[279] *Henryk Urban and Ryszard Urban v. Poland*, no. 23614/08, § 53, 30 November 2010.

[280] *Micallef v. Malta* [GC], no. 17056/06, § 93, ECHR 2009; *Fey v. Austria*, 24 February 1993, Series A no. 255, §§ 27, 28 and 30; *Wettstein v. Switzerland*, no. 33958/96, § 42, ECHR 2000-XII.

[281] *Gautrin and Others v. France*, § 58, 20 May 1998, *Reports of Judgments and Decisions* 1998-III; *Marguš v. Croatia*, no. 4455/10, § 43, 13 November 2012.

[282] *Micallef v. Malta* [GC], no. 17056/06, § 95, ECHR 2009; *Kyprianou v. Cyprus* [GC], no. 73797/01, § 119, ECHR 2005-XIII.

[283] *Marguš v. Croatia* [GC], no. 4455/10, § 85, 27 May 2014; *Hauschildt v. Denmark*, 24 May 1989, § 50, Series A no. 154; *Romero Martin v. Spain* (dec.), no. 32045/03, 12 June 2006; *Ringeisen v. Austria*, 16 July 1971, Series A no. 13, § 97; *Diennet v. France*, 26 September 1995, Series A no. 325-A, § 38; *Vaillant v. France*, no. 30609/04, §§ 29–35, 18 December 2008; *Craxi III v. Italy* (dec.), no. 63226/00, 14 June 2001; *Ferrantelli and Santangelo v. Italy*, 7 August 1996, § 59, *Reports of Judgments and Decisions* 1996-III.

[284] *Thomann v. Switzerland*, 10 June 1996, §§ 35–36, *Reports of Judgments and Decisions* 1996-III.

judge re-considers a case that he or she has already examined at first instance but where the initial decision was quashed on appeal.[285]

There is a strong presumption that a professional judge in the domestic legal system is impartial, absent evidence to the contrary.[286] The presumption may be rebutted if there is evidence to establish that the judge has shown personal bias, for example by displaying hostility or ill will.[287] It is a very rare occurrence for the Court to conclude that the presumption of personal impartiality has been rebutted. Exceptionally, a majority of the European Court noted several factors that compromised the impartiality of Cypriot judges in a contempt of court proceeding: the judges stated that they had been personally insulted and offended by the applicant's words; their emphatic language 'conveyed a sense of indignation and shock'; they deemed a sentence of five days' imprisonment to be the only adequate response for the contempt in question; early in the hearing they expressed the view that a contempt had been committed.[288] Dissenting judges Bratza and Pellonpää considered that 'none of these factors, whether considered individually or cumulatively, are sufficient to rebut the strong presumption, consistently applied by the Court, that professional judges are free from personal bias'.[289]

It may be difficult to produce evidence capable of rebutting the presumption of impartiality in a subjective sense. For this reason, the requirement of objective impartiality provides an additional guarantee.[290] The objective test focuses on the existence of hierarchical or other links between the judge and participants in the proceedings that justify misgivings about impartiality.[291] Other factors include the existence of national procedures that are aimed at ensuring impartiality, such as rules governing the withdrawal of judges.[292] The fear of bias by the applicant is not irrelevant, but something more objective is required.[293] Nevertheless, appearances are important because 'justice must not only be done, it must also be seen to be done'.[294] The reason for this is the need for public confidence in the courts.[295]

[285] *Marguš v. Croatia* [GC], no. 4455/10, § 86, 27 May 2014.
[286] *Wettstein v. Switzerland*, no. 33958/96, § 43, ECHR 2000-XII; *Micallef v. Malta* [GC], no. 17056/06, § 94, ECHR 2009; *Kyprianou v. Cyprus* [GC], no. 73797/01, § 119, ECHR 2005-XIII.
[287] *Micallef v. Malta* [GC], no. 17056/06, § 94, ECHR 2009; *De Cubber v. Belgium*, 26 October 1984, § 25, Series A no. 86.
[288] *Kyprianou v. Cyprus* [GC], no. 73797/01, § 130, ECHR 2005-XIII.
[289] *Kyprianou v. Cyprus* [GC], no. 73797/01, Concurring Opinion of Judges Sir Nicolas Bratza and Pellonpää, ECHR 2005-XIII.
[290] *Micallef v. Malta* [GC], no. 17056/06, § 95, ECHR 2009; *Pullar v. the United Kingdom*, 10 June 1996, § 32, *Reports of Judgments and Decisions* 1996-III.
[291] *Micallef v. Malta* [GC], no. 17056/06, § 97, ECHR 2009. See court martial cases, for example, *Miller and Others v. the United Kingdom*, nos 45825/99, 45826/99, and 45827/99, 26 October 2004. See also cases regarding the dual role of a judge, for example, *Mežnarić v. Croatia*, no. 71615/01, § 36, 15 July 2005; *Wettstein v. Switzerland*, no. 33958/96, § 47, ECHR 2000-XII (where the lawyer representing the applicant's opponents subsequently judged the applicant in a single set of proceedings and overlapping proceedings, respectively).
[292] *Micallef v. Malta* [GC], no. 17056/06, § 99, ECHR 2009; *Pescador Valero v. Spain*, no. 62435/00, §§ 24–29, ECHR 2003-VII.
[293] *Ferrantelli and Santangelo v. Italy*, 7 August 1996, § 58, *Reports of Judgments and Decisions* 1996-III; *Wettstein v. Switzerland*, no. 33958/96, § 44, ECHR 2000-XII; *Micallef v. Malta*, no. 17056/06, § 74, 15 January 2008.
[294] *De Cubber v. Belgium*, 26 October 1984, § 26, Series A no. 86; *Mežnarić v. Croatia*, no. 71615/01, § 32, 15 July 2005; *Micallef v. Malta*, no. 17056/06, § 75, 15 January 2008.
[295] *Micallef v. Malta* [GC], no. 17056/06, § 98, ECHR 2009; *Castillo Algar v. Spain*, 28 October 1998, § 45, *Reports of Judgments and Decisions* 1998-VIII; *Mežnarić v. Croatia*, no. 71615/01, § 27, 15 July 2005.

Reasoned decision

A court or tribunal contemplated by article 6(1) is 'under a duty to conduct a proper examination of the submissions, arguments and evidence adduced by the parties, without prejudice to its assessment of whether they are relevant for its decision'.[296] The purpose of this is to satisfy the parties that they have been heard, 'thereby contributing to a more willing acceptance of the decision on their part'.[297] It also obliges judges to base their reasoning on objective arguments as well as preserving the rights of the defence.[298] A reasoned judgment is very much of a prerequisite for a meaningful appeal, something that is required in the case of a criminal conviction by article 2 of Protocol No. 7.

The scope of the obligation to provide reasons will vary according to the nature of the decision and must be determined in the light of the circumstances of the case.[299] The European Court takes into account 'the diversity of the submissions that a litigant may bring before the courts and the differences existing in the Contracting States with regard to statutory provisions, customary rules, legal opinion and the presentation and drafting of judgments'.[300] A detailed answer to every argument that has been raised is not required.[301] But where a higher court only provides sparse reasons, for example by incorporating the reasons of a lower court in its decision, it must be clear that it addressed the essential issues and did not merely endorse the findings of the lower court. This requirement is particularly important where the litigant has not been able to make oral representations.[302]

In many Council of Europe States, lay juries sit in judgment, particularly for serious crimes. This is 'guided by the legitimate desire to involve citizens in the administration of justice'.[303] The configurations of such juries and their tasks vary considerably from one country to another, something that is often a function of history, culture, and traditions. Where juries sit in so-called 'assize courts', they are generally not required and are sometimes expressly forbidden to provide reasons for their decisions. In such cases, article 6 obviously does not require a detailed judgment but it does dictate an assessment that there are sufficient safeguards to avoid a risk of arbitrariness and to enable the accused to understand the reasons for his or her conviction.[304] Examples of such safeguards are the

---

[296] *Perez v. France* [GC], no. 47287/99, § 80, ECHR 2004-I; *Buzescu v. Romania*, no. 61302/00, § 63, 24 May 2005.

[297] *Taxquet v. Belgium* [GC], no. 926/05, § 91, ECHR 2010.

[298] Ibid.

[299] *Lăcătuş and Others v. Romania*, no. 12694/04, § 97, 13 November 2012; *Ruiz Torija v. Spain*, 9 December 1994, § 29, Series A no. 303-A; *Hiro Balani v. Spain*, 9 December 1994, § 27, Series A 303-B; *Helle v. Finland*, 19 December 1997, § 55, *Reports of Judgments and Decisions* 1997-VIII.

[300] *Ruiz Torija v. Spain*, 9 December 1994, § 29, Series A no. 303-A; *Boldea v. Romania*, no. 19997/02, § 29, 15 February 2007.

[301] *Van de Hurk v. the Netherlands*, 19 April 1994, §§ 59, 61, Series A no. 288; *Burg v. France* (dec.), no. 34763/02, ECHR 2003-II.

[302] *Taxquet v. Belgium* [GC], no. 926/05, § 91, ECHR 2010; *Helle v. Finland*, 19 December 1997, § 60, *Reports of Judgments and Decisions* 1997-VIII; *Boldea v. Romania*, no. 19997/02, § 30, 15 February 2007; *Segame SA v. France*, no. 4837/06, § 62, ECHR 2012 (extracts).

[303] *Taxquet v. Belgium* [GC], no. 926/05, § 83, ECHR 2010.

[304] *Goktepe v. Belgium*, no. 50372/99, § 28, 2 June 2005; *Voica v. France*, no. 60995/09, § 46, 10 January 2013; *Rache and Ozon v. Romania*, no. 21468/03, §§ 29030, 31 March 2009; *Papon v. France (no. 2)* (dec.), no 54210/00, ECHR 2001-XII; *Bellerín Lagares v. Spain* (dec.), no. 31548/02, 4 November 2003; *R. v. Belgium*, no. 15957/90, Commission decision of 30 March 1992, DR 72, p. 195; *Zarouali v. Belgium*, no. 20664/92, Commission decision of 29 June 1994, DR 78-B, p. 97; *Planka v. Austria*, no. 25852/94, Commission decision of 15 May 1996.

requirement that the presiding judge provide direction or guidance on the legal and factual issues and that questions from the jury be answered in a precise and unequivocal manner.[305]

Presumption of innocence (art. 6(2))

The presumption of innocence benefits everyone charged with a criminal offence until proved guilty according to law. Enshrined in a distinct provision, the presumption of innocence is nevertheless a constituent element of the right to a fair trial in criminal proceedings set out more generally in article 6(1).[306] It is a fundamental feature of criminal justice first stated in the context of international law in article 11(1) of the Universal Declaration of Human Rights: 'Everyone charged with a penal offence has the right to be presumed innocent until proved guilty according to law...' The wording of article 6(2) of the Convention is largely identical, although it may be argued that the Universal Declaration provision is slightly broader in scope due to its reference to 'penal offence' in contrast with the Convention's 'criminal offence'. In the French version, the Declaration refers to *acte délictueux* and the Convention to *infraction*.

In its General Comment on fair trial rights, issued in 2007, the United Nations Human Rights Committee said, in respect of the presumption of innocence:

The presumption of innocence, which is fundamental to the protection of human rights, imposes on the prosecution the burden of proving the charge, guarantees that no guilt can be presumed until the charge has been proved beyond reasonable doubt, ensures that the accused has the benefit of doubt, and requires that persons accused of a criminal act must be treated in accordance with this principle. It is a duty for all public authorities to refrain from prejudging the outcome of a trial, e.g. by abstaining from making public statements affirming the guilt of the accused. Defendants should normally not be shackled or kept in cages during trials or otherwise presented to the court in a manner indicating that they may be dangerous criminals. The media should avoid news coverage undermining the presumption of innocence. Furthermore, the length of pre-trial detention should never be taken as an indication of guilt and its degree. The denial of bail or findings of liability in civil proceedings do not affect the presumption of innocence.[307]

Onus and burden of proof

Most of article 6 concerns rights that are essentially procedural or evidentiary in nature. But by entrenching the presumption of innocence in the Convention, article 6 confirms that fairness also has a substantive dimension. The central manifestation of the presumption of innocence in the criminal trial is the imposition of an onus or burden of proof upon the prosecution.[308] This is a particular aspect of a more general principle of law by which the party that invokes a right has the burden of proof: *Ei incumbit probatio qui dicit, non qui negat*. In the criminal law context, it is elevated to a norm of more fundamental importance. Within criminal justice, the presumption of innocence extends well beyond

---

[305] *Taxquet v. Belgium* [GC], no. 926/05, § 92, ECHR 2010.

[306] *Karaman v. Germany*, no. 17103/10, § 41, 17 February 2014; *Deweer v. Belgium*, 27 February 1980, § 56, Series A no. 35; *Allenet de Ribemont v. France*, 10 February 1995, § 35, Series A no. 308; *G.C.P. v. Romania*, no. 20899/03, § 54, 20 December 2011.

[307] General Comment No. 32, Article 14: Right to equality before courts and tribunals and to a fair trial, UN Doc. CCPR/C/GC/32.

[308] *Barberà, Messegué and Jabardo v. Spain*, 6 December 1988, § 77, Series A no. 146; *Telfner v. Austria*, no. 33501/96, § 15, 20 March 2001.

the actual trial as such. For example, it applies to government officials who make statements or declarations about the guilt of a person when trial is pending, and even to the media. It also extends after the trial in cases where the accused is acquitted[309] or the proceedings discontinued.[310]

Sometimes, criminal justice legislation or judicial practice reverses the burden of proof, with the consequence that the accused is obliged to produce evidence, and often to testify, in order to rebut a presumption of fact or of law. Obviously, this raises problems with respect to the presumption of innocence. The Convention does not prohibit presumptions of fact or of law in criminal cases. Some evidentiary presumptions are almost inherent in the fact-finding process and result from common sense rather than a legislated provision. An example is the presumption that individuals intend the consequences of their acts or the presumption than an individual is legally sane at the time of the alleged crime.

However, the presumption of innocence requires States 'to remain within certain limits in this respect', in that they must 'take into account the importance of what is at stake and maintain the rights of the defence'.[311] Legislation by which the director of a media firm is presumed to be liable for dissemination of defamatory statements by virtue of his or her position, 'having regard to what [is] at stake', was not deemed to be within 'reasonable limits' and therefore not contrary to article 6(2).[312] Presumptions created to deal with smuggling have been deemed compatible with the Convention, notably because judges mitigated their strictness and did not automatically rely upon them.[313] Tax legislation imposing various surcharges on the basis of presumptions was deemed to be within reasonable limits, in part because 'an efficient system of taxation is important to the State's financial interests' but also because they allowed for 'certain means of defence based on subjective elements'.[314] In drug prosecutions, presumptions that property was derived from the proceeds of trafficking have also been deemed compatible with the Convention, bearing in mind how the courts applied them.[315] On the other hand, presumptions of law and fact that led to an automatic conviction for false denunciation of a person who complained of sexual assault because the prosecutor had decided to discontinue the case was judged to breach article 6(2) of the Convention.[316] The Court held there was a violation of the presumption of innocence in a prosecution for driving too

[309] *Sekanina v. Austria*, 25 August 1993, Series A no. 266-A; *Rushiti v. Austria*, no. 28389/95, 21 March 2000; *Lamanna v. Austria*, no. 28923/95, 10 July 2001.
[310] *Minelli v. Switzerland*, 25 March 1983, Series A no. 62; *Englert v. Germany*, 25 August 1987, Series A no. 123-B; *Nölkenbockhoff v. Germany*, 25 August 1987, Series A no. 123-C.
[311] *Salabiaku v. France*, 7 October 1988, § 28, Series A no. 141-A; *Willcox and Hurford v. The United Kingdom* (dec.), nos 43759/10 and 43771/12, § 96, ECHR 2013; *Radio France and Others v. France*, no. 53984/00, ECHR 2004-II; *Hardy v. Ireland* (dec.), no. 23456/94, 29 June 1994; *Telfner v. Austria*, no. 33501/96, § 16, 20 March 2001; *Nicoleta Gheorghe v. Romania*, no. 23470/05, § 30, 3 April 2012; *Haxhishabani v. Luxembourg*, no. 52131/07, § 38, 20 January 2011; *Phillips v. the United Kingdom*, no. 41087/98, § 40, ECHR 2001-VII; *Krumpholz v. Austria*, no. 13201/05, § 34, 18 March 2010; *Müller v. Austria*, no. 12555/03, § 32, 5 October 2006.
[312] *Radio France and Others v. France*, no. 53984/00, § 71, ECHR 2004-II.
[313] *Pham Hoang v. France*, 25 September 1992, § 36, Series A no. 243.
[314] *Janosevic v. Sweden*, no. 34619/97, § 104, ECHR 2002-VII. Also *Västberga Taxi Aktiebolag and Vulic v. Sweden*, no. 36985/97, §§ 114–122, 23 July 2002; *King v. the United Kingdom*, no. 13881/02, 8 April 2003.
[315] *Phillips v. the United Kingdom*, no. 41087/98, §§ 41–47, ECHR 2001-VII. Also *Grayson and Barnham v. the United Kingdom*, nos 19955/05 and 15085/06, §§ 42–50, 23 September 2008.
[316] *Klouvi v. France*, no. 30754/03, §§ 42–54, 30 June 2011.

fast where the only evidence was a speed recording of the car of which the accused person was the registered keeper, but there was no evidence as to the identity of the driver. The registered keeper presented evidence that he had not been driving the car and was not even in the country at the time, but this was inadequate to overturn the legislated presumption. The Court said it could not find 'that in such a situation the only common-sense conclusion was that the applicant himself had been the driver'.[317] In traffic offences where fines are imposed on the owner on the grounds that at the very least he or she has been negligent in letting others use the vehicle, there should not be a problem with article 6(2).[318]

Although not strictly speaking a presumption of fact or law, so-called strict or absolute liability offences make it impossible for an accused person to argue that he or she did not have knowledge of an element of the crime and therefore lacked the criminal intent. For example, in prosecutions for rape of a child, many national criminal codes do not require evidence that the perpetrator had knowledge of the child's age. The Court has held that this does not raise issues under article 6 of the Convention.[319]

The burden of proof should not be confused with the standard of proof. Within the Council of Europe, the formulation of the standard of proof in a criminal trial varies somewhat. Common law jurisdictions generally refer to the notion of proof beyond reasonable doubt, whereas continental systems of the Romano-Germanic tradition use formulations like the *intime conviction* of the judge of fact. The Court has not explicitly recognized the 'beyond reasonable doubt' standard, a norm whose international status is confirmed by its inclusion in the Rome Statute of the International Criminal Court.[320] It has nevertheless stated that the presumption of innocence requires that 'any doubt should benefit the accused'.[321] Reversal of the burden of proof is closely related to guarantees against self-incrimination and the right to silence, which are not explicitly addressed in the European Convention and the Protocols. In practice, a reversed burden is generally aimed at forcing the accused to testify. The rationale is that the accused is in possession of information that cannot be obtained otherwise.

Protection against self-incrimination

One facet of the presumption of innocence is the privilege against self-incrimination. It is closely related to the notion of burden of proof and the idea that the accused person should not contribute to or participate in meeting the evidentiary threshold. The Court has referred to a 'right not to incriminate oneself',[322] explaining that it is primarily concerned with 'respecting the will of an accused person to remain silent'.[323] It has

---

[317] *Krumpholz v. Austria*, no. 13201/05, § 40, 18 March 2010. The decision seems based upon a violation of the right to silence in that the accused person was required to testify to rebut the presumption, but in fact it seems preferable to view this as a case of an unreasonable or disproportionate presumption of fact whereby the registered owner of a vehicle is conclusively or irrebuttably presumed to be the driver. It is probably no longer good law: *Weh v. Austria*, no. 38544/97, §§ 46–48, 8 April 2004.

[318] *Falk v. the Netherlands* (dec.), no. 66273/01, 19 October 2004.

[319] *G. v. the United Kingdom* (dec.), no. 37334/08, §§ 28–30, 30 August 2011.

[320] Rome Statute of the International Criminal Court, (2002) 2187 UNTS 90, art. 66.

[321] *Barberà, Messegué and Jabardo v. Spain*, 6 December 1988, § 77, Series A no. 146. Also *Anghel v. Romania*, no. 28183/03, § 54, 4 October 2007.

[322] *Saunders v. the United Kingdom*, 17 December 1996, § 69, *Reports of Judgments and Decisions* 1996-VI; *Radio France and Others v. France*, no. 53984/00, § 24, ECHR 2004-II.

[323] *Saunders v. the United Kingdom*, 17 December 1996, § 69, Reports of Judgments and Decisions 1996-VI.

identified the right within the general scope of article 6(1), while acknowledging that it is 'closely linked to the presumption of innocence'.[324] Article 14(3)(g) of the International Covenant on Civil and Political Rights provides explicitly for the right of a person charged with a criminal offence '[n]ot to be compelled to testify against himself or to confess guilt'. Several cases before the European Court have applied the 'right not to incriminate oneself' to proceedings involving prosecution of car owners for moving vehicle infractions whereby they would be convicted unless they identified the driver.[325] But 'as commonly understood', the principle does not extend to the use of material obtained from the accused through use of compulsion but which exists independently of the will of the accused, such as documents acquired pursuant to a warrant, breath, blood, and urine samples and bodily tissue for the purpose of DNA testing.[326] Protection against self-incrimination is also related to access to counsel at the earliest stage in an investigation, at a time when the suspect is most vulnerable and susceptible to infringements of the right not to incriminate oneself.[327] It is often at that point that the accused person makes an incriminating statement to the authorities, something that more or less tips the balance against him or her in all subsequent proceedings.

The right not to incriminate oneself is not confined to admissions of wrongdoing and directly incriminating remarks. Some statements obtained through legal compulsion may not be incriminating on their face yet later be relevant in a criminal prosecution in such a way as to contribute to proof of guilt, for example when it is used to discredit other testimony of an accused. This may be especially harmful in a trial by jury; where professional judges are the triers of fact, the danger of a violation is much less apparent.[328] Consequently, 'what is of the essence in this context is the use to which evidence obtained under compulsion is put in the course of the criminal trial'.[329]

It is not uncommon for individuals accused of participating in the same crime to be tried separately. As a consequence, in the trial of one of the suspects there may be expressions about the guilt of others who have not yet been tried. In principle, this may result in infringements of the presumption of innocence.[330] Statements in the first trial may have a prejudicial effect upon subsequent proceedings involving other defendants who are not present or directly involved and who are without means to contest allegations that directly concern them.[331] The Court has said that it accepts the fact that 'in complex criminal proceedings involving several persons who cannot be tried together, references by the trial court to the participation of third persons, who may later be tried separately, may be indispensable for the assessment of the guilt of those who are on trial'. However, where

[324] Ibid., § 68; *Heaney and McGuinness v. Ireland*, no. 34720/97, § 40, ECHR 2000-XII. In *Funke v. France*, 25 February 1993, § 45, Series A no. 256-A, the Court held that punishing a person for refusing to reveal information breached the protection against self-incrimination, assured by article 6(1), and that it was therefore unnecessary to consider the application of article 6(2).

[325] For example, *Weh v. Austria*, no. 38544/97, 8 April 2004; *Krumpholz v. Austria*, no. 13201/05, § 40, 18 March 2010; *Tora Tolmos v. Spain*, no. 23816/94, Commission decision of 17 May 1995, DR 81, p. 82; *J.P., K.R., and G. H. v. Austria*, nos 15135/89, 15136/89, and 15137/89, Commission decision of 5 September 1989, DR 62, p. 319. See also *Weh v. Austria*, no. 38544/97, Joint Dissenting Opinion of Judges Lorenzen, Levits, and Hajiyev, 8 April 2004.

[326] *Saunders v. the United Kingdom*, 17 December 1996, § 69, *Reports of Judgments and Decisions* 1996-VI.

[327] *Salduz v. Turkey* [GC], no. 36391/02, § 54, ECHR 2008.

[328] *Akay v. Turkey* (dec.), no. 34501/97, 19 February 2002.

[329] Ibid.

[330] *Karaman v. Germany*, no. 17103/10, § 42, 17 February 2014.

[331] Ibid., § 43.

such facts must be introduced, 'the court should avoid giving more information than necessary for the assessment of the legal responsibility of those persons who are accused in the trial before it'.[332]

Negative comments and publicity

Negative pre-trial publicity may compromise the presumption of innocence. It can influence public opinion about the guilt of the accused person and directly impact on the impartiality of jurors.[333] There is a tension with the right to information, to which the general public is entitled pursuant to article 10(1) of the European Convention. But this must be balanced with the right to a fair trial, and specifically the presumption of innocence. Where a virulent press campaign surrounds a trial, 'what is decisive is not the subjective apprehensions of the suspect concerning the absence of prejudice required of the trial courts, however understandable, but whether, in the particular circumstances of the case, his fears can be held to be objectively justified'.[334]

In a case involving prosecution for corruption of a senior Turkish official, the Court considered the seriousness of the case and noted that although 'certaines appellations dont le requérant a fait l'objet puissent sembler destinées à impressionner le public', the press coverage consisted essentially of reports of objective facts and of the public reaction. It added that 'dans une société démocratique, des commentaires sévères faits par la presse sont parfois inévitables dans une affaire sensible faisant référence à des événements qui concernent l'intérêt public'.[335] It reached a similar result in a Georgian case.[336] Factors that will be considered will include the temporal proximity of the negative publicity to the trial itself,[337] and the involvement of professional judges rather than lay jurors as finders of fact.[338]

The Court has explained that article 6(2) 'is aimed at preventing the undermining of a fair criminal trial by prejudicial statements made in close connection with those proceedings'.[339] It does not 'prevent the authorities from informing the public of criminal investigations in progress, but it requires that they do so with all the discretion and circumspection necessary if the presumption of innocence is to be respected'.[340] A fundamental distinction is made between a statement indicating that an individual is suspected of having committed a crime and a clear declaration, absent a final conviction, that the person is criminally responsible.[341] According to the Court, 'the presumption of

[332] Ibid., § 64.
[333] *Wloch v. Poland* (dec.), no. 27785/95, 30 March 2000; *Baragiola v. Switzerland*, no. 17265/90, Commission decision of 21 October 1993, (1993) 36 YB 90, DR 75, p. 76; *Berns and Ewert v. Luxembourg*, no. 13251/87, Commission decision of 6 March 1991, (1991) 34 YB 65, DR 68, p. 147.
[334] *G.C.P. v. Romania*, no. 20899/03, § 46, 20 December 2011; *Del Giudice v. Italy* (dec.), no. 42351/98, 6 July 1999.
[335] *Akay v. Turkey* (dec.), no. 34501/97, 19 February 2002. Also *Priebke v. Italy* (dec.), no. 48799/99, 5 April 2001.
[336] *Natsvlishvili and Togonidze v. Georgia*, no. 9043/05, § 105, 29 April 2014.
[337] *G.C.P. v. Romania*, no. 20899/03, § 47, 20 December 2011.
[338] Ibid., § 48; *Akay v. Turkey* (dec.), no. 34501/97, 19 February 2002.
[339] *G.C.P. v. Romania*, no. 20899/03, § 54, 20 December 2011.
[340] Ibid.; *Allenet de Ribemont v. France*, 10 February 1995, § 38, Series A no. 308.
[341] *Virabyan v. Armenia*, no. 40094/05, § 185, 2 October 2012; *Matijašević v. Serbia*, no. 23037/04, § 48, ECHR 2006-X; *Khaydarov v. Russia*, no. 21055/09, § 149, 20 May 2010; *Garycki v. Poland*, no. 14348/02, § 67, 6 February 2007.

innocence will be violated if a judicial decision or a statement by a public official concerning a person charged with a criminal offence reflects an opinion that he is guilty before he has been proved guilty according to law'.[342] In assessing the content of impugned declarations there can be a breach of the presumption of innocence even in the absence of any formal finding to the extent 'that there is some reasoning suggesting that the court or the official regards the accused as guilty'.[343] Not only does article 6(2) prohibit any premature finding by the court or tribunal itself,[344] the presumption of innocence also covers statements made by public officials about criminal investigations that encourage a public belief in the guilt of the individual in question as well as prejudge the findings of the competent judicial authority.[345] More generally, the presumption of innocence imposes restrictions upon the conduct of authorities of the State outside of the courtroom.[346] Public officials, including prosecutors and judges, may make statements about the guilt of an accused prior to any judicial determination and therefore while the individual still benefits from the presumption of innocence.[347] Where a prosecutor explained that a criminal case was being discontinued but that there was no doubt about the guilt of the accused person, the Court said there was a violation of the presumption of innocence. But in another case where the prosecutor issued a decision stating that guilt had been 'proved' before the judgment had been rendered, the Court said that although the choice of the word was 'unfortunate', when 'seen in its proper context, the term signified no more than the prosecution's view that the case file disclosed sufficient evidence of the applicant's guilt to justify proceeding to trial'.[348] Public officials must choose their words carefully when they speak about pending criminal proceedings.[349] The Court will be more exigent when the statement is made by politicians who are also acting in their capacity as public officials because it is more difficult to dismiss their comments as 'part of a legitimate political debate, which might arguably allow a certain degree of exaggeration and liberal use of value judgments with reference to political rivals'.[350]

Related proceedings

When criminal proceedings terminate in either discontinuance or an acquittal, the individual concerned is in principle no longer charged with a criminal offence. This does not, however, mean that article 6(2) cannot apply. The Court has considered its application in a number of subsequent proceedings concerning such matters as an

[342] *G.C.P. v. Romania*, no. 20899/03, § 55, 20 December 2011.
[343] Ibid.
[344] *Něšták v. Slovakia*, no. 65559/01, § 89, 27 February 2007; *Minelli v. Switzerland*, 25 March 1983, § 38, Series A no. 62.
[345] *Allenet de Ribemont v. France*, 10 February 1995, § 41, Series A no. 308; *Daktaras v. Lithuania*, no. 42095/98, §§ 41–43, ECHR 2000-X; *Samoilă and Cionca v. Romania*, no. 33065/03, § 92, 4 March 2008; *Něšták v. Slovakia*, no. 65559/01, § 88, 27 February 2007; *G.C.P. v. Romania*, no. 20899/03, § 54, 20 December 2011.
[346] *X v. Austria*, no. 9295/81, Commission decision of 6 October 1982, DR 30, p. 227; *Sekanina v. Austria*, 25 August 1993, § 21, Series A no. 266-A.
[347] *Virabyan v. Armenia*, no. 40094/05, §§ 187–193, 2 October 2012.
[348] *Kuvikas v. Lithuania*, no. 21837/02, § 55, 27 June 2006. Also *Daktaras v. Lithuania*, no. 42095/98, §§ 13 and 39–45, ECHR 2000-X.
[349] *G.C.P. v. Romania*, no. 20899/03, § 57, 20 December 2011; *Khuzhin and Others v. Russia*, no. 13470/02, § 94, 23 October 2008; *Butkevičius v. Lithuania*, no. 48297/99, § 49, ECHR 2002-II.
[350] *G.C.P. v. Romania*, no. 20899/03, § 59, 20 December 2011.

obligation to bear the costs of the court and the prosecution,[351] confiscation of assets,[352] compensation for detention or other consequences of wrongful prosecution,[353] a request for defence costs,[354] civil liability to compensate the victim,[355] claims against insurers,[356] child-care orders relating to allegations of child abuse,[357] disciplinary and dismissal issues,[358] and revocation of a right to social housing.[359] In explaining why the presumption of innocence would be applicable despite the fact that the person was no longer charged with an offence, the Court explained that it was relevant to compensation proceedings and an entitlement to costs because these are 'a direct sequel to' the termination of the criminal proceedings.[360] It described compensation as being linked 'to such a degree that the decision on the latter issue could be regarded as a consequence and, to some extent, the concomitant of the decision on the former'.[361] A claim for compensation 'not only followed the criminal proceedings in time, but was also tied to those proceedings in legislation and practice, with regard to both jurisdiction and subject matter'.[362] Summarizing its jurisprudence on this subject, in a 2013 decision the Grand Chamber held that:

the presumption of innocence means that where there has been a criminal charge and criminal proceedings have ended in an acquittal, the person who was the subject of the criminal proceedings is innocent in the eyes of the law and must be treated in a manner consistent with that innocence.

---

[351] *Minelli v. Switzerland*, 25 March 1983, §§ 30–32, Series A no. 62; *McHugo v. Switzerland* (dec.), no. 55705/00,12 May 2005.

[352] *Geerings v. the Netherlands*, no. 30810/03, §§ 41–51, 1 March 2007.

[353] *Englert v. Germany*, 25 August 1987, § 35, Series A no. 123; *Nölkenbockhoff v. Germany*, 25 August 1987, § 35, Series A no. 123; *Sekanina v. Austria*, 25 August 1993, § 22, Series A no. 266-A; *Rushiti v. Austria*, no. 28389/95, § 27, 21 March 2000; *Mulaj and Sallahi v. Austria* (dec.). no. 48886/99, 27 June 2002; *O. v. Norway*, no. 29327/95, §§ 33–38, ECHR 2003-II; *Hammern v. Norway*, no. 30287/96, §§ 41–46, 11 February 2003; *Baars v. the Netherlands*, no. 44320/98, § 21, 28 October 2003; *Capeau v. Belgium* (dec.), no. 42914/98, 6 April 2004; *Del Latte v. the Netherlands*, no. 44760/98, § 30, 9 November 2004; *A.L. v. Germany*, no. 72758/01, §§ 31–33, 28 April 2005; *Puig Panella v. Spain*, no. 1483/02, § 50, 25 April 2006; *Tendam v. Spain*, no. 25720/05, §§ 31, 36, 13 July 2010; *Bok v. the Netherlands*, no. 45482/06, §§ 37–48, 18 January 2011; *Lorenzetti v. Italy*, no. 32075/09, § 43, 10 April 2012; *Panteleyenko v. Ukraine*, no. 11901/02, § 67, 29 June 2006; *Grabchuk v. Ukraine*, no. 8599/02, § 42, 21 September 2006.

[354] *Lutz v. Germany*, 25 August 1987, §§ 56–57, Series A no. 123; *Leutscher v. the Netherlands*, 26 March 1996, § 29, *Reports of Judgments and Decisions* 1996-II; *Yassar Hussain v. the United Kingdom*, no. 8866/04, § 19, ECHR 2006-III; *Ashendon and Jones v. the United Kingdom* (revision), nos 35730/07 and 4285/08, §§ 42, 49, 15 December 2011.

[355] *Ringvold v. Norway*, no. 34964/97, § 36, ECHR 2003-II; *Y. v. Norway*, no. 56568/00, § 39, ECHR 2003-II (extracts); *Orr v. Norway*, no. 31283/04, §§ 47–49, 15 May 2008; *Erkol v. Turkey*, no. 50172/06, §§ 33, 37, 19 April 2011; *Vulakh and Others v. Russia*, no. 33468/03, § 32, 10 January 2012; *Diacenco v. Romania*, no. 124/04, §55, 7 February 2012; *Lagardère v. France*, no. 18851/07, §§ 73, 76, 12 April 2012; *Constantin Florea v. Romania*, no. 21534/05, §§ 50, 52, 19 June 2012.

[356] *Lundkvist v. Sweden* (dec.), no, 48518/99, ECHR 2003-XI; *Reeves v. Norway* (dec.), no. 4248/02, 8 July 2004.

[357] *O.L. v. Finland* (dec.), no. 61110/00, 5 July 2005.

[358] *Moullet v. France* (dec.), no. 27521/0413 September 2007; *Taliadorou and Stylianou v. Cyprus*, nos 39627/05 and 39631/05, § 25, 16 October 2008; *Šikić v. Croatia*, no. 9143/08, §§ 42–47, 15 July 2010; *Çelik (Bozkurt) v. Turkey*, no. 34388/05, § 32, 12 April 2011.

[359] *Vassilios Stavropoulos v. Greece*, no. 35522/04, §§ 28–32, 27 September 2007.

[360] *Englert v. Germany*, 25 August 1987, § 35, Series A no. 123; *Nölkenbockhoff v. Germany*, 25 August 1987, § 35, Series A no. 123; *Lutz v. Germany*, 25 August 1987, § 56, Series A no. 123.

[361] *Sekanina v. Austria*, 25 August 1993, § 22, Series A no. 266-A; *Rushiti v. Austria*, no. 28389/95, § 27, 21 March 2000; *Weixelbraun v. Austria*, no. 33730/96, § 24, 20 December 2001.

[362] *Hammern v. Norway*, no. 30287/96, § 46, 11 February 2003; *O. v. Norway*, no. 29327/95, §§ 39–41, ECHR 2003-II.

To this extent, therefore, the presumption of innocence will remain after the conclusion of criminal proceedings in order to ensure that, as regards any charge which was not proven, the innocence of the person in question is respected. This overriding concern lies at the root of the Court's approach to the applicability of Article 6 § 2 in these cases.[363]

A review of the case law shows that 'there is no single approach to ascertaining the circumstances in which that Article will be violated in the context of proceedings which follow the conclusion of criminal proceedings'.[364] Much depends on the nature and context of the proceedings.

In order to avail of article 6(2) under such circumstances, the individual must be able to demonstrate that there is a link between the concluded criminal proceedings and the subsequent proceedings. According to the Grand Chamber, '[s]such a link is likely to be present, for example, where the subsequent proceedings require examination of the outcome of the prior criminal proceedings and, in particular, where they oblige the court to analyse the criminal judgment; to engage in a review or evaluation of the evidence in the criminal file; to assess the applicant's participation in some or all of the events leading to the criminal charge; or to comment on the subsisting indications of the applicant's possible guilt'.[365] In particular, the Court will look to the language used by the decision-maker to determine whether the presumption of innocence has been breached. Where the domestic court said it was 'clearly probable' that the person had 'committed the offences . . . with which he was charged', it considered that doubts had been cast on the acquittal and that the presumption of innocence had thereby been compromised.[366] The European Court does not look favourably on decisions that refer to the earlier decision of the criminal court as having failed to dispel suspicions of guilt.[367] However, 'even the use of some unfortunate language may not be decisive'.[368]

In some legal systems, a civil claim by the victim may be lodged even after the person who is allegedly responsible for the act has been acquitted. The Court considers that 'while exoneration from criminal liability ought to be respected in the civil compensation proceedings, it should not preclude the establishment of civil liability to pay compensation arising out of the same facts on the basis of a less strict burden of proof'.[369] Nor do disciplinary proceedings arising out of the same facts as a criminal charge become impossible simply because the person in question has been acquitted at trial or the case discontinue. Disciplinary bodies may make their own independent findings of fact based upon a different standard of proof.[370]

Compensation

The presumption of innocence does not entitle a person who is detained prior to and during trial to claim compensation if ultimately acquitted. A considerably limited right to

---

[363] *Allen v. the United Kingdom* [GC], no. 25424/09, § 103, 12 July 2013.
[364] Ibid., § 125, 12 July 2013.
[365] *Allen v. the United Kingdom* [GC], no. 25424/09, § 104, 12 July 2013.
[366] *Y v. Norway*, no. 56568/00, § 46, ECHR 2003-II (extracts). Also *Orr v. Norway*, no. 31283/04, § 51, 15 May 2008; *Diacenco v. Romania*, no. 124/04, § 64, 7 February 2012.
[367] *Sekanina v. Austria*, 25 August 1993, §§ 29–30, Series A no. 266-A; *Rushiti v. Austria*, no. 28389/95, §§ 30–31, 21 March 2000.
[368] *Allen v. the United Kingdom* [GC], no. 25424/09, § 126, 12 July 2013.
[369] Ibid., § 123.
[370] *Vanjak v. Croatia*, no. 29889/04, §§ 68–71, 14 January 2010.

compensation is recognized by article 5(5) of the Convention, but it requires more than an acquittal because the applicant must show that the detention itself was wrongful in the sense of article 5.[371] In the event of detention following a miscarriage of justice, article 3 of Protocol No. 7 also entitles a victim to compensation. Again, however, this is not in any sense a corollary of the presumption of innocence. A refusal of compensation does not in and of itself raise an issue concerning the presumption of innocence.[372] The Court has noted that there is great diversity among European States on compensation for a person who is detained during the proceedings and then acquitted. It has found that in most States, compensation is conditional on the applicant's conduct prior to or during trial, or it is simply left to the discretion of the courts.[373]

In States where some form of compensation is not infrequently granted when a person who has been detained is then acquitted by a final judgment, it is not permissible for national courts to speculate about the guilt of the individual. An acquittal is not necessarily a finding of innocence. But if the individual is presumed innocent until convicted in accordance with article 6(2), then the presumption is left undisturbed by the acquittal. The Court has said that 'the voicing of suspicions regarding an accused's innocence is conceivable as long as the conclusion of criminal proceedings has not resulted in a decision on the merits of the accusation. However, it is no longer admissible to rely on such suspicions once an acquittal has become final.'[374] Nor can an applicant for compensation following an acquittal be required to prove he or she is innocent. In compensation proceedings, '[r]equiring a person to establish his or her innocence, which suggests that the court regards that person as guilty, is unreasonable and discloses an infringement of the presumption of innocence'.[375]

Article 6(2) also protects individuals who have been acquitted of a crime, or where prosecution has been discontinued, from being treated by public officials as if they are actually guilty.[376] Failure to ensure respect for the acquittal or the discontinuation decision could make the protection of article 6(2) theoretical and illusory, threatening the person's reputation and how the public perceives him or her. One of the functions of article 6(2) is 'to protect an acquitted person's reputation from statements or acts that follow an acquittal which would seem to undermine it'.[377] In this context, the Court has said that to a certain extent article 6(2) overlaps with the protection provided by article 8(1).[378] But in a case involving accusations by a government minister that persons

---

[371] *Englert v. Germany*, 25 August 1987, § 36, Series A no. 123; *Sekanina v. Austria*, 25 August 1993, § 25, Series A no. 266-A.

[372] *Nölkenbockhoff v. Germany*, 25 August 1987, § 36, Series A no. 123; *Minelli v. Switzerland*, 25 March 1983, §§ 34–35, Series A no. 62; *Capeau v. Belgium*, no. 42914/98, § 23, ECHR 2005-I.

[373] *Sekanina v. Austria*, 25 August 1993, § 25, Series A no. 266-A.

[374] Ibid., § 30. Also *Rushiti v. Austria*, no. 28389/95, § 31, 21 March 2000; *Weixelbraun v. Austria*, no. 33730/96, §§ 27–31, 20 December 2001; *Lamanna v. Austria*, no. 28923/95, §§ 38–40, 10 July 2001; *O. v. Norway*, no. 29327/95, §§ 39–41, ECHR 2003-II; *Hammern v. Norway*, no. 30287/96, §§ 47–49, 11 February 2003; *Allen v. the United Kingdom* [GC], no. 25424/09, § 122, 12 July 2013. The *Sekanina* decision distinguishes earlier precedents where suspicions were expressed but no final judgment entered: *Englert v. Germany*, 25 August 1987, §§ 37–39, Series A no. 123; *Nölkenbockhoff v. Germany*, 25 August 1987, §§ 37–39, Series A no. 123.

[375] *Capeau v. Belgium*, no. 42914/98, § 25, ECHR 2005-I.

[376] *Allen v. the United Kingdom* [GC], no. 25424/09, § 94, 12 July 2013.

[377] *Taliadorou and Stylianou v. Cyprus*, nos 39627/05 and 39631/05, § 26, 16 October 2008.

[378] *Allen v. the United Kingdom* [GC], no. 25424/09, § 94, 12 July 2013.

had breached United Nations Security Council resolutions, the Court found the link with a 'criminal offence' to be too remote and held that article 6(2) did not apply.[379]

Minimum guarantees in criminal prosecutions

In criminal trials, the general rules about fairness that apply to all judicial proceedings in accordance with article 6(1) are complemented by special rules, some of which are set out expressly in article 6(3) and some of which have been developed in the case law of the Court given the special nature of criminal trials. The English text of article 6(3) refers to 'minimum guarantees', indicating clearly that there is no intention to exclude other protections of an accused person. The French text uses the word *notamment*, implying that article 6(3) is a non-exhaustive enumeration and that the Court may add rights to the provision that are not expressly set out.[380] In criminal proceedings the Court generally examines fairness applying paragraphs 1 and 3 of article 6 together,[381] treating the requirements of article 6(3) as particular aspects of the right to a fair trial guaranteed by paragraph 1. Article 6(3) applies to anyone 'charged with a criminal offence', possibly a larger formulation than that used in article 6(1) ('[i]n the determination of... any criminal charge against him'). Arguably, article 6(1) applies to the criminal trial itself, whereas article 6(3) is clearly operative well before the trial and from the moment when the individual is 'charged'. The case law has not insisted upon this distinction, however, as can be seen in 'reasonable time' cases under article 6(1), where the clock starts to run from the moment the person is charged and not from the beginning of the trial itself.[382] One judgment states that 'Article 6—especially paragraph 3—may be relevant before a case is sent for trial if and so far as the fairness of the trial is likely to be seriously prejudiced by an initial failure to comply with its provisions.'[383]

The right of access to a court, held to be a general principle as part of the right to a fair trial under article 6, 'is no more absolute in criminal than in civil matters'.[384] Examples of implied limitations include a decision not to prosecute and an order for discontinuance of proceedings.[385] Nor is there any right under article 6 to a particular outcome of criminal proceedings, such as a formal conviction or an acquittal after charges have been laid.[386]

Information about nature and cause of charge (art. 6(3)(a))

The first of the minimum rights to which a person charged with a criminal offence is entitled is 'to be informed promptly, in a language which he understands and in detail, of the nature and cause of the accusation against him'. As the Grand Chamber has explained, '[p]articulars of the offence play a crucial role in the criminal process, in that it is from the

[379] *Zollmann v. the United Kingdom* (dec.), no. 62902/00, 27 November 2003, ECHR 2003-XII.
[380] *Deweer v. Belgium*, 27 February 1980, § 56, Series A no. 35; *Artico v. Italy*, 13 May 1980, § 32, Series A no. 37.
[381] *F.C.B. v. Italy*, 28 August 1991, § 29, Series A no. 208-B; *Van Geyseghem v. Belgium* [GC], no. 26103/95, § 27, ECHR 1999-I; *Poitrimol v. France*, 23 November 1993, § 29, Series A no. 277-A; *Lala v. the Netherlands*, 22 September 1994, § 26, Series A no. 297-A; *Krombach v. France*, no. 29731/96, § 82, ECHR 2001-II,
[382] *Imbrioscia v. Switzerland*, 24 November 1993, § 36, Series A no. 275.
[383] *Berliński v. Poland*, nos 27715/95 and 30209/96, § 75, 20 June 2002.
[384] *Deweer v. Belgium*, 27 February 1980, § 49, Series A no. 35.
[385] *Deweer v. Belgium*, no. 6903/75, § 58, Commission report of 5 October 1978.
[386] *Withey v. the United Kingdom* (dec.), no. 59493/00, 26 August 2003; *Kart v. Turkey* [GC], no. 8917/05, § 56, ECHR 2009 (extracts).

moment of their service that the suspect is formally put on notice of the factual and legal basis of the charges against him'.[387] The defendant must not only be informed of the cause of the charge, which is to say the acts alleged and on which the charge is based, but also their legal characterization.[388] An accused person who is not familiar with the language used by the criminal tribunal is at a particular disadvantage.[389] In order to avoid contestation on this point, the authorities will often include, in any statement by the suspect or accused person following questioning, a reference to the fact that he or she has been informed of the charges.[390]

The scope of article 6(3)(a) must be assessed within the framework of the general right to a fair trial enshrined in article 6(1).[391] Paragraphs (a) and (b) of article 6(3) are connected because the right to be informed of the nature and the cause of the charges is related to the right to prepare the defence.[392] Article 6(3)(a) does not, however, impose any particular form in which this information is to be communicated.[393] Although there is no specific requirement that the information be provided in writing or that a translation be given in writing, article 6(3)(a) 'does point to the need for special attention to be paid to the notification of the "accusation" to the defendant. An indictment plays a crucial role in the criminal process, in that it is from the moment of its service that the defendant is formally put on notice of the factual and legal basis of the charges against him.'[394]

Adequate time and facilities for defence (art. 6(3)(b))

Any person charged with a criminal offence is entitled to 'to have adequate time and facilities for the preparation of his defence'. The provision implies that substantive defence activity on behalf of the accused may comprise everything 'necessary' to prepare the main trial.[395] The French text makes this clearer, using the word *nécessaires*, as the European Commission of Human Rights observed.[396] The accused must have the opportunity to organize his or her defence in an appropriate way and without restriction as to the opportunity to put all relevant defence arguments before the trial court and thus to influence the outcome of the proceedings.[397] This includes the opportunity to become

---

[387] *Pélissier and Sassi v. France* [GC], no. 25444/94, § 51, ECHR 1999-II. Also *Kamasinski v. Austria*, 19 December 1989, § 79, Series A no. 168.

[388] *Mulosmani v. Albania*, no. 29864/03, § 123, 8 October 2013; *Pélissier and Sassi v. France* [GC], no. 25444/94, § 51, ECHR 1999-II; *Kamasinski v. Austria*, 19 December 1989, § 79, Series A no. 168; *Drassich v. Italy*, no 25575/04, § 34, 11 December 2007.

[389] *Protopapa v. Turkey*, no. 16084/90, § 78, 24 February 2009; *Sejdovic v. Italy* [GC], no. 56581/00, § 89, ECHR 2006-II; *Kamasinski v. Austria*, 19 December 1989, § 79, Series A no. 168; *Tabaï v. France* (dec.), no. 73805/01, 17 February 2004.

[390] *Niculescu v. Romania*, no. 25333/03, § 119, 25 June 2013.

[391] *Pélissier and Sassi v. France* [GC], no. 25444/94, § 52, ECHR 1999-II; *D.M.T. and D.K.I. v. Bulgaria*, no. 29476/06, § 75, 24 July 2012; *Deweer v. Belgium*, 27 February 1980, § 56, Series A no. 35; *Artico v. Italy*, 13 May 1980, § 32, Series A no. 37; *Goddi v. Italy*, 9 April 1984, § 28, Series A no. 76; *Colozza v. Italy*, 12 February 1985, § 26, Series A no. 89.

[392] *Block v. Hungary*, no. 56282/09, § 21, 25 January 2011; *Pélissier and Sassi v. France* [GC], no. 25444/94, §§ 52–54, ECHR 1999-II.

[393] *Pélissier and Sassi v. France* [GC], no. 25444/94, §§ 53–54, ECHR 1999-II; *D.M.T. and D.K.I. v. Bulgaria*, no. 29476/06, § 75, 24 July 2012;

[394] *Hermi v. Italy* [GC], no. 18114/02, § 68, ECHR 2006-XII.

[395] *Vyerentsov v. Ukraine*, no. 20372/11, § 75, 11 April 2013; *Galstyan v. Armenia*, no. 26986/03, § 84, 15 November 2007.

[396] *Can v. Austria*, no. 9300/81, Commission report of 12 July 1984, § 5, DR 35, p. 523.

[397] *Connolly v. the United Kingdom* (dec.), no. 27245/95, 26 June 1996; *Mayzit v. Russia*, no. 63378/00, § 78, 20 January 2005; *Galstyan v. Armenia*, no. 26986/03, § 84, 15 November 2007.

acquainted with results of investigations carried out throughout the proceedings.[398] The defendant should have unrestricted access to the case file and unrestricted use of any notes, including, if necessary, the possibility of obtaining copies of relevant documents.[399]

Sub-paragraph (b) of article 6(3) is connected to sub-paragraph (a), in that the right to be informed of the nature and the cause of the charge is necessary for the preparation of the defence.[400] It is also related to sub-paragraph (c) in that denial of access to counsel may also be associated with insufficient time and facilities to prepare a defence.[401] In particular, 'an applicant who represents himself must be given time and facilities for the preparation of his defence that would be adequate in his particular circumstances'.[402]

The Court has explained that 'national judges have a very difficult task in balancing the need to ensure that the defendant has adequate time to prepare his case and the need to ensure that the trial progresses in a reasonably expeditious way'.[403] The main concern should be fair treatment of the accused, but 'this does not mean that the court must accede to every request made by the defendant'.[404]

The adequacy of the time and facilities afforded to an accused must be assessed in the light of the circumstances of each particular case.[405] A period of a few hours in an administrative case that was 'not a complex one' was nevertheless judged inadequate and a violation of the right protected by article 6(3)(b).[406] Four days for an applicant who was self-represented, and who moreover had to remain handcuffed when studying a file consisting of twenty-eight volumes, was incompatible with article 6(3)(b).[407] In a case involving a minor theft that was 'neither legally nor factually complex', the applicant knew of the charges two months before the trial, but was not informed about the hearing in time to prepare to participate. The Court considered her right to adequate time had been breached.[408]

Although waiver of rights to a fair trial is not in principle contrary to article 6, it must be unequivocal and accompanied by minimum safeguards commensurate with its importance, and not run counter to any important public interest.[409] In the case of the right to time and facilities for preparation of the defence, the Court has said there is no public policy reason opposed to waiver 'because the question of time depends primarily on the assessment of the persons concerned; different counsel need different amounts of time to prepare for a case'.[410]

---

[398] *C.G.P. v. the Netherlands* (dec.), no. 29835/96, 15 January 1997; *Foucher v. France*, 18 March 1997, §§ 26–38, *Reports of Judgments and Decisions* 1997-II.

[399] *Matyjek v. Poland*, no. 38184/03, §§ 59 and 63, ECHR 2007-V; *Luboch v. Poland*, no. 37469/05, §§ 64 and 68, 15 January 2008; *Beraru v. Romania*, no. 40107/04, § 70, 18 March 2014.

[400] *Pélissier and Sassi v. France* [GC], no. 25444/94, §§ 52–54, ECHR 1999-II; *Block v. Hungary*, no. 56282/09, § 21, 25 January 2011.

[401] *Luchaninova v. Ukraine*, no. 16347/02, § 67, 9 June 2011.

[402] *Naviede v. the United Kingdom* (dec.), no. 38072/97, 7 September 1999.

[403] Ibid.; *Tsonyo Tsonev v. Bulgaria (no. 2)*, no. 2376/03, § 36, 14 January 2010.

[404] *Naviede v. the United Kingdom* (dec.), no. 38072/97, 7 September 1999.

[405] *Vyerentsov v. Ukraine*, no. 20372/11, § 75, 11 April 2013; *Galstyan v. Armenia*, no. 26986/03, § 84, 15 November 2007.

[406] *Vyerentsov v. Ukraine*, no. 20372/11, § 76, 11 April 2013. Similarly: *Hakobyan and Others v. Armenia*, no. 34320/04, § 113, 10 April 2012; *Galstyan v. Armenia*, no. 26986/03, §§ 85–88, 15 November 2007; *Ashughyan v. Armenia*, no. 33268/03, § 66, 17 July 2008.

[407] *Iglin v. Ukraine*, no. 39908/05, §§ 69–73, 12 January 2012.

[408] *Luchaninova v. Ukraine*, no. 16347/02, §§ 64–67, 9 June 2011.

[409] *Tsonyo Tsonev v. Bulgaria (no. 2)*, no. 2376/03, § 36, 14 January 2010; *Hermi v. Italy* [GC], no. 18114/02, § 73, ECHR 2006-XII.

[410] *Tsonyo Tsonev v. Bulgaria (no. 2)*, no. 2376/03, § 36, 14 January 2010.

In the course of criminal proceedings, the tribunal may decide to reclassify the offence. The European Court considers that this does not violate the right to a fair trial provided that the accused person has sufficient opportunity to defend himself or herself.[411]

In principle, fairness requires adequate disclosure to the defence, prior to the trial and in sufficient time to enable its effective use in preparing the defence, of any material capable of assisting the defence.[412] In some cases, such as those involving national security issues, an exception to the general rules about disclosure of evidence is allowed on public interest grounds.[413] One recognized procedure is for the trial judge to examine the sensitive evidence *ex parte* so as to rule on whether the public interest in secrecy outweighs the value of the material to the defendant.[414] The issue is whether so-called counterbalancing measures will adequately remedy the lack of a full adversarial procedure.[415]

Defence in person or legal assistance (art. 6(3)(c))

Sub-paragraph (c) of article 6(3) entitles a person charged with a criminal offence 'to defend himself in person or through legal assistance of his own choosing or, if he has not sufficient means to pay for legal assistance, to be given it free when the interests of justice so require'. The right of the accused to participate in the criminal trial, something underscored by the right to be present, also includes the right to receive legal assistance and to follow the proceedings effectively. As the Court has explained, '[s]uch rights are implicit in the very notion of an adversarial procedure', in addition to specific formulations of them in sub-paragraphs (c) and (3) of article 6(3).[416]

The right to a lawyer should be available from the initial stages of the proceedings.[417] The issue of access to counsel at an early stage in the proceedings is of particular importance, and the Court has said that this is an important factor in assessing matters such as the protection against self-incrimination. The Court has underlined the importance of the investigation stage for the preparation of the criminal proceedings, in particular because evidence obtained then may determine the framework of the trial, especially with regard to issues of self-incrimination.[418] This is because 'an accused often

---

[411] *Dallos v. Hungary*, no. 29082/95, §§ 47–53, 1 March 2001; *Sipavičius v. Lithuania*, no. 49093/99, § 30, 21 February 2002; *Haxhia v. Albania*, no. 29861/03, 8 October 2013. For debate on this issue before the International Criminal Court, where the reclassification of offences has been examined in light of the case law of the European Court of Human Rights, see *Prosecutor v. Katanga* (ICC 01/04-01/07), Décision relative à la mise en œuvre de la norme 55 du Règlement de la Cour et prononçant la disjonction des charges portées contre les accusés, 21 November 2012, para. 16; *Prosecutor v. Katanga* (ICC 01/04-01/07), Dissenting Opinion of Judge Christine Van Den Wyngaert, 21 November 2012, paras 47, 57.

[412] *Jespers v. Belgium*, no. 8403/78, Commission decision of 15 October 1980, DR 22, p. 116; *Rowe and Davis v. the United Kingdom* [GC], no. 28901/95, § 60, ECHR 2000-II; *Edwards v. the United Kingdom*, 16 December 1992, § 36, Series A no. 247-B.

[413] *A. and Others v. the United Kingdom* [GC], no. 3455/05, § 206, ECHR 2009; *Rowe and Davis v. the United Kingdom* [GC], no. 28901/95, §§ 60–63, ECHR 2000-II; *McKeown v. the United Kingdom*, no. 6684/05, §§ 40–47, 11 January 2011.

[414] *Jasper v. the United Kingdom* [GC], no. 27052/95, §§ 51–53, ECHR 2000-II; *Edwards and Lewis v. the United Kingdom* [GC], nos 39647/98 and 40461/98, §§ 46–48, ECHR 2004-X.

[415] *A. and Others v. the United Kingdom* [GC], no. 3455/05, § 207, ECHR 2009.

[416] *Lagerblom v. Sweden*, no. 26891/95, § 49, 14 January 2003; *Stanford v. the United Kingdom*, 23 February 1994, § 26, Series A no. 282-A.

[417] *Salduz v. Turkey* [GC], no. 36391/02, § 52, ECHR 2008; *Aras v. Turkey (no. 2)*, no. 15065/07, § 40, 18 November 2014; *Yiğitdoğan v. Turkey*, no. 72174/10, § 63, 3 June 2014; *Yaremenko v. Ukraine*, no. 32092/02, §§ 90–91, 12 June 2008; *Luchaninova v. Ukraine*, no. 16347/02, § 63, 9 June 2011.

[418] *Salduz v. Turkey* [GC], no. 36391/02, § 54, 27 November 2008.

finds himself in a particularly vulnerable position at that stage of the proceedings, the effect of which is amplified by the fact that legislation on criminal procedure tends to become increasingly complex, notably with respect to the rules governing the gathering and use of evidence'.[419] The vulnerability of the suspect 'can only be properly compensated for by the assistance of a lawyer whose task it is, among other things, to help to ensure respect of the right of an accused not to incriminate himself'.[420]

Article 6(3)(c) speaks of 'assistance' and not of 'nomination' or 'appointment', an important distinction because mere nomination or appointment does not ensure effective assistance.[421] A lawyer appointed by legal aid may become indisposed or otherwise be prevented from fulfilling the task of representation.[422] The fact of assigning counsel 'does not in itself ensure the effectiveness of the assistance he may afford an accused'.[423] At the same time, the State cannot be held responsible for any shortcomings of a legal aid lawyer or a court-appointed counsel. Conduct of the defence 'is essentially a matter between the defendant and his counsel, whether counsel be appointed under a legal aid scheme or be privately financed'.[424] This is a consequence of the independence of the legal profession from the State. The authorities are required to intervene pursuant to article 6(3)(c) only where the failings of a legal aid lawyer in provision of effective representation is 'manifest or sufficiently brought to their attention in some other way'.[425]

Although an accused is entitled to be defended by counsel 'of his own choosing', the Court has not viewed this as absolute but rather subject to limitations when free legal aid is being provided. The accused does not have a free choice of funded counsel, although the relationship between lawyer and client is important, and consideration must be given to the wishes of the accused in this respect.[426]

The 'interests of justice' will require that counsel be appointed when effective assistance is necessary, for example where there is a complex written procedure that can only really be completed by a qualified professional.[427] A requirement of the law that the accused be assisted by counsel is not incompatible with the Convention, despite the express terms of article 6(3)(c) recognizing the right 'to defend himself in person'.[428]

---

[419] Ibid.
[420] Ibid.
[421] *Artico v. Italy,* 13 May 1980, § 33, Series A no. 37; *Luchaninova v. Ukraine,* no. 16347/02, § 63, 9 June 2011; *Kamasinski v. Austria,* 19 December 1989, § 65, Series A no. 168.
[422] *Iglin v. Ukraine,* no. 39908/05, § 67, 12 January 2012; *Kahraman v. Turkey,* no. 42104/02, § 35 *in fine,* 26 April 2007
[423] *Imbrioscia v. Switzerland,* 24 November 1993, § 38, Series A no. 275.
[424] *Kamasinski v. Austria,* 19 December 1989, § 65, Series A no. 168.
[425] *Janyr v. Czech Republic,* no. 42937/08, § 68, 31 October 2013; *Falcão dos Santos v. Portugal,* no. 50002/08, §§ 43–46, 3 July 2012; *Bogumil v. Portugal,* no 35228/03, § 46, 7 October 2008; *Czekalla v. Portugal,* no. 38830/97, § 60, ECHR 2002-VIII; *Pavlenko v. Russia,* no. 42371/02, § 99, 1 April 2010.
[426] *Lagerblom v. Sweden,* no. 26891/95, § 54, 14 January 2003; *Croissant v. Germany,* 25 September 1992, § 29, Series A no. 237-B.
[427] *Artico v. Italy,* 13 May 1980, § 34, Series A no. 37.
[428] *Croissant v. Germany,* 25 September 1992, § 27, Series A no. 237-B; *Lagerblom v. Sweden,* no. 26891/95, § 137, 14 January 2003. For debates on this issue at the International Criminal Tribunal for the former Yugoslavia, where the European Court's case law was widely discussed, see *Prosecutor v. Milošević* (IT-02-54-T), Reasons for Decision on Assignment of Defence Counsel, 22 September 2004; *Prosecutor v. Milošević* (IT-02-54-AR73.7), Decision on Interlocutory Appeal of the Trial Chamber's Decision on the Assignment of Defence Counsel, 1 November 2004.

Examination of witnesses (art. 6(3)(d))

A person charged with a criminal offence has the right 'to examine or have examined witnesses against him and to obtain the attendance and examination of witnesses on his behalf under the same conditions as witnesses against him'. This is a specific aspect of the right to a fair hearing set out in article 6(1), and the two provisions are therefore examined together.[429] The formulation of paragraph (d) reflects the notion of 'equality of arms', an over-arching value that applies to article 6 more generally. Paragraph (d) reflects the need to take into account the variety of criminal procedural regimes within Europe, where the rules governing witness testimony vary considerably. Thus, there is no right to any particular form of availability or examination of witnesses, but the standards must be the same whether they apply to the prosecution or the defence. Admissibility of evidence is primarily a matter for national law, where the domestic courts are best equipped to decide whether it is necessary or advisable to hear a witness. Article 6 does not provide an accused with an unlimited right to secure the appearance of the witness in the court.[430]

Article 6(3(d) is considered to require that the accused person 'be given an adequate and proper opportunity to challenge and question a witness against him, either at the time the witness was making his statement or at some later stage of the proceedings'.[431] Accordingly, '[a]ll evidence must normally be produced in the presence of the accused at a public hearing with a view to adversarial argument'.[432] Although some legal systems, including that of the English common law, generally require personal attendance of witnesses and regard as inadmissible 'hearsay' statements that are made outside of court, the European Court does not consider that evidence of statements obtained at the stage of police inquiry or judicial investigation is in principle incompatible with article 6(3)(d), as long as the rights of the defence are respected.[433]

This means, as a rule, that the accused person be provided with 'an adequate and proper opportunity to challenge and question a witness against him either when he or she was testifying or at a later stage of the proceedings'.[434] In one case, the Court noted that many prosecution witnesses did not attend the hearing, depriving the defendant of the possibility of questioning them in person. It said the State had not shown convincingly that the non-attendance was justified, that a reasonable effort had been made to secure their presence, and that 'there were sufficient counterbalancing factors permitting a fair and proper assessment of the reliability of those statements'.[435]

---

[429] *Asch v. Austria*, 26 April 1991, § 25, Series A no. 203; *S.N. v. Sweden*, no. 34209/96, § 43, ECHR 2002-V.

[430] *Gani v. Spain*, no. 61800/08, § 37, 19 February 2013; *S.N. v. Sweden*, no. 34209/96, § 44, ECHR 2002-V.

[431] *Asadbeyli and Others v. Azerbaijan*, nos 3653/05, 14729/05, 20908/05, 26242/05, 36083/05, and 16519/06, § 134, 11 December 2012; *Al-Khawaja and Tahery v. the United Kingdom* [GC], nos 26766/05 and 22228/06, §§ 118–19, ECHR 2011; *Kostovski v. the Netherlands*, 20 November 1989, § 41, Series Ano. 166.

[432] *Gani v. Spain*, no. 61800/08, § 38, 19 February 2013; *Lucà v. Italy*, no. 33354/96, § 39, ECHR 2001-II; *Asch v. Austria*, 26 April 1991, § 27, Series A no. 203.

[433] *Kuvikas v. Lithuania*, no. 21837/02, § 424, 27 June 2006; *Scheper v. the Netherlands* (dec.), no. 39209/02, 5 April 2005.

[434] *Gani v. Spain*, no. 61800/08, § 38, 19 February 2013; *Unterpertinger v. Austria*, 24 November 1986, § 31, Series A no. 110.

[435] *Asadbeyli and Others v. Azerbaijan*, nos 3653/05, 14729/05, 20908/05, 26242/05, 36083/05, and 16519/06, § 134, 11 December 2012.

Three particular contexts dealing with difficulties in the application of article 6(3)(d) have been identified in the case law of the Court: 'anonymous witnesses' who have their identity concealed as a protective measure;[436] 'absent witnesses', where a statement is admitted even though the witness is not present because of death, unavailability, or some other reason;[437] and witnesses who invoke a privilege against self-incrimination.[438] Related to the problem of absent witnesses is that of particularly vulnerable witnesses, for example in cases of sexual assault. The Court will respect the need for special measures of protection, particularly when the victim is confronted with the presumed aggressor.[439] In such circumstances, the Court conducts an overall examination of the fairness of the proceedings, including 'an examination of both the significance of the untested evidence for the case against the accused, namely whether the untested evidence constituted the sole or decisive evidence brought against the applicant . . . and of the counterbalancing measures taken by the judicial authorities to compensate the handicaps under which the defence had laboured'.[440] A conviction that is based solely or to a decisive extent on statements by a witness whom the accused has not been able to examine or have examined is as a general rule incompatible with the guarantee set out in paragraph (d) of article 6(3).[441] Described as the 'sole or decisive rule', the Court has said it should nevertheless not be applied in an inflexible manner, as this 'would transform the rule into a blunt and indiscriminate instrument that runs counter to the traditional way in which the Court approaches the issue of the overall fairness of proceedings, namely by weighing in the balance the competing interests of the defence, the victim, and witnesses, and the public interest in the effective administration of justice'.[442] Accordingly, if a conviction is based solely or decisively on witnesses who cannot be examined by the defence, 'the Court must subject the proceedings to the most searching scrutiny. Because of the dangers of the admission of such evidence, it would constitute a very important factor to balance in the scales and one which would require sufficient counterbalancing factors, including the existence of strong procedural safeguards.'[443]

Article 6(3)(d) also governs the right of the accused person to obtain the testimony of witnesses. In this respect, the State has a positive obligation,[444] one that is of means rather than of result. If they show due diligence, the authorities cannot be blamed for the failure to obtain defence witnesses such that the trial will necessarily be deemed unfair.[445]

---

[436] *Doorson v. the Netherlands*, 26 March 1996, *Reports of Judgments and Decisions* 1996-II; *Kostovski v. the Netherlands*, 20 November 1989, Series A no. 166.

[437] *Craxi v. Italy (no. 1)*, no. 34896/97, 5 December 2002; *Al-Khawaja and Tahery v. the United Kingdom* [GC], nos 26766/05 and 22228/06, ECHR 2011.

[438] *Vidgen v. the Netherlands*, no. 29353/06, 10 July 2012.

[439] *Şandru v. Romania*, no. 3382/05, § 61, 15 October 2013; *S.N. v. Sweden*, no. 34209/96, § 47, ECHR 2002-V; *V.D. v. Romania*, no. 7078/02, § 112, 16 February 2010.

[440] *Gani v. Spain*, no. 61800/08, § 41, 19 February 2013.

[441] *Lucà v. Italy*, no. 33354/96, § 40, ECHR 2001-II; *Al-Khawaja and Tahery v. the United Kingdom* [GC], nos 26766/05 and 22228/06, § 119, ECHR 2011.

[442] *Al-Khawaja and Tahery v. the United Kingdom* [GC], nos 26766/05 and 22228/06, § 146, ECHR 2011.

[443] *Gani v. Spain*, no. 61800/08, § 42, 19 February 2013.

[444] *Sadak and Others v. Turkey (no. 1)*, nos 29900/96, 29901/96, 29902/96, and 29903/96, § 67, ECHR 2001-VIII.

[445] *Gani v. Spain*, no. 61800/08, § 39, 19 February 2013; *Artner v. Austria*, 28 August 1992, § 21, Series A no. 242-A; *Mayali v. France*, no. 69116/01, § 32, 14 June 2005; *Ž. v. Latvia*, no. 14755/03, § 94, 24 January 2008.

Interpreter (art. 6(3)(e))

The final sub-paragraph of article 6(3) recognizes the right of a person charged with a criminal offence to have the free assistance of an interpreter if he cannot understand or speak the language used in court. Like other components of the right to a fair trial, it is possible to waive the right to an interpreter.[446]

An evaluation of the linguistic abilities of the person charged with an offence is obviously vital to the application of article 6(3)(e). The Court will consider the nature of the offence and communications to the accused person by the domestic authorities so as to assess whether they are sufficiently complex as to require detailed knowledge of the language used during the trial proceedings.[447] Assessing the language skills of the accused person is primarily a matter for the domestic authorities. In principle, the European Court will not intervene in such determinations. On occasion, however, it makes its own evaluation. Finding that the right to an interpreter of an applicant who was a native Russian speaker was not violated by France, the Court noted that he had been represented by a lawyer at trial and had made no request for an interpreter, he had been assisted by an interpreter in another proceeding six years earlier so he was aware that the request could be made, he had lived and worked in France for six years, and the record relating to his detention indicated that he spoke French.[448] In a United Kingdom case, problems of comprehension were signalled to the judge by defence counsel when an Italian-speaking accused decided to plead guilty. The judge agreed, although he decided to make do without one, at the invitation of the defence counsel, when a proper interpreter did not attend before the criminal court. Agreeing that this was in principle a matter between the accused and his counsel, the European Court found that 'the ultimate guardian of the fairness of the proceedings was the trial judge who had been clearly apprised of the real difficulties which the absence of interpretation might create for the applicant', holding there was a violation of article 6(3)(e).[449]

The possible need for assistance of an interpreter may arise at the earliest stages in the proceedings. It may even be necessary at the investigation stage. Certainly, article 6(3)(a), requiring that the accused person be informed of the charges, and with which there is a close relationship to article 6(3)(e),[450] can only operate in a meaningful way if the person actually understands the language in which the communication is provided. The Court has explained that a defendant 'may be at a practical disadvantage if the indictment is not translated into a language which he understands'.[451]

The assistance of an interpreter should be provided during the investigating stage unless it is demonstrated in the light of the particular circumstances of each case that there are compelling reasons to restrict this right.[452] In this respect, attention should be drawn to

---

[446] *Sardinas Albo v. Italy* (dec.), no. 56271/00, ECHR 2004-I; *Özcan v. Turkey* (dec.), no. 12822, 21 November 2006.

[447] *Şaman v. Turkey*, no. 35292/05, § 30, 5 April 2011.

[448] *Katritsch v. France*, no. 22575/08, § 45, 4 November 2010.

[449] *Cuscani v. the United Kingdom*, no. 32771/96, § 39, 24 September 2002.

[450] *Kamasinski v. Austria*, 19 December 1989, § 79, Series A no. 168; *Horvath v. Belgium* (dec.), no. 6224/07, 24 January 2012.

[451] *Hermi v. Italy* [GC], no. 18114/02, § 68, ECHR 2006-XII. Also *Sejdovic v. Italy* [GC], no. 56581/00, § 89, ECHR 2006-II; *Kamasinski v. Austria*, 19 December 1989, § 79, Series A no. 168; *Tabaï v. France* (dec.), no. 73805/01, 17 February 2004; *Vakili Rad v. France*, no. 31222/96, Commission decision of 10 September 1997.

[452] *Baytar v. Turkey*, no. 45440/04, § 50, 14 October 2014; *Diallo v. Sweden* (dec.), no. 13205/07, § 25, 5 January 2010; *Şaman v. Turkey*, no. 35292/05, § 30, 5 April 2011.

article 55(1)(c) of the Rome Statute of the International Criminal Court providing that any person questioned during an investigation shall, 'if questioned in a language other than a language the person fully understands and speaks, have, free of any cost, the assistance of a competent interpreter and such translations as are necessary to meet the requirements of fairness'.

The right to an interpreter applies not only to oral statements made at trial, but also to documentary material. This means the accused person who cannot understand or speak the language of the court has 'the right to the free assistance of an interpreter for the translation or interpretation of all those documents or statements in the proceedings instituted against him which it is necessary for him to understand or to have rendered into the court's language in order to have the benefit of a fair trial'.[453]

The European Court has said that Article 6(3)(e) 'does not go so far as to require a written translation of all items of written evidence or official documents in the procedure'.[454] In a case file of 400,000 pages, the Court said it could not blame the Belgian government for refusing to translate everything into Armenian.[455] Attention has been drawn to the use of the term 'interpreter' and not 'translator' (in French, the Convention speaks of an *interprète*), suggesting that oral linguistic assistance may be adequate.[456] However, interpretation must be sufficient to enable the accused to have knowledge of the case and mount a proper defence, in particular by being able to present the court with his or her version of the events.[457] Because the right must be practical and effective, the obligation of the competent authorities is not limited to the appointment of an interpreter but, if they are put on notice in the particular circumstances, it may also extend to a degree of subsequent control over the adequacy of the interpretation provided.[458]

Use of the word 'free' (in French, *gratuitement*) is 'clear and determinate', bearing 'the unqualified meaning they ordinarily have in both of the Court's official languages'.[459] The case law is unequivocal that the State cannot subsequently attempt to recover the costs from an accused person who is subsequently convicted.[460] Any contrary interpretation would 'leave in existence the disadvantages that an accused who does not understand or speak the language used in court suffers as compared with an accused who is familiar with that language'.[461] Moreover, in marginal cases an accused person concerned about the costs might forego interpretation, thereby prejudicing the fairness of the proceedings.[462]

---

[453] *Luedicke, Belkacem and Koç v. Germany*, 28 November 1978, § 48, Series A no. 29; *Diallo v. Sweden* (dec.), no. 13205/07, § 23, 5 January 2010. Also *Hermi v. Italy* [GC], no. 18114/02, §§ 69–70, ECHR 2006-XII.

[454] *Diallo v. Sweden* (dec.), no. 13205/07, § 23, 5 January 2010; *X v. Austria*, no. 6185/73, Commission decision of 29 May 1975, DR 2, p. 68.

[455] *Khatchadourian v. Belgium* (dec.), no. 22738/08, 12 January 2010.

[456] *Diallo v. Sweden* (dec.), no. 13205/07, § 23, 5 January 2010; *Katritsch v. France*, no. 22575/08, § 41, 4 November 2010; *Protopapa v. Turkey*, no. 16084/90, § 80, 24 February 2009; *Husain v. Italy* (dec.), no. 18913/03, 24 February 2005.

[457] *Güngör v. Germany* (dec.), no. 31540/96, 17 May 2001; *Katritsch v. France*, no. 22575/08, § 42, 4 November 2010.

[458] *Kamasinski v. Austria*, 19 December 1989, § 54, Series A no. 168.

[459] *Luedicke, Belkacem and Koç v. Germany*, 28 November 1978, § 42, Series A no. 29.

[460] Ibid., § 46; *Öztürk v. Germany*, 21 February 1984, § 58, Series A no. 73; *Işyar v. Bulgaria*, no. 391/03, § 45, 20 November 2008; *Hovanesian v. Bulgaria*, no. 31814/03, § 48, 21 December 2010.

[461] *Luedicke, Belkacem and Koç v. Germany*, 28 November 1978, § 42.

[462] Ibid.

The right to an interpreter is a special form of a more general human rights protection that relates to a person's membership in a minority group.

Presence at trial

Nowhere does article 6 declare explicitly that a person 'charged with a criminal offence' is entitled to take part in the hearing, but this is a consequence of 'the object and purpose of the Article taken as a whole'.[463] This is confirmed by sub-paragraphs (c), (d), and (e) of paragraph 3. They guarantee to 'everyone charged with a criminal offence' the right 'to defend himself in person', 'to examine or have examined witnesses', and 'to have the free assistance of an interpreter if he cannot understand or speak the language used in court'. The Grand Chamber has said that 'it is difficult to see how he could exercise these rights without being present'.[464] The Court has said the duty to guarantee the right of a criminal defendant to be present in the courtroom—either during the original proceedings or in a retrial—ranks as one of the essential requirements of Article 6.[465] Article 14(3)(d) of the International Covenant on Civil and Political Rights provides for the right of an accused person '[t]o be tried in his presence'.

Criminal trial proceedings in the absence of the accused are not incompatible with article 6, and in one form or another take place in most European States.[466] As the Court has said, 'the impossibility of holding a trial by default may paralyse the conduct of criminal proceedings, in that it may lead, for example, to dispersal of the evidence, expiry of the time-limit for prosecution or a miscarriage of justice'.[467] But there is a violation of article 6 if a person who is convicted *in absentia* is unable subsequently to obtain a fresh determination of the merits of the charge, with respect both to questions of law and of fact, if it is not established that the person convicted had earlier waived the right to appear and to defend himself[468] or had attempted to escape trial.[469] If proceedings have been conducted *in absentia*, the refusal to reopen them, absent evidence that the accused has waived the right to be present, has been described as a 'flagrant denial of justice' rendering the proceedings 'manifestly contrary to the provisions of Article 6 or the principles embodied therein'.[470] The person convicted *in absentia* must be entitled to participate in new proceedings or proceedings on appeal with the possibility of obtaining admission of new evidence, and obtaining a fresh factual and legal determination.[471]

At the same time, the Court has stressed the importance of the accused's appearance, 'both because of his right to a hearing and because of the need to verify the accuracy of his statements and compare them with those of the victim—whose interests need to be protected—and of the

---

[463] *Sejdovic v. Italy* [GC], no. 56581/00, § 81, ECHR 2006-II.

[464] Ibid. Also *Colozza v. Italy*, 12 February 1985, § 27, Series A no. 89; *T. v. Italy*, 12 October 1992, § 26, Series A no. 245-C; *F.C.B. v. Italy*, 28 August 1991, § 3, Series A no. 208-B; *Belziuk v. Poland*, 25 March 1998, § 37, *Reports of Judgments and Decisions* 1998-II.

[465] *Sejdovic v. Italy* [GC], no. 56581/00, § 81, § 84, ECHR 2006-II; *Stoichkov v. Bulgaria*, no. 9808/02, § 56, 24 March 2005.

[466] *Krombach v. France*, no. 29731/96, § 85, ECHR 2001-II.

[467] *Colozza v. Italy*, 12 February 1985, § 29, Series A no. 89.

[468] *Sejdovic v. Italy* [GC], no. 56581/00, § 82, ECHR 2006-II; *Colozza v. Italy*, 12 February 1985, § 29, Series A no. 89; *Einhorn v. France* (dec.), no. 71555/01, § 33, ECHR 2001-XI; *Krombach v. France*, no. 29731/96, § 85, ECHR 2001-II; *Somogyi v. Italy*, no. 67972/01, § 66, ECHR 2004-IV.

[469] *Medenica v. Switzerland*, no. 20491/92, § 55, ECHR 2001-VI.

[470] *Stoichkov v. Bulgaria*, no. 9808/02, §§ 54–58, 24 March 2005; *Sejdovic v. Italy* [GC], no. 56581/00, § 84, ECHR 2006-II.

[471] *Sejdovic v. Italy* [GC], no. 56581/00, § 85, ECHR 2006-II; *Jones v. the United Kingdom* (dec.), no. 30900/02, 9 September 2003.

witnesses'.[472] As a result, legislation can discourage unjustified absences, as long as sanctions are not disproportionate and the accused is not deprived of the right to counsel.[473]

Like other fundamental fair trial rights, the right to be present at trial can be waived by the accused person. This must be established in an unequivocal manner and be attended by safeguards commensurate with its importance.[474] If an accused person has not been notified in person of the trial, waiver cannot simply be inferred from his or her status as a 'fugitive'.[475] Even where there is evidence of waiver based upon the conduct of the accused, the consequences of this must have been reasonably foreseeable.[476] The person concerned must not bear the burden of proving he or she sought to evade justice or that the absence was due to force majeure.[477] But national authorities are entitled to assess whether the accused showed good cause for absence or whether there was anything to warrant a finding that the absence was due to circumstances beyond his or her control.[478] There is always the possibility that certain established facts might prove unequivocally that the accused knew of the criminal proceedings and of the nature and cause of the charges, and intentionally avoided appearance. An example might be where the accused states publicly or in writing an intent to defy summonses to appear.[479] Of course, another example of clear waiver is when the accused misbehaves during the proceedings and is excluded as a result of such conduct.[480] Even then, the Court bears the responsibility to see that the defence is properly represented and that counsel have been appointed to ensure the trial is fair.[481] Where *in absentia* proceedings are possible under national law, the right to a defence remains in force and the accused is entitled to be represented by counsel even if he or she is not present in the courtroom.[482]

Other fundamental fair trial rights are also relevant to criminal proceedings conducted in the absence of the accused. For there to be any legitimacy to a waiver, the accused must have been informed of the accusations, a right assured to criminal defendants by article 6(3)(a).[483] The right to be defended by a lawyer, set out in article 6(3)(c), must remain even if the accused is absent.[484]

While attendance of the accused at the trial is fundamental, practice suggests that this is far less important at the appeal stage, where it 'does not take on the same crucial significance'.[485]

---

[472] *Sejdovic v. Italy* [GC], no. 56581/00, § 92, ECHR 2006-II; *Mariani v. France*, no. 43640/98, § 40, 31 March 2005; *Krombach v. France*, no. 29731/96, § 86, ECHR 2001-II.

[473] *Krombach v. France*, no. 29731/96, §§ 84, 89 and 90, ECHR 2001-II; *Van Geyseghem v. Belgium* [GC], no. 26103/95, § 34, ECHR 1999-I; *Poitrimol v. France*, 23 November 1993, § 35, Series A no. 277-A.

[474] *Sejdovic v. Italy* [GC], no. 56581/00, § 86, ECHR 2006-II; *Poitrimol v. France*, 23 November 1993, § 31, Series A no. 277-A.

[475] *Sejdovic v. Italy* [GC], no. 56581/00, § 87, ECHR 2006-II; *Colozza v. Italy*, 12 February 1985, § 28, Series A no. 89.

[476] *Sejdovic v. Italy* [GC], no. 56581/00, § 87, ECHR 2006-II; *Jones v. the United Kingdom* (dec.), no. 30900/02, 9 September 2003.

[477] *Sejdovic v. Italy* [GC], no. 56581/00, § 88, ECHR 2006-II; *Colozza v. Italy*, 12 February 1985, § 30, Series A no. 89.

[478] *Sejdovic v. Italy* [GC], no. 56581/00, § 88, ECHR 2006-II; *Medenica v. Switzerland*, no. 20491/92, § 57, ECHR 2001-VI.

[479] *Sejdovic v. Italy* [GC], no. 56581/00, § 9, ECHR 2006-II; *Iavarazzo v. Italy* (dec.), no. 50498/99, 4 December 2001.

[480] *Marguš v. Croatia*, no. 4455/10, §§ 50–54, 13 November 2012.

[481] *Lala v. the Netherlands*, 22 September 1994, §§ 33–34, Series A no. 297-A; *Pelladoah v. the Netherlands*, 22 September 1994, §§ 40–41, Series A no. 297-B; *Krombach v. France*, no. 29731/96, § 84, ECHR 2001-II.

[482] *Krombach v. France*, no. 29731/96, §§ 87–91, ECHR 2001-II.

[483] *Sejdovic v. Italy* [GC], no. 56581/00, § 89, ECHR 2006-II.

[484] Ibid., § 91; *Mariani v. France*, no. 43640/98, § 91, 31 March 2005.

[485] *Kamasinski v. Austria*, 19 December 1989, § 106, Series A no. 168; *Ekbatani v. Sweden*, 26 May 1988, § 31, Series A no. 134.

Age of criminal responsibility

Nowhere in the fair trial guarantees of the Covenant or the other major international human rights conventions is a minimum age of criminal responsibility set out. That it belongs within the realm of human rights is clear from article from article 40(3)(a) of the Convention on the Rights of the Child: 'the establishment of a minimum age below which children shall be presumed not to have the capacity to infringe the penal laws'.[486] The Convention on the Rights of the Child presents this as an issue of 'capacity' and in that sense it is analogous to the issue of fitness to stand trial. However, issues relating to minimum age might also be raised under article 3 or article 8 of the Convention.

A challenge arose in two cases concerning conviction of 11-year-olds for murder in England, where the age of criminal responsibility is set at 10. The Grand Chamber rejected a challenge based upon article 3, where a number of factors, of which age was only one, were raised by the applicant. On the issue of a minimum age for criminal trial, the Grand Chamber noted that there was no commonly accepted minimum age for criminal responsibility in Europe. It acknowledged that most States Parties had an age limit higher than that in force in England and Wales, although some States, such as Cyprus, Ireland, Liechtenstein, and Switzerland, had one that was lower.[487] The Grand Chamber observed that neither the Convention on the Rights of the Child nor the Beijing Rules[488] give any indication as to what the minimum age might be. It said that 'the age of ten cannot be said to be so young as to differ disproportionately from the age-limit followed by other European States'.[489]

Nevertheless, in a case involving an 11-year-old who was described as 'intellectually backward' the Court held that he was not able to participate effectively in the trial, resulting in a violation of article 6(1) of the Convention. 'In the case of a child, it is essential that he be dealt with in a manner which takes full account of his age, level of maturity and intellectual and emotional capacities, and that steps are taken to promote his ability to understand and participate in the proceedings', the Court said.[490] The Court acknowledged that even adults cannot often fully understand complex courtroom proceedings, something that justifies the importance of the right to counsel. However, 'effective participation' requires that 'the accused has a broad understanding of the nature of the trial process and of what is at stake for him or her, including the significance of any penalty which may be imposed'.[491] The Court added that 'when the decision is taken to deal with a child, such as the applicant, who risks not being able to participate effectively because of his young age and limited intellectual capacity, by way of criminal proceedings rather than some other form of disposal directed primarily at determining the child's best

---

[486] Convention on the Rights of the Child, (1990) 1577 UNTS 3.

[487] *T. v. The United Kingdom* [GC], no. 24724/94, § 71, 16 December 1999 ; *V. v. the United Kingdom* [GC], no. 24888/94, § 73, ECHR 1999-IX.

[488] United Nations Standard Minimum Rules for the Administration of Juvenile Justice ('The Beijing Rules'), UN Doc. A/RES/40/33.

[489] *T. v. the United Kingdom* [GC], no. 24724/94, § 72, 16 December 1999; *V. v. the United Kingdom* [GC], no. 24888/94, § 74, ECHR 1999-IX.

[490] *S.C. v. the United Kingdom*, no. 60958/00, § 28, ECHR 2004-IV. See, nevertheless, ibid., Dissenting Opinion of Judge Pellonpää Joined by Judge Sir Nicolas Bratza, ECHR 2004-IV.

[491] Ibid., § 29.

interests and those of the community, it is essential that he be tried in a specialist tribunal which is able to give full consideration to, and make proper allowance for, the handicaps under which he labours, and adapt its procedure accordingly'.[492] More generally, when juvenile defendants are on trial, the proceedings must be organized so as to respect the principle of the best interests of the child. According to the Court, '[i]t is essential that a child charged with an offence is dealt with in a manner which takes full account of his age, level of maturity and intellectual and emotional capacities, and that steps are taken to promote his ability to understand and participate in the proceedings'.[493]

Protection against self-incrimination

The right to silence and the protection against self-incrimination are not explicitly set out in article 6, but the Court has deemed them part of its implied content because they are 'generally recognised international standards that lie at the heart of the notion of fair procedure under Article 6'.[494] In *Saunders*, the European Court of Human Rights held that the protection against self-incrimination did not apply only to admissions of wrongdoing or to remarks that are directly incriminating. 'Testimony obtained under compulsion which appears on its face to be of a non-incriminating nature—such as exculpatory remarks or mere information on questions of fact—may later be deployed in criminal proceedings in support of the prosecution case, for example to contradict or cast doubt upon other statements of the accused or evidence given by him during the trial to otherwise undermine his credibility', the Court said.[495] In another case, this finding was extended to the production of documents.[496]

The rationale is to protect the accused against improper compulsion by the authorities, 'thereby contributing to the avoidance of miscarriages of justice'.[497] The right not to incriminate oneself 'presupposes that the prosecution in a criminal case seek to prove their case against the accused without resort to evidence obtained through methods of coercion or oppression in defiance of the will of the accused'.[498] The right is closely related to the presumption of innocence enshrined in article 6(2).[499]

[492] Ibid., § 35.
[493] *Blokhin v. Russia*, no. 47152/06, § 157, 14 November 2013; *Martin v. Estonia*, no. 35985/09, § 92, 30 May 2013; *Panovits v. Cyprus*, no. 4268/04, § 67, 11 December 2008; *Adamkiewicz v. Poland*, no. 54729/00, § 70, 2 March 2010.
[494] *Saunders v. the United Kingdom*, 17 December 1996, § 68, *Reports of Judgments and Decisions* 1996-VI. Also *Murray v. the United Kingdom*, 28 October 1994, § 45, Series A no. 300-A; *Heaney and McGuinness v. Ireland*, no. 34720/97, § 40, ECHR 2000-XII.
[495] *Saunders v. the United Kingdom*, 17 December 1996, § 71, *Reports of Judgments and Decisions* 1996-VI.
[496] *J.B. v. Switzerland*, no. 31827/96, § 66, ECHR 2001-III.
[497] *Saunders v. the United Kingdom*, 17 December 1996, § 68, *Reports of Judgments and Decisions* 1996-VI; *Heaney and McGuinness v. Ireland*, no. 34720/97, § 40, ECHR 2000-XII; *John Murray v. the United Kingdom*, 8 February 1996, § 45, *Reports of Judgments and Decisions* 1996-I; *Bykov v. Russia* [GC], no. 4378/02, § 89, 10 March 2009; *Allan v. the United Kingdom*, no. 48539/99, § 44, ECHR 2002-IX; *Jalloh v. Germany* [GC], no. 54810/00, §§ 94–117, ECHR 2006-IX; *O'Halloran and Francis v. the United Kingdom* [GC], nos 15809/02 and 25624/02, §§ 53–63, ECHR 2007-III.
[498] *Bykov v. Russia* [GC], no. 4378/02, § 89, 10 March 2009; *Saunders v. the United Kingdom*, 17 December 1996, § 68, *Reports of Judgments and Decisions* 1996-VI; *Heaney and McGuinness v. Ireland*, no. 34720/97, § 40, ECHR 2000-XII.
[499] *Saunders v. the United Kingdom*, 17 December 1996, § 68, *Reports of Judgments and Decisions* 1996-VI; *Heaney and McGuinness v. Ireland*, no. 34720/97, § 40, ECHR 2000-XII.

Admissibility of evidence

Article 6 does set out any rules on the admissibility of evidence as such. The matter has been treated by the European Court as something to be regulated by national law.[500] It is 'not the role of the Court to determine, as a matter of principle, whether particular types of evidence—for example, evidence obtained unlawfully in terms of domestic law—may be admissible or, indeed, whether the applicant was guilty or not'.[501] Moreover, the Court has often said that it 'cannot exclude as a matter of principle and in the abstract that unlawfully obtained evidence . . . may be admissible'.[502] The question for the Court is 'whether the proceedings as a whole, including the way in which the evidence was obtained, were fair'.[503]

The obtaining of evidence often raises issues under article 8 of the Convention. However, it is immaterial whether the violation of article 8 results from failure to comply with 'domestic law' or with the Convention.[504] In *Schenk v. Switzerland*, a case involving an illegal telephone recording that was used as incriminating evidence, a majority of the Plenary Court concluded that the use of a disputed recording as evidence had not deprived the applicant of a fair trial. It said it 'attache[d] weight to the fact that the recording of the telephone conversation was not the only evidence on which the conviction was based'.[505] The minority insisted that '[n]o court can, without detriment to the proper administration of justice, rely on evidence which has been obtained not only by unfair means but, above all, unlawfully. If it does so, the trial cannot be fair within the meaning of the Convention.'[506] These views were echoed two decades later by several judges of the Grand Chamber.[507]

The same issue was perhaps more difficult when the illegality of the evidence concerned a violation not of article 8 but of article 3. In *Jalloh v. Germany*, the Court ruled that the use in criminal proceedings of evidence obtained through torture raised serious issues as to the fairness of such proceedings, even if the admission of the evidence in question had not

---

[500] *Bykov v. Russia* [GC], no. 4378/02, § 88, 10 March 2009; *Schenk v. Switzerland*, 12 July 1988, § 45, Series A no. 140; *Teixeira de Castro v. Portugal*, 9 June 1998, § 34, *Reports of Judgments and Decisions* 1998-IV; *Jalloh v. Germany* [GC], no. 54810/00, §§ 94–96, ECHR 2006-IX.

[501] *Bykov v. Russia* [GC], no. 4378/02, § 89, 10 March 2009; *Khan v. the United Kingdom*, no. 35394/97, § 34, ECHR 2000-V; *P.G. and J.H. v. the United Kingdom*, no. 44787/98, § 76, ECHR 2001-IX; *Heglas v. the Czech Republic*, no. 5935/02, §§ 89–92, 1 March 2007; *Allan v. the United Kingdom*, no. 48539/99, § 42, ECHR 2002-IX.

[502] *Schenk v. Switzerland*, 12 July 1988, § 46, Series A no. 140.

[503] *Bykov v. Russia* [GC], no. 4378/02, § 89, 10 March 2009; *Khan v. the United Kingdom*, no. 35394/97, § 34, ECHR 2000-V; *P.G. and J.H. v. the United Kingdom*, no. 44787/98, § 76, ECHR 2001-IX; *Heglas v. the Czech Republic*, no. 5935/02, §§ 89–92, 1 March 2007; *Allan v. the United Kingdom*, no. 48539/99, § 42, ECHR 2002-IX; *Haxhia v. Albania*, no. 29861/03, § 128, 8 October 2013.

[504] *Khan v. the United Kingdom*, no. 35394/97, § 26, ECHR 2000-V. Also *Heglas v. the Czech Republic*, no. 5935/02, 1 March 2007.

[505] *Schenk v. Switzerland*, 12 July 1988, § 48, Series A no. 140. See also *Khan v. the United Kingdom*, no. 35394/97, § 26, ECHR 2000-V; *Heglas v. The Czech Republic*, no. 5935/02, 1 March 2007.

[506] *Schenk v. Switzerland*, 12 July 1988, Joint Dissenting Opinion of Judges Pettiti, Spielmann, De Meyer, and Carrillo Salcedo, Series A no. 140. See also *Khan v. the United Kingdom*, no. 35394/97, Partly Concurring, Partly Dissenting Opinion of Judge Loucaides, ECHR 2000-V; *P.G. and J.H. v. the United Kingdom*, no. 44787/98, Partly Dissenting Opinion of Judge Tulkens, ECHR 2001-IX; *Bykov v. Russia* [GC], no. 4378/02, Partly Dissenting Opinion of Judge Spielmann joined by Judges Rozakis, Tulkens, Casadevall, and Mijović, § 6, 10 March 2009.

[507] *Bykov v. Russia* [GC], no. 4378/02, Partly Dissenting Opinion of Judge Spielmann joined by Judges Rozakis, Tulkens, Casadevall, and Mijović, § 6, 10 March 2009; *Bykov v. Russia* [GC], no. 4378/02, Concurring Opinion of Judge Cabral Barretto, 10 March 2009.

been decisive in securing the suspect's conviction.[508] It seems that the use of evidence obtained through torture will always breach article 6, even if it is not decisive in the conviction. Article 15 of the United Nations Convention against Torture and Other Cruel, Inhuman and Degrading Treatment or Punishment provides the following: 'Each State Party shall ensure that any statement which is established to have been made as a result of torture shall not be invoked as evidence in any proceedings, except against a person accused of torture as evidence that the statement was made.'[509] The Torture Convention does not expressly dictate the exclusion of evidence obtained as a result of cruel, inhuman, and degrading treatment or punishment, and the European Court has not taken a position on this point.[510]

Discrimination

Article 14, prohibiting discrimination, applies to article 6 in the same complementary way as it does to the other substantive provisions of the Convention, and it has frequently been invoked in litigation before the Convention organs. However, it appears to have had no real practical application. Sometimes, after finding a violation of article 6, the Court declares that it is unnecessary to examine the complaint separately from the perspective of article 14. On several occasions it has determined that the tribunal was not independent and impartial,[511] or that it was not 'established by law',[512] and from this it has proceeded to hold it unnecessary to look further at any other specific violations of article 6 or of article 14.

Sometimes, courts have expressed racist or discriminatory sentiments. This has led to findings of a violation of article 14 combined with article 6. In a case concerning anti-Roma violence that took place in Romania in 1993, the applicants complained that remarks made by the Târgu-Mureş County Court 'contained clear anti-Roma sentiment'. In criminal prosecution relating to the violence, which resulted in deaths of some Roma, the local court had spoken of 'the marginal lifestyle' of certain Roma, or their 'rejection of the moral values accepted by the rest of the population', and of a propensity to crime.[513] In the European Court, the applicants argued that 'remarks made by the Târgu-Mureş County Court in its judgment of 17 July 1998, although made in the course of the criminal proceedings after the severance of the civil and criminal cases, could have had consequences for the outcome of the civil case, having regard to the close relation in Romanian law between the criminal proceedings and the civil claims'.[514] They noted that the civil court, in dismissing their claims, characterized them as 'liars and tax evaders'.[515]

---

[508] *Jalloh v. Germany* [GC], no. 54810/00, ECHR 2006-IX.

[509] Convention Against Torture and Other Cruel, Inhuman and Degrading Treatment or Punishment, (1984) 1465 UNTS 85.

[510] See, on this issue *Bykov v. Russia* [GC], no. 4378/02, Concurring Opinion of Judge Cabral Barretto, 10 March 2009.

[511] *Tutmaz and Others v. Turkey*, no. 51053/99, §§ 31–32, 23 October 2003; *Peker v. Turkey*, no. 53014/99, § 26, 23 October 2003.

[512] *Coëme and Others v. Belgium*, nos 32492/96, 32547/96, 32548/96, 33209/96, and 33210/96, § 108, ECHR 2000-VII.

[513] *Moldovan and Others v. Romania (no. 2)*, nos 41138/98 and 64320/01, § 44, ECHR 2005-VII (extracts).

[514] Ibid., § 133.

[515] Ibid., § 134.

Concluding that article 14 had been breached, in conjunction with article 6, the Court noted that:

> the applicants' Roma ethnicity appears to have been decisive for the length and the result of the domestic proceedings, after the entry into force of the Convention in respect of Romania. It further notes the repeated discriminatory remarks made by the authorities throughout the whole case determining the applicants' rights under Article 8, when rejecting claims for goods or furnishings, and their blank refusal until 2004 to award non-pecuniary damages for the destruction of the family homes. As to the judgment of 24 February 2004, confirmed by the Court of Cassation on 25 February 2005, the decision to reduce the non-pecuniary damages granted was motivated by remarks related directly to the applicants' ethnic specificity.[516]

In a subsequent case dealing with the same episode of racist violence, the Court confirmed its finding of discrimination based upon ethnicity in the relevant judicial proceedings.[517]

In sentencing a Roma defendant for fraud, a Romanian court spoke of a 'sentiment d'impunité, surtout parmi les membres des groupes minoritaires', explaining that this argued against imposing a suspended sentence.[518] The European Court refused to speculate on the outcome of the proceedings had these remarks not been made, or even the extent to which they might have influenced the Romanian judges, but it had no difficulty concluding that equal treatment had been denied the applicant.[519]

Violations of article 14 in conjunction with article 6 have been found in cases dealing with access to a court. In a Spanish case, the Court concluded that article 14 had been violated, on the basis of sex, in conjunction with article 6, because of the failure to provide access to a court in order to establish discrimination in the workplace.[520] Greek Catholics in Romania successfully challenged a situation where they were unable to obtain access to a court in order to establish their right to access religious facilities.[521]

A refusal of legal aid to a person without legal status in Belgium for a case contesting paternity on the grounds that the legislation only permitted non-residents to have legal aid if there was a reciprocal agreement with their State of nationality was deemed discriminatory. The European Court noted the importance of the case ('des questions graves liées au droit de la famille') for the private and family life of the applicant, explaining that there would have to be 'des raisons particulièrement impérieuses pour justifier une différence de traitement entre la requérante, qui ne possédait pas de carte de séjour, et les personnes qui en possédaient une'.[522]

In a case dealing with contestation of paternity by the presumed father of a child, the Court held that article 6 had been breached because the applicant was denied access to a court after the expiry of certain time limits that did not apply to other 'interested parties'.[523] Where an insurance tribunal charged with ruling upon eligibility for benefit referred to 'an "assumption based on experience of everyday life", namely that many married women give up their jobs when their first child is born and resume it only later',

---

[516] *Moldovan and Others v. Romania (no. 2)*, nos 41138/98 and 64320/01, § 139, ECHR 2005-VII (extracts).

[517] *Lăcătuş and Others v. Romania*, no. 12694/04, § 135–138, 13 November 2012.

[518] *Paraskeva Todorova v. Bulgaria*, no. 37193/07, § 10, 25 March 2010.

[519] Ibid., §§ 44–46.

[520] *García Mateos v. Spain*, no. 38285/09, §§ 42–49, 19 February 2013.

[521] *Sâmbata Bihor Greco-Catholic Parish v. Romania*, no. 48107/99, §§ 79–82, 12 January 2010.

[522] *Anakomba Yula v. Belgium*, no. 45413/07, §§ 37–39, 10 March 2009.

[523] *Mizzi v. Malta*, no. 26111/02, §§ 131–136, ECHR 2006-I (extracts).

the Court concluded that there was a violation of article 6 in conjunction with article 14. '[T]he equality of the sexes is today a major goal in the member States of the Council of Europe and very weighty reasons would have to be put forward before such a difference of treatment could be regarded as compatible with the Convention', it said.[524]

Many legal systems provide for different procedural regimes and different jurisdictions, depending upon the infraction. The Court has rejected challenges claiming that this constitutes discrimination contrary to article 14.[525] In an early decision, the European Commission held that differential treatment of elected officials in criminal proceedings could not be considered contrary to article 14.[526]

Reservations and declarations

The requirement of a public hearing has prompted several reservations. Austria's reservation concerning constitutional provisions on public hearings[527] was applied by the Court in a number of cases.[528] Eventually, the Court held that the reservation was invalid, noting that the conformity of the reservation with article 57 had never been properly examined.[529] The Austrian reservation referred to a permissive, non-exhaustive provision of the constitution and lacked the statement of the relevant law to which it was to apply, as required by article 57(2). A reservation by Liechtenstein, subsequently modified nine years after ratification,[530] to both the public hearing and public pronouncement of the judgment, with precise references to the applicable legislation, has been declared compatible with the Convention.[531] Both Croatia[532] and Serbia and Montenegro[533] have made a reservation concerning the right to a public hearing before the Administrative Court. Estonia formulated a reservation concerning public hearings at the appellate court level.[534]

Serbia and Montenegro made a reservation to article 6, declaring that it was subject to its legislation governing minor offences, although the statement did not make it clear what the precise problem was. The declaration stated that the reservation would be

[524] *Schuler-Zgraggen v. Switzerland*, 24 June 1993, §§ 64–67, Series A no. 263.
[525] *Comak v. Turkey* (dec.), no. 225/02, 4 October 2005. For similar reasoning in an article 5 case: *Gerger v. Turkey* [GC], no. 24919/94, § 69, 8 July 1999.
[526] *Crociani, Palmiotti, Tanassi, and Lefebvre d'Ovidio v. Italy*, nos 8603/79, 8722/79, 8723/79, and 8729/79, Commission decision of 18 December 1980, § 56, (1981) 24 YB 222, DR 22, p. 192.
[527] (1958–59) 2 YB 88–91.
[528] *Ringeisen v. Austria*, 16 July 1971, §§ 98–99, Series A no. 13; *Ettl and Others v. Austria*, 23 April 1987, § 42, Series A no. 117; *Bulut v. Austria*, 22 February 1996, § 43, *Reports of Judgments and Decisions* 1996-II; *Fischer v. Austria*, 26 April 1995, § 41, Series A no. 312; *Stallinger and Kuso v. Austria*, 23 April 1997, § 48, *Reports of Judgments and Decisions* 1997-II; *Pauger v. Austria*, 28 May 1997, § 54, *Reports of Judgments and Decisions* 1997-III; *Szücs v. Austria*, 24 November 1997, § 40, *Reports of Judgments and Decisions* 1997-VII; *Werner v. Austria*, 24 November 1997, § 42, *Reports of Judgments and Decisions* 1997-VII.
[529] *Eisenstecken v. Austria*, no. 29477/95, § 30, ECHR 2000-X; *Kolb and Others v. Austria*, nos 35021/97 and 45774/99, § 59, 17 April 2003. This view had earlier been expressed in *Fischer v. Austria*, 26 April 1995, Separate Opinion of Judge Martens, Series A no. 312.
[530] (1991) 34 YB 5–6.
[531] *Steck-Risch v. Liechtenstein* (dec.), no. 63151/00, ECHR 2004-II; *Schädler-Eberle v. Liechtenstein*, no. 56422/09, § 75, 18 July 2013.
[532] (1997) 49 YB 34.
[533] (2004) 47 YB 22.
[534] (1996) 39 YB 20.

withdrawn as soon as the legislation was amended.[535] In 2011, Serbia withdrew this reservation.[536]

Reservations have also been made concerning the right to an oral hearing. Finland's reservation on the lack of an oral hearing in certain proceedings,[537] part of which has since been withdrawn,[538] was considered by the Court[539] and subsequently declared valid.[540] Switzerland's reservation concerning the right to a hearing[541] was declared invalid for failing to include a 'brief statement of the law', as required by article 57.[542] Switzerland withdrew the reservation in 2000.[543]

At the time of ratification, Ireland formulated a reservation to article 6(3)(c) stating that it did not interpret the text 'as requiring the provision of free legal assistance to any wider extent than is now provided in Ireland'.[544] The Netherlands also made a reservation to article 6(3)(c), but applicable only to Surinam and the Netherlands Antilles.[545] It later withdrew the reservation with respect to the Netherlands Antilles.[546] Switzerland made an interpretative declaration stating that it considers the guarantee of free legal assistance, as well as that of an interpreter set out in paragraph 3(e), 'as not permanently absolving the beneficiary from payment of the resulting costs'.[547]

Hungary's reservation respecting the right to access to administrative courts[548] was declared valid in a decision of the European Commission of Human Rights.[549] It was withdrawn in 2000.[550]

Several States have formulated general reservations to article 6 respecting military discipline: Azerbaijan, Czech Republic,[551] France,[552] Slovakia,[553] and Spain.[554] Ireland made a reservation confined to article 6(3)(c) to the effect that it does not require the provision of free legal assistance 'wider extent than is now provided in Ireland'. Monaco made a reservation to article 6(1), but also to articles 8 and 14, with respect to its

---

[535] (2004) 48 YB 22.
[536] (2011) 54 YB 8–9.
[537] (1990) 33 YB 9.
[538] (1997) 40 YB 35; (1998) 41 YB 9; (2001) 44 YB 12–15.
[539] *V. v. Finland*, no. 40412/98, § 58–59, 24 April 2007; *Laaksonen v. Finland*, no. 70216/01, §§ 22–25, 32, 12 April 2007.
[540] *Helle v. Finland*, 19 December 1997, § 44, *Reports of Judgments and Decisions* 1997-VIII; *Hopia v. Finland* (dec.), no. 30632/96, 25 November 1999; *Tamminen and Tammelin v. Finland* (dec.), no. 33003/96, 28 September 1999; *TH-tekniikka Oy:n Konkurssipesä v. Finland* (dec.), no. 35897/97, 28 September 1999; *Kangasniemi v. Finland* (dec.), no. 43828/98, 1 June 1999; *Laukkanen and Manninen v. Finland* (dec.), no. 50230/99, § 31, 3 February 2004; *M.C. v. Finland* (dec.), no. 28460/95, 25 January 2001; *Thomasi v. Finland* (dec.), no. 28339/95, 19 March 2002; *P.K. v. Finland* (dec.), no. 37442/97, 9 July 2002 *Suominen v. Finland* (dec.), no. 37801/97, 26 February 2002; *T.K. v. Finland* (dec.), no. 29347/95, 13 September 2001; *A.W. and F.W. v. Finland*, no. 26570/95, 25 January 2001.
[541] (1974) 17 YB 6–7.
[542] *Weber v. Switzerland*, 22 May 1990, § 38, Series A no. 177.
[543] (2000) 43 YB 14.
[544] (1955–56–57) 1 YB 40.
[545] (1965) 8 YB 20–21.
[546] (1980) 23 YB 8–9.
[547] (1974) 17 YB 8–9.
[548] (1992) 35 YB 4–5.
[549] *Rékási v. Hungary*, no. 31506/96, Commission decision of 25 November 1996.
[550] (2000) 43 YB 14.
[551] As Czechoslovakia: (1992) 35 YB 4. Confirmed by Czech Republic: (1993) 36 YB 6–7.
[552] (1974) 17 YB 4–5.
[553] As Czechoslovakia: (1992) 35 YB 4.
[554] (1979) 22 YB 22–25.

legislation restricting the employment of non-nationals.[555] A reservation made by Serbia and Montenegro excludes legislation governing prosecution of minor offences before magistrates' courts from the application of the Convention. Serbia later withdrew the reservation, although presumably it continues to apply to Montenegro.

Ukraine made the following reservation: 'Ukraine fully recognises on its territory the validity of Article 6, paragraph 3.d, of the Convention for the Protection of Human Rights and Fundamental Freedoms of 1950 in regard to the defendant's right to obtain the attendance and examination of witnesses (Articles 263 and 303 of the Criminal Procedure Code of Ukraine) and as regards the rights of the suspect and persons charged in pre-trial proceedings to submit petitions for the attendance and examination of witnesses and the confrontation with them in accordance with Articles 43, 43[1] and 142 of the above-mentioned Code.'[556] The purpose of this reservation is not very clear. The provisions of the Code that accompany it set out several procedural rights of the suspect.[557]

Malta made a declaration to article 6(2) to the effect that the presumption of innocence does not 'preclude any particular law from imposing upon any person charged under such law the burden of proving particular facts'.[558]

At the time of ratification, in 1974, Switzerland made a declaration with respect to article 6(1), stating that the guarantee of a fair trial 'is intended solely to ensure ultimate control by the judiciary over the acts or decisions of the public authorities relating to such rights or obligations or the determination of such a charge'.[559] Switzerland's intention was apparently to address the consequences of the European Court's decision in *Ringeisen v. Austria*.[560] In *Belilos v. Switzerland*, the Court held that Switzerland's 'interpretative declaration' was, in effect, a reservation. It then concluded that it was inconsistent with the requirements of article 57, and consequently invalid.[561] Switzerland then submitted what it called a 'clarification of the interpretative declaration': 'The Swiss Federal Council considers that the guarantee of fair trial in Article 6, paragraph 1 of the Convention in the determination of civil rights and obligations is intended solely to ensure ultimate control by the judiciary over the acts or decisions of the public authorities relating to such rights or obligations. For the purpose of the present declaration, "ultimate control by the judiciary" shall mean a control by the judiciary limited to the application of the law, such as a cassation control.'[562] Several months later, Switzerland submitted a compilation of federal and cantonal legislation that it said was covered by the revised declaration, although it said the 'continuing uncertainty' created by the case law meant that the list could not be taken to be exhaustive.[563]

Further reading

Rebecca P. Barnes, '*Al-Khawaja & Tahery v. United Kingdom* (Eur. Ct. H.R.), Introductory Note', (2012) 51 *International Legal Materials* 477.

---

[555] (2005) 48 YB 9.
[556] (1997) 40 YB 44.
[557] Ibid., pp. 45–9.
[558] (1966) 9 YB 24–25.
[559] (1974) 17 YB 8–9.
[560] *Belilos v. Switzerland*, no. 10328/83, §§ 96–104, Commission report of 7 May 1986; *Belilos v. Switzerland*, 29 April 1988, § 41, Series A no. 132.
[561] *Belilos v. Switzerland*, 29 April 1988, § 60, Series A no. 132.
[562] (1988) 31 YB 5.
[563] (1988) 31 YB 5.

Eva Brems, 'Conflicting Human Rights: An Exploration in the Context of the Right to a Fair Trial in the European Convention for the Protection of Human Rights and Fundamental Freedoms', (2005) 27 *Human Rights Quarterly* 294.

J.-P. Costa, 'Le tribunal de la Rote et l'article 6 de la Convention européenne des droits de l'homme', [2002] *RTDH* 470.

J.J. Cremona, 'The Public Character of Trial and Judgment in the Jurisprudence of the European Court of Human Rights', in F. Matscher and H. Petzold, eds, *Protecting Human Rights: The European Dimension*, Cologne: Carl Heymanns, 1988, pp. 107–14.

Nicholas Croquet, 'The International Criminal Court and the Treatment of Defence Rights: A Mirror of the European Court of Human Rights' Jurisprudence?', (2011) 11 *HRLR* 91.

J.-A. Epp and D. O'Brien, 'Defending the Right to Choose: Legally Aided Defendants and Choice of Legal Representative', [2001] *EHRLR* 409.

J.J. Fawcett, 'The Impact of Article 6(1) of the ECHR on Private International Law', (2007) 56 *ICLQ* 1.

Frowein/Peukert, *MenschenRechtsKonvention*, pp. 140–268.

Grabenwarter, *European Convention*, pp. 98–170.

Marc Henzelin and Héloïse Rordorf, 'When Does the Length of Criminal Proceedings Become Unreasonable According to the European Court of Human Rights?', (2014) 5 *New Journal of European Criminal Law* 78.

Sverre Erik Jebens, 'The Scope of the Presumption of Innocence in Article 6§2 of the Convention—Especially on its Reputation-Related Aspect', in Lucius Caflisch, Johan Callewaert, Roderick Liddell, Paul Mahoney, and Mark Villiger, eds, *Liber Amicorum Luzius Wildhaber*, Kehl, Germany: N.P. Engel, 2007, pp. 207–28.

Harris et al., *Law of the European Convention*, pp. 201–330.

Chris Jenks, '*Şahin v. Turkey* (Eur. Ct. H.R.), Introductory Note', (2012) 51 *International Legal Materials* 268.

Patrick Kinsch, 'The Impact of Human Rights on the Application of Foreign Law and on the Recognition of Foreign Judgments—A Survey of the Cases Decided by the European Human Rights Institutions', in T. Einhorn and K Siehr, eds, *Intercontinental Cooperation Through Private International Law, Essays in Memory of Peter E. Nygh*, The Hague: T.M.C. Asser Press, 2004, pp. 197–228.

Patrick Kinsch, 'Le droit international privé au risque de la hiérarchie des normes: l'exemple de la jurisprudence de la Cour européenne des droits de l'homme en matière de reconnaissance des jugements', [2007] *Annuaire de droit européen* 958.

Paul Lemmens, 'The Right to a Fair Trial and its Multiple Manifestation: Article 6(1) ECHR', in Eva Brems and Janneke Gerards, eds, *Shaping Rights in the ECHR*, Cambridge: Cambridge University Press, 2013, pp. 294–314.

Roderick Liddell, 'Reflections on Certain Aspecs of the Kyprianou Judgment', in Lucius Caflisch, Johan Callewaert, Roderick Liddell, Paul Mahoney, and Mark Villiger, eds, *Liber Amicorum Luzius Wildhaber*, Kehl, Germany: N.P. Engel, 2007, pp. 247–62.

F. Marchadier, *Les objectifs généraux du droit international privé à l'épreuve de la Convention européenne des droits de l'homme*, Brussels, Bruylant, 2007.

Jeremy McBride, *Human Rights and Criminal Procedure: The Case Law of the European Court of Human Rights*, Strasbourg: Council of Europe, 2009.

Aileen McHarg, 'Reconciling Human Rights and the Public Interest: Conceptual Problems and Doctrinal Uncertainty in the Jurisprudence of the European Court of Human Rights' (1999) 62 *Modern Law Review* 671.

H. Murray and M.-J. Beloff, 'The Green Paper on Legal Aid and International Human Rights Law', [1996] *EHRLR* 5.

Kurt H. Nadelmann, 'Due Process of Law Before the European Court of Human Rights: The Secret Deliberation', (1972) 66 *AJIL* 509.

Ovey/White, *Jacobs and White, European Convention*, pp. 139–97.

Jörg Polakiewicz, 'European Union Action on Procedural Rights and the European Convention on Human Rights', (2009–2010) 30 *HRLJ* 12.

Michael Ramsden and Imran Aslam, 'EC Dawn Raids: A Human Rights Violation?', (2008) 5 *Competition Law Review* 61.

Katie Quinn, 'Jury Bias and the European Convention on Human Rights: A Well-Kept Secret?', [2004] *Criminal Law Review* 998.

Karen Reid, *A Practitioner's Guide to the European Convention on Human Rights*, London: Sweet & Maxwell, 2011, pp. 81–268.

Paul Roberts, 'Does Article 6 of the European Convention on Human Rights Require Reasoned Verdicts in Criminal Trials?', (2011) 11 *HRLR* 213.

S. Shipman, 'Defamation and Legal Aid in the European Court of Human Rights', (2005) 24 *Civil Justice Quarterly* 23.

Jean-Claude Soyer and Michel de Salvia, 'Article 6', in Pettiti et al., *La Convention européenne*, pp. 239–92.

Dean Spielmann, 'Recognition and Enforcement of Foreign Judicial Decisions, Requirements Under the European Convention on Human Rights, An Overview', (2012) 1 *Cyprus Human Rights Law Review* 4.

Stephanos Stavros, *The Guarantees for Accused Persons under Article 6 of the European Convention on Human Rights*, Dordrecht/Boston/London: Martinus Nijhoff, 1993.

Sarah J. Summers, *Fair Trials: The European Criminal Procedural Tradition and the European Court of Human Rights,* Oxford: Hart Publishing, 2007.

P.J. Sutherland and C.A. Gearty, 'Insanity and the European Court of Human Rights', [1992] *Criminal Law Review* 418.

Paul Tavernier, 'Faut-il reviser l'article 6 de la Convention européenne des droits de l'homme? (A propos du champ d'application de l'article 6', in G. Flécheux, ed., *Mélanges en hommage à Louis Edmond Pettiti*, Brussels: Bruylant, 1998, pp. 707–20.

Pieter van Dijk and Marc Viering, 'Right to a Fair and Public Hearing (Article 5)', in Van Dijk et al., *Theory and Practice*, pp. 511–650.

Sébastien Van Drooghenbroek, 'Labour Law Litigation and Fair Trial under Article 6 ECHR', in Filip Dorssemont, Klaus Lörcher, and Isabelle Schömann, eds, *The European Convention on Human Rights and the Employment Relation*, Oxford and Portland, OR: Hart, 2013, pp. 159–82.

Walter B.J. Van Overbeek, 'The Right to Remain Silent in Competition Investigations: The Funke Decision of the Court of Human Rights makes Revision of the ECJ's Case Law Necessary', (1994) 15 *European Competition Law Review* 127.

Panayotis Voyatzis, 'The Right to Legal Assistance Free of Charge in the Case-law of the European Court of Human Rights', (2012) 1 *Cyprus Human Rights Law Review* 42.

Stuart Wallace, 'The Empire Strikes Back: Hearsay Rules in Common Law Legal Systems and the Jurisprudence of the European Court of Human Rights', [2010] *EHRLR* 408.

Article 7. No punishment without law/Pas de peine sans loi

1. No one shall be held guilty of any criminal offence on account of any act or omission which did not constitute a criminal offence under national or international law at the time when it was committed. Nor shall a heavier penalty be imposed than the one that was applicable at the time the criminal offence was committed.

2. This article shall not prejudice the trial and punishment of any person for any act or omission which, at the time when it was committed, was criminal according to the general principles of law recognised by civilised nations.

1. Nul ne peut être condamné pour une action ou une omission qui, au moment où elle a été commise, ne constituait pas une infraction d'après le droit national ou international. De même il n'est infligé aucune peine plus forte que celle qui était applicable au moment où l'infraction a été commise.

2. Le présent article ne portera pas atteinte au jugement et à la punition d'une personne coupable d'une action ou d'une omission qui, au moment où elle a été commise, était criminelle d'après les principes généraux de droit reconnus par les nations civilisées.

Introductory comments

The direct ancestor of article 7 of the European Convention is article 11(2) of the Universal Declaration of Human Rights: 'No one shall be held guilty of any penal offence on account of any act or omission which did not constitute a penal offence, under national or international law, at the time when it was committed.' The principle is consecrated in a familiar Latin expression: *nullum crimen nulla poena sine lege*. As one of a handful of rights that are not subject to derogation under the Convention and the relevant clauses of the other main human rights treaties, it is sometimes spoken of as being part of the *noyau dur* of human rights law. Often called the principle of legality, it was described recently by the Appeals Chamber of the Special Tribunal for Lebanon as a peremptory norm (*jus cogens*).[1]

That there can be no punishment without law is a principle recognized long before it was codified in the Universal Declaration of Human Rights and the European Convention. It was set out in article 8 of the French *Déclaration des droits de l'homme et du citoyen*, adopted on 26 August 1789: 'no one shall suffer punishment except it be legally inflicted in virtue of a law passed and promulgated before the commission of the offense'. In international law, it may have first arisen at the Paris Peace Conference in 1919. Delegates from the United States objected to plans to prosecute violations of the 'laws and principles of humanity' that were too uncertain to have any place in a court of criminal justice.[2] They said they 'were of the opinion that an act could not be a crime in the legal sense of the word, unless it were made so by law, and that the commission of an act declared to be a crime by law could not be punished unless the law prescribed the penalty to be inflicted'.[3] Despite their objections, the Treaty of Versailles proposed a trial of the

---

[1] *Unnamed defendant* (STL-11-01/I), Interlocutory Decision on the Applicable Law: Terrorism, Conspiracy, Homicide, Perpetration, Cumulative Charging, 16 February 2011, para. 45.

[2] 'Memorandum of Reservations Presented by the Representatives of the United States to the Report of the Commission on Responsibilities', (1920) 14 *AJIL* 127, at p. 134.

[3] Ibid., p. 145.

German Emperor for breaches of 'a supreme offence against international morality and the sanctity of treaties', but the Netherlands, where he had sought refuge, refused to extradite for the reason that this would violate the maxim *nullum crimen sine lege.*

The principle of legality was discussed in a 1935 precedent of the Permanent Court of International Justice condemning Nazi decrees in Danzig that allowed courts to punish new crimes where they were 'deserving of penalty according to the fundamental conceptions of a penal law and sound popular feeling'. The Permanent Court said this was incompatible with the prohibition on retroactive punishment in the Constitution of the Free City, which was guaranteed by the League of Nations. The Nazi lawyer arguing before the Permanent Court contended that under the new legislation, 'real justice will take the place of formal justice, and that henceforth the rule will be *nullum crimen sine poena* instead of *nullum crimen sine lege*'.[4]

The Nazis themselves invoked the principle of legality when they were tried before the International Military Tribunal. Their lawyers filed a motion challenging the indictment because the charge of crimes against peace, which had never before been codified, was 'repugnant to a principle of jurisprudence sacred to the civilised world, the partial violation of which by Hitler's Germany has been vehemently discountenanced outside and inside the Reich'. They noted that the maxim *nullum crimen sine lege* 'is precisely not a rule of expediency but it derives from the recognition of the fact that any defendant must needs [sic] consider himself unjustly treated if he is punished under an *ex post facto* law'.[5] The final judgment dismissed their objection, stating that 'it is to be observed that the maxim *nullum crimen sine lege* is not a limitation of sovereignty, but is in general a principle of justice'. The French version of the judgment is more qualified: '[n]ullum crimen sine lege *ne limite pas la souveraineté des États; elle ne formule qu'une règle généralement suivie*'. The judgment continues:

To assert that it is unjust to punish those who in defiance of treaties and assurances have attacked neighbouring states without warning is obviously untrue, for in such circumstances the attacker must know that he is doing wrong, and so far from it being unjust to punish him, it would be unjust if his wrong were allowed to go unpunished . . . [The Nazi leaders] must have known that they were acting in defiance of all international law when in complete deliberation they carried out their designs of invasion and aggression.[6]

In other words, the Tribunal admitted that there was a retroactive dimension to prosecution for crimes against peace, but said leaving such wrongs unpunished would be unjust. Commenting on the issue, Hens Kelsen argued that 'the retroactivity of the law applied to them can hardly be considered as absolutely incompatible with justice'. He said that justice required that the Nazi leaders be brought to book: 'to punish those who were morally responsible for the international crime of the Second World War may certainly be

---

[4] *Consistency of Certain Danzig Legislative Decrees with the Constitution of the Free City*, PCIJ, Series A/B, No. 65, p. 52. See Dean Spielmann, 'Une internationalisation avant la lettre des droit de l'homme ?/À propos de l'avis consultatif de la Cour permanente de Justice internationale du 4 décembre 1935', in Lucius Caflisch, Johan Callewaert, Roderick Liddell, Paul Mahoney, and Mark Villiger, eds, *Liber Amicorum Luzius Wildhaber*, Kehl, Germany: N.P. Engel, 2007, pp. 403–22.
[5] Motion adopted by all defense counsel, 19 November 1945, (1948) 1 IMT 168–170.
[6] *France et al. v. Goering et al.*, (1948) 22 IMT 411, p. 462.

considered as more important than to comply with the rather relative rule against *ex post facto* laws, open to so many exceptions'.[7]

The Documented Outline prepared by the Secretariat of the United Nations Commission on Human Rights in June 1947 as part of the drafting process of the Universal Declaration of Human Rights identified thirty-five national constitutions containing provisions formulating the non-retroactivity norm in one form or another, including six of the ten founding members of the Council of Europe: Belgium, France, Luxembourg, the Netherlands, Norway, and Sweden.[8] In the United Kingdom, with no written constitution, it was an interpretative presumption. The principle was also present in the constitutions of Ireland and Italy, but these countries were not listed in the United Nations Outline because they were not yet Member States.

It would seem that what was a rather flexible approach to the *nullum crimen* principle at the time of the post-Second-World-War prosecutions has hardened into a more rigid and uncompromising prohibition. Yet the case law of the European Court of Human Rights pursuant to article 7 of the Convention in many ways reflects the spirit of the Nuremberg judges. Insisting that the crime be 'accessible' and 'foreseeable' to the accused person at the time of the punishable act, the Court has upheld prosecutions based upon unwritten norms, in particular when they concern serious crimes that violate human dignity.[9]

The equivalent provision in the International Covenant on Civil and Political Rights clearly reflects the text of article 7 of the European Convention. However, there is one addition, the recognition of the right to the lesser penalty if the law has been changed since the commission of the alleged act (*lex mitior*).[10] The European Charter of Fundamental Rights relies upon the text of the Covenant but also makes an addition, setting out the principle of proportionate sentencing in paragraph 3:

Article 49. Principles of legality and proportionality of criminal offences and penalties
1. No one shall be held guilty of any criminal offence on account of any act or omission which did not constitute a criminal offence under national law or international law at the time when it was committed. Nor shall a heavier penalty be imposed than that which was applicable at the time the criminal offence was committed. If, subsequent to the commission of a criminal offence, the law provides for a lighter penalty, that penalty shall be applicable.
2. This Article shall not prejudice the trial and punishment of any person for any act or omission which, at the time when it was committed, was criminal according to the general principles recognised by the community of nations.
3. The severity of penalties must not be disproportionate to the criminal offence.

According to the drafters of the European Charter, paragraph 1 of article 49 (with the exception of the last sentence), and paragraph 2 are meant to have the same meaning and scope as article 7 of the European Convention.[11]

---

[7] Hans Kelsen, 'Will the Judgment in the Nuremberg Trial Constitute a Precedent in International Law?', (1947) 1 *International Law Quarterly* 153, at p. 165. For an endorsement of Kelsen's approach, see the reasons of Justice Peter Cory in *R. v. Finta*, (1994) 1 SCR 701, at p. 874.

[8] UN Doc. E/CN.4/AC.1/3/Add.1, pp. 220–34.

[9] *C.R. v. the United Kingdom*, 22 November 1995, § 42, Series A no. 335-C.

[10] International Covenant on Civil and Political Rights, (1976) 999 UNTS 171, art. 15.

[11] Explanation Relating to the Charter of Fundamental Rights, Official Journal of the European Union, C 303/34, 14 December 2007.

Drafting of the provision

The initial draft European Convention on Human Rights was prepared by the International Juridical Section of the European Movement, chaired by Pierre-Henri Teitgen, with David Maxwell Fyfe and Fernand Dehousse as rapporteurs. Both Maxwell Fyfe and Dehousse had been involved in the adoption of the Universal Declaration of Human Rights at the United Nations the previous year. Asked to prepare a text for discussion in the Committee on Legal and Administrative Questions at the first session of the Consultative Assembly, held from 22 August to 5 September 1949, Teitgen proposed the following: 'Immunity from arbitrary arrest, detention and exile, in accordance with Articles 9, 10 and 11 of the United Nations Declaration'.[12] The annex contained the relevant provisions of the Universal Declaration of Human Rights, including article 11(2), where the *nullum crimen* principle is set out. The draft report submitted by Teitgen contained the following: 'Immunity from all arbitrary arrest, detention, exile and other arbitrary measures, in accordance with Articles 9, 10 and 11 of the Declaration of the United Nations'.[13] With some small changes, this was the text adopted by the Consultative Assembly and forwarded to the Committee of Ministers.[14]

Meeting in November 1950, the Committee of Ministers decided to refer the draft to a Committee of Experts, with instructions that it should pay 'due attention' to the draft Covenant that had been adopted by the United Nations Commission of Human Rights in June 1949.[15] On the *nullum crimen* issue, the Commission draft was identical to that of article 11(2) of the Declaration.[16] Prior to the meeting of the Committee of Experts, the United Kingdom circulated its critical comments on the United Nations draft: 'His Majesty's Government consider that the latest text of this Article might be thought to impugn the validity of the judgments of the Nuremberg Tribunal. They therefore suggest that the Commission might wish to consider the desirability of adding a second paragraph to this Article on the following lines: "Nothing in this Article shall prejudice the trial and punishment of any person for the commission of any act which, at the time it was committed, was criminal according to the general principles of law recognised by civilised nations."'[17] In fact, the additional paragraph proposed by the United Kingdom had been present in an earlier version of the draft Covenant[18] and was removed at the 1949 session on the proposal of France.[19]

[12] Proposals by Mr P.H. Teitgen, Rapporteur, 29 August 1949, Doc. A 116, I *TP* 166–8.
[13] Report presented by Mr P.H. Teitgen, 5 September 1949, Doc. A 290, I *TP* 192–213, at p. 206. See also Report [of the Committee on Legal and Administrative Questions], 5 September 1949, Doc. AS (1) 77, I *TP* 216–39, at p. 228.
[14] Recommendation No. 38 to the Committee of Ministers adopted 8 September 1949 on the conclusion of the debates, Doc. AS (1) 108, II *TP* 274–83, at p. 276.
[15] Letter addressed on 18 November 1949 by the Secretary General to the Ministers for Foreign Affairs of the Member States, Ref. D 26/2/49, II *TP* 302–5.
[16] Report of the Fifth Session of the Commission on Human Rights to the Economic and Social Council, UN Doc. E/1371(Supp.), p. 33.
[17] Comments of Governments on the Draft International Covenant on Human Rights and Measures of Implementation [UN Doc. E/CN.4/353/Add.1-3], Doc. A 770, III *TP* 156–79, at p. 162.
[18] UN Doc. E/800, Annex B, p. 27. On the drafting of article 15 of the International Covenant on Civil and Political Rights at the fifth session of the Commission on Human Rights, see Kenneth S. Gallant, *The Principle of Legality in International and Comparative Criminal Law*, Cambridge: Cambridge University Press, 2009, pp. 178–88; David Weissbrodt, *The Right to a Fair Trial under the Universal Declaration of Human Rights and the International Covenant on Civil and Political Rights*, The Hague/Boston/London: Martinus Nijhoff, 2001, pp. 78–83.
[19] UN Doc. E/CN.4/SR.112.

In preparation for the Committee of Experts meeting, Luxembourg raised a similar concern to that of the United Kingdom. Noting that article 11(2) of the Universal Declaration appeared 'absolutely to exclude the retrospective application of penal laws, whether they are laws defining crimes or laws governing punishment', Luxembourg said that '[c]onceived in this way, the prohibition appears to be too absolute'. It noted that the principle had been 'rejected' in legislation adopted subsequent to the Second World War. Luxembourg suggested that the absolute formulation of the Universal Declaration be 'attenuated' by the addition of a 'more subtle phraseology' and proposed this text: 'No one shall be guilty of any act or omission which, at the time when it was committed, did not constitute a delinquent act, either under national or international law, nor according to the general principles of law as recognised by civilised nations.'[20]

Sweden also had a proposal: 'As regards reference to Article 11, para. 2 of the United Nations Declaration, it is pointed out that each Member State reserves the right to apply to a crime or to an act or delinquent omission only that law which is in force in its territory at the time the act was committed.'[21] The amendment was subsequently withdrawn, Sweden being satisfied with a statement in the Report of the Committee of Experts 'that the Convention does not compel Member States to apply, as a criminal measure, a rule of international law which is not incorporated in the national law'.[22]

At the conclusion of its first session, in February 1950, the Committee of Experts adopted the text found in article 11(2) of the Universal Declaration.[23] The report of the Committee explains that instead of enumerating rights by reference to the relevant provision in the Universal Declaration, as had been done by the Consultative Assembly, it was better to incorporate the text verbatim. Accordingly, the Committee 'scrupulously adhered to the text of the Universal Declaration'.[24] At the second session of the Committee of Experts, in March 1950, the United Kingdom representative renewed efforts to add a second paragraph, submitting a text similar to what it had proposed to the United Nations Commission on Human Rights except that the words 'for any act or omission which' replaced 'for the commission of any act which'.[25] The United Kingdom provision was left unchanged by a Drafting Committee designated to review the text.[26] Shortly thereafter, the United Kingdom also prevailed with the same amendment in the drafting of the United Nations Covenant at the Sixth Session of the Commission on Human Rights. In that forum, several States considered that the issue of crimes under international law had already been addressed with the addition of the words 'international law'

---

[20] Amendment to Article 2, para. 3 of the Recommendation of the Consultative Assembly proposed by the Expert of Luxembourg, Doc. A 784, III *TP* 192–4, at p. 194.

[21] Amendments to Article 2, paras 3, 5, and 6 of the Recommendation of the Consultative Assembly proposed by the Swedish expert, Doc. A 777, III *TP* 184.

[22] Ibid.

[23] Preliminary Draft Convention for the Maintenance and Further Realisation of Human Rights and Fundamental Freedoms, 15 February 1950, Doc. A 833, III *TP* 236–46, at p. 236. Also Draft text of the first section of a draft Convention based on the work of the Consultative Assembly, Doc. A 809, III *TP* 220–31, at p. 222.

[24] Preliminary draft of the Report to the Committee of Ministers, 24 February 1950, Doc. CM/WP 1 (50) 1, A 847, III *TP* 246–79, at pp. 260–2.

[25] Amendments to Articles 1, 2, 4, 5, 6, 8, and 9 of the Committee's Preliminary Draft proposal by the Expert of the United Kingdom, Doc. CM/WP 1 (50) 2, A 915, III *TP* 280–9, at p. 286.

[26] Amendments to the British draft proposed by the Drafting Committee composed of Sir Oscar Dowson, MM le Quesne, Dons Moeller and Salén, Doc. CM/WP 1 (50) 10, p. 3, A 919, III *TP* 288–95, at pp. 290–2.

to the first sentence, in accordance with the Universal Declaration text, and thought the United Kingdom addition to be unnecessary. The United Kingdom replied that paragraph 2 would cover acts implicitly recognized by international law, even if they were not expressly addressed. Its proposal was accepted in the Commission on Human Rights by a vote of seven to six, with two abstentions.[27]

The Committee of Experts of the Council of Europe concluded its work with the submission to the Committee of Ministers of two different drafts. The first, 'Alternatives A and A/2', was text adopted by the Committee of Experts at its first session.[28] The second, labelled 'Alternatives B and B/2', contained the text that had been proposed by the United Kingdom.[29] Referring to the principle of non-retroactivity, the Report of the Committee of Experts to the Committee of Ministers 'stressed' that what was being proposed 'did not affect the laws which, under the very exceptional circumstances at the end of the second world war, were passed in order to suppress war crimes, treason and collaboration with the enemy, and did not aim at any legal or moral condemnation of these laws'.[30] The wording had been sharpened somewhat by comparison with the draft report, which read: '. . . did not affect laws passed at the end of the world war to suppress war-crimes, treason and collaboration with the enemy, and did not imply any legal or moral condemnation of these laws'.[31]

The Conference of Senior Officials that convened in June 1950 assigned a Drafting Committee to attempt to reconcile the competing versions. It prepared a new formulation that essential merged the two proposals.

1) No one shall be held guilty of any criminal offence on account of any act or omission which did not constitute a penal offence under national or international law at the time when it was committed. Nor shall a heavier penalty be imposed than the one that was applicable at the time the criminal offence was committed.
2) Nothing in this article shall prejudice the trial and punishment of any person for any act or omission which, at the time it was committed, was criminal according to the general principles of law recognised by civilised nations.[32]

---

[27] UN Doc. E/CN.4/SR.159. The Report of the Commission on Human Rights provides the following explanation for the second paragraph: 'It was argued that the second paragraph of the article was superfluous: if, as was claimed, it was intended as a confirmation of the principles applied by the war crimes tribunals after the Second World War, it might have the opposite effect of calling into question the validity of the judgments of those tribunals; if it was intended as a guarantee that no alleged war criminal in the future would be able to argue that there were no positive principles of international law or of relevant national law qualifying his acts as crimes, it merely reiterated what was already contained in the expression "international law" in the first paragraph, since that term included "the generally recognised principles of law" mentioned at the end of the second paragraph. On the other hand, the view was heard that the saving provision set forth in paragraph 2 had no application to past convictions for war crimes, nor was it fully covered by the term "international law" contained in the first paragraph.' UN Doc. E/CN.4/694/Add.7, para. 96.

[28] Report to the Committee of Ministers submitted by the Committee of Experts Instructed to Draw Up a Draft Convention of Collective Guarantee of Human Rights and Fundamental Freedoms, Doc. CM/WP 1 (5) 15, A 924, IV *TP* 2–55, at p. 52. See also Preliminary Draft Convention, Doc. CM/WP 1 (50) 14, A 932, III *TP* 312–35, at p. 320.

[29] Report to the Committee of Ministers submitted by the Committee of Experts Instructed to Draw Up a Draft Convention of Collective Guarantee of Human Rights and Fundamental Freedoms, Doc. CM/WP 1 (5) 15, A 924, IV *TP* 2–55, at p. 62. See also Preliminary Draft Convention, Doc. CM/WP 1 (50) 14, A 932, III *TP* 312–35, at p. 316.

[30] Report to the Committee of Ministers submitted by the Committee of Experts Instructed to Draw Up a Draft Convention of Collective Guarantee of Human Rights and Fundamental Freedoms, Doc. CM/WP 1 (5) 15, A 924, IV *TP* 2–55, at p. 22.

[31] Preliminary Draft of the Report to the Committee of Ministers, 24 February 1950, Doc. CM/WP 1 (50) 1, A 847, III *TP* 246–79, at p. 262.

[32] New draft alternatives B and B/2, Doc. CM/WP 4 (50) 9, A 1372, IV *TP* 182–91, at pp. 186–8.

A change in wording from 'penal offence' to 'criminal offence' does not seem to have been intended to modify the meaning. In the French version, the original British proposal referred to *'des actions ou omissions'*[33] and this became, in the Drafting Committee text, *'une action ou omission'*.[34] The remaining reference to 'penal offence' in paragraph 1 was subsequently changed to 'criminal offence' in the final version adopted by the Conference.[35]

At its fifth meeting in early August 1950, the Committee of Ministers removed the word 'when' from the first sentence of paragraph 1. Paragraph 2 was altered slightly by the Committee of Ministers, replacing the words 'Nothing in this article' with 'This article shall not'.[36] There were no further modifications of the text, and the version confirmed at the fifth session of the Committee of Ministers is the definitive one.

The heading 'No punishment without law' was added according to the provisions of Protocol No. 11.[37]

Analysis and interpretation

Article 7 of the European Convention on Human Rights sets out, 'in general terms, the principle that only the law can define a crime and prescribe a penalty (*nullum crimen, nulla poena sine lege*) and prohibits in particular the retrospective application of the criminal law where it is to an accused's disadvantage'.[38] It is known as the 'principle of legality' in national law as well as in some international instruments,[39] such as the European Charter of Fundamental Rights, but the term is not generally used in the case law of the European Court of Human Rights.[40] The Court has insisted that 'the Convention is not confined to prohibiting the retrospective application of the criminal law to an accused's disadvantage'. Article 7 of the Convention also embodies, more generally, 'the principle that only the law can define a crime and prescribe a penalty (*nullum crimen, nulla poena sine lege*) and the principle that the criminal law must not be extensively construed to an accused's detriment, for instance by analogy; it follows from this that an offence must be clearly defined in law'.[41]

---

[33] Amendments to Articles 1, 2, 4, 5, 6, 8, and 9 of the Committee's Preliminary Draft Proposal by the Expert of the United Kingdom, Doc. CM/WP 1 (50) 2, A 915, III *TP* 280–9, at p. 287.
[34] New draft alternatives B and B/2, Doc. CM/WP 4 (50) 9, A 1372, IV *TP* 182–91, at p. 187.
[35] Draft Convention appended to the Draft Report, Doc. CM/WP 4 (50) 16, appendix, A 1445, IV *TP* 218–40, at p. 222.
[36] Draft Convention adopted by the Sub-Committee, Doc. CM 1 (50) 52, A 1884, V *TP* 76–99, at p. 80; Draft Convention adopted by the Committee of Ministers, 7 August 1950, Doc. A 1937, V *TP* 120–45, at p. 126.
[37] Protocol No. 11 to the Convention for the Protection of Human Rights and Fundamental Freedoms, restructuring the control machinery established thereby, ETS 155, art. 2(2).
[38] *Kokkinakis v. Greece*, 25 May 1993, § 51, Series A no. 260-A; *Kononov v. Latvia* [GC], no. 36376/04, § 185, ECHR 2010; *Del Río Prada v. Spain* [GC], no. 42750/09, § 78, 21 October 2013.
[39] *Del Río Prada v. Spain* [GC], no. 42750/09, § 23, 21 October 2013; *Custers and Others v. Denmark*, nos 11843/03, 11847/03, and 11849/03, § 43, 3 May 2007.
[40] There are isolated references to the term in some individual opinions with reference to article 7: *Streletz, Kessler, and Krenz v. Germany* [GC], nos 34044/96, 35532/97, and 44801/98, Concurring Opinion of Judge Zupančić, ECHR 2001-II; *Maktouf and Damjanović v. Bosnia and Herzegovina* [GC], nos 2312/08 and 34179/08, Concurring Opinion of Judge Pinto de Albuquerque, Joined by Judge Vučinić, ECHR 2013; *Achour v. France* [GC], no. 67335/01, Concurring Opinion of Judge Zupančić, ECHR 2006-IV (extracts).
[41] *Kokkinakis v. Greece*, 25 May 1993, § 52, Series A no. 260-A; *Scoppola v. Italy (no. 2)* [GC], no. 10249/03, § 93, 17 September 2009; *Coëme and Others v. Belgium*, nos 32492/96, 32547/96, 32548/96, 33209/96, and 33210/96, § 145, ECHR 2000-VII.

The guarantee enshrined in article 7 is 'an essential element of the rule of law',[42] a notion also set out in recital 5 of the Preamble of the Convention. The provision requires a sufficiently elevated degree of legal precision so that the possibility of commission of an offence is 'foreseeable'. The criminal law must also be 'accessible'. In an example of extending definitions of crimes by analogy, two Romanian bank employees were prosecuted for passive corruption pursuant to legislation that referred only to 'civil servants' and 'other employees'. They argued that the law did not contemplate persons like themselves who worked in the private sector, and the Court agreed. It indicated that it would have been acceptable to apply a provision broadly in this manner but only if previous case law provided support, which it did not.[43] Article 7 also appears to confirm the principle of strict interpretation of criminal law.[44] Furthermore, '[i]t should be construed and applied, as follows from its object and purpose, in such a way as to provide effective safeguards against arbitrary prosecution, conviction and punishment'.[45] The 'prominent place' of article 7 in the Convention is 'underlined' by the fact that no derogation is permitted under article 15 in time of war or other public emergency.[46]

The text of article 7(1) makes it very clear that this provision only applies to criminal proceedings. There is no prohibition of retroactive, or retrospective, legislation outside of the prescription of crimes and punishments. Indeed, the Court has repeatedly ruled that in civil disputes 'in principle, the legislature is not prevented from regulating, through new retrospective provisions, rights derived from the laws in force'.[47] Retroactive provisions may even apply to criminal procedure where, to the extent they do not impact upon the definitions of criminal conduct and the available penalties, they do not appear to be prohibited by article 7. Nor is retroactive or retrospective application of the law prohibited when this is to the advantage of an accused or convicted person.[48] However, 'the principle of the rule of law and the notion of fair trial enshrined in Article 6 preclude, except for compelling public-interest reasons, interference by the legislature with the administration of justice designed to influence the judicial determination of a dispute'.[49] More generally, legal certainty has been identified as a fundamental component of the rule of law, and

[42] *Ould Dah v. France* (dec.), no. 13113/03, ECHR 2009.

[43] *Dragotoniu and Militaru-Pidhorni v. Romania*, nos 77193/01 and 77196/01, §§ 42–43, 24 May 2007.

[44] Ibid., § 40.

[45] *Scoppola v. Italy (no. 2)* [GC], no. 10249/03, § 92, 17 September 2009; *S.W. v. the United Kingdom*, 22 November 1995, § 32, Series A no. 335-B; *C.R. v. The United Kingdom*, 22 November 1995, § 32, Series A no. 335-C; *Kafkaris v. Cyprus* [GC], no. 21906/04, § 137, ECHR 2008.

[46] *Ould Dah v. France* (dec.), no. 13113/03, ECHR 2009.

[47] *Scoppola v. Italy (no. 2)* [GC], no. 10249/03, § 132, 17 September 2009; *Stran Greek Refineries and Stratis Andreadis v. Greece*, 9 December 1994, § 49, Series A no. 301-B, *National & Provincial Building Society, Leeds Permanent Building Society and Yorkshire Building Society v. the United Kingdom*, 23 October 1997, § 112, *Reports of Judgments and Decisions* 1997-VII; *Zielinski and Pradal and Gonzalez and Others v. France* [GC], nos 24846/94 and 34165/96 to 34173/96, § 57, ECHR 1999-VII; *Scordino v. Italy (no. 1)* [GC], no. 36813/97, § 126, ECHR 2006-V.

[48] *Maktouf and Damjanović v. Bosnia and Herzegovina* [GC], nos 2312/08 and 34179/08, Concurring Opinion of Judge Pinto de Albuquerque, Joined by Judge Vučinić, ECHR 2013 (extracts), citing in this regard article 15 of the revised Arab Charter of Human Rights.

[49] *Scoppola v. Italy (no. 2)* [GC], no. 10249/03, § 132, 17 September 2009; *Stran Greek Refineries and Stratis Andreadis v. Greece*, 9 December 1994, § 49, Series A no. 301-B; *National & Provincial Building Society, Leeds Permanent Building Society, and Yorkshire Building Society v. The United Kingdom*, 23 October 1997, § 112, *Reports of Judgments and Decisions* 1997-VII; *Zielinski and Pradal and Gonzalez and Others v. France* [GC], nos 24846/94 and 34165/96 to 34173/96, § 57, ECHR 1999-VII; *Scordino v. Italy (no. 1)* [GC], no. 36813/97, § 126, ECHR 2006-V.

something necessary to encourage the trust of litigants in the justice system as a whole.[50] Thus, retrospective or retroactive legislation outside the criminal sphere requires close scrutiny.

The first sentence of the first paragraph of article 7 sets out the principle of non-retroactivity of crimes, referring to both national and international law. The second sentence of the paragraph states a variant on the rule against retroactive punishment by prohibiting the imposition of a penalty that is heavier than what was applicable at the time of the commission of the offence. The second paragraph of article 7 establishes a special rule intended to shelter from challenge under the Convention a prosecution based upon acts that were 'criminal according to the general principles of law recognised by civilised nations'.

Problems arise in the case of a 'continuing crime', where some acts are perpetrated before the entry into force of the crime and some after. To the extent that the applicant is convicted without distinction as to the acts prior to and subsequent to the relevant legislation, there is a violation of article 7(1), because of concern that the earlier conduct influenced the severity of the penalty or had other tangible negative consequences.[51]

Article 17, preventing the Convention being interpreted as implying a right to engage in activity aimed at the destruction of fundamental rights, cannot be used to prevent a physical person from invoking the provisions of article 7.[52]

'Law'

The term 'law' in article 7 is used in the same sense as when it appears elsewhere in the Convention, for example in articles 2, 5, 6, 8, 9, 10, and 11. Interpreting the phrase 'prescribed by law' that is used in article 10(2), the Court said that a norm could not be regarded as 'law' unless it was 'formulated with sufficient precision to enable the citizen to regulate his conduct'.[53] The Court said this did not mean the consequences had to be foreseeable with 'absolute certainty', deeming this unattainable. It acknowledged that law should not be excessively rigid so as to permit it 'to keep pace with changing circumstances'.[54] These general principles have informed the understanding of 'law' as the term is used in article 7, but with probably greater rigour given that criminal law is the focus of the provision and the consequences for the individual often involve deprivation of freedom.

There are important 'qualitative requirements', principally accessibility and foreseeability.[55] The European Court found that retrospective imposition of a heavier penalty relating to release after service of part of a life sentence was a question of 'quality of law'. The relevant legislation in Cyprus 'taken as a whole was not formulated with sufficient

---

[50] *Unedic v. France*, no. 20153/04, § 74, 18 December 2008.
[51] *Veeber v. Estonia (no. 2)*, no. 45771/99, §§ 31, 36, 21 January 2003.
[52] *Ould Dah v. France* (dec.), no. 13113/03, ECHR 2009.
[53] *The Sunday Times v. the United Kingdom (no. 1)*, 26 April 1979, § 49, Series A no. 30.
[54] Ibid.
[55] *Scoppola v. Italy (no. 2)* [GC], no. 10249/03, § 99, 17 September 2009; *Kokkinakis v. Greece*, 25 May 1993, §§ 40–41, Series A no. 260-A; *Cantoni v. France*, 15 November 1996, § 29, *Reports of Judgments and Decisions* 1996-V; *Coëme and Others v. Belgium*, nos 32492/96, 32547/96, 32548/96, 33209/96, et 33210/96, § 145, ECHR 2000-VII; *E.K. v. Turkey*, no. 28496/95, § 51, 7 February 2002; *E.K. v. Turkey*, no. 28496/95, § 51, 7 February 2002; *Custers and Others v. Denmark*, nos 11843/03, 11847/03, and 11849/03, § 77, 3 May 2007; *Achour v. France* [GC], no. 67335/01, §§ 41–43, ECHR 2006-IV; *Camilleri v. Malta*, no. 42931/10, § 34, 22 January 2013.

precision as to enable the applicant to discern, even with appropriate advice, to a degree that was reasonable in the circumstances, the scope of the penalty of life imprisonment and the manner of its execution'.[56]

Although rarely invoked by the European Court, the content of the law is also relevant to the concept of 'law'. In a case dealing with a sham trial of political opponents held in Czechoslovakia in 1950, the European Court said 'the practice of eliminating opponents to a political regime through the death penalty, imposed at the end of trials which flagrantly infringed the right to a fair trial and, in particular, the right to life, can not be described as "law" within the meaning of Article 7 of the Convention'.[57]

Certainly 'law' as the word is used in article 7 must be appreciated in its substantive rather than its formal sense.[58] It is construed to refer to law in many different forms, including both written and unwritten law, and to both positive legislative enactments and to case law.[59] It has thus included enactments of lower rank than statutes as well as unwritten law that has emerged through judicial pronouncement.[60] In two celebrated cases, the Court examined the crime of rape under the legal system of England and Wales, where there is no formal codification and where judges apply an offense defined as part of the common law, that is to say, as elucidated in prior judicial decisions. The Court explained that '[i]n a common law system, not only written statutes but also rules of common or other customary law may provide sufficient legal basis for the criminal convictions envisaged in Article 7'.[61] It said that where criminal law was developed in such a way, the law-making function of the Courts 'must remain within reasonable limits'.[62] A judicial evolution by which rape could be perpetrated by a man against his wife, something previously excluded by the common law, was upheld as acceptable by the Court.

As a general principle, the European Court of Human Rights does not intrude in the interpretation of national laws given by the relevant domestic courts, unless there is 'flagrant non-observance or arbitrariness' in their application.[63] Nor does it have any authority to determine whether the person in question is criminally liable, something that is reserved exclusively for the national courts.[64] Such deference does not apply in the same way when article 7 is concerned. However, in applying article 7, the European Court will review the interpretation of criminal law provisions that has been conducted by the national courts.[65] According to an early decision of the Commission: 'Although it is not normally for the Commission to ascertain the proper interpretation of municipal law by national courts, the case is otherwise in matters where the Convention expressly refers to municipal law, as it does in Article 7.'[66] The power of review in such cases must be

---

[56] *Kafkaris v. Cyprus* [GC], no. 21906/04, § 150, ECHR 2008.

[57] *Polednová v. Czech Republic* (dec.), no. 2615/10, 21 June 2011.

[58] *Kafkaris v. Cyprus* [GC], no. 21906/04, § 139, ECHR 2008.

[59] *The Sunday Times v. the United Kingdom (no. 1)*, 26 April 1979, §§ 48–49, Series A no. 30.

[60] *Kafkaris v. Cyprus* [GC], no. 21906/04, § 139, ECHR 2008.

[61] *S.W. v. the United Kingdom*, 22 November 1995, § 46, Series A no. 335-B.

[62] Ibid.

[63] *Société Colas Est and Others v. France*, no. 37971/97, § 43, ECHR 2002-III.

[64] *K.A. and A.D. v. Belgium*, no. 42758/98 and 45558/99, § 52, 17 February 2005; *Streletz, Kessler, and Krenz v. Allemagne* [GC], nos 34044/96, 35532/97, and 44801/98, § 51, ECHR 2001-II.

[65] *K.A. and A.D. v. Belgium*, no. 42758/98 and 45558/99, § 52, 17 February 2005.

[66] *Murphy v. the United Kingdom*, no. 4681/70, Commission decision of 3 and 4 October 1972, DR 43, p. 1.

greater than normal because it is the law itself, and its application by national courts, that is the essence of the right in question. According to the Grand Chamber, 'Article 7 § 1 requires the Court to examine whether there was a contemporaneous legal basis for the applicant's conviction and, in particular, it must satisfy itself that the result reached by the relevant domestic courts... was compatible with Article 7 of the Convention, even if there were differences between the legal approach and reasoning of this Court and the relevant domestic decisions. To accord a lesser power of review to this Court would render Article 7 devoid of purpose.'[67]

Sometimes, laws confer discretion on officials who are then responsible for their application, and to that extent the actual scope of the law may not be entirely foreseeable. According to the Court, such laws are not inconsistent with article 7 'provided that the scope of the discretion and the manner of its exercise are indicated with sufficient clarity, having regard to the legitimate aim in question, to give the individual adequate protection against arbitrary interference'.[68]

The requirement of 'law' imposes upon the Court the duty to verify that there was in fact a legal provision making an act punishable, and that the penalty imposed did not exceed what was fixed by that provision.[69] In a case involving trespass regulations in Greenland where protesters at the American base were prosecuted, the Court considered that a provision of the Penal Code authorizing enactment of delegated legislation 'in accordance with established practice' was sufficient to meet the requirement of a sufficient legal basis. The provision provided legal authority to a range of administrative rules adopted by the Provincial Council of Greenland.[70]

Role of judicial interpretation and case law

In a simplistic sense, any new interpretation by courts of existing law has the potential to violate the rule against retroactive application. Such a rigid approach would deny the courts any contribution in the progressive development of the law. In any case, regardless of how clear a legal text may seem, there is always an element of legal interpretation involved in understanding the scope of an enactment.[71] Moreover, as the Court has often noted, 'the wording of statutes is not always precise'.[72] Legislators frequently regulate conduct by general categorizations rather than through exhaustive codification, with the consequence that 'many laws are inevitably couched in terms which, to a greater or lesser extent are, and their interpretation and application depend on practice'.[73] This makes judicial

[67] *Kononov v. Latvia* [GC], no. 36376/04, § 198, ECHR 2010. Also *K.A. and A.D. v. Belgium,* no. 42758/98 and 45558/99, § 52, 17 February 2005.
[68] *Margareta and Roger Andersson v. Sweden,* 25 February 1992, § 75, Series A no. 226-A.
[69] *Scoppola v. Italy (no. 2)* [GC], no. 10249/03, § 95, 17 September 2009; *Coëme and Others v. Belgium,* nos 32476/96, 32547/96, 32548/96, 33209/96, and 33210/96, § 145, ECHR 2000-VII; *Achour v. France* [GC], no. 67335/01, § 43, ECHR 2006-IV.
[70] *Custers and Others v. Denmark,* nos 11843/03, 11847/03, and 11849/03, § 84, 3 May 2007.
[71] *K.A. and A.D. v. Belgium,* no. 42758/98 and 45558/99, § 52, 17 February 2005.
[72] *Scoppola v. Italy (no. 2)* [GC], no. 10249/03, § 100, 17 September 2009; *Cantoni v. France,* 15 November 1996, § 31, *Reports of Judgments and Decisions* 1996-V; *Kokkinakis v. Greece,* 25 May 1993, § 40, Series A no. 260-A; *Camilleri v. Malta,* no. 42931/10, § 36, 22 January 2013; *Del Río Prada v. Spain,* no. 42750/09, § 47, 10 July 2012.
[73] *Scoppola v. Italy (no. 2)* [GC], no. 10249/03, § 100, 17 September 2009; *Cantoni v. France,* 15 November 1996, § 31, *Reports of Judgments and Decisions* 1996-V; *Kokkinakis v. Greece,* 25 May 1993, § 40, Series A no. 260-A; *Camilleri v. Malta,* no. 42931/10, § 36, 22 January 2013; *Del Río Prada v. Spain,* no. 42750/09, § 47,

interpretation an indispensable part of the process of making law foreseeable and accessible.

The Convention organs have repeatedly stated that 'it is a firmly established part of the legal tradition of the States party to the Convention that case-law, as one of the sources of the law, necessarily contributes to the gradual development of the criminal law'.[74] Moreover, it actually contributes to greater legal certainty, which is obviously one of the central values underpinning article 7. In effect, '[t]he role of adjudication vested in the courts is precisely to dissipate such interpretational doubts as remain'.[75] Indeed, the lack of accessible and reasonably foreseeable judicial interpretation may actually result in a breach of article 7.[76] The Grand Chamber has explained that:

in any system of law, however clearly drafted a legal provision may be, including a criminal law provision, there is an inevitable element of judicial interpretation. There will always be a need for elucidation of doubtful points and for adaptation to changing circumstances. Again, whilst certainty is highly desirable, it may bring in its train excessive rigidity and the law must be able to keep pace with changing circumstances.[77]

Article 7 does not inhibit the 'gradual clarification of the rules of criminal liability through judicial interpretation from case to case', although the development that results must be 'consistent with the essence of the offence' and be reasonably foreseeable.[78] The Grand Chamber has distinguished 'an interpretation of criminal law pursuing a perceptible line of case-law development' that it identified in the spousal rape cases from the United Kingdom, discussed earlier, and a new and unexpected turn in Spanish case law respecting remission of sentence.[79] In the latter case, the Grand Chamber considered that 'at the time when the applicant was convicted and at the time when she was notified of the decision to combine her sentences and set a maximum term of imprisonment, there was no indication of any perceptible line of case-law development' by which the effective length of the sentence would be increased.[80] An absence of case law with respect to a given crime may be a factor favouring the applicant in an article 7 case.[81]

10 July 2012; *Dragotoniu and Militaru-Pidhorni v. Romania*, nos 77193/01 and 77196/01, § 36, 24 May 2007; *Van Anraat v. the Netherlands* (dec.), no. 65389/09, § 83, 6 July 2010.

[74] *Scoppola v. Italy (no. 2)* [GC], no. 10249/03, § 101, 17 September 2009; *Kruslin v. France*, 24 April 1990, § 29, Series A no. 176-A); *Camilleri v. Malta*, no. 42931/10, § 37, 22 January 2013; *Del Río Prada v. Spain*, no. 42750/09, § 47, 10 July 2012.

[75] *Scoppola v. Italy (no. 2)* [GC], no. 10249/03, § 101, 17 September 2009; *Kafkaris v. Cyprus* [GC], no. 21906/04, § 141, ECHR 2008; *Del Río Prada v. Spain*, no. 42750/09, § 47, 10 July 2012.

[76] *Pessino v. France*, no. 40403/02, §§ 35–36, 10 October 2006; *Dragotoniu and Militaru-Pidhorni v. Romania*, nos 77193/01 and 77196/01, §§ 43–44, 24 May 2007; *Alimuçaj v. Albania*, no. 20134/05, §§ 154–162, 7 February 2012.

[77] *Scoppola v. Italy (no. 2)* [GC], no. 10249/03, § 100, 17 September 2009; *S.W. v. the United Kingdom*, 22 November 1995, § 36, Series A no. 335-B; *Camilleri v. Malta*, no. 42931/10, § 36, 22 January 2013.

[78] *S.W. v. the United Kingdom*, 22 November 1995, § 36, Series A no. 335-B; *Camilleri v. Malta*, no. 42931/10, § 37, 22 January 2013; *Streletz, Kessler, and Krenz v. Germany* [GC], nos 34044/96, 35532/97, and 44801/98, § 50, ECHR 2001-II; *Delbos and Others v. France* (dec.), no. 60819/00, ECHR 2004-IX; *Eurofinacom v. France* (dec.), no. 58753/00, ECHR 2004-VII (extracts); *Radio France and Others v. France*, no. 53984/00, § 20, ECHR 2004-II.

[79] *Del Río Prada v. Spain* [GC], no. 42750/09, § 115, 21 October 2013. Also *Del Río Prada v. Spain* [GC], no. 42750/09, Concurring Opinion of Judge Nicolaou, § 10, 21 October 2013.

[80] *Del Río Prada v. Spain* [GC], no. 42750/09, § 117, 21 October 2013.

[81] *Plechkov v. Romania*, no. 1660/03, § 73, 16 September 2014.

Administrative practice in the implementation of law, and in particular sentencing provisions, may create a 'legitimate expectation'.[82] But a tolerance or a practice by which legal provisions may not have been applied in a thorough manner cannot justify a claim that article 7 has been violated. Even if criminal law provisions have not been applied for many years, they remain in force and can be activated by a change in prosecutorial policy and even, where laws permit this, at the initiative of an individual complainant.[83] The relationship between policy and law is especially acute in the case of offences such as assault, where general principles seem to give way to customs and traditions that are highly influenced by culture. Starting with a broad prohibition by which the application of force to another person that causes bodily harm is prohibited by law, there is a multitude of exceptions and special understandings that govern the relationship between the criminal law and practices such as consensual fighting, duelling, violent sports like boxing and wrestling, tattooing and other forms of body mutilation, ritual disfiguring of the sexual organs, and cosmetic surgery. In a Belgian case, the applicants did not challenge the legal text itself, which was a rather classic prohibition of assault, but claimed instead that there was a tolerance of such conduct in the 'liberal, permissive and individualistic society' of modern-day Belgium. To the argument that there was no relevant case law interpreting the provision as a prohibition on such behaviour, the Court said this was not significant because the practices themselves were both very violent and very rare.[84]

Foreseeability and accessibility

The Convention organs have employed the words 'foreseeability' and 'accessibility' to describe the requirements of law imposed by article 7 of the Convention. The scope of these concepts 'depends to a considerable degree on the content of the instrument in issue, the field it is designed to cover and the number and status of those to whom it is addressed'.[85] The European Court concluded that legislation was not 'foreseeable' where a crime established by Maltese law could be punished before two different courts, at the discretion of the prosecutor, with the consequence that two different sentencing scales applied. In deciding where to try the case, the Court agreed that the prosecutor might have given weight to a number of criteria, but these were not specified in a legislative text, nor were they clarified through case law over the years. Consequently, the decision was 'inevitably subjective and left room for arbitrariness, particularly given the lack of procedural safeguards'.[86]

According to the Convention organs, law may still satisfy the requirement of foreseeability 'where the person concerned has to take appropriate legal advice to assess, to a degree that is reasonable in the circumstances, the consequences which a given action may entail'.[87] On occasion, the Court has noted the impossibility, even with the help of

---

[82] *Del Río Prada v. Spain*, no. 42750/09, § 54, 10 July 2012.

[83] *Norris v. Ireland*, 26 October 1988, § 38, Series A no. 142.

[84] *K.A. and A.D. v. Belgium*, no. 42758/98 and 45558/99, § 55, 17 February 2005.

[85] *Groppera Radio AG and Others v. Switzerland*, 28 March 1990, § 68, Series A no. 173; *Camilleri v. Malta*, no. 42931/10, § 38, 22 January 2013; *K.A. and A.D. v. Belgium*, nos 42758/98 and 45558/99, § 53, 17 February 2005.

[86] *Camilleri v. Malta*, no. 42931/10, § 43, 22 January 2013.

[87] *Scoppola v. Italy (no. 2)* [GC], no. 10249/03, § 102, 17 September 2009; *Achour v. France* [GC], no. 67335/01, § 54, ECHR 2006-IV; *Sud Fondi srl and Others v. Italy*, no. 75909/01, § 110, 20 January 2009; *Camilleri v. Malta*, no. 42931/10, § 38, 22 January 2013.

professional legal advice, of foreseeing a change in judicial interpretation of criminal law provisions.[88] In *Groppera Radio AG*, the relevant provisions of international telecommunications law were highly technical and complex, and intended for specialists. The Court said it was to be expected of a business engaging in broadcasting across a frontier that it would seek to inform itself fully about the applicable rules with the help of advisers.[89] In a Georgian prosecution for the crime of being a 'thief in law', that is today, 'a member of the thieves' underworld who, using any type of methods, directly runs or coordinates the running of the thieves' underworld', the European Court noted that this rather colloquial description of the crime was not only well-known to the general public in Georgia, it was apparently done 'to ensure that the essence of the newly criminalised offences would be grasped more easily by the general public'.[90]

The case law speaks of crimes that are 'reasonably' foreseeable, implying that the assessment is an objective one. Nevertheless, the Court will sometimes consider the personal circumstances of the applicant when deciding whether a crime was foreseeable. There are higher expectations with respect to foreseeability and accessibility with respect to persons carrying on a professional activity, as they are used to proceeding with a high degree of caution with respect to legal norms. Thus, they should 'take special care in assessing the risks that such activity entails'.[91] In a Belgian case, the Court noted that one of the applicants was a magistrate who could be expected to be familiar with relevant case law.[92]

Although the case law is sparse on this point, as a general proposition it seems proper that the accessibility and foreseeability of criminal offences within the framework of an article 7 analysis must also take into account available defences, excuses, and justifications, and modes of liability. These matters are not strictly speaking components of the definitions of the offences, but they nevertheless can have a substantial impact on whether or not there is individual criminal liability. As a general rule, domestic courts refuse to entertain a defence of mistake or ignorance of the law (*ignorantia juris non excusat*), in effect making the individual face the consequences of a penal provision regardless of how accessible the law may have been.

In some of the cases concerning atrocity crimes the Court has had to consider the availability of the defence of superior orders. The defence of superior orders was simply prohibited by the Charter of the International Military Tribunal,[93] but it is probably fair to say that soldiers and other persons required to obey orders from superiors may avail of the defence to the extent that the order is not manifestly unlawful. This is the way the matter was formulated in early decisions[94] and it is also presented in this manner in the Rome Statute of the International Criminal Court.[95] The Court has taken the view that 'even a private soldier could not show total, blind obedience to orders which flagrantly

---

[88] *Dragotoniu and Militaru-Pidhorni v. Romania*, nos 77193/01 and 77196/01, § 44, 24 May 2007.

[89] *Groppera Radio AG and Others v. Switzerland*, 28 March 1990, § 68, Series A no. 173.

[90] *Ashlarba v. Georgia*, no. 45554/08, § 38, 15 July 2014.

[91] *Cantoni v. France*, 15 November 1996, § 35, *Reports of Judgments and Decisions* 1996-V.

[92] *K.A. and A.D. v. Belgium*, no. 42758/98 and 45558/99, §§ 55, 58, 17 February 2005.

[93] Agreement for the Prosecution and Punishment of Major War Criminals of the European Axis, and Establishing the Charter of the International Military Tribunal (I.M.T.), annex, (1951) 82 UNTS 279, art. 8.

[94] *Empire* v. *Dithmar and Boldt* (Hospital Ship 'Llandovery Castle'), (1922) 16 *AJIL* 708.

[95] Rome Statute of the International Criminal Court, (2002) 2187 UNTS 90, art. 33. See William A. Schabas, *The International Criminal Court: A Commentary on the Rome Statute*, Oxford: Oxford University Press, 2010, pp. 507–14.

infringed not only the [German Democratic Republic's] own legal principles but also internationally recognised human rights, in particular the right to life'.[96] Despite being ordered to do so, it considered that a soldier was not justified in firing on unarmed persons who were merely trying to leave the country. In *Kononov*, the Court examined whether an order to murder civilians suspected of complicity in Nazi atrocities could furnish a defence to charges of war crimes. The Grand Chamber said that 'even the most cursory reflection by the applicant, would have indicated that, at the very least, the impugned acts risked being counter to the laws and customs of war as understood at that time and, notably, risked constituting war crimes for which, as commander, he could be held individually and criminally accountable'.[97] In another case concerning atrocities perpetrated during the wars in the former Yugoslavia, the Court said that 'having in mind the flagrantly unlawful nature of his acts, which included murders and torture of Bosniacs within the context of a widespread and systematic attack against the Bosniac civilian population of the Višegrad Municipality, even the most cursory reflection by the applicant would have indicated that they risked constituting a crime against humanity for which he could be held criminally accountable'.[98] It held that national legislation based upon the definition of crimes against humanity in the Rome Statute, which was adopted in 1998 and entered into force in 2002, can be applied to acts perpetrated in 1992 without offending article 7.[99] In another case dealing with atrocities perpetrated in Africa, the Court held that 'at the time when the offences were committed, the applicant's actions constituted offences that were defined with sufficient accessibility and foreseeability under French law and international law, and that the applicant could reasonably, if need be with the help of informed legal advice, have foreseen the risk of being prosecuted and convicted for acts of torture committed by him between 1990 and 1991'.[100]

Statutory limitation

Where statutory limitation may apply to a particular offence, a question arises as to whether a change that would be to the detriment of an individual falls within the ambit of article 7(1). Statutory limitation is often involved in *nullum crimen* issues, especially when there has been a change of regime, as is the case in the countries of Eastern and Central Europe. According to the Court, 'it is legitimate for a State governed by the rule of law to bring criminal proceedings against persons who have committed crimes under a former regime'.[101] The words of Judge Nicolas Bratza, albeit in a somewhat different context, seem relevant to the issue. Referring to prosecution of German border guards for murdering fugitives, he said that he accepted 'that the situation in the [German Democratic Republic] was such that the applicant could hardly have foreseen at the time that his actions would result in his prosecution for the offence of intentional homicide'. But, said

---

[96] *K.-H.W. v. Germany* [GC], no. 37201/97, § 75, ECHR 2001-II (extracts).

[97] *Kononov v. Latvia* [GC], no. 36376/04, § 238, ECHR 2010.

[98] *Šimšić v. Bosnia and Herzegovina* (dec.), no. 51552/10, § 24, 10 April 2012.

[99] Ibid.

[100] *Ould Dah v. France* (dec.), no. 13113/03, ECHR 2009. Also *Achour v. France* [GC], no. 67335/01, § 54, ECHR 2006-IV; *Jorgić v. Germany*, no. 74613/01, § 113, ECHR 2007-III; *Korbely v. Hungary* [GC], no. 9174/02, § 70, ECHR 2008.

[101] *Polednová v. Czech Republic* (dec.), no. 2615/10, 21 June 2011; *Streletz, Kessler, and Krenz v. Germany* [GC], nos 34044/96, 35532/97, and 44801/98, § 81, ECHR 2001-II.

Judge Bratza, that is not at all the same question as 'whether the applicant could reasonably have foreseen that his actions amounted to such an offence'.[102]

In *Kononov*, the Grand Chamber addressed the issue of statutory limitation indirectly, answering the applicant's argument that his prosecution was time-barred by concluding that there was no statutory limitation applicable to war crimes at the time the offence was committed.[103] The better view was expressed by four judges in a joint concurring opinion. They explained:

Article 7 of the Convention and the principles it enshrines require that in a rule-of-law system anyone considering carrying out a particular act should be able, by reference to the legal rules defining crimes and the corresponding penalties, to determine whether or not the act in question constitutes a crime and what penalty he or she faces if it is carried out. Hence no one can speak of retroactive application of substantive law, when a person is convicted, even belatedly, on the basis of rules existing at the time of the commission of the act. Considering, as the Court leaves one to believe, that the procedural issue of the statute of limitations is a constituent element of the applicability of Article 7, linked to the question of retroactive application and sitting alongside, with equal force, the conditions of the existence of a crime and a penalty, can lead to unwanted results which could undermine the very spirit of Article 7.[104]

In effect, the entitlement of an accused person is to be prosecuted only with respect to crimes and punishments in existence at the time of the impugned act. This is not at all the same, however, as a right to benefit from changes to legal terms on statutory limitation. The *Kononov* case was a particularly difficult manifestation of the problem, because the applicant's argument was that war crimes were subject to statutory limitation when committed in 1944, while acknowledging this to have changed subsequently.

International law

Like article 11(2) of the Universal Declaration of Human Rights and article 15(1) of the International Covenant on Civil and Political Rights, article 7(1) of the Convention refers to criminal offences under 'international law' as well as under 'national law'. Given that the European Court exercises jurisdiction essentially over national proceedings pursuant to national law, issues arise when criminal offences under national law are prosecuted using retrospective or retroactive provisions but where the government insists that the crimes in question already existed under international law.

When the Convention was adopted, the notion of 'crimes under international law' was already fairly well developed. For example, in 1946 the United Nations General Assembly adopted a resolution affirming that 'genocide is a crime under international law' ('*le génocide est un crime du droit des gens*').[105] The Charter of the International Military Tribunal, a document that was widely ratified and whose principles were also confirmed by a General Assembly resolution,[106] codified three categories of international crime: war crimes, crimes against peace, and crimes against humanity. In addition to these offences,

---

[102] *K.-H.W. v. Germany* [GC], no. 37201/97, Concurring Opinion of Judge Sir Nicolas Bratza, Joined by Judge Vajić, ECHR 2001-II.

[103] *Kononov v. Latvia* [GC], no. 36376/04, §§ 230, 233, ECHR 2010.

[104] *Kononov v. Latvia* [GC], no. 36376/04, Joint Concurring Opinion of Judge Rozakis, Tulkens, Spielmann and Jebens, § 6, ECHR 2010.

[105] UN Doc. A/RES/96(I), OP1.

[106] UN Doc. A/RES/95(I).

which concern atrocities and human rights violations, international law also recognizes a variety of offences many of which are also characterized as 'transnational', in the areas of piracy, terrorism, and drug trafficking.

The identification of the content of the offences under international law poses particular problems. Because of the increasing codification of international crimes, reference to written texts of international law may be sufficient, at least for crimes committed in the recent past. According to the Court, article 7 remains 'wholly valid where . . . an international instrument for the protection of human rights of universal scope has been enacted'.[107] In identifying 'universal scope', near-universal ratification, for example of the Geneva Conventions, may be relevant. Sometimes, crimes are punished as international offences but by national courts, despite the fact that they were not codified in a relevant international instrument at the time of the act. Reliance is placed upon the existence of the crime under customary international law in somewhat the same manner that some national courts recognizzed crimes of common law.

When the international crimes are codified, there can be disputes relating from differing definitions. There is, for example, rather significant variation in the definition of crimes against humanity in the various international texts, as well as in the reflections of these crimes when they are incorporated into national law. In *Jorgić v. Germany*, the Court noted that a broad concept of genocide was being applied by the national courts of Germany that was not consistent with the prevailing interpretation of the crime by international tribunals, notably the International Criminal Tribunal for the former Yugoslavia and the International Court of Justice. Nevertheless,

while many authorities had favoured a narrow interpretation of the crime of genocide, there had already been several authorities at the material time which had construed the offence of genocide in the same wider way as the German courts. In these circumstances, the Court finds that the applicant, if need be with the assistance of a lawyer, could reasonably have foreseen that he risked being charged with and convicted of genocide for the acts he had committed in 1992.[108]

The Court noted, in this context, that Jorgić had been convicted of several killings, detention and ill-treatment as leader of a paramilitary group pursuing a policy of ethnic cleansing. Consequently, 'the national courts' interpretation of the crime of genocide could reasonably be regarded as consistent with the essence of that offence and could reasonably be foreseen by the applicant at the material time'.[109]

The International Military Tribunal said that international criminal law was 'not static, but by continual adaptation follows the needs of a changing world'.[110] Because of the evolution in the notion of international crimes, problems with respect to article 7(1) may arise because of the need to fix the relevant law at the time the crimes was committed and to determine, using the general notions applicable to that provision of the Convention, whether the international law was foreseeable and accessible. Examples have been presented with respect to prosecutions by courts of Eastern and Central Europe during the 1990s and 2000s of crimes committed half a century earlier in association with the Second World War and with the post-war regimes. Although crimes against humanity were

---

[107] *Ould Dah v. France* (dec.), no. 13113/03, ECHR 2009.
[108] *Jorgić v. Germany*, no. 74613/01, § 114, ECHR 2007-III.
[109] Ibid., § 115.
[110] *France et al. v. Goering et al.*, (1948) 22 IMT 411, at p. 464.

recognized under international law at Nuremberg, they were severely restricted by the requirement of a nexus with international armed conflict and aggressive war. It is beyond debate that by the 1990s, this restriction on crimes against humanity had disappeared, and they could be prosecuted even when committed in peacetime. The European Court has dismissed complaints founded on article 7(1) with respect to prosecution for crimes against humanity in peacetime dating from the 1940s and 1950s.[111] However, as Antonio Cassese wrote in an article criticizing the case law of the European Court, 'the indispensable link between those crimes and war had not yet been severed' in the late 1940s. He said it was only later, in the late 1960s, that a general rule gradually began to evolve, prohibiting crimes against humanity even when committed in time of peace.[112] Similar issues arise with respect to war crimes. The Grand Chamber has acknowledged that 'in 1944 a nexus with an international armed conflict was required to prosecute acts as war crimes'.[113] Obviously, that nexus is no longer mandatory because article 8 of the Rome Statute of the International Criminal Court recognizes individual liability for war crimes perpetrated in non-international armed conflict. At what point between 1944 and 1998, when the Rome Statute was adopted, the nexus disappeared is a matter of debate in relevant cases.

In some cases, the legal provisions of national law are inspired by international law but reflect it in an inexpert and sometimes inaccurate manner. For example, Hungarian law refers to the notion of crimes against humanity set out in common article 3 of the Geneva Conventions. Yet common article 3 does not purport to define criminal offences. The Court said that it was not its role 'to seek to establish authoritatively the meaning of the concept of "crime against humanity" as it stood in 1956'.[114] The rather clumsy and idiosyncratic definition in the Hungarian law probably contributed to the finding of a violation by the Grand Chamber in an application submitted by a former police chief who had been convicted for a killing that took place during the 1956 revolution.[115]

Heavier penalty

The principle of legality concerns the penalty as well as the crime itself, as the second sentence of article 7(1) affirms: 'Nor shall a heavier penalty be imposed than the one that was applicable at the time the criminal offence was committed.' The relevant Latin maxim is *nulla poena sine lege*, although strictly speaking it affirms the requirement that the penalty be foreseeable and accessible to the perpetrator at the time the criminal act takes place. The 'qualitative requirements' of accessibility and foreseeability apply to the penalty as well as to the definition of the offence.[116] The concept of penalty in article 7(1) is autonomous, like the notions of 'civil rights and obligations' and 'criminal charge' in article 6(1), in that the European Court is free to determine whether a particular measure

---

[111] *Kolk and Kislyiy v. Estonia* (dec.), nos 23052/04 and 24018/04, ECHR 2006-I; *Penart v. Estonia* (dec.), no. 14685/04, 24 January 2006; *Korbely v. Hungary* [GC], no. 9174/02, § 83, ECHR 2008.

[112] Antonio Cassese, 'Balancing the Prosecution of Crimes against Humanity and Non-Retroactivity of Criminal Law, The *Kolk and Kislyiy v. Estonia* Case before the ECHR', (2006) 4 *Journal of International Criminal Justice* 410, at p. 413.

[113] *Kononov v. Latvia* [GC], no. 36376/04, § 211, ECHR 2010.

[114] *Korbely v. Hungary* [GC], no. 9174/02, § 78, ECHR 2008.

[115] Ibid.

[116] *Kafkaris v. Cyprus* [GC], no. 21906/04, § 140, ECHR 2008; *Achour v. France* [GC], no. 67335/01, § 41, ECHR 2006-IV.

is a penalty regardless of the qualification that it may be given under national law.[117] The Court is free to go behind appearances and make its own assessment as to the substantive nature of a particular measure.[118]

The starting point in determining whether something is a penalty is whether it is imposed following conviction for a 'criminal offence'.[119] The Court may also take other factors into account, such as the nature and purpose of the measure in question, the way it is characterized under national law, the relevant procedures, and the severity.[120] 'The severity of the measure is not, however, in itself decisive', the Court has said, because 'for instance, many non-penal measures of a preventive nature may have a substantial impact on the person concerned'.[121] Considering the claim that listing of an individual on the Sex Offenders Register might lead to some public stigmatization, the European Commission said this could not be relevant to 'whether the Act imposes a "penalty" as they stem from the public's reaction to particular types of offence, rather than from the registration requirements'.[122]

Although conviction for a criminal offence is a starting point for consideration of an issue of retroactive punishment, it does not follow that every legal consequence of the conviction amounts to punishment within the meaning of article 7(1). Legislation in the Netherlands imposed a requirement of DNA sampling on convicted criminals. According to the Court,

> the purpose of the measure in question is to assist in the solving of crimes, including bringing their perpetrators to justice, since, with the help of the database, the police may be able to identify perpetrators of offences faster, and to contribute towards a lower rate of reoffending, since a person knowing that his or her DNA profile is included in a national database may dissuade him or her from committing further offences. The Court considers that, seen in this light, the Act merely employs the applicant's conviction as a criterion by means of which he could be identified as a person who has shown himself capable of committing an offence of a certain severity, rather than that the measure in question is to be seen as intending to inflict a punishment upon him in relation to the particular offences of which he has been convicted.[123]

Fines and similar measures pose particular problems. It is important to ascertain whether they are imposed essentially to inflict punishment and deter future breaches, or rather to provide pecuniary reparation for damages. If a fine appears to be both deterrent and punitive, the conclusion may well be that it is criminal in nature.[124] It is common for justice systems to provide for imprisonment in the case of failure to pay a fine, although

---

[117] *Scoppola v. Italy (no. 2)* [GC], no. 10249/03, § 96, 17 September 2009; *M. v. Germany*, no. 19359/04, § 126, ECHR 2009; *Gurguchiani v. Spain*, no. 16012/06, § 31, 15 December 2009.

[118] *Del Río Prada v. Spain* [GC], no. 42750/09, § 81, 21 October 2013; *Del Río Prada v. Spain*, no. 42750/09, § 48, 10 July 2012; *Welch v. the United Kingdom*, 9 February 1995, § 27, Series A no. 307-A; *Jamil v. France*, 8 June 1995, § 30, Series A no. 317-B.

[119] *Gurguchiani v. Spain*, no. 16012/06, § 31, 15 December 2009; *Del Río Prada v. Spain*, no. 42750/09, § 48, 10 July 2012.

[120] *Scoppola v. Italy (no. 2)* [GC], no. 10249/03, § 97, 17 September 2009; *Welch v. the United Kingdom*, 9 February 1995, § 28, Series A no. 307-A; *Del Río Prada v. Spain*, no. 42750/09, § 48, 10 July 2012.

[121] *M. v. Germany*, no. 19359/04, § 120, ECHR 2009. Also *Welch v. the United Kingdom*, 9 February 1995, § 32, Series A no. 307-A.

[122] *Ibbotson v. the United Kingdom*, no. 40146/98, Commission decision of 21 October 1998; *Adamson v. the United Kingdom* (dec.), no. 42293/98, 26 January 1999.

[123] *Van der Velden v. the Netherlands* (dec.), no. 29514/05, ECHR 2006-XV.

[124] *Öztürk v. Germany*, 21 February 1984, § 53, Series A no. 73.

the fact that a financial penalty cannot be converted into a prison sentence in case of default is not decisive in determining whether it is criminal in nature.[125] In *Jamil v. France*, legislation providing for imprisonment following default on payment of a customs fine was challenged under article 7(1). The Court noted that the regime was harsher than for sentences of imprisonment under ordinary criminal law because it was not mitigated by parole, pardon, and similar measures. 'Imprisonment in default is a survival of the ancient system of imprisonment for debt', said the judgment. '[I]t now exists only in respect of debts to the State and does not absolve the debtor from the obligation to pay which led to his committal to prison.' Noting that the sanction was ordered by a criminal court, was intended as a deterrent and could lead to deprivation of liberty, the Court concluded that the fine was indeed a penalty and subject to article 7(1).[126]

In cases involving changes to provisions for parole eligibility that are to the detriment of a convicted person serving a sentence of imprisonment, there has been some fluctuation in the case law. A line of cases holds that this is not the modification of a 'penalty'.[127] According to the Grand Chamber, 'the manner of their implementation and the reasoning behind' early release or parole policies are matters for domestic criminal justice policy.[128] In the important case of *Kafkaris v. Cyprus*, a provision by which life imprisonment was the mandatory sentence for murder, but where release after twenty years had been served was possible, was modified subsequent to the crime with the effect that the convicted person would not be eligibile for release. According to the Grand Chamber, such a measure concerning remission of a sentence or a change in a regime for early release was not part of the 'penalty' within the meaning of Article 7:

However, as regards the fact that as a consequence of the change in the prison law ... the applicant, as a life prisoner, no longer has a right to have his sentence remitted, the Court notes that this matter relates to the execution of the sentence as opposed to the 'penalty' imposed on him, which remains that of life imprisonment. Although the changes in the prison legislation and in the conditions of release may have rendered the applicant's imprisonment effectively harsher, these changes cannot be construed as imposing a heavier 'penalty' than that imposed by the trial court ...[129]

In subsequent cases, the Court distinguished *Kafkaris*. For example, in one decision it viewed expulsion from territory as a substitute for a prison sentence then being served to be a 'penalty' within the meaning of article 7: '[L]e remplacement de la peine de prison de dix-huit mois infligée au requérant par son expulsion et l'interdiction de territoire pour une durée de dix ans, sans qu'il ait été entendu et sans qu'il ait été tenu compte des circonstances autres que l'application quasi automatique de la nouvelle rédaction de l'article 89 du code pénal en vigueur depuis le 1er octobre 2003, doit s'analyser en une peine au même titre que celle fixée lors de la condamnation de l'intéressé.'[130]

---

[125] *Valico S.r.l. v. Italy* (dec.), no. 70074/01, ECHR 2006-III; *Lauko v. Slovakia*, 2 September 1998, § 58, Reports of Judgments and Decisions 1998-VI.

[126] *Jamil v. France*, 8 June 1995, Series A no. 317-B.

[127] The United States Supreme Court has taken a different position on this: *Marrero v. Warden of Louisberg Penitentiary*, (1974) 417 U.S. 653.

[128] *Kafkaris v. Cyprus* [GC], no. 21906/04, § 151, ECHR 2008.

[129] Ibid. Also *Hosein v. the United Kingdom*, no. 26293/95, Commission decision of 28 February 1996; *Uttley v. the United Kingdom* (dec.), no. 36946/03, 29 November 2005; *Hogben v. the United Kingdom*, no. 11653/85, Commission decision of 3 March 1986, DR 46, p. 231.

[130] *Gurguchiani v. Spain*, no. 16012/06, § 40, 15 December 2009.

In a German case, the extension of preventive detention was extended from ten years to an unlimited period of time. In Germany, preventive detention is not considered a penalty subject to the prohibition on retrospective punishment but rather a measure of correction and prevention.[131] At the time of the offence, a preventive detention order could be made for a maximum of ten years. The law changed, with the consequence that applicant's preventive detention was prolonged with retrospective effect after six years in preventive detention had been served.[132] In *Kafkaris*, it could not be assumed at the time sentence was imposed that if would actually amount to twenty years' imprisonment. By contrast, in the German case when the crime was committed the law 'clearly and unambiguously fixed the duration of a first period of preventive detention at a maximum of ten years'.[133]

The Grand Chamber returned to this issue in *Del Rio Prado v. Spain*. It explained that the term 'imposed' in the second sentence of article 7(1) was not to be interpreted as excluding all measures introduced after the pronouncement of the sentence.[134] It said it would 'not rule out the possibility that measures taken by the legislature, the administrative authorities or the courts after the final sentence has been imposed or while the sentence is being served may result in the redefinition or modification of the scope of the "penalty" imposed by the trial court'.[135] Judges Mahoney and Vehabović did not see the distinction with the earlier case law of the Court and dissented, while acknowledging 'the humanitarian thinking behind the reasoning of the majority' and recognizing 'that the circumstances of the present case are quite extraordinary and, indeed, disquieting from the point of view of the fairness of treatment of prisoners, especially those who have the prospect of spending a large part of their life incarcerated'.[136]

Placement of offenders on registers for sex offenders has also been the subject of applications to the Court. These are deemed to be 'public-order measures' rather than penalties. The French Sex Offenders Register 'is designed to prevent persons who have committed sexual offences or violent crimes from reoffending and to ensure that they can be identified and traced'.[137] Therefore, according to the Court, it has a preventive and deterrent purpose and cannot be considered punitive or as constituting a sanction.[138]

When prisoners are moved from one jurisdiction to another pursuant to a transfer agreement such as the Council of Europe Transfer Convention and its Additional Protocol,[139] the new system may be harsher in some respects, leading to charges that a breach of article 7(1) may be involved. In several cases the Court has dismissed such claims on the grounds that changes should not be considered a penalty because they concern the execution of a sentence rather than a sentence itself.[140] As a more general proposition, the Court has insisted upon the distinction between a measure that is a

---

[131] *M. v. Germany*, no. 19359/04, § 125, ECHR 2009.

[132] Ibid., §§ 121–123.

[133] Ibid., § 136.

[134] *Del Río Prada v. Spain* [GC], no. 42750/09, § 88, 21 October 2013.

[135] Ibid. See also ibid., §§ 109–110.

[136] *Del Río Prada v. Spain* [GC], no. 42750/09, Joint Partly Dissenting Opinion of Judges Mahoney and Vehabović, 21 October 2013.

[137] *Gardel v. France*, no. 16428/05, § 42, ECHR 2009.

[138] Ibid., § 43.

[139] Additional Protocol to the Convention on the Transfer of Sentenced Persons, ETS 167; Convention on the Transfer of Sentenced Persons, ETS 112.

[140] *Csoszánszki v. Sweden* (dec.), no. 22318/02, 27 June 2006; *Szabó v. Sweden* (dec.), no. 28578/03, 27 June 2006; *Müller v. Czech Republic* (dec.), no. 48058/09, 6 September 2011.

penalty in a substantive sense, and to which article 7 clearly applies, and one that concerns its execution or enforcement.[141] But it has also acknowledged that 'in practice, the distinction between the two may not always be clear-cut'.[142] Of course, the sentence imposed following transfer may also be challenged as inhuman or degrading treatment or punishment under article 3, although 'where a measure of international cooperation is directed at promoting and protecting the fundamental rights of those subject to criminal sanctions abroad, the benefit enjoyed by the applicant as a result of the execution of that measure is an important factor in favour of finding that the manner and method of the execution of the sentence do not subject the applicant to distress or hardship exceeding the unavoidable level of suffering inherent in detention'.[143]

The notion of 'heavier' penalty in article 7(1) may present difficulties when the nature of the penalty is changed. It may not be obvious that one type of penalty is more or less severe than another. In a Spanish case, the law allowed a judge, at his or her discretion, to replace a sentence of detention with expulsion from the territory and a prohibition of return for a period of time. New legislation made expulsion the rule, and allowed a custodial sentence only in exceptional circumstances. Moreover, the prohibition of return was for ten years rather than for three to ten years, constituting a penalty that was 'bien plus sévère que celle prévue par l'ancienne version de la même disposition du code pénal'.[144]

In an Austrian case before the European Commission, the applicant had been sentenced to three years' imprisonment followed by detention in a labour camp. Subsequently, the courts converted the applicant's labour camp sentence into imprisonment in an institution for dangerous recidivists, because labour camps had been abolished in the meantime. The Commission referred to a previous case where it had held that it had not been substantiated that the character of the detention in an institution for recidivists was essentially different from the conditions in the former labour camps, and in particular that more restrictive conditions of confinement were imposed.[145] Decades later, the Court considered *X. v. Austria*, noting that it concerned two different types of penalty, namely a prison sentence and a labour camp, and even then the Commission did not consider the character of the penalty as 'essentially different'.[146]

In countries where the death penalty has been abolished, it is invariably replaced with a lengthy term of imprisonment. In a Bulgarian case, the Court held that in replacing capital punishment with a sentence of life imprisonment, 'the amendment of the forms of penalties envisaged in the Criminal Code for the most severe offence for which the applicant was found guilty operated in the applicant's favour and he received a more lenient penalty than was envisaged for that offence at the time it was committed'.[147] The issue was considered in a case directed against Azerbaijan but without the Court making

---

[141] *Scoppola v. Italy (no. 2)* [GC], no. 10249/03, § 98, 17 September 2009; *Kafkaris v. Cyprus* [GC], no. 21906/04, § 142, ECHR 2008; *Grava v. Italy*, no. 43522/98, § 51, 10 July 2003; *Saccoccia v. Austria* (dec.), no. 69917/01, 5 July 2007; *Del Río Prada v. Spain*, no. 42750/09, § 48, 10 July 2012; *Hosein v. the United Kingdom*, no. 26293/95, Commission decision of 28 February 1996; *M. v. Germany*, no. 19359/04, § 121, 17 December 2009.

[142] *Del Río Prada v. Spain*, no. 42750/09, § 48, 10 July 2012; *Kafkaris v. Cyprus* [GC], no. 21906/04, § 142, ECHR 2008; *Gurguchiani v. Spain*, no. 16012/06, § 31, 15 December 2009.

[143] *Willcox and Hurford v. the United Kingdom* (dec.), nos 43759/10 and 43771/12, § 76, ECHR 2013.

[144] *Gurguchiani v. Spain*, no. 16012/06, § 32, 15 December 2009.

[145] *X. v. Austria* (dec.), no. 7720/76, 8 May 1978.

[146] *Müller v. Czech Republic* (dec.), no. 48058/09, 6 September 2011.

[147] *Karmo v. Bulgaria* (dec.), no. 76965/01, 9 February 2006.

any firm pronouncement.[148] In *Öcalan v. Turkey (no. 2)*, a Chamber held that the replacement of capital punishment with a sentence of life imprisonment where there was no possibility of release did not breach article 7.[149] Nevertheless, such an incompressible life sentence was in breach of article 3.[150]

It is quite normal for criminal justice systems to provide more severe penalties in the case of recidivism. The Court has insisted that in 'matters relating to the existence of such rules [on recidivism], the manner of their implementation and the reasoning behind them fall within the power of the High Contracting Parties to determine their own criminal policy, which is not in principle a matter for [the Court] to comment on'.[151] French law required that the second crime be committed within a statutory period for the consequences of recidivism to be considered in sentencing, in effect establishing a form of statutory limitation with respect to the aggravation of sentence.[152] The Court noted that well-established principles had been recognized by the Court of Cassation with respect to the consequence of new legislation concerning recidivism, and this was 'manifestly capable of enabling the applicant to regulate his conduct'.[153]

Lex mitior

In contrast with the International Covenant on Civil and Political Rights, the text of the European Convention does not set out the *lex mitior* principle. Article 15(1) of the Covenant ensures that '[i]f, subsequent to the commission of the offence, provision is made by law for the imposition of the lighter penalty, the offender shall benefit thereby'. A 1978 decision of the European Commission of Human Rights held that the right to a more lenient penalty was not implied within article 7 of the European Convention.[154] That ruling was then confirmed by the European Court on several occasions[155] until, in 2009, the Grand Chamber reversed the position and held that article 7 could sustain the right of an offender to application of a more favourable criminal law.[156] In *Scoppola v. Italy (no. 2)*, the Grand Chamber noted that in addition to recognition in the International Covenant and the American Convention on Human Rights, the *lex mitior* principle was also set out in the Rome Statute of the International Criminal Court[157] and in the Charter of Fundamental Rights of the European Union.[158] Furthermore, the Grand Chamber noted that it had been recognized by the Court of Justice of the European Communities as forming part of the constitutional traditions common to the member States and, therefore, a part of the general principles of Community law.[159]

---

[148] *Hummatov v. Azerbaijan* (dec.), nos 9852/03 and 13413/04, 29 November 2007.

[149] *Öcalan v. Turkey (no. 2)*, nos 24069/03, 197/04, 6201/06, and 10464/07, § 186, 18 March 2014.

[150] Ibid., § 207, following *Vinter and Others v. the United Kingdom* [GC], nos 66069/09, 130/10, and 3896/10, §§ 111–113, ECHR 2013 (extracts).

[151] *Achour v. France* [GC], no. 67335/01, § 44, ECHR 2006-IV.

[152] Ibid., § 46.

[153] Ibid., § 53.

[154] *X v. Federal Republic of Germany*, no. 7900/77, Commission decision of 6 March 1978, DR 13, p. 70.

[155] *Le Petit v. the United Kingdom* (dec.), no. 35574/97, 5 December 2000; *Zaprianov v. Bulgaria* (dec.), no. 41171/98, 6 March 2003.

[156] *Scoppola v. Italy (no. 2)* [GC], no. 10249/03, § 103, 17 September 2009.

[157] Rome Statute of the International Criminal Court, (2002) 2187 UNTS 90, art. 24(2).

[158] Charter of Fundamental Rights of the European Union, 2010 OJ C 83/02, art. 49(1).

[159] *Berlusconi and Others*, 3 May 2005, C-387/02, C-391/02, and C-403/02, paras 66–69.

In reversing existing precedent, the Grand Chamber said that 'a long time has elapsed since the Commission gave the above-mentioned *X v. Germany* decision and that during that time there have been important developments internationally'.[160] Consequently, it concluded that since the Commission decision in *X v. Germany* 'a consensus has gradually emerged in Europe and internationally around the view that application of a criminal law providing for a more lenient penalty, even one enacted after the commission of the offence, has become a fundamental principle of criminal law'.[161] It said that the lack of express mention of such an obligation in article 7 of the Convention was not a 'decisive' argument.[162] The Court said that this conclusion was 'consistent with the principle of the rule of law, of which Article 7 forms an essential part' in that a trial court should apply the punishment that the legislator considers proportionate.[163]

Inflicting a heavier penalty for the sole reason that it was prescribed at the time of the commission of the offence would mean applying to the defendant's detriment the rules governing the succession of criminal laws in time. In addition, it would amount to disregarding any legislative change favourable to the accused which might have come in before the conviction and continuing to impose penalties which the State—and the community it represents—now consider excessive. The Court notes that the obligation to apply, from among several criminal laws, the one whose provisions are the most favourable to the accused is a clarification of the rules on the succession of criminal laws, which is in accord with another essential element of Article 7, namely the foreseeability of penalties.[164]

Several members of the Grand Chamber dissented, disputing the notion that the *lex mitior* principle had some visceral link with the principle of legality enshrined in article 7(1). They described *lex mitior* as a 'different kind of norm' that did no more than express a choice in the criminal law policy of States.[165] They noted that the drafters of article 7(1) had considered including the *lex mitior* principle but that they had decided against it. Citing *Johnston and Others v. Ireland*, they acknowledged the importance of evolutive interpretation but said that it did not permit the Court 'to derive from these instruments a right which was not included therein at the outset. This is particularly so here, where the omission was deliberate.'[166]

General principles of law recognized by civilized nations

Paragraph 2 of article 7 declares: 'This article shall not prejudice the trial and punishment of any person for any act or omission which, at the time when it was committed, was criminal according to the general principles of law recognised by civilised nations.' There is a corresponding provision in the International Covenant on Civil and Political Rights, although the wording differs slightly: 'Nothing in this article shall prejudice the trial and punishment of any person for any act or omission which, at the time when it was committed, was criminal according to the general principles of law recognised by the

---

[160] *Scoppola v. Italy (no. 2)* [GC], no. 10249/03, § 105, 17 September 2009.
[161] Ibid., § 106.
[162] Ibid., § 107.
[163] Ibid., § 108.
[164] Ibid.
[165] *Scoppola v. Italy (no. 2)* [GC], no. 10249/03, Partly Dissenting Opinion of Judge Nicolaou, Joined by Judges Bratza, Lorenzen, Jočiené, Villiger, and Sajó, 17 September 2009.
[166] *Scoppola v. Italy (no. 2)* [GC], no. 10249/03, Partly Dissenting Opinion of Judge Nicolaou, Joined by Judges Bratza, Lorenzen, Jočiené, Villiger, and Sajó, 17 September 2009, referring to *Johnston and Others v. Ireland*, 18 December 1986, § 53, Series A no.112.

community of nations.' According to a Chamber of the Court, the provision consists of 'une clause de dérogation exceptionnelle au principe général contenu dans le premier'.[167] The two paragraphs of article 7 'are interlinked and are to be interpreted in a concordant manner'.[168]

The wording evokes article 38(1)(c) of the Statute of the International Court of Justice, where 'the general principles of law recognised by civilised nations' are identified as one of three sources of international law, the others being treaty and customary law. In that context, while apparently of equal status to the other two categories, in reality 'general principles' is very much of a subsidiary or supplementary source of law. It was apparently introduced into the formulation of sources of law in order to ensure that there were no gaps in the applicable international law.[169] Public international law jurisprudence has never found specific crimes to be contemplated by the notion of 'general principles of law'. Somewhat analogous expressions have been used to describe genuinely international crimes. In the *Corfu Channel* case, the International Court of Justice spoke of 'elementary considerations of humanity, even more exacting in peace than in war'.[170] In its Advisory Opinion on Reservations to the Genocide Convention, the Court said the Convention contained 'principles which are recognised by civilised nations as binding on States, even without any conventional obligation'.[171]

According to the Convention organs, the *travaux préparatoires* of the European Convention indicate that the intent behind this provision was to shelter the Nuremberg principles from attack on the grounds that they were contrary to the principle of legality set out in paragraph 1. The European Commission on Human Rights explained its understanding of the drafting of article 7(2) as follows:

The Commission recalls that it transpires from the preparatory work to the Convention that the purpose of paragraph 2 of Article 7 is to specify that this Article does not affect laws which, in the wholly exceptional circumstances at the end of the Second World War, were passed in order to punish war crimes, and collaboration with the enemy and does not in any way aim to pass legal or moral judgment on those laws.[172]

The Court subsequently endorsed this position.[173] The words are drawn from a report by the Committee of Experts to the Committee of Ministers.[174] The simplistic statement

---

[167] *Tess v. Latvia* (dec.), no. 34854/02, 3 December 2002; *Kononov v. Latvia*, no. 36376/04, § 115, 24 July 2008.

[168] *Kononov v. Latvia* [GC], no. 36376/04, § 186, ECHR 2010; *Tess v. Latvia* (dec.), no. 34854/02, 3 December 2002; *Maktouf and Damjanović v. Bosnia and Herzegovina* [GC], nos 2312/08 and 34179/08, § 72, ECHR 2013 (extracts). Also *Van Anraat v. the Netherlands* (dec.), no. 65389/09, § 186, 6 July 2010.

[169] Alain Pellet, 'Article 38', in Andreas Zimmermann, Christian Tomuschat, and Karin Oellers-Frahm, eds, *The Statute of the International Court of Justice, A Commentary*, Oxford: Oxford University Press, 2006, pp. 677–792, at pp. 764–73.

[170] *Corfu Channel case*, Judgment of April 9th, 1949, I.C.J. Reports 1949, p. 4, at p. 22.

[171] *Reservations to the Convention on Genocide*, Advisory Opinion, I.C.J. Reports 1951, p. 15, at p. 23.

[172] *Touvier v. France*, no. 29420/95, Commission decision of 13 January 1997, DR 88-B, p. 161.

[173] *Kononov v. Latvia*, no. 36376/04, § 115, 24 July 2008; *Kononov v. Latvia*, no. 36376/04, Joint Dissenting Opinion of Judges Fura-Strandström, Davíd Thór Björgvinsson, and Ziemele, § 2, 24 July 2008; *Van Anraat v. the Netherlands* (dec.), no. 65389/09, § 186, 6 July 2010. See also *Linkov v. the Czech Republic*, no. 10504/03, §§ 41–42, 7 December 2006.

[174] Report to the Committee of Ministers submitted by the Committee of Experts Instructed to Draw Up a Draft Convention of Collective Guarantee of Human Rights and Fundamental Freedoms, Doc. CM/WP 1 (5) 15, A 924, IV *TP* 2–55, at p. 22.

about the significance of the *travaux*, based upon a sentence in the report of the Committee of Experts and without regard to the broader history of the provision, has ricocheted through the case law over the decades. It is not apparent, however, that this is a correct understanding of the *travaux*, and of the intent of those who drafted and adopted article 7(2).

The *travaux préparatoires* are examined earlier in this chapter. They indicate that the real debate about the text and the relationship between paragraphs 1 and 2 took place in sessions of the United Nations Commission on Human Rights concerning what was to become article 15 of the International Covenant on Civil and Political Rights.[175] The concern was to ensure that crimes under international law, both codified and those that were emerging, as they had done at Nuremberg, would not be deemed contrary to the *nullum crimen* principle. The two paragraphs are largely redundant, as some delegates in the Commission insisted, because crimes under international law are already addressed in paragraph 1 and general principles of law are a source of international law.[176] To the extent that paragraph 2 contributes to the normative framework, in keeping with the principle of effectivity of treaty provisions, it seems appropriate to consider that it contemplates prosecutions for international crimes before they have in fact been codified. This was the situation with respect to both crimes against peace and crimes against humanity at the International Military Tribunals that sat in Nuremberg and Tokyo. There are some contemporary examples at the *ad hoc* international criminal tribunals, where judges have addressed the *nullum crimen* challenge by referring to customary international law rather than 'general principles'.[177] The suggestion in the formulaic phrase of the European Commission that it is meant to cover 'war crimes, and collaboration with the enemy' is not sustainable. Simply put, 'collaboration with the enemy' is not an international crime. To the extent that prosecutions took place following the Second World War for such an offence in the absence of legal provisions that were foreseeable and accessible, there is indeed a conflict with the principles stated in article 7 of the Convention. In this respect, it is of interest that when the scope of article 7(2) was considered by the Grand Chamber, the words 'war crimes, and collaboration with the enemy' were replaced by '*inter alia* war crimes'.[178]

As early as 1957, the European Commission referred to article 7(2) in declaring inadmissible an application by a Belgian journalist who had been convicted as a Nazi collaborator, although the decision did not indicate of what consisted the 'general principles' he was alleged to have violated.[179] The reasoning is not very clear. Following the interpretation proposed above, that ruling by the European Commission was wrong. In several subsequent decisions involving Second World War crimes where the Court has

---

[175] See the discussion in *Maktouf and Damjanović v. Bosnia and Herzegovina*, nos 2312/08 and 34179/08, Concurring Opinion of Judge Pinto de Albuquerque, Joined by Judge Vučinić, ECHR 2013 (extracts), especially fn. 33.

[176] Antonio Cassese, 'Balancing the Prosecution of Crimes against Humanity and Non-Retroactivity of Criminal Law, The *Kolk and Kislyiy v. Estonia* Case before the ECHR', (2006) 4 *Journal of International Criminal Justice* 410, at p. 414.

[177] *Prosecutor* v. *Kordić et al.* (IT-95-14/2-T), Judgment, 26 February 2001, para. 20; *Prosecutor* v. *Norman* (SCSL-04-14-AR72(E), Decision on Preliminary Motion based on Lack of Jurisdiction (Child Recruitment), 31 May 2004.

[178] *Kononov* v. *Latvia* [GC], no. 36376/04, § 187, ECHR 2010.

[179] *De Becker* v. *Belgium*, no. 214/56, Commission decision of 9 June 1958.

dismissed the application, it has confined itself to article 7(1) and declared that it was unnecessary to consider article 7(2).[180]

In *Kononov v. Latvia*, the Chamber did not find there had been a breach of article 7(1). Consequently, it was unnecessary to address the question of article 7(2). Nevertheless, it opined that 'even supposing that that paragraph was applicable in the instant case, the operation of 27 May 1944 cannot be regarded as "criminal according to the general principles of law recognised by civilised nations"'.[181] The act in question was a summary execution conducted against non-combatants who were apparent enemy sympathizers and who had arguably participated actively in the hostilities, although they were obviously *hors de combat* at the time of the killing. In *Kolk and Kislyiy v. Estonia*, the Court invoked article 7(2) as a response to a charge that prosecution of crimes against humanity in the immediate post-Second-World-War period was contrary to article 7(1). In this connection, the Court asserted that the Charter of the International Military Tribunal affirmed that crimes against humanity could not be time-barred.[182]

Some interpreters of the Convention have argued against the suggestion that article 7(2) be confined solely to prosecutions related to the Second World War. They point to a substantial evolution in international criminal law and to the on-going work of codification, insisting that 'general principles of law' should not be cast in post-Second-World-War stone, but rather should take account of future developments.[183] The recent tendency of the Court, however, has been to disregard article 7(2) entirely.[184] In a case concerning the State Court of Bosnia and Herzegovina, it dismissed an argument from the government invoking article 7(2) as being 'inconsistent with the travaux préparatoires which imply that Article 7 § 1 can be considered to contain the general rule of non-retroactivity and that Article 7 § 2 is only a contextual clarification of the liability limb of that rule, included so as to ensure that there was no doubt about the validity of prosecutions after the Second World War in respect of the crimes committed during that war'. The Grand Chamber said: 'It is thus clear that the drafters of the Convention did not intend to allow for any general exception to the rule of non-retroactivity. Indeed,

---

[180] *Kononov v. Latvia* [GC], no. 36376/04, § 187, ECHR 2010; *Streletz, Kessler, and Krenz v. Germany* [GC], nos 34044/96, 35532/97, and 44801/98, § 108, ECHR 2001-II; *Polednová v. Czech Republic* (dec.), no. 2615/10, 21 June 2011; *Ould Dah v. France* (dec.), no. 13113/03, ECHR 2009; *Kononov v. Latvia*, no. 36376/04, § 147, 24 July 2008. Also *Achour v. France* [GC], no. 67335/01, § 54, ECHR 2006-IV; *Jorgić v. Germany*, no. 74613/01, § 113, ECHR 2007-III.

[181] *Kononov v. Latvia*, no. 36376/04, § 147, 24 July 2008.

[182] *Kolk and Kislyiy v. Estonia* (dec.), nos 23052/04 and 24018/04, ECHR 2006-I. The reference is puzzling, because the International Military Tribunal laid down no such principle, nor would it have any reason for doing so, given the temporal proximity of the crimes it was dealing with. In support of this affirmation, the Court invoked a decision of the Commission, *Touvier v. France*, no. 29420/95, Commission decision of 13 January 1997, DR 88-B, p. 161, where reference is made to an opinion by the French Minister of Foreign Affairs that 'it could be inferred from the Charter of the Nuremberg International Military Tribunal that the prosecution of crimes against humanity was not subject to limitation'. The finding of the Commission was subsequently adopted by a Chamber of the Court in *Papon v. France (no. 2)* (dec.), no. 54210/00, 15 November 2001, and in turn by Judge Myjer in his concurring opinion in *Kononov v. Latvia*, no. 36376/04, 24 July 2008.

[183] Patrice Rolland, 'Article 7', in Pettiti et al., *La Convention européenne*, pp. 293–303, at pp. 300–1.

[184] There is one curious and isolated exception: *Naletilić v. Croatia* (dec.), no. 51891/99, 4 May 2000, described by Judge Pinto de Albuquerque as an 'unfortunate decision': *Damjanović v. Bosnia and Herzegovina*, nos 2312/08 and 34179/08, Concurring Opinion of Judge Pinto de Albuquerque, Joined by Judge Vučinić, ECHR 2013 (extracts).

the Court has held in a number of cases that the two paragraphs of Article 7 are interlinked and are to be interpreted in a concordant manner.'[185]

Whether or not any useful autonomous role can be found for paragraph 2, legal history shows that the concerns of some experts involved in the drafting were misplaced. Article 7(1) of the Convention (and, consequently, article 11(2) of the Universal Declaration of Human Rights) is entirely sufficient to shelter the post-war prosecutions for atrocity crimes from attack. To the extent there was uncertainty about the scope of international law in the 1940s, this has entirely dissipated in modern times. If the scope of article 7(2) is confined to international crimes, it seems unnecessary and redundant. International crimes do not raise issues of retroactivity because of the explicit reference to them in article 7(1). However, most of the discussion of article 7(2) seems to concern international offences, particularly war crimes and crimes against humanity.[186] No doubt this vision of article 7(2) is nourished by the reference to 'general principles of law', language that pertains to sources of international law. But within international law, 'general principles of law' is actually a reference to norms found in national law. This apparent tautology is useful as a way to incorporate broadly accepted principles such as *res judicata* and *lis pendens* into the international forum but it does not work in the same way when national courts rely upon international law sources derived from national law as an answer to complaints of retroactive prosecution.

Some of the early jurisprudence of the European Commission refers to crimes of treason and collaboration with the enemy. While of some importance in the 1950s and 1960s, such crimes are rarely seen in modern times. Even here, it is not apparent why article 7(2) would be necessary. Presumably, European states at the time of the Second World War had adequate criminal legislation dealing with treason and assisting the enemy in wartime.

Discrimination

There do not appear to have been any findings of discrimination by which article 7 and article 14 of the Convention are associated. It has rarely been invoked by applicants, and complaints are almost invariably dismissed in a summary manner.[187]

In the German border guards cases, the Court briefly considered the argument that article 7 had been breached in a discriminatory manner, the differential treatment being a consequence of the applicants' status as citizens of the German Democratic Republic. The European Court considered that the principles applied by the Federal Constitutional Court in Germany were of 'general scope and were therefore equally valid in respect of persons who were not former nationals of the GDR'.[188]

---

[185] *Maktouf and Damjanović v. Bosnia and Herzegovina* [GC], nos 2312/08 and 34179/08, § 72, ECHR 2013 (extracts).

[186] *Kononov v. Latvia*, no. 36376/04, Joint Dissenting Opinion of Judges Fura-Sandström, Davíd Thór Björgvinsson, and Ziemele, § 2, 24 July 2008.

[187] *Giza v. Poland* (dec.), no. 1997/11, § 14, 23 November 2012; *Stanculescu v. Romania and Chitac v. Romania* (dec.), nos 22555109 and 42204/109, § 77, 3 July 2012; *Mignon v. Belgium* (dec.), no. 20022/09, 5 June 2012; *Asproftas v. Turkey*, no. 16079/90, §§ 124–129, 27 May 2010; *Petrakidou v. Turkey*, no. 16081/90, §§ 121–126, 27 May 2010; *Olymbiou v. Turkey*, no. 16091/90, §§ 138–139, 27 October 2009; *Doinov v. Bulgaria* (dec.), no. 68358/01, 3 November 2005; *P. v. France*, no. 12514/86, Commission decision of 12 December 1988.

[188] *Streletz, Kessler, and Krenz v. Germany* [GC], nos 34044/96, 35532/97, and 44801/98, §§ 112–113, ECHR 2001-II. Also *K.-H.W. v. Germany* [GC], no. 37201/97, §§ 118–120, ECHR 2001-II (extracts).

The application of laws on statutory limitation were also challenged on the grounds of a discriminatory effect. In an earlier decision, the Court had considered statutory limitation to be a matter of procedure rather than substance.[189] It upheld this approach, noting that such laws do not define crimes and punishments, and only establish conditions of admissibility.[190] As for the article 14 claim, the Court said the applicant was treated in the same manner as those similarly situated, that is, whose trials were at the same stage.[191]

Reservations

There have been two reservations to article 7, rare examples of such a practice with respect to a non-derogable right. At the time of ratification, in 1952, Germany formulated a reservation with respect to article 7(2):

Conformément à l'article 64 de la Convention, la République Fédérale d'Allemagne fait la réserve qu'elle n'appliquera la disposition de l'article 7, alinéa 2 de la Convention que dans les limites de l'article 103, alinée 2 de la Loi Fondamentale de la République Fédérale d'Allemagne. Cette dernière disposition stipule : 'Un acte ne peut être puni que si la loi le déclarait punissable avant qu'il ai été commis.[192]

Upon ratification of the International Covenant on Civil and Political Rights, Germany did not make any reservation to article 15(2), which is similar in import to article 7(2) of the European Convention. Germany withdrew its reservation to article 7(2) in 2001.[193]

Portugal made a reservation to article 7 respecting a provision of its Constitution governing indictment and trial of officers and personnel of the State Police Force.[194]

Further reading

J. Arnold, N. Karsten, and H. Kreicker, 'The German Border Guard Cases before the European Court of Human Rights', (2003) 11 *European Journal of Crime, Criminal Law and Criminal Justice* 67.

S. Atrill, 'Nulla Poena Sine Lege in Comparative Perspective: Retrospectivity Under the ECHR and the US Constitution', [2005] *Public Law* 107.

A. Austin, 'Punishing Mass Crimes: Joint Criminal Enterprise/Joint Criminal Action, The Principle of Legality under the European Convention on Human Rights', in O. de Frouville, ed., *Punir les crimes de masse: entreprise criminelle commune ou coaction?*, Actes de la journée d'études du 14 mai 2010, Brussels: Bruylant, 2011, pp. 143–63.

Edwin Bleichrodt, 'Freedom from Retrospective Effect of Penal Legislation', in Van Dijk et al., *Theory and Practice*, pp. 651–62.

Michael Bohlander, 'Retrospective Reductions in the Severity of Substantive Criminal Law—The Lex Mitior Principle and the Impact of *Scoppola v Italy No. 2*', (2011) 8 *Criminal Law Review* 627.

---

[189] *Coëme and Others v. Belgium* (nos 32492/96, 32547/96, 32548/96, 33209/96, and 33210/96, § 149, ECHR 2000-VII.

[190] *Previti v. Italy* (dec.), no. 1845/08, § 80, 12 February 2013.

[191] Ibid., § 88.

[192] (1955–56–57) 1 YB 41. Cited in *K.-H.W. v. Germany* [GC], no. 37201/97, § 40, ECHR 2001-II (extracts).

[193] (2001) 44 YB 15.

[194] (1978) 21 YB 14–15.

Antonio Cassese, 'Balancing the Prosecution of Crimes against Humanity and Non-Retroactivity of Criminal Law: The *Kolk and Kislyiy v. Estonia* Case before the ECHR', (2006) 4 *Journal of International Criminal Justice* 415.

Jean-Paul Costa and Michael O'Boyle, 'The European Court of Human Rights and International Humanitarian Law', in Dean Spielmann, Marialena Tsirli and Panayotis Voyatzis, eds, *La Convention européenne des droits de l'homme, un instrument vivant, Mélanges en l'honneur de Christos L. Rozakis*, Brussels: Bruylant, 2011, pp. 107–31.

P. von Feuerbach, 'The Foundations of Criminal Law and the *Nullum Crimen* Principle', (2007) 5 *Journal of International Criminal Justice* 1005.

Frowein/Peukert, *MenschenRechtsKonvention*, pp. 269–78.

Kenneth S. Gallant, *The Principle of Legality in International and Comparative Criminal Law*, Cambridge: Cambridge University Press, 2009.

Grabenwarter, *European Convention*, pp. 171–82.

Harris et al., *Law of the European Convention*, pp. 331–40.

Ben Juratowitch, 'Retroactive Criminal Liability and International Human Rights Law', (2004) 75 *British Year Book of International Law* 337.

Renée Koering-Joulin, 'Pour un retour à une interprétation stricte … du principe de la légalité criminelle (A propos de l'article 7(1) de la Convention européenne des droits de l'homme)', in *Liber Amicorum Marc-André Eissen*, Brussels: Bruylant, 1995, pp. 247–54.

Triestino Mariniello, 'The 'Nuremberg Clause' and Beyond: Legality Principle and Sources of International Criminal Law in the European Court's Jurisprudence', (2013) 82 *Nordic Journal of International Law* 221.

Cian V. Murphy, 'The Principle of Legality in Criminal Law under the European Convention on Human Rights', [2010] *EHRLR* 192.

Ovey/White, *Jacobs and White, European Convention*, pp. 187–95.

Giulia Pinzauti, 'The European Court of Human Rights' Incidental Application of International Criminal Law and Humanitarian Law', (2008) 6 *Journal of International Criminal Justice* 1043.

P.E. Quint, 'The Border Guard Trials and the East German Past-Seven Arguments', (2000) 4 *AJIL* 541.

Patrice Rolland, 'Article 7', in Pettiti et al., *La Convention européenne*, pp. 293–303.

D. Scalia, 'Constat sur le respect du principe *nulla poena sine lege* par les tribunaux pénaux internationaux', [2006] *Revue international de droit comparé* 185.

B.V. Schaack, 'Crimen *Sine Lege:* Judicial Lawmaking at the Intersection of Law and Morals', (2008) 97 *Georgetown Law Journal* 119.

William Schabas, 'Synergy or Fragmentation?: International Criminal Law and the European Convention on Human Rights', (2011) 9 *Journal of International Criminal Justice* 615.

M. Shahabuddeen, 'Does the Principle of Legality Stand in the Way of Progressive Development of Law?', (2004) 2 *Journal of International Criminal Justice* 1007.

Frédéric Sudre, 'Le principe de la légalité et la jurisprudence de la Cour européenne des droits de l'homme', [2001] *Revue pénitentiaire et de droit pénal* 349.

Jacques Velu and Rusen Ergec, *La Convention européenne des droits de l'homme*, Brussels: Bruylant, 1990, pp. 510–17.

Marten Zwanenburg and Guido den Dekker, 'Introductory Note to European Court of Human Rights: *Van Anraat v. The Netherlands*', (2010) 49 *International Legal Materials* 1268.

Article 8. Right to respect for private and family life/Droit au respect de la vie privée et familiale

1. Everyone has the right to respect for his private and family life, his home and his correspondence.	1. Toute personne a droit au respect de sa vie privée et familiale, de son domicile et de sa correspondance.
2. There shall be no interference by a public authority with the exercise of this right except such as is in accordance with the law and is necessary in a democratic society in the interests of national security, public safety or the economic well-being of the country, for the prevention of disorder or crime, for the protection of health or morals, or for the protection of the rights and freedoms of others.	2. Il ne peut y avoir ingérence d'une autorité publique dans l'exercice de ce droit que pour autant que cette ingérence est prévue par la loi et qu'elle constitue une mesure que, dans une société démocratique, est nécessaire à la sécurité nationale, à la sûreté publique, au bien-être économique du pays, à la défense de l'ordre et à la prévention des infractions pénales, à la protection de la santé ou de la morale, ou à la protection des droits et libertés d'autrui.

Introductory comments

The ancestor of the right to private and family life would appear to be the fourth amendment to the Constitution of the United States: 'The right of the people to be secure in their persons, houses, papers, and effects, against unreasonable searches and seizures...'. In a creative interpretation of that provision, Louis Brandeis discerned a 'right to privacy', or 'a right to be left alone'.[1] In 1947, when John Humphrey canvassed the provisions of national constitutions and various draft human rights declarations and charters in his preparation of an initial draft of the Universal Declaration of Human Rights, he identified a distinct category that he labelled 'Liberty of and respect for private life'. The text that Humphrey proposed read: 'No one shall be subjected to arbitrary searches or seizures, or to unreasonable interference with his person, home, family relations, reputation, privacy, activities, or personal property. The secrecy of correspondence shall be respected.'[2] Of the European sources considered, there was something loosely resembling this formulation in the constitutions of Belgium, Denmark, Greece, Iceland, Luxembourg, the Netherlands, Norway, and Sweden. When the negotiating process was completed some two years later, the final version of article 12 of the Universal Declaration read: 'No one shall be subjected to arbitrary interference with his privacy, family, home or correspondence, nor to attacks upon his honour and reputation. Everyone has the right to the protection of the law against such interference or attacks.'

This is an area where technological developments have had a huge impact. Expectations by previous generations of a sphere of anonymity have changed as a result of various forms

---

[1] Samuel Warren and Louis Brandeis, 'The Right to Privacy', (1890) 4 *Harvard Law Review* 193; *Olmstead v. United States*, 277 US 438 (1928).

[2] Draft Outline of International Bill of Rights (prepared by the Division of Human Rights), UN Doc. E/CN.4/AC.1/3, pp. 3–4. See also UN Doc. E/CN.4/W.16, p. 4; UN Doc. A/CN.4/W.18, p. 2.

of collection and transfer of data. For many people, concerns about privacy that once seemed important have become insignificant. Today, in massive numbers individuals seek to share information about their lives and those around them with the virtually limitless audience that social media provide. Whereas once the taking of a photograph was an event surrounded by planning and almost invariably a degree of implied consent, the proliferation of cameras makes the capture and sharing of images essentially uncontrollable. Where once intrusions into the private sphere seemed exceptional and rare, technology has made them common and mundane. For many, the sensitivities of the past no longer seem so important.

The corresponding provision in the Charter of Fundamental Rights differs very slightly in formulation:

Article 7. Respect for private and family life
Everyone has the right to respect for his or her private and family life, home and communications.

It is meant to have the same meaning and scope as article 8 of the European Convention.[3]

Drafting of the provision

Both paragraphs of article 8 of the Convention can be traced directly to provisions of the Universal Declaration of Human Rights, adopted on 10 December 1948 by the United Nations General Assembly. Article 8(1) is derived from article 12 of the Declaration: 'No one shall be subjected to arbitrary interference with his privacy, family, home or correspondence, nor to attacks upon his honour and reputation. Everyone has the right to the protection of the law against such interference or attacks.' The progenitor of article 8(2) is article 29(2) of the Declaration: 'In the exercise of his rights and freedoms, everyone shall be subject only to such limitations as are determined by law solely for the purpose of securing due recognition and respect for the rights and freedoms of others and of meeting the just requirements of morality, public order and the general welfare in a democratic society.'

The 'Liste des Droits de l'Homme à protéger par la Cour européenne (présentée comme base d'étude' adopted by the International Council of the European Movement, in February 1949, included '[l]a protection contre toute immixtion dans la famille' and '[l]a protection du caractère sacré du foyer'.[4] The draft convention adopted by the International Juridical Section of the European Movement on 12 July 1949 recognized '[t]he natural rights deriving from marriage and paternity and those pertaining to the family' and '[t]he sanctity of the home'.[5] The European Movement draft also contained a restrictions or limitations clause: 'The rights specified in Articles 1 and 2 shall be subject only to such limitations as are in conformity with the general principles of law recognized by civilised nations and as are prescribed by law for: a) Protecting the legal rights of

---

[3] Explanation Relating to the Charter of Fundamental Rights, Official Journal of the European Union, C 303/33, 14 December 2007.

[4] Recommendations adopted at the meeting of the International Council of the European Movement held at Brussels in February 1949, INF/2/F, p. 3. This is reproduced in CDH (67) 5, at pp. 2–3, with the indication that the original English version no longer exists.

[5] Convention for the Collective Protection of Individual Rights and Democratic Liberties by the States, Members of the Council of Europe, and for the establishment of a European Court of Human Rights to ensure observance of the Convention, Doc. INF/5/E/R, I *TP* 296–303, at p. 296, art. I(h).

others; b) Meeting the just requirements of morality, public order (including the safety of the community), and the general welfare.'[6]

At the first session of the Consultative Assembly, which met in August and September 1949, Pierre-Henri Teitgen called for adoption of a convention that was to include 'the natural rights deriving from marriage and paternity and those pertaining to the family, the sanctity of the home...'[7] Contributing to the introductory debate in the Assembly, Mario Cingolani of Italy spoke of 'unbelievable encroachments on our rights' such as 'the violation of the sanctity of the home'.[8] James Everett of Ireland referred to the fact that in many countries 'raiding of citizen's homes without warrant is also practised by governments on minorities',[9] while Ireland's Sean MacEntee urged the inclusion of article 12 of the Universal Declaration 'without reservation'.[10]

In the Committee on Legal and Administrative Questions of the Consultative Assembly, Teitgen presented a list that questioned the inclusion of 'natural rights appertaining to marriage, paternity and the family' and 'inviolability of domicile'.[11] Asked to prepare a text for discussion in the Committee, Teitgen proposed the following: 'Inviolability of privacy, home, correspondence and family, in accordance with Article 12 of the United Nations Declaration.'[12]

One of the United Kingdom delegates, Lord Layton, argued for exclusion of the provision. According to the draft report, the inclusion of 'family rights', including arbitrary interference family life, 'raised, within the Committee, various objections based on the fact that in this case no fundamental "political" rights were at stake... This argument did not prevail, since the majority of the Committee thought that the racial restrictions on the right of marriage made by the totalitarian regimes as also the forced regimentation of children and young persons organised by these regimes should be absolutely prohibited.'[13] Layton's resolution was rejected by sixteen votes against to three in favour. The Committee then voted to amend Teitgen's proposal as follows: 'Immunity from arbitrary interference in his private life, his home, his correspondence and his family as laid down in Article 12 of the Declaration of the United Nations'.[14]

In the report of the Committee on Legal and Administrative Questions to the plenary Consultative Assembly, the word 'all' was added before 'arbitrary' and the masculine pronouns removed.[15] Something was being lost in translation from the French, which

[6] Convention for the Collective Protection of Individual Rights and Democratic Liberties by the States, Members of the Council of Europe, and for the establishment of a European Court of Human Rights to ensure observance of the Convention, Doc. INF/5/E/R, I *TP* 296–303, at p. 298, art. 3.

[7] Report of the Sitting [of the Consultative Assembly, 19 August 1949], I *TP* 38–154, at p. 46.

[8] Ibid., p. 62.

[9] Ibid., p. 104.

[10] Ibid., p. 142.

[11] Sitting [of the Committee on Legal and Adminsitrative Question], 22 August 1949, I *TP* 154–63, at p. 160.

[12] Proposals by Mr P.H. Teitgen, Rapporteur, 29 August 1949, Doc. A 116, I *TP* 166–8. Also Report presented by Mr P.H. Teitgen, 5 September 1949, Doc. A 290, I *TP* 192–213, at p. 206. See also Report [of the Committee on Legal and Administrative Questions], 5 September 1949, Doc. AS (1) 77, I *TP* 216–39, at p. 228.

[13] Report presented by Mr P.H. Teitgen, 5 September 1949, Doc. A 290, I *TP* 192–213, at p. 198. Also Report [of the Committee on Legal and Administrative Questions], 5 September 1949, Doc. AS (1) 77, I *TP* 216–39, at p. 220.

[14] Minutes of the Sitting [of the Committee for Legal and Administrative Affairs of the Consultative Assembly, 29 August 1949], Doc. A 142, I *TP* 170–73, at p. 172.

[15] Report presented by Mr P.H. Teitgen, 5 September 1949, Doc. A 290, I *TP* 192–213, at p. 206.

appears to have been the primary language of the negotiations. Some of the problems were fixed in the Committee's final report to the Consultative Assembly. The word 'all' disappeared and 'immunity' (from the French *immunité*) was replaced by the more appropriate 'freedom': 'Freedom from arbitrary interference in private and family life, home and correspondence, in accordance with Article 12 of the Declaration of the United Nations'.[16] This was not in fact in accordance with article 12 because the words 'nor to attacks upon his honour and reputation' were omitted.

Presenting the report of the Committee to the plenary Consultative Assembly, Teitgen explained that there had been discussion in the Committee about including 'family rights', as he called them:

No one in the Committee, I hasten to add, has denied the vital importance of these family rights. Some have said that they would prefer to see the guarantee confined for the moment to essential civic freedoms, to those which are the necessary conditions for the functioning of democratic institutions, and that it would be better for the time being to exclude all other freedoms and all other fundamental rights which would include, in spite of their importance, family rights.

The Committee recalled the time in the recent past when, in some countries, certain people were denied the right to marry on account of race or religious convictions. It also recalled the legislation, under which some countries suffered during cruel years, which subordinated the child to the benefit of the state.

On account of these memories, the majority of the Committee considered it desirable to include these fundamental rights in the list of guaranteed freedoms. It considered that the father of a family cannot be an independent citizen, cannot feel free within his own country, if he is menaced in his own home and if, every day, the State steals from his soul, or the conscience of his children.[17]

Layton resumed the debate, explaining that the proposed list of fundamental rights for the convention was 'not intended to be anything like a complete list of human rights. It is a selected list of rights which should be the subject of collective guarantee, and guaranteed now.'[18] Layton insisted upon a short list that 'should be limited to the absolute minimum necessary to constitute the cardinal principles for the functioning of political democracy'.[19] He pointed to the much longer list in the Universal Declaration of Human Rights, adding that he thought that all of the States represented in the Consultative Assembly were already 'parties to this Declaration'.[20] In fact, there are no 'parties' to the Universal Declaration, which is a resolution of the United Nations General Assembly; moreover, two members of the Consultative Assembly, Ireland and Italy, were not yet members of the United Nations.

Layton's proposal was criticized by Sean MacEntee of Ireland, who said its adoption would 'seal the triumph of the totalitarian ideologies'. For MacEntee, '[t]he outstanding feature of the totalitarian regimes was the ruthless and savage way in which they endeavoured to wipe out the concept of the family as the natural unit of society'.[21]

---

[16] Report [of the Committee on Legal and Administrative Questions], 5 September 1949, Doc. AS (1) 77, I *TP* 216–39, at p. 228.
[17] Report of the Sitting [of the Consultative Assembly, 7 September 1949], I *TP* 258–95, at p. 270.
[18] Official Report of the Sitting [of the Consultative Assembly, 8 September 1949], II *TP* 14–274, at p. 50.
[19] Ibid., p. 52.
[20] Ibid., p. 50.
[21] Ibid., p. 90.

Delegates from the Netherlands,[22] Italy,[23] and France[24] made similar statements. Recognizing the isolation of his position, Layton agreed to its withdrawal.[25] The Consultative Assembly adopted the text proposed by the Committee.[26]

Teitgen had also included a general provision on the restriction or limitation of rights that was based upon the text in the European Movement Draft.[27] After a short debate without a vote, the Consultative Assembly adopted the following text:

In the exercise of these rights, and in the enjoyment of the freedoms guaranteed by the Convention, no limitations shall be imposed except those established by law, with the sole object of ensuring the recognition and respect for the rights and freedoms of others, or with the purpose of satisfying the just requirement of public morality, order and security in a democratic society.[28]

Although bearing a close affinity to article 12 of the Universal Declaration, the words 'nor to attacks upon his honour and reputation' had been excluded from the Consultative Assembly draft.[29] This discrepancy was noted in a report prepared by the Secretariat-General of the Council of Europe. It considered that incorporation of the entire text of article 12 of the Universal Declaration was implied by the fact that it was annexed to the report prepared by Teitgen for the Consultative Assembly.[30]

The Committee of Experts, meeting in February and March 1950, was divided on the general approach to the formulation of human rights in the Convention, with some members favouring a relatively laconic enumeration based upon the Universal Declaration, while others preferred a more expansive and detailed text akin to that of the draft Covenant then being negotiated in the United Nations Commission on Human Rights. The current version of the draft Covenant did not then include any provision dealing with private and family life. Pursuing the simplified enumeration approach, the Committee of Experts adopted the following provision: 'No one shall be subjected to arbitrary interference with his privacy, family, home or correspondence. Everyone has the right to the protection of the law against such interference.'[31] The report of the Committee explains

---

[22] Ibid., p. 96. See also the statement by de Valera, ibid., p. 102.

[23] Ibid., p. 100.

[24] Ibid., p. 108.

[25] Ibid., p. 132.

[26] Recommendation No. 38 to the Committee of Ministers adopted 8 September 1949 on the conclusion of the debates, Doc. AS (1) 108, II *TP* 274–83, at p. 276.

[27] Proposals by Mr P.H. Teitgen, Rapporteur, 29 August 1949, Doc. A 116, I *TP* 166–68. Also Report presented by Mr P.H. Teitgen, 5 September 1949, Doc. A 290, I *TP* 192–213, at p. 206. See also Report [of the Committee on Legal and Administrative Questions], 5 September 1949, Doc. AS (1) 77, I *TP* 216–39, at p. 228.

[28] Official Report of the Sitting [of the Consultative Assembly, 8 September 1949], II *TP* 14–274, at pp. 134–42. See also Recommendation No. 38 to the Committee of Ministers adopted 8 September 1949 on the conclusion of the debates, Doc. AS (1) 108, II *TP* 274–83, at p. 278; Report [of the Committee on Legal and Administrative Questions], 5 September 1949, Doc. AS (1) 77, I *TP* 216–39, at p. 230; Preparatory Report by the Secretariat-General concerning a Preliminary Draft Convention to Provide a Collective Guarantee of Human Rights, Doc. B 22, III *TP* 2–37, at pp. 16–18.

[29] Jacques Velu, 'La Convention européenne des droits de l'homme et le droit au respect de la vie privée, du domicile et des communications', in *Vie privée et droits de l'homme*, Brussels: Bruylant, 1973, pp. 35–138, at p. 39.

[30] Preparatory Report by the Secretariat-General concerning a Preliminary Draft Convention to Provide a Collective Guarantee of Human Rights, Doc. B 22, III *TP* 2–37, at p. 8.

[31] Preliminary Draft Convention for the Maintenance and Further Realisation of Human Rights and Fundamental Freedoms, 15 February 1950, Doc. A 833, III *TP* 236–46, at p. 236. Also Draft text of the first section of a draft Convention based on the work of the Consultative Assembly, Doc. A 809, III *TP* 220–31, at p. 222.

that instead of listing rights with reference to the relevant provision in the Universal Declaration, as had been done by the Consultative Assembly, it was better to incorporate the text verbatim. Accordingly, the Committee of Experts, as it explained in its Report, 'scrupulously adhered to the text of the Universal Declaration'.[32] The text it adopted is, of course, very close to that of article 12 of the Universal Declaration of Human Rights. Nevertheless, the Committee of Experts removed the words 'or attacks' that follow 'interference' in the Universal Declaration, and it maintained the exclusion of the reference to honour and reputation that it had inherited from the Consultative Assembly. The report of the Committee of Experts to the Committee of Ministers notes that '[i]n accordance with the Assembly's intentions, only a certain part of the rights mentioned in [Article 12] of the Universal Declaration were included'.[33] The second, contending approach considered by the Committee of Experts was formulated in a draft submitted by the United Kingdom. It dispensed entirely with the provision on private and family life.[34]

The Committee of Experts also adopted a general provision on restrictions or limitations:

In the exercise of these rights and in the enjoyment of the freedoms secured by the Convention, no limitation shall be imposed except those established by the law, with the sole object of ensuring the recognition and respect for the rights and freedoms of others, or with the purpose of satisfying the just requirements of public morality and order and national security and integrity (and solidarity) as well as the functioning of administration and justice in a democratic society.[35]

The Report of the Committee of Experts explained that it had decided to add 'to the number of higher interests, the demands of which might justify the limitation of human rights, two further restrictions: a) territorial integrity; b) the smooth working of administration and justice'.[36] It said that the first of these had been introduced on the proposal of the Turkish representative 'in order to make provision for the need of States to be able to defend themselves against all activities which might lead to the disintegration of the nation'.[37] This was accepted by the Committee of Experts 'on the clear understanding that it did not permit a restriction on the rights of national minorities to press their views by democratic means', to which the Turkish representative responded that the proposal 'had no connection with the question of the rights of national minorities, a question which, moreover, would be outside the scope of the Convention'.[38] The second limitation, 'the smooth working of administration and justice', was introduced by the Swedish

[32] Preliminary Draft of the Report to the Committee of Ministers, 24 February 1950, Doc. CM/WP I (50) 1, A 847, III *TP* 246–79, at pp. 260–2.

[33] Report to the Committee of Ministers submitted by the Committee of Experts Instructed to Draw Up a Draft Convention of Collective Guarantee of Human Rights and Fundamental Freedoms, Doc. CM/WP 1 (5) 15, A 924, IV *TP* 2–79, at p. 22. Also Preliminary Draft of the Report to the Committee of Ministers, III *TP* 246–79, at p. 262.

[34] Amendments to Articles 1, 2, 4, 5, 6, 8, and 9 of the Committee's Preliminary Draft Proposal by the Expert of the United Kingdom, Doc. CM/WP I (50) 2, A 915, III *TP* 280–9, at pp. 286–8.

[35] Preliminary Draft Convention for the Maintenance and Further Realisation of Human Rights and Fundamental Freedoms, 15 February 1950, Doc. A 833, III *TP* 236–46, at p. 236. Also Draft text of the first section of a draft Convention based on the work of the Consultative Assembly, Doc. A 809, III *TP* 220–31, at p. 222.

[36] Report to the Committee of Ministers submitted by the Committee of Experts Instructed to Draw Up a Draft Convention of Collective Guarantee of Human Rights and Fundamental Freedoms, Doc. CM/WPI (5) 15, A 924, IV *TP* 2–79, at p. 24.

[37] Ibid.

[38] Ibid., pp. 24–6.

expert so as to make provision for the fact that sometimes 'certain information should be kept secret'.[39]

The Committee of Experts concluded its work with the submission to the Committee of Ministers of two different drafts. The first, 'Alternatives A and A/2', consisted of the text adopted by the Committee of Experts at its first session derived generally from the Universal Declaration of Human Rights.[40] The second, labelled 'Alternatives B and B/2', was essentially the draft of the Convention proposed by the United Kingdom, a text based on the 1949 draft of the International Covenant adopted by the United Nations Commission on Human Rights.[41]

The Conference of Senior Officials that convened in June 1950 assigned a Drafting Committee to attempt to reconcile the competing approaches, using the British text as its starting point. In the case of the right to private and family life there was nothing to reconcile, given the absence of any provision in the British draft. The Drafting Committee prepared new versions of the various substantive provisions, melding the formulation of rights in the two versions, with the exception of private and family life, which was left blank in its initial report.[42] When the issue was pointed out by the President of the Conference of Senior Officials, Sir Samuel Hoare explained that the contents of the provision were covered by other articles dealing with freedom of association and information.[43]

It then fell to the United Kingdom to propose a new provision on private and family life:

1. Everyone shall have the right to freedom from governmental interference with his privacy, family, house or correspondence.
2. No restrictions shall be placed on the exercise of this right other than such as are in accordance with law and are necessary in a democratic society in the interests of national security, public safety, for the prevention of disorder or crime or for the protection of health or morals.[44]

This text was changed significantly by the Drafting Committee, notably in the elimination of the limitation of the right to 'government interference': 'The right to privacy in respect of family, home and correspondence shall be recognised.'[45] The second paragraph was also altered by replacing '[n]o restrictions shall be placed on' with '[t]here shall be no interference by a public authority with' and a change from 'and are necessary' to 'and is necessary'. The plenary Conference of Senior Officials further reworked the

---

[39] Ibid., p. 26. Also Amendments to Article 2, paras 3, 5, and 6 of the Recommendation of the Consultative Assembly Proposed by the Swedish Expert, Doc. A 777, III *TP* 184.

[40] Report to the Committee of Ministers submitted by the Committee of Experts Instructed to Draw Up a Draft Convention of Collective Guarantee of Human Rights and Fundamental Freedoms, Doc. CM/WPI (5) 15, A 924, IV *TP* 2–79, at p. 52. See also Preliminary Draft Convention, Doc. CM/WP 1 (50) 14, A 932, III *TP* 312–35, at p. 320.

[41] Report to the Committee of Ministers submitted by the Committee of Experts Instructed to Draw Up a Draft Convention of Collective Guarantee of Human Rights and Fundamental Freedoms, Doc. CM/WPI (5) 15, A 924, IV *TP* 2–79, at p. 62. See also Preliminary Draft Convention, Doc. CM/WP 1 (50) 14, A 932, III *TP* 312–35, at p. 316.

[42] New draft alternatives B and B/2, Doc. CM/WP 4 (50) 9, A 1372, IV *TP* 182–91, at p. 188.

[43] Minutes [of the 9 June 1950 sitting of the Conference of Senior Officials], Doc. CM/WP 1 (50) 16, IV *TP* 102–11, at p. 110.

[44] Proposal submitted by the United Kingdom Delegation, Doc. CM/WP 4 (50) 14, A 1377, IV *TP* 202.

[45] Draft Convention appended to the Draft report, Doc. CM/WP 4 (50) 16, appendix, A 1445, IV *TP* 218–40, at p. 222. Also Text of the report submitted by the Conference [of Senior Officials] to the Committee of Ministers, Doc. CM/WP IV (50) 19, CM/WP IV (50) 16 rev., A 1431, IV *TP* 242–73, at p. 258.

text: 'Everyone's right to respect for his private and family life, his home and his correspondence shall be recognised.'[46] The words 'this right' were changed to 'these rights'.

Earlier, in their 'definitional' proposal within the Committee of Experts, the British had introduced the idea of distinct clauses concerning restriction or limitation specifically tailored to the right and freedom in question. However, there was no limitations clause for the right to private or family life because the right had been omitted entirely in the British draft. Once the British draft was accepted by the Conference of Senior Officials as a basis for further negotiation, any work on a general limitations clause was essentially set aside in favour of specific provisions applicable to individual rights. The British duly presented a draft paragraph 2 governing the right to private and family life:

No restrictions shall be placed on the exercise of this right other than such as are in accordance with law and are necessary in a democratic society in the interests of national security, public safety, for the prevention of disorder or crime or for the protection of health or morals.[47]

The Drafting Committee changed this text significantly, essentially by the inclusion of the notion of 'interference by a public authority' that the British had placed in paragraph 1:

There shall be no interference by a public authority with the exercise of these rights except such as is in accordance with law and is necessary in a democratic society in the interests of national security, public safety, for the prevention of disorder or crime or for the protection of health or morals.[48]

By this change, the Drafting Committee opened up the right to private and family life to positive obligations, in that the interference need not be the work of a public authority, although, of course, the obligation to enforce the right remains with the State and its institutions.

The text of article 8(1) was modified yet again by the Committee of Ministers: 'Everyone has the right to respect for his private and family life, his home and his correspondence.'[49] The United Kingdom commented upon the draft text of article 8(2), which of course it had itself proposed only weeks earlier:

In its present form this Article does not provide either for the rules under which the party to a civil action may be compelled to give disclosure of his documents to the other party or for the powers of inspection (for example the opening of letters which are suspected of attempting to export currency in breach of Exchange Control Regulations) which may be necessary in order to safeguard the economic well-being of the country. H.M. Government, therefore, propose an amendment to paragraph 2 of this Article to read: '... in the interests of national security, public safety *or the economic well-being* of the country, for the prevention of disorder or crime, for the protection of health or morals, *or for the protection of the rights and freedoms of others*'.[50]

---

[46] Draft Convention annexed to the Report, Doc. CM/WP 4 (50) 19 annex, CM/WP 4 (50) 16 rev., A 1452, IV *TP* 274–95, at p. 278.

[47] Proposal submitted by the United Kingdom Delegation, Doc. CM/WP 4 (50) 14, A 1377, IV *TP* 202.

[48] Draft Convention appended to the Draft Report, Doc. CM/WP 4 (50) 16, appendix, A 1445, IV *TP* 218–40, at p. 222. Also Text of the Report submitted by the Conference [of Senior Officials] to the Committee of Ministers, Doc. CM/WP IV (50) 19, CM/WP IV (50) 16 rev., A 1431, IV *TP* 242–73, at p. 258.

[49] Draft Convention adopted by the Committee of Ministers, 7 August 1950, Doc. A 1937, V *TP* 120–45, at p. 126. Note that the French version also underwent these modifications. In the text adopted by the Conference of Senior Officials, article 8(1) read: 'Le droit de toute personne au respect de sa vie privée et familiale, son domicile ou sa correspondance est reconnu.'

[50] Amendments proposed by the United Kingdom Delegation, Doc. CM 1 (50) 6, A 1867, V *TP* 66–70 (italics in the original).

The draft text of paragraph 2 was then amended by a Sub-Committee of the Committee of Ministers:

There shall be no interference by a public authority with the exercise of this right except such as is in accordance with law and is necessary in a democratic society in the interests of national security, public safety or the economic well-being of the country, for the prevention of disorder or crime, for the protection of health or morals, or for the protection of the rights and freedoms of others.[51]

The only subsequent modification to article 8 by the Committee of Ministers was replacing 'rights' with 'right' in the final words of paragraph 2.[52]

The provision on private and family life did not give rise to discussion in the August 1950 session of the Consultative Assembly. The version confirmed at the fifth session of the Committee of Ministers in August 1950 is therefore the definitive one. Only two very minor changes were introduced at Rome in November 1950: the addition of the article 'the' before 'law' in paragraph 2, and the replacement of 'right' with 'rights' in the final words of the provision.

The heading of article 8, 'Right to respect for private and family life', was added pursuant to Protocol No. 11.[53]

Analysis and interpretation

The Court's judgments have stated again and again that '[t]he essential object of Article 8 is to protect the individual against arbitrary interference by public authorities'.[54] The wording suggests a profoundly negative 'right to be left alone', and yet most of the case law has focused on the positive dimension of the right. The State is required, by article 8, to ensure a broad range of entitlements in areas ranging from housing to medical treatment, from the control of stray dogs to bullying at school to ensuring that people may end their lives in dignity. According to the Court, 'it is under Article 8 that notions of the quality of life take on significance'.[55] The constantly expanding protection of private and family life has taken litigation under the European Convention on Human Rights deep into the realm of private law. In recent years, article 8 has proven to be one of the richest areas of legal development by the Court.

The provision is divided into four categories: private life; family life; home; and correspondence. The heading of article 8 narrows this to 'private and family life' and indeed the jurisprudence of the first two categories is overwhelming by comparison with the relatively few cases that concern home and correspondence. There is no neat dividing line between private and family life, and certain problems, such as the right of settled migrants to remain where they are,[56] an entitlement to registration of marriage,[57]

---

[51] Text of amended articles after deliberation at the sitting of 4 August 1950, Doc. CM I (50) 9), V *TP* 74–7, at p. 74; Draft Convention adopted by the Sub-Committee, Doc. CM 1 (50) 52, A 1884, V *TP* 76–99, at p. 80.

[52] Draft Convention adopted by the Committee of Ministers, 7 August 1950, Doc. A 1937, V *TP* 120–45, at p. 126.

[53] Protocol No. 11 to the Convention for the Protection of Human Rights and Fundamental Freedoms, restructuring the control machinery established thereby, ETS 155, art. 2(2).

[54] *P. and S. v. Poland*, no. 57375/08, § 94, 30 October 2012; *Nunez v. Norway*, no. 55597/09, § 68, 28 June 2011.

[55] *Pretty v. the United Kingdom*, no. 2346/02, § 65, ECHR 2002-III.

[56] *Samsonnikov v. Estonia*, no. 52178/10, § 81, 3 July 2012.

[57] *Dadouch v. Malta*, no. 38816/07, § 48, 20 July 2010.

childbirth,[58] and matters concerning the dead,[59] may be examined under both rubrics.[60] Some settled migrants will not have adequate family ties in the country, so their claim will have to be based upon the right to private life.[61] In practice, the proportionality analysis is likely to be much the same.[62] In the case of an applicant who had been adopted and who contested her inability to obtain information about her birth and origins, the Court chose 'to examine the case from the perspective of private life, not family life, since the applicant's claim to be entitled, in the name of biological truth, to know her personal history is based on her inability to gain access to information about her origins and related identifying data'.[63]

Like articles 9, 10, and 11, the definition of the right in the first paragraph of article 8 is complemented by a second paragraph that restricts or limits the scope of the right. The restriction or limitation clauses in the four articles have many broad similarities but they are also somewhat distinct, each having been specifically tailored to the right in question. In its application of article 8, the Court first proceeds to consider whether there has been an 'interference' with a right within the scope of paragraph 1. It then, as a general rule, examines the criteria set out in paragraph 2 in order to determine whether the 'interference' is also a violation of the Convention. Occasionally, however, judgments of the Court with respect to article 8 do not present any detailed discussion of the criteria in paragraph 2. After deciding that article 8 is applicable, they attempt to assess the 'inconvenience' that the interference creates for the applicant, sometimes concluding that it is significant enough to find a violation,[64] while in other cases adopting the view that it is not.[65]

This chapter proceeds with consideration of the scope of the right set out in article 8(1), followed by a section dealing with restrictions or limitations that may be imposed in accordance with paragraph 2.

Respect—negative and positive obligations

Article 8(1) is the only substantive provision of the Convention where the word 'respect' is employed. The word also appears in the title of article 1, a consequence of Protocol No. 11. Article 12 of the Universal Declaration of Human Rights, from which article 8(1) of the Convention was derived, does not use the word 'respect' either. The Court has said that the notion of 'respect' is not 'clear-cut', 'especially where the positive obligations implicit in that concept are concerned'.[66] One of the aspects of 'respect' that has been highlighted in the case law is the rule of law. It is one of the fundamental principles of a

---

[58] *Hanzelkovi v. Czech Republic*, no. 43643/10, § 67, 11 December 2014.

[59] *Elli Poluhas Dödsbo v. Sweden*, no. 61564/00, § 24, ECHR 2006-I.

[60] *Samsonnikov v. Estonia*, no. 52178/10, § 81, 3 July 2012; *Dadouch v. Malta*, no. 38816/07, § 48, 20 July 2010.

[61] *Slivenko v. Latvia* [GC], no.48321/99, §97, ECHR 2003-X; *Kwakye-Nti and Dufie v. the Netherlands* (dec.), no. 31519/96, 7 November 2000; *Anam v. the United Kingdom* (dec.), no. 21783/08, 7 June 2011; *A.H. Khan v. the United Kingdom*, no. 6222/10, § 32, 20 December 2011.

[62] *A.A. v. the United Kingdom*, no. 8000/08, § 49, 20 September 2011.

[63] *Odièvre v. France* [GC], no. 42326/98, § 28, ECHR 2003-III.

[64] *B. v. France*, 25 March 1992, § 62, Series A no. 232-C.

[65] *Guillot v. France*, 24 October 1996, § 23, *Reports of Judgments and Decisions* 1996-V.

[66] *B. v. France*, 25 March 1992, § 44, Series A no. 232-C; *Rees v. the United Kingdom*, 17 October 1986, § 37, Series A no. 106; *Abdulaziz, Cabales, and Balkandali v. the United Kingdom*, 28 May 1985, § 67, Series A no. 94; *Tysiąc v. Poland*, no. 5410/03, § 112, ECHR 2007-I; *Mosley v. the United Kingdom*, no. 48009/08, § 108, 10 May 2011.

democratic society and inherent in all provisions of the Convention.[67] The rule of law dictates the existence of measures of legal protection against arbitrary interference by public authorities with the right protected by the Convention.[68] To the extent that it encapsulates the obligatory nature of article 8, at the heart of the word 'respect' sit both positive and negative dimensions. The State must not only abstain from interference with private and family life, but it must also protect individuals from infringements of their right to private and family life that are attributable to others.[69]

Despite the distinction between positive and negative obligations under article 8, the applicable principles in the two contexts are similar in nature. It is not always evident whether an interference results from a denial of a right in a negative sense or a failure of the State to provide an adequate regulatory framework, nor does the Court always find it necessary to decide on which basis the matter should be studied.[70] Whether private and family life is approached from a positive or negative perspective, due regard must be had to 'the fair balance that has to be struck between the competing interests of the individual and of the community as a whole'.[71]

Whether a negative or positive understanding of article 8 is adopted, in both the State enjoys a certain margin of appreciation. In cases requiring the State to strike a balance between competing rights, the margin of appreciation will be greater if one individual's right to private and family life may be infringed as a result of exercise by another of a fundamental right.[72] On the other hand, '[w]here a particularly important facet of an individual's existence or identity is at stake, the margin allowed to the State is correspondingly narrowed. The same is true where the activities at stake involve a most intimate aspect of private life.'[73] Difficulties arise in particular with respect to freedom of expression. Here a proper balance must be struck between the private and family life of the individual and the public interest in access to information through a free media.[74]

Where relations between individuals are concerned, the means chosen by a State to address this are in principle something within their margin of appreciation.[75] Certainly,

[67] *Iatridis v. Greece* [GC], no. 31107/96, § 58, ECHR 1999-II; *Carbonara and Ventura v. Italy*, no. 24638/94, § 63, ECHR 2000-VI; *Capital Bank AD v. Bulgaria*, no. 49429/99, § 133, ECHR 2005-XII (extracts).

[68] *Malone v. the United Kingdom*, 2 August 1984, § 67, Series A no. 82; *Hasan and Chaush v. Bulgaria* [GC], no. 30985/96, § 84, ECHR 2000-XI.

[69] *Söderman v. Sweden* [GC], no. 5786/08, § 78, 12 November 2013; *Airey v. Ireland*, 9 October 1979, § 32, Series A no. 32; *X and Y v. the Netherlands*, 26 March 1985, § 23, Series A no. 91; *Aksu v. Turkey* [GC], nos 4149/04 and 41029/04, § 59, ECHR 2012; *Tavlı v. Turkey*, no. 11449/02, § 28, 9 November 2006; *Ciubotaru v. Moldova*, no. 27138/04, § 50, 27 April 2010.

[70] *Nunez v. Norway*, no. 55597/09, § 69, 28 June 2011; *Dickson v. the United Kingdom* [GC], no. 44362/04, § 71, ECHR 2007-V.

[71] *Aksu v. Turkey* [GC], nos 4149/04 and 41029/04, § 59, ECHR 2012; *Hristozov and Others v. Bulgaria*, nos 47039/11 and 358/12, § 117, 13 November 2012; *Keegan v. Ireland*, 26 May 1994, § 49, Series A no. 290; *Botta v. Italy*, 24 February 1998, § 33, *Reports of Judgments and Decisions* 1998-I; *Gurgenidze v. Georgia*, no. 71678/01, § 38, 17 October 2006; *Evans v. the United Kingdom* [GC], no. 6339/05, §§ 75–76, ECHR 2007-I; *Rommelfanger v. Federal Republic of Germany*, no. 12242/86, Commission decision of 6 September 1989, (1989) 32 YB 57, DR 62, p. 151; *Fuentes Bobo v. Spain*, no. 39293/98, § 38, 29 February 2000.

[72] *Fernández Martínez v. Spain*, no. 56030/07, § 78, 15 May 2012.

[73] *E.S. v. Sweden*, no. 5786/08, § 58, 21 June 2012; *Evans v. the United Kingdom* [GC], no. 6339/05, § 77, ECHR 2007-I; *Mosley v. the United Kingdom*, no. 48009/08, § 109, 10 May 2011.

[74] *MGN Limited v. the United Kingdom*, no. 39401/04, § 142, 18 January 2011; *Hachette Filipacchi Associés (ICI PARIS) v. France*, no. 12268/03, § 41, 23 July 2009; *Mosley v. the United Kingdom*, no. 48009/08, § 111, 10 May 2011.

[75] *Von Hannover v. Germany (no. 2)* [GC], nos 40660/08 and 60641/08, § 104, ECHR 2012; *E.S. v. Sweden*, no. 5786/08, § 58, 21 June 2012; *Söderman v. Sweden* [GC], no. 5786/08, § 79, 12 November 2013;

States are required to have an adequate legal framework providing protection against acts of violence by others,[76] although recourse to the criminal law is not necessarily the only approach, especially for acts of lesser seriousness.[77] Where 'fundamental values and essential aspects of private life are at stake... [e]ffective deterrence is indispensable in this area and it can be achieved only by criminal-law provisions'.[78] In assessing the adequacy of the criminal justice system, the Court will consider whether there were 'significant flaws' in the investigation of the alleged crime.[79] When the legislation comes to be examined, however, the issue is no longer whether there are 'significant flaws', but rather 'whether the respondent State had in place an adequate legal framework in compliance with its positive obligations under Article 8 of the Convention since the issue before the Court concerns the question of whether the law afforded an acceptable level of protection to the applicant in the circumstances'.[80]

Private life

The Court has explained that 'private life' is a broad term encompassing the sphere of personal autonomy within which everyone can freely pursue the development and fulfilment of his or her personality and establish and develop relationships with other persons and the outside world.[81] The Parliamentary Assembly has described 'the right to privacy' as set out in article 8 as 'the right to live one's own life with a minimum of interference'.[82] The Convention organs have explained that the right to private life is not susceptible to precise or exhaustive definition.[83] The Universal Declaration of Human Rights as well as the International Covenant on Civil and Political Rights enshrine a right to 'privacy', whereas the European Convention speaks of 'private life'. This difference, which does not seem to have any legal consequences, may be related to the important role of the French language in the drafting of the European Convention, 'private life' being a somewhat awkward rendering of 'vie privée'.

Odièvre v. France [GC], no. 42326/98, § 46, ECHR 2003-III; *Evans v. the United Kingdom* [GC], no. 6339/05, § 77, ECHR 2007-I; *Mosley v. the United Kingdom*, no. 48009/08, § 109, 10 May 2011.

[76] *Söderman v. Sweden* [GC], no. 5786/08, § 80, 12 November 2013; *Z and Others v. the United Kingdom* [GC], no. 29392/95, § 73, ECHR 2001-V; *M.P. and Others v. Bulgaria*, no. 22457/08, § 108, 15 November 2011.

[77] *A v. Croatia*, no. 55164/08, § 60, 14 October 2010; *M.C. v. Bulgaria*, no. 39272/98, § 150, ECHR 2003-XII; *K.U. v. Finland*, no. 2872/02, § 43, ECHR 2008; *Söderman v. Sweden* [GC], no. 5786/08, § 108, 12 November 2013.

[78] *X and Y v. the Netherlands*, 26 March 1985, § 27, Series A no. 91.

[79] *M.C. v. Bulgaria*, no. 39272/98, § 167, ECHR 2003-XII.

[80] *Söderman v. Sweden* [GC], no. 5786/08, § 91, 12 November 2013.

[81] *Jehovah's Witnesses of Moscow v. Russia*, no. 302/02, § 117, 10 June 2010; *Hadri-Vionnet v. Switzerland*, no. 55525/00, § 51, 14 February 2008; *Pretty v. the United Kingdom*, no. 2346/02, § 61, ECHR 2002-III; *Gillberg v. Sweden* [GC], no. 41723/06, § 66, 3 April 2012; *S. and Marper v. the United Kingdom* [GC], nos 30562/04 and 30566/04, § 66, ECHR 2008; *Haas v. Switzerland*, no. 31322/07, § 50, ECHR 2011; *Friedl v. Austria*, no. 15225/89, § 44, Commission report of 19 May 1994; *A.H. v. the United Kingdom*, no. 3868/68, Collection 34, p. 10; *X. v. Iceland*, no. 6825/74, Commission decision of 18 May 1976, (1976) 19 YB 342, DR 5, p. 86; *Brüggemann and Scheuten v. Federal Republic of Germany*, §§ 55–58, Commission report of 12 July 1977, DR 10, p. 100.

[82] Resolution 428 (1970) containing a declaration on mass communication media and human rights.

[83] *Nada v. Switzerland* [GC], no. 10593/08, § 151, ECHR 2012; *Aksu v. Turkey* [GC], nos 4149/04 and 41029/04, § 58, ECHR 2012; *Glor v. Switzerland*, no. 13444/04, § 52, ECHR 2009; *Tysiąc v. Poland*, no. 5410/03, § 107, ECHR 2007-I, ECHR 2007-I; *Pretty v. the United Kingdom*, no. 2346/02, § 61, ECHR 2002-III; *S. and Marper v. the United Kingdom* [GC], nos 30562/04 and 30566/04, § 66, ECHR 2008.

With respect to 'private life', the interpretation of article 8 is 'underpinned by the notions of personal autonomy and quality of life'.[84] According to the Court's case law, private life encompasses 'a person's physical and psychological integrity; the guarantee afforded by Article 8 of the Convention is primarily intended to ensure the development, without outside interference, of the personality of each individual in his relations with other human beings'.[85] It is not limited to the protection of an 'inner circle', where 'the individual may live his own personal life as he chooses and to exclude therefrom entirely the outside world not encompassed within that circle. It also protects the right to establish and develop relationships with other human beings and the outside world.'[86] This has sometimes been described as a 'zone of interaction between a person and others which, even in a public context, may fall within the scope of "private life"'.[87]

Physical, psychological, and moral integrity

Private life includes the 'physical and psychological integrity' of the individual. Somewhat less frequently, reference has also been made to 'moral integrity'.[88] The positive aspect of the obligation is of particular significance, and article 8 requires the State 'to maintain and apply in practice an adequate legal framework affording protection against acts of violence by private individuals'.[89] Article 8 may also extend to questions relating to the effectiveness of a criminal investigation.[90] Especially when physical, psychological, and moral integrity are concerned, there is a relationship between article 8 and article 3.[91] The latter imposes a threshold of a minimum level of severity for its application.[92] When this is not met, treatment that is not a violation of article 3 may nevertheless breach the private life aspect of article 8 if the effects are sufficiently adverse.[93]

The extent of the State's positive obligation to protect against attacks on physical and psychological integrity may even extend to problems of bullying in schools.[94] The failure of the authorities in Bucharest to take sufficient measures to address an endemic problem of stray dogs, some of them dangerous to humans, was held to infringe upon the respect of private life.[95]

---

[84] *Pretty v. the United Kingdom*, no. 2346/02, §§ 61 *in fine* and 65, ECHR 2002-III; *Christine Goodwin v. the United Kingdom* [GC], no. 28957/95, § 90, ECHR 2002-VI.

[85] *Costello-Roberts v. the United Kingdom*, 25 March 1993, § 36, Series A no. 247-C; *X and Y v. the Netherlands*, 26 March 1985, § 22, Series A no. 91.

[86] *Shimovolos v. Russia*, no. 30194/09, § 64, 21 June 2011.

[87] *Gillan and Quinton v. the United Kingdom*, no. 4158/05, § 61, ECHR 2010 (extracts); *Mółka v. Poland* (dec.), no. 56550/00, ECHR 2006-IV.

[88] *E.S. v. Sweden*, no. 5786/08, § 40, 21 June 2012; *Von Hannover v. Germany (no. 2)* [GC], nos 40660/08 and 60641/08, § 95, ECHR 2012; *Gillberg v. Sweden* [GC], no. 41723/06, § 68, 3 April 2012.

[89] *Đurđević v. Croatia*, no. 52442/09, § 107, ECHR 2011 (extracts); *X and Y v. the Netherlands*, 26 March 1985, §§ 22–23, Series A no. 91; *Costello-Roberts v. the United Kingdom*, 25 March 1993, § 36, Series A no. 247-C; *D.P. and J.C. v. the United Kingdom*, no. 38719/97, § 118, 10 October 2002; *M.C. v. Bulgaria*, no. 39272/98, §§ 150 and 152, ECHR 2003-XII; *Bevacqua and S. v. Bulgaria*, no. 71127/01, § 65, 12 June 2008; *Sandra Janković v. Croatia*, no. 38478/05, § 45, 5 March 2009; *Isaković Vidović v. Serbia*, no. 41694/07, § 59, 1 July 2014.

[90] *M. and C. v. Romania*, no. 29032/04, § 110, 27 September 2011; *Osman v. the United Kingdom*, 28 October 1998, § 128, *Reports of Judgments and Decisions* 1998-VIII.

[91] *M. and V. v. Romania*, no. 29032/04, § 111, 27 September 2011.

[92] See the chapter on article 3 in this Commentary.

[93] *Costello-Roberts v. the United Kingdom*, 25 March 1993, § 36, Series A no. 247-C; *Raninen v. Finland*, 16 December 1997, § 63, *Reports of Judgments and Decisions* 1997-VIII.

[94] *Đurđević v. Croatia*, no. 52442/09, § 105, ECHR 2011 (extracts).

[95] *Georgel and Georgeta Stoicescu v. Romania*, no. 9718/03, § 62, 26 July 2011.

Health and medical care

Together with physical and moral integrity, health falls within the scope of private life.[96] Although it cannot be excluded that medical care may result in violations of article 3 of the Convention, the Court generally prefers to consider these matters from the standpoint of article 8.[97] Here there are conflicts between the State's interest in protecting the lives and health of its citizens and the individual's right to personal autonomy.[98] According to the Court, although the Convention does not guarantee 'any specific level of medical care', private life 'includes a person's physical and psychological integrity'. Moreover, 'the State is also under a positive obligation to secure to its citizens their right to effective respect for this integrity'.[99]

Issues arise with respect to consent to medical treatment. As the Court has explained, 'a medical intervention in defiance of the subject's will gives rise to an interference with respect for his or her private life, and in particular his or her right to physical integrity'.[100] According to the Court, '[i]n the sphere of medical assistance, even where the refusal to accept a particular treatment might lead to a fatal outcome, the imposition of medical treatment without the consent of a mentally competent adult patient would interfere with his or her right to physical integrity contrary to article 8'.[101] Similarly, forced administration of drugs will constitute an interference with the right to private life, subject to justification according to the criteria of article 8(2).[102] An exception to this general principle might be vaccination during an epidemic, as it would be necessary to protect third parties. Otherwise, 'the State must abstain from interfering with the individual freedom of choice in the sphere of health care, for such interference can only lessen and not enhance the value of life'.[103]

Competing interests also present themselves where patients with a dismal prognosis seek authorization to use medication that is not generally available, because it has not obtained regulatory approval. In some European jurisdictions, exceptions are available for such cases, and the Court said 'there is now a clear trend in the Contracting States towards allowing, under certain exceptional conditions, the use of unauthorised medicinal products'.[104]

---

[96] *Nada v. Switzerland* [GC], no. 10593/08, § 151, ECHR 2012.

[97] *Tysiąc v. Poland*, no. 5410/03, § 66, ECHR 2007-I.

[98] *Pretty v. the United Kingdom*, no. 2346/02, § 62 et seq., ECHR 2002-III.

[99] *Tysiąc v. Poland*, no. 5410/03, § 107, ECHR 2007-I; *Glass v. the United Kingdom*, no. 61827/00, §§ 74–83, ECHR 2004-II; *Sentges v. the Netherlands* (dec.) no. 27677/02, 8 July 2003; *Pentiacova and Others v. Moldova* (dec.), no. 14462/03, ECHR 2005-I; *Nitecki v. Poland* (dec.), no. 65653/01, 21 March 2002.

[100] *X v. Finland*, no. 34806/04, § 212, ECHR 2012 (extracts); *Glass v. the United Kingdom*, no. 61827/00, § 70, ECHR 2004-II; *Y.F. v. Turkey*, no. 24209/94, § 33, ECHR 2003-IX; *X. v. Austria*, 8278/78, Commission decision of 13 December 1979, DR 18, p. 154; *X v. the Netherlands*, no. 8239/78, Commission decision of 4 December 1978, DR 16, p. 184; *Acmanne and Others v. Belgium*, no. 10435/83, Commission decision of 10 December 1984, DR 40, p. 251; *Storck v. Germany*, no. 61603/00, §§ 143–144, ECHR 2005-V; *Jehovah's Witnesses of Moscow v. Russia*, no. 302/02, § 135, 10 June 2010; *Shopov v. Bulgaria*, no. 11373/04, § 41, 2 September 2010.

[101] *Jehovah's Witnesses of Moscow v. Russia*, no. 302/02, § 135, 10 June 2010; *Pretty v. the United Kingdom*, no. 2346/02, § 63, ECHR 2002-III; *Glass v. the United Kingdom*, no. 61827/00, §§ 70–72, ECHR 2004-II.

[102] *X v. Finland*, no. 34806/04, §§ 220–221, ECHR 2012 (extracts).

[103] *Jehovah's Witnesses of Moscow v. Russia*, no. 302/02, § 135, 10 June 2010, citing decisions of the Ontario Court of Appeal, *Malette v. Shulman*, (1990) 72 OR 417 (CA), and the Court of Appeals of New York, *Fosmire v. Nicoleau*, 75 NY2d 218, 551 NE2d 77, 551 NYS2d 876 (1990).

[104] *Hristozov and Others v. Bulgaria*, nos 47039/11 and 358/12, § 123, 13 November 2012.

Nevertheless, it granted that the somewhat inflexible approach in Bulgaria was permitted by its margin of appreciation.[105]

Reproductive health is an area of special importance in the protection of private and family life. It is an area of some sensitivity because of fascist practices in Europe during the first half of the twentieth century. The decision to have a child, as well as the decision not to have a child, certainly falls within the right to private life.[106] In a case dealing with sterilization of a Roma woman following childbirth without full and informed consent, the Court held there was a breach of article 3, but also insisted on examining whether, pursuant to article 8, the State had put in place effective legal safeguards to protect the reproductive health of women of Roma origin.

The Court notes that the documents before it indicate that the issue of sterilisations and its improper use affected vulnerable individuals belonging to various ethnic groups. However, the Council of Europe Commissioner for Human Rights was convinced that the Roma population of eastern Slovakia had been at particular risk. This was due, *inter alia*, to the widespread negative attitudes towards the relatively high birth rate among the Roma compared to other parts of the population, often expressed as worries of an increased proportion of the population living on social benefits. In the Commissioner's view, the Slovakian Government had an objective responsibility in the matter because of systemic shortcomings in the procedures permitted and, in particular, for failing to put in place adequate legislation and exercise appropriate supervision of sterilisation practices.[107]

Noting a systematic mention of Roma origin in the medical dossier, the Court said that 'the reference in the record to the applicant's ethnic origin, without more, indicates, in the view of the Court, a certain mindset on the part of the medical staff as to the manner in which the medical situation of a Roma woman should be managed'. It certainly did not indicate that 'special care was to be, or was in fact, exercised to ensure that the full and informed consent of such a patient was obtained before any sterilisation was contemplated or that the patient was involved in the decision-making process to a degree permitting her interests to be effectively protected'.[108]

Private life incorporates a right to become a parent. In cases where access to artificial insemination facilities has been refused, it has been held that article 8 incorporates the right of a couple to respect for their decision to become genetic parents.[109] More generally, the Grand Chamber has stated 'the right of a couple to conceive a child and to make use of medically assisted procreation for that purpose'.[110] In addition, 'the right concerning the decision to become a parent includes the right of choosing the circumstances of becoming a parent', such as giving birth at home rather than in a hospital.[111]

[105] Ibid.
[106] *Evans v. the United Kingdom* [GC], no. 6339/05, § 71, ECHR 2007-I; *A, B, and C v. Ireland* [GC], no. 25579/05, § 212, ECHR 2010; *Knecht v. Romania*, no. 10048/10, § 54, 2 October 2012; *S. H. and Others v. Austria* [GC], no. 57813/00, § 82, 3 November 2011.
[107] *V.C. v. Slovakia*, no. 18968/07, § 146, ECHR 2011 (extracts).
[108] Ibid.
[109] *Dickson v. the United Kingdom* [GC], no. 44362/04, § 66, ECHR 2007-V; *E.L.H. and P.B.H. v. the United Kingdom*, nos 32094/96 and 32568/96, Commission decision of 22 October 1997, DR 91-A, p. 61; *Kalashnikov v. Russia* (dec.), no. 47095/99, ECHR 2001-XI; *Aliev v. Ukraine*, no. 41220/98, § 187–189, 29 April 2003; *Evans v. the United Kingdom* [GC], no. 6339/05, § 71–72, ECHR 2007-I.
[110] *S.H. and Others v. Austria* [GC], no. 57813/00, § 82, ECHR 2011.
[111] *Ternovszky v. Hungary*, no. 67545/09, § 22, 14 December 2010.

Legislation regulating the interruption of pregnancy concerns private life because 'whenever a woman is pregnant her private life becomes closely connected with the developing foetus'.[112] But pregnancy is not exclusively about a woman's private life, which 'must be weighed against other competing rights and freedoms invoked including those of the unborn child'.[113] State regulations dealing with therapeutic abortion must be 'assessed against the positive obligations of the State to secure the physical integrity of mothers-to-be'.[114] The abortion cases before the Convention organs have generally arisen in European jurisdictions where the practice is severely restricted, notably Poland[115] and Ireland.[116] While the Court has held that article 8 cannot be interpreted as conferring a right to abortion, it has found that the prohibition of abortion when sought for reasons of health and well-being falls within the scope of the right to respect for private life.[117] In *A, B, and C*, the Grand Chamber declared that there is 'a consensus amongst a substantial majority of the Contracting States of the Council of Europe towards allowing abortion on broader grounds than accorded under Irish law', but said this could not displace Ireland's margin of appreciation on the subject.[118]

According to the Court, the first requirement of such strict regulation is that it 'ensure clarity of the pregnant woman's legal position'.[119] It has warned that a broad legal prohibition on abortion, subject to therapeutic exceptions, coupled with a threat of criminal prosecution for those who perform abortions, 'can well have a chilling effect on doctors when deciding whether the requirements of legal abortion are met in an individual case'.[120] Thus, '[o]nce the legislature decides to allow abortion, it must not structure its legal framework in a way which would limit real possibilities to obtain it'.[121] Procedures to determine availability of a legal abortion must be accessible to the pregnant woman and undertaken diligently, bearing in mind the time-sensitive nature of such determinations. A failure to provide genuine possibilities of determination according to law may result in a violation of article 8.[122]

The unavailability in Italy of assisted pregnancy accompanied by genetic tests was successfully challenged by parents of a child afflicted with cystic fibrosis. The government expressed its concerns about eugenic practices, as well as the protection of the health of mother and child, together with the dignity and freedom of conscience of health-care professionals. Noting that Italy allowed the abortion of a foetus where cystic fibrosis was present, the Court cited a 'manque de cohérence' in the applicable legislation.[123]

---

[112] *Tysiąc v. Poland*, no. 5410/03, § 106, ECHR 2007-I; *Brüggemann and Scheuten v. Federal Republic of Germany*, no. 6959/75, Commission report of 12 July 1977, DR 10, p. 100.

[113] *A, B and C v. Ireland* [GC], no. 25579/05, § 213, ECHR 2010; *Vo v. France* [GC], no. 53924/00, §§ 76, 80, 82, ECHR 2004-VIII.

[114] *Tysiąc v. Poland*, no. 5410/03, § 107, ECHR 2007-I.

[115] Ibid.; *R.R. v. Poland*, no. 27617/04, ECHR 2011 (extracts); *P. and S. v. Poland*, no. 57375/08, 30 October 2012.

[116] *A, B, and C v. Ireland* [GC], no. 25579/05, ECHR 2010.

[117] Ibid., § 245; *P. and S. v. Poland*, no. 57375/08, § 96, 30 October 2012; *Tysiąc v. Poland*, no. 5410/03, § 110, ECHR 2007-I.

[118] *A, B, and C v. Ireland* [GC], no. 25579/05, § 235, ECHR 2010.

[119] *Tysiąc v. Poland*, no. 5410/03, § 116, ECHR 2007-I; *A, B, and C v. Ireland* [GC], no. 25579/05, § 245, ECHR 2010; *R.R. v. Poland*, no. 27617/04, § 184, ECHR 2011 (extracts).

[120] *Tysiąc v. Poland*, no. 5410/03, § 116, ECHR 2007-I.

[121] Ibid.

[122] Ibid., §§ 117–118.

[123] *Costa and Pavan v. Italy*, no. 54270/10, § 64, 28 August 2012.

Associated with the health aspect of private life is the right of effective access to information concerning health and reproductive status. This is similar in nature to the right to information concerning environmental hazards, discussed elsewhere in this chapter. But it also seems related to an entitlement to consult one's own medical records. The Court has acknowledged that the authority or individual detaining the file may determine the arrangements for consultation, as well as provisions concerning the cost of copying. The data subject should not be required to justify a specific request in order to obtain a copy of a personal file; rather, it is for the authorities to justify any refusal of such access.[124]

Employment and professional activities

The Court has often applied article 8 in the area of employment law and to the exercise of professional and business activities.[125] According to the Court, '[r]estrictions on an individual's professional life may fall within Article 8 where they have repercussions on the manner in which he or she constructs his or her social identity by developing relationships with others'.[126] Moreover, the Court has pointed out that it is in the course of their working lives that the majority of people are able to develop relationships with the outside world:

[P]rofessional life often overlaps with private life, in the strict sense of the term, such that it is not always easy to distinguish clearly in what capacity an individual is acting at a given moment of time. In sum, professional life is part of the zone of interaction between a person and others which, even in a public context, may fall within the scope of 'private life'.[127]

Nevertheless, the application of article 8 to professional activities is not open-ended. For example, it does not guarantee a right to recruitment to the civil service[128] or to freedom of profession.[129] But when the law society in Athens had initially allowed a non-citizen to proceed with qualification to become a practicing lawyer, apparently by mistake, only to refuse her the right to continue subsequently, the Court said that the 'comportement des autorités compétentes a manqué de cohérence et de respect pour la personne et la vie professionnelle de la requérante', concluding that article 8 had been infringed.[130]

There are many cases of the application of article 8 in the employment context. For example, the decisions of Jehovah's Witnesses whether to take full-time or part-time and paid or unpaid employment were matters that fell within the sphere of their private

---

[124] *K.H. and Others v. Slovakia*, no. 32881/04, §§ 44–58, ECHR 2009 (extracts).

[125] *Fernández Martínez v. Spain*, no. 56030/07, §§ 56–57, 15 May 2012; *Bigaeva v. Greece*, no. 26713/05, § 23, 28 May 2009; *Turán v. Hungary*, no. 33068/05, § 19, 6 July 2010; *Sidabras and Džiautas v. Lithuania*, nos 55480/00 and 59330/00, §§ 47–50, ECHR 2004-VIII; *Halford v. the United Kingdom*, 25 June 1997, § 44, *Reports of Judgments and Decisions* 1997-III; *Niemietz v. Germany*, 16 December 1992, § 29, Series A no. 251-B.

[126] *Fernández Martínez v. Spain* [GC], no. 56030/07, §§ 109–112, 12 June 2014; *Fernández Martínez v. Spain*, no. 56030/07, § 57, 15 May 2012.

[127] *Fernández Martínez v. Spain*, no. 56030/07, § 57, 15 May 2012. Also *Evans v. the United Kingdom* [GC], no. 6339/05, § 71, ECHR 2007-I; *Niemietz v. Germany*, 16 December 1992, § 29, Series A no. 251-B.

[128] *Vogt v. Germany*, 26 September 1995, § 43, Series A no. 323; *Vilho Eskelinen and Others v. Finland* [GC], no. 63235/00, § 57, ECHR 2007-II. But see *Sidabras and Džiautas v. Lithuania*, nos 55480/00 and 59330/00, §§ 46–47, ECHR 2004-VIII; *D.M.T. and D.K.I. v. Bulgaria*, no. 29476/06, § 103, 24 July 2012.

[129] *Thlimmenos v. Greece* [GC], no. 34369/97, § 41, ECHR 2000-IV.

[130] *Bigaeva v. Greece*, no. 26713/05, § 36, 28 May 2009. But see *Bigaeva v. Greece*, no. 26713/05, Partly Dissenting Opinion of Judges Vajić, Malinverni, and Nicolaou, 28 May 2009.

lives.[131] A Spanish priest, married with five children, claimed he lost his job because of his views on Catholic celibacy. The Court considered that the issue was balancing the State's positive obligation to protect his private life against the Catholic Church's decision to refuse renewal of his contract, bearing in mind the latter's rights under articles 9 and 11.[132] The Court described a prohibition on seeking employment outside of the civil service that lasted more than six years placed upon a senior police official who was suspended on suspicion of corruption as 'néfaste et prolongé' and said it affected his private life.[133]

The Convention organs have been cautious in applying article 8 to political activities.[134] They have taken the view that article 8 must be read in harmony with article 3 of Protocol No. 1 and that it should not take its place when, for example, a State has withdrawn the application of article 3 to a particular territory.[135] Referring to its case law on freedom of expression concerning media coverage of the lives of political figures, the Court noted that political activity 'is very much a matter of public life, to which Article 8 can have only limited application'.[136]

Personal autonomy and identity

The notion of personal autonomy plays an important role in the application of article 8. It provides protection to the personal sphere of an individual, including the right to establish details of his or her identity as a human being.[137] This extends to various aspects of an individual's 'social identity', including name and image as well as religion, ethnicity, and sexual orientation.[138]

Although article 8 does not explicitly refer to the protection of the name as part of private life, the Convention organs have often considered it to be applicable to this issue.[139] Name is important because it links an individual to the family, with its special role in both articles 8 and 12. It is also germane to the identity of the individual within a community defined by nationality, ethnicity, and religion. However, the right of women to inherit titles of nobility was held to fall outside the scope of article 8; a claim that reserving such titles to male descendants constituted discrimination was inadmissible for this reason.[140] Latvian legislation requiring that when a woman takes the name of her husband upon marriage it must be spelled in accordance with Latvian linguistic rules was deemed to infringe article 8 because 'when a couple choose to use the same name, that name assumes importance as a testimony to their reciprocal attachment and to the unity

---

[131] *Jehovah's Witnesses of Moscow v. Russia*, no. 302/02, § 117, 10 June 2010.

[132] *Fernández Martínez v. Spain*, no. 56030/07, §§ 82–89, 15 May 2012. Also *Schüth v. Germany*, no. 1620/03, § 74, ECHR 2010.

[133] *D.M.T. and D.K.I. v. Bulgaria*, no. 29476/06, § 113, 24 July 2012.

[134] *Baškauskaitė v. Lithuania*, no. 41090/98, Commission decision of 21 October 1998; *Mółka v. Poland* (dec.), no. 56550/00, ECHR 2006-IV.

[135] *Misick v. the United Kingdom* (dec.), no. 10781/10, § 22, 16 October 2012.

[136] Ibid.

[137] *Ciubotaru v. Moldova*, no. 27138/04, § 49, 27 April 2010; *Burghartz v. Switzerland*, 22 February 1994, § 24, Series A no. 280-B; *Christine Goodwin v. the United Kingdom* [GC], no. 28957/95, § 90, ECHR 2002-VI.

[138] *Aksu v. Turkey* [GC], nos 4149/04 and 41029/04, § 58, ECHR 2012.

[139] *Negrepontis-Giannisis v. Greece*, no. 56759/08, § 55, 3 May 2011; *Znamenskaya v. Russia*, no. 77785/01, § 23, 2 June 2005; *Cerva Osorio de Moscoso and Others v. Spain* (dec.), nos 41127/98, 41503/98, 41717/98, and 45726/99, 28 October 1999; *Mentzen v. Latvia* (dec.), no. 71074/01, 7 December 2004.

[140] *Cerva Osorio de Moscoso and Others v. Spain* (dec.), nos 41127/98, 41503/98, 41717/98, and 45726/99, 28 October 1999.

of the family' and 'when the applicant and her husband use their respective passports, which contain different written forms of their surname, their joint identification as a family unit may, in certain situations, become difficult'.[141] The role of the name in the respect of private life extends to the given name.[142]

Respect for the right to private life requires that every individual be able to determine the details of his or her identity.[143] According to the Court, the right to private life comprises acknowledgement that individuals have 'a vital interest, protected by the Convention, in establishing the biological truth about an important aspect of their private and family life and having it recognised in law'.[144] This necessarily involves the determination of paternity, which falls under the scope of article 8.[145] Sometimes the identity of the mother is also unknown. As the child matures, he or she may seek to learn about the biological parents. The child has a right to know his or her origins, something that is a component of private life; the failure to obtain such information may imply mental and psychological suffering.[146] The origins go beyond birth and extend to 'the information necessary to know and to understand their childhood and early development'.[147] Nevertheless, the mother may have a right 'in remaining anonymous in order to protect her health by giving birth in appropriate medical conditions'.[148] Even if the mother cannot be compelled to reveal her identity, a child should have access to mechanisms so that this can be explored and in order to obtain certain relevant information.[149] The right to this personal and social identity comprises an entitlement to registration of a marriage.[150]

Dress and other features of personal appearance are matters that concern private life. According to the Grand Chamber, 'personal choices as to an individual's desired appearance, whether in public or in private places, relate to the expression of his or her personality and thus fall within the notion of private life'.[151] There have also been many decisions of the Court concerning clothing (and the lack of it) in application of articles 9 and 10 of the Convention. The Court has already held that shaving the head of a prison inmate constitutes a breach of article 3.[152] The less drastic measure of a haircut may not have reached the required level of seriousness and was therefore addressed under article 8.[153] A measure that emanates from a public authority that restricts a choice of dress, such as a ban on wearing clothing designed to conceal the face in public places, is in

---

[141] *Mentzen v. Latvia* (dec.), no. 71074/01, 7 December 2004. See also *Güzel Erdagöz v. Turkey*, no. 37483/02, § 43, 21 October 2008.

[142] *Guillot v. France*, 24 October 1996, §§ 21–22, *Reports of Judgments and Decisions* 1996-V.

[143] *A.M.M. v. Romania*, no. 2151/10, § 51, 14 February 2012; *Gaskin v. the United Kingdom*, 7 July 1989, § 39, Series A no. 160.

[144] *Kruškovic v. Croatia*, no. 46185/08, § 34, 21 June 2011.

[145] Ibid., § 18; *A.M.M. v. Romania*, no. 2151/10, § 51, 14 February 2012; *Mikulic v. Croatia*, no. 53176/99, § 51, ECHR 2002-I; *Rasmussen v. Denmark*, 28 November 1984, §33, Series A no. 87; *Keegan v. Ireland*, 26 May 1994, § 45, Series A no. 290.

[146] *Godelli v. Italy*, no. 33783/09, § 56, 25 September 2012.

[147] *Odièvre v. France* [GC], no. 42326/98, §42, ECHR 2003-III.

[148] *Godelli v. Italy*, no. 33783/09, §§ 47, 50, 25 September 2012.

[149] *Odièvre v. France* [GC], no. 42326/98, §49, ECHR 2003-III.

[150] *Dadouch v. Malta*, no. 38816/07, § 48, 20 July 2010.

[151] *S.A.S. v. France* [GC], no. 43835/11, § 107, 1 July 2014. Also *McFeeley and Others v. the United Kingdom*, no. 8317/78, Commission decision of 15 May 1980, (1980) 23 YB 256, DR 20, p. 44; *Kara v. the United Kingdom*, no. 36528/97, Commission decision of 22 October 1998.

[152] *Yankov v. Bulgaria*, no. 39084/97, §§ 108–121, ECHR 2003-XII (extracts).

[153] *Popa v. Romania* (dec.), no. 4233/09, §§ 32–33, 18 June 2013.

principle an interference with article 8.[154] In the case of the 'naked rambler', who chose to go without clothes in public so as to make a public statement of his belief in the inoffensive nature of the human body, the Court said that article 8 could not be taken to protect every conceivable personal choice about one's desired appearance in public. '[T]here must presumably be a de minimis level of seriousness as to the choice of desired appearance in question', it said, adding that '[w]hether the requisite level of seriousness has been reached in relation to the applicant's choice to appear fully naked on all occasions in all public places without distinction may be doubted, having regard to the absence of support for such a choice in any known democratic society in the world'.[155]

A person's image is an important attribute of personality 'as it reveals the person's unique characteristics and distinguishes the person from his or her peers'.[156] Consequently, the individual is entitled to control the use of the image, including the right to refuse publication of a photograph and to object to the recording, conservation, and reproduction of the image by another person. Otherwise, as the Court has explained, 'an essential attribute of personality would be retained in the hands of a third party and the person concerned would have no control over any subsequent use of the image'.[157] There are particular concerns about technical developments in filming and photography that make it possible to store and reproduce personal data.[158] In some European States, measures have been considered in order to address the phenomenon of illicit or covert filming of individuals, including criminalization where personal integrity is compromised.[159] Video surveillance by an employer in order to detect theft by employees was held to infringe article 8(1), although the Court considered that it struck an appropriate balance bearing in mind the rights of the employer and the probability of success in catching a dishonest worker. But in rejecting the application, the Court said that this 'might well be given a different weight in the future, having regard to the extent to which intrusions into private life are made possible by new, more and more sophisticated technologies'.[160]

Publication of photos involves a balancing of freedom of expression, including the rights of a free press with the right to private life. One of the factors to be considered by the Court in determining whether there has been an interference with article 8 is a contribution to an area of general interest. Obviously political issues and crime falls in the category of general interest,[161] but it also includes sporting issues and performing artists.[162] But rumours of marital problems of a head of State and financial troubles of a performing artist do not meet this criterion.[163] Nor is the fact that a person is the subject

---

[154] *S.A.S. v. France* [GC], no. 43835/11, § 107, 1 July 2014.
[155] *Gough v. the United Kingdom*, no. 49327/11, § 184, 24 October 2014.
[156] *Reklos and Davourlis v. Greece*, no. 1234/05, § 40, 15 January 2009.
[157] Ibid.
[158] *Von Hannover v. Germany*, no. 59320/00, § 70, ECHR 2004-VI.
[159] *E.S. v. Sweden*, no. 5786/08, § 71, 21 June 2012.
[160] *Köpke v. Germany* (dec.), no. 420/07, 5 October 2010.
[161] *White v. Sweden*, no. 42435/02, § 29, 19 September 2006; *Egeland and Hanseid v. Norway*, no. 34438/04, § 58, 16 April 2009; *Leempoel & S.A. ED. Ciné Revue v. Belgium*, no. 64772/01, § 72, 9 November 2006.
[162] *Nikowitz and Verlagsgruppe News GmbH v. Austria*, no. 5266/03, § 25, 22 February 2007; *Colaço Mestre and SIC—Sociedade Independente de Comunicação, S.A. v. Portugal*, nos 11182/03 and 11319/03, § 28, 26 April 2007; *Sapan v. Turkey*, no.44102/04, § 34, 8 June 2010.
[163] *Standard Verlags GmbH v. Austria (no. 2)*, no. 21277/05, § 48, 4 June 2009; *Hachette Filipacchi Associés (ICI PARIS) v. France*, no. 12268/03, § 53, 23 July 2009.

of criminal proceedings sufficient to curtail the protection of article 8 with respect to publication of a photo.[164]

A second factor concerns the notoriety of the person and the nature of the activities in the photograph. The Court operates a distinction between political or public figures and private individuals who may be acting in a public context. Consequently, 'whilst a private individual unknown to the public may claim particular protection of his or her right to private life, the same is not true of public figures'.[165] Along the same lines, the Court distinguishes between reporting facts that may contribute to democratic debate about the activities of politicians exercising their functions and the reporting of details of the private life of a person with no public functions.[166] Prior conduct of the individual may also be significant, although previous cooperation with the media does not automatically deprive the person of protection against publication.[167] Also, the Court will consider the content and form of the publication,[168] and the extent of its dissemination.[169] Finally, the manner in which the photo was taken will be taken into account: did the person consent or was it done surreptitiously?[170]

Identity documents are essential in modern life. Issues relating to their issuance may result in an interference with article 8. A passport or identity card is essential for international travel, but also for routine requirements of the daily life of a person living abroad. Confiscation and non-restitution of a passport may raise issues under article 8,[171] although the provision does not guarantee an entitlement to a passport.[172] The failure to invalidate a driving licence promptly after it was reported missing made possible the abuse of an individual's identity by others and constituted an interference with article 8.[173] According to the Court, 'swift administrative action to deprive a driving license of its usefulness as an identity document was possible and practicable', and was something the Government failed to do, with the consequence that article 8 was breached.[174]

The European Convention on Human Rights does not contain a right to nationality[175] comparable to what is found in article 15 of the Universal Declaration of

---

[164] *Sciacca v. Italy*, no. 50774/99, § 29, ECHR 2005-I.

[165] *Von Hannover v. Germany (no. 2)* [GC], nos 40660/08 and 60641/08, § 110, ECHR 2012; *Minelli v. Switzerland* (dec.), no. 14991/02, 14 June 2005; *Petrenco v. Moldova*, no. 20928/05, § 55, 30 March 2010.

[166] *Von Hannover v. Germany (no. 2)* [GC], nos 40660/08 and 60641/08, § 110, ECHR 2012; *Von Hannover v. Germany*, no. 59320/00, § 63, ECHR 2004-VI; *Standard Verlags GmbH v. Austria (no. 2)*, no. 21277/05, § 47, 4 June 2009.

[167] *Egeland and Hanseid v. Norway*, no. 34438/04, § 62, 16 April 2009; *Hachette Filipacchi Associés (ICI PARIS) v. France*, no. 12268/03, §§ 52–53, 23 July 2009.

[168] *Wirtschafts-Trend Zeitschriften-Verlagsgesellschaft m.b.H. v. Austria (no. 3)*, nos 66298/01 and 15653/02, § 47, 13 December 2005; *Reklos and Davourlis v. Greece*, no. 1234/05, § 42, 15 January 2009; *Jokitaipale and Others v. Finland*, no. 43349/05, § 68, 6 April 2010.

[169] *Karhuvaara and Iltalehti v. Finland*, no. 53678/00, § 47, ECHR 2004-X; *Gurguenidze v. Georgia*, no. 71678/01, § 55, 17 October 2006.

[170] *Gurguenidze v. Georgia*, no. 71678/01, § 56, 17 October 2006; *Reklos and Davourlis v. Greece*, no. 1234/05, § 41, 15 January 2009; *Hachette Filipacchi Associés (ICI PARIS) v. France*, no. 12268/03, § 47, 23 July 2009; *Flinkkilä and Others v. Finland*, no. 25576/04, § 81, 6 April 2010.

[171] *Iletmiş v. Turkey*, no. 29871/96, § 42, ECHR 2005-XII; *Smirnova v. Russia*, nos 46133/99 and 48183/99, §§ 95–97, ECHR 2003-IX (extracts). Passport issues have also been considered under article 2 of Protocol No. 4: *Bartik v. Russia*, no. 55565/00, ECHR 2006-XV and *Napijalo v. Croatia*, no. 66485/01, 13 November 2003.

[172] *M. v. Switzerland*, no. 41199/06, § 67, 26 April 2011.

[173] *Romet v. the Netherlands*, no. 7094/06, § 37, 14 February 2012.

[174] Ibid., § 43.

[175] The right to a nationality is enshrined in article 4(a) of the European Convention on Nationality, ETS 166.

Human Rights.[176] Nor does it contain a right to legal personality, set out in article 6 of the Universal Declaration.[177] To some extent, however, these rights can be vindicated through article 8 of the European Convention. The Slovenian citizenship legislation case provides a good example. Following the breakup of the former Yugoslavia, legislation governed the grant of Slovenian nationality to citizens of the Socialist Federal Republic of Yugoslavia. Within a few years, the legislation resulted in several thousand residents within Slovenia who belonged to other ethnic groups within the former Yugoslavia becoming stateless. The situation was addressed in reports of the Council of Europe's Commission of Human Rights and the European Commission against Racism and Intolerance, as well as the United Nations Committee for the Elimination of Racial Discrimination and the Committee Against Torture. Ultimately, the Grand Chamber found that the citizenship scheme and the resulting statelessness for certain individuals violated article 8 as well as article 14 of the Convention.[178]

Ethnicity is a component of an individual's identity that is protected by article 8.[179] The European Commission took the view that 'a minority group is, in principle, entitled to claim the right to respect for the particular life style it may lead as being "private life", "family life" or "home"'.[180] Not only is this an entitlement of the person's own dignity and integrity, it may also be relevant to identity documents and with respect to entitlements in areas such as schooling. Whether ethnicity is a matter of individual choice, and therefore entirely subjective, or something that has an objective existence subject to proof is a matter that has vexed international law for nearly a century.[181] The Court has acknowledged that in recognizing the ethnicity of an individual, objective evidence of what is claimed may be required. Moreover, 'it should be open to the authorities to refuse a claim to be officially recorded as belonging to a particular ethnicity where such a claim is based on purely subjective and unsubstantiated grounds'.[182] Nevertheless, where an individual can provide objective evidence of belonging to an ethnic group or minority, the State should provide a mechanism so that the identity can be established officially.[183]

Although issues concerning ethnicity often manifest themselves in claims for various rights related to identity, and to that extent they are not 'private', although they may belong to the 'private sphere', article 8 should also protect those who do not wish to divulge their ethnic origins or identity. In the case of religion, the Court has already affirmed that 'information about personal religious and philosophical conviction concerns some of the most intimate aspects of private life'. Therefore, imposing an obligation upon

---

[176] *Fehér and Dolník v. Slovakia* (dec.), nos 14927/12 and 30415/12, § 41, 21 May 2013; *Karassev and family v. Finland* (dec.), no. 31414/96, ECHR 1999-II.

[177] See *Kurić and Others v. Slovenia* [GC], no. 26828/06, Partly Concurring, Partly Dissenting Opinion of Judge Vučinić, ECHR 2012 (extracts).

[178] *Kurić and Others v. Slovenia* [GC], no. 26828/06, ECHR 2012 (extracts).

[179] *Aksu v. Turkey* [GC], nos 4149/04 and 41029/04, § 58, ECHR 2012; *S. and Marper v. the United Kingdom* [GC], nos 30562/04 and 30566/04, § 66, 4 December 2008; *Ciubotaru v. Moldova*, no. 27138/04, § 49, 27 April 2010; *Chapman v. the United Kingdom* [GC], no. 27238/95, §§ 73–74, ECHR 2001-I.

[180] *G. and E. v. Norway*, nos 9278/81 and 9415/81, Commission decision of 3 October 1983, DR 35, p. 30.

[181] *Rights of Minorities in Upper Silesia (Minority Schools)*, PCIJ, Series A No. 15; *German Settlers in Poland*, PCIJ, Series B No. 6; *Access to German Minority Schools in Upper Silesia*, PCIJ, Series A/B, No. 40; *Minority Schools in Albania*, PCIJ, Series A/B, No. 64; *Advisory Opinion of 31 July 1930 on the Greco-Bulgarian Community*, PCIJ, Series B No. 17.

[182] *Ciubotaru v. Moldova*, no. 27138/04, § 57, 27 April 2010.

[183] Ibid., § 59.

parents to provide school authorities with information about their religion or their philosophical beliefs might well be an interference with article 8.[184]

Any negative stereotyping, when it reaches a certain level, is capable of impacting on the group's sense of identity and the feelings of self-worth and self-confidence of its members. It is in this sense that the private life of members of the group may be affected.[185] In the case of a Turkish book presenting somewhat stereotyped views of Roma, the Court did not find the comments excessive, and rejected the application. At the heart of the debate was a balancing of article 8 and the right to freedom of expression set out in article 10.[186] The Court concluded likewise with respect to a related complaint about negative stereotypes of Roma found in a dictionary prepared for Turkish students. The Court said it would have been preferable to indicate 'pejorative' or 'insulting' next to the impugned definitions, but that alone was not enough to support a violation of article 8.[187]

In a few cases, the Court has accepted the relationship between article 8 and the rights of persons with disabilities. For example, the requirement that a disabled person pay a military service exemption tax that was imposed on persons deemed unfit to serve in the army for health reasons, 'that is, a factor outside the person's control', was clearly covered by article 8, 'even if the consequences of the measure are above all pecuniary'.[188] However, in the case of holiday access to a private beach and to the sea by a disabled person, the Court said the matter 'concerns interpersonal relations of such broad and indeterminate scope that there can be no conceivable direct link between the measures the State was urged to take in order to make good the omissions of the private bathing establishments and the applicant's private life'.[189]

Sexual life and activity

Gender identification, sexual orientation, and sexual life are details of individual identity that come within the sphere protected by article 8.[190] Unlike nationality and ethnicity, this is a 'most intimate aspect of private life', where the Court has said 'there must exist particularly serious reasons before interferences on the part of the public authorities can be legitimate'.[191] After initially rejecting applications by transsexuals seeking recognition of their new identity in official documents,[192] on the grounds that this fell within the margin of appreciation of States, the Court moved towards recognition of a positive obligation to recognize the gender change in transsexuals who had undergone surgery.[193] It moved still

[184] *Folgerø and Others v. Norway* [GC], no. 15472/02, § 98, ECHR 2007-III.
[185] *Aksu v. Turkey* [GC], nos 4149/04 and 41029/04, § 58, ECHR 2012.
[186] Ibid., §§ 69–79.
[187] Ibid., §§ 85–86.
[188] *Glor v. Switzerland*, no. 13444/04, § 54, ECHR 2009.
[189] *Botta v. Italy*, 24 February 1998, § 35, *Reports of Judgments and Decisions* 1998-I.
[190] *Bensaid v. the United Kingdom*, no. 44599/98, § 47, ECHR 2001-I; *Peck v. the United Kingdom*, no. 44647/98, § 57, ECHR 2003-I; *Stübing v. Germany*, no. 43547/08, § 55, 12 April 2012.
[191] *Dudgeon v. the United Kingdom*, 22 October 1981, § 52, Series A no. 45.
[192] *Rees v. the United Kingdom*, 17 October 1986, § 47, Series A no. 106; *Cossey v. the United Kingdom*, 27 September 1990, § 42, Series A no. 184; *Sheffield and Horsham v. the United Kingdom*, 30 July 1998, §§ 58–61, *Reports of Judgments and Decisions* 1998-V; *X, Y, and Z v. the United Kingdom*, 22 April 1997, § 62, *Reports of Judgments and Decisions* 1997-II.
[193] Beginning with *B. v. France*, 25 March 1992, §§ 59–63, Series A no. 232-C, followed by *Christine Goodwin v. the United Kingdom* [GC], no. 28957/95, §§ 71–93, ECHR 2002-VI; *Grant v. the United Kingdom*, no. 32570/03, §§ 39–44, ECHR 2006-VII.

further, finding a violation of article 8 where gender change surgery had not been completed, the delays being attributable to legal inadequacies and shortcomings in the public health system.[194]

In a series of cases, the Court held that legislation criminalizing homosexual activity between two consenting adults was a violation of article 8.[195] The influence of its jurisprudence in this area was felt as far away as the United States, where three judgments of the European Court of Human Rights were cited approvingly in an exceedingly rare reference to international human rights law by the majority of the Supreme Court.[196] Subsequently, the European Court of Human Rights enlarged this finding to include criminalization of sexual activity involving more than two participants.[197]

Presumably, article 8 now protects most adult sexual activity of any sort as long as it is in private and there are no public health considerations. There are still some exceptions, however—'not every sexual activity carried out behind closed doors necessarily falls within the scope of Article 8'[198]—although legal history may suggest that they will not last very much longer. One remaining taboo is the incestuous relationship, where the Court has observed that 'a broad consensus transpires that sexual relationships between siblings are neither accepted by the legal order nor by society as a whole'.[199] Indeed, 'domestic authorities enjoy a wide margin of appreciation in determining how to confront incestuous relationships between consenting adults, notwithstanding the fact that this decision concerns an intimate aspect of an individual's private life'.[200] The Court has also used article 8 to address forms of discrimination and inequality based upon identity, including sexual orientation. It held that the inquiry and subsequent expulsion into sexual orientation of members of the United Kingdom armed forces was an interference with the right to private life.[201]

In a case involving a sexual orgy with rather disturbing forms of sado-masochism, on its own motion the Court asked whether this even fell within the scope of private life, given that there were many participants and the proceedings were recorded on a video-tape that was then circulated.[202] Many years later, the Court noted that this issue had not been contested between the parties to the litigation, and that all it had done was 'raise a question' about the matter. In a case involving the filming of homosexual activity of several men, where there was no evidence to suggest the materials would ever be made public, the Court considered that article 8 was applicable.[203]

---

[194] *L. v. Lithuania*, no. 27527/03, §§ 58–60, ECHR 2007-IV.

[195] *Dudgeon v. the United Kingdom*, 22 October 1981, Series A no. 45; *Norris v. Ireland*, 26 October 1988, Series A no. 142; *Modinos v. Cyprus*, 22 April 1993, Series A no. 259.

[196] *Lawrence et al. v. Texas*, 539 US 558 (2003). See William N. Eskridge Jr, 'United States: Lawrence v. Texas and the Imperative of Comparative Constitutionalism', (2004) 2 *International Journal of* Constitutional Law 555–60.

[197] *A.D.T. v. the United Kingdom*, no. 35765/97, ECHR 2000-IX.

[198] *Laskey, Jaggard, and Brown v. the United Kingdom*, 19 February 1997, § 36, *Reports of Judgments and Decisions* 1997-I. Also *Laskey, Jaggard, and Brown v. the United Kingdom*, 19 February 1997, Concurring Opinion of Judge Pettiti, *Reports of Judgments and Decisions* 1997-I.

[199] *Stübing v. Germany*, no. 43547/08, § 61, 12 April 2012.

[200] Ibid., § 61.

[201] *Smith and Grady v. the United Kingdom*, nos 33985/96 and 33986/96, § 71, ECHR 1999-VI.

[202] *Laskey, Jaggard, and Brown v. the United Kingdom*, 19 February 1997, § 36, *Reports of Judgments and Decisions* 1997-I. Also *Gillberg v. Sweden* [GC], no. 41723/06, § 69, 3 April 2012.

[203] *A.D.T. v. the United Kingdom*, no. 35765/97, § 25, ECHR 2000-IX.

Death and dying

The right to decide when and by what means one's life will end is part of private life protected by the Convention, subject to the person being capable of freely making such a decision and acting upon it.[204] Dealing with the especially difficult case of a person at the terminal stage of an incurable degenerative disease who argued that she had a right to prevent what she considered to be 'an undignified and distressing end to her life', the Court said it was 'not prepared to exclude' that preventing a person from exercising a choice to avoid dying in such a way was an interference with her right to respect for private life and therefore within the ambit of article 8.[205] A decade later it took a more certain position, holding 'that an individual's right to decide by what means and at what point his or her life will end, provided he or she is capable of freely reaching a decision on this question and acting in consequence, is one of the aspects of the right to respect for private life within the meaning of Article 8 of the Convention'.[206] It has explained that '[w]ithout in any way negating the principle of sanctity of life protected under the Convention, the Court considered that, in an era of growing medical sophistication combined with longer life expectancies, many people were concerned that they should not be forced to linger on in old age or in states of advanced physical or mental decrepitude which conflicted with strongly held ideas of self and personal identity'.[207] However, the Court has declined to extend its reasoning to a full-blown 'freedom to die'. It has stopped short of recognizing that someone who is not infirm may nevertheless have a right to commit suicide with dignity.[208]

In cases involving death and dying, the applicants are often close relatives of the deceased person. The Court has often made no distinction as to whether the matter concerns private life or family life. Article 8 was held to apply when the authorities delayed the return of a child's body to the parents following an autopsy.[209] Similarly, it was relevant to the wish of an individual that his ashes be spread over his own land.[210] Regulations prohibiting the removal of an urn from one gravesite to another so that it could be closer to the home of surviving relatives was deemed an interference with article 8.[211] The Court has also held that article 8 entitles the mother of a stillborn child 'to attend the burial of her child, possibly accompanied by a ceremony, and to have the child's remains transported in an appropriate vehicle'.[212]

Data and information

The storage of information relating to an individual's private life and the release of such information is governed by article 8.[213] Protection of personal data is addressed explicitly in a provision of the Charter of Fundamental Rights of the European Union:

---

[204] *Haas v. Switzerland*, no. 31322/07, § 51, ECHR 2011.

[205] *Pretty v. the United Kingdom*, no. 2346/02, § 67, ECHR 2002-III.

[206] *Haas v. Switzerland*, no. 31322/07, § 51, ECHR 2011.

[207] *Koch v. Germany*, no. 497/09, § 51, 19 July 2012.

[208] *Haas v. Switzerland*, no. 31322/07, § 52, ECHR 2011.

[209] *Pannullo and Forte v. France*, no. 37794/97, §§ 31–35, ECHR 2001-X.

[210] *X v. Federal Republic of Germany*, no. 8741/79, Commission decision of 10 March 1981, DR 24, p. 137.

[211] *Elli Poluhas Dödsbo v. Sweden*, no. 61564/00, § 24, ECHR 2006-I.

[212] *Hadri-Vionnet v. Switzerland*, no. 55525/00, § 52, 14 February 2008.

[213] *Leander v. Sweden*, 26 March 1987, § 48, Series A no. 116; *Amann v. Switzerland* [GC], no. 27798/95, §§ 65 and 69–70, ECHR 2000-II; *Rotaru v. Romania* [GC], no. 28341/95, § 43, ECHR 2000-V; *S. and Marper v. the United Kingdom* [GC], nos 30562/04 and 30566/04, § 67, ECHR 2008; *Khelili v. Switzerland*, no. 16188/07, § 55, 18 October 2011; *M.M. v. the United Kingdom*, no. 24029/07, § 90, 13 November 2012.

1. Everyone has the right to the protection of personal data concerning him or her.
2. Such data must be processed fairly for specified purposes and on the basis of the consent of the person concerned or some other legitimate basis laid down by law. Everyone has the right of access to data which has been collected concerning him or her, and the right to have it rectified.
3. Compliance with these rules shall be subject to control by an independent authority.[214]

The right to private life protects individuals against disclosure of information concerning them that is in the possession of public authorities.[215] The counterpart of the protection of confidential data is its availability to the individual under appropriate circumstances. For example, according to the Court there is a positive obligation on the authorities to make a full, frank, and complete disclosure of the medical records of a deceased child to the latter's parents.[216]

To fall within the scope of article 8, the information or data in question need not be private in the sense that it is confidential. Where public information is systematically collected and stored in official files, article 8 may be engaged.[217] This includes information collected in public, such as photographs and other materials gathered and stored by security services.[218] Medical data brings with it special issues:

Respecting the confidentiality of health data is crucial not only for the protection of a patient's privacy but also for the maintenance of that person's confidence in the medical profession and in the health services in general. Without such protection, those in need of medical assistance may be deterred from seeking appropriate treatment, thereby endangering their own health.[219]

In a Polish case where the availability of legal abortion had stimulated considerable public interest, the hospital in question issued a press release about the situation and provided information to journalists. The hospital said it did not reveal the name of the individual concerned, but she was apparently readily identifiable and was in fact contacted by many people. For the Court, 'the fact that the issue of the availability of legal abortion in Poland is a subject of heated debate does not confer on the State a margin of appreciation so wide as to absolve the medical staff from their uncontested professional obligations regarding medical secrecy'.[220] The collection and storage of data by means of a satellite navigation device attached to a person's car has been held to constitute an interference with private life.[221]

Here the Court insists, as it does in other areas of private and family life, upon the existence of a proper legislative framework for the collection and protection of information and data of a personal nature. It is important to have 'minimum safeguards

[214] Charter of Fundamental Rights of the European Union, 2010 OJ C 83/02, art. 8.

[215] *C.C. v. Spain*, no. 1425/06, § 33, 6 October 2009.

[216] *Powell and Powell v. the United Kingdom* (dec.), no. 45305/99, ECHR 2000-V. Also *K.H. and Others v. Slovakia*, no. 32881/04, § 44, ECHR 2009.

[217] *Rotaru v. Romania* [GC], no. 28341/95, §§ 43, 47, ECHR 2000-V; *P.G. and J.H. v. the United Kingdom*, no. 44787/98, § 57, ECHR 2001-IX; *Segerstedt-Wiberg and Others v. Sweden*, no. 62332/00, § 72, ECHR 2006-VII; *Cemalettin Canlı v. Turkey*, no. 22427/04, § 33, 18 November 2008.

[218] *Peck v. the United Kingdom*, no. 44647/98, § 59, ECHR 2003-I; *P.G. and J.H. v. the United Kingdom*, no. 44787/98, §§ 57–59, ECHR 2001-IX.

[219] *P. and S. v. Poland*, no. 57375/08, § 128, 30 October 2012. See also *Z v. Finland*, 25 February 1997, §§ 95–96, *Reports of Judgments and Decisions* 1997-I; *Biriuk v. Lithuania*, no. 23373/03, § 43, 25 November 2008.

[220] *P. and S. v. Poland*, no. 57375/08, § 133, 30 October 2012.

[221] *Shimovolos v. Russia*, no. 30194/09, § 65, 21 June 2011; *Uzun v. Germany*, no. 35623/05, §§ 51–53, ECHR 2010 (extracts).

concerning, *inter alia*, duration, storage, usage, access of third parties, procedures for preserving the integrity and confidentiality of data and procedures for their destruction, thus providing sufficient guarantees against the risk of abuse and arbitrariness'.[222] The need for proper regulation is all the greater if data are processed automatically. According to the Court, there must be regulations to ensure that 'such data are relevant and not excessive in relation to the purposes for which they are stored; and preserved in a form which permits identification of the data subjects for no longer than is required for the purpose for which those data are stored'.[223] The importance of a regulatory framework is imposed both by the notion of the rule of law, which is in the background of every provision of the Convention, and by the requirement that any restrictions on private life be 'in accordance with law', as set out in article 8(2).

Information in the form of fingerprints, cellular samples, and DNA may be collected and retained for the purposes of prevention and detection of criminal activity. In this regard, '[t]he interests of the data subjects and the community as a whole in protecting the personal data, including fingerprint and DNA information, may be outweighed by the legitimate interest in the prevention of crime'.[224] Nevertheless, what the Court has called the 'intrinsically private character of this information' dictates careful scrutiny of any measures that authorize its retention and use without the consent of the individual concerned.[225] Information about minor forms of misconduct and criminal activity may be stored centrally and over time become forgotten by everyone involved, only to return inadvertently because of some form of automatic disclosure. Yet as this information 'recedes into the past, it becomes a part of the person's private life which must be respected'.[226] Thus, over time, data that was not part of a person's private life may become so. A requirement that persons convicted of sexual offences inform the police of their name, address, and other personal details falls within the scope of article 8.[227]

Honour and reputation

The thief of my purse steals trash, explains Iago in Shakespeare's Othello, 'but he that filches from me my good name/Robs me of that which not enriches him, And makes me poor indeed'.[228] Article 12 of the Universal Declaration of Human Rights, from which article 8 of the Convention is derived, provides explicit protection against attacks upon 'honour and reputation'. The absence of these words in article 8—apparently an intentional omission by the drafters—does not mean, however, that the matter is not comprised within the scope of private life. In particular, issues arise because of the tension between article 8 and article 10, where the freedom of the press is at stake. Perhaps somewhat surprisingly, it was only in 2004 that the Court explicitly recognized 'the right of the persons attacked . . . to protect their reputation, a right which is protected by Article 8 of

[222] *M.M. v. the United Kingdom*, no. 24029/07, § 95, 13 November 2012.
[223] *S. and Marper v. the United Kingdom* [GC], nos 30562/04 and 30566/04, § 103, ECHR 2008.
[224] Ibid., § 104.
[225] Ibid.
[226] *M.M. v. the United Kingdom*, no. 24029/07, § 194, 13 November 2012. Also *Khelili v. Switzerland*, no. 16188/07, § 68, 18 October 2011.
[227] *Adamson v. the United Kingdom* (dec.), no. 42293/98, 26 January 1999; *Gardel v. France*, no. 16428/05, § 58, ECHR 2009.
[228] *William Shakespeare, Othello, III.3, lines 155–161.*

the Convention as part of the right to respect for private life'.[229] Subsequently, it framed this as a positive obligation to protect the reputation of the individual.[230]

Threats to honour and reputation do not only result from media activity. In one case, the Court considered that a domestic judgment 'conveyed information to the effect that the High Court, having regard to the state of the evidence, held a suspicion that the applicant had sexually abused' his son. As an authoritative judicial decision, it was likely to carry great significance by the way it stigmatized him and was capable of having a major impact on his personal situation, as well as his honour and reputation, thereby engaging article 8.[231]

Not every attack on honour and reputation will amount to an interference with private and family life. The attack 'must attain a certain level of gravity and in a manner causing prejudice to personal enjoyment of the right to respect for private life'.[232] In another formulation, the Court said 'reputation had been deemed to be an independent right mostly when the factual allegations were of such a seriously offensive nature that their publication had an inevitable direct effect on the applicant's private life'.[233]

In a Slovakian case involving domestic violence, where the wife had attacked her husband, no criminal charge was laid because he refused to make a formal complaint. Then, the insurance company learned of the allegation from the police file and sought recovery of medical expenses from her. Noting that she had not been charged 'but was nevertheless placed on record as a criminal offender', the Court expressed its concern about 'the risk of stigmatisation of individuals stemming from such practices and the threat which they represent to the principle of the presumption of innocence'.[234] It added that 'the damage which may be caused to the reputation of the individual concerned through the communication of inaccurate or misleading information cannot be ignored'.[235] In one case it referred to the 'humiliation or injury' resulting from publication of articles, photographs, and video images of the applicant participating in sexual acts.[236]

Conviction for a crime in and of itself may impact upon a person's honour and reputation, but the Court has said that article 8 cannot be invoked to address the foreseeable consequences of one's actions such as perpetration of a criminal offence.[237] Distinguishing the judgment in *Laskey, Jaggard, and Brown*, where article 8 was held to apply in the context of a conviction for sado-masochistic activities, the Court noted that it was 'the result of an unforeseeable application of a provision of the criminal law'.[238]

Search and seizure

In the development of human rights law, the origin of the right to private life seems to be the protection against 'arbitrary search and seizure' set out in article 4 of the United States

[229] *Chauvy and Others v. France*, no. 64915/01, § 70, ECHR 2004-VI.
[230] *Pfeifer v. Austria*, no. 12556/03, § 38, ECHR 2007-XII.
[231] *Sanchez Cardenas v. Norway*, no. 12148/03, § § 33 and 38, 4 October 2007.
[232] *A. v. Norway*, no. 28070/06, § 64, 9 April 2009; *Sidabras and Džiautas v. Lithuania*, nos 55480/00 and 59330/00, § 49, ECHR 2004-VIII.
[233] *Mikolajová v. Slovakia*, no. 4479/03, § 55, 18 January 2011; *Karakó v. Hungary*, no. 39311/05, § 23, 28 April 2009; *Polanco Torres and Movilla Polanco v. Spain*, no. 34147/06, § 40, 21 September 2010.
[234] *Mikolajová v. Slovakia*, no. 4479/03, § 61, 18 January 2011. Also *S. and Marper v. the United Kingdom* [GC], nos 30562/04 and 30566/04, § 122, ECHR 2008.
[235] *Mikolajová v. Slovakia*, no. 4479/03, § 61, 18 January 2011.
[236] *Mosley v. the United Kingdom*, no. 48009/08, § 71, 10 May 2011.
[237] *Gillberg v. Sweden* [GC], no. 41723/06, §§ 67–68, 3 April 2012; *Sidabras and Džiautas v. Lithuania*, nos 55480/00 and 59330/00, § 49, ECHR 2004-VIII; *Mikolajová v. Slovakia*, no. 4479/03, § 57, 18 January 2011.
[238] *Gillberg v. Sweden* [GC], no. 41723/06, § 69, 10 May 2011.

Constitution. This is the foundation upon which the right to privacy in American law has been built. Article 12 of the Universal Declaration of Human Rights recognizes protection against search and seizure explicitly but the notion was removed by the drafters of article 8 of the European Convention on Human Rights. Nevertheless, there seems to be no doubt that the general formulation of article 8 encompasses a protection against 'arbitrary search and seizure'.[239]

In assessing whether domestic law and practice provide adequate and effective safeguards to protect against arbitrary search and seizure,[240] factors to be considered include whether the search was based on a warrant issued by a judge, grounded in reasonable suspicion, and of reasonably limited scope. The search of a lawyer's office requires the presence of an independent observer in order to protect the confidentiality of materials subject to professional secrecy.[241] The fact that the person subject to the search and seizure may subsequently be acquitted is of no consequence in assessing the search and seizure, whose reasonableness must be assessed at the time it is conducted or authorized.[242] The fact that a search takes place in public does not remove it from the scope of private life. Indeed, 'the public nature of the search may, in certain cases, compound the seriousness of the interference because of an element of humiliation and embarrassment. Items such as bags, wallets, notebooks and diaries may, moreover, contain personal information which the owner may feel uncomfortable about having exposed to the view of his companions or the wider public.'[243]

Prior judicial authorization of search and seizure may not always be possible. It is not contrary to article 8 provided that sufficient safeguards are in place to prevent abuse.[244] The Court will impose an enhanced level of scrutiny when searches are undertaken without prior judicial authorization, for example when a stop-and-search policy is imposed under specific circumstances.[245] In Amsterdam, the designation of certain areas where the authorities could do preventive searches essentially at random as a result of high levels of crime was justified by relevant and sufficient reasons and therefore necessary in a democratic society.[246]

Law enforcement authorities may use covert listening devices or 'bugs' in order to monitor conversations in a private residence or on the telephone. Clearly, issues relating to private life arise.[247] With respect to telephone conversations,[248] the Court has made a distinction between metering by the service provider, for billing and similar purposes,

[239] *Robathin v. Austria*, no. 30457/06, § 39, 3 July 2012; *Funke v. France*, 25 February 1993, § 48, Series A no. 256-A.
[240] *Société Colas Est and Others v. France*, no. 37971/97, § 48, ECHR 2002-III.
[241] *Niemietz v. Germany*, 16 December 1992, § 37, Series A no. 251-B; *Tamosius v. the United Kingdom* (dec.), no. 62002/00, ECHR 2002-VIII; *Wieser and Bicos Beteiligungen GmbH v. Austria*, no. 74336/01, § 57, ECHR 2007-IV.
[242] *Robathin v. Austria*, no. 30457/06, § 46, 3 July 2012.
[243] *Gillan and Quinton v. the United Kingdom*, no. 4158/05, § 63, ECHR 2010 (extracts).
[244] *Klass and Others v. Germany*, 6 September 1978, § 56, Series A no. 28; *Rotaru v. Romania* [GC], no. 28341/95, § 59, ECHR 2000-V.
[245] *Colon v. the Netherlands* (dec.), no. 49458/06, § 74, 15 May 2012; *Gillan and Quinton v. the United Kingdom*, no. 4158/05, §§ 83–86, ECHR 2010 (extracts).
[246] *Colon v. the Netherlands* (dec.), no. 49458/06, 15 May 2012.
[247] *P.G. and J.H. v. the United Kingdom*, no. 44787/98, § 37, ECHR 2001-IX.
[248] See: *Klass and Others v. Germany*, 6 September 1978, § 41, Series A no. 28; *Malone v. the United Kingdom*, 2 August 1984, § 64, Series A no. 82; *Lambert v. France*, 24 August 1998, § 21, *Reports of Judgments and Decisions* 1998-V.

which does not per se offend article 8, and use of telephone data by law enforcement officials for the purposes of investigation. Release to the police of information about numbers that were telephoned by the telephone provider constitutes an interference with the right to private life.[249] Nevertheless, although users of telecommunications and Internet services are entitled to the protection of their private lives, this may be limited when the resources themselves are used to violate the rights of others. In a Finnish case in which the Internet had been used for defamatory purposes, a legal impediment preventing the victim from uncovering the identity of the perpetrator was an interference with the rights protected by article 8.[250]

Monitoring and surveillance outside the home raise special issues. The Court has explained that because there are occasions 'when people knowingly or intentionally involve themselves in activities which are or may be recorded or reported in a public manner, a person's reasonable expectations as to privacy may be a significant, although not necessarily conclusive, factor' in establishing an interference with private life.[251] Thus, a person walking along the street is normally visible to all. Monitoring such a scene using technological means, such as closed-circuit television, 'is of a similar character'.[252] Article 8 only arises when a systematic, permanent record is made, such as video recording of public places[253] and surveillance using GPS,[254] because only then can the material that is gathered be made available subsequently to the general public.[255]

In the case of communications in the workplace by telephone or e-mail, and use of the Internet, employees may have a reasonable expectation of privacy.[256]

Environment

Issues concerning the environment have been addressed under article 8, where they may concern both private life and home. Cases have dealt with noise from nightclubs,[257] passing aircraft,[258] electric transformers,[259] wind turbines,[260] commercial and industrial establishments,[261] a military shooting range,[262] a bar,[263] a computer club,[264] ferries,[265] a

---

[249] *Malone v. the United Kingdom*, 2 August 1984, § 84, Series A no. 82.

[250] *K.U. v. Finland*, no. 2872/02, § 49, ECHR 2008.

[251] *Uzun v. Germany*, no. 35623/05, § 44, ECHR 2010 (extracts).

[252] Ibid.

[253] *Peck v. the United Kingdom*, no. 44647/98, §§ 57–63, ECHR 2003-I.

[254] *Uzun v. Germany*, no. 35623/05, §§ 48–52, ECHR 2010 (extracts).

[255] *Herbecq and the Association « Ligue des droits de l'homme » v. Belgium*, nos 32200/96 and 32201/96, Commission decision of 14 January 1998, (1998) 41 YB 60, DR 92-B, p. 92.

[256] *Copland v. the United Kingdom*, no. 62617/00, § 42, ECHR 2007-I; *Halford v. the United Kingdom*, 25 June 1997, § 45, *Reports of Judgments and Decisions* 1997-III.

[257] *Moreno Gómez v. Spain*, no. 4143/02, §§ 9–19, 45 and 58–60, ECHR 2004-X.

[258] *Hatton and Others v. the United Kingdom* [GC], no. 36022/97, §§ 11–27 and 116–18, ECHR 2003-VIII; *Ashworth and Others v. the United Kingdom* (dec.), no. 39561/98, 20 January 2004; *Arrondelle v. the United Kingdom*, no. 7889/77, Commission decision of 15 July 1980, (1980) 23 YB 166, DR 19, p. 186; *Baggs v. the United Kingdom*, no. 9310/81, Commission decision of 16 October 1985, DR 44, p. 13; *Rayner v. the United Kingdom*, no. 9310/81, Commission decision of 16 July 1986, DR 47, p. 5.

[259] *Ruano Morcuende v. Spain* (dec.), no. 75287/01, 6 September 2005.

[260] *Fägerskiöld v. Sweden* (dec.), no. 37664/04, 26 February 2008.

[261] *Leon and Agnieszka Kania v. Poland*, no. 12605/03, §§ 5 and 101–03, 21 July 2009; *Borysiewicz v. Poland*, no. 71146/01, §§ 5 and 52–55, 1 July 2008.

[262] *G. Vearncombe, W. Herbst, L. Clemens, and E. Spielhagen v. the United Kingdom and the Federal Republic of Germany*, no. 12816/87, Commission decision of 18 January 1989, (1989) 32 YB 74, DR 59, p. 186.

[263] *Oluić v. Croatia*, no. 61260/08, §§ 52–62, 20 May 2010.

[264] *Mileva and Others v. Bulgaria*, nos 43449/02 and 21475/04, § 97, 25 November 2010.

[265] *G.A. v. Sweden*, no. 12671/87, Commission decision of 13 March 1989.

nuclear power station,[266] road works,[267] and a dental clinic.[268] Several applications have concerned smells, attributable to such places as a waste-treatment plant,[269] a pigsty,[270] and a dump.[271] Where the municipal authorities in Italy failed to provide an adequate system of garbage collection, the Court concluded that there was a breach of article 8, even if the applicants could not demonstrate that this had consequences in terms of their own health.[272] Generally, such environmental issues will involve positive obligations, whereby the State is required to have an appropriate regulatory framework suitable of ensuring a safe and healthy environment.

The Court has used the term 'nuisance' to describe a variety of phenomena, involving noise, smell, and health hazards. For the matter to engage article 8, the alleged nuisance must attain 'the minimum level of severity required for it to amount to an interference with the applicants' rights to respect for their private lives and their homes'.[273] The assessment of that minimum is relative and depends on all the circumstances: 'the intensity and duration of the nuisance, its physical or mental effects, the general context, and whether the detriment complained of was negligible in comparison to the environmental hazards inherent to life in every modern city'.[274]

With respect to the environment, the Court has attached special importance to the right of the public to access information enabling it to assess the dangers to which it may be exposed.[275] Sometimes it has described this as the 'procedural aspect' of article 8.[276]

Family life

The notion of 'family' has an important place in international human rights law. The Universal Declaration of Human Rights describes the family as 'the natural and fundamental group unit of society', adding that it 'is entitled to protection by society and the State'.[277] In addition to the important reference in article 8, family is central to the right set out in article 12 of the European Convention on Human Rights: 'Men and women of marriageable age have the right to marry and to found a family, according to the national laws governing the exercise of this right.' The obligations with respect to the right to family life are both negative and positive in nature: 'States are under an obligation to "act

---

[266] *S. v. France*, no. 13728/88, Commission decision of 17 May 1990, DR 65, p. 250.
[267] *Deés v. Hungary*, no. 2345/06, § 24, 9 November 2010; *Trouche v. France*, no. 19867/92, Commission decision of 1 September 1993.
[268] *Galev and Others v. Bulgaria* (dec.), no. 18324/04, 29 December 2009.
[269] *López Ostra v. Spain*, 9 December 1994, §§ 7, 8, 49, 50, and 52, Series A no. 303-C.
[270] *Wałkuska v. Poland* (dec.), no. 6817/04, 29 April 2008.
[271] *Brânduşe v. Romania*, no. 6586/03, §§ 9–18, 66, and 67, 7 April 2009.
[272] *Di Sarno and Others v. Italy*, no. 30765/08, §§ 104–108, 10 January 2012.
[273] *Galev and Others v. Bulgaria* (dec.), no. 18324/04, 29 December 2009.
[274] *Mileva and Others v. Bulgaria*, nos 43449/02 and 21475/04, § 90, 25 November 2010; *Fadeyeva v. Russia*, no. 55723/00, §§ 66–70, ECHR 2005-IV.
[275] *Guerra and Others v. Italy*, 19 February 1998, § 60, *Reports of Judgments and Decisions* 1998-I; *Taşkın and Others v. Turkey*, no. 46117/99, § 119, ECHR 2004-X; *Giacomelli v. Italy*, no. 59909/00, § 83, ECHR 2006-XII; *Tătar v. Romania*, no. 67021/01, § 113, 27 January 2009; *Di Sarno and Others v. Italy*, no. 30765/08, § 113, 10 January 2012.
[276] *Di Sarno and Others v. Italy*, no. 30765/08, § 113, 10 January 2012; *Airey v. Ireland*, 9 October 1979, § 32, Series A no. 32; *Tysiąc v. Poland*, no. 5410/03, §§ 107–113, ECHR 2007-I; *A.M.M. v. Romania*, no. 2151/10, § 40, 14 February 2012; *Saleck Bardi v. Spain*, no. 66167/09, § 31, 24 May 2011; *A, B, and C v. Ireland* [GC], no. 25579/05, §§ 247–249, ECHR 2010; *V.C. v. Slovakia*, no. 18968/07, § 141, ECHR 2011 (extracts); *Koch v. Germany*, no. 497/09, § 65, 19 July 2012.
[277] Universal Declaration of Human Rights, GA Res. 217 A (III), UN Doc. A/810, art. 16(3).

in a manner calculated to allow those concerned to lead a normal family life".'[278] Although the suggestion in article 12 might be that 'family' is about monogamous relationships between persons of opposite sex focused upon procreation, it is obvious that such a narrow conception bears no resemblance to the immense diversity in form and content of modern families in contemporary Europe. But article 8 does not guarantee the right to found a family.[279] However, the Grand Chamber has found a violation of article 8 in the refusal of prison authorities to provide artificial insemination so that two people, one of whom was detained, could become genetic parents.[280]

The protection of family life presupposes the existence of a 'family'.[281] Family life is much broader than the relationship between a 'couple' with or without children. Early in its case law, the Court confirmed that a single mother and her child constituted a 'family'.[282] Similarly, 'family life' applies to the relationship between a single father and his adopted son.[283] In other words, despite the terms of article 12, which might be taken to imply that a man and a woman of marriageable age is the starting point for a 'family', nothing of the sort emerges from the Court's case law. Rejecting an objection *ratione materiae* from France, the Court recognized the existence of 'family life' between a father and his son-and-law.[284] Family life may also exist between siblings,[285] and between grandparents and grandchildren, although 'in normal circumstances the relationship between grandparents and grandchildren is different in nature and degree from the relationship between parent and child'.[286]

Whether or not 'family life' exists is a question of fact that depends upon the existence of close family ties.[287] The Court has said that 'the notion of "family life" in Article 8 is not confined solely to marriage-based relationships but may also encompass other *de facto* "family ties" where sufficient constancy is present'.[288] In determining whether a relationship amounts to 'family life' several factors may be considered, including whether a couple lives together, the length of their relationship, and whether they have demonstrated their commitment to each other by having children together or by any other means.[289] The fact that a marriage may not be in accordance with national legislation does not in any way

---

[278] *Popov v. France*, nos 39472/07 and 39474/07, § 102, 19 January 2012; *Marckx v. Belgium*, 13 June 1979, § 31, Series A no. 31.

[279] *Harroudj v. France*, no. 43631/09, § 41, 4 October 2012; *E.B. v. France* [GC], no. 43546/02, 22 January 2008.

[280] *Dickson v. the United Kingdom* [GC], no. 44362/04, § 66, ECHR 2007-V; *E.L.H. and P.B.H. v. the United Kingdom*, nos 32094/96 and 32568/96, Commission decision of 22 October 1997, DR 91-A, p. 61; *Kalashnikov v. Russia* (dec.), no. 47095/99, ECHR 2001-XI; *Aliev v. Ukraine*, no. 41220/98, § 187–89, 29 April 2003; *Evans v. the United Kingdom* [GC], no. 6339/05, § 71–72, ECHR 2007-I.

[281] *Marckx v. Belgium*, 13 June 1979, § 31, Series A no. 31.

[282] Ibid.

[283] *Negrepontis-Giannisis v. Greece*, no. 56759/08, § 55, 3 May 2011.

[284] *Mallah v. France*, no. 29681/08, § 31, 10 November 2011.

[285] *Moustaquim v. Belgium*, 18 February 1991, § 36, Series A no. 193; *Mustafa and Armağan Akın v. Turkey*, no. 4694/03, § 19, 6 April 2010.

[286] *Angela and Rodney Price v. the United Kingdom*, no. 12402/86, Commission decision of 9 March 1988, DR 55, p. 224. Also *Bronda v. Italy*, 9 June 1998, § 51, *Reports of Judgments and Decisions* 1998-IV.

[287] *K. and T. v. Finland* [GC], no. 25702/94, § 150, ECHR 2001-VII; *Mallah v. France*, no. 29681/08, § 29, 10 November 2011.

[288] *Krušković v. Croatia*, no. 46185/08, § 18, 21 June 2011; *Kroon and Others v. the Netherlands*, 27 October 1994, § 30, Series A no. 297-C.

[289] *Van der Heijden v. the Netherlands* [GC], no. 42857/05, § 50, 3 April 2012.

conflict with the existence of family life.[290] However, in a case where a prisoner corresponded with a woman outside the prison, meeting her in person on one occasion, followed by the engagement of the two, the European Commission considered that 'more substantial ties' were required for family life between the couple and the woman's children to exist.[291]

The Court initially resisted the idea that same-sex couples can invoke the protection of 'family life'.[292] Then, noting that 'rapid evolution of social attitudes towards same-sex couples has taken place in many member States', manifested in legislation giving legal recognition to the phenomenon within member States and the European Union, the Court said it was 'artificial to maintain the view that, in contrast to a different-sex couple, a same-sex couple cannot enjoy "family life" for the purposes of Article 8'. Therefore, 'a cohabiting same-sex couple living in a stable de facto partnership, falls within the notion of "family life", just as the relationship of a different-sex couple in the same situation would'.[293]

A child born from a relationship where the parties are living together 'out of wedlock' 'is ipso jure part of that "family" unit from the moment, and by the very fact, of the birth'.[294] Nevertheless, biological kinship between a natural parent and a child is insufficient to constitute family life as it is meant by article 8 in the absence of further legal or factual elements that indicate the existence of a close personal relationship.[295] Family life may also fall within the scope of article 8 even if it is only inchoate, notably when the fact that it has not crystallized is not attributable to the applicant.[296] It is not unknown for the father of a child to be denied access altogether. In such cases, the fact that a relationship has not yet developed does not exclude the protection by article 8 of the rights of the father to have meaningful contact with the child.

Cases have arisen in various countries as a result of a rather ancient rule, whose influence seems derived from its inclusion in the French *Code civil* whereby, when a woman is married, no man other than the husband can has legal standing to assert paternity:

Having regard to the realities of family life in the 21st century . . . the Court is not convinced that the best interest of children living with their legal father but having a different biological father can be truly determined by a general legal assumption. Consideration of what lies in the best interest of the child concerned is, however, of paramount importance in every case of this kind . . . Having regard to the great variety of family situations possibly concerned, the Court therefore considers that a fair balancing of the rights of all persons involved necessitates an examination of the particular circumstances of the case.[297]

Relevant factors would be the existence of a close personal relationship between the biological parents and a 'demonstrable interest in and commitment by the father . . .

---

[290] *Abdulaziz, Cabales and Balkandali v. the United Kingdom*, 28 May 1985, § 63, Series A no. 94.

[291] *Wakefield v. the United Kingdom*, no. 5817/89, Commission decision of 1 October 1990, DR 66, p. 251.

[292] *Mata Estevez v. Spain* (dec.), no. 56501/00, ECHR 2001-VI.

[293] *Vallianatos and Others v. Greece* [GC], nos 29381/09 and 32684/09, § 74, ECHR 2013; *Schalk and Kopf v. Austria*, no. 30141/04, §§ 93–94, ECHR 2010; *P.B. and J.S. v. Austria*, no. 18984/02, § 30, 22 July 2010.

[294] *Schneider v. Germany*, no. 17080/07, § 79, 15 September 2011; *Keegan v. Ireland*, 26 May 1994, § 44, Series A no. 290; *L. v. the Netherlands*, no. 45582/99, § 35, ECHR 2004-IV; *Znamenskaya v. Russia*, no. 77785/01, § 26, 2 June 2005.

[295] *Schneider v. Germany*, no. 17080/07, § 80, 15 September 2011.

[296] *Pini and Others v. Romania*, nos 78028/01 and 78030/01, §§ 143 and 146, ECHR 2004-V.

[297] *Schneider v. Germany*, no. 17080/07, § 100, 15 September 2011.

before and after the birth'.[298] In a Maltese case where the presumption of paternity prevented the husband of the mother who was determined by DNA testing not to be the father, the Court questioned the Government's argument that 'such a radical restriction of the applicant's right to institute proceedings to deny paternity was "necessary in a democratic society". In particular, it has not been shown why society as a whole would benefit from such a situation.'[299] It said the interest of the child in enjoying the 'social reality' of being the presumed father's child could not outweigh the latter's legitimate right to have the opportunity to contest paternity. It said that 'a situation in which a legal presumption is allowed to prevail over biological reality might not be compatible, even having regard to the margin of appreciation left to the State, with the obligation to secure effective "respect" for private and family life'.[300]

Close relationships that fall short of 'family life' will be entitled to protection within the scope of 'private life' rather than 'family life'.[301] The determination of the legal relationship between a man and a child where paternity is contested may involve 'family life', but it most certainly involves 'private life', and it is under that heading that the Court has generally addressed the issue.[302] Inheritance rights are closely linked to family life and fall under the scope of article 8.[303]

Relationships between parents and their children

The mutual enjoyment by parent and child of each other's company is 'a fundamental element of "family life" within the meaning of Article 8 of the Convention'.[304] When they are separated, parents have a right to be reunited with their children, with a corresponding obligation on the State to facilitate such a reunion.[305] However, the fact that the family is united does not mean that family life is assured, in particular if it is detained as a unit. The detention of a family in difficult conditions may be an interference with the right to family life under article 8 of the Convention.[306]

The right is not absolute, however, and there may well be circumstances where family life does not entitle one or another of the parents, or both of them, to be together with their children. Nevertheless, 'restrictions placed by the domestic authorities on parental

---

[298] Ibid., §§ 81, 84, 87–90; *Nylund v. Finland* (dec.), no. 27110/95, ECHR 1999-VI; *Nekvedavicius v. Germany* (dec.), no. 46165/99, 19 June 2003; *L. v. the Netherlands*, no. 45582/99; *Hülsmann v. Germany* (dec.), no. 33375/03, 18 March 2008; *Anayo v. Germany*, no. 20578/07, 21 December 2010; *Różański v. Poland*, no. 55339/00, § 64, 18 May 2006.

[299] *Mizzi v. Malta*, no. 26111/02, § 112, ECHR 2006-I (extracts).

[300] Ibid., § 113.

[301] *Schneider v. Germany*, no. 17080/07, § 82, 15 September 2011; *Znamenskaya v. Russia*, no. 77785/01, § 27, 2 June 2005.

[302] *Rasmussen v. Denmark*, 28 November 1984, § 33, Series A no. 87; *Nylund v. Finland* (dec.), no. 27110/95, ECHR 1999-VI; *Yildirim v. Austria* (dec.), no. 34308/96, 19 October 1999; *Backlund v. Finland*, no. 36498/05, § 37, 6 July 2010; *Schneider v. Germany*, no. 17080/07, § 82, 15 September 2011.

[303] *Negrepontis-Giannisis v. Greece*, no. 56759/08, § 55, 3 May 2011; *Marckx v. Belgium*, 13 June 1979, § 51, Series A no. 31.

[304] *Gluhaković v. Croatia*, no. 21188/09, § 54, 12 April 2011; *Monory v. Romania and Hungary*, no. 71099/01, § 70, 5 April 2005; *Fuşcă v. Romania*, no. 34630/07, § 32, 13 July 2010; *Olsson v. Sweden (no. 1)*, 24 March 1988, § 59, Series A no. 130; *Popov v. France*, nos 39472/07 and 39474/07, § 103, 19 January 2012; *M. and C. v. Romania*, no. 29032/04, § 125, 27 September 2011; *Eriksson v. Sweden*, 22 June 1989, § 58, Series A no. 156.

[305] *Ignaccolo-Zenide v. Romania*, no. 31679/96, § 94, ECHR 2000-I; *Nuutinen v. Finland*, no. 32842/96, § 127, ECHR 2000-VIII; *Iglesias Gil and A.U.I. v. Spain*, no. 56673/00, § 49, ECHR 2003-V; *Shaw v. Hungary*, no. 6457/09, § 64, 26 July 2011.

[306] *Popov v. France*, nos 39472/07 and 39474/07, § 103, 19 January 2012.

rights of access call for strict scrutiny as they entail the danger that the family relations between a young child and a parent will be effectively curtailed'.[307] Splitting up a family 'is an interference of a very serious order' and it 'must be supported by sufficiently sound and weighty considerations in the interests of the child'.[308]

Difficulties arise in this respect when there are disputes about custody and access between the parents and sometimes with other members of the child's family,[309] as well as when children are removed from their parents and taken into public care.[310] The natural family relationship is not terminated simply because the child has been taken into public care.[311] Sometimes there is an international dimension, with parents and children separated as a consequence of abduction[312] or the vagaries of immigration legislation. The paramount factor must be the best interest of the child.[313] Depending upon their nature and seriousness, the best interests of the child may prevail over that of the parents.[314] Assessing the child's best interests involves a number of factors and circumstances, notably the age and level of maturity, the wishes of the child, the presence or absence of the parents, and the environment and experiences.[315] It in the child's best interests that ties with his family be maintained except in cases where the family has proved particularly unfit and it is in the child's best interests to ensure his or her development in a safe and secure environment.[316] The Court has taken international conventions, especially the Convention on the Rights of the Child, into consideration in examining the issue of the best interests of the child.[317]

Making assessments and determinations about the best interests of the child is not an exact science. Those with responsibility to protect children who make such judgments and assessments 'cannot be held liable every time genuine and reasonably held concerns about the safety of children vis-à-vis members of their family are proved, retrospectively, to have been misguided'.[318] As for the Court, it can rarely go much beyond the procedural

---

[307] *Schneider v. Germany*, no. 17080/07, § 94, 15 September 2011; *Elsholz v. Germany* [GC], no. 25735/94, §§ 48–49, ECHR 2000-VIII; *Sommerfeld v. Germany* [GC], no. 31871/96, §§ 62–63, ECHR 2003-VIII (extracts); *A.D. and O.D. v. the United Kingdom*, no. 28680/06, § 83, 16 March 2010; *T.P. and K.M. v. the United Kingdom* [GC], no. 28945/95, §§ 71–72, ECHR 2001-V (extracts).

[308] *M. and C. v. Romania*, no. 29032/04, § 124, 27 September 2011; *Olsson v. Sweden (no. 1)*, 24 March 1988, § 72, Series A no. 130.

[309] *Hokkanen v. Finland*, 23 September 1994, § 55, Series A no. 299.

[310] *Olsson v. Sweden (no. 2)*, 27 November 1992, § 90, Series A no. 250.

[311] *M. and C. v. Romania*, no. 29032/04, § 125, 27 September 2011; *Eriksson v. Sweden*, 22 June 1989, § 58, Series A no. 156.

[312] In the area of international child abduction, particular account is to be given to the provisions of the Hague Convention on the Civil Aspects of International Child Abduction, (1983) 1343 UNTS 98: *V.P. v. Russia*, no. 61362/12, § 129, 23 October 2014; *Ignaccolo-Zenide v. Romania*, no. 31679/96, § 95, ECHR 2000-I; *Karrer v. Romania*, no. 16965/10, § 41, 21 February 2012; *Maire v. Portugal*, no. 48206/99, § 72, ECHR 2003-VII; *Šneersone and Kampanella v. Italy*, no. 14737/09, § 85(ii), 12 July 2011; *B. v. Belgium*, no. 4320/11, § 56, 10 July 2012. The Court is 'competent to ascertain whether the domestic court, in applying and interpreting the Hague Convention, secured the guarantees set forth in Article 8 of the Convention': *X v. Latvia*, no. 27853/09, § 68, 13 December 2011.

[313] *Yousef v. the Netherlands*, no. 33711/96, § 73.

[314] *Sommerfeld v. Germany* [GC], no. 31871/96, § 66, ECHR 2003-VIII (extracts); *Görgülü v. Germany*, no. 74969/01, § 43, 26 February 2004; *Hokkanen v. Finland*, 23 September 1994, § 55, Series A no. 299-A.

[315] *Šneersone and Kampanella v. Italy*, no. 14737/09, § 84(v), 12 July 2011; *Y.C. v. the United Kingdom*, no. 4547/10, § 135, 13 March 2012.

[316] *Y.C. v. the United Kingdom*, no. 4547/10, § 134, 13 March 2012.

[317] *Popov v. France*, nos 39472/07 and 39474/07, § 116, 19 January 2012.

[318] *A.D. and O.D. v. the United Kingdom*, no. 28680/06, § 84, 16 March 2010; *R.K. and A.K. v. the United Kingdom*, no. 38000/05, § 36, 30 September 2008.

dimension, striving to ensure that the process of determining the right of the parties under national law is fair, and not arbitrary.[319] It must ascertain 'whether the domestic courts conducted an in-depth examination of the entire family situation and of a whole series of factors, in particular of a factual, emotional, psychological, material and medical nature, and made a balanced and reasonable assessment of the respective interests of each person'.[320] The Court is poorly equipped for the task, given the notorious length of proceedings in Strasbourg. Because children grow and evolve both physically and emotionally, meaningful determinations concerning access and custody must be made very quickly, indeed too quickly for the Court to react in a useful way. To take one example, in July 2011 a Chamber of the European Court of Human Rights declared that a June 2006 order of the Rome Youth Court giving custody to the father of a child, and ordering the return from Latvia where he had been taken by the mother in mid-2005, was in breach of article 8. When the impugned judgment was issued, the child was about four years old; by the time the European Court responded by affirming his rights and those of his mother under the Convention, he was nine.[321] Indeed, the Court itself has acknowledged that 'time is of the essence' in its oversight of national institutions: '[T]he adequacy of a measure is to be judged by the swiftness of its implementation, as the passage of time can have irremediable consequences for relations between the child and the parent who does not live with the child.'[322]

In contrast with custody and access disputes driven by the parents and relatives, when public authorities intervene to protect and sometimes remove children from their parents there must be a strong presumption that they are attempting to implement the best interests of the child. There is no debate in such cases about the existence of an interference with family life, which is obvious.[323] The principles for assessing whether the interference can be justified are essentially the same as in access and custody cases; that is, the grounds invoked by the authorities for the restriction must be shown to be 'relevant and sufficient' and the decision-making process must be fair, affording due respect for the rights of the applicant.[324] In determining the margin of appreciation, the Court normally distinguishes between infringements that are attributable to the State and those resulting from the acts of other individuals, whose rights must also be considered in striking the right balance. It does not seem to do this here, however, perhaps because of the overwhelming importance of the 'best interests of the child'.

Beyond limitations on access to children, there are more extreme forms of separation that may break the link altogether and permanently, including removal of parental rights

[319] *Ignaccolo-Zenide v. Romania*, no. 31679/96, § 99, ECHR 2000-I; *Tiemann v. France and Germany* (dec.), nos 47457/99 and 47458/99, ECHR 2000-IV.
[320] *Karrer v. Romania*, no. 16965/10, § 40, 21 February 2012; *Neulinger and Shuruk v. Switzerland* [GC], no. 41615/07, § 139, ECHR 2010.
[321] *Šneersone and Kampanella v. Italy*, no. 14737/09, 12 July 2011.
[322] *Gluhaković v. Croatia*, no. 21188/09, § 59, 12 April 2011; *Ignaccolo-Zenide v. Romania*, no. 31679/96, § 102, ECHR 2000-I; *Karrer v. Romania*, no. 16965/10, § 54, 21 February 2012; *Shaw v. Hungary*, no. 6457/09, § 66, 26 July 2011.
[323] *M.D. and Others v. Malta*, no. 64791/10, § 73, 17 July 2012; *Y.C. v. the United Kingdom*, no. 4547/10, § 130, 13 March 2012; *Sabou and Pircalab v. Romania*, no. 46572/99, § 46, 28 September 2004.
[324] *K. and T. v. Finland* [GC], no. 25702/94, § 154, ECHR 2001-VII; *R.K. and A.K. v. the United Kingdom*, no. 38000/05, § 34, 30 September 2008; *T.S. and D.S. v. the United Kingdom* (dec.), no. 61540/09, 19 January 2010; *A.D. and O.D. v. the United Kingdom*, no. 28680/06, § 82, 16 March 2010; *Neulinger and Shuruk v. Switzerland* [GC], no. 41615/07, § 134, ECHR 2010; *R. and H. v. the United Kingdom*, no. 35348/06, §§ 75 and 81, 31 May 2011.

and, ultimately, adoption. Removal of parental rights is 'a particularly far-reaching measure which deprives a parent of his or her family life with the child and is inconsistent with the aim of reuniting them'. Such measures are only to be applied in 'exceptional circumstances and can only be justified if they are motivated by an overriding requirement pertaining to the child's best interests'.[325] In a case where deprivation was an automatic consequence of a conviction for a serious crime, the Court felt that the absence of access to a court to challenge or review the matter in the future failed to strike a fair balance between the interests of the child, the applicant, and society at large.[326]

Adoption entails a permanent rupture in the bond between natural parents and their offspring. Any decision in this area must be taken in the best interests of the child. Once adoption has been completed, the relationship between the child and the adopting parents becomes one contemplated by 'family life' and subject to article 8.[327] From the standpoint of the Convention, a child who has been adopted is in the same legal position as if he or she were the natural or biological child of the adopting parents.[328] Refusal by the courts to recognize a foreign judgment of adoption constitutes an interference with family life.[329] Nevertheless, article 8 does not provide a right to adopt.[330] Likewise, it does not provide a right of an adopting parent to bring an end to the adoption.[331]

Some intermediate forms of adoption where the link with the biological parents is not entirely broken exist within certain legal systems. One of these is *kefala*, a type of Islamic adoption. The European Court of Human Rights has welcomed attempts to use such a system as a way to encourage the integration of children of foreign origin, thereby respecting cultural pluralism and balancing the public interest.[332] In adoption matters, the interpretation of article 8 is to be guided by the special provisions in the United Nations Convention on the Rights of the Child.[333]

Expulsion and deportation

Article 8 has been applied in many cases involving non-citizens who have invoked its provisions as a basis for a right to remain in the country. In principle, only a citizen has the right to remain within a country unconditionally.[334] The Convention does not ensure an

---

[325] *M.D. and Others v. Malta*, no. 64791/10, § 76, 17 July 2012; *Sabou and Pircalab v. Romania*, no. 46572/99, § 47, 28 September 2004; *Johansen v. Norway*, 7 August 1996, §§ 64, 78, *Reports of Judgments and Decisions* 1996-III.

[326] *M.D. and Others v. Malta*, no. 64791/10, § 79, 17 July 2012,

[327] *Negrepontis-Giannisis v. Greece*, no. 56759/08, § 55, 3 May 2011.

[328] *Pla and Puncernau v. Andorra*, no. 69498/01, § 61, ECHR 2004-VIII.

[329] *Negrepontis-Giannisis v. Greece*, no. 56759/08, §§ 60, 75–76, 3 May 2011; *Wagner and J.M.W.L. v. Luxembourg*, no. 76240/01, § 210, 28 June 2007.

[330] *Harroudj v. France*, no. 43631/09, § 41, 4 October 2012; *Fretté v. France*, no. 36515/97, § 32, ECHR 2002-I; *E.B. v. France* [GC], no. 43546/02, § 41, 22 January 2008; *Pini and Others v. Romania*, nos 78028/01 and 78030/01, §§ 140 and 142, ECHR 2004-V (extracts). On human rights and adoption generally, see the Issue Paper published by the Commissioner on Human Rights of the Council of Europe: Adoption and Children: A Human Rights Perspective, CommDH/IssuePaper(2011)2.

[331] *Goția v. Romania* (dec.), no. 24315/06, § 35, 5 October 2010.

[332] *Harroudj v. France*, no. 43631/09, § 51, 4 October 2012. But see *Chbihi Loudoudi and Others v. Belgium*, no. 52265/10, §§ 94–105, 16 December 2014.

[333] *Pini and Others v. Romania*, nos 78028/01 and 78030/01, § 139, ECHR 2004-V (extracts); *Goția v. Romania* (dec.), no. 24315/06, § 32, 5 October 2010. See Convention on the Rights of the Child, (1990) 1577 UNTS 3, arts. 20, 21.

[334] *Kane v. Cyprus* (dec.), no. 33655/06, 13 September 2011; *H. v. the Netherlands* (dec.), no. 37833/10, 18 October 2011; *Djokaba Lambi Longa v. the Netherlands* (dec.), no. 33917/12, § 81, 9 October 2012.

absolute right for any category of non-citizen not to be removed from the country. However, that does not mean that expulsion of a non-citizen (or alien) cannot result, depending upon the circumstances, in a breach of article 8. The case law of the Court is replete with examples.[335]

International law recognizes the right of refugees to protection against *refoulement* but that is not the same thing at all as a right to remain within the country of asylum. As the European Court has often pointed out, 'a State is entitled, as a matter of international law and subject to its treaty obligations, to control the entry of aliens into its territory and their residence there'.[336] Furthermore, nothing in the Convention guarantees a non-citizen the right to enter or reside in a particular country. Although article 14(1) of the Universal Declaration of Human Rights recognizes the right of everyone 'to seek and enjoy in other countries asylum from persecution', there is no echo of this provision in the European Convention.[337]

Expulsion cases arise in a number of circumstances. Sometimes it is the country to which the individual is being expelled that presents a problem because of the threat of torture or inhuman or degrading treatment, or of a violation of the right to life or a flagrant abuse of the right to a fair trial.[338] Such cases will generally be dealt with pursuant to articles 2, 3, and 6. Cases of refugees in the sense of the 1951 Convention on the Status of Refugees and its Protocol also involve concerns about the country of origin. It must be shown that there is a well-founded fear of persecution for reasons of race, religion, nationality, membership of a particular social group, or political opinion if the asylum seeker is returned. Special mechanisms exist in all European countries for the implementation of obligations under international refugee law. The European Court provides a level of subsidiary or complementary protection for individuals who find themselves unprotected because of various limitations in refugee law.

Many migrants who have settled in a European country may find themselves threatened with expulsion because they have lost their legal entitlement to remain. This may be the consequence of criminal activity. It may also result from some other infringement of the legal framework governing residence within the country. In some cases, where citizenship is not automatically the right of a person born in the country but rather depends upon the nationality of the parents, someone who has lived their entire life in a European country may be threatened with expulsion. The Parliamentary Assembly of the Council of Europe has recommended that long-term migrants who were born or raised in the host country not be expelled under any circumstances.[339] The Court has not taken such an inflexible position, and has sometimes found that there is no violation of article 8 when, as a result of criminal activity, a person born in Europe is expelled to a country even if the connections with it are very limited.[340]

---

[335] *Moustaquim v. Belgium*, 18 February 1991, Series A no. 193; *Beldjoudi v. France*, 26 March 1992, Series A no. 234-A; *Boultif v. Switzerland*, no. 54273/00, ECHR 2001-IX; *Amrollahi v. Denmark*, no. 56811/00, 11 July 2002; *Yilmaz v. Germany*, no. 52853/99, 17 April 2003; *Keles v. Germany*, 32231/02, 27 October 2005.

[336] *Abdulaziz, Cabales, and Balkandali v. the United Kingdom*, 28 May 1985, § 67, Series A no. 94; *Boujlifa v. France*, 21 October 1997, § 42, *Reports of Judgments and Decisions* 1997-VI; *Nunez v. Norway*, no. 55597/09, § 66, 28 June 2011.

[337] *Vilvarajah and Others v. the United Kingdom*, 30 October 1991, § 102, Series A no. 215; *Chahal v. The United Kingdom*, 15 November 1996, § 73, *Reports of Judgments and Decisions* 1996-V.

[338] *Soering v. the United Kingdom*, 7 July 1989, § 113, Series A no. 161.

[339] Recommendation 1504 (2001). See also Rec(2000)15 of the Committee of Ministers.

[340] *Mutlag v. Germany*, no. 40601/05, 25 March 2010.

In all of these cases, issues may arise with respect to private and family life. Most of the litigation has focused on family life because the expulsion disrupts the family relationship. However, even where there are no substantial family ties, other attachments to the country may be examined under the heading of private life. That is because article 8 also protects the right 'to establish and develop relationships with other human beings and the outside world and can sometimes embrace aspects of an individual's social identity [and] it must be accepted that the totality of social ties between settled migrants and the community in which they are living constitutes part of the concept of "private life"'.[341] In practice, the analysis conducted by the Court will be the same. Although exceptionally, the State may be unable to show that the measure was provided by law or pursued a legitimate aim, in the vast majority of cases the issue will be the necessity of the expulsion and whether it was proportionate to the aim pursued.

If the commission of criminal offences in the home State is the justification for expulsion, the relevant considerations in making such determinations were set out in 2001 in *Boultif v. Switzerland* and have become known as the '*Boultif* criteria':

- the nature and seriousness of the offence committed by the applicant;
- the length of the applicant's stay in the country from which he or she is to be expelled;
- the time elapsed since the offence was committed and the applicant's conduct during that period;
- the nationalities of the various persons concerned;
- the applicant's family situation, such as the length of the marriage, and other factors expressing the effectiveness of a couple's family life;
- whether the spouse knew about the offence at the time when he or she entered into a family relationship;
- whether there are children of the marriage, and if so, their age; and
- the seriousness of the difficulties which the spouse is likely to encounter in the country to which the applicant is to be expelled.[342]

There are additional factors in non-criminal cases, such as those involving issues of immigration status and regulation, including whether there are insurmountable obstacles in the way of the family living in the country of origin of one or more of them and whether there are factors of immigration control (for example, a history of breaches of immigration law) or other considerations of public order weighing in favour of exclusion.[343] Subsequent case law has added some precision and developed new dimensions to this, especially in terms of the strength of social, cultural, and family ties with the European state by comparison with the country of destination and the role of the best interests of children affected by the measure.

The Court has said that 'it will be a rare case where a settled migrant will be unable to demonstrate that his or her deportation would interfere with his or her private life as

[341] *A.A. v. the United Kingdom*, no. 8000/08, § 49, 20 September 2011; *Samsonnikov v. Estonia*, no. 52178/10, § 82, 3 July 2012.
[342] *Boultif v. Switzerland*, no. 54273/00, § 48, ECHR 2001-IX; *Üner v. the Netherlands* [GC], no. 46410/99, § 57, ECHR 2006-XII; *Samsonnikov v. Estonia*, no. 52178/10, § 86, 3 July 2012.
[343] *Nunez v. Norway*, no. 55597/09, § 83, 28 June 2011; *Ajayi and Others v. the United Kingdom* (dec.), no. 27663/95, 22 June 1999; *Solomon v. the Netherlands* (dec.), no. 44328/98, 5 September 2000.

guaranteed by Article 8'.[344] This is mainly because 'the totality of social ties between settled migrants such as the applicant and the community in which they are living constitutes part of the concept of "private life" within the meaning of Article 8.'[345] Thus, while family ties are very important and are emphasized in the *Boultif* criteria, other factors concerning general integration into European society are of great significance.

The fact that the individual was born in the host country or moved there at an early age is important.[346] In a Danish case, a young person of Somali origin had moved to Denmark with her family, where she had a residence permit. She had spent much of her life, from about seven to fifteen, in Denmark, had attended school there, spoke the language, and had important family ties in the country. When she was fifteen, her father took her to Kenya in order to care for her grandmother, who was in a refugee camp, and the applicant remained there for more than two years. When she sought to return, the Danish authorities refused to renew her residence permit. The Court held that 'it cannot be said that the applicant's interests have sufficiently been taken into account in the authorities' refusal to reinstate her residence permit in Denmark or that a fair balance was struck between the applicants' interests on the one hand and the State's interest in controlling immigration on the other'.[347] As the Grand Chamber said in another case, 'it is self-evident that the Court will have regard to the special situation of aliens who have spent most, if not all, their childhood in the host country, were brought up there and received their education there'.[348]

Although family ties are not essential, and the issue of expulsion can be addressed solely from the standpoint of private life, in practice it is almost invariably an important aspect of the case. There has been considerable debate about the nature of the family ties. The Court has held that 'family life' cannot be invoked by adults who do not belong to the 'core family' and who have not been dependent members of the applicants' family.[349] However, there are many cases concerning relatively young adults who base their claims on relationships with their parents and siblings and who are apparently not fully autonomous with families of their own making. In a deportation case concerning a 20-year-old who lived with his mother, step-father, and siblings, the Court accepted the existence of 'family life'.[350] It made the same finding with an applicant who was 28 years old when proceedings began. He had moved to France at the age of five, where his parents and siblings also lived, and had resided there all his life with the exception of a period of imprisonment in Switzerland.[351] Some cases have required evidence of an 'additional

---

[344] *A.H. Khan v. the United Kingdom*, no. 6222/10, § 32, 20 December 2011; *Miah v. the United Kingdom* (dec.), no. 53080/07, § 17, 27 April 2010.

[345] *Maslov v. Austria* [GC], no. 1638/03, § 63, ECHR 2008; *Üner v. the Netherlands* [GC], no. 46410/99, § 59, ECHR 2006-XII.

[346] *Mokrani v. France*, no. 52206/99, § 31, 15 July 2003.

[347] *Osman v. Denmark*, no. 38058/09, § 77, 14 June 2011.

[348] *Üner v. the Netherlands* [GC], no. 46410/99, § 58, ECHR 2006-XII.

[349] *Slivenko v. Latvia* [GC], no.48321/99, §97, ECHR 2003-X; *Kwakye-Nti and Dufie v. the Netherlands* (dec.), no. 31519/96, 7 November 2000; *A.W. Khan v. the United Kingdom*, no. 47486/06, § 32, 12 January 2010; *Anam v. the United Kingdom* (dec.), no. 21783/08, 7 June 2011.

[350] *Bouchelkia v. France*, 29 January 1997, §41, *Reports of Judgments and Decisions* 1997-I. Also *Maslov v. Austria* [GC], no. 1638/03, § 62, ECHR 2008; *Bousarra v. France*, no. 25672/07, §§ 38–39, 23 September 2010.

[351] *Boujlifa v. France*, 21 October 1997, § 36, *Reports of Judgments and Decisions* 1997-VI.

element of dependence' in order to recognize the strength of 'family life' of adults and their parents.[352] If 'family life' was created at a time when those involved were aware of the uncertain immigration status and therefore the precarious nature of the relationship,[353] exceptional circumstances will be required for the Court to hold that there has been a breach of article 8.[354]

In *Nunez v. Norway*, there was nothing compelling about the applicant's objection to expulsion, as she had repeatedly lied on her applications. But she had given birth to two minor children in Norway and it was the best interests of these children that tipped the balance in her favour. In this respect, the Court has created indirect rights for children that protect their parents from expulsion. Two dissenting judges expressed concern 'that this case will send the wrong signal, namely that persons who are illegally in a country can somehow contrive to have their residence "legitimised" through the expedient of marriage and of having children'.[355]

Imprisonment of parents

Detention or other measures depriving an individual of freedom necessarily entails limitations on private and family life. Nevertheless, 'it is an essential part of a detainee's right to respect for family life that the authorities enable him or, if need be, assist him, in maintaining contact with his close family'.[356] The State may impose limitations on the number of visits and may require that they be supervised, possibly taking into account the nature of the offence, but this interference with 'family life' must meet the tests imposed by article 8(2) of the Convention.[357]

In an Italian case, two family visits per month were not deemed to violate article 8.[358] But a prisoner in Ukraine, who was allowed a supervised visit of a few hours every three months for three family members, whereas he had a close 'inner' family of four people, was held by the Court to be contrary to the Convention.[359] Extenuating circumstances, such as the presence of organized crime, may dictate more limited access rights. The Court has explained that 'given the specific nature of the phenomenon of organised crime, particularly of the Mafia type, and the fact that family visits have frequently served as a means of conveying orders and instructions to the outside, the —admittedly substantial— restrictions on visits, and the accompanying controls, could not be said to be disproportionate to the legitimate aims pursued'.[360]

---

[352] *Slivenko v. Latvia* [GC], no. 48321/99, §97, ECHR 2003-X; *Onur v. the United Kingdom*, no. 27319/07, §§ 43–45, 17 February 2009; *A.W. Khan v. the United Kingdom*, no. 47486/06, § 32, 12 January 2010.

[353] *Jerry Olajide Sarumi v. the United Kingdom* (dec.), no. 43279/98, 26 January 1999; *Sheabashov v. Latvia* (dec.), no. 50065/99, 22 May 1999.

[354] *Nunez v. Norway*, no. 55597/09, § 70, 28 June 2011; *Abdulaziz, Cabales and Balkandali v. the United Kingdom*, 28 May 1985, § 68, Series A no. 94; *Mitchell v. the United Kingdom* (dec.), no. 40447/98, 24 November 1998; *Ajayi and Others v. the United Kingdom* (dec.), no. 27663/95, 22 June 1999; *Rodrigues da Silva and Hoogkamer v. the Netherlands*, no. 50435/99, § 39, ECHR 2006.

[355] *Nunez v. Norway*, no. 55597/09, Joint Dissenting Opinion of Judges Mojović and De Gaetano, 28 June 2011.

[356] *Trosin v. Ukraine*, no. 39758/05, § 39, 23 February 2012.

[357] *Moiseyev v. Russia*, no. 62936/00, § 246, 9 October 2008.

[358] *Messina v. Italy (no. 2)*, no. 25498/94, §§ 62–74, ECHR 2000-X.

[359] *Trosin v. Ukraine*, no. 39758/05, § 47, 23 February 2012.

[360] *Enea v. Italy* [GC], no. 74912/01, § 126, ECHR 2009; *Salvatore v. Italy* (dec.), no. 42285/98, 7 May 2002; *Bastone v. Italy* (dec.), no. 59638/00, ECHR 2005-II.

Home

The 'home' that is protected by article 8 is an autonomous notion. It is not dependent upon the qualification of the term in domestic law.[361] The notion of home is defined with respect to factual circumstances, in particular the existence of sufficient, continuous links with a given location.[362] It is also independent of the lawfulness of the occupation of the premises under domestic law, applying for example to improvised or makeshift accommodation[363] and to non-traditional residences such as caravans or trailers.[364] It is closely related to the other categories protected by article 8 because the home is normally the physical space where private and family life develops.[365] The actual address of the 'home' is protected as a component of private life. Revealing the address of a public personality in a national newspaper was a violation both of privacy and home.[366]

The French version of the Convention, where the word *domicile* is employed, has a 'broader connotation than the word "home" and may extend, for example, to a professional person's office'.[367] Despite a European Court of Justice ruling that article 8 of the European Convention is not applicable to business premises,[368] the European Court of Human Rights ruled that it applied to an office because 'it is not always possible to distinguish clearly which of an individual's activities form part of his professional or business life and which do not'.[369] In the case of corporate entities, they seem to be able to invoke the concept of 'home' to their business premises.[370] However, the Court has refused to apply the notion to a laundry that did not serve as a residence.[371] It was dubious about whether 'home' might extend to an orchestra conductor's dressing room.[372]

Article 8 not only protects the physical existence of the 'home', it also ensures a quality of life that involves peaceful enjoyment.[373] Many issues have arisen concerning various forms of nuisance that disrupt the peaceful enjoyment of home. These are also considered earlier in this chapter under the heading 'Environment'. The occupant of a home may or may not be its owner. Where the occupant also owns the property where his or her home is located, problems related to peaceful enjoyment may be raised under both article 8 of

---

[361] *Buckley v. the United Kingdom*, no. 20348/92, § 63, Commission report of 11 January 1995; *Prokopovich v. Russia*, no. 58255/00, § 36, ECHR 2004-XI (extracts); *Gillow v. the United Kingdom*, 24 November 1986, § 46, Series A no. 109.

[362] *Hartung v. Germany* (dec.), no. 10231/07, 3 November 2009; *Prokopovitch v. Russia*, no. 58255/00, § 36, ECHR 2004-XI; *Chelu v. Romania*, no. 40274/04, § 43, 12 January 2010.

[363] *Yordanova and Others v. Bulgaria*, no. 25446/06, § 103, 24 April 2012; *McCann v. the United Kingdom*, no. 19009/04, § 46, 13 May 2008.

[364] *Buckley v. the United Kingdom*, no. 20348/92, § 63, Commission report of 11 January 1995; *Chapman v. the United Kingdom* [GC], no. 27238/95, §§ 71–74, ECHR 2001-I.

[365] *Moreno Gómez v. Spain*, no. 4143/02, § 53, ECHR 2004-X; *Yordanova and Others v. Bulgaria*, no. 25446/06, § 105, 24 April 2012; *Chapman v. the United Kingdom* [GC], no. 27238/95, § 73, ECHR 2001-I.

[366] *Alkaya v. Turkey*, no. 42811/06, §§ 40–41, 9 October 2012.

[367] *Niemietz v. Germany*, 16 December 1992, § 30, Series A no. 251-B.

[368] *Hoechst AG v. Commission*, [1989] ECR 2839, para. 10.

[369] *Niemietz v. Germany*, 16 December 1992, § 29, Series A no. 251-B.

[370] *Chappell v. the United Kingdom*, 30 March 1989, §§ 26 and 63, Series A no. 152-A; *Niemietz v. Germany*, 16 December 1992, § 30, Series A no. 251-B; *Société Colas Est and Others v. France*, no. 37971/97, § 41, ECHR 2002-III.

[371] *Chelu v. Romania*, no. 40274/04, §§ 45–46, 12 January 2010.

[372] *Hartung v. Germany* (dec.), no. 10231/07, 3 November 2009.

[373] *Alkaya v. Turkey*, no. 42811/06, § 29, 9 October 2012; *Moreno Gómez v. Spain*, no. 4143/02, § 53, ECHR 2004-X.

the Convention and article 1 of Protocol No. 1. In some cases, the Court will find a violation of article 8 and then decline to pronounce itself on article 1 of Protocol No. 1.[374] In others, for example where expropriation is concerned, it may apply article 1 of Protocol No. 1 and consider that there is no need to look at article 8.[375] Legal issues relating to tenancy may also arise, although the Court will generally consider that a dispute concerning a lease does not fall within the scope of article 8.[376]

When housing issues relate to social policy, especially in an urban or rural planning context, '[i]n so far as the exercise of discretion involving a multitude of local factors is inherent in the choice and implementation of planning policies, the national authorities in principle enjoy a wide margin of appreciation'.[377] But 'where the right at stake is crucial to the individual's effective enjoyment of intimate or key rights', the margin of appreciation is not as broad.[378] If the loss of the home is possible, some remedy or procedural vehicle should be available in order to ensure that rights under article 8 are not violated. The official tolerance of a community for a considerable period of time in spite of the fact that its title to property may not have been very certain is relevant and must be taken into consideration. Although the residents of an illegal community may not be able to claim a legitimate expectation to remain, '[t]he principle of proportionality requires that such situations, where a whole community and a long period are concerned, be treated as being entirely different from routine cases of removal of an individual from unlawfully occupied property'.[379] If the State is the owner of the property, the exercise is simplified because there is no need to balance the rights of the occupant with those of another occupant with a possibly valid claim.[380]

Probably the most extreme form of a breach of the right to protection of the home takes place during conflict, when there may be mass expulsions and internal displacement. In *Cyprus v. Turkey*, the Grand Chamber condemned 'the complete denial of the right of displaced persons to respect for their homes', noting that it had no basis in law within the meaning of article 8(2) of the Convention. It said that the violation at issue had endured 'as a matter of policy since 1974' and that it was a continuing violation of article 8 'by reason of the refusal to allow the return of any Greek-Cypriot displaced persons to their homes in northern Cyprus'.[381]

Correspondence

Both traditional mail and electronic messages, including those made in the context of business or professional relationships, fall within the ambit of 'correspondence' as well as generally under 'private life',[382] as do telephone calls[383] and similar forms

---

[374] *Surugiu v. Romania*, no. 48995/99, §§ 67–69, 75, 20 April 2004.

[375] *Mehmet Salih and Abdülsamet Çakmak v. Turkey*, no. 45630/99, § 22, 29 April 2004; *Mutlu v. Turkey*, no. 8006/02, § 23, 10 October 2006.

[376] *Langborger v. Sweden*, 22 June 1989, §§ 38–39, Series A no. 155.

[377] *Buckley v. the United Kingdom*, 25 September 1996, § 75 *in fine*, *Reports of Judgments and Decisions* 1996-IV; *Ćosić v. Croatia*, no. 28261/06, § 18, 15 January 2009.

[378] *Yordanova and Others v. Bulgaria*, no. 25446/06, § 120, 24 April 2012.

[379] Ibid., § 121.

[380] *Gladysheva v. Russia*, no. 7097/10, §§ 94–96, 6 December 2011.

[381] *Cyprus v. Turkey* [GC], no. 25781/94, §§ 174–175, ECHR 2001-IV.

[382] *Kennedy v. the United Kingdom*, no. 26839/05, § 118, 18 May 2010.

[383] *Dumitru Popescu v. Romania (no. 2)*, no. 71525/01, § 61, 26 April 2007; *Association '21 December 1989' and Others v. Romania*, nos 33810/07 and 18817/08, §167, 24 May 2011; *Weber and Saravia v. Germany*

of communication.[384] Special issues arise here concerning contestation of measures that interfere with correspondence when these are secret in nature.[385] The matter is considered in the chapter of this volume dealing with article 34 of the European Convention on Human Rights.

Correspondence of prisoners is routinely monitored. This amounts to an interference with the right to correspondence enshrined in article 8(1),[386] although one that will often be acceptable through the application of article 8(2).[387] The actual content of the correspondence is immaterial to the determination of whether there has been an interference with the right.[388] Stringent standards apply to legal correspondence because it is in principle privileged in nature.[389] Depending upon the circumstances, a similar strict approach may apply to medical correspondence of prisoners.[390]

Prison authorities need not assume the cost of all prison correspondence, although a problem will arise if financial hardship means an inmate is entirely deprived of the possibility of communication with the outside.[391] Turkish prison authorities invoked the cost of translation when they refused to transmit correspondence written in Kurdish. They said the prison had neither the staff nor the money to undertake translation. They explained that letters could be translated, at the applicants' expense, by a sworn translator. The letters could then be sent if they were deemed to be inoffensive. The Court noted that the conduct of the prison authorities was not in fact governed by any relevant regulations.[392] Consequently, it held that there was a violation of article 8 without having to rule on the core issue, which was whether correspondence could be withheld because of the language that was used.

Restriction and limitation (art. 8(2))

Article 8(2) authorizes 'interference' (in French, *ingérence*) with the rights to private and family life and to home and correspondence set out in paragraph 1. The paragraph is similar to, although not identical with, corresponding second paragraphs in articles 9, 10, and 11 of the Convention. Article 9(2) speaks of 'limitations', article 10(2) of 'formalities, conditions, restrictions or penalties', and article 11(2) of 'restrictions'. These differences in terminology do not appear to have had any practical or substantive consequences in their

---

(dec.), no. 54934/00, § 77, ECHR 2006-XI; *Iordachi and Others v. Moldova*, no. 25198/02, § 29, 10 February 2009.

[384] *Bykov v. Russia* [GC], no. 4378/02, § 79, 10 March 2009.

[385] *Klass and Others v. Germany*, 6 September 1978, §§ 34–38, 41, Series A no. 28; *Malone v. the United Kingdom*, 2 August 1984, § 64, Series A no. 82; *Kennedy v. the United Kingdom*, no. 26839/05, §§ 120–124, 18 May 2010; *Iordachi and Others v. Moldova*, no. 25198/02, § 34, 10 February 2009.

[386] *Mehmet Nuri Özen v. Turkey*, no. 37619/05, § 40, 2 February 2010; *Calogero Diana v. Italy*, 15 November 1996, § 28, *Reports of Judgments and Decisions* 1996-V.

[387] *Szuluk v. the United Kingdom*, no. 36936/05, § 46, ECHR 2009; *Silver and Others v. the United Kingdom*, 25 March 1983, § 98, Series A no. 61; *Kwiek v. Poland*, no. 51895/99, § 39, 30 May 2006; *Ostrovar v. Moldova*, no. 35207/03, § 105, 13 September 2005.

[388] *Frerot v. France*, no. 70204/01, 12 June 2007, § 54; *Mehmet Nuri Özen v. Turkey*, no. 37619/05, § 41, 2 February 2010.

[389] *Petrov v. Bulgaria*, no. 15197/02, § 43, 22 May 2008; *Campbell v. the United Kingdom*, 25 March 1992, § 48, Series A no. 233.

[390] *Szuluk v. the United Kingdom*, no. 36936/05, §§ 53–54, ECHR 2009.

[391] *Gagiu v. Romania*, no. 63258/00, § 88, 24 February 2009; *Cotleţ v. Romania*, no. 38565/97, § 61, 3 June 2003.

[392] *Mehmet Nuri Özen v. Turkey*, no. 37619/05, § 58, 2 February 2010.

application and interpretation by the Convention organs. Nevertheless, the somewhat different formulation of the clauses is not without consequences, depending upon the provision that the Court employs in analysing a given situation. For example, in the French *burqa* case, the Court noted that although 'public order' was a lawful ground for restriction under article 9(2), they were not mentioned in article 8(2).[393]

The ancestor of the four provisions is article 29(2) of the Universal Declaration of Human Rights: 'In the exercise of his rights and freedoms, everyone shall be subject only to such limitations as are determined by law solely for the purpose of securing due recognition and respect for the rights and freedoms of others subject only to such limitations as are determined by law solely for the purpose of securing due recognition and respect for the rights and freedoms of others and of meeting the just requirements of morality, public order and the general welfare in a democratic society.' The limitation clause in the Universal Declaration applies generally to all rights set out in the instrument, whereas the specific clauses of this nature in the European Convention, of which article 8(2) is an example, are tailored to the right at issue. It is noteworthy that although the International Covenant on Civil and Political Rights has clauses similar to those of the European Convention in its formulation of the freedoms of religion, expression, peaceful assembly, and association, there is no restriction clause associated with the right to private and family life.[394]

The Convention organs have developed a flexible methodology for the interpretation and application of paragraph 2 in determining whether or not the interference with a right set out in the first paragraph of articles 8, 9, 10, and 11 is actually in breach of the Convention. The general framework is identical for each of the four provisions. Similar texts are also used with respect to some of the provisions in the Protocols: article 1 of Protocol No. 1 (protection of property); article 2(3) of Protocol No. 4 (freedom of movement); art. 2(2) of Protocol No. 7 (right of appeal in criminal matters).

In accordance with the law

An interference with article 8 must be, in the words of article 8(2), 'in accordance with the law'. The other three articles use the expression 'prescribed by law'. The French text of the four provisions uses the same wording (*prévue par la loi*), and this provides confirmation that the different formulations in the English text are without any legal significance.[395] A decade after the adoption of the Convention, when Protocol No. 4 was being drafted, the Committee of Experts preferred the expression 'in accordance with the law' over 'provided by law' for the limitations clause dealing with freedom of movement, noting the text of article 8(2). It said that 'in accordance with law' was 'better', and that it allowed for administrative action, provided it were taken in accordance with internal legislation.[396]

The requirement that a restriction or limitation be prescribed by or in accordance with law has both a formal or technical sense and a substantive one. The interference must, of

---

[393] *S.A.S. v. France* [GC], no. 43835/11, § 117, 1 July 2014.

[394] International Covenant on Civil and Political Rights, (1976) 999 UNTS 171, art. 17. Attempts by some European States to introduce a paragraph in article 17 of the Covenant similar to article 8(2) of the Convention were rejected. See Manfred Nowak, *UN Covenant on Civil and Political Rights, CCPR Commentary*, 2nd rev. edn, Kehl, Germany: N.P. Engel, 2005, p. 381.

[395] *The Sunday Times v. the United Kingdom (no. 1)*, 26 April 1979, § 48, Series A no. 30; *Silver and Others v. the United Kingdom*, 25 March 1983, § 85, Series A no. 61.

[396] Explanatory Report on Protocol No. 4, para. 13.

course, be authorized by a rule recognized in the national legal order. This includes 'written law', including various forms of delegated legislation, and unwritten law as interpreted and applied by the courts.[397] But there is also a qualitative requirement for the legal rule. It must be accessible and foreseeable. There may be higher expectations in applying the condition depending upon the individuals involved, in light of their training, professional activity, and experience. It may be reasonable to expect them to obtain expert advice on the law, depending upon the circumstances. The law must also be subject to mechanisms so that it can be applied in a manner that is genuine and not arbitrary. If the law grants discretion to public authorities, it must be framed with sufficient clarity and specify the manner in which it is to be exercised.[398] The Court is not prescriptive in this respect, acknowledging that States have a 'margin of appreciation' in deciding upon the legal mechanisms by which they limit or restrict the rights set out in the Convention. In effect, the words 'in accordance with the law' refer to the broad, general notion of the 'rule of law'. Often the Court will conclude that the interference is not made 'in accordance with law' or 'provided by law', and find that the Convention has been violated, without considering whether the measure complies with the other two facets of its analysis under paragraph 2.

The degree of precision required of 'law' depends upon the subject-matter. When secret surveillance of communications is concerned, 'it would be contrary to the rule of law for the legal discretion granted to the executive—or to a judge—to be expressed in terms of an unfettered power'. The law must frame the discretion in such a way as to provide adequate protection against arbitrary interference.[399] Such secret measures also present problems with respect to the requirement that the legal measure be 'foreseeable', where the Court has held on several occasions that special circumstances exist.[400] According to the Court,

[F]oreseeability in the special context of secret measures of surveillance, such as the interception of communications, cannot mean that an individual should be able to foresee when the authorities are likely to intercept his communications so that he can adapt his conduct accordingly. However, especially where a power vested in the executive is exercised in secret, the risks of arbitrariness are evident. It is therefore essential to have clear, detailed rules on interception of telephone conversations, especially as the technology available for use is continually becoming more sophisticated. The domestic law must be sufficiently clear in its terms to give citizens an adequate indication as to the circumstances in which and the conditions on which public authorities are empowered to resort to any such measures. Moreover, since the implementation in practice of measures of secret surveillance of communications is not open to scrutiny by the individuals concerned or the public at large, it would be contrary to the rule of law for the legal discretion granted to the executive or to a judge to be expressed in terms of an unfettered power. Consequently, the law must indicate the scope of

---

[397] *Leyla Şahin v. Turkey* [GC], no. 44774/98, § 88, ECHR 2005-XI; *Sanoma Uitgevers B.V. v. the Netherlands* [GC], no. 38224/03, § 83, 14 September 2010.

[398] *The Sunday Times v. the United Kingdom (no. 1)*, 26 April 1979, § 49, Series A no. 30; *Tolstoy Miloslavsky v. the United Kingdom*, 13 July 1995, § 37, Series A no. 316-B; *Rotaru v. Romania* [GC], no. 28341/95, § 52, ECHR 2000-V; *Hasan and Chaush v. Bulgaria* [GC], no. 30985/96, § 84, ECHR 2000-XI; *Maestri v. Italy* [GC], no. 39748/98, § 30, ECHR 2004-I.

[399] *Bykov v. Russia* [GC], no. 4378/02, § 78, 10 March 2009; *Huvig v. France*, 24 April 1990, §§ 29 and 32, Series A no. 176-B; *Amann v. Switzerland* [GC], no. 27798/95, § 56, ECHR 2000-II; *Valenzuela Contreras v. Spain*, 30 July 1998, § 46, *Reports of Judgments and Decisions* 1998-V.

[400] *Malone v. the United Kingdom*, 2 August 1984, § 67, Series A no. 82; *Leander v. Sweden*, 26 March 1987, § 51, Series A no. 116; *Association for European Integration and Human Rights and Ekimdzhiev v. Bulgaria*, no. 62540/00, § 79, 28 June 2007; *Al-Nashif v. Bulgaria*, no. 50963/99, § 121, 20 June 2002.

any such discretion conferred on the competent authorities and the manner of its exercise with sufficient clarity to give the individual adequate protection against arbitrary interference.[401]

Some cases of interference have failed the test, obviating the need for the Court to apply the two other criteria. In the Slovenian 'erasure' case, the Court found the legislation to be insufficient and held there was a violation.[402] Although the monitoring of legal correspondence of prisoners in Italy was ordered by a judge, the European Court held that the legal prescriptions had not been followed and that consequently the measures were not in accordance with law.[403] When a Polish hospital provided information about a patient involved in a controversial abortion decision, the Court noted that there was no provision of national law allowing for such public disclosure, and as a consequence the impugned measure was not 'in accordance with law'.[404]

Legitimate purpose

The issue of the legitimate aim or purpose of an interference is rarely very significant, given the breadth of what is permissible under article 8. It seems that the assessment under article 8(2) does not depend upon what is submitted by the respondent State and apparently sometimes the governments have nothing to say on this point. Article 8(2) permits interference with family and private life, home, and correspondence 'in the interests of national security, public safety or the economic well-being of the country, for the prevention of disorder or crime, for the protection of health or morals, or for the protection of the rights and freedoms of others'. The Grand Chamber has explained that it is the Court's practice 'to be quite succinct when it verifies the existence of a legitimate aim within the meaning of the second paragraphs of Articles 8 to 11 of the Convention'.[405] The list is large enough to cover most government activity, whether it is oppressive or benign. The Court has tended to espouse a rather broad and liberal application of the terms, often finding that more than one of the purposes applies to a specific form of interference.

In a case against Moldova concerning the government's refusal to modify the ethnic identity on official records, no specific legitimate aim was proposed, yet the Court said it was prepared to accept that the measure was to safeguard national security and prevent disorder.[406] Often several grounds appear to justify the measures in question. In a case involving entry and residence of aliens, the Court thought that several grounds might apply, including the interests of national security, the economic well-being of the country, and the prevention of disorder or crime.[407] In contrast with the other restriction clauses in the Convention, article 8(2) does not include 'public order' in the list.[408]

A rare example of violation of the Convention being declared because the impugned measure did not serve any legitimate purpose is found in the disclosure by a Polish

---

[401] *Weber and Saravia v. Germany* (dec.), no. 54934/00, §§ 93–94, ECHR 2006-XI (references omitted). See also *Shimovolos v. Russia*, no. 30194/09, §§ 68–71, 21 June 2011.

[402] *Kurić and Others v. Slovenia* [GC], no. 26828/06, § 349, ECHR 2012 (extracts).

[403] *Enea v. Italy* [GC], no. 74912/01, § 142, ECHR 2009.

[404] *P. and S. v. Poland*, no. 57375/08, § 134, 30 October 2012.

[405] *S.A.S. v. France* [GC], no. 43835/11, § 114, 1 July 2014.

[406] *Ciubotaru v. Moldova*, no. 27138/04, § 5, 27 April 2010.

[407] *Popov v. France*, nos 39472/07 and 39474/07, § 106, 19 January 2012.

[408] *S.A.S. v. France* [GC], no. 43835/11, Joint Partly Dissenting Opinion of Judges Nußburger and Jäderblom, § 11, 1 July 2014.

hospital of medical information about a patient who was awaiting determination of eligibility for an abortion. The Court said it could not see how release of information about the patient's unwanted pregnancy and the subsequent refusal by hospital authorities to terminate it could fulfil a legitimate aim listed in article 8(2).[409]

In the case concerning statelessness in Slovenia, the Court concluded that legislation requiring citizens of the Socialist Federated Republic of Yugoslavia to opt quickly for Slovenian citizenship at the time of the breakup, in order to create a 'corpus of Slovenian citizens', could be explained by the legitimate purpose of protection of the country's national security.[410]

The 'interests of economic well-being' are listed in article 8(2). It is the only one of the four limitations clauses to contain such a reference, although logically there is no good reason why this might not also be applicable in the case of freedom of expression and freedom of association. Occasionally the Court has accepted 'interests of economic well-being' as an acceptable purpose for measures that infringe upon the rights in article 8(1). In a case involving violation of the 'home' of a Roma community, the Court considered there was sufficient evidence of genuine plans for urban development in the area that 'economic well-being' could be considered legitimate.[411]

A deportation order was justified by the United Kingdom government using several categories of legitimate aim, including 'public safety', 'prevention of disorder or crime', and 'protection of the rights of others'.[412] The Court noted that it had consistently viewed that such expulsion measures fell within the legitimate aim of 'prevention of disorder or crime'.[413] It referred to authority where the other two grounds had been accepted, but noted that these were not contested by the applicants and therefore of limited authority.[414]

In the French *burqa* case, the Grand Chamber recognized that 'public safety' had been invoked by the legislator as part of the rationale for the ban on covering the face. According to France, the prohibition 'satisfied the need to identify individuals in order to prevent danger for the safety of persons and property and to combat identity fraud'.[415] Protection of 'the rights and freedoms of others' is a legitimate aim that may encompass the promotion of gender equality.[416] In its consideration of the French ban on wearing clothing that covers the face, the Court said it accepted 'that the barrier raised against others by a veil concealing the face is perceived by the respondent State as breaching the right of others to live in a space of socialisation which makes living together easier'.[417]

---

[409] *P. and S. v. Poland*, no. 57375/08, § 133, 30 October 2012. See also the section entitled 'No legitimate aim under the Convention', in *S.A.S. v. France* [GC], no. 43835/11, Joint Partly Dissenting Opinion of Judges Nußberger and Jäderblom, 1 July 2014.

[410] *Kurić and Others v. Slovenia* [GC], no. 26828/06, § 353, ECHR 2012 (extracts).

[411] *Yordanova and Others v. Bulgaria*, no. 25446/06, § 115, 24 April 2012.

[412] *A.A. v. the United Kingdom*, no. 8000/08, § 40, 20 September 2011.

[413] Ibid., § 53. Referring to *Bouchelkia v. France*, 29 January 1997, § 4, *Reports of Judgments and Decisions* 1997-I; *Boujlifa v. France*, 21 October 1997, § 39, *Reports of Judgments and Decisions* 1997-VI; *Boultif v. Switzerland*, no. 54273/00, § 45, ECHR 2001-IX; *Maslov v. Austria* [GC], no. 1638/03, § 67, ECHR 2008; *Omojudi v. the United Kingdom*, no. 1820/08, § 40, 24 November 2009; *Bousarra v. France*, no. 25672/07, § 42, 23 September 2010.

[414] *A.A. v. the United Kingdom*, no. 8000/08, § 54, 20 September 2011.

[415] *S.A.S. v. France* [GC], no. 43835/11, § 115, 1 July 2014.

[416] *Staatkundig Gereformeerde Partij v. the Netherlands* (dec.), 10 July 2012; *S.A.S. v. France* [GC], no. 43835/11, § 115, 1 July 2014.

[417] *S.A.S. v. France* [GC], no. 43835/11, § 122, 1 July 2014.

This aim was subsumed within the general concept of 'protection of the rights and freedoms of others'.

Necessary in a democratic society

Most decisions concerning the second paragraph of article 8 involve the third component of the analysis, namely whether the impugned measure is 'necessary in a democratic society'. The objective is to consider whether the authorities have struck 'a fair balance between the competing interests of the individual and of society as a whole'.[418] It is the most subjective part of the application of paragraph 2, involving subtle distinctions about the proportionality of measures taken by the State that limit or restrict human rights. There is an important relationship between 'necessity' and 'democratic society', of which the hallmarks are pluralism, tolerance, and broadmindedness.[419]

The Court frequently begins its consideration of this element by questioning whether the interference responds to a 'pressing social need'. The term seems to be not much more than a gloss on the word 'necessity'. It employs two other notions in this context, insisting that the measure in question be 'relevant and sufficient'. The interference must also respond to an assessment of its proportionality, something that necessitates balancing the right of the individual against the interest of the State and the society that it represents. Where the Court is considering the positive dimension of the right in question, in other words, the obligation upon the State to take measures to ensure enforcement of the right, it must usually consider the rights of others in the balance as well. If other less severe measures could have fulfilled the same objective, there will be a problem with proportionality.

Nevertheless, in applying the 'necessary in a democratic society' test, the Court will allow the State a margin of appreciation, recognizing that its role is not to sit as a tribunal of fourth instance and that it is in one sense not as well positioned as the national legal institutions to assess many of the relevant factors. Often, especially in sensitive matters that concern morality, ethics, and social policy, the Court refers to the practice in European jurisdictions in determining whether or not any consensus exists. Where there is none, the margin of appreciation will almost invariably be much greater. But although the national authorities make the initial assessment of necessity, 'the final evaluation as to whether the reasons cited for the interference are relevant and sufficient remains subject to review by the Court for conformity with the requirements of the Convention'.[420]

Beyond a general presentation of the factors employed by the Court in considering whether an interference is 'necessary in a democratic society', it is difficult to extract any broad themes concerning the application of this concept to the right to private and family life. Certainly, it is under this rubric where significant evolution is likely to take place to the extent that the Court considers controversial moral and ethical issues, such as abortion, sexual orientation and practices, and the termination of life. The Court has said that when intimate areas such as sexual life are in question, the margin of appreciation is narrow.[421]

---

[418] *Keegan v. Ireland*, 26 May 1994, § 49, Series A no. 290.

[419] *Smith and Grady v. the United Kingdom*, nos 33985/96 and 33986/96, § 87, ECHR 1999-VI; *Vereinigung demokratischer Soldaten Österreichs and Gubi v. Austria*, 19 December 1994, § 36, Series A no. 302; *Dudgeon v. the United Kingdom*, 22 October 1981, § 53, Series A no. 45.

[420] *Szuluk v. the United Kingdom*, no. 36936/05, § 45, ECHR 2009.

[421] *Dudgeon v. the United Kingdom*, 22 October 1981, § 52, Series A no. 45; *A.D.T. v. The United Kingdom*, no. 35765/97, § 37, ECHR 2000-IX; *Pretty v. the United Kingdom*, no. 2346/02, § 71, ECHR 2002-III.

Discrimination

With respect to discrimination concerning private and family life, home, and correspondence, article 8 is no different than the other provisions of the Convention. Article 14 plays a subsidiary role and in practice it is rarely applied. In many cases, where article 14 has been invoked together with article 8, the Court has found a violation of article 8 and then declared there was no need for a separate discussion or analysis pursuant to article 14.[422]

The Court considered that article 14 had been violated in conjunction with article 8 in the case concerning statelessness in Slovenia. As a result of legislation enacted in the aftermath of the breakup of Yugoslavia, there was differential treatment of 'real' aliens—that is, nationals of a State other than the former Yugoslavia—and those who had been nationals of the former Yugoslavia with citizenship in one of its component republics other than Slovenia. The victims, who had become stateless persons, were known as the 'erased'. Noting this differential treatment, which it said was based upon national origin, the Court held that the Convention had been breached.[423] However, the Court rejected a claim based on article 14 in conjunction with article 8 that discrimination based on citizenship in access to the legal profession was contrary to the Convention.[424]

Upon the death of the lawful tenant, Austrian legislation concerning residential tenancy enabled a lease to pass to a close relative, but this did not apply to the same-sex partner of the deceased. The Court concluded that there was a violation of article 14 in conjunction with article 8.[425]

In a Greek case, an unmarried member of the clergy adopted a son, who was already an adult at the time, while the two were in the United States. Later, siblings successfully challenged the adoption before the Greek courts, with the consequence of disinheriting the adopted child following the death of the adopting father. The Court held that there was discrimination and applied articles 8 and 14 together. The adopting father had been entitled to marry and to have a family, with the consequence that his natural children would have been heirs, so it was discriminatory for the Greek courts to deny the validity of the adoption and thereby exclude the adopted son from sharing in the estate.[426]

A person's name belongs to the sphere of private and family life protected by article 8 of the Convention. Legislation requiring a change of name in the case of a woman upon marriage constitutes a violation of article 8 taken together with article 14. The State argued that the requirement promoted family unity by imposing a joint family name, but the Court said this 'cannot provide a justification for the gender-based difference in treatment complained of in the instant case'.[427]

The Court held that there was a violation of article 14 in conjunction with article 8 with respect to Greek legislation authorizing civil union or civil partnership that excluded

---

[422] *Yordanova and Others v. Bulgaria*, no. 25446/06, § 148, 24 April 2012; *Dudgeon v. the United Kingdom*, 22 October 1981, § 70, Series A no. 45; *Tysiąc v. Poland*, no. 5410/03, § 144, ECHR 2007-I; *Smith and Grady v. the United Kingdom*, nos 33985/96 and 33986/96, § 116, ECHR 1999-VI; *A.D.T. v. the United Kingdom*, no. 35765/97, § 41, ECHR 2000-IX.

[423] *Kurić and Others v. Slovenia* [GC], no. 26828/06, §§ 394–396, ECHR 2012 (extracts).

[424] *Bigaeva v. Greece*, no. 26713/05, § 41, 28 May 2009.

[425] *Karner v. Austria*, no. 40016/98, §§ 42–43, ECHR 2003-IX.

[426] *Negrepontis-Giannisis v. Greece*, no. 56759/08, § 84, 3 May 2011.

[427] *Ünal Tekeli v. Turkey*, no. 29865/96, § 69, ECHR 2004-X (extracts). Also *Tuncer Güneş v. Turkey*, no. 26268/08, 3 September 2013; *Losonci Rose and Rose v. Switzerland*, no. 664/06, §§ 49–53, 9 November 2010.

same-sex relationships. Citing an emerging trend in Europe, it noted that of the nineteen States that authorize a form of partnership other than marriage, Lithuania and Greece are the only ones to reserve it exclusively to different-sex couples. 'In other words', said the Court, 'with two exceptions, Council of Europe member States, when they opt to enact legislation introducing a new system of registered partnership as an alternative to marriage for unmarried couples, include same-sex couples in its scope.'[428] Greece had insisted that the main purpose of its legislation was to provide protection for children of unmarried couples, but the Court said it had not offered 'convincing and weighty reasons capable of justifying the exclusion of same-sex couples'.[429]

Issues concerning discrimination against same-sex couples have also arisen with respect to what are called 'second-parent adoptions', whereby the partner of the natural parent in such a relationship becomes the adoptive parent of the child. According to a study by the Commissioner on Human Rights, second-parent adoptions benefit the child by providing for two legal guardians. Moreover,

Second-parent adoptions also protect the parents by giving both of them legally recognised parental status. The lack of second-parent adoption deprives the child and the non-biological parent of rights if the biological parent dies or in the case of divorce, separation, or other circumstances that would bar the parent from carrying out parental responsibilities. The child also has no right to inherit from the non-biological parent. Moreover, at an everyday level, the lack of second-parent adoption rules out parental leave, which can be harmful financially for LGBT families. The third procedure is joint adoption of a child by a same sex couple.[430]

In Austria, where same-sex partnership but not same-sex marriage is authorized by law, the Grand Chamber held that legislation preventing second-parent adoption in same-sex couples violated article 14 in conjunction with article 8. It insisted that the issue arose because the prohibition on such adoptions prevented the courts from examining 'in any meaningful manner' whether the requested adoption was in the interests of the child.[431] It referred to recent judgments finding a breach of article 14 together with article 8, where the father of a child born outside marriage could not obtain an examination by the domestic courts of whether the award of joint custody to both parents or sole custody to him was in the child's interests.[432]

Reservations

Upon ratification in 1982, Liechtenstein made a lengthy reservation to article 8. The first portion stated that article 8 'shall be exercised, with regard to homosexuality, in accordance with the principles at present embodied in paragraphs 129 and 130 of the Liechtenstein Criminal Code of 27 May 1852'. The second part reserved Liechtenstein's

---

[428] *Vallianatos and Others v. Greece* [GC], nos 29381/09 and 32684/09, § 91, ECHR 2013.

[429] Ibid., § 92.

[430] Council of Europe Commissioner for Human Rights, *Discrimination on Grounds of Sexual Orientation and Gender Identity in Europe*, Strasbourg: Council of Europe Publishing, 2011.

[431] *X and Others v. Austria* [GC], no. 19010/07, §§ 152–153, ECHR 2013. But see *X and Others v. Austria* [GC], no. 19010/07, Joint Partly Dissenting Opinion of Judges Casadevall, Ziemele, Kovler, Jočiené, Šikuta, De Gaetano, and Sicilianos, ECHR 2013; *Vallianatos and Others v. Greece* [GC], nos 29381/09 and 32684/09, Joint Concurring Opinion of Judges Casadevall, Ziemele, Jočiené, and Sicilianos, ECHR 2013.

[432] *Zaunegger v. Germany*, no. 22028/04, §§ 61–63, 3 December 2009; *Sporer v. Austria*, no. 35637/03, §§ 88–90, 3 February 2011.

legislation relating to 'the status of illegitimate children' and 'the status of women in matrimonial and family law'. The third reservation to article 8 stated that 'the right to respect for family life, as guaranteed by Article 8 of the Convention, shall be exercised, with regard to aliens, in accordance with the principles at present embodied in the Ordinance of 9 September 1980'. The 1991 Yearbook of the European Convention on Human Rights says that the reservation in respect of article 8 'with regard to homosexuality' had been withdrawn but made no mention of the other reservations.[433] The compilation of reservations in the 1994 Yearbook indicates that the entire reservation to article 8 had been withdrawn in 1991.[434] However, this must certainly have been an error, something that was confirmed when in 1999 Liechtenstein withdrew the second of its reservations dealing with 'illegitimate children'.[435]

Monaco has also formulated a complex reservation that it says applies to articles 6, 8, and 14. It concerns legislation governing authorization to exercise a professional activity and creates a preference for citizens of the country.[436]

Further reading

Antje du Bois-Pedain, 'The Right to Family Life in Extradition Cases: More Defendant-Friendly than Strasbourg Requires', (2010) 69 *Cambridge Law Journal* 223.

Christiane Bourloyannis-Vrailas, '*Aksu v. Turkey* (Eur. Ct. H.R.), Introductory Note', (2012) 51 *International Legal Materials* 685.

Stephan Breitenmoser, *Der Schutz der Privatsphäre gemäss Art. 8 EMRK. Das Recht auf Achtung des Privat- und Familienlebens, der Wohnung und des Briefverkehrs*, Basel: Helbing & Lichtenbahn, 1986.

Patrick Breyer, 'Telecommunications Data Retention and Human Rights: The Compatibility of Blanket Traffic Data Retention with the ECHR', (2005) 11 *European Law Journal* 365.

Maris Burbergs, 'How the Right to Respect for Private and Family Life, Home and Correspondence became the Nursery in which New Rights are Born: Article 8 ECHR', in Eva Brems and Janneke Gerards, eds, *Shaping Rights in the ECHR*, Cambridge: Cambridge University Press, 2013, pp. 315–29.

A.M. Connelly, 'Problems of Interpretation of Article 8 of the European Convention on Human Rights', (1986) 25 *ICLQ* 567.

Vincent Coussirat-Coustere, 'Article 8§2', in Pettiti et al., *La Convention européenne*, pp. 323–351.

Kathryn F. Deringer, 'Privacy and the Press: The Convergence of British and French Law in Accordance with the European Convention of Human Rights', (2003) 22 *Penn State International Law Review* 191.

P. Nikiforos Dimandouros, 'Vers la reconnaissance d'un droit d'accès aux informations détenues par les autorités', in Dean Spielmann, Marialena Tsirli, and Panayotis Voyatzis, eds, *La Convention européenne des droits de l'homme, un instrument vivant, Mélanges en l'honneur de Christos L. Rozakis*, Brussels: Bruylant, 2011, pp. 131–54.

Louise Doswald-Beck, 'The Meaning of the "Right to Respect for Private Life" under the European Convention on Human Rights', (1983) 4 *HRLJ* 4, 283.

Markus Dirk Dubber, 'Homosexual Privacy Rights before the United States Supreme Court and the European Court of Human Rights: A Comparison of Methodologies', (1990–91) 27 *Stanford Journal of International Law* 189.

---

[433] (1991) 34 YB 5.
[434] (1994) 33A YB 75.
[435] (1999) 42 YB 7.
[436] (2005) 48 YB 11.

Jochen Abr. Frowein, 'Les guaranties offertes par les mécanismes institutionnels de la Convention', in *Vie privée et droits de l'homme*, Brussels: Bruylant, 1973, pp. 411–36.

Frowein/Peukert, *MenschenRechtsKonvention*, pp. 287–317.

Grabenwarter, *European Convention*, pp. 813–33.

Tomás Gómez-Arostegui, 'Defining Private Life Under the European Convention on Human Rights by Referring to Reasonable Expectations', (2005) 35 *California Western Journal of International Law* 153.

Michele Grigolo, 'Sexualities and the ECHR: Introducing the Universal Sexual Legal Subject', (2003) 14 *European Journal of International Law* 1023.

John Hedigan, 'The Princess, the Press and Privacy. Observations on *Caroline von Hannover v. Germany*', in Lucius Caflisch, Johan Callewaert, Roderick Liddell, Paul Mahoney, and Mark Villiger, eds, *Liber Amicorum Luzius Wildhaber*, Kehl, Germany: N.P. Engel, 2007, pp. 193–206.

A. Heldrich, 'Persönlichkeitsschutz und Pressefreiheit nach der Europäischen Menschenrechtskonvention', [2004] *Neue Juristische Wochenschrift* 2634.

Laurence R. Helfer, 'Finding a Consensus on Equality: The Homosexual Age of Consent and the European Convention on Human Rights', (1990) 65 *New York University Law Review* 1044.

Frank Hendrikx and Aline Van Bever, 'Article 8 ECHR: Judicial Patterns of Employment Policy', in Filip Dorssemont, Klaus Lörcher, and Isabelle Schömann, eds, *The European Convention on Human Rights and the Employment Relation*, Oxford / Portland, OR: Hart, 2013, pp. 183–208.

Aalt Willem Herringa and Leo Zwaak, 'Right to Respect for Privacy (Article 8)', in Van Dijk et al., *Theory and Practice*, pp. 663–750.

Jeremy Hyam, '*Hatton v. United Kingdom* in the Grand Chamber: One Step Forward, Two Steps Back?', [2003] *EHRLR* 631.

Paul Johnson, '"An Essentially Private Manifestation of Human Personality": Constructions of Homosexuality in the European Court of Human Rights', (2010) 10 *HRLR* 67.

Ursula Kilkelly, 'Article 8: The Right to Respect for Private and Family Life, Home, and Correspondence', in Harris et al., *Law of the European Convention*, pp. 361–424.

Renée Koering-Joulin, 'Public Morals', in Mireille Delmas-Marty, ed., *The European Convention for the Protection of Human Rights*, Dordrecht/Boston/London: Martinus Nijhoff, 1992, pp. 83–98.

Timo Koivurova, 'Jurisprudence of the European Court of Human Rights Regarding Indigenous Peoples: Retrospect and Prospects', (2011) 18 *International Journal on Minority and Group Rights* 1.

H. Lambert, 'The European Court of Human Rights and the Right of Refugees and Other Persons in Need of Protection to family Reunion', (1999) 11 *International Journal of Refugee Law* 427.

L. G. Loucaides, 'Personality and Privacy under the European Convention on Human Rights', (1990) 61 *British Yearbook of International Law* 175.

J. De Meyer, 'Le droit au respect de la vie privée et familiale, du domicile et des communciations dans les relations entre personnes privées et les obligations qui en résultent pour les États Parties à la Convention', in *Vie privée et droits de l'homme*, Brussels: Bruylant, 1973, pp. 363–86.

Leslie J. Moran, '*Laskey v. The United Kingdom*: Learning the Limits of Privacy', (1998) 61 *Modern Law Review* 77.

N. A. Moreham, 'The Right to Respect for Private Life in the European Convention on Human Rights: A Re-examination', [2008] *EHRLR* 44.

T. Opsahl, 'La Convention et le droit au respect de la vie familiale spécialement en ce qui concerne l'unité de la famille et la protection des droits des parents et tuteurs familiaux dans l'éducation des enfants', in *Vie privée et droits de l'homme*, Brussels: Bruylant, 1973, pp. 243–322.

Kath O'Donnell, 'Protection of Family Life: Positive Approaches and the ECHR', (1995) 17 *Journal of Social Welfare and Family Law* 261.

Ovey/White, *Jacobs and White, European Convention*, pp. 217–63.

Daniel Reitiker, '*Neulinger and Shuruk v. Switzerland* (No. 41615/07)—Grand Chamber Judgment of 6 July 2010', (2012) 1 *Cyprus Human Rights Law Review* 98.

Carlo Russo, 'Article 8§1', in Pettiti et al., *La Convention européenne*, pp. 305–21.

M.A. Sanderson, 'Is Von Hannover v Germany a Step Backward for the Substantive Analysis of Speech and Privacy Interest?', (2004) 6 *EHRLR* 631.

Dean Spielmann and Leto Carioulou, 'The Right to Protection of Reputation under the European Convention on Human Rights', in Dean Spielmann, Marialena Tsirli, and Panayotis Voyatzis, eds, *La Convention européenne des droits de l'homme, un instrument vivant, Mélanges en l'honneur de Christos L. Rozakis*, Brussels: Bruylant, 2011, pp. 571–96.

Helen Stalford, 'Concepts of Family under EU Law—Lessons from the ECHR', (2002) 16 *International Journal of Law, Policy and the Family* 410.

Charlotte Steinorth, '*Üner v. The Netherlands:* Expulsion of Long-term Immigrants and the Right to Respect for Private and Family Life', (2008) 8 *HRLR* 1.

Frédéric Sudre, 'Les aléas de la notion de "vie privée" dans la jurisprudence de la Cour européenne des droits de l'homme', in G. Flécheux, ed., *Mélanges en hommage à Louis Edmond Pettiti*, Brussels: Bruylant, 1998, pp. 687–706.

Pierre Thielbörger, 'Positive Obligations in the ECHR after the Stoicesco Case: A Concept in Search of Content?', in Wolfgang Benedek, Florence Benoît-Rohmer, Wolfram Karl, and Manfred Nowak, eds, *European Yearbook on Human Rights*, Antwerp: Intersentia and Vienna-Graz, Neuer Wissenschaftlicher Verlag, 2012, pp. 259–68.

Daniel Thym, 'Respect for Private and Family Life under Article 8 ECHR in Immigration Cases: A Human Right to Regularize Illegal Stay?', (2008) 57 *ICLQ* 87.

Jacques Velu, 'La Convention européenne des droits de l'homme et le droit au respect de la vie privée, du domicile et des communications', in *Vie privée et droits de l'homme*, Brussels: Bruylant, 1973, pp. 35–138.

Guido Westkamp, '*Axel Springer AG v. Germany; Von Hannover v. Germany (no. 2)* (Eur. Ct. H.R.), Introductory Note', (2012) 51 *International Legal Materials* 631.

Article 9. Freedom of thought, conscience and religion/Liberté de pensée, de conscience et de religion

1. Everyone has the right to freedom of thought, conscience and religion; this right includes freedom to change his religion or belief and freedom, either alone or in community with others and in public or private, to manifest his religion or belief, in worship, teaching, practice and observance.

2. Freedom to manifest one's religion or beliefs shall be subject only to such limitations as are prescribed by law and are necessary in a democratic society in the interests of public safety, for the protection of public order, health or morals, or for the protection of the rights and freedoms of others.

1. Toute personne a droit à la liberté de pensée, de conscience et de religion; ce droit implique la liberté de changer de religion ou de conviction, ainsi que la liberté de manifester sa religion ou sa conviction individuellement ou collectivement, en public ou en privé, par le culte, l'enseignement, les pratiques et l'accomplissement des rites.

2. La liberté de manifester sa religion ou ses convictions ne peut faire l'objet d'autres restrictions que celles qui, prévues par la loi, constituent des mesures nécessaires, dans une société démocratique, à la sécurité publique, à la protection de l'ordre, de la santé ou de la morale publiques, ou à la protection des droits et libertés d'autrui.

Introductory comments

The second of Franklin D. Roosevelt's four freedoms, proclaimed in his 1941 State of the Union Address, is 'freedom of every person to worship God in his own way—everywhere in the world'. The four freedoms are invoked in the Preamble of the Universal Declaration of Human Rights, where the second of the freedoms is formulated as 'freedom of religion'. The four freedoms reappear yet again in the preambles of the two International Covenants. In those instruments, the first freedom (of expression) and the second are collectively referred to as 'civil and political freedoms'. There is no reference to God in the Universal Declaration or, for that matter, in the European Convention on Human Rights. Roosevelt's point was not to focus on monotheistic beliefs but rather to affirm the importance of the freedom of all to their own beliefs, and to that extent the instruments that echo his words are faithful to his intent.

During the drafting of the Universal Declaration, some European states, notably the Netherlands, urged unsuccessfully that a reference to God be included. Ultimately, the Universal Declaration addresses this by reaching a 'a bargain about God and nature', as one scholar has described it.[1] René Cassin later attributed much of its success to '[c]et œcuménisme de la Déclaration. A laquelle les Églises et les Confessions ont donné leur adhésion solonelle, sans abdiquer aucunement leurs dogmes et principes.'[2] Ireland, which was not yet a member of the United Nations and had therefore not participated in the

---

[1] Johannes Morsink, *The Universal Declaration of Human Rights, Origins, Drafting and Intent*, Philadelphia: University of Pennsylvania Press, 1999, p. 284.

[2] René Cassin, 'Historique de la Déclaration Universelle de 1948', in René Cassin, *La Pensée et l'action*, Paris: Lalou, 1972, at p. 116.

drafting of the Universal Declaration, favoured some religious references in the European Convention. The founding members of the Council of Europe had a degree of cultural homogeneity that was absent in the United Nations General Assembly, making this in principle considerably easier to accommodate. But like the Universal Declaration of Human Rights, the European Convention on Human Rights is a secular instrument. The Court has said that secularism is 'consistent with the values underpinning the Convention'.[3] Not only does it remain neutral in terms of any particular religion or confession, it advances visions of human dignity and values that, while certainly compatible with those of established religions, are not essentially spiritual. The role of religion in the lives of many, if not most, Europeans has undoubtedly declined significantly since 1950. Nevertheless, it remains important to many. Some religions, notably Islam, seem to have a new vigour.

Freedom of religion is one of the earliest concerns relating to human rights within the body of public international law. Article XIV of the Treaty of Utrecht of 1713 ceded territory in North America from France to the Britain, but at the same time ensured that French-speaking Catholics who wished to remain were entitled 'to enjoy the free exercise of their religion, according to the usage of the church of Rome, as far as the laws of Great Britain do allow the same'. Freedom of religion was protected by the minorities treaties adopted in the aftermath of the First World War. The 1919 Treaty of Peace with Poland, sometimes called the 'Little Treaty of Versailles', provided that '[a]ll inhabitants of Poland shall be entitled to the free exercise, whether public or private, of any creed, religion or belief, whose practices are not inconsistent with public order or public morals'.[4] In the letter to President Paderewski of Poland transmitting the treaty, Georges Clemenceau described the article as guaranteeing 'those elementary rights, which are, as a matter of fact, secured in every civilised State'.[5] Detailed provisions addressed the rights of Jews to public funding of parochial schools and respect for the Jewish Sabbath.[6] Inevitably, freedom of religion was set out as the first of the fundamental freedoms in the Universal Declaration of Human Rights. Article 18 states: 'Everyone has the right to freedom of thought, conscience and religion; this right includes freedom to change his religion or belief, and freedom, either alone or in community with others and in public or private, to manifest his religion or belief in teaching, practice, worship and observance.'

One of the first human rights conventions in the United Nations system is the International Convention on the Elimination of All Forms of Racial Discrimination. At the time it was proposed, in 1962, there were plans for a companion instrument dealing with religious discrimination.[7] The subject-matter proved more difficult than racial discrimination. No Convention has ever been completed, although the General Assembly did succeed in adopting the United Nations Declaration on the Elimination of All Forms of Intolerance and of Discrimination Based on Religion or Belief, in 1981. That

---

[3] *Leyla Şahin v. Turkey* [GC], no. 44774/98, § 114, ECHR 2005-XI.

[4] Treaty of Peace between the United States of America, the British Empire, France, Italy, and Japan and Poland, [1919] TS 8, art. 2.

[5] Letter addressed to Mr Paderewski by the President of the Conference transmitting to him the Treaty to be signed by Poland under Article 93 of the Treaty of Peace with Germany, Paris, 25 June 1919.

[6] Treaty of Peace between the United States of America, the British Empire, France, Italy, and Japan and Poland, [1919] TS 8, arts. 10–11.

[7] Preparation of a Draft Declaration and a Draft Convention on the Elimination of All Forms of Religious Intolerance, GA Res. 1781 (XVII).

document enumerates several components of 'the right to freedom of thought, conscience, religion or belief':

In accordance with article I of the present Declaration, and subject to the provisions of article 1, paragraph 3, the right to freedom of thought, conscience, religion or belief shall include, inter alia, the following freedoms:
(a) To worship or assemble in connection with a religion or belief, and to establish and maintain places for these purposes;
(b) To establish and maintain appropriate charitable or humanitarian institutions;
(c) To make, acquire and use to an adequate extent the necessary articles and materials related to the rites or customs of a religion or belief;
(d) To write, issue and disseminate relevant publications in these areas;
(e) To teach a religion or belief in places suitable for these purposes;
(f) To solicit and receive voluntary financial and other contributions from individuals and institutions;
(g) To train, appoint, elect or designate by succession appropriate leaders called for by the requirements and standards of any religion or belief;
(h) To observe days of rest and to celebrate holidays and ceremonies in accordance with the precepts of one's religion or belief;
(i) To establish and maintain communications with individuals and communities in matters of religion and belief at the national and international levels.[8]

The Charter of Fundamental Rights of the European Union also proclaims the right to freedom of thought, conscience, and religion. The text differs very slightly in formulation compared with article 9 of the European Convention on Human Rights:

Article 10. Freedom of thought, conscience and religion
1. Everyone has the right to freedom of thought, conscience and religion. This right includes freedom to change religion or belief and freedom, either alone or in community with others and in public or in private, to manifest religion or belief, in worship, teaching, practice and observance.

According to the explanatory notes, article 10 of the Charter is meant to have the same meaning and scope as article 9 of the European Convention.[9] Paragraph 2 of article 10 of the Charter recognizes a right of conscientious objection.

Drafting of the provision

The initial draft European Convention on Human Rights, prepared by the International Juridical Section of the European Movement, contained the following: 'Every State a party to this Convention shall guarantee to all persons within its territory the following rights: . . . e) Freedom of religious belief, practice and teaching.'[10] The European Movement draft also contained a restrictions or limitations clause, inspired by article 29 of the Universal Declaration of Human Rights: 'The rights specified in Articles 1 and 2 shall be

---

[8] GA Res. 36/55, art. 6.
[9] Explanation Relating to the Charter of Fundamental Rights, Official Journal of the European Union, C 303/33, 14 December 2007.
[10] Convention for the Collective Protection of Individual Rights and Democratic Liberties by the States, Members of the Council of Europe, and for the establishment of a European Court of Human Rights to ensure observance of the Convention, Doc. INF/5/E/R, I *TP* 296–303, at p. 296, art. I(e).

subject only to such limitations as are in conformity with the general principles of law recognised by civilised nations and as are prescribed by law for: a) Protecting the legal rights of others; b) Meeting the just requirements of morality, public order (including the safety of the community), and the general welfare.'[11]

At the first session of the Consultative Assembly, Pierre-Henri Teitgen called for adoption of a convention that would include 'freedom of religious belief, practice and teaching'.[12] Asked to prepare a text for discussion in the Committee on Legal and Administrative Questions at the first session of the Consultative Assembly, Teitgen proposed these words: 'Freedom of religious practice and teaching, in accordance with Article 18 of the United Nations Declaration.'[13] The Committee adopted the following text: 'Freedom of thought, conscience and religion, in accordance with Article 18 of the Declaration of the United Nations.'[14] In presenting the report of the Commission on Legal and Administrative Questions to the plenary Consultative Assembly, Teitgen said that 'in recommending a collective guarantee not only of freedom to express convictions, but also of thought, conscience, religion and opinion, the Committee wished to protect all nationals of any member State, not only from breaches of obligation for so-called reasons of State, but also from those abominable methods of police enquiry or judicial process which rob the suspected or accused person of control of his intellectual faculties and of conscience'.[15] The sentence proposed by the Committee was adopted without debate by the Consultative Assembly.[16]

Teitgen also included a general provision on the restriction or limitation of rights that was based upon the text in the European Movement Draft.[17] After a short debate without a vote, the Consultative Assembly adopted the following text:

In the exercise of these rights, and in the enjoyment of the freedoms guaranteed by the Convention, no limitations shall be imposed except those established by law, with the sole object of ensuring the recognition and respect for the rights and freedoms of others, or with the purpose of satisfying the just requirement of public morality, order and security in a democratic society.[18]

[11] Ibid., p. 296, art. 3.
[12] Report of the Sitting (Reports of the Consultative Assembly, First Session, Part I, 8th Sitting, pp. 210–41), I *TP* 38–154, at p. 46.
[13] Proposals by Mr P.H. Teitgen, Rapporteur, 29 August 1949, Doc. A 116, I *TP* 166–8. Also Report presented by Mr P.H. Teitgen, 5 September 1949, Doc. A 290, I *TP* 192–213, at p. 206. See also I *TP* 228.
[14] Report [of the Committee on Legal and Administrative Questions] to the fifteenth sitting of the Consultative Assembly, 5 September 1949, Doc. AS (1) 77, I *TP* 216–39, at p. 228. See also Minutes of the Sitting [of the Committee on Legal and Administrative Questions, Consultative Assembly, 30 August 1949], Doc. A 167, I TP 174–80, at p. 174.
[15] Report presented by Mr P.H. Teitgen, 5 September 1949, Doc. A 290, I *TP* 192–213, at pp. 198–200.
[16] Recommendation No. 38 to the Committee of Ministers adopted 8 September 1949 on the conclusion of the debates, Doc. AS (1) 108, II *TP* 274–83, at p. 276.
[17] Proposals by Mr P.H. Teitgen, Rapporteur, 29 August 1949, Doc. A 116, I *TP* 166–8. Also Report presented by Mr P.H. Teitgen, 5 September 1949, Doc. A 290, I *TP* 192–213, at p. 206; Report to the fifteenth sitting of the Consultative Assembly, 5 September 1949, Doc. AS (1) 77, I *TP* 216–39, at p. 228.
[18] Official Report of the Sitting (Reports of the Consultative Assembly, First Session, part II. 18th Sitting, pp. 1164–299 and 1308–27), II *TP* 14–274, at pp. 134–42. See also Recommendation No. 38 to the Committee of Ministers adopted 8 September 1949 on the conclusion of the debates, Doc. AS (1) 108, II *TP* 274–83, at p. 278; Report to the fifteenth sitting of the Consultative Assembly, 5 September 1949, Doc. AS (1) 77, I *TP* 216–39, at p. 230; Preparatory Report by the Secretariat-General concerning a Preliminary Draft Convention to Provide a Collective Guarantee of Human Rights, Doc. B 22, III *TP* 2–37, at pp. 16–18.

An early draft prepared by Teitgen had included a phrase that was removed in the final version: 'These rights and freedoms may in no case be exercised contrary to the aims and principles of the Council of Europe.'[19]

Several amendments to the freedom of religion provision were proposed in the Committee of Experts, which convened in February 1950. From the United Kingdom expert, Sir Oscar Dowson, an amendment that was identical to the draft freedom of religion provision adopted by the Commission on Human Rights for the Covenant on human rights the previous year[20] was submitted:

1) Everyone has the right to freedom of thought, conscience and religion; this right includes freedom to change his religion or belief, and freedom, either alone or in community with others and in public or private, to manifest his religion or belief in teaching, practice, worship and observance.
2) Freedom to manifest one's religion or beliefs shall be subject only to such limitations as are pursuant to law and are reasonable and necessary to protect public safety, order, health, or morals or the fundamental rights and freedoms of others.[21]

At the conclusion of its first session, in February 1950, the Committee of Experts adopted the following provision: 'Everyone has the right to freedom of thought, conscience and religion; this right includes freedom to change his religion or belief, and freedom, either alone or in community with others and in public or private, to manifest his religion or belief in teaching, practice, worship and observance.'[22] The report of the Committee explains that instead of enumerating rights by reference to the relevant provision in the Universal Declaration of Human Rights, as had been done by the Consultative Assembly, it was better to incorporate the text verbatim. Accordingly, the Committee 'scrupulously adhered to the text of the Universal Declaration'.[23] The text it adopted is identical to that of article 18 of the Universal Declaration of Human Rights.

The Committee of Experts also adopted a new provision of relevance to the exercise of religious freedom that said nothing in the convention could be considered 'as derogating from already existing national rules as regards religious institutions and foundations or membership of certain confessions'.[24] It was derived from proposals made by the

---

[19] Proposals by Mr P.H. Teitgen, Rapporteur, 29 August 1949, Doc. A 116, I *TP* 166–8. Also Report presented by Mr P.H. Teitgen, 5 September 1949, Doc. A 290, I *TP* 192–213, at p. 206; Report to the fifteenth sitting of the Consultative Assembly, 5 September 1949, Doc. AS (1) 77, I *TP* 216–39, at p. 228.

[20] Report of the Fifth Session of the Commission on Human Rights to the Economic and Social Council, UN Doc. E/1371(Supp.), p. 21.

[21] Amendments to Article 2 of the Recommendation of the Consultative Assembly proposed by the Expert of the United Kingdom, Doc. A 798, III *TP* 204–7, at p. 206.

[22] Preliminary Draft Convention for the Maintenance and Further Realisation of Human Rights and Fundamental Freedoms, 15 February 1950, Doc. A 833, III *TP* 236–46, at p. 236. Also Draft text of the first section of a draft Convention based on the work of the Consultative Assembly, Doc. A 809, III *TP* 220–31, at p. 222.

[23] Preliminary Draft of the Report to the Committee of Ministers, 24 February 1950, Doc. CM/WP 1 (50) 1, A 847, III *TP* 246–79, at pp. 260–2.

[24] Preliminary Draft Convention for the Maintenance and Further Realisation of Human Rights and Fundamental Freedoms, 15 February 1950, Doc. A 833, III *TP* 236–46, at p. 238. Also Draft text of the first section of a draft Convention based on the work of the Consultative Assembly, Doc. A 809, III *TP* 220–31, at p. 224; First part of the Report of the Sub-Committee Instructed to Make a Preliminary Study of the Amendments Proposed by the Members of the Committee, Doc. A 796, III *TP* 200–3.

Swedish expert[25] and the Turkish expert,[26] both of whom invoked 'the existence in their countries of certain national laws which might be considered contrary to the right of the free exercise of religion'.[27] The report of the Committee of Experts explained that the paragraph 'only applies to existing laws, and may not be invoked to justify new restrictions which might be imposed on the free exercise of religion at a future date'.[28] The expert of the Netherlands, with the support of the United Kingdom, objected to the provision, noting that 'the guaranteeing of certain situations of fact, which this provision tends to ensure, do [sic] not justify the incorporation in the text of the Convention of a derogation of such a considerable extent, in spite of the importance they might have'.[29]

At the second session of the Group of Experts, in March 1950, the United Kingdom representative renewed efforts to promote a text similar to that of the draft United Nations Covenant:

1) Everyone has the right to freedom of thought, conscience and religion; this right includes freedom to change his religion or belief and freedom, either alone or in community with others and in public or private, to manifest his religion or belief in teaching, practice, worship and observance.
2) Freedom to manifest one's religion or beliefs shall be subject only to such limitations as are prescribed by law and are necessary in the interests of public safety, or for the protection of public order, health, or morals, or for the protection of the rights and freedoms of others.[30]

Paragraph 1 was unchanged from Britain's earlier proposal. In paragraph 2, the words 'pursuant to law' were replaced with 'prescribed by law', the words 'reasonable and necessary' became 'necessary', the words 'interests of' had been added immediately before 'public safety', 'order' was replaced with 'or for the protection of public order', and 'the fundamental rights and freedoms of others' replaced by 'the protection of the rights and freedoms of others'. A drafting committee revised the text, adding to paragraph 2 a phrase reflecting the initiatives of the Turkish and Swedish experts: 'provided that nothing in this convention may be considered as derogating from already existing national rules as regards religious institutions, or membership of certain confessions'.[31] The Committee explained that this was 'intended to cover those reasonable restrictions on the eligibility for public office of members of certain religious faiths which are prescribed in the constitutions of certain States and which, it was recognised, could not be removed immediately'. The

[25] Amendments to Article 2, para. 3, 5, and 6 of the Recommendation of the Consultative Assembly proposed by the Swedish Expert, Doc. A 777, III *TP* 184: 'This provision does not effect [sic] existing national laws as regards rules relating to religious practice and membership of certain faiths.'
[26] Amendment to Article 2 para. 5 of the Recommendation of the Consultative Assembly proposed by the Turkish Expert, Doc. A 787, III *TP* 196: 'Subject to reservations as regards the measures required for ensuring security and public order, as well as those restrictions which, for reasons of history, it has been considered necessary, by the States, signatories of this Convention, to place on the exercise of this right.'
[27] Report to the Committee of Ministers submitted by the Committee of Experts Instructed to Draw Up a Draft Convention of Collective Guarantee of Human Rights and Fundamental Freedoms, Doc. CM/WP 1 (5) 15, A 924, IV *TP* 2–55, at p. 26.
[28] Ibid.
[29] Ibid., pp. 26–8.
[30] Amendments to Articles 1, 2, 4, 5, 6, 8, and 9 of the Committee's Preliminary Draft Proposal by the Expert of the United Kingdom, Doc. CM/WP 1 (50) 2, A 915, III *TP* 280–9, at p. 286.
[31] Amendments to the British draft proposed by the Drafting Committee composed of Sir Oscar Dowson, MM le Quesne, Dons Moeller, and Salén, Doc. CM/WP 1 (50) 10, p. 3, A 919, III *TP* 288–95, at p. 292.

Report went on to say that the provision was also meant 'to cover similar regulations regarding the membership and the activity of certain religious institutions'.[32]

The Committee of Experts concluded its work with the submission to the Committee of Ministers of two different drafts. The first, 'Alternatives A and A/2', consisted of the text reflecting the Universal Declaration of Human Rights provision that had been adopted by the Committee of Experts at its first session.[33] The second, labelled 'Alternatives B and B/2', contained a text derived from the draft United Nations Covenant that had been proposed by the United Kingdom.[34]

The Committee of Experts also adopted a general provision on restrictions or limitations:

In the exercise of these rights and in the enjoyment of the freedoms secured by the Convention, no limitation shall be imposed except those established by the law, with the sole object of ensuring the recognition and respect for the rights and freedoms of others, or with the purpose of satisfying the just requirements of public morality and order and national security and integrity (and solidarity) as well as the functioning of administration and justice in a democratic society.[35]

The Report of the Committee of Experts explained that it had decided to add 'to the number of higher interests, the demands of which might justify the limitation of human rights, two further restrictions: a) territorial integrity; b) the smooth working of administration and justice'.[36] It said that the first of these had been added on the proposal of the Turkish representative 'in order to make provision for the need of States to be able to defend themselves against all activities which might lead to the disintegration of the nation'.[37] This was accepted by the Committee of Experts 'on the clear understanding that it did not permit a restriction on the rights of national minorities to press their views by democratic means', to which the Turkish representative responded that the proposal 'had no connection with the question of the rights of national minorities, a question which, moreover, would be outside the scope of the Convention'.[38] The second limitation, 'the smooth working of administration and justice', was introduced by the Swedish expert so as to make provision for the fact that sometimes 'certain information should be kept secret'.[39]

---

[32] Report to the Committee of Ministers submitted by the Committee of Experts Instructed to Draw Up a Draft Convention of Collective Guarantee of Human Rights and Fundamental Freedoms, Doc. CM/WP 1 (5) 15, A 924, IV *TP* 2–55, at p. 32.

[33] Ibid., p. 52. See also Preliminary Draft Convention, Doc. CM/WP 1 (50) 14, A 932, III *TP* 312–35, at p. 320.

[34] Report to the Committee of Ministers submitted by the Committee of Experts Instructed to Draw Up a Draft Convention of Collective Guarantee of Human Rights and Fundamental Freedoms, Doc. CM/WP 1 (5) 15, A 924, IV *TP* 2–55, p. 62. See also Preliminary Draft Convention, Doc. CM/WP 1 (50) 14, A 932, III *TP* 312–335, at pp. 316–18.

[35] Preliminary Draft Convention for the Maintenance and Further Realisation of Human Rights and Fundamental Freedoms, 15 February 1950, Doc. A 833, III *TP* 236–46, at p. 236. Also Draft text of the first section of a draft Convention based on the work of the Consultative Assembly, Doc. A 809, III *TP* 220–31, at p. 222.

[36] Report to the Committee of Ministers submitted by the Committee of Experts Instructed to Draw Up a Draft Convention of Collective Guarantee of Human Rights and Fundamental Freedoms, Doc. CM/WP 1 (5) 15, A 924, IV *TP* 2–55, at p. 24.

[37] Ibid., p. 24.

[38] Ibid., pp. 24–6.

[39] Report to the Committee of Ministers submitted by the Committee of Experts Instructed to Draw Up a Draft Convention of Collective Guarantee of Human Rights and Fundamental Freedoms, Doc. CM/WP 1 (5) 15, A 924, IV *TP* 2–55, at p. 26. Also Amendments to Article 2, para. 3, 5, and 6 of the Recommendation of the Consultative Assembly proposed by the Swedish Expert, Doc. A 777, III *TP* 184.

The Conference of Senior Officials that convened in June 1950 assigned a Drafting Committee to attempt to reconcile the competing versions. It prepared a new formulation on freedom of religion based largely on the British proposal, with a few very minor stylistic changes and the addition of the words 'in a democratic society' to paragraph 2.

1) Everyone has the right to freedom of thought, conscience and religion; this right includes freedom to change his religion or belief and freedom, either alone or in community with others and in public or private, to manifest his religion or belief, in teaching, practice, worship and observance.

2) Freedom to manifest one's religion or beliefs shall be subject only to such limitations as are prescribed by law and are necessary in the interests of public safety, or for the protection of public order, health, or morals in a democratic society, or for the protection of the rights and freedoms of others, provided that nothing in this Convention may be considered as derogating from already existing national rules as regards religious institutions and foundations, or membership of certain confessions.[40]

The Drafting Committee revised paragraph 2, removing the final clause that had been proposed initially by experts from Sweden and Turkey and that had provoked so much controversy. The provision then read as follows:

2) Freedom to manifest one's religion or beliefs shall be subject only to such limitations as are prescribed by law and are necessary in a democratic society, in the interests of public safety, or for the protection of public order, health, or morals, or for the protection of the rights and freedoms of others.[41]

The texts of the two paragraphs were subsequently confirmed by the Committee of Ministers at its fifth session, in early August 1950. There were only two minor changes: the comma after 'democratic society' in paragraph 2 and the word 'or' after 'public safety' were removed.[42] There were no further modifications to the text.

The heading, 'Freedom of thought, conscience and religion', was added by Protocol No. 11.[43]

Analysis and interpretation

As the heading of the provisions indicates, freedom of thought, of conscience, and of religion are all protected by article 9 of the European Convention. Although paragraph 1 of article 9 begins with reference to 'thought, conscience and religion' it subsequently refers, on two occasions, to 'religion and belief' (in French, *de religion ou de conviction, sa religion ou sa conviction*), and again to 'religion and beliefs' (*sa religion ou ses convictions*) in paragraph 2. Article 2 of Protocol No. 1 to the Convention, which deals with parental choice of education for their children, speaks of 'religious and philosophical convictions'.

---

[40] New draft alternatives B and B/2, Doc. CM/WP 4 (50) 9, A 1372, IV *TP* 182–91, at p. 188.

[41] Draft Convention appended to the Draft Report, Doc. CM/WP 4 (50) 16, appendix, A 1445, IV *TP* 218–40, at pp. 222–4; Draft Convention annexed to the Report, Doc. CM/WP 4 (50) 19 annex, CM/WP 4 (50) 16 rev., A 1452, IV *TP* 274–95, at p. 278.

[42] Draft Convention adopted by the Sub-Committee, Doc. CM (50) 52, A 1884, V *TP* 76–99, at pp. 80–2; Draft Convention adopted by the Committee of Ministers, 7 August 1950, Doc. A 1937, V *TP* 120–45, at p. 126.

[43] Protocol No. 11 to the Convention for the Protection of Human Rights and Fundamental Freedoms, restructuring the control machinery established thereby, ETS 155, art. 2(2).

Most of the case law is about religion, but the importance of freedom of thought and conscience cannot be overlooked.[44] It is said that '[r]eligious freedom is primarily a matter of individual thought and conscience',[45] a useful way of linking the three concepts in the first sentence of article 9(1). But freedom of thought and conscience also go beyond being a rationale for the protection of religious freedom.

There are three components of the freedom defined in article 9(1): the freedom of thought, conscience, and religion as such; the freedom to change one's religion or belief; and the freedom to manifest religion or belief. Unlike the other fundamental freedoms set out in articles 8, 9, 10, and 11 of the Convention, freedom of thought, conscience, and religion, as well as the freedom to change one's religion or belief, have an absolute nature.[46] In practice, they do not often create much difficulty. They cannot be limited or restricted in any way. '[A] State cannot dictate what a person believes or take coercive steps to make him change his beliefs',[47] the Court has said. This can be seen when paragraph 1 of article 9 is juxtaposed against paragraph 2, a provision that applies only to freedom to manifest religion or belief.[48] Indeed, it is essentially the third component—the manifestation of religion or belief—that raises difficulties. Because manifestation of religious belief may impact upon others, paragraph 2 of article 9 provides for limitations to be imposed using a formulation similar to that in the equivalent paragraphs of articles 8, 10, and 11. Any limitation must be prescribed by law, it must have a legitimate purpose, and it must be necessary in a democratic society.

In theory, although freedom of thought, conscience, and religion, and the freedom to change religion or belief, are not subject to limitations or restrictions, they could still be subject to derogation under article 15(1) of the Convention. It is unclear what this would entail. In one of its General Comments, the United Nations Human Rights Committee observed that derogation from certain rights cannot have any real or practical consequences, giving freedom of conscience as an example.[49]

In its religious dimension, the right set out in article 9 is 'one of the most vital elements that go to make up the identity of believers and their conception of life, but it is also a precious asset for atheists, agnostics, sceptics and the unconcerned'.[50] It entails 'freedom to hold or not to hold religious beliefs and to practise or not to practise a religion'.[51] Article 9 primarily protects 'the sphere of personal beliefs and religious creeds, that is, the

[44] On freedom of conscience, see *Eweida and Others v. the United Kingdom*, no. 48420/10, Joint Partly Dissenting Opinion of Judges Vučinić and De Gaetano, § 2, ECHR 2013 (extracts).

[45] *Eweida and Others v. the United Kingdom*, no. 48420/10, § 80, ECHR 2013 (extracts).

[46] Ibid.

[47] *Ivanova v. Bulgaria*, no. 52435/99, § 79, 12 April 2007; *Masaev v. Moldova*, no. 6303/05, § 23, 12 May 2009.

[48] On this point, see *Eweida and Others v. the United Kingdom*, no. 48420/10, Joint Partly Dissenting Opinion of Judges Vučinić and De Gaetano, § 3, ECHR 2013 (extracts).

[49] General Comment No. 24: Issues relating to reservations made upon ratification or accession to the Covenant or the Optional Protocols thereto, or in relation to declarations under article 41 of the Covenant, UN Doc. CCPR/C/21/Rev.1/Add.6, para. 10.

[50] *Kokkinakis v. Greece*, 25 May 1993, § 31, Series A no. 260-A; *Church of Scientology Moscow v. Russia*, no. 18147/02, § 64, 5 April 2007; *Metropolitan Church of Bessarabia and Others v. Moldova*, no. 45701/99, § 114, ECHR 2001-XII.

[51] *Bayatyan v. Armenia* [GC], no. 23459/03, § 118, ECHR 2011; *Buscarini and Others v. San Marino* [GC], no. 24645/94, § 34, ECHR 1999-I; *Kokkinakis v. Greece*, 25 May 1993, § 31, Series A no. 260-A; *Leyla Şahin v. Turkey* [GC], no. 44774/98, § 104, ECHR 2005-XI.

area which is sometimes called the forum internum'.[52] The Court has held that the term 'beliefs' in article 9, like the term 'convictions' in article 2 of Protocol No. 1, denotes views that attain a certain level of cogency, seriousness, cohesion, and importance.[53] For the Grand Chamber, 'supporters of secularism are able to lay claim to views attaining the "level of cogency, seriousness, cohesion and importance" required for them to be considered "convictions" within the meaning of Articles 9 of the Convention and 2 of Protocol No. 1'.[54]

Freedom of thought, conscience, and religion is one of the foundations of a 'democratic society' within the meaning of the Convention. As the Court has often said, '[t]he pluralism indissociable from a democratic society, which has been dearly won over the centuries, depends on it'.[55] In promoting this value, the role of the authorities is not 'to remove the cause of tension by eliminating pluralism, but to ensure that the competing groups tolerate each other'.[56] But pluralism also brings with it the need for restraints: '[I]n a democratic society, in which several religions coexist within one and the same population, it may be necessary to place restrictions on this freedom in order to reconcile the interests of the various groups and ensure that everyone's beliefs are respected.'[57]

An early decision of the European Commission holds that article 9 can only be invoked by a natural person.[58]

Positive obligation or interference

The methodology for examining whether article 9 has been observed involves initially determining whether the provision applies at all. Once this has been established, it is generally necessary to examine whether a positive obligation has been involved or whether there has been an interference with the right. When the alleged violation cannot directly be attributed to the State, it may nevertheless have a positive obligation to secure rights under article 9 to those within its jurisdiction.

In matters involving a positive obligation, the Court will determine whether measures have been taken that are reasonable and appropriate. For example, where a religious meeting held by Jehovah's Witnesses was broken up with considerable violence, the Court found that there had been a violation of the Convention because 'the relevant authorities

---

[52] *Skugar and Others v. Russia* (dec.), no. 40010/04, 3 December 2009; *Blumberg v. Germany* (dec.), no. 14618/03, 18 March 2008.

[53] *Campbell and Cosans v. the United Kingdom*, 25 February 1982, Series A no. 48, § 36; *Bayatyan v. Armenia* [GC], no. 23459/03, § 110, ECHR 2011; *Leela Förderkreis e.V. and Others v. Germany*, no. 58911/00, § 80, 6 November 2008; *Jakóbski v. Poland*, no. 18429/06, § 44, 7 December 2010; *Blumberg v. Germany* (dec.), no. 14618/03, 18 March 2008.

[54] *Lautsi and Others v. Italy* [GC], no. 30814/06, § 58, ECHR 2011 (extracts). Article 9(1) does not use the word 'convictions'. Perhaps something has been lost in translation, given that the French version of article 9(1) uses the word '*convictions*' where the English version speaks of 'belief'.

[55] *Bayatyan v. Armenia* [GC], no. 23459/03, § 118, ECHR 2011; *Church of Scientology Moscow v. Russia*, no. 18147/02, § 64, 5 April 2007; *Metropolitan Church of Bessarabia and Others v. Moldova*, no. 45701/99, § 114, ECHR 2001-XII.

[56] *Serif v. Greece*, no. 38178/97, § 53, ECHR 1999-IX; *Members of the Gldani Congregation of Jehovah's Witnesses and Others v. Georgia*, no. 71156/01, § 132, 3 May 2007; *Leyla Şahin v. Turkey* [GC], no. 44774/98, Dissenting Opinion of Judge Tulkens, § 106, ECHR 2005-XI.

[57] *Leyla Şahin v. Turkey* [GC], no. 44774/98, § 106, ECHR 2005-XI; *Kokkinakis v. Greece*, 25 May 1993, § 33, Series A no. 260-A.

[58] *Church of X. v. the United Kingdom*, no. 3798/68, Commission decision of 17 December 1968, (1969) 12 YB 306, Collection 29, p. 70.

failed in their duty to take the necessary measures to ensure that the group of Orthodox extremists led by Father Basil tolerated the existence of the applicants' religious community and enabled them to exercise freely their rights to freedom of religion'.[59]

Otherwise, the question to be addressed is whether there has been an interference with the right by the State. If this is the conclusion, the analysis then proceeds to article 9(2), where the Court begins by inquiring as to whether the interference has been 'provided by law'. If the Court concludes there is no interference, the application will be dismissed without paragraph 2 even being considered. In *Skugar v. Russia*, the applicant objected to a taxpayer identification number that she said contained a number that 'was a forerunner of the mark of the Antichrist'. The Court held that 'general legislation which applies on a neutral basis without any link whatsoever with an applicant's personal beliefs cannot in principle be regarded as an interference'.[60] The European Commission reached a similar conclusion dealing with an application from a Quaker who refused to pay taxes destined for military expenditure. The Commission said 'the obligation to pay taxes is a general one which has no specific conscientious implications in itself'. It held that 'Article 9 does not confer on the applicant the right to refuse to abide by legislation . . . which applies neutrally and generally in the public sphere, without impinging on the freedoms guaranteed by Article 9.'[61]

Obviously, in the case of a positive obligation where a non-State actor is involved there can be no question about the interference being 'provided by law'. The whole point is whether the violation attributable to a third party is addressed by the State. However, the Court has often said that although 'the boundary between the State's positive and negative obligations under the Convention does not lend itself to precise definition, the applicable principles are, nonetheless, similar'. In other words, a fair balance must be struck between the competing interests of the individual and of the community as a whole, subject to the margin of appreciation enjoyed by the State.[62] Although not directly applicable, 'in relation to the positive obligations flowing from the first paragraph of Article 9, in striking the required balance the aims mentioned in the second paragraph may be of a certain relevance'.[63]

The Court has invoked the notion of positive obligations as a justification for measures that attempt to educate or warn the public about what it considers to be dangerous religious practices or activities. In a German case, it referred to 'the increasing number of new religious and ideological movements [that] generated conflict and tension in German society, raising questions of general importance', and said that the German authorities, 'by providing people in good time with explanations it considered useful at that time, was aiming to settle a burning public issue and attempting to warn citizens against phenomena it viewed as disturbing, for example, the appearance of numerous new religious movements and their attraction for young people'.[64] In so doing, it was addressing an 'interference imputable to private individuals within non-State entities'.[65]

---

[59] *Members of the Gldani Congregation of Jehovah's Witnesses and Others v. Georgia*, no. 71156/01, § 134, 3 May 2007.

[60] *Skugar and Others v. Russia* (dec.), no. 40010/04, 3 December 2009.

[61] *C. v. the United Kingdom*, no. 10358/83, Commission decision of 15 December 1983, DR 37, p. 142.

[62] *Eweida and Others v. the United Kingdom*, no. 48420/10, § 84, ECHR 2013 (extracts).

[63] *Jakóbski v. Poland*, no. 18429/06, § 47, 7 December 2010.

[64] *Leela Förderkreis e.V. and Others v. Germany*, no. 58911/00, § 98, 6 November 2008.

[65] Ibid., § 99.

Freedom of thought

Benjamin Franklin said that 'Without freedom of thought there can be no such thing as wisdom...' In the constitutional case law of the United States, the right to freedom of thought has been linked to freedom of speech. The two were described by Supreme Court Justice Benjamin Cardozo as 'the matrix, the indispensable condition, of nearly every other form of freedom. With rare aberrations a pervasive recognition of this truth can be traced in our history, political and legal.'[66]

Within European human rights law, very little has been said on freedom of thought as such. Loukis Loucaides, who served as both a judge on the Court and a member of the Commission, has suggested that '[t]his may be attributed to the fact that freedom of thought as a general rule may create a problem only when manifested through the expression of ideas or beliefs in which case other safeguarded rights, such as the freedom of expression or the freedom to manifest one's religion or beliefs come into play and may be invoked and applied instead of freedom of thought'.[67] Reference has been made to Pierre-Henri Teitgen's comment during the drafting of article 9. He explained that the intent was 'to protect all nationals of any member State, not only from breaches of obligation for so-called reasons of State, but also from those abominable methods of police enquiry or judicial process which rob the suspected or accused person of control of his intellectual faculties and of conscience',[68] although more in terms of the relevance to articles 3 and 5 than to article 9.[69]

In its General Comment on article 18 of the International Covenant on Civil and Political Rights, which is very similar in wording to article 9 of the European Convention, the Human Rights Committee 'draws the attention of States parties to the fact that the freedom of thought and the freedom of conscience are protected equally with the freedom of religion and belief'.[70]

Freedom of conscience

'Conscience' seems to be much closer to religion than 'thought' in the sense that religious ideas may emerge from one's 'conscience'. Religious beliefs have been described as 'a matter of individual conscience'.[71] By contrast, 'thoughts' about scientific issues, about whether or not the earth is flat and whether it may revolve around the sun, and of what matter may be composed, and how wealth is created, may be derived from the study of facts rather than probing of the conscience. There may be some preference for the term 'freedom of conscience' instead of 'freedom of religion' because it clarifies the position of atheists and agnostics, and those who profess no religion, yet are possessed of an

---

[66] *Palko v. State of Connecticut*, 302 US 319, 326 (1937).
[67] Loukis G. Loucaides, 'The Right to Freedom of Thought as Protected by the European Convention on Human Rights', (2012) 1 *Cyprus Human Rights Law Review* 79, at p. 80.
[68] Report presented by Mr P.H. Teitgen, 5 September 1949, Doc. A 290, I *TP* 192–213, at pp. 198–200.
[69] Yannis Ktistakis, 'The Protection of Forum Internum under Article 9 of the ECHR', in Dean Spielmann, Marialena Tsirli, and Panayotis Voyatzis, eds, *La Convention européenne des droits de l'homme, un instrument vivant, Mélanges en l'honneur de Christos L. Rozakis*, Brussels: Bruylant, 2011, pp. 285–303, at p. 287; Loukis G. Loucaides, 'The Right to Freedom of Thought as Protected by the European Convention on Human Rights', (2012) 1 *Cyprus Human Rights Law Review* 79, at p. 80.
[70] UN Doc. HRI/GEN/1/Rev.1, p. 35.
[71] *Grzelak v. Poland*, no. 7710/02, § 93, 15 June 2010; *Dogru v. France*, no. 27058/05, § 61, 4 December 2008.

'individual conscience'. The moral or ethical dimension of 'conscience' may be under-scored by the reference in the Preamble of the Hague Conventions of 1899 and 1907 to 'the protection and the rule of the principles of the law of nations, as they result from the usages established among civilised peoples, from the laws of humanity, and the dictates of the public conscience'.[72] The Preamble to the Rome Statute of the International Criminal Court refers to 'unimaginable atrocities that deeply shock the conscience of humanity'.[73]

Like freedom of thought, there is very little in the case law of the Convention organs on freedom of conscience *per se*. In an individual opinion concerning the refusal of a local official to officiate at same-sex civil partnership ceremonies, Judges Vučinić and De Gaetano insisted that this was not a case of freedom of religion so much as one of freedom of conscience. They said there was a fundamental difference between the two, something evident by the presence of the word 'conscience' in paragraph 1 of article 9 but not in paragraph 2, where it is 'conspicuously absent'. They wrote:

Conscience—by which is meant moral conscience—is what enjoins a person at the appropriate moment to do good and to avoid evil. In essence it is a judgment of reason whereby a physical person recognises the moral quality of a concrete act that he is going to perform, is in the process of performing, or has already completed. This rational judgment on what is good and what is evil, although it may be nurtured by religious beliefs, is not necessarily so, and people with no particular religious beliefs or affiliations make such judgments constantly in their daily lives. The pre-eminence (and the ontological roots) of conscience is underscored by the words of a nineteenth century writer who noted that '. . . Conscience may come into collision with the word of a Pope, and is to be followed in spite of that word.'[74]

They omission of 'conscience' in article 9(2) was explained by the fact that religious prescription, such as dietary laws, dress codes, and display of religious symbols, may be subject to limitations whereas prescriptions of conscience may not. 'We are of the view that once that a genuine and serious case of conscientious objection is established, the State is obliged to respect the individual's freedom of conscience both positively (by taking reasonable and appropriate measures to protect the rights of the conscientious objector) and negatively (by refraining from actions which punish the objector or discriminate against him or her)', they wrote.[75] 'In our view the State's margin of appreciation, whether wide or narrow, does not enter into the equation in matters of individual moral conscience.'[76]

In a decision relating to objections to hunting of animals, Judge Pinto de Albuquerque referred to the German federal Constitutional Court's pronouncement that a decision of conscience is a 'serious ethical decision, i.e., one based on the categories of "good" and "bad", by which an individual in a certain situation feels unconditionally bound in his or her innermost self, so that he or she could not act against it without serious qualms of conscience'.[77]

---

[72] Hague Convention (No. II) Respecting the Laws and Customs of War on Land, 32 Stat. 1803, TS 403, preamble; Hague Convention (No. IV) Respecting the Laws and Customs of War on Land (and Annex Regulations Concerning the Laws and Customs of War on Land), 36 Stat. 2277, TS 539, preamble.
[73] Rome Statute of the International Criminal Court, (2002) 2187 UNTS 90, preamble.
[74] *Eweida and Others v. the United Kingdom*, no. 48420/10, Join Partly Dissenting Opinion of Judges Vučinić and De Gaetano, § 2, ECHR 2013 (extracts). The reference is to Cardinal Newman.
[75] Ibid., § 3.
[76] Ibid., § 5.
[77] *Herrmann v. Germany* [GC], no. 9300/07, Partly Concurring and Partly Dissenting Opinion of Judge Pinto de Albuquerque, 26 June 2012, citing BVerfGE 12, 45—Kriegsdienstverweigerung I, 20 December 1960.

Freedom of religion (and belief)

The first sentence of article 9, as well as the title, refers to 'freedom of... religion'. Subsequently, the word 'religion' is linked to the word 'belief' (in French, *convictions*), a word that is not present in the first sentence. The word 'belief' is used in the plural alongside religion. According to the Court, in principle the right to freedom of religion for the purposes of the Convention excludes assessment by the State of the legitimacy of religious beliefs or the ways in which those beliefs are expressed.[78]

Determining whether something constitutes 'thought' or 'conscience' has not posed particular difficulties, but the same cannot be said of religion. There are established or traditional religions in Europe and several States have official religions. Alongside the major religions are religious groups that result from schisms within the mainstream organization or confession. For a significant period in the history of modern Europe the continent was wracked by religious wars associated with such divisions. In addition, there are so-called sects that generally emerge from outside the traditional religions and often do not really resemble them. Such sects may claim to be recognized as a religion and thereby benefit from certain legal advantages.[79]

The 'Church of Scientology' has been active throughout the continent since its establishment half a century ago. According to the European Court, whether Scientology may be called a 'religion' is a matter of controversy among member States.[80] It has taken the view that absent a European consensus on the religious nature of certain 'teachings', and 'being sensitive to the subsidiary nature of its role, the Court considers that it must rely on the position of the domestic authorities in the matter and determine the applicability of Article 9 of the Convention accordingly'.[81] Because the Russian authorities have treated Scientology as a religion, the Court has examined allegations of interference under the rubric of article 9.[82] On the other hand, the Court has been far less prepared to tolerate resistance in some States to the recognition of the Jehovah's Witnesses as a fully fledged religion.[83]

In a German case involving the Osho movement, the Court avoided the issue by referring to 'belief' rather than religion. It said that the applicant association operated meditation centres, organized seminars, and carried out joint work projects. According to its teachings, 'the aim of spiritual development is enlightenment'. Its conception of the world was 'based on the idea of achieving transcendence in all essential areas of life and is continuously shared by them and their community'. These were, said the Court, 'the

---

[78] *Metropolitan Church of Bessarabia and Others v. Moldova*, no. 45701/99, § 117, ECHR 2001-XII.

[79] For a discussion, see *Leela Förderkreis e.V. and Others v. Germany*, no. 58911/00, §§ 7–10, 25, 6 November 2008, as well as the Partly Dissenting Opinion of Judge Lazarova Trajakovska.

[80] A decision by the Court included the following: 'Many European countries, including Belgium, France, Germany and the United Kingdom, have refused to grant Scientology religious recognition, whereas such recognition has been obtained through the courts in other States, such as Spain and Portugal.' The sentence was removed as a result of a rectification of the judgment: *Kimlya and Others v. Russia*, nos 76836/01 and 32782/03, § 79, ECHR 2009.

[81] *Church of Scientology Moscow v. Russia*, no. 18147/02, § 64, 5 April 2007; *Kimlya and Others v. Russia*, nos 76836/01 and 32782/03, § 79, ECHR 2009.

[82] *Kimlya and Others v. Russia*, nos 76836/01 and 32782/03, § 81, ECHR 2009. Similarly, for the Unification Church: *Nolan and K. v. Russia*, no. 2512/04, 12 February 2009.

[83] *Association Les Témoins de Jéhovah v. France*, no. 8916/05, § 50, 30 June 2011; *Kuznetsov and Others v. Russia*, no. 184/02, § 75, 11 January 2007; *Members of the Gldani Congregation of Jehovah's Witnesses and Others v. Georgia*, no. 71156/01, § 134, 3 May 2007; *Religionsgemeinschaft der Zeugen Jehovas and Others v. Austria*, no. 40825/98, § 98, 31 July 2008.

manifestation of the applicant associations' belief' and consequently of matters within the ambit of article 9.[84]

Noting that opinion in democratic societies about the relationship between the State and religions differs widely, the Court has emphasized the margin of appreciation and said that 'special importance' must be given to national decision-making bodies.[85] This is because it is 'not possible to discern throughout Europe a uniform conception of the significance of religion in society'[86] and 'the meaning or impact of the public expression of a religious belief will differ according to time and context'.[87] The variation in rules and traditions from one country to another imposes upon the Court a duty of considerable deference.

Freedom to change religion

Freedom to change one's religion was incorporated in article 18 of the Universal Declaration of Human Rights, from which article 9 of the European Convention is derived. Like freedom of opinion, conscience, and religion, freedom to change one's religion or belief is absolute and is not subject to any interference by the State.[88] Of significance in some parts of the world where change in religion is not a simple matter, or where it is plainly prohibited, within Europe this does not seem to be an issue of importance. There have been several decisions holding that pressuring an individual to change religious beliefs is at variance with article 9.[89] However, there do not appear to be any cases before the Convention organs dealing directly with freedom to change one's religion.

The closest that the Court has come to the issue is in a proselytizing case, *Kokkinakis v. Greece.* At the time, Greece was the only Member State in the Council of Europe to make proselytizing an offence. The applicant was an elderly Greek businessman who, as a Jehovah's Witness, had spent many months in prison in the course of his lifetime as a result of convictions for proselytizing. The Court linked the issue to freedom to change religion or belief: 'in principle the right to try to convince one's neighbour, for example through "teaching", failing which, moreover, "freedom to change [one's] religion or belief", enshrined in Article 9 (art. 9), would be likely to remain a dead letter'.[90] In that sense, proselytizing was protected as a form of freedom to manifest one's religion.

The Court was cautious, however, and did not condemn the Greek legislation; rather, it held that it had not been properly applied to the applicant. It insisted upon a distinction between 'bearing Christian witness and improper proselytism', describing the former as 'true evangelism' and the latter as 'a corruption or deformation of it' that might 'take the form of activities offering material or social advantages with a view to gaining new

---

[84] *Leela Förderkreis e.V. and Others v. Germany*, no. 58911/00, § 81, 6 November 2008.

[85] *Leyla Şahin v. Turkey* [GC], no. 44774/98, § 109, ECHR 2005-XI.

[86] *Otto-Preminger-Institut v. Austria*, 20 September 1994, § 50, Series A no. 295-A.

[87] *Dahlab v. Switzerland* (dec.), no. 42393/98, ECHR 2001-V.

[88] *Kokkinakis v. Greece*, 25 May 1993, Partly Dissenting Opinion of Judge Martens, § 14, Series A no. 260-A.

[89] *Knudsen v. Norway*, no. 11045/84, Commission decision of 8 March 1985, (1985) 28 YB 129, DR 42, p. 247; *Konttinen v. Finland*, no. 24949/94, Commission decision of 3 December 1996, (1997) 40 YB 94, DR 87-A, p. 68; *Francesco Sessa v. Italy*, no. 28790/08, § 37, ECHR 2012 (extracts); *Ivanova v. Bulgaria*, no. 52435/99, § 80, 12 April 2007.

[90] *Kokkinakis v. Greece*, 25 May 1993, § 31, Series A no. 260-A. Also *Ivanova v. Bulgaria*, no. 52435/99, § 78, 12 April 2007; *Jehovah's Witnesses of Moscow v. Russia*, no. 302/02, § 139, 10 June 2010.

members for a Church or exerting improper pressure on people in distress or in need; it may even entail the use of violence or brainwashing'. It said that 'improper proselytism' was 'not compatible with respect for the freedom of thought, conscience and religion of others'.[91] In a subsequent decision, the Court said that article 9 does not 'protect improper proselytism, such as the offering of material or social advantage or the application of improper pressure with a view to gaining new members for a Church'.[92] Some judges were prepared to condemn the Greek anti-proselytizing law outright as a breach of article 9.[93]

Freedom to manifest religion or belief

In addition to freedom of belief, conscience, and religion, and freedom to change religion or belief, the first paragraph of article 9 recognizes 'freedom, either alone or in community with others and in public or private, to manifest his religion or belief, in worship, teaching, practice and observance'. According to the text, this freedom has several components. It may be exercised 'alone or in community with others' and 'in public or private'. The freedom may involve 'teaching, practice and observance'. However, article 9(1) of the Convention 'does not protect every act motivated or inspired by a religion or belief. Moreover, in exercising his freedom to manifest his religion, an individual may need to take his specific situation into account.'[94] Paragraph 2 of article 9 applies to freedom to manifest religion or belief in contrast with the other main components of article 9(1).

Freedom to manifest religion or belief is enshrined in article 9(1), although in a sense this reference is superfluous because '[w]hile religious freedom is primarily a matter of individual conscience, it also implies, inter alia, freedom to "manifest [one's] religion" alone and in private or in community with others, in public and within the circle of those whose faith one shares. Bearing witness in words and deeds is bound up with the existence of religious convictions.'[95] Article 9 lists four forms that manifestation of religion or belief may take: worship; teaching; practice; and observance. It does not protect all acts that are motivated or inspired by religion or belief.[96]

To fall within the concept of 'manifest', as the term is used in article 9(1), there must be an intimate link to the religion or belief, for example 'an act of worship or devotion which forms part of the practice of a religion or belief in a generally recognised form'.[97] There is no requirement that the impugned act constitute a religious duty, but there must be a sufficiently close and direct nexus between the act and the underlying belief, something that is determined on the facts of each case.[98]

---

[91] *Kokkinakis v. Greece*, 25 May 1993, § 48, Series A no. 260-A.

[92] *Larissis and Others v. Greece*, 24 February 1998, § 45, *Reports of Judgments and Decisions* 1998-I.

[93] *Kokkinakis v. Greece*, 25 May 1993, Partly Concurring Opinion of Judge Pettiti, Series A no. 260-A; *Kokkinakis v. Greece*, 25 May 1993, Partly Dissenting Opinion of Judge Martens, § 20, Series A no. 260-A.

[94] *Kalaç v. Turkey*, 1 July 1997, § 27, *Reports of Judgments and Decisions* 1997-IV. Also *Porter v. the United Kingdom* (dec.), no. 15814/02, 8 April 2003; *Zaoui v. Switzerland* (dec.), no. 41615/98, 18 January 2001; *Blumberg v. Germany* (dec.), no. 14618/03, 18 March 2008.

[95] *Metropolitan Church of Bessarabia and Others v. Moldova*, no. 45701/99, § 114, ECHR 2001-XII. Also *Kokkinakis v. Greece*, 25 May 1993, § 31, Series A no. 260-A; *Leyla Şahin v. Turkey* [GC], no. 44774/98, § 105, ECHR 2005-XI.

[96] *Kalaç v. Turkey*, 1 July 1997, § 27, *Reports of Judgments and Decisions* 1997-IV.

[97] *Eweida and Others v. the United Kingdom*, no. 48420/10, § 82, ECHR 2013 (extracts).

[98] *Cha'are Shalom Ve Tsedek v. France* [GC], no. 27417/95, §§ 73–74, ECHR 2000-VII; *Leyla Şahin v. Turkey* [GC], no. 44774/98, §§ 78, 105, ECHR 2005-XI; *Bayatyan v. Armenia* [GC], no. 23459/03, § 111,

There is a negative aspect to the freedom to manifest religion or belief. Individuals have the right not to be required to reveal their faith or religious beliefs and not to be compelled to assume a stance from which it may be inferred whether or not they have such beliefs. Consequently, 'there will be an interference with the negative aspect of this provision when the State brings about a situation in which individuals are obliged—directly or indirectly—to reveal that they are non-believers. This is all the more important when such obligation occurs in the context of the provision of an important public service such as education.'[99]

In some States, identity cards have indicated religious domination. Unhappy when the reference to religion on Greek identity cards was eliminated in 2000, the applicants invoked article 9 before the Court. The Court said that identity cards were not intended to provide the devout with a means to manifest their religion.[100] The right to manifest one's religion does not include an entitlement that religion be mentioned on an individual's identity card. Because identity cards are used regularly for a range of services, there is a concern that this might contribute to discriminatory situations.[101] The problem is not resolved by allowing a person to leave the reference to religion blank. But although the Court has found that reference to religion on public identity cards is contrary to article 9,[102] it has accepted the mention on German tax documents, whose public exposure was quite minimal.[103]

The Court found that there had been a violation of article 9 in Greece with respect to the swearing-in of a lawyer. There was a presumption that an oath would be taken on the Bible, forcing those for whom it was not a sacred text to declare their religion or belief, or the absence of one. According to the Court, '[i]l n'est pas loisible aux autorités étatiques de s'immiscer dans la liberté de conscience d'une personne en s'enquérant de ses convictions religieuses ou en l'obligeant à les manifester, et spécialement à le faire, notamment à l'occasion d'une prestation de serment, pour pouvoir exercer certaines fonctions'.[104] In another case, the Court found that the Greek legislation governing civil procedure created a presumption that the oath of a witness to tell the truth be taken on the Bible, with a solemn declaration being possible for those making such a request. This, too, was held to be incompatible with the negative dimension of article 9.[105] On the relatively rare occasions when a witness is heard by the European Court of Human Rights, he or she may 'swear' or 'solemnly declare on my honour and conscience' that 'I shall speak the truth, the whole truth and nothing but the truth'.[106]

The Court has also examined issues relating to manifestation of religion or belief as a positive obligation. This means the State must take reasonable and appropriate measures

ECHR 2011; *Skugar and Others v. Russia* (dec.), no. 40010/04, 3 December 2009; *Pichon and Sajous v. France* (dec.), no. 49853/99, *Reports of Judgments and Decisions* 2001-X.

[99] *Grzelak v. Poland*, no. 7710/02, § 87, 15 June 2010.

[100] *Sofianopoulos and Others v. Greece* (dec.), nos 988/02, 1997/02, and 1977/02, 12 December 2002.

[101] *Sinan Işık v. Turkey*, no. 21924/05, § 43, ECHR 2010.

[102] Ibid., §§ 51–53.

[103] *Wasmuth v. Germany*, no. 12884/03, §§ 61–63, 17 February 2011.

[104] *Alexandridis v. Greece*, no. 19516/06, § 38, 21 February 2008; *Dimitras and Others v. Greece*, nos 42837/06, 3237/07, 3269/07, 35793/07, and 6099/08, § 78, 3 June 2010; *Wasmuth v. Germany*, no. 12884/03, § 50, 17 February 2011; *Sinan Işık v. Turkey*, no. 21924/05, § 41, ECHR 2010.

[105] *Dimitras and Others v. Greece*, nos 42837/06, 3237/07, 3269/07, 35793/07, and 6099/08, §§ 84–88, 3 June 2010.

[106] Rules of Court, Rule 6A(1).

to secure rights under article 9(1), although the analysis is broadly similar to that under article 9(2) when the permissibility of an interference is considered.[107] A 'fair balance' must be struck between the competing interests of the individual and the community. The State has a margin of appreciation in this respect.

Alone or in community

Freedom to manifest religion or belief may be exercised alone or in community with others. According to the Court, this 'encompasses the expectation that believers will be allowed to associate freely, without arbitrary State intervention. Indeed, the autonomous existence of religious communities is indispensable for pluralism in a democratic society and is thus an issue at the very heart' of article 9.[108] For this reason, the reference to 'community' in article 9 points to article 11, which safeguards associative life against unjustified State interference. There have been many cases involving religious institutions and their freedom of association and peaceful assembly. The Court has said that 'where the organisation of the religious community is at issue, Article 9 of the Convention must be interpreted in the light of Article 11'.[109] Furthermore, 'one of the means of exercising the right to manifest one's religion, especially for a religious community, in its collective dimension, is the possibility of ensuring judicial protection of the community, its members and its assets, so that Article 9 must be seen not only in the light of Article 11, but also in the light of Article 6'.[110]

Refusal of the authorities to grant a legal-entity status to a religious association or church is an interference with freedom of association. This will also amount to an interference with the right to manifest religion or belief, both for the community and the individual members.[111] Some countries reserve various rights to religious organizations that have legal-entity status such as establishing places of worship, holding religious services in places accessible to the public, producing, obtaining, and distributing religious literature, creating educational institutions, and maintaining contacts for international exchanges and conferences.[112] Questions relating to the tax status of buildings used for religious purposes may have important repercussions on the exercise of the right to manifest religious belief by members of religious groups.[113]

States are entitled to verify whether a movement or association carries on, ostensibly in pursuit of religious aims, activities that are harmful to the population or to

---

[107] *Jakóbski v. Poland*, no. 18429/06, § 47, 7 December 2010.

[108] *Church of Scientology Moscow v. Russia*, no. 18147/02, § 64, 5 April 2007; *Jehovah's Witnesses of Moscow v. Russia*, no. 302/02, § 100, 10 June 2010; *Metropolitan Church of Bessarabia and Others v. Moldova*, no. 45701/99, §§ 118–123, ECHR 2001-XII; *Religionsgemeinschaft der Zeugen Jehovas and Others v. Austria*, no. 40825/98, § 61, 31 July 2008; *Hasan and Chaush v. Bulgaria* [GC], no. 30985/96, § 62, ECHR 2000-XI.

[109] *Schüth v. Germany*, no. 1620/03, § 58, ECHR 2010; *Siebenhaar v. Germany*, no. 18136/02, § 42, 3 February 2011; *Svyato-Mykhaylivska Parafiya v. Ukraine*, no. 77703/01, § 112, 14 June 2007.

[110] *Religionsgemeinschaft der Zeugen Jehovas and Others v. Austria*, no. 40825/98, § 63, 31 July 2008.

[111] *Church of Scientology of St. Petersburg and Others v. Russia*, no. 47191/06, §§ 37–38, 2 October 2014; *Religionsgemeinschaft der Zeugen Jehovas and Others v. Austria*, no. 40825/98, §§ 79–80, 31 July 2008; *Jehovah's Witnesses of Moscow v. Russia*, no. 302/02, § 101, 10 June 2010; *Metropolitan Church of Bessarabia and Others v. Moldova*, no. 45701/99, § 105, ECHR 2001-XII; *Kimlya and Others v. Russia*, nos 76836/01 and 32782/03, § 81, ECHR 2009.

[112] *Jehovah's Witnesses of Moscow v. Russia*, no. 302/02, § 102, 10 June 2010; *Kimlya and Others v. Russia*, nos 76836/01 and 32782/03, §§ 54–55, 86, ECHR 2009.

[113] *Cumhuriyetçi Eğitim Ve Kültür Merkezi Vakfi v. Turkey*, no. 32093/10, § 41, 2 December 2014; *The Church of Jesus Christ of Latter-Day Saints v. the United Kingdom*, no. 7552/09, § 30, 4 March 2014.

public safety.[114] Because of the special importance of religion and the protection offered by article 9, when religious associations apply for legal status the State must act with particular diligence and ensure that proceedings are not excessively prolonged.[115] If a religious community is divided, the State should not take measures favouring one particular leader or group, nor should it compel the community, or part of it, to place itself under a single leadership.[116]

In public or private

Most of the litigation concerning freedom to manifest religion or belief necessarily involves activities that take place in public. The reference to 'in private' suggests a relationship with article 8 of the Convention and the protection of private life. In a case involving persecution of Jehovah's Witnesses in Russia, the respondent government attempted to justify denial of legal-entity status on the grounds that the activities of the religious group breached the privacy of its members. Examples that were given were the determination of the place and nature of employment, a preference for part-time work allowing time to preach, unpaid work at the community centre, regulation of leisure activities, a ban on celebrating holidays and birthdays and mandatory missionary activity, and 'door-to-door' preaching.[117] The Court concluded that 'what was taken by the Russian courts to constitute an infringement by the applicant community of the right of its members to respect for their private life was in fact a manifestation of their beliefs in their private lives in the sense protected by Article 9'.[118]

Many religions impose standards of behaviour and conduct upon their adherents who are expected to abide by these in their private lives. The Court has provided several examples of manifesting religion or relief in private life, including regular attendance at church services, performance of certain rituals such as communion or confession, observance of religious holidays or abstention from work on specific days of the week, wearing specific clothes, and dietary regulations.[119] By following such practices and customs in their daily lives, believers manifest their desire 'to comply strictly with the religious beliefs they professed and their liberty to do so was guaranteed by Article 9 of the Convention in the form of the freedom to manifest religion, alone and in private'.[120] Sometimes, such practices may be injurious: 'The Court observes, on a general note, that the rites and rituals of many religions may harm believers' well-being, such as, for example, the practice of fasting, which is particularly long and strict in Orthodox Christianity, or circumcision practised on Jewish or Muslim male babies.'[121]

---

[114] *Metropolitan Church of Bessarabia and Others v. Moldova*, no. 45701/99, § 113, ECHR 2001-XII; *Stankov and the United Macedonian Organisation Ilinden v. Bulgaria*, nos 29221/95 and 29225/95, § 84, ECHR 2001-IX.

[115] *Kimlya and Others v. Russia*, nos 76836/01 and 32782/03, § 99, ECHR 2009; *Religionsgemeinschaft der Zeugen Jehovas and Others v. Austria*, no. 40825/98, §§ 78–80, 31 July 2008.

[116] *Supreme Holy Council of the Muslim Community v. Bulgaria*, no. 39023/97, §§ 76, 96, 16 December 2004; *Serif v. Greece*, no. 38178/97, §§ 49, 52, and 53, ECHR 1999-IX; *Hasan and Chaush v. Bulgaria* [GC], no. 30985/96, § 78, ECHR 2000-XI; *Svyato-Mykhaylivska Parafiya v. Ukraine*, no. 77703/01, § 123, 14 June 2007; *Mirolubovs and Others v. Latvia*, no. 798/05, § 80, 15 September 2009; *Fernández Martínez v. Spain*, no. 56030/07, § 80, 15 May 2012.

[117] *Jehovah's Witnesses of Moscow v. Russia*, no. 302/02, § 116, 10 June 2010.

[118] Ibid., § 121.

[119] Ibid., § 118.

[120] Ibid.

[121] Ibid., § 144.

Worship, teaching, practice, and observance

The Convention organs have recognized many 'aspects of the practice of a religion or belief in a generally recognised form'[122] by which individuals may manifest their beliefs including the reading of sacred texts,[123] assembling with others for a service of worship,[124] participation in the life of the community,[125] proselytizing,[126] wearing specific clothes,[127] respecting dietary restrictions,[128] and the consumption of hallucinogenic drugs.[129] Respect for the freedom to practice religion cannot provide the State with a pretext to avoid ensuring the protection of fundamental rights, however. When the Polish government attempted to justify its failure to provide access to abortion where this was governed by law for the reason that physicians refused to provide the service on the grounds of conscience, the Court recalled that 'the word "practice" used in Article 9 § 1 does not denote each and every act or form of behaviour motivated or inspired by a religion or a belief... States are obliged to organise their health service system in such a way as to ensure that the effective exercise of freedom of conscience by health professionals in a professional context does not prevent patients from obtaining access to services to which they are entitled under the applicable legislation.'[130]

The term 'teaching' in article 9(1) implies 'in principle the right to try to convince one's neighbour'.[131] It certainly goes beyond the restrictive notion, proposed by a dissenting judge, that 'the term "teaching" in Article 9 (art. 9) undoubtedly refers to religious teaching in school curricula or in religious institutions, and not to personal door-to-door canvassing'.[132] The word 'teaching' is certainly used in a more narrow school classroom sense in article 2 of Protocol No. 1.

The enumeration of the four forms of manifesting religion indicates that the freedom is not unlimited. Indeed, not every act that may be inspired, motivated, or influenced by religion or belief can be taken as a 'manifestation' in the sense of article 9(1).[133] Acts or omissions that do not directly express the belief concerned or which are only remotely connected to a precept of faith are excluded from the scope of article 9(1).[134]

---

[122] *Kuznetsov and Others v. Russia*, no. 184/02, § 57, 11 January 2007; *Kalaç v. Turkey*, 1 July 1997, § 27, *Reports of Judgments and Decisions* 1997-IV.

[123] *Kuznetsov and Others v. Russia*, no. 184/02, § 57, 11 January 2007.

[124] *Barankevich v. Russia*, no. 10519/03, § 20, 26 July 2007.

[125] *Supreme Holy Council of the Muslim Community v. Bulgaria*, no. 39023/97, § 73, 16 December 2004.

[126] *Kokkinakis v. Greece*, 25 May 1993, § 36, Series A no. 260-A.

[127] *Leyla Şahin v. Turkey* [GC], no. 44774/98, § 78, ECHR 2005-XI; *Phull v. France* (dec.), no. 35753/03, 11 January 2005; *Ahmet Arslan and Others v. Turkey*, no. 41135/98, § 35, 23 February 2010.

[128] *Cha'are Shalom Ve Tsedek v. France* [GC], no. 27417/95, § 73, ECHR 2000-VII; *Jakóbski v. Poland*, no. 18429/06, § 44, 7 December 2010.

[129] *Alida Maria Fränklin-Beentjes and CEFLU-Luz da Floresta v. the Netherlands* (dec.), no. 28167/07, 6 May 2014.

[130] *P. and S. v. Poland*, no. 57375/08, § 106, 30 October 2012. Also *R.R. v. Poland*, no. 27617/04, § 206, ECHR 2011 (extracts).

[131] *Kokkinakis v. Greece*, 25 May 1993, § 31, Series A no. 260-A; *Ivanova v. Bulgaria*, no. 52435/99, § 78, 12 April 2007; *Larissis and Others v. Greece*, 24 February 1998, § 45, Reports of Judgments and Decisions 1998-I; *Jehovah's Witnesses of Moscow v. Russia*, no. 302/02, § 139, 10 June 2010.

[132] *Kokkinakis v. Greece*, 25 May 1993, Dissenting Opinion of Judge Valtikos, Series A no. 260-A.

[133] *Eweida and Others v. the United Kingdom*, no. 48420/10, § 82, ECHR 2013 (extracts); *Kalaç v. Turkey*, 1 July 1997, § 27, *Reports of Judgments and Decisions* 1997-IV; *Kosteski v. 'the former Yugoslav Republic of Macedonia'*, no. 55170/00, § 37, 13 April 2006.

[134] *Skugar and Others v. Russia* (dec.), no. 40010/04, 3 December 2009; *Arrowsmith v. the United Kingdom*, no. 7050/75, Commission report of 12 October 1978, DR 19, p. 5; *C. v. the United Kingdom*, no. 10358/83,

The Convention organs have refused to recognize many practices that were allegedly motivated by religion or belief, such as having one's ashes scattered on one's own land,[135] putting a photograph on a graveyard memorial,[136] giving a specific name to a child,[137] an exemption from a general prohibition on divorce,[138] assisted suicide,[139] mandatory participation in a school parade,[140] a refusal of pharmacists to sell contraceptive pills,[141] and a refusal to have a tax number because it had a pejorative religious connotation.[142]

Interference with freedom to manifest religion or belief

Freedom to manifest religion often involves conflicts between employers and their employees with respect to working conditions and conduct in the workplace. All European States recognize various public holidays or rest days; indeed, the right to rest and leisure is required by article 24 of the Universal Declaration of Human Rights and a score of other international human rights and specialized labour instruments. The European Social Charter acknowledges the role of 'tradition or custom in the country or region concerned' in setting rest days.[143] But in a pluralist Europe, not everyone shares the same 'traditions or customs'.

The Convention organs have held that article 9 does not protect a public servant who is a member of the Seventh-day Adventist Church from being dismissed for refusing to work after sunset on Friday in accordance with requirements of religious observance.[144] Similarly, a private-sector employee who objected to working on Sundays could not avail of article 9.[145] Nor did article 9 protect a Jewish lawyer who was refused adjournment of a case because the hearing conflicted with Yom Kippur.[146] In concluding there was no infringement on the right to manifest religion, the Court explained that it was not disputed that the lawyer was able to perform his religious duties. It said he could have expected his request for an adjournment would be refused and arranged be represented at the hearing so as to comply with his professional obligations.[147]

The Convention organs have generally viewed measures taken against employees in such circumstances to be based not on their religious beliefs but rather justified by the specific contractual obligations between the persons concerned and their respective employers. But in one case, the dismissal of an employee was preceded by an attempt of government employees to convince her to abandon her affiliation with a Christian evangelical group known as the Word of Life. This was associated with a more

Commission decision of 15 December 1983, DR 37, p. 142; *Zaoui v. Switzerland* (dec.), no. 41615/98, 18 January 2001.

[135] *X. v. Federal Republic of Germany*, no. 8741/79, Commission decision of 10 March 1981, 24, p. 137.
[136] *Jones v. the United Kingdom* (dec.), no. 42639/04, 13 September 2005.
[137] *Salonen v. Finland*, no. 27868/95, Commission decision of 2 July 1997.
[138] *Johnston and Others v. Ireland*, 18 December 1986, § 63, Series A no. 112.
[139] *Pretty v. the United Kingdom*, no. 2346/02, § 82, ECHR 2002-III.
[140] *Valsamis v. Greece and Efstratiou v. Greece*, 18 December 1996, § 37, *Reports of Judgments and Decisions* 1996-VI.
[141] *Pichon and Sajous v. France* (dec.), no. 49853/99, *Reports of Judgments and Decisions* 2001-X.
[142] *Skugar and Others v. Russia* (dec.), no. 40010/04, 3 December 2009.
[143] European Social Charter, ETS 35, art. 2(5).
[144] *Konttinen v. Finland*, no. 24949/94, Commission decision of 3 December 1996, (1997) 40 YB 94, DR 87-A, p. 68.
[145] *Stedman v. the United Kingdom*, no. 29107/95, Commission decision of 9 April 1997, DR 89-A, p. 104.
[146] *Francesco Sessa v. Italy*, no. 28790/08, § 35, ECHR 2012 (extracts).
[147] Ibid., § 37.

widespread policy of intolerance towards the religion that included the breaking up of meetings and the dismissal of the former principal of the school because she was alleged to have tacitly approved of religious activities in the school.[148]

In the field of education, the Court considers that article 2 of Protocol No. 1, which deals with the rights of parents in the choice of schools for their children, is the *lex specialis* of article 9. At least, that should be the approach if 'the dispute concerns the obligation laid on Contracting States by the second sentence of Article 2 to respect, when exercising the functions they assume in that area, the right of parents to ensure such education and teaching in conformity with their own religious and philosophical convictions'.[149] Thus, in cases concerning religion and education, it prefers to premise the analysis primarily on article 2 of Protocol No. 1. In the Italian case concerning the crucifix in the classroom, the Court concluded there had been no violation of article 2 and that no separate issue arose under article 9.[150]

Article 4(3)(b) of the Convention, concerning slavery and servitude, states that the term 'forced or compulsory labour' shall not include 'any service of a military character or, in case of conscientious objectors in countries where they are recognised, service exacted instead of compulsory military service'. The term 'conscientious objector' also evokes the word conscience in article 9(1). As early as 1967, the Parliamentary Assembly of the Council of Europe affirmed a right of conscientious objection to military service, explicitly associating this with article 9 of the European Convention on Human Rights;

1. Persons liable to conscription for military service who, for reasons of conscience or profound conviction arising from religious, ethical, moral, humanitarian, philosophical or similar motives, refuse to perform armed service shall enjoy a personal right to be released from the obligation to perform such service.
2. This right shall be regarded as deriving logically from the fundamental rights of the individual in democratic Rule of Law States which are guaranteed in Article 9 of the European Convention on Human Rights.[151]

A formal right to conscientious objection is recognized in article 10(2) of the European Union Charter of Fundamental Rights within the freedom of belief, conscience, and religion provision: '2. The right to conscientious objection is recognised, in accordance with the national laws governing the exercise of this right.'[152] This addition to a text that is clearly inspired by article 9(1) of the European Convention 'reflects the unanimous recognition of the right to conscientious objection by the member States of the European Union, as well as the weight attached to that right in modern European society'.[153]

In early cases filed by conscientious objectors, the European Commission of Human Rights took the view that a right to conscientious objection could not be sustained precisely because the matter was dealt with in article 4.[154] This was similar to the position

---

[148] *Ivanova v. Bulgaria*, no. 52435/99, §§ 84–85, 12 April 2007.
[149] *Lautsi and Others v. Italy* [GC], no. 30814/06, § 58, ECHR 2011 (extracts); *Folgerø and Others v. Norway* [GC], no. 15472/02, § 84, ECHR 2007-VIII, § 84.
[150] *Lautsi and Others v. Italy* [GC], no. 30814/06, § 77, ECHR 2011.
[151] Resolution 337 (1967) on the right of conscientious objection.
[152] Charter of Fundamental Rights of the European Union, 2010 OJ C 83/02, art. 10;(2).
[153] *Bayatyan v. Armenia* [GC], no. 23459/03, § 106, ECHR 2011.
[154] *Grandrath v. Federal Republic of Germany*, no. 2299/64, Commission report of 12 December 1966, (1967) 10 YB 630. Similarly *X v. Austria*, no. 5591/72, Commission decision of 2 April 1973, Collection 43, p. 161; *X v. Federal Republic of Germany*, no. 7705/76, Commission decision of 5 July 1977, DR 9, p. 196;

taken with respect to capital punishment by which it could not be challenged under article 3 of the Convention given the explicit recognition of its permissibility under article 2.[155] Revisiting this case law, the Grand Chamber referred to the *travaux préparatoires* to confirm its impression that 'the sole purpose of sub-paragraph (b) of Article 4 § 3 is to provide a further elucidation of the notion "forced or compulsory labour". In itself it neither recognises nor excludes a right to conscientious objection and should therefore not have a delimiting effect on the rights guaranteed by Article 9.'[156] The Grand Chamber took the view that the refusal of a Jehovah's Witness in Armenia to report for military service upon being conscripted amounted to a manifestation of religion or belief.[157] The Court concluded that 'opposition to military service, where it is motivated by a serious and insurmountable conflict between the obligation to serve in the army and a person's conscience or his deeply and genuinely held religious or other beliefs, constitutes a conviction or belief of sufficient cogency, seriousness, cohesion and importance to attract the guarantees of Article 9'.[158] Since the *Bayatyan* case, the Court has held that although many conscientious objectors invoke religious beliefs, there is no reason why the right cannot also protect an individual with pacifist views or other beliefs that make military service unacceptable.[159]

The Convention organs were for many years quite reluctant to allow article 9 to be applied in cases relating to immigration, deportation, and expulsion. The European Commission, in a case involving Swami Omkarananda, the leader of a sect known as the Divine Light Zentrum, explained that article 9 'does not in itself grant a right for an alien to stay in a given country'. While acknowledging that the expulsion was 'likely to deeply shake' the organization, the Commission held that there could be no interference with article 9 'unless it can be established that the measure was designed to repress the exercise of such rights and stifle the spreading of the religion or philosophy of the followers'.[160] In another case, the Commission stated that 'freedom of religion does not as such encompass the right to a residence permit for the purposes of taking employment, even if the employer is a religious association'.[161] More recently, the Court has been inclined to conclude that there is an interference with article 9 in such cases. In a Latvian case involving the American pastor of an evangelical Christian group known as Morning Star International, the Court concluded that the refusal to renew a residence permit did indeed constitute an interference with article 9.[162] It adopted a similar view in a Russian case.[163] In a case

---

Conscientious objectors v. Denmark, no. 7565/76, Commission decision of 7 March 1977, DR 9, p. 117; *A. v. Switzerland*, no. 10640/83, Commission decision of 9 May 1984, DR 38, p. 219; *N. v. Sweden*, no. 10410/83, Commission decision of 11 October 1984, DR 40, p. 203.

[155] See, for example, *Soering v. the United Kingdom*, 7 July 1989, § 102, Series A no. 161.

[156] *Bayatyan v. Armenia* [GC], no. 23459/03, § 100, ECHR 2011.

[157] Ibid., § 102.

[158] Ibid., § 110.

[159] *Savda v. Turkey*, no. 42730/05, § 96, 12 June 2012.

[160] *Swami Omkarananda and the Divine Light Zentrum v. Switzerland*, no. 8118/77, Commission decision of 19 March 1981, DR 25, p. 105.

[161] *Öz v. Germany*, no. 32168/96, Commission decision of 3 December 1996. See also *El Majjaoui and Stichting Touba Moskee v. the Netherlands* (striking out) [GC], no. 25525/03, Joint Dissenting Opinion of Judges Zupančič, Zagrebelsky, and Myjer, § 2, 20 December 2007; *Eweida and Others v. the United Kingdom*, no. 48420/10, Joint Partly Dissenting Opinion of Judges Bratza and Davíd Thór Björgvinsson, § 2, ECHR 2013 (extracts).

[162] *Perry v. Latvia*, no. 30273/03, § 56, 8 November 2007.

[163] *Nolan and K. v. Russia*, no. 2512/04, § 62, 12 February 2009.

involving a Muslim fundamentalist who was being deported from Bulgaria, the Court found a violation of the right to family life, and said that it was unnecessary to pronounce itself on the article 9 issue.[164] Another Bulgarian case concerning the expulsion of Jehovah's Witnesses was declared admissible.[165]

The Court considered the case of a prisoner serving a lengthy sentence who insisted upon being provided a vegetarian diet, in compliance with his religious beliefs. The authorities had refused this saying that the cost would be excessive, given that only one prisoner was involved. The Court did not find the explanation very convincing and held that article 9(1) had been violated.[166]

Limitations (art. 9(2))

Article 9 is one of four provisions of the European Convention with a restrictions or limitations clause. Paragraph 2 of article 9 states: 'Freedom to manifest one's religion or beliefs shall be subject only to such limitations as are prescribed by law and are necessary in a democratic society in the interests of public safety, for the protection of public order, health or morals, or for the protection of the rights and freedoms of others.' There are similar but not identical clauses in articles 8, 10, and 11. Comparable texts are also used with respect to some of the provisions in the Protocols: article 1 of Protocol No. 1 (protection of property); article 2(3) of Protocol No. 4 (freedom of movement); and article 2(2) of Protocol No. 7 (right of appeal in criminal matters). The Convention organs have developed a flexible methodology for the interpretation and application of paragraph 2 in determining whether or not the interference with a right set out in the first paragraph of articles 8, 9, 10, and 11 is actually in breach of the Convention.

The ancestor of the four provisions is article 29(2) of the Universal Declaration of Human Rights: 'In the exercise of his rights and freedoms, everyone shall be subject only to such limitations as are determined by law solely for the purpose of securing due recognition and respect for the rights and freedoms of others and of meeting the just requirements of morality, public order and the general welfare in a democratic society.' The limitation clause in the Universal Declaration applies generally to all rights set out in the instrument, whereas the specific clauses of this nature in the European Convention, of which article 9(2) is an example, are tailored to the right at issue. A provision comparable in content to article 9(2) appears in the International Covenant on Civil and Political Rights.

Prescribed by law

It is a preliminary condition for any restriction upon the rights set out in article 9(1) that the measure be 'prescribed by law'. The interference must, of course, be authorized by a rule recognized in the national legal order. This encompasses 'written law', including various forms of delegated legislation, and unwritten law as interpreted and applied by the courts.[167] But there is also a qualitative requirement for the legal rule. It must be accessible and foreseeable. There may be higher expectations in applying the condition depending

---

[164] *Al-Nashif v. Bulgaria*, no. 50963/99, § 142, 20 June 2002.

[165] *Lotter and Lotter v. Bulgaria* (dec.), no. 39015/97, 6 February 2003.

[166] *Jakóbski v. Poland*, no. 18429/06, §§ 52–55, 7 December 2010.

[167] *Leyla Şahin v. Turkey* [GC], no. 44774/98, § 88, ECHR 2005-XI; *Sanoma Uitgevers B.V. v. the Netherlands* [GC], no. 38224/03, § 83, 14 September 2010.

upon the individuals involved, in light of their training, professional activity, and experience. It may be reasonable to expect them to obtain expert advice on the law depending upon the circumstances. The law must also be subject to mechanisms so that it can be applied in a manner that is genuine and not arbitrary. If the law grants discretion to public authorities, it must be framed with sufficient clarity and specify the manner in which it is to be exercised.[168] The Court is not prescriptive in this respect, acknowledging that States have a 'margin of appreciation' in deciding upon the legal mechanisms by which they limit or restrict the rights set out in the Convention. In effect, the words 'prescribed by law' refer to the broad, general notion of the 'rule of law'.

Accordingly, the domestic law must provide protection against arbitrary interference by the authorities with rights that are enshrined in the Convention. This is fundamental to the rule of law, a seminal concept that is basic to democratic governance. If the law grants discretion to public authorities, it must be framed with sufficient clarity and specify the manner in which it is to be exercised.[169]

Where authorities essentially broke up a meeting being held by Jehovah's Witnesses, the Court noted that 'the legal basis for breaking up a religious event conducted on the premises lawfully rented for that purpose was conspicuously lacking' and held that there had been a violation of the Convention because the interference was not prescribed by law.[170] An application directed against Turkey involved the conviction of two persons for 'la propagande en faveur d'une organisation terroriste'. The applicants had organized a memorial ceremony on behalf of members of a terrorist organization who had been killed in action. The Court found the charge of 'propaganda' was not sufficiently precise. As a result, the requirement that the restriction be 'prescribed by law' was not met and there was a violation of article 9.[171]

Legitimate purpose

The second component of the analysis is the existence of a legitimate purpose or aim. The inquiry involves the enumeration of purposes set out in paragraph 2, namely the interests of public safety, for the protection of public order, health, or morals, or for the protection of the rights and freedoms of others. These exceptions to freedom of religion are to be interpreted narrowly.[172] Nevertheless, examples of violations of article 9(1) because of the failure of the State to put forward a plausible legal and factual justification for the interference are relatively isolated.[173] In practice, this part of the analysis is rarely very important. It is not uncommon for the Court to simply pass over the issue entirely and move to the heart of the debate, which takes place under the rubric of 'necessary in a democratic society', finding that it violates the final component of the test regardless of whether it fulfils a legitimate purpose.[174] The Grand Chamber has explained that it is the

---

[168] *Hasan and Chaush v. Bulgaria* [GC], no. 30985/96, § 84, ECHR 2000-XI; *Maestri v. Italy* [GC], no. 39748/98, § 30, ECHR 2004-I.

[169] *Hasan and Chaush v. Bulgaria* [GC], no. 30985/96, § 84, ECHR 2000–XI

[170] *Kuznetsov and Others v. Russia*, no. 184/02, § 74, 11 January 2007.

[171] *Güler and Uğur v. Turkey*, nos 31706/10 33088/10, §§ 45–57, 2 December 2014.

[172] *Nolan and K. v. Russia*, no. 2512/04, § 73, 12 February 2009; *Svyato-Mykhaylivska Parafiya v. Ukraine*, no. 77703/01, § 132, 14 June 2007.

[173] For example, *Nolan and K. v. Russia*, no. 2512/04, § 75, 12 February 2009.

[174] For example, *Bayatyan v. Armenia* [GC], no. 23459/03, § 117, ECHR 2011; *Erçep v. Turkey*, no. 43965/04, § 53, 22 November 2011.

Court's practice 'to be quite succinct when it verifies the existence of a legitimate aim within the meaning of the second paragraphs of Articles 8 to 11 of the Convention'.[175]

In *Leyla Şahin v. Turkey*, for example, concerning the headscarf ban in public universities, the Grand Chamber made a perfunctory reference to 'public order' and 'the rights and freedoms of others', noting that this issue was not in dispute between the parties.[176] Similarly, a campaign by German government authorities against so-called sects was deemed to respond to the legitimate aim of the protection of public safety and public order and the protection of the rights and freedoms of others.[177] The same grounds were invoked in a case dealing with measures to deal with a leadership conflict in the Muslim community.[178] The rights and freedoms of others was also deemed to be a legitimate purpose in a case involving a lawyer's request to adjourn a hearing because it conflicted with a Jewish holiday. The Court referred to 'the public's right to the proper administration of justice and the principle that cases be heard within a reasonable time'.[179]

In the French full-face veil or *burqa* case, the government invoked 'public safety' as well as 'respect for the minimum set of values of an open and democratic society'. France explained that the second ground was composed of three elements: respect for equality between men and women; respect for human dignity; and respect for the minimum requirements of life in society. After noting that this second ground was not expressly mentioned in article 9(2), the Grand Chamber proceeded to dismiss the elements of gender equality and human dignity. It attributed some credence to the third element, which it said could be associated with 'the rights and freedoms of others'. 'The Court is therefore able to accept that the barrier raised against others by a veil concealing the face is perceived by the respondent State as breaching the right of others to live in a space of socialisation which makes living together easier', the Grand Chamber concluded.[180]

In contrast with the limitations clauses in articles 8, 10, and 11, article 9(2) does not recognize 'national security' as a legitimate purpose for an interference with freedom to manifest religion or belief. According to the Court, this is '[f]ar from being an accidental omission'. The Court has explained that the non-inclusion of national security in article 9(2) 'reflects the primordial importance of religious pluralism as "one of the foundations of a 'democratic society' within the meaning of the Convention" and the fact that a State cannot dictate what a person believes or take coercive steps to make him change his beliefs'.[181]

Necessary in a democratic society

Most decisions concerning the application of article 9(2) to infringements of the right to manifest religion or belief involve assessing whether the impugned measure is 'necessary in a democratic society'. The objective is to consider whether the authorities have struck 'a fair balance between the competing interests of the individual and of society as

[175] *S.A.S. v. France* [GC], no. 43835/11, § 114, 1 July 2014.
[176] *Leyla Şahin v. Turkey* [GC], no. 44774/98, § 99, ECHR 2005-XI. Also *Ahmet Arslan and Others v. Turkey*, no. 41135/98, § 43, 23 February 2010; *Karaduman v. Turkey*, no. 16278/90, Commission decision of 3 May 1993, (1993) 36 YB 66, DR 74, p. 93; *Dahlab v. Switzerland* (dec.), no. 42393/98, ECHR 2001-V.
[177] *Leela Förderkreis e.V. and Others v. Germany*, no. 58911/00, § 94, 6 November 2008.
[178] *Supreme Holy Council of the Muslim Community v. Bulgaria*, no. 39023/97, § 92, 16 December 2004. Also *Religionsgemeinschaft der Zeugen Jehovas and Others v. Austria*, no. 40825/98, §§ 75–76, 31 July 2008.
[179] *Francesco Sessa v. Italy*, no. 28790/08, § 35, ECHR 2012 (extracts).
[180] *S.A.S. v. France* [GC], no. 43835/11, §§ 114–122, 1 July 2014.
[181] *Nolan and K. v. Russia*, no. 2512/04, § 73, 12 February 2009.

a whole'.[182] It is the most subjective part of the application of paragraph 2, involving subtle distinctions about the proportionality of measures taken by the State that limit or restrict human rights. There is an important relationship between 'necessity' and 'democratic society', of which the hallmarks are pluralism, tolerance, and broadmindedness.[183]

The Court frequently begins its consideration of this element by questioning whether the interference responds to a 'pressing social need'. The term seems to be little more than a gloss on the word 'necessity'. It employs two other notions in this context, insisting that the measure in question be 'relevant and sufficient'. The interference must also respond to an assessment of its proportionality, something that involves balancing the right of the individual against the interest of the State and the society that it represents. Where the Court is considering the positive dimension of the right in question—in other words, the obligation upon the State to take measures to ensure enforcement of the right—it must usually consider the rights of others in the balance as well. If other less severe measures could have fulfilled the same objective, there will be a problem with proportionality.

Nevertheless, in applying the 'necessary in a democratic society' test, the Court will allow the State a margin of appreciation, recognizing that its role is not to sit as a tribunal of fourth instance and that it is in one sense not as well positioned as the national legal institutions to assess many of the relevant factors. Often, especially in sensitive matters that concern morality, ethics, and social policy, the Court refers to the practice in European jurisdictions in determining whether or not any consensus exists. Where there is none, the margin of appreciation will almost invariably be much greater. But although the national authorities make the initial assessment of necessity, 'the final evaluation as to whether the reasons cited for the interference are relevant and sufficient remains subject to review by the Court for conformity with the requirements of the Convention'.[184]

Restrictions on religious activity may be necessary in democratic societies in which several religions coexist within one and the same population, so as to reconcile the interests of the various groups and ensure that everyone's beliefs are respected.[185] The Court has 'frequently emphasised the State's role as the neutral and impartial organiser of the exercise of various religions, faiths and beliefs, and stated that this role is conducive to public order, religious harmony and tolerance in a democratic society'.[186] Interference with the activities of religious organizations may be justified in order to protect 'key principles underlying the Convention' such as a prohibition on polygamous or underage marriage[187] and the use of force or coercive practices.[188] In a case where the employee of a private firm objected on religious grounds to providing counselling to homosexuals, the Court said that 'the most important factor to be taken into account is that the employer's action was intended to secure the implementation of its policy of providing a service

---

[182] *Keegan v. Ireland*, 26 May 1994, § 49, Series A no. 290.

[183] *Smith and Grady v. the United Kingdom*, nos 33985/96 and 33986/96, § 87, ECHR 1999-VI; *Vereinigung demokratischer Soldaten Österreichs and Gubi v. Austria*, 19 December 1994, § 36, Series A no. 302; *Dudgeon v. the United Kingdom*, 22 October 1981, § 53, Series A no. 45.

[184] *Szuluk v. the United Kingdom*, no. 36936/05, § 45, ECHR 2009.

[185] *Kokkinakis v. Greece*, 25 May 1993, § 33, Series A no. 260-A.

[186] *Refah Partisi (the Welfare Party) and Others v. Turkey* [GC], nos 41340/98, 41342/98, 41343/98, and 41344/98, §§ 90–95, ECHR 2003-II.

[187] *Khan v. the United Kingdom*, no. 11579/85, Commission decision of 7 July 1986, DR 48, p. 253; *Kasymakhunov and Saybatalov v. Russia*, nos 26261/05 and 26377/06, § 110, 14 March 2013.

[188] *Jehovah's Witnesses of Moscow v. Russia*, no. 302/02, § 119, 10 June 2010.

without discrimination. The State authorities therefore benefitted from a wide margin of appreciation in deciding where to strike the balance between Mr McFarlane's right to manifest his religious belief and the employer's interest in securing the rights of others.'[189]

There have been many cases concerning clothing, head-covering, and jewellery. These may also involve issues under the right to private life and article 8 of the Convention, although the Court has indicated a preference for dealing with such matters under article 9.[190] One factor is the degree to which clothing and jewellery are used to manifest religion or belief. Noting 'the value to an individual who has made religion a central tenet of his or her life to be able to communicate that belief to others', the Court upheld the right of an airline employee to wear a 'discrete' cross on a necklace in a context where other forms of religious manifestation, such as the wearing of a *hidjab* or headscarf, had been accommodated.[191] It reached the opposite conclusion where the applicant was a nurse working in a public hospital and where there were safety concerns about the wearing of any chain or necklace.[192] In fact, States often invoke concerns about health, safety, and security in justifying measures that limit wearing of clothing with religious significance. There is nevertheless the suspicion that restrictive measures are really directed at the manifestation of religion or belief, although it is not always simple, in practice, to establish this with clear evidence.

The turban, which Sikh men are required to wear, has resulted in several applications to the Convention organs, all of them dismissed. One concerned a requirement that all motorcycle drivers wear a protective helmet.[193] With respect to a rule by which the turban had to be removed for a driver's licence photo, the Court said that the measure was justifiable because of an increase in the risk of fraud and falsification of drivers' licences and that the implementation of such controls was within the State's margin of appreciation.[194] It declared manifestly unfounded an application by a Sikh who objected to removing his turban as part of the security control at a French airport.[195]

Reasonable accommodation is a rich concept developed mainly within the context of equality law, principally as a way to address so-called 'indirect discrimination'. It is a way of addressing problems that arise where an ostensibly neutral rule or standard has a discriminatory effect upon an individual or group. It is also a way of confronting what amounts to intentional discrimination that is concealed behind apparently neutral rules, such as a height requirement for certain jobs which unduly excludes women, or strict rules about working hours and working days that exclude members of religious minorities. Flexibility must be shown in attempting to accommodate the differences so as to minimize the discriminatory effect. In a dissenting opinion in a case involving religious holidays, Judges Tulkens, Popović and Keller argued that 'reasonable accommodation' should be considered within the proportionality determination. 'By dint of a few concessions, this would have made it possible to avoid interfering with the applicant's religious

---

[189] *Eweida and Others v. the United Kingdom*, no. 48420/10, § 109, ECHR 2013 (extracts).
[190] *S.A.S. v. France* [GC], no. 43835/11, § 109, 1 July 2014.
[191] *Eweida and Others v. the United Kingdom*, no. 48420/10, § 94, ECHR 2013 (extracts).
[192] Ibid., § 99 (extracts).
[193] *X v. the United Kingdom*, no. 7992/77, Commission decision of 12 July 1978, DR 14, p. 234.
[194] *Shingara Mann Singh v. France* (dec.), no. 24479/07, 13 November 2008.
[195] *Phull v. France* (dec.), no. 35753/03, 11 January 2005. Also *El Morsli v. France* (dec.), no. 15585/06, 4 March 2008.

freedom without compromising the achievement of the clearly legitimate aim of ensuring the proper administration of justice', they wrote.[196]

Frequently, the Court makes a 'reasonable accommodation' determination without actually using the expression. For example, dealing with the demand of a Polish prisoner who was a Buddhist and who insisted upon a vegetarian diet, the Court said it was 'not persuaded that the provision of a vegetarian diet to the applicant would have entailed any disruption to the management of the prison or to any decline in the standards of meals served to other prisoners'.[197]

Discrimination

Protection against discrimination based upon religion or membership in a religious group is quite central to recognition and enforcement of this fundamental right. In that sense, article 9 is related to article 14 in a special way, unlike the cognate provisions dealing with privacy, expression, assembly, and association in articles 8, 10, and 11. A reaction to discrimination against and persecution of a religious group was central to the political impetus for the creation of the Council of Europe and the adoption of the European Convention on Human Rights.

Many applicants before the European Court have invoked article 14 in conjunction with article 9. As a general rule, the Court has chosen to examine the complaints under article 9 first. Ruling that there has been a breach of article 9, it then notes the subsidiary dimension of article 14 and concludes that there is no need for a separate examination under that provision.[198] However, occasionally there are distinctly different issues relating specifically to article 14 and justifying a separate treatment. Recently, the Court has opted to consider the violation of article 9 in conjunction with article 14 before looking at the stand-alone issue of a violation of article 9.[199]

In a case involving the exceedingly prolonged waiting period for recognition of legal-entity status of a Jehovah's Witness community, which resulted in a finding that article 9 had been breached, the Court also considered the subsequent recognition of the community from the perspective of article 14 in conjunction with article 9. The community alleged that the status it was granted was allegedly limited and insufficient, putting it at a disadvantage vis-à-vis other religious communities. The Austrian system did not treat all religious communities in the same way. It distinguished between 'religious societies' and 'religious communities', the latter being subject to more severe State control in terms of religious doctrine, membership rules, and administration of their assets. The Court insisted that because article 9 requires State authorities to remain neutral in the regulation of religious organisations, 'if a State sets up a framework for conferring legal personality on religious groups to which a specific status is linked, all religious groups which so wish must have a fair opportunity to apply for this status and the criteria established must be applied

---

[196] *Francesco Sessa v. Italy*, no. 28790/08, Joint Dissenting Opinion of Judges Tulkens, Popović and Keller, § 10, ECHR 2012 (extracts).

[197] *Jakóbski v. Poland*, no. 18429/06, § 52, 7 December 2010.

[198] *Ivanova v. Bulgaria*, no. 52435/99, § 92, 12 April 2007; *Jakóbski v. Poland*, no. 18429/06, § 59, 7 December 2010; *Metropolitan Church of Bessarabia and Others v. Moldova*, no. 45701/99, § 134, ECHR 2001-XII; *Sidiropoulos and Others v. Greece*, 10 July 1998, § 52, *Reports of Judgments and Decisions* 1998-IV; *Nolan and K. v. Russia*, no. 2512/04, § 79, 12 February 2009; *Lautsi and Others v. Italy* [GC], no. 30814/06, § 81, ECHR 2011 (extracts).

[199] *Cumhuriyetçi Eğitim Ve Kültür Merkezi Vakfı v. Turkey*, no. 32093/10, §§ 53–54, 2 December 2014.

in a non-discriminatory manner'.[200] In the Austrian case, a ten-year waiting period had been imposed upon the Jehovah's Witnesses before they could be considered for religious society status. According to the Court,

such a period might be necessary in exceptional circumstances such as would be in the case of newly established and unknown religious groups. But it hardly appears justified in respect of religious groups with a long-standing existence internationally which are also long established in the country and therefore familiar to the competent authorities, as is the case with the Jehovah's Witnesses. In respect of such a religious group, the authorities should be able to verify whether it fulfils the requirements of the relevant legislation within a considerably shorter period. Further, the example of another religious community cited by the applicants shows that the Austrian State did not consider the application on an equal basis of such a waiting period to be an essential instrument for pursuing its policy in that field.[201]

There was, consequently, a violation of article 14 in conjunction with article 9.

Reservations and declarations

Norway formulated the following reservation: 'L'article 2 de la Constitution de la Norvège du 17 mai 1814 contenant une disposition selon laquelle les Jésuites ne sont pas tolérés, une réserve correspondante est faite en ce qui concerne l'application de l'article 9 de la Convention.'[202] On 4 December 1956, Norway informed the Secretary General of the Council of Europe that as a result of the repeal of the constitutional provision, a Royal Decree of 30 November 1956 had revoked the reservation to the Convention.[203]

Further reading

Benjamin Bleiberg, 'Unveiling the Real Issue: Evaluating the European Court of Human Rights' Decision to Enforce the Turkish Headscarf Ban *in Leyla Sahin v. Turkey*', (2005–2006) 91 *Cornell Law Review* 129.

Christiane Bourloyannis-Vrailas, 'European Court of Human Rights: *Lautsi and Others v. Italy*, Introductory Note', (2011) 50 *International Legal Materials* 894.

Kevin Boyle and Anneliese Baldaccini, 'A Critical Evaluation of International Human Rights Approaches to Racism', in Sandra Fredman, ed., *Discrimination and Human Rights the Case of Racism*, Oxford: Oxford University Press, 2001, pp. 135–91.

Nicolas Bratza, 'The "Precious Asset": Freedom of Religion under the European Convention on Human Rights', (2012) 14 *Ecclesiastical Law Journal* 256.

Zachary R. Calo, 'Pluralism, Secularism and the European Court of Human Rights', (2010) 26 *Journal of Law and Religion* 101.

Nusrat Choudhury, 'From the Stasi Commission to the European Court of Human Rights: L'Affaire du Foulard and the Challenge of Protecting the Rights of Muslim Girls', (2007) 16 *Columbia Journal of Gender & Law* 199.

Vincent Coussirat-Couxtere, 'Article 9§2', in Pettiti et al., *La Convention européenne*, pp. 361–3.

Peter Cumper, 'Article 9: Freedom of Religion', in Harris et al., eds., *Law of the European Convention*, pp. 425–42.

---

[200] *Religionsgemeinschaft der Zeugen Jehovas and Others v. Austria,* no. 40825/98, § 92, 31 July 2008.
[201] Ibid., § 98.
[202] (1955–56–57) 1 YB 41.
[203] Ibid., p. 42.

Peter W. Edge, 'The European Court of Human Rights and Religious Rights', (1998) 47 *ICLQ* 680.

Carolyn Evans, *Freedom of Religion Under* the *European Convention on Human Rights*, Oxford: Oxford University. Press 2001.

Carolyn Evans, 'The Islamic Scarf in the European Court of Human Rights', (2006) 7 *Melbourne Journal of International Law* 52.

M.D. Evans, *Religious Liberty and International Law in Europe*, Cambridge: Cambridge University Press, 1997.

Jochen Abr. Frowein, 'Article 9§1', in Pettiti et al., *La Convention européenne*, pp. 353–60.

Frowein/Peukert, *MenschenRechtsKonvention*, pp. 318–38.

Nicholas Gibson, 'An Unwelcome Trend: Religious Dress and Human Rights Following *Leila Şahin vs Turkey*', (2007) 25 *Netherlands Quarterly of Human Rights* 599.

Grabenwarter, *European Convention*, pp. 234–50.

T.J. Gunn, 'Adjudicating Rights of Conscience under the European Convention on Human Rights', in Johan D. Van der Vyver and John Witte, eds, *Religious Human Rights in Global Perspective: Legal Perspectives*, The Hague: Martinus Nijhoff, 1996, pp. 305–30.

Erica Howard, 'Bans on the Wearing of Religious Symbols in British Schools: A Violation of the Right to Non-Discrimination?', (2011) 6 *Religion and Human Rights* 127.

Renée Koering-Joulin, 'Public Morals', in Mireille Delmas-Marty, ed., *The European Convention for the Protection of Human Rights*, Dordrecht/Boston/London: Martinus Nijhoff, 1992, pp. 83–98.

Yannis Kristakis, 'The Protection of *forum internum* under Article 9 of the ECHR', in Dean Spielmann, Marialena Tsirli, and Panayotis Voyatzis, eds, *La Convention européenne des droits de l'homme, un instrument vivant, Mélanges en l'honneur de Christos L. Rozakis*, Brussels: Bruylant, 2011, pp. 285–304.

Sylvie Langlaude, 'Indoctrination, Secularism, Religious Liberty, and the ECHR', (2006) 55 *ICLQ* 929.

Ian Leigh, 'Balancing Religious Autonomy and Other Human Rights under the European Convention', (2012) 1 *Oxford Journal of Law and Religion* 109.

Tom Lewis, 'What not to Wear: Religious Rights, the European Court, and the Margin of Appreciation', (2007) 56 *ICLQ* 395.

Titia Loenen, 'The Headscarf Debate Approaching the Intersection of Sex, Religion and Race under the European Convention on Human Rights and EU Equality Law', in Dagmar Schiek and Victoria Chege, eds, *European Non-Discrimination Law Comparative Perspectives on Multi-dimensional Equality Law*, London/New York: Routledge 2009, pp. 313–27.

Loukis G. Loucaides, 'The Right to Freedom of Thought as Protected by the European Convention on Human Rights', (2012) 1 *Cyprus Human Rights Law Review* 79.

Jill Marshall, 'Freedom of Religious Expression and Gender Equality: *Sahin v. Turkey*', (2006) 69 *Modern Law Review* 460.

Javier Martínez-Torrón, 'Limitations on Religious Freedom in the Case Law of the European Court of Human Rights', (2005) 19 *Emory International Law Review* 587.

Dominic McGoldrick, *Human Rights and Religion: The Islamic Headscarf Debate in Europe*, Oxford/Portland: Hart Publishing, 2006.

Dominic McGoldrick, 'Religion in the Public Square and in European Public Life— Crucifixes in the Classroom?', (2011) 11 *HRLR* 451.

Ovey/White, *Jacobs and White, European Convention*, pp. 264–75.

Carlo Panara, '*Lautsi v Italy*: The Display of Religious Symbols by the State', (2011) 17 *European Public Law* 139.

Megan Pearson, 'Article 9 at a Crossroads: Interference Before and After *Eweida*', (2013) 13 *HRLR* 580.

Ted Stahnke, 'Proselytism and Freedom to Change Religion in International Human Rights Law', [1999] *Brigham Young University Law Review* 251.

James Sweeney, 'Freedom of Religion and Democratic Transition', in Antoine Buyse and Michael Hamilton, eds, *Transitional Jurisprudence and the ECHR*, Cambridge: Cambridge University Press, 2011, pp. 103–30.

Paul M. Taylor, *Freedom of Religion: UN and European Human Rights Law and Practice*, Cambridge: Cambridge University Press, 2005.

Anastasia Vakulenko, ' "Islamic Headscarves" and the European Convention On Human Rights: an Intersectional Perspective', (2007) 16 *Social Legal Studies* 183.

Ben Vermeulen, 'Freedom of Thought, Conscience and Religion (Article 9)', in Van Dijk et al., *Theory and Practice*, pp. 751–71.

Lucy Vickers, 'Freedom of Religion and Belief, Article 9 ECHR and the EU Equality Directive', in Filip Dorssemont, Klaus Lörcher, and Isabelle Schömann, eds, *The European Convention on Human Rights and the Employment Relation*, Oxford / Portland, OR: Hart, 2013, pp. 209–236.

Article 10. Freedom of expression/Liberté d'expression

1. Everyone has the right to freedom of expression. This right shall include freedom to hold opinions and to receive and impart information and ideas without interference by public authority and regardless of frontiers. This article shall not prevent States from requiring the licensing of broadcasting, television or cinema enterprises.

2. The exercise of these freedoms, since it carries with it duties and responsibilities, may be subject to such formalities, conditions, restrictions or penalties as are prescribed by law and are necessary in a democratic society, in the interests of national security, territorial integrity or public safety, for the prevention of disorder or crime, for the protection of health or morals, for the protection of the reputation or rights of others, for preventing the disclosure of information received in confidence, or for maintaining the authority and impartiality of the judiciary.

1. Toute personne a droit à la liberté d'expression. Ce droit comprend la liberté d'opinion et la liberté de recevoir ou de communiquer des informations ou des idées sans qu'il puisse y avoir ingérence d'autorités publiques et sans considération de frontière. Le présent article n'empêche pas les États de soumettre les entreprises de radiodiffusion, de cinéma ou de télévision à un régime d'autorisations.

2. L'exercice de ces libertés comportant des devoirs et des responsabilités peut être soumis à certaines formalités, conditions, restrictions ou sanctions, prévues par la loi, qui constituent des mesures nécessaires, dans une société démocratique, à la sécurité nationale, à l'intégrité territoriale ou à la sûreté publique, à la défense de l'ordre et à la prévention du crime, à la protection de la santé ou de la morale, à la protection de la réputation ou des droits d'autrui, pour empêcher la divulgation d'informations confidentielles ou pour garantir l'autorité et l'impartialité du pouvoir judiciaire.

Introductory comments

'Give me the liberty to know, to utter, and to argue freely according to conscience, above all liberties', wrote John Milton in the *Areopagitica*, his challenge to attempts in Parliament to require the licensing of printers and thereby State control of free speech. He was writing at the height of the English revolution, of which he was a supporter. The importance of freedom of expression echoed through the writings of the Enlightenment thinkers such as Voltaire, Locke, and Diderot.

The right also featured in the early codifications of human rights. For example, the English Bill of Rights of 1688 declared: 'That the freedom of speech and debates or proceedings in Parliament ought not to be impeached or questioned in any court or place out of Parliament.' The pre-eminence of freedom of expression can also be seen in the French *Déclaration des droits de l'homme et du citoyen*, adopted at the same time as the United States Constitution, where '[l]a libre communication des pensées et des opinions' is described as 'un des droits les plus précieux de l'Homme'. The first amendment to the United States Constitution declares that 'Congress shall make no law...abridging the freedom of speech, or of the press.'

The first of Franklin D. Roosevelt's 'four essential freedoms', proclaimed in his 1941 State of the Union Address at the dawn of modern human rights law, was 'freedom of speech and expression—everywhere in the world'. Article 19 of the Universal Declaration of Human Rights affirms 'Everyone has the right to freedom of opinion and expression; this right includes freedom to hold opinions without interference and to seek, receive and impart information and ideas through any media and regardless of frontiers.' It was the inspiration for the text of article 10 of the European Convention on Human Rights, to which it bears a very close resemblance. Article 10(1) adds a second sentence dealing with licensing and article 10(2) sets out the permissible limitations on freedom of expression in a text modelled on article 29(1) of the European Convention on Human Rights.

The association between free speech and political democracy has always been fundamental. The European Court has said that 'freedom of expression constitutes one of the essential foundations of a democratic society and one of the basic conditions for its progress and each individual's self-fulfilment'.[1] Yet in its implementation and enforcement, it remains a complex right, bedevilled with limitations and exceptions. Just as free speech seems essential to the survival of democracy, its abusive exercise may also threaten to destroy it. 'Militant democracy' calls for limits on those who use words to threaten the rule of law and promote fascism and totalitarianism. On very important aspects, such as the repression of so-called 'hate speech', views still vary greatly on the appropriate measures that may be justifiable in order to ensure respect for the rights and freedoms of others.

The corresponding provision in the European Union Charter of Fundamental Rights, article 11(1), is identical to the first sentence of article 10(1) of the European Convention. It is meant to have the same meaning and scope but 'without prejudice to any restrictions which Union law may impose on Member States' right to introduce the licensing arrangements referred to in the third sentence of Article 10(1) of the ECHR'.[2]

Drafting of the provision

The initial draft European Convention on Human Rights was prepared by the International Juridical Section of the European Movement, chaired by Pierre-Henri Teitgen, with David Maxwell Fyfe and Fernand Dehousse as rapporteurs. Both Maxwell Fyfe and Dehousse had been involved in the adoption of the Universal Declaration of Human Rights at the United Nations the previous year. The enumeration of rights in the draft contained the following: 'Every State a party to this Convention shall guarantee to all persons within its territory the following rights: . . . d) Freedom of speech and of expression of opinion generally.'[3] The European Movement draft also contained a restrictions or limitations clause, inspired by article 29 of the Universal Declaration of Human Rights: 'The rights specified in Articles 1 and 2 shall be subject only to such limitations as are in conformity with the general principles of law recognised by civilised nations and as are prescribed by law for: a) Protecting the legal rights of others; b) Meeting the just requirements of morality, public order (including the safety of the community), and the general welfare.'[4]

---

[1] *Rekvényi v. Hungary* [GC], no. 25390/94, § 42, ECHR 1999-III.
[2] Explanation Relating to the Charter of Fundamental Rights, Official Journal of the European Union, C 303/33, 14 December 2007.
[3] Convention for the Collective Protection of Individual Rights and Democratic Liberties by the States, Members of the Council of Europe, and for the establishment of a European Court of Human Rights to ensure observance of the Convention, Doc. INF/5/E/R, I *TP* 296–303, at p. 296, art. I(d).
[4] Convention for the Collective Protection of Individual Rights and Democratic Liberties by the States, Members of the Council of Europe, and for the establishment of a European Court of Human Rights to ensure observance of the Convention, Doc. INF/5/E/R, I *TP* 296–303, art. 3.

At the first session of Consultative Assembly of the Council of Europe, in August 1949, Teitgen called for adoption of a convention that would include 'freedom of speech and expression'.[5] Asked to prepare a text for discussion in the Committee on Legal and Administrative Questions at the first session of the Consultative Assembly, held from 22 August to 5 September 1949, Teitgen proposed the following: 'Freedom to hold opinions without interference and to express them in speech or writing.'[6] Teitgen also submitted a text based upon article 29(2) of the Universal Declaration of Human Rights. It is the forerunner of paragraph 2 of article 10: 'In the exercise of these rights, and in the enjoyment of the freedoms guaranteed by the Convention, no limitations will be imposed except those established with the sole object of ensuring recognition and respect for the rights and freedoms of others, or with the purpose of satisfying the just requirements of public morality, order and security and general welfare in a democratic society. These rights and freedoms may in no case be exercised contrary to the aims and principles of the Council of Europe.'[7]

At the 30 August 1949 meeting of the Committee on Legal and Administrative Questions, Teitgen proposed the following: 'The right not to be molested on account of his opinions and the freedom to express them by word of mouth and through the press'. The Committee preferred an alternative version, submitted by Henri Rolin of Belgium: 'Freedom of opinion and expression, in accordance with Article 19 of the Declaration of the United Nations'.[8] It was changed slightly in the final report of the Committee on Legal and Administrative Questions to the plenary Consultative Assembly: 'Freedom of opinion and expression, in accordance with Article 19 of the United Nations Declaration.'[9] There was no particular discussion in the Assembly and the text proposed by the Committee was adopted without debate.[10] The restrictions or limitation clause, still then a general provision applicable to the entire draft convention, was somewhat altered by the Consultative Assembly: 'In the exercise of these rights, and in the enjoyment of the freedoms guaranteed by the Convention, no limitations shall be imposed except those established by law, with the sole object of ensuring the recognition and respect for the rights and freedoms of others, or with the purpose of satisfying the just requirement of public morality, order and security in a democratic society.' It was adopted without a vote after a short debate.[11]

Following adoption of a draft convention by the Consultative Assembly, the Committee of Ministers decided to convene a Committee of Experts. In preparation for the Committee of Experts, the Secretariat-General of the Council of Europe prepared a report that discussed and compared the draft with the Covenant on human rights that was then

---

[5] Report of the Sitting [of the Consultative Assembly, 19 August 1949], I *TP* 38–154, at p. 46.

[6] Proposals by Mr P.H. Teitgen, Rapporteur, 29 August 1949, Doc. A 116, I *TP* 166–8. Also Report presented by Mr P.H. Teitgen, 5 September 1949, Doc. A 290, I *TP* 192–213, at p. 206. See also I *TP* 228.

[7] Proposals by Mr P.H. Teitgen, Rapporteur, 29 August 1949, Doc. A 116, I *TP* 166–8. Also Report presented by Mr P.H. Teitgen, 5 September 1949, Doc. A 290, I *TP* 192–213, at p. 206. See also I *TP* 228.

[8] Minutes of the Sitting [of the Committee on Legal and Administrative Questions, Consultative Assembly, 30 August 1949], Doc. A 167, I *TP* 174–80, at p. 174.

[9] Report [of the Committee on Legal and Administrative Questions], 5 September 1949, Doc. AS (1) 77, I *TP* 216–39, at p. 228.

[10] Recommendation No. 38 to the Committee of Ministers adopted 8 September 1949 on the conclusion of the debates, Doc. AS (1) 108, II *TP* 274–83, at p. 276.

[11] Official Report of the Sitting [of the Consultative Assembly, 8 September 1949], II *TP* 14–274, at pp. 134–42.

being considered by the United Nations Commission on Human Rights. It noted a text proposed by France to the Commission on Human Rights, explaining that while generally in accordance with article 19 of the Universal Declaration of Human Rights, it espoused a 'very broad notion' of information.[12] France had proposed the following: 'Every person shall be free to receive and disseminate information of all kinds, including facts, critical comment and ideas, by the medium of books, newspapers, oral instruction or in any other manner.'[13] As the report noted, no definitive text had been agreed by the United Nations. Commission on Human Rights. It had decided to wait for the results in the United Nations General Assembly on the Convention on Freedom of Information.[14] The report also contained a comment from the United Kingdom prepared within the context of the United Nations debate, noting with approval the recommendation of the United Nations General Assembly that a provision on freedom of information be included in the Covenant. The United Kingdom said it supported 'wholeheartedly the proposal to enumerate the specific limitations on the right to freedom of information which are to be permitted'. The following was suggested:

1. Every person shall have the right to freedom of thought and the right to freedom of expression without governmental interference: these rights shall include freedom to hold opinions, to receive and impart information and ideas, without government interference, regardless of frontiers, either orally, in writing or in print, in the form of art, or by duly licensed visual or auditory devices.
2. The exercise of these freedoms carries with it duties and responsibility and may therefore be subject to certain penalties, liabilities and restrictions provided by law, which are necessary in the interests of national security, for prevention of disorder or crime, for the protection of public safety, health or morals, for the protection of the reputations or rights of other persons, for preventing the disclosure of information received in confidence, or for maintaining the authority and impartiality of the judiciary.[15]

The Committee of Experts met in February and March 1950. Two Turkish experts, Cavat Ustun and Ilhan Lutem, tabled the following amendment: 'Freedom of opinion and expression, in accordance with Article 19 of the United Nations Declaration, *to the extent that this can be reconciled with the principles set forth in paragraph 3 of the Preamble to the Statute of the Council of Europe*'.[16] The Sub-Committee that examined the proposal said it was difficult to approve as it imposed a restriction on freedom of opinion and expression 'which would be too extensive'. Cavat Ustun said he had made the proposal because 'there is in

[12] Preparatory Report by the Secretariat-General concerning a Preliminary Draft Convention to Provide a Collective Guarantee of Human Rights, Doc. B 22, III *TP* 2–37, at p. 30.
[13] Report of the Fifth Session of the Commission on Human Rights to the Economic and Social Council, UN Doc. E/1371(Supp.), p. 21.
[14] The United Nations Conference on Freedom of Information, held in early 1948, adopted the text of a Convention on Freedom of Information. There had been 'divergent views' about the draft convention in the Third Committee of the United Nations General Assembly meeting in late 1948 and the plenary Assembly postponed debate on adoption of the draft convention until its fourth session in 1949 (see GA Res. 277 B (III)). Work on the Convention on Freedom of Information was again postponed by the General Assembly at its 1949 session. The relevant resolution recommended that a provision on freedom of information be included in the draft Covenant on human rights under consideration in the Commission on Human Rights (see GA Res. 313 (IV)). The issue of a Convention was postponed at a subsequent session and ultimately abandoned.
[15] Comments of Governments on the Draft International Covenant on Human Rights and Measures of Implementation [UN Doc. E/CN.4/353/Add.1-3], Doc. A 770, III *TP* 156–79, at pp. 162–4.
[16] Amendments to Articles 2 (paras 5 and 6) and 6 proposed by the Turkish Experts concerning the Consultative Assembly's Draft Convention, Doc. A 775, III *TP* 182–4, at p 182 (emphasis in the original).

Turkey a law which forbids the diffusion of propaganda on extremist ideas'. To this, the Sub-Committee explained that the imposition of special conditions was authorized by other provisions in the draft Convention.[17] The Swedish expert, Torsten Salén, proposed the following addition to the text of the Consultative Assembly: 'These freedoms can only be subjected to the restrictions, sanctions and responsibilities defined by law in the interest of public order, national security and the good functioning of public administration and justice, as well as for the safeguarding of the good traditions and respect for the freedom of others.'[18]

At the conclusion of its first session, in February 1950, the Committee of Experts adopted the following provision: 'Everyone has the right of freedom of opinion and expression; this right includes freedom to hold opinions without interference and to seek, receive and impart information and ideas through any media and regardless of frontiers.'[19] The Committee explained that instead of enumerating rights by reference to the relevant provision in the Universal Declaration, as had been done by the Consultative Assembly, it was better to incorporate the text verbatim. Accordingly, the Committee 'scrupulously adhered to the text of the Universal Declaration'.[20] There are two small differences in the Committee text: the fifth word is 'to' rather than 'of' and the word 'opinion' is in the singular.

At the second session of the Committee of Experts, in March 1950, the United Kingdom representative submitted an amendment that was very similar to the text it had proposed in the United Nations Commission on Human Rights:

1) Everyone has the right to freedom of thought, and to freedom of expression without governmental interference; these rights shall include freedom to hold opinions and to receive and impart information and ideas without government interference regardless of frontiers, either orally, in writing or in print, in the form of art or by duly licensed visual or auditory devices.
2) The exercise of these freedoms carries with it duties and responsibilities and may therefore be subject to such penalties, liabilities and restrictions as are prescribed by law and are necessary in the interests of national security or public safety, for the prevention of disorder or crime, for the protection of health or morals, for the protection of the reputations and rights of other persons, for preventing the disclosure of information received in confidence, or for maintaining the authority and impartiality of the judiciary.[21]

The redundant reference to 'freedom of thought' already present in the freedom of religion text submitted by the United Kingdom was removed by the Drafting Committee in its revision of the proposal. The Committee made several small stylistic changes to the second paragraph and added reference to 'territorial integrity' after 'national security'.[22]

[17] Continuation of the Report of the Sub-Committee Instructed to Make a Preliminary Study of the Amendments proposed by the Members of the Committee, Doc. A 802, III *TP* 206–13, at p. 208.
[18] Amendments to Article 2, para. 3, 5, and 6 of the Recommendation of the Consultative Assembly proposed by the Swedish Expert, Doc. A 777, III *TP* 184.
[19] Preliminary Draft Convention for the Maintenance and Further Realisation of Human Rights and Fundamental Freedoms, 15 February 1950, Doc. A 833, III *TP* 236–46, at p. 236. Also Draft text of the first section of a draft Convention based on the work of the Consultative Assembly, Doc. A 809, III *TP* 220–31, at p. 222.
[20] Preliminary Draft of the Report to the Committee of Ministers, 24 February 1950, Doc. CM/WP 1 (50) 1, A 847, III *TP* 246–79, at pp. 260–2.
[21] Amendments to Articles 1, 2, 4, 5, 6, 8, and 9 of the Committee's Preliminary Draft Proposal by the Expert of the United Kingdom, Doc. CM/WP 1 (50) 2, A 915, III *TP* 280–9, at p. 286.
[22] Amendments to the British draft proposed by the Drafting Committee composed of Sir Oscar Dowson, MM le Quesne, Dons Moeller, and Salén, Doc. CM/WP 1 (50) 10, p. 3, A 919, III *TP* 288–95, at p. 292.

The Report of the Committee of Experts explained that '[t]he permission accorded in this paragraph to the imposition of certain restrictions in the interests of territorial integrity was accepted by the Committee on the clear understanding that it did not permit a restriction on the rights of national minorities to advocate their views by democratic means'.[23] The Committee of Experts prepared two different drafts. The first, 'Alternatives A and A/2', consisted of the text derived from the Consultative Assembly draft that had been adopted by the Committee of Experts at its first session.[24] The second, labelled 'Alternatives B and B/2', contained the text that had been proposed by the United Kingdom.[25]

The Conference of Senior Officials that convened in June 1950 assigned a Drafting Committee to attempt to reconcile the competing versions. It prepared a new formulation on freedom of expression based on the British proposal as amended by the Drafting Committee of the Committee of Experts, with a few changes. The reference to 'without governmental interference' in the first phrase was removed, probably because it was deemed redundant given a similar expression later in the paragraph.

1) Everyone shall have the right to freedom of expression; these rights shall include freedom to hold opinions and to receive and impart information and ideas without government interference, regardless of frontiers, either orally, in writing or in print, in the form of art or by duly licensed visual or auditory devices.
2) The exercise of these freedoms, since it carries with it duties and responsibilities, may be subject to such penalties, liabilities and restrictions as are prescribed by law and are necessary in the interests of national security (territorial integrity), or public safety, for the prevention of disorder or crime, for the protection of health or morals, for the protection of the reputation or rights of others, for preventing the disclosure of information received in confidence, or for maintaining the authority and impartiality of the judiciary.[26]

Small changes were made by the Drafting Committee: the replacement of 'governmental interference' with 'interference by public authority' and the addition of 'in a democratic society' after 'necessary'.[27] The text was further modified by the plenary Conference of Senior Officials. The semi-colon in paragraph 1 was changed in favour of a new sentence and the parentheses in paragraph 2 surrounding territorial integrity were removed. The final version of the Conference of Senior Officials read:

1) Everyone has the right to freedom of expression. This right shall include freedom to hold opinions and to receive and impart information and ideas without interference by public authority, regardless of frontiers, either orally, in writing or in print, in the form of art or by duly licensed visual or auditory devices.
2) The exercise of these freedoms, since it carries with it duties and responsibilities, may be subject to such penalties, liabilities and restrictions as are prescribed by law and are necessary in a

---

[23] Report to the Committee of Ministers submitted by the Committee of Experts Instructed to Draw Up a Draft Convention of Collective Guarantee of Human Rights and Fundamental Freedoms, Doc. CM/WP 1 (5) 15, A 924, IV *TP* 2–55, at p. 32.

[24] Ibid., p. 52. See also Preliminary Draft Convention, Doc. CM/WP 1 (50) 14, A 932, III *TP* 312–35, at pp. 320–2.

[25] Report to the Committee of Ministers submitted by the Committee of Experts Instructed to Draw Up a Draft Convention of Collective Guarantee of Human Rights and Fundamental Freedoms, Doc. CM/WP 1 (5) 15, A 924, IV TP 2–55, at pp. 62–4. See also Preliminary Draft Convention, Doc. CM/WP 1 (50) 14, A 932, III *TP* 312–35, at p. 318.

[26] New draft alternatives B and B/2, Doc. CM/WP 4 (50) 9, A 1372, IV *TP* 182–91, at p. 188.

[27] Draft Convention appended to the draft report, Doc. CM/WP 4 (50) 16, appendix, A 1445, IV *TP* 218–40, at p. 224.

democratic society, in the interests of national security, territorial integrity, or public safety, for the prevention of disorder or crime, for the protection of health or morals, for the protection of the reputations or rights of others, for preventing the disclosure of information received in confidence, or for maintaining the authority and impartiality of the judiciary.[28]

The Report of the Conference attributes the reference to 'territorial integrity' to the Turkish delegate's insistence that these words be retained.[29] It also mentions '[i]n this connection' the reservations of the Danish delegate 'according to which it was well understood that no restriction should be introduced which would interfere with the right of national minorities to give expression to their aspirations by democratic means'.[30] The implication is that Turkey's concerns were with the exercise of freedom of expression by minorities to promote autonomy and secession.

The text was further revised by the Committee of Ministers at its fifth session, in early August 1950. The United Kingdom had proposed some minor changes to the punctuation of the English version that were of no substantive significance.[31] The Irish government recommended '[t]hat Article 10(2) of the present draft be amended to stipulate that no restriction should be imposed on the right of national minorities to give expression to their aspiration by democratic means'.[32] The Committee of Ministers removed the phrase 'either orally, in writing or in print, in the form of art or by duly licensed visual or auditory devices' at the end of paragraph 1. A third sentence was added to paragraph 1: 'This article shall not prevent States from requiring the licensing of broadcasting, television or cinema enterprises.' The *travaux préparatoires* provide no indication of the source of this amendment or of any debate surrounding it. In paragraph 2, the words 'penalties, liabilities and restrictions' were replaced with 'formalities, liabilities, restrictions or penalties'.[33] The provision did not give rise to any discussion in the Consultative Assembly at its 1950 session.

Immediately prior to adoption of the Convention, in Rome in November, two small modifications to the English version of the text of article 10 were made: the word 'and' replaced the comma between 'public authority' and 'regardless' in the second sentence of paragraph 1; 'conditions' replaced 'liabilities' in paragraph 2.

The heading 'Freedom of expression' was added according to the provisions of Protocol No. 11.[34]

Analysis and interpretation

Freedom of expression is said to constitute 'one of the essential foundations of a democratic society and one of the basic conditions for its progress and for each

---

[28] Draft Convention annexed to the Report, Doc. CM/WP 4 (50) 19 annex, CM/WP 4 (50) 16 rev., A 1452, IV *TP* 274–95, at p. 280.

[29] Text of the Report submitted by the Conference [of Senior Officials] to the Committee of Ministers, Doc. CM/WP 4 (50) 19, CM/WP 4 (50) 16 rev., A 1431, IV *TP* 242–73, at p. 262.

[30] Ibid.

[31] Comments by the United Kingdom Delegation on the Report of the Conference of Senior Officials and the text of the Draft Convention, Doc. A 1690, p. 3.

[32] Amendments proposed by the Irish Government (4 August 1950), Doc. CM 1 (50) 2, A 1863, V *TP* 58–61, at p. 60.

[33] Draft Convention adopted by the Sub-Committee, Doc. CM 1 (50) 52, A 1884, V *TP* 76–99, at p. 82; Draft Convention adopted by the Committee of Ministers, 7 August 1950, Doc. A 1937, V *TP* 120–45, at pp. 126–8.

[34] Protocol No. 11 to the Convention for the Protection of Human Rights and Fundamental Freedoms, restructuring the control machinery established thereby, ETS 155, art. 2(2).

individual's self-fulfilment'.[35] It applies both to 'information' and 'ideas' that may be favourably received or regarded as inoffensive or as a matter of indifference as well as to those that offend, shock, or disturb.[36] It is 'all the more important when it comes to conveying ideas which offend, shock or challenge the established order'.[37] This is a requirement of pluralism, tolerance, and broadmindedness 'without which there is no "democratic society"'.[38]

Although the relationship of freedom of expression to democracy is profound, its importance as a fundamental right goes well beyond speech of a political nature. Freedom to receive and impart information and ideas also extends to artistic expression. Indeed, it 'affords the opportunity to take part in the public exchange of cultural, political and social information and ideas of all kinds'.[39] There is an association between artistic and political speech in that '[t]hose who create, perform, distribute or exhibit works of art contribute to the exchange of ideas and opinions which is essential for a democratic society'.[40] Because of the important relationship between freedom of expression and democracy, publications that relate to a debate on a matter of general concern, and that constitute political or militant expression, are entitled to 'a high level of protection of the right to freedom of expression'.[41]

Article 10 consists of two paragraphs. It is similar in form to articles 8, 9, and 11 of the Convention, in that the right is set out in the first paragraph and the permissible limitations defined in the second. Paragraph 1 comprises three sentences. The first two are derived from and closely based on article 19 of the Universal Declaration of Human Rights. The third, referring to licensing of broadcasting, television, or cinema, was an innovation of the drafters of the Convention. Paragraph 2 is modelled on article 29(2) of the Universal Declaration of Human Rights. It sets out the limitations on freedom of expression.

The European Court of Human Rights exercises a supervisory function. Its purpose is not to replace competent national authorities. In applying article 10, the Court goes beyond simply ascertaining whether the State exercised its discretion reasonably, carefully, and in good faith. It is required to examine the interference in light of the case as a whole, considering whether this was proportionate to the legitimate aim and whether the reasons provided by the national authorities to justify the interference are 'relevant and sufficient'. The Court must 'satisfy itself that the national authorities applied standards which were in

---

[35] *Palomo Sánchez and Others v. Spain* [GC], nos 28955/06, 28957/06, 28959/06, and 28964/06, § 53, ECHR 2011; *Lingens v. Austria*, 8 July 1986, § 41, Series A no. 103.

[36] *Palomo Sánchez and Others v. Spain* [GC], nos 28955/06, 28957/06, 28959/06, and 28964/06, § 53, ECHR 2011; *Handyside v. the United Kingdom*, 7 December 1976, § 49, Series A no. 24; *Lehideux and Isorni v. France*, 23 September 1998, § 55, *Reports of Judgments and Decisions* 1998-VII; *Murphy v. Ireland*, no. 44179/98, § 72, ECHR 2003-IX; *Monnat v. Switzerland*, no. 73604/01, § 55, ECHR 2006-X.

[37] *Women On Waves and Others v. Portugal*, no. 31276/05, § 42, 3 February 2009.

[38] *Handyside v. the United Kingdom*, 7 December 1976, § 49, Series A no. 24; *Lindon, Otchakovsky-Laurens and July v. France* [GC], nos 21279/02 and36448/02, § 45, ECHR 2007-IV; *Verein gegen Tierfabriken Schweiz (VgT) v. Switzerland (no. 2)* [GC], no. 32772/02, § 96, ECHR 2009; *Palomo Sánchez and Others v. Spain* [GC], nos 28955/06, 28957/06, 28959/06, and 28964/06, § 53, ECHR 2011; *Axel Springer AG v. Germany* [GC], no. 39954/08, § 78, 7 February 2012.

[39] *Karataş v. Turkey* [GC], no. 23168/94, § 49, ECHR 1999-IV.

[40] Ibid.

[41] *Lindon, Otchakovsky-Laurens and July v. France* [GC], nos 21279/02 and 36448/02, § 48, ECHR 2007-IV. Also *Müller v. Switzerland*, no. 41202/98, § 27, 5 November 2002.

conformity with the principles embodied in Article 10 and, moreover, that they relied on an acceptable assessment of the relevant facts'.[42]

The freedom of expression provision of the American Convention on Human Rights provides expressly, in article 13(2), that freedom of expression 'shall not be subject to prior censorship but shall be subject to subsequent imposition of liability'. This is the notion of prior restraint, deeply rooted in American law, where the first amendment to the Constitution creates a strong presumption against any 'preventive' limits on free speech.[43] The European Convention is not explicit on the subject, although the Court has held that 'prior restraints on publication entail such dangers that they call for the most careful scrutiny'.[44] It has also said that article 10 does not prohibit prior restraints on publication as such, noting that this is clear from use of the words 'conditions', 'restrictions', 'preventing', and 'prevention' that appear in that provision.[45] Concerns about prior restraint are especially acute with respect to the press 'for news is a perishable commodity and to delay its publication, even for a short period, may well deprive it of all its value and interest. This danger also applies to publications other than periodicals that deal with a topical issue.'[46] The Court has carefully distinguished situations of individualized or targeted prior restraint, where the presumption this is a violation will be strong, and general measures that restrict freedom of expression.[47] A general measure applies to pre-defined situations regardless of the individual facts of each case 'even if this might result in individual hard cases'.[48]

The scope of freedom of expression is larger with respect to criticism of government than it may be when a private citizen is the target, or even an individual politician. Democracy requires that the acts or omissions of government be scrutinized closely, not only by the legislative and judicial arms of the State but also by public opinion. The dominant position held by government dictates that it show restraint when it resorts to efforts to stifle its adversaries, including the use of criminal proceedings, and particularly where other means are available, even if the attacks and criticisms appear unjustified.[49] Because 'thought and opinions on public matters are of a vulnerable nature', the mere possibility that the authorities will interfere, or that there will be interference by private parties who are not subject to proper control or who have the support of the authorities, is capable of imposing 'a serious burden on the free formation of ideas and democratic debate and have a effect'.[50]

Freedom of expression cases will often involve issues that overlap with other freedoms protected by the Convention, notably privacy, religion, assembly and association, set out in articles 8, 9, and 11, respectively. The Court often makes a determination to focus its

---

[42] *Mouvement raëlien suisse v. Switzerland*, no. 16354/06, § 49, 13 January 2011; *Mouvement raëlien suisse v. Switzerland* [GC], no. 16354/06, § 48, ECHR 2012 (extracts).

[43] *Near v. Minnesota*, 283 US 697 (1931).

[44] *Verein gegen Tierfabriken Schweiz (VgT) v. Switzerland (no. 2)* [GC], no. 32772/02, § 93, ECHR 2009; *The Sunday Times v. the United Kingdom (no. 2)*, 26 November 1991, § 51, Series A no. 217; *Dammann v. Switzerland*, no. 77551/01, §52, 25 April 2006.

[45] *Ahmet Yıldırım v. Turkey*, no. 3111/10, § 47, ECHR 2012.

[46] Ibid. Also *RTBF v. Belgium*, no. 50084/06, § 105, ECHR 2011 (extracts).

[47] *Animal Defenders International v. the United Kingdom* [GC], no. 48876/08, § 106, ECHR 2013 (extracts); *Observer and Guardian v. the United Kingdom*, 26 November 1991, § 60, Series A no. 216.

[48] *Ždanoka v. Latvia* [GC], no. 58278/00, §§ 112–115, ECHR 2006-IV.

[49] *Fatullayev v. Azerbaijan*, no. 40984/07, § 116, 22 April 2010.

[50] *Altuğ Taner Akçam v. Turkey*, no. 27520/07, § 81, 25 October 2011.

examination of an application on article 10, generally without any elaborate explanation for its decision.[51]

Positive obligation or interference?

Once it has been established that article 10 is applicable, consideration must be given to the negative or positive nature of the obligation in question. If the obligation is negative and not positive, the question to be addressed is whether there has been an interference with the right by the State. Where this is the conclusion, the analysis then proceeds to article 10(2), where the Court begins by inquiring as to whether the interference has been 'prescribed by law'. In cases of negative obligations, when the Court concludes there is no interference the application will be dismissed without paragraph 2 even being considered.

If the alleged violation cannot directly be attributed to the State, the latter may nevertheless have a positive obligation to secure rights under article 10 to those within its jurisdiction.[52] For example, Turkey was held to have a positive obligation to investigate and provide protection when journalists and staff of a newspaper that supported the Kurdistan Workers Party were victims of violence and intimidation.[53] The Court has also examined the obligation to protect freedom of expression in the employment context[54] and where exercise of free speech may infringe upon property rights.[55] More generally, States have a positive obligation to create 'un environnement favorable à la participation aux débats publics de toutes les personnes concernées, leur permettant d'exprimer sans crainte leurs opinions et idées, même si celles-ci vont à l'encontre de celles défendues par les autorités officielles ou par une partie importante de l'opinion publique, voire même sont irritantes ou choquantes pour ces dernières'.[56]

Positive obligations may also require the State to facilitate access to various media. The Court has said that in order to ensure that there is true pluralism in the audio-visual sector, it is insufficient that provision be made for several channels or for 'the theoretical possibility for potential operators to access the audio-visual market'. It is also necessary 'to allow effective access to the market so as to guarantee diversity of overall programme content, reflecting as far as possible the variety of opinions encountered in the society at which the programmes are aimed'.[57] The Court has held that the lack of any adequate legislative framework enabling journalists to use on-line material without threat of legal consequences is in itself a violation of article 10.[58]

Assessing the existence of a positive obligation involves striking a 'fair balance' between the general interest of the community and the interests of the individual. The search for this balance has been described as being 'inherent throughout the Convention'.[59] The obligation will vary depending upon the diversity of situations in States Parties as well as

[51] *Karademirci and Others v. Turkey*, nos 37096/97 and 37101/97, § 26, ECHR 2005-I.
[52] *Fuentes Bobo v. Spain*, no. 39293/98, § 38, 29 February 2000; *Palomo Sánchez and Others v. Spain* [GC], nos 28955/06, 28957/06, 28959/06, and 28964/06, § 59, ECHR 2011; *Appleby and Others v. the United Kingdom*, no. 44306/98, §§ 39–40, ECHR 2003-VI.
[53] *Özgür Gündem v. Turkey*, no. 23144/93, §§ 42–46, ECHR 2000-III.
[54] *Wojtas-Kaleta v. Poland*, no. 20436/02, § 43, 16 July 2009.
[55] *Appleby and Others v. the United Kingdom*, no. 44306/98, ECHR 2003-VI.
[56] *Dink v. Turkey*, nos 2668/07, 6102/08, 30079/08, 7072/09, and 7124/09, § 137, 14 September 2010.
[57] *Centro Europa 7 S.R.L. and di Stefano v. Italy* [GC], no. 38433/09, § 129, ECHR 2012.
[58] *Editorial Board of Pravoye Delo and Shtekel v. Ukraine*, no. 33014/05, § 64, ECHR 2011 (extracts).
[59] *Verein gegen Tierfabriken Schweiz (VgT) v. Switzerland (no. 2)* [GC], no. 32772/02, § 81, ECHR 2009.

their choices with respect to priorities and resources. In freedom of expression cases, the Court has taken into account the nature of the freedom in question, its contribution to the public debate, the nature and scope of restrictions on freedom of expression, the existence of alternatives, and the weight to be given to the rights of others.[60]

In matters involving positive obligations, the Court will determine whether measures have been taken that are reasonable and appropriate. This should not impose an impossible or disproportionate burden on the authorities.[61] Obviously, in the case of a positive obligation, where a non-State actor is involved, there can be no question about the interference being 'prescribed by law'. The whole point is that the violation is not being addressed by the State. However, the Court has often said that although 'the boundary between the State's positive and negative obligations under the Convention does not lend itself to precise definition, the applicable principles are, nonetheless, similar'. In other words, a fair balance must be struck between the competing interests of the individual and of the community as a whole, subject to the margin of appreciation enjoyed by the State.[62] In striking this balance, the aims set out in article 10(2) are not without relevance.

There are dissident voices on the Court with respect to the extent of positive obligations. In an article 10 case involving access to media, several judges warned that developing the concept of positive obligations could result in losing sight of 'the fundamental negative obligation of the State to abstain from interfering':

The very initiative to legislate on the exercise of freedom in the name of broadcasting freedom, and in order to promote democracy in general terms, and for aims which may not necessarily fully conform to one or more of the legitimate aims of Article 10 § 2, remains problematic. The ban itself creates the condition it is supposedly trying to avert—out of fear that small organisations could not win a broadcast competition of ideas, it prevents them from competing at all. It is one thing to level a pitch; it is another to lock the gates to the cricket field.[63]

Special scrutiny is required when criminal punishment is imposed for offences related to freedom of expression. After noting that sentencing was in principle a matter for national courts, the European Court said that 'the imposition of a prison sentence for an offence in the area of political speech will be compatible with freedom of expression as guaranteed by Article 10 of the Convention only in exceptional circumstances, notably where other fundamental rights have been seriously impaired, as, for example, in the case of hate speech or incitement to violence'.[64] Punishment of a journalist for disseminating statements made by another person during an interview 'would seriously hamper the contribution of the press to discussion of matters of public interest and should not be envisaged unless there are particularly strong reasons for doing so'.[65]

[60] *Frăsilă and Ciocîrlan v. Romania*, no. 25329/03, § 54, 10 May 2012; *Remuszko v. Poland*, no. 1562/10, § 65, 16 July 2013.
[61] *Rees v. the United Kingdom*, 17 October 1986, § 37, Series A no. 106; *Osman v. the United Kingdom*, 28 October 1998, § 116, *Reports of Judgments and Decisions* 1998-VIII.
[62] *Verein gegen Tierfabriken Schweiz (VgT) v. Switzerland (no. 2)* [GC], no. 32772/02, § 81, ECHR 2009.
[63] *Animal Defenders International v. the United Kingdom* [GC], no. 48876/08, Joint Dissenting Opinion of Judges Ziemele, Sajó, Kalaydjieva, Vučinić and De Gaetano, § 12, ECHR 2013 (extracts).
[64] *Bingöl v. Turkey*, no. 36141/04, § 41, 22 June 2010.
[65] *Björk Eiðsdóttir v. Iceland*, no. 46443/09, § 80, 10 July 2012.

Scope of freedom of expression

Article 10 guarantees freedom of expression to 'everyone'. It applies to both natural and legal persons and has frequently been invoked by the latter, notably by publishing houses and media outlets. No distinction is made with respect to the role played by those who exercise freedom of expression,[66] or whether the aim pursued is to make profit.[67] In addition to books, newspapers, magazines, and similar publications, freedom of expression will apply to a speech,[68] a poem,[69] a brochure,[70] a leaflet,[71] a flag,[72] a press conference,[73] a letter,[74] a slogan,[75] a caricature,[76] a painting,[77] a photograph,[78] the constitution of an organization,[79] submissions by lawyers in court,[80] an advertisement,[81] a website,[82] and SMS or text messages sent by mobile phone.[83] Imaginative and unconventional forms of expression are also covered by article 10. For example, a display of dirty clothing near the Hungarian Parliament as a representation of the 'dirty laundry of the nation' was deemed a form of political expression encompassed within article 10.[84] Likewise, public nudity as a way of affirming the 'inoffensiveness of the human body' constitutes expression of views or opinions.[85] Blowing a hunting horn so as to disrupt a fox hunt was a form of expression of opinion covered by article 10.[86] Similarly, it applied to the pouring of red paint on statues of Ataturk as a means of expressing 'lack of affection' for the iconic Turkish leader.[87] The removal of a ribbon from a wreath that had just been laid by the president of Ukraine on the country's independence day as a way of

---

[66] *Çetin and Others v. Turkey*, nos 40153/98 and 40160/98, § 57, ECHR 2003-III (extracts).

[67] *Société de conception de presse et d'édition and Ponson v. France*, no. 26935/05, § 34, 5 March 2009; *Autronic AG v. Switzerland*, 22 May 1990, § 47, Series A no. 178.

[68] *Karkın v. Turkey*, no. 43928/98, § 10, 23 September 2003.

[69] *Karataş v. Turkey* [GC], no. 23168/94, § 49, ECHR 1999-IV.

[70] *Baran v. Turkey*, no. 48988/99, § 29, 10 November 2004.

[71] *Unabhängige Initiative Informationsvielfalt v. Austria*, no. 28525/95, § 9, ECHR 2002-I; *Özer v. Turkey*, nos 35721/04 and 3832/05, § 6, 5 May 2009.

[72] *Fáber v. Hungary*, no. 40721/08, §§ 57–59, 24 July 2012.

[73] *Çetinkaya v. Turkey*, no. 75569/01, § 28, 27 June 2006.

[74] See the discussion in *Gąsior v. Poland*, no. 34472/07, Dissenting Opinion of Judge Davíd Thór Björgvinsson, 21 February 2012.

[75] *Savgın v. Turkey*, no. 13304/03, § 32, 2 February 2010.

[76] *Cumpǎnǎ and Mazǎre v. Romania* [GC], no. 33348/96, § 22, ECHR 2004-XI; *Leroy v. France*, no. 36109/03, §§ 6 and 27, 2 October 2008.

[77] *Müller and Others v. Switzerland*, 24 May 1988, § 27, Series A no. 133; *Vereinigung Bildender Künstler v. Austria*, no. 68354/01, § 27, 25 January 2007.

[78] *Mosley v. the United Kingdom*, no. 48009/08, § 115, 10 May 2011; *Österreichischer Rundfunk v. Austria* (dec.), no. 57597/00, 25 May 2004; *Verlagsgruppe News GmbH v. Austria (no. 2)*, no 10520/02, §§ 29 and 40, 14 December 2006.

[79] *Eğitim ve Bilim Emekçileri Sendikası v. Turkey*, no. 20641/05, §§ 73–77, 25 September 2012.

[80] *Kyprianou v. Cyprus* [GC], no. 73797/01, § 151, ECHR 2005-XIII; *Nikula v. Finland*, no. 31611/96, § 30, ECHR 2002-II; *Steur v. the Netherlands*, no. 39657/98, ECHR 2003-XI.

[81] *Krone Verlag GmbH & Co. KG v. Austria (no. 3)*, no. 39069/97, § 11, ECHR 2003-XII.

[82] *Neij and Sunde Kolmisoppi v. Sweden* (dec.), no. 40397/12, 19 February 2013; *Editorial Board of Pravoye Delo and Shtekel v. Ukraine*, no. 33014/05, § 63, ECHR 2011 (extracts); *Ahmet Yıldırım v. Turkey*, no. 3111/10, §§ 48–49, 18 December 2012. For a detailed review of the human rights considerations associated with the Internet and its regulation, see *Ahmet Yıldırım v. Turkey*, no. 3111/10, Concurring Opinion of Judge Pinto de Albuquerque, ECHR 2012.

[83] *Bahçeci and Turan v. Turkey*, no. 33340/03, §§ 5–6, 16 June 2009.

[84] *Tatár and Fáber v. Hungary*, no. 26005/08 and 26160/08, § 36, 12 June 2012.

[85] *Gough v. the United Kingdom*, no. 49327/11, § 147, 24 October 2014.

[86] *Hashman and Harrup v. the United Kingdom* [GC], no. 25594/94, § 28, ECHR 1999-VIII.

[87] *Murat Vural v. Turkey*, no. 9540/07, § 56, 21 October 2014.

manifesting the view that he was not the legitimate head of State was viewed in the same way. The Court noted that the applicant was an activist in the opposition party whose leader, Yulia Tymoshenko, was then in prison.[88]

Article 10 guarantees not only the right to impart information but also the right of the public to receive it.[89]

Because the concept of 'expression' in article 10 is mainly concerned with the expression of opinion and the receiving and imparting of information and ideas, '[c]ertain classes of speech, such as lewd and obscene speech have no essential role in the expression of ideas. An offensive statement may fall outside the protection of freedom of expression where the sole intent of the offensive statement is to insult.'[90] However, 'the use of vulgar phrases in itself is not decisive in the assessment of an offensive expression as it may well serve merely stylistic purposes'.[91] The application by a Croatian soldier who had been convicted of 'tarnishing the reputation of the Republic of Croatia' because of his use of obscene language to speak of the origin of Croats was held to fall outside the protection of article 10 'because it amounted to wanton denigration and its sole intent was to insult'.[92] Nevertheless, 'providing increased protection by means of a special law on insults will not, as a rule, be in keeping with the spirit of the Convention'.[93]

Freedom of expression applies to the means of dissemination and not just to the content because restrictions on the former necessarily interfere with the right to receive and impart information.[94] The 'style' constitutes part of the communication as the form of expression.[95] The freedom to receive and impart information and ideas protected by article 10 is concerned with the language itself. The Court has said it applies to any language that 'affords the opportunity to take part in the public exchange of cultural, political and social information and ideas of all kinds'.[96] However, it does not guarantee the right to use a language for interaction with the public administration[97] or in elected institutions.[98]

The European Commission of Human Rights held that 'the right to freedom of expression by implication also guarantees a "negative right" not to be compelled to express oneself, that is, to remain silent'.[99] The Grand Chamber has declined to rule out the possibility that article 10 may extend to a right not to express oneself.[100] However, in a case where an academic challenged a conviction for refusing to provide information the

---

[88] *Shvydka v. Ukraine*, no. 17888/12, §§ 37–38, 30 October 2014.
[89] *Observer and Guardian v. the United Kingdom*, 26 November 1991, § 59(b), Series A no. 216; *Guerra and Others v. Italy*, 19 February 1998, § 53, *Reports of Judgments and Decisions* 1998-I.
[90] *Rujak v. Croatia* (dec.), no. 57942/10, § 29, 2 October 2012.
[91] *Uj v. Hungary*, no. 23954/10, § 20, 19 July 2011.
[92] *Rujak v. Croatia* (dec.), no. 57942/10, § 30, 2 October 2012.
[93] *Otegi Mondragon v. Spain*, no. 2034/07, § 55, ECHR 2011.
[94] *Ahmet Yıldırım v. Turkey*, no. 3111/10, § 50, ECHR 2012; *De Haes and Gijsels v. Belgium*, 24 February 1997, § 48, *Reports of Judgments and Decisions* 1997-I.
[95] *Uj v. Hungary*, no. 23954/10, § 20, 19 July 2011.
[96] *Eğitim ve Bilim Emekçileri Sendikası v. Turkey*, no. 20641/05, § 99, 25 September 2012.
[97] *Inhabitants of Leeuw-Saint-Pierre v. Belgium*, no. 2333/64, Commission decision of 16 December 1968, (1968) 11 YB 228, Collection 28, p. 1; *Fryske nationale partij v. the Netherlands*, no. 11100/84, Commission decision of 12 December 1985, DR 45, p. 240; *Samo Pahor v. Italy*, no. 19927/92, Commission decision of 29 June 1994.
[98] *Clerfayt, Legros, and Alii v. Belgium*, no. 10650/83, Commission decision of 17 May 1985, DR 42, p. 218; *Birk-Levy v. France* (dec.), no. 39416/06, 21 September 2010.
[99] *Strohal v. Austria*, no. 20871/92, Commission decision of 7 April 1994.
[100] *Gillberg v. Sweden* [GC], no. 41723/06, § 86, 3 April 2012.

Court did not consider that article 10 had been breached.[101] In a case concerning a refusal to give evidence, it held that article 10 was not applicable.[102]

Freedom of expression is, of course, subject to derogation in accordance with article 15. Along with the protection against arbitrary detention, freedom of expression is commonly given as one of the classic examples of a right that may be reduced or suspended during public emergencies such as war. However, in the State practice of derogation there do not appear to be any examples of declarations suspending article 10. Freedom of expression is also a right that may interact with article 17, where it is provided that nothing in the Convention may be interpreted as implying for any State, group, or person any right to engage in any activity or perform any act aimed at the destruction of any of the rights and freedoms set forth herein or at their limitation to a greater extent than is provided for in the Convention.

Article 10(1) refers specifically to the 'freedom to hold opinions'. This formulation echoes the guarantee, in article 9(1) of the Convention, of 'freedom of thought'. It has not given rise to any particular difficulties of interpretation or application. Like article 9(1), interference by the State or by other individuals with the freedom to hold opinions can only become an issue when such opinions are expressed, communicated, and disseminated. These matters fall under the freedom to impart information and ideas. The Court has said that the freedom to receive and impart information and ideas 'basically prohibits a Government from restricting a person from receiving information that others wish or may be willing to impart to him'.[103]

Press

Freedom of expression is intimately related to freedom of the press. Indeed, the two rights are often presented as if they are synonymous. The notion of 'freedom of the press' is probably as old as Gutenberg and the invention of moveable type. Early legal scholars, such as William Blackstone, took strong positions supportive of freedom of the press:

The liberty of the press is indeed essential to the nature of a free state; but this consists in laying no previous restraints upon publications, and not in freedom from censure for criminal matter when published. Every freeman has an undoubted right to lay what sentiments he pleases before the public; to forbid this, is to destroy the freedom of the press; but if he publishes what is improper, mischievous or illegal, he must take the consequence of his own temerity.[104]

Today, of course, 'press' is a generic term that refers to various forms of print and electronic media. We continue to use the old term 'press' in much the same way that we refer to 'fonts' and 'upper and lower case', linguistic remnants of an earlier technology. Audiovisual media, including radio and television, are particularly important: '[b]ecause of their power to convey messages through sound and images, such media have a more immediate and powerful effect than print'.[105] The impact of television and radio as

---

[101] Ibid., § 94.

[102] *Ezelin v. France*, 26 April 1991, § 33, Series A no. 202.

[103] *Gillberg v. Sweden* [GC], no. 41723/06, § 82, 3 April 2012; *Leander v. Sweden*, 26 March 1987, § 74, Series A no. 116; *Gaskin v. the United Kingdom*, 7 July 1989, § 52, Series A no. 160.

[104] *Blackstone's Commentaries on the Laws of England*, Book IV, pp. 151, 152.

[105] *Jersild v. Denmark*, 23 September 1994, § 31, Series A no. 298; *Pedersen and Baadsgaard v. Denmark* [GC], no. 49017/99, § 79, ECHR 2004-XI.

familiar sources of entertainment, often received in the intimacy of the listener's or viewer's home, further reinforces their impact.[106]

The European Court of Human Rights has frequently insisted upon the importance of the press because of its role in imparting information and ideas of public interest, and in discovering and forming an opinion of the ideas and attitudes of political leaders.[107] For this reason, it plays a vital role of 'public watchdog' in the proper functioning of democratic societies.[108] Not only does the press 'have the task of imparting such information and ideas: the public also has a right to receive them'.[109] The responsibility of the press in this respect includes reporting on opposition gatherings and demonstrations.[110] Caution is required when measures or sanctions may dissuade the press from taking part in a discussion of matters of public interest.[111]

Journalists have the freedom to resort to a degree of exaggeration and even to provocation.[112] Neither the national courts nor the European Court are entitled to substitute their own view for those of the press as to the reporting techniques to be adopted in any particular case.[113] Journalists are afforded great protection by article 10 subject to the condition that they are acting in good faith in order to provide accurate and reliable information in accordance with the ethics of journalism.[114] In the context of a public debate on an important issue, journalists cannot be required to prove the veracity of statements, only that they have acted with due diligence in order to establish this.[115] Article 10 does not grant them wholly unrestricted freedom of expression, even when matters of serious public concern are involved.[116] They must not overstep certain bounds, in particular when respect of the reputation and rights of others is required.[117]

---

[106] *Murphy v. Ireland*, no. 44179/98, § 74, ECHR 2003-IX.

[107] *De Haes and Gijsels v. Belgium*, 24 February 1997, § 37, *Reports of Judgments and Decisions* 1997-I; *Colombani and Others v. France*, no. 51279/99, § 55, ECHR 2002-V; *Fatullayev v. Azerbaijan*, no. 40984/07, § 88, 22 April 2010.

[108] *Goodwin v. the United Kingdom*, 27 March 1996, § 39, *Reports of Judgments and Decisions* 1996-II; *Axel Springer AG v. Germany* [GC], no. 39954/08, § 79, 7 February 2012; *Aquilina and Others v. Malta*, no. 28040/08, § 43, 14 June 2011; *De Haes and Gijsels v. Belgium*, 24 February 1997, *Reports of Judgments and Decisions* 1997-I, pp. 233–4, § 37.

[109] *Handyside v. the United Kingdom*, 7 December 1976, § 49, Series A no. 24; *Lingens v. Austria*, 8 July 1986, §§ 41–42, Series A no. 103; *Axel Springer AG v. Germany* [GC], no. 39954/08, § 79, 7 February 2012; *Thorgeir Thorgeirson v. Iceland*, 25 June 1992, Series A no. 239, p. 27, § 63; *Bladet Tromsø and Stensaas v. Norway* [GC], no. 21980/93, § 62, ECHR 1999-III; *Gawęda v. Poland*, no. 26229/95, § 34, ECHR 2002-II.

[110] *Najafli v. Azerbaijan*, no. 2594/07, § 63, 2 October 2012.

[111] *Kaperzyński v. Poland*, no. 43206/07, § 70, 3 April 2012; *Standard Verlags GmbH v. Austria*, no. 13071/03, § 49, 2 November 2006; *Kuliś and Różycki v. Poland*, no. 27209/03, § 37, 6 October 2009.

[112] *Pedersen and Baadsgaard v. Denmark* [GC], no. 49017/99, § 71, ECHR 2004-XI; *Prager and Oberschlick v. Austria*, 26 April 1995, § 38, Series A no. 313; *Bladet Tromsø and Stensaas v. Norway* [GC], no. 21980/93, § 59, ECHR 1999-III.

[113] *Axel Springer AG v. Germany* [GC], no. 39954/08, § 81, 7 February 2012; *Jersild v. Denmark*, 23 September 1994, § 31, Series A no. 298; *Eerikäinen and Others v. Finland*, no. 3514/02, § 65, 10 February 2009.

[114] *Radio France and Others v. France*, no. 53984/00, § 37, ECHR 2004-II; *Colombani and Others v. France*, no. 51279/99, § 65, ECHR 2002-V.

[115] *Braun v. Poland*, no. 30162/10, §§ 50–51, 4 November 2014.

[116] *Kaperzyński v. Poland*, no. 43206/07, § 57, 3 April 2012.

[117] *De Haes and Gijsels v. Belgium*, 24 February 1997, § 37, *Reports of Judgments and Decisions* 1997-I; *Colombani and Others v. France*, no. 51279/99, § 55, ECHR 2002-V; *Fatullayev v. Azerbaijan*, no. 40984/07, § 88, 22 April 2010; *Pedersen and Baadsgaard v. Denmark* [GC], no. 49017/99, § 78, ECHR 2004-X; *Times Newspapers Ltd v. United Kingdom* (nos 1 and 2), no. 3002/03 and 23676/03, § 42, ECHR 2009; *MGN Limited v. the United Kingdom*, no. 39401/04, § 1341, 18 January 2011; *Mosley v. the United Kingdom*, no. 48009/08, § 113, 10 May 2011.

An important protection for journalists deemed necessary to ensure the effectiveness of their work is the ability to protect the confidentiality of their sources of information. This is sometimes described as a 'privilege' in the sense that in the course of legal proceedings they are entitled to refuse to divulge their sources so as to protect the identity of informants.[118] Because of the importance of the confidentiality of sources in the protection of freedom of the press in a democratic society, 'an interference cannot be compatible with Article 10 of the Convention unless it is justified by an overriding requirement in the public interest'.[119]

The Committee of Ministers of the Council of Europe has adopted a Recommendation on the protection of journalistic sources that declares: 'Domestic law and practice in member States should provide for explicit and clear protection of the right of journalists not to disclose information identifying a source in accordance with Article 10 of the Convention for the Protection of Human Rights and Fundamental Freedoms...'[120] Referring to that instrument, the Court has said that it understands that the concept of journalistic 'source' refers to 'any person who provides information to a journalist'. As for 'information identifying a source', this includes both 'the factual circumstances of acquiring information from a source by a journalist' and 'the unpublished content of the information provided by a source to a journalist'.[121] The Court has expressed its concern about the chilling effect that will result if journalists are seen to assist in the identification of anonymous sources.[122] The protection of sources is important even when they are unaware that they are generating material to be used in a journalistic investigation, for example when they are filmed surreptitiously.[123]

International human rights law provides explicit support for a right of reply to a person who is injured by inaccurate or offensive statements disseminated by the press.[124] Despite the absence of any formulation in the European Convention similar to that in the American Convention on Human Rights, the European Court has held that an obligation to publish a rectification or a reply may be considered a normal element of the legal framework governing the exercise of freedom of expression. Moreover, this may extend to an obligation to inform the individual concerned about the reasons why a media outlet has refused to publish a reply or rectification. According to the Court, '[s]uch an obligation makes it possible, for example, for the person who feels aggrieved by a press article to present his reply in a manner compatible with the editorial practice of the newspaper concerned'.[125] Thus, although the Convention does not guarantee a right of

---

[118] *Van der Heijden v. the Netherlands* [GC], no. 42857/05, § 64, 3 April 2012; *Goodwin v. the United Kingdom*, 27 March 1996, § 45, *Reports of Judgments and Decisions* 1996-II. For a review of the case law, see *Sanoma Uitgevers B.V. v. the Netherlands* [GC], no. 38224/03, §§ 59–63, 14 September 2010.

[119] *Sanoma Uitgevers B.V. v. the Netherlands* [GC], no. 38224/03, § 18, 14 September 2010; *Goodwin v. the United Kingdom*, 27 March 1996, § 39, *Reports of Judgments and Decisions* 1996-II; *Roemen and Schmit v. Luxembourg*, no. 51772/99, § 46, ECHR 2003-IV; *Voskuil v. the Netherlands*, no. 64752/01, § 65, 22 November 2007; *Telegraaf Media Nederland Landelijke Media B.V. and Others v. the Netherlands*, no. 39315/06, §§ 86–88, 22 November 2012.

[120] Recommendation No. R (2000) 7, Appendix, principle 1.

[121] *Nagla v. Latvia*, no. 73469/10, § 81, 16 July 2013.

[122] *Financial Times Ltd and Others v. the United Kingdom*, no. 821/03, § 70, 15 December 2009; *Nordisk Film & TV A/S v. Denmark* (dec.), no. 40485/02, ECHR 2005-XII; *Sanoma Uitgevers B.V. v. the Netherlands* [GC], no. 38224/03, § 65, 14 September 2010.

[123] *Nordisk Film & TV A/S v. Denmark* (dec.), no. 40485/02, ECHR 2005-XIII.

[124] American Convention on Human Rights, (1978) 1144 UNTS 123, art. 14.

[125] *Kaperzyński v. Poland*, no. 43206/07, § 66, 3 April 2012.

reply or rectification, the freedom of expression of the media outlet cannot be invoked if the national law imposes a requirement of rectification. The Committee of Ministers of the Council of Europe has recommended that member governments provide an individual about whom information has been published, in any medium, with 'an effective possibility for the correction, without undue delay, of incorrect facts relating to him which he has a justified interest in having corrected, such correction being given, as far as possible, the same prominence as the original publication'.[126] According to the Court, in certain cases there may be a positive obligation for the State, even in the case of privately owned media, to ensure that an individual has 'a reasonable opportunity to exercise his right of reply by submitting a response to the newspaper for publication and, secondly, that he had an opportunity to contest the newspaper's refusal'.[127]

If the links between democratic governance, the rule of law, and freedom of expression are important, there is also an important connection with the right to a fair trial and the proper operation of the judicial system. Media contribute to this by reporting upon trial proceedings and on justice more generally. Article 6 of the Convention guarantees the right to a 'public trial'. In practice, this right is ensured with the help of the media. A particular dimension of the reputation or rights of others is the reporting of criminal proceedings. In this area, the Committee of Ministers has adopted Principles concerning the provision of information through the media in relation to criminal proceedings.[128] It seeks a balance among a number of factors, including the public interest in being informed about criminal proceedings, the protection of the presumption of innocence, accuracy of the information that is published, and the protection of privacy.

The duty of the press in a democratic society 'extends to the reporting and commenting on court proceedings which, provided that they do not overstep the bounds set out above, contribute to their publicity and are thus consonant with the requirement under Article 6 § 1 of the Convention that hearings be public'.[129] The Court has described as 'inconceivable' the possibility that there be no prior or contemporaneous discussion of the subject matter of trials, explaining that '[n]ot only do the media have the task of imparting such information and ideas; the public also has a right to receive them'.[130]

Nevertheless, 'the public nature of court proceedings does not function as a carte blanche relieving the media of their duty to show due care in communicating information received in the course of those proceedings'.[131] There is considerable deference to the role of the judiciary, which may be subject to legitimate criticism of its shortcomings but without losing sight of its special role in society.[132] In one case, the media breached a

---

[126] Resolution (74) 26 of the Committee of Ministers of the Council of Europe on the right of reply— Position of the individual in relation to the press. See also Recommendation Rec(2004)16 of the Committee of Ministers to member States on the right of reply in the new media environment.

[127] *Melnychuk v. Ukraine* (dec.), no. 28743/03, ECHR 2005-IX.

[128] Rec(2003)13 of the Committee of Ministers, Appendix.

[129] *Axel Springer AG v. Germany* [GC], no. 39954/08, § 80, 7 February 2012; *News Verlags GmbH & Co. KG v. Austria*, no. 31457/96, § 56, ECHR 2000-I; *Dupuis and Others v. France*, no. 1914/02 § 35, ECHR 2007-VII; *Campos Dâmaso v. Portugal*, no. 17107/05, § 31, 24 April 2008.

[130] *Axel Springer AG v. Germany* [GC], no. 39954/08, § 80; *News Verlags GmbH & Co. KG v. Austria*, no. 31457/96, § 56, ECHR 2000-I; *Dupuis and Others v. France*, no. 1914/02 § 35, ECHR 2007-VII; *Campos Dâmaso v. Portugal*, no. 17107/05, § 31, 24 April 2008.

[131] *Kurier Zeitungsverlag und Druckerei GmbH v. Austria*, no. 3401/07, § 44, 17 January 2012; *Eerikäinen and Others v. Finland*, no. 3514/02, § 63, 10 February 2009.

[132] *Prager and Oberschlick v. Austria*, 26 April 1995, § 34, Series A no. 313; *Falter Zeitschriften GmbH v. Austria (no. 2)*, no. 3084/07, §§ 38–39, 18 September 2012.

prohibition on photographing a convicted person without her consent as she left the hearing where the verdict was pronounced. The European Court said the presentation of the individual in the press had been 'particularly intrusive', finding that the applicant's interest in restricting publication outweighed that of the media in informing the public.[133] In the United Kingdom, jurors are forbidden to divulge the content of their deliberations. *The Times* was prosecuted for publishing an account of jury deliberations by a disgruntled juror. Noting that divulgation of jury deliberations had not been conducted as part of research into jury methods, or where disclosure might be justified by the interests of justice, but rather with the aim of contributing to the 'serious debate concerning the use of expert medical evidence in criminal trials', the Court declared the case inadmissible.[134]

Physical ill-treatment by State agents of journalists who are performing their professional work may constitute interference with article 10, in addition, of course, to raising issues with respect to article 3. The Court has held that the intent of those who perpetrate such abuse is not important because 'what matters is that the journalist was subjected to the unnecessary and excessive use of force, amounting to ill-treatment under Article 3 of the Convention, despite having made clear efforts to identify himself as a journalist who was simply doing his work and observing the event'.[135]

The quality of journalism varies enormously. For some newspapers, the public interest in promoting democratic discussion about the issues of the day is rather remote. A distinction has been made between 'reporting facts—even if controversial—capable of contributing to a debate of general public interest in a democratic society' and the making of 'tawdry allegations about an individual's private life'.[136] For this reason, while the contribution of the press to public debate weighs heavily in considerations about acceptable limitations on freedom of expression, the same factors do not apply to 'press reports concentrating on sensational and, at times, lurid news, intended to titillate and entertain, which are aimed at satisfying the curiosity of a particular readership regarding aspects of a person's strictly private life'.[137] Such reports 'are often taken in a climate of continual harassment which may induce in the person concerned a very strong sense of intrusion into their private life or even of persecution',[138] leading to obvious conflicts with the right to private life, enshrined in article 8 of the Convention.[139] In such cases, 'the focus must be on whether the publication is in the interest of the public and not whether the public might be interested in reading it'.[140] The public interest in matters involving the private life of important public officials may increase as time elapses.[141] Public interest

---

[133] *Egeland and Hanseid v. Norway*, no. 34438/04, §§ 61 and 63, 16 April 2009.

[134] *Seckerson v. The United Kingdom and Time Newspapers Limited v. the United Kingdom* (dec.), nos 32844/10 and 33510/10, 24 January 2012.

[135] *Najafli v. Azerbaijan*, no. 2594/07, § 68, 2 October 2012

[136] *Mosley v. the United Kingdom*, no. 48009/08, § 114, 10 May 2011. Also *Armonienė v. Lithuania*, no. 36919/02, § 39, 25 November 2008.

[137] *Von Hannover v. Germany*, no. 59320/00, § 65, ECHR 2004-VI; *Hachette Filipacchi Associés (ICI PARIS) v. France*, no. 12268/03, § 40, 23 July 2009; *MGN Limited v. the United Kingdom*, no. 39401/04, § 143, 18 January 2011; *Société Prisma Presse v. France* (dec.), nos 66910/01 and 71612/01, 1 July 2003; *Leempoel & S.A. ED. Ciné Revue v. Belgium*, no. 64772/01, § 77, 9 November 2006.

[138] *Von Hannover v. Germany (no. 2)* [GC], nos 40660/08 and 60641/08, § 103, ECHR 2012.

[139] See, in particular *Lindon, Otchakovsky-Laurens and July v. France* [GC], nos 21279/02 and 36448/02, Concurring Opinion of Judge Loucaides, ECHR 2007-IV.

[140] *Mosley v. the United Kingdom*, no. 48009/08, § 114, 10 May 2011.

[141] *Von Hannover v. Germany*, no. 59320/00, §§ 59–60, ECHR 2004-VI; *Editions Plon v. France*, no. 58148/00, § 53, ECHR 2004-IV.

is not confined to political figures or criminal activity; it also extends to sporting issues and performance artists.[142] Nevertheless, the justification for press freedom that is rooted in the role as 'public watchdog' is obviously not relevant in the same way.[143] According to the Court, 'as a matter of principle' the rights enshrined in articles 8 and 10 'deserve equal respect' and therefore the margin of appreciation accorded to States should be the same.[144]

The Internet

When the European Convention was adopted, the Internet was still the stuff of science fiction. Its enormous importance today in the expression of ideas, their dissemination, and in access to information needs no demonstration. It has become 'one of the principal means by which individuals exercise their right to freedom of expression and information, providing as it does essential tools for participation in activities and discussions concerning political issues and issues of general interest'.[145] As one judge noted, '[i]f streets and parks of a city are the historical quintessential public fora, the Internet is today's global marketplace of ideas'.[146] The Committee of Ministers has explained that information and communication technologies 'provide unprecedented opportunities for all to enjoy freedom of expression'.[147] In important ways, the Internet has democratized access to the media, greatly reducing—if not eliminating—barriers in terms of both cost and regulatory framework that served in the past as practical obstacles to the expression of opinions and ideas. Consequently, because of technological progress there is immensely greater genuine freedom of expression today than there was in 1950, when the European Convention was adopted.

The Internet raises particular problems in terms of the protection of freedom of expression.[148] The Court has explained that '[i]n light of its accessibility and its capacity to store and communicate vast amounts of information, the Internet plays an important role in enhancing the public's access to news and facilitating the dissemination of information generally'.[149] For example, '[t]he risk of harm posed by content and communications on the Internet to the exercise and enjoyment of human rights and freedoms, particularly the right to respect for private life, is certainly higher than that posed by the press. Therefore, the policies governing reproduction of material from the printed media and the Internet may differ.'[150]

---

[142] *Nikowitz and Verlagsgruppe News GmbH v. Austria*, no. 5266/03, § 25, 22 February 2007; *Colaço Mestre and SIC—Sociedade Independente de Comunicação, S.A. v. Portugal*, nos 11182/03 and 11319/03, § 28, 26 April 2007; *Sapan v. Turkey*, no. 44102/04, § 34, 8 June 2010.

[143] *Axel Springer AG v. Germany* [GC], no. 39954/08, § 91, 7 February 2012.

[144] Ibid., § 87; *Hachette Filipacchi Associés (ICI PARIS) v. France*, no. 12268/03, § 41, 23 July 2009; *Timciuc v. Romania* (dec.), no. 28999/03, § 144, 12 October 2010; *Mosley v. the United Kingdom*, no. 48009/08, § 111, 10 May 2011.

[145] *Ahmet Yıldırım v. Turkey*, no. 3111/10, § 54, ECHR 2012.

[146] *Mouvement raëlien suisse v. Switzerland* [GC], no. 16354/06, Dissenting Opinion of Judge Pinto de Albuquerque, ECHR 2012 (extracts).

[147] Declaration CM(2005)56 final. See also Recommendation CM/Rec(2007)16; Recommendation CM/Rec(2007)11; Recommendation CM/Rec(2008)6; Recommendation CM/Rec(2012)3.

[148] See, generally, Council of Europe Commissioner on Human Rights, The rule of law on the Internet and in the wider digital world, Council of Europe Issue Paper, December 2014.

[149] *Times Newspapers Ltd v. the United Kingdom (nos. 1 and 2)*, nos 3002/03 and 23676/03, § 27, ECHR 2009.

[150] *Editorial Board of Pravoye Delo and Shtekel v. Ukraine*, no. 33014/05, § 63, ECHR 2011 (extracts).

Referring specifically to issues concerning the application of article 8 of the Convention and the protection of private life, the Court said:

> Although freedom of expression and confidentiality of communications are primary considerations and users of telecommunications and Internet services must have a guarantee that their own privacy and freedom of expression will be respected, such guarantee cannot be absolute and must yield on occasion to other legitimate imperatives, such as the prevention of disorder or crime or the protection of the rights and freedoms of others. Without prejudice to the question whether the conduct of the person who placed the offending advertisement on the Internet can attract the protection of Articles 8 and 10, having regard to its reprehensible nature, it is nonetheless the task of the legislator to provide the framework for reconciling the various claims which compete for protection in this context.[151]

One of the features of the Internet is the 'hyperlink' by which texts and documents are connected so that the reader is referred to related materials. In one sense, this fulfils the same function as a footnote or a bibliographic reference in traditional publications. At the same time, the 'hyperlink' is a form of publication that may contribute to disseminating information that threatens the rights and freedoms of others. In *Mouvement Raëlien Suisse*, seven dissenting judges explained that '[a] reference is not an endorsement or an identification, and even an endorsement would not create a clear danger of committing a crime. Otherwise the "referring" person would be obliged to distance himself all the time and that would impose a considerable burden on freedom of speech in the world of the Internet.' They described as 'unrealistic' the imposition of responsibility on a person who uses a hyperlink to reference another website where that website can easily be found using a search engine.[152]

Literary and artistic expression

Artistic expression 'affords the opportunity to take part in the public exchange of cultural, political and social information and ideas of all kinds'.[153] Noting that article 10 does not specifically contemplate artistic expression, the Court has said this can be implied from the reference to 'broadcasting, television or cinema enterprises' in the second sentence as these are media whose activities extend to the field of art. The Court also referred to the reference in article 19(2) of the International Covenant on Civil and Political Rights to information and ideas 'in the form of art' to support its conclusion that artistic expression is also included in article 10(1) of the Convention, despite the silence of the provision.[154]

A novel is a form of artistic expression contemplated by article 10 because 'it affords the opportunity to take part in the public exchange of cultural, political and social information and ideas of all kinds. Those who create or distribute a work, for example of a literary nature, contribute to the exchange of ideas and opinions which is essential for a democratic society.'[155] Indeed, because of the important relationship between freedom of expression and democracy, publications that relate to a debate on a matter of general concern, and that constitute political or militant expression, are entitled to 'a high level of

---

[151] *K.U. v. Finland*, no. 2872/02, § 49, ECHR 2008.
[152] *Mouvement raëlien suisse v. Switzerland* [GC], no. 16354/06, Joint Dissenting Opinion of Judges Tulkens, Sajó, Lazarova Trajkovska, Bianku, Power-Force, Vučinić, and Yudkivska, ECHR 2012 (extracts).
[153] *Müller and Others v. Switzerland*, 24 May 1988, § 27, Series A no. 133.
[154] Ibid., § 27.
[155] *Lindon, Otchakovsky-Laurens, and July v. France* [GC], nos 21279/02 and 36448/02, § 48, ECHR 2007-IV; *Karataş v. Turkey* [GC], no. 23168/94, § 49, ECHR 1999-IV.

protection of the right to freedom of expression'.[156] Often, literary creation has been associated with political activism, and it is this that has provoked the ire of the authorities. In Turkey, poems were prohibited that 'through the frequent use of pathos and metaphors, called for self-sacrifice for "Kurdistan" and included some particularly aggressive passages directed at the Turkish authorities'. While acknowledging that '[t]aken literally, the poems might be construed as inciting readers to hatred, revolt and the use of violence', in deciding whether this was in fact the case the Court said 'it must nevertheless be borne in mind that the medium used by the applicant was poetry, a form of artistic expression that appeals to only a minority of readers'.[157] It made a similar comment about a novel providing a fictional account of ill-treatment and atrocities perpetrated by the Turkish authorities.[158]

But artistic works or publications need not have political content or contribute to democratic debate in order to be deserving of protection under article 10. In a Turkish case concerning the censorship of an erotic novel by French author Guillaume Apollinaire, the Court noted that it had earlier been published in the distinguished *La Pléiade* collection and that it had become 'une œuvre figurant dans le patrimoine littéraire européen'.[159] The right of everyone 'to enjoy the arts' is affirmed in article 27(1) of the Universal Declaration of Human Rights. It can only be honoured to the extent that there is genuine freedom of artistic expression.

Freedom of expression in the workplace

Freedom of expression is one of the main ways of ensuring the effective enjoyment of freedom of assembly and association, and is of special importance to the activities of trade unions.[160] There is much authority for the application of article 10 to the workplace when the freedom of expression of civil or public servants is concerned.[161] Article 10 also applies when the employer is not the State and the relations between employer and employee are governed by private law. Then the State has a positive obligation to protect the right to freedom of expression, even in the sphere of relations between individuals.

Although trade union rights enjoy special protection under article 11 of the Convention, where this is made explicit in the final words of paragraph 1, the relationship with article 10 is also quite fundamental. Trade union rights are, of course, also ensured by a specialized body of international law developed under the aegis of the International Labour Organisation, a United Nations agency whose existence can be traced to the establishment of the League of Nations. Citing the case law of the Inter-American Court of Human Rights, the Grand Chamber of the European Court has insisted that freedom of expression was 'a *conditio sine qua non* for the development of ... trade unions'.[162]

---

[156] *Lindon, Otchakovsky-Laurens, and July v. France* [GC], nos 21279/02 and 36448/02, § 48, ECHR 2007-IV. Also *Müller v. Switzerland*, no. 41202/98, § 27, 5 November 2002.

[157] *Karataş v. Turkey* [GC], no. 23168/94, § 49, ECHR 1999-IV.

[158] *Alınak v. Turkey*, no. 40287/98, § 41, 29 March 2005.

[159] *Akdaş v. Turkey*, no. 41056/04, §§ 28–30, 16 February 2010. But see *Lautsi and Others v. Italy* [GC], no. 30814/06, Concurring Opinion of Judge Bonello, § 4.1, ECHR 2011 (extracts), where Judge Bonello sarcastically described the novel as a 'smear of transcendental smut'.

[160] *Vellutini and Michel v. France*, no. 32820/09, § 32, 6 October 2011; *Zima v. Hungary*, no. 29723/11, § 28, 9 October 2012.

[161] *Kudeshkina v. Russia*, no. 29492/05, § 85, 26 February 2009; *Vogt v. Germany*, 26 September 1995, § 53, Series A no. 323; *Guja v. Moldova* [GC], no. 14277/04, § 52, ECHR 2008.

[162] *Palomo Sánchez and Others v. Spain* [GC], nos 28955/06, 28957/06, 28959/06, and 28964/06, §§ 26, 56, ECHR 2011, citing Advisory Opinion OC-5/85193.

Consequently, wrote the Grand Chamber, 'for the purpose of guaranteeing the meaningful and effective nature of trade union rights, the national authorities must ensure that disproportionate penalties do not dissuade trade union representatives from seeking to express and defend their members' interests'.[163]

So-called 'whistleblowing' raises issues of freedom of expression, notably in the context of employer–employee relations. The Grand Chamber has spoken of 'the right of civil servants and other employees to report illegal conduct and wrongdoing at their place of work'.[164] According to the Court, 'the signalling by an employee in the public sector of illegal conduct or wrongdoing in the workplace should, in certain circumstances, enjoy protection. This may be called for in particular where the employee or civil servant concerned is the only person, or part of a small category of persons, aware of what is happening at work and is thus best placed to act in the public interest by alerting the employer or the public at large.'[165] Six criteria have been identified in assessing the necessity of an infringement with article 10 in such circumstances: '(a) public interest involved in the disclosed information; (b) authenticity of the information disclosed; (c) the damage, if any, suffered by the authority as a result of the disclosure in question; (d) the motive behind the actions of the reporting employee; (e) whether, in the light of duty of discretion owed by an employee toward his or her employer, the information was made public as a last resort, following disclosure to a superior or other competent body; and (f) severity of the sanction imposed'.[166]

Indeed, employees also owe a duty of loyalty to the employer, notably in the protection of reputation and of commercial interests, which may limit the scope of their freedom of expression.[167] 'This is particularly so in the case of civil servants since the very nature of civil service requires that a civil servant is bound by a duty of loyalty and discretion', the Court has said.[168] Civil servants in a democratic society have a mission of assisting the government in discharging its functions. Because members of the public have a right 'to expect that they will help and not hinder the democratically elected government, the duty of loyalty and reserve assumes special significance for them'.[169]

Even members of the military are entitled to invoke article 10, although 'the proper functioning of the armed forces is hardly imaginable without legal rules designed to prevent servicemen from undermining the requisite discipline, for example by writings'.[170]

---

[163] Ibid., § 56, citing I/A Court H.R., *Compulsory Membership in an Association Prescribed by Law for the Practice of Journalism (Arts 13 and 29 American Convention on Human Rights)*, Advisory Opinion OC-5/85 of November 13, 1985. Series A No. 5. For a more spirited defence of the importance of freedom of expression for trade unions, see *Palomo Sánchez and Others v. Spain* [GC], nos 28955/06, 28957/06, 28959/06, and 28964/06, Joint Dissenting Opinion of Juges Tulkens, Davíd Thór Björgvinsson, Jočienė, Popović, and Vučinić, ECHR 2011.

[164] *Guja v. Moldova* [GC], no. 14277/04, § 97, ECHR 2008.

[165] *Heinisch v. Germany*, no. 28274/08, § 63, ECHR 2011 (extracts); *Vogt v. Germany*, 26 September 1995, § 53, Series A no. 323; *Ahmed and Others v. the United Kingdom*, 2 September 1998, § 55, *Reports of Judgments and Decisions* 1998-VI; *De Diego Nafría v. Spain*, no. 46833/99, § 37, 14 March 2002, no. 4063/04, § 46, 19 February 2009.

[166] *Matúz v. Hungary*, no. 73571/10, § 34, 21 October 2014.

[167] *Heinisch v. Germany*, no. 28274/08, § 64, ECHR 2011 (extracts).

[168] *Guja v. Moldova* [GC], no. 14277/04, § 70, ECHR 2008.

[169] Ibid., § 71.

[170] *Szima v. Hungary*, no. 29723/11, § 25, 9 October 2012; *Vereinigung demokratischer Soldaten Österreichs and Gubi v. Austria*, 19 December 1994, § 36, Series A no. 302; *Hadjianastassiou v. Greece*, 16 December 1992, § 39, Series A no. 252.

Regardless of frontiers

Freedom of expression may be exercised 'regardless of frontiers' (*sans considération de frontière*). This language was inherited from article 19 of the Universal Declaration of Human Rights and received no particular attention during the drafting of the European Convention. It can be traced to proposals in the United Nations Sub-Commission on Freedom of Information and of the Press, where it was initially associated with the idea that any abuses of freedom of expression could only be those 'determined by the law of nations'.[171] Although the term was adopted with almost no discussion, one of the drafters of the Universal Declaration stated that '[b]y implication, the words "regardless of frontiers" implied ideological barriers as well as physical frontiers'.[172] Another participant in the negotiations 'wondered whether "regardless of frontiers" referred to geographical or moral frontiers'.[173]

Turkish legislation blocking access to an internet site was described by the Court as being 'in direct conflict with the actual wording of paragraph 1 of Article 10 of the Convention, according to which the rights set forth in that Article are secured "regardless of frontiers"'.[174] Similarly, a 'direct conflict' with article 10(1) was signalled by the Court with respect to French legislation conferring on the Minister of the Interior broad powers to issue administrative bans on the dissemination of publications of foreign origin or written in a foreign language. The Government had argued that the legislation was justified by the difficulty in instituting proceedings against authors or publishers located abroad. The Court said that 'the exceptional circumstances in 1939, on the eve of the Second World War, might have justified tight control over foreign publications' but that 'the argument that a system that discriminated against publications of that sort should continue to remain in force would appear to be untenable'.[175]

Licensing of broadcasting, television, or cinema enterprises

Licensing of broadcasting, television, or cinema enterprises is specifically authorized by the third sentence of article 10(1). There can be no claim that freedom of expression, as guaranteed by article 10, is breached merely because such licensing measures have been adopted by a State. This provision is unique to the European Convention on Human Rights, added by the Committee of Ministers at the very end of the drafting process without debate or discussion to shed light on the purpose or intent. Nothing similar appears in the freedom of expression provisions of the other major human rights treaties.

The Court has said that licensing is permitted by article 10(1) 'particularly in its technical aspects'.[176] However, granting of a licence may also be made conditional on considerations such as 'the nature and objectives of a proposed channel, its potential audience at national, regional or local level, the rights and needs of a specific audience and the obligations deriving from international legal instruments'.[177] The imposition of such

---

[171] UN Doc. E/CN.4/Sub.1/45. Also: UN Doc. E/CN.4/Sub.1/48.

[172] *Official Records of the General Assembly,* Third Session, 1948, p. 409 (Aquino, Philippines).

[173] UN Doc. E/CN.4/SR.63, p. 13 (Pavlov, Soviet Union).

[174] *Ahmet Yıldırım v. Turkey,* no. 3111/10, § 67, ECHR 2012.

[175] *Association Ekin v. France,* no. 39288/98, § 62, ECHR 2001-VIII.

[176] *Centro Europa 7 S.R.L. and di Stefano v. Italy* [GC], no. 38433/09, § 139, ECHR 2012; *Demuth v. Switzerland,* no. 38743/97, § 33, ECHR 2002-IX.

[177] *Centro Europa 7 S.R.L. and di Stefano v. Italy* [GC], no. 38433/09, § 139, ECHR 2012.

conditions may result in interference with freedom of expression that may not correspond to one of the legitimate aims permitted by paragraph 2 of article 10. Nevertheless, the other criteria in paragraph 2 will be applied to the interference in assessing whether it is permissible.[178]

For example, replying to an application that challenged the denial of a license for a station of a religious nature, the United Kingdom explained that the capacity for national radio service was 'very limited' and that the measure was consistent with a policy 'to promote the efficient use of scarce resources in order to safeguard pluralism in the media, cater for a variety of tastes and interests and avoid discrimination as between the many different religions practised in the United Kingdom'. It added that there was no restriction on licenses for local or satellite radio stations because the same constraints on spectrum capacity did not apply. The Court, by a majority, declared the application inadmissible.[179] In another case, the Court accepted the explanation by Switzerland that its licensing system was 'capable of contributing to the quality and balance of programmes through the powers conferred on the government'.[180]

In such a sensitive sector as the audio-visual media, the State has a positive obligation to establish a regulatory framework capable of guaranteeing 'effective pluralism'.[181] The licensing of media outlets should not permit powerful economic or political groups to obtain a position of dominance, something that may exercise pressure on broadcasters and 'eventually curtail their editorial freedom', thereby undermining 'the fundamental role of freedom of expression in a democratic society as enshrined in Article 10 of the Convention, in particular where it serves to impart information and ideas of general interest, which the public is moreover entitled to receive'.[182] Similarly, where the dominant position is held by public broadcasters that are owned by the State, the licensing regime must be justified by a pressing social need.[183]

Formalities, conditions, restrictions, or penalties

Article 10 is one of four provisions of the European Convention with a restrictions or limitations clause. Paragraph 2 of article 10 states: 'The exercise of these freedoms, since it carries with it duties and responsibilities, may be subject to such formalities, conditions, restrictions or penalties as are prescribed by law and are necessary in a democratic society, in the interests of national security, territorial integrity or public safety, for the prevention of disorder or crime, for the protection of health or morals, for the protection of the reputation or rights of others, for preventing the disclosure of information received in confidence, or for maintaining the authority and impartiality of the judiciary.' There are similar but not identical clauses in articles 8, 9, and 11. Comparable texts are also used

---

[178] *Demuth v. Switzerland*, no. 38743/97, § 33, ECHR 2002-IX; *Tele 1 Privatfernsehgesellschaft mbH v. Austria*, no. 32240/96, § 25, 21 September 2000; *Radio ABC v. Austria*, 20 October 1997, § 28, *Reports of Judgments and Decisions* 1997-VI; *Groppera Radio AG and Others v. Switzerland*, 28 March 1990, § 61, Series A no. 173.

[179] *United Christian Broadcasters Ltd. v. the United Kingdom* (dec.), no. 44802/98, 7 December 2000.

[180] *Demuth v. Switzerland*, no. 38743/97, § 35, ECHR 2002-IX.

[181] *Centro Europa 7 S.R.L. and di Stefano v. Italy* [GC], no. 38433/09, § 134, ECHR 2012.

[182] Ibid., § 133; *VgT Verein gegen Tierfabriken v. Switzerland*, no. 24699/94, §§ 73, 75, ECHR 2001-VI; *De Geillustreerde v. the Netherlands*, no. 5178/71, Commission decision of 6 July 1976, DR 8, p. 13.

[183] *Informationsverein Lentia and Others v. Austria*, 24 November 1993, § 39, Series A no. 276; *Centro Europa 7 S.R.L. and di Stefano v. Italy* [GC], no. 38433/09, § 133, ECHR 2012.

with respect to some of the provisions in the Protocols: article 1 of Protocol No. 1 (protection of property); article 2(3) of Protocol No. 4 (freedom of movement); and article 2(2) of Protocol No. 7 (right of appeal in criminal matters). The Convention organs have developed a flexible methodology for the interpretation and application of paragraph 2 in determining whether or not the interference with a right set out in the first paragraph of articles 8, 9, 10, and 11 is actually in breach of the Convention. The formalities, conditions, restrictions, and penalties that apply to freedom of expression are to be construed strictly,[184] with any need for restriction to be 'established convincingly'.[185]

The ancestor of the four provisions is article 29(2) of the Universal Declaration of Human Rights: 'In the exercise of his rights and freedoms, everyone shall be subject only to such limitations as are determined by law solely for the purpose of securing due recognition and respect for the rights and freedoms of others and of meeting the just requirements of morality, public order and the general welfare in a democratic society.' The limitation clause in the Universal Declaration applies generally to all rights set out in the instrument, whereas the specific clauses of this nature in the European Convention, of which article 10(2) is an example, are tailored to the right at issue.

A provision comparable in content to article 10(2) appears in the International Covenant on Civil and Political Rights. It is quite laconic by comparison with article 10(2) of the Convention.[186] The Covenant does not admit territorial integrity or public safety, the prevention of disorder or crime, preventing the disclosure of information received in confidence, and maintaining the authority and impartiality of the judiciary as permissible grounds justifying restriction or limitation of freedom of expression.

Duties and responsibilities

Paragraph 2 of article 10 begins with the following words: 'The exercise of these freedoms, since it carries with it duties and responsibilities, may be subject to such formalities, conditions, restrictions or penalties . . .' The provision is similar in its general formulation to the second paragraphs of articles 8, 9, and 11. However, the reference to 'duties and responsibilities' that accompanies the exercise of freedom of expression is the only one of its kind in the Convention. The rights to private and family life, to opinion, belief, and religion, and to freedom of assembly and association are not made subject to duties and responsibilities. The Court has often invoked the notion of duties and responsibilities, especially with respect to the media.[187] Nevertheless, it applies to all who exercise freedom of expression.[188]

In reporting on issues of general interest, journalists have the duty and responsibility to act in good faith so as to provide accurate and reliable information 'in accordance with the

---

[184] *Stoll v. Switzerland* [GC], no. 69698/01, § 61, ECHR 2007-V.

[185] *Janowski v. Poland* [GC], no. 25716/94, § 30, ECHR 1999-I; *Nilsen and Johnsen v. Norway* [GC], no. 23118/93, § 43, ECHR 1999-VIII; *Lingens v. Austria*, 8 July 1986, § 41, Series A no. 103.

[186] International Covenant on Civil and Political Rights, (1976) 999 UNTS 171, art. 19(3).

[187] *Aquilina and Others v. Malta*, no. 28040/08, § 44, 14 June 2011; *McVicar v. the United Kingdom*, no. 46311/99, § 84, ECHR 2002-III; *Bladet Tromsø and Stensaas v. Norway* [GC], no. 21980/93, § 66, ECHR 1999-III.

[188] *Lindon, Otchakovsky-Laurens and July v. France* [GC], nos 21279/02 and 36448/02, § 51, ECHR 2007-IV.

ethics of journalism'.[189] The duties and responsibilities associated with freedom of expression 'are liable to assume significance when there is a question of attacking the reputation of a named individual and infringing the "rights of others"', the Court has said.[190] The media has an ordinary obligation to verify factual statements[191] and can only be dispensed from this where special grounds exist. This will depend on the reasonableness of reliance upon the sources of the information.[192]

Duties and responsibilities may also arise in an employment context. An example of such 'duties and responsibilities' would be the duty of loyalty owed by an employee to the employer in the protection of reputation and commercial interests. A 'whistleblower' employee who chooses to disclose information must carefully verify, to the extent permitted by the circumstances, that it is accurate and reliable.[193] Along the same lines, a senior police officer who had considerable influence on trade union members and other servicemen 'should have had to exercise her right to freedom of expression in accordance with the duties and responsibilities which that right carries with it in the specific circumstances of her status and in view of the special requirement of discipline in the police force'.[194]

Prescribed by law

It is a preliminary condition for any restriction upon the fundamental right that is protected by article 10 that the measure be 'prescribed by law'. This term 'alludes to the very same concept of lawfulness as that to which the Convention refers elsewhere when using the same or similar expressions, notably the expressions "in accordance with the law" and "lawful" found in the second paragraph of Articles 8 to 11'.[195] This means that the impugned measure must have a basis in domestic law, a condition that goes beyond matters of form and that speaks to the quality of the law in question. It includes 'written law', including various forms of delegated legislation, and unwritten law as interpreted and applied by the courts.[196] If the law grants discretion to public authorities, it must be framed with sufficient clarity and specify the manner in which it is to be exercised.[197] The law must be accessible and foreseeable, meaning that it must be

[189] *Kaperzyński v. Poland*, no. 43206/07, § 57, 3 April 2012; *Goodwin v. the United Kingdom*, 27 March 1996, §39, *Reports of Judgments and Decisions* 1996-II; *Fressoz and Roire v. France* [GC], no. 29183/95, § 54, ECHR1999-I; *Wołek, Kasprów, and Łęski v. Poland* (dec.), no. 20953/06, 21 October 2008; *Eerikäinen and Others v. Finland*, no. 3514/02, § 60, 10 February 2009; *Brunet-Lecomte and Lyon Mag' v. France*, no. 17265/05, § 42, 6 May 2010.

[190] *Axel Springer AG v. Germany* [GC], no. 39954/08, § 82, 7 February 2012; *Aquilina and Others v. Malta*, no. 28040/08, § 44, 14 June 2011; *McVicar v. the United Kingdom*, no. 46311/99, § 84, ECHR 2002-III; *Bladet Tromsø and Stensaas v. Norway* [GC], no. 21980/93, § 66, ECHR 1999-III.

[191] *Wizerkaniuk v. Poland*, no. 18990/05, § 66, 5 July 2011.

[192] *Axel Springer AG v. Germany* [GC], no. 39954/08, § 82, 7 February 2012; *McVicar v. the United Kingdom*, no. 46311/99, § 84, ECHR 2002-III; *Bladet Tromsø and Stensaas v. Norway* [GC], no. 21980/93, § 66, ECHR 1999-III; *Tønsbergs Blad A.S. and Haukom v. Norway*, no. 510/04, § 89, ECHR 2007-III.

[193] *Heinisch v. Germany*, no. 28274/08, § 67, ECHR 2011 (extracts).

[194] *Szima v. Hungary*, no. 29723/11, § 32, 9 October 2012. Also *Rekvényi v. Hungary* [GC], no. 25390/94, § 43 *in fine*, ECHR 1999-III.

[195] *Kenedi v. Hungary*, no. 31475/05, § 44, 26 May 2009.

[196] *Leyla Şahin v. Turkey* [GC], no. 44774/98, § 88, ECHR 2005-XI; *Sanoma Uitgevers B.V. v. the Netherlands* [GC], no. 38224/03, § 83, 14 September 2010.

[197] *The Sunday Times v. the United Kingdom (no. 1)*, 26 April 1979, § 49, Series A no. 30; *Tolstoy Miloslavsky v. the United Kingdom*, 13 July 1995, § 37, Series A no. 316-B; *Rotaru v. Romania* [GC], no. 28341/95, § 52, ECHR 2000-V; *Hasan and Chaush v. Bulgaria* [GC], no. 30985/96, § 84, ECHR 2000-XI; *Maestri v. Italy*

sufficiently precise in its formulation to enable an individual to regulate his or her conduct.

There is a subjective dimension here, because there may be higher expectations of individuals depending upon their training, professional activity, and experience, and it may be reasonable to expect them to obtain expert advice on the law depending upon the circumstances. In a French case, the Court agreed that the relevant case law was dated and rather scant, but it also took into account the fact that the applicants were senior officials of a publishing company. 'Being professionals in the field of publishing it was incumbent on them to apprise themselves of the relevant legal provisions and case-law in such matters, even if it meant taking specialised legal advice', it concluded.[198]

There are many examples in the case law of measures taken that infringe the protection of freedom of expression yet that are not prescribed by law. For example, in a Ukrainian case, the applicable legislation concerning defamation authorized a judicial order that the offending statement be retracted but did not entitle the national courts to require an apology, yet one of the applicants was condemned to make one. The European Court held that the infringement was therefore not prescribed by law.[199] Under legislation in the Netherlands, the public prosecutor and not an independent judge had the authority to require surrender of materials obtained by journalists from confidential sources. Acknowledging that 'the public prosecutor, like any public official, is bound by requirements of basic integrity', the Grand Chamber noted that 'in terms of procedure he or she is a "party" defending interests potentially incompatible with journalistic source protection and can hardly be seen as objective and impartial so as to make the necessary assessment of the various competing interests'.[200] It concluded: 'Such a situation is scarcely compatible with the rule of law.'[201] The Court said that 'the quality of the law was deficient in that there was no procedure attended by adequate legal safeguards for the applicant company in order to enable an independent assessment as to whether the interest of the criminal investigation overrode the public interest in the protection of journalistic sources'.[202]

Italian legislation governing allocation of telecommunications frequencies 'did not enable the applicant company to foresee, with sufficient certainty, the point at which it might be allocated the frequencies and be able to start performing the activity for which it had been granted a licence, this notwithstanding the successive findings of the Constitutional Court and the CJEU'. Consequently, the foreseeability requirements established by the Court in its case law were not met.[203]

The criminal offence of 'denigrating Turkishness', set out in article 301 of the Criminal Code of Turkey, was held to lack the required clarity and therefore to fail the 'quality of law' test. According to the Court, 'while the legislator's aim of protecting and preserving values and State institutions from public denigration can be accepted to a certain extent, the scope of the terms under Article 301 of the Criminal Code, as interpreted by the

[GC], no. 39748/98, § 30, ECHR 2004-I; *Amann v. Switzerland* [GC], no. 27798/95, § 50, ECHR 2000-II; *Vajnai v. Hungary*, no. 33629/06, § 46, 8 July 2008.

[198] *Lindon, Otchakovsky-Laurens, and July v. France* [GC], nos 21279/02 and 36448/02, § 42, ECHR 2007-IV.

[199] *Editorial Board of Pravoye Delo and Shtekel v. Ukraine*, no. 33014/05, §§ 54–59, ECHR 2011 (extracts).

[200] *Sanoma Uitgevers B.V. v. the Netherlands* [GC], no. 38224/03, § 92, 14 September 2010.

[201] Ibid., § 98.

[202] Ibid., § 100.

[203] *Centro Europa 7 S.R.L. and di Stefano v. Italy* [GC], no. 38433/09, § 153, ECHR 2012.

judiciary, is too wide and vague and thus the provision constitutes a continuing threat to the exercise of the right to freedom of expression'.[204] It said that the wording of the provision did not enable individuals to govern their conduct or to foresee the consequences of their acts. In reality, as the Court noted, 'any opinion or idea that is regarded as offensive, shocking or disturbing can easily be the subject of a criminal investigation by public prosecutors'.[205] In an earlier case involving article 301 of the Turkish Criminal Code, the Court had declined to rule on the foreseeability issue, taking the view that it was closely related to the nature of the interference and of the right considered in the context of the necessity of the interference.[206]

Applying legislation in such a way as to extend its application by analogy will fall foul of the requirement that an interference be prescribed by law. For example, Turkish legislation imposed certain formalities to be followed by associations, such as trade unions, wishing to publish or distribute leaflets, statements, or similar publications. The applicants were prosecuted under this provision because they did not follow the procedure in the case of a press conference. The European Court held that in convicting the applicants, the Turkish judicial authorities went beyond what was reasonably foreseeable and thereby 'extended the scope of a criminal statute by applying it by analogy'.[207]

Legitimate aim

The second component of the analysis is the existence of a legitimate purpose or aim. The inquiry involves the enumeration of purposes set out in paragraph 2, namely the interests of national security, territorial integrity or public safety, the prevention of disorder or crime, the protection of health or morals, the protection of the reputation or rights of others, preventing the disclosure of information received in confidence, and maintaining the authority and impartiality of the judiciary. In practice, this part of the analysis is rarely very important. It is not uncommon for the Court to simply pass over the issue entirely and move to the heart of the debate which takes place under the rubric of 'necessary in a democratic society', finding that it violates the final component of the test regardless of whether it fulfils a legitimate purpose.[208] The Grand Chamber has explained that it is the Court's practice 'to be quite succinct when it verifies the existence of a legitimate aim within the meaning of the second paragraphs of Articles 8 to 11 of the Convention'.[209]

The first of the legitimate aims listed in article 10(2) is national security, territorial integrity, or public safety (*à la sécurité nationale, à l'intégrité territoriale ou à la sûreté publique*). Public safety also appears in the limitations clauses of articles 8, 9, and 11, and national security in articles 8 and 11, but article 10 is the only provision to include territory integrity. In a Turkish case where a sympathizer of Kurdish activist Abdullah Öcalan was prosecuted under the Law on Associations for signing a declaration in 2001 in support of lifting the ban on activities of the Kurdistan Workers' Party (PKK) imposed by

---

[204] *Dink v. Turkey*, nos 2668/07, 6102/08, 30079/08, 7072/09, and 7124/09, § 116, 14 September 2010. Also *Tatár and Fáber v. Hungary*, no. 26005/08 and 26160/08, § 31, 12 June 2012.

[205] *Altuğ Taner Akçam v. Turkey*, no. 27520/07, §§ 93–95, 25 October 2011.

[206] *Dink v. Turkey*, nos 2668/07, 6102/08, 30079/08, 7072/09, and 7124/09, § 116, 14 September 2010. Also *Tatár and Fáber v. Hungary*, no. 26005/08 and 26160/08, § 31, 12 June 2012.

[207] *Karademirci and Others v. Turkey*, nos 37096/97 and 37101/97, § 42, ECHR 2005-I.

[208] For example, *Bayatyan v. Armenia* [GC], no. 23459/03, § 117, ECHR 2011; *Erçep v. Turkey*, no. 43965/04, § 53, 22 November 2011.

[209] *S.A.S. v. France* [GC], no. 43835/11, § 114, 1 July 2014.

virtue of an Order of the Minister of Interior, the Court recognized a legitimate aim that it said was 'to protect public order and safety'.[210] In a case dealing with the security situation in south-east Turkey, measures limiting freedom of expression were said to have been 'in furtherance of certain of the aims mentioned by the Government, namely the protection of national security and territorial integrity and the prevention of disorder and crime'.[211]

The second legitimate aim or purpose justifying a limitation on article 10(1) is the prevention of disorder or crime (*à la défense de l'ordre et à la prévention du crime*). In a case concerning artistic expression, where planning regulations were in dispute, the Court considered that the protection of the cultural heritage fell under this rubric as a legitimate purpose.[212] A ban on display of sectarian emblems in a Northern Irish prison was deemed to fulfil the legitimate aim of prevention of disorder or crime.[213] The notion has also been applied in the case of disciplinary matters within the armed forces, such as instigation to insubordination, because this may lead to 'disorder'.[214]

The issue of protection of health or morals (*à la protection de la santé ou de la morale*), the third of the categories, has arisen mainly in cases involving artistic expression. For example, when publication of Guillaume Appolinaire's *Les onze mille verges* led to prosecution by Turkish authorities, it was common ground that the legitimate purpose was the protection of morals.[215] However, in judicial proceedings against a Viennese art gallery for displaying a collage of various public figures in sexual positions, including Mother Teresa, the Austrian cardinal Hermann Groer and the former head of the Austrian Freedom Party Jörg Haider, the Government's argument that the legitimate purpose was the protection of morals was rejected. The Court said that this aim was not referred to in the relevant legislation or court decisions.[216] In a Swiss case involving prosecution for displaying obscene works of art, the Court had no difficulty with the claim that this pursued the protection of public morals.[217]

The fourth category of legitimate aim set out in article 10(2) is the protection of the reputation or rights of others (*la protection de la réputation ou des droits d'autrui*). The other three limitations paragraphs, in articles 8, 9, and 11, use a similar, although somewhat distinct, expression: 'the protection of the rights and freedoms of others'. The protection of the reputation or rights of others is unique among the enumerated purposes permitting restriction of freedom of expression in that it is also contemplated by a distinct provision of the Convention, article 8.[218] Legislation governing defamation claims pursues the legitimate aim of protecting the reputation or rights of others.[219] In one of the leading cases, *Otto-Preminger-Institut v. Austria*, the Court considered section

[210] *Aydin v. Germany*, no. 16637/07, §§ 66–67, 27 January 2011.
[211] *Karataş v. Turkey* [GC], no. 23168/94, § 44, ECHR 1999-IV.
[212] *Ehrmann and SCI VHI v. France* (dec.), no. 2777/10, § 2, 7 June 2011.
[213] *Donaldson v. The United Kingdom* (dec.), no. 56975/09, § 23, 25 January 2011.
[214] *Szima v. Hungary*, no. 29723/11, § 24, 9 October 2012; *Engel and Others v. the Netherlands*, 8 June 1976, § 98, Series A no. 22; *Vereinigung demokratischer Soldaten Österreichs and Gubi v. Austria*, 19 December 1994, § 32, Series A no. 302.
[215] *Akdaş v. Turkey*, no. 41056/04, §§ 23–24, 16 February 2010.
[216] *Vereinigung Bildender Künstler v. Austria*, no. 68354/01, § 31, 25 January 2007.
[217] *Müller and Others v. Switzerland*, 24 May 1988, § 39, Series A no. 133.
[218] *Axel Springer AG v. Germany* [GC], no. 39954/08, § 83, 7 February 2012; *Chauvy and Others v. France*, no. 64915/01, § 70, ECHR 2004-VI; *Pfeifer v. Austria*, no. 12556/03, § 35, 15 November 2007; *Polanco Torres and Movilla Polanco v. Spain*, no. 34147/06, § 40, 21 September 2010.
[219] *Aquilina and Others v. Malta*, no. 28040/08, § 39, 14 June 2011.

188 of the Austrian Penal Code, whose objective is the suppression of behaviour directed against objects of religious veneration that is likely to cause 'justified indignation', to be pursuing the legitimate purpose of protecting the right of citizens not to be insulted in their religious feelings by the public expression of views of other persons.[220] The term 'others' has been used to apply to political parties[221] and to companies and commercial enterprises,[222] as well as to individuals.

The Grand Chamber has said that 'a clear distinction must be made between criticism and insult'.[223] Dealing with dismissal of trade union officials for publishing a cartoon mocking a firm's human resources manager, the Grand Chamber referred to the International Labour Office's Committee on Freedom of Association, stating that 'in expressing their opinions, trade union organisations should respect the limits of propriety and refrain from the use of insulting language'.[224] Accordingly, the dismissal was compatible with the legitimate aim of protecting the reputation of others.

Preventing the disclosure of information received in confidence (*pour empêcher la divulgation d'informations confidentielles*), the fifth category of legitimate purpose set out in article 10(2), is without equivalent in any of the other restriction or limitation clauses of the Convention. There is a difference in the English and French texts that has attracted judicial attention. The English wording 'might suggest that the provision relates only to the person who has dealings in confidence with the author of a secret document and that, accordingly, it does not encompass third parties, including persons working in the media'.[225] But the Court has rejected such an interpretation as being unduly restrictive, and has considered it 'appropriate to adopt an interpretation of the phrase "preventing the disclosure of information received in confidence" which encompasses confidential information disclosed either by a person subject to a duty of confidence or by a third party and ... by a journalist'.[226] Punishment of a journalist for revealing information received in confidence about a Swiss diplomat was considered compatible with this legitimate aim.[227] In a whistleblowing case, where a senior prosecutor released documents to the media, the Court accepted that the legitimate purpose was preventing the disclosure of information received in confidence. 'In so deciding, the Court finds it significant that at the time of his dismissal the applicant refused to disclose the source of the information, which suggests that it was not easily or publicly available', it said.[228]

The final category of legitimate purpose listed in article 10(2) is the maintenance of the authority and impartiality of the judiciary. Because this phrase is to be understood 'within the meaning of the Convention', account is to be taken 'of the central position occupied in this context by Article 6 (art. 6), which reflects the fundamental principle of the rule

[220] *Otto-Preminger-Institut v. Austria*, 20 September 1994, § 48, Series A no. 295-A. Also *Wingrove v. the United Kingdom*, 25 November 1996, §§ 46–51, *Reports of Judgments and Decisions* 1996-V.
[221] *Lindon, Otchakovsky-Laurens and July v. France* [GC], nos 21279/02 and 36448/02, § 47, ECHR 2007-IV.
[222] *Uj v. Hungary*, no. 23954/10, § 22, 19 July 2011.
[223] *Palomo Sánchez and Others v. Spain* [GC], nos 28955/06, 28957/06, 28959/06, and 28964/06, § 67, ECHR 2011.
[224] Ibid.
[225] *Stoll v. Switzerland* [GC], no. 69698/01, § 58, ECHR 2007-V.
[226] Ibid., §§ 59–61.
[227] Ibid., § 56.
[228] *Guja v. Moldova* [GC], no. 14277/04, § 59, ECHR 2008. Also *Haseldine v. the United Kingdom*, no. 18957/91, Commission decision of 13 May 1992, (1992) 35 YB 47.

of law'.[229] The term 'judiciary' (*pouvoir judiciaire*) is interpreted broadly so as to include 'the machinery of justice or the judicial branch of government as well as the judges in their official capacity'.[230] The term 'authority of the judiciary' includes the notion that 'the courts are, and are accepted by the public at large as being, the proper forum for the settlement of legal disputes and for the determination of a person's guilt or innocence on a criminal charge'.[231] The Court has said that '[w]hat is at stake as regards protection of the authority of the judiciary is the confidence which the courts in a democratic society must inspire in the accused, as far as criminal proceedings are concerned, and also in the public at large'.[232]

Necessity in a democratic society

Any infringement on freedom of expression, to the extent that it is prescribed by law and responds to a legitimate aim, can only restrict the right if it is 'necessary in a democratic society'. The Convention organs have often said that the 'necessity' for any restriction on freedom of expression must be 'established convincingly'.[233] The first step in this analysis of necessity involves determining whether there is a 'pressing social need'.[234] The pressing social need must be appreciated in the context of the interests of a democratic society. For example, when press freedom is at issue, the importance for a democratic society of ensuring and maintaining a free press must be weighed in the balance.[235] Where freedom of the press is at stake, the national authorities have only a limited margin of appreciation to decide whether there is a 'pressing social need' to take such measures.[236] The Court has often insisted that there can be little scope for restrictions on political speech or on debates about questions of public interest.[237]

In assessing this pressing social need, States enjoy 'a certain margin of appreciation'. This margin of appreciation goes hand in hand with European supervision, embracing both the legislation and the decisions applying it, even those given by an independent tribunal. The Court is therefore empowered to give the final ruling on whether any 'formalities, conditions, restrictions or penalties' are reconcilable with freedom of expression as protected by article 10.

In supervising the respect for freedom of expression, the Court does not take the place of domestic courts. Rather, it reviews the decisions they have taken in light of their own power of appreciation, ensuring that this has been done reasonably, carefully, and in good faith. The European Court looks at the interference complained of in the light of the case as a whole, assessing whether the reasons given by the national authorities to justify the

---

[229] *The Sunday Times v. the United Kingdom (no. 1)*, 26 April 1979, § 55, Series A no. 30.
[230] Ibid.
[231] *Kyprianou v. Cyprus* [GC], no. 73797/01, § 172, ECHR 2005-XIII; *Worm v. Austria*, 29 August 1997, § 40, *Reports of Judgments and Decisions* 1997-V.
[232] *Kyprianou v. Cyprus* [GC], no. 73797/01, § 172, ECHR 2005-XIII.
[233] *Steel and Morris v. the United Kingdom*, no. 68416/01, § 87, ECHR 2005-II; *Mouvement raëlien suisse v. Switzerland* [GC], no. 16354/06, § 48, ECHR 2012 (extracts).
[234] *Otegi Mondragon v. Spain*, no. 2034/07, § 49, ECHR 2011.
[235] *Fatullayev v. Azerbaijan*, no. 40984/07, § 82, 22 April 2010.
[236] *Wizerkaniuk v. Poland*, no. 18990/05, § 65, 5 July 2011.
[237] *Verein gegen Tierfabriken Schweiz (VgT) v. Switzerland (no. 2)* [GC], no. 32772/02, § 92, ECHR 2009; *Lingens v. Austria*, 8 July 1986, § 42, Series A no. 103; *Castells v. Spain*, 23 April 1992, § 43, Series A no. 236; *Thorgeir Thorgeirson v. Iceland*, 25 June 1992, § 63, Series A no. 239; *Wingrove v. the United Kingdom*, 25 November 1996, § 58, *Reports of Judgments and Decisions* 1996-V; *Monnat v. Switzerland*, no. 73604/01, § 58, ECHR 2006-X.

interference were 'relevant and sufficient' and whether the measure taken was 'proportionate to the legitimate aims pursued'.[238] In doing so, the Court has to satisfy itself that the national authorities applied standards which were in conformity with the principles embodied in article 10 and, moreover, that they relied on an acceptable assessment of the relevant facts.[239]

Gravity is an important issue in determining the proportionality of interferences. A prohibition upon prisoners wearing an Easter lily outside their cells, something considered to be a sectarian emblem, was considered in light of the fact that it constituted a 'relatively minor interference' with freedom of expression.[240] In a whistleblowing case involving a public servant, the Court identified several following factors to be balanced in determining whether the interference was proportional: the public interest involved in the disclosed information; the authenticity of the information disclosed; the damage, if any, suffered by the public authority as a result of the disclosure; the motive behind the actions of the reporting employee; and the penalty imposed.[241]

The nature and severity of any penalties are factors that are often considered in assessing the proportionality of an interference.[242] As a general principle, the nature and severity of any sanction imposed are relevant factors in assessing the proportionality of an interference.[243] Civil sanctions such as an injunction are generally viewed to be less serious than criminal punishments.[244] The Grand Chamber said a sentence of five days' imprisonment, to be served immediately, imposed upon a senior lawyer for contempt of court, was 'harsh' and disproportionate. It constituted a breach of article 10 in that it was imposed as a reaction to comments made by the lawyer on behalf of his client during a trial.[245] The severity of sanctions is of special importance when the press is involved because of the danger that this may deter its engagement in matters of legitimate public concern.[246]

Sometimes, harsh sentences have been imposed for acts of political protest that, absent the political dimension, would never have attracted such punishment. A sentence of ten days' administrative detention, the maximum allowed by the law, on a 63-year-old woman with no criminal record for 'petty hooliganism', imposed because she had removed a ribbon from a memorial wreath as a form of political protest, failed the necessity test and constituted a violation of article 10.[247] A sentence of more than

---

[238] *Hertel v. Switzerland*, 25 August 1998, § 46, *Reports of Judgments and Decisions* 1998-VI; *Steel and Morris v. the United Kingdom*, no. 68416/01, § 87, ECHR 2005-II; *Stoll v. Switzerland* [GC], no. 69698/01, § 101, ECHR 2007-V.

[239] *Mamère v. France*, no. 12697/03, § 19, ECHR 2006-XIII; *Lindon, Otchakovsky-Laurens, and July v. France* [GC], nos 21279/02 and36448/02, § 45, ECHR 2007-IV; *Perna v. Italy* [GC], no. 48898/99, § 39, ECHR 2003-V; *Zana v. Turkey*, 25 November 1997, *Reports of Judgments and Decisions* 1997-VII, pp. 2547–8, § 51; *Aquilina and Others v. Malta*, no. 28040/08, §§ 40–42, 14 June 2011.

[240] *Donaldson v. the United Kingdom* (dec.), no. 56975/09, §§ 31–33, 25 January 2011.

[241] *Guja v. Moldova* [GC], no. 14277/04, § 74, ECHR 2008. Also *Heinisch v. Germany*, no. 28274/08, §§ 71–92, ECHR 2011 (extracts).

[242] *Otegi Mondragon v. Spain*, no. 2034/07, § 58, ECHR 2011.

[243] *PETA Deutschland v. Germany*, no. 43481/09, § 50, 8 November 2012; *Ceylan v. Turkey* [GC], no. 23556/94, § 37, ECHR 1999-IV; *Annen II v. Germany* (dec.), nos 2373/07 and 2396/07, 30 March 2010; *Skałka v. Poland*, no. 43425/98, §§ 41–42, 27 May 2003; *Pedersen and Baadsgaard v. Denmark* [GC], no. 49017/99, § 93, ECHR 2004-XI.

[244] *PETA Deutschland v. Germany*, no. 43481/09, § 50, 8 November 2012.

[245] *Kyprianou v. Cyprus* [GC], no. 73797/01, §§ 178–180, ECHR 2005-XIII.

[246] *Cumpănă and Mazăre v. Romania* [GC], no. 33348/96, § 111, ECHR 2004-XI.

[247] *Shvydka v. Ukraine*, no. 17888/12, §§ 35–42, 30 October 2014.

13 years' imprisonment for vandalizing statues of Ataturk was 'grossly disproportion-ate'.[248] In general, 'peaceful and non-violent forms of expression should not be made subject to the threat of imposition of a custodial sentence'.[249]

Some interferences are inherently serious because of what is at stake. Thus, 'an attack on the respectability of individuals by using grossly insulting or offensive expressions in the professional environment is, on account of its disruptive effects, a particularly serious form of misconduct capable of justifying severe sanctions'.[250] But in a defamation case, the Court thought a €1,000 fine was disproportionate.[251] According to the Court, given the margin of appreciation allowed to States, criminal sanctions for defamation cannot be considered disproportionate.[252] A criminal sentence depriving a media professional of the right to exercise his or her profession was described as 'very harsh' because it heightens the risk of a chilling effect on public debate. According to the Court, this has potentially 'an enormous dissuasive effect for an open and unhindered public debate on matters of public interest'.[253] Imposition of a fine upon parliamentarians for a rather innocuous protest that purportedly disrupted a official session threatened to have a 'chilling effect on the parliamentary opposition' and was consequently contrary to article 10.[254]

Politicians have a right to the protection of their reputation, even when not acting in a private capacity, 'but the requirements of that protection have to be weighed against the interests of open discussion of political issues, since exceptions to freedom of expression must be interpreted narrowly'.[255] They are expected to have a thick skin, especially when they have themselves shown little respect for others.[256] But this does not mean 'that politicians should not be given an opportunity to defend themselves when they consider that publications about them are erroneous and capable of misleading public opinion'.[257]

Public officials are also subject to wider limits of criticism than private individuals, although the criteria applied to them cannot be the same as for politicians.[258] The State is also entitled to protect its own institutions from abuses that may be associated with expression. The Court has said that although 'it is perfectly legitimate for the institutions of the State, as guarantors of the institutional public order, to be protected by the

---

[248] *Murat Vural v. Turkey*, no. 9540/07, § 68, 21 October 2014.

[249] Ibid., citing *Akgöl and Göl v. Turkey*, nos 28495/06 and 28516/06, § 43, 17 May 2011.

[250] *Palomo Sánchez and Others v. Spain* [GC], nos 28955/06, 28957/06, 28959/06, and 28964/06, § 76, ECHR 2011; *Editions Plon v. France*, no. 58148/00, § 44, ECHR 2004-IV.

[251] *Vellutini and Michel v. France*, no. 32820/09, § 43, 6 October 2011.

[252] *Lindon, Otchakovsky-Laurens and July v. France* [GC], nos 21279/02 and 36448/02, § 59, ECHR 2007-IV; *Radio France and Others v. France*, no. 53984/00, §40, ECHR 2004-II; *Rumyana Ivanova v. Bulgaria*, no. 36207/03, § 68, 14 February 2008; *Reinboth and Others v. Finland*, no. 30865/08, § 90, 25 January 2011; *Kaperzyński v. Poland*, no. 43206/07, § 69, 3 April 2012.

[253] *Kaperzyński v. Poland*, no. 43206/07, § 74, 3 April 2012; *Cumpănă and Mazăre v. Romania* [GC], no. 33348/96, § 118, ECHR 2004-XI.

[254] *Szél and Others v. Hungary*, no. 44357/13, § 85, 16 September 2014. Also *Karácsony and Others v. Hungary*, no. 42461/13, § 88, 16 September 2014.

[255] *Artun and Güvener v. Turkey*, no. 75510/01, § 26, 26 June 2007; *Otegi Mondragon v. Spain*, no. 2034/07, § 50, ECHR 2011; *Pakdemirli v. Turkey*, no. 35839/97, § 45, 22 February 2005.

[256] *Lindon, Otchakovsky-Laurens, and July v. France* [GC], nos 21279/02 and 36448/02, § 56, ECHR 2007-IV; *Wirtschafts-Trend Zeitschriften-Verlags GmbH v. Austria*, no. 58547/00, § 37, 27 October 2005; *Oberschlick v. Austria (no. 2)*, 1 July 1997, § 34, *Reports of Judgments and Decisions* 1997-IV.

[257] *Gąsior v. Poland*, no. 34472/07, § 43, 21 February 2012; *Sanocki v. Poland*, no. 28949/03, §§ 61–62, 17 July 2007.

[258] *Janowski v. Poland* [GC], no. 25716/94, § 33, ECHR 1999-I.

competent authorities, the dominant position occupied by those institutions requires the authorities to display restraint in resorting to criminal proceedings'.[259]

Another relevant factor in the proportionality determination is the extent to which the impugned expression is disseminated. For example, in assessing whether an interference was 'necessary' in the case of a work of fiction, the Court noted that a novel is a form of artistic expression that, 'although potentially maintaining its readership for a longer period, appeals generally to a relatively narrow public compared with the print media'. This meant that the number of persons exposed to the offending remarks and the potential damage to rights and reputation was limited.[260] There is a higher level of tolerance when statements are made spontaneously, for example at a press conference,[261] rather than in a publication, where there has been time for sober reflection.[262] Legislation often exonerates the press in cases of defamation when the impugned statement is merely reproduced verbatim from another source. The Court has suggested that this is a fairly general approach.[263]

There is an important distinction between statements of fact and value judgments. According to the Court, '[w]hile the existence of facts can be demonstrated, the truth of value judgments is not susceptible of proof. The requirement to prove the truth of a value judgment is impossible to fulfil and infringes freedom of opinion itself, which is a fundamental part of the right secured by Article 10.'[264] Nevertheless, even a value judgment must have some factual basis. Otherwise, it is excessive.[265] The requirement that facts be produced to support a value judgment is less stringent if the information is well known.[266]

When fiction is concerned, there can obviously be no requirement that the statements be 'true'. However, sometimes 'fiction' introduces real characters or facts, and when this is the case the author or publisher may be required to show that passages in a novel found to be defamatory have a 'sufficient factual basis'. They are more than mere value judgments.[267]

The extent of acceptable criticism will be narrower when private individuals are concerned than when it is directed at politicians or civil servants acting in the exercise of their functions.[268] Unlike a private citizen, the politician 'inevitably and knowingly lays himself open to close scrutiny of his every word and deed by both journalists and the

[259] *Otegi Mondragon v. Spain*, no. 2034/07, § 58, ECHR 2011.

[260] *Lindon, Otchakovsky-Laurens, and July v. France* [GC], nos 21279/02 and 36448/02, § 47, ECHR 2007-IV.

[261] *Otegi Mondragon v. Spain*, no. 2034/07, § 53, ECHR 2011.

[262] *Palomo Sánchez and Others v. Spain* [GC], nos 28955/06, 28957/06, 28959/06, and 28964/06, Joint Dissenting Opinion of Juges Tulkens, Davíd Thór Björgvinsson, Jočienė, Popović, and Vučinić, ECHR 2011.

[263] *Editorial Board of Pravoye Delo and Shtekel v. Ukraine*, no. 33014/05, § 61, ECHR 2011 (extracts), citing *Jersild v. Denmark*, 23 September 1994, § 35, Series A no. 298; *Thoma v. Luxembourg*, no. 38432/97, § 62, ECHR 2001-III.

[264] *Otegi Mondragon v. Spain*, no. 2034/07, § 54, ECHR 2011; *Fuentes Bobo v. Spain*, no. 39293/98, § 46, 29 February 2000; *Birol v. Turkey*, no. 44104/98, § 30, 1 March 2005; *Prager and Oberschlick v. Austria*, 26 April 1995, § 36, Series A no. 313.

[265] *Lindon, Otchakovsky-Laurens, and July v. France* [GC], nos 21279/02 and 36448/02, § 55, ECHR 2007-IV.

[266] *Feldek v. Slovakia*, no. 29032/95, § 86, ECHR 2001-VIII.

[267] *Lindon, Otchakovsky-Laurens and July v. France* [GC], nos 21279/02 and 36448/02, § 55, ECHR 2007-IV.

[268] *Palomo Sánchez and Others v. Spain* [GC], nos 28955/06, 28957/06, 28959/06, and 28964/06, § 71, ECHR 2011.

public at large, and he must consequently display a greater degree of tolerance'.[269] In a case involving defamation proceedings against an Icelandic journalist by the owner of a strip club, the Court said that:

> by having engaged in the particular kind of business in question and bearing in mind also the legitimate public concern highlighted in paragraph 67 above, Mr Y must be considered to have inevitably and knowingly entered the public domain and lain himself open to close scrutiny of his acts. The limits of acceptable criticism must accordingly be wider than in the case of a private individual or an ordinary professional.'[270]

The Court dealt with a case of *lèse majesté* directed at the King of Spain as if he were a political figure and did not attach any special significance to the position as head of State.[271] It said that 'while some of the remarks made in the applicant's speech portrayed the institution embodied by the King in a very negative light, with a hostile connotation, they did not advocate the use of violence, nor did they amount to hate speech, which in the Court's view is the essential element to be taken into account'.[272] According to the Court, the fact that 'the King occupies a neutral position in political debate and acts as an arbitrator and a symbol of State unity should not shield him from all criticism in the exercise of his official duties or— as in the instant case—in his capacity as representative of the State which he symbolises, in particular from persons who challenge in a legitimate manner the constitutional structures of the State, including the monarchy'.[273] In *Colombani*, French legislation that made foreign heads of State and diplomats immune to criticism solely because of their status was considered. The Court said this 'could not be reconciled with modern practice and political conceptions', concluding that it was the special protection afforded to foreign heads of State that undermined freedom of expression.[274] In making the assessment with respect to public figures, it is relevant whether the impugned remarks concern private or personal matters,[275] or personal honour,[276] or whether they constitute a gratuitous attack.[277]

The prohibition of hate speech is a limitation on freedom of expression that is dictated by international law. A general rule appears in article 7 of the Universal Declaration of Human Rights: 'All are entitled to equal protection against any discrimination in violation of this Declaration and against any incitement to such discrimination.' A more specific obligation concerning the prohibition of incitement to hatred appears in article 20(2) of the International Covenant on Civil and Political Rights: 'Any advocacy of national, racial or religious hatred that constitutes incitement to discrimination, hostility or violence shall be prohibited by law.' The Committee of Ministers of the Council of Europe has defined the notion of 'hate speech' as covering 'all forms of expression which spread, incite,

---

[269] *Otegi Mondragon v. Spain*, no. 2034/07, § 50, ECHR 2011; *Lingens v. Austria*, 8 July 1986, § 42, Series A no. 103; *Vides Aizsardzības Klubs v. Latvia*, no. 57829/00, § 40, 27 May 2004; *Lopes Gomes da Silva v. Portugal*, no. 37698/97, § 30, ECHR 2000-X.

[270] *Björk Eiðsdóttir v. Iceland*, no. 46443/09, § 68, 10 July 2012.

[271] *Otegi Mondragon v. Spain*, no. 2034/07, § 54, ECHR 2011.

[272] Ibid.

[273] *Otegi Mondragon v. Spain*, no. 2034/07, § 56, ECHR 2011.

[274] *Colombani and Others v. France*, no. 51279/99, § 69, ECHR 2002-V. Also *Artun and Güvener v. Turkey*, no. 75510/01, § 31, 26 June 2007; *Pakdemirli v. Turkey*, no. 35839/97, § 52, 22 February 2005.

[275] *Standard Verlags GmbH v. Austria (no. 2)*, no. 21277/05, 4 June 2009; *Von Hannover v. Germany*, no. 59320/00, § 64, ECHR 2004-VI.

[276] *Otegi Mondragon v. Spain*, no. 2034/07, § 57, ECHR 2011.

[277] *Pakdemirli v. Turkey*, no. 35839/97, § 46, 22 February 2005.

promote or justify racial hatred, xenophobia, anti-Semitism or other forms of hatred based on intolerance . . .'.[278]

The European Court has examined the proportionality of measures directed at restricting hate speech in a number of decisions. The Court has noted that inciting to hatred does not necessarily entail a call for an act of violence, or other criminal acts. Consequently, '[a]ttacks on persons committed by insulting, holding up to ridicule or slandering specific groups of the population can be sufficient for the authorities to favour combating racist speech in the face of freedom of expression exercised in an irresponsible manner'.[279] Political speeches that incite hatred based upon religious, ethnic, or cultural prejudice 'représentent un danger pour la paix sociale et la stabilité politique dans les États démocratiques'.[280] Frequently, cases concerning hate speech have been declared inadmissible pursuant to article 17 of the European Convention.[281]

One particular form of legislation dealing with incitement of hatred is directed at 'denialism'. The most familiar example is provided by measures in a number of States directed at those who contest the existence or scale of the destruction of the European Jews by the Nazi regime. In a German case, the prohibition by a civil court of public display of pamphlets denying the Holocaust was deemed necessary in a democratic society, given that it rests upon 'principles of tolerance and broadmindedness which the pamphlets in question clearly failed to observe'. The European Commission further addressed the fact that German legislation dealt specifically with Holocaust denial: 'The fact that collective protection against defamation is limited to certain specific groups including Jews is based on objective considerations and does not involve any element of discrimination contrary to Article 14 of the Convention.'[282] In another case, the Court noted the importance of the specific 'historical and social context in which the expression of opinion takes place', noting 'that a reference to the Holocaust must also be seen in the specific context of the German past . . . and respects the Government's stance that they deem themselves under a special obligation towards the Jews living in Germany'.[283]

The measures directed at denialism are, of course, intimately related to the protection of minorities against racism. When Swiss legislation directed at denial of genocide in a more general sense, the Court considered that the prosecution of a Turkish extremist for contesting the Armenian genocide of 1915 was not consistent with the Convention, noting that it had not been alleged by the applicants that the denial was intended to incite

---

[278] Recommendation No. R (97) 20.

[279] *Vejdeland v. Sweden*, no. 1813/07, § 55, 9 February 2012; *Féret v. Belgium*, no. 15615/07, § 73, 16 July 2009.

[280] *Féret v. Belgium*, no. 15615/07, § 73, 16 July 2009.

[281] *J. Glimmerveen and J. Hagenbeek v. the Netherlands*, nos 8348/78 and 8406/78 (joined), Commission decision of 11 October 1979, (1980) 23 YB 366, DR 18, p. 187; *Marais v. France*, no. 31159/96, Commission decision of 24 June 1996, DR 86, p. 184; *Lehideux and Isorni v. France*, 23 September 1998, §§ 47 and 53, *Reports of Judgments and Decisions* 1998–VII.

[282] *X. v. Federal Republic of Germany*, no. 9235/81, Commission decision of 16 July 1982, DR 29, p. 194. See also *B.H., M.W., H.P., and G.K. v. Austria*, no. 12774/87, Commission decision of 12 October 1989, DR 62, p. 216; *Honsik v. Austria*, no. 25062/94, Commission decision of 18 October 1995, DR 83-A, p. 77; *Nationaldemokratische Partei Deutschlands Bezirksverband München-Oberbayern v. Germany*, no. 25992/94, Commission decision of 29 November 1995, DR 84, p. 149; *D.I. v. Germany*, no. 26551/95, Commission decision of 29 June 1996.

[283] *PETA Deutschland v. Germany*, no. 43481/09, § 49, 8 November 2012. For a note of caution about such relativism, see *PETA Deutschland v. Germany*, no. 43481/09, Concurring Opinion of Judge Zupančič, Joined by Judge Spielmann, 8 November 2012.

hatred against Armenians or that manifestations of racism had taken place during the relevant period.[284] The Court has insisted that it does not 'arbitrate the underlying historical issues which are part of a continuing debate between historians that shapes opinion as to the events which took place and their interpretation'.[285] The case of 'established historical facts', of which the Holocaust is pre-eminent, stands as an exception to this general rule.[286]

Protection of copyright obviously results in possible interference with the exercise of freedom of expression. The Court has explained that balancing of rights is involved, given that the interest of protecting intellectual property is contemplated by article 1 of Protocol No. 1.[287] The positive obligation upon States to protect intellectual property through the enforcement of copyright provides 'weighty reasons' to justify interference with freedom of expression.[288]

Discrimination

It does not appear that the Convention organs have ever found a violation of article 14 in association with article 10.

A media outlet alleged discriminatory treatment when it was excluded from attending a trial involving juvenile offenders. The judge authorized a limited number of journalists to attend, chosen by drawing lots, but the applicant was not among the successful ones. The Court held that although there was a difference there was no unjustified discriminatory treatment, in that it was necessary to limit access to the hearing and the method of selection chosen fell within the margin of appreciation.[289]

An Irish republican detainee in a British prison complained of discrimination in his freedom of expression when he sought to wear an Easter lily as a manifestation of his political views. He argued that loyalist prisoners were allowed to wear poppies to honour war victims, a tradition that was not followed by Irish nationalists, and that he should be allowed to do the same. The Court noted that the Prison Service had differentiated on the basis that the Easter lily was an emblem directly related to the community conflict, whereas the poppy was an emblem that distinguished one community from the other in Northern Ireland but was not directly connected with the conflict. The Court said States were entitled to a wide margin of appreciation in assessing the emblems that might inflame existing tensions if displayed publicly and those that should not. Therefore, prisoners who wore a poppy were not in an analogous situation to the applicant and there was no prohibited discrimination related to article 10.[290]

A French magazine complained of discrimination because it was prosecuted for publishing photos associated with an article on remuneration of professional athletes because they included tobacco advertising. It argued that similar restrictions were not

---

[284] *Perinçek v. Switzerland*, no. 27510/08, §§ 51–54, 17 December 2013.
[285] *Fatullayev v. Azerbaijan*, no. 40984/07, § 87, 22 April 2010; *Chauvy and Others v. France*, no. 64915/01, § 69, ECHR 2004-VI; *Karsai v. Hungary*, no. 5380/07, § 35, 1 December 2009; *Giniewski v. France*, no. 64016/00,§§ 50–51, ECHR 2006-I.
[286] *Garaudy v. France* (dec.), no. 65831/01, ECHR 2003-IX; *Lehideux and Isorni v. France*, 23 September 1998, § 47, *Reports of Judgments and Decisions* 1998-VII.
[287] *Anheuser-Busch Inc. v. Portugal* [GC], no. 73049/01, § 72, ECHR 2007-I.
[288] *Neij and Sunde Kolmisoppi v. Sweden* (dec.), no. 40397/12, 19 February 2013.
[289] *Axel Springer AG v. Germany* (dec.), no. 44585/10, 13 March 2012.
[290] *Donaldson v. the United Kingdom* (dec.), no. 56975/09, §§ 38–39, 25 January 2011.

placed on audio-visual media. The Court dismissed the complaint because it said that the print media were not similarly situated.[291]

Reservations and declarations

There have been four reservations to article 10 of the Convention. Azerbaijan formulated a reservation concerning a requirement of a certain level of national ownership of mass media.[292] Malta made a reservation concerning restrictions upon the political activity of public officers during working hours or on official premises.[293] Monaco made a reservation with respect to a State monopoly on radio and television broadcasting.[294]

Portugal formulated the following reservation: 'Article 10 of the Convention will be applied subject to Article 38(6) of the Constitution of the Portuguese Republic, which provides that television may not be privately owned.'[295] It was withdrawn in 1987.[296]

Spain formulated an interpretative declaration specifying that the final sentence of article 10(1) is to be interpreted as being compatible with the system governing the organization of radio and television broadcasting then in effect.[297] At the time of ratification, in 1974, France formulated the following interpretative declaration: 'The Government of France declares that it interprets the provisions of Article 10 as being compatible with the system established in France under Act No. 72-553 of 10 July 1972, determining the legal status of the French Radio and Television.'[298] France withdrew the declaration in 1988.[299]

None of these reservations or declarations appears to have been at issue in any litigation.

Further reading

Yutaka Arai, 'Article 10: Freedom of Expression', in Harris et al., eds, *Law of the European Convention*, pp. 443–514.

Eduardo Andres Bertoni, 'The Inter-American Court of Human Rights and the European Court of Human Rights: A Dialogue on Freedom of Expression Standards', [2009] *EHRLR* 332.

Violeta Beširević, 'A Short Guide to Militant Democracy: Some Remarks on the Strasbourg Jurisprudence', in Wolfgang Benedek, Florence Benoît-Rohmer, Wolfram Karl, and Manfred Nowak, eds, *European Yearbook on Human Rights*, Antwerp: Intersentia and Vienna-Graz, Neuer Wissenschaftlicher Verlag, 2012, pp. 243–57.

Antoin Buyse, 'The Truth, the Past and the Present: Article 10 and Situations of Transition', in Antoine Buyse and Michael Hamilton, eds, *Transitional Jurisprudence and the ECHR*, Cambridge: Cambridge University Press, 2011, pp. 131–50.

Josep Casadevall, Egbert Myjer, Michael O'Boyle, and Anna Austin, eds, *Freedom of Expression, Essays in Honour of Nicolas Bratza*, Oisterwijk: Wolf Publishers, 2012.

Marina Castellaneta, *La libertà di stampa nel diritto internazionale ed europeo*, Bari: Cacucci, 2012.

---

[291] *Société de conception de presse et d'édition and Ponson v. France*, no. 26935/05, § 80, 5 March 2009. Also *Hachette Filipacchi Presse Automobile and Dupuy v. France*, no. 13353/05, § 65, 5 March 2009.

[292] (2002) 45 YB 17.

[293] (1966) 9 YB 24–25.

[294] (2005) 48 YB 11.

[295] (1978) 21 YB 14–15.

[296] (1987) 30 YB 4–5.

[297] (1979) 22 YB 22–25.

[298] (1974) 17 YB 4.

[299] (1988) 31 YB 4.

Gérard Cohen-Jonathan, 'Article 10', in Pettiti et al., *La Convention européenne*, pp. 365–418.

Margaret de Merieux, 'The German Competition Law and Article 10 ECHR', (1995) 20 *European Law Review* 388.

Frowein/Peukert, *MenschenRechtsKonvention*, pp. 339–72.

Grabenwarter, *European Convention*, pp. 251–96.

Mauro Gatti, '*Mouvement Raëlien Suisse v. Switzerland* (Eur. Ct. H.R.), Introductory Note', (2012) 51 *International Legal Materials* 925.

John Hedigan, 'The Princess, the Press and Privacy. Observations on Caroline von Hannover v. Germany', in Lucius Caflisch, Johan Callewaert, Roderick Liddell, Paul Mahoney, and Mark Villiger, eds, *Liber Amicorum Luzius Wildhaber*, Kehl, Germany: N.P. Engel, 2007, pp. 193–206.

Christian Jacq and Francis Teitgen, 'The Press', in Mireille Delmas-Marty, ed., *The European Convention for the Protection of Human Rights*, Dordrecht/Boston/London: Martinus Nijhoff, 1992, pp. 59–81.

Renée Koering-Joulin, 'Public Morals', in Mireille Delmas-Marty, ed., *The European Convention for the Protection of Human Rights*, Dordrecht/Boston/London: Martinus Nijhoff, 1992, pp. 83–98.

Katrien Lefever, Hannes Cannie, and Peggy Valcke, 'Watching Live Sport on Television: A Human Right?', [2010] *EHRLR* 396.

Loukis G. Loucaides, 'The Right to Information', in Loukis G. Loucaides, *Essays on the Developing Law of Human Rights*, The Hague: Brill, 1995, pp. 3–31.

Darragh Murray, 'Freedom of Expression, Counter-Terrorism and the Internet in Light of the UK Terrorist Act 2006 and the Jurisprudence of the European Court of Human Rights', (2009) 27 *Netherlands Quarterly of Human Rights* 331.

M. O'Boyle, 'Right to Speak and Associate under Strasbourg Case-Law with Reference to Eastern and Central Europe', (1993) 8 *Connecticut Journal of International Law* 282.

Mario Oetheimer, 'Protecting Freedom of Expression: The Challenge of Hate Speech in the European Court of Human Rights Case Law', (2009) 17 *Cardozo Journal of International & Comparative Law* 427.

Ovey/White, *Jacobs and White, European Convention*, pp. 276–89.

Karen Reid, *A Practitioner's Guide to the European Convention on Human Rights*, London: Sweet & Maxwell, 2011, pp. 464–503.

Arjen van Rijn, 'Freedom of Expression (Article 10)', in Van Dijk et al., *Theory and Practice*, pp. 773–816.

M.A. Sanderson, 'Is *Von Hannover v Germany* a Step Backward for the Substantive Analysis of Speech and Privacy Interest?', (2004) 6 *EHRLR* 631.

Jasper P. Sluijs, 'From Competition to Freedom of Expression: Introducing Article 10 ECHR in the European Network Neutrality Debate', (2012) 12 *HRLR* 509.

Albert Verdoodt, 'The Right to Use a Language of One's Choice', (1995) 38 A YB 50.

D. Voorhoof and J. Englebert, 'La liberté d'expression syndicale mise à mal par la Cour européenne des droits de l'homme', (2010) 83 *RTDH* 743.

Dirk Voorhoof and Patrick Humblet, 'The Right to Freedom of Expression in the Workplace under Article 10 ECHR', in Filip Dorssemont, Klaus Lörcher, and Isabelle Schömann, eds, *The European Convention on Human Rights and the Employment Relation*, Oxford/Portland: OR: Hart, 2013, pp. 237–86.

Patrick Wachsmann, 'Liberté d'expression et négationnisme', [2001] *RTDH* 585.

Guido Westkamp, '*Axel Springer AG v. Germany; Von Hannover v. Germany (no. 2)* (Eur. Ct. H.R.), Introductory Note', (2012) 51 *International Legal Materials* 631.

Katja J. Ziegler, 'The Princess and the Press: Privacy After *Caroline van Hannover v. Germany*', in Katja S. Ziegler, ed., *Human Rights and Private Law: Privacy as Autonomy*, Oxford: Hart Publishing, 2007, pp. 189–208.

Article 11. Freedom of assembly and association/Liberté de réunion et d'association

1. Everyone has the right to freedom of peaceful assembly and to freedom of association with others, including the right to form and to join trade unions for the protection of his interests.

2. No restrictions shall be placed on the exercise of these rights other than such as are prescribed by law and are necessary in a democratic society in the interests of national security or public safety, for the prevention of disorder or crime, for the protection of health or morals or for the protection of the rights and freedoms of others. This article shall not prevent the imposition of lawful restrictions on the exercise of these rights by members of the armed forces, of the police or of the administration of the State.

1. Toute personne a droit à la liberté de réunion pacifique et à la liberté d'association, y compris le droit de fonder avec d'autres des syndicats et de s'affilier à des syndicats pour la défense de ses intérêts.

2. L'exercice de ces droits ne peut faire l'objet d'autres restrictions que celles qui, prévues par la loi, constituent des mesures nécessaires, dans une société démocratique, à la sécurité nationale, à la sûreté publique, à la défense de l'ordre et à la prévention du crime, à la protection de la santé ou de la morale, ou à la protection des droits et libertés d'autrui. Le présent article n'interdit pas que des restrictions légitimes soient imposées à l'exercice de ces droits par les membres des forces armées, de la police ou de l'administration de l'État.

Introductory comments

Although freedom of association and peaceful assembly are often grouped with the other two great freedoms, religion and expression, in a sense they are adjectival rights in that they provide a means to implement the other freedoms. In his seminal 'four freedoms' speech, Franklin D. Roosevelt listed religion and expression but not association and peaceful assembly. Freedom of peaceful assembly and association are closely related to the exercise of political rights as part of modern democracy, although they also take on significance with respect to the practice of religion. They were widely recognized in national constitutions well before their codification in international human rights instruments.[1] An early formulation appears in the first amendment to the Constitution of the United States: 'Congress shall make no law ... abridging ... the right of the people peaceably to assemble.'

Within the Universal Declaration of Human Rights, they are formulated in a succinct sentence, article 20(1): 'Everyone has the right to freedom of peaceful assembly and association.' It is followed by a second, related provision: '(2) No one may be compelled to belong to an association.' During the drafting of the Declaration, the right to freedom of association was closely related to important debates about the rights of trade unions, and the second sentence of article 20 was obviously directed at issues relating to compulsory membership in unions. In addition to a general recognition of freedom of association, the

---

[1] UN Doc. E/CN.4/AC.1/3/Add.1, pp 147–58.

Declaration also affirms, in article 23(4): 'Everyone has the right to form and to join trade unions for the protection of his interests.'

The close relationship between freedom of association and trade unions is reinforced by a very substantial body of law generated within the International Labour Organisation. Its central instrument is Convention No. 87 on Freedom of Association and Protection of the Right to Organise, adopted in 1948.[2] The influence of Convention No. 87 was certainly felt by the drafters of the Universal Declaration of Human Rights. A more contemporary assertion of freedom of association appears in the Charter of Fundamental Rights of the European Union: 'Everyone has the right to freedom of peaceful assembly and to freedom of association at all levels, in particular in political, trade union and civic matters, which implies the right of everyone to form and to join trade unions for the protection of his or her interests.'[3] The scope of article 12 of the Charter is wider than article 11 of the Convention because it may be extended to the European Union level.[4]

Within the Council of Europe system, the European Social Charter of 1961 and the revised European Social Charter of 1996 affirm that 'workers and employers have the right to freedom of association in national or international organisations for the protection of their economic and social interests'. Detailed provisions of the Charters set out the right to organize and to collective bargaining.[5] The European Commission for Democracy through Law (the Venice Commission) has devoted considerable attention to freedom of assembly and freedom of association, issuing many opinions on detailed issues and legislative provisions. Of particular interest is its opinion interpreting the guidelines of the Organisation for Security and Cooperation in Europe and the Office of Democratic Initiatives and Human Rights dealing with freedom of peaceful assembly.[6] The Venice Commission has issued guidelines on the financing of political parties,[7] on their dissolution,[8] and on a range of related issues.[9] Freedom of assembly and association has also featured in work of the Parliamentary Assembly of the Council of Europe.[10]

Drafting of the provision

The initial draft European Convention on Human Rights was prepared by the International Juridical Section of the European Movement, chaired by Pierre-Henri Teitgen, with David Maxwell Fyfe and Fernand Dehousse as rapporteurs. Both Maxwell Fyfe and Dehousse had been involved in the adoption of the Universal Declaration of Human

---

[2] International Labour Organisation Convention No. 87 on Freedom of Association and Protection of the Right to Organise, (1950), 68 UNTS 17.

[3] See, for example, *Sindicatul 'Păstorul cel Bun' v. Romania*, no. 2330/09, § 33, 31 January 2012.

[4] Explanation relating to the Charter of Fundamental Rights, Official Journal of the European Union, C 303/34, 14 December 2007.

[5] European Social Charter, ETS 35, arts 5, 6.

[6] CDL(2008)062. Cited in *Oya Ataman v. Turkey*, no. 74552/01, § 16, ECHR 2006-XIII.

[7] CDL-INF (2001) 8. Cited in *Parti nationaliste basque—Organisation régionale d'Iparralde v. France*, no. 71251/01, § 16, ECHR 2007-II.

[8] CDL-INF(2000)1.

[9] Guidelines and Explanatory Report on Legislation on Political Parties: Some Specific Issues, CDL-AD(2004)007rev; Report on the Participation of Political Parties in Elections, CDL-AD(2006)025; Code of Good Practice in Electoral Matters, CDL-AD(202)23.

[10] For example, Recommendation 1516 (2001) on the financing of political parties. Cited in *Parti nationaliste basque—Organisation régionale d'Iparralde v. France*, no. 71251/01, § 17, ECHR 2007-II.

Rights at the United Nations the previous year. The enumeration of rights in the draft affirmed '[f]reedom of association and assembly'.[11] The European Movement draft also contained a restrictions or limitations clause, inspired by article 29 of the Universal Declaration of Human Rights: 'The rights specified in Articles 1 and 2 shall be subject only to such limitations as are in conformity with the general principles of law recognised by civilised nations and as are prescribed by law for: a) Protecting the legal rights of others; b) Meeting the just requirements of morality, public order (including the safety of the community), and the general welfare.'[12]

At the first session of the Consultative Assembly of the Council of Europe, Pierre-Henri Teitgen called for adoption of a convention that would include 'freedom of association and assembly'.[13] Mandated to prepare a text for discussion for the Committee on Legal and Administrative Questions at the first session of the Consultative Assembly, held from 22 August to 5 September 1949, Teitgen proposed the following: 'Freedom of assembly, in accordance with Article 20 of the United Nations Declaration. Freedom of association, in accordance with Article 20 of the United Nations Declaration. Freedom to unite in trade unions, in accordance with Article 23(4) of the United Nations Declaration.'[14] Teitgen's draft provision on freedom of assembly and association was adopted by the Committee on Legal and Administrative Questions at its 30 August 1949 meeting.[15] The texts in the draft report adopted by the Committee read: 'Freedom of meeting, in accordance with Article 20 of the Declaration of the United Nations. Freedom of association, in accordance with Article 20 (paragraphs 1 and 2) of the Declaration of the United Nations. Freedom to unite in trade unions, in accordance with paragraph 4 of Article 23 of the Declaration of the United Nations.'[16] In the final report to the Consultative Assembly the awkward translation of *réunion* in French was changed from meeting to assembly and Declaration of the United Nations changed to United Nations Declaration in all three paragraphs.[17] The texts proposed by the Committee were adopted without debate by the Consultative Assembly.[18]

In the Committee on Legal and Administrative Questions of the Consultative Assembly, Teitgen had also proposed a limitations clause of general application: 'In the exercise of these rights, and in the enjoyment of the freedoms guaranteed by the Convention, no limitations will be imposed except those established with the sole object of ensuring recognition and respect for the rights and freedoms of others, or with the purpose of satisfying the just requirements of public morality, order and security and general welfare

[11] Convention for the Collective Protection of Individual Rights and Democratic Liberties by the States, Members of the Council of Europe, and for the establishment of a European Court of Human Rights to ensure observance of the Convention, Doc. INF/5/E/R, I *TP* 296–303, at p. 296, art. I(f).

[12] Ibid., art. 3.

[13] Report of the Sitting [of the Consultative Assembly, 19 August 1949], I *TP* 38–154, at p. 46.

[14] Proposals by Mr P.H. Teitgen, Rapporteur, 29 August 1949, Doc. A 116, I *TP* 166–8. Also Report presented by Mr P.H. Teitgen, 5 September 1949, Doc. A 290, I *TP* 192–213, at p. 206. See also Report [of the Committee on Legal and Administrative Questions], 5 September 1949, Doc. AS (1) 77, I *TP* 216–39, at p. 228.

[15] Minutes of the Sitting [of the Committee on Legal and Administrative Questions, Consultative Assembly, 30 August 1949], Doc. A 167, I TP 174–80, at p. 176.

[16] Report presented by Mr P.H. Teitgen, 5 September 1949, Doc. A 290, I *TP* 192–213, at p. 208.

[17] Report [of the Committee on Legal and Administrative Questions], 5 September 1949, Doc. AS (1) 77, I *TP* 216–39, at p. 228.

[18] Recommendation No. 38 to the Committee of Ministers adopted 8 September 1949 on the conclusion of the debates, Doc. AS (1) 108, II *TP* 274–83, at p. 276.

in a democratic society. These rights and freedoms may in no case be exercised contrary to the aims and principles of the Council of Europe.' The restrictions or limitation clause, still then a general provision applicable to the entire draft convention, was somewhat altered by the Consultative Assembly: 'In the exercise of these rights, and in the enjoyment of the freedoms guaranteed by the Convention, no limitations shall be imposed except those established by law, with the sole object of ensuring the recognition and respect for the rights and freedoms of others, or with the purpose of satisfying the just requirement of public morality, order and security in a democratic society.' It was adopted after a short debate without a vote.[19]

The Committee of Ministers decided to refer consideration of the Consultative Assembly draft to a Committee of Experts. In the meantime, the United Nations Commission on Human Rights had produced provisions on freedom of assembly and association for the draft Covenant on human rights. The relevant texts are as follows:

Article 18
Everyone has the right to freedom of peaceful assembly. No restrictions shall be placed on the exercise of this right other than those prescribed by law and which are necessary to ensure national security, public order, the protection of health or morals, or the protection of the rights and freedoms of others.

Article 19
1. Everyone has the right to freedom of association with others.
2. This freedom shall be subject only to such limitations as are pursuant to law and as are necessary for the protection of national security, public order, public safety, health or morals, or the fundamental rights and freedoms of others.
3. National legislation shall neither prejudice, nor be applied in such a manner as to prejudice, the guarantees provided for in the International Convention on Freedom of Association and Protection of the Right to Organise, in so far as States parties to that Convention are concerned.[20]

In preparation for the Committee of Experts, the Secretariat of the Council of Europe prepared comments comparing the draft Covenant with the draft convention adopted by the Consultative Assembly:

Article 18
Article 2, paragraph 7 and Article 6 [the general limitations clause] of the Resolution cover this provision, except for the reservations as above under Article 16 [on freedom of thought, conscience and religion] regarding the control of State restrictions on this freedom.

Article 19
This provision is covered by paragraph 8 of Article 2 and Article 6 [the general limitations clause] of the Resolution. However, the aim and character of the international control have been give [sic] a definition which is not found in Article 6 of the Resolution. As for paragraph 3, there is a choice to be made between this Universal Declaration text to which paragraph 9 of Article 2 of the Resolution refers, and the provisions of paragraph 3 of the draft Covenant.[21]

[19] Official Report of the Sitting [of the Consultative Assembly, 8 September 1949], II *TP* 14–274, at pp. 134–42. See also Preparatory Report by the Secretariat-General concerning a Preliminary Draft Convention to Provide a Collective Guarantee of Human Rights, Doc. B 22, III *TP* 2–37, at pp. 16–18.

[20] Report of the Fifth Session of the Commission on Human Rights to the Economic and Social Council, UN Doc. E/1371(Supp.), p. 23.

[21] Preparatory Report by the Secretariat-General concerning a Preliminary Draft Convention to Provide a Collective Guarantee of Human Rights, Doc. B 22, III *TP* 2–37, at pp. 20–1.

The United Kingdom also submitted comments on the draft Covenant:

Art. 19(a). It has been the consistent view of H.M. Government that the terms of the Covenant should define the obligations of States which accede to it in clear and precise terms. H.M. Government consider it reasonable to provide for the possibility of certain restrictions on the full freedom of association of members of the armed forces, of the police and of the administration of the State and it does not seem clear that such restrictions are necessarily permissible under paragraph 2 of this Article as at present drafted.

(b) Further, His Majesty's Government consider that the language used to describe the limitations in this Article should be the same as that used in Article 18. They therefore propose that paragraph 2 should be amended to read:

(2) No restrictions shall be placed on the exercise of this right other than those prescribed by law and which are necessary to ensure national security, public order, the protection of health or morals, or the protection of the rights and freedoms of others, provided that this Article shall not prevent the imposition of restrictions on the exercise of this right by members of the armed forces, the police or the administration of a State.[22]

At the first session of the Committee of Experts, in February 1950, Sir Oscar Dowson of the United Kingdom proposed that the draft provision on freedom of assembly be replaced with the following text:

1) Everyone has the right to freedom of peaceful assembly. No restrictions shall be placed on the exercise of this right other than those prescribed by law and which are necessary to ensure national security, public order, the protection of health or morals, or the protection of the rights and freedoms of others.[23]

However, the Committee of Experts concluded its first session with the adoption of the following, essentially reflecting the text adopted by the Consultative Assembly: 'Everyone has the right of freedom of peaceful assembly. Everyone has the right of freedom of peaceful association. No one may be compelled to belong to an association. Everyone has the right to form and to join trade unions for the protection of his interests.'[24]

The report of the Committee explains that instead of enumerating rights by reference to the relevant provision in the Universal Declaration, as had been done by the Consultative Assembly, it was better to incorporate the text verbatim. Accordingly, the Committee 'scrupulously adhered to the text of the Universal Declaration'.[25] The texts it adopted are very similar to those of articles 20 and 23(4) of the Universal Declaration of Human Rights. What the Declaration labels 'peaceful assembly and association' became two distinct sentences, with the dubious addition of 'peaceful' before association.

At the second session of the Committee of Experts, in March 1950, the United Kingdom representative submitted amendments:

Everyone has the right to freedom of peaceful assembly. No restrictions shall be placed on the exercise of this right other than such as are prescribed by law and are necessary in the interests of

[22] Comments of Governments on the draft International Covenant on Human Rights and Measures of Implementation [UN Doc. E/CN.4/353/Add.1-3], Doc. A 770, III *TP* 156–79, at p. 164.

[23] Amendments to Article 2 of the Recommendation of the Consultative Assembly proposed by the Expert of the United Kingdom, Doc. A 798, III *TP* 204–7, at p. 206.

[24] Preliminary Draft Convention for the Maintenance and Further Realisation of Human Rights and Fundamental Freedoms, 15 February 1950, Doc. A 833, III *TP* 236–46, at p. 238. Also Draft text of the first section of a draft Convention based on the work of the Consultative Assembly, Doc. A 809, III *TP* 220–31, at p. 224.

[25] Preliminary draft of the Report to the Committee of Ministers, 24 February 1950, Doc. CM/WP 1 (50) 1, A 847, III *TP* 246–79, at pp. 260–2.

national security or public safety, or for the prevention of disorder or crime, for the protection of health or morals, or for the protection of the rights and freedoms of others.[26]

This text differed slightly from the earlier proposal in minor ways. The words 'other than those' were replaced by 'such as are', 'to ensure' became 'in the interests of', the words 'national security, public order,' became 'national security or public safety, or for the prevention of disorder or crime, for', and the word 'for' was added before 'the protection of the rights and freedoms of others'. The British experts also proposed a new provision on freedom of association:

1) Everyone has the right to freedom of association with others.
2) No restrictions shall be placed on the exercise of this right other than such as are prescribed by law and are necessary in the interests of national security or public safety, or for the prevention of disorder or crime, for the protection of health or morals, or for the protection of the rights and freedoms of others; provided that this article shall not prevent the imposition of restrictions on the exercise of this right by members of the armed forces, the police or the administration of the State.[27]

The United Kingdom proposal did not include the text on trade unions derived from article 23(4) of the Universal Declaration. Nevertheless, the Report of the Committee of Experts explained its understanding that '[t]he rights defined in this Article include the right to associate in trade unions'.[28]

The United Kingdom proposal was revised by a Drafting Committee and the rights of peaceful assembly and association combined in a single sentence:

1) Everyone has the right to freedom of peaceful assembly and to freedom of association with others.
2) No restrictions shall be placed on the exercise of this right other than such as are prescribed by law and are necessary in the interests of national security, public safety or for the prevention of disorder or crime, for the protection of health or morals, or for the protection of the rights and freedoms of others; provided that this article shall not prevent the imposition of lawful restrictions on the exercise of this right by members of the armed forces, the police or the administration of the State.[29]

The Committee of Experts concluded its work with the submission to the Committee of Ministers of two different drafts. The first, labelled 'Alternative A', contained the texts in the report of the first session of the Committee of Experts.[30] The second, 'Alternative B', contained the British text as amended by the Drafting Committee.[31]

---

[26] Amendments to Articles 1, 2, 4, 5, 6, 8, and 9 of the Committee's preliminary draft proposal by the Expert of the United Kingdom, Doc. CM/WP 1 (50) 2, A 915, III *TP* 280–9, at p. 286.

[27] Ibid., pp. 286–8.

[28] Report to the Committee of Ministers submitted by the Committee of Experts Instructed to Draw Up a Draft Convention of Collective Guarantee of Human Rights and Fundamental Freedoms, Doc. CM/WP 1 (5) 15, A 924, IV *TP* 2–55, at p. 32.

[29] Amendments to the British draft proposed by the Drafting Committee composed of Sir Oscar Dowson, MM le Quesne, Dons Moeller, and Salén, Doc. CM/WP 1 (50) 10, p. 3, A 919, III *TP* 288–95, at p. 292.

[30] Preliminary Draft Convention, Doc. CM/WP 1 (50) 14, A 932, III *TP* 312–35, at p. 322; Report to the Committee of Ministers submitted by the Committee of Experts Instructed to Draw Up a Draft Convention of Collective Guarantee of Human Rights and Fundamental Freedoms, Doc. CM/WP 1 (5) 15, A 924, IV *TP* 2–55, at p. 64.

[31] Preliminary Draft Convention, Doc. CM/WP 1 (50) 14, A 932, III *TP* 312–35, p. 318; Report to the Committee of Ministers submitted by the Committee of Experts Instructed to Draw Up a Draft Convention of Collective Guarantee of Human Rights and Fundamental Freedoms, Doc. CM/WP 1 (5) 15, A 924, IV *TP* 2–55, at p. 52.

The Conference of Senior Officials that convened in June 1950 assigned a Drafting Committee to attempt to reconcile the competing versions that had been prepared by the Committee of Experts. It prepared a new formulation on freedom of peaceful assembly and association based on the British proposal as amended by the Drafting Committee of the Committee of Experts, but with the addition of a new phrase in the first sentence explicitly acknowledging the role of trade unions drawn from article 23(4) of the Universal Declaration of Human Rights. A reference to 'democratic society' was also introduced in paragraph 2.

1) Everyone has the right to freedom of peaceful assembly and to freedom of association with others, including the right to form and to join trade unions for the protection of his interests.
2) No restrictions shall be placed on the exercise of these rights other than such as are prescribed by law and are necessary in the interests of national security, public safety, or for the prevention of disorder or crime, for the protection of health or morals in a democratic society, or for the protection of the rights and freedoms of others; provided that this article shall not prevent the imposition of lawful restrictions on the exercise of this right by members of the armed forces, the police or the administration of the State.[32]

A few modifications were made in the final version adopted by the Conference:

2) No restrictions shall be placed on the exercise of these rights other than such as are prescribed by law and are necessary in a democratic society in the interests of national security, public safety, or for the prevention of disorder or crime, for the protection of health or morals in a democratic society, or for the protection of the rights and freedoms of others; provided that this Article shall not prevent the imposition of lawful restrictions on the exercise of this right by members of the armed forces, the police or the administration of the State.[33]

The Report of the Conference contained a detailed comment on the reference to trade unions that had been added in paragraph 1:

In this Article, the Conference has introduced express reference to the right to form trade unions, so as to bring this Article into confirmation with the United Nations Universal Declaration. This Declaration mentions the right to form trade unions as a right distinct from the right of association in general. Certain delegates considered, however, that the right to form trade unions was also included in the right of association.

On account of the difficulties raised by the 'closed shop system' in certain countries, the Conference in this connection considered that it was undesirable to introduce into the Convention a rule under which 'no one may be compelled to belong to an association' which features in the United Nations Universal Declaration.[34]

After the work of the Conference had concluded, the United Kingdom proposed the following: 'Insert "or" between "national security" and "public safety" (deleting the comma) and delete "or" after "public safety"'.[35]

---

[32] New draft alternatives B and B/2, Doc. CM/WP 4 (50) 9, A 1372, IV *TP* 182–91, at pp. 188–90.

[33] Draft Convention annexed to the Report, Doc. CM/WP 4 (50) 19 annex, CM/WP 4 (50) 16 rev., A 1452, IV *TP* 274–95, at p. 280. Also Draft Convention appended to the draft report, Doc. CM/WP 4 (50) 16, appendix, A 1445, IV *TP* 218–40, at p. 224.

[34] Text of the report submitted by the Conference [of Senior Officials] to the Committee of Ministers, Doc. CM/WP 4 (50) 19, CM/WP 4 (50) 16 rev., A 1431, IV *TP* 242–73, at p. 262.

[35] Comments by the United Kingdom Delegation on the Report of the Conference of Senior Officials and the text of the draft Convention, Doc. A 1690, p. 3.

The Committee of Ministers, at its fifth session in early August 1950, revised the text and made some small stylistic adjustments to paragraph 2:

2) No restrictions shall be placed on the exercise of these rights other than such as are prescribed by law and are necessary in a democratic society in the interests of national security or public safety, for the prevention of disorder or crime, for the protection of health or morals or for the protection of the rights and freedoms of others. This Article shall not prevent the imposition of lawful restrictions on the exercise of this right by members of the armed forces, the police or the administration of the State.[36]

Prior to adoption of the final text of the Convention, in November 1950, the Committee of Legal Experts added the word 'of' before 'the police' and 'the administration' in the final phrase of paragraph 2.[37]

The heading 'Freedom of assembly and association' was added by Protocol No. 11.[38]

Analysis and interpretation

Like articles 8, 9, and 10, article 11 consists of two paragraphs, the first describing the two rights in question and the second their permissible restrictions or limitations. In its analysis of alleged violations, the Court initially considers whether there has been an infringement of one of the rights. Then it proceeds to examine the possibility that the infringement is subject to an acceptable restriction. In contrast with the restriction clauses of articles 8, 9, and 10, article 11(2) contains a second sentence that reflects its special focus on labour relations: 'This article shall not prevent the imposition of lawful restrictions on the exercise of these rights by members of the armed forces, of the police or of the administration of the State.'

The freedoms set out in article 11 are closely associated with democracy, something that is a 'fundamental feature of the European public order'.[39] The Convention was designed to promote and maintain the ideals and values of a democratic society.[40] The Court has stressed that democracy is the only political model contemplated by the Convention or compatible with it.[41] It has spoken of the hallmarks of democratic society, attaching special importance to pluralism, tolerance, broadmindedness,[42] and social

---

[36] Draft Convention adopted by the Sub-Committee, Doc. CM 1 (50) 52, A 1884, V *TP* 76–99, at p. 82; Draft Convention adopted by the Committee of Ministers, 7 August 1950, Doc. A 1937, V *TP* 120–45, at p. 128.

[37] Report of the Committee of Legal Experts held at Rome, 2 and 3 November 1950 (revised text), Doc. CM/Adj (50) 3 rev., A 2531, VII *TP* 10–13.

[38] Protocol No. 11 to the Convention for the Protection of Human Rights and Fundamental Freedoms, restructuring the control machinery established thereby, ETS 155, art. 2(2).

[39] *Staatkundig Gereformeerde Partij v. the Netherlands* (dec.), no. 58369/10, § 70, 10 July 2012; *United Communist Party of Turkey and Others v. Turkey*, 30 January 1998, § 45, *Reports of Judgments and Decisions* 1998-I.

[40] *Bączkowski and Others v. Poland*, no. 1543/06, § 61, 3 May 2007.

[41] Ibid.

[42] *Stankov and the United Macedonian Organisation Ilinden v. Bulgaria*, nos 29221/95 and 29225/95, § 86, ECHR 2001-IX; *Handyside v. the United Kingdom*, 7 December 1976, § 49, Series A no. 24; *Gerger v. Turkey* [GC], no. 24919/94, § 46, 8 July 1999; *Association of Citizens Radko and Paunkovski v. 'the former Yugoslav Republic of Macedonia'*, no. 74651/01, § 64, ECHR 2009 (extracts); *Gorzelik and Others v. Poland* [GC], no. 44158/98, § 90, ECHR 2004-I; *Bączkowski and Others v. Poland*, no. 1543/06, § 63, 3 May 2007; *Skiba v. Poland* (dec.), no. 10659/03, 7 July 2009; *Christian Democratic People's Party v. Moldova*, no. 28793/02, § 64, ECHR 2006-II; *Hyde Park and Others v. Moldova (nos 5 and 6)*, nos 6991/08 and 15084/08, § 69, 14 September 2010.

cohesion.[43] Although 'individual interests must on occasion be subordinated to those of a group, democracy does not simply mean that the views of a majority should always prevail: a balance must be achieved which ensures the fair and proper treatment of minorities and avoids any abuse of a dominant position'.[44] Freedom of association 'is particularly important for persons belonging to minorities, including national and ethnic minorities, and that, as laid down in the Preamble to the Council of Europe Framework Convention, "a pluralist and genuinely democratic society should not only respect the ethnic, cultural, linguistic and religious identity of each person belonging to a national minority, but also create appropriate conditions enabling them to express, preserve and develop this identity"'.[45] According to the Court, States must refrain from applying arbitrary measures that interfere with the rights protected by article 11(1). Because of 'the essential nature of freedom of assembly and association and its close relationship with democracy there must be convincing and compelling reasons to justify an interference with this right'.[46]

Article 11 has important links with the freedoms of religion and expression set out in articles 9 and 10. Although its scope extends well beyond the exercise of the freedoms of assembly and association in the exercise of freedom of religion and expression, the visceral connection is undeniable. The Court has noted that 'the protection of personal opinions guaranteed by Articles 9 and 10 of the Convention is one of the purposes of the guarantee of freedom of association'[47] and of peaceful assembly.[48] Moreover, this 'applies all the more in relation to political parties in view of their essential role in ensuring pluralism and the proper functioning of democracy'.[49]

In practice, although the Court frequently insists upon the 'autonomous role' of article 11, freedom of association and peaceful assembly are often linked by the Court to issues of freedom of religion and expression, and less frequently to some other rights such as privacy[50] and property. Sometimes, the Court specifies that there is a violation of article 11 'interpreted in the light of' article 9[51] or article 10,[52] or simply that it has 'taken

---

[43] *Ouranio Toxo and Others v. Greece*, no. 74989/01, § 42, ECHR 2005-X (extracts).

[44] *Chassagnou and Others v. France* [GC], nos 25088/95 and 28443/95, § 112, ECHR 1999-III, p. 65.

[45] *Gorzelik and Others v. Poland* [GC], no. 44158/98, § 93, ECHR 2004-I.

[46] *Barankevich v. Russia*, no. 10519/03, § 25, 26 July 2007; *Ouranio Toxo v. Greece*, no. 74989/01, § 36, ECHR 2005-X (extracts); *Makhmudov v. Russia*, no. 35082/04, § 64, 26 July 2007; *Adalı v. Turkey*, no. 38187/97, § 267, 31 March 2005.

[47] *Vörður Ólafsson v. Iceland*, no. 20161/06, § 46, ECHR 2010; *Chassagnou and Others v. France* [GC], nos 25088/94, 28331/95, and 28443/95, § 103, ECHR 1999-III; *Young, James and Webster v. the United Kingdom*, 13 August 1981, § 57, Series A no. 44; *Partidul Comunistilor (Nepeceristi) and Ungureanu v. Romania*, no. 46626/99, § 44, ECHR 2005; *Freedom and Democracy Party (ÖZDEP) v. Turkey* [GC], no. 23885/94, § 37, ECHR 1999-VIII; *Zhechev v. Bulgaria*, no. 57045/00, § 33, 21 June 2007.

[48] *Ezelin v. France*, 26 April 1991, § 37, Series A no. 202; *Djavit An v. Turkey*, no. 20652/92, § 39, ECHR 2003-III.

[49] *Herri Batasuna and Batasuna v. Spain*, nos 25803/04 and 25817/04, § 74, ECHR 2009. Also *Communist Party of Turkey and Others v. Turkey*, 30 January 1998, §§ 42–43, *Reports of Judgments and Decisions* 1998-I; *Christian Democratic People's Party v. Moldova*, no. 28793/02, § 62, ECHR 2006-II.

[50] *N.F. v. Italy*, no. 37119/97, §§ 35–40, ECHR 2001-IX.

[51] *Barankevich v. Russia*, no. 10519/03, § 35, 26 July 2007; *Church of Scientology Moscow v. Russia*, no. 18147/02, § 98, 5 April 2007; *Skiba v. Poland* (dec.), no. 10659/03, 7 July 2009.

[52] *Association of Citizens Radko and Paunkovski v. 'the former Yugoslav Republic of Macedonia'*, no. 74651/01, § 63, ECHR 2009 (extracts); *Association of Citizens Radko and Paunkovski v. 'the former Yugoslav Republic of Macedonia'*, no. 74651/01, § 63, ECHR 2009 (extracts); *Skiba v. Poland* (dec.), no. 10659/03, 7 July 2009; *Schwabe and M.G. v. Germany*, nos 8080/08 and 8577/08, § 101, ECHR 2011 (extracts); *Berladir and Others v. Russia*, no. 34202/06, § 36, 10 July 2012; *Galstyan v. Armenia*, no. 26986/03, § 96, 15 November 2007;

account' of the other provisions of the Convention.[53] It also does this in the other direction, noting that article 9[54] or article 10[55] must be 'interpreted in the light of' article 11. In a case involving a form of performance art where two individuals displayed dirty laundry in front of the Hungarian legislative assembly, the State argued that this was an 'assembly', and thereby subject to specific legislation requiring authorization for such a manifestation. The Court said it was satisfied that the event 'constituted predominantly an expression . . . all the more so since it involved only two persons and lasted a very short time' and that it should be considered under article 10.[56] In another case where a press release was delivered in public with twenty-five people present, the Court preferred to address the matter under article 10 rather than article 11.[57] Occasionally, the Court has also addressed issues related to article 11 within the frame of article 3 of Protocol No. 1,[58] sometimes with a degree of controversy.[59] The Court speaks of one or the other provisions being the *lex specialis*.[60] When making its determination of the relevant provision, the Court says that it is 'having regard to the specific circumstances of the case and the way in which the applicants formulated their complaints'.[61]

Frequently, if the Court concludes that if there is an infringement of article 11, it will forego further separate analysis of a violation under the other provisions of the Convention.[62] In *Appleby and Others v. the United Kingdom*, which concerned the right of an environmental group to set up stands and disseminate information, the Court ruled that there was no violation of article 10, and then summarily dismissed the complaint under article 11, saying that 'largely identical considerations' applied.[63]

Positive obligation or interference

Judgments affirm that 'although the essential object of Article 11 is to protect the individual against arbitrary interference by public authorities with the exercise of the

Herri Batasuna and Batasuna v. Spain, nos 25803/04 and 25817/04, § 74, ECHR 2009; *Öllinger v. Austria,* no. 76900/01, § 38, ECHR 2006-IX.

[53] *Young, James and Webster v. the United Kingdom,* 13 August 1981, § 66, Series A no. 44.

[54] *Moscow Branch of the Salvation Army v. Russia,* no. 72881/01, § 58, ECHR 2006-XI; *Hasan and Chaush v. Bulgaria* [GC], no. 30985/96, § 91, ECHR 2000-XI.

[55] *Palomo Sánchez and Others v. Spain* [GC], nos 28955/06, 28957/06, 28959/06, and 28964/06, §61, ECHR 2011; *Szima v. Hungary,* no. 29723/11, § 13, 9 October 2012.

[56] *Tatár and Fáber v. Hungary,* no. 26005/08 and 26160/08, § 29, 12 June 2012.

[57] *Karademirci and Others v. Turkey,* nos 37096/97 and 37101/97, § 26, ECHR 2005-I.

[58] *Silay v. Turkey,* no. 8691/02, §§ 22–23, 5 April 2007; *Sadak and Others v. Turkey (no. 2),* nos 25144/94, 26149/95 to 26154/95, 27100/95, and 27101/95, § 47, ECHR 2002-IV. See also *Ždanoka v. Latvia* [GC], no. 58278/00, § 141, ECHR 2006-IV.

[59] *Ždanoka v. Latvia* [GC], no. 58278/00, Partly Dissenting Opinion of Judge Wildhaber, ECHR 2006-IV; *Ždanoka v. Latvia* [GC], no. 58278/00, Partly Dissenting Opinion of Judges Spielmann and Jaeger, ECHR 2006-IV; *Ždanoka v. Latvia* [GC], no. 58278/00, Dissenting Opinion of Judge Rozakis, ECHR 2006-IV.

[60] *Trade Union of the Police in the Slovak Republic and Others v. Slovakia,* no. 11828/08, § 52, 25 September 2012; *Skiba v. Poland* (dec.), no. 10659/03, 7 July 2009; *Schwabe and M.G. v. Germany,* nos 8080/08 and 8577/08, § 99, ECHR 2011 (extracts); *Galstyan v. Armenia,* no. 26986/03, § 96, 15 November 2007; *Ždanoka v. Latvia* [GC], no. 58278/00, § 141, ECHR 2006-IV.

[61] *Schwabe and M.G. v. Germany,* nos 8080/08 and 8577/08, § 100, ECHR 2011 (extracts); *Djavit An v. Turkey,* no. 20652/92, § 36, ECHR 2003-III.

[62] *N.F. v. Italy,* no. 37119/97, § 39, ECHR 2001-IX; *Wilson, National Union of Journalists and Others v. the United Kingdom,* nos 30668/96, 30671/96, and 30678/96, § 50, ECHR 2002-V; *Patyi v. Hungary,* no. 35127/08, § 47, 17 January 2012.

[63] *Appleby and Others v. the United Kingdom,* no. 44306/98, § 52, ECHR 2003-VI.

rights protected, there may in addition be positive obligations on the State to secure the effective enjoyment of such rights'.[64] This does not mean that as a matter of principle the negative and positive aspects of article 11 may not be entitled to the same level of protection. Saying the matter was difficult to describe in the abstract, the Court added:

The boundaries between the State's positive and negative obligations under Article 11 of the Convention do not lend themselves to precise definition. The applicable principles are nonetheless similar. Whether the case is analysed in terms of a positive duty on the State or in terms of interference by a public authority which needs to be justified, the criteria to be applied do not differ in substance. In both contexts regard must be had to the fair balance to be struck between the competing interests of the individual and of the community as a whole.[65]

In one case, the Court determined that 'both approaches are possible given the mixture of action and inaction on the part of the authorities with which it is confronted'.[66]

The Court first addressed the question of positive obligations with respect to freedom of association in a trade union case involving the closed shop. The collective agreement between union and employer, rather than the government, was responsible for depriving the applicants of a right not to associate. Noting that the contract was the 'proximate cause', the Court said that 'it was the domestic law in force at the relevant time that made lawful the treatment of which the applicants complained. The responsibility of the respondent State for any resultant breach of the Convention is thus engaged on this basis.'[67] A few years later, it addressed the matter of positive obligations with respect to freedom of peaceful assembly, recognizing a duty on the State to ensure that it can be exercised without interference or disruption by individuals and groups opposed to those seeking to exercise their rights. Austria argued that it was under no positive obligation to protect a demonstration protesting the availability of abortion. Noting that it did 'not have to develop a general theory of the positive obligations which may flow from the Convention', the Court said:

A demonstration may annoy or give offence to persons opposed to the ideas or claims that it is seeking to promote. The participants must, however, be able to hold the demonstration without having to fear that they will be subjected to physical violence by their opponents; such a fear would be liable to deter associations or other groups supporting common ideas or interests from openly expressing their opinions on highly controversial issues affecting the community. In a democracy the right to counter-demonstrate cannot extend to inhibiting the exercise of the right to demonstrate. Genuine, effective freedom of peaceful assembly cannot, therefore, be reduced to a mere duty on the part of the State not to interfere: a purely negative conception would not be compatible with the object and purpose of Article 11.[68]

---

[64] *Barankevich v. Russia*, no. 10519/03, § 33, 26 July 2007; *Wilson, National Union of Journalists and Others v. the United Kingdom*, nos 30668/96, 30671/96, and 30678/96, § 41, ECHR 2002-V; *Demir and Baykara v. Turkey* [GC], no. 34503/97, § 110, ECHR 2008; *Gustafsson v. Sweden*, 25 April 1996, § 45, *Reports of Judgments and Decisions* 1996-II.

[65] *Sørensen and Rasmussen v. Denmark* [GC], nos 52562/99 and 52620/99, § 58, ECHR 2006-I. See also *Hatton and Others v. the United Kingdom* [GC], no. 36022/97, § 98, ECHR 2003-VIII; *Demir and Baykara v. Turkey* [GC], no. 34503/97, § 111, ECHR 2008.

[66] *Demir and Baykara v. Turkey* [GC], no. 34503/97, § 116, ECHR 2008.

[67] *Young, James and Webster v. the United Kingdom*, 13 August 1981, § 49, Series A no. 44.

[68] *Plattform 'Ärzte für das Leben' v. Austria*, 21 June 1988, § 32, Series A no. 139.

The Court has described the positive obligations as being 'of particular importance for persons holding unpopular views or belonging to minorities, because they are more vulnerable to victimisation'.[69]

Subsequently, many decisions have affirmed the positive obligations associated with the right enshrined in article 11. In a trade union case, the Court applied the concept of positive obligations where employers had de-recognized unions for collective-bargaining purposes and had offered more favourable terms of employment to those prepared to work without union representation.[70] Where an employee protested the closed shop by which he was forced to belong to a trade union, the Court held 'that national authorities may, in certain circumstances, be obliged to intervene in the relationships between private individuals by taking reasonable and appropriate measures to secure the effective enjoyment' of the right not to belong to an association.[71] The positive obligation has been affirmed in cases involving meetings or demonstrations concerning gay rights, nationalist and irredentist claims[72] and those of national minorities,[73] and membership in racist organizations.[74] Difficult issues arise because typically these cases involve conflicts between rival groups, and protecting one of them may often involve restricting or denying the rights of assembly of others.[75] The positive obligation may also be relevant when States deny the right to hold a meeting or a demonstration on the pretext that it could provoke violent reactions and counter-demonstrations.[76]

Freedom of peaceful assembly

Freedom of assembly is 'a fundamental right in a democratic society and, like the right to freedom of expression, is one of the foundations of such a society'.[77] It covers both private and public meetings, including those that take place in public thoroughfares and static meetings that take place in fixed venues. Often, it involves a demonstration, a march, or a parade. Nevertheless, the 'mere fact that an expression occurs in the public space does not necessarily turn such an event into an assembly'.[78] The term 'assembly' may be defined in national legislation, but it has its own autonomous meaning under the Convention.[79]

[I]n qualifying a gathering of several people as an assembly, regard must be had to the fact that an assembly constitutes a specific form of communication of ideas, where the gathering of an indeterminate number of persons with the identifiable intention of being part of the communicative process can be in itself an intensive expression of an idea. The support for the idea in question is

[69] *Bączkowski and Others v. Poland*, no. 1543/06, § 64, 3 May 2007.

[70] *Wilson, National Union of Journalists and Others v. the United Kingdom*, nos 30668/96, 30671/96, and 30678/96, § 41, ECHR 2002-V.

[71] *Gustafsson v. Sweden*, 25 April 1996, § 45, *Reports of Judgments and Decisions* 1996-II.

[72] *Stankov and the United Macedonian Organisation Ilinden v. Bulgaria*, nos 29221/95 and 29225/95, ECHR 2001-IX.

[73] *Ouranio Toxo and Others v. Greece*, no. 74989/01, ECHR 2005-X (extracts).

[74] *Redfearn v. the United Kingdom*, no. 47335/06, 6 November 2012.

[75] *Öllinger v. Austria*, no. 76900/01, ECHR 2006-IX.

[76] *Alekseyev v. Russia*, nos 4916/07, 25924/08, and 14599/09, §§ 72, 77, 21 October 2010; *Makhmudov v. Russia*, no. 35082/04, § 67, 26 July 2007; *Barankevich v. Russia*, no. 10519/03, § 33, 26 July 2007; *Christians against Racism and Fascism v. the United Kingdom*, no. 8440/78, Commission decision of 16 July 1980, DR 21, p. 138.

[77] *Djavit An v. Turkey*, no. 20652/92, § 56, ECHR 2003-III.

[78] *Tatár and Fáber v. Hungary*, nos 26005/08 and 26160/08, § 38, 12 June 2012.

[79] Ibid., § 38.

being expressed through the very presence of a group of people, particularly—as in the present case—at a place accessible to the general public. Furthermore, an assembly may serve the exchange of ideas between the speakers and the participants, intentionally present, even if they disagree with the speakers.[80]

Because of its fundamental role in democratic life, the right of peaceful assembly is not to be interpreted restrictively.[81] The right may be invoked by individual participants as well as by those who have organized the assembly.[82] It avails to both physical persons and organizations, and applies to all assemblies 'except those where the organisers and partici-pants have violent intentions or otherwise deny the foundations of a "democratic society"'.[83] According to the Court, 'any measures interfering with the freedom of assembly and expression other than in cases of incitement to violence or rejection of democratic principles—however shocking and unacceptable certain views or words used may appear to the authorities—do a disservice to democracy and often even endanger it'.[84]

Although it is often expressed in abbreviated form as the 'right of assembly', the adjective 'peaceful' is an important qualifier.[85] The right belongs to everyone to the extent that they do not have violent intentions.[86] The possibility of violent counter-demonstrations does not neutralize the right, nor may it be restricted because of the possibility that extremists with violent intentions who are not involved in the organization of the meeting may join a demonstration.[87] Thus, '[e]ven if there is a real risk of a public procession resulting in disorder by developments outside the control of those organising it, such procession does not for this reason fall outside the scope of Article 11(1)'.[88] The fact that a protest, demonstration, or sit-in takes place in the absence of official notifica-tion or authorization, and that it may involve unlawful disruption of traffic, does not mean that it is violent in nature and therefore deprived of the protection of article 11(1).[89] Moreover, 'peaceful protest against legislation which has been contravened does not consti-tute a legitimate aim for a restriction on liberty within the meaning of Article 11 § 2'.[90] In a case where the government said slogans of demonstrators had incited violence, the Court

---

[80] Ibid.

[81] *Djavit An v. Turkey*, no. 20652/92, § 56, ECHR 2003-III; *Skiba v. Poland* (dec.), no. 10659/03, 7 July 2009; *Rassemblement jurassien and Unité jurassienne v. Switzerland*, no. 8191/78, Commission decision of 10 October 1979, DR 17, p. 93; *Christians against Racism and Fascism v. the United Kingdom*, no. 8440/78, Commission decision of 16 July 1980, DR 21, p. 138; *Barraco v. France*, no. 31684/05, § 41, 5 March 2009; *Schwabe and M.G. v. Germany*, nos 8080/08 and 8577/08, § 110, ECHR 2011 (extracts).

[82] *Adalı v. Turkey*, no. 38187/97, § 266, 31 March 2005; *Barankevich v. Russia*, no. 10519/03, § 25, 26 July 2007.

[83] *Alekseyev v. Russia*, nos 4916/07, 25924/08, and 14599/09, § 80, 21 October 2010.

[84] *Sergey Kuznetsov v. Russia*, no. 10877/04, § 45, 23 October 2008. Also *Association of Citizens Radko and Paunkovski v. 'the former Yugoslav Republic of Macedonia'*, no. 74651/01, § 76, ECHR 2009 (extracts).

[85] The African Charter of Human and Peoples' Rights is the only major international human rights treaty not to include the adjective 'peaceful' in the relevant provision on freedom of assembly: African Charter of Human and Peoples' Rights, (1981) 1520 UNTS 217, art. 11.

[86] *Stankov and the United Macedonian Organisation Ilinden v. Bulgaria*, nos 29221/95 and 29225/95, § 77, ECHR 2001-IX; *G. v. Germany*, no. 13079/87, Commission decision of 6 March 1989, DR 60, p. 256; *Galstyan v. Armenia*, no. 26986/03, § 101, 15 November 2007; *Barankevich v. Russia*, no. 10519/03, § 32, 26 July 2007.

[87] *Schwabe and M.G. v. Germany*, nos 8080/08 and 8577/08, § 103, ECHR 2011 (extracts).

[88] *Christians against Racism and Fascism v. the United Kingdom*, no. 8440/78, Commission decision of 16 July 1980, DR 21, p. 138.

[89] *G. v. Germany*, no. 13079/87, Commission decision of 6 March 1989, DR 60, p. 256.

[90] *Cisse v. France*, no. 51346/99, § 50, ECHR 2002-III.

found that 'the slogans could be considered ambiguous and that the applicants could thus have negligently incited others to violence by displaying the slogans during certain demonstrations'.[91]

Interference with freedom of peaceful assembly

Freedom of assembly protects 'the abstract possibility of holding an undisturbed peaceful assembly'. Consequently, the organizers of a meeting may contend that there is an interference with their rights if the authorities deny permission to hold the meeting.[92] The issue is more difficult with respect to prospective participants in a meeting that does not take place. In a Hungarian case, although conceding 'the obvious difficulties of proving an intention to participate in events which never materialised', the Court ruled inadmissible a complaint by forty-seven applicants who had been victims of the situation that the meeting was designed to protest. It said it bore in mind evidence that the organizer never expected more than twenty to attend.[93] Where a government challenged the existence of an infringement because children had participated in a gathering, the Court said children are entitled to exercise freedom of assembly: '[I]t was rather a matter of personal choice for the parents to decide whether to allow their children to attend those gatherings and it would appear to be contrary to the parents' and children's freedom of assembly to prevent them from attending such events which, it must be recalled, were to protest against government policy on schooling.'[94]

The European Convention on Human Rights does not recognize freedom of movement, a lacuna that was eventually addressed in Protocol No. 4. Nevertheless, freedom of movement arises indirectly to the extent that an individual needs to move freely in order to exercise freedom of peaceful assembly. The Court found a violation in the repeated denial of travel authorization to a Turkish Cypriot who wished to cross the 'green line', the ceasefire line dividing the limits of occupied Cyprus. The refusal to grant permits to the applicant in order to cross into southern Cyprus had the consequence of impeding participation in bi-communal meetings with Greek Cypriots, 'preventing him consequently from engaging in peaceful assembly with people from both communities'.[95]

Criminal prosecution and conviction for activities related to participation in a peaceful assembly will constitute an interference with the right,[96] as will arrest during a peaceful demonstration.[97] In reaching this conclusion, the Court will consider whether the demonstration was prohibited or not authorized[98] and if there was an attempt to order its dispersal on the grounds that it was illegal or obstructed traffic.[99] Prohibition of a meeting of residents to protest against a municipal planning policy, followed by dispersal by the police when it was attempted, were held to constitute an interference.[100] Where

---

[91] *Schwabe and M.G. v. Germany*, nos 8080/08 and 8577/08, § 115, ECHR 2011 (extracts).

[92] *Patyi and Others v. Hungary*, no. 5529/05, § 27, 7 October 2008; *Bączkowski and Others v. Poland*, no. 1543/06, § 73, 3 May 2007.

[93] *Patyi and Others v. Hungary*, no. 5529/05, § 26, 7 October 2008.

[94] *Christian Democratic People's Party v. Moldova*, no. 28793/02, § 74, ECHR 2006-II.

[95] *Djavit An v. Turkey*, no. 20652/92, § 61, ECHR 2003-III.

[96] *Mkrtchyan v. Armenia*, no. 6562/03, § 37, 11 January 2007.

[97] *Galstyan v. Armenia*, no. 26986/03, § 102, 15 November 2007.

[98] *Ziliberberg v. Moldova* (dec.), no. 61821/00, 4 May 2004.

[99] *Steel and Others v. the United Kingdom*, 23 September 1998, § 7, *Reports of Judgments and Decisions* 1998-VII; *Lucas v. the United Kingdom* (dec.), no. 39013/02, 18 March 2003.

[100] *Makhmudov v. Russia*, no. 35082/04, § 56, 26 July 2007.

Bulgarian authorities prevented a nationalist group from holding meetings, save one occasion when it allowed a public demonstration provided there were no speeches, posters, and slogans, the Court said there had 'undoubtedly' been an interference with freedom of assembly.[101]

The holding of a meeting or demonstration may be made conditional upon obtaining authorization from the authorities.[102] Nor does a requirement of prior notification violate article 11(1), provided that it is not a disguised means of restricting freedom of assembly.[103] Exceptional circumstances may compel the need to allow an essentially spontaneous and unplanned meeting that responds to very recent developments. In such circumstances, the right to hold such a meeting may prevail over the need to provide the authorities with prior notice.[104] Respect for official notice periods may have the consequence of making such a meeting practically impossible, because by its very nature the demonstration must be a prompt reaction to unforeseen developments.[105] For that reason, 'regulations of this nature should not represent a hidden obstacle to the freedom of peaceful assembly as it is protected by the Convention',[106] and in exceptional circumstances they will not warrant an infringement of freedom of peaceful assembly. Nevertheless, it cannot be excluded that absence of prior notification or authorization, where this is a requirement, may provide a justification to disperse a demonstration.[107]

Provision of various security measures, including first aid services, is also important,[108] as well as the 'prevention of disorder or crime'.[109] The Court has insisted that associations and others who organize demonstrations respect the rules of democratic life in which they participate.[110] If States have the right to require authorization or notification, then they are also entitled to impose sanctions when these formalities are not observed.[111] The government may regulate the free movement of people at public meetings.[112] There is no automatic right to demonstrate in a particular place. In a Russian case, the Court criticized

---

[101] *Stankov and the United Macedonian Organisation Ilinden v. Bulgaria,* nos 29221/95 and 29225/95, § 80, ECHR 2001-IX.

[102] *Güneri and Others v. Turkey,* nos 42853/98, 43609/98, and 44291/98, § 79, 12 July 2005; *Bukta and Others v. Hungary,* no. 25691/04, § 35, ECHR 2007-III; *Oya Ataman v. Turkey,* no. 74552/01, § 39, ECHR 2006-XIII; *Rassemblement Jurassien Unité v. Switzerland,* no. 8191/78, Commission decision of 10 October 1979, DR 17, p. 119; *Plattform 'Ärzte für das Leben' v. Austria,* 21 June 1988, §§ 32 and 34, Series A no. 139; *Sergey Kuznetsov v. Russia,* no. 10877/04, § 42, 23 October 2008; *Çiloğlu and Others v. Turkey,* no. 73333/01, § 47, 6 March 2007; *Rai and Evans v. the United Kingdom* (dec.), nos 26258/07 and 26255/07, 17 November 2009.

[103] *Balçık and Others v. Turkey,* no. 25/02, § 49, 29 November 2007; *Skiba v. Poland* (dec.), no. 10659/03, 7 July 2009.

[104] *Skiba v. Poland* (dec.), no. 10659/03, 7 July 2009; *Berladir and Others v. Russia,* no. 34202/06, § 43, 10 July 2012; *Éva Molnár v. Hungary,* no. 10346/05, § 36, 7 October 2008.

[105] *Éva Molnár v. Hungary,* no. 10346/05, § 38, 7 October 2008.

[106] *Oya Ataman v. Turkey,* no. 74552/01, § 38, ECHR 2006-XIII; *Samüt Karabulut v. Turkey,* no. 16999/04, § 35, 27 January 2009; *Berladir and Others v. Russia,* no. 34202/06, § 39, 10 July 2012.

[107] *Éva Molnár v. Hungary,* no. 10346/05, §§ 37 and 38, 7 October 2008.

[108] *Oya Ataman v. Turkey,* no. 74552/01, § 39, ECHR 2006-XIII.

[109] *Berladir and Others v. Russia,* no. 34202/06, § 42, 10 July 2012.

[110] *Oya Ataman v. Turkey,* no. 74552/01, § 38, ECHR 2006-XIII; *Skiba v. Poland* (dec.), no. 10659/03, 7 July 2009; *Samüt Karabulut v. Turkey,* no. 16999/04, § 36, 27 January 2009.

[111] *Berladir and Others v. Russia,* no. 34202/06, § 41, 10 July 2012; *Ziliberberg v. Moldova* (dec.), no. 61821/00, 4 May 2004; *Rai and Evans v. the United Kingdom* (dec.), nos 26258/07 and 26255/07, 17 November 2009.

[112] *Djavit An v. Turkey,* no. 20652/92, §§ 66–67, ECHR 2003-III; *Rune Andersson v. Sweden,* no. 12781/87, §§ 2–3, Commission decision of 13 December 1998, DR 59, p. 171; *Skiba v. Poland* (dec.), no. 10659/03, 7 July 2009.

the lack of diligence on the part of the organizers of a demonstration, noting that the authorities had suggested a venue for their activity that was not accepted 'without any valid reason'.[113]

The formalities associated with holding a meeting or a demonstration find some justification in the positive obligation imposed upon governments to ensure that freedom of assembly is ensured. Possible disruption of traffic is another reason supporting the reasonableness of prior notice or authorization.[114] Almost inevitably, a demonstration in a public place will lead to a degree of disruption of traffic,[115] and a restriction on public assembly for this reason alone may often be disproportionate. Although recognizing that some disruption of traffic is a rather normal and acceptable feature of the exercise of freedom of association, this is not to be equated with deliberate attempts to obstruct vehicles, something that the Court may frown upon.[116]

Sometimes, the Court will conclude that the government has exaggerated the claim that traffic is disturbed or impeded.[117] In a very general sense, States should exercise a high level of tolerance of demonstrations, bearing in mind that 'any demonstration in a public place may cause a certain level of disruption to ordinary life and encounter hostility'.[118] For example, shouting of slogans 'is a well established feature of peaceful protest'.[119] On occasion, the Court has recognized the tolerance of the authorities.[120] A case from Moldova involved the arrest of demonstrators who were, quite ironically, protesting harassment by the Ministry of the Interior. The alleged purpose of the arrest was to ensure that authorization for the demonstration had been given. According to the Court,

even assuming that such a check were necessary, as the applicants have observed, it could have been carried out at the demonstration, or shortly after it had ended. Instead, by arresting the demonstrators and taking them to the police station, the demonstration was ended prematurely. Furthermore, in terms of the justification for the arrests, the Court finds that little relevance can be attached to the provocative nature of the demonstration. The applicants sought to protest against alleged harassment by the Ministry of Internal Affairs. The street outside the Ministry was clearly the most appropriate place to carry out such a protest. Even if their signs and chants were calculated to insult the Minister, he was clearly a public figure of some prominence in Moldova. In a democratic society, greater tolerance should be shown to those expressing opinions which are critical of such figures, even if those opinions are expressed inarticulately or intemperately.[121]

If the necessary permission has not been obtained or notification given, 'where demonstrators do not engage in acts of violence it is important for the public authorities to show a certain degree of tolerance towards peaceful gatherings if the freedom of assembly guaranteed by Article 11 of the Convention is not to be deprived of all substance'.[122]

---

[113] *Berladir and Others v. Russia*, no. 34202/06, § 56, 10 July 2012.

[114] *Skiba v. Poland* (dec.), no. 10659/03, 7 July 2009; *Éva Molnár v. Hungary*, no. 10346/05, § 34, 7 October 2008.

[115] *Patyi v. Hungary*, no. 35127/08, § 40, 17 January 2012; *Nurettin Aldemir and Others v. Turkey*, nos 32124/02, 32126/02, 32129/02, 32132/02, 32133/02, 32137/02, and 32138/02, § 43, 18 December 2007.

[116] *Barraco v. France*, no. 31684/05, § 46, 5 March 2009.

[117] *Patyi v. Hungary*, no. 35127/08, § 41–42, 17 January 2012.

[118] *Oya Ataman v. Turkey*, no. 74552/01, § 38, ECHR 2006-XIII.

[119] *Hyde Park and Others v. Moldova (nos 5 and 6)*, nos 6991/08 and 15084/08, § 49, 14 September 2010.

[120] *Barraco v. France*, no. 31684/05, § 47, 5 March 2009.

[121] *Hyde Park and Others v. Moldova (nos 5 and 6)*, nos 6991/08 and 15084/08, § 43, 14 September 2010.

[122] *Oya Ataman v. Turkey*, no. 74552/01, § 40, ECHR 2006-XIII. Also *Berladir and Others v. Russia*, no. 34202/06, § 38, 10 July 2012; *Galstyan v. Armenia*, no. 26986/03, §§ 116 and 117, 15 November 2007;

Freedom of association

The Court has said that 'the way in which national legislation enshrines [freedom of association] and its practical application by the authorities reveal the state of democracy in the country concerned'[123]. Article 11 applies to organizations, including political parties as well as to individuals.[124] Organizations are not excluded from the protection of the Convention merely because the government considers that it threatens the constitutional structures of the State.[125]

Litigation about freedom of association before the Convention organs has focused on three main categories of organization, their members, and potential members: religious groups; political parties; and trade unions. For each type of association, other fundamental rights are generally at issue. In the case of religious organizations, issues concerning freedom of thought and religion arise, notably in light of article 9 of the Convention.[126] With respect to political parties, election rights as set out in article 3 of Protocol No. 1, as well as freedom of expression, enshrined in article 10 of the Convention, are important. According to the Court, 'the protection of opinions and the freedom to express them is one of the objectives of the freedom of association as enshrined in Article 11'.[127] As for trade unions, the right to work and related issues is usually associated with economic, social, and cultural rights. These are not part of the European Convention framework, although their protection is ensured through other instruments of the Council of Europe, notably the European Social Charter.[128]

In addition to this synergy with other fundamental rights, freedom of association may also be a source of conflicts with them. A case involving the Romanian Orthodox Church raised an interesting problem about the right to form an association within an association, in that this was a trade union within a church. Two dissenting judges took the view that allowing clergy and lay employees of the Romanian Orthodox Church to organize a union threatened the integrity of the Church itself. In this way, article 9 was employed to restrict the scope of article 11.[129]

Article 11 recognizes an intrinsic value in freedom of association, regardless of its association with other rights specifically set out in the Convention, its Protocols, and other sources of international human rights law. According to the Court, '[i]t is only natural that, where a civil society functions in a healthy manner, the participation of citizens in the democratic process is to a large extent achieved through belonging to associations in

---

Bukta and Others v. Hungary, no. 25691/04, § 37, ECHR 2007-III; *Akgöl and Göl v. Turkey*, nos 28495/06 and 28516/06, § 43, 17 May 2011; *Barraco v. France*, no. 31684/05, § 43, 5 March 2009.

[123] *Sidiropoulos and Others v. Greece*, 10 July 1998, § 40, *Reports of Judgments and Decisions* 1998-IV; *Republican Party of Russia v. Russia*, no. 12976/07, § 75, 12 April 2011; *Eğitim ve Bilim Emekçileri Sendikası v. Turkey*, no. 20641/05, § 48, 25 September 2012; *Zhechev v. Bulgaria*, no. 57045/00, § 34, 21 June 2007; *Jehovah's Witnesses of Moscow v. Russia*, no. 302/02, § 100, 10 June 2010; *Church of Scientology Moscow v. Russia*, no. 18147/02, § 73, 5 April 2007; *Koretskyy and Others v. Ukraine*, no. 40269/02, § 38, 3 April 2008.

[124] *United Communist Party of Turkey and Others v. Turkey*, 30 January 1998, *Reports of Judgments and Decisions* 1998-I; *Socialist Party and Others v. Turkey*, 25 May 1998, *Reports of Judgments and Decisions* 1998-III.

[125] *United Communist Party of Turkey and Others v. Turkey*, 30 January 1998, § 27, *Reports of Judgments and Decisions* 1998-I.

[126] *Metropolitan Church of Bessarabia and Others v. Moldova*, no. 45701/99, § 105, ECHR 2001-XII.

[127] *Ouranio Toxo and Others v. Greece*, no. 74989/01, § 35, ECHR 2005-X (extracts).

[128] European Social Charter, ETS 35.

[129] *Sindicatul 'Păstorul cel Bun' v. Romania*, no. 2330/09, Joint Dissenting Opinion of Judges Ziemele and Tsotsoria, 31 January 2012.

which they may integrate with each other and pursue common objectives collectively'.[130] This is associated with pluralism, built upon recognition of the 'diversity and the dynamics of cultural traditions, ethnic and cultural identities, religious beliefs, artistic, literary and socio-economic ideas and concepts'. Furthermore, '[t]he harmonious interaction of persons and groups with varied identities is essential for achieving social cohesion'.[131] Freedom of association protects a broad range of organizations created for various purposes, such as protection of cultural heritage, social and economic objectives, ethnic identity, and the manifestation of a minority consciousness.[132]

Victims of an infringement may include those who do not belong to an organization but who are discouraged from joining it by an official act. In the Slovak Republic, the Minister of the Interior made statements that threatened the activity of a police union. This intimidated the applicants and was 'a situation which could have thus had a chilling effect and discouraged them from pursuing activities within the first applicant trade union, including organising or taking part in similar meetings'.[133]

Interference with freedom of association

Associations of individuals for various legitimate purposes should be able to be formed and to operate informally. Nevertheless, there may be important advantages for such associations in obtaining a form of legal status. Thus, 'the ability to establish a legal entity in order to act collectively in a field of mutual interest is one of the most important aspects of freedom of association, without which that right would be deprived of any meaning'.[134] The refusal of government authorities to recognize an association as a legal entity may constitute an interference with freedom of association.[135] Violations of freedom of association have arisen because of government-imposed requirements that associations be registered.[136]

Official registration may be crucial to the ability of an organization to function properly. Without legal entity status, the association may be deprived of grants as well as the possibility of receiving financial donations and of engaging in charitable activities. Significant delays in obtaining legal entity status may amount to an interference with article 11.[137] Recognition as a legal entity may also be necessary for an association to own or rent property, to maintain bank accounts, to hire employees, and to ensure judicial

---

[130] *Alekseyev v. Russia*, nos 4916/07, 25924/08, and 14599/09, § 62, 21 October 2010; *Gorzelik and Others v. Poland* [GC], no. 44158/98, § 92, ECHR 2004-I.

[131] *Zhechev v. Bulgaria*, no. 57045/00, § 35, 21 June 2007; *Tebieti Mühafize Cemiyyeti and Israfilov v. Azerbaijan*, no. 37083/03, § 53, ECHR 2009.

[132] *Gorzelik and Others v. Poland* [GC], no. 44158/98, § 92, ECHR 2004-I; *Bekir-Ousta and Others v. Greece*, no. 35151/05, § 36, 11 October 2007.

[133] *Trade Union of the Police in the Slovak Republic and Others v. Slovakia*, no. 11828/08, §§ 60–61, 25 September 2012.

[134] *Church of Scientology Moscow v. Russia*, no. 18147/02, § 81, 5 April 2007; *Bozgan v. Romania*, no. 35097/02, § 19, 11 October 2007; *IPSD and Others v. Turkey*, no. 35832/97, § 35, 25 October 2005; *Sidiropoulos and Others v. Greece*, 10 July 1998, § 40, *Reports of Judgments and Decisions* 1998-IV.

[135] *Gorzelik and Others v. Poland* [GC], no. 44158/98, § 52, ECHR 2004-I; *Sidiropoulos and Others v. Greece*, 10 July 1998, § 31, *Reports of Judgments and Decisions* 1998-IV; *Partidul Comunistilor (Nepeceristi) and Ungureanu v. Romania*, no. 46626/99, § 27, ECHR 2005-I (extracts); *The United Macedonian Organisation Ilinden and Others v. Bulgaria*, no. 59491/00, § 53, 19 January 2006; *Tsonev v. Bulgaria*, no. 45963/99, § 43, 13 April 2006; *Ramazanova and Others v. Azerbaijan*, no. 44363/02, § 60, 1 February 2007; *Bozgan v. Romania*, no. 35097/02, § 19, 11 October 2007.

[136] *Zhechev v. Bulgaria*, no. 57045/00, § 37, 21 June 2007.

[137] *Ramazanova and Others v. Azerbaijan*, no. 44363/02, §§ 58–61, 1 February 2007.

protection of the community, its members, and its assets.[138] In the case of religious organizations, registration may be essential for entitlements such as the right to establish places of worship, to hold religious services in places accessible to the public, to the production and distribution of religious literature, to the creation of educational institutions, and to the maintenance of contacts for international exchanges and conferences.[139]

Several cases in Russia have resulted from the 1997 Religions Act by which organizations previously benefitting from legal-entity status were required to amend their founding documents and 're-register' within a specific period of time, failing which they could be dissolved by judicial decision. For the Court, this was an interference with article 11.[140] The Court rejected the argument of the government that a religious organization could not claim to be the victim of a violation of freedom of association because it had not been dissolved and had retained its status as a legal entity. The issue was whether the body could be re-registered. The Court said that 'even in the absence of prejudice and damage, the religious association may claim to be a "victim" since the refusal of re-registration directly affected its legal position'.[141]

Where an organization exists already, its dissolution constitutes an interference with freedom of association.[142] The Committee of Ministers has recommended to Member States that '[t]he legal personality of [non-governmental organisations (NGOs)] can only be terminated pursuant to the voluntary act of their members—or in the case of non-membership-based NGOs, its governing body—or in the event of bankruptcy, prolonged inactivity or serious misconduct'.[143] The termination of an NGO 'should only be ordered by a court where there is compelling evidence that the grounds specified . . . above have been met. Such an order should be subject to prompt appeal.'[144]

Article 11 may be infringed when measures impact upon individuals because of their membership in an association. For example, the ability of an association to attract members, or its image and prestige, may be challenged. An Italian masonic lodge successfully argued against a requirement that public employees declare that they are not its members constituted an interference with freedom of association. The Court said this had the consequence either of discouraging membership or of imposing an unfair hardship on those who remained members because they were denied the possibility of public employment.[145] Legislation in Turkey required official authorization from the Interior Ministry for members of associations to travel abroad. When members of an association did so without permission, their organization was dissolved by the courts.

---

[138] *Koretsky and Others v. Ukraine*, no. 40269/02, § 40, 3 April 2008; *Jehovah's Witnesses of Moscow v. Russia*, no. 302/02, § 102, 10 June 2010.

[139] *Jehovah's Witnesses of Moscow v. Russia*, no. 302/02, § 102, 10 June 2010.

[140] *Church of Scientology Moscow v. Russia*, no. 18147/02, §§ 83–85, 5 April 2007; *Moscow Branch of the Salvation Army v. Russia*, no. 72881/01, §§ 64–65, ECHR 2006-XI; *Jehovah's Witnesses of Moscow v. Russia*, no. 302/02, § 173, 10 June 2010.

[141] *Church of Scientology Moscow v. Russia*, no. 18147/02, §§ 77–80, 5 April 2007.

[142] *United Communist Party of Turkey and Others v. Turkey*, 30 January 1998, §§ 32–34, *Reports of Judgments and Decisions* 1998-I; *Association Rhino and Others v. Switzerland*, no. 48848/07, § 44–45, 11 October 2011.

[143] Recommendation CM/Rec(2007)14 of the Committee of Ministers to member States on the legal status of non-governmental organisations in Europe, para. 44. Cited in *Tebieti Mühafize Cemiyyeti and Israfilov v. Azerbaijan*, no. 37083/03, § 39, ECHR 2009.

[144] Recommendation CM/Rec(2007)14 of the Committee of Ministers to member States on the legal status of non-governmental organisations in Europe, para. 72. See also *Association Rhino and Others v. Switzerland*, no. 48848/07, § 62, 11 October 2011.

[145] *Grande Oriente d'Italia di Palazzo Giustiniani v. Italy*, no. 35972/97, § 135, ECHR 2001-VIII.

Noting that similar legislation did not exist in other Council of Europe States, the Court found this to be an interference with article 11.[146] Article 11 also restricts the possibility of penalizing past membership in a political party.[147]

Associations are in principle entitled to choose their members and to exclude those whom they do not accept. A British trade union was successful in challenging a tribunal decision ordering it to accept as a member someone affiliated with the British National Party, an extreme right wing and racist formation. The applicable legislation prohibited a trade union from expelling an individual based solely upon that person's membership in a political party. The Court stated that it had 'some sympathy with the notion that any worker should be able to join a trade union'. At the same time, it noted that:

[h]istorically, trade unions in the United Kingdom, and elsewhere in Europe, were, and though perhaps to a lesser extent today are, commonly affiliated to political parties or movements, particularly those on the left. They are not bodies solely devoted to politically-neutral aspects of the well-being of their members, but are often ideological, with strongly held views on social and political issues.

The Court concluded that there had been a violation of article 11 because the law prevented the trade union from excluding someone from membership based upon political opinion.[148]

Freedom of association has a negative dimension in that it protects the right of a person not to be required to join an association.[149] Although 'compulsion to join a particular trade union may not always be contrary to the Convention', forms of pressure that strike at the very substance of freedom of association would constitute an interference with article 11.[150] In this respect, 'regard must also be had in this context to the fact that the protection of personal opinions guaranteed by Articles 9 and 10 of the Convention is one of the purposes of the guarantee of freedom of association, and that such protection can only be effectively secured through the guarantee of both a positive and a negative right to freedom of association'.[151] Personal autonomy, which is described as 'an important principle underlying the interpretation of the Convention guarantees' supports the individual's freedom of choice that is 'implicit in Article 11 and confirmation of the importance of the negative aspect of that provision'.[152]

---

[146] *İzmir Savaşa Karşıtları Derneği and Others v. Turkey*, no. 46257/99, § 32, 2 March 2006.

[147] *Ždanoka v. Latvia* [GC], no. 58278/00, Partly Dissenting Opinion of Judges Spielmann and Jaeger, § 5, ECHR 2006-IV.

[148] *Associated Society of Locomotive Engineers and Firemen (ASLEF) v. the United Kingdom*, no. 11002/05, §§ 47–53, 27 February 2007.

[149] *Sigurður A. Sigurjónsson v. Iceland*, 30 June 1993, § 35, Series A no. 264.

[150] *Vörður Ólafsson v. Iceland*, no. 20161/06, § 45, ECHR 2010; *Gustafsson v. Sweden*, 25 April 1996, § 45, Reports of Judgments and Decisions 1996-II; *Young, James, and Webster v. the United Kingdom*, 13 August 1981, § 55, Series A no. 44; *Sigurður A. Sigurjónsson v. Iceland*, 30 June 1993, § 36, Series A no. 264; *Sørensen and Rasmussen v. Denmark* [GC], nos 52562/99 and 52620/99, § 54, ECHR 2006-I.

[151] *Sørensen and Rasmussen v. Denmark* [GC], nos 52562/99 and 52620/99, § 54, ECHR 2006-I; *Chassagnou and Others v. France* [GC], nos 25088/94, 28331/95, and 28443/95, § 103, ECHR 1999-III; *Young, James, and Webster v. the United Kingdom*, 13 August 1981, § 57, Series A no. 44; *Sigurður A. Sigurjónsson v. Iceland*, 30 June 1993, § 37, Series A no. 264.

[152] *Sørensen and Rasmussen v. Denmark* [GC], nos 52562/99 and 52620/99, § 54, ECHR 2006-I.

Political parties

Political parties possess a special place within the guarantee of freedom of association because of their central role in the functioning of democratic government. The Grand Chamber has spoken of 'the primordial role played in a democratic regime by political parties enjoying the freedoms and rights enshrined in Article 11 and also in Article 10 of the Convention'.[153] But 'even more persuasive than the wording of Article 11, in the Court's view, is the fact that political parties are a form of association essential to the proper functioning of democracy. In view of the importance of democracy in the Convention system ... there can be no doubt that political parties come within the scope of Article 11.'[154] Indeed, democracy is central to the entire vision of the European Convention on Human Rights.

That is apparent, firstly, from the Preamble to the Convention, which establishes a very clear connection between the Convention and democracy by stating that the maintenance and further realisation of human rights and fundamental freedoms are best ensured on the one hand by an effective political democracy and on the other by a common understanding and observance of human rights ... The Preamble goes on to affirm that European countries have a common heritage of political tradition, ideals, freedom and the rule of law. The Court has observed that in that common heritage are to be found the underlying values of the Convention ... ; it has pointed out several times that the Convention was designed to maintain and promote the ideals and values of a democratic society ...

In addition, Articles 8, 9, 10 and 11 of the Convention require that interference with the exercise of the rights they enshrine must be assessed by the yardstick of what is 'necessary in a democratic society'. The only type of necessity capable of justifying an interference with any of those rights is, therefore, one which may claim to spring from 'democratic society'. Democracy thus appears to be the only political model contemplated by the Convention and, accordingly, the only one compatible with it.[155]

Political parties have an 'essential role in ensuring pluralism', without which 'there can be no democracy'.[156] Moreover, 'the notion of "democratic society" is devoid of any meaning if there is no pluralism, tolerance or open-mindedness'.[157] Pluralism is built on 'the genuine recognition of, and respect for, diversity and the dynamics of traditions and of ethnic and cultural identities, religious beliefs, artistic, literary and socio-economic ideas and concepts'.[158] Moreover, '[t]he harmonious interaction of persons and groups with varied identities is essential for achieving social cohesion'.[159] However, '[p]luralism and democracy are based on a compromise that requires various concessions by

---

[153] *Refah Partisi (the Welfare Party) and Others v. Turkey* [GC], nos 41340/98, 41342/98, 41343/98, and 41344/98, § 87, ECHR 2003-II; *Linkov v. the Czech Republic*, no. 10504/03, § 34, 7 December 2006; *Redfearn v. the United Kingdom*, no. 47335/06, § 55, 6 November 2012.

[154] *United Communist Party of Turkey and Others v. Turkey*, 30 January 1998, § 25, *Reports of Judgments and Decisions* 1998-I; *Ouranio Toxo and Others v. Greece*, no. 74989/01, § 34, ECHR 2005-X (extracts).

[155] *United Communist Party of Turkey and Others v. Turkey*, 30 January 1998, § 45. *Reports of Judgments and Decisions* 1998–I.

[156] *Refah Partisi (the Welfare Party) and Others v. Turkey* [GC], nos 41340/98, 41342/98, 41343/98, and 41344/98, §§ 88–89, ECHR 2003-II; *Partidul Comunistilor (Nepeceristi) and Ungureanu v. Romania*, no. 46626/99, § 45, ECHR 2005-I (extracts).

[157] *Ouranio Toxo and Others v. Greece*, no. 74989/01, § 35, ECHR 2005-X (extracts).

[158] *Gorzelik and Others v. Poland* [GC], no. 44158/98, § 92, ECHR 2004-I.

[159] *Ouranio Toxo and Others v. Greece*, no. 74989/01, § 35, ECHR 2005-X (extracts).

individuals or groups of individuals, who must sometimes agree to limit some of the freedoms they enjoy in order to guarantee greater stability of the country as a whole'.[160]

Because of the role played by political parties within democratic political systems, measures taken against them affect not only freedom of association but democracy as such:

It is in the nature of the role they play that political parties, the only bodies which can come to power, also have the capacity to influence the whole of the regime in their countries. By the proposals for an overall societal model which they put before the electorate and by their capacity to implement those proposals once they come to power, political parties differ from other organisations which intervene in the political arena.[161]

In a case involving dissolution of a political party because it failed to maintain minimum requirements for the number of members, the Court was not impressed with the government's claim that the party was entitled to reorganize itself into an association. This was 'a legal shape its founders and members did not seek', and the solution 'would reduce the freedom of association of the founders and members so as to render it either non-existent or of no practical value'.[162] The Court noted the uniqueness of political parties and their position as the only actors capable of nominating candidates for election.

In several European states, minimum membership requirements are imposed upon political parties. In Russia, where the requirements are the highest in Europe, a political party that was not alleged to have encouraged violence or otherwise acted so as to undermine the democratic and pluralist system, or to pursue racist objectives, was dissolved because it did not comply with requirements of minimum membership and regional representation. The Court said it was not convinced by the justifications provided, namely that the condition was necessary 'to strengthen political parties and limit their number in order to avoid disproportionate expenditure from the budget during electoral campaigns and prevent excessive parliamentary fragmentation and, in so doing, promote stability of the political system'.[163] It rejected the financial argument, noting that no support was given to marginal parties if they failed to get 3 per cent of the vote, and that 'financial considerations cannot serve as a justification for limiting the number of political parties and allowing the survival of large, popular parties only'.[164] The Court viewed the fragmentation argument as being overly protective of large political parties, noting that 'small minority groups must also have an opportunity to establish political parties and participate in elections with the aim of obtaining parliamentary representation ... [D]emocracy does not simply mean that the views of the majority must always prevail.'[165]

The Russian legislation also required that political parties demonstrate a minimum number of regional branches. The apparent purpose of the measure was to discourage regional parties that might threaten the country's unity and territorial activity.[166] The Court noted that 'there can be no justification for hindering a public association or political party solely because it seeks to debate in public the situation of part of the State's

---

[160] *Refah Partisi (the Welfare Party) and Others v. Turkey* [GC], nos 41340/98, 41342/98, 41343/98, and 41344/98, § 99, ECHR 2003-II.

[161] Ibid., § 87.

[162] *Republican Party of Russia v. Russia*, no. 12976/07, § 105, 12 April 2011. Also *Zhechev v. Bulgaria*, no. 57045/00, § 56, 21 June 2007.

[163] *Republican Party of Russia v. Russia*, no. 12976/07, § 111, 12 April 2011.

[164] Ibid., § 112.

[165] Ibid., § 114.

[166] Ibid., § 123.

population, or even advocates separatist ideas by calling for autonomy or requesting secession of part of the country's territory'.[167] The Court said that a review of practice in Council of Europe states showed a consensus allowing the establishment of regional parties, although it has accepted that 'a different approach may be justified where special historical or political considerations exist which render a more restrictive practice necessary'.[168] For example, it did not exclude the claim that in the immediate aftermath of the disintegration of the Soviet Union, some restriction on regional political parties might have been justifiable at the time.[169] In making the assessment, the historical context is important.[170]

Many States have legislation concerning the funding of political parties and this may have an impact upon freedom of association.[171] Legislation that prevented a French-based political party associated with the Spanish Basque Nationalist Party receiving funding from foreign legal entities was recognized as an interference with article 11.[172] The Conseil d'État had concluded that the legislation was intended to 'preclude the possibility of creating a relationship of dependency which would be detrimental to the expression of national sovereignty'. The Court therefore held that the aim was protection of the 'institutional order'.[173] It said it had no difficulty accepting a prohibition on funding by foreign States in order to preserve national sovereignty, but the same rationale did not seem valid with respect to foreign political parties.[174]

Trade unions

The right to form and join trade unions is specifically mentioned in article 11(1). The language derives from the Universal Declaration of Human Rights and recognizes that '[e]veryone has the right to form and to join trade unions for the protection of his interests', although this appears in a provision dealing with the rights of workers rather than with freedom of association.[175] The Court has treated the right to form and join trade unions as 'a special aspect of freedom of association which also protects, first and foremost, against State action',[176] while nevertheless insisting that '[t]he essential object of Article 11 is to protect the individual against arbitrary interference by public authorities

---

[167] Ibid.

[168] Ibid., § 126; *Tănase v. Moldova* [GC], no. 7/08, § 172, ECHR 2010.

[169] *Republican Party of Russia v. Russia*, no. 12976/07, § 127, 12 April 2011.

[170] *Refah Partisi (the Welfare Party) and Others v. Turkey* [GC], nos 41340/98, 41342/98, 41343/98, and 41344/98, § 104, ECHR 2003-II; *Partidul Comunistilor (Nepeceristi) and Ungureanu v. Romania*, no. 46626/99, § 48, ECHR 2005-I (extracts).

[171] Within the Council of Europe, there are relevant materials from the Venice Commission (Guidelines and Report on the Financing of Political Parties) and the Committee of Ministers (Recommendation Rec(2003) 4 of 8 April 2003 on common rules against corruption in the funding of political parties and electoral campaigns).

[172] *Parti nationaliste basque—Organisation régionale d'Iparralde v. France*, no. 71251/01, §§ 37–38, ECHR 2007-II.

[173] Ibid., § 43.

[174] Ibid., § 47. See, however, *Parti nationaliste basque—Organisation régionale d'Iparralde v. France*, no. 71251/01, Dissenting Opinion of Judge Rozakis, ECHR 2007-II.

[175] Universal Declaration of Human Rights, GA Res. 217 A (III), UN Doc. A/810, art. 23(4).

[176] *Young, James, and Webster v. the United Kingdom*, 13 August 1981, § 52, Series A no. 44; *Vörður Ólafsson v. Iceland*, no. 20161/06, § 45, ECHR 2010; *National Union of Belgian Police v. Belgium*, 27 October 1975, § 38, Series A no. 19; *Swedish Engine Drivers' Union v. Sweden*, 6 February 1976, § 39, Series A no. 20; *Demir and Baykara v. Turkey* [GC], no. 34503/97, § 109, ECHR 2008.

with the exercise of the rights protected'.[177] Article 11 'safeguards freedom to protect the occupational interests of trade union members by trade union action, the conduct and development of which the Contracting States must both permit and make possible'.[178] Attention is drawn to the words 'for the protection of his interests' in article 11(1) of the Convention. These words are 'not redundant' and are deemed to safeguard 'freedom to protect the occupational interests of trade-union members by trade-union action, the conduct and development of which the Contracting States must both permit and make possible'.[179] The case law has identified three 'essential elements' of freedom of association in the context of trade union activities: the right to form and join a trade union;[180] the prohibition of closed-shop agreements;[181] and the right for a trade union to seek to persuade the employer to hear what it has to say on behalf of its members.[182] The Grand Chamber has explained that the list is not finite but is 'subject to evolution depending on particular developments in labour relations'.[183]

Pointing to the more detailed provisions concerning trade unions in the European Social Charter of 1961, the Court has insisted that article 11(1) 'does not secure any particular treatment of trade unions, or their members, by the State, such as the right that the State should conclude any given collective agreement with them'. In its early case law, the Court said such a right is not 'indispensable for the effective enjoyment of trade union freedom' nor is it 'an element necessarily inherent in a right guaranteed by the Convention'.[184] Later, it took a more nuanced view: 'even if collective bargaining was not indispensable for the effective enjoyment of trade-union freedom, it might be one of the ways by which trade unions could be enabled to protect their members' interests. The union had to be free, in one way or another, to seek to persuade the employer to listen to what it had to say.'[185]

The Court found the legislative framework of labour relations within the United Kingdom to be inadequate to the extent that employers were not required to recognize trade unions and could provide financial incentives to employees who would agree not to be represented by the relevant union. The Court explained that a corollary of this was authorization under United Kingdom law to treat less favourably employees who were not prepared to renounce a freedom that was an essential feature of union membership. 'Such conduct constituted a disincentive or restraint on the use by employees of union membership to protect their interests', it said.[186] Thus, 'by permitting employers to use financial incentives to induce employees to surrender important union rights, the

---

[177] *Associated Society of Locomotive Engineers and Firemen (ASLEF) v. the United Kingdom*, no. 11002/05, § 37, 27 February 2007.

[178] *Sindicatul 'Păstorul cel Bun' v. Romania*, no. 2330/09, § 58, 31 January 2012; *Demir and Baykara v. Turkey* [GC], no. 34503/97, § 140, ECHR 2008; *National Union of Belgian Police v. Belgium*, 27 October 1975, §§ 39–40, Series A no. 19; *Swedish Engine Drivers' Union v. Sweden*, 6 February 1976, §§ 40–41, Series A no. 20; *Schmidt and Dahlström v. Sweden*, 6 February 1976, § 36, Series A no. 21.

[179] *Tüm Haber Sen and Çınar v. Turkey*, no. 28602/95, § 28, ECHR 2006-II.

[180] Ibid., §§ 30–32.

[181] *Sørensen and Rasmussen v. Denmark* [GC], nos. 52562/99 and 52620/99, §§ 75–77, ECHR 2006-I.

[182] *Wilson, National Union of Journalists and Others v. the United Kingdom*, nos 30668/96, 30671/96, and 30678/96, § 44, ECHR 2002-V.

[183] *Demir and Baykara v. Turkey* [GC], no. 34503/97, § 146, ECHR 2008.

[184] *Swedish Engine Drivers' Union v. Sweden*, 6 February 1976, § 39, Series A no. 20.

[185] *Wilson, National Union of Journalists and Others v. the United Kingdom*, nos 30668/96, 30671/96, and 30678/96, § 44, ECHR 2002-V; *Demir and Baykara v. Turkey* [GC], no. 34503/97, § 143, ECHR 2008.

[186] *Wilson, National Union of Journalists and Others v. the United Kingdom*, nos 30668/96, 30671/96, and 30678/96, § 47.

respondent State has failed in its positive obligation to secure the enjoyment of the rights under Article 11 of the Convention. This failure amounted to a violation of Article 11, as regards both the applicant trade unions and the individual applicants.'[187]

The Court's refusal to recognize collective bargaining as a component of article 11 remained controversial and eventually, in 2008, led to a reversal of its case law. In a Turkish case, the Grand Chamber stated:

[T]he Court considers that, having regard to the developments in labour law, both international and national, and to the practice of Contracting States in such matters, the right to bargain collectively with the employer has, in principle, become one of the essential elements of the 'right to form and to join trade unions for the protection of [one's] interests' set forth in Article 11 of the Convention, it being understood that States remain free to organise their system so as, if appropriate, to grant special status to representative trade unions.[188]

A 'closed shop' is 'an undertaking or workplace in which, as a result of an agreement or arrangement between one or more trade unions and one or more employers or employers' associations, employees of a certain class are in practice required to be or become members of a specified union. The employer is not under any legal obligation to consult or obtain the consent of individual employees directly before such an agreement or arrangement is put into effect.'[189] Undoubtedly influenced by the strong position of industrial and trade unions, particularly in the social-democratic parties present in the Consultative Assembly, as well as in some Western European governments at the time the European Convention of Human Rights was being prepared, the drafters of the Convention deliberately excluded a provision equivalent to that found in article 20(2) of the Universal Declaration of Human Rights, which affirms that 'no one may be compelled to belong to an association'. The issue of the 'closed shop' is directly addressed in the *travaux préparatoires* of the Convention. The report of the 19 June 1950 meeting of the Conference of Senior Officials states: 'On account of the difficulties raised by the "closed shop system" in certain countries, the Conference in this connection considered it undesirable to intro-duce into the Convention a rule under which "no one may be compelled to belong to an association" which features in [Article 20 § 2] of the United Nations Universal Declar-ation.'[190] This passage has generated much debate and no consensus before the Court.[191] According to one individual opinion, '[t]he "travaux préparatoires" of the Convention—which anyway are not conclusive—speak only of "undesirability" and so do not enable one to conclude that the negative aspect of trade union freedom was intended to be excluded from the ambit of Article 11'.[192] Nevertheless, the case law is quite clear that

---

[187]   Ibid., § 48.

[188]   *Demir and Baykara v. Turkey* [GC], no. 34503/97, § 154, ECHR 2008.

[189]   *Young, James, and Webster v. the United Kingdom,* 13 August 1981, § 13, Series A no. 44.

[190]   Report of 19 June 1950 of the Conference of Senior Officials, Collected Edition of the *travaux préparatoires*, vol. IV, p. 262.

[191]   *Young, James, and Webster v. the United Kingdom,* 13 August 1981, § 51, Series A no. 44; Ibid., Dissenting Opinion of Judge Sørensen, Joined by Judges Thór, Vilhjálmsson, and Lagergren, § 2; *Sørensen and Rasmussen v. Denmark* [GC], nos 52562/99 and 52620/99, § 33, ECHR 2006-I; *Sørensen and Rasmussen v. Denmark* [GC], nos 52562/99 and 52620/99, Dissenting Opinion of Judge Lorenzen, § 2, ECHR 2006-I.

[192]   Ibid., Concurring Opinion of Judges Ganshof van der Meersch, Bindschedler-Robert, Liesch, Gölcüklü, Matscher, Pinheiro Farinha, and Pettiti.

closed-shop agreements whereby a monopoly is granted to one trade union as a repre-sentative of employees are not permitted.[193]

In some legal systems, an individual may not be required to join the trade union but must nevertheless contribute financially to it, either directly or indirectly. According to one decision, 'the imposition on non-union members of an obligation to pay fees to a trade union and Government measures entailing favouritism towards or discrimination against a trade union may in certain circumstances be considered incompatible with the right to organise and the right to join an organisation of one's own choosing'.[194]

There is no explicit right to strike in the European Convention, nor has the Court considered it to be implied by article 11(1). According to the Court, '[t]here is no express inclusion of a right to strike or an obligation on employers to engage in collective bargaining. At most, Article 11 may be regarded as safeguarding the freedom of trade unions to protect the occupational interests of their members.'[195] The Court has said that while 'the ability to strike represents one of the most important of the means by which trade unions can fulfil this function, there are others'.[196] A right to strike is set out in other international human rights and labour instruments, such as the International Covenant on Economic, Social and Cultural Rights, where it is explicit,[197] and International Labour Organisation Convention No. 87, where it has been deemed incorporated by interpret-ation as something inherent in the right to organize.[198] Article 28 of the European Union's Charter of Fundamental Rights provides: 'Workers and employers, or their respective organisations, have, in accordance with Community law and national laws and practices, the right to negotiate and conclude collective agreements at the appropriate levels and, in cases of conflicts of interest, to take collective action to defend their interests, including strike action.' In a recent judgment, the Court referred to the importance of these international law sources for the construction of article 11, stating that it would be 'inconsistent for the Court to adopt in relation to Article 11 an interpretation of the scope of freedom of association of trade unions that is much narrower than that which prevails in international law'.[199] Accordingly, the Court said, 'the taking of secondary industrial action by a trade union, including strike action, against one employer in order to further a

---

[193] *Demir and Baykara v. Turkey* [GC], no. 34503/97, § 145, ECHR 2008; *Sørensen and Rasmussen v. Denmark* [GC], nos 52562/99 and 52620/99, § 54, ECHR 2006-I. For dissenting views on this difficult and controversial issue, see the opinions of Judges Rozakis, Bratza, Vajić, Zupančič, and Lorenzen in *Sørensen and Rasmussen v. Denmark* [GC], nos 52562/99 and 52620/99, Joint Partly Dissenting Opinion of Judges Rozakis, Bratza, and Vajić, ECHR 2006-I.

[194] *Vörður Ólafsson v. Iceland*, no. 20161/06, § 53, ECHR 2010.

[195] *UNISON v. the United Kingdom* (dec.), no. 53574/99, ECHR 2002-I.

[196] Ibid. Also *Wilson, National Union of Journalists and Others v. the United Kingdom*, nos 30668/96, 30671/96, and 30678/96, § 45, ECHR 2002-V; *Schmidt and Dahlström v. Sweden*, 6 February 1976, § 36, Series A no. 21; *Enerji Yapı-Yol Sen v. Turkey*, no. 68959/01, § 28, 21 April 2009.

[197] (1976) 993 UNTS 3, art. 8(1)(d). On the right to strike and international law, see *Hrvatski liječnički sindikat v. Croatia*, no. 36701/09, Concurring Opinion of Judge Pinto de Albuquerque, §§ 3–6, 27 November 2014.

[198] Report of the Committee of Experts on the Application of Conventions and Recommendations, ILC, 43rd Session, 1959, Part I, Report III, pp. 114–15, relying upon International Labour Organisation Convention No. 87 on Freedom of Association and Protection of the Right to Organise, (1950) 68 UNTS 17, arts 3, 8, and 10.

[199] *National Union of Rail, Maritime, and Transport Workers v. the United Kingdom*, no. 31045/10, § 76, 8 April 2014. See also *Hrvatski liječnički sindikat v. Croatia*, no. 36701/09, Concurring Opinion of Judge Pinto de Albuquerque, § 9, 27 November 2014.

dispute in which the union's members are engaged with another employer must be regarded as part of trade union activity covered by Article 11'.[200]

No distinction is made between the State as the instrument of public power and the State as employer; those who work for the State are entitled to the same freedom of assembly as those who work in the private sector.[201] If confirmation is required, this is made apparent in the final words of article 11(2).

Restrictions on freedom of peaceful assembly and of association

Like articles 8, 9, and 10 of the Convention, article 11 contains a second paragraph setting out the scope of permissible restrictions on freedom of peaceful assembly and association. Article 11(2) is the longest of the four restriction clauses in the Convention, mainly because of the final sentence of paragraph 2 dealing with limitations on freedom of association in the armed forces and the police. The term 'restrictions' as it is used in article 11(2) may apply to measures taken before an assembly, during an assembly, and after it, for example punitive measures.[202] Such restrictions are only acceptable to the extent that they are prescribed by law, pursue a legitimate aim listed in article 11(2), and are deemed necessary in a democratic society.

The ancestor of the restrictions and limitations clauses is article 29(2) of the Universal Declaration of Human Rights: 'In the exercise of his rights and freedoms, everyone shall be subject only to such limitations as are determined by law solely for the purpose of securing due recognition and respect for the rights and freedoms of others and of meeting the just requirements of morality, public order and the general welfare in a democratic society.' The limitations clause in the Universal Declaration applies generally to all rights set out in the instrument, whereas the specific clauses of this nature in the European Convention, of which article 11(2) is an example, are tailored to the right at issue.

The restriction clauses in the International Covenant on Civil and Political Rights are similar to article 11(2). There are two separate provisions, one dealing with freedom of peaceful and assembly and the other with freedom of association.[203] Where the European Convention speaks of 'the prevention of disorder or crime' the Covenant refers to 'public order (*ordre public*)'. The Covenant also allows lawful restrictions on members of the armed forces and the police, but it does not extend this to the administration of the State. Also, the Covenant's freedom of association provision contains an additional paragraph: 'Nothing in this article shall authorize States Parties to the International Labour Organisation Convention of 1948 concerning Freedom of Association and Protection of the Right to Organize to take legislative measures which would prejudice, or to apply the law in such a manner as to prejudice the guarantees provided for in that Convention.'[204] Article 11(2) of the European Convention is also more extensive than the restriction

---

[200] National Union of Rail, Maritime, and Transport Workers v. the United Kingdom, no. 31045/10, § 77, 8 April 2014.

[201] *Tüm Haber Sen and Çınar v. Turkey,* no. 28602/95, § 29, ECHR 2006-II; *Demir and Baykara v. Turkey* [GC], no. 34503/97, § 109, ECHR 2008; *Swedish Engine Drivers' Union v. Sweden,* 6 February 1976, § 37, Series A no. 20.

[202] *Sergey Kuznetsov v. Russia,* no. 10877/04, § 35, 23 October 2008; *Ezelin v. France,* 26 April 1991, § 39, Series A no. 202.

[203] International Covenant on Civil and Political Rights, (1976) 999 UNTS 171, arts 21, 22(2).

[204] Ibid., art. 22(3).

clauses dealing with labour rights in the International Covenant on Economic, Social and Cultural Rights.[205]

Prescribed by law

It is a preliminary condition for any restriction upon freedom of peaceful assembly that the interference be 'prescribed by law'. The restriction must be authorized by a rule recognized in the national legal order. This includes 'written law', including various forms of delegated legislation, and unwritten law as interpreted and applied by the courts.[206] But there is also a qualitative requirement for the legal rule. It must be accessible and foreseeable and be formulated with sufficient precision to enable the citizen to regulate his or her conduct.[207] Factors such as a failure by national courts to refer to a legal provision in support of the interference and inconsistencies between the legislation itself and case law may inform the Court's conclusion that the measure is not prescribed by law.[208] If the law grants discretion to public authorities, it must be framed with sufficient clarity and specify the manner in which it is to be exercised.[209] Accordingly, the domestic law must provide protection against arbitrary interference by the authorities with rights that are enshrined in the Convention. This is fundamental to the rule of law, a seminal concept that is basic to democratic governance.

If the Court determines that there is no legal authorization for a restriction on freedom of assembly, it will conclude there has been a breach of article 11 without further consideration of the proportionality. Where the participation of a Turkish Cypriot in bi-communal meetings was stymied by the denial of permits to cross the green line into southern Cyprus, the Court concluded that there was no law applicable to the issuance of permits.[210] Measures preventing meetings and a march to promote equality for gays were not founded on legal provisions.[211] In a case concerning the Non-governmental Organisation Act in force in Azerbaijan, the Court raised serious questions about the foreseeability of the law in question, notably because it allowed for warnings by the Ministry of Justice that activities were 'incompatible with the objectives' of the legislation. This could result in the dissolution of an association. The Court did not reach a definitive conclusion on the issue, however.[212]

---

[205] International Covenant on Economic, Social, and Cultural Rights, (1976) 993 UNTS 3, arts. 8(1)(a), (c). See *Hrvatski liječnički sindikat v. Croatia*, no. 36701/09, Concurring Opinion of Judge Pinto de Albuquerque, § 9, fn. 32, 27 November 2014, with the references to Matthew Craven, *The International Covenant on Economic, Social and Cultural Rights, A Perspective on its Development*, Oxford: Clarendon Press, 1995, p. 258 and Ben Saul, David Kinley, and Jaqueline Mowbray, *The International Covenant on Economic, Social and Cultural Rights, Commentary, Cases and Materials*, Oxford: Oxford University Press, 2014, p. 581.

[206] *Leyla Şahin v. Turkey* [GC], no. 44774/98, § 88, ECHR 2005-XI; *Sanoma Uitgevers B.V. v. the Netherlands* [GC], no. 38224/03, § 83, 14 September 2010.

[207] *Rekvényi v. Hungary* [GC], no. 25390/94, § 34, ECHR 1999-III; *Mkrtchyan v. Armenia*, no. 6562/03, § 39, 11 January 2007; *Association of Citizens Radko and Paunkovski v. 'the former Yugoslav Republic of Macedonia'*, no. 74651/01, § 64, ECHR 2009 (extracts); *Gorzelik and Others v. Poland* [GC], no. 44158/98, § 64, ECHR 2004-I; *N.F. v. Italy*, no. 37119/97, § 29, ECHR 2001-IX.

[208] *Mkrtchyan v. Armenia*, no. 6562/03, §§ 39–43, 11 January 2007.

[209] *The Sunday Times v. the United Kingdom (no. 1)*, 26 April 1979, § 49, Series A no. 30; *Tolstoy Miloslavsky v. the United Kingdom*, 13 July 1995, § 37, Series A no. 316-B; *Rotaru v. Romania* [GC], no. 28341/95, § 52, ECHR 2000-V; *Hasan and Chaush v. Bulgaria* [GC], no. 30985/96, § 84, ECHR 2000-XI; *Maestri v. Italy* [GC], no. 39748/98, § 30, ECHR 2004-I.

[210] *Djavit An v. Turkey*, no. 20652/92, § 67, ECHR 2003-III.

[211] *Bączkowski and Others v. Poland*, no. 1543/06, §§ 69–73, 3 May 2007.

[212] *Tebieti Mühafize Cemiyyeti and Israfilov v. Azerbaijan*, no. 37083/03, §§ 60–65, ECHR 2009.

The Court held that the 'prescribed by law' requirement was not met when the authorities failed to register an association within time limits set by the legislation. The law did not specify with sufficient precision the consequences of this failure to respond within the legal time limits, in effect enabling an arbitrary prolongation of the registration procedure. As a result, 'the law did not afford the applicants sufficient legal protection against the arbitrary actions of the Ministry of Justice'.[213] Russian law governing the requirements for amending the State Register of political parties did not provide applications with sufficient provision enabling them to foresee which documents they would need to submit and the adverse consequences if the submission as deemed defective by the authorities.[214] By declining to provide a religious institution with clear reasons for the rejection of its application for re-registration, the Court said the Moscow Justice Department had 'acted in an arbitrary manner'[215] and breached an express requirement of domestic law that such refusal should be reasoned.[216] Russian authorities also denied registration to the Salvation Army, invoking a legal provision that prohibited foreign nationals from being founders of a Russian religious institution. But the Court did not find this to be the case and said the refusal of registration had 'no legal foundation'.[217]

In a case dealing with disciplinary action taken against a judge who belonged to a legal Masonic lodge, the Court said that legislation prohibiting membership of secret associations was insufficient to meet the foreseeability requirement.[218] In another Italian case involving the secret masonic lodge known as P2, the Court said that disciplinary provisions concerning judges were not sufficiently foreseeable. A general text imposed punishment upon a judge who 'fails to fulfil his duties'. Guidelines adopted by the National Council of the Judiciary addressed the issue of membership in masonic lodges, saying that this 'raises delicate problems'. The Court concluded that the guidelines were 'not sufficiently clear to enable the users, who, being judges, were nonetheless informed and well-versed in the law, to realise—even in the light of the preceding debate—that their membership of an official Masonic lodge could lead to sanctions being imposed on them'.[219]

In a Macedonian case where a political association denied the Macedonian ethnic identity, the Court found provisions in the Constitution dealing with violent destruction of the constitutional order, or to the encouragement of or incitement to military aggression or ethnic, racial, or religious hatred or intolerance, to be sufficiently precise.[220]

Legitimate purpose

The second component of the analysis under article 11(2) is the existence of a legitimate purpose or aim. The inquiry involves the enumeration of purposes set out in paragraph 2, namely the interests of national security or public safety, the prevention of disorder or

[213] *Ramazanova and Others v. Azerbaijan*, no. 44363/02, § 66, 1 February 2007.
[214] *Republican Party of Russia v. Russia*, no. 12976/07, § 85, 12 April 2011.
[215] *Jehovah's Witnesses of Moscow v. Russia*, no. 302/02, § 176, 10 June 2010.
[216] Ibid., § 175; *Church of Scientology Moscow v. Russia*, no. 18147/02, § 91, 5 April 2007.
[217] *Moscow Branch of the Salvation Army v. Russia*, no. 72881/01, §§ 82–86, ECHR 2006-XI.
[218] *Maestri v. Italy* [GC], no. 39748/98, §§ 37–42, ECHR 2004-I.
[219] *N.F. v. Italy*, no. 37119/97, § 31, ECHR 2001-IX.
[220] *Association of Citizens Radko and Paunkovski v. 'the former Yugoslav Republic of Macedonia'*, no. 74651/01, § 59, ECHR 2009 (extracts).

crime, the protection of health or morals, and the protection of the rights and freedoms of others. The enumeration is exhaustive, and is to be interpreted narrowly.[221]

In practice, this issue is rarely very important. It is not uncommon for the Court simply to pass over the issue entirely and move to the heart of the debate, which takes place under the rubric 'necessary in a democratic society', finding that it violates the final component of the test regardless of whether it fulfils a legitimate purpose.[222] The Grand Chamber has explained that it is the Court's practice 'to be quite succinct when it verifies the existence of a legitimate aim within the meaning of the second paragraphs of Articles 8 to 11 of the Convention'.[223]

Often several of the legitimate aims listed in article 11(2) may be relevant. In a Turkish case involving dissolution of a political party because of its threat to 'the importance of the principle of secularism for the democratic system in Turkey', the Court cited protection of national security and public safety, prevention of disorder or crime, and protection of the rights and freedoms of others.[224] Italian legislation required candidates for public office to declare that they were not members of a masonic lodge. The government explained that this measure had been introduced in order to 'reassure' the public at a time when there was controversy about the role certain freemasons played in public life. The Court considered this purpose as legitimate for the protection of national security and prevention of disorder.[225]

The first of the listed objectives is the interests of national security or public safety. These two grounds appear in the three other limitations clauses of the Convention with the exception of freedom of religion, where national security is not a legitimate purpose for limitation of the right. Within this context, the Court has also accepted as a legitimate purpose the State's territorial integrity, a concept closely linked with the protection of national security.[226] The Court has been especially strict in admitting 'national security' as a legitimate purpose for interference with freedom of peaceful assembly or association. In the context of meetings of a secessionist group, it said that '[d]emanding territorial changes in speeches and demonstrations does not automatically amount to a threat to the country's territorial integrity and national security'.[227] In a Bulgarian case, the Court said that an organization's position favouring 'abolition' or 'opening' of the country's border with Macedonia could not be thought to 'jeopardise in any conceivable way those countries' territorial integrity or national security'.[228] The Court rejected Turkey's claim that the imposition of a legislative requirement upon members of organizations

---

[221] *Sidiropoulos and Others v. Greece*, 10 July 1998, §§ 37–39, *Reports of Judgments and Decisions* 1998-IV; *Stankov and the United Macedonian Organisation Ilinden v. Bulgaria*, nos 29221/95 and 29225/95, § 84, ECHR 2001-IX; *Galstyan v. Armenia*, no. 26986/03, § 114, 15 November 2007.

[222] For example, *Bayatyan v. Armenia* [GC], no. 23459/03, § 117, ECHR 2011; *Erçep v. Turkey*, no. 43965/04, § 53, 22 November 2011.

[223] *S.A.S. v. France* [GC], no. 43835/11, § 114, 1 July 2014.

[224] *Refah Partisi (the Welfare Party) and Others v. Turkey* [GC], nos 41340/98, 41342/98, 41343/98, and 41344/98, § 67, ECHR 2003-II.

[225] *Grande Oriente d'Italia di Palazzo Giustiniani v. Italy*, no. 35972/97, § 26, ECHR 2001-VIII. Also *Grande Oriente d'Italia di Palazzo Giustiniani v. Italy (no. 2)*, no. 26740/02, § 51, 31 May 2007.

[226] *Republican Party of Russia v. Russia*, no. 12976/07, § 101, 12 April 2011; *United Communist Party of Turkey and Others v. Turkey*, 30 January 1998, § 40, *Reports of Judgments and Decisions* 1998-I.

[227] *Stankov and the United Macedonian Organisation Ilinden v. Bulgaria*, nos 29221/95 and 29225/95, § 97, ECHR 2001-IX.

[228] *Zhechev v. Bulgaria*, no. 57045/00, § 48, 21 June 2007.

seeking to travel abroad that they inform the government of their plans fulfilled a legitimate purpose of protecting national security and public safety.[229]

The prevention of disorder or crime also appears in the limitations clauses governing the right to private and family life and freedom of expression. Instead, article 9(2) uses the expression 'the protection of public order'. An interesting distinction has been made between the English and French versions of article 11(2). One of the justifications for restrictions in the English version is 'the prevention of disorder or crime', while in the French version the text refers to 'la défense de l'ordre et à la prévention du crime'. The Court has said that 'the protection of a State's democratic institutions and constitutional foundations relates to "the prevention of disorder", the concept of "order" within the meaning of the French version of Article 11 encompassing the "institutional order"'.[230] A religious organization occupying a church, with some members conducting a hunger strike, was evacuated on the grounds of a number of public order considerations. Concluding that 'the evacuation was ordered to put an end to the continuing occupation of a place of worship by persons, including the applicant, who had broken French law', the Court said that this measure pursued the legitimate aim of the prevention of disorder.[231]

The protection of the rights and freedoms of others was invoked in a case involving squatters who operated as part of an organization. The Swiss authorities dissolved the applicant association, a measure the Court noted was quite inadequate to deal with the circumstances, and to address the rights of the property owners.[232] In a case involving dissolution of a separatist organization, the Court referred to the Constitutional Court, holding that the real objective of the group violated 'the free expression of the national affiliation of the Macedonian people'. It said this fulfilled the legitimate aim of protection of the rights and freedoms of others.[233]

Necessary in a democratic society

Most decisions concerning the application of article 11(2) to infringements of freedom of peaceful assembly and association involve assessing whether the impugned measure is 'necessary in a democratic society'. The objective is to consider whether the authorities have struck 'a fair balance between the competing interests of the individual and of society as a whole'.[234] It is the most subjective part of the application of paragraph 2, involving subtle distinctions about the proportionality of measures taken by the State that limit or restrict human rights. There is an important relationship between 'necessity' and 'democratic society', of which the hallmarks are pluralism, tolerance, and broadmindedness.[235] Indeed, because democracy is 'the only political model contemplated in the Convention and the only one compatible with it... the only necessity capable of justifying an

---

[229] *İzmir Savaş Karşıtları Derneği and Others v. Turkey*, no. 46257/99, §§ 36–37, 2 March 2006.

[230] *Republican Party of Russia v. Russia*, no. 12976/07, § 101, 12 April 2011. Also *Parti nationaliste basque— Organisation régionale d'Iparralde v. France*, no. 71251/01, § 43, ECHR 2007-II.

[231] *Cisse v. France*, no. 51346/99, § 22, ECHR 2002-III.

[232] *Association Rhino and Others v. Switzerland*, no. 48848/07, § 62–63, 11 October 2011.

[233] *Association of Citizens Radko and Paunkovski v. 'the former Yugoslav Republic of Macedonia'*, no. 74651/01, § 62, ECHR 2009 (extracts).

[234] *Keegan v. Ireland*, 26 May 1994, § 49, Series A no. 290.

[235] *Smith and Grady v. the United Kingdom*, nos 33985/96 and 33986/96, § 87, ECHR 1999-VI; *Vereinigung demokratischer Soldaten Österreichs and Gubi v. Austria*, 19 December 1994, § 36, Series A no. 302; *Dudgeon v. the United Kingdom*, 22 October 1981, § 53, Series A no. 45.

interference with any of the rights enshrined in those Articles is one that may claim to spring from a "democratic society".[236]

The term 'necessary' does not have the flexibility of such expressions as 'useful' or 'desirable'.[237] Although individual interests may sometimes be subordinated to those of a group, democracy cannot be reduced to a simplistic proposition by which the majority always prevails. There must be a balance that ensures 'the fair and proper treatment of minorities and avoids any abuse of a dominant position'.[238] Disciplinary measures imposed upon civil servants who posted announcements on the walls of their offices of an event commemorating the first of May was not necessary in a democratic society. The employees did not engage in 'un affichage sauvage générant une pollution visuelle dans l'ensemble du lieu de travail', the event being announced was a peaceful one, and nothing on the posters was unlawful or susceptible of shocking the public.[239] The Court found that a decision transferring a civil servant from one part of the country to another on the grounds of his membership in a legally constituted trade union was not necessary in a democratic society.[240]

Punishment of individuals for being 'present and proactive' at a demonstration but who were not charged with doing 'anything illegal, violent or obscene', and where the demonstration itself was not prohibited, threatened to impair 'the very essence of the right to freedom of peaceful assembly' and was therefore not necessary in a democratic society.[241] According to the Court, 'where demonstrators do not engage in acts of violence, it is important for the public authorities to show a certain degree of tolerance towards peaceful gatherings if the freedom of assembly guaranteed by Article 11 of the Convention is not to be deprived of all substance'.[242]

Pressing social need

The Court frequently begins its consideration of 'necessity in a democratic society' by questioning whether the interference responds to a 'pressing social need'. The term seems to be little more than a gloss on the word 'necessity'.[243] For example, in determining whether a restriction of the right to organize meets a 'pressing social need', there must be plausible evidence that the establishment or activities of a trade union represent 'a sufficiently imminent threat to the State or to a democratic society'.[244]

The assessment of whether there is a 'pressing social need' is primarily for the national authorities. They are entitled to a margin of appreciation, but this cannot displace judicial supervision by the European Court of Human Rights. The Court is concerned both with

[236] *Bączkowski and Others v. Poland*, no. 1543/06, § 61, 3 May 2007.
[237] *Associated Society of Locomotive Engineers and Firemen (ASLEF) v. the United Kingdom*, no. 11002/05, § 42, 27 February 2007.
[238] *Young, James, and Webster v. the United Kingdom*, 13 August 1981, § 53, Series A no. 44; *Chassagnou and Others v. France* [GC], nos 25088/94, 28331/95, and 28443/95, § 112, ECHR 1999-III; *Gorzelik and Others v. Poland* [GC], no. 44158/98, § 90, ECHR 2004-I.
[239] *Şişman and Others v. Turkey*, no. 1305/05, §§ 29–37, 27 September 2011.
[240] *Metin Turan v. Turkey*, no. 20868/02, § 31, 14 November 2006.
[241] *Galstyan v. Armenia*, no. 26986/03, § 117, 15 November 2007.
[242] *Oya Ataman v. Turkey*, no. 74552/01, 5 December 2006, §§ 41–42; *Patyi v. Hungary*, no. 35127/08, § 43, 17 January 2012.
[243] *Trade Union of the Police in the Slovak Republic and Others v. Slovakia*, no. 11828/08, § 66, 25 September 2012; *Herri Batasuna and Batasuna v. Spain*, nos 25803/04 and 25817/04, § 119, ECHR 2009.
[244] *Sindicatul 'Păstorul cel Bun' v. Romania*, no. 2330/09, § 69, 31 January 2012; *Koretskyy and Others v. Ukraine*, no. 40269/02, § 55, 3 April 2008.

the law and the decisions that apply it at the national level. It does not substitute its own view for that of the national authorities, who are deemed better placed to rule on matters of legislative policy and measures of implementation. As the Grand Chamber has explained,

This does not mean that it has to confine itself to ascertaining whether the respondent State exercised its discretion reasonably, carefully and in good faith; it must look at the interference complained of in the light of the case as a whole and determine whether it was 'proportionate to the legitimate aim pursued' and whether the reasons adduced by the national authorities to justify it are "relevant and sufficient". In so doing, the Court has to satisfy itself that the national authorities applied standards which were in conformity with the principles embodied in Article 11 and, moreover, that they based their decisions on an acceptable assessment of the relevant facts.[245]

The Court has accepted that where an association is permitted by law to participate in elections with the possibility of acceding to power, it may be necessary to require its registration as a political party. In this way, rules concerning financing, public control, and transparency may be brought to bear. But if the association cannot participate in elections, the Court has said there is no 'pressing social need' to require it to register as a political party, something that 'would mean forcing the association to take a legal shape which its founders did not seek'.[246] In a Polish case concerning the refusal to allow an association to call itself an 'organisation of a national minority', because of possible consequences in terms of participation in elections, the Grand Chamber said the national authorities 'did not overstep their margin of appreciation in considering that there was a pressing social need, at the moment of registration, to regulate the free choice of associations to call themselves an "organisation of a national minority", in order to protect the existing democratic institutions and election procedures in Poland and thereby, in Convention terms, prevent disorder and protect the rights of others'.[247]

In determining whether the dissolution of a political party responds to a pressing social need, the Grand Chamber has said that the analysis should focus on three points: the imminence of a risk to democracy; the attribution of the acts of leaders to the party itself; and 'whether the acts and speeches imputable to the political party formed a whole which gave a clear picture of a model of society conceived and advocated by the party which was incompatible with the concept of a "democratic society"'.[248] A Turkish trade union for civil servants invoked article 11 when it was dissolved by the courts on the ground that civil servants were not entitled to form trade unions. The Court said that Turkey had failed to demonstrate a 'pressing social need'. The fact that the law did not permit such unions was not sufficient to justify 'a measure as radical as the dissolution of a trade union'.[249] The Court took into account Turkey's ratification of International Labour Organisation Convention No. 87 where the right of all workers to form trade unions without distinction between the private and public sectors is acknowledged. It also noted the interpretation of article 5 of the European Social Charter by the Committee of

---

[245] *Gorzelik and Others v. Poland* [GC], no. 44158/98, § 96, ECHR 2004-I.

[246] *Zhechev v. Bulgaria*, no. 57045/00, § 56, 21 June 2007.

[247] *Gorzelik and Others v. Poland* [GC], no. 44158/98, § 104, ECHR 2004-I.

[248] *Refah Partisi (the Welfare Party) and Others v. Turkey* [GC], nos 41340/98, 41342/98, 41343/98, and 41344/98, § 104, ECHR 2003-II; *Partidul Comunistilor (Nepeceristi) and Ungureanu v. Romania*, no. 46626/99, § 48, ECHR 2005-I (extracts); *Linkov v. the Czech Republic*, no. 10504/03, § 37, 7 December 2006.

[249] *Tüm Haber Sen and Çinar v. Turkey*, no. 28602/95, § 36, ECHR 2006-II.

Independent Experts recognizing a right of public employees to form unions, saying it could 'only subscribe to this interpretation by a particularly well-qualified committee'.[250]

Prohibition of the right to form certain types of associations, notably trade unions, also raises issues under article 11. Clergy and laity working for the Orthodox Church in Romania were prohibited from forming a trade union, with the local court basing its refusal of registration upon an ecclesiastical rule that it said was necessary to protect religious tradition. The Court said that priests and lay staff who worked for the Church under individual employment contracts could not simply be excluded from the ambit of article 11.[251]

Proportionality

The interference must respond to an assessment of its proportionality, something that involves balancing the right of the individual against the interest of the State and the society that it represents. Furthermore, the reasons given by the national authorities must be 'relevant and sufficient', which means that the national authorities 'applied standards which were in conformity with the principles embodied in article 11 and, moreover, that they based their decisions on an acceptable assessment of the relevant facts'.[252] Where the Court is considering the positive dimension of the right in question, in other words, the obligation upon the State to take measures to ensure enforcement of the right, it must usually consider the rights of others in the balance as well. If other less severe measures could have fulfilled the same objective, there will be a problem with proportionality.

In its assessment of the proportionality of measures that interfere with a public demonstration, where a requirement of authorization has not been respected, the Court will take into account the genuineness of the claim of urgency,[253] the level of fine or other sanction imposed,[254] security concerns relating to the location of the demonstration,[255] the length of time of the demonstration before its dispersal by the authorities,[256] the fact that despite the absence of notice the authorities were in fact well informed of the planned demonstration,[257] and the impatience of the authorities in resorting to force.[258]

Part of the proportionality assessment involves determining whether there existed 'effective, less intrusive measures' capable of achieving the legitimate aim.[259] In one case, the Court said that rather than suppress a demonstration because the police judged

---

[250] Ibid., § 38.

[251] *Sindicatul 'Păstorul cel Bun' v. Romania*, no. 2330/09, §§ 60–65, 31 January 2012.

[252] *Sidiropoulos and Others v. Greece*, 10 July 1998, *Reports of Judgments and Decisions* 1998-IV; *United Communist Party of Turkey and Others v. Turkey*, 30 January 1998, § 47, *Reports of Judgments and Decisions* 1998-I; *Partidul Comunistilor (Nepeceristi) and Ungureanu v. Romania*, no. 46626/99, § 49, ECHR 2005-I (extracts).

[253] *Bukta and Others v. Hungary*, no. 25691/04, § 35, ECHR 2007-III; *Éva Molnár v. Hungary*, no. 10346/05, § 38, 7 October 2008.

[254] *Ziliberberg v. Moldova*, no. 61821/00, 1 February 2005; *Skiba v. Poland* (dec.), no. 10659/03, 7 July 2009; *Rai and Evans v. the United Kingdom* (dec.), nos 26258/07 and 26255/07, 17 November 2009; *Hyde Park and Others v. Moldova (nos 5 and 6)*, nos 6991/08 and 15084/08, § 47, 14 September 2010.

[255] *Rai and Evans v. the United Kingdom* (dec.), nos 26258/07 and 26255/07, 17 November 2009; *Hyde Park and Others v. Moldova (nos 5 and 6)*, nos 6991/08 and 15084/08, § 47, 14 September 2010.

[256] *Éva Molnár v. Hungary*, no. 10346/05, § 34, 7 October 2008.

[257] *Barraco v. France*, no. 31684/05, § 45, 5 March 2009.

[258] *Oya Ataman v. Turkey*, no. 74552/01, ECHR 2006-XIII; *Balçık and Others v. Turkey*, no. 25/02, 29 November 2007; *Ekşi and Ocak v. Turkey*, no. 44920/04, 23 February 2010; *Aytaş and Others v. Turkey*, no. 6758/05, 8 December 2009; *Skiba v. Poland* (dec.), no. 10659/03, 7 July 2009.

[259] *Schwabe and M.G. v. Germany*, nos 8080/08 and 8577/08, § 118, ECHR 2011 (extracts).

the slogans on banners to be illegal, they could simply have seized the banners in question. This might have had a 'chilling effect' on the production of new banners, thereby restricting freedom of expression, but it would not have made the demonstration impossible.[260] Where an organization of squatters was dissolved, the Court noted that given a lengthy period in which occupation of buildings had been tolerated by the authorities, as well as the association's statutory objectives, the State had failed to show that the actions taken were the only available option.[261] Even if the harm done by an infringement on freedom of association is quite minimal, this does not necessarily assist in arguing for its proportionality. Where Italian law required candidates for public office to declare they were not members of a masonic lodge, the government argued that the damage this might do to the organization by discouraging people to join was quite minimal. But the Court said freedom of association 'is of such importance that it cannot be restricted in any way, even in respect of a candidate for public office, so long as the person concerned does not himself commit any reprehensible act by reason of his membership of the association'.[262]

In assessing proportionality, the nature and severity of the sanction imposed are important factors to be considered.[263] Dissolution of an association is a drastic measure that will often fail the proportionality test.[264] Less severe measures, such as a fine or withdrawal of tax benefits, are alternatives that may adequately fulfil the legitimate purpose.[265] When small fines were imposed on demonstrators after their refusal to move the venue of a protest was deemed an administrative offence, the Court said 'the decisions of the national authorities in the present case were based on an acceptable assessment of the relevant facts and contained relevant and sufficient reasons which justified the interference with the applicants' right of assembly and freedom of expression' and was therefore proportionate and necessary to prevent disorder or protect the rights and freedoms of others.[266]

Margin of appreciation

In applying the 'necessary in a democratic society' test, the Court will allow the State a margin of appreciation, recognizing that its role is not to sit as a Tribunal of fourth instance and that it is in one sense not as well positioned as the national legal institutions to assess many of the relevant factors. Often, especially in sensitive matters that concern morality, ethics, and social policy, the Court refers to the practice in European jurisdictions in determining whether or not any consensus exists. Where there is none, the margin of appreciation will almost invariably be much greater. But although the national authorities make the initial assessment of necessity, 'the final evaluation as to whether the reasons cited for the interference are relevant and sufficient remains subject to review by the Court for conformity with the requirements of the Convention'.[267]

Invoking the notion of margin of appreciation, the Court often shows considerable deference to States in how they deal with problems related to public assemblies. This is

[260] Ibid.

[261] *Association Rhino and Others v. Switzerland*, no. 48848/07, § 66, 11 October 2011.

[262] *Grande Oriente d'Italia di Palazzo Giustiniani v. Italy*, no. 35972/97, § 26, ECHR 2001-VIII.

[263] *Tebieti Mühafize Cemiyyeti and Israfilov v. Azerbaijan*, no. 37083/03, § 82, ECHR 2009; *Jehovah's Witnesses of Moscow v. Russia*, no. 302/02, § 154, 10 June 2010.

[264] *Biblical Centre of the Chuvash Republic v. Russia*, no. 33203/08, § 60, 12 June 2014.

[265] *Tebieti Mühafize Cemiyyeti and Israfilov v. Azerbaijan*, no. 37083/03, § 82, ECHR 2009.

[266] *Berladir and Others v. Russia*, no. 34202/06, § 61, 10 July 2012.

[267] *Szuluk v. the United Kingdom*, no. 36936/05, § 45, ECHR 2009.

especially true where there is evidence of incitement to violence against an individual or a public official or a sector of the population, in which case the margin of appreciation is broader. Otherwise, there is little scope under the Convention for restrictions that impact upon political activities.[268]

Typically, States rely upon the margin of appreciation as a final argument in defence against charges they have violated the Convention. Russia invoked the lack of a European consensus on issues relating to the treatment of sexual minorities in response to a complaint of interference with an advocacy organization that planned to hold a public demonstration. The Court noted that there was in fact consensus on a number of important matters concerning sexual orientation, such as the impermissibility of criminal sanctions for homosexual relations between adults, access to the armed forces, and the granting of parental rights. But in any case, the Court said, 'the absence of a European consensus on these questions is of no relevance to the present case because conferring substantive rights on homosexual persons is fundamentally different from recognising their right to campaign for such rights'. Rejecting the margin of appreciation argument, the Court said that '[t]he only factor taken into account by the Moscow authorities was the public opposition to the event, and the officials' own views on morals'.[269]

The Court has accepted that 'in certain cases, the States' margin of appreciation may include a right to interfere—subject to the condition of proportionality—with an association's internal organisation and functioning in the event of non-compliance with reasonable legal formalities applying to its establishment, functioning or internal organisational structure'.[270] It may also be justified in intervening in the case of a serious and prolonged internal conflict of the organization.[271] However, 'the authorities should not intervene in the internal organisational functioning of associations to such a far-reaching extent as to ensure observance by an association of every single formality provided by its own charter'.[272] The observance of internal formalities 'should be primarily up to the association itself and its members, and not the public authorities'.[273]

In a Polish case concerning the refusal to allow an association to call itself an 'organisation of a national minority', because of possible consequences in terms of participation in elections, the Grand Chamber said the national authorities 'did not overstep their margin of appreciation in considering that there was a pressing social need, at the moment of registration, to regulate the free choice of associations to call themselves an "organisation of a national minority", in order to protect the existing democratic institutions and election procedures in Poland and thereby, in Convention terms, prevent disorder and protect the rights of others'.[274]

[268] *Schwabe and M.G. v. Germany,* nos 8080/08 and 8577/08, § 113, ECHR 2011 (extracts); *Stankov and the United Macedonian Organisation Ilinden v. Bulgaria,* nos 29221/95 and 29225/95, § 88, ECHR 2001-IX.
[269] *Alekseyev v. Russia,* nos 4916/07, 25924/08 and 14599/09, §§ 83–85, 21 October 2010.
[270] *Ertan and Others v. Turkey* (dec.), no. 57898/00, 21 March 2006; *Baisan and Liga Apararii Drepturilor Omului din Romania v. Romania* (dec.), no. 28973/95, 30 October 1995; *Carmuirea Spirituala a Musulmanilor din Republica Moldova v. Moldova* (dec.), no. 12282/02, 14 June 2005.
[271] *Holy Synod of the Bulgarian Orthodox Church (Metropolitan Inokentiy) and Others v. Bulgaria,* nos 412/03 and 35677/04, § 131, 22 January 2009.
[272] *Tebieti Mühafize Cemiyyeti and Israfilov v. Azerbaijan,* no. 37083/03, § 78, ECHR 2009.
[273] *Republican Party of Russia v. Russia,* no. 12976/07, § 88, 12 April 2011.
[274] *Gorzelik and Others v. Poland* [GC], no. 44158/98, § 104, ECHR 2004-I.

Militant democracy

The term 'militant democracy' was introduced by the German philosopher, Karl Loewenstein.[275] His perspective was providing democratic societies with the means to deal with anti-democratic elements in general and fascists in particular in light of the threat that they would exploit freedoms of assembly and association in order to destroy democratic government.[276] Judgments of the Court have referred to the term 'militant democracy', although it has never been formally endorsed.[277] There is an inherent tension between the protection of democracy and recognition of freedom of association to the extent that political parties may advocate dramatic change to the established order. Recalling that '[f]reedom of association is not absolute', the Court has said that where an association jeopardizes the State's institutions or the rights and freedoms of others, article 11 does not deprive the State of the power to protect those institutions and persons. It has noted that this follows both from article 11(2) and from the State's positive obligations under article 1 of the Convention.[278] In addition, of course, article 17 is a means by which the Convention can resist being exploited by groups determined to undermine its very principles. Invoking article 17, the Court held that a racist organization known as the National and Patriotic Association of Polish Victims of Bolshevism and Zionism, claiming to represent persons persecuted by Jews, could not invoke article 11 in order to contest its prohibition.[279]

According to the Court,

[O]ne of the principal characteristics of democracy [is] the possibility it offers of resolving a country's problems through dialogue, without recourse to violence, even when they are irksome. Democracy thrives on freedom of expression. From that point of view, there can be no justification for hindering a political group solely because it seeks to debate in public the situation of part of the State's population and to take part in the nation's political life in order to find, according to democratic rules, solutions capable of satisfying everyone concerned.[280]

The Court has said that a political party may promote a change in the law or the legal and constitutional structures of the State on two conditions: first, the means used to that end must be legal and democratic; second, the change proposed must itself be compatible with fundamental democratic principles. A political party 'is not excluded from the protection afforded by the Convention simply because its activities are regarded by the national authorities as undermining the constitutional structures of the State and calling for the imposition of restrictions'.[281] But where a political party incites violence or puts forward a policy that does not respect democracy or is aimed at its destruction, and that flouts the rights and freedoms recognized in a democracy, it cannot demand the protection of

---

[275] K. Loewenstein, 'Militant Democracy and Fundamental Rights I,' (1995) 31 *American Political Science Review* 417.

[276] P. Harvey, 'Militant Democracy and the European Convention on Human Rights', (2004) 29 *European Law Review* 407.

[277] *Refah Partisi (the Welfare Party) and Others v. Turkey*, nos 41340/98, 41342/98, 41343/98, and 41344/98, § 62, 31 July 2001; *Herri Batasuna and Batasuna v. Spain*, nos 25803/04 and 25817/04, §§ 20, 21, 30, 45, ECHR 2009.

[278] *Gorzelik and Others v. Poland* [GC], no. 44158/98, § 94, ECHR 2004-I.

[279] *W.P. and Others v. Poland* (dec.), no. 42264/98, ECHR 2004-VII (extracts).

[280] *United Communist Party of Turkey and Others v. Turkey*, 30 January 1998, § 57, *Reports of Judgments and Decisions* 1998-I.

[281] Ibid., § 27; *Herri Batasuna and Batasuna v. Spain*, nos 25803/04 and 25817/04, § 79, ECHR 2009.

the Convention.[282] As the Court has noted, 'it is not at all improbable that totalitarian movements, organised in the form of political parties, might do away with democracy, after prospering under the democratic regime, there being examples of this in modern European history'.[283] Furthermore,

a State cannot be required to wait, before intervening, until a political party has seized power and begun to take concrete steps to implement a policy incompatible with the standards of the Convention and democracy, even though the danger of that policy for democracy is sufficiently established and imminent. The Court accepts that where the presence of such a danger has been established by the national courts, after detailed scrutiny subjected to rigorous European supervision, a State may 'reasonably forestall the execution of such a policy, which is incompatible with the Convention's provisions, before an attempt is made to implement it through concrete steps that might prejudice civil peace and the country's democratic regime'.[284]

In determining the objectives and intentions of a political party as justification for restrictions on its activity, the constitution and the programme are not the only factors to be considered in evaluating whether the political party may invoke article 11. History has shown that 'political parties with aims contrary to the fundamental principles of democracy have not revealed such aims in their official publications until after taking power'.[285] The programme of a political party 'may conceal objectives and intentions different from the ones it proclaims'.[286] Analysis of the actions and stances of the leaders of the party must also be considered.[287] In a case dealing with a Basque nationalist party, the Court referred to conduct that bore 'a strong resemblance to explicit support for violence and the commendation of people seemingly linked to terrorism'.[288] In addition, a 'refusal to condemn violence against a backdrop of terrorism that had been in place for more than thirty years and condemned by all the other political parties amounted to tacit support for terrorism'.[289]

However, if the impugned decision by a State is based solely on the programme of a political party, the Court will not consider statements by its leaders in determining whether the measures were proportionate.[290] Political parties 'animated by the moral values imposed by a religion cannot be regarded as intrinsically inimical to the

---

[282] *Refah Partisi (the Welfare Party) and Others v. Turkey* [GC], nos 41340/98, 41342/98, 41343/98, and 41344/98, § 98, ECHR 2003-II; *Yazar and Others v. Turkey*, nos 22723/93, 22724/93, and 22725/93, § 49, ECHR 2002-II; *Partidul Comunistilor (Nepeceristi) and Ungureanu v. Romania*, no. 46626/99, § 46, ECHR 2005-I (extracts); *Linkov v. the Czech Republic*, no. 10504/03, § 36, 7 December 2006.
[283] *Refah Partisi (the Welfare Party) and Others v. Turkey* [GC], nos 41340/98, 41342/98, 41343/98, and 41344/98, § 99.
[284] *Herri Batasuna and Batasuna v. Spain*, nos 25803/04 and 25817/04, § 81, ECHR 2009; *Refah Partisi (the Welfare Party) and Others v. Turkey* [GC], nos 41340/98, 41342/98, 41343/98, and 41344/98, § 102, ECHR 2003-II.
[285] *Refah Partisi (the Welfare Party) and Others v. Turkey* [GC], nos 41340/98, 41342/98, 41343/98, and 41344/98, § 101, ECHR 2003-II.
[286] Ibid., § 44.
[287] *United Communist Party of Turkey and Others v. Turkey*, 30 January 1998, § 58, *Reports of Judgments and Decisions* 1998-I; *Socialist Party and Others v. Turkey*, 25 May 1998, § 38, *Reports of Judgments and Decisions* 1998-III.
[288] *Herri Batasuna and Batasuna v. Spain*, nos 25803/04 and 25817/04, § 86, ECHR 2009.
[289] Ibid., § 88.
[290] *Partidul Comunistilor (Nepeceristi) and Ungureanu v. Romania*, no. 46626/99, §§ 51–52, ECHR 2005-I (extracts); *Dicle for the Democracy Party (DEP) v. Turkey*, no. 25141/94, § 50, 10 December 2002; *IPSD and Others v. Turkey*, no. 35832/97, § 34, 25 October 2005; *Bozgan v. Romania*, no. 35097/02, § 22, 11 October 2007.

fundamental principles of democracy, as set forth in the Convention'.[291] The Court has applied article 11 in recognizing the right to establish new communist parties in Central and Eastern Europe as part of the democratic debate.[292]

Where political parties are concerned, the exceptions set out in article 11 are to be strictly construed.[293] Restrictions on the freedom of association of political parties can only be justified by 'convincing and compelling reasons'. Accordingly, a variety of sanctions 'may be imposed on those political parties that use illegal or undemocratic methods, incite to violence or put forward a policy which is aimed at the destruction of democracy and flouting of the rights and freedoms recognised in a democracy'.[294] The most drastic forms of restriction on political parties involve their dissolution or prohibitions on the political activities of their leaders. Such measures may only be taken 'in the most serious cases'.[295] Moreover, 'the Court must scrutinise very carefully the necessity for imposing a ban on a parliamentary political party's activities, even a ban of fairly short duration'.[296] In determining whether restrictions are necessary, in accordance with article 11(2), States have only a limited margin of appreciation. Still, the European Court 'must exercise rigorous supervision embracing both the law and the decisions applying it, including those given by independent courts'.[297]

The Court acknowledges that national authorities may be better placed than an international court to assess of matters such as the appropriate timing for interference.[298] An assessment needs to be made of the danger a political party may pose for democracy before irreparable damage is done. In this assessment, the Court is prepared to show considerable deference to the national courts. The Court has associated such preventive intervention with the positive obligations upon the State to control the conduct of non-State entities: 'A Contracting State may be justified under its positive obligations in imposing on political parties, which are bodies whose raison d'être is to accede to power and direct the work of a considerable portion of the State apparatus, the duty to respect and safeguard the rights and freedoms guaranteed by the Convention and the obligation not to put forward a political programme in contradiction with the fundamental principles of democracy.'[299]

[291] *Refah Partisi (the Welfare Party) and Others v. Turkey* [GC], nos 41340/98, 41342/98, 41343/98, and 41344/98, § 100, ECHR 2003-II.

[292] *Partidul Comunistilor (Nepeceristi) and Ungureanu v. Romania*, no. 46626/99, § 55, ECHR 2005-I (extracts).

[293] *Refah Partisi (the Welfare Party) and Others v. Turkey* [GC], nos 41340/98, 41342/98, 41343/98, and 41344/98, § 100, ECHR 2003-II; *Christian Democratic People's Party v. Moldova*, no. 28793/02, § 68, ECHR 2006-II.

[294] *Republican Party of Russia v. Russia*, no. 12976/07, § 129, 12 April 2011; *Herri Batasuna and Batasuna v. Spain*, nos 25803/04 and 25817/04, § 79, ECHR 2009.

[295] *Refah Partisi (the Welfare Party) and Others v. Turkey* [GC], nos 41340/98, 41342/98, 41343/98, and 41344/98, § 100, ECHR 2003-II; *Freedom and Democracy Party (ÖZDEP) v. Turkey* [GC], no. 23885/94, § 45, ECHR 1999-VIII; *United Communist Party of Turkey and Others v. Turkey*, 30 January 1998, § 46, *Reports of Judgments and Decisions* 1998-I; *Socialist Party and Others v. Turkey*, 25 May 1998, § 50, *Reports of Judgments and Decisions* 1998-III; *The United Macedonian Organisation Ilinden—PIRIN and Others v. Bulgaria*, no. 59489/00, § 56, 20 October 2005. Also, for other associations, *Association Rhino and Others v. Switzerland*, no. 48848/07, § 62, 11 October 2011.

[296] *Christian Democratic People's Party v. Moldova*, no. 28793/02, § 68, ECHR 2006-II.

[297] *Refah Partisi (the Welfare Party) and Others v. Turkey* [GC], nos 41340/98, 41342/98, 41343/98, and 41344/98, § 100, ECHR 2003-II; *Christian Democratic People's Party v. Moldova*, no. 28793/02, § 68, ECHR 2006-II.

[298] *Refah Partisi (the Welfare Party) and Others v. Turkey* [GC], nos 41340/98, 41342/98, 41343/98, and 41344/98, § 100, ECHR 2003-II; *Christian Democratic People's Party v. Moldova*, no. 28793/02, § 68, ECHR 2006-II.

[299] *Refah Partisi (the Welfare Party) and Others v. Turkey* [GC], nos 41340/98, 41342/98, 41343/98, and 41344/98, § 103, ECHR 2003-II; *Herri Batasuna and Batasuna v. Spain*, nos 25803/04 and 25817/04, § 82, ECHR 2009.

Lawful restrictions on public employees

The final sentence of article 11(2) states that 'the imposition of lawful restrictions on the exercise of these rights by members of the armed forces, of the police or of the administration of the State' is not prohibited. According to the Court, 'the restrictions imposed on the three groups mentioned in Article 11 are to be construed strictly and should therefore be confined to the "exercise" of the rights in question. However, these restrictions must not impair the very essence of the right to organise.'[300] As a result, civil servants are entitled to form trade unions and to exercise their rights under article 11(1) of the Convention like any other worker.[301]

Pursuant to the final sentence of article 11(2), employers are entitled, in certain circumstances, to place restrictions on freedom of association of employees in order to maintain the political neutrality of civil servants.[302] When civil servants are concerned, the right to strike may not be absolute, and it is possible for some categories of public employees to be prohibited from taking such industrial action.[303] A prohibition on a police officer belonging to a political party was considered an acceptable restriction on freedom of association.[304]

Article 22 of the International Covenant on Civil and Political Rights is worded in a similar manner to article 11(2) of the European Convention except that it only restricts the exercise of freedom of association to members of the armed forces and of the police and makes no reference to members of the administration of the State. There is a similar provision, applicable to the police and members of the armed forces, in the European Social Charter (revised).[305] Other international law sources, notably International Labour Organisation Conventions No. 87 and No. 98 and the European Code of Police Ethics, provide confirmation that it has been 'generally acknowledged that the duties and responsibilities inherent in the position and role of the police justify particular arrangements as regards the exercise of their trade union rights'.[306]

If the notion of members of the armed forces and the police seems to raise no great problems of interpretation, the same cannot be said of 'the administration of the State'. Construed broadly, it has the potential to provide a huge loophole in the protection provided by article 11. In this respect, the Court has taken note of the practice of European states:

[I]n the vast majority of them, the right of civil servants to bargain collectively with the authorities has been recognised, subject to various exceptions so as to exclude certain areas regarded as sensitive or certain categories of civil servants who hold exclusive powers of the State. In particular, the right of public servants employed by local authorities and not holding State powers to engage in collective bargaining in order to determine their wages and working conditions has been recognised in the

---

[300] *Demir and Baykara v. Turkey* [GC], no. 34503/97, § 97, ECHR 2008.

[301] See also *Tüm Haber Sen and Çınar v. Turkey*, no. 28602/95, § 38, ECHR 2006-II.

[302] *Ahmed and Others v. the United Kingdom*, 2 September 1998, § 63, *Reports of Judgments and Decisions* 1998-VI; *Redfearn v. the United Kingdom*, no. 47335/06, § 44, 6 November 2012.

[303] *Enerji Yapı-Yol Sen v. Turkey*, no. 68959/01, § 32, 21 April 2009.

[304] *Rekvényi v. Hungary* [GC], no. 25390/94, § 61, ECHR 1999-III. See, however, *Rekvényi v. Hungary* [GC], no. 25390/94, Partly Dissenting Opinion of Judge Fischbach, ECHR 1999-III.

[305] European Social Charter (revised), ETS 163, art. 5.

[306] *Trade Union of the Police in the Slovak Republic and Others v. Slovakia*, no. 11828/08, § 67, 25 September 2012.

majority of Contracting States. The remaining exceptions can be justified only by particular circumstances.[307]

Basing itself on these and other sources, the Grand Chamber has in effect removed the words 'or of the administration of the State' from the final sentence of article 11(2).[308]

Consequently, the notion of 'administration of the State' is to be interpreted narrowly and the position of the victim of an infringement of article 11(1) scrutinized carefully in order to determine whether it falls under the exception of the final sentence of article 11(2). For example, teachers are public employees but they are not considered to be part of the 'administration of the State'.[309] Similarly, nominations and appointments to regional organizations do not follow under the exception.[310] In the context of article 6(1) of the Convention, the Grand Chamber has adopted a functional criterion for determining the scope of 'public servants', a notion that seems cognate with 'administration of the State'. Adopting a restrictive interpretation, it has said that this applies only to persons 'whose duties typify the specific activities of the public service in so far as the latter is acting as the depositary of public authority responsible for protecting the general interests of the State or other public authorities', adding that '[a] manifest example of such activities is provided by the armed forces and the police'.[311]

The term 'lawful' in the second sentence of article 11(2) denotes the same concept of lawfulness found elsewhere in the Convention, where the expressions 'in accordance with the law' and 'prescribed by law' are employed, in articles 9, 10, and 11.[312] This implies qualitative requirements, notably foreseeability and an absence of arbitrariness. The European Commission of Human Rights took the position that the word 'lawful' meant that a restriction need only have a basis in national law and need not be arbitrary, and that it did not also entail a requirement of proportionality.[313] The Grand Chamber adopted a more progressive position, considering that the State was required to show the legitimacy of any restrictions to the right to organize. In particular, it said that municipal civil servants who are not engaged in the administration of the State as such should not be treated as 'members of the administration of the State'.[314]

Discrimination

Article 14 of the Convention sets out a protection against discrimination that is subsidiary in that it requires a relationship with the enjoyment of the rights and freedoms set out elsewhere in the Convention. Even if there is no breach of article 11 taken alone, the Strasbourg organs may consider that there is an infringement of the Convention when article 11 is associated with article 14, as if article 14 formed an integral part of article 11.[315]

---

[307] *Demir and Baykara v. Turkey* [GC], no. 34503/97, § 151, ECHR 2008.

[308] Ibid., § 107.

[309] *Vogt v. Germany*, 26 September 1995, § 67, Series A no. 323.

[310] *Grande Oriente d'Italia di Palazzo Giustiniani v. Italy*, no. 35972/97, § 31, ECHR 2001-VIII.

[311] *Pellegrin v. France* [GC], no. 28541/95, § 66, ECHR 1999-VIII.

[312] *Rekvényi v. Hungary* [GC], no. 25390/94, § 59, ECHR 1999-III; *Grande Oriente d'Italia di Palazzo Giustiniani v. Italy*, no. 35972/97, § 30, ECHR 2001-VIII.

[313] *Council of Civil Service Unions and Others v. the United Kingdom*, no. 11603/85, Commission decision of 20 January 1987, DR 50, p. 228.

[314] *Demir and Baykara v. Turkey* [GC], no. 34503/97, § 98, ECHR 2008.

[315] *National Union of Belgian Police v. Belgium*, 27 October 1975, § 44, Series A no. 19. *Contra*: *National Union of Belgian Police v. Belgium*, 27 October 1975, Separate Opinion of Sir Gerald Fitzmaurice, Series A no. 19.

The general principles for the application of article 14 include recognition that there is prohibited discrimination only if different treatment lacks a reasonable and objective justification.[316] Different treatment must not only pursue a legitimate aim or purpose but there must also be a reasonable relationship of proportionality between the means that are employed and the objective of the measures.[317] States enjoy a margin of appreciation in this respect, although the Court remains the final arbiter.[318] As a general rule, if the Court finds that there is a violation of article 11 it will not also consider the case under article 14 unless 'a clear inequality of treatment in the enjoyment of the right in question is a fundamental aspect of the case'.[319]

The Court held there was a violation of article 11 and article 14 with respect to Italian legislation applicable in Friuli-Venezia Giulia that required members of an association of freemasons to declare their affiliation in applying for public positions given the absence of any similar obligation on members of other secret organizations.[320] However, in Tuscany, where the requirement that membership in secret organizations be revealed only applied in a general sense, the Court did not consider this to be contrary to the Convention. Nor was there discrimination because the same rule did not apply to similar positions in other regions of Italy because the possibility that certain issues be addressed differently from one region to another was merely the natural consequence of administrative autonomy.[321] The Court did not rule out the possibility that prohibited discrimination might result from exceptionally strict or rigid application to certain groups of regulations that were not in themselves discriminatory,[322] but it held that in the circumstances this had not been proven satisfactorily.[323]

In a labour relations context, the Swedish Engine Drivers complained that they were victims of discrimination because the Swedish National Collective Bargaining Office (*Statens Avtalsverk*), which favoured larger trade union bodies in the conclusion of collective agreements, would not negotiate with them. Because of the high degree of centralization in the Swedish trade union movement, the government argued that it preferred to reach collective agreements with the most representative organizations. The Court considered this to be legitimate and said there was 'no reason to think that the Swedish State had other and ill-intentioned designs in the matter'.[324] Similar conclusions were reached in a case concerning Belgium.[325] In neither of these cases was one of the

---

[316] *Zarb Adami v. Malta*, no. 17209/02, § 71, ECHR 2006-VIII; *Ünal Tekeli v. Turkey*, no. 29865/96, § 49, ECHR 2004-X (extracts).

[317] *Petrovic v. Austria*, 27 March 1998, § 30, *Reports of Judgments and Decisions* 1998-II; *Lithgow and Others v. the United Kingdom*, 8 July 1986, § 77, Series A no. 102.

[318] *Rasmussen v. Denmark*, 28 November 1984, § 40, Series A no. 87; *Inze v. Austria*, 28 October 1987, § 41, Series A no. 126.

[319] *Redfearn v. the United Kingdom*, no. 47335/06, § 66, 6 November 2012; *Moscow Branch of the Salvation Army v. Russia*, no. 72881/01, § 101, ECHR 2006-XI; *Church of Scientology Moscow v. Russia*, no. 18147/02, § 101, 5 April 2007; *Demir and Baykara v. Turkey* [GC], no. 34503/97, §§ 171–172, ECHR 2008; *Chassagnou and Others v. France* [GC], nos 25088/94, 28331/95, and 28443/95, § 89, ECHR 1999-III; *Dudgeon v. the United Kingdom*, 22 October 1981, § 67, Series A no. 45.

[320] *Grande Oriente d'Italia di Palazzo Giustiniani v. Italy (no. 2)*, no. 26740/02, §§ 51–57, 31 May 2007.

[321] *Siveri and Chiellini v. Italy* (dec.), no. 13148/04, 3 June 2008.

[322] *Zarb Adami v. Malta*, no. 17209/02, §§ 75–79, ECHR 2006-VIII.

[323] *Siveri and Chiellini v. Italy* (dec.), no. 13148/04, 3 June 2008.

[324] *Swedish Engine Drivers' Union v. Sweden*, 6 February 1976, § 46, Series A no. 20.

[325] *National Union of Belgian Police v. Belgium*, 27 October 1975, § 48, Series A no. 19. *Contra: National Union of Belgian Police v. Belgium*, 27 October 1975, Joint Separate Opinion of Judges Wiarda, Ganshof van der Meersch, and Bindschedler-Robert, Series A no. 19.

enumerated grounds listed in article 14 invoked or discussed by the Court. The assumption seems to have been that a discussion on discrimination should proceed based upon the differential treatment of a union without the need to specify the prohibited ground.

A requirement that candidates for public office declare their membership in a masonic lodge was deemed discriminatory and a breach of article 11 in conjunction with article 14. In an earlier case, the Court had held that a prohibition on membership in a masonic lodge for holders of public office was a breach of article 11 taken alone. Italy argued that in the second case there was no prohibition and all that was required was a form of public disclosure. The Court said the measure was discriminatory because it only applied to freemasons, whereas if the justification of protection of national security advanced by the State were applied consistently, it should also be used for members of political parties and groups with racist or xenophobic ideas, and this was not the case.[326]

The mayor of Warsaw refused permission to hold a demonstration from the Foundation for Equality, whose aim was to alert public opinion to the issue of discrimination against minorities—sexual, national, ethnic, and religious—and also against women and disabled persons. At the same time, permits were granted for six other demonstrations on the following themes: 'For more stringent measures against persons convicted of paedophilia'; 'Against any legislative work on the law on partnerships'; 'Against propaganda for partnerships'; 'Education in Christian values, a guarantee of a moral society'; 'Christians respecting God's and nature's laws are citizens of the first rank'; 'Against adoption of children by homosexual couples'. Bearing in mind that the mayor had expressed his negative views on 'propaganda about homosexuality', the Court said 'that it may be reasonably surmised that his opinions could have affected the decision-making process in the present case and, as a result, impinged on the applicants' right to freedom of assembly in a discriminatory manner'. Consequently, there was a violation of article 14 in conjunction with article 11.[327]

Reservations

Andorra formulated a reservation with respect to its legislation governing professional and trade union organizations.[328] San Marino made a reservation concerning the two active trade unions in the country and the requirement that they obtain registration with the Law Court.[329] Spain's reservation makes article 11 subject to two provisions of the Spanish Constitution. These permit restricting the right to organize within the armed forces and prevent serving judges, law officers, and prosecutors from belonging to trade unions.[330] Portugal formulated two reservations to article 11, sheltering provisions of its Constitution that prohibit lock-outs and that forbid organizations with allegiance to a fascist ideology.[331] Portugal's reservations were withdrawn in 1987.[332]

---

[326] *Grande Oriente d'Italia di Palazzo Giustiniani v. Italy (no. 2)*, no. 26740/02, §§ 55–56, 31 May 2007. But see *Siveri and Chiellini v. Italy* (dec.), no. 13148/04, 3 June 2008, where the facts are similar and there is no finding of a violation.

[327] *Bączkowski and Others v. Poland*, no. 1543/06, §§ 101–102, 3 May 2007.

[328] (1996) 39 YB 19.

[329] (1989) 32 YB 5.

[330] (1979) 22 YB 24–25.

[331] (1978) 21 YB 14–17.

[332] (1987) 30 YB 4–5.

Further reading

Charles Barrow, '*Demir and Baykara v Turkey*: Breathing Life into Article 11', [2010] *EHRLR* 419.

Violeta Beširević, 'A Short Guide to Militant Democracy: Some Remarks on the Strasbourg Jurisprudence', in Wolfgang Benedek, Florence Benoît-Rohmer, Wolfram Karl, and Manfred Nowak, eds, *European Yearbook on Human Rights*, Antwerp: Intersentia and Vienna-Graz, Neuer Wissenschaftlicher Verlag, 2012, pp. 243–57.

Antoine Buyse, 'Contested Contours: The Limits of Freedom of Expression from an Abuse of Rights Perspective—Article 10 and 17 ECHR', in Eva Brems and Janneke Gerards, eds, *Shaping Rights in the ECHR*, Cambridge: Cambridge University Press, 2013, pp. 183–210.

Council of Europe, *Freedom of Association*, Dordrecht/Boston/London: Martinus Nijhoff, 1994.

Vincent Coussirat-Coustere, 'Article 11§2', in Pettiti et al., *La Convention européenne*, pp. 431–2.

Filip Dorssemont, 'The Right to Take Collective Action under Article 11 ECHR', in Filip Dorssemont, Klaus Lörcher, and Isabelle Schömann, eds, *The European Convention on Human Rights and the Employment Relation*, Oxford and Portland, OR: Hart, 2013, pp. 333–66.

Andrew Drzemczewski and Frank Wooldridge, 'The Closed Shop Case in Strasbourg', (1982) 31 *ICLQ* 396.

K.D. Ewing and J. Hendy, 'The Dramatic Implications of Demir and Baykara', (2010) 39 *Industrial Law Journal* 2.

Frowein/Peukert, *MenschenRechtsKonvention,* pp. 373–85.

Grabenwarter, *European Convention*, pp. 297–318.

Harris et al., *Law of the European Convention*, pp. 515–48.

P. Harvey, 'Militant Democracy and the European Convention on Human Rights', (2004) 29 *European Law Review* 407.

Aalt Willem Heringa and Fried van Hoof, 'Freedom of Association and Assembly (Article 11)', in Van Dijk et al., *Theory and Practice*, pp. 817–40.

Antoine Jacobs, 'Article 11 ECHR: The Right to Bargain Collectively under Article 11 ECHR', in Filip Dorssemont, Klaus Lörcher, and Isabelle Schömann, eds, *The European Convention on Human Rights and the Employment Relation*, Oxford and Portland, OR: Hart, 2013, pp. 309–32.

Paul Johnson, 'Homosexuality, Freedom of Assembly and the Margin of Appreciation Doctrine of the European Court of Human Rights: Alekseyev v Russia', (2011) 11 *HRLR* 578.

Mustafa Koçak and Esin Örücü, 'Dissolution of Political Parties in the Name of Democracy, Cases from Turkey and the European Court of Human Rights', (2003) 9 *European Public Law* 399.

Renée Koering-Joulin, 'Public Morals', in Mireille Delmas-Marty, ed., *The European Convention for the Protection of Human Rights*, Dordrecht/Boston/London: Martinus Nijhoff, 1992, pp. 83–98.

Klaus Lörcher, 'The New Social Dimension in the Jurisprudence of the European Court of Human Rights (ECtHR): The *Demir and Baykara* Judgment, its Methodology and Follow-up', in Filip Dorssemont, Klaus Lörcher, and Isabelle Schömann, eds, *The European Convention on Human Rights and the Employment Relation*, Oxford and Portland, OR: Hart, 2013, pp. 3–46.

J.P. Marguénaud and J. Mouly, 'La Cour européenne des droits de l'homme à la conquête du droit de grève', (2009) 9 *Revue de Droit du Travail* 499.

M. O'Boyle, 'Right to Speak and Associate under Strasbourg Case-Law with Reference to Eastern and Central Europe', (1993) 8 *Connecticut Journal of International Law* 282.

P. O'Higgins, 'The Closed Shop and the European Convention on Human Rights', [1981] *Revue des droits de l'homme* 22.

Ovey/White, *Jacobs and White, European Convention*, pp. 290–9.

R. Pelloux, 'Trois affaires syndicales devant la Cour européenne des droits de l'homme', [1976] *Annaire français de droit international* 122.

Karen Reid, *A Practitioner's Guide to the European Convention on Human Rights*, London: Sweet & Maxwell, 2011, pp. 444–63.

Stefan Sottiaux, 'Anti-Democratic Associations: Content and Consequences in Article 11 Adjudication', (2004) 22 *Netherlands Quarterly of Human Rights* 585.

Nicolas Valticos, 'Article 11§1', in Pettiti et al., *La Convention européenne*, pp. 419–35.

Isabelle Van Hiel, 'The Right to Form and Join Trade Unions Protected by Article 11 ECHR', in Filip Dorssemont, Klaus Lörcher, and Isabelle Schömann, eds, *The European Convention on Human Rights and the Employment Relation*, Oxford and Portland, OR: Hart, 2013, pp. 287–308.

Jacques Velu and Rusen Ergec, *La Convention européenne des droits de l'homme*, Brussels: Bruylant, 1990, pp. 643–59.

Ferdinand von Prondzynski, 'Freedom of Association and the Closed Shop: The European Perspective', (1982) 41 *Cambridge Law Journal* 256.

D. Voorhoof and J. Englebert, 'La liberté d'expression syndicale mise à mal par la Cour européenne des droits de l'homme', (2010) 83 *RTDH* 743.

Article 12. Right to marry/Droit au mariage

Men and women of marriageable age have the right to marry and to found a family, according to the national laws governing the exercise of this right.

A partir de l'âge nubile, l'homme et la femme ont le droit de se marier et de fonder une famille selon les lois nationales régissant l'exercice de ce droit.

Introductory comments

The right to marry was largely an invention of the Commission on Human Rights in the preparation of the Universal Declaration of Human Rights. It had not figured previously in the draft human rights declarations proposed by bodies like the Institut de droit international or by prominent individuals like H.G. Wells or Hersch Lauterpacht. The original draft of the Universal Declaration, prepared by the Secretariat of the Commission on Human Rights, read: 'Everyone has the right to contract marriage in accordance with the laws of the State.'[1] The Secretariat had analysed the constitutions of United Nations Member States, several draft declarations proposed by States, and a text submitted by the American Federation of Labor, collating the various texts and then setting out draft provisions for the future declaration based upon what it found. The right to marry appeared in only a handful of domestic constitutions, essentially confined to Latin America.[2] From the modest proposal of the Secretariat, a much more elaborate provision eventually emerged. The changes were largely the result of work by the Commission on the Status of Women.[3] It used the text to address issues of women's inequality related to the institution of marriage. For example, the words 'men and women' replaced 'everyone' in order to ensure equal treatment and not—this is the modern-day gloss based on a simplistic reading of the text rather than the intent of those who crafted the provision[4]—so as to reserve marriage to persons of opposite sex. Many of the classic inequalities relating to married women that were concerns of the Commission on the Status of Women have now declined in importance. They were also addressed in some detail in treaties negotiated under the auspices of the United Nations during the 1950s.[5]

Article 16 of the Universal Declaration consists of three paragraphs:

1. Men and women of full age, without any limitation due to race, nationality or religion, have the right to marry and to found a family. They are entitled to equal rights as to marriage, during marriage and at its dissolution.
2. Marriage shall be entered into only with the free and full consent of the intending spouses.

---

[1] E/CN.4/AC.1/3.

[2] E/CN.4/AC.1/3/Add.1, pp. 98–9.

[3] Draft Report of the Commission on the Status of Women to the Economic and Social Council Lake Success, 5 to 16 January 1948, E/CN.6/74, pp. 13–14.

[4] See, e.g., EU Network of Independent Experts on Fundamental Rights, Commentary of the Charter of Fundamental Rights of the European Union, June 2006, pp. 101–2.

[5] Convention on the Political Rights of Women, (1954) 193 UNTS 135; Convention on the Nationality of Married Women, (1958) 309 UNTS 65; Convention on Consent to Marriage, Minimum Age for Marriage and Registration of Marriages, (1964) 521 UNTS 232.

3. The family is the natural and fundamental group unit of society and is entitled to protection by society and the State.

Article 12 of the European Convention is derived from article 16 of the Universal Declaration of Human Rights. As a general rule, the provisions of the Declaration are more laconic than the detailed texts of the subsequent treaties whose content it has inspired, but this is not the case with article 12. From seventy-seven words in the Declaration, the right to marry generates only twenty-seven words in the Convention.

Article 23 of the International Covenant on Civil and Political Rights is the equivalent provision to article 12 of the European Convention:

1. The family is the natural and fundamental group unit of society and is entitled to protection by society and the State.
2. The right of men and women of marriageable age to marry and to found a family shall be recognised.
3. No marriage shall be entered into without the free and full consent of the intending spouses.
4. States Parties to the present Covenant shall take appropriate steps to ensure equality of rights and responsibilities of spouses as to marriage, during marriage and at its dissolution. In the case of dissolution, provision shall be made for the necessary protection of any children.[6]

In 1985, article 5 of Protocol No. 7 to the European Convention on Human Rights added a provision based broadly on article 23(4) of the Covenant.

Other international legal instruments are also of relevance to article 12 of the Convention. The European Social Charter, adopted in 1961, contains provisions dealing with the social, legal, and economic protection of the family.[7] The European Charter of Fundamental Rights contains a similar provision but with a wider scope:

Article 9. Right to marry and right to found a family
The right to marry and the right to found a family shall be guaranteed in accordance with the national laws governing the exercise of these rights.

Thus, the scope of article 9 of the Charter may be extended to other forms of marriage if these are established by national legislation.[8]

Drafting of the provision

The initial draft European Convention on Human Rights prepared by the International Juridical Section of the European Movement contained the following: 'Every State a party to this Convention shall guarantee to all persons within its territory the following rights: . . . g) The natural rights deriving from marriage and paternity and those pertaining to the family.'[9]

---

[6] For a comparison of article 12 with the corresponding provision of the Covenant, see A.H. Robertson, 'The United Nations International Covenant on Civil and Political Rights and the European Convention on Human Rights', (1968–1969) 32 *British Yearbook of International Law* 21, at pp. 34–5.

[7] European Social Charter, ETS 35, art. 16.

[8] Explanation relating to the Charter of Fundamental Rights, Official Journal of the European Union, C 303/34, 14 December 2007.

[9] Convention for the Collective Protection of Individual Rights and Democratic Liberties by the States, Members of the Council of Europe, and for the establishment of a European Court of Human Rights to ensure observance of the Convention, Doc. INF/5/E/R, I *TP* 296–303, at p. 296, art. I(g).

At the first session of the Consultative Assembly of the Council of Europe, in August–September 1949, Pierre-Henri Teitgen called for adoption of a convention that would include 'the natural rights deriving from marriage and paternity . . .'.[10] Asked to prepare a text for discussion in the Assembly's Committee on Legal and Administrative Questions, Teitgen proposed the following: 'Right to marry with free and full consent and to found a family, in accordance with Article 16 of the United Nations Declaration.'[11] The proposal met with opposition within the Committee. A motion by Lord Layton to delete the entire provision was defeated, with six in favour, nine against, and one abstention. Subsequently, an amendment to remove the reference to free and full consent succeeded, with eight in favour, four against, and three abstentions.[12] The Committee proposed the following: 'The right to marry and to found a family, in accordance with Article 16 of the United Nations Declaration.'[13]

In the plenary Consultative Assembly, Teitgen explained that the Committee had intended to 'make use, as far as possible, of the definitions set out in the "Universal Declaration of Human Rights"'.[14] The draft convention 'did not relate to all the provisions of the article in question, but only to those specifying the content of the liberty'.[15] He provided article 16 of the Declaration as an example: 'In mentioning the particular Article of the Universal Declaration, we have used only that part of the paragraph of the Article which affirms the right to marry and to found a family, but not the subsequent provisions of the Article concerning equal rights after marriage, since we only guarantee the right to marry.'[16] Teitgen also elaborated upon the inclusion of 'family rights' in the draft, noting that the subject had given rise to discussion in the Committee:

There were first of all those rights which I shall call 'family rights.' I might explain that by this I mean those rights which we had in mind when we refer in paragraph (4) of Article 2, to 'freedom from all arbitrary interference in private and family life'; and also those which we mentioned in paragraph (10) where we ask for protection of 'the right to marry and found a family,' and finally those which we defined in paragraph (11) where we speak of 'the right of parents to have prior right regarding the kind of education to be given to their children.'

No one in the Committee, I hasten to add, has denied the vital importance of these family rights. Some have said that they would prefer to see the guarantee confined for the moment to essential civic freedoms, to those which are the necessary conditions for the functioning of democratic institutions, and that it would be better for the time being to exclude all other freedoms and all other fundamental rights which would include, in spite of their importance, family rights.

---

[10] Report of the Sitting [of the Consultative Assembly, 19 August 1949], I *TP* 38–154, at p. 46.

[11] Proposals by Mr P.H. Teitgen, Rapporteur, 29 August 1949, Doc. A 116, I *TP* 166–8. Also Report presented by Mr P.H. Teitgen, 5 September 1949, Doc. A 290, I *TP* 192–213, at p. 206. See also Report [of the Committee on Legal and Administrative Questions], 5 September 1949, Doc. AS (1) 77, I *TP* 216–39, at p. 228.

[12] Minutes of the Sitting [of the Committee on Legal and Administrative Questions, 30 August 1949], Doc. A 167, I TP 174–80, at p. 176.

[13] Report [of the Committee on Legal and Administrative Questions], 5 September 1949, Doc. AS (1) 77, I *TP* 216–39, at p. 230. Also Report presented by Mr P.H. Teitgen, 5 September 1949, Doc. A 290, I *TP* 192–213, at p. 208.

[14] Report presented by Mr P.H. Teitgen, 5 September 1949, Doc. A 290, I *TP* 192–213, at p. 194.

[15] Ibid., p. 194. Also Report [of the Committee on Legal and Administrative Questions], 5 September 1949, Doc. AS (1) 77, I *TP* 216–39, at p. 218.

[16] Report of the Sitting [of the Consultative Assembly, 7 September 1949], I *TP* 258–95, at p. 268. Cited in *Johnston and Others v. Ireland*, 18 December 1986, § 52, Series A no. 112.

The Committee recalled the time in the recent past when, in some countries, certain people were denied the right to marry on account of race or religious convictions. It also recalled the legislation, under which some countries suffered during cruel years, which subordinated the child to the benefit of the State.

On account of these memories, the majority of the Committee considered it desirable to include these fundamental rights in the list of guaranteed freedoms. It considered that the father of a family cannot be an independent citizen, cannot feel free within his own country, if he is menaced in his own home and if, every day, the State steals from his soul, or the conscience of his children.[17]

There was a proposal to delete the entire provision.[18] Lord Layton of the United Kingdom took the lead, explaining that the proposed list of fundamental rights for the convention was 'not intended to be anything like a complete list of human rights. It is a selected list of rights which should be the subject of collective guarantee, and guaranteed now.'[19] Layton insisted upon a short list that 'should be limited to the absolute minimum necessary to constitute the cardinal principles for the functioning of political democracy'.[20] He pointed to the much longer list in the Universal Declaration of Human Rights, adding that he thought that all of the States represented in the Consultative Assembly were already 'parties to this Declaration'.[21] In fact there are no 'parties' to the Universal Declaration, which is a resolution of the United Nations General Assembly; moreover, at the time of Layton's remarks two members of the Consultative Assembly of the Council of Europe, Ireland and Italy, were not yet members of the United Nations.

Layton's proposal was criticized by Sean MacEntee of Ireland, who said that its adoption would 'seal the triumph of the totalitarian ideologies'. For MacEntee, '[t]he outstanding feature of the totalitarian regimes was the ruthless and savage way in which they endeavoured to wipe out the concept of the family as the natural unit of society'.[22] Similar statements were made by delegates from the Netherlands,[23] Italy,[24] and France.[25] Recognizing the isolation of his position, Layton agreed to its withdrawal.[26] The text that the Committee proposed was adopted by the Consultative Assembly.[27]

The Committee of Ministers decided to refer the draft adopted by the Consultative Assembly to a Committee of Experts. It held two sessions, in February and March 1950. At the conclusion of its first session, the Committee of Experts adopted the following provision: 'Men and women of full age have the right to marry and to found a family.'[28] The text it adopted is similar to that of the first sentence of article 16 of the Declaration except that the words 'without any limitation due to race, nationality or religion' that

---

[17] Report of the Sitting [of the Consultative Assembly, 7 September 1949], I *TP* 258–95, at p. 270.
[18] Amendment proposed by Lord Layton, Doc. AS (1) 93, I *TP* 254.
[19] Official Report of the Sitting [of the Consultative Assembly, 8 September 1949], II *TP* 14–274, at p. 50.
[20] Ibid., p. 52.
[21] Ibid., p. 50.
[22] Ibid., p. 90.
[23] Ibid., p. 96. See also the statement by Eamonn de Valera, ibid., p. 102.
[24] Ibid., p. 100.
[25] Ibid., p. 108.
[26] Ibid., p. 132.
[27] Recommendation No. 38 to the Committee of Ministers adopted 8 September 1949 on the conclusion of the debates, Doc. AS (1) 108, II *TP* 274–83, at p. 276.
[28] Preliminary Draft Convention for the Maintenance and Further Realisation of Human Rights and Fundamental Freedoms, 15 February 1950, Doc. A 833, III *TP* 236–46, at p. 238. Also Draft text of the first section of a draft Convention based on the work of the Consultative Assembly, Doc. A 809, III *TP* 220–31, at p. 224.

follow 'full age' are omitted. At the second session of the Committee, the United Kingdom made a proposal to dispense with the provision altogether.[29] A Drafting Committee charged with reviewing the United Kingdom proposal added a second sentence to the draft: 'Each State party hereto shall be entitled to establish rules governing the exercise of these rights.'[30] The Committee of Experts concluded its work with the submission to the Committee of Ministers of two different drafts. The first, labelled 'Alternative A', contained the text from the Drafting Committee.[31] The second, 'Alternative B', contained the text in the report of the first session of the Committee of Experts.[32] The report of the Committee to the Committee of Ministers explains that instead of enumerating rights by reference to the relevant provision in the Universal Declaration, as had been done by the Consultative Assembly, it was thought better to incorporate the text verbatim. Nevertheless, '[i]n accordance with the Assembly's intentions, only a certain part of the rights mentioned in [Article 16] of the Universal Declaration were included'.[33]

The Conference of Senior Officials that convened in June 1950 assigned a Drafting Committee to attempt to reconcile the competing versions. It prepared a new formulation on the right to marry based upon that of the Drafting Committee of the Committee of Experts with the addition of a phrase concerning national laws: 'Men and women of full age have the right to marry and to found a family, according to the national laws governing the exercise of these rights.'[34] There were no changes in the final version adopted by the Conference of Senior Officials.[35] In the text adopted by the Committee of Ministers at its fifth session, in early August 1950, the words 'these rights' were changed to 'this right'.[36]

It seems that minor changes continued to be discussed until the very last minute prior to the official adoption. On 21 October 1950, two weeks before the ceremony in Rome at which the Convention was to be signed, A.H. Robertson of the Secretariat wrote to H.J. Downing, a Foreign Office official in London, as follows:

There is one point to which I would like particularly to draw your attention—this is in Article 14 [article 12]. The French phrase 'à partir de l'âge nubile' has been translated 'of full age'. The latter, however, in my view, means 'who have attained their majority' which is quite different from 'l'âge nubile'. Consequently, I have suggested 'who may have reached the age of consent'. You may care to consider whether this is the most appropriate translation. An alternative would be 'of marriageable age', but it is less precise and would not make a good sentence.[37]

---

[29] Amendments to Articles 1, 2, 4, 5, 6, 8, and 9 of the Committee's preliminary draft proposal by the Expert of the United Kingdom, Doc. CM/WP 1 (50) 2, A 915, III *TP* 280–9, at pp. 286–8.

[30] Amendments to the British draft proposed by the Drafting Committee composed of Sir Oscar Dowson, MM le Quesne, Dons Moeller, and Salén, Doc. CM/WP 1 (50) 10, p. 3, A 919, III *TP* 288–95, at p. 292.

[31] Preliminary Draft Convention, Doc. CM/WP 1 (50) 14, A 932, III *TP* 312–35, at pp. 318–20.

[32] Ibid., p. 322.

[33] Report to the Committee of Ministers submitted by the Committee of Experts Instructed to Draw Up a Draft Convention of Collective Guarantee of Human Rights and Fundamental Freedoms, Doc. CM/WP 1 (5) 15, A 924, IV *TP* 2–55, at p. 22. Also Preliminary Draft of the Report to the Committee of Ministers, 24 February 1950, Doc. CM/WP 1 (50) 1, A 847, III *TP* 246–79, at p. 262.

[34] New draft alternatives B and B/2, Doc. CM/WP 4 (50) 9, A 1372, IV *TP* 182–91, at p. 190.

[35] Draft Convention appended to the draft report, Doc. CM/WP 4 (50) 16, appendix, A 1445, IV *TP* 218–40, at p. 224.

[36] Draft Convention adopted by the Sub-Committee, Doc. CM 1 (50) 52, A 1884, V *TP* 76–99, at p. 82; Draft Convention adopted by the Committee of Ministers, 7 August 1950, Doc. A 1937, V *TP* 120–45, at p. 128.

[37] Letter addressed 21 October 1950 by Mr Robertson (Member of the Secretariat) to Mr Downing (Official of the Western Organisations Department, Foreign Office, London), VI *TP* 184–7, at p. 286.

Downing answered:

[T]he phrase 'age of consent' is ambiguous in English. The word 'nubility' does exist in English but is not usual. I am unable to suggest any translation that would be entirely satisfactory. I think, however, that the solution is to omit any reference to age in both the English and French versions. These references are not necessary because the whole Article is governed by the concluding words 'according to the national laws' etc., and the age at which a person may marry with or without consent of parent or guardian will, of course, be provided for in the national laws.[38]

These exchanges did not result in any further changes to the text of article 12, however. The heading 'Right to marry' was added by Protocol No. 11.[39]

Analysis and interpretation

The wording of article 12 'makes it clear', a unanimous European Court of Human Rights sitting in Plenary has said, 'that Article 12 is mainly concerned to protect marriage as the basis of the family'.[40] In one of its judgments, the Court slightly rephrased article 12, stating that it 'secures the fundamental right of a man and woman to marry and to found a family'.[41] Exercise of the right gives rise to social, personal, and legal consequences. Marriage 'remains an institution which is widely accepted as conferring a particular status on those who enter it'.[42] Despite analogies with long-term relationships of unmarried couples, the Court has pointed to the distinct feature of a legally binding agreement associated with a public undertaking.[43]

Article 12 contains no limitation clause setting out permissible grounds for interference with the right that it enshrines, in contrast with articles 8 to 11. This 'underlines the fundamental character of the right to marry and to found a family', according to an individual opinion.[44] However, it does not mean the right is absolute, 'but rather that the Court would have to determine, regard being had to the State's margin of appreciation, the impugned interference was arbitrary or disproportionate'.[45] Although subject to national laws, as the final words of article 12 make explicit, 'the limitations thereby introduced must not restrict or reduce the right in such a way or to such an extent that the very essence of the right is impaired'.[46] Limitations arise at the procedural level, for

[38] Response to the preceding Letter, addressed 28 October 1950 by Mr Downing to Mr Roberson (US 17311/102), VI *TP* 286–91, at p. 288.
[39] Protocol No. 11 to the Convention for the Protection of Human Rights and Fundamental Freedoms, restructuring the control machinery established thereby, ETS 155, art. 2(2).
[40] *Rees v. the United Kingdom*, 17 October 1986, § 49, Series A no. 106; *Cossey v. the United Kingdom*, 27 September 1990, § 43, Series A no. 184.
[41] *B. and L. v. the United Kingdom*, no. 36536/02, § 34, 13 September 2005.
[42] *Şerife Yiğit v. Turkey* [GC], no. 3976/05, § 72, 2 November 2010; *Shackell v. the United Kingdom* (dec.), no. 45851/99, 27 April 2000; *Burden v. the United Kingdom* [GC], no. 13378/05, § 63, ECHR 2008.
[43] *Burden v. the United Kingdom* [GC], no. 13378/05, § 65, ECHR 2008.
[44] *W. v. the United Kingdom*, no. 11095/84, Commission report of 7 March 1989, Partially dissenting opinion of Mr Schermers.
[45] *Frasik v. Poland*, no. 22933/02, § 90, ECHR 2010 (extracts); *Jaremowicz v. Poland*, no. 24023/03, § 49, 5 January 2010; *O'Donoghue and Others v. the United Kingdom*, no. 34848/07, § 84, ECHR 2010 (extracts).
[46] *B. and L. v. the United Kingdom*, no. 36536/02, § 34, 13 September 2005; *Rees v. the United Kingdom*, 17 October 1986, § 50, Series A no. 106; *F. v. Switzerland*, 18 December 1987, § 32, Series A no. 128; *Muñoz Díaz v. Spain*, no. 49151/07, § 78, ECHR 2009; *Jaremowicz v. Poland*, no. 24023/03, § 48, 5 January 2010.

example with respect to publicity and solemnization of marriage, and at the substantive level, where there are issues of capacity, consent, and certain impediments.[47]

Limitations on the right are not left entirely to the margin of appreciation of States, something that 'would be tantamount to finding that the range of options open to a Contracting State included an effective bar on any exercise of the right to marry. The margin of appreciation cannot extend so far.'[48] On the other hand, 'given the sensitive moral choices concerned and the importance to be attached to the protection of children and the fostering of secure family environments, this Court must not rush to substitute its own judgment in place of the authorities who are best placed to assess and respond to the needs of society'.[49]

Article 8 of the Convention, which ensures the right to respect of family life, is closely related to article 12,[50] and frequently applications to the Convention organs invoke both provisions. The Court has held that if an interference with family life is justified under article 8(2) of the Convention, it cannot then be deemed a breach of article 12.[51] If the Court concludes that there is a violation of article 8 with respect to family life, it finds it unnecessary to examine separately a complaint under article 12.[52] It has occasionally described article 12 as the *lex specialis* of the right to marry, thereby implying, though perhaps unintentionally, that article 12 actually limits the scope of article 8.[53]

The Court has treated article 12 as if it recognizes one right, to marry and found a family, rather than two distinct rights, the first to marry and the second to found a family. There is a right to marry, but the right to found a family is contingent upon marriage.[54] Thus, no right of unmarried people to found a family is recognized by article 12. That does not mean that the Court denies the term 'family' to single parents or unmarried couples, but it considers their rights to be located within article 8, rather than granting them a right to 'found a family' pursuant to article 12.[55] At the same time, marriage is not dependent upon the intention to found a family. It exists even if there is no possibility or likelihood of procreation.[56] The right to found a family does not imply any right to procreate, nor does it entitle grandparents to any right to have grandchildren.[57]

---

[47] *F. v. Switzerland*, 18 December 1987, § 32, Series A no. 128; *O'Donoghue and Others v. the United Kingdom*, no. 34848/07, § 83, ECHR 2010 (extracts).

[48] *Frasik v. Poland*, no. 22933/02, § 88, ECHR 2010 (extracts). Also *R. and F. v. the United Kingdom* (dec.), no. 35748/05, 28 November 2006.

[49] *B. and L. v. the United Kingdom*, no. 36536/02, § 36, 13 September 2005.

[50] *Frasik v. Poland*, no. 22933/02, § 90, ECHR 2010 (extracts); *V.C. v. Slovakia*, no. 18968/07, § 159, ECHR 2011 (extracts).

[51] *Boso v. Italy* (dec.), no. 50490/99, ECHR 2002 VII; *Dickson v. the United Kingdom*, no. 44362/04, § 41, 18 April 2006.

[52] *V.C. v. Slovakia*, no. 18968/07, § 160, ECHR 2011 (extracts); *Lashin v. Russia*, no. 33117/02, § 124, 22 January 2013.

[53] *Hämäläinen v. Finland* [GC], no. 37359/09, § 96, 16 July 2014; *H. v. Finland*, no. 37359/09, § 38, 13 November 2012; *De Francesco v. Italy*, no. 13741/88, Commission decision of 12 March 1990; *De Luca v. Italy*, no. 13823/88, Commission decision of 12 March 1990; *R. and F. v. the United Kingdom* (dec.), no. 35748/05, 28 November 2006; *Parry v. the United Kingdom* (dec.), no. 42971/05, ECHR 2006-XV.

[54] *Rees v. the United Kingdom*, 17 October 1986, § 49, Series A no. 106; *Christine Goodwin v. the United Kingdom* [GC], no. 28957/95, § 98, ECHR 2002-VI.

[55] *Marckx v. Belgium*, 13 June 1979, § 31, Series A no. 31.

[56] *Hamer v. the United Kingdom*, no. 7114/75, Commission decision of 13 October 1977, (1978) 21 YB 302, DR 24, p. 5; *Christine Goodwin v. the United Kingdom* [GC], no. 28957/95, § 98, ECHR 2002-VI; *I. v. the United Kingdom* [GC], no. 25680/94, § 78, 11 July 2002.

[57] *Sijakova v. 'the former Yugoslav Republic of Macedonia'* (dec.), no. 67914/01, 6 March 2003.

'Men and women'

Attitudes towards gender and marriage have changed dramatically in recent times, both within Europe and throughout the world, since the European Court of Human Rights, in 1986, said that 'the right to marry guaranteed by Article 12 refers to the traditional marriage between persons of opposite biological sex'.[58] For example, same-sex marriage is now authorized in several Member States of the Council of Europe as a result of legislative changes. Constitutional courts in some countries have ruled that same-sex marriage must be allowed despite legislation that does not permit this.[59]

There can be little doubt that at the time of adoption of article 12 and of its direct ancestor, article 16 of the Universal Declaration of Human Rights, the suggestion that marriage could be anything but the 'traditional' union of a man and a woman was not given very much thought. Of course, same-sex relationships similar to marriage existed, but they were generally shrouded in euphemistic expressions such as 'roommate'. In terms of marriage other than that of a woman and a man, the main concern at the time was with non-monogamous relationships.[60] Attention has focused on use of the words 'men and women' in the relevant provisions. Speaking to the point in a 2011 decision rejecting an application by a same-sex couple, the Court explained why it persisted in its view that marriage necessarily involved a man and a woman:

The Court observes that, looked at in isolation, the wording of Article 12 might be interpreted so as not to exclude the marriage between two men or two women. However, in contrast, all other substantive Articles of the Convention grant rights and freedoms to 'everyone' or state that 'no one' is to be subjected to certain types of prohibited treatment. The choice of wording in Article 12 must thus be regarded as deliberate.[61]

The wording of article 12 repeats the formulation in article 16 of the Universal Declaration of Human Rights. In that instrument, the term 'everyone' is strongly favoured in formulations of fundamental rights. It is replaced with 'men and women' in two places, in article 16 and in the Preamble, where the reference is to 'equal rights of men and women'. The drafters of the Universal Declaration of Human Rights were quite 'deliberate' in recognizing the right to marry of men and women, as the Court noted, but the reason was not to exclude marriage of same-sex couples or transsexuals. It was to ensure the equality of women in the formation of the marital bond, during marriage, and at its dissolution, and had nothing at all to do with the gender of the partners.

The Court developed its understanding of the relationship between gender and marriage in a series of cases dealing with transsexuals. The issue is not strictly identical to that of same-sex marriage, but it is similar to the extent that before the change in gender of the transsexual, the two partners are of the same sex. An issue also arises if one of the partners in a 'traditional' marriage undergoes a change in gender, with the result that the

---

[58] *Rees v. the United Kingdom*, 17 October 1986, § 49, Series A no. 106. Also *Hämäläinen v. Finland* [GC], no. 37359/09, § 96, 16 July 2014.

[59] *Minister of Home Affairs v. Fourie (2005) and Lesbian and Gay Equality Project and Eighteen Others v. Minister of Home Affairs*, (2006) 3 BCLR 355 (CC); *Halpern v. Canada (Attorney General)*, (2003) 85 OR (3rd) 161 (CA).

[60] See, e.g., UN Doc. E/CN.6/SR.28, p. 7; UN Doc. E/CN.6/SR.29, pp. 6–7; E/CN.6/69; E/CN.6/74, p. 14.

[61] *Schalk and Kopf v. Austria*, no. 30141/04, § 55, ECHR 2010. See also *Alekseyev v. Russia*, nos 4916/07, 25924/08, and 14599/09, § 83, 21 October 2010.

couple are then of the same sex. The Court has held that the regulation of the consequences of a sex change in such circumstances falls within the margin of appreciation of
States.[62]

Under the English common law, marriage is confined to a man and a woman, and this
position has subsequently been codified by statute. In *Rees v. The United Kingdom*, the
Court rather summarily dismissed a challenge by an individual who was registered as a
woman at birth but who was living as a man. The Court referred to the reference to
national laws in article 12, noting that although they 'must not restrict or reduce the right
in such a way or to such an extent that the very essence of the right is impaired . . . the legal
impediment in the United Kingdom on the marriage of persons who are not of the
opposite biological sex cannot be said to have an effect of this kind'.[63]

A few years later, a similar issue was presented to the Court but with the distinction that
the transsexual applicant had a partner who was ready for marriage, something that had
not been the case in *Rees*, where the impediment to marriage was somewhat hypothetical.
The Court observed that this had not been a material issue in its earlier ruling, and saw no
reason to modify the position it had taken previously, adding that 'whether a person has
the right to marry depends not on the existence in the individual case of such a partner
or a wish to marry, but on whether or not he or she meets the general criteria laid down
by law'.[64]

It would take the Court more than another decade to change its mind. In a case dealing
with a 'post-operative transsexual', it said it was 'not persuaded that at the date of this case
it can still be assumed that these terms must refer to a determination of gender by purely
biological criteria'. The Court said there had been 'major social changes in the institution
of marriage since the adoption of the Convention as well as dramatic changes brought
about by developments in medicine and science in the field of transsexuality'. It also
pointed to the recently adopted Charter of Fundamental Rights of the European Union,
which refers, in its provision on marriage, to a right to marry and found a family with no
mention of men and women, 'no doubt deliberately'.[65]

In *Christine Goodwin*, the Court confronted an argument, quickly dismissed in *Cossey*,
that the right to marry was not breached because the transsexual could always marry
someone of the sex opposite to his or her former gender. The Court described this
suggestion as 'artificial', noting that the applicant 'lives as a woman, is in a relationship
with a man and would only wish to marry a man'. Denying her the right to marry, a man
thereby infringes 'the very essence of the right to marry'.[66] Speaking to the margin of
appreciation issue, the Court said that while a State may determine 'the conditions under
which a person claiming legal recognition as a transsexual establishes that gender
re-assignment has been properly effected or under which past marriages cease to be
valid and the formalities applicable to future marriages (including, for example, the

---

[62] *Parry v. the United Kingdom* (dec.), no. 42971/05, ECHR 2006-XV; *R. and F. v. the United Kingdom*
(dec.), no. 35748/05, 28 November 2006; *Schalk and Kopf v. Austria*, no. 30141/04, § 53, ECHR 2010.

[63] *Rees v. the United Kingdom*, 17 October 1986, § 50, Series A no. 106.

[64] *Cossey v. the United Kingdom*, 27 September 1990, § 32, Series A no. 184. Also *Sheffield and Horsham v.
the United Kingdom*, 30 July 1998, *Reports of Judgments and Decisions* 1998-V.

[65] *Christine Goodwin v. the United Kingdom* [GC], no. 28957/95, § 100, ECHR 2002-VI. Also *I. v. the
United Kingdom* [GC], no. 25680/94, § 80, 11 July 2002.

[66] *Christine Goodwin v. the United Kingdom* [GC], no. 28957/95, § 101, ECHR 2002-VI. Also *I. v. the
United Kingdom* [GC], no. 25680/94, § 81, 11 July 2002.

information to be furnished to intended spouses)',[67] this cannot justify 'barring the transsexual from enjoying the right to marry under any circumstances'.[68] However, in cases involving opposite-sex couples that choose to remain married after one has undergone a change of gender, the Court has said that the refusal of the State to recognize fully the new gender as long as the couple remains married remains within the margin appreciation.[69]

With its new and more modern approach, it would seem a small step for the Court to recognize same-sex marriage as being protected by article 12. But this was a step too far. The idea had been mooted as early as 1989 in a dissenting opinion by a member of the European Commission:

The right to live in a family and—when of marriageable age—to found a family is of paramount importance for the individual. Denial of this right means condemnation to solitude and loneliness. There must be strong arguments to justify such a condemnation. In my opinion the fundamental human right underlying Article 12 should also be granted to homosexual and lesbian couples. They should not be denied the right to found a family without good reasons.[70]

Ruling on an application in 2010, the Court said that there was no European consensus on same-sex marriage and that it was permitted in only six of forty-seven Convention States.[71] The Court returned to article 9 of the European Union Charter of Fundamental Rights and said that by referring to national law the drafters had left the decision whether to allow same-sex marriage to individual States. It referred to the Commentary: '... it may be argued that there is no obstacle to recognise same-sex relationships in the context of marriage. There is however, no explicit requirement that domestic laws should facilitate such marriages.'[72] Concluding that same-sex marriage lies within the scope of article 12, but that there was no violation of the provision because of a lack of consensus within Europe,[73] the Court's position on same-sex marriage must now be considered analogous to the view it takes of divorce with regard to article 12. It considers that States are not required to authorize same-sex marriage but, it seems, if they do, they must ensure that there are no unrealistic impediments or rules that might be discriminatory in nature.

Marriageable age

The term 'marriageable age' (*âge nubile*) does not seem to have led to any litigation. It would seem to be 18 throughout Europe, with the exception of Scotland, where it is 16. In many European countries, marriage as low as 15 or 16 is possible with parental consent.

---

[67] *Christine Goodwin v. the United Kingdom* [GC], no. 28957/95, § 103, ECHR 2002-VI.
[68] Ibid. Also *I. v. the United Kingdom* [GC], no. 25680/94, § 83, 11 July 2002.
[69] *R. and F. v. the United Kingdom* (dec.), no. 35748/05, 28 November 2006; *Parry v. the United Kingdom* (dec.), no. 42971/05, 28 November 2006.
[70] *W. v. the United Kingdom*, no. 11095/84, Commission report of 7 March 1989, Partially dissenting opinion of Mr Schermers.
[71] Belgium, the Netherlands, Norway, Portugal, Spain, and Sweden: *Schalk and Kopf v. Austria*, no. 30141/04, § 58, ECHR 2010.
[72] *Schalk and Kopf v. Austria*, no. 30141/04, § 90, ECHR 2010.
[73] But see *Schalk and Kopf v. Austria*, no. 30141/04, Concurring Opinion of Judge Malinverni, Joined by Judge Kovler, § 2, ECHR 2010.

The right to marry

The Court has said that '[t]he essence of the right to marry is the formation of a legal union of a man and a woman'.[74] Consequently, the focus is on 'legal' marriage. Couples who cohabit in marriage-like relationships are excluded from the scope of article 12. According to the Grand Chamber, '[m]arriage is characterised by a corpus of rights and obligations that differentiate it markedly from the situation of a man and woman who cohabit'.[75] For the Court, '[t]he choice of a partner and the decision to marry him or her, whether at liberty or in detention, is a strictly private and personal matter and there is no universal or commonly accepted pattern for such a choice or decision'.[76] The Court has not taken kindly to speculation by the authorities as to the motivation behind a marriage, for example the claim that it was to permit the partner to invoke spousal privilege and refuse to testify or that the relationship was 'superficial' or 'unworthy'.[77] In an early case dealing with a prisoner who sought to marry, the European Commission said it was not relevant whether the applicant could have 'consummated his marriage' while serving his sentence. Consequently, the 'essence' of the right to marry is the formation of a 'legally binding association between a man and a woman', without any requirement that they be able to or even desire to cohabit.[78] Some European legal systems may also recognize a form of *de facto* marriage, like the so-called common law marriage known in English law. The Court has dismissed a claim by which 'all the legal effects attaching to marriage should apply equally to situations that are in certain respects comparable to marriage', saying it falls outside the scope of article 12.[79]

It is probably better to speak of the freedom not to marry rather than a right not to marry, as was alleged by the unmarried mother of a child in *Marckx v. Belgium*. The case concerned distinctions between 'legitimate' and 'illegitimate' children. It was contended that the mother would be forced to marry in order to confer upon her daughter 'legitimate' status. The Court said there was 'no legal obstacle confronting the first applicant in the exercise of the freedom to marry or to remain single; consequently, the Court has no need to determine whether the Convention enshrines the right not to marry'.[80]

The Convention organs have not had to rule on whether article 12 includes a right to polygamous marriage. In *Johnston and Others v. Ireland*, the Court said that '[i]n any society espousing the principle of monogamy' it would be 'inconceivable' for marriage to take place as long as one of the partners was already married to another person.[81] In another case, it noted that 'the Croatian legal system adheres to the principle of monogamy, and does not allow individuals who are already married to conclude

---

[74] *Jaremowicz v. Poland*, no. 24023/03, § 60, 5 January 2010.

[75] *Şerife Yiğit v. Turkey* [GC], no. 3976/05, § 72, 2 November 2010. Also *Van der Heijden v. the Netherlands* [GC], no. 42857/05, § 69, 3 April 2012; *Nylund v. Finland* (dec.), no. 27110/95, ECHR 1999-VI; *D.G. and D.W. Lindsay v. the United Kingdom*, no. 11089/84, Commission decision of 11 November 1986, (1986) 29 YB 102, DR 49, p. 181.

[76] *Frasik v. Poland*, no. 22933/02, § 95, ECHR 2010 (extracts); *Jaremowicz v. Poland*, no. 24023/03, § 59, 5 January 2010.

[77] *Jaremowicz v. Poland*, no. 24023/03, § 56, 5 January 2010.

[78] *Hamer v. the United Kingdom*, no. 7114/75, Commission decision of 13 October 1977, § 71, (1978) 21 YB 302, DR 10, p. 174.

[79] *Marckx v. Belgium*, 13 June 1979, § 67, Series A no. 31.

[80] Ibid.

[81] *Johnston and Others v. Ireland*, 18 December 1986, § 50, Series A no. 112.

another marriage'.[82] The implication seems to be that polygamy is not in fact contrary to the Convention, but that States are entitled to make provision prohibiting it within their national laws as allowed by article 12.[83]

National legislation contains various obstacles to marriage among persons who are related either by blood or marriage. In one case, a man and the woman who had previously been married to his son lived together in a permanent and longstanding relationship. They were prohibited from marriage as long as the man's former wife and his son were still alive. This impediment to marriage had been criticized by a prestigious advisory committee as 'based simply on tradition' and no longer justifiable 'on any logical, rational or practical ground'. A minority report argued for retention of the prohibition because its removal 'would condone sexual rivalry between father and son, or mother and daughter, which, within the close confines of the family, would be destructive of the father and son, or mother and daughter, relationships'. Parliament agreed, and the norm was included in new legislation adopted in 1986.[84]

The Court held that the prohibition violated article 12. It considered that the prohibition pursued a legitimate aim in that it was to protect the integrity of the family by preventing sexual rivalry between parents and children as well as preventing harm to children who might be affected by such changing relationships. But it noted that the prohibition on marriage did not in fact prevent the relationships from developing, as the case at bar demonstrated. The government's suggestion that exceptions might be allowed where an inquiry demonstrated that there was no risk of harm did not impress the Court, which said that 'a cumbersome and expensive vetting process of this kind would not appear to offer a practically accessible or effective mechanism for individuals to vindicate their rights. It would also view with reservation a system that would require a person of full age in possession of his or her mental faculties to submit to a potentially intrusive investigation to ascertain whether it is suitable for them to marry.'[85]

Several cases involving prisoners and marriage have been addressed by the Convention organs. Early decisions of the European Commission denied the right of prisoners to marry,[86] but views evolved, and later it accepted the principle.[87] The European Commission even recognized the right to marry of a prisoner sentenced to life imprisonment with no foreseeable prospect of release on licence or parole.[88] There are many practical difficulties with prison marriages. But, as the Court has explained, '[w]hat needs to be solved in a situation where a detained person wishes to get married is not whether or not it is reasonable for him to marry in prison but the practical aspects of timing and making the necessary arrangements'.[89] In *Dickson v. The United Kingdom*, which concerned a prison detainee, the applicants argued that the denial of access to artificial insemination facilities breached the right to found a family found in article 12. The Chamber referred to 'the wide margin of appreciation afforded to the national authorities' and said that the refusal

[82] *V.K. v. Croatia*, no. 38380/08, § 100, 27 November 2012.
[83] See *Frasik v. Poland*, no. 22933/02, § 89, ECHR 2010 (extracts).
[84] *B. and L. v. the United Kingdom*, no. 36536/02, §§ 17–19, 13 September 2005.
[85] Ibid., § 37.
[86] *X v. Federal Republic of Germany*, no. 892/60, (1961) 4 YB 240, at pp. 254–7, Collection 6, p. 17.
[87] *Hamer v. the United Kingdom*, no. 7114/75, Commission decision of 13 October 1977, (1978) 21 YB 302, DR 24, p. 5.
[88] *Draper v. the United Kingdom*, no. 8186/78, Commission decision of 1 May 1979, DR 24, p. 72.
[89] *Frasik v. Poland*, no. 22933/02, § 95, ECHR 2010 (extracts).

of such access was not arbitrary or unreasonable, nor did it fail to strike a fair balance between competing interests.[90]

The phenomenon of the 'marriage of convenience' is well known in the field of international migration, and has even been the subject of comic cinematic treatments. States attempt to regulate through a range a measures the use of marriage that is undertaken solely for the purpose of permitting one of the partners to immigrate or to regularize a particular status.

The Court has said that States are entitled 'to prevent marriages of convenience, entered solely for the purpose of securing an immigration advantage'.[91] For example, it is permissible to require that a foreign national obtain a certificate of capacity before marriage in the country of immigration is allowed, and that evidence to confirm the genuineness of the marriage be provided.[92] Nevertheless, such legislation must meet the standards of accessibility and clarity that the Convention requires, and they may not otherwise deprive a person or a category of persons of full legal capacity to marry the partners of their choice.[93]

The Court objected to the scheme in force in the United Kingdom, noting that approval did not seem to be based solely on the genuineness of the marriage. It also found fault with a regulatory framework that imposed a blanket ban on marriage by individuals whose authorization to reside had almost expired, apparently on the presumption that such last-minute marriages were inherently suspect.[94] Such measures restricted the right to marry to such an extent that they encroached upon its very essence, the Court held. It also considered that the application fee was set at a level that a needy applicant might not be able to afford, constituting an additional impairment of the right to marry.[95]

The words 'at its dissolution' were included in article 16 of the Universal Declaration at the insistence of the Commission on the Status of Women over the opposition of some States that were concerned these words might imply a right to divorce. The drafting history of the Universal Declaration is indecisive as to whether 'at its dissolution' actually recognizes divorce or only ensures protection of the rights of the spouses at the end of marriage, where divorce is recognized by law.[96]

The leading case on the subject is *Johnston and Others v. Ireland*. The applicants contended that the impossibility of obtaining dissolution of marriage under Irish law prevented them from remarrying, thereby denying their rights under article 12 as well as under article 8. Ireland's Constitution contained the following: 'No law shall be enacted providing for the grant of a dissolution of marriage.' The applicants urged the Court not to consider whether the Convention allowed a right to divorce, but it said that it could not separate that notion from the right to remarry, given the principle of monogamy in Irish society. Interpreting article 12, the Court said that the ordinary meaning of the words

---

[90] *Dickson v. the United Kingdom*, no. 44362/04, §§ 39, 41, 18 April 2006. Also ibid., §§ 57, 86, ECHR 2007-V.

[91] *O'Donoghue and Others v. the United Kingdom*, no. 34848/07, §§ 83, 87, ECHR 2010 (extracts); *Sanders v. France*, no. 31401/96, Commission decision of 16 October 1996, DR 87-B, p. 160.

[92] *Klip and Krüger v. the Netherlands* (dec.), no. 33257/96, 3 December 1997; *Sanders v. France* (dec.), 31401/96, 16 October 1996; *Frasik v. Poland*, no. 22933/02, § 89, ECHR 2010 (extracts).

[93] *O'Donoghue and Others v. the United Kingdom*, no. 34848/07, § 83, ECHR 2010 (extracts).

[94] Ibid., § 88.

[95] Ibid., § 90.

[96] UN Doc. E/CN.6/SR.28, p. 7; UN Doc. E/CN.6/SR.29, p. 7; UN Doc. E/CN.4/SR.58, p. 10; UN Doc. E/CN.4/SR.62, pp. 10–12; *Official Records of the General Assembly*, Third Session, 1948, pp. 359–79.

'right to marry' covered the formation of marital relationships, but not their dissolution. In addition, the Court noted the reference to 'national laws', stating that 'even if, as the applicants would have it, the prohibition on divorce is to be seen as a restriction on capacity to marry, the Court does not consider that, in a society adhering to the principle of monogamy, such a restriction can be regarded as injuring the substance of the right guaranteed by Article 12'.[97]

Turning to the *travaux préparatoires*, the Court observed that article 12 was based on article 16(1) of the Universal Declaration of Human Rights. It cited the remarks of the rapporteur of the Committee on Legal and Administrative Questions during drafting of the European Convention, who explained that paragraph 1 of article 16 had been incorporated in the draft, but not the subsequent paragraphs 'concerning equal rights after marriage, since we only guarantee the right to marry'.[98] There, 'the travaux préparatoires disclose no intention to include in Article 12 (art. 12) any guarantee of a right to have the ties of marriage dissolved by divorce'.[99] It described the omission of the right to divorce as 'deliberate'.[100] The Court added that no right to divorce was included in Protocol No. 7, which was opened for signature in 1984. It observed that although the Protocol guaranteed certain additional rights to spouses, notably in the event of dissolution of marriage, its drafters did not use the opportunity to recognize a right to divorce. The Court cited the Explanatory Report on the Protocol that said that the words 'in the event of its dissolution' in article 5 'do not imply any obligation on a State to provide for dissolution of marriage or to provide any special forms of dissolution'.[101]

In *Johnston and Others*, Judge Pinheiro Farinha made a separate declaration expressing the hope that an additional sentence would have been added to the judgment: 'The Court recognises that support and encouragement of the traditional family is in itself legitimate or even praiseworthy.'[102] Judge de Meyer appended a lengthy separate, partly dissenting and partly concurring opinion in which he said the prohibition of divorce in Ireland was contrary to articles 8 and 12 of the Convention. He alluded to the fact that the rule was dictated by the Catholic majority, yet it applied to others like the applicants, who were protestant, citing article 9 of the Convention.[103]

In 1995, not quite a decade after the *Johnston and Others* judgment, the Irish constitution was amended following a popular referendum, opening the door to legislation that allowed for divorce. In countries where divorce is permitted, there is a right to remarry without unreasonable restrictions.[104] Delays in such proceedings have led to complaints of a violation of article 12 because this prevented remarriage.[105] In the context of article 6, the Court has said that 'special diligence is required in cases relating to civil status and capacity'.[106] The Convention organs have insisted that there be a realistic

---

[97] *Johnston and Others v. Ireland*, 18 December 1986, § 52, Series A no. 112.
[98] Ibid.
[99] Ibid.
[100] Ibid., § 53.
[101] Ibid.
[102] Ibid., Declaration by Judge Pinheiro Farinha.
[103] Ibid., Separate Opinion, Partly Dissenting and Partly Concurring, of Judge de Meyer.
[104] *F. v. Switzerland*, 18 December 1987, § 38, Series A no. 128.
[105] *V.K. v. Croatia*, no. 38380/08, §§ 106–107, 27 November 2012; *Aresti Charalambous v. Cyprus*, no. 43151/04, § 56, 19 July 2007; *S.D.P. v. Italy*, no. 27962/95, Commission decision of 16 April 1996.
[106] *Maciariello v. Italy*, 27 February 1992, § 18, Series A no. 230-A. Also *Bock v. Germany*, 29 March 1989, § 49, Series A no. 15.

possibility of remarriage rather than some abstract desire by the applicant.[107] Nevertheless, a delay in divorce proceedings as such may constitute a violation of article 6.[108]

Article 12 does not distinguish between the right to marriage and a right to remarriage.[109] Although the Court does not consider a right to divorce to fall within the scope of article 12, when legislation recognizes divorce the exercise of the right to marry, or rather, to remarry, may be contingent upon effective and relatively expedited divorce proceedings. According to the Court, 'a failure to conduct divorce proceedings within a reasonable time could in certain circumstances raise an issue under Article 12 of the Convention'.[110]

In many national legislative schemes, it has been common to impose a waiting period after the divorce before the former partners are in a position to remarry. This was meant as a period of reflection, premised on the idea that they might well change their mind and return to cohabitation, although in practice it rarely happened. It also seems to have been viewed as a sanction; in some legal systems, it could be imposed upon the party deemed to be at fault for the rupture of the marriage.[111] When Swiss legislation allowing the imposition upon the party deemed at fault of a three-year period between dissolution of one marriage and remarriage was contested, the Court noted that most States had done away with such measures. However, the Court said, 'the fact that, at the end of a gradual evolution, a country finds itself in an isolated position as regards one aspect of its legislation does not necessarily imply that that aspect offends the Convention, particularly in a field—matrimony—which is so closely bound up with the cultural and historical traditions of each society and its deep-rooted ideas about the family unit'.[112] The Court agreed that the three-year waiting period interfered with the right to marry but said it did not impair the very essence of the right. The Swiss approach was explained as intended to protect the institution of marriage as well as the rights of others, and even the person upon whom the temporary prohibition of marriage was imposed.[113] Concluding that article 12 had been violated, the Court affirmed that the stability of marriage was a legitimate aim that was in the public interest but said it doubted that the means being used were appropriate.[114]

Right to found a family

The family is a notion that is not only culturally specific but also one that is being transformed as unconventional and innovative forms of social relationship similar to traditional nuclear families but with marked differences emerge. The Court takes a fairly broad approach to the notion of family when it considers the concept from the standpoint of article 8, but within the framework of article 12 its vision is rather more conservative. There, the main concern is 'to protect marriage as the basis of the family'.[115] The right to

[107] *Capoccia v. Italy*, no. 16479/90, Commission decision of 13 October 1993; *Bolignari v. Italy*, no. 37175/97, Commission decision of 22 April 1998; *Bacuzzi v. Italy* (dec.), no. 43817/04, 24 May 2011.
[108] *Chau v. France* (dec.), no. 39144/02, 14 June 2005.
[109] *F. v. Switzerland*, 18 December 1987, § 33, Series A no. 128.
[110] *Aresti Charalambous v. Cyprus*, no. 43151/04, § 56, 19 July 2007.
[111] *F. v. Switzerland*, 18 December 1987, § 13, Series A no. 128.
[112] Ibid., § 33.
[113] Ibid., § 35.
[114] Ibid., § 36.
[115] *Rees v. the United Kingdom*, 17 October 1986, § 49, Series A no. 106.

found a family is not viewed as an autonomous right but rather one that is an attribute or a consequence of the right to marry. However, the intent to found a family is not necessary for the right to marry to be exercised. The Court has said that '[t]he second aspect is not however a condition of the first and the inability of any couple to conceive or parent a child cannot be regarded as per se removing their right to enjoy the first limb of this provision'.[116] To view the matter otherwise would deprive women of the possibility of founding a family once they have reached an age when they can no longer have children. Younger women, and men too, may find themselves infertile for various reasons, or may be advised against procreation because of a predisposition to genetically transmitted illnesses and disabilities.

The classic solution in such cases is adoption. Nevertheless, the case law of the European Commission has not recognized a right of adoption as a component of article 12. According to the European Commission, article 12 'implies the existence of a couple and cannot be construed as including the right of an unmarried person to adopt'.[117] For the Commission, adoption of a child and its integration into a family could, 'in some circumstances, be said to constitute the foundation of a family by that couple. It is quite conceivable that a "family" might be "founded" in such a way.' However, the article 'does not as such guarantee a right to adopt or otherwise integrate into a family a child which is not the natural child of the couple concerned'.[118]

A State policy preventing births through sterilization or forced abortion would almost certainly fall foul of article 12, although there are no examples in case law. An attempt to invoke the provision where infertility resulted from nuclear tests was found to be inadmissible *ratione temporis*.[119] The Court rejected a claim by a man who claimed that the State, by allowing his wife to have an abortion, was violating his right to found a family on the grounds that the abortion was justified by her health. It said that in applying the Convention to such situations, the Court indicated that the rights of the woman should generally prevail over those of the man, 'as she is the person primarily concerned by the pregnancy and its continuation or termination'.[120]

Discrimination

The Convention addresses issues of discrimination through article 14. However, because article 14 has no independent existence, any violation of that provision must be related to another right set out in the Convention. As it does with other provisions of the Convention, when the Court finds there is a violation of the substantive article, it may exercise discretion and decline to make a separate ruling on the application of article 14.[121]

The Court did not conclude that there was discrimination in relation to article 12 in a case involving a Roma marriage conducted in accordance with customs and cultural traditions and recognized by the community. For the Roma community, such marriage generates social effects, notably an obligation to live together, as well as other rights and

[116] *Christine Goodwin v. the United Kingdom* [GC], no. 28957/95, § 98, ECHR 2002-VI.
[117] *X v. Belgium and the Netherlands*, no. 6482/74, Commission decision of 10 July 1975, DR 7, p. 76; *Di Lazzaro v. Italy*, no. 31924/96, Commission decision of 10 July 1997, DR 90-B, p. 134.
[118] *X and Y v. the United Kingdom*, no. 7229/75, Commission decision of 15 December 1977, DR 12, p. 32.
[119] *McGinley and Egan v. the United Kingdom*, nos 21825/93 and 23414/95, Commission decision of 28 November 1995.
[120] *Boso v. Italy* (dec.), no. 50490/99, §§ 2–3, ECHR 2002-VII.
[121] See, e.g., *B. and L. v. the United Kingdom*, no. 36536/02, § 14, 13 September 2005.

duties that are inherent in the institution of marriage. However, Roma marriage is not recognized under Spanish law, whereas other forms of marital rites, such as those of the Catholic, Protestant, Jewish, and Muslim confessions, produce legal effects. The Court noted that Catholic, Protestant, Jewish, and Muslim marriages benefited from legal recognition as a result of special agreements with the State giving them the same status as civil marriage, something available in Spain since 1981 to all without distinction.[122]

In *Johnston and Others v. Ireland*, which concerned whether a right to divorce could be found within article 12, dissenting Judge de Meyer said that the prohibition of divorce in Irish law was discriminatory, in that Irish people who obtained divorces while residing abroad could return home, where they could then remarry. He said the distinction the law made between Irish citizens depending upon whether they were domiciled in Ireland or elsewhere lacked an objective and reasonable justification.[123] The majority did not speak to the article 14 issue.

United Kingdom legislation dealing with so-called marriages of convenience was not applicable to marriages in the Church of England, apparently premised on the logic that such marriages were inherently sound, while those of other denominations were inherently suspect. The Court concluded that the government had failed to adduce any reasons capable of offering an objective and reasonable justification for a difference in treatment between those prepared to marry in the Church of England and those who were not.[124]

A failure to apply the same rules, for example in the area of testimonial privilege of spouses, to persons who are married and to those who live in stable relationships similar to marriage such as civil partnerships, does not constitute discrimination under the Convention.[125]

It is common for special rules to apply to couples who cohabit as opposed to single persons with respect to various social benefits. This may include eligibility for social welfare and state-funded housing, for example, as well as entitlements to certain transfers in pension benefits and a distinct taxation regime. Although increasingly States follow policies in this respect that minimize any distinctions in the treatment of couples that cohabit depending upon whether they are married or not, some disparities continue. Given that cohabiting couples and married couples are not 'similarly situated', the Convention organs have considered complaints based on differing regimes in these areas to be inadmissible under article 14.[126]

The Court has held that measures applied to transsexuals that related to the right to marry were not discriminatory because the group was not similarly situated to cissexuals.[127]

The requirement in Switzerland that married spouses and their children, as long as they are minors, bear the same name fulfils a legitimate aim of their identification vis-à-vis third parties. The European Commission considered this to be a suitable measure, proportionate to the aim it sought to realize, and therefore not contrary to article 14.[128]

---

[122] *Muñoz Díaz v. Spain*, no. 49151/07, §§ 79–81, ECHR 2009.

[123] *Johnston and Others v. Ireland*, 18 December 1986, Separate Opinion, Partly Dissenting and Partly Concurring, of Judge de Meyer, Series A no. 112.

[124] *O'Donoghue and Others v. the United Kingdom*, no. 34848/07, § 101, ECHR 2010 (extracts).

[125] *Van der Heijden v. the Netherlands* [GC], no. 42857/05, § 84, 3 April 2012.

[126] *D.G. and D.W. Lindsay v. the United Kingdom*, no. 11089/84, Commission decision of 11 November 1986, (1986) 29 YB 102, DR 49, p. 181.

[127] *Hämäläinen v. Finland* [GC], no. 37359/09, § 112, 16 July 2014.

[128] *Hagmann-Hüsler v. Switzerland*, no. 8042/77, Commission decision of 15 December 1977, DR 12, p. 202.

Reservations

There have been no reservations or declarations with respect to article 12 of the Convention.

Further reading

Christina M. Cerna, '*Schalk & Kopf v. Austria* (Eur. Ct. H.R.), Introductory Note', (2010) 49 *International Legal Materials* 1302.

Pieter van Dijk, 'The Right to Marry and to Found a Family (Article 12)', in Van Dijk et al., *Theory and Practice*, pp. 841–62.

Frowein/Peukert, *MenschenRechtsKonvention*, pp. 386–90.

Grabenwarter, *European Convention*, pp. 319–26.

Harris et al., *Law of the European Convention*, pp. 549–56.

Loveday Hodson, 'A Marriage by Any Other Name? *Schalk and Kopf v Austria*', (2011) 11 *HRLR* 170.

Paul Johnson, '"An Essentially Private Manifestation of Human Personality": Constructions of Homosexuality in the European Court of Human Rights', (2010) 10 *HRLR* 67.

Paul Johnson, 'Challenging the Heteronormativity of Marriage: The Role of Judicial Interpretation and Authority', (2011) 20 *Social and Legal Studies* 349.

Paul Johnson, *Homosexuality and the European Court of Human Rights*, Abingdon, UK: Routledge, 2013.

Montserrat Enrich Mas, 'Article 12', in Pettiti et al., *La Convention européenne*, pp. 437–54.

Rebekka Wiemann, 'Keine Verpflichtung der Konventionsstaaten zur Einführung gleichgeschlecht-licher Ehe / Schalk und Kopf gegen Österreich', (2010) 37 *Europaische grundrechte zeitschrift* 445.

Article 13. Right to an effective remedy/Droit à un recours effectif

Everyone whose rights and freedoms as set forth in this Convention are violated shall have an effective remedy before a national authority notwithstanding that the violation has been committed by persons acting in an official capacity.	Toute personne dont les droits et libertés reconnus dans la présente Convention ont été violés, a droit à l'octroi d'un recours effectif devant une instance nationale, alors même que la violation aurait été commise par des personnes agissant dans l'exercice de leurs fonctions officielles.

Introductory comments

The Universal Declaration of Human Rights guarantees, in article 8, the right to an effective remedy: 'Everyone has the right to an effective remedy by the competent national tribunals for acts violating the fundamental rights granted him by the constitution or by law.' One of the earliest drafts of the international bill of rights, proposed by the United Kingdom to the United Nations Commission on Human Rights, set this out as one of the core obligations: '*Article 2.* Every state is, by international law, under an obligation to ensure:... (b) that any person whose rights or freedoms are violated should have an effective remedy, notwithstanding that the violation has been committed by persons acting in an official capacity.'[1] However, the proposal that the right be incorporated in the Universal Declaration only emerged rather late in the negotiations, during the debates in the Third Committee of the General Assembly.[2] It resulted from attempts to amend the text that became article 7, dealing with equality before the law and protection against discrimination.

Article 8 of the Universal Declaration inspired the drafters of the European Convention, as it did those who prepared the International Covenant on Civil and Political Rights. Article 2(3) of the latter instrument has a close affinity with article 8 of the Universal Declaration of Human Rights. It states:

3. Each State Party to the present Covenant undertakes:
   (a) To ensure that any person whose rights or freedoms as herein recognized are violated shall have an effective remedy, notwithstanding that the violation has been committed by persons acting in an official capacity;
   (b) To ensure that any person claiming such a remedy shall have his right thereto determined by competent judicial, administrative or legislative authorities, or by any other competent authority provided for by the legal system of the State, and to develop the possibilities of judicial remedy;
   (c) To ensure that the competent authorities shall enforce such remedies when granted.

---

[1] Text of Letter from Lord Dukeston, the United Kingdom Representative on the Human Rights Commission, to the Secretary General of the United Nations, UN Doc. E/CN.4/AC.1/4, p. 6.

[2] Mexico: Amendment to Article 6 of the Draft Declaration (E/800), UN Doc. A/C.3/308; Mexico, Chile, Venezuela: Amendment to Article 6 of the Draft Declaration (E/800), UN Doc. A/C.3/309; Cuba: Addendum to Article 6 of the Draft Declaration (E/800), UN Doc. A/C.3/310; Official Records of the General Assembly, Third Session, 1948, p. 235.

The Charter of Fundamental Rights of the European Union combines articles 13 and 6 of the European Convention in a provision that heads the section entitled 'Justice' and is labelled 'Right to an effective remedy and to a fair trial':

Article 47. Right to an effective remedy and to a fair trial
Everyone whose rights and freedoms guaranteed by the law of the Union are violated has the right to an effective remedy before a tribunal in compliance with the conditions laid down in this Article.

Everyone is entitled to a fair and public hearing within a reasonable time by an independent and impartial tribunal previously established by law. Everyone shall have the possibility of being advised, defended and represented.

Legal aid shall be made available to those who lack sufficient resources in so far as such aid is necessary to ensure effective access to justice.

Drafting of the provision

The initial list of rights included in a working paper prepared by the International Council of the European Movement, meeting in Brussels in February 1949, contained a reference to freedom of petition or appeal against a violation of fundamental rights.[3] However, the draft convention presented by the European Movement to the Committee of Ministers in June 1949 did not contain any relevant provision.[4]

A trace of article 13 of the European Convention on Human Rights appears in the proposal by Pierre-Henri Teitgen to the Consultative Assembly of the Council of Europe, in August 1949: 'Security of person, in accordance with Articles 3, 5 and 8 of the Universal Declaration of Human Rights approved by the General Assembly of the United Nations.'[5] Article 3 concerned life, liberty, and security of person and article 5 dealt with torture and cruel, inhuman, and degrading treatment or punishment. Article 8 was the 'right to an effective remedy' provision of the Universal Declaration of Human Rights. The proposal was retained in the text adopted by the Committee and, subsequently, by the plenary Consultative Assembly.[6] The reference to article 8 did not give rise to any particular comment or to a reference in the explanatory memorandum.

The Committee of Ministers decided to refer the draft of the Consultative Assembly to a Committee of Experts. In the meantime, work in the United Nations Commission on Human Rights on the draft covenant had advanced. The Commission had agreed on the following draft:

Article 2, para. 2: Each State party hereto undertakes to ensure that any persons whose rights or freedoms as herein defined are violated shall have an effective remedy before the competent national tribunals notwithstanding that the violation has been committed by persons acting in an official capacity.[7]

---

[3] Recommendations adopted at the meeting of the International Council of the European Movement held at Brussels in February 1949, INF/2/F, p. 3.

[4] Convention for the Collective Protection of Individual Rights and Democratic Liberties by the States, Members of the Council of Europe, and for the establishment of a European Court of Human Rights to ensure observance of the Convention, Doc. INF/5/E/R, I *TP* 296–303.

[5] Proposals by Mr P.H. Teitgen, Rapporteur, 29 August 1949, Doc. A 116, I *TP* 166–8.

[6] Minutes of the Sitting [of the Committee for Legal and Administrative Affairs of the Consultative Assembly, 29 August 1949], Doc. A 142, I *TP* 170–3; Report presented by Mr P.H. Teitgen, 5 September 1949, Doc. A 290, I *TP* 192–213.

[7] Report of the Fifth Session of the Commission on Human Rights to the Economic and Social Council, UN Doc. E/1371(Supp.), p. 18.

The United Kingdom's comments on the draft covenant were circulated in preparation for the first session of the Committee of Experts of the Council of Europe. According to the United Kingdom:

b) The phrase 'an effective remedy before the competent national tribunal' in paragraph 2 appears to be too much compressed. The guarantee of the individual's rights against abuse comprises three distinct elements, viz.,

   1) The possession of a legal remedy.
   2) The grant of this remedy by an independent tribunal. (His Majesty's Government consider it desirable to mention specifically in the Covenant that the tribunal should be independent.)
   3) The enforcement of the remedy granted by the Courts by the police or executive authorities responsible.

c) His Majesty's Government therefore consider that this paragraph should be expanded to read as follows:

'2. Each State party hereto undertakes to ensure:

   a) *that any person whose rights or freedom as herein defined are violated shall have an effective remedy, notwithstanding that the violation has been committed by persons acting in an official capacity,*

   b) *that any person claiming such a remedy shall have his right thereto determined by national tribunals, whose independence is secured,* and

   c) *that the police and executive authorities shall enforce such remedies when granted.*[8]

Oscar Dowson, the United Kingdom delegate to the Committee of Experts, proposed an amendment to the draft European Convention along almost identical lines.[9]

A Sub-Committee of the Committee of Experts assigned to study the amendments that had been proposed reported that it 'considered it advisable to give due consideration to these proposals as being of interest even to those who adhere to the definition of Human Rights as proposed by the Assembly. This Article could, in fact, be included as an addition to Article 4 of the Assembly Draft.'[10] The Italian expert said the reference to article 8 was unnecessary.[11] The Sub-Committee did not take up the British proposal and instead suggested something rather different, inspired by the text of article 8 of the Universal Declaration of Human Rights but with significant differences:

Article 8. The High Contracting Parties must ensure that all persons within their jurisdiction shall have an effective remedy by an independent tribunal for acts violating the rights and freedoms accorded to them under this Convention.[12]

It was modified by the replacement of the words 'independent tribunal' with 'independent judicial authority'.[13] The preliminary draft report of the Committee of Experts, prepared at the conclusion of its first session in February 1950, stated:

---

[8] Comments of Governments on the Draft International Covenant on Human Rights and Measures of Implementation [UN Doc. E/CN.4/353/Add.1-3], Doc. A 770, III *TP* 156–79, at pp. 156–8 (emphasis added).

[9] Amendments to Articles 4 and 7 of the Recommendation of the Consultative Assembly proposed by the Expert of the United Kingdom, Doc. A 782, III *TP* 188–91.

[10] First part of the Report of the Sub-Committee Instructed to Make a Preliminary Study of the Amendments Proposed by the Members of the Committee, Doc. A 796, III *TP* 200–5, at p. 202. Article 4 laid down the principle that every member State 'shall be entitled to establish the rules by which the guaranteed rights and freedoms shall be organised and protected within its territory'.

[11] Ibid.

[12] Corrigendum to preceding document, Doc. A 815, III *TP* 226–7.

[13] Preliminary Draft Convention for the Maintenance and Further Realisation of Human Rights and Fundamental Freedoms, 15 February 1950, Doc. A 833, III *TP* 236–46, at p. 240.

2. With regard to the right mentioned in Article 2, para. 1, the Committee did not copy the text of Article 8 of the Universal Declaration, to which the Assembly Draft refers, because this Article is concerned with the right of remedy through national tribunals in cases of violation of fundamental rights, a question which the Committee thought should be placed elsewhere in the Convention (cf. Article 8).

...

Article 8 is new and replaces the reference to Article 8 of the Universal Declaration contained in Article 2, paragraph 1, of the Assembly draft.[14]

At the second session of the Committee of Experts, in March 1950, the United Kingdom revived the proposal it had put forward the previous month.[15] The Committee of Experts prepared two drafts. Alternatives A and A/2, which were broadly based upon the Consultative Assembly draft, contained the following: 'The High Contracting Parties must ensure that all persons within their jurisdiction, shall have an effective remedy by a national independent authority for acts violating the rights and freedoms accorded to them under this Convention, notwithstanding that the violation has been committed by persons acting in an official capacity.'[16] Alternatives B and B/2, originating with the British proposals, included this text: 'The High Contracting Parties undertake to ensure that any person whose rights and freedoms as herein defined are violated shall have an effective remedy notwithstanding that the violation has been committed by persons acting in an official capacity.'[17]

The Report of the Committee of Experts to the Committee of Ministers said:

a) Comments on Alternatives A and A/2:
– Article 2
...

With regard to the right mentioned in Article 2, paragraph 1, the Committee did not copy the text of article 8 of the Universal Declaration, to which the Assembly draft refers, because this Article is concerned with the right of remedy through national tribunals in cases of violation of fundamental rights. This is not a Human Right in itself, but a mode to secure these rights. The Committee thought this question should be placed elsewhere in the Convention (cf. Article 9).[18]

– Article 9
Article 9 is new and replaced the reference to Article 8 of the Universal Declaration, contained in Article 2, paragraph 1 of the Assembly draft (Cf. comments on Art. 2, para. 2).

The national authority envisaged in this Article may be an administrative or legal court. For recourse to it to be effective, it was obvious that the court concerned must be in a position to judge the case impartially.[19]

The draft proposed for Alternatives B and B/2 was similar in scope.[20] In effect, the Committee of Experts had reached agreement on a provision common to the two drafts.

---

[14] Preliminary Draft of the Report to the Committee of Ministers, 24 February 1950, Doc. CM/WP 1 (50) 1, A 847, III *TP* 246–79, at pp. 262, 266.
[15] Amendments to Articles 1, 2, 4, 5, 6, 8, and 9 of the Committee's preliminary draft proposal by the Expert of the United Kingdom, Doc. CM/WP 1 (50) 2, A 915, III *TP* 280–9, at p. 280.
[16] Appendix to the Report of the Committee of Experts to the Committee of Ministers—Draft Convention (16 March 1950), Doc. CM/WP 1 (50) 14 revised, A 925, IV *TP* 50–79, at p. 56.
[17] Ibid.
[18] Report to the Committee of Ministers submitted by the Committee of Experts Instructed to Draw Up a Draft Convention of Collective Guarantee of Human Rights and Fundamental Freedoms, Doc. CM/WP 1 (5) 15, A 924, IV *TP* 2–55, at p. 22.
[19] Ibid., p. 30.
[20] Ibid.

The Conference of Senior Officials, meeting in June 1950, made a small change, adding the words 'before a national authority' after 'effective remedy'.[21] The Report of the Conference of Senior Officials to the Committee of Ministers explained that the new provision had become article 15 in its draft: 'This is a question of the right to bring cases before national courts in respect of the rights protected by this Convention. This Article should therefore be placed after the Articles defining these rights.'[22]

At the fifth session of the Committee of Ministers, in August 1950, the text was further modified, the words 'The High Contracting Parties undertake to ensure that any person' being replaced by 'Everyone'[23] and the word 'defined' changed to 'secured': 'Article 13. Everyone whose rights and freedoms as herein secured are violated shall have an effective remedy before a national authority notwithstanding that the violation has been committed by persons acting in an official capacity.'[24]

No comments were made on the provision at the August 1950 session of the Consultative Assembly. The text that became article 13 of the Convention underwent one further modification at Rome, in November 1950, immediately prior to adoption of the final text, where the words 'as in herein secured' became 'as set forth in this Convention'.

The heading 'Right to an effective remedy' was added by Protocol No. 11.[25]

Analysis and interpretation

Article 13 enshrines the right to enforcement at the national level of the substance of the rights and freedoms set out in the Convention, regardless of the form in which these rights may be secured within the domestic legal order. It requires the national authorities to ensure that there is a domestic remedy that allows the competent national authority to address the substance of a complaint under the Convention and to provide appropriate relief. Thereby, article 13, 'giving direct expression to the States' obligation to protect human rights first and foremost within their own legal system, establishes an additional guarantee for an individual in order to ensure that he or she effectively enjoys those rights'.[26]

According to the Court, 'the place of Article 13 in the scheme of human rights protection set up by the Convention would argue in favour of implied restrictions of Article 13 being kept to a minimum'.[27] States have some discretion in the manner in which they abide by this obligation, whose scope will vary depending upon the nature of the complaint of a violation of the Convention.[28] However, the remedy must be effective in practice as well as in law, 'in particular in the sense that its exercise must not be unjustifiably hindered by the acts or omissions of the authorities of the respondent State'.[29] For example, if no effective criminal investigation is

---

[21] Draft Convention annexed to the Report [of the Conference of Senior Officials], Doc. CM/WP 4 (50) 19 annex, CM/WP 4 (50) 16 rev., A 1452, IV *TP* 274–95, at p. 282.

[22] Text of the Report submitted by the Conference [of Senior Officials] to the Committee of Ministers, Doc. CM/WP 4 (50) 19, CM/WP 4 (50) 16 rev., A 1431, IV *TP* 242–73, at p. 260.

[23] Draft Convention adopted by the Sub-Committee, Doc. CM 1 (50) 52, A 1884, V *TP* 76–99, at p. 82.

[24] Letter dated 7 August 1950 sent by Mr MacBride, Chairman of the Committee of Ministers, to M. Spaak, President of the Consultative Assembly, Doc. No. 11, p. 600–19, V *TP* 144–71, at pp. 152–4.

[25] Protocol No. 11 to the Convention for the Protection of Human Rights and Fundamental Freedoms, restructuring the control machinery established thereby, ETS 155, art. 2(2).

[26] *Kudła v. Poland* [GC], no. 30210/96, § 152, ECHR 2000-XI.

[27] Ibid.

[28] *Church of Jesus Christ of Latter-Day Saints v. the United Kingdom*, no. 7552/09, § 41, 4 March 2014.

[29] *Husayn (Abu Zubaydah) v. Poland*, no. 7511/13, § 540, 24 July 2014; *Kaya v. Turkey*, 19 February 1998, § 106, *Reports of Judgments and Decisions* 1998-I; *Mahmut Kaya v. Turkey*, no. 22535/93, § 124, ECHR 2000-III.

carried out in a case involving issues of violence, it may foreclose the possibility of any other remedy, including damages. According to the Court, in certain circumstances '[w]hile the civil courts have the capacity to make an independent assessment of fact, in practice the weight attached to a preceding criminal inquiry is so important that even the most convincing evidence to the contrary furnished by a plaintiff would often be discarded and such a remedy would prove to be only theoretical and illusory'.[30]

Article 13 does not, however, guarantee a remedy allowing a challenge to primary legislation before a national authority on the ground of being contrary to the Convention.[31] The Convention does not impose any obligation that it be incorporated into domestic law. However, by virtue of article 1 the substance of the rights and freedoms that it sets out must be secured within the domestic legal order in one form or another.[32] Article 13 is also related to article 35, where the rule of exhaustion of domestic remedies is enshrined.[33] There is a presumption that an effective remedy exists in order to deal with an arguable complaint under the Convention, one that is capable of providing appropriate relief.[34] Article 13 is also related to article 6(1), whereby a right to access to a court is ensured.[35] The right to trial within a reasonable time, in the determination of a criminal charge or of the rights and obligations of an individual, is 'reinforced' by article 13 'rather than being absorbed by the general obligation imposed by [article 6(1)] not to subject individuals to inordinate delays in legal proceedings'.[36] Finally, article 13 is bound up with the principle of subsidiarity,[37] now explicitly mentioned in recital 6 of the Preamble to the Convention, as amended by Protocol No. 15. The issue was first highlighted in one of the very early decisions of the Court, where reference was made to the 'subsidiary nature of the international machinery of collective enforcement established by the Convention'.[38] The Court has declared that '[i]t is fundamental to the machinery of protection established by the Convention that the national systems themselves provide redress for breaches of its provisions, with the Court exercising a supervisory role subject to the principle of subsidiarity'.[39]

The right to an effective remedy arises if the applicant has an 'arguable complaint' that there has been a violation of a Convention right. Even if the Court concludes that the substantive right has not been violated, this does not preclude a complaint under article 13 from being 'arguable'. The Court has said that even notwithstanding the terms of article 13 suggesting, read literally, that an actual breach of another 'substantive' provision is necessary for the provision to be applicable, this is in fact not a prerequisite as long as the alleged violation is 'arguable'.[40] This is because article 13 guarantees 'the availability of a

---

[30] *Cobzaru v. Romania*, no. 48254/99, § 83, 26 July 2007; *Menesheva v. Russia*, no. 59261/00, § 77, ECHR 2006-III; *Corsacov v. Moldova*, no. 18944/02, § 82, 4 April 2006.

[31] *A. and Others v. the United Kingdom* [GC], no. 3455/05, § 135, ECHR 2009.

[32] *Ireland v. the United Kingdom*, 18 January 1978, § 239, Series A no. 25.

[33] *Kudła v. Poland* [GC], no. 30210/96, § 152, ECHR 2000-XI.

[34] *Nemtsov v. Russia*, no. 1774/11, § 112, 31 July 2014.

[35] *De Geouffre de la Pradelle v. France*, 16 December 1992, § 37, Series A no. 253-B.

[36] *Kudła v. Poland* [GC], no. 30210/96, § 152, ECHR 2000-XI.

[37] *M.S.S. v. Belgium and Greece* [GC], no. 30696/09, § 288, ECHR 2011; *Kudła v. Poland* [GC], no. 30210/96, § 152, ECHR 2000-XI; *Handyside v. the United Kingdom*, 7 December 1976, § 48, Series A no. 24.

[38] *Case 'relating to certain aspects of the laws on the use of languages in education in Belgium'* (merits), 23 July 1968, p. 32, § 10, Series A no. 6.

[39] *A. and Others v. the United Kingdom* [GC], no. 3455/05, § 174, ECHR 2009; *Z. and Others v. the United Kingdom*, no. 29392/95, § 103, ECHR 2001-V.

[40] *Boyle and Rice v. the United Kingdom*, 27 April 1988, § 52, Series A no. 131.

remedy at national level to enforce—and hence to allege non-compliance with—the substance of the Convention rights and freedoms in whatever form they may happen to be secured in the domestic legal order'.[41] The 'arguable claim' standard means that there is no right to require a remedy with respect to any supposed grievance, regardless of how frivolous it may be.[42]

The requirement of an 'effective remedy' means that in addition to the payment of compensation, if this is appropriate, there must also be 'a thorough and effective investigation capable of leading to the identification and punishment of those responsible and including effective access for the complainant to the investigatory procedure'.[43] Here there are similarities to the procedural obligation imposed by articles 2 and 3 of the Convention, but the requirements of article 13 are said to be broader.[44] The leading case involves a claim by relatives of a victim with an arguable claim that he had been unlawfully killed by agents of the State. According to the Court, 'the notion of an effective remedy for the purposes of Article 13 entails, in addition to the payment of compensation where appropriate, a thorough and effective investigation capable of leading to the identification and punishment of those responsible and including effective access for the relatives to the investigatory procedure ... Seen in these terms the requirements of Article 13 are broader than a Contracting State's procedural obligation under Article 2 to conduct an effective investigation.'[45]

In practice, the Court examines the effectiveness of a domestic remedy proposed by the government, often finding 'that even though review by a supervising prosecutor plays an important part in securing appropriate conditions of detention, a report or order by a prosecutor is primarily a matter between the supervising authority and the supervised body and is not geared towards providing preventive or compensatory redress to the aggrieved individual. Since the complaint to a prosecutor about unsatisfactory conditions of detention does not give the person using it a personal right to the exercise by the State of its supervisory powers, it cannot be regarded as an effective remedy.'[46]

Discrimination

The protection against discrimination provided by the Convention in accordance with article 14 is a 'subsidiary right'. It must be related to a substantive right under the Convention. This includes article 13, although it too is in a sense a subsidiary right as well. In practice, the Court does not appear to have found violations of article 14 with respect to article 13 in the absence of a violation of a substantive article, such as article 3. Indeed, it is difficult to see how this could be otherwise, given the role of articles 13 and 14 in the scheme of the Convention.

---

[41] Ibid.; *James and Others v. the United Kingdom*, 21 February 1986, § 84, Series A no. 98.

[42] *Leander v. Sweden*, 26 March 1987, § 77, Series A no. 116.

[43] *Husayn (Abu Zubaydah) v. Poland*, no. 7511/13, § 541, 24 July 2014; *Anguelova v. Bulgaria*, no. 38361/97, §§ 161–162, ECHR 2002-IV; *Assenov and Others v. Bulgaria*, 28 October 1998, § 114, *Reports of Judgments and Decisions* 1998-VIII; *El Masri v. 'the former Yugoslav Republic of Macedonia'* [GC], no. 39630/09, § 255, ECHR 2012; *Süheyla Aydın v. Turkey*, no. 25660/94, § 208, 24 May 2005.

[44] *Husayn (Abu Zubaydah) v. Poland*, no. 7511/13, § 542, 24 July 2014; *El Masri v. 'the former Yugoslav Republic of Macedonia'* [GC], no. 39630/09, § 255, ECHR 2012; *Khashiyev and Akayeva v. Russia*, nos 57942/00 and 57945/00, § 183, 24 February 2005; *Kurt v. Turkey*, 25 May 1998, § 140, *Reports of Judgments and Decisions* 1998-III; *Orhan v. Turkey*, no. 25656/94, § 384, ECHR 2002, ECHR 2002; *Kiliç v. Turkey*, no 22492/93, § 93, ECHR 2000-III.

[45] *Kaya v. Turkey*, 19 February 1998, § 107, *Reports of Judgments and Decisions* 1998-I.

[46] *Nemtsov v. Russia*, no. 1774/11, § 114, 31 July 2014; *Dirdizov v. Russia*, no. 41461/10, § 76, 27 November 2012; *Ananyev and Others v. Russia*, nos 42525/07 and 60800/08, § 104, 10 January 2012.

In one of the rare findings of a violation of article 14 taken together with article 13, the applicant complained that he was deprived of an adequate remedy in a case of ill-treatment because he was of Roma origin, something that was known to the police officers. He said that while in the police station, 'his ethnic origin was openly and repeatedly referred to by the investigating authorities as a factor militating against his complaint of police abuse'. Noting that racial violence 'is a particular affront to human dignity and, in view of its perilous consequences, requires from the authorities special vigilance and a vigorous reaction', the Court said that 'when investigating violent incidents, State authorities have the additional duty to take all reasonable steps to unmask any racist motive and to establish whether or not ethnic hatred or prejudice may have played a role in the events'.[47] The Court said that the applicant did not refer to any particular facts substantiating the claim that the violence he sustained was racially motivated (although it had observed, only a few paragraphs earlier, that the applicant had indicated that his ethnic origin had in fact been regularly referred to by investigating authorities). Instead, the Court said, 'he claimed that his allegation should be evaluated within the context of documented and repeated failure by the Romanian authorities to remedy instances of anti-Roma violence and to provide redress for discrimination'.[48] The Court referred to official programmes directed at eradicating anti-Roma conduct that should have been well known to the investigating authorities. Yet, '[n]ot only was there no attempt on the part of the prosecutors to verify the behaviour of the policemen involved in the violence, ascertaining, for instance, whether they had been involved in the past in similar incidents or whether they had been accused of displaying anti-Roma sentiment, but the prosecutors made tendentious remarks in relation to the applicant's Roma origin throughout the investigation'.[49] This, it said, disclosed 'a general discriminatory attitude of the authorities, which reinforced the applicant's belief that any remedy in his case was purely illusory'.[50] The Court concluded that 'the failure of the law enforcement agents to investigate possible racial motives in the applicant's ill-treatment combined with their attitude during the investigation constitutes a discrimination with regard to the applicant's rights contrary to Article 14 taken in conjunction with Articles 3 in its procedural limb and 13 of the Convention'.[51]

In a similar case, the Court found there was a violation of the procedural limb of article 3 and said it did not, consequently, need to rule on the complaint based upon article 13. It went on to rule that there had been a violation of article 14 because of racism in the conduct of the investigatory authorities.[52] In yet another case, while acknowledging the systematic racism against Roma in the Bulgarian justice system, the Court said there was no evidence in the file indicating that racist attitudes had played a part in the events in question.[53]

[47] *Cobzaru v. Romania*, no. 48254/99, §§ 86–89, 26 July 2007.
[48] Ibid., § 94.
[49] Ibid., § 98.
[50] Ibid.
[51] Ibid., § 100.
[52] *Nachova and Others v. Bulgaria* [GC], nos 43577/98 and 43579/98, §§ 120–123, ECHR 2005-VII.
[53] *Ognyanova and Choban v. Bulgaria*, no. 46317/99, §§ 146–149, 23 February 2006. See also *Yaşar v. Turkey*, no. 46412/99, §§ 72–74, 24 January 2006.

Reservations

Two reservations have been formulated with respect to article 13. Serbia and Montenegro made a reservation to article 13 stating that it was not applicable to the jurisdiction of the Court of Serbia and Montenegro until that Court became operational.[54] Monaco has declared that article 13 (as well as article 6(1)) does not apply to provisions of its Constitution providing for immunity of the Prince from legal proceedings and those governing his royal prerogatives in the areas of naturalization and re-instatement of nationality.[55]

Further reading

Yutaki Arai, 'Right to an Effective Remedy before a National Authority (Article 13), in Van Dijk et al., *Theory and Practice*, pp. 997–1026.

Andrew Drzemczewski and Christos Giakoumopoulos, 'Article 13', in Pettiti et al., *La Convention européenne*, pp. 455–74.

Frowein/Peukert, *MenschenRechtsKonvention*, pp. 391–400.

Françoise Hampson, 'The Concept of an "Arguable Claim" under Article 13 of the European Convention on Human Rights', (1990) 39 *ICLQ* 891.

Harris et al., *Law of the European Convention*, pp. 557–76.

Patricia Mallia, 'European Court of Human Rights: *M.S.S. v. Belgium & Greece*, Introductory Note', (2011) 50 *International Legal Materials* 364.

---

[54] (2004) 48 YB 22.
[55] (2005) 48 YB 9.

Article 14. Prohibition of discrimination/Interdiction de discrimination

The enjoyment of the rights and freedoms set forth in this Convention shall be secured without discrimination on any ground such as sex, race, colour, language, religion, political or other opinion, national or social origin, association with a national minority, property, birth or other status.

La jouissance des droits et libertés reconnus dans la présente Convention doit être assurée, sans distinction aucune, fondée notamment sur le sexe, la race, la couleur, la langue, la religion, les opinions politiques ou toutes autres opinions, l'origine nationale ou sociale, l'appartenance à une minorité nationale, la fortune, la naissance ou toute autre situation.

Introductory comments

The prohibition of discrimination based upon race, sex, language, religion, and other analogous grounds stands at the heart of the modern human rights corpus. It is the only substantive human right set out in the Charter of the United Nations. Article 1(3) of the Charter lists as one of the purposes of the United Nations the promotion and encouragement of 'respect for human rights and for fundamental freedoms for all without distinction as to race, sex, language, or religion'. The Preamble of the Charter also speaks of 'the equal rights of men and women'. An earlier attempt at the condemnation of racial discrimination, proposed by Japan at the Paris Peace Conference of 1919, was unsuccessful, apparently vetoed by President Wilson of the United States.[1]

Pursuing the logic of the Charter of the United Nations, the Universal Declaration of Human Rights gives equality and non-discrimination pride of place. The core provision is article 2, appearing even before the right to life and the prohibition of torture. The first sentence of article 2 of the Universal Declaration of Human Rights states: 'Everyone is entitled to all the rights and freedoms set forth in this Declaration, without distinction of any kind, such as race, colour, sex, language, religion, political or other opinion, national or social origin, property, birth or other status.' The list was expanded from that of the Charter in two ways. It was made non-exhaustive by virtue of the words 'such as' and several prohibited grounds were added to the succinct enumeration in article 1(3) of the Charter. The Universal Declaration also addresses equality and non-discrimination in article 7: 'All are equal before the law and are entitled without any discrimination to equal protection of the law. All are entitled to equal protection against any discrimination in violation of this Declaration and against any incitement to such discrimination.' Other provisions are also relevant, notably article 16 in its recognition of the right to marry to 'men and women' and article 23(2): 'Everyone, without any discrimination, has the right to equal pay for equal work.'

Subsequent human rights treaties adopted at the universal level have addressed specific facets of discrimination: the International Convention on the Elimination of All Forms of

---

[1] Paul Gordon Lauren, *The Evolution of Human Rights: Visions Seen*, Philadelphia: University of Pennsylvania Press, 1998, pp. 90–22.

Racial Discrimination, the Convention on the Elimination of All Forms of Discrimination against Women and the Convention on the Rights of Persons with Disabilities. Treaties of general application or scope, such as the International Covenant on Civil and Political Rights or the Convention on the Rights of the Child, incorporate general non-discrimination clauses similar to what is found in the Universal Declaration of Human Rights.

As one commentary has noted quite perceptively, '[n]on-discrimination does not have the same, specific, foundational designation in the Statute of the Council of Europe or Preamble to the Convention as it does in the UN Charter'[2] or, for that matter, in the Universal Declaration of Human Rights. Even the European Social Charter, adopted a decade after the European Convention, contains an equality clause in its short Preamble: 'Considering that the enjoyment of social rights should be secured without discrimination on grounds of race, colour, sex, religion, political opinion, national extraction or social origin'.[3] It would seem that the drafters of the European Convention on Human Rights did not have equality at the centre of their priorities in codifying fundamental rights and freedoms. One terrible lapse was the omission of discrimination on the ground of sex in the first draft of the Convention proposed by the European Movement.[4] Perhaps the drafters hadn't read the Charter of the United Nations, with its prominent reference to gender equality, but this is an unlikely hypothesis. It seems more likely that they didn't think the equality of men and women to be important enough.

The somewhat secondary role of equality and non-discrimination is also reflected in the European Union Charter of Fundamental Rights. Article 21 of the Charter is the counterpart of article 14(1) of the Convention: 'Any discrimination based on any ground such as sex, race, colour, ethnic or social origin, genetic features, language, religion or belief, political or any other opinion, membership of a national minority, property, birth, disability, age or sexual orientation shall be prohibited.' Some grounds have been added to this more modern instrument: disability, age, and sexual orientation. An important one, in terms of the broad interpretation that has been given by the European Court to article 14, has been removed: 'other status'.

Article 14 of the European Convention on Human Rights plays an adjectival role in that its relevance is conditioned on the application of one of the other substantive rights listed in the Convention. Thus, while discrimination on one of the prohibited grounds with respect to the right to private and family life may amount to a breach of the Convention, the same would not be the case with respect to nationality because there is no right to nationality in the Convention. A non-discrimination clause of more general application results from Protocol No. 12 of the Convention. The difficulty this raises for States Parties is manifested in the relatively modest number of ratifications of the Protocol, which only entered into force in 2005.

---

[2] Harris et al., *Law of the European Convention*, at p. 577.
[3] European Social Charter, (1965) 529 UNTS 89, PP 4.
[4] Convention for the Collective Protection of Individual Rights and Democratic Liberties by the States, Members of the Council of Europe, and for the establishment of a European Court of Human Rights to ensure observance of the Convention, Doc. INF/5/E/R, I *TP* 296–303, at p. 296.

Drafting of the provision

The International Council of the European Movement, meeting in Brussels in February 1949, adopted a list of human rights to be assured by the European Court that included '[l]'égalité devant la loi' and '[l]a protection contre toute discrimination basée sur la religion, la race, l'origine nationale, la profession d'une opinion politique ou de toute autre opinion'.[5] The initial draft European Convention on Human Rights was prepared by the International Juridical Section of the European Movement, chaired by Pierre-Henri Teitgen, with David Maxwell Fyfe and Fernand Dehousse as rapporteurs. Both Maxwell Fyfe and Dehousse had been involved in the adoption of the Universal Declaration of Human Rights at the United Nations the previous year. The enumeration of rights in the draft contained the following: 'Every State a party to this Convention shall guarantee to all persons within its territory the following rights: ... i) Equality before the law. j) Freedom from discrimination on account of religion, race, national origin or political or other opinion.'[6] Quite remarkably, and inexplicably, the European Movement draft omitted discrimination based on sex, despite the references to this form of inequality in article 2 of the Universal Declaration of Human Rights, as well as in the Charter of the United Nations.

Many speakers at the first session of the Council of Europe's Consultative Assembly spoke about the importance of non-discrimination. Pierre-Henri Teitgen called for adoption of a convention to include 'the natural rights ... pertaining to ... equality before the law, protection from discrimination on account of religion, race, national origin, political or philosophical opinion ...'[7] Again, note the absence of 'sex' within the enumeration. Italy's Mario Cingolani condemned 'the violation of the ... principle of equality before the law; the horrible triumph of discrimination on grounds of race or political opinions'.[8] Rolf Edberg of Sweden said '[a]nother fundamental right is that no individual should be persecuted or discriminated against on account of his opinions'.[9] The United Kingdom's John Foster referred to difficulties faced by some countries in negotiating the text of the Universal Declaration of Human Rights, explaining that one of these came from 'certain countries where, for reasons of internal policy, certain discriminations on, we will say, race or religion, were in existence and they did not feel themselves in a position to sign the Declaration of Human Rights without considerable compromise'. Foster added that 'we in Europe do not have the same difficulties'.[10] Gérard Jaquet of France said '[a]ll individuals must be free and equal before the law, whatever their race, their colour, their sex, their language, their religion, or their social position'.[11]

---

[5] Recommendations adopted at the meeting of the International Council of the European Movement held at Brussels in February 1949, INF/2/F, p. 3. Two decades later, the Council of Europe provided an unofficial English translation of these provisions: '[e]quality before the law' and '[f]reedom from discrimination on account of religion, race, national origin or political or other opinion'. Preparatory work on Article 14 of the European Convention on Human Rights, CDH (67) 3, p. 3.

[6] Convention for the Collective Protection of Individual Rights and Democratic Liberties by the States, Members of the Council of Europe, and for the establishment of a European Court of Human Rights to ensure observance of the Convention, Doc. INF/5/E/R, I *TP* 296–303, at p. 296, art. I(i) and (j).

[7] Report of the Sitting [of the Consultative Assembly, 19 August 1949], I *TP* 38–154, at p. 46.

[8] Ibid., p. 62.

[9] Ibid., p. 76.

[10] Ibid., pp. 94–6.

[11] Ibid., p. 134.

Sean MacEntee of Ireland cited article 2 of the Universal Declaration of Human Rights, saying that the Consultative Assembly should approve it 'without reservation'.[12]

The only constructive proposal for amendment came from Hermod Lannung of Denmark, who insisted upon the importance of the status of women: 'The draft Convention which the European Movement has worked out, and which is a very remarkable piece of work, has not the word "sex" [in its freedom from discrimination provision]. I consider this to be a mistake . . .' he said.[13] He pointed to inclusion of sex as a prohibited ground in the Universal Declaration of Human Rights and the draft covenant on human rights.

Be it in relation to marriage, politics, education, opportunities in trades, etc., the principle followed should be that of no discrimination on account of sex. Something is lacking in political democracy if women do not have equal rights with men. Even if some countries do not today fulfil this condition, it would be natural that they should take steps towards it as soon as possible.[14]

Lannung also stated that 'we should stress the very important point that human rights should also include national minority rights and their protection . . . in order that national minorities may secure the right to a free national life and protection against persecution . . .'[15]

A few speakers used the occasion to score political points. One of the Danish members, Ole Bjorn Kraft, said that the Danish national group living in South Schleswig 'must have secured to them the right to lead their national life and to work for their national goals without discrimination, without persecution and without injury'.[16] An Irish delegate, James Everett, condemned discrimination based upon religious or political opinion, noting that it was 'practised in every walk of life. Jobs, the type of employment and even the allocation of houses are often determined on the basis of the religious views of the applicant.' He added, referring to Northern Ireland, that '[s]uch injustices as I have referred to are known to exist in certain countries in Europe, and some of them even in a portion of my own country, cut off from the Motherland'.[17]

As rapporteur of the Committee on Legal and Administrative Questions, Teitgen prepared an initial list of questions. He asked whether the convention should include 'equality before the law' and 'protection against all discrimination based on religion, race, national origin, profession or political or other opinion'.[18] Teitgen's proposal to the Committee, dated 29 August 1949, included the following: 'The fundamental rights and freedoms enumerated above will be guaranteed without distinction on any ground such as race, colour, sex, language, religion, political or other opinion professed with violence, national or social origin, membership of a national minority, fortune or birth.'[19] There were two attempts at amendment when the proposal was discussed in the Committee. The first, to insert 'physical violence or incitement to' after 'without', was rejected by twelve to three, with one abstention. The second, to delete 'professed without

---

[12] Ibid., p. 142.
[13] Ibid., p. 54.
[14] Ibid.
[15] Ibid. See also the remarks of Kraft of Denmark, ibid., p. 68.
[16] Ibid., p. 68.
[17] Ibid., pp. 104–6.
[18] Letter addressed 22 August 1949 by Mr P.H. Teitgen to the Chairman of the Legal Committee with a list of questions for examination by the Legal Committee as appendix, Doc. A 14, I *TP* 156–61, at p. 160.
[19] Proposals by Mr P.H. Teitgen, Rapporteur, 29 August 1949, Doc. A 116, I *TP* 166–8.

violence', was adopted by fourteen to one, with one abstention. As amended, the text was adopted by seventeen votes to nil.[20]

The Report of the Commission on Legal and Administrative Questions to the first session of the Consultative Assembly noted that the draft did not contain a prohibition of discrimination based on membership of a national minority. It explained that there had been discussion on a report by Hermod Lannung, and the Committee had 'unanimously recognised the importance of this problem'. The Report said the Committee had considered that its task was not to draw up a list of fundamental rights to be defined in a general declaration but only 'those which appeared suitable for inclusion in an immediate international guarantee'. The Committee had agreed to draw the attention of the Committee of Ministers to the need for subsequent examination and 'defining more exactly the rights of national minorities'.[21] The draft recommendation of the Committee read as follows: 'The fundamental rights and freedoms enumerated above shall be guaranteed without any distinction based on race, colour, sex, language, religion, political or other opinion, national or social origin, affiliation to a national minority, fortune or birth.'[22] Presenting the report to the plenary Consultative Assembly, Teitgen explained:

[E]ach country will maintain the right to determine the means by which the guaranteed freedoms are exercised within its territory, but—and this is Article 5 of the draft Resolution—its legislation, in defining the measures for the achievement of these freedoms, cannot make any distinction based on race, colour, sex, language, religion, political or other opinion, national or social origin, affiliation to a national minority, fortune or birth. Any national legislation which, under pretext of organising freedom, makes any such discrimination, falls within the scope of the international guarantee.[23]

Article 5 was adopted by the Consultative Assembly without amendment or dissenting vote.[24]

The Committee of Ministers decided to refer the draft convention prepared by the Consultative Assembly to a Committee of Experts. In the meantime, the Commission on Human Rights had adopted a draft text on equality as part of its work on the International Covenant on human rights:

Article 20
1. All are equal before the law and shall be accorded equal protection of the law.
2. Everyone shall be accorded all the rights and freedoms defined in this Covenant without discrimination on any ground such as race, colour, sex, language, religion, political or other opinion, national or social origin, property, birth or other status.
3. Everyone shall be accorded equal protection against any incitement to such discrimination.[25]

---

[20] Minutes of the Sitting [of the Committee on Legal and Administrative Questions, Consultative Assembly, 30 August 1949], Doc. A 167, I TP 174–80, at p. 176.

[21] Report presented by Mr P.H. Teitgen, 5 September 1949, Doc. A 290, I TP 192–213, at p. 200.

[22] Report [of the Committee on Legal and Administrative Questions], 5 September 1949, Doc. AS (1) 77, I TP 216–39, at p. 230.

[23] Report of the Sitting [of the Consultative Assembly, 7 September 1949], I TP 250–95, at p. 278.

[24] Recommendation No. 38 to the Committee of Ministers adopted 8 September 1949 on the conclusion of the debates, Doc. AS (1) 108, II TP 274–83, at p. 278.

[25] Report of the Fifth Session of the Commission on Human Rights to the Economic and Social Council, UN Doc. E/1371(Supp.), p. 24.

In preparation for the Committee of Experts meeting, the Council of Europe's Secretariat General compared the draft covenant to the draft European convention:

Paragraph 1 [of article 20 of the draft Covenant] is not provided for by the Resolution [of the Consultative Assembly]. Paragraph 2 is covered by Article 5 of the Resolution except the differences relating to association with a national minority and to any other situation. Paragraph 3 is not provided for by the Resolution. In the light of article 5 of the Resolution, paragraphs 1 and 3 seem even to have been excluded intentionally.[26]

The comments of the United Kingdom on the draft Covenant were also circulated in anticipation of the Committee of Experts' meeting:

The first paragraph of [article 20 of the draft Covenant] appears not to take account of the permissible legal disabilities to which minors and persons of unsound mind may be subject. His Majesty's Government consider therefore that the paragraph should be amended to read:
1. All are equal before the law and shall be accorded equal protection of the law *provided that this Article shall not be held to forbid the imposition of reasonable legal disabilities of minors and persons of unsound mind.*[27]

The Committee of Experts held two sessions, the first in February and the second in March 1950. A Sub-Committee assigned to study the amendments submitted a report at the first session, noting that some rights could not be recognized to aliens without restriction and suggesting that a reference to this effect was inserted in the text of article 5.[28] This was not adopted, however, because of a decision to draw up a separate provision on aliens, the ancestor of article 16 of the Convention. At the conclusion of its first session, the Committee of Experts adopted the following: 'Article 6. The aforesaid rights and freedoms shall be guaranteed without discrimination on any ground such as race, colour, sex, language, religion, political or other opinion, national or social origin, affiliation to a national minority, fortune or birth.'[29] In the final version, the Committee changed the first words of the text to 'These fundamental rights and freedoms . . .' It also changed the word 'guaranteed' to 'secured', based on the notion that 'the aim of the Convention was not to set up an international guarantee to be undertaken by the signatory States themselves'.[30]

For the second session of the Committee of Experts, the British submitted the following text:

Article 14
1. All are equal before the law and shall be accorded equal protection of the law; provided that this Article shall not be held to forbid the imposition of reasonable legal disabilities on minors and persons of unsound mind.

---

[26] Preparatory Report by the Secretariat-General concerning a Preliminary Draft Convention to Provide a Collective Guarantee of Human Rights, Doc. B 22, III *TP* 2–37, at pp. 18, 21.

[27] Comments of Governments on the Draft International Covenant on Human Rights and Measures of Implementation [UN Doc. E/CN.4/353/Add.1-3], Doc. A 770, III *TP* 156–79, at p. 164 (emphasis in the original).

[28] First part of the Report of the Sub-Committee Instructed to Make a Preliminary Study of the Amendments Proposed by the <embers of the Committee, Doc. A 796, III *TP* 200–5, at p. 200.

[29] Draft text of the first section of a draft Convention based on the work of the Consultative Assembly, Doc. A 809, III *TP* 220–31, at p. 224.

[30] Preliminary draft of the Report to the Committee of Ministers, 24 February 1950, Doc. CM/WP 1 (50) 1, A 847, III *TP* 246–79, at p. 264.

2. Everyone shall be accorded all the rights and freedoms defined in this Convention without discrimination on any grounds such as race, colour, sex, language, religion, political or other opinion, national or social origin, property, birth or other status.[31]

The Drafting Committee proposed that 'association with a national minority' be added to the second paragraph.[32]

The Committee of Experts submitted two draft conventions in its Report. The first, labelled A and A/2, stated: 'These fundamental rights and freedoms shall be secured without any distinction based on race, colour, sex, language, religion, political or other opinion, national or social origin, belonging to a national minority, fortune or birth.' The second, labelled B and B/2, derived from the United Kingdom proposal, said:

1. All are equal before the law.
2. Everyone shall be accorded all the rights and freedoms defined in this Convention without discrimination on any grounds such as sex, race, colour, language, religion, political or other opinion, national or social origin, association with a national minority, property, birth or other status.[33]

The two competing drafts adopted by the Committee of Experts were subsequently studied by the Conference of Senior Officials. It was agreed to attempt to amalgamate the two texts. With respect to the non-discrimination provision, the Conference took the second draft (B and B/2) and reworked it, removing the first paragraph and making slight changes to the second: 'The rights and freedoms defined in this Convention shall be secured without discrimination on any grounds such as sex, race, colour, language, religion, political or other opinion, national or social origin, association with a national minority, property, birth or other status.'[34] The Committee of Ministers, meeting in August 1950, added the words 'The enjoyment of' at the beginning of the provision. It also replaced the word 'defined' with 'secured'.[35] No further changes were made to article 14.

The Committee's final draft was then considered by the Consultative Assembly. Hermod Lannung of Denmark, whose had insisted the previous year that sex be added as one of the prohibited grounds and that the protection of national minorities be addressed, spoke with enthusiasm about the provision:

In the name of justice, let us not forget, when we study the draft Convention before us, that on two points it is still an improvement on the original draft of the European Movement, namely, as regards the additions to Article 14, according to which 'the enjoyment of the rights and freedoms secured in this Convention shall be secured without discrimination on any ground'—I quote the additions— 'such as sex...' and 'association with a national minority...' I welcome this with the greatest satisfaction.[36]

---

[31] Amendments to Articles 1, 2, 4, 5, 6, 8, and 9 of the Committee's preliminary draft proposal by the Expert of the United Kingdom, Doc. CM/WP 1 (50) 2, A 915, III *TP* 280–9, at p. 288.

[32] Amendments to the British draft proposed by the Drafting Committee composed of Sir Oscar Dowson, MM le Quesne, Dons Moeller, and Salén, Doc. CM/WP 1 (50) 10, p. 3, A 919, III *TP* 288–95, at p. 294.

[33] Appendix to the Report of the Committee of Experts on Human Rights: Draft Convention of Protection of Human Rights and Fundamental Freedoms, 16 March 1950, Doc. C/WP 1 (50) 15 appendix, CM/WP 1 (50) 14 revised, A 925, IV *TP* 50–79, at p. 64.

[34] New draft alternatives B and B/2, Doc. CM/WP 4 (50) 9, A 1372, IV *TP* 182–91, at p 190.

[35] Draft Convention adopted by the Sub-Committee, Doc. CM 1 (50) 52, A 1884, V *TP* 76–99, at p. 84.

[36] Report of the sitting [of the Consultative Assembly, 14 August 1950], V *TP* 216–71, at p. 240.

A more cautious statement, testifying perhaps to the difficulty associated with gender equality at the time, came from a British delegate, Gilbert Mitchison:

> There are bound to be many of us in this Assembly who will feel that on this point or that we would have had matters otherwise, and that we would have gone further. Perhaps some of us, as was pointed out just now, might not have gone quite so far in some respects—I refer to the inclusion of sex and national minorities in the Article to which Mr. Lannung referred. At any rate, there is agreement in a most difficult field, reached after the fullest examination.[37]

Emrys Roberts, also of the United Kingdom, welcomed the reference to national minorities in article 14: 'Central Governments sometimes regard national minorities purely as nuisance and like to try to level them out. As a member of the Welsh nation . . . I believe that the cultures and customs of the small nations enrich the pattern of European civilisation.'[38]

Finally, Léopold Senghor, who was part of the French parliamentary delegation but who went on to be the first president of Senegal, complained that article 14 was in conflict with article 63, by which European States had the freedom to extend the protection of the Convention to their colonies. Beginning with the admonition 'Let the Assembly beware!', Senghor noted that article 14 of the Convention reproduced the first sentence of article 2 of the Universal Declaration of Human Rights but not the second—'the lines which the experts of our Committee of Ministers set aside'—by which the benefits of the Declaration are applied with distinction, regardless of the political, jurisdictional, or international status of the territory to which the individual belongs.[39]

The heading 'Prohibition of discrimination' was added according to the provisions of Protocol No. 11.[40]

Analysis and interpretation

Subsidiary nature of article 14

Article 14 provides protection against discrimination in the enjoyment of rights and freedoms guaranteed by the other substantive provisions of the Convention. It is a subsidiary provision in that it complements the other substantive provisions of the Convention and its Protocols. Article 14 does not have an independent existence because it applies only to 'the enjoyment of the rights and freedoms' safeguarded by other provisions of Convention law. Nevertheless, it is autonomous to the extent that it does not require that there be a breach of one of the other substantive provisions. Article 14 is applicable when 'the facts at issue fall "within the ambit" of one or more of the latter'.[41] Consequently, a measure that 'in itself is in conformity with the requirements of the

[37] Ibid., p. 256.

[38] Report of the Sitting [of the Consultative Assembly, 25 August 1950, morning], VI *TP* 74–143, at p. 86.

[39] Report of the Sitting [of the Consultative Assembly, 25 August 1950, afternoon], VI *TP* 142–91, at p. 174.

[40] Protocol No. 11 to the Convention for the Protection of Human Rights and Fundamental Freedoms, restructuring the control machinery established thereby, ETS 155, art. 2(2).

[41] *Church of Jesus Christ of Latter-Day Saints v. the United Kingdom*, no. 7552/09, § 39, 4 March 2014; *Sejdić and Finci v. Bosnia and Herzegovina* [GC], nos 27996/06 and 34836/06, § 39, ECHR 2009; *Abdulaziz, Cabales, and Balkandali v. the United Kingdom*, 28 May 1985, § 71, Series A no. 94; *Petrovic v. Austria*, 27 March 1998, § 22, *Reports of Judgments and Decisions* 1998-II; *Şahin v. Germany* [GC], no. 30943/96, § 85, ECHR 2003-VIII; *Case 'relating to certain aspects of the laws on the use of languages in education in Belgium'*

Article enshrining the right or freedom in question may therefore infringe this Article when read in conjunction with Article 14' because of its discriminatory nature. It is, the Court has said, as if article 14 was 'an integral part of each of the Articles laying down rights and freedoms whatever their nature'.[42] Another consequence of this broad view is that article 14 extends 'beyond the enjoyment of the rights and freedoms which the Convention and Protocols require each State to guarantee. It applies also to those additional rights, falling within the general scope of any Convention article, for which the State has voluntarily decided to provide.'[43]

Findings of a violation of article 14 are always associated with one of the other rights set out in the Convention or the protocols. For this reason, admissibility issues concerning article 14 may be assessed separately from those concerning the substantive right concerned.[44] Sometimes the Court will conclude that the two provisions have been violated, that is, article 14 and the substantive provision with which it is related, such as article 8. On other occasions, it will satisfy itself with declaring that there has been a violation of article 14. Most often, it establishes a violation of the substantive provision in the Convention or the protocols and then says there is no need to address separately the issue of article 14.

The prohibition of discrimination in article 14 thus extends beyond the enjoyment of the rights and freedoms that the Convention and the Protocols require each State to guarantee. It applies also to those additional rights falling within the general scope of any Convention article, for which the State has voluntarily decided to provide.[45] For example, although there may be no obligation under the Convention for a State to provide a scheme for benefits or pension, if it does it must do so in a manner that is compliant with article 14 of the Convention.[46] Similarly, a State is not required by article 9 to allow religious institutions to perform marriages, but if it does it cannot discriminate between religious groups or denominations, allowing some but not others to exercise this function.[47] Nor are States required to give religious organizations any particular status, benefits, or privileges; if they do, however, it must be without discrimination.[48]

Extreme forms of discrimination may go beyond article 14 and constitute ill-treatment that violates article 3 of the Convention. Both the Court and the Commission have taken the view that discrimination may also constitute inhuman treatment in breach of article 3 of the Convention where it attains a sufficient level of severity.[49] Interferences with

(merits), 23 July 1968, p. 30, § 9, Series A no. 6; *Van Buitenen v. the Netherlands*, no. 11775/85, Commission decision of 2 March 1987; *Cha'are Shalom Ve Tsedek v. France* [GC], no. 27417/95, § 86, ECHR 2000-VII.

[42] *National Union of Belgian Police v. Belgium,* 27 October 1975, § 44, Series A no. 19.

[43] *Anderle v. the Czech Republic,* no. 6268/08, § 28, 17 February 2011.

[44] *Đorđević v. Croatia,* no. 41526/10, § 158, ECHR 2012.

[45] *Sejdić and Finci v. Bosnia and Herzegovina* [GC], nos 27996/06 and 34836/06, § 39, ECHR 2009; *Andrejeva v. Latvia* [GC], no. 55707/00, § 74, ECHR 2009; *Case 'relating to certain aspects of the laws on the use of languages in education in Belgium'* (merits), 23 July 1968, p. 30, § 9, Series A no. 6; *Stec and Others v. the United Kingdom* (dec.) [GC], nos 65731/01 and 65900/01, § 40, ECHR 2005-X; *E.B. v. France* [GC], no. 43546/02, § 48, 22 January 2008.

[46] *Stec and Others v. the United Kingdom* [GC], nos 65731/01 and 65900/01, § 53, ECHR 2006-VI.

[47] *Savez crkava 'Riječ života' and Others v. Croatia,* no. 7798/08, § 58, 9 December 2010.

[48] *Cumhuriyetçi Eğitim Ve Kültür Merkezi Vakfı v. Turkey,* no. 32093/10 § 48, 2 December 2014.

[49] *Abdulaziz, Cabales, and Balkandali v. the United Kingdom,* 28 May 1985, §§ 90–92, Series A no. 94; *East African Asians v. the United Kingdom,* nos 4403/70-4419/70, 4422/70, 4423/70, 4434/70, 4443/70, 4476/70-4478/70, 4486/70, 4501/70, and 4526/70-4530/70, Commission report of 14 December 1973, § 208, DR 78-A, p. 5.

fundamental rights directed at the Karpas Greek-Cypriot 'class of persons' by the Turkish occupying government could only be explained by the 'the features which distinguish them from the Turkish-Cypriot population, namely their ethnic origin, race and religion'. They were compelled to live in conditions where they were 'isolated, restricted in their movements, controlled and with no prospect of renewing or developing their community'. These conditions were 'debasing and violate the very notion of respect for the human dignity of its members'.[50] The Court said that such 'discriminatory treatment attained a level of severity which amounted to degrading treatment' and was consequently a violation of article 3.[51]

Meaning of 'discrimination'

Discrimination means treating persons in analogous situations differently without an objective and reasonable justification.[52] The requirement of an 'analogous position' does not mean that the situations must be identical, but they must be 'relevantly similar'.[53] Thus, not every difference in treatment constitutes a violation of article 14. The justification provided to account for a distinction must be assessed with regard to principles that normally prevail in democratic societies. In addition to pursuing a legitimate aim, a difference in treatment will not be discriminatory to the extent that there is a 'reasonable relationship of proportionality between the means employed and the aim sought to be realised'.[54]

The other important provision concerning discrimination in the law of the Convention is found in article 1(1) of Protocol No. 12. Article 14 of the Convention and the text in Protocol No. 12 are very similar, although the latter is broader in scope, covering rights that may not be addressed within the Convention and its Protocols. The Explanatory Report on Protocol No. 12 states that '[t]he meaning of the term "discrimination" in Article 1 is intended to be identical to that in Article 14 of the Convention',[55] something confirmed in the case law.[56] The plenary European Court adopted an opinion on the draft text of Protocol No. 12 that includes a discussion of the concept of discrimination and that is therefore also germane to the interpretation of article 14 of the Convention:

As regards the substantive content of the Protocol, it notes, in relation to Article 1, that the draft Explanatory Report (see paragraph 18) refers to the notion of discrimination as consistently

---

[50] *Cyprus v. Turkey* [GC], no. 25781/94, § 309, ECHR 2001-IV.

[51] Ibid., § 310.

[52] *D.H. and Others v. the Czech Republic* [GC], no. 57325/00, § 75, ECHR 2007-IV; *Willis v. the United Kingdom*, no. 36042/97, § 48, ECHR 2002-IV; *Okpisz v. Germany*, no. 59140/00, § 33, 25 October 2005; *National & Provincial Building Society, Leeds Permanent Building Society and Yorkshire Building Society v. the United Kingdom*, 23 October 1997, § 88, *Reports of Judgments and Decisions* 1997-VII; *Timishev v. Russia*, nos 55762/00 and 55974/00, § 56, ECHR 2005-XII; *Nachova and Others v. Bulgaria* [GC], nos 43577/98 and 43579/98, § 145, ECHR 2005-VII; *Sejdić and Finci v. Bosnia and Herzegovina* [GC], nos 27996/06 and 34836/06, § 42, ECHR 2009.

[53] *Clift v. the United Kingdom*, no. 7205/07, § 66, 13 July 2010.

[54] *Petrovic v. Austria*, 27 March 1998, § 30, *Reports of Judgments and Decisions* 1998-II; *Lithgow and Others v. the United Kingdom*, 8 July 1986, § 177, Series A no. 102; *Sejdić and Finci v. Bosnia and Herzegovina* [GC], nos 27996/06 and 34836/06, § 42, ECHR 2009; *Rejeva v. Latvia* [GC], no. 55707/00, § 81, ECHR 2009; *Stec and Others v. the United Kingdom* [GC], nos 65731/01 and 65900/01, § 51, ECHR 2006-VI.

[55] Explanatory Report on Protocol No. 12, para. 18.

[56] *Sejdić and Finci v. Bosnia and Herzegovina* [GC], nos 27996/06 and 34836/06, § 55, ECHR 2009; *Šimšić v. Bosnia and Herzegovina* (dec.), no. 51552/10, § 31, 10 April 2012; *Maktouf and Damjanović v. Bosnia and Herzegovina* [GC], nos 2312/08 and 34179/08, § 81, ECHR 2013 (extracts).

interpreted in the case-law of the Court, namely that a difference of treatment is discriminatory if it has no objective and reasonable justification, that is if it does not pursue a legitimate aim or if there is not a reasonable relationship of proportionality between the means employed and the aim sought to be realised. As the Court put it in the Belgian Linguistic case, 'the competent national authorities are frequently confronted with situations and problems which, on account of differences inherent therein, call for different legal solutions' (judgment of 23 July 1968, Series A no. 6, p. 34, § 10). This is further reflected, consistently with the subsidiary character of the Convention system, in the margin of appreciation accorded to the national authorities in assessing whether and to what extent differences in otherwise similar situations justify a difference of treatment in law (see, among other authorities, *Rasmussen v. Denmark*, judgment of 28 November 1984, Series A no. 87, p. 15, § 40).[57]

The French text of article 14 of the Convention employs a 'very general wording' (*sans distinction aucune*), but the Court has said that if interpreted literally this could generate 'absurd results' in that it appears to prohibit all distinctions. The Court warned this could lead to a violation of 'every one of the many legal or administrative provisions which do not secure to everyone complete equality of treatment in the enjoyment of the rights and freedoms recognised'. It noted that national authorities must frequently deal with situations and problems that 'call for different legal solutions; moreover, certain legal inequalities tend only to correct factual inequalities'. The Court said that the French text must be read in light of the 'more restrictive text' of the English version ('without discrimination').[58]

Discrimination is present if a person or group is treated less favourably than another, without justification, even if the Convention does not require such favourable treatment.[59] Differential treatment that appears to be founded on an objective assessment of essentially different factual circumstances that strike a fair balance between protection of the interests of the community and respect for the rights and freedoms safeguarded by the Convention are not contrary to article 14.[60] The applicant must be a victim of differential treatment based upon personal features. The Court declared manifestly unfounded an allegation that a person had been sentenced for fraud more severely than others because the victims of his crime were Jewish.[61]

The notion of proportionality is central to the Court's analysis in evaluating whether a distinction is to be deemed discriminatory and therefore contrary to article 14. An important factor in the assessment is whether there is a possibility of alternative means for achieving the same end.[62] In *Sejdić and Finci*, the Grand Chamber held that deprivation of the right to be a candidate for president to persons from ethnic groups other than the Serbs, Croats, and Bosniaks who were comprised in the power-sharing regime of the Dayton Agreement did not comply with the requirements of reasonableness

---

[57] Opinion of the European Court of Human Rights on draft Protocol No. 12 adopted at the plenary administrative session of the Court on 6 December 1999, para. 5.

[58] Case *'relating to certain aspects of the laws on the use of languages in education in Belgium'* (merits), 23 July 1968, p. 31, § 10, Series A no. 6. See also *National Union of Belgian Police v. Belgium*, 27 October 1975, § 46, Series A no. 19.

[59] *Abdulaziz, Cabales, and Balkandali v. the United Kingdom*, 28 May 1985, § 82, Series A no. 94.

[60] *Zarb Adami v. Malta*, no. 17209/02, § 73, ECHR 2006-VIII; *G.M.B. and K.M. v. Switzerland* (dec.), no. 36797/97, 27 September 2001.

[61] *Gruber v. Germany* (dec.), no. 45198/04, 20 November 2007.

[62] *Glor v. Switzerland*, no. 13444/04, § 94, 30 April 2009. Cited with approval in *Sejdić and Finci v. Bosnia and Herzegovina* [GC], nos 27996/06 and 34836/06, § 48, ECHR 2009.

and proportionality. It said that although 'the time may still not be ripe for a political system which would be a simple reflection of majority rule, there exist mechanisms of power-sharing which do not automatically lead to the total exclusion of representatives of the other communities'.[63] For this reason, the measure lacked an 'objective and reasonable justification'.[64] In *Andrejeva*, where the applicant was a stateless person resident in Latvia, and where pensions for labour performed outside the country were only payable to citizens, the government's exclusion of non-citizens was deemed not proportionate.[65]

It is unnecessary to establish that discrimination is intentional for there to be a breach of article 14. It may be the consequence of a general policy or a measure that has disproportionately prejudicial effects on a particular group even in the absence of evidence that the group has been targeted.[66] When the discrimination is indirect rather than intentional, and it is the result of a practice rather than a discriminatory legislative provision, the Court does not distinguish between proportionality and a legitimate aim. In a Maltese case, statistics showed that women and men were not called for jury duty in equal numbers. The government argued that a legislative provision allowed an exemption from jury duty because the person had to take care of a family, and the Court acknowledged 'more women than men could successfully rely on such a provision'. The government also said that defence lawyers would have a tendency to challenge female jurors 'for cultural reasons'.[67] These arguments did not impress the Court as they failed to indicate the disproportion of men and women in the pool of jurors.[68]

Differential treatment of groups directed at correction of 'factual inequalities' between them is not prohibited discrimination.[69] In certain circumstances, 'a failure to attempt to correct inequality through different treatment may in itself give rise to a breach'.[70] Such measures are sometimes called 'positive discrimination' or 'affirmative action', although the United Nations Committee for the Elimination of Racial Discrimination has said that the term is inappropriate and urged that the phenomenon be labelled 'special measures'.[71] Special measures to deal with inequalities are authorized by international conventions dealing with discrimination. The International Convention on the Elimination of All Forms of Racial Discrimination permits such measures 'taken for the sole purpose of securing adequate advancement of certain racial or ethnic groups or individuals', provided

---

[63] *Sejdić and Finci v. Bosnia and Herzegovina* [GC], nos 27996/06 and 34836/06, § 48, ECHR 2009.
[64] Ibid., § 50.
[65] *Andrejeva v. Latvia* [GC], no. 55707/00, §§ 88–89, ECHR 2009.
[66] *D.H. and Others v. the Czech Republic* [GC], no. 57325/00, § 75, ECHR 2007-IV; *Hugh Jordan v. the United Kingdom*, no. 24746/94, § 154, ECHR 2001-III (extracts); *Hoogendijk v. the Netherlands* (dec.), no. 58461/00, 6 January 2005.
[67] *Zarb Adami v. Malta*, no. 17209/02, § 81, ECHR 2006-VIII.
[68] Ibid., §§ 82–83.
[69] *D.H. and Others v. the Czech Republic* [GC], no. 57325/00, § 175, ECHR 2007-IV; *Kurić and Others v. Slovenia* [GC], no. 26828/06, § 388, ECHR 2012 (extracts); *Case 'relating to certain aspects of the laws on the use of languages in education in Belgium' v. Belgium (merits)*, 23 July 1968, p. 34, § 10, Series A no. 6; *Thlimmenos v. Greece* [GC], no. 34369/97, § 44, ECHR 2000-IV; *Stec and Others v. the United Kingdom* [GC], no. 65731/01, § 51, ECHR 2006-VI; *Sejdić and Finci v. Bosnia and Herzegovina* [GC], nos 27996/06 and 34836/06, § 44, ECHR 2009.
[70] *Case 'relating to certain aspects of the laws on the use of languages in education in Belgium' v. Belgium (merits)*, 23 July 1968, p. 34, § 10, Series A no. 6; *Thlimmenos v. Greece* [GC], no. 34369/97, § 44, ECHR 2000-IV; *Religionsgemeinschaft der Zeugen Jehovas and Others v. Austria*, no. 40825/98, § 96, 31 July 2008; *Thlimmenos v. Greece* [GC], no. 34369/97, § 44, ECHR 2000-IV.
[71] The meaning and scope of special measures in the International Convention on the Elimination of Racial Discrimination, General Recommendation No. 32, UN Doc. CERD/C/GC/32, para. 14.

they do not 'lead to the maintenance of separate rights for different racial groups and that they shall not be continued after the objectives for which they were taken have been achieved'.[72] The Convention on the Elimination of All Forms of Discrimination against Women permits 'temporary special measures aimed at accelerating *de facto* equality between men and women'.[73] Although not explicitly permitted by article 14, special measures are undoubtedly consistent with the Convention.

Dealing with differences in pensionable ages between men and women in the United Kingdom, the Grand Chamber noted that these were introduced in 1940, and were intended to address a situation of financial inequality and hardship arising out of the situation of women who traditionally were not paid for their role in caring for the family in the home rather than remunerated employment in the workplace. 'At their origin, therefore, the differential pensionable ages were intended to correct "factual inequalities" between men and women and appear therefore to have been objectively justified under Article 14 of the Convention', said the Court.[74] Such differences continued to be justified until social conditions had evolved to the point where women were no longer victims of such prejudice because their working lives outside the home were shorter than those of men. The Court noted that '[t]his change, must, by its very nature, have been gradual, and it would be difficult or impossible to pinpoint any particular moment when the unfairness to men caused by differential pensionable ages began to outweigh the need to correct the disadvantaged position of women'.[75]

A margin of appreciation is granted to States in determining whether and to what extent different treatment is justified with respect to otherwise similar circumstances. The extent of the margin of appreciation varies depending on the background, circumstances, and subject-matter.[76] This will also evolve over time because of the need to consider changing conditions and respond to an emerging consensus among the Member States of the Council of Europe.[77] The presence or absence of a common denominator within the Member States is relevant in assessing the extent of the margin of appreciation.[78]

One of the important factors in determining the extent of this margin relates to the rights that are at issue. When measures involving social and economic policy are involved, the margin is described as being 'wide'.[79] The Court has explained that '[b]ecause of their

---

[72] International Convention on the Elimination of All Forms of Racial Discrimination, (1966) 660 UNTS 195, art. 1(4).

[73] Convention on the Elimination of All Forms of Discrimination against Women, (1980) 1249 UNTS 13, art. 4(1).

[74] *Stec and Others v. the United Kingdom* [GC], nos 65731/01 and 65900/01, § 61, ECHR 2006-VI.

[75] Ibid., § 62, ECHR 2006-VI.

[76] *Rasmussen v. Denmark,* 28 November 1984, § 40, Series A no. 87; *Inze v. Austria,* 28 October 1987, § 41, Series A no. 126; *Sejdić and Finci v. Bosnia and Herzegovina* [GC], nos 27996/06 and 34836/06, § 42, ECHR 2009; *Rejeva v. Latvia* [GC], no. 55707/00, § 82, ECHR 2009; *Stec and Others v. the United Kingdom* [GC], nos 65731/01 and 65900/01, §§ 51–52, ECHR 2006-VI; *Van Raalte v. the Netherlands,* 21 February 1997, § 39, *Reports of Judgments and Decisions* 1997-I; *Zarb Adami v. Malta,* no. 17209/02, § 74, ECHR 2006-VIII; *Gaygusuz v. Austria,* 16 September 1996, § 42, *Reports of Judgments and Decisions* 1996-IV; *Petrovic v. Austria,* 27 March 1998, § 38, *Reports of Judgments and Decisions* 1998-II; *Inze v. Austria,* 28 October 1987, § 41, Series A no. 126.

[77] *Zarb Adami v. Malta,* no. 17209/02, § 74, ECHR 2006-VIII; *Stafford v. the United Kingdom* [GC], no. 46295/99, § 68, ECHR 2002-IV; *Ünal Tekeli v. Turkey,* no. 29865/96, § 54, ECHR 2004-X (extracts).

[78] *Glor v. Switzerland,* no. 13444/04, § 75, ECHR 2009.

[79] *James and Others v. the United Kingdom,* 21 February 1986, § 46, Series A no. 98; *National & Provincial Building Society, Leeds Permanent Building Society, and Yorkshire Building Society v. the United Kingdom,* 23 October 1997, § 80, *Reports of Judgments and Decisions* 1997-VII.

direct knowledge of their society and its needs, the national authorities are in principle better placed than the international judge to appreciate what is in the public interest on social or economic grounds, and the Court will generally respect the legislature's policy choice unless it is "manifestly without reasonable foundation"'.[80] In a case dealing with pension schemes, the Court said that 'the precise timing and means of putting right the inequality were not so manifestly unreasonable as to exceed the wide margin of appreciation allowed it in such a field'.[81]

Indirect discrimination

The term 'indirect discrimination' is often used to denote policies or measures that are ostensibly neutral but that have disproportionately prejudicial effects on individuals or a group protected by article 14. The European Union's Racial Equality Directive defines it as follows: '[I]ndirect discrimination shall be taken to occur where an apparently neutral provision, criterion or practice would put persons of a racial or ethnic origin at a particular disadvantage compared with other persons, unless that provision, criterion or practice is objectively justified by a legitimate aim and the means of achieving that aim are appropriate and necessary.'[82]

Sometimes, references to 'indirect discrimination' include the notion that it is not 'targeted at the group'[83] or that it does not require a discriminatory intent.[84] This is also described sometimes as 'effects discrimination'. A confusion in concepts may result. In some cases, facially neutral measures with prejudicial effects on groups can well have been motivated by discriminatory intentions. Nevertheless, proof of such intent may be very difficult because the apparent neutrality of the measure or policy effectively conceals the intent. The same problem does not arise when discrimination is direct. Discrimination need not necessarily result from legislation, but may also be a consequence of a 'de facto situation'.[85]

The first case of indirect discrimination considered by the Court concerned a Jehovah's Witness who was denied appointment as a chartered accountant on the ground that he had previously been convicted of insubordination in the armed forces because of his anti-militarist beliefs. The Court noted that 'such difference of treatment does not generally come within the scope of Article 14 in so far as it relates to access to a particular profession, the right to freedom of profession not being guaranteed by the Convention'.[86] But the applicant's claim was not about the distinction made by the professional body regarding persons with criminal convictions. Rather, it was because 'in the application of the relevant law no distinction is made between persons convicted of offences committed exclusively because of their religious beliefs and persons convicted of other offences'.[87]

---

[80] *James and Others v. the United Kingdom*, 21 February 1986, § 46, Series A no. 98; *National & Provincial Building Society, Leeds Permanent Building Society, and Yorkshire Building Society v. the United Kingdom*, 23 October 1997, § 80, *Reports of Judgments and Decisions* 1997-VII.

[81] *Stec and Others v. the United Kingdom* [GC], nos 65731/01 and 65900/01, § 66, ECHR 2006-VI.

[82] Racial Equality Directive 2000/43/EC, art. 2.

[83] *D.H. and Others v. the Czech Republic* [GC], no. 57325/00, § 175, ECHR 2007-IV; *Hoogendijk v. the Netherlands* (dec.), no. 58461/00, 6 January 2005; *Zarb Adami v. Malta*, no. 17209/02, § 81, ECHR 2006-VIII; *McShane v. the United Kingdom*, no. 43290/98, § 135, 28 May 2002.

[84] *D.H. and Others v. the Czech Republic* [GC], no. 57325/00, § 194, ECHR 2007-IV.

[85] *Zarb Adami v. Malta*, no. 17209/02, § 76, ECHR 2006-VIII.

[86] *Thlimmenos v. Greece* [GC], no. 34369/97, § 41, ECHR 2000-IV. Also *Bigaeva v. Greece*, no. 26713/05, § 39, 28 May 2009.

[87] *Thlimmenos v. Greece* [GC], no. 34369/97, § 42, ECHR 2000-IV.

Finding that there had been a violation of article 14 in conjunction with article 9, the Grand Chamber said that the relevant legislation failed 'to introduce appropriate exceptions to the rule barring persons convicted of a serious crime from the profession of chartered accountants'.[88]

Yet another example, this one based on the category of disability which is not explicitly enumerated in article 14, concerns a diabetic who was alleged to be a victim of indirect or effects discrimination. The applicant was not eligible for military service, despite his expressed wish to do so, because of his medical problems. At the same time, he was ineligible for alternative civil service because he was not a conscientious objector. As a result, he was subject to a tax levied upon those exempted from military service. The Court held that article 14 had been violated because the State had failed to respond to the individual circumstances of the applicant by, for example, allowing him to fill less strenuous posts within the military.[89]

The Court's conclusions in these cases seems inspired by a related concept known as 'reasonable accommodation' that is often part of the discussion about indirect discrimination. Noting that 'reasonable accommodation' is a familiar notion in various national legal systems, the Court has considered the issue but declined to apply it to the Convention.[90] In a case involving religious observance, three dissenting judges held that a 'reasonable accommodation' was a way of achieving proportionality, in that 'for a measure to be proportionate, the authorities, when choosing between several possible means of achieving the legitimate aim pursued, must opt for the measure that is least restrictive of rights and freedoms'.[91]

An example of indirect discrimination is provided by a case where Roma children were assigned to special schools on the basis of tests that appeared objective. The Grand Chamber said there was a danger that the tests were biased. Consequently, 'the results were not analysed in the light of the particularities and special characteristics of the Roma children who sat them'. The Grand Chamber said that as a result 'the tests in question cannot serve as justification for the impugned difference in treatment'.[92] The Grand Chamber found this to be a form of indirect discrimination. It held there was a violation of article 14 taken in conjunction with article 2 of Protocol No. 1.[93] The Grand Chamber's conclusion that this was 'indirect discrimination' is not entirely convincing. If the tests given to Roma children were not properly interpreted and misapplied, it is a problem of direct and not indirect discrimination. Genuine indirect discrimination would result from ostensibly fair and accurate tests that nevertheless impacted negatively on the education of Roma children.

Proof of discrimination

The general rule set out in the case law of the European Court of Human Rights is that proof must be made 'beyond reasonable doubt'.[94] However, this expression, while very

---

[88] Ibid., § 48.

[89] *Glor v. Switzerland*, no. 13444/04, §§ 77–98, ECHR 2009.

[90] *Eweida and Others v. the United Kingdom*, no. 48420/10, §§ 48, 49, 78, ECHR 2013 (extracts).

[91] *Francesco Sessa v. Italy*, no. 28790/08, Joint Dissenting Opinion of Judges Tulkens, Popović, and Keller, §§ 9–10, ECHR 2012 (excerpts).

[92] *D.H. and Others v. the Czech Republic* [GC], no. 57325/00, § 201, ECHR 2007-IV.

[93] Ibid., § 210.

[94] *Avşar v. Turkey*, no. 25657/94, § 282, ECHR 2001.

familiar in criminal proceedings, especially those of the common law tradition, is not used in quite the same sense by the European Court, whose role is not to rule on guilt or innocence or on civil liability, but rather on the responsibility of States Parties under the Convention.[95] In litigation concerning discrimination,

> there are no procedural barriers to the admissibility of evidence or predetermined formulae for its assessment. The Court adopts the conclusions that are, in its view, supported by the free evaluation of all evidence, including such inferences as may flow from the facts and the parties' submissions. According to its established case-law, proof may follow from the coexistence of sufficiently strong, clear and concordant inferences or of similar unrebutted presumptions of fact. Moreover, the level of persuasion necessary for reaching a particular conclusion and, in this connection, the distribution of the burden of proof are intrinsically linked to the specificity of the facts, the nature of the allegation made and the Convention right at stake.[96]

There is a shifting burden of proof in the area of discrimination. The general principle *affirmanti incumbit probatio* (he or she who alleges something must prove that allegation) is therefore not applied in a rigorous manner.[97] The initial burden, of course, falls upon the applicant to establish that there is a difference in treatment. Once this has been done, the burden moves to the government, where the responsibility is to demonstrate that the measure in question was justified.[98] This approach seems straightforward enough when legislation or a judicial decision and their effects are being considered. However, discrimination cases may concern allegations of ill-treatment that result from conduct of the authorities motivated by prohibited grounds. Then, the applicant must do something more than establish 'differential treatment' and provide some *prima facie* demonstration of the discriminatory conduct of the authorities. If the events in contention lie wholly, or in large part, within the exclusive knowledge of the authorities, for example when a person dies in custody, the burden of proof may shift to the authorities to provide a satisfactory and convincing explanation.[99] Although the shifting of the burden of proof in this way may be more suited to violations of articles 2 and 3, the Grand Chamber has not ruled out the possibility that 'in certain cases of alleged discrimination it may require the respondent Government to disprove an arguable allegation of discrimination and—if they fail to do so—find a violation of Article 14 of the Convention on that basis'.[100]

Nevertheless, in a case where it was alleged that the authorities had failed to carry out an effective investigation into the supposedly racist motive for a killing, the Grand Chamber reversed the findings of the Chamber and rejected the idea of a shift in the burden of proof. The applicants had explained that a law enforcement official had discharged bursts of automatic fire in a populated area, disregarding public safety. Absent any rational explanation for this, they said that 'racist hatred . . . was the only plausible explanation and

---

[95] *Nachova and Others v. Bulgaria* [GC], nos 43577/98 and 43579/98, § 147, ECHR 2005-VII.

[96] *D.H. and Others v. the Czech Republic* [GC], no. 57325/00, § 178, ECHR 2007-IV; *Nachova and Others v. Bulgaria* [GC], nos 43577/98 and 43579/98, § 147, ECHR 2005-VII.

[97] *Aktaş v. Turkey*, no. 24351/94, § 272, ECHR 2003-V (extracts).

[98] *Oršuš and Others v. Croatia* [GC], no. 15766/03, § 150, ECHR 2010; *Chassagnou and Others v. France* [GC], nos 25088/94, 28331/95, and 28443/95, §§ 91–92, ECHR 1999-III; *Timishev v. Russia*, nos 55762/00 and 55974/00, § 57, ECHR 2005-XII; *D.H. and Others v. the Czech Republic* [GC], no. 57325/00, § 177, ECHR 2007-IV; *Rejeva v. Latvia* [GC], no. 55707/00, § 84, ECHR 2009.

[99] *Salman v. Turkey* [GC], no. 21986/93, § 100, ECHR 2000-VII.

[100] *Nachova and Others v. Bulgaria* [GC], nos 43577/98 and 43579/98, § 157, ECHR 2005-VII.

that he would not have acted in that manner in a non-Roma neighbourhood'.[101] The Grand Chamber did not find this to be persuasive. Nor was it convinced by the suggestion that the attitude of the military police was influenced by their knowledge of the Roma origin of the victims, something it described as speculative. In the same way, evidence of a racial slur uttered in connection with a violent act should have prompted the authorities to verify the statement but was 'in itself an insufficient basis for concluding that the respondent State is liable for a racist killing'.[102] The Grand Chamber explained that reversing the burden in such a case would 'amount to requiring the respondent Government to prove the absence of a particular subjective attitude on the part of the person concerned'.[103]

In what appears to be the only finding of a violation of article 14 taken together with article 13, the applicant complained that he was deprived of an adequate remedy in a case of ill-treatment because he was of Roma origin, something that was known to the police officers. He said that while in the police station, 'his ethnic origin was openly and repeatedly referred to by the investigating authorities as a factor militating against his complaint of police abuse'. Noting that racial violence 'is a particular affront to human dignity and, in view of its perilous consequences, requires from the authorities special vigilance and a vigorous reaction', the Court said that 'when investigating violent incidents, State authorities have the additional duty to take all reasonable steps to unmask any racist motive and to establish whether or not ethnic hatred or prejudice may have played a role in the events'.[104] The Court said that the applicant did not refer to any particular facts substantiating the claim that the violence he sustained was racially motivated (although it had observed, only a few paragraphs earlier, that the applicant had indicated that his ethnic origin had in fact been regularly referred to by investigating authorities). Instead, the Court said, 'he claimed that his allegation should be evaluated within the context of documented and repeated failure by the Romanian authorities to remedy instances of anti-Roma violence and to provide redress for discrimination'.[105] The Court referred to official programmes directed at eradicating anti-Roma conduct that should have been well known to the investigating authorities. Yet, '[n]ot only was there no attempt on the part of the prosecutors to verify the behaviour of the policemen involved in the violence, ascertaining, for instance, whether they had been involved in the past in similar incidents or whether they had been accused of displaying anti-Roma sentiment, but the prosecutors made tendentious remarks in relation to the applicant's Roma origin throughout the investigation'.[106] This, it said, disclosed 'a general discriminatory attitude of the authorities, which reinforced the applicant's belief that any remedy in his case was purely illusory'.[107] The Court concluded that 'the failure of the law enforcement agents to investigate possible racial motives in the applicant's ill-treatment combined with their attitude during the investigation constitutes a discrimination with regard to the applicant's rights contrary to Article 14'.[108]

[101] Ibid., § 149.
[102] Ibid., §§ 152–153.
[103] Ibid.
[104] *Cobzaru v. Romania*, no. 48254/99, §§ 86–89, 26 July 2007.
[105] Ibid., § 94.
[106] Ibid., § 98.
[107] Ibid.
[108] Ibid., § 100.

Evidentiary issues often lie at the heart of litigation about indirect discrimination. Many discriminatory measures are ostensibly neutral, applying to all in a general sense yet in practice in a differential manner. An example would be a height requirement for certain employment, in that it might result in differential treatment of women. Differential treatment is not difficult to establish when the measure makes this clear, for example a prohibition upon women working in certain jobs or a distinct difference in treatment, such as unequal salaries. According to the European Court, 'less strict evidential rules should apply in cases of alleged indirect discrimination'.[109] Usually, proof of indirect discrimination will involve statistical materials, although this is not essential.[110] Statistical evidence is especially useful in demonstrating such indirect discrimination, where the allegation is based not on the intention but on the effects of the measure in dispute. In *Hoogendijk v. The Netherlands*, the Court stated:

[W]here an applicant is able to show, on the basis of undisputed official statistics, the existence of a prima facie indication that a specific rule—although formulated in a neutral manner—in fact affects a clearly higher percentage of women than men, it is for the respondent Government to show that this is the result of objective factors unrelated to any discrimination on grounds of sex. If the onus of demonstrating that a difference in impact for men and women is not in practice discriminatory does not shift to the respondent Government, it will be in practice extremely difficult for applicants to prove indirect discrimination.[111]

The Court has relied upon statistics in a similar manner in other cases,[112] although previously it had been rather unimpressed by statistical evidence as evidence of a discriminatory practice.[113] Moreover, it has said that 'statistics are not in themselves sufficient to disclose a practice which could be classified as discriminatory'.[114]

Grounds of discrimination

The list of protected categories is clearly inspired by article 2 of the Universal Declaration of Human Rights, with the addition of the reference to 'association with a national minority'. The words 'such as' indicate that the list is not exhaustive. Although a plausible interpretation would restrict the non-enumerated categories to those that are analogous to what is listed in the provision, the Court has not favoured any such limitation that might be imposed by an *ejusdem generis* interpretation and seems to have taken a very broad approach, recognizing a prohibition of discrimination going well beyond 'personal characteristics'.[115] It has said that article 14 prohibits, within the ambit of the rights and freedoms guaranteed, 'discriminatory treatment having as its basis or reason a personal characteristic ("status") by which persons or groups of persons are distinguishable from each other'.[116]

[109] *D.H. and Others v. the Czech Republic* [GC], no. 57325/00, § 184, ECHR 2007-IV.
[110] Ibid., § 188.
[111] *Hoogendijk v. the Netherlands* (dec.), no. 58641/00, 6 January 2005. Cited in *D.H. and Others v. the Czech Republic* [GC], no. 57325/00, § 180, ECHR 2007-IV; *Opuz v. Turkey*, no. 33401/02, § 183, ECHR 2009.
[112] *Zarb Adami v. Malta*, no. 17209/02, §§ 77–78, ECHR 2006-VIII.
[113] *Hugh Jordan v. the United Kingdom*, no. 24746/94, § 154, ECHR 2001-III (extracts).
[114] *Zarb Adami v. Malta*, no. 17209/02, § 76, ECHR 2006-VIII; *Hugh Jordan v. the United Kingdom*, no. 24746/94, § 154, ECHR 2001-III (extracts).
[115] *Clift v. the United Kingdom*, no. 7205/07, § 56, 13 July 2010.
[116] *Kjeldsen, Busk Madsen, and Pedersen v. Denmark*, 7 December 1976, § 56, Series A no. 23; *Berezovskiy v. Ukraine* (dec.), no. 70908/01, 15 June 2004; *Carson and Others v. the United Kingdom* [GC], no. 42184/05, §§ 61, 70, ECHR 2010.

Case law has already recognized several non-enumerated categories as falling within the scope of article 14. The issue of codifying this arose when Protocol No. 12 was being drafted. The Explanatory Report states that 'expressly including certain additional non-discrimination grounds (for example, physical or mental disability, sexual orientation or age) [appeared to the drafters of the Protocol as] unnecessary from a legal point of view since the list of non-discrimination grounds is not exhaustive, and because inclusion of any particular additional ground might give rise to unwarranted *a contrario* interpretations as regards discrimination based on grounds not so included'.[117] The European Union Charter of Fundamental Rights, adopted in 2000 like Protocol No. 12, takes the list in article 14 of the Convention and adds genetic features, disability, age, and sexual orientation.

In some cases a line has been drawn premised upon the requirement that the distinctions be related to personal characteristics or status. For example, where two different criminal court systems had jurisdiction over the same offenders, the selection of defendants by prosecuting authorities was challenged as discriminatory. In Bosnia and Herzegovina, the sentencing regime differed depending upon the court system that was chosen. Although this was criticized for creating uncertainty in the criminal law, the European Court held that differences in treatment were not to be explained in terms of personal characteristics and therefore did not amount to discriminatory treatment.[118] Along similar lines, an applicant argued that article 14 was breached because he was tried in one part of the country where different procedural rules applied to a criminal trial than in another. The Court explained that any difference in treatment was not to be explained 'in terms of personal characteristics, such as national origin or association with a national minority, but on the geographical location where the individual is arrested and detained'.[119] The Court suggested that it was even desirable that legislation takes account of regional differences and characteristics of an objective and reasonable nature.[120] The Court dismissed an argument by a woman of forty-seven who had been denied the right to adopt a child because of her age on the grounds that she was being treated differently than women her age who could have biological children. According to the Court, 'the State has no influence over a woman's ability or inability to have biological children'.[121]

But the Court has also pointed out that not all grounds of discrimination relate to personal characteristics, giving property as an example.[122] It has applied article 14 to discrimination between different categories of property owners[123] and between large and small landowners,[124] non-commissioned officers and ordinary soldiers in the military,[125] holders of fishing rights,[126] place of residence,[127] and tenants of the State and those of

---

[117] Explanatory Report on Protocol No. 12, para. 20.

[118] *Maktouf and Damjanović v. Bosnia and Herzegovina* [GC], nos 2312/08 and 34179/08, § 83, ECHR 2013 (extracts).

[119] *Magee v. the United Kingdom*, no. 28135/95, § 50, ECHR 2000-VI.

[120] Ibid.

[121] *Schwizgebel v. Switzerland*, no. 25762/07, § 84, ECHR 2010 (extracts).

[122] *Clift v. the United Kingdom*, no. 7205/07, § 56, 13 July 2010.

[123] *James and Others v. the United Kingdom*, 21 February 1986, § 74, Series A no. 98.

[124] *Chassagnou and Others v. France* [GC], nos 25088/94, 28331/95, and 28443/95, §§ 90 and 95, ECHR 1999-III.

[125] *Engel and Others v. the Netherlands*, 8 June 1976, § 72, Series A no. 22.

[126] *Alatulkkila and Others v. Finland*, no. 33538/96, § 67, 28 July 2005.

[127] *Carson and Others v. the United Kingdom* [GC], no. 42184/05, §§ 70–71, ECHR 2010. See also *Carson and Others v. the United Kingdom* [GC], no. 42184/05, Joint Dissenting Opinion of Judges Tulkens, Vajić, Spielmann, Jaeger, Jočienė, and López Guerra, ECHR 2010.

private landlords.[128] Dealing with a prohibition on employment of former Soviet intelligence officers in both the public and private sectors, the Court said this lacked proportionality. In effect, the differential treatment depended upon whether or not the person had worked for the KGB.[129] When a French magazine complained of discrimination because it was prosecuted for publishing photos on the basis of legislation that applied to print but not audio-visual media, the Court dismissed the complaint because it said that the two types of media were not similarly situated.[130]

On occasion, the case law has referred to 'suspect grounds',[131] suggesting some sort of hierarchy within the grounds prohibited by article 14. In one case, the court referred to 'suspect categories', offering sex, sexual orientation, ethnic origin, and nationality as examples.[132] In another, it spoke of 'suspect grounds of race and ethnicity'.[133] One judge spoke of 'national origin' as a 'suspect class'.[134] This may be more a reference to the issue of proportionality, in the sense that certain grounds such as race and sex are almost inherently disproportionate. There is isolated support for the proposition that all of the enumerated categories in article 14 are 'suspect', an observation that seems to deprive the notion of any real utility.[135] Even when the Court has not spoken of 'suspect grounds' it has sometimes, in the proportionality analysis, suggested that certain forms of distinction require 'very weighty reasons' or 'particularly serious and weighty reasons' before they may be justifiable. The Court has said this about discrimination based upon birth outside of marriage,[136] nationality,[137] sex,[138] sexual orientation,[139]

---

[128] *Larkos v. Cyprus* [GC], no. 29515/95, § 58, ECHR 1999-I.
[129] *Sidabras and Džiautas v. Lithuania*, nos 55480/00 and 59330/00, §§ 41, 56–62, ECHR 2004-VIII. But see the objections to the application of article 14 in the three concurring or dissenting opinions in this case. *Sidabras and Džiautas* was followed in *Rainys and Gasparavičius v. Lithuania*, nos 70665/01 and 74345/01, § 40, 7 April 2005.
[130] *Société de conception de presse et d'édition and Ponson v. France*, no. 26935/05, § 80, 5 March 2009. Also *Hachette Filipacchi Presse Automobile and Dupuy v. France*, no. 13353/05, § 65, 5 March 2009.
[131] *Clift v. the United Kingdom*, no. 7205/07, § 72, 13 July 2010.
[132] *Eweida and Others v. the United Kingdom*, no. 48420/10, § 71, ECHR 2013 (extracts).
[133] *Sejdić and Finci v. Bosnia and Herzegovina* [GC], nos 27996/06 and 34836/06, § 37, ECHR 2009.
[134] *Ždanoka v. Latvia* [GC], no. 58278/00, Dissenting Opinion of Judge Zupančič, ECHR 2006-IV.
[135] *Oršuš and Others v. Croatia*, no. 15766/03, § Joint Partly Dissenting Opinion of Judges Jungwiert, Vajić, Kovler, Gyulumyan, Jaeger, Myjer, Berro-Lefèvre, and Vučinić, 17 July 2008; *Burden v. the United Kingdom* [GC], no. 13378/05, Dissenting Opinion of Judge Zupančič, ECHR 2008.
[136] *Fabris v. France* [GC], no. 16574/08, § 59, ECHR 2015 (extracts); *Camp and Bourimi v. the Netherlands*, no. 28369/95, § 38, ECHR 2000-X; *Mazurek v. France*, no. 34406/97, § 49, ECHR 2000-II; *Inze v. Austria*, 28 October 1987, § 41, Series A no. 126; *Sahin v. Germany*, no. 30943/96, § 94, 11 October 2001; *Sommerfeld v. Germany* [GC], no. 31871/96, § 93, ECHR 2003-VIII (extracts).
[137] *Gaygusuz v. Austria*, 16 September 1996, § 42, *Reports of Judgments and Decisions* 1996-IV; *Rejeva v. Latvia* [GC], no. 55707/00, § 87, ECHR 2009; *Koua Poirrez v. France*, no. 40892/98, § 46, ECHR 2003-X; *Bah v. the United Kingdom*, no. 56328/07, § 37, ECHR 2011.
[138] *Abdulaziz, Cabales, and Balkandali v. the United Kingdom*, 28 May 1985, § 78, Series A no. 94; *Bah v. the United Kingdom*, no. 56328/07, § 84, ECHR 2011; *Ünal Tekeli v. Turkey*, no. 29865/96, § 53, ECHR 2004-X (extracts); *Stec and Others v. the United Kingdom* [GC], nos 65731/01 and 65900/01, § 52, ECHR 2006-VI; *Van Raalte v. the Netherlands*, 21 February 1997, § 39, *Reports of Judgments and Decisions* 1997-I; *Schuler-Zgraggen v. Switzerland*, 24 June 1993, § 67, Series A no. 263; *Burghartz v. Switzerland*, 22 February 1994, § 27, Series A no. 280-B; *Karlheinz Schmidt v. Germany*, 18 July 1994, § 24, Series A no. 291-B; *Petrovic v. Austria*, 27 March 1998, § 37, *Reports of Judgments and Decisions* 1998-II; *Zarb Adami v. Malta*, no. 17209/02, § 80, ECHR 2006-VIII; *Willis v. the United Kingdom*, no. 36042/97, § 39, ECHR 2002-IV; *Rangelov v. Germany*, no. 5123/07, § 102, 22 March 2012.
[139] *Vallianatos and Others v. Greece* [GC], no. 29381/09 and 32684/09, § 76, ECHR 2013; *Smith and Grady v. the United Kingdom*, nos 33985/96 and 33986/96, § 90, ECHR 1999-VI; *Karner v. Austria*, no. 40016/98, §§ 37 and 42, ECHR 2003-IX; *X and Others v. Austria* [GC], no. 19010/07, § 99, ECHR 2013.

and ethnic origin.[140] The references to 'non-suspect' or 'less-suspect' categories are very rare. But in *Carson v. The United Kingdom*, the Court explained that 'the individual does not require the same high level of protection against differences in treatment based on [residence] as is needed in relation to differences based on an inherent characteristic, such as gender or racial or ethnic origin'.[141] In cases before the Court, the United Kingdom has argued that the alleged discrimination did not concern 'suspect grounds' such as sex or race, suggesting that this would justify a wide margin of appreciation.[142]

It is unlikely that any distinction on racial or ethnic origin could ever be deemed proportionate. For example, the Court has said that 'no difference in treatment which is based exclusively or to a decisive extent on a person's ethnic origin is capable of being objectively justified in a contemporary democratic society built on the principles of pluralism and respect for different cultures'.[143] The Court will be very demanding with respect to a margin of appreciation, and is likely to insist on a demonstration that the impugned measure is not only pursuing a legitimate aim but also that it is necessary. On the other hand, distinctions based on age or disability are common and accepted. This does not mean, of course, that discrimination based upon these categories cannot take place, but the exercise in assessing proportionality may not be as straightforward.

Sex

The term 'sex', used in the equality rights provisions of the Charter of the United Nations and the Universal Declaration of Human Rights and in many subsequent instruments, including article 14 of the European Convention on Human Rights, has gradually been supplanted by 'gender'. Early cases referred to 'gender' but only with respect to gender reassignment, rather than discrimination as such.[144] The terminology began to change in the 1990s. In recent judgments, the Court has spoken of discrimination on the basis of 'gender' when it was quite clearly referring to discrimination attributable to the sex of the applicants.[145]

As the discussion of the *travaux préparatoires* at the beginning of this chapter indicates, sex did not even appear in the original list of prohibited grounds considered by the Consultative Assembly. The Court has said that 'gender equality' is one of the 'key principles underlying the Convention',[146] but while that may be the contemporary interpretation the drafting history shows that it was far from the minds of most of those who negotiated it. The Council of Europe in 1949 and 1950 contrasts rather markedly

---

[140] *Oršuš and Others v. Croatia* [GC], no. 15766/03, § 149, ECHR 2010.

[141] *Carson and Others v. the United Kingdom*, no. 42184/05, § 80, 4 November 2008.

[142] *Hode and Abdi v. the United Kingdom*, no. 22341/09, § 51, 6 November 2012; *Clift v. The United Kingdom*, no. 7205/07, § 72, 13 July 2010.

[143] *D.H. and Others v. the Czech Republic* [GC], no. 57325/00, § 176, ECHR 2007-IV; *Timishev v. Russia*, nos 55762/00 and 55974/00, § 58, ECHR 2005-XII.

[144] *Sheffield and Horsham v. the United Kingdom*, 30 July 1998, § 12, *Reports of Judgments and Decisions* 1998-V; *Cossey v. the United Kingdom*, 27 September 1990, § 11, Series A no. 184; *Rees v. the United Kingdom*, no. 9532/81, Commission decision of 15 March 1983, DR 36, p. 78.

[145] *Opuz v. Turkey*, no. 33401/02, § 177, ECHR 2009; *Carson and Others v. The United Kingdom*, no. 42184/05, § 80, 4 November 2008; *Leyla Şahin v. Turkey*, no. 44774/98, § 107, 29 June 2004; *Leyla Şahin v. Turkey* [GC], no. 44774/98, § 115, ECHR 2005-XI; *Smith and Grady v. the United Kingdom*, nos 33985/96 and 33986/96, § 81, 102, ECHR 1999-VI ; *Van Raalte v. the Netherlands*, 21 February 1997, § 40, *Reports of Judgments and Decisions* 1997-I .

[146] *Şahin v. Turkey*, no. 44774/98, § 107, 29 June 2004; *Leyla Şahin v. Turkey* [GC], no. 44774/98, § 115, ECHR 2005-XI.

with the United Nations. Reference to 'the equal rights of men and women' had been inserted in the Preamble to the Charter of the United Nations only a few years earlier. One explanation for the omission of sex discrimination in the initial drafts of the European Convention may be the rather glaring absence of women in the negotiation of the European Convention on Human Rights.[147] This stands in sharp contrast with the standard setting within the United Nations at the time, where the Commission on Human Rights was presided by Eleanor Roosevelt, and where many distinguished and dynamic women participated in the drafting of the Universal Declaration of Human Rights and the early versions of the International Covenants.

In 1985, the European Court said 'that the advancement of the equality of the sexes is today a major goal in the member States of the Council of Europe'.[148] Reiterating this statement two decades later, the Court pointed to a 1978 resolution of the Committee of Ministers on the equality of spouses in civil law and the Committee's recommendation adopted in 1985 on legal protection against sex discrimination as 'the main examples of this'.[149] Much more recently, it has declared that 'the advancement of the equality of the sexes in the member States of the Council of Europe prevents the State from lending its support to views of the man's role as primordial and the woman's as secondary'.[150]

Much of the case law concerning discrimination and women's equality involves violations in the private sphere rather than as a result of legislation, judicial decisions, or the conduct of government authorities. This raises issues of the State's positive obligations. Such matters arise, for example, in the case of violence against women. The Court has held that an inadequate legal framework for the investigation and prosecution of rape, rooted in stereotypes about the behaviour of women, may result in a violation of article 3, although without reference to article 14 and issues of women's equality.[151] More recently, it has confronted the issue of domestic violence, referring to the international law background on this issue and especially the pronouncements of the United Nations Committee on the Elimination of Discrimination against Women and the Human Rights Committee as well as the specialized treaty of the Organisation of American States known as the Belém do Pará Convention.[152] These sources indicate that 'the State's failure to protect women against domestic violence breaches their right to equal protection of

---

[147] There is virtually no evidence in the *travaux préparatoires* of women participating actively in the negotiations. Kirsten Gloerfelt-Tarp, the only female member of the Legal Committee, was the alternate of Hermod Lannung, the Danish representative who challenged the absence of a reference to sex discrimination. The only reference to her participation is in a footnote to the Report of the Committee, where its composition is described: Report [of the Committee on Legal and Administrative Questions], 5 September 1949, Doc. AS (1) 77, I *TP* 216–39, at p. 216, fn. 1. Gloerfelt-Tarp was a Danish politician and activist for women's social, political, and economic rights. The 1949 Consultative Assembly consisted of ninety-five men and six women. During the debate on the Convention in the 1950 session of the Consultative Assembly, Helene Weber of Germany intervened to call for the liberation of prisoners of war who were still detained: Report of the Sitting [of the Consultative Assembly, 25 August 1950, afternoon], VI *TP* 144–91, at pp. 144–6. Also, Alice Bacon, a British Labour Party delegate, intervened briefly on the issue of the right to property and the right to education: Report of the sitting [of the Consultative Assembly, 25 August 1950, morning], VI *TP* 74–141, at p. 138.

[148] *Abdulaziz, Cabales, and Balkandali v. the United Kingdom*, 28 May 1985, § 78, Series A no. 94. Also *Schuler-Zgraggen v. Switzerland*, 24 June 1993, § 67, Series A no. 263; *Burghartz v. Switzerland*, 22 February 1994, § 27, Series A no. 280-B; *Petrovic v. Austria*, 27 March 1998, § 37, *Reports of Judgments and Decisions* 1998-II; *Konstantin Markin v. Russia*, no. 30078/06, § 47, 7 October 2010.

[149] *Ünal Tekeli v. Turkey*, no. 29865/96, § 59, ECHR 2004-X (extracts).

[150] *Staatkundig Gereformeerde Partij v. the Netherlands* (dec.), no. 58369/10, § 73, 10 July 2012.

[151] *M.C. v. Bulgaria*, no. 39272/98, §§ 151–169, ECHR 2003-XII.

[152] *Opuz v. Turkey*, no. 33401/02, §§ 184–191, ECHR 2009.

the law and that this failure does not need to be intentional'.[153] The Court concluded that 'the general and discriminatory judicial passivity in Turkey [to domestic violence against women] created a climate that was conducive to domestic violence'.[154] The violence suffered by the applicants was to be regarded 'as gender-based violence which is a form of discrimination against women'.[155] The Court said this amounted to a violation of article 14 taken in conjunction with articles 2 and 3.[156]

Dismissing an application by a conservative clergyman who invoked article 9 of the Convention in an objection to a new policy of the Church of England permitting the ordination of women, the Commission referred to article 14 and noted that 'one of the aims of the Church of England in permitting the ordination of women was undoubtedly to achieve greater equality between men and women in that Church's hierarchy'. It also said that 'the Synod's wish to treat women equally can be regarded as necessary for "the protection of the rights and freedoms of others"'.[157]

Race, colour, and ethnic origin

The second and third terms in the enumeration of discriminatory grounds in article 14 of the Convention are race and colour. In practice, they belong together and overlap considerably. Moreover, neither term is used very much in modern times because most discrimination that may be associated with race or colour is generally considered under the non-enumerated category of 'ethnic origin' or 'ethnicity'. Race, in particular, has come to be viewed as an archaic and even inappropriate term that is itself rooted in racist notions.

While eschewing the notion of 'race', international human rights continues to speak of 'racism' and 'racial discrimination'. Interpreting the category of 'race' in article 14, the Court has referred to the definition of 'racial discrimination' in article 1 of the authoritative International Convention on the Elimination of All Forms of Racial Discrimination:[158]

In this Convention, the term 'racial discrimination' shall mean any distinction, exclusion, restriction or preference based on race, colour, descent, or national or ethnic origin which has the purpose or effect of nullifying or impairing the recognition, enjoyment or exercise, on an equal footing, of human rights and fundamental freedoms in the political, economic, social, cultural or any other field of public life.[159]

The Court has also referred to General Policy Recommendation no. 7 on national legislation to combat racism and racial discrimination, adopted by the Council of Europe's European Commission against Racism and Intolerance:[160]

1. For the purposes of this Recommendation, the following definitions shall apply:
    ...
    (b) 'direct racial discrimination' shall mean any differential treatment based on a ground such as race, colour, language, religion, nationality or national or ethnic origin, which has no objective and reasonable justification....

[153] Ibid., § 191.
[154] Ibid., § 198.
[155] Ibid., § 200.
[156] Ibid., § 202.
[157] *Williamson v. the United Kingdom*, no. 27008/95, 17 May 1995.
[158] *Timishev v. Russia*, nos 55762/00 and 55974/00, § 33, ECHR 2005-XII; *Sejdić and Finci v. Bosnia and Herzegovina* [GC], nos 27996/06 and 34836/06, § 43, ECHR 2009.
[159] International Convention on the Elimination of All Forms of Racial Discrimination, (1966) 660 UNTS 195, art. 1.
[160] *Timishev v. Russia*, nos 55762/00 and 55974/00, § 34, ECHR 2005-XII.

(c) 'indirect racial discrimination' shall mean cases where an apparently neutral factor such as a provision, criterion or practice cannot be as easily complied with by, or disadvantages, persons belonging to a group designated by a ground such as race, colour, language, religion, nationality or national or ethnic origin, unless this factor has an objective and reasonable justification . . ."

The Court has held that discrimination on the basis of 'ethnic origin'[161] or of 'actual or perceived ethnicity'[162] constitutes racial discrimination. The Court has explained that 'the notion of race is rooted in the idea of biological classification of human beings into subspecies on the basis of morphological features such as skin colour or facial characteristics', whereas 'ethnicity has its origin in the idea of societal groups marked in particular by common nationality, religious faith, shared language, or cultural and traditional origins and backgrounds'.[163]

Racial discrimination has been described in the case law as 'a particularly invidious kind of discrimination and, in view of its perilous consequences, requires from the authorities special vigilance and a vigorous reaction'.[164] They have a positive duty to combat racism, 'thereby reinforcing democracy's vision of a society in which diversity is not perceived as a threat but as a source of enrichment'.[165] A large number of the recent cases before the Court dealing with racism relate to abuse directed at Roma. The Court has explained that 'as a result of their turbulent history and constant uprooting, the Roma have become a specific type of disadvantaged and vulnerable minority. They therefore require special protection.'[166]

Race, colour, and ethnic origin are clearly 'suspect categories' where it is difficult to think of examples or distinctions ever being proportionate. Although the Court will not rule this out, it has said that '[w]here the difference in treatment is based on race, colour or ethnic origin, the notion of objective and reasonable justification must be interpreted as strictly as possible'.[167]

As in the case of discrimination on the basis of sex, violence directed at groups identified on the basis of race, colour, or ethnic origin engages the responsibility of the State, even when this is the work of third parties. The procedural obligation that flows from articles 2 and 3 of the Convention has a special dimension in this respect, in that the authorities are required to investigate possible racist motives for acts of violence.[168] According to the Grand Chamber, 'the authorities' duty to investigate the existence of a possible link between racist attitudes and an act of violence is an aspect of their procedural obligations arising under Article 2 of the Convention, but may also be seen as implicit in

---

[161] *D.H. and Others v. the Czech Republic* [GC], no. 57325/00, § 176, ECHR 2007-IV.

[162] *Timishev v. Russia*, nos 55762/00 and 55974/00, § 56, ECHR 2005-XII; *Sejdić and Finci v. Bosnia and Herzegovina* [GC], nos 27996/06 and 34836/06, § 43, ECHR 2009.

[163] *Sejdić and Finci v. Bosnia and Herzegovina* [GC], nos 27996/06 and 34836/06, § 43, ECHR 2009.

[164] *D.H. and Others v. the Czech Republic* [GC], no. 57325/00, § 176, ECHR 2007-IV; *Nachova and Others v. Bulgaria* [GC], nos 43577/98 and 43579/98, § 145, ECHR 2005-VII; *Timishev v. Russia*, nos 55762/00 and 55974/00, § 56, ECHR 2005-XII; *Sampanis and Others v. Greece*, no. 32526/05, § 69, 5 June 2008.

[165] *D.H. and Others v. the Czech Republic* [GC], no. 57325/00, § 176, ECHR 2007-IV; *Nachova and Others v. Bulgaria* [GC], nos 43577/98 and 43579/98, § 145, ECHR 2005-VII; *Timishev v. Russia*, nos 55762/00 and 55974/00, § 56, ECHR 2005-XII.

[166] *Horváth and Kiss v. Hungary*, no. 11146/11, § 102, 29 January 2013.

[167] *Oršuš and Others v. Croatia* [GC], no. 15766/03, § 156, ECHR 2010; *D.H. and Others v. the Czech Republic* [GC], no. 57325/00, § 196, ECHR 2007-IV; *Sejdić and Finci v. Bosnia and Herzegovina* [GC], nos 27996/06 and 34836/06, § 43, ECHR 2009.

[168] *Nachova and Others v. Bulgaria* [GC], nos 43577/98 and 43579/98, § 160, ECHR 2005-VII.

their responsibilities under Article 14 of the Convention taken in conjunction with Article 2 to secure the enjoyment of the right to life without discrimination'.[169]

Language

The first major case considered by the European Court of Human Rights pursuant to article 14 involved discrimination on the basis of language. The Court decided that a Belgian law enacted in 1963 violated article 14, read in conjunction with article 2 of Protocol No. 1, on the right to education, because it prevented certain children from attending French-language schools in suburban Brussels solely because of the residence of their parents.[170] The Convention does not guarantee the right to use a language in, for example, relations with the public administration[171] or in elected institutions.[172]

Religion

Discrimination based upon religion has played an important part in the case law under article 14. Like discrimination based upon political or other opinion, it is closely related to the substantive protection of freedom of opinion, belief, and religion set out in article 9 of the Convention. Historically, the Christian religion predominated in Europe. Discrimination within that broad church, by one branch of the religion against another, accounted for much violence and abuse over the centuries and indeed through to modern times, as the many cases before the Court related to the conflict in Northern Ireland confirm. Indeed, the first case to come before the European Court of Human Rights concerned a conflict that had such sectarianism at its roots.[173] Of course, the origins of the Council of Europe are found in the Second World War and the efforts by a European government to exterminate a group identified by religion. These examples highlight the close relationship between discrimination based upon race or ethnicity and discrimination based upon religion. In practice, the line between these categories is often quite blurred, and it is not uncommon to speak of discrimination based upon religion as 'racism'.

In a case involving custody of minor children, when Austrian courts took into consideration the fact that one of the parents was a Jehovah's Witness, the European Court of Human Rights said 'a distinction based essentially on a difference in religion alone is not acceptable' and concluded that there had been a violation of article 14 in conjunction with article 8.[174] Similarly, French courts took the religion of one parent, a Jehovah's Witness, into account in determining custody, thereby breaching article 14 combined with article 9. The Court of Appeal had 'treated the parents differently on the basis of the applicant's religion, on the strength of a harsh analysis of the principles regarding child-rearing allegedly imposed by this religion'.[175] But in another case, the

---

[169] Ibid., § 161.

[170] *Case 'relating to certain aspects of the laws on the use of languages in education in Belgium'* (merits), 23 July 1968, Series A no. 6. See Marc Bossuyt, *L'interdiction de la discrimination dans le droit international des droits de l'homme*, Brussels: Bruylant, 1976.

[171] *Inhabitants of Leeuw-Saint-Pierre v. Belgium*, no. 2333/64, Commission decision of 16 December 1968, (1968) 11 YB 228, Collection 28, p. 1; *Fryske nationale partij v. the Netherlands*, no. 11100/84, Commission decision of 12 December 1985, DR 45, p. 240; *Samo Pahor v. Italy*, no. 19927/92, Commission decision of 29 June 1994.

[172] *Clerfayt, Legros, and Alii v. Belgium*, no. 10650/83, Commission decision of 17 May 1985, DR 42, p. 218; *Birk-Levy v. France* (dec.), no. 39416/06, 21 September 2010.

[173] *Lawless v. Ireland (no. 1)*, 14 November 1960, Series A no. 1.

[174] *Hoffmann v. Austria*, 23 June 1993, § 36, Series A no. 255-C.

[175] *Palau-Martinez v. France*, no. 64927/01, § 38, ECHR 2003-XII.

Court dismissed these precedents and upheld the national courts' custody decisions because they were based upon 'religious practices' and not religion as such.[176]

Historically, schools in many countries in Europe were controlled or dominated by the predominant religious groups. To some extent this still continues, raising issues about discrimination when children from other religious groups or non-believers are concerned. For example, where children were expected to attend religious instruction as part of the school curriculum but had the possibility of opting out of such classes, the absence of a mark for 'religion/ethics' was deemed to be 'a form of unwarranted stigmatisation'. The Court held that article 14 was violated in conjunction with article 9, given that it was not satisfied that there was an objective and reasonable justification for the measure.[177]

Case law concerning the application of article 14 to opinion, belief, and religion is discussed in detail in the chapter on article 9 of the Convention.

Political or other opinion

Discrimination based upon political or other opinion is closely related to the issues that arise with respect to freedom of expression under article 10 of the Convention. It is also associated with the profoundly democratic orientation of the Convention, a requirement of the pluralism, tolerance, and broadmindedness 'without which there is no "democratic society"'.[178] Because of the word 'other', the prohibition on discrimination applies to any form of opinion whatsoever. Indeed, it might be said that the adjective 'political' is entirely superfluous. Nevertheless, its presence confirms the special place reserved in the Convention for the protection of political opinion. It seems this was indeed the intention when the words 'political or other opinion' were first proposed during drafting of the Universal Declaration of Human Rights within the Sub-Commission on Prevention of Discrimination and Protection of Minorities.[179]

Case law concerning the application of article 14 to political or other opinion is discussed in detail in the chapters on articles 9, 10, and 11 of the Convention.

National or social origin

Only two forms of 'origin' are listed in article 14. The first, national origin, is undoubtedly related to the prohibited grounds of race and colour, listed earlier in the provision. The notion of 'social origin' is somewhat different, however. It appears that the term originated in the 1936 Constitution of the Soviet Union.[180] The categories of 'national or social origin' were first proposed for inclusion in article 2 of the Universal Declaration of Human Rights by the Soviet representative in the Sub-Commission on Prevention of Discrimination and Protection of Minorities.[181]

There does not appear to be any case law of the Court concerning discrimination based on 'social origin'. The case law of the Court has tended to confound 'nationality' with

---

[176] *Ismailova v. Russia*, no. 37614/02, §§ 62–63, 29 November 2007.

[177] *Grzelak v. Poland*, no. 7710/02, §§ 100–101, 15 June 2010.

[178] *Handyside v. the United Kingdom*, 7 December 1976, § 49, Series A no. 24; *Lindon, Otchakovsky-Laurens, and July v. France* [GC], nos 21279/02 and36448/02, § 45, ECHR 2007-IV; *Verein gegen Tierfabriken Schweiz (VgT) v. Switzerland (no. 2)* [GC], no. 32772/02, § 96, ECHR 2009; *Palomo Sánchez and Others v. Spain* [GC], nos 28955/06, 28957/06, 28959/06, and 28964/06, § 53, ECHR 2011; *Axel Springer AG v. Germany* [GC], no. 39954/08, § 78, 7 February 2012.

[179] UN Doc. E/CN.4/Sub.2/SR.4, p. 7.

[180] Cited in UN Doc. E/CN.4/AC.1/3/Add.1, pp. 264, 271.

[181] UN Doc. E/CN.4/Sub.2/21.

'national origin'. The Court has said that 'very weighty reasons would have to be put forward before the Court could regard a difference of treatment based exclusively on the ground of nationality as compatible with the Convention'.[182] In *Bigaeva*, a case concerning a resident in Greece of Russian nationality who was denied the possibility of becoming a lawyer, the Court said that determining whether or not to let non-nationals practise law was something that fell within the margin of appreciation, absent evidence that arbitrary factors were involved.[183] Here too, the Court referred to discrimination based on 'nationality', which was quite correct. Of course 'nationality' and 'national origin' are not unrelated concepts, but they are not identical either.[184] An individual may change his or her nationality, in the sense of citizenship—this is expressly authorized by article 15(1) of the Universal Declaration of Human Rights—without changing the 'national origin', which presumably remains constant throughout one's lifetime.

When Slovenian citizenship legislation left some nationals of the former Yugoslav republics in a situation of statelessness, the Court found that there was a difference of treatment depending upon whether a person was a 'real' alien from a third State rather than from one of the component republics of the former Yugoslavia or a citizen of the former Yugoslavia. Court held it was discrimination based upon nationality. This was a difference in treatment based upon national origin, because former citizens of the Socialist Federal Republic of Yugoslavia were treated differently to other foreigners in the absence of any legitimate purpose.[185]

Association with a national minority

Although article 14 of the European Convention prohibits discrimination based upon 'association with a national minority', neither the Convention nor its Protocols contain a dedicated minority rights provision comparable to article 27 of the International Covenant on Civil and Political Rights.[186] As early as 1961, the Assembly had proposed an amendment to the Convention, adding a provision on minorities as part of Protocol No. 4.[187] In 1993, it submitted a draft text[188] but this was not pursued by the Committee of Ministers. In the early 1990s, the Council of Europe adopted the Framework Convention for the Protection of National Minorities and the European Charter for Minority or Regional Languages. Nearly two decades later, the Parliamentary Assembly complained that these instruments were not universally accepted by Member States, and furthermore that there were 'numerous shortcomings' in their implementation.[189] In 2012, the

---

[182] *Gaygusuz v. Austria*, 16 September 1996, § 42, *Reports of Judgments and Decisions* 1996-IV; *Rejeva v. Latvia* [GC], no. 55707/00, § 87, ECHR 2009; *Koua Poirrez v. France*, no. 40892/98, § 46, ECHR 2003-X.
[183] *Bigaeva v. Greece*, no. 26713/05, § 40, 28 May 2009.
[184] The distinction was quite intentional, as can be seen from the *travaux préparatoires* of the Universal Declaration of Human Rights, which is the model on which article 14 of the European Convention is based. See, e.g., UN Doc. E/CN.4/Sub.2/SR.5, pp. 7, 9–10; UN Doc. E/CN.4/Sub.2/SR.6, pp. 3, 5–6; UN Doc. E/CN.4/Sub.2/SR.11, p. 16–18; UN Doc. E/CN.4/52, p. 5.
[185] *Kurić and Others v. Slovenia* [GC], no. 26828/06, §§ 394–396, ECHR 2012 (extracts).
[186] *G. and E. v. Norway*, nos 9278/81 and 9415/81, Commission decision of 3 October 1983, DR 35, p. 30.
[187] Recommendation 285 (1961).
[188] Recommendation 1201 (1993).
[189] Minority protection in Europe: best practices and deficiencies in implementation of common standards, Resolution 1713 (2010).

rapporteur of the Assembly lamented 'the precarious situation of numerous national minority groups in Europe'.[190]

The Court has touched on issues relating to national minorities in a number of contexts. An application filed against Poland contested the denial of registration to an association named the 'Union of People of Silesian Nationality', described by its organizers as an 'organisation of the Silesian national minority'. The government insisted that the nomenclature was misleading because the Silesians, who live near the borders of Poland, Germany, and the Czech Republic and speak a language that is a mixture of Polish, German, and Czech, were not considered to be a national minority. The Court took a cautious position, noting the difficulty in formulating a definition of 'national minority' given that 'the notion is not defined in any international treaty'. Moreover, said the Grand Chamber, 'practice regarding official recognition by States of national, ethnic or other minorities within their population varies from country to country or even within countries'. It said the matter 'must, by the nature of things, be left largely to the State concerned, as it will depend on particular national circumstances'.[191] Moreover, continued the Court:

While it appears to be a commonly shared European view that, as laid down in the preamble to the Framework Convention, 'the upheavals of European history have shown that the protection of national minorities is essential to stability, democratic security and peace on this continent' and that respect for them is a condition *sine qua non* for a democratic society, it cannot be said that the Contracting States are obliged by international law to adopt a particular concept of 'national minority' in their legislation or to introduce a procedure for the official recognition of minority groups.[192]

Yet the Court has also acknowledged 'an emerging international consensus among the Contracting States of the Council of Europe recognising the special needs of minorities and an obligation to protect their security, identity and lifestyle, not only for the purpose of safeguarding the interests of the minorities themselves but to preserve a cultural diversity of value to the whole community'.[193]

In this respect, the Court's attention has been focused on Roma, Sinti, Gypsies, and Travellers, described as 'a specific type of disadvantaged and vulnerable minority' because of 'their turbulent history and constant uprooting'.[194] In a variety of contexts, but notably in the recognition of the right to education secured by article 2 of Protocol No. 1, the Court has spoken of 'the vulnerable position of Roma/Gypsies', saying this means that 'special consideration should be given to their needs and their different lifestyle both in the relevant regulatory framework and in reaching decisions in particular cases'.[195]

Property, birth, or other status

The category of 'property, birth or other status', derived directly from article 2 of the Universal Declaration of Human Rights, appeared rather late in the drafting of that

---

[190] An Additional Protocol to the European Convention on Human Rights on National Minorities, Doc. 12879, 23 February 2012, para. 5.

[191] *Gorzelik and Others v. Poland* [GC], no. 44158/98, § 47, ECHR 2004-I.

[192] Ibid., § 48.

[193] *Chapman v. the United Kingdom* [GC], no. 27238/95, §§ 93–94, ECHR 2001-I; *D.H. and Others v. the Czech Republic* [GC], no. 57325/00, § 181, ECHR 2007-IV.

[194] *D.H. and Others v. the Czech Republic* [GC], no. 57325/00, § 182, ECHR 2007-IV.

[195] Ibid., § 181; *Chapman v. the United Kingdom* [GC], no. 27238/95, § 96, ECHR 2001-I; *Connors v. the United Kingdom*, no. 66746/01, § 84, 27 May 2004.

instrument. In the Third Committee of the General Assembly, in October 1948, Cuba proposed a reformulation of the non-discrimination text that included the phrase 'without distinction of race, birth, sex, language, religion, political opinion, or property or other status'.[196] In the ensuing debate, there were suggestions that 'birth' might be replaced by 'social status' or by 'caste', but these were not pursued.[197] The text adopted by the Third Committee used the phrase 'race, colour, sex, language, religion, political or other opinion, property or other status, birth, or national or social origin'.[198] The text of the Drafting Committee was worded slightly differently: 'race, colour, sex, language, religion, birth, national or social origin, political or other opinion, property or other status'.[199] One of the very last debates about the text of the Declaration concerned these words. A compromise, proposed by the Lebanese Karim Azkoul, produced the final text.[200]

In several cases, the Court has considered the application of article 14 to distinctions based upon property.[201] Discrimination grounded on 'birth' has been the basis of cases dealing with legislation distinguishing between 'legitimate' and 'illegitimate' children.[202] The term 'other status' has permitted the Court to give a very broad scope to article 14. It has described the other grounds in article 14, such as sex, race, and property, as being 'illustrative and not exhaustive', pointing not only to the words 'any ground such as' that precede the enumeration but also to the words 'any other status' with which it concludes.[203] Several examples of this broad approach to 'other status' are discussed earlier in this chapter. Three categories that are listed in the corresponding provision of the European Union Charter of Fundamental Rights, disability, age, and sexual orientation, have been added to article 14. The Court has also recognized marital status and gender reassignment.

A Chamber of the Court has held that disability is an analogous ground contemplated by article 16.[204] It said there was a European and universal consensus on the need to protect disabled persons from discrimination,[205] invoking in support a 2003 Recommendation of the Parliamentary Assembly of the Council of Europe[206] and the United Nations Convention on the Rights of Persons with Disabilities.[207]

The European Union Charter of Fundamental Rights explicitly includes age as one of the prohibited grounds of discrimination. Age discrimination is also prohibited by the European Union Employment Equality Directive adopted in 2000.[208] The Convention itself could be said to discriminate on the basis of age by setting an upper limit for judges, a matter considered in the chapter of this Commentary dealing with article 21. The issue

[196] Cuba: Amendments to the first nine Articles of the Draft Declaration (E/800), UN Doc. A/C.3/224.
[197] *Official Records of the General Assembly,* Third Session, 1948, pp. 137–8.
[198] UN Doc. A/C.3/320.
[199] UN Doc. A/C.3/SC.4/7.
[200] *Official Records of the General Assembly,* Third Session, 1948, pp. 852–3.
[201] *James and Others v. the United Kingdom,* 21 February 1986, § 74, Series A no. 98; *Chassagnou and Others v. France* [GC], nos 25088/94, 28331/95, and 28443/95, §§ 90 and 95, ECHR 1999-III; *Larkos v. Cyprus* [GC], no. 29515/95, § 58, ECHR 1999-I.
[202] *Marckx v. Belgium,* 13 June 1979, § 34, Series A no. 31; *Inze v. Austria,* 28 October 1987, §§ 41–45, Series A no. 126; *Mazurek v. France,* no. 34406/97, §§ 44–46, ECHR 2000-II; *Vermeire v. Belgium,* 29 November 1991, § 28, Series A no. 214-C.
[203] *Clift v. the United Kingdom,* no. 7205/07, § 55, 13 July 2010.
[204] *Glor v. Switzerland,* no. 13444/04, § 80, ECHR 2009.
[205] Ibid., § 53.
[206] Towards full social inclusion of people with disabilities, Recommendation 1592 (2003).
[207] UN Doc. A/RES/61/106, Annex I.
[208] 2000/78/EC.

of age discrimination has only rarely come before the European Court of Human Rights. The Court appeared to recognize age as an analogous ground in a case concerning a woman of forty-seven who had been refused the possibility of adopting a child because she was deemed to be too old. It said she was being treated differently from 'a younger single woman who, in the same circumstances, would be likely to obtain authorisation to receive a second child with a view to its adoption' and that she was therefore 'a victim of a difference in treatment between persons in analogous situations'.[209] The Court considered practice in European States with respect to age limits upon adoption and concluded that there was no 'uniform principle'.[210] It held that the impugned distinction was not disproportionate, bearing in mind a broad margin of appreciation and the significance of the best interests of the child.[211] In a Latvian case based on a mandatory retirement age, the Court dismissed the complaint because the applicant failed to show that other persons who were similarly situated had been treated differently.[212]

It is not discrimination to provide a different detention regime for adults than for children. Admittedly, the treatment of the two categories is different, but there is an objective and reasonable justification in the protective rather than punitive nature of juvenile detention.[213] If it were otherwise, even the Convention could be deemed discriminatory as a consequence of article 5(1)(d), allowing for detention of children for 'educational purposes', something that is not permitted in the case of adults.

The Court declared that sexual orientation as a prohibited ground was 'undoubtedly covered' by article 14 in a case involving child custody where a father had been denied parental rights because he was homosexual.[214] It has since elevated the category to one that is 'suspect', saying that '[w]here sexual orientation is in issue, there is a need for particularly convincing and weighty reasons to justify a difference in treatment regarding rights falling within Article 8'.[215] It has gone still further: '[D]iscrimination based on sexual orientation is as serious as discrimination based on "race, origin or colour"'.[216] Moreover, 'the Court would not exclude that treatment which is grounded upon a predisposed bias on the part of a heterosexual majority against a homosexual minority of the nature described above could, in principle, fall within the scope of Article 3'.[217]

Reservations

Only one reservation has been formulated with respect to article 14. Monaco declared that article 14 (as well as articles 6(1) and 8) does not apply to provisions of its national law,

---

[209] *Schwizgebel v. Switzerland*, no. 25762/07, § 85, ECHR 2010 (extracts).

[210] Ibid., § 90.

[211] Ibid., § 97.

[212] *Jokšas v. Lithuania*, no. 25330/07, §§ 73–74, 12 November 2013.

[213] *Bouamar v. Belgium*, 29 February 1988, § 66, Series A no. 129.

[214] *Salgueiro da Silva Mouta v. Portugal*, no. 33290/96, § 28, ECHR 1999-IX.

[215] *E.B. v. France* [GC], no. 43546/02, § 91, 22 January 2008; *L. and V. v. Austria*, nos 39392/98 and 39829/98, § 45, ECHR 2003-I; *Eweida and Others v. the United Kingdom*, no. 48420/10, § 105, ECHR 2013 (extracts); *Karner v. Austria*, no. 40016/98, § 37, ECHR 2003-IX; *Schalk and Kopf v. Austria*, no. 30141/04, § 97, ECHR 2010.

[216] *Vejdeland v. Sweden*, no. 1813/07, § 55, 9 February 2012; *Smith and Grady v. The United Kingdom*, nos 33985/96 and 33986/96, § 97, ECHR 1999-VI.

[217] *Smith and Grady v. the United Kingdom*, nos 33985/96 and 33986/96, § 153, ECHR 1999-VI.

including the Constitution, that provide for preferential conditions of employment of Monagesque nationals.

Further reading

Oddný Mjöll Arnadóttir, *Equality and Non-discrimination under the European Convention on Human Rights*, The Hague: Martinus Nijhoff, 2003.

Oddný Mjöll Arnadóttir, 'Discrimination as a Magnifying Lens: Scope and Ambit under Article 14 and Protocol No. 12', in Eva Brems and Janneke Gerards, eds, *Shaping Rights in the ECHR*, Cambridge: Cambridge University Press, 2013, pp. 330–49.

Sam Bardutzky, 'The Strasbourg Court on the Dayton Constitution Judgment in the Case of *Sejdić and Finci v. Bosnia and Herzegovina*, 22 December 2009', (2010) 6 *European Constitutional Law Review* 309.

Marc Bossuyt, *L'interdiction de la discrimination dans le droit international des droits de l'homme*, Brussels: Bruylant, 1976.

Marc Bossuyt, 'Article 14', in Pettiti et al., *La Convention européenne*, pp. 475–88.

Kevin Boyle and Anneliese Baldaccini, 'A Critical Evaluation of International Human Rights Approaches to Racism', in Sandra Fredman, ed., *Discrimination and Human Rights the Case of Racism*, Oxford: Oxford University Press, 2001, pp. 135–91.

Niklas Bruun, 'The Prohibition of Discrimination under Article 14 ECHR', in Filip Dorssemont, Klaus Lörcher, and Isabelle Schömann, eds, *The European Convention on Human Rights and the Employment Relation*, Oxford and Portland, OR: Hart, 2013, pp. 367–80.

Luke Clements and Janet Read, *Disabled People and European Human Rights*, Bristol, UK: The Policy Press, 2003.

E. Debout, 'Vers une protection de l'égalité "collective" par la Cour européenne des droits de l'homme?', [2006] *RTDH* 851.

J.-Fr. Flauss, 'Discrimination positive et Convention européenne des droits de l'homme', in *Pouvoir et liberté. Mélanges offerts à Jacques Mourgeon*, Brussels, Bruylant, 1998, pp. 415–22.

Frowein/Peukert, *MenschenRechtsKonvention*, pp. 401–18.

Janneke Gerards, 'The Application of Article 14 ECHR by the European Court of Human Rights', in J. Niessen and Isabelle Chopin, eds, *The Development of Legal Instruments to Combat Racism in a Diverse Europe*, Leiden/Boston: Martinus Nijhoff, 2004, pp. 3–60.

Janneke Gerards, 'Intensity of Judicial Review in Equal Treatment Cases', [2004] *Netherlands International Law Review* 135.

Janneke Gerards, 'The Discrimination Grounds of Article 14 of the European Convention on Human Rights', (2013) 13 *HRLR* 99.

Grabenwarter, *European Convention*, pp. 340–63.

Harris et al., *Law of the European Convention*, pp. 577–616.

Aalt Willem Heringa and Fried van Hoof, 'Prohibition of Discrimination (Article 14)', in Van Dijk et al., *Theory and Practice*, pp. 1027–51.

Erica Howard, 'Bans on the Wearing of Religious Symbols in British Schools: A Violation of the Right to Non-Discrimination?', (2011) 6 *Journal of Religion and Human Rights* 127.

Timo Koivurova, 'Jurisprudence of the European Court of Human Rights regarding Indigenous Peoples: Retrospect and Prospects', (2011) 18 *International Journal on Minority and Group Rights* 1.

P. Lambert, 'Vers une évolution de l'interprétation de l'article 14 de la Convention européenne des droits de l'homme ?', [1998] RTDH 497.

Titia Loenen, 'The Headscarf Debate Approaching the Intersection of Sex, Religion and Race under the European Convention on Human Rights and EU Equality Law', in Dagmar Schiek and Victoria Chege, eds, *European Non-discrimination Law Comparative Perspectives on Multi-dimensional Equality Law*, London/New York: Routledge 2009, pp. 313–28.

Jill Marshall, 'Freedom of Religious Expression and Gender Equality: *Sahin v. Turkey*', (2006) 69 *Modern Law Review* 460.

Dominic McGoldrick, *Human Rights and Religion: The Islamic Headscarf Debate in Europe,* Oxford/ Portland: Hart Publishing, 2006.

Denis Martin, *Egalité et non-discrimination dans la jurisprudence communautaire. Etude critique à la lumière d'une approche comparatiste*, Brussels: Bruylant, 2006.

Ovey/White, *Jacobs and White, European Convention*, pp. 347–60.

Erick Acuña Pereda, 'The Institutionalization of People with Mental Disabilities: Comparative Analysis between its Treatment under the Inter-American and European System of Human Rights', (2012) 5 *Inter-American and European Human Rights Journal* 72.

Ivana Radacic, 'Gender Equality Jurisprudence of the European Court of Human Rights', (2008) 19 *European Journal of International Law* 841.

Luzius Wildhaber, 'Protection Against Discrimination under the European Convention on Human Rights—A Second-class Guarantee?', [2002] *Baltic Yearbook of International Law* 5.

Robert Wintemute, '"Within the Ambit": How Big *Is* the "Gap" in Article 14 European Convention on Human Rights?', (2004) *EHRLR* 366.

Article 15. Derogation in time of emergency/Dérogation en cas d'état d'urgence

1. In time of war or other public emergency threatening the life of the nation any High Contracting Party may take measures derogating from its obligations under this Convention to the extent strictly required by the exigencies of the situation, provided that such measures are not inconsistent with its other obligations under international law.

2. No derogation from Article 2, except in respect of deaths resulting from lawful acts of war, or from Articles 3, 4 (paragraph 1) and 7 shall be made under this provision.

3. Any High Contracting Party availing itself of this right of derogation shall keep the Secretary General of the Council of Europe fully informed of the measures which it has taken and the reasons therefor. It shall also inform the Secretary General of the Council of Europe when such measures have ceased to operate and the provisions of the Convention are again being fully executed.

1. En cas de guerre ou en cas d'autre danger public menaçant la vie de la nation, toute Haute Partie Contractante peut prendre des mesures dérogeant aux obligations prévues par la présente Convention, dans la stricte mesure où la situation l'exige et à la condition que ces mesures ne soient pas en contradiction avec les autres obligations découlant du droit international.

2. La disposition précédente n'autorise aucune dérogation à l'article 2, sauf pour le cas de décès résultant d'actes licites de guerre, et aux articles 3, 4 (paragraphe 1) et 7.

3. Toute Haute Partie Contractante qui exerce ce droit de dérogation tient le Secrétaire Général du Conseil de l'Europe pleinement informé des mesures prises et des motifs qui les ont inspirées. Elle doit également informer le Secrétaire Général du Conseil de l'Europe de la date à laquelle ces mesures ont cessé d'être en vigueur et les dispositions de la Convention reçoivent de nouveau pleine application.

Introductory comments

Derogation clauses are a feature of some modern international human rights instruments, notably the general treaties that deal primarily with civil and political rights. In addition to article 15 of the European Convention on Human Rights, derogation clauses may be found in the European Social Charter, where the text is identical to that of article 15(1),[1] the International Covenant on Civil and Political Rights,[2] and the American Convention on Human Rights.[3] Many find the whole idea that human rights may be suspended to be offensive and unacceptable. It is arguable that without allowing States the possibility of temporarily opting out of their human rights treaty obligations in time of emergency it would have been much harder to obtain their adherence to the relevant instruments. Yet with a few notable exceptions, such as the United Kingdom, States rarely comply with the formalities and resort to derogation. Moreover, most human rights treaties do not allow

---

[1] European Social Charter, (1965) 529 UNTS 89, art. 30(1); Revised European Social Charter 1999, ETS 163, 529 UNTS 89, art. F(1).
[2] International Covenant on Civil and Political Rights, (1976) 999 UNTS 171, art. 5.
[3] American Convention on Human Rights, (1978) 1144 UNTS 123, art. 27.

for derogation, suggesting that the possibility of suspending their obligations in time of crisis may not be as important as some make this out to be.

The Parliamentary Assembly of the Council of Europe has called upon Member States not to derogate from the Convention 'in their fight against terrorism'. In particular, it has urged States to 'refrain from using Article 15 of the European Convention on Human Rights (derogation in time of emergency) to limit the rights and liberties guaranteed under its Article 5 (right to liberty and security)'.[4] All Member States seem to have heeded the call with one exception, the United Kingdom. In the twenty-first century, it is the only State to have invoked article 15 in order to derogate from the Convention. However, in recent years, several European states have derogated from the International Covenant on Civil and Political Rights: Armenia, 6 March 2008 (for 20 days); France, 15 November 2005 (from 8 November 2005 to 4 January 2006); Georgia, 8 November 2007 (from 7 November 2007 and still in effect). Why they choose to derogate from the Covenant and not the Convention is a mystery.

Researchers have identified nearly 600 acts of derogation from the three international human rights treaties taken as a whole. The European Social Charter was not included in the study, but it has apparently never been subject to derogation. Nearly half of all derogations are attributable to Peru and about ten per cent to the United Kingdom, followed by Turkey, Colombia, Equador, Algeria, Russia, and Israel. Altogether, thirty-three States have derogated from the treaties.[5] The researchers theorize that countries with weak democratic governance rarely bother with derogation because they are not concerned about domestic repercussions. On the other hand, 'derogation is resorted to by stable democracies and countries with strong judiciaries [who] derogate to buy time and reduce censure from voters, interest groups, and judges'.[6]

Derogation provisions are sometimes presented as a rationale for the importance of international humanitarian law. The latter is applicable in time of armed conflict, when States may be most likely to derogate from their human rights obligations. No derogation is permitted under international humanitarian law, however. But this may be oversimplifying the relationship between international human rights law and international humanitarian law, partly because most States do not in fact resort to derogation and partly because many of the most fundamental rights are not subject to derogation. Most derogations seem to be concerned with detention issues.

Drafting of the provision

The Universal Declaration of Human Rights does not contain a derogation clause. The issue never received any attention when the Declaration was being drafted. There is an obvious explanation: the Declaration was intended as an aspirational text rather than a source of binding conventional obligation. Nor was there anything of the sort in the draft prepared by the European Movement at the outset of the negotiations of the European Convention on Human Rights. In the work of the Consultative Assembly, questions arose concerning measures that a State was permitted to employ in order to protect itself against

---

[4] Resolution 1271 (2002), para. 9.
[5] Emilie M. Hafner-Burton, Laurence R. Helfer, and Christopher J. Fariss, 'Emergency and Escape: Explaining Derogations from Human Rights Treaties', (2011) 65 *International Organization* 673, at p. 679.
[6] Ibid., p. 703.

subversive and anti-democratic groups. The answer was that this issue was adequately addressed in the general limitation clause, resembling article 29(2) of the Universal Declaration of Human Rights, that had been proposed. Pierre-Henri Teitgen said the reply was 'quite simple' and was 'stated clearly' in the limitation clause.[7]

The Committee of Ministers decided to refer the draft adopted by the Consultative Assembly to a Committee of Experts. The Committee of Ministers had instructed the Committee of Ministers to take account of work then underway within the United Nations on the draft covenant on human rights.[8] Earlier in 1949, the United Nations Commission on Human Rights had adopted the following preliminary text:

Article 4

1. In time of war or other public emergency threatening the interests of the people, a State may take measures derogating from its obligations under part II of the Covenant to the extent strictly limited by the exigencies of the situation.
2. No derogation from Articles ... can be made under this provision.
3. Any State party hereto availing itself of this right of derogation shall inform the Secretary-General of the United Nations fully of the measures which it has thus enacted and the reasons therefor. It shall also inform him as and when such measures cease to operate and the provisions of part II of the Covenant are being fully executed.[9]

In comments on the draft, the United Kingdom suggested that paragraph 2 be changed as follows: '[N]o derogation from Article 6, except in respect of deaths resulting from lawful acts of war, or from Articles 6, 7 8 (paragraphs 1 and 2) or 14 can be made under this provision.'[10]

A report from the Secretariat-General of the Council of Europe to the Committee of Experts said that such a provision 'would seem unnecessary in the European system' because the Consultative Assembly draft contained a limitations clause.[11] A submission from the United Kingdom to the Committee of Experts proposed a provision similar to that of article 4 of the draft preliminary covenant.[12] The Committee of Experts held two sessions, in February and in March 1950. A Sub-Committee charged with analysing the various amendments that had been proposed reacted favourably to the British text:

The first Article ... is aimed at the national protection of Human Rights. The Sub-Committee considered it advisable to give due consideration to these proposals as being of interest even to those who adhere to the definition of Human Rights as proposed by the Assembly. This Article could, in fact, be included as an addition to Article 4 of the Assembly draft.[13]

---

[7] Official Report of the Sitting [of the Consultative Assembly, 8 September 1949], II *TP* 14–274, at p. 32.

[8] Letter addressed on 18 November 1949 by the Secretary-General to the Ministers for Foreign Affairs of the Member States, Ref. D 26/2/49, II *TP* 302–5.

[9] Report of the Fifth Session of the Commission on Human Rights to the Economic and Social Council, UN Doc. E/1371(Supp.), p. 18.

[10] Comments of Governments on the draft International Covenant on Human Rights and Measures of Implementation [UN Doc. E/CN.4/353/Add.1-3], Doc. A 770, III *TP* 156–79, at p. 158. The provisions concern the right to life, the prohibition of torture and slavery, and the rule against retroactive criminal prosecution.

[11] Preparatory Report by the Secretariat-General concerning a Preliminary Draft Convention to Provide a Collective Guarantee of Human Rights, Doc. B 22, III *TP* 2–37, at p. 18.

[12] Amendments to Articles 4 and 7 of the Recommendation of the Consultative Assembly proposed by the Expert of the United Kingdom, Doc. A 782, III *TP* 188, at pp. 188–190.

[13] First part of the Report of the Sub-Committee Instructed to Make a Preliminary Study of the Amendments Proposed by the Members of the Committee, Doc. A 796, III *TP* 200–5.

Article 4 of the Assembly draft reserved to States the competence to organize the protection of human rights within their territories. At the March session, the Committee concluded its work by adopting two different versions of the Convention, one based upon British proposals that provided detailed definitions of fundamental rights and the other based upon the Consultative Assembly draft that largely reflected the Universal Declaration of Human Rights. However, the Committee of Experts adopted essentially identical approaches when it came to the derogation clause. Thus, the draft that relied upon the Consultative Assembly version contained the following:

1. In time of war or other public emergency threatening the interests of the people, a State may take measures derogating from its obligations under this Convention to the extent strictly limited by the exigencies of the situation provided that such measures are not inconsistent with its other obligations under international law.
2. No derogation from Articles 3, except in respect of deaths resulting from lawful acts of war, 4, 5 (paragraph 1) or 8 can be made under this provision.
3. Any State party hereto availing itself of this right of derogation shall inform the Secretary-General of the Council of Europe fully of the measures which it has thus enacted and the reasons therefor. It shall also inform the Secretary-General of the Council of Europe when such measures have ceased to operate and the provisions of the Convention are again being fully executed.[14]

A similar text was proposed for the draft based upon the detailed British proposals (Alternatives B and B/2). An explanatory report prepared by the Committee of Experts for the Committee of Ministers made the following comment:

This Article was taken from the Proposals of the British Government... The French and Italian representatives stated that they were opposed to its insertion in the text of Alternatives A and A/2. They considered that this provision was contrary to the system of these Alternatives, since it provides detailed regulations concerning the kind of case already covered by the general provisions of Articles 6, 7 and 10.

Other members of the Committee considered that it was, nevertheless, important to include Article 8 in the text of Alternatives A and A/2, since it had the advantage of excluding, even in the case of war or threat to the life of the nation, any derogation of certain fundamental rights, and because the procedure laid down in paragraph 3 could prove to be useful for the protection of Human Rights in exceptional circumstances.[15]

The Committee of Ministers referred the drafts adopted by the Committee of Experts to the Conference of Senior Officials, which met in June. It combined the two drafts, basing itself upon the derogation clause contained in the version derived from the Consultative Assembly text. In paragraph 1, the words 'the interests of the people' were changed to 'the life of the nation' and a comma was inserted after the word 'situation'. The numbers of the articles listed in paragraph 2 were also changed to take into account other modifications to the draft.[16] The Committee decided that the derogation provision belonged after the

---

[14] Appendix to the Report of the Committee of Experts on Human Rights: Draft Convention of Protection of Human Rights and Fundamental Freedoms, 16 March 1950, Doc. C/WP 1 (50) 15 appendix, CM/WP 1 (50) 14 revised, A 925, IV *TP* 50–79, at p. 56.

[15] Report to the Committee of Ministers submitted by the Committee of Experts Instructed to Draw Up a Draft Convention of Collective Guarantee of Human Rights and Fundamental Freedoms, Doc. CM/WP 1 (5) 15, A 924, IV *TP* 2–55, at p. 30.

[16] Draft Convention annexed to the Report [of the Conference of Senior Officials], Doc. CM/WP 4 (50) 19 annex, CM/WP 4 (50) 16 rev., A 1452, IV *TP* 274–95, at pp. 280–2.

articles in which the rights were defined.[17] The Committee of Ministers itself made some further amendments when it met in August. In paragraph 1, the word 'limited' became 'required', the words 'or from Articles' were added to paragraph 2, and in paragraph 3 the phrase 'shall inform the Secretary-General of the Council of Europe fully' was changed to 'shall keep the Secretary-General of the Council of Europe fully informed'.[18]

The Consultative Assembly met again in August 1950 to consider the final version of the Convention. Speaking as rapporteur of the Legal Committee, Sir David Maxwell Fyfe of the United Kingdom explained to the plenary Assembly:

There are certain rights which even in time of war or national emergency the Committee of Ministers do not suggest should be abrogated. They are the rights of safety of life, freedom from torture, and fundamental rights of that sort. Therefore, we took that as our guide, and we suggest that with regard to these rights there cannot be serious argument that the individual should not have the right to complain. If these rights are so fundamental that they must exist even in time of war, then surely they are equally fundamental from the point of view of the individual having the right to complain.[19]

Henri Rolin of Belgium added the following comment:

In the course of an exchange of views some Members pointed out that in times of civil strife or of a threat of civil war some exceptional measures could, by virtue of Article 15 of the draft, be decided upon to deal with doubtful elements in the population which it would be intolerable to see brought up before an international authority on the appeal of those concerned . . . We were obliged, in view of this, to try to provide for a restriction of the right of appeal, whilst safeguarding it in the essential cases. In order to define these cases, we relied on the definition put forward by the Committee of Ministers itself, in the text of Article 15 relative to the state of war or state of siege. It recognised that even in these hypothetical cases some rights were so essential to our self-respect as well as to the respect for other persons, that, really, under no conditions could we permit any departure therefrom.[20]

On 21 October 1950, two weeks before the ceremony in Rome at which the Convention was to be signed, A.H. Robertson of the Secretariat wrote to H.J. Downing, a Foreign Office official in London, proposing a few changes to the text of article 15.[21] These were implemented by the Committee of Ministers prior to signature of the text. The references to 'any State' in paragraph 1 was replaced with 'High Contracting Party', the word 'can' in paragraph 2 became 'shall', the opening words of paragraph 3 were changed to 'Any High Contracting Party availing . . .' and the word 'enacted' replaced with 'taken'.

The heading 'Derogation in time of emergency' was added according to the provisions of Protocol No. 11.[22]

There is no evidence that any consideration was given to enlarging the list of non-derogable rights when the various Protocols to the Convention were being adopted. Article 1 of Protocol No. 4, prohibiting imprisonment for debt, was intended to enlarge

[17] Text of the Report submitted by the Conference [of Senior Officials] to the Committee of Ministers, Doc. CM/WP 4 (50) 19, CM/WP 4 (50) 16 rev., A 1431, IV *TP* 242–73, at p. 260.

[18] Draft Convention adopted by the Sub-Committee, Doc. CM 1 (50) 52, A 1884, V *TP* 76–99, at p. 84.

[19] Report of the Sitting [of the Consultative Assembly, 25 August 1950, morning], VI *TP* 74–143, at p. 80.

[20] Ibid., p. 126.

[21] Letter addressed 21 October 1950 by Mr Robertson (Member of the Secretariat) to Mr Downing (Official of the Western Organisations Department, Foreign Office, London), VI *TP* 184–7, at p. 286.

[22] Protocol No. 11 to the Convention for the Protection of Human Rights and Fundamental Freedoms, restructuring the control machinery established thereby, ETS 155, art. 2(2).

the scope of the Convention in order to align it better with the provisios of the draft International Covenant on Civil and Political Rights. The equivalent provision in the Covenant cannot be subject to derogation.

Analysis and interpretation

In declaring that some rights may never be subject to derogation, article 15 implies a hierarchy of rights. Paragraph 2 of article 15 excludes the possibility of derogation with respect to four substantive provisions, articles 2, 3, 4(1), and 7. In the case of the right to life enshrined in article 2, this is subject to 'deaths resulting from lawful acts of war'. Two other rights introduced by the Protocols to the Convention are made non-derogable: the abolition of the death penalty[23] and the protection against double jeopardy.[24] The derogation clauses in the other international instruments are somewhat more extensive. Like the European Convention, the International Covenant on Civil and Political Rights forbids derogation with respect to the right to life and the prohibition of torture, slavery, and retroactive criminal prosecution, but it also does this for imprisonment for debt, the right to recognition as a person before the law, and freedom of religion.[25] The American Convention on Human Rights builds on this list, adding the right to family life, name, nationality, participation in government, and the rights of the child.[26] Unlike the European Convention, neither of the others excludes 'deaths resulting from lawful acts of war' from the right to life.

Invoking article 15(2) of the European Convention, it is often suggested that the non-derogable rights are especially sacrosanct and that they form a hard core or *noyau dur* within the broader universe of fundamental human rights.[27] In this sense, the European Court has sometimes pointed to the non-retroactivity of criminal prosecution enshrined in article 7 ('No derogation is allowed from that provision even in time of public emergency threatening the life of the nation'[28]) in order to underscore its importance. It has made the same point with respect to the prohibition of torture and inhuman or degrading treatment and punishment, noting the impermissibility of derogation as evidence that '[u]nlike most of the substantive clauses of the Convention and of Protocols Nos 1 and 4, Article 3 [it] makes no provision for exceptions and no derogation from it is permissible under Article 15 § 2 notwithstanding the existence of a public emergency threatening the life of the nation'.[29] The non-derogable status of certain rights is

---

[23] Protocol No. 6 to the Convention for the Protection of Human Rights and Fundamental Freedoms concerning the Abolition of the Death Penalty, ETS 114, art. 3; Protocol No. 13 to the Convention for the Protection of Human Rights and Fundamental Freedoms, concerning the abolition of the death penalty in all circumstances, ETS 187, art. 2.

[24] Protocol No. 7 to the Convention for the Protection of Human Rights and Fundamental Freedoms, ETS 117, art. 4(3).

[25] International Covenant on Civil and Political Rights, (1976) 999 UNTS 171, art. 5(2).

[26] American Convention on Human Rights, (1978) 1144 UNTS 123, art. 27(2).

[27] See, e.g., Gérard Cohen-Jonathan, 'Universalité et singularité des droits de l'homme', [2003] *RTDH* 3, at p. 7.

[28] *K. v. Germany*, no. 61827/09, § 88, 7 June 2012; *G. v. Germany*, no. 65210/09, § 79, 7 June 2012; *Jendrowiak v. Germany*, no. 30060/04, § 48, 14 April 2011; *O.H. v. Germany*, no. 4646/08, § 107, 24 November 2011.

[29] *A. and Others v. the United Kingdom* [GC], no. 3455/05, § 126, ECHR 2009; *Ramirez Sanchez v. France* [GC], no. 59450/00, § 116, ECHR 2006-IX; *Labita v. Italy* [GC], no. 26772/95, § 119, ECHR 2000-IV; *Selmouni v. France* [GC], no. 25803/94, § 95, ECHR 1999-V; *Assenov and Others v. Bulgaria*, 28 October 1998, § 93, *Reports of Judgments and Decisions* 1998-VIII.

also offered as evidence of their position as norms of customary international law and even peremptory norms (*jus cogens*).

The Human Rights Committee considered whether the non-derogable status of rights is relevant to determining whether they were immune to reservation. Its position is certainly germane to the interpretation of article 15 of the European Convention, given the broad similarities between the relevant provisions. The Committee explained that although 'there is no hierarchy of importance of rights under the Covenant', the fact that certain rights may not be suspended, even in times of national emergency, 'underlines the great importance of non-derogable rights'. The Committee noted that 'not all rights of profound importance, such as articles 9 [arbitrary detention] and 27 [minority rights] of the Covenant, have in fact been made non-derogable'. Moreover, it seems that the fact some rights are non-derogable does not indicate they are of such importance. According to the Committee, '[o]ne reason for certain rights being made non-derogable is because their suspension is irrelevant to the legitimate control of the state of national emergency (for example, no imprisonment for debt, in article 11). Another reason is that derogation may indeed be impossible (as, for example, freedom of conscience).'[30] It is of interest, however, that although freedom of conscience is non-derogable under the International Covenant, this is not the case under the European Convention. As for the principle of legality set out in article 7 of the European Convention, its inclusion in article 15(2) would seem to be at least partially explained by the fact that its suspension is irrelevant to the state of national emergency rather than its hierarchically superior importance.

The non-derogable status of certain rights is also associated with their claim to be *jus cogens* or peremptory. A *jus cogens* rule is defined in the Vienna Convention on the Law of Treaties as 'a norm accepted and recognized by the international community of States as a whole as a norm from which no derogation is permitted'.[31] The United Nations Human Rights Committee has noted that some non-derogable rights, in particular the prohibition of torture and arbitrary deprivation of life, are indeed encompassed in the *jus cogens* category.[32] Their inclusion in the non-derogable category 'is to be seen partly as recognition of the peremptory nature of some fundamental rights ensured in treaty form in the Covenant'. But further caution is dictated in attempts to equate the two, because the category of peremptory norms extends beyond the list in article 4(1) of the Covenant, as it may also do with respect to article 15 of the European Convention.[33] Claims of peremptory status possess a certain logic when the right to life and the prohibition of torture and ill-treatment are concerned, but a note of caution should be struck in generalizing about an equation between *jus cogens* and non-derogable norms.

The Convention makes no explicit requirement that declarations of derogation be subject to some form of effective domestic scrutiny although, as the Council of Europe Commissioner on Human Rights has pointed out, '[t]he requirement is, however, easily discerned'.[34] According to the Commissioner, effective domestic scrutiny by the legislature and the judiciary represents 'essential guarantees against the possibility of an arbitrary

---

[30] General Comment 23, UN Doc. CCPR/C/21/Rev.1/Add.6, para. 10.
[31] Vienna Convention on the Law of Treaties, (1980) 1155 UNTS 331, art. 53.
[32] General Comment 23, UN Doc. CCPR/C/21/Rev.1/Add.6, para. 10.
[33] General Comment 29, UN Doc. CCPR/C/21/Rev.1/Add.11, para. 11.
[34] Opinion of the Commissioner for Human Rights, Mr Alvaro Gil-Robles, on certain aspects of the United Kingdom 2001 derogation from Article 5 par. 1 of the European Convention on Human Rights, CommDH (2002)7, para. 5.

assessment by the executive and the subsequent implementation of disproportionate measures'.[35] Mere parliamentary approval is not sufficient because 'the effectiveness of the parliamentary scrutiny of derogations depends in large measure on the access of at least some of its members to the information on which the decision to derogate is based'.[36]

Time of war or other emergency

Article 15(1) permits derogation from some of the rights listed in the Convention '[i]n time of war or other public emergency threatening the life of the nation'. The International Covenant on Civil and Political Rights allows derogation '[i]n time of public emergency which threatens the life of the nation'.[37] The corresponding provision in the American Convention on Human Rights refers to 'time of war, public danger, or other emergency that threatens the independence or security of a State Party'.[38] In the European Convention, the words 'or other public emergency' indicate that a 'time of war' is also one of 'public emergency threatening the life of the nation'. Put otherwise, a State should not invoke article 15 during 'time of war' unless there is also a 'public emergency threatening the life of the nation'. There is no case law confirming this interpretation of article 15 because no derogation has ever been claimed to react to a 'time of war'.[39]

The derogation provision of the European Social Charter uses the same wording as article 15(1) of the Convention except that it specifies, in the Appendix, that '[t]he term "in time of war or other public emergency" shall be so understood as to cover also the threat of war'.[40] Protocol No. 6 to the European Convention does not exclude capital punishment 'in time of war or of imminent threat of war'.[41] There is no guidance on the interpretation of these provisions in the case law or the Explanatory Report on Protocol No. 6.

According to Rusen Ergec, war as it is contemplated by article 15 of the European Convention '. . . peut être définie comme un affrontement armé d'une certaine envergure et d'une certaine durée conduite par des armées organisées sous la responsabilité des gouvernements respectifs dont elles relèvent'.[42] When the Convention was being drafted, the concept of 'war' under international law was still a rather meaningful one, but it has since fallen into desuetude. Today, the preferred term is 'armed conflict'.[43] A widely accepted definition developed by the Appeals Chamber of the International Criminal Tribunal for the former Yugoslavia states that 'an armed conflict exists whenever there is a

---

[35] Ibid., para. 8.
[36] Ibid., para. 12.
[37] International Covenant on Civil and Political Rights, (1976) 999 UNTS 171, art. 5(1).
[38] American Convention on Human Rights, (1978) 1144 UNTS 123, art. 27(1).
[39] For discussion of this issue under the International Covenant on Civil and Political Rights, see General Comment 29, UN Doc. CCPR/C/21/Rev.1/Add.11, para. 11.
[40] European Social Charter, (1965) 529 UNTS 89, Appendix, art. 30; Revised European Social Charter, ETS 163, (1999) 529 UNTS 89, Appendix, art. F(1).
[41] Protocol No. 6 to the Convention for the Protection of Human Rights and Fundamental Freedoms concerning the Abolition of the Death Penalty, ETS 114, art. 2.
[42] K.J. Parsch, 'Experiences Regarding the War and Emergency Clause (art. 15) of the European Convention of Human Rights', (1971) 1 *Israel Yearbook on Human Rights* 327.
[43] See *Cyprus v. Turkey*, nos 6780/74 and 6950/75, Separate Opinion of Mr F. Ermacora, § 6, Commission report of 10 July 1976.

resort to armed force between States or protracted armed violence between governmental authorities and organized armed groups or between such groups within a State'.[44]

The words 'public emergency threatening the life of the nation' were initially interpreted in *Lawless v. Ireland*, the very first case to come before the European Court of Human Rights. The Court said that 'the natural and customary meaning of the words "other public emergency threatening the life of the nation" is sufficiently clear' and that 'they refer to an exceptional situation of crisis or emergency which affects the whole population and constitutes a threat to the organised life of the community of which the State is composed'.[45] In the *Greek case*, the European Commission referred to this passage and noted that the French version, which was to be deemed the authentic one and 'given weight', was slightly different: 'une situation de crise ou de danger exceptionnel et imminent...' The word 'imminent' was not found in the English translation.[46] Accordingly, it was held that the emergency must be 'actual or imminent', its effects must involve the whole nation, the continuance of the organized life of the community must be threatened, and the crisis or danger should be exceptional, in that the normal measures or restrictions, permitted by the Convention for the maintenance of public safety, health, and order, must be plainly inadequate.[47]

Decades later, following the terrorist attacks of 11 September 2001, the European Court specified that '[t]he requirement of imminence cannot be interpreted so narrowly as to require a State to wait for disaster to strike before taking measures to deal with it'.[48] That case involved a notice of derogation submitted in December 2001, but the Court noted that the validity of the concerns of the British authorities were confirms by the terrorist attacks in London in July 2005. It noted that the purpose of derogation was to protect against future risks. Therefore, the existence of a threat to the life of the nation was to be assessed primarily with regard to the facts known at the time of derogation. Nevertheless, the Court said it was not precluded from considering subsequent developments.[49] It also rejected a narrow construction of the words 'threatening the life of the nation' by which this must go beyond 'a threat of serious physical damage and loss of life' so as to menace 'our institutions of government or our existence as a civil community'. According to the European Court, a much broader range of factors may be taken into consideration, noting early decisions concluding that emergency situations exist although the institutions of the State do not appear to be seriously imperilled.[50]

In its General Comment on states of emergency, the United Nations Human Rights Committee said that measures derogating from rights set out in the International Covenant on Civil and Political Rights 'must be of an exceptional and temporary nature'.[51] However, the European Court has distanced itself from this proposition, noting

---

[44] *Prosecutor v. Tadic* (IT-94-1-AR72), Decision on the Defence Motion for Interlocutory Appeal on Jurisdiction, 2 October 1995, para. 70.

[45] *Lawless v. Ireland (no. 3)*, 1 July 1961, p. 27, § 28, Series A no. 3.

[46] *Denmark, Norway, Sweden, and the Netherlands v. Greece*, nos 3321/67, 3322/67, 3323/67, and 3344/67, Commission report of 5 November 1969, § 112, (1969) 12 YB 'The Greek Case' 1.

[47] Ibid., § 113.

[48] *A. and Others v. the United Kingdom* [GC], no. 3455/05, § 177, ECHR 2009.

[49] Ibid.

[50] Ibid., § 179.

[51] General Comment No. 29, UN Doc. CCPR/C/21/Rev.1/Add.11, para. 2.

the possibility that measures of derogation continue for many years and that they cannot be held to be impermissible simply because they are not temporary in nature.[52]

Not every emergency will constitute a threat to the life of the nation. The Court considers that the assessment of such threats falls primarily to the States Parties, a matter about which there is a wide margin of appreciation. 'By reason of their direct and continuous contact with the pressing needs of the moment, the national authorities are in principle better placed than the international judge to decide both on the presence of such an emergency and on the nature and scope of the derogations necessary to avert it,' the Court has said.[53] Such deference to the national authorities includes Parliament and the executive, but also the national courts.[54] However, the discretion accorded to States is not absolute and the Court retains a residual role of supervision where it weighs relevant factors, notably the nature of the rights affected by the derogation, the circumstances leading to the emergency, and its duration.[55]

Practice

The United Kingdom has issued several notices of derogation concerning public emergency. The Convention had barely entered into force when, on 24 May 1954, the United Kingdom informed the Council of Europe of a state of emergency in Malaysia, Singapore, Kenya, British Guiana, and the Buganda Province of Uganda. It explained that the governments had 'exercised or are exercising powers to detain persons which involve derogating in certain respects from the obligations imposed by Article 15 of the Convention... [A]ll persons now in detention have been permitted in accordance with the provisions of the relevant Regulations to have their cases reviewed by a Committee under a judicially qualified chairman.'[56] In 1955 and 1956 it made similar declarations with respect to Cyprus, and in 1957 with respect to Northern Ireland and Northern Rhodesia.[57] For many years, the United Kingdom continued to submit notices of derogation and withdrawal of derogation with respect to Aden,[58] British Guiana,[59] Cyprus,[60] Kenya,[61] Mauritius,[62] Northern Rhodesia,[63] Nyasaland,[64] Singapore,[65] and Zanzibar.[66] Recently, the Grand Chamber observed that with the exception of these declarations by the United Kingdom between 1954 and 1966 respecting colonial uprisings, 'derogations made by Contracting States under Article 15 of the Convention have all made reference to emergencies arising within the territory of the derogating State'.[67]

---

[52] *A. and Others v. the United Kingdom* [GC], no. 3455/05, § 178, ECHR 2009.
[53] Ibid., § 173.
[54] Ibid., § 180.
[55] *Brannigan and McBride v. the United Kingdom*, 26 May 1993, § 43, Series A no. 258-B.
[56] (1955–56–57) 1 YB 48–49.
[57] Ibid., pp. 49–51.
[58] (1960) 3 YB 68–73; (1966) 9 YB 16–21.
[59] (1958–59) 2 YB 78; (1964) 7 YB 28–31; (1965) 8 YB 10–15.
[60] (1958–59) 2 YB, pp. 78–85.
[61] (1960) 3 YB 82–91.
[62] (1965) 8 YB 14–17
[63] (1962) 5 YB 8–11.
[64] (1958–59) 2 YB 84–87.
[65] (1960) 3 YB 74–81.
[66] (1961) 4 YB 44–54, withdrawn (1963) 6 YB 32.
[67] *Hassan v. the United Kingdom* [GC], no. 29750/09, §40, 16 September 2014.

With the beginning of 'the troubles' in Northern Ireland, on 25 September 1969, the United Kingdom filed the first of several derogations.[68] The last of them was withdrawn in respect of the United Kingdom and Northern Ireland in 2001[69] and for Jersey, Guernsey, and the Isle of Man in 2006.[70] In *Ireland v. the United Kingdom*, the Court considered the existence of an emergency threatening the life of the nation to be 'perfectly clear',[71] given the existence of 'a particularly far-reaching and acute danger for the territorial integrity of the United Kingdom, the institutions of the six counties and the lives of the province's inhabitants'.[72] After the *Brogan* decision, declaring the regime of detention for a maximum of seven days without the possibility of judicial control to be contrary to article 5(3), the United Kingdom made a declaration of derogation on 23 December 1988 and yet another one on 12 December 1989.

Following the terrorist attacks in the United States of 11 September 2001, the United Kingdom made a notice of derogation declaring the existence of 'a terrorist threat to the United Kingdom from persons suspected of involvement in international terrorism', noting in particular the presence within the country of foreign nationals involved in terrorist activities who constituted 'a threat to the national security of the United Kingdom'.[73] This declaration of derogation was sharply criticized by the Council of Europe Commissioner on Human Rights who said 'general appeals to an increased risk of terrorist activity post September 11 2001 cannot, on their own be sufficient to justify derogating from the Convention'.[74] The Commissioner noted that several European States long faced with recurring terrorist activity had not deemed it necessary to derogate from Convention rights. He said that '[d]etailed information pointing to a real and imminent danger to public safety in the United Kingdom will, therefore, have to be shown'.[75] The Commissioner pointed to the detention scheme in the relevant legislation: 'In so far as these measures are applicable only to non-deportable foreigners, they might appear, moreover, to be ushering in a two-track justice, whereby different human rights standards apply to foreigners and nationals.'[76] After issuing his Opinion, the Commissioner visited the United Kingdom. In his report, he said that terrorist activity 'not only must but can be combated within the existing framework of human rights guarantees, which provide precisely for a balancing, in questions concerning national security, of individual rights and the public interest and allow for the use of proportionate special powers'. He also noted that 'in the Terrorist [sic] Act 2000, the United Kingdom already has amongst the toughest and most comprehensive anti-terror legislation in Europe'.[77]

---

[68] (1969) 12 YB 72–75. Other declarations were to follow: (1971) 14 YB 32–33; (1973) 16 YB 24–29; (1975) 18 YB 18–19; (1978) 21 YB 22–23; (1988) 31 YB 15–16; (1989) 32 YB 8; (1998) 41 YB 11.

[69] (2001) 44 YB 15–18.

[70] (2006) 49 YB 9.

[71] *Ireland v. the United Kingdom*, 18 January 1978, § 205, Series A no. 25.

[72] Ibid., § 212.

[73] (2001) 44 YB 20–23. Withdrawn (2005) 48 YB 12. See *A. and Others v. The United Kingdom* [GC], no. 3455/05, § 11, ECHR 2009.

[74] Opinion of the Commissioner for Human Rights, Mr Alvaro Gil-Robles, on certain aspects of the United Kingdom 2001 derogation from Article 5 par. 1 of the European Convention on Human Rights, CommDH (2002)7, para. 33.

[75] Ibid.

[76] Ibid., para. 40.

[77] Report by Mr Alvaro Gil-Robles, Commission for Human Rights, on his Visit to the United Kingdom, 4–12 November 2004, CommDH(2005)6, para. 6.

Ireland made a notice of derogation on 20 July 1957 concerning the Offences Against the State (Amendment) Act, 1940.[78] On 3 April 1962 it informed the Council of Europe that the derogation was withdrawn.[79] It made another derogation in 1976 with respect to the Emergency Powers Act 1976. Ireland said it was necessary to authorize the police to hold terrorism suspects in custody for up to seven days.[80]

Turkey made its first derogation on 28 February 1961, explaining that the armed forces had taken over the country as a result of a 'revolutionary movement'.[81] Two years later, Turkey submitted a notice of derogation informing the Commission that a state of siege had been proclaimed following a failed *coup d'état*.[82] Many others were to follow.[83] Turkey notified the Secretary General of derogation on 6 August 1990 with respect to disturbances in South-East Anatolia associated with Kurdish separatist activity. Subsequent notices were issued in 1991 and 1992. The Court considered 'that the particular extent and impact of PKK terrorist activity in South-East Turkey has undoubtedly created, in the region concerned, a "public emergency threatening the life of the nation"'.[84]

Following the seizure of power by the Greek military regime in 1967, a notice of derogation was issued.[85] Inter-state proceedings were taken by several European governments against Greece, in which the validity of the notice was contested. After a detailed examination, the Commission concluded that the evidence did not satisfy the requirement of a public emergency threatening the life of the nation. The Commission said that a situation of political unrest in the country was not 'beyond the control of the public authorities using normal measures' nor was it 'on a scale threatening the organised life of the community'.[86]

Limitations on the right of derogation

States Parties do not have an absolute right to derogate from the Convention. Paragraphs 1 and 2 of article 15 impose limitations on the right of derogation. They must be 'strictly required by the exigencies of the situation', they must not be inconsistent with other obligations under international law, and they cannot apply to certain provisions deemed to be non-derogable. In addition, the Court has determined that measures of derogation cannot be discriminatory. In exercising its supervisory role, the limits on the Court's powers are 'particularly apparent' when article 15 is concerned.[87]

---

[78] (1955–56–57) 1 YB 47–48.

[79] (1962) 5 YB 6.

[80] (1976) 19 YB 21–25. Withdrawn (1977) 20 YB 28–31.

[81] (1961) 4 YB 54–58. Withdrawn (1961) 4 YB 58–63.

[82] (1963) 6 YB 28–31. It was later extended: (1964) 7 YB 22–27. Withdrawn (1964) 7 YB 26–27.

[83] (1970) 13 YB 18–23; (1971) 14 YB 24–33; (1972) 15 YB 16–23; (1973) 16 YB 16–25; (1974) 17 YB 24–29 (1975) 18 YB 8–17; (1978) 21 YB 20–21; (1979) 22 YB 26–31; (1980) 23 YB 1017; (1986) 29 YB 12–13; (1987) 39 YB 18–19; (1990) 33 YB 14–15; (1991) 34 YB 14–15; (1992) 35 YB 16; (2002) 45 YB 17–18.

[84] *Aksoy v. Turkey*, 18 December 1996, § 70, *Reports of Judgments and Decisions* 1996-VI; *Bilen v. Turkey*, no. 34482/97, § 46, 21 February 2006.

[85] (1967) 10 YB 26–45. For subsequent correspondence relating to the derogation by Greece, see (1968) 11 YB 10–35; (1969) 12 YB 38–73.

[86] *Denmark, Norway, Sweden and the Netherlands v. Greece*, nos 3321/67, 3322/67, 3323/67, and 3344/67, Commission report of 5 November 1969, §§ 143–144, (1969) 12 YB 'The Greek Case' 1.

[87] *Ireland v. the United Kingdom*, 18 January 1978, § 207, Series A no. 25.

'Strictly required by the exigencies of the situation'

The measures that are taken must be 'strictly required by the exigencies of the situation'. Although the Court shows very considerable deference to States in assessing the permissibility of measures of derogation, under the margin of appreciation doctrine it nevertheless exercises a degree of judicial supervision. The United Nations Human Rights Committee gave considerable attention to this restriction on the right of derogation in General Comment No. 29. It explained that the strict requirements of the exigencies of the situation relate to the duration, geographical coverage, and material scope of the state of emergency and any measures of derogation resorted to because of the emergency. Although derogation is 'clearly distinct' from restrictions or limitations allowed under other provisions, 'the obligation to limit any derogations to those strictly required by the exigencies of the situation reflects the principle of proportionality which is common to derogation and limitation powers'.[88] Although some provisions are specifically excluded from derogation, this does not mean that derogation is permitted to any other provision more or less at will. Indeed, in practice some other provisions may be non-derogable. The Human Rights Committee has said that it should be sufficient to impose limitations on freedom of movement or freedom of association, making derogation unnecessary.[89] According to the Committee, '[t]he legal obligation to narrow down all derogations to those strictly required by the exigencies of the situation establishes both for States parties and for the Committee a duty to conduct a careful analysis under each article of the Covenant based on an objective assessment of the actual situation'.

In the *Lawless* case, the Court examined the provisions of Irish law governing detention without trial, noting that they were complemented by various safeguards, concluding that this was consistent with the 'exigencies of the situation'.[90] However, in the *Greek case*, the Commission considered that deprivation of liberty without regard for the limits imposed by article 5, maintenance of extraordinary courts martial and denial of a right of re-hearing before the Court of Appeal to offenders against national security or *ordre public* was not strictly required by the exigencies of the situation.[91] In *Ireland v. the United Kingdom*, the Court observed:

Above all, one is dealing with special legislation designed to combat a public emergency threatening the life of the nation; such provisions cannot be torn out of context without leading to arbitrary results. It was hardly possible for this legislation to forecast in a rigid and inflexible manner the frontiers of the demands of an inherently fluid and changing situation; the massive scale of the outrages and the large number of the persons arrested, detained and interned prevented the provision of guarantees similar to those required by the Convention. In 1972 and 1973, the British authorities attenuated the severity of the original legislation, thereby demonstrating their concern not to go beyond the "extent strictly required by the exigencies" of the circumstances. On this, a question of fact rather than of law, the said authorities enjoyed a margin of appreciation which they do not seem to have exceeded.[92]

---

[88] General Comment No. 29, para. 4.
[89] Ibid., para. 5.
[90] *Lawless v. Ireland (no. 3)*, 1 July 1961, pp. 28–30, §§ 31–38, Series A no. 3.
[91] *Denmark, Norway, Sweden, and the Netherlands v. Greece*, nos 3321/67, 3322/67, 3323/67, and 3344/67, Commission report of 5 November 1969, §§ 201, 234, (1969) 12 YB 'The Greek case' 1.
[92] *Ireland v. the United Kingdom*, 18 January 1978, § 243, Series A no. 25.

In another case relating to the conflict in Northern Ireland, *Brannigan and McBride*, the Court confirmed its assessment, holding that the United Kingdom had not gone beyond the strict exigencies of the situation when it authorized detention of suspects for up to seven days without any judicial control.[93] The applicants had argued that the measures were introduced in order to neutralize a judgment of the European Court holding such lengthy detention without access to a court to be contrary to article 5(3).[94]

Then, in a Turkish case, the Court held that detention without judicial supervision for fourteen days was not strictly required by the exigencies of the situation. It found the period to be 'exceptionally long', leaving the applicant vulnerable to torture as well as to arbitrary interference with his right to liberty. The Court said the government had not adduced 'detailed reasons... as to why the fight against terrorism in South-East Turkey rendered judicial intervention impracticable'.[95] Referring to the discussion of the exigencies question in one of the Turkish cases, Judge De Meyer said that this showed the 'inanity' of the 'fallacious concept' of margin of appreciation in the context of article 15: 'Where human rights are concerned, States may permit themselves only what the Court considers permissible.'[96]

Non-discrimination

The derogation provision of the International Covenant on Civil and Political Rights contains a phrase that is not found in article 15(1) of the European Convention on Human Rights: '... provided that such measures are not inconsistent with their other obligations under international law and do not involve discrimination solely on the ground of race, colour, sex, language, religion or social origin'. Although it did not refer to article 4(1) of the Covenant, the European Court found a similar condition to be implicit within the Convention pursuant to the principle of proportionality. It said measures concerning expulsion of terrorists 'were disproportionate in that they discriminated unjustifiably between nationals and non-nationals'.[97]

Consistency with other obligations under international law

The drafters of the Convention were probably not particularly concerned about the existence of other human rights treaty regimes, where the provisions might not be the same. However, the great majority of States Parties are also subject to the International Covenant on Civil and Political Rights, which has its own derogation regime, one that is arguably somewhat more restrictive than that of the European Convention. In particular, article 4 of the International Covenant on Civil and Political Rights requires that a public emergency be 'officially proclaimed', a condition not explicitly included in article 15 of the European Convention. According to the Human Rights Committee, this requirement 'is essential for the maintenance of the principles of legality and rule of law at times when they are most needed'. The Committee has explained that if derogation may be associated

[93] *Brannigan and McBride v. the United Kingdom*, 26 May 1993, § 66, Series A no. 258-B. Also *Marshall v. the United Kingdom* (dec.), no. 41571/98, 10 July 2001.

[94] *Brogan and Others v. the United Kingdom*, 29 November 1988, Series A no. 145-B.

[95] *Aksoy v. Turkey*, 18 December 1996, §§ 77–78, *Reports of Judgments and Decisions* 1996-VI. Also *Bilen v. Turkey*, no. 34482/97, §§ 47–50, 21 February 2006; *Demir and Others v. Turkey*, 23 September 1998, §§ 49–57, *Reports of Judgments and Decisions* 1998-VI.

[96] *Demir and Others v. Turkey*, 23 September 1998, Concurring Opinion of Judge De Meyer, *Reports of Judgments and Decisions* 1998-VI.

[97] *A. and Others v. the United Kingdom* [GC], no. 3455/05, § 190, ECHR 2009.

with proclamation of a state of emergency with consequences, States must act within their constitutional and other provisions of law that govern such proclamation and the exercise of emergency powers.[98] The Council of Europe Commissioner on Human Rights has also addressed this issue to the extent that he has insisted upon the availability of mechanisms for domestic scrutiny of the proclamation of emergency measures.[99]

In *Brannigan and McBride v. the United Kingdom*, the applicants contended that because official proclamation was a requirement of the Covenant, it was in a sense imported into the European Convention by virtue of the requirement of consistency with other obligations imposed by international law. The Court noted that the Secretary of State for the Home Department had made a statement in the House of Commons explaining in detail the government's decision to derogate from the Convention, adding that there was 'a public emergency within the meaning of these provisions in respect of terrorism connected with the affairs of Northern Ireland in the United Kingdom'. The Court said that the statement met the requirements of article 4 of the Covenant in that 'it was formal in character and made public the Government's intentions as regards derogation, was well in keeping with the notion of an official proclamation'.[100]

Other obligations relevant to situations of war and national emergency may arise under treaties governing the law of armed conflict, as well as from sources such as resolutions of the United Nations Security Council.

Lawful acts of war

Derogation from four provisions of the Convention is not permitted. However, there is an exception with respect to article 2 of the Convention in that deaths resulting from lawful acts of war ('*d'actes licites de guerre*') may be excluded. This provision has not resulted in any case law. Nothing in the drafting history of article 15 assists in its construction. Nor is there any parallel reference in the derogation clause of the International Covenant on Civil and Political Rights that might be of assistance for the purposes of interpretation. If nothing else, the reference to 'lawful acts of war' in article 15(2) of the Convention confirms that those who drafted the instrument turned their minds to its possible application in wartime. This is also apparent from the reference to wartime in article 2 of Protocol No. 6. If the intent had been to exclude the application of the Convention during armed conflict, these provisions would not exist.

The term 'acts of war' does not appear in any of the relevant treaties, whether they date from before or after the adoption of the European Convention on Human Rights. It was used very occasionally during the negotiations of the Geneva Conventions in August 1949.[101] The term also appears, but rarely, in national military manuals.[102] Historically, the term 'act of war' had significance in the context of the *jus ad bellum*. It described conduct such as an armed attack that would initiate a state of war even in the absence of a

---

[98] General Comment 29, UN Doc. CCPR/C/21/Rev.1/Add.11, para. 2.

[99] Opinion of the Commissioner for Human Rights, Mr Alvaro Gil-Robles, on certain aspects of the United Kingdom 2001 derogation from article 5 par. 1 of the European Convention on Human Rights, CommDH(2002)7, paras 5, 8, and 12.

[100] *Brannigan and McBride v. the United Kingdom*, 26 May 1993, § 73, Series A no. 258-B.

[101] Final Record of the Diplomatic Conference of Geneva of 1949, Vol. II, Section A, pp. 56, 57, 492.

[102] Jean-Marie Henckaerts and Louise Doswald-Beck, eds, *Customary International Humanitarian Law, Vol. II: Practice*, Part I, Cambridge: Cambridge University Press, 2005, pp. 117, 676, 677, 858, 1014, 1382; Jean-Marie Henckaerts and Louise Doswald-Beck, eds, *Customary International Humanitarian Law, Vol. III: Practice*, Part II, Cambridge: Cambridge University Press, 2005, pp. 2548, 3103, 3622.

declaration of war. Even prior to adoption of the European Convention, the legality of the use of force by one State against another had been confined to the exceptional circumstances laid out in the Charter of the United Nations, namely measures authorized by the Security Council in the interests of international peace and security and the inherent right of self defence. Consequently, to avail of the 'lawful acts of war' exception to killing in the course of armed conflict, the use of force itself must be consistent with international law. In other words, a declaration of derogation from to the right to life by a State with respect to the use of force against another State that is not in the exercise of the inherent right of self-defence or authorized by the Security Council would be ineffective. The lawfulness of the use of force would be assessed in light of international case law, notably the judgment of the International Military Tribunal,[103] the General Assembly resolution on aggression,[104] and the definition of aggression in the Rome Statute of the International Criminal Court.[105]

It is also possible to consider the term 'lawful acts of war' from the standpoint of the *jus in bello*. In this context, it refers essentially to means and methods of warfare. There is a very large body of treaty law as well as customary law applicable in this area, the primary instruments being the Regulations annexed to the fourth Hague Convention of 1907, the Additional Protocols to the Geneva Conventions of 1977, and the definition of war crimes contained in article 8 of the Rome Statute. There is a *jus in bello* reference to the term 'lawful acts of war' in the British Military Manual of 1958 that may well have been inspired by article 15 of the Convention: 'Assassination, the killing or wounding of a selected individual behind the line of battle by enemy agents or partisans, and the killing or wounding by treachery of individuals belonging to the opposing nation or army, are not lawful acts of war.'[106]

Notification of derogation

A State Party availing itself of the 'right of derogation' is required to keep the Secretary General of the Council of Europe 'fully informed of the measures which it has taken and the reasons therefor'. It is also required to notify the Secretary General when the measures have ceased to operate and the provisions of the Convention are again being fully executed. Article 15(3), together with the principle of proportionality, impose upon States 'a process of continued reflection' on the necessity of the measures that they have taken in derogation from the Convention.[107]

There are no formal requirements for the notice of derogation. Whether a declaration is necessary at all in order for a State to avail of article 15 is a question that has never been definitively determined and that was left open explicitly by the European Commission of Human Rights in *Lawless*.[108] In *Cyprus v. Turkey*, the European Commission declined to

[103] *France et al. v. Goering et al.*, (1948) 22 IMT 411.
[104] Definition of Aggression, GA Res. 3314 (XXIX), annex.
[105] The crime of aggression, RC/Res.6, Annex I.
[106] United Kingdom Military Manual, 1958, para. 115, cited in Jean-Marie Henckaerts and Louise Doswald-Beck, eds, *Customary International Humanitarian Law, Vol. II: Practice*, Part I, Cambridge: Cambridge University Press, 2005, p. 1382. For other references to 'acts of war', see ibid., pp. 117, 676, 677, 858, 1014; Jean-Marie Henckaerts and Louise Doswald-Beck, eds, *Customary International Humanitarian Law, Vol. III: Practice*, Part II, Cambridge: Cambridge University Press, 2005, pp. 2548, 3103, 3622.
[107] *Brannigan and McBride v. the United Kingdom*, 26 May 1993, § 54, Series A no. 258-B.
[108] *Lawless v. Ireland*, no. 332/57, Commission report of 19 December 1959, p. 75.

rule on the necessity of a declaration deposited with the Secretary General, but it held that article 15 'requires some formal and public act of derogation, such as a declaration of martial law or state of emergency, and that, where no such act has been proclaimed by the High Contracting Party concerned, although it was not in the circumstances prevented from doing so, Art. 15 cannot apply'.[109] Two members of the Commission dissented on this point, holding that article 15(3) imposed 'an autonomous obligation in the sense that its violation does not affect the valid exercise of the right of derogation flowing from the same article'.[110]

In *Lawless*, the applicant challenged the validity of Ireland's notification because it did not adduce the existence of a time of war or public emergency, nor did it 'properly' define the nature of the measure the government had taken.[111] Dismissing the argument, the Court noted that Ireland had provided a copy of the relevant legislation and that it had explained that the measures were necessary 'to prevent the commission of offences against public peace and order and to prevent the maintaining of military or armed forces other than those authorised by the Constitution'.[112] Although the Convention does not impose any time limit for the deposit of a notice of derogation,[113] in *Lawless* the Court noted that notification was submitted without delay, in that case twelve days after the entry into force of the impugned measures.[114]

However, in the *Greek case*, the Commission found that Greece had failed to comply with the requirements of article 15(3). In particular, it had not communicated the texts of several of the relevant legislative measures, nor had it provided full information about administrative measures, including the number of persons arrested and detained without court order. In addition, the Commission considered that a delay of more than four months from the time the measures were taken to the filing of the notification of derogation was not consistent with article 15(3).[115]

In Turkish cases, the Court rejected the claim that measures were sheltered by legislation contemplated by a declaration of derogation. The legislation Turkey had listed in its derogation did not apply to the provinces or urban centres where the alleged infringements of the Convention had occurred. The Court said it 'would be working against the object and purpose of that provision if, when assessing the territorial scope of the derogation concerned, it were to extend its effects to a part of Turkish territory not explicitly named in the notice of derogation'.[116]

In contrast with article 4(3) of the International Covenant on Civil and Political Rights, article 15 of the Convention does not formally oblige the Secretary General to inform the

---

[109] *Cyprus v. Turkey*, nos 6780/74 and 6950/75, § 527, Commission report of 10 July 1976.

[110] Ibid., Dissenting Opinion of Mr G. Sperduti, Joined by Mr S. Trechsel, on art. 15 of the Convention, § 3.

[111] *Lawless v. Ireland (no. 3)*, 1 July 1961, p. 31, § 44, Series A no. 3.

[112] Ibid., § 47.

[113] *Denmark, Norway, Sweden, and the Netherlands v. Greece*, nos 3321/67, 3322/67, 3323/67, and 3344/67, Commission report of 5 November 1969, § 43, (1969) 12 YB 'The Greek case' 1.

[114] *Lawless v. Ireland (no. 3)*, 1 July 1961, p. 32, § 47, Series A no. 3.

[115] *Denmark, Norway, Sweden, and the Netherlands v. Greece*, nos 3321/67, 3322/67, 3323/67, and 3344/67, Commission report of 5 November 1969, § 45, (1969) 12 YB 'The Greek case' 1.

[116] *Sakık and Others v. Turkey*, 26 November 1997, § 39, *Reports of Judgments and Decisions* 1997-VII; *Abdülsamet Yaman v. Turkey*, no. 32446/96, § 69, 2 November 2004; *Bilen v. Turkey*, no. 34482/97, § 44, 21 February 2006; *Şimşek v. Turkey*, no. 28010/95, § 47, Commission report of 1 March 1999.

other States parties of a notice of derogation. However, the case law of the European Commission on Human Rights declares this to be a requirement.[117]

Reservations and declarations

France formulated a reservation to the Convention:

to the effect, firstly, that the circumstances specified in Article 16 of the Constitution regarding the implementation of that Article, in Section I of the Act of 3 April 1878 and the Act of 9 August 1849 regarding proclamation of a state of siege, and in Section I of Act No. 55-385 of 3 April 1955 regarding proclamation of a state of emergency, and in which it is permissible to apply the provisions of those texts, must be understood as complying with the purpose of Article 15 of the Convention and that, secondly, for the interpretation and application of Article 16 of the Constitution of the Republic, the terms 'to the extent strictly required by the exigencies of the situation' shall not restrict the power of the President of the Republic to take 'the measures required by the circumstances'.[118]

Because of the objective nature of the Convention, the Court did not consider that France was barred from making an application against Turkey in which it challenged the validity of Turkey's derogation based upon article 15.[119]

Spain made an interpretative declaration to the effect that article 15 permits adoption of measures contemplated in articles 55 and 116 of the Spanish Constitution.[120] Andorra made a reservation to article 15 by which it is to be applied within the limits provided for in its own constitution. Article 42 of the Constitution sets out the mechanism for declaring an emergency and the length of time it may remain in force.[121]

Further reading

Jean Allain, 'Derogation from the European Convention of Human Rights in Light of "Other Obligations under International Law"', (2005) 10 *EHRLR* 480.

Edward Crysler, '*Brannigan and McBride v. U.K.*: A New Direction on Article 15 Derogations under the European Convention on Human Rights?', (1996) 65 *Nordic Journal of International Law* 91.

Joan Fitzpatrick, *Human Rights in Crisis: The International System for Protecting Human Rights during States of Emergency*, Philadelphia: University of Pennsylvania Press, 1994.

Cees Flinterman, 'Derogation from the Rights and Freedoms in Case of a Public Emergency (Article 15)', in Van Dijk et al., *Theory and Practice*, pp. 1053–75.

Frowein/Peukert, *MenschenRechtsKonvention*, pp. 419–26.

L.C. Green, 'Derogation of Human Rights in Emergency Situations', (1978) 16 *Canadian Yearbook of International Law* 92.

Oren Gross, 'Once More unto the Breach: The Systemic Failure of Applying the European Convention on Human Rights to Entrenched Emergencies', (1998) 23 *Yale Journal of International Law* 437.

---

[117] *Denmark, Norway, Sweden, and the Netherlands v. Greece*, nos 3321/67, 3322/67, 3323/67, and 3344/67, Commission decision of 24 January 1968, (1968) 11 YB 690, Collection 25, p. 92, § 45.
[118] (1974) 17 YB 4–5.
[119] *France, Norway, Denmark, Sweden, and the Netherlands v. Turkey*, nos 9940–9944/82, Commission decision of 6 December 1983, (1983) 26 YB COMM.EUR.JURIS. 1, DR 35, p. 143, at p. 169.
[120] (1979) 22 YB 24–25.
[121] (1996) 39 YB 19.

Oren Gross and Fionnuala Ní Aoláin, 'From Discretion to Scrutiny: Revisiting the Application of the Margin of Appreciation Doctrine in the Context of Article 15 of the European Convention on Human Rights', (2001) 23 *Human Rights Quarterly* 625.

Oren Gross and Fionnuala Ní Aoláin, *Law in Times of Crisis: Emergency Powers in Theory and Practice*, Cambridge: Cambridge University Press, 2006.

Harris et al., *Law of the European Convention*, pp. 617–43.

Joan F. Hartman, 'Derogation from Human Rights Treaties in Public Emergencies—A Critique of Implementation by the European Commission and Court of Human Rights and the Human Rights Committee of the United Nations', (1981) 22 *Harvard International Law Journal* 1.

Virginia Helen Henning, 'Anti-Terrorism, Crime and Security Act 2001: Has the United Kingdom Made a Valid Derogation from the European Convention on Human Rights?', (2001–2) 17 *American University International Law Review* 1263.

Stefan Kirchner, 'Human Rights Guarantees During States of Emergency: The European Convention on Human Rights', (2010) 3 *Baltic Journal of Law and Politics* 1.

Ronald St. J. Macdonald, 'Protecting Human Rights in Emergency Situations: Making Article 15 work', in Mahoney et al., *Mélanges Ryssdal*, pp. 817–36.

Susan Marks, 'Civil Liberties at the Margin: The UK Derogation and the European Court of Human Rights', (1995) 15 *Oxford Journal of Legal Studies* 69.

Aly Mokhtar, 'Human Rights Obligations v. Derogations: Article 15 of the European Convention on Human Rights', (2004) 8 *International Journal of Human Rights* 64.

M. O'Boyle, 'The Margin of Appreciation and Derogation under Article 15: Ritual Incantation or Principle', (1998) *HRLJ* 23.

Jaime Oràà, *Human Rights in States of Emergency in International Law*, New York: Oxford University Press, 1992.

K.J. Parsch, 'Experiences Regarding the War and Emergency Clause (art. 15) of the European Convention of Human Rights', (1971) 1 *Israel Yearbook on Human Rights* 327.

João de Deus Pinheiro Farinha, 'L'article 15 de la Convention', in Franz Matscher and Herbert Petzold, eds, *Protection des droits de l'homme: La dimension européenne. Mélanges en l'honneur de Gérard J. Wiarda*, Cologne: Carl Heymanns, 1988, pp. 521–9.

A.H. Robertson, 'The First Case before the European Court of Human Rights: *Lawless v. The Government of Ireland*', (1960) 36 *British Year Book of International Law* 343.

Christoph Schreuer, 'Derogation of Human Rights in Situations of Public Emergency: The Experience of the European Convention on Human Rights', (1982) 9 *Yale Journal of World Public Order* 113.

Paul Tavernier, 'Article 15', in Pettiti et al., *La Convention européenne*, pp. 489–503.

Mohamed M. El Zeidy, 'ECHR and States of Emergency: Article 15—A Domestic Power of Derogation from Human Rights Obligations', (2003) 4 *San Diego International Law Journal* 277.

Article 16. Restrictions on political activity of aliens/Restrictions à l'activité politique des étrangers

Nothing in Articles 10, 11 and 14 shall be regarded as preventing the High Contracting Parties from imposing restrictions on the political activity of aliens.	Aucune des dispositions des articles 10, 11 et 14 ne peut être considérée comme interdisant aux Hautes Parties Contractantes d'imposer des restrictions à l'activité politique des étrangers.

Introductory comments

The prohibition on political activity of 'aliens' (in French, *étrangers*) is unique to the European Convention within the corpus of international human rights law. In a report issued in 1994, the European Commission of Human Rights as much as described article 16 as an anachronism, a provision that reflected 'une conception prédominante à l'époque en droit international, autorisant de façon générale et illimitée des restrictions aux activités politiques des étrangers'.[1] It is not without interest that the European Union Charter of Fundamental Rights contemplates no similar limitation on political participation. Only one provision of the Universal Declaration of Human Rights, concerning participation in democratic elections, expressly excludes non-nationals.[2]

Drafting of the provision

The notion that the Convention might not apply equally to everyone within the jurisdiction of a State Party had been contemplated by the Consultative Assembly, but in the context of the ancestor of article 1 of the Convention. There were discussions about whether it would only cover those who were resident or domiciled within the country.[3]

The Committee of Ministers established a Committee of Experts to study the draft of the Consultative Assembly, with the instruction that it should consider the work of the United Nations Commission on Human Rights on the human rights Covenant. But there was nothing in the draft Covenant of any relevance to the issue of excluding the political activity of aliens. The Committee of Experts, meeting in February 1950, introduced a provision by which some rights could be subject to 'particular rules' with respect to non-nationals.[4] The proposal originated in the Sub-Committee established to assess proposed

---

[1] *Piermont v. France*, nos 15773/89 and 15774/89, § 58, Commission report of 20 January 1994.
[2] Universal Declaration of Human Rights, GA Res. 217 A (III), UN Doc. A/810, art. 21.
[3] Proposals by Mr P.H. Teitgen, Rapporteur, 29 August 1949, Doc. A 116, I *TP* 166–8; Minutes of the Sitting [of the Committee for Legal and Administrative Affairs of the Consultative Assembly, 29 August 1949], Doc. A 142, I *TP* 170–3, at pp. 170–2; Minutes of the Sitting [of the Committee for Legal and Administrative Affairs of the Consultative Assembly, 31 August 1949], Doc. A 199, I *TP* 182–3.
[4] Draft text of the first section of a draft Convention based on the work of the Consultative Assembly, Doc. A 809, III *TP* 220–31, at p. 224; Preliminary Draft Convention for the Maintenance and Further Realisation of Human Rights and Fundamental Freedoms, 15 February 1950, Doc. A 833, III *TP* 236–46, at p. 238; Preliminary Draft Convention, Doc. CM/WP 1 (50) 14, A 932, III *TP* 312–35, at pp. 322–4.

amendments. Its Report explained that 'since certain of the rights enumerated under Article 2 cannot be guaranteed to aliens without restrictions...a reference to these restrictions should be inserted'.[5] The Committee proposed the following: 'Each state shall be competent to establish the particular rules applicable within its territory for the ensurement [sic] and exercise of the rights enumerated in Article 2, para. 3, 6, 7, 8 and 9 by persons who are not its nationals, subject to the principles set out in Article 9.'[6] The substantive provisions referred to dealt with the prohibition of slavery, servitude and the slave trade, freedom of expression, freedom of peaceful assembly and association, and the right to form and join trade unions. Article 9, which said 'the protection provided by this Convention [should] ensure that the rules issued by each State for the organisation of the exercise of these secured rights and freedoms within its territory, as well as the application of these rules, are in accordance with the general principles of law as recognised by civilised nations', did not survive to the final draft of the Convention. In its report on its first session, the Committee of Experts said that the aim of the text was 'to make provision for the fact that, in accordance with a universally admitted practice, the exercise of the fundamental rights by foreigners (non-nationals) may be subject to certain restrictions not applicable to nationals. These restrictions, however, must not violate the general principles of law as recognised by civilised nations.'[7]

A more modest form of this provision, stating that the protections of freedom of expression and freedom of peaceful assembly did not prevent imposing 'such restrictions as may be necessary to prohibit persons who are not nationals of that State from engaging in political activities', was submitted by Sweden during the second session of the Committee of Experts.[8] The Committee decided to present two drafts of the Convention to the Committee of Ministers. The first, A and A/1, was close to the draft adopted by the Consultative Assembly that was in turn aligned with the text of the Universal Declaration of Human Rights. The Committee of Experts proposed the following clause for draft A and A/1: 'The State shall be competent to establish the particular rules applicable within its territory for the enjoyment and exercise of the rights enumerated in Article 2, paragraphs 3(a) and (b), 6, 7, 8 and 9 by persons who are not its Nationals, subject to the principles set out in article 10.'[9] The second draft Convention, labelled B and B/1, was very largely based on British proposals that were themselves a reflection of the draft covenant being prepared by the United Nations Commission on Human Rights. The draft for B and B/2 read: 'Nothing in Articles 10 [freedom of expression] and 11 [freedom

---

[5] First part of the Report of the Sub-Committee Instructed to Make a Preliminary Study of the Amendments Proposed by the Members of the Committee, Doc. A 796, III *TP* 200–5, at p. 200.

[6] Preliminary Draft Convention for the Maintenance and Further Realisation of Human Rights and Fundamental Freedoms, 15 February 1950, Doc. A 833, III *TP* 236–46, at p. 238.

[7] Preliminary draft of the Report to the Committee of Ministers, 24 February 1950, Doc. CM/WP 1 (50) 1, A 847, III *TP* 246–79, at p. 266; Report to the Committee of Ministers submitted by the Committee of Experts Instructed to Draw Up a Draft Convention of Collective Guarantee of Human Rights and Fundamental Freedoms, Doc. CM/WP 1 (5) 15, A 924, IV *TP* 2–55, at p. 28; Appendix to the Report of the Committee of Experts on Human Rights: Draft Convention of Protection of Human Rights and Fundamental Freedoms, 16 March 1950, Doc. C/WP 1 (50) 15 appendix, CM/WP 1 (50) 14 revised, A 925, IV *TP* 50–79, at p. 54.

[8] Amendment to the British draft proposed by the Swedish Expert, Doc. CM/WP 1 (50) 12, A 921, III *TP* 308–9.

[9] Appendix to the Report of the Committee of Experts on Human Rights: Draft Convention of Protection of Human Rights and Fundamental Freedoms, 16 March 1950, Doc. C/WP 1 (50) 15 appendix, CM/WP 1 (50) 14 revised, A 925, IV *TP* 50–79, at p. 54.

of assembly] shall be regarded as preventing the High Contracting Parties from imposing restrictions to the political activity of aliens.'[10]

In principle, the Conference of Senior Officials, meeting in June 1950, agreed to consolidate the two texts. In practice, the text it adopted was essentially identical to the second version adopted by the Committee of Experts: 'Nothing in Articles 10 and 11 shall be regarded as preventing the High Contracting Parties from imposing restrictions on the political activity of aliens.'[11] This was revised with the addition of a reference to article 13, which at the time was the non-discrimination clause.[12] No other changes were made subsequently aside from renumbering, and there does not appear to have been any further discussion of the provision by the Committee of Ministers or the Consultative Assembly.

The heading 'Restriction on political activity of aliens' was added by Protocol No. 11.[13]

Analysis and interpretation

Article 16's prohibition on political activity of 'aliens' is specifically addressed to articles 10, 11, and 14 of the Convention. It operates as an additional limitation to what is already set out in paragraph 2 of articles 10 and 11. Its formulation suggests an admissibility issue, permitting the State to object to an application on the grounds that the individual concerned is an 'alien'. The term 'alien' is also used in article 4 of Protocol No. 4 and in article 1 of Protocol No. 7. As an exception to some of the most fundamental provisions of the Convention and more generally because of its interference with participatory democracy, article 16 requires a strict construction.[14]

The provision of the Convention where the issue of discrimination against non-nationals is most important is probably article 3 of Protocol No. 1. 'Political activity' involves various aspects of the electoral process, including the right to stand for office, and to vote. Non-nationals are generally excluded, at least partially, from participation in democratic elections. It would have seemed logical to include a reference to article 3 of Protocol No. 1 in article 16 of the Convention, but of course there is an obvious chronological explanation why this is not the case. Article 16 was drafted and adopted first. Perhaps restrictions on the political activity of non-nationals in the electoral process seemed an obvious implied limitation for which mention was not even necessary. Possibly the drafters did not consider participation in elections to be 'political activity'.

Article 16 has been invoked only very rarely before the Convention organs. The leading case, *Piermont v. France*, concerned the expulsion of an environmental activist and pacifist who was also a Member of the European Parliament from the French overseas territory of New Caledonia. The Court dismissed France's attempt to rely on article 16, stating that this was not allowed because she possessed the nationality of a European Union Member

---

[10] Ibid., p. 64.

[11] New draft alternatives B and B/2, Doc. CM/WP 4 (50) 9, A 1372, IV *TP* 182–91, at p. 190; Draft Convention appended to the Draft Report, Doc. CM/WP 4 (50) 16, appendix, A 1445, IV *TP* 218–40, at p. 226.

[12] Draft Convention annexed to the Report, Doc. CM/WP 4 (50) 19 annex, CM/WP 4 (50) 16 rev., A 1452, IV *TP* 274–95, at p. 282.

[13] Protocol No. 11 to the Convention for the Protection of Human Rights and Fundamental Freedoms, restructuring the control machinery established thereby, ETS 155, art. 2(2).

[14] *Piermont v. France*, nos 15773/89 and 15774/89, Commission report of 20 January 1994, Concurring Opinion of Mr L. Loucaides Joined by Mr M. Pellonpää and Opinion partiellement dissidente de M. H. Danelius à laquelle se rallient MM. E. Busuttil, G. Jörundsson, Mme J. Liddy, et M. B. Marxer.

State. Moreover, the people of France's overseas territories participate in European Parliament elections.[15] The majority of the Commission had been more explicit, finding article 16 to be inapplicable because she was not an 'alien'.[16] Three judges of the Court dissented from the majority, insisting that Piermont was undoubtedly an 'alien' in the eyes of French law and that the term in article 16 was unambiguous. But they said that even if article 16 applied, it did not follow that the State had unfettered discretion to limit political expression without breaching article 10. They acknowledged 'the increased internationalisation of politics in modern circumstances' and said that article 16 should be considered within the analysis of permitted restrictions pursuant to article 10(2).[17]

Because article 16 has no equivalent in the International Covenant on Civil and Political Rights, several States formulated reservations at the time of ratification so that the same legal regime would be applicable under the Covenant as under the Convention. Thus, Austria made the following reservation: 'Articles 19, 21 and 22 in connection with article 2 (1) of the Covenant will be applied provided that they are not in conflict with legal restrictions as provided for in article 16 of the European Convention for the Protection of Human Rights and Fundamental Freedoms.' Belgium, France, and Germany submitted essentially identical reservations. Similarly, Malta formulated a reservation invoking article 16: 'The Government of Malta also reserves the right not to apply article 19 to the extent that this may be fully compatible with Act 1 of 1987 entitled "An act to regulate the limitations on the political activities of aliens", and this in accordance with Article 16 of the Convention of Rome (1950) for the protection of Human Rights and Fundamental Freedoms or with Section 41 (2) (a) (ii) of the Constitution of Malta.'

Emmanuel Decaux has noted the frequent suggestions that article 16 be removed from the Convention.[18] Among them is a proposal from the Parliamentary Assembly urging the Committee of Ministers '[t]o instruct the competent committee of experts to make proposals of the amendment of the European Convention for the protection of Human Rights and Fundamental Freedoms in such a way as to exclude restrictions at present authorised by Article 16 with respect to political activity on the exercise by aliens of freedoms guaranteed by Article 10 (freedom of expression) and Article 11 (freedom of association)'.[19]

Within the Member States of the European Union, legislation frequently allows for broad participation of non-nationals, at least those who are nationals of a European Union State, at various levels of local government. The Charter of Fundamental Rights of the European Union entitles 'every citizen of the Union' the right to vote and be a candidate in municipal elections to the extent that he or she is a resident 'under the same conditions as nationals of that State'. Citizens of the European Union are not to be considered as aliens in the scope of the application of Union law because of the prohibition of any discrimination on grounds of nationality in the European Charter of Fundamental Rights.

---

[15] *Piermont v. France*, 27 April 1995, § 64, Series A no. 314.

[16] *Piermont v. France*, nos 15773/89 and 15774/89, Commission report of 20 January 1994, § 69.

[17] *Piermont v. France*, 27 April 1995, Joint Partly Dissenting Opinion of Judges Ryssdal, Matscher, Sir John Freeland, and Jungwiert, § 5, Series A no. 314. Similarly, *Piermont v. France*, nos 15773/89 and 15774/89, Commission report of Report 20 January 1994, Opinion concordante de M. C. A. Nørgaard et de Mme G.H. Thune.

[18] Emmanuel Decaux, 'Article 16', in Pettiti et al., *La Convention européenne*, pp. 505–7, at p. 507.

[19] Recommendation 799 (1977) on the political rights and position of aliens, 15 January 1977.

Article 16 does not therefore apply to European Union citizens in this context as regards the rights of aliens.[20]

Perhaps there will come a time when European values have progressed to the extent that the right of non-nationals to be a full part of the democratic process is not contested, regardless of whether they are citizens of the European Union. This will be based on evidence of a commitment to be part of civil society, manifested through residence rather than nationality.

Further reading

Juan Fernando Durán Alba, 'Restrictions on the Political Activity of Aliens under Article 16 ECHR', in Javier García Roca and Pablo Santolaya, eds, *Europe of Rights: A Compendium on the European Convention of Human Rights*, Leiden/Boston: Martinus Nijhoff, 2012, pp. 497–502.

Yutaka Arai, 'Restrictions on the Political Activity of Aliens (Article 16)', in Van Dijk et al., *Theory and Practice*, pp. 1077–86.

Emmanuel Decaux, 'Article 16', in Pettiti et al., *La Convention européenne*, pp. 505–7.

Frowein/Peukert, *MenschenRechtsKonvention*, pp. 427–9.

Harris et al., *Law of the European Convention*, pp. 647–8.

Hélène Lambert, *The Position of Aliens in Relation to the European Convention on Human Rights*, Strasbourg: Council of Europe Publishing, 2007.

Richard B. Lillich, *The Human Rights of Aliens in Contemporary International Law*, Manchester: Manchester University Press, 1984.

Carmen Tiburcio, *The Human Rights of Aliens under International and Comparative Law*, The Hague/Boston/London: Martinus Nijhoff, 2001.

---

[20] Explanation relating to the Charter of Fundamental Rights, Official Journal of the European Union, C 303/34, 14 December 2007.

Article 17. Prohibition of abuse of rights/Interdiction d'abus de droit

Nothing in this Convention may be interpreted as implying for any State, group or person any right to engage in any activity or perform any act aimed at the destruction of any of the rights and freedoms set forth herein or at their limitation to a greater extent than is provided for in the Convention.

Aucune des dispositions de la présente Convention ne peut être interprétée comme impliquant pour un État, un groupement ou un individu, un droit quelconque de se livrer à une activité ou d'accomplir un acte visant à la destruction des droits ou libertés reconnus dans la présente Convention ou à des limitations plus amples de ses droits et libertés que celles prévues à ladite Convention.

Introductory comments

The memory of the Second World War sits heavily on Europe to this day. It was the most devastating conflict in history, leaving tens of millions of Europeans dead, their towns and cities destroyed. It was the work of totalitarian regimes that had implanted themselves within some of the greatest nations of the continent. The Council of Europe was established in order to ensure there could be no repetition. As Rolv Ryssdal, a president of the European Court of Human Rights, once said the Court's role was both to provide a bulwark to totalitarian ideas and to 'sound the alarm at their resurgence'.[1] In one decision, the Court commented on the experience of Weimer Germany and the aftermath of its collapse. Adopting the Basic Law in 1949, post-war Germany 'wished to avoid a repetition of those experiences by founding its new State on the idea that it should be a "democracy capable of defending itself"'.[2] Or, as the French revolutionary Saint-Just put it in his legendary declaration, '[p]as de liberté pour les ennemis de la liberté'.

The European Convention's prohibition of the abuse of rights is derived from article 30 of the Universal Declaration of Human Rights: 'Nothing in this Declaration may be interpreted as implying for any State, group or person any right to engage in any activity or to perform any act aimed at the destruction of any of the rights and freedoms set forth herein.' Charles Malik of Lebanon was author of the provision, first proposed during the December 1947 session of the Commission on Human Rights.[3] Article 17 of the European Convention is almost identical to article 5(1) of the International Covenant on Civil and Political Rights: 'Nothing in the present Covenant may be interpreted as implying for any State, group or person any right to engage in any activity or perform any act aimed at the destruction of any of the rights and freedoms recognised herein or at their limitation to a greater extent than is provided for in the present Covenant.' A text that is

---

[1] Rolv Ryssdal, 'The Expanding Role of the European Court of Human Rights', in Asbjørn Eide and Jan Helgesen, eds, *The Future of Human Rights Protection in a Changing World*, Oslo: Norwegian University Press, 1991.

[2] *Vogt v. Germany*, 26 September 1995, § 59, Series A no. 323.

[3] Proposals submitted by the Representative of Lebanon, UN Doc. E/CN.4/74; UN Doc. E/CN.4/SR.41, p. 7.

very similar to article 17 appears as the final provision of the European Union Charter of Fundamental Rights.[4]

Drafting of the provision

Nothing resembling article 17 appears in the European Movement text that constitutes the starting point of the drafting of the European Convention on Human Rights. However, the issue was certainly a live one from the first session of the Consultative Assembly. In the Assembly's Committee on Legal and Administrative Questions, David Maxwell Fyfe insisted that '[w]e do not desire by sentimentality in drafting to give evilly disposed persons the opportunity to create a totalitarian government which will destroy Human Right altogether . . .'[5] Leon Maccas of Greece spoke at length about the threats to democratic rule and the importance of recognizing duties as well as rights.[6] Even Pierre-Henri Teitgen warned that '[a] certain brand of anti-communism, which claims to fight communism not with democratic methods but with dictatorial methods, sometimes puts in jeopardy the very principles of democracy'.[7]

As rapporteur of the Committee, Teitgen proposed the following: 'These rights and freedoms may in no case be exercised contrary to the aims and principles of the Council of Europe.' In addition, he moved a text patterned on article 30 of the Universal Declaration: 'Nothing in the Convention may be interpreted as implying for any State, group or person any right to engage in any activity or perform any act aimed at the destruction of any of the rights and freedoms set forth therein.'[8] In the Committee, an amendment to replace the reference to 'Council of Europe' with 'United Nations' was defeated, eight votes to eight. A second amendment to omit the entire sentence was adopted by fourteen to two, with one abstention. A third, to delete the second sentence, was adopted by seventeen to nought.[9] Explaining the decision to remove any such reference, the explanatory memorandum said:

M. Callias would have liked to word Article 5 of the draft Resolution in such a way that it would expressly authorise the States signatory to the proposed Convention to take special measures to deal with those who, under pretext of expressing their opinions have resort to violence, or else try to provoke it.[10]

The report said that the Committee considered that this point was covered by the general limitation clause, which is the ancestor of articles 8(2), 9(2), 10(2) and 11(2) and whose text resembles article 29(2) of the Universal Declaration of Human Rights.[11]

---

[4] Charter of Fundamental Rights of the European Union, 2010 OJ C 83/02, art. 54. See Explanation relating to the Charter of Fundamental Rights, Official Journal of the European Union, C 303/34, 14 December 2007.

[5] Report of the Sitting [of the Consultative Assembly, 19 August 1949], I *TP* 38–154, at p. 118.

[6] Ibid., p. 110.

[7] Ibid., p. 40.

[8] Proposals by Mr P.H. Teitgen, Rapporteur, 29 August 1949, Doc. A 116, I *TP* 166–8. Also Report presented by Mr P.H. Teitgen, 5 September 1949, Doc. A 290, I *TP* 192–213, at p. 206. See also Report [of the Committee on Legal and Administrative Questions], 5 September 1949, Doc. AS (1) 77, I *TP* 216–39, at p. 228.

[9] Minutes of the Sitting [of the Committee on Legal and Administrative Questions, Consultative Assembly, 30 August 1949], Doc. A 167, I *TP* 174–80, at p. 180.

[10] Report presented by Mr P.H. Teitgen, 5 September 1949, Doc. A 290, I *TP* 192–213, at p. 201.

[11] Ibid.

Lodovico Benvenuti of Italy complained:

Every time that we, in our country, modify our free institutions, in order to protect ourselves against preparatory activity on the part of the totalitarian parties, these latter raise an outcry and say that we violate Human Rights and the fundamental rights of freedom. The implementation of the proposed uniform law would also result in introducing into the constitution of every country the principles adopted by the United Nations in Article 30 of their Declaration of Human Rights . . . I am frankly surprised that such an important and fundamental principle, relating to the subject which we are discussing at this moment, has not been introduced into our Convention.

Last night I intended to submit an amendment to this effect, drafted as follows: 'No provision of the proposed Convention may imply the recognition of the right of a State or of an individual to undertake activity aimed at the destruction of the freedoms which are contained in it.' Unfortunately, I arrived half an hour after the expiry of the time-limit and the Bureau relentlessly rejected my draft Amendment. If the Rapporteur wished to propose it, he would perhaps be more fortunate . . . [12]

At Teitgen's request, Benvenuti withdrew his proposal and there was no such initiative. [13] The Consultative Assembly draft convention contained no provision resembling article 30 of the Universal Declaration. [14]

The Committee of Ministers referred the Consultative Assembly draft to a Committee of Experts with the instruction that it was to take account of the work underway on the United Nations draft covenant within the Commission on Human Rights. In its 1949 draft, the Commission had included the following:

Nothing in this Covenant may be interpreted as implying for any State, group or person any right to engage in any activity or perform any act aimed at the destruction of any of the rights and freedoms defined herein or at their limitation to a greater extent than is already provided for in this Covenant. [15]

A report prepared by the Secretariat-General of the Council noted this discrepancy between the United Nations text and that prepared by the Consultative Assembly of the Council of Europe. [16] In preparation for the first session of the Committee of Experts, in February 1950, Sir Oscar Dowson of the United Kingdom proposed a text similar to the one in the draft covenant. [17] The Committee of Experts accepted the proposal, noting in the report of its February session that the aim was to protect States Parties from 'activities which threaten the preservation of the democratic rights and freedoms themselves. This provision was inserted at the request of the Turkish representative and was taken from the Draft Covenant of the United Nations.' [18] It adopted the following text:

None of the preceding provisions may be interpreted as implying for any state, group or person, any right to engage in any activity or perform any act aimed at the destruction of any of the rights and

[12] Official Report of the Sitting [of the Consultative Assembly, 8 September 1949], II *TP* 14–274, at pp. 140–142.

[13] Ibid., p. 208.

[14] Recommendation No. 38 to the Committee of Ministers adopted 8 September 1949 on the conclusion of the debates, Doc. AS (1) 108, II *TP* 274–83.

[15] Report of the Fifth Session of the Commission on Human Rights to the Economic and Social Council, UN Doc. E/1371(Supp.), p. 25.

[16] Preparatory Report by the Secretariat-General concerning a Preliminary Draft Convention to Provide a Collective Guarantee of Human Rights, Doc. B 22, III *TP* 2–37, at p. 21.

[17] Amendments to Article 2 of the Recommendation of the Consultative Assembly proposed by the Expert of the United Kingdom, Doc. A 798, III *TP* 204–7.

[18] Preliminary Draft of the Report to the Committee of Ministers, 24 February 1950, Doc. CM/WP 1 (50) 1, A 847, III *TP* 246–79, at p. 266.

freedoms set forth herein or at their limitation to a greater extent than is already provided for in this Convention.[19]

At its second session, in March 1950, the Committee of Experts made only one minor change to the text, deleting the word 'already' between 'than is' and 'provided for'.[20] The report of the Committee contains the following comment:

The Turkish representative had mentioned the fact that there is in Turkey a law which forbids the diffusion of propaganda in favour of extremist ideas. In this connection the Committee stated that if, in any country, there exist special circumstances justifying certain exceptional restrictions of the freedom of expression, the right to apply these restrictions would be covered by Articles 4 and 6.[21]

The Conference of Senior Officials restored the words 'Nothing in this Convention' at the start of the provision, consistent with the original British proposal.[22] There were no further changes of any significance to the text of article 17. In the Consultative Assembly, which met in August 1950, both Turkish and Greek representatives returned to the importance of measures directed at the protection of democracy. On 21 October 1950, two weeks before the ceremony in Rome at which the Convention was to be signed, A.H. Robertson of the Secretariat wrote to H.J. Downing, a Foreign Office official in London, proposing that the comma following 'group or person' be deleted.[23] This change was implemented by the Committee of Ministers prior to signature of the text.

The heading 'Prohibition on the abuse of rights' was added according to the provisions of Protocol No. 11.[24]

Analysis and interpretation

There is some uncertainty as to whether article 17 operates as a principle of interpretation aimed at other provisions of the Convention or as an exception to admissibility. The opening words of article 17—'may be interpreted'—seem to indicate that the prohibition on abuse of rights is a principle of interpretation. Manfred Nowak, writing on the equivalent provision in the International Covenant on Civil and Political Rights, has described the norm as a 'rule of interpretation'.[25] Thus, it is to be taken into account in the application of the substantive rights set out in the Convention. As a rule of interpretation, it is of comparable legal value or authority to other rules of interpretation that are

[19] Draft text of the first section of a draft Convention based on the work of the Consultative Assembly, Doc. A 809, III *TP* 220–31, at p. 224.

[20] Appendix to the Report of the Committee of Experts to the Committee of Ministers—Draft Convention (16 March 1950), Doc. CM/WP 1 (50) 14 revised, A 925, IV *TP* 50–79, at p. 54.

[21] Report to the Committee of Ministers submitted by the Committee of Experts Instructed to Draw Up a Draft Convention of Collective Guarantee of Human Rights and Fundamental Freedoms, Doc. CM/WP 1 (5) 15, A 924, IV *TP* 2–55, at p. 18.

[22] Draft Convention annexed to the Report [of the Conference of Senior Officials], Doc. CM/WP 4 (50) 19 annex, CM/WP 4 (50) 16 rev., A 1452, IV *TP* 274–95, at p. 282.

[23] Letter addressed 21 October 1950 by Mr Robertson (Member of the Secretariat) to Mr Downing (Official of the Western Organisations Department, Foreign Office, London), VI *TP* 184–7, at p. 286.

[24] Protocol No. 11 to the Convention for the Protection of Human Rights and Fundamental Freedoms, restructuring the control machinery established thereby, ETS 155, art. 2(2).

[25] Manfred Nowak, *UN Covenant on Civil and Political Rights, CCPR Commentary*, 2nd rev. edn, Kehl, Germany: N.P. Engel, 2005, pp. 112–17, on art. 5, para. 1.

considered in the application of the Convention. Possibly it benefits from some special status among rules of interpretation because it is set out explicitly in a distinct provision. Nevertheless, States often invoke article 17 as if it is an exception to admissibility. They contend that the issue of abuse of rights is a matter to be determined at a preliminary stage prior to addressing the application on the merits.

There is some basis for both approaches in the case law of the Convention organs. Although certain of the decisions do not say explicitly that abuse of rights is being considered as a principle of interpretation, they decline to consider the article 17 issue as a preliminary question and turn immediately to the merits, saying that they 'begin by considering the question of compliance with [the relevant substantive provision of the Convention], whose requirements it will however assess in the light of Article 17'.[26] Sometimes consideration of abuse of rights is postponed and the substantive right, generally freedom of expression or freedom of association, is addressed first because '[o]nly when that review is complete will the Court be in a position to decide, in the light of all the circumstances of the case, whether Article 17 of the Convention should be applied'.[27] Usually in such cases the Court will then conclude that there is no violation of the substantive provision and consequently that it is unnecessary to consider article 17.[28]

Support for the approach whereby article 17 functions as a principle of interpretation can also be found in a dissenting opinion of three judges who stated that the applicant's expression was too remote for article 17 to apply but that 'the principle which underlies Article 17 is a factor which can properly be taken into account in the assessment of the exercise of the margin of appreciation and the existence of necessity'. The principle at stake, they said, was 'firm discouragement of the promotion of values hostile to those embodied in the Convention'.[29] In effect, they appeared to view article 17 as both a preliminary exception and an interpretative principle.

Some of the case law confirms an approach whereby article 17 is a preliminary issue going to the admissibility of the application in the strict sense. From this perspective, if article 17 applies, then there is no need for the Court to inquire as to whether or not the relevant substantive provisions of the Convention have been violated. Indeed, there may well be a violation, but the applicant is foreclosed from claiming a 'right to engage in any activity or perform any act aimed at the destruction of any of the rights and freedoms' in the Convention. Concern has been expressed that the application of article 17 in this way may 'disable the applicants from relying on Article 10',[30] implying that the article 17 determination not only precedes the examination of article 10 but obviates it entirely where article 17 applies. France successfully invoked article 17 as a preliminary issue in a case involving Holocaust denial.[31]

---

[26] *Lehideux and Isorni v. France*, 23 September 1998, § 38, *Reports of Judgments and Decisions* 1998-VII.

[27] *United Communist Party of Turkey and Others v. Turkey*, 30 January 1998, § 32, *Reports of Judgments and Decisions* 1998-I.

[28] Ibid., § 58.

[29] *Lehideux and Isorni v. France*, 23 September 1998, Joint Dissenting Opinion of Judges Foighel, Loizou and Sir Sir John Freeland, § 6, *Reports of Judgments and Decisions* 1998-VII.

[30] *Lehideux and Isorni v. France*, 23 September 1998, Joint Dissenting Opinion of Judges Foighel, Loizou, and Sir John Freeland, § 6, *Reports of Judgments and Decisions* 1998-VII.

[31] *Garaudy v. France* (dec.), no. 65831/01, ECHR 2003-IX. Also *Pierre Marais v. France*, no. 31159/96, Commission decision of 24 June 1996, DR 86, p. 184.

The prohibition on abuse of rights applies to 'any State, group or person'. Frequently, individual litigants invoke article 17 in support of their applications to the Court, sometimes together with article 13, but always in conjunction with a reference to the article containing the substantive right that they invoke. These are dismissed at the admissibility stage, with the Court's decision simply acknowledging that article 17 was alleged without any additional comment. Possibly, some applicants who invoke article 17 also have the final words of the provision in mind, contending that the State has limited their rights to a greater extent than is provided for in the Convention.

In practice, article 17 primarily serves to shelter actions by States directed at individuals and groups that advocate terrorism, the overthrow of democracy, racism, and other forms of discrimination. Yet the words of article 17 indicate that it also applies to States that may themselves be charged with the abuse of rights. This might arise in the context of an inter-State application to the Court. Moreover, the text concerns 'any State' and not only a Contracting State to the European Convention on Human Rights. This may take on more relevance as the extraterritorial reach of the Convention continues to grow. Referring to the equivalent text in the International Covenant on Civil and Political Rights, Christian Tomuschat described 'a provision designed to cover instances where formally rules under the Covenant seem to legitimise actions which substantially run counter to its purposes and general spirit. Thus, Governments may never use the limitation clauses supplementing the protected rights and freedoms to such an extent that the very substance of those rights and freedoms would be annihilated...'[32]

The destruction of Convention rights

The provision concerning abuse of rights was considered in the first case to come before the Court. In *Lawless v. Ireland*, the Court said that:

> the purpose of Article 17, in so far as it refers to groups or to individuals, is to make it impossible for them to derive from the Convention a right to engage in any activity or perform any act aimed at destroying any of the rights and freedoms set forth in the Convention;... therefore, no person may be able to take advantage of the provisions of the Convention to perform acts aimed at destroying the aforesaid rights and freedoms...[33]

These words have been cited repeatedly in cases concerning article 17.[34] The rationale for article 17 is deeply rooted in Europe's past and its experience with totalitarian and un-democratic regimes. The Court has referred to 'the very clear link between the Convention and democracy' and insisted that 'no one may be authorised to rely on the Convention's provisions in order to weaken or destroy the ideals and values of a democratic society'. It is not 'improbable that totalitarian movements might do away with democracy, after prospering under the democratic regime, there being examples of this in modern European history'.[35] According to the Court, 'the general purpose of

[32] *Delia Saldias de Lopez v. Uruguay*, no. 52/1979, UN Doc. CCPR/C/OP/1, p. 88 § 12.3; *Lilian Celiberti de Casariego v. Uruguay*, no. 56/1979, UN Doc. CCPR/C/OP/1, p. 92, § 10.3.

[33] *Lawless v. Ireland*, 1 July 1961, § 7, pp. 45–6, Series A no. 3.

[34] *Ould Dah v. France* (dec.), no. 13113/03, ECHR 2009; *Paksas v. Lithuania* [GC], no. 34932/04, § 87, ECHR 2011 (extracts); *Leroy v. France*, no. 36109/03, § 26, 2 October 2008; *United Communist Party of Turkey and Others v. Turkey*, 30 January 1998, § 60, *Reports of Judgments and Decisions* 1998-I.

[35] *Kasymakhunov and Saybatalov v. Russia*, nos 26261/05 and 26377/06, § 104, 14 March 2013; *Refah Partisi (the Welfare Party) and Others v. Turkey* [GC], nos 41340/98, 41342/98, 41343/98, and 41344/98, § 99, ECHR 2003-II.

Article 17 is to prevent totalitarian groups from exploiting in their own interests the principles enunciated by the Convention'.[36]

Because of its relationship to the fundamental values underlying the Convention, article 17 does not apply to reprehensible views or expressions that do not fit within this perspective.[37] A case filed against France concerning a satirical cartoon published in a Basque nationalist journal following the attacks on the World Trade Centre in September 2001 illustrates this. The cartoon showed the collapsed buildings with a caption, apparently inspired by a commercial advertising campaign, saying 'Nous en avions tous rêvé... Le Hamas l'a fait'. The applicant submitted that he wanted to depict the destruction of the American empire. He was prosecuted, together with the publisher, for 'apologie du terrorisme'. Declaring that article 17 was not applicable, the Court said that 'le message de fond visé par le requérant—la destruction de l'impérialisme américain—ne vise pas la négation de droits fondamentaux et n'a pas d'égal avec des propos dirigés contre les valeurs qui sous-tendent la Convention tels que le racisme, l'antisémitisme ou l'islamophobie'.[38] Then, examining the restriction on freedom of expression within the framework of article 10(2), the Court concluded that there was no violation of the Convention.[39] The provision was not applicable to a challenge to impeachment based upon article 3 of Protocol No. 1 by the former head of State of Lithuania.[40]

Article 17 is obviously most relevant in cases involving articles 8, 9, 10, and 11 of the Convention. Indeed, while it may not be necessary 'to take away every one of the rights and freedoms guaranteed from groups and persons engaged in activities contrary to the text and spirit of the Convention, the Court has found that the freedoms of religion, expression and association guaranteed by Articles 9, 10 and 11 of the Convention are covered by Article 17'.[41] In one decision involving restrictions on broadcasting interviews with leaders of the Sinn Fein Party in Ireland, the European Commission explicitly linked articles 10(2) and 17: 'By allowing, in Article 10 para. 2 (Art. 10-2), certain restrictions on the exercise of the freedom of expression, the Convention recognises the principle that no group or person has the right to pursue activities which aim at the destruction of any of the rights and freedom enshrined in it (cf. Article 17 (Art. 17) of the Convention).'[42] Article 17 is negative in scope, and cannot be invoked by a State in order to deprive a physical person of fundamental individual rights such as those in articles 5 and 6.[43] Article 17 'is applicable only on an exceptional basis and in extreme cases'.[44]

---

[36] *W.P. and Others v. Poland* (dec.), no.42264/98, ECHR 2004-VII; *Norwood v. the United Kingdom* (dec.), no. 23131/03, 16 November 2004, *Reports of Judgments and Decisions* 2004-VII (extracts); *Witzsch v. Germany* (dec.), no. 7485/03, 13 December 2005; *Kasymakhunov and Saybatalov v. Russia*, nos 26261/05 and 26377/06, § 103, 14 March 2013.

[37] *Paksas v. Lithuania* [GC], no. 34932/04, § 88, ECHR 2011 (extracts); *Lehideux and Isorni v. France*, 23 September 1998, § 53, *Reports of Judgments and Decisions* 1998-VII.

[38] *Leroy v. France*, no. 36109/03, § 27, 2 October 2008.

[39] Ibid., § 48.

[40] *Paksas v. Lithuania* [GC], no. 34932/04, § 89, ECHR 2011 (extracts).

[41] *W.P. and Others v. Poland* (dec.), no.42264/98, ECHR 2004-VII (extracts); *Garaudy v. France* (dec.), no. 65831/01, ECHR 2003-IX; *Pavel Ivanov v. Russia* (dec.), no. 35222/04, 20 February 2007; *Hizb ut-Tahrir and Others v. Germany* (dec.), no. 31098/08, §§ 72–75 and 78, 12 June 2012; *Kasymakhunov and Saybatalov v. Russia*, nos 26261/05 and 26377/06, § 103, 14 March 2013.

[42] *Purcell and Others. v. Ireland*, no. 15404/89, Commission decision of 16 April 1991, (1991) 34 YB 90.

[43] *Ould Dah v. France* (dec.), no. 13113/03, ECHR 2009; *Varela Geis v. Spain*, no. 61005/09, § 40, 5 March 2013.

[44] *Paksas v. Lithuania* [GC], no. 34932/04, § 87, ECHR 2011 (extracts).

There is a relationship between article 17 and the restrictions clauses that comprise the second paragraphs of articles 9, 10, and 11. Arguably, article 17 might be deemed unnecessary if the position that activities amounting to promotion of anti-democratic and discriminatory views may be restricted pursuant to the well-recognized principles of proportionality and necessity. Indeed, sometimes the Court will respond to article 17 by noting the close relationship with the issue of restrictions and limitations.[45] In a Belgian case involving racist propaganda, the Court said the content of the offending materials did not justify the application of article 17, but went on to hold that in prosecuting the applicants for disseminating the material Belgium had not breached article 10.[46] In that case, three members of the Chamber dissented[47] and it may well be that it was easier for the majority to address the matter under article 10, where there is more room for nuance in the proportionality analysis, than article 17.

In a Turkish case concerning dissolution of a political party, the Grand Chamber examined the matter under article 11(2). Concluding that the impugned measures were proportionate, it said there was no need for a separate discussion of the applicability of article 17.[48] Sometimes it seems artificial or awkward to separate the analysis under article 10 from that concerning article 17. In a case concerning two persons accused of the crime of 'publicly defending collaboration' by expressing sympathy for the collaborationist Vichy regime during wartime, the Grand Chamber said it would begin 'by considering the question of compliance with Article 10, whose requirements it will however assess in the light of Article 17'.[49] It proceeded by concluding that the conviction breached article 10(1) and was not justified by article 10(2); consequently, there was no need to examine the application of article 17.[50] The Court has reached similar conclusions in a case involving dissolution of a political party with anti-democratic views. The measures taken by the State were justified by article 11(2), and as a result there was no need to consider the application of article 17.[51]

In other cases, the Court has found insufficient evidence or an absence of evidence that the applicant had relied upon the Convention to engage in activity or perform acts aimed at the destruction of any of the rights and freedoms set forth in it.[52] The Court refused to apply article 17 in the case of a racist organisation threatened with dissolution. It distinguished the case from decisions of the Commission and the Court concerning freedom of expression. It said that '[i]n these circumstances, the Court cannot conclude that the Association's activities were intended to justify or propagate totalitarian oppression serving "totalitarian groups"'.[53]

---

[45] *Féret v. Belgium*, no. 15615/07, § 52, 16 July 2009.

[46] Ibid., § 82.

[47] Ibid., Opinion dissidente du Juge Andràs Sajó laquelle declarant se rallier les Juges Vladimiro Zagrebelsky et Nona Tsotsoria.

[48] *Refah Partisi (the Welfare Party) and Others v. Turkey* [GC], nos 41340/98, 41342/98, 41343/98, and 41344/98, § 137, ECHR 2003-II.

[49] *Lehideux and Isorni v. France*, 23 September 1998, § 14, *Reports of Judgments and Decisions* 1998-VII.

[50] Ibid., § 58.

[51] *Refah Partisi (the Welfare Party) and Others v. Turkey* [GC], nos 41340/98, 41342/98, 41343/98, and 41344/98, §§ 136–137, ECHR 2003-II. Also *Refah Partisi (the Welfare Party) and Others v. Turkey*, nos 41340/98, 41342/98, 41343/98, and 41344/98, §§ 84–85, 31 July 2001.

[52] *Association of Citizens Radko and Paunkovski v. 'the former Yugoslav Republic of Macedonia'*, no. 74651/01, § 77, ECHR 2009 (extracts); *United Communist Party of Turkey and Others v. Turkey*, 30 January 1998, § 60, *Reports of Judgments and Decisions* 1998-I.

[53] *Vona v. Hungary*, no. 35943/10, § 37, 9 July 2013.

Hungary invoked article 17 in response to a charge that it had violated freedom of expression by prosecuting a person for wearing a red star as a symbol of the international workers' movement. Hungarian law makes use of totalitarian symbols, including the hammer and sickle or red star associated with communist and socialist movements, a crime. The Court distinguished the case from decisions dealing with Nazi sympathizers. It noted that the Hungarian government had not argued that the applicant expressed contempt for the victims of a totalitarian regime or that he belonged to a group with totalitarian ambitions. According to the Court, the applicant was an official in a registered left-wing political party who wore the contested red star at one of its lawful demonstrations. In these circumstances, the Court could not conclude that its display was intended to justify or propagate totalitarian oppression serving 'totalitarian groups'. It was merely the symbol of lawful left-wing political movements. Unlike other article 17 cases, the expression that was sanctioned in the instant case was unrelated to racist propaganda.[54]

The Court has applied article 17 to Islamophobic[55] or anti-Semitic[56] statements and organizations,[57] racist expression,[58] and to the advocacy of a political regime that discriminates against women.[59] It has also been invoked against an organization whose programme challenged the right of the State of Israel to exist, that called for its violent destruction and banishment and killing of its inhabitants.[60] The Court used article 17 with respect to an organization that called for establishing a regime that rejected political freedoms, proposing to ban all political parties that were not based on Islam and to introduce capital punishment for apostasy.[61] Statements pursuing the unequivocal aim of justifying war crimes such as torture or summary executions likewise amounted to deflecting article 10 from its real purpose.[62]

The Grand Chamber has spoken of a 'category of clearly established historical facts—such as the Holocaust—whose negation or revision would be removed from the protection of Article 10 by Article 17'.[63] Revisionist or 'denialist' writing that challenges the historic truth of the Nazi crimes has been held to run 'counter to the fundamental values of the Convention and of democracy, namely justice and peace'.[64] But the Court has resisted the proposition that when it is a feature of the historical context or the legal qualification and the responsibilities that are in dispute rather than the underlying facts, freedom of expression cannot be removed from the protection of the Convention by virtue of article 17.[65]

[54] *Vajnai v. Hungary*, no. 33629/06, § 25, ECHR 2008.
[55] *Norwood v. the United Kingdom* (dec.), no. 23131/03, *Reports of Judgments and Decisions* 2004-VII.
[56] *Pavel Ivanov v. Russia* (dec.), no. 35222/04, 20 February 2007.
[57] *Paksas v. Lithuania* [GC], no. 34932/04, §§ 81–89, ECHR 2011 (extracts); *W.P. and Others v. Poland* (dec.), no. 42264/98, ECHR 2004-VII (extracts).
[58] *J. Glimmerveen and J. Hagenbeek v. the Netherlands*, nos 8348/78 and 8406/78 (joined), Commission decision of 11 October 1979, (1980) 23 YB 366, DR 18, p. 187.
[59] *Kasymakhunov and Saybatalov v. Russia*, nos 26261/05 and 26377/06, § 110, 14 March 2013.
[60] *Hizb Ut-Tahrir and others v. Germany*, no. 31098/08, § 73, 12 June 2012; *Kasymakhunov and Saybatalov v. Russia*, nos 26261/05 and 26377/06, §§ 106–107, 14 March 2013.
[61] *Kasymakhunov and Saybatalov v. Russia*, nos 26261/05 and 26377/06, § 109, 14 March 2013.
[62] *Orban and Others v. France*, no. 20985/05, § 35, 15 January 2005.
[63] *Lehideux and Isorni v. France*, 23 September 1998, § 47, *Reports of Judgments and Decisions* 1998-VII.
[64] *Garaudy v. France* (dec.), no. 65831/01, ECHR 2003-IX; *Witzsch v. Germany* (dec.), no. 4785/03, 13 December 2005.
[65] *Fatullayev v. Azerbaijan*, no. 40984/07, § 82, 22 April 2010.

It seems that the actual motive of the applicant is germane to the analysis. Where cases concern freedom of expression, the Court seems concerned about what the applicants intend, rather than whether or not the impugned speech or publication is in fact properly subject to limitation or restriction in accordance with article 10(2) of the Convention. Evidence of this can be found in some judgments, where the Court speaks of activity or acts *aimed* at the destruction of any of the rights and freedoms set forth in the Convention.[66] In a case involving an extremist political party in Turkey, the Court said that 'it cannot be ruled out that the passages concerned may conceal a different political design from the publicly proclaimed one'. Nevertheless, 'given the absence of any concrete acts suggesting otherwise' it found no reason to doubt the genuineness of the party's programme.[67] Consequently, the State could not avail of article 17 because there was nothing to suggest the applicant 'relied on the Convention to engage in activity or perform acts aimed at the destruction of any of the rights and freedoms set forth in it'.[68]

'Limitation to a greater extent'

The final words of article 17 prohibit 'any State, group or person' from engaging in an activity or performing an act aimed at limitation to a greater extent than is provided for in the Convention. In reality, and in contrast with the abuse of rights norm set out earlier in the provision, this is directed at States. It is in this context that many litigants invoke article 17, generally as an adjunct argument to a claim that one of the substantive rights has been violated. Almost invariably, the Court simply ignores such references to article 17. There are only a few examples in the case law of the interpretation and application of the final portion of article 17. They concern the claim that in spite of the absence of an explicit restriction or limitation clause, similar to what is found in articles 8, 9, 10, and 11, certain other rights enshrined in the Convention are not absolute, but are subject to implicit limitations.

In *Golder v. The United Kingdom*, the Court examined whether the right of access to a court was not only implied within the Convention but was also unlimited:

The Court considers, accepting the views of the Commission and the alternative submission of the Government, that the right of access to the courts is not absolute. As this is a right which the Convention sets forth (see Articles 13, 14, 17 and 25) (art. 13, art. 14, art. 17, art. 25) without, in the narrower sense of the term, defining, there is room, apart from the bounds delimiting the very content of any right, for limitations permitted by implication.[69]

Judge Zekia spoke to the matter in his separate opinion:

Article 17 (art. 17) provides, inter alia, that no limitation to a greater extent than is provided for in the Convention is allowed to the rights and freedoms set forth therein. The relevance of this Article (art. 17) lies in the fact that, if right of access is to be read into Article 6 para. 1 (art. 6-1), such right of access will have to be an absolute one because no restrictions or limitations are mentioned in regard to this right. No one can seriously argue that the Convention contemplates an absolute and unfettered right of access to courts.[70]

---

[66] *Freedom and Democracy Party* (ÖZDEP) *v. Turkey* [GC], no. 23885/94, §§ 46–47, ECHR 1999-VIII.
[67] Ibid., § 42.
[68] Ibid.
[69] *Golder v. the United Kingdom*, 21 February 1975, § 38, Series A no. 18.
[70] Ibid., Separate Opinion of Judge Zekia.

The Court returned to the point, with a less enigmatic discussion of article 17, in a case concerning the requirement that hearings be held in public:

It is true that the Court has recognised that to a certain extent the right of access to the courts secured by Article 6 (art. 6) may be subject to limitations permitted by implication (see the above-mentioned Golder judgment, Series A no. 18, pp. 18–19, para. 38). However, that recognition resulted from the fact that the right in question was inherent in the first sentence of Article 6 para. 1 (art. 6-1) but was not defined therein. Again, unlike the first sentence, the second sentence does already contain a detailed list of express exceptions. Bearing in mind the terms of Article 17 (art. 17) and the importance of the principle of publication (see, inter alia, the Sutter judgment of 22 February 1984, Series A no. 74, p. 12, para. 26), the Court does not consider that that principle may be regarded as subject to an implied limitation as suggested by the Government.[71]

With respect to article 5, the Court again considered whether there were implied limitations in *Ireland v. the United Kingdom*:

Paragraph 1 of Article 5 (art. 5-1) contains a list of the cases in which it is permissible under the Convention to deprive someone of his liberty. Subject to Article 15 (art. 15)—and without prejudice to Article 1 of Protocol No. 4 (P4-1) which the United Kingdom has not ratified—, that list is exhaustive: this appears from the words 'save in the following cases' and is confirmed by Article 17 (art. 17).[72]

Case law of the Court recognizes that rights considered to be implicit may also be subject to implied restrictions or limitations. This seems merely logical. But the import of article 17 *in fine* is that no right set out explicitly in the Convention may be limited by implication.[73] The 'implied limitation' that the Court will acknowledge with respect to certain rights has another consequence. The Court does not apply the traditional notions of 'necessity' or 'pressing social need' in assessing the permissibility of such a limitation. Instead, it tends to look in a general sense at whether the limitation is arbitrary or lacks proportionality.[74]

Contrasting approaches can be seen in the decision of the Commission and the judgment of the Court in *Sporrong and Lönnroth*. The Commission noted that it had already found that permits and prohibitions related to expropriation were lawful measures imposed in the general interest and with respect for proportionality. It said that the applicants had produced no evidence to show that the restrictions on their right to peaceful enjoyment of possessions were aimed at its 'limitation to a greater extent than is provided for in the Convention', and that consequently there was no violation of articles 17.[75] The Court adopted what has been called the 'absorption approach'.[76]

---

[71] *Campbell and Fell v. the United Kingdom*, 28 June 1984, § 90, Series A no. 80.

[72] *Ireland v. the United Kingdom*, 18 January 1978, § 194, Series A no. 25.

[73] Jacques Velu and Rusen Ergec, *La Convention européenne des droits de l'homme*, Brussels: Bruylant, 1990, p. 155.

[74] *Ždanoka v. Latvia* [GC], no. 58278/00, § 115, ECHR 2006-IV; *Saccomanno and Others v. Italy*, no. 11583/08, § 49, 13 March 2012.

[75] *Sporrong and Lönnroth v. Sweden*, nos 7151/75 and 7152/75, Commission report of 8 October 1980, § 123.

[76] Yutaka Arai, 'Prohibition of Abuse of the Rights and Freedoms Set Forth in the Convention and of their Limitation to a Greater Extent than is Provided for in the Convention (Article 17)', in Van Dijk et al., *Theory and Practice*, pp. 1083–92, at p. 1092.

It dismissed any relevance of article 17 given that it had already ruled there was no violation of article 1 of Protocol No. 1.[77]

Declarations

Spain made an interpretative declaration to the effect that article 17 permits adoption of measures contemplated in articles 55 and 116 of the Spanish Constitution.[78]

Further reading

Yutaka Arai, 'Prohibition of Abuse of the Rights and Freedoms Set Forth in the Convention and of their Limitation to a Greater Extent than is Provided for in the Convention (Article 17)', in Van Dijk et al., *Theory and Practice*, pp. 1083–92.

Antoine Buyse, 'Contested Contours: The Limits of Freedom of Expression from an Abuse of Rights Perspective—Article 10 and 17 ECHR', in Eva Brems and Janneke Gerards, eds, *Shaping Rights in the ECHR*, Cambridge: Cambridge University Press, 2013, pp. 183–210.

Hannes Cannie and Dirk Voorhoof, 'The Abuse Clause and Freedom of Expression in the European Human Rights Convention: An Added Value for Democracy and Human Rights Protection?', (2011) 29 *Netherlands Quarterly of Human Rights* 54.

S. van Drooghenbroek, 'L'article 17 de la Convention européenne des droits de l'homme est-il indispensable?', (2001) 46 *RTDH* 541.

Frowein/Peukert, *MenschenRechtsKonvention*, pp. 430–3.

David Keane, 'Attacking Hate Speech under Article 17 of the European Convention on Human Rights', (2007) 25 *Netherlands Quarterly of Human Rights* 641.

Pierre Le Mire, 'Article 17', in Pettiti et al., *La Convention européenne*, pp. 509–22.

Harris et al., *Law of the European Convention*, pp. 648–51.

Javier García Roca, 'Abuse of Fundamental Rights and Defence of Democracy (Art. 17 ECHR)', in Javier García Roca and Pablo Santolaya, *Europe of Rights: A Compendium on the European Convention of Human Rights*, Leiden/Boston: Martinus Nijhoff, 2012, pp. 503–26.

Alphonse Spielmann, 'La Convention européenne des droits de l'homme et l'abus de droit', in G. Flécheux, ed., *Mélanges en hommage à Louis Edmond Pettiti*, Brussels: Bruylant, 1998, pp. 673–86.

Jacques Velu and Rusen Ergec, *La Convention européenne des droits de l'homme*, Brussels: Bruylant, 1990, pp. 153–5.

---

[77] *Sporrong and Lönnroth v. Sweden*, 23 September 1982, § 76, Series A no. 52.
[78] (1979) 22 YB 24–25.

Article 18. Limitation on use of restrictions on rights/Limitation de l'usage des restrictions aux droits

The restrictions permitted under this Convention to the said rights and freedoms shall not be applied for any purpose other than those for which they have been prescribed.	Les restrictions qui, aux termes de la présente Convention, sont apportées auxdits droits et libertés ne peuvent être appliquées que dans le but pour lequel elles ont été prévues.

Introductory comments

Article 18 is one of the strangest provisions in the Convention. It has no counterpart in the Universal Declaration of Human Rights or in the human rights treaties adopted within the United Nations, nor is it reproduced in the European Union Charter of Fundamental Rights. The drafting history provides virtually no insight to assist in its interpretation. The case law is exceedingly sparse. Francis Jacobs wrote that article 18 adds little to the Convention other than confirming what is already set out explicitly or implicitly in other provisions or what is established under general principles of international law.[1] Vincent Coussirat-Coustere described it as 'une disposition apparemment inutile', although one that had served a role by influencing the interpretation of the Convention.[2]

Drafting of the provision

No doubt inspired by article 29(2) of the Universal Declaration of Human Rights, whereby limitations are permitted in a general sense upon all rights, the European Movement draft recognized that rights were 'subject only to such limitations as are in conformity with the general principle of law recognised by civilised nations and as are prescribed by law for: (a) protecting the legal rights of others; (b) meeting the just requirements of morality public order (including the safety of the community), and the general welfare'.[3] The Committee of Experts, which met in February and March 1950, began to develop specialized limitations clauses applicable to certain provisions in the draft convention. These are the ancestors of article 8(2), 9(2), 10(2), and 11(2).

Only in the Conference of Senior Officials on Human Rights, convened by the Committee of Ministers in June 1950, did the beginnings of article 18 appear. The proposal read as follows: 'The restrictions to the said rights and freedoms shall not be applied for any other purpose than those for which they have been adopted.'[4] It was

---

[1] Francis Jacobs, 'To What Extent Have Restrictions on the Enjoyment of Freedoms Evolved?', in *Proceedings of the 4th International Colloquy about the European Convention on Human Rights*, Strasbourg: Council of Europe, 1976, pp. 187–210, at p. 199.

[2] Vincent Coussirat-Coustere, 'Article 18', in Pettiti et al., *La Convention européenne*, pp. 523–7, at p. 527.

[3] Convention for the Collective Protection of Individual Rights and Democratic Liberties by the States, Members of the Council of Europe, and for the establishment of a European Court of Human Rights to ensure observance of the Convention, Doc. INF/5/E/R, I *TP* 296–303, at p. 298, art. 3.

[4] New draft alternatives B and B/2, Doc. CM/WP 4 (50) 9, A 1372, IV *TP* 182–91, at p. 190.

placed as the second paragraph of draft article 15, the first paragraph being the non-discrimination provision that eventually became article 14 in the final version. A revised version prepared by the Conference replaced 'the said' with 'these' and 'adopted' with 'prescribed'.[5] The Report listed it as one of the 'general principles' of the Convention, describing it as 'the application of the theory of the misapplication of power'.[6]

The Committee of Ministers, meeting in August 1950, revised the text somewhat: 'The restrictions permitted under this Convention to these rights and freedoms shall not be applied for any purpose other than those for which they have been prescribed.'[7] When the Committee of Ministers met in Rome in November 1950 to adopt the final text of the Convention, a Committee of Experts made a slight amendment to article 18, re-introducing the term 'the said rights and freedoms' in replacement of 'these rights and freedoms'.[8]

The heading 'Limitation on use of restriction on rights' was added according by Protocol No. 11.[9]

Analysis and interpretation

Article 18 imposes a limitation on the limitations, declaring that 'restrictions permitted under this Convention to the said rights and freedoms shall not be applied for any purpose other than those for which they have been prescribed'. The European Commission described article 18 as a provision dealing with 'abuse of restrictions', focusing its consideration on the purpose for which the State was imposing restrictions on a Convention right.[10] Article 18 confirms a component of intention or purpose with respect to restrictions under the Convention: they may only be imposed for the purposes that are permitted under the relevant provision. For example, the Court has indicated that article 18 may inform the debate about 'lawfulness' in article 5(1) in this way.[11] It requires that restrictions not be 'arbitrary or effected for an ulterior purpose'.[12]

Subsidiary in nature, article 18 can only be invoked with respect to another provision of the Convention. It has no autonomous role.[13] As the European Commission noted in an early Report,

Art. 18, like Art. 14 of the Convention, does not have an autonomous role. It can only be applied in conjunction with other Articles of the Convention. There may, however, be a violation of Art. 18 in

---

[5] Draft Convention annexed to the Report [of the Conference of Senior Officials], Doc. CM/WP 4 (50) 19 annex, CM/WP 4 (50) 16 rev., A 1452, IV *TP* 274–295, at p. 282.

[6] Text of the report submitted by the Conference [of Senior Officials] to the Committee of Ministers, Doc. CM/WP 4 (50) 19, CM/WP 4 (50) 16 rev., A 1431, IV *TP* 242–73, at p. 258.

[7] Draft Convention adopted by the Sub-Committee, Doc. CM 1 (50) 52, A 1884, V *TP* 76–99, at p. 84; Draft Convention adopted by the Committee of Ministers, 7 August 1950, Doc. A 1937, V *TP* 120–45, at p. 130.

[8] Report of the Committee of Legal Experts, 2–3 November 1950, Doc. CM/Adj. (50) 3 Rev., A 2531, VII *TP* 10–13.

[9] Protocol No. 11 to the Convention for the Protection of Human Rights and Fundamental Freedoms, restructuring the control machinery established thereby, ETS 155, art. 2(2).

[10] *Sporrong and Lönnroth v. Sweden*, nos 7151/75 and 7152/75, Commission report of 8 October 1980, § 123.

[11] *Ashingdane v. the United Kingdom*, 28 May 1985, § 45, Series A no. 93.

[12] Ibid., § 48.

[13] *Ilgar Mammadov v. Azerbaijan*, no. 15172/13, § 137, 22 May 2014; *Gusinskiy v. Russia*, no. 70276/01, § 75, ECHR 2004-IV.

connection with another Article, although there is no violation of that Article taken alone. It follows further from the terms of Art. 18 that a violation can only arise where the right or freedom concerned is subject to 'restrictions permitted under this Convention'.[14]

The Convention allows rights to be restricted in a number of explicit provisions, of which the most classic are the restriction or limitations clauses in the second paragraphs of articles 8, 9, 10, and 11 of the Convention, and the equivalent provision in article 2(3) of Protocol No. 4. But there are many other ways in which Convention rights are limited. For example, the right to life, set out in article 2, is subject to the most notorious of all limitations, the possibility of capital punishment. Article 1(2) of Protocol No. 7 allows for expulsion of aliens even when procedural safeguards have not been fully complied with when this is deemed 'necessary in the interests of public order or is grounded on reasons of national security'. Moreover, implied restrictions or limitations on Convention rights have been recognized in the case law of the Convention organs with respect to many provisions, including the right to a fair trial[15] and to free and fair elections.[16] Finally, and perhaps most significant of all, are the restrictions and limitations contained in the provisions contiguous to article 18: the non-application of certain Convention provisions to the political activity of non-nationals in article 16 and the prohibition of abuse of rights in article 17. Arguably, derogation under article 15 might also be deemed a 'restriction' permitted under the Convention.

For example, in *Kamma v. The Netherlands*, the European Commission considered article 18 with regard to article 5, assessing whether detention was imposed for any reasons other than those permitted in the Convention. The applicant had been detained on remand in one criminal investigation. He claimed that this situation was exploited by the police in order to facilitate the investigation of another matter, with the result that detention was improperly protracted. After analysing the facts, and without any discussion about the interpretation and application of article 18, the Commission concluded that 'there has been no breach of Art. 18 read in conjunction with Art. 5 of the Convention'.[17]

There are few examples of violations of article 18 in the case law of the Court. Clearly, there is a simmering dispute among members of the Court about the evidentiary requirements. Some judgments speak of 'a very exacting standard of proof' with respect to allegations that article 18 has been breached. An applicant who charges that the State has a 'hidden agenda' or an improper reason for restricting rights 'must convincingly show that the real aim of the authorities was not the same as that proclaimed or which could be reasonably inferred from the context'.[18] Mere suspicion that purposes other than those defined in the Convention lie behind an infringement are insufficient.[19] The reason for

---

[14] *Kamma v. the Netherlands*, no. 4774/71, Commission report of 14 July 1974, (1975) 18 YB 301, at pp. 316–22, DR 1, p. 4. Also *Bozano v. France*, no. 9990/82, Commission decision of 15 May 1984, (1984) 27 YB 118; *Oates v. Poland* (dec.), no. 35036/97, 11 May 2000; *Gusinskiy v. Russia*, no. 70276/01, § 73, ECHR 2004-IV; *Ramishvili and Kokhreidze v. Georgia* (dec.), no. 1704/06, 27 June 2007.

[15] *Golder v. the United Kingdom*, 21 February 1975, § 38, Series A no. 18; *Campbell and Fell v. the United Kingdom*, 28 June 1984, § 90, Series A no. 80.

[16] *Ždanoka v. Latvia* [GC], no. 58278/00, § 115, ECHR 2006-IV; *Saccomanno and Others v. Italy*, no. 11583/08, § 49, 13 March 2012.

[17] *Kamma v. the Netherlands*, no. 4774/71, Commission report of 14 July 1974, (1975) 18 YB 300, at pp. 316–22, DR 1, p. 4.

[18] *Ilgar Mammadov v. Azerbaijan*, no. 15172/13, § 138, 22 May 2014; *Lutsenko v. Ukraine*, no. 6492/11, §§ 108–109, 3 July 2012.

[19] *Khodorkovskiy v. Russia*, no. 5829/04, § 255, 31 May 2011.

this is that 'the whole structure of the Convention rests on the general assumption that public authorities in the member States act in good faith', although the presumption is certainly rebuttable.[20] Were the standard of proof not so high, 'the Court would have to find violations in every high-profile case where the applicant's status, wealth, reputation, etc. gives rise to a suspicion that the driving force behind his or her prosecution was improper'.[21] On the other hand, direct knowledge of what the Court has called a 'hidden agenda' will almost invariably lie with the authorities. Evidence of improper motives necessarily relies on 'inferences drawn from the concrete circumstances and the context of the case'.[22]

One of the handful of cases of a breach of article 18 concerned the criminal investigation of a Russian businessman who was in a bitter conflict with a State gas company. The Court concluded that the applicant had been arrested 'for the purpose of bringing him before the competent legal authority on reasonable suspicion of having committed an offence', as authorized by article 5(1)(c) of the Convention. In fact, he was being detained in order to pressure him to transfer shares in his business. Concluding that there was a violation of article 18 in conjunction with article 5, the Court said 'it is not the purpose of such public-law matters as criminal proceedings and detention on remand to be used as part of commercial bargaining strategies'.[23] In another finding of violation of article 18, also involving complex commercial matters, the Court considered that there was no reasonable suspicion a crime had been committed and that the arrest of the applicant was in reality directed to a lawsuit that he had filed.[24] But in a Russian case involving prosecution of very wealthy businessmen, the Court recognized elements of 'improper motivation' but said that this did not make the prosecution illegitimate 'from the beginning to the end'. It said the accusations against the applicants remained serious and that they had a 'healthy core', despite the 'mixed intent' of the authorities.[25]

Some cases have involved political opponents of the government, although there has been some reluctance to ascribe the motivation of the authorities as being the targeting of their adversaries. Rather, it has focused on disputes related to the operation of the criminal justice system. The Court found that 'both the factual context and the reasoning advanced by the authorities' showed the actual purpose for the detention of the former Prime Minister of Ukraine, Yuliya Volodymyrivna Tymoshenko, to be 'to punish the applicant for a lack of respect towards the court which it was claimed she had been manifesting by her behaviour during the proceedings'.[26] In another Ukrainian case, the Court cited the reasoning of the prosecuting authorities as evidence they sought to punish the applicant 'for publicly disagreeing with accusations against him and for asserting his innocence, which he had the right to do'.[27]

---

[20] *Ilgar Mammadov v. Azerbaijan*, no. 15172/13, § 137, 22 May 2014.

[21] *Khodorkovskiy and Lebedev v. Russia*, nos 11082/06 and 13772/05, § 903, 25 July 2013.

[22] *Tymoshenko v. Ukraine*, no. 49872/11, Joint Concurring Opinion of Judges Jungwiert, Nussberger, and Potocki, 30 April 2013. Also *Georgia v. Russia (I)* [GC], no. 13255/07, Partly Dissenting Opinion of Judge Tsotsoria, 3 July 2014.

[23] *Gusinskiy v. Russia*, no. 70276/01, §§ 73–78, ECHR 2004-IV.

[24] *Cebotari v. Moldova*, no. 35615/06, § 53, 13 November 2007.

[25] *Khodorkovskiy and Lebedev v. Russia*, nos 11082/06 and 13772/05, § 908, 25 July 2013.

[26] *Tymoshenko v. Ukraine*, no. 49872/11, § 299, 30 April 2013.

[27] *Lutsenko v. Ukraine*, no. 6492/11, § 109, 3 July 2012.

In the *Tymoshenko case*, three judges wished to take this a step further, holding that the measures of detention resulted from 'the applicant's identity and influence as a leading opposition politician in Ukraine'.[28] In an application filed against Azerbaijan, a unanimous Chamber of the Court concluded that measures restricting the liberty of an individual were not applied for the purposes authorized by article 5(1)(c) of the Convention, that is, to bring him before a competent legal authority on reasonable suspicion of having committed an offence, but rather 'that the actual purpose of the impugned measures was to silence or punish the applicant for criticising the Government and attempting to disseminate what he believed was the true information that the Government were trying to hide'.[29]

In the first *Georgia v. Russia* inter-State case, dissenting Judge Tsotsoria considered that article 18 had been violated with respect to the 'anti-Georgian campaign', whose real purpose was 'retaliation, employed for ulterior motives contrary to the rules of international law rather than a legitimate migration control measure as claimed by the respondent State'.[30] She relied upon the concurring opinion of Judges Jungwiert, Nußberger and Potocki in *Tymoshenko v. Ukraine*, where they said that 'in interpreting Article 18 of the Convention the direct link between human rights protection and democracy must be taken into account'.[31]

Litigants frequently invoke article 18 in support of claims that are founded in other provisions of the Convention and its Protocols. Almost invariably, the Court acknowledges the reference to article 18 but determines that it is unnecessary to address the provision separately.[32] In one case, it briefly described the applicant's complaint, noted that the government had made no answer or submission on the point, and dismissed the claim.[33] In another, it observed that the Commission had found allegations based on article 18 to be 'unsubstantiated' and said only that it agreed.[34] The Commission had done no more than dismiss the complaint under article 18 without explanation.[35] In a case where an article 18 complaint was dismissed by the Commission with respect to one of two litigants, the Court said it would not consider the issue on its own motion with respect to the other applicant.[36]

---

[28] *Tymoshenko v. Ukraine*, no. 49872/11, Joint Concurring Opinion of Judges Jungwiert, Nußberger, and Potocki, 30 April 2013.

[29] *Ilgar Mammadov v. Azerbaijan*, no. 15172/13, § 143, 22 May 2014.

[30] *Georgia v. Russia (I)* [GC], no. 13255/07, Partly Dissenting Opinion of Judge Tsotsoria, 3 July 2014.

[31] Ibid., citing *Tymoshenko v. Ukraine*, no. 49872/11, Joint Concurring Opinion of Judges Jungwiert, Nußberger, and Potocki, 30 April 2013.

[32] *Navalnyy and Yashin v. Russia*, no. 76204/11, § 117, 4 December 2014; *Öcalan v. Turkey* [GC], no. 46221/99, § 206, ECHR 2005-IV; *Refah Partisi (the Welfare Party) and Others v. Turkey* [GC], nos 41340/98, 41342/98, 41343/98, and 41344/98, § 137, ECHR 2003-II; *Orhan v. Turkey*, no. 25656/94, § 402, ECHR 2002; *Beyeler v. Italy* [GC], no. 33202/96, §§ 127–129, ECHR 2000-I; *Socialist Party and Others v. Turkey*, 25 May 1998, § 55, *Reports of Judgments and Decisions* 1998-III; *Bozano v. France*, 18 December 1986, § 61, Series A no. 111.

[33] *Tahsin Acar v. Turkey* [GC], no. 26307/95, § 245, ECHR 2004-III. Also *Menteş and Others v. Turkey* (Article 50), 24 July 1998, §§ 93–96, *Reports of Judgments and Decisions* 1998-IV.

[34] *Çakıcı v. Turkey* [GC], no. 23657/94, §§ 115–117, ECHR 1999-IV. Also *Akdivar and Others v. Turkey*, 16 September 1996, §§ 98–99, *Reports of Judgments and Decisions* 1996-IV.

[35] *Çakıcı v. Turkey*, no. 23657/94, Commission report of 12 March 1998, § 293.

[36] *Sürek and Özdemir v. Turkey* [GC], nos 23927/94 and 24277/94, §§ 65–66, 8 July 1999.

Further reading

Yutaka Arai, 'Prohibition of Misuse of Power in Restricting the Rights and Freedoms (Article 18)', in Van Dijk et al., *Theory and Practice*, pp. 1093–100.

Vincent Coussirat-Coustere, 'Article 18', in Pettiti et al., *La Convention européenne*, pp. 523–7.

Frowein/Peukert, *MenschenRechtsKonvention,* pp. 434–6.

Harris et al., *Law of the European Convention*, pp. 652–4.

Pablo Santolaya, 'Limiting Restrictions on Rights. Art. 18 ECHR (A Generic Limit on Limits According to Purpose)', in Javier García Roca and Pablo Santolaya, *Europe of Rights: A Compendium on the European Convention of Human Rights*, Leiden/Boston: Martinus Nijhoff, 2012, pp. 527–36.

SECTION II
EUROPEAN COURT OF HUMAN RIGHTS

Article 19. Establishment of the Court/Institution de la Cour

To ensure the observance of the engagements undertaken by the High Contracting Parties in the Convention and the Protocols thereto, there shall be set up a European Court of Human Rights, hereinafter referred to as 'the Court'. It shall function on a permanent basis.

Afin d'assurer le respect des engagements résultant pour les Hautes Parties contractantes de la présente Convention et de ses Protocoles, il est institué une Cour européenne des droits de l'homme, ci-dessous nommée « la Cour ». Elle fonctionne de façon permanente.

Introductory comments

The idea of an international court of human rights has inspired international lawyers and activists for at least a century. The Permanent Court of International Justice, created in the aftermath of the First World War, exercised jurisdiction over a limited range of human rights violations set out in treaties that had been adopted as part of the protection of national or ethnic minorities in Central and Eastern Europe. The Permanent Court's case law addressed issues such as access to schools and the use of language,[1] matters that lie within the protection of minorities, but also questions falling within the general scope of international human rights, such as the principle of legality and the prohibition of retroactive prosecution.[2]

As the United Nations developed its first instruments of international human rights law, proposals for a world human rights court emerged. Australia was the flag-bearer for the project.[3] It submitted a proposal for an international court of human rights to the 1946 Paris Peace Conference.[4] An early draft of the International Covenant on Civil and Political Rights adopted by the Commission on Human Rights included the Australian proposal, as an annex, entitled a 'Draft Statute of the International Court of Human Rights'.[5] Ultimately, the United Nations adopted rather modest mechanisms for implementation of the treaties adopted in the wake of the Universal Declaration of Human Rights. The international human rights court project remains alive, yet there seems to be little support for it.[6]

The great innovation of the European Convention on Human Rights was its machinery. Two primary organs were established by article 19 of the text adopted in November 1950, the European Commission of Human Rights and the European Court of Human Rights. There was no unanimity among the Member States of the Council of Europe on the subject. Indeed, a convincing majority was opposed to the establishment of a Court

---

[1] For example, *Access to German Minority Schools in Upper Silesia*, Series A/B, No. 40.

[2] *Consistency of Certain Danzig Legislative Decrees with the Constitution of the Free City*, Series A/B, No. 65.

[3] Draft Resolution for an International Court of Human Rights submitted by the Representative from Australia, UN Doc. E/CN.4/15; UN Doc. E/CN.4/SR.16, pp. 1–5.

[4] See UN Doc. E/CN.4/SR.15, p. 2.

[5] Report of the Fifth Session of the Commission on Human Rights to the Economic and Social Council, UN Doc. E/1371, E/CN.4/350, pp. 63–9.

[6] Manfred Novak, 'The Need for a World Court of Human Rights', (2007) 7 *HRLR* 251; Stefan Trechsel, 'A World Court for Human Rights?', (2004) 1 *Northwestern Journal of International Human Rights* 3.

until a compromise was worked out allowing States to recognize its jurisdiction by means of an optional clause, similar to what is found in the Statute of the International Court of Justice. There was more agreement on the establishment of the European Commission of Human Rights. Nevertheless, agreement on the right of individual petition remained in dispute until the end of the negotiations. This impasse was also resolved by means of an optional clause.

Both the Commission and the Court became operational during the 1950s. The Court was born somewhat later than the Commission. The Court's establishment was contingent on a minimum number of States Parties declaring their acceptance of its jurisdiction, whereas the Commission was created as a consequence of entry into force of the Convention itself. Under the 1950 Convention, individual applications were submitted to the Commission, and only then if the State had recognized the right of petition. The only function of the Commission in contentious cases that flowed automatically from the Convention was the inter-State application.

In the vast majority of cases, the Commission ruled the application inadmissible, a decision from which there was no appeal. If the Commission determined otherwise, it then prepared a report with its findings on the merits. If the respondent State Party had accepted the Court's jurisdiction, the Commission was empowered to refer the case to the Court. There, the Commission took charge of the proceedings on behalf of the applicant. If the Commission issued a report but did not refer the case to the Court, the matter was dealt with by the Committee of Ministers. Over the years, as the Commission and the Court prospered and became increasingly active, there were calls to reconfigure the Convention machinery. The first proposal to 'merge' the Court and the Commission was considered in 1982 at a meeting of the Committee of Experts for the Improvement of the Procedure under the European Convention on Human Rights. It was revived at the European Ministerial Conference on Human Rights, held in 1985.[7] In 1990, Sweden and the Netherlands independently put forward similar proposals by which opinions of the Commission, issued with respect to individual applications under article 31 of the 1950 text of the Convention, would be legally binding. The Commission would thereby operate as a tribunal of first instance, with the Court sitting on appeal in appropriate cases.[8] But despite considerable support, consensus on these proposals could not be reached.

Negotiations continued and in May 1993 the Committee of Ministers adopted *ad hoc* terms of reference for the Steering Committee for Human Rights, requiring it to prepare a draft protocol 'restructuring the existing supervisory mechanism' and replacing it with a single institution, the Court, 'it being understood that [the competence of the Committee of Ministers] to deal with individual applications under the present Article 32 of the Convention is abolished'.[9] After consultation with the European Commission and the European Court, as well as with the Parliamentary Assembly, the draft protocol was adopted in April 1994 by the Ministers' Deputies.

The Explanatory Report does not provide any significant discussion of the actual drafting of the Protocol. It does, however, explain the rationale for the decision to replace the enforcement machinery of the Convention with a single Court. It refers to an

---

[7] Explanatory Report on Protocol No. 11, para. 10.
[8] Ibid., para. 15.
[9] Ibid., para. 4.

'increasingly urgent' need for reform resulting from a growing number of complaints to the Commission, as well as an increase in membership of the Council of Europe. It notes that the number of applications registered annually with the Commission increased from 404 in 1981 to more than 2,000 in 1993. Moreover, it anticipated that by the year 2000 the size of the Council of Europe might increase to as many as 35 or 40 Member States (in fact, there were 41 Member States by 2000).[10] The Report said that '[t]he increasing workload of the Commission has also resulted in more cases being referred to the Court in the last few years'.[11] Until 1988, the Court had never had more than twenty-five cases referred to it in any given year. By the early 1990s the number had doubled.

According to the Explanatory Report, '[t]he reform proposed is thus principally aimed at restructuring the system, so as to shorten the length of Strasbourg proceedings. There is need for a supervising machinery that can work efficiently and at acceptable costs even with forty member States and which can maintain the authority and quality of the case-law in the future.'[12] It cited the 'Vienna Declaration' of the Council of Europe's Heads of State and Government of 9 October 1993:

Since the Convention entered into force in 1953 the number of contracting States has almost tripled and more countries will accede after becoming members of the Council of Europe. We are of the opinion that it has become urgently necessary to adapt the present control mechanism to this development in order to be able to maintain in the future effective international protection for human rights. The purpose of this reform is to enhance the efficiency of the means of protection, to shorten procedures and to maintain the present high quality of human rights protection.[13]

The Report continued: 'The creation of a single Court is intended to prevent the overlapping of a certain amount of work and also to avoid certain delays which are inherent in the present system.'[14] It also said the Protocol was aimed 'at strengthening the judicial elements of the system'.[15]

According to the Explanatory Report, '[t]he new single Court will replace two of the existing supervisory organs created by the European Convention on Human Rights and will perform the functions carried out by these organs. The Committee of Ministers will retain its competence under former Article 54; its competence under former Article 32 of the Convention will be abolished.'[16] The 'new Court' would have jurisdiction 'in all matters concerning the interpretation and application of the Convention including inter-State cases as well as individual applications. In addition, the Court will, as at present, be able to give advisory opinions when so requested by the Committee of Ministers.'[17]

[10] Ibid., para. 20.
[11] Ibid., para. 19.
[12] Ibid., para. 23.
[13] Ibid., para. 23.
[14] Ibid., para. 24.
[15] Ibid., para. 25.
[16] Ibid., para. 26.
[17] Ibid., para. 27.

Drafting of the provision

The Draft Convention prepared by the European Movement and presented to the Committee of Ministers of the Council of Europe in July 1949 was accompanied by a commentary on the rationale for a European Court of Human Rights:

The success of the European Court of Human Rights, like that of the International Court of Justice at The Hague, will depend not so much upon the powers it wields as upon the overall prestige it enjoys. In most cases the pressure of public opinion will be quite sufficient to secure respect for its decisions.

Governments will be reluctant to be regarded as violators of their people's liberties and will usually prefer to comply with the judgments of the Court, even if they do not always agree with them, rather than face the loss of popularity and electoral support which refusal would probably involve. With this in mind, the framers of the Draft Convention have included in Article 11 the provision that every signatory State 'must, by all means available to it, ensure the widest possible publicity for the judgments of the Court and for any statements published by the Commission'.

States in which democracy has been completely overthrown and in which an absolute dictator-ship has been established, admittedly present a much harder problem. However, it must be remembered that it is rare indeed for a democratic society to go over to a totalitarian system in a day. There is almost always a period during which liberty is being progressively curtailed. It is in this critical transition stage that the publication of the Court's judgments could exercise such an important and perhaps even decisive influence.

Germany, for example, was not suddenly transformed from a state of freedom to a state of serfdom on the thirtieth day of January 1933. The democratic institutions of the Weimar Republic were already beginning to be seriously undermined some time before the Nazis came to power. If a European Court of Human Rights had been in existence in 1932 it would without doubt have condemned many of the authoritarian acts of Herr von Papen's government. Yet the German press was at the time still free and would have given the widest publicity to any such judgments of the Court. This would have stimulated much public resentment against the Government and would undoubtedly have had the effect of winning great numbers of voters for the democratic parties of the Centre and Left. This might well have offered to President Hindenburg the possibility of forming a democratic government and have spared him the necessity of appointing Adolf Hitler as Chancellor the Reich.

It is, of course, impossible in retrospect to assess with any degree of certainty how changed circumstances would have affected subsequent events. If, however, there is even a remote chance that the existence of a European Court of Human Rights would have prevented Hitler's rise to power, with all its dire consequences for mankind, this project surely cannot be dismissed as negligible or unrealistic.[18]

The draft Convention provided for the right of any natural or corporate person in the territory of a State Party to petition the Council of Europe about an infringement of fundamental rights. Such petitions were to be dealt with by a European Human Rights Commission 'and in proper cases by a European Court of Human Rights'.[19] The Commission would have an investigatory function. Cases could be brought before the Court by the Commission, by an 'affected party' with the authorization of the Commission, and by a State Party.[20] The Court was given the following authority:

---

[18] Convention for the Collective Protection of Individual Rights and Democratic Liberties by the States, Members of the Council of Europe, and for the establishment of a European Court of Human Rights to ensure observance of the Convention, Doc. INF/5/E/R.

[19] Ibid., I *TP* 296–303, at p. 298, art. 7(b).

[20] Ibid., p. 300, art. 12.

a) The Court shall have jurisdiction to determine all cases concerning the infringement of Part I of this Convention arising out of executive, legislative or juridical acts.

b) The Court may either prescribe a measure of reparation or it may require that the State concerned shall take penal or administrative action in regard to the persons responsible for the infringement, or it may demand the repeal, cancellation or amendment of the act.[21]

At the same time, a very detailed Draft Statute of the European Court of Human Rights was proposed. The Statute said explicitly that it was 'based on the Statute of the International Court of Justice'.[22] It provided for a Court that was to remain permanently in session.[23] The Court was to be assisted by the European Human Rights Commission, whose members it was to select.[24]

The draft convention was first considered by the Committee on Legal and Administrative Questions of the Consultative Assembly. It used the European Movement draft as a basis, together with the following motion:

The Committee notes that it must be made known at once that in order to guarantee the list of human rights:

1) There shall be a Court of Justice or an [sic] European Court of Human Rights;
2) That this Court shall be composed of nine Members. It shall not include more than one national of the same State. Members of the Court shall be elected by the Committee of Ministers and by the Consultative Assembly by an absolute majority of the votes obtained in each of these bodies;
3) That before the Court examines petitions submitted to it, they shall be previously submitted to a (European) Commission;
4) That the Court shall have power to determine all cases of violation of the rights mentioned on the list of human rights, resulting from legislative, judicial or executive acts;
5) That the rules for the functioning of the Court and the Commission, as regards the carrying out of their decisions, shall be studied by the Committee and submitted for discussion at the next session.[25]

Presenting the matter to the Committee on Legal and Administrative Questions of the Consultative Assembly, Pierre-Henri Teitgen said that in order to ensure the operation of the 'collective guarantee' of human rights pledged by the Council of Europe, it was necessary to envisage 'the creation of an appropriate European Court, since the Permanent Court of International Justice may only consider a complaint made by a State'.[26]

The proposal for a court met with controversy in the Consultative Assembly.[27] One of the delegates, Henri Rolin of Belgium, described it as 'not only useless, but also illogical and harmful' and an institution that would find itself in competition with the International Court of Justice.[28] Teitgen spoke passionately in defence of the proposed court.[29] The amendment aimed at rejecting the court was defeated without a recorded

---

[21] Ibid., pp. 300–2, art. 13.

[22] Draft Statute of the European Court of Human Rights, INF/5/E/R, I *TP* 302–21, at p. 302, art. 1.

[23] Ibid., p. 308, art. 22(a).

[24] Ibid., p. 320, Part V.

[25] Preparatory Report by the Secretariat-General concerning a Preliminary Draft Convention to Provide a Collective Guarantee of Human Rights, Doc. B 22, III *TP* 2–37, at p. 4.

[26] Report presented by Mr P.H. Teitgen, 5 September 1949, Doc. A 290, I *TP* 192–213, at p. 204.

[27] See the account by Ed Bates, *The Evolution of the European Convention on Human Rights*, Oxford: Oxford University Press, 2010, pp. 70–4.

[28] Official Report of the Sitting [of the Consultative Assembly, 8 September 1949], II *TP* 14–274, at p. 150.

[29] Ibid., pp. 170–80.

vote.[30] The heart of the debate was not the idea of a court as such but the proposal to allow individual petitions, even if only through the indirect route of reference by the preliminary commission.[31] Lynn Ungoed-Thomas of the United Kingdom expressed concern about 'politically-inspired application . . . which invites action by those on the extreme right and those on the extreme left, with whom none of us here have sympathy'.[32] But Lord Layton, also of the United Kingdom, pointed to the practice before the United Nations Commission on Human Rights, saying that the proposed European Commission of Human Rights would be quite capable of sifting through petitions and identifying those without merit.[33] The proposal to eliminate individual petitions was rejected.[34]

The draft statute adopted by the Consultative Assembly contained the following:

Art. 8. To ensure the observance, in accordance with Articles 4, 5, 6 and 7 of the engagements subscribed to by the Member States in application of Articles 2 and 3, the Convention shall establish:
1) A European Court of Justice (hereafter referred to as the Court);
2) A European Commission of Human Rights (hereafter referred to as the Commission).[35]

Several provisions followed with details about the establishment, structure, and jurisdiction of the two organs that were proposed. If the Commission held a petition to be admissible, it was to try to effect a conciliation of the opposing parties, failing which it had the discretion to refer the matter to the Court for 'a legal ruling'.[36]

The Consultative Assembly draft was forwarded to the Committee of Ministers. The Committee of Ministers, in turn, chose to refer the draft for further study to a Committee of Experts that met in February and March 1950. An initial draft, adopted by the Committee of Experts at its February session, was similar to the text of article 8 of the Consultative Assembly draft. The major difference was that the order of the two organs was reversed, the Commission being listed in paragraph 1 and the Court in paragraph 2. It had also taken on the name 'European Court of Human Rights'.[37] According to the Report, all members of the Committee, with the exception of the British expert, agreed with the idea of a Commission. On the Court, however, there was considerable division, with only a minority in support. The representatives of Luxembourg, Norway, Denmark, Turkey, Greece, and the United Kingdom were opposed to a Court, while the French, Italian, Belgian, and Irish members were in favour.[38] The Report did not discuss the arguments for and against a Court, these having been 'fully developed in the debates of the Consultative Assembly'.[39] Indeed, the Committee of Experts did not take a position on

---

[30] Ibid., p. 184. See also Preparatory Report by the Secretariat-General concerning a Preliminary Draft Convention to Provide a Collective Guarantee of Human Rights, Doc. B 22, III *TP* 2–37, at pp. 18–20.

[31] Official Report of the Sitting [of the Consultative Assembly, 8 September 1949], II *TP* 14–274, at p. 166.

[32] Ibid., p. 188.

[33] Ibid., p. 196.

[34] Ibid., p. 202. See also Preparatory Report by the Secretariat-General concerning a Preliminary Draft Convention to Provide a Collective Guarantee of Human Rights, Doc. B 22, III *TP* 2–37, at p. 22.

[35] Recommendation No. 38 to the Committee of Ministers adopted 8 September 1949 on the conclusion of the debates, Doc. AS (1) 108, II *TP* 274–83, at p. 278.

[36] Ibid., pp. 278–83.

[37] Preliminary Draft Convention for the Maintenance and Further Realisation of Human Rights and Fundamental Freedoms, 15 February 1950, Doc. A 833, III *TP* 236–46, at p. 240.

[38] Preliminary Draft of the Report to the Committee of Ministers, 24 February 1950, Doc. CM/WP 1 (50) 1, A 847, III *TP* 246–79, at p. 268.

[39] Ibid.

the subject of whether or not to establish the Court 'since, in its opinion, this matter was also of a political nature'.[40]

The Committee of Ministers referred the drafts adopted by the Committee of Experts to a Conference of Senior Officials that met in June 1950. It assigned a number of 'political' issues to the Conference, although the issue of establishing a Court was not one of them.[41] Nevertheless, the matter could not be avoided by the Conference of Senior Officials. Views were as divided as they had been in the Consultative Assembly. A compromise solution began to emerge whereby jurisdiction of the Court would be subject to an optional clause, inspired by article 36 of the Statute of the International Court of Justice, thereby allowing States that accepted the Court to recognize its jurisdiction while at the same time sheltering from its authority those that did not.[42] The Conference also developed the mechanism of referral by the Commission to the Committee of Ministers.[43]

Italy proposed a text with a provision entitled 'Optional Court', by which the Committee of Ministers would not act if the Commission, the respondent State Party, or a State Party referring the application requested that the case be submitted to the Court.[44] During the debate, the chairman suggested that six ratifications would be necessary for the optional clause to come into force.[45] When a vote was taken on the proposal for a Court, the same four States that had earlier supported the proposal were the only ones in favour, and seven States were opposed. But when the compromise with an optional clause was put to a vote, there were nine States in favour and only three opposed, Norway, the Netherlands, and the United Kingdom.[46]

Sweden, which was opposed to the Court as such but which favoured one if there was an optional clause, submitted a series of provisions that began with the following: 'Art. . . . Apart from the European Commission of Human Rights, there shall be set up a European Court of Human Rights, on condition however that at least six States give their adherence to this Section (IV).'[47] Italy made an elaborate proposal for a Court with competence on 'all questions concerning the interpretation of the present Convention which the High Contracting Parties shall lay before it'. It was accompanied by an optional clause that was very similar to that of the Statute of the International Court of Justice.[48]

---

[40] Report to the Committee of Ministers submitted by the Committee of Experts Instructed to Draw Up a Draft Convention of Collective Guarantee of Human Rights and Fundamental Freedoms, Doc. CM/WP 1 (5) 15, A 924, IV *TP* 2–55, at p. 16.

[41] Letter of 11 May 1950 from the Secretary General to the Foreign Ministers of Member States, IV *TP* 92–95.

[42] Minutes of the morning sitting [of 9 June 1950 of the Conference of Senior Officials], Doc. CM/WP 4 (50) 3, IV *TP* 110–19; Minutes of the afternoon sitting [of 9 June 1950 of the Conference of Senior Officials], unreferenced document, IV *TP* 120–31; Minutes of the morning sitting [of 10 June 1950], unreferenced document, IV *TP* 132–41.

[43] Proposal submitted by the French, Irish, and United Kingdom Delegations (Original text), Doc. CM/WP 4 (50) 5, A 1366, IV *TP* 160–1; Proposal submitted by the French, Irish, and United Kingdom Delegations (Revised text), Doc. CM/WP 4 (50) 5 rev., A 1369, IV *TP* 160–1.

[44] Proposal submitted by the Italian Delegation, Doc. CM/WP 4 (50) 6, A 1367, IV *TP* 162–3.

[45] Minutes of the afternoon setting [of 12 June 1950 of the Conference of Senior Officials], unreferenced document, IV *TP* 170–81, at p. 174.

[46] Ibid., p. 178.

[47] Proposal submitted by the Swedish Delegation, Doc. CM/WP 4 (50) 10, A 1373, IV *TP* 190–5.

[48] Proposal submitted by the Italian Delegation (Original text), Doc. CM/WP 4 (50) 12, A 1375, IV *TP* 198–201; Proposal submitted by the Italian Delegation (Revised text), Doc. CM/WP 4 (50) 12 rev., A 1427, IV *TP* 200–3.

The Report of the Conference of Senior Officials noted that 'it has not yet been agreed that the creation of a European Court of Human Rights at the present time corresponds to a real need of the Member States of the Council of Europe'. Nevertheless, it recognized that four States considered that 'only a Court, having all the characteristics of an impartial tribunal, would be able to ensure the efficient protection of human rights'. The Report pointed to the 'compromise suggestion' from the Swedish delegation and the support that had emerged for a Court based upon an optional clause. The drafting Sub-Committee had favoured a solution by which a European Court was to be created but with optional jurisdiction.[49] The draft Convention adopted by the Conference of Senior Officials contained the following provision:

To ensure the observance of the engagements undertaken by the High Contracting Parties in the present Convention, there shall be set up:
a) a European Commission of Human Rights hereafter referred to as the 'Commission';
b) A European Court of Human Rights, hereafter referred to as the 'Court'.[50]

Jurisdiction of the Court would be based upon an optional clause and its members would not be elected until it had been accepted by nine States.[51]

The Report of the Conference of Senior Officials was considered a few days later at a meeting of the Committee on Legal and Administrative Questions of the Consultative Assembly. The compromise seemed to be favourably received, the only significant change being a proposal to reduce the number of States necessary for entry into force of the provision 'since this figure was too large and would unnecessarily delay the establishment of the Court'.[52]

The text adopted by the Conference of Senior Officials was accepted without change by the Committee of Ministers at its fifth session[53] and subsequently by the Consultative Assembly.[54] The Consultative Assembly changed the threshold for establishment of the Court to eight declarations from the nine in the earlier versions.[55] Ireland had proposed that it be set as low as five.[56] In November 1950, the Committee of Legal Experts of the

[49] Text of the Report submitted by the Conference [of Senior Officials] to the Committee of Ministers, Doc. CM/WP 4 (50) 19, CM/WP 4 (50) 16 rev., A 1431, IV *TP* 242–73, at pp. 248–53. Also Draft Report to the Committee of Ministers, Doc. CM/WP 4 (50) 16, A 1426, IV *TP* 204–17, at p. 210, at pp. 210–13.

[50] Draft Convention annexed to the Report, Doc. CM/WP 4 (50) 19 annex, CM/WP 4 (50) rev., A 1452, IV *TP* 274–95, at pp. 282–3. Also Draft Convention appended to the Draft Report, Doc. CM/WP 4 (50) 16, appendix, A 1445, IV *TP* 218–40, at pp. 226–7.

[51] Draft Convention annexed to the Report, Doc. CM/WP 4 (50) 19 annex, CM/WP 4 (50) rev., A 1452, IV *TP* 274–95, pp. 290–2.

[52] Minutes of the meeting [of 23 June 1950 of the Committee on Legal and Administrative Questions of the Consultative Assembly], Doc. AS/JA (2) PV I, A 1840, V *TP* 2–11, at p. 8. Also Report of the sitting [of the Consultative Assembly, 14 August 1950], V *TP* 216–71, at p. 266; Letter of 24 June 1950 from Sir David Maxwell Fyfe, Chairman of the Committee on Legal and Administrative Questions, to the Chairman of the Committee of Ministers, Doc. CM (50) 29, V *TP* 32–41, at p. 38.

[53] Draft Convention adopted by the Sub-Committee, Doc. CM 1 (50) 52, A 1884, V *TP* 76–99, at p. 84; Draft Convention adopted by the Committee of Ministers, 7 August 1950, Doc. A 1937, V *TP* 120–45, at p. 130; Letter dated 7 August 1950 sent by Mr MacBride, Chairman of the Committee of Ministers, to M. Spaak, President of the Consultative Assembly, Doc. No. 11, p. 600–19, V *TP* 144–71, at p. 154.

[54] Text of the draft amended by the Consultative Assembly including notes on the articles not yet approved by the Committee of Ministers and the adoption of which is urged by the Consultative Assembly, Doc. A 2838, VI *TP* 238–73, at p. 252.

[55] Ibid., p. 266.

[56] Amendments proposed by the Irish Government (4 August 1950), Doc. CM 1 (50) 2, A 1863, V *TP* 58–61.

Committee of Ministers agreed to the figure 'eight'.[57] The word 'hereafter' appeared in the final version of article 19 of the Convention as 'hereinafter'.

Protocol No. 11 was responsible for major changes in article 19 of the Convention. The two paragraphs referring to the European Commission and the European Court were replaced, consistent with the decision to merge the institutions into a 'new Court'. There were two other changes: the words 'and the Protocols thereto' were added after the reference to the Convention and a second sentence was added declaring that the Court would function on a permanent basis.

The Explanatory Report on Protocol No. 11 provides very little information about the drafting of amended article 19. Referring to the words 'and the Protocols thereto', it states that 'this addition reflects developments after the adoption of the Convention in 1950. Obviously, States will be bound only by the protocols they have ratified.'[58] The Explanatory Report also confirms that, despite appearances, the drafters intended that the single institution be a 'new Court' and not a modified version of the 'former Court': 'The same title as that of the former Court has been retained for the supervisory institution. This, however, should not disguise the fact that it is a new institution. The new Court is to be a permanent Court, whose seat is in Strasbourg.'[59]

Analysis and interpretation

The Rules of Court refer to the pre-Protocol No. 11 institution as the 'former Court'.[60] The reform was intended to reduce the length of proceedings and to reinforce their judicial character.[61] Nevertheless, the reform has been broadly understood as the end of the Commission and the continuation of a much-reformed Court. The reference to it operating on a 'permanent basis' demarcates it from the earlier Court, whose judges were not resident in Strasbourg and who only attended for one week per month. In addition to requiring full-time residency in Strasbourg, Protocol No. 11 made other significant changes to the Court, including reforms in the mode of election. Judgments of the 'new Court' refer to the case law of the 'former' Court without even a hint that two different institutions are involved.

Behind the seemingly modest changes to article 19 is a more important modification of the Convention. Articles 25 and 46 of the Convention as adopted in 1950, the provisions that framed the mechanisms for individual applications to the Commission and the Court, respectively, were repealed by Protocol No. 11. They provided for a system of optional declarations establishing jurisdiction in the case of individual petitions. With their removal from the Convention, the role that they played is to a large extent assumed by article 19. As the Court explained in the *Loizidou v. Turkey* case, referencing article 19 together with article 25 and 46 of the 1950 Convention:

The Court observes that Articles 25 and 46 of the Convention are provisions which are essential to the effectiveness of the Convention system since they delineate the responsibility of the

---

[57] Report of the Committee of Legal Experts held at Rome, 2 and 3 November 1950 (revised text), Doc. CM/Adj (50) 3 rev., A 2531, VII *TP* 10–13.
[58] Explanatory Report on Protocol No. 11, para. 57.
[59] Ibid., para. 58.
[60] Rules of Court, Rule 1(t).
[61] Explanatory Report on Protocol No. 14, para. 4.

Commission and Court 'to ensure the observance of the engagements undertaken by the High Contracting Parties' (Article 19), by determining their competence to examine complaints concerning alleged violations of the rights and freedoms set out in the Convention. In interpreting these key provisions it must have regard to the special character of the Convention as a treaty for the collective enforcement of human rights and fundamental freedoms.[62]

At the same time, the Court noted an earlier precedent where it had stated that '[u]nlike international treaties of the classic kind, the Convention comprises more than mere reciprocal engagements between Contracting States. It creates, over and above a network of mutual, bilateral undertakings, objective obligations which, in the words of the Preamble benefit from a "collective enforcement".'[63] Other references to article 19 in the case law of the Court note how it 'must bear in mind the special character of the Convention as an instrument of European public order (*ordre public*) for the protection of individual human beings and its mission, as set out in Article 19, "to ensure the observance of the engagements undertaken by the High Contracting Parties"'.[64]

Article 19 has also been cited to support a role for the Court in determining issues on public policy grounds in the common interest, and not merely as an arbiter of human rights applications filed by individuals. In so doing, it is 'thereby raising the general standards of protection of human rights and extending human rights jurisprudence throughout the community of Convention States'.[65]

On several occasions, article 19 has been invoked to confirm that the Court is not a tribunal of fourth instance, established to revise the findings of the apex courts in European States in a general sense. Many decisions have affirmed that it is not the Court's function 'to deal with errors of fact or law allegedly committed by a national court, unless and in so far as they may have infringed the rights and freedoms protected by the Convention. It is primarily for the domestic courts to interpret and apply domestic law.'[66] Some of these decisions invoke article 19 as the basis for such an affirmation.[67]

Article 19 has been invoked in the context of the pilot-judgment procedure, a mechanism designed to alleviate the case load of the Court by addressing applications that deal with systemic problems and that are similar and repetitive. Specifically, referring to article 19, the Court said:

A requirement to deliver, continually, individual decisions in cases where there is no longer any live Convention issue cannot be said to be compatible with this task. Nor does this judicial exercise

---

[62] *Loizidou v. Turkey* (Preliminary objections), 23 March 1995, § 70, Series A no. 310.

[63] Ibid., citing *Ireland v. the United Kingdom*, 18 January 1978, § 239, Series A no. 25.

[64] Ibid., § 93. See also § 96.

[65] *Djokaba Lambi Longa v. the Netherlands* (dec.), no. 33917/12, § 58, 9 October 2012.

[66] *Polednová v. Czech Republic* (dec.), no. 2615/10, 21 June 2011; *Streletz, Kessler, and Krenz v. Germany* [GC], nos 34044/96, 35532/97, and 44801/98, § 81, ECHR 2001-II.

[67] *L.H. v. Latvia*, no. 52019/07, § 49, 29 April 2014; *Glykantzi v. Greece*, § 39, no. 40150/09, 30 October 2012; *Nechiporuk and Yonkalo v. Ukraine*, no. 42310/04, § 273, 21 April 2011; *Ocone v. Italy* (dec.), no. 48889/99, 19 February 2004; *Akay v. Turkey* (dec.), no. 34501/97, 19 February 2002; *García Ruiz v. Spain* [GC], no. 30544/96, § 28, ECHR 1999-I; *Lehto v. Finland*, no. 31043/96, Commission decision of 4 March 1998; *Lupander v. Finland*, no. 28941/95, Commission decision of 3 December 1997; *D.S. v. the United Kingdom*, no. 14067/88, Commission decision of 6 July 1989; *Schenk v. Switzerland*, 12 July 1988, § 45, Series A no. 140; *E. v. Sweden*, no. 11453/85, Commission decision of 7 July 1986; *X v. Belgium*, no. 458/59, Commission decision of 29 March 1960, (1960) 3 YB 222; *X v. Austria*, no. 1140/61, Commission decision of 19 December 1961, Collection 8, p. 57; *Andorfer Tonwerke v. Austria*, no. 7987/77, Commission decision of 19 December 1978, (1980) 23 YB 190, DR 18, p. 31; *Ziegler v. Switzerland*, no. 19890/92, Commission decision of 3 May 1993, (1993) 36 YB 73, DR 74, p. 234.

contribute usefully or in any meaningful way to the strengthening of human rights protection under the Convention; indeed, it cannot be ruled out that in the future the Court may wish to redefine its role in this respect and decline to examine such cases.[68]

The Court has also said that 'elle ne s'acquitte pas forcément au mieux de sa tâche, qui consiste selon l'article 19 de la Convention à « assurer le respect des engagements résultant pour les Hautes Parties contractantes de la (...) Convention et de ses Protocoles », en répétant les mêmes conclusions dans un grand nombre d'affaires'.[69]

In the first *Georgia v. Russia* inter-State case, the Grand Chamber spoke of the 'specificity' of the Court's task under article 19 of the Convention, namely 'to ensure the observance by the High Contracting Parties of their engagements to secure the fundamental rights enshrined in the Convention'. The Grand Chamber said this conditioned the Court's approach. It said 'there are no procedural barriers to the admissibility of evidence or predetermined formulae for its assessment' and that it adopts 'conclusions that are, in its view, supported by the free evaluation of all evidence, including such inferences as may flow from the facts and the parties' submissions'.[70]

Reference to article 19 has also been made in order to distinguish the Court and the Commission from other organs of the Council of Europe. In the inter-State application by several European States against Greece following the 1967 coup, the Commission dismissed the relevance of action and inaction by the Consultative Assembly of the Council of Europe.[71]

The European Convention does not provide for the seat of the Court.[72] The Rules of Court state the following:

Rule 19—Seat of the Court
1. The seat of the Court shall be at the seat of the Council of Europe at Strasbourg. The Court may, however, if it considers it expedient, perform its functions elsewhere in the territories of the member States of the Council of Europe.
2. The Court may decide, at any stage of the examination of an application, that it is necessary that an investigation or any other function be carried out elsewhere by it or one or more of its members.

The Court's jurisdiction is confined to the interpretation and application of the European Convention on Human Rights. It cannot pronounce itself on alleged violations of other international treaties.[73] Despite this jurisdictional limitation, the Court frequently refers to other international treaties in its interpretation of provisions of the Convention. For example, in *Hassan v. the United Kingdom*, it referred to the third and fourth Geneva Conventions of 1949 in establishing the scope of article 5 of the Convention.[74] In this

---

[68] *E.G. v. Poland and 175 Other Bug River Applications* (dec.), no. 50425/99, § 27, 23 September 2008.
[69] *Demiroğlu and Others v. Turkey* (dec.), no. 56125/10, 4 June 2013.
[70] *Georgia v. Russia (I)* [GC], no. 13255/07, § 94, 3 July 2014. The evidentiary principles applied by the Court are discussed in detail in the chapter on article 38 of this Commentary.
[71] *Government of Denmark v. the Government of Greece; Denmark, Norway, Sweden, and the Netherlands v. Greece*, nos 3321/67, 3322/67, 3323/67, and 3344/67, Commission decision of 24 January 1968, (1968) 11 YB 690, Collection 25, pp. 92.
[72] Compare: Statute of the International Court of Justice, art. 22(1); Rome Statute of the International Criminal Court, (2002) 2187 UNTS 90, art. 3.
[73] *Occhetto v. Italy* (dec.), no. 14507/07, 12 November 2013; *Di Giovine v. Portugal* (dec.), no. 39912/98, 31 August 1999; *Hermida Paz v. Spain* (dec.), no. 4160/02, 28 January 2003.
[74] *Hassan v. the United Kingdom*, [GC], no. 29750/09, §§ 102–103, 16 September 2014.

context, it has relied on article 31(3)(c) of the Vienna Convention on the Law of Treaties by which a treaty may be interpreted in light of 'any relevant rules of international law applicable in the relations between the parties'.[75]

Further reading

Frowein/Peukert, *MenschenRechtsKonvention*, pp. 437–8.
Inete Ziemele, 'International Courts and *Ultra Vires* Acts', in Lucius Caflisch, Johan Callewaert, Roderick Liddell, Paul Mahoney, and Mark Villiger, eds, *Liber Amicorum Luzius Wildhaber*, Kehl, Germany: N.P. Engel, 2007, pp. 537–56.

---

[75] The role of other sources of international law in the interpretation of the Convention is discussed in detail in the introductory chapter of this Commentary.

Article 20. Number of judges/Nombre de juges

The Court shall consist of a number of judges equal to that of the High Contracting Parties.

La Cour se compose d'un nombre de juges égal à celui des Hautes Parties contractantes.

Introductory comments

The number of judges on the European Court is equal to the number of States Parties. The original choice of a Court whereby the number of judges corresponded to the number of States Parties was made at a time when only ten countries were involved. Perhaps the decision would have been different if there had been forty-seven, as is the case today. No other similar international court has followed this model. The International Court of Justice has fifteen, the International Criminal Court has eighteen, the African Court on Human and Peoples' Rights has eleven, and the Inter-American Court of Human Rights has seven.

The judges of the European Court no longer sit on cases in a plenary formation, even on an exceptional basis. The largest bench currently allowed by the Convention is the seventeen-judge Grand Chamber. Much of the work of the judges of the Court involves highly routine processing of the tens of thousands of applications that make up its enormous caseload. To that extent, it is radically different from other international courts and tribunals that never consider more than a small number of cases.

Drafting of the provision

The initial draft European Convention on Human Rights prepared by the International Juridical Section of the European Movement provided for a European Court of Human Rights that was 'to be composed of nine members, no two of whom may be nationals of the same State'.[1] The Consultative Assembly adopted a proposal along these lines.[2]

The Committee of Experts initially agreed that the Court should consist of nine judges 'in order to make it clear that the Court was a Court of Justice and not a political council of Member States'.[3] There were objections from several smaller States based upon concerns that their interests might not be properly represented. According to the Report of the Committee, '[i]t was felt that, by force of circumstances, the bigger powers would always have one of their nationals acting as judge to the Court, whereas the chances of

---

[1] Convention for the Collective Protection of Individual Rights and Democratic Liberties by the States, Members of the Council of Europe, and for the establishment of a European Court of Human Rights to ensure observance of the Convention, Doc. INF/5/E/R, I *TP* 296–303, at p. 300, art. 9(b); Draft Statute of the European Court of Human Rights, INF/5/E/R, I *TP* 302–21, at p. 302, art. 3.

[2] Report [of the Committee on Legal and Administrative Questions], 5 September 1949, Doc. AS (1) 77, I *TP* 216–39, at p. 234; Official Report of the Sitting [of the Consultative Assembly, 8 September 1949], II *TP* 14–274, at p. 218.

[3] Report to the Committee of Ministers Submitted by the Committee of Experts Instructed to Draw Up a Draft Convention of Collective Guarantee of Human Rights and Fundamental Freedoms, Doc. CM/WP 1 (5) 15, A 924, IV *TP* 2–55, at p. 42.

nations [sic] from the smaller States being nominated to the Court would be slighter'. The Committee of Experts recommended that the Court be composed of a number of judges equal to the number of States Parties.[4] The draft provision it adopted read as follows: 'The European Court of Human Rights shall consist of a number of judges equal to that of the High Contracting Parties not [sic] two of the judges may be nationals of the same State.'[5]

The Committee of Ministers referred the drafts that were adopted by the Committee of Experts to a Conference of Senior Officials that convened in June 1950. The Conference of Senior Officials reached a degree of consensus on establishing a Court but one whose jurisdiction would be based upon an optional clause similar to that of the International Court of Justice.[6] This provoked Sweden to present an amended version of the provision on the number of judges by which this would be equal to the number of States that had accepted the jurisdiction of the Court.[7] But its vision of a Court that was in effect reserved to those States that had accepted its jurisdiction, including control over the election of judges, was rejected. The Report of the Conference explained that '[c]onfronted with the choice between a Court which would be set up only for those States which so desire, and a Court which would be set up by all the High Contracting Parties, but the jurisdiction of which would be binding only on States which had expressly accepted it, the Conference decided in favour of the second Alternative'. It said that several delegates felt a Court set up only for some Member States 'would be contrary to the basic idea of the Statute. Such a Court would constitute a factor of division rather than of union between the Member States.'[8] Accordingly, the words 'High Contracting Parties' were replaced with 'Member States of the Council of Europe'.[9]

The provision, as amended by the Conference of Senior Officials, was not subject to further amendment and there is no evidence of any debate in the Committee of Ministers or the Consultative Assembly prior to adoption of the Convention in November.[10] Article 38 of the 1950 text of the Convention reads as follows: 'The European Court of Human Rights shall consist of a number of judges equal to that of the Members of the Council of Europe. No two judges may be nationals of the same State.'

Article 20 of the Convention replaced article 38 of the 1950 text of the Convention pursuant to Protocol No. 11 with two substantive changes: the words 'the Members of the Council of Europe' were changed for 'the High Contracting Parties' and the second sentence ('No two judges may be nationals of the same State') was eliminated. The Explanatory Report says that '[i]n this respect it was considered preferable to follow the

---

[4] Ibid.

[5] Appendix to the Report of the Committee of Experts to the Committee of Ministers—Draft Convention (16 March 1950), Doc. CM/WP 1 (50) 14 revised, A 925, IV *TP* 50–79, at p. 70.

[6] This is discussed in more detail in the chapter on article 19 of this Commentary.

[7] Proposal submitted by the Swedish Delegation, Doc. CM/WP 4 (50) 10, A 1373, IV *TP* 190–5, at pp 190–2.

[8] Text of the report submitted by the Conference [of Senior Officials] to the Committee of Ministers, Doc. CM/WP 4 (50) 19, CM/WP 4 (50) 16 rev., A 1431, IV *TP* 242–73, at p. 266.

[9] Draft Convention annexed to the Report, Doc. CM/WP 4 (50) 19 annex, CM/WP 4 (50) rev., A 1452, IV *TP* 274–95, at p. 288.

[10] Draft Convention adopted by the Sub-Committee, Doc. CM 1 (50) 52, A 1884, V *TP* 76–99, at p. 90; Letter dated 7 August 1950 sent by Mr MacBride, Chairman of the Committee of Ministers, to M. Spaak, President of the Consultative Assembly, Doc. No. 11, p. 600–19, V *TP* 144–71, at p. 162; Text of the draft amended by the Consultative Assembly including notes on the articles not yet approved by the Committee of Ministers and the adoption of which is urged by the Consultative Assembly, Doc. A 2838, VI *TP* 238–73, at p. 262.

procedure relating to the appointment of members of the Commission (see Article 20 of the former text of the Convention)'.[11] The Explanatory Report does not indicate why this was considered preferable, although it seems clear that it was related to the understanding that no new member could join the Council of Europe without ratifying the Convention. According to the 1950 text, a State was entitled to a judge on the Court even if it had not ratified the Convention. The most striking example of this is René Cassin, who served as the French judge and even President of the Court despite the fact that at the time his country, which hosted the Court in Strasbourg, had not only failed to accept the jurisdiction of the Court, it was not even a party to the Convention.[12]

The Explanatory Report discusses the elimination of the rule by which no two judges of the Court may be nationals of the same State. It notes that '[i]n principle, there should be no more than two judges of the same nationality on the Court'. It continues: 'A State Party will have the possibility to put forward the name of a judge who is a national of another State Party rather than propose a judge from a State which has not ratified the Convention.'[13]

During the drafting of Protocol No. 14, there were proposals to increase the number of judges. The Parliamentary Assembly objected on the grounds that it might create inequalities between countries and it questioned the expediency of such a measure.[14] The Explanatory Report on Protocol No. 14 says that the idea was dropped in light of the Parliamentary Assembly's Opinion.[15]

Analysis and interpretation

The number of judges of the European Court of Human Rights is set at a number equal to that of the High Contracting Parties. A somewhat archaic term, 'High Contracting Parties' was employed in 1950 but is rarely used in modern treaty language, where the preferred term today would be 'States Parties'. Indeed, 'States Parties' rather than 'High Contracting Parties' is used frequently in the Explanatory Report on Protocol No. 11.[16] Acceptance of the European Convention on Human Rights is not a requirement for membership set out in the Statute of the Council of Europe. Most of the founding members of the Council ratified the Convention within a few years of its adoption, although France did not take this step until 1974. In 1993, the Committee of Ministers adopted, as a condition for membership in the Council of Europe, an undertaking by a candidate State to sign the European Convention on Human Rights and accept the Convention's supervisory machinery in its entirety within a short period.[17]

The 1950 text of the European Convention prevented two judges of the same nationality from serving on the Court. If, for whatever reason, a State chose not to

---

[11] Explanatory Report on Protocol No. 11, para. 59.
[12] See Karel Vasak, 'Historique des problèmes de la ratification de la Convention par la France', (1970) 3 *Revue des droits de l'homme* 558.
[13] Ibid.
[14] Draft Protocol No. 14 to the Convention for the Protection of Human Rights and Fundamental Freedoms amending the control system of the Convention, Opinion No. 251 (2004), Parliamentary Assembly, para. 7.
[15] Explanatory Report on Protocol No. 14, para. 34.
[16] See the discussion of the term 'High Contracting Parties' in the chapter on article 1 of this Commentary.
[17] Vienna Declaration, Vienna, 9 October 1993.

propose its own nationals for judgeship, it would then have little option but to look outside the membership in the Council of Europe. This happened only once, when Ronald St John MacDonald, a citizen of Canada, was elected to two terms at the Court, from 1980 to 1998, as judge for Liechtenstein. The sentence in article 38 of the 1950 text of the Convention prohibiting two nationals of the same State from serving on the Court was removed as a consequence of Protocol No. 11. Since the entry into force of article 20 as amended by Protocol No. 11 there have been two judges of the same nationality on four occasions: Luigi Ferrari Bravo and Benedetto Conforti of Italy served as a judges for San Marino and Italy, respectively, from 1998 to 2001; Lucius Caflish and Luzius Wildhaber of Switzerland served as judges for Liechtenstein and Switzerland, respectively from 1998 to 2006; Mark Villiger and Giorgio Malinverni of Switzerland served as a judges for Liechtenstein and Switzerland, respectively from 2006 to 2011; and Mark Villiger and Helen Keller of Switzerland have served as a judges for Liechtenstein and Switzerland, respectively from 2011 to the present.

Further reading

Johan Callewaert, 'Article 38', in Pettiti et al., *La Convention européenne*, pp. 743–5.
Frowein/Peukert, *MenschenRechtsKonvention*, pp. 439–40.

Article 21. Criteria for office/Conditions d'exercice des fonctions

1. The judges shall be of high moral character and must either possess the qualifications required for appointment to high judicial office or be jurisconsults of recognised competence.

2. Candidates shall be less than 65 years of age at the date by which the list of three candidates has been requested by the Parliamentary Assembly, further to Article 22.[1]

2. The judges shall sit on the Court in their individual capacity.

3. During their term of office the judges shall not engage in any activity which is incompatible with their independence, impartiality or with the demands of a full-time office; all questions arising from the application of this paragraph shall be decided by the Court.

1. Les juges doivent jouir de la plut haute considération morale et réunir les conditions requises pour l'exercice de hautes fonctions judiciaires ou être des jurisconsultes possédant une compétence notoire.

2. Les candidats doivent être âgés de moins de 65 ans à la date à laquelle la liste de trois candidats est attendue par l'Assemblée parlementaire, en vertu de l'article 22.

2. Les juges siègent à la Cour à titre individuel.

3. Pendant la durée de leur mandat, les juges ne peuvent exercer aucune activité incompatible avec les exigences d'indépendance, d'impartialité ou de disponibilité requise par une activité exercée à plein temps; toute question soulevée en application de ce paragraphe est tranchée par la Cour.

Introductory comments

The first international judges were political figures, sometimes heads of State. Sitting as arbitrators, they addressed inter-State disputes more as diplomats than as jurists. Gradually, the requirement that international arbitrators or judges should be selected primarily for their legal expertise took hold.[2] The requirements were first codified in the Hague Convention on the Peaceful Settlement of International Disputes, adopted in 1899. It stated that arbitrators at the Permanent Court of Arbitration be persons 'of known competency in questions of international law' and 'of the highest moral reputation'. Article 2 of the Statute of the Permanent Court of International Justice, as amended in 1929, required that the Court 'be composed of a body of independent judges, elected regardless of their nationality from amongst persons of high moral character, who possess the qualifications required in their respective countries for appointment to the highest judicial offices, or are jurisconsults of recognised competence in international law'.

At the international level, all judges should be expected to demonstrate independence and impartiality, but also a very high level of expertise in the relevant bodies of law. Issues of independence and impartiality are fundamentally the same as they are before domestic

---

[1] This paragraph, added pursuant to article 2 of Protocol No. 15 amending the Convention for the Protection of Human Rights and Fundamental Freedoms, ETS 213, is not yet in force. When it enters into force, paragraphs 2 and 3 of the existing provision will be renumbered paragraphs 3 and 4.

[2] Mariano J. Aznar-Gómez, 'Article 2', in Andreas Zimmermann, Christian Tomuschat, and Karin Oellers-Frahm, eds, *The Statute of the International Court of Justice, A Commentary*, Oxford: Oxford University Press, 2006, pp. 205–18, at pp. 206–7.

courts. There is a huge body of case law, much of it emanating from the European Court of Human Rights pursuant to article 6 of the Convention, that deals with these issues.

Drafting of the provision

Paragraph 1 of article 21 can be traced to article 39 of the 1950 text of the Convention. It concerns the election of judges. What is today article 21(1) was the second paragraph of the original article 39 of the Convention.

The initial Draft Statute of the European Court of Human Rights prepared by the International Juridical Section of the European Movement provided that the Court was to be composed 'of a body of independent judges, elected regardless of their nationality from among persons of high moral character, who possess the qualifications required in their respective countries for appointment to the highest judicial offices or are jurisconsults of recognised competence in international law'.[3] The text replicated article 2 of the Statute of the International Court of Justice, adopted a few years previously.

The Consultative Assembly draft of the Convention adopted in September 1949 did not contain a provision concerning the criteria for judges of the Court. The Committee of Experts, meeting in February and March 1950, noted in its Report that it had not copied the provision in the Statute of the International Court of Justice forbidding members of the Court from exercising other functions. The Committee explained that it anticipated 'the possibility of only a very limited number of cases' being brought to the Court and was concerned that judges might 'find themselves condemned to idleness while drawing a fixed salary'. Its solution was to pay them an allowance for every day of service.[4] In the draft provision governing election of judges, the Committee of Experts added that members of the Court 'shall be of high moral character and must possess the qualifications required for appointment to high judicial offices, or shall be jurisconsults of recognised competence'.[5] There was no debate on this and no subsequent modifications were made. Article 39(3) of the Convention adopted in 1950 reads: 'The candidates shall be of high moral character and must either possess the qualifications required for appointment to high judicial office or be jurisconsults of recognised competence.'

Paragraph 2 of article 21 can be traced directly to Protocol No. 8 of the Convention. More indirectly, it is derived from a provision in the 1950 text of the Convention that applied to the European Commission of Human Rights but not to the Court. Article 23 of the 1950 text of the Convention stated: 'The members of the Commission shall sit on the Commission in their individual capacity. During their term of office they shall not hold any position which is incompatible with their independence and impartiality as members of the Commission or the demands of this office.'

Detailed provisions about the Commission were only first considered by the Committee of Experts that met in February and March 1950. In the provision dealing with election to the Commission, the Committee of Experts proposed the following paragraph: 'The members of the Commission shall sit on the Commission in their individual

---

[3] Draft Statute of the European Court of Human Rights, INF/5/E/R, I *TP* 302–21, at p. 302, art. 2.
[4] Report to the Committee of Ministers submitted by the Committee of Experts Instructed to Draw Up a Draft Convention of Collective Guarantee of Human Rights and Fundamental Freedoms, Doc. CM/WP 1 (5) 15, A 924, IV *TP* 2–55, at pp. 42–4.
[5] Ibid., p. 72.

capacity.'[6] The Commentary did not address this sentence specifically, but it noted concerns about the 'somewhat political character of the Commission'. This may explain why the reference to individual capacity was included.[7] The paragraph was retained without change or debate by the Conference of Senior Officials that met in June 1950.[8] The Committee of Ministers, meeting in August, moved the paragraph from the provision dealing with election to the Commission and made it a distinct article, subsequently numbered as article 23.[9]

Protocol No. 8, adopted in 1985 and in force in 1990, added the following paragraph to article 40(7) of the Convention: 'The members of the Court shall sit on the Court in their individual capacity. During their term of office they shall not hold any position which is incompatible with their independence and impartiality as members of the Court or the demands of this office.'[10] According to the Explanatory Report on Protocol No. 8, the purpose was simply to make the provision dealing with the Court consistent with article 23, which applied to the Commission.[11] It continued:

With regard to the first sentence of this provision, that judges sit in an individual capacity is inherent in the very concept of a court. Nevertheless, the authors of the Protocol thought it appropriate to mention this requirement in the Convention, in particular as the latter already contained such a provision in relation to members of the Commission. Reasons of textual consistency also spoke in favour of including the second sentence following the insertion in the Convention of such a provision for Commission members. The Court has previously, through its Rules, laid down that a judge may not exercise his functions while he holds a post or exercises a profession which is incompatible with his independence and impartiality; the new paragraph 7 of Article 40 strengthens this rule by placing an obligation on a judge holding such a position to resign from the Court.[12]

Protocol No. 11 consolidated these provisions and somewhat reconfigured them. Thus, article 39(2) became article 21(1), with the word 'judges' replacing 'candidates'. The first sentence of article 40(7) became article 21(2), with the word 'judges' replacing 'members of the Court'. The second sentence of article 40(7) formed the basis of article 39(3), although changes were made. A proposal from the Parliamentary Assembly to add the words 'as well as the length of their term of office' at the end of paragraph 3 was not adopted.[13] The Explanatory Report on Protocol No. 11 provides little information about the drafting of article 21. It states:

Paragraphs 1 and 2 of Article 21 follow closely paragraph 3 of former Article 39 and paragraph 7 of former Article 40 of the Convention. The provision in paragraph 3 concerns incompatibility 'with

---

[6] Appendix to the Report of the Committee of Experts to the Committee of Ministers—Draft Convention (16 March 1950), Doc. CM/WP 1 (50) 14 revised, A 925, IV *TP* 50–79, at p. 70.

[7] Report to the Committee of Ministers submitted by the Committee of Experts Instructed to Draw Up a Draft Convention of Collective Guarantee of Human Rights and Fundamental Freedoms, Doc. CM/WP 1 (5) 15, A 924, IV *TP* 2–55, at p. 36.

[8] Draft Convention annexed to the Report, Doc. CM/WP 4 (50) 19 annex, CM/WP 4 (50) rev., A 1452, IV *TP* 274–95, at p. 284.

[9] Draft Convention adopted by the Sub-Committee, Doc. CM 1 (50) 52, A 1884, V *TP* 76–99, at p. 86.

[10] Protocol No. 8 to the Convention for the Protection of Human Rights and Fundamental Freedoms, ETS 118, art. 9.

[11] Explanatory Report on Protocol No. 8, para. 11.

[12] Ibid., para. 43.

[13] Draft Protocol No. 14 to the Convention for the Protection of Human Rights and Fundamental Freedoms amending the control system of the Convention, Opinion No. 251 (2004), Parliamentary Assembly, para. 14.i.

the demands' of this office and means that judges must be able fully to assume all the duties inherent in membership of the new permanent Court; this is an indispensable requirement for the efficient working of the Court. During their term of office judges may not engage in any activity incompatible with the full-time character of their office.[14]

The heading 'Criteria for office' was also introduced by Protocol No. 11.

Protocol No. 15, which is not yet in force, introduces a new paragraph 2 to article 21 dealing with the maximum age of candidates for election to the Court and, by ricochet, the maximum age of a judge of the Court.[15] The origins of the Protocol can be traced to the Brighton High Level Conference on the Future of the Court of April 2012. The Conference Declaration noted that '[a] stable judiciary promotes the consistency of the Court. It is therefore in principle undesirable for any judge to serve less than the full term of office provided for in the Convention,'[16] The Conference resolved that 'article 23(2) of the Convention should be amended to replace the age limit for judges by a requirement that judges must be no older than 65 years of age at the date on which their term of office commences'.[17] According to the Explanatory Report on Protocol No. 15, the modification is aimed at enabling 'highly qualified judges to serve the full nine-year term of office and thereby reinforce the consistency of the membership of the Court'. It notes that '[t]he age limit applied under Article 23, paragraph 2 of the Convention, as drafted prior to the entry into force of this Protocol, had the effect of preventing certain experienced judges from completing their term of office. It was considered no longer essential to impose an age limit, given the fact that judges' terms of office are no longer renewable.'[18] The Court itself welcomed the amendment, stating that the former age limit of 70 'no longer seems imperative in the present day'.[19]

As the Explanatory Report notes, because the process of election of a judge can be long, it was felt necessary to foresee a date that was sufficiently certain for the purpose of determining the age of the candidate. The concern was that a candidate might initially qualify but then exceed the date because of the length of the election proceedings. 'For this practical reason, the text of the Protocol departs from the exact wording of the Brighton Declaration, whilst pursuing the same end. It was thus decided that the age of the candidate should be determined at the date by which the list of three candidates has been requested by the Parliamentary Assembly', the Explanatory Report states.[20] Instead of amending article 23, the Protocol deletes paragraph 23(2), as it is superseded by the amendment to article 21.[21]

---

[14] Explanatory Report on Protocol No. 11, para. 60.

[15] Protocol No. 15 amending the Convention for the Protection of Human Rights and Fundamental Freedoms, ETS 213, art 2.

[16] High Level Conference on the Future of the European Court of Human Rights, Brighton Declaration, para. 24.

[17] Ibid., para. 25.f.

[18] Explanatory Report on Protocol No. 15, para. 12.

[19] Opinion of the European Court of Human Rights on Draft Protocol No. 15 to the European Convention on Human Rights, para. 6.

[20] Explanatory Report on Protocol No. 15, para. 13.

[21] Ibid., para. 14.

Analysis and interpretation

The 1950 Convention dealt with election of judges and their criteria for office in a single provision, article 39. The revision of the Convention effected by Protocol No. 11 divided these two notions into two distinct provisions. Article 21 governs criteria for office and article 22 addresses election of judges. The first two paragraphs of article 21 'follow closely' articles 39(3) and 40(7) of the 1950 text of the Convention, respectively.[22]

The Brighton Declaration, adopted in 2012 at the High Level Conference on the Future of the European Court of Human Rights, affirmed: 'The high calibre of judges elected to the Court depends on the quality of the candidates that are proposed to the Parliamentary Assembly for election. The States Parties' role in proposing candidates of the highest possible quality is therefore of fundamental importance to the continued success of the Court ... '[23]

High moral character and qualifications for appointment to high judicial office

According to the Grand Chamber, 'Article 21 § 1 and Article 22 of the Convention are intended to ensure the election, as members of the Court, of judges who are of high moral character and possess the qualifications required for appointment to high judicial office'.[24] In assessing candidates for election as judges of the Court, the Parliamentary Assembly will not consider lists containing candidates who 'do not appear to be of the stature to meet the criteria in Article 21, paragraph 1, of the European Convention on Human Rights'.[25]

The requirement that 'candidates shall be of high moral character and must either possess the qualifications required for appointment to high judicial office or be jurisconsults of recognised competence' is derived from article 2 of the Statute of the International Court of Justice. Article 21(1) closely resembles the provision that one commentator has described as having attained customary status.[26] The Guidelines of the Committee of Ministers say this means that 'behaviour and personal status must be compatible with holding judicial office'.[27]

The Statute of the International Court of Justice requires that judges possess qualifications for appointment to 'the highest judicial offices', whereas the European Convention speaks of 'high judicial office'. The Statute of the International Court also specifies that 'recognised competence' be in 'international law'. That seems logical at a court that applies international law but less obvious at a specialized human rights court.

---

[22] Explanatory Report on Protocol No. 11, para. 60.

[23] High Level Conference on the Future of the European Court of Human Rights, Brighton Declaration, para. 22.

[24] *Advisory Opinion on certain legal questions concerning the lists of candidates submitted with a view to the election of judges to the European Court of Human Rights (no. 2)* [GC], §38, 22 January 2010.

[25] Candidates for the European Court of Human Rights, Parliamentary Assembly, Resolution 1366 (2004), para. 3(b).

[26] Mariano J. Aznar-Gómez, 'Article 2', in Andreas Zimmermann, Christian Tomuschat, and Karin Oellers-Frahm, eds, *The Statute of the International Court of Justice, A Commentary*, Oxford: Oxford University Press, 2006, pp. 205–18, at p. 218.

[27] Guidelines of the Committee of Ministers on the Selection of Candidates for the Post of Judge at the European Court of Human Rights, CM(2012)40 addendum final, para. 20.

The dictionary meaning of the term 'jurisconsult' is 'expert in law'. In an advertisement for candidates for the position of judge at the European Court, the United Kingdom explained that the term meant 'academic lawyers and practitioners'.

The Guidelines of the Committee of Ministers suggest as examples of good practice in this regard that judges 'have at least a Master's degree in law and practical experience in legal affairs', and that they 'show a high level of achievement and experience'.[28]

When it advertised for candidates for the position of judge at the European Court, the United Kingdom included as criteria '[a] proven and consistently high level of achievement in the areas of law in which candidates have been engaged, and experience relevant to the post', '[t]he capacity to learn and understand quickly other legal, constitutional and political systems', and '[t]he ability to communicate effectively both orally and on paper, particularly in the role of judge rapporteur, and to work well in a chamber of international judges'. It also insisted upon '[c]ommitment to the principles of the European Convention on Human Rights'.

Legal knowledge

The European Convention requires 'recognised competence' but does not say in what. The Interlaken Declaration, adopted by the High Level Conference of the Council of Europe in 2010, refers to 'full satisfaction of the Convention's criteria for office as a judge of the Court, including knowledge of public international law and of the national legal systems'.[29] A call for applications by the Government of Ireland said that '[c]andidates need to have knowledge of the national legal system(s) and of public international law. Practical legal experience is also desirable.'[30]

The Guidelines prepared by the Committee of Ministers provide some indications in this area:

Although this criterion does not supersede Article 21 of the Convention, a high level of knowledge in these fields should be taken as an implicit requirement for candidates for judge at the Court and relative levels of knowledge could be taken into account when choosing between applicants of otherwise equal merits. As the judges sit on an international court playing a subsidiary role in supervising national implementation of the Convention, it is important for them to have knowledge of both public international law and the national legal system(s). Although the Court's composition benefits from a range of legal expertise, it is generally advantageous that applicants have expertise in human rights, notably the Convention and the Court's case-law.[31]

Fluency in official languages

The working languages of the Court are English and French and it is inconceivable that a judge could serve effectively without adequate fluency in at least one of these. Nevertheless, with the expansion in membership in the Court in the 1990s concerns were expressed that some of the judges were deficient in this respect. A Recommendation on the subject

---

[28] Ibid., para. 23.

[29] High Level Conference on the Future of the European Court of Human Rights, Interlaken Declaration, 19 February 2010, para. 8(a).

[30] Department of Foreign Affairs and Trade, Judge of the European Court of Human Rights with Respect to Ireland, Information Sheet, September 2014.

[31] Guidelines of the Committee of Ministers on the Selection of Candidates for the Post of Judge at the European Court of Human Rights, CM(2012)40 addendum final, para. 27.

from the Parliamentary Assembly in 1999 noted that the candidates put forward by States Parties for election to the Court 'did not always meet the criteria established by the Convention' and that in particular some of them 'were not sufficiently fluent in at least one of the Council of Europe's two official languages'.[32]

There is no formal requirement in this respect within the Convention itself, nor does it seem one has ever been seriously proposed. However, to the extent that the Parliamentary Assembly is the gatekeeper to the Court because it elects the judges, it is in a position to impose requirements that may only be implicit in the Convention. That is precisely what it has done with respect to linguistic competence. As the Grand Chamber of the Court noted in its first Advisory Opinion, 'a sufficient knowledge of at least one of the official languages is necessary in order to make a useful contribution to the Court's work, given that the Court uses only those two languages'.[33] In 1999, the Parliamentary Assembly recommended that the Committee of Ministers invite governments to apply criteria additional to those listed in article 21, notably that they 'ensure that the candidates are in fact fluent in either French or English and are capable of working in one of these two languages'.[34] In 2004, it made a similar recommendation, although in perhaps a less peremptory manner, requesting 'that the candidates have a sufficient knowledge of at least one of the two official languages'.[35] This was accompanied by a Resolution stating that the Assembly would not consider lists of candidates that 'do not appear to have sufficient knowledge of at least one of the two official languages'.[36] It made this slightly more demanding in 2009 with the criterion that 'candidates should possess an active knowledge of one official language of the Council of Europe and a passive knowledge of the other'.[37] Yet the model curriculum vitae that it asks candidates to complete, as revised in 2009, suggests a less stringent approach: 'In the event that you do not meet the level of language proficiency required for the post of judge in an official language, please confirm your intention to follow intensive language classes of the language concerned prior to, and if need be also at the beginning of, your term of duty if elected a judge on the Court.'[38]

The Guidelines of the Committee of Ministers also consider this requirement:

The Court's working methods involve many documents in either English or French only and relatively few in both. This requires that judges be able to read and assimilate technical, complex and nuanced documents in both languages. They must be able to direct and supervise the drafting of such documents in one of the official languages. Their language abilities must be such as to inspire confidence on the part of other courts, lawyers, applicants to the Court and the general public.

[32] National procedures for nominating candidates for election to the European Court of Human Rights, Parliamentary Assembly, Recommendation 1429 (1999), para. 5.

[33] Advisory Opinion on certain legal questions concerning the lists of candidates submitted with a view to the election of judges to the European Court of Human Rights [GC], § 47, 12 February 2008.

[34] National procedures for nominating candidates for election to the European Court of Human Rights, Parliamentary Assembly, Recommendation 1429 (1999).

[35] Candidates for the European Court of Human Rights, Parliamentary Assembly, Recommendation 1649 (2004), para. 19(4).

[36] Candidates for the European Court of Human Rights, Parliamentary Assembly, Resolution 1366 (2004), para. 3.

[37] Nomination of candidates and election of judges to the European Court of Human Rights, Parliamentary Assembly, Resolution 1646 (2009), para. 4.4.

[38] Ibid., Appendix.

Between otherwise equivalent candidates, States should therefore prefer those with the relevant levels of ability in both languages.[39]

The United Kingdom's advertisement for candidates for the position of judge at the European Court required '[a]n operational working knowledge of French'. It seems that the United Kingdom presumed an 'operational working knowledge' of English was so obvious as not to require mention!

Experience in the field of human rights

The Convention does not impose any requirement that candidates for judicial office possess relevant experience or knowledge in the field of human rights. Nevertheless, this criterion has been added by the Parliamentary Assembly. In 1999, the Parliamentary Assembly invited governments to ensure that candidates 'have experience in the field of human rights, either as practitioners or as activists in non-governmental organisations working in this area'.[40] The model curriculum vitae annexed to the 1999 Resolution referred to '[a]ctivities and experience in the field of human rights'.[41] This requirement was stated more generally in another Recommendation adopted in 2004, requiring that 'candidates have experience in the field of human rights'.[42] At the same time, the Parliamentary Assembly adopted a Resolution stating that it would not consider lists of candidates where 'the areas of competence of the candidates appear to be unduly restricted'.[43] In 2009, the Assembly returned to the question, proposing a list of criteria additional to those in article 21 similar to what it had provided earlier but without any reference to 'experience in the field of human rights'.[44]

The Committee of Ministers Guidelines designed to assist States in selecting and vetting candidates for the Court devote considerable attention to such matters as legal knowledge, language skills, and age, while virtually ignoring the issue of activities and experience in the field of human rights.[45]

Age

The 1950 Convention did not impose any minimum or maximum age limit for members of the judiciary. Protocol No. 11 introduced a requirement that judges be required to retire at age 70.[46] The Explanatory Report on Protocol No. 11 said that '[s]ince the Court

---

[39] Guidelines of the Committee of Ministers on the Selection of Candidates for the Post of Judge at the European Court of Human Rights, CM(2012)40 addendum final, para. 25.

[40] National procedures for nominating candidates for election to the European Court of Human Rights, Parliamentary Assembly, Recommendation 1429 (1999), para. 6.ii.

[41] Election of judges to the European Court of Human Rights, Parliamentary Assembly, Resolution 1200 (1999), Appendix I, Model curriculum vitae for candidates seeking election to the European Court of Human Rights.

[42] Candidates for the European Court of Human Rights, Parliamentary Assembly, Recommendation 1649 (2004), para. 19(2).

[43] Candidates for the European Court of Human Rights, Parliamentary Assembly, Resolution 1366 (2004), para. 3.

[44] Nomination of candidates and election of judges to the European Court of Human Rights, Parliamentary Assembly, Resolution 1646 (2009), para. 4.

[45] Guidelines of the Committee of Ministers on the Selection of Candidates for the Post of Judge at the European Court of Human Rights, CM(2012)40 addendum final, para. 25.

[46] Protocol No. 11 to the Convention for the Protection of Human Rights and Fundamental Freedoms, restructuring the control machinery established thereby, ETS 155, art. 1 (new article 23(6)). The provision was

will function on a permanent basis, it was deemed appropriate to introduce an age limit, as exists in most domestic legal systems'.[47] While this may be true, it is also the case that international tribunals do not, as a general rule, establish any such criterion. There is no age limit at the International Court of Justice, the International Criminal Court, and Inter-American Court of Human Rights, for example. At the International Criminal Tribunal for the former Yugoslavia, Mohamed Shahabuddeen was re-elected a judge by the United Nations General Assembly at the age of 78. Theodor Meron was re-elected president of the Tribunal at the age of 83. At the European Court of Human Rights itself, René Cassin served as president until the age of 81. The age limit in national tribunals is often a relic of the past, at a time when life expectancy was considerably lower than it is today. Arguably, the discriminatory age limit for judges is itself incompatible with article 14 of the Convention and Protocol No. 12.

Historically, the average age of judges at the European Court of Human Rights has been about 65. This began to change as membership in the Council of Europe expanded during the 1990s. By 2012, the average age had dropped to 55, with several judges aged less than 40. According to a study, '[o]ne driver for this change was the appointment of several very young judges from Eastern Europe, as states preferred to put forward candidates who had received their education in the years after the break-up of the Soviet Union'. However, a similar phenomenon was observable in States that had joined the Council of Europe prior to 1992, 'suggesting that the trend toward nominating much younger judges was a wider phenomenon'.[48]

Protocol No. 15, not yet in force, in effect raises the maximum age for judges by requiring that at the age the Parliamentary Assembly requests a list of candidates they be less than 65 years of age. In practice, this will mean that a judge could be about a year over the age of 65 at the time of taking office and therefore serve until the age of 75. There is a transitional provision by which the new rule does not apply to pending elections, and to judges who are in office or who have been elected at the time of entry into force of the amendment.[49]

There is no minimum age for election as a judge to the European Court of Human Rights or, for that matter, to any other international court or tribunal. The idea has been mooted by the Rapporteur of the Committee on Legal Affairs and Human Rights of the Parliamentary Assembly. He has suggested that rather than impose a minimum starting age, something that 'may not in itself be a firm indicator of judicial capacity', it might be appropriate to impose a requirement of 12 to 15 years of relevant experience of candidates for election to the European Court of Human Rights.[50]

---

renumbered as article 23(2) by Protocol No. 14 to the Convention for the Protection of Human Rights and Fundamental Freedoms, amending the control system of the Convention, ETS 194.

[47] Explanatory Report on Protocol No. 11, para. 63.

[48] Leigh Swigart and Daniel Terris, 'Who are International Judges?', in Cesare P.R. Romano, Karen J. Alter, and Yuval Shany, eds, *The Oxford Handbook of International Adjudication*, Oxford: Oxford University Press, 2014, pp. 619–38, at p. 631.

[49] Protocol No. 15 amending the Convention for the Protection of Human Rights and Fundamental Freedoms, ETS 213, art. 8. See also Explanatory Report on Protocol No. 15, para. 15.

[50] Draft Protocol No. 15 amending the Convention for the Protection of Human Rights and Fundamental Freedoms, Report, Committee on Legal Affairs and Human Rights, Doc. 13154, para. 11. Also Nomination of candidates and election of judges to the European Court of Human Rights, Report, Committee on Legal Affairs and Human Rights, Doc. 11767, paras. 5, 32.

Individual capacity

Judges sit in their 'individual capacity'. The text is rather more elaborate than its predecessors in the 1950 version of the Convention. That the two were linked in article 40 of the 1950 Convention suggests that the requirement judges serve in their individual capacity is related to the prohibition on 'incompatible activities'. The notion of 'individual capacity' confirms that judges do not represent a State or act on its behalf. In this respect, attention must be given to the rule set out in article 26(4) of the Convention whereby the judge elected from the respondent State sits in cases before the Court.

Incompatible activities

The final paragraph of article 21 'concerns incompatibility "with the demands" of this office and means that judges must be able fully to assume all the duties inherent in membership of the new permanent Court; this is an indispensable requirement for the efficient working of the Court. During their term of office judges may not engage in any activity incompatible with the full-time character of their office.'[51] The provision is a somewhat expanded version of the second sentence of article 40(7) in the 1950 text of the Convention.

'Incompatible activities' are set out in Rule 4 of the Rules of Court. It is probably not an exhaustive description. According to Rule 4:

1. In accordance with Article 21 § 3 of the Convention, the judges shall not during their term of office engage in any political or administrative activity or any professional activity which is incompatible with their independence or impartiality or with the demands of a full-time office. Each judge shall declare to the President of the Court any additional activity. In the event of a disagreement between the President and the judge concerned, any question arising shall be decided by the plenary Court.
2. A former judge shall not represent a party or third party in any capacity in proceedings before the Court relating to an application lodged before the date on which he or she ceased to hold office. As regards applications lodged subsequently, a former judge may not represent a party or third party in any capacity in proceedings before the Court until a period of two years from the date on which he or she ceased to hold office has elapsed.

The requirement that 'all questions arising from the application of this paragraph shall be decided by the Court' was not part of the predecessor texts in the 1950 version of the Convention. Added by Protocol No. 11, it seems intended to strengthen the independence of the Court by discouraging any other body from attempting to intervene, although no guidance to its interpretation is offered by the explanatory report.

Oath of office

Judges are required to take the following oath or solemn declaration either at the first session of the plenary Court that they attend or before the President: 'I swear'—or 'I solemnly declare'—'that I will exercise my functions as a judge honourably, independently and impartially and that I will keep secret all deliberations.'[52]

---

[51] Explanatory Report on Protocol No. 11, para. 60.
[52] Rules of Court, Rule 3.

Further reading

Johan Callewaert, 'Article 39', in Pettiti et al., *La Convention européenne*, pp. 747–8.

Johan Callewaert, 'Article 40', in Pettiti et al., *La Convention européenne*, pp. 749–50.

J.A. Carrillo-Salcedo, 'Quels juges pour la nouvelle Cour européenne des droits de l'homme?', (1997) 9 *Revue universelle des droits de l'homme* 1–3.

Andrew Drzemczewski, 'Election of Judges to the Strasbourg Court: An Overview', [2010] EHRLR 377.

Frowein/Peukert, *MenschenRechtsKonvention*, pp. 441–2.

N. Vajić, 'Some Remarks Linked to the Independence of International Judges and the Observance of Ethics Rules in the European Court of Human Rights', in C. Hohmann-Dennhardt, P. Masuch and M. Villiger, eds, *Grundrechte und Solidarität: Festschrift für Renate Jaeger*, Kehl, Germany: N.P. Engel, 2011, pp. 179–93.

Nicolas Valticos, 'Quels juges pour la prochaine Cour européenne des droits de l'homme', in *Liber Amicorum Marc-André Eissen*, Brussels: Bruylant, 1995, pp. 415–34.

Erik Voeten, 'The Impartiality of International Judges: Evidence from the European Court of Human Rights', (2008) 102 *American Political Science Review* 417.

Article 22. Election of judges/Election des juges

The judges shall be elected by the Parliamentary Assembly with respect to each High Contracting Party by a majority of votes cast from a list of three candidates nominated by the High Contracting Party.

Les juges sont élus par l'Assemblée parlementaire au titre de chaque Haute Partie contractante, à la majorité des voix exprimées, sur une liste de trois candidats présentés par la Haute Partie contractante.

Introductory comments

Judges of international courts and tribunals are, by and large, elected to office, although there are exceptions. The judges of the International Military Tribunal were appointed by each of the four powers that had created the Tribunal. Judges at two United Nations criminal tribunals, the Special Court for Sierra Leone and the Special Tribunal for Lebanon, are subject to a complex appointment procedure but there is no election. Judges at the *ad hoc* tribunals for the former Yugoslavia and Rwanda created by the United Nations Security Council have, once elected, had their terms extended by resolution of the Security Council.

Where international judges are elected, the process is often accompanied by unseemly campaigning and bartering of votes. This situation is especially acute when the election is conducted in a body like the United Nations General Assembly. That each State Party to the European Convention on Human Rights is entitled to one judge eliminates some of this unpleasantness. The Parliamentary Assembly of the Council of Europe continues to reflect on techniques intended to enhance the quality, independence, and impartiality of the judges of the Court.

Drafting of the provision

The initial draft European Convention on Human Rights prepared by the International Juridical Section of the European Movement provided that judges of the European Court of Human Rights would 'be elected by the Committee of Ministers and the Consultative Assembly, by an absolute majority of votes in each body'.[1] The model for this was the Statute of the International Court of Justice whereby judges are elected in both the Security Council and the General Assembly, acting independently of each other.[2] The Draft Statute of the European Court of Human Rights, proposed at the same time, set out very detailed rules for the election of judges.[3] The Consultative Assembly adopted the following proposal: 'Art. 23. Members of the Court shall be elected by the Committee of Ministers and by the Consultative Assembly of the Council of Europe by a

---

[1] Convention for the Collective Protection of Individual Rights and Democratic Liberties by the States, Members of the Council of Europe, and for the establishment of a European Court of Human Rights to ensure observance of the Convention, Doc. INF/5/E/R, I *TP* 296–303, at p. 300, art. 9(b).

[2] Statute of the International Court of Justice, arts 4(1), 8.

[3] Draft Statute of the European Court of Human Rights, INF/5/E/R, I *TP* 302–21, at pp. 302–7, arts 4–13.

simple majority cast in each of these bodies.'[4] The initial proposal was for elections to take place in both the Consultative Assembly and the Committee of Ministers, with separate votes in each forum.[5]

The Committee of Experts, meeting in February and March 1950, agreed upon the following: 'The members of the Court shall be elected by the Consultative Assembly and by the Committee of Ministers of the Council of Europe from a list of persons nominated by the High Contracting Parties; each Party shall nominate three candidates.'[6] The accompanying commentary said '[t]his system is essentially the same as that contained in the Assembly draft'.[7] The provision was subsequently modified by the Conference of Senior Officials by appending, at the very end, the words 'of whom two at least shall be its nationals'.[8] The reason was 'to prevent a group of representatives submitting the name of a single candidate of their nationality, and thus limiting the choice of the Committee of Ministers to that one candidate'.[9]

The major modification to the provision, by which the Committee of Ministers was removed and the election of judges made the sole prerogative of the Consultative Assembly, took place at the fifth session of the Committee of Ministers in August 1950. The text then read: 'The members of the Court shall be elected by the Consultative Assembly by a majority of the votes cast from a list of persons nominated by the Members of the Council of Europe; each Member shall nominate three candidates, of whom two at least shall be its nationals.'[10]

Meeting in Rome immediately before adoption of the Convention, the Committee of Legal Experts agreed on the addition of a paragraph specifying that '[a]s far as applicable, the same procedure shall be followed to complete the Court in the event of the admission of new members of the Council of Europe, and in filling casual vacancies'.[11] Article 39, as adopted in 1950, read as follows:

1. The members of the Court shall be elected by the Consultative Assembly by a majority of the votes cast from a list of persons nominated by the Members of the Council of Europe; each Member shall nominate three candidates, of whom two at least shall be its nationals.

[4] Report presented by Mr P.H. Teitgen, 5 September 1949, Doc. A 290, I *TP* 192–213, at p. 198. Also Report [of the Committee on Legal and Administrative Questions], 5 September 1949, Doc. AS (1) 77, I *TP* 216–39, at p. 234; Official Report of the Sitting [of the Consultative Assembly, 8 September 1949], II *TP* 14–274, at p. 218.

[5] Ibid., p. 210.

[6] Appendix to the Report of the Committee of Experts on Human Rights: Draft Convention of Protection of Human Rights and Fundamental Freedoms, 16 March 1950, Doc. C/WP 1 (50) 15 appendix, CM/WP 1 (50) 14 revised, A 925, IV *TP* 50–79, at p. 71.

[7] Report to the Committee of Ministers submitted by the Committee of Experts Instructed to Draw Up a Draft Convention of Collective Guarantee of Human Rights and Fundamental Freedoms, Doc. CM/WP 1 (5) 15, A 924, IV *TP* 2–55, p. 42.

[8] Draft Convention annexed to the Report, Doc. CM/WP 4 (50) 19 annex, CM/WP 4 (50) rev., A 1452, IV *TP* 274–95, at p. 288.

[9] Text of the report submitted by the Conference [of Senior Officials] to the Committee of Ministers, Doc. CM/WP 4 (50) 19, CM/WP 4 (50) 16 rev., A 1431, IV *TP* 242–73, at pp. 262, 266.

[10] Draft Convention adopted by the Sub-Committee, Doc. CM 1 (50) 52, A 1884, V *TP* 76–99, at p. 90; Draft Convention adopted by the Committee of Ministers, 7 August 1950, Doc. A 1937, V *TP* 120–45, at pp. 120–36; Letter dated 7 August 1950 sent by Mr MacBride, Chairman of the Committee of Ministers, to M. Spaak, President of the Consultative Assembly, Doc. No. 11, p. 600–19, V *TP* 144–71, at p. 162.

[11] Report of the Committee [of Legal Experts, 2–3 November 1950], Doc. CM/Adj (50) 3 revised, A 2531, VII *TP* 10–13, p. 12.

2. As far as applicable, the same procedure shall be followed to complete the Court in the event of the admission of new Members of the Council of Europe, and in filling casual vacancies.

3. The candidates shall be of high moral character and must either possess the qualifications required for appointment to high judicial office or be jurisconsults of recognized competence.

A week after adoption of the Convention, A.H. Robertson of the Secretariat General circulated a note observing that there were two possible interpretations on paragraph 2, one by which the new Member State would propose a list of three candidates and the other by which all Members of the Council, including the new Members State, would each nominate three candidates. Robertson did not indicate how he thought the interpretative difficulty should be resolved.[12]

The provision was renumbered article 22 by Protocol No. 11 and given the title 'Election of judges'. In the words of the Explanatory Report, the new article 22 is 'virtually identical' to article 39 of the 1950 text. The reference to 'Consultative Assembly' in the 1950 version was changed to 'Parliamentary Assembly', reflecting the new terminology adopted by the Council of Europe in 1974. The Explanatory Report also states with respect to article 22: 'The judges of the new permanent Court will be elected in respect of each State Party in the same manner as those of the Court, prior to the Convention's amendment by this Protocol, namely by the Parliamentary Assembly.'[13]

Both the 1950 text of the Convention and the subsequent provision in Protocol No. 11 on the election of judges made special provision for the election of judges from new States Parties and the filling of casual vacancies. This was removed by Protocol No. 14, given changes that were made to article 23, which in effect eliminated the notion of casual vacancies. Pursuant to Protocol No. 14, when a judge does not complete a full term, an election is held according to the general procedure described in the sole remaining paragraph of article 22.[14] A proposal from the Parliamentary Assembly to add the words 'containing at least one candidature from a person of each gender' after 'Contracting Party' was not adopted.[15]

Analysis and interpretation

An important dimension of the credibility of the European Court of Human Rights depends upon the integrity of the election process. It involves the interaction of two bodies, the State Party, which is responsible for nominating candidates, and the Parliamentary Assembly, which elects them. The Grand Chamber of the Court has spoken of a 'balance and division of powers' between the States Parties and the Parliamentary Assembly in the appointment process.[16] The system 'seeks to ensure that the entities involved—the State concerned and the Assembly—enjoy a certain autonomy, within the limits of their respective powers, allowing them to determine how the procedural rules laid

---

[12] Note of Mr Robertson dated 14 November 1950, VII *TP* 12–23, at pp. 14–19.

[13] Explanatory Report on Protocol No. 11, para. 61.

[14] Explanatory Report on Protocol No. 14, para. 48.

[15] Draft Protocol No. 14 to the Convention for the Protection of Human Rights and Fundamental Freedoms, amending the control system of the Convention, Opinion No. 251 (2004), Parliamentary Assembly, para. 14.ii.

[16] *Advisory Opinion on certain legal questions concerning the lists of candidates submitted with a view to the election of judges to the European Court of Human Rights (no. 2)* [GC], §39, 22 January 2010.

down in Article 22 are to be applied'.[17] However, 'none of the entities involved in the procedure for electing judges—the High Contracting Parties and the Parliamentary Assembly—may exercise the powers they enjoy in this matter to the detriment of the others' powers'.[18] A tension necessarily results to the extent that States may attempt to neutralize the role of the Parliamentary Assembly by using the nomination process to make the outcome of the election rather predictable by, for example, including two evidently incompetent candidates on their list. For some time, Ukraine attempted to emasculate the Parliamentary Assembly by simply refusing to nominate a three-judge slate and instead relying upon *ad hoc* judges designated in accordance with article 26(4). The Parliamentary Assembly has taken the view that '[i]n the absence of a real choice among the candidates submitted by a state party to the Convention, the Assembly shall reject lists submitted to it. In addition, in the absence of a fair, transparent and consistent national selection procedure, the Assembly may reject such lists.'[19]

The Parliamentary Assembly has insisted that 'the process of appointment must reflect the principles of democratic procedure, the rule of law, non-discrimination, accountability and transparency'.[20] In 1999, following the first elections to the 'new Court', the Parliamentary Assembly expressed dissatisfaction with certain aspects of the nomination process. It found that the method of selection of candidates varied considerably from one country to another and that 'in the majority of cases there are no rules governing the selection of candidates'. Moreover, 'the candidates put forward did not always meet the criteria established by the Convention: either they lacked experience in human rights, had never held judicial office, or were not sufficiently fluent in at least one of the Council of Europe's two official languages'.[21]

Reviewing experience a decade later, the Parliamentary Assembly said that 'despite a marked improvement in national selection procedures in several countries, there is still significant variance as concerns fairness, transparency and consistency'.[22] A harsher critique came from a former judge of the Court: 'Lawyers who had no training or even a background acquaintance with human rights and/or did not have essential or adequate knowledge of one, and on some occasions of both, official working languages of the Court, namely English and French, became members of the Court with self-evident negative consequences.'[23]

The Grand Chamber has stated that 'the provisions of the Convention—including those relating to the organisation and functioning of the Court—must be interpreted in such a way as to ensure their effectiveness and, in the context of Articles 21 and 22, to

---

[17] Ibid. Also Advisory Opinion on certain legal questions concerning the lists of candidates submitted with a view to the election of judges to the European Court of Human Rights [GC], §§ 43–44, 12 February 2008.

[18] *Advisory Opinion on certain legal questions concerning the lists of candidates submitted with a view to the election of judges to the European Court of Human Rights (no. 2)* [GC], §44, 22 January 2010.

[19] Nomination of candidates and election of judges to the European Court of Human Rights, Parliamentary Assembly, Resolution 1646 (2009), para. 2.

[20] Candidates for the European Court of Human Rights, Parliamentary Assembly, Recommendation 1649 (2004).

[21] National procedures for nominating candidates for election to the European Court of Human Rights, Parliamentary Assembly, Recommendation 1429 (1999), para. 5.

[22] Nomination of candidates and election of judges to the European Court of Human Rights, Parliamentary Assembly, Resolution 1646 (2009), para. 2.

[23] Loukis Loukaides, 'Reflections of a Former European Court of Human Rights Judge on his Experiences as a Judge', (2010) 1 *Roma Rights Quarterly* 61.

ensure the prompt filling of all vacancies in the composition of the Court'.[24] Furthermore, 'Article 21 § 1 and Article 22 of the Convention are intended to ensure the election, as members of the Court, of judges who are of high moral character and possess the qualifications required for appointment to high judicial office.'[25]

Procedure

The Parliamentary Assembly has urged governments to have appropriate national selection procedures 'to ensure that the authority and credibility of the Court are not put at risk by *ad hoc* and politicised processes in the nomination of candidates'.[26] It has indicated that States should 'issue a call for candidatures through the specialised press, so as to obtain candidates who are indeed eminent jurists satisfying the criteria' of the Convention.[27] The Assembly has also invited governments to ensure the selection panels or bodies and those advising on selection are 'as gender-balanced as possible'.[28]

The Parliamentary Assembly has developed guidelines for States with respect to the nomination of candidates for the Court. The starting point for the engagement of the Parliamentary Assembly is the list of three candidates proposed by the State for whom a vacancy must be filled. One simple requirement is that the list be in alphabetical order, a mechanism to discourage the State from ranking the candidates or expressing a preference.[29] The list is to be accompanied by a curriculum vitae following a model adopted by the Assembly.[30] It has said that '[i]n principle, the list of candidates for the election of judges, once submitted to the Parliamentary Assembly, should not be modified'.[31] Only exceptionally will the Assembly accept partial or complete modification of the list on the initiative of the government concerned.[32]

---

[24] *Advisory Opinion on certain legal questions concerning the lists of candidates submitted with a view to the election of judges to the European Court of Human Rights (no. 2)* [GC], §37, 22 January 2010.

[25] Ibid., §38.

[26] Nomination of candidates and election of judges to the European Court of Human Rights, Parliamentary Assembly, Resolution 1646 (2009).

[27] National procedures for nominating candidates for election to the European Court of Human Rights, Parliamentary Assembly, Recommendation 1429 (1999), para. 6.i. Also Candidates for the European Court of Human Rights, Parliamentary Assembly, Recommendation 1649 (2004), para. 19.i.

[28] Nomination of candidates and election of judges to the European Court of Human Rights, Parliamentary Assembly, Resolution 1646 (2009).

[29] National procedures for nominating candidates for election to the European Court of Human Rights, Parliamentary Assembly, Recommendation 1429 (1999), para. 6.v; Candidates for the European Court of Human Rights, Parliamentary Assembly, Recommendation 1649 (2004), para. 19.v; Modalities for the election procedure of judges to the European Court of Human Rights and the Council of Europe Commissioner for Human Rights, Parliamentary Assembly, Appendix to Resolution 1432 (2005), para. 3.

[30] Nomination of candidates and election of judges to the European Court of Human Rights, Parliamentary Assembly, Resolution 1646, Appendix, Model curriculum vitae for candidates seeking election to the European Court of Human Rights. This replaces an earlier version: Election of judges to the European Court of Human Rights, Parliamentary Assembly, Resolution 1200 (1999), Appendix I, Model curriculum vitae for candidates seeking election to the European Court of Human Rights.

[31] Modalities for the election procedure of judges to the European Court of Human Rights and the Council of Europe Commissioner for Human Rights, Parliamentary Assembly, Appendix to Resolution 1432 (2005), para. 1.

[32] Procedure for elections held by the Parliamentary Assembly other than those of its President and Vice-Presidents, Parliamentary Assembly, Resolution 1432 (2005); Modalities for the election procedure of judges to the European Court of Human Rights and the Council of Europe Commissioner for Human Rights, Parliamentary Assembly, Appendix to Resolution 1432 (2005).

As early as 1996, in the election of judges for the 'new Court' established pursuant to Protocol No. 11, the Parliamentary Assembly began to interview the three judges on the list submitted by a State Party. Interviews are now conducted by the Sub-Committee on the Election of Judges to the European Court of Human Rights of the Committee on Legal Affairs and Human Rights. According to the Assembly, the interviews are 'most helpful in order to obtain a better insight into the qualities of the candidates and thus facilitate a better-informed choice'.[33] The Sub-Committee considers the candidates 'not only as individuals but also with an eye to a harmonious composition of the Court, taking into account, for example, their professional backgrounds and a gender balance'.[34]

In a report on its work, the Sub-Committee indicated that the interview enabled an assessment of the following characteristics: knowledge and awareness of European Convention jurisprudence; general legal knowledge and experience; intellectual and analytical ability; maturity and soundness of judgment; decisiveness and authority; communication and listening skills; integrity and independence; fairness and impartiality; understanding of people and society; courtesy and humanity; commitment to public service; conscientiousness and diligence.[35] The Sub-Committee submits a recommendation to the Bureau of the Assembly. The Bureau forwards to the Assembly members and may decide to make it public.[36]

The Assembly elects the judges to the European Court of Human Rights during its part-sessions. It interrupts the procedure if one of the candidates withdraws before the first ballot. Should that happen, it asks the government to complete the list of candidates.[37] However, once the process is underway the State concerned cannot arbitrarily withdraw a candidate from those it has nominated.[38] If a candidate withdraws for reasons outside the control of the nominating State, the latter cannot then prepare a new list, but is confined to replacing the absent candidate.[39] To be elected, the candidate must obtain an absolute majority of votes cast. If no candidate obtains an absolute majority, a second ballot is held, after which the candidate who has obtained a relative majority of votes cast is declared elected. Election results are publicly announced by the President of the Assembly.[40] The Committee of Ministers has published a document entitled 'Guidelines of the Committee of Ministers on the Selection of Candidates for the Post of Judge at the European Court of

---

[33] Election of judges to the European Court of Human Rights, Parliamentary Assembly, Resolution 1200 (1999), para. 3. Also Candidates for the European Court of Human Rights, Parliamentary Assembly, Resolution 1366 (2004), para. 4.

[34] Procedure for electing judges to the European Court of Human Rights, Sub-Committee on the election of Judges to the European Court of Human Rights, Committee on Legal Affairs and Human Rights AS/Jur (2010) 12, para. 6.

[35] Report of the Committee on Legal Affairs and Human Rights concerning Resolution 1366, Doc. 9963 (2003).

[36] Procedure for electing judges to the European Court of Human Rights, Sub-Committee on the election of Judges to the European Court of Human Rights, Committee on Legal Affairs and Human Rights AS/Jur (2010) 12, para. 6.

[37] Modalities for the election procedure of judges to the European Court of Human Rights and the Council of Europe Commissioner for Human Rights, Parliamentary Assembly, Appendix to Resolution 1432 (2005), para. 2.

[38] *Advisory Opinion on certain legal questions concerning the lists of candidates submitted with a view to the election of judges to the European Court of Human Rights (no. 2)* [GC], §§ 47–49, 22 January 2010.

[39] Ibid., § 57.

[40] Procedure for electing judges to the European Court of Human Rights, Sub-Committee on the election of Judges to the European Court of Human Rights, Committee on Legal Affairs and Human Rights AS/Jur (2010) 12, para. 7.

Human Rights' setting out its interpretation of the relevant provisions of the Convention concerning the election of judges.[41]

In 2010, pursuant to the Interlaken Declaration, the Committee of Ministers established an 'Advisory Panel of Experts on Candidates for Election as Judge to the European Court of Human Rights'. The mandate of the Panel is 'to advise the High Contracting Parties whether candidates for election as judges of the European Court of Human Rights meet the criteria stipulated in Article 21 § 1 of the European Convention on Human Rights'. Its seven members include judges of the highest national courts, former judges of international courts, including the European Court of Human Rights, and lawyers. Before the list of three candidates is submitted to the Parliamentary Assembly in accordance with article 22, each State is to provide the panel with the names and curricula vitae of the candidates it intends to propose. The panel assesses the candidates in order to ensure that they are suitable. If it concludes that one or more of the candidates is not suitable, it informs the State. Its opinion on the list of candidates is subsequently communicated to the Parliamentary Assembly.[42] According to the Plenary Court, the Advisory Panel has 'enhanced the procedure for the election of judges, to the benefit of States and the Parliamentary Assembly as they exercise their respective powers under Article 22 of the Convention'.[43]

Gender balance

Like other international courts, the European Court of Human Rights has struggled with the issue of gender balance. According to the Explanatory Report on Protocol No. 14, a proposal to amend article 22 so as to require that the lists of three candidates contain representatives of both sexes was rejected, 'since that might have interfered with the primary consideration to be given to the merits of potential candidates. However, Parties should do everything possible to ensure that their lists contain both male and female candidates.'[44] At present, approximately one-third of the judges of the Court are women. This compares somewhat poorly with the International Criminal Court, which has had a feminine majority for some years, but favourably with the International Court of Justice, which has never had more than three women in a cohort of fifteen. At the 'former' European Court of Human Rights, which closed its doors in 1998 when it was replaced by the 'new Court', only two women had ever been elected as judges: Denise Bindschedler-Robert of Switzerland (1975–1991) and Elizabeth Palm of Sweden (1988–2003).

The Parliamentary Assembly began to address the challenge of gender balance at the Court during the 1990s. By its Order No. 519, the Assembly instructed the Committee on Legal Affairs and Human Rights to examine the question of the qualifications and manner of appointment of judges to the European Court of Human Rights, with a view to achieving a balanced representation of the sexes. Noting that a 'substantial number of

---

[41] CM(2012)40 addendum final.
[42] Resolution CM/Res(2010)26 on the establishment of an Advisory Panel of Experts on Candidates for Election as Judge to the European Court of Human Rights.
[43] Opinion on the CDDH report on the Advisory Panel, 15 April 2014, para. 5.
[44] Explanatory Report on Protocol No. 14, para. 49.

governments' did not include a woman on their list,[45] the Parliamentary Assembly recommended that the Committee of Ministers invite States, when drawing up lists of candidates, to 'select candidates of both sexes in every case'.[46]

In 2004, it proposed that the Committee of Ministers amend article 22 so as to require that the three-judge list submitted by States Parties contain at least one candidate of each sex.[47] However, no action was taken on this initiative. The Committee of Ministers took the view that 'circumstances may exceptionally arise in which, as a result of the correct application of the other five criteria, a Contracting Party may find itself obliged to submit a list containing candidates of only one sex in derogation from that rule, and that it would therefore be undesirable to give such a rule binding force under the Convention'. The Committee drew attention 'to the danger that such an obligation could under certain circumstances give rise to difficulties in satisfying the requirements of Article 21 of the Convention'.[48]

Nevertheless, without amendment of the Convention, the Parliamentary Assembly can have a serious impact by rejecting lists that do not contain at least one woman. The Assembly determined that in assessing the three candidates, in the case of equal merit the Sub-Committee should give precedence 'to a candidate of the sex under-represented at the Court'.[49] It also decided not to consider lists of candidates that did not include at least one candidate of each sex.[50] This rather mechanistic approach had a serious shortcoming in that it did not permit a list of three women, 'even if this would obviously contribute to furthering the Assembly's purpose of achieving a more balanced representation of both sexes in the Court', as was noted subsequently.[51] Therefore, the Assembly amended the rule to allow a same-sex list if 'the candidates belong to the sex which is under-represented in the Court, that is the sex to which under 40% of the total number of judges belong'.[52]

The requirement did not in practice pose any difficulty for the vast majority of States. The possibility that a State could include a non-national on the list meant there could be no valid reason for a failure to identify a suitable female candidate. When Malta's list consisting of three male candidates was rejected as being inconsistent with the requirement of the Parliamentary Assembly, an advisory opinion of the Court was sought as to whether the Parliamentary Assembly had such authority under the Convention. After a thorough review of the applicable law and the development of the debate within the

---

[45] National procedures for nominating candidates for election to the European Court of Human Rights, Parliamentary Assembly, Recommendation 1429 (1999), para. 5.

[46] Ibid. Also Candidates for the European Court of Human Rights, Parliamentary Assembly, Recommendation 1649 (2004), para. 19.iii.

[47] Candidates for the European Court of Human Rights, Parliamentary Assembly, Recommendation 1649 (2004).

[48] Candidates for the European Court of Human Rights, Parliamentary Assembly Recommendation 1649 (2004) (Reply adopted by the Committee of Ministers on 20 April 2005 at the 924th meeting of the Ministers' Deputies), CM/AS(2005)Rec1649, para. 8.

[49] Candidates for the European Court of Human Rights, Parliamentary Assembly, Resolution 1366 (2004), para. 4(vi).

[50] Ibid., para. 3(ii).

[51] Candidates for the European Court of Human Rights, Parliamentary Assembly, Resolution 1426 (2005), para. 4.

[52] Ibid., para. 5.

Council of Europe, the Court ruled that the Assembly was required to contemplate exceptions and that it could not impose the strict rule that it had adopted. According to the Court:

> In any event it is clear that, in not allowing any exceptions to the rule that the under-represented sex must be represented, the current practice of the Parliamentary Assembly is not compatible with the Convention: where a Contracting Party has taken all the necessary and appropriate steps with a view to ensuring that the list contains a candidate of the under-represented sex, but without success, and especially where it has followed the Assembly's recommendations advocating an open and transparent procedure involving a call for candidatures..., the Assembly may not reject the list in question on the sole ground that no such candidate features on it.[53]

The Court indicated that 'exceptions to the principle that lists must contain a candidate of the under-represented sex should be defined as soon as possible'.[54] The Assembly acted promptly to allow derogation from the general rule in exceptional circumstances if a State has taken 'all the necessary and appropriate steps to ensure that the list contains a candidate of the under-represented sex, but has not been able to find a candidate of that sex who satisfies the requirements' of the Convention.[55]

Further reading

Johan Callewaert, 'Article 39', in Pettiti et al., *La Convention européenne*, pp. 747–8.

J.A. Carrillo-Salcedo, 'Quels juges pour la nouvelle Cour européenne des droits de l'homme?', (1997) 9 *Revue universelle des droits de l'homme* 1.

Andrea Coomber, 'Judicial Independence: Law and Practice of Appointments to the European Court of Human Rights' [2003] *European Human Rights Law Revies* 486.

Andrew Drzemczewski, 'Election of Judges to the Strasbourg Court: An Overview', [2010] *EHRLR* 377.

Andrew Drzemczewski, 'L'élection du juge de l'Union européenne à la Cour européenne des droits de l'homme', (2013) 24 *RTDH* 551.

Frowein/Peukert, *MenschenRechtsKonvention*, pp. 443–5.

Hans Christian Krüger, 'Procédure de selection des juges de la nouvelle Cour européenne des droits de l'homme', (1991) 8 *Revue universelle des droits de l'homme* 113.

M. Kuijer, 'Voting Behaviour and National Bias in the European Court of Human Rights and the International Court of Justice', (1997) 10 *Leiden Journal of International Law* 49.

P. Lambert, 'Les Juges ad hoc à la Court européenne des Droits de l'Homme', [1999] *RTDH* 479.

Jutta Limbach, Pedro Cruz Villalón, Roger Errera, Anthony Lester, Tamara Morshchakova, Steven Sedley, and Andrzej Zoll, *Judicial Independence: Law and Practice of Appointments to the European Court of Human Rights*, London: Interights, 2003.

H.G. Schermers, 'Election of Judges to the European Court of Human Rights', [1998] *European Law Review* 575.

N. Vajic, 'Some Remarks Linked to the Independence of International Judges and the Observance of Ethical Rules in the ECHR', in Christine Hohmann-Dennhardt, Peter Masuch, and Mark

---

[53] Advisory Opinion on certain legal questions concerning the lists of candidates submitted with a view to the election of judges to the European Court of Human Rights [GC], § 54, 12 February 2008.

[54] Ibid.

[55] Candidates for the European Court of Human Rights, Parliamentary Assembly, Resolution 1627 (2008).

Villiger, eds, *Grundrechte und Solidarität. Durchsetzung und Verfahren: Festschrift für Renate Jaeger*, Kehl, Germany: N.P. Engel, 2011, pp. 179–93.

E. Voeten, 'The Politics of International Judicial Appointments: Evidence from the European Court of Human Rights', (2007) 61 *International Organization* 669.

E. Voeten, 'The Impartiality of International Judges: Evidence from the European Court of Human Rights', (2008) 102 *American Political Science Review* 417.

Article 23. Terms of office and dismissal/Durée du mandat et révocation

1. The judges shall be elected for a period of nine years. They may not be re-elected.

2. The terms of office of judges shall expire when they reach the age of 70.[1]

3. The judges shall hold office until replaced. They shall, however, continue to deal with such cases as they already have under consideration.

4. No judge may be dismissed from office unless the other judges decide by a majority of two-thirds that that judge has ceased to fulfil the required conditions.

1. Les juges sont élus pour une durée de neuf ans. Ils ne sont pas rééligibles.

2. Le mandat des juges s'achève dès qu'ils atteignent l'âge de 70 ans.

3. Les juges restent en fonction jusqu'à leur remplacement. Ils continuent toutefois de connaître des affaires dont ils sont déjà saisis.

4. Un juge ne peut être relevé de ses fonctions que si les autres juges décident, à la majorité des deux tiers, que ce juge a cessé de répondre aux conditions requises.

Introductory comments

Unlike national justice systems, where judges are frequently appointed for life or until some specified retirement age, international courts and tribunals usually specify a fixed term of a number of years with provision for a short extension in order to complete pending cases. Nine-year terms are prescribed for judges at the International Court of Justice and the International Criminal Court. At temporary or *ad hoc* institutions the terms may be much shorter; judges at the International Criminal Tribunal for the former Yugoslavia and the International Criminal Tribunal for Rwanda were elected to terms of four years and judges at the Special Court for Sierra Leone and the Special Tribunal for Lebanon to terms of three years. As a general proposition, the longer the term, the better the protection of the independence and impartiality of the judge. The restriction to a single term is also a valuable feature that contributes to independence and impartiality. If judges can be re-elected, there is a concern that their views may be influenced by inappropriate concerns, especially as the renewal date approaches.

Dismissal is a very rare event and there are only a few examples of this even being considered by international courts and tribunals. In May 2012, the plenary of the judges of the Special Court for Sierra Leone declared a judge 'unfit to sit' and recommended that the case be dealt with further by the appointing authority.[2] In another case, at the International Criminal Tribunal for the former Yugoslavia, a judge was disqualified from a case, in effect ending his term because he had been appointed *at litem*.[3]

---

[1] Paragraph 2 is deleted pursuant to article 2 of Protocol No. 15 amending the Convention for the Protection of Human Rights and Fundamental Freedoms, ETS 213, not yet in force. When Protocol No. 15 enters into force, paragraphs 3 and 4 will become paragraphs 2 and 3.

[2] Resolution on Complaint by Trial Chamber II against Justice Malick Sow, cited in *Prosecutor v. Taylor* (SCSL-03-01-A), Separate Opinion of Justice George Gelaga King on Decision on Charles Ghankay Taylor's Motion for Partial Voluntary Withdrawal or Disqualification of Appeals Chamber Judges, 13 September 2012.

[3] *Prosecutor v. Šešelj* (IT-03-67-T), Decision on Defence Motion for Disqualification of Judge Frederik Harhoff and Report to Vice President, 28 August 2013; UN Doc. S/2013/678, para. 14.

Drafting of the provision

The initial Draft Statute of the European Court of Human Rights prepared by the International Juridical Section of the European Movement provided for election to nine-year terms, with the possibility of re-election.[4] A member of the Court could only be dismissed if 'in the unanimous opinion of the other members, he has ceased to fulfil the required conditions'.[5]

Although the draft Convention adopted by the Consultative Assembly in September 1949 contained provisions governing establishment of the Court and the election of its judges, the term of office was nowhere specified, nor did any provision contemplate removal from office.[6] The Committee of Experts, meeting in February and March 1950, introduced a provision that provided for a nine-year term of office with the possibility of re-election. As an exception, the terms of four of the first judges to be elected would expire after three years and the terms of another four after three years. In this way, a system whereby approximately one-third of the judges would be elected every three years would be put in place.[7] The Conference of Senior Officials added yet another paragraph to the text: 'A member of the Court shall hold office until replaced. After having been replaced, he shall continue to deal with such cases as he already had under consideration.'[8]

As the text of the Convention was being finalized, H.J. Downing of the United Kingdom's Foreign Office drew the attention of the Secretariat General to a discrepancy in the Convention. He noted that the provision dealing with terms of office of members of the European Commission was essentially identical to that for the Court except that there was an additional paragraph in the former specifying that a member elected to replace a member whose term of office had not expired was to hold office for the remainder of the term (and not, presumably, begin a new three-year term). 'Was it intended that the terms of office should be parallel?', Downing inquired.[9] Meeting in Rome immediately before adoption of the Convention, the Committee of Legal Experts agreed on the addition of a paragraph equivalent to the one applicable to the Commission.[10]

The antecedent of article 23 adopted as part of the 1950 Convention read as follows:

Article 40
1. The members of the Court shall be elected for a period of nine years. They may be re-elected. However, of the members elected at the first election the terms of four members shall expire at the end of three years, and the terms of four more members shall expire at the end of six years.
2. The members whose terms are to expire at the end of the initial periods of three and six years shall be chosen by lot by the Secretary-General immediately after the first election has been completed.

---

[4] Draft Statute of the European Court of Human Rights, INF/5/E/R, I *TP* 302–21, at p. 304, art. 12(a).

[5] Ibid., p. 306, art. 17.

[6] Recommendation No. 38 to the Committee of Ministers adopted 8 September 1949 on the conclusion of the debates, Doc. AS (1) 108, II *TP* 274–83.

[7] Appendix to the Report of the Committee of Experts to the Committee of Ministers—Draft Convention (16 March 1950), Doc. CM/WP 1 (50) 14 revised, A 925, IV *TP* 50–79, at p. 72.

[8] Draft Convention appended to the Draft Report, Doc. CM/WP 4 (50) 16, appendix, A 1445, IV *TP* 218–40, at p. 234.

[9] Letter addressed 28 October 1950 by Mr Downing (United Kingdom) to Mr Robertson (Secretariat), CDH (70) 30, VI *TP* 286–91, at p. 290.

[10] Report of the Committee [of Legal Experts, 2–3 November 1950], Doc. CM/Adj (50) 3 revised, A 2531, VII *TP* 10–13, p. 12.

3. A member of the Court elected to replace a member whose terms of office has not expired shall hold office for the remainder of his predecessor's term.
4. The members of the Court shall hold office until replaced. After having been replaced, they shall continue to deal with such cases as they already have under consideration.

A week after adoption of the Convention, A.H. Robertson of the Secretariat General circulated a note concerning the term of office of judges elected from new Member States. He said the Committee of Legal Experts contemplated two possible solutions, one whereby after a new Member State is admitted no new judge should be elected until the next triennial election, the other by which there would be a judicial election immediately following admission of a new Member State but the term would be less than the full nine years so as to expire at the time of a triennial election. Robertson noted the suggestion that this might be addressed in the Rules of Court.[11]

Article 40 was amended in 1966 by Protocol No. 5. The following paragraphs were added:

1. In order to ensure that, as far as possible, one third of the membership of the Court shall be renewed every three years, the Consultative Assembly may decide, before proceeding to any subsequent election, that the term or terms of office of one or more members to be elected shall be for a period other than nine years but not more than twelve and not less than six years.
2. In cases where more than one term of office is involved and the Consultative Assembly applies the preceding paragraph, the allocation of the terms of office shall be effected by the drawing of lots by the Secretary General immediately after the election.

These paragraphs were inserted after paragraph 2, and paragraphs 3 and 4 of the original text were renumbered as paragraph 5 and 6. The provision was similar to one adopted at the same time with respect to the European Commission of Human Rights. According to the Explanatory Report on Protocol No. 5:

In the case of the Court, it is the Consultative Assembly which may fix terms of office between six and twelve years for judges in order to ensure that, as far as possible, one-third of the membership of the Court shall be renewed every three years. The new provision also applies to elections of judges on the accession of a new Member State to the Council of Europe, in order that they may fit into the new pattern.[12]

Article 23 in its present form results from Protocol No. 11. It introduced a term of six years for members of the 'new Court'. The Explanatory Report did not provide any information on the rationale for this change.[13] Six years had been the term for members of the European Commission of Human Rights pursuant to article 22(1) of the 1950 text of the Convention. As in the 'former Court', judges remained eligible for re-election. The new article introduced by Protocol No. 11 also contained transitional provisions, necessary in order to establish a rotation of judges so that all of their terms did not expire at the same time. These provisions are no longer relevant and were removed by Protocol No. 14. Finally, Protocol No. 11 introduced an age limit, requiring judges to retire at the age of 70.

The term of judges was again changed by Protocol No. 14, returning to the nine-year term of the original 1950 Convention but without the possibility of renewal. According to the Explanatory Report on Protocol No. 14, '[t]hese changes are intended to reinforce

---

[11] Note of Mr Robertson dated 14 November 1950, VII *TP* 12–23, at pp. 18–21.
[12] Explanatory Report on Protocol No. 5, para. 16.
[13] Explanatory Report on Protocol No. 11, paras 29, 62.

their independence and impartiality, as desired notably by the Parliamentary Assembly in its Recommendation 1649 (2004)'.[14] Under the 1950 Convention and Protocol No. 11, a judge elected to replace an incumbent who did not complete the term would only sit for the remainder of the term. That system was abolished by Protocol No. 14, by rewording paragraph 1 of article 23 and removing paragraphs 2 to 5 (and the consequential renumbering of paragraphs 6 and 7 as paragraphs 2 and 3, respectively). Henceforth, a new judge begins a full nine-year term, even in the case of a casual vacancy. The Explanatory Report says that this is 'to ensure that the introduction of a non-renewable term of office does not threaten the continuity of the Court'.[15]

The age limit of 70 imposed by Protocol No. 11 was retained. According to the Explanatory Report, paragraphs 1 and 2, when read together, 'may not be understood as excluding candidates who, on the date of election, would be older than 61'.[16] It notes that such an interpretation 'would be tantamount to unnecessarily depriving the Court of the possibility of benefiting from experienced persons, if elected'.[17] Nevertheless, 'it is generally recommended that High Contracting Parties avoid proposing candidates who, in view of their age, would not be able to hold office for at least half the nine-year term before reaching the age of 70'.[18] Finally, Protocol No. 14 incorporated the former article 24, dealing with dismissal, within article 23. The reason was purely technical: to avoid renumbering a large number of provisions as a result of the insertion of a new article 27.[19]

Pursuant to Protocol No. 15, which is not yet in force, the age limit of 70 is replaced by a requirement that candidates for the Court be under 65. The relevant provision will become paragraph 2 of article 22. With the entry into force of Protocol No. 15 and the elimination of paragraph 2, paragraphs 3 and 4 will be renumbered as paragraphs 2 and 3.

Analysis and interpretation

Terms of office

Judges of the European Court of Human Rights are elected for a term of nine years. They may not be re-elected. If the seat is vacant on the date of the election of the judge, or if it takes place less than three months before the vacancy, the term of office begins from the date of taking up office. This shall not be later than three months after the date of election. On the other hand, if it takes place more than three months before the seat becomes vacant, the term begins on the date the seat becomes vacant.[20] The incumbent judge remains in office until the successor has taken the oath or made the solemn declaration.[21]

Even if the term has expired, or if the judge has resigned, he or she continues to sit in pending cases.[22] Resignation of a judge is to be notified to the President of the Court, who must transmit this to the Secretary General of the Council of Europe.[23]

---

[14] Explanatory Report on Protocol No. 14, para. 50.
[15] Ibid.
[16] Ibid., para. 53.
[17] Ibid.
[18] Ibid.
[19] Ibid., para. 56.
[20] Rules of Court, Rule 2.
[21] Ibid., Rule 2(3).
[22] Ibid., Rules 6, 24(4), 26(3).
[23] Ibid., Rule 6.

The term of a judge comes to an end if the State withdraws from the Council of Europe. This was the case of the Greek judge, Georges Maridakis, when his country denounced the European Convention and quit the Council of Europe in 1970. The Court held that 'as the withdrawal of Greece from the Council of Europe becomes effective on 31 December 1970, the office for which Mr. Maridakis was elected by the Consultative Assembly on the nomination of the Greek Government cannot continue to operate beyond that date'.[24] When Czechoslovakia broke into two, on 31 December 1992, B. Repik ceased being the judge elected for that country. He was re-elected to the Court the following September as the judge for Slovakia.

The Grand Chamber has stated that 'the provisions of the Convention—including those relating to the organisation and functioning of the Court—must be interpreted in such a way as to ensure their effectiveness and, in the context of Articles 21 and 22, to ensure the prompt filling of all vacancies in the composition of the Court'.[25]

Age

Judges are required to retire from office when they reach the age of 70. Protocol No. 15 repeals this rule, replacing it with a requirement that they be aged less than 65 at the time of the call for nominations by the Parliamentary Assembly, a provision that will be article 22(2) when the Protocol enters into force. The new rule will enable judges to serve until about the age of 75. This issue of age limits is discussed in more detail in the chapter on article 21 in this Commentary.

Dismissal

The 1950 text of the Convention did not have a provision governing dismissal. This was introduced by Protocol No. 11 with a text modelled upon article 18(1) of the Statute of the International Court of Justice. Unlike article 18(1), however, which postulates unanimity, article 23 of the Convention requires a majority of two-thirds of the judges of the Court. Rule 7 of the Rules of Court specifies that in dismissal proceedings, the judge 'must first be heard by the plenary Court'. Furthermore, proceedings for dismissal may be 'set in motion' by any judge, suggesting that this is the only way for this to take place. The procedure itself is not specified anywhere in the Convention or the Rules of Court. Although rare in practice—it seems that no such proceedings have ever been initiated—in the unusual circumstances where they might arise greater precision about the procedure would be desirable. The Explanatory Report on Protocol No. 11 states that the provision was added 'in order to ensure the independence of the Court'.[26] But the rights of a judge threatened with dismissal must also be ensured in order to avoid a situation where personal rivalries and prejudices might contribute to an attempt at removal.

Status and working conditions of judges

The status and conditions of service of judges of the European Court of Human Rights are set by the Committee of Ministers, acting pursuant to article 16 of the Statute of the

---

[24] Resolution of the Court, 29 September 1970, (1970) 13 YB 43.
[25] *Advisory Opinion on certain legal questions concerning the lists of candidates submitted with a view to the election of judges to the European Court of Human Rights (no. 2)* [GC], §37, 22 January 2010.
[26] Explanatory Report on Protocol No. 11, para. 64.

Council of Europe.[27] Salaries of judges were raised in 2009 to a net amount of approximately €163,160 per annum, with additional sums payable for relocation and a small premium for the President and the Vice-presidents. In 2009, the Committee of Ministers also introduced an annual pension for judges of the Court, varying from about €22,151 to €44,301 depending upon a minimum of six and a maximum of twelve years of service.[28] The Committee of Ministers requires that judges reside 'at or near the seat of the Court'.[29] The Committee has also addressed what it calls 'Recognition of service as a judge of the European Court of Human Rights' by calling upon States 'to address appropriately the situation of judges of the Court, once their term of office has expired, by seeking to ensure, to the extent possible within the applicable national legislation, that former judges have the opportunity to maintain their career prospects at a level consistent with the office that they have exercised'.[30] This becomes more important to the extent that judges are younger. In the past, when the average age of judges was about 65, most of them were not particularly concerned with employment prospects upon the completion of their terms.

The Parliamentary Assembly also takes an interest in the employment conditions of judges. In particular, it has insisted on the need to: ensure that the status and remuneration of judges is commensurate with the dignity of their profession and burden of responsibilities; provide adequate support staff and equipment to ensure that judges can act efficiently and without undue delay; take all necessary measures to ensure the safety of judges, including the presence of security guards on Court premises or providing police protection for judges who are, or may become, victims of serious threats; ensure that judges of the Court are entitled to freedom of expression and association, providing that they exercise these rights in a manner that preserves the dignity of their office, impartiality, and independence.[31]

Precedence

Nothing in the Convention suggests any relevance to the issue of 'precedence' of members of the Court. However, Rule 5 of the Rules of Court provides a mechanism for determining this issue. It is a combination of the position they hold within the Court, the date of taking up office, and chronological age. The President comes first, followed by the Vice-Presidents of the Court and the Presidents of the Sections. If the Vice-Presidents and the President of the Sections have been elected on the same date, then the length of time since they took office determines their position. If this is the same, chronological age resolves the issue. It they were born on the same day, the Rules provide no answer. Elected

[27] Resolution CM/Res(2013)4 amending Resolution CM/Res(2009)5 on the status and conditions of service of judges of the European Court of Human Rights and of the Commissioner for Human Rights; Resolution CM/Res(2009)5 on the status and conditions of service of judges of the European Court of Human Rights and of the Commissioner for Human Rights, Committee of Ministers, 23 September 2009; Resolution Res(2004)50 on the status and conditions of service of judges of the European Court of Human Rights, Committee of Ministers, 15 December 2004.

[28] Resolution CM/RES(2009)5 on the status and conditions of service of judges of the European Court of Human Rights and of the Commissioner for Human Rights, Committee of Ministers, 23 September 2009, art. 10.

[29] Ibid., art. 5.

[30] Recognition of service as a judge of the European Court of Human Rights, DD(2013)1321 and DD (2014)302.

[31] Candidates for the European Court of Human Rights, Parliamentary Assembly, Recommendation 1649 (2004).

judges take precedence according to the date of their taking up office in accordance with Rule 2. Judges who have served the same length of time shall take precedence according to age. *Ad hoc* judges take precedence after the elected judges according to their date of birth.

Further reading

Johan Callewaert, 'Article 40', in Pettiti et al., *La Convention européenne*, pp. 749–50.
Frowein/Peukert, *MenschenRechtsKonvention*, pp. 446–7.

Article 24. Registry and rapporteurs/Greffe et rapporteurs

1. The Court shall have a Registry, the functions and organisation of which shall be laid down in the rules of the Court.

2. When sitting in a single-judge formation, the Court shall be assisted by rapporteurs who shall function under the authority of the President of the Court. They shall form part of the Court's Registry.

1. La Cour dispose d'un greffe dont les tâches et l'organisation sont fixées par le règlement de la Cour.

2. Lorsqu'elle siège en formation de juge unique, la Cour est assistée de rapporteurs qui exercent leurs fonctions sous l'autorité du président de la Cour. Ils font partie du greffe de la Cour.

Introductory comments

The Registry is the administrative pillar of the Court. This is a feature of the structure of virtually all international courts and tribunals.

Drafting of the provision

There was no provision concerning the Registry and legal secretaries in the 1950 text of the Convention. Protocol No. 11 introduced the ancestor of article 24. It was numbered article 25, and consisted of one paragraph containing two sentences. The first sentence was derived from Rules 11 and 12 of the former Rules of Court.[1] The second sentence read: 'The Court shall be assisted by legal secretaries.' According to the Explanatory Report on Protocol No. 11, it was inserted 'in order to ensure that members of the Court can, if they so wish, be assisted by legal secretaries (law clerks). Such assistants, who may be appointed upon the proposal of the judges, must have the required qualifications and practical experience to carry out the duties assigned to them by the judges.'[2]

The provision became article 24 when articles 22 and 23 were combined, an amendment dictated by Protocol No. 14. The second sentence of the original provision was deleted. The Explanatory Report on Protocol No. 14 noted that 'the legal secretaries, created by Protocol No. 11, have in practice never had an existence of their own, independent from the registry, as is the case at the Court of Justice of the European Communities'.[3]

Paragraph 2 was added by Protocol No. 14 'so as to introduce the function of rapporteur as a means of assisting the new single-judge formation provided for in the new Article 27'.[4] The Explanatory Report continues:

58. ... While it is not strictly necessary from a legal point of view to mention rapporteurs in the Convention text, it was none the less considered important to do so because of the novelty of rapporteur work being carried out by persons other than judges and because it will be indispensable

---

[1] Explanatory Report on Protocol No. 11, para. 65.
[2] Ibid., para. 67.
[3] Explanatory Report on Protocol No. 14, para. 58.
[4] Ibid., para. 58.

to create these rapporteur functions in order to achieve the significant potential increase in filtering capacity which the institution of single-judge formations aims at. The members of the registry exercising rapporteur functions will assist the new single-judge formations. In principle, the single judge should be assisted by a rapporteur with knowledge of the language and the legal system of the respondent Party. The function of rapporteur will never be carried out by a judge in this context.

59. It will be for the Court to implement the new paragraph 2 by deciding, in particular, the number of rapporteurs needed and the manner and duration of appointment. On this point, it should be stressed that it would be advisable to diversify the recruitment channels for registry lawyers and rapporteurs. Without prejudice to the possibility to entrust existing registry lawyers with the rapporteur function, it would be desirable to reinforce the registry, for fixed periods, with lawyers having an appropriate practical experience in the functioning of their respective domestic legal systems. Since rapporteurs will form part of the Court's registry, the usual appointment procedures and relevant staff regulations will apply. This would make it possible to increase the work capacity of the registry while allowing it to benefit from the domestic experience of these lawyers. Moreover, it is understood that the new function of rapporteur should be conferred on persons with a solid legal experience, expertise in the Convention and its case-law and a very good knowledge of at least one of the two official languages of the Council of Europe and who, like the other staff of the registry, meet the requirements of independence and impartiality.

Analysis and interpretation

The Registry

The Registry provides the Court with legal and administrative support so that it can conduct its judicial functions. The Registry processes and prepares applications for adjudication by Court. It has a staff of more than 600, including nearly 300 legal professionals. Members of the staff of the Registry correspond with applicants, States, and other participants in the litigation process. The activities of the Registry are governed by General Instructions. These are drawn up by the Registrar and approved by the President of the Court.[5]

The Registry consists of Section Registries for each of the Sections set up by the Court, as well as of administrative units necessary for the legal and administrative services of the Court.[6] A Section Registrar and a Deputy Section Registrar assist each of the Court's five judicial Sections. Case-processing divisions within the Registry prepare the files and analytical notes to assist the judges. Besides the case-processing divisions, the Registry also has administrative units responsible for such matters as information technology; case-law information and publications; research and the library; just satisfaction; press and public relations; language department; and internal administration.

The Registrar is the head of the Registry.[7] The functions of the Registrar are set out in Rule 17. The Registrar is to 'assist the Court in the performance of its functions and shall be responsible for the organisation and activities of the Registry under the authority of the President of the Court'. The Registrar has custody of the archives of the Court and is 'the channel for all communications and notifications made by, or addressed to, the Court in connection with the cases brought or to be brought before it'.[8] Subject to the duty of

---

[5] Rules of Court, Rule 17(4).
[6] Ibid., Rule 18(1).
[7] Ibid., Rule 15(1).
[8] Ibid., Rule 17(2).

discretion, the Registrar has the responsibility to reply to requests for information concerning the work of the Court, particularly enquiries from the press.[9] The Registrar 'shall be of high moral character and must possess the legal, managerial and linguistic knowledge and experience necessary to carry out the functions attaching to the post'.[10]

The Registrar is elected for a term of five years, which may be renewed. Elections for the position are held by secret ballot and only elected judges who are present may take part. If no candidate receives an absolute majority of the elected judges present, a second ballot is held for the two candidates who have received the most votes. If there is a tie, preference is to be given to a female candidate and, secondly, to the older candidate.[11] Before taking office, the Registrar takes an oath or solemn declaration to exercise his or her functions 'loyally, discreetly and conscientiously'.[12] The Registrar may only be dismissed on the basis of a vote in which a majority of two-thirds of the elected judges decides, meeting in plenary session, 'that the person concerned has ceased to fulfil the required conditions'. The procedure may be set in motion by any judge. The Registry 'must be heard by the plenary Court'.[13]

The Explanatory Report on Protocol No. 11 states that 'one or more Deputy Registrars are elected by the Court'.[14] The Rules of Court state that two Deputy Registrars are elected in similar fashion.[15] In practice, there is only one Deputy Registrar.

Rapporteurs

Non-judicial rapporteurs assist the Court when it sits in a single-judge formation. They are appointed by the President of the Court on the proposal of the Registrar. Section Registrars and Deputy Section Registrars act *ex officio* as non-judicial rapporteurs.[16] The rapporteur provided for by article 24 should not be confused with Judge rapporteurs who are assigned to oversee the preparation of a case in accordance with Rules 48 to 50 of the Rules of Court.

Further reading

Norbert Paul Engel, 'Status, Ausstattung und Personalhoheit des Inter-Americanischen und des Europäischen Gerichtshofs für Menschenrechte', (2003) 30 *EuGRZ* 122.

Frowein/Peukert, *MenschenRechtsKonvention*, p. 448.

Erik Fribergh, 'The Authority over the Court's Registry within the Council of Europe', in Lucius Caflisch, Johan Callewaert, Roderick Liddell, Paul Mahoney, and Mark Villiger, eds, *Liber Amicorum Luzius Wildhaber*, Kehl, Germany: N.P. Engel, 2007, pp. 145–58.

Paul Mahoney, 'The Status of the Registry of the European Court of Human Rights: Past, Present and Future', in Mahoney et al., *Mélanges Ryssdal*, pp. 845–62.

Paul Mahoney, 'Separation of Powers in the Council of Europe: The Status of the Euroepan Court of Human Rights vis-à-vis the Authorities of the Council of Europe', (2003) 24 *HRLJ* 152.

---

[9] Ibid., Rule 17(3).
[10] Ibid., Rule 15(1).
[11] Ibid., Rule 15(3).
[12] Ibid., Rule 15(4).
[13] Ibid., Rule 15(2).
[14] Explanatory Report on Protocol No. 11, para. 66.
[15] Ibid., Rule 16.
[16] Ibid., Rule 18A.

Article 25. Plenary Court/Assemblée plénière

The plenary Court shall	La Cour réunie en Assemblée plénière
(a) elect its President and one or two Vice-Presidents for a period of three years; they may be re-elected;	a) élit, pour une durée de trois ans, son président et un ou deux vice-présidents; ils sont rééligibles;
(b) set up Chambers, constituted for a fixed period of time;	b) constitue des chambres pour une période déterminée;
(c) elect the Presidents of the Chambers of the Court; they may be re-elected;	c) élit les présidents des chambres de la Cour, qui sont rééligibles;
(d) adopt the rules of the Court;	d) adopte le règlement de la Cour;
(e) elect the Registrar and one or more Deputy Registrars;	e) élit le greffier et un ou plusieurs greffiers adjoints;
(f) make any request under Article 26, paragraph 2.	f) fait toute demande au titre de l'article 26, paragraphe 2.

Introductory comments

The Plenary Court, consisting of all forty-seven judges, does not sit as a judicial body. This was the case previously, when the Court was smaller, prior to the adoption of Protocol No. 11. Since that time, the largest judicial formation is the Grand Chamber, made up of seventeen judges. The competence of the Plenary Court is now confined to the matters set out in article 25.

Drafting of the provision

A provision in the 1949 draft statute of the European Court of Human Rights prepared by the European Movement said that 'the full Court shall sit except when it is expressly provided otherwise'. The term 'full Court' was rendered in French as '*séance plénière*'.[1] During its 1949 session, the Consultative Assembly does not appear to have considered the possibility that the European Court would sit in plenary session. Indeed, it was not particularly concerned with the detailed operations of the Court at all. That discussion really began in the Committee of Experts that met in February and March 1950. It proposed that the Court 'shall consist of one Chamber composed of 7 judges, to consider cases brought before it'.[2] The draft referred to three functions of 'the Court', namely electing the President and Vice-President, the development of rules, and the

---

[1] Draft Statute of the European Court of Human Rights, INF/5/E/R, I *TP* 302–21, at p. 308, art. 24.

[2] Appendix to the Report of the Committee of Experts on human rights: Draft Convention of protection of human rights and fundamental freedoms, 16 March 1950, Doc. CM/WP 1 (50) 15 appendix, CM/WP 1 (50) 14 revised, A 925, IV *TP* 50–79, at p. 72, art. 34. Also: Preliminary draft convention for the maintenance and further realisation of human rights and fundamental freedoms, 15 February 1950, Doc. A 833, III *TP* 236–46, at p. 244, art. 31; Preliminary Draft Convention, Doc. CM/WP 1 (50) 14, A 932, III *TP* 312–35, at p. 330, art. 38.

determination of the procedure.[3] Subsequently these provisions, subject to a few minor changes, became articles 41 and 55 of the final version of the Convention.[4]

Article 41
The Court shall elect its President and one or two Vice-Presidents for a period of three years. They may be re-elected.

Article 55
The Court shall draw up its own rules and shall determine its own procedure.

It seems obvious from the context of articles 41 and 55 of the 1950 text of the Convention that what is meant by 'the Court' is the 'plenary Court' in the sense of all elected judges. Nevertheless, elsewhere in the Convention the term 'the Court' is used in a context indicating a reference to the relevant Chamber dealing with a particular case. For example, article 49 states that if there is a dispute about 'whether the Court has jurisdiction, the matter shall be settled by the decisions of the Court'. It is clear from the context that this is not the plenary Court, but rather the Chamber in question.

The expression 'plenary Court' was employed in the first version of the Rules of Court, adopted in 1959. Rule 1(b) said that 'the expression "plenary Court" means the European Court of Human Rights sitting in plenary session'. The Rules specified that the elections of the President and the Vice-President, in accordance with article 41, were to be conducted by the 'plenary Court'.[5] Indeed, the Rules referred to the office as 'Presidency of the Plenary Court'. The Rules required that a session of the plenary Court be convened at least once annually and that there be a quorum of nine of the elected judges.[6]

The original Rules of Court gave the plenary Court an adjudicative role in three situations: '[i]n the case of doubt or dispute as to whether a Contracting Party has the right... to bring a case before the Court';[7] dispute about the existence of a common interest justifying designation of a single common-interest judge;[8] cases where the Chamber had relinquished jurisdiction because of the existence of a 'serious question affecting the interpretation of the Convention' and those 'where the resolution of such question might have a result inconsistent with a judgment previously delivered by a Chamber or by the plenary Court'.[9]

The 1950 text of the Convention authorized only one Vice-President. The possibility of a second Vice-President was introduced by Protocol No. 8.[10] According to the Explanatory Report, the relevant provision 'has been rendered more flexible so as to allow for a second vice-presidency. This is justified by both the increase over recent years in the number of the Court's members and the build-up in its workload.'[11]

---

[3] Appendix to the Report of the Committee of Experts on human rights: Draft Convention of protection of human rights and fundamental freedoms, 16 March 1950, Doc. CM/WP 1 (50) 15 appendix, CM/WP 1 (50) 14 revised, A 925, IV TP 50–79, at p. 72, arts. 31, 33.

[4] Note that article 55 of the 1950 text was amended by Protocol No. 2, art. 4. In this respect, see the Explanatory Report on Protocol No. 11, para. 69.

[5] Rules of Court (adopted 18 September 1959), Rule 7(2).

[6] Ibid., Rules 16, 17.

[7] Ibid., Rule 21(4).

[8] Ibid., Rule 25(2).

[9] Ibid., Rule 48.

[10] Protocol No. 8 to the Convention for the Protection of Human Rights and Fundamental Freedoms, ETS 118, art. 9.

[11] Explanatory Report on Protocol No. 8, para. 44.

Article 25 was introduced by Protocol No. 11, although at the time of entry into force it bore the number 26.[12] The provision was renumbered as article 25 by Protocol No. 14, consequent upon the combining of articles 22 and 23 in a single provision. It was also given the heading 'Plenary Court'. Protocol No. 11 determined that the plenary Court would deal only with matters of organization and that judicial functions like those that it had exercised in the 'former Court' would henceforth be the realm of the Grand Chamber.[13]

According to the Explanatory Report on Protocol No. 14:

It is understood that the term "Chambers" appearing in paragraphs b and c refers to administrative entities of the Court (which in practice are referred to as "Sections" of the Court) as opposed to the judicial formations envisaged by the term "Chambers" in new Article 26, paragraph 1, first sentence. It was not considered necessary to amend the Convention in order to clarify this distinction.[14]

Paragraph (f) was added to article 25 by Protocol No. 14 'in order to reflect the new function attributed to the plenary Court by this protocol'.[15]

Analysis and interpretation

The Court sits in plenary session in order to exercise a variety of functions, most of them of an administrative rather than a judicial nature. For example, the plenary Court is responsible for the election of the President, the Vice-Presidents, the Registrar, and the Deputy-Registrars. Removal of the Registrar, the Deputy-Registrars, and the judges themselves also falls under the authority of the plenary Court.

The list of functions of the plenary Court in article 25 is not exhaustive. For example, the plenary Court has issued opinions on the adoption of new protocols to the Convention.[16] The Court has also expressed opinions in response to requests from the Committee of Ministers and the Steering Committee on Human Rights dealing with execution of judgments, reducing the caseload of the Court and the election of judges.[17] The plenary Court is charged by the Sixth Protocol to the General Agreement on Privileges and Immunities of the Council of Europe with responsibility respecting the waiver of immunity:

The plenary Court alone shall be competent to waive the immunity of judges; it has not only the right, but is under a duty, to waive the immunity of a judge in any case where, in its opinion, the immunity would impede the course of justice, and where it can be waived without prejudice to the purpose for which the immunity is accorded.[18]

---

[12] See Explanatory Report on Protocol No. 11, paras 68–69.

[13] Ibid., para. 80.

[14] Explanatory Report on Protocol No. 14, para. 60.

[15] Ibid., para. 60.

[16] Opinion of the Court on Draft Protocol No. 15 to the European Convention on Human Rights, 6 February 2013; Opinion of the Court on Draft Protocol No. 16 to the Convention extending its competence to give advisory opinions on the interpretation of the Convention, 6 May 2013.

[17] Opinion on the CDDH report on the Advisory Panel, 15 April 2014; Reply to Committee of Ministers request for comments on the CDDH Report on Execution, 9 May 2014; Response of the Court to the 'CDDH report containing conclusions and possible proposals for action on ways to resolve the large numbers of applications arising from systemic issues identified by the Court', 20 October 2014.

[18] Sixth Protocol to the General Agreement on Privileges and Immunities of the Council of Europe, ETS 162, art. 4.

In 2011, the plenary Court issued a decision on a request by Romania for waiver of immunity. The Court partially granted the application with respect to the judge's spouse and denied it with respect to the judge himself.[19]

Sessions of the plenary Court are convened by the President at least once a year, either on his or her initiative or, if so requested, by at least one-third of the judges.[20] A quorum of the plenary Court consists of two-thirds of the elected judges in office.[21] Some decisions of the plenary Court must be taken by a two-thirds majority of the elected judges and not simply a majority of those present at the meeting of the plenary Court. This is the case with dismissal of a judge, in accordance with article 23(4),[22] and with removal of the Registrar or a Deputy-Registrar.[23] In other cases, decisions are taken by a majority of the elected judges who are present.[24]

'[A] point of procedure or any other question' may be decided outside of a scheduled meeting of the plenary Court by tacit agreement. The President circulates a draft decision and, if there is no objection after a certain lapse of time, it will be deemed adopted.[25]

President and Vice-Presidents of the Court

According to article 41 of the 1950 text of the Convention, the Court is to elect its President and one or two Vice-Presidents for a period of three years. This became article 25(a) pursuant to Protocol No. 11, with the explicit requirement that the election be by the 'plenary Court' rather than 'the Court'. Article 25(a) sets the term of office of the President and the Vice-Presidents at three years. Rule 8(5) of the Rules of Court sets out the procedure for the election of President and Vice-Presidents:

The elections referred to in paragraph 1 of this Rule shall be by secret ballot. Only the elected judges who are present shall take part. If no candidate receives an absolute majority of the elected judges present, an additional round or rounds shall take place until one candidate has achieved an absolute majority. At each round, any candidate receiving less than five votes shall be eliminated. Of the remaining candidates, the one who has received the least number of votes shall also be eliminated. If there is more than one candidate in this position, only the candidate who is lowest in the order of precedence in accordance with Rule 5 shall be eliminated. In the event of a tie between two candidates in the final round, preference shall be given to the judge having precedence in accordance with Rule 5.

In electing judges to the Presidency, the Rules of Court direct the Court to 'pursue a policy aimed as securing a balanced representation of the sexes'.[26] Pursuant to an amendment to the Rules adopted in 2005, a judge who is elected President or Vice-President may be re-elected, but only once to the same level of office.[27] The President and Vice-Presidents shall continue to hold office until their successors are elected.[28] Rule 8(1)

---

[19] Press release, ECHR 265 (2011), 29 November 2011.
[20] Rules of Court, Rule 20(1).
[21] Ibid., Rule 20(2).
[22] Ibid., Rule 7.
[23] Ibid., Rule 15(2).
[24] Ibid., Rule 8(5), for the election of the President and the Vice-Presidents.
[25] Ibid., Rule 23A.
[26] Ibid., Rule 14.
[27] Ibid., Rule 8(3).
[28] Ibid., Rule 8(4).

of the Rules of Court adds the proviso that the members of the Presidency 'shall not exceed the duration of their terms of office as judges'.

There have been 12 Presidents of the Court: Arnold McNair (1959–1965), René Cassin (1965–1968), Henri Rolin (1968–1971), Humphrey Waldock (1971–1974), Giorgio Balladore Pallieri (1974–1980), Gérard Wiarda (1981–1985), Rolv Ryssdal (1985–1998), Rudolf Bernhardt (1998), Luzius Wildhaber (1998–2007), Jean-Paul Costa (2007–2011), Nicolas Bratza (2011–2012), and Dean Spielmann (2012–). No woman has served as president of the Court. Three of the Presidents were nationals of the United Kingdom, two of France, and one each of Belgium, Germany, Italy, Luxembourg, the Netherlands, Norway, and Switzerland. Under the 'former Court' there was only one Vice-President at any given time. Since Protocol No. 11 entered into force in 1998, there have always been two Vice-Presidents. Altogether, there have been nineteen Vice-Presidents of the Court, of whom two were women: René Cassin (1959–1965), Henri Rolin (1965–1968), Humphrey Waldock (1968–1971), Giorgio Balladore Pallierei (1971–1974), Hermann Mosler (1974–1977), Gérard J. Wiarda (1977–1980), Rolv Ryssdal (1981–1985), Walter-Jean Ganshof van der Meersch (1985–1986), Jean Cremona (1986–1992), Rudolf Bernhardt (1992–1998), Thór Vilhjálmsson (1998), Elisabeth Palm (1998–2001), Christos Rozakis (1998–2011), Jean-Paul Costa (2001–2006), Nicolas Bratza (2007–2011), Françoise Tulkens (2011–2012), Josep Casadevall (2011–), Dean Spielmann (2012), and Guido Raimondi (2012–). Three Vice-Presidents have been nationals of Belgium, two have been nationals of France, Italy, Germany, and the United Kingdom, and one each has been a national of Andorra, Greece, Iceland, Luxembourg, Malta, the Netherlands, Norway, and Sweden.

The President directs the work and administration of the Court. The President represents the Court and, in particular, is responsible for its relations with the authorities of the Council of Europe.[29] The President presides over the plenary meetings of the Court, the meetings of the Grand Chamber, and the meetings of the panel of five judges.[30] The President does not take part in consideration of cases being heard by the Chambers unless he or she is the judge elected with respect to a State Party concerned with the case.[31]

The Vice-Presidents assist the President, taking the place of the President if he or she cannot carry out the duties of the office or if the position of President is vacant. They also act as presidents of Sections.[32] If the President or the Vice-Presidents of the Court are unable to carry out their duties or if their offices are vacant, the office of President is assumed by a President of a Section or, if none is available, by another elected judge, in accordance with the order of precedence.[33]

Chambers (Sections)

The 'Sections' are not contemplated by the Convention itself. They are an administrative unit constituted pursuant to the Rules of Court, although their composition largely overlaps with that of the Chambers. The term 'Section' is used with respect to a Chamber

---

[29] Ibid., Rule 9(1).
[30] Ibid., Rule 9(2).
[31] Ibid., Rule 9(3).
[32] Ibid., Rule 10.
[33] Ibid., Rule 11.

set up by the plenary Court for a fixed period in accordance with article 25(b).[34] As noted in the Explanatory Report on Protocol No. 14, the term 'Chambers' in paragraphs (b) and (c) of article 25 'refers to administrative entities of the Court (which in practice are referred to as "Sections" of the Court) as opposed to the judicial formations envisaged by the term "Chambers" in new Article 26, paragraph 1, first sentence. It was not considered necessary to amend the Convention in order to clarify this distinction.'[35]

The plenary Court has the responsibility to 'set up' the Chambers (Sections). The plenary Court is also responsible for electing the Presidents of the Chambers (Sections). There are five Sections of the Court (a minimum of four is required by the Rules[36]), each made up of seven judges as well as a President and a Vice-President. They are required to be 'geographically and gender balanced and shall reflect the different legal systems among the Contracting Parties'.[37]

The plenary Court elects the Section President for a three-year term.[38] A Section Vice-President is elected by the Section itself.[39] The President of the Section is responsible for directing the work of the Section.[40] The President presides at the sittings of the Section.[41] Each Section also has a Section Registry that is directed by a Section Registrar, who may be assisted by a Deputy Section Registrar.[42]

Bureau

There is no reference to the Bureau in the Convention itself. The Bureau is provided for by the Rules of Court, pursuant to an amendment adopted in 2003. It is composed of the President of the Court, the Vice-Presidents, and the Section Presidents. Where a Vice-President or a Section President is unable to attend a Bureau meeting, he or she is replaced by the Section Vice-President or, failing that, by the next most senior member of the Section according to the order of precedence.[43] The Bureau may request the attendance of any other member of the Court or any other person whose presence it considers necessary.[44] It is assisted by the Registrar and the Deputy Registrars.[45]

The task of the Bureau is to assist the President in carrying out the functions of the office with respect to the Court's work and administration. The President may submit to the Bureau 'any administrative or extra-judicial matter which falls within his or her competence'.[46] The Bureau is also charged with facilitating coordination between the Court's Sections.[47] The President may consult the Bureau before issuing practice

---

[34] Ibid., Rules 1(d), 25.
[35] Explanatory Report on Protocol No. 14, para. 60.
[36] Rules of Court, Rule 25(2).
[37] Ibid., Rule 25(2).
[38] Ibid., Rule 8(1).
[39] Ibid., Rule 8(2).
[40] Ibid., Rule 12.
[41] Ibid.
[42] Ibid., Rule 18.
[43] Ibid., Rule 9A(1)(a).
[44] Ibid., Rule 9A(1)(b).
[45] Ibid., Rule 9A(2).
[46] Ibid., Rule 9A(3).
[47] Ibid., Rule 9A(4).

decisions and before approving general instructions drawn up by the Registrar.[48] The Bureau may report on any matter and make proposals to the plenary Court.[49]

Rules of Court

The plenary Court is responsible for drafting the Rules of Court. The 1950 text of the Convention included a distinct article authorizing adoption of the Rules of Court: 'Article 55. The Court shall draw up its own rules and shall determine its own procedure.' The provision was removed by Protocol No. 11. The first version of the Rules of Court was adopted in 1959. The judges were inspired by similar instruments from other international tribunals, notably the International Court of Justice, as well as by the Rules of the Commission that had already been adopted pursuant to article 36 of the 1950 text of the Convention.[50] The Rules have since been frequently amended.

The Rules of Court are subordinate legislation and must, of course, be consistent with the Convention itself. Because they are adopted by the judges sitting in plenary it is unlikely that the judges sitting in judicial formations will contest their validity. Nevertheless, challenges to the legality of the Rules of Court cannot be excluded entirely. In the first judgment of the Court, the Greek judge, Georges Maridakis, insisted that Rule 76, by which the Commission appeared to maintain a residual role even after a case had been referred to the Court, was incompatible with provisions of the Convention. Perhaps he was merely reviving an argument that he had lost in the plenary when the Rules were being adopted. Judge Maridakis agreed that the Court was without authority to declare the impugned Rule null and void, but it said 'there is no doubt that the Court has the right, and is in duty bound, to refuse to apply any of these rules which it regards as contrary to the terms of the Convention, in accordance with the principle of domestic law, whereby it is a judge's duty to refrain from applying any legal provision which contravenes the Constitution or any regulation which is contrary to law'.[51]

The Rules of Court are not 'a mere "act of an internal nature" but they emanate from the Court's treaty-given power set forth in Article 25(d) of the Convention to adopt its own rules regarding the conduct of the judicial proceedings before it'.[52] They deal with a range of matters mainly of an administrative and organizational nature. There are only a few references to the content of the Rules within the Convention itself. Article 24(1) says that the functions and organization of the Registry are to be laid down in the Rules. Article 26(5) requires that judges are to be designated to sit in the Grand Chamber 'in accordance with the rules'. Several Practice Directions, issued by the President, supplement and complete the Rules on the following subjects: requests for interim measures; institution of proceedings; written pleadings; just satisfaction claims; secured electronic filing; and requests for anonymity.

---

[48] Ibid., Rule 9A(5).

[49] Ibid., Rule 9A(6).

[50] Preparatory working paper drafted by the Directorate of Human Rights, 16 February 1959, CDH (59) 1.

[51] *Lawless v. Ireland (no. 1)*, 14 November 1960, Dissenting Opinion of Mr G. Maridakis, p. 17, Series A no. 1.

[52] *Husayn (Abu Zubaydah) v. Poland*, no. 7511/13, § 364, 24 July 2014; *Al Nashiri v. Poland*, no. 28761/11, § 371, 24 July 2014.

Suggestions with respect to the Rules of Court appeared in the Explanatory Report on Protocol No. 11:

70. The rules of Court will have to be adapted to the new structure and, in particular, to be supplemented on the following points: the role of the registry; the functions of the plenary Court; the constitution and the composition of the Grand Chamber, Chambers and committees; procedure on questions of admissibility and procedure concerning friendly settlement negotiations. The Rules of Procedure of the Commission will be of assistance in this connection.

71. Another matter for the rules of the new Court will be the question of publicity. The Court's proceedings (unlike those of the Commission; see former Article 33 of the Convention) will, save in exceptional circumstances, be public (see Article 40). Material relating to the friendly settlement negotiations will remain confidential (see Article 38, paragraph 2; see also Article 40, paragraph 2).

The failure by a State to observe a provision of the Rules may result in a finding that the Convention has been breached, provided that this can be related to a provision of the Convention itself.[53] Absent such a link, the Rules themselves cannot give rise to an independent binding obligation.[54]

Further reading

Frowein/Peukert, *MenschenRechtsKonvention*, p. 449.

---

[53] *Mamatkulov and Askarov v. Turkey* [GC], nos 46827/99 and 46951/99, § 129, ECHR 2005-I.
[54] *Cruz Varas and Others v. Sweden*, 20 March 1991, § 98, Series A no. 201.

Article 26. Single-judge formation, Committees, Chambers, and Grand Chamber/Formations de juge unique, comités, chambres et Grande Chambre

1. To consider cases brought before it, the Court shall sit in a single-judge formation, in committees of three judges, in Chambers of seven judges and in a Grand Chamber of seventeen judges. The Court's Chambers shall set up committees for a fixed period of time.

2. At the request of the plenary Court, the Committee of Ministers may, by a unanimous decision and for a fixed period, reduce to five the number of judges of the Chambers.

3. When sitting as a single judge, a judge shall not examine any application against the High Contracting Party in respect of which that judge has been elected.

4. There shall sit as an *ex-officio* member of the Chamber and the Grand Chamber the judge elected in respect of the High Contracting Party concerned. If there is none or if that judge is unable to sit, a person chosen by the President of the Court from a list submitted in advance by that Party shall sit in the capacity of judge.

5. The Grand Chamber shall also include the President of the Court, the Vice-Presidents, the Presidents of the Chambers and other judges chosen in accordance with the rules of the Court. When a case is referred to the Grand Chamber under Article 43, no judge from the Chamber which rendered the judgment shall sit in the Grand Chamber, with the exception of the President of the Chamber and the judge who sat in respect of the High Contracting Party concerned.

1. Pour l'examen des affaires portées devant elle, la Cour siège en formations de juge unique, en comités de trois juges, en chambres de sept juges et en une Grande Chambre de dix-sept juges. Les chambres de la Cour constituent les comités pour une période déterminée.

2. A la demande de l'Assemblée plénière de la Cour, le Comité des Ministres peut, par une décision unanime et pour une période déterminée, réduire à cinq le nombre de juges des chambres.

3. Un juge siégeant en tant que juge unique n'examine aucune requête introduite contre la Haute Partie contractante au titre de laquelle ce juge a été élu.

4. Le juge élu au titre d'une Haute Partie contractante partie au litige est membre de droit de la chambre et de la Grande Chambre. En cas d'absence de ce juge, ou lorsqu'il n'est pas en mesure de siéger, une personne choisie par le président de la Cour sur une liste soumise au préalable par cette partie siège en qualité de juge.

5. Font aussi partie de la Grande Chambre, le président de la Cour, les vice-présidents, les présidents des chambres et d'autres juges désignés conformément au règlement de la Cour. Quand l'affaire est déférée à la Grande Chambre en vertu de l'article 43, aucun juge de la chambre qui a rendu l'arrêt ne peut y siéger, à l'exception du président de la chambre et du juge ayant siégé au titre de la Haute Partie contractante intéressée.

Introductory comments

Since it began operations, the Court has experimented with a variety of judicial formations. Over the years, as the volume of cases increased, choices about the composition and size of chambers were increasingly driven by the need for efficient case management. At the same time, it has always been important to ensure an adequate level of consistency in the case law.

Drafting of the provision

Using a summary procedure before a chamber of reduced size is an idea that has been considered since the earliest stages of drafting of the European Convention on Human Rights. The initial Draft Statute of the European Court of Human Rights prepared by the International Juridical Section of the European Movement authorized the Court '[w]ith a view to the speedy despatch of business' to establish chambers composed of two or more judges, although this required the consent of the parties.[1] Participation of the national judge *ex officio* was also contemplated in this early draft.[2]

During its 1949 session, the Consultative Assembly does not appear to have examined the subject. Indeed, it was not particularly concerned with the detailed operations of the Court. That discussion really began in the Committee of Experts that met in February and March 1950. At its February session, the Committee of Experts adopted a provision by which the Court 'shall consist of one Chamber composed of 7 judges, to consider cases brought before it'. The Chamber was to be composed by drawing lots. Judges of the nationality of the parties were automatically members of the Chamber.[3] If there was no judge of the nationality of one of the parties, it could designate an *ad hoc* judge for the case.[4] The following month, the Committee revised the text, eliminating the mechanism for appointment of *ad hoc* judges and specifying instead that '[j]udges, nationals of the States parties to the dispute, shall take ex officio their seats in the Court; the names of the other judges shall be decided before the opening of the case'.[5]

At the June 1950 session of the Conference of Senior Officials Sweden submitted an amendment that contemplated a chamber of five rather than seven judges.[6] The Conference revised the text adopted by the Committee of Experts, reviving the concept of *ad hoc* judges. It said it was 'desirable' to complete the text with a provision 'allowing a judge to be appointed *ad hoc* in cases where any State implicated does not have a judge who is one of its nationals among the members of the Court'. The Report of the Conference added that the Danish delegate reserved the position of his Government on this question.[7] The Conference adopted the following text:

The Court shall consist of one Chamber composed of 7 judges, to consider cases brought before it. Any State party concerned shall be represented by the Member of the Court who is its national, or,

---

[1] Draft Statute of the European Court of Human Rights, INF/5/E/R, I *TP* 302–21, at p. 308, arts 25, 26.

[2] Ibid., p. 310, art. 28.

[3] See Amendment to Articles 21 and 28 of the Recommendation of the Consultative Assembly proposed by the Greek Expert, Doc. A 811, III *TP* 226–29.

[4] Preliminary Draft Convention for the Maintenance and Further Realisation of Human Rights and Fundamental Freedoms, 15 February 1950, Doc. A 833, III *TP* 236–46, at p. 244, art. 31. Also Preliminary Draft Convention, Doc. CM/WP 1 (50) 14, A 932, III *TP* 312–35, at p. 330, art. 38.

[5] New text suggested for Sections II, III, and IV, Doc. CM/WP 1 (50) 4, A 917, III *TP* 294–302, at p. 300; Preliminary Draft Convention, Doc. CM/WP 1 (50) 14, A 932, III *TP* 312–35, at p. 330, art. 38; Report to the Committee of Ministers submitted by the Committee of Experts Instructed to Draw Up a Draft Convention of Collective Guarantee of Human Rights and Fundamental Freedoms, Doc. CM/WP 1 (5) 15, A 924, IV *TP* 2–55, at p. 42; Appendix to the Report of the Committee of Experts on Human Rights: Draft Convention of Protection of Human Rights and Fundamental Freedoms, 16 March 1950, Doc. CM/WP 1 (50) 15 appendix, CM/WP 1 (50) 14 revised, A 925, IV *TP* 50–79, at p. 72, art. 34.

[6] Proposal submitted by the Swedish Delegation, Doc. CM/WP 4 (50) 10, A 1373, IV *TP* 190–95, at p. 192.

[7] Text of the report submitted by the Conference [of Senior Officials] to the Committee of Ministers, Doc. CM/WP 4 (50) 19, CM/WP 4 (50) 16 rev., A 1431, IV *TP* 242–73, at p. 266.

failing such a person of its choice who shall act as a judges; the names of the other judges shall be drawn by lot by the President before the opening of the case.[8]

This text was modified by the Committee of Ministers at its August 1950 meeting.

For the consideration of each case brought before it the Court shall consist of a Chamber composed of seven judges. There shall sit as an ex officio member of the Chamber the judge who is a national of any State party concerned, or, if there is none, a person of its choice who shall sit in the capacity of judge; the names of the other judges shall be chosen by lot by the President before the opening of the case.[9]

According to the *travaux* there was no further debate on the subject. The text adopted by the Committee of Ministers became article 43 of the 1950 final text of the Convention.

In 1990, with the entry into force of Protocol No. 8, the Chambers were enlarged from seven to nine judges.[10] According to the Explanatory Report, the gradual increase in the number of members of the Court had made the seven-judge Chamber 'progressively less representative of the Court as a whole'. A consequence of this had been an increase in the frequency of relinquishment of jurisdiction in favour of the plenary Court. 'To counter this, the number of members of Chambers has been increased to nine', the Report said.[11] Shortly after the entry into force of Protocol No. 8, the provision of the Rules of Court providing for relinquishment to the plenary Court was changed to allow for relinquishment to a 'Grand Chamber' consisting of the President, the Vice-President, the judges of the Chamber that had relinquished jurisdiction, and additional judges, so that it would comprise nineteen members.[12] The amendment entered into force on 27 October 1993 and the first hearings before a Grand Chamber took place in 1994.[13]

Article 26 of the Convention was introduced by Protocol No. 11. At the time, it was numbered article 27:

Committees, Chambers and Grand Chamber
1. To consider cases brought before it, the Court shall sit in committees of three judges, in Chambers of seven judges and in a Grand Chamber of seventeen judges. The Court's Chambers shall set up committees for a fixed period of time.
2. There shall sit as an *ex officio* member of the Chamber and the Grand Chamber the judge elected in respect of the State Party concerned or, if there is none or if he is unable to sit, a person of its choice who shall sit in the capacity of judge.
3. The Grand Chamber shall also include the President of the Court, the Vice-Presidents, the Presidents of the Chambers and other judges chosen in accordance with the rules of the Court. When a case is referred to the Grand Chamber under Article 43, no judge from the Chamber

---

[8] Draft Convention annexed to the Report, Doc. CM/WP 4 (50) 19 annex, CM/WP 4 (50) rev., A 1452, IV *TP* 274–95, at p. 290, art. 43.
[9] Draft Convention adopted by the Sub-Committee, Doc. CM 1 (50) 52, A 1884, V *TP* 76–99, at p. 92; Draft Convention adopted by the Committee of Ministers, 7 August 1950, Doc. A 1937, V *TP* 120–45, at p. 138.
[10] Protocol No. 8 to the Convention for the Protection of Human Rights and Fundamental Freedoms, ETS 118, art. 11.
[11] Explanatory Report on Protocol No. 8, para. 45.
[12] Rules of Court A (as in force at 1 February 1994), Rule 51 (Relinquishment of jurisdiction by the Chamber in favour of the Grand Chamber and by the Grand Chamber in favour of the plenary Court).
[13] *Murray v. the United Kingdom*, 28 October 1994, § 6, Series A no. 300-A; *Jersild v. Denmark*, 23 September 1994, § 6, Series A no. 298.

which rendered the judgment shall sit in the Grand Chamber, with the exception of the President of the Chamber and the judge who sat in respect of the State Party concerned.

The Chambers and the Grand Chamber had existed under the 'former Court', although their size was adjusted: from nine to seven for the Chambers and from nineteen to seventeen for the Grand Chamber. The Committee was an innovation. According to the new article 28, this three-judge formation was empowered to declare cases inadmissible or strike them from the list.

The text of article 26 was substantially amended by Protocol No. 14. To the judicial formations of the Court, it introduced the single-judge formation. Flexibility concerning the size of the Chambers was established by article 26(2). The Explanatory Report says this 'will reduce, for a fixed period, the size of Chambers generally; it should not allow, however, for the setting up of a system of Chambers of different sizes which would operate simultaneously for different types of cases'.[14]

The system of appointment of *ad hoc* judges was also changed by Protocol No. 14. By virtue of the new rule, contained in article 26(4), each State Party provides a reserve list of *ad hoc* judges from which the President of the Court appoints an *ad hoc* judge when this is required. The Explanatory Report states that '[t]his new system is a response to criticism of the old system, which allowed a High Contracting Party to choose an *ad hoc* judge after the beginning of proceedings'.[15] It notes that '[c]oncerns about this had also been expressed by the Parliamentary Assembly',[16] although the amendment does not fully respond to them. The Parliamentary Assembly had wanted to add, after the words 'by that party' in the final phrase of paragraph 4, the following: 'containing at least one candidature from a person of each gender, and approved by the Parliamentary Assembly'.[17] The Parliamentary Assembly said it 'welcomes the proposals as an improvement on the present practice regarding the category of persons "chosen by the President of the Court from a list submitted in advance" by the High Contracting Party, where the judge sitting in respect of this party is unavoidably detained. But the Assembly still considers such *ad hoc* judges as lacking legitimacy unless approved by the Assembly.'[18] The Explanatory Report says that it 'is understood that the list of potential *ad hoc* judges may include names of judges elected in respect of other High Contracting Parties'.[19]

Temporary provisions governing the single judge and the three-judge formation were applied pursuant to Protocol No. 14*bis* until the entry into force of Protocol No. 14 in 2010.

Analysis and interpretation

Article 26 concerns the judicial formations of the Court. Its provisions identify the bodies within the Court that are involved in the process of adjudication. For each formation, one

---

[14] Explanatory Report on Protocol No. 14, para. 63.
[15] Ibid., para. 64.
[16] Ibid.
[17] Draft Protocol No. 14 to the Convention for the Protection of Human Rights and Fundamental Freedoms amending the control system of the Convention, Opinion No. 251 (2004), Parliamentary Assembly, para. 14.iv.
[18] Ibid., para. 10.
[19] Explanatory Report on Protocol No. 14, para. 64.

or more articles of the Convention complement and develop the description of the judicial functions. These provisions are completed by the Rules of Court.

The Grand Chamber, the Chambers and the Committees sit 'full time', although the Court may fix session periods each year. Outside of those periods, the Grand Chamber and the Chambers may be convened by their Presidents in cases of urgency.[20]

Single-judge formation

The single-judge formation was introduced by Protocol No. 14 and has only been in operation since 2010. The functions of the single-judge formation are described in article 27 of the Convention and Rule 27A of the Rules of Court. An exception to the general rule by which a judge from a State concerned in the case participates is made by paragraph 3 of article 26.

After consulting the Bureau, the President of the Court decides upon the number of single judges and appoints them. They sit for a term of twelve months,[21] during which they also exercise their other functions as members of a Section. Several members of the Court act as single judges *ex officio*: the Presidents of the Section, when exercising certain functions under Rule 54 and Vice-Presidents of the Section appointed to decide on requests for interim measures.[22] The President prepares a list of States Parties in respect of which the single judge is authorized to examine applications.[23] Single judges are assisted by a non-judicial rapporteur, appointed pursuant to article 24(2) of the Convention.[24] In cases where the material submitted by the applicant 'is on its own sufficient to disclose that the application is inadmissible or should be struck out of the list', the application should be considered by a single-judge formation 'unless there is some special reason to the contrary'.[25]

Committees

The three-judge Committee was introduced by Protocol No. 11. The Committees are set up within the Sections of the Court. They are constituted for a period of twelve months, with the members of the Section, excepting the President of the Section, each taking a turn.[26] The President of the Court decides on the number of Committees after consulting the Presidents of the Sections.[27] The Explanatory Report on Protocol No. 11 notes that although the judge elected in respect to a State involved in a particular case is present *ex officio* in the Chamber and the Grand Chamber, this does not apply to Committees.[28]

Chambers

The Chambers are the main judicial unit of the Court. As noted in the Explanatory Report on Protocol No. 11, subject to powers attributed to other judicial formations,

---

[20] Rules of Court, Rule 29.
[21] Ibid., Rule 27A(1), (3).
[22] Ibid., Rule 27A(2).
[23] Ibid., Rule 27A(1).
[24] Ibid., Rule 27A(4). See also Rule 18A(1).
[25] Ibid., Rule 49(1).
[26] Ibid., Rule 27(2), (3).
[27] Ibid., Rule 27(1).
[28] Explanatory Report on Protocol No. 11, paras 32, 72.

'Chambers will have inherent competence to examine the admissibility and the merits of all individual and inter-State applications.'[29] The term 'Chambers' is also used in article 25, but in a different sense. There it refers to the administrative unit that is more commonly described by the term 'Section'. When Protocol No. 14 was being adopted, '[i]t was not considered necessary to amend the Convention in order to clarify this distinction'.[30] Composed of seven judges (with a possibility that the number be reduced to five), they rule on the merits of the vast bulk of admissible applications.

In any particular case, the seven judges of the Chamber are drawn from the members of the Section constituted pursuant to article 25. The Chamber constituted under article 26 consists of the President of the Section and the judge of the nationality of the State Party concerned in the litigation. Normally, the 'national judge' will be a member of the Section, although exceptionally the judge may belong to another Chamber.[31] This issue is even more likely to arise if there are two States Parties with an interest in the case. The other members of the Chamber are designated by the President of the Section following a rotation. Those members of the Section who are not judges of the Chamber sit in the case as substitute judges.[32]

Grand Chamber

The Grand Chamber considers approximately twenty to twenty-five cases each year. It sits when a Chamber decides to relinquish jurisdiction because the case raises 'a serious question affecting the interpretation of the Convention or the Protocols' or where there is the possibility that the result may be inconsistent with an earlier judgment of the Court (art. 30), when following a judgment by the Chamber one of the parties refers the case to it (art. 43), when the Committee of Ministers refers a situation of non-compliance with a judgment of the Court (art. 46(4)), and in the case of a request for an advisory opinion (art. 47).

The Grand Chamber is composed of seventeen judges and at least three substitute judges.[33] Several of its members sit *ex officio*: the President and the Vice-Presidents of the Court and the Presidents of the Sections constituted in accordance with article 25. The Explanatory Report on Protocol No. 11 says that the Presidents of the Sections sit in the Grand Chamber so as to 'ensure the consistency of the Court's case-law'.[34] A Vice-President of the Court who cannot sit is replaced by the Vice-President of the relevant Section.[35] The 'national judge' is also automatically a member of the Grand Chamber,[36] a measure that the Explanatory Report on Protocol No. 11 says was intended to avoid *ad hoc* judges sitting in the Grand Chamber.[37] In cases where a Chamber has relinquished jurisdiction, in accordance with article 30, the members of that Chamber also sit as members of the Grand Chamber. The President of the Court completes the required complement of seventeen judges by a drawing of lots from among the remaining judges of

---

[29] Ibid., para. 42.
[30] Explanatory Report on Protocol No. 14, para. 60.
[31] Rules of Court, Rule 26(1)(a).
[32] Ibid., Rule 26(1).
[33] Ibid., Rule 24(1).
[34] Explanatory Report on Protocol No. 11, para. 74.
[35] Rules of Court, Rule 24(2)(a).
[36] Ibid., Rule 24(2)(b).
[37] Explanatory Report on Protocol No. 11, para. 74.

the Court. The Rules of Court specify that 'modalities for the drawing of lots shall be laid down by the Plenary Court, having due regard to the need for a geographically balanced composition reflecting the different legal systems among the Contracting Parties'.[38] The judgments of the Grand Chamber indicate those who have been drawn by lots but give no information about how the composition was 'balanced'.

If the case is referred to the Grand Chamber by one of the parties following judgment by a Chamber, the Grand Chamber does not include the judges who sat as members of the Chamber or those who may have ruled on the admissibility of the application, with the exception of the President of that Chamber and the 'national judge'.[39] The rationale, according to the Explanatory Report on Protocol No. 11, is '[t]o make sure that the Grand Chamber looks into the matter afresh when examining a case referred to it under Article 43'.[40] If the case results from a referral by the Committee of Ministers concerning failure to implement a judgment, pursuant to article 46(4), the Grand Chamber includes the members of the Chamber that issued the original judgment or, if the case had already been heard by the Grand Chamber, the members of the Grand Chamber in the original judgment.[41] Thus, although the Rules of Court seek to avoid judges sitting in the same case in the Chamber and in the Grand Chamber, where they participate *ex officio* this is unavoidable, placing those judges in a 'disconcerting position'.[42] It is not inconceivable that they change their position.[43] In the case of a request for an advisory opinion, pursuant to article 47, the Grand Chamber consists of the Presidents and the Vice-Presidents, with the remaining judges drawn by lots.[44]

Referral of a case to the Grand Chamber by one of the parties is subject to authorization of a five-judge panel of the Grand Chamber, in accordance with article 43. This panel consists of the President, two Presidents of Sections designated by rotation, and two judges designated by rotation from among the judges elected by the remaining Sections.[45] Nevertheless, a judge who previously participated in the determination of the admissibility of the case or the merits is excluded.[46] The 'national judge' is also excluded from the five-judge panel.[47]

Ex officio or 'national' judges (art. 26(4))

The elected judge of a State concerned with the proceedings sits *ex officio* as a member of the Chamber or the Grand Chamber. Various justifications have been offered to explain the approach of the European Convention. It is said that the presence of the 'national judge' ensures that the Chamber benefits from expertise as to the law and practice in the respondent State.[48] Prior to the entry into force of Protocol No. 11, the jurisdiction of the

---

[38] Rules of Court, Rule 24(2)(f).
[39] Ibid., Rule 24(2)(d).
[40] Explanatory Report on Protocol No. 11, para. 73.
[41] Rules of Court, Rule 24(2)(g).
[42] *Kyprianou v. Cyprus* [GC], no. 73797/01, Partly Dissenting Opinion of Judge Costa, § 2, ECHR 2005-XIII.
[43] Ibid., §§ 4, 9; *Dickson v. the United Kingdom* [GC], no. 44362/04, Concurring Opinion of Judge Bratza, ECHR 2007-XV; *Sanoma Uitgevers B.V. v. the Netherlands* [GC], no. 38224/03, Concurring Opinion of Judge Myjer, 14 September 2010.
[44] Rules of Court, Rule 24(2)(f).
[45] Ibid., Rule 24(5)(a).
[46] Ibid., Rule 24(5)(b).
[47] Ibid., Rule 24(5)(c).
[48] See, e.g., Explanatory Report on Protocol No. 14, para. 71.

Court was not mandatory, and the presence of a 'national judge' may have reassured some States that were hesitant about making the relevant declaration of acceptance of jurisdiction. It may also enhance the willingness of States to comply with the judgment.[49]

The institution of the *ex officio* judge seems to have been 'conceived in international law for the resolution of classic disputes between States' rather than human rights litigation usually involving an individual applicant and a respondent State.[50] It is 'intended to preserve the procedural equity between the parties, constituted by two or more sovereign States equal under the law and whose relations are governed by the principle of reciprocity'.[51] Notably, it is the norm at the International Court of Justice, where a State that is a party to proceedings may designate a judge *ad hoc* if there is no judge of its nationality on the Court.[52] Similar provisions to those of the European Convention can be found in the American Convention on Human Rights. However, they have been interpreted by the Inter-American Court as being applicable only to inter-State complaints and not to apply when applications originate from individuals.[53]

The presence of the 'national judge' may raise concerns about independence and impartiality in a Court where, unlike the situation at the International Court of Justice, the State is always the respondent with the exception of the rare inter-State application. At the International Court of Justice, litigation in contentious cases takes place between two or more States, and each is on the same footing in terms of the right to the presence of a judge of their nationality. So-called 'national judges' do not necessarily vote in favour of their own State, and the likelihood of this is probably reduced to the extent that judges may sit for only one term and need not, therefore, fear that they will not be nominated for re-election. According to one study, when a ruling of the European Court was favourable to the respondent State, 95 per cent of 'national judges' (and 100 per cent of *ad hoc* judges appointed to replace the 'national judge') voted with the majority, compared with 81 per cent of other judges. Where the State was found to be in violation of the Convention, 16 per cent of 'national judges' (and 33 per cent of *ad hoc* judges) were in dissent, compared with only 8 per cent of other judges.[54]

The approach of the European Convention is in striking contrast with practice at the United Nations Human Rights Committee and other bodies, where the national representative is excused from sitting if the State of his or her nationality is the respondent in a contentious case.[55] The Inter-American Court has also concluded that the 'national judge' should not sit in cases where his or her State is respondent.[56]

---

[49] M. Kuijer, 'Voting Behaviour and National Bias in the ECHR and the ICJ', (1997) 10 *Leiden Journal of International Law* 49, at p. 52.

[50] I/A Court H.R., '*Article 55 of the American Convention on Human Rights*', Advisory Opinion OC-20/ 09 of 29 September 2009. Series A, No. 20, para. 34.

[51] Ibid., para. 36.

[52] Statute of the International Court of Justice, art. 31.

[53] I/A Court H.R., '*Article 55 of the American Convention on Human Rights*', Advisory Opinion OC-20/09 of 29 September 2009. Series A No. 20, para. 45.

[54] E. Voeten, 'The Impartiality of International Judges: Evidence from the European Court of Human Rights', (2008) 102 *American Political Science Review* 417, at p. 422.

[55] International Covenant on Civil and Political Rights, (1976) 999 UNTS 171, art. 42(2). Also International Convention on the Elimination of All Forms of Racial Discrimination, (1966) 660 UNTS 195, art. 12 (2); Protocol to the African Charter on Human and Peoples' Rights on the Establishment of an African Court on Human and Peoples' Rights, OAU Doc. OAU/LEG/EXP/AFCHPR/PROT (III), art. 22.

[56] I/A Court H.R., '*Article 55 of the American Convention on Human Rights*', Advisory Opinion OC-20/09 of 29 September 2009, Series A No. 20, para. 86.

Rule 13 of the Rules of Court prohibits a judge from presiding in cases in which he or she has been appointed an *ex officio* judge.

Where two or more States are entitled to the participation of their national judge *ex officio*, the President of the Chamber may invite them to agree on the appointment of a single judge elected in respect to one of them. If the parties cannot agree, the President chooses the common-interest judge by lot from the judges proposed by the parties.[57] This provision is only used on very rare occasions.[58]

Ad hoc judges (art. 26(4))

If the elected judge of a State concerned with the proceedings is unable to sit *ex officio* as a member of the Chamber or the Grand Chamber, for example because of a conflict of interest or on account of illness, an *ad hoc* judge may be designated.[59] Similarly, a judge may leave office permanently before a replacement is elected, creating an absence for a period of time that will be filled by an *ad hoc* judge. States are encouraged to nominate candidates for elected office who are not likely to require the designation of *ad hoc* judges.[60]

In accordance with article 26(4), in cases where the judge of a particular State should sit *ex officio*, the President of the Court is to select the *ad hoc* judge from a list submitted in advance by the State in question. The requirement of a prior list of candidates was imposed as a result of Protocol No. 14. Previously, if the need arose the State had the freedom to designate an *ad hoc* judge,[61] an unsatisfactory situation that resulted in delayed proceedings and that had in some situations raised issues concerning independence and impartiality.[62] According to Rule 29 of the Rules of Court, the list is to consist of three to five persons deemed eligible. The list is to include candidates of both sexes. Persons on the list may not represent a party or a third party in any capacity in proceedings before the Court. Where the State has not submitted a list, or where the list is inadequate because it does not contain a minimum of three candidates who are genuinely eligible, the President may appoint another elected judge to set as an *ad hoc* judge.

Rule 13 of the Rules of Court prohibits a judge from presiding in cases in which he or she has been appointed an *ad hoc* judge.

---

[57] Rules of Court, Rule 30(1).

[58] *Artemi and Gregory v. Cyprus, Austria, Belgium, the Czech Republic, Denmark, Estonia, Finland, France, Germany, Hungary, Ireland, Italy, Latvia, Lithuania, Luxembourg, Malta, the Netherlands, Poland, Portugal, Slovakia, Slovenia, and Sweden* (dec.), no. 35524/06, 30 November 2010; *Behrami and Behrami v. France* [GC] (dec.), no. 71412/01; and *Saramati v. France, Germany, and Norway* [GC] (dec.), no. 78166/01, 2 May 2007.

[59] *Application of the Convention on the Prevention and Punishment of the Crime of Genocide, Provisional Measures*, Order of 13 September 1993, I.C.J. Reports 1993, p. 325, Separate Opinion of Judge Lauterpacht, paras 4–6; I/A Court H.R., '*Article 55 of the American Convention on Human Rights*', Advisory Opinion OC-20/09 of 29 September 2009, Series A No. 20.

[60] Candidates for the European Court of Human Rights, Parliamentary Assembly, Recommendation 1649 (2004), para. 19(vi); Nomination of candidates and election of judges to the European Court of Human Rights, Parliamentary Assembly, Resolution 1646 (2009), para. 4.5.

[61] Pursuant to article 43 of the 1950 text of the Convention and article 27(2) of the Convention as amended by Protocol No. 11.

[62] Ad hoc judges at the European Court of Human Rights: an overview, Parliamentary Assembly, Doc. 12827, para. 10.

Excusal and recusal

A judge may not sit in cases where he or she has a personal interest in the case, where he or she has previously acted in the case, and where he or she has expressed opinions publicly that 'are objectively capable of adversely affecting his or her impartiality'. In the case of *ad hoc* judges or judges who have completed their terms but remain to complete a case, they must not sit if they are engaged in incompatible professional activities. More generally, judges must not sit if 'for any other reason, his or her independence or impartiality may legitimately be called into doubt'.[63] The Rules specify that '[i]n the event of any doubt on the part of the judge concerned or the President', the matter is decided by the Chamber.[64]

Evidence of excusal and recusal in the case law of the Court is rather rare. It is very unusual for a challenge to independence and impartiality to be reported. The reasons are not given. For example, in the *Cyprus v. Turkey* inter-State case, the judgment reports that the elected judge for Cyprus was challenged by Turkey. The Grand Chamber 'requested' that the elected judge withdraw and an *ad hoc* judge was then designated to replace him.[65] In the same case, the elected judge for Turkey withdrew without explanation. The *ad hoc* judge appointed as a replacement was challenged by Cyprus, but he had already indicated 'his intention to withdraw from the case'. When objections were raised about his replacement, 'the Grand Chamber decided that Mrs Ferdi was prevented from taking part in the consideration of the case'.[66]

Further reading

Johan Callewaert, 'Article 43', in Pettiti et al., *La Convention européenne*, pp. 755–8.
Frowein/Peukert, *MenschenRechtsKonvention*, p. 450.

---

[63] Rules of Court, Rule 15(2).
[64] Ibid., Rule 15(3).
[65] *Cyprus v. Turkey* [GC], no. 25781/94, § 8, ECHR 2001-IV.
[66] Ibid.

Article 27. Competence of single judges/Compétence des juges uniques

1. A single judge may declare inadmissible or strike out of the Court's list of cases an application submitted under Article 34, where such a decision can be taken without further examination.	1. Un juge unique peut déclarer une requête introduite en vertu de l'article 34 irrecevable ou la rayer du rôle lorsqu'une telle décision peut être prise sans examen complémentaire.
2. The decision shall be final.	2. La décision est définitive.
3. If the single judge does not declare an application inadmissible or strike it out, that judge shall forward it to a committee or to a Chamber for further examination.	3. Si le juge unique ne déclare pas une requête irrecevable ou ne la raye pas du rôle, ce juge la transmet à un comité ou à une chambre pour examen complémentaire.

Introductory comments

'Spectacular' was the word used by the President of the European Court of Human Rights, Nicolas Bratza, to describe the impact of the single-judge procedure on the filtering of non-meritorious cases in a speech he delivered in January 2012 on the occasion of the opening of the judicial year.[1] Since their introduction, the single judges account for about half of the Court's caseload. An indication of the impact can be seen from statistics on the number of cases declared inadmissible or struck out of the list by single judge. In 2010, for which Protocol No. 14 only applied during seven months, 22,260 applications where eliminated by the single judges.[2] In 2011, the number increased to 46,928,[3] and in 2012 to 81,700.[4] Much of this involved clearing a backlog of cases. At the end of 2010, 88,407 cases were pending before the single-judge formation.[5] That number increased to 92,050 the following year,[6] but had dropped to 59,850 by the end of 2012.[7]

Single judges may be particularly effective in repetitive cases where the Court has issued a pilot judgment pursuant to article 46 of the Convention. Once the applicant State has developed satisfactory mechanisms to address the systemic problem, the single judge may then rule on similar applications, usually declaring them inadmissible for failure to exhaust domestic remedies. In an opinion addressed to the Steering Committee on Human Rights of the Council of Europe, the Court referred to measures taken by Romania in response to such a pilot judgment concerning compensation for property confiscated under the previous regime.[8] In a subsequent judgment, the Court concluded

---

[1] Speech given by Sir Nicolas Bratza, President of the European Court of Human Rights, on the occasion of the opening of the judicial year, 27 January 2012, *Annual Report 2012*, pp. 31–8, at p. 33.

[2] *Annual Report 2010*, p. 67.

[3] *Annual Report 2011*, p. 67.

[4] *Annual Report 2012*, p. 60.

[5] *Annual Report 2010*, p. 67.

[6] *Annual Report 2011*, p. 67.

[7] *Annual Report 2012*, p. 60.

[8] *Maria Atanasiu and Others v. Romania*, nos 30767/05 and 33800/06, 12 October 2010.

that legislation enacted in 2013 in response to what it had indicated in the pilot judgment were satisfactory.[9] As a result, some 2,600 similar applications that had been held in abeyance were rejected, mainly by decision of the single judge.[10]

Drafting of the provision

There was no authority given by the 1950 Convention to a single judge, sitting alone, nor for that matter was any such power given to a single member of the Commission either. The function of a single judge, described in article 27, was introduced by Protocol No. 14, which came into force in 2010.[11] The Preamble to Protocol No. 14 notes 'the urgent need to amend certain provisions of the Convention in order to maintain and improve the efficiency of the control system for the long term, mainly in the light of the continuing increase in the workload of the European Court of Human Rights and the Committee of Ministers of the Council of Europe'. In order to achieve this objective, amendments were introduced to reinforce 'the Court's filtering capacity in respect of the mass of unmeritorious applications'.[12]

According to the Explanatory Report on Protocol No. 14,

The filtering capacity is increased by making a single judge competent to declare inadmissible or strike out an individual application. This new mechanism retains the judicial character of the decision-making on admissibility. The single judges will be assisted by non-judicial rapporteurs, who will be part of the registry.[13]

The Explanatory Report further develops the vision of the drafters:

Adequate assistance to single judges requires additional resources. The establishment of this system will thus lead to a significant increase in the Court's filtering capacity, on the one hand, on account of the reduction, compared to the old committee practice, of the number of actors involved in the preparation and adoption of decisions (one judge instead of three; the new rapporteurs who could combine the functions of case-lawyer and rapporteur), and, on the other hand, because judges will be relieved of their rapporteur role when sitting in a single-judge formation and, finally, as a result of the multiplication of filtering formations operating simultaneously.[14]

Analysis and interpretation

The single judge may declare a case inadmissible or strike it out of the Court's list where such a decision can be taken 'without further examination'. This decision is final, subject to the possibility of reopening an examination of admissibility where the Court itself has committed an error.[15] These summary decisions are not reported on the Court's on-line

---

[9] *Preda and Others v. Romania*, nos 9584/02, 33514/02, 38052/02, 25821/03, 29652/03, 3736/03, 17750/03, and 28688/04, § 142, 29 April 2014.

[10] Response of the Court to the 'CDDH report containing conclusions and possible proposals for action on ways to resolve the large numbers of applications arising from systemic issues identified by the Court', para. 4.

[11] Protocol No. 14 to the Convention for the Protection of Human Rights and Fundamental Freedoms, amending the control system of the Convention, ETS 194, art. 8.

[12] Explanatory Report on Protocol No. 14, para. 36.

[13] Ibid., para. 38.

[14] Ibid., para. 62.

[15] *Storck v. Germany*, no. 61603/00, § 67, ECHR 2005-V; *Storck v. Germany* (dec.), no. 61603, 26 October 2004; *Ölmez v. Turkey* (dec.), no. 39464/98, 5 July 2005; *Des Fours Walderode v. Czech Republic* (dec.), no. 40057/98, ECHR 2004-V; *Harrach v. Czech Republic* (dec.), no. 77532/01, 18 May 2004; *Le Syndicat des*

database. The applicant is to receive a letter explaining that the application has been judged inadmissible.[16] In accordance with article 26(3) of the Convention, the single judge may not sit in a case involving the State for which he or she has been elected.[17] The Explanatory Report on Protocol No. 14 draws attention to the limitation on the authority of the single judge to taking decisions of inadmissibility or decisions to strike the case out of the list 'where such a decision can be taken without further examination'.[18] Consequently, 'the judge will take such decisions only in clear-cut cases, where the inadmissibility of the application is manifest from the outset'.[19]

Protocol No. 14 also introduced a new admissibility criterion for cases where 'the applicant has not suffered a significant disadvantage'.[20] This necessitated a transitional solution, given that single judges could not be expected to determine manifest inadmissibility in the absence of guidance from the case law of the Chambers and the Grand Chamber on the scope of this new concept. For this reason, a two-year grace period was provided following entry into force of Protocol No. 14 during which the single judge was not empowered to declare an application inadmissible solely on the basis of the ground.[21] As the Explanatory Report confirms, referring to article 35(3)(b) of the Convention, '[i]n case of doubt as to the admissibility, the judge will refer the application to a committee or a Chamber'.[22]

At the time of signature and ratification of Protocol No. 14, several States formulated declarations concerning the application of the new admissibility criterion and the role of the single-judge formation. This is discussed in the chapter of this Commentary concerning article 35, under the heading 'Declarations'.

It seems that in declining to rule a case inadmissible, the single judge is also required to make an assessment as to whether the case concerns an underlying issue that is the subject of well-established case law, in which case the three-judge Committee should receive the case. Otherwise, the single judge should send the case to the seven-judge Chamber.

Further reading

Frowein/Peukert, *MenschenRechtsKonvention*, pp. 451–2.

---

copropriétaires du 20 bd de la Mer à Dinard v. France (dec.), no. 47339/99, 22 May 2003; *Wortmann v. Germany* (dec.), no. 70929/01, 18 November 2003; *Appietto v. France* (dec.), no. 56927/00, § 8, 26 February 2002.

[16] Rules of Court, Rule 52A(1).
[17] Also Rules of Court, Rule 52(A)(2).
[18] Explanatory Report on Protocol No. 14, para. 67.
[19] Ibid., para. 67.
[20] European Convention on Human Rights, art. 35(3)(b).
[21] Protocol No. 14 to the Convention for the Protection of Human Rights and Fundamental Freedoms, amending the control system of the Convention, ETS 194, art. 20(2).
[22] Explanatory Report on Protocol No. 14, para. 67.

Article 28. Competence of Committees/Compétence des comités

1. In respect of an application submitted under Article 34, a committee may, by a unanimous vote,

(a) declare it inadmissible or strike it out of its list of cases, where such decision can be taken without further examination; or

(b) declare it admissible and render at the same time a judgment on the merits, if the underlying question in the case, concerning the interpretation or the application of the Convention or the Protocols thereto, is already the subject of well-established case-law of the Court.

2. Decisions and judgments under paragraph 1 shall be final.

3. If the judge elected in respect of the High Contracting Party concerned is not a member of the committee, the committee may at any stage of the proceedings invite that judge to take the place of one of the members of the committee, having regard to all relevant factors, including whether that Party has contested the application of the procedure under paragraph 1.b.

1. Un comité saisi d'une requête individuelle introduite en vertu de l'article 34 peut, par vote unanime,

a) la déclarer irrecevable ou la rayer du rôle lorsqu'une telle décision peut être prise sans examen complémentaire; ou

b) la déclarer recevable et rendre conjointement un arrêt sur le fond lorsque la question relative à l'interprétation ou à l'application de la Convention ou de ses Protocoles qui est à l'origine de l'affaire fait l'objet d'une jurisprudence bien établie de la Cour.

2. Les décisions et arrêts prévus au paragraphe 1 sont définitifs.

3. Si le juge élu au titre de la Haute Partie contractante partie au litige n'est pas membre du comité, ce dernier peut, à tout moment de la procédure, l'inviter à siéger en son sein en lieu et place de l'un de ses membres, en prenant en compte tous facteurs pertinents, y compris la question de savoir si cette partie a contesté l'application de la procédure du paragraphe 1.b.

Introductory comments

From the beginning of its operations, the function of filtering applications for the Court had been performed mainly by the European Commission of Human Rights. Until the entry into force of Protocol No. 9, in 1994, cases could only come before the Court if the Commission had not declared them to be inadmissible. Protocol No. 9 introduced the right of individual application to the Court. But even then, a case could only be brought to the Court by an individual if it had already been declared admissible by the Commission.

With the abolition of the Commission in accordance with Protocol No. 11, which entered into force in 1998, the filtering function had to be assumed by the Court itself. The intent of the drafters of Protocol No. 11 was that the summary elimination of cases that were obviously inadmissible would largely be the work of three-judge Committees. This mechanism did not prove to be entirely satisfactory. Within only a few years Protocol No. 14 was adopted in order to assign this filtering function to single judges. Article 27 was introduced for this purpose by Protocol No. 14, which entered into force in 2010.

Drafting of the provision

Under article 20(3) of the 1950 text of the Convention, the Commission was entitled to sit in a committee 'composed of at least three members, with the power, exercisable by a unanimous vote, to declare inadmissible or strike from its list of cases a petition ... when such a decision can be taken without further examination'. According to the Explanatory Report on Protocol No. 11, this is the basis of the committee mechanism for the Court set out in article 28.[1]

The original draft Convention proposed by the Consultative Assembly contemplated a Commission but it did not specify whether it would sit in plenary or in some smaller unit.[2] The Conference of Senior Officials was concerned that the plenary Commission would be 'an unduly cumbersome body for the purpose of fact-finding and for making the efforts necessary to obtain a friendly solution'. Its proposal to establish a seven-member Sub-Commission[3] became article 29 of the 1950 text of the Convention. The Committees described in former article 20(3) were introduced by Protocol No. 8.[4] The principal reform of Protocol No. 8 was its authorization for the Commission to sit in Chambers, but the establishment of Committees was described as '[a]nother significant change'. According to the Explanatory Report, the Committees 'offer a double advantage: the plenary Commission and Chambers will be freed from the task of dealing with such petitions, thereby allowing them more time for the consideration of serious cases, and the waiting-time for a decision on manifestly inadmissible petitions will be considerably reduced, in particular as the committees will be able to meet at frequent intervals'.[5]

The judicial function of the three-judge Committee was introduced by Protocol No. 11 as a component of the 'new Court' that began operations in 1998. Article 28, as introduced by Protocol No. 11, read as follows:

Declarations of inadmissibility by committees
A committee may, by a unanimous vote, declare inadmissible or strike out of its list of cases an individual application submitted under Article 34 where such a decision can be taken without further examination. The decision shall be final.[6]

The Report noted that the Rules the Court might provide for the immediate transfer of applications to the Chamber, when appropriate.[7]

This provision was substantially modified by Protocol No. 14. As amended, it enabled the Committees to rule on the merits as well as admissibility in repetitive cases where the

---

[1] Explanatory Report on Protocol No. 11, para. 76.

[2] Recommendation No. 38 to the Committee of Ministers adopted 8 September 1949 on the conclusion of the debates, Doc. AS (1) 108, II *TP* 274–83, at pp. 278–80, arts 9–17.

[3] Text of the report submitted by the Conference to the Committee of Ministers, Doc. CM/WP 4 (50) 19, CM/WP 4 (50) 16 rev., A 1431, IV *TP* 242–73, at p. 264; Draft Convention annexed to the Report [of the Conference of Senior Officials], Doc. CM/WP 4 (50) 19 annex, CM/WP 4 (50) 16 rev., A 1452, IV *TP* 274–95, at p. 286, art. 28.

[4] Protocol No. 8 to the Convention for the Protection of Human Rights and Fundamental Freedoms, ETS 118, art. 1.

[5] Explanatory Report on Protocol No. 8, para. 9. On the operation of the Committees established by the Commission, see Caroline Ravaud, 'Article 20', in Pettiti et al., *La Convention européenne*, at pp. 551–3.

[6] Protocol No. 11 to the Convention for the Protection of Human Rights and Fundamental Freedoms, restructuring the control machinery established thereby, ETS 155, art. 1.

[7] Explanatory Report on Protocol No. 11, para. 40. But no such rule appears to have been adopted.

case law of the Court is well established.[8] Even the title was changed, reflecting the assignment of other functions to the Committees and at the same time the transfer of the primary filtering responsibility to the single judge formation pursuant to article 27. The Explanatory Report said that the Rules of Court should deal with practical questions concerning composition of the committee and 'plan its working methods in a way that optimises the new procedure's effectiveness'.[9] The Explanatory Report promised that '[t]he implementation of the new procedure will increase substantially the Court's decision-making capacity and effectiveness, since many cases can be decided by three judges, instead of the seven currently required when judgments or decisions are given by a Chamber'.[10]

Paragraph 3 allows an exception to the rule by which the 'national judge' does not participate in the Committee. The rationale for the provision is described in the Explanatory Report:

[I]t was considered important to have at least some reference in the Convention itself to the possibility for respondent Parties to contest the application of the simplified procedure... For example, a respondent Party may contest the new procedure on the basis that the case in question differs in some material respect from the established case-law cited. It is likely that the expertise of the 'national judge' in domestic law and practice will be relevant to this issue and therefore helpful to the committee. Should this judge be absent or unable to sit, the procedure provided for in the new Article 26, paragraph 4 *in fine* applies.[11]

The Parliamentary Assembly had requested that the words 'including whether that Party has contested the application of the procedure under paragraph 1.b' at the end of article 28(3) be deleted.[12]

Analysis and interpretation

The Committees were initially introduced as part of the 'new Court' by Protocol No. 11 in order to operate the filtering function that had previously been undertaken by the European Commission. This role largely changed as a result of Protocol No. 14. It transferred the main burden of the filtering function to the single-judge formation provided by article 17, but at the same time enlarged the powers of the three-judge chamber to enable it to declare cases admissible as well as inadmissible, and then proceed to examine the merits of those applications deemed admissible. The competence of the three-judge Committees to rule on the merits is limited to repetitive cases where the case law of the Court is well established.

According to article 28(2), the decision of the Committee is final,[13] subject to the possibility of reopening an examination of admissibility where the Court itself has

---

[8] Protocol No. 14 to the Convention for the Protection of Human Rights and Fundamental Freedoms, amending the control system of the Convention, ETS 194, art. 8.

[9] Explanatory Report on Protocol No. 14, para. 72.

[10] Ibid., para. 70.

[11] Explanatory Report on Protocol No. 14, para. 71.

[12] Draft Protocol No. 14 to the Convention for the Protection of Human Rights and Fundamental Freedoms amending the control system of the Convention, Opinion No. 251 (2004), Parliamentary Assembly, para. 14.v.

[13] Also Rules of Court, Rule 53(4).

committed an error.[14] Consequently, only if the Committee declines to take a decision is the case even eligible to be considered by a Grand Chamber.

Ruling on inadmissibility

The Committee has the authority to declare a case inadmissible or to strike it out of its list of cases if it can decide on this 'without further examination'. The Committee may do this 'by a unanimous vote and at any stage of the proceedings'.[15] The jurisdiction in this regard is identical to that of the single-judge formation provided for by article 27. Since introduction of the single-judge formation in 2010, with the entry into force of Protocol No. 14, this aspect of the work of the Committees has become much less significant. In 2008, the final year before the new mechanisms of Protocol No. 14 began to become operational, the Committees declared inadmissible or struck out of the list some 28,202 cases.[16] By 2011, when Protocol No. 14 had become fully operational, that number had dropped to 1,187.[17] The applicant, as well as the Contracting Parties concerned where these have previously been involved in the application in accordance with the present Rules, shall be informed of the decision by letter 'unless the Committee decides otherwise'.[18]

Joint decision on admissibility and merits

Since the entry into force of Protocol No. 14, Committees have issued decisions on both the admissibility and the merits in several hundred cases. For example, in 2012, seven-judge Chambers delivered 861 judgments (concerning 1,119 applications) while three-judge Committees delivered 206 judgments (concerning 509 applications).[19] Applications that did not result in judgments were declared inadmissible. Thus, the Committees account for about 31 per cent of the total number of applications that are not already inadmissible by the single-judge formation.

The inadmissibility decisions of the Committees look no different compared to those of seven-judge Chambers in the sense that they do not provide any explanation or justification for the exercise of jurisdiction by the Committee. There is no systematic attempt to explain why the matter is a repetitive one involving well-established case law. Sometimes, a Committee judgment will note that its ruling is consistent with 'well-established case-law',[20] but this seems to be the exception rather than the rule. According to the Explanatory Report, the expression 'well-established case-law' should be construed to

---

[14] *Storck v. Germany*, no. 61603/00, § 67, ECHR 2005-V; *Storck v. Germany* (dec.), no. 61603, 26 October 2004; *Ölmez v. Turkey* (dec.), no. 39464/98, 5 July 2005; *Des Fours Walderode v. Czech Republic* (dec.), no. 40057/98, ECHR 2004-V; *Harrach v. Czech Republic* (dec.), no. 77532/01, 18 May 2004; *Le Syndicat des copropriétaires du 20 bd de la Mer à Dinard v. France* (dec.), no. 47339/99, 22 May 2003; *Wortmann v. Germany* (dec.), no. 70929/01, 18 November 2003; *Appietto v. France* (dec.), no. 56927/00, § 8, 26 February 2002.

[15] Rules of Court, Rule 53(1).

[16] *Annual Report 2008*, pp. 55–7.

[17] *Annual Report 2011*, pp. 65–6.

[18] Rules of Court, Rule 53(5).

[19] *Annual Report 2012*, p. 60.

[20] *Vinnik and Others v. Ukraine*, no. 13977/05 and 45 other applications, § 65, 7 November 2013; *Rooney v. Ireland*, no. 32614/10), § 2, 31 October 2013; *Kiselyov v. Ukraine*, no. 42953/04, § 21, 13 June 2013; *FEYA, MPP and Others v. Ukraine*, no. 27617/06 and 126 other applications, 21 February 2013; *Themeli v. Albania*, no. 63756/09, §§ 24, 31, 15 January 2013; *Tushaj v. Albania*, no. 13620/10, §§ 30, 37, 15 January 2013; *Hasdemir v. Turkey*, no. 44027/09, § 4, 22 May 2012.

contemplate case law that has been consistently applied by a Chamber. However, exceptionally 'it is conceivable that a single judgment on a question of principle may constitute "well-established case-law", particularly when the Grand Chamber has rendered it'.[21] The Explanatory Report considered that the parties might debate whether case law was in fact 'well established' before the Committee.[22] But they cannot 'veto the use of this procedure which lies within the committee's sole competence'.[23]

This new procedure is 'both simplified and accelerated, although it preserves the adversarial character of proceedings and the principle of judicial and collegiate decision-making on the merits'.[24] The judges of the Committee must be unanimous on each aspect. If they do not agree, no decision is taken and the case is dealt with under the general procedure before a Chamber set out in article 29.[25] The decision by the Committee to proceed under article 28(1)(b) does not preclude a subsequent finding that the case is inadmissible. This could arise when the State demonstrates a failure to exhaust domestic remedies, for example.[26]

The 'national judge' does not participate in the Committee. This constitutes a significant new exception to the general rule that has existed since the Court began its work by which the judge of the nationality of the concerned State Party is included in the bench. The Explanatory Report justified this by observing that '[t]he presence of this judge would not appear necessary, since committees will deal with cases on which well-established case-law exists'.[27] There is an exception to the exception, as the Explanatory Report notes:

However, a committee may invite the judge elected in respect of the High Contracting Party concerned to replace one of its members as, in some cases, the presence of this judge may prove useful. For example, it may be felt that this judge, who is familiar with the legal system of the respondent Party, should join in taking the decision, particularly when such questions as exhaustion of domestic remedies need to be clarified.[28]

The Committee may decide to proceed in this way. A unanimous vote is required. It invites the national judge to take the place of one of its members, 'having regard to all relevant factors, including whether that Party has contested the application of the procedure under Article 28 § 1 (b) of the Convention'.[29]

Declarations

Upon signature of Protocol No. 14, Russia made the following declaration: 'the application of Article 28, paragraph 3, of the Convention as amended by Article 8 of the Protocol does not exclude the right of a High Contracting Party concerned, if the judge elected in

---

[21] Explanatory Report on Protocol No. 14, para. 68.
[22] Ibid., para. 68.
[23] Ibid., para. 69.
[24] Ibid.
[25] Ibid.
[26] Ibid.
[27] Ibid., para. 71.
[28] Ibid.
[29] Rules of Court, Rule 53(3).

its respect is not a member of the committee, to request that he or she be given the possibility to take the place of one of the members of the Committee'.[30]

Further reading

Frowein/Peukert, *MenschenRechtsKonvention*, p. 453.
Caroline Ravaud, 'Article 20', in Pettiti et al., *La Convention européenne*, at pp. 551–3.

---

[30] (2006) 49 YB 11. The statement was renewed upon ratification: (2010) 53 YB 28.

Article 29. Decisions by Chambers on admissibility and merits/ Décisions des chambres sur la recevabilité et le fond

1. If no decision is taken under Article 27 or Article 28, or no judgment rendered under Article 28, a Chamber shall decide on the admissibility and merits of individual applications submitted under Article 34. The decision on admissibility may be taken separately.

2. A Chamber shall decide on the admissibility and merits of inter-State applications submitted under Article 33. The decision on admissibility shall be taken separately unless the Court, in exceptional cases, decides otherwise.

1. Si aucune décision n'a été prise en vertu des articles 27 ou 28, ni aucun arrêt rendu en vertu de l'article 28, une chambre se prononce sur la recevabilité et le fond des requêtes individuelles introduites en vertu de l'article 34. La décision sur la recevabilité peut être prise de façon séparée.

2. Une chambre se prononce sur la recevabilité et le fond des requêtes étatiques introduites en vertu de l'article 33. Sauf décision contraire de la Cour dans des cas exceptionnels, la décision sur la recevabilité est prise séparément.

Introductory comments

Although most, if not all tribunals, be they national or international, grapple with the distinction between the admissibility of an application and its assessment on the merits, the matter is of particular importance at the international level. It is very common for international tribunals to address these issues separately, making formal rulings on admissibility before even beginning to examine the substance of a claim. In some cases, the procedural stage of determining admissibility is set out in the foundational instrument of the institution.[1] At the International Court of Justice, it is quite normal for there to be a hearing followed by a ruling on jurisdiction and admissibility. Then, depending upon the result, the case may proceed to a second hearing and a judgment on the merits of the case. The distinction is recognized in the Rules of Court.[2]

The Convention organs have not generally distinguished between jurisdiction and admissibility. The two concepts operate in a similar manner in that they require an initial determination before the substance of an application can be determined. In a general sense, jurisdiction indicates a *sine qua non*, without which a tribunal cannot proceed, whereas admissibility implies a degree of discretion available to a judicial institution that already properly exercises jurisdiction. The European Court addresses both jurisdiction and admissibility when it makes a ruling that it calls an 'admissibility decision'.[3] It also delves rather deeply into the merits at this stage, exercising its authority under article 35(3) to declare inadmissible any application that it deems to be 'manifestly ill-founded'.

---

[1] Rome Statute of the International Criminal Court, (2002) 2187 UNTS 90, art. 17.
[2] Rules of Court [of the International Court of Justice], Rule 79(1).
[3] Among many examples, see *Galić v. the Netherlands* (dec.), no. 22617/07, § 44, 9 June 2009.

Drafting of the provision

The 1950 text of the Convention made the distinction between admissibility and merits with respect to the procedure of the European Commission of Human Rights. Under article 27, the Commission was to make an initial assessment of admissibility. Only then would it assess the merits of the application and, assuming it had not managed to effect a friendly settlement, prepare a report on the merits of the application. It then had the discretion to refer the case to the Court. The Court was entitled to rule on the issue of jurisdiction pursuant to article 49 of the Convention. Arguably it was not to assess issues of admissibility that were not jurisdictional in nature, this being reserved to the Commission by the Convention.[4] But in an early decision it ruled otherwise and held that it was competent to reconsider the decision of the Commission on admissibility.[5]

There was no equivalent of article 29 in the 1950 text of the Convention with respect to the Court. The provision, which codifies a practice established by the Court from its earliest cases, was introduced to the Convention by Protocol No. 11. The original version of article 29 read as follows:

Decisions by Chambers on admissibility and merits
1. If no decision is taken under Article 28, a Chamber shall decide on the admissibility and merits of individual applications submitted under Article 34.
2. A Chamber shall decide on the admissibility and merits of inter-State applications submitted under Article 33.
3. The decision on admissibility shall be taken separately unless the Court, in exceptional cases, decides otherwise.[6]

The reference to article 28 concerned the provision introduced by Protocol No. 11 by which the Committee filtered cases, eliminating those that were inadmissible or striking them from the list, but without the ability to rule a case admissible and consider the merits.[7]

This text was amended pursuant to Protocol 14.[8] The third paragraph of the provision that had been introduced by Protocol No. 11, making a combined admissibility and merits ruling the exception, was removed. In its place is a phrase at the end of paragraph 1 implying that such combined decisions are in fact encouraged.[9] The reverse applies to inter-State cases, where the admissibility and merits stages require distinct rulings except in exceptional circumstances.[10] For this purpose, a second sentence was added to paragraph 2.

---

[4] Francis G. Jacobs and Robin C.A. White, *The European Convention on Human Rights*, 2nd edn, Oxford: Clarendon Press, 1996, p. 384.

[5] *De Wilde, Ooms, and Versyp v. Belgium*, 18 June 1971, §§ 47–52, Series A no. 12.

[6] Protocol No. 11 to the Convention for the Protection of Human Rights and Fundamental Freedoms, restructuring the control machinery established thereby, ETS 155, art. 1.

[7] Explanatory Report on Protocol No. 11, para. 77.

[8] Protocol No. 14 to the Convention for the Protection of Human Rights and Fundamental Freedoms, amending the control system of the Convention, ETS 194, art. 9.

[9] Explanatory Report on Protocol No. 14, paras 41, 73.

[10] Ibid., para. 74.

Analysis and interpretation

Article 29 confirms the role of the seven-judge Chamber as the central adjudicative body of the Court. It has general jurisdiction to rule on both the admissibility and the merits of all applications submitted to the Court. The other judicial organs—the single judge, the Committee, and the Grand Chamber—are all subject to special conditions that limit their jurisdiction.

The two paragraphs of article 29 distinguish between individual applications and inter-State applications. Since the amendments introduced in 2010 by Protocol No. 14, it is clear that the Chambers are encouraged to rule on both the admissibility and the merits at the same time when individual applications are concerned. When the Court informs the parties that it intends to procede in this way, they are invited to include in their observations any submissions concerning just satisfaction and any proposals for a friendly settlement.[11] If no friendly settlement is reached and if the Chamber is satisfied the case is admissible and ready to be determined on the merits, it then adopts a judgment that includes its admissibility decision.[12] Although the separation of these two stages is the exception in individual applications, the Chambers remain free to proceed otherwise, should they prefer to take a separate decision on admissibility.[13] The Rules of Court specify that the Court may decide 'at any stage, if necessary, to take a separate decision on admissibility'.[14]

Initially, article 29 created a presumption in favour of separate decisions for both individual and inter-State cases. The Explanatory Report on Protocol No. 11 suggested this was desirable because it could assist the parties in friendly settlement negotiations.[15] Nevertheless, even before the entry into force of Protocol No. 14, a practice of taking joint decisions on the admissibility and the merits of individual applications had already taken hold within the Court.[16] It was not at all uncommon for it to reserve its ruling on the admissibility issue of failure to exhaust domestic remedies to the merits stage, especially in cases dealing with procedural matters and the procedural obligation of articles 2 and 3.[17]

The Explanatory Report on Protocol No. 14 does not indicate why the rule was changed for individual applications yet retained for inter-State applications. In the only inter-State cases submitted to the Court since the entry into force of Protocol No. 11 in 1998, the Chamber decided to join the issue of admissibility with the merits: '[I]n the instant case the question of the application of the rule of exhaustion of domestic remedies and compliance with it are so closely related to that of the existence of an administrative practice that they must be considered jointly during an examination of the merits of the case.'[18]

---

[11] Rules of Court, Rule 54A(1).

[12] Ibid., Rule 54A(2).

[13] Explanatory Report on Protocol No. 14, paras 41, 73.

[14] Rules of Court, Rule 54A(1).

[15] Explanatory Report on Protocol No. 11, para. 78.

[16] Explanatory Report on Protocol No. 14, para. 73. See in this respect *Perişan and Others v. Turkey*, no. 12336/03, §§ 68–72, 20 May 2010.

[17] *Dink v. Turkey*, nos 2668/07, 6102/08, 30079/08, 7072/09, and 7124/09, §§ 56–58, 14 September 2010; *Scoppola v. Italy (no. 2)* [GC], no. 10249/03, § 126, 17 September 2009; *A, B and C v. Ireland* [GC], no. 25579/05, § 155, ECHR 2010; *M.S.S. v. Belgium and Greece* [GC], no. 30696/09, § 336, ECHR 2011.

[18] *Georgia v. Russia* (dec.), no. 13255/07, § 50, 30 June 2009. Also *Georgia v. Russia* (dec.), no. 38263/08, §§ 68, 75, 94, 13 December 2011.

The decision of the Chamber that a case is inadmissible is final, subject to the possibility of reopening an examination of admissibility where the Court itself has committed an error.[19]

Further reading

Frowein/Peukert, *MenschenRechtsKonvention*, p. 454.
Leo Zwaak, 'The Procedure before the European Court of Human Rights', in Van Dijk et al., *Theory and Practice*, pp. 95–290.

---

[19] *Storck v. Germany*, no. 61603/00, § 67, ECHR 2005-V; *Storck v. Germany* (dec.), no. 61603, 26 October 2004; *Ölmez v. Turkey* (dec.), no. 39464/98, 5 July 2005; *Des Fours Walderode v. Czech Republic* (dec.), no. 40057/98, ECHR 2004-V; *Harrach v. Czech Republic* (dec.), no. 77532/01, 18 May 2004; *Le Syndicat des copropriétaires du 20 bd de la Mer à Dinard v. France* (dec.), no. 47339/99, 22 May 2003; *Wortmann v. Germany* (dec.), no. 70929/01, 18 November 2003; *Appietto v. France* (dec.), no. 56927/00, § 8, 26 February 2002.

Article 30. Relinquishment of jurisdiction to the Grand Chamber/Dessaisissement en faveur de la Grande Chambre

Where a case pending before a Chamber raises a serious question affecting the interpretation of the Convention or the Protocols thereto, or where the resolution of a question before the Chamber might have a result inconsistent with a judgment previously delivered by the Court, the Chamber may, at any time before it has rendered its judgment, relinquish jurisdiction in favour of the Grand Chamber, unless one of the parties to the case objects.[1]

Si l'affaire pendante devant une chambre soulève une question grave relative à l'interprétation de la Convention ou de ses Protocoles, ou si la solution d'une question peut conduire à une contradiction avec un arrêt rendu antérieurement par la Cour, la chambre peut, tant qu'elle n'a pas rendu son arrêt, se dessaisir au profit de la Grande Chambre, à moins que l'une des parties ne s'y oppose.

Introductory comments

The largest judicial formation of the European Court of Human Rights is the Grand Chamber. Its judgments are especially authoritative. Cases may come before the Grand Chamber following a decision by a seven-judge Chamber upon the request of one of the parties. Known as referral, it is governed by article 43. However, they may also be submitted to the Grand Chamber by the Chamber itself, on its own initiative, before it has issued a judgment. This is the purpose of article 30.

Drafting of the provision

The ancestor of article 30 was in the original Rules of Court adopted in 1959. It authorized the Chamber to relinquish jurisdiction in favour of the plenary Court where a case 'raised serious questions affecting the interpretation of the Convention'.[2] The *Belgian Linguistic case* was the first occasion when the Court sat on this basis in plenary, which at the time consisted of fourteen judges.[3]

Many years later, the provision of the Rules of Court providing for relinquishment to the plenary Court was changed to allow for relinquishment to a 'Grand Chamber' consisting of the President, the Vice-President, the judges of the Chamber that had relinquished jurisdiction, and additional judges so that it would comprise

---

[1] The words 'unless one of the parties to the case objects' are deleted pursuant to article 3 of Protocol No. 15 amending the Convention for the Protection of Human Rights and Fundamental Freedoms, ETS 213, which is not yet in force.

[2] Rules of Court, (adopted 18 September 1959), Rule 48 (Relinquishment of jurisdiction by the Chamber in favour of the plenary Court). This became Rule 50 pursuant to Revised Rules of Court (adopted on 24 November 1982) and then Rule 51 pursuant to Rules of Court (adopted on 24 November 1982 and amended on 26 January 1989).

[3] Case 'relating to certain aspects of the laws on the use of languages in education in Belgium' (merits), 23 July 1968, Series A no. 6.

nineteen members.[4] The amendment entered into force on 27 October 1993 and the first hearings before a Grand Chamber were held in 1994.[5] Relinquishment by a Chamber in favour of the Grand Chamber was mandatory where the resolution of 'one or more serious questions affecting the interpretation of the Convention . . . might have a result inconsistent with a judgment previously delivered by the Court'. Reasons were not required for the decision to relinquish jurisdiction. The Grand Chamber could then rule on the case, or return it to the Chamber for judgment, or relinquish jurisdiction to the plenary Court 'exceptionally, when the issues raised are particularly serious or involve a significant change of existing case-law'.

Protocol No. 11 transferred the relinquishment procedure from the Rules of Court to the Convention. The new article 30 is clearly derived from the provision in the Rules of Court. However, contrary to the situation under the Rules, article 30 does not oblige the Chamber to relinquish jurisdiction.[6] The Explanatory Report also includes the following explanation:

The reason for making relinquishment subject to the approval of the parties should be seen in the light of the introduction of the concept of 're-hearing', in accordance with the decision of the Committee of Ministers on 28 May 1993 . . . The provision is designed so as to secure the possibility that such a 're-hearing' not be adversely affected. This procedure of relinquishment, the use of which can be made any time prior to judgment, must thus be distinguished from that of a re-hearing as provided for in Article 43.[7]

Protocol No. 15, not yet in force, amends article 30 by eliminating the final words: 'unless one of the parties to the case objects'.[8] The Explanatory Report says this measure is 'intended to contribute to consistency in the case-law of the Court, which had indicated that it intended to modify its Rules of Court (Rule 72) so as to make it obligatory for a Chamber to relinquish jurisdiction where it envisages departing from settled case-law'.[9] The Report says that '[r]emoval of the parties' right to object to relinquishment will reinforce this development'.[10] The Explanatory Report also said that 'removal of this right would also aim at accelerating proceedings before the Court in cases which raise a serious question affecting the interpretation of the Convention or the Protocols thereto or a potential departure from existing case-law'.[11] Furthermore, the Report says 'it would be expected that the Chamber will consult the parties on its intentions and it would be preferable for the Chamber to narrow down the case as far as possible, including by finding inadmissible any relevant parts of the case before relinquishing it'.[12] The amendment is made 'in the expectation that the Grand Chamber will in future give more specific

---

[4] Rules of Court A (as in force at 1 February 1994), Rule 51 (Relinquishment of jurisdiction by the Chamber in favour of the Grand Chamber and by the Grand Chamber in favour of the plenary Court).

[5] *Murray v. the United Kingdom*, 28 October 1994, § 6, Series A no. 300-A; *Jersild v. Denmark*, 23 September 1994, § 6, Series A no. 298.

[6] Explanatory Report on Protocol No. 11, para. 79.

[7] Ibid.

[8] Protocol No. 15 amending the Convention for the Protection of Human Rights and Fundamental Freedoms, ETS 213, art. 3.

[9] Explanatory Report on Protocol No. 15, para. 16.

[10] Ibid., para. 16.

[11] Ibid., para. 17.

[12] Ibid., para. 18.

indication to the parties of the potential departure from existing case-law or serious question of interpretation of the Convention or the Protocols thereto'.[13]

The Court itself issued an Opinion addressing the comments in the Explanatory Report. With respect to the desire that before relinquishing the case it consult the parties, the Court said '[t]his can be accommodated'. As for narrowing the case by rejecting inadmissible aspects of the complaint before relinquishing jurisdiction, the Court agreed this was desirable, pointing to existing practice. It also noted amended Rule 27A whereby when a case is communicated to the respondent State, the President of the Section may strike out manifestly ill-founded or plainly inadmissible complaints. 'This will be in the interests of a more focussed procedure before the Chamber and, in case of relinquishment, before the Grand Chamber', the Court said. On the third issue raised in the Explanatory Report, concerning the need for specific indications to the parties about the possible change in case law or the serious question of interpretation involved, the Court said '[i]t is in the interests of the procedure that it be clear to the parties what issues they should address in depth before the Grand Chamber. In most cases, these issues should be clear enough. Where a party has a doubt, it may raise the matter with the Court's Registry, which can provide assistance.'[14]

Analysis and interpretation

Perhaps slightly less than half of the cases that come to the Grand Chamber result from relinquishment by a Chamber, in accordance with article 30 of the Convention. The number of cases relinquished each year does not reach ten. Relinquishment must be distinguished from referral, the other door to the Grand Chamber. Under article 43, referral may be granted upon the application by one of the parties on grounds that are similar, but not identical, to those for relinquishment.

Two grounds justify relinquishment of jurisdiction: 'a serious question affecting the interpretation of the Convention or the Protocols', and 'where the resolution of a question before the Chamber might have a result inconsistent with a judgment previously delivered by the Court'. The Chamber need not relinquish jurisdiction in the first situation, whereas in the second relinquishment is mandatory. Serious questions of interpretation are addressed constantly by the Chambers and it would be absurd for them to defer to the Grand Chamber systematically. Numerous dissenting and separate opinions within the Chambers confirm that serious questions of interpretation often arise, yet there is no relinquishment of jurisdiction. There does not seem to be any method or principle that can enable an observer to predict when a case will be relinquished on this basis and when it will not.

With respect to the possibility of a result inconsistent with previous authority, there is thereby established a principle akin to *stare decisis* in that a Chamber is formally prohibited from reversing precedent. By relinquishing jurisdiction the members of the Chamber may appear already to have taken a position favouring reversal of an earlier precedent. Nevertheless, to the extent that they may be inclined to depart from previously decided authority, they have no choice but to relinquish jurisdiction to the Grand Chamber.

---

[13] Ibid., para. 19.
[14] Opinion of the Court on Draft Protocol No. 15 to the European Convention on Human Rights, 6 February 2013, paras 9–11.

Reasons are not required by the Rules of Court and generally they are not given.[15] Nor do the judgments on the Grand Chamber indicate whether the case came to it because of an issue of interpretation or the possibility of a result inconsistent with previous authority. In a case involving consideration of a controversial ruling by the Grand Chamber on immunities issued thirteen years previously, with a narrow majority and where there had been important subsequent legal developments, a Chamber has said that '[w]here the precedent in question is a relatively recent and comprehensive judgment of the Grand Chamber, as in the present case, a Chamber which is not prepared to follow the established precedent should propose relinquishment of the case before it to the Grand Chamber'.[16] One member of the Chamber clearly disagreed, contending in a separate opinion that the jurisdiction should have been relinquished to the Grand Chamber 'in order to give it the opportunity to consider whether Al-Adsani still remains good law'.[17]

It is open to the parties to contest relinquishment by the Chamber. The Registrar is to notify the parties of the Chamber's intention. They have one month in which to provide a 'duly reasoned objection',[18] a requirement that suggests the objection does not function as a veto and that the Chamber is then to consider the arguments of the parties in taking a final decision. Nevertheless, it seems that the Court treats the objection to relinquishment as an absolute right of the parties and it does not appear to consider the merits of the objection.[19] Once the relinquishment decision has been taken, an objection cannot subsequently be raised in the proceedings before the Grand Chamber.[20] These provisions are slated for removal when Protocol No. 15 enters into force.

Although the Court's practice is to consider issues of admissibility and merits at the same time, in accordance with article 29(1), it is possible for a Chamber to declare part of an application inadmissible and then relinquish jurisdiction in favour of the Grand Chamber.[21]

Further reading

Frowein/Peukert, *MenschenRechtsKonvention*, p. 455.
Leo Zwaak, 'The Procedure before the European Court of Human Rights', in Van Dijk et al., *Theory and Practice*, pp. 238–9.

---

[15] Rules of Court, Rule 72(3). For example, '[t]he Court does not see any reason to relinquish jurisdiction in favour of the Grand Chamber': *Lordos and Others v. Turkey* (just satisfaction), no. 15973/90, § 9, 10 January 2012; 'the Chamber rejected the applicant's request that it relinquish jurisdiction in favour of the Grand Chamber': *Mateescu v. Romania*, no. 1944/10, § 5, 14 January 2014.

[16] *Jones and Others v. the United Kingdom*, nos 34356/06 and 40528/06, § 104, 14 January 2014.

[17] Ibid., Concurring Opinion of Judge Bianku, 14 January 2014. Also *Bayatyan v. Armenia*, no. 23459/03, Concurring Opinion of Judge Fura, 27 October 2009.

[18] Rules of Court, Rule 72(4).

[19] *Al-Dulimi and Montana Management Inc. v. Switzerland*, no. 5809/08, § 9, 26 November 2013; *Ivanţoc and Others v. Moldova and Russia*, no. 23687/05, § 4, 15 November 2011; *Herri Batasuna and Batasuna v. Spain*, nos 25803/04 and 25817/04, § 6, ECHR 2009.

[20] *Scoppola v. Italy (no. 2)* [GC], no. 10249/03, §§ 58–59, 17 September 2009.

[21] *Catan and Others v. Moldova and Russia* (dec.), nos 43370/04, 8252/05, and 18454/06, 15 June 2010 and *Catan and Others v. the Republic of Moldova and Russia* [GC], nos 43370/04, 8252/05, and 18454/06, § 3, ECHR 2012 (extracts); *Scoppola v. Italy (no. 2)* (dec.), no. 10249/03, §§ 1–4, 8 September 2005 and *Scoppola v. Italy (no. 2)* [GC], no. 10249/03, § 4, 17 September 2009.

Article 31. Powers of the Grand Chamber/Attributions de la Grande Chambre

The Grand Chamber shall

(a) determine applications submitted either under Article 33 or Article 34 when a Chamber has relinquished jurisdiction under Article 30 or when the case has been referred to it under Article 43;
(b) decide on issues referred to the Court by the Committee of Ministers in accordance with Article 46, paragraph 4; and
(c) consider requests for advisory opinions submitted under Article 47.

La Grande Chambre

a) se prononce sur les requêtes introduites en vertu de l'article 33 ou de l'article 34 lorsque l'affaire lui a été déférée par la chambre en vertu de l'article 30 ou lorsque l'affaire lui a été déférée en vertu de l'article 43;
b) se prononce sur les questions dont la Cour est saisie par le Comité des Ministres en vertu de l'article 46, paragraphe 4; et
c) examine les demandes d'avis consultatifs introduites en vertu de l'article 47.

Introductory comments

There is a certain redundancy about article 31 in that it appears to do no more than confirm the jurisdiction of the Grand Chamber that is set out in other provisions of the Convention. In effect, the Grand Chamber has jurisdiction with respect to individual applications and inter-State applications, whether these come to it through relinquishment or by application of one of the parties. It also has competence to deal with matters referred by the Committee of Ministers in accordance with article 46(4). Finally, it is competent to deliver advisory opinions, as set out in article 47.

Drafting of the provision

The Grand Chamber did not exist under the 1950 text of the Convention. The 'Grand Chamber' was initially created by the Rules of Court, essentially to replace the function of the plenary Court as an apex bench hearing cases when the Chamber had relinquished jurisdiction.[1] Article 31 was introduced by Protocol No. 11:

Powers of the Grand Chamber
The Grand Chamber shall
(a) determine applications submitted either under Article 33 or Article 34 when a Chamber has relinquished jurisdiction under Article 30 or when the case has been referred to it under Article 43; and
(b) consider requests for advisory opinions submitted under Article 47.

Noting that the plenary would consist of more than thirty judges, the Report said this 'could work only with difficulty' and that a Grand Chamber composed of seventeen judges would be 'sufficiently representative'. The Grand Chamber would, 'as far as

---

[1] Rules of Court A (as in force at 1 February 1994), Rule 51.

possible, provide a balanced representation of judges from each Chamber as well as a diversity of legal systems'.[2]

Paragraph (b) was added to article 31 by Protocol No. 14, with the consequential renumbering of the former paragraph (b) and paragraph (c).[3] It confirms the jurisdiction of the Grand Chamber when the Committee of Ministers votes to bring proceedings against a State Party that refuses to comply with a judgment of the Court.[4]

Analysis and interpretation

There is no matter before the Court over which the Grand Chamber may not exercise jurisdiction, with one exception. It is bound by the admissibility decision of the Chamber to the extent that it may not consider issues already judged inadmissible. It may only examine the case that has been declared admissible.[5] Thus, '[w]ithin the compass thus delimited, the Grand Chamber may deal with any issue of fact or law that arises during the proceedings before it'.[6]

Further reading

Frowein/Peukert, *MenschenRechtsKonvention*, p. 456.
Katharina Pabel, 'Die Rolle des Großen Kammer des EGMR bei Überprüfung von Kammer-Urteilen im Lichte der bisherigen Praxis / Kopftuch-Fall Leyla Şahin', (2006) 33 *Europäische Grundrechte Zeitschrift* 3.
Leo Zwaak, 'The Procedure before the European Court of Human Rights', in Van Dijk et al., *Theory and Practice*, pp. 237–40.

---

[2] Explanatory Report on Protocol No. 11, para. 80.
[3] Protocol No. 14 to the Convention for the Protection of Human Rights and Fundamental Freedoms, amending the control system of the Convention, ETS 194, art. 10.
[4] Explanatory Report on Protocol No. 14, paras 42, 75.
[5] *Gillberg v. Sweden* [GC], no. 41723/06, § 53, 3 April 2012; *K. and T. v. Finland* [GC], no. 25702/94, §§ 140–141, ECHR 2001-VII; *Göç v. Turkey* [GC], no. 36590/97, §§ 35–37, ECHR 2002-V; *Perna v. Italy* [GC], no. 48898/99, §§ 23–24, ECHR 2003- V; *D.H. and Others v. the Czech Republic* [GC], no. 57325/00, § 109, ECHR-2007-IV.
[6] *Scoppola v. Italy (no. 2)* [GC], no. 10249/03, § 48, 17 September 2009; *Philis v. Greece (no. 1)*, 27 August 1991, § 56, Series A no. 209; *Guerra and Others v. Italy*, 19 February 1998, § 44 *in fine, Reports of Judgments and Decisions* 1998-I.

Article 32. Jurisdiction of the Court/Compétence de la Cour

1. The jurisdiction of the Court shall extend to all matters concerning the interpretation and application of the Convention and the Protocols thereto which are referred to it as provided in Articles 33, 34, 46 and 47.

2. In the event of dispute as to whether the Court has jurisdiction, the Court shall decide.

1. La compétence de la Cour s'étend à toutes les questions concernant l'interprétation et l'application de la Convention et de ses Protocoles qui lui seront soumises dans les conditions prévues par les articles 33, 34, 46 et 47.

2. En cas de contestation sur le point de savoir si la Cour est compétente, la Cour décide.

Introductory comments

The concept of jurisdiction refers to the power of a court 'to decide a matter in controversy and presupposes the existence of a duly constituted court with control over the subject matter and the parties'.[1]

Drafting of the provision

The 1949 draft of the European Movement contained the following: 'La Cour sera compétente pour juger de toute violation des droits précités, résultant d'un acte législatif, administratif ou juridictionnel, ou d'une voie de fait . . .'[2] The draft adopted for submission to the Committee of Ministers of the Council of Europe read: 'The Court shall have jurisdiction to determine all cases concerning the infringement of this Convention arising out of executive, legislative or juridical acts.'[3] The European Movement also prepared a draft statute for a European Court of Human Rights. It contained the following:

Part II. Competence
Article 31
a) The jurisdiction of the Court is defined in the Convention on Human Rights.
b) In the event of a dispute as to whether the Court has jurisdiction the matter shall be settled by decision of the Court.

---

[1] *Prosecutor v. Tadić* (IT-94-1-AR72), Decision on the Defence Motion for Interlocutory Appeal on Jurisdiction, 2 October 1995, para. 10, citing *Black's Law Dictionary*, 712 (6th edn, 1990).

[2] Recommendations adopted at the meeting of the International Council of the European Movement held at Brussels in February 1949, INF/2/F, p. 3. This is reproduced in CDH (67) 5, at pp. 2–3, with the indication that the original English version no longer exists.

[3] Convention for the Collective Protection of Individual Rights and Democratic Liberties by the States, Members of the Council of Europe, and for the establishment of a European Court of Human Rights to ensure observance of the Convention, Doc. INF/5/E/R, I *TP* 296–303, at p. 300, art. 13(a).

Article 32

a) The Court, whose function is to decide in accordance with international law (subject to the qualification contained in Articles 4 and 5 of the Convention on Human Rights) such questions or issues as are submitted to it, shall apply:
  (i) the provisions of the Convention on Human Rights;
  (ii) the general principles of law recognised by civilised nations;
  (iii) judicial decisions and the teachings of the most highly qualified publicists of the various nations as subsidiary means for the determination of rules of law;
  (iv) international conventions, whether general or particular, establishing rules expressly recognised by any State concerned.

b) This provision shall not prejudice the power of the Court to decide a case *ex aequo et bono*.[4]

Articles 36 and 38 of the Statute of the International Court of Justice were the inspiration for these provisions.

The Legal Committee of the Consultative Assembly proposed that the following provision be included in the Convention:

The jurisdiction of the Court shall extend to all violations of the obligations defined by the Convention, whether they result from legislative, executive or judicial acts. Nevertheless, where objection is taken to a judicial decision, that decision cannot be impugned unless it was given in disregard of the fundamental rights defined in Article 2 by reference to Articles 9, 10 and 11 of the United Nations Declaration.[5]

Presenting this text to the plenary Consultative Assembly, Pierre-Henri Teitgen explained that the Committee:

proposes that the guarantee exercised either by the Commission or, later, by the jurisdiction of the European Court of Human Rights, shall extend to all violations of the obligations defined in the Convention, whether they are the result of legislative, executive or judicial acts. But in this connection, and especially as regards judicial acts, [your] Committee takes care to point out that the Court will not in any way operate as a Supreme Court of Appeal having jurisdiction to review any errors of laws or of fact which are alleged against a national Court.[6]

Teitgen went to considerable pains to insist that the proposed Court would not interfere with the decisions of domestic courts except in the case of what he called a 'pseudo-judgment', that is, 'when there has been a travesty of justice or a verdict given in disregard of all fundamental individual rights, or all elementary guarantees of procedure...'[7] An amendment was submitted to insert the word 'finally' after the words 'unless it was'. The proposers said this was 'to avoid any possibility of conflict between supra-national jurisdiction and national jurisdiction', adding that it prevented a matter being brought before the Court unless all instances of national jurisdiction were exhausted. 'This amendment should help to reassure those who fear an infringement of national sovereignty', they said.[8] The amendment was accepted and the draft article adopted by the Consultative Assembly.[9]

---

[4] Draft Statute of the European Court of Human Rights, INF/5/E/R, I *TP* 302–21, at p. 312.
[5] Report presented by Mr P.H. Teitgen, 5 September 1949, Doc. A 290, I *TP* 192–213, at p. 198. Also Report [of the Committee on Legal and Administrative Questions], 5 September 1949, Doc. AS (1) 77, I *TP* 216–39, at p. 234, art. 24.
[6] Report of the Sitting [of the Consultative Assembly, 7 September 1949], I *TP* 258–95, p. 288.
[7] Ibid., p. 290.
[8] Amendment proposed by Mr Dominedo and Mr Benvenuti (Italy) (8 September 1949), Doc. 105, II *TP* 12–13.
[9] Official Report of the Sitting [of the Consultative Assembly, 8 September 1949], II *TP* 14–274, at p. 218–20.

The Committee of Ministers referred the Consultative Assembly draft to a Committee of Experts for further consideration. Prior to its meetings, the Secretariat General of the Council of Europe prepared a detailed study on the notion of 'denial of justice' to assist in the discussions on the jurisdictional provision.[10] In the first session of the Committee of Experts, in February 1950, a proposal emerged that begins to resemble the final result:

Article A
The competence of the Court shall cover the following matters:
1) Any disputes arising out of the interpretation and application of the present Convention which is brought before the Court by one of the Contracting Parties;
2) Any questions concerning the application, by the parties to the present Convention, of the provisions of Article 2 to...of this Convention, which is referred to the Court by the Commission of Human Rights.

In the event of dispute as to whether or not the Court possesses competence, it is for the Court to decide.[11]

After noting that the concern of the Consultative Assembly with the relationship between national jurisdictions and the European court had been resolved by formulation of a rule of exhaustion of domestic remedies, the Committee of Experts adopted the following provisions in the report on its first session, held in February 1950:

Article 32
The competence of the Court shall cover all cases of violation of individual rights protected by the application of Articles 2, 4, 5, 6, 7, 8 and 9 of this Convention.

Article 35
In the event of dispute as to whether the Court has jurisdiction, the matter shall be settled by the decision of the Court.[12]

With respect to article 35, the accompanying commentary said no explanation was required. As for article 32, the following was provided:

This Article gives rulings on the competence of the Court.
Contrary to the Assembly draft, the Committee of Experts considered that in no case should the Court be competent to give a ruling on cases of violation of article 3, relating to the safeguarding of democratic institutions. Such cases were not the kind which it was suitable to settle by judgment of a court. The measures to be taken for remedying them came exclusively with the political sphere. According to the Committee of Experts' system, moreover, the Court should only be permitted to give a ruling on cases of violation of the *individual* rights protected by the Convention, and not of cases of violation of the Convention by legislative acts as such.[13]

---

[10] Documentation of the Secretary General on the denial of justice such as it is understood by general international public law in the framework of the responsibility of the State for acts of its judicial organs (undated), cited in CDH (70) 32, p. 23. Also Preparatory Report by the Secretariat-General concerning a Preliminary Draft Convention to Provide a Collective Guarantee of Human Rights, Doc. B 22, III *TP* 2–37, at p. 34.

[11] Amendments to various articles of the Recommendation of the Consultative Assembly proposed by the Italian Expert, Doc. A 812, III *TP* 228–31.

[12] Preliminary Draft Convention for the Maintenance and Further Realisation of Human Rights and Fundamental Freedoms, 15 February 1950, Doc. A 833, III *TP* 236–46, at p. 246.

[13] Preliminary Draft of the Report to the Committee of Ministers, 24 February 1950, Doc. CM/WP 1 (50) 1, A 847, III *TP* 246–79, at pp. 274–6 (emphasis in the original).

At its second session, the Committee of Experts made slight changes to the report:

This Article defines the competence of the Court.

Contrary to the Assembly draft, the Committee of Experts considered that in no case should the Court be competent to give a ruling on cases of violation of article 3, relating to the safeguarding of democratic institutions. Such cases were not the kind which it was suitable to settle by judgment of a court. The measures to be taken for remedying them are political measures and therefore should fall within the exclusive competence of the Commission of Human Rights and the Committee of Ministers.

According to the Committee of Experts' system, moreover, the Court should only be permitted to give a ruling on cases of violation of the *individual* rights protected by the Convention, and not of cases of violation of the Convention simply by promulgation of legislative acts.[14]

The draft prepared by the Committee of Experts was then studied by the Conference of Senior Officials on Human Rights, in June 1950. Articles 32 and 35 of the draft were considered in the context of concern about the proliferation of international courts and tribunals. Members of the Committee stressed the importance of confining the remit of the Court to matters arising from the Convention.[15] The Conference adopted an initial draft containing the following provisions:

Article 46

The jurisdiction comprises all cases concerning the interpretation and application of the present Convention which the High Contracting Parties shall refer to it, in accordance with the provisions hereafter...

Article 50

In the event of dispute as to whether the Court has jurisdiction, the matter shall be settled by the decision of the Court.[16]

There were no further changes to article 50, which became article 49 in the final text of the Convention. Article 46 of the earlier draft (it had become article 45) was revised by the Conference of Senior Officials: 'The jurisdiction of the Court comprises all cases concerning the interpretation and application of the present Convention which the High Contracting Parties or the Commission shall refer to it in accordance with article 48.'[17] Article 48, to which reference was made, was in draft form very similar to the final version of article 48. It set out the sources of referrals to the Court. The text of article 46, as adopted by the Conference, was identical to that of article 45 in the final version of the Convention except that the words 'comprises all cases' were changed to 'shall extend to all cases' on a proposal of the British delegate.[18]

A theme throughout the debates in all of the bodies engaged in drafting the Convention was whether to include a provision derived from the original article 32 of the

---

[14] Appendix to the Report of the Committee of Experts on Human Rights: Draft Convention of Protection of Human Rights and Fundamental Freedoms, 16 March 1950, Doc. CM/WP 1 (50) 15 appendix, CM/WP 1 (50) 14 revised, A 925, IV *TP* 50–79, at p. 44 (emphasis in the original).

[15] Non-official report of the sessions, cited in CDH (70) 32, pp. 34–7.

[16] Draft Convention appended to the draft report, Doc. CM/WP 4 (50) 16, appendix, A 1445, IV *TP* 218–40, at pp. 234–6.

[17] Draft Convention annexed to the Report [of the Conference of Senior Officials], Doc. CM/WP 4 (50) 19 annex, CM/WP 4 (50) 16 rev., A 1452, IV *TP* 274–95, at p. 290.

[18] Draft Convention adopted by the Sub-Committee, Doc. CM 1 (50) 52, A 1884, V *TP* 76–99, at p. 92.

European Movement text.[19] This would have invited the Court to apply 'general principles of law recognised by civilised nations', an expression taken from article 38 of the Statute of the International Court of Justice. It was really an applicable law provision rather than a provision on jurisdiction as such. The line between the two concepts may not always be entirely clear. In practice, the European Court of Human Rights has applied 'general principles of law recognised by civilised nations' (note the reference in article 7(2) of the Convention) as well as other relevant sources of international law but only as guidance for the interpretation of the Convention, in accordance with article 31(3)(c) of the Vienna Convention on the Law of Treaties, a matter discussed in the introductory chapter of this book.

In its report to the Consultative Assembly, in August 1950, the Legal Committee wrote the following:

The Committee, while recognising the importance of the proposal that the European Commission and Court should apply the general principles of law recognised among civilised States, as referred to in Article 38 of the Statute of the International Court, were of the opinion that the insertion of a specific clause to this effect was unnecessary, but wished to recommend to the Assembly that in transmitting the draft Convention to the Committee of Ministers the attention of the latter might be drawn to this point. It is anticipated that the Commission and the Court must necessarily apply such principles in coming to a decision.[20]

In the plenary Assembly, David Maxwell Fyfe of the United Kingdom explained that the Legal Committee had not insisted on requiring the Court to apply general principles of law because it 'could not contemplate the organs or the machinery doing anything else. If they are going to work they must apply these principles, and it is in that spirit that we have made no suggestion for a specific inclusion.'[21]

Article 32 of the Convention results from Protocol No. 11. The first paragraph of article 32 closely resembles article 45 of the 1950 text. The mention of the Commission disappeared, and the reference to article 48 in the concluding words was modified so as to list the provisions in the revised Convention governing referral of cases to the Court. The second sentence of article 32 is identical to article 49 of the 1950 Convention.[22] The provision was amended by Protocol No. 14 with the addition of article 46 to the enumeration of provisions in the concluding words of paragraph 1 so as to take into account the new procedure introduced in that text.[23]

Analysis and interpretation

'[I]t follows from [article 32] that the Court may exercise its jurisdiction only in regard to cases which have been duly brought before it', the Plenary Court has said.[24] The

---

[19] See, for example, the speech by P.-H. Teitgen in the 1950 session of the Consultative Assembly, Report of the Sitting [of the Consultative Assembly, 7 September 1949], I *TP* 250–95, at p. 280.

[20] First Report [of the Committee on Legal and Administrative Questions], Doc. AS/JA (2) 15, A 2298, VI *TP* 46–52, at p. 50; Second Report [of the Committee on Legal and Administrative Questions], Doc. AS/JA (2) rev., A 2493, VI *TP* 52–58, at p. 56; Text of the Report [of the Committee on Legal and Administrative Questions], Doc. AS (2) 93, VI *TP* 58–72, at p. 62.

[21] Report of the Sitting [of the Consultative Assembly, 25 August 1950, morning], VI *TP* 74–143, at p. 78.

[22] Explanatory Report on Protocol No. 11, para. 82.

[23] Protocol No. 14 to the Convention for the Protection of Human Rights and Fundamental Freedoms, amending the control system of the Convention, ETS 194, art. 11.

[24] *De Wilde, Ooms, and Versyp v. Belgium*, 18 June 1971, § 49, Series A no. 12.

consequence is that the Court 'cannot interpret the Convention in an abstract manner, but only in relation to such specific cases as are referred to it'.[25] But '[o]nce a case is duly referred to it, however, the Court is endowed with full jurisdiction and may thus take cognisance of all questions of fact and of law which may arise in the course of the consideration of the case'.[26]

Issues of jurisdiction, in particular temporal, territorial, and personal jurisdiction, are also addressed in the context of article 1 of the Convention. Article 32 is concerned primarily with the subject-matter jurisdiction of the Court.

The Court invoked article 32 in a case dealing with succession to the European Convention on Human Rights. After Montenegro seceded from Serbia and Montenegro, in June 2006, an application raised the issue of attribution of responsibility for observance of the Convention within Montenegro prior to that date. When it invited Montenegro to join the Council of Europe, the Committee of Ministers adopted a resolution stating that Montenegro was to be regarded as a Party to the European Convention on Human Rights and its Protocols No. 1, 4, 6, 7, 12, 13, and 14 thereto with effect from 6 June 2006.[27] In its judgment, the Court noted that the Committee of Ministers had accepted, 'apparently because of the earlier ratification of the Convention by the State Union of Serbia and Montenegro, that it was not necessary for Montenegro to deposit its own formal ratification of the Convention'.[28] Holding Montenegro responsible for a breach of article 1 of Protocol No. 1 prior to 6 June 2006, the Court said that notwithstanding article 54 of the Convention, it has 'the sole competence under Article 32 thereof to determine all issues concerning "the interpretation and application of the Convention", including those involving its temporal jurisdiction and/or the compatibility of the applicants' complaints ratione personae'.[29]

Jurisdiction of the Court (para. 1)

In its very first decision, the Court explained that 'the exact meaning' of article 32 (then article 45) was defined in other articles of the Convention, specifically referring to the former article 47, which required the failure of efforts by the Commission to reach a friendly settlement, and article 46(1) (then article 53) by which States Parties 'undertake to abide by the decision of the Court in any case to which they are parties'.[30]

The presence of article 32 in the Convention is the result of a very substantial debate around the inclusion of a more elaborate provision governing applicable law analogous to article 38 of the Statute of the International Court of Justice. Article 32 (articles 45 and 49 in the 1950 text of the Convention) is what remained when the detailed text on applicable law, with its reference to 'general principles of law recognised by civilised nations', was not retained. When the Convention was revised by Protocol No. 11 and Protocol No. 14, the provision underwent amendment, but only of the most perfunctory nature. It did not attract any attention in a substantive sense.

[25] *Lawless v. Ireland (no. 1)*, 14 November 1960, p. 8, Series A no. 1.
[26] *De Wilde, Ooms, and Versyp v. Belgium*, 18 June 1971, § 49, Series A no. 12.
[27] Resolution CM/Res(2007)7 inviting the Republic of Montenegro to become a member of the Council of Europe.
[28] *Bijelić v. Montenegro and Serbia*, no. 11890/05, § 68, 28 April 2009.
[29] Ibid., § 67.
[30] *Lawless v. Ireland (no. 1)*, 14 November 1960, p. 8, Series A no. 1.

In one case, a Chamber of the Court said that it 'would reiterate, as clearly as possible, that it alone is competent to decide on its jurisdiction to interpret and apply the Convention and its Protocols (Article 32 of the Convention), in particular with regard to the issue of whether the person in question is an applicant within the meaning of Article 34 of the Convention and whether the application fulfils the requirements of that provision'.[31] In another, where Latvia contested the authority of the Court to consider measures taken by the State in order to implement a treaty concluded prior to entry into force of the Convention, the Court said it 'must therefore first address the question of its own jurisdiction (Article 32 § 2 of the Convention)'.[32] The Court said:

Under the terms of Article 32 § 1 its jurisdiction extends to all matters concerning the interpretation and application of the Convention and Protocols which are referred to it, inter alia by way of an individual application lodged under Article 34. In accordance with its established case-law, the Court's power of interpretation is not limited to the text itself of the Convention and Protocols, but also embraces the interpretation of reservations and other unilateral declarations made by a Contracting Party in relation thereto.[33]

Article 32 has also been invoked in the context of the *jura novit curiae* doctrine, by which the Court may address substantive provisions of the Convention even if these have not been raised by the parties. The Court 'is master of the characterisation to be given in law to the facts of the case' and 'it does not consider itself bound by the characterisation given by an applicant, a government or the Commission'.[34]

Disputes about jurisdiction (para. 2)

Paragraph 2 of article 32, reproducing article 49 of the 1950 text of the Convention, specifies that 'In the event of dispute as to whether the Court has jurisdiction, the Court shall decide.' This does not mean that the Court must await a challenge to its jurisdiction before considering the matter. If there are doubts about the jurisdiction, the Court may raise the issue *proprio motu*. Otherwise, it would be possible for parties to consent to the intervention of the Court even when it did not in fact have jurisdiction. The Court must 'satisfy itself that it has jurisdiction in any case brought before it, and is therefore obliged to examine the question of its jurisdiction at every stage of the proceedings'.[35]

Preliminary objections by governments that a provision is outside the jurisdiction *ratione materiae* have occasionally been dismissed by the Court, invoking article 32 as authority for dealing with the merits of disputes about the interpretation and application of the Convention.[36] In the *Ireland v. the United Kingdom* case, the Court referred to article 32 (then article 49) as a basis for the need to interpret the admissibility decision of

---

[31] *Shamayev and Others v. Georgia and Russia*, no. 36378/02, § 293, ECHR 2005-III.

[32] Ibid., §§ 53, 56.

[33] Ibid., § 57 (extracts).

[34] *Akdeniz v. Turkey*, no. 25165/94, §§ 87–88, 31 May 2005. *Jura novit curia* is discussed in detail in the chapter on article 38 of this Commentary.

[35] *Blečić v. Croatia* [GC], no. 59532/00, § 67, ECHR 2006-III; *Šilih v. Slovenia* [GC], no. 71463/01, § 139, 9 April 2009; *Shamayev and Others v. Georgia and Russia*, no. 36378/02, § 293, ECHR 2005-III. Also *Nielsen v. Denmark*, no. 343/57, Commission decision of 2 September 1959, (1958–59) YB 412, at p. 454.

[36] *Bozano v. France*, 18 December 1986, § 42, Series A no. 111; *Glasenapp v. Germany*, 28 August 1986, § 41, Series A no. 104; *Kosiek v. Germany*, 28 August 1986, § 32, Series A no. 105.

the Commission, given that the Court could only exercise jurisdiction over those parts of the application that had been declared admissible by the Commission.[37]

Further reading

Johan Callewaert, 'Article 45', in Pettiti et al., *La Convention européenne*, pp. 767–75.
Johan Callewaert, 'Article 49', in Pettiti et al., *La Convention européenne*, pp. 805–7.
Frowein/Peukert, *MenschenRechtsKonvention*, p. 457.

---

[37] *Ireland v. the United Kingdom*, 18 January 1978, § 157, Series A no. 25.

Article 33. Inter-State cases/Affaires interétatiques

Any High Contracting Party may refer to the Court any alleged breach of the provisions of the Convention and the Protocols thereto by another High Contracting Party.

Toute Haute Partie contractante peut saisir la Cour de tout manquement aux dispositions de la Convention et de ses Protocoles qu'elle croira pouvoir être imputé à une autre Haute Partie contractante.

Introductory comments

When the Rome Statute of the International Criminal Court was being negotiated, the very limited recourse to inter-State applications before the European Court of Human Rights was frequently invoked as an argument favouring an autonomous power of an independent prosecutor to launch investigations. Early drafts of the Statute had confined the power to trigger a prosecution to the United Nations Security Council and to States Parties. It was argued that one State would almost never refer another State to the Court, the experience of the European human rights system being given as evidence to support such a claim. Indeed, more than a decade into the operation of the International Criminal Court, that observation is indeed valid.[1]

Some of the architects of the European system may well have thought that the inter-State petition mechanism would constitute the main act before the Convention organs. They manifested considerable anxiety about the possibility of overlapping jurisdiction with the International Court of Justice. Article 55 of the Convention testifies to that concern. In the 1950 Convention, jurisdiction of the European Commission of Human Rights to consider inter-State applications was the automatic consequence of ratification of the Convention. A right of individual petition required the State party to make a separate declaration. That distinction eventually disappeared with the reforms implemented by Protocol No. 11 in the 1990s. Perhaps this stands as confirmation of the change in vision, by which the individual application became far and away the major activity of the Court. In practice, the inter-State petition, on the other hand, has always sat on the margins of the system. Its use is idiosyncratic and recourse to it remains unpredictable.

Drafting of the provision

The initial draft European Convention on Human Rights prepared by the International Juridical Section of the European Movement provided that applications could be initiated by any State Party to the Convention, thereby implying that such proceedings would be

---

[1] There has only been one referral by a State Party against a third State, that of Comoros concerning the obstruction of the Gaza flotilla by Israeli forces: Statement of the Prosecutor of the International Criminal Court, Fatou Bensouda, on concluding the preliminary examination of the situation referred by the Union of Comoros: 'Rome Statute legal requirements have not been met', 6 November 2014. Several States have invoked the Statute in order to confer jurisdiction on the Court, but this has been directed at their own territory and has been generally intended to focus on rebel or opposition movements or groups.

directed against another State party.[2] The Draft Statute of the Court that was annexed to the Convention was clearly inspired by the Statute of the International Court of Justice. Thus, there were several provisions that seemed to contemplate inter-State cases. For example, the parties were to be represented by 'agents' and there was the possibility of a case being brought before the Court by 'special agreement', implying some form of *compromis* between two States Parties.[3] It was also specified that nothing in the Convention was to be understood as preventing States Parties from referring any matter to the International Court of Justice.[4] It is also important to bear in mind that the negotiations that took place in 1950 were strongly influenced by the parallel work of the United Nations Commission on Human Rights with respect to the draft Covenant. It did not contemplate an individual petition mechanism at all and was solely concerned with inter-State complaints.[5]

The draft Convention adopted by the Consultative Assembly in September 1949 recognized the right of a State Party to 'appeal to the [European] Commission [of Human Rights] on any supposed breach of the provisions of the Convention by another Member State'.[6] A similar provision was adopted by the Committee of Experts at its February and March 1950 sessions: 'Any High Contracting Party may refer to the Commission through the Secretary-General of the Council of Europe the matter of any alleged breach of the provisions of the Convention by another High Contracting Party.'[7] It was slightly modified by the Conference of Senior Officials, where it took a form very close to the final version.[8] Article 24 of the Convention, adopted in November 1950, reads: 'Any High Contracting Party may refer to the Commission, through the Secretary-General of the Council of Europe, any alleged breach of the provisions of the Convention by another High Contracting Party.'

Under the 1950 text of the Convention, no supplementary declaration or acceptance of the mechanism was required with respect to inter-State petitions. All States Parties were subject to the possibility of an application from another State, although very few were actually filed. After issuance of the Commission's report, an inter-State case could then be brought before the European Court either by the Commission or by one of the parties

---

[2] Convention for the Collective Protection of Individual Rights and Democratic Liberties by the States, Members of the Council of Europe, and for the establishment of a European Court of Human Rights to ensure observance of the Convention, Doc. INF/5/E/R, I *TP* 296–303, at p. 298, art. 7(a).

[3] Draft Statute of the European Court of Human Rights, INF/5/E/R, I *TP* 302–21, at p. 314, art. 34(a).

[4] Convention for the Collective Protection of Individual Rights and Democratic Liberties by the States, Members of the Council of Europe, and for the establishment of a European Court of Human Rights to ensure observance of the Convention, Doc. INF/5/E/R, I *TP* 296–303, at p. 302, art. 15.

[5] See, e.g., Minutes of the afternoon sitting [of 9 June 1950 of the Conference of Senior Officials], IV *TP* 120–31, at pp. 124–8.

[6] Recommendation No. 38 to the Committee of Ministers adopted 8 September 1949 on the conclusion of the debates, Doc. AS (1) 108, II *TP* 274–83, at p. 278, art. 11.

[7] Appendix to the Report of the Committee of Experts on Human Rights: Draft Convention of Protection of Human Rights and Fundamental Freedoms, 16 March 1950, Doc. C/WP 1 (50) 15 appendix, CM/WP 1 (50) 14 revised, A 925, IV *TP* 50–79, at p. 68, art. 16(20). See also Preliminary Draft Convention for the Maintenance and Further Realisation of Human Rights and Fundamental Freedoms, 15 February 1950, Doc. A 833, III *TP* 236–46, at pp. 240–3, art. 14; Preliminary Draft of the Report to the Committee of Ministers, 24 February 1950, Doc. CM/WP 1 (50), A 847, III *TP* 246–79, at p. 270; Report to the Committee of Ministers submitted by the Committee of Experts Instructed to Draw Up a Draft Convention of Collective Guarantee of Human Rights and Fundamental Freedoms, Doc. CM/WP 1 (5) 15, A 924, IV *TP* 2–55, at p. 36.

[8] Draft Convention annexed to the Report, Doc. CM/WP 4 (50) 19 annex, CM/WP 4 (50) rev., A 1452, IV *TP* 274–95, at p. 284, art. 22.

pursuant to article 48 of the Convention to the extent that the States concerned had accepted the jurisdiction of the Court over such matters in accordance with article 46. In the first forty years of the Court, until the reform effected by Protocol No. 11, this happened only twice.[9]

Article 33 was introduced by Protocol No. 11. The Explanatory Report noted: 'This Article on inter-State cases reflects the former system whereby proceedings could be instituted before the Commission by one or more States against another State that had ratified the Convention, without the necessity for any additional acceptance of competence on the latter's part. States are, of course, bound only by the protocols they have ratified.'[10]

Analysis and interpretation

The inter-State complaint mechanism established by the Convention is a 'vehicle' for the 'collective enforcement' of rights contemplated by the Convention.[11] The existence of the inter-State application procedure—indeed, its obligatory nature was binding within the Convention system long before the individual petition mechanism became mandatory—confirms that the rights and obligations set out are *erga omnes*. In one of the first inter-State applications, the European Commission on Human Rights stated that:

the purpose of the High Contracting parties in concluding the Convention was not to concede to each other reciprocal rights and obligations in pursuance of their individual national interests but to realise the aims and ideals of the Council of Europe, as expressed in its Statute, and to establish a common public order of the free democracies of Europe with the object of safeguarding their common heritage of political traditions, ideals, freedom and the rule of law...'[12]

In that case, however, Austria's application against Italy was concerned with the rights of German speakers in a portion of pre-First-World-War Austria that was annexed by Italy. Austria was not acting on behalf of its nationals in the strict sense, but nor can it be said that this was a neutral and disinterested attempt to apply the Convention in order to enforce Europe's common public order. A similar observation can be made about the inter-State applications filed by Greece against the United Kingdom concerning violations related to the independence movement of Greek speaking Cypriots during the 1950s.[13] These cases, and others that followed, are similar in philosophy to the phenomenon of diplomatic protection by which a State invokes international law on behalf of its nationals in another State. One of the first cases before the Permanent Court of International Justice, filed in the early 1920s, involved diplomatic protection in a commercial matter.[14] But there are also some very recent examples of international human rights treaties being invoked on behalf of a State's nationals before the International Court of Justice.[15]

---

[9] *Ireland v. the United Kingdom*, 18 January 1978, § 2, Series A no. 25; *Cyprus v. Turkey* [GC], no. 25781/94, § 1, ECHR 2001-IV.

[10] Explanatory Report on Protocol No. 11, para. 83.

[11] *Austria v. Italy*, no. 788/60, p. 138, Commission decision of 11 January 1961, (1961) 4 YB 116; *Cyprus v. Turkey*, no. 25781/94, § 70, Commission report of 4 June 1999.

[12] *Austria v. Italy*, no. 788/60, Commission decision of 11 January 1961, (1961) 4 YB 116, at p. 138.

[13] *Greece v. the United Kingdom*, no. 176/56, Commission decision of 2 June 1956, (1958–59) 2 YB 182; *Greece v. the United Kingdom*, no. 299/57, Commission decision of 12 October 1957, (1958–59) 2 YB 186.

[14] *Mavrommatis Palestine Concessions*, Series A, No. 2.

[15] *Ahmadou Sadio Diallo (Republic of Guinea v. Democratic Republic of the Congo)*, Compensation, Judgment, I.C.J. Reports 2012, p. 324.

The early Strasbourg cases filed by Greece and Austria were not diplomatic protection in the strict sense because the alleged victims were subjects of the respondent State, not the applicant State. Only one case really resembles a classic matter of diplomatic protection. Denmark filed an application on behalf of one of its nationals alleging ill-treatment at the hands of the Turkish authorities. The case resulted in a friendly settlement.[16] Such cases have many similarities with individual applications. Under the 1950 text of the Convention, an inter-State application might have been the only available remedy if a State had not accepted the individual petition mechanism before the Commission and the Court. However, since Protocol No. 11 there seems to be little practical difference between an individual application taken under article 34 and an inter-State one filed under article 33.

A few inter-State cases are more genuinely examples of States acting without any direct interest, in a bi-lateral sense, but rather in the enforcement of European public order. The *Greek case* is probably the best example, an application by several Council of Europe members dealing with a range of human rights violations attributable to the fascist junta that took power in Athens in 1967.[17] Similarly, several European States took proceedings against Turkey in the 1980s.[18]

Attempts to classify inter-State cases into precise categories, mainly for the purpose of determining whether or not the applicant State may claim just satisfaction under article 41, do not lead to entirely satisfactory results.[19] As Judge Pinto de Albuquerque explained, 'Article 33 claims are not exclusively aimed at upholding the European public order, but may also simultaneously seek to protect and satisfy the interests of one or more nationals of the applicant State.'[20]

One confirmation of the *erga omnes* nature of the inter-State application is the absence of any requirement that a State demonstrate any particular interest, such as claiming that the impugned measure has prejudiced one of its nationals.[21] Legal interest arises in an inter-State case only 'insofar as the same matters may also be the subject of individual applications'.[22] The inter-State application does not need to seek redress for any particular individual, but rather it serves to address the protection of 'the public order of Europe'.[23] It need not be made on behalf of an individual. In contrast with the individual applicant, who must show a legal interest as a victim, be it direct, indirect, or potential, a State is not required to demonstrate any particular legal interest when it files an application against another State. The application is admissible because of 'the general interest attaching to the observance of the Convention'.[24]

---

[16] *Denmark v. Turkey* (friendly settlement), no. 34382/97, ECHR 2000-IV.

[17] *Denmark, Norway, Sweden, and the Netherlands v. Greece*, nos 3321/67, 3322/67, 3323/67, and 3344/67, Commission report of 5 November 1969, (1969) 12 YB 'The Greek case' 1. Also *Denmark, Norway, and Sweden v. Greece*, no. 4448/70, Commission decision of 16 July 1970, (1970) 13 YB 122, Collection 34, p. 70.

[18] *France, Norway, Denmark, Sweden, and the Netherlands v. Turkey*, nos 9940–9944/82, Commission decision of 6 December 1983, (1983) 26 YB COMM.EUR.JURIS. 1, DR 35, p. 143.

[19] *Cyprus v. Turkey* (just satisfaction) [GC], no. 25781/94, §§ 44–45, 12 May 2014; ibid., Partly Concurring and Partly Dissenting Opinion of Judge Casadevall.

[20] Ibid., Concurring Opinion of Judge Pinto de Albuquerque, Joined by Judge Vučinić, § 4.

[21] *Ireland v. the United Kingdom*, 18 January 1978, § 239, Series A no. 25.

[22] *Cyprus v. Turkey*, no. 25781/94, § 77, Commission report of 4 June 1999.

[23] *Austria v. Italy*, no. 788/60, p. 138, Commission decision of 11 January 1961, (1961) 4 YB 116.

[24] *Karner v. Austria*, no. 40016/98, § 24, ECHR 2003-IX.

Citing the purpose of article 33 (formerly article 24), the Commission dismissed an objection by Turkey that the Government of Cyprus was not legitimate under the country's Constitution. It said that 'the protection of the rights and freedoms of the people of Cyprus under the Convention should not be impaired by any constitutional defect of its Government'.[25] In another case, the Commission said that 'to accept that a Government may avoid "collective enforcement" of the Convention under Article 24, by asserting that they do not recognise the Government of the applicant State, would defeat the purpose of the Convention'.[26]

The scope of an inter-State application is larger than that of an individual application. The Court 'has the power to examine the conformity with the Convention of legislative measures and administrative practices as such', and even if there is no identifiable individual victim.[27] Nevertheless, the Court has said, 'the institutions established by the Convention may find a breach of this kind only if the law challenged pursuant to [article 33] is couched in terms sufficiently clear and precise to make the breach immediately apparent; otherwise, the decision of the Convention institutions must be arrived at by reference to the manner in which the respondent State interprets and applies *in concreto* the impugned text or texts'.[28]

Although there is an admissibility phase to the determination of inter-State complaints, it is more limited in scope than is the case for individual applications. The distinction can be seen in article 35 of the Convention; paragraphs 1 and 4 apply to all applications, whereas paragraphs 2 and 3 only apply to individual applications. In other words, several of the admissibility criteria that are relevant to individual applications are not examined in the case of inter-State complaints.[29] Specifically, the Court has no authority to declare an inter-State application to be 'manifestly ill-founded'.[30] However, the text of article 35 'cannot prevent the Court from establishing already at this preliminary stage, under general principles governing the exercise of jurisdiction by international tribunals, whether it has any competence at all to deal with the matter laid before it'.[31]

It seems that there is a very limited authority to assess whether there exists *prima facie* evidence capable of sustaining the application.[32] The Court would then be required to ascertain whether the allegations in the application are 'wholly unsubstantiated' (*pas du tout étayées*) or are 'lacking the requirements of a genuine allegation in the sense of Article 33

---

[25] *Cyprus v. Turkey*, no. 25781/94, § 71, Commission report of 4 June 1999. Also *Cyprus v. Turkey*, nos 6780/74 and 6950/75, Commission decision of 26 May 1975, (1975) 18 YB 84, DR 2, p. 125.

[26] *Cyprus v. Turkey*, no. 8007/77, Commission decision of 10 July 1978, (1978) 21 YB 101, DR 13, p. 85.

[27] *Cyprus v. Turkey*, no. 25781/94, § 313, Commission report of 4 June 1999.

[28] *Ireland v. the United Kingdom*, 18 January 1978, § 240, Series A no. 25.

[29] *Georgia v. Russia (I)* (dec.), no. 13255/07, § 44, 30 June 2009. Also *France, Norway, Denmark, Sweden, and the Netherlands v. Turkey*, nos 9940–9944/82, Commission decision of 6 December 1983, (1983) 26 YB COMM.EUR.JURIS. 1, DR 35, p. 143; *Cyprus v. Turkey*, no. 25781/94, Commission decision of 28 June 1996, (1996) 39 YB 130, DR 86, p. 104; *Denmark v. Turkey* (dec.), no. 34382/97, 8 June 1999; *Denmark, Norway, Sweden, and the Netherlands v. Greece*, nos 3321/67, 3322/67, 3323/67, and 3344/67, Commission decision of 24 January 1968, (1968) 11 YB 690, Collection 25, p. 92; *Denmark, Norway, Sweden, and the Netherlands v. Greece*, nos 3321/67, 3322/67, 3323/67, and 3344/67, § 113, Commission report of 5 November 1969, (1969) 12 YB 'The Greek case' 1.

[30] *Ireland v. the United Kingdom*, nos 5310/71 and 5451/72, Commission decision of 1 October 1972, (1972) 15 YB 80; *Georgia v. Russia (II)* (dec.), no. 38263/08, § 64, 13 December 2011.

[31] *Georgia v. Russia (II)* (dec.), no. 38263/08, § 64, 13 December 2011.

[32] *France, Norway, Denmark, Sweden, and the Netherlands v. Turkey*, nos 9940–9944/82, Commission decision of 6 December 1983, (1983) 26 YB COMM.EUR.JURIS. 1, DR 35, p. 143.

of the Convention' (*feraient défaut les éléments constitutifs d'une véritable allégation au sens de l'article 33 de la Convention*).[33] An early decision of the European Commission held that an allegation of a breach of the Convention is sufficient for the purposes of determining admissibility.[34]

The requirement of exhaustion of domestic remedies applies, in principle, to inter-State applications as well as to individual cases. In the *Ireland v. The United Kingdom* case, the European Commission granted an exception to admissibility raised by the respondent State with respect to an allegation of a violation of article 2 of the Convention for which domestic remedies had not been exhausted.[35] However, the rule of exhaustion does not always operate in the same way in inter-State proceedings as it does with individual petitions. It does not apply to the extent that 'the applicant State complains of a practice as such, with the aim of preventing its continuation or recurrence, but does not ask the Court to give a decision on each of the cases put forward as proof or illustrations of that practice'.[36] On the other hand, 'when the applicant State does no more than denounce a violation or violations allegedly suffered by individuals whose place is taken by the State', the exhaustion requirement applies in exactly the same way as it does with respect to an individual petition.[37]

For the purposes of the exception to the general rule, an administrative practice is said to have two distinct elements: a repetition of acts and official tolerance.[38] A repetition of acts is 'an accumulation of identical or analogous breaches which are sufficiently numerous and inter-connected not to amount to merely isolated incidents or exceptions but to a pattern or system'.[39] An official tolerance means that:

illegal acts are tolerated in that the superiors of those immediately responsible, though cognisant of such acts, take no action to punish them or to prevent their repetition; or that a higher authority, in face of numerous allegations, manifests indifference by refusing any adequate investigation of their truth or falsity, or that in judicial proceedings a fair hearing of such complaints is denied.[40]

---

[33] *Georgia v. Russia (I)* (dec.), no. 13255/07, § 43, 30 June 2009; *Georgia v. Russia (II)* (dec.), no. 38263/08, § 88, 13 December 2011.

[34] *France, Norway, Denmark, Sweden, and the Netherlands v. Turkey*, nos 9940–9944/82, Commission decision of 6 December 1983, (1983) 26 YB COMM.EUR.JURIS. 1, DR 35, p. 143.

[35] *Ireland v. the United Kingdom*, nos 5310/71 and 5451/72, Commission decision of 1 October 1972, (1972) 15 YB 80; *Ireland v. the United Kingdom*, 18 January 1978, § 159, Series A no. 25.

[36] *Georgia v. Russia (I)* (dec.), no. 13255/07, § 40, 30 June 2009; *Ireland v. the United Kingdom*, 18 January 1978, § 159, Series A no. 25; *Cyprus v. Turkey*, no. 25781/94, Commission decision of 28 June 1996, (1996) 39 YB 130, DR 86, p. 104; *Denmark v. Turkey* (dec.), no. 34382/97, 8 June 1999; *Greece v. the United Kingdom*, no. 176/56, Commission decision of 2 June 1956, (1958-59) 2 YB 182; *Denmark, Norway, Sweden, and the Netherlands v. Greece*, nos 3321/67, 3322/67, 3323/67, and 3344/67, Commission decision of 24 January 1968, (1968) 11 YB 690, at pp. 726, 730, 768–70, Collection 25, p. 92; *Denmark, Norway, and Sweden v. Greece*, no. 4448/70, Commission decision of 16 July 1970, (1970) 13 YB 122, Collection 34, p. 70, at p. 73.

[37] *Denmark v. Turkey* (dec.), no. 34382/97, 8 June 1999.

[38] *Georgia v. Russia (I)* (dec.), no. 13255/07, § 40, 30 June 2009; *France, Norway, Denmark, Sweden, and the Netherlands v. Turkey*, nos 9940–9944/82, Commission decision of 6 December 1983, (1983) 26 YB COMM. EUR.JURIS. 1, DR 35, p. 143.

[39] *Georgia v. Russia (I)* [GC], no. 13255/07, § 123, 4 July 2014; *Ireland v. the United Kingdom*, 18 January 1978, § 122, Series A no. 25; *Cyprus v. Turkey* [GC], no. 25781/94, § 99, ECHR 2001-IV.

[40] Georgia v. Russia (I) [GC], no. 13255/07, § 123, 4 July 2014; Ireland v. the United Kingdom, 18 January 1978, § 124, 4 July 2014.

Furthermore, 'any action taken by the higher authority must be on a scale which is sufficient to put an end to the repetition of acts or to interrupt the pattern or system'.[41] According to the Court,

it is inconceivable that the higher authorities of a State should be, or at least should be entitled to be, unaware of the existence of such a practice. Furthermore, under the Convention those authorities are strictly liable for the conduct of their subordinates; they are under a duty to impose their will on subordinates and cannot shelter behind their inability to ensure that it is respected.[42]

In order to exclude application of the rule concerning exhaustion of domestic remedies, the applicant State must do more than simply allege an administrative practice. It must show the existence of such a practice by means of 'substantial evidence'.[43] This does not, however, mean 'full proof'. That is because:

whether the existence of an administrative practice is established or not can only be determined after an examination of the merits. At the stage of admissibility prima facie evidence, while required, must also be considered as sufficient . . . There is prima facie evidence of an alleged administrative practice where the allegations concerning individual cases are sufficiently substantiated, considered as a whole and in the light of the submissions of both the applicant and the respondent Party. It is in this sense that the term 'substantial evidence' is to be understood.[44]

In *Georgia v. Russia*, the respondent State complained that the application did not fulfil the requirements of Rule 46 of the Rules of Court, governing the contents of an inter-State application, because it was 'abstract (largely based on anonymous witness statements), [and] essentially private'.[45] The Court concluded that 'the content and scope of the application and the written and oral submission by the applicant Government are sufficiently clear to allow a judicial examination under the Convention'.[46] Specific regulations on the contents of an inter-State application are set out in the Rules of Court.[47] When there is an application under article 33, the Chamber assigned to the case designates one or more of its judges as Judge Rapporteur charged with preparing a report on admissibility once the written observations of the concerned States have been received.[48]

It is possible to obtain a request for interim measures in an inter-State case. In March and June 2014, the Court issued interim measures with respect to applications filed by Ukraine against Russia.[49] The second order, which concerned the abduction of children, was lifted once the children were returned to safety.

---

[41] Ibid.; *France, Norway, Denmark, Sweden, and the Netherlands v. Turkey*, nos. 9940–9944/82, Commission decision of 6 December 1983, (1983) 26 YB COMM.EUR.JURIS. 1, DR 35, p. 143.

[42] *Georgia v. Russia (I)* [GC], no. 13255/07, § 123, 4 July 2014; *Ireland v. the United Kingdom*, 18 January 1978, § 159, Series A no. 25.

[43] *Denmark, Norway, Sweden, and the Netherlands v. Greece*, nos 3321/67, 3322/67, 3323/67, and 3344/67, Commission decision of 24 January 1968, (1968) 11 YB 690, at p. 770, Collection 25, p. 92; *Ireland v. the United Kingdom*, nos 5310/71 and 5451/72, Commission decision of 1 October 1972, (1972) 15 YB 80.

[44] *France, Norway, Denmark, Sweden, and the Netherlands v. Turkey*, nos 9940–9944/82, Commission decision of 6 December 1983, (1983) 26 YB COMM.EUR.JURIS. 1, DR 35, p. 143, cited in *Georgia v. Russia (I)* (dec.), no. 13255/07, § 41, 30 June 2009.

[45] *Georgia v. Russia (I)* (dec.), no. 13255/07, §§ 15, 32, 30 June 2009.

[46] Ibid. § 34.

[47] Rules of Court, Rule 46.

[48] Ibid., Rule 48.

[49] *Ukraine v. Russia (I)* (interim measures), no. 20958/14, not yet reported; *Ukraine v. Russia (II)* (interim measures), no. 43800/14, not yet reported.

Further reading

Emmanuel Decaux, 'L'avenir du règlement des différends interétatiques au sein du Conseil de l'Europe', in Mahoney et al., *Mélanges Ryssdal*, pp. 387–96.

Frowein/Peukert, *MenschenRechtsKonvention*, pp. 458–66.

Menno Kamminga, *Inter-State Accountability for Violations of Human Rights*, Philadelphia: University of Pennsylvania Press, 1992.

Henri Labayle, 'Article 24', in Pettiti et al., *La Convention européenne*, pp. 571–8.

Aisling O'Sullivan and William Schabas, 'Of Politics and Poor Weather: How Ireland Decided to Sue the United Kingdom Under the European Convention on Human Rights', (2007) 2 *Irish Yearbook of International Law* 3.

Article 34. Individual applications/Requêtes individuelles

The Court may receive applications from any person, non-governmental organisation or group of individuals claiming to be the victim of a violation by one of the High Contracting Parties of the rights set forth in the Convention or the Protocols thereto. The High Contracting Parties undertake not to hinder in any way the effective exercise of this right.	La Cour peut être saisie d'une requête par toute personne physique, toute organisation non gouvernementale ou tout groupe de particuliers qui se prétend victime d'une violation par l'une des Hautes Parties contractantes des droits reconnus dans la Convention ou ses Protocoles. Les Hautes Parties contractantes s'engagent à n'entraver par aucune mesure l'exercice efficace de ce droit.

Introductory comments

Traditionally, individuals were not viewed as subjects of international law. International law governed the rights and obligations of States. The rights of the individual might be addressed in terms of international law but only to the extent that the State was acting to protect its own national from a violation perpetrated by a third State under what is usually known as 'diplomatic protection'.[1] For example, in one of the earliest cases at the Permanent Court of International Justice, Greece sued the United Kingdom because of the alleged refusal by the government of Palestine, then a League of Nations mandate of the United Kingdom, to recognize property rights of a Greek subject under agreements he had reached with the Ottoman authorities.[2] Today, if such a dispute were to arise in Europe it would probably lead to litigation before the European Court of Human Rights based upon articles 6 and 13 of the Convention and article 1 of Protocol No. 1. To a limited extent, there was a more direct recourse by individuals to the Permanent Court of International Justice with respect to enforcement of the minorities treaties. Individuals would complain to the Council of the League of Nations alleging a violation of their rights. The Council might then request an advisory opinion of the Permanent Court.[3]

The possibility of individual application was originally intended as an optional part of the system of protection, but has 'over the years become of high importance and is now a key component of the machinery for protecting the rights and freedoms set forth in the Convention'.[4]

Drafting of the provision

The initial draft European Convention on Human Rights prepared by the International Juridical Section of the European Movement was premised on the existence of two

---

[1] For a recent example, see *Ahmadou Sadio Diallo (Republic of Guinea* v. *Democratic Republic of the Congo)*, Merits, Judgment, I.C.J. Reports 2010, p. 639.

[2] *The Mavromattis Palestine Concessions*, PCIJ Series A, No. 2.

[3] *Minority Schools in Albania*, PCIJ, Series A/B No. 64; *Rights of Minorities in Upper Silesia (Minority Schools)*, PCIJ, Series A No. 15.

[4] *Mamatkulov and Abdurasulovic v. Turkey*, nos 46827/99 and 46951/99, § 122, 6 February 2003.

institutions, a Commission, and a Court. According to article 7, '[a]ny State a party to this Convention and any natural or corporate person in the territory of any such State, shall have the right to petition the Council of Europe in respect of any infringement of Part I of this Convention'.[5] Petitions were initially to be dealt with by the European Human Rights Commission 'and in proper cases by a European Court of Human Rights'. Access to the Court was available to the Commission, as well as to '[a]ny affected party, with the authorisation of the Commission which shall be entitled to withhold such authorisation without stating any reason'.[6] The Draft Statute empowered the human rights court to indicate provisional measures if it considered that circumstances so required.[7]

The draft Convention adopted by the Consultative Assembly in September 1949 provided that 'any person, or corporate body, which claims to have been the victim of a violation of the Convention by one of the signatory States, may petition the [European] Commission [of Human Rights] in a request presented through legal channels'.[8] Access to the Court was available to the Commission and to any State Party, but there was no such right for individuals.[9]

The Committee of Ministers referred the Consultative Assembly draft to a Committee of Experts. It met in February and March 1950. Provisions that were similar to those of the Assembly were adopted by a drafting sub-committee[10] and included in the Report of the Committee. In addition to individuals and non-governmental organizations, the Committee added 'or any group of individuals'.[11] The Report noted that '[t]he Committee insisted that it was never proper for an individual to refer to the Court. The interests of individuals would always be defended either by the Commission ... or by a State.'[12]

The Committee of Ministers decided to convene a Conference of Senior Officials, primarily in order to take decisions about the political issues that had been left unresolved by the Committee of Experts. Writing to the Foreign Ministers of Member States on 11 May 1950, the Secretary General noted that among the issues the Conference of Senior Officials should consider was the access of individuals to the Commission, something on which it pointed out the United Kingdom had reserved its position.[13] The issue of the

---

[5] Convention for the Collective Protection of Individual Rights and Democratic Liberties by the States, Members of the Council of Europe, and for the establishment of a European Court of Human Rights to ensure observance of the Convention, Doc. INF/5/E/R, I *TP* 296–303, at p. 298, art. 7(a).

[6] Ibid., p. 300, art. 12(c).

[7] Draft Statute of the European Court of Human Rights, INF/5/E/R, I *TP* 302–21, at p. 314.

[8] Recommendation No. 38 to the Committee of Ministers adopted 8 September 1949 on the conclusion of the debates, Doc. AS (1) 108, II *TP* 274–83, at p. 278, art. 11.

[9] Ibid., p. 280, arts 18, 19.

[10] First part of the proposals of the Drafting Sub-Committee concerning Sections II and III put forward by MM. Perassi, Salen and Chaumont, Doc. A 806, III *TP* 212–17, at p. 214, arts. 11, 12.

[11] Preliminary Draft Convention for the Maintenance and Further Realisation of Human Rights and Fundamental Freedoms, 15 February 1950, Doc. A 833, III *TP* 236–46, arts 14, 15, 34; Appendix to the Report of the Committee of Experts on Human Rights: Draft Convention of Protection of Human Rights and Fundamental Freedoms, 16 March 1950, Doc. C/WP 1 (50) 15 appendix, CM/WP 1 (50) 14 revised, A 925, IV *TP* 50–79, at pp. 68, 74, arts 16(2), 17(21), 37(41). See also Preliminary Draft of the Report to the Committee of Ministers, 24 February 1950, Doc. CM/WP 1 (50), A 847, III *TP* 246–79, at p. 270.

[12] Report to the Committee of Ministers submitted by the Committee of Experts Instructed to Draw Up a Draft Convention of Collective Guarantee of Human Rights and Fundamental Freedoms, Doc. CM/WP 1 (5) 15, A 924, IV *TP* 2–55, at p. 44. See also Preliminary Draft of the Report to the Committee of Ministers, 24 February 1950, Doc. CM/WP 1 (50), A 847, III *TP* 246–79, at p. 276.

[13] Letter of 11 May 1950 from the Secretary General to the Foreign Ministers of Member States, Ref. D 281/6/50, IV *TP* 92–5.

'right of petition' of individuals was discussed in depth by the Conference of Senior Officials.[14] Only Greece, the Netherlands, and the United Kingdom maintained any reservations on the point, 'fearing that the right of petition might easily lead to abuse, particularly in the interests of subversive propaganda'.[15] The Conference of Senior Officials added a sentence to the provision governing access to the Commission: 'The High Contracting Parties undertake not to hinder in any way the effective exercise of this right.'[16] It also introduced a new article stating explicitly that only States Parties and the Commission could bring a case before the Court.[17]

The Consultative Assembly's Committee on Legal and Administrative Questions convened in June to consider the report of the Conference of Senior Officials. It affirmed its attachment to granting individuals the right to seek a remedy. It indicated its dislike of the term 'right of petition', saying it was incorrect and noting that it was 'in reality, the right of individuals to seek remedy directly, in certain cases'.[18] The Committee renewed its attachment to the draft proposed the previous year by the Assembly, underscoring the importance of the idea that the petition or application be a 'request presented through legal channels'.[19]

The 'right of petition' remained a controversial issue when the Committee of Ministers met in August 1950 with a view to adopting a final version of the text. Belgium proposed that the relevant provision simply be deleted from the Convention.[20] Greece was of a similar view, explaining that '[t]he possession of this right by ill-intentioned persons could rapidly degenerate into a dangerous arm that could be used against the freedoms which we seek to guarantee and against our established democratic systems'.[21] The Netherlands reiterated its view that 'the right of petition might easily lead to abuse, particularly in the interest of subversive propaganda'.[22] The United Kingdom announced that it had instructions to reconsider the provision on individual petition,[23] noting the 'grave danger, in the present state of the world, in the inclusion of such an Article'.[24] Instead of proposing deletion of the article, the United Kingdom suggested an optional clause

[14] Minutes of the morning sitting [of 10 June 1950] (unreferenced document), IV *TP* 132–41, at pp. 132–7.

[15] Text of the Report submitted by the Conference [of Senior Officials] to the Committee of Ministers, Doc. CM/WP 4 (50) 19, CM/WP 4 (50) 16 rev., A 1431, IV *TP* 242–73, at p. 252; Draft Report to the Committee of Ministers, Doc. CM/WP 4 (50) 16, A 1426, IV *TP* 204–17, at p. 214; Minutes of the morning sitting [of 10 June 1950] (unreferenced document), IV *TP* 132–41, at pp. 132–7, at p. 136; Minutes of the afternoon setting [of 12 June 1950], unreferenced document, IV *TP* 170–81, at p. 180.

[16] Draft Convention annexed to the Report, Doc. CM/WP 4 (50) 19 annex, CM/WP 4 (50) rev., A 1452, IV *TP* 274–95, at p. 284, art. 23.

[17] Ibid., p. 290, art. 44; Text of the Report submitted by the Conference to the Committee of Ministers, Doc. CM/WP 4 (50) 19, CM/WP 4 (50) 16 rev., A 1431, IV *TP* 242–73, at p. 266.

[18] Letter of 24 June 1950 from Sir David Maxwell Fyfe, Chairman of the Committee on Legal and Administrative Questions, to the Chairman of the Committee of Ministers, Doc. CM (50) 29, V *TP* 32–41, at p. 36; Draft of a letter to the Chairman of the Committee of Ministers, Doc. AS/JA (2) 2, A 1579, V *TP* 10–15, at p. 12.

[19] Minutes of the meeting [of 23 June 1950 of the Committee on Legal and Administrative Questions of the Consultative Assembly], Doc. AS/JA (2) PV I, A 1840, V *TP* 2–11, at p. 8.

[20] Revised text, Doc. CM 1 (50) 3 rev., A 1872, V *TP* 62–3.

[21] Amendments proposed by the Greek Delegation, Doc. CM 1 (50) 4, A 1865, V *TP* 62–5.

[22] Amendments proposed by the Netherlands Delegation, Doc. CM 1 (50) 5, A 1866, V *TP* 64–5.

[23] Report of the meeting [of 3 August 1950 of the Committee of Ministers], V *TP* 52–7, at p. 54.

[24] Amendments proposed by the United Kingdom Delegation, Doc. CM 1 (50) 6, A 1867, V *TP* 66–70, at p. 68.

similar to what had already been agreed to as a solution for including the European Court of Human Rights within the framework of the Convention.[25]

In an attempt at rallying support for a right of petition that was not subject to an optional clause, Robert Schuman of France suggested adding the words 'being nationals of the High Contracting Parties'. He explained that the amendment would 'limit the right of petition to nationals of those states which actually signed the Convention'.[26] Seán MacBride, Ireland's Foreign Minister, said that '[a] Convention on Human Rights which did not grant any right of redress to individuals was not worth the paper it was written on. It was obvious that no Government would come before the Commission to accuse itself.' MacBride said he would accept Schuman's proposal and would appeal to the minority among his colleagues to do the same.[27] The proposal obtained nine votes in favour to four against.[28] The Ministers then considered the compromise suggested by the United Kingdom of a right of individual petition to the Commission but with an optional clause. Twelve ministers were in favour, with Ireland opposed. MacBride said he was prepared for his vote to be recorded as an abstention.[29]

There was much dissatisfaction with this result when the Consultative Assembly convened later in August 1950 to consider the draft of the Committee of Ministers. David Maxwell Fyfe noted 'considerable and natural pessimism as to whether any State will make such a declaration and lay up trouble for itself'. He said it was felt the optional clause was 'a retrogressive step in that the general modern tendency of international law has been to emphasise the rights and duties of an individual as a subject of international law'.[30] Hermod Lannung described the optional clause as a 'most serious retrograde step'.[31] Various amendments were proposed on the subject, notably the idea of an 'opt-out' clause.[32] Eventually, the Consultative Assembly adopted a revised provision that recognized a right of petition but made it subject to a declaration by which States could withdraw jurisdiction for certain provisions of the Convention. The rights set out in articles 2, 3, 4, and 7 could never be excluded, however.[33]

The Committee of Ministers ignored the recommendation of the Consultative Assembly. With a few minor modifications, the text adopted by the Committee of Ministers became article 25 of the Convention. It allowed a person, a non-governmental organization, or group of individuals claiming to be a victim of a violation to petition the European Commission. This was conditional upon a State Party making a declaration recognizing the right of petition. The right would become operational only when six States Parties had made the declaration.

---

[25] Ibid.

[26] Report of the meeting [of 7 August 1950 of the Committee of Ministers], V *TP* 110–21, at p. 112.

[27] Ibid.

[28] Ibid., p. 114.

[29] Ibid. Also Minutes of the meeting [of 7 August 1950 of the Committee of Ministers], V *TP* 108–11, at p. 110.

[30] Official report of the sixth sitting [of 14 August 1950 of the Consultative Assembly], VI *TP* 216–70, at p. 226.

[31] Ibid., p. 236.

[32] Draft Motion submitted by M. Teitgen, Revised Draft, Doc. AS/JA (2) 6 rev., A 2238, VI *TP* 10–15, at p. 12; Proposed by Mr Pernot, Doc. AS/JA (2) 8, Doc. A 2252, VI *TP* 20–1; Revised Draft [Proposed by M. Lannung], Doc. AS/JA (2) 11 rev., A 2367, VI *TP* 20–3; Doc. A 2290, VI *TP* 34–5; Doc. A 2299, VI *TP* 34–7.

[33] Text published in the Collected Documents of the Consultative Assembly, Doc. AS (2) 104, VI *TP* 198–229, at p. 214.

Some States made the declaration at the time of ratification of the Convention, in the early 1950s, while others waited decades. In the 1950 text, there was no corresponding right of access to the European Court of Human Rights. In the first place, another declaration recognizing the jurisdiction of the Court was required, in accordance with article 46. In the second place, cases could only be taken to the Court by the Commission itself or by a State Party and not by the individual applicant. If neither opted to bring the case to the Court, the enforcement of the Commission's findings was left to the Committee of Ministers.

By the 1990s, declarations accepting the individual petition mechanism before the Commission in accordance with article 25 had become a *de facto* condition for membership in the Council of Europe. Protocol No. 9 to the Convention revised the Convention so as to allow a right of individual application to the Court after the matter had been adjudicated by the European Commission of Human Rights.[34] The stage was set for the biggest reform of all. Protocol No. 11 abolished the Commission and with it the individual petition to that body. When Protocol No. 11 entered into force in 1998, individuals, non-governmental organizations, and groups of individuals were given direct recourse to the European Court of Human Rights in accordance with the new article 34.

Compared with article 25 of the 1950 text of the Convention, article 34 of the current text applies without the need for any additional or supplementary declaration by a State Party. Aside from this substantive change in the individual petition mechanism, there are some minor technical and linguistic adjustments. The individual, non-governmental organization, or group presents an 'application' rather than a 'petition', as was the case in the former system. The application is submitted to the Court and not the Secretary General of the Council of Europe. Finally, the provision refers to the 'Protocols' as well as the Convention itself, it being understood that States are bound only by the Protocols that they have ratified.[35]

Analysis and interpretation

Article 34 is one of the 'the keystones in the machinery for the enforcement of the rights and freedoms set forth in the Convention'.[36] It provides 'one of the fundamental guarantees of the effectiveness of the Convention system of human rights protection'.[37] According to the Grand Chamber, '[i]n interpreting such a key provision, the Court must have regard to the special character of the Convention as a treaty for the collective enforcement of human rights and fundamental freedoms'.[38] The Court has explained that unlike 'international treaties of the classic kind', the Convention comprises more than mere reciprocal engagements between Contracting States. It creates, over and above a network of mutual, bilateral undertakings, objective obligations that, in the words of the Preamble, benefit from a 'collective enforcement'.[39]

---

[34] Protocol No. 9 to the Convention for the Protection of Human Rights and Fundamental Freedoms, ETS 140.

[35] Explanatory Report on Protocol No. 11, para. 75.

[36] *Klass and Others v. Germany*, 6 September 1978, § 34, Series A no. 28.

[37] *Mamatkulov and Askarov v. Turkey* [GC], nos 46827/99 and 46951/99, § 100, ECHR 2005-I.

[38] Ibid.; *Paladi v. Moldova* [GC], no. 39806/05, § 84, 10 March 2009.

[39] *Mamatkulov and Askarov v. Turkey* [GC], nos 46827/99 and 46951/99, § 100, ECHR 2005-I; *Ireland v. The United Kingdom*, 18 January 1978, § 239, Series A no. 25. See also, with respect to the 1950 text of the Convention, *Loizidou v. Turkey* (Preliminary objections), 23 March 1995, § 70, Series A no. 310.

Individual, organization, or group

In order to avail of article 34 of the Convention, two conditions must be met: the applicant must be a 'person, non-governmental organisation or group of individuals' and must 'make out a case that he or she is the victim of a violation of the Convention'.[40] Recourse to the Court is not restricted in any way by such factors as nationality, residency, civil status, or legal capacity. For example, minors and persons deprived of legal capacity, who may be subject to special rules before the national courts in terms of their capacity to take legal proceedings, are in no way prevented from making an application to the European Court of Human Rights. The Court has not ruled out allowing a person who lacks legal capacity under domestic law to file an application pursuant to article 34. Noting that article 34 applies to 'any person', the Court has said that '[t]here is no obligation in general, or for persons lacking legal capacity in particular, to be represented at the initial stage of the proceedings'.[41] An individual who alleges arbitrary detention but who later absconds and leaves the country is still entitled to pursue an application.[42]

The notion of 'non-governmental organisations' is broad and flexible and is not subject to any formalities of registration. The Court has held that the removal of legal registration and of corporate status to a non-governmental organization has no consequence in terms of its ability to invoke article 34.[43]

The Convention does not expressly refer to corporate bodies; these are subsumed under the rubric of 'non-governmental organisations'. On this basis, a corporation or similar entity has *locus standi* before the Court in accordance with article 34.[44] The Court is not particularly strict about the formalities of representation either, although the individual acting on behalf of a corporation will have to show some form of legal authorization.[45] Disregarding the legal personality of a company is only allowed exceptionally, for example when it cannot act through the organs set up by its own instruments of incorporation or through a bankruptcy trustee.[46] The Court will only lift the corporate veil in exceptional circumstances.[47] Luxembourg contested the *locus standi* of a shell company without assets or activities, insisting it did not fulfil the requirements of article 34. The Court noted that the company's existence had not been contested in the national proceedings and that it had been subject to a search in the lawyer's office where it had its head office.[48]

---

[40] *Vallianatos and Others v. Greece* [GC], no. 29381/09, § 47, ECHR 2013.

[41] *Zehentner v. Austria*, no. 20082/02, § 39, 16 July 2009.

[42] *Van der Tang v. Spain*, 13 July 1995, § 53, Series A no. 321.

[43] *Hyde Park and Others v. Moldova (no. 4)*, no. 18491/07, § 33, 7 April 2009; *Hyde Park and Others v. Moldova (nos 5 and 6)*, nos 6991/08 and 15084/08, § 31, 14 September 2010; *Christians against Racism and Fascism v. the United Kingdom*, no. 8440/78, Commission decision of 16 July 1980, (1981) 24 YB 178, DR 21, p. 138.

[44] *Agrotexim and Others v. Greece*, 24 October 1995, § 66, Series A no. 330-A; *Société Faugyr Finance S.A. v. Luxembourg* (dec.), no. 38788/97, 23 March 2000; *Unédic v. France*, no. 20153/04, §§ 48–59, 18 December 2008; *Radio France and Others v. France* (dec.), no. 53984/00, § 26, 23 September 2003.

[45] *Nosov v. Russia* (dec.), no. 30877/02, 20 October 2005.

[46] *Capital Bank AD v. Bulgaria* (dec.), no. 49429/99, 9 September 2004; *Camberrow MM5 AD v. Bulgaria* (dec.), no. 50357/99, 1 April 2004; *G.J. v. Luxembourg*, no. 21156/93, § 23, 26 October 2000; *Meltex Ltd and Movsesyan v. Armenia*, no. 32283/04, § 66, 17 June 2008; *CDI Holding Aktiengesellschaft and Others v. Slovakia* (dec.), no. 37398/97, 18 October 2001; *Amat-G Ltd and Mebaghishvili v. Georgia*, no. 2507/03, § 33, ECHR 2005-VIII).

[47] *Agrotexim and Others v. Greece*, 24 October 1995, § 66, Series A no. 330-A, citing *Barcelona Traction, Light and Power Company, Limited*, Judgment, I.C.J. Reports 1970, p. 3, at pp. 39 and 41, paras 56–58 and 66; *Matrot S.A. and Others v. France* (dec.), no. 43798/98, 3 February 2000.

[48] *Société Faugyr Finance S.A. v. Luxembourg* (dec.), no. 38788/97, 23 March 2000.

Governmental bodies or public corporations under the strict control of a State are not entitled to bring an application under article 34 of the Convention.[49] The Court has explained that 'the idea behind this principle is to prevent a Contracting Party acting as both an applicant and a respondent party before the Court'.[50] Commercial corporations without public service mandates fall within the scope of non-governmental organizations as the term is meant by article 34, even if they are wholly owned by the State.[51] In addition to the central organs of the State, governmental organizations, as opposed to non-governmental organizations, include decentralized authorities that exercise public functions, regardless of their degree of autonomy.[52] Among such bodies are various municipal and territorial institutions,[53] as well as professional corporations that exercise 'des fonctions officielles... attribuées par la Constitution et par la loi'[54] and national railway companies under State control in a monopolistic situation.[55]

Greece contested the *locus standi* of the Holy Monasteries. These are ancient institutions belonging generally within the sphere of the Orthodox Church, which itself has long-standing and profound connections, both legal and financial, with the government of the country. But the Court noted that the Holy Monasteries are 'ascetic religious institutions' that 'do not exercise governmental powers', holding them to be non-governmental organizations.[56] France challenged the non-governmental status of Radio France, the national television company, distinguishing the case from that of the Holy Monasteries. It noted that the existence of the company was governed by public law, that its mission was to broadcast 'dans l'intérêt général, des missions de service public', and that it was financed by public funds.[57] But the Court noted the independence of the institution, something expressly guaranteed in the enabling legislation as evidenced by the fact that only four of its twelve directors were government officials, and the lack of a monopoly over television broadcasting.[58]

Victim status

A person, non-governmental organization, or group of individuals that files an application under article 34 must claim to be 'a victim' of a violation of the rights set forth in the Convention or its Protocols. To be a victim, the applicant must be directly affected by the impugned measure.[59] An individual applicant cannot undertake an

---

[49] *Islamic Republic of Iran Shipping Lines v. Turkey*, no. 40998/98, § 81, ECHR 2007-V.

[50] Ibid.

[51] *Österreichischer Rundfunk v. Austria*, no. 35841/02, § 53, 7 December 2006; *Islamic Republic of Iran Shipping Lines v. Turkey*, no. 40998/98, §§ 80–81, ECHR 2007-V.

[52] *Radio France and Others v. France* (dec.), no. 53984/00, § 26, 23 September 2009.

[53] *Commune de Rothenthurm v. Switzerland*, no. 13252/87, Commission decision of 14 December 1988, DR 59, p. 251; *Section de commune d'Antilly v. France* (dec.), no. 42129/98, 23 November 1999; *The Province of Bari, Sorrentino, and Messeni Nemagna v. Italy* (dec.), no. 41877/98, 22 March 2001; *Ayuntamiento de Mula v. Spain* (dec.), no. 55346/00, 1 February 2001; *Danderyds Kommun v. Sweden* (dec.) no. 52559199, 7 June 2001; *Döşemealtı Belediyesi v. Turkey* (dec.), no. 50108/06, 23 March 2010.

[54] *Consejo General de Colejos Ociciales de Economista de España v. Spain*, nos 26114/95 and 26455/95, Commission decision of 28 June 1995, DR 82-B, p. 150.

[55] *RENFE v. Spain*, no. 35216/97, Commission decision of 8 September 1997, DR 90-B, p. 179.

[56] *The Holy Monasteries v. Greece*, 9 December 1994, § 49, Series A no. 301-A.

[57] *Radio France and Others v. France* (dec.), no. 53984/00, § 24, 23 September 2009.

[58] Ibid., § 26.

[59] *Vallianatos and Others v. Greece* [GC], no. 29381/09, § 47, ECHR 2013; *Micallef v. Malta* [GC], no. 17056/06, § 44, ECHR 2009; *Burden v. the United Kingdom* [GC], no. 13378/05, § 33, ECHR 2008;

actio popularis.[60] This is in distinction with the inter-State application authorized by article 33, whereby the State may act in order to enforce the European public order and not because it has any particular interest. The victim criterion 'is not to be applied in a rigid, mechanical and inflexible way'[61] or with excessive formalism.[62] The notion of 'victim' within the meaning of article 34 has an autonomous and independent meaning that does not depend upon concepts of national law such as the legal interest and the *locus standi* or standing.[63] In effect, 'the conditions governing individual applications are not necessarily the same as national criteria relating to *locus standi*. National rules in this respect may serve purposes different from those contemplated by Article 34 of the Convention and, whilst those purposes may sometimes be analogous, they need not always be so.'[64] According to the established case law of the Court, the existence of a violation of the Convention is sufficient for the applicant to be a victim without the need to demonstrate a prejudice.[65] Prejudice arises only in the context of article 41 concerning the determination of just satisfaction.

A dead person cannot file an application even through a legally authorized representative.[66] Exceptionally, the Court will allow the next-of-kin of persons who have died in certain circumstances to submit applications where issues under article 2 arise, but 'this is a particular situation governed by the nature of the violation alleged and considerations of the effective implementation of one of the most fundamental provisions in the Convention system'.[67] In authorizing next-of-kin applications, the Court has recognized spouses, children, and nephews, as well as unmarried partners.[68] Whether the applicant is the legal heir of the deceased person is without relevance.[69] In such cases, the application is

---

Gorraiz Lizarraga and Others v. Spain, no. 62543/00, § 35, ECHR 2004-III; *SARL du Parc d'Activités de Blotzheim v. France*, no. 72377/01, § 20, 11 July 2006.

[60] *Sejdić and Finci v. Bosnia and Herzegovina* [GC], nos 27996/06 and 34836/06, § 28, ECHR 2009; *La Ligue des Musulmans de Suisse v. Switzerland* (dec.), no. 66274/09, 28 June 2011; *Norris v. Ireland*, 26 October 1988, § 31, Series A no. 142; *Klass and Others v. Germany*, 6 September 1978, § 33, Series A no. 28; *The Georgian Labour Party v. Georgia* (dec.), no. 9103/04, 22 May 2007; *Burden v. the United Kingdom* [GC], no. 13378/05, § 33, ECHR 2008.

[61] *Micallef v. Malta* [GC], no. 17056/06, § 45, ECHR 2009; *Karner v. Austria*, no. 40016/98, § 25, ECHR 2003-IX.

[62] *Gorraiz Lizarraga and Others v. Spain*, no. 62543/00, § 38, ECHR 2004-III; *Monnat v. Switzerland*, no. 73604/01, §§ 30–33, ECHR 2006-X; *Stukus and Others v. Poland*, no. 12534/03, § 35, 1 April 2008; *Zietal v. Poland*, no. 64972/01, §§ 54–59, 12 May 2009.

[63] *Sanles Sanles v. Spain* (dec.), no. 48335/99, ECHR 2000-XI; *Gorraiz Lizarraga and Others v. Spain*, no. 62543/00, § 35, ECHR 2004-III; *Tourkiki Enosi Xanthis and Others v. Greece*, no. 26698/05, § 38, 27 March 2008.

[64] *Scozzari and Giunta v. Italy* [GC], nos 39221/98 and 41963/98, § 139, ECHR 2000-VIII; *A.V.* [Velikova] *v. Bulgaria* (dec.), no. 41488/98, 18 May 1999; *Norris v. Ireland*, 26 October 1988, § 31, Series A no. 142.

[65] *Nada v. Switzerland* [GC], no. 10593/08, § 128, ECHR 2012.

[66] *Varnava and Others v. Turkey* [GC], nos 16064/90, 16065/90, 16066/90, 16068/90, 16069/90, 16070/90, 16071/90, 16072/90, and 16073/90, § 111, ECHR 2009; *Fairfield and Others v. the United Kingdom* (dec.), no. 24790/04, ECHR 2005-VI.

[67] *Fairfield and Others v. the United Kingdom* (dec.), no. 24790/04, ECHR 2005-VI.

[68] *A.V.* [Velikova] *v. Bulgaria* (dec.), no. 41488/98, 18 May 1999.

[69] *Yaşa v. Turkey*, 2 September 1998, § 66, *Reports of Judgments and Decisions* 1998-VI; *Andreas and Pareskevoula Andronicou and Yiolanda Constantinou v. Cyprus*, no. 25052/94, Commission decision of 5 July 1995, (1995) 38 YB 120, DR 82, p. 102; *Wolfgram v. Federal Republic of Germany*, no. 11257/84, Commission decision of 6 October 1986, DR 49, p. 213; *H. v. United Kingdom and Ireland*, no. 9833/82, Commission decision of 7 March 1985, DR 42, p. 53. But see *McCann, Farrell, and Savage v. the United Kingdom*, no. 18984/91, Commission decision of 3 September 1993 and *McCann and Others v. the United Kingdom*,

registered in the name of the living applicant,[70] although the Court will sometimes refer to the original victim as the applicant.[71] In a case involving the killing of a Kurdish newspaper vendor, the Court admitted an application filed by his nephew, who had himself also been the victim of attacks that formed part of the case. Turkey contested the standing of the nephew to submit an application on behalf of his deceased uncle, claiming there was no proof that they were in fact related but that even if they were they were not 'direct relatives'. The delegate of the European Commission had said before the Court that 'if a relative wished to complain about a question as serious as the murder of one of his close relations, that ought to suffice to show that he felt personally concerned by the incident', a view that the Court endorsed.[72] Because Turkey had not disputed whether the applicant was the victim's nephew before the Commission, the Court considered it was estopped from raising the issue.[73] In one very exceptional case involving a severely disabled victim of Roma ethnicity with no next-of-kin, the Court recognized the *locus standi* of a non-governmental organization to pursue a wrongful death application.[74]

In disappearance cases, the Court may apply a presumption of death where there is no reliable information about the person over a period of several years.[75] It may also recognize close relatives of the disappeared person as victims of breaches of article 3 because of the anguish and distress that they suffer,[76] although there is no 'general principle that a family member of a "disappeared person" is thereby a victim of treatment contrary to Article 3'.[77] For a family member to be a victim of a disappearance, there must be special factors that give the suffering of the applicant 'a dimension and character distinct from the emotional distress which may be regarded as inevitably caused to relatives of a victim of a serious human rights violation'.[78] These will include the closeness of the relationship ('a certain weight will attach to the parent–child bond'), the extent to which the family member witnessed the abduction, and the involvement of the family member in attempts to learn about the whereabouts of the disappeared person. The Court has said that 'the essence of such a violation does not so much lie in the fact of the "disappearance" of the family member but rather concerns the authorities' reactions and

---

27 September 1995, § 1, Series A no. 324, where the applicants are identified as representatives of the estate of the deceased person.

[70] *Varnava and Others v. Turkey* [GC], nos 16064/90, 16065/90, 16066/90, 16068/90, 16069/90, 16070/90, 16071/90, 16072/90, and 16073/90, § 111, ECHR 2009; *Fairfield v. the United Kingdom* (dec.), no. 24790/04, ECHR 2005-VI.

[71] *Asadbeyli and Others v. Azerbaijan,* nos 3653/05, 14729/05, 20908/05, 26242/05, 36083/05, and 16519/06, § 106, 11 December 2012.

[72] *Yaşa v. Turkey,* 2 September 1998, §§ 61–65, *Reports of Judgments and Decisions* 1998-VI.

[73] Ibid., § 65.

[74] *Centre for Legal Resources on behalf of Valentin Câmpeanu v. Romania* [GC], no. 47848/08, § 114, 17 July 2014.

[75] *Janowiec and Others v. Russia* [GC], nos 55508/07 and 29520/09, § 154, ECHR 2013; *Aslakhanova and Others v. Russia,* nos 2944/06, 8300/07, 50184/07, 332/08, and 42509/10, §§ 103–115, 18 December 2012; *Imakayeva v. Russia,* no. 7615/02, § 155, ECHR 2006-XIII (extracts).

[76] *Kurt v. Turkey,* 25 May 1998, §§ 130–134, *Reports of Judgments and Decisions* 1998-III; *Varnava and Others v. Turkey* [GC], nos 16064/90, 16065/90, 16066/90, 16068/90, 16069/90, 16070/90, 16071/90, 16072/90, and 16073/90, § 112, ECHR 2009; *Imakayeva v. Russia,* no. 7615/02, ECHR 2006-XIII (extracts).

[77] *Çakıcı v. Turkey* [GC], no. 23657/94, § 98, ECHR 1999-IV.

[78] *Sabanchiyeva and Others v. Russia,* no. 38450/05, § 113, ECHR 2013 (extracts); *Tahsin Acar v. Turkey* [GC], no. 26307/95, § 238, ECHR 2004-III.

attitudes to the situation when it is brought to their attention. It is especially in respect of the latter that a relative may claim directly to be a victim of the authorities' conduct.'[79]

As it does with right-to-life cases, in disappearance cases the Court will generally list the case as being in the name of the next of kin who is the actual applicant.[80] This has been criticized as being inconsistent with its view that enforced disappearance is a continuing violation of the Convention and thereby distinct from right-to-life cases where the death is admitted. Thus, 'for as long as the fate of the missing men is not known it would be contrary to the very nature of a particular continuing obligation if the Court were to accept that they could be presumed dead, in which case the relevant legal consequences would include their lack of standing before the Court'.[81] The significance of recognizing the disappeared person as a full victim has been related to the right to be recognized as a person before the law, something set out explicitly in article 6 of the Universal Declaration of Human Rights and that is arguably implicit in the European Convention.[82]

The death of an applicant during proceedings before the Court is treated differently to a case in which the applicant is dead before the filing of the application at the Court. In principle, the relatives of the applicant are generally entitled to pursue the matter.[83] The Court takes into account the statements of the applicant's heirs or close family members expressing the wish to continue the proceedings.[84] In article 6 cases, the Court has acknowledged the legitimate interest of the heirs in pursuing the application[85] 'or on the basis of the direct effect on the applicant's patrimonial rights'.[86] If there is no close relative or heir interested in continuing the case, the Court will usually strike it from the list.[87] However, article 37(1) of the Convention allows the Court to decline to strike out an application 'if respect for human rights . . . so requires'. It will continue with a case even in the absence of heirs or family members interested in the subject where there is some broader interest in a judgment being issued.

In deportation and expulsion cases, where an application may be based upon a real risk of a violation of articles 2 and 3 of the Convention, the fact that the actual threat is no longer present does not mean that the applicant is no longer a victim of a violation of the

[79] *Çakıcı v. Turkey* [GC], no. 23657/94, § 98, ECHR 1999-IV.
[80] *Varnava and Others v. Turkey* [GC], nos 16064/90, 16065/90, 16066/90, 16068/90, 16069/90, 16070/90, 16071/90, 16072/90, and 16073/90, § 111, ECHR 2009.
[81] *Varnava and Others v. Turkey* [GC], nos 16064/90, 16065/90, 16066/90, 16068/90, 16069/90, 16070/90, 16071/90, 16072/90, and 16073/90, Concurring Opinion of Judge Ziemele, § 3, ECHR 2009.
[82] Ibid., § 4.
[83] *Dalban v. Romania* [GC], no. 28114/95, § 39, ECHR 1999-VI; *Raimondo v. Italy*, 22 February 1994, § 2, Series A no. 281-A; *Malhous v. the Czech Republic* (dec.) [GC], no. 33071/96, ECHR 2000-XII; *Statileo v. Croatia*, no. 12027/10, §§ 88–90, 10 July 2014.
[84] *Janowiec and Others v. Russia*, nos 55508/07 and 29520/09, §§ 57–58, 16 April 2012; *Janowiec and Others v. Russia* [GC], nos 55508/07 and 29520/09, §§ 98–101, ECHR 2013; *Karner v. Austria*, no. 40016/98, § 25, ECHR 2003-IX; *Dalban v. Romania* [GC], no. 28114/95, § 39, ECHR 1999-VI; *Toteva v. Bulgaria*, no. 42027/98, § 45, 19 May 2004; *Mutlu v. Turkey*, no. 8006/02, §§ 13–14, 10 October 2006; *Yakovenko v. Ukraine*, no. 15825/06, § 65, 25 October 2007; *Getiren v. Turkey*, no. 10301/03, §§ 60–62, 22 July 2008.
[85] *Micallef v. Malta* [GC], no. 17056/06, § 48, ECHR 2009; *Loyen and Others v. France*, no. 55926/00, § 29, 29 April 2003.
[86] *Micallef v. Malta* [GC], no. 17056/06, § 48, ECHR 2009; *Ressegatti v. Switzerland*, no. 17671/02, § 29, 13 July 2006.
[87] *Malhous v. the Czech Republic* (dec.) [GC], no. 33071/96, ECHR 2000-XII; *Scherer v. Switzerland*, 25 March 1994, § 31, Series A no. 287; *Öhlinger v. Austria*, no. 21444/93, § 15, Commission report of 14 January 1997.

right to a remedy. Even if the substantive claim has become inadmissible, a grievance under article 13 cannot be excluded.[88]

Although corporate bodies and non-governmental organizations are entitled to make applications under article 34, there are some circumstances where they cannot be victims because of the nature of the right. For example, it is difficult to conceive of a corporation being denied the right to marry, something that applies to 'men and women' pursuant to article 12. Nor can a corporation or association be a victim of a violation of article 3 of Protocol No. 1 to the extent that it is ineligible to stand for elected office.[89] On the other hand, corporations can obviously be victims of deprivation of property contrary to article 1 of Protocol No. 1, or of freedom of expression as enshrined in article 10 of the Convention. The Court has rejected the argument of some governments that an association or organization cannot be a victim of freedom of association.[90] Even if a corporation may be a victim of a violation, this does not automatically mean that its shareholders have the same status. For example, if the alleged violation concerns the length of judicial proceedings involving a corporation, one of its shareholders cannot also be a victim.[91] Explaining the distinction between interests of the shareholder and those of the corporation, the Court noted that a wrong done to the latter may cause prejudice to the former but that this does not imply both are entitled to claim compensation. Citing the International Court of Justice in *Barcelona Traction*, the Court said:

Whenever a shareholder's interests are harmed by a measure directed at the company, it is up to the latter to take appropriate action. An act infringing only the company's rights does not involve responsibility towards the shareholders, even if their interests are affected. Such responsibility arises only if the act complained of is aimed at the rights of the shareholder as such . . . or if the company has been wound up.[92]

Nevertheless, the sole owner of a company can claim to be a victim of damage suffered by the company because 'there is no risk of differences of opinion among shareholders or between shareholders and a board of directors as to the reality of infringements of the Convention rights or the most appropriate way of reacting to such infringements'.[93]

An advocacy organization or association cannot itself be a victim under the Convention simply because the individuals on whose behalf it acts are direct victims.[94] An organization whose chief aim was to provide psychological and moral support to gays and lesbians

---

[88] *M.A. v. Cyprus*, no. 41872/10, §§ 118–119, 23 July 2013; *I.M. v. France*, no. 9152/09, §§ 94–95, 2 February 2012; *Gebremedhin [Gaberamadhien] v. France*, no. 25389/05, § 56, ECHR 2007-II. Similarly, with respect to article 8: *De Souza Ribeiro v. France* [GC], no. 22689/07, §§84–100, 13 December 2012; *De Souza Ribeiro v. France*, no. 22689/07, §§ 22–26, 30 June 2011.

[89] *The Georgian Labour Party v. Georgia* (dec.), no. 9103/04, 22 May 2007.

[90] *Hyde Park and Others v. Moldova (nos 5 and 6)*, nos 6991/08 and 15084/08, § 32, 14 September 2010; *Gypsy Council and Others v. the United Kingdom* (dec.), no. 66336/01, 14 May 2002; *Plattform 'Ärzte für das Leben' v. Austria*, 21 June 1988, Series A no. 139; *Christians against Racism and Fascism v. the United Kingdom*, no. 8440/78, Commission decision of 16 July 1980, (1981) 24 YB 178, DR 21, p. 138.

[91] *F. Santos, Lda. and Fachadas v. Portugal* (dec.), no. 49020/99, ECHR 2000-X.

[92] *Olczak v. Poland*, no. 30417/96, § 59, 7 November 2002, citing *Barcelona Traction, Light and Power Company, Limited*, Judgment, I.C.J. Reports 1970, p. 3, at pp. 39 and 41, paras 56–58 and 66.

[93] *Groppera Radio AG and Others v. Switzerland*, 28 March 1990, § 49, Series A no. 173; *Ankarcrona v. Sweden* (dec.), no. 35178/97, 27 June 2000; *Dyrwold v. Sweden*, no. 12259/86, Commission decision of 7 September 1990; *Glas Nadezhda EOOD and Anatoliy Elenkov v. Bulgaria*, no. 14134/02, § 40, 11 October 2007; *Nosov v. Russia* (dec.), no. 30877/02, 20 October 2005.

[94] *Čonka and Others, la ligue des droits de l'homme v. Belgium* (dec.) no. 51564/99, 13 March 2001; *Grande Oriente d'Italia di Palazzo Giustiniani v. Italy* (dec.), no. 35972/97, 21 October 1999.

could not claim to be a victim of denial of a right of same-sex couples to enter into civil union.[95] However, an association can be a victim if the violation of the Convention to which its members are subjected results in the departure of a significant number of them or a loss of its standing and prestige.[96] An association may also be a victim if the impugned measure can prevent the achievement of its objectives. There must be clear evidence of this, and more than mere conjecture. When a religious group argued that it would be victimized if a parliamentary report were tabled, the Court claimed this was speculative and denied victim status to the organization.[97] For the same reason, an Islamic organization in Switzerland was denied victim status to contest a constitutional amendment preventing the construction of minarets.[98] A member of an ethnic group who complains about racist remarks and expressions that allegedly debase the community to which he or she belongs may not have been targeted personally but is entitled to claim to be a victim because 'he could, however, have felt offended by the remarks concerning the ethnic group to which he belonged'.[99]

There is a certain hierarchy in the way the Court assesses the status of victims. First and foremost are direct victims, that is, persons who are directly affected by the alleged infringement of rights protected by the Convention.[100] The organizer of a demonstration that does not take place may claim to be denied the right freedom of assembly.[101] But a person who 'would have gone' to a demonstration if it had taken place cannot claim to be a victim of a breach of freedom of assembly. This would stretch the concept of a victim too far in that it would 'allow an indeterminate number of people to complain that their Article 11 rights had been violated'.[102]

Exceptionally, a person who is indirectly affected by the violation may be an applicant under article 34.[103] For example, the Court has recognized victim status to the spouse of a woman who was forced to submit to a gynaecological examination[104] and to the nephew of a person who died in suspicious circumstances.[105] In right-to-life cases, close family members, such as parents, may be applicants before the Court because they are themselves 'indirect victims' of the breach of article 2. It is irrelevant whether legally they are deemed the heirs of the deceased person.[106] As a general rule, a corporate body cannot be an indirect victim of an infringement of the Convention.[107]

---

[95] *Vallianatos and Others v. Greece* [GC], no. 29381/09, § 48, ECHR 2013.

[96] *Grande Oriente d'Italia di Palazzo Giustiniani v. Italy*, no. 35972/97, § 15, ECHR 2001-VIII.

[97] *Fédération chrétienne des témoins de Jéhovah de France v. France* (dec.), no. 53430/99, 6 November 2011.

[98] *La Ligue des Musulmans de Suisse v. Switzerland* (dec.), no. 66274/09, 28 June 2011.

[99] *Aksu v. Turkey* [GC], nos 4149/04 and 41029/04, §§ 50–54, ECHR 2012.

[100] *Norris v. Ireland*, 26 October 1988, § 31, Series A no. 142; *Open Door and Dublin Well Woman v. Ireland*, 29 October 1992, § 43, Series A no. 246-A; *Otto-Preminger-Institut v. Austria*, 20 September 1994, §§ 39–41, Series A no. 295-A; *Tanrıkulu and Others v. Turkey* (dec.), no. 40150/98, 6 November 2001; *SARL du Parc d'Activités de Blotzheim v. France*, no. 72377/01, § 20, 11 July 2006.

[101] *Patyi and Others v. Hungary*, no. 5529/05, §§ 25–28, 7 October 2008.

[102] *Hyde Park and Others v. Moldova (nos 5 and 6)*, nos 6991/08 and 15084/08, § 32, 14 September 2010.

[103] *Vatan v. Russia*, no. 47978/99, § 48, 7 October 2004.

[104] *Fidan v. Turkey* (dec.), no. 24209/94, 29 February 2000.

[105] *Yaşa v. Turkey*, 2 September 1998, §§ 61–66, *Reports of Judgments and Decisions* 1998-VI.

[106] Ibid., § 66; *A.V. v. Bulgaria* (dec.), no. 41488/98, 18 May 1999; *Keenan v. the United Kingdom*, no. 27229/95, ECHR 2001-III; *Paul and Audrey Edwards v. the United Kingdom*, no. 46477/99, ECHR 2002-II; *Koku v. Turkey*, no. 27305/95, 31 May 2005; *Opuz v. Turkey*, no. 33401/02, ECHR 2009.

[107] *La Ligue des Musulmans de Suisse v. Switzerland* (dec.), no. 66274/09, 28 June 2011.

Finally, the Court has, 'very exceptionally', recognized a 'potential victim' status to persons likely to be affected by an alleged infringement of fundamental rights. It is reticent in this respect because:

the exercise of the right of individual petition could not be used to prevent a potential violation of the Convention: in theory the organs designated by Article 19 to ensure the observance of the engagements undertaken by the Contracting Parties in the Convention could not examine—or, if applicable, find—a violation other than a posteriori, once that violation had occurred. . . . It was only in highly exceptional circumstances that an applicant could nevertheless claim to be a victim of a violation of the Convention owing to the risk of a future violation.[108]

An applicant who claims to be a 'potential victim' is required to provide 'reasonable and convincing evidence of the likelihood that a violation affecting him personally will occur; mere suspicion or conjecture is insufficient'.[109] For example, if a potential breach of the Convention would take place as a consequence of expulsion or deportation, the proceedings must have reached a stage where there is a real threat to the applicant, or when the expulsion or deportation has already taken place. This will normally be reached once a formal expulsion order has been issued.[110]

Potential victimization has been recognized in situations where an individual is obliged to change behaviour because of a threat of criminal prosecution based upon legislation that breaches the right to private life or that is discriminatory.[111] A potential applicant may also be someone belonging to a category of persons at risk of being directly subject to legislation alleged to be contrary to the Convention.[112] For example, French legislation prohibiting the wearing of a full-face veil in public presented individuals wishing to do so for religious reasons with a dilemma: 'either they comply with the ban and thus refrain from dressing in accordance with their approach to religion; or they refuse to comply and face prosecution'.[113] As Judge Pinto de Albuquerque has explained, 'when a law or regulation confers a Convention right solely on one group of people based on an identifiable characteristic of that group, by implication depriving another group of people in the same or similar situation of the enjoyment of the said right without any objective justification, the Convention compliance of that law or regulation may be reviewed *in*

---

[108] *Fédération chrétienne des témoins de Jéhovah de France v. France* (dec.), no. 53430/99, 6 November 2011; *Ada Rossi and Others v.* Italy (dec.), nos 55185/08, 55483/08, 55516/08, 55519/08, 56010/08, 56278/08, 58420/08, and 58424/08, 16 December 2008; *Noël Narvii Tauira and 18 Others v. France*, no. 28204/95, Commission decision of 4 December 1995, (1995) 38 YB 155, DR 83, p. 112.

[109] *Senator Lines GmbH v. Austria, Belgium, Denmark, Finland, France, Germany, Greece, Ireland, Italy, Luxembourg, the Netherlands, Portugal, Spain, Sweden, and the United Kingdom* (dec.) [GC], no. 56672/00, ECHR 2004-IV; *Segi and Gestoras Pro-Amnistia and Others v. Austria, Belgium, Denmark, Finland, France, Germany, Greece, Ireland, Italy, Luxembourg, the Netherlands, Portugal, Spain, Sweden, and the United Kingdom* (dec.), nos 6422/02 and 9916/02, ECHR 2002-V.

[110] *Vijayanathan and Pusparajah v. France*, nos 17550/90 and 17825/91, § 46, 27 August 1992.

[111] *Dudgeon v. the United Kingdom*, 22 October 1981, §§ 40–41, Series A no. 45; *Norris v. Ireland*, 26 October 1988, § 29, Series A no. 142; *Bowman v. the United Kingdom*, 19 February 1998, § 29, *Reports of Judgments and Decisions* 1998-I; *Altuğ Taner Akçam v. Turkey*, no. 27520/07, § 66, 25 October 2011; *S.A.S. v. France* [GC], no. 43835/11, § 57, 1 July 2014.

[112] *Sejdić and Finci v. Bosnia and Herzegovina* [GC], nos 27996/06 and 34836/06, § 29, ECHR 2009; *Marckx v. Belgium*, 13 June 1979, § 27, Series A no. 31; *Johnston and Others v. Ireland*, 18 December 1986, § 42, Series A no. 112; *Open Door and Dublin Well Woman v. Ireland*, 29 October 1992, §§ 43–44, Series A no. 246-A; *S.L. v. Austria* (dec.), no. 45330/99, 22 November 2001; *Burden v. the United Kingdom* [GC], no. 13378/05, § 35, ECHR 2008.

[113] *S.A.S. v. France* [GC], no. 43835/11, § 57, 1 July 2014.

abstracto by the Court on the basis of a complaint lodged by any member of the deprived group of people'.[114] In some cases, owing to the secrecy of measures that are the object of an application, an individual may be unable to point to any specific or concrete measure affecting him or her.[115] The Court has said that 'the effectiveness (*l'effet utile*) of the Convention implies in such circumstances some possibility of having access' to the Convention organs. If this were not so, the efficiency of the Convention's enforcement machinery would be materially weakened.'[116]

The victim issue is relevant at all stages of the proceedings before the Court and may change in the course of the litigation.[117] The fact that a decision or measure has been taken that is favourable to the applicant does not deprive him or her of victim status unless the authorities have acknowledged the violation and then provided redress.[118] The issue of 'appropriate' and 'sufficient' redress will depend upon the circumstances.[119] The amount of compensation that is offered is an important factor,[120] notably in cases of unreasonable delay during judicial proceedings.[121] A person may no longer claim to be a victim of a violation of the right to a fair trial if the proceedings have resulted in an acquittal or were discontinued.[122] However, if the sentence has begun before the acquittal and time was served in detention, the applicant may remain a victim.[123] A decision to acquit a person convicted after an allegedly unfair trial, where the final ruling was based on an issue quite distinct from the violation during the proceedings and did not even mention the earlier rulings, was deemed to be insufficient acknowledgment and unable to deprive the applicant of victim status.[124] In cases dealing with deportation or

[114] *Vallianatos and Others v. Greece* [GC], nos 29381/09 and 32684/09, Partly Concurring, Partly Dissenting Opinion of Judge Pinto de Albuquerque, ECHR 2013.

[115] *Klass and Others v. Germany*, 6 September 1978, § 35, Series A no. 28; *Weber and Saravia v. Germany* (dec.), no. 54934/00, § 78, ECHR 2006-XI; *Association for European Integration and Human Rights and Ekimdzhiev v. Bulgaria*, no. 62540/00, §§ 58 to 60, 28 June 2007; *Iliya Stefanov v. Bulgaria*, no. 65755/01, § 49, 22 May 2008; *Liberty and Others v. The United Kingdom*, no. 58243/00, §§ 56–57, 1 July 2008; *Iordachi and Others v. Moldova*, no. 25198/02, §§ 30 to 35, 10 February 2009.

[116] *Klass and Others v. Germany*, 6 September 1978, § 35, Series A no. 28.

[117] *Burdov v. Russia*, no. 59498/00, § 30, ECHR 2002-III; *Burdov v. Russia (no. 2)*, no. 33509/04, § 55, ECHR 2009.

[118] *Brumărescu v. Romania* [GC], no. 28342/95, § 50, ECHR 1999-VII; *Nada v. Switzerland* [GC], no. 10593/08, § 129, ECHR 2012; *Gäfgen v. Germany* [GC], no. 22978/05, § 115, ECHR 2010; *Association Ekin v. France* (dec.), no. 39288/98, 18 January 2000; *Amuur v. France*, 25 June 1996, § 36, *Reports of Judgments and Decisions* 1996-III; *Eckle v. Germany*, 15 July 1982, § 66, Series A no. 51; *Dalban v. Romania* [GC], no. 28114/95, § 44, ECHR 1999-VI; *Scordino v. Italy (no. 1)* [GC], no. 36813/97, §§ 179–180, ECHR 2006-V; *Kurić and Others v. Slovenia* [GC], no. 26828/06, § 259, ECHR 2012 (extracts); *Kopylov v. Russia*, no. 3933/04, § 150, 29 July 2010.

[119] *Gäfgen v. Germany* [GC], no. 22978/05, § 116, ECHR 2010.

[120] *Kurić and Others v. Slovenia* [GC], no. 26828/06, § 261, ECHR 2012 (extracts); *Normann v. Denmark* (dec.), no. 44704/98, 14 June 2001; *Scordino v. Italy (no. 1)* [GC], no. 36813/97, § 202, ECHR 2006-V; *Jensen and Rasmussen v. Denmark* (dec.), no. 52620/99, 20 March 2003.

[121] *Stokić v. Serbia* (dec.), no. 54689/12, 12 February 2013; *Vidaković v. Serbia* (dec.), 16231/07, § 29, 24 May 2011; *Dubjakova v. Slovakia* (dec.), no. 67299/01, 19 October 2004; *Gäfgen v. Germany* [GC], no. 22978/05, § 116, ECHR 2010.

[122] *Oleksy v. Poland* (dec.), no. 1379/06, 16 May 2009; *Üstün v. Turkey*, no. 37685/02, § 24, 10 May 2007; *Sharomov v. Russia*, no. 8927/02, § 36, 15 January 2009; *Komyakov v. Russia* (dec.), no. 7100/02, 8 January 2009; *X v. the United Kingdom*, no. 8083/77, Commission decision of 13 March 1980, DR 19, p. 223; *Eğinlioğlu v. Turkey*, no. 31312/96, Commission decision of 21 October 1998; *Osmanov and Yuseinov v. Bulgaria* (dec.), nos 54178/00 and 59901/00, 4 September 2003; *Witkowski v. Poland* (dec.), no. 53804/00, 3 February 2003; *Bouglame v. Belgium* (dec.), no. 16147/08, 2 March 2010.

[123] *Arat v. Turkey*, no. 10309/03, § 47, 10 November 2009.

[124] *Constantinescu v. Romania*, no. 28871/95, § 42, ECHR 2000-VIII.

extradition of non-nationals, regularization of an applicant's stay or removal of the threat of deportation or extradition has been deemed to be enough to bring victim status to an end.[125] Where a Romanian court deprived a minor of the right to leave the country, thereby infringing article 2 of Protocol No. 4, the European Court of Human Rights considered the subsequent reversal of the ruling to provide adequate redress and acknowledgement.[126] In double jeopardy cases, where article 4 of Protocol No. 7 is invoked, if there are two sets of proceedings but the authorities terminate or cancel one set of them and remove its effects, the Court may consider the applicant to have lost the status of a victim: 'Were it otherwise it would be impossible for the national authorities to remedy alleged violations of Article 4 of Protocol No. 7 at the domestic level and the concept of subsidiarity would lose much of its usefulness.'[127]

Content of the application

An application must be submitted in writing and be signed by the applicant or the applicant's representative.[128] It must be submitted by mail, the postmark providing the submission date.[129] It appears that if it is submitted otherwise, by facsimile for example, the Registry will request that the applicant resubmit an application using the post, although the date the fax is received will be sufficient to interrupt the six-month time limit for the filing of an application that is imposed by article 35(1).[130]

An application from a non-governmental organization must be signed by the authorized representative.[131] If the applicant is represented, a power of attorney or similar written authorization must be provided,[132] signed by the applicant.[133] Formalities are not too important here; what is at issue is clarifying the genuine intention of the alleged victim to submit the application.[134] The Court considers that it is 'essential for representatives to demonstrate that they have received specific and explicit instructions from the alleged victim(s) within the meaning of Article 34 of the Convention on whose behalf they purport to act'.[135] The date that this is received by the Court is not decisive for the purposes of the six-month delay. In other words, the legal representative can submit an application without the signed authorization, although it must be provided subsequently.[136]

---

[125] *Kurić and Others v. Slovenia* [GC], no. 26828/06, § 261, ECHR 2012 (extracts); *Pančenko v. Latvia* (dec.), no. 40772/98, 28 October 1999; *Yang Chun Jin alias Yang Xiaolin v. Hungary* (striking out), no. 58073/00, §§ 20–23, 8 March 2001; *Mikheyeva v. Latvia* (dec.), no. 50029/99, 12 September 2002; *Fjodorova and Others v. Latvia* (dec.), no. 69405/01, 6 April 2006; *Sisojeva and Others v. Latvia* (striking out) [GC], no. 60654/00, §§ 102–104, ECHR 2007-I; *Shevanova v. Latvia* (striking out) [GC], no. 58822/00, §§ 48–50, 7 December 2007; *Kaftailova v. Latvia* (striking out) [GC], no.59643/00, §§ 52–54, 7 December 2007.

[126] *D.J. and A.-K. R. v. Romania* (dec.), no. 34175/05, § 74, 20 October 2009.

[127] *Sergey Zolotukhin v. Russia* [GC], no. 14939/03, § 115, ECHR 2009.

[128] Rules of Court, Rule 45(1). See also Practice Direction, Institution of Proceedings (Individual applications under article 34 of the Convention), 1 November 2003 and amended on 22 September 2008 and on 24 June 2009.

[129] Rules of Court, Rule 47(6).

[130] *Post v. the Netherlands* (dec.), no. 21727/08, 20 January 2009.

[131] Rules of Court, Rule 45(2).

[132] Ibid., Rule 45(3).

[133] For a contestation of the applicant's signature, see *Aliev v. Georgia*, no. 522/04, §§ 44–50, 13 January 2009.

[134] *Velikova v. Bulgaria*, no. 41488/98, § 52, ECHR 2000-VI.

[135] *Post v. the Netherlands* (dec.), no. 21727/08, 20 January 2009.

[136] *Fitzmartin and Others v. the United Kingdom* (dec.), 34953/97, 21 January 2003; *Post v. the Netherlands* (dec.), no. 21727/08, 20 January 2009.

The application must provide a succinct statement of the alleged violation and the relevant arguments, as well as a brief explanation of the applicant's compliance with the admissibility criteria. Relevant documents are to be included with the application.[137] A form provided by the Court is to be used by individual applicants.[138] The application should be in one of the official languages of the Member States of the Council of Europe.[139]

It has been clear from the outset of the Court's work that in the application process too much 'strictness would lead to unjust consequences' because 'the vast majority of "individual" petitions are received from laymen' who apply without the assistance of a lawyer.[140] Individual applicants must claim to be victim of 'a violation of the rights set forth in the Convention' but they are not required to specify the relevant provisions of the Convention or even the right that they are invoking. In any case, the Court can make its own determination of the relevant provisions. The complaint is characterized primarily by the facts that it alleges rather than by the legal grounds or arguments invoked by the applicant.[141]

At the time the application is made, the applicant may indicate a desire that his or her identity not be disclosed. Reasons must be provided justifying this departure from the normal rule of public access to information in proceedings before the Court. The President of the Chamber is empowered to authorize anonymity or grant it of his or her own motion.[142]

Effective exercise of the right of application

The final words of article 34 refer to 'this right' in a manner that can only mean the submission of an application. There is a legal obligation upon States to respect the right of application to the Court, and 'not to hinder' its exercise 'in any way'. According to the Grand Chamber, this 'obligation set out in Article 34 *in fine* requires the Contracting States to refrain not only from exerting pressure on applicants, but also from any act or omission which, by destroying or removing the subject matter of an application, would make it pointless or otherwise prevent the Court from considering it under its normal procedure'.[143] The Court has described the purpose of the rule as being 'to ensure the effectiveness of the right of individual petition'.[144] Consequently, 'the intentions or reasons underlying the acts or omissions in question are of little relevance when assessing whether Article 34 of the Convention was complied with . . . What matters is whether the situation created as a result of the authorities' act or omission conforms to Article 34.'[145]

---

[137] Rules of Court, Rule 47.
[138] Ibid., Rule 48.
[139] Ibid., Rule 34(2).
[140] *Guzzardi v. Italy*, 6 November 1980, § 61, Series A no. 39. Also *Ringeisen v. Austria*, 16 July 1971, § 92, Series A no. 13.
[141] *Guerra and Others v. Italy*, 19 February 1998, § 44, *Reports of Judgments and Decisions* 1998-I; *Powell and Rayner v. the United Kingdom*, 21 February 1990, § 29, Series A no. 172; *Scoppola v. Italy (no. 2)* [GC], no. 10249/03, § 54, 17 September 2009.
[142] Rules of Court, Rule 47(3); Practice Direction, Requests for Anonymity (Rules 33 and 47 of the Rules of Court), 14 January 2010.
[143] *Mamatkulov and Askarov v. Turkey* [GC], nos 46827/99 and 46951/99, § 102, ECHR 2005-I.
[144] *Paladi v. Moldova* [GC], no. 39806/05, § 87, 10 March 2009.
[145] Ibid.

The right conferred by article 34 is procedural in nature and thereby distinguishable from the substantive rights set out under Section I of the Convention.[146] As a result, issues of admissibility are not engaged.[147] Probably for this reason, the Court usually describes an infringement of article 34 as 'a failure to comply with obligations',[148] although on occasion it speaks of 'violation'.[149] Some complaints about obstruction of communication with the Convention organs by a State party with respect to prisoners have been examined under article 8 rather than article 34.[150]

The obligation set out in article 34 is completed by a distinct treaty, the European Agreement relating to Persons Participating in Proceedings of the European Court of Human Rights.[151] It provides for such matters as immunity from suit with respect to the contents of applications and for unimpeded travel to and from the seat of the Court in Strasbourg. The Committee of Ministers has called upon all Member States to ratify the Convention.[152]

According to the Court, applicants or potential applicants should be able to communicate freely with the Convention organs 'without being subjected to any form of pressure from the authorities to withdraw or modify their complaints'.[153] The expression 'any form of pressure' covers 'direct coercion and flagrant acts of intimidation of applicants or potential applicants or their families or legal representatives' as well as 'other improper indirect acts or contacts designed to dissuade or discourage them from pursuing a Convention remedy'.[154] Relevant circumstances in assessing this include 'the vulnerability of the complainant and his or her susceptibility to influence exerted by the authorities'.[155] In one case, the Court referred to the 'chilling effect' of a letter from the authorities to a lawyer engaged in an application.[156] Criminal or disciplinary proceedings and other forms of inquiry directed against lawyers have also been found not to comply

---

[146] *Shamayev and Others v. Georgia and Russia*, no. 36378/02, § 470, ECHR 2005-III; *Paladi v. Moldova* [GC], no. 39806/05, § 85, 10 March 2009.

[147] *Ryabov v. Russia*, no. 3896/04, § 56, 31 January 2008; *Cooke v. Austria*, no. 25878/94, § 46, 8 February 2000; *Ergi v. Turkey*, 28 July 1998, § 105, *Reports of Judgments and Decisions* 1998-IV; *Enukidze and Girgvliani v. Georgia*, no. 25091/07, § 295, 26 April 2011.

[148] *McShane v. the United Kingdom*, no. 43290/98, § 152, 28 May 2002; *Colibaba v. Moldova*, no. 29089/06, § 69, 23 October 2007; *Ryabov v. Russia*, no. 3896/04, § 65, 31 January 2008; *Fedotova v. Russia*, no. 73225/01, § 52, 13 April 2006.

[149] *Iambor v. Romania (no. 1)*, no. 64536/01, § 217, 24 June 2008; *Cotleţ v. Romania*, no. 38565/97, § 72, 3 June 2003; *Oferta Plus SRL v. Moldova*, no. 14385/04, § 156, 19 December 2006; *Boicenco v. Moldova*, no. 41088/05, § 158, 11 July 2006; *Al-Saadoon and Mufdhi v. the United Kingdom*, no. 61498/08, § 166, ECHR 2010 (extracts).

[150] *Peers v. Greece*, no. 28524/95, § 84, ECHR 2001-III; *Kornakovs v. Latvia*, no. 61005/00, § 157, 15 June 2006.

[151] ETS 161.

[152] Resolution CM/Res(2010)25 on member States' duty to respect and protect the right of individual application to the Court.

[153] *Petra v. Romania*, 23 September 1998, § 43, *Reports of Judgments and Decisions* 1998-VII.

[154] Ibid.

[155] *Kurt v. Turkey*, 25 May 1998, §§ 159–160, *Reports of Judgments and Decisions* 1998-III; *Iambor v. Romania (no. 1)*, no. 64536/01, § 217, 24 June 2008; *Aksoy v. Turkey*, 18 December 1996, § 105, *Reports of Judgments and Decisions* 1996-VI; *Akdivar and Others v. Turkey*, 16 September 1996, § 105, *Reports of Judgments and Decisions* 1996-IV.

[156] *Colibaba v. Moldova*, no. 29089/06, § 68, 23 October 2007.

with article 34 of the Convention.[157] A denial of confidentiality of solicitor–client meetings was deemed contrary to article 34,[158] as was access to a lawyer.[159]

The obligation is positive as well as negative, a dimension that is of particular importance to applicants who are in particularly vulnerable situations.[160] With respect to persons detained seeking to make a submission to the Court, the authorities are required to assist in obtaining relevant documents,[161] to facilitate necessary medical examinations,[162] and not to obstruct the actual filing of the submission.[163] Article 34 operates as a *lex generalis* with respect to article 38 whereby States are required to furnish 'all necessary facilities' for the investigation of a case.[164] Linking the two provisions, the Court has said that 'it is of the utmost importance for the effective operation of the system of individual petition instituted under Article 34 of the Convention that States should furnish all necessary facilities to make possible a proper and effective examination of applications'.[165]

Prisoners are in a special situation, dependent upon the cooperation of the authorities in order not only to communicate with the Court but also to obtain the relevant documents in support of their applications. In this respect, the Court has recalled Rule 47(1)(h) requiring that an application be supported by 'copies of any relevant documents and in particular the decisions, whether judicial or not, relating to the object of the application', noting that a failure to do so may result in its rejection. Consequently, 'l'examen de la requête par la Cour pourrait être sérieusement entravé si, par manque de moyens, un requérant détenu n'était pas en mesure de fournir les copies susvisées'.[166] Nevertheless, The Court rejected a petition based on article 34 by an inmate of a Bulgarian penitentiary who could not post his petition to Strasbourg because he had no money for stamps and the authorities refused to assist. Despite this, however, the Court said he was able to file his application and obtain the necessary documents with the assistance of a non-governmental organization.[167]

Legal aid

Legal aid for persons who submit applications to the Court in accordance with article 34 is available at the discretion of the President of the Chamber.[168] It is only granted if the President of the Chamber is satisfied that legal aid is necessary for the proper conduct of the case and that the applicant has insufficient means to cover all or part of the costs that are involved.[169]

---

[157] *McShane v. the United Kingdom*, no. 43290/98, § 152, 28 May 2002; *Kurt v. Turkey*, 25 May 1998, §§ 159–165, *Reports of Judgments and Decisions* 1998-III; *Şarli v. Turkey*, no. 24490/94, §§ 85–86, 22 May 2001; *Ryabov v. Russia*, no. 3896/04, §§ 53–65, 31 January 2008; *Fedotova v. Russia*, no. 73225/01, §§ 45–52, 13 April 2006.
[158] *Oferta Plus SRL v. Moldova*, no. 14385/04, § 156, 19 December 2006.
[159] *Shtukaturov v. Russia*, no. 44009/05, §§ 138 et seq., ECHR 2008.
[160] *Amirov v. Russia*, no. 51857/13, § 65, 27 November 2014; *Iulian Popescu v. Romania*, no. 24999/04, § 33, 4 June 2013.
[161] *Naydyon v. Ukraine*, no. 16474/03, § 68, 14 October 2010.
[162] *Boicenco v. Moldova*, no. 41088/05, § 158, 11 July 2006.
[163] *Nurmagomedov v. Russia*, no. 30138/02, § 61, 7 June 2007.
[164] *Bazorkina v. Russia*, no. 69481/01, § 175, 27 July 2006.
[165] Ibid., § 171; *Tanrıkulu v. Turkey* [GC], no. 23763/94, § 70, ECHR 1999-IV.
[166] *Gagiu v. Romania*, no. 63258/00, § 96, 24 February 2009.
[167] *Dimcho Dimov v. Bulgaria*, no. 57123/08, §§ 92–103, 16 December 2014.
[168] Rules of Court, Rule 100.
[169] Ibid., Rule 101.

Interim measures

Although the Convention and its Protocols do not make explicit provision for the issuance of interim measures, the Court is authorized to issue them in accordance with Rule 39 of the Rules of Court.[170] Interim measures 'play a vital role in avoiding irreversible situations that would prevent the Court from properly examining the application and, where appropriate, securing to the applicant the practical and effective benefit of the Convention rights asserted'.[171] As the Court has explained,

The crucial significance of interim measures is further highlighted by the fact that the Court issues them, as a matter of principle, only in truly exceptional cases and on the basis of a rigorous examination of all the relevant circumstances. In most of these cases, the applicants face a genuine threat to life and limb, with the ensuing real risk of grave, irreversible harm in breach of the core provisions of the Convention. The vital role played by interim measures in the Convention system not only underpins their binding legal effect on the States concerned, as upheld by the established case-law, but also commands that the utmost importance be attached to the question of the States Parties' compliance with the Court's indications in that regard.[172]

Interim measures allow the Court 'to carry out an effective examination of the application but also to ensure that the protection afforded to the applicant by the Convention is effective'.[173] They thereby facilitate supervision of the execution of a final judgment and enable the State to discharge its obligations.[174] They may be issued by the Chamber or, where appropriate, the President of the Section or a duty judge, either at the request of a party or 'other person concerned' or on their own motion.[175] An interim order may consist of any measure 'in the interests of the parties or of the proper conduct of the proceedings'.[176]

For many years the issue was controversial, with a very close vote of the plenary Court in 1991 (ten judges to nine) holding that the authority of the European Commission of Human Rights to order binding interim measures could not be inferred from the text of the Convention.[177] Largely inspired by a judgment of the International Court of Justice determining interim measures to be inherent in the authority of a judicial body,[178] the European Court changed its position in 2003. In *Mamatkulov and Askarov v. Turkey*, it quite explicitly took into account 'general principles of international law and the view expressed on this subject by other international bodies since *Cruz Varas and Others*'.[179] There is today no doubt that interim measures are binding upon States and that a failure

---

[170] See also Practice Direction, Requests for Interim Measures (Rule 39 of the Rules of Court), 5 March 2003 and amended on 16 October 2009 and on 7 July 2011.

[171] *Al-Saadoon and Mufdhi v. the United Kingdom*, no. 61498/08, § 160, ECHR 2010 (extracts); *Mamatkulov and Askarov v. Turkey* [GC], nos 46827/99 and 46951/99, § 125, ECHR 2005-I; *Paladi v. Moldova* [GC], no. 39806/05, § 86, 10 March 2009; *Savriddin Dzhurayev v. Russia*, no. 71386/10, §§ 211–213, ECHR 2013 (extracts); *Trabelsi v. Belgium*, no. 140/10, §§ 144–150, 4 September 2014.

[172] *Kasymakhunov v. Russia*, no. 296041/12, § 181, 14 November 2013.

[173] *Mamatkulov and Askarov v. Turkey* [GC], nos 46827/99 and 46951/99, § 125, ECHR 2005-I; *Paladi v. Moldova* [GC], no. 39806/05, § 86, 10 March 2009.

[174] *Mamatkulov and Askarov v. Turkey* [GC], nos 46827/99 and 46951/99, § 125, ECHR 2005-I; *Paladi v. Moldova* [GC], no. 39806/05, § 86, 10 March 2009.

[175] Rules of Court, Rule 39(1).

[176] Ibid..

[177] *Cruz Varas and Others v. Sweden*, 20 March 1991, §§ 102–103, Series A no. 201.

[178] *LaGrand (Germany v. United States of America)*, Judgment, I.C.J. Reports 2001, p. 466, para. 109.

[179] *Mamatkulov and Abdurasulovic v. Turkey*, nos 46827/99 and 46951/99, § 110, 6 February 2003.

to implement them may result in a breach of article 34.[180] The Final Declaration of the High Level Conference on the Future of the Court, held in İzmir on 26–27 April 2011, reaffirmed the requirement that States Parties comply with interim measures indications:

[The Conference] stresses the importance of States Parties providing national remedies, where necessary with suspensive effect, which operate effectively and fairly and provide a proper and timely examination of the issue of risk in accordance with the Convention and in light of the Court's case law; and, while noting that they may challenge interim measures before the Court, reiterates the requirement for States Parties to comply with them.

Nevertheless, some governments continue to defy the Court's indication of interim measures. In 2013, Russia contended that 'the legally binding force of the interim measure issued under Rule 39 of the Rules of Court may not be drawn from Article 34 of the Convention or "from any other source"'. Moreover, it said that the Rules of Court and accordingly the interim measure applied did not have a binding force on the State Party.[181] Also in 2013, Belgium extradited an alleged terrorist to the United States despite an interim measure from the Court. Four times Belgium had attempted to convince the Court to lift the measure, with no success. In defence of its actions it claimed that the Court ought to have realized that the application was not well founded. In addition, Belgium said it felt obliged to honour its treaty obligations with the United States.[182] In 2008, the United Kingdom did not comply with interim measures of the Court when it transferred two detainees to the Iraqi authorities, although there was a threat that they would be subject to capital punishment. 'An indication under Rule 39 could not require a Contracting State to violate the law and sovereignty of a non-Contracting State', the United Kingdom claimed, insisting that it was required to make the transfer under Iraqi law. It said the case was 'exceptional' because the facts arose outside of its own territory, noting that the United Kingdom government 'were proud of their long history of cooperation with the Court and their compliance with previous Rule 39 indications. They had failed to comply with the indication in this case only because there was an objective impediment preventing compliance.'[183]

The Court may find that article 34 is infringed if a State fails 'to take all steps which could reasonably have been taken in order to comply with the interim measure indicated by the Court'.[184] In its examination of an alleged breach of article 34, the Court does not reconsider the correctness of its decision on interim measures.[185] In the practice of the Court, interim measures are indicated only in limited spheres. An order will be made only if there is an imminent risk of irreparable damage. Interim measures usually concern the right to life, the right not to be subjected to torture or inhuman treatment and, more exceptionally, the right to respect for private and family life.[186] By their very nature,

---

[180]   *Paladi v. Moldova* [GC], no. 39806/05, § 85, 10 March 2009.

[181]   *Amirov v. Russia*, no. 51857/13, § 62, 27 November 2014.

[182]   *Trabelsi v. Belgium*, no. 140/10, §§ 142–143, 4 September 2014.

[183]   *Al-Saadoon and Mufdhi v. the United Kingdom*, no. 61498/08, § 155, ECHR 2010 (extracts).

[184]   *Paladi v. Moldova* [GC], no. 39806/05, § 88, 10 March 2009; *Al-Saadoon and Mufdhi v. the United Kingdom*, no. 61498/08, § 161, ECHR 2010 (extracts).

[185]   *Paladi v. Moldova* [GC], no. 39806/05, § 92, 10 March 2009; *Al-Saadoon and Mufdhi v. the United Kingdom*, no. 61498/08, § 161, ECHR 2010 (extracts).

[186]   *Al-Saadoon and Mufdhi v. the United Kingdom*, no. 61498/08, § 160, ECHR 2010 (extracts); *Mamatkulov and Askarov v. Turkey* [GC], nos 46827/99 and 46951/99, § 104, ECHR 2005-I; *Paladi v. Moldova* [GC], no. 39806/05, § 86, 10 March 2009.

interim measures are ordered on the basis of a plausible assertion of a risk of irreparable damage. Later, as evidence is produced in the course of the proceedings, this may prove not to correspond to the reality. But '[i]t is precisely for the purpose of preserving the Court's ability to render such a judgment after an effective examination of the complaint that such measures are indicated'.[187] If subsequently it becomes evident that the interim measure may not have been required, this fact does not absolve the State for its failure to respect the order and thereby fulfil its obligations under article 34.[188] The respondent State has the onus to show compliance with the interim measures order or to explain 'that there was an objective impediment which prevented compliance and that the Government took all reasonable steps to remove the impediment and to keep the Court informed about the situation'.[189] The State is certainly not entitled to substitute its own judgment for that of the Court as to the legitimacy of the measures, or to decide on how and when they are to be complied with. A State that considers it has materials that justify cancelling the interim measure is to inform the Court accordingly.[190]

Declarations

When it ratified the Convention, Monaco made a declaration stating that it 'rules out any implication of its international responsibility with regard to Article 34 of the Convention, concerning any act or any decision, any fact or event prior to the entry into force of the Convention and its Protocols in respect of the Principality'.[191]

Further reading

Ronny Abraham, 'Article 25', in Pettiti et al., *La Convention européenne*, pp. 579–90.

Ledi Bianku, 'For Whom the Alarm Bells Ring?', (2012) 1 *Cyprus Human Rights Law Review* 42.

Clara Burbano-Herrera and Yves Haeck, 'Letting States off the Hook? The Paradox of the Legal Consequences following State Non-compliance with Provisional Measures in the Inter-American and European Human Rights Systems', [2010] *Netherlands Quarterly of Human Rights* 332.

Gérard Cohen-Jonathan, 'De l'effet juridique des "mesures provisoires" dans certaines circonstances et de l'efficacité du droit de recours individuels', [1991] *Revue universelle des droits de l'homme* 205.

Frowein/Peukert, *MenschenRechtsKonvention*, pp. 467–94.

Yves Haeck, Clara Burbano Herrera and Leo Zwaak, 'Strasbourg Takes Away any Remaining Doubts and Broadens its Pan-European Protection: Non-compliance with a Provisional Measure Automatically Leads to a Violation of the Right of Individual Application . . . or Doesn't It?', (2008) 4 *European Constitutional Law Review* 41.

Yves Haeck, Clara Burbano-Herrera, and Leo Zwaak, 'Strasbourg's Interim Measures Under Fire: Does the Rising Number of State Incompliances with Interim Measures Pose a Threat to the European Court of Human Rights?', (2008) 4 *European Constitutional Law Review* 41.

---

[187] *Paladi v. Moldova* [GC], no. 39806/05, § 89, 10 March 2009.
[188] *Salakhov and Islyamova v. Ukraine*, no. 28005/08, § 223, 14 March 2013; *Paladi v. Moldova* [GC], no. 39806/05, § 89, 10 March 2009.
[189] *Paladi v. Moldova* [GC], no. 39806/05, § 92, 10 March 2009.
[190] Ibid., § 90; *Olaechea Cahuas v. Spain*, no. 24668/03, § 70, ECHR 2006-X; *Tanrıkulu v. Turkey* [GC], no. 23763/94, § 131, ECHR 1999-IV; *Orhan v. Turkey*, no. 25656/94, § 409, ECHR 2002; *Kasymakhunov v. Russia*, no. 29604/12, § 182, 14 November 2013.
[191] (2005) 38 YB 8.

Yves Haeck, Clara Burbano-Herrera, and Leo Zwaak, 'Strasbourg's Interim Measures Under Fire: Does the Rising Number of State Incompliances with Interim Measures Pose a Threat to the European Court of Human Rights?', (2011) 11 *European Yearbook on Human Rights* 1.

V. Harby, 'The Changing Nature of Interim Measures before the European Court of Human Rights, (2010) 16 *EHRLR* 80.

Henrik Jorem, 'Protecting Human Rights in Cases of Urgency: Interim Measures and the Right of Individual Application under Article 34 ECHR', (2012) 30 *Nordic Journal of Human Rights* 404.

Helen Keller and C. Marti, 'Interim Measures Compared: Use of Interim Measures by the Un Human Rights Committee and the European Court of Human Rights', (2013) 73 *Heidelberg Journal of International Law* 2013.

Astrid Kjeldgaard-Pedersen, 'The Evolution of the Right of Individuals to Seise the European Court of Human Rights', (2010) 12 *Journal of the History of International Law* 267.

Philip Leach, *Taking a Case to the European Court of Human Rights*, London: Blackstone, 2001.

George Letsas, 'International Human Rights and the Binding Force of Interim Measures', (2003) 5 *EHRLR* 527.

R. St J. MacDonald, 'Interim Measures in International Law, with Special Reference to the European System for the Protection of Human Rights, (1992) 52 *Zeitschrift für ausländisches öffentliches Recht und Völkerrecht* 703.

Alastair Mowbray, 'A New Strasbourg Approach to the Legal Consequences of Interim Measures', (2005) 5 *HRLR* 377.

Christian J. Tams, 'Interim Orders by the European Court of Human Rights: Comments on *Mamatkulov and Abdurasulovic v. Turkey*', (2003) 63 *Zeitschrift für ausländisches öffentliches Recht und Völkerrecht* 681.

N. Vajić, '*Interim* Measures and the Mamatkulov Judgement of the European Court of Human Rights', in M. Kohen, ed., *Liber Amicorum Lucius Caflisch*, Leiden: Brill, 2007, pp. 601–22.

Leo Zwaak, 'The Procedure before the European Court of Human Rights', in Van Dijk et al., *Theory and Practice*, pp. 110–20.

Article 35. Admissibility criteria/Conditions de recevabilité

1. The Court may only deal with the matter after all domestic remedies have been exhausted, according to the generally recognised rules of international law, and within a period of six months[1] from the date on which the final decision was taken.

2. The Court shall not deal with any application submitted under Article 34 that

(a) is anonymous; or
(b) is substantially the same as a matter that has already been examined by the Court or has already been submitted to another procedure of international investigation or settlement and contains no relevant new information.

3. The Court shall declare inadmissible any individual application submitted under Article 34 if it considers that:

a) the application is incompatible with the provisions of the Convention or the Protocols thereto, manifestly ill-founded, or an abuse of the right of individual application; or
b) the applicant has not suffered a significant disadvantage, unless respect for human rights as defined in the Convention and the Protocols thereto requires an examination of the application on the merits and provided that no case may be rejected on this ground which has not been duly considered by a domestic tribunal.[2]

4. The Court shall reject any application which it considers inadmissible under this Article. It may do so at any stage of the proceedings.

1. La Cour ne peut être saisie qu'après l'épuisement des voies de recours internes, tel qu'il est entendu selon les principes de droit international généralement reconnus, et dans un délai de six mois à partir de la date de la décision interne définitive.

2. La Cour ne retient aucune requête individuelle introduite en application de l'article 34, lorsque

a) elle est anonyme; ou
b) elle est essentiellement la même qu'une requête précédemment examinée par la Cour ou déjà soumise à une autre instance internationale d'enquête ou de règlement, et si elle ne contient pas de faits nouveaux.

3. La Cour déclare irrecevable toute requête individuelle introduite en application de l'article 34 lorsqu'elle estime:

a) que la requête est incompatible avec les dispositions de la Convention ou de ses Protocoles, manifestement mal fondée ou abusive; ou
b) que le requérant n'a subi aucun préjudice important, sauf si le respect des droits de l'homme garantis par la Convention et ses Protocoles exige un examen de la requête au fond et à condition de ne rejeter pour ce motif aucune affaire qui n'a pas été dûment examinée par un tribunal interne.

4. La Cour rejette toute requête qu'elle considère comme irrecevable par application du présent article. Elle peut procéder ainsi à tout stade de la procédure.

---

[1] The words 'within a period of six months' are changed to 'within a period of four months', pursuant to article 4 of Protocol No. 15 amending the Convention for the Protection of Human Rights and Fundamental Freedoms, ETS 213, not yet in force.

[2] The words 'and provided that no case may be rejected on this ground which has not been duly considered by a domestic tribunal' are deleted pursuant to article 5 of Protocol No. 15, ibid., not yet in force.

Introductory comments

When the Convention organs were being first conceived, in the Consultative Assembly of the Council of Europe in August 1949, one of the architects of the European Convention on Human Rights, Pierre-Henri Teitgen, signalled the need for the enforcement mechanisms to have 'a kind of barrier—a practical necessity well known to all jurists—which would weed out frivolous or mischievous petitions'.[3] David Maxwell Fyfe spoke of the proposed European Commission of Human Rights acting as 'a sieve or filter to stop the Court from being flooded out by numerous petitions for vexatious reference to the Court. It will be for the Commission to say whether a case shall go to the Court. There is, therefore, a good answer to the criticism that the Court will be inundated with frivolous litigation.'[4] It is perhaps a little harsh to characterize the applications under the Convention with such words, even if many of them may be wide of the mark in a legal sense, perhaps because they have been prepared by victims who were well intentioned and genuinely aggrieved but not fully informed about the law. The lack of formalism in the requirements for formulation of an individual petition under article 34 has been explained by the Court's desire to encourage applications. At the same time, the requirement of exhaustion of domestic remedies in article 35 makes it highly probable that professionals have been involved in the case as it proceeds through the national courts prior to any submission to Strasbourg.

The vast majority of applications to the Convention organs have been and continue to be declared inadmissible. Some of the criteria reflect general principles of law such as the requirement that an application not be substantially the same as a matter that has already been examined by the Court or one that is also pending before another adjudicative body, and that domestic remedies have been exhausted. Others are more particular to the European human rights system, such as the rule by which the application must be filed within six months of the decision by which the victim has exhausted the domestic remedies.

Drafting of the provision

The initial draft European Convention on Human Rights was prepared by the International Juridical Section of the European Movement provided for the right of any natural or corporate person in the territory of a State party to petition the Council of Europe in respect of an infringement of fundamental rights. Such petitions were not to be considered 'until the internal juridical processes of the State concerned have been exhausted, provided that these function without unreasonable delay'.[5] The Draft Statute that was annexed to the Convention did not contemplate any particular admissibility phase as part of the proceedings.

The draft report of the Legal Committee, prepared by Pierre-Henri Teitgen, contained the following proposal for inclusion in the Convention: 'After all other means of redress

---

[3] Report of the Sitting [of the Consultative Assembly, 19 August 1949], I *TP* 38–154, at p. 48.

[4] Ibid., p. 112.

[5] Convention for the Collective Protection of Individual Rights and Democratic Liberties by the States, Members of the Council of Europe, and for the establishment of a European Court of Human Rights to ensure observance of the Convention, Doc. INF/5/E/R, I *TP* 296–303, at p. 298, art. 7(c).

within a State have been tried, any person, or corporate body, which claims to have been a victim of a violation of the Convention by one of the signatory States may petition the Commission in a request presented through legal channels.[6] The accompanying explanatory memorandum said:

The Commission shall not deal with an individual complaint until after the plaintiff has exhausted 'all other means of redress within a State'. Long practice in international procedure has defined the meaning of this expression as being resort to the ordinary legal channels to the exclusion, for example, of a request for retrial of the case.[7]

The draft provision and the explanatory memorandum he proposed were adopted by the Committee.[8] Presenting the Committee's Report to the plenary Consultative Assembly, Teitgen explained:

The Commission would have set aside all complaints which it considered to be irreceivable [sic] and obviously ill-founded, and would investigate the serious complaints. If it did not, by its own means, manage to solve the case, it would transmit the dossier to a court which, acting as a court of second instance, would pronounce judgment according to judicial procedure... We have added that the Commission, which is responsible in the first place for the procedure of guarantee, could not deal with a complaint by the victim until the plaintiff has exhausted all other means of redress within a State. This goes without saying.[9]

After some debate, the Consultative Assembly adopted the following provisions:

Article 12
After all other means of redress within a State have been tried, any person or corporate body, which claims to have been the victim of a violation of the Convention by one of the signatory States, may petition the Commission in a request presented through legal channels.

Article 14
The Commission shall reject petitions which are irregular or manifestly ill-founded.[10]

The Committee of Ministers referred the draft convention adopted by the Consultative Assembly to a Committee of Experts. In preparation for that body, the Secretariat of the Council of Europe assembled a review of the notion of exhaustion of domestic remedies.[11] The United Kingdom submitted a document it had prepared in the context of the drafting of the international covenant by the United Nations Commission on Human Rights:

The provision regarding the enforcement of the Covenant should be confined to complaints laid by Contracting States. His Majesty's Government do not consider that due attention has been paid to the practical difficulties to which the admission of individual petition would give rise. Thus it would be necessary to elaborate rules regarding the form and content of such petitions; to determine what would happen with regard to petitions submitted anonymously or under a *nom de plume*; to make

---

[6] Report presented by Mr P.H. Teitgen, 5 September 1949, Doc. A 290, I *TP* 192–213, at p. 210, art. 12.
[7] Ibid., p. 204.
[8] Ibid., p. 198. Also Report [of the Committee on Legal and Administrative Questions], 5 September 1949, Doc. AS (1) 77, I *TP* 216–39.
[9] Report of the Sitting [of the Consultative Assembly, 7 September 1949], I *TP* 250–95, at pp. 284, 288.
[10] Recommendation No. 38 to the Committee of Ministers adopted 8 September 1949 on the conclusion of the debates, Doc. AS (1) 108, II *TP* 274–83.
[11] Documents assembled by the Secretary General relating to the rule on the exhaustion of domestic remedies as known in general public international law in the context of the procedure known as diplomatic protection of nationals abroad, Doc. B 27, III *TP* 38–74.

clear that no immunity could be claimed by petitioners who disclosed State secrets, encouraged the overthrow of a government by force or uttered a malicious libel about an individual; and to prevent the submission of frivolous or malicious complaints. Constitutional problems of some complexity would be raised by petitions which appealed from the decision of the highest tribunal of a State. And above all, it would be likely to overburden the machinery established for the enforcement of the Covenant with trivial matters to the prejudice of important issues.[12]

The Committee of Experts was also presented with an amendment by the Norwegian representative: 'Before appealing to the Commission, all normal forms of redress must have been tried, in accordance with the general principles of international law. The Commission will itself decide whether it has competence to consider the case.'[13] The French representative proposed an amendment: 'The Commission will reject petitions which it considers to be irregular, under the provisions of Articles 11 and 12 and those which it considers to be manifestly unfounded.'[14] The two amendments were combined by the Drafting Sub-Committee of the Committee of Experts during its February meeting.[15] At the conclusion of the February meeting, the Committee of Experts adopted the following texts:

Article 16
The Commission may only be petitioned after all legal remedies within a State have been exhausted.

Article 17
The Commission shall reject any application which it considers irregular under the provisions of Articles 14 [inter-State petition], 15 [individual petition] and 16, and those which it considers to be manifestly ill-founded.[16]

The accompanying commentary noted:

With regard to the fear expressed by the Assembly concerning the large number of petitions which would be referred to the Commission, the Committee was of the opinion that the majority of these petitions would be irregular or manifestly ill-founded and that the Commission might easily make provision on its Rules of procedure to dispose of such affaires without needless less [sic] of time.[17]

When it met for its second session in March 1950, the Committee of Experts made minor changes to the two provisions. Article 16 was completed with the phrase 'according to the generally recognised rules of international law'. In article 17, the word 'irregular' was replaced by 'inadmissible'.[18] This was explained in the commentary:

The Committee has added to the text of the Assembly draft the words 'according to the generally reocgnised rules of international law' to indicate that, in order to decide whether all domestic legal

[12] Comments of Governments on the draft International Covenant on Human Rights and Measures of Implementation [UN Doc. E/CN.4/353/Add.1-3], Doc. A 770, III *TP* 156–79, at p. 172.

[13] Amendments to Article 12 of the Recommendation No. 38 of the Consultative Assembly presented by Mr Roed (Norway), 4 February 1950, Doc. A 789.

[14] Amendment to Article 14 of Recommendation No. 38 of the Consultative Assembly proposed by Mr Chaumont (France), 4 February 1950, Doc. A 793.

[15] Proposals of the Drafting Sub-Committee concerning Sections II and III, 6 February 1950, Doc. A 866.

[16] Preliminary Draft Convention for the Maintenance and Further Realisation of Human Rights and Fundamental Freedoms, 15 February 1950, Doc. A 833, III *TP* 236–46, at p. 242.

[17] Preliminary draft of the Report to the Committee of Ministers, 24 February 1950, Doc. CM/WP 1 (50) 1, A 847, III *TP* 246–79, at pp. 272–4.

[18] New text suggested for Sections II, III, and IV, Doc. CM/WP 1 (50) 4, A 917, III *TP* 294–302, at pp. 296–8.

remedies had been exhausted, it would be necessary to take into account the jurisprudence established in this respect, according to which cases where national tribunals improperly delay taking their decisions are considered as an exhaustion of legal remedies.[19]

It then developed a much more elaborate version of the second of the two articles:

1. The Commission shall not consider any application submitted under Article 21 (17) which
   (a) is anonymous;
   (b) is substantially the same as a previous application and contains no important new information.
2. The Commission shall reject any application which it considers inadmissible under article 22 (18) [for failure to exhaust domestic remedies].
3. The Commission shall reject any application submitted under Article 21 (17) [individual petitions], which it considers
   (a) incompatible with the provisions of the present Convention;
   (b) manifestly ill-founded.[20]

This subsequently underwent some minor revisions: in paragraph 1(b), 'important' was changed to 'relevant'; in paragraph 2, 'reject any application which it considers inadmissible' became 'consider inadmissible'.[21] In the commentary, the Committee said that it had replaced the shorter provision in the Assembly draft with 'a more detailed regulation of the methods of procedure which should enable the Commission to deal with the requests which were inadmissible or manifestly ill-founded without enquiry'. It explained that '[c]ertain members of the Committee had expressed doubt as to the possibility, from the legal point of view, of allowing the Commission the right to regulate these details in its rules of procedure'. The commentary also noted that the Committee had considered it desirable to distinguish between inter-State petitions and individual applications, 'in as much as the Commission should not be able to reject a petition from one of the High Contracting Parties without preliminary enquiry'.[22]

In June 1950, the Conference of Senior Officials of Human Rights developed a new draft in which the first of the two provisions, dealing with exhaustion, included a six-month time limit: 'The Commission may only deal with the matter after all domestic legal remedies have been exhausted according to the generally recognised rules of international law and only if the petition is made after six months from the final domestic decision.'[23] The text was subsequently revised: 'The Commission may only deal with the matter after all domestic legal remedies have been exhausted according to the generally recognised rules of international law and only if the petition is made after six months from the final domestic decision.'[24] The Report of the Conference explained the addition: 'The Conference considered it useful to fix a time-limit during which recourse to the Commission

---

[19] Amendments to the Report of the Committee, Doc. CM/WP 1 (50) 6, A 907, III *TP* 304–5.

[20] Preliminary Draft Convention, Doc. CM/WP 1 (50) 14, A 932, III *TP* 312–35, at p. 328.

[21] Draft Convention of Protection of Human Rights and Fundamental Freedoms, 16 March 1950, Doc. CM/WP 1 (50) 15 appendix, CM/WP 1 (50) 14 revised, A 925, IV *TP* 50–79, at p. 68.

[22] Report to the Committee of Ministers submitted by the Committee of Experts Instructed to Draw up a Draft Convention of Collective Guarantee of Human Rights and Fundamental Freedoms, 16 March 1950, Doc. CM/WP 1 (50) 15, A 924, IV *TP* 2–51, at p. 38.

[23] New draft Section III prepared by the Drafting Sub-Committee, Doc. CM/WP 4 (50) 11, A 1374, IV *TP* 194–9, at p. 196, art. f.

[24] Draft Convention appended to the draft report, Doc. CM/WP 4 (50) 16, appendix, A 1445, IV *TP* 218–40, at p. 230.

should be formulated, in accordance with the provision to this effect in Article 31, para. 2, of the General Act of Geneva.'[25] This was a reference to the General Act for the Pacific Settlement of International Disputes where a one-year time limit was set out.[26] The second provision, with the detailed rules on rejection of applications, was modified slightly by the addition of the words 'or an abuse of the right of application' after 'manifestly ill-founded'.[27]

On 24 June 1950, the Legal Committee of the Consultative Assembly wrote to the Committee of Ministers about the provision:

> The rule that all domestic remedies must first have been exhausted, and the power which the Commission of Human Rights is recognised to possess to reject *de plano* applications which it considers inadmissible, are sufficient to protect States against any risks of abuse. The Committee has, however, insisted on the maintenance of the proposal contained in Article 12 of the Recommendation of the Assembly, namely that applications must be made through legal channels, in its opinion, a necessary precaution to prevent the Committee [sic] of Human Rights from being inundated by a flood of irregular requests.[28]

The Committee of Ministers revised the second of the two provisions by adding a requirement concerning pending applications before other international dispute settlement mechanisms. The United Kingdom proposed a text that is the ancestor of article 55 of the Convention; it prevents States Parties from availing of other mechanisms than those set out in the Convention. The United Kingdom had signalled the need for a provision 'providing against the possibility of the submission of two complaints arising out of one incident to two systems of international settlement'. But since individuals and groups were not be bound by such a provision, as it applies only to States Parties, 'it would be necessary to add a further provision preventing the Commission from entertaining any question which has already been submitted to another international mode of settlement'.[29] The Sub-Committee of Human Rights of the Committee of Ministers settled on the following provisions:

Article 26
The Commission may only deal with the matter after all domestic remedies have been exhausted according to the generally recognised rules of international law and within a period of six months from the date on which the final decision was taken.

Article 27
1. The Commission shall not deal with any petition submitted under Article 25 which:
   (a) is anonymous;
   (b) is substantially the same as a matter which has already been examined by the Commission or has already been submitted to another procedure of international investigation or settlement and if it contains no relevant new information.

---

[25] Text of the report submitted by the Conference to the Committee of Ministers, Doc. CM/WP 4 (50) 19, CM/WP 4 (50) 16 rev., A 1431, IV *TP* 242–73, at p. 264.

[26] (1929) 93 LNTS 344, art. 31(2).

[27] New draft Section III prepared by the Drafting Sub-Committee, Doc. CM/WP 4 (50) 11, A 1374, IV *TP* 194–9, at p. 196, art. f; Draft Convention appended to the draft report, Doc. CM/WP 4 (50) 16, appendix, A 1445, IV *TP* 218–40, at p. 230.

[28] Letter of 24 June 1950 from Sir David Maxwell Fyfe, Chairman of the Committee on Legal and Administrative Questions, to the Chairman of the Committee of Ministers, Ref. D 280/3/50, Doc. CM (50) 29, V *TP* 32–41, at p. 346. Also Draft of a letter to the Chairman of the Committee of Ministers, Doc. AS/JA (50) 2, A 1579, V *TP* 10–15, at p. 10.

[29] Amendments proposed by the United Kingdom Delegation, Doc. CM 1 (50) 6, A 1867, V *TP* 66–71, at p. 70.

2. The Commission shall consider inadmissible any petition submitted under Article 25 which it considers incompatible with the provisions of the present Convention, manifestly ill-founded, or an abuse of the right of application.

3. The Commission shall reject any matter referred to it which it considers inadmissible under Article 26.[30]

In the Consultative Assembly, which convened in August 1950, a proposal to allow the Committee of Ministers to overrule an inadmissibility decision by the Commission[31] was not adopted. No changes were subsequently introduced to article 26 in the final version of the Convention adopted in Rome in November 1950. There were a few minor modifications to article 27 following a British proposal:[32] the word 'or' was added to paragraph 1(a) and the word 'petition' replaced 'application' in paragraphs 2 and 3.

Protocol No. 11 reformulated the admissibility criteria in articles 26 and 27 into a single provision, article 35. The Explanatory Report said that '[t]he admissibility criteria remain unchanged', and that the Court would henceforth exercise the 'effective filter function, as presently performed by the Commission'.[33] The new text read as follows:

Article 35—Admissibility criteria

1. The Court may only deal with the matter after all domestic remedies have been exhausted, according to the generally recognised rules of international law, and within a period of six months from the date on which the final decision was taken.

2. The Court shall not deal with any individual application submitted under Article 34 that:
   a. is anonymous; or
   b. is substantially the same as a matter that has already been examined by the Court or has already been submitted to another procedure of international investigation or settlement and contains no relevant new information.

3. The Court shall declare inadmissible any individual application submitted under Article 34 which it considers incompatible with the provisions of the Convention or the protocols thereto, manifestly ill-founded, or an abuse of the right of application.

4. The Court shall reject any application which it considers inadmissible under this Article. It may do so at any stage of the proceedings.[34]

According to the Explanatory Report on Protocol No. 11:

87. Paragraph 1 of Article 35 is derived from former Article 26 of the Convention and paragraphs 2 to 4 from former Article 27. The intention here is to continue practice based on the former Commission's Rules of Procedure. Grounds of inadmissibility, as they existed under the former system, have been left unchanged in order to provide the new Court with an effective filter mechanism. An application which is patently inadmissible can be so declared at the initial stage of the proceedings by a committee, as provided for in Article 28. The decision declaring an application inadmissible will be final. The decision on admissibility will, in most cases, be taken separately (see Article 29, second sentence).

---

[30] Draft Convention adopted by the Sub-Committee, Doc. CM 1 (50) 52, A 1884, V *TP* 76–99, at p. 86–8.

[31] Proposed by M. Lanning, Doc. AS/JA (2) 11, A 2320, VI *TP* 20–23 and Doc. AS/JA (2) 11 rev., A 2367, VI *TP* 22–25.

[32] Letter addressed 28 October 1950 by Mr Downing (United Kingdom) to Mr Robertson (Secretariat), CDH (70) 30, VI *TP* 286–91, at p. 290.

[33] Explanatory Report on Protocol No. 11, para. 41.

[34] Protocol No. 11 to the Convention for the Protection of Human Rights and Fundamental Freedoms, restructuring the control machinery established thereby, ETS 155, art. 1.

88. Paragraph 4 of Article 35 does not signify that a State is able to raise an admissibility question at any stage of the proceedings, if it could have been raised earlier. It is nevertheless important to stress that the Court will be able to reject an application at any stage of the proceedings—even without an oral hearing—if it finds the existence of one of the grounds of non- acceptance provided in Article 35 (see Article 29 of the Convention's former text).

89. Copies of all decisions declaring applications inadmissible should be transmitted to the States concerned for information.

Paragraph 3 of article 35 was amended by Protocol No. 14. It added the new admissibility requirement of 'significant damage' to sub-paragraph (b).[35] Introduction of the new criterion was not without controversy. The Parliamentary Assembly objected, arguing that the proposal was 'vague, subjective and liable to do the applicant a serious injustice, and would exclude only 1.6% of existing cases'. Moreover, 'it may have the unintentional effect of discriminating against female applicants to the Court, by, for example, putting a premium on financial disadvantages suffered'.[36] The Parliamentary Assembly said that if the Committee of Ministers insisted on the new provision, 'it would recommend that the Court be empowered to declare an application inadmissible if it is satisfied that the application has been duly examined by a domestic tribunal in accordance with the provisions of the Convention and the protocols thereto'.[37] This concern is reflected in the final phrase of the new provision. The Assembly noted that this element would encourage States to incorporate the Convention and its Protocols into their domestic legislation.

The Explanatory Report describes the scope of the amendment:

39. A new admissibility requirement is inserted in Article 35 of the Convention. The new requirement provides the Court with an additional tool which should assist it in concentrating on cases which warrant an examination on the merits, by empowering it to declare inadmissible applications where the applicant has not suffered a significant disadvantage and which, in terms of respect for human rights, do not otherwise require an examination on the merits by the Court. Furthermore, the new requirement contains an explicit condition to ensure that it does not lead to rejection of cases which have not been duly considered by a domestic tribunal. It should be stressed that the new requirement does not restrict the right of individuals to apply to the Court or alter the principle that all individual applications are examined on their admissibility. While the Court alone is competent to interpret the new admissibility requirement and decide on its application, its terms should ensure that rejection of cases requiring an examination on the merits is avoided. The latter will notably include cases which, notwithstanding their trivial nature, raise serious questions affecting the application or the interpretation of the Convention or important questions concerning national law.

According to the Explanatory Report,

the purpose of this amendment is to provide the Court with an additional tool which should assist it in its filtering work and allow it to devote more time to cases which warrant examination on the merits, whether seen from the perspective of the legal interest of the individual applicant or considered from the broader perspective of the law of the Convention and the European public

---

[35] Protocol No. 14 to the Convention for the Protection of Human Rights and Fundamental Freedoms, amending the control system of the Convention, ETS 194, art. 12.

[36] Draft Protocol No. 14 to the Convention for the Protection of Human Rights and Fundamental Freedoms amending the control system of the Convention, Opinion No. 251 (2004), Parliamentary Assembly, para. 11.

[37] Ibid., paras 11–12.

order to which it contributes. The new criterion therefore pursues the same aim as some other key changes introduced by this protocol and is complementary to them.[38]

The Explanatory Report explains that the introduction of the new criterion 'was considered necessary in view of the ever-increasing caseload of the Court. In particular, it is necessary to give the Court some degree of flexibility in addition to that already provided by the existing admissibility criteria, whose interpretation has become established in the case-law that has developed over several decades and is therefore difficult to change.'[39] The Report continues:

78. This is so because it is very likely that the numbers of individual applications to the Court will continue to increase, up to a point where the other measures set out in this protocol may well prove insufficient to prevent the Convention system from becoming totally paralysed, unable to fulfil its central mission of providing legal protection of human rights at the European level, rendering the right of individual application illusory in practice.

79. The new criterion may lead to certain cases being declared inadmissible which might have resulted in a judgment without it. Its main effect, however, is likely to be that it will in the longer term enable more rapid disposal of unmeritorious cases. Once the Court's Chambers have developed clear-cut jurisprudential criteria of an objective character capable of straightforward application, the new criterion will be easier for the Court to apply than some other admissibility criteria, including in cases which would at all events have to be declared inadmissible on another ground.

80. The main element contained in the new criterion is the question whether the applicant has suffered a significant disadvantage. These terms are open to interpretation (this is the additional element of flexibility introduced); the same is true of many other terms used in the Convention, including some other admissibility criteria. Like those other terms, they are legal terms capable of, and requiring, interpretation establishing objective criteria through the gradual development of the case-law of the Court.

81. The second element is a safeguard clause to the effect that, even where the applicant has not suffered a significant disadvantage, the application will not be declared inadmissible if respect for human rights as defined in the Convention or the protocols thereto requires an examination on the merits. The wording of this element is drawn from the second sentence of Article 37, paragraph 1, of the Convention where it fulfils a similar function in the context of decisions to strike applications out of the Court's list of cases.

82. A second safeguard clause is added to this first one. It will never be possible for the Court to reject an application on account of its trivial nature if the case has not been duly considered by a domestic tribunal. This clause, which reflects the principle of subsidiarity, ensures that, for the purposes of the application of the new admissibility criterion, every case will receive a judicial examination whether at the national level or at the European level.

83. The wording of the new criterion is thus designed to avoid rejection of cases warranting an examination on the merits. As was explained in paragraph 39 above, the latter will notably include cases which, notwithstanding their trivial nature, raise serious questions affecting the application or interpretation of the Convention or important questions concerning national law.

84. As explained in paragraph 67 above, it will take time for the Court's Chambers or Grand Chamber to establish clear case-law principles for the operation of the new criterion in concrete contexts. It is clear, having regard to the wording of Articles 27 and 28, that single-judge formations and committees will not be able to apply the new criterion in the absence of such guidance. In

---

[38] Explanatory Report on Protocol No. 14, para. 77.
[39] Ibid., para. 78.

accordance with Article 20, paragraph 2, second sentence, of this protocol, single-judge formations and committees will be prevented from applying the new criterion during a period of two years following the entry into force of this protocol.

Two changes to article 35 were introduced by Protocol No. 15, which is not yet in force. The time limit for submitting applications that was set at six months following the final domestic decision by the original 1950 version of the Convention is reduced to four months.[40] According to the Explanatory Report, '[t]he development of swifter communications technology, along with the time limits of similar length in force in the member States, argue for the reduction of the time limit'.[41] This provision will enter into force six months after the entry into force of the Protocol[42] 'in order to allow potential applicants to become fully aware of the new deadline'.[43] The amendment will not apply to applications in respect of which the final domestic decision was taken prior to entry into force of the Protocol.[44] Protocol No. 15 also amends article 35(3)(b)—containing the 'significant disadvantage' criterion introduced by Protocol No. 14—so as to remove the proviso that the case first be considered by a domestic tribunal.[45] According to the Explanatory Report, '[t]he requirement remains of examination of an application on the merits where required by respect for human rights. This amendment is intended to give greater effect to the maxim *de minimis non curat praetor.*'[46] Unlike the other amendment to article 35, there is no delay in the entry into force of this amendment 'in order not to delay the impact of the expected enhancement of the effectiveness of the system. It will therefore apply also to applications on which the admissibility decision is pending at the date of entry into force of the Protocol.'[47]

Analysis and interpretation

Admissibility must be determined as a preliminary condition for examination of the case on the merits. Most applications to the European Court of Human Rights are declared inadmissible based upon one or more of the grounds listed in article 35. The first paragraph of article 35 governs all applications to the Court, whether they are formulated by one State against another according to article 33 or by an individual pursuant to article 34. Paragraphs 2 and 3 only apply to individual applications.

Procedure concerning admissibility

The procedure for determination of admissibility is somewhat different, depending upon whether the Court is dealing with an inter-State application or an individual application. This is reflected not only in the relevant provisions of the Convention itself but also in the Rules of Court.

---

[40] Protocol No. 15 amending the Convention for the Protection of Human Rights and Fundamental Freedoms, art. 4.

[41] Explanatory Report on Protocol No. 15, para. 22.

[42] Protocol No. 15 amending the Convention for the Protection of Human Rights and Fundamental Freedoms, art. 8(3).

[43] Explanatory Report on Protocol No. 15, para. 21.

[44] Protocol No. 15 amending the Convention for the Protection of Human Rights and Fundamental Freedoms, art. 8(4).

[45] Ibid., art. 5.

[46] Ibid., para. 23.

[47] Ibid., para. 24.

An inter-State application must contain a statement on compliance with the admissibility criteria set out in article 35(1), that is, the exhaustion of domestic remedies and the six-month rule.[48] Upon receipt of the application, the President of the Court notifies the respondent State and assigns the case to one of the Sections.[49] The President of the Section constitutes a Chamber to hear the case and at the same time invites the respondent State to make submissions on the admissibility of the application.[50] Before ruling on admissibility, the Chamber or its President may request that the parties make additional written observations.[51] Once the written observations have been submitted, the Judge Rapporteur of the Chamber is to prepare a written report on admissibility.[52] A hearing will be held upon the request of one of the parties or by decision of the Chamber acting on its own motion.[53]

An individual application to the Court submitted in accordance with article 34 must contain a concise and legible statement on compliance with the first two of the listed admissibility criteria, namely exhaustion of domestic remedies and the six-month rule that is set out in article 35(1).[54] The application must also be accompanied by relevant information, and notably documents and decisions, relevant to the exhaustion of domestic remedies and the six-month rule.[55] The applicant must also provide copies of documents relating to any procedure of international investigation or settlement where appropriate.[56] An individual application is first considered by a single judge, who may rule on its admissibility if this can be done 'without further examination', in accordance with article 27(1) of the Convention, 'unless there is some special reason to the contrary'.[57] A very large number of applications are dismissed in this manner. If the single judge does not take such a decision, the judge is to forward the case either to a three-judge Committee for a determination of admissibility pursuant to article 28(1) or to a seven-judge Chamber acting pursuant to article 29.[58] If the committee takes no decision, article 29 dictates that the matter of admissibility be adjudicated by a seven-judge Chamber.[59] The Chamber may decide to take a distinct decision on admissibility, although there is a presumption in favour of joint rulings on both admissibility and merits. Should the Chamber agree on the bifurcated approach, it may also decide to hold a hearing, either at the request of a party or on its own motion, 'if it considers that the discharge of its functions under the Convention so requires'.[60]

Eventually, the issue of admissibility may come before the Grand Chamber pursuant to article 31, but only with respect to matters that have not been declared inadmissible by the Chamber.[61] The Grand Chamber has no authority to re-activate elements of an

---

[48] Rules of Court, Rule 46(d).
[49] Ibid., Rule 51(1).
[50] Ibid., Rule 51(3).
[51] Ibid., Rule 51(4).
[52] Ibid., Rule 48(1).
[53] Ibid., Rule 51(5).
[54] Ibid., Rule 47(1)(f).
[55] Ibid., Rule 47(3.1)(b).
[56] Ibid., Rule 47(3.1)(c).
[57] Ibid., Rules 49(1), 52A(1).
[58] Ibid., Rule 52A(3).
[59] Also ibid., Rule 53(6).
[60] Ibid., Rule 53(5).
[61] *Sisojeva and Others v. Latvia* (striking out) [GC], no. 60654/00, §§ 61–62, ECHR 2007-I.

application that have already been found to be inadmissible at an earlier stage in the proceedings. On the other hand, in accordance with article 35(4) the Grand Chamber may find a case inadmissible even at the merits stage, and thereby reconsider a ruling by the Chamber favouring admissibility.[62]

Rule 55 of the Rules of Court states that '[a]ny plea of inadmissibility must, in so far as its character and the circumstances permit, be raised by the respondent Contracting Party in its written or oral observations on the admissibility of the application...' The government that fails to do this may be estopped from challenging admissibility subsequently.[63] However, there are exceptional circumstances where this can be dispensed with, notably when the reason leading to the objection to admissibility only became known at a later stage.[64]

Exhaustion of domestic remedies (art. 35(1))

The first of the admissibility criteria listed in article 35 is the requirement that domestic remedies be exhausted. It is a rule that is to be applied with 'some degree of flexibility and without excessive formalism'.[65] The Grand Chamber has explained that:

the rule of exhaustion is neither absolute nor capable of being applied automatically; for the purposes of reviewing whether it has been observed, it is essential to have regard to the circumstances of the individual case. This means, in particular, that the Court must take realistic account not only of the existence of formal remedies in the legal system of the Contracting State concerned but also of the general context in which they operate, as well as the personal circumstances of the applicant. It must then examine whether, in all the circumstances of the case, the applicant did everything that could reasonably be expected of him or her to exhaust domestic remedies.[66]

The flexibility is justified by the fact that the rule of exhaustion of domestic remedies 'is being applied in the context of machinery for the protection of human rights'.[67]

In substance, the rule 'obliges applicants to use first the remedies that are available and sufficient in the domestic legal system to afford redress for the violation complained of'.[68] The purpose of the rule is to provide States with the opportunity to prevent or 'put right' the alleged violations before the matter is submitted to the international court.[69] As the

---

[62] *Gillberg v. Sweden* [GC], no. 41723/06, § 54, 3 April 2012; *Azinas v. Cyprus* [GC], no. 56679/00, § 32, ECHR 2004-III.

[63] *Andrejeva v. Latvia* [GC], no. 55707/00, §§ 49, 55, ECHR 2009; *Sergey Zolotukhin v. Russia* [GC], no. 14939/03, § 46, ECHR 2009; *Prokopovitch v. Russia*, no. 58255/00, § 29, ECHR 2004-XI; *K. and T. v. Finland* [GC], no. 25702/94, § 145, ECHR 2001-VII; *N.C. v. Italy* [GC], no. 24952/94, § 44, ECHR 2002-X.

[64] *Mooren v. Germany* [GC], no. 11364/03, § 57, 9 July 2009; *N.C. v. Italy* [GC], no. 24952/94, § 44, ECHR 2002-X; *Sejdovic v. Italy* [GC], no. 56581/00, § 41, ECHR 2006-II; *Lebedev v. Russia*, no. 4493/04, §§ 39–40, 25 October 2007.

[65] *Eberhard and M. v. Slovenia*, no. 8673/05 and 9733/05, § 104, 1 December 2009; *Scoppola v. Italy (no. 2)* [GC], no. 10249/03, § 69, 17 September 2009; *Fressoz and Roire v. France* [GC], no. 29183/95, § 37, ECHR 1999-I; *Azinas v. Cyprus* [GC], no. 56679/00, § 38, ECHR 2004-III; *Ankerl v. Switzerland*, 23 October 1996, § 34, *Reports of Judgments and Decisions* 1996-V.

[66] *D.H. and Others v. the Czech Republic* [GC], no. 57325/00, § 116, ECHR 2007-IV.

[67] *Aksoy v. Turkey*, 18 December 1996, § 53, *Reports of Judgments and Decisions* 1996-VI.

[68] *Mooren v. Germany* [GC], no. 11364/03, § 118, 9 July 2009; *Airey v. Ireland*, 9 October 1979, § 19, Series A no. 32; *Iatridis v. Greece* [GC], no. 31107/96, § 47, ECHR 1999-II; *Ilhan v. Turkey* [GC], no. 22277/93, § 58, ECHR 2000-VII.

[69] *Micallef v. Malta* [GC], no. 17056/06, § 55, ECHR 2009; *Ananyev and Others v. Russia*, nos 42525/07 and 60800/08, § 93, 10 January 2012; *Selmouni v. France* [GC], no. 25803/94, § 74, ECHR 1999-V; *E.S. v.*

European Commission explained in a very early case, '[t]he respondent State must first have an opportunity to redress by its own means within the framework of its own domestic legal system the wrong alleged to have been done to the individual'.[70] According to the Grand Chamber, '[t]he object of the rule on exhaustion of domestic remedies is to allow the national authorities (primarily the judicial authorities) to address the allegation made of violation of a Convention right and where appropriate, to afford redress before that allegation is submitted to the Court'.[71]

The requirement of article 35(1) has 'a close affinity' with article 13 in that both are based on the assumption 'that there is an effective remedy available to deal with the substance of an "arguable complaint" under the Convention and to grant appropriate relief'.[72] This is related to the principle that the Convention machinery is subsidiary to that of the national legal systems for the protection of human rights.[73] One practical reason for this is to enable the European Court to 'have the benefit of the views of the national courts, as being in direct and continuous contact with the forces of their countries'.[74]

The existence of the remedies must be sufficiently certain both in theory and in practice, failing which they will lack the requisite accessibility and effectiveness.[75] There is no obligation to have recourse to remedies that are inadequate or ineffective. It is incumbent on the respondent Government claiming non-exhaustion to indicate to the Court with sufficient clarity the remedies to which the applicants have not had recourse and to satisfy the Court that the remedies were effective and available in theory and in practice at the relevant time, that is to say that they were accessible, capable of providing redress in respect of the applicants' complaints, and offered reasonable prospects of success.[76] If a proposed remedy does not offer reasonable prospects of success, taking into account the domestic case law, then there is no need to exhaust this for a case to be admissible.[77] But although an

Sweden, no. 5786/08, § 43, 21 June 2012; *Remli v. France*, 23 April 1996, § 33, *Reports of Judgments and Decisions* 1996-II; *Scoppola v. Italy (no. 2)* [GC], no. 10249/03, § 69, 17 September 2009; *Varnava and Others v. Turkey* [GC], nos 16064/90, 16065/90, 16066/90, 16068/90, 16069/90, 16070/90, 16071/90, 16072/90, and 16073/90, § 164, ECHR 2009.

[70] *Nielsen v. Denmark*, no. 343/57, Commission decision of 2 September 1959, (1958–59) 2 YB 412, at p. 438.

[71] *Azinas v. Cyprus* [GC], no. 56679/00, § 38, ECHR 2004-III.

[72] *Ananyev and Others v. Russia*, nos 42525/07 and 60800/08, § 93, 10 January 2012; *Vallianatos and Others v. Greece* [GC], no. 29381/09 and 32684/09, § 51, ECHR 2013; *Kudła v. Poland* [GC], no. 30210/96, § 152, ECHR 2000-XI; *Hasan and Chaush v. Bulgaria* [GC], no. 30985/96, §§ 96–98, ECHR 2000-XI.

[73] *Ananyev and Others v. Russia*, nos 42525/07 and 60800/08, § 93, 10 January 2012; *Kudła v. Poland* [GC], no. 30210/96, § 152, ECHR 2000-XI; *Handyside v. the United Kingdom*, 7 December 1976, § 48, Series A no. 24; *Varnava and Others v. Turkey* [GC], nos 16064/90, 16065/90, 16066/90, 16068/90, 16069/90, 16070/90, 16071/90, 16072/90, and 16073/90, § 164, ECHR 2009; *Scoppola v. Italy (no. 2)* [GC], no. 10249/03, § 68, 17 September 2009; *Akdivar and Others v. Turkey*, 16 September 1996, § 65, *Reports of Judgments and Decisions* 1996-IV.

[74] *Burden v. the United Kingdom* [GC], no. 13378/05, § 42, ECHR 2008.

[75] *Scoppola v. Italy (no. 2)* [GC], no. 10249/03, § 70, 17 September 2009; *Sofri and Others v. Italy* (dec.), no. 37235/97, ECHR 2003-VIII; *Dalia v. France*, 19 February 1998, § 38, *Reports of Judgments and Decisions* 1998-I.

[76] *Mooren v. Germany* [GC], no. 11364/03, § 118, 9 July 2009; *McFarlane v. Ireland* [GC], § 107, 10 September 2010; *Akdivar and Others v. Turkey*, 16 September 1996, § 68, *Reports of Judgments and Decisions* 1996-IV; *Kleyn and Others v. the Netherlands* [GC], nos 39343/98, 39651/98, 43147/98, and 46664/99, § 156, ECHR 2003-VI; *Aksoy v. Turkey*, 18 December 1996, §§ 51–52, *Reports of Judgments and Decisions* 1996-VI; *Cennet Ayhan and Mehmet Salih Ayhan v. Turkey*, no. 41964/98, § 64–65, 27 June 2006; *Scoppola v. Italy (no. 2)* [GC], no. 10249/03, § 71, 17 September 2009; *Sejdovic v. Italy* [GC], no. 56581/00, § 46, ECHR 2006-II.

[77] *Pressos Compania Naviera S.A. and Others v. Belgium*, 20 November 1995, § 27, Series A no. 332; *Carson and Others v. the United Kingdom* [GC], no. 42184/05, § 58, ECHR 2010.

applicant need not pursue an evidently unproductive remedy, 'the existence of mere doubts as to the prospects of success of a particular remedy which is not obviously futile is not a valid reason for failing to exhaust domestic remedies'.[78]

The requirement of exhaustion is inapplicable 'where an administrative practice consisting of a repetition of acts incompatible with the Convention and official tolerance by the State authorities has been shown to exist, and is of such a nature as to make proceedings futile or ineffective'.[79] In some cases, the Court has found the remedies proposed by the government to be unreasonable or disproportionate, such as the suggestion that a special procedure be undertaken in reaction to administrative delays that had taken more than eighteen years.[80] In an inter-State case, the requirement of exhaustion of domestic remedies does not apply if it is a legislative or administrative practice that is being challenged by the applicant State. The latter cannot be expected to undertake its own litigation before the national courts of the respondent State.[81] This issue does not arise with individual applications because of the refusal to allow the *actio popularis*.

There is a certain sharing of the burden of proof in the exhaustion determination. Once the State has established the existence of a feasible remedy,[82] the burden of proof shifts to the applicant to show that the remedy proposed by the State was exhausted or was inadequate and ineffective or that there were special circumstances making it unnecessary to meet this requirement.[83] Of course, the applicant must first have submitted the complaint, at least in substance, to the appropriate national tribunal in respecting all of the formalities, including time limits.[84] Even when the domestic tribunals dismiss the case for failure to observe certain technical rules, if they have considered the substance of the complaint then the exhaustion requirement will be satisfied.[85] Domestic law may provide two or more potentially effective remedies to deal with the issue. An applicant need make

---

[78] *Scoppola v. Italy (no. 2)* [GC], no. 10249/03, § 70, 17 September 2009; *Brusco v. Italy* (dec.), no. 69789/01, ECHR 2001-IX; *Sardinas Albo v. Italy* (dec.), no. 56271/00, ECHR 2004-I; *Epözdemir v. Turkey* (dec.), no. 57039/00, 31 January 2002; *Milošević v. the Netherlands* (dec.), no. 77631/01, 19 March 2002; *Whiteside v. the United Kingdom*, no. 20357/92, Commission decision of 7 March 1994, DR 76, p. 80.

[79] *Aksoy v. Turkey*, 18 December 1996, § 52, *Reports of Judgments and Decisions* 1996-VI; *Akdivar and Others v. Turkey*, 16 September 1996, §§ 66–67, *Reports of Judgments and Decisions* 1996-IV.

[80] *Veriter v. France*, no. 31508/07, § 59, 14 October 2010. Also *Vaney v. France*, no. 53946/00, § 53, 30 November 2004.

[81] *Greece v. the United Kingdom*, no. 176/56, Commission decision of 2 June 1956, (1958–59) 2 YB 182; *Ireland v. the United Kingdom*, nos 5310/71 and 5451/72, Commission decision of 1 October 1972, 15 YB 80, at p. 242.

[82] *Dalia v. France*, 19 February 1998, § 38, *Reports of Judgments and Decisions* 1998-I; *McFarlane v. Ireland* [GC], no. 31333/06, § 107, 10 September 2010.

[83] *Mooren v. Germany* [GC], no. 11364/03, § 118, 9 July 2009; *Akdivar and Others v. Turkey*, 16 September 1996, § 68, *Reports of Judgments and Decisions* 1996-IV; *Kleyn and Others v. the Netherlands* [GC], nos 39343/98, 39651/98, 43147/98, and 46664/99, § 156, ECHR 2003-VI.

[84] *Zarb Adami v. Malta* (dec.), no. 17209/02, 24 May 2005; *Merger and Cros v. France* (dec.), no. 68864/01, 11 March 2004; *Cardot v. France*, 19 March 1991, § 36, Series A no. 200; *Le Compte v. Belgium*, no. 6878/75, Commission decision of 6 October 1976, (1977) 20 YB 254, DR 6, p. 79; *T. v. Switzerland*, no. 18079/91, Commission decision of 4 December 1991, DR 72, p. 263.

[85] *Voggenreiter v. Germany* (dec.), no. 47169/99, 28 November 2002; *Verein gegen Tierfabriken Schweiz (VgT) v. Switzerland (no. 2)* [GC], no. 32772/02, §§ 43–45, ECHR 2009; *Huber v. Switzerland*, no. 12794/87, Commission decision of 9 July 1988, DR 57, p. 259; *Chammas v. Switzerland*, no. 35438/97, Commission decision of 30 May 1997; *Jamal-Aldin v. Switzerland*, no. 19959/92, Commission decision of 23 May 1996; *Thaler v. Austria* (dec.), no. 58141/00, 15 September 2003; *Atik v. Germany* (dec.), no. 67500/01, 13 May 2004.

use of only one of them.[86] The applicant cannot be required to exercise a legal remedy that would have been directed to essentially the same end as the one he or she pursued and that had no better chance of success.[87]

Article 35(1) specifies that the domestic remedies be exhausted 'according to the generally recognised rules of international law'. This is one of only four references to international law in the Convention and its Protocols.[88] The reference to 'generally recognised rules of international law' may have seemed useful to the drafters of the Convention, who obviously thought it important to add some precision to the general notion of exhaustion of domestic remedies. Similar rules can be found in the other international human rights treaties.[89] In one of its very early rulings, the European Commission noted, but without citing any authority, that 'the generally recognised rules of international law required the Applicant to exhaust not merely the remedies in the ordinary Courts but the whole system of legal remedies available in the Republic'.[90] In one of its very early rulings, the Court noted 'a long established international practice from which the Convention has definitely not departed' of admitting waiver by the State of the exhaustion rule. In that decision, the Court specifically referred to the reference to 'generally recognised rules of international law' in the Convention.[91] In another, it noted with respect to the exhaustion rule and the reference to rules of international law that 'international courts have on various occasions held that international law cannot be applied with the same regard for matters of form as is sometimes necessary in the application of national law'.[92] In some of the early case law there were rare and essentially perfunctory references to rulings on the issue of exhaustion from the International Court of Justice,[93] the Permanent Court of

---

[86] *Aquilina v. Malta* [GC], no. 25642/94, § 39, ECHR 1999-III; *Moreira Barbosa v. Portugal* (dec.), no. 65681/01, 29 April 2004; *Jeličić v. Bosnia and Herzegovina* (dec.), no. 41183/02, 15 November 2005; *Wójcik v. Poland*, no. 26757/95, Commission decision of 7 July 1997, DR 90, p. 24; *Günaydin v. Turkey* (dec.), no. 27526/95, 25 April 2002.

[87] *Mooren v. Germany* [GC], no. 11364/03, § 118, 9 July 2009; *Iatridis v. Greece* [GC], no. 31107/96, § 47, ECHR 1999-II; *Miailhe v. France (no. 1)*, 25 February 1993, § 27, Series A no. 256-C; *Micallef v. Malta* [GC], no. 17056/06, § 58, ECHR 2009; *Kozacıoğlu v. Turkey* [GC], no. 2334/03, § 40, 19 February 2009; *Riad and Idiab v. Belgium*, nos 29787/03 and 29810/03, § 84, 24 January 2008; *Jasinskis v. Latvia*, no. 45744/08, §§ 50–54, 21 December 2010.

[88] International law is also referred to in articles 7(1) and 15(1) of the European Convention and article 1 of Protocol No. 1.

[89] International Covenant on Civil and Political Rights, (1976) 999 UNTS 171, art. 41(1)(c); Optional Protocol to the International Covenant on Civil and Political Rights, (1976) 999 UNTS 171, arts. 2, 5(2)(b); American Convention on Human Rights, (1978) 1144 UNTS 123, art. 46; African Charter on Human and Peoples' Rights, arts 50, 56(5). See also Rome Statute of the International Criminal Court, (2002) 2187 UNTS 90, art. 17.

[90] *Lawless v. Ireland*, no. 332/57, Commission report of 19 December 1959, p. 37; *Lawless v. Ireland*, no. 332/57, Commission decision of 30 August 1958, (1958–59) 2 YB 308.

[91] *De Wilde, Ooms, and Versyp v. Belgium*, 18 June 1971, § 55, Series A no. 12.

[92] *Ringeisen v. Austria*, 16 July 1971, § 89, Series A no. 13.

[93] *Interhandel Case (Switzerland v. the United States)*, Judgment, I.C.J. Reports 1959, p. 6, at p. 29. See *Austria v. Italy*, no. 788/60, Commission decision of 11 January 1961, (1961) 4 YB 116, at p. 148; *Retimag SA v. Federal Republic of Germany*, no. 712/60, Commission decision of 16 December 1961, (1961) 4 YB 384, at p. 400; *Ringeisen. v. Austria*, no. 2614/65, Commission decision of 18 July 1968, (1968) 11 YB 268; *Fifty-five inhabitants of Louvain and Environs v. Belgium*, no. 1994/63, Commission decision of 5 March 1964, (1964) 7 YB 252, at p. 260. More recent decisions of the International Court of Justice dealing with exhaustion of domestic remedies (*Barcelona Traction, Light and Power Company, Limited*, Judgment, I.C.J. Reports 1970, p. 3, at p. 26; *Elettronica Sicula S.P.A. (ELSI)*, Judgment, I.C.J. Reports 1989, p. 15, paras 56–63) have not been cited by the European Court of Human Rights.

International Justice[94] and arbitral tribunals,[95] as well as to resolutions of the Institut de droit international.[96] Such references to international authorities has long been without any particular relevance, given that the international tribunal with the richest case law on the subject is without any doubt the European Court of Human Rights itself.

There is a formulaic phrase in some of the judgments stating that 'according to the "generally recognised rules of international law", there may be special circumstances which absolve applicants from the obligation to exhaust the domestic remedies at their disposal'.[97] In fact, the Court does not draw upon international law in this context. An example of such special circumstances would be the situation where the national authorities fail to act on serious allegations of misconduct by State agents. Then, 'the burden of proof shifts once again, so that it becomes incumbent on the respondent Government to show what they have done in response to the scale and seriousness of the matters complained of'.[98]

The remedies referred to in paragraph 1 are domestic, as opposed to international. International remedies are addressed under paragraph 2 of article 35, where admissibility is contingent on an option for the European Court should the applicant have two or more possibilities to choose from. Within the context of both provisions, disputes may arise as to whether a remedy is in fact domestic or international. The Court will make its determination in light of the legal character of the instrument founding the body, but also the body's composition, its competence, its place (if any) in an existing legal system, and its funding. It held that the Human Rights Chamber in Bosnia and Herzegovina, which was a creation of the 1995 Dayton Agreement and was comprised of several 'international' judges, was nevertheless part of the national legal order and therefore a 'domestic remedy' contemplated by article 35(1) rather than a 'procedure of international investigation or settlement' within the meaning of article 35(2)(b).[99]

Most European States provide for the constitutional protection of human rights. In those circumstances, the applicant is required to test the extent of that protection. In a common law system, rights are often developed by the domestic court through

---

[94] *The Panevezys-Saldutiskis Railway*, Series A/B no. 75 (cited in *Austria v. Italy*, no. 788/60, Commission decision of 11 January 1961, (1961) 4 YB 116, at pp. 148, 172 and *Retimag SA v. Federal Republic of Germany*, no. 712/60, Commission decision of 16 December 1961, (1961) 4 YB 384, at p. 400).

[95] *The Ambatielos Claim (Greece, United Kingdom of Great Britain, and Northern Ireland)*, (1956) 12 *Reports of International Arbitral Awards* 83, at p. 118 (cited in *Retimag SA v. Federal Republic of Germany*, no. 712/60, Commission decision of 16 December 1961, (1961) 4 YB 384, at p. 400; *Cardot v. France*, 19 March 1991, § 34, Series A no. 200); *Finnish Ships case (Finland v. the United Kingdom)*, (1934) 3 *Reports of International Arbitral Awards* 1479 (cited in *Retimag SA v. Federal Republic of Germany*, no. 712/60, Commission decision of 16 December 1961, (1961) 4 YB 384, at p. 400).

[96] Resolution adopted by the Institut de droit international at Grenada, 1956 (cited in *Austria v. Italy*, no. 788/60, Commission decision of 11 January 1961, (1961) 4 YB 116, at p. 172; *Retimag SA v. Federal Republic of Germany*, no. 712/60, Commission decision of 16 December 1961, (1961) 4 YB 384, at p. 400; and *Fifty-five inhabitants of Louvain and Environs v. Belgium*, no. 1994/63, Commission decision of 5 March 1964, (1964) 7 YB 252, at p. 260). Generally on this subject, see John Dugard, 'Diplomatic Protection', in Rüdiger Wolfrum, ed., *the Max Planck Encyclopedia of Public International Law*, Vol. III, Oxford: Oxford University Press, 2012, pp. 114–34, at pp. 125–7.

[97] *Scoppola v. Italy (no. 2)* [GC], no. 10249/03, § 70, 17 September 2009; *Aksoy v. Turkey*, 18 December 1996, § 52, *Reports of Judgments and Decisions* 1996-VI; *Öcalan v. Turkey* [GC], no. 46221/99, § 67, ECHR 2005-IV; *Van Oosterwijck v. Belgium*, 6 November 1980, §§ 36–41, Series A no. 40.

[98] *Selmouni v. France* [GC], no. 25803/94, § 76, ECHR 1999-V.

[99] *Jeličić v. Bosnia and Herzegovina* (dec.), no. 41183/02, 15 November 2005.

interpretation, notably by declaratory action.[100] The role of constitutional remedies depends on the law of the national jurisdiction, where it is difficult to make too many generalizations. In Italy, there is no direct access to the Constitutional Court by an individual litigant. The latter must raise constitutional issues before the regular courts, failing which the application to the European Court may be deemed inadmissible on the exhaustion ground.[101] Exceptionally, a constitutional remedy might be deemed effective where the impugned decision of the domestic courts was one that directly applied an unconstitutional provision of the national law.[102] As a general rule, resort to discretionary or extraordinary remedies as part of the exhaustion of domestic remedies is not expected of applicants.[103]

What is important is that the complaint be raised 'at least in substance',[104] although the Convention itself need not necessarily be invoked at the domestic level. In cases filed by Greek Cypriots against Turkey regarding property in the occupied zone of the island, the Court rejected an argument from Cyprus, which intervened in the proceedings pursuant to article 36. Cyprus contended that 'property owners who had not voluntarily submitted to the jurisdiction of Turkey could not be required to use Turkish remedies in respect of acts which were in violation of their rights outside Turkey's lawful jurisdiction'. It argued that to do otherwise would suggest that 'the aggressor would be treated as if it had the power to abrogate private rights and create new legal procedures; it was thus contrary to principle to insist that victims of an illegal armed invasion must first exhaust procedures imposed on them by the invader'.[105] The Grand Chamber held that 'there is no direct, or automatic correlation of the issue of recognition of the "[Turkish Republic of Northern Cyprus]" and its purported assumption of sovereignty over northern Cyprus on an international plane and the application of Article 35 § 1 of the Convention'.[106]

Where the procedural law imposed a fine upon the losing party in an application to revise a judgment, even where no misconduct or abuse was alleged or present, the European Court considered this to be incompatible with article 35(1).[107]

Normally, the Court will assess the issue of exhaustion as of the date when the application is filed with the Court, but this rule is subject to exceptions if new remedies are created.[108]

---

[100] *A, B, and C v. Ireland* [GC], no. 25579/05, § 142, ECHR 2010; *Patrick Holland v. Ireland*, no. 24827/94, Commission decision of 14 April 1998, (1998) 41 YB 90, DR 93, p. 15; *Independent News and Media and Independent Newspapers Ireland Limited v. Ireland* (dec.), no. 55120/00, 19 June 2003; *D v. Ireland* (dec.), no. 26499/02, 28 June 2006.

[101] *Scoppola v. Italy (no. 2)* [GC], no. 10249/03, § 75, 17 September 2009; *Brozicek v. Italy*, 19 December 1989, § 34, Series A no. 167; *C.I.G.L. and Cofferati v. Italy*, no. 46967/07, § 48, 24 February 2009.

[102] *Szott-Medyńska v. Poland* (dec.), no. 47414/99, 9 October 2003; *Pachla v. Poland* (dec.), no. 8812/02, 8 November 2005.

[103] *Kiiskinen v. Finland* (dec.) no. 26323/95, ECHR 1999-V; *Prystavska v. Ukraine*, no. 21287/02, 17 December 2002.

[104] *Castells v. Spain*, 23 April 1992, § 32, Series A no. 236; *Ahmet Sadık v. Greece*, 15 November 1996, § 33, *Reports of Judgments and Decisions* 1996-V; *Fressoz and Roire v. France* [GC], no. 29183/95, §§ 40–41, ECHR 1999–1; *Azinas v. Cyprus* [GC], no. 56679/00, §§ 40–41, ECHR 2004-III.

[105] *Demopoulos and Others v. Turkey* (dec.) [GC], nos 46113/99, 3843/02, 13751/02, 13466/03, 10200/04, 14163/04, 19993/04, and 21819/04, § 101, ECHR 2010.

[106] Ibid., § 100.

[107] *Prencipe v. Monaco*, no. 43376/06, § 96, 16 July 2009.

[108] *Demiroğlu and Others v. Turkey* (dec.), no. 56125/10, 4 June 2013; *Demopoulos and Others v. Turkey* (dec.) [GC], nos 46113/99, 3843/02, 13751/02, 13466/03, 10200/04, 14163/04, 19993/04, and 21819/04, § 87, ECHR 2010; *Baumann v. France*, no. 33592/96, § 47, ECHR 2001-V; *Brusco v. Italy* (dec.), no. 69789/

Six-month rule (art. 35(1))

The Court may only deal with a case 'within a period of six months from the date on which the final decision was taken'. Protocol No. 15, not yet in force, amends article 35(1), reducing the time limit from six months to four.[109] As legal time limits go with respect to challenging adverse decisions in the course of litigation, even four months is rather generous. The object of the Convention's time limit is to promote legal certainty and security of the law, thereby ensuring 'that cases raising issues under the Convention are dealt with in a reasonable time and that past decisions are not continually open to challenge'.[110] Because the six-month time limit serves such interests, it cannot be waived by the State. The Court will enforce the rule even if the State has not made a preliminary objection on the point.[111] It also 'protect[s] the authorities and other persons concerned from being under uncertainty for a prolonged period of time'.[112] Furthermore, '[t]he rule also affords the prospective applicant time to consider whether to lodge an application and, if so, to decide on the specific complaints and arguments to be raised'.[113] The six-month time limit 'marks out the temporal limits of supervision carried out by the organs of the Convention and signals to both individuals and State authorities the period beyond which such supervision is no longer possible'.[114] According to the Court, 'the purpose of limitations *ratione temporis* is to preclude the possibility of submitting to the Court, by means of an application, facts dating from a period when the respondent State was not in a position to foresee the international responsibility or legal proceedings to which these facts might give rise'.[115] Judgments of the Court have also said that the six-month rule 'ensures that, insofar as possible, matters are examined while they are still fresh, before the passage of time makes it difficult to ascertain the pertinent facts and renders a fair examination of the question at issue almost impossible'.[116] In cases 'where time is of the essence', there is a burden on the applicant to ensure that his or her claims are raised

---

01, ECHR 2001-IX; *Andrášik and Others v. Slovakia* (dec.), nos 57984/00, 60226/00, 60237/00, 60242/00, 60679/00, 60680/00, and 68563/01, ECHR 2002-IX; *İçyer v. Turkey* (dec.) no. 18888/02, ECHR 2006-I.

[109] Protocol No. 15 amending the Convention for the Protection of Human Rights and Fundamental Freedoms, art. 4.

[110] *Varnava and Others v. Turkey* [GC], nos 16064/90, 16065/90, 16066/90, 16068/90, 16069/90, 16070/90, 16071/90, 16072/90, and 16073/90, § 156, ECHR 2009; *Walker v. the United Kingdom* (dec.), no. 34979/97, ECHR 2000-I.

[111] *Blečić v. Croatia* [GC], no. 59532/00, § 67, ECHR 2006-III; *Belaousof and Others v. Greece*, no. 66296/01, § 38, 27 May 2004; *Walker v. the United Kingdom* (dec.), no. 34979/97, ECHR 2000-I; *Šilih v. Slovenia* [GC], no. 71463/01, § 139, 9 April 2009; *Benet Praha, Spol S.R.O. v. Czech Republic* (dec.), no. 38354/06, 28 September 2010.

[112] *P.M. v. the United Kingdom* (dec.), no. 6638/03, 24 August 2004.

[113] *O'Loughlin and Others v. the United Kingdom* (dec.), no. 23274/04, 25 August 2005. Also *Worm v. Austria*, 29 August 1997, § 32, *Reports of Judgments and Decisions* 1997-V; *Edwards v. the United Kingdom* (dec.), 46477/99, 7 June 2001.

[114] *Varnava and Others v. Turkey* [GC], nos 16064/90, 16065/90, 16066/90, 16068/90, 16069/90, 16070/90, 16071/90, 16072/90, and 16073/90, § 156, ECHR 2009; *Walker v. the United Kingdom* (dec.), no. 34979/97, ECHR 2000-I; *Di Giorgio and Others v. Italy* (dec.), no. 35808/03, 29 September 2009; *Cheilas v. Greece* (dec.), no. 9693/03, 12 May 2005.

[115] *Varnava and Others v. Turkey* [GC], nos 16064/90, 16065/90, 16066/90, 16068/90, 16069/90, 16070/90, 16071/90, 16072/90, and 16073/90, § 157, ECHR 2009; *Dennis and Others v. the United Kingdom* (dec.), no. 76573/01, 2 July 2002; *Blečić v. Croatia* [GC], no. 59532/00, § 68, ECHR 2006-III.

[116] *Williams v. the United Kingdom* (dec.), no. 32567/06, 17 February 2009; *Baybora and Others v. Cyprus* (dec.), no. 77116/01, 22 October 2002; *Denisov v. Russia* (dec.), no. 33408/03, 6 May 2004; *Kelly v. the United Kingdom*, no. 10626/83, Commission decision of 7 May 1985.

before the Court with the necessary expedition to ensure that they may be properly, and fairly, resolved'.[117]

The six-month period begins when the domestic remedies have been exhausted.[118] The operative date (the *dies a quo*) should be when the parties are in a position to know the full content of the decision and not just the conclusions or the result.[119] In establishing the date of the final decision in order to determine when the six-month period starts, the Court relies upon national procedural law. For example, where the domestic law clearly and expressly provides that a litigant is entitled to be served with a written copy of a final judgment as a condition for its validity, the six-month period to file an application will only begin when this has taken place.[120] The applicant cannot contend that he or she was not specifically informed if the lawyer had been made aware of the contents of the judgment.[121] The legal representative, and the applicant, must show due diligence in obtaining the judgment.[122]

The applicant is only required to undertake remedies that are likely to be effective and sufficient, a matter discussed above in this chapter with respect to the requirement of exhaustion of domestic remedies. The applicant cannot prolong or delay the six-month time limit by filing appeals or similar proceedings that have no hope of success.[123] In a case against the United Kingdom, after losing an appeal to the Court of Appeal the applicant then filed yet another appeal to the House of Lords. However, the House of Lords was without jurisdiction and this final appeal was futile and to no avail. The Court held that the six months began to run with the judgment of Court of Appeal rather than the final dismissal by the House of Lords. '[A]n applicant cannot extend the strict time-limit imposed under the Convention by seeking to make inappropriate or misconceived applications to bodies or institutions which have no power or competence to offer effective redress for the complaint in issue under the Convention', said the Court.[124] Similar principles apply with respect to extraordinary remedies, retrial, and other procedural mechanisms,[125] as well as remedies that depend upon administrative discretion.[126] These are not required by the rule of exhaustion of domestic remedies and therefore do

---

[117] *El Masri v. 'the former Yugoslav Republic of Macedonia'* [GC], no. 39630/09, § 134, ECHR 2012; *Varnava and Others v. Turkey* [GC], nos 16064/90, 16065/90, 16066/90, 16068/90, 16069/90, 16070/90, 16071/90, 16072/90, and 16073/90, § 160, ECHR 2009.

[118] *Kadiÿis v. Latvia (no. 2)* (dec.), no. 62393/00, 25 September 2003.

[119] *Perry v. Latvia* (dec.), no. 30273/03, 18 January 2007; *Papachelas v. Greece* [GC], no. 31423/96, § 30, ECHR 1999-II; *Z.Y. v. Turkey* (dec.), no. 27532/95, 19 June 2001; *Haralambidis and Others v. Greece*, no. 36706/97, § 38, 29 March 2001; *Käns and Others v. Latvia* (dec.), no. 57823/00, 9 October 2003. But see *Koç and Tosun v. Turkey* (dec.), no. 23852/04, §§ 6–9, 13 November 2008.

[120] *Worm v. Austria*, 29 August 1997, §§ 32–34, *Reports of Judgments and Decisions* 1997-V.

[121] *Çelik v. Turkey* (dec.), no. 52991/99, 23 September 2004; *Keskin and Others v. Turkey* (dec.), no. 36091/97, 7 September 1999; *Bölükbaş and Others v. Turkey* (dec.), no. 37793/97, 12 October 1999; *Pejic v. Croatia* (dec.), no. 66894/01, 19 December 2002; *Martinus Godefridus Aarts v. the Netherlands*, no. 14056/88, Commission decision of 28 May 1991, DR 70, p. 208.

[122] *Ölmez v. Turkey* (dec.), no. 39464/98, 1 February 2005 (revised by *Ölmez v. Turkey* (dec.), no. 39464/98, 5 July 2005.

[123] *Şahmo v. Turkey* (dec.), no. 37415/97, 1 April 2003; *Moyo Alvarez v. Spain* (dec.), no. 44677/98, 23 November 1999.

[124] *Fernie v. the United Kingdom* (dec.), no. 14881/04, 5 January 2006.

[125] *Williams v. the United Kingdom* (dec.), no. 32567/06, 17 February 2009; *Galstyan v. Armenia*, no. 26986/03, § 39, 15 November 2007; *Denisov v. Russia* (dec.), no. 33408/03, 6 May 2004.

[126] *Tumilovich v. Russia* (dec.), no. 47033/99, 2 June 1999; *Gurepka v. Ukraine*, no. 61406/00, § 60, 6 September 2005.

not interrupt the six-month time limit.[127] The Court is not impressed by the claim of a self-represented litigant alleging ignorance of the scope and modalities of available domestic remedies.[128]

In some circumstances, it will be clear from the outset that there is no effective remedy available to the applicant. In such cases, the six-month period starts to run from the date of the acts or measures complained of, or from the date of knowledge of that act or its effect on, or prejudice to, the applicant.[129] An applicant may proceed to exhaust domestic remedies only to become aware subsequently that the mechanism is ineffective. Under such circumstances, it may be appropriate to take the start of the six-month period from the date when the applicant first became or ought to have become aware of those circumstances.[130]

The Court considers that the time limit is interrupted when the applicant sends an initial letter indicating an intention to lodge an application that provides some indication of the nature of the application.[131] Nevertheless, the applicant must then proceed with diligence in providing further information about the application and in submitting the application form.[132] As the Court has noted, '[i]t would be contrary to the spirit and aim of the six-month rule if, by any initial communication, an application could set into motion the proceedings under the Convention and then remain inactive for an unexplained and unlimited length of time'.[133] The Court will therefore 'examine the particular circumstances of the case to determine what date should be regarded as the date of introduction with a view to calculating the running of the six month period imposed by Article 35 of the Convention'.[134] Among the factors that it will consider are the originality of the complaint and the need for legal research to be conducted, the overall complexity of the case, and the number of parties involved.[135] The time limit is calculated in calendar months. It starts to run the day following the final decision, and expires on the same day of the month six months later. Unlike the situation in some domestic systems, there is no rule at the Court whereby if the final day falls on a weekend or a holiday this is not counted and the time limit expires on the next working day.[136]

---

[127] *Williams v. the United Kingdom* (dec.), no. 32567/06, 17 February 2009; *Galstyan v. Armenia*, no. 26986/03, § 39, 15 November 2007.

[128] *Fernie v. the United Kingdom* (dec.), no. 14881/04, 5 January 2006.

[129] *Varnava and Others v. Turkey* [GC], nos 16064/90, 16065/90, 16066/90, 16068/90, 16069/90, 16070/90, 16071/90, 16072/90, and 16073/90, § 157, ECHR 2009; *Dennis and Others v. the United Kingdom* (dec.), no. 76573/01, 2 July 2002; *O'Loughlin and Others v. the United Kingdom* (dec.), no. 23274/04, 25 August 2005.

[130] *Varnava and Others v. Turkey* [GC], nos 16064/90, 16065/90, 16066/90, 16068/90, 16069/90, 16070/90, 16071/90, 16072/90, and 16073/90, § 157, ECHR 2009; *Edwards v. the United Kingdom* (dec.), no. 46477/99, 4 June 2001; *Keenan v. the United Kingdom*, no. 27229/95, Commission decision of 22 May 1998.

[131] *P.M. v. the United Kingdom* (dec.), no. 6638/03, 24 August 2004; *Kemevuaku v. the Netherlands* (dec.), no. 65938/09, § 19, 1 June 2010; *Barankevich v. Russia* (dec.), no. 10519/03, 20 October 2005; *Chalkley v. the United Kingdom* (dec.), no. 63831/00, 26 September 2002; *Sergey Kuznetsov v. Russia*, no. 10877/04, § 27, 23 October 2008.

[132] *Olivier Gaillard v. France* (dec.), no. 47337/99, 11 July 2000; *Franz Hofstädter v. Austria* (dec.), no. 25407/94, 12 September 2000; *Bulut and Yavuz v. Turkey* (dec.), no. 73065/01, 28 May 2002.

[133] *P.M. v. the United Kingdom* (dec.), no. 6638/03, 24 August 2004.

[134] Ibid.

[135] *Nee v. Ireland* (dec.), no. 52787/99, 30 January 2003.

[136] *Otto v. Germany* (dec.), no. 21425/06, 10 November 2009; *Benet Praha, Spol S.R.O. v. Czech Republic* (dec.), no. 38354/06, 28 September 2010; *Poslu and Others v. Turkey*, nos 6162/04, 6297/04, 6304/04, 6305/04, 6149/04, 9724/04, and 9733/04, § 5, 8 June 2010.

Where there is a continuing violation, the six-month time limit does not apply.[137] Because there is an on-going breach, 'the time-limit in effect starts afresh each day and it is only once the situation ceases that the final period of six months will run to its end'.[138]

Cases involving the procedural obligations associated with articles 2 and 3 of the Convention raise special issues. Given that the complaint is based on the failure to pursue an adequate investigation, the date at which it became clear that the State was not taking the appropriate steps falls to be determined. In a case involving the procedural obligation associated with the right to life, where relatives of the victim invoke the duty on the State to investigate the circumstances of a death in suspicious circumstances, the applicants must 'take steps to keep track of the investigation's progress, or lack thereof, and to lodge their applications with due expedition once they are, or should have become, aware of the lack of any effective criminal investigation'.[139] A similar approach applies in disappearance cases,[140] where applicants 'cannot wait indefinitely before coming to Strasbourg'.[141] According to the Grand Chamber, applications concerning disappearances can be rejected as out of time where there has been excessive or unexplained delay by the applications. As long as there are initiatives being pursued, or some 'meaningful contact between families and authorities concerning complaints and requests for information', the issue of undue delay will not arise. But there will come a moment when it is apparent that there will be no effective investigation. If the applicants fail to react at this point by filing their application with the Court, they risk losing their rights under the Convention.[142] Dissenting on this point, Judge Ziemele wrote: 'Non-application of the six months rule to breaches of international obligations having a continuing character, especially when we deal with such crimes as enforced disappearance, serves the important purpose of preventing the perpetrators from enjoying impunity for such acts.'[143]

Anonymous applications (art. 35(2)(a))

An anonymous application is not to be dealt with by the Court. This condition, which should not in principle raise any particular problems, has nevertheless given rise to some judicial decisions. The Rules of Court permit an applicant to request anonymity.[144] This seems to be granted upon request without much difficulty.[145] Although the applicant is

---

[137] *Varnava and Others v. Turkey* [GC], nos 16064/90, 16065/90, 16066/90, 16068/90, 16069/90, 16070/90, 16071/90, 16072/90, and 16073/90, § 159, ECHR 2009; *Agrotexim Hellos S.A., Biotex S.A., Hymofix Hellas S.A., Kykladiki S.A., Mepex S.A., and Texema S.A. v. Greece*, no. 14807/89, Commission decision of 12 February 1991, (1992) 35 YB 39, DR 71, p. 148; *Cone v. Romania*, no. 35935/02, § 22, 24 June 2008.

[138] *Varnava and Others v. Turkey* [GC], nos 16064/90, 16065/90, 16066/90, 16068/90, 16069/90, 16070/90, 16071/90, 16072/90, and 16073/90, § 159, ECHR 2009.

[139] Ibid., § 158; *Bulut and Yavuz v. Turkey* (dec.), no. 73065/01, 28 May 2002; also *Bayram and Yıldırım v. Turkey* (dec.), no. 38587/97, ECHR 2002-III.

[140] *Eren and Others v. Turkey* (dec.), no. 42428/98, 4 July 2002; *Üçak and Kargili and Others v. Turkey* (dec.), nos 75527/01 and 11837/02, 28 March 2006.

[141] *Varnava and Others v. Turkey* [GC], nos 16064/90, 16065/90, 16066/90, 16068/90, 16069/90, 16070/90, 16071/90, 16072/90, and 16073/90, § 158, ECHR 2009.

[142] Ibid., § 165. See also *Gutiérrez Dorado and Dorado Ortiz v. Spain* (dec.), no 30141/09, §§ 37–42, 27 March 2012.

[143] *Varnava and Others v. Turkey* [GC], nos 16064/90, 16065/90, 16066/90, 16068/90, 16069/90, 16070/90, 16071/90, 16072/90, and 16073/90, Concurring Opinion of Judge Ziemele, § 10, ECHR 2009. But see *Varnava and Others v. Turkey* [GC], nos 16064/90, 16065/90, 16066/90, 16068/90, 16069/90, 16070/90, 16071/90, 16072/90, and 16073/90, Concurring Opinion of Judge Villiger, ECHR 2009.

[144] Rules of Court, Rule 47(4).

[145] *A v. Croatia*, no. 55164/08, § 1, 14 October 2010; *A, B, and C v. Ireland* [GC], no. 25579/05, § 1, ECHR 2010.

required to sign the application form, if this has been omitted it does not lead to inadmissibility as long as the materials submitted to the Court contain personal details sufficient for the person to be identified.[146] An application introduced by an organization claiming to act on behalf of its members, who were not named or otherwise identified, but that invoked no violation against itself amounted to an anonymous application.[147]

In *'Blondje' v. the Netherlands*, the Court issued a decision declaring the case inadmissible because the applicant's identity was not disclosed. It noted that in the forms and documents submitted, the applicant—whom the Court called 'he', possibly implying that it knew something about 'him'—was referred to only as 'Blondje', 'NN cel 07', and 'Nn. PI09.m.20081101.1100'. The authority to act that was submitted was signed 'X'.[148] A very early decision of the European Commission declared inadmissible an application that was signed 'lover of tranquility', but only because there was nothing in the materials to permit proper identification of the applicant.[149]

Russia challenged several applications that had been submitted by allegedly authorized representatives who used simulated signatures on the grounds that they were anonymous. The State contended that applications introduced by persons using multiple identities or pseudonyms were in fact anonymous. In fact, much information had been provided about the applicants, who were quite open about the fact that their initial submission employed pseudonyms. The Court rejected Russia's objection, noting that '[à] l'exception de leurs vrais noms, les requérants fournirent un grand nombre d'éléments factuels et juridiques permettant à la Cour de les identifier par rapport aux faits litigieux et aux griefs invoqués'.[150] Acknowledging that pseudonyms were used in the application, and that real names were only provided subsequently, the Court said that 'derrière les tactiques de dissimulation des vraies identités pour des raisons que l'on peut comprendre, se trouvent des personnes réelles, concrètes et identifiables par un nombre suffisant d'indices, autres que leurs noms'.[151]

Substantially the same (art. 35(2)(b))

The Court will not consider an application that is 'substantially the same as a matter that has already been examined by the Court'. In applying this rule concerning redundant cases, the Court is required to ascertain whether two applications brought before it 'relate essentially to the same person, the same facts and the same complaints'.[152] In order to be 'substantially the same', the application must be introduced by the same persons.[153]

---

[146] *Kusnetsova v. Russia* (dec.), no. 67579/01, 19 January 2006.

[147] *Federation of French Medical Trade Unions and the National Federation of Nurses v. France*, no. 10983/84, Commission decision of 12 May 1986.

[148] *'Blondje' v. the Netherlands* (dec.), no. 7245/09, 15 September 2009.

[149] *X v. Ireland*, no. 361/58, Commission decision of 1 September 1958.

[150] *Shamayev and Others v. Georgia and Russia* (dec.), no. 36378/02, 16 September 2002. Also *Shamayev and Others v. Georgia and Russia*, no. 36378/02, § 275, ECHR 2005-III.

[151] *Shamayev and Others v. Georgia and Russia* (dec.), no. 36378/02, 16 September 2002.

[152] *Verein gegen Tierfabriken Schweiz (VgT) v. Switzerland (no. 2)* [GC], no. 32772/02, § 63, ECHR 2009; *Pauger v. Austria*, no. 24872/94, Commission decision of 9 January 1995, DR 80-A, p. 170; *Folgerø and Others v. Norway* (dec.), no. 15472/02, 14 February 2006.

[153] *Varnava and Others v. Turkey* [GC], nos 16064/90, 16065/90, 16066/90, 16068/90, 16069/90, 16070/90, 16071/90, 16072/90, and 16073/90, § 118, ECHR 2009; *Folgerø and Others v. Norway* (dec.), no. 15472/02, 14 February 2006; *Malsagova and Others v. Russia* (dec.), no. 27244/03, 6 March 2008.

Consequently, an inter-State application cannot form an obstacle to an individual application, even if the subject matter is quite similar.[154]

In considering whether a complaint is substantially the same, it should be borne in mind that the Court is not bound by the characterization given by the applicant. It can raise legal issues that arise from the facts, even if these have not been invoked by the parties.[155] The Court can address the issue on its own initiative even before the respondent State has been informed of the application to the extent that part or all of a complaint is substantially similar to an earlier filing.[156] In an application dealing with provisional detention, an objection by Turkey based upon redundancy was dismissed. The applicant was the same in three cases, but the subject matter was quite different.[157]

The owner of an apartment building in Berlin filed successive applications to the European Commission concerning essentially the same complaint about taxation, but after the first application was declared inadmissible he submitted a second concerning a different tenant. The Commission noted that 'le fond de la cause étant essentiellement le même, celle-ci a donné lieu à une procédure identique devant les Tribunaux berlinois' and that the applicant 'réitère les griefs, dirigés notamment contre la législation des loyers, régissant son immeuble, qu'il a déjà formulés dans la requête No. 1169/61, que l'argumentation du requérant n'apporte aucun élément de nature à modifier essentiellement les données de base de la situation légale à la vue de laquelle la Commission avait décliné sa compétence quant à la requête'.[158]

If new information is submitted with the subsequent filing, the application will not be viewed as 'essentially the same'. In *Chappex v. Switzerland*, the European Commission accepted a second application concerning violations of article 6 in the dismissal of an employee. The applicant complained about different judicial proceedings than those addressed in the first submission.[159] In another case where new information was submitted, the Commission said it found 'nothing in this information which could alter the basis on which its previous decisions, in particular the decision on Application No. 16964/90, were taken and does not see any reason to reopen the case'.[160] On the other hand, the Commission declined to declare inadmissible individual applications concerning missing persons in occupied Cyprus, despite the existence of an inter-State application dealing with the same issue, because new information had been submitted.[161]

[154] Ibid.

[155] *Guerra and Others v. Italy*, 19 February 1998, § 44, *Reports of Judgments and Decisions* 1998-I; *Powell and Rayner v. the United Kingdom*, 21 February 1990, § 29, Series A no. 172; *Scoppola v. Italy (no. 2)* [GC], no. 10249/03, § 54, 17 September 2009.

[156] *Dinç v. Turkey* (dec.), no. 42437/98, 22 November 2001; *Clinique Mozart SARL v. France* (dec.), no. 46098/99, 1 July 2003; *Rupa v. Romania* (dec.), no. 37971/02, 23 February 2010; *Coscodar v. Romania* (dec.), no. 36020/06, § 27, 9 March 2010; *Serves v. France* (dec.), no. 38642/97, 4 May 2000.

[157] *Sadak v. Turkey*, nos 251421/94 and 27099/95, §§ 30–33, 8 April 2004 (regarding *Sadak and Others v. Turkey (no. 1)*, nos 29900/96, 29901/96, 29902/96, and 29903/96, ECHR 2001-VIII and *Sadak and Others v. Turkey (no. 2)*, nos 25144/94, 26149/95 to 26154/95, 27100/95, and 27101/95, ECHR 2002-IV.) Also *Yurttas v. Turkey*, nos 25143/94 and 27098/95, §§ 36–37, 27 May 2004 (regarding *Sadak and Others v. Turkey (no. 2)*, nos 25144/94, 26149/95 to 26154/95, 27100/95, and 27101/95, ECHR 2002-IV.)

[158] *X v. Federal Republic of Germany*, no. 2606/65, Commission decision of 1 April 1968.

[159] *Chappex v. Switzerland*, no. 20338/92, Commission decision of 12 October 1994.

[160] *Adesina v. France*, no. 31398/96, Commission decision of 13 September 1996.

[161] *Varnava and Others v. Turkey*, nos 16064/90, 16065/90, 16066/90, 16068/90, 16069/90, 16070/90, 16071/90, 16072/90, and 16073/90, Commission decision of 14 April 1998.

Submission to another international body (art. 35(2)(b))

When the European Convention was adopted in 1950 it was difficult to speak of international procedures for the enforcement of human rights. The United Nations Commission on Human Rights had already stumbled on the point as it was negotiating the International Bill of Rights. A number of proposals existed, including one for the establishment of a world human rights court,[162] but while the United Nations organs were able to adopt rather quickly a concise declaration of rights without any implementation mechanism, the issue of enforcement was postponed for almost two decades. The drafters of the European Convention were mainly concerned with recourse to the International Court of Justice as well as to international arbitration. Moreover, they were thinking essentially of inter-State complaints rather than individual petitions. They could not have imagined the proliferation of human rights mechanisms that would be created over the decades that followed. Nevertheless, they anticipated something that was barely an issue in 1950 but that is today a very real challenge when they declared that the Convention organs could not deal with any application that had already been investigated or was being investigated by an international body. According to the case law, the purpose of the provision is to avoid a multiplicity of international procedures concerning the same case.[163]

The rule does not apply if the applicant before the Court and the complainant before the other international body are not the same,[164] or if one of the petitions was formulated by a non-governmental organization without clear authorization by the actual victim.[165] In establishing whether the complaint is the same, the factors considered by the Court in application of the first part of article 35(2)(b) are very relevant.[166] These include the time frame of the complaint.[167] In a case where an organization representing the interests of employers challenged legislation and measures before the European Committee of Social Rights, individual petitions from workers dealing with the same issue were not held to be inadmissible because the organization did not represent their interests.[168] Where trade unions have applied to the International Labour Organisation, the case law is inconsistent with respect to individual applications to the Convention organs filed by individual workers.[169]

The provision is only applicable if another 'international body' has been involved in a complaint concerning the right. In establishing this, the Court has said that the legal

---

[162]   An unfulfilled idea that is still alive: Manfred Nowak, 'It's Time for a World Court of Human Rights', in Cherif Bassiouni and William Schabas, eds, *New Challenges for the UN Human Rights Machinery, What Future for the UN Treaty Body System and the Human Rights Council Procedures?*, Antwerp: Intersentia, 2011, pp. 17–34.

[163]   *Celniku v. Greece*, no. 21449/04, § 39, 5 July 2007; *Calcerrada Fornieles et Cabeza Mato v. Spain*, no. 17512/90, Commission decision of 6 July 1992, (1992) 35 YB 63, DR 73, p. 214; *Cereceda Martin v. Spain*, no. 16358/90, Commission decision of 12 October 1992, DR 73, p. 120; *Smirnova and Smirnova v. Russia* (dec.), nos 46133/99 and 48183/99, 3 October 2002.

[164]   *Celniku v. Greece*, no. 21449/04, § 40, 5 July 2007; *Folgerø and Others v. Norway* (dec.), no. 15472/02, 14 February 2006.

[165]   *Malsagova and Others v. Russia* (dec.), no. 27244/03, 6 March 2008. Also *Illiu and Others v. Belgium* (dec.), no. 14301/08, 19 May 2009.

[166]   *OAO Neftyanaya Kompaniya Yukos v. Russia*, no. 14902/04, §§ 519–526, 20 September 2011.

[167]   *Patera v. Czech Republic* (dec.), no. 25326/03, § 2.2, 10 January 2006.

[168]   *Evaldsson and Others v. Sweden* (dec.), no. 75252/01, 28 March 2006.

[169]   *Cereceda Martin v. Spain*, no. 16358/90, Commission decision of 12 October 1992, DR 73, p. 120; *Council of Civil Service Unions and Others v. the United Kingdom*, no. 11603/85, Commission decision of 20 December 1987, DR 50, p. 228.

character of the instrument founding the body is the logical starting-point for its assessment. It will take into account the body's composition, its competence, its place (if any) in an existing legal system, and its funding. The purpose of the exercise is to identify 'the essential nature of the body', something the Court says is 'determinative of the issue'.[170] For example, the Human Rights Chamber of Bosnia and Herzegovina did not constitute an international body contemplated by article 35(2)(b), although it was created as a consequence of an international treaty, had an international composition involving foreign judges, and received international funding.[171] A complaint to a non-governmental organization does not fall within the scope of the provision of the Convention. Admissibility objections concerning bodies like the Inter-Parliamentary Union have been rejected.[172]

The procedure itself must be judicial or quasi-judicial and similar to what is offered under the Convention.[173] The Court must determine 'si la nature de l'organe de contrôle, la procédure suivie par celui-ci et l'effet de ses décisions sont tels que l'article 35 § 2 b) exclut la compétence de la Cour'.[174] They must be 'procedures in which a matter is submitted by way of "a petition" lodged formally or substantively by the applicant'.[175] The Convention organs have recognized that the United Nations Human Rights Committee,[176] the Committee on Freedom of Association of the International Labour Organisation[177] and the United Nations Working Group on Arbitrary Detention[178] provide such a procedure. However, the so-called '1503 Procedure', an early mechanism for monitoring gross violations of human rights by the United Nations Commission on Human Rights and the Human Rights Council set up by the Economic and Social Council in 1970,[179] has been considered to deal with situations rather than individual

---

[170] *Jeličić v. Bosnia and Herzegovina* (dec.), no. 41183/02, 15 November 2005.

[171] Ibid.

[172] *Andrei Karlov Lukanov v. Bulgaria*, no. 21915/93, Commission decision of 12 January 1995, (1995) 38 YB 55, DR 80-B, p. 108.

[173] *Mikolenko v. Estonia* (dec.), no. 16944/03, 5 January 2006; *Zagaria v. Italy* (dec.), no. 24408/03, 3 June 2008; *Andrei Karlov Lukanov v. Bulgaria*, no. 21915/93, Commission decision of 12 January 1995, (1995) 38 YB 55, DR 80-B, p. 108.

[174] *Peraldi v. France* (dec.), no. 2096/05, 7 April 2009.

[175] *Varnava and Others v. Turkey*, nos 16064–66/90 and 16068–73/90, Commission decision of 14 April 1998, DR 93-A, p. 5; *Malsagova and Others v. Russia* (dec.), no. 27244/03, 6 March 2008.

[176] *Patera v. Czech Republic* (dec.), no. 25326/03, § 2.1, 10 January 2006; *Calcerrada Fornieles et Cabeza Mato v. Spain*, no. 17512/90, Commission decision of 6 July 1992, (1992) 35 YB 63, DR 73, p. 214; *Pauger v. Austria*, no. 24872/94, Commission decision of 9 January 1995, DR 80-A, p. 170; *C.W. v. Finland*, no. 17230/90, Commission decision of 9 October 1991. In *Yağmurdereli v. Turkey* (dec.), no. 29590/96, 13 February 2001, the Court noted that the State had not ratified the Optional Protocol to the International Covenant on Civil and Political Rights. Consequently, the applicant before the Court could not have availed himself of the right of individual petition provided to the Human Rights Committee by the Protocol. Several decisions by the Human Rights Committee have dealt with related applications to the European Convention organs: *Kollar v. Austria*, no. 989/2001, UN Doc. CCPR/C/78/D/989/2001; *Peterson v. Germany*, no. 1115/2002, UN Doc. CCPR/C/80/D/1115/2002; *Mahabir v. Austria*, no. 944/2000, UN Doc. CCPR/C/82/D/944/2000; *Loth v. Germany*, no. 1754/2008, UN Doc. CCPR/C/98/D/1754/2008.

[177] *Council of Civil Service Unions and Others v. the United Kingdom*, no. 11603/85, Commission decision of 20 January 1987, DR 50, p. 228; *Cereceda Martin and Others v. Spain*, no. 16358/90, Commission decision of 12 October 1992, DR 73, p. 120.

[178] *Peraldi v. France* (dec.), no. 2096/05, 7 April 2009; *Illiu and Others v. Belgium* (dec.), no. 14301/08, 19 May 2009.

[179] UN Doc. E/RES/1504 (XLVIII). In 2006, the Human Rights Council replaced the Commission on Human Rights. The Council introduced a new complaint procedure to address consistent patterns of gross and reliably attested violations of all human rights and all fundamental freedoms occurring in any part of the world

complaints and therefore falls outside the scope of article 35(2)(b). The European Court characterized the United Nations Commission on Human Rights as an inter-governmental organ composed of State representatives rather than an independent body comprised of experts or judges.[180] Similarly, the Working Group on Enforced or Involuntary Disappearances set up by the United Nations Commission on Human Rights fails to fulfil the requirements of article 35(2)(b). It does not investigate disappearances or provide relatives with legal means of redress, and cannot attribute responsibility.[181] Nor is the European Committee for the Prevention of Torture and Inhuman or Degrading Treatment or Punishment, a Council of Europe organ with a preventive mission, a body falling under article 35(2)(b). Individual complainants have no right to participate in the procedure before the European Committee, nor are they entitled to be informed of recommendations that it makes unless a decision is taken to the contrary.[182] Similarly, a complaint to the European Commission, which is the executive organ of the European Union, is not a mechanism contemplated by article 35(2)(b).[183] The fact that a special rapporteur established by a United Nations body may interview and report on the case of an individual does not suffice to obstruct admissibility under article 35(2)(b).[184]

If there has been no final decision from the other international body to which an application has been made, the application to the Court will survive to the extent that the competing petition is discontinued. According to the Court, 'it is not the date of such a step that is decisive, but whether a decision on the merits has already been taken by the time the Court examines the case'.[185]

Incompatible with provisions of the Convention (art. 35(3)(a))

Sub-paragraph 3(a) of article 35 lists three grounds of inadmissibility that apply to individual applications, of which the first is incompatibility with the provisions of the Convention. This refers to jurisdictional matters rather than the merits of the application, something considered under the 'manifestly ill-founded' heading. The main dimensions of jurisdiction—personal (*ratione personae*), territorial (*ratione loci*) and temporal (*ratione temporis*)—are considered in detail in the chapter on article 1 of the Convention in this Commentary. Subject-matter (*ratione materiae*) jurisdiction, which is governed by article 32 of the Convention, is addressed in the individual chapters of this Commentary dealing

---

and under any circumstances: Institution-building of the United Nations Human Rights Council, UN Doc. A/CHR/RES/5/1, Annex, paras. 85–87.

[180] *Mikolenko v. Estonia* (dec.), no. 16944/03, 5 January 2006; *Celniku v. Greece*, no. 21449/04, § 40, 5 July 2007.

[181] *Malsagova and Others v. Russia* (dec.), no. 27244/03, 6 March 2008.

[182] *De Pace v. Italy*, no. 22728/03, §§ 24–29, 17 July 2008; *Gallo v. Italy* (dec.), no. 24406/03, 7 July 2009; *Zagaria v. Italy* (dec.), no. 24408/03, 3 June 2008; *Annunziata v. Italy* (dec.), no. 24423/03, 7 July 2009; *Genovese v. Italy* (dec.), no. 24407/03, 10 November 2009; *Stolder v. Italy*, no. 24418/03, §§ 16–19, 1 December 2009.

[183] *Karoussiotis v. Portugal*, no. 23205/08, §§ 65–76, ECHR 2011 (extracts).

[184] *Yağmurdereli v. Turkey* (dec.), no. 29590/96, 13 February 2001; *Illiu and Others v. Belgium* (dec.), no. 14301/08, 19 May 2009.

[185] *National Union of Rail, Maritime, and Transport Workers v. the United Kingdom*, no. 31045/10, § 48, 8 April 2014; *Peraldi v. France* (dec.), no. 2096/05, 7 April 2009; *Professional Trades Union for Prison, Correctional, and Secure Psychiatric Workers and Others v. the United Kingdom* (dec.), no. 59253/11, 21 May 2013.

with substantive rights. When jurisdiction is concerned, the Court must address the question even if the parties do not.[186]

Manifestly ill-founded application (art. 35(3)(a))

The second criterion of inadmissibility listed in article 35(3)(a) is the manifestly ill-founded nature of the application. This provision has provided the Convention organs with broad authority to dismiss applications that did not disclose any likelihood of a violation of a protected right. In that sense, when the Court examines whether an application is manifestly ill-founded, in reality it is making a preliminary ruling on the merits of the application. The essence of this stage of the proceedings can only be fully understood with reference to the drafting history of the Convention. It is quite clear that the manifestly ill-founded criterion of inadmissibility was intricately bound up with the role ascribed to the European Commission of Human Rights in filtering or 'sifting' cases that did not deserve the attention of the European Court. The decision of the Commission was final. If it declared part of an application inadmissible, the Court could not revive that part of the petition; it was bound by the inadmissibility ruling of the Commission. When the Convention organs were reformed by Protocol No. 11 and the Commission abolished, the filtering function pursuant to the manifestly ill-founded criterion passed to the Chambers and committees of the Court itself. The Court has continued to struggle with the application of the criterion, torn between the requirements of an increasingly burdensome caseload and the imperative of providing individualized justice to a huge number of applicants.

The vast majority of applications are found to be inadmissible on the ground that they are manifestly ill-founded, primarily by single judges or three-judge committees. Nevertheless, such a finding can also be made by a seven-judge Chamber and even, but only occasionally, by the Grand Chamber.[187] In some cases, there is a detailed examination of the entire case that makes a ruling on inadmissibly virtually indistinguishable from a full judgment on the merits.[188] It is only in the final words of such decisions, where the Court declares the application inadmissible rather than declaring that there is no violation of the Convention, that the distinction becomes apparent. The Court may declare some but not other parts of an application to be manifestly ill-founded.

Rejection of an application or a portion of an application on the grounds that it is ill-founded may be premised on the view that it is a 'fourth-instance' complaint. The Court is an institution that applies and enforces the Convention; it is not a court of appeal from decisions of the highest level of national courts. In other words, 'it is not the Court's role to assess itself the facts which have led a national court to adopt one decision rather than another. If it were otherwise, the Court would be acting as a court of third or fourth instance, which would be to disregard the limits imposed on its action.'[189] This is often misunderstood by litigants.

[186] *Sejdić and Finci v. Bosnia and Herzegovina* [GC], nos 27996/06 and 34836/06, § 27, ECHR 2009.

[187] *Demopoulos and Others v. Turkey* (dec.) [GC], nos 46113/99, 3843/02, 13751/02, 13466/03, 10200/04, 14163/04, 19993/04, and 21819/04, § 101, ECHR 2010; *Von Maltzan and Others v. Germany* (dec.) [GC], nos 71916/01, 71917/01, and 10260/02, ECHR 2005-V; *Gratzinger and Gratzingerova v. the Czech Republic* (dec.) [GC], no. 39794/98, ECHR 2002-VII.

[188] For example, *Mentzen alias Mencena v. Latvia* (dec.), no. 71041/01, 7 December 2004.

[189] *Kemmache v. France (no. 3)*, 24 November 1994, § 44, Series A no. 296-C; *Mkrtchyan v. Armenia*, no. 6562/03, § 43, 11 January 2007.

Applications that cite one or more provisions of the Convention but that do not explain the nature of the breach, unless this is obvious from the facts, will usually be regarded as manifestly ill-founded.[190] The Court considered a petition to be manifestly ill-founded when the applicant had been detained 'for only a few days' and where there was no evidence 'that during that time he suffered any hardship beyond that inherent in detention'.[191]

Abuse of the right of individual application (art. 35(3)(a))

Dismissal of a petition for abuse of the right of application is an 'exceptional procedural measure' that the Court will use with caution.[192] If there is any hesitation, the option is to declare an application inadmissible on the ground that it is manifestly ill-founded.[193] The concept of abuse is to be taken in its ordinary meaning, namely, the harmful exercise of a right by its holder in a manner that is inconsistent with the purpose for which such right is granted.[194] A conclusion that the applicant has acted abusively 'requires not only manifest inconsistency with the purpose of the right of application but also some hindrance to the proper functioning of the Court or to the smooth conduct of the proceedings before it'.[195]

Four categories of situation have been identified in the case law concerning abuse of the right of application. The first are applications involving outright dishonesty, or at the very least serious negligence in relations with the Court. A conclusion that the applicant has intentionally misled the Court must be established with sufficient certainty.[196] Examples include applications knowingly based upon untrue facts,[197] applications submitted under a false identity,[198] falsification of documents,[199] and a failure by the applicant to inform the Court of essential evidence[200] or of major developments of significance in the course of the proceedings.[201] The Rules of Court require the applicant to provide notification of relevant developments.[202]

In the second category, an applicant will have used 'particularly vexatious, contemptuous, threatening or provocative expressions in his correspondence with the Court'.[203]

---

[190] *Trofimchuk v. Ukraine* (dec.), no. 4241/03, 31 May 2005.

[191] *A. and Others v. the United Kingdom* [GC], no. 3455/05, § 123, ECHR 2009.

[192] *S.A.S. v. France* [GC], no. 43835/11, § 66, 1 July 2014; *Mirolubovs and Others v. Latvia*, no. 798/05, § 62, 15 September 2009.

[193] *Baillard v. France* (dec.), no. 6032/04, 25 September 2008.

[194] *S.A.S. v. France* [GC], no. 43835/11, § 66, 1 July 2014; *Mirolubovs and Others v. Latvia*, no. 798/05, § 62, 15 September 2009.

[195] *S.A.S. v. France* [GC], no. 43835/11, § 66, 1 July 2014; *Mirolubovs and Others v. Latvia*, no. 798/05, § 65, 15 September 2009.

[196] *Melnik v. Ukraine*, no. 72286/01, §§ 58–60, 28 March 2006; *Nold v. Germany*, no. 27250/02, § 87, 29 June 2006; *Miszczyński v. Poland* (dec.), no. 23672/07, 8 February 2011.

[197] *Varbanov v. Bulgaria*, no. 31365/96, § 36, ECHR 2000-X.

[198] *Drijfhout v. the Netherlands* (dec.), no. 51721/09, §§ 27–29, 22 February 2011.

[199] *Jian v. Romania* (dec.), no. 46640/99, 30 March 2004; *Bagheri and Maliki v. the Netherlands* (dec.), no. 30164/06, 15 May 2007; *Poznanski and Others v. Germany* (dec.), no. 25101/05, 3 July 2007.

[200] *Komatinović v. Serbia* (dec.), no. 75381/10, 29 January 2013; *Al-Nashif v. Bulgaria*, no. 50963/99, § 89, 20 June 2002; *Kerechashvili v. Georgia* (dec.), no. 5667/02, 2 May 2006; *Grande Stevens and Others v. Italy*, nos 18640/10, 18647/10, 18663/10, 18668/10, and 18698/10, § 66, 4 March 2014; *Hüttner v. Germany* (dec.), no. 23130/04, 19 June 2006; *Basileo and Others v. Italy* (dec.), no. 11303/02, 23 August 2011.

[201] *Predescu v. Romania*, no. 21447/03, §§ 25–27, 2 December 2008.

[202] Rules of Court, Rule 47(6).

[203] *S.A.S. v. France* [GC], no. 43835/11, § 66, 1 July 2014 For examples, *Řehák v. Czech Republic* (dec.), no. 67208/01, 18 May 2004; *Duringer and Grunge v. France* (dec.), nos 61164/00 and 18589/02, ECHR 2003-II; *Stamoulakatos v. Greece*, no. 27567/95, Commission decision of 9 April 1997.

This must involve language that goes well beyond 'the bounds of normal civil and legitimate criticism' and not merely talk that is polemical, sarcastic, or ironic.[204] An applicant warned by the Court about the use of inappropriate language may correct the situation by withdrawing offensive remarks or by an apology to the Court.[205]

Third, the applicant will have deliberately breached the confidentiality of friendly settlement negotiations.[206] Rule 38(2) of the Rules of Court as well as article 39(2) of the Convention itself impose an obligation to respect the confidential nature of such exchanges. The breach must, of course, be an intentional one. It is important to bear in mind the purpose of the confidentiality rule, which is to facilitate negotiations between the parties. The rule is not applied too strictly. A 'technical' breach will not necessarily be deemed abusive. Mainly, the principle applies to a situation where the applicant publicizes the contents of friendly settlement discussions.[207]

Applications in the fourth category consist of petty, vexatious, quibbling, and manifestly ill-founded applications that are similar to earlier submissions already declared inadmissible.[208]

The Court has also held that 'even though an application motivated by publicity or propaganda is not, by that very fact alone, an abuse of the right of application, the situation is different where the applicant, driven by political interests, gives an interview to the press or television showing an irresponsible and frivolous attitude towards proceedings that are pending before the Court'.[209]

De minimis non curat praetor (art. 35(3)(b))

The lack of a *de minimis* rule, enabling the dismissal of applications dealing with petty or trivial issues, had been lamented in dissenting opinions dating to the time of the European Commission.[210] For example, in a case dealing with a 'trivial dispute' about laundry hanging over a neighbour's courtyard, several dissenting judges said they would have refused to consider the case on grounds of an abuse of the right of application.[211] 'The

---

[204] *Di Salvo v. Italy* (dec.), no. 16098/05, 11 January 2007; *Aleksanyan v. Russia*, no. 46468/06, §§ 116–118, 22 December 2008.

[205] *Chernitsyn v. Russia*, no. 5964/02, §§ 25–28, 6 April 2006.

[206] *Hadrabová and Others* (dec.), nos 42165/02 and 466/03, 25 September 2007; *Popov v. Moldova (no. 1)*, no. 74153/01, § 48, 18 January 2005; *Andrejeva v. Latvia* [GC], no 55707/00, § 99, ECHR 2009; *Pérez de Rada Cavanilles v. Spain*, 28 October 1998, § 45, *Reports of Judgments and Decisions* 1998-VIII; *Malige v. France*, no. 26135/95, Commission decision of 5 March 1996.

[207] *Miroļubovs and Others v. Latvia*, no. 798/05, § 68, 15 September 2009.

[208] *Anibal Vieira & Filhos LDA and Maria Rosa Ferreira da Costa LDA v. Portugal* (dec.), nos 980/12 and 18385/12, 13 November 2012; *M. v. the United Kingdom*, no. 13284/87, Commission decision of 15 October 1987; *Philis v. Greece*, no. 28970/95, Commission decision of 17 October 1996; *X v. Austria and Federal Republic of Germany*, no. 3479/68, Commission decision of 14 December 1968.

[209] *S.A.S. v. France* [GC], no. 43835/11, § 67, 1 July 2014; *Miroļubovs and Others v. Latvia*, no. 798/05, § 62, 15 September 2009; *McFeeley and Others v. the United Kingdom*, no. 8317/78, Commission decision of 15 May 1980, (1980) 23 YB 256, DR 20, p. 44; *Georgian Labour Party v. Georgia* (dec.), no. 9103/04, 22 May 2007.

[210] *Dudgeon v. the United Kingdom*, 22 October 1981, Dissenting Opinion of Judge Matscher, Series A no. 45; *O'Halloran and Francis v. the United Kingdom* [GC], nos 15809/02 and 25624/02, Dissenting Opinion of Judge Myjer, ECHR 2007-III.

[211] *Micallef v. Malta* [GC], no. 17056/06, Joint Dissenting Opinion of Judges Costa, Jungwiert, Kovler and Fura, § 1, ECHR 2009.

disproportion between the triviality of the facts and the extensive use—or rather over-use—of court proceedings is an affront to good sense, especially as serious human-rights violations subsist in a number of States Parties. Is it really the role of our Court to determine cases such as this?' they wrote.[212] Nevertheless, the Court has quite clearly refused to apply the *de minimis* principle in cases where it was explicitly invoked by the respondent State.[213]

The issue has finally been addressed with the new admissibility criterion of 'significant disadvantage', introduced by Protocol No. 14. Shortly before it entered into force on 1 June 2010, the Action Plan adopted by States Parties at the Interlaken Conference invited the Court to give full effect to the new criterion, as well as to consider other possibilities of applying the principle *de minimis non curat praetor*.[214] The new provision is applicable to all pending applications except those already declared admissible. The Court may consider this admissibility ground even if it has not been raised by the respondent State.[215] Its purpose is 'in the long run, to enable more rapid disposal of unmeritorious cases and thus to allow it to concentrate on the Court's central mission of providing legal protection of human rights at the European level'.[216]

Pursuant to the provision, the Court may declare inadmissible an individual application if the applicant has not suffered a significant disadvantage. Two provisos are associated with the rule. First, the Court may not apply the provision if respect for human rights requires an examination of the application on the merits. Second, the new criterion does not apply to cases that have not been duly considered by a domestic authority. For the first two years following entry into force of the amendment, its application was reserved to Chambers and to the Grand Chamber.[217] Judgments have noted that although there is no formal hierarchy among the three elements of article 35(3)(b), 'the question of whether the applicant has suffered a "significant disadvantage" is at the core of this admissibility criterion'.[218]

Sometimes the Court will conclude that an issue of admissibility is intricately linked to the merits and decide to proceed, reserving its opinion on admissibility. It seems contrary to the very purpose of the admissibility criterion, which is to reduce the caseload by eliminating undeserving applications. But in a case concerning the *de minimis* rule, the Court said 'cette exception du Gouvernement est étroitement liée à la substance du grief énoncé sur le terrain de l'article 6 § 1 de la Convention dans la mesure où elle porte précisément sur la question de savoir si l'absence de communication du rapport médical a porté atteinte au droit du requérant à un procès équitable. Elle décide donc de la joindre au fond'.[219] The case concerned an allegation that a fair hearing had been denied. In other

[212] Ibid.

[213] *Koumoutsea and Others v. Greece* (dec.), no. 56625/00, 13 December 2011.

[214] Action Plan adopted by the High Level Conference on the Future of the European Court of Human Rights, Interlaken, 19 February 2010, para. 9(c), cited in *Korolev v. Russia* (dec.), no. 25551/05, ECHR 2010.

[215] *Adrian Mihai Ionescu v. Romania* (dec.), no. 36659/04, § 30, 1 June 2010; *Rinck v. France* (dec.), no. 18774/09, 19 October 2010.

[216] *Korolev v. Russia* (dec.), no. 25551/05, 1 July 2010.

[217] Protocol No. 14 to the Convention for the Protection of Human Rights and Fundamental Freedoms, amending the control system of the Convention, ETS 194, art. 20(2).

[218] *Shefer v. Russia* (dec.), no. 45175/04, 13 March 2012. Also *Ladygin v. Russia* (dec.), no. 35365/05, 30 August 2011.

[219] *Martins Silva v. Portugal*, no. 12959/10, § 32, 28 May 2014.

cases concerning judicial remedies, the Court said it was unable to determine the 'duly considered' issue without proceeding to the merits.[220]

The notion of 'significant disadvantage' is said to be 'open to interpretation'.[221] It is a criterion that gives the Court 'some degree of flexibility' and that is 'not susceptible to exhaustive definition'.[222] The new criterion 'hinges on the idea that a violation of a right, however real from a purely legal point of view, should attain a minimum level of severity to warrant consideration by an international court'.[223] The Court should take into account 'both the applicant's subjective perceptions and what is objectively at stake in a particular case'.[224] It may be that the applicant considers the matter to be of the utmost significance, but this factor alone is obviously insufficient to rebut application of the criterion.[225]

The concept of 'significant disadvantage' has been considered in several cases with respect to the amount of money in dispute. The Court declared an application inadmissible *proprio motu* where the amount of financial loss was estimated at €90.[226] In another, a €150 fine and loss of one penalty point, for driving very slightly over the speed limit, was deemed *de minimis*.[227] But the Court has cautioned that 'even modest pecuniary damage may be significant in the light of the person's specific condition and the economic situation of the country or region in which he or she lives'.[228] In a case involving €129,000, the Court said this was 'tout sauf modique', rejecting the exception raised by the respondent State.[229] An expropriation involving sums in the range of €30,000 to €76,000 led the Court to conclude that the prejudice was significant.[230] In an Italian case involving imposition of fines ranging from €500,000 to €3,000,000, as well as a possibility of detention and a prohibition on managing or directing companies listed on the stock exchange for a period of months, the Court considered there was a significant disadvantage and rejected the admissibility challenge.[231]

Significant disadvantage cannot be assessed purely in monetary terms. There are cases where the amount at stake is insignificant, yet other factors must also be taken into account in applying the admissibility criterion. The Court has said there are two main aspects to this, the subjective importance of the case to the applicant and what is objectively at stake. Moreover, 'a violation of the Convention may concern important questions of principle and thus cause a significant disadvantage without affecting

---

[220] *Bannikov v. Latvia*, no. 19279/03, § 59, 11 June 2013; *Maravić Markeš v. Croatia*, no. 70923/11, § 43, 9 January 2014.

[221] *Korolev v. Russia* (dec.), no. 25551/05, ECHR 2010.

[222] Ibid.; *Rinck v. France* (dec.), no. 18774/09, 19 October 2010.

[223] *Korolev v. Russia* (dec.), no. 25551/05, 1 July 2010; *Rinck v. France* (dec.), no. 18774/09, 19 October 2010.

[224] *Korolev v. Russia* (dec.), no. 25551/05, 1 July 2010; *Stefanescu v. Roumanie* (déc.), no. 11774/04, § 35, 12 April 2011; *Gagliano Giorgi v. Italy*, no. 23563/07, § 54, ECHR 2012 (extracts).

[225] *Rinck v. France* (dec.), no. 18774/09, 19 October 2010.

[226] *Adrian Mihai Ionescu v. Romania* (dec.), no. 36659/04, § 36, 1 June 2010.

[227] *Rinck v. France* (dec.), no. 18774/09, 19 October 2010.

[228] *Korolev v. Russia* (dec.), no. 25551/05, ECHR 2010.

[229] *Avotiņš v. Latvia*, no. 17502/07, § 36, 25 February 2014.

[230] *Sancho Cruz and 14 other 'Agrarian Reform' cases v. Portugal*, nos 8851/07, 8854/07, 8856/07, 8865/07, 10142/07, 10144/07, 24622/07, 32733/07, 32744/07, 41645/07, 19150/08, 22885/08, 22887/08, 26612/08, and 202/09, § 35, 18 January 2011.

[231] *Grande Stevens and Others v. Italy*, nos 18640/10, 18647/10, 18663/10, 18668/10, and 18698/10, § 74, 4 March 2014.

pecuniary interest'.[232] It has signalled the importance of 'honorabilité professionnelle' as a non-monetary factor relevant to the assessment.[233] In a case where the financial implications were minimal, the Court took into account the importance of the issue to the applicant, who had pursued the proceedings to their conclusion, even after being refused legal aid.[234] Where an applicant does not act diligently, however, the Court may conclude that 'conduct demonstrates apparent absence of significant interest in the outcome of the proceedings'.[235] In terms of the objective dimension, the Court has noted widespread media attention given to a case involving whether insulting the head of State should remain a criminal offence, a matter that was regularly raised in Parliament.[236]

The respect for human rights exception is expressed in language that is drawn from article 37(1) of the Convention. There, it fulfils a similar function in the context of decisions to strike applications from the list. The same criterion is also used in article 39(1) as a basis for a friendly settlement between the parties. Consequently, there is much case law on which to rely in the interpretation of the new provision.[237] The European Commission considered that the concept would apply to an application raising questions of a general character affecting the observance of the Convention.[238] The human rights exception will apply 'where there is a need to clarify the States' obligations under the Convention or to induce the respondent State to resolve a structural deficiency affecting other persons in the same position as the applicant'.[239] For example, in one of the first cases under the new criterion, this proviso was held to be not applicable where the impugned legislation had been repealed, given that the issue was then of only 'historical interest'.[240] Where a novel question is raised, for example with respect to a new procedural mechanism in the domestic system, the Court will be inclined to apply the human rights exception because its ruling on a question of principle will provide guidance to national courts and tribunals.[241]

The second proviso is the fact that the issue was already submitted to the domestic courts. The purpose of the provision, according to the Court, 'is to ensure that every case receives a judicial examination whether at the national level or at the European level, in other words, to avoid a denial of justice'.[242] It is closely related to the notion of subsidiarity, something implied by article 13 and set out explicitly in recital 6 of the Convention's Preamble. Article 35(3)(b) speaks of a 'case', rather than an 'application' (in

---

[232] *Korolev v. Russia* (dec.), no. 25551/05, ECHR 2010. Also *Giuran v. Romania*, no. 24360/04, § 32, ECHR 2011 (extracts).

[233] *Grande Stevens and Others v. Italy*, nos 18640/10, 18647/10, 18663/10, 18668/10, and 18698/10, § 74, 4 March 2014.

[234] *Eon v. France*, no. 26118/10, § 34, 14 March 2013.

[235] *Shefer v. Russia* (dec.), no. 45175/04, 13 March 2012.

[236] *Eon v. France*, no. 26118/10, § 34, 14 March 2013.

[237] For example, *Can v. Austria*, 30 September 1985, §§ 15–18, Series A no. 96; *Léger v. France* (striking out) [GC], no. 19324/02, § 51, 30 March 2009; *Van Houten v. the Netherlands* (striking out), no. 25149/03, § 33, ECHR 2005-IX; *Kavak v. Turkey* (dec.), no. 34719/04 et 37472/05, 19 May 2009.

[238] *Tyrer v. the United Kingdom*, no. 5856/72, Commission report of 14 December 1976.

[239] *Korolev v. Russia* (dec.), no. 25551/05, ECHR 2010.

[240] *Adrian Mihai Ionescu v. Romania* (dec.), no. 36659/04, § 39, 1 June 2010.

[241] *Grande Stevens and Others v. Italy*, nos 18640/10, 18647/10, 18663/10, 18668/10, and 18698/10, 4 March 2014. Similarly *Vlad and Others v. Romania*, nos 40756/06, 41508/07, and 50806/07, § 99, 16 November 2013, *Finger v. Bulgaria*, no. 37346/05, §§ 75–77, 10 May 2011; *Nicoleta Gheorghe v. Romania*, no. 23470/05, § 24, 3 April 2012.

[242] *Korolev v. Russia* (dec.), no. 25551/05, ECHR 2010.

French, *l'affaire* and *la requête*). Noting this distinction, the Court has held that it is to determine whether the claims of the applicant were considered by a domestic tribunal rather than the actual content of the petition filed in Strasbourg. The difficulty arises because normally the applicant will undertake more than one proceeding at the national level, if for no other reason than to exhaust domestic remedies. Article 35(3)(b) only requires that there be an examination at one level. According to the Court,

En effet, s'il fallait entendre ici la notion de 'l'affaire' comme synonyme de 'la requête', on aboutirait à une situation où il existerait des griefs se rapportant aux agissements des instances internes ultimes (comme en l'espèce la Cour constitutionnelle mais aussi d'autres tribunaux dans les pays qui n'ont pas mis en place les juridictions, accessibles aux particuliers, chargées de vérifier le respect de la constitution, voire de la Convention), qui ne pouvaient plus être examinés au niveau national et à l'égard desquels la Cour ne pourrait donc plus décliner sa compétence en raison de la banalité de la requête. Or, la Cour n'est pas convaincue qu'elle devrait être dotée d'une telle compétence générale de super-révision.[243]

As the Court explained, were it to adopt the alternative approach, this would mean that it would be unable to apply the *de minimis* criterion in any case where a violation of fundamental rights by the highest court in the country was alleged.

At the time of signature and ratification of Protocol No. 14, several States made declarations concerning the interpretation and application of the new criterion. This is discussed below under the heading 'Declarations'.

Rejection 'at any stage of the proceedings' (art. 35(4))

Issues of admissibility may present themselves at any stage of the proceedings.[244] Article 35(4) allows the Court, even when it is judging the merits, 'to reconsider a decision to declare an application admissible where it concludes that it should have been declared inadmissible for one of the reasons given in the first three paragraphs of Article 35, including that of incompatibility with the provisions of the Convention (Article 35 § 3 taken together with Article 34)'.[245] Even the Grand Chamber may reconsider the admissibility issue, ruling a case inadmissible that had previously been examined on the merits by the Chamber.[246] The provision results from Protocol No. 11 but it was inspired by article 29 of the 1950 text of the Convention. The Explanatory Report on Protocol No. 11 stressed that 'the Court will be able to reject an application at any stage of the proceedings—even without an oral hearing—if it finds the existence of one of the grounds of non-acceptance provided in Article 35 (see Article 29 of the Convention's former text)'.[247]

For example, article 35(4) may apply if the applicant cannot or can no longer assert status as a victim under the Convention.[248] Article 35(4) does not mean that a State can

---

[243] *Holub v. Czech Republic* (dec.), no. 24880/05, 14 December 2010.
[244] *Scoppola v. Italy (no. 2)* [GC], no. 10249/03, § 56, 17 September 2009; *K. and T. v. Finland* [GC], no. 25702/94, §§ 140–141, ECHR 2001-VII; *Perna v. Italy* [GC], no. 48898/99, §§ 23–24, ECHR 2003-V.
[245] *Pisano v. Italy* (striking out) [GC], no. 36732/97, § 34, 24 October 2002.
[246] *Scoppola v. Italy (no. 2)* [GC], no. 10249/03, § 56, 17 September 2009; *Azinas v. Cyprus* [GC], no. 56679/00, § 32, ECHR 2004-III; *Blečić v. Croatia*, no. 59532/00 [GC], § 65, ECHR 2006-III; *Odièvre v. France* [GC], no. 42326/98, § 22, ECHR 2003-III; *Mooren v. Germany* [GC], no. 11364/03, § 57, 9 July 2009.
[247] Explanatory Report on Protocol No. 11, para. 88. Cited in *Pisano v. Italy* (striking out) [GC], no. 36732/97, § 34, 24 October 2002.
[248] *İlhan v. Turkey* [GC], no. 22277/93, § 52, ECHR 2000-VII.

raise an objection to admissibility at any point in the proceedings.[249] The State may be estopped from raising the issue if it has not done so early in the proceedings, absent exceptional circumstances,[250] although there is nothing to prevent the Court from doing this on its own motion.

Declarations

At the time of signature of Protocol No. 14, Belgium made a declaration indicating that with respect to the amendment to article 35, adding a new admissibility criterion,

it understands this provision within the meaning specified in particular in paragraphs 79, 80, 83 and 84 of the Explanatory Report, from which it results that:

– the Court shall apply the new admissibility criterion by establishing a case-law allowing to define the legal terms which state this criterion on the basis of an interpretation establishing objective criteria of definition (paragraphs 79 and 80);
– the new criterion is designed to avoid rejection of cases warranting an examination on the merits (paragraph 83);
– the single-judge formations and committees will not be able to apply the new criteria in the absence of a clear and well-established case-law of the Court's Chambers and Grand Chamber (paragraph 64).[251]

Poland also made a declaration at the time of signature stating that it interprets the amendments in accordance with article 59(3) of the Convention, 'following the general principle of non-retroactivity of treaties, contained in Article 28 of the Vienna Convention on the Law of Treaties of 23 May 1969'.[252] Russia made a similar declaration, although it relied upon article 19 of the Convention as the basis of the principle of non-retroactivity of treaties.[253]

In its instrument of ratification of Protocol No. 14, by which article 35 was amended, Latvia made the following declaration:

1. The new admissibility criterion may not be applied to reject such applications, which examination would otherwise be important for the protection of human rights and fundamental freedoms as defined in the Convention and the Protocols thereto, as well as to reject such applications, which have not been duly considered by a domestic tribunal.
2. The single-judge formations and committees will be able to apply the new admissibility criterion only after the Court's Chamber and Grand Chamber develop their case-law on this subject.
3. The new admissibility criterion will not be applied to the applications declared admissible before the entry into force of this Protocol in accordance with the general principle of non-retroactivity of treaties, contained in Article 28 of the Vienna Convention on the Law of Treaties of 23 May 1969.[254]

---

[249] *Velikova v. Bulgaria*, no. 41488/98, § 57, ECHR 2000-VI.
[250] *Mooren v. Germany* [GC], no. 11364/03, § 57, 9 July 2009; *N.C. v. Italy* [GC], no. 24952/94, § 44, ECHR 2002-X; *Sejdovic v. Italy* [GC], no. 56581/00, § 41, ECHR 2006-II; *Lebedev v. Russia*, no. 4493/04, §§ 39–40, 25 October 2007.
[251] (2005) 48 YB 13–14.
[252] (2004) 47 YB 26.
[253] (2006) 49 YB 12. The statement was renewed upon ratification: (2010) 53 YB 28.
[254] (2006) 49 YB 10.

Further reading

A.A. Cançado Trindade, *The Application of the Rule of Exhaustion of Local Remedies in International Law. Its Rationale in the International Protection of Individual Rights*, Cambridge: Cambridge University Press, 1983.

Jean-François Flauss, 'La condition de l'épuisement des griefs au sens de l'article 26 CEDH: les enseignements de l'arrêt Cardot', (1991) 3 *Revue universelle des droits de l'homme* 529.

Jean-François Flauss, 'De l'abus de droit dans le cadre de la Convention européenne des droits de l'homme', (1992) 4 *Revue universelle des droits de l'homme* 461.

Frowein/Peukert, *MenschenRechtsKonvention,* pp. 495–520.

Michael O'Boyle, '*Ne bis in idem* for the Benefit of States?', in Lucius Caflisch, Johan Callewaert, Roderick Liddell, Paul Mahoney, and Mark Villiger, eds, *Liber Amicorum Luzius Wildhaber*, Kehl, Germany: N.P. Engel, 2007, pp. 285–308.

Etienne Picard, 'Article 26', in Pettiti et al., *La Convention européenne*, pp. 591–620.

Stefan Trechsel, 'Article 27', in Pettiti et al., *La Convention européenne*, pp. 621–47.

Harmen van der Wilt and Sandra Lyngdorf, 'Procedural Obligations Under the European Convention on Human Rights: Useful Guidelines for the Assessment of 'Unwillingness' and 'Inability' in the Context of the Complementarity Principle', (2009) 9 *International Criminal Law Review* 39.

Leo Zwaak, 'The Procedure before the European Court of Human Rights', in Van Dijk et al., *Theory and Practice*, pp. 98–203.

Article 36. Third-party intervention/Tierce intervention

1. In all cases before a Chamber or the Grand Chamber, a High Contracting Party one of whose nationals is an applicant shall have the right to submit written comments and to take part in hearings.	1. Dans toute affaire devant une chambre ou la Grande Chambre, une Haute Partie contractante dont un ressortissant est requérant a le droit de présenter des observations écrites et de prendre part aux audiences.
2. The President of the Court may, in the interest of the proper administration of justice, invite any High Contracting Party which is not a party to the proceedings or any person concerned who is not the applicant to submit written comments or take part in hearings.	2. Dans l'intérêt d'une bonne administration de la justice, le président de la Cour peut inviter toute Haute Partie contractante qui n'est pas partie à l'instance ou toute personne intéressée autre que le requérant à présenter des observations écrites ou à prendre part aux audiences.
3. In all cases before a Chamber or the Grand Chamber, the Council of Europe Commissioner for Human Rights may submit written comments and take part in hearings.	3. Dans toute affaire devant une chambre ou la Grande Chambre, le Commissaire aux droits de l'homme du Conseil de l'Europe peut présenter des observations écrites et prendre part aux audiences.

Introductory comments

Paragraph 1 of article 36 has been described as a 'vestige de la traditionnelle protection diplomatique ou judiciaire des nationaux'[1] by which a State is give the opportunity 'to protect its nationals in a situation where they suffer an injury as a result of a breach of public international law by another Member State'.[2] Under article 48(b) of the 1950 text of the Convention, 'a High Contracting Party whose national is alleged to be a victim' had the right to bring a case before the European Court of Human Rights. This could only happen if the case had already been considered by the Commission and had been found to be admissible. In practice, this happened only twice.[3] The State of nationality of a victim could also initiate an application before the Commission under the general provision dealing with inter-State cases. It, too, has hardly ever been invoked (see the chapter on article 33 in this Commentary).

The Court began admitting *amici curiae* in 1979, initially allowing a State Party other than the respondent to make written submissions.[4] Two years later, in the 'closed shop case', the Court 'decided *proprio motu*, in pursuance of Rule 38 par. 1 of the Rules of Court, that during the oral proceedings it would hear, on certain questions of fact (including English law and practice) and for the purpose of information, a representative

---

[1] Ireneu Cabral Barreto, 'Article 48', in Pettiti et al., *La Convention européenne*, pp. 793–803, at p. 796.

[2] *I v. Sweden*, no. 61204/09, § 42, 5 September 2013.

[3] *Soering v. the United Kingdom*, 7 July 1989, § 1, Series A no. 161; *Loizidou v. Turkey* (Preliminary objections), 23 March 1995, § 1, Series A no. 310.

[4] *Winterwerp v. the Netherlands*, 24 October 1979, § 7, Series A no. 33.

of the British Trades Union Congress'.[5] The Court now routinely authorizes qualified interveners to submit briefs on specific questions.

Drafting of the provision

The Draft Statute that was annexed to the initial of the text European Convention on Human Rights prepared by the International Juridical Section of the European Movement empowered the proposed Court to 'entrust any individual, body, bureau, commission, or other organisation that it may select, with the task of carrying out an inquiry or giving an expert opinion'.[6] Another provision authorized a State to 'submit a request to the Court to be permitted to intervene' if the State considered 'it has an interest of a legal nature which may be affected by the decision in the case'. The Court was to rule upon the request.[7] The Consultative Assembly did not consider the issue and its final draft had no such provision.

The Committee of Ministers assigned a Committee of Experts to study the Consultative Assembly draft, noting that it should in particular address the '[l]egal scope of judgments: grounds, revision, appeal, effect on third parties and intervening parties'.[8] What became article 48(b) appeared in an early draft adopted by the Committee of Experts in March 1950.[9] The Report noted that '[t]he Committee insisted that it was never proper for an individual to refer to the Court. The interests of individuals would always be defended either by the Commission . . . or by a State . . . '[10] There appears to have been no subsequent debate on this provision and no changes were made.

Other than this right of referral by the States of nationality, the 1950 text of the Convention did not explicitly authorize intervention or participation in the proceedings before the Court. Rule 38 of the original Rules of Court, adopted in 1959, was entitled 'Enquiry, expert opinion and other measures for obtaining information'. Paragraph 1 allowed that a Chamber 'at the request of a Party or of delegates of the Commission or *proprio motu*, decide to hear as a witness or expert or in any other capacity any person whose evidence or statements seem likely to assist it in the carrying out of its task'. The Rule appears to have been used first in 1981 when the Chamber, acting *proprio motu*, decided that during the oral proceedings it would hear 'on certain questions of fact (including English law and practice) and for the purpose of information' a representative of the British Trades Union Congress.[11] The Rules of Court were amended in 1982 to authorize the President, 'in the interest of the proper administration of justice', to 'invite or grant leave to any Contracting State which is not a Party to the proceedings to submit written comments within a time-limit and on issues which he shall specify. He may

---

[5] *Young, James, and Webster v. the United Kingdom*, 13 August 1981, § 8, Series A no. 44.

[6] Draft Statute of the European Court of Human Rights, INF/5/E/R, I *TP* 302–21, at p. 316, art. 44.

[7] Ibid., p. 318, art. 55.

[8] Preparatory Report by the Secretariat-General concerning a Preliminary Draft Convention to Provide a Collective Guarantee of Human Rights, Doc. B 22, III *TP* 2–37, at p. 36.

[9] New text suggested for Sections II, III, and IV, Doc. CM/WP 1 (50) 4, A 917, III *TP* 294–302, at p. 300, art 34(b).

[10] Report to the Committee of Ministers submitted by the Committee of Experts Instructed to Draw Up a Draft Convention of Collective Guarantee of Human Rights and Fundamental Freedoms, Doc. CM/WP 1 (5) 15, A 924, IV *TP* 2–55, at p. 44. See also Preliminary Draft of the Report to the Committee of Ministers, 24 February 1950, Doc. CM/WP 1 (50), A 847, III *TP* 246–79, at p. 276.

[11] *Young, James, and Webster v. the United Kingdom*, 13 August 1981, § 8, Series A no. 44.

extend such an invitation or grant such leave to any person concerned other than the applicant.'[12] The new Rule was applied in another trade union case when the Post Office Engineering Union was granted permission to make submissions, albeit of a narrower scope than what it had requested.[13] The Rule does not appear to have been invoked by a State Party. It was used in the years that followed by such organizations as Amnesty International,[14] Liberty,[15] Human Rights Watch,[16] the Federation of Italian Lawyers' Unions,[17] the Confederazione Generale Italiana del Lavoro,[18] JUSTICE (the British section of the International Commission of Jurists),[19] the Italian Association of Young Barristers,[20] the Campaign for Freedom of Information,[21] the Conseil d'État and Court of Cassation Bar,[22] the Rome Lawyers' Association,[23] the International Press Institute,[24] and the Standing Advisory Commission on Human Rights of Northern Ireland.[25]

These two features of the Court's practice were both modified and codified in the first two paragraphs of article 36, which were added to the Convention by Protocol No. 11. The Explanatory Report noted that paragraph 1 had been based on article 48(b) of the former Convention,[26] and that paragraph 2 'follows closely' Rule 37(2) of the Rules of Court. The Explanatory Report clarified that '[t]he person concerned may be a natural or a legal person'. It added that 'States and persons taking part in such proceedings are not parties to the proceedings'.[27]

It was the Commissioner of Human Rights himself who proposed that the Convention be amended to recognize expressly the right of intervention in the proceedings,[28] an idea that was supported by the Parliamentary Assembly.[29] Paragraph 3 was added by Protocol 14.[30] The Explanatory Report on Protocol No. 14 noted that article 36, as adopted by Protocol No. 11, already permitted the Commissioner to intervene with the authorization of the President of the Court. The Explanatory Report states:

---

[12] Rules of Court, Rule 37(2) (as amended, 24 November 1982).
[13] *Malone v. the United Kingdom*, 2 August 1984, § 8, Series A no. 82.
[14] *Soering v. the United Kingdom*, 7 July 1989, § 8, Series A no. 161; *Aydın v. Turkey*, 25 September 1997, § 6, *Reports of Judgments and Decisions* 1997-VI; *Kurt v. Turkey*, 25 May 1998, § 5, *Reports of Judgments and Decisions* 1998-III.
[15] *McGinley and Egan v. the United Kingdom*, 9 June 1998, § 5, *Reports of Judgments and Decisions* 1998-III; *Ahmed and Others v. the United Kingdom*, 2 September 1998, § 5, *Reports of Judgments and Decisions* 1998-VI.
[16] *Jersild v. Denmark*, 23 September 1994, § 5, Series A no. 298.
[17] *Capuano v. Italy*, 25 June 1987, § 6, Series A no. 119.
[18] *Caleffi v. Italy*, 24 May 1991, § 6, Series A no. 206-B.
[19] *Monnell and Morris v. the United Kingdom*, 2 March 1987, § 6, Series A no. 115.
[20] *Capuano v. Italy*, 25 June 1987, § 6, Series A no. 119.
[21] *McGinley and Egan v. the United Kingdom*, 9 June 1998, § 5, *Reports of Judgments and Decisions* 1998-III.
[22] *Pham Hoang v. France*, 25 September 1992, § 5, Series A no. 243.
[23] *Capuano v. Italy*, 25 June 1987, § 6, Series A no. 119. An earlier application by the Council of the Rome Bar Association was denied because it was made too late: *Goddi v. Italy*, 9 April 1984, § 7, Series A no. 76.
[24] *Lingens v. Austria*, 8 July 1986, § 5, Series A no. 103.
[25] *Tinnelly & Sons Ltd and Others and McElduff and Others v. the United Kingdom*, 10 July 1998, § 6, *Reports of Judgments and Decisions* 1998-IV.
[26] Explanatory Report on Protocol No. 11, para. 90.
[27] Ibid., para. 91.
[28] 3rd Annual Report on the Activities of the Council of Europe Commissioner for Human Rights (1 January–31 December 2002), adopted on 26 January 2004.
[29] Parliamentary Assembly in its Recommendation 1640 (2004).
[30] Protocol No. 14 to the Convention for the Protection of Human Rights and Fundamental Freedoms, amending the control system of the Convention, ETS 194, art. 13.

With a view to protecting the general interest more effectively, the third paragraph added to Article 36 for the first time mentions the Commissioner for Human Rights in the Convention text by formally providing that the Commissioner has the right to intervene as third party. The Commissioner's experience may help enlighten the Court on certain questions, particularly in cases which highlight structural or systemic weaknesses in the respondent or other High Contracting Parties.[31]

According to the Explanatory Report on Protocol No. 14, other amendments to article 36 were not considered necessary: 'In particular, it was decided not to provide for a possibility of third party intervention in the new committee procedure under the new Article 28, paragraph 1.b, given the straightforward nature of cases to be decided under that procedure.'[32]

Analysis and interpretation

Intervention as of right (art. 36(1))

The right of the State of nationality to request referral to the Court if the Commission found a case involving one of its citizens to be admissible, set out in article 48(b) of the 1950 text of the Convention, obviously disappeared with the abolition of the European Commission in accordance with Protocol No. 11. The provision was only invoked for the first time in 1989, in *Soering v. the United Kingdom*,[33] and once more prior to its repeal in 1998.[34] Otherwise, States were systematically informed of the possibility and more or less systematically declined to get involved.[35] Article 36(1) stands in its place, permitting the State of nationality to intervene in proceedings at the Court. However, in contrast with the situation under the former Convention, the State of nationality does not become a party to the proceedings. There have been several cases of such intervention,[36] but States

---

[31] Explanatory Report on Protocol No. 14, para. 87.

[32] Ibid., para. 89.

[33] *Soering v. the United Kingdom*, 7 July 1989, § 1, Series A no. 161. Prior to *Soering*, States had been informed of the possibility but did not show any interest: *Bozano v. France*, 18 December 1986, § 2, Series A no. 111; *Johnston and Others v. Ireland*, 18 December 1986, § 2, Series A no. 112; *O. v. the United Kingdom*, 8 July 1987, § 3, Series A no. 120.

[34] *Loizidou v. Turkey* (Preliminary objections), 23 March 1995, § 1, Series A no. 310.

[35] *John Murray v. the United Kingdom*, 8 February 1996, § 2, *Reports of Judgments and Decisions* 1996-I; *Hornsby v. Greece*, 19 March 1997, § 2, *Reports of Judgments and Decisions* 1997-II; *Bizzotto v. Greece*, 15 November 1996, § 2, *Reports of Judgments and Decisions* 1996-V; *Gül v. Switzerland*, 19 February 1996, § 2, *Reports of Judgments and Decisions* 1996-I; *Piermont v. France*, 27 April 1995, § 2, Series A no. 314; *Gasus Dosier- und Fördertechnik GmbH v. the Netherlands*, 23 February 1995, § 2, Series A no. 306-B; *Brannigan and McBride v. the United Kingdom*, 26 May 1993, § 2, Series A no. 258-B; *Paskhalidis and Others v. Greece*, 19 March 1997, § 2, *Reports of Judgments and Decisions* 1997-II; *Helmers v. Sweden*, 29 October 1991, § 2, Series A no. 212-A; *Scott v. Spain*, 18 December 1996, § 2, *Reports of Judgments and Decisions* 1996-VI; *Hamer v. France*, 7 August 1996, § 2, *Reports of Judgments and Decisions* 1996-III; *Bulut v. Austria*, 22 February 1996, § 2, *Reports of Judgments and Decisions* 1996-II; *British-American Tobacco Company Ltd v. the Netherlands*, 20 November 1995, § 2, Series A no. 331; *Van der Tang v. Spain*, 13 July 1995, § 2, Series A no. 321; *Brincat v. Italy*, 26 November 1992, § 2, Series A no. 249-A; *Rieme v. Sweden*, 22 April 1992, § 2, Series A no. 226-B; *Imbrioscia v. Switzerland*, 24 November 1993, § 2, Series A no. 275; *Quaranta v. Switzerland*, 24 May 1991, § 2, Series A no. 205; *Dobbertin v. France*, 25 February 1993, § 2, Series A no. 256-D; *Fey v. Austria*, 24 February 1993, § 2, Series A no. 255-A; *Vernillo v. France*, 20 February 1991, § 2, Series A no. 198.

[36] E.g., *Varnava and Others v. Turkey*, nos 16064/90, 16065/90, 16066/90, 16068/90, 16069/90, 16070/90, 16071/90, 16072/90, and 16073/90, § 7, 10 January 2008; *Kononov v. Latvia*, no. 36376/04, § 2, 24 July 2008; *Varnava and Others v. Turkey* [GC], nos 16064/90, 16065/90, 16066/90, 16068/90, 16069/90, 16070/90, 16071/90, 16072/90, and 16073/90, §§ 7, 16, ECHR 2009; *Kononov v. Latvia* [GC], no. 36376/04, § 2, ECHR 2010; *Demopoulos and Others v. Turkey* (dec.) [GC], nos 46113/99, 3843/02, 13751/02, 13466/03,

do not intervene systematically in cases where their nationals are involved.[37] The Rules of Court provide that the Registrar is to notify any State other than the respondent State if one of its nationals is a party.[38] The Registrar is also required to notify such a State if there is to be an oral hearing in the case.[39]

Although it was probably never contemplated by those who conceived of the right to intervene, situations have arisen where an individual alleges a real risk of violation of fundamental rights, notably those enshrined in articles 2 and 3, if that person is returned to the State of nationality. This is certainly not a situation that at all resembles the notion of diplomatic protection, from which article 36(1) was derived. According to the Court, in such cases the State of nationality 'does not appear objectively in a position to support its nationals. Moreover, Article 36 § 1 does not encompass a Member State's right to defend itself before the Court unless the applicants in their application claim to be victims of a violation of their rights by that Member State as well.'[40] It is, of course, open to an applicant to sue two States in the same proceeding, and to the extent that one of them is the State of nationality then it has no need to intervene because it is already a party.[41] Thus, it has been held that article 36(1) does not apply 'in cases where the applicants' reason for applying to the Court is fear of being returned to the relevant Member State, which allegedly will subject them to a treatment contrary to Articles 2 and 3 of the Convention. Consequently, in such circumstances, applications are not transmitted to the applicants' State of origin inviting their Government to intervene.'[42]

Intervention with leave (art. 36(2))

According to article 36(2), the President of the Court may, 'in the interest of the proper administration of justice', invite a State Party that is not a party to the proceedings or any person concerned who is not the applicant to submit written comments or take part in hearings.[43] On occasion, the Court has referred to this as a 'right to intervene',[44] but it seems clear from the Convention that this is overstating the situation. The contrast with article 36(1), where a genuine right is set out, is evident. Article 36(2) requires that the President of the Court authorize the intervention. The Rules of Court permit a Chamber to 'ask any person or institution of its choice to express an opinion or make a written report on any matter considered by it to be relevant to the case'.[45]

Rule 44(3)(b) of the Rules of Court states that requests for leave to intervene be 'duly reasoned' and submitted no later than twelve weeks after the notice of application has been given to the respondent State. It appears that authorization is routinely granted. It is

---

10200/04, 14163/04, 19993/04, and 21819/04, § 3, ECHR 2010; *Janowiec and Others v. Russia*, nos 55508/07 and 29520/09, § 4, 16 April 2012; *Janowiec and Others v. Russia* [GC], nos 55508/07 and 29520/09, § 4, ECHR 2013.

[37] *Krombach v. France*, no. 29731/96, § 7, ECHR 2001-II; *Hutten-Czapska v. Poland*, no. 35014/97, § 10, 22 February 2005.

[38] Rules of Court, Rule 44(1)(a).

[39] Ibid.

[40] *I. v. Sweden*, no. 61204/09, § 41, 5 September 2013.

[41] E.g., *Rantsev v. Cyprus and Russia*, no. 25965/04, ECHR 2010 (extracts); *M.S.S. v. Belgium and Greece* [GC], no. 30696/09, § ECHR 2011.

[42] *I. v. Sweden*, no. 61204/09, §§ 45–46, 5 September 2013.

[43] E.g., *Sejdovic v. Italy* [GC], no. 56581/00, § 8, ECHR 2006-II.

[44] *Saadi v. Italy* [GC], no. 37201/06, § 7, ECHR 2008.

[45] Rules of Court, Annex to the Rules (concerning investigations), Rule A 1(2).

not at all uncommon for several non-governmental organizations to intervene in a particular case, sometimes individually and sometimes collectively.[46] Much more unusual is an intervention by individuals.[47] Even governmental[48] and intergovernmental organizations[49] have been known to intervene in proceedings. In the case concerning CIA detention sites in Poland, the Chamber invited the United Nations Special Rapporteur on the promotion and protection of human rights and fundamental freedoms while countering terrorism to participate in the hearing.[50] The European Commission for Democracy through Law (Venice Commission) produced an opinion[51] at the request of a Chamber in a case concerning funding of a political party.[52] It has submitted *amicus curiae* briefs in a number of other cases.[53]

States intervene less frequently, generally when there is an issue that may concern them in other pending cases.[54] During the drafting of Protocol No. 14, there was 'wide agreement' about 'the need to encourage more frequent third party interventions by other states in cases pending before the Court which raise important general issues...'[55] Although actual participation in the hearing is rarely, if ever, accorded to individuals and

[46] See, e.g., *D.H. and Others v. the Czech Republic* [GC], no. 57325/00, § 9, ECHR 2007-IV; *Pini and Others v. Romania*, nos 78028/01 and 78030/01, § 7, ECHR 2004-V (extracts); *Al-Skeini and Others v. the United Kingdom* [GC], no. 55721/07, § 6, ECHR 2011.

[47] *Py v. France*, no. 66289/01, § 7, ECHR 2005-I (extracts); *Z and Others v. the United Kingdom* [GC], no. 29392/95, § 7, ECHR 2001-V; *T.P. and K.M. v. the United Kingdom* [GC], no. 28945/95, § 7, ECHR 2001-V (extracts); *Koua Poirrez v. France*, no. 40892/98, § 7, ECHR 2003-X; *Feldek v. Slovakia*, no. 29032/95, § 7, ECHR 2001-VIII.

[48] E.g., the Northern Ireland Human Rights Commission: *McKerr v. the United Kingdom*, no. 28883/95, § 7, ECHR 2001-III; *Hugh Jordan v. the United Kingdom*, no. 24746/94, § 7, ECHR 2001-III (extracts); *Shanaghan v. the United Kingdom*, no. 37715/97, § 7, 4 May 2001.

[49] E.g., the Organisation for Security and Cooperation in Europe: *Blečić v. Croatia*, no. 59532/00, § 6, 29 July 2004; the Office of the United Nations High Commissioner for Refugees: *M.S.S. v. Belgium and Greece* [GC], no. 30696/09, § 7, ECHR 2011 and *Ahmed Ali v. the Netherlands* (dec.), no. 26494, § 7, 24 January 2012; the Office of the United Nations High Commissioner for Human Rights: *M.S.S. v. Belgium and Greece* [GC], no. 30696/09, § 7, ECHR 2011.

[50] *Husayn Abu Zubaydah v. Poland*, no. 7511/13, § 8, 24 July 2014.

[51] Opinion on the Prohibition of Financial Contributions to Political Parties from Foreign Sources (*amicus curiae* opinion for the European Court of Human Rights) adopted by the Venice Commission at its 66th Plenary Session (Venice, 17–18 March 2006), CDL-AD(2006)014.

[52] *Parti nationaliste basque—Organisation régionale d'Iparralde v. France*, no. 71251/01, § 3, ECHR 2007-II.

[53] *Amicus curiae* brief in the case of *Rywin v. Poland* (Application nos 6091/06, 4047/07, and 4070/07) pending before the European Court of Human Rights (on Parliamentary Committees of inquiry) adopted by the Venice Commission at its 98th plenary session (Venice, 21–22 March 2014), CDL-AD(2014)013; *Amicus curiae* brief in the cases of *Sejdić and Finci v. Bosnia and Herzegovina* (Application nos 27996/06 and 34836/06) pending before The European Court of Human Rights adopted by the Venice Commission at its 76th Plenary Session (Venice, 17–18 October 2008), CDL-AD(2008)027; *Amicus curiae* brief in the case of *Bijelić v. Montenegro and Serbia* (Application N° 11890/05) pending before the European Court of Human Rights adopted by the Venice Commission at its 76th Plenary Session (Venice, 17–18 October 2008), CDL-AD(2008)021; *Amicus curiae* Opinion (Proceedings before the European Court of Human Rights) on the nature of proceedings before the Human Rights Chamber and the Constitutional Court of Bosnia and Herzegovina adopted by the Commission at its 63rd plenary session (Venice, 10–11 June 2005), CDL-AD(2005)020 (*in Jeličić v. Bosnia and Herzegovina*, no. 41183/02, ECHR 2006-XII).

[54] See, e.g., *Taxquet v. Belgium* [GC], no. 926/05, § 7, ECHR 2010; *Nada v. Switzerland* [GC], no. 10593/08, § 5, ECHR 2012; *S.A.S. v. France* [GC], no. 43835/11, §§ 8, 36–38, 1 July 2014; *Hirst v. the United Kingdom (no. 2)* [GC], no. 74025/01, § 9, ECHR 2005-IX.

[55] Explanatory Report on Protocol No. 14, para. 19.

non-governmental organizations, this has been allowed to States Parties in some cases.[56] Both the United Nations High Commissioner for Human Rights and the United Nations High Commissioner for Refugees participated in the oral hearing after making written submissions in one case.[57]

The submissions of interveners, especially non-governmental organizations, have been cited approvingly by the Court on some occasions. In *Soering*, the Court explicitly borrowed words from the Amnesty International submission to the effect that the 'virtual consensus in Western European legal systems that the death penalty is, under current circumstances, no longer consistent with regional standards of justice'.[58] It has also cited the submissions of Liberty, a London-based non-governmental organization, in assessing the existence of a European or international consensus on specific issues.[59] In one case, the Court noted the intervention by several non-governmental organizations in proceedings as something that 'highlights the general importance of the issue'.[60]

Intervention of the Commissioner for Human Rights (art. 36(3))

The Council of Europe Commissioner for Human Rights was established by the Committee of Ministers on 7 May 1999.[61] The Commissioner may intervene in proceedings as of right pursuant to article 36(3). The Commissioner is to advise the Registrar of the Court no later than twelve weeks after transmission of the application to the respondent State or notification to it of the decision to hold an oral hearing. The President of the Court may fix another time limit 'for exceptional reasons'. The Commissioner is also entitled to participate in the proceedings before the Court, either in person or, if unable to do so, by a person or persons so designated. The Commissioner may be assisted by an advocate.[62]

The Commissioner has only exercised this right to intervene in proceedings on one occasion. Of course, the Court has often cited reports of the Commissioner for Human Rights,[63] although it does not always heed the views of the Commissioner.[64] In a case concerning treatment of persons with disability, on the basis of article 36(3) the Commissioner submitted written observations to the Court and subsequently participated in the hearing with oral submissions.[65] The intervention by the Commissioner was confined to an admissibility issue, the standing of a non-governmental organization to submit an application on behalf of a severely disabled man who was already dead at the time of the application, and who did not apparently have any close relatives. The Commissioner

---

[56] *S.A.S. v. France* [GC], no. 43835/11, § 8, 1 July 2014; *M.S.S. v. Belgium and Greece* [GC], no. 30696/09, § 8, ECHR 2011. But not *Taxquet v. Belgium* [GC], no. 926/05, §§ 7–8, ECHR 2010; *Nada v. Switzerland* [GC], no. 10593/08, § 5, ECHR 2012.

[57] *M.S.S. v. Belgium and Greece* [GC], no. 30696/09, §§ 7–88, ECHR 2011.

[58] *Soering v. the United Kingdom*, 7 July 1989, § 102, Series A no. 161. Also *Chahal v. the United Kingdom*, 15 November 1996, §§ 99, 102, 145, *Reports of Judgments and Decisions* 1996-V; *Brannigan and McBride v. the United Kingdom*, 26 May 1993, Concurring Opinion of Judge Martens, § 1, Series A no. 258-B.

[59] *I. v. the United Kingdom* [GC], no. 25680/94, §§ 64, 83, 11 July 2002; *Sheffield and Horsham v. the United Kingdom*, 30 July 1998, § 57, *Reports of Judgments and Decisions* 1998-V.

[60] *Karner v. Austria*, no. 40016/98, § 28, ECHR 2003-IX.

[61] Resolution (99) 50.

[62] Rules of Court, Rule 44(2). See also Explanatory Report on Protocol No. 14, para. 88.

[63] E.g., *Oleksandr Volkov v. Ukraine*, no. 21722/11, § 80, 9 January 2013.

[64] *S.A.S. v. France* [GC], no. 43835/11, §§ 37, 147, 149, 1 July 2014.

[65] CommDH(2011)37, in *Centre for Legal Resources on behalf of Valentin Câmpeanu v. Romania* [GC], no. 47848/08, §§ 5, 6, 17 July 2014.

argued in favour of expanding the Court's approach to legal standing, 'recognising the invaluable contribution made by NGOs in the field of human rights for people with disabilities'.[66]

The Commissioner has also intervened in cases at the invitation of the Court. In a case involving expulsion of asylum seekers, the Commissioner made written submissions and participated in the oral hearing.[67] Information on the length of proceedings submitted by the Commissioner was accepted by the Court as evidence.[68] In a dissenting opinion, Judge Nicolas Bratza spoke of the 'powerful submissions' of the Commissioner for Human Rights.[69]

Further reading

Hervé Ascensio, '*L'amicus curiae* devant les juridictions internationales', [2001] *Revue générale de droit international public* 897.

Ireneu Cabral Barreto, 'Article 48', in Pettiti et al., *La Convention européenne*, pp. 793–803.

Nicole Bürli, '*Amicus curiae* as a Means to Reinforce the Legitimacy of the European Court of Human Rights', in Spyridon Flogaitis, Tom Zwart, and Julie Fraser, eds, *The European Court of Human Rights and its Discontents, Turning Criticism into Strength*, Cheltenham, UK/Northampton, MA: Edward Elgar, 2013, pp. 135–46.

Frowein/Peukert, *MenschenRechtsKonvention*, pp. 521–2.

Janneke Gerards and Ashley Terlouw, 'Solutions for the European Court of Human Rights: The *Amicus Curiae* Project', in Spyridon Flogaitis, Tom Zwart, and Julie Fraser, eds, *The European Court of Human Rights and its Discontents, Turning Criticism into Strength*, Cheltenham, UK / Northampton, MA: Edward Elgar, 2013, pp. 158–82.

Antony Lester, '*Amici curiae*: Third Party Interventions before the European Court of Human Rights', in F. Matscher and H. Petzold, eds, *Protecting Human Rights: The European Dimension*, Cologne: Carl Heymanns, 1988, pp. 341–9.

J.H. Gerards and A. Terlouw, eds, *Amici curiae. Adviezen aan het Europees Hof voor de Rechten van de Mens*, Nijmegen: Wolf Legal Publishers, 2012.

Leo Zwaak, 'The Procedure before the European Court of Human Rights', in Van Dijk et al., *Theory and Practice*, pp. 204–6.

---

[66] *Centre for Legal Resources on behalf of Valentin Câmpeanu v. Romania* [GC], no. 47848/08, §§ 92–93, 17 July 2014.

[67] CommDH(2010)22, in *M.S.S. v. Belgium and Greece* [GC], no. 30696/09, §§ 7–8, ECHR 2011. See also *Ahmed Ali v. the Netherlands and Greece* (dec.), no. 26494/09, § 7, 24 January 2012; *Djelani Sufi, Hassan Guduud, and Others v. the Netherlands and Greece* (dec.), no. 28631/09, § 7, 20 September 2011.

[68] *M.S.S. v. Belgium and Greece* [GC], no. 30696/09, § 320, ECHR 2011.

[69] *M.S.S. v. Belgium and Greece* [GC], no. 30696/09, Partly Dissenting Opinion of Judge Bratza, § 9, ECHR 2011.

Article 37. Striking out applications/Radiation

1. The Court may at any stage of the proceedings decide to strike an application out of its list of cases where the circumstances lead to the conclusion that

(a) the applicant does not intend to pursue his application; or

(b) the matter has been resolved; or

(c) for any other reason established by the Court, it is no longer justified to continue the examination of the application.

However, the Court shall continue the examination of the application if respect for human rights as defined in the Convention and the Protocols thereto so requires.

2. The Court may decide to restore an application to its list of cases if it considers that the circumstances justify such a course.

1. A tout moment de la procédure, la Cour peut décider de rayer une requête du rôle lorsque les circonstances permettent de conclure

a) que le requérant n'entend plus la maintenir; ou

b) que le litige a été résolu; ou

c) que, pour tout autre motif dont la Cour constate l'existence, il ne se justifie plus de poursuivre l'examen de la requête.

Toutefois, la Cour poursuit l'examen de la requête si le respect des droits de l'homme garantis par la Convention et ses Protocoles l'exige.

2. La Cour peut décider la réinscription au rôle d'une requête lorsqu'elle estime que les circonstances le justifient.

Introductory comments

All courts require some mechanism enabling them to dispose of cases when the parties no longer wish to proceed, or when the dispute has been settled, or when the facts have changed rendering the continuation of proceedings to be of no practical use. Because human rights issues may be of significance that goes well beyond the interests and wishes of the parties, the Convention circumscribes this power somewhat, authorizing the Court to proceed with cases under specific circumstances even if this is not the wish of the parties.

Drafting of the provision

Nothing resembling article 37 is found in the 1950 text of the Convention. A provision authorizing the European Commission of Human Rights to strike out an application was introduced as article 30 by Protocol No. 8, which entered into force in 1990.[1] The provision was described as 'thereby confirming what is already a long-established practice'.[2] Indeed, the only substantive change to the practice then followed by the Commission was the introduction of paragraph 1(c). The Explanatory Report notes that the Commission had assumed the power to do this from its creation. It said that 'it was felt

---

[1] Protocol No. 8 to the Convention for the Protection of Human Rights and Fundamental Freedoms, ETS 118, art. 6.

[2] Explanatory Report on Protocol No. 8, para. 10.

appropriate' to regulate the power of the Commission in this area, although detailed rules concerning the striking out of applications would be left to the Commission's rules of procedure. The Explanatory Report says that it was not considered necessary to adopt a similar provision for the Court, noting that the power had also been introduced into the Rules of Court.[3]

Protocol No. 11 made only very minor changes to the text. The second paragraph of article 30, which dealt with the procedure of the European Commission, was removed. Otherwise, the first and third paragraphs were altered by replacing the word 'Commission' with 'Court'. The word 'petition' in the first sentence of former article 30 was replaced with 'application' wherever it occurred. Finally, the term 'Convention' was changed to 'Convention and its Protocols'. The title of the provision, 'Striking-out applications', was also added by Protocol No. 11, and it was renumbered as article 37. According to the Explanatory Report:

As was the case under former Article 30 of the Convention, the power to strike out is extended to applications submitted by a State under Article 33 as well as applications submitted by an individual under Article 34. Although it could be argued that an inherent power to strike out cases is vested in any court, this article has been included to avoid any doubts on the matter.[4]

Thus, there was no significant modification in the provision introduced by Protocol No. 11 that would suggest a change in interpretation.

Analysis and interpretation

At any stage of the proceedings, the Court may decide to strike an application out of its list of cases in accordance with article 37 of the Convention.[5] Striking out of a case from the list may take place when an applicant has lost the status of a victim within the meaning of article 34, when the matter has been resolved, and for any other reason deemed appropriate by the Court. Sub-paragraph (a) of paragraph 1 is dependent upon the will of the applicant, whereas sub-paragraphs (b) and (c) may apply regardless of the applicant's intention and even if he or she is still a victim within the meaning of article 34 of the Convention.[6] In inter-State cases, when an applicant State Party notifies the Registrar of its intention not to proceed with the case, the Chamber is empowered to strike the application out of the Court's list pursuant to article 37 of the Convention if the other State Party or Parties concerned in the case agree to such discontinuance.[7]

If there is a friendly settlement pursuant to article 39, the application is struck out of the Court's list by means of a decision. Article 39(4) of the Convention declares that the decision is transmitted to the Committee of Ministers for the supervision of its execution. In other cases contemplated by article 37, if the application has already been declared admissible it is struck out by a judgment. If it has not yet been declared admissible, it is struck out by a decision. In the case of a judgment, the President of the Chamber forwards

---

[3] Explanatory Report on Protocol No. 8, para. 34.
[4] Explanatory Report on Protocol No. 11, para. 92.
[5] Rules of Court, Rule 43(1).
[6] *Pisano v. Italy* (striking out) [GC], no. 36732/97, § 34, 24 October 2002; *Akman v. Turkey* (striking out), no. 37453/97, ECHR 2001-VI; *Tanda-Muzinga v. France*, no. 2260/10, § 57, 10 July 2014.
[7] Rules of Court, Rule 43(2). See *Denmark, Norway, and Sweden v. Greece*, no. 4448/70, Commission report of 4 October 1976.

the judgment, once it has become final, to the Committee of Ministers for supervision, pursuant to article 46(2), the execution of any undertakings that were made as part of the settlement of the case.[8]

Failure to pursue an application (art. 37(1)(a))

Neither the Convention nor the Rules contemplate expressly the possibility of a discontinuance. Indeed, use of the word 'may' in the opening sentence of article 37(1) as well as the final sentence in paragraph 37(1) confirms that the Court is not bound to strike out a case simply because the applicant has indicated a desire to stop the proceedings. Nevertheless, in practice the Court will often strike out a case if the applicant had made clear an intent not to pursue the case.[9] This may be indicated implicitly, by a failure to respond to communications from the Court.[10] Sometimes the Court will conclude that an applicant has 'lost interest' in pursuing the case and strike it from the list.[11] If the applicant dies during the proceedings, it may be possible for next of kin to continue the case. But if no relative wishes to do this, article 37(1)(a) will apply.[12]

Matter resolved (art. 37(1)(b))

The Court may strike a case from the list if 'the matter has been resolved'. This requires the Court to address two issues. First, it must determine that the circumstances that form the basis of the application no longer obtain. Second, it must confirm that the effects of a possible violation of the Convention resulting from such circumstances have been redressed.[13] The fact that a decision or measure favourable to the applicant has been taken by the government does not in itself remove the 'victim status' unless it is shown that the national authorities both acknowledged the violation of the Convention and provided some form of redress.[14] Developments subsequent to the submission of the application may be taken into account. For example, where an asylum seeker was separated from his family for several years, the decision to enable family reunification did not sufficiently address the violation of the Convention that had taken place.[15]

[8] Ibid., Rule 43(3).
[9] *D.D. v. France* (striking out), no. 3/02, §§ 28–29, 8 November 2005; *Zanguropol v. Romania* (striking out), no. 29959/96, §§ 31–32, 8 April 2003; *Duveau v. France* (striking out), no. 77403/01, § 20, 26 April 2005; *Teret v. Belgium* (striking out), no. 49497/99, §§ 13–14, 15 November 2002.
[10] *Witczak v. Poland* (striking out), no. 47404/99, §§ 15–18, 6 May 2003.
[11] *Berdji v. France* (striking out), no. 74184/01, §§ 19–29, 7 March 2006; *Baldi v. Italy* (striking out), no. 32584/96, §§ 19–21, 11 December 2003; *Mróz v. Poland* (striking out), no. 35192/97, §§ 51–53, 9 December 2003; *Istituto Nazionale Case Srl v. Italy* (striking out), nos 41479/78, §§ 16–19, 6 November 2003.
[12] *Bitsinas v. Greece* (striking out), no. 33076/02, § 12, 15 November 2005.
[13] *Pisano v. Italy* (striking out) [GC], no. 36732/97, § 42, 24 October 2002; *Sisojeva and Others v. Latvia* (striking out) [GC], no. 60654/00, § 97, ECHR 2007-I; *El Majjaoui and Stichting Touba Moskee v. the Netherlands* (striking out) [GC], no. 25525/03, § 30, 20 December 2007; *Shevanova v. Latvia* (striking out) [GC], no. 58822/00, § 45, 7 December 2007.
[14] *Amuur v. France*, 25 June 1996, § 36, *Reports of Judgments and Decisions* 1996-III; *Dalban v. Romania* [GC], no. 28114/95, § 44, ECHR 1999-VI; *Ilaşcu and Others v. Moldova and Russia* (dec.) [GC], no. 48787/99, 4 July 2001.
[15] *Tanda-Muzinga v. France*, no. 2260/10, § 58, 10 July 2014.

No longer justified (art. 37(1)(c))

A case may be struck out from the list where the State has made a unilateral declaration that the Court deems to be an acceptable offer of settlement, even if it is not considered adequate by the applicant.[16] Nevertheless, the Grand Chamber may reverse a decision taken by a Chamber to strike out a case because of a unilateral declaration by a State. According to the Grand Chamber, the application of article 37(1)(c) in a situation of unilateral declaration depends upon whether it offers a sufficient basis for finding that respect for human rights does not require it to continue an examination of the case. The Grand Chamber said:

Relevant factors in this respect include the nature of the complaints made, whether the issues raised are comparable to issues already determined by the Court in previous cases, the nature and scope of any measures taken by the respondent Government in the context of the execution of judgments delivered by the Court in any such previous cases, and the impact of these measures on the case at issue. It may also be material whether the facts are in dispute between the parties, and, if so, to what extent, and what prima facie evidentiary value is to be attributed to the parties' submissions on the facts. In that connection it will be of significance whether the Court itself has already taken evidence in the case for the purposes of establishing disputed facts. Other relevant factors may include the question of whether in their unilateral declaration the respondent Government have made any admission(s) in relation to the alleged violations of the Convention and, if so, the scope of such admissions and the manner in which they intend to provide redress to the applicant. As to the last-mentioned point, in cases in which it is possible to eliminate the effects of an alleged violation (as, for example, in some property cases) and the respondent Government declare their readiness to do so, the intended redress is more likely to be regarded as appropriate for the purposes of striking out the application, the Court, as always, retaining its power to restore the application to its list as provided in Article 37 § 2 of the Convention and Rule 44 § 5 of the Rules of Court.[17]

The Grand Chamber noted that the list it was proposing was not meant to be exhaustive and that further considerations might come into play in the future.[18]

The Court has wide discretion to identify grounds that fall within article 37(1)(c).[19] Such grounds must 'reside in the particular circumstances of each case'.[20] When the provision was first introduced into the Convention, in Protocol No. 8, the Explanatory Report said that '[t]he authors of the Protocol considered that the scope of this sub-paragraph should be limited to cases which are comparable to those mentioned in sub-paragraphs a and b, for example, where the applicant has died and his heirs do not have a sufficient legal interest to justify the further examination of the petition on their behalf'.[21]

It is not unusual for an applicant to wish to withdraw the case because the source of the complaint has been resolved. The Court applies article 37(1)(c) in granting such a

---

[16] *T.A. v. Turkey*, no. 26307/95, § 64, 9 April 2002; *Haran v. Turkey* (striking out), no. 25754/94, § 23, 26 March 2002; *Tahsin Acar v. Turkey* (preliminary issue) [GC], no. 26307/95, § 75, ECHR 2003-VI; *Meriakri v. Moldova* (striking out), no. 53487/99, § 31, 1 March 2005. See also *Tahsin Acar v. Turkey* (preliminary issue) [GC], no. 26307/95, Joint Concurring Opinion of Judges Sir Nicolas Bratza, Tulkens, and Vajić, ECHR 2003-VI; *Tahsin Acar v. Turkey* (preliminary issue) [GC], no. 26307/95, Concurring Opinion of Judge Ress, ECHR 2003-VI.

[17] *Tahsin Acar v. Turkey* (preliminary issue) [GC], no. 26307/95, § 76, ECHR 2003-VI.

[18] Ibid., § 77.

[19] *Sergey Zolotukhin v. Russia* [GC], no. 14939/03, § 115, ECHR 2009.

[20] *Association SOS Attentats and de Boery v. France* [GC] (dec.), no. 76642/01, § 37, 2006-XIV; *M.H. and A.S. v. the United Kingdom* (dec.), nos 38267/07 and 14293/07, 16 December 2008.

[21] Explanatory Report on Protocol No. 8, para. 35.

request.[22] In such cases, it may be that subparagraphs (a) and (c) both apply.[23] The Court accepted a unilateral declaration by the United Kingdom in a case concerning nearly 200 Somali asylum seekers.[24]

Respect for human rights (art. 37(1) *in fine*)

Even if the other conditions are fulfilled, the Court will not strike out a case 'if respect for human rights as defined in the Convention and the Protocols thereto so requires'. The same expression is used in article 35(3)(b), whereby the Court may apply the *de minimis* principle and find an application to be inadmissible, and in article 39, governing a friendly settlement. In effect, once an application has been filed, even the consent of the parties is not enough, as a matter of law, to ensure that there is no assessment by the Court. The Explanatory Report on Protocol No. 8, from which this provision originated, states that in assessing the issue of respect for human rights, 'the views of the respondent state as to the general interest in continuing with the examination of a petition should be given due weight'.[25]

The *raison d'être* of this exception is that 'human rights cases before the Court generally also have a moral dimension, which must be taken into account when considering whether the examination of an application after the applicant's death should be continued. All the more so if the main issue raised by the case transcends the person and the interests of the applicant.'[26] Thus, '[a]lthough the primary purpose of the Convention system is to provide individual relief, its mission is also to determine issues on public-policy grounds in the common interest, thereby raising the general standards of protection of human rights and extending human rights jurisprudence throughout the community of Convention States'.[27]

Before the human rights exception had been codified by Protocol No. 8 to the Convention, the European Commission of Human Rights had already recognized something similar. In *Tyrer*, a leading case dealing with corporal punishment, the Commission decided 'not to accede to the applicant's purported withdrawal of the application . . . since the case raised questions of a general character affecting the observance of the Convention which necessitated a further examination of the issues involved'.[28] In a case concerning differential treatment of homosexuals with respect to succession to tenancies, the Court considered that the application raised 'an important question of general interest not only for Austria but also for other States Parties to the Convention'. Rejecting the government's application to strike the case, the Court said that 'continued examination of the present application would contribute to elucidate, safeguard and develop the standards of protection under the Convention'.[29] Usually, however, the Court will make a perfunctory

---

[22] *Asadov and Others v. Azerbaijan* (striking out), no. 138/03, §§ 14–15, 26 October 2006; *Fazilet Partisi and Kutan v. Turkey* (striking out), no. 1444/02, §§ 9–10, 27 April 2006.

[23] *Koroniotis v. Germany* (striking out), no. 66046/01, § 21, 21 April 2005.

[24] *Musa and Others v. the United Kingdom* (striking out), no. 8276/07, 26 June 2012.

[25] Explanatory Report on Protocol No. 8, para. 36.

[26] *Karner v. Austria*, no. 40016/98, § 25, ECHR 2003-IX; *Micallef v. Malta* [GC], no. 17056/06, § 45, ECHR 2009; *Malhous v. the Czech Republic* [GC] (dec.), no. 33071/96, ECHR 2000-XII.

[27] *Karner v. Austria*, no. 40016/98, § 26, ECHR 2003-IX; *Marie-Louise Loyen and Bruneel v. France*, no. 55929/00, § 29, 5 July 2005.

[28] *Tyrer v. the United Kingdom*, no. 5856/72, Commission report of 14 December 1976, Appendix I, p. 25, referring to a Commission decision of 9 March 1976.

[29] *Karner v. Austria*, no. 40016/98, §§ 24–25, ECHR 2003-IX.

statement to the effect that 'no particular reason relating to respect for human rights as defined in the Convention requires it to continue the examination of the application'.[30]

Restoration to the list (art. 37(2))

Exceptional circumstances allow the Court to restore a case to its list if it has previously been struck out.[31] It may do this with respect to part of an application and not all of it.[32] Although the Convention provides no specifics on the legal consequences, it would seem that the applicant is thereby restored to the position that he or she was in at the time the case was struck out. The Explanatory Report on Protocol No. 8, in which the ancestor of this provision was first introduced to the Convention, says that 'bearing in mind the general requirement of legal certainty, it is to be expected that this power will be exercised very rarely'.[33] Indeed, there are very few examples in the case law of the provision being considered.

The Court will restore a case that was struck out because there was a friendly settlement whose terms and conditions were not then respected by the State.[34] The Court applied the provision where the State transferred the settlement sum to the account of two disabled applicants. However, the applicants could not themselves access the account and the money was not being spent on their welfare by those responsible for their care.[35] A case was also restored where a detainee dropped his application because it was a condition for a plea bargain with the prosecution that was to result in release. He claimed to have been misled by the authorities, renewing his allegations about the absence of appropriate medical care in prison. The Court agreed to restore the portion of the original application that was based upon violations of article 3 of the Convention.

In a case dealing with entitlement to social insurance that was submitted by several applicants, the representative of one of them informed the Court that for personal reasons she did not wish to continue. This was confirmed in a second letter and the Court agreed to grant the request, acknowledging her desire and considering that respect for human rights did not compel it to continue. Some weeks later, the applicant's representative said she had changed her mind. Noting that the original request to withdraw from the case was clear and unequivocal and that there was nothing to suggest the decision of the applicant had not been made freely, and considering that the issues were in any event being pursued by the other applicants, the Court said there was no reason to restore the application to the list.[36]

The Court has taken into consideration the passage of a considerable lapse of time—several years—between the consent that a case be struck out and a request that it be restored in dismissing such an application.[37]

---

[30] *Sisojeva and Others v. Latvia* (striking out) [GC], no. 60654/00, § 103, ECHR 2007-I; *El Majjaoui and Stichting Touba Moskee v. the Netherlands* (striking out) [GC], no. 25525/03, § 35, 20 December 2007; *Pisano v. Italy* (striking out) [GC], no. 36732/97, § 49, 24 October 2002.

[31] Rules of Court, Rule 45.

[32] *Jashi v. Georgia*, no. 10799/06, 9 December 2008.

[33] Explanatory Report on Protocol No. 8, para. 39.

[34] *Aleksentseva and 28 Others v. Russia* (dec.), no. 75025/01, ECHR, 23 March 2006.

[35] *Katić and Katić v. Serbia*, no. 13920/04, 7 July 2009.

[36] *Stec and Others v. the United Kingdom* (dec.) [GC], nos 65731/01 and 65900/01, §§ 29–32, ECHR 2005-X.

[37] *Matyar v. Turkey*, no. 23423/94, §§ 134–135, 21 February 2002.

Costs

If an application is struck out from the list pursuant to article 37, any award of costs to the applicant is at the discretion of the Court.[38] If costs are awarded in a decision striking out an application that was not previously declared admissible, the President of the Chamber is required to forward the decision to the Committee of Ministers.[39]

Further reading

Fiona Ang and Eva Berghmans, 'Friendly Settlements and Striking Out of Applications', in Paul Lemmens and Wouter Vandenhole, eds, *Protocol No. 14 and the Reform of the European Court of Human Rights*, Antwerp: Intersentia, 2005, pp. 89–104.

Frowein/Peukert, *MenschenRechtsKonvention*, pp. 523–6.

Stefan Trechsel, 'Article 30', in Pettiti et al., *La Convention européenne*, pp. 687–90.

Leo Zwaak, 'The Procedure before the European Court of Human Rights', in Van Dijk et al., *Theory and Practice*, pp. 207–13.

---

[38] Rules of Court, Rule 44(3).
[39] Ibid., Rule 43(4).

Article 38. Examination of the case/Examen contradictoire de l'affaire

The Court shall examine the case together with the representatives of the parties and, if need be, undertake an investigation, for the effective conduct of which the High Contracting Parties concerned shall furnish all necessary facilities.	La Cour examine l'affaire de façon contradictoire avec les représentants des parties et, s'il y a lieu, procède à une enquête pour la conduite efficace de laquelle les Hautes Parties contractantes intéressées fourniront toutes facilités nécessaires.

Introductory comments

There is no detailed provision in the Convention for the procedure to be followed and the evidentiary rules that are to be applied. It is relatively simple in nature and therefore well suited to an institution that receives litigants from scores of different legal systems, many of them without experience before the Convention organs and even, in some cases, without legal training or qualification. To some extent, the procedural regime has been developed within the Rules of Court. As for the rules of evidence, they are largely the result of evolving practice as developed in the case law.

Drafting of the provision

The ancestor of article 38 is article 28 of the 1950 Convention. It concerned the European Commission, not the European Court, however. It was the former that had the primary responsibility for fact-finding under the former Convention, although the possibility of the Court not only hearing evidence but even soliciting it, *proprio motu*, could not be excluded.[1]

The Draft Statute that was annexed to the initial draft European Convention on Human Rights prepared by the International Juridical Section of the European Movement made detailed provision for the conduct of proceedings, including the presentation of evidence.[2] In Section III of its draft Convention, dealing with the functions of the European Commission, the Consultative Assembly adopted the following provision:

The Commission shall then undertake:
1) An investigation of the application with the assistance of the representatives of either party;
2) If necessary, an enquiry.[3]

The Consultative Assembly text was referred by the Committee of Ministers to a Committee of Experts that met in February and March 1950. The French expert, Charles

---

[1] See, for example, *Ireland v. the United Kingdom*, 18 January 1978, § 184, Series A no. 25.

[2] Draft Statute of the European Court of Human Rights, INF/5/E/R, I *TP* 302–321, at pp. 314–16, arts. 36–49.

[3] Recommendation No. 38 to the Committee of Ministers adopted 8 September 1949 on the conclusion of the debates, Doc. AS (1) 108, II *TP* 274–83, at p. 280, art. 13.

Chaumont, proposed that paragraph 2 be replaced with: 'If need be, an enquiry; the State concerned shall furnish all facilities necessary for the efficient conduct of this enquiry.'[4] It was incorporated in the draft adopted by the Committee of Experts.

In the event of the Commission accepting the application, it shall then undertake:
a) an investigation of the application with the assistance of the representative of either party;
b) if need be, an enquiry; the State concerned shall furnish all facilities necessary for the efficient conduct of this enquiry, after an exchange of views with the Commission.[5]

The Committee of Ministers referred the draft to a Conference of Senior Officials, Its drafting Sub-Committee made a number of changes to the provision.[6] The final version adopted by the Conference stated:

In the event of the Commission accepting the application, it shall then undertake:
a) an examination of the application with the representatives of the parties of the application;
b) if need be, an investigation, for the effective conduct of which, the States concerned shall furnish all facilities after an exchange of views with the Commission.[7]

The Committee of Ministers consolidated the two paragraphs:

In the event of the Commission accepting a matter referred to it:
a) it shall, with a view to ascertaining the facts, undertake an examination, together with the representatives of the parties, of the matter and, if need be, an investigation, for the effective conduct of which the States concerned shall furnish all facilities after an exchange of views with the Commission.[8]

The final version of article 28(a), adopted in November 1950, reads as follows:

1. In the event of the Commission accepting a petition referred to it:
   (a) it shall, with a view to ascertaining the facts, undertake together with the representatives of the parties an examination of the petition and, if need be, an investigation, for the effective conduct of which the States concerned shall furnish all necessary facilities, after an exchange of views with the Commission;

As a consequence of Protocol No. 11, article 28 was replaced by article 38:

Examination of the case and friendly settlement proceedings
1. If the Court declares the application admissible, it shall:
   a. pursue the examination of the case, together with the representatives of the parties, and if need be, undertake an investigation, for the effective conduct of which the States concerned shall furnish all necessary facilities;

---

[4] Amendments to Articles 20 and 27 of the Recommendation of the Consultative Assembly proposed by the French Expert, Doc. A 794, III *TP* 198–201.

[5] Appendix to the Report of the Committee of Experts on Human Rights: Draft Convention of Protection of Human Rights and Fundamental Freedoms, 16 March 1950, Doc. CM/WP 1 (50) 15 appendix, CM/WP 1 (50) 14 revised, A 925, IV *TP* 50–79, at p. 68, art. 20(24). Also Preliminary Draft Convention for the Maintenance and Further Realisation of Human Rights and Fundamental Freedoms, 15 February 1950, Doc. A 833, III *TP* 236–46, at p. 242, art. 18; First part of the proposals of the Drafting Sub-Committee concerning Sections II and III put forward by MM. Perassi, Salen, and Chaumont, Doc. A 806, III *TP* 212–17, at p. 214, art. 14.

[6] New draft Section III prepared by the Drafting Sub-Committee, Doc. CM/WP 4 (50) 11, A 1374, IV *TP* 194–9, at p. 196, art. H.

[7] Draft Convention annexed to the Report, Doc. CM/WP 4 (50) 19 annex, CM/WP 4 (50) rev., A 1452, IV *TP* 274–95, at p. 286, art. 26.

[8] Draft Convention adopted by the Committee of Ministers, 7 August 1950, Doc. A 1937, V *TP* 120–45, at p. 134, art. 28; Draft Convention adopted by the Sub-Committee, Doc. CM 1 (50) 52, A 1884, V *TP* 76–99, at p. 88, art. 28.

Paragraph 1 of article 38 is based on paragraph 1 of article 28 of the 1950 text of the Convention, as the Explanatory Report to Protocol No. 11 makes clear. It adds that the paragraph has been 'somewhat shortened'. According to the Report, '[t]he Court is responsible for the establishment of the facts and may conduct an investigation on the understanding that the parties furnish the Court with all the relevant information'.[9]

Article 38 was modified by Protocol No. 14. The second paragraph of article 38, dealing with friendly settlement proceedings, became a distinct provision, article 39. According to the Explanatory Report,

Article 38 incorporates the provisions of paragraph 1.a of former Article 38. The changes are intended to allow the Court to examine cases together with the Parties' representatives, and to undertake an investigation, not only when the decision on admissibility has been taken, but at any stage in the proceedings. They are a logical consequence of the changes made in Articles 28 and 29, which encourage the taking of joint decisions on the admissibility and merits of individual applications. Since this provision applies even before the decision on admissibility has been taken, High Contracting Parties are required to provide the Court with all necessary facilities prior to that decision. The Parties' obligations in this area are thus reinforced. It was not considered necessary to amend Article 38 (or Article 34, last sentence) in other respects, notably as regards possible non-compliance with these provisions. These provisions already provide strong legal obligations for the High Contracting Parties and, in line with current practice, any problems which the Court might encounter in securing compliance can be brought to the attention of the Committee of Ministers so that the latter take any steps it deems necessary.[10]

Analysis and interpretation

Article 38 sets out several principles concerning the examination of the case by the European Court of Human Rights. First, it establishes that the Court is to examine the case 'together with the representatives of the parties'. The French version is slightly more detailed in this respect: 'de façon contradictoire avec les représentants des parties', although it seems that the two versions state 'en substance la même idée'.[11] The details on how this examination is to be conducted are left to the Rules of Court.

The possibility that the Court may undertake an investigation is recognized. Finally, the obligation on the parties to 'furnish all necessary facilities' to facilitate 'the effective conduct' of any investigation is affirmed. Investigations by the Court are quite unusual. Detailed provision for their conduct is found in the Rules of Court.

Conduct of the examination

With respect to individual applications, upon receipt of an application, a number is assigned and a legal officer of the Court makes a preliminary review of the petition. At this pre-judicial stage, a large number of applications appear to be 'disposed of administratively', according to statistical information published by the Court. Each case is then assigned to a single judge, a three-judge Committee, or a seven-judge Chamber. Each one of these judicial formations may reject the application summarily based upon an initial assessment.[12] Those that pass this initial filtering are 'communicated' to the respondent State. The Court may request the parties to provide factual information, documents, and other

---

[9] Explanatory Report on Protocol No. 11, para. 93.
[10] Explanatory Report on Protocol No. 14, para. 90.
[11] Stefan Trechsel, 'Article 28§1-a', in Pettiti et al., *La Convention européenne*, pp. 649–59, at p. 652.
[12] Rules of Court, Rules 52A(1), 53(1), 54(1).

materials considered relevant.[13] It will also give notice of the application, or that part that it does not consider to be evidently inadmissible, inviting the respondent State to submit written observations. These are then transmitted to the applicant, who is invited to submit observations in reply.[14] The Court may then seek additional submissions from the parties.[15] Upon the request of one of the parties or on its own motion, the Chamber may decide to hold an oral hearing.[16]

With respect to inter-State cases, there is no initial screening. Notice of the application is given immediately to the respondent State.[17] The respondent State is invited to submit its observations on the issue of admissibility. The applicant State may make written observations in reply.[18] Further submissions on the issue of admissibility may be requested by the Court.[19] If the Court decides to admit the application, it sets down time limits for filing of written submissions on the merits and the production of additional evidence.[20] An oral hearing on both admissibility and the merits may be held if requested by one of the parties or if the Chamber so decides.[21]

In the vast majority of cases, the submissions are entirely written and no hearing is conducted.[22] Pleadings may be filed with the Court in hard copy, by fax, or electronically.[23] When a hearing takes place, it is in principle open to the public, although in exceptional circumstances some or all of it may be held *in camera*.[24] The President of the Chamber organizes and directs the hearings, prescribing the order in which the parties address the Court.[25] Typically, each of the parties is given 30 minutes in which to make submissions. This is followed by questions from members of the Chamber.[26] After a brief pause, the parties have a short period of time in which to reply to the submissions of the other party and to respond to the questions from the bench, if any. Very exceptionally, the hearing may also involve testimony of material or expert witnesses.[27] At the hearing, any judge may put questions to a person appearing before the Chamber.[28] If a party or any other person due to appear fails to do so or declines to appear, the Chamber may nevertheless proceed with the hearing 'provided that it is satisfied that such a course is consistent with the proper administration of justice'.[29] The President may require that a verbatim record of the hearing be prepared, the contents of which are prescribed in the Rules of Court.[30]

---

[13] Ibid., Rules 53(2), 54(2)(a).
[14] Ibid., Rule 54(2)(b).
[15] Ibid., Rules 54(2)(c), 59(1).
[16] Ibid., Rules 54(5), 59(3).
[17] Ibid., Rule 51(1).
[18] Ibid., Rule 51(3).
[19] Ibid., Rule 51(4).
[20] Ibid., Rule 58(1).
[21] Ibid., Rules 51(5), 58(2).
[22] See Practice Direction, Written Pleadings, 10 December 2007.
[23] See Practice Direction, Secured Electronic Filing, 22 September 2008.
[24] Rules of Court, Rule 63. See *Husayn (Abu Zubaydah) v. Poland*, no. 7511/13, § 8, 24 July 2014.
[25] Rules of Court, Rule 64.
[26] Ibid., Rule 64(2).
[27] E.g., *Husayn (Abu Zubaydah) v. Poland*, no. 7511/13, § 8, 24 July 2014.
[28] Rules of Court, Rule 64(2).
[29] Ibid., Rule 65.
[30] Ibid., Rule 70.

Pursuant to the Rules of Court, a Chamber may 'ask any person or institution of its choice to express an opinion or make a written report on any matter considered by it to be relevant to the case'.[31] For example, the European Commission for Democracy through Law (Venice Commission) produced an opinion[32] at the request of a Chamber in a case concerning funding of a political party.[33] This seems essentially the same as the *amicus curiae* function provided for in article 36(2) of the Convention.

Investigations and fact-finding

The vast majority of cases that come before the Court raise issues concerning the application of national legislation, its consistency with the Convention, and the operation of the judicial system. Because of the requirement of exhaustion of domestic remedies, which is itself rooted in the principle of subsidiarity, the factual underpinning of cases has usually been well established at the domestic level before it gets to the European Court. Not only does the European Court of Human Rights not sit as a tribunal of fourth instance, it also 'has consistently recognised that it must be cautious in taking on the role of a first-instance tribunal of fact, where this is not rendered unavoidable by the circumstances of a particular case'.[34] There is great deference for the findings of fact by domestic courts.[35] Although the Court is not bound by such conclusions at the national level and remains free to reach its own view of the facts, 'in normal circumstances it requires cogent elements to lead it to depart from the findings of fact reached by the domestic courts'.[36] In some circumstances, the Court has found it necessary to undertake fact-finding, notably, although not exclusively, in inter-State cases. This function of the Court is expressly provided by article 38 in the reference to its authority to 'undertake an investigation'.

The investigative function of the Court is framed in the Annex to the Rules (concerning investigations). This document provides that a Chamber may, at the request of a party or *proprio motu*, 'adopt any investigative measure which it considers capable of clarifying the facts of the case'. Specifically, it says such measures may include 'inviting' the parties to produce documentary evidence and the hearing of witnesses or experts.[37] The Annex to the Rules refers to conducting an inquiry, carrying out an on-site visit, and 'tak[ing] evidence in some other manner'.[38]

The investigation may be conducted by the Chamber itself[39] or by a 'delegate' or 'delegates' who compose a 'delegation'. These are judges of the Court, normally members

---

[31] Ibid., Annex to the Rules (concerning investigations), Rule A 1(2).

[32] Opinion on the Prohibition of Financial Contributions to Political Parties from Foreign Sources (*amicus curiae* opinion for the European Court of Human Rights) adopted by the Venice Commission at its 66th Plenary Session (Venice, 17–18 March 2006), CDL-AD(2006)014.

[33] *Parti nationaliste basque—Organisation régionale d'Iparralde v. France*, no. 71251/01, § 3, ECHR 2007-II.

[34] *Husayn (Abu Zubaydah) v. Poland*, no. 7511/13, § 393, 24 July 2014; *Imakayeva v. Russia*, no. 7615/02, § 113, ECHR 2006-XIII (extracts); *Aslakhanova and Others v. Russia*, nos 2944/06, 8300/07, 50184/07, 332/08, and 42509/10, § 96, 18 December 2012; *El-Masri v. the former Yugoslav Republic of Macedonia* [GC], no. 39630/09, § 154, ECHR 2012; *McKerr v. the United Kingdom* (dec.), no. 28883/95, 4 April 2000.

[35] *Edwards v. the United Kingdom*, 16 December 1992, § 34, Series A no. 247-B; *Klaas v. Germany*, 22 September 1993, § 29, Series A no. 269.

[36] *Giuliani and Gaggio v. Italy*, no. 23458/02, § 180, 24 March 2011; *Avşar v. Turkey*, no. 25657/94, § 283, ECHR 2001-VII (extracts); *Barbu Anghelescu v. Romania*, no. 46430/99, § 52, 5 October 2004.

[37] Rules of Court, Annex to the Rules (concerning investigations), Rule A1(1).

[38] Ibid., Rule A1(3).

[39] Ibid., Rule A1(4).

of the Chamber assigned to the case, but the Chamber is also entitled to 'appoint any person or institution of its choice to assist the delegation in such manner as it sees fit'.[40] In principle, proceedings that make up the investigation by a Chamber or its delegation are held *in camera*, although the President of the Chamber or the head of the delegation may decide otherwise.[41]

The Annex to the Rules imposes an obligation on the applicant and any States that are 'concerned' in the case to 'assist the Court as necessary in implementing any investigative measures'.[42] In the case of an on-site visit to a State Party, the latter is required to 'extend to the delegation the facilities and cooperation necessary for the proper conduct of the proceedings'.[43] The binding nature of such an obligation has not been tested before the Court, although it would seem likely it will view this by analogy with orders of interim measures. Both mechanisms are set out in the Rules and not the Convention itself, but they are a necessary corollary of the operation of the Court and implied or inherent in its authority.[44]

In contrast with the imperative language used to describe the obligation to assist an investigation by the Court, the Rules are rather modest with respect to the conduct of hearings and the appearance of witnesses. For example, the Annex to the Rules speaks of a witness who fails to appear or 'declines to do so',[45] implying that there is nothing mandatory about a summons to testify before the Court. The State Party where the witness resides is 'responsible for servicing any summons sent to it by the Chamber for service'.[46]

An on-site investigation was conducted in one of the very earliest cases to come before the Convention organs. In 1957, the European Commission of Human Rights decided to send a six-member 'Investigation Party' to visit Cyprus in order to inquire into the curfew then in force.[47] The Investigation Party conducted an inquiry over two weeks in January 1958, hearing witnesses from the Greek and Turkish communities, as well as British witnesses.[48] The Commission returned to Cyprus in in 1975 and again in 1997 and 1998. The 1975 visit was described as being conducted both for the purpose of gathering information and also to put themselves as the disposal of the parties with a view to reaching a friendly settlement.[49] In 1997 and 1998, delegates of the Commission heard witnesses on the situation of Greek Cypriots and Maronites in the occupied portion of northern Cyprus.[50] Hearings were conducted in Strasbourg, London, and Cyprus.[51] The Commission travelled to the occupied territory, visiting schools and churches.[52] When it assessed the evidence gathered by the delegates of the Commission, the European Court

---

[40] Ibid., Rule A1(3).
[41] Ibid., Rule A1(5).
[42] Ibid., Rule A2(1).
[43] Ibid., Rule A2(2).
[44] *Bazorkina v. Russia*, no. 69481/01, § 179, 27 July 2006. On interim measures, see: *Paladi v. Moldova* [GC], no. 39806/05, § 85, 10 March 2009.
[45] Rules of Court, Annex to the Rules (concerning investigations), Rule A3.
[46] Ibid., Rule A5(4).
[47] *Greece v. the United Kingdom*, no. 176/56, § 284, Commission report of 26 September 1958.
[48] Ibid., §§ 242–245, 285–288, 315–317.
[49] *Cyprus v. Turkey*, nos 6780/74 and 6950/75, §§ 4, 30–40, Commission report of 10 July 1976.
[50] *Cyprus v. Turkey*, no. 25781/94, §§ 391–406, 542–55, Commission report of 4 June 1999; *Cyprus v. Turkey* [GC], no. 25781/94, §§ 37, 107–110, ECHR 2001-IV.
[51] *Cyprus v. Turkey*, no. 25781/94, § 542, Commission report of 4 June 1999.
[52] Ibid., §§ 407–409.

noted that when they took evidence they complied with the fairness requirements of article 6 of the Convention.[53]

The Commission also heard evidence in the *Ireland v. The United Kingdom* case. A total of 119 witnesses testified before delegates of the Commission. Three witnesses proposed by the United Kingdom were heard in London in the absence of representatives of the parties and without being cross-examined.[54] Witnesses from the British armed forces and the Royal Ulster Constabulary were heard at the Stavanger Military Base in Norway. A delegation was also dispatched to Turkey in the case filed by several European States. It met with a number of senior government officials and visited detention centres.[55] Much more recently, the European Court has appointed delegates to hear evidence in the inter-State case between Georgia and Russia. This consisted of witness testimony in Strasbourg; there was no on site visit.[56]

Investigation in individual petition cases is relatively rare.[57] In a case concerning prisoners in Northern Ireland, the delegates of the Commission first heard evidence in Strasbourg, then travelled to Northern Ireland, where they took the testimony of detainees in the Maze prison.[58] The Commission also conducted *in situ* investigations with respect to allegations of torture in Turkey.[59] As long as the European Commission of Human Rights was operating, the European Court was generally deferential towards it as the designated fact-finding body.[60] There were exceptions, however, when the Court decided to hear witnesses. Two judges were delegated to take the evidence; one witness who had difficulty attending in Strasbourg was permitted to submit a written statement. A handwriting expert was also consulted by the Court.[61]

Since the abolition of the Commission, the Court has conducted investigations in several individual cases.[62] In the case concerning detention sites in Poland, the Court heard several witnesses in Strasbourg.[63] The Grand Chamber conducted an on site visit to Transdniestria in another case, hearing scores of witnesses. In its judgment, the Grand Chamber said it 'deplore[d] the fact' that a government witness had failed to appear, finding it 'hard to believe, in view of his high profile, that it was impossible to contact him in order to summon him to give evidence'. The Court reserved the right to draw 'the

---

[53] *Cyprus v. Turkey* [GC], no. 25781/94, § 6, ECHR 2001-IV.

[54] *Ireland v. the United Kingdom*, 18 January 1978, § 146, Series A no. 25.

[55] *France, Norway, Denmark, Sweden, and the Netherlands v. Turkey*, nos 9940-9944/82, §§ 27–28, Commission report of 7 December 1985, DR 35, p. 143.

[56] *Georgia v. Russia (I)* [GC], no. 13255/07, §§ 13–17, 86–92, 3 July 2014.

[57] *Arthur Hilton v. the United Kingdom*, no. 5613/72, pp. 1–2, Commission report of 6 March 1978; *Simon Herold v. Austria*, no. 4340/69, p. 6, Commission report of 19 December 1972.

[58] *Donnelly and Others v. the United Kingdom*, nos 5577-5583/72, Commission decision of 15 December 1975, (1976) 19 YB 84, DR 4, p. 4.

[59] *Aksoy v. Turkey*, 18 December 1996, § 23, *Reports of Judgments and Decisions* 1996-VI; *Aksoy v. Turkey*, no. 21987/93, §§ 12, 16, 73–116, Commission report of 23 October 1995; *Kurt v. Turkey*, 25 May 1998, §§ 13, 45, *Reports of Judgments and Decisions* 1998-III; *Kurt v. Turkey*, no. 24276/94, §§ 30–50, Commission report of 5 December 1996; *Çakıcı v. Turkey* [GC], no. 23657/94, §§ 13, 43–55, ECHR 1999-IV; *Çakıcı v. Turkey*, no. 23657/94, §§ 11–32, Commission report of 12 March 1998.

[60] *Stocké v. Germany*, 19 March 1991, § 53, Series A no. 199.

[61] *Brozicek v. Italy*, 19 December 1989, §§ 5–7, Series A no. 167.

[62] For example, *İpek v. Turkey*, no. 25760/94, § 8, ECHR 2004-II (extracts); *Davydov and Others v. Ukraine*, nos 17674/02 and 39081/02, §§ 6–9, 1 July 2010.

[63] *Husayn (Abu Zubaydah) v. Poland*, no. 7511/13, §§ 8, 12, 24 July 2014.

necessary inferences'.[64] The Court, sitting as a Chamber and not as a delegation, heard several witnesses in the cases concerning secret detention sites in Poland.[65]

When witnesses testify before the Court, they are required to take an oath or solemn declaration.[66] Rules that are customary to the examination of witnesses in judicial proceedings apply.[67]

Evidence

Although in most cases before the Court the facts themselves are not in dispute, when the parties advance conflicting accounts of the events, the Court 'is inevitably confronted when establishing the facts with the same difficulties as those faced by any first-instance court'.[68] The Court has 'complete freedom in assessing not only the admissibility and relevance but also the probative value of each item of evidence before it'.[69] The Court has often stated that it adopts the 'beyond reasonable doubt' standard, an expression borrowed from the common law. Nevertheless it has couched this in caveats, insisting that 'it has never been its purpose to borrow the approach of the national legal systems that use that standard' because it is not ruling on criminal guilt or civil liability.[70] Its task is to assess the responsibility of States under the European Convention. It insists that there are 'no procedural barriers to the admissibility of evidence or pre-determined formulae for its assessment'.[71] Rather, '[i]t adopts the conclusions that are, in its view, supported by the free evaluation of all evidence, including such inferences as may flow from the facts and the parties' submissions'.[72] The Court has said that 'proof may follow from the coexistence of sufficiently strong, clear and concordant inferences or of similar unrebutted presumptions of fact'.[73] The Court has said it is 'attentive to the seriousness that attaches to a ruling that a Contracting State has violated fundamental rights'.[74]

It is probably a general principle of international law that *affirmanti incumbit probatio*: the burden of proof rests on the party making the claim. But the Court has said that Convention proceedings do not in all cases lend them to a strict application of this principle. In cases concerning the right to life and the prohibition of torture, 'where the events in issue lie wholly, or in large part, within the exclusive knowledge of the authorities, for instance as in the case of persons under their control in custody, strong presumptions of fact will arise in respect of injuries and death occurring during that

---

[64] *Ilaşcu and Others v. Moldova and Russia* [GC], no. 48787/99, §§ 12–14, ECHR 2004-VII.

[65] *Husayn (Abu Zubaydah) v. Poland*, no. 7511/13, § 8, 14, 24 July 2014; *Al Nashiri v. Poland*, no. 28761/11, § 344, 24 July 2014.

[66] Rules of Court, Annex to the Rules (concerning investigations), Rule A6.

[67] Ibid., Rules A7, A8.

[68] *Georgia v. Russia (I)* [GC], no. 13255/07, § 104, 3 July 2014.

[69] Ibid., § 138; *Ireland v. the United Kingdom*, 18 January 1978, § 210, Series A no. 25.

[70] *Husayn (Abu Zubaydah) v. Poland*, no. 7511/13, § 394, 24 July 2014; *Georgia v. Russia (no. 1)* [GC], no. 31255/07, § 93, 3 July 2014.

[71] *Husayn (Abu Zubaydah) v. Poland*, no. 7511/13, § 394, 24 July 2014.

[72] Ibid.

[73] Ibid.

[74] *Ireland v. the United Kingdom*, 18 January 1978, § 161, Series A no. 25; *Nachova and Others v. Bulgaria* [GC], nos 43577/98 and 43579/98, § 147, ECHR 2005-VII; *Creangă v. Romania* [GC], no. 29226/03, § 88, 23 February 2012; *El-Masri v. the former Yugoslav Republic of Macedonia* [GC], no. 39630/09, § 151, ECHR 2012; *Giuliani and Gaggio v. Italy*, no. 23458/02, § 181, 24 March 2011; *Ribitsch v. Austria*, 4 December 1995, § 32, Series A no. 336; *Nachova and Others v. Bulgaria* [GC], nos 43577/98 and 43579/98, § 147, ECHR 2005-VII.

detention'.[75] There is a reversal of the burden of proof: 'Lorsqu'il se trouve établi ou lorsqu'il n'est pas contesté qu'un décès dénoncé au regard de l'article 2 § 2 a résulté d'un usage délibéré de la force meurtrière par des agents de l'Etat, la charge de la preuve incombe au gouvernement défendeur, auquel il appartient de réfuter les allégations de la partie requérante par des moyens appropriés et convaincants.'[76]

When considering the existence of an administrative practice in an inter-State case, the Court does not consider that either of the two States involved bears a burden of proof; rather, it will 'study all the material before it, from whatever source it originates'.[77] In both inter-State and individual cases, satisfactory proof may result from 'the coexistence of sufficiently strong, clear and concordant inferences or of similar unrebutted presumptions of fact'.[78] This is especially true in disappearance cases, where the applicant is generally in possession of little evidence. The Court has said that 'strong presumptions of fact will arise in respect of injuries, death or disappearances' when persons have been detained and they are not accounted for.[79] In such circumstances, it is sufficient for applicants to make a *prima facie* case of abduction by officials under the control of the authorities 'and it would then be for the Government to discharge their burden of proof either by disclosing the documents in their exclusive possession or by providing a satisfactory and convincing explanation of how the events in question occurred'.[80] In some cases, the Court has also drawn the presumption that a missing person is actually dead if an individual has been detained by unidentified State agents without any subsequent acknowledgement of the detention.[81] In discrimination cases, if the applicant has established the existence of a differential treatment, the State has the burden to prove that this is justified.[82]

The Court may draw inferences that are unfavourable to the respondent State in the absence of an explanation, even if the latter does not in the strict sense have any burden of proof.[83] More generally, the conduct of the parties with respect to any efforts of the Court

[75] *Husayn (Abu Zubaydah) v. Poland*, no. 7511/13, § 396, 24 July 2014; *Çakıcı v. Turkey* [GC], no. 23657/94, § 85, ECHR 1999-IV; *Salman v. Turkey* [GC], no. 21986/93, § 100, ECHR 2000-VII; *Imakayeva v. Russia*, no. 7615/02, §§ 114–115, ECHR 2006-XIII (extracts).

[76] *Mansuroğlu v. Turkey*, no. 43443/98, § 77, 26 February 2008.

[77] *Georgia v. Russia (no. 1)* [GC], no. 31255/07, § 95, 3 July 2014; *Ireland v. the United Kingdom*, 18 January 1978, § 160, Series A no. 25; *Cyprus v. Turkey* [GC], no. 25781/94, § 113, ECHR 2001-IV.

[78] *Varnava and Others v. Turkey* [GC], nos 16064/90, 16065/90, 16066/90, 16068/90, 16069/90, 16070/90, 16071/90, 16072/90, and 16073/90, § 148, ECHR 2009; *Salman v. Turkey* [GC], no. 21896/93, § 100, ECHR 2000-VII; *Akdeniz and Others v. Turkey*, no. 23954/94, §§ 85–89, 31 May 2000.

[79] *Varnava and Others v. Turkey* [GC], nos 16064/90, 16065/90, 16066/90, 16068/90, 16069/90, 16070/90, 16071/90, 16072/90, and 16073/90, § 148, ECHR 2009; *Salman v. Turkey* [GC], no. 21896/93, § 100, ECHR 2000-VII; *Akdeniz and Others v. Turkey*, no. 23954/94, §§ 85–89, 31 May 2000.

[80] *Akhmatov and Others v. Russia*, nos 38828/10, 2543/11, 2650/11, 2685/11, 7409/11, 14321/11, and 26277/11, § 202, 16 January 2014; *Bopayeva and Others v. Russia*, no. 40799/06, § 70, 7 November 2013; *Aziyevy v. Russia*, no. 7626/01, § 74, 20 March 2008; *Utsayeva and Others v. Russia*, no. 29133/03, § 160, 29 May 2008; *Khutsayev and Others v. Russia*, no. 16622/05, § 104, 27 May 2010.

[81] *Bopayeva and Others v. Russia*, no. 40799/06, §§ 71–75, 7 November 2013; Bazorkina v. Russia, no. 69481/01, 27 July 2006; *Imakayeva v. Russia*, no. 7615/02, ECHR 2006-XIII (extracts); *Luluyev and Others v. Russia*, no. 69480/01, ECHR 2006-XIII (extracts); *Akhmadova and Sadulayeva v. Russia*, no. 40464/02, 10 May 2007; *Velkhiyev and Others v. Russia*, no. 34085/06, 5 July 2011; *Akhmatov and Others v. Russia*, nos. 38828/10, 2543/11, 2650/11, 2685/11, 7409/11, 14321/11, and 26277/11, § 203, 16 January 2014.

[82] *Chassagnou and Others v. France* [GC], nos 25088/94, 28331/95, and 28443/95, § 70, ECHR 1999-III; *Timishev v. Russia*, nos. 55762/00 and 55974/00, § 57, ECHR 2005-XII.

[83] *Husayn (Abu Zubaydah) v. Poland*, no. 7511/13, § 396, 24 July 2014; *El-Masri v. the former Yugoslav Republic of Macedonia* [GC], no. 39630/09, § 152, ECHR 2012; *Varnava and Others v. Turkey* [GC], nos 16064/90, 16065/90, 16066/90, 16068/90, 16069/90, 16070/90, 16071/90, 16072/90, and 16073/90, § 184, ECHR 2009; *Kadirova and Others v. Russia*, no. 5432/07, § 94, 27 March 2012; *Aslakhanova and Others v. Russia*, nos 2944/06, 8300/07, 50184/07, 332/08, and 42509/10, § 97, 18 December 2012.

to obtain evidence will be taken into account.[84] If the respondent State has exclusive information capable of corroborating or refuting the allegations of the applicant, the Court may draw inferences as to their validity if there is a lack of cooperation by the Government without a satisfactory explanation.[85]

The Court has often attached importance to information found in reports of international human rights organizations as well as government sources.[86] In determining the reliability of such materials, 'the relevant criteria are the authority and reputation of their authors, the seriousness of the investigations by means of which they were compiled, the consistency of their conclusions and whether they are corroborated by other sources'.[87]

Obligation to cooperate

Although not stated explicitly in article 38, the Court has considered that States have a general obligation to furnish documents to the Court. The duty to cooperate is spelled out in the Rules of Court:

The parties have a duty to cooperate fully in the conduct of the proceedings and, in particular, to take such action within their power as the Court considers necessary for the proper administration of justice. This duty shall also apply to a Contracting Party not party to the proceedings where such cooperation is necessary.[88]

This obligation is also 'a corollary of the undertaking not to hinder the effective exercise of the right of individual application under Article 34 of the Convention'. Effective exercise of this right 'may be thwarted by a Contracting Party's failure to assist the Court in conducting an examination of all circumstances relating to the case, including in particular by not producing evidence which the Court considers crucial for its task'. The two provisions, article 34 and article 38, 'work together to guarantee the efficient conduct of the judicial proceedings and they relate to matters of procedure rather than to the merits of the applicants' grievances under the substantive provisions of the Convention or its Protocols'.[89] The Court may establish that there has been a failure by the respondent State to comply with its procedural obligations even in the absence of any admissible complaint about a violation of a substantive Convention right.[90] The procedural obligations resulting from articles 34 and 38 'must be enforced irrespective of the eventual outcome of the

[84] *Ireland v. the United Kingdom*, 18 January 1978, § 161, Series A no. 25; *Ilaşcu and Others v. Moldova and Russia* [GC], no. 48787/99, §§ 26, ECHR 2004-VII; *Davydov and Others v. Ukraine*, nos 17674/02 and 39081/02, § 158, 1 July 2010.
[85] *Georgia v. Russia (I)* [GC], no. 13255/07, § 104, 3 July 2014; *Imakayeva v. Russia*, no. 7615/02, § 111, ECHR 2006-XIII (extracts); *Taniş and Others v. Turkey*, no. 65899/01, § 160, ECHR 2005–VIII; *Nolan and K. v. Russia*, no. 2512/04, § 69, 12 February 2009; *Makhmudov v. Russia*, no. 35082/04, § 68, 26 July 2007; *Fadeyeva v. Russia*, no. 55723/00, § 79, ECHR 2005-IV; *Ahmet Özkan and Others v. Turkey*, no. 21689/93, § 426, 6 April 2004.
[86] *Georgia v. Russia (I)* [GC], no. 13255/07, § 138, 3 July 2014, 4 July 2014; *Saadi v. Italy* [GC], no. 37201/06, § 131, ECHR 2008; *NA. v. the United Kingdom*, no. 25904/07, § 119, 17 July 2008; *M.S.S. v. Belgium and Greece* [GC], no. 30696/09, §§ 227 and 255, ECHR 2011; *Hirsi Jamaa and Others v. Italy* [GC], no. 27765/09, § 118, ECHR 2012.
[87] *Georgia v. Russia (I)* [GC], no. 13255/07, § 138, 3 July 2014; *Saadi v. Italy* [GC], no. 37201/06, § 143, ECHR 2008; *NA. v. the United Kingdom*, no. 25904/07, § 120, 17 July 2008; *Sufi and Elmi v. the United Kingdom*, nos 8319/07 and 11449/07, § 230, 28 June 2011.
[88] Rules of Court, Rule 44A.
[89] *Janowiec and Others v. Russia* [GC], nos 55508/07 and 29520/09, § 209, ECHR 2013.
[90] Ibid.; *Poleshchuk v. Russia*, no. 60776/00, 7 October 2004.

proceedings and in such a manner as to avoid any actual or potential chilling effect on the applicants or their representatives'.[91]

The Grand Chamber has explained:

[I]t is of the utmost importance for the effective operation of the system of individual petition instituted under Article 34 of the Convention that States should furnish all necessary facilities to make possible a proper and effective examination of applications. This obligation requires the Contracting States to furnish all necessary facilities to the Court, whether it is conducting a fact-finding investigation or performing its general duties as regards the examination of applications.[92]

The obligation to provide evidence if requested by the Court binds the State from the moment it is formulated, regardless of the stage of the proceedings.[93] The State must furnish the requested material in its entirety. It must properly account for any missing elements.[94] For example, 'the Government's failure to respond diligently to the Court's requests for the evidence it considered necessary for the examination of the application, such as an unexpurgated copy of the investigation file, and the fact that it was unable to take evidence from Levent Ersöz, the commanding officer of the Şırnak gendarmerie regiment at the material time, or from the person, whose name has been withheld, who telephoned Serdar Tanış on 25 January 2001 ... cannot be reconciled with the Government's obligations under Article 38 § 1 (a) of the Convention'.[95] The Court has found violations of article 38 where the respondent State did not explain a refusal to submit documents it had requested[96] or submitted an incomplete or distorted copy while refusing to produce the original document for the Court's inspection.[97] Failure to provide documents or to obtain the attendance of witnesses 'prejudices the establishment of facts in a case, both before and after the decision on admissibility'.[98]

In addition to a finding that the State has breached article 38, the Court may also draw adverse evidentiary inferences from a failure to comply with its requests for cooperation. According to the Rules of Court, '[w]here a party fails to comply with an order of the Court concerning the conduct of the proceedings, the President of the Chamber may take any steps which he or she considers appropriate'.[99] If there is 'a substantial and unexplained delay' in producing evidentiary materials, this may lead the Court 'to find the

---

[91] *Janowiec and Others v. Russia* [GC], nos 55508/07 and 29520/09, § 209, ECHR 2013.

[92] Ibid., § 202.

[93] *Janowiec and Others v. Russia* [GC], nos 55508/07 and 29520/09, § 209, ECHR 2013., § 203; *Enukidze and Girgvliani v. Georgia*, no. 25091/07, § 295, 26 April 2011; *Bekirski v. Bulgaria*, no. 71420/01, §§ 111–113, 2 September 2010.

[94] *Janowiec and Others v. Russia* [GC], nos 55508/07 and 29520/09, § 209, ECHR 2013; *Damir Sibgatullin v. Russia*, no.1413/05, §§ 65–68, 24 April 2012; *Enukidze and Girgvliani v. Georgia*, no. 25091/07, §§ 299–300, 26 April 2011; *Davydov and Others v. Ukraine*, nos 17674/02 and 39081/02, §§ 167 et seq., 1 July 2010.

[95] *Tanış and Others v. Turkey*, no. 65899/01, § 164, ECHR 2005–VIII. Also *Benzer and Others v. Turkey*, no. 23502/06, 12 November 2013; *Yasin Ateş v. Turkey*, no. 30949/96, §§ 84–7, 31 May 2005; *Kişmir v. Turkey*, no. 27306/95, §§ 77–80, 31 May 2005; *Koku v. Turkey*, no. 27305/95, §§ 103–109, 31 May 2005; *Süheyla Aydın v. Turkey*, no. 25660/94, §§ 137–143, 24 May 2005; *Akkum and Others v. Turkey*, no. 21894/93, §§ 185–190, ECHR 2005-II (extracts).

[96] *Bekirski v. Bulgaria*, no. 71420/01, § 115, 2 September 2010; *Tigran Ayrapetyan v. Russia*, no. 75472/01, § 64, 16 September 2010; *Maslova and Nalbandov v. Russia*, no. 839/02, §§ 128–129, 24 January 2008.

[97] *Trubnikov v. Russia*, no. 49790/99, §§ 50–57, 5 July 2005.

[98] *Bazorkina v. Russia*, no. 69481/01, § 171, 27 July 2006; *Timurtaş v. Turkey*, no. 23531/94, §§ 66, 70, ECHR 2000-VI; *Orhan v. Turkey*, no. 25656/94, § 266, ECHR 2002.

[99] Rules of Court, Rule 44B. For application of the Rule, see *Benzer and Others v. Turkey*, no. 23502/06, 12 November 2013.

respondent State's explanations unconvincing'.[100] In the inter-State case between Georgia and Russia, following a finding of a breach of article 38 by the respondent State the Court held that there was 'a strong presumption that the applicant Government's allegations regarding the content of the circulars ordering the expulsion specifically of Georgian nationals are credible'.[101]

Governments have advanced confidentiality or security considerations to explain a failure to produce materials requested by the Court. In such cases, the Court must satisfy itself of the existence of 'reasonable and solid grounds for treating the documents in question as secret or confidential'.[102] In examining the validity of the State's position, the Court will consider whether the document was in fact known to persons outside the secret intelligence services and the highest State officials. If this is the case, doubt is cast on the claim that the material in question is highly sensitive.[103] The Court has said that 'a mere reference to the structural deficiency of the domestic law which rendered impossible communication of sensitive documents to international bodies is an insufficient explanation to justify the withholding of information requested by the Court'.[104] States are reminded of the principle *pacta sunt servanda*, codified in article 26 of the Vienna Convention on the Law of Treaties, by which they must perform their conventional obligations in good faith, and of article 27 of the Convention by which provisions of internal law may not be invoked to justify the failure to comply with such obligations.[105]

The Court will show considerable deference to a domestic judicial process by which documents are deemed to be sensitive and confidential. It does not consider that it is 'well equipped to challenge' such judgments.[106] Nevertheless, 'even where national security is at stake, the concepts of lawfulness and the rule of law in a democratic society require that measures affecting fundamental human rights must be subject to some form of adversarial proceedings before an independent body competent to review the reasons for the decision and the relevant evidence'.[107] The Court will not be satisfied with a perfunctory or incomplete assessment by national authorities. It has also offered to accommodate the concerns of States by, for example, ensuring restricted access to documents and even holding *in camera* hearings.[108]

Estoppel

The requirement of the exhaustion of domestic remedies has the consequence of compelling the applicant to raise challenges based upon Convention rights before the national

---

[100] *Janowiec and Others v. Russia* [GC], nos 55508/07 and 29520/09, § 203, ECHR 2013; *Damir Sibgatullin v. Russia*, no.1413/05, § 68, 24 April 2012; *Enukidze and Girgvliani v. Georgia*, no. 25091/07, §§ 297, 301, 26 April 2011.

[101] *Georgia v. Russia (I)* [GC], no. 13255/07, § 140, 3 July 2014.

[102] *Janowiec and Others v. Russia* [GC], nos 55508/07 and 29520/09, § 205, ECHR 2013.

[103] Ibid., § 206.

[104] *Janowiec and Others v. Russia* [GC], nos 55508/07 and 29520/09, § 211, ECHR 2013; *Nolan and K. v. Russia*, no. 2512/04, § 56, 12 February 2009.

[105] *Janowiec and Others v. Russia* [GC], nos 55508/07 and 29520/09, § 211, ECHR 2013; *Davydov and Others v. Ukraine*, nos 17674/02 and 39081/02, § 170, 1 July 2010; *Nolan and K. v. Russia*, no. 2512/04, § 56, 12 February 2009; *Georgia v. Russia (no. 1)* [GC], no. 31255/07, § 105, 3 July 2014; *Shakhgiriyeva and Others v. Russia*, no. 27251/03, §§ 136–140, 8 January 2009; *Al Nashiri v. Poland*, no. 28761/11, § 366, 24 July 2014; *Husayn (Abu Zubaydah) v. Poland*, no. 7511/13, § 358, 24 July 2014.

[106] *Janowiec and Others v. Russia* [GC], nos 55508/07 and 29520/09, § 213, ECHR 2013.

[107] Ibid.

[108] Ibid., § 215; *Nolan and K. v. Russia*, no. 2512/04, § 51, 12 February 2009; *Al Nashiri v. Poland*, no. 28761/11, § 365, 24 July 2014; *Husayn (Abu Zubaydah) v. Poland*, no. 7511/13, § 357, 24 July 2014.

courts. Although obviously a condition of admissibility in the strict sense, the respondent State should also raise its objections to the challenge in the course of the national litigation. The arguments put by the State in proceedings before the European Court should be consistent with the position it adopted before the national courts.[109] Although unusual, there is no rule against a government disagreeing with the conclusions of its highest court in its submissions before the European Court.[110] Where the highest courts in Britain found a notice of derogation from the Convention to be invalid, the European Court did not consider this to be an obstacle when the United Kingdom attempted to rely upon the notice in the Strasbourg proceedings.[111]

Jura novit curiae

The Court is the master of the legal debate. It is entitled, by virtue of the *jura novit curia* principle, to consider provisions of the Convention that have not been invoked by the parties. 'A complaint is characterised by the facts alleged in it and not merely by the legal grounds or arguments relied on', it has said.[112] For example, on its own motion the Court raised a complaint under article 8 of the Convention, namely whether the facts of the case disclosed a breach of the State's positive obligation to ensure effective respect for the applicants' private life within the meaning of that provision.[113] In a case of police violence, an applicant relied upon article 6 of the Convention but, invoking *jura novit curia*, the Court said that it would examine the case under article 3.[114] In a wrongful death case, the Court took the perspective of article 2, although the applicant's submission had been based upon articles 6 and 8.[115]

Bibliography

Frowein/Peukert, *MenschenRechtsKonvention*, pp. 527–32.
Stefan Trechsel, 'Article 28§1-a', in Pettiti et al., *La Convention européenne*, pp. 649–59.
Leo Zwaak, 'The Procedure before the European Court of Human Rights', in Van Dijk et al., *Theory and Practice*, pp. 213–21.

[109] *A. and Others v. the United Kingdom* [GC], no. 3455/05, § 154, ECHR 2009; *Pine Valley Developments Ltd and Others v. Ireland*, 29 November 1991, § 47, Series A no. 222; *Kolompar v. Belgium*, 24 September 1992, §§ 31–32, Series A no. 235-C.

[110] *A. and Others v. the United Kingdom* [GC], no. 3455/05, § 157, ECHR 2009.

[111] Ibid., §§ 156–157.

[112] *Scoppola v. Italy (no. 2)* [GC], no. 10249/03, § 54, 17 September 2009; *Powell and Rayner v. the United Kingdom*, 21 February 1990, § 29, Series A no. 172; *Guerra and Others v. Italy*, 19 February 1998, § 44, *Reports of Judgments and Decisions* 1998-I; *Bouchacourt v. France*, no. 5335/06, § 56, 17 December 2009; *Şerife Yiğit v. Turkey* [GC], no. 3976/05, §§ 52–53, 2 November 2010; *M.M. v. the United Kingdom*, no. 24029/07, § 150, 13 November 2012.

[113] *Grzelak v. Poland*, no. 7710/02, § 49, 15 June 2010.

[114] *Grămadă v. Romania*, no. 14974/09, § 51, 11 February 2014.

[115] *Pleşca v. Romania*, no. 2158/08, § 34, 18 June 2013.

Article 39. Friendly settlements/Règlements amiables

1. At any stage of the proceedings, the Court may place itself at the disposal of the parties concerned with a view to securing a friendly settlement of the matter on the basis of respect for human rights as defined in the Convention and the Protocols thereto.	1. A tout moment de la procedure, la Cour peut se mettre à la disposition des intéressés en vue de parvenir à un règlement amiable de l'affaire s'inspirant du respect des droits de l'homme tels que les reconnaissent la Convention et ses Protocoles.
2. Proceedings conducted under paragraph 1 shall be confidential.	2. La procédure décrite au paragraphe 1 est confidentielle.
3. If a friendly settlement is effected, the Court shall strike the case out of its list by means of a decision which shall be confined to a brief statement of the facts and of the solution reached.	3. En cas de règlement amiable, la Cour raye l'affaire du rôle par une décision qui se limite à un bref exposé des faits et de la solution adoptée.
4. This decision shall be transmitted to the Committee of Ministers, which shall supervise the execution of the terms of the friendly settlement as set out in the decision.	4. Cette décision est transmise au Comité des Ministres qui surveille l'exécution des termes du règlement amiable tels qu'ils figurent dans la décision.

Introductory comments

The European Convention encourages the applicant and the respondent State to reach a 'friendly settlement'. In a sense, this is merely an extension of the philosophy of subsidiarity underpinning the entire Convention, highlighted particularly in the rule of exhaustion of domestic remedies. If a victim of a violation of the Convention reaches a friendly settlement with the State prior to an application being made to the European Court, the Court obviously has no involvement at all. Once the threshold of an application to the Court is crossed, however, the Convention organs have a role in ensuring the legitimacy of the friendly settlement as well as ensuring that it is actually carried out. According to the Parliamentary Assembly, the friendly settlement, 'while remaining a matter left entirely to the discretion of the parties to the case, may constitute a means of alleviating the workload of the Court, as well as a means of providing a rapid and satisfactory solution for the parties'.[1]

Drafting of the provision

That an application might be resolved through a 'friendly settlement' was contemplated in article 28 of the 1950 text of the Convention:

1. In the event of the Commission accepting a petition referred to it:
   (a) it shall, with a view to ascertaining the facts, undertake together with the representatives of the parties an examination of the petition and, if need be, an investigation, for the effective

---

[1] Resolution Res(2002)59 concerning the practice in respect of friendly settlements.

conduct of which the States concerned shall furnish all necessary facilities, after an exchange of views with the Commission;

(b) it shall at the same time place itself at the disposal of the parties concerned with a view to securing a friendly settlement of the matter on the basis of respect for Human Rights as defined in this Convention.

2. If the Commission succeeds in effecting a friendly settlement, it shall draw up a Report which shall be sent to the States concerned, to the Committee of Ministers and to the Secretary General of the Council of Europe for publication. This Report shall be confined to a brief statement of the facts and of the solution reached.

The notion that petitions or applications to the Convention organs should ideally result in a settlement or reconciliation had been present from the first drafts in the Consultative Assembly. The Committee on Legal and Administrative Questions of the Consultative Assembly proposed the following text: 'If it does not reject the petition, the Commission shall try to effect a reconciliation of the opposing parties.' Then, if reconciliation was not successful, the Commission could publish a report on the facts of the case.[2] There was some debate about this in the plenary Assembly. A motion to delete the provision on reconciliation was rejected.[3] The Committee's text was included in the Assembly's final draft.[4]

The Committee of Experts was undecided on whether the Convention should contain a provision on friendly settlement. Its final draft provided a text, but it was in square brackets indicating a lack of agreement: 'If it does not reject the application, the Commission shall try to effect a settlement of the matter.'[5] Norway, the Netherlands, and the United Kingdom had taken the view that if there was to be no Court, then it should not be the task of the Commission to encourage a friendly settlement. According to the experts from these three countries,

[t]he Convention provides for a minimum standard of protection of human rights. If the protection accorded by a State is found by the Commission to be below that standard, there is clearly a violation of the Convention. It seemed to them that, in such circumstances, it is inappropriate to introduce the notion of conciliation. A denial of the enjoyments of human rights could not be rectified by a process of compromise.[6]

Other experts thought it useful to retain the provision because friendly settlement might involve determining the amount of compensation due to a victim.[7] The Report also noted that the Committee preferred replacing the French term *'conciliation'* with *'règlement amiable'* because 'this first term is used primarily in the case of disputes between States,

---

[2] Report presented by Mr P.H. Teitgen, 5 September 1949, Doc. A 290, I *TP* 192–213, at p. 198. Also Report [of the Committee on Legal and Administrative Questions], 5 September 1949, Doc. AS (1) 77, I *TP* 216–39, at p. 232, arts 14, 15.

[3] Official Report of the Sitting [of the Consultative Assembly, 8 September 1949], II *TP* 14–274, at p. 208.

[4] Recommendation No. 38 to the Committee of Ministers adopted 8 September 1949 on the conclusion of the debates, Doc. AS (1) 108, II *TP* 274–83, at p. 280, art. 15.

[5] Appendix to the Report of the Committee of Experts on Human Rights: Draft Convention of Protection of Human Rights and Fundamental Freedoms, 16 March 1950, Doc. C/WP 1 (50) 15 appendix, CM/WP 1 (50) 14 revised, A 925, IV *TP* 50–79, at p. 68, art. 21(25).

[6] Report to the Committee of Ministers submitted by the Committee of Experts Instructed to Draw Up a Draft Convention of Collective Guarantee of Human Rights and Fundamental Freedoms, Doc. CM/WP 1 (5) 15, A 924, IV *TP* 2–55, at p. 40.

[7] Ibid.

whereas the Commission is equally concerned with disputes between States and individuals'.[8]

At the Conference of Senior Officials, the United Kingdom supported the idea that 'conciliation' be among the functions of the Commission. 'In the case of a "technical" violation or of negligence or inadvertence a friendly settlement could prove useful', said Samuel Hoare.[9] But to make conciliation its essential function was not acceptable. 'Conciliation should be a secondary, ancillary, matter', he said.[10] Charles Chaumont of France considered the meaning of the term 'friendly settlement'. For Chaumont, this was 'a form of settlement that stopped short of a decision finding a violation and consisted in the State at fault voluntarily making amends'.[11] France, Ireland, and the United Kingdom proposed the following text: 'If it succeeds in effecting a friendly settlement of the case in accordance with Article 21 the Commission shall draw up a report...'[12] A revised version dropped the word 'friendly'.[13] The Conference of Senior Officials adopted the following text: 'If it does not reject the application, the Commission shall ascertain the facts and place itself at the disposal of the parties concerned with a view to securing a friendly solution of the matter on the basis of respect for human rights as defined in this Convention.'[14] The Report drew attention to the change whereby friendly settlement was encouraged, although it 'should in all cases be on the basis of respect for human rights as defined in this Convention'.[15] This was incorporated in the draft Convention adopted by the Conference of Senior Officials.[16]

Meeting in August 1950, the Committee of Ministers modified the provision:

Art. 28. In the event of the Commission accepting a matter referred to it...

b) it shall place itself at the disposal of the parties concerned with a view to securing a friendly solution of the matter on the basis of respect for human rights as defined in this Convention.[17]

If it 'succeed[ed] in effecting a settlement', the Commission was to prepare a summary Report.[18] The word 'solution' was changed to 'settlement' in the final text of article 28(b) adopted in November.

---

[8] Ibid. Also Preliminary Draft of the Report to the Committee of Ministers, 24 February 1950, Doc. CM/WP 1 (50), A 847, III *TP* 246–79, at pp. 270–2.

[9] Minutes of the morning sitting [of 9 June 1950 of the Conference of Senior Officials], Doc. CM/WP 4 (50) 3, IV *TP* 110–19, at pp. 114–16.

[10] Ibid., p. 116.

[11] Ibid.

[12] Proposal submitted by the French, Irish, and United Kingdom Delegations (Original text), Doc. CM/WP 4 (50) 5, A 1366, IV *TP* 160–1.

[13] Proposal submitted by the French, Irish, and United Kingdom Delegations (Revised text), Doc. CM/WP 4 (50) 5 rev., A 1369, IV *TP* 160–1.

[14] Draft Convention annexed to the Report, Doc. CM/WP 4 (50) 19 annex, CM/WP 4 (50) rev., A 1452, IV *TP* 274–95, at p. 286, art. 29.

[15] Draft Report to the Committee of Ministers, Doc. CM/WP 4 (50) 16, A 1426, IV *TP* 204–16, at p. 216; Text of the report submitted by the Conference to the Committee of Ministers, Doc. CM/WP 4 (50) 19, CM/WP 4 (50) 16 rev., A 1431, IV *TP* 242–57, at p. 264.

[16] Draft Convention annexed to the Report, Doc. CM/WP 4 (50) 19 annex, CM/WP 4 (50) rev., A 1452, IV *TP* 274–95, at p. 286, art. 29.

[17] Draft Convention adopted by the Committee of Ministers, 7 August 1950, Doc. A 1937, V *TP* 120–45, at p. 134; Draft Convention adopted by the Sub-Committee, Doc. CM 1 (50) 52, A 1884, V *TP* 76–99, at p. 88.

[18] Draft Convention adopted by the Committee of Ministers, 7 August 1950, Doc. A 1937, V *TP* 120–45, at p. 134, art. 30.

The Rules of Court of the former Court also considered the issue of friendly settlement in a provision entitled 'discontinuance': 'When the Commission, after having brought a case before the Court, informs the Court that a friendly settlement which satisfies the conditions of Article 28 of the Convention has subsequently been reached, the Chamber may, after having obtained the opinion, if necessary, of the delegates of the Commission, strike the case out of its list.'[19] This provision was later amended: 'When the Chamber is informed of a friendly settlement, arrangement or other fact of a kind to provide a solution of the matter, it may, after consulting, if necessary, the Parties, the Delegates of the Commission and the applicant, strike the case out of the list.'[20]

Protocol No. 11 introduced two new provisions on the subject of friendly settlement:

Article 38—Examination of the case and friendly settlement proceedings
1. If the Court declares the application admissible, it shall
    a) pursue the examination of the case, together with the representatives of the parties, and if need be, undertake an investigation, for the effective conduct of which the States concerned shall furnish all necessary facilities;
    b) place itself at the disposal of the parties concerned with a view to securing a friendly settlement of the matter on the basis of respect for human rights as defined in the Convention and the protocols thereto.
2. Proceedings conducted under paragraph 1.b shall be confidential.

Article 39—Finding of a friendly settlement
If a friendly settlement is effected, the Court shall strike the case out of its list by means of a decision which shall be confined to a brief statement of the facts and of the solution reached.

Article 38(1) was based on the former article 28(1), although it had been somewhat shortened. The Explanatory Report said that the text of article 39 was modelled on Rule 49(2) of the former Rules of Court. The Report said that '[t]he second part of this Article is virtually identical to the last sentence of paragraph 2 of former Article 28 of the Convention'.[21]

The Explanatory Report noted that experience had shown 'the great utility of the conciliation element in Convention proceedings'. It considered that '[f]riendly settlement negotiations could be "guided", or even encouraged, by a judge (with the help of the registry of the Court). Also, during friendly settlement negotiations, parties may call upon the services of the Court's registry to help them in these negotiations.' The Report said a Chamber might at any stage assist the parties in settling their case.[22] According to the Explanatory Report, '[p]arties to friendly settlement proceedings will not be at liberty to disclose to anyone the nature and content of any communication made with a view to and in connection with a friendly settlement'.[23]

The current text of article 39 results from Protocol No. 14. According to the Explanatory Report, it was decided to address the friendly settlement procedure in a specific article in order '[t]o make the Convention easier to read'.[24] Article 39 was an amalgam of the

---

[19] Rules of Court (adopted 18 September 1959), Rule 47(3).
[20] Rules of Court (adopted 27 August 1974), Rule 47(2). Later, this became Rules of Court 'A' (in force 1 February 1994), Rule 49(2).
[21] Explanatory Report on Protocol No. 11, para. 95.
[22] Ibid., para. 94.
[23] Ibid., para. 93.
[24] Explanatory Report on Protocol No. 14, para. 91.

relevant provisions of articles 38 and 39 of the previous version of the Convention, which itself was a result of Protocol No. 11. The Report said that the amendments should result in fewer separate admissibility decisions because the friendly settlement had been made more flexible, allowing the Court to promote settlement discussions at any stage in the proceedings.[25] As a result, '[f]riendly settlements are therefore encouraged, and may prove particularly useful in repetitive cases, and other cases where questions of principle or changes in domestic law are not involved'.[26]

Analysis and interpretation

The Court may strike out a case from its list if a friendly settlement has been reached between the parties. Although the friendly settlement negotiations are confidential, if a case has already been declared admissible and an agreement is reached subsequently, the Court must issue a decision that is public. The friendly settlement agreements provide satisfaction for the application in terms of personal interests but often they also involve policy commitments by governments.

For example, as part of a friendly settlement agreement the Irish Government confirmed that its programme contained a commitment 'to modernise and reform outdated elements of family law', adding that new legislation 'will respect the public policy objective of treating children equally, regardless of the marital status of their parents'.[27] In a case directed against Cyprus concerning the unavailability of civil marriage for Turkish Cypriots, a friendly settlement was reached with the applicant that involved payment of a sum of money. But Cyprus also informed the Court of legislative measures being taken to rectify the situation. In deciding to strike out the case from the list on the basis of the friendly settlement, the Court took into account the reforms that Cyprus had undertaken to make, although the relevant legislation had not yet been adopted.[28] In a case directed against Andorra where the applicant complained about being denied access to a constitutional appeal, the Court confirmed the friendly settlement, noting amendments to the relevant legislation to correct the situation, including a provision giving them retroactive effect.[29]

Even an inter-State case may conclude with a friendly settlement. Denmark and Turkey agreed to resolve a dispute concerning the torture of a Danish national by the Turkish authorities. In approving the settlement, the Court 'emphasise[d], with reference to Turkey's continued participation in the Council of Europe's police-training project, the importance of the training of Turkish police officers and in addition provides for the establishment of a new bilateral project in this area'. The Court noted the commitment of the parties, as part of the friendly settlement, of a continuous political dialogue focusing on human rights issues within which individual cases could be raised.[30] The Court also considered changes to Turkey's legal and administrative framework, introduced in response to issues of torture and ill treatment, and the government's undertaking to

---

[25] Ibid., para. 92.
[26] Ibid., para. 93.
[27] *E. v. Ireland* (friendly settlement), no. 42734/09, § 4, 1 October 2013.
[28] *Selim v. Cyprus* (friendly settlement), no. 47293/99, § 16, 16 July 2002.
[29] *Millan I Tornes v. Andorra* (friendly settlement), no. 35052/97, § 21, ECHR 1999-IV.
[30] *Denmark v. Turkey* (friendly settlement), no. 34382/97, § 23, ECHR 2000-IV.

make further improvements. Finally, it noted the commitment of the Turkish authorities 'to continue their co-operation with international human rights bodies, in particular the Committee for the Prevention of Torture'.[31]

Role of the Court in encouraging settlement

As the opening words of article 39(1) explain, the Court may place itself at the disposal of the parties '[a]t any stage of the proceedings'. This is a change introduced by Protocol No. 14. Previously, the Convention provision governing friendly settlement was only operative if a case had been declared admissible. The dramatic change that this provision has brought about can be seen in the statistics of the Court's activity. These show that the number of friendly settlements has declined dramatically. In fact there are probably many more friendly settlements than in the past, but they are not recorded as such because this takes place prior to the admissibility stage and therefore no decision is issued. According to the Annual Report of the Court for 2012, there were only nine friendly settlements out of 1,093 cases that were adjudicated over the course of the year, less than 0.1 per cent of the total.[32] Over the entire life of the Court, there have been 1,063 friendly settlements out of a total of 15,947 cases adjudicated, or about 6.6 per cent of the total.[33]

Even before a case is declared admissible, when the Chamber decides to give notice of the application to the respondent State the parties are 'invited to include in their observations any submissions concerning just satisfaction and any proposals for a friendly settlement'.[34] Once an application is declared admissible, the Registrar is to contact the parties 'with a view to securing a friendly settlement'. The Registrar is to be 'acting on the instructions of the Chamber or its President'.[35] The Rules state that '[t]he Chamber shall take any steps that appear appropriate to facilitate such a settlement'.[36]

Striking out by means of a decision (art. 39(3))

Rule 43(3) states that 'the application shall be struck out of the Court's list of cases by means of a decision'. Prior to the entry into force of Protocol No. 14, the Rules of Court required the Court to strike out the case by means of a 'judgment'.[37] The Explanatory Report on Protocol No. 14 justifies the change in terminology:

The new Article 39 provides for supervision of the execution of friendly settlements by the Committee of Ministers. This new provision was inserted to reflect a practice which the Court had already developed. In the light of the text of former Article 46, paragraph 2, the Court used to endorse friendly settlements through *judgments* and not—as provided for in former Article 39 of the Convention—through *decisions,* whose execution was not subject to supervision by the Committee of Ministers. The practice of the Court was thus in response to the fact that only the execution of *judgments* was supervised by the Committee of Ministers (former Article 39). It was recognised,

[31] Ibid., § 24.
[32] *Annual Report 2012*, p. 155.
[33] Ibid., p. 159.
[34] Rules of Court, Rule 54A.
[35] Ibid., Rule 62(1).
[36] Ibid.
[37] The earlier version of the Rules of Court said: 'The striking of a case shall be effected by means of a judgment...' (Rules of Court (as in force at 1 February 1994), Rule 49(3)). This was amended: 'the decision to strike out an application which has been declared admissible shall be given in the form of a judgment' (Rules of Court (amended by the Court on 17 June and 8 July 2002), Rule 44(3)).

however, that adopting a judgment, instead of a decision, might have negative connotations for respondent Parties, and make it harder to secure a friendly settlement. The new procedure should make this easier and thus reduce the Court's workload. For this reason, the new Article 39 gives the Committee of Ministers authority to supervise the execution of *decisions* endorsing the terms of friendly settlements. This amendment is in no way intended to reduce the Committee's present supervisory powers, particularly concerning the strike-out decisions covered by Article 37. It would be advisable for the Committee of Ministers to distinguish more clearly, in its practice, between its supervision function by virtue of the new Article 39, paragraph 4 (friendly settlements), on the one hand and that under Article 46, paragraph 2 (execution of judgments), on the other.[38]

The observation that a 'decision' rather than a 'judgment' may attach less stigma to the respondent State may be correct, although it is not clear that this promotes settlement. As one textbook has observed, '[w]hile this may be true as regards certain governments, the fact that a settlement can be adopted by way of a judgment can also be an incentive for applicants to settle on the basis that a judgment is more likely to attract media interest'.[39]

Nevertheless, the authority conferred by article 39 is not solely dependent on the will of the parties. Echoing the words of article 37(1) of the Convention, the Rules of Court require that if the Chamber is informed that a settlement has been reached it shall only strike out the case from the list 'after verifying that the settlement has been reached on the basis of respect for human rights as defined in the Convention and the Protocols thereto'.[40] As a consequence, the Grand Chamber has insisted that 'the Court may strike an application out of its list only if it is satisfied that the solution of the matter embodied in the settlement arrived at between the parties is based on "respect for human rights as defined in the Convention and the Protocols thereto"'.[41] This is discussed in more depth in the chapter on article 37 of this Commentary. The settlement must be 'equitable' within the meaning of Rule 75 of the Rules of Court.[42]

Confidentiality (art. 39(2))

Friendly settlement proceedings are 'confidential', subject to the possibility of a unilateral declaration by the respondent State. The Rules note that the principle of confidentiality is without prejudice to the parties' arguments in the contentious proceedings. No written or oral communication and no offer or concession made in the framework of the attempt to secure a friendly settlement may be referred to or relied on in the contentious proceedings.[43] The rule of confidentiality 'is absolute and does not allow for an individual assessment of how much detail was disclosed'.[44] According to the Court, 'la règle de confidentialité des négociations du règlement amiable revêt une importance particulière dans la mesure où elle vise à préserver les parties et la Cour elle-même de toute tentative de pression politique ou de quelque autre ordre que ce soit'.[45] If an applicant does not respect

---

[38] Explanatory Report on Protocol No. 14, para. 94 (emphasis in the original).

[39] Harris et al., *Law of the European Convention*, p. 833.

[40] Rules of Court, Rule 62(3).

[41] *Broniowski v. Poland* (friendly settlement) [GC], no. 31443/96, § 33, ECHR 2005-IX.

[42] *Fabris v. France* (just satisfaction - striking out) [GC], no. 16574/08, § 7, 28 June 2013.

[43] Rules of Court, Rules 33(1).

[44] *Balenović v. Croatia* (dec.), no. 28369/07, 30 September 2010; *Lesnina Veletrgovina d.o.o. v. the Former Yugoslav Republic of Macedonia* (dec.), no. 37619/04, 2 March 2010; *Mandil v. France* (dec.), no. 67037/09, 13 December 2011.

[45] *Miroļubovs and Others v. Latvia*, no. 798/05, § 66, 15 September 2009; *Mandil v. France* (dec.), no. 67037/09, 13 December 2011.

the rule, the Court may declare the application to be admissible as an abuse of the right of application.[46] Before sanctioning the applicant for violating the norm, liability must be established with 'suffisamment de certitude, une simple suspicion ne suffisant pas pour déclarer la requête abusive au sens de l'article 35 § 3 de la Convention'.[47]

Unilateral declaration

If a proposal by the respondent State for a friendly settlement is refused by an applicant, the State may then file with the Court a request to strike the application out of the list.[48] Such a 'unilateral declaration' by a State must 'be accompanied by a declaration clearly acknowledging that there has been a violation of the Convention in the applicant's case together with an undertaking to provide adequate redress and, as appropriate, to take necessary remedial measures'.[49] If justified by 'exceptional circumstances', the request may be filed even if there has been no prior attempt to reach a friendly settlement.[50] With the filing of such a declaration, the friendly settlement proceedings that have hitherto been confidential take on a degree of publicity. The unilateral declaration by a State 'must be made in public and adversarial proceedings', although with 'due respect for the confidentiality of any friendly-settlement proceedings'.[51] If the applicant does not accept the State's offer, the Court may then strike out the case from the list, in accordance with article 37(1)(c), either in whole or in part, '[i]f it is satisfied that the declaration offers a sufficient basis for finding that respect for human rights as defined in the Convention and the Protocols thereto does not require it to continue its examination of the application'.[52]

Sometimes, the applicant accepts the unilateral declaration by the State as an appropriate offer. In such cases, providing the Court is itself satisfied, the matter is treated as a friendly settlement.[53] However, the applicant may also contest the State's request that the unilateral declaration be accepted by the Court and the case struck from the list. If the unilateral declaration is contested, the Court will disregard statements made within the 'strictly confidential' context of friendly settlement negotiations.[54]

Further reading

Fiona Ang and Eva Berghmans, 'Friendly Settlements and Striking Out of Applications', in Paul Lemmens and Wouter Vandenhole, eds, *Protocol No. 14 and the Reform of the European Court of Human Rights*, Antwerp: Intersentia, 2005, pp. 89–104.

---

[46] *Mandil v. France* (dec.), no. 67037/09, 13 December 2011; *Miroļubovs and Others v. Latvia*, no. 798/05, § 66, 15 September 2009; *Hadrabová and Hadrabová v. Czech Republic* (dcc.), no. 42165/02, 25 September 2007; *Popov v. Moldova*, no. 74153/01, § 48, 18 January 2005; *Balenović v. Croatia* (dec.), no. 28369/07, 30 September 2010.

[47] *Miroļubovs and Others v. Latvia*, no. 798/05, § 66, 15 September 2009; *Mandil v. France* (dec.), no. 67037/09, 13 December 2011.

[48] Rules of Court, Rule 62A(1)(a). See also the discussion of unilateral declaration in the chapter in this Commentary on article 37.

[49] Ibid., Rule 62A(1)(b).

[50] Ibid., Rule 62A(2).

[51] Ibid., Rule 62A(1)(c).

[52] Ibid., Rule 62A(3).

[53] *Huseynov v. Azerbaijan* (friendly settlement), no. 36666/11, 22 October 2013; *H. v. the United Kingdom* (friendly settlement), no. 22241/08, 18 September 2012.

[54] *Tahsin Acar v. Turkey* (preliminary issue) [GC], no. 26307/95, § 74, ECHR 2003-VI.

Vincent Berger, 'Le règlement amiable devant la Cour', in Pettiti et al., *La Convention européenne*, pp. 783–92.

Sally Dollé, 'Friendly Settlement 14 Years on in the European Commission of Human Rights', in Michele de Salvia and Mark E. Villiger, eds, *The Birth of European Human Rights Law—Liber Amicorum Carl Aage Nørgaard*, Baden-Baden: Nomos, 1998, pp. 243–4.

Frowein/Peukert, *MenschenRechtsKonvention*, p. 533.

Helen Keller, Magdalena Forowicz, and Lorenz Engi, *Friendly Settlement before the European Court of Human Rights, Theory and Practice*, Oxford: Oxford University Press, 2010.

Hans Christian Krüger and Carl Aage Nørgaard, 'Reflections concerning Friendly Settlement under the European Convention on Human Rights', in Franz Matscher and Herbert Petzold, eds, *Protecting Human Rights: The European Dimension—Studies in Honour of Gérard J. Wiarda*, Cologne: Heymann, 1988, pp. 329–34.

Egbert Myjer, 'It is Never too Late for the State—Friendly Settlements and Unilateral Declarations', in Lucius Caflisch, Johan Callewaert, Roderick Liddell, Paul Mahoney, and Mark Villiger, eds, *Liber Amicorum Luzius Wildhaber*, Kehl, Germany: N.P. Engel, 2007, pp. 309–27.

Carl Aage Nørgaard and Hans Christian Krüger, 'Article 28§1-b and §2', in Pettiti et al., *La Convention européenne*, pp. 661–79.

Torkel Opsahl, 'Settlement based on Respect of Human Rights under the European Convention on Human Rights', in *Proceedings of the Sixth International Colloquy About the European Convention on Human Rights*, Strasbourg: Council of Europe, 1988, pp. 966–97.

Christos L. Rozakis, 'Unilateral Declarations as a Means of Settling Human Rights Disputes: A New Tool for the Resolution of Disputes in the ECHR's Procedure', in Marcelo G. Kohen, ed., *Promoting Justice, Human Rights and Conflict Resolution through International Law. Liber Amicorum Lucius* Caflisch, Leiden: Nijhoff, 2007, pp. 1003–14.

Olivier de Schutter, 'Le règlement amiable dans la Convention européenne des droits de l'homme: entre théorie de la fonction de juger et théorie de la négociation', in Patrick de Fontbressin et al., eds, *Les droits de l'homme au seuil du troisième millénaire. Mélanges en homage à Pierre Lambert*, Brussels: Bruylant, 2000, pp. 225–61.

Adam Tomkins, 'The Committee of Ministers: Its Roles under the European Convention on Human Rights', (1995) 1 *EHRLR* 50.

Greogry S. Weber, 'Who Killed the Friendly Settlement? The Decline of Negotiated Resolutions at the European Court of Human Rights', (2007) 7 *Pepperdine Dispute Resolution Law Journal* 215.

Leo Zwaak, 'The Procedure before the European Court of Human Rights', in Van Dijk et al., *Theory and Practice*, pp. 222–36.

Article 40. Public hearings and access to documents/Audience publique et accès aux documents

1. Hearings shall be in public unless the Court in exceptional circumstances decides otherwise.	1. L'audience est publique à moins que la Cour n'en décide autrement en raison de circonstances exceptionnelles.
2. Documents deposited with the Registrar shall be accessible to the public unless the President of the Court decides otherwise.	2. Les documents déposés au greffe sont accessibles au public à moins que le président de la Cour n'en décide autrement.

Introductory comments

That judicial proceedings be public is a general principle of law, confirmed by its recognition in article 10 of the Universal Declaration of Human Rights as well as in article 6(1) of the European Convention on Human Rights. Nevertheless, it cannot be an absolute principle.

Drafting of the provision

The original draft provisions concerning the European Court of Human Rights were proposed by the International Juridical Section of the European Movement. Its draft Statute included the following: 'The hearing in Court shall be public, unless the Court shall for a special reason decide otherwise, or unless the parties demand that the public be not admitted.'[1] However, no such provision appeared in the draft of the Consultative Assembly or any of the subsequent versions of the 1950 text Convention.

Under the 'former Court', prior to entry into force of Protocol No. 11, the public hearing was ensured by two provisions of the Rules of Court:

Rule 18 (Public character of the hearings)
The hearings shall be public unless, the Court shall in exceptional circumstances decide otherwise.[2]
Rule 56 (Publication of judgments and other documents)
2. Documents deposited with the Registrar and not published shall be accessible to the public unless otherwise decided by the President either on his own initiative or at the request of a Party, of the Commission, of the applicant or of any other person concerned.[3]

A note of explanation published in the *Yearbook* said of Rule 56(2): 'While the former Rule 52 simply authorised the publication of judgments and other decisions and documents of the Court, the new rule lays down the conditions for such publication and furthermore, it deals with the documents which are not published.'[4]

---

[1] Draft Statute of the European Court of Human Rights, INF/5/E/R, I *TP* 302–21, at p. 314, art. 40.
[2] Rules of Court (adopted 18 September 1959), Rule 18. The comma seems to have disappeared in 1989: Rules of Court (adopted on 24 November 1982 and amended on 26 January 1989).
[3] Amendments to the Rules of Court (adopted 23–25 October 1962), Rule 56(2).
[4] (1961) 4 YB 12.

Article 40 was introduced to the Convention by Protocol No. 11. The Explanatory Report on Protocol No. 11 notes that 'proceedings, where oral, are, in principle, to be conducted in public'. According to the Report, because article 40 specifies that documents submitted in the written proceedings (memorials and formal written information) are also, in principle, accessible to the public, 'documents deposited with the Registrar and not published will be accessible to the public unless otherwise decided by the President either on his own initiative or at the request of a party, or of any other person concerned'.[5]

Analysis and interpretation

The proceedings at the Court have always been public, although it was not until the adoption of Protocol No. 11 that the principle was set out explicitly in the Convention. The public nature of the Court's proceedings was in quite marked distinction with what applied to the European Commission. Article 33 of the original text of the European Convention said bluntly: 'The Commission shall meet in camera.'

In the first case to come before the Court, the respondent State objected because the Commission had sent a copy of its report to the applicant when the matter was transferred to the Court. Dismissing Ireland's objection, the Court noted that in its opinion, the procedure in a case brought before it under the Convention was different from that prevailing at the Commission or, for that matter, the Committee of Ministers. It explained that when a case came before the Court, the proceedings assumed 'a judicial character'. According to the Court, 'in any democratic society, within the meaning of the Preamble and the other clauses of the Convention, proceedings before the judiciary should be conducted in the presence of the parties and in public'. Moreover, such a 'fundamental principle' was upheld in article 6 of the Convention. The Court used an *a contrario* argument, citing the absence of a provision comparable to article 33 within the Section of the Convention governing procedure before the Court.[6]

Public character of hearings (art. 40(1))

The Court may derogate from the general rule that hearings are public, acting either on its own motion or at the request of a party or of 'a person concerned'.[7] An application to exclude the public is to provide reasons and specify whether it envisages all or part of the hearing.[8] In language that is inspired by article 6(1) of the Convention, Rule 63(2) states:

The press and the public may be excluded from all or part of a hearing in the interests of morals, public order or national security in a democratic society, where the interests of juveniles or the protection of the private life of the parties so require, or to the extent strictly necessary in the opinion of the Chamber in special circumstances where publicity would prejudice the interests of justice.

There are only a few examples of hearings before the Court being held *in camera*. In five cases directed against the United Kingdom concerning matters of child custody and adoption, all heard at the same time, the Court 'decided that, in view of the exceptional circumstances, the hearings should be held in camera', but no further reasons were

---

[5] Explanatory Report on Protocol No. 11, para. 96.
[6] *Lawless v. Ireland (no. 1)*, 14 November 1960, p. 10, Series A no. 1.
[7] Rules of Court, Rule 63(1).
[8] Ibid., Rule 63(3).

provided.[9] In an application involving medical records and infection with HIV, the Court granted the government's request for an *in camera* hearing given 'the sensitive nature of the case'.[10] Cases raising issues of private and family life, often concerning children and vulnerable victims in cases of sexual assault, are an everyday affair at the Court. It is difficult to understand why such rare resort to exclusion of the public should have been ordered in the few cases in which the Court has decided to sit *in camera*. In any event, the issues are well known because they are inevitably explored in the judgment. The identities of victims remain protected by the very common resort to pseudonyms, in accordance with art. 47(3).

The Court has proposed that States take advantage of the possibility of *in camera* proceedings when evidence that they deem to be sensitive, for reasons of national security, is to be examined. According to the Court, 'legitimate national security concerns may be accommodated in its proceedings by means of appropriate procedural arrangements, including restricted access to the document in question under Rule 33 of the Rules of Court and, *in extremis*, the holding of a hearing behind closed doors'.[11] This is indeed what took place in the applications directed against Poland by persons detained at secret prisons operated by the United States. An *in camera* hearing was held at the Human Rights Building in Strasbourg.[12] The Court declined Poland's invitation for it to examine documents *ex parte*, that is, without them being shown to the applicant and his counsel, noting that this was not authorized by the Rules of Court.[13]

Public character of documents

Documents that are deposited with the Registry by the parties or by a third party with respect to an application are accessible to the public, unless the President of the Chamber decides otherwise. According to Rule 33 of the Rules of Court:

Rule 33—Public character of documents

1. All documents deposited with the Registry by the parties or by any third party in connection with an application, except those deposited within the framework of friendly-settlement negotiations as provided for in Rule 62, shall be accessible to the public in accordance with arrangements determined by the Registrar, unless the President of the Chamber, for the reasons set out in paragraph 2 of this Rule, decides otherwise, either of his or her own motion or at the request of a party or any other person concerned.
2. Public access to a document or to any part of it may be restricted in the interests of morals, public order or national security in a democratic society, where the interests of juveniles or the protection of the private life of the parties or of any person concerned so require, or to the extent strictly necessary in the opinion of the President of the Chamber in special circumstances where publicity would prejudice the interests of justice.
3. Any request for confidentiality made under paragraph 1 of this Rule must include reasons and specify whether it is requested that all or part of the documents be inaccessible to the public.

---

[9] *H. v. the United Kingdom*, 8 July 1987, § 6(c), Series A no. 120; *O. v. the United Kingdom*, 8 July 1987, § 6(c), Series A no. 120; *R. v. the United Kingdom*, 8 July 1987, § 6(c), Series A no. 121; *B. v. the United Kingdom*, 8 July 1987, § 6(c), Series A no. 121; *W. v. the United Kingdom*, 8 July 1987, § 5(c), Series A no. 121.

[10] *Z and Others v. the United Kingdom* [GC], no. 29392/95, § 6, ECHR 2001-V.

[11] *Janowiec and Others v. Russia* [GC], nos 55508/07 and 29520/09, § 215, ECHR 2013.

[12] *Al Nashiri v. Poland*, no. 28761/11, §§ 12, 14, 367, 378, 24 July 2014; *Husayn (Abu Zubaydah) v. Poland*, no. 7511/13, §§ 10, 12, 360, 372, 24 July 2014.

[13] *Al Nashiri v. Poland*, no. 28761/11, §§ 25, 27, 24 July 2014; *Husayn (Abu Zubaydah) v. Poland*, no. 7511/13, §§ 23, 25, 24 July 2014.

4. Decisions and judgments given by a Chamber shall be accessible to the public. Decisions and judgments given by a Committee, including decisions covered by the proviso to Rule 53 § 5, shall be accessible to the public. The Court shall periodically make accessible to the public general information about decisions taken by single-judge formations pursuant to Rule 52A § 1 and by Committees in application of Rule 53 § 5.

The Court has used its authority to derogate from the public nature of the dossier in appropriate cases dealing, for example, with refugee and asylum claims[14] and psychiatric patients.[15] The Court has indicated that this is a useful mechanism by which States can address concerns about the production of documents that they deem to be sensitive, because of national security concerns.[16] In the two Polish cases concerning secret detention centres, the Court requested the State to provide documents on a confidentiality basis pursuant to Rule 33(2) of the Rules of Court. In particular, it noted allegations of the existence of an agreement concerning the operation of a secret CIA prison on Polish territory, asking that it be produced on a confidentiality basis 'in case that document existed'.[17] Invoking Rule 33(2), the Court declared that it applied to 'any documents that might be produced by the Government in the future relating to the alleged CIA rendition operations in Poland or other States and the alleged participation of Poland or other States in that operation' as well as documents relating to the investigation.[18] Poland objected that 'the general provisions contained in the Court's Rules of procedure do not indicate in any way the manner in which fragile documents produced by the parties, especially states, to the Court are to be protected. This situation is hardly comparable with internal regulations of other international judicial bodies.'[19] Poland mentioned the International Criminal Court as an example of better practice in this respect.[20] In other cases, Russia has also objected that Rule 33 does not provide any sanction for its breach.[21]

The European Court responded:

The absence of specific, detailed provisions for processing confidential, secret or otherwise sensitive information in the Rules of Court—which, in the Government's view justified their refusal to produce evidence—does not mean that the Court in that respect operates in a vacuum. On the contrary ... over many years the Convention institutions have established sound practice in handling cases involving various highly sensitive matters, including national-security related issues. Examples of procedural decisions emerging from that practice demonstrate that the Court is sufficiently well equipped to address adequately any concerns involved in processing confidential evidence by adopting a wide range of practical arrangements adjusted to the particular circumstances of a given case.[22]

---

[14] *Mohammad Hassan v. the Netherlands and Italy* (dec.), no. 40524/10, §§ 74, 139, 27 August 2013; *S.H. v. the Netherlands* (dec.), no. 47607/07, § 8, 5 March 2013.

[15] *A.E.L. v. Finland* (dec.), no. 59435/10, § 1, 10 December 2013; *G. v. Germany*, no. 65210/09, § 1, 7 June 2012.

[16] *Janowiec and Others v. Russia* [GC], nos 55508/07 and 29520/09, § 215, ECHR 2013.

[17] *Husayn (Abu Zubaydah) v. Poland*, no. 7511/13, § 15, 24 July 2014; *Al Nashiri v. Poland*, no. 28761/11, § 17, 24 July 2014.

[18] *Husayn (Abu Zubaydah) v. Poland*, no. 7511/13, § 16, 24 July 2014; *Al Nashiri v. Poland*, no. 28761/11, § 18, 24 July 2014.

[19] *Husayn (Abu Zubaydah) v. Poland*, no. 7511/13, § 33, 24 July 2014; *Al Nashiri v. Poland*, no. 28761/11, § 35, 24 July 2014.

[20] *Husayn (Abu Zubaydah) v. Poland*, no. 7511/13, § 341, 24 July 2014; *Al Nashiri v. Poland*, no. 28761/11, § 348, 24 July 2014.

[21] *Janowiec and Others v. Russia* [GC], nos 55508/07 and 29520/09, § 193, ECHR 2013; *Sasita Israilova and Others v. Russia*, no. 35079/04, §§ 79, 142, 28 October 2010.

[22] *Husayn (Abu Zubaydah) v. Poland*, no. 7511/13, § 364, 24 July 2014; *Al Nashiri v. Poland*, no. 28761/11, § 371, 24 July 2014.

In a case concerning detention of extradited suspects to Russia, the Court asked for the name and address of detention facilities where the applicants were being held. Russia requested written assurances that the information would remain confidential and would not be 'improperly divulged'. After the President of the Section was made personally responsible for ensuring the confidentiality of the information, Russia complied 'in conditions of strict confidentiality'.[23] Subsequently, the Court has pointed to this example in order to reassure States of its ability to ensure confidentiality pursuant to Rule 33(2).[24]

Further reading

Frowein/Peukert, *MenschenRechtsKonvention*, pp. 534–5.
Leo Zwaak, 'The Procedure before the European Court of Human Rights', in Van Dijk et al., *Theory and Practice*, pp. 109–10.

---

[23] *Shamayev and Others v. Georgia and Russia*, no. 36378/02, §§ 15–17, ECHR 2005-III.
[24] *Georgia v. Russia (I)* [GC], no. 13255/07, § 108, 3 July 2014. Also *Shokkarov and Others v. Russia*, no. 41009/04, § 4, 3 May 2011; *Tsechoyev v. Russia*, no. 39358/05, § 3, 15 March 2011.

Article 41. Just satisfaction/Satisfaction équitable

If the Court finds that there has been a violation of the Convention or the Protocols thereto, and if the internal law of the High Contracting Party concerned allows only partial reparation to be made, the Court shall, if necessary, afford just satisfaction to the injured party.	Si la Cour déclare qu'il y a eu violation de la Convention ou de ses Protocoles, et si le droit interne de la Haute Partie contractante ne permet d'effacer qu'imparfaitement les conséquences de cette violation, la Cour accorde à la partie lésée, s'il y a lieu, une satisfaction équitable.

Introductory comments

'Just satisfaction' is the term used by the European Convention when it addresses the issue of reparation or compensation. The principle is that an applicant who has suffered a loss as a result of a violation of the Convention—the injured party—is entitled to be placed back in the situation before the loss occurred, to the extent that this is possible. As the drafting history of the Convention demonstrates, the award of 'just satisfaction' was a weak substitute for a more robust power enabling the Court to declare national legislation invalid being advocated by some members of the Consultative Assembly of the Council of Europe. Over the decades, however, 'just satisfaction' has become only one feature of the intervention of the Court as it has addressed systemic violations of human rights within States Parties.

Drafting of the provision

The initial draft European Convention on Human Rights prepared by the International Juridical Section of the European Movement declared that the European Court of Human Rights 'may either prescribe measures of reparation or it may require that the State concerned shall take penal or administrative action in regard to the persons responsible for the infringement, or it may demand the repeal, cancellation or amendment of the act'.[1]

After a protracted debate,[2] the Consultative Assembly adopted the following provision:

The jurisdiction of the Court shall extend to all violations of the obligations defined by the Convention, whether they result from legislative, executive or judicial acts. Nevertheless, where objection is taken to a judicial decision, that decision cannot be impugned unless it was finally given in disregard of the fundamental rights defined in Article 2 by reference to Articles 9, 10 and 11 of the United Nations Declaration.[3]

---

[1] Convention for the Collective Protection of Individual Rights and Democratic Liberties by the States, Members of the Council of Europe, and for the establishment of a European Court of Human Rights to ensure observance of the Convention, Doc. INF/5/E/R, I *TP* 296–303, at pp. 300–302, art. 13(b).

[2] See the chapter in this Commentary dealing with article 46, 'Drafting of the provision'.

[3] Amendment proposed by Mr Dominedo and Mr Benvenuti (Italy) (8 September 1949), Doc. 105, II *TP* 12–13.

The beginnings of article 41 can be traced to the Committee of Experts that met at the behest of the Committee of Ministers in February and March 1950. Tomasso Perassi of Italy proposed the following:

If the Court finds that a decision or a measure taken by a legal authority or any other authority of one of the Contracting Parties, [sic] is completely or partially opposed to the obligations arising from the present Convention, and if the constitutional law of the said Party only allows the consequences of this decision or measure to be superficially regained, the decisions of the Court shall, if necessary, accord just satisfaction to the injured party.[4]

This was modified by the Drafting Sub-Committee:

If the Court finds that a decision or a measure taken by a legal authority, or of any other authority of one of the Contracting Parties is completely or partially opposed to the obligations arising from the present Convention, and if the internal law of the said Party only allows partial reparation to be made for the consequences of this decision or measure, the decision of the Court shall, if necessary, accord just satisfaction to the injured party.[5]

A draft commentary accompanying this text made it quite clear that the Committee of Experts was rejecting the approach of the Consultative Assembly. It said that '[c]ontrary to the Assembly draft, the Committee of Experts considered that in no case should the Court be competent to give a ruling on cases of violation of Article 3, relating to the safeguarding of democratic institutions'. Challenges to legislation 'were not the kind which it was suitable to settle by judgment of a court' but rather a matter that came 'exclusively within the political sphere'. The draft report added that '[a]ccording to the Committee of Experts' system, moreover, the Court should only be permitted to give a ruling on cases of violations of the *individual* rights protected by the Convention and not of cases of violation of the Convention by legislative acts as such'.[6]

A few very minor modifications were made in the final draft adopted by the Committee of Experts, the words 'legal authority, or of any other authority of one of the Contracting Parties' being changed to 'legal authority or of any authority of one of the High Contracting Parties'.[7] Also, the comma after 'if necessary' in the final phrase was deleted. The Commentary read as follows:

This provision is in accordance with the actual international law relating to the violation of an obligation by a State. In this respect, jurisprudence of a European Court will never, therefore, introduce any new element or one contrary to existing international law. In particular, the Court will not have the power to declare null and void or amend Acts emanating from the public bodies of the signatory States.[8]

---

[4] Amendments to various articles of the Recommendation of the Consultative Assembly proposed by the Italian Expert, Doc. A 812, III *TP* 228–31.

[5] Continuation and end of the proposals of the Drafting Sub-Committee concerning Section III, Doc. A 813, III *TP* 230–3.

[6] Preliminary Draft of the Report to the Committee of Ministers, 24 February 1950, Doc. CM/WP 1 (50) 1, A 847, III *TP* 246–79, at pp. 274–6 (emphasis in the original).

[7] Preliminary Draft Convention for the Maintenance and Further Realisation of Human Rights and Fundamental Freedoms, 15 February 1950, Doc. A 833, III *TP* 236–46, at p. 246, art. 36.

[8] Preliminary Draft of the Report to the Committee of Ministers, 24 February 1950, Doc. CM/WP 1 (50) 1, A 847, III *TP* 246–79, at p. 276; Appendix to the Report of the Committee of Experts on Human Rights: Draft Convention of Protection of Human Rights and Fundamental Freedoms, 16 March 1950, Doc. CM/WP 1 (50) 15 appendix, CM/WP 1 (50) 14 revised, A 925, IV *TP* 50–79, at p. 44.

The Conference of Senior Officials on Human Rights, which met in June 1950, made only a few technical changes to the provision, restoring the comma after 'necessary' and deleting the word 'of' before 'any authority'.[9] No further changes were made by the Committee of Ministers at its August 1950 session.[10]

The Consultative Assembly returned to the provision in August 1950. Antonio Azara of Italy spoke of the provision,

which enables the Court to grant redress to the injured party if the domestic law of the State to which the injured party belongs allows of only a partial reparation of the consequences of an ordinance, legal or otherwise, issued by an authority representing one of the Member States of the Council of Europe which happens to be in conflict with the obligations arising from the Covnention . . . It is therefore in this last Article that is to be found the sanction to be used if one of the rights indicated in the list of human rights is violated. Substantially and fundamentally, therefore, this list of rights acquires a value which is not only moral and philosophical, but also legal. And the Council of Europe, by giving its approval, will be achieving a glorious phase in its onward march towards international brotherhood, civilisation and progress of our peoples.[11]

Pierre-Henri Teitgen was less enthusiastic. He recalled that the previous year the Consultative Assembly had proposed a Court with the power to annul all legislative or statutory measures contrary to the Convention, something he said was 'essential'. He said the Committee of Ministers had 'very cleverly' substituted for this 'a rather confused' provision.

To begin with, it contains an important error, for it seems to assume that the principal duties of the Court will be in the control of judicial decisions. But that is precisely the view that we have unanimously rejected. What we are afraid of in our countries is not judicial errors. These certainly occur in all our countries: judges are not infallible, but these judicial errors are the exception, the minute exception.

But, Teitgen said, 'the Committee of Ministers is now inserting at the head of the list of powers of the European Court this control of judicial decisions, and it does so without any further explanation—a fact which might lead to regrettable confusion'. He said the draft provision had 'another outstanding defect' because it suggested that 'the only form of reparations will be compensation'. He added that '[i]t seems to suggest that the European Court will be able to grant indemnities to victims, damages and interests, or reparation or this kind. It does not say that the Euroepan Court will be able to pronounce the nullity or invalidity of the rule or the law, or the decree which constitutes a violation of the Convention.'

'That, Ladies and Gentlemen, is something very grave', said Teitgen. He acknowledged that 'reparation in kind may be advisable where the victim is a specified individual' and that 'satisfaction may be given in the form of reparation in cash or the awarding of an indemnity'. But, said Teitgan, 'can the graver form of violation which consists in removing a fundamental law guaranteeing a specific freedom for the whole nation, from the laws of a country in virtue of some law or decree, can such a violation be redressed by

---

[9] Draft Convention annexed to the Report [of the Conference of Senior Officials], Doc. CM/WP 4 (50) 19 annex, CM/WP 4 (50) 16 rev., A 1452, IV *TP* 274–95, at p. 292, art. 50.

[10] Draft Convention adopted by the Sub-Committee, Doc. CM 1 (50) 52, A 1884, V *TP* 76–99, at p. 94, art. 50.

[11] Report of the sitting [of the Consultative Assembly, 14 August 1950], V *TP* 216–71, at p. 248.

awarding a symbolic farthing damages to the citizens of the country?'. Teitgen asked whether, if France were to 'sink into a dictatorship' and suppress the freedom of the press, the European Court would 'award a franc damage to all Frenchmen so as to compensate for the injury which the suppression of this fundamental freedom had caused them? Such a proceeding would not make sense.'[12]

Teitgen proposed replacing the draft provision of the Committee of Ministers with the following:

The Court shall have jurisdiction to deal with any violation of the obligations defined in the Convention, whether they result from legislative, executive or judicial acts. Nevertheless, when an appeal is lodged against a judicial decision, such a decision cannot be challenged unless it was definitely pronounced in disregard of the fundamental rights defined in Articles 5, 6 and 7.

The Court may declare the impugned legislative, executive or judicial acts to be null and void.

Where necessary the Court shall grant just compensation to the injured party.[13]

But Teitgen was unsuccessful in the Legal Committee, where the draft of the Committee of Ministers was retained.[14] The plenary Consultative Assembly agreed with the Committee of Ministers, the only change being the removal of the word 'only' before 'allows'.[15] Immediately prior to final adoption of the Convention, a Committee of Experts reviewed the text of the Convention, reinserting the word 'only'.[16]

The text of article 50 of the 1950 version of the Convention read as follows:

If the Court finds that a decision or a measure taken by a legal authority or any other authority of a High Contracting Party is completely or partially in conflict with the obligations arising from the present Convention, and if the internal law of the said Party allows only partial reparation to be made for the consequences of this decision or measure, the decision of the Court shall, if necessary, afford just satisfaction to the injured party.

It was modified by Protocol No. 11 and renumbered as article 41. The Explanatory Report on Protocol No. 11 describes article 41 as a 'simplified and shortened version' of its predecessor.[17] The heading 'Just satisfaction' was also added by Protocol No. 11.

Analysis and interpretation

If there is no friendly settlement and the Court then finds there has been a violation of the Convention, it may award the applicant 'just satisfaction'. Article 41 of the Convention says it is to do this 'if the internal law of the High Contracting Party concerned allows only partial reparation to be made'. The exercise is similar in nature to that undertaken by civil courts when they award damages to a plaintiff. Of course, within the European Convention system it is the State rather than a private party that is required to pay the amount that has been awarded. Although certain principles have been developed in the case law of

---

[12] *Rep.* 1950, II, p. 512.

[13] Draft Motion submitted by M. Teitgen, Revised Draft, Doc. AS/JA (2) 6 rev., A 2238, VI *TP* 10–15.

[14] First Report [of the Committee on Legal and Administrative Questions], Doc. AS/JA (2) 15, A 2298, VI *TP* 46–52.

[15] Text published in the Collected Documents of the Consultative Assembly, Doc. AS (2) 104, VI *TP* 198–229, at p. 222.

[16] Report of the Committee [of Legal Experts], Doc. CM/Adj (50) 3, A 2530, VII *TP* 8; Doc. CM/Adj (50) 3 revised, A 2531, VII *TP* 10.

[17] Explanatory Report on Protocol No. 11, para. 97.

the Court, there is no entitlement of an applicant to the award of just satisfaction. This remains subject to the discretion of the Court.

The Court has only been asked to apply article 41 in an inter-State case on one occasion following many years of defiance of its judgment on the merits in *Cyprus v. Turkey*.[18] In *Ireland v. the United Kingdom*, at the request of the Court the applicant State answered that 'while not wishing to interfere with the *de bene esse* jurisdiction of the Court' its object had not been obtaining compensation, nor did it invite the Court to accord just satisfaction in the form of monetary compensation to any individual victim of a breach of the Convention. The Court accordingly said it was not necessary to address the question.[19]

During the just satisfaction proceedings, Turkey argued that article 41 did not in principle apply to inter-State cases. It referred to the early pronouncement of the European Commission in the *Austria v. Italy* case to the effect that applicant States do not enforce their own rights or those of their nationals, but rather they vindicate the public order of Europe.[20] Rejecting Turkey's contention, the Grand Chamber referred to the *travaux préparatoires* of article 41 and more precisely to a reference in the Report of the Committee of Experts to the consistency of the provision with 'the actual international law relating to the violation of an obligation by a State'. The Grand Chamber described '[t]he most important principle of international law relating to the violation, by a State, of a treaty obligation' as being 'that the breach of an engagement involves an obligation to make reparation in an adequate form'.[21] According to the Grand Chamber, '[d]espite the specific character of the Convention, the overall logic of Article 41 is not substantially different from the logic of reparations in public international law, according to which "it is a well-established rule of international law that an injured State is entitled to obtain compensation from the State which has committed an internationally wrongful act for the damage caused by it"'.[22] The Court described article 41 as '*lex specialis* in relation to the general rules and principles of international law', saying it could not therefore be interpreted 'in such a narrow and restrictive way so as to exclude inter-State applications from its scope'.[23]

The Grand Chamber acknowledged that in some cases an applicant State might complain about general issues in another State Party, such as systemic problems and administrative practices. In those circumstances, where the applicant State is acting in the interests of European public order, it might not be appropriate to award just satisfaction.[24] However, the Grand Chamber said that there was another category of inter-State complaint where the applicant State is denouncing violations of the rights of its own nationals. Such cases are substantially not only similar to those of individual applicants but are also consistent with the long-standing practice of diplomatic protection under

[18] *Cyprus v. Turkey* [GC], no. 25781/94, ECHR 2001-IV.

[19] *Ireland v. the United Kingdom*, 18 January 1978, §§ 245–246, Series A no. 25.

[20] *Cyprus v. Turkey* (just satisfaction) [GC], no. 25781/94, §§ 36–38, 12 May 2014, citing *Austria v. Italy*, no. 788/60, p. 140, Commission decision of 11 January 1961, (1961) 4 YB 116.

[21] *Cyprus v. Turkey* (just satisfaction) [GC], no. 25781/94, § 41, 12 May 2014, citing *Factory at Chorzów (Jurisdiction)*, PCIJ, Series A, No. 9, p. 21.

[22] Cyprus v. Turkey (just satisfaction) [GC], no. 25781/94, § 41, 12 May 2014, citing *Gabčíkovo-Nagymaros Project (Hungary/Slovakia)*, Judgment, I.C.J. Reports 1997, p. 7, para. 152.

[23] Cyprus v. Turkey (just satisfaction) [GC], no. 25781/94, § 42, 12 May 2014. See, for a somewhat different view, ibid., Partly Concurring and Partly Dissenting Opinion of Judge Casadevall.

[24] Ibid., § 44.

international law.[25] In this context, the Court insisted that any award of just satisfaction must always be for the benefit of individual victims. It set a sum of €30 million as non-pecuniary damage for surviving relatives of missing persons and €60 million as non-pecuniary damage for the suffering of enclaved residents of the Karpas peninsula, specifying that the sums were to be distributed by Cyprus to the individual victims of the violations.[26]

'The internal law of the High Contracting Party concerned...'

Noting in a separate opinion that the words 'the internal law of the High Contracting Party concerned...' have never been interpreted by the Convention organs, Judge Zupančič referred to the origins of article 41 in the amendment proposed by Tomasso Perassi in the Committee of Experts in February 1950. He explained that:

[t]he provision was inspired by the 1921 German-Swiss Treaty on Arbitration and Conciliation (Article 10) and the Geneva General Act for the Pacific Settlement of International Disputes of 1928 (Article 32). Of course, these provisions were meant to deal with specific inter-State situations in which the State party to an arbitration agreement was unable to change its internal law but was willing to pay an equitable satisfaction of another kind. The basis for the arbitrage was extra-judicial compensation for the damage suffered by an individual caused to him by an alien State. The reference to "the internal law of the...Party [which] allows only partial reparation to be made" makes sense in inter-State disputes in which the State was politically willing to compensate for the restitution to the aggrieved individual, but was unable to do so due to specific provisions of its internal, usually constitutional, law. The intent of the provision, therefore, was to by-pass the internal legal impediments and to transpose the compensation question to the inter-State diplomatic protection level. This is also why, as we shall see, the language is difficult to interpret in the context of the Convention.[27]

Judge Zupančič underscored the difficulty of interpreting a provision derived from an inter-State arbitration agreement within the context of human rights protection, explaining, as had done Pierre-Henri Teitgen in the Consultative Assembly in August 1950, that '[m]any procedural violations of human rights cannot be compensated for by pecuniary "just satisfaction". The fears concerning the infringement of national sovereignty which hung over the Committee of Experts for Human Rights in 1949 are clearly out of date today.'[28] Describing the approach of the Court as 'too timid',[29] he urged the following interpretation of the phrase 'if the internal law of the High Contracting Party concerned allows only partial reparation to be made':

Before the Court awards pecuniary just satisfaction, this critical phrase logically (*argumento a contrario*) presupposes that the High Contracting Party's legal system will have done everything in its power to correct the violation in question. Since the domestic remedies have been exhausted

---

[25] Ibid., § 45.

[26] Ibid., § 58.

[27] *Lucà v. Italy*, no. 33354/96, Partly Concurring Opinion of Judge Zupančič, ECHR 2001-II.

[28] Ibid.

[29] *Pétur Thór Sigurðsson v. Iceland*, no. 39731/98, Concurring Opinion of Judge Zupančič, ECHR 2003-IV. Also *Cable and Others v. The United Kingdom* [GC], nos 24436/94, 24582/94, 24583/94, 24584/94, 24895/94, 25937/94, 25939/94, 25940/94, 25941/94, 26271/95, 26525/95, 27341/95, 27342/95, 27346/95, 27357/95, 27389/95, 27409/95, 27760/95, 27762/95, 27772/95, 28009/95, 28790/95, 30236/96, 30239/96, 30276/96, 30277/96, 30460/96, 30461/96, 30462/96, 31399/96, 31400/96, 31434/96, 31899/96, 32024/96, and 32944/96, Partly Dissenting Opinion of Judge Zupančič, 18 February 1999.

through the hierarchy of legal appeals before the case has reached the Court, this in most cases implies that the "the internal law of the High Contracting Party concerned" did not "allow ... [for any] ... reparation to be made".[30]

Just satisfaction

Pursuant to article 41, the Court may award monetary compensation if it considers this to be 'necessary'. The Court has wide discretion in making this determination. In the exercise of its discretion, 'the Court will have regard to all the circumstances of the case including the nature of the violations found as well as any special circumstances pertaining to the context of the case'.[31] The discretionary nature of the power to award just satisfaction is confirmed by the adjective 'just' and the phrase 'if necessary'.[32]

There can only be a finding of just satisfaction if the Court concludes that there has been a violation of the Convention. An award cannot be made for damage caused by events or situations that have not been found in breach of the Convention or for complaints declared inadmissible at an earlier stage in the proceedings. The existence of a causal link between the damage claimed and the violation of the Convention is a *sine qua non* for an award of just satisfaction.[33] The Court will not be satisfied if there is a 'merely tenuous connection between the alleged violation and the damage, nor by mere speculation as to what might have been'.[34]

A ruling on article 41 will only be included in the Court's judgment if a specific claim has been submitted in accordance with Rule 60 of the Rules of Court[35] and if the question is ready for decision. The Court will reserve its jurisdiction with respect to just satisfaction if the question is not yet ready for decision.[36] If the Court makes a separate, subsequent ruling on just satisfaction, it shall endeavour to reconstitute the Chamber or the Committee that made the ruling on the violation itself.[37] In establishing the amount of just satisfaction, the Court normally considers 'local economic circumstances'. It may also take guidance from domestic standards, although it is not bound by these.

Nevertheless, the Court may, 'for reasons of equity', award less than the amount of damage that has actually been sustained, for example in a case where the applicant bears some degree of responsibility for the actual damage, the costs, and the expenses. Frequently, the Court concludes that the finding of a violation is sufficient satisfaction and makes no monetary award.[38] In a case involving suspected terrorists, for example, the Court held 'that the circumstances justify the making of an award substantially lower than that which it has had occasion to make in other cases of unlawful detention'.[39] But in the case concerning Al Qaeda leaders detained in Poland for several months, the Court

---

[30] *Lucà v. Italy*, no. 33354/96, Partly Concurring Opinion of Judge Zupančič, ECHR 2001-II.

[31] *A. and Others v. the United Kingdom* [GC], no. 3455/05, § 250, ECHR 2009.

[32] *Guzzardi v. Italy*, 6 November 1980, § 114, Series A no. 39; *Arvanitaki-Roboti and Others v. Greece* [GC], no. 27278/03, § 32, 15 February 2008.

[33] *Andrejeva v. Latvia* [GC], no. 55707/00, § 111, ECHR 2009; *Nikolova v. Bulgaria* [GC], no. 31195/96, § 73, ECHR 1999-II.

[34] Practice Direction, Just Satisfaction Claims, 28 March 2007, para. 7.

[35] For technical requirements, see also Practice Direction, Just Satisfaction Claims, 28 March 2007.

[36] Rules of Court, Rule 75(1).

[37] Ibid., Rule 75(2).

[38] *A. and Others v. the United Kingdom* [GC], no. 3455/05, § 250, ECHR 2009; *Nikolova v. Bulgaria* [GC], no. 31195/96, § 76, ECHR 1999-II.

[39] Ibid., § 253.

awarded €100,000 plus any tax chargeable on the amount.[40] The wrongful extradition of a terror suspect from Belgium to the United States resulted in an award of €60,000.[41] The Court has explained that there are situations where public vindication of the wrong suffered is 'a powerful form of redress in itself. In many cases where a law, procedure or practice has been found to fall short of Convention standards this is enough to put matters right.'[42]

When it makes an award of just satisfaction, the Court may direct that if settlement is not made within a specific time, the sums awarded will be subject to interest.[43] Normally, this will be three months from the date when the judgment becomes final and binding. The rate will be equal to the marginal lending rate of the European Central Bank during the default period plus three percentage points.[44]

Pecuniary damages

The Court has explained that 'the principle underlying the provision of just satisfaction is that the applicant should, as far as possible, be put in the position he or she would have enjoyed had the violation of the Convention not occurred'.[45] This is the ancient principle of *restitutio in integrum*, confirmed in international case law[46] as well as in article 35 of the Draft Articles on State Responsibility adopted by the United Nations International Law Commission.[47] Not all cases will lend themselves to assessing just satisfaction on this basis. However, '[i]f the nature of the breach allows of *restitutio in integrum*, it is for the respondent State to effect it, the Court having neither the power nor the practical possibility of doing so itself'.[48] In establishing the amount of compensation for the purposes of pecuniary damages, the Court will consider the loss actually suffered (*damnum emergens*), but it may also take into account the loss, or diminished gain, to be expected in the future (*lucrum cessans*).[49]

In an expropriation case, the applicants sought the revocation of the expropriation order but did not make any additional claim for just satisfaction. The Court acknowledged that *restitutio in integrum* was possible to the extent the national jurisdictions revoked the order.[50] In cases involving expropriation, the Court may consider not only

---

[40] *Al Nashiri v. Poland*, no. 28761/11, § 595, 24 July 2014; *Husayn (Abu Zubaydah) v. Poland*, no. 7511/13, § 567, 45 July 2014. See also *El Masri v. 'the former Yugoslav Republic of Macedonia'* [GC], no. 39630/09, § 270, ECHR 2012.

[41] *Trabelsi v. Belgium*, no. 140/10, § 176, 4 September 2014.

[42] *Varnava and Others v. Turkey* [GC], nos 16064/90, 16065/90, 16066/90, 16068/90, 16069/90, 16070/90, 16071/90, 16072/90, and 16073/90, § 224, ECHR 2009; *Christine Goodwin v. the United Kingdom* [GC], no. 28957/95, § 120, ECHR 2002-VI; *Saadi v. Italy* [GC], no. 37201/06, § 188, ECHR 2008; *S. and Marper v. the United Kingdom* [GC], nos. 30562/04 and 30566/04, § 134, 4 December 2008.

[43] Rules of Court, Rule 75(3).

[44] Practice Direction, Just Satisfaction Claims, 28 March 2007, para. 15.

[45] *Andrejeva v. Latvia* [GC], no. 55707/00, § 111, ECHR 2009; *Kingsley v. the United Kingdom* [GC], no. 35605/97, § 40, ECHR 2002-IV.

[46] *Texaco Overseas Petroleum Company and California Asiatic Oil Company v. Libya*, (1977) 104 *Journal de droit international* 350, cited in *Guiso-Gallisay v. Italy* (just satisfaction) [GC], no. 58858/00, § 52, 22 December 2009.

[47] UN Doc. A/RES/56/83, annex, cited in *Guiso-Gallisay v. Italy* (just satisfaction) [GC], no. 58858/00, § 53, 22 December 2009; *Verein gegen Tierfabriken Schweiz (VgT) v. Switzerland (no. 2)* [GC], no. 32772/02, § 86, ECHR 2009.

[48] *Kozacıoğlu v. Turkey* [GC], no. 2334/03, § 80, 19 February 2009; *Turgut and Others v. Turkey* (just satisfaction), no. 1411/03, § 12, 13 October 2009.

[49] Practice Direction, Just Satisfaction Claims, 28 March 2007, para. 10.

[50] *Fakiridou and Schina v. Greece*, no. 6789/06, § 61, 14 November 2008.

the market value of the property in question but also 'on an equitable basis' an amount in compensation for loss of opportunities.[51] In some cases where *restitutio in integrum* is possible in the form of a restoration of property, the Court will reserve its decision on just satisfaction. This is governed by Rule 75 of the Rules of Court.

Non-pecuniary or moral damages

The European Convention contains no express reference to non-pecuniary damages. This has not, however, prevented the Court from making awards on this basis as part of the just satisfaction. The case law has identified situations where the applicant has 'suffered evident trauma, whether physical or psychological, pain and suffering, distress, anxiety, frustration, feelings of injustice or humiliation, prolonged uncertainty, disruption to life, or real loss of opportunity'.[52] These are situations where 'the impact of the violation may be regarded as being of a nature and degree as to have impinged so significantly on the moral well-being of the applicant as to require something further'.[53] Referring to Greek Cypriot residents of the Karpas peninsula in northern Cyprus, enclaved since the 1974 invasion, the Grand Chamber said it had 'no doubt about the protracted feelings of helplessness, distress and anxiety' of the victims.[54]

In assessing moral damages, the Court has noted that this is an area that does not lend itself to 'a process of calculation or precise quantification'.[55] The amount 'is intended to make reparation for the state of distress, inconvenience and uncertainty resulting from the violation in question'.[56] The Court does not function like a mechanism for establishing tort or civil liability in a domestic legal system. Rather, '[i]ts guiding principle is equity, which above all involves flexibility and an objective consideration of what is just, fair and reasonable in all the circumstances of the case, including not only the position of the applicant but the overall context in which the breach occurred'. The non-pecuniary awards 'serve to give recognition to the fact that moral damage occurred as a result of a breach of a fundamental human right and reflect in the broadest of terms the severity of the damage; they are not, nor should they be, intended to give financial comfort or sympathetic enrichment at the expense of the Contracting Party concerned'.[57]

Costs and expenses

The European Court of Human Rights applies article 41 in awarding costs and expenses to applicants. In order to receive them, the Court requires that the injured party have actually and necessarily incurred them.[58] Under Rule 60(2) of the Rules of Court,

---

[51] *Guiso-Gallisay v. Italy* (just satisfaction) [GC], no. 58858/00, § 107, 22 December 2009.

[52] *Varnava and Others v. Turkey* [GC], nos 16064/90, 16065/90, 16066/90, 16068/90, 16069/90, 16070/90, 16071/90, 16072/90, and 16073/90, § 224, ECHR 2009; *Elsholz v. Germany* [GC], no. 25735/94, § 70, ECHR 2000-VIII; *Selmouni v. France* [GC], no. 25803/94, § 123, ECHR 1999-V; *Smith and Grady v. the United Kingdom* (just satisfaction), nos 33985/96 and 33986/96, § 12, ECHR 2000-IX.

[53] *Varnava and Others v. Turkey* [GC], nos 16064/90, 16065/90, 16066/90, 16068/90, 16069/90, 16070/90, 16071/90, 16072/90, and 16073/90, § 224, ECHR 2009.

[54] *Cyprus v. Turkey* (just satisfaction) [GC], no. 25781/94, § 57, 12 May 2014.

[55] *Varnava and Others v. Turkey* [GC], nos 16064/90, 16065/90, 16066/90, 16068/90, 16069/90, 16070/90, 16071/90, 16072/90, and 16073/90, § 224, ECHR 2009.

[56] *Arvanitaki-Roboti and Others v. Greece* [GC], no. 27278/03, § 27, 15 February 2008; *Comingersoll S.A. v. Portugal* [GC], no. 35382/97, § 29, ECHR 2000-IV.

[57] *Varnava and Others v. Turkey* [GC], nos 16064/90, 16065/90, 16066/90, 16068/90, 16069/90, 16070/90, 16071/90, 16072/90, and 16073/90, § 224, ECHR 2009.

[58] *A. and Others v. the United Kingdom* [GC], no. 3455/05, § 256, ECHR 2009; *Kingsley v. the United Kingdom* [GC], no. 35605/97, § 49, ECHR 2002-IV; *Micallef v. Malta* [GC], no. 17056/06, § 115, ECHR 2009.

itemized particulars of any claim are required along with supporting documents or vouchers. If the documentation is not sufficient, sometimes the Court will recognize that substantial costs and expenses will have been incurred. In those circumstances, it may make an award on an 'equitable basis'.[59]

The costs and expenses must actually relate to the violation of the Convention.[60] They are only awarded to a successful applicant.

Punitive damages

The European Court of Human Rights does not award punitive damages, at least explicitly.[61] According to the Grand Chamber, there is 'little, if any, scope under the Convention for directing Governments to pay penalties to applicants which are unconnected with damage shown to be actually incurred in respect of past violations of the Convention; in so far as such sums would purport to compensate for future suffering of the applicants, this would be speculative in the extreme'.[62] Nevertheless, the Court seems to have left the door open to awarding punitive damages by stating, for example, that it has 'until now, considered it inappropriate to accept claims for damages with labels such as "punitive", "aggravated" or "exemplary"'.[63]

Judge Pinto de Albuquerque has pointed to many examples of the award of just satisfaction where there is a lack of genuine correspondence between the actual damage suffered and the amount, suggesting that in practice this amounts to a form of punishment imposed upon the respondent State. '[P]unitive damages are an appropriate and necessary instrument for fulfilling the Court's mission to uphold human rights in Europe and ensuring the observance of the engagements undertaken by the Contracting Parties in the Convention and the Protocols thereto (Article 19 of the Convention)', he has written.[64]

Further reading

Gabriella Citroni, 'Measures of Reparation for Victims of Gross Human Rights Violations: Developments and Challenges in the Jurisprudence of Two Regional Human Rights Courts', (2012) 5 *Inter-American and European Human Rights Journal* 49.

Frowein/Peukert, *MenschenRechtsKonvention*, pp. 536–95.

Alastair Mowbray, 'The European Court of Human Rights' Approach to Just Satisfaction', [1997] *Public Law* 647.

Karen Reid, *A Practitioner's Guide to the European Convention on Human Rights*, London: Sweet & Maxwell, 2011, pp. 831–70.

---

[59] *Andrejeva v. Latvia* [GC], no. 55707/00, § 116, ECHR 2009; *Svipsta v. Latvia*, no. 66820/01, § 170, ECHR 2006-III (extracts); *Zaicevs v. Latvia*, no. 65022/01, § 64, 31 July 2007.

[60] *Andrejeva v. Latvia* [GC], no. 55707/00, § 115, ECHR 2009; *Iatridis v. Greece* (just satisfaction) [GC], no. 31107/96, § 54, ECHR 2000-XI; *Beyeler v. Italy* (just satisfaction) [GC], no. 33202/96, § 27, 28 May 2002; *Svipsta v. Latvia*, no. 66820/01, § 170, ECHR 2006-III (extracts); *J.L. and Others v. The United Kingdom* (just satisfaction), nos 29522/95, 30056/96, and 30574/96, § 18, 25 September 2001.

[61] *Akdivar and Others v. Turkey* (Article 50), 1 April 1998, § 38, *Reports of Judgments and Decisions* 1998-II; *Orhan v. Turkey*, no. 25656/94, § 448, ECHR 2002.

[62] *Varnava and Others v. Turkey* [GC], nos 16064/90, 16065/90, 16066/90, 16068/90, 16069/90, 16070/90, 16071/90, 16072/90, and 16073/90, § 223, ECHR 2009.

[63] Practice Direction, Just Satisfaction Claims, 28 March 2007, para. 9.

[64] *Cyprus v. Turkey* (just satisfaction) [GC], no. 25781/94, Concurring Opinion of Judge Pinto de Albuquerque, Joined by Judge Vučinić, § 19, 12 May 2014.

Christian Tomuschat, 'Just Satisfaction under Article 50 of the European Convention on Human Rights', in Mahoney et al., *Mélanges Ryssdal*, pp. 1409–30.

Luzius Wildhaber, 'Article 41 of the European Convention on Human Rights: Just Satisfaction under the European Convention on Human Rights', [2003] *Baltic Yearbook of International Law* 1.

Leo Zwaak, 'The Procedure before the European Court of Human Rights', in Van Dijk et al., *Theory and Practice*, pp. 245–78.

Article 42. Judgments of Chambers/Arrêts des chambres

Judgments of Chambers shall become final in accordance with the provisions of Article 44, paragraph 2.	Les arrêts des chambres deviennent définitifs conformément aux dispositions de l'article 44, paragraphe 2.

Introductory comments

Under the 1950 text of the Convention, the judgment of a Chamber was final, subject to the possibility of a request for interpretation or revision in accordance with the Rules of Court. When the mechanism of referral to the Grand Chamber was introduced by Protocol No. 11, it became necessary to revise the original provision. Accordingly, the judgment of a Chamber only becomes final once the issue of referral to the Grand Chamber has been resolved pursuant to article 44(2).

Drafting of the provision

According to article 52 of the 1950 text of the Convention, '[t]he judgment of the Court shall be final'. The drafting of this provision is discussed in the chapter of this Commentary on article 44.

Protocol No. 11 replaced article 52 with the current article 42. According to the Explanatory Report:

The Chamber will decide, as the Court had done in the past, by means of a judgment. This judgment will not—contrary to the former system—be immediately definitive, but will become so later in accordance with Article 44, paragraph 2. The judgment will have to be reasoned (Article 45, paragraph 1). It shall be transmitted to the parties but will not be published until it has become final (Article 44, paragraph 3). Further details may be determined in the rules of the Court.[1]

The heading of the provision, 'Judgments of Chambers', was also introduced by Protocol No. 11.

Analysis and interpretation

'[I]ts sole object is to make the Court's judgments not subject to any appeal to another authority', the Court stated in an early judgment with reference to article 42.[2] Article 42 needs to be read in conjunction with article 44(2), by which a judgment of a Chamber becomes final once it has become clear that the case will not be examined by the Grand Chamber. Thus, if a case is heard by a Grand Chamber, the judgment of the Chamber never becomes 'final'.

---

[1] Explanatory Report on Protocol No. 11, para. 42.
[2] *Ringeisen v. Austria* (Article 50), 22 June 1972, § 17, Series A no. 15; *Ringeisen v. Austria* (interpretation), 23 June 1973, § 13, Series A no. 16.

A judgment that has become final is deemed to be *res judicata*. Article 35(2)(b) reflects the same notion by making inadmissible any application that 'is substantially the same as a matter that has already been examined by the Court'. The Convention uses the term 'judgment' to refer to a ruling on the merits whereas the term 'decision' is reserved for rulings on admissibility. Only a 'judgment' is subject to execution by the Committee of Ministers.

The rule set out in article 42 must also be understood in conjunction with article 46 whereby a judgment of the Court may be 'interpreted' at the request of the Committee of Ministers. The Rules of Court allow for both 'interpretation' and 'revision' of a final judgment upon the request of one of the parties and for 'rectification' upon the request of the Chamber that issued the judgment.

Further reading

Frowein/Peukert, *MenschenRechtsKonvention,* p. 596.

Janneke Gerards, 'Judicial Deliberations in the European Court of Human Rights', in N. Huls, M. Adams, and J.A. Bomhoff, eds, *The Legitimacy of Highest Courts' Rulings,* The Hague: TMC Asser, 2009, pp. 407–36.

Leo Zwaak, 'The Procedure before the European Court of Human Rights', in Van Dijk et al., *Theory and Practice,* pp. 241–4.

Article 43. Referral to the Grand Chamber/Renvoi devant la Grande Chambre

1. Within a period of three months from the date of the judgment of the Chamber, any party to the case may, in exceptional cases, request that the case be referred to the Grand Chamber.

2. A panel of five judges of the Grand Chamber shall accept the request if the case raises a serious question affecting the interpretation or application of the Convention or the Protocols thereto, or a serious issue of general importance.

3. If the panel accepts the request, the Grand Chamber shall decide the case by means of a judgment.

1. Dans un délai de trois mois à compter de la date de l'arrêt d'une chambre, toute partie à l'affaire peut, dans des cas exceptionnels, demander le renvoi de l'affaire devant la Grande Chambre.

2. Un collège de cinq juges de la Grande Chambre accepte la demande si l'affaire soulève une question grave relative à l'interprétation ou à l'application de la Convention ou de ses Protocoles, ou encore une question grave de caractère général.

3. Si le collège accepte la demande, la Grande Chambre se prononce sur l'affaire par un arrêt.

Introductory comments

The function of the Grand Chamber is to provide rulings in cases that raise serious questions affecting the interpretation or application of the Convention and its Protocols, or a serious issue of general importance. Its judgments carry great authority because of the enlarged composition of the bench, consisting of seventeen judges rather than seven for a Chamber. Moreover, the Grand Chamber is also comprised of the President of the Court, the Vice-Presidents, and the Presidents of the Chambers. The determination of cases that are examined by the Grand Chamber is governed by article 43.

Drafting of the provision

Article 43 of the Convention was introduced by Protocol No. 11. The 1950 text of the Convention did not contemplate Chambers of different configurations. Article 43 of the 1950 Convention read:

For the consideration of each case brought before it the Court shall consist of a Chamber composed of seven judges. There shall sit as an ex officio member of the Chamber the judge who is a national of any State party concerned, or, if there is none, a person of its choice who shall sit in the capacity of judge; the names of the other judges shall be chosen by lot by the President before the opening of the case.[1]

---

[1] Draft Convention adopted by the Sub-Committee, Doc. CM 1 (50) 52, A 1884, V *TP* 76–99, at p. 92; Draft Convention adopted by the Committee of Ministers, 7 August 1950, Doc. A 1937, V *TP* 120–45, at p. 138. For the full drafting history, see the chapter on article 26 in this Commentary.

Nevertheless, the Rules of Court adopted in 1959 provided that the 'plenary Court' consisting of all of the judges would fulfil not only an administrative function but also a judicial role. The plenary Court exercised jurisdiction in three situations, including cases where the Chamber had relinquished jurisdiction because of the existence of a 'serious question affecting the interpretation of the Convention' and those 'where the resolution of such question might have a result inconsistent with a judgment previously delivered by a Chamber or by the plenary Court'.[2] However, there was no possibility of a referral to the plenary Court at the request of a party to the proceedings.

With the entry into force of Protocol No. 11, the plenary Court ceased to have any judicial function and the Grand Chamber became the largest judicial unit. The Explanatory Report referred to instructions from the Committee of Ministers to draft a Protocol that would include the following features: 'an appropriate structure to ensure the quality and consistency of its case-law and to enable a re-hearing in exceptional cases, for example those raising serious questions affecting the interpretation or application of the Convention; provision should be made for the presence of a national judge in any such re-hearing'.[3] The language in article 43(2) was drawn from a provision introduced by Protocol No. 9 authorizing a three-judge panel to deal with a case submitted to a Court that did not 'raise a serious question affecting the interpretation or application of the Convention' and that did not 'for any other reason warrant consideration by the Court'.[4]

Analysis and interpretation

The rehearing of a case that is governed by article 43 is to be distinguished from the relinquishment of jurisdiction by a Chamber in favour of the Grand Chamber pursuant to article 30 of the Convention. In the latter case, the Chamber has not yet issued a judgment. In the former, the proceeding is more like a classic appeal in the sense that the initiative rests entirely with the parties and seeks to modify or reverse the judgment of the Chamber. A consequence of the Grand Chamber decision is that 'the Chamber judgment, as *res judicata*, is invalidated with retrospective effect' and is henceforth 'only of historical value'.[5]

There are some curious differences in the criteria allowing for referral under article 43 and relinquishment under article 30, although they do not appear to have provoked any reflection in the case law. Referral may be authorized 'if the case raises a serious question affecting the interpretation or application of the Convention or the protocols thereto'. Relinquishment, on the other hand, is justified if the case 'raises a serious question affecting the interpretation' but not, apparently, 'the 'application'. Referral under article 43 may also be ordered for 'a serious issue of general importance', something that is absent in article 30 dealing with relinquishment. Relinquishment is also possible 'where the

---

[2] Rules of Court, (Adopted 18 September 1959), Rule 48 (Relinquishment of jurisdiction by the Chamber in favour of the plenary Court). This became Rule 50 pursuant to Revised Rules of Court (adopted on 24 November 1982) and then Rule 51 pursuant to Rules of Court (Adopted on 24 November 1982 and amended on 26 January 1989).

[3] Explanatory Report on Protocol No. 11, para. 4. Also paras 47, 99.

[4] Ibid., para. 99. See Protocol No. 9 to the Convention for the Protection of Human Rights and Fundamental Freedoms, art. 5(2); Explanatory Report on Protocol No. 9, paras. 24–25.

[5] *Kyprianou v. Cyprus* [GC], no. 73797/01, Partly Dissenting Opinion of Judge Costa, § 2, ECHR 2005-XIII.

resolution of a question before the Chamber might have a result inconsistent with a judgment previously delivered by the Court'. Referral does not seem to be allowed when the judgment of the Chamber actually as a result inconsistent with a judgment previously delivered by the Court.

The 'case'

Paragraphs 1 and 3 of article 43 refer to 'the case'. It is 'the case' that is referred to the Grand Chamber and 'the case' that is dealt with in the final judgment of the Grand Chamber. The case that is referred to the Grand Chamber consists of those aspects of the application that have been declared admissible by the Chamber or by some other formation of the Court. In other words, the Grand Chamber may not review a decision holding part of the application to be inadmissible.[6] Otherwise, the scope of the 'case' before the Grand Chamber is 'limited only by the Chamber's decision on admissibility'.[7] Thus, 'whilst the existence of "a serious question affecting the interpretation or application of the Convention or the Protocols thereto, or a serious issue of general importance" (paragraph 2) is a prerequisite for acceptance of a party's request, the consequence of acceptance is that the whole "case" is referred to the Grand Chamber to be decided afresh by means of a new judgment (paragraph 3)'.[8] The Grand Chamber remains free to rule that the entire application or portions of it are inadmissible. Its power in this respect is ensured by article 35(4), which gives the Court the power to 'reject any application which it considers inadmissible . . . at any stage of the proceedings'.[9]

It is not possible for a party to request the referral of only part of 'the case'.[10] To that extent, the procedure is quite different from a classic appeal, where grounds of appeal frame the authority of the higher court.[11] If there are two applicants but only one of them requests the referral to the Grand Chamber, this does not mean that the Grand Chamber does not rule on the entire case declared admissible by the Chamber, including that portion concerning the applicant who has not requested referral. This approach is said to be 'in keeping with the spirit and the letter of Article 37 § 1 *in fine* of the Convention, by which the Court is entitled to continue the examination of an application if respect for human rights as defined in the Convention and the Protocols so requires'.[12] One consequence of this is that the party that seeks the re-hearing may end up losing those parts of the Chamber judgment with which it is satisfied. For example, in *Janowiec v. Poland*, the applicants had been successful in the Chamber with a portion of the original claim concerning article 3 of the Convention; this was reconsidered and rejected by the Grand Chamber along with the rest of their application.[13]

---

[6] *Sanoma Uitgevers B.V. v. the Netherlands* [GC], no. 38224/03, § 47, 14 September 2010; *K. and T. v. Finland* [GC], no. 25702/94, § 141, ECHR 2001-VII; *Šilih v. Slovenia* [GC], no. 71463/01, § 120, 9 April 2009; *Kafkaris v. Cyprus* [GC], no. 21906/04, § 124, ECHR 2008; *Kovačić and Others v. Slovenia* [GC], nos 44574/98, 45133/98, and 48316/99, § 194, 3 October 2008.

[7] *Azinas v. Cyprus* [GC], no. 56679/00, § 32, ECHR 2004-III.

[8] *Perna v. Italy* [GC], no. 48898/99, § 23, ECHR 2003-V.

[9] *Šilih v. Slovenia* [GC], no. 71463/01, § 120, 9 April 2009.

[10] *K. and T. v. Finland* [GC], no. 25702/94, §§ 137–141, ECHR 2001-VII.

[11] *Mooren v. Germany* [GC], no. 11364/03, § 101, 9 July 2009; *K. and T. v. Finland* [GC], no. 25702/94, §§ 140–41, ECHR 2001-VII; *Göç v. Turkey* [GC], no. 36590/97, § 36, ECHR 2002-V; *Azinas v. Cyprus* [GC], no. 56679/00, §§ 31–33, ECHR 2004-III.

[12] *Cumpǎnǎ and Mazǎre v. Romania* [GC], no. 33348/96, § 67, ECHR 2004-XI.

[13] *Janowiec and Others v. Russia* [GC], nos 55508/07 and 29520/09, §§ 162–189, ECHR 2013.

Authorization of referral

Any party to the proceedings may, 'in exceptional cases', request referral to the Grand Chamber. The party must specify in its request 'the serious question affecting the interpretation or application of the Convention or the Protocols thereto, or the serious issue of general importance, which in its view warrants consideration by the Grand Chamber'.[14] The application must be made within three months of the date of the judgment of the Chamber. Approximately 5 per cent of applications for referral are granted.

The request for referral to the Grand Chamber is decided by a five-judge Panel. The Panel is made up of the President of the Court, two Presidents of Sections designated by rotation, two judges designated by rotation from among judges elected by the remaining Sections to sit on the Panel for a period of six months, and at least two substitute judges.[15] Excluded from the Panel are judges who took part in the consideration of the admissibility or merits of the case in question, a judge elected in respect of a State Party concerned by the referral request, and a judge who is a national of such a State Party.[16] The Panel examines the request solely on the basis of the existing case file.[17] The request may be refused without any reasons given.[18] It is not the practice of the Court to give reasons. This is justified by article 45 of the Convention requiring reasons to be given only for judgments and for decisions on admissibility. The Explanatory Report on Protocol No. 11 states that article 45 'does not concern decisions taken by the Panel of five judges of the Grand Chamber in accordance with Article 43'.[19] No appeal or review of this decision is possible.[20] According to article 44(2)(c), if the Panel rejects the application for rehearing, then the judgment of the Chamber becomes final.

If the Panel decides to accept the request, article 43(3) dictates that the Grand Chamber *shall* decide the case. Consequently, 'the Grand Chamber has no option but to examine the case' if the request has been accepted by the Panel.[21] It is not possible for the Grand Chamber to refer a case back to a Section of the Court once the Panel has ruled on referral.[22] According to the Grand Chamber, 'it must assess the facts as they appear at the time of its decision by applying the appropriate legal solution. Once a case is referred to it the Grand Chamber may accordingly employ the full range of judicial powers conferred on the Court.'[23]

If re-hearing of the case is authorized by the five-judge Panel, the Grand Chamber may render a judgment on the merits, but it may also apply other provisions of the Convention enabling it to terminate proceedings, in particular the approval of a friendly settlement under article 39 or striking out of the case pursuant to article 37.[24] Although the

---

[14] Rules of Court, Rule 73(1).

[15] Ibid., Rule 24(5)(a).

[16] Ibid., Rules 24(5)(b) and (c).

[17] Ibid., Rule 73(2).

[18] *Mateescu v. Romania*, no. 1944/10, § 5, 14 January 2014; *Lordos and Others v. Turkey* (just satisfaction), no. 15973/90, § 9, 10 January 2012; *Yuriy Nikolayevich Ivanov v. Ukraine*, no. 40450/04, § 6, 15 October 2009.

[19] Explanatory Report on Protocol No. 11, para. 105.

[20] *Pisano v. Italy* (striking out) [GC], no. 36732/97, § 29, 24 October 2002.

[21] Ibid., § 26.

[22] *Tahsin Acar v. Turkey* [GC], no. 26307/95, § 199, ECHR 2004-III.

[23] *Pisano v. Italy* (striking out) [GC], no. 36732/97, § 28, 24 October 2002.

[24] Ibid., §§ 40–50; *Kovačić and Others v. Slovenia* (striking out) [GC], nos 44574/98, 45133/98, and 48316/99, § 266, 3 October 2008.

judgment of the Grand Chamber is final, replacing the judgment of the Chamber that precedes it, even a judgment of the Grand Chamber, may be subject to a request for interpretation or revision. Subject to these exceptional circumstances, in the normal course of events a judgment of the Grand Chamber is definitive and has immediate effect.[25]

Serious questions and serious issues

The Convention authorizes re-hearing by a Grand Chamber 'if the case raises a serious question affecting the interpretation or application of the Convention or the Protocols thereto, or a serious issue of general importance'. Some guidance to the scope of the text, at least as it was intended to be applied by the drafters of Protocol No. 11, appears in the Explanatory Report:

100. Serious questions affecting the interpretation of the Convention are raised when a question of importance not yet decided by the Court is at stake, or when the decision is of importance for future cases and for the development of the Court's case-law. Moreover, a serious question may be particularly evident when the judgment concerned is not consistent with a previous judgment of the Court.

101. A serious question concerning the application of the Convention may be at stake when a judgment necessitates a substantial change to national law or administrative practice but does not itself raise a serious question of interpretation of the Convention.

102. A serious issue considered to be of general importance could involve a substantial political issue or an important issue of policy.[26]

Because these matters are not subject to debate before the Grand Chamber, and in the absence of reported case law from the Panel making the determination, it is difficult to assess how the provision is being interpreted. It is not particularly helpful to look at the cases where authorization is granted, as they invariably contain elements indicating the 'serious questions' about the interpretation and application of the Convention. It is more difficult to understand the rationale for the rejection of the many applications where serious questions also appear to be present. The actual judgment of the Grand Chamber in cases where leave has been granted may not necessarily clarify the reason for referral because the composition of the Panel and the Grand Chamber is not the same. The reasoning of the Panel about the importance of the issue or issues may not be shared by the Grand Chamber.

In the İzmir Declaration, Member States said that decisions of the five-judge panels on authorization should be 'clearly reasoned', something avoiding 'repetitive [referral] requests and ensuring better understanding of Chamber judgments'.[27] A background document issued by the Court notes that it is not enough to demonstrate that a case is factually complex, politically delicate, or has given rise to dissenting opinions.[28] Although article 43 does not refer to the issue of consistency of the case law, in contrast with article 30 dealing with relinquishment, the Panel will indeed be likely to refer the case to the Grand Chamber if the Chamber judgment departs from established jurisprudence. In

---

[25] Explanatory Report on Protocol No. 11, para. 104.

[26] Ibid., paras 100–102.

[27] Final Declaration of the High Level Conference on the Future of the Court, held in İzmir on 26–27 April 2011, para. 2(e).

[28] The General Practice Followed by the Panel of the Grand Chamber When Deciding on Requests for Referral in Accordance with Article 43 of the Convention, October 2011.

one case, the Grand Chamber noted that the Chamber had 'departed from the case-law on the application of Article 41 in cases of constructive expropriation'.[29] Other judgments confirm earlier and sometimes controversial precedents set by the Grand Chamber.[30]

The Panel has occasionally referred cases raising similar issues to those of other recent Grand Chamber judgments, presumably in order to clarify or limit the scope of imprecise pronouncements on such matters as the temporal scope of the procedural obligation contained in article 2.[31] Another rationale for the referral will be the development of the case law, pursuing a dynamic and evolutive approach to interpretation of the Convention. For example, in *Bayatyan v. Armenia*, the Grand Chamber completely revised the interpretation of the Convention with respect to the right to conscientious objection after the Chamber had taken a more conservative stance.[32]

Referral to the Grand Chamber is also the occasion for important judgments on new issues in the area of human rights. Examples include the ban on the wearing of headscarves in Turkish universities[33] and reproductive rights.[34] Examples of a 'serious issue of general importance' include protection against transnational crime on the high seas,[35] discrimination directed against Roma,[36] the death penalty,[37] and the legitimacy and legality of amnesty for serious international crimes.[38] Finally, there are what have been called the 'high-profile cases', such as those involving notorious crimes and criminals,[39] religious symbols in public places,[40] and the killing of a demonstrator during a protest against the G8.[41]

Further reading

Robert Badinter, 'Du Protocol no 11 au Protocole no 12', in G. Flécheux, ed., *Mélanges en hommage à Louis Edmond Pettiti*, Brussels: Bruylant, 1998, pp. 103–12.
Jean-Paul Costa, 'Les arrêts de la Grande Chambre rendus après renvoi (article 43 de la ECHR)', in Lucius Caflisch, Johan Callewaert, Roderick Liddell, Paul Mahoney, and Mark Villiger, eds, *Liber Amicorum Luzius Wildhaber*, Kehl, Germany: N.P. Engel, 2007, pp. 133–44.
Frowein/Peukert, *MenschenRechtsKonvention*, pp. 597–8.
Leo Zwaak, 'The Procedure before the European Court of Human Rights', in Van Dijk et al., *Theory and Practice*, pp. 238–9.

---

[29] *Guiso-Gallisay v. Italy* (just satisfaction) [GC], no. 58858/00, § 56, 22 December 2009.
[30] *Scoppola v. Italy (no. 3)* [GC], no. 126/05, § 96, 22 May 2012, affirming *Hirst v. the United Kingdom (no. 2)* [GC], no. 74025/01, ECHR 2005-IX.
[31] *Janowiec and Others v. Russia* [GC], nos 55508/07 and 29520/09, §§ 149–151, ECHR 2013, *Šilih v. Slovenia* [GC], no. 71463/01, § 163 *in fine*, 9 April 2009 and *Blečić v. Croatia* [GC], no. 59532/00, §§ 77–82, ECHR 2006-III.
[32] *Bayatyan v. Armenia* [GC], no. 23459/03, §§ 98–111, ECHR 2011. See *Bayatyan v. Armenia*, no. 23459/03, § 63, 27 October 2009.
[33] *Leyla Şahin v. Turkey* [GC], no. 44774/98, ECHR 2005-XI.
[34] *Evans v. the United Kingdom* [GC], no. 6339/05, ECHR 2007-I; *Dickson v. The United Kingdom* [GC], no. 44362/04, ECHR 2007-V; *S.H. and Others v. Austria* [GC], no. 57813/00, ECHR 2011.
[35] *Medvedyev and Others v. France* [GC], no. 3394/03, ECHR 2010.
[36] *D.H. and Others v. the Czech Republic* [GC], no. 57325/00, ECHR 2007-IV; *Oršuš and Others v. Croatia* [GC], no. 15766/03, ECHR 2010; *Aksu v. Turkey* [GC], nos 4149/04 and 41029/04, ECHR 2012.
[37] *Öcalan v. Turkey* [GC], no. 46221/99, ECHR 2005-IV.
[38] *Marguš v. Croatia* [GC], no. 4455/10, 27 May 2014.
[39] *Gäfgen v. Germany* [GC], no. 22978/05, ECHR 2010; *Öcalan v. Turkey* [GC], no. 46221/99, ECHR 2005-IV; *Ramirez Sanchez v. France* [GC], no. 59450/00, ECHR 2006-IX.
[40] *Lautsi and Others v. Italy* [GC], no. 30814/06, ECHR 2011 (extracts).
[41] *Giuliani and Gaggio v. Italy* [GC], no. 23458/02, ECHR 2011 (extracts).

Article 44. Final judgments/Arrêts définitifs

1. The judgment of the Grand Chamber shall be final.

2. The judgment of a Chamber shall become final

(a) when the parties declare that they will not request that the case be referred to the Grand Chamber; or

(b) three months after the date of the judgment, if reference of the case to the Grand Chamber has not been requested; or

(c) when the panel of the Grand Chamber rejects the request to refer under Article 43.

3. The final judgment shall be published.

1. L'arrêt de la Grande Chambre est définitif.

2. L'arrêt d'une chambre devient définitif

a) lorsque les parties déclarent qu'elles ne demanderont pas le renvoi de l'affaire devant la Grande Chambre; ou

b) trois mois après la date de l'arrêt, si le renvoi de l'affaire devant la Grande Chambre n'a pas été demandé; ou

c) lorsque le collège de la Grande Chambre rejette la demande de renvoi formulée en application de l'article 43.

3. L'arrêt définitif est publié.

Introductory comments

Article 44 embodies 'the principle of the finality of judgments'.[1] Known by the Latin expression *res judicata*, it has been described as a general principle of law as this notion is meant by article 38 of the Statute of the International Court of Justice.[2] As noted by three judges of the Court in a dissenting opinion, 'it is an elemental requirement in judicial conflict-resolution to resolve disputes with finality and irrevocability. The doctrines of *res judicata*, legal certainty, *ne bis in idem* (in criminal procedure), for example, and ultimately the principle of the rule of law, call for no less.'[3]

In a sense, of course, nothing is really final, and the European Court of Human Rights is no exception. The Court may return to issues of law decided definitively in earlier cases and decide to revise its interpretation quite dramatically.[4] There is also an apparently residual power, not specified in the Convention or the Rules, allowing for revision of a judgment where the Court itself has committed an error.[5]

---

[1] *McGinley and Egan v. the United Kingdom* (revision), nos 21825/93 and 23414/94, § 30, ECHR 2000-I.

[2] *Interpretation of Judgments Nos 7 and 8 (Chorzów Factory)*, Series A, No. 13, Dissenting Opinion by M. Anzilotti, para. 7. See also *Effect of awards of compensation made by the U.N. Administrative Tribunal*, Advisory Opinion, I.C.J. Reports 1954, p. 47, at pp. 53, 59.

[3] *Nuutinen v. Finland*, no. 32842/96, Dissenting Opinion of Judge Zupančić, Joined by Judges Pânţiru and Türmen, ECHR 2000-VIII.

[4] *Scoppola v. Italy (no. 2)* [GC], no. 10249/03, § 104, 17 September 2009; *Sergey Zolotukhin v. Russia* [GC], no. 14939/03, § 80, ECHR 2009; *Vilho Eskelinen and Others v. Finland* [GC], no. 63235/00, § 56, ECHR 2007-II.

[5] *Storck v. Germany*, no. 61603/00, § 67, ECHR 2005-V; *Storck v. Germany* (dec.), no. 61603, 26 October 2004; *Ölmez v. Turkey* (dec.), no. 39464/98, 5 July 2005; *Des Fours Walderode v. Czech Republic* (dec.), no. 40057/98, ECHR 2004-V; *Harrach v. Czech Republic* (dec.), no. 77532/01, 18 May 2004; *Le Syndicat des copropriétaires du 20 bd de la Mer à Dinard v. France* (dec.), no. 47339/99, 22 May 2003; *Wortmann v. Germany* (dec.), no. 70929/01, 18 November 2003; *Appietto v. France* (dec.), no. 56927/00, § 8, 26 February 2002.

Drafting of the provision

The 1950 text of the Convention contained a laconic provision on the subject of 'final judgments': 'Article 52. The judgment of the Court shall be final.'

The initial draft proposal for a European Convention, adopted by the European Movement, contained the following: 'The judgment is final and without appeal. In the event of dispute as to the meaning or scope of the judgment, the Court shall construe it upon the request of any party.'[6] It also had a separate provision authorizing revision of a judgment based upon the discovery of a fact of such a nature as to be a decisive factor unknown to the parties or the Court at the time of the judgment.[7]

The Consultative Assembly did not consider the issue, and its final draft had no such provision. The Committee of Ministers assigned a Committee of Experts to study the Consultative Assembly draft, noting that it should in particular address '[t]he legal scope of judgments: grounds, revision, appeal, effect on third parties intervening parties'.[8] At its first session, in February 1950, the Committee of Experts adopted this text: 'The judgment of the Court is final.'[9] The provision also appeared in the final draft of the Committee of Experts.[10] The Report of the Committee of Experts stated that it '[r]equire[d] no comment'.[11] The provision was adopted without change by the Conference of Senior Officials,[12] although the United Kingdom commented that is should read '[t]he judgment of the Court shall be final'.[13] The change was adopted by the Committee of Ministers when it met in August 1950.[14] There were no further changes and the text appears in the final version of the Convention as article 52.

The current version of article 44 was introduced to the Convention by Protocol No. 11. According to the Explanatory Report, article 44(1) is taken from article 52 of

---

[6] Convention for the Collective Protection of Individual Rights and Democratic Liberties by the States, Members of the Council of Europe, and for the establishment of a European Court of Human Rights to ensure observance of the Convention, Doc. INF/5/E/R, I *TP* 296–303, at p. 318, art. 54.

[7] Ibid., art. 55.

[8] Preparatory Report by the Secretariat-General concerning a Preliminary Draft Convention to Provide a Collective Guarantee of Human Rights, Doc. B 22, III *TP* 2–37, at p. 36.

[9] Preliminary Draft Convention for the Maintenance and Further Realisation of Human Rights and Fundamental Freedoms, 15 February 1950, Doc. A 833, III *TP* 236–46, at p. 246. See also Amendments to various articles of the Recommendation of the Consultative Assembly proposed by the Italian Expert, Doc. A 812, III *TP* 228–31, art. E; Continuation and end of the proposals of the Drafting Sub-Committee concerning Section III, Doc. A 813, III *TP* 230–3.

[10] Appendix to the Report of the Committee of Experts on Human Rights: Draft Convention of Protection of Human Rights and Fundamental Freedoms, 16 March 1950, Doc. CM/WP 1 (50) 15 appendix, CM/WP 1 (50) 14 revised, A 925, IV *TP* 50–79, at p. 74, art. 41(4). Also New text suggested for Sections II, III, and IV, Doc. CM/WP 1 (50) 4, A 917, III *TP* 294–302, at p. 302, art. 38.

[11] Report to the Committee of Ministers submitted by the Committee of Experts Instructed to Draw Up a Draft Convention of Collective Guarantee of Human Rights and Fundamental Freedoms, Doc. CM/WP 1 (5) 15, A 924, IV *TP* 2–55, at p. 44.

[12] Draft Convention annexed to the Report, Doc. CM/WP 4 (50) 19 annex, CM/WP 4 (50) rev., A 1452, IV *TP* 274–95, at p. 292, art. 52; Draft Convention appended to the draft report, Doc. CM/WP 4 (50) 16, appendix, A 1445, IV *TP* 218–40, at p. 236, art. 53. Also Proposal submitted by the Swedish Delegation, Doc. CM/WP 4 (50) 10, A 1373, IV *TP* 190–5.

[13] Comments by the United Kingdom Delegation on the Report of the Conference of Senior Officials and the text of the draft Convention, Doc. A 1690, p. 4.

[14] Draft Convention adopted by the Sub-Committee, Doc. CM 1 (50) 52, A 1884, V *TP* 76–99, at p. 94, art. 52; Draft Convention adopted by the Committee of Ministers, 7 August 1950, Doc. A 1937, V *TP* 120–45, at p. 140, art. 52.

the Convention.[15] The heading, 'Final judgments', was also introduced by Protocol No. 11. Nothing of interest with respect to the drafting of this provision can be found in the Explanatory Report.

The 1950 text of the Convention did not contain any provision requiring the publication of judgments, despite the fact that wide dissemination of judgments of the Court was part of the vision of those who originally proposed its establishment. Publication of the judgments of the Court was contemplated by the Rules, adopted in 1959. In the original version, publication of judgments was not mandatory: 'The Registrar shall be responsible for the publication of judgments and of such other decisions and documents whose publication may have been authorised by the Court.'[16] This provision later became more elaborate, mentioning publication not only of judgments but also of documents relating to the proceedings 'but excluding any document which the President considers unnecessary or inadvisable to publish', verbatim records of public hearings, and 'any document which the President considers useful to publish'.[17] Publication of judgments was to take place in the two official languages.

Analysis and interpretation

Article 44 must be read in conjunction with two other provisions governing the definitive nature of decisions and judgments issued by a single judge formation and a three-judge Committee. Article 27(2) says that the decision of the single judge that an application is inadmissible or that it should be struck out of the list 'shall be final'. Similarly, pursuant to article 28(2), a decision taken by a three-judge Committee, whether to declare the application inadmissible or rule on admissibility and on the merits, 'shall be final'. The combined effect of these texts indicates that article 44 only concerns 'judgments' of the Grand Chamber and of Chambers. Use of the term 'judgment' also suggests that article 44 does not apply to 'decisions', which are judicial pronouncements dealing with admissibility and striking out of the list that may bring an end to a case.

Article 44(2) specifies the conditions under which a judgment of a seven-judge Chamber also becomes definitive. The first involves a declaration by the parties that they will not request that the case be referred to the Grand Chamber. Such declarations have been made in the case of friendly settlements.[18] The second takes effect by the simple passage of time, if referral of the case to the Grand Chamber has not been sought within three months from the date of the judgment. The third is a consequence of the dismissal by a panel of the Grand Chamber of a request that the case be referred to it, in accordance with article 43.

Interpretation of a judgment

A request for interpretation of a judgment by a party to the proceedings is governed by Rule 79 of the Rules of Court. The provision is derived from a similar text in the 1959

[15] Explanatory Report on Protocol No. 11, para. 104.
[16] Rules of Court, (Adopted 18 September 1959), Rule 52 (Publication of judgments and other decisions).
[17] Rules of Court (as amended on 24 October 1961), Rule 52 (Publication of judgments, decisions and other documents); Revised Rules of Court (Adopted on 24 November 1982), Rule 56 (Publication of judgments and other documents).
[18] See, e.g., *Toimi v. Sweden* (friendly settlement), no. 55164/00, § 10, 22 March 2005; *Samy v. the Netherlands* (friendly settlement), no. 36499/97, § 15, 18 June 2002.

version of the Rules of Court.[19] Interpretation of a judgment at the request of the Committee of Ministers is contemplated by article 46(3) of the Convention. The request for interpretation governed by Rule 79 must be filed within a period of one year following the delivery of the judgment. An attempt is made to reconstitute the original Chamber, failing which the President completes or composes the Chamber by drawing lots.[20]

The request for interpretation pursuant to Rule 79 is not an appeal. That is because it is addressed to the same Chamber that rendered the initial judgment. In considering the request, the Court has been described as exercising 'inherent jurisdiction'. This has been described as going 'no further than to clarify the meaning and scope which [the Court] intended to give to a previous decision which issued from its own deliberations, specifying if need be what it thereby decided with binding force'.[21] For that reason, the Rule authorizing an application for interpretation is 'in no wise irreconcilable' with article 42 of the Convention.[22] If the application is aimed not at clarifying 'the meaning and scope' of a judgment but rather at modifying it 'in respect of an issue which the Court decided', the interpretation judgment will be denied.[23]

Revision of a judgment

An application for revision of a judgment is authorized 'in the event of the discovery of a fact which might by its nature have a decisive influence and which, when a judgment was delivered, was unknown to the Court and could not reasonably have been known to that party'.[24] The provision is derived from article 61(1) of the Statute of the International Court of Justice. It dictates a two-stage procedure by which the Court initially rules on the admissibility of the application for revision, and this was copied in the initial version of the Rules of Court.[25] The revised Rules of Court that came into force with Protocol No. 11 removed the two-stage procedure, allowing the original Chamber to refuse to consider the request, acting on its own motion, 'on the ground that there is no reason to warrant considering it'.[26] As with an application for interpretation, the original Chamber is reconvened. Where this is not possible, the President completes the Chamber or composes a new Chamber by drawing lots.[27] The application for revision to the European Court of Human Rights must be made within six months of the acquisition of knowledge of the fact.[28]

Because an application for revision 'calls into question the final character of judgments' set out in article 42 of the Convention, the possibility of revision, 'which is not provided for in the Convention but was introduced by the Rules of Court, is an exceptional

---

[19] Rules of Court (Adopted 18 September 1959), Rule 53 (Request for interpretation of a judgment).
[20] Ibid.
[21] *Ringeisen v. Austria* (interpretation), 23 June 1973, § 13, Series A no. 16; *Allenet de Ribemont v. France* (interpretation), 7 August 1996, § 17, *Reports of Judgments and Decisions* 1996-III.
[22] *Ringeisen v. Austria* (Interpretation), 23 June 1973, § 13, Series A no. 16.
[23] *Hentrich v. France* (interpretation), 3 July 1997, § 16, *Reports of Judgments and Decisions* 1997-IV.
[24] Rules of Court, Rule 80(1).
[25] Rules of Court, (adopted 18 September 1959), Rule 54(4).
[26] Rules of Court, Rule 80(3).
[27] Ibid.
[28] Ibid., Rule 80(1).

procedure'. For that reason, 'the admissibility of any request for revision of a judgment of the Court under this procedure is subject to strict scrutiny'.[29]

Revision was requested by a respondent State when it was unable to execute the judgment because the applicant died before the judgment had been adopted. The death of the applicant was a fact that 'might by its nature have a decisive influence on the judgment delivered by the Court'.[30] Requests to revise a judgment so as to direct that the sums awarded to a deceased applicant be received by the heirs have sometimes been granted by the Court.[31] But the Court has also revised a judgment in order to remove an award of just satisfaction given the death of the applicant prior to issuance of the judgment, although it maintained the rest of the ruling because of its general importance for the respect of human rights.[32]

Revision has been granted in situations where the Court has made a mistake in the treatment of the application. For example, revision was authorized where the Chamber itself misunderstood or misinterpreted the submissions of the respondent State with respect to the costs that were payable. The 'fact' discovered subsequently was the misunderstanding that only became knowable when the judgment was delivered. The Court distinguished this from rectification based upon a clerical error, an error in calculation, or an obvious mistake, something governed by Rule 81.[33] In another case, it revised the judgment because it had 'overlooked' a relevant document.[34] When the Court neglected to invite the respondent State to comment on claims made by the applicant with respect to just satisfaction, it agreed the absence of submissions in rebuttal had a 'decisive influence' on the judgment. The applicant's submissions had been filed outside of the time limit and in the absence of an indication from the Court the respondent State assumed that there was no need to respond. There was no real change to the result, but the judgment was altered by adding the following sentence: 'Le Gouvernement a commenté les prétentions des requérants et formulé ses observations les 15 et 20 janvier 2009.'[35] In a case involving failure to comply with article 38, a finding of a violation was revised after Russia demonstrated that it had actually submitted documents as required but that they failed to reach the Court because of shortcomings in its information processing systems. It agreed that Russia could not 'reasonably' have

[29] *Pardo v. France* (revision—admissibility), 10 July 1996, § 21, *Reports of Judgments and Decisions* 1996-III; *Gustafsson v. Sweden* (revision—merits), 30 July 1998, § 25, *Reports of Judgments and Decisions* 1998-V; *McGinley and Egan v. the United Kingdom* (revision), nos 21825/93 and 23414/94, § 14, ECHR 2000-I; *Cernescu and Manolache v. Romania* (revision), no. 28607/04, § 7, 30 November 2010; *Damir Sibgatullin v. Russia* (revision), no. 1413/05, § 12, 28 May 2014.

[30] *Bajrami v. Albania* (revision), no. 35853/04, §§ 5–8, 18 December 2007.

[31] *Bolovan v. Romania* (revision), no. 64541/01, §§ 6–11, 20 September 2011; *Armando Grasso v. Italy* (revision), no. 48411/99, §§ 4–8, 29 April 2003; *Carolla v. Italy* (revision), no. 51127/99, §§ 5–8, 28 November 2002; *D'Ammassa and Frezza v. Italy* (revision), no. 44513/98, §§ 5–9, 9 January 2003; *Erdoğan and Fırat v. Turkey* (revision), nos. 15121/03 and 15127/03, §§ 5–10, 20 July 2010; *Armando Grasso v. Italy* (revision), no. 48411/99, §§ 5–8, 29 April 2003; *Gülbahar Özer and Others v. Turkey* (revision), no. 44125/06, §§ 5–12, 10 June 2014.

[32] *C.B. v. Romania* (revision), no. 21207/03, §§ 5–11, 19 July 2011.

[33] *Baumann v. Austria* (revision), no. 76809/01, §§ 10–14, 9 June 2005.

[34] *Fonyódi v. Hungary* (revision), no. 30799/04, § 8, 7 April 2009. Along similar lines, *Naumoski v. the former Yugoslav Republic of Macedonia* (revision), no. 25248/05, §§ 5–11, 5 December 2013.

[35] *Bortesi and Others v. Italy* (revision), no. 71399/01, § 13, 8 December 2009. Note, however, the partially dissenting opinion of Judges Zagrebelsky and Sajó. See also *Adamczuk v. Poland* (revision), no. 30523/07, §§ 82–85, 15 June 2010.

known that the documents in question had not reached the Court within the required time limit.[36]

Some revision cases have involved a failure by the applicant to disclose relevant documents to the Court. In a case concerning property rights, the applicant had not been entirely forthcoming, conduct that the Court described as 'improper'. But there had been nothing to prevent the respondent State making its own inquiries as the information in question was available to the public in the land registers, something it had failed to do. The Court rejected the application for revision.[37] In a similar case, it granted the request for revision after concluding that the State could not 'reasonably' have known of the fact that the applicant had failed to disclose, despite the fact that it was in the public domain.[38] In a case involving the applicant's failure to disclose relevant information, the Court granted the application for revision and declared the claim to be inadmissible because it was an abuse of the right of individual application, contrary to article 35(3)(a) of the Convention.[39] In a case against Turkey concerning access to property in occupied Cyprus, the Court had ruled in favour of the applicant but reserved a ruling on just satisfaction so that evidence about the value of the asset could be produced. Evidence emerged that the property had been transferred to the applicant's children prior to the filing of the claim. The Court revised the judgment and found it to be inadmissible.[40] In December 2014, Ireland filed an application for revision of the 1978 judgment of the Court concerning treatment of detainees in Northern Ireland[41] based upon information that the United Kingdom had not disclosed at the time and that was unknown to the applicant State and the Court.[42]

The Rules of Court require that the new fact 'could not reasonably have been known to that party'. The earlier version used the phrase 'was unknown both to the Court and to that Party or the Commission'.[43] The Court has held that '[t]he express mention of this objective element in Rule 80 § 1 accords, in the Court's view, with the meaning likely to have been given to the word "unknown" in Rule 58 of former Rules of Court A'.[44] The Court said that although the applicants may not have actually possessed certain documents at the time of the judgment, their existence 'could reasonably have been known', with the consequence that the request for revision was denied.[45]

Rectification of errors in decisions and judgments

Errors in decisions and judgments that are clerical in nature or involve miscalculation, or are 'obvious mistakes', may be rectified by the Court of its own motion or at the request of a party. The application by a party for rectification must be made within one month of the

---

[36] *Damir Sibgatullin v. Russia* (revision), no. 1413/05, §§ 18–22, 28 May 2014.

[37] *Bugajny and Others v. Poland* (revision), no. 22531/05, §§ 24–27, 15 December 2009. Similarly: *De Luca v. Italy* (revision), no. 43870/04, §§ 16–20, 8 July 2014.

[38] *Cernescu and Manolache v. Romania* (revision), no. 28607/04, §§ 13–14, 30 November 2010.

[39] *Gardean and S.C. Grup 95 SA v. Romania* (revision), no. 25787/04, § 22, 30 April 2013.

[40] *Nicola v. Turkey* (revision), no. 18404/91, § 26, 26 October 2010.

[41] *Ireland v. the United Kingdom*, 18 January 1978, Series A no. 25.

[42] Henry McDonald, 'Ireland to Clash with UK at Human Rights Court over Hooded Men Judgment', *The Guardian*, 2 December 2014; Philip Leach, *Ireland v. UK: Revisiting the Treatment of the 'Hooded Men'*, JURIST—Student Commentary, 6 December 2014.

[43] Rules of Court, (adopted 18 September 1959), Rule 54(1).

[44] *McGinley and Egan v. the United Kingdom* (revision), nos 21825/93 and 23414/94, § 17, ECHR 2000-I.

[45] Ibid., § 36.

delivery of a decision or a judgment.[46] It seems that the Court may rectify an error at any time.[47]

Examples of rectification indicate the relatively anodyne nature of this procedure. The Court rectified the *dispositif* of judgment that said 'Holds by a majority', changing this to 'Holds by six votes to one'.[48] It has rectified the *dispositif* in order to add reference to an article that was violated.[49] The name of the applicant was changed by rectification from 'Doğan Sorguç' to 'Vehbi Doğan Sorguç'.[50] The name of a witness was modified from 'Ve.M.' to 'V.M.'[51] The initials 'D.Š.' were changed to 'the two officers in question'.[52] Rectification has been used to add a separate or dissenting opinion to a judgment.[53]

The distinction between rectification and revision is not always clear. In one case, the Court had not considered the applicant's full claim for costs. It granted the request in revision and revised the amount.[54] In similar cases, however, it has viewed such mistakes as requiring revision of the decision under Rule 80, as discussed earlier in this chapter.[55]

Publication and dissemination

The Convention decrees that '[t]he final judgment shall be published'. The Rules of Court specify that this is the responsibility of the Registrar, and that it is to be done 'in an appropriate form'.[56] The Rules also declare that the Registrar is responsible 'for the publication of official reports of selected judgments and decisions and of any document which the President of the Court considers it useful to publish'.[57] Publication of judgments in the official reports of the Court, as set out in Rule 78 of the Rules of Court, is to be in both of the official languages.[58]

Judgments are given in either English or in French unless the Court decides that they shall be given in both official languages.[59] They are signed by the President of the Chamber or the Committee and the Registrar, distributed to the parties and any third party, and transmitted to the Committee of Ministers.[60] Before electronic publication, provisions governing the dissemination of judgments may have been of greater significance than they are today. In practice, they are now instantly available on the website of the Court.

[46] Rules of Court, Rule 81.
[47] For example, *K.H. and Others v. Slovakia*, no. 32881/04, ECHR 2009 (extracts), which was rectified nearly two years after the judgment had become final.
[48] *K.H. and Others v. Slovakia*, no. 32881/04, *dispositif*, fn. 1, ECHR 2009 (extracts).
[49] *Barišić v. Slovenia*, no. 32600/05, §§ 48, 49, *dispositif*, fn. 2, 18 October 2012.
[50] *Sorguç v. Turkey*, no. 17089/03, § 1, 23 June 2009.
[51] *D.J. v. Croatia*, no. 42418/10, §§ 16, 18, 21, 24, 30, 103, 24 July 2012.
[52] Ibid., § 59.
[53] *M.S. v. the United Kingdom*, no. 24527/08, Declaration of Judge Kalaydjieva, fn. 1, 3 May 2012.
[54] *Tsfayo v. the United Kingdom*, no. 60860/00, §§ 9, 57–59, 14 November 2006.
[55] *Baumann v. Austria* (revision), no. 76809/01, §§ 12–14, 9 June 2005.
[56] Rules of Court, Rule 78.
[57] Ibid.
[58] Ibid., Rule 76(2).
[59] Ibid., Rule 76(1).
[60] Ibid., Rule 77.

Further reading

Frowein/Peukert, *MenschenRechtsKonvention,* pp. 599–600.

Alastair Mowbray, 'No Violations but Interesting: A Study of the Strasbourg Court's Jurisprudence in Cases where no Breach of the Convention has been Found', (2008) 14 *European Public Law* 237.

Leo Zwaak, 'The Procedure before the European Court of Human Rights', in Van Dijk et al., *Theory and Practice,* pp. 241–4, 279–86.

Article 45. Reasons for judgments and decisions/Motivation des arrêts et décisions

1. Reasons shall be given for judgments as well as for decisions declaring applications admissible or inadmissible.	1. Les arrêts, ainsi que les décisions déclarant des requêtes recevables ou irrecevables, sont motivés.
2. If a judgment does not represent, in whole or in part, the unanimous opinion of the judges, any judge shall be entitled to deliver a separate opinion.	2. Si l'arrêt n'exprime pas en tout ou en partie l'opinion unanime des juges, tout juge a le droit d'y joindre l'exposé de son opinion séparée.

Introductory comments

The justification for a rule requiring that reasons be given for judgments and decisions can be found in the case law of the Convention organs themselves. In an early decision, the European Commission of Human Rights said that it 'accepts the view expressed by the applicants that Art. 6 requires reasons to be given by a court for its decision and considers that this applies to civil as well as criminal proceedings'.[1] The principle has often been reaffirmed by the Court, with the proviso that the requirement of a reasoned judgment 'cannot be understood as requiring a detailed answer to every argument'.[2] According to the Grand Chamber, reasoned decisions 'also serve the purpose of demonstrating to the parties that they have been heard, thereby contributing to a more willing acceptance of the decision on their part. In addition, they oblige judges to base their reasoning on objective arguments...'[3] Many legal systems prohibit or discourage separate or dissenting opinions. However, in the practice of international tribunals they are very much the rule rather than the exception. Article 45 of the European Convention is clearly modelled on article 57 of the Statute of the International Court of Justice.

Drafting of the provision

The Draft Statute of the European Court of Human Rights proposed by the International Juridical Section of the European Movement included the following:

Art. 50.
a) The judgment shall state the reasons on which it is based.
b) It shall contain the names of the judges who have taken part in the decision.

---

[1] *The Firestone Tire and Rubber Co., Firestone Tyre and Rubber Co. Ltd and the International Synthetic Rubber Co. v. the United Kingdom*, no. 5460/72, Commission decision of 2 April 1973, Collection 43, p. 99.

[2] *Haxhia v. Albania*, no. 29861/03, § 126, 8 October 2013; *Taxquet v. Belgium*, no. 926/05, § 40, 13 January 2009; *Hiro Balani v. Spain*, 9 December 1994, § 27, Series A no. 303-B; *Van de Hurk v. the Netherlands*, 19 April 1994, § 61, Series A no. 288; *Helle v. Finland*, 19 December 1997, § 55, *Reports of Judgments and Decisions* 1997-VIII; *Burg v. France* (dec.), no. 34763/02, ECHR 2003-II.

[3] *Taxquet v. Belgium* [GC], no. 926/05, § 91, ECHR 2010.

Art. 51.

If the judgment in whole or in part does not represent the unanimous opinion of the judges, any judge shall be entitled to deliver a separate opinion.[4]

The Consultative Assembly draft adopted in September 1949 did not contain detailed provisions on the operation of the Court. There was no provision governing the reasons for judgments.

The Greek delegate to the Committee of Experts that met in February and March 1950 proposed a text that is very similar to the final version: 'Reasons shall be given for the findings of the Court. If the findings do not express all or part of the opinion of the judges, any judge has the right to attach to it a statement of his individual opinion.'[5] The provision was slightly reformulated by the Committee in the drafts it adopted in February and March. The word 'judgment' replaced 'findings' and 'separate opinion' replaced 'individual opinion'.[6] The Committee of Experts text was left unchanged in the draft of the Conference of Senior Officials[7] and of the Committee of Ministers when it met in August 1950.[8]

Article 51 of the 1950 text of the Convention read as follows:

1. Reasons shall be given for the judgment of the Court.
2. If the judgment does not represent in whole or in part the unanimous opinion of the judges, any judge shall be entitled to deliver a separate opinion.

As a consequence of Protocol No. 11, it was renumbered as article 45 and given the heading 'Reasons for judgment and decision'. The only significant modification is the additional phrase in article 45(1) requiring that reasons also be given for decisions declaring applications admissible or inadmissible. The Explanatory Report says that it is 'understood that reasons for decisions rejecting or accepting applications can be given in summary form'.[9] In addition, the Report declares that article 45 'does not concern decisions taken by the panel of five judges of the Grand Chamber in accordance with Article 43'.[10]

Analysis and interpretation

Article 45 sets out a 'general rule' by which 'all judgments and most decisions of the Court must be reasoned, whether they relate to its jurisdiction, a question of procedure, the

---

[4] Draft Statute of the European Court of Human Rights, INF/5/E/R, I *TP* 302–21, at p. 316.

[5] Amendments to Article 21 and 28 of the Recommendation of the Consultative Assembly proposed by the Greek Expert, Doc. A 811, III *TP* 226–9, art. A.

[6] Preliminary Draft Convention for the Maintenance and Further Realisation of Human Rights and Fundamental Freedoms, 15 February 1950, Doc. A 833, III *TP* 236–46, art. 37; Appendix to the Report of the Committee of Experts on Human Rights: Draft Convention of Protection of Human Rights and Fundamental Freedoms, 16 March 1950, Doc. C/WP 1 (50) 15 appendix, CM/WP 1 (50) 14 revised, A 925, IV *TP* 50–79, at p. 74, art. 40 (44).

[7] Draft Convention annexed to the Report, Doc. CM/WP 4 (50) 19 annex, CM/WP 4 (50) rev., A 1452, IV *TP* 274–95, at p. 292, art. 51.

[8] Draft Convention adopted by the Sub-Committee, Doc. CM 1 (50) 52, A 1884, V *TP* 76–99, at p. 94, art. 51.

[9] Explanatory Report on Protocol No. 11, para. 105.

[10] Ibid.

merits of the case or the award of just satisfaction to the applicant'.[11] The Rules of Court provide detailed guidance on the content of the judgment:

Rule 74—Contents of the judgment
1. A judgment as referred to in Articles 28, 42 and 44 of the Convention shall contain
    (a) the names of the President and the other judges constituting the Chamber or the Committee concerned, and the name of the Registrar or the Deputy Registrar;
    (b) the dates on which it was adopted and delivered;
    (c) a description of the parties;
    (d) the names of the Agents, advocates or advisers of the parties;
    (e) an account of the procedure followed;
    (f) the facts of the case;
    (g) a summary of the submissions of the parties;
    (h) the reasons in point of law;
    (i) the operative provisions;
    (j) the decision, if any, in respect of costs;
    (k) the number of judges constituting the majority;
    (l) where appropriate, a statement as to which text is authentic.

This guidance is quite formalist, however, and the requirement in the Convention that the judgment be 'reasoned' is only amplified by the words 'the reasons in point of law'.

A distinction is made between decisions and judgments. The Rules of Court provide for voting on decisions, adding that in the event of a tie the President has a casting vote.[12] In the Chambers and the Grand Chamber, both decisions and judgments are taken by majority vote of the sitting judges.[13] Abstentions are not allowed in final votes on the admissibility and merits of cases.[14]

Dissenting and concurring separate opinions are not at all uncommon. The Rules of Court expressly provide for this in the case of judgments, but not decisions.[15] There are no dissenting opinions with respect to decisions on admissibility even if some of the members of the Chamber may be in profound disagreement with the result. To the extent that there is dissent in a decision on admissibility, this is acknowledged in the *dispositif* with the words '*Decides* by a majority...'[16] or '*Declares* admissible, by a majority...'[17]

Pursuant to Protocol No. 2 to the Convention, reasons are also required for advisory opinions of the Court issued in accordance with article 47. In advisory opinions, judges are entitled to deliver separate opinions.[18]

---

[11] Ibid.
[12] Rules of Court, Rule 23(1).
[13] Ibid., Rule 23(2).
[14] Ibid., Rule 23(2).
[15] Ibid., Rule 74.
[16] See, e.g., *Demopoulos and Others v. Turkey* (dec.) [GC], nos 46113/99, 3843/02, 13751/02, 13466/03, 10200/04, 14163/04, 19993/04, and 21819/04, *dispositif*, ECHR 2010.
[17] *Stec and Others v. the United Kingdom* (dec.) [GC], nos 65731/01 and 65900/01, *dispositif*, ECHR 2005-X.
[18] Protocol No. 2 to the Convention for the Protection of Human Rights and Fundamental Freedoms, conferring upon the European Court of Human Rights competence to give advisory opinions, ETS 44, art. 3.

Further reading

Fred J. Bruinsma, 'The Room at the Top: Separate Opinions in the Grand Chamber of the ECHR (1998–2006)', [2008] *Ancilla Juris* 32.

Fred J. Bruinsma and Matthits de Blois, 'Rules of Law from Westport to Wladiwostok: Separate Opinions in the European Court of Human Rights', (1997) 15 *Netherlands Quarterly of Human Rights* 175.

Johan Callewaert, 'Article 51', in Pettiti et al., *La Convention européenne*, p. 842.

Frowein/Peukert, *MenschenRechtsKonvention*, p. 601.

Florence Rivière, *Les opinions séparées des juges à la Cour européenne des droits de l'homme*, Brussels: Bruylant, 2004.

Robin C.A. White and Iris Boussiakou, 'Separate Opinions in the European Court of Human Rights', (2009) 9 *HRLR* 37.

Luzius Wildhaber, 'Opinion dissidentes et concordantes de juges individuels à la Cour européenne des droits de l'homme', in René-Jean Dupuy, ed., *Droit et Justice. Mélanges en l'honneur de Nicolas Valticos*, Paris: Pedone, 19991 pp. 529–35.

Article 46. Binding force and execution of judgments/Force obligatoire et exécution des arrêts

1. The High Contracting Parties undertake to abide by the final judgment of the Court in any case to which they are parties.

2. The final judgment of the Court shall be transmitted to the Committee of Ministers, which shall supervise its execution.

3. If the Committee of Ministers considers that the supervision of the execution of a final judgment is hindered by a problem of interpretation of the judgment, it may refer the matter to the Court for a ruling on the question of interpretation. A referral decision shall require a majority vote of two thirds of the representatives entitled to sit on the committee.

4. If the Committee of Ministers considers that a High Contracting Party refuses to abide by a final judgment in a case to which it is a party, it may, after serving formal notice on that Party and by decision adopted by a majority vote of two thirds of the representatives entitled to sit on the committee, refer to the Court the question whether that Party has failed to fulfil its obligation under paragraph 1.

5. If the Court finds a violation of paragraph 1, it shall refer the case to the Committee of Ministers for consideration of the measures to be taken. If the Court finds no violation of paragraph 1, it shall refer the case to the Committee of Ministers, which shall close its examination of the case.

1. Les Hautes Parties Contractantes s'engagent à se conformer aux arrêts définitifs de la Cour dans les litiges auxquels elles sont parties.

2. L'arrêt définitif de la Cour est transmis au Comité des Ministres qui en surveille l'exécution.

3. Lorsque le Comité des Ministres estime que la surveillance de l'exécution d'un arrêt définitif est entravée par une difficulté d'interprétation de cet arrêt, il peut saisir la Cour afin qu'elle se prononce sur cette question d'interprétation. La décision de saisir la Cour est prise par un vote à la majorité des deux tiers des représentants ayant le droit de siéger au Comité.

4. Lorsque le Comité des Ministres estime qu'une Haute Partie contractante refuse de se conformer à un arrêt définitif dans un litige auquel elle est partie, il peut, après avoir mis en demeure cette partie et par décision prise par un vote à la majorité des deux tiers des représentants ayant le droit de siéger au Comité, saisir la Cour de la question du respect par cette Partie de son obligation au regard du paragraphe 1.

5. Si la Cour constate une violation du paragraphe 1, elle renvoie l'affaire au Comité des Ministres afin qu'il examine les mesures à prendre. Si la Cour constate qu'il n'y a pas eu violation du paragraphe 1, elle renvoie l'affaire au Comité des Ministres, qui décide de clore son examen.

Introductory comments

Judgments of the European Court of Human Rights are not directly enforceable in a manner similar to that of judgments of domestic courts. That is not to say that execution of a judgment is not central to the scheme of the European Convention: it is 'an integral part of the Convention system'.[1] States Parties are required to abide by judgments, but the way in which they do so is left largely to their own discretion. Some judgments require legislative changes while others may require administrative changes in order to alter a

---

[1] Explanatory Report on Protocol No. 11, para. 16.

policy that violates the Convention. The execution of a final judgment is supervised by the Committee of Ministers of the Council of Europe.

Drafting of the provision

The Recommendations adopted by the International Council of the European Movement in February 1949 included the following:

10. In the event of failure to comply with a recommendation of the Commission or a judgment of the Court, the matter may be brought before the Council of Europe. The Council shall order the party to effect execution and, in case of persistent failure to execute, shall decide on such measures as are appropriate.[2]

In July 1949, the European Movement presented a draft convention to the Committee of Ministers of the Council of Europe containing the following provision: 'Article 14. In the event of failure to comply with a judgment of the Court the matter shall be brought before the Council of Europe, which shall take such action as it may consider appropriate.'[3]

Speaking in the Consultative Assembly, in August 1949, Winston Churchill referred to the establishment of a European Court 'before which cases of the violation of these rights in our own body of twelve nations might be brought to the judgment of the civilized world'. He explained that such a court 'would have no sanctions and would depend for the enforcement of their judgments on the individual decisions of the States'. However, Churchill said he had 'no doubt that the great body of public opinion in all these countries would press for action in accordance with the freely given decision'.[4] Another member of the Assembly, Francesco Dominedo of Italy, described a court with 'the power to declare the law' and with 'the acquisition of the necessary prestige to enable it to apply indirect sanction for the enforcement of judgments'.[5] Henri Fayat of Belgium explained that 'the question of the means of enforcing [the proposed court's] judgments appears of only subsidiary importance. Are we not States by right of law? And can it be supposed that States existing by right of law will fail to yield to the authority of a European Court of Justice whose jurisdiction it has deliberately recognised and accepted?'[6] William Norton of Ireland spoke of a court 'with the power and authority to compel, by moral pressure, the affiliated nations to respect the Convention to which they have subscribed'.[7]

The Legal Committee of the Consultative Assembly prepared a draft recommendation containing a text based on the draft of the European Movement: 'Article 27. In case of non-execution of a verdict of the Court, the latter shall appeal to the Council of Europe which shall take appropriate measures.'[8] This was modified in the final version of the Report: 'Article 27. These findings [of the Court] shall be transmitted to the Council of

[2] Recommendations adopted at the meeting of the International Council of the European Movement held at Brussels in February 1949, INF/2/F, p. 3. This is reproduced in CDH (67) 5, at pp. 2–3, with the indication that the original English version no longer exists.
[3] Convention for the Collective Protection of Individual Rights and Democratic Liberties by the States, Members of the Council of Europe, and for the establishment of a European Court of Human Rights to ensure observance of the Convention, Doc. INF/5/E/R, I *TP* 296–303, at p. 302.
[4] Report of the Sitting [of the Consultative Assembly, 17 August 1949], I *TP* 32–5, at p. 35.
[5] Eighth sitting [of the Consultative Assembly] held 19 August 1949, I TP 36–154, at p. 72.
[6] Ibid., p. 90.
[7] Ibid., p. 132.
[8] Report presented by Mr P.H. Teitgen, 5 September 1949, Doc. A 290, I *TP* 192–213, at p. 212, art. 27.

Europe, if necessary, for action.'[9] In the plenary Assembly, Arthur Sundt of Norway proposed that the text be replaced with something more modest: 'The findings of the Court shall be transmitted to the Committee of Ministers.'[10] Sundt said he had submitted the amendment 'because the proposal in the report is not in accordance with the decision of the Committee at the meeting on Tuesday night'.[11] The rapporteur of the Committee, Pierre-Henri Teitgen, accepted the amendment, and it was duly adopted by the Consultative Assembly.[12]

The Committee of Ministers delegated the examination of the draft convention that had been adopted by the Consultative Assembly to a Committee of Experts that met in February and March 1950. Amendments were proposed to the Consultative Assembly draft. Charles Chaumont of France moved that article 27 be preceded by the following text: 'Each member of the Council of Europe undertakes to abide by the decisions of the Court.'[13] Article 17 was to be redrafted: 'The findings of the Court shall be transmitted to the Committee of Ministers, who, in conjunction with the Consultative Assembly, will ensure their execution.'[14] Tomasso Perassi of Italy also put forward amendments:

Article F.
Each Contracting Party shall undertake to abide by the decision of the Court in any case to which it is a party.

...

Article H.
If one of the Parties does not abide by the findings of the Court, the other party to the dispute, or the Commission on Human Rights, can refer the matter to the Committee of Ministers which, if it considers it necessary to do so, may make recommendations to implement the Court's findings.[15]

A drafting committee composed of Chaumont, Perassi, and Torsten Salén of Sweden prepared the following:

Article 30—(new)
Each Contracting Party shall undertake to abide by the decision of the Court in any case to which it is a party.

...

Article 31 – (new)
The findings of the Court shall be transmitted to the Committee of Ministers which shall supervise its implementation.[16]

Very minor modifications were made to the text at the conclusion of the February 1950 session. The word 'High' was inserted before 'Contracting Party' in article 30 and 'findings' was changed to 'judgment' in article 31. The accompanying commentary

[9] Report [of the Committee on Legal and Administrative Questions], 5 September 1949, Doc. AS (1) 77, I *TP* 216–39.
[10] Amendment presented by Mr Sundt, Doc. 1949, No. 103, II *TP* 10–11.
[11] Official Report of the Sitting [of the Consultative Assembly, 8 September 1949], II *TP* 14–274, at p. 220.
[12] Ibid., p. 222.
[13] Amendments to Articles 20 and 27 of the Recommendation of the Consultative Assembly proposed by the French Expert, Doc. A 794, III *TP* 198–201.
[14] Ibid.
[15] Amendments to various articles of the Recommendation of the Consultative Assembly proposed by the Italian Expert, Doc. A 812, III *TP* 228–31.
[16] Continuation and end of the proposals of the Drafting Sub-Committee concerning Section III, Doc. A 813, III *TP* 230–3.

explained that the provisions 'are concerned with the question of the Court's decisions. It is expressly stipulated here that it is for the Committee of Ministers to supervise their execution.'[17] The provisions remained unchanged at the March session of the Committee.[18]

Small alterations were made to the first of the two provisions by the Committee of Ministers at its August 1950 session: 'The High Contracting Parties undertake to abide by the decision of the Court in any case to which they are parties.'[19] No further changes were made to what became articles 53 and 54 of the Convention text adopted in November 1950:

Article 53
The High Contracting Parties undertake to abide by the decision of the Court in any case to which they are parties.

Article 54
The judgment of the Court shall be transmitted to the Committee of Ministers which shall supervise its execution.

Protocol No. 11 to the Convention reconfigured articles 53 and 54 of the Convention as article 46.

Article 46—Binding force and execution of judgments
1. The High Contracting Parties undertake to abide by the final judgment of the Court in any case to which they are parties.
2. The final judgment of the Court shall be transmitted to the Committee of Ministers, which shall supervise its execution.

In the first sentence, the word 'decision' was changed to 'final judgment'. In the second, the word 'final' was added before judgment. The title 'Binding force and execution of judgments' was given to the new provision. According to the Explanatory Report, 'no change of substance' was involved.[20]

The current text of article 46 contains three new paragraphs that were introduced by Protocol No. 14. These were 'designed to improve and accelerate the execution process'. According to the Explanatory Report:

16. Execution of the Court's judgments is an integral part of the Convention system. The measures that follow are designed to improve and accelerate the execution process. The Court's authority and the system's credibility both depend to a large extent on the effectiveness of this process. Rapid and adequate execution has, of course, an effect on the influx of new cases: the more rapidly general measures are taken by States Parties to execute judgments which point to a structural problem, the fewer repetitive applications there will be. In this regard, it would be desirable for states, over and above their obligations under Article 46, paragraph 1, of the Convention, to give retroactive effect to such measures and remedies . . . In addition, it would be useful if the Court and, as regards the supervision of the execution of judgments, the Committee of Ministers, adopted a special procedure

---

[17] Preliminary Draft Convention for the Maintenance and Further Realisation of Human Rights and Fundamental Freedoms, 15 February 1950, Doc. A 833, III *TP* 236–46, at p. 246.

[18] Appendix to the Report of the Committee of Experts on Human Rights: Draft Convention of Protection of Human Rights and Fundamental Freedoms, 16 March 1950, Doc. CM/WP 1 (50) 15 appendix, CM/WP 1 (50) 14 revised, A 925, IV *TP* 50–79, at p. 74, arts 42(46) and 43(47).

[19] Draft Convention adopted by the Sub-Committee, Doc. CM 1 (50) 52, A 1884, V *TP* 76–99, at p. 94, arts 53 and 54.

[20] Explanatory Report on Protocol No. 11, para. 106.

so as to give priority treatment to judgments that identify a structural problem capable of generating a significant number of repetitive applications, with a view to securing speedy execution of the judgment. The most important Convention amendment in the context of execution of judgments of the Court involves empowering the Committee of Ministers to bring infringement proceedings in the Court against any state which refuses to comply with a judgment.

17. The measures referred to in the previous paragraph are also designed to increase the effectiveness of the Convention system as a whole. While the supervision of the execution of judgments generally functions satisfactorily, the process needs to be improved to maintain the system's effectiveness.[21]

The first change introduced by Protocol No. 14, in article 46(3), empowers the Committee of Ministers to ask the Court to interpret a final judgment for the purpose of facilitating the supervision of its execution. According to the Explanatory Report,

96. ... The Committee of Ministers' experience of supervising the execution of judgments shows that difficulties are sometimes encountered due to disagreement as to the interpretation of judgments. The Court's reply settles any argument concerning a judgment's exact meaning. The qualified majority vote required by the last sentence of paragraph 3 shows that the Committee of Ministers should use this possibility sparingly, to avoid over-burdening the Court.

97. The aim of the new paragraph 3 is to enable the Court to give an interpretation of a judgment, not to pronounce on the measures taken by a High Contracting Party to comply with that judgment. No time-limit has been set for making requests for interpretation, since a question of interpretation may arise at any time during the Committee of Ministers' examination of the execution of a judgment. The Court is free to decide on the manner and form in which it wishes to reply to the request. Normally, it would be for the formation of the Court which delivered the original judgment to rule on the question of interpretation. More detailed rules governing this new procedure may be included in the Rules of Court.[22]

The second modification, resulting from the addition of paragraphs 4 and 5 of article 46, is to enable the Committee of Ministers to bring infringement proceedings in the Court:

98. Rapid and full execution of the Court's judgments is vital. It is even more important in cases concerning structural problems, so as to ensure that the Court is not swamped with repetitive applications. For this reason, ever since the Rome ministerial conference of 3 and 4 November 2000 (Resolution I), it has been considered essential to strengthen the means given in this context to the Committee of Ministers. The Parties to the Convention have a collective duty to preserve the Court's authority—and thus the Convention system's credibility and effectiveness—whenever the Committee of Ministers considers that one of the High Contracting Parties refuses, expressly or through its conduct, to comply with the Court's final judgment in a case to which it is party.

99. Paragraphs 4 and 5 of Article 46 accordingly empower the Committee of Ministers to bring infringement proceedings in the Court (which shall sit as a Grand Chamber—see new Article 31, paragraph b), having first served the state concerned with notice to comply. The Committee of Ministers' decision to do so requires a qualified majority of two thirds of the representatives entitled to sit on the Committee. This infringement procedure does not aim to reopen the question of violation, already decided in the Court's first judgment. Nor does it provide for payment of a financial penalty by a High Contracting Party found in violation of Article 46, paragraph 1. It is felt that the political pressure exerted by proceedings for non-compliance in the Grand Chamber and by

---

[21] Explanatory Report on Protocol No. 14, paras 16–17.
[22] Ibid., paras 96–97.

the latter's judgment should suffice to secure execution of the Court's initial judgment by the state concerned.

100. The Committee of Ministers should bring infringement proceedings only in exceptional circumstances. None the less, it appeared necessary to give the Committee of Ministers, as the competent organ for supervising execution of the Court's judgments, a wider range of means of pressure to secure execution of judgments. Currently the ultimate measure available to the Committee of Ministers is recourse to Article 8 of the Council of Europe's Statute (suspension of voting rights in the Committee of Ministers, or even expulsion from the Organisation). This is an extreme measure, which would prove counter-productive in most cases; indeed the High Contracting Party which finds itself in the situation foreseen in paragraph 4 of Article 46 continues to need, far more than others, the discipline of the Council of Europe. The new Article 46 therefore adds further possibilities of bringing pressure to bear to the existing ones. The procedure's mere existence, and the threat of using it, should act as an effective new incentive to execute the Court's judgments. It is foreseen that the outcome of infringement proceedings would be expressed in a judgment of the Court.[23]

Analysis and interpretation

'Binding force' is in the title of the provision, added by Protocol No. 11, but the words do not appear in the text itself. The notion of 'binding force' is closely related to that of *res judicata*,[24] although the first paragraph of article 46 suggests here that this is not what is really meant by the term 'binding'. The only other use of the term 'binding' in the law of the Convention is in article 5 of Protocol No. 16 where, according to the Explanatory Report, the meaning appears related to the *res judicata* principle.[25] Nor does 'binding' in the context of article 46 apply to the notion of judicial precedent. In principle, there is no rule of *stare decisis* at the European Court of Human Rights.

The Court has described findings of a violation in its judgments as being 'essentially declaratory'.[26] By article 46 of the Convention, States Parties have undertaken to abide by final judgments of the Court in cases to which they were parties, with execution being supervised by the Committee of Ministers.[27] The obligation set out in paragraph 1 of article 46 is a specific formulation of the general principle *pacta sunt servanda*.[28] It is codified in article 26 of the Vienna Convention on the Law of Treaties as well as in the third recital of its Preamble: 'Every treaty in force is binding upon the parties to it and must be performed by them in good faith.' The Convention regime for the observance of *pacta sunt servanda* is self-contained, a consequence of article 55. Otherwise, it would be possible for failure to observe a judgment of the Court to be raised in an application before a body like the International Court of Justice, to the extent that States Parties to the Convention have accepted its jurisdiction.

---

[23] Ibid., paras 98–100 (reference omitted).
[24] Rudolf Bernhardt, 'Article 59', in Andreas Zimmermann, Christian Tomuschat, and Karin Oellers-Frahm, eds, *The Statute of the International Court of Justice, A Commentary*, Oxford: Oxford University Press, 2006, pp. 1232–51.
[25] Explanatory Report on Protocol No. 16, paras 25–27.
[26] *Verein gegen Tierfabriken Schweiz (VgT) v. Switzerland (no. 2)* [GC], no. 32772/02, § 61, ECHR 2009; *Marckx v. Belgium*, 13 June 1979, § 58, Series A no. 31; *Lyons and Others v. the United Kingdom* (dec.), no. 15227/03, ECHR 2003-IX; *Krčmář and Others v. the Czech Republic* (dec.), no. 69190/01, 30 March 2004; *Öcalan v. Turkey* [GC], no. 46221/99, § 210, ECHR 2005-IV.
[27] *Verein gegen Tierfabriken Schweiz (VgT) v. Switzerland (no. 2)* [GC], no. 32772/02, § 61, ECHR 2009.
[28] Ibid., § 87.

In the inter-State case filed by Cyprus against Turkey relating to the 1974 invasion and its consequences, judgment was issued in 2001 finding violations of articles 2, 3, 5, 9, and 13 of the Convention and article 1 of Protocol No. 1 with respect to missing persons and their relatives and Greek Cypriots living in an enclave in the occupied northern part of the island.[29] When Turkey did not address the situation for many years, Cyprus applied to the Court to rule on just satisfaction in accordance with article 41 of the Convention, a matter that it had expressly reserved in the judgment on the merits ('Holds unanimously that the issue of the possible application of Article 41 of the Convention is not ready for decision and adjourns consideration thereof').[30] Turkey did nothing to implement and enforce the judgment. Several years later, Cyprus applied to the Court on the basis of article 41. In principle, this was only the continuation of the proceedings on the merits. But in reality, Turkey's failure to respect the judgment was the *leitmotif* of the judgment on just satisfaction. One judge went so far as to suggest that the extraordinary sum of €90 million awarded against Turkey as just satisfaction was a form of punishment because it 'deliberately failed year after year to comply with the Grand Chamber's judgment on the merits delivered a long time ago with regard to these specific violations'.[31]

In the just satisfaction proceedings, Cyprus asked the Court to apply article 46 and issue a 'declaratory judgment' as part of its ruling on just satisfaction. The Grand Chamber said this was unnecessary, 'since it is clear that the respondent Government is, in any event, formally bound by the relevant terms of the main judgment... It thus falls to the Committee of Ministers to ensure that this holding which is binding in accordance with the Convention, and which has not yet been complied with, is given full effect by the respondent Government.'[32] Several judges distanced themselves from a controversial sentence in the judgment suggesting a role for the Court in enforcing the judgment. They said that it sought 'to extend the powers of the Court and runs counter to Article 46 § 2 of the Convention by encroaching on the powers of the Committee of Ministers of the Council of Europe, to which the Convention has entrusted the task of supervising execution of the Court's judgments'. In this respect, they said the Court was without jurisdiction, warning of the creation of 'an imbalance in the distribution of powers between the two institutions that was envisaged by the authors of the Convention'.[33]

Freedom to determine means of discharging obligations

If the Court finds that there is a violation, the respondent State remains free to determine the means by which it will discharge the legal obligation that arises from the judgment, subject to the proviso that such means are compatible with the conclusions of the

[29] *Cyprus v. Turkey* [GC], no. 25781/94, *dispositif*, ECHR 2001-IV.
[30] Ibid.
[31] *Cyprus v. Turkey* (just satisfaction) [GC], no. 25781/94, Concurring Opinion of Judge Pinto de Albuquerque, Joined by Judge Vučinić, § 19, 12 May 2014.
[32] *Cyprus v. Turkey* (just satisfaction) [GC], no. 25781/94, § 63, 12 May 2014. But see *Cyprus v. Turkey* (just satisfaction) [GC], no. 25781/94, Concurring Opinion of Judge Pinto de Albuquerque, Joined by Judge Vučinić, §§ 20–23, 12 May 2014.
[33] *Cyprus v. Turkey* (just satisfaction) [GC], no. 25781/94, Partly Concurring Opinion of Judges Tulkens, Vajić, Raimondi, and Bianku, Joined by Judge Karakaş, §§ 6, 9.

Court.[34] The Committee of Ministers has described this as 'the discretion of the High Contracting Party concerned to choose the means necessary to comply with the judgment'.[35]

In principle, the finding of a breach by the Court 'imposes on the respondent State a legal obligation to put an end to the breach and make reparation for its consequences in such a way as to restore as far as possible the situation existing before the breach'.[36] The State Party must not only pay to those concerned the sums that have been awarded but also take individual and general measures, where appropriate, in its domestic legal order 'to put an end to the violation found by the Court and to redress the effects, the aim being to put the applicant, as far as possible, in the position he would have been in had the requirements of the Convention not been disregarded'.[37] Despite the principle of freedom in determining the means of implementation of obligations, there are cases where the nature of the violation leaves no choice about the measures that must be taken.[38]

Thus, 'a total or partial failure to execute a judgment of the Court can engage the State Party's international responsibility'.[39] The obligations in the Convention in this respect are a manifestation of principles of international law by which a State responsible for a wrongful act is required to make restitution. According to article 35 of the Draft Articles on State Responsibility, which is the authoritative statement on the issue:

A State responsible for an internationally wrongful act is under an obligation to make restitution, that is, to re-establish the situation which existed before the wrongful act was committed, provided and to the extent that restitution:

(*a*) is not materially impossible;

(*b*) does not involve a burden out of all proportion to the benefit deriving from restitution instead of compensation.[40]

This is the principle of *restitutio in integrum* accompanied by its exceptions. The Parliamentary Assembly has insisted that the execution of a judgment should bring about *restitutio in integrum* to the extent that this is at all possible.[41] Judgments of the Court have also insisted that 'the aim of individual measures should be to put the applicant, as far as possible, in the position he would have been in had the requirements of the Convention not been disregarded'.[42]

The measures taken by the State in fulfilment of its obligation may be individual or general in nature. They must address the specific violation of which the applicant has been

---

[34] *Andrejeva v. Latvia* [GC], no. 55707/00, § 110, ECHR 2009; *Scozzari and Giunta v. Italy* [GC], nos 39221/98 and 41963/98, § 249, ECHR 2000-VIII; *Verein gegen Tierfabriken Schweiz (VgT) v. Switzerland (no. 2)* [GC], no. 32772/02, § 88, ECHR 2009.

[35] Committee of Ministers' Rules for the supervision of the execution of judgments and of the terms of friendly settlements, Rule 6(2)(b).

[36] *Papamichalopoulos and Others v. Greece* (Article 50), 31 October 1995, § 34, Series A no. 330-B.

[37] *Verein gegen Tierfabriken Schweiz (VgT) v. Switzerland (no. 2)* [GC], no. 32772/02, § 82, ECHR 2009; *Scozzari and Giunta v. Italy* [GC], nos 39221/98 and 41963/98, § 249, ECHR 2000-VIII; *Assanidze v. Georgia* [GC], no. 71503/01, § 198, ECHR 2004-II.

[38] *Verein gegen Tierfabriken Schweiz (VgT) v. Switzerland (no. 2)* [GC], no. 32772/02, § 88, ECHR 2009; *Assanidze v. Georgia* [GC], no. 71503/01, § 202, ECHR 2004-II.

[39] *Verein gegen Tierfabriken Schweiz (VgT) v. Switzerland (no. 2)* [GC], no. 32772/02, § 85, ECHR 2009.

[40] UN Doc. A/RES/56/83, annex, cited in *Verein gegen Tierfabriken Schweiz (VgT) v. Switzerland (no. 2)* [GC], no. 32772/02, § 86, ECHR 2009; *Guiso-Gallisay v. Italy* (just satisfaction) [GC], no. 58858/00, § 53, 22 December 2009.

[41] Recommendation No. R (2000) 2 and Explanatory memorandum on Recommendation R (2000) 2.

[42] *Scoppola v. Italy (no. 2)* [GC], no. 10249/03, § 150, 17 September 2009; *Piersack v. Belgium* (Article 50), 26 October 1984, § 12, Series A no. 85.

a victim, but they must also be taken 'in respect of other persons in the applicant's position, notably by solving the problems that have led to the Court's findings'.[43] Measures taken by a respondent State to remedy a violation may in certain circumstances raise a new issue that was undecided by the initial judgment.[44] This can lead to a new application. For example, a retrial by national courts that is intended to implement a judgment may give rise to a new breach of the Convention.[45]

Although infrequent, there are cases where States Parties to the Convention have broken up, and where problems arise concerning the attribution of responsibility where the alleged violation took place prior to the breakup but where the claim is being made after.[46]

Role of the Court

The Court 'may propose various options and leave the choice of measure and its implementation to the discretion of the State concerned'.[47] Where there is no real option in terms of the measures that may be adopted, the Court may decide to indicate only one measure.[48] Although the Court does not have jurisdiction to order the reopening of trial, in its judgment on proceedings involving a criminal conviction following proceedings that have entailed breaches of the requirements of Article 6 of the Convention it may indicate retrial or reopening of the case as 'in principle an appropriate way of redressing the violation'[49] or even 'the most appropriate remedy'.[50]

Despite the principle of freedom of choice of means of execution of judgments, in 'certain special circumstances' the Court has 'found it useful' and suggested it may be of assistance to the respondent State for it to offer an indication of the types of measures that may be taken in order to remedy a situation that has resulted in a violation.[51] This is notably the case where there is a systemic problem.[52] The Court generally invokes article 46 when making such indications. It has done so in about 150 cases, ranging from 'quite general suggestions intended to guide the Government in the execution of the judgment

[43] *Manushaqe Puto and Others v. Albania*, nos 604/07, 43628/07, 46684/07, and 34770/09, § 102, 31 July 2012; *Burdov v. Russia (no. 2)*, no. 33509/04, § 125, ECHR 2009.

[44] *Mehemi v. France (no. 2)*, no. 53470/99, § 43, ECHR 2003-IV; *Pailot v. France*, 22 April 1998, § 57, *Reports of Judgments and Decisions* 1998-II; *Leterme v. France*, 29 April 1998, § 70, *Reports of Judgments and Decisions* 1998-III; *Rando v. Italy*, no. 38498/97, § 17, 15 February 2000.

[45] *Verein gegen Tierfabriken Schweiz (VgT) v. Switzerland* (no. 2) [GC], no. 32772/02, § 62, ECHR 2009; *Hertel v. Switzerland* (dec.), no. 3440/99, ECHR 2002-I; *Mehemi v. France (no. 2)*, no. 53470/99, § 43, ECHR 2003-IV; *Pailot v. France*, 22 April 1998, § 57, *Reports of Judgments and Decisions* 1998-II; *Rando v. Italy*, no. 38498/97, § 17, 15 February 2000.

[46] *Bijelić v. Montenegro and Serbia*, no. 11890/05, § 69, 28 April 2009.

[47] *Öcalan v. Turkey*, no. 46221/99, § 210 *in fine*, ECHR 2005-IV.

[48] *Scoppola v. Italy (no. 2)* [GC], no. 10249/03, § 148, 17 September 2009; *Aleksanyan v. Russia*, no. 46468/06, § 239, 22 December 2008; *Abbasov v. Azerbaijan*, no. 24271/05, § 37, 17 January 2008.

[49] *Verein gegen Tierfabriken Schweiz (VgT) v. Switzerland* (no. 2) [GC], no. 32772/02, § 86, ECHR 2009; *Gençel v. Turkey*, no. 53431/99, § 27, 23 October 2003; *Claes and Others v. Belgium*, nos 46825/99, 47132/99, 47502/99, 49010/99, 49104/99, 49195/99, and 49716/99, § 53, 2 June 2005.

[50] *Scoppola v. Italy (no. 2)* [GC], no. 10249/03, § 150, 17 September 2009.

[51] *Verein gegen Tierfabriken Schweiz (VgT) v. Switzerland (no. 2)* [GC], no. 32772/02, § 88, ECHR 2009; *Öcalan v. Turkey*, no. 46221/99, § 210 *in fine*, ECHR 2005-IV; *Broniowski v. Poland* [GC], no. 31443/96, § 194, ECHR 2004-V; *Popov v. Russia*, no. 26853/04, § 263, 13 July 2006; *Scoppola v. Italy (no. 2)* [GC], no. 10249/03, § 148, 17 September 2009; *Broniowski v. Poland* [GC], no. 31443/96, § 194, ECHR 2004-V.

[52] *Öcalan v. Turkey*, no. 46221/99, § 210 *in fine*, ECHR 2005-IV; *Broniowski v. Poland* [GC], no. 31443/96, § 194, ECHR 2004-V; *Popov v. Russia*, no. 26853/04, § 263, 13 July 2006.

to cases in which specific directives are included in the operative provisions of the judgment, thereby binding the respondent State'.[53] However, the Court does not always invoke article 46, and may simply draw the respondent's attention to arrangements made in other States Parties or to international practice.[54]

In its judgment on an application concerning 'erased' persons in Slovenia, the Court noted that although there were only a few similar applications pending, a potential inflow of future cases was anticipated. The Court indicated, in accordance with Rule 61(3), that the State should set up 'within one year' a domestic compensation scheme.[55] In a case involving retrospective application where the Court found that retrospective application of the law to the detriment of the applicant meant he received a sentence of life imprisonment rather than one of thirty years, that '[h]aving regard to the particular circumstances of the case and the urgent need to put an end to the breach of Articles 6 and 7 of the Convention, the Court therefore considers that the respondent State is responsible for ensuring that the applicant's sentence of life imprisonment is replaced by a penalty consistent with the principles set out in the present judgment, which is a sentence not exceeding thirty years' imprisonment'.[56] In a case involving disappearances, the European Court concluded that the domestic tribunals should have required 'that an effective investigation into the matter should be held. Accountability for the fate of the missing men includes carrying out an investigation into the events and those responsible and offering the possibility of claiming redress to the victims and the relatives.'[57]

The 'pilot-judgment procedure' provides the Court with a means of indicating measures to resolve 'a structural or system problem or other similar dysfunction' that is at the origin of a violation of the Convention.[58] The object of the procedure 'is to facilitate the speediest and most effective resolution of a dysfunction affecting the protection of the Convention right in question in the national legal order'. The aim 'is to induce the respondent State to resolve large numbers of individual cases arising from the same structural problem at the domestic level, thus implementing the principle of subsidiarity which underpins the Convention system'.[59]

The pilot-judgment procedure may be initiated by one of the parties or by the Court acting on its own motion.[60] In a pilot judgment, the Court is to identify the nature of the problem and to indicate the type of remedial measures that the State Party is required to take.[61] The Court may indicate the time frame for implementation of remedial measures, 'bearing in mind the nature of the measures required and the speed with which the problem which it has identified can be remedied at the domestic level'.[62] If the parties in a

---

[53] Reply to Committee of Ministers request for comments on the CDDH Report on Execution, 9 May 2014, para. 12.
[54] *Vinter and Others v. the United Kingdom* [GC], nos 66069/09, 130/10 and 3896/10, § 120, ECHR 2013 (extracts).
[55] *Kurić and Others v. Slovenia* [GC], no. 26828/06, §§ 414–415, ECHR 2012 (extracts).
[56] *Scoppola v. Italy (no. 2)* [GC], no. 10249/03, § 154, 17 September 2009.
[57] *Varnava and Others v. Turkey* [GC], nos 16064/90, 16065/90, 16066/90, 16068/90, 16069/90, 16070/90, 16071/90, 16072/90, and 16073/90, Concurring Opinion of Judge Spielmann, Joined by Judges Ziemele and Kaladjieva, § 3, ECHR 2009.
[58] Rules of Court, Rule 61(1).
[59] *Manushaqe Puto and Others v. Albania*, nos 604/07, 43628/07, 46684/07, and 34770/09, § 104, 31 July 2012; *Maria Atanasiu and Others v. Romania*, nos 30767/05 and 33800/06, § 212, 12 October 2010.
[60] Rules of Court, Rule 61(2)(b).
[61] Ibid.
[62] Ibid., Rule 61(4).

pilot case reach agreement on a friendly settlement, the agreement is taken as a declaration by the respondent State on the general measures to be taken and the redress to be offered to actual or potential applicants.[63]

Supervision of execution by the Committee of Ministers

The *travaux préparatoires* of the Convention demonstrate the development of the idea of supervision of the enforcement of judgments of the Court by the Committee of Ministers. The initial vision in the Consultative Assembly had been a treaty with an essentially moral force, relying upon the political pressure of civil society within States Parties in order to enforce the judgments of the Court. It is set out in article 46(2) of the Convention According to the Court, '[s]uch a mechanism demonstrates the importance of effective implementation of judgments'.[64]

The Committee of Ministers has adopted a set of Rules for the supervision of the execution of judgments and of the terms of friendly settlements. In the first place, respondent States are required to provide the Committee of Ministers with 'detailed, up-to-date information on developments in the process of executing judgments that are binding on them'.[65] The Committee of Ministers holds four regular meetings each year at which the execution of judgments is considered. The Committee concludes each case with the adoption of a final resolution. In some cases it will also adopt interim resolutions.

Ultimately, of course, the system still falls back upon the political pressure of civil society, combined with the disapproval and condemnation of the States Parties when there is a failure to implement the rulings of the Court. In recent years, the Committee of Ministers has condemned States Parties for their failure to comply. For example, five years after Bosnia and Herzegovina was required by the Grand Chamber to amend its constitution in order to allow all citizens to stand for election to the presidency,[66] the Committee of Ministers '[f]irmly call[ed] upon all authorities and political leaders of Bosnia and Herzegovina to ensure that the constitutional and legislative framework is immediately brought in line with the Convention requirements so that the elections in October 2014 are held without any discrimination against those citizens who are not affiliated with any of the "constituent peoples"'.[67] In the *Varnava* case,[68] concerning Greek Cypriots missing since the 1974 invasion, more than four years after the Grand Chamber judgment Turkey was '[e]xhort[ed] to pay, without further delay, the sums awarded in respect of just satisfaction in the Court's judgment of 18 September 2009, as well as the default interest due'.[69]

---

[63] Ibid., Rule 61(7).

[64] *Verein gegen Tierfabriken Schweiz (VgT) v. Switzerland* (no. 2) [GC], no. 32772/02, § 84, ECHR 2009.

[65] Committee of Ministers' Rules for the supervision of the execution of judgments and of the terms of friendly settlements, Rule 6. See also *Verein gegen Tierfabriken Schweiz (VgT) v. Switzerland* (no. 2) [GC], no. 32772/02, § 87, ECHR 2009.

[66] *Sejdić and Finci v. Bosnia and Herzegovina* [GC], nos 27996/06 and 34836/06, ECHR 2009.

[67] Interim Resolution CM/ResDH(2013)259. See also Interim Resolution CM/ResDH(2012)233; Interim Resolution CM/ResDH(2011)291.

[68] *Varnava and Others v. Turkey* [GC], nos 16064/90, 16065/90, 16066/90, 16068/90, 16069/90, 16070/90, 16071/90, 16072/90, and 16073/90, ECHR 2009.

[69] Interim Resolution CM/ResDH(2013)201.

Interpretation (art. 46(3))

The Committee of Ministers may seek a ruling of the Court if it considers that supervision of the execution of a final judgment is hindered by a problem of interpretation. This provision was introduced by Protocol No. 14. The request for interpretation is to be considered by the Grand Chamber, the Chamber or the Committee that rendered the initial judgment, failing which the President is to complete or compose a Chamber by drawing lots.[70] The decision on the question of interpretation is final. Like an admissibility decision, separate opinions of judges are not permitted.[71] This provision has not yet been invoked by the Committee of Ministers. As several judges recently commented, for article 46(3) to be invoked, 'the Committee of Ministers must have taken the referral decision by a qualified majority of two thirds of the representatives entitled to sit on the committee'.[72]

Failure to fulfil an obligation (art. 46(4) and (5))

If the Committee of Ministers considers that a State Party refuses to abide by a final judgment in a case to which it is party, it may refer the question of the failure to fulfil the obligation to the Court. The case is to be considered by the Grand Chamber.[73] If the Court concludes that there has been such a failure, it shall refer the case back to the Committee of Ministers 'for consideration of the measures to be taken'. Paragraphs 4 and 5 were introduced by Protocol No. 14.[74] They have not yet been invoked by the Committee of Ministers.

Further reading

Johan Callewaert, 'Article 53', in Pettiti et al., *La Convention européenne*, pp. 847–56.
Valerio Colandrea, 'On the Power of the European Court of Human Rights to Order Specific Non-monetary Measures: Some Remarks in Light of the Assanidze, Broniowski and Sejdovic Cases', (2007) 7 *HRLR* 396.
P. Ducolombier, '"Arrêts pilotes" et efficacité des nouveaux recours internes', in P. Dourneau-Josette and E. Lambert-Abdelgawad, eds, *Quel filtrage des requêtes par la Cour européenne des droits de l'homme?*, Strasbourg: Editions du Conseil de l'Europe, 2011, pp. 255–92.
Frowein/Peukert, *MenschenRechtsKonvention*, pp. 602–10.
Markus Fyrnys, 'Expanding Competences of Judicial Lawmaking: The Pilot Judgment Procedure of the European Court of Human Rights', (2011) 12 *German Law Journal* 1231.
Lech Garlicki, 'Broniowski and After: On the Dual Nature of "Pilot Judgments"', in Lucius Caflisch, Johan Callewaert, Roderick Liddell, Paul Mahoney, and Mark Villiger, eds, *Liber Amicorum Luzius Wildhaber*, Kehl, Germany: N.P. Engel, 2007, pp. 177–92.
Dominik Haider, *The Pilot-Judgment Procedure of the European Court of Human Rights*, The Hague: Martinus Nijhoff, 2013.

---

[70] Rules of Court, Rule 92.
[71] Ibid., Rule 93.
[72] *Cyprus v. Turkey* (just satisfaction) [GC], no. 25781/94, Partly Concurring Opinion of Judges Tulkens, Vajić, Raimondi, and Bianku, Joined by Judge Karakaş, § 8, § 19, 12 May 2014.
[73] Rules of Court, Rule 96.
[74] See also Rules of Court, Rules 94–99.

Philip Leach, Helen Hardman, Svetlana Stephenson, and Brad K. Blitz, *Responding to Systemic Human Rights Violations: An Analysis of the 'Pilot Judgments' of the European Court of Human Rights and their Impact at National Level*, Antwerp: Intersentia, 2010.

Georg Ress, 'Article 54', in Pettiti et al., *La Convention européenne*, pp. 857–69.

Georg Ress, 'The Effect of Decisions and Judgments of the European Court of Human Rights in the Domestic Legal Order', (2004) 40 *Texas International Law Journal* 359.

Frederik G.E. Sundberg, 'Control of Execution of Decisions Under the ECHR—Some Remarks on the Committee of Ministers' Control of the Proper Implementation of Decisions Finding Violations of the Convention', in Gudmundur Alfredsson, Jonas Grimheden, Bertram G. Ramcharan, and Alfred de Zayas, eds, *International Human Rights Monitoring Mechanisms: Essays in Honour of Jakob Th. Möller*, The Hague/Boston/London: Kluwer Law International, 2002, pp. 561–85.

Vladimiro Zagrebelsky, 'Questions autour de Broniowski', in Lucius Caflisch, Johan Callewaert, Roderick Liddell, Paul Mahoney, and Mark Villiger, eds, *Liber Amicorum Luzius Wildhaber*, Kehl, Germany: N.P. Engel, 2007, pp. 521–6.

Leo Zwaak, 'The Supervisory Task of the Committee of Ministers', in Van Dijk et al., *Theory and Practice*, pp. 291–321.

Article 47. Advisory opinions/Avis consultatifs

1. The Court may, at the request of the Committee of Ministers, give advisory opinions on legal questions concerning the interpretation of the Convention and the Protocols thereto.

2. Such opinions shall not deal with any question relating to the content or scope of the rights or freedoms defined in Section I of the Convention and the Protocols thereto, or with any other question which the Court or the Committee of Ministers might have to consider in consequence of any such proceedings as could be instituted in accordance with the Convention.

3. Decisions of the Committee of Ministers to request an advisory opinion of the Court shall require a majority vote of the representatives entitled to sit on the Committee.

1. La Cour peut, à la demande du Comité des Ministres, donner des avis consultatifs sur des questions juridiques concernant l'interprétation de la Convention et de ses protocoles.

2. Ces avis ne peuvent porter ni sur les questions ayant trait au contenu ou à l'étendue des droits et libertés définis au titre I de la Convention et dans les protocoles ni sur les autres questions dont la Cour ou le Comité des Ministres pourraient avoir à connaître par suite de l'introduction d'un recours prévu par la Convention.

3. La décision du Comité des Ministres de demander un avis à la Cour est prise par un vote à la majorité des représentants ayant le droit de siéger au Comité.

Introductory comments

Many international courts and tribunals have a jurisdiction to issue advisory opinions. The Permanent Court of International Justice was the first international tribunal with the express power to issue advisory opinions. Initially this resulted from article 14 of the Covenant of the League of Nations, but it was subsequently included in amendments to the Statute of the Court.[1] The Charter of the United Nations allows for the issuance of an advisory opinion by the International Court of Justice at the request of the General Assembly or the Security Council 'on any legal question'.[2] Under certain conditions, other United Nations organs and specialized agencies may seek advisory opinions 'on legal questions arising within the scope of their activities'.[3] In one form or another, a comparable mechanism exists in many domestic legal orders, whereby a political body such as a legislative assembly may seek an opinion on a legal issue from a constitution court or similar body.

The other main international human rights court, the Inter-American Court of Human Rights, also has jurisdiction to issue advisory opinions.[4] In the course of its activities, it has issued several advisory opinions, many of them at the request of States Parties.[5] Article 47 of the European Convention is quite clear that only the Committee of Ministers is entitled to seek an advisory opinion. In 2013, the Committee of Ministers adopted

---

[1] Statute of the Permanent Court of International Justice, arts 65–68.
[2] Charter of the United Nations, art. 96(1).
[3] Ibid., art. 96(2).
[4] American Convention on Human Rights, (1978) 1144 UNTS 123, art. 64.
[5] Ibid.

Protocol No. 16 in order to give the Court jurisdiction to issue advisory opinions at the request of national courts and tribunals.[6]

Drafting of the provision

The original 1950 version of the European Convention did not provide the authority for the Court to issue advisory opinions. This had initially been proposed by the International Juridical Section of the European Movement in its Draft Statute of the European Court of Human Rights whereby the European Commission of Human Rights would have the authority to request advisory opinions.[7]

In 1960, a resolution of the Consultative Assembly of the Council of Europe recommending that the competence of the Court be extended 'as regards the interpretation of the Convention on Human Rights' lies at the origin of article 47.[8] Over the course of the next few years, the Committee of Experts on Human Rights prepared a draft Protocol for this purpose.[9] During the drafting process, the European Commission of Human Rights proposed that it be allowed to request advisory opinions, but the suggestion was not adopted.[10]

The competence of the European Court to deliver advisory opinions was introduced by Protocol No. 2, which amended the text of the Convention.[11] Adopted in 1963, it entered into force in 1970. The operative provisions were as follows:

Article 1
1. The Court may, at the request of the Committee of Ministers, give advisory opinions on legal questions concerning the interpretation of the Convention and the Protocols thereto.
2. Such opinions shall not deal with any question relating to the content or scope of the rights or freedoms defined in Section 1 of the Convention and in the Protocols thereto, or with any other question which the Commission, the Court or the Committee of Ministers might have to consider in consequence of any such proceedings as could be instituted in accordance with the Convention.
3. Decisions of the Committee of Ministers to request an advisory opinion of the Court shall require a two-thirds majority vote of the representatives entitled to sit on the Committee.

Article 2
The Court shall decide whether a request for an advisory opinion submitted by the Committee of Ministers is within its consultative competence as defined in Article 1 of this Protocol.

Article 3
1. For the consideration of requests for an advisory opinion, the Court shall sit in plenary session.
2. Reasons shall be given for advisory opinions of the Court.
3. If the advisory opinion does not represent in whole or in part the unanimous opinion of the judges, any judge shall be entitled to deliver a separate opinion.
4. Advisory opinions of the Court shall be communicated to the Committee of Ministers.

---

[6] See the chapters on Protocol No. 16 in this Commentary.
[7] Draft Statute of the European Court of Human Rights, INF/5/E/R, I *TP* 302–21, at p. 318, art. 58.
[8] Recommendation 232, Consultative Assembly, 22 January 1960.
[9] Explanatory Report on Protocol No. 2, paras 2–6.
[10] Explanatory Report on Protocol No. 2, paras 5, 7. See the individual statement protesting the exclusion of the Commission by one of the members of the Committee of Experts: Explanatory Report on Protocol No. 2, para. 6.
[11] Protocol No. 2 to the Convention for the Protection of Human Rights and Fundamental Freedoms, conferring upon the European Court of Human Rights competence to give advisory opinions, ETS 44.

Article 4

The powers of the Court under Article 55 of the Convention shall extend to the drawing up of such rules and the determination of such procedure as the Court may think necessary for the purposes of this Protocol.

Articles 1 to 4 of Protocol No. 2 did not assume consecutive numbers within the Convention itself, although from the moment the Protocol entered into force they were deemed to be provisions of the Convention.[12]

Protocol No. 11 incorporated the provisions of Protocol No. 2 into the Convention itself. As amended, articles 47 to 49 are 'virtually identical' to articles 1, 2, 3(2), and 3(4) of Protocol No. 2.[13] The word 'two-thirds' in article 1(3) of Protocol No. 2 was deleted in article 47(3), a consequence of a change made by Protocol No. 10 to article 32 of the Convention. Also, mention of the Commission was removed in article 47. The reference to the plenary Court in Article 3(1) of Protocol No. 2 was changed to the Grand Chamber. The headings of the three provisions were also added by Protocol No. 11.

Analysis and interpretation

The Committee of Ministers waited more than thirty years after the entry into force of the procedure before requesting an advisory opinion.[14] Over the years there were complaints that Protocol No. 2 was for all practical purposes inert. At one point, the Committee of Experts suggested that if the scope of the consultative opinion jurisdiction was not expanded in order to make it more effective, the alternative might be to repeal Protocol No.2 altogether.[15] There were occasional attempts to invoke the procedure. In 1972, the Netherlands asked the Committee of Ministers to request an opinion concerning proposed legislation on military discipline. The Committee decided not to pursue this, given objections from some governments about whether this really fell within the scope of Protocol No. 2, given the exceptions it contained.[16] In 1983, the Committee of Ministers also considered whether to request an opinion about the scope of its role under the Convention, although in the end it abandoned the idea.[17]

The first application for an advisory opinion was submitted by the Committee of Ministers on 9 January 2002. It was provoked by a Recommendation from the Parliamentary Assembly addressed to the Committee of Ministers to seek the Court's opinion on the relationship between the European Convention and the Convention on Human Rights adopted by the Commonwealth of Independent States.[18] A second request concerned a conflict between Malta and the Parliamentary Assembly, when the former failed to submit the name of a woman on its list of candidates for election as a judge of the Court. The Committee of Ministers formulated the request after being asked to do so by

---

[12] Ibid., para. 1.

[13] Explanatory Report on Protocol No. 11, para. 107.

[14] Decision on the Competence of the Court to Give an Advisory Opinion [GC], §§ 1, 15, 21, ECHR 2004-VI.

[15] Andrew Drzemczewski, 'Protocol No. 2, Article 1-4', in Pettiti et al., *La Convention européenne*, pp. 1028–36, at p. 1031.

[16] Documents of the Parliamentary Assembly, 1972–1973, Vol. 1, no. 3 117, pp. 13–14.

[17] Andrew Drzemczewski, 'Protocol No. 2, Article 1-4', in Pettiti et al., *La Convention européenne*, pp. 1028–36, at p. 1035.

[18] Recommendation 1519 (2001).

the Maltese government.[19] The third concerned whether a State could withdraw a list of candidates for judgeship that it had already submitted from the election process by the Parliamentary Assembly.[20] Like the first request, it was instigated by a Recommendation of the Parliamentary Assembly.[21]

In the case law, there is a hint that even when the request meets the criteria set out in article 47, the Court has a degree of discretion as whether or not to issue the advisory opinion. In the second request, after discussing the jurisdictional issues the Court said that it 'considers it appropriate to give a ruling on this question in the interests of the proper functioning of the Convention system, as there is a need to ensure that the situation which gave rise to the request for an opinion does not cause a blockage in the system'.[22] The fact that article 47 begins with the words 'the Court may...' adds weight to the suggestion that the Court has the discretion not to provide an advisory opinion. The language is very similar to what appears in article 65(1) of the Statute of the International Court of Justice, the provision governing advisory opinions before that body.[23] Although the International Court of Justice has never refused a request for an advisory opinion, it has regularly noted that it is a 'permissive' or 'discretionary' function.[24]

Neither Protocol No. 2 nor the amended provisions derived from it that were introduced to the Convention by Protocol No. 11 consider whether or not advisory opinions are 'binding'. At the International Court of Justice, where the Statute is also silent on the point, the case law supports the position that an advisory opinion is not binding. The rationale for this is that the advisory opinion originates with the General Assembly or the Security Council and not with a State; thus the binding or non-binding nature does not arise.[25]

Article 5 of the new Protocol No. 16, not yet in force, states: 'Advisory opinions shall not be binding.' Protocol No. 16 concerns advisory opinions requested by the highest courts at the national level and not by the Committee of Ministers. Even when this provision is in force, following ten ratifications of the Protocol, it would not seem that it could apply to article 47 because Protocol No. 16 is an additional protocol and not an amending protocol. In practice this is of no significance to the extent that advisory opinions under article 47 are not binding in any case. The reason it may have been thought necessary to include the provision in Protocol No. 16 is precisely the same as the reason for interpreting article 47 in the manner explained above.

---

[19] *Advisory opinion on certain legal questions concerning the lists of candidates submitted with a view to the election of judges to the European Court of Human Rights* [GC], §§ 8–14, 12 February 2008.

[20] *Advisory opinion on certain legal questions concerning the lists of candidates submitted with a view to the election of judges to the European Court of Human Rights (no. 2)* [GC], §§ 7–18, 22 January 2010.

[21] Recommendation 1875 (2009).

[22] *Advisory opinion on certain legal questions concerning the lists of candidates submitted with a view to the election of judges to the European Court of Human Rights* [GC], § 39, 12 February 2008.

[23] Jochen Abr. Frowein and Karin Oellers-Frahm, 'Article 65', in Andreas Zimmermann, Chrstiain Tomuschat, and Karin Oellers-Frahm, eds, *The Statute of the International Court of Justice; A Commentary*, Oxford: Oxford University Press, 2006, pp. 1401–26, at paras 30–42.

[24] *Legality of the Threat or Use of Nuclear Weapons*, Advisory Opinion, I.C.J. Reports 1996, p. 226, § 14; *Legal Consequences of the Construction of a Wall in the Occupied Palestinian Territory*, Advisory Opinion, I.C.J. Reports 2004, p. 136, § 44.

[25] *Interpretation of Peace Treaties*, Advisory Opinion, [1950] I.C.J. Reports 65, p. 76.

Content of advisory opinion

The Explanatory Report on Protocol No. 2 says that the term 'legal question' should be 'understood as having the same meaning as is given to this term in similar international conventions'.[26] The term is used in the provision on advisory opinions in the Statute of the International Court of Justice, as well as in article 96(2) of the Charter of the United Nations.[27] For the International Court of Justice, the expression refers to questions 'framed in terms of law and rais[ing] problems of international law ... [that]. are by their very nature susceptible of a reply based on law ... [and] appear ... to be questions of a legal character'.[28] That a matter may also have political aspects is not sufficient to deny it status as a 'legal question' and thereby 'deprive the Court of a competence expressly conferred on it by its Statute'.[29] The existence of political motives for requesting an opinion and political implications that may result 'are of no relevance in the establishment of its jurisdiction to give such an opinion'.[30] Therefore, '[w]hatever its political aspects, the Court cannot refuse to admit the legal character of a question which invites it to discharge an essentially judicial task, namely, an assessment of the legality of the possible conduct of States with regard to the obligations imposed upon them by international law'.[31]

Accordingly, 'this rules out, on the one hand, questions which would go beyond the mere interpretation of the text and tend by additions, improvements or corrections to modify its substance; and, on the other hand, questions whose solution would in any way involve matters of policy'.[32] Interpreting the provision, the Grand Chamber has turned to the *travaux préparatoires* of Protocol No. 2, from which article 47 originates. It has cited a report presented on behalf of the Legal Committee of the Consultative Assembly:

It is for consideration, consequently, whether the Court should not be given a general jurisdiction to interpret the Convention, which would therefore include matters arising out of the application of the Convention but not resulting from contentious proceedings brought under Article 48.

If the Court is given jurisdiction to give an authoritative interpretation on matters of this sort, it is important to keep it within proper limits. Its new competence should be limited to questions of a legal character. There are no doubt gaps in the Convention which will need to be filled; some of them require legal decisions and might well be left to the Court, but others are of a political character and we should put the Court in a false position if we asked it to take political decisions.

. . .

Within the limits thus laid down, there are a certain number of problems of interpretation of a legal character on which it would be useful to have an authoritative ruling. The following are just

---

[26] Explanatory Report on Protocol No. 2, para. 6.

[27] Statute of the International Court of Justice, art. 65(1).

[28] *Western Sahara*, Advisory Opinion, I.C.J. Reports 1975, p. 18, para. 15.

[29] *Application for Review of Judgement No. 158 of the United Nations Administrative Tribunal*, Advisory Opinion, I.C.J. Reports 1973, p. 172, para. 14; *Application for Review of Judgement No. 158 of the United Nations Administrative Tribunal*, Advisory Opinion, I.C.J. Reports 1973, p. 172, para. 14.

[30] *Legality of the Threat or Use of Nuclear Weapons*, Advisory Opinion, I.C.J. Reports 1996, p. 226 § 13.

[31] *Conditions of Admission of a State to Membership in the United Nations (Article 4 of the Charter)*, Advisory Opinion, I.C.J. Reports 1947–1948, pp. 61–2; *Competence of the General Assembly for the Admission of a State to the United Nations, Advisory Opinion*, I.C.J. Reports 1950, pp. 6–7; *Certain Expenses of the United Nations (Article 17, paragraph 2, of the Charter)*, Advisory Opinion, I.C.J. Reports 1962, p. 155.

[32] Explanatory Report on Protocol No. 2, para. 6.

two examples of problems of a legal character about which the interpretation of the Convention is not clear:

1. Whether a simple majority or an absolute majority is required for the election of the judges under Article 39....
2. The procedure by which the Committee of Ministers should discharge its obligations under Article 32 of the Convention....[33]

These examples, the Grand Chamber has noted, 'illustrate the type of questions which might fall within this general jurisdiction related mainly to procedural points concerning, among other subjects, the election of judges and the procedure followed by the Committee of Ministers in monitoring the execution of judgments'.[34]

The Grand Chamber also referred to discussion in the Committee of Experts, where the utility of the term 'legal' was challenged because 'a question concerning the interpretation of a Convention should be considered as being of necessity a legal one. Conversely, it was said that the use of this term would underline the Committee's desire to exclude any questions whose terms or whose solution would involve matters of policy'.[35] It concluded that the restriction of its advisory opinion jurisdiction to 'legal questions' had been 'stressed' during the drafting of Protocol No. 2, when 'it was decided to maintain the adjective "legal" in order to rule out any jurisdiction on the Court's part regarding matters of policy'.[36]

In the first request for an advisory opinion, the Grand Chamber considered whether a 'legal question' was involved. The Committee of Ministers had referred only in general terms to the coexistence of the European Convention and the Convention on Human Rights of the Commonwealth of Independent States, but the Court took into account the Recommendation of the Parliamentary Assembly that had led to the request. It was clear that the issue was not abstract but rather whether the Commission of the Commonwealth of Independent States could be considered 'another procedure of international investigation or settlement' within the meaning of Article 35(2)(b) of the Convention. The Grand Chamber said it was satisfied 'that the request for an advisory opinion concerns a legal question concerning the interpretation of the Convention'.[37] The second request concerned the rights and obligations of the Parliamentary Assembly in the election of judges pursuant to the provisions of article 22 of the Convention and in the Convention system in general. Thus, concluded the Court, 'whatever its implications, it is of a legal character and as such falls within the scope of the Court's jurisdiction under Article 47 § 1 of the Convention'.[38]

---

[33] Doc. 1061 of 24 November 1959, cited in: *Advisory opinion on certain legal questions concerning the lists of candidates submitted with a view to the election of judges to the European Court of Human Rights* [GC], § 18, 12 February 2008.

[34] *Advisory opinion on certain legal questions concerning the lists of candidates submitted with a view to the election of judges to the European Court of Human Rights* [GC], § 37, 12 February 2008; *Advisory opinion on certain legal questions concerning the lists of candidates submitted with a view to the election of judges to the European Court of Human Rights (no. 2)* [GC], § 29, 22 January 2010.

[35] *Advisory opinion on certain legal questions concerning the lists of candidates submitted with a view to the election of judges to the European Court of Human Rights* [GC], § 19, 12 February 2008; *Advisory opinion on certain legal questions concerning the lists of candidates submitted with a view to the election of judges to the European Court of Human Rights (no. 2)* [GC], § 29, 22 January 2010.

[36] *Advisory opinion on certain legal questions concerning the lists of candidates submitted with a view to the election of judges to the European Court of Human Rights* [GC], § 36, 12 February 2008.

[37] *Decision on the Competence of the Court to Give an Advisory Opinion* [GC], § 24, ECHR 2004-VI.

[38] *Advisory opinion on certain legal questions concerning the lists of candidates submitted with a view to the election of judges to the European Court of Human Rights* [GC], § 38, 12 February 2008.

The second condition set out in paragraph 1 of article 47 is that the request for an advisory opinion directed to 'the interpretation of the Convention and the Protocols thereto'. In the second advisory request, one of the questions concerned whether two resolutions of the Parliamentary Assembly were in breach of its responsibilities under article 22 of the Convention concerning the examination of a list of candidates for judgeship. The Court said that '[i]n so far as this question ultimately concerns the effects of the two Parliamentary Assembly resolutions in question, the Court has doubts as to whether it relates solely to "the interpretation of the Convention and the Protocols thereto" within the meaning of Article 47 § 1"'.[39] Under the circumstances, it did not find it necessary to answer this part of the request. The Court returned to the issue in the third advisory opinion where one of the questions it was asked was about the compatibility of resolutions of the Parliamentary Assembly with the European Convention. It said it could not exclude the possibility that it might, in certain circumstances 'be called upon to interpret one or more provisions of an instrument such as the one cited in this instance in order to clarify its answers to questions on which an advisory opinion has been sought from it'. But it said it could not 'express a view on the compatibility with the Convention of such provisions themselves' because this would not involve an advisory opinion about 'the interpretation of the Convention and the protocols thereto'.[40]

Limitations (art. 47(2))

Paragraph 2 of article 47 imposes two limitations on the scope of a legal question that may be the object of an advisory opinion. According to the Court, 'the purpose of the provisions excluding its advisory jurisdiction is to avoid the potential situation in which the Court adopts in an advisory opinion a position which might prejudice its later examination of an application brought under Articles 33 or 34 of the Convention'.[41] In this respect, the Court cited the *travaux préparatoires* of Protocol No. 2, where it was stated that it was necessary 'to ensure that the Court shall never be placed in the difficult position of being required, as the result of a request for its opinion, to make a direct or indirect pronouncement on a legal point with which it might subsequently have to deal as a main consideration in some case brought before it'.[42]

In submissions to the Court respecting the first advisory opinion, some governments contended that the Court was not prevented from issuing an advisory opinion because the request was not related to a specific application pending before it. To that argument, the Grand Chamber noted the wording of article 47(2), speaking of 'such proceedings as could be instituted in accordance with the Convention', emphasizing the word 'could'. It said it was 'irrelevant that such an application has not and may never be lodged'. The Explanatory Report had spoken of proceedings that were 'past, present, future or merely hypothetical', the Court noted.[43] Consequently, the Grand Chamber considered 'that it suffices to exclude its advisory jurisdiction that the legal question submitted to it is one

[39] Ibid., § 40.
[40] *Advisory opinion on certain legal questions concerning the lists of candidates submitted with a view to the election of judges to the European Court of Human Rights (no. 2)* [GC], § 30, 22 January 2010.
[41] *Decision on the Competence of the Court to Give an Advisory Opinion* [GC], § 28, ECHR 2004-VI.
[42] CM(61)91.
[43] *Decision on the Competence of the Court to Give an Advisory Opinion* [GC], § 28, ECHR 2004-VI.

which it might be called upon to address in the future in the exercise of its primary judicial function, that is in the examination of the admissibility or merits of a concrete case'.[44]

The first of the two restrictions or exclusions set out in paragraph 2 consists of 'any question relating to the content or scope of the rights or freedoms defined in Section I of the Convention and the Protocols thereto'. According to the Explanatory Report on Protocol No. 2, the object of this limitation 'is to prevent exercise of the consultative competence of the Court in questions which could come within the Court's primary function, namely, its judicial function'.[45] The Report said the reasons for this limitation were 'self-evident'.[46]

The second limitation in article 47(2) concerns 'any other question which the Court or the Committee of Ministers might have to consider'. The Explanatory Report on Protocol No. 2 noted the intent to 'exclude all questions of substance which, while they do not concern the content or scope of the rights and freedoms, involve obligations on the Contracting Parties'.[47] A detailed discussion of this provision was provided in the Explanatory Report:

In the first place the Committee intended to exclude all questions of substance which, while they do not concern the content or scope of the rights and freedoms, involve obligations on the Contracting Parties.

Thus, Article 25, paragraph 1 [now article 34 *in fine*] of the Convention in fine provides that Contracting Parties which have recognised the right of individual application undertake not to hinder in any way the effective exercise of this right.

Article 57 [now article 52] stipulates that Contracting Parties must furnish, on request from the Secretary General, an explanation of the manner in which their internal law ensures the effective implementation of any of the provisions of the Convention.

According to Article 24 [now article 33] of the Convention any Contracting Party may refer to the Commission "any alleged breach" of the provisions of the Convention by another Contracting Party. Owing to the general terms in which this provision is cast, it would be possible for the bodies provided for by the Convention to have to consider breaches of the Convention which do not necessarily result from a violation of the rights and freedoms defined in Section 1 of the Convention and the Protocols, namely, violations of Articles 25, paragraph 1 and 57.

The Committee also intended to rule out questions of competence or of procedure which might come before one of the bodies provided for by the Convention in consequence of the institution of proceedings.

Thus, for example, the consultative competence of the Court does not extend to questions regarding the conditions of admissibility of applications before the Commission, which are defined in Articles 26 and 27 of the Convention.

The Committee has employed the phrase in French 'par suite de l'introduction d'un recours' ('in consequence of... proceedings') rather than the phrase 'à l'occasion de l'introduction d'un recours' ('in the course of proceedings') because it considered that the latter phrase was too wide.

The questions which are excluded are those which the Commission, the Court or the Committee of Ministers might have to consider in consequence of the institution of proceedings provided for in the Convention whether such proceedings are past, present, future or merely hypothetical.

In its first advisory opinion, the Court considered as a preliminary matter whether the request from the Committee of Ministers about the coexistence of the European

---

[44] Ibid.
[45] Explanatory Report on Protocol No. 2, para. 9.
[46] Ibid., para. 9.
[47] Ibid., para. 11.

Convention and the Convention on Human Rights of the Commonwealth of Independent States might fall under this exception. The submissions of the many States Parties that intervened in the proceedings were relatively divided on the point.[48] The Court noted that the notion of 'any other question' could only refer to questions that did not relate to the content or scope of the rights set out in the Convention and its Protocols because this was explicitly ruled out by the first exclusion defined in article 47(2).[49] The Court turned to the extensive discussion of the scope of the second exclusion in article 47(2) found in the Explanatory Report on Protocol No. 2, cited above, and notably to the statement that 'the consultative competence of the Court does not extend to questions regarding the conditions of admissibility'.[50] Yet the heart of the legal question that was asked by Committee of Ministers concerned a matter of admissibility, and the Court concluded that as a result it did not have jurisdiction to issue an advisory opinion.

Procedure

Technical requirements concerning the request for an advisory opinion are set out in further detail in the Rules of Court.[51]

As an exception to the general principle that intervention in proceedings is by application and remains at the discretion of the President, the Rules of Court require that the Registrar inform States Parties that they are entitled to submit written comments.[52] There is no right, however, to an oral hearing. Holding an oral hearing is at the discretion of the President.[53] In the three advisory opinion requests that have come before the Court there has been no oral hearing.[54]

Under Protocol No. 2, a request for an advisory opinion required a two-thirds majority vote of the representatives entitled to sit on the Committee of Ministers,[55] replicating the norm in article 32 of the original text of the Convention concerning the special majority required in the Committee of Ministers for adoption of a report of the Commission. Article 32 of the 1950 text of the Convention was amended by Protocol No. 10 so as to provide for a simple majority.[56] This was described by the Explanatory Report as a 'logical development of the Convention's system of control' intended to ensure that all three control organs would take decision by means of a simple majority.[57] Perhaps the rule in Protocol No. 2 had been forgotten. In any event, a few years later, with the adoption of Protocol No. 11, the two-thirds majority required for an advisory opinion was also amended.[58]

---

[48] *Decision on the Competence of the Court to Give an Advisory Opinion* [GC], §§ 22–23, ECHR 2004-VI.
[49] Ibid., § 27.
[50] Ibid., § 28.
[51] Rules of Court, Rules 82–86.
[52] Ibid., Rule 84(2).
[53] Ibid., Rule 86.
[54] *Decision on the Competence of the Court to Give an Advisory Opinion* [GC], § 5, ECHR 2004-VI; *Advisory opinion on certain legal questions concerning the lists of candidates submitted with a view to the election of judges to the European Court of Human Rights* [GC], § 6, 12 February 2008; *Advisory opinion on certain legal questions concerning the lists of candidates submitted with a view to the election of judges to the European Court of Human Rights (no. 2)* [GC], § 5, 22 January 2010.
[55] Explanatory Report on Protocol No. 2, para. 8.
[56] Protocol No. 10 to the Convention for the Protection of Human Rights and Fundamental Freedoms, ETS 146, art. 1.
[57] Explanatory Report on Protocol No. 10, para. 6.
[58] Explanatory Report on Protocol No. 11, para. 107.

The advisory opinion is issued by the Grand Chamber in accordance with article 31(c) of the Convention. At the former Court, the responsibility for consideration of an advisory opinion lay with the plenary Court.[59] The Committee of Experts that drafted Protocol No. 2 had 'considered that the power conferred on the Court to give advisory opinions was such an important one that it ought to be exercised by the Court sitting in plenary session'.[60]

Further reading

Andrew Drzemczewski, 'Protocol No. 2, Article 1-4', in Pettiti et al., *La Convention européenne*, pp. 1028–36.

M.A. Eissen, 'La France et le Protocole no 2 à la Convention européenne des droits de l'homme', in *Mélanges Balladore Pallieri*, Vol. II, Milan: Università Cattolica, 1978, pp. 249–79.

Frowein/Peukert, *MenschenRechtsKonvention*, pp. 611–12.

A.H. Robertson, 'Advisory Opinions of the Court of Human Rights', in Marceau Long and François Monnier, eds, *René Cassin Amicorum Discipulorumque Liber, I, Problèmes de protection international des droits de l'homme*, Paris: Pedone, 1969, pp. 225–40.

Leo Zwaak, 'The Procedure before the European Court of Human Rights', in Van Dijk et al., *Theory and Practice*, pp. 287–90.

---

[59] Protocol No. 2 to the Convention for the Protection of Human Rights and Fundamental Freedoms, conferring upon the European Court of Human Rights competence to give advisory opinions, ETS 44, art. 3(1); Explanatory Report on Protocol No. 11, para. 81.

[60] Explanatory Report on Protocol No. 2, para. 17.

Article 48. Advisory jurisdiction of the Court/Compétence consultative de la Cour

The Court shall decide whether a request for an advisory opinion submitted by the Committee of Ministers is within its competence as defined in Article 47.	La Cour décide si la demande d'avis consultatif présentée par le Comité des Ministres relève de sa compétence telle que définie par l'article 47.

Introductory comments

Article 47 is no more than a specific formulation of the very general principle that a Court may determine its own competence: *kompetenz-kompetenz* or *la compétence de la compétence*. Put otherwise, the Committee of Ministers is not entitled to an advisory opinion from the Court simply because it so requests. The Court must also have jurisdiction, and it has the authority to rule on this issue.

Drafting of the provision

The advisory opinion procedure was introduced into the Convention system by Protocol No. 2. Article 2 of Protocol No. 2 became article 48 of the European Convention as a consequence of Protocol No. 11. The Explanatory Report on Protocol No. 2 indicates that article 2 was itself based upon article 49 of the 1950 text of the Convention: 'in the event of disputes as to whether the Court has jurisdiction, the matter shall be settled by the decision of the court'. Why it was felt necessary to repeat the same notion in the Protocol to the Convention is not explained.[1] According to the Explanatory Report to Protocol No. 2: 'Thus, the Court has both the right and the obligation to refuse a request for an advisory opinion which the Committee of Ministers has asked to give if it comes to the conclusion that the request made is not within the scope of the Court's power as defined in this Agreement.'[2]

Analysis and interpretation

In the first request for an advisory opinion, the Court considered 'in the light of Article 48 of the Convention, that it is required to examine, as a preliminary issue', whether it has jurisdiction to give an advisory opinion.[3] The Grand Chamber sought the views of States Parties in its request for written comments:

Does the Court have jurisdiction to deal with the Committee of Ministers' request (Article 48 of the Convention and Rule 87)? In particular, does the request relate to a question which the Court might

---

[1] Explanatory Report on Protocol No. 2, para. 12.

[2] Ibid. See Andrew Drzemczewski, 'Protocol No. 2, Article 1-4', in Pettiti et al., *La Convention européenne*, pp. 1028–36, at pp. 1028–31.

[3] *Decision on the Competence of the Court to Give an Advisory Opinion* [GC], § 21, ECHR 2004-VI.

have to consider in consequence of any such proceedings which could be instituted before it in accordance with the Convention (Article 47 § 2 of the Convention), and more precisely, in the context of the examination of the admissibility of an individual application under Article 35 § 2 of the Convention?[4]

Several governments replied that the Court did not in fact have competence to issue the advisory opinion requested by the Committee of Ministers,[5] which dealt with whether the European Convention could coexist with the Convention on Human Rights and Fundamental Freedoms of the Commonwealth of Independent States. The Grand Chamber concluded that 'the request for an advisory opinion relates to a question which the Court might have to consider in consequence of proceedings instituted in accordance with the Convention and that it therefore does not have competence to give an advisory opinion on the matter referred to it'.[6]

In the first advisory opinion on lists of candidates for election as judges of the Court, the Grand Chamber dealt with the issue of jurisdiction quite summarily and without any specific reference to article 48. It wrote:

Accordingly, whatever its implications, [the question] is of a legal character and as such falls within the scope of the Court's jurisdiction under Article 47 § 1 of the Convention. Furthermore, it does not appear—nor has any government claimed—that the opinion requested concerns one of the matters excluded from the Court's jurisdiction by the second paragraph of Article 47. Consequently, the Court has jurisdiction to answer the first question.[7]

The Grand Chamber expressed doubts about whether it had jurisdiction to answer the second question, but concluded that the matter was moot given the answer to the first question.[8] In the second advisory opinion, the Court addressed the issue of jurisdiction in a distinct section of its judgment but, once again, did not refer explicitly to article 48.[9]

These decisions tend to confirm the totally superfluous role played by article 48 in the Convention. It merely echoes what is stated in article 32(2) of the Convention with respect to the powers of the Court in a more general sense.

Rule 87(2) of the Rules of Court states: 'If the Grand Chamber considers that the request is not within its competence as defined in Article 47 of the Convention, it shall so declare in a reasoned decision.'

Further reading

Andrew Drzemczewski, 'Protocol No. 2, Article 1-4', in Pettiti et al., *La Convention européenne*, pp. 1028–36.
Frowein/Peukert, *MenschenRechtsKonvention*, p. 614.

---

[4] Ibid.
[5] Ibid., § 22.
[6] Ibid., § 35.
[7] *Advisory opinion on certain legal questions concerning the lists of candidates submitted with a view to the election of judges to the European Court of Human Rights* [GC], § 38, 12 February 2008.
[8] Ibid., § 40.
[9] *Advisory opinion on certain legal questions concerning the lists of candidates submitted with a view to the election of judges to the European Court of Human Rights (no. 2)* [GC], §§ 29–34, 22 January 2010.

A.H. Robertson, 'Advisory Opinions of the Court of Human Rights', in Marceau Long and
    François Monnier, eds, *René Cassin Amicorum Discipulorumque Liber, I, Problèmes de protection
    internationale des droits de l'homme*, Paris: Pedone, 1969, pp. 225–40.
Leo Zwaak, 'The Procedure before the European Court of Human Rights', in Van Dijk et al.,
    Theory and Practice, pp. 287–90.

Article 49. Reasons for advisory opinions/Motivation des avis consultatifs

1. Reasons shall be given for advisory opinions of the Court.	1. L'avis de la Cour est motivé.
2. If the advisory opinion does not represent, in whole or in part, the unanimous opinion of the judges, any judge shall be entitled to deliver a separate opinion.	2. Si l'avis n'exprime pas en tout ou en partie l'opinion unanime des juges, tout juge a le droit d'y joindre l'exposé de son opinion séparée.
3. Advisory opinions of the Court shall be communicated to the Committee of Ministers.	3. L'avis de la Cour est transmis au Comité des Ministres.

Introductory comments

Article 49 is nothing more than a confirmation that the rules applicable to judgments of the Court, set out in articles 45 and 46(2) of the Convention, also apply to advisory opinions.

Drafting of the provision

The text of article 49 is drawn from Protocol No. 2 to the European Convention on Human Rights, which entered into force in 1970. Article 49 was introduced into the Convention by Protocol No. 11. Article 49 is identical to paragraphs 2–4 of article 3 of Protocol No. 2.

Analysis and interpretation

There have been no separate or dissenting opinions in the two advisory opinions issued by the Court. The Court has said that it has been its practice, when issuing advisory opinions, 'to endeavour to speak with one voice'.[1] At the International Court of Justice, when advisory opinions have been issued it is almost *de rigueur* for there to be separate and dissenting opinions. The International Court of Justice has never issued a unanimous advisory opinion. In one advisory opinion, every member of the Court issued a separate or dissenting opinion or made a declaration.[2]

---

[1] Opinion of the European Court of Human Rights on Draft Protocol No. 16 to the European Convention on Human Rights extending its competence to give advisory opinions on the interpretation of the Convention, 6 May 2013, para. 11.

[2] *Legality of the Threat or Use of Nuclear Weapons*, Advisory Opinion, I.C.J. Reports 1996, p. 226.

Further reading

Andrew Drzemczewski, 'Protocol No. 2, Article 1–4', in Pettiti et al., *La Convention européenne*, pp. 1028–36.

Frowein/Peukert, *MenschenRechtsKonvention*, p. 616.

A.H. Robertson, 'Advisory Opinions of the Court of Human Rights', in Marceau Long and François Monnier, eds, *René Cassin Amicorum Discipulorumque Liber, I, Problèmes de protection internationale des droits de l'homme*, Paris: Pedone, 1969, pp. 225–40.

Leo Zwaak, 'The Procedure before the European Court of Human Rights', in Van Dijk et al., *Theory and Practice*, pp. 287–90.

Article 50. Expenditure on the Court/Frais de fonctionnement de la Cour

The expenditure on the Court shall be borne by the Council of Europe.	Les frais de fonctionnement de la Cour sont à la charge du Conseil de l'Europe.

Introductory comments

Given that all Member States of the Council of Europe are also States Parties to the European Convention on Human Rights, and that it is impossible to join without ratifying the Convention, it may seem superfluous to specify that the Council of Europe is responsible for the costs of its human rights Court. But in 1949 and 1950, when a majority of Member States were initially opposed to the Court altogether, and only changed their views when acceptance of the jurisdiction of the Court required an optional declaration, the financial responsibility for the institution was a matter of debate. The Committee of Ministers might well have left the financing of the Court to the States that had accepted the Court's jurisdiction or, alternatively, those States that had ratified the Convention.

Drafting of the provision

The original draft Statute of the European Court of Human Rights proposed by the International Juridical Section of the European Movement included the following provision: 'The expenses of the Court shall be borne by the States parties to the Convention on Human Rights in such manner as they shall decide.'[1] The Consultative Assembly draft did not contain any such provision. The March 1950 draft adopted by the Committee of Experts included this text: 'The expenses of the Commission and the Court shall be borne by the Council of Europe.'[2] It did not undergo any subsequent amendment and was included in the final text of the Convention adopted in November 1950 as article 58.

Pursuant to Protocol No. 11, the provision was renumbered as article 50 and given the title 'Expenditure on the Court'.[3] The Explanatory Report states: 'Article 50 follows closely the text of former Article 58 of the Convention. The "expenditure" on the new Court will include, in addition to items relating to staff and equipment, the salaries and social security contributions which will be paid to or for the judges in lieu of the allowances provided for in former Article 42 of the Convention.'[4]

---

[1] Draft Statute of the European Court of Human Rights, INF/5/E/R, I *TP* 302–21, at p. 312, art. 30.

[2] Appendix to the Report of the Committee of Experts on Human Rights: Draft Convention of Protection of Human Rights and Fundamental Freedoms, 16 March 1950, Doc. C/WP 1 (50) 15 appendix, CM/WP 1 (50) 14 revised, A 925, IV *TP* 50–79, at p. 74, art. 44 (48). See also Proposed final provisions—Section V, Doc. CM/WP 1 (50) 5, A 906, III *TP* 302–3.

[3] Protocol No. 11 to the Convention for the Protection of Human Rights and Fundamental Freedoms, restructuring the control machinery established thereby, ETS 155, art. 2(2).

[4] Explanatory Report on Protocol No. 11, para. 50.

Analysis and interpretation

The European Court of Human Rights does not have a separate budget. It is funded by the Council of Europe, in accordance with article 50, where it comprises a distinct and important component of the overall budget of the Council. The budget of the Council of Europe is approved by the Committee of Ministers.

For the 2014–2015 biennium, the amount budgeted for the European Court of Human Rights was set at about €68 million.[5] Of this sum, about €54 million is taken up in remuneration of the judges and members of the Court's personnel.

Further reading

Johan Callewaert, 'Article 58', in Pettiti et al., *La Convention européenne*, pp. 893–4.
Frowein/Peukert, *MenschenRechtsKonvention*, p. 615.

---

[5] Programme and Budget 2014–2015, CM(2014)1E, p. 21.

Article 51. Privileges and immunities of judges/Privilèges et immunités des juges

The judges shall be entitled, during the exercise of their functions, to the privileges and immunities provided for in Article 40 of the Statute of the Council of Europe and in the agreements made thereunder.	Les juges jouissent, pendant l'exercice de leurs fonctions, des privilèges et immunités prévus à l'article 40 du Statut du Conseil de l'Europe et dans les accords conclus au titre de cet article.

Introductory comments

The Statute of the International Court of Justice states that judges 'when engaged on the business of the Court, shall enjoy diplomatic privileges and immunities'. But the role of a judge is not at all that of a diplomat. The *raison d'être* for the protection of international judges is to ensure their independence and impartiality rather than to promote international comity, which is the usual justification for diplomatic immunity. Judicial immunity is a feature of most domestic legal systems. It ensures that a judge cannot be sued or prosecuted for acts committed in the exercise of the judicial function.

Drafting of the provision

The original draft Statute of the European Court of Human Rights proposed by the International Juridical Section of the European Movement included the following provision: 'The members of the Court, when engaged on the business of the Court, shall enjoy diplomatic privileges and immunities.'[1] The Consultative Assembly draft adopted in September 1949 did not contain detailed provisions on the operation of the Court. There was no provision governing immunities. The Greek delegate to the Committee of Experts that met in February and March 1950 made a proposal in this area but it was not adopted: 'In the exercise of their duties, members of the Court shall enjoy diplomatic privileges and immunities.'[2]

The Convention's provision on privileges and immunities of judges was only added to the draft by the Committee of Ministers at its August 1950 meeting: 'The members of the Commission and of the Court shall be entitled, during the discharge of their functions, to the privileges and immunities provided for in Article 40 of the Statute of the Council of Europe and in the agreements made thereunder.'[3] This became article 59 of the 1950 text of the Convention.

The provision was slightly revised by Protocol No. 11 to take into account the disappearance of the Commission. Instead of '[t]he members of . . . the Court', the current

---

[1] Draft Statute of the European Court of Human Rights, INF/5/E/R, I *TP* 302–21, at p. 306, art. 18.
[2] Amendments to Article 21 and 28 of the Recommendation of the Consultative Assembly proposed by the Greek Expert, Doc. A 811, III *TP* 226–9, art. B.
[3] Draft Convention adopted by the Sub-Committee, Doc. CM 1 (50) 52, A 1884, V *TP* 76–99, at p. 96,

text speaks of '[t]he judges'. It was renumbered as article 51 and given the heading 'Privileges and immunities of judges'.[4]

Analysis and interpretation

According to the Explanatory Report on Protocol No. 11, the word 'agreements' refers to the Fourth Protocol to the General Agreement on Privileges and Immunities of the Council of Europe and any further treaties ratified by States Parties on related subjects.[5] Following adoption of Protocol No. 11 and its signature by all Member States of the Council of Europe, the Committee of Ministers authorized the amendment and consolidation of the Fourth and Fifth Protocols to the General Agreement on Privileges and Immunities of the Council of Europe. The Sixth Protocol was adopted on 9 February 1996. It entered into force on 1 November 1998.[6] Its application to judges of the Court is confirmed by Resolutions of the Committee of Ministers.[7] The Preamble to the Protocol, which applies only to judges of the Court, makes reference to article 51 of the Convention as revised by Protocol No. 11. According to the Sixth Protocol, the immunities that protect judges are those of 'diplomatic envoys in accordance with international law'.[8] They apply to judges of the Court, including *ad hoc* judges, and to their spouses and minor children.[9] The Sixth Protocol also applies to the Registrar and the Deputy Registrar.[10] Other officials of the Court benefit from the provisions of the General Agreement on Privileges and Immunities of the Council of Europe.[11]

Article 51 confirms the immunity of judges because this is an important component of judicial independence. The Court itself has held that national legislation granting immunity to judges manifests 'a long-standing practice intended to ensure the proper administration of justice'.[12] The Sixth Protocol also highlights the rationale for judicial immunity: 'Privileges and immunities are accorded to judges not for the personal benefit of the individuals themselves but in order to safeguard the independent exercise of their functions.'[13] Although it is a functional immunity that applies, according to article 51, 'during the exercise of their functions', it remains effective even after the judge's term is completed.[14]

[4] Protocol No. 11 to the Convention for the Protection of Human Rights and Fundamental Freedoms, restructuring the control machinery established thereby, ETS 155, art. 2(2).

[5] Explanatory Report on Protocol No. 11, para. 111.

[6] Sixth Protocol to the General Agreement on Privileges and Immunities of the Council of Europe, ETS 162. See also Explanatory Report on the Sixth Protocol to the General Agreement on Privileges and Immunities of the Council of Europe.

[7] Resolution CM/Res(2009)5 on the status and conditions of service of judges of the European Court of Human Rights and of the Commissioner for Human Rights, art. 2.

[8] Sixth Protocol to the General Agreement on Privileges and Immunities of the Council of Europe, ETS 162, art. 1.

[9] Ibid., art. 4.

[10] Ibid., art. 5.

[11] General Agreement on Privileges and Immunities of the Council of Europe, ETS 2, art. 18.

[12] *Ernst and Others v. Belgium*, no. 33400/96, § 50, 15 July 2003.

[13] Sixth Protocol to the General Agreement on Privileges and Immunities of the Council of Europe, ETS 162, arts. 1–2.

[14] *Zoernsch v. Waldock*, [1964] 1 WLR 675, [1964] 2 All ER 256.

In 2011, Romanian authorities searched the house of judge Corneliu Bîrsan as part of an investigation into corruption concerning the judge's spouse, a judge at the national level. On 19 October 2011, the President of the Court issued a statement of concern:

The immunities of the judges of the European Court of Human Rights are provided for in the Sixth Protocol to the General Agreement on Privileges and Immunities of the Council of Europe and Article 51 of the European Convention on Human Rights. Immunities extend also to their spouses and minor children.

Such immunities are an essential component of judicial independence under the rule of law and attach to judges of every international court. In the specific context of the European Convention on Human Rights they must operate so as to allow judges to carry out their duties in accordance with the independence and impartiality required of them by that instrument.

The Court is concerned that in carrying out a search in the home of the Romanian judge as part of an inquiry concerning allegations about his wife the rules on immunity may not have been respected. The Court has requested the Romanian Government to indicate whether they have grounds for asking the Court to waive the judge's immunity. Under the terms of Article 4 of the Sixth Protocol only the plenary Court is empowered to waive a judge's immunity.

At the present time no request for a waiver of the immunity has been presented to the Court.[15]

Shortly thereafter, Romania asked for a waiver of the judge's immunity. The plenary Court's authority to waive immunity under the Sixth Protocol is formulated as a duty as well as a right, to be exercise 'where, in its opinion, the immunity would impede the course of justice, and where it can be waived without prejudice to the purpose for which the immunity is accorded'.[16] In a decision issued on 29 November 2011, the plenary Court agreed to waive immunity for the judge's spouse but not for himself, and only to the extent that this was 'strictly necessary for the investigation'. With respect to Judge Bîrsan, the plenary Court said it was 'not satisfied that the immunity would impede the course of justice or that the immunity could be waived without prejudice to the purpose for which it is accorded'. The waiver was without retroactive effect, thereby confirming that the initial search was contrary to Protocol No. 6.[17]

Further reading

Johan Callewaert, 'Article 59', in Pettiti et al., *La Convention européenne*, pp. 895–6.
Frowein/Peukert, *MenschenRechtsKonvention*, p. 616.

---

[15] Statement by the President of the European Court of Human Rights, ECHR 200 (2011), 19 October 2011.

[16] Sixth Protocol to the General Agreement on Privileges and Immunities of the Council of Europe, ETS 162, art. 4.

[17] Press release, ECHR 265 (2011), 29 November 2011.

SECTION III
MISCELLANEOUS PROVISIONS

Article 52. Inquiries by the Secretary General/Enquêtes du Secrétaire Général

On receipt of a request from the Secretary General of the Council of Europe any High Contracting Party shall furnish an explanation of the manner in which its internal law ensures the effective implementation of any of the provisions of the Convention.

Toute Haute Partie contractante fournira sur demande du Secrétaire Général du Conseil de l'Europe les explications requises sur la manière dont son droit interne assure l'application effective de toutes les dispositions de cette Convention.

Introductory comments

The role of the Secretary General of the Council of Europe within the European Convention on Human Rights is essentially confined to administrative functions. In particular, as depositary of the treaty itself, the Secretary General receives notifications of derogation, territorial application, denunciation, ratification, and legislation authorizing capital punishment in time of war. The Secretary General's responsibility as depositary, only implicit in the Convention itself, is spelled out in detail in the Protocols.

The position of Secretary General is established by article 38 of the Statute of the Council of Europe. The Secretary General is appointed by the Parliamentary Assembly upon the recommendation of the Committee of Ministers. The description of the responsibilities of the position in the Statute is quite vague, stating only that the Secretary General 'is responsible to the Committee of Ministers for the work of the Secretariat' and that he or she shall 'provide such secretariat and other assistance as the [Parliamentary] Assembly may require'. Although the Secretary General's powers are not clearly defined, in practice the office holder has overall responsibility for the strategic management of the Council of Europe's work programme and budget. The Secretary General also oversees the day-to-day running of the organization and Secretariat.

Article 52 is a rather exceptional provision and can in no way be considered to be implicit in the Secretary General's status as depositary of the Convention. Nothing comparable to this power exists with respect to the role of the Secretary General of the United Nations in the implementation of that body's human rights treaties.

Drafting of the provision

The text of article 52 originates from a proposal by the United Kingdom at the February 1950 session of the Committee of Experts: 'On receipt of a request to this effect from the Secretary General of the Council of Europe, made under the authority of the Resolution of the Consultative Assembly of the Council of Europe the Government of any party to this Convention shall supply an explanation as to the manner in which the law of that State gives effect to any of the provisions of this Convention.'[1] The text was identical in

<hr />

[1] Amendments to Articles 4 and 7 of the Recommendation of the Consultative Assembly proposed by the Expert of the United Kingdom, Doc. A 782, III *TP* 188–91.

substance to one considered the previous year by the United Nations Commission on Human Rights for inclusion in the draft covenant.[2] The Commission had voted to postpone consideration of the text and, in the end, no such provision was included in either of the Covenants.

The British proposal was accepted by the Committee of Experts but with the deletion of the reference to a resolution of the Consultative Assembly: 'On receipt of a request to that effect from the Secretary General of the Council of Europe the Government of any State Party to this Convention shall supply an explanation of the manner in which the law of that State gives effect to any of the provisions in this Convention.'[3] The Committee's report said that the provision 'tends to strengthen the safeguards of the rights listed in the Convention'.[4]

The text was left unchanged and without comment by the Committee of Senior Officials, although it was moved to the final provisions of the Convention.[5] It became article 57 in the final text adopted in November 1950.

The provision was renumbered as article 52 and the heading 'Inquiries by the Secretary General' was added according to the provisions of Protocol No. 11.[6]

Analysis and interpretation

The European Convention on Human Rights authorizes the Secretary General of the Council of Europe to request that a State Party furnish an explanation of the manner in which its internal law ensures the effective implementation of any of the provisions of the Convention. The language used—'furnish an explanation'—is rather imperative, an impression that is further enhanced by the title given to the provision as a result of the amendments contained in Protocol No. 11: 'Inquiries by the Secretary General.'

Although it has been compared to the reporting procedures provided for under various human rights treaties, including the European Social Charter, the 'unique characteristic feature is the fact that the Secretary General's power to request explanations under Article 52 is discretionary in nature'.[7] The Secretary General is free to determine the nature of the

---

[2] Report of the Fifth Session of the Commission on Human Rights to the Economic and Social Council, UN Doc. E/1371, E/CN.4/350, pp. 28–9.

[3] Appendix to the Report of the Committee of Experts on Human Rights: Draft Convention of Protection of Human Rights and Fundamental Freedoms, 16 March 1950, Doc. C/WP 1 (50) 15 appendix, CM/WP 1 (50) 14 revised, A 925, IV *TP* 50–79, at p. 66, art. 12(16). See also New articles, Doc. CM/WP 1 (50) 9, A 910, III *TP* 306–9; Preliminary Draft Convention, Doc. CM/WP 1 (50) 14, A 932, III *TP* 312–35, at p. 324–6, art. 16(12).

[4] Report to the Committee of Ministers submitted by the Committee of Experts Instructed to Draw Up a Draft Convention of Collective Guarantee of Human Rights and Fundamental Freedoms, Doc. CM/WP 1 (5) 15, A 924, IV *TP* 2–55, at p. 34.

[5] Text of the report submitted by the Conference [of Senior Officials] to the Committee of Ministers, Doc. CM/WP 4 (50) 19, CM/WP 4 (50) 16 rev., A 1431, IV *TP* 242–73, at p. 262. Also New draft alternatives B and B/2, Doc. CM/WP 4 (50) 9, A 1372, IV *TP* 182–91, at p. 190; Draft Convention annexed to the Report, Doc. CM/WP 4 (50) 19 annex, CM/WP 4 (50) rev., A 1452, IV *TP* 274–95, at p. 292, art. 56; Text of the report submitted by the Conference to the Committee of Ministers, Doc. CM/WP 4 (50) 19, CM/WP 4 (50) 16 rev., A 1431, IV *TP* 242–73, at p. 270.

[6] Protocol No. 11 to the Convention for the Protection of Human Rights and Fundamental Freedoms, restructuring the control machinery established thereby, ETS 155, art. 2(2).

[7] Consolidated Report containing an Analysis of the Correspondence between the Secretary General of the Council of Europe and the Russian Federation under Article 52 of the European Convention on Human

request and the States to whom it is directed. Moreover, nothing in article 52 prevents the Secretary General from addressing the request to a single State Party.[8]

The procedure has only rarely been invoked. On nine occasions, the Secretary General directed a request on the basis of article 52. All but two of the requests have been directed to all States Parties to the Convention: on the manner in which their internal law ensures the effective implementation of any of the provisions of this Convention, 9 October 1964; on the application of the Convention and its first Protocol, 10 September 1965; on the right to compensation (art. 5(5)), 23 July 1970; on articles 8, 9, 10, and 11, 9 April 1975; on the implementation of the Convention in respect of children and young persons placed in care, 25 March 1983; on fair trial proceedings, 7 July 1988; and on secret detention sites in Europe related to CIA activities, 21 November 2005. On 13 December 1999, a request was directed to Russia concerning implementation of the Convention in Chechnya. On 4 February 2002, a request was directed to Moldova concerning implementation of the Convention on its territory.

When article 52 was first invoked by the Secretary General, in 1964, he made a statement about its scope. The Secretary General explained that the purpose of article 52 was to strengthen the protection of the rights provided for by the Convention and that, in the minds of the drafters it 'was apparently of particular importance'. He noted that the wording of the provision had been taken from the draft human rights Covenant then under discussion within the United Nations Commission on Human Rights. According to the United Nations draft, the Secretary General of the United Nations had a 'right of interrogation' but only on the basis of a resolution of the General Assembly. The requirement of such authorization was not retained in the European Convention. The Secretary General said the wording of article 52 was 'absolutely clear and unequivocal', noting that as a corollary the States Parties are under an obligation to provide the explanation requested. He said that when invoking article 52, the Secretary General would be 'acting on his own responsibility and at his own discretion, in virtue of powers conferred upon him by the Convention independently of any powers he may have in virtue of the Statute of the Council of Europe'. This power of the Secretary General 'is not subject to control or instruction'. He said that while it may have been wise not to use the power in the early years of the Convention, 'the time is now ripe for a modest beginning to be made in developing the procedure'.[9]

Decades later, the Secretary General described the obligations placed upon States Parties when they receive a request under article 52:

The State has the obligation to provide truthful explanations. It appears clearly from the wording of Article 52 that this obligation is unconditional. The scope of the obligation is defined by Article 52 itself. The State must furnish the requested explanations about 'the manner in which its internal law ensures the effective implementation of any of the provisions of this Convention'. The State has an obligation of result to provide explanations about the effective implementation of the Convention in its internal law: the State cannot, therefore, confine itself to providing explanations of a formal nature. On the contrary, bearing in mind also the obligation to execute treaty obligations in good

---

Rights, Prepared by Mr Tamas Bán, Mr Frédéric Sudre, and Mr Pieter Van Dijk, SG/Inf(2000)24, 26 June 2000, para. 4.

[8] Ibid.

[9] Statement by the Secretary General on Article 57 of the European Human Rights Convention, (1964) 7 YB 38–43.

faith (Article 26 of the Vienna Convention on the Law of Treaties of 23 May 1969), a State has the obligation to furnish precise and adequate explanations which make it possible to verify whether the Convention is actually implemented in its internal law. This necessarily implies that the State must furnish information of a sufficiently detailed nature about the national law and the practice of the national authorities, in particular the judicial authorities, and about their conformity with the Convention as interpreted in the case-law of the European Court of Human Rights (hereinafter 'the Court'). The case-law has given a concrete expression to the rights and freedoms laid down in the Convention and has specified the conditions for an effective application of the rights guaranteed by the Convention: as the European Court of Human Rights has stated: 'The Convention is intended to guarantee not rights that are theoretical or illusory but rights that are practical and effective' (*Airey* judgment of 9 October 1979, Series A, No. 32, paragraph 24).[10]

The Secretary General considers that '[i]t goes without saying that under Article 52 States Parties are also bound to provide the explanations requested by the time-limit indicated in the request, provided that the time given is not unreasonably short in relation to the scope of the explanations sought'.[11]

With respect to the request directed at Russia concerning application of the Convention in Chechnya, three independent experts concluded 'that replies given were not adequate and that the Russian Federation has failed in its legal obligations as a Contracting State under Article 52 of the Convention'.[12] The most recent of the requests, relating to allegations of secret detention sites operated by the CIA in European States, have been discussed in judgments of the Court. Poland replied on 10 March 2006 indicating that 'findings of the Polish Government's internal enquiry into the alleged existence in Poland of secret detention centres and related over flights fully deny the allegations in the debate'.[13] The Court concluded that 'Poland knew of the nature and purposes of the CIA's activities on its territory at the material time and that, by enabling the CIA to use its airspace and the airport, by its complicity in disguising the movements of rendition aircraft and by its provision of logistics and services, including the special security arrangements, the special procedure for landings, the transportation of the CIA teams with detainees on land, and the securing of the Stare Kiejkuty base for the CIA's secret detention, Poland cooperated in the preparation and execution of the CIA rendition, secret detention and interrogation operations on its territory'.[14] Macedonia answered the request of the Secretary General with specific information about the case of Khaled El-Masri, indicating that he had been allowed to enter the country on 31 December 2003 and that he 'left the Republic of Macedonia on 23 January 2004 at the Blace border

---

[10] Report by the Secretary General on the Use of his Powers under Article 52 of the European Convention on Human Rights, in the light of reports suggesting that individuals, notably persons suspected of involvement in acts of terrorism, may have been arrested and detained, or transported while deprived of their liberty, by or at the instigation of foreign agencies, with the active or passive co-operation of States Parties to the Convention or by States Parties themselves at their own initiative, without such deprivation of liberty having been acknowledged, SG/Inf (2006) 5, 28 February 2006, para. 12.

[11] Ibid., para. 13.

[12] Consolidated Report containing an Analysis of the Correspondence between the Secretary General of the Council of Europe and the Russian Federation under Article 52 of the European Convention on Human Rights, Prepared by Mr Tamas Bán, Mr Frédéric Sudre, and Mr Pieter Van Dijk, SG/Inf(2000)24 26 June 2000, para. 32.

[13] *Al Nashiri v. Poland*, no. 28761/11, § 242, 24 July 2014; *Husayn (Abu Zubaydah) v. Poland*, no. 7511/13, § 236, 24 July 2014.

[14] *Al Nashiri v. Poland*, no. 28761/11, § 442, 24 July 2014; *Husayn (Abu Zubaydah) v. Poland*, no. 7511/13, § 444, 24 July 2014.

crossing to the State Union of Serbia and Montenegro (on the Kosovo section)'.[15] In judgment of the Court, both submissions were rejected as being untrue. The Grand Chamber accepted the applicant's version that he had been 'subjected to extraordinary rendition by CIA agents assisted, to a large extent, by agents of the respondent State' and that he did not leave Macedonia voluntarily, as the report to the Secretary General had claimed.[16]

Further reading

Frowein/Peukert, *MenschenRechtsKonvention*, pp. 617–18.

Monica Hakimi, 'The Council of Europe Addresses CIA Rendition and Detention Program', (2007) 101 *AJIL* 442.

Paul Mahoney, 'Does Article 57 of the European Convention on Human Rights Serve Any Useful Purpose?', in F. Matscher and H. Petzold, eds, *Protecting Human Rights: The European Dimension*, Cologne: Carl Heymanns, 1988, pp. 373–93.

Jeroen Schokkenbroek, 'The Supervisory Function of the Secretary General of the Council of Europe', in Van Dijk et al., *Theory and Practice*, pp. 323–32.

---

[15] *El Masri v. 'the former Yugoslav Republic of Macedonia'* [GC], no. 39630/09, § 39, ECHR 2012.
[16] Ibid., §§ 149, 167.

Article 53. Safeguard for existing human rights/Sauvegarde des droits de l'homme reconnus

Nothing in this Convention shall be construed as limiting or derogating from any of the human rights and fundamental freedoms which may be ensured under the laws of any High Contracting Party or under any other agreement to which it is a Party.

Aucune des dispositions de la présente Convention ne sera interprétée comme limitant ou portant atteinte aux droits de l'homme et aux libertés fondamentales qui pourraient être reconnus conformément aux lois de toute Partie contractante ou à toute autre Convention à laquelle cette Partie contractante est partie.

Introductory comments

The title 'Safeguard for existing human rights', which was only added to article 53 in the 1990s as a result of Protocol No. 11 and did not appear in the original 1950 version of the Convention, suggests that this is a kind of 'savings clause' intended to protect pre-existing human rights. The French title is probably closer to the real meaning of article 53, making clear that the Convention cannot be interpreted so as to limit or derogate from rights recognized by other sources in national or international law. The text was based on a British proposal in the United Nations Commission on Human Rights[1] that, as modified, became article 5(2) of the International Covenant on Civil and Political Rights. According to article 5(2) of the Covenant: 'There shall be no restriction upon or derogation from any of the fundamental human rights recognised or existing in any State Party to the present Covenant pursuant to law, conventions, regulations or custom on the pretext that the present Covenant does not recognize such rights or that it recognizes them to a lesser extent.'

Similar provisions are also present in other international treaties. For example, article 1 of the 1984 Convention against Torture and Other Cruel, Inhuman or Degrading Treatment or Punishment states: 'This article is without prejudice to any international instrument or national legislation which does or may contain provisions of wider application.' According to article 23 of the Convention on the Elimination of All Forms of Discrimination Against Women: 'Nothing in the present Convention shall affect any provisions that are more conducive to the achievement of equality between men and women which may be contained: (a) In the legislation of a State Party; or (b) In any other international convention, treaty or agreement in force for that State.'

Drafting of the provision

Article 53 originated in an Italian proposal to the February 1950 session of the Committee of Experts: 'This Convention shall in no way affect the rights and obligations arising

---

[1] UN Doc. E/CN.4/317: 'Nothing in this Covenant may be construed as limiting or derogating from any of the rights and freedoms which may be guaranteed to all under the law of any contracting State or any conventions to which it is a party.'

from the conventions in force between the High Contracting Parties.'[2] At the March session, the United Kingdom adopted the concept, submitting an amended version: 'Nothing in this Convention shall be construed as limiting or derogating from any of the rights and freedoms which may be guaranteed under the laws of any State party to the Convention or under any other agreement to which it is a party.'[3] It was incorporated in the draft adopted by the Committee of Experts.[4] The commentary noted that it reproduced the United Kingdom proposal and that '[t]he experts unanimously considered that the precisions given by this Article were necessary'.[5] As drafted by the Committee of Experts, it became article 60 of the text adopted in November 1950.

The provision was renumbered as article 53 and the heading 'Safeguard for existing human rights' added by Protocol No. 11.[6]

Analysis and interpretation

By virtue of article 53, the Convention cannot be interpreted so as to prejudice the protection of human rights enshrined in the national law of a State Party or as a result of agreements to which it is a party. In one of the very rare references to the provision, Judge Wojtyczek wrote:

> The Convention clearly envisages in this provision a situation in which different instruments may provide a higher level of protection than the Convention itself. Such a situation cannot be seen as an example of fragmentation, let alone of incoherence, of international law. The nature of the Convention as a minimum standard for a limited catalogue of rights limits the risk of contradictions with other treaties. A situation in which other treaties guarantee broader rights or offer a higher standard of protection of the same rights cannot be seen as a conflict of treaties. Nor does it change per se the scope of the rights protected under the Convention. While there is no doubt that the Convention has to be interpreted in the context of other rules of international law, the scope of its protection does not automatically align on the highest standard set up by other rules of international law binding the Parties to the Convention.[7]

In one case, involving article 10 of the Convention, the Court dismissed the argument of the applicant that the provision was narrower than article 25 of the Belgian constitution.[8]

---

[2] Amendments to various articles of the Recommendation of the Consultative Assembly proposed by the Italian Expert, Doc. A 812, III *TP* 228–31, Art. 1.

[3] New articles, Doc. CM/WP 1 (50) 9, A 910, III *TP* 306–309; Amendments to Articles 1, 2, 4, 5, 6, 8, and 9 of the Committee's Preliminary Draft Proposal by the Expert of the United Kingdom, Doc. CM/WP 1 (50) 2, A 915, III *TP* 280–9, at p. 288, art. 15; Amendments to the British draft proposed by the Drafting Committee composed of Sir Oscar Dowson, MM le Quesne, Dons Moeller, and Salén, Doc. CM/WP 1 (50) 10, p. 3, A 919, III *TP* 288–95, at p. 294, art. 15.

[4] Appendix to the Report of the Committee of Experts to the Committee of Ministers—Draft Convention (16 March 1950), Doc. CM/WP 1 (50) 14 revised, A 925, IV *TP* 50–79, at p. 76, art. 46(5). See also Preliminary Draft Convention, Doc. CM/WP 1 (50) 14, A 932, III *TP* 312–35, at p. 334, art. 51(47).

[5] Report to the Committee of Ministers submitted by the Committee of Experts Instructed to Draw Up a Draft Convention of Collective Guarantee of Human Rights and Fundamental Freedoms, Doc. CM/WP 1 (5) 15, A 924, IV *TP* 2–55, at p. 46.

[6] Protocol No. 11 to the Convention for the Protection of Human Rights and Fundamental Freedoms, restructuring the control machinery established thereby, ETS 155, art. 2(2).

[7] *National Union of Rail, Maritime, and Transport Workers v. the United Kingdom*, no. 31045/10, Concurring Opinion of Judge Wojtyczek, § 1, 8 April 2014.

[8] *Leempoel & S.A. ED. Ciné Revue v. Belgium*, no. 64772/01, §§ 86–87, 9 November 2006. See also *Okyay and Others v. Turkey*, no. 36220/97, § 68, ECHR 2005-VII; *Martynov v. Ukraine*, no. 36202/03, §§ 16–17, 14 December 2006.

It is probably not surprising that there have been almost no citations to article 53 in the jurisprudence of the Convention organs. The provision is really addressed elsewhere, to courts and tribunals at the domestic or international level where the Convention is enlisted in support of arguments aimed at restricting rights and freedoms secured by other legal instruments.[9]

Article 53 deals with two sources of law: 'the laws of any High Contracting Party' and 'any other agreement to which [the High Contracting Party] is a Party'. The first category concerns the applicable domestic law about which, according to Emmanuel Decaux, the provision has hardly any practical significance. He has described it as 'une formule rituelle' from treaty law added to the Convention to address the anxieties of diplomats.[10] With respect to international 'agreements', which is to say treaties and conventions, article 53 may have some relevance to the extent that there are attempts to 'harmonize' obligations that may be secured by other treaties using formulations that differ from those of the European Convention. Although article 53 is, strictly speaking, of no relevance when the Court refers to other treaties in its interpretation of the Convention, the tendency to use such sources in order to enlarge, rather than restrict, the protection of human rights is certainly remarkable. One notable example is found in the very creative reading by the Grand Chamber of article 7 in such a way as to incorporate the *lex mitior* principle.[11]

Further reading

Emmanuel Decaux, 'Article 60', in Pettiti et al., *La Convention européenne*, pp. 897–903.
Frowein/Peukert, *MenschenRechtsKonvention*, p. 619.
J. de Meyer, 'Brèves réflexions à propos de l'article 60 de la Convention européenne des droits de l'homme', in Franz Matscher and Herbert Petzold, eds, *Protection des droits de l'homme: La dimension européenne. Mélanges en l'honneur de Gérard J. Wiarda*, Cologne: Carl Heymanns, 1988, pp. 125–9.

---

[9] J. de Meyer, 'Brèves réflexions à propos de l'article 60 de al Convention européenne des droits de l'homme', in Franz Matscher and Herbert Petzold, eds, *Protection des droits de l'homme: La dimension européenne. Mélanges en l'honneur de Gérard J. Wiarda*, Cologne: Carl Heymanns, 1988, pp. 125–9, at p. 125.

[10] Emmanuel Decaux, 'Article 60', in Pettiti et al., *La Convention européenne*, pp. 897–903, at p. 900.

[11] *Scoppola v. Italy (no. 2)* [GC], no. 10249/03, 17 September 2009.

Article 54. Powers of the Committee of Ministers/Pouvoirs du Comité des Ministres

Nothing in this Convention shall prejudice the powers conferred on the Committee of Ministers by the Statute of the Council of Europe.

Aucune disposition de la présente Convention ne porte atteinte aux pouvoirs conférés au Comité des Ministres par le Statut du Conseil de l'Europe.

Introductory comments

The Statute of the Council of Europe and the European Convention on Human Rights are the two primary instruments of the Council of Europe system. The authority of the Committee of Ministers is defined in both of these treaties. In the Convention, article 46, giving the Committee responsibility for the execution of judgments of the Court, is the main provision. Article 54 is a provision of little real significance, as can be seen by the only judicial consideration it has received. The Court begins with the words 'notwithstanding article 54 of the Convention . . .'.[1]

Drafting of the provision

The origin of article 54 is an Italian proposal submitted to the June 1950 session of the Conference of Senior Officials: 'No provision of the present Convention prejudices the powers conferred on the Committee of Ministers by the Statute of the Council of Europe.'[2] Italy renewed its efforts at the fifth session of the Committee of Ministers, in August 1950, with the following proposal: 'Nothing in this Convention shall prejudice the powers conferred on the Committee of Ministers by the Statute of the Council of Europe.'[3] The text was incorporated in the draft Convention adopted by the Committee of Ministers.[4] It was article 61 of the final text adopted in November.

The provision was renumbered as article 58 and given the heading 'Powers of the Committee of Ministers' by Protocol No. 11.[5]

Analysis and interpretation

The Council of Europe is composed of two organs, the Committee of Ministers and the Parliamentary Assembly.[6] The Committee of Ministers consists of one representative

---

[1] *Bijelić v. Montenegro and Serbia*, no. 11890/05, § 67, 28 April 2009.

[2] Proposal submitted by the Italian Delegation, Doc. CM/WP 4 (50) 6, A 1367, IV *TP* 162–3.

[3] Amendments proposed by the Italian Delegation, Doc. CM 1 (50) 7, V *TP* 70–3.

[4] Draft Convention adopted by the Committee of Ministers, 7 August 1950, Doc. A 1937, V *TP* 120–45, at p. 142. Also Draft Convention adopted by the Sub-Committee, Doc. CM 1 (50) 52, A 1884, V *TP* 76–99, at p. 97.

[5] Protocol No. 11 to the Convention for the Protection of Human Rights and Fundamental Freedoms, restructuring the control machinery established thereby, ETS 155, art. 2(2).

[6] Statute of the Council of Europe, ETS 1, art. 10.

from each Member State. This is in principle the Minister of Foreign Affairs, although in practice a member of the government may be delegated to represent the State.[7] According to article 13 of the Statute of the Council of Europe, the Committee of Ministers 'is the organ which acts on behalf of the Council of Europe'.

According to article 8 of the Statute of the Council of Europe, '[a]ny member of the Council of Europe which has seriously violated Article 3 may be suspended from its rights of representation and requested by the Committee of Ministers to withdraw under Article 7. If such member does not comply with this request, the Committee may decide that it has ceased to be a member of the Council as from such date as the Committee may determine.' It is probably this power that is principally contemplated by article 54 of the European Convention. As Peter Leuprecht has explained,[8] article 8 must be read in conjunction with article 3 of the Statute, where it is affirmed that '[e]very member of the Council of Europe must accept the principles of the rule of law and of the enjoyment by all persons within its jurisdiction of human rights and fundamental freedoms, and collaborate sincerely and effectively in the realisation of the aim of the Council'.

There appears to be only one reference to article 54 in the case law of the Court. It concerns the attribution of responsibility under the Convention in a case concerning alleged violations of article 1 of Protocol No. 1 in Montenegro before June 2006, when the country seceded from Serbia and Montenegro. In its resolution inviting Montenegro to join the Council of Europe, the Committee of Ministers adopted a resolution stating that Montenegro was to be regarded as a Party to the European Convention on Human Rights and its Protocols Nos. 1, 4, 6, 7, 12, 13, and 14 thereto with effect from 6 June 2006.[9] The Court said that notwithstanding article 54 of the Convention, it has 'the sole competence under Article 32 thereof to determine all issues concerning "the interpretation and application of the Convention", including those involving its temporal jurisdiction and/or the compatibility of the applicants' complaints ratione personae'.[10]

Further reading

Frowein/Peukert, *MenschenRechtsKonvention,* p. 620.
Peter Leuprecht, 'Article 61', in Pettiti et al., *La Convention européenne,* pp. 905–7.

---

[7] Ibid., art. 14.

[8] Peter Leuprecht, 'Article 61', in Pettiti et al., *La Convention européenne,* pp. 905–7, at p. 906.

[9] Resolution CM/Res(2007)7 inviting the Republic of Montenegro to become a member of the Council of Europe.

[10] *Bijelić v. Montenegro and Serbia,* no. 11890/05, § 67, 28 April 2009.

Article 55. Exclusion of other means of dispute settlement/Renonciation à d'autres modes de règlement des différends

The High Contracting Parties agree that, except by special agreement, they will not avail themselves of treaties, conventions or declarations in force between them for the purpose of submitting, by way of petition, a dispute arising out of the interpretation or application of this Convention to a means of settlement other than those provided for in this Convention.

Les Hautes Parties contractantes renoncent réciproquement, sauf compromis spécial, à se prévaloir des traités, conventions ou déclarations existant entre elles, en vue de soumettre, par voie de requête, un différend né de l'interprétation ou de l'application de la présente Convention à un mode de règlement autre que ceux prévus par ladite Convention.

Introductory comments

The proliferation in recent years of international courts and tribunals has provoked much discussion about 'fragmentation'. Although the term was not used at the time, those who drafted the European Convention on Human Rights addressed the issue when they ensured the autonomy of the European Court of Human Rights. In effect, article 55 grants the Convention organs a form of monopoly with respect to the interpretation and application of the Convention. To that extent, 'fragmentation' is prevented because only the Convention organs are competent to address inter-State disputes regarding the Convention.

Drafting of the provision

This provision results from debates within the Consultative Assembly about the relationship between the proposed European Court of Human Rights and the existing international dispute settlement mechanisms, in particular the International Court of Justice.[1] The initial draft European Convention on Human Rights prepared by the International Juridical Section of the European Movement contained a provision specifying that nothing in the Convention was to be understood as preventing States Parties from referring any matter to the International Court of Justice.[2]

There was much debate within the Consultative Assembly on the issue of whether or not to establish a European Court of Human Rights. If no European Court was established, then the jurisdiction of existing international dispute mechanisms, notably the International Court of Justice but also arbitration tribunals, would remain untouched. There would be no need for provisions of the Convention to address possible conflicts

---

[1] Emmanuel Decaux, 'Article 62', in Pettiti et al., *La Convention européenne*, pp. 909–14, at pp. 909–11.

[2] Convention for the Collective Protection of Individual Rights and Democratic Liberties by the States, Members of the Council of Europe, and for the establishment of a European Court of Human Rights to ensure observance of the Convention, Doc. INF/5/E/R, I *TP* 296–303, at p. 302, art. 15.

in jurisdiction. The Assembly's Legal Committee opted for a compromise position, whereby disputes between States were to be settled by the future European Court. However, States Parties would retain the alternative of litigating issues before the International Court of Justice. The objections to the latter approach were summarized by the chairman of the Legal Committee, Pierre-Henri Teitgen, in his report to the plenary Consultative Assembly. He explained that the International Court of Justice was 'composed of judges who are nationals of countries outside the European Union and sometimes nationals of countries whose general policy or, more exactly, general spirit are opposed to current European ideals'. At the same time, it was important 'not to set European order in opposition to world order'.[3]

In the plenary Consultative Assembly, Henri Rolin led the debate favouring recognition of a role for the International Court of Justice.[4] Rolin was opposed to the entire idea of a European Court of Human Rights. He warned of the fragmentation of case law, something that could undermine the International Court of Justice to which European States, as members of the United Nations, were committed. Rolin dismissed the argument about the political or philosophical leanings of non-European judges, noting that as a general rule the International Court addressed disputes relating to treaties that were not adhered to by countries of which its judges were nationals. 'I think that those who have followed the work of the International Court of Justice, even in its recent composition, must recognise that in fact the fears which have been expressed on account of the political division of the world, have not had the repercussions which might have been feared in the Court, and that in this connection, the judges of the International Court of Justice have shown themselves as a whole to be perfectly worthy of our confidence', Rolin told the Assembly.[5] Although he did not make any direct reference, Rolin might have had in mind the judgment in the *Corfu Channel case*, the first contentious case to come before the International Court of Justice, issued only months earlier on 9 April 1949. It was an early skirmish in the Cold War, pitting Albania against the United Kingdom. The Court found both sides to be at fault, condemning the United Kingdom for violating the sovereignty of Albania and holding Albania responsible for failing to respect 'elementary considerations of humanity even more exacting in peace than in war'.[6]

The Consultative Assembly retained the approach of the Legal Committee. It adopted two relevant provisions:

Article 19
If reconciliation fails, any Member State, signatory to the Convention, may submit the matter to the Court for judicial decision. In that case, the Commission shall immediately pass the case over the Court.

Article 20
The States concerned may also, if they prefer, petition the International Court of Justice in accordance with their reciprocal agreements.[7]

The Court that was referred to in article 19 was the proposed European Court of Human Rights.

---

[3] Report of the Sitting [of the Consultative Assembly, 7 September 1949], I *TP* 250–95, at p. 270.
[4] Amendment proposed by MM. Rolin and Ungoed-Thomas, Doc. 84, I *TP* 242–5.
[5] Official Report of the Sitting [of the Consultative Assembly, 8 September 1949], II *TP* 14–274, at p. 150.
[6] *Corfu Channel case*, Judgment, I.C.J. Reports 1949, p. 4, at p. 22.
[7] Recommendation No. 38 to the Committee of Ministers adopted 8 September 1949 on the conclusion of the debates, Doc. AS (1) 108, II *TP* 274–83, at p. 280.

The Committee of Ministers referred the Consultative Assembly draft to a Committee of Experts that met in February and March 1950. In a preparatory memorandum, the Secretariat General identified a list of issues for consideration by the Committee of Experts that included '[d]emarcation of jurisdiction between the International Court of Justice and the European Court'.[8] It must be borne in mind that at this point in the negotiations of the Convention, the majority of States represented at the Committee of Experts was opposed altogether to the establishment of a court. In the Committee of Experts, the representative of France, Charles Chaumont, proposed that article 20 of the Consultative Assembly draft be replaced with the following: 'No provision of this Convention may be interpreted in such a way as to prevent Member States from bringing a case before the International Court of Justice, in accordance with the Statute of the Court and their international engagements relating to its competence.'[9] At the end of its first session, in February, the Committee of Experts agreed upon the following: 'No provisions of this Convention can be interpreted in such a way as to prevent the States concerned, provided they agree to do so, from bringing the case before the International Court of Justice, in accordance with the Statutes [sic] of that Court.'[10]

At its first session, the Committee of Experts also adopted a draft report explaining that 'the Convention must not prevent the signatory States from referring conflict resulting from the application of the Convention to the International Court of Justice, if they prefer to have recourse to this tribunal'. Nevertheless, by virtue of the optional clause in the Statute of the International Court of Justice, the consent of both States would be necessary for there to be jurisdiction. The draft report said that if there was no such consent, 'it is the European Court which shall be empowered to deal with the matter, as a special tribunal, the competence of which shall derogate from the general competence of the International Court of Justice'. Thus, any possible conflict of jurisdiction was avoided, 'at least in theory', said the draft report.[11]

At this point in the work of the Committee of Experts, the positions of States took a turn. A new text emerged that made dispute settlement by the European Court the rule and litigation elsewhere the exception: 'The High Contracting Parties reciprocally agree, except as otherwise specified, not to take advantage of treaties, conventions or declarations, with a view to submitting, by means of petition, any dispute arising out of the application of this Convention to any means of settlement other than those laid down in this Convention.'[12] In the final version adopted by the Committee of Experts, the words 'by special agreement' replaced 'as otherwise specified'.[13] Thus, what had begun as a

---

[8] Preparatory Report by the Secretariat-General concerning a Preliminary Draft Convention to Provide a Collective Guarantee of Human Rights, Doc. B 22, III *TP* 2–37, at p. 34.

[9] Amendments to Articles 20 and 27 of the Recommendation of the Consultative Assembly proposed by the French Expert, Doc. A 794, III *TP* 198.

[10] Continuation and end of the proposals of the Drafting Sub-Committee concerning Section III, Doc. A 813, III *TP* 230–3; Preliminary Draft Convention for the Maintenance and Further Realisation of Human Rights and Fundamental Freedoms, 15 February 1950, Doc. A 833, III *TP* 236–46, at p. 246, art. 41.

[11] Preliminary Draft of the Report to the Committee of Ministers, 24 February 1950, Doc. CM/WP 1 (50) 1, A 847, III *TP* 246–79, at p. 276.

[12] Final provisions. New articles, Doc. CM/WP 1 (50) 11, A 920, III *TP* 308–9. Also New text of Article 41, Doc. CM/WP 1 (50) 7, A 908, III *TP* 304–5.

[13] Appendix to the Report of the Committee of Experts to the Committee of Ministers—Draft Convention (16 March 1950), Doc. CM/WP 1 (50) 14 revised, A 925, IV *TP* 50–79, at pp. 74–6, art. 45(49); Report to the Committee of Ministers submitted by the Committee of Experts Instructed to Draw Up a Draft Convention of

presumption in favour of the jurisdiction of the International Court of Justice was now being formulated as an exception, the rule being the jurisdiction of the European Court of Human Rights.

The texts adopted by the Committee of Experts were next examined by the Conference of Senior Officials, in June 1950. By this point, the debate was inexorably favourable to establishment of a Court, albeit one with jurisdiction based upon an optional clause. Referring to the issue of jurisdiction of the International Court of Justice in disputes concerning the European Convention, the Italian representative, Tomasso Perassi, said that '[i]f we wish to avoid going before the Hague Court by virtue of the optional clause, as regards disputes arising from the Convention, the only solution is to create a European Court'.[14] Belgium agreed with the Italians, asking whether 'the creation of a European Court would not be more satisfactory for psychological reasons. Besides, this point of view would be supported easily by the close relationship existing between the European countries.'[15] Sir Samuel Hoare of the United Kingdom said his country remained opposed to the Court, warning of 'proliferation of organs with tremendous difficulties for the definition of their respective jurisdiction'.[16] The Conference revised the existing draft provision as follows: 'The High Contracting Parties declare that disputes relating to the application of this Convention can only be submitted to a procedure of arbitration or legal settlement, by means of treaties, conventions or declarations in force among them, six months after the decision taken by the Committee of Ministers, in accordance with article 31.'[17] This was a reference to the proposal whereby the Commission would refer matters to the Committee of Ministers, rather than to a European Court, for a final decision. In its Report, the Conference of Senior Officials said that it was unable to reach agreement on a single text governing dispute settlement and notably as to whether an appeal could be taken against a decision by the Committee of Ministers. It had, however, agreed on certain principles: 'so long as a case is under discussion by the Commission of Human Rights or the Committee of Ministers, it shall not be brought before any other Court' and '[n]o appeal shall be possible against the decision of a European Court for Human Rights'. It added:

Certain delegates consider that all possibility of appeal should be excluded as the decision of the Committee of Ministers was fixed.

Other delegates thought there was no need to thus restrict the competence of the International Court of Justice, as far as concerned States which had signed the optional clause provided for in Article 36 of the Statute of the Court.

Finally, certain delegates considered that member States of the Council of Europe would more readily accept the powers given to the Committee of Ministers in the draft Convention attached to the present Report, if the comeptence of the International Court of Justice were left intact on this matter.[18]

Collective Guarantee of Human Rights and Fundamental Freedoms, Doc. CM/WP 1 (5) 15, A 924, IV *TP* 2–55, at p. 46.

[14] Minutes of the morning sitting [of 9 June 1950 of the Conference of Senior Officials], Doc. CM/WP 4 (50) 3, IV *TP* 110–19, at p. 118.

[15] Ibid.

[16] Minutes of the afternoon sitting [of 9 June 1950], unreferenced document, IV *TP* 120–31, at p. 124.

[17] Draft Convention appended to the draft report, Doc. CM/WP 4 (50) 16, appendix, A 1445, IV *TP* 218–40, at p. 236, art. 58.

[18] Text of the report submitted by the Conference to the Committee of Ministers, Doc. CM/WP 4 (50) 19, CM/WP 4 (50) 16 rev., A 1431, IV *TP* 242–73, at p. 272.

During the fifth session of the Committee of Ministers, in August 1950, Sweden presented its view that the procedure instituted by the Convention should be exclusive. It said that '[u]nless some special clause is inserted to exclude such other international tribunals, the adoption of the new convention would have unexpected results'. Sweden proposed that the following clause be inserted: 'The Commission and the European Court having been created to settle disputes relating to the interpretation and the application of this Convention, such disputes shall not be submitted to other judicial or arbitral tribunals established by treaties or declarations in force, unless the Parties concerned shall so decide by an agreement expressly relating to the dispute in question.'[19] There was a competing proposal from the United Kingdom: 'The High Contracting Parties agree not to submit disputes relating to the interpretation or application of this Convention to other procedures of arbitration or legal settlement established by other treaties, conventions or declarations to which they are parties.'[20] But the United Kingdom said that a further clause was necessary on possible submission of complaints applicable to individuals who were not parties to the Convention. This became the admissibility criterion in article 35. The Netherlands also had a proposal: 'As to the possibility of appeal against a decision of the Committee of Ministers, it is considered that the competence of the International Court of Justice should be left intact as far as States are concerned which have signed the optional clause provided for in Article 36 of the Statute of the Court.'[21] Finally, Italy too had a proposal: 'The High Contracting Parties agree that, except by special agreement, they will not avail themselves of texts, conventions or declarations in force between them for the purpose of submitting by way of petition, a dispute arising out of the application of this Convention to a means of settlement other than those provided for in this Convention.'[22]

Within the Sub-Committee on Human Rights of the Committee of Ministers, which met on 4 August 1950, agreement was reached by all delegations but one, the Netherlands, on the following: 'The High Contracting Parties agree that, except by special agreement, they will not avail themselves of treaties, conventions or declarations in force between them for the purpose of submitting, by way of petition, a dispute arising out of the interpretation or application of this Convention to a means of settlement other than those provided for in this Convention.'[23] The Netherlands later withdrew its opposition and the text was adopted.[24]

There appears to have been no further discussion. The text approved by the Committee of Ministers in August 1950 became article 62 of the Convention. It was renumbered as

---

[19] Amendments proposed by the Swedish Delegation, Doc. CM 1 (50) 1, CM 1 (50) 8, A 1862, V *TP* 56–9.

[20] Amendments proposed by the United Kingdom Delegation, Doc. CM I (50) 6, A 1867, V *TP* 66–71, at p. 70.

[21] Amendments proposed by the Netherlands Delegation, Doc. CM I (50) 5, A 11866, V *TP* 64–5.

[22] Amendments proposed by the Italian Delegation, Doc. CM I (50) 7, V *TP* 70–3.

[23] Also Provisions of the Draft Convention about which agreement was not reached in the Sub- Committee, First version, Doc. CM 1 (50) 11, A 1688, IV *TP* 98–103, at p. 100; Provisions of the Draft Convention about which agreement was not reached in the Sub-Committee, Final version, Doc. CM 1 (50) 53, A 1889, IV *TP* 102–7, at p. 104.

[24] Draft Convention adopted by the Committee of Ministers, 7 August 1950, Doc. A 1937, V *TP* 120–45, at p. 142, art. 62.

article 55 by Protocol No. 11. The heading 'Exclusion of other means of dispute settlement' was also added according to the provisions of Protocol No. 11.[25]

Analysis and interpretation

Article 55 prevents States Parties from submitting a dispute about the interpretation and application of the Convention to means of settlement other than those provided by the Convention. In practice, it means that such disputes are confined to the inter-State application procedure. It also presents an obstacle to any attempt by a State Party dissatisfied with a ruling of the Court in an inter-State case to appeal the decision to the International Court of Justice.

Within the treaty system of the Council of Europe, care has been taken to respect the principle set out in article 55. For example, the European Convention for the Peaceful Settlement of Disputes declares: 'This Convention shall in no way affect the application of the provisions of the Convention for the Protection of Human Rights and Fundamental Freedoms signed on 4th November 1950, or of the Protocol thereto signed on 20th March 1952.'[26] Along similar lines, the European Convention for the Prevention of Torture and Inhuman or Degrading Treatment or Punishment states: 'Nothing in this Convention shall be construed as limiting or derogating from the competence of the organs of the European Convention on Human Rights or from the obligations assumed by the Parties under that Convention.'[27] The Explanatory Report notes:

This paragraph addresses the particular relationship between the new Convention and the European Convention on Human Rights, to which all member States of the Council of Europe are party and a connection with which is acknowledged in the Preamble. The obligations of the Parties under the European Convention on Human Rights are not affected. Nor is the competence entrusted by that Convention to the European Court and Commission of Human Rights and the Committee of Ministers. Accordingly, in respecting the established competence of these organs, the committee set up by the present Convention will not concern itself with matters raised in proceedings pending before them, and will not itself formulate interpretations of the provisions of the European Convention on Human Rights.[28]

Problems in the interpretation of article 55 arose in the late 1960s as European states were considering ratification of the International Covenant on Civil and Political Rights, adopted by the United Nations General Assembly in 1966. Unlike the European Convention, the Covenant has no exclusivity clause. Indeed, the Covenant states explicitly that its provisions 'shall not prevent the States Parties to the present Covenant from having recourse to other procedures for settling a dispute in accordance with general or special international agreements in force between them'.[29] The Covenant establishes an optional inter-State petition mechanism to the Human Rights Committee.

---

[25] Protocol No. 11 to the Convention for the Protection of Human Rights and Fundamental Freedoms, restructuring the control machinery established thereby, ETS 155, art. 2(2).

[26] European Convention for the Peaceful Settlement of Disputes, ETS 23, art. 28(2).

[27] European Convention for the Prevention of Torture and Inhuman or Degrading Treatment or Punishment, ETS 126, art. 17(2).

[28] Explanatory Report on the European Convention for the Prevention of Torture and Inhuman or Degrading Treatment or Punishment, para. 91.

[29] International Covenant on Civil and Political Rights, (1976) 999 UNTS 171, art. 44. See Manfred Nowak, *CCPR Commentary*, 2nd rev. edn, Kehl, Germany: N.P. Engel, 2005, pp. 791–2; Alexandre-Linos

In 1970, the Committee of Ministers adopted a resolution in order to address situations where States Parties to the European Convention ratified the Covenant and accepted the jurisdiction of the Human Rights Committee with respect to inter-State applications. The Preamble to the resolution noted that 'there are a certain number of rights which in substance are covered both by the UN Covenant and by the European Convention' and that the inter-State procedure set out in the Convention 'provides an effective system for the protection of human rights, including binding decisions by the Court of Human Rights or by the Committee of Ministers'. It acknowledged 'the value of the procedure established by the UN Covenant for the protection of rights not included in the European Convention and its protocol', adding 'that Article 33 of the Charter of the United Nations emphasises the importance of regional settlement of inter-State disputes'. But, said the Committee, 'differences of opinion appear to exist as regards the exact scope of the obligation' created by article 55 (it was then article 62) of the Convention. The Committee declared that:

as long as the problem of interpretation of Article 62 of the European Convention is not resolved, States Parties to the Convention which ratify or accede to the UN Covenant on Civil and Political Rights and make a declaration under Article 41 of the Covenant should normally utilise only the procedure established by the European Convention in respect of complaints against another Contracting Party to the European Convention relating to an alleged violation of a right which in substance is covered both by the European Convention (or its protocols) and by the UN Covenant on Civil and Political Rights, it being understood that the UN procedure may be invoked in relation to rights not guaranteed in the European Convention (or its protocols) or in relation to States which are not Parties to the European Convention.[30]

Many States Parties to the European Convention have also formulated declarations accepting the jurisdiction of the Human Rights Committee pursuant to article 41 of the Covenant, but the mechanism has never been invoked, in Europe or elsewhere, so the problem anticipated in the resolution of the Committee of Ministers has never arisen. None of the declarations by European States has made reference directly or indirectly to the article 55 issue.

Article 55 does not entirely exclude the possibility that disputes involving human rights issues as well as related matters are addressed in other fora. Professor Emmanuel Decaux gives two examples of States Parties to the European Convention who addressed their differences before the European Court of Human Rights but also took aspects of the dispute elsewhere.[31] The first is the conflict between Austria and Italy about minority rights in the Süd Tirol/Alto Adige, a matter submitted to the European Commission on Human Rights in one of the first inter-State applications.[32] In 1969, the two States reached an agreement that granted a degree of autonomy to the region. In a compromissory clause, they agreed to submit disputes to the International Court of Justice.[33]

Sicilianos and Elias Kastanas, 'Article 44', in Emmanuel Decaux, ed., *Le Pacte international relative aux droits civils et politiques, Commentaire article par article*, Paris: Economica, 2011, pp. 752–65.

[30] UN Covenant on Civil and Political Rights and the European Convention on Human Rights: Procedure for dealing with inter-state complaints, Committee of Ministers Resolution (70) 17, 15 May 1970.
[31] Emmanuel Decaux, 'Article 62', in Pettiti et al., *La Convention européenne*, pp. 909–14, at pp. 912–13.
[32] (1960) 3 YB 168–171.
[33] A. Fenet, 'La fin du litige italo-autrichien sur le Haut Adige-Tyrol du Sud', (1993) 39 *Annuaire français de droit international* 357.

The second is the dispute between Cyprus and Turkey, a matter that has come before the Convention organs in a variety of forms but that is also addressed in various other institutions. In one of the applications filed by Cyprus against Turkey, the respondent State invoked article 55, referring to various mechanisms under the aegis of the United Nations Security Council addressing the occupation of the northern part of the island. Rejecting Turkey's argument, the European Commission on Human Rights said 'the possibility for a High Contracting Party of withdrawing a case from the jurisdiction of the Convention organs on the ground that it has entered into a special agreement with the other High Contracting Party concerned, is given only in exceptional circumstances'. The Commission said that '[e]ven assuming that both Turkey and Cyprus are bound by international obligations concerning the intercommunal talks and the Committee on Missing Persons, it is difficult to see how this could amount to a "special agreement" between them to resort exclusively to these means of settlement precluding the Convention organs from performing their normal functions'.[34]

A third and more recent example is the dispute between Georgia and Russia at the International Court of Justice. Georgia relied upon the compromissory clause in the International Convention on the Elimination of All Forms of Racial Discrimination, although it also reserved the right to invoke the Convention on the Prevention and Punishment of the Crime of Genocide. Georgia charged that Russia was responsible for the ethnic cleansing of ethnic Georgians in two breakaway Georgian provinces, South Ossetia and Abkhazia, in August 2008. On 15 October 2008, the Court granted an application for interim measures, calling upon the parties to refrain from acts of racial discrimination, not to sponsor, defend, or support racial discrimination by any persons or organisations, and a range of other measures that might just as well have been included in a interim measures order by the European Court of Human Rights pursuant to articles 3, 8, and 14 of the European Convention.[35] Three years later, the International Court of Justice granted a preliminary objection by Russia, ruling that Georgia had failed to attempt to settle the dispute by negotiation.[36] In the meantime, Georgia also initiated proceedings against Russia at the European Court of Human Rights, where Russia raised an objection about the similarity of those proceedings with the application at the International Court of Justice. The European Court noted that the proceedings in The Hague had come to an end in April 2011 and that there was therefore no ground to object on the basis of *lis pendens*. The Court added that the rule against similar proceedings set out in article 35 of the European Convention did not apply to inter-State cases and it did not consider the application of article 55 to the case.[37] Georgia may well have breached article 55 of the Convention, although it is hard to see what consequence this could have in judicial proceedings. Jurisdiction before either the International Court of Justice or the European Court of Human Rights could not be defeated merely because one of the States had failed to respect article 55 of the Convention.

---

[34] *Cyprus v. Turkey*, no. 25781/94, Commission decision of 28 June 1996, (1996) 39 YB 130, DR 86, p. 104.

[35] *Application of the International Convention on the Elimination of all Forms of Racial Discrimination* (*Georgia v. Russian Federation*), Provisional Measures, Order of 15 October 2008, I.C.J. Reports 2008, p. 353, paras. 46, 47.

[36] *Application of the International Convention on the Elimination of All Forms of Racial Discrimination* (*Georgia v. Russian Federation*) (Preliminary objections), Judgment, I.C.J. Reports 2011, p. 70.

[37] *Georgia v. Russia* (dec.), no. 38263/08, § 79, 13 December 2011.

In 2007, the Human Rights Council of the United Nations introduced the human rights monitoring mechanism known as 'Universal Periodic Review'. It is an inter-State process, whereby States submit reports on human rights compliance and then are questioned about this by their peers, often very critically. They are invited to undertake commitments and often agree to do so. In that sense, it is a mechanism of dispute resolution. The basis of the Universal Periodic Review is outlined in a resolution of the Council that includes 'Human rights instruments to which a State is party'.[38] For European States, this obviously includes the European Convention. Some European States report on issues relating to litigation before the European Court. For example, in its second report to the Council the United Kingdom discussed the issue of prisoner voting, making explicit reference to the case law of the Court and its requirement that legislative changes be undertaken.[39] When challenged about legislation restricting free-dom of expression on issues relating to sexual orientation, Russia answered by invoking article 10(2) of the European Convention on Human Rights.[40] When Turkey was being discussed, Greece recommended that it '[i]mplement the large number of European Court of Human Rights decisions like the one concerning the Orphanage on Prince Island, which belongs to the Orthodox Ecumenical Patriarchate, or the ones that have found that Turkey is liable for numerous violations of ECHR articles in Cyprus, namely in the occupied northern part'.[41]

The examples from the Universal Periodic Review process demonstrate the difficulty of imposing a watertight separation between the system of the European Convention and other international human rights mechanisms. The scope of article 55 of the European Convention is probably best confined to the very traditional vision that prevailed in 1950 of inter-State litigation, something that has been a rare occurrence in any event, as the case law pursuant to article 33 of the Convention demonstrates. European States will only undertake an inter-State application in the most serious of circumstances. Indeed, it is for this reason that mechanisms for States to deal with differences and disputes about compliance with fundamental human rights, whatever the normative source, be addressed in the sort of environment that the Universal Periodic Review provides.

Further reading

Emmanuel Decaux, 'Article 62', in Pettiti et al., *La Convention européenne*, pp. 909–14.
Frowein/Peukert, *MenschenRechtsKonvention*, p. 620.

---

[38] Institution-building of the United Nations Human Rights Council, UN Doc. A/HRC/RES/5/1, Annex, para. 19c).
[39] A/HRC/WG.6/13/GBR/1, paras 38–39.
[40] UN Doc. A/HRC/24/14/Add.1, p. 13.
[41] UN Doc. A/HRC/15/13, para. 103.7.

Article 56. Territorial application/Application territoriale

1. Any State may at the time of its ratification or at any time thereafter declare by notification addressed to the Secretary General of the Council of Europe that the present Convention shall, subject to paragraph 4 of this Article, extend to all or any of the territories for whose international relations it is responsible.

2. The Convention shall extend to the territory or territories named in the notification as from the thirtieth day after the receipt of this notification by the Secretary General of the Council of Europe.

3. The provisions of this Convention shall be applied in such territories with due regard, however, to local requirements.

4. Any State which has made a declaration in accordance with paragraph 1 of this article may at any time thereafter declare on behalf of one or more of the territories to which the declaration relates that it accepts the competence of the Court to receive applications from individuals, non-governmental organisations or groups of individuals as provided by Article 34 of the Convention.

1. Tout Etat peut, au moment de la ratification ou à tout autre moment par la suite, déclarer, par notification adressée au Secrétaire Général du Conseil de l'Europe, que la présente Convention s'appliquera, sous réserve du paragraphe 4 du présent article, à tous les territoires ou à l'un quelconque des territoires dont il assure les relations internationales.

2. La Convention s'appliquera au territoire ou aux territoires désignés dans la notification à partir du trentième jour qui suivra la date à laquelle le Secrétaire Général du Conseil de l'Europe aura reçu cette notification.

3. Dans lesdits territoires les dispositions de la présente Convention seront appliquées en tenant compte des nécessités locales.

4. Tout Etat qui a fait une déclaration conformément au premier paragraphe de cet article, peut, à tout moment par la suite, déclarer relativement à un ou plusieurs des territoires visés dans cette déclaration qu'il accepte la compétence de la Cour pour connaître des requêtes de personnes physiques, d'organisations non gouvernementales ou de groupes de particuliers, comme le prévoit l'article 34 de la Convention.

Introductory comments

It is one of the enduring paradoxes of the development of modern human rights law that the first comprehensive convention was developed in the bosom of the world's great colonial empires. Several of the founding members of the Council of Europe, but notably the United Kingdom and France, had far-flung 'possessions'. At the time, perhaps even they did not understand how ephemeral their empires would be. Their pioneering work in developing the international law of human rights stands alongside anxiety about possible application of the legal regime to their colonies, where brutality, persecution, and exploitation continued to reign.

The issue of application of international human rights principles to colonial territories had already arisen during the drafting of the Universal Declaration of Human Rights. An awkward formulation appears in article 2 of the Declaration, immediately following a general affirmation of the right to equality: 'Furthermore, no distinction shall be made on the basis of the political, jurisdictional or international status of the country or territory to which a person belongs, whether it be independent, trust, non-self-governing or under any other limitation of sovereignty.' The clause was initially a distinct article resulting from a proposal by Yugoslavia.[1] Literally hours before adoption of the Declaration by the General Assembly, the United Kingdom successfully argued to reposition the sentence, describing it as 'one of the most serious blemishes' on the text about which otherwise there could be no doubt as to its universal application.[2] Yugoslavia, the Soviet Union, and others may have pushed for an explicit reference to 'non-self-governing territories' not so much to ensure universal application of the Declaration as to embarrass the colonial powers.

Nevertheless, in contrast with the United Nations Declaration, there is no doubt that the European Convention does not apply with the same degree of universality. Known as the 'colonial clause', although later baptised with the less pejorative title '[t]erritorial application' by Protocol No. 11, article 56 of the Convention was introduced at the insistence of the British, 'who made it clear they would not accept the Convention without it'.[3] Marko Milanovic has noted that '[s]ince colonies are historically primarily a European problem, it makes sense that only European human rights treaties have colonial clauses'.[4] According to Brian Simpson, '[s]o far as the Colonial Office was concerned the real belief of the officials was that British involvement in the whole human rights exercise had been regrettable and was potentially harmful to British interests'.[5] British negotiators masked their real concerns by suggesting that a colonial clause was necessary out of respect for local self-governance.[6] But as the Haitian diplomat Emile St Lot had said about such clauses, when the Universal Declaration of Human Rights was being drafted, they were inserted in treaties by colonial powers 'under the pretext that signatories could not impose their will upon their colonies', but this 'had, however, never prevented such Powers from imposing their will when they had so desired'.[7]

Eventually, and possibly encouraged by a 1953 resolution in the Consultative Assembly recommending extension of the Convention to colonies, the United Kingdom invoked article 56 with respect to forty-two of its overseas territories and colonies.[8] Denmark and the Netherlands made similar 'Declarations of extension'.[9] Germany, bereft of colonies since 1918, used article 56 to extend the Convention to West Berlin.[10] Both Belgium and the Netherlands also made declarations indicating that were they to formulate such declarations of extension, they reserved the right to 'faire accompagner cette déclaration de réserves imposées par les nécessités locales'.[11]

In the 1960s, the United Kingdom informed the Council of Europe that its responsibilities for several of the overseas territories, including Cyprus, Ghana, Jamaica, Kenya,

---

[1] Yugoslavia: Amendments to the draft Declaration (E/800), UN Doc. A/C.3/233.

[2] UN Doc. A/PV.181; United Kingdom: Amendment to Article 3 of the Draft Declaration proposed by the Third Committee (A/777), UN Doc. A/778/Rev.1.

[3] Ed Bates, *The Evolution of the European Convention on Human Rights*, Oxford: Oxford University Press, 2010, at p. 93.

[4] Marko Milanovic, *Extraterritorial Application of Human Rights Treaties*, Oxford: Oxford University Press, 2011, at p. 13.

[5] A.W. Brian Simpson, *Human Rights and the End of Empire, Britain and the Genesis of the European Convention*, Oxford: Oxford University Press, 2001, p. 824.

[6] L. Moor and A.W. Brian Simpson, 'Ghosts of Colonialism in the European Convention on Human Rights', (2006) 76 *British Yearbook of International law* 121, at pp. 136–58.

[7] UN Doc. A/C.3/SR.163.

[8] (1955–56–57) 1 YB 46–47.

[9] Ibid., pp. 45–6.

[10] (1955–56–57) 1 YB 52.

[11] (1955–56–57) 1 YB 51, 53.

and Nigeria, had 'lapsed'. Periodically, it has provided a revised list of States for whose international relations it was responsible and to which it was extending the European Convention on Human Rights.[12] It has also extended the application of the Convention to territories not earlier covered by its initial declaration.[13]

Drafting of the provision

The initial draft European Convention on Human Rights prepared by the International Juridical Section of the European Movement addressed the issue of territorial application in a provision stating that each State Party 'shall guarantee to all persons within its territory' the rights therein set out. This is the ancestor of article 1 of the European Convention. The draft also set out an obligation 'to respect the fundamental principles of political democracy, and, in particular, within its metropolitan territory'.[14] Inspired by the European Movement draft, the Legal Committee of the Consultative Assembly, meeting in August 1949, adopted a text by which 'the Member States shall undertake to ensure to all persons residing within their territories...' the benefit of the Convention.[15] The report noted that with respect to extension of the rights 'not only to all persons residing within its metropolitan territory, but also to all persons residing within its overseas territories or in its colonial possessions, the majority of the Committee replied in the affirmative'. It added that 'reservations were made on this point by some members of the Committee, who were not able to appreciate exactly the difficulties which this solution might raise'.[16]

The Committee of Ministers referred the draft Convention prepared by the Consultative Assembly to a Committee of Experts that met in February and March 1950. The Belgian expert, Etienne de la Vallée-Poussin, proposed the following amendment: 'The rules given above shall be applied within the overseas territories, in conformity with local needs and the standard of civilization of the native population, which may not yet have been able to reach the conditions necessary for the practice of democratic freedom.'[17] The first session of the Committee of Experts agreed upon a summary clause: 'In the overseas territories, the provisions of this Convention shall be applicable with due regard, however, to local necessities.'[18] The emergence of the expression 'local necessities', which is present in the final version, was not entirely a benign measure of respect for autonomy. Rather, as the accompanying commentary explained, it was felt that 'the state of civilisation of certain overseas territories does not permit the application of fundamental rights under

---

[12] (1963) 7 YB 32–39; (1966) 9 YB 20–23; (1967) 10 YB 46–49; (1969) 12 YB 74–77; (1980) 23 YB 8–9; (1981) 24 YB 26–27; (1983) 26 YB CONV.EUR.DECL.63 1.

[13] (1967) 10 YB 12–17; (1976) 18 YB 20–21; (2004) 47 YB 23.

[14] Convention for the Collective Protection of Individual Rights and Democratic Liberties by the States, Members of the Council of Europe, and for the establishment of a European Court of Human Rights to ensure observance of the Convention, Doc. INF/5/E/R, I *TP* 296–303, at p. 296.

[15] Report [of the Committee on Legal and Administrative Questions], 5 September 1949, Doc. AS (1) 77, I *TP* 216–39, at p. 228.

[16] Report presented by Mr P.H. Teitgen, 5 September 1949, Doc. A 290, I *TP* 192–213, at p. 202; Report [of the Committee on Legal and Administrative Questions], 5 September 1949, Doc. AS (1) 77, I *TP* 216–39.

[17] Amendment to Article 6 of the Recommendation of the Consultative Assembly proposed by the Belgian Expert, Doc. A 803, III *TP* 210–11.

[18] Preliminary Draft Convention for the Maintenance and Further Realisation of Human Rights and Fundamental Freedoms, 15 February 1950, Doc. A 833, III *TP* 236–46, at p. 238, art. 7(d).

the same condition as for European territories. The States concerned have, however, to perform the task of bringing civilisation to their overseas territories, a task of which the aim is precisely that of making the human rights applicable to these territories.'[19] There was also a second provision that was referred to as the 'colonial clause': 'This Convention shall only apply to territories of the High Contracting Parties possessing jurisdiction within the fields covered by the present Convention when the consent of the appropriate authorities of these territories has been obtained. The High Contracting Parties responsible for these territories shall, if necessary, take steps to obtain this consent.'[20] Small changes were made to the draft at the second session of the Committee of Experts. A note was added in the final report explaining that the provision on local necessities or requirements had been introduced in order 'to make provision for the political autonomy accorded to certain overseas territories'.[21]

The Committee of Ministers referred the draft developed by the Committee of Experts to a Conference of Senior Officials that met in June 1950. It did not reach agreement on the clause. In addition to the 'colonial clause' adopted by the Committee of Experts, the United Kingdom had a competing proposal that it entitled 'Draft Colonial Application Clause':

1. Any State may at the time of accession or at any time thereafter declare by notification addressed to the Secretary-General of the Council of Europe that the present Convention shall extend to all or any of the territories for which it has international responsibility.
2. The Convention shall extend to the territory or territories named in the notification as from the thirtieth day after the receipt of this notification by the Secretary-General of the Council of Europe.[22]

The Report of the Conference included both drafts. It noted that the United Kingdom said it could not accept the version prepared by the Committee of Experts 'for constitutional reasons'. The Italian delegate insisted upon the Committee of Experts' draft noting that its aim was to extend the benefits of the Convention 'as far as possible to all the inhabitants of overseas territories'. To this, the United Kingdom answered that this was also the purpose of its draft. The Report did not take a position, one way or the other.[23] Later in the month, the Legal Committee of the Consultative Assembly adopted 'the more liberal solution' of the Committee of Experts, expressing the hope 'that the Committee of Ministers will find a way of overcoming the constitutional objections raised by certain members'.[24]

At the meeting of the Committee of Ministers in early August 1950, the United Kingdom explained that it could not accept international commitments on behalf of many of the British colonies without first consulting and obtaining agreement of the local

---

[19] Preliminary draft of the Report to the Committee of Ministers, 24 February 1950, Doc. CM/WP 1 (50) 1, A 847, III *TP* 246–79, at p. 266.

[20] Preliminary Draft Convention for the Maintenance and Further Realisation of Human Rights and Fundamental Freedoms, 15 February 1950, Doc. A 833, III *TP* 236–46, at p. 246, art. 42.

[21] Appendix to the Report of the Committee of Experts on Human Rights: Draft Convention of Protection of Human Rights and Fundamental Freedoms, 16 March 1950, Doc. C/WP 1 (50) 15 appendix, CM/WP 1 (50) 14 rev., A 925, IV *TP* 50–79, at p. 76, art. 47(51).

[22] Proposal submitted by the United Kingdom Delegation, Doc. CM/WP 4 (50) 8, A 1371, IV *TP* 180–3.

[23] Text of the report submitted by the Conference to the Committee of Ministers, Doc. CM/WP 4 (50) 19, CM/WP 4 (50) 16 rev., A 1431, IV *TP* 242–73, at p. 270.

[24] Letter of 24 June 1950 from Sir David Maxwell Fyfe, Chairman of the Committee on Legal and Administrative Questions, to the Chairman of the Committee of Ministers, Doc. CM (50) 29, V *TP* 32–41.

governments. The United Kingdom wanted a text that would enable it to ratify the Convention immediately and deposit subsequent ratifications later upon obtaining the agreement of the colonial governments. If the Convention provided for immediate application, then the United Kingdom would not be able to ratify the Convention until it had conducted such a consultation. Moreover, if any colonial governments rejected the Convention, 'the United Kingdom would be prevented from ratifying at all'.[25] The Committee of Ministers agreed upon the text proposed by the United Kingdom:

1. Any State may at the time of its ratification or accession or at any time thereafter declare by notification addressed to the Secretary-General of the Council of Europe that the present Convention shall extent to all or any of the territories for whose international relations it is responsible.
2. The Convention shall extend to the territory or territories named in the notification as from the thirtieth day after the receipt of this notification by the Secretary-General of the Council of Europe.
3. The provisions of this Convention shall be applied in the overseas territories with due regard, however, to local requirements.
4. Any State which has made a declaration in accordance with paragraph 1 of this Article may at any time thereafter declare on behalf of one or more of those territories to which the Convention extends that it accepts the competence of the Commission to receive petitions from individuals, non-governmental organisations or groups of individuals, in accordance with Article 25 of the present Convention.[26]

Subsequently, the 'colonial clause' in the draft adopted by the Committee of Ministers only underwent very minor changes.

Nevertheless, there was great dissatisfaction and a fierce debate on the subject in the Consultative Assembly. Noting that the clause was 'recast in a considerably less liberal form than we asked for in Committee, and a still less liberal form than the proposal of the Assembly', Hermod Lannung of Denmark warned that any colonial clause would provide 'invaluable opportunities for Communist propaganda'. By excluding colonial territories from the protection of the Convention, it would 'inevitably provide a weapon which can be used with considerable success against the Council of Europe and the Western Democracies, first and foremost in their overseas territories, but also in all ex-colonial territories in Asia, Africa and South America'. Giovanni Persico of Italy proposed that the colonial clause should be mandatory rather than permissive, following the example of the Universal Declaration of Human Rights.[27] Italy had done this with respect to Somaliland because of a human rights provision in the Trusteeship Agreement, he explained. 'As you can see, we have already agreed to extend all of the rights specified in the Universal Declaration of Human Rights to the natives of Somaliland, which means

---

[25] Report of the meeting [of 7 August 1950 of the Committee of Ministers], V *TP* 110–21, at p. 118. See also Provisions of the Draft Convention about which agreement was not reached in the Sub-Committee, First version, Doc. CM 1 (50) 11, A 1688, IV *TP* 98–103, at pp. 100–3; Provisions of the Draft Convention about which agreement was not reached in the Sub-Committee, Final version, Doc. CM 1 (50) 53, A 1889, IV *TP* 102–7, at pp. 104–7.

[26] Report of the meeting [of 7 August 1950 of the Committee of Ministers], V *TP* 110–121, at pp. 110, 118–21; Draft Convention adopted by the Committee of Ministers, 7 August 1950, Doc. A 1937, V *TP* 120–45, at p. 142.

[27] He later withdrew the amendment: Minutes of the sitting [of the Consultative Assembly, 23 August 1950], VI *TP* 36–41, at p. 40.

that these are more favoured than the Italians themselves since there is no such clause yet laid down in our Constitution.'[28]

In support of the provision adopted by the Committee of Ministers, David Maxwell Fyfe of the United Kingdom pleaded with the Assembly 'not to jeopardise the Convention as a whole by pressing matters which may seem superficially attractive but which may cause great difficulty to those whose life-work is the improvement of the peoples in our territories abroad'.[29] Henri Rolin of Belgium said he acknowledged 'how distressing, and even at first sight shocking, this method of *de jure* discrimination will be for some of our colleagues'. He could only urge 'that the Governments may use in the most liberal fashion the option-extending clause'.[30]

The most eloquent voice was that of Léopold Senghor, the Senegalese poet who would go on to become his country's president upon its independence. He sat in the Consultative Assembly by virtue of his membership in the French *Assemblée nationale*, where he served as deputy for Sénégal-Mauritanie. He charged that the colonial clause in the Committee of Ministers' draft was contrary to the Universal Declaration of Human Rights. Senghor described it as 'a rather clumsy way of excluding overseas territories' and 'an echo of the Colonial Pact'. But he said the more important reason to exclude it was 'moral'. The clause 'would transform the European Declaration of Human Rights into the Declaration of European Human Rights', thereby 'betraying the spirit of European Civilisation'.[31] Senghor's amendment to delete the provision entirely was adopted by the Consultative Assembly, by forty-seven votes to thirty-seven.[32]

In preparation for the final approval of the Convention, the Secretariat General proposed some changes of a technical nature to article 56. The reference to 'accession' in paragraph 1 was dropped, in accordance with a more general decision to remove the term from the Convention. The Secretariat General proposed using the words 'overseas territories' in paragraph 3 in place of 'territories for whose international relations it is responsible', given that the latter term was used in the fourth paragraph. In the fourth paragraph, 'for the purposes of greater clarity', it proposed replacing 'those territories to which the Convention extends' with 'the territories to which the declaration relates'.[33] These changes were accepted.

Immediately prior to adoption of the Convention, the British and French members of the Committee of Legal Experts noted that the Convention did not clarify whether a declaration pursuant to the colonial clause automatically conferred jurisdiction upon the Court. As adopted in 1950, the Convention required States to confer jurisdiction upon the Court by means of a separate declaration, something that was subsequently removed by Protocol No. 11. The British and French experts thought that jurisdiction of the Court would not follow automatically from a declaration extending the Convention to an overseas territory. They believed a distinct provision was required and that it had been simply omitted by oversight. However, they apparently chose not to 'press for its inclusion in Rome in order not to raise contentious issues at the last moment, having regard

[28] Report of the sitting [of the Consultative Assembly, 14 August 1950], V *TP* 216–71, at p. 258.
[29] Report of the sitting [of the Consultative Assembly, 25 August 1950, afternoon], VI *TP* 144–91, at pp. 180–2.
[30] Ibid., p. 182.
[31] Ibid., pp. 173–6.
[32] Ibid., p. 182.
[33] Drafting changes proposed by the Secretariat-General, Doc. A 2520, no date, VI *TP* 274–9, at p. 278.

particularly to the very contentious history' of the colonial clause.[34] The provision, as amended, became article 63 of the 1950 text of the Convention.

Article 63 was renumbered as article 56 by Protocol No. 11. The heading 'Territorial application' was also added.[35] The Explanatory Report on Protocol No. 11 explains that paragraph 1 of article 56 'enables States to extend the Convention to territories for whose international relations States are responsible' and that paragraph 4 'enables States to make declarations in respect of territories accepting the competence of the Court to receive individual applications', such declarations being possible for a specific period as is the case with Protocol No. 4 and Protocol No. 7. Protocol No. 11 added the words 'subject to paragraph 4' in paragraph 1 and it replaced the reference to the 'Commission' with 'Court'. The Explanatory Report notes that '[t]he provision in paragraph 3, that regard should be had to local requirements, is retained'.[36]

Analysis and interpretation

The general rule of international law, codified in article 29 of the Vienna Convention on the Law of Treaties, is that a treaty is binding upon each party in respect of its entire territory unless a contrary intention is indicated.[37] Article 56 of the Convention is a clear example of such a contrary intention. It is an example of what has been labelled a 'negative colonial clause' because it establishes the inapplicability of the treaty to non-metropolitan territories in the absence of a distinct declaration.[38] Article 56 appears to establish the inapplicability of the Convention to territories for whose international relations the State Party is responsible in the absence of a declaration made to that effect in accordance with paragraphs 1 and 2 of article 56. Even when a State Party has made such a declaration, the Convention is still to be applied 'with due regard . . . to local circumstances' (art. 56(3)). Finally, pursuant to article 56(4), a State Party may by declaration extend the jurisdiction of the European Court of Human Rights for individual applications concerning alleged violations of the Convention on the territory in question, in accordance with article 34.

The Convention organs have rejected applications that concern 'territories' for which the State Party was responsible but where no article 56 declaration had been formulated. For example, the European Commission of Human Rights declared inadmissible an application concerning Hong Kong, before it was returned to China, given the absence of any declaration by the United Kingdom pursuant to article 56.[39] Similarly, the Court declared an application concerning Macao to be inadmissible because Portugal had not made such a declaration.[40] The same principle applies if the State Party has declared the Convention applicable but not all of the Protocols, to the extent that the application

[34] Note of Mr Robertson dated 14 November 1950, VII *TP* 12–23, at pp. 14–19.
[35] Protocol No. 11 to the Convention for the Protection of Human Rights and Fundamental Freedoms, restructuring the control machinery established thereby, ETS 155, art. 2(2).
[36] Explanatory Report on Protocol No. 11, para. 113.
[37] Syméon Karagiannis, 'Article 29. Territorial Scope of Treaties', in Olivier Corten and Pierre Klein, eds, *The Vienna Convention on the Law of Treaties, A Commentary*, Vol. I, Oxford: Oxford University Press, 2011, pp. 731–63, at p. 732.
[38] J.E.S. Fawcett, 'Treaty Relations of British Overseas Territories', (1949) 26 *British Yearbook of International Law* 86, at pp. 96–7.
[39] *Bui van Thanh and Others v. the United Kingdom*, no. 16137/90, Commission decision of 12 March 1990, (1990) 33 YB 59, DR 65-A, p. 330.
[40] *Yonghong v. Portugal* (dec.), no. 50887/99, ECHR 1999–IX.

concerns one of the Protocols not contemplated by the declaration.[41] Besides the issue of a declaration accepting the application of the Convention there is also the matter of acceptance of the jurisdiction of the Court, something contemplated by paragraph 4 of article 56. The Court will declare inadmissible an application concerning a territory even if the State Party has declared that it accepts the application of the Convention to the extent that there is no supplementary declaration recognising the jurisdiction of the Court.[42]

There can today be little doubt that article 56 of the Convention is an anachronism. As applicants have pointed out, it is inconsistent with the approach the Court has taken to the territorial jurisdiction of the Convention, pursuant to article 1, by which it is applicable even where the State Party bears no responsibility with respect to the international relations of the territory to the extent that it exercises some form of effective control over that territory. On this basis, the Court has held the United Kingdom responsible for the treatment of prisoners in Iraq.[43] However, despite this legal development in the application and interpretation of article 1 of the Convention, the Court subsequently refused to apply Protocol No. 1 of the Convention to a British Overseas Territory, the South Georgia and South Sandwich Islands, because no declaration pursuant to article 56 had been formulated. To applicants who argued that the regime of article 56 is 'outdated, geared to the colonial systems in the aftermath of the Second World War', and that 'the Convention should not be interpreted so as to allow the United Kingdom to escape responsibility for its unlawful actions where there is no objective justification for failing to extend the Convention and its Protocols fully', the Court replied:

The Court can only agree that the situation has changed considerably since the time that the Contracting Parties drafted the Convention, including former Article 63. Interpretation, albeit a necessary tool to render the protection of Convention rights practical and effective, can only go so far. It cannot unwrite provisions contained in the Convention. If the Contracting States wish to bring the declarations system to an end, this can only be possible through an amendment to the Convention to which those States agree and give evidence of their agreement through signature and ratification. Since there is no dispute as to the status of the SGSSI as a territory for whose international relations the United Kingdom is responsible within the meaning of Article 56, the Court finds that the Convention and its Protocols cannot apply unless expressly extended by declaration. The fact that the United Kingdom has extended the Convention itself to the territory gives no ground for finding that Protocol No. 1 must also apply or for the Court to require the United Kingdom somehow to justify its failure to extend that Protocol. There is no obligation under the Convention for any Contracting State to ratify any particular Protocol or to give reasons for their decisions in that regard concerning their national jurisdictions. Still less can there be any such obligation as regards the territories falling under the scope of Article 56 of the Convention.[44]

Similarly, the Court explained that the 'effective control' principle of jurisdiction, applied to address cases of armed occupation and to avoid leaving a gap in the protection within the 'Convention space', does not replace the regime established by article 56.[45] 'The situations covered by the "effective control" principle are clearly separate and distinct from circumstances where a Contracting State has not, through a declaration under Article 56,

---

[41] *Quark Fishing Ltd v. the United Kingdom* (dec.), no. 15305/06, ECHR 2006-XIV.
[42] *Chagos Islanders v. the United Kingdom* (dec.), no. 35622/04, §§ 61–62, 11 December 2012.
[43] E.g., *Al-Saadoon and Mufdhi v. the United Kingdom*, no. 61498/08, § 165, ECHR 2010 (extracts).
[44] *Quark Fishing Ltd v. the United Kingdom* (dec.), no. 15305/06, ECHR 2006-XIV.
[45] *Chagos Islanders v. the United Kingdom* (dec.), no. 35622/04, § 39, 11 December 2012.

extended the Convention or any of its Protocols to an overseas territory for whose international relations it is responsible', it said.[46]

The Court has held out the possibility of amendment of the Convention in order to remove the anomaly of article 56. But there seems little support for such a change. Indeed, Protocol No. 16 to the Convention, adopted in 2013, expressly contemplates the special jurisdictional regime set up by article 56 in that it allows the 'highest courts and tribunals' to make territorial exceptions when they submit requests for advisory opinions to the Court. According to the Explanatory Report, '[i]n order to accommodate the provisions of article 56 of the Convention, whereby it may apply to some territories of a State and not to others, article 1 of Protocol No. 16 authorises a State to make a declaration at the time of ratification of Protocol No. 16 by which it excludes certain territories'.[47]

With the acquisition of independence, any declaration extending the application of the Convention to a territory and granting jurisdiction to the European Court of Human Rights comes to an end.[48] Where formerly dependent territories are part of Europe, they may subsequently join the Council of Europe in their own right, as Cyprus and Malta have done. In 1963, the United Kingdom informed the Council of Europe that Cyprus had become independent as of 16 August 1960 and that accordingly the responsibilities assumed by Her Majesty's Government under the Convention had 'lapsed' as of that date. Cyprus had been subject to the Convention prior to its independence by virtue of a declaration of extension formulated by the United Kingdom in 1953.[49] Cyprus became a State Party to the Convention on 6 October 1962. In 2004, the United Kingdom submitted a declaration of extension with regard to its two Sovereign Base Areas in Cyprus, adding that it accepted the competence of the Court to receive applications.[50]

'Territories for whose international relations it is responsible'

Although colloquially referred to as the 'colonial clause', the nomenclature adopted in article 56 is 'territories for whose international relations it is responsible'. The expression is similar to what is employed in article 13 of the 1948 Genocide Convention: 'the territories for the conduct of whose foreign relations that Contracting Party is responsible'. During negotiations of the Genocide Convention, Gerald Fitzmaurice of the United Kingdom argued that such clauses had been customary in multilateral treaties for the previous twenty or thirty years, although in recent times they had raised difficulties 'based on purely political motives and designed to create difficulties for the colonial powers'.[51] When the International Law Commission was drafting the Convention on the Law of Treaties, Fitzmaurice, then acting as rapporteur, distinguished between 'metropolitan' and 'dependent' territories. The term 'metropolitan territory' denoted 'all

---

[46] *Al-Skeini and Others v. the United Kingdom* [GC], no. 55721/07, § 140, ECHR 2011; *Hassan v. the United Kingdom* [GC], no. 29750/09, § 74, 16 September 2014.

[47] Explanatory Report on Protocol No. 16, para. 8.

[48] *X v. the Netherlands*, no. 7230/75, DR 7, p. 109.

[49] (1955–56–57) 1 YB 46–47.

[50] (2004) 47 YB 23. The two Sovereign Base Areas are deemed British Overseas Territories. They were retained by Britain pursuant to the Treaty of Establishment, (1960) 382 UNTS 160, adopted at the time of the independence of Cyprus in 1960. See the report by the rapporteur of the Parliamentary Assembly of the Council of Europe on the application of human rights law, including the European Convention on Human Rights, in the Sovereign Base Areas: Situation of the inhabitants of the Sovereign Base Areas of Akrotiri and Dhekelia, Explanatory Memorandum by Mr Andreas Gross, Doc. 11232, paras 10–12.

[51] UN Doc. A/C.6/SR.107.

those territories of a contracting party which are administered directly by its central government under the basic constitution of the State, in such a manner that this government is not subject, either in the domestic or in the international field, to any other or ulterior authority'. A 'dependent territory' was a territory that was not a 'metropolitan territory'.[52] In a very early case, the European Commission noted that the phrase 'territories for whose international relations it is responsible' had 'succeeded other, more restrictive terms employed such as "colonies", or "non-metropolitan areas"'. It said 'this change represents an effort to facilitate, although without rendering compulsory, the application of the more important international treaties to territories the status of which is as varied as it is changeable but without assigning a final degree of importance to any one such status'.[53]

In *Loizidou v. Turkey*, the Court offered a rather charitable explanation of the object and purpose of the colonial clause, suggesting that it sheltered a State Party from responsibility for the acts of another entity merely because it assumed responsibility for its foreign relations.[54] Indeed, there are certainly examples, even in modern times, of such relationships. British documents indicate that the United Kingdom considered the rule, subsequently codified in article 29 of the Vienna Convention on the Law of Treaties, was a customary norm that could only be set aside with an express provision.[55]

Determining whether a territory is properly described as a 'territory for whose international relations a State is responsible' raises problems of its own. In litigation before the Court, an applicant seeking to establish jurisdiction may argue that a territory does not in fact fall within such a category, with the consequence that it is thereby deemed to be part of the State's 'metropolitan' territory or, alternatively, a territory over which it exercises control. Either conclusion results in jurisdiction, whereas if the State can establish that the territory is a 'territory for whose international relations a State is responsible' it may then be able to invoke the absence of an article 56 declaration. The scope of the term 'territory for whose international relations a State is responsible' was considered by the European Commission of Human Rights in an early case concerning the Belgian Congo. The Commission rejected a claim by the applicants that the Congo was in fact part of Belgian territory and that as a result article 56 did not apply. The application was dismissed given the absence of any declaration by Belgium.[56] In a case against the United Kingdom concerning Guernsey, the Court referred to a statement made in 1950 by the United Kingdom and circulated widely, including within the Council of Europe, concerning the position of the Channel Islands in relation to treaties and international agreements applicable to the United Kingdom. The Court said that '[i]t was thereby established that the island of Guernsey should be regarded as a "territory for the international relations of which [the United Kingdom] is responsible"' for the purposes of treaty provisions. Because the United Kingdom had made no declaration concerning Guernsey with respect to Protocol No. 1, which was one basis of the litigation, the Court held that part of the application to be inadmissible.[57] In another application, the Commission had reached a similar conclusion with respect to Jersey.[58]

---

[52] UN Doc. A/CN.4/Ser.A/1959/Add.1, Vol. II, p. 48.

[53] *X v. Belgium*, no. 1065/61, Commission decision of 30 May 1961, (1961) 4 YB 260.

[54] *Loizidou v. Turkey* (Preliminary objections), 23 March 1995, § 67, Series A no. 310.

[55] L. Moor and A.W. Brian Simpson, 'Ghosts of Colonialism in the European Convention on Human Rights', (2006) 76 *British Yearbook of International Law* 121, at pp. 151–2.

[56] *X v. Belgium*, no. 1065/61, Commission decision of 30 May 1961, (1961) 4 YB 260.

[57] *Gillow v. the United Kingdom*, 24 November 1986, § 62, Series A no. 109.

[58] *X v. the United Kingdom*, no. 8873/80, Commission decision of 13 May 1982, DR 99, p. 99.

'Due regard for local requirements' (art. 56(3))

The Convention is to be applied in territories contemplated by article 56 'with due regard, however, to local requirements'. On the one hand, this offends notions of universality in the protection of human rights. It leaves the suspicion that European colonial powers intended that even when human rights protections were extended to their dependent territories, adjustments would be made in deference to the colonial relationship. At the same time, the recognition of local requirements 'may prove a prescient insight by its drafters in favour of a place for minorities and indigenous peoples inhabiting the last "colonies" of European Powers'.[59]

France insisted upon the 'local requirements' condition in a declaration associated with its instrument of ratification: 'The Government of the Republic further declares that the Convention shall apply to the whole territory of the Republic, having due regard, where the overseas territories are concerned, to local requirements, as mentioned in Article 63 [now article 56]'.[60] France later invoked the declaration before the Court, claiming that it amounted to a reservation. With reference to overseas territories in the Pacific Ocean, France contended that 'local requirements 'were the indisputable special features of protecting public order in the Pacific territories, namely their island status and distance from metropolitan France'.[61]

The messages in the case law of the Court as to the rationale behind paragraph 3 have not been entirely consistent. In *Tyrer v. the United Kingdom*, the Court opined 'that the system established by Article 63 (art. 63) was primarily designed to meet the fact that, when the Convention was drafted, there were still certain colonial territories whose state of civilisation did not, it was thought, permit the full application of the Convention'.[62] Yet at about the same time, the European Commission said that the purpose of article 56 was not only the territorial extension of the Convention but 'its adaptation to the measure of self-government attained in particular non-metropolitan territories and to the cultural and social differences in such territories'.[63] In another, more recent, case, the Court limited itself to explaining the features of article 63 as being included in the Convention for 'historical reasons'.[64] France has argued before the Court that the purpose of article 56, and especially paragraph 3, is to 'take into account the autonomy afforded in such matters to certain overseas territories'.[65]

The notion of 'local requirements' was invoked by the United Kingdom in the *Tyrer* case, where the use of corporal punishment for juveniles was challenged as a violation of article 3 of the Convention. The United Kingdom had extended the Convention to the Isle of Man in 1953. The European Commission of Human Rights said it did not find 'any significant social or cultural differences between the Isle of Man and the United

---

[59] Syméon Karagiannis, 'Article 29. Territorial Scope of Treaties', in Olivier Corten and Pierre Klein, eds, *The Vienna Convention on the Law of Treaties, A Commentary*, Vol. I, Oxford: Oxford University Press, 2011, pp. 731–63, at p. 743.

[60] Cited in *Piermont v. France*, 27 April 1995, §§ 28, 44, Series A no. 314; *Py v. France*, no. 66289/01, § 59, ECHR 2005-I (extracts).

[61] *Piermont v. France*, 27 April 1995, §56, Series A no. 314.

[62] *Tyrer v. the United Kingdom*, 25 April 1978, § 38, Series A no. 26.

[63] *Cyprus v. Turkey*, nos 6780/74 and 6950/75, Commission decision of 26 May 1975, (1975) 18 YB 84, DR 2, p. 125.

[64] *Al-Skeini and Others v. the United Kingdom* [GC], no. 55721/07, § 140, ECHR 2011; *Hassan v. the United Kingdom*, [GC], no. 29750/09, § 74, 16 September 2014.

[65] *Py v. France*, no. 66289/01, § 26, ECHR 2005-I (extracts).

Kingdom which could be relevant to the application of Art. 3 in the present case'.[66] When the case proceeded to the Court, the United Kingdom asked the Chamber to conduct an *in situ* examination on the Isle of Man so that it could 'become acquainted at first hand with local circumstances and requirements in the Isle of Man, having regard to Article 63 para. 3 (art. 63-3) of the Convention, by meeting... leading members of the Manx community'.[67] Indeed, counsel for the United Kingdom insisted upon the role of local public opinion, saying it strongly endorsed the virtues of judicial corporal punishment for young offenders. Agreeing with the Commission, the Court held that 'undoubtedly sincere beliefs on the part of members of the local population afford some indication that judicial corporal punishment is considered necessary in the Isle of Man as a deterrent and to maintain law and order'.[68] But for article 56(3) to apply, 'more would be needed: there would have to be positive and conclusive proof of a requirement and the Court could not regard beliefs and local public opinion on their own as constituting such proof'.[69] In a French case, the Court concluded that '[a] political situation, admittedly a sensitive one but also one which could occur in the mother country, does not suffice in order to interpret the phrase "local requirements" as justifying an interference' with freedom of expression.[70]

In only one case has the Court actually applied the 'local requirements' exception. It dealt with legislation in New Caledonia that restricted the right to vote to certain individuals. This was associated with an increasing autonomy of the local authorities. The Court said that 'the history and status of New Caledonia are such that they may be said to constitute "local requirements" warranting the restrictions imposed on the applicant's right to vote'.[71] In a subsequent decision, when the Court refused to allow restrictions on the right of prisoners to vote in the United Kingdom, Judge Costa raised the issue of 'double standards'. He acknowledged that the New Caledonia decision might have found support in 'local requirements' but noted another incompatible ruling within a European State.[72]

Individual applications to the Court (art. 56(4))

Not only does article 56 of the Convention require a declaration by States in order to extend the jurisdiction of the Court to their dependent territories, it also imposes a further condition for the right of individual petition to the Court to be permitted. The scheme is

---

[66] *Tyrer v. the United Kingdom*, no. 5856/72, § 47, Commission report of 14 December 1976. See also, with respect to Guernsey: *Gillow v. the United Kingdom*, 24 November 1986, § 62, Series A no. 109; *Wiggins v. the United Kingdom*, no. 7456/76, Commission decision of 8 February 1978, DR 13, p. 40, at p. 48. To Gibraltar: *Matthews v. the United Kingdom* [GC], no. 24833/94, § 59, ECHR 1999-I.

[67] *Tyrer v. the United Kingdom*, 25 April 1978, § 6, Series A no. 26.

[68] Ibid. Also *Py v. France*, no. 66289/01, § 60, ECHR 2005-I (extracts); *Matthews v. the United Kingdom* [GC], no. 24833/94, § 59, ECHR 1999-I.

[69] *Tyrer v. the United Kingdom*, 25 April 1978, § 6, Series A no. 26.

[70] *Piermont v. France*, 27 April 1995, § 59, Series A no. 314.

[71] *Py v. France*, no. 66289/01, § 64, ECHR 2005-I (extracts). See also *Piermont v. France*, 27 April 1995, Joint Partly Dissenting Opinion of Judges Ryssdal, Matscher, Sir John Freeland and Jungwiert, § 3, Series A no. 314. Along similar lines, see *Matthews v. the United Kingdom*, no. 24833/94, Commission report of 29 October 1997, Concurring Opinion of Mr E. Busuttil and Concurring Opinion of Mr L. Loucaides.

[72] *Hirst v. the United Kingdom (no. 2)* [GC], no. 74025/01, Dissenting Opinion of Judge Costa, § 6, ECHR 2005-IX.

similar to what existed under the 1950 text of the Convention, whereby States were required to accept the jurisdiction of the Court by a declaration that was additional to their actual ratification or accession to the Convention. But paragraph 4 'hardly appears justifiable' because Protocol No. 11 generalizes and broadens the right of individual recourse to the European Court of Human Rights.[73]

When the United Kingdom recognized the right of individual petition to the European Commission of Human Rights, in 1966, it included the following declaration: 'This declaration does not extend to petitions in relation to anything done or occurring in any territory in respect of which the competence of the European Commission of Human Rights to receive petitions has not been recognised by the Government of the United Kingdom or to petitions in relation to anything done or occurring in the United Kingdom in respect of such a territory or of matters arising there.'[74]

Since Protocol No. 11 entered into force, the United Kingdom has made several declarations recognizing the competence of the Court with respect to individual petitions from territories to which the Convention has been extended. In 2001, it made such declarations valid for a period of five years with respect to several islands in the Atlantic Ocean and the Caribbean Sea, as well as the Bailiwick of Guernsey and Gibraltar. It subsequently made declarations 'on a permanent basis' with respect to the Bailiwick of Jersey, the Isle of Man, the Sovereign Base Areas of Aktrotiri and Dhekelia in Cyprus, the Falkland Islands, Gibraltar, South Georgia and South Sandwich Islands, the Turks and Caicos Islands, the British Virgin Islands, Anguilla, Bermuda, Montserrat, St. Helena, Ascension, and Tristan de Cunha.[75]

A potential difficulty arose in a case filed before the Commission against the United Kingdom concerning corporal punishment on the Isle of Man. An article 56 declaration was in force at the time the application was filed but it had lapsed when the Commission had dealt with the matter. The Commission considered that jurisdiction was established because a declaration had been in force at the time the initial application was filed. The United Kingdom said that it did not object to jurisdiction but 'it was not to be inferred that they necessarily agreed with the reasoning in the Commission's request'.[76]

Further reading

F. Coomans and M. Kamminga, eds, *Extraterritorial Application of Human Rights Treaties*, Antwerp: Intersentia, 2004.
Frowein/Peukert, *MenschenRechtsKonvention*, pp. 623–7.
Syméon Karagiannis, 'L'aménagement des droits de l'homme outre-mer: la clause des « nécessités locales » de la Convention européenne', in [1995] *Revue belge de droit international* 224.
C. Lush, 'The Territorial Application of the European Convention on Human Rights: Recent Case Law', (1993) 42 *ICLQ* 897.

---

[73] Syméon Karagiannis, 'Article 29. Territorial Scope of Treaties', in Olivier Corten and Pierre Klein, eds, *The Vienna Convention on the Law of Treaties, A Commentary*, Vol. I, Oxford: Oxford University Press, 2011, pp. 731–63, at p. 743.
[74] Cited in *Bui van Thanh and Others v. the United Kingdom*, no. 16137/90, Commission decision of 12 March 1990, (1990) 33 YB 59, DR 65-A, p. 330.
[75] (2004) 47 YB 24; (2006) 49 YB 9; (2009) 52 YB 8; (2010) 53 YB 26–27.
[76] *Tyrer v. the United Kingdom*, 25 April 1978, § 27, Series A no. 26.

Barbara Miltner, 'Revisiting Extraterritoriality after Al-Skeini: The ECHR and Its Lessons', (2012) 33 *Michigan Journal of International Law* 693.

Louise Moor and A.W. Brian Simpson, 'Ghosts of Colonialism in the European Convention on Human Rights', (2006) 76 *British Yearbook of International Law* 121.

Michael Wood, 'Article 63', in Pettiti et al., *La Convention européenne*, pp. 915–21.

Article 57. Reservations/Réserves

1. Any State may, when signing this Convention or when depositing its instrument of ratification, make a reservation in respect of any particular provision of the Convention to the extent that any law then in force in its territory is not in conformity with the provision. Reservations of a general character shall not be permitted under this Article.	1. Tout Etat peut, au moment de la signature de la présente Convention ou du dépôt de son instrument de ratification, formuler une réserve au sujet d'une disposition particulière de la Convention, dans la mesure où une loi alors en vigueur sur son territoire n'est pas conforme à cette disposition. Les réserves de caractère général ne sont pas autorisées aux termes du présent article.
2. Any reservation made under this Article shall contain a brief statement of the law concerned.	2. Toute réserve émise conformément au présent article comporte un bref exposé de la loi en cause.

Introductory comments

Reservations are a feature of multilateral treaty practice, although some Conventions prohibit them altogether.[1] Many treaties, however, recognize the flexibility that a reservations regime brings to them, enabling States that are in agreement with most but not all of the provisions to ratify or accede to the instrument. Some of them impose conditions of substance as well as form, such as that they be consistent with the 'object and purpose' of the treaty,[2] or restrict the possibility of reservation to certain provisions of the treaty.[3] If the treaty is silent on the subject of reservations, the general rule set out in the Vienna Convention on the Law of Treaties is that they must be compatible with the instrument's 'object and purpose'.[4]

The European Convention on Human Rights may well be the human rights treaty with the most generous approach to reservations. It imposes no real requirements of substance, not even that the reservation be compatible with the instrument's object and purpose. The Convention only imposes formal requirements upon the formulation of reservations.

In the 1990s, the issue of reservations was a real preoccupation of human rights institutions. This was provoked by a large number of exceedingly broad reservations to human rights treaties within the United Nations system. The problem did not really arise

---

[1] Rome Statute of the International Criminal Court, (2002) 2187 UNTS 90, art. 120.

[2] American Convention on Human Rights, (1978) 1144 UNTS 123, art. 75; Convention on the Rights of the Child, (1990) 1577 UNTS 3, art. 51.

[3] Second Optional Protocol to the International Covenant on Civil and Political Rights Aimed at Abolition of the Death Penalty, (1991) 1642 UNTS 414, art. 2: Convention on the Political Rights of Women, (1953) 193 UNTS 135, art. VII; Convention Relating to the Status of Refugees, (1951) 189 UNTS 137, art. 42(1); Convention on the Nationality of Married Women, (1957) 309 UNTS 65, art. 8; International Convention on the Elimination of All Forms of Racial Discrimination, (1966) 660 UNTS 195, art. 20; Protocol Relating to the Status of Refugees, (1969) 606 UNTS 267, art. VII; Convention on the Elimination of All Forms of Discrimination Against Women, (1980) 1249 UNTS 13, art. 28.

[4] (1980) 1155 UNTS 331, art. 19(b).

under the European Convention on Human Rights because article 57 prohibits reservations of a general nature. In any case, the concern with reservations to human rights
treaties has probably diminished in recent years, perhaps because of the growing effectiveness of mechanisms like the Universal Periodic Review of the Human Rights Council,
where reservations to human rights norms are rarely, if ever, invoked by States and, for all
practical purposes, appear to be virtually irrelevant.

Within the European system, there have been calls for States Parties to withdraw
reservations that are no longer relevant or that have become obsolete because of legislative
changes. As early as 1993, the Parliamentary Assembly said the number of reservations to
Council of Europe treaties should be 'considerably reduced'.[5] In 2004, the Parliamentary
Assembly said that reservations 'should not therefore be of a permanent nature and should
be confined to the period required to bring the legislation in question into conformity
with the Convention'.[6] It noted that numerous States had withdrawn reservations 'as is
the intended practice'.[7] The Committee of Ministers confirmed the position taken by the
Parliamentary Assembly about the desirability of withdrawal of reservations, although it
did not endorse the Assembly's proposal that a three-year deadline be set.[8]

Drafting of the provision

The idea of a reservations clause first surfaced in discussions within the Committee of
Experts, in March 1950, where a favourable reference was made by some members to a
Danish proposal in the debates on the draft Covenant on Human Rights in the United
Nations Commission on Human Rights.[9]

At the Conference of Senior Officials, which met in June 1950, the United Kingdom
proposed the following:

Article concerning reservations.
1) Any State may, when signing this Convention or when depositing its instrument of ratification
   or accession, make a reservation in respect of any provision of the Convention to the extent that
   any law then in force on its territory is not in conformity with that provision.
2) Any reservation made under this article shall contain a brief statement of the law concerned.
3) Reservations of a general character shall not be permitted.[10]

The tenor of the debates indicates that this was viewed as a transitional provision, whereby
States might ratify the Convention even if their legislation was not entirely consistent with
the Convention. For example, the author of the provision on reservations, Samuel Hoare,
described it as 'illogical' to provide that a State could retain legislation incompatible with

---

[5] Recommendation 1223 (1993) on reservations made by member states to Council of Europe
Convention.

[6] Ratification of protocols and withdrawal of reservations and derogations made in respect of the European
Convention on Human Rights, Recommendation 1671 (2004), para. 7.

[7] Ibid., para. 9.

[8] Ibid., para. 2.

[9] Report to the Committee of Ministers submitted by the Committee of Experts Instructed to Draw Up a
Draft Convention of Collective Guarantee of Human Rights and Fundamental Freedoms, Doc. CM/WP 1 (5)
15, A 924, IV *TP* 2–55, at pp. 48–50.

[10] Proposal submitted by the United Kingdom Delegation, Doc. CM/WP 4 (50) 7, A 1368, IV *TP* 162–5.

the Convention. He favoured imposing a time limit for a State to adjust its legislation.[11] During the debate, the representative of the Netherlands said 'his government would not wish there to be any reservations with regard to application of the Convention in the matter of religious freedom, except where existing legislation was concerned'.[12] The Conference adopted a provision based upon the United Kingdom's proposal, the only significant change involving moving the text of paragraph 3 to the end of paragraph 1.[13] Related to the issue of reservations was a proposal by which States were required to make a solemn declaration to the effect that their domestic legislation gave full effect to the Convention. The Conference of Senior Officials decided not to include such a provision given that allowance was being made for States Parties to make reservations 'with respect to the maintenance of certain existing laws which might not be in accordance with a particular provision of the Convention'.[14]

The report of the Conference of Senior Officials was considered by the Committee on Legal and Administrative Questions of the Consultative Assembly. Concerns were expressed about the provision on reservations. Members of the Committee said they should be made only 'exceptionally' and that they should be accompanied by a 'statement of reasons'. The Committee decided that States making reservations 'should undertake to send to the Secretary General of the Council of Europe periodical Reports which pointed out the reasons for which the law in question was maintained; and that this procedure should be followed until the situation was changed'.[15] In its comments on the draft, the Committee said it would object if 'States were allowed unlimited power to reserve the least "ne varietur" in their legislation on each of the matters dealt with in the Convention. Such a power would threaten to deprive the latter of its practical effect and in any case of its moral authority.' The Committee added that the validity of ratifications should be subject to the acceptance of a qualified majority of the other States Parties and that it would be advisable that the motives for such reservations be stated.[16]

Meeting in August 1950, the Committee of Ministers formulated this text:

1) Any State may when signing this Convention or when depositing its instrument of ratification or accession, make a reservation in respect of any particular provision of the Convention to the extent that any law then in force in its territory is not in conformity with that provision. Reservations of a general character shall not be permitted under this Article.

2) Any reservation made under this article shall contain a brief statement of the law concerned.[17]

[11] Minutes of the afternoon setting [of 12 June 1950], unreferenced document, IV *TP* 170–81, at pp. 170–2.

[12] Ibid., p. 172.

[13] Draft Convention appended to the draft report, Doc. CM/WP 4 (50) 16, appendix, A 1445, IV *TP* 218–40, at p. 238, art. 61.

[14] Text of the report submitted by the Conference [of Senior Officials] to the Committee of Ministers, Doc. CM/WP 4 (50) 19, CM/WP 4 (50) 16 rev., A 1431, IV *TP* 242–73, at p. 256; Draft report to the Committee of Ministers, Doc. CM/WP 4 (50) 16, A 1426, IV *TP* 204–17, at p. 216.

[15] Minutes of the morning meeting [of 24 June 1950, of the Committee on Legal and Administrative Questions of the Consultative Assembly], Doc. AS/JA (50) PV 2, A 1841, V *TP* 14–21, at p. 18.

[16] Letter of 24 June 1950 from Sir David Maxwell Fyfe, Chairman of the Committee on Legal and Administrative Questions, to the Chairman of the Committee of Ministers, Doc. CM (50) 29, V *TP* 32–41, at p. 40. Also Additions to the draft letter proposed by M. Rolin, Doc. AS/JA (50) 3, A 1544, V *TP* 26–29, at p. 28; Further additions, Doc. AS/JA (50) 4, A 1546, pp. 28–31.

[17] Draft Convention adopted by the Sub-Committee, Doc. CM 1 (50) 52, A 1884, V *TP* 76–99, at p. 88.

Adopted as article 63 in the 1950 text of the Convention, the provision was renumbered as article 57 by Protocol No. 11. The heading 'Reservations' was also added by Protocol No. 11.[18]

Analysis and interpretation

The Vienna Convention on the Law of Treaties defines a reservation as 'a unilateral statement, however phrased or named, made by a State, when signing, ratifying, accepting, approving or acceding to a treaty, whereby it purports to exclude or to modify the legal effect of certain provisions of the treaty in their application to that State'.[19] States may also make 'interpretative declarations'. The suggestion is that these are not reservations as such. However, the Court will look behind the nomenclature that the State has employed, considering the intention behind the declaration and whether or not it was in substance a reservation.[20] There is no substantive requirement in the sense that certain reservations are prohibited because of the rights involved.[21] In principle, a State could even make a reservation to such fundamental rights as those set out in articles 2, 3, and 4. Nevertheless, the power to make reservations is 'a limited one, being confined to particular provisions of the Convention'.[22]

The text of article 57(1) of the Convention, read in conjunction with article 1, confirms that 'ratification of the Convention by a State presupposes that any law then in force in its territory should be in conformity with the Convention'.[23] Reservations are therefore an exception to this general principle and are, consequently, subject to narrow interpretation.[24] However, there is no requirement that reservations to the Convention be compatible with its object and purpose, as is the case with most multilateral human rights treaties, either because they require this explicitly or because they are governed by article 31 of the Vienna Convention on the Law of Treaties. A descendent of the Italian royal family contended before the Court that a reservation to article 3(2) of Protocol No. 4 respecting legislation that prevented his return to Italy was invalid because it was inspired by discriminatory grounds based on birth and sex, thereby violating the universal scope of the Convention. The Court said that serious questions of fact and in law were raised, in particular concerning the validity of the reservation.[25] However, the case never did proceed to the merits. In 2002, as part of the settlement of these proceedings, Italy

---

[18] Protocol No. 11 to the Convention for the Protection of Human Rights and Fundamental Freedoms, restructuring the control machinery established thereby, ETS 155, art. 2(2).

[19] (1980) 1155 UNTS 331, art. 2(1)(*d*).

[20] *Belilos v. Switzerland*, 29 April 1988, § 49, Series A no. 132; *Temeltasch v. Switzerland*, no. 9116/80, Commission report of 5 May 1982, DR 31, p. 147, § 73; *Ilaşcu and Others v. Moldova and Russia* (dec.) [GC], no. 48787/99, 4 July 2001.

[21] But see *Belilos v. Switzerland*, 29 April 1988, Concurring Opinion of Judge de Meyer, Series A no. 132.

[22] *Loizidou v. Turkey* (Preliminary objections), 23 March 1995, § 76, Series A no. 310.

[23] *Slivenko v. Latvia* [GC], no. 48321/99, § 60, ECHR 2003-X.

[24] *Schmautzer v. Austria*, 23 October 1995, § 31, Series A no. 328-A; *Umlauft v. Austria*, 23 October 1995, § 34, Series A no. 328-B.

[25] *Victor-Emmanuel De Savoie v. Italy* (dec.), no. 53360/99, 13 September 2001.

notified the Secretary General of the Council of Europe, as well as the Court itself,[26] that it had withdrawn the declaration in question.

The Vienna Convention on the Law of Treaties contemplates a system whereby States Parties themselves determine the legality of reservations through the mechanism of objections. This does not correspond to practice under the European Convention where the Court 'always retains the power to examine whether or not a purported reservation has been validly made in conformity with the requirements of Article 57'.[27] The silence of the depositary and States Parties does not prevent the Court from making its own assessment.[28] If the Court determines that a reservation is valid, it is without jurisdiction *ratione materiae* to consider the conformity of the legal provisions governed by the reservation with the rights set out in the Convention.[29]

The Court has noted the relevance of reservations to the interpretation of the Convention in a more general sense. It has said with respect to article 2 of Protocol No. 1 that the existence of reservations tends to confirm the fact that the final draft of the provision 'does not seem to settle a number of doubts about its application'.[30]

Formulation at time of signature or ratification

A reservation to the European Convention on Human Rights must be made at the time the State signs or ratifies the treaty, as article 57(1) makes quite clear. There are examples in the practice of States Parties to the European Convention of modification of a reservation subsequent to signature or ratification. This would seem to be prohibited by the Convention. In one case concerning the modification by Liechtenstein of its reservation, the Court declined to pronounce itself on this issue, noting that the change in the reservation was not relevant to the dispute.[31]

When Greece ratified Protocol No. 1 for the second time (having denounced the Convention and the Protocols in 1970), it formulated the following reservation: 'For the application of Article 2 of the 1952 Protocol, the Government of Greece, in view of certain provisions of the Education Acts in force in Greece, formulates a reservation according to which the principle affirmed in the second sentence of Article 2, is accepted only so far as it is compatible with the provision of efficient instruction and training, and the avoidance of unreasonable public expenditure.'[32] Four years later, it informed the Council of Europe that the reservation had been entered by mistake and that it should be removed and replaced with the following: 'The application of the word *philosophical* which is the penultimate word of the second sentence of Article 2, will, in Greece, conform with the relevant provisions of internal legislation.'[33] The new reservation was in fact equivalent to the one made by Greece at the time of signature of the Protocol, in 1952. The depositary of the Convention replied to Greece that the 1952 reservation had

---

[26] *Victor-Emmanuel De Savoie v. Italy* (striking out), no. 53360/99, § 21, 24 April 2003.

[27] *Slivenko v. Latvia* [GC], no. 48321/99, § 60, ECHR 2003-X.

[28] *Belilos v. Switzerland*, 29 April 1988, § 47, Series A no. 132.

[29] *Slivenko v. Latvia* [GC], no. 48321/99, § 60, ECHR 2003-X; *Labzov v. Russia* (dec.), no. 62208/00, 28 February 2002.

[30] *Kjeldsen, Busk Madsen and Pedersen v. Denmark*, nos 5095/71, 5920/72, and 5926/72, Commission report of 21 March 1975, § 154.

[31] *Schädler-Eberle v. Liechtenstein*, no. 56422/09, § 74, 18 July 2013.

[32] (1976) 19 YB 20–21.

[33] (1979) 22 YB 14–15.

not been included in a recent publication because 'it was supposed that the reservation of 1974 to the same article had replaced the previous one'. The letter confirmed that it was the intention of Greece to withdraw the 1974 text and to 'retain the reservation made in 1952'. The depositary said that this would be brought to the attention of Council of Europe Member States.[34]

Law then in force

A reservation must relate to specific laws in force at the moment of ratification; although the case law is not entirely clear on this, it seems that the requirement that the reservation applies only to the law then in force means that it cannot cover future amendments or changes or new legislation in the same field.[35] If a new legislative provision is not essentially identical to the provision in force at the time of ratification, but extends the measures covered by the reservation, article 57 is not respected.[36]

An interesting problem arose in a Lithuanian case concerning the temporal scope of a reservation. At the time of ratification, Lithuania had formulated a reservation to article 5(3) that expired one year after entry into force of the Convention. The fact that the applicant was not brought before an appropriate officer when detention on remand was ordered, during the period when the reservation applied, could not therefore be a violation of the Convention.[37] The applicant argued that once the reservation had expired he was then entitled to be 'brought promptly' before an appropriate officer. The Court held that the term 'brought promptly' referred to the time when the individual was first deprived of liberty, and that only then was a State required to implement the obligation to bring the individual promptly before an appropriate officer. It said: 'A reservation under Article 57 of the Convention would be devoid of purpose if, upon its expiry, the State were required to enforce the right retroactively for the period covered by the reservation.'[38] Therefore, 'when the reservation expired Lithuania was no longer under an obligation to bring the applicant promptly before an appropriate officer. Consequently, there was no scope under Article 5 § 3 for a renewed obligation after the expiry of the reservation.'[39]

Prohibition of reservations of a general character

Reservations are only permissible if they respond to criteria of precision and clarity.[40] Paragraph 1 prohibits reservations of a general character. According to the European Commission of Human Rights, 'a reservation is of a general nature . . . when it is worded in such a way that it does not allow its scope to be determined'.[41] According to the Court, the 'general character' criterion denotes 'in particular a reservation which does not refer to

[34] Ibid., pp. 14–17.

[35] *Shestjorkin v. Estonia* (dec.), no. 49450/99, 15 June 2000; *Põder and Others v. Estonia* (dec.), no. 67723/01, 26 April 2005.

[36] *Fischer v. Austria*, 26 April 1995, § 41, Series A no. 312; *Stallinger and Kuso v. Austria*, 23 April 1997, § 48, *Reports of Judgments and Decisions* 1997-II; *Eisenstecken v. Austria*, no. 29477/95, § 25, ECHR 2000-X; *Dacosta Silva v. Spain*, no. 69966/01, § 37, ECHR 2006-XIII.

[37] *Jėčius v. Lithuania*, no. 34578/97, § 82, ECHR 2000-IX.

[38] Ibid., § 85.

[39] Ibid., § 86. Also *Grauslys v. Lithuania*, no. 36743/97, § 49, 10 October 2000.

[40] *Schädler-Eberle v. Liechtenstein*, no. 56422/09, § 62, 18 July 2013.

[41] *Temeltasch v. Switzerland*, no. 9116/80, § 84, Commission report of 5 May 1982, DR 31, p. 147.

a specific provision of the Convention or is couched in terms that are too vague or broad for it to be possible to determine their exact meaning and scope'.[42]

Examining Switzerland's 'declaration' concerning article 6(3)(e), the European Commission noted that it was 'clearly worded' and that it 'expressly refers to a provision of the Convention'. Thus, it could not be deemed a reservation of a general character.[43] But subsequently, the European Court said that Switzerland's reservation to article 6(1) did not meet the general character criterion. It was 'couched in terms that are too vague or broad for it to be possible to determine their exact meaning and scope'.[44]

Need for a brief statement of the law

In the absence of a brief statement of the law, a reservation will be declared non-compliant with the provisions of article 57 and invalid. The reservation will not apply to a law that it does not mention.[45] The Special Rapporteur on reservations of the International Law Commission has described this as a 'requirement to give reasons (or to explain)'.[46] Noting the absence of such a statement accompanying a general reservation to article 6 formulated by Austria in 1958, at the time of ratification, the Court said that 'a reservation which merely refers to a permissive, non-exhaustive, provision of the Constitution and which does not refer to, or mention, those specific provisions of the Austrian legal order which exclude public hearings, does not "afford to a sufficient degree 'a guarantee … that [it] does not go beyond the provision expressly excluded' by Austria"'.[47] In *Belilos v. Switzerland*, the Court held that the requirement that a reservation shall contain a brief statement of the law concerned is not a 'purely formal requirement but a condition of substance which constitutes an evidential factor and contributes to legal certainty'.[48] Such a 'stricter approach' was confirmed in subsequent judgments.[49]

The requirement of a brief statement is both an evidential factor and something that contributes to legal certainty. According to the Court, '[t]he purpose of Article 57 § 2 is to provide a guarantee—in particular for the other Contracting Parties and the Convention institutions—that a reservation does not go beyond the provisions expressly excluded by the State concerned. This is not a purely formal requirement, but a condition of substance.'[50]

It is not necessary to provide a description, even a concise one, of the substance of the texts governed by the reservation.[51] The requirements of article 57 were considered to

---

[42] *Schädler-Eberle v. Liechtenstein*, no. 56422/09, § 62, 18 July 2013; *Belilos v. Switzerland*, 29 April 1988, § 55, Series A no. 132; *Koslova and Smirnova v. Latvia* (dec.), no. 57381/00, 23 October 2001; *Shestjorkin v. Estonia* (dec.), no. 49450/99, 15 June 2000; *Steck-Risch v. Liechtenstein* (dec.), no. 63151/00, ECHR 2004-II.

[43] *Temeltasch v. Switzerland*, no. 9116/80, § 84, Commission report of 5 May 1982, DR 31, p. 147.

[44] *Belilos v. Switzerland*, 29 April 1988, § 55, Series A no. 132.

[45] *Pūpēdis v. Latvia* (dec.), no. 53631/00, 15 February 2001.

[46] Report of the International Law Commission, Sixtieth session (5 May–6 June and 7 July–8 August 2008), UN Doc. A/63/10, p. 185.

[47] *Eisenstecken v. Austria*, no. 29477/95, § 29, ECHR 2000-X, citing *Gradinger v. Austria*, 23 October 1995, § 51, Series A no. 328-C and *Chorherr v. Austria*, 25 August 1993, § 20, Series A no. 266-B.

[48] *Belilos v. Switzerland*, 29 April 1988, § 59, Series A no. 132.

[49] *Weber v. Switzerland*, 22 May 1990, § 38, Series A no. 177; *Eisenstecken v. Austria*, no. 29477/95, § 24, ECHR 2000-X.

[50] *Schädler-Eberle v. Liechtenstein*, no. 56422/09, § 63, 18 July 2013; *Belilos v. Switzerland*, 29 April 1988, § 59, Series A no. 132; *Weber v. Switzerland*, 22 May 1990, § 38, Series A no. 177; *Steck-Risch v. Lichtenstein* (dec.), no. 63151/00, ECHR 2004-II; *Dacosta Silva v. Spain*, no. 69966/01, § 37, ECHR 2006-XIII.

[51] *Schädler-Eberle v. Liechtenstein*, no. 56422/09, § 64, 18 July 2013.

have been met when the title of each law cited in a reservation was followed by a reference to the Official Gazette, 'so that anyone can identify precisely which laws are concerned and obtain information about them'. In addition, the annex briefly outlined the main aim and scope of each law contemplated by the reservation.[52] However, practical difficulties, such as listing and briefly describing all applicable legal enactments, do not justify a failure to comply with the requirements of article 57.[53]

When States formulate what amount to disguised reservations, labelling them 'interpretative declarations', they may not include a specific reference to legislation, with the consequence that what amounts to a reservation in substance is incompatible with the terms of article 57.[54] For example, upon signature Monaco made the following declaration: 'The Principality of Monaco undertakes to respect the provisions of the Convention while emphasising that the fact that it forms a State with limited territorial dimensions requires paying special attention to the issues of residence and work as well as to social measures in respect of foreigners, even if these matters are not covered by the Convention.'[55] Similar declarations were made by San Marino[56] and by Andorra.[57]

States have occasionally made reservations with respect to international treaties in force at the time of ratification. For example, Austria made a reservation to article 1 of Protocol No. 1 with respect to the provisions of the 1955 State Treaty. The Court has acknowledged that reservations concerning international treaties are permissible under article 57.[58]

Territorial reservations

Article 29 of the Vienna Convention on the Law of Treaties states that '[u]nless a different intention appears from the treaty or is otherwise established, a treaty is binding upon each party in respect of its entire territory'. The European Convention does not expressly provide for territorial reservations. It is, of course, possible to restrict the application of the Convention to a State's metropolitan territory, in accordance with article 56 of the Convention. However, where article 56 is not applicable, a State may not use a reservation to limit the territorial scope of the Convention. The Court has noted that the situation is different before the International Court of Justice but considers that such a distinction is explained by the 'fundamental difference in the role and purpose of the respective tribunals'.[59]

When Turkey accepted the jurisdiction of the Court under the provisions of the Convention in effect prior to the entry into force of Protocol No. 11, it claimed to restrict this to its metropolitan territory. Turkey was without colonies and therefore article

---

[52] *Koslova and Smirnova v. Latvia* (dec.), no. 57381/00, 23 October 2001; *Chorherr v. Austria*, 25 August 1993, § 20, Series A no. 266-B; *Steck-Risch v. Lichtenstein* (dec.), no. 63151/00, ECHR 2004-II; *Rékási v. Hungary*, no. 31506/96, Commission decision of 25 November 1996.

[53] *Grande Stevens and Others v. Italy*, nos 18640/10, 18647/10, 18663/10, 18668/10, and 18698/10, § 210, 4 March 2014; *Liepājnieks v. Latvia* (dec.), no. 37586/06, § 45, 2 November 2010; *Belilos v. Switzerland*, 29 April 1988, § 59, Series A no. 132.

[54] *Ilaşcu and Others v. Moldova and Russia* (dec.) [GC], no. 48787/99, 4 July 2001; *Gradinger v. Austria*, 23 October 1995, § 50, Series A no. 328-C.

[55] (2004) 47 YB 21.

[56] (1989) 32 YB 5.

[57] (1996) 39 YB 20.

[58] *Slivenko v. Latvia* [GC], no. 48321/99, § 61, ECHR 2003-X.

[59] *Loizidou v. Turkey* (Preliminary objections), 23 March 1995, § 85, Series A no. 310.

56 could not apply. Nevertheless, it apparently anticipated the possible application of the Convention to the territory it has occupied in Cyprus since the 1974 invasion. The Court referred to article 57 and its restriction of the scope of reservations as evidence that 'States could not qualify their acceptance of the optional clauses thereby effectively excluding areas of their law and practice within their "jurisdiction" from supervision by the Convention institutions'.[60] It raised the spectre of an inequality between States Parties that such qualified acceptance of jurisdiction might create, noting that this would also 'run counter to the aim, as expressed in the Preamble to the Convention, to achieve greater unity in the maintenance and further realisation of human rights'.[61]

Some States that do not fully control their own territory have made declarations explaining that they are not to be held responsible for violations of the Convention in such places. Moldova formulated a declaration at the time of ratification indicating that 'it will be unable to guarantee compliance with the provisions of the Convention in respect of omissions and acts committed by the organs of the self-proclaimed Trans-Dniester republic within the territory actually controlled by such organs, until the conflict in the region is finally settled'.[62] Upon ratification of Protocol No. 13, Moldova declared that 'until the full re-establishment of the territorial integrity of the Republic of Moldova, the provisions of the Protocol shall be applied only on the territory controlled effectively by the authorities of the Republic of Moldova'. Before the European Court of Human Rights, Moldova maintained that its declaration was a reservation satisfying the terms of article 57 of the Convention.[63] The Grand Chamber noted that the declaration itself did not purport to be a 'reservation', although it acknowledged a line of cases requiring that it look behind the title to determine the real intent.[64] The Court said that the Moldovan declaration did not comply with the terms of article 57 because it was general in nature, concluding that it could not be deemed a reservation.[65]

Azerbaijan made a similar declaration with respect to Mountainous Karabakh, stating at the time of ratification 'that it is unable to guarantee the application of the provisions of the Convention in the territories occupied by the Republic of Armenia until these territories are liberated from that occupation'. When it ratified Protocol No. 12 and Protocol No. 13, Georgia declared that it was not responsible for violations on the territories of Abkhazia and Tskhinvali Region 'until the full jurisdiction of Georgia is restored'.[66]

Objections

The Convention does not provide expressly for the possibility of objections to reservations. The Vienna Convention on the Law of Treaties codifies a reservations regime based upon the consent of other States Parties. It presents itself in a negative manner, in that the other States Parties to a multilateral treaty are deemed to consent in the absence of an objection that is formulated promptly. The relevant provision of the Convention states that '[a] reservation expressly authorized by a treaty does not require any subsequent

---

[60] Ibid., § 77.

[61] Ibid.

[62] (1997) 40 YB 35, 52.

[63] *Ilaşcu and Others v. Moldova and Russia* (dec.) [GC], no. 48787/99, 4 July 2001.

[64] Referring to *Belilos v. Switzerland*, 29 April 1988, § 49, Series A no. 132; *Temeltasch v. Switzerland*, no. 9116/80, § 73, Commission report of 5 May 1982, DR 31, p. 147.

[65] *Ilaşcu and Others v. Moldova and Russia* (dec.) [GC], no. 48787/99, 4 July 2001.

[66] (2001) 44 YB 24; (2003) 46 YB 13.

acceptance by the other contracting States unless the treaty so provides'.[67] It seems that the objections regime contemplated by article 20 of the Vienna Convention is inapplicable to the European Convention system. There have been only a few examples of a practice that resembles objections to reservations.

In 1987, Turkey formulated a declaration pursuant to what was then article 24 of the Convention, recognizing the jurisdiction of the European Commission of Human Rights to receive individual petitions but limited to 'the boundaries of the territory to which the Constitution of the Republic of Turkey is applicable'. This was contested by several States Parties. Greece was the most insistent of them, describing the 'reservation' as being 'null and void'. Other States issued declarations indicating their doubts about the validity of the Turkish position.[68] When it ruled the Turkish 'reservation' to be invalid, the Court did not describe the various statements as 'objections'. Rather, it viewed them as evidence of a practice among the States Parties by which territorial exceptions to declarations recognizing the jurisdiction of the Commission to receive individual petitions were not acceptable under the Convention.[69]

At the time of ratification, Portugal formulated a rather militant reservation: 'Article 1 of the Protocol will be applied subject to Article 82 of the Constitution of the Portuguese Republic, which provides that expropriations of large landowners, big property owners and entrepreneurs or shareholders may be subject to no compensation under the conditions to be laid down by the law.'[70] The United Kingdom reacted to the reservation with a letter to the Secretary General of the Council of Europe 're-affirm[ing] the view of the Government of the United Kingdom that the general principles of international law require the payment of prompt, adequate and effective compensation in respect of the expropriation of foreign property'.[71] Similar statements were made by Germany and France. The Secretary General replied to each country noting that the letters did not constitute a formal objection to the Portuguese reservation but that they would nevertheless be circulated to Member States.[72] The Special Rapporteur on reservations of the International Law Commission presented this as an example of a reaction to a reservation that does not constitute an objection.[73]

Further reading

Henry J. Bourguignon, 'The *Belilos* Case: New Light on Reservations to Multilateral Treaties', (1989) 29 *Virginia Journal of International Law* 347.

Iain Cameron and Frank Horn, 'Reservations to the European Convention on Human Rights: the Belilos Case', (1990) 33 *German Yearbook of International Law* 97–109.

Gérard Cohen-Jonathan, 'Les réserves à la Convention européenne des droits de l'homme (à propos de l'arrêt Belilos du 29 avril 1988)', (1989) 93 *Revue générale de droit international public* 273.

---

[67] Vienna Convention on the Law of Treaties, (1980) 1155 UNTS 331, art. 20.

[68] *Loizidou v. Turkey* (Preliminary objections), 23 March 1995, §§ 15–24, Series A no. 310.

[69] Ibid., § 81.

[70] (1978) 21 YB 16–19.

[71] (1979) 22 YB 16–17.

[72] Ibid., pp. 16–23.

[73] Report of the International Law Commission, Fifty-seventh session, (2 May–3 June and 11 July–5 August 2005), UN Doc. A/60/10, pp. 191–2.

Gérard Cohen-Jonathan, 'Les réserves dans les traités institutionnels relatifs aux droits de l'homme. Nouveaux aspects européens et internationaux', [1996] *Revue générale de droit international public* 915.

Jean-François Flauss, 'Le contentieux de la validité des réserves à la CEDH devant le tribunal fédéral suisse: Requiem pour la déclaration interprétative relative à l'article 6§1', (1993) 5 *Revue universelle des droits de l'homme* 297.

Cees Flinterman, 'Reservations (Article 57)', in Van Dijk et al., *Theory and Practice*, pp. 1101–15.

Johcen Abr. Frowein, 'Reservations to the European Convention on Human Rights', in F. Matscher and H. Petzold, eds, *Protecting Human Rights: The European Dimension*, Cologne: Carl Heymanns, 1988, pp. 193–200.

Frowein/Peukert, *MenschenRechtsKonvention*, pp. 628–33.

P.-H. Imbert, 'Reservations to the European Convention on Human Rights before the Strasbourg Commission: The *Temeltasch* Case', (1984) 33 *ICLQ* 558.

Susan Marks, 'Reservations Unhinged: The Belilos Case before the European Court of Human Rights', (1990) 39 *ICLQ* 300.

Ronald St J. Macdonald, 'Reservations under the European Convention on Human Rights', (1988) 21 *Revue belge de droit international* 428.

J.G. Merrills, 'Belilos Case'. (1988) 69 *British Yearbook of International Law* 386.

William Schabas, 'Article 64', in Pettiti et al., *La Convention européenne*, pp. 923–42.

Article 58. Denunciation/Dénonciation

1. A High Contracting Party may denounce the present Convention only after the expiry of five years from the date on which it became a party to it and after six months' notice contained in a notification addressed to the Secretary General of the Council of Europe, who shall inform the other High Contracting Parties.

2. Such a denunciation shall not have the effect of releasing the High Contracting Party concerned from its obligations under this Convention in respect of any act which, being capable of constituting a violation of such obligations, may have been performed by it before the date at which the denunciation became effective.

3. Any High Contracting Party which shall cease to be a member of the Council of Europe shall cease to be a Party to this Convention under the same conditions.

4. The Convention may be denounced in accordance with the provisions of the preceding paragraphs in respect of any territory to which it has been declared to extend under the terms of Article 56.

1. Une Haute Partie contractante ne peut dénoncer la présente Convention qu'après l'expiration d'un délai de cinq ans à partir de la date d'entrée en vigueur de la Convention à son égard et moyennant un préavis de six mois, donné par une notification adressée au Secrétaire Général du Conseil de l'Europe, qui en informe les autres Parties contractantes.

2. Cette dénonciation ne peut avoir pour effet de délier la Haute Partie contractante intéressée des obligations contenues dans la présente Convention en ce qui concerne tout fait qui, pouvant constituer une violation de ces obligations, aurait été accompli par elle antérieurement à la date à laquelle la dénonciation produit effet.

Sous la même réserve cesserait d'être Partie à la présente Convention toute Partie contractante qui cesserait d'être membre du Conseil de l'Europe.

La Convention peut être dénoncée conformément aux dispositions des paragraphes précédents en ce qui concerne tout territoire auquel elle a été déclarée applicable aux termes de l'article 56.

Introductory comments

In contrast with the International Covenant on Civil and Political Rights, the European Convention expressly allows a State to denounce the Convention. The United Nations Human Rights Committee has taken the view that a human rights treaty like the Covenant is 'not the type of treaty which, by its nature, implies a right of denunciation'.[1] But even many very modern international human rights treaties permit denunciation, including the Convention on the Rights of Persons with Disabilities[2] and the Optional Protocols to the Convention on the Rights of the Child dealing with Child Soldiers[3] and Pornography.[4] In practice, denunciation of human rights treaties is an exceeding rare

---

[1] General Comment on Issues relating to the Continuity of Obligations to the International Covenant on Civil and Political Rights, UN Doc. CCPR/C/21/Rev.1/Add.8/Rev.1, para. 3.

[2] Convention on the Rights of Persons with Disabilities, UN Doc. A/RES/61/106, Annex I, art. 48.

[3] Optional Protocol to the Convention on the Rights of the Child on the involvement of children in armed conflict, (2002) 2173 UNTS 222, art. 11.

[4] Optional Protocol to the Convention on the Rights of the Child on the Sale of Children, Child Prostitution, and Child Pornography, (2002) 2171 UNTS 227, art. 15.

phenomenon, possibly because of the flexibility that treaties offer States in terms of limitations, restrictions, and derogation.

Drafting of the provision

A text dealing with denunciation of the Convention was proposed by the United Kingdom at the penultimate session of the Committee of Ministers, in early August 1950. It read as follows: 'Any Contracting State may denounce the present Convention by notification to the Secretary General of the Council of Europe. Denunciation shall take effect as from the thirtieth day after the receipt of this notification by the Secretary General of the Council of Europe.'[5] The United Kingdom said that if a denunciation clause was agreed to, it would also be necessary to provide for declarations of denunciation with respect to colonial territories.[6] A Sub-Committee initially adopted a provision consisting of three paragraphs of article 58, the second and third of which are identical to that of article 58(2) and (3). The text of paragraph 1 contained slight differences of no significance compared with that of article 58(1).[7] In discussion about the 'colonial clause', the United Kingdom noted that, depending upon the text that was adopted, it might be necessary to include an additional provision in the article on denunciation: 'The Convention may be denounced in accordance with the provisions of the preceding paragraph in respect of any territory to which it has been declared to extend under the terms of article 62.'[8] When the 'colonial clause' was finalized, the fourth paragraph of the denunciation clause was also adopted.[9]

The provision was renumbered as article 58 and given the heading 'Denunciation' by Protocol No. 11. An amendment to the numbering of the article in paragraph 4 also resulted from Protocol No. 11.[10]

Analysis and interpretation

Although political figures within States Parties have occasionally invoked the spectre of denunciation of the Convention,[11] it has in fact taken place only once. On 12 December 1969, Greece announced its decision to withdraw from the Council of Europe. This came on the heels of the adoption of a report by the European Commission of Human Rights that the fascist junta that had taken power in Greece in 1967 had violated several

---

[5] Amendments proposed by the United Kingdom Delegation, Doc. CM 1 (50) 6, A 1867, V *TP* 66–71, at pp. 68–70.

[6] Ibid., p. 70.

[7] Draft Convention adopted by the Sub-Committee, Doc. CM 1 (50) 52, A 1884, V *TP* 76–99, at p. 97, art 64.

[8] Provisions of the Draft Convention about which agreement was not reached in the Sub Committee, Final version, Doc. CM 1 (50) 53, A 1889, IV *TP* 102–7, at p. 106.

[9] Minutes of the meeting [of 7 August 1950 of the Committee of Ministers], V *TP* 108–11, at p. 110; Report of the meeting [of 7 August 1950 of the Committee of Ministers], V *TP* 110–21, at p. 120.

[10] Protocol No. 11 to the Convention for the Protection of Human Rights and Fundamental Freedoms, restructuring the control machinery established thereby, ETS 155, art. 2(2).

[11] Joshua Rozenberg, 'Tory Plans for European Human Rights Convention will Take UK Back 50 years', *The Guardian*, 3 October 2014; L.R. Helfer, 'Not Fully Committed? Reservations, Risk, and Treaty Design', (2006) 31 *Yale Journal of International Law* 367, at p. 374.

provisions of the Convention.[12] In accordance with article 7 of the Statute of the Council of Europe, Greece's withdrawal would take place on 31 December 1970. The consequence of this would be withdrawal from the European Convention on Human Rights in accordance with article 58(3). However, invoking article 58 of Convention, the Greek regime also denounced the Convention on 12 December 1969.[13] In accordance with article 58(1), such a measure would become effective on 13 June 1970.[14]

On 10 April 1970, Denmark, Norway, and Sweden introduced a second inter-State application directed against Greece. The European Commission of Human Rights considered it was competent to consider the pending application directed against Greece.[15] However, it subsequently reported to the Committee of Ministers that, given the circumstances created by a military coup, it could not 'adequately continue its functions in this case with a view to the eventual adoption of a Report'.[16] When Greece again joined the Council of Europe in 1974, the Commission renewed its consideration of the application.[17] It was eventually struck from the list when the applicant States and Greece indicated they did not wish to proceed.[18] The Committee of Ministers had already decided not to continue its examination of the earlier report of the Commission given 'the fundamental changes which have since occurred in Greece, as illustrated by the procedure already initiated for the readmission of Greece to the Council of Europe'.[19]

Paragraph 4 of article 58 permits a State Party to withdraw a declaration of territorial application that it may have made pursuant to article 56. No State Party has invoked this provision.

Further reading

Frowein/Peukert, *MenschenRechtsKonvention*, pp. 634–6.
Pierre-Henri Imbert, 'Article 65', in Pettiti et al., *La Convention européenne*, pp. 943–56.
A.-Ch. Kiss and Ph. Vegleris, 'L'affaire grèque devant le Conseil de l'Europe et la Commission européenne des droits de l'hommeè, [1971] *Annuaire français de droit international* 889.
Yogesh Tyagi, 'The Denunciation of Human Rights Treaties', (2008) 79 *British Yearbook of International Law* 86.

---

[12] *Denmark, Norway, Sweden, and the Netherlands v. Greece*, nos 3321/67, 3322/67, 3323/67, and 3344/67, Commission report of 5 November 1969, (1969) 12 YB 'The Greek case' 1. See Yogesh Tyagi, 'The Denunciation of Human Rights Treaties', (2008) 79 *British Yearbook of International Law* 86, at pp. 157–60.

[13] Note verbale, 12 December 1970, (1969) 12 YB 79–83.

[14] Note verbale, 17 December 1970, (1969) 12 YB 82–85.

[15] *Denmark, Norway, and Sweden v. Greece*, no. 4448/70, Commission decision of 26 May 1970, (1970) 13 YB 108; *Denmark, Norway, and Sweden v. Greece*, no. 4448/70, Commission decision of 16 July 1970, (1970) 13 YB 122, Collection 34, p. 70. See A.-Ch. Kiss and Ph. Vegleris, 'L'affaire grèque devant le Conseil de l'Europe et la Commission européenne des drotis de l'homme', [1971] *Annuaire français de droit international* 889.

[16] *Denmark, Norway, and Sweden v. Greece*, no. 4448/70, Report of the Commission on the Present State of the Proceedings, 5 October 1970.

[17] *Denmark, Norway, and Sweden v. Greece*, no. 4448/70, Commission report of 4 October 1976, para. 6.

[18] Ibid., para. 10.

[19] Resolution DH (74) 2, 26 November 1974.

Article 59. Signature and ratification/Signature et ratification

1. This Convention shall be open to the signature of the members of the Council of Europe. It shall be ratified. Ratifications shall be deposited with the Secretary General of the Council of Europe.

2. The European Union may accede to this Convention.

3. The present Convention shall come into force after the deposit of ten instruments of ratification.

4. As regards any signatory ratifying subsequently, the Convention shall come into force at the date of the deposit of its instrument of ratification.

5. The Secretary General of the Council of Europe shall notify all the members of the Council of Europe of the entry into force of the Convention, the names of the High Contracting Parties who have ratified it, and the deposit of all instruments of ratification which may be effected subsequently.

1. La présente Convention est ouverte à la signature des membres du Conseil de l'Europe. Elle sera ratifiée. Les ratifications seront déposées près le Secrétaire général du Conseil de l'Europe.

2. L'Union européenne peut adhérer à la présente Convention.

3. La présente Convention entrera en vigueur après le dépôt de dix instruments de ratification.

4. Pour tout signataire qui la ratifiera ultérieurement, la Convention entrera en vigueur dès le dépôt de l'instrument de ratification.

5. Le Secrétaire général du Conseil de l'Europe notifiera à tous les membres du Conseil de l'Europe l'entrée en vigueur de la Convention, les noms des Hautes Parties contractantes qui l'auront ratifiée, ainsi que le dépôt de tout instrument de ratification intervenu ultérieurement.

Introductory comments

All international treaties and conventions make provision for the means by which a State establishes on the international plane its consent to be bound by a treaty. In the case of multilateral treaties, as a general rule the number of ratifications or accessions necessary for entry into force is also specified. It is also customary to indicate a depositary of the treaty. The European Convention does this only implicitly.

Drafting of the provision

The early drafts of the Convention prepared by the European Movement and the Consultative Assembly did not contain provisions dealing with ratification and entry into force. The text first emerged in the March 1950 draft adopted by the Committee of Experts:

1. This Convention shall be submitted for ratification. The ratifications shall be deposited with the Secretariat General of the Council of Europe.
2. This Convention shall come into force after the deposit of [nine] instruments of ratification.
3. As regards any signatory State ratifying subsequently, the Convention shall come into force at the date of the deposit of the instrument of ratification.[1]

---

[1] Appendix to the Report of the Committee of Experts on Human Rights: Draft Convention of Protection of Human Rights and Fundamental Freedoms, 16 March 1950, Doc. C/WP 1 (50) 15 appendix, CM/WP 1

The Commentary on the text explained that '[h]aving regard to the fact that the expenses of the Commission (and of the Court) are to be borne by the Council of Europe, it appeared right that the Convention should not enter into force until after its ratification by a certain number of the Member States of the Council of Europe'. The Committee recommended that the number be nine, but acknowledged that the decision was 'of a political nature'.[2] The initial proposal had contemplated the possibility of accession by Member States of the Council of Europe but the idea was not initially pursued.[3]

The Conference of Senior Officials debated this issue, with opinions ranging from six to nine ratifications.[4] The text was significantly revised, and lengthened, by the Conference of Senior Officials, meeting in June 1950. It adopted this text as article 64, the final provision of the Convention aside from the signature clause:

1. This Convention shall be open to the signature of the Member States of the Council of Europe and submitted for ratification. The ratification shall be deposited with the Secretariat General of the Council of Europe.
2. This Convention shall come into force after the deposit of ten instruments of ratification.
3. As regards any signatory ratifying subsequently the Convention shall come into force at the date of the deposit of its instrument of ratification.
4. Any Members of the Council of Europe may accede thereafter to this Convention by depositing their instrument of accession with the Secretariat General of the Council of Europe.
5. The Secretary-General of the Council of Europe shall notify all the High Contracting Parties of the entry into force of the Convention, the names of the High Contracting Parties who have ratified it, and the deposit of all instruments of ratification which may be effected subsequently.[5]

In preparation for adoption of the Convention in November 1950, the Secretariat General proposed a number of drafting or technical adjustments. It suggested that references to accession be deleted. One change that this occasioned was the removal of the fourth paragraph of the article.[6]

At the Sixth Session of the Committee of Ministers held in Rome on 2–3 November 1950, the Committee of Legal Experts agreed on the following signature clause:

Done at Rome this...day of November 1950 in English and French, both texts being equally authentic, in a single copy which shall remain deposited in the archives of the Council of Europe. The Secretary-General shall transmit certified copies to each of the signatories.

For the Government of the Kingdom of Belgium...

Etc., etc.[7]

---

(50) 14 revised, A 925, IV *TP* 50–79, at p. 76, art. 48. An earlier draft had suggested seven as the number for entry into force: Proposed final provisions—Section V, Doc. CM/WP 1 (50) 5, A 906, III *TP* 302–3.

[2] Report to the Committee of Ministers submitted by the Committee of Experts Instructed to Draw Up a Draft Convention of Collective Guarantee of Human Rights and Fundamental Freedoms, Doc. CM/WP 1 (5) 15, A 924, IV *TP* 2–55, at p. 46.

[3] Proposed final provisions—Section V, Doc. CM/WP 1 (50) 5, A 906, III *TP* 302–3.

[4] Minutes of the afternoon setting [of 12 June 1950], unreferenced document, IV *TP* 170–81, at p. 174.

[5] Draft Convention annexed to the Report, Doc. CM/WP 4 (50) 19 annex, CM/WP 4 (50) rev., A 1452, IV *TP* 274–95, at p. 294, art. 61.

[6] Drafting changes proposed by the Secretariat-General, Doc. A 2520, VI *TP* 274–9, at p. 276.

[7] Report of the Committee [of Legal Experts], Doc. CM/Adj (50) 3 rev., A 2531, VII *TP* 8–22, at p. 12. For the proposal, see Draft Preamble and draft signature clause, Doc. A 2518, VI *TP* 272–5.

Article 64 was renumbered as article 59 and the heading 'Signature and ratification' added according to the provisions of Protocol No. 11.[8]

Paragraph 2 of article 59, enabling accession to the Convention by the European Union, was added by Protocol 14. The other paragraphs were then renumbered as a consequence.[9]

Analysis and interpretation

Signature and ratification (art. 59(1))

The Convention is 'open to the signature of the members of the Council of Europe'. Membership in the Council of Europe is governed by Chapter II of the Statute of the Council of Europe. Only a 'European State' is eligible for membership in the Council of Europe. It may join if invited by the Committee of Ministers. To be eligible for membership, a State must 'accept the principles of the rule of law and of the enjoyment by all persons within its jurisdiction of human rights and fundamental freedoms, and collaborate sincerely and effectively in the realisation of the aim of the Council'.[10]

The Statute provides for associate membership in the Council of Europe '[i]n special circumstances'.[11] For the purposes of article 59 of the Convention, the concept of membership includes associate members. Initially, the Federal Republic of Germany and Saarland were invited to join the Council of Europe as associate members. Both States signed and ratified the European Convention on Human Rights. Saarland even elected a member of the European Commission of Human Rights, Irmgard Fuerst. Her term concluded on 1 January 1957 upon Saarland's integration with the Federal Republic of Germany.

Of the more than 200 Council of Europe treaties, dealing with a range of issues including mutual legal assistance, the environment, criminal justice, culture, education, and sports, as well as human rights, the European Convention on Human Rights is very much the exception in its exclusion of the possibility of ratification by non-European States. Upon obtaining independence, Malawi, which had formerly been known as the protectorate of Nyasaland, informed the Secretary General of the United Nations that it considered itself bound by the European Convention as an inherited treaty. Some years later, it informed the Secretary General of the Council of Europe that it no longer considered itself bound by the European Convention on Human Rights.[12] When Surinam announced that upon independence it considered that it was a party to the European Convention as a consequence of rules of succession to treaties, the Secretary General of the Council of Europe answered that this was not possible because article 59 of the Convention restricted ratification to European States.[13]

---

[8] Protocol No. 11 to the Convention for the Protection of Human Rights and Fundamental Freedoms, restructuring the control machinery established thereby, ETS 155, art. 2(4)(a).

[9] Protocol No. 14 to the Convention for the Protection of Human Rights and Fundamental Freedoms, amending the control system of the Convention, ETS 194, art. 17. See also Explanatory Report on Protocol No. 14, paras 101–102.

[10] Statute of the Council of Europe, ETS 1, art. 3.

[11] Ibid., art. 5(a).

[12] (1968) 11 YB 36.

[13] M.-A. Eissen, 'Surinam and the European Convention on Human Rights', (1978) 49 *British Yearbook of International Law* 200.

There have been many proposals that the Convention be changed in order to permit the enlargement of its scope to non-member States. In 1962, at a time when the completion of the United Nations Covenants on human rights seemed uncertain, and when the independence of former colonies threatened to remove certain territories from the Convention regime, the Parliamentary Assembly adopted a recommendation 'that the Committee of Ministers should instruct the Committee of Experts which is already examining various questions relating to the European Convention on Human Rights to draft amendments to the Convention providing for the possibility of accession by non-member States which possess the necessary qualifications, on the invitation of the Committee of Ministers, after consultation of the Assembly'.[14] The Committee of Ministers decided not to pursue the recommendation, explaining that Switzerland had indicated its intention to join the Council of Europe and that there were no other European States that seemed to be in a position to ratify the Convention.[15] A similar proposal emerged from the Parliamentary Assembly in 1989.[16]

The first sentence of paragraph 1 of article 59 specifies that the Convention 'shall be open to the signature' of Council of Europe Member States. This is a preliminary step that must be followed by ratification in order for the State to be bound by the Convention. Nevertheless, signature alone brings with its certain legal obligations. In particular, according to article 18 of the Vienna Convention on the Law of Treaties, a State that has signed a treaty may not 'defeat the object and purpose of a treaty prior to its entry into force' for that State.[17] The European Court of Human Rights referred to article 18 in a Ukrainian case in which the respondent State argued that it was not bound by the 1951 Refugee Convention because it had not yet entered into force at the relevant time, although it had been signed.[18]

The Vienna Convention on the Law of Treaties specifies that 'the consent of a State to be bound by a treaty may be expressed by signature, exchange of instruments constituting a treaty, ratification, acceptance, approval or accession, or by any other means if so agreed'.[19] It also declares: 'The consent of a State to be bound by a treaty is expressed by ratification when: (a) the treaty provides for such consent to be expressed by means of ratification'.[20] This is the case of the European Convention on Human Rights, as the second sentence of article 59(1) makes clear.

The Convention was opened for signature on 4 November 1950. That day, thirteen of the fifteen Member States of the Council of Europe signed the Convention: Belgium, Denmark, France, Germany, Ireland, Iceland, Italy, Luxembourg, the Netherlands, Norway, Saarland, Turkey, and the United Kingdom. Greece and Sweden said they could not sign on that day 'for technical reasons' but they would do so soon afterwards,[21] and in fact they signed later in the same month. The United Kingdom was the first signatory State to ratify the Convention, on 8 March 1951.

---

[14] Recommendation 316 (1962).

[15] (1963) 6 YB 75.

[16] Accession of non-member states to the Convention for the Protection of Human Rights and Fundamental Freedoms, Doc. 6046.

[17] Vienna Convention on the Law of Treaties, (1980) 1155 UNTS 331, art. 12.

[18] *Melnychenko v. Ukraine*, no. 17707/02, § 47, ECHR 2004-X.

[19] Vienna Convention on the Law of Treaties, (1980) 1155 UNTS 331, art. 11.

[20] Ibid., art. 14.

[21] Minutes of the Meeting [of the Committee of Ministers, 3 November 1950], VII *TP* 22–24, at p. 24.

European Union accession (art. 59(2))

Paragraph 2 of article 59, which was added by Protocol No. 14, authorizes the European Union to accede to the Convention. The Vienna Convention on the Law of Treaties states that 'ratification' and 'accession' are terms that 'mean in each case the international act so named whereby a State establishes on the international plane its consent to be bound by a treaty'.[22] It seems that the only real difference between the two is that ratification describes the act that confirms the signature of the treaty, whereas accession is the term used when there is no preliminary signature.

All twenty-eight members of the European Union are parties to the European Convention on Human Rights. In its early years, the forerunners of the European Union were concerned almost exclusively with economic integration. Questions of human rights protection did not seem to warrant any special provision. However, by the 1970s the European Court of Justice found itself compelled to consider human rights issues, referring to various sources of human rights law, including the European Convention on Human Rights.[23] On many occasions, the European Court of Human Rights has been required to consider European Union legislation to the extent that it is applied indirectly within the legal systems of some of the Member States of the Council of Europe. In a general sense, it has shown considerable deference for European Union law. The Strasbourg Court's view has been that as long as fundamental rights are protected by European Union law in a manner equivalent to that offered by the Convention, State action that is taken in compliance with legal obligations flowing from membership of the European Union is consistent with the requirements of the Convention.[24]

Accession by the European Union has been under discussion since the late 1970s.[25] In 1996, the European Court of Justice held that the European Union treaties could not, unless they were amended, permit accession to the Convention.[26] Article 6(2) of the Treaty on European Union, as amended by the Lisbon Treaty, which entered into force in 2009, declares that 'the Union shall accede' to the European Convention on Human Rights.[27] When Protocol No. 14 to the European Convention on Human Rights was drafted, in 2002–2003, the European Union lacked the competence to accede to the Convention, and as a result it was not possible to negotiate additional provisions that might have been included in the Protocol.[28] According to the Explanatory Report on Protocol No. 14, 'further modifications to the Convention will be necessary in order to make such accession possible from a legal and technical point of view'.[29] The Steering Committee for Human Rights of the Council of Europe has said that this could be effected either by an amending

---

[22] Vienna Convention on the Law of Treaties, (1980) 1155 UNTS 331, art. 2(1)(b). See also article 11.

[23] *J. Nold v. Commission of the E.C.*, Case 4/73, [1974] 2 C.M.L.R. 354, at p. 355.

[24] *Bosphorus Hava Yolları Turizm ve Ticaret Anonim Şirketi v. Ireland* [GC], no. 45036/98, § 156, ECHR 2005-VI; *Cooperatieve Producentenorganisatie van de Nederlandse Kokkelvisserij U.A. v. the Netherlands* (dec.), no. 13645/05, ECHR 2009; *Stichting Mothers of Srebrenica and Others v. the Netherlands* (dec.), no. 65542/12, § 151, ECHR 2013 (extracts).

[25] European Commission's memorandum of 4 April 1979, Supplement no. 2/79, Bulletin of the EC and the communication it published on 19 November 1990 (Sec(90)2087 final).

[26] Opinion no. 2/94 [1996] ECR I-1759.

[27] J.-P. Jacqué, 'The Accession of the European Union to the European Convention on Human Rights and Fundamental Freedoms', (2011) 48 *Common Market Law Review* 995.

[28] Explanatory Report on Protocol No. 14, para. 102.

[29] Ibid., para. 101.

protocol to the Convention or by an accession agreement with the European Union.[30] A Draft agreement on the Accession of the EU to the European Convention on Human Rights was published by the Steering Committee for Human Rights of the Council of Europe in 2011.

The European Union will not join the Council of Europe as such, but this is a superfluous gesture in one sense because all members of one institution are also members of the other. Nevertheless, consideration has been given to whether the European Union should be represented at the Committee of Ministers of the Council of Europe. A related issue concerns whether the European Union would be entitled to nominate a judge for election to the European Court of Human Rights. In principle, the European Court of Human Rights will be empowered to review all European Union legislation, including the treaties that constitute its fundamental law. This is the same situation that prevails with respect to national legislation, where the European Court may consider the compatibility of the European Convention with both ordinary legislation and the constitution itself.[31] Whether the inter-State petition mechanism can apply to disputes between States Parties relating to European Union law is also a matter of some debate, given article 344 of the Treaty on the Functioning of the European Union prohibiting Member States of the European Union from 'submit[ing] a dispute concerning the interpretation or application of the Treaties to any method of settlement other than those provided for therein'. There are also legal difficulties with the exhaustion of domestic remedies, given the role of the European Court of Justice, and with the identification of the correct respondent in litigation.

Entry into force (art. 59(3) and (4))

The tenth ratification of the European Convention was deposited on 3 September 1953. This brought the Convention immediately into force. The initial ten States Parties, in order of ratification, are the United Kingdom, Norway, Sweden, Germany, Saarland, Ireland, Greece, Denmark, Iceland, and Luxembourg. The Convention does not indicate what might happen if, as a result of denunciation or disappearance of the State, the number of States Parties were to fall below ten. Given the large number of ratifications, this seems to be of purely theoretical interest today. Article 59(3) no longer serves any useful purpose and might well have been removed as part of the amendment process effect by Protocol No. 11 or Protocol No. 14.

With respect to States that became parties to the Convention subsequent to 3 September 1953, the Convention enters into force for those States upon the deposit of the instrument of ratification. Many international treaties provide for a delay of a few months between ratification and entry into force but this is not the case with the European Convention, where the effect is immediate.

The date of entry into force is relevant in the establishment of the temporal scope of the Convention and has given rise to much litigation. For example, it has been possible for the Court to consider the application of the Convention to acts that took place prior to

---

[30] Ibid., para. 101.
[31] See, e.g., *Sejdić and Finci v. Bosnia and Herzegovina* [GC], nos 27996/06 and 34836/06, ECHR 2009.

the entry into force for a particular State under certain conditions,[32] a subject discussed in more detail in the chapter of this Commentary dealing with article 1.

Notification by the Secretary General (art. 59(5))

The European Convention does not designate a depositary of the treaty, although some of the functions that are customarily attributed to the depositary are assigned to the Secretary General of the Council of Europe by article 59(5). One commentator has concluded that by specifying that the Secretary General is to receive instruments of ratification, article 59(1) implicitly designates that person as the depositary.[33] Protocol No. 6 to the Convention contains a provision entitled 'depositary functions', a provision that has been repeated in subsequent Protocols. The Vienna Convention on the Law of Treaties declares that unless otherwise provided in the treaty or agreed by the contracting States, the functions of the depositary include keeping custody of the original text of the treaty, preparing certified copies of the original text, receiving signatures to the treaty, receiving and keeping custody of any instruments, notifications, and communications relating to it, examining whether the signature or any instrument, notification, or communication relating to the treaty is in due and proper form and, if need be, bringing the matter to the attention of the State in question, informing the parties and the States entitled to become parties to the treaty of acts, notifications, and communications relating to the treaty, and registering the treaty with the Secretariat of the United Nations.[34]

Succession to the European Convention

The Convention does not expressly deal with the issue of succession when a State breaks apart. In the history of the Council of Europe, this has happened in the case of two Member States. With active secessionist movements in a number of Member States, future cases cannot be ruled out.

Czechoslovakia joined the Council of Europe on 21 February 1991 and ratified the Convention on 18 March 1992. The State broke into two on 31 December 1992. The following day, the Czech Republic and Slovakia informed the Secretary General of the Council of Europe that they considered themselves to be bound by the Convention and its Protocols. The two new States were admitted to the Council of Europe on 30 June 1993. The Committee of Ministers took note of the declarations and considered the two States to be parties to the Convention as of 1 January 1993.[35] However, the Court has considered the operative date applicable to continuing violations that arose before the creation of the two States to be 18 March 1992 and not 1 January 1993.[36]

On 3 June 2006, following a referendum, Montenegro declared independence, thereby seceding from Serbia and Montenegro. Three days later, it informed the Secretary General of the Council of Europe of its intention to succeed to various international obligations of Serbia and Montenegro, including the European Convention on Human Rights.

---

[32] See, e.g., *Šilih v. Slovenia* [GC], no. 71463/01, 9 April 2009; *Varnava and Others v. Turkey* [GC], nos 16064/90, 16065/90, 16066/90, 16068/90, 16069/90, 16070/90, 16071/90, 16072/90, and 16073/90, ECHR 2009; *Janowiec and Others v. Russia* [GC], nos 55508/07 and 29520/09, ECHR 2013.

[33] Pierre-Henri Imbert, 'Article 66', in Pettiti et al., *La Convention européenne*, pp. 957–68, at p. 959.

[34] Vienna Convention on the Law of Treaties, (1980) 1155 UNTS 331, art. 77.

[35] Notification by Secretary General, 13 July 1993.

[36] *Konečný v. the Czech Republic*, nos 47269/99, 64656/01, and 65002/01, § 62, 26 October 2004.

The Parliamentary Assembly stated that it was 'particularly satisfied to note in this connection that Montenegro considers that since 3 June 2006 it is bound by the obligations stemming from the European Convention on Human Rights'.[37] The following year, the Committee of Ministers decided to invite Montenegro to become a member of the Council of Europe. It also decided that Montenegro was to be regarded as a Party to the European Convention on Human Rights and its Protocols Nos 1, 4, 6, 7, 12, 13, and 14 thereto with effect from 6 June 2006.[38] Montenegro was admitted as a full member of the Council of Europe on 11 May 2007. The Court has noted that the Committee of Ministers accepted, 'apparently because of the earlier ratification of the Convention by the State Union of Serbia and Montenegro, that it was not necessary for Montenegro to deposit its own formal ratification of the Convention'.[39] In a case before the Court concerning alleged violations in Montenegro that had taken place prior to secession, the Venice Commission submitted an *amicus curiae* brief contending that it would further the protection of European human rights and be in accordance with the Court's earlier practice were Montenegro to be held responsible.[40] The Court agreed: '[G]iven the practical requirements of Article 46 of the Convention, as well as the principle that fundamental rights protected by international human rights treaties should indeed belong to individuals living in the territory of the State party concerned, notwithstanding its subsequent dissolution or succession . . . the Court considers that both the Convention and Protocol No. 1 should be deemed as having continuously been in force in respect of Montenegro' from the date of entry into force for Serbia and Montenegro.[41]

Signature clause

The Convention concludes with a signature clause indicating that the original is to be deposited in the archives of the Council of Europe and that the Secretary General is to transmit certified copies to each of the signatories.

Further reading

F. Benoît-Rohmer, 'À propos de l'arrêt *Bosphorus Airlines* du 30 juin 2005: l'adhésion contrainte de l'Union à la Convention', [2005] *RTDH* 827.

Frowein/Peukert, *MenschenRechtsKonvention,* pp. 637–8.

Paul Gragl, *The Accession of the European Union to the European Convention on Human Rights,* Oxford: Hart, 2013.

P. Grigoriou, 'L'adhésion de l'Union européenne à la Convention européenne des droits de l'Homme à l'ère du traité de Lisbonne', in Olivier Delas and Michaela Leuprecht, eds, *Liber Amicorum Peter Leuprecht,* Brussels: Bruylant, 2012, pp. 131–49.

Pierre-Henri Imbert, 'Article 66', in Pettiti et al., *La Convention européenne,* pp. 957–68.

---

[37] Opinion No. 261 (2007), Accession of the Republic of Montenegro to the Council of Europe, para. 10.

[38] Resolution CM/Res(2007)7 inviting the Republic of Montenegro to become a member of the Council of Europe.

[39] *Bijelić v. Montenegro and Serbia,* no. 11890/05, § 68, 28 April 2009.

[40] *Amicus curiae* Brief in the case of Bijelić against Montenegro and Serbia (Application N° 11890/05) pending before the European Court of Human Rights adopted by the Venice Commission at its 76th Plenary Session (Venice, 17–18 October 2008), CDL-AD(2008)021, para. 45.

[41] *Bijelić v. Montenegro and Serbia,* no. 11890/05, § 69, 28 April 2009. Also *Šabanović v. Montenegro and Serbia,* no. 5995/06, § 28, 31 May 2011; *Lakićević and Others v. Montenegro and Serbia,* nos 27458/06, 37205/06, 37207/06, and 33604/07, § 41, 13 December 2011.

J.-P. Jacqué, 'The Accession of the European Union to the European Convention on Human Rights and Fundamental Freedoms', (2011) 48 *Common Market Law Review* 995.

Jean Rossetto, 'Quelques observations sur les conditions de l'adhésion de l'Union européenne à la CEDH', in *La Constitution, l'Europe et le droit, Mélanges en l'honneur de Jean-Claude Masclet*, Paris: Publications de la Sorbonne, 2013, pp. 927–40.

Paul Tavernier, 'De la protection équivalente. La jurisprudence *Bosphorus* à l'heure de l'adhésion de l'Union européenne à la Convention européenne des droits de l'homme', in *La Constitution l'Europe et le droit, Mélanges en l'honneur de Jean-Claude Masclet*, Paris: Publications de la Sorbonne, 2013, pp. 1003–18.

PART THREE

PROTOCOL NO. 1 TO THE CONVENTION FOR THE PROTECTION OF HUMAN RIGHTS AND FUNDAMENTAL FREEDOMS

Preamble/Préambule

The Governments signatory hereto, being Members of the Council of Europe,

Being resolved to take steps to ensure the collective enforcement of certain rights and freedoms other than those already included in Section I of the Convention for the Protection of Human Rights and Fundamental Freedoms signed at Rome on 4th November, 1950 (hereinafter referred to as 'the Convention'),

Have agreed as follows:

Les Gouvernements signataires Membres du Conseil de l'Europe,

Résolus à prendre des mesures propres à assurer la garantie collective de droits et libertés autres que ceux qui figurent déjà dans le Titre I de la Convention de sauvegarde des Droits de l'homme et des libertés fondamentales, signée à Rome le 4 November 1950 (ci-après dénommée «la Convention»).

Sont convenus de ce qui suit:

Introductory comments

Like the Convention itself, each of the additional Protocols begins with a preamble. The Convention's Preamble is relatively lengthy, with provisions clearly intended to frame the substantive provisions of the treaty. Indeed, Protocol No. 15 to the Convention actually amends the Preamble of the Convention, adding two paragraphs. In the case of the Protocols, the Preambles tend to be more perfunctory. Moreover, because the Preamble is deemed to be additional to the Convention itself—a consequence of article 5 of Protocol No. 1—the Preamble of the Convention also applies to the provisions of the Protocol.

Article 31 of the Vienna Convention on the Law of Treaties sets out, as the 'general rule' for the interpretation of treaties: 'The context for the purpose of the interpretation of a treaty shall comprise, in addition to the text, including its preamble ...'[1] Although the Vienna Convention was drafted many years after the European Convention, and it is not binding upon all States Parties because it has not been ratified by them, the European Court has nevertheless made reference to its provisions dealing with interpretation on many occasions. Noting the relevant provision in the Vienna Convention, the Court has described the preamble as being 'generally very useful for the determination of the "object" and "purpose" of the instrument to be construed'.[2] This is discussed in detail in the chapter on the Preamble of the Convention in this Commentary.

Although the instrument is commonly referred to as the 'First Protocol' or 'Protocol No. 1', this does not appear in its official title. The reason should be obvious: because it came first, when no second protocol was yet considered, it was simply *the* additional protocol to the Convention.

Drafting of the provision

A draft Protocol prepared for the February 1951 meeting of the Committee of Experts by the United Kingdom contained the following preamble:

---

[1] Vienna Convention on the Law of Treaties, (1980) 1155 UNTS 331, art. 2.
[2] *Golder v. the United Kingdom*, 21 February 1975, § 34, Series A no. 18.

The Governments signatory hereto, being Members of the Council of Europe,

Considering that certain additions should be made to the rights and freedoms defined in Section I of the Convention for the Protection of Human Rights and Fundamental Freedoms, signed at Rome on the fourth day of November 1950 (hereinafter referred to as 'the Convention'),

Have agreed as follows:[3]

A very substantially revised version was prepared by the Committee of Experts at its April 1951 meeting:

The Governments signatory hereto, being Members of the Council of Europe and Parties to the Convention on Human Rights and Fundamental Freedoms signed at Rome on 4th November 1950,

Desirous of adding to the rights and freedoms protected by the said Convention other rights and freedoms whose protection is within the scope of the aims and purposes of the said Convention,

Have agreed as follows:[4]

This was changed yet again by the Committee of Experts at its June 1951 meeting:

The Governments signatory hereto, being Members of the Council of Europe,

Being resolved to take steps to ensure the collective enforcement of certain rights and freedoms other than those already included in Section I of the Convention on Human Rights and Fundamental Freedoms signed at Rome on 4th November 1950 (hereinafter referred to as 'the Convention'),

Have agreed as follows:[5]

There is no evidence in the *travaux* of any discussion or debate as the formulation of the Preamble evolved.

The heading 'Preamble' was added according to the provisions of Protocol No. 11.[6]

Analysis and interpretation

The first and third paragraphs of the Preamble of Protocol No. 1 are essentially formalist in nature and raise no issues of application or interpretation. They do recall that there was agreement by all of the States Parties to the Convention as to the adoption of the text of Protocol No. 1, even if its ratification and extension to dependent territories was only optional.

The second paragraph of the Preamble recalls recital 5 of the Preamble of the Convention itself, which reads: 'Being resolved, as the governments of European countries which are like-minded and have a common heritage of political traditions, ideals, freedom and the rule of law, to take the first steps for the collective enforcement of certain of the rights stated in the Universal Declaration'. Unlike the Preamble to the Convention, that of Protocol No. 1 does not make explicit reference to the Universal Declaration of Human Rights as the

---

[3] Draft Protocol extending Section I of the Convention (14 February 1951), Doc. CM/WP 1 (51) 23, p. 1, CM/WP VI (51) 1, p. 1, VII *TP* 188–91. Also Proposal of the United Kingdom Delegation, Doc. CM/WP VI (51) 12, A 4387, VII *TP* 234–43, at pp. 234–5.

[4] Revised version, Doc. CM/WP VI (51) 9, A 4405, VII *TP* 228–9.

[5] Report of the Committee of Experts to the Committee of Ministers (6 June 1951), Doc. CM/WP VI (51) 20 final, Appendix, VII *TP* 300–9, at pp. 304–5. Also Recommendations of the Ministers' Advisers relating to the Agenda for the Session (1 August 1951), Doc. CM (51) 64 rev., A 5578 VII *TP* 326–33, at pp. 328–9.

[6] Protocol No. 11 to the Convention for the Protection of Human Rights and Fundamental Freedoms, restructuring the control machinery established thereby, ETS 155, art. 4(a).

source of the rights whose collective enforcement is being ensured. Nevertheless, there is no doubt about their origin: the Universal Declaration recognizes the right to property (art. 17), the right to education (art. 26), and the right to democratic elections (art. 21). It was unnecessary to state this because the Preamble of the Convention is also applicable to Protocol No. 1 as a result of article 5 of the Protocol. There appears to be no case law of the Convention organs in which the Preamble of the Convention has been consulted with respect to Protocol No. 1.

The importance of the idea that the Convention system is centred on the 'collective enforcement of certain rights and freedoms' is discussed in the chapter of this Commentary dealing with the Preamble to the Convention itself. The reference to 'collective enforcement' in recital 5 of the Preamble has been used by the Grand Chamber to support the position that article 6 of the Convention does not apply to measures of expulsion.[7]

There is apparently only one reference in the case law of the Convention organs to the Preamble of Protocol No. 1. In the *Belgian Linguistic case*, the Court noted that the object of the Protocol, as set out in the Preamble, 'lies in the collective enforcement of "rights and freedoms". There is therefore no doubt that Article 2 (P1-2) does enshrine a right.'[8]

---

[7] *Maaouia v. France* [GC], no. 39652/98, § 36, ECHR 2000-X.
[8] Case *'relating to certain aspects of the laws on the use of languages in education in Belgium'* (merits), 23 July 1968, pp. 30–2, § 3, Series A no. 6.

Article 1. Protection of property/Protection de la propriété

Every natural or legal person is entitled to the peaceful enjoyment of his possessions. No one shall be deprived of his possessions except in the public interest and subject to the conditions provided for by law and by the general principles of international law.

The preceding provisions shall not, however, in any way impair the right of a State to enforce such laws as it deems necessary to control the use of property in accordance with the general interest or to secure the payment of taxes or other contributions or penalties.

Toute personne physique ou morale a droit au respect de ses biens. Nul ne peut être privé de sa propriété que pour cause d'utilité publique et dans les conditions prévues par la loi et les principes généraux du droit international.

Les dispositions précédentes ne portent pas atteinte au droit que possèdent les États de mettre en vigueur les lois qu'ils jugent nécessaires pour réglementer l'usage des biens conformément à l'intérêt général ou pour assurer le paiement des impôts ou d'autres contributions ou des amendes.

Introductory comments

Property figures in the earliest declarations of human rights. The French *Déclaration des droits de l'homme et du citoyen* of 1789 recognized the right to property as being one of the 'droits naturels et imprescriptibles'. Article 17 of the *Déclaration* stated: 'La propriété étant un droit inviolable et sacré, nul ne peut en être privé, si ce n'est lorsque la nécessité publique, légalement constatée, l'exige évidemment, et sous la condition d'une juste et préalable indemnité.'[1] But this profoundly *bourgeois* right was also contested, famously by the anarchist Pierre-Joseph Proudhon: 'la propriété, c'est le vol'.[2] In the Communist Manifesto, Marx and Engels said that 'the theory of the Communists may be summed up in the single sentence: Abolition of private property.'[3]

To some extent, the philosophical differences about the sanctity of private property that characterized the formulation of the right in the Universal Declaration and that persist to the present day find their reflection in the case law of the European Court of Human Rights under article 1 of Protocol No. 1, notably in cases involving control or deprivation of property in pursuit of social policy in such matters as rent control. The Universal Declaration of Human Rights, in article 17, recognizes a right to property:

(1) Everyone has the right to own property alone as well as in association with others.
(2) No one shall be arbitrarily deprived of his property.

This text results from a compromise, an attempt to reconcile different social systems and their corresponding approaches to private property.[4] The Universal Declaration of

---

[1] See also article 16 of the 23 June 1793 version of the *Déclaration*, cited by Judge Borrego Borrego: *Stec and Others v. the United Kingdom* [GC], nos 65731/01 and 65900/01, Concurring Opinion of Judge Borrego Borrego, ECHR 2006-VI.

[2] Pierre-Joseph Proudhon, *Qu'est-ce que la propriété?*, Paris: Bibliothèque internationale, 1867, at p. 13.

[3] Karl Marx and Friedrich Engels, *The Communist Manifesto*, Oxford: Oxford University Press, 2008, p. 24.

[4] See Johannes Morsink, *The Universal Declaration of Human Rights, Origins, Drafting, and Intent*, Philadelphia: University of Pennsylvania Press, 1999, at pp. 146–56.

Human Rights also enshrines respect for intellectual property, described in article 27(2) as 'the right to the protection of the moral and material interests resulting from any scientific, literary or artistic production of which he is the author'.

There is no right to property in the two United Nations Covenants. Agreement both on where it belonged and the proper formulation could not be reached, and the matter was dropped by the Commission on Human Rights, never to return in the course of the negotiations.[5] However, the importance of the right to property has resurfaced in debates about indigenous peoples, extreme poverty, and women's equality. The United Nations Special Rapporteur on adequate housing has referred to the 'social function of property' in the Guiding Principles on Security of Tenure for the Urban Poor:

Policies that promote the social function of property aim to ensure that land is allocated, used and regulated in a manner that serves both individual and collective needs. Limitations are placed on private property rights for the purpose of promoting social interests and the general welfare. States inherently recognize the social function of land through, inter alia, the collection of property taxes, the exercise of expropriation powers for the public good, adverse possession laws, and urban planning that designates spaces for public use and environmental protection. States should take further measures to ensure both private and public land is used optimally to give effect to its social function, including adequate housing of the urban poor.[6]

The African Commission on Human and Peoples' Rights has addressed the importance of the right to property in its Principles and Guidelines on the Implementation of Economic, Social and Cultural Rights. Accordingly,

The right to property is a broad right that includes the protection of the real rights of individuals and peoples in any material thing which can be possessed as well as any right which may be part of a person's patrimony. The concept also includes the protection of a legitimate expectation of the acquisition of property. It encompasses the rights of the individual, group or people to peaceful enjoyment of the property. The right may be limited by the State in a non-arbitrary manner, according to the law and the principle of proportionality.[7]

The Convention concerning Indigenous and Tribal Peoples in Independent Countries of the International Labour Organisation provides that 'the rights of ownership and possession of the peoples concerned over the lands which they traditionally occupy shall be recognised'.[8] The United Nations Declaration on the Rights of Indigenous Peoples protects 'cultural, intellectual, religious and spiritual property' and the right of indigenous peoples to 'maintain, control, protect and develop their intellectual property over such cultural heritage, traditional knowledge, and traditional cultural expressions'.[9]

---

[5] William Schabas, 'The Omission of the Right to Property in the International Covenants', (1991) 4 *Hague Yearbook of International Law* 135.

[6] Report of the Special Rapporteur on Adequate Housing as a Component of the Right to an Adequate Standard of Living, and on the Right to Non-discrimination in this Context, Raquel Rolnik, UN Doc. A/HRC/25/54, para. 42.

[7] Principles and Guidelines on the Implementation of Economic, Social and Cultural Rights in the African Charter of Human and Peoples' Rights, November 2010, para. 53.

[8] International Labour Convention No. 169 concerning Indigenous and Tribal Peoples in Independent Countries, (1991) 1650 UNTS 383, art. 14(1).

[9] United Nations Declaration on the Rights of Indigenous Peoples, UN Doc. A/RES/61/295, annex, arts. 11(2), 31(1).

The Charter of Fundamental Rights of the European Union recognizes a right to property in the following terms:

Art. 17. Right to property

1. Everyone has the right to own, use, dispose of and bequeath his or her lawfully acquired possessions. No one may be deprived of his or her possessions, except in the public interest and in the cases and under the conditions provided for by law, subject to fair compensation being paid in good time for their loss. The use of property may be regulated by law in so far as is necessary for the general interest.
2. Intellectual property shall be protected.

It is meant to have the same meaning and scope as it does in article 1 of Protocol No. 1 to the European Convention.[10]

Drafting of the provision

The initial draft European Convention on Human Rights was prepared by the International Juridical Section of the European Movement, chaired by Pierre-Henri Teitgen, with David Maxwell Fyfe and Fernand Dehousse as rapporteurs. Both Maxwell Fyfe and Dehousse had been involved in the drafting of the Universal Declaration of Human Rights the previous year. The text enshrined '[f]reedom from arbitrary deprivation of property'.[11] Teitgen, at the first session of Consultative Assembly, called for adoption of a convention that was to include 'freedom from arbitrary deprivation of property'.[12]

There was no general agreement in the Commission on Legal and Administrative Questions of the Consultative Assembly on the inclusion of a right to property. Some members contended 'that there was no reason to differentiate between the right to own property and the other social and economic rights, and that it would be preferable, therefore, to exclude it from the guarantee, since in principle the [Convention] did not cover rights of this nature'.[13] However, the majority considered that it should be included 'having regard to the importance of the part played by the right to own property in the independence of the individual and of the family'.[14] The Commission proposed the following text: 'In this Convention, the Member States shall undertake to ensure to all persons residing within their territories: ... The right to own property, in accordance with article 17 of the United Nations Declaration.'[15] In the plenary Assembly, the debate continued, with Lord Layton of the United Kingdom arguing against including a right to

---

[10] Explanation relating to the Charter of Fundamental Rights, Official Journal of the European Union, C 303/34, 14 December 2007.

[11] Convention for the Collective Protection of Individual Rights and Democratic Liberties by the States, Members of the Council of Europe, and for the establishment of a European Court of Human Rights to ensure observance of the Convention, Doc. INF/5/E/R, I *TP* 296–303, at p. 296, art. 1(k).

[12] Eighth sitting [of the Consultative Assembly] held 19 August 1949, I *TP* 36–154, at p. 46.

[13] Report presented by Mr. P.H. Teitgen, 5 September 1949, Doc. A 290, I *TP* 192–213, at pp. 198–200; Report [of the Committee on Legal and Administrative Questions], 5 September 1949, Doc. AS (1) 77, I *TP* 216–39, at pp. 228–9.

[14] Report presented by Mr. P.H. Teitgen, 5 September 1949, Doc. A 290, I *TP* 192–213, at pp. 198–200; Report [of the Committee on Legal and Administrative Questions], 5 September 1949, Doc. AS (1) 77, I *TP* 216–39, at pp. 228–9.

[15] Report presented by Mr. P.H. Teitgen, 5 September 1949, Doc. A 290, I *TP* 192–213, at pp. 198–200.

property in the Convention: 'I urge that the list of rights should be limited to the absolute minimum necessary to constitute the cardinal principles for the functioning of political democracy.'[16] It appears that this was an issue upon which the deputies were divided on political lines, with the socialists contending that to recognize the right to property but not any other economic and social rights, such as the right to work, would send the wrong message about the substance of human rights.[17] Faced with a lack of any agreement on including the right to property, the Consultative Assembly voted to refer its draft to the Committee of Ministers and not include it in its proposed text of the Convention.[18]

In the Committee of Experts, which met in February 1950, Ireland and Turkey proposed that the provision be restored.[19] A Sub-Committee assigned to examine the matter proposed the Committee of Ministers be informed that the Committee of Experts, 'or certain of its members', believed that the Convention should include the right to property.[20] In fact, the Report adopted by the Committee said the view was held by '[m]ost of the Members of the Committee'. The Report drew the Ministers' attention to the importance of the right to property, noting 'that the totalitarian regimes had a tendency to interfere with the right to own property as a means of exercising illegitimate pressure on its nationals'.[21]

The Conference of Senior Officials did not consider the issue when it met in June 1950, to the dismay of the Legal Committee of the Consultative Assembly.[22] Ireland formally proposed the addition of a right to property provision when the Committee of Ministers met in August 1950,[23] but no action appears to have been taken. The debate returned to the Consultative Assembly at its August 1950 session. Basing itself on a proposal from Henri Rolin,[24] the Committee on Legal and Administrative Questions agreed on the following:

All individuals and corporate bodies are entitled to respect for their property. Such property shall not be liable to arbitrary confiscation. This shall not, however, in any way prejudice the right of the different States to enact such laws as may be necessary to ensure the use of this property for the public good.[25]

---

[16] Official Report of the Sitting [of the Consultative Assembly, 8 September 1949], II *TP* 14–274, at p. 52.

[17] For the extensive debate, see Official Report of the Sitting [of the Consultative Assembly, 8 September 1949], II *TP* 14–274, notably pp. 54–6, 60–2, 70–4, 76–86, 92–4, 98–100, 104–8.

[18] Ibid., p. 134.

[19] Amendment to Article 2 of the Recommendation of the Consultative Assembly proposed by the Experts of Ireland and Turkey, Doc. A 776, III *TP* 184–5; Amendment to Articles 2 and 3 of the Recommendation of the Consultative Assembly, proposed by the Irish Expert, Doc. A 778, III *TP* 184–5.

[20] First part of the Report of the Sub-Committee Instructed to Make a Preliminary Study of the Amendments Proposed by the Members of the Committee, Doc. A 796, III *TP* 200–5, at p. 204.

[21] Report to the Committee of Ministers submitted by the Committee of Experts Instructed to Draw Up a Draft Convention of Collective Guarantee of Human Rights and Fundamental Freedoms, Doc. CM/WP 1 (5) 15, A 924, IV *TP* 2–55, at p. 18.

[22] Letter of 24 June 1950 from Sir David Maxwell Fyfe, Chairman of the Committee on Legal and Administrative Questions, to the Chairman of the Committee of Ministers, Doc. CM (50) 29, V *TP* 32–41, at p. 36.

[23] Amendments proposed by the Irish Government, Doc. CM 1 (50) 2, A 1863, V *TP* 58–61.

[24] Text proposed by M. Rolin, Doc. AS/JA/WP 1 (2) 1, A 1942, V *TP* 204–5.

[25] Progress Report, Doc. AS/JA (2) 1, A 2041, V *TP* 206–7; Supplementary Report of 8 August 1950 on the Draft Convention for the Protection of Human Rights and Fundamental Freedoms Presented on Behalf of the Committee by M. P.H. Teitgen, Doc. AS/JA (2) 30, V *TP* 208–9.

After a resumed debate in the plenary Consultative Assembly,[26] the Committee on Legal and Administrative Questions continued its work on the matter. Teitgen had a revised text:

Every natural or legal person is entitled to the peaceful enjoyment of his possessions. Such possessions cannot be subjected to arbitrary confiscation. The present measures shall not however be considered as infringing, in any way, the right of a State to pass necessary legislation to ensure that the said possessions are utilised in accordance with the general interest.[27]

The text met with agreement in the Committee.[28] Its Report to the plenary Consultative Assembly described the text as 'a fair definition of an essential right, arrived at after much discussion'. The Report noted that 'certain members of the Committee felt that it was wrong to include this social right and exclude others such as the right to work and the right to rest and leisure, and had doubts as to the form in which the right was stated'. It noted that the text had been adopted by fifteen votes to four.[29] After further debate in the plenary Consultative Assembly,[30] the provision adopted by the Legal Committee was endorsed, by ninety-seven votes, with eleven abstentions[31] and the recommendation duly transmitted to the Committee of Ministers.[32] A memorandum on the Consultative Assembly discussions prepared by the Secretariat General described the text as 'a compromise' produced by a Sub-Committee 'the members of which held varying political views'.[33]

Meeting in Rome immediately prior to adoption of the Convention, on 3 November 1950, the Committee of Ministers was unable to agree on inclusion of the right to property in the Convention. The United Kingdom representative moved that proposals from the Consultative Assembly, including the right to property provision, be referred to a Committee of Experts 'with a view to the preparation of a Protocol to the Convention'. This was adopted by ten votes to one. An attempt by the Irish representative, Seán

[26] Report of the sitting [of the Consultative Assembly, 14 August 1950], V *TP* 216–71, at pp. 244–6; Report of the sitting [of the Consultative Assembly, 16 August 1950], V *TP* 272–351, at p. 312–14, 324; Motion relative to the right to own property proposed by Mr. MacEntee and several of his colleagues, Doc. AS/JA (2) 59, V *TP* 272–73.

[27] Draft Motion submitted by M. Teitgen, Original Draft, Doc. AS/JA (2) 6, A 2207, VI *TP* 6–11; Draft Motion submitted by M. Teitgen, Revised Draft, Doc. AS/JA (2) 6 rev., A 2238, VI *TP* 10–15.

[28] Draft Recommendation submitted to the Consultative Assembly, Doc. AS/JA (2) 20, A 2491, VI *TP* 42–7.

[29] Text of the Report [of the Committee on Legal and Administrative Questions], Doc. AS (2) 93, VI *TP* 58–72, at pp. 60–2, 68; First Report [of the Committee on Legal and Administrative Questions], Doc. AS/JA (2) 15, A 2298, VI *TP* 46–52, at p. 48; Second Report Doc. AS/JA (2) rev., A 2493, VI *TP* 52–9, at p. 54. See also Note of 14 December 1950 prepared by the Secretariat-General on the reasons for the Amendments to the Convention for the Protection of Human Rights and Fundamental Freedoms adopted by the Consultative Assembly on 15 August 1950, Doc. CM (50) 96, A 3503, VII *TP* 130–41, at pp. 132–6.

[30] Report of the sitting [of the Consultative Assembly, of 25 August 1950, morning], VI *TP* 74–141, at pp. 86–8, 94–8, 104–10, 116–20, 134–40; Report of the Sitting [of the Consultative Assembly, 25 August 1950, afternoon], VI *TP* 144–91, at pp. 148–64.

[31] Report of the Sitting [of the Consultative Assembly, 25 August 1950, afternoon], VI *TP* 144–91, at p. 164. See also Note of 14 December 1950 prepared by the Secretariat-General on the reasons for the Amendments to the Convention for the Protection of Human Rights and Fundamental Freedoms adopted by the Consultative Assembly on 15 August 1950, Doc. CM (50) 96, A 3503, VII *TP* 130–41, at pp. 136–41.

[32] Text published in the Collected Documents of the Consultative Assembly, Doc. AS (2) 104, VI *TP* 198–229, at p. 208.

[33] Explanatory Note by the Secretariat General, 9 September 1950, Doc. CM (50) 57, A 2781, VI *TP* 230–9, at p. 232.

MacBride, to enlarge the Committee so as to include representatives of the Consultative Assembly was not accepted.[34]

There was much discontent in the Consultative Assembly about the turn of events. On 5 November 1950, the Standing Committee expressed 'regret' that the amendments, including the right to property provision, were not included in the Convention.[35] Later in November, when the plenary Assembly convened, anger was expressed with the United Kingdom, to whom responsibility for omission of the right to property was attributed. The Assembly grudgingly accepted the fact that work would continue on a protocol where its concerns could be addressed.[36]

The Secretariat-General prepared a memorandum noting that the Assembly had drafted a text 'as a statement of general principles rather than as an exact definition' and that this approach had generally been rejected by the Committee of Ministers. 'It therefore appears necessary to define as accurately as possible what is meant by "arbitrary confiscation" and what exceptions are to be permitted in the general interest to the individual rights of enjoyment of one's possessions.' The Secretariat-General said definitions would need to take into account national legislation on such matters as nationalization, requisition in time of war, expropriation for public use, agrarian reform, confiscation in criminal law, death duties, and reversion to the State on intestacy.[37] The Secretary General wrote to Member States inviting them to prepare proposals for discussion by a Committee of Experts in February 1951 in view of adoption of a protocol to the Convention by the Committee of Ministers the following month.[38] He wrote again to Member States in early February, conveying a draft right to property provision proposed by the United Kingdom:

Every natural or legal person is entitled to the peaceful enjoyment of his possessions. This provision, however, shall not be considered as infringing in any way the right of a state to enforce such laws as it deems necessary either to serve the ends of justice or to secure the payment of monies due whether by way of taxes or otherwise, or to ensure the acquisition or use of property in accordance with the general interest.[39]

The United Kingdom subsequently proposed a change to its text 'in order to protect the principle of compensation' that changed the last phrase by inserting between 'or to ensure' and 'the acquisition' the words '... subject to compensation,...'. Alternatively, it

[34] Report of the Meeting [of the Committee of Ministers, 3 November 1950], VII *TP* 24–34, at p. 34.

[35] Minutes of the meeting held by the Standing Committee of the Consultative Assembly in Rome on 5 November 1950 (morning), Doc. AS/CP (2) PV 5, p. 2, A 3057, VII *TP* 82–4; Minutes of the fourth meeting held in the afternoon of 5 November 1950 [by the Standing Committee of the Consultative Assembly], Doc. AS/CP (2) PV 6, p. 2, A 3058, VII *TP* 84–5; Second Report on the work of the Standing Committee presented in accordance with the Resolution adopted by the Assembly on 6 September 1949, Doc. AS (2) 137, pp. 1126–7, VII *TP* 86–9.

[36] Report of the Consultative Assembly, 2nd session, 18 November 1950, VII *TP* 90–121.

[37] Note on the amendments to the Convention on Human Rights proposed by the Consultative Assembly about which the Committee of Ministers was not able to reach unanimous agreement, Doc. CM (50) 90, A 3034, VII *TP* 126–30, at pp. 126–8.

[38] Letter from the Secretary General of the Council of Europe to the Foreign Ministers of Member States, 18 November 1950, Doc. D 280/9/50, VII *TP* 180–1.

[39] Memorandum by the Secretariat setting forth the different texts proposed, Doc. CM/WP 4 (50) 3, CM/WP 1 (51) 29, A 4005, VII *TP* 192–7, at pp. 192–3. Also Letter from the Secretary General of the Council of Europe to the Foreign Ministers of Member States, 7 February 1951, Doc. D 1357, VII *TP* 184–7.

suggested adding at the end, following 'general interest', the words 'subject to such compensation as shall be determined by law'.[40]

In addition to the Consultative Assembly draft and the British text, Belgium submitted its own version:

Every natural or legal person is entitled to the peaceful enjoyment of his possession. No-one shall be deprived of his possessions except in the public interest, in such cases and by such procedure as may be established by law and subject to fair compensation which shall be fixed in advance. The penalty of total confiscation of property shall not be permitted.

The present measures shall not however infringe in any way the right possessed by states to pass legislation to control the use of property in accordance with the general interest or to impose texts or other contributions.[41]

Belgium also proposed a modification that placed a full stop in the second sentence after the words 'subject to fair compensation' and deleted the remainder of the first paragraph.[42]

The Committee of Experts met from 21 to 24 February 1951. The Report of the Committee of Experts to the Committee of Ministers indicates that it reached unanimity on the following sentence: 'Every natural or legal person is entitled to the peaceful enjoyment of his possessions.' However, the Committee did not find consensus on whether the Protocol should protect a right to compensation in the case of acquisition of private property in the public interest. France considered the phrase 'such possessions cannot be subjected to arbitrary confiscation' in the Consultative Assembly draft to be the most satisfactory. The majority of delegations supported the Belgian proposal. The United Kingdom was opposed to stating a general principle because it:

did not think it possible to express this principle in terms which would be appropriate to all the various types of case which might arise, nor could it admit that decisions taken on this matter by the competent national authorities should be subject to revision by international organs. On the other hand, the words 'arbitrary confiscation' in the text proposed by the Assembly were imprecise, and if 'arbitrary' meant 'not in accordance with law' the idea was completely covered by the United Kingdom draft.[43]

France said it could accept the British proposal on the condition that the second sentence of the Assembly draft ('Such possessions cannot be subjected to arbitrary confiscation') be added after the first sentence of the British draft. The other delegations were also prepared to accept the British draft, but on the condition that the last two lines were replaced with the following: 'or to ensure the acquisition or use of property in accordance with the general interest, subject, in the case of acquisition, to such compensation as shall be determined in accordance with the conditions provided for by law'.[44]

[40] Proposed addition to the text of the United Kingdom Delegation, Doc. CM/WP 1 (51) 30, CM/WP VI (51) 4, VII *TP* 196–9.

[41] Proposal of the Belgian Government, Doc. CM/WP 1 (51) 25, CM/WP VI (51) 5, VII *TP* 192–3.

[42] Ibid.

[43] Report of the Committee of Experts to the Committee of Ministers, Doc. CM/WP 1 (51) 40, CM/WP VI (51) 7, A 4024, VII *TP* 204–13, at p. 208.

[44] Report of the Committee of Experts to the Committee of Ministers, Doc. CM/WP 1 (51) 40, CM/WP VI (51) 7, A 4024, VII *TP* 204–13, at pp. 206–9.

The Committee of Experts met again in April 1951. At the outset, Belgium, Denmark, Germany, Greece, Ireland, Italy, Luxembourg, the Netherlands, and Norway said they could accept a draft based on the Belgian proposal:

Every natural or legal person is entitled to the peaceful enjoyment of his possessions. No-one shall be deprived of his possessions except in the public interest, in such cases and by such procedure as are established by law and subject to such compensation as shall be determined in accordance with the conditions provided for by law.

The present measures shall not however infringe, in any way, the right of a State to pass legislation to control the use of property in accordance with the general interest or to impose taxes or other contributions.

France, the United Kingdom, and the Saar could not agree, while Sweden and Turkey reserved their positions.[45] No progress was made at the meeting in resolving the differences.[46]

The Committee of Experts met yet again in June. By this point, the only outstanding issue in negotiations to adopt the Protocol concerned the right to property. The Committee was able to submit a proposal based upon the text cited above that had obtained broad support. However, the final phrase in the second sentence, following the words 'except in the public interest,' were replaced with: 'and subject to the conditions provided for by law and by the general principles of international law'. Also, the words 'The present measures' in the final sentence were replaced with 'The preceding provisions'.[47]

Advisers to the Ministers of Foreign Affairs met in Strasbourg on 17 July 1951 to see if a final agreement could be reached. The United Kingdom returned with yet another amendment. It proposed replacing the second paragraph with the following: 'The preceding provisions shall not, however, in any way infringe the right of a state to enforce such laws as it deems necessary to control the use of property in accordance with the general interest or to secure the payment of taxes or other contributions or of penalties imposed by the Courts.'[48] Acting on a letter from Germany seeking the record indicate 'the general principles of international law entail the obligation to pay compensation in cases of expropriation',[49] the Advisers stated that at the request of Germany and Belgium, it was agreed that 'the general principles of international law, in their present connotation, entailed the obligation to pay compensation to non-nationals in cases of expropriation'.[50] The Report also indicated that Sweden had requested that the conclusions mention 'that the general principles of international law referred to under Article 1 of the Protocol only applied to relations between a State and non-nationals'.[51] The Ministers' Advisers recommended the following text for consideration by the Committee of Ministers:

---

[45] Note relating to the right of property, Doc. CM/WP VI (51) 11, A 4388, VII *TP* 232–5.

[46] Report of the Committee of Experts to the Committee of Ministers (19 April 1951), Doc. CM (51) 33 final, A 4421, VII *TP* 250–5, at pp. 250–1.

[47] Report of the Committee of Experts to the Committee of Ministers (6 June 1951), Doc. CM/WP VI (51) 20 final, Appendix, VII *TP* 300–9, at pp. 304–5.

[48] Amendments proposed by the Government of the United Kingdom, Doc. CM/Adj. (51) 34, VII *TP* 314–15.

[49] Letter from M Blankenhorn [on behalf of the Minister for Foreign Affairs of the Federal Republic of Germany to the Secretary General of the Council of Europe (10 July 1951)], Doc. A 4652, VII *TP* 312–13.

[50] Conclusions of the Meeting of the Ministers' Advisers, Doc. CM, Point II, pp. 300–3, VII *TP* 324–7.

[51] Ibid.

Every natural or legal person is entitled to the peaceful enjoyment of his possessions. No one shall be deprived of his possessions except in the public interest, and subject to the conditions provided for by law and by the general principles of international law.

The present measures shall not, however, in any way infringe the right of a State to enforce such property in accordance with the general interest or to impose taxes, other contributions or penalties.[52]

The Committee of Ministers agreed on this text.

In preparation for examination of the text by the Consultative Assembly, the Secretariat-General prepared a commentary on the draft Protocol. Comments were made on three aspects of the draft text. The Commentary noted that the sentence '[s]uch possessions cannot be subjected to arbitrary confiscation' in the Consultative Assembly draft had been replaced, 'principally because the phrase "arbitrary confiscation" was thought to be too unprecise [sic] in a legal text, as it is subject to very varying interpretations'. The Commentary referred to the debate about whether to make deprivation of property 'subject to compensation'. It noted that at one time a majority of governments favoured such a reference but that others had made objections. However, even in the absence of an explicit reference, the Commentary said 'the phrase "subject to the conditions provided for by law" would normally require the payment of compensation, since it is normally provided for in legislation on the nationalisation or expropriation of property'. The reference to international law would guarantee compensation to foreigners even if it were not paid to nationals. Finally, the Commentary noted that the final sentence of the Assembly's text had been extended 'to make it clear that this article does not prevent the State from collecting taxes, or other penalties such as fines, even though they might constitute the whole of the property of the individual in question'.[53]

The Legal Committee of the Consultative Assembly adopted the right to property proposed by the Committee of Ministers.[54] But the debate was not quite over. At the December 1951 meeting of the Consultative Assembly, a radically altered version of article 1 was proposed as an amendment by one of the French deputies, Claude Hettier de Boislambert.[55] It was aimed at protecting rights of inheritance. Pierre-Henri Teitgen took the floor to confirm that although the text adopted by the Committee of Ministers differed in several details from the Assembly text, 'we have no objections as regards this Article guaranteeing the right to property'.[56] At his urging, Hettier de Boislambert agreed to withdraw the amendment.[57]

The Committee of Ministers finally adopted Protocol No. 1 in March 1952, a year after it was promised. Pursuant to Germany's request, it reiterated that 'as regards

---

[52] Recommendations of the Ministers' Advisers relating to the Agenda for the Session (1 August 1951), Doc. CM (51) 64 revised, A 5578 VII *TP* 326–33, at pp. 328–9.

[53] Commentary by the Secretariat General on the Draft Protocol (18 September 1951), Doc. AS/JA (3) 13, pp. 2–4, VIII *TP* 4–17, at pp. 8–11.

[54] Minutes of the Meeting of 1 October 1951 [of the Committee on Legal and Administrative Questions of the Consultative Assembly], Doc. AS/JA (3) PV 3, p. 2, VIII *TP* 16–19, at pp. 18–19; Report on the Draft Protocol to the Convention presented by the Committee on Legal and Administrative Questions, Doc. AS (3) 81, VIII *TP* 28–37, at pp. 34–5.

[55] Doc. AS (3) 93, Amendment No. 1, VIII *TP* 76–7.

[56] Consultative Assembly Sitting of 7 December 1951 (afternoon), VIII *TP* 76–115, at pp. 82–3.

[57] Consultative Assembly Sitting of 8 December 1951 (afternoon), VIII *TP* 114–71, at pp. 160–7.

Article 1, the general principles of international law in their present connotation entail the obligation to pay compensation to non-nationals in cases of expropriation'.[58]

The heading 'Protection of property' was added pursuant to Protocol No. 11.[59]

Analysis and interpretation

'[T]he first and most important requirement of Article 1 of Protocol No. 1 is that any interference by a public authority with the peaceful enjoyment of possessions should be lawful', the Court has said.[60] Three distinct rules are set out in article 1 of Protocol No. 1. The first sentence of the first paragraph presents the principle of peaceful enjoyment of possessions. This is a right recognized to every natural and legal person. The second sentence of the first paragraph prohibits the deprivation of possessions, but only 'in the public interest and subject to the conditions provided for by law and by the general principles of international law'. The second paragraph of article 1 recognizes that States Parties may control the use of property in accordance with the public interest. The Court has explained that the three rules 'are not, however, distinct in the sense of being unconnected'. The second and third rules deal with particular forms of interference with the right to peaceful enjoyment of property 'and should therefore be construed in the light of the general principle enunciated in the first rule'.[61] It has been said that all three rules 'are not to be seen as watertight or unconnected' and that they import 'a requirement of proportionality and the necessity of striking a fair balance between the demands of the community as a whole and the protection of the rights and interests of the individual'.[62]

The distinction between an interference with the peaceful enjoyment of possessions, under the first sentence, and the deprivation of possessions, under the second, is not always crystal clear. For example, in a case involving litigation directed against the State, it had been possible for the lawyer to recover fees due from the client directly from the State under a provision in the Code of Civil Procedure. This mode of payment had been agreed between the lawyer and her client. Subsequently, in the midst of the proceedings and after the client had been successful at first instance, the State enacted legislation to extinguish the claim, thereby preventing the lawyer from recovering the amount due for professional services. The Court considered this to be an interference with enjoyment of possessions and not a deprivation of them. The claim by the lawyer for her fees had not been brought to an end by the legislation, merely the possibility under the Code of Civil Procedure of recovering them by offsetting them against the amount payable by the State to the lawyer's client.[63]

---

[58] Resolution CM (52) 1, VIII *TP* 202–5.

[59] Protocol No. 11 to the Convention for the Protection of Human Rights and Fundamental Freedoms, restructuring the control machinery established thereby, ETS 155, art. 4(a).

[60] *Khodorkovskiy and Lebedev v. Russia*, nos 11082/06 and 13772/05, § 869, 25 July 2013.

[61] *Kozacıoğlu v. Turkey* [GC], no. 2334/03, § 48, 19 February 2009; *James and Others v. the United Kingdom*, 21 February 1986, § 37, Series A no. 98; *Sporrong and Lönnroth v. Sweden*, 23 September 1982, § 61, Series A no. 52; see also *The Holy Monasteries v. Greece*, 9 December 1994, § 56, Series A no. 301-A; *Iatridis v. Greece* [GC], no. 31107/96, § 55, ECHR 1999-II; *Beyeler v. Italy* [GC], no. 33202/96, § 106, ECHR 2000-I.

[62] *Brosset-Triboulet and Others v. France* [GC], no. 34078/02, Joint Dissenting Opinion of Judges Bratza, Vajić, David Thòr Björgvinsson, and Kalaydjieva, § 2, 29 March 2010.

[63] *Ambruosi v. Italy*, no. 31227/96, § 27, 19 October 2000.

Like other rights enshrined in the Convention and its Protocols the protection of property also has positive dimensions. This is underscored by the phrase 'shall secure to everyone within [its] jurisdiction the rights and freedoms defined in [the] Convention'. According to the Grand Chamber, 'this general duty may entail positive obligations inherent in ensuring the effective exercise of the rights guaranteed by the Convention. In the context of Article 1 of Protocol No. 1, those positive obligations may require the State to take the measures necessary to protect the right of property.'[64] In a very broad and general formulation, the Court said:

> When an interference with the right to peaceful enjoyment of possessions is perpetrated by a private individual, a positive obligation arises for the State to ensure in its domestic legal system that property rights are sufficiently protected by law and that adequate remedies are provided whereby the victim of an interference can seek to vindicate his rights, including, where appropriate, by claiming damages in respect of any loss sustained.[65]

Such measures may be either preventive or remedial.

The State is not, of course, directly liable in the case of private disputes. Its obligations 'are limited to providing the necessary assistance to the creditor in the enforcement of the respective court awards, for example, through a bailiff service or bankruptcy procedures'.[66] States are required to provide judicial procedures accompanied by the appropriate procedural guarantees so as to enable effective and fair adjudication of disputes between private parties including the possibility of claims to recover damages.[67] Even when it is the horizontal relations between private parties that are concerned, 'there may be public-interest considerations involved which may impose some obligations on the State'.[68] Moreover, although the Court does not in principle deal with disputes of a purely private nature, 'it cannot remain passive where a national court's interpretation of a legal act, be it a testamentary disposition, a private contract, a public document, a statutory provision or an administrative practice appears unreasonable, arbitrary or blatantly inconsistent with the prohibition of discrimination established by Article 14 and more broadly with the principles underlying the Convention'.[69] The boundaries between positive and negative obligations of the State with respect to article 1 do not lend themselves to precise definition. A case may be analysed in terms of a positive duty of the State or an interference by a public authority; in either case, the applicable criteria are substantively the same. 'In both contexts regard must be had to the fair balance to be struck between the competing interests of the individual and of the community as a whole', according to the Grand Chamber.[70]

---

[64] *Ališić and Others v. Bosnia and Herzegovina, Croatia, Serbia, Slovenia, and 'the former Yugoslav Republic of Macedonia'* [GC], no. 60642/08, § 100, 16 July 2014; *Broniowski v. Poland* [GC], no. 31443/96, § 143, ECHR 2004-V; *Likvidējamā p/s Selga and Vasiļevska v. Latvia* (dec.), nos 17126/02 and 24991/02, §§ 94–113, 1 October 2013.

[65] *Blumberga v. Latvia*, no. 70930/01, § 67, 14 October 2008.

[66] *Shestakov v. Russia* (dec.), no. 48757/99, 18 June 2002; *Krivonogova v. Russia* (dec.), no. 74694/01, 1 April 2004; *Kesyan v. Russia*, no. 36496/02, 19 October 2006.

[67] *Sovtransavto Holding v. Ukraine*, no. 48553/99, § 96, ECHR 2002-VII.

[68] *Zolotas v. Greece (no. 2)*, no. 66610/09, § 39, ECHR 2013 (extracts); *Broniowski v. Poland* [GC], no. 31443/96, § 143, ECHR 2004-V.

[69] *Fabris v. France* [GC], no. 16574/08, § 60, ECHR 2013 (extracts); *Pla and Puncernau v. Andorra*, no. 69498/01, § 59, ECHR 2004-VIII.

[70] *Ališić and Others v. Bosnia and Herzegovina, Croatia, Serbia, Slovenia, and 'the former Yugoslav Republic of Macedonia'* [GC], no. 60642/08, § 101, 16 July 2014; *Broniowski v. Poland* [GC], no. 31443/96, § 144, ECHR 2004-V.

Natural or legal person

The right to peaceful enjoyment of possessions is ensured to '[e]very natural or legal person'. It is the only right in the Convention and the Protocols where the protection is formally extended to corporate bodies. Article 34 of the Convention authorizes the Court to receive applications from 'any person, non-governmental organisation or group of individuals', a notion that must be larger than 'natural or legal persons' because a non-governmental organization may be an informal body without legal status and a group of individuals may not necessarily have a legal existence separate from that of its component members.[71] There does not appear to be any case law on the concept of 'legal person' within the scope of article 1 of Protocol No. 1.

Possessions

Even if it is 'possessions', and not 'property', that are protected by the first paragraph of article 1 of Protocol No. 1, the provision is 'in substance guaranteeing the right of property'.[72] The second paragraph, in which the exception to the general rule is stated, speaks of the 'use of property'. In the French version of the text, 'possessions' and 'property' are rendered as *biens* and *propriété*, suggesting that the two English terms are synonymous. The word 'Property' is also used in the title, added by Protocol No. 11.

'Possessions' may be 'existing possessions' in the sense of assets. If a property interest contemplated by article 1 of Protocol No. 1 is in dispute, it falls to the European Court to determine the applicant's legal position.[73] Article 1 does not enshrine any right to acquire property,[74] although in one case the Grand Chamber seemed to recognize the possibility of this taking place through 'adverse possession', despite the impossibility of such a thing happening under domestic law.[75] Article 1 may apply where a person has 'at least a "legitimate expectation" of obtaining effective enjoyment of a property right'.[76] By 'legitimate expectation' is meant something grounded in 'a legislative provision or a legal act bearing on the property interest in question'.[77] The Court does not apply the concepts of 'genuine dispute' and 'arguable claim' in determining whether a 'legitimate expectation' exists.[78]

---

[71] *Hyde Park and Others v. Moldova (no. 4)*, no. 18491/07, § 33, 7 April 2009; *Hyde Park and Others v. Moldova (nos 5 and 6)*, nos 6991/08 and 15084/08, § 31, 14 September 2010; *Christians against Racism and Fascism v. the United Kingdom*, no. 8440/78, Commission decision of 16 July 1980, (1981) 24 YB 178, DR 21, p. 138.

[72] *Marckx v. Belgium*, 13 June 1979, § 63, Series A no. 31.

[73] *J.A. Pye (Oxford) Ltd and J.A. Pye (Oxford) Land Ltd v. the United Kingdom* [GC], no. 44302/02, § 61, ECHR 2007-III.

[74] *Kopecký v. Slovakia* [GC], no. 44912/98, § 35, ECHR 2004-IX; *Slivenko and Others v. Latvia* (dec.) [GC], § 121, 23 January 2002.

[75] *Brosset-Triboulet and Others v. France* [GC], no. 34078/02, § 71, 29 March 2010: 'in the present case the time that elapsed had the effect of vesting in the applicants a proprietary interest in peaceful enjoyment of the house'. See also *Brosset-Triboulet and Others v. France* [GC], no. 34078/02, Concurring Opinion of Judge Casadevall, § 5, 29 March 2010.

[76] *J.A. Pye (Oxford) Ltd and J.A. Pye (Oxford) Land Ltd v. the United Kingdom* [GC], no. 44302/02, § 61, ECHR 2007-III; *Von Maltzan and Others v. Germany* (dec.) [GC], nos 71916/01, 71917/01, and 10260/02, § 74, ECHR 2005-V; *Prince Hans-Adam II of Liechtenstein v. Germany* [GC], no. 42527/98, § 83, ECHR 2001-VIII.

[77] *Saghinadze and Others v. Georgia*, no. 18768/05, § 103, 27 May 2010.

[78] *Kopecký v. Slovakia* [GC], no. 44912/98, § 52, ECHR 2004-IX; *Vilho Eskelinen and Others v. Finland* [GC], no. 63235/00, § 94, ECHR 2007-II.

From a temporal jurisdiction standpoint, there is no obligation under article 1 for the State to compensate the former owners or to return property transferred to it prior to ratification of the Convention and of Protocol No. 1. 'Deprivation of ownership or of another right *in rem* is in principle an instantaneous act and does not produce a continuing situation of "deprivation of a right"', the Grand Chamber has explained.[79] Thus, a property confiscated prior to entry into force of the Protocol is not a 'possession' that falls within the scope of article 1. Nor does article 1 apply where there is only a hope that 'an old property right which it has long been impossible to exercise effectively' may have survived.[80] However, it may extend to a particular benefit of which the persons concerned have been deprived on the basis of a discriminatory condition of entitlement.[81]

Although most States in Central and Eastern Europe have enacted some form of restitution legislation concerning property confiscated by former regimes, some have opted to do nothing in this respect, while others have made provision within certain limits.[82] If they chose to do so, States Parties are free to establish the scope of property restitution and the conditions under which it will be conducted.[83] For example, they may exclude categories of property owners from eligibility for restitution.[84] If, however, they enact a scheme by which formerly confiscated property is to be restored, this generates a new property right protected by article 1 for beneficiaries of the legislation.[85] Even if the relevant arrangements for restitution or compensation pre-date the ratification of Protocol No. 1, if the legislation has subsequently remained in force, then Protocol No. 1 may be applicable.[86]

The application of article 1 to various categories of assets has been discussed in the case law. The notion has an autonomous meaning that is not limited to ownership of physical goods, and 'certain other rights and interests constituting assets can also be regarded as "property rights", and thus as "possessions"'.[87] The scope of 'possessions' is independent of formal classifications found in domestic law.[88] According to the Court, 'the issue that needs to be examined is whether the circumstances of the case, considered as a whole, may

[79] *Von Maltzan and Others v. Germany* (dec.) [GC], nos 71916/01, 71917/01, and 10260/02, §§ 74, 81–82, ECHR 2005-V; *Malhous v. the Czech Republic* (dec.) [GC], no. 33071/96, ECHR 2000-XII; *Gisela Mayer, Hans-Christoph Weidlich, and Bernd-Joachim Fullbrecht, Ortwin A. Hasenkamp, Hartwig Golf, Werner Klaussner v. Germany*, nos 18890/91, 19048/91, 19342/92, and 19549/92, Commission decision of 4 March 1996, (1996) 39 YB 86, DR 85, p. 5; *Ladislav and Aurel Brežny v. Slovakia*, no. 23131/93, Commission decision of 4 March 1996, (1996) 39 YB 96, DR 85, p. 65.
[80] *Malhous v. the Czech Republic* (dec.) [GC], no. 33071/96, ECHR 2000-XII; *Prince Hans-Adam II of Liechtenstein v. Germany* [GC], no. 42527/98, § 85, ECHR 2001-VIII; *Nerva and Others v. the United Kingdom*, no. 42295/98, § 43, ECHR 2002-VIII; *Stretch v. the United Kingdom*, no. 44277/98, § 32, 24 June 2003.
[81] *Andrejeva v. Latvia* [GC], no. 55707/00, § 79, ECHR 2009; *Fabris v. France* [GC], no. 16574/08, § 50, ECHR 2013 (extracts).
[82] *Maria Atanasiu and Others v. Romania*, nos 30767/05 and 33800/06, §§ 85–106, 12 October 2010.
[83] *Von Maltzan and Others v. Germany* (dec.) [GC], nos 71916/01, 71917/01, and 10260/02, §§ 74, 81–82, ECHR 2005-V; *Jantner v. Slovakia*, no. 39050/97, § 34, 4 March 2003.
[84] *Gratzinger and Gratzingerova v. the Czech Republic* (dec.) [GC], no. 39794/98, § 69, ECHR 2002-VII.
[85] *Maria Atanasiu and Others v. Romania*, nos 30767/05 and 33800/06, § 136, 12 October 2010; *Kopecký v. Slovakia* [GC], no. 44912/98, § 35, ECHR 2004-IX; *Manushaqe Puto and Others v. Albania*, nos 604/07, 43628/07, 46684/07, and 34770/09, § 92, 31 July 2012.
[86] *Broniowski v. Poland* [GC], no. 31443/96, § 125, ECHR 2004-V.
[87] *Gasus Dosier- und Fördertechnik GmbH v. the Netherlands*, 23 February 1995, § 53, Series A no. 306-B.
[88] See, e.g., *Brosset-Triboulet and Others v. France* [GC], no. 34078/02, § 71, 29 March 2010.

be regarded as having conferred on the applicant title to a substantive interest protected by that provision'.[89]

As a general principle, a proprietary interest that constitutes a claim or a debt must be rooted in national law, for example where the case law of the courts confirms its validity.[90] If there is no debt, article 1 does not apply.[91] In the case of an attempt to recover a sum that was unduly paid, the debtor cannot invoke article 1 because the sum owed cannot be considered a 'possession'.[92] An enforceable judgment debt is a 'possession' within the terms of article 1.[93] Future income constitutes a 'possession' pursuant to article 1 of Protocol No. 1 only if it has been earned or where an enforceable claim to it exists.[94] But there is no right to become the owner of property.[95]

With respect generally to non-physical assets, the Court will consider 'whether the legal position in question gave rise to financial rights and interests and thus had an economic value'.[96] Accordingly, article 1 has been applied to professional practices and their clientele,[97] to intellectual property,[98] to business permits and licences,[99] trade marks and copyright,[100] the right to use an internet domain name,[101] and to shares in limited liability companies.[102]

The European Convention does not generally deal with economic and social rights, and there is no obligation on States Parties to provide social security payments, or to any particular amount of such benefit.[103] In practice, all States Parties have such schemes for

---

[89] *Saghinadze and Others v. Georgia*, no. 18768/05, § 103, 27 May 2010; *Depalle v. France* [GC], no. 34044/02, § 62, ECHR 2010; *Anheuser-Busch Inc. v. Portugal* [GC], no. 73049/01, § 63, ECHR 2007-I; *Öneryıldız v. Turkey* [GC], no. 48939/99, § 123, ECHR 2004-XII.

[90] *Plechanow v. Poland*, no. 22279/04, § 83, 7 July 2009; *Vilho Eskelinen and Others v. Finland* [GC], no. 63235/00, § 94, ECHR 2007-II; *Anheuser-Busch Inc. v. Portugal* [GC], no. 73049/01, § 65, ECHR 2007-I; *Kopecký v. Slovakia* [GC], no. 44912/98, § 52, ECHR 2004-IX; *Draon v. France* [GC], no. 1513/03, § 68, 6 October 2005.

[91] *Van der Mussele v. Belgium*, 23 November 1983, § 48, Series A no. 70.

[92] *Cheminade v. France* (dec.), no. 31599/96, 19 January 1999.

[93] *Kotov v. Russia* [GC], no. 54522/00, § 90, 3 April 2012; *Stran Greek Refineries and Stratis Andreadis v. Greece*, 9 December 1994, § 59, Series A no. 301-B; *Burdov v. Russia*, no. 59498/00, § 40, ECHR 2002-III.

[94] *Ambruosi v. Italy*, no. 31227/96, § 20, 19 October 2000; *Anheuser-Busch Inc. v. Portugal* [GC], no. 73049/01, § 64, ECHR 2007-I.

[95] *Slivenko v. Latvia* (dec.) [GC], no. 48321/99, § 121, ECHR 2002-II; *Kopecký v. Slovakia* [GC], no. 44912/98, § 35 (b), ECHR 2004-IX; *Andrejeva v. Latvia* [GC], no. 55707/00, § 77, ECHR 2009; *Stec and Others v. the United Kingdom* [GC], nos 65731/01 and 65900/01, § 53, ECHR 2006-VI.

[96] Paeffgen *GmbH v. Germany* (dec.), nos 25379/04, 21688/05, 21722/05, and 21770/05, 18 September 2007.

[97] *Lederer v. Germany* (dec.), no. 6213/03, 22 May 2006; *Buzescu v. Romania*, no. 61302/00, § 81, 24 May 2005; *Wendenburg and Others v. Germany* (dec.), no. 71630/01, 6 February 2003; *Olbertz v. Germany* (dec.) no. 37592/97, 25 May 1999; *Döring v. Germany* (dec.), no. 37595/97, 9 November 1999; *Van Marle and Others v. the Netherlands*, 26 June 1986, § 41, Series A no. 101.

[98] *Anheuser-Busch Inc. v. Portugal* [GC], no. 73049/01, §§ 72, 78, ECHR 2007-I.

[99] *Megadat.com SRL v. Moldova*, no. 21151/04, §§ 62–63, ECHR 2008; *Bimer S.A. v. Moldova*, § 49; *Rosenzweig and Bonded Warehouses Ltd v. Poland*, no. 51728/99, § 49, 28 July 2005; *Capital Bank AD v. Bulgaria*, no. 49429/99, § 130, ECHR 2005-XII (extracts); *Tre Traktörer AB v. Sweden*, 7 July 1989, § 53, Series A no. 159.

[100] *Melnychuk v. Ukraine* (dec.), no. 28743/03, ECHR 2005-IX.

[101] Paeffgen *GmbH v. Germany* (dec.), nos 25379/04, 21688/05, 21722/05, and 21770/05, 18 September 2007.

[102] *Olczak v. Poland* (dec.), no. 30417/96, § 60, 7 November 2002; *Sovtransavto Holding v. Ukraine*, no. 48553/99, § 91, ECHR 2002-VII.

[103] *Andrejeva v. Latvia* [GC], no. 55707/00, § 77, ECHR 2009; *Kjartan Ásmundsson v. Iceland*, no. 60669/00, § 39, ECHR 2004-IX; *Domalewski v. Poland* (dec.), no. 34610/97, ECHR 1999-V; *Janković v. Croatia* (dec.), no. 43440/98, ECHR 2000-X.

the payment of social benefits. This generates a property interest that falls under the scope of article 1.[104] It has also been applied to pensions and other forms of social security benefit[105] to the extent that some tangible and definable proprietary interest can be demonstrated. Previously, the Court and the Commission distinguished between contributory and non-contributory pension benefits for the purposes of applying article 1, but that has now been abandoned.[106] It now takes the view that 'when a State chooses to set up a pension scheme, the individual rights and interests deriving from it fall within the ambit of that provision, irrespective of the payment of contributions and the means by which the pension scheme is funded'.[107]

Peaceful enjoyment of property

The first rule, set out in the first sentence of the first paragraph, is of a general nature and enunciates the principle of the peaceful enjoyment of property: *usus, fructus, abusus*,[108] to invoke the categories of Roman law that are reflected in all legal systems in one form or another. Provided there is a proprietary interest, the right to be protected against interference, even if it does not involve deprivation, is ensured by article 1. The protection of peaceful enjoyment of property must be read together with the second paragraph of article 1, where measures necessary to control the use of property are authorized. When the Court concludes that there has been an interference with the peaceful enjoyment of property, it will first examine whether the measures have a 'reasonable basis' and then assess whether or not 'the applicants have had to bear an individual and excessive burden which has upset the fair balance which should be struck between the requirements of the general interest and the protection of the right to the peaceful enjoyment of one's possessions'.[109] Any interference with the right to the peaceful enjoyment of possessions 'must achieve a "fair balance" between the demands of the general interest of the community and the requirements of the protection of the individual's fundamental rights'.[110] The Court has explained that '[t]he concern to achieve this balance is reflected in the structure of Article 1 of Protocol No. 1 as a whole, including, therefore, the second sentence, which is to be read in the light of the general principle enunciated in the first sentence'. In particular, 'there must be a reasonable relationship of proportionality between the means employed and the aim sought to be realised by any measures applied by the State, including measures depriving a person of his of her possessions'.[111]

---

[104] *Stec and Others v. the United Kingdom* (dec.) [GC], nos 65731/01 and 65900/01, §§ 53–55, ECHR 2005-X; *Andrejeva v. Latvia* [GC], no. 55707/00, § 77, ECHR 2009; *Moskal v. Poland*, no. 10373/05, § 38, 15 September 2009.

[105] *Stec and Others v. the United Kingdom* (dec.) [GC], nos 65731/01 and 65900/01, §§ 53–55, ECHR 2005-X; *Andrejeva v. Latvia* [GC], no. 55707/00, § 77, ECHR 2009; *Moskal v. Poland*, no. 10373/05, § 38, 15 September 2009.

[106] *Stec and Others v. the United Kingdom* (dec.) [GC], nos 65731/01 and 65900/01, §§ 47–53, ECHR 2005-X

[107] *Andrejeva v. Latvia* [GC], no. 55707/00, § 76, ECHR 2009.

[108] *Mosteanu and Others v. Romania*, no. 33176/96, § 61, 26 November 2002; *Hirschhorn v. Romania*, no. 29294/02, § 57, 26 July 2007; *Chassagnou and Others v. France* [GC], nos 25088/94, 28331/95, and 28443/95, Dissenting Opinion of Judge Costa, § 9, ECHR 1999-III.

[109] *Matos e Silva, Lda., and Others v. Portugal*, 16 September 1996, § 72, *Reports of Judgments and Decisions* 1996-IV.

[110] *Kozacıoğlu v. Turkey* [GC], no. 2334/03, § 63, 19 February 2009; *Sporrong and Lönnroth v. Sweden*, 23 September 1982, § 69, Series A no. 52.

[111] *Kozacıoğlu v. Turkey* [GC], no. 2334/03, § 63, 19 February 2009; *Pressos Compania Naviera S.A. and Others v. Belgium*, 20 November 1995, § 38, Series A no. 332; *The former King of Greece and Others v. Greece*

The Court concluded that there was a violation of article 1 when the owner of property in occupied Cyprus had been unable to use, control, and enjoy her property as a result of the Turkish invasion. As the judgment explains, this could not be regarded as either deprivation of property or a control of use of property, falling instead within the meaning of the first sentence of article 1 as an interference with the peaceful enjoyment of possessions.[112] But in a case involving a citizen of Yugoslavia residing in Germany who did not take Croatian citizenship following the breakup of the country but who retained property within Croatia, the Court distinguished this with the situation in Cyprus. It said 'the rights entailed in the provisions of Article 1 of Protocol No. 1 do not encompass the right for a foreign citizen who owns property in another country to permanently reside in that county in order to use his property'.[113]

Withdrawal of a licence to conduct business activities constitutes interference with the right to peaceful enjoyment of possessions.[114] Even if it is not fully withdrawn, limitation of the licence may amount to depriving the right of its substance.[115]

The issue of peaceful enjoyment has also arisen in a series of cases involving hunting rights. Several States have legislation authorizing the vesting of hunting rights in private associations despite the objections of the actual landowners, who may be morally and ethically opposed to the practice as such. For example, in France the *Loi Verdeille* of 1964 compelled small landowners to transfer hunting rights to hunters' associations without compensation. It did not deprive them of property rights, but rather it interfered with the peaceful enjoyment by the owners. The European Court said this 'upset the fair balance to be struck between protection of the right of property and the requirements of the general interest'.[116] In a similar case from Luxembourg, there was some financial compensation for the landowners but the Court did not feel this to be decisive—it amounted to €3.25 per annum—and again concluded that the right to peaceful enjoyment had been breached.[117] It reached the same result in other cases.[118]

The right to dispose of one's property, the *abusus*, 'constitutes a traditional and fundamental aspect of the right of property'.[119] When Poland revised its rent control policy in order to deal with housing problems, it lowered the rent payable to such an extent that owners could not cover their operating expenses out of the income from tenants. This resulted in the reduction of the value of the tenement houses and 'entailed

---

[GC], no. 25701/94, §§ 89–90, ECHR 2000-XII; *Sporrong and Lönnroth v. Sweden*, 23 September 1982, § 73, Series A no. 52; *Beyeler v. Italy* [GC], no. 33202/96, § 107, ECHR 2000-I.

[112] *Loizidou v. Turkey* (merits), 18 December 1996, § 63, *Reports of Judgments and Decisions* 1996-VI; *Cyprus v. Turkey* [GC], no. 25781/94, §§ 186–189, ECHR 2001-IV.

[113] *Ilić v. Croatia* (dec.), no. 42389/98, 19 September 2000.

[114] *Tre Traktörer AB v. Sweden*, 7 July 1989, § 53, Series A no. 159; *Capital Bank AD v. Bulgaria*, no. 49429/99, § 130, ECHR 2005-XII (extracts); *Rosenzweig and Bonded Warehouses Ltd v. Poland*, no. 51728/99, § 49, 28 July 2005; *Bimer S.A. v. Moldova*, no. 15084/03, § 49, 10 July 2007.

[115] *Centro Europa 7 S.r.l. and Di Stefano v. Italy* [GC], no. 38433/09, § 177, ECHR 2012.

[116] *Chassagnou and Others v. France* [GC], nos 25088/94, 28331/95, and 28443/95, §§ 79, 82–85, ECHR 1999-III. Measures subsequently taken by France allowing for a form of 'conscientious objection' were approved by the Committee of Ministers: ResDH(2005)26 and *Chabauty v. France* [GC], no. 57412/08, § 25, 4 October 2012.

[117] *Schneider v. Luxembourg*, no. 2113/04, § 49, 10 July 2007.

[118] *Herrmann v. Germany* [GC], no. 9300/07, § 93, 26 June 2012; *Baudinière and Vauzelle v. France*, nos 25708/03 and 25719/03, 6 December 2007; *Piippo v. Sweden*, no. 70518/01, 21 March 2006; *Nilsson v. Sweden*, no. 11811/05, 26 February 2008.

[119] *Marckx v. Belgium*, 13 June 1979, § 63, Series A no. 31.

consequences similar to expropriation'. Although the owners were not deprived of their possessions, their right to enjoyment was infringed.[120] In other cases, the Court has rejected the '*de facto* expropriation' thesis to describe restrictions imposed on the right of property that have the consequence of reducing the value and thereby encroaching upon the possibility of disposing of the asset. Such measures do not amount to deprivation and are to be examined from the standpoint of the second sentence of the first sentence of paragraph 1 of article 1.[121] In some cases involving forfeiture and seizure for tax liability, the Court has taken the perspective of interference with control over possessions under paragraph 2, rather than deprivation of property under paragraph 1.[122]

Limitations periods are a common feature of national legislation. They are designed 'to ensure legal certainty and finality and prevent the injustice which might arise if courts were required to decide upon events which took place in the distant past'.[123] In a case concerning provisions of the Greek Civil Code, whereby a twenty-year limitation period applied to bank deposits, the Court noted that 'the twenty-year limitation period for agreements on the deposit of fungible goods was justified by an aim in the public interest, namely that of terminating, in the interests of the community, legal relationships that had been created so long before that their existence had become uncertain'.[124] This interference with the enjoyment of possessions was 'a drastic measure', especially because it applied to ordinary people who were not versed in the law. As a result, the Court said the State had a positive obligation 'to require that banks, in view of the potentially adverse consequences of limitation periods, should inform the holders of dormant accounts when the limitation period is due to expire and thus afford them the possibility to stop the limitation period running, for instance by performing a transaction on the account'.[125] Law applicable in the United Kingdom providing that the registered owner lost control of property where there had been 'adverse possession' for twelve years was deemed proportionate, although there were many dissenters in the Grand Chamber.[126]

Deprivation of possessions

At the heart of article 1 is the protection against deprivation of possessions. This is the second rule of the provision, set out in the second sentence of the first paragraph. Deprivation of possessions is subjected to certain conditions. It must be 'in the public interest', and 'subject to the conditions provided for by law and by the general principles

---

[120] *Hutten-Czapska v. Poland*, no. 35014/97, § 176, 22 February 2005; *Hutten-Czapska v. Poland* [GC], no. 35014/97, §§ 202–203, ECHR 2006-VII.

[121] *Anthony Aquilina v. Malta*, no. 3851/12, § 54, 11 December 2014; *Elia S.r.l. v. Italy*, no. 37710/97, §§ 57–58, ECHR 2001-IX; *Sporrong and Lönnroth v. Sweden*, 23 September 1982, § 65, Series A no. 52; *Erkner and Hofauer v. Austria*, 23 April 1987, § 74, Series A no. 117; *Poiss v. Austria*, 23 April 1987, § 6, Series A no. 117.

[122] *AGOSI v. the United Kingdom*, 24 October 1986, § 51, Series A no. 108; *Air Canada v. The United Kingdom*, 5 May 1995, § 34, Series A no. 316-A; *C.M. v. France* (dec.), no. 28078/95, ECHR 2001-VII; *Gasus Dosier- und Fördertechnik GmbH v. the Netherlands*, 23 February 1995, § 59, Series A no. 306-B.

[123] *Zolotas v. Greece (no. 2)*, no. 66610/09, § 43, ECHR 2013 (extracts); *J.A. Pye (Oxford) Ltd and J.A. Pye (Oxford) Land Ltd v. the United Kingdom* [GC], no. 44302/02, § 68, ECHR 2007-III; *Stubbings and Others v. the United Kingdom*, 22 October 1996, § 51, *Reports of Judgments and Decisions* 1996-IV.

[124] *Zolotas v. Greece (no. 2)*, no. 66610/09, § 48, ECHR 2013.

[125] Ibid., § 53.

[126] *J.A. Pye (Oxford) Ltd et J.A. Pye (Oxford) Land Ltd v. the United Kingdom* [GC], no. 44302/02, §§ 75–85, ECHR 2007-III; ibid., Joint Dissenting Opinion of Judges Rozakis, Bratza, Tsatsa-Nikolovska, Gylumyan, and Šikuta; ibid., Dissenting Opinion of Judge Loucaides Joined by Judge Kovler.

of international law'. The Court will also consider whether deprivation of property was 'proportionate'. In determining whether there is a deprivation of possessions governed by the second rule, the Court will look behind the appearances and investigate the realities of the situation complained of. Because 'the Convention is intended to guarantee rights that are "practical and effective", it has to be ascertained whether the situation amounted to a *de facto* expropriation'.[127]

In the public interest

The concept of 'public interest', which permits States to deprive persons of their property, has been distinguished with the necessity tests that are so familiar to the jurisprudence of the European Convention on Human Rights. The discretion accorded pursuant to the 'public interest' is wider in scope. As the European Commission of Human Rights explained in *Handyside v. The United Kingdom*, '[c]learly, the public or general interest encompasses measures which would be preferable or advisable, and not only essential, in a democratic society'. It considered that its duty under the Convention was 'to review the actions of member States purporting to be in the public or general interest, in order to establish that they have acted reasonably and in good faith'.[128] The Commission's view was endorsed by the Court. It added that in contrast with article 10(2) of the Convention, article 1 of Protocol No. 1 'sets the Contracting States up as sole judges of the "necessity" for an interference. Consequently, the Court must restrict itself to supervising the lawfulness and the purpose of the restriction in question.'[129]

In a subsequent decision, the Court referred to *Handyside*, noting that under the Convention system 'it is thus for the national authorities to make the initial assessment both of the existence of a problem of public concern warranting measures of deprivation of property and of the remedial action to be taken'. It said that '[b]ecause of their direct knowledge of their society and its needs, the national authorities are in principle better placed than the international judge to appreciate what is "in the public interest"'. The Court explained that the notion of 'public interest' was necessarily extensive, given that decisions to enact legislation expropriating property commonly involved controversial political, economic, and social issues. It said the Court would 'respect the legislature's judgment as to what is "in the public interest" unless that judgment be manifestly without reasonable foundation'.[130] That there may exist alternative solutions does not impugn the contested legislation. As long as the legislature remains within the bounds of its margin of appreciation, 'it is not for the Court to say whether the legislation represented the best solution for dealing with the problem or whether the legislature's discretion should have been exercised in another way'.[131]

---

[127] *Brosset-Triboulet and Others v. France* [GC], no. 34078/02, § 81, 29 March 2010; *Brumărescu v. Romania* [GC], no. 28342/95, § 76, ECHR 1999-VII; *Sporrong and Lönnroth v. Sweden*, 23 September 1982, §§ 63, 69–74, Series A no. 52.

[128] *Handyside v. the United Kingdom*, no. 5493/72, Commission report of 30 September 1979, § 167. Also *Håkansson and Sturesson v. Sweden*, no. 11855/85, Commission decision of 15 July 1987, DR 53, p. 190.

[129] *Handyside v. the United Kingdom*, 7 December 1976, § 62, Series A no. 24.

[130] *James and Others v. the United Kingdom*, 21 February 1986, § 46, Series A no. 98. Also *Kozacıoğlu v. Turkey* [GC], no. 2334/03, § 53, 19 February 2009; *Beyeler v. Italy* [GC], no. 33202/96, § 112, ECHR 2000-I.

[131] *Zolotas v. Greece (no. 2)*, no. 66610/09, § 44, ECHR 2013 (extracts); *J.A. Pye (Oxford) Ltd. v. the United Kingdom*, no 44302/02, §§ 43–45, 15 November 2005.

Conditions provided by law

The second sentence of article 1 provides that in addition to a deprivation of property being in the 'public interest' it must also be 'provided by law'. The relevant provisions must satisfy the requirements of accessibility, precision, and foreseeability.[132] But the Court 'has limited power, however, to review compliance with domestic law'.[133] Its review is generally confined to considering whether national courts applied the applicable law in a manifestly erroneous manner or in such a way as to reach arbitrary conclusions.[134] It will also look at the aim pursued to ensure that it is legitimate. For example, it has taken the view that 'the proper conduct of criminal proceedings and, more generally, of fighting and preventing crime...undoubtedly falls within the general interest as envisaged in Article 1 of Protocol No. 1'.[135] Also, 'the protection of a country's cultural heritage is a legitimate aim capable of justifying the expropriation by the State of a building listed as "cultural property"'.[136] The disbarment of a lawyer had the effect of depriving him of his clientele and therefore was an interference with the enjoyment of possessions. The Court said that this pursued an aim that was in the general interest 'since it appeared to be legitimate for the FRG to review retrospectively the behaviour of persons, who after reunification, were authorised to practise the professions of lawyer, notary or lay judge throughout Germany, and who, by the nature of their work, were required to meet particularly high standards of integrity and morality, given that they were considered to be officers of the court and guarantors of the rule of law'. Such checks were designed to protect the public by verifying the integrity and morality of legal practitioners.[137]

Finally, the Court considers the proportionality of the measure, something described in the case law as striking a 'fair balance' between the demands of the general interest of the community and the requirements of the protection of the individual's fundamental rights. The issue of 'fair balance' only becomes relevant 'once it has been established that the interference in question satisfied the requirement of lawfulness and was not arbitrary'.[138] This is where the issue of compensation arises. According to the Court, 'the taking of property without payment of an amount reasonably related to its value will normally constitute a disproportionate interference'.[139] But article 1 of Protocol No. 1 does not, however, guarantee a right to full compensation in all circumstances. Legitimate objectives of 'public interest' may call for less than reimbursement of the full market value of the

[132] *Beyeler v. Italy* [GC], no. 33202/96, §§ 108–109, ECHR 2000-I; *Hentrich v. France*, 22 September 1994, § 42, Series A no. 296-A; *Lithgow and Others v. the United Kingdom*, 8 July 1986, § 110, Series A no. 102.

[133] *Håkansson and Sturesson v. Sweden*, 21 February 1990, § 47, Series A no. 171-A.

[134] *Tre Traktörer AB v. Sweden*, 7 July 1989, § 58, Series A no. 159.

[135] *Lavrechov v. the Czech Republic*, no. 57404/08, § 46, ECHR 2013; *Denisova and Moiseyeva v. Russia*, no. 16903/03, § 58, 1 April 2010.

[136] *Kozacıoğlu v. Turkey* [GC], no. 2334/03, § 54, 19 February 2009; *SCEA Ferme de Fresnoy v. France* (dec.), no. 61093/00, ECHR 2005-XIII; *Debelianovi v. Bulgaria*, no. 61951/00, § 54, 29 March 2007.

[137] *Döring v. Germany* (dec.), no. 37595/97, 9 November 1999.

[138] *Iatridis v. Greece* [GC], no. 31107/96, § 58, ECHR 1999-II.

[139] *Pyrantienė v. Lithuania*, no. 45092/07, § 40, 12 November 2013; *Kozacıoğlu v. Turkey* [GC], no. 2334/03, § 64, 19 February 2009; *Lithgow and Others v. the United Kingdom*, 8 July 1986, § 121, Series A no. 102; *Broniowski v. Poland* [GC], no. 31443/96, § 182, ECHR 2004-V; *Scordino v. Italy (no. 1)* [GC], no. 36813/97, § 95, ECHR 2006-V.

expropriated property.[140] Indeed, there may be exceptional circumstances where no compensation is provided.[141] For example, interference with property will be in the public interest when the impugned measures are designed to correct mistakes of the authorities and restore the rights of ownership of former owners.[142]

The Court has said that 'where an issue in the general interest is at stake, in particular when the matter affects fundamental human rights such as those involving property, the public authorities must act in good time and in an appropriate and above all consistent manner'.[143] Described as the 'good governance principle',[144] it does not 'as a general rule, prevent the authorities from correcting occasional mistakes, even those resulting from their own negligence'.[145] In cases involving revocation of ownership of property that has been transferred erroneously, the Court has invoked the 'good governance principle'. It has said that 'where an issue in the general interest is at stake, in particular when the matter affects fundamental human rights such as those involving property, the public authorities must act in good time and in an appropriate and above all consistent manner'.[146] The authorities may be required not only to act promptly in correcting the mistake but also some form of compensation or reparation to the former *bona fide* holder of the property may be dictated.[147]

Under Turkish law, it was not possible to take into account that part of the value related to the architectural and historical features of a building for the purposes of compensation in the case of expropriation. The Court described such a valuation system as unfair because it enabled depreciation resulting from a property's listed status to be taken into account during expropriation, although any eventual appreciation was deemed irrelevant in determining the compensation for expropriation. 'Thus, not only is such a system likely to penalise those owners of listed buildings who assume burdensome maintenance costs, it deprives them of any value that might arise from the specific features of their property', it said.[148]

General principles of international law

Aside from article 1 of Protocol No. 1, there are only three other references to international law in the European Convention. In article 1, the clear intent of the drafters was to engage the international law concerning the expropriation of property. Customary international law 'permits States to expropriate foreign property if it is in the public

---

[140] *Pyrantienė v. Lithuania*, no. 45092/07, § 64, 12 November 2013; *Lithgow and Others v. the United Kingdom*, 8 July 1986, § 121, Series A no. 102; *Broniowski v. Poland* [GC], no. 31443/96, § 182, ECHR 2004-V; *Scordino v. Italy (no. 1)* [GC], no. 36813/97, § 95, ECHR 2006-V.

[141] *Sociedad Anónima del Ucieza v. Spain*, no. 38963/08, § 76, 4 November 2014; *The Holy Monasteries v. Greece*, 9 December 1994, § 71, Series A no. 301-A; *Broniowski v. Poland* [GC], no. 31443/96, § 186, ECHR 2004-V.

[142] *Romankevic v. Lithuania*, no. 25747/07, § 35, 2 December 2014; *Pyrantienė v. Lithuania*, no. 45092/07, §§ 44–48, 12 November 2013.

[143] *Bogdel v. Lithuania*, no. 41248/06, § 65, 26 November 2013; *Moskal v. Poland*, no. 10373/05, § 51, 15 September 2009 .

[144] For the origins of the principle, before it was given the name 'good governance': *Beyeler v. Italy* [GC], no. 33202/96, § 120, ECHR 2000-I; *Megadat.com SRL v. Moldova*, no. 21151/04, § 72, ECHR 2008.

[145] *Bogdel v. Lithuania*, no. 41248/06, § 66, 26 November 2013.

[146] Ibid., § 65.

[147] *Romankevic v. Lithuania*, no. 25747/07, § 35, 2 December 2014; *Maksymenko and Gerasymenko v. Ukraine*, no. 49317/07, § 64, 16 May 2013.

[148] *Kozacıoğlu v. Turkey* [GC], no. 2334/03, § 70, 19 February 2009.

interest or for a public purpose, accomplished in a non-discriminatory fashion, and in conformity with due process'.[149] There has been controversy in international law with respect to the issue of compensation, although the debate has been mainly about the level or amount rather than about the existence of an obligation itself. A 1962 General Assembly resolution speaks of 'appropriate compensation',[150] whereas another resolution with the same title, adopted a decade later, says that 'each State is entitled to determine the amount of possible compensation and the mode of payment...'[151]

In early cases, the European Commission took the view that the principles of international law referred to in article 1 were inapplicable to nationals of the respondent State.[152] The Commission later adjusted its view that article 1 'requires member States to respect the property of "every natural or legal person" within their jurisdiction, which of necessity includes nationals. To decide otherwise would be to render the Article meaningless.'[153] Subsequently, the Court explained that the reference to international law serves at least two purposes:

Firstly, it enables non-nationals to resort directly to the machinery of the Convention to enforce their rights on the basis of the relevant principles of international law, whereas otherwise they would have to seek recourse to diplomatic channels or to other available means of dispute settlement to do so. Secondly, the reference ensures that the position of non-nationals is safeguarded, in that it excludes any possible argument that the entry into force of Protocol No. 1 (P1) has led to a diminution of their rights. In this connection, it is also noteworthy that Article 1 (P1-1) expressly provides that deprivation of property must be effected 'in the public interest': since such a requirement has always been included amongst the general principles of international law, this express provision would itself have been superfluous if Article 1 (P1-1) had had the effect of rendering those principles applicable to nationals as well as to non-nationals.[154]

The Court concluded that the negotiating history as a whole shows 'that the reference to the general principles of international law was not intended to extend to nationals'.[155]

According to Luigi Condorelli, when there is a reference to 'principles of international law' in a treaty, it can only be in order to resolve a profound difficulty among the drafters in reaching a consensus, who were unable to reconcile positions about the extent to which an obligation of compensation should be a condition for lawful taking of property.[156] Professor Condorelli notes that this debate has since been resolved to the extent that the Court has established a strong presumption in favour of compensation regardless of the nationality of the owner of the possessions in question. Indeed, in recent decades there does not appear to have been any litigation of any significance at the European Court

---

[149] Ursula Kriebaum and August Reinisch, 'Property, Right to, International Protection', in Rüdiger Wolfrum, ed., *The Max Planck Encyclopedia of Public International Law*, Vol. III, Oxford: Oxford University Press, 2012, pp. 522–33, at p. 525.

[150] Permanent Sovereignty over Natural Resources, UN Doc. A/RES/1803 (1962), para. 4.

[151] Permanent Sovereignty over Natural Resources, UN Doc. A/RES/3171 (1973), para. 3.

[152] *Gudmundsson v. Iceland*, no. 511/59, Commission decision of 20 December 1960, (1960) 3 YB 394, at p. 426; *X v. Federal Republic of Germany*, no. 1870/63, Commission decision of 16 December 1965, (1965) 8 YB 218.

[153] *Handyside v. the United Kingdom*, no. 5493/72, Commission report of 30 September 1979, § 163.

[154] *James and Others v. the United Kingdom*, 21 February 1986, § 62, Series A no. 98; *Lithgow and Others v. the United Kingdom*, 8 July 1986, § 115, Series A no. 102.

[155] *James and Others v. the United Kingdom*, 21 February 1986, §§ 64, 66, Series A no. 98; *Lithgow and Others v. The United Kingdom*, 8 July 1986, § 115, Series A no. 102.

[156] Luigi Condorelli, 'Premier Protocole Additionnel, Article 1', in Pettiti et al., *La Convention européenne*, pp. 971–97, at p. 986.

concerning the issue of 'principles of international law' as it relates to the property rights of non-nationals.

Control of the use of property

The second paragraph of article 1 enables the State Party to 'enforce such laws as it deems necessary to control the use of property in accordance with the general interest or to secure the payment of taxes or other contributions or penalties'. The distinction with deprivation of the right to enjoy one's possessions, governed by the first paragraph of article 1, is not always evident, and the parties may admit that article 1 applies but disagree about whether it is a question of deprivation or merely of control.[157] In practice, the methodology used in examining cases where this provision applies is not significantly different from that of the other two rules set out in article 1.[158] The interference must be prescribed by law and it must pursue one or more legitimate aims. There must be a relationship of proportionality between the means that are employed and the aim or aims of the legislation. This involves assessing whether a 'fair balance' has been struck between the requirements of the 'general interest' and those of the individual concerned.[159] The second paragraph of paragraph 1 invokes the criterion of 'general interest', whereas the first paragraph refers to 'public interest'. The case law has not attempted to make any meaningful distinction between the two.[160]

The State has a broad margin of appreciation in this area. Its power to review whether domestic law has been complied with is limited.[161] The Court has said that '[i]t is in the first place for the national authorities, notably the courts, to interpret and apply domestic law, even in those fields where the Convention "incorporates" the rules of that law, since the national authorities are, in the nature of things, particularly qualified to settle the issues arising in this connection'.[162] The deference for national courts is especially robust when difficult questions of interpretation of domestic law are involved.[163] Where the general interest of the community is pre-eminent, for example in cases involving regional planning and environmental conservation policies, the margin of appreciation is greater than where civil rights alone are at stake.[164]

A classic example of control of the use of property 'in accordance with the general interest' concerns legislation governing residential tenancies.[165] This is the area where the Court may come the closest to ruling on economic and social rights. The Court has held 'that in spheres such as housing, States necessarily enjoy a wide margin of appreciation not

---

[157] E.g., *Lindheim and Others v. Norway*, nos 13221/08 and 2139/10, §§ 75–78, 12 June 2012.

[158] *N.K.M. v. Hungary*, no. 66529/11, § 44, 14 May 2013; *R.Sz. v. Hungary*, no. 41838/11, § 32, 2 July 2013.

[159] *AGOSI v. the United Kingdom*, 24 October 1986, § 51, Series A no. 108; *Sporrong and Lönnroth v. Sweden*, 23 September 1982, §§ 69–73, Series A no. 52; *Handyside v. the United Kingdom*, 7 December 1976, §§ 62–63, Series A no. 24.

[160] *Hutten-Czapska v. Poland* [GC], no. 35014/97, § 165, ECHR 2006-VIII.

[161] *Allan Jacobsson v. Sweden (no. 2)*, 19 February 1998, § 57, *Reports of Judgments and Decisions* 1998-I.

[162] *Pavlinović and Tonić v. Croatia* (dec.), no. 17124/05 and 17126/05, 3 September 2009.

[163] *Anheuser-Busch Inc. v. Portugal* [GC], no. 73049/01, § 83, ECHR 2007-I.

[164] *Gorraiz Lizarraga and Others v. Spain*, no.62543/00, §70, ECHR 2004-III; *Alatulkkila and Others v. Finland*, no. 33538/96, § 67, 28 July 2005; *Valico S.r.l. v. Italy* (dec.), no. 70074/01, ECHR 2006-III; *Lars and Astrid Fägerskiöld v. Sweden* (dec.), no. 37664/04, 26 February 2008.

[165] *Hutten-Czapska v. Poland* [GC], no. 35014/97, §§ 160–168, ECHR 2006-VIII; *Edwards v. Malta*, no. 17647/04, §§ 52–78, 24 October 2006; *Srpska pravoslavna Opština na Rijeci v. Croatia* (dec.), no. 38312/02, 18 May 2006.

only in regard to the existence of a problem of public concern warranting measures for control of individual property but also to the choice of the measures and their implementation'.[166] It has also noted that 'State control over levels of rent is one such measure and its application may often cause significant reductions in the amount of rent chargeable.' Moreover, the principles that govern the matter 'apply equally, if not *a fortiori*, to measures adopted in the course of the fundamental reform of a country's political, legal and economic system in the transition from a totalitarian regime to a democratic State'.[167] According to the Court, 'where the operation of the rent-control legislation involves wide-reaching consequences for numerous individuals and has economic and social consequences for the country as a whole, the authorities must have considerable discretion not only in choosing the form and deciding on the extent of control over the use of property, but also in deciding on the appropriate timing for the enforcement of the relevant laws'.[168] The Court has indicated its sensitivity to the 'reconciliation of the conflicting interests of landlords and tenants', observing that the State authorities are required 'on the one hand, to secure the protection of the property rights of the former and, on the other, to respect the social rights of the latter, often vulnerable individuals'.[169]

The Court has often ruled in favour of the landlord, probably too often. With regard to Croatian legislation governing rent control, it referred to factors such as the small amount of protected rent to which the applicant was entitled, the statutory burdens placed upon him, the low level of profit, the fact that he had not been able to recover possession of the flat for fifty-five years, and 'the absence of adequate procedural safeguards for achieving a balance between the competing interests of landlords and protected'. The Court said there were no discernable demands of general interest that could justify such restrictions and that there was 'not a fair distribution of the social and financial burden resulting from the reform of the housing sector. Rather, a disproportionate and excessive individual burden was placed on the applicant as a landlord'.[170] A similar conclusion was reached with respect to legislation in Slovakia,[171] and in a case dealing with ground rent in Norway.[172] In a Maltese case, the Court considered that rent control legislation no longer corresponded to the economic reality of the country, and as a result could no longer be justified.[173]

Taxation, contemplated by the second paragraph of article 1, 'is in principle an interference with the right guaranteed by the first paragraph of Article 1 of Protocol No. 1, since it deprives the person concerned of a possession, namely the amount of money which must be paid'.[174] Noting that 'the interference is generally justified under the second paragraph of this Article, which expressly provides for an exception as regards the payment of taxes or other contributions', the Grand Chamber has insisted that 'the

---

[166] *Statileo v. Croatia*, no. 12027/10, § 140, 10 July 2014.
[167] *Bittó and Others v. Slovakia*, no. 30255/09, § 96, 28 January 2014.
[168] *Anthony Aquilina v. Malta*, no. 3851/12, § 61, 11 December 2014.
[169] Ibid., § 114.
[170] *Statileo v. Croatia*, no. 12027/10, § 143, 10 July 2014. See also *Ghigo v. Malta*, no. 31122/05, § 69, 26 September 2006; *Edwards v. Malta*, no. 17647/04, § 78, 24 October 2006.
[171] *Bittó and Others v. Slovakia*, no. 30255/09, §§ 115–117, 28 January 2014.
[172] *Lindheim and Others v. Norway*, nos 13221/08 and 2139/10, § 134, 12 June 2012.
[173] *Anthony Aquilina v. Malta*, no. 3851/12, § 65, 11 December 2014.
[174] *Buffalo S.r.l. en liquidation v. Italy*, no. 38746/97, § 32, 3 July 2003.

issue is nonetheless within the Court's control, since the correct application of Article 1 of Protocol No. 1 is subject to its supervision'.[175]

The approach to the second exception in the second paragraph of article 1, 'to secure the payment of taxes or other contributions or penalties', is much the same as it is with the 'general interest'. The measures must strike a 'fair balance' between the demands of the general interest of the community and the requirements of the protection of the individual's fundamental rights. A reasonable relationship of proportionality between the means employed and the aims pursued is required.[176] Thus, 'the financial liability arising out of the raising of tax or contributions may adversely affect the guarantee secured under this provision if it places an excessive burden on the person or the entity concerned or fundamentally interferes with his or its financial position'.[177] For example, where Swedish authorities sold a valuable asset at auction that had been seized in order to enforce tax liability, obtaining a sum that was dramatically lower than the actual value of the property in question, the Court held that article 1 had been breached because an individual and excessive burden had been imposed upon the applicant.[178] In this area, there is considerable deference to the national legislature. The Court has explained that '[d]ecisions in this area normally involve, in addition, an assessment of political, economic and social problems which the Convention leaves to the competence of the member States, as the domestic authorities are clearly better placed than the Convention organs to assess such problems'.[179]

The term 'contributions' has been interpreted as covering court costs.[180]

It is not uncommon for laws imposing taxes to be given a retrospective effect. The Court has confirmed that this is not inconsistent with the lawfulness requirement imposed by article 1 of Protocol No. 1.[181]

Discrimination

The Grand Chamber has noted that article 14 does not expressly prohibit distinctions based 'on the ground of property'. It is not deemed a criterion of distinction that is unacceptable as a matter of principle, as is the case with racial or ethnic origin, or unacceptable in the absence of very weighty reasons, as is the case with gender and sexual orientation.[182] This does not mean, however, that there can never be a violation of the Convention related to article 1 of Protocol No. 1 in conjunction with article 14.

The area of social benefits—which are recognized as 'possessions' and therefore within the ambit of article 1—is fraught with distinctions and therefore with allegations of

---

[175] *Burden v. the United Kingdom* [GC], no. 13378/05, § 59, ECHR 2008.

[176] *National & Provincial Building Society, Leeds Permanent Building Society and Yorkshire Building Society v. the United Kingdom*, 23 October 1997, § 80, *Reports of Judgments and Decisions* 1997-VII.

[177] *Ferretti v. Italy*, no. 25083/94, Commission decision of 26 February 1997; *Buffalo S.r.l. in liquidation v. Italy*, no. 38746/97, § 32, 3 July 2003.

[178] *Rousk v. Sweden*, no. 27183/04, § 126, 25 July 2013.

[179] *Azienda Agricola Silverfunghi S.a.s. and Others v. Italy*, nos 48357/07, 52677/07, 52687/07, and 52701/07, § 103, 24 June 2014; *Musa v. Austria*, no. 40477/98, Commission decision of 10 September 1998; *Baláž v. Slovakia* (dec.), no. 60243/00, 16 September 2003.

[180] *Perdigão v. Portugal* [GC], no. 24768/06, § 61, 16 November 2010; *Aires v. Portugal*, no. 21775/93, Commission decision of 25 May 1995, DR 81, p. 48.

[181] *Maggio and Others v. Italy*, nos 46286/09, 52851/08, 53727/08, 54486/08, and 56001/08, § 60, 31 May 2011; *Arras and Others v. Italy*, no. 17972/07, § 81, 14 February 2012.

[182] *Chabauty v. France* [GC], no. 57412/08, § 50, 4 October 2012.

982 Part Three: Protocol No. 1

prohibited discrimination. The Court insists that although there is no restriction on the freedom of States Parties to decide whether to have in place any form of social security scheme, nor any obligation to do so, if a State creates a benefits or pension scheme this must comply with article 14 of the Convention.[183] The leading case, *Stec and Others v. The United Kingdom*, concerns differences in pensionable age between men and women. The Grand Chamber noted that the rationale for such a distinction was to mitigate the 'financial inequality and hardship arising out of women's traditional unpaid role of caring for the family in the home rather than earning money in the workplace' and that as a measure to correct 'factual inequalities' between men and women it was objectively justified under Article 14.[184] Over time, this changed but, as the Grand Chamber explained, 'the development of parity in the working lives of men and women has been a gradual process, and one which the national authorities are better placed to assess'.[185]

Ukraine imposed a rule whereby retirement pensions were not payable to persons living abroad. The Court considered that this constituted a distinction based on personal status in accordance with article 14 of the Convention. It said that Ukraine had provided no justification for the measure, adding that 'the Government has not relied on considerations of international cooperation to justify treating pensioners living in Ukraine differently from those living abroad'. Referring to the 1952 International Labour Organisation's Social Security (Minimum Standards) Convention that authorizes suspension of pension benefits to non-residents, the European Court said it was 'not prevented from defining higher standards on the basis of the Convention than those contained in other international legal instruments'. It went on to say that '[t]he rise of population mobility, the higher levels of international cooperation and integration, as well as developments in the area of banking services and information technologies no longer justify largely technically motivated restrictions in respect of beneficiaries of social security payments living abroad, which may have been considered reasonable in the early 1950s'. Consequently, there was a breach of article 14 in conjunction with article 1 of Protocol No. 1.[186]

The Court rejected the claim of two elderly sisters who had lived together all their lives. They argued that property taxes imposed on the surviving sister following the death of one of them would pose a discriminatory burden because married cohabiting couples as well as same-sex couples were not exposed to the same liability. 'States, in principle, remaining free to devise different rules in the field of taxation policy', the Grand Chamber said.[187] Cohabiting sisters could not be equated with married or same-sex couples.

In a case concerning hunting rights, a small landowner invoked the Court's judgment finding a violation because French legislation had assigned the rights to associations without regard to the views of some owners who were opposed to the practice on ethical reasons. The applicant argued, unsuccessfully, that this was discrimination because it did not take into account the encroachment on the rights of landowners who had principles opposed to hunting.

---

[183] *Stec and Others v. the United Kingdom* (dec.) [GC], nos 65731/01 and 65900/01, §§ 54–55, ECHR 2005-X; *Stec and Others v. the United Kingdom* [GC], nos 65731/01 and 65900/01, § 53, ECHR 2006-VI.
[184] *Stec and Others v. the United Kingdom* [GC], nos 65731/01 and 65900/01, § 61, ECHR 2006-VI.
[185] Ibid., § 63.
[186] *Pichkur v. Ukraine*, no. 10441/06, §§ 52–54, 7 November 2013.
[187] *Burden v. the United Kingdom* [GC], no. 13378/05, § 65, ECHR 2008.

Reservations and declarations

Upon ratification, Luxembourg made the following reservation: 'Désirant éviter toute incertitude en ce qui concerne l'application de l'article 1ᵉʳ du Protocole additionnel par rapport à la loi luxembourgeoise du 26 avril 1951 qui concerne la liquidation de certains biens, droits et intérêts ci-devant ennemis, soumis à des mesures de séquestre, *Déclare* réserver les dispositions de la loi du 26 avril 1951 désignée ci-dessus.'[188]

Austria made a reservation to Protocol No. 1 that was associated with the obligations it assumed under the State Treaty: 'being desirous of avoiding any uncertainty concerning the application of Article 1 of the Protocol in connection with the State Treaty of 15th May 1955 for the Restoration of and Independent and Democratic Austria, declares the Protocol ratified with the reservations that there shall be no interference with the provisions of Part IV "Claims arising out of the War" and Part V "Property, Rights and Interests" of the abovementioned State Treaty'.[189] However, the law itself was not referred to in the reservation. The Commission held that in making the reservation, 'Austria must necessarily have had the intention of excluding from the scope of the First Protocol everything forming the subject matter of Parts IV and V of said Treaty'. Accordingly, Austria's reservation must be interpreted as intended to cover all legislative and administrative measures directly related to the subject matter of Parts IV and V of the State Treaty'.[190] Later, the Commission expressed its intent to reconsider its position.[191]

Portugal formulated the following reservation: 'Article 1 of the Protocol will be applied subject to Article 82 of the Constitution of the Portuguese Republic, which provides that expropriations of large landowners, big property owners and entrepreneurs or shareholders may be subject to no compensation under the conditions to be laid down by the law.'[192] The United Kingdom reacted to the reservation with a letter to the Secretary General of the Council of Europe 're-affirm[ing] the view of the Government of the United Kingdom that the general principles of international law require the payment of prompt, adequate and effective compensation in respect of the expropriation of foreign property'.[193] Similar statements were made by Germany and France. The Secretary General replied to each country, noting that the letters did not constitute a formal objection to the Portuguese reservation but that they would nevertheless be circulated to Member States.[194] The Portuguese reservation to article 1 of Protocol No. 1 was withdrawn in 1987.[195]

San Marino formulated a reservation declaring that 'having regard to the provisions of law in force which govern the use of goods in conformity with the general interest', the principle set forth in article 1 'has no bearing on the regulations in force concerning the real estate of foreigners'.[196]

[188] (1955–56–57) 1 YB 42.
[189] (1958–59) 2 YB 88–91.
[190] *F. H. jr. v. Austria*, no. 1452/62, Commission decision of 18 December 1963, (1963) 6 YB 268, at p. 276. Also *Association X v. Austria*, no. 473/59, Commission decision of 29 August 1959, (1958–59) 2 YB 400.
[191] *X v. Austria*, no. 8180/78, Commission decision of 10 May 1979, DR 20, p. 26.
[192] (1978) 21 YB 16–19.
[193] (1979) 22 YB 16–17.
[194] Ibid., pp. 16–23.
[195] (1987) 30 YB 4–5.
[196] (1989) 32 YB 5.

Invoking article 33 of its Constitution, Spain made three reservations to article 1: '1. The right to private property and to inheritance is recognised. 2. The social function of these rights shall determine their scope, as provided for by law. 3. No person shall be deprived of their property or their rights except for a cause recognised as being in the public interest or in the interest of society and in exchange for fitting compensation as provided for by law.'[197]

Bulgaria made a reservation stating that article 1 of Protocol No. 1 'shall not affect the scope or content of Article 22, paragraph 1 of the Constitution of the Republic of Bulgaria, which states that: "No foreign physical person or foreign legal entity shall acquire ownership over land, except through legal inheritance. Ownership thus acquired shall be duly transferred."'[198]

Upon ratification on 16 April 1996, Estonia formulated the following reservation:

> In accordance with Article 64 [now article 57] of the Convention, the Republic of Estonia declares that the provisions of Article 1 of the First Protocol shall not apply to the laws on property reform which regulate the restoration or compensation of property nationalised, confiscated, requisitioned, collectivised or otherwise unlawfully expropriated during the period of Soviet annexation; the restructuring of collectivised agriculture and privatisation of state owned property.

The reservation was completed with a lengthy list of relevant legislation.[199] The Court has upheld the validity of the Estonian reservation.[200] But it has also observed: 'The reservation only covers laws in force at the material time and does not extend to later amendments to the restitution laws which might subsequently be subjected to Convention scrutiny. Moreover it only concerns substantive as opposed to procedural questions in the field of the property issues encompassed by its terms.'[201] It has suggested that the reservation cannot apply to subsequent amendments to the Property Reform (Principles) Act.[202] Upon ratification in 1997, Latvia made a similar reservation to Protocol No. 1.[203] It has also been upheld by the Court.[204]

Georgia has made several reservations to article 1 of Protocol No. 1. Georgia stated that article 1 'shall not apply to persons who have or will obtain status of "internally displaced persons" until the elimination of circumstances motivating the granting of this status (until the restoration of the territorial integrity of Georgia)'. There are several other detailed reservations relating to Georgian legislation.[205]

---

[197] (1990) 33 YB 9.

[198] (1992) 35 YB 5.

[199] (1996) 39 YB 23–25.

[200] *Shestjorkin v. Estonia* (dec.), no. 49450/99, 15 June 2000; *Põder and Others v. Estonia* (dec.), no. 67723/01, 26 April 2005. Also *Vesterby v. Estonia*, no. 34476/97, 1 July 1998; *Stalas v. Estonia*, no. 40108/98, Commission decision of 21 October 1998; *Elias v. Estonia*, no. 41456/98, Commission decision of 21 October 1998.

[201] Ibid.; *Põder and Others v. Estonia* (dec.), no. 67723/01, 26 April 2005.

[202] *Põder and Others v. Estonia* (dec.), no. 67723/01, 26 April 2005.

[203] (1997) 40 YB 49–52.

[204] *Koslova and Smirnova v. Latvia* (dec.), no. 57381/00, 23 October 2001; *Liepājnieks v. Latvia* (dec.), no. 37586/06, § 45, 2 November 2010.

[205] (2002) 45 YB 19.

Further reading

Corneliu Bîrsan, 'La protection du droit de propriété: développements récents de la jurisprudence de la Cour européenne des droits de l'homme', in Lucius Caflisch, Johan Callewaert, Roderick Liddell, Paul Mahoney, and Mark Villiger, eds, *Liber Amicorum Luzius Wildhaber*, Kehl, Germany: N.P. Engel, 2007, pp. 5–24.

Ali Riza Çoban, *Protection of Property Rights within the European Convention on Human Rights*, Farnham, UK: Ashgate, 2004.

Luigi Condorelli, 'Premier Protocole Additionnel, Article 1', in Pettiti et al., *La Convention européenne*, pp. 971–97.

Hélène Ruiz Fabri, 'The Approach taken by the European Court of Human Rights to the Assessment of Compensation for Regulatory Expropriations of the Property of Foreign Investors', (2002–2003) 1 *New York University Environmental Law Journal* 148.

Frowein/Peukert, *MenschenRechtsKonvention* Vladimiro Zagrebeslsky, pp. 639–70.

Grabenwarter, *European Convention*, pp. 365–80.

Harris et al., *Law of the European Convention*, pp. 655–96.

Timo Koivurova, 'Jurisprudence of the European Court of Human Rights regarding Indigenous Peoples: Retrospect and Prospects', (2011) 18 *International Journal on Minority and Group Rights* 1.

Richard Lang, 'Unlocking the First Protocol: Protection of Property and the European Court of Human Rights', (2008) 29 *HRLJ* 1.

Helen Mountfield, 'Regulatory Expropriations in Europe: The Approach of the European Court of Human Rights', (2002–2003) 11 *New York University Environmental Law Journal* 136.

Petra Herzfeld Olsson, 'Every Natural or Legal Person is Entitled to the Peaceful Enjoyment of His or Her Possessions: Article 1, Protocol 1 to the Euroepan Convention on Human Rights', in Filip Dorssemont, Klaus Lörcher, and Isabelle Schömann, eds, *The European Convention on Human Rights and the Employment Relation*, Oxford/Portland, OR: Hart, 2013, pp. 381–416.

Kudret Özersay and Ayla Gürel, 'Property and Human Rights in Cyprus: The European Court of Human Rights as a Platform of Political Struggle', (2008) 44 *Middle Eastern Studies* 291.

Ovey/White, *Jacobs and White, European Convention*, pp. 300–19.

Arjen van Rijn, 'Right to the Peaceful Enjoyment of One's Possessions (Article 1 of Protocol No. 1)', in Van Dijk et al., *Theory and Practice*, pp. 863–93.

Egon Schwelb, 'The Protection of the Right of Property of Nationals under the First Protocol to the European Convention on Human Rights', (1964) 13 *American Journal of Comparative Law* 518.

Maya Sigron, *Legitimate Expectations Under Article 1 of Protocol No. 1 to the European Convention on Human Rights*, Antwerp: Intersentia, 2014.

Article 2. Right to education/Droit à l'instruction

No person shall be denied the right to education. In the exercise of any functions which it assumes in relation to education and to teaching, the State shall respect the right of parents to ensure such education and teaching in conformity with their own religious and philosophical convictions.

Nul ne peut se voir refuser le droit à l'instruction. L'État, dans l'exercice des fonctions qu'il assumera dans le domaine de l'éducation et de l'enseignement, respectera le droit des parents d'assurer cette éducation et cet enseignement conformément à leurs convictions religieuses et philosophiques.

Introductory comments

The right to education is the only right set out in the Convention and its Protocols that without any dispute can be said to belong to the category of economic, social, and cultural rights. Of the other two rights in Protocol No. 1, the right to elections is clearly among the civil and political rights, while the right to property seems to straddle the two categories. Economic, social, and cultural rights are sometimes regarded as being less important or essential, or comprising norms that are not suitable for formulation in an absolute fashion. Yet the education of young children provided by the State is about as absolute a right as can be found. Nowhere in the modern world, and certainly not in Europe, is this right contested. Of course, debate remains about the age and level when the right to education starts to become less absolute and less of an obligation as well as a right.

During the drafting of the European Convention and Protocol No. 1, more attention was devoted to the provision on the right to education than to any other right. In most cases, the drafters did little more than import the formulation of fundamental rights from the Universal Declaration of Human Rights, adding some detail as to the scope of the rights and the permissible restrictions. The problems in drafting the right of education provision mainly involved the struggle between universal public education and the protection of private systems, generally of a confessional nature. Often, it was not at all a question of the right to education as such but rather of the right of parents, rather than the State, to control the education of children. A judgment of the European Court of Human Rights speaks of 'lengthy and impassioned discussions'.[1] The drafting history of article 2 of Protocol No. 1 reveals a complex confrontation between the Consultative Assembly and the Committee of Ministers about the content of the Protocol, with the Consultative Assembly finally prevailing. But even in the Committee of Ministers, there was sharp division among the delegates.

Article 26 of the Universal Declaration of Human Rights states:

(1) Everyone has the right to education. Education shall be free, at least in the elementary and fundamental stages. Elementary education shall be compulsory. Technical and professional education shall be made generally available and higher education shall be equally accessible to all on the basis of merit.

---

[1] *Kjeldsen, Busk Madsen, and Pedersen v. Denmark*, 7 December 1976, § 50, Series A no. 23.

(2) Education shall be directed to the full development of the human personality and to the strengthening of respect for human rights and fundamental freedoms. It shall promote understanding, tolerance and friendship among all nations, racial or religious groups, and shall further the activities of the United Nations for the maintenance of peace.

(3) Parents have a prior right to choose the kind of education that shall be given to their children.

It is the longest of the thirty articles in the Declaration, testimony not so much to the importance of the rights it enshrines—the right to life, in article 3, takes all of eleven words—as to the difficulties of the drafters in reaching agreement on a succinct formulation.

When the United Nations General Assembly decided to divide the 'covenant on human rights' into two distinct instruments, there was no debate about consigning the right to education to the one dealing with economic, social, and cultural rights. Articles 14 and 15 of the International Covenant on Economic, Social, and Cultural Rights make detailed provision for the right to education, reproducing in somewhat more detail the content of paragraphs 1 and 2 of article 16 of the Universal Declaration. Paragraph 3 of the Universal Declaration is reflected in paragraphs 3 and 4 of article 14:

3. The States Parties to the present Covenant undertake to have respect for the liberty of parents and, when applicable, legal guardians to choose for their children schools, other than those established by the public authorities, which conform to such minimum educational standards as may be laid down or approved by the State and to ensure the religious and moral education of their children in conformity with their own convictions.

4. No part of this article shall be construed so as to interfere with the liberty of individuals and bodies to establish and direct educational institutions, subject always to the observance of the principles set forth in paragraph 1 of this article and to the requirement that the education given in such institutions shall conform to such minimum standards as may be laid down by the State.

The right to education is recognized in other specialized treaties of the United Nations system. The first of them, in a chronological sense, is the Convention against Discrimination in Education adopted by the United Nations Educational, Scientific, and Cultural Organization in 1960.[2] Although the International Convention on the Elimination of All Forms of Racial Discrimination contains only a reference to the right to education, nestled amongst other economic, social, and cultural rights,[3] the Convention on the Elimination of All Forms of Discrimination Against Women devotes a detailed provision to the subject. It addresses the importance of equality in terms of career and vocational guidance at all levels of education, access to the same curricula and examinations, equal opportunities for scholarships and study grants, and the reduction of drop-out rates. Inspired by article 26(2) of the Universal Declaration, it also addresses the content of education: 'The elimination of any stereotyped concept of the roles of men and women at all levels and in all forms of education by encouraging coeducation and other types of education which will help to achieve this aim and, in particular, by the revision of textbooks and school programmes and the adaptation of teaching methods.'[4] Not surprisingly, the Convention on the Rights of the Child also dedicates great attention to the subject of education.[5]

---

[2] (1962) 429 UNTS 93.

[3] International Convention on the Elimination of All Forms of Racial Discrimination, (1966) 660 UNTS 195, 5(e)(v).

[4] Convention on the Elimination of All Forms of Discrimination Against Women, (1980) 1249 UNTS 13, art. 10.

[5] Convention on the Rights of the Child, (1990) 1577 UNTS 3, arts. 28–29.

The European Union Charter of Fundamental Rights reads as follows:

Article 14. Right to education.
1. Everyone has the right to education and to have access to vocational and continuing training.
2. This right includes the possibility to receive free compulsory education.
3. The freedom to found educational establishments with due respect for democratic principles and the right of parents to ensure the education and teaching of their children in conformity with their religious, philosophical and pedagogical convictions shall be respected, in accordance with the national laws governing the exercise of such freedom and right.

The ambit of article 14(1) of the Charter is wider than that of article 2 of Protocol No. 1 to the Convention because it may be extended to cover access to vocational and continuing training.[6] The scope of article 14(3) corresponds to that of article 2 of Protocol No. 1 as regards the rights of parents.[7]

Drafting of the provision

The initial draft European Convention on Human Rights prepared by the International Juridical Section of the European Movement did not deal with education and the rights of parents. Nevertheless, it contained a provision on family life,[8] a forerunner of article 8 of the Convention. As is the case with the other rights added by Protocol No. 1, there was substantial discussion of the issues during the drafting of the Convention itself. This resumed after the Convention was adopted as the Council of Europe struggled to find an acceptable text dealing with the rights of parents in the education of their children.

Drafting of the European Convention

Asked to prepare a text for discussion in the Committee on Legal and Administrative Questions at the first session of the Consultative Assembly, held from 22 August to 5 September 1949, Pierre-Henri Teitgen proposed the following: 'Rights of parents in regard to the education of their children, in accordance with Article 26(3) of the United Nations Declaration.'[9] Teitgen also elaborated upon the inclusion of 'family rights' in the draft, noting that the subject had given rise to discussion in the Committee:

There were first of all those rights which I shall call 'family rights.' I might explain that by this I mean those rights which we had in mind when we refer in paragraph (4) of Article 2, to 'freedom from all arbitrary interference in private and family life'; and also those which we mentioned in paragraph (10) where we ask for protection of 'the right to marry and found a family,' and finally

---

[6] Explanation relating to the Charter of Fundamental Rights, Official Journal of the European Union, C 303/34, 14 December 2007.

[7] Ibid.

[8] Convention for the Collective Protection of Individual Rights and Democratic Liberties by the States, Members of the Council of Europe, and for the establishment of a European Court of Human Rights to ensure observance of the Convention, Doc. INF/5/E/R, I *TP* 296–303, at p. 296, art. I(g). Also Recommendations adopted at the meeting of the International Council of the European Movement held at Brussels in February 1949, INF/2/F, p. 3. This is reproduced in CDH (67) 5, at pp. 2–3, with the indication that the original English version no longer exists.

[9] Proposals by Mr P.H. Teitgen, Rapporteur, 29 August 1949, Doc. A 116, I *TP* 166–8. Also Report presented by Mr P.H. Teitgen, 5 September 1949, Doc. A 290, I *TP* 192–213, at p. 206; Report [of the Committee on Legal and Administrative Questions], 5 September 1949, Doc. AS (1) 77, I *TP* 216–39, at p. 228.

those which we defined in paragraph (11) where we speak of 'the right of parents to have prior right regarding the kind of education to be given to their children.'

No one in the Committee, I hasten to add, has denied the vital importance of these family rights. Some have said that they would prefer to see the guarantee confined for the moment to essential civic freedoms, to those which are the necessary conditions for the functioning of democratic institutions, and that it would be better for the time being to exclude all other freedoms and all other fundamental rights which would include, in spite of their importance, family rights.

The Committee recalled the time in the recent past when, in some countries, certain people were denied the right to marry on account of race or religious convictions. It also recalled the legislation, under which some countries suffered during cruel years, which subordinated the child to the benefit of the State.

On account of these memories, the majority of the Committee considered it desirable to include these fundamental rights in the list of guaranteed freedoms. It considered that the father of a family cannot be an independent citizen, cannot feel free within his own country, if he is menaced in his own home and if, every day, the State steals from his soul, or the conscience of his children.[10]

The matter was hotly debated in the plenary sessions of the Consultative Assembly.[11] Indeed, it was the most contentious right of the entire draft convention. A proposal to refer the draft on the right of parents to the education of their children, together with the right to property, to the Legal Committee and not to include it in the draft adopted by the Consultative Assembly was adopted by a very close margin, forty-three votes to forty.[12]

The Committee of Ministers sent the Consultative Assembly draft to a Committee of Experts that met in February and March 1950. Delegates from Ireland and Turkey proposed that the provision on the rights of parents be restored.[13] The Report of the Committee said that 'most' of its members supported inclusion of a right of parents to the education of their children. The Committee considered that a decision to reinstate the right was a political question outside of its own competence, although it noted the importance of the right, given the propensity of 'totalitarian regimes' that 'sought systematically to expose the children to their ideological propaganda, by depriving them of the rightful influence of their parents'.[14]

The next substantive discussion of the issue occurred at the second session of the Consultative Assembly, in August 1950. Basing itself on a proposal from Henri Rolin,[15] the Committee on Legal and Administrative Questions adopted the following, by eight votes to nil, with three abstentions: 'All persons are entitled to education. The responsibilities assumed by the State with regard to education may not encroach on the right of parents to ensure the spiritual and moral instruction of their children in accordance with

[10] Report of the Sitting [of the Consultative Assembly, 7 September 1949], I *TP* 250–95, at p. 270.

[11] Official Report of the sitting [of the Consultative Assembly, 8 September 1949], II *TP* 14–274, at pp. 64–8.

[12] Ibid., p. 132. For the draft Convention as a whole, see Recommendation No. 38 to the Committee of Ministers adopted 8 September 1949 on the conclusion of the debates, Doc. AS (1) 108, II *TP* 274–83.

[13] Amendment to Article 2 of the Recommendation of the Consultative Assembly proposed by the Experts of Ireland and Turkey, Doc. A 776, III *TP* 184–5; Amendment to Articles 2 and 3 of the Recommendation of the Consultative Assembly, proposed by the Irish Expert, Doc. A 778, III *TP* 184–5.

[14] Report to the Committee of Ministers submitted by the Committee of Experts Instructed to Draw Up a Draft Convention of Collective Guarantee of Human Rights and Fundamental Freedoms, Doc. CM/WP 1 (5) 15, A 924, IV *TP* 2–55, at pp. 18–20.

[15] Text proposed by M. Rolin, Doc. AS/JA/WP 1 (2) 1, A 1942, V *TP* 204–5.

their own religious and philosophical beliefs.'[16] After debate in the plenary Consultative Assembly,[17] the matter returned again to the Committee on Legal and Administrative Questions, where Pierre-Henri Teitgen had a revised text: 'Every person has a right to education. The functions assumed by the State in respect of education and of teaching may not encroach upon the right of parents to ensure the spiritual and moral education and the teaching of their children in conformity with their own religious and philosophical convictions.'[18] The text was adopted in the Committee by seventeen votes to three.[19] After further debate in the plenary Consultative Assembly,[20] the provision adopted by the Legal Committee was endorsed, by ninety-seven votes, with fifteen abstentions,[21] and the recommendation duly transmitted to the Committee of Ministers.[22] A memorandum on the Consultative Assembly discussions prepared by the Secretariat General described the text as 'a compromise' produced by a Sub-Committee 'the members of which held varying political views'.[23]

Meeting in Rome immediately prior to adoption of the Convention, on 3 November 1950, the Committee of Ministers was unable to agree on inclusion of the right in the Convention. The United Kingdom representative moved that that proposals from the Consultative Assembly, including the provision on the right of parents to education of their children, be referred to a Committee of Experts 'with a view to the preparation of a Protocol to the Convention'. This was adopted by ten votes to one. An attempt by the Irish representative, Seán MacBride, to enlarge the Committee so as to include representatives of the Consultative Assembly was not accepted.[24]

There was much discontent in the Consultative Assembly about the turn of events. On 5 November 1950, the Standing Committee expressed 'regret' that the amendments,

---

[16] Progress Report, Doc. AS/JA (2) 1, A 2041, V *TP* 206–7; Supplementary Report of 8 August 1950 on the Draft Convention for the Protection of Human Rights and Fundamental Freedoms Presented on Behalf of the Committee by M. P.H. Teitgen, Doc. AS/JA (2) 30, V *TP* 208–9.

[17] Report of the sitting [of the Consultative Assembly, 14 August 1950], V *TP* 216–71, at p. 250; Report of the sitting [of the Consultative Assembly, 16 August 1950], V *TP* 272–351, at pp. 278, 326–8; Motion relative to the right to own property proposed by Mr MacEntee and several of his colleagues, Doc. AS/JA (2) 55, V *TP* 216–17.

[18] Draft Motion submitted by M. Teitgen, Original Draft, Doc. AS/JA (2) 6, A 2207, VI *TP* 6–11; Draft Motion submitted by M. Teitgen, Revised Draft, Doc. AS/JA (2) 6 rev., A 2238, VI *TP* 10–15.

[19] Minutes of the sitting [of the Committee on Legal and Administrative Questions, 18 August 1950], Doc. AS/JA (2) PV 4, A 2265, VI *TP* 16–20, at p. 20; Draft Recommendation submitted to the Consultative Assembly, Doc. AS/JA (2) 20, A 2491, VI *TP* 42–7, at p. 44; Text of the Report [of the Committee on Legal and Administrative Questions], Doc. AS (2) 93, VI *TP* 58–72, at pp. 62, 68; First Report [of the Committee on Legal and Administrative Questions], Doc. AS/JA (2) 15, A 2298, VI *TP* 46–52; Second Report Doc. AS/JA (2) rev., A 2493, VI *TP* 52–9, at p. 56.

[20] Report of the sitting [of the Consultative Assembly, of 25 August 1950, morning], VI *TP* 74–141, at pp. 78, 88, 104–10, 138–40; Report of the sitting [of the Consultative Assembly, 25 August 1950, afternoon], VI *TP* 144–91, at pp. 152–62.

[21] Report of the sitting [of the Consultative Assembly, 25 August 1950, afternoon], VI *TP* 144–91, at p. 164. See also Note of 14 December 1950 prepared by the Secretariat-General on the reasons for the Amendments to the Convention for the Protection of Human Rights and Fundamental Freedoms adopted by the Consultative Assembly on 15 August 1950, Doc. CM (50) 96, A 3503, VII *TP* 130–41, at pp. 136–41.

[22] Text published in the Collected Documents of the Consultative Assembly, Doc. AS (2) 104, VI *TP* 198–229, at p. 208.

[23] Explanatory Note by the Secretariat General, 9 September 1950, Doc. CM (50) 57, A 2781, VI *TP* 230–9, at p. 232.

[24] Report of the meeting [of the Committee of Ministers, 3 November 1950], VII *TP* 24–34, at p. 34.

including the provision on education, were not included in the Convention.[25] Later in November, when the plenary Assembly convened, anger was expressed at the United Kingdom, to whom responsibility for omission of the provision was attributed. The Assembly grudgingly accepted the fact that work would continue on a protocol where its concerns could be addressed.[26]

The Secretariat prepared a memorandum suggesting that the right required more exact definition. In particular, it identified two questions for clarification: the extent to which governments may be required to organize or subsidize teaching in response to the religious or philosophical convictions of parents and whether 'political groups which aim at the destruction of any of the rights and freedoms set forth in the Convention shall have the right to educate their children in accordance with such aims'.[27] The Secretariat described the views as being divided between those who were satisfied with the text and those who felt it did not go far enough in safeguarding the rights of parents with respect to religious education of their children. It noted that those who wanted no change included many 'advocates of a completely secular education, who felt they had already made sufficient compromise in agreeing to the text before them'.[28]

Preparation of Protocol No. 1

Drafting of the Protocol was assigned to a Committee of Experts that met in Paris in February 1951. In addition to the Consultative Assembly text that had been passed over by the Committee of Ministers, two other proposals had been submitted for consideration. The United Kingdom submitted the following:

No person should be denied the right to education. In the exercise of any functions which the State may assume in relation to education and to teaching it shall have regard to the liberty of the parents to ensure the religious education of their children in conformity with their own convictions.[29]

A Belgian draft read as follows:

No person shall be denied the right to education. In the exercise of any functions which the State may assume in relation to education and to teaching it shall have regard to the liberty of the parents to ensure the religious education of their children in conformity with their own convictions.[30]

---

[25] Minutes of the meeting held by the Standing Committee of the Consultative Assembly in Rome on 5 November 1950 (morning), Doc. AS/CP (2) PV 5, p. 2, A 3057, VII *TP* 82–4; Minutes of the fourth meeting held in the afternoon of 5 November 1950 [by the Standing Committee of the Consultative Assembly], Doc. AS/CP (2) PV 6, p. 2, A 3058, VII *TP* 84–5; Second Report on the Work of the Standing Committee presented in accordance with the Resolution adopted by the Assembly on 6th September 1949, Doc. AS (2) 137, pp. 1126–7, VII *TP* 86–9.

[26] Reports of the Consultative Assembly, 2nd session, 18 November 1950, VII *TP* 90–121.

[27] Note on the amendments to the Convention on Human Rights proposed by the Consultative Assembly about which the Committee of Ministers was not able to reach unanimous agreement, Doc. CM (50) 90, A 3034, VII *TP* 126–30, at p. 128.

[28] Note of 14 December 1950 prepared by the Secretariat-General on the reasons for the Amendments to the Convention for the Protection of Human Rights and Fundamental Freedoms adopted by the Consultative Assembly on 25 August 1950, Doc. CM (50) 96, A 3503, VII *TP* 130–79, at p. 144.

[29] Memorandum by the Secretariat setting forth the different texts proposed, Doc. CM/WP 4 (50) 3, CM/WP 1 (51) 29, A 4005, VII *TP* 192–7, at pp. 192–3. Also Letter from the Secretary General of the Council of Europe to the Foreign Ministers of Member States, 7 February 1951, Doc. D 1357, VII *TP* 184–7.

[30] Memorandum by the Secretariat setting forth the different texts proposed, Doc. CM/WP 4 (50) 3, CM/WP 1 (51) 29, A 4005, VII *TP* 192–7, pp. 194–6.

The Committee's Report noted that 'certain delegations' agreed on a positive statement of the right, in accordance with the Consultative Assembly and the Belgian delegation, while others agreed with the British preference for a negative statement of the right. The British were supported by Denmark, Germany, and Norway in their concern that a positive statement of the right 'might be interpreted as imposing on the governments the obligation to take effective measures to ensure that everybody could receive the education which he desired'. Others insisted that the provision recognized the obligation of the State to provide education to all children who were not in receipt of private education. A second issue was whether the Convention should guarantee the right of parents to choose the religious education or all of the education of their children. A text, based upon the British proposal, met with wide acceptance:

Everybody has the right to education. (No person shall be denied the right to education). In the exercise of any functions which it may assume in relation to education and to teaching, the State must respect the liberty of parents to ensure the religious education of their children in conformity with their own convictions.[31]

The Belgian, French, Saar, and Swedish delegations found this text acceptable but preferred one expressly endorsing the principle of the freedom of private teaching. Denmark proposed an additional sentence: 'Parents or children in charge of the education of children shall have the right to decide freely that children in their charge shall attend recognised schools with another teaching language than the language of the country in question.' Turkey moved the following amendment: 'The State shall also refrain from interfering in the education of minors for political purposes.'[32]

The Committee of Experts met again in June 1951. It reported that the majority, although having no objection in principle to the Danish proposal, felt that the Convention 'was not the most appropriate medium for settling the question'. Denmark agreed to withdraw its proposal. The majority did not support the Turkish proposal. The Committee accepted the following provision:

No person shall be denied the right to education. In the exercise of any functions which it may assume in relation to education and to teaching, the State shall have regard to the liberty of parents to ensure the religious education of their children in conformity with their own creeds, and to the right of parents to send their children to schools, other than those established by the State, which conform to the standards laid down by law.[33]

At the meeting of Ministers' Advisers, in June 1951, the United Kingdom proposed deletion of the sentence following the word 'creeds' and its replacement with the following: 'and, where schools have been established by the State, to send their children to any other school of their choice, provided that such school conforms with the requirements of law'.[34] Turkey proposed deletion of the last sentence, beginning with the words 'and to the right of parents to send...'[35] The Ministers' Advisers agreed on the

---

[31] Report of the Committee of Experts to the Committee of Ministers, Doc. CM/WP 1 (51) 40, CM/WP VI (51) 7, A 4024, VII *TP* 204–13, at pp. 208–11.

[32] Report of the Committee of Experts to the Committee of Ministers [of 19 April 1951], Doc. CM (51) 33 final, A 4421 with corrigendum A 4475, VII *TP* 250–5, at p. 252.

[33] Ibid.

[34] Amendments proposed by the United Kingdom Government, Doc. CM/Adj. (51) 34, A 5444, VII *TP* 314.

[35] Amendments proposed by the Turkish Government, Doc. CM/Adj. (51) 36, A 5461, VII *TP* 314.

following: 'No person shall be denied the right to education. In the exercise of any functions which it may assume in relation to education and to teaching, the State shall have regard to the right of parents to ensure the religious education of their children in conformity with their own creeds.'[36] The text was endorsed in August 1951 by the Committee of Ministers.[37]

The Secretariat-General prepared an opinion on the provision noting the negative formulation of the right, a consequence of concern that 'the positive formulation proposed by the Assembly might be interpreted to impose on the State the positive duty to provide education'. The Secretariat-General said that although education was provided by the State for children as a matter of course, 'it is still not possible for them to give an unlimited guarantee to apply to illiterate adults for whom no facilities exist, or to types or standards of education which the State cannot furnish for one reason or another'. It noted that the Assembly draft's reference to 'religious and moral education' and to 'religious and philosophical convictions' had been changed to 'religious education' because the Assembly text 'could be construed to mean that parents whose "philosophical convictions" are fundamentally opposed to the conceptions of democracy and human rights would have the right to educate their children in the same beliefs'.[38]

The Legal Committee of the Consultative Assembly submitted an opinion to the Committee of Ministers that addressed several aspects of the proposed text. It objected to the term 'have regard to' as being 'a phrase which is too elastic to secure the supervision which is the aim of the Convention'. It noted the restriction of the guarantee to religious education, saying this would 'undoubtedly be interpreted in the majority of States as an appreciable retreat, which it will be difficult to accept, from the traditional conception of freedom of education'. It seems the concern here was about the language of education rather than ideology or belief. As for concerns that this might result in promotion of undemocratic ideologies, the Committee said this concern was already addressed in article 17 of the Convention. The Assembly recommended the following text: 'No person shall be denied the right to education. In the exercise of any functions which it assumes in relation to education and to teaching, the State shall respect the right of parents to ensure such education and teaching in conformity with their own religious and philosophical convictions.'[39]

In response to the concerns of the Legal Committee of the Consultative Assembly, and so as to comply with its concern that the principle of the independent school be recognized, the Committee of Ministers agreed to add the following to its draft article 2: '. . . and, where schools have been established by the State, to send their children to any other school of their choice, provided that such school conforms with the requirements of the law'. The following text was proposed: 'No person shall be denied the right to education. In the exercise of any functions which it assumes in relation to education and to teaching, the State shall respect the right of parents to ensure such education and in

---

[36] Recommendations of the Ministers' Advisers relating to the Agenda of the ninth Session of the Committee of Ministers, Doc. CM (51) 54 rev., A 5578, VII *TP* 326–33.

[37] Text of the Draft Protocol approved by the Committee of Ministers on 3 August 1951, VII *TP* 338–43.

[38] Commentary by the Secretariat-General on the Draft Protocol, Doc. AS/JA (3) 13, A 5904, VIII *TP* 4–17.

[39] Draft letter to be submitted to the President of the Consultative Assembly concerning the Draft Protocol, Doc. AS/JA (3) 17, A 6131, VIII *TP* 20–29.

conformity with their own religious and philosophical convictions.'[40] The plenary Consultative Assembly convened in December 1951. By this point, article 2 was the only outstanding issue of Protocol No. 1. Once again, there was a lengthy debate in the Assembly. The Legal Committee's text was adopted by seventy-five votes, with twenty-three abstentions.[41]

The Secretariat-General addressed the impasse that seemed to confront the Consultative Assembly and the Committee of Ministers. It noted that there appeared to be division on two points. The first was the complaint of the Assembly that 'have regard to' was not precise enough and should be replaced by 'respect'. The second was whether the guarantee involved only religious education or also covered 'philosophical' convictions. The Secretariat-General noted that both sides agreed that the question of according grants to private schools should be kept outside the framework of the Convention. However, recognition of a right of parents 'belonging to no creed to be free from the obligation to have their children given any religious instruction whatsoever' appeared to be 'insoluble owing to the constitutional or legal difficulties which the Assembly's solution would present to certain States'.[42]

In a note on article 2 that is not dated but that clearly was issued in December 1951, entitled 'The right to education and the question of denominational schools', A.H. Robertson of the Secretariat-General criticized the Consultative Assembly draft. If it were to be adopted, he said, 'the terms "religious and *moral* education and *teaching*" would guarantee to the parents the right to ensure as they thought fit the complete education of their children (and not only their relgious education), without the State being bound to provide or support the schools necessary to this end'. Robertson noted that at the Committee of Experts meeting in February 1951, 'most delegations voted against such a far-reaching undertaking'. In April, he pointed out, a majority of the Committee of Experts accepted the British proposal that did not apply to education in general but only to religious education. Then, in June, in order to achieve unanimity, the Experts agreed to modify the British draft so as to recognize explicitly a right to general education in denominational schools, although it imposed no obligation on the State to support such schools. Robertson noted that the Experts also substituted the word 'creeds' for 'convictions', thereby clarifying the right of parents to ensure religious education but no correspondiing right of those with no religion to have their children instructed in atheism or in agnosticism. Finally, in July, the Ministers' Advisers accepted a Turkish amendment that narrowed the right by limiting the right of parents to choose the education of their children to religious education and only then when the parents belong to a religious denomination. Robertson said that in terms of protecting denominational schools, this was the most restrictive of all the texts that had been examined during the negotiations.[43]

---

[40] Letter dated 28 November 1951 from the Chairman of the Committee of Ministers to the President of the Consultative Assembly, Doc. AS (3) 84, VIII *TP* 48–59.

[41] Report of the sitting [of the Consultative Assembly, 8 December 1951], VIII *TP* 76–169, at p. 168.

[42] Note of 12 December 1951 by the Secretariat-General relating to the Draft Protocol, Doc. CM (51) 81, A 7194, VIII *TP* 174–91.

[43] Note (not dated) by Mr Robertson, member of the Secretariat-General, on Article 2 of the draft Protocol (unreferenced document), VIII *TP* 190–5 (emphasis in the original).

The text of article 2 was finalized in late February 1952 at the meeting of Ministers' Advisers. The United Kingdom made yet another proposal:

No person shall be denied the right to education. In the exercise of any functions which it assumes in relation to education and to teaching, the State shall respect the right of parents to ensure that their children shall be educated and taught in conformity with the parents' own (religious or philosophical) convictions, provided that the education to be given to the children is efficient and does not involve unreasonable public expenditure.

However, the Ministers' Advisers opted for the Consultative Assembly text.

The heading 'Right to education' was added according to the provisions of Protocol No. 11.[44]

Analysis and interpretation

In contrast with what is the general rule in the Convention, the right to education is set out in rather more succinct terms in article 2 of Protocol No. 1 than it is in the corresponding provisions of the Universal Declaration of Human Rights, on which it is based. Thus, there is no explicit reference to either free or compulsory education of any kind, or to access to higher education. Nor does Protocol No. 1 contemplate the purposes of education: the full development of the human personality; the strengthening of respect for human rights and fundamental freedoms; the promotion of understanding, tolerance, and friendship among all nations, racial or religious groups; and furtherance of the activities of the United Nations for the maintenance of peace. Protocol No. 1 formulates education in a negative sense, prohibiting that it be denied rather than asserting it as a right. Essentially, it addresses what the State should not do rather than what it should do by insisting upon respect of the right of parents to education compatible with their religious and philosophical convictions. All told, it is a much more conservative provision than article 26 of the Universal Declaration of Human Rights. In Protocol No. 1, the right is more 'civil and political' in nature, whereas in the Universal Declaration it is primarily 'economic, social and cultural'.

The structure of article 2 is similar to that of articles 2, 3, 4(1), and 7 of the Convention ('no one shall ...'), 'which together enshrine the most fundamental values of democratic societies making up the Council of Europe'.[45] As the Court has explained, '[i]n a democratic society, the right to education, which is indispensable to the furtherance of human rights, plays such a fundamental role that a restrictive interpretation of the first sentence of Article 2 of Protocol No. 1 would not be consistent with the aim or purpose of that provision.[46]

Right to education

Article 2 of Protocol No. 1 must be read as a whole, although it is 'dominated by its first sentence'.[47] The obligation not to 'deny the right to education' means that States

---

[44] Protocol No. 11 to the Convention for the Protection of Human Rights and Fundamental Freedoms, restructuring the control machinery established thereby, ETS 155, art. 4(a).

[45] *Timishev v. Russia*, nos 55762/00 and 55974/00, § 64, ECHR 2005-XII.

[46] Ibid.; *Leyla Şahin v. Turkey* [GC], no. 44774/98, § 137, ECHR 2005-XI.

[47] *Kjeldsen, Busk Madsen, and Pedersen v. Denmark*, 7 December 1976, § 52, Series A no. 23.

guarantee 'a right of access to educational institutions existing at a given time'. This includes 'the possibility of drawing', by 'official recognition of the studies ... profit from the education received'.[48] The Court has described 'education of children' as 'the whole process whereby, in any society, adults endeavour to transmit their beliefs, culture and other values to the young, whereas teaching or instruction refers in particular to the transmission of knowledge and to intellectual development'.[49]

Although article 2 'has no stated exceptions',[50] it is not an absolute right, and finds itself subject to implied limitations.[51] The limitations must be foreseeable ('provided by law')[52] and pursue a legitimate purpose although, in contrast with articles 8 to 11 of the Convention, there is no defined list of such legitimate aims. Ultimately, there must be 'a reasonable relationship of proportionality between the means employed and the aim sought to be achieved'.[53]

The negative formulation of the right does not imply that there are no positive obligations associated with it.[54] By its very nature, education calls for regulation by the State that 'may vary in time and place according to the needs and resources of the community and of individuals'.[55] Such regulation 'must never injure the substance of the right nor conflict with other rights enshrined in the Convention or its Protocols'.[56]

Education continues, in different forms, at all stages of life, although it is usually understood as featuring primarily during childhood and adolescence. Article 26(1) of the Universal Declaration of Human Rights makes specific reference to 'elementary education', and although primary education is not reserved exclusively to children, they are far and away its main beneficiaries. The Universal Declaration also affirms that the right to education belongs to '[e]veryone', an idea that seems lost with the negative formulation of article 2 of Protocol No. 1. Of course, nothing in article 2 confines its scope to children, who are not even mentioned in the provision. The second sentence refers to the rights of 'parents' and rather obviously assumes that this is with respect to their children rather than to themselves, although a purely literal reading of the provision might lead to a different interpretation. The Convention on the Rights of the Child recognizes a right to education that belongs to children without reference to parents.[57]

---

[48] Case 'relating to certain aspects of the laws on the use of languages in education in Belgium' (merits), 23 July 1968, p. 28, § 4, Series A no. 6; *Kjeldsen, Busk Madsen, and Pedersen v. Denmark*, 7 December 1976, § 52, Series A no. 23.

[49] *Campbell and Cosans v. the United Kingdom*, 25 February 1982, § 33, Series A no. 48.

[50] *Timishev v. Russia*, nos 55762/00 and 55974/00, § 64, ECHR 2005-XII.

[51] *Tarantino and Others v. Italy*, nos 25851/09, 29284/09, and 64090/09, § 44, ECHR 2013 (extracts); *Altinay v. Turkey*, no. 37222/04, § 33, 9 July 2013; *Catan and Others v. the Republic of Moldova and Russia* [GC], nos 43370/04, 8252/05, and 18454/06, § 140, ECHR 2012 (extracts).

[52] *Tarantino and Others v. Italy*, nos 25851/09, 29284/09, and 64090/09, § 47, 2 April 2013.

[53] Ibid., § 45; *Altinay v. Turkey*, no. 37222/04, § 33, 9 July 2013; *Leyla Şahin v. Turkey* [GC], no. 44774/98, § 154, ECHR 2005-XI.

[54] Case 'relating to certain aspects of the laws on the use of languages in education in Belgium' (merits), 23 July 1968, p. 28, § 3, Series A no. 6.

[55] Ibid., p. 29, § 5; *Altinay v. Turkey*, no. 37222/04, § 33, 9 July 2013.

[56] Case 'relating to certain aspects of the laws on the use of languages in education in Belgium' (merits), 23 July 1968, p. 29, § 5, Series A no. 6. *Campbell and Cosans v. the United Kingdom*, 25 February 1982, § 41, Series A no. 48.

[57] Convention on the Rights of the Child, (1990) 1577 UNTS 3, art. 28. The closest that the Convention on the Rights of the Child comes to the language in the second sentence of article 2 of Protocol No. 1 is article 29(2): 'No part of the present article or article 28 shall be construed so as to interfere with the liberty of individuals and bodies to establish and direct educational institutions, subject always to the observance of the principles set forth in paragraph 1 of the present article and to the requirements that the education given in such institutions shall conform to such minimum standards as may be laid down by the State.'

Article 2 of Protocol 1 establishes 'a right of access to educational institutions existing at a given time'.[58] Although stopping short of affirming a right to free primary education set out in other international instruments, the Court has declared that 'there is no doubt that the right to education guarantees access to elementary education which is of primordial importance for a child's development'.[59] It has referred to other international instruments concerning the right to education, including article 26 of the Universal Declaration of Human Rights and article 13 of the International Covenant on Economic, Social and Cultural Rights, as 'relevant rules and principles of international law applicable in relations between the Contracting Parties' for the purpose of interpreting article 2 of Protocol No. 1.[60] The Court has invoked the preparatory work of the Protocol to support the conclusion that article 2 does not 'require them to establish at their own expense, or to subsidise, education of any particular type or at any particular level'.[61] Where an individual is denied enrolment in a university, despite succeeding in the required admissions examination, because the authorities appeared to suspect that he had cheated, without nevertheless formulating or proving such an accusation, the Court considered there was a violation of the first sentence of article 2 of Protocol No. 1.[62]

The Court has referred to article 28 of the Convention on the Rights of the Child as authority for differentiating between different levels of education.[63] Primary education is the most fundamental, as it 'provides basic literacy and numeracy—as well as integration into and first experiences of society—and is compulsory in most countries'.[64] Early decisions of the Commission took the view that the right to education contemplated by article 2 of Protocol No. 1 'mainly concerns elementary education and not necessarily specialist advanced studies',[65] but that is a view that no longer prevails. The right to education set out in article 2 of Protocol No. 1 also includes secondary[66] and tertiary[67] education, and may even extend to courses for professional accreditation.[68] There is support in the case law of the Court for the view that 'university education is a human right'.[69] Obviously, Protocol No. 1 'permits limiting access to universities to those who duly applied for entrance and passed the examination'.[70] According to the Court, 'assessing candidates through relevant tests in order to identify the most meritorious

---

[58] Case 'relating to certain aspects of the laws on the use of languages in education in Belgium' (merits), 23 July 1968, p. 28, § 4, Series A no. 6.

[59] Timishev v. Russia, nos 55762/00 and 55974/00, § 64, ECHR 2005-XII.

[60] Catan and Others v. the Republic of Moldova and Russia [GC], nos 43370/04, 8252/05, and 18454/06, § 138, ECHR 2012 (extracts).

[61] Case 'relating to certain aspects of the laws on the use of languages in education in Belgium' (merits), 23 July 1968, p. 28, § 3, Series A no. 6.

[62] Mürsel Eren v. Turkey, no. 60856/00, § 50, ECHR 2006-II.

[63] Ponomaryovi v. Bulgaria, no. 5335/05, § 57, ECHR 2011.

[64] Ibid., § 56.

[65] X v. the United Kingdom, no. 5962/72, Commission decision of 13 March 1975; 15 Foreign Students v. the United Kingdom, no. 7671/76 and fourteen other applications, Commission decision of 19 May 1977; Yanasik v. Turkey, no. 14524/89, Commission decision of 6 January 1993, DR 74, p. 14.

[66] Ponomaryovi v. Bulgaria, no. 5335/05, § 49, ECHR 2011.

[67] Leyla Şahin v. Turkey [GC], no. 44774/98, §§ 134–142, ECHR 2005-XI; Mürsel Eren v. Turkey, no. 60856/00, §§ 40–41, ECHR 2006-II; Tarantino and Others v. Italy, nos 25851/09, 29284/09, and 64090/09, § 43, ECHR 2013 (extracts); Altinay v. Turkey, no. 37222/04, 9 July 2013.

[68] Kök v. Turkey, no. 1855/02, §§ 56–60, 19 October 2006.

[69] Tarantino and Others v. Italy, nos 25851/09, 29284/09, and 64090/09, Partly Dissenting Opinion of Judge Pinto de Albuquerque, ECHR 2013 (extracts).

[70] Lukach v. Russia (dec.), no. 48041/99, 16 November 1999.

students is a proportionate measure designed to ensure a minimum and adequate education level in the universities'.[71] The right of access to higher education is subject to restrictions based upon resource limitations within the State. It may invoke such considerations in imposing a quota or *numerus clausus* limiting access to certain programmes, such as medical and dentistry school, given the huge investment that is required.[72] In dissent, Judge Pinto de Albuquerque described the Italian regulations as 'groundless and even arbitrary'.[73]

One of the familiar limitations on access to education consists of disciplinary measures imposed by an institution that restrict or deny attendance to certain students on behavioural and related grounds. The right to education set out in article 2 of Protocol No. 1 does not exclude recourse to such measures, including suspension and expulsion. According to the Court, 'imposition of disciplinary penalties is an integral part of the process whereby a school seeks to achieve the object for which it was established, including the development and moulding of the character and mental powers of its pupils'.[74] Suspension and expulsion is one of the implied limitations on the right to education, and it must therefore meet criteria of foreseeability and proportionality. The Court will consider factors such as procedural safeguards in enabling the exclusion to be challenged and to avoid arbitrariness, the length of the exclusion, the extent of co-operation manifested by the pupil and the parents with attempts at re-integration, whether adequate measures to provide alternative education during exclusion were provided, and consideration for the rights of third parties.[75] The suspension of students by a Turkish university for one or two terms because they had submitted petitions demanding that instruction in Kurdish language and culture be provided was held not to meet the tests of reasonableness and proportionality.[76]

Several cases before the Convention organs have concerned the right of prisoners to education. In 2006, the Committee of Ministers adopted revisions to the European Prison Rules that address the issue of education of prisoners. They specify that '[e]very prison shall seek to provide all prisoners with access to educational programmes which are as comprehensive as possible and which meet their individual needs while taking into account their aspirations'. Priority is to be given to prisoners with literacy and numeracy needs and those who lack basic or vocational education.[77] While acknowledging this pronouncement of the Committee of Ministers, the Court has said that article 2 of Protocol No. 1 'does not place an obligation on Contracting States to organise educational facilities for prisoners where such facilities are not already in place'.[78] In a case where there was an education system in place within a prison, the Court held that restrictions upon access to it were not sufficiently foreseeable. Consequently, the Court considered that the refusal to enrol the applicant in the prison school was not sufficiently foreseeable, that it

---

[71] *Tarantino and Others v. Italy*, nos 25851/09, 29284/09, and 64090/09, § 49, ECHR 2013 (extracts).

[72] Ibid., §§ 51–56.

[73] Ibid., Partly Dissenting Opinion of Judge Pinto de Albuquerque, 2 April 2013.

[74] *Ali v. the United Kingdom*, no. 40385/06, § 54, 11 January 2011; *Sulak v. Turkey*, no. 24515/94, Commission decision of 17 January 1996, DR 84-A, p. 98; *Campbell and Cosans v. the United Kingdom*, 25 February 1982, p. 14, § 33, Series A no. 48; *Yanasik v. Turkey*, no. 14524/89, Commission decision of 6 January 1993, DR 74, p. 14.

[75] *Ali v. the United Kingdom*, no. 40385/06, § 58, 11 January 2011.

[76] *Irfan Temel and Others v. Turkey*, no. 36458/02, § 46, 3 March 2009.

[77] Recommendation R (2006) 2 on the European Prison Rules, para. 28.

[78] *Velyo Velev v. Bulgaria*, no. 16032/07, § 34, 27 May 2014.

did not pursue a legitimate aim, and that it was not proportionate.[79] Protocol No. 1 has not been construed as imposing an obligation on prison authorities to set up *ad hoc* courses[80] or to ensure teaching programmes in certain areas.[81] It cannot be said that article 2 of Protocol No. 1 is breached simply because prisoners are prevented from continuing in full-time education during a period of lawful detention following conviction.[82] A similar approach has been taken to the argument that lawful deportation would prevent a person from continuing with their education.[83]

The language of education was one of the first human rights issues to be litigated at the international level. Cases adjudicated by the Permanent Court of International Justice under the minorities treaties dealt with the language of instruction.[84] The first case before the European Court under article 2 of Protocol No. 1 concerned language. The Court held that although article 2 'does not specify the language in which education must be conducted, the right to education would be meaningless if it did not imply in favour of its beneficiaries, the right to be educated in the national language or in one of the national languages, as the case may be'.[85] In the interstate case of *Cyprus v. Turkey*, the applicant argued that Greek Cypriot children in occupied Cyprus were denied the right to education because there were no secondary schools offering instruction in the medium of Greek. The Court acknowledged that because the Turkish authorities did not prevent them attending Turkish-language secondary schools, '[i]n the strict sense, accordingly, there is no denial of the right to education'.[86] However,

the option available to Greek-Cypriot parents to continue their children's education in the north is unrealistic in view of the fact that the children in question have already received their primary education in a Greek-Cypriot school there. The authorities must no doubt be aware that it is the wish of Greek-Cypriot parents that the schooling of their children be completed through the medium of the Greek language. Having assumed responsibility for the provision of Greek-language primary schooling, the failure of the 'TRNC' authorities to make continuing provision for it at the secondary-school level must be considered in effect to be a denial of the substance of the right at issue. It cannot be maintained that the provision of secondary education in the south in keeping with the linguistic tradition of the enclaved Greek Cypriots suffices to fulfil the obligation laid down in Article 2 of Protocol No. 1, having regard to the impact of that option on family life.[87]

In a case involving the breakaway Moldavian Republic of Transdniestria, the Court found that a requirement by the authorities that children be educated in Moldavian but using Cyrillic script breached the rights of their parents:

---

[79] Ibid., § 42, 27 May 2014.

[80] *Natoli v. Italy*, no. 26161/95, Commission decision of 18 May 1998.

[81] *X v. the United Kingdom*, no. 5962/72, Commission decision of 13 March 1975, DR 2, p. 50.

[82] *Epistatu v. Romania*, no. 29343/10, § 62, 24 September 2013; *Durmaz and Others v. Turkey* (dec.), nos 46506/99, 46569/99, 46570/99, and 46939/99, 4 September 2001; *Georgiou v. Greece* (dec.), no. 45138/98, 13 January 2000.

[83] *15 Foreign Students v. the United Kingdom*, no. 7671/76 and fourteen other applications, Commission decision of 19 May 1977; *Sorabjee v. the United Kingdom*, no. 23938, Commission decision of 23 October 1995.

[84] *Minority Schools in Albania*, PCIJ, Series A/B No. 64; *Rights of Minorities in Upper Silesia (Minority Schools)*, PCIJ, Series A No. 15.

[85] *Case 'relating to certain aspects of the laws on the use of languages in education in Belgium'* (merits), 23 July 1968, p. 28, § 3, Series A no. 6; *Catan and Others v. the Republic of Moldova and Russia* [GC], nos 43370/04, 8252/05, and 18454/06, § 137, ECHR 2012 (extracts).

[86] *Cyprus v. Turkey* [GC], no. 25781/94, § 277, ECHR 2001-IV.

[87] Ibid., § 278.

The applicant parents in this case wanted their children to be educated in the official language of their country, which was also their own mother tongue. Instead, they were placed in the invidious position of having to choose, on the one hand, between sending their children to schools where they would face the disadvantage of pursuing their entire secondary education in a combination of language and alphabet which they consider artificial and which is unrecognised anywhere else in the world, using teaching materials produced in Soviet times or, alternatively, subjecting their children to long journeys and/or substandard facilities, harassment and intimidation.[88]

In this case, the Court applied article 2 of Protocol No. 1 in light of article 8 of the Convention.

Respect for parents' religious and philosophical convictions

The second sentence 'is an adjunct'[89] that is 'grafted'[90] onto the 'fundamental right to education'.[91] It acknowledges the primary responsibility of parents for 'education and teaching' of their children. It is intimately linked with the first sentence in that where parents cannot accept that their children be educated under circumstances that breach the second sentence of article 2, there is also a violation of the first sentence to the extent that the child is denied the right to education if the parents refuse to allow attendance.[92] The right of parents to insist upon respect for their religious and philosophical convictions 'corresponds to a responsibility closely linked to the enjoyment and the exercise of the right to education'.[93] The second sentence of Article 2 of Protocol No. 1 aims at 'safeguarding the possibility of pluralism in education, which possibility is essential for the preservation of the "democratic society" as conceived by the Convention'.[94]

References in the case law to the existence of any tension between the rights of parents and those of their children are rare. In one decision, the European Commission noted that the convictions of the parents must not conflict with the child's fundamental right to education: 'Where, instead of supporting the child's right to education, the parents' rights come into conflict with it, the child's rights must prevail.'[95]

There has been no litigation or dispute about the scope of the term 'parents'. This is the only use of the term in the Convention and its Protocols. There is at least one example of a grandparent invoking the second sentence of article 2 without objection.[96] The child cannot claim to be a victim of a violation of the second sentence of article 2.[97]

The Court has explained that the second sentence of article 2 of Protocol No. 1 speaks of the 'right' of parents concerning the education of their children, but has held that they

---

[88] *Catan and Others v. the Republic of Moldova and Russia* [GC], nos 43370/04, 8252/05, and 18454/06, § 143, ECHR 2012 (extracts). But see *Catan and Others v. the Republic of Moldova and Russia* [GC], nos 43370/04, 8252/05, and 18454/06, Partly Dissenting Opinion of Judge Kovler, ECHR 2012 (extracts).

[89] *Kjeldsen, Busk Madsen, and Pedersen v. Denmark*, 7 December 1976, § 52, Series A no. 23.

[90] *Folgerø and Others v. Norway* [GC], no. 15472/02, § 84, ECHR 2007-III.

[91] *Campbell and Cosans v. the United Kingdom*, 25 February 1982, § 41, Series A no. 48.

[92] Ibid.

[93] *Kjeldsen, Busk Madsen, and Pedersen v. Denmark*, 7 December 1976, § 52, Series A no. 23.

[94] *Folgerø and Others v. Norway* [GC], no. 15472/02, § 84, ECHR 2007-III; *Kjeldsen, Busk Madsen, and Pedersen v. Denmark*, 7 December 1976, § 50, Series A no. 23.

[95] *Zénon Bernard and Others v. Luxembourg*, no. 17187/90, Commission decision of 8 September 1993, (1993) 36 YB 83, DR 75, p. 57; *Graeme v. the United Kingdom*, no. 13887/88, 5 February 1990, DR 64, p. 158.

[96] *Lee v. the United Kingdom* [GC], no. 25289/94, §§ 122–125, 18 January 2001.

[97] *Eriksson v. Sweden*, 22 June 1989, § 93, Series A no. 156.

have 'a natural duty towards their children—parents being primarily responsible for the "education and teaching" of their children'.[98] The right of parents 'corresponds to a responsibility closely linked to the enjoyment and the exercise of the right to education'.[99] The duty set out in the second sentence of article 2 of Protocol No. 1 'is broad in its extent as it applies not only to the content of education and the manner of its provision but also to the performance of all the "functions" assumed by the State'.[100] The two sentences that comprise article 2 of Protocol No. 1 are to be interpreted both in light of each other and also in conjunction with other provisions of the European Convention, particularly those dealing with respect for private and family life, for freedom of thought, conscience, and religion, and freedom to receive and impart information and ideas.[101]

According to the Court, the term 'respect' in the second sentence implies a positive as well as a negative obligation, meaning more than 'acknowledge' or 'take into account'.[102] The term 'respect' is also used in article 8 of the Convention. The Court has taken a very broad approach to the notion of 'respect', acknowledging a considerable margin of appreciation. In particular, the duty to respect in the second sentence of article 2 of Protocol No. 1 'cannot be interpreted to mean that parents can require the State to provide a particular form of teaching'.[103] The provision only ensures 'a right to *respect* for those convictions' and not 'an absolute right to have children educated in accordance with parents' philosophical convictions'.[104]

The Court has explained that the term 'conviction', which is not used elsewhere in the Convention or its Protocols, is not synonymous with the words 'opinions' and 'ideas' that appear in article 10 on freedom of expression. Rather, the term is 'more akin to the term "beliefs"'. The Court has noted that the French version of article 9 uses the term 'convictions'. It 'denotes views that attain a certain level of cogency, seriousness, cohesion and importance'.[105] To the extent that article 2 concerns 'religious convictions', it should be viewed as the *lex specialis* with respect to article 9 of the Convention.[106] Consequently, the second sentence of article 2 of Protocol 1 should be read taking into account article 9 of the Convention, held to impose upon States a 'duty of neutrality and impartiality'.[107]

The scope of the adjective 'philosophical' (or philosophy) can run the gamut from a fully fledged system of thought to views on trivial matters. The Court has said that neither of these extremes should be applied to article 2 of Protocol No. 1 because 'the former would too narrowly restrict the scope of a right that is guaranteed to all parents and the latter might result in the inclusion of matters of insufficient weight or substance'.[108] For

---

[98] *Kjeldsen, Busk Madsen, and Pedersen v. Denmark*, 7 December 1976, § 52, Series A no. 23.

[99] Ibid.

[100] *Valsamis v. Greece*, 18 December 1996, § 27, *Reports of Judgments and Decisions* 1996-VI; *Campbell and Cosans v. the United Kingdom*, 25 February 1982, §§ 36, Series A no. 48.

[101] *Kjeldsen, Busk Madsen, and Pedersen v. Denmark*, 7 December 1976, § 52, Series A no. 23.

[102] *Valsamis v. Greece*, 18 December 1996, § 27, *Reports of Judgments and Decisions* 1996-VI; *Campbell and Cosans v. the United Kingdom*, 25 February 1982, §§ 36, Series A no. 48.

[103] *Lautsi and Others v. Italy* [GC], no. 30814/06, § 61, ECHR 2011 (extracts); *Bulski v. Poland* (dec.), nos 46254/99 and 31888/02, 9 May 2006.

[104] *Family H. v. the United Kingdom*, no. 10233/83, Commission decision of 6 March 1983 (emphasis in the original).

[105] *Valsamis v. Greece*, 18 December 1996, § 27, *Reports of Judgments and Decisions* 1996-VI; *Campbell and Cosans v. the United Kingdom*, 25 February 1982, § 36, Series A no. 48.

[106] *Lautsi and Others v. Italy* [GC], no. 30814/06, § 59, ECHR 2011 (extracts).

[107] Ibid., § 60.

[108] *Campbell and Cosans v. the United Kingdom*, 25 February 1982, § 36, Series A no. 48.

the Court, 'philosophical convictions' denotes those that 'are worthy of respect in a "democratic society"', 'are not incompatible with human dignity', and do not conflict with the fundamental right of the child to education.[109] Views that 'relate to a weighty and substantial aspect of human life and behaviour' include the propriety of corporal punishment[110] and secularism.[111]

Implementation of the second sentence of article 2 of Protocol No. 1 may involve private or separate schooling, or even 'home schooling'. Some countries have permitted parents to 'home school' their children, subject to supervision by the State in order to ensure that it is of adequate quality,[112] while others have not. Noting Germany's concern about 'the emergence of parallel societies based on separate philosophical convictions and the importance of integrating minorities into society' as a justification for refusing to permit 'home schooling', the Court said this was 'in accordance with its own case-law on the importance of pluralism for democracy'.[113]

The provision clearly applies to State schools accessible to all children, although article 2 of Protocol No. 1 makes no distinction between State and private teaching.[114] Nor can it be said that the second sentence is concerned with religious instruction as opposed to other subjects. The second sentence 'enjoins the State to respect parents' convictions, be they religious or philosophical, throughout the entire State education programme'.[115] For this reason, the 'setting and planning of the curriculum fall in principle within the competence of the Contracting States'.[116]

States are not prevented by the second sentence of article 2 from 'imparting through teaching or education information or knowledge of a directly or indirectly religious or philosophical kind'.[117] Parents cannot object when such material is integrated into the school curriculum 'for otherwise all institutionalised teaching would run the risk of proving impracticable'.[118] Nevertheless, there must be a 'fair and proper treatment of minorities' that 'avoids any abuse of a dominant position'.[119] In setting the school curriculum, the State 'must take care that information or knowledge included in the curriculum is conveyed in an objective, critical and pluralistic manner'.[120] It may not 'pursue an aim of indoctrination that might be considered as not respecting parents' religious and philosophical convictions'.[121] Admittedly, 'abuses can occur as to the manner in which the provisions in force are applied by a given school or teacher and the competent authorities have a duty to take the utmost care to see to it that parents' religious and philosophical convictions are not disregarded at this level by carelessness, lack of judgment or misplaced proselytism'.[122]

---

[109] Ibid.

[110] Ibid., § 36. But see ibid., Partly Dissenting Opinion of Judges Sir Vincent Evans, § 4.

[111] *Lautsi and Others v. Italy* [GC], no. 30814/06, § 58, ECHR 2011 (extracts).

[112] *Family H. v. the United Kingdom*, no. 10233/83, 6 March 1984.

[113] *Konrad v. Germany* (dec.), no. 35504/03, § 1, ECHR 2006-XIII.

[114] *Folgerø and Others v. Norway* [GC], no. 15472/02, § 84, ECHR 2007-III.

[115] Ibid.; *Kjeldsen, Busk Madsen, and Pedersen v. Denmark*, 7 December 1976, § 51, Series A no. 23.

[116] *Kjeldsen, Busk Madsen, and Pedersen v. Denmark*, 7 December 1976, § 53, Series A no. 23.

[117] Ibid.

[118] Ibid; *Hasan and Eylem Zengin v. Turkey*, no. 1448/04, § 51, ECHR 2007-XI.

[119] *Valsamis v. Greece*, 18 December 1996, § 27, *Reports of Judgments and Decisions* 1996-VI.

[120] Ibid.

[121] Ibid., § 28; *Kjeldsen, Busk Madsen, and Pedersen v. Denmark*, 7 December 1976, § 53, Series A no. 23.

[122] *Kjeldsen, Busk Madsen, and Pedersen v. Denmark*, 7 December 1976, § 54, Series A no. 23.

Nevertheless, the Court has been prepared to show considerable deference where the presence and visibility of the majority religion is emphasized within State schools. For example, it held that the fact that Norway's school syllabus gave a larger share to knowledge of the Christian religion than to that of other religions and philosophies could not in itself be viewed as a departure from the principles of pluralism and objectivity amounting to indoctrination.[123] Likewise, in one case it did not find a violation with respect to 'religious culture and ethics' classes in Turkish schools where Islam was given prominence because, although the State was secular in nature, Islam was the religion of the majority.[124] In a subsequent application, filed by parents of Alevi confession, the Turkish system was found to breach article 2. The Court found that 'dans le système éducatif turc, aucune possibilité de choix appropriée n'a été envisagée pour les enfants des parents ayant une conviction religieuse ou philosophique autre que l'islam sunnite, et que le mécanisme de dispense très limité est susceptible de soumettre les parents d'élève à une lourde charge et à la nécessité de dévoiler leur convictions religieuses ou philosophiques afin que leurs enfants soient dispensés de suivre les cours de religion'.[125]

An application from parents who objected to sexual education programmes was declared inadmissible. According to the Court, the impugned programme provided students with information that was objective and scientific about sexual activity and sexually transmitted diseases, as well as unwanted pregnancy and methods of contraception. It was a general programme that could hardly be deemed 'une tentative d'endoctrinement visant à préconiser un comportement sexuel déterminé'.[126]

The scope of the second sentence of article 2 may extend beyond the curriculum itself and include the presence of religious or other symbols in schools and classrooms. Dealing with a challenge to Italian legislation requiring that a crucifix be placed in schoolrooms, the Court said such decisions were in principle matters that fell within the margin of appreciation of the State, adding that the absence of a European consensus on the presence of religious symbols in State schools supported the approach it was taking.[127] It acknowledged, nevertheless, that by prescribing the presence of crucifixes in State-school classrooms, with their undoubted religious significance, Italy's regulations conferred 'preponderant visibility in the school environment' to Christianity.[128] The Court attached importance to the fact that a crucifix on a wall was an 'essentially passive symbol' that 'cannot be deemed to have an influence on pupils comparable to that of didactic speech or participation in religious activities'.[129]

The 'respect' required by article 2 of Protocol No. 1 extends beyond the content of education as such and includes such aspects as discipline. The Court concluded there was a violation when the Scottish school system did not accommodate the views of parents who objected to the imposition of corporal punishment on adolescent children. In terms of a solution, it rejected the viability of a dual system of education based upon whether or

---

[123] *Folgerø and Others v. Norway* [GC], no. 15472/02, § 89, ECHR 2007-III.
[124] *Hasan and Eylem Zengin v. Turkey*, no. 1448/04, §§ 51 and 52, ECHR 2007-XI.
[125] *Mansur Yalçın and Others v. Turkey*, no. 21163/11, § 77, 16 September 2014.
[126] *Jimnez Alonso and Jimenez Merino v. Spain* (dec.), no. 51188/99, 25 May 2000.
[127] *Lautsi and Others v. Italy* [GC], no. 30814/06, § 70, ECHR 2011 (extracts).
[128] Ibid., § 71.
[129] Ibid., § 72.

not the parents accepted corporal punishment, but considered that a system of exemption of students in particular schools might be acceptable.[130]

An obligation imposed upon pupils to participate in a national day parade was contested by parents who were Jehovah's Witnesses. The Court did not consider the national day parade to be necessarily militaristic and said it could 'discern nothing, either in the purpose of the parade or in the arrangements for it, which could offend the applicants' pacifist convictions to an extent prohibited by the second sentence of Article 2 of Protocol No. 1'. But it said it was 'surprised that pupils can be required on pain of suspension from school— even if only for two days—to parade outside the school precincts on a holiday'.[131]

Discrimination in education

There is much evidence of discrimination directed towards Roma children with respect to access to education. In a case involving access to education, the Court noted that 'la minorité rom était un type particulier de minorité vulnérable ayant besoin d'une protection spéciale'.[132] Without necessarily condemning this as intentional discrimination by the State based upon race and ethnicity, the Court has observed that 'a number of European States encounter serious difficulties in providing adequate schooling for Roma children'.[133] It has often turned to studies and reports on this issue by the European Commission against Racism and Intolerance and the Commissioner on Human Rights.[134]

In some countries, discrimination in the area of access to education has taken the form of assigning them to remedial or special schools formally designated for the disabled. According to the Court, 'the misplacement of Roma children in special schools has a long history across Europe'.[135] This has often resulted from bias in placement procedures and discriminatory practices disguised as neutral tests. In this context, the Czech Republic and Hungary have been found to be in breach of article 14 of the Convention taken in conjunction with article 2 of Protocol 1.[136]

Discrimination against Roma children with respect to education also takes on other forms. In Greece, the educational authorities attempted to address a situation that had developed whereby in practice certain schools were only attended by Roma children. Their efforts met with opposition from the parents of non-Roma children. According to the Court, despite the absence of any discriminatory intent on the part of the State, a situation that had been allowed to exist whereby Roma children went to schools where they were the only pupils where effective anti-segregationist measures were not being imposed, such as distributing the Roma children in mixed classes in other schools

---

[130] *Campbell and Cosans v. the United Kingdom*, 25 February 1982, § 37, Series A no. 48.

[131] *Efstratiou v. Greece*, 18 December 1996, § 32, *Reports of Judgments and Decisions* 1996-VI.

[132] *Lavida and Others v. Greece*, no. 7973/10, 30 May 2013. Also *Oršuš and Others v. Croatia* [GC], no. 15766/03, § 147, ECHR 2010; *Chapman v. the United Kingdom* [GC], no. 27238/95, § 96, ECHR 2001-I; *Connors v. the United Kingdom*, no. 66746/01, § 84, 27 May 2004; *Sampanis and Others v. Greece*, no. 32526/05, § 72, 5 June 2008.

[133] *Oršuš and Others v. Croatia* [GC], no. 15766/03, § 180, ECHR 2010.

[134] Final Report by Mr Alvaro Gil-Robles on the Human-Rights Situation of the Roma, Sinti, and Travellers in Europe, CommDH(2006)1, 15 February 2006, paras 44–59.

[135] *Horváth and Kiss v. Hungary*, no. 11146/11, § 115, 29 January 2013.

[136] *D.H. and Others v. the Czech Republic* [GC], no. 57325/00, § 210, ECHR 2007-IV. Also *Horváth and Kiss v. Hungary*, no. 11146/11, §§ 109–121, 29 January 2013.

or a realignment of school districts, could not be objectively justified by a legitimate purpose.[137]

Similarly, in Croatia the explanation for the segregation of Roma children into separate schools was based on shortcomings in mastering the language of education. The Grand Chamber accepted that 'temporary placement of children in a separate class on the grounds that they lack an adequate command of the language is not, as such, automatically contrary to Article 14 of the Convention'.[138] But in the case of Croatia, 'while recognising the efforts made by the Croatian authorities to ensure that Roma children receive schooling, the Court considers that there were at the relevant time no adequate safeguards in place capable of ensuring that a reasonable relationship of proportionality between the means used and the legitimate aim said to be pursued was achieved and maintained'.[139]

The Court has also addressed an application concerning discrimination in university admission based upon changes in regulations governing access related to the weighting of grades obtained in secondary education. These had the consequence of restricting university admission to students who had followed a professional training profile as opposed to a more traditionally academic one. Agreeing that the applicant had been subject to differential treatment as a result, the Court explained that States have a considerable margin of appreciation in regulating access to universities and similar institutions to the extent that they are selecting candidates based on the likelihood that they will succeed in their studies.[140] Nevertheless, the Court said it was incumbent on the Court to ascertain 'whether the system complained of pursued a legitimate aim and whether there was a reasonable relationship of proportionality between the means employed and the aim pursued. Applying these two criteria to the facts of the case will enable the Court to decide whether the measures at issue constituted discrimination incompatible with Article 14 of the Convention and/or impaired the very essence of the right to education as secured under Article 2 of Protocol No. 1.'[141] In the case of an applicant who was denied access to a Turkish university based upon changes in admissions policy with respect to courses he had taken at secondary school, the Court found that this was not reasonably proportionate to the purpose of the measure and held that there was a violation of article 14 of the Convention combined with article 2 of Protocol No. 1.[142] A separate opinion noted that Turkish policies were not consistent with obligations under the so-called 'Bologna process' and the 'Copenhagen process'.[143]

Bulgaria required non-citizens to pay fees for secondary education, something that was free to citizens. The Court noted that 'a State may have legitimate reasons for curtailing the use of resource-hungry public services—such as welfare programmes, public benefits and health care—by short-term and illegal immigrants, who, as a rule, do not contribute

---

[137] *Lavida and Others v. Greece*, no. 7973/10, § 73, 30 May 2013. Also *Sampani and Others v. Greece*, no. 59608/09, §§ 90–105, 11 December 2012; *Sampanis and Others v. Greece*, no. 32526/05, § 96, 5 June 2008.

[138] *Oršuš and Others v. Croatia* [GC], no. 15766/03, § 157, ECHR 2010.

[139] Ibid., § 184, ECHR 2010.

[140] *Altinay v. Turkey*, no. 37222/04, § 41, 9 July 2013.

[141] Ibid., § 40.

[142] Ibid., §§ 51–61.

[143] Ibid., Opinion en partie dissidente commune aux juges Vučinić et Pinto de Albuquerque, 9 July 2013. On the 'Copenhagen process'; see also *Tarantino and Others v. Italy*, nos 25851/09, 29284/09, and 64090/09, Partly Dissenting Opinion of Judge Pinto de Albuquerque, ECHR 2013 (extracts).

to their funding'.[144] However, unlike some of these public services, education is a right directly enshrined in the law of the Convention. Moreover, '[i]t is also a very particular type of public service, which not only directly benefits those using it but also serves broader societal functions'.[145] The Court concluded that requiring non-citizens to pay fees to attend secondary school was not justified and amounted to a violation of article 14 of the Convention read in conjunction with article 2 of Protocol No. 1.[146]

Reservations and declarations

Article 57 of the Convention authorizes States to make reservations at the time of signature as well as upon ratification. Reservations at the time of signature are relatively rare. A reservation respecting article 2 of Protocol No. 1 was formulated at the time of signature by Greece and the United Kingdom. The Greek reservation reads as follows: 'Au moment de la signature du présent Protocole, le Gouvernement hellénique, se prévalent de l'article 64 de ladite Convention, formule la réserve suivante, portant sur l'article 2 du Protocole: "Le mot 'philosophique', par lequel se termine le second paragraphe de l'article 2, recevra en Grèce une application conforme aux dispositions y relatives de la législation intérieure."'[147] The United Kingdom formulated the following reservation: 'At the time of signing the present Protocol, I declare that in view of certain provisions of the Education Acts in force in the United Kingdom, the principle affirmed in the second sentence of Article 2 is accepted by the United Kingdom only so far as it is compatible with the provision of efficient instruction and training, and the avoidance of unreasonable public expenditure.'[148]

Three States made declarations at the time of signature. Ireland declared the following: 'At the time of signing the Protocol, the Irish delegate puts on record that, in the view of the Irish Government, Article 2 of the Protocol is not sufficiently explicit in ensuring to parents the right to provide education for their children in their homes or in schools of the parents' own choice, whether or not such schools are private schools or are schools recognised or established by the State.'[149] The Netherlands also made a declaration: 'In the opinion of the Netherlands Government, the State should not only respect the rights of parents in the matter of education but, if need be, ensure the possibility of exercising those rights by appropriate financial measures.'[150]

Both Greece and the United Kingdom made reservations at the time of ratification. When Greece ratified Protocol No. 1 for the second time, having denounced the Convention and the Protocols in 1970, it formulated the following reservation: 'For the application of Article 2 of the 1952 Protocol, the Government of Greece, in view of certain provisions of the Education Acts in force in Greece, formulates a reservation according to which the principle affirmed in the second sentence of Article 2, is accepted only so far as it is compatible with the provision of efficient instruction and training, and

[144] *Ponomaryovi v. Bulgaria*, no. 5335/05, § 54, ECHR 2011.
[145] Ibid., § 55, ECHR 2011.
[146] Ibid., § 63.
[147] (1955–56–57) 1 YB 44. See also Note by the Greek Delegation, Doc. CM/Adj. (52) 41, A 8015, VIII *TP* 202–3.
[148] Note by the United Kingdom Delegation, Doc. CM/Adj. 39, A 8013, VIII *TP* 200–3.
[149] Minutes of the meeting [of the Committee of Ministers, 19 March 1952], VIII *TP* 202–5.
[150] Ibid.

the avoidance of unreasonable public expenditure.'[151] Four years later, it informed the Council of Europe that the reservation had been entered by mistake and that it should be removed and replaced with the following: 'The application of the word *philosophical* which is the penultimate word of the second sentence of Article 2, will, in Greece, conform with the relevant provisions of internal legislation.'[152] The new reservation was in fact equivalent to the one formulated by Greece at the time of signature of the Protocol, in 1952. The depository of the Convention replied to Greece that the 1952 reservation had not been included in a recent publication because 'it was supposed that the reservation of 1974 to the same article had replaced the previous one'. The letter confirmed that it was the intention of Greece to withdraw the 1974 text and to 'retain the reservation made in 1952'. The depository said that this would be brought to the attention of Council of Europe Member States.[153]

At the time of ratification, the United Kingdom confirmed the reservation that it had made when it signed the Protocol.[154] In a dissenting opinion, the country's judge said that because of the reservation, article 2 of Protocol No. 1 'must be interpreted and applied as modified by the reservation. This means that the obligation thereunder to respect the right of parents has been assumed by the United Kingdom only so far as this can be done compatibly with the provision of efficient instruction and training and the avoidance of unreasonable public expenditure.'[155] The United Kingdom also made a reservation to article 2 with respect to several of its overseas territories so that administration of corporal punishment, sometimes described as 'moderate and reasonable', is sheltered from scrutiny. In addition, it made a reservation concerning Guernsey and Gibraltar accepting 'the principle affirmed in the second sentence of Article 2 is accepted by the United Kingdom only so far as it is compatible with the provision of efficient instruction and training, and the avoidance of unreasonable public expenditure in Guernsey and Gibraltar'.[156] It made a similar reservation with respect to the Isle of Man in 2001.[157]

There are several other reservations to article 2 of Protocol No. 1.

Sweden made the following reservation: 'A ces causes et fins Nous avons voulu ratifier, approuver et accepter ledit Protocole additionnel avec tous ses articles, points et clauses, sous réserve toutefois relative à l'article 2 du Protocole, réserve portant que la Suède ne peut accorder aux parents le droit d'obtenir, en se référant à leur conviction philosophique, dispense pour leurs enfants de l'obligation de prendre part à certaines parties de l'enseignement des écoles publiques et portant aussi que la dispense de l'obligation de prendre part à l'enseignement du christianisme dans ces écoles ne peut être accordée que pour les enfants d'une autre profession de foi que l'église suédoise, en faveur desquels une instructions religeuse satisfaisante a été organisée, cette réserve se fondant sur les dispositions du règlement nouveau du 17 mars 1933 pour les établissements d'enseignement secondaire du Royaume et les dispositions analogues concernant les autres établissements

[151] (1976) 19 YB 20–21.
[152] (1979) 22 YB 14–15 (emphasis in the original).
[153] Ibid., pp. 14–17.
[154] (1955–56–57) 1 YB 45.
[155] *Campbell and Cosans v. the United Kingdom*, 25 February 1982, Partly Dissenting Opinion of Judges Sir Vincent Evans, § 5, Series A no. 48.
[156] (1988) 31 YB 6.
[157] (2001) 44 YB 23.

d'enseignement.'[158] The European Commission of Human Rights said it found 'no indication that the reservation is contrary to Article 64 of the Convention. It must therefore be regarded as a valid reservation.'[159] The Commission applied the reservation, saying it concluded that 'Sweden has not undertaken to grant any exemption from parts of the education in the public schools be it for religious, philosophical or other reasons, except in respect of children who belong to a religious faith other than the Swedish Church and for whom other satisfactory religious instruction has been arranged.'[160] Referring to the Swedish reservation, the Court has said that Sweden 'has obviously interpreted Art. 2 in a very wide sense . . . giving almost complete freedom to the Swedish Government to organise child education regardless of the religion and philosophical convictions of parents'.[161] Sweden withdrew its reservation in 1994.[162]

Turkey made the following reservation: 'Ayant vu et examiné la Convention précitée et le Protocole additionnel, Nous les avons approuvés sous réserve formulée dans le deuxième article du Protocole additionnel, en vertu de dispositions de la Loi No 6366 votée par la Grande Assemblée Nationale de Turquie en date du 10 mars 1954.' Annexed to the reservation was a copy of the legislation, the operative paragraph of which reads as follows: 'L'article 2 du Protocole additionnel ne porte pas atteinte aux dispositions de la Loi No 430 du 3 mars 1924 relative à l'unification de l'enseignement.'[163]

Portugal formulated the following reservation: 'Article 2 of the Protocol will be applied subject to Articles 43 and 75 of the Constitution of the Portuguese Republic, which provide for the non-denominationality of public education, the supervision of private education by the State and the validity of legal provisions concerning the setting up of private educational establishments.'[164] It was withdrawn in 1987.[165]

Macedonia made a reservation to article 2 in the following terms: 'Pursuant to Article 45 of the Constitution of the Republic of Macedonia, the right of parents to ensure education and teaching in conformity with their own religious and philosophical convictions cannot be realised through primary private education, in the Republic of Macedonia.'[166] Article 45 of the Constitution reads: 'Citizens have a right to establish private schools at all levels of education, with the exception of primary education, under conditions determined by law.'

There have been several interpretative declarations. There are also some regional declarations relevant to article 2 of Protocol No. 1. These are discussed in the chapter on article 4 of Protocol No. 1.

Germany made a declaration at the time of ratification of the Protocol:

The Federal Republic of Germany adopts the opinion according to which the second sentence of Article 2 of the Protocol entails no obligation on the part of the State to finance schools of a religious

---

[158] (1955–56–57) 1 YB 44.

[159] *Lena and Anna Angelini v. Sweden*, no. 10491/83, Commission decision of 3 December 1986, (1986) 29 YB 113.

[160] Ibid.

[161] *Kjeldsen, Busk Madsen, and Pedersen v. Denmark*, Nos 5095/71, 5920/72 and 5926/72, Commission Report of 21 March 1975, § 154.

[162] (1994) 37 YB 16; (1995) 38 YB 17.

[163] (1955–56–57) 1 YB 43.

[164] (1978) 21 YB 18ß–19.

[165] (1987) 30 YB 4–5.

[166] (1997) 40 YB 52.

or philosophical nature, or to assist in financing such schools, since this question, as confirmed by the concurring declaration of the Legal Committee of the Consultative Assembly and the Secretary General of the Council of Europe, lies outside the scope of the Convention for the Protection of Human Rights and Fundamental Freedoms and of its Protocol.[167]

Similar declarations have been made by Azerbaijan,[168] Bulgaria,[169] Georgia,[170] Moldova,[171] and Romania.[172]

Malta made an interpretative declaration that is arguably tantamount to a reservation, especially because it invokes the provision of the Convention governing reservations (article 64, now article 57): 'The Government of Malta, having regard to Article 64 of the Convention, declares that the principle affirmed in the second sentence of Article 2 of the Protocol is accepted by Malta only in so far as it is compatible with the provision of efficient instruction and training, and the avoidance of unreasonable public expenditure, having regard to the fact that the population of Malta is overwhelmingly Roman Catholic.'[173]

Andorra made a declaration affirming that it allows 'Catholic religion lessons in all educational centres, on an optional basis, outside the school timetable. Other religions can offer teaching in educational centres, outside the school timetable, with the approval of the government and the education representatives and without involving public expenditure.'[174]

Further reading

Klaus Dieter Beiter, *The Protection of the Right to Education by International Law: Including a Systematic Analysis of Article 13 of the International Convenant on Economic, Social and Cultural Rights*, The Hague: Martinus Nijhoff, 2006.

Pierre-Marie Dupuy and Laurence Boisson de Chazournes, 'Premier Protocole Additionnel, Article 2', in Pettiti et al., *La Convention européenne*, pp. 999–1010.

Thomas Englund, Ann Quennerstedt, and Ninni Wahlström, 'Education as a Human and a Citizenship Right—Parents' Rights, Children's Rights, or...? The Necessity of Historical Contextualization', (2009) 8 *Journal of Human Rights* 133.

Roger Errera, 'La Convention et les problèmes de la laïcité et de l'enseignement', (1970) 3 *Revue des droits de l'homme* 572.

Frowein/Peukert, *MenschenRechtsKonvention*, pp. 671–9.

Harris et al., *Law of the European Convention*, pp. 697–710.

Grabenwarter, *European Convention*, pp. 389–98.

Douglas Hodgson, *The Human Right to Education*, Farnham, UK: Ashgate, 1998.

G. Lauwers, *The Impact of the European Convention on Human Rights on the Rights to Education in Russia: 1992–2004*, Nijmegen: Wolf Legal Publishers, 2005.

Jane Liddy, 'European Convention of Human Rights: Case Law on the Right to Education', in Jan de Groof and Hilde Penneman, eds, *The Legal Status of Pupils in Europe*, The Hague: Kluwer Law, 1998, pp. 131–6.

---

[167] (1955–56–57) 1 YB 52.
[168] (2002) 45 YB 18–19.
[169] (1992) 35 YB 5.
[170] (2002) 45 YB 19–20.
[171] (1997) 40 YB 36.
[172] (1994) 37 YB 16.
[173] (1966) 9 YB 26–27.
[174] (2008 51 YB 8.

J. Lonbay, 'Rights in Education under the European Convention on Human Rights', (1983) 46 *Modern Law Review* 345–50.

Ovey/White, *Jacobs and White, European Convention*, pp. 320–30.

Ben Vermeulen, 'The Right to Education (Article 2 of Protocol No. 1)', in Van Dijk et al., *Theory and Practice*, pp. 895–910.

Ninni Wahlström, 'The Struggle for the Right to Education in the European Convention on Human Rights', (2009) 8 *Journal of Human Rights* 150.

Article 3. Right to free elections/Droit à des élections libres

The High Contracting Parties undertake to hold free elections at reasonable intervals by secret ballot, under conditions which will ensure the free expression of the opinion of the people in the choice of the legislature.

Les Hautes Parties Contractantes s'engagent à organiser, à des intervalles raisonnables, des élections libres au scrutin secret, dans les conditions qui assurent la libre expression de l'opinion du peuple sur le choix du corps législatif.

Introductory comments

When the Council of Europe was established, in 1949, democracy as we know it based upon universal suffrage was well established, although for some of the founding members this was a fairly recent phenomenon. France was the first country to introduce universal suffrage for men, in 1792, but it was not until 1944 that this became truly universal with recognition of the right to vote for women. Belgium, another founding member of the Council of Europe, achieved universal suffrage for men in 1892, but not until 1948 were women entitled to vote. Greece did not allow women to vote in national elections until 1952, three years after it had helped found the Council of Europe.

Winston Churchill, who participated in the earliest discussions about the European Convention on Human Rights, famously stated that 'democracy is the worst form of government except all the others that have been tried'. Political democracy is central to the entire vision of the European Convention on Human Rights and of the institution to which it belongs, the Council of Europe. The Preamble of the Statute of the Council of Europe speaks of 'devotion to the spiritual and moral values which are the common heritage of their peoples and the true source of individual freedom, political liberty and the rule of law, principles which form the basis of all genuine democracy'.[1] The European Court of Human Rights has frequently recalled the centrality of democracy, particularly in cases involving freedom of expression and freedom of association. According to the Court:

Democracy is without doubt a fundamental feature of the European public order...That is apparent, firstly, from the Preamble to the Convention, which establishes a very clear connection between the Convention and democracy by stating that the maintenance and further realisation of human rights and fundamental freedoms are best ensured on the one hand by an effective political democracy and on the other by a common understanding and observance of human rights ...The Preamble goes on to affirm that European countries have a common heritage of political traditions, ideals, freedom and the rule of law. The Court has observed that in that common heritage are to be found the underlying values of the Convention...; it has pointed out several times that the Convention was designed to maintain and promote the ideals and values of a democratic society...[2]

---

[1] *Bartik v. Russia*, no. 55565/00, § 50, ECHR 2006-XV.
[2] *United Communist Party of Turkey and Others v. Turkey*, 30 January 1998, § 45, *Reports of Judgments and Decisions* 1998-I.

Moreover, 'the rights guaranteed under Article 3 of Protocol No. 1 are crucial to establishing and maintaining the foundations of an effective and meaningful democracy governed by the rule of law'.[3]

The right to free elections is set out in article 21 of the Universal Declaration of Human Rights:

(1) Everyone has the right to take part in the government of his country, directly or through freely chosen representatives.
(2) Everyone has the right of equal access to public service in his country.
(3) The will of the people shall be the basis of the authority of government; this will shall be expressed in periodic and genuine elections which shall be by universal and equal suffrage and shall be held by secret vote or by equivalent free voting procedures.

It is also enshrined in article 25 of the International Covenant on Civil and Political Rights.

Every citizen shall have the right and the opportunity, without any of the distinctions mentioned in article 2 and without unreasonable restrictions:
(a) To take part in the conduct of public affairs, directly or through freely chosen representatives;
(b) To vote and to be elected at genuine periodic elections which shall be by universal and equal suffrage and shall be held by secret ballot, guaranteeing the free expression of the will of the electors;
(c) To have access, on general terms of equality, to public service in his country.

The Grand Chamber of the European Court of Human Rights has said that article 25 of the Covenant sets out 'the same rights' as article 3 of Protocol No. 1.[4]

Chapter V of the European Union Charter of Fundamental Rights is entitled 'Citizen's rights'. It contains provisions guaranteeing the right to vote and to stand as a candidate in elections for the European Parliament as well as in municipal elections within European Union Member States.

Drafting of the provision

The European Movement, which met in The Hague in May 1948, considered a proposal for a 'Declaration of Rights' comprised in a report from the International Committee of the Movements for European Union. Speaking of membership qualifications for the future Council of Europe, it said governments should 'subscribe to a common Declaration guaranteeing the fundamental personal and civil rights essential for the maintenance of democracy'. It also contemplated a European Court with 'power to send representatives to investigate any relevant matter, such as the conduct of elections or political trials'. Finally, the Council was to have the authority to send 'a mixed European armed force ... to assure conditions in which free elections could be held, and so afford to the population the possibility of electing a new parliament that would restore their liberties'.[5]

---

[3] *Hirst v. the United Kingdom (no. 2)* [GC], no. 74025/01, § 58, ECHR 2005-IX.
[4] *Scoppola v. Italy (no. 3)* [GC], no. 126/05, § 82, 22 May 2012.
[5] Political Report from the International Committee of the Movements for European Union submitted to The Hague Congress, May 1948.

The initial draft European Convention on Human Rights, prepared by the International Juridical Section of the European Movement and submitted to the Council of Europe in July 1949, contained the following:

Every State a party to this Convention undertakes faithfully to respect the fundamental principles of political democracy, and, in particular, within its metropolitan territory:
a) To hold at reasonable intervals free elections by universal suffrage and secret ballot, so that governmental action and legislation may accord with the expressed will of the people.
b) To take no action which will interfere with the right of political criticism and the right to organise a political opposition.[6]

The Consultative Assembly of the Council of Europe met in August and September 1949. Following a preliminary discussion in which the importance of a provision guaranteeing free elections was underscored by several delegates,[7] the rapporteur of the Legal Committee, Pierre-Henri Teitgen, prepared the following draft:

The Convention will include an undertaking by member States to respect the fundamental principles of democracy in all good faith, and, in particular, within their metropolitan territory:
A. To hold at reasonable intervals free elections, by universal suffrage and secret ballot so that governmental action and legislation may accord with the expressed will of the people.
B. To take no action which will interfere with the right of criticism or the right to organise a political opposition.[8]

In presenting the report of the Commission on Legal and Administrative Questions to the first Session of the Consultative Assembly, Teitgen said that the proposal:

[a]nticipates the undertaking by the Members States to respect the fundamental principles of democracy in all good faith, and particularly, in their metropolitan territory, to hold, at reasonable intervals, free elections by universal suffrage and secret ballot *'so as to ensure that Government action is indeed an expression of the will of the people'*. An amendment to delete this phrase was rejected by the Committee, since it was considered that this was not a theory of political philosophy and therefore a subject of dispute, but rather a fundamental requirement of democracy.[9]

The text proposed by the Legal Committee was modified by the Consultative Assembly:

The Convention shall include the undertaking by Member States to respect the fundamental principles of democracy in all good faith, and in particular, as regards their metropolitan territory:
1) To hold free elections at reasonable intervals, with universal suffrage and secret ballot, so as to ensure that Government action and legislation is, in fact, an expression of the will of the people.
b) To take no action which shall interfere with the right of criticism and the right to organise a political opposition.[10]

---

[6] Convention for the Collective Protection of Individual Rights and Democratic Liberties by the States, Members of the Council of Europe, and for the establishment of a European Court of Human Rights to ensure observance of the Convention, Doc. INF/5/E/R, I *TP* 296–303, at pp. 296–8, art. 2.

[7] Report of the Sitting sitting [of the Consultative Assembly, 19 August 1949], I *TP* 38–154, at p. 76.

[8] Proposals by Mr P.H. Teitgen, Rapporteur, 29 August 1949, Doc. A 116, I *TP* 166–8. Also Report presented by Mr P.H. Teitgen, 5 September 1949, Doc. A 290, I *TP* 192–213, at p. 202.

[9] Report presented by Mr P.H. Teitgen, 5 September 1949, Doc. A 290, I *TP* 192–213, at pp. 198–200 (emphasis in the original).

[10] Recommendation No. 38 to the Committee of Ministers adopted 8 September 1949 on the conclusion of the debates, Doc. AS (1) 108, II *TP* 274–83, at p. 276.

The provision was adopted by the plenary Consultative Assembly without a recorded vote.[11]

The Committee of Ministers decided to convene a Committee of Experts with the mandate to study the Consultative Assembly draft. In preparation, the Secretariat-General of the Council of Europe produced a memorandum that addressed the distinction between article 2, consisting of an enumeration of rights to be protected by the Convention drawn from provisions of the Universal Declaration of Human Rights, and article 3, which was the free elections provision adopted by the Assembly. The Secretariat-General said that the rights listed in article 2 needed to be 'ensured' by the State, because they could be breached by individuals or groups, whereas article 3 was a direct function of government action. Also, most of article 2 concerned individual freedoms, whereas article 3 dealt with political freedoms, it explained. In any event, the Secretariat-General said that article 3 'requires a more solemn and unequivocal commitment (specific reference to the rule of "good faith")'.[12]

When the Committee of Experts first met, in February 1950, the United Kingdom proposed the deletion of the undertakings concerning electoral machinery and the right of political opposition. It said these were of a constitutional and political character, adding that it would be difficult to reach agreement on the notion of 'fundamental principles of democracy'. The United Kingdom also objected to a reference to 'universal suffrage', observing that it was not unusual or unacceptable for a state to impose restrictions in this area.[13] The Committee of Experts endorsed amendments proposed by the Irish that altered the final phrase of paragraph 1[14] and added the word 'arbitrary' to paragraph 2. It also shortened considerably the chapeau of the provision because it felt this duplicated what appeared in articles 1 and 2, 'in particular the reference to the fundamental principles of democracy', and instead drew up a text which only provided for the safeguarding of the democratic institutions of the signatory States.[15]

The High Contracting Parties furthermore undertake, as regards their metropolitan territory:
1. to hold free elections at reasonable intervals, with universal suffrage and secret ballot, under conditions which will ensure that the Government and the legislature represent the people;
2. to take no arbitrary action which will interfere with the right of criticism and the right to organise a political opposition.[16]

The Committee explained that 'reasonable intervals' was meant as meaning intervals 'which are customary in free States'. The United Kingdom's expert said his government opposed such a provision as it related 'to matters of a constitutional and political nature which should not be included in a Convention for the protection of Human Rights'. He warned of 'practical difficulties', in particular with respect to 'universal suffrage', given

---

[11] Official Report of the Sitting [of the Consultative Assembly, 8 September 1949], II *TP* 14–274, at p. 132.

[12] Preparatory Report by the Secretariat-General concerning a Preliminary Draft Convention to Provide a Collective Guarantee of Human Rights, Doc. B 22, III *TP* 2–37, at p. 16.

[13] Amendment to Article 3 of the Recommendation of the Consultative Assembly proposed by the Expert of the Untied Kingdom, Doc. A 774, III *TP* 182–3.

[14] Amendment presented by Mr Lavery (Ireland) (4 February 1950), Doc. A 778, III *TP* 184–6.

[15] Report to the Committee of Ministers submitted by the Committee of Experts Instructed to Draw Up a Draft Convention of Collective Guarantee of Human Rights and Fundamental Freedoms, Doc. CM/WP 1 (5) 15, A 924, IV *TP* 2–55, at pp. 23–5.

[16] Appendix to the Report of the Committee of Experts to the Committee of Ministers—Draft Convention (16 March 1950), Doc. CM/WP 1 (50) 14 revised, A 925, IV *TP* 50–79.

that the right to vote was subject to restrictions in all countries. He also said that universal suffrage and a secret ballot did not, in all cases, 'ensure that the Government and legislature really represented the people'.[17]

The Conference of Senior Officials that met in June manifested the extent of the divided opinions within the Council of Europe on including a provision ensuring the protection of democratic institutions. Denmark, Greece, the Netherlands, Norway, Sweden, and the United Kingdom were all opposed to its inclusion. They took the position that such a provision 'went outside the scope of a Convention, the aim of which was to protect the fundamental rights of individuals'. Denmark thought the principle in question might be recognized in the preamble. In the opposite camp, France, Ireland, Italy, Luxembourg, and Turkey favoured a provision because 'the maintenance of democratic institutions in a country constitutes an indispensable guarantee of the protection of Human Rights'. Belgium reserved its position.[18] There was, as a consequence, no provision on free elections in the draft Convention adopted by the Conference.

What amounted to a decision not to include a text in the Convention on the right to free elections provoked an angry reaction from the Legal Committee of the Consultative Assembly. It informed the Committee of Ministers that 'it would gravely weaken the Convention if no reference were made in the Convention to democratic institutions'.[19] Ireland also wrote to the Committee of Ministers expressing its disappointment with the negotiations in a general sense, but in particular complaining about the possible omission of a free elections provision.[20] The unhappiness continued in the Consultative Assembly when it gathered for its second session in August 1950.[21] The Consultative Assembly voted by twenty-one to zero, with two abstentions, to request the Committee of Ministers to include in the Convention a text that was rather different from what it had proposed the previous year, focusing on the political rights of individuals rather than the protection of democratic institutions: 'The High Contracting Parties undertake to respect the political liberty of their nationals and in particular, with regard to their home territories, to hold free elections at reasonable intervals by secret ballot under conditions which will ensure that the government and legislature shall represent the opinion of the people.'[22] The text the Assembly had adopted the previous year was amended, redefining the right in an attempt to address the objections of the Committee of Experts and the Conference of Senior Officials.[23]

---

[17] Report to the Committee of Ministers submitted by the Committee of Experts Instructed to Draw Up a Draft Convention of Collective Guarantee of Human Rights and Fundamental Freedoms, Doc. CM/WP 1 (5) 15, A 924, IV *TP* 2–55, at pp. 23–5.

[18] Text of the report submitted by the Conference [of Senior Officials] to the Committee of Ministers, Doc. CM/WP 4 (50) 19, CM/WP 4 (50) 16 rev., A 1431, IV *TP* 242–73, at pp. 252–4.

[19] Letter from Sir David Maxwell Fyfe, Chairman of the Committee to Chairman of the Committee of Ministers (23 June 1950), Doc. AS (2) 6, V *TP* 32–4.

[20] Amendments proposed by the Irish Government (4 August 1950), Doc. CM 1 (50) 2, A 1863, V *TP* 58–61.

[21] Plenary sitting [of the Consultative Assembly] on 11 August 1950, Rep., 1950, I, pp. 212, 282–3, V *TP* 210–12; Report of the sitting [of the Consultative Assembly, 14 August 1950], V *TP* 216–71, at pp. 224–6, 236, 266–8; Consultative Assembly sitting of 16 August 1950 (morning), Rep., 1950, II, pp. 504–8, 518, 526–8, 534, V *TP* 286–94, 308–10, 322, 326, 336.

[22] Text published in the Collected Documents of the Consultative Assembly, Doc. AS (2) 104, VI *TP* 198–229, at p. 210.

[23] Report of the Committee on Legal and Administrative Questions to the Consultative Assembly (24 August 1950), Doc. AS (2) 93, VI *TP* 61–73.

But there was still no agreement within the Committee of Ministers. The United Kingdom representative moved that proposals from the Consultative Assembly, including the free elections provision, be referred to a Committee of Experts 'with a view to the preparation of a Protocol to the Convention'. This was adopted by ten votes to one. An attempt by the Irish representative, Seán MacBride, to enlarge the Committee so as to include representatives of the Consultative Assembly was not accepted.[24]

On 5 November 1950, the Standing Committee expressed 'regret' that the amendments, including the free elections provision, were not included in the Convention.[25] Later in November, when the plenary Assembly convened, there was much unhappiness with the rejection of the Consultative Assembly's proposals. '[W]ere the decisions of the Committee of Ministers deliberately intended to cause consternation?' asked Pierre-Henri Teitgen. 'If this was their aim, they have achieved it.'[26] The Assembly grudgingly accepted the fact that work would continue on a Protocol where its concerns could be addressed.[27]

The Secretariat-General prepared a memorandum suggesting that the right required more precise definition. In particular, it noted that the requirement of elections 'under conditions which will ensure that the government and legislature shall represent the opinion of the people' could be taken, 'if literally construed, to impose an obligation to adopt a system of proportional representation, even though this was presumably not the intention of the Assembly'.[28] The Secretary General wrote to Member States inviting them to prepare proposals for discussion by a Committee of Experts in February 1951 in view of adoption of a Protocol to the Convention by the Committee of Ministers the following month.[29] He wrote again to Member States in early February, conveying a draft-free elections provision proposed by the United Kingdom: 'Signatory Governments undertake to respect the political liberty of their nationals and, in particular, to hold free elections at reasonable intervals by secret ballot under conditions which will ensure the free expression of the opinion of the people in the choice of government legislation.'[30]

The Committee of Experts that met in February 1951 reached agreement on a text based upon the British proposal. The delegation of the United Kingdom told the Committee that its concern was to avoid the danger of the Convention being interpreted as imposing a specific system of parliamentary representation. Satisfied with this explanation, the Committee agreed on the following text: 'Signatory governments undertake to respect the political liberty of their nationals and, in particular, to hold free elections at reasonable intervals by secret ballot, under conditions which will ensure the free

[24] Report of the Meeting [of the Committee of Ministers, 3 November 1950], VII *TP* 24–34, at p. 34.
[25] Minutes of the meeting held by the Standing Committee of the Consultative Assembly in Rome on 5 November 1950 (morning), Doc. AS/CP (2) PV 5, p. 2, A 3057, VII *TP* 82–4; Minutes of the fourth meeting held in the afternoon of 5 November 1950 [by the Standing Committee of the Consultative Assembly], Doc. AS/CP (2) PV 6, p. 2, A 3058, VII *TP* 84–5; Second Report on the Work of the Standing Committee Presented in Accordance with the Resolution adopted by the Assembly on 6 September 1949, Doc. AS (2) 137, pp. 1126–7, VII *TP* 86–9.
[26] Reports of the Consultative Assembly, 2nd session, 18 November 1950, VII *TP* 90–121, at pp. 93–7.
[27] Ibid., pp. 90–121.
[28] Note on the amendments to the Convention on Human Rights proposed by the Consultative Assembly about which the Committee of Ministers was not able to reach unanimous agreement, Doc. CM (50) 90, A 3034, VII *TP* 126–30, at p. 30.
[29] Letter from the Secretary General of the Council of Europe to the Foreign Ministers of Member States (18 November 1950), Doc. D 280/9/50, VII *TP* 180–1.
[30] Letter from the Secretary General of the Council of Europe to the Foreign Ministers of Member States (7 February 1951), Doc. D 1357, VII *TP* 184–7.

expression of the opinion of the people in the choice of legislature and government.'
According to the Report to the Committee of Ministers, the majority of the Committee
considered that the text 'expressed sufficiently clearly the fact that choice of the government is not necessarily made directly by the people'. It added that Norway and Sweden
did not agree that this was clear enough.[31] The Committee of Ministers considered the
text again at its April 1951 session. It made some small amendments, changing 'Signatory
governments' to 'The High Contracting Parties' and deleting the final two words, 'and
government'.[32] Although this was accepted unanimously, the Irish delegate regretted that
reference in the text to 'political freedom' had been eliminated. Other delegations said this
would add nothing and might even lead to difficulties of interpretation.[33]

The organs of the Council of Europe laboured on for several more months before
agreeing on the three substantive provisions in Protocol No. 1. However, the text on free
elections adopted by the Committee of Experts seemed to meet with general agreement.
This was noted in the debate in the Consultative Assembly in May 1951.[34] In September
1951, the Secretariat-General prepared a commentary on the draft provision. It explained
that the reference to 'political liberty' in the Consultative Assembly draft had been
removed for two reasons: 'insofar as it relates to such rights as freedom of opinion,
freedom of assembly and freedom of association, these rights are already provide for in
the Convention itself'; 'insofar as it relates to other rights, the phrase "political liberty" is
too unprecise [sic] in a legal text'. The reference to 'home territories' was deleted because
the issue was dealt with in the territorial application provision of the Convention (article
56). Finally, the clause dealing with 'the opinion of the people' had been reformulated to
avoid any implication that it required the institution of a form of proportional
representation.[35]

Despite apparent satisfaction with the free elections text, the Legal Committee,
meeting in Brussels in early October 1951, took another stab at amendment. It proposed
the following: 'The High Contracting Parties undertake to hold free elections for the
legislature at reasonable intervals by secret ballot, under conditions which will ensure the
free expression of the will of the people.'[36] By way of explanation, the Committee said it
accepted the view of the Committee of Experts that the statement of political liberty was
not sufficiently precise and noted concern that the idea of representation could be
interpreted narrowly.[37] The Ministers' Advisers, meeting in Strasbourg in November
1951, said that although the new wording 'respected the substance of the text approved by
the Committee of Ministers', it had the defect of not taking into account the situation of

---

[31] Report of the Committee of Experts to the Committee of Ministers (24 Febraury 1951), CM/WP VI (51)
7, Doc. CM/WP 1 (51) 40, VII *TP* 210–12.
[32] Revised version (18 April 1951) and final version (19 April 1951), Doc. CM/WP (51) 9 (revised) and
(final) VII *TP* 228–30.
[33] Report of the Committee of Experts to the Committee of Minsters, Doc. CM (51) 33 (final), VII *TP*
250–4. Ireland returned to the point in the Committee of Ministers: Conclusions of the meeting held from
17–19 July 1951, Doc. CM/Adj (51) 38, VII *TP* 324–7.
[34] Official Report of the Sitting [of the Consultative Assembly, 10 May 1951, morning], VII *TP* 276–9.
[35] Commentary by the Secretarial General on the draft Protocol (18 September 1951), Doc. AS/JA (3) 13,
A 5904, VIII *TP* 4–14, at p. 14.
[36] Minutes of the meeting of 1 October 1951 [of the Committee on Legal and Administrative Questions],
Doc. AS/JA (3) PV 3, VIII *TP* 16–21.
[37] Draft letter to be submitted to the President of the Consultative Assembly concerning the draft Protocol,
Doc. AS/JA (3) 17, A 6131, VIII *TP* 20–9, at p. 26.

parliaments with non-elected chambers.[38] The Chairman of the Committee of Ministers wrote to the President of the Consultative Assembly explaining the position, referring to upper chambers in the United Kingdom where some members inherit their position and in Belgium where some are appointed. 'The text adopted by the Committee of Ministers in August had been carefully drafted to avoid this difficulty, and the Committee has therefore felt it necessary to maintain the earlier text', he said.[39] The Legal Committee demurred,[40] and its view was endorsed by the plenary Assembly.[41]

The heading 'Right to free elections' was added pursuant to Protocol No. 11.[42]

Analysis and interpretation

In an effective political democracy, the State is the ultimate guarantor of pluralism. It bears the responsibility pursuant to article 3 of Protocol No. 1 to 'organize' democratic elections 'under conditions which will ensure the free expression of the opinion of the people in the choice of the legislature'.[43] Its primary obligation is 'not one of abstention or non-interference, as with the majority of civil and political rights, but one of adoption by the State of positive measures to "hold" democratic elections'.[44] Three conditions are attached to the right to free elections set out in article 3 of Protocol No. 1: elections must be held at reasonable intervals; there must be a secret ballot; and they must take place 'under conditions which will ensure the free expression of the opinion of the people in the choice of the legislature'. Article 3 has been held to guarantee certain so-called 'subjective rights' that are not set out explicitly, in particular the right to vote and to stand for election.[45]

Article 3 of Protocol No. 1 is 'akin to other Convention provisions protecting various forms of civic and political rights', notably article 10 on freedom of expression and article 11 on freedom of association, including membership in political parties.[46] According to the Court, there is 'undoubtedly a link between all of these provisions, namely the need to guarantee respect for pluralism of opinion in a democratic society through the exercise of civic and political freedoms'.[47]

Although most of the substantive provisions of the Convention and the Protocols open with the words 'Everyone has the right' or 'No one shall', article 3 of Protocol No. 1

---

[38] Conclusions of the meeting of 23 November 1951 [of the Ministers' Advisers], Doc. CM/Adj (51) 68 (final), A 6678, VIII *TP* 45–7.

[39] Letter dated 28 November 1951 from the Chairman of the Committee of Ministers to the President of the Consultative Assembly, Doc. AS (3) 84, VIII *TP* 48–59.

[40] Minutes of the 4th meeting held on 29 November 1951 [of the Legal and Administrative Committee of the Consultative Assembly], Doc. AS/JA (3) PV 4 rev., VIII *TP* 64.

[41] Consultative Assembly sitting of 8 December 1951 (morning), VIII *TP* 169.

[42] Protocol No. 11 to the Convention for the Protection of Human Rights and Fundamental Freedoms, restructuring the control machinery established thereby, ETS 155, art. 4(a).

[43] *Mathieu-Mohin and Clerfayt v. Belgium*, 2 March 1987, § 54, Series A no. 113; *Özgürlük ve Dayanışma Partisi (ÖDP) v. Turkey*, no. 7819/03, § 27, 10 May 2012.

[44] *Sitaropoulos and Giakoumopoulos v. Greece* [GC], no. 42202/07, § 60, ECHR 2012.

[45] *Scoppola v. Italy (no. 3)* [GC], no. 126/05, § 81, 22 May 2012; *Labita v. Italy* [GC], no. 26772/95, § 201, ECHR 2000-IV; *Sadak and Others v. Turkey (no. 2)*, nos 25144/94, 26149/95 to 26154/95, 27100/95, and 27101/95, § 31, ECHR 2002-IV; *Ahmed and Others v. the United Kingdom*, 2 September 1998, § 75, *Reports of Judgments and Decisions* 1998-VI.

[46] *Ždanoka v. Latvia* [GC], no. 58278/00, § 115, ECHR 2006-IV.

[47] Ibid.

begins with the phrase 'The High Contracting Parties undertake'. In its first judgment dealing with article 3, the Court described this as the 'inter-State colouring' of the provision.[48] However, it rejected a restrictive interpretation whereby individuals could not invoke the provision as victims of a violation of their electoral rights.[49] The Court noted that nothing in the *travaux préparatoires* indicated an intent of the drafters to exclude the right of individual petition, adding that 'for a long time the idea was canvassed—only to be finally abandoned—of withholding the subject from the Court's jurisdiction. The *travaux préparatoires* also frequently refer to "political freedom", "political rights", "the political rights and liberties of the individual", "the right to free elections" and "the right of election".'[50] The rather unique wording of article 3 is explained by 'the desire to give greater solemnity to the commitment undertaken and in the fact that the primary obligation in the field concerned is not one of abstention or non-interference, as with the majority of the civil and political rights, but one of adoption by the State of positive measures to "hold" democratic elections'.[51]

For this reason, the Court has cautioned that alleged interferences with article 3 of Protocol No. 1 do not 'automatically adhere to the same criteria' as those set out in the restriction or limitation clauses of articles 8 to 11 of the Convention. It has said that '[b]ecause of the relevance of Article 3 of Protocol No. 1 to the institutional order of the State, this provision is cast in very different terms from Articles 8 to 11 of the Convention'. Article 3 employs collective and general terms even though it has been applied by the Court so as to enshrine individual rights. The consequence of this perspective is that standards of compliance with article 3 are 'less stringent' than those of article 8 to 11 of the Convention.[52]

The right to vote and to stand for election is not set out explicitly in article 3 of Protocol No. 1, unlike article 25 of the International Covenant on Civil and Political Rights. The European Commission of Human Rights initially adopted an 'institutional' approach to free elections, rejecting the idea that article 3 of Protocol No. 1 encompassed a right to vote and to stand for election.[53] Its position evolved to one apparently recognizing 'universal suffrage'[54] and then to the acceptance of the 'subjective rights' of the right to vote and to stand for election.[55] In its first judgment dealing with article 3 of Protocol No. 1, the Court endorsed the Commission's position.[56]

Organization of elections

The State has a duty to organize free elections. These must be held 'at reasonable intervals by secret ballot, under conditions which will ensure the free expression of the opinion of the people in the choice of the legislature'. This 'free expression' referred to in article 3 of Protocol No. 1 'is inconceivable without the participation of a plurality of political parties

---

[48] *Mathieu-Mohin and Clerfayt v. Belgium*, 2 March 1987, § 50, Series A no. 113.
[49] Ibid., § 49; *Karimov v. Azerbaijan*, no. 12535/06, § 34, 25 September 2014.
[50] *Mathieu-Mohin and Clerfayt v. Belgium*, 2 March 1987, § 49, Series A no. 113.
[51] Ibid., § 50; *Hirst v. the United Kingdom (no. 2)* [GC], no. 74025/01, § 57, ECHR 2005-IX.
[52] *Ždanoka v. Latvia* [GC], no. 58278/00, § 115, ECHR 2006-IV.
[53] *X v. Belgium*, no. 1038/61, Commission decision of 18 September 1961, (1961) 4 YB 338.
[54] *X v. Federal Republic of Germany*, no. 2728/66, Commission decision of 6 October 1967, (1967) 10 YB 336, Collection 25, pp. 38–41.
[55] *W, X, Y, and Z v. Belgium*, nos 6745/76 and 6746/76, Commission decision of 30 May 1975, (1975) 18 YB 237, DR 2, p. 111.
[56] *Mathieu-Mohin and Clerfayt v. Belgium*, 2 March 1987, § 51, Series A no. 113.

representing the different shades of opinion to be found within a country's population'.[57] Most of the case law has concerned the implied content of article 3. The only significant debates about the text itself have involved the notion of 'legislature'. There appears to be no litigation whatsoever on the issue of 'secret ballot'. The term 'reasonable intervals' seems to have been discussed only rarely in the jurisprudence. In terms of the actual conduct of elections, 'it is important for the authorities in charge of electoral administration to function in a transparent manner and to maintain impartiality and independence from political manipulation'.[58]

The European Commission of Human Rights said that the question of what constitutes a reasonable interval is to be determined by reference to the purpose of parliamentary elections. 'That purpose is to ensure that fundamental changes in prevailing public opinion are reflected in the opinions of the representatives of the people', it said. Thus, 'Parliament must in principle be in a position to develop and execute its legislative intentions—including longer term legislative plans.' According to the Commission, '[t]oo short an interval between elections may impede political planning for the implementation of the will of the electorate; too long an interval can lead to the petrification of political groupings in Parliament which may no longer bear any resemblence to the prevailing will of the electorate'. Under the circumstances, it said that a five-year interval between elections was not objectionable.[59]

The only free elections that are protected by article 3 are those involving the 'choice of the legislature'. The term 'legislature' is to be construed in the light of the constitutional structure of the State concerned[60] bearing in mind, 'in particular, its constitutional traditions and the scope of the legislative powers of the chamber in question'.[61] The provision 'was carefully drafted so as to avoid terms which could be interpreted as an absolute obligation to hold elections for both chambers in each and every bicameral system'.[62] The drafters took account of the situation in certain parliaments where there are non-elective chambers. In such cases, article 3 of Protocol No. 1 is only applicable to the chamber that is filled by direct elections.[63] Where a legislature results from indirect elections, 'the extent of the legislative powers enjoyed by it is a decisive factor'.[64] Matters to be considered included the extent of its powers to control the passage of legislation, its role in determining the budget, and its importance in a treaty ratification process.

The term 'legislature' does not necessarily mean the national parliament.[65] The provision has been declared applicable to regional elected assemblies, such as the *diets* of the German *Länder*,[66] the Austrian *landtag* or regional parliament,[67] and the legislative

[57] *Christian Democratic People's Party v. Moldova*, no. 28793/02, § 66, ECHR 2006-II.
[58] *Namat Aliyev v. Azerbaijan*, no. 18705/06, § 73, 8 April 2010; *The Georgian Labour Party v. Georgia*, no. 9103/04, § 101, 8 July 2008.
[59] *Timke v. Germany*, no. 27311/95, Commission decision of 11 September 1995.
[60] *Matthews v. the United Kingdom* [GC], no. 24833/94, § 40, ECHR 1999-I.
[61] *Sejdić and Finci v. Bosnia and Herzegovina* [GC], nos 27996/06 and 34836/06, § 40, ECHR 2009.
[62] *Mathieu-Mohin and Clerfayt v. Belgium*, 2 March 1987, § 53, Series A no. 113.
[63] *Sejdić and Finci v. Bosnia and Herzegovina* [GC], nos 27996/06 and 34836/06, § 40, ECHR 2009.
[64] Ibid., § 41.
[65] *Matthews v. the United Kingdom* [GC], no. 24833/94, § 40, ECHR 1999-I; *Boškoski v. 'the former Yugoslav Republic of Macedonia'* (dec.), no. 11676/04, ECHR 2004-VI.
[66] *Timke v. Germany*, no. 27311/95, Commission decision of 11 September 1995; *X v. Federal Republic of Germany*, no. 2728/66, Commission decision of 6 October 1967, (1967) 10 YB 336, Collection 25, pp. 38–41.
[67] *X v. Austria*, no. 7008/75, Commission decision of 12 July 1976, DR 6, p. 120.

assembly of the Autonomous Community of the Canary Islands,[68] as well as to the Flemish and Walloon community councils in the Belgian system.[69] Municipal councils do not fit under the rubric of 'legislature' as the term is meant in article 3.[70] As a general rule, if the body enacts delegated or subordinate legislation, framed by statutes adopted by the legislature of the country, it will not fit within article 3.[71] Since adoption of the Maastricht Treaty in 1992,[72] the European Parliament has moved from a purely consultative body to one exercising a decisive legislative role within the European Union. According to the Court, it 'represents the principal form of democratic, political accountability in the Community system', deriving 'democratic legitimation from the direct elections by universal suffrage'. Accordingly, elections for the European Parliament now fall within the ambit of article 3 of Protocol No. 1.[73]

A referendum or plebiscite is not covered by article 3, according to the jurisprudence.[74] The rationale seems rooted only in a literal reading of the text. After all, a referendum may certainly be legislative in the sense that it may change the laws of the country, and perhaps even the constitution. It does not seem reasonable to think that the drafters of the Convention actually meant to exclude such democratic manifestations from article 3.

By contrast, the case law has been more flexible with respect to presidential elections. The Court has said it does not exclude the possibility that article 3 of Protocol No. 1 may be applicable in such circumstances:

Should it be established that the office of Head of State has been given the power to initiate and adopt legislation or enjoys wide powers to control the passage of legislation or the power to censure the principal lawmaking authorities, then that office could arguably be considered to be a 'legislature' within the meaning of Article 3 of Protocol No. 1.[75]

However, the Court has fairly systematically declared inadmissible applications relating to elections for the Head of State on the ground that the function is without significant legislative power.[76]

---

[68] *Federación Nacionalista Canaria v. Spain* (dec.), no. 56618/00, 7 June 2001.

[69] *Mathieu-Mohin and Clerfayt v. Belgium*, 2 March 1987, § 53, Series A no. 113. Earlier, the European Commission had reached the opposite conclusion: *W, X, Y, and Z v. Belgium*, nos 6745/76 and 6746/76, Commission decision of 30 May 1975, (1975) 18 YB 237, DR 2, p. 111.

[70] *Salleras Llinares v. Spain* (dec.), no. 52226/99, 12 October 2000; *Malarde v. France* (dec.), no. 46813/99, 5 September 2000; *Clerfayt, Legros and Alii v. Belgium*, no. 10650/83, Commission decision of 17 May 1985, DR 42, p. 218.

[71] *Xuereb v. Malta* (dec.), no. 52492/99, 15 June 2000; *Booth-Clibborn and Others v. the United Kingdom*, no. 11391/85, Commission decision of 5 July 1985, DR 43, p. 236; *X v. the United Kingdom*, no. 5155/71, Commission decision of 12 July 1976, DR 6, p. 13.

[72] In early cases, the Convention organs considered that the European Parliament was not a 'legislature' within the meaning of article 3: *Marcel Fournier v. France*, no. 11406/85, Commission decision of 10 March 1988, (1988) 31 YB 45, DR 55, p. 130.

[73] *Matthews v. the United Kingdom* [GC], no. 24833/94, §§ 52–54, ECHR 1999-I. Also *Occhetto v. Italy* (dec.), no. 14507/07, 12 November 2013.

[74] *Hilbe v. Liechtenstein* (dec.), no. 31981/96, ECHR 1999-VI; *Borghi v. Italy* (dec.), no. 54767/00, 20 June 2002; *Bader v. Austria*, no. 26633/95, Commission decision of 15 March 1996.

[75] *Krivobokov v. Ukraine* (dec.), no. 38707/04, 19 February 2013. Also *Boškoski v. 'the former Yugoslav Republic of Macedonia'* (dec.), no. 11676/04, ECHR 2004-VI; *Sejdić and Finci v. Bosnia and Herzegovina* [GC], nos 27996/06 and 34836/06, § 54, ECHR 2009.

[76] *Anchugov and Gladkov v. Russia*, nos 11157/04 and 15162/05, §§ 55, 4 July 2013; *Paksas v. Lithuania* [GC], no. 34932/04, § 72, ECHR 2011 (extracts); *Niedźwiedź v. Poland* (dec.), no. 1345/06, 11 March 2008; *Krivobokov v. Ukraine* (dec.), no. 38707/04, 19 February 2013; *Baskauskaite v. Lithuania*, no. 41090/98,

In a case concerning Azerbaijan, the Court noted that the legislative power was exercised by the Milli Mejlis (the Parliament) whereas the President of Azerbaijan was head of the executive power. The President was vested with limited powers relating to the enactment of legislation, including the authority to sign and veto laws adopted by the Parliament. Furthermore, the President had the authority to issue presidential decrees and orders although these could not contradict or supersede legislation adopted by Parliament and they were confined to implementation of legislation. The Court said such powers were to be distinguished from the legislative power, concluding that elections for the position of President were not contemplated by article 3 of Protocol No. 1.[77] The Court reached the same conclusion with respect to the President of Macedonia after analysing the scope of the limited powers that position exercises with respect to lawmaking.[78]

In most European States, there is a very significant amount of regulation of the electoral process in areas such as financing of campaigns and access to the media. The purpose of such legislation is, in principle, to ensure that the election actually constitutes 'the free expression of the opinion of the people'. The Convention does not guarantee a right to such funding, at least according to the prevailing interpretation of article 3 of Protocol No. 1.[79] The Court has noted that although political parties were funded traditionally by contributions from their members, this is no longer adequate given 'a background of political competition and complex and costly modern means of communication'. It has observed that 'in Europe, as in the rest of the world, State funding for political parties is aimed at preventing corruption and avoiding excessive reliance by parties on private donors. It follows that this funding is intended to strengthen political pluralism and contributes to the proper functioning of democratic institutions.'[80] There are two main systems, one by which funds are allocated equally to political parties and the other by which they vary depending on performance of the party in the previous elections. Where funds are divided equally, a minimum threshold of votes is generally required in order for a party to be eligible. In Turkey, a minimum of 7 per cent of the votes in the preceding elections is a requirement for funding; this is at the high end of European practice. However, the Court declared inadmissible an application by a political party that had received between 0.8 per cent and 0.15 per cent of the valid votes cast, noting that the impugned difference in treatment was reasonably proportionate to the aim pursued.[81]

Similar issues arise with respect to other features of the regulation of elections, such as the need for a minimum number of signatures in order to stand for elected office, the deposit of a sum of money that will be refunded only if a significant result is obtained in the election, and a minimum threshold in order to obtain seats within a proportional representation system. It has been held that 'even a system which fixes a relatively high threshold, e.g. as regards the number of signatures required in order to stand for election or, as in the present case, a minimum percentage of votes on the national level, may be

---

Commission decision of 21 October 1998; *Habsburg-Lothringen v. Austria*, no. 15344/89, Commission decision of 14 December 1989, (1989) 32 YB 116, DR 64-B, p. 211.

[77] *Guliyev v. Azerbaijan* (dec.), no. 35584/02, 27 May 2004.

[78] *Boškoski v. 'the former Yugoslav Republic of Macedonia'* (dec.), no. 11676/04, ECHR 2004-VI.

[79] *Özgürlük ve Dayanışma Partisi (ÖDP) v. Turkey*, no. 7819/03, Joint Partly Dissenting Opinion of Judges Tulken and Sajó, § 2, 10 May 2012.

[80] *Özgürlük ve Dayanışma Partisi (ÖDP) v. Turkey*, no. 7819/03, § 37, 10 May 2012.

[81] Ibid., §§ 46–48.

regarded as not exceeding the margin of appreciation permitted to States in the matter'.[82] Restrictions on the access to the media by which air time is apportioned to political parties, thereby denying this to independent candidates, has been considered to meet the proportionality requirements of article 3.[83]

Implied limitations

As it has done with other provisions in the Convention and its Protocols, the European Court of Human Rights has applied a theory of 'implied limitations'.[84] Unlike articles 8 to 11 of the Convention, it contains no restriction or limitation clause. Moreover, the Court has recognized certain subjective rights, in particular the right to vote and to stand for election, deriving them from the text of article 3. However, this does not mean that the rights set out in article 3 of Protocol No. 1, either explicitly or by implication, are absolute.

Because of the absence of a restriction or limitation clause containing an enumeration of 'legitimate aims', such as public safety, national security, and the protection of the rights and freedoms of others, States Parties are not constrained in the identification of purposes justifying an infringement on article 3.[85] For example, the disenfranchisement of prisoners as a form of supplementary penalty has been held to pursue aims of preventing crime and enhancing civic responsibility and respect for the rule of law.[86] Similarly, the preservation of the democratic order[87] and 'encouraging citizen-like conduct'[88] have been recognized as legitimate aims. But the Grand Chamber hesitated when it came to 'loyalty', stating that it accepted the principle of loyalty to a State but that loyalty to a government was something else: 'In a democratic State committed to the rule of law and respect for fundamental rights and freedoms, it is clear that the very role of MPs, and in particular those members from opposition parties, is to represent the electorate by ensuring the accountability of the government in power and assessing their policies.'[89]

The European Commission of Human Rights recognized the protection of linguistic minorities as a legitimate aim for restrictions on the right to free elections, noting its importance 'for stability, democratic security and peace, which has been shown by the upheavals of European history, and as a source of cultural wealth and traditions'. The Commission cited 'the growing commitment concerning the protection of minorities on the European and international levels', reflected in documents such as the Declaration of the Heads of State and Government of the member States of the Council of Europe, the Copenhagen Document of the Conference on Security and Co-operation in Europe, the

---

[82] *Silvius Magnago and Südtiroler Volkspartei v. Italy*, no. 25035/94, Commission decision of 15 April 1996, (1996) 39 YB 117, DR 85-A, p. 112. Also *Federación Nacionalista Canaria v. Spain* (dec.), no. 56618/00, 7 June 2001; *Tête v. France*, no. 11123/84, Commission decision of 9 December 1987, DR 54, p. 52.

[83] *Oran v. Turkey*, nos 28881/07 and 37920/07, 15 April 2014.

[84] *Karimov v. Azerbaijan*, no. 12535/06, § 34, 25 September 2014; *Matthews v. the United Kingdom* [GC], no. 24833/94, § 63, ECHR 1999-I; *Labita v. Italy* [GC], no. 26772/95, § 201, ECHR 2000-IV; *Podkolzina v. Latvia*, no. 46726/99, § 33, ECHR 2002-II.

[85] *Hirst v. the United Kingdom (no. 2)* [GC], no. 74025/01, § 74, ECHR 2005-IX; *Frodl v. Austria*, no. 20201/04, § 28, 8 April 2010.

[86] *Scoppola v. Italy (no. 3)* [GC], no. 126/05, § 90, 22 May 2012; *Hirst v. The United Kingdom (no. 2)* [GC], no. 74025/01, §§ 74–75, ECHR 2005-IX; *Frodl v. Austria*, no. 20201/04, § 30, 8 April 2010.

[87] *Paksas v. Lithuania* [GC], no. 34932/04, § 100, ECHR 2011 (extracts).

[88] *Söyler v. Turkey*, no. 29411/07, § 37, 17 September 2013.

[89] *Tănase v. Moldova* [GC], no. 7/08, § 166, ECHR 2010.

European Charter for Regional and Minority Languages, and the Framework Convention for the Protection of National Minorities.[90]

In contrast with the relevant provisions of the Convention, there is no express reference in article 3 of Protocol No. 1 to the 'lawfulness' of measures taken by the State to restrict or limit the right to free elections. Yet the rule of law, affirmed in the Preamble of the Convention and inherent in all of its provisions, 'entails a duty on the part of the State to put in place a legislative framework for securing its obligations under the Convention in general and Article 3 of Protocol No. 1 in particular, and to ensure that its public officials charged with executing those obligations do not act outside the law, but exercise their powers in accordance with the applicable legal rules'.[91] Article 3 of Protocol No. 1 requires that 'the compatibility of that aim with the principle of the rule of law and the general objectives of the Convention is proved in the particular circumstances of a case'.[92]

More generally, the Court must ensure that restrictions or limitations 'do not curtail the rights in question to such an extent as to impair their very essence and deprive them of their effectiveness; that they are imposed in pursuit of a legitimate aim; and that the means employed are not disproportionate'.[93] The nature and severity of the interferences are factors to be taken into account when assessing their proportionality.[94] Where a suspected mafia personality was denied the right to vote although he had been acquitted at trial, the European Court said the evidence of guilt had been rebutted. Although the removal of his name from the electoral list fulfilled a legitimate purpose, given the verdict of the trial court it could not be considered proportionate.[95] The dissolution of a political party, having as a consequence the removal of its members as elected officials in the legislature, could not be regarded as proportionate to any legitimate aim. Moreover, it was 'incompatible with the very substance of the applicants' right to be elected and sit in parliament under Article 3 of Protocol No. 1 and infringed the sovereign power of the electorate who elected them as members of parliament'.[96] A permanent and irreversible nature of the applicant's disqualification from holding parliamentary office was deemed disproportionate.[97]

Because of the specificities of the 'implied limitations' concept as it applies to article 3, the Court does not apply the 'necessity' or 'pressing social need' criteria that are also part of the methodology used with respect to articles 8 to 11 of the Convention. Instead, in article 3 cases the Court has tended to focus on two factors: 'whether there has been arbitrariness or a lack of proportionality, and whether the restriction has interfered with the free expression of the opinion of the people'.[98] A wide margin of appreciation is involved.[99] This is because '[t]here are numerous ways of organising and running electoral

---

[90] *Polacco and Garofalo v. Italy*, no. 23450/94, Commission decision of 15 September 1997, (1998) 41 YB 42, DR 90-B, p. 5.

[91] *Karimov v. Azerbaijan*, no. 12535/06, § 42, 25 September 2014.

[92] *Ždanoka v. Latvia* [GC], no. 58278/00, § 115, ECHR 2006-IV.

[93] *Hirst v. The United Kingdom (no. 2)* [GC], no. 74025/01, § 62, ECHR 2005-IX; *Mathieu-Mohin and Clerfayt v. Belgium*, 2 March 1987, § 52, Series A no. 113.

[94] *Silay v. Turkey*, no. 8691/02, § 32, 5 April 2007.

[95] *Labita v. Italy* [GC], no. 26772/95, § 203, ECHR 2000-IV.

[96] *Sadak and Others v. Turkey (no. 2)*, nos 25144/94, 26149/95 to 26154/95, 27100/95, and 27101/95, § 40, ECHR 2002-IV.

[97] *Paksas v. Lithuania* [GC], no. 34932/04, § 112, ECHR 2011 (extracts).

[98] *Ždanoka v. Latvia* [GC], no. 58278/00, § 115, ECHR 2006-IV.

[99] *Podkolzina v. Latvia*, no. 46726/99, § 33, ECHR 2002-II.

systems and a wealth of differences, inter alia, in historical development, cultural diversity and political thought within Europe which it is for each Contracting State to mould into their own democratic vision'.[100] There exist a great variety of electoral systems within the territory of the Council of Europe. Article 3 of Protocol No. 1 does not impose any particular system. Both the 'simple majority system' and 'proportional representation', in its various forms, are compatible with article 3.[101] The Court has also explained that electoral legislation must be assessed in the light of the political evolution of the country concerned. Features considered unacceptable in the context of one system may be justified in the context of another so long as the system adopted ensures the 'free expression of the opinion of the people in the choice of the legislature'.[102] At the same time, the Court must bear in mind changing conditions within both the respondent State and other States Parties, responding to an emerging consensus about appropriate standards.[103]

The Grand Chamber has also noted that the need for 'individualisation of a legislative measure alleged by an individual to be in breach of the Convention, and the degree of that individualisation where it is required by the Convention, depend on the circumstances of each particular case, namely the nature, type, duration and consequences of the impugned statutory restriction'.[104] A lesser degree of individualization may be sufficient in electoral rights cases than in situations concerning regarding articles 8 to 11 of the Convention.[105]

Article 3 of Protocol No. 1 does not require the Court to verify whether every irregularity in an election is a breach of national law.[106] However, it must satisfy itself 'from a more general standpoint' that the respondent State has 'complied with its obligation to hold elections under free and fair conditions and ensured that individual electoral rights were exercised effectively'.[107] The Court has stressed 'the need to avoid arbitrary decisions and abuse of power in various electoral contexts and has emphasised that the relevant procedures for such decisions must be characterised by procedural fairness and legal certainty'.[108]

Accordingly, an assessment is necessary when there is an allegation that a breach of national regulations governing elections is such as to seriously undermine the legitimacy of the election as a whole.[109] If the appropriate domestic institutions have already examined the matter, the Court may only be required to determine whether their findings were arbitrary.[110] For this to take place, there must be in place a national institution capable of an effective examination of individual complaints and appeals in matters concerning electoral rights. 'Such a system ensures an effective exercise of individual rights to vote and to stand for election, maintains general confidence in the State's administration of the electoral process and constitutes an important device at the State's

---

[100] *Hirst v. the United Kingdom (no. 2)* [GC], no. 74025/01, § 61, ECHR 2005-IX.
[101] *Lindsay v. the United Kingdom*, no. 8364/78, Commission decision of 8 March 1979, (1979) 22 YB 344, DR 15, p. 247, at p. 251; *X v. the United Kingdom*, no. 7140/75, DR 7, p. 95.
[102] *Ždanoka v. Latvia* [GC], no. 58278/00, § 115, ECHR 2006-IV.
[103] *Karimov v. Azerbaijan*, no. 12535/06, § 37, 25 September 2014.
[104] *Yumak and Sadak v. Turkey* [GC], no. 10226/03, § 111, ECHR 2008; *Ždanoka v. Latvia* [GC], no. 58278/00, § 115, ECHR 2006-IV.
[105] *Ždanoka v. Latvia* [GC], no. 58278/00, § 115, ECHR 2006-IV.
[106] *I.Z. v. Greece*, no. 18997/91, Commission decision of 28 February 1994, DR 76-B, p. 65.
[107] *Namat Aliyev v. Azerbaijan*, no. 18705/06, § 77, 8 April 2010.
[108] *Orujov v. Azerbaijan*, no. 4508/06, § 42, 26 July 2011.
[109] *Karimov v. Azerbaijan*, no. 12535/06, § 43, 25 September 2014.
[110] *Babenko v. Ukraine* (dec.), no. 43476/98, 4 May 1999.

disposal in achieving the fulfilment of its positive duty under Article 3 of Protocol No. 1', the Court has said.[111]

Right to vote

The case law of the Court refers to the right to vote as the 'active' aspect of article 3 and to the right to stand as a candidate as the passive aspect of the provision. The Court has insisted that the right to vote is not a privilege. 'In the twenty-first century, the presumption in a democratic State must be in favour of inclusion', the Court has explained with reference to the parliamentary history of the United Kingdom and other countries 'where the franchise was gradually extended over the centuries from select individuals, elite groupings or sections of the population approved of by those in power'. Today, '[u]niversal suffrage has become the basic principle'.[112] Departure from the principle of universal suffrage 'risks undermining the democratic validity of the legislature thus elected and the laws it promulgates'.[113] Although exclusion of groups or categories of the general population is not ruled out, such measures must be reconcilable with the underlying principles of article 3.[114]

Eligibility for the vote necessarily imposes restrictions or limitations on the right to participate in free elections. The free elections provision of the American Convention on Human Rights addresses this issue explicitly, stating the right as belonging to 'every citizen' and affirming: 'The law may regulate the exercise of the rights and opportunities referred to in the preceding paragraph only on the basis of age, nationality, residence, language, education, civil and mental capacity, or sentencing by a competent court in criminal proceedings.'[115]

As a general rule, States do not allow non-citizens to vote in national elections. Although there may be exceptions to this, no cases dealing with the matter have come before the Convention organs. With respect to age, within Europe, Scotland has the youngest age, 16, at which persons are eligible to vote. The norm appears to be 18 years of age. For example, the imposition of a minimum age may be envisaged with a view to ensuring the maturity of those participating in the electoral process or, in some circumstances, eligibility may be geared to criteria, such as residence, to identify those with sufficiently continuous or close links to, or a stake in, the country concerned.[116] Again, there appears to be no case law concerning the lower age limit for voting. Disenfranchisement may be part of lustration measures of the sort taken in Central and Eastern Europe in the 1990s.[117]

An application concerning the right to vote in a particular election will be declared inadmissible, in accordance with article 35 of the Convention, if it is not lodged within six months of the election in question.[118]

---

[111] *Namat Aliyev v. Azerbaijan*, no. 18705/06, § 81, 8 April 2010.
[112] *Hirst v. the United Kingdom (no. 2)* [GC], no. 74025/01, § 59, ECHR 2005-IX.
[113] *Oran v. Turkey*, nos 28881/07 and 37920/07, § 54, 15 April 2014; *Sukhovetskyy v. Ukraine*, no. 13716/02, § 52, ECHR 2006-VI; *Russian Conservative Party of Entrepreneurs and Others v. Russia*, nos 55066/00 and 55638/00, § 49, 11 January 2007; *Krasnov and Skuratov v. Russia*, nos 17864/04 and 21396/04, § 41, 19 July 2007; *Kovach v. Ukraine*, no. 39424/02, § 50, ECHR 2008.
[114] *Hirst v. the United Kingdom (no. 2)* [GC], no. 74025/01, § 62, ECHR 2005-IX.
[115] American Convention on Human Rights, (1978) 1144 UNTS 123, art. 23(2).
[116] *Hirst v. the United Kingdom (no. 2)* [GC], no. 74025/01, § 62, ECHR 2005-IX.
[117] *Ādamsons v. Latvia*, no. 3669/03, § 116, 24 June 2008.
[118] *McLean and Cole v. the United Kingdom* (dec.), nos 12626/13 and 2522/12, § 24, 11 June 2013; *Dunn and Others v. the United Kingdom* (dec.), no. 566/10, § 11, 13 May 2014.

Non-residents

In 1982, the Parliamentary Assembly of the Council of Europe noted that as many as nine million nationals of Member States live outside their country of nationality in another Member State.[119] The territory of the Council of Europe (not to mention the European Union) was then a much smaller place, and that number has no doubt increased by orders of magnitude. The question of non-resident voting is part of a much larger debate about migration. In recent years, there has been a very concerted effort to facilitate the participation of non-residents in elections of their countries of nationality, although restrictions remain and 'there is a clear trend in favour of allowing voting by non-residents'.[120] Nevertheless, it cannot be said that any absolute principle has emerged. The Convention organs have consistently recognized that as a general rule having to satisfy a residence requirement in order to have or exercise the right to vote in parliamentary elections is not an arbitrary restriction of the right to vote.[121] Various reasons have been deemed to justify the exclusion of non-residents from voting. There is a presumption that non-residents are not as involved in concerns about public affairs and know less about them, that they have less influence on the choice of candidates and the development of their programmes, and that they should not be in a position to have significant issues on matters that do not really affect them. The impracticability for and sometimes the undesirability of candidates presenting the issues to non-residents is also a relevant factor.[122] In some countries, votes by non-residents are treated differently, as in Turkey, where such electors may only select a political party and not independent candidates. The Court has held that the Turkish rule 'meets the legislature's legitimate concern to ensure the political stability of the country and of the government which will be responsible for leading it after the elections'.[123]

In a recent decision, the Grand Chamber said that measures to allow expatriates to exercise their right to vote from their place of residence, although not provided for in article 3 of Protocol No. 1, was nevertheless 'consonant with that provision'.[124] The Grand Chamber went on to analyse whether, in a State where the legislation authorizes the vote for non-residents, article 3 imposes an obligation to organize this effectively. It considered the practice of European States as well as applicable legal instruments, concluding that as the law now stands, there is nothing to conclude that States are

---

[119] Recommendation 951 (1982) on voting rights of nationals of Council of Europe member states. For a review of the relevant intiatives within the Parliamentary Assembly as well as those of the Venice Commission, see *Shindler v. the United Kingdom*, no. 19840/09, §§ 39–71, 111, 7 May 2013.

[120] *Shindler v. the United Kingdom*, no. 19840/09, § 115, 7 May 2013.

[121] *Hilbe v. Liechtenstein* (dec.), no. 31981/96, ECHR 1999-VI; *X and Association Y v. Italy*, no. 8987/80, Commission decision of 6 May 1981, DR 24, p. 192; *X v. the United Kingdom*, no. 7730/76, Commission decision of 28 February 1979, DR 15, p. 137; *Luksch v. Germany*, no. 35385/97, Commission decision of 21 May 1997, DR 89-B, p. 175.

[122] *Oran v. Turkey*, nos 28881/07 and 37920/07, § 53, 15 April 2014; *Sitaropoulos and Giakoumopoulos v. Greece* [GC], no. 42202/07, § 66, ECHR 2012; *Doyle v. the United Kingdom* (dec.), no. 30158/06, 6 February 2007; *Hilbe v. Liechtenstein* (dec.), no. 31981/96, ECHR 1999-VI; *Polacco and Garofalo v. Italy*, no. 23450/94, Commission decision of 15 September 1997, (1998) 41 YB 42, DR 90-B, p. 5; *Luksch v. Germany*, no. 35385/97, Commission decision of 21 May 1997, DR 89-B, p. 175; *X and Association Y v. Italy*, no. 8987/80, Commission decision of 6 May 1981, DR 24, p. 192; *X v. The United Kingdom*, no. 7730/76, Commission decision of 28 February 1979, DR 15, p. 137.

[123] *Oran v. Turkey*, nos 28881/07 and 37920/07, § 66, 15 April 2014.

[124] *Sitaropoulos and Giakoumopoulos v. Greece* [GC], no. 42202/07, § 71, ECHR 2012.

under an obligation to enable citizens living abroad to exercise the right to vote.[125] Consequently, Greece's failure to facilitate voting for expatriates in their place of residence was not a breach of article 3 of Protocol No. 1.[126]

Convicted persons

Deprivation of the right to vote is imposed in some States Parties to the Convention as a consequence of conviction of a criminal offence, regardless of whether or not they are detained in prison. In others, the denial of voting is confined to those in detention. Slightly less than half the States Parties place no restrictions on the voting rights of persons convicted of criminal offences.[127] Seven States parties—Armenia, Bulgaria, Estonia, Georgia, Hungary, Russia, and the United Kingdom—have a blanket ban on voting by convicted persons. In some early decisions of the European Commission of Human Rights, applications by prisoners with respect to voting rights were declared inadmissible.[128] But more recently, describing such bans as a 'blunt instrument',[129] the Court has concluded that applications by prisoners in two of these States breached article 3 of Protocol No. 1.[130]

The automatic denial of the right to vote to prisoners, whatever the length of their sentence and without regard to the nature or gravity of their offence and their individual circumstances, falls 'outside any acceptable margin of appreciation, however wide that margin might be' and is consequently incompatible with article 3 of Protocol No. 1.[131] Obviously, the same finding applies to convicted persons who are not even incarcerated or who are released before their custodial sentence has been completed.[132] A prisoner does not forfeit Convention rights merely because of his or her status as a person detained following conviction. 'Nor is there any place under the Convention system, where tolerance and broadmindedness are the acknowledged hallmarks of democratic society, for automatic disenfranchisement based purely on what might offend public opinion', the Grand Chamber has said.[133]

In its Code of Good Practice in Electoral Matters, the Venice Commission has said that deprivation of the right to vote 'must be based on mental incapacity or a criminal conviction for a serious offence'.[134] The Court has said that disenfranchisement 'may only be envisaged for a rather narrowly defined group of offenders serving a lengthy term of imprisonment; there should be a direct link between the facts on which a conviction is based and the sanction of disenfranchisement; and such a measure should preferably be imposed not by operation of a law but by the decision of a judge following judicial proceedings'.[135] Moreover, disenfranchisement based upon mere suspicion of

---

[125] Ibid., § 75.

[126] Ibid., § 60.

[127] *Scoppola v. Italy (no. 3)* [GC], no. 126/05, § 45, 22 May 2012.

[128] *X v. the Netherlands*, no. 6573/74, Commission decision of 19 December 1974, DR 1, p. 87; *H. v. the Netherlands*, no. 9914/82, Commission decision of 4 July 1983, DR 33, p. 246; *Patrick Holland v. Ireland*, no. 24827/94, Commission decision of 14 April 1998, (1998) 41 YB 90, DR 93, p. 15.

[129] *Hirst v. the United Kingdom (no. 2)* [GC], no. 74025/01, § 82, ECHR 2005-IX.

[130] Ibid., § 85; *Anchugov and Gladkov v. Russia*, nos 11157/04 and 15162/05, § 100, 4 July 2013.

[131] *Hirst v. the United Kingdom (no. 2)* [GC], no. 74025/01, § 82, ECHR 2005-IX.

[132] *Söyler v. Turkey*, no. 29411/07, § 47, 17 September 2013.

[133] *Hirst v. the United Kingdom (no. 2)* [GC], no. 74025/01, § 70, ECHR 2005-IX.

[134] European Commission for Democracy through Law, Code of Good Practice in Electoral Matters, CDL-AD (2002) 23 rev., para. 1.1.d.iv.

[135] *Frodl v. Austria*, no. 20201/04, § 28, 8 April 2010.

involvement in organized crime cannot be a proportionate measure.[136] Where disenfranchisement for a period of more than ten years was imposed upon an individual who had poured red paint on statues of Atatürk, the Court held that there was a violation of article 3.[137] It has in a more general sense found the Turkish legislation on disenfranchisement to be indiscriminate in application as it fails to take into account the nature or gravity of the offence, the length of the sentence, and the individual circumstances of the convicted person.[138]

Right to stand for election

The right to stand for election to the legislature is the 'passive' dimension of the individual right to free elections enshrined in article 3 of Protocol No. 1. It is not a right to a successful result, but rather one to participate as a candidate under fair and democratic conditions. Article 3 requires the Court 'not to ascertain merely that the election outcome as such was not prejudiced, but to verify that the applicant's individual right to stand for election was not deprived of its effectiveness and that its essence had not been impaired'.[139] Although there is no right to a favourable outcome, in one case the Court concluded that as a result of tampering with votes in violation of article 3 the applicant was denied a seat in the Parliament. She was awarded compensation based on the difference in her salary as a deputy and what she might otherwise have earned.[140]

Restrictions and limitations on the right to stand for election are broadly similar to those regarding the 'active' wing of the right, the right to vote. The right is thinner, and the scope of permissible restrictions and limitations is thicker, with respect to the passive aspect than the active one.[141] Consequently, although the 'active' aspect of article 3 dictates a larger appreciation of the proportionality of restrictions on the right to vote of certain categories, the 'passive' aspect is generally confined to assessing whether arbitrary factors have prevented an individual from being a candidate.[142] The problem may arise from legislation that is not sufficiently precise or from an interpretation of the domestic law that is marked by arbitrariness. In one case, a Chamber of the Court was divided, four judges considering that legislation excluding 'clergymen' from elected office was insufficiently clear and precise to prevent arbitrary decisions by electoral authorities, and three judges finding the legislation acceptable but its application to be marked by arbitrariness in the application under consideration.[143]

A variety of grounds for disqualification from holding office can be found in national legal systems. Some disqualifications are related to the separation of powers. For example,

---

[136] *Labita v. Italy* [GC], no. 26772/95, § 203, ECHR 2000-IV.

[137] *Murat Vural v. Turkey* no. 9540/07, §§ 77–80, 21 October 2014.

[138] *Söyler v. Turkey*, no. 29411/07, §§ 36–47, 17 September 2013.

[139] *Namat Aliyev v. Azerbaijan*, no. 18705/06, § 75, 8 April 2010.

[140] *Kerimova v. Azerbaijan*, no. 20799/06, § 64, 30 September 2010.

[141] *Occhetto v. Italy* (dec.), no. 14507/07, § 47, 12 November 2013; *Melnychenko v. Ukraine*, no. 17707/02, § 57, ECHR 2004-X; *Seyidzade v. Azerbaijan*, no. 37700/05, § 29, 3 December 2009. See also European Commission for Democracy through Law, Code of Good Practice in Electoral Matters, CDL-AD (2002) 23 rev., para. 1.1.d.iii.

[142] *Ādamsons v. Latvia*, no. 3669/03, § 111, 24 June 2008; *Ždanoka v. Latvia* [GC], no. 58278/00, § 127, ECHR 2006-IV.

[143] *Seyidzade v. Azerbaijan*, no. 37700/05, §§ 36–39, 3 December 2009; *Seyidzade v. Azerbaijan*, no. 37700/05, Concurring Opinion of Judge Malinverni, Joined by Judges Vajić and Kovler, 3 December 2009.

it may be deemed incompatible to hold simultaneously a seat in Parliament and a senior office in the executive or judicial branch.[144] Disqualification may also exist in order to protect the independence of parliamentarians. For this reason, in most countries judges and prosecutors, police officers, members of the armed forces, and diplomats are not permitted to sit in Parliament. Individuals may also be disqualified from holding office because of conflicts of interest with the private sector, and because they cannot be available full time for their parliamentary duties.[145]

Given that the Court has considered residence requirements for voting to be justified on a number of grounds, as discussed above, it would not make sense for it to impose a more stringent standard with respect to the right to run for elected office. It has said that it would not 'preclude outright a five-year continuous residency requirement for potential parliamentary candidates'. Such a condition 'may be deemed appropriate to enable such persons to acquire sufficient knowledge of the issues associated with the national parliament's tasks'.[146]

The Court has intervened in the case of a prohibition on elected office to persons with dual nationality. Noting that only four Council of Europe Member States impose such a restriction on eligibility for elected office, two of which altogether prohibit candidates with dual nationality, the Court said that there was 'a consensus that where multiple nationalities are permitted, the holding of more than one nationality should not be a ground for ineligibility to sit as an MP, even where the population is ethnically diverse and the number of MPs with multiple nationalities may be high'.[147] It acknowledged that a 'special historico-political context' might justify such a restriction, noting that it could not exclude that 'in the immediate aftermath of the Declaration of Independence by Moldova in 1991, a ban on multiple nationals sitting as MPs could be justified'.[148] But it noted that the measure was only put in place in 2008 and that no explanation of the rationale was provided by the respondent State. It added that it must 'examine with particular care any measure which appears to operate solely, or principally, to the disadvantage of the opposition, especially where the nature of the measure is such that it affects the very prospect of opposition parties gaining power at some point in the future'.[149]

It is quite usual for legislation to require that eligibility as a candidate depend upon some demonstration of significant support in the form of signatures of electors. Case law of the Convention organs has established that a certain minimum number of signatures does not constitute an infringement on the right of the people to choose their representatives.[150] In an Austrian case, the European Commission said that a requirement of 200 certified signatures 'which can easily be satisfied by any political party with a reasonable chance of success cannot be said to hinder the free expression of the people in the choice of the legislature within the meaning of the said Article'.[151]

[144] *Ahmed and Others v. the United Kingdom*, 2 September 1998, §§ 73, 75, *Reports of Judgments and Decisions* 1998-VI; *Gitonas and Others v. Greece*, 1 July 1997, §§ 29, 44, *Reports of Judgments and Decisions* 1997-IV; *Brike v. Latvia* (dec.), no. 47135/99, 29 June 2000.
[145] *Lykourezos v. Greece*, no. 33554/03, §§ 21–27, ECHR 2006-VIII.
[146] *Melnychenko v. Ukraine*, no. 17707/02, § 57, ECHR 2004-X.
[147] *Tănase v. Moldova* [GC], no. 7/08, § 172, ECHR 2010.
[148] Ibid., § 173.
[149] Ibid., § 179.
[150] *Magnago and Südtiroler Volkspartei v. Italy* (dec.), no. 25035/94, 15 April 1996; *Asensio Serqueda v. Spain*, no. 23151/94, Commission decision of 9 May 1994, DR 77-B, p. 122.
[151] *X v. Austria*, no. 7008/75, Commission decision of 12 July 1976, DR 6, p. 120.

Discrimination

The only findings of a violation of article 14 of the Convention in conjunction with article 3 of Protocol No. 1 concern the constitution of Bosnia and Herzegovina. It reserves the Presidency and membership in the House of Peoples to members of the three 'constituent peoples', namely Bosniacs, Croats, and Serbs. In the leading case, the two applicants described themselves as being of Roma and Jewish origin and said they did not wish to declare affiliation with one of the 'constituent peoples'. As a result, they were excluded from running for election to the House of Peoples. The Grand Chamber accepted that the impugned restriction pursued:

at least one aim which is broadly compatible with the general objectives of the Convention, as reflected in the Preamble to the Convention, namely the restoration of peace. When the impugned constitutional provisions were put in place a very fragile cease-fire was in effect on the ground. The provisions were designed to end a brutal conflict marked by genocide and 'ethnic cleansing'. The nature of the conflict was such that the approval of the 'constituent peoples' (namely, the Bosniacs, Croats and Serbs) was necessary to ensure peace. This could explain, without necessarily justifying, the absence of representatives of the other communities (such as local Roma and Jewish communities) at the peace negotiations and the participants' preoccupation with effective equality between the 'constituent peoples' in the post-conflict society.[152]

The Grand Chamber concluded that the exclusion of groups or individuals from election to the House of Peoples based on race or ethnicity lacked an objective and reasonable justification. As a result, there was a breach of article 14 of the Convention in conjunction with article 3 of Protocol No. 1.[153] In a subsequent case, the Court reached the same conclusion with respect to an individual who claimed no particular ethnic or racial identity but who declined to declare affiliation with a 'constituent people'.[154]

Reservations

Albania is the only State to have made a reservation to article 3 of Protocol No. 1. Its reservation was temporary in nature, formulated for a period of five years. The legislation in question concerned denial of democratic rights to persons associated with the former regime.[155]

Some States have made territorial declarations applicable to Protocol No. 1 as a whole; these are discussed in the chapter in this Commentary dealing with article 4 of Protocol No. 1.

Following serious concerns about corruption within the local government, in 2009 the United Kingdom imposed direct rule and accordingly withdrew the application of article 3 of Protocol No. 1 to the Turks and Caicos Islands.[156] On 19 December 2012, it declared that following elections that international observers deemed to be transparent and accountable, with results reflecting the will of the people, these 'welcome and significant developments' resulted in it 'end[ing] its withdrawal of the application of

---

[152] *Sejdić and Finci v. Bosnia and Herzegovina* [GC], nos 27996/06 and 34836/06, § 45, ECHR 2009.
[153] Ibid., § 51.
[154] *Zornić v. Bosnia and Herzegovina*, no. 3681/06, §§ 30, 15 July 2014.
[155] (1996) 39 YB 21–22.
[156] (2009) 52 YB 9; (2010) 53 YB 27. See *Misick v. the United Kingdom* (dec.), no. 10781/10, §§ 16, 22, 16 October 2012.

Article 3 of Protocol No. 1 to the Turks and Caicos Islands, in such a way that Article 3 of Protocol No. 1 will once again apply to this territory'.[157]

Further reading

John J. Cremona, 'The Right to Free Elections in the European Convention on Human Rights' in Mahoney et al., *Mélanges Ryssdal*, pp. 309–24.

Donald Davis, 'Britain must Defy the European Court of Human Rights on Prisoner Voting as Strasbourg is Exceeding its Authority', in Spyridon Flogaitis, Tom Zwart, and Julie Fraser, eds, *The European Court of Human Rights and its Discontents, Turning Criticism into Strength*, Cheltenham, UK: Edward Elgar, 2013, pp. 65–70.

Achiles V. Emilianides, 'Do Minimum Age Requirements Violate the Right to Stand for Election under the European Convention on Human Rights?', [2010] *EHRLR* 670.

Frowein/Peukert, *MenschenRechtsKonvention*, pp. 680–9.

Sergey Golubok, 'Right to Free Elections: Emerging Guarantees or Two Layers of Protection?', (2009) 27 *Netherlands Quarterly of Human Rights* 36.

Grabenwarter, *European Convention*, pp. 399–409.

Heather Lardy, 'Article 3, First Protocol: The Right to Free Elections', in Harris et al., eds, *Law of the European Convention*, pp. 711–34.

Silvio Marcus-Helmons, 'Premier Protocole Additionnel, Article 3', in Pettiti et al., *La Convention européenne*, pp. 1011–20.

Michael O'Boyle, 'Electoral Disputes and the ECHR: An Overview', (2009–2010) 30 *HRLJ* 1.

Ovey/White, *Jacobs and White, European Convention*, pp. 331–8.

Jeroen Schokkenbroek, 'Free Elections by Secret Ballot (Article 3 of Protocol No. 1)', in Van Dijk et al., *Theory and Practice*, pp. 911–35.

---

[157] (2012) 55 YB 8.

Article 4. Territorial application/Application territoriale

Any High Contracting Party may at the time of signature or ratification or at any time thereafter communicate to the Secretary General of the Council of Europe a declaration stating the extent to which it undertakes that the provisions of the present Protocol shall apply to such of the territories for the international relations of which it is responsible as are named therein.

Any High Contracting Party which has communicated a declaration in virtue of the preceding paragraph may from time to time communicate a further declaration modifying the terms of any former declaration or terminating the application of the provisions of this Protocol in respect of any territory.

A declaration made in accordance with this Article shall be deemed to have been made in accordance with paragraph 1 of Article 56 of the Convention.

Toute Haute Partie contractante peut, au moment de la signature ou de la ratification du présent protocole ou à tout moment par la suite, communiquer au Secrétaire Général du Conseil de l'Europe une déclaration indiquant la mesure dans laquelle elle s'engage à ce que les dispositions du présent protocole s'appliquent à tels territoires qui sont désignés dans ladite déclaration et dont elle assure les relations internationales.

Toute Haute Partie contractante qui a communiqué une déclaration en vertu du paragraphe précédent peut, de temps à autre, communiquer une nouvelle déclaration modifiant les termes de toute déclaration antérieure ou mettant fin à l'application des dispositions du présent protocole sur un territoire quelconque.

Une déclaration faite conformément au présent article sera considérée comme ayant été faite conformément au paragraphe 1 de l'article 56 de la Convention.

Introductory comments

Territorial application of the Convention itself is governed by article 56 of the Convention. Clauses governing territorial application also appear in several of the Protocols. They are known as 'colonial clauses' and have in practice been applicable to only a small number of European States with dependent territories. Such clauses constitute an exception to the general law of treaties, codified in article 29 of the Vienna Convention on the Law of Treaties, by which a convention applies to the entire territory of a State Party. They have been criticized for permitting double standards but, in theory at least, they also permit the European State to show some deference for local autonomy.

Drafting of the provision

The draft Protocol prepared for the February 1951 meeting of the Committee of Experts by the United Kingdom included a provision dealing with territorial application:

1. Any signatory Government may at the time of signature or ratification or at any time thereafter communicate to the Secretary-General of the Council of Europe a declaration stating the extent to which it undertakes that the provisions of the present Protocol shall apply to such of the territories for the international relations of which it is responsible as are named therein.
2. Any signatory Government which has communicated a declaration in virtue of the preceding paragraph may from time to time communicate a further declaration modifying the terms of any

former declaration or terminating the application of the provision of this Protocol in respect of any territory.[1]

This provision was substantially revised by the Committee of Experts at its April 1951 meeting:

The High Contracting Parties shall declare at the time of signature or ratification whether their acceptance of the present Protocol relates to all three of Articles 2, 3 and 5 or to one or two of them. Any High Contracting Party which has not accepted all the provisions in question may, by a subsequent declaration extend its acceptance to others. The declarations provided for in the preceding paragraph shall be communicated to the Secretary-General of the Council of Europe.[2]

At the same time, the United Kingdom submitted a far more elaborate text governing application to dependent territories.[3]

The first paragraph of the April text was substantially revised by the Committee of Experts at its June 1951 session:

Any High Contracting Party which is not in a position to extend the application of one or more of the foregoing Articles to all or any of the territories for whose international relations it is responsible may make a declaration to this effect at the time of the notification referred to in paragraph 1 of Article 63 of the Convention. Any High Contracting Party which has made such a declaration may subsequently revoke it in whole or in part.[4]

This provision was revised yet again by the Ministers' Advisers as a result of their July 1951 meeting:

Any High Contracting Party may at the time of signature or ratification or at any time therefore communicate to the Secretary-General of the Council of Europe a declaration stating the extent to which it undertakes that the provisions of the present Protocol shall apply to such of the territories for the international relations of which it is responsible as are named herein.

Any High Contracting Party which has communicated a declaration in virtue of the preceding paragraph may from time to time communicate a further declaration modifying the terms of any former declaration or terminating the application of the provisions of this Protocol in respect of any territory.[5]

The text figured in the draft Protocol adopted in August 1951 by the Committee of Ministers. The draft then returned to the Consultative Assembly for its opinion. The Secretariat-General prepared a Commentary on the draft Protocol. Describing article 4 as the 'colonial clause', the Commentary noted that it was based on article 63 (now article 56) of the Convention. It was included because 'certain member States could not ratify the Protocol without previous consultation with the overseas territories affected, which would greatly delay the process of ratification'. The Commentary explained that

---

[1] Draft Protocol extending Section I of the Convention (14 February 1951), Doc. CM/WP 1 (51) 23, p. 1, CM/WP VI (51) 1, p. 1, VII *TP* 188–91.

[2] Revised version, Doc. CM/WP VI (51) 9, A 4405, VII *TP* 228–33.

[3] Proposal of the United Kingdom Delegation, Doc. CM/WP VI (51) 12, A 4387, VII *TP* 234–43, at pp. 238–9.

[4] Report of the Committee of Experts to the Committee of Ministers (6 June 1951), Doc. CM/WP VI (51) 20 final, Appendix, VII *TP* 300–9, at pp. 306–37.

[5] Recommendations of the Ministers' Advisers relating to the Agenda for the Session (1 August 1951), Doc. CM (51) 64 rev., A 5578 VII *TP* 326–33, at pp. 330–1.

ratification could be *à la carte*, and it would be 'feasible for the Articles on property and education to be thus extended, without including the undertaking about free elections'.[6]

The Legal Committee of the Consultative Assembly voted to delete the provision. It concluded instead that provision for oversees territories should be made in article 5(4), proposing the following:

However, when use is made of the option provided for in Article 63 of the Convention of declaring that the Convention shall extend to the territories for whose international relations a State is responsible, exception may be made of Articles 1, 2 or 3 of the present Protocol.

Such an exception may be revoked at any time. It may also be incorporated at any time in the declaration.[7]

The Committee explained that its amendment was intended to 'remove all doubts' about where article 63 (now article 56) of the Convention was among the provisions applicable to the Protocol as a consequence of draft article 5.[8]

Instead of accepting the suggestion of the Legal Committee of the Assembly, the Advisers to the Ministers of Foreign Affairs proposed that the problem could be solved by adding a final paragraph to article 4: 'a declaration made in accordance with this Article shall be deemed to have been made in accordance with paragraph 1 of Article 63 of the Convention'.[9] A letter from the President of the Committee of Ministers to the President of the Consultative Assembly explained that the text previously adopted by the Committee of Ministers required a positive declaration by a State Party. This would be reversed if the Legal Committee's proposal were adopted. The President of the Committee of Ministers noted that 'this procedure would put the Governments concerned in an invidious position, as compared with the procedure contemplated in the earlier draft'.[10] When it reconvened in late November, the Legal Committee of the Assembly accepted the proposal from the Committee of Ministers.[11] Speaking in the plenary Assembly in December 1951, Pierre-Henri Teitgen explained that the Ministers had ignored the advice of the Legal Committee on its 'awkward wording' and the 'clumsiness of certain formulae', but said that no question of principle was involved and that therefore the provisions should be accepted 'in spite of their defects'.[12]

The third paragraph was amended by Protocol No. 11 to take into account the renumbering of the Convention provisions.[13] The heading 'Territorial application' was added by Protocol No. 11.[14]

[6] Commentary by the Secretariat General on the Draft Protocol (18 September 1951), Doc. AS/JA (3) 13, pp. 2–4, VIII *TP* 4–17, at pp. 8–11.

[7] Minutes of the Meeting of 1 October 1951 [of the Committee on Legal and Administrative Questions of the Consultative Assembly], Doc. AS/JA (3) PV 3, p. 2, VIII *TP* 16–19, at pp. 18–19.

[8] Report on the Draft Protocol to the Convention presented by the Committee on Legal and Administrative Questions, Doc. CA no. 81, VIII *TP* 28–37, at pp. 34–5.

[9] Conclusions of the meeting [of Advisers to the Ministers for Foreign affairs, 21–23 November 1951], VIII *TP* 44–7, at pp. 46–7.

[10] Letter dated 28 November 1951 from the Chairman of the Committee of Ministers to the President of the Consultative Assembly, Doc. CA No. 84, VIII *TP* 48–59, at pp. 52–3.

[11] Report on the Communication from the Committee of Ministers relating to the Protocol to the Convention presented on behalf of the Committee on Legal and Administrative Questions, Doc. CA 93, VIII *TP* 66–75.

[12] Consultative Assembly sitting of 7 December 1951 (afternoon), VIII *TP* 76–115, at pp. 84–5.

[13] Protocol No. 11 to the Convention for the Protection of Human Rights and Fundamental Freedoms, restructuring the control machinery established thereby, ETS 155, art. 4(b).

[14] Ibid., art. 4(a).

Analysis and interpretation

The territorial application provision in Protocol No. 1 refers to article 56 of the Convention, with which it is closely related. Article 4 of the Protocol confirms the presumption that the instrument applies only to a State's metropolitan territory and that it can only be extended to dependent territories by way of a declaration. Article 4 of Protocol No. 1 goes even further than article 56 of the Protocol. It enables a State Party to declare 'the extent to which it undertakes that the provisions of the present Protocol shall apply'.

In 1986, The European Court of Human Rights declared inadmissible a portion of an application based on Protocol No. 1 directed at the United Kingdom concerning Guernsey, given that no declaration pursuant to article 4 had been formulated.[15] By a declaration dated 22 February 1988, the United Kingdom extended application of Protocol No. 1 to the following territories: The Bailiwick of Guernsey; The Bailiwick of Jersey; Anguilla; British Virgin Islands; Cayman Islands; Gibraltar; Montserrat; St. Helena, Ascension, and Tristan da Cunha (renamed St Helena and Dependencies in 2009); and Turks and Caicos Islands. On 9 October 2001, the United Kingdom extended application of Protocol No. 1 to the Isle of Man.[16] On 19 December 2012, the United Kingdom informed the Secretary General of the Council of Europe that it was ending its withdrawal of the application of article 3 of Protocol No. 1 to the Turks and Caicos Islands, 'such as that the Article 3 of the Protocol No. 1 will once again apply there'.

The Netherlands accompanied its instrument of ratification of the Protocol with a declaration respecting application to Surinam and the Netherlands Antilles. It has not applied to Surinam since it became·independent on 25 November 1975. In 1985, the Netherlands informed the Secretary General of the Council of Europe that the island of Aruba, which was a part of the Netherlands Antilles, would obtain 'internal autonomy' on 1 January 1986, although it would remain part of the Kingdom of the Netherlands. Consequently, Protocol No. 1 would henceforth apply to the Netherlands, the Netherlands Antilles, and Aruba.[17]

At the time of its ratification of Protocol No. 1, France declared that it was to apply 'to the whole territory of the Republic, having due regard, where the overseas territories are concerned, to local requirements, as mentioned in Article 63 of the Convention for the Protection of Human Rights and Fundamental Freedoms'.

Further reading

Michael Wood, 'Premier Protocole Additionnel, Article 4', in Pettiti et al., *La Convention européenne*, pp. 1021–2.

---

[15] *Gillow v. the United Kingdom*, 24 November 1986, § 62, Series A no. 109.
[16] (2001) 44 YB 23 (Isle of Man).
[17] (1986) 29 YB 4.

Article 5. Relationship to the Convention/Relations avec la Convention

As between the High Contracting Parties the provisions of Articles 1, 2, 3 and 4 of this Protocol shall be regarded as additional Articles to the Convention and all the provisions of the Convention shall apply accordingly.

Les Hautes Parties contractantes considérer-ont les articles 1, 2, 3 et 4 de ce protocole comme des articles additionnels à la Convention et toutes les dispositions de la Convention s'appliqueront en conséquence.

Introductory comments

Protocols to the Convention come in two varieties: additional and amending. An amending protocol changes the Convention and can only enter into force when it has been accepted by all States Parties. An additional protocol, on the other hand, applies only to those States that have accepted it. Article 5 confirms that Protocol No. 1 is an additional protocol.

Drafting of the provision

Article 1 of the draft Protocol prepared for the February 1951 meeting of the Committee of Experts by the United Kingdom stated: 'Section I of the present Protocol shall be considered to have been added to Section I of the Convention.'[1] Section I of the Protocol consisted of three articles, corresponding to what became articles 1, 2, and 3 in the final version of the Protocol. This provision was substantially revised by the Committee of Experts at its April 1951 meeting: 'This Protocol shall form an integral part of the Convention for the Protection of Human Rights and Fundamental Freedoms signed at Rome on 4th November 1950 (hereinafter referred to as "the Convention").'[2] At the same time, the United Kingdom presented a very elaborate series of provisions governing the status of declarations respecting the jurisdiction of the European Commission and the Court, as well as distinct texts governing denunciation and reservations.[3]

In the text of the draft Protocol prepared by the Committee of Experts at its June 1951 session, a new provision appeared, as article 5: 'This protocol shall form an integral part of the Convention.'[4] This provision was significantly revised by the Ministers' Advisers as a result of their July 1951 meeting: 'As between the High Contracting Parties the provisions

---

[1] Draft Protocol extending Section I of the Convention (14 February 1951), Doc. CM/WP 1 (51) 23, p. 1, CM/WP VI (51) 1, p. 1, VII *TP* 188–91. Also Proposal of the United Kingdom Delegation, Doc. CM/WP VI (51) 12, A 4387, VII *TP* 234–43, at pp. 234–5.

[2] Revised version, Doc. CM/WP VI (51) 9, A 4405, VII *TP* 228–33.

[3] Proposal of the United Kingdom Delegation, Doc. CM/WP VI (51) 12, A 4387, VII *TP* 234–43.

[4] Report of the Committee of Experts to the Committee of Ministers (6 June 1951), Doc. CM/WP VI (51) 20 final, Appendix, VII *TP* 300–9, at pp. 306–7.

of Articles 1, 2 3 and 4 of this Protocol shall be regarded as additional Articles to the Convention and all provisions of the Convention shall apply accordingly.'[5]

The text proposed by the Advisers was included in the draft Protocol adopted in August 1951 by the Committee of Ministers. The draft then returned to the Consultative Assembly for its opinion. The Secretariat General prepared a Commentary on the draft Protocol, where it was explained succinctly that '[t]his Article incorporates in the Protocol by reference the general provisions of the Convention itself'.[6] The Legal Committee of the Consultative Assembly had no difficulty with the provision.[7]

The heading 'Relationship to the Convention' was added by Protocol No. 11.[8]

Analysis and interpretation

For States Parties to Protocol No. 1, article 5 confirms that its provisions become an 'integral part' of the Convention.[9] According to the Grand Chamber, 'the Convention and its Protocols must be read as a whole, and interpreted in such a way as to promote internal consistency and harmony between their various provisions'.[10]

Questions have been raised about whether denunciation of the Convention, authorized by article 58 of the Convention, automatically results in denunciation of Protocol No. 1 (or, for that matter, any other protocol to the Convention that has been accepted by the State Party).[11] When Greece denounced the European Convention, in 1969, it also denounced Protocol No. 1.

Further reading

Pierre-Henri Imbert, 'Premier Protocole Additionnel, Article 5', in Pettiti et al., *La Convention européenne*, p. 1023.

---

[5] Recommendations of the Ministers' Advisers relating to the Agenda for the Session (1 August 1951), Doc. CM (51) 64 rev., A 5578 VII *TP* 326–33, at pp. 332–3.

[6] Commentary by the Secretariat General on the Draft Protocol (18 September 1951), Doc. AS/JA (3) 13, pp. 2–4, VIII *TP* 4–17, at pp. 8–11.

[7] Minutes of the Meeting of 1 October 1951 [of the Committee on Legal and Administrative Questions of the Consultative Assembly], Doc. AS/JA (3) PV 3, p. 2, VIII *TP* 16–19, at pp. 18–21.

[8] Protocol No. 11 to the Convention for the Protection of Human Rights and Fundamental Freedoms, restructuring the control machinery established thereby, ETS 155, art. 4(a).

[9] J.W. Fawcett, *The Application of the European Convention on Human Rights*, Oxford: Clarendon Press, 1987, p. 420.

[10] *Marguš v. Croatia* [GC], no. 455/10, § 128, 27 May 2014; *Austin and Others v. the United Kingdom* [GC], nos 39692/09, 40713/09, and 41008/09, § 54, ECHR 2012; *Stec and Others v. the United Kingdom* [GC], nos 65731/01 and 65900/01, § 48, ECHR 2006-VI.

[11] Pierre-Henri Imbert, 'Article 65', in Pettiti et al., *La Convention européenne*, pp. 943–56, at pp. 946–9.

Article 6. Signature and ratification/Signature et ratification

This Protocol shall be open for signature by the members of the Council of Europe, who are the signatories of the Convention; it shall be ratified at the same time as or after the ratification of the Convention. It shall enter into force after the deposit of ten instruments of ratification. As regards any signatory ratifying subsequently, the Protocol shall enter into force at the date of the deposit of its instrument of ratification.

The instruments of ratification shall be deposited with the Secretary General of the Council of Europe, who will notify all members of the names of those who have ratified.

Le présent protocole est ouvert à la signature des membres du Conseil de l'Europe, signataires de la Convention; il sera ratifié en même temps que la Convention ou après la ratification de celle-ci. Il entrera en vigueur après le dépôt de dix instruments de ratification. Pour tout signataire qui le ratifiera ultérieurement, le protocole entrera en vigueur dès le dépôt de l'instrument de ratification.

Les instruments de ratification seront déposés près le Secrétaire Général du Conseil de l'Europe qui notifiera à tous les membres les noms de ceux qui l'auront ratifié.

Introductory comments

This article is closely related to article 59 of the Convention, also entitled 'Signature and ratification'.

Drafting of the provision

The draft Protocol prepared for the February 1951 meeting of the Committee of Experts by the United Kingdom included a provision dealing with signature and ratification:

1. The present Protocol shall be open for signature by such Members of the Council of Europe as have signed the Convention. This Protocol shall be ratified. It shall come into force upon a ratification by ten members and, as regards any member ratifying subsequently, upon ratification.
2. The Secretary-General of the Council of Europe shall notify all Members of the Council of Europe of the entry into force of this Protocol and the names of the Members which have ratified it.[1]

This text was substantially revised by the Committee of Experts at its April 1951 meeting. On the condition that the Convention itself had entered into force, the Protocol would enter into force for a ratifying State without any requirement of a minimum number of ratifications for entry into force:

1. This Protocol shall be open for signature by such Members of the Council of Europe, who are the signatories of the Convention. This Protocol shall be ratified at the same time as the Convention or thereafter. It shall enter into force for each member at the time of deposit of its instrument of ratification, on condition that the Convention itself has then entered into force.

---

[1] Draft Protocol extending Section I of the Convention (14 February 1951), Doc. CM/WP 1 (51) 23, p. 1, CM/WP VI (51) 1, p. 1, VII *TP* 188–91.

2. The instruments of ratification shall be deposited with the Secretary-General of the Council of Europe, who will notify all members of the names of those who have ratified.[2]

The first paragraph of the April text was revised by the Committee of Experts at its June 1951 session. It made entry into force conditional on ten ratifications of the Protocol. There was no need to specify the prior entry into force of the Convention, given that States could not ratify the Protocol unless they had also ratified the Convention:

This Protocol shall be open for signature by the Members of the Council of Europe, who are the signatories of the Convention; it shall be ratified at the same time as or after the ratification of the Convention. It shall enter into force after the deposit of ten instruments of ratification. As regards any signatory ratifying subsequently, the Protocol shall enter into force at the date of the deposit of its instrument of ratification.[3]

The text was included in the draft Protocol adopted in August 1951 by the Committee of Ministers. The Legal Committee of the Consultative Assembly approved of the text.[4]

The heading 'Signature and ratification' was added by Protocol No. 11.[5]

Analysis and interpretation

The signature and ratification provision of Protocol No. 1 deals with some of the issues that also arise with respect to article 59 of the Convention. The reader is referred to the relevant chapter in this Commentary. However, there are also some differences. In particular, article 6 of Protocol No. 1 addresses the subsidiary nature of the instrument, in the sense that it can only be signed and ratified by a State that is also taking or has already taken this step with respect to the Convention itself. Accordingly, it was impossible for the Protocol to fulfil the condition of entry into force of ten ratifications without this also being the case for the Convention. In fact, the Convention entered into force a year before Protocol No. 1. Like the Convention, Protocol No. 1 enters into force for ratifying States immediately and without any grace period.

Protocol No. 1 was opened for signature on 20 March 1952. All of the Member States of the Council of Europe signed the Protocol on that date. The United Kingdom was the first State to ratify Protocol No. 1, followed by Norway, Saarland,[6] Ireland, Greece, Denmark, Sweden, Iceland, Luxembourg, and Turkey. It entered into force on 18 May 1954. All States Parties to the Convention have signed Protocol No. 1. Monaco, which signed on 5 October 2004, and Switzerland, which signed on 19 May 1976, have yet to

---

[2] Revised version, Doc. CM/WP VI (51) 9, A 4405, VII *TP* 228–33.

[3] Report of the Committee of Experts to the Committee of Ministers (6 June 1951), Doc. CM/WP VI (51) 20 final, Appendix, VII *TP* 300–9, at pp. 306–7.

[4] Minutes of the Meeting of 1 October 1951 [of the Committee on Legal and Administrative Questions of the Consultative Assembly], Doc. AS/JA (3) PV 3, p. 2, VIII *TP* 16–19, at pp. 20–1; Report on the Draft Protocol to the Convention presented by the Committee on Legal and Administrative Questions, Doc. CA no. 81, VIII *TP* 28–37, at pp. 36–7. See also Commentary by the Secretariat General on the Draft Protocol (18 September 1951), Doc. AS/JA (3) 13, pp. 2–4, VIII *TP* 4–17, at pp. 16–17.

[5] Protocol No. 11 to the Convention for the Protection of Human Rights and Fundamental Freedoms, restructuring the control machinery established thereby, ETS 155, art. 4(a).

[6] With respect to signature of the Protocol by the Saar, as well as to the use of the terms 'signatory Governments' and 'High Contracting Parties', the German federal government raised objections concerning the position of the Saar in the field of international law. See Report of the Committee of Experts to the Committee of Ministers (6 June 1951), Doc. CM/WP VI (51) 20 (final), VII *TP* 301–7.

ratify Protocol No. 1. When the Council of Europe was enlarged during the 1990s with the membership of many States from Central and Eastern Europe, ratification of Protocol No. 1 within a year of becoming a member of the organization was one of the undertakings made by new Member States.[7]

The final paragraph of article 6 concerns the role of the depositary. This text is rather more summary than the corresponding provision in article 59 of the Convention.

Further reading

Pierre-Henri Imbert, 'Premier Protocole Additionnel, Article 6', in Pettiti et al., *La Convention européenne*, pp. 1025–6.

---

[7] E.g., Application by Ukraine for membership of the Council of Europe, Opinion 190 (1995), para. 12.1; Application by Russia for membership of the Council of Europe, Opinion 193 (1996), para. 10.1; Application by Croatia for membership of the Council of Europe, Opinion 195 (1996), para. 9.2.

PART FOUR

PROTOCOL NO. 4 TO THE CONVENTION FOR THE PROTECTION OF HUMAN RIGHTS AND FUNDAMENTAL FREEDOMS, SECURING CERTAIN RIGHTS AND FREEDOMS OTHER THAN THOSE ALREADY INCLUDED IN THE CONVENTION AND IN THE FIRST PROTOCOL THERETO

Preamble/Préambule

The Governments signatory hereto, being Members of the Council of Europe,

Being resolved to take steps to ensure the collective enforcement of certain rights and freedoms other than those already included in Section I of the Convention for the Protection of Human Rights and Fundamental Freedoms signed at Rome on 4th November 1950 (hereinafter referred to as the 'Convention') and in Articles 1 to 3 of the First Protocol to the Convention, signed at Paris on 20th March 1952,

Have agreed as follows:

Les gouvernements signataires, membres du Conseil de l'Europe,

Résolus à prendre des mesures propres à assurer la garantie collective de droits et libertés autres que ceux qui figurent déjà dans le titre I de la Convention de sauvegarde des Droits de l'Homme et des Libertés fondamentales, signée à Rome le 4 novembre 1950 (ci-après dénommée «la Convention») et dans les articles 1 à 3 du premier Protocole additionnel à la Convention, signé à Paris le 20 March 1952,

Sont convenus de ce qui suit:

Introductory comments

Like the Convention itself, each of the additional Protocols begins with a preamble. The Convention's Preamble is relatively lengthy, with provisions clearly intended to frame the substantive provisions of the treaty. Indeed, Protocol No. 15 to the Convention actually amends the Preamble of the Convention, adding two paragraphs. In the case of the protocols, the preambles tend to be more perfunctory. It seems this has been driven by a concern that innovation in the preambles may complicate their interpretation as well as that of the Convention itself. Moreover, because the Preamble is deemed to be additional to the Convention itself, as a result of article 6 of Protocol No. 4, the Preamble of the Convention also applies to the provisions of the Protocol.

Article 31 of the Vienna Convention on the Law of Treaties sets out, as the 'general rule' for the interpretation of treaties: 'The context for the purpose of the interpretation of a treaty shall comprise, in addition to the text, including its preamble...'[1] Although the Vienna Convention was drafted many years after the European Convention, and it is not binding upon all States Parties because it has not been ratified by them, the European Court has nevertheless made reference to its provisions on interpretation on many occasions.[2] Indeed, noting the provision in the Vienna Convention, it has described the

---

[1] Vienna Convention on the Law of Treaties, (1980) 1155 UNTS 331, art. 2.

[2] *Golder v. the United Kingdom*, 21 February 1975, § 29, Series A no. 18; *Johnston and Others v. Ireland*, 18 December 1986, §§ 51 et seq., Series A no. 112; *Lithgow and Others v. the United Kingdom*, 8 July 1986, §§ 114 and 117, Series A no. 102; *Witold Litwa v. Poland*, no. 26629/95, paras 57–59, ECHR 2000-III; *Banković and Others v. Belgium and Others* (dec.) [GC], no. 52207/99, §§ 16–17, ECHR 2001-XII; *Mamatkulov and Askarov v. Turkey* [GC], nos 46827/99 and 46951/99, ECHR 2005-I; *Saadi v. Italy* [GC], no. 37201/06, § 61, ECHR 2008; *Demir and Baykara v. Turkey* [GC], no. 34503/97, § 65, ECHR 2008.

preamble as being 'generally very useful for the determination of the "object" and "purpose" of the instrument to be construed'.[3]

Drafting of the provision

The draft protocol prepared by the Consultative Assembly contained a fairly elaborate Preamble. The Consultative Assembly draft alluded to the Preamble of the Convention itself, noting that it was a 'first step' for the collective enforcement of fundamental rights and freedoms. The Assembly's draft also stated that it was '[t]aking account of the work being done at the United Nations to draw up an international covenant on civil and political rights'. Finally, it described the objective of the protocol as being to 'extend the collective guarantee provided by the Convention to other political rights which are also part of their common spiritual and legal heritage and their common conception of democracy'.[4]

Most of it was deleted by the Committee of Experts in favour of a succinct text modelled on that of Protocol No. 1. The Committee was concerned that if the preambles of the two Protocols differed too widely 'for no good reason' the consequence might be difficulties in the interpretation of the two instruments. Members of the Committee also expressed doubts about a reference to the International Covenant on Civil and Political Rights given the absence of any such mention in the Preambles to the Convention and Protocol No. 1.[5]

The heading 'Preamble' was added by Protocol No. 11.[6]

Analysis and interpretation

In its use of the phrase 'to take steps to ensure the collective enforcement of certain rights and freedoms', the laconic Preamble of Protocol No. 4 references recital 5 of the Preamble to the Convention that states: 'Being resolved, as the governments of European countries which are like-minded and have a common heritage of political traditions, ideals, freedom and the rule of law, to take the first steps for the collective enforcement of certain of the rights stated in the Universal Declaration.' Unlike Protocol No. 1, where the additional rights had in fact been proclaimed in the Universal Declaration of Human Rights, two of the four new rights set out in Protocol No. 4 do not derive directly from that instrument. The prohibition of imprisonment for debt, set out in article 1 of the Protocol, is not enshrined in the Declaration. It constitutes article 11 of the International Covenant on Civil and Political Rights; it was the draft of that instrument that inspired the Committee of Ministers to add such a right to the Convention system. The text on collective

---

[3] *Golder v. the United Kingdom*, 21 February 1975, § 34, Series A no. 18.

[4] Recommendation 234 (1960), Draft for a Second Protocol to the Convention for the Protection of Human Rights and Fundamental Freedoms. See Preparatory Work on the Draft Second Protocol to the Convention on Human Rights, Appended to Recommendation 234 (1960) of the Consultative Assembly, Preamble to the Draft, Memorandum by the Directorate of Human Rights, DH/Exp (60) 10, 26 October 1960.

[5] Memorandum of the Human Rights Directorate on the Committee's third meeting, 2 to 11 October 1961, DH/Exp (61) 35 Final, 17 October 1961, para. 8; Explanatory Report on Protocol No. 4, para. 1.

[6] Protocol No. 11 to the Convention for the Protection of Human Rights and Fundamental Freedoms, restructuring the control machinery established thereby, ETS 155, art. 2(5)(a).

expulsion of aliens, in article 4 of the Protocol, has no equivalent in any of the contemporary human rights instruments, although it may be viewed as a corollary of article 3, which is derived from article 13(2) of the Universal Declaration.

Further reading

M. Sand, 'Le quatrième protocole additionnel à la Convention européenne des droits de l'homme', [1964] *Annuaire français de droit international* 569.

Article 1. Prohibition of imprisonment for debt/Interdiction de l'emprisonnement pour dette

No one shall be deprived of his liberty merely on the ground of inability to fulfil a contractual obligation.	Nul ne peut être privé de sa liberté pour la seule raison qu'il n'est pas en mesure d'exécuter une obligation contractuelle.

Introductory comments

Although it was practised for many centuries,[1] the phenomenon of imprisonment for debt has virtually disappeared in modern times. At the age of twelve, Charles Dickens underwent the grief and humiliation associated with his father's detention in the Marshelsea Prison for failure to pay debts. He wrote about the place in *Little Dorrit.*

The prohibition of imprisonment for debt is set out in article 11 of the International Covenant on Civil and Political Rights, where it is deemed a non-derogable norm. It was one of the innovations during the drafting of the Covenant, as there is no comparable provision in the Universal Declaration of Human Rights. Indeed, it seems that the issue did not even arise when the Universal Declaration of Human Rights was being drafted. Its inclusion in the Protocol is rather anachronistic and no violations of article 11 have ever been registered by the Convention organs.

Drafting of the provision

Inclusion of a provision dealing with imprisonment for debt had been briefly considered at the time the Convention was being adopted, in 1949 and 1950. The provision that became article 11 of the International Covenant on Civil and Political Rights already appeared in the 1949 draft examined by the United Nations Commission on Human Rights.[2] The Committee of Ministers instructed its Committee of Experts to give 'due attention' to the draft Covenant.[3] A document prepared by the Secretariat-General of the Council of Europe to assist the Committee of Experts said: 'To the knowledge of the Secretary-General, and subject to correction, imprisonment for the non-payment of debts between individuals does not exist in any European country.'[4] The proposal returned in the Committee of Experts in early 1950. The British representative, Sir Oscar Dowson, urged that such a text be inserted. He actually proposed what was at the time the current draft in the United Nations Covenant: 'No one shall be imprisoned merely on the grounds

---

[1] Jay Cohen, 'The History of Imprisonment for Debt and its Relation to the Development of Discharge in Bankruptcy', (1982) 3 *Journal of Legal History* 153; Richard Ford, 'Imprisonment for Debt', (1926) 25 *Michigan Law Review* 24.

[2] Report of the Fifth Session of the Commission on Human Rights to the Economic and Social Council, UN Doc. E/1371(Supp.), p. 19.

[3] Letter addressed on 18 November 1949 by the Secretary General to the Ministers for Foreign Affairs of the Member States, Ref. D 26/2/49, II *TP* 302–5.

[4] Preparatory Report by the Secretariat-General concerning a Preliminary Draft Convention to Provide a Collective Guarantee of Human Rights, Doc. B 22, III *TP* 2–37, at pp. 18–19.

of inability to fulfil a contractual obligation.'[5] The provision was not reproduced in the proposals submitted by the United Kingdom to the second session of the Committee of Experts in 1950,[6] and nothing further appears on this subject in the *travaux préparatoires* of the Convention.

In 1958, when the Legal Committee of the Consultative Assembly began consideration of an additional protocol, the list of rights that might be included began with freedom from imprisonment on the ground of inability to fulfil a contractual obligation. As the Preliminary Report of the Committee noted, it was already included in the draft United Nations Covenant.[7] The rapporteur, Hermod Lannung, argued that the text would strengthen the provisions of article 5 of the Convention. He explained that the provision would only apply to contractual obligations and not to all civil debts, nor to cases of fraudulent non-performance. Accordingly, it would cover 'neither public obligations (fiscal, military etc.) nor civil obligations imposed by statute or court order (e.g. maintenance obligations of parents or spouses, whether divorced or not, a judgment debt for damages, etc.)'.[8] The text adopted by the Consultative Assembly replicated verbatim the draft provision in the United Nations Covenant: 'No-one shall be imprisoned merely on the ground of inability to fulfil a contractual obligation.'[9]

The Committee of Experts decided to depart slightly from the initial draft of the Consultative Assembly. It proposed that the word 'imprisoned' be replaced with 'deprived of his liberty' so as to cover loss of liberty for any length of time, whether by detention or arrest. The Committee of Experts recognized that the proposed wording was designed to reinforce the terms of article 5 of the Convention. Article 5(1) uses the expression 'no-one shall be deprived of his liberty'. Moreover, the term 'deprived' covers arrest as well as detention. For that reason, it was therefore thought to be more precise. The Committee of Experts noted that article 5(4) of the Convention used the phrase 'person deprived of his liberty by arrest or detention'.[10]

The Explanatory Report confirms that the text is intended to relate to failure to fulfil contractual obligations of any kind and not only money debts. Thus, it may apply to 'non-delivery, non-performance or non-forbearance'. Nevertheless, the obligation must arise from a contract and not from legislation in public or private law.[11]

---

[5] Amendments to Article 2 of the Recommendation of the Consultative Assembly proposed by the Expert of the United Kingdom, Doc. A 798, III *TP* 204–7.

[6] Amendments to Articles 1, 2, 4, 5, 6, 8, and 9 of the Committee's Preliminary Draft Proposal by the Expert of the United Kingdom, Doc. CM/WP 1 (50) 2, A 915, III *TP* 280–9.

[7] Preliminary Report by M. Lannung, Rapporteur, AS/Jur XII (10) 1, 21 August 1958; Minutes of the meeting [of the Legal Committee, Consultative Assembly], held on 9 and 10 June 1958, AS/Jur (10) PV 2 rev., 22 September 1958; Minutes of the meeting [of the Legal Committee, Sub-Committee No. 12 (Human Rights), Consultative Assembly], held on Tuesday 16 September, 1958, AS/Jur XII (10) PV 1, 7 October 1958.

[8] Second Protocol to the Convention on Human Rights, Second Preliminary Report presented by M. Lannung, Rapporteur, AS/Jur XII (10) 3, 10 November 1958; Second Protocol to the Convention on Human Rights, Third Report presented by M. Lannung, Rapporteur, AS/Jur XII (11) 1, 8 June 1959.

[9] Recommendation 234 (1960), Draft for a Second Protocol to the Convention for the Protection of Human Rights and Fundamental Freedoms; Preparatory work on the Draft Second Protocol to the Convention on Human Rights, appended to Recommendation 234 (1960) of the Consultative Assembly. III. Article 1 of the Draft—Contractual Obligations—Memorandum presented by the Directorate of Human Rights, DH/Exp (60) 11 and Appendix I to VI, 27 October 1960.

[10] Memorandum by the Human Rights Directorate on the proceedings of the Committee's first meeting, 7 to 11 November 1960, DX/Exp (60) 27, 10 February 1961. Also Memorandum by the Human Rights Directorate on the Committee's second meeting, 24 to 29 April 1961, DH/Exp (61) 15, 7 August 1961, paras 11–14.

[11] Explanatory Report on Protocol No. 4, paras 3–4.

According to the Committee of Experts, the provision 'aimed at prohibiting, as contrary to the concept of human liberty and dignity, any deprivation of liberty for the sole reason that the individual had not the material means to fulfil his contractual obligations'. But it said that if the inability to fulfil a contractual obligation was accompanied by some other factor, such as malicious or fraudulent intent, or deliberate refusal to fulfil an obligation, or inability due to negligence, the right does not apply. For this reason, the Committee thought that the provision could not be interpreted as a prohibition on deprivation of liberty as a penalty 'for a proved criminal offence or as a necessary preventive measure before trial for such an offence, even if criminal law recognised as an offence an act or omission which was at the same time a failure to fulfil a contractual obligation'. It gave some examples of situations where law would not be in conflict with the provision: a person who orders food and drink in a cafe or restaurant and leaves without paying for them, knowing beforehand that he or she cannot pay; an individual, through negligence, fails to supply goods to the army when under contract to do so; someone preparing to leave the country to avoid meeting his commitments. A suggestion to replace the word 'contractual' with 'civil' was rejected.[12]

The heading 'Prohibition of imprisonment for debt' was added according to the provisions of Protocol No. 11.[13]

Analysis and interpretation

The Court has said that article 1 of Protocol No. 4 'completes' article 5(1) of the Convention.[14] When inclusion of the right was being considered by the Consultative Assembly, in 1958 and 1959, some members did not think the provision to be very useful because, they said, imprisonment for debt was no longer practised in Europe. Indeed, the Court's database of case law does not identify a single finding of a violation of article 1 by either the Court or the Commission. Applications based upon article 1 of Protocol No. 4 have often been rejected summarily, without discussion.[15] The Commission dismissed a complaint by an applicant who was required to post a bond (*une caution*), failing which he would be arrested. It said the obligation to provide the bond resulted from a judicial decision and not a contractual obligation.[16] Similarly, it held that the French procedure of 'contrainte par corps', whereby payment of a fine could be compelled by threat of imprisonment, did not fall within the scope of article 1 of Protocol No. 4, which dealt with civil matters and not with criminal or penal law.[17] In a Polish case, it dismissed the application of a man charged with 'abuse of property' who was detained pending trial at

---

[12] Examination of the Draft, Article 1, DH/Exp. (61) 3, 26 April 1961.
[13] Protocol No. 11 to the Convention for the Protection of Human Rights and Fundamental Freedoms, restructuring the control machinery established thereby, ETS 155, art. 2(5)(a).
[14] *Luordo v. Italy* (dec.), no. 32190/96, 23 May 2002.
[15] E.g., *Ursu v. Romania*, no. 21949/04, § 43, 4 June 2013; *Miulescu v. Romania*, no. 35493/06, 9 April 2013.
[16] *Raimondo v. Italy*, no. 12954/87, § 4, Commission decision of 6 December 1991.
[17] *Hunter v. France*, no. 22247/93, § 2, Commission decision of 22 February 1995. Also *Jamil v. France*, no.15917/89, § 51, Commission decision of 10 March 1994; *Barajas v. France*, no. 26241/95, Commission decision of 12 April 1996; *Mattelin v. France*, no. 22238/93, Commission decision of 9 April 1996; *J.-M. B. v. France*, no. 26198/95, Commission decision of 15 May 1996; *Bitti v. France*, no. 28645/95, Commission decision of 15 May 1996; *Ninin v. France*, no. 27373/95, Commission decision of 15 May 1996.

the request of the public prosecutor.[18] It noted that article 1 did not apply to the case where an individual was detained for non-payment of support for his family.[19]

According to the European Commission, article 1 of Protocol No. 4 does not prohibit imprisonment of a person 'if there are reasons apart from the material incapacity to fulfil contractual obligations, e.g. if the person concerned deliberately refuses to fulfil an obligation'.[20] The Court has held that 'deprived of his liberty' does not encompass measures restricting freedom of movement, such as the order of a bankruptcy court not to change one's residence without judicial authorization.[21]

Article 11 of the International Covenant on Civil and Political Rights is one of a handful of rights that are not subject to derogation.[22] It is in august company there, alongside such fundamental rights as the right to life and the prohibition of torture and slavery. It does not seem that consideration was ever given to including article 1 of Protocol No. 4 in the short list of non-derogable rights set out in article 15(2) of the European Convention.

Further reading

Frowein/Peukert, *MenschenRechtsKonvention*, p. 690.
Grabenwarter, *European Convention*, pp. 410.
Harris et al., *Law of the European Convention*, p. 735.
Jacques Mourgeon, 'Protocole No 4, Article 1', in Pettiti et al., *La Convention européenne*, p. 1041–2.
Jeroen Schokkenbroek, 'Prohibition of Deprivation of Liberty on the Ground of Inability to Fulfil a Contractual Obligation (Article 1 of Protocol No. 4)', in Van Dijk et al., *Theory and Practice*, pp. 937–8.

---

[18] *Pietrzyk v. Poland*, no. 28346/95, Commission decision of 26 February 1997.
[19] *R.R. v. Italy* (dec.), no. 42191/02, 2 December 2004.
[20] *Christakis v. Cyprus*, no. 34399/97, Commission decision of 21 May 1997, citing *X v. Federal Republic of Germany*, no. 5025/71, Commission decision of 18 December 1971, (1971) 14 YB 692.
[21] *A.Q. v. Italy* (dec.), no. 44994/98, 14 March 2002.
[22] International Covenant on Civil and Political Rights, (1976) 999 UNTS 171, art. 4(2).

Article 2. Freedom of movement/Liberté de circulation

1. Everyone lawfully within the territory of a State shall, within that territory, have the right to liberty of movement and freedom to choose his residence.

2. Everyone shall be free to leave any country, including his own.

3. No restrictions shall be placed on the exercise of these rights other than such as are in accordance with law and are necessary in a democratic society in the interests of national security or public safety, for the maintenance of ordre public, for the prevention of crime, for the protection of health or morals, or for the protection of the rights and freedoms of others.

4. The rights set forth in paragraph 1 may also be subject, in particular areas, to restrictions imposed in accordance with law and justified by the public interests in a democratic society.

1. Quiconque se trouve régulièrement sur le territoire d'un État a le droit d'y circuler librement et d'y choisir librement sa résidence.

2. Toute personne est libre de quitter n'importe quel pays, y compris le sien.

3. L'exercice de ces droits ne peut faire l'objet d'autres restrictions que celles qui, prévues par la loi, constituent des mesures nécessaires, dans une société démocratique, à la sécurité nationale, à la sûreté publique, au maintien de l'ordre public, à la prévention des infractions pénales, à la protection de la santé ou de la morale, ou à la protection des droits et libertés d'autrui.

4. Les droits reconnus au paragraphe 1er peuvent également, dans certaines zones déterminées, faire l'objet de restrictions qui, prévues par la loi, sont justifiées par l'intérêt public dans une société démocratique.

Introductory comments

As Protocol No. 4 was being negotiated, a wall was erected dividing one of Europe's great cities. Freedom of movement, already prohibited by law, was being inhibited with a massive barrier of concrete, barbed wire, and lethal gunfire.[1] Three decades later, the Berlin Wall came down when a public official announced that residents of the German Democratic Republic had 'freedom of movement'. In a very general sense, there has probably never been so much freedom of movement in Europe as there is today nor has the population of the continent ever been so mobile. Europeans often travel from State to State without showing identity documents. Frequently, they establish residences in other States without any particular formalities. Technology has also made its contribution in the form of low-cost air travel and high-speed trains.

This was unheard of at the time when Protocol No. 4 to the European Convention was negotiated, even in Western Europe. In Central and Eastern Europe, of course, there were huge restrictions on both internal and external mobility until the end of the Cold War. That is not to say that there are no problems in the enforcement of the rights set out in article 2 of Protocol No. 4. Measures such as Security Council-imposed travel bans, taken in the name of counterterrorism, have introduced new restrictions on freedom of movement. According to an Issue Paper published by the Commissioner on Human Rights, 'we are seeing the development of policies which mimic Cold War obstacles to

---

[1] *Streletz, Kessler, and Krenz v. Germany* [GC], nos 34044/96, 35532/97, and 44801/98, ECHR 2001-II.

movement of people but which are being put into place at the behest of those states which had been among the greatest critics of this practice by the Communist regimes'.[2] Nevertheless, very generally the landscape has undoubtedly been transformed for the better, and it is likely to continue to change in favour of still greater freedom in this area.

Freedom of movement is enshrined in article 13 of the Universal Declaration of Human Rights:

(1) Everyone has the right to freedom of movement and residence within the borders of each state.
(2) Everyone has the right to leave any country, including his own, and to return to his country.

The right did not appear in the drafts of the European Convention. Freedom of movement is recognized in article 12 of the International Covenant on Civil and Political Rights:

1. Everyone lawfully within the territory of a State shall, within that territory, have the right to liberty of movement and freedom to choose his residence.
2. Everyone shall be free to leave any country, including his own.
3. The above-mentioned rights shall not be subject to any restrictions except those which are provided by law, are necessary to protect national security, public order (ordre public), public health or morals or the rights and freedoms of others, and are consistent with the other rights recognised in the present Covenant.
4. No one shall be arbitrarily deprived of the right to enter his own country.

The Universal Declaration of Human Rights also recognized a right of asylum. Article 14(1) states: 'Everyone has the right to seek and to enjoy in other countries asylum from persecution.' This right was never transposed into the International Covenant on Civil and Political Rights. Likewise, it is not found in the European Convention on Human Rights or its Protocols. The matter is addressed in part within the context of the 1951 Convention on the Status of Refugees[3] and its Protocol.[4] Despite the absence of a right of asylum as such, many provisions concerning the process of seeking asylum and the treatment of asylum seekers have been addressed within the framework of the European Convention on Human Rights.

Article 45 of the Charter of Fundamental Rights of the European Union affirms 'freedom of movement and residence', specifying that it is reserved to a 'citizen of the Union'.

1. Every citizen of the Union has the right to move and reside freely within the territory of the Member States.
2. Freedom of movement and residence may be granted, in accordance with the Treaty establishing the European Community, to nationals of third countries legally resident in the territory of a Member State.

But freedom of movement also exists in much of the European Union as a result of the Schengen Agreement, adopted in 1985. It virtually eliminates border controls among European States, making it as easy to move from one country to another as it is to travel from one state to another in the United States. The Schengen zone is a territory of more than four million square kilometres with some 400 million residents.

---

[2] Commissioner on Human Rights, *The Right to Leave a Country*, Strasbourg: Council of Europe, 2013, p. 11.
[3] (1951) 189 UNTS 137.
[4] Protocol Relating to the Status of Refugees, (1967) 606 UNTS 267.

Drafting of the provision

In 1958, when the Legal Committee of the Consultative Assembly began consideration of an additional protocol, the list of rights that might be included contained freedom of movement, freedom to choose one's residence, freedom to emigrate, prohibition of arbitrary exile, and the right to enter one's own country. As the Committee's Report noted, these were already included in provisions of the draft United Nations Covenant on Civil and Political Rights.[5] The relevant provision in the draft prepared by the Consultative Assembly was entitled 'Liberty of movement'. The first two paragraphs of the original draft article 2 proposed by the Consultative Assembly were modelled on the text in the draft Covenant, as the rapporteur explained. He said it had been re-worded in order to bring it into line with other provisions of the European Convention. Thus, the rights in question were defined in the first paragraph and then the permissible restrictions set out in the second.[6] There were two small differences: the word 'lawfully' in paragraph 1 was replaced by 'legally', and the word 'country' in paragraph 2 was replaced by 'State'. The third paragraph, dealing with restrictions, was similar in content but somewhat more extensive in terms of allowable criteria: 'No restrictions shall be placed on the exercise of these rights other than such as are prescribed by law and constitute a measure which in a democratic society, is necessary for national security, public safety, economic welfare of the country, the maintenance of law and order, the prevention of crime and the protection of health or morals, or rights and freedoms of others.' The Legal Committee agreed that the draft 'would not in any way restrict the right of a court to order a person to leave his place of residence while his case was *sub judice*'.[7] The Consultative Assembly dropped altogether the final paragraph 4 of the draft Covenant recognizing a right to enter one's own country.[8]

The Committee of Experts returned to the exact language of paragraph 1 of article 12 of the draft Covenant in the English version. In the French version, it replaced the word 'légalement' with 'régulièrement'. This was because 'in most States, the administrative authorities enjoy considerable discretionary powers enabling them to admit or refuse entry to foreigners and to control their stay'.[9] It rejected a proposal to replace the words 'se trouve' with 'réside' in the French version and to insert the term 'residing' between the words 'lawfully' and 'within' in the English text. The consequence of such an amendment would have been to extend the protection of paragraph 1 to someone who was not permanently resident in the State but only passing through or temporarily living there. The Committee considered 'that an alien admitted under certain conditions of entry (not

---

[5] Preliminary Report by M. Lannung, Rapporteur, AS/Jur XII (10) 1, 21 August 1958; Minutes of the meeting [of the Legal Committee, Consultative Assembly], held on 9 and 10 June 1958, AS/Jur (10) PV 2 rev., 22 September 1958; Minutes of the meeting [of the Legal Committee, Sub-Committee No. 12 (Human Rights), Consultative Assembly], held on Tuesday 16 September, 1958, AS/Jur XII (10) PV 1, 7 October 1958.

[6] Report on the Second Protocol to the Convention on Human Rights, M. Lannung, Rapporteur, Doc. 1057, 17 November 1959.

[7] Ibid.

[8] Recommendation 234 (1960), Draft for a Second Protocol to the Convention for the Protection of Human Rights and Fundamental Freedoms. See Preparatory work on the Draft Second Protocol to the Convention on Human Rights, appended to Recommendation 234 (1960) of the Consultative Assembly. IV. Article 2 of the Draft—Liberty of Movement—Memorandum by the Directorate of Human Rights, DH/Exp (60) 12 and Appendix I, II, 28 October 1960.

[9] Memorandum by the Human Rights Directorate on the proceedings of the Committee's first meeting, 7 to 11 November 1960, DX/Exp (60) 27, 10 February 1961.

necessarily conditions about residence or movement) which he transgresses or fails to comply with, can no longer be regarded as being "lawfully" in the country'. The Committee also rejected a proposal to add 'of a Contracting party' after 'territory of a State'. Such language would have been superfluous because the Convention cannot bind a third State in any case, but the Explanatory Report says it was rejected 'on the ground that in a Human Rights Convention it was preferable from a psychological point of view to use words in their widest possible sense when laying down regulations equivalent to broad general principles of law'.[10]

In paragraph 2, the Committee of Experts replaced the word 'State' with 'country', rendering the text consistent with the equivalent provisions in the Universal Declaration of Human Rights and the International Covenant on Civil and Political Rights. The Committee said that it 'meant to give the greatest possible scope to the freedom to leave a region, whether or not it is a State; the Committee considered further that, from a psychological point of view, the notion of "country" was preferable to that of "State", as having deeper emotional implications'.[11] The Committee also thought it not impossible for a Court to have to rule on the legality of emigration of a person who had left the territory of a non-party State. It said that in such a case, 'it might be asked whether the court should not decide that reference to the law of the other State was authorised only insofar as that law did not prejudice the principle of freedom to leave a country'.[12]

Several modifications were made to the Consultative Assembly draft of article 3, providing for restrictions upon the application of the article as a whole. The Consultative Assembly draft already differed somewhat from article 12(3) of the International Covenant. The Committee of Experts opted for the expression 'in accordance with law', noting the similarity with the text of article 8(2) of the Convention and explaining that this was 'better' than the expression 'prescribed by law' found in articles 9(2), 10(2), and 11(2) of the Convention. In particular, the Committee of Experts noted that this covered 'administrative action, provided it were taken in accordance with internal legislation'.[13] However, in the French version it retained the expression 'prévues par la loi' so as to avoid difficulties of interpretation that might arise if there was a departure from the standard phrase found in the Convention. The Committee of Experts changed the words 'and constitute a measure which, in a democratic society, is necessary for' to 'and are necessary in a democratic society in the interests of', making the paragraph more consistent with its counterparts in the Convention itself. Similarly, in the French version, the Committee changed 'constituent une mesure nécessaire' to 'constituent des mesures nécessaires'.

The Committee of Experts replaced the reference to 'law and order' in the English version with *ordre public*, set within inverted commas. The formulation is similar, but not identical, to article 12(3) of the International Covenant on Civil and Political Rights, which uses the term 'public order (*ordre public*)', with the French in parentheses following the English term. The Explanatory Report refers to the Committee's view that 'the notion of "*ordre public*" should be understood in the broad sense in general use in continental countries'.[14] A third change to paragraph 3 only concerned the French version. The

[10] Explanatory Report on Protocol No. 4, para. 9.
[11] Ibid., para. 10.
[12] Ibid., para. 11.
[13] Ibid., para. 13.
[14] Ibid., para. 16.

Committee of Experts preferred the expression 'prévention des infractions pénales' to 'prévention du crime'. To the suggestion that the provision also address the punishment of crime, the Committee felt this was covered by the notion of maintenance of 'ordre public'.[15]

With respect to the enumeration of legitimate purposes justifying a restriction on the rights in paragraphs 1 and 2, the Committee of Experts removed one of the grounds proposed by the Assembly, 'economic welfare of the country'.[16] There was a division of opinion in the Committee, with one position advocating the total exclusion of economic welfare of the country and the other allowing it with respect to paragraph 1 but not paragraph 2.[17] Ultimately, the first of the two approaches prevailed.[18] Subsequently, the Committee of Experts decided to reconcile the two positions by adding a fourth paragraph for which there was no ancestor in the draft of the Consultative Assembly nor any equivalent in article 12 of the International Covenant on Civil and Political Rights: 'The rights set forth in paragraph 1 may also be subject in particular areas to restrictions imposed in accordance with law and justified by the public interest in a democratic society.'[19] According to the Explanatory Report: 'The term "area", as used in this article, does not refer to any definite geographical or administrative unit. The meaning of this provision is that the restrictions in question must be localised within a well-defined area.'[20]

The heading 'Freedom of movement' was added in accordance with Protocol No. 11.[21]

Analysis and interpretation

Article 2 of Protocol No. 4 is intended to secure to any person the right to liberty of movement within a territory and the right to leave that territory. Thus, the Court has explained, 'freedom of movement prohibits any measure liable to infringe that right or to restrict the exercise thereof which is not "in accordance with the law" and does not satisfy the requirement of a measure which can be considered "necessary in a democratic society" in the pursuit of the legitimate aims' set out in paragraphs 3 and 4.[22]

Article 2 of Protocol No. 4 is related to article 5(1) of the Convention to the extent that it concerns restrictions on the freedom movement of individuals. However, article 5(1) is not concerned with 'mere restrictions on liberty of movement'.[23] The distinction between

---

[15] Ibid., para. 17.

[16] Memorandum by the Human Rights Directorate on the Committee's second meeting, 24 to 29 April 1961, DH/Exp (61) 15, 7 August 1961, para. 28.

[17] Memorandum of the Human Rights Directorate on the Committee's third meeting, 2 to 11 October 1961, DH/Exp (61) 35 Final, 17 October 1961, para. 18; Explanatory Report on Protocol No. 4, para. 15.

[18] Text adopted by the majority in April 1961, DH/Exp (61) 33, 7 October 1961; Memorandum of the Human Rights Directorate on the Committee's third meeting, 2 to 11 October 1961, DH/Exp (61) 35 Final, 17 October 1961, paras 10–12.

[19] Memorandum of the Human Rights Directorate on the Committee's third meeting, 2 to 11 October 1961, DH/Exp (61) 35 Final, 17 October 1961, para. 19; Memorandum of the Human Rights Directorate on the Committee's fourth meeting, 2 to 10 March 1962, DH/Exp/Misc (62) 11, 9 March 1962, para. 19.

[20] Explanatory Report on Protocol No. 4, para. 18.

[21] Protocol No. 11 to the Convention for the Protection of Human Rights and Fundamental Freedoms, restructuring the control machinery established thereby, ETS 155, art. 2(5)(a).

[22] *Diamante and Pelliccioni v. San Marino*, no. 32250/08, § 210, 27 September 2011; *Baumann v. France*, no. 33592/96, § 61, ECHR 2001-V (extracts).

[23] *Engel and Others v. the Netherlands*, 8 June 1976, § 38, Series A no. 22; *Guzzardi v. Italy*, 6 November 1980, § 92, Series A no. 39; *Ashingdane v. the United Kingdom*, 28 May 1985, § 41, Series A no. 93; *Nada v.*

deprivation of liberty, falling under article 5(1) of the Convention, and restriction on freedom of movement, coming within the ambit of article 2 of Protocol No. 4, is 'nonetheless merely one of degree or intensity, and not one of nature or substance'.[24] Admittedly, 'the process of classification into one or other of these categories sometimes proves to be no easy task in that some borderline cases are a matter of pure opinion'.[25] Several factors must be considered, such as the type, duration, effects, and manner of implementation of the measure in question.[26]

Lawfully within the territory (art. 2(1))

The words 'lawfully within the territory' impose a condition for the application of the rights set out in article 2(1). Article 2(1) adds that the right to liberty of movement and freedom to choose the residence of a person 'lawfully within the territory' is only applicable 'within that territory'. This second criterion seems to be largely redundant. It is difficult to see in practice how it could be invoked and, in reality, it does not seem to have been addressed in any case law of the Convention organs. These restrictions on the rights set out in article 2(1) clearly apply to non-citizens, as they may be 'lawfully within the territory' even if they do not possess its citizenship.

In applying article 2, regard must be had to article 5(4) of the Protocol: 'The territory of any State to which this Protocol applies by virtue of ratification or acceptance by that State, and each territory to which this Protocol is applied by virtue of a declaration by that State under this Article, shall be treated as separate territories for the purpose of the references in Articles 2 and 3 to the territory of a State.'

The expression is subject to strict construction. In an application filed against Russia, a stateless person who was formerly a citizen of the Soviet Union was denied a residence permit. Before the Court, Russia argued that she could not avail of article 2(1) of Protocol No. 4 because she was not 'lawfully within the territory'. The Court found that there was no factual basis for Russia's objection.[27]

Article 7(1) of Protocol No. 7 applies to persons who are 'lawfully resident' on the territory of a State Party. The concept is similar to 'lawfully on the territory' but it is obviously somewhat narrower. A traveller in transit may be 'lawfully on the territory' of a State without being 'lawfully resident'. The case law under article 7(1) of Protocol No. 7 is obviously relevant to the interpretation of article 2 of Protocol No. 4. Cases falling within the scope of article 7(1) of Protocol No. 7 are subsumed within article 2 of Protocol No. 4.

Freedom of movement (art. 2(1))

Paragraph 1 of article 2 of Protocol No. 4 recognizes the right to 'liberty of movement' to '[e]veryone lawfully within the territory of a State . . . within that territory'. The expression 'liberty of movement' is rephrased as 'freedom of movement' in the title of the provision that was added by Protocol No. 11. Restrictions on internal travel within European States

---

Switzerland [GC], no. 10593/08, § 225, ECHR 2012; *Villa v. Italy*, no. 19675/06, § 41, 20 April 2010; *E.M.B. v. Romania*, no. 4488/03, § 31, 13 November 2012.

[24] *Villa v. Italy*, no. 19675/06, § 41, 20 April 2010.
[25] *Guzzardi v. Italy*, 6 November 1980, § 93, Series A no. 39.
[26] *Engel and Others v. the Netherlands*, 8 June 1976, §§ 38–39, Series A no. 22.
[27] *Tatishvili v. Russia*, no. 1509/02, § 43, ECHR 2007-I.

are generally confined to a criminal law context, where they are imposed as a condition for interim release or, more unusually, as a form of sanction. According to the Convention organs, any 'measure by means of which an individual is dispossessed of an identity document such as, for example, a passport, undoubtedly amounts to an interference with the exercise of liberty of movement'.[28]

The Grand Chamber has applied article 2 of Protocol No. 4 only once, and it did not provide any significant interpretative guidance on the provision in that case.[29] The applicant had been acquitted of criminal charges related to organized crime, but measures of supervision were imposed upon him nevertheless. These restricted his freedom of movement within the country. Amongst other things, he was required to reside in a specific town, could not leave his home without informing the authorities, he had to be at home at certain hours, and he had to report to the police regularly. The State justified this on the basis of family ties with known Mafia members, but the Grand Chamber said it could not see how 'the mere fact that the applicant's wife was the sister of a Mafia boss, since deceased, could justify such severe measures being taken against him in the absence of any other concrete evidence to show that there was a real risk that he would offend'. It said such restrictions on freedom of movement could not have been regarded as having been 'necessary in a democratic society' and concluded that there was a violation of article 2 of Protocol No. 4.[30]

It is common in criminal proceedings for interim release or bail to include a requirement not to change residence. In principle, this amounts to an interference with the right to freedom of movement.[31] Because of the nature of criminal proceedings, such a condition for interim release will generally meet the proportionality test. As the Court has explained, in criminal proceedings an obligation not to leave an area of residence is a proportionate restriction on an accused's liberty.[32] Of course, the duration of the proceedings must be taken into account in assessing the proportionality of such measures, but the Court has found no violation of the Convention where such a restriction lasted for more than five years.[33] In another case, restrictions on movement that lasted between four and five years were not held to be contrary to article 2 of Protocol No. 2.[34]

However, where an accused was being investigated for obstructing police at an unauthorized demonstration, restrictions on freedom of movement imposed with respect to criminal proceedings that lasted more than three years were found to be incompatible

---

[28] *Baumann v. France*, no. 33592/96, § 62, ECHR 2001-V. Also *Nalbantski v. Bulgaria*, no. 30943/04, § 61, 10 February 2011; *M. v. Federal Republic of Germany*, no. 10307/83, Commission decision of 6 March 1984, (1984) 27 YB 161, DR 37, p. 113; *Peltonen v. Finland*, no. 19583/92, Commission decision of 20 February 1995, DR 80-A, p. 38; *Napijalo v. Croatia*, no. 66485/01, § 69, 13 November 2003; *Ignatov v. Russia*, no. 27193/02, § 33, 24 May 2007; *Soltysyak v. Russia*, no. 4663/05, § 37, 10 February 2011; *Bartik v. Russia*, no. 55565/00, § 36, ECHR 2006-XV; *Timishev v. Russia* (dec.), nos 55762/00 and 55974/00, 30 March 2004.

[29] *Labita v. Italy* [GC], no. 26772/95, §§ 196–197, ECHR 2000-IV. In *Assanidze v. Georgia* [GC], no. 71503/01, § 194, ECHR 2004-II, it found it unnecessary to pronounce itself on an alleged violation of article 2 of Protocol No. 4. In *Nada v. Switzerland* [GC], no. 10593/08, ECHR 2012, it did not apply Protocol No. 4, which had not been ratified by Switzerland: see § 225.

[30] *Labita v. Italy* [GC], no. 26772/95, §§ 196–197, ECHR 2000–IV.

[31] *Antonenkov and Others v. Ukraine*, no. 14183/02, § 52, 22 November 2005; *Raimondo v. Italy*, 22 February 1994, § 39, Series A no. 281-A; *Hannak v. Austria*, no. 17208/90, Commission decision of 13 October 1993; *Hajibeyli v. Azerbaijan*, no. 16528/05, § 58, 10 July 2008.

[32] *Antonenkov and Others v. Ukraine*, no. 14183/02, § 61, 22 November 2005.

[33] Ibid., § 64.

[34] *Fedorov and Fedorova v. Russia*, no. 31008/02, §§ 32–47, 13 October 2005.

with article 2 of Protocol No. 2. The Court considered that the process was 'unreasonably lengthy while the case did not appear to be particularly complex' and found it 'difficult to see, in the circumstances of the present case, any plausible justification for the continued restriction of the applicant's freedom of movement, especially without any review of the necessity for it either when the investigation was suspended or when the applicant specifically complained of the restriction'.[35] In another case of restriction on movement lasting more than ten years respecting a 'medium grave offence', the Court said 'its mere duration could be sufficient to conclude that it was disproportionate'.[36]

The Court has held that the requirement to report to the police a change of residence or a visit to family friends constitutes an interference with freedom of movement.[37] Even the refusal of domestic authorities to certify or register residency has been deemed an interference.[38] The existence of a mechanism by which permission can be granted for exceptions to such prohibitions is no answer to the charge that there is an infringement of freedom of movement.[39]

In a case involving an order not to frequent certain areas in Amsterdam known for high levels of criminality, the government conceded that there was an infringement of freedom of movement. But the Court accepted its justification and considered the infringement to meet the proportionality test: the applicant had defied earlier prohibition orders, returning to the area to use hard drugs in public, and had been warned of a longer ban if he did not comply.[40]

In a Russian case, the Court agreed that article 2 was engaged when traffic police at a checkpoint in the North Caucasus region prevented a person from crossing the administrative border between two regions of the country, Ingushetia and Kabardino-Balkaria.[41] The Court did not rule 'on the general question whether the political and social situation in Ingushetia or Kabardino-Balkaria at the material time called for the introduction of checkpoints on a federal motorway and thorough identity checks', because the order establishing the checkpoint had not been properly formulated. Consequently, the restriction on freedom of movement was not 'in accordance with the law'.[42]

Where a person would not return to her home country because there was an outstanding warrant, alleging 'she needs to hide and cannot leave the country hosting her for fear of being arrested', the Court noted that this was a 'personal choice of the applicant not to make use of her right to freedom of movement in order to avoid confronting the justice system'.[43]

The Court declared manifestly unfounded an application by a Sikh who objected to removing his turban as part of the security control at a French airport, explaining that 'les contrôles de sécurité auxquels les passagers sont astreints dans les aéroports avant d'embarquer ne sont pas constitutifs de restrictions à la liberté de circulation'.[44]

---

[35] *Hajibeyli v. Azerbaijan*, no. 16528/05, § 66, 10 July 2008.

[36] *Ivanov v. Ukraine*, no. 15007/02, § 96, 7 December 2006.

[37] *Denizci and Others v. Cyprus*, nos 25316-25321/94 and 27207/95, §§ 346–347 and 403–404, ECHR 2001-V; *Bolat v. Russia*, no. 14139/03, § 65, ECHR 2006-XI (extracts).

[38] *Tatishvili v. Russia*, no. 1509/02, §§ 45–46, ECHR 2007-I.

[39] *Ivanov v. Ukraine*, no. 15007/02, § 85, 7 December 2006. Also *Rosengren v. Romania*, no. 70786/01, §§ 38–41, 24 April 2008.

[40] *Olivieira v. the Netherlands*, no. 33129/96, § 65, ECHR 2002-IV.

[41] *Timishev v. Russia*, nos 55762/00 and 55974/00, § 44, ECHR 2005-XII.

[42] Ibid., §§ 47–49.

[43] *E.M.B. v. Romania* (dec.), no. 4488/03, §§ 32–33, 28 September 2010.

[44] *Phull v. France* (dec.), no. 35753/03, 11 January 2005.

Freedom to choose residence (art. 2(1))

Freedom to choose one's residence is presented in article 2(1) as a right distinct from 'liberty of movement'. The term 'residence' has not been interpreted in the case law. Obviously, it is related to the notion of 'home' that appears in article 8(1) of the Convention.

In several Italian cases, the Court has addressed judicial orders not to leave one's place of residence. The *Luordo* case involved bankruptcy proceedings, and the Court concluded that the restriction was disproportionate because of the duration of the proceedings, of fourteen years and eight months. In that case, there had been no indication of the desire of the applicant to leave the place of residence or of a refusal of permission to do so.[45]

A Russian case involved a refusal to allow an individual to establish a residence in a 'closed administrative and territorial entity', so designated because of the presence of industrial enterprises specializing in development, production, storage, and disposal of weapons of mass destruction, the processing of radioactive materials, and military facilities. That this was an infringement upon freedom to choose one's residence had even been confirmed by the Russian courts.[46]

Freedom to leave a country (art. 2(2))

'Everyone shall be free to leave any country, including his own', states article 2(2) of Protocol No. 4. The right to leave one's country is set out in several international instruments, including the Universal Declaration of Human Rights and the International Covenant on Civil and Political Rights, both of them cited in the introduction to this chapter, but also the International Convention on the Elimination of All Forms of Racial Discrimination[47] and the Convention on the Rights of the Child.[48] The International Convention on the Protection of the Rights of All Migrant Workers and Members of Their Families affirms that '[m]igrant workers and members of their families shall be free to leave any State, including their State of origin'.[49]

The right applies to 'everyone'. It applies even to a minor, despite the fact that the minor's right to leave the country may depend upon consent from persons exercising parental authority.[50] Article 2(2) does not refer to the country of nationality, but rather to 'his own' country. Clearly, the use of the word 'including' before 'his own' confirms the application of the right to leave with respect to non-citizens. Thus, 'his own' is an inclusive expression that merely adds to the breadth of the provision. Difficulties might arise if the Convention also included a right to return, along the lines of the International Covenant on Civil and Political Rights. But there is no right of return in the European Convention, be it for non-citizens who have made the country their own or for citizens. In article 3 of Protocol No. 4, the expulsion of 'nationals' is prohibited, a norm that is related to but not identical with a right of return.

---

[45] *Luordo v. Italy*, no. 32190/96, § 96, ECHR 2003-IX. Also *Forte v. Italy*, no. 77986/01, §§ 30–32, 10 November 2005.

[46] *Karpacheva and Karpachev v. Russia*, no. 34861/04, §§ 25–27, 27 January 2011.

[47] International Convention on the Elimination of All Forms of Racial Discrimination, (1966) 660 UNTS 195, art. 5(2).

[48] Convention on the Rights of the Child, (1990) 1577 UNTS 3, art. 37(c), art. 10(2).

[49] (1990) 1577 UNTS 3.

[50] *Diamante and Pelliccioni v. San Marino*, no. 32250/08, § 204, 27 September 2011. See also *Pini and Others v. Romania*, nos 78028/01 and 78030/01, §§ 190–198, ECHR 2004-V (extracts).

In one decision, the Court spoke of 'a fundamental right, namely the applicant's freedom to come and go as he pleased'.[51] An obligation to obtain authorization for each departure from a country 'does not correspond to the sense of the concept "freedom of movement"'.[52] Indeed, the right to leave is really a specialized aspect of freedom of movement set out in article 2(1). Arguably, even if the Protocol did not provide explicitly for freedom to leave a country, it would almost certainly be considered to be implied by the liberty of movement set out in article 2(1). In the case of a French citizen convicted of a crime who was temporarily prevented from leaving the country after serving his sentence, the Court said there was a breach of article 2, without specifying the relevant paragraph. It held that the restriction on freedom of movement was disproportionate, 'particularly given that [the applicant] was forced to stay for all that period in a foreign country and was not allowed to leave even for a short period of time'.[53]

The general considerations and approaches taken in the interpretation of article 2(1), and in particular the criteria considered when applying the restrictions authorized by article 2(3), are broadly similar when article 2(2) is applicable. The State must ensure 'that a restriction of an individual's right to leave his or her country is, from the outset and throughout its duration, justified and proportionate'.[54] For example, the Court has considered restrictions on foreign travel to be justified by the need to prevent convicted offenders from re-engaging in criminal conduct, and has allowed measures restricting movement on individuals suspected of being members of the Mafia even in the absence of a criminal conviction.[55]

Problems in the implementation of this right generally arise as a result of some form of administrative or judicial order denying a person the right to leave the country, or simply by the refusal to issue the appropriate travel documents necessary for foreign travel. The right may be infringed by a formal travel ban as well as indirectly, by the seizure of a passport.[56] The international dimension may also arise when the right bearer has important ties with another country. In a Polish case, the Court noted that the applicant was a French national, with family, friends, and business, as well as a right to medical care, located in France. 'Such a situation cannot be compared to a restriction on an applicant's freedom of movement imposed on him or her in his or her own country', noted the Court.[57]

Freedom to leave a country has been addressed in cases concerning criminal sanctions,[58] pending criminal proceedings,[59] bankruptcy,[60] taxation claims,[61] judgment

---

[51] *Raimondo v. Italy*, 22 February 1994, § 39, Series A no. 281-A.

[52] *Diamante and Pelliccioni v. San Marino*, no. 32250/08, § 211, 27 September 2011; *Ivanov v. Ukraine*, no. 15007/02, § 85, 7 December 2006.

[53] *Miażdżyk v. Poland*, no. 23592/07, § 41, 24 January 2012.

[54] *Nalbantski v. Bulgaria*, no. 30943/04, § 64, 10 February 2011.

[55] *Raimondo v. Italy*, 22 February 1994, § 39, Series A no. 281-A; *Labita v. Italy* [GC], no. 26772/95, § 195, ECHR 2000-IV.

[56] *Baumann v. France*, no. 33592/96, §§ 62–63, ECHR 2001-V; *Napijalo v. Croatia*, no. 66485/01, §§ 69–73, 13 November 2003; *Nalbantski v. Bulgaria*, no. 30943/04, § 61, 10 February 2011; *Stamose v. Bulgaria*, no. 29713/05, § 30, ECHR 2012.

[57] *Miażdżyk v. Poland*, no. 23592/07, § 39, 24 January 2012.

[58] *M. v. Federal Republic of Germany*, no. 10307/83, Commission decision of 6 March 1984, DR 37, p. 113.

[59] *Miażdżyk v. Poland*, no. 23592/07, 24 January 2012; *Prescher v. Bulgaria*, no. 6767/04, 7 June 2011; *A.E. v. Poland*, no. 14480/04, 31 March 2009; *Bessenyei v. Hungary*, no. 37509/06, 21 October 2008; *Földes and Földesné Hajlik v. Hungary*, no. 41463/02, ECHR 2006-XII; *Baumann v. France*, no. 33592/96, ECHR 2001-V (extracts); *Schmidt v. Austria*, no. 10670/83, Commission decision of 9 July 1985, DR 44, p. 195.

[60] *Luordo v. Italy*, no. 32190/96, ECHR 2003-IX.

[61] *Napijalo v. Croatia*, no. 66485/01, 13 November 2003; *Riener v. Bulgaria*, no. 46343/99, 23 May 2006.

debts,[62] knowledge of State secrets,[63] military service,[64] lack of rehabilitation in respect of criminal offences,[65] mental illness combined with a lack of appropriate care in the destination country,[66] and child custody disputes.[67] Recently, Bulgaria prevented one of its nationals from leaving the country in order to prevent him violating the immigration laws of the United States![68]

Russia is the only State Party to the Convention to have retained restrictions on international travel for private purposes on the grounds that the individual has been privy to 'State secrets'. Countries in Central and Eastern Europe generally abolished such limitations as part of their transition to democratic governance.[69] As a condition for joining the Council of Europe in 1996, Russia pledged to eliminate such restrictions, but it has not done so. Such restrictions were imposed at a time when the State had the power to control means of communication with the outside world by means of restrictions on correspondence and prohibition of unsupervised contacts with foreigners within the country. But with all of this having disappeared in modern times, 'the necessity of restriction on international travel for private purposes by persons aware of "State secrets" became less obvious. In these circumstances, in so far as the ban on international travel for private reasons purported to prevent the applicant from communicating information to foreign nationals, in a contemporary democratic society such a restriction fails to achieve the protective function previously assigned to it.'[70] Finding a violation of article 2(2) of Protocol No. 4, the Court said: 'Having regard to the established common European and international standard, the Court considers that the Russian Government were under an obligation to provide a particularly compelling justification for maintaining the restriction in question.'[71]

Restrictions (art. 2(3) and art. 2(4))

Article 2(3) authorizes 'restrictions' (in French, *ingérence*) with the rights set out in paragraphs 1 and 2. The paragraph is similar to, although not identical with, corresponding second paragraphs in articles 9, 10, and 11 of the Convention. In contrast with the four Convention provisions with restriction clauses, article 2(4) of Protocol No. 4 imposes an additional restriction, but only with regard to paragraph 1: 'The rights set forth in paragraph 1 may also be subject, in particular areas, to restrictions imposed in accordance with law and justified by the public interests in a democratic society.' This provision, which was quite unique, was added by the drafters in order to resolve a difficulty in the formulation of article 2(3). It has been without practical application and does not appear to have ever been invoked, applied, or interpreted by the Convention organs.

---

[62] *Khlyustov v. Russia*, no. 28975/05, 11 July 2013; *Ignatov v. Bulgaria*, no. 50/02, 2 July 2009; *Gochev v. Bulgaria*, no. 34383/03, 26 November 2009.

[63] *Bartik v. Russia*, no. 55565/00, ECHR 2006-XV.

[64] *Peltonen v. Finland*, no. 19583/92, Commission decision of 20 February 1995, DR 80-A, p. 38; *Marangos v. Cyprus*, no. 31106/96, Commission decision of 20 May 1997.

[65] *Nalbantski v. Bulgaria*, no. 30943/04, 10 February 2011.

[66] *Nordblad v. Sweden*, no. 19076/91, Commission decision of 13 October 1993.

[67] *Roldan Texeira and Others v. Italy* (dec.), no. 40655/98, 26 October 2000; *Diamante and Pelliccioni c. San Marino*, no. 27 September 2011.

[68] *Stamose v. Bulgaria*, no. 29713/05, ECHR 2012.

[69] *Soltysyak v. Russia*, no. 4663/05, § 51, 10 February 2011.

[70] *Bartik v. Russia*, no. 55565/00, § 49, ECHR 2006-XV.

[71] *Soltysyak v. Russia*, no. 4663/05, § 51, 10 February 2011.

In accordance with the law

An interference with the rights set out in paragraphs 1 and 2 of article 2 must be, in the words of article 2(3), 'in accordance with the law'. The drafters of Protocol No. 4 made a deliberate choice favouring 'in accordance with the law', which is the term used in article 8(2) of the Convention, rather than 'prescribed by law', which is used in articles 9(2), 10(2), and 11(2). It was deemed the 'better' formulation in that it allowed for administrative action, provided this was taken in accordance with internal legislation.[72]

The requirement that a restriction or limitation be prescribed by or in accordance with law has both a formal or technical sense and a substantive one. The interference must, of course, be authorized by a rule recognized in the national legal order. This includes 'written law', including various forms of delegated legislation, and unwritten law as interpreted and applied by the courts.[73] But there is also a qualitative requirement for the legal rule. It must be accessible and foreseeable.

Legitimate purpose

The issue of the legitimate aim or purpose of an interference is rarely very significant. Article 2(3) permits interference with freedom of movement 'in the interests of national security or public safety, for the maintenance of ordre public, for the prevention of crime, for the protection of health or morals, or for the protection of the rights and freedoms of others'. The Grand Chamber has explained that it is the Court's practice 'to be quite succinct when it verifies the existence of a legitimate aim'.[74] The list is large enough to cover most government activity, whether it is oppressive or benign. The Court has tended to a rather broad and liberal application of the terms, often finding that more than one of the purposes applies to a specific form of interference.

A measure restricting a convicted and not yet rehabilitated offender from travelling abroad was said to pursue the legitimate aims of maintenance of public order and prevention of crime.[75] Travel bans imposed to secure payment of private judgment debts were deemed to pursue the protection of the rights of others.[76] Refusal of authorization for children to leave a country out of concerns about abduction have as a purpose the maintenance of 'ordre public' as well as the protection of the rights of others.[77]

Necessary in a democratic society

Most decisions concerning the paragraph 3 of article 4 involve the third component of the analysis, namely whether the impugned measure is 'necessary in a democratic society'. The objective is to consider whether the authorities have struck 'a fair balance between the competing interests of the individual and of society as a whole'.[78] It is the most subjective part of the application of paragraph 3, involving subtle distinctions about the proportionality of measures taken by the State that limit or restrict human rights. There is an

---

[72] Explanatory Report on Protocol No. 4, para. 13.

[73] *Leyla Şahin v. Turkey* [GC], no. 44774/98, § 88, ECHR 2005-XI; *Sanoma Uitgevers B.V. v. the Netherlands* [GC], no. 38224/03, § 83, 14 September 2010.

[74] *S.A.S. v. France* [GC], no. 43835/11, § 114, 1 July 2014.

[75] *Nalbantski v. Bulgaria*, no. 30943/04, § 61, 10 February 2011.

[76] *Khlyustov v. Russia*, no. 28975/05, § 80, 11 July 2013; *Ignatov v. Bulgaria*, no. 50/02, § 35, 2 July 2009; *Gochev v. Bulgaria*, no. 34383/03, § 48, 26 November 2009.

[77] *Diamante and Pelliccioni v. San Marino*, no. 32250/08, § 213, 27 September 2011.

[78] *Keegan v. Ireland*, 26 May 1994, § 49, Series A no. 290.

important relationship between 'necessity' and 'democratic society', of which the hall-marks are pluralism, tolerance, and broadmindedness.[79]

The Court frequently begins its consideration of this element by questioning whether the interference responds to a 'pressing social need'. The term seems to be not much more than a gloss on the word 'necessity'. It employs two other notions in this context, insisting that the measure in question be 'relevant and sufficient'. The interference must also respond to an assessment of its proportionality, something that necessitates balancing the right of the individual against the interest of the State and the society that it represents. Where the Court is considering the positive dimension of the right in question, in other words, the obligation upon the State to take measures to ensure enforcement of the right, it must usually consider the rights of others in the balance as well. If other less severe measures could have fulfilled the same objective, there will be a problem with proportionality.

There must be a clear and foreseeable legal procedure for the imposition restrictions on freedom of movement such as foreign travel bans, failing which the Court will find a violation without considering the proportionality of the measure.[80] An 'automatic approach' to a travel ban, imposed without explanation or an examination of the personal circumstances of the individuals concerned, the result of a discretionary decision by the police not subject to any substantive judicial review, was not acceptable.[81]

Measures restricting freedom of movement may become unjustifiable with the passage of time For example, with regard to the proportionality of a restriction imposed on leaving a country on account of unpaid debts, the Court has held that 'even were it justified at the outset, a measure restricting an individual's freedom of movement may become disproportionate and breach that individual's rights if it is automatically extended over a long period'[82] Where the ban is related to ongoing criminal investigations or proceedings that do not proceed with reasonable diligence, the 'fair balance' between the right and the public interest will be upset.[83] A delay of six months in examining a request for permission to leave the country was deemed unacceptable.[84]

A two-year travel ban was imposed by Bulgaria upon one of its nationals who had been deported from the United States. Bulgaria explained that the measure was necessary in order to prevent Bulgarian citizens from breaching the immigration laws of other countries. The legislation had been adopted largely to assuage the concerns of European Union members and in a more general context of illegal immigration by Bulgarian nationals. The Court said that such a travel ban, imposed in 'such a blanket and indiscriminate measure', could not be considered proportionate and therefore was not

[79] *Smith and Grady v. the United Kingdom*, nos 33985/96 and 33986/96, § 87, ECHR 1999-VI; *Vereinigung demokratischer Soldaten Österreichs and Gubi v. Austria*, 19 December 1994, § 36, Series A no. 302; *Dudgeon v. the United Kingdom*, 22 October 1981, § 53, Series A no. 45.

[80] *Dzhaksybergenov v. Ukraine*, no. 12343/10, §§ 60–61, 10 February 2011.

[81] *Sarkizov and Others v. Bulgaria*, nos 37981/06, 38022/06, 39122/06, and 44278/06, § 67, 17 April 2012.

[82] *Gochev v. Bulgaria*, no. 34383/03, § 49, 26 November 2009; *Diamante and Pelliccioni v. San Marino*, no. 32250/08, § 214, 27 September 2011; *Makedonski v. Bulgaria*, no. 36036/04, § 45, 20 January 2011; *Luordo v. Italy*, no. 32190/96, § 96, ECHR 2003-IX; *Földes and Földesné Hajlik v. Hungary*, no. 41463/02, § 35, ECHR 2006-XII; *Riener v. Bulgaria*, no. 46343/99, § 121, 23 May 2006; *Bessenyei v. Hungary*, no. 37509/06, §§ 21–24, 21 October 2008.

[83] *Makedonski v. Bulgaria*, no. 36036/04, § 42, 20 January 2011.

[84] Ibid.

'necessary in a democratic society'.[85] It said that the normal consequences of a breach of immigration laws would be removal from the country in question and a prohibition on re-entry. It said that '[i]t appears quite draconian for the Bulgarian State—which could not be regarded as directly affected by the applicant's infringement—to have also prevented him from travelling to any other foreign country for a period of two years'.[86] The Court concluded that 'the automatic imposition of such a measure without any regard to the individual circumstances of the person concerned [could] be characterised as necessary in a democratic society'.[87]

Discrimination

As a consequence of article 6 of Protocol No. 4, article 14 of the Convention is applicable to freedom of movement as set out in article 2 of Protocol No. 4. Article 14 of the Convention does not have an independent existence. It can only be invoked with respect to a right protected elsewhere in the Convention or the Protocols. There appears to be only one case that has dealt with the application of article 14 in the context of article 2 of Protocol No. 4.

A senior police officer in the Russian republic of Kabardino-Balkar gave instructions to traffic police officers not to admit 'Chechens'. Given that ethnic origin is not listed on Russian identity documents, the order affected individuals who were perceived as belonging to the Chechen ethnic group as well as those who were genuine ethnic Chechens. There was no evidence that other ethnic groups were subjected to similar prohibitions. The Court said this represented a clear inequality of treatment in the enjoyment of the right to liberty of movement on account of one's ethnic origin.[88] No justification for such differential treatment was offered by Russia. The Court said that in any event 'no difference in treatment which is based exclusively or to a decisive extent on a person's ethnic origin is capable of being objectively justified in a contemporary democratic society built on the principles of pluralism and respect for different cultures'.[89]

Reservations and declarations

Reservations to Protocol No. 4 are governed by the principles of article 57 of the Convention. Monaco made a declaration that amounts to a reservation in its instrument of ratification, deposited on 30 November 2005. The reservation concerns conditions of entry and stay of foreigners in Monaco. It protects the right of the State Minister to, 'by measure of police or by issuing an expulsion warrant, enjoin any foreigner to leave immediately the Monegasque territory or to forbid him/her to enter it'.[90]

On 28 September 2010, the Netherlands made the following declaration:

In reference to the declaration made by the Kingdom of the Netherlands on ratifying Protocol No. 4 to the Convention for the Protection of Human Rights and Fundamental Freedoms on 23 June 1982, the Kingdom of the Netherlands wishes to make the following declaration:

---

[85] *Stamose v. Bulgaria*, no. 29713/05, § 34, ECHR 2012.
[86] Ibid.
[87] Ibid., § 36.
[88] *Timishev v. Russia*, nos 55762/00 and 55974/00, § 54, ECHR 2005-XII.
[89] Ibid., § 58.
[90] (2005) 48 YB 12.

The Kingdom of the Netherlands, consisting as per 10 October 2010 of the European part of the Netherlands, the Caribbean part of the Netherlands (the islands of Bonaire, Sint Eustatius and Saba), Aruba, Curaçao and Sint Maarten, regards these parts as separate territories for the applications of Articles 2 and 3 of the Protocol.[91]

Further reading

Frowein/Peukert, *MenschenRechtsKonvention,* pp. 691–5.

Grabenwarter, *European Convention,* pp. 411–17.

Harris et al., *Law of the European Convention,* pp. 736–42.

Nuria Arenas Hidalgo, 'Liberty of Movement within the Territory of a State (Article 2 of Additional Protocol No. 4 ECHR)', in Javier García Roca and Pablo Santolaya, eds, *Europe of Rights: A Compendium on the European Convention of Human Rights,* Leiden/Boston: Martinus Nijhoff, 2012, pp. 607–24.

Jacques Mourgeon, 'Protocole No 4, Article 2', in Pettiti et al., *La Convention européenne,* p. 1043–51.

Ovey/White, *Jacobs and White, European Convention,* pp. 339–46.

Ben Vermeulen, 'The Right to Liberty of Movement (Article 2 of Protocol No. 4)', in Van Dijk et al., *Theory and Practice,* pp. 939–45.

---

[91] (2010) 53 YB 27–28.

Article 3. Prohibition of expulsion of nationals/Interdiction de l'expulsion des nationaux

1. No one shall be expelled, by means either of an individual or of a collective measure, from the territory of the State of which he is a national.

2. No one shall be deprived of the right to enter the territory of the State of which he is a national.

1. Nul ne peut être expulsé, par voie de mesure individuelle ou collective, du territoire de l'État dont il est le ressortissant.

2. Nul ne peut être privé du droit d'entrer sur le territoire de l'État dont il est le ressortissant.

Introductory comments

European history during the first half of the twentieth century testifies to a widespread phenomenon of expulsion of nationals described at the time with the euphemism 'population transfers'.[1] Today, 'ethnic cleansing' would be the more suitable term. These so-called population transfers were often given the blessing of international law, sometimes in bilateral agreements, but also multilateral treaties associated with peace processes. For example, populations were 'exchanged' in 1923 by Greece and Turkey in accordance with the Convention Concerning the Exchange of Greek and Turkish Populations.[2] Article XII of the Potsdam Protocol, adopted by the victorious Allies in July 1945, provides for the transfer of German populations from Poland, Czechoslovakia, and Hungary, adding the condition that it take place 'in an orderly and humane manner'.[3] A few years later, when the United Nations General Assembly was preparing the Genocide Convention, an American delegate urged that care be taken in drafting the definition of the crime out of concern that it 'might be extended to embrace forced transfers of minority groups such as have already been carried out by members of the United Nations'.[4]

---

[1] See the recent statement by the Parliamentary Assembly: Resolution 1863 (2012), Enforced population transfer as a human rights violation.

[2] (1923) 32 LNTS 76. See also *Exchange of Greek and Turkish Populations*, Series B, No. 10.

[3] A. De Zayas, 'International Law and Mass Population Transfers', (1975) 16 *Harvard International Law Journal* 207; Freiherr Von Braun, 'Germany's Eastern Border and Mass Expulsions', (1964) 58 *AJIL* 747.

[4] Comments by Governments on the Draft Convention prepared by the Secretariat, Communications from non-Governmental Organisations, UN Doc. E/623. The United States cited specifically paragraph 3(b), '[d]estroying the specific characteristics of the group by: (b) Forced and systematic exile of individuals representing the culture of a group . . .' The fears of the United States were not totally misplaced. One academic writer has said that 'the expulsion of Germans and of persons of German descent living in the former eastern provinces of Germany and in eastern and south-eastern European countries frequently took place under conditions that are classifiable as genocide': Hans-Heinrich Jescheck, 'Genocide', in Rudolph Bernhardt, ed., *Encyclopedia of Public International Law*, Vol. II, Amsterdam: North-Holland Elsevier, 1995, pp. 541–4, p. 541. During United States Senate consideration of the Genocide Convention in 1950, James Finucane of the National Council for the Prevention of War testified about the United States' 'genocidal intent, or genocidal carelessness, at Potsdam': United States of America, *Hearings Before a Subcommittee of the Committee on Foreign Relations, United States Senate, Jan. 23, 24, 25, and Feb. 9, 1950*, Washington: United States Government Printing Office, 1950, p. 312.

The legality of population transfer treaties was considered by the prestigious Institut de Droit International at its 1952 session. Rapporteur Giorgio Balladore Pallieri listed twenty 'population transfer' treaties between 1913 and 1945, admitting that 'il n'y a jamais de transfert vraiment volontaire des populations'.[5] Pallieri concluded that there was nothing in international law to challenge the legitimacy of population transfers and that they were even, in certain circumstances, desirable. They were the consequences of the legitimate desire of all modern States to have loyal citizens, he said.[6] Pallieri's analysis was well received by most of the members of the Institute, including Max Huber, Jean Spiropoulos, and Fernand de Visscher, with the notable exception of Georges Scelle, who said it was incompatible with the emerging law of human rights.

The great contribution of article 3 of Protocol No. 4 is to confirm Scelle's observation and to codify it. The Explanatory Report leaves no doubt that Europe's sad history in this respect was in the minds of the drafters.[7] Protocol No. 4 distinguishes between the expulsion of non-nationals (or 'aliens'), a matter addressed in article 4, and the expulsion of nationals, which is governed by article 3. Article 3 of Protocol No. 4 is an intriguing hybrid of norms derived to some extent from the other relevant international instruments, but with its own originality. Article 13(2) of the Universal Declaration of Human Rights recognizes that '(2) Everyone has the right to leave any country, including his own, and to return to his country.' The first part of this provision is addressed in article 2 of Protocol No. 4. It is the second part, recognizing the right 'to return to his country', that finds an incomplete and somewhat distorted reflection in article 3(2) of Protocol No. 4. The silence of the Universal Declaration of Human Rights on the issue of expulsion may not be all that significant, because it can be argued that if there is a right to return, then expulsion makes no sense in any case.

Although the International Covenant on Civil and Political Rights generally expands upon the provisions in the Universal Declaration, it also innovates in some respects. Article 13 is one of the examples of this:

An alien lawfully in the territory of a State Party to the present Covenant may be expelled therefrom only in pursuance of a decision reached in accordance with law and shall, except where compelling reasons of national security otherwise require, be allowed to submit the reasons against his expulsion and to have his case reviewed by, and be represented for the purpose before, the competent authority or a person or persons especially designated by the competent authority.

Not formally adopted until 1966, the provision had nonetheless been drafted and debated within the Third Committee of the United Nations General Assembly before Protocol No. 4 was adopted. Based on the text, the drafters of Protocol No. 4 made their own contribution with the reference to 'collective' expulsions, a subject dealt with in article 4 of Protocol No. 4.

Drafting of the provision

In 1958, when the Legal Committee of the Consultative Assembly began consideration of an additional protocol, the list of rights that might be included contained prohibition of

---

[5] Giorgia Balladore Pallieri, 'Les transferts internationaux de populations', [1952] II *Annuaire de l'Institut de droit international* 138, at pp. 142–3.

[6] Ibid., p. 149.

[7] Explanatory Report on Protocol No. 4, paras 31–33.

arbitrary exile. As the report noted,[8] this was already comprised in article 12(2) of the draft United Nations Covenant,[9] where it echoed article 9 of the Universal Declaration of Human Rights ('No one shall be subjected to arbitrary arrest, detention or exile'). The rapporteur of the Legal Committee, Hermod Lannung, explained that 'in the homogenous circle of the Council of Europe, the prohibition of *exile* ought to be *absolute*—which would be difficult in the wider context of the United Nations'. He said for this reason he had omitted the word 'arbitrary', used in the draft Covenant. Moreover, '[d]esirous, secondly, of avoiding all confusion between exile of nationals and expulsion of aliens, I added the words "from the country of which he is a national"'.[10] The Consultative Assembly draft read as follows: 'No-one shall be exiled from the State of which he is a national. Everyone shall be free to enter the State of which he is a national.'[11]

Some members of the Committee of Experts were concerned about use of the word 'exiled'. They raised the likelihood of it being taken to cover extradition, and even expulsion. The hypothesis of a State wishing to exile a national after denaturalization was raised. There were suggestions that the Protocol might also include recognition of a right to nationality along the lines of article 15 of the Universal Declaration of Human Rights.[12] The Committee opted for a text that 'would prohibit any constitutional, legislative or administrative or judicial authority from expelling nationals from their own country'. According to the Explanatory Report, expulsion of nationals, whether as individuals or as groups, was 'more often than not... inspired by political motives'. For this reason, the majority of the Committee 'thought it preferable not to use the term "exile" which is open to various difficulties of interpretation. It was agreed to speak of expulsion, although it was recognised that in normal technical usage this term applies to aliens only'.[13] The Explanatory Report notes that '[t]he word "expulsion" is to be understood here in the generic meaning, in current use (to drive away from a place)'.[14] Incidentally, the reference to 'exile' also disappeared in the final version of the International Covenant on Civil and Political Rights.[15] To the objection that some countries had laws banishing members of former reigning houses, the representatives of the countries concerned said they would have to make reservations to article 3.[16]

---

[8] Preliminary Report by M. Lannung, Rapporteur, AS/Jur XII (10) 1, 21 August 1958; Minutes of the meeting [of the Legal Committee, Consultative Assembly], held on 9 and 10 June 1958, AS/Jur (10) PV 2 rev., 22 September 1958; Minutes of the meeting [of the Legal Committee, Sub-Committee No. 12 (Human Rights), Consultative Assembly], held on Tuesday 16 September, 1958, AS/Jur XII (10) PV 1, 7 October 1958.
[9] Draft international Covenant on Civil and Political Rights, UN Doc. A/3824, art. 12(2)(a).
[10] Second Protocol to the Convention on Human Rights, Second Preliminary Report presented by M. Lannung, Rapporteur, AS/Jur XII (10) 3, 10 November 1958 (emphasis in the original); Second Protocol to the Convention on Human Rights, Third Report presented by M. Lannung, Rapporteur, AS/Jur XII (11) 1, 8 June 1959; Report on the Second Protocol to the Convention on Human Rights, M. Lannung, Rapporteur, Doc. 1057, 17 November 1959.
[11] Recommendation 234 (1960), Draft for a Second Protocol to the Convention for the Protection of Human Rights and Fundamental Freedoms. See Preparatory work on the Draft Second Protocol to the Convention on Human Rights, appended to Recommendation 234 (1960) of the Consultative Assembly. V. Article 3 of the Draft—Prohibition of exile—Memorandum by the Directorate of Human Rights, DH/Exp (60) 13, 28 October 1960.
[12] Memorandum by the Human Rights Directorate on the proceedings of the Committee's first meeting, 7 to 11 November 1960, DX/Exp (60) 27, 10 February 1961, para. 46.
[13] Explanatory Report on Protocol No. 4, para. 21.
[14] Ibid.
[15] Manfred Nowak, *UN Covenant on Civil and Political Rights, CCPR Commentary*, 2nd rev. edn, Kehl, Germany: N.P. Engel, 2005, p. 283.
[16] Memorandum by the Human Rights Directorate on the proceedings of the Committee's first meeting, 7 to 11 November 1960, DX/Exp (60) 27, 10 February 1961, para. 49.

The addition of the notion of collective expulsion was made by the Committee of Experts in order to reconcile article 3 with article 4 concerning the collective expulsion of aliens. The Committee of Experts thought it important to prohibit explicitly the collective expulsion of nationals as well as of aliens. The Explanatory Report notes that 'paragraph 1 of Article 3 could in no way be interpreted as in any way justifying measures of collective expulsion which may have been taken in the past'.[17]

The Committee of Experts also preferred the formulation 'the territory of a State' to 'the State'. The Explanatory Report says this was 'for drafting purposes only'.[18] A proposal to use the words 'his own country'—the term employed in the International Covenant on Civil and Political Rights—in place of 'state of which he is a national' was not accepted. Most of the experts thought 'state of which he is a national' to have 'a more precise legal meaning'.[19]

The Committee of Experts understood extradition to be outside the scope of paragraph 1.[20] It also considered that the provision could not be invoked in order to avoid 'certain obligations which are not contrary to the Convention', such as military service.[21] The Committee also discussed the possibility of a State expelling one of its nationals after depriving him or her of nationality. The following text was proposed: 'a State would be forbidden to deprive a national of his nationality for the purpose of expelling him'. The Explanatory Report says that the principle behind this proposal was approved of by the Committee, but that the majority of experts did not think it advisable 'to touch on the delicate question of the legitimacy of measures depriving individuals of nationality'. They also thought that in practice it would be difficult to establish that denaturalization had been undertaken with the intention of expelling the person in question.[22]

The Consultative Assembly draft of article 3(2) read: 'Everyone shall be free to enter the State of which he is a national.' Quite explicitly borrowing the language of article 12(4) of the draft International Covenant on Civil and Political Rights, the Committee of Experts changed the opening phrase of the provision to 'No-one shall be deprived of the right to'. According to the Explanatory Report:

This wording seemed a better solution than the other to a matter of twofold concern to the Committee:

a) On the one hand, paragraph 2 should not relieve persons who wish to enter the territory of the State of which they were nationals, of the obligation to prove their nationality if so required. (A State is not obliged to admit an individual who claims to be a national unless he can make good his claim.)

b) On the other hand, such temporary measures as quarantine should not be interpreted as a refusal of entry.[23]

The Committee also opted for the words 'enter the territory of the State' that it found preferable to 'enter the State'. This was 'purely a drafting change'.[24]

---

[17] Explanatory Report on Protocol No. 4, para. 33.

[18] Ibid., para. 22.

[19] Memorandum of the Human Rights Directorate on the Committee's third meeting, 2 to 11 October 1961, DH/Exp (61) 35 Final, 17 October 1961, para. 28.

[20] Ibid., para. 25.

[21] Ibid., para. 26.

[22] Explanatory Report on Protocol No. 4, para. 23.

[23] Ibid., para. 26.

[24] Ibid., para. 27.

Although article 12(4) of the draft International Covenant was the model for article 3(2) of the Protocol, the Committee of Experts did not think it appropriate to include the word 'arbitrarily'. The Explanatory Report states:

It was understood, however, that an individual's right to enter the territory of the State of which he was a national could not be interpreted as conferring on him an absolute right to remain in that territory. For example, a criminal who, having been extradited by the State of which he was a national, then escaped from prison in the other State, would not have an unconditional right to seek refuge in his own country. Similarly, a soldier serving on the territory of a State other than that of which he is a national, would not have a right to repatriation in order to remain in his own country.[25]

Although this does not appear in the text of the provision itself, the Committee of Experts agreed that the terms of paragraph 2 could be invoked only in relation to the State of which the victim of any violation of this provision was a national.[26]

The heading 'Prohibition of expulsion of nationals' was added by Protocol No. 11.[27]

Analysis and interpretation

There is very little case law respecting article 3 of Protocol No. 4. Almost all of the reported cases involve summary dismissal of complaints at the admissibility level on the grounds that they are manifestly unfounded, often for failure to exhaust domestic remedies or lack of jurisdiction *ratione temporis*. The Court's database, HUROC, does not indicate a single violation of the provision in the case law of the Court and the Commission. The explanation would appear to be that States Parties to the Protocol respect its terms without exception or that, at any rate, in the event of disputes, their legislation is adequate to address the matter effectively.[28] It must also be borne in mind that other instruments of international law are also applicable in circumstances concerning the right of citizens to mobility in and out of the territory, including the European Convention on Establishment, the provisions of European Union law governing movement within the territory of the union,[29] and prohibitions in the treaties on the reduction of statelessness. Any mass expulsion, be it of nationals or non-nationals, might also result in charges of the crime against humanity of deportation and lead to prosecutions under article 7(1)(d) of the Rome Statute of the International Criminal Court. The crime against humanity of deportation is defined as 'forced displacement of the persons concerned by expulsion or other coercive acts from the area in which they are lawfully present, without grounds permitted under international law'.[30]

A rare example of a dispute in which the provision was invoked that was found to be admissible concerned a descendant of the Italian royal family. A citizen of Italy living in

---

[25] Ibid., para. 28. Also Memorandum of the Human Rights Directorate on the Committee's third meeting, 2 to 11 October 1961, DH/Exp (61) 35 Final, 17 October 1961, para. 30.

[26] Ibid., para. 29; Memorandum of the Human Rights Directorate on the Committee's third meeting, 2 to 11 October 1961, DH/Exp (61) 35 Final, 17 October 1961, para. 32.

[27] Protocol No. 11 to the Convention for the Protection of Human Rights and Fundamental Freedoms, restructuring the control machinery established thereby, ETS 155, art. 2(5)(a).

[28] E.g., *Rosengren v. Romania* (dec.), no. 70786/01, 4 May 2006; *Oudrhiri v. France*, no. 19554/92, Commission decision of 31 March 1993.

[29] Charter of Fundamental Rights of the European Union, 2010 OJ C 83/02, arts 15(2), 45.

[30] Rome Statute of the International Criminal Court, (2002) 2187 UNTS 90.

Switzerland, he was nevertheless forbidden from returning to his country because of post-Second World War legislation targeted at the monarchy. Aware of the possible conflict with article 3 of Protocol No. 4, Italy had formulated a declaration at the time of ratification, something discussed below under the heading 'Reservations and declarations'. In its submissions to the Court with respect to the legislative prohibition on the return of the royal family, Italy noted the specific historic context of such a measure, explaining that this had been chosen as an alternative to a law ordering the former King's exile.[31]

The Court avoided application of article 3 of Protocol No. 4 in a case involving expulsion of Turkish Cypriots to Northern Cyprus. It had already found there was a breach of article 2 and considered it unnecessary to determine whether article 3 might also apply.[32]

Article 3 is only applicable to cases of expulsion. This involves an obligation to leave the territory of which one is a national without the possibility of returning subsequently. It does not apply to situations where an individual feels obliged to leave the country of nationality in a child custody dispute, where the custodial parent has left the country of nationality of the non-custodial parent.[33] Although there is no explicit reference to extradition in article 3, it is understood that a national cannot invoke the provision as an obstacle in such proceedings.

Article 3 of Protocol No. 4 applies only to 'nationals' (in French, *ressortissants*). The Court always insists that it may make an autonomous interpretation of the terms of the Convention and that it is not bound by the determinations of national jurisdictions or authorities. Nevertheless, it is obvious that the status of nationality must be governed by the laws of the relevant country. The terms for the recognition of citizenship, and for its denial, remain a prerogative of national law. Thus, for the purposes of article 3 of Protocol No. 4, the nationality of an applicant is determined by reference to the national law.[34] Article 3 can only be invoked by a natural person.[35]

The European Convention does not guarantee a right to a nationality,[36] something that is recognized in article 15 of the Universal Declaration of Human Rights. Arbitrary deprivation of nationality could raise issues under article 8 of the Convention.[37] A European Commission decision suggests that an issue respecting article 3 of Protocol No. 4 might arise in a situation where an application to obtain nationality was refused where there was a relationship to an expulsion order, such that there was a presumption that the purpose of refusing nationality was expulsion.[38] In 2014, the Government of the United Kingdom indicated it would consider proposing legislation to remove nationality from British citizens who travel abroad to join terrorist organizations.

[31] *Victor-Emmanuel De Savoie v. Italy* (dec.), no. 53360/99, 13 September 2001.

[32] *Denizci and Others v. Cyprus*, nos 25316–25321/94 and 27207/95, § 411, ECHR 2001-V.

[33] *A.B. v. Poland* (dec.), no. 33878/96, 13 March 2003. Along similar lines: *Sadet v. Romania* (dec.), no. 36416/02, 20 September 2007; *Schober v. Austria* (dec.), no. 34891/97, 9 November 1999.

[34] *Slivenko and Others v. Latvia* [GC] (dec.), no. 48321/99, § 77, ECHR 2002-II (extracts); *Nagula v. Estonia* (dec.), no. 39203/02, § 8, 25 October 2005; *Fedorova and Others v. Latvia* (dec.), no. 69405/01, 9 October 2003; *Gribenko v. Latvia* (dec.), no. 76878/01, 15 May 2003.

[35] *Association 'Regele Mhai' v. Romania*, no. 26916/95, Commission decision of 4 September 1995.

[36] *Slivenko and Others v. Latvia* [GC] (dec.), no. 48321/99, § 77, 23 January 2002.

[37] *Karassev and family v. Finland* (dec.), no. 31414/96, ECHR 1999-II; *Naumov v. Albania* (dec.), no. 10513/03, 3 December 2002.

[38] *X v. Federal Republic of Germany*, no. 3745/68, Commission decision of 15 December 1969, Collection 31, p. 107.

In applying article 3, regard must be had to article 5(4) of the Protocol: 'The territory of any State to which this Protocol applies by virtue of ratification or acceptance by that State, and each territory to which this Protocol is applied by virtue of a declaration by that State under this Article, shall be treated as separate territories for the purpose of the references in Articles 2 and 3 to the territory of a State.'

Reservations and declarations

Two States Parties, Austria and Italy, have made reservations or declarations in order to address the denial of return to the country by members of the former royal family. Upon signing the Protocol, on 16 September 1963, Austria made a reservation to article 3 specifying that it did not apply to legislation regarding the banishment of the House of Habsbourg-Lorraine and the confiscation of their property. It was renewed upon deposit of the instrument of ratification, in 1969. Its conformity with article 57 of the Convention was upheld by the European Commission of Human Rights.[39] Upon ratification of Protocol No. 4 in 1982, Italy made a declaration respecting the constitutional prohibition of the return of the Italian royal family to the territory: 'Le paragraphe 2 de l'article 3 ne peut faire obstacle à l'application de la disposition transitoire XIII de la Constitution italienne concernant l'interdiction d'entrée et de séjour de certains membres de la Maison de Savoie sur le territoire de l'Etat.' The son of Italy's last king, Victor-Emmanuel de Savoie, attacked the 'reservation' on the grounds that it was inspired by discriminatory grounds based on birth and sex, thereby violating the universal scope of the Convention. He said that it was contrary to the object and purpose of the Convention and should not therefore be applied by the Court.[40] In 2002, as part of the settlement of these proceedings, Italy notified the Secretary General of the Council of Europe, as well as the Court itself,[41] that it had withdrawn the declaration.[42]

Ireland formulated a declaration at the time of signature, on 16 September 1963: 'The reference to extradition contained in paragraph 21 of the Report of the Committee of Experts on this Protocol[43] and concerning paragraph 1 of Article 3 of the Protocol includes also laws providing for the execution in the territory of one Contracting party of warrants of arrest issued by the authorities of another Contracting Party.'

The Netherlands made a declaration at the time of ratification, on 23 June 1982, concerning the territorial application of articles 2 and 3 of Protocol No. 4 with respect to the Netherlands Antilles:

Under Article 3, no one may be expelled from or deprived of the right to enter the territory of the State of which he is a national. There is, however, only one nationality (Netherlands) for the whole of the Kingdom. Accordingly, nationality cannot be used as a criterion in making a distinction between the 'citizens' of the Netherlands and those of the Netherlands Antilles, a distinction which is unavoidable since Article 3 applies separately to each of the parts of the Kingdom. This being so, the Netherlands reserve the right to make a distinction in law, for purpose of the application of

---

[39] *Habsburg-Lothringen v. Austria*, no. 15344/89, Commission decision of 14 December 1989, (1989) 32 YB 116, DR 64-B, p. 211.

[40] *Victor-Emmanuel De Savoie v. Italy* (dec.), no. 53360/99, 13 September 2001.

[41] *Victor-Emmanuel De Savoie v. Italy* (striking out), no. 53360/99, § 21, 24 April 2003.

[42] (2002) 45 YB 20.

[43] Report of the Committee of Experts on Human Rights to the Committee of Ministers, CM (63) 39, 21 February 1963: '21. . . . It was understood that extradition was outside the scope of this paragraph . . .'

Article 3 of the Protocol, between Netherlands nationals residing in the Netherlands and Netherlands nationals residing in the Netherlands Antilles.[44]

On 28 September 2010, the Netherlands made the following declaration:

In reference to the declaration made by the Kingdom of the Netherlands on ratifying Protocol No. 4 to the Convention for the Protection of Human Rights and Fundamental Freedoms on 23 June 1982, the Kingdom of the Netherlands wishes to make the following declaration:

The Kingdom of the Netherlands, consisting as per 10 October 2010 of the European part of the Netherlands, the Caribbean part of the Netherlands (the islands of Bonaire, Sint Eustatius and Saba), Aruba, Curaçao and Sint Maarten, regards these parts as separate territories for the applications of Articles 2 and 3 of the Protocol.[45]

Further reading

Juan Fernando Durán Alba, 'The Prohibition on Expelling and Depriving Nationals of the Right to Enter in Their Own State (Article 3 of Protocol 4)', in Javier García Roca and Pablo Santolaya, eds, *Europe of Rights: A Compendium on the European Convention of Human Rights*, Leiden/Boston: Martinus Nijhoff, 2012, pp. 625–8.
Frowein/Peukert, *MenschenRechtsKonvention*, pp. 696–7.
Grabenwarter, *European Convention*, pp. 418–20.
Harris et al., *Law of the European Convention*, p. 743.
Danièle Lochak, 'Protocole No 4, Article 3', in Pettiti et al., *La Convention européenne*, p. 1053–5.
Jeroen Schokkenbroek, 'Prohibition of Expulsion of Nationals and the Right of Nationals to Enter their own Country (Article 3 of Protocol No. 4)', in Van Dijk et al., *Theory and Practice*, pp. 947–51.

---

[45] (2010) 53 YB 27–28.
[44] (1982) 25 YB EUR.CONV.RES./DECL. 1.

Article 4. Prohibition of collective expulsion of aliens/ Interdiction des expulsions collectives d'étrangers

Collective expulsion of aliens is prohibited.   Les expulsions collectives d'étrangers sont interdites.

Introductory comments

Article 4 of Protocol No. 4 must be read together with article 3, which deals with the expulsion of nationals. The main consequence of the distinction between the expulsion of nationals and the expulsion of non-nationals (or 'aliens') is that the former are protected against individual expulsions as well as collective expulsions. The Charter of Fundamental Rights of the European Union contains a similar provision:

Article 19. Protection in the event of removal, expulsion or extradition
1. Collective expulsions are prohibited.

It is meant to have the same meaning and scope as article 4 of Protocol No. 4 to the European Convention.[1]

The drafting history of articles 3 and 4 of Protocol No. 4 reveals the inability to agree on a more extensive protection of the rights of non-nationals in the context of expulsion. Ironically, the importance of such a provision was justified at the time on the basis of the lessons of 'recent history'.[2] To a large extent, the inadequacy of article 4 of Protocol No. 4 is alleviated by other provisions of the Convention, notably articles 5, 6, and 13, as well as by the expansive interpretation that the Court has given to article 4 of Protocol No. 4.

Drafting of the provision

The Consultative Assembly proposed a detailed draft provision prohibiting the expulsion of an alien who was lawfully resident in a country:

1. An alien lawfully residing in the territory of a High Contracting Party may be expelled only if he endangers national security or offends against *ordre public* or morality.
2. Except where imperative considerations of national security otherwise require, an alien who has been lawfully residing for more than two years in the territory of a Contracting Party shall not be expelled without first being allowed to avail himself of an effective remedy before a national authority, within the meaning of Article 13 of the Convention.
3. An alien who has been lawfully residing for more than ten years in the territory of a Contracting Party may be expelled only for reasons of national security or if the other reasons mentioned in paragraph 1 of this Article are of a particularly serious nature.[3]

---

[1] Explanation relating to the Charter of Fundamental Rights, Official Journal of the European Union, C 303/34, 14 December 2007.
[2] Memorandum of the Human Rights Directorate on the Committee's third meeting, 2 to 11 October 1961, DH/Exp (61) 35 Final, 17 October 1961, para. 53.
[3] Recommendation 234 (1960), Draft for a Second Protocol to the Convention for the Protection of Human Rights and Fundamental Freedoms. See Preparatory work on the Draft Second Protocol to the Convention on Human Rights, appended to Recommendation 234 (1960) of the Consultative Assembly.

The rapporteur noted that this provision raised some difficulties because the expulsion of aliens was also dealt with in the European Convention on Establishment, adopted on 13 December 1955. Indeed, article 4 of the Assembly draft bore a close resemblance to article 3 of the Convention on Establishment.[4] The question was whether article 4 'serves any useful purpose'. The rapporteur noted 'considerable difficulty at the drafting stage' of article 3 of the Convention on Establishment, 'although it only concerned the treatment of nationals of the Contracting Parties'. However, the proposed article 4 of the Protocol applied to everyone, regardless of nationality, and was therefore 'more advantageous than Article 33 of the Convention on Establishment'.[5]

The Committee had several problems with the broad proposal of the Consultative Assembly. Members of the Committee were opposed to the concept in principle because 'the State concerned should alone be competent, in applying such a provision, to judge of the reasons which, according to its internal law, could motivate expulsion and that such decisions should not be subject to control by the organs envisaged by the Convention'. Germany proposed an amendment governing the conditions on which an alien lawfully resident in a territory could be expelled, referring to 'considerations of national security' and recognizing the right to an effective remedy before a national authority.[6] The Secretariat also came up with an amendment by which protection against expulsion would apply to an alien who had been lawfully resident for more two years.[7] A Working Party presented the Committee with alternative proposals, one of which included a new paragraph: 'In no circumstances shall a measure of collective expulsion be taken.'[8]

The Committee of Experts thought it desirable to prohibit formally 'collective expulsions of the kind which was a matter of recent history'.[9] The Committee insisted that 'the adoption of this article could in no way be interpreted as justifying such measures of collective expulsion taken in the past either against nationals or against foreigners'.[10] This text was in fact all that survived of draft article 4 when the Committee decided not to include any provision in the Protocol governing the individual expulsion of aliens. It justified this with reference to article 3 of the Convention on Establishment, expressing concerns about possible conflicts between the two treaties. The Committee recognized that it might have been able to agree upon a text stating that a 'decision of expulsion must be taken in accordance with law'. However, 'the majority of the Committee maintained that only the State concerned should be competent, in applying such a provision, to judge

---

VI. Article 4 of the Draft—Prohibition of arbitrary expulsion—Memorandum by the Directorate of Human Rights, DH/Exp (60) 14 and Appendix I and II, 28 October 1960.

[4] European Convention on Establishment, ETS 19, art. 3. Given the importance of the Convention in the debates concerning drafting of article 4 of Protocol No. 4 (and, later, article 1 of Protocol No. 7), it is interesting to note that there are only twelve ratifications, the last being that of Turkey in 1990.

[5] Report on the Second Protocol to the Convention on Human Rights, M. Lannung, Rapporteur, Doc. 1057, 17 November 1959, para. 11.

[6] Amendment proposed by the Federal Republic of Germany, DH/Exp (61) 26, 3 October 1961.

[7] Amendment proposed by the Secretariat, DH/Exp (61) 27, 4 October 1961.

[8] Report of the Working Party, DH/Exp (61) 30 Revised, 6 October 1961. Also Draft text (meeting of 5 October 1961), DH/Exp (61) 31, 6 October 1961; Draft text (meeting of 6 October 1961), DH/Exp (61) 32, 6 October 1961.

[9] Memorandum of the Human Rights Directorate on the Committee's third meeting, 2 to 11 October 1961, DH/Exp (61) 35 Final, 17 October 1961, para. 53.

[10] Memorandum of the Human Rights Directorate on the Committee's fourth meeting, 2 to 10 March 1962, DH/Exp/Misc (62) 11, 9 March 1962, para. 35.

of the reasons which, according to its internal law, could motivate expulsion and that such judgment should not be subject to the bodies provided for by the Convention'.[11] The Committee considered replacing the draft provision with a text ensuring certain procedural guarantees for non-nationals threatened with expulsion, but felt 'a provision limited to guarantees of a procedural character would be insufficient, and that it would be preferable to have no provision at all'. It reasoned as follows:

First of all, these procedural rights would have no application whenever the State 'considered' that compelling reasons of national security required otherwise. According to this system it would be for the State concerned alone to judge whether such compelling reasons of national security did exist. This situation would prevent the exercise of the powers vested by the Convention in the bodies which it instituted for the purpose of ensuring that Contracting Parties would respect their commitments.

Furthermore, the 'competent authority' before which the alien would have the right to have his case examined could be the same as that which was empowered to take the decision of expulsion; in that case, the alien would have no assurance of the impartiality of the authority.[12]

The heading 'Prohibition of collective expulsion of aliens' was added pursuant to Protocol No. 11.[13]

Analysis and interpretation

'Collective expulsion', as the term is used in article 4 of Protocol No. 4, 'is to be understood as any measure compelling aliens, as a group, to leave a country, except where such a measure is taken on the basis of a reasonable and objective examination of the particular case of each individual alien of the group'.[14] Therefore, 'that a number of aliens are subject to similar decisions does not in itself lead to the conclusion that there is a collective expulsion if each person concerned has been given the opportunity to put arguments against his expulsion to the competent authorities on an individual basis'.[15] There is no violation of article 4 if the lack of an individual expulsion decision is a consequence of the applicant's culpable conduct.[16] If an applicant's asylum claim is

---

[11] Ibid., para. 36.

[12] Explanatory Report on Protocol No. 4, para. 35.

[13] Protocol No. 11 to the Convention for the Protection of Human Rights and Fundamental Freedoms, restructuring the control machinery established thereby, ETS 155, art. 2(5)(a).

[14] *Hirsi Jamaa and Others v. Italy* [GC], no. 27765/09, § 167, ECHR 2012; *Čonka v. Belgium*, no. 51564/99, § 59, ECHR 2002-I; *Andric v. Sweden* (dec.), no. 45917/99, 23 February 1999; *Henning Becker v. Denmark*, no. 7011/75, Commission decision of 3 October 1975, (1976) 19 YB 416, DR 4, p. 215; *Alibaks and Others v. the Netherlands*, no. 14209/88, Commission decision of 16 December 1988, DR 59, p. 274; *Davydov v. Estonia* (dec.), no. 16387/03, 31 May 2005; *Berisha and Haljiti v. 'the former Yugoslav Republic of Macedonia'* (dec.)., no. 18670/03, 16 June 2005; *Sultani v. France*, no. 45223/05, ECHR 2007-IV; *Ghulami v. France* (dec.), no. 45302/05, 7 April 2009; *Dritsas v. Italy* (dec.), no. 2344/02, 1 February 2011; *M.A. v. Cyprus*, no. 41872/10, § 245, 23 July 2013.

[15] *M.A. v. Cyprus*, no. 41872/10, § 246, 23 July 2013; *Hirsi Jamaa and Others v. Italy* [GC], no. 27765/09, § 184, ECHR 2012; *Sultani v. France*, no. 45223/05, § 81, ECHR 2007-IV (extracts); *Ghulami v. France* (dec.), no. 45302/05, 7 April 2009; *Andric v. Sweden* (dec.) no. 45917/99, 23 February 1999; *Tahiri v. Sweden*, no. 25129/94, Commission decision of 11 January 1995; *B. and Others v. the Netherlands*, no. 14457/88, Commission decision of 16 December 1988; *Georgia v. Russia (I)* [GC], no. 13255/07, § 167, 3 July 2014.

[16] *Berisha and Haljiti v. 'the former Yugoslav Republic of Macedonia'* (dec.), no. 18670/03, 16 June 2005; *Dritsas v. Italy* (dec.), no. 2344/02, 1 February 2011.

treated individually and an individual decision is issued, it cannot be considered to be a collective expulsion.[17]

However, even when there is such an examination, the background to expulsion orders may still be considered in assessing compliance with article 4.[18] In a Belgian application concerning large-scale expulsion of Slovakian Roma from the country, allegedly on the basis of individual determinations of breaches of immigration law, the Court said that 'in view of the large number of persons of the same origin who suffered the same fate as the applicants' it could not 'eliminate all doubt that the expulsion might have been collective'.[19] It said its doubt was 'reinforced by a series of factors', including statements by the political authorities referring to plans for 'collective repatriation', orders to report to the police at the same time, documents drafted in identical terms, and the fact that asylum applications had not been examined completely.[20]

In the *Georgia v. Russia* inter-State case, the Grand Chamber observed that Russian authorities had made thousands of expulsion orders over a relatively brief period. It said that even if in a formal sense there had been a court decision in respect of each individual concerned, 'the conduct of the expulsion procedures during that period, after the circulars and instructions had been issued, and the number of Georgian nationals expelled—from October 2006—made it impossible to carry out a reasonable and objective examination of the particular case of each individual'. The collective nature of the expulsions was confirmed by evidence of a 'coordinated policy of arresting, detaining and expelling Georgian nationals'.[21]

The Grand Chamber has extended the application of article 4 of Protocol No. 4 to cover the *refoulement* of migrants who are stopped before they enter the national territory. 'A long time has passed since Protocol No. 4 was drafted', it said, in proposing an expansive and evolutive interpretation of article 4. 'Since that time, migratory flows in Europe have continued to intensify, with increasing use being made of the sea, although the interception of migrants on the high seas and their removal to countries of transit or origin are now a means of migratory control, in so far as they constitute tools for States to combat irregular immigration.'[22] The Grand Chamber observed that if article 4 of Protocol No. 4 were to apply only to collective expulsions from the national territory, 'a significant component of contemporary migratory patterns would not fall within the ambit of that provision, notwithstanding the fact that the conduct it is intended to prohibit can occur outside national territory and in particular, as in the instant case, on the high seas'.[23] Consequently, article 4 of Protocol No. 4 would be ineffective in practice.

The Court considered whether such an interpretation could be excluded by the *travaux préparatoires* of Protocol No. 4. It cited the Explanatory Report containing the views of the Committee of Experts that article 4 was intended to prohibit 'collective expulsions of aliens of the kind which was a matter of recent history'. For the Grand Chamber, the

---

[17] *Mikolenko v. Estonia* (dec.), no. 10664/05, § 4, 8 January 2008.

[18] *Čonka v. Belgium*, no. 51564/99, § 59, ECHR 2002-I; *Georgia v. Russia (I)* [GC], no. 13255/07, § 167, 3 July 2014.

[19] Ibid., § 61.

[20] Ibid., § 62.

[21] *Georgia v. Russia (I)*[GC], no. 13255/07, §§ 175–176, 3 July 2014.

[22] *Hirsi Jamaa and Others v. Italy* [GC], no. 27765/09, § 173, ECHR 2012.

[23] Ibid., § 177.

Explanatory Report indicates that 'the aliens to whom the Article refers are not only those lawfully resident on the territory but "all those who have no actual right to nationality in a State, whether they are passing through a country or reside or are domiciled in it, whether they are refugees or entered the country on their own initiative, or whether they are stateless or possess another nationality"'. The Grand Chamber also noted that the word 'expulsion' was intended to be interpreted 'in the generic meaning, in current use (to drive away from a place)'.[24]

Nor did it find any obstacle to such an interpretation in the text itself. The Court noted that it contained no reference to 'territory', in contrast with article 3 of the Protocol. It also noted that article 1 of Protocol No. 7 also referred to territory. The absence of the term in article 4 of Protocol No. 4 could not be ignored, it said.[25] The Court said that while the notion of 'jurisdiction' was 'principally territorial', it said it did not 'see any obstacle to accepting that the exercise of extraterritorial jurisdiction by that State took the form of collective expulsion'.[26] It also said that 'the special nature of the maritime environment cannot justify an area outside the law where individuals are covered by no legal system capable of affording them enjoyment of the rights and guarantees protected by the Convention which the States have undertaken to secure to everyone within their jurisdiction'.[27]

Interpreting article 4 of Protocol No. 4 in light of the Grand Chamber judgment in *Hirsi Jamaa*, the Court said that 'les rapports entre l'interprétation du champ d'application de l'article 4 du Protocole no 4 retenue par la Grande Chambre et l'étendue du principe du non-refoulement [as set out in international refugee law] ne sont pas non plus dépourvus d'intérêt'.[28] Here, the Court was referring to a statement on the *refoulement* of asylum seekers issued by the United Nations High Commissioner for Refugees:

The obligation of States not to expel, return or *refoule* refugees to territories where their life or freedom would be threatened is a cardinal protection principle enshrined in the Convention, to which no reservations are permitted. In many ways, the principle is the logical complement to the right to seek asylum recognized in the Universal Declaration of Human Rights. It has come to be considered a rule of customary international law binding on all States. In addition, international human rights law has established *non-refoulement* as a fundamental component of the absolute prohibition of torture and cruel, inhuman or degrading treatment or punishment. The duty not to *refoule* is also recognized as applying to refugees irrespective of their formal recognition, thus obviously including asylum-seekers whose status has not yet been determined. It encompasses any measure attributable to a State which could have the effect of returning an asylum-seeker or refugee to the frontiers of territories where his or her life or freedom would be threatened, or where he or she would risk persecution. This includes rejection at the frontier, interception and indirect *refoulement*, whether of an individual seeking asylum or in situations of mass influx.[29]

Finding that Italy was in breach of article 4 by the *refoulement* of migrants who had reached its shores by boat from Greece, the Court rejected the respondent State's contention that because 'le but de l'interdiction prévue par cette disposition serait de

[24] Ibid., § 174; *Georgia v. Russia (I)*[GC], no. 13255/07, § 168, 3 July 2014.
[25] *Hirsi Jamaa and Others v. Italy* [GC], no. 27765/09, § 173, ECHR 2012.
[26] Ibid., § 178.
[27] *Hirsi Jamaa and Others v. Italy* [GC], no. 27765/09, § 178, ECHR 2012.
[28] *Sharifi and Others v. Italy and Greece*, no. 16643/09, § 211, 21 October 2014.
[29] Note on International Protection, A/AC.96/951, para. 16.

conjurer l'horreur historique des pogroms, . . . celle-ci ne concerne pas les refoulements ou les refus d'admission sur le territoire des États parties à la Convention'.[30]

Reservations and declarations

At the time of signature, in 1988, Cyprus made a declaration[31] that was confirmed upon ratification a year later, to the effect that 'according to a proper interpretation of the provisions of Article 4 of the Protocol, they are not applicable to aliens unlawfully in the Republic of Cyprus as a result of the situation created by the continuing invasion and military occupation of part of the territory of the Republic of Cyprus by Turkey'.

Further reading

Juan Fernando Durán Alba, 'Prohibition on the Collective Expulsion of Aliens (Article 4 of Protocol 4)', in Javier García Roca and Pablo Santolaya, eds, *Europe of Rights: A Compendium on the European Convention of Human Rights*, Leiden/Boston: Martinus Nijhoff, 2012, pp. 629–34.
Frowein/Peukert, *MenschenRechtsKonvention*, pp. 698–9.
Grabenwarter, *European Convention*, pp. 421–2.
E. Guild and P. Minderhoud, eds, *Security of Residence and Expulsion: Protection of Aliens in Europe*, The Hague: Martinus Nijhoff, 2001.
Harris et al., *Law of the European Convention*, p. 744.
Danièle Lochak, 'Protocole No 4, Article 4', in Pettiti et al., *La Convention européenne*, pp 1057–9.
Jeroen Schokkenbroek, 'Prohibition of Collective Expulsion of Aliens (Article 4 of Protocol No. 4)', in Van Dijk et al., *Theory and Practice*, pp. 953–7.

---

[30] *Sharifi and Others v. Italy and Greece*, no. 16643/09, § 193, 21 October 2014.
[31] (1988) 31 YB 8.

Article 5. Territorial application/Application territoriale

1. Any High Contracting Party may, at the time of signature or ratification of this Protocol, or at any time thereafter, communicate to the Secretary-General of the Council of Europe a declaration stating the extent to which it undertakes that the provisions of this Protocol shall apply to such of the territories for the international relations of which it is responsible as are named therein.

2. Any High Contracting Party which has communicated a declaration in virtue of the preceding paragraph may, from time to time, communicate a further declaration modifying the terms of any former declaration or terminating the application of the provisions of this Protocol in respect of any territory.

3. A declaration made in accordance with this Article shall be deemed to have been made in accordance with paragraph 1 of Article 56 of the Convention.

4. The territory of any State to which this Protocol applies by virtue of ratification or acceptance by that State, and each territory to which this Protocol is applied by virtue of a declaration by that State under this Article, shall be treated as separate territories for the purpose of the references in Articles 2 and 3 to the territory of a State.

5. Any State which has made a declaration in accordance with paragraph 1 or 2 of this Article may at any time thereafter declare on behalf of one or more of the territories to which the declaration relates that it accepts the competence of the Court to receive applications from individuals, non-governmental organisations or groups of individuals as provided in Article 34 of the Convention in respect of all or any of Articles 1 to 4 of this Protocol.

1. Toute Haute Partie contractante peut, au moment de la signature ou de la ratification du présent Protocole ou à tout moment par la suite, communiquer au Secrétaire Général du Conseil de l'Europe une déclaration indiquant la mesure dans laquelle elle s'engage à ce que les dispositions du présent Protocole s'appliquent à tels territoires qui sont désignés dans ladite déclaration et dont elle assure les relations internationales.

2. oute Haute Partie contractante qui a communiqué une déclaration en vertu du paragraphe précédent peut, de temps à autre, communiquer une nouvelle déclaration modifiant les termes de toute déclaration antérieure ou mettant fin à l'application des dispositions du présent Protocole sur un territoire quelconque.

3. Une déclaration faite conformément au présent article sera considérée comme ayant été faite conformément au paragraphe 1 de l'article 56 de la Convention.

4. Le territoire de tout Etat auquel le présent Protocole s'applique en vertu de sa ratification ou de son acceptation par ledit Etat, et chacun des territoires auxquels le Protocole s'applique en vertu d'une déclaration souscrite par ledit Etat conformément au présent article, seront considérés comme des territoires distincts aux fins des références au territoire d'un Etat faites par les articles 2 et 3.

5. Tout Etat qui a fait une déclaration conformément au paragraphe 1 ou 2 du présent article peut, à tout moment par la suite, déclarer relativement à un ou plusieurs des territoires visés dans cette déclaration qu'il accepte la compétence de la Cour pour connaître des requêtes de personnes physiques, d'organisations non gouvernementales ou de groupes de particuliers, comme le prévoit l'article 34 de la Convention, au titre des articles 1 à 4 du présent Protocole ou de certains d'entre eux.

Introductory comments

Territorial application of the Convention itself is governed by article 56 of the Convention. Clauses governing territorial application also appear in several of the Protocols. They are known as 'colonial clauses' and have actually been applicable to only the small number of European States with dependent territories. Such clauses constitute an exception to the general law of treaties, codified in article 29 of the Vienna Convention on the Law of Treaties, by which a convention applies to the entire territory of a State Party. They have been criticized for permitting double standards but, in theory at least, they also permit the European State to show some deference for local autonomy.

Drafting of the provision

The Consultative Assembly draft of Protocol No. 4 contained a territorial application clause based on article 56 of the Convention and article 4 of Protocol No. 1. The rapporteur of the Legal Committee, Hermod Lannung, explained that in 1950 the Assembly had been opposed to such a colonial clause. However, he said, its objections did not convince the governments. As a result, he said, 'however regretfully' there was 'no alternative for the time being but to bow to that decision'.[1] Responding to the Consultative Assembly draft in a general sense, the United Kingdom objected that the Protocol 'does not seem to have been drawn up with much regard to the needs of dependent or non-metropolitan territories, and any Committee of Experts which may further consider [the draft protocol] should be instructed to bear such problems particularly in mind'.[2]

The Committee of Experts left the first three articles of the draft proposed by the Consultative Assembly essentially unchanged. There were concerns that the terms 'territory' and 'national of a state' in articles 2, 3, and 4 of the draft Protocol might lead to problems of interpretation in non-metropolitan territories.[3] The Explanatory Report notes, for example, that the United Kingdom recognized a common citizenship designated 'citizenship of the United Kingdom and Colonies'. Nevertheless, this did not entitle them to move freely or to resist expulsion from one territory to another.[4] Paragraph 4 was added in order to address this issue.[5]

Paragraph 5 was added by Protocol No. 11.[6] It provides for declarations accepting the jurisdiction of the Court and is equivalent to similar provisions introduced with respect to article 56 of the Convention and the other protocols.[7] The reference to an article of the

---

[1] Second Protocol to the Convention on Human Rights, Third Report presented by M. Lannung, Rapporteur, AS/Jur XII (11) 1, 8 June 1959, para. 15; Report on the Second Protocol to the Convention on Human Rights, M. Lannung, Rapporteur, Doc. 1057, 17 November 1959, para. 16.

[2] Memorandum by the United Kingdom, DH/Exp (60) 20, 28 October 1960.

[3] Memorandum by the Human Rights Directorate on the proceedings of the Committee's first meeting, 7 to 11 November 1960, DX/Exp (60) 27, 10 February 1961, para. 25; Memorandum by the Human Rights Directorate on the Committee's second meeting, 24 to 29 April 1961, DH/Exp (61) 15, 7 August 1961, para. 18; Memorandum of the Human Rights Directorate on the Committee's third meeting, 2 to 11 October 1961, DH/Exp (61) 35 Final, 17 October 1961, para. 62.

[4] Explanatory Report on Protocol No. 4, para. 38. Also ibid., paras 39–42.

[5] Memorandum of the Human Rights Directorate on the Committee's third meeting, 2 to 11 October 1961, DH/Exp (61) 35 Final, 17 October 1961, para. 63.

[6] Protocol No. 11 to the Convention for the Protection of Human Rights and Fundamental Freedoms, restructuring the control machinery established thereby, ETS 155, art. 5.

[7] Explanatory Report on Protocol No. 11, para. 113.

Convention in paragraph 3 was changed because of the renumbering of the Convention, and the heading 'Territorial application' was added by Protocol No. 11.[8]

Analysis and interpretation

Articles 2, 3, and 4 of Protocol No. 4 concern mobility rights and therefore the issue of territorial application inevitably arises in a unique manner. The issue of territorial application of article 4 was addressed by the Court for the first time in 2012 in a case concerning *refoulement* of migrants who had not yet entered the territory of the State Party. The Grand Chamber concluded that 'removal of aliens carried out in the context of interceptions on the high seas by the authorities of a State in the exercise of their sovereign authority, the effect of which is to prevent migrants from reaching the borders of the State or even to push them back to another State, constitutes an exercise of jurisdiction within the meaning of Article 1 of the Convention which engages the responsibility of the State in question under Article 4 of Protocol No. 4'.[9] It did not refer to article 5 of Protocol No. 4. Clearly, article 5 could not apply because the high seas do not constitute a territory for the international relations of which the State Party is responsible. Nevertheless, article 5 highlights the conundrum of the application of the Convention outside the metropolitan territory of the State Party, whereby it may be held responsible for application of the Convention except in the territories to which article 5 applies. Only then is a declaration under article 5 necessary for the Court to exercise jurisdiction. A State Party with dependent territories that has ratified Protocol No. 4 is thus responsible for its observance outside the territory except in such territories to the extent that it has not made a declaration.

This anachronistic provision is only relevant to a few European States. The most important of those to whom it might be relevant is the United Kingdom. The Explanatory Report on Protocol No. 4 indicates that article 5 was adopted primarily to address the concerns of the United Kingdom.[10] But the United Kingdom has yet to ratify Protocol No. 4. Another European State with significant dependent territories is France, a State Party to Protocol No. 4. The Court applied article 5 in a case dealing with expulsion from French Polynesia of a European parliamentarian and environmental activist. According to the Court, article 5(4) 'requires that Polynesia should be regarded as a separate territory'.[11] The Court noted the French declaration, made at the time of ratification on 3 May 1984.[12]

Declarations

At the time of ratification, on 1 June 1968, Germany made a declaration pursuant to article 5 extending Protocol No. 4 to the territory of Land Berlin. It is no longer of any significance.

---

[8] Protocol No. 11 to the Convention for the Protection of Human Rights and Fundamental Freedoms, restructuring the control machinery established thereby, ETS 155, art. 5.
[9] *Hirsi Jamaa and Others v. Italy* [GC], no. 27765/09, § 174, ECHR 2012.
[10] Explanatory Report on Protocol No. 4, paras 39–42.
[11] *Piermont v. France*, 27 April 1995, § 44, Series A no. 314.
[12] Ibid., § 28.

France made a declaration at the time of ratification: 'The Protocol shall apply to the whole territory of the Republic, having due regard, where the overseas territories are concerned, to local requirements...'[13]

The Netherlands formulated a declaration on 23 June 1982, at the time of ratification, providing for application of the Protocol to the Kingdom in Europe and the Netherlands Antilles.[14] Three years later, it informed the Secretariat-General that Aruba would obtain internal autonomy as of 1 January 1986, but that this would not affect the consequences in international law of treaties that applied previously to Aruba as a component of the Netherlands Antilles, including Protocol No. 4.[15]

At the time of ratification, on 16 September 2009, Spain made a declaration concerning the legal consequences were the Protocol to be extended by the United Kingdom to Gibraltar.

Further reading

Michael Wood, 'Protocole No 4, Article 5', in Pettiti et al., *La Convention européenne*, p. 1061.

---

[13] Ibid., § 28.
[14] (1982) 25 YB EUR.CONV.RES./DECL. 1.
[15] (1986) 29 YB 4.

Article 6. Relationship to the Convention/Relations avec la Convention

As between the High Contracting Parties the provisions of Articles 1 to 5 of this Protocol shall be regarded as additional Articles to the Convention, and all the provisions of the Convention shall apply accordingly.

Les Hautes Parties contractantes considérer-ont les articles 1 à 5 de ce Protocole comme des articles additionnels à la Convention et toutes les dispositions de la Convention s'appliqueront en conséquence.

Introductory comments

Protocols to the Convention come in two varieties: additional and amending. An amending protocol changes the Convention and can only enter into force after it has been accepted by all States Parties. An additional protocol, on the other hand, applies only to those States that have accepted it. Article 6 confirms that Protocol No. 4 is an additional protocol.

Drafting of the provision

The first draft of article 6 of Protocol No. 4 was prepared by the Legal Committee of the Consultative Assembly.[1] It proposed two options, one by which jurisdiction of the European Commission to receive applications from individuals and jurisdiction of the Court was automatic upon ratification, the other by which a supplementary declaration was required of a State that accepted Protocol No. 4. When the final draft of the Protocol was being considered by the Committee of Experts, paragraph 1 was endorsed without change by the Committee of Experts. In the Committee of Experts there was a preference for the second alternative, by which jurisdiction of the Convention organs would be subject to a supplementary declaration.[2] The second paragraph of article 6, concerning 'à la carte' acceptance of the jurisdiction to submit individual petitions, read as follows:

Nevertheless, the right of individual recourse recognised by a declaration made under Article 25 of the Convention, or the acceptance of the compulsory jurisdiction of the Court by a declaration made under Article 46 of the Convention, shall not be effective in relation to this Protocol unless the High Contracting Party concerned has made a statement recognising such right, or accepting such jurisdiction, in respect of all or any of Articles 1 to 4 of the Protocol.

Paragraph 2 was removed by Protocol No. 11, making it henceforth impossible for a State to ratify the Protocol but exclude the jurisdiction of the Court to consider individual

---

[1] Resolution (60) 6, 22 March 1960.
[2] Memorandum by the Human Rights Directorate on the proceedings of the Committee's first meeting, 7 to 11 November 1960, DX/Exp (60) 27, 10 February 1961, paras 70–72; Memorandum of the Human Rights Directorate on the Committee's third meeting, 2 to 11 October 1961, DH/Exp (61) 35 Final, 17 October 1961, para. 64; Explanatory Report on Protocol No. 4, paras 43–44.

applications, except with respect to non-metropolitan territories.[3] No State Party ever made a partial acceptance of jurisdiction as authorized by paragraph 2. The heading 'Relationship to the Convention' was also added by Protocol No. 11.[4]

Analysis and interpretation

Article 6(2) of Protocol No. 4 was invoked by Turkey in the *Loizidou* case to bolster its claim to be able to make an *à la carte* declaration recognizing the jurisdiction of the Commission to receive individual applications that was confined to its metropolitan territory.[5] The Court rejected Turkey's argument, noting that 'even if it had been established, which is not the case, that restrictions, other than those *ratione temporis*, were considered permissible under Articles 25 and 46 (art. 25, art. 46) at a time when a minority of the present Contracting Parties adopted the Convention, such evidence could not be decisive'.[6]

Further reading

Pierre-Henri Imbert, 'Protocole No 4, Article 6', in Pettiti et al., *La Convention européenne*, p. 1063–4.

---

[3] Protocol No. 11 to the Convention for the Protection of Human Rights and Fundamental Freedoms, restructuring the control machinery established thereby, ETS 155, art. 2(5)(c).
[4] Ibid., art. 2(5)(a).
[5] *Loizidou v. Turkey* (Preliminary objections), 23 March 1995, § 67, Series A no. 310.
[6] Ibid., § 71.

Article 7. Signature and ratification/Signature et ratification

1. This Protocol shall be open for signature by the Members of the Council of Europe who are the signatories of the Convention; it shall be ratified at the same time as or after the ratification of the Convention. It shall enter into force after the deposit of five instruments of ratification. As regards any signatory ratifying subsequently, the Protocol shall enter into force at the date of the deposit of its instrument of ratification.

2. The instruments of ratification shall be deposited with the Secretary-General of the Council of Europe, who will notify all Members of the names of those who have ratified.

1. Le présent Protocole est ouvert à la signature des membres du Conseil de l'Europe, signataires de la Convention; il sera ratifié en même temps que la Convention ou après la ratification de celle-ci. Il entrera en vigueur après le dépôt de cinq instruments de ratification. Pour tout signataire qui le ratifiera ultérieurement, le Protocole entrera en vigueur dès le dépôt de l'instrument de ratification.

2. Les instruments de ratification seront déposés près le Secrétaire Général du Conseil de l'Europe qui notifiera à tous les membres les noms de ceux qui l'auront ratifié.

Introductory comments

This article is closely related to article 59 of the Convention, also entitled 'Signature and ratification'.

Drafting of the provision

The text of article 7 proposed by the Consultative Assembly was based on article 6 of Protocol No. 1. The number of ratifications required for entry into force was set at five rather than ten, as it was in Protocol No. 1.[1] The rapporteur summarily justified this by stating that entry into force 'should be expedited'.[2] The text proposed by the Parliamentary Assembly was retained without change by the Committee of Experts and, according to the Explanatory Report, 'requires no comment'.[3] The heading 'Signature and ratification' was added pursuant to the provisions of Protocol No. 11.[4]

Analysis and interpretation

The signature and ratification provision of Protocol No. 4 deals with some of the issues that also arise with respect to article 59 of the Convention and with article 6 of Protocol

---

[1] Recommendation 234 (1960), Draft for a Second Protocol to the Convention for the Protection of Human Rights and Fundamental Freedoms; Preparatory work on the Draft Second Protocol to the Convention on Human Rights, Appended to Recommendation 234 (1960) of the Consultative Assembly. XI. Article 9 of the Draft—Signature, Ratification, Entry into Force—Memorandum presented by the Directorate of Human Rights, DH/Exp (60) 19, 28 October 1960.

[2] Report on the Second Protocol to the Convention on Human Rights, M. Lannung, Rapporteur, Doc. 1057, 17 November 1959.

[3] Explanatory Report on Protocol No. 4, para. 45.

[4] Protocol No. 11 to the Convention for the Protection of Human Rights and Fundamental Freedoms, restructuring the control machinery established thereby, ETS 155, art. 2(5)(a).

No. 1. The reader is referred to the relevant chapters in this Commentary. The only difference with the corresponding provision of Protocol No. 1 is the requirement in article 7 of five ratifications rather than ten for entry into force.

Protocol No. 4 was opened for signature on 16 September 1963. Ten of the fourteen Member States of the Council of Europe signed the Protocol on that date: Austria, Belgium, Denmark, Germany, Ireland, Italy, Luxembourg, Norway, the United Kingdom, and Sweden. Norway was the first State to ratify Protocol No. 4, followed by Sweden, Denmark, Iceland, and Luxembourg. It entered into force on 2 May 1968. All States Parties to the Convention have signed Protocol No. 4 with the exception of Greece and Switzerland. The United Kingdom, which signed on 16 September 1963, and Turkey, which signed on 19 October 1992, have yet to ratify Protocol No. 4. When the Council of Europe was enlarged during the 1990s with the membership of many States from Central and Eastern Europe, ratification of Protocol No. 4 within a year of becoming a member of the organization was one of the undertakings that were made.[5]

The final paragraph of article 7 concerns the role of the depositary. This text is shorter than the corresponding provision in article 59 of the Convention. Although this is not specified, the Secretary General assumes the role of depositary and fulfils the various functions associated with that role in addition to those explicitly set out in article 7.

Further reading

Pierre-Henri Imbert, 'Protocole No 4, Article 7', in Pettiti et al., *La Convention européenne*, p. 1065–6.

---

[5] E.g., Application by Ukraine for membership of the Council of Europe, Opinion 190 (1995), para. 12.1; Application by Russia for membership of the Council of Europe, Opinion 193 (1996), para. 10.1; Application by Croatia for membership of the Council of Europe, Opinion 195 (1996), para. 9.2.

PART FIVE

PROTOCOL NO. 6 TO THE CONVENTION FOR THE PROTECTION OF HUMAN RIGHTS AND FUNDAMENTAL FREEDOMS, CONCERNING THE ABOLITION OF THE DEATH PENALTY

Preamble/Préambule

The member States of the Council of Europe, signatory to this Protocol to the Convention for the Protection of Human Rights and Fundamental Freedoms, signed at Rome on 4 November 1950 (hereinafter referred to as 'the Convention'),

Considering that the evolution that has occurred in several member States of the Council of Europe expresses a general tendency in favour of abolition of the death penalty;

Have agreed as follows:

Les États membres du Conseil de l'Europe, signataires du présent Protocole à la Convention de sauvegarde des Droits de l'homme et des Libertés fondamentales, signée à Rome le 4 novembre 1950 (ci-après dénommée 'la Convention'),

Considérant que les développements intervenus dans plusieurs États membres du Conseil de l'Europe expriment une tendance générale en faveur de l'abolition de la peine de mort;

Sont convenus de ce qui suit:

Introductory comments

'Dans l'Europe unie de demain . . . l'abolition solennelle de la peine de mort devrait être le premier article du Code européen que nous espérons tous', wrote Albert Camus in 1957, the year he received the Nobel Prize for literature. These words appeared in an essay entitled 'Réflexions sur la guillotine' that was part of a volume Camus co-edited with Arthur Koestler.[1] Already, a movement towards universal abolition within the Member States of the Council of Europe was discernible. Yet, article 2(1) of the European Convention expressly acknowledges the death penalty as an exception to the right to life. Abolition came in stages rather than in one fell swoop. Adopted in 1983, Protocol No. 6 effectively amends this provision for ratifying States and imposes two obligations with respect to the death penalty in time of peace: not to pronounce it and not to implement it. The Committee of Ministers, in the Explanatory Report on Protocol No. 13, described Protocol No. 6 as a 'landmark stage' in the 'evolution in domestic and international law towards abolition of the death penalty'.[2]

Protocol No. 6 was widely but not unanimously accepted by Member States at the time of its adoption, in 1983. Writing in 1989, the Plenary Court said:

De facto the death penalty no longer exists in time of peace in the Contracting States to the Convention. In the few Contracting States which retain the death penalty in law for some peacetime offences, death sentences, if ever imposed, are nowadays not carried out. This 'virtual consensus in Western European legal systems that the death penalty is, under current circumstances, no longer consistent with regional standards of justice', to use the words of Amnesty International, is reflected in Protocol No. 6 to the Convention, which provides for the abolition of the death penalty in time of peace. Protocol No. 6 was opened for signature in April 1983, which in the practice of the Council of Europe indicates the absence of objection on the part of any of the Member States of the

---

[1] Albert Camus, 'Réflexions sur la guillotine', in *Œuvres complètes*, IV, 1957–1959, Paris: Gallimard, 2008, pp. 124–67, at p. 165.
[2] Explanatory Report on Protocol No. 13, paras 3–4.

Organisation; it came into force in March 1985 and to date has been ratified by thirteen
Contracting States to the Convention ...[3]

Protocol No. 6 provided a valuable legal tool that brought rapid change to new Member
States such as Russia and Ukraine, where hundreds of people were executed annually in
the years preceding the accession to the Council of Europe.[4] When they joined the
organization, in 1996, executions stopped abruptly and they have never resumed.

In the first years of the new century, Protocol No. 6 was surpassed by Protocol No. 13,
which abolishes the death penalty at all times. Virtually all Member States in the Council
of Europe have ratified Protocol No. 13. In 2010, a Chamber of the European Court of
Human Rights held that in light both of Protocol No. 13 and consistent State practice,
'Article 2 has been amended so as to prohibit the death penalty in all circumstances'.[5]
Indeed, both Protocols concerning abolition of the death penalty have become obsolete as
a result of the evolving interpretation of the Convention itself by the European Court of
Human Rights.

Even at the time of its adoption, several members of the Council of Europe had either
recently abolished the death penalty or were actively considering taking this step.
A broader global movement towards abolition gathered momentum during the 1950s
and 1960s. By the mid-1950s, increasingly progressive attitudes on the subject were
visible in the negotiations of article 6 of the International Covenant on Civil and Political
Rights. The Covenant's draft provision in 1949 on the right to life had inspired those who
wrote the European Convention on Human Rights. But the drafting of the Covenant was
not completed until 1966. Over the 1950s, as the right-to-life provision of the Covenant
was reworked, it took on an increasingly restrictive approach to capital punishment, and
even added a final phrase pointing to the goal of abolition. This development was largely
the contribution of European States within the United Nations. Probably if the European
Convention on Human Rights had been adopted in 1960 rather than in 1950, the text of
article 2(1) of the Convention would have looked very different. Thus, within a few years
of the adoption of the European Convention article 2(1) presented itself as a rather archaic
and outdated provision.

Within the law of the European Union, the Final Act of the Amsterdam Treaty, which
was adopted on 2 October 1997 and came into force on 1 May 1999, contains a
'Declaration on the abolition of the death penalty':

With reference to Article F(2) of the Treaty on European Union, the Conference recalls that
Protocol No. 6 to the European Convention for the Protection of Human Rights and Fundamental
Freedoms signed in Rome on 4 November 1950, and which has been signed and ratified by a large
majority of Member States, provides for the abolition of the death penalty. In this context, the
Conference notes the fact that since the signature of the abovementioned Protocol on 28 April 1983,
the death penalty has been abolished in most of the Member States of the Union and has not been
applied in any of them.[6]

---

[3] *Soering v. the United Kingdom*, 7 July 1989, § 102, Series A no. 161.
   [4] Capital punishment and implementation of the safeguards guaranteeing protection of the rights of those
facing the death penalty, Report of the Secretary General, UN Doc. E/2000/3, p. 13.
   [5] *Al-Saadoon and Mufdhi v. the United Kingdom*, no. 61498/08, § 120, ECHR 2010 (extracts).
   [6] Treaty of Amsterdam amending the Treaty on European Union, the Treaties establishing the European
Communities and Certain Related Acts, OJ C 340, 10 November 1997.

It was soon follow by the Charter of Fundamental Rights of the European Union. The text of article 2 of the Charter is clearly inspired by article 1 of Protocol No. 6, but it is broader in scope because there it is not confined to time of peace:

1. Everyone has the right to life.
2. No one shall be condemned to the death penalty, or executed.

Additionally, article 19(2) declares: 'No one may be removed, expelled or extradited to a State where there is a serious risk that he or she would be subjected to the death penalty, torture or other inhuman or degrading treatment or punishment.'[7]

The impact of Protocol No. 6 has been felt far beyond Europe. For example, Protocol No. 6 inspired lawmakers in the United Nations and the Organisation of American States to adopt comparable abolitionist protocols within their human rights treaty regimes.[8] Protocol No. 6 has been cited before domestic courts of non-European states, such as Canada, Zimbabwe, and South Africa.[9] In *United States v. Burns*, decided in February 2001, the Supreme Court of Canada noted that 'a significant number of countries' had either signed or ratified Protocol No. 6 since it had last considered the issue of capital punishment, a decade earlier. This was taken as evidence of the international trend towards abolition of capital punishment.[10]

Drafting of the provision

In 1980, the Committee of Ministers asked the Steering Committee on Human Rights and the European Committee on Crime Problems to prepare an opinion on action to be taken with the aim of abolition of the death penalty, referring directly to the idea of an 'additional protocol'. The two Committees drafted a joint opinion concluding that it would be difficult to adopt an amending protocol because it seemed very unlikely to rally the support of all parties to the Convention. Instead, it recommended that an additional or optional protocol be considered. The two Committees observed that they had no mandate to draft such an instrument. In their joint opinion, the two steering committees reached the conclusion that 'the adoption of an additional protocol to the European convention on human rights, modelled on protocols 1 and 4, would be a possible solution'. During these meetings both the United Kingdom and Turkey manifested their opposition to the idea of any protocol. The United Kingdom insisted this was a matter for the conscience of individual parliamentarians. Turkey, where capital punishment was still being practised, simply did not feel it was in a position to abolish the death penalty.

In light of these reports, on 25 September 1981 the Committee of Ministers mandated the Steering Committee on Human Rights to prepare a draft additional protocol concerning abolition of the death penalty 'in peacetime',[11] setting a deadline of June 1982.

---

[7] Charter of Fundamental Rights of the European Union, 2010 OJ C 83/02.

[8] Second Optional Protocol to the International Covenant on Civil and Political Rights, (1991) 1642 UNTS 414; Protocol to the American Convention on Human Rights to Abolish the Death Penalty, OASTS No. 73.

[9] *Kindler v. Canada*, [1991] 2 SCR 779, pp. 809, 833; *S. v. Makwanyane and Another*, [1995] ZACC 3; *Catholic Commission for Justice and Peace in Zimbabwe v. Attorney-General et al.*, [1993] 14 HRLJ 323.

[10] *United States v. Burns*, [2001] 1 SCR 283, para. 87.

[11] Explanatory Report on Protocol No. 6.

The Steering Committee met in November 1981 and again in April 1982, when it completed its report together with a draft additional protocol for submission to the Committee of Ministers.[12] At a meeting of Deputies in September 1982, the Steering Committee's draft additional protocol to the Convention was discussed and approved. The Secretariat was asked to prepare a synoptic report for the Committee of Ministers meeting in December 1982. The Committee of Ministers made no changes to the draft that had been accepted by the Deputies in September and formally adopted the text of the protocol in December 1982. Protocol No. 6 was opened for signature on 28 April 1983. It entered into force on 1 March 1985.

The Explanatory Report provides little insight into the substantive discussions concerning the drafting of Protocol No. 6. According to a United Nations document, during the drafting of Protocol No. 6 there had been suggestions that the Preamble be more extensive and that it include reference to both article 2(1) of the European Convention and to the right to life, similar to the approach followed in the Preamble to the Second Optional Protocol to the International Covenant on Civil and Political Rights.[13]

The heading, 'Preamble', was added by Protocol No. 11.[14]

Analysis and interpretation

The Preamble is succinct and makes no reference whatsoever to any substantive law. The contrast with the more elaborate provisions of Protocol No. 13 is apparent. The Preamble of Protocol No. 6 does not, for example, mention articles 2(1) or 3 of the Convention or suggest the relationship between these provisions and the Protocol. Nor does it refer either to the right to life or to the issue of inhuman treatment. The suggestion that capital punishment might be incompatible with substantive provisions of the Convention itself was probably avoided out of deference to the few Member States of the Council of Europe where the death penalty had not yet been abolished. Furthermore, a reference to the prohibition of inhuman treatment might be difficult to explain in an instrument that only partially abolished the death penalty.

Two important ideas are expressed in the second recital of the Preamble of Protocol No. 6: that there has been 'evolution' in 'several' member States, and that this evolution 'expresses a general tendency in favour of abolition of the death penalty'.

Evolution that has occurred

The second recital of the Preamble of Protocol No. 6 speaks of 'evolution that has occurred in several member States of the Council of Europe'. Certainly, at the time the European Convention on Human Rights was adopted the death penalty was still rather widely practised by member States. Although it had been in decline through much of Europe prior to the Second World War, capital punishment revived briefly for the post-war trials of war criminals and collaborators. Twelve of the defendants before the International Military Tribunal were sentenced to death and ten of them were actually

---

[12] Doc. H/INF (82) 1, p. 20.
[13] UN Doc. A/C.3/35/L.75.
[14] Protocol No. 11 to the Convention for the Protection of Human Rights and Fundamental Freedoms, restructuring the control machinery established thereby, ETS 155, art. 2(6)(a).

executed. Alongside the brief post-War resurgence of the death penalty in certain States of Western Europe, the States of the former European axis, namely the Federal Republic of Germany, Austria, and Italy, quickly abolished capital punishment, largely to distance themselves from the terrible excesses of the fascist regimes. Several German judges and prosecutors were convicted by an American Military Tribunal of crimes against humanity for the abusive use of capital punishment associated with their blind obedience to Nazi law.[15]

Of the original States Parties to the European Convention when it entered into force in 1953, only the United Kingdom and Ireland conducted executions subsequently. Ireland's last execution took place in 1954, although courts in the country continued to sentence people to death into the 1980s. The last executions in the United Kingdom took place in 1964. The Death Penalty Act of 1965 abolished capital punishment in the United Kingdom for an experimental period that became permanent following 1969 resolutions of both Houses of Parliament. In the case of Germany, a constitutional provision adopted in 1949 prohibited capital punishment. Several of the first States Parties were *de facto* abolitionist, retaining capital punishment in legal texts that had fallen into disuse, or that only applied in time of war or emergency. Swedish law allowed capital punishment for military offences; the relevant provisions were repealed in 1973, followed by a constitutional prohibition in 1975. Norway had abolished the death penalty in peacetime in 1902, but it executed collaborators after the Second World War and only removed capital punishment from its legislation in 1979.

Some other Member States of the Council of Europe that were not yet States Parties to the Convention when it entered into force also retained capital punishment. Belgium and the Netherlands had recently carried out executions related to the Second World War. Greece imposed the death penalty during the early 1970s; by then, it was no longer democratic and had briefly withdrawn from the Council of Europe. Turkey continued the practice of capital punishment until late 1984. It did not repeal the death penalty in law until 2004. France held its last execution in 1977 and removed capital punishment from the Penal Code in 1981. By 1983, when the text of Protocol No. 6 was adopted, seven more States had joined the Council of Europe. In none—Austria, Switzerland, Cyprus, Malta, Portugal, Spain, Liechtenstein—was the death penalty still being practised, although relevant legislative provisions remained in force for some of them.

The first United Nations quinquennial report on capital punishment, published in 1974, indicated the status of the death penalty for Member States, including those in the Council of Europe. Only five Council of Europe Member States were deemed to be fully abolitionist: Austria, Finland, Germany, Iceland, and Sweden. Several others were described as 'abolitionist by law for ordinary crimes only': Denmark, Italy, Malta, the Netherlands, Norway, and the United Kingdom. Belgium and Luxembourg were labelled 'abolitionist by custom'. Four States were considered 'retentionist': Cyprus, France, Ireland, and Turkey.[16] Switzerland was not listed as it did not then belong to the United Nations. In his conclusions, the Secretary General said that '[i]t remains extremely doubtful whether there is any progression towards the restriction of the Use of the death penalty'. Nevertheless, 'in the face of a considerable upsurge in terrorism, the

---

[15] *United States v. Altstötter et al.*(Justice case), (1951) 3 TWC 954 (US Military Tribunal), at pp. 1025, 1028, 1154–5.

[16] Capital Punishment, Report of the Secretary General, UN Doc. E/5616, Annex I, pp. 2–3.

British Parliament voted overwhelmingly against the reintroduction of capital punishment and urged other countries to follow its example'.[17]

The United Nations Secretary General again reported on changes to the status of capital punishment in the world, including Western Europe, in 1979 and 1984. According to the 1979 report,

Major legal changes leading towards the abolition of capital punishment were reported by countries in Western Europe and North America, where Portugal in 1977, Denmark in 1978, and Luxembourg and Norway in 1979 became completely abolitionist. In 1978, Spain abolished the death penalty under ordinary penal law, and replaced it by 30 years' imprisonment...Legislative initiatives seeking the general abolition of capital punishment in the Netherlands were announced in 1977 and in France legislative initiatives seeking the reduction and the total abolition of the death penalty were undertaken during the period under review...In the United Kingdom a motion that the death penalty be made available to the courts was defeated in the House of Commons in 1979.[18]

According to the 1984 report:

In Western Europe, France, the Netherlands and Norway totally abolished capital punishment. Norway, however, only reaffirmed in 1981 its decision of 1902 to abolish the death penalty, while the Netherlands in 1983 extended the abolition of capital punishment to military crimes...France first renounced its retentionist position four years ago. In the reply of France, it was stated that: 'Rejection of capital punishment—constantly called for by major philosophical trends and recommended by international authorities (United Nations, Council of Europe, Assemblies of the European Communities)—was one of the objectives of the candidates for the presidential and legislative elections in favour of whom the French electorate decided in 1981.'[19]

Liechtenstein and Turkey were the only Council of Europe Member States to be indicated as retentionist. All the others were described as abolitionist either in law or in practice. Thus, when Protocol No. 6 was adopted there was indeed a very noticeable evolution in the law and practice of 'several' of the member States of the Council of Europe.

The only real exception at the time was Turkey (Liechtenstein's last reported execution was in 1789), where no significant progressive development on the subject had yet taken place.[20] After the adoption of Protocol No. 6, Turkey continued to pronounce the penalty for another fifteen years. On 29 June 1999, Abdullah Öcalan was sentenced to death by the Second State Security Court, pursuant to article 125 of the Turkish Penal Code. The Turkish Court of Cassation confirmed the death sentence on 25 November 1999. On 30 November 1999, the European Court of Human Rights requested Turkey 'to take all necessary measures to ensure that the death penalty is not carried out so as to enable the Court to proceed effectively with the examination of the admissibility and merits of the applicant's complaints under the Convention'.[21] Turkey signed and ratified Protocol No. 6 in 2003.

---

[17] Ibid., para. 48.

[18] UN Doc. E/1980/9, para. 26.

[19] UN Doc. E/1985/43, paras 18–19.

[20] Semih Gemilmaz, 'The Death Penalty in Turkey (1920–2001): Facts, Truths and Illusions', (2002) 13 *Criminal Law Forum* 91.

[21] *Öcalan v. Turkey* (interim measures), no. 46221/99, 30 November 1999.

A general tendency in favour of abolition

That there is 'a general tendency in favour of abolition of the death penalty' is also stated in the second recital of the Preamble to Protocol No. 6. This proposition is, of course, linked to the preceding affirmation of the evolution in the law and practice of 'several' Member States. Seemingly obvious, especially with the hindsight of three decades and the confirmation of the 'general tendency' around the globe, in 1983 this represented an assessment of the situation that might not have been universally shared. Pessimists have frequently considered that progressive developments on capital punishment are fragile and ephemeral. But even the most optimistic of those who drafted Protocol No. 6 would probably have hesitated if it was suggested that by 2000 the death penalty would have disappeared totally, not only from western Europe but also from virtually all of central and eastern Europe. Yet it did.

The 2009 report of the United Nations Secretary General confirms the 'general tendency' in Europe but also in much of the rest of the world. Moreover, the report demonstrates that the tendency is solid and, apparently, irreversible. A reversion to capital punishment, whether abolished *de jure* or as a result of consistent practice, is almost unknown. It has never taken place in modern Europe. The 'tendency' is consolidated through constitutional amendments, judicial decisions, and additional legal instruments, including Protocol No. 13 to the European Convention, the Second Optional Protocol to the International Covenant on Civil and Political Rights, and the Charter of Fundamental Rights of the European Union.

Further reading

A. Adinolfi, 'Premier instrument international sur l'abolition de la peine de mort', (1987) 58 *Revue internationale de droit pénal* 321.

Gilbert Guillaume, 'Protocole No 6, Articles 1–4', in Pettiti et al., *La Convention européenne*, pp. 1067–72.

Erik Harremoes, 'The Council of Europe and Its Efforts to Promote the Abolition of the Death Penalty', (1986) 12–13 *Crime Prevention and Criminal Justice Newsletter* 62.

Harris et al., *Law of the European Convention*, pp. 745–6.

Peter Leuprecht, 'The First International Instrument for the Abolition of the Death Penalty', (1983) 2 *Forum* 2.

William A. Schabas, *The Abolition of the Death Penalty in International Law*, 3rd edn, Cambridge: Cambridge University Press, 2003.

William A. Schabas, 'A Step to Universal Abolition of the Death Penalty: Protocol No. 6 to the European Convention', in Olivier Delas and Michaela Leuprecht, eds, *Liber Amicorum Peter Leuprecht*, Brussels: Bruylant, 2012, pp. 297–320.

Jon Yorke, 'The Right to Life and Abolition of the Death Penalty in the Council of Europe,' (2009) 34 *European Law Review* 205.

Jon Yorke, 'Inhuman and Degrading Punishment and Abolition of the Death Penalty in the Council of Europe', (2010) 16 *European Public Law* 77.

Article 1. Abolition of the death penalty/Abolition de la peine de mort

The death penalty shall be abolished. No one shall be condemned to such penalty or executed.

La peine de mort est abolie. Nul ne peut être condamné à une telle peine ni exécuté.

Introductory comments

Article 1 of Protocol No. 6 establishes three principles: the death penalty shall be abolished; no one may be condemned to death; and no one may be executed. The Explanatory Report says that article 1 'affirms the principle of the abolition of the death penalty'. Nevertheless, article 1 cannot be read without bearing in mind the exception in article 2 by which the death penalty may be imposed in wartime.

Drafting of the provision

The history of the drafting of the Protocol is discussed in the introductory chapter of this Commentary. Nothing in the Explanatory Report assists in understanding the drafting of article 1.

The heading, 'Abolition of the death penalty', was added by Protocol No. 11.[1]

Analysis and interpretation

The texts of article 1 of Protocol No. 6 and article 1 of Protocol No. 13 are identical. This discussion of the analysis and interpretation applies to both provisions.

The English version of article 1 of Protocol No. 6 declares that 'the death penalty shall be abolished'. The Explanatory Report states that '[s]ubject to the situations envisaged in Article 2, a state must, where appropriate, delete this penalty from its law in order to become a Party to the Protocol'. The French version of the first sentence of article 1 seems somewhat different from the English: 'La peine de mort est abolie.' The French language formulation is clearly self-executing; in countries where the constitution provides for direct implementation of international treaties, the French version is of some assistance.[2]

Abolition of the death penalty

Article 1 'affirms the principle of the abolition of the death penalty'.[3] In Protocol No. 6, of course, this 'principle' is subject to the wartime exception set out in article 2. In Protocol No. 13, the principle is stated in a more absolute manner. When Protocol No. 13 was

---

[1] Protocol No. 11 to the Convention for the Protection of Human Rights and Fundamental Freedoms, restructuring the control machinery established thereby, ETS 155, art. 2(6)(a).

[2] Gilbert Guillaume, 'Protocole No 6, Articles 1–4', in Pettiti et al., *La Convention européenne*, pp. 1067–72, at p. 1068.

[3] Explanatory Report on Protocol No. 6; Explanatory Report on Protocol No. 13, para. 14.

being adopted, the Rapporteur of the Parliamentary Assembly argued that it should include an explicit repeal of the reference to capital punishment that is comprised in article 2(1) of the Convention. In effect, the Protocol would be of a mixed nature, additional from its entry into force and amending once all States Parties to the Convention had deposited their instruments of ratification.[4]

The abolition of the death penalty requires that a State delete the penalty from its domestic law in order to become a Party to the Protocol.[5] The Explanatory Report on Protocol No. 13 states that the first sentence of article 1 'entails the obligation to abolish this penalty in all circumstances, including for acts committed in time of war or of imminent threat of war'.[6]

The right not to be subjected to the death penalty

The Explanatory Reports on both Protocols state that '[t]he second sentence of this article aims to underline the fact that the right guaranteed is a subjective right of the individual'.[7] The second sentence leaves no doubt that an alleged violation of article 1 provides a person with recourse to the Convention organs for what the Court has described as 'the right not to be subjected to the death penalty'.[8] According to the Court,

Judicial execution involves the deliberate and premeditated destruction of a human being by the State authorities. Whatever the method of execution, the extinction of life involves some physical pain. In addition, the foreknowledge of death at the hands of the State must inevitably give rise to intense psychological suffering. The fact that the imposition and use of the death penalty negates fundamental human rights has been recognised by the Member States of the Council of Europe.[9]

Direct violations of article 1 by States Parties to one or both of the Protocols, in the sense that they have failed to abolish the death penalty, have not taken place. The very modest amount of litigation concerning the provision has involved the extraterritorial application of capital punishment by a third State resulting from extradition or *refoulement* by a State Party. Early decisions of the European Commission under Protocol No. 6 expressed some hesitation on its application in extradition and *refoulement* cases.[10] The position the Commission adopted was more conservative than the view taken by the French Conseil d'État, which expressed the view that Protocol No. 6 established a European *ordre public* prohibiting extradition in capital cases.[11] On similar lines, the Supreme Court of the

---

[4] Draft Protocol to the European Convention on Human Rights concerning the Abolition of the Death Penalty in All Circumstances, Report, Doc. 9316, para. 11.

[5] Explanatory Report on Protocol No. 6.

[6] Explanatory Report on Protocol No. 13, para. 14.

[7] Explanatory Report on Protocol No. 6; Explanatory Report on Protocol No. 13, para. 14.

[8] *Al-Saadoon and Mufdhi v. the United Kingdom*, no. 61498/08, § 115, ECHR 2010 (extracts).

[9] Ibid.; *Al Nashiri v. Poland*, no. 28761/11, § 577, 24 July 2014.

[10] *X v. the Netherlands*, no. 15216/89, Commission decision of 16 January 1991; *Y v. the Netherlands*, no. 16531/90, Commission decision of 16 January 1991, (1991) 34 YB 31, DR 68, p. 299; *Aylor-Davis v. France*, no. 22742/93, Commission decision of 20 January 1994, DR 76, p. 164; *Alla Raidl v. Austria*, no. 25342/94, Commission decision of 4 September 1995, (1995) 38 YB 132, DR 82-A, p. 134.

[11] *Fidan*, (1987) II *Rec. Dalloz-Sirey* 305 (Conseil d'État); *Gacem*, (1988) I *Semaine juridique* IV-86 (Conseil d'État), 14 December 1987. *Fidan* was cited by Judge De Meyer in his concurring opinion in *Soering v. the United Kingdom*, 7 July 1989, Concurring opinion of Judge de Meyer, fns 6, 7, Series A no. 161. See also the reference to *Fidan*, invoked by the French government, in *B. v. France*, no. 13706/88, Commission decision of 9 December 1988, and to both *Fidan* and *Gacem* in *Drozd and Janousek v. France and Spain*, 26 June 1992, § 110, Series A no. 240.

Netherlands invoked the Protocol in refusing to return a United States serviceman to the custody of his country,[12] although required to do so by the NATO Status of Forces Agreement, because of the threat the death penalty would be imposed. The Dutch Court considered that Protocol No. 6 took precedence over the other treaty.[13]

The European Court of Human Rights has always had a clear position by which article 1 of the Protocols is violated in cases involving a real risk of execution in a third country. Several decisions hold that extradition may raise an issue under article 1 of Protocols Nos 6 and 13 if there is a real risk that the individual concerned may be sentenced to death by the receiving State.[14] A detailed examination of the status of the death penalty in the receiving State must be undertaken in order to assess whether or not the risk of capital punishment is in fact genuine. In a case involving extradition from Ukraine to Kazakhstan, the Court looked at a range of sources, including reports from Amnesty International and the Organisation for Security and Cooperation in Europe, reaching the conclusion that there was no real risk.[15] The Court reached a similar conclusion in a case involving extradition from Russia to Uzbekistan.[16]

When diplomatic assurances that the death penalty will not be imposed are provided, the Court has generally considered this sufficient to eliminate the risk.[17] For example, in an Italian case, the Court said that nothing in the assurances given by the United States Attorney General suggested that 'en l'espèce les assurances en question n'étaient pas sérieuses et fiables'.[18] This contrasts with the Court's very chary attitude to diplomatic assurances respecting torture and ill-treatment.[19] The distinction can be explained by the fact that undertakings not to impose capital punishment take place within a fully legal framework, given that the death penalty itself is provided by law in certain States. Torture, on the other hand, is never authorized by law, and an undertaking not to conduct it is ultimately rather meaningless. If an undertaking is considered necessary, the situation in the third State suspected of conducting torture is already too dire. According to the United Nations Independent Expert on the Protection of Human Rights and Fundamental Freedoms while Countering Terrorism, 'unlike assurances on the use of the death

---

[12] *Short v. The Netherlands*, Supreme Court of the Netherlands, 30 March 1990, (1990) 76 *Rechtspraak van de Week* 358, (1990) 29 *International Legal Materials* 1378.

[13] Agreement between the Parties to the 1949 North Atlantic Treaty regarding the Status of Their Forces, (1951) 199 UNTS 67. In 1995, the States Parties to the NATO treaty finalized the Agreement among the States Parties to the North Atlantic Treaty and the Other States Participating in the Partnership for Peace regarding the Status of Their Forces together with an Additional Protocol. Article 1 of the Additional Protocol states: 'Insofar as it has jurisdiction according to the provisions of the agreement, each State party to the present additional protocol shall not carry out a death sentence with regard to any member of a force and its civilian component, and their dependents from any other state party to the present additional protocol.'

[14] *Ismaili v. Germany* (dec.), no. 58128/00, 15 March 2001; *Bader and Kanbor v. Sweden*, no. 13284/04, § 42, ECHR 2005-XI; *Saoudi v. Spain* (dec.), no. 22871/06, 18 September 2006; *Hakizimana v. Sweden* (dec.), no. 37913/05, 27 March 2008; *Salem v. Portugal* (dec.), no. 26844/04, 9 May 2006; *Al Shari v. France* (dec.), no. 57/03, 5 July 2005; *Nivette v. France* (dec.), no. 44190/98, ECHR 2001-VII; *Einhorn v. France* (dec.), no. 71555/01, ECHR 2001-XI; *Al Shari v. France* (dec.), no. 57/03, 5 July 2005.

[15] *Kaboulov v. Ukraine*, no. 41015/04, §§ 101–103, 19 November 2009.

[16] *Ismoilov and Others v. Russia*, no. 2947/06, § 119, 24 April 2008.

[17] *Boumediène and Others v. Bosnia and Herzegovina* (dec.), nos 38703/06, 40123/06, 43301/06, 43302/06, 2131/07, and 2141/07, §§ 46, 67, 18 November 2008; *Chentiev and Ibragimov v. Slovakia* (dec.), nos 21022/08 and 51946/08, 14 September 2010; *Salem v. Portugal* (dec.), no. 26844/04, 9 May 2006; *Nivette v. France* (dec.), no. 44190/98, ECHR 2001-VII.

[18] *Cipriani v. Italy* (dec.), no. 22142/07, 30 March 2010.

[19] *Saadi v. Italy* [GC], no. 37201/06, §§ 55, 148, ECHR 2008.

penalty or trial by a military court, which are readily verifiable, assurances against torture and other abuse require constant vigilance by competent and independent personnel'.[20]

In a case involving extradition from Sint Maarten, a Dutch territory in the Caribbean, to the United States, where an applicant complained of the threat of execution for murder in the State of Georgia, the Court summarily decided to strike the case. The reason was that counsel for the applicant had not replied to requests from the Court for documents. Nevertheless, this involved the Court concluding that there were 'no special circumstances regarding respect for human rights as defined in the Convention and its Protocols which require the continued examination of the case', in accordance with article 37(1) of the Convention.[21] The decision does not indicate whether the Netherlands had obtained assurances from the United States that the death penalty would not be imposed. However, it states that the President of the Court had put factual questions to the respondent State and that, upon receipt of its reply, had decided not to indicate an interim measure in order to block the extradition.[22]

On two occasions, the European Court of Human Rights has concluded that there was a violation of article 1. In *Al-Saadoon and Mufdhi v. The United Kingdom*, the Court found a breach of article 1 of Protocol No. 13 in circumstances where government authorities had handed over two suspects to Iraqi authorities without obtaining assurances that the death penalty would not be imposed.[23] In *Al Nashiri v. Poland*, of 24 July 2014, it held that by facilitating the transfer of an individual to the United States, where there was a real risk capital punishment might be imposed, Poland had violated articles 2 and 3 of the Convention taken together with Article 1 of Protocol No. 6 to the Convention.[24] The Court observed that the proceedings before American courts were still incomplete and that the risk to the applicant of capital punishment remained a reality. It held that 'compliance with their obligations under Articles 2 and 3 of the Convention taken together with Article 1 of Protocol No. 6 to the Convention requires the Government to seek to remove that risk as soon as possible, by seeking assurances from the US authorities that he will not be subjected to the death penalty'.[25] By the time the judgment was issued, Poland had ratified Protocol No. 13. However, it was not applicable *ratione temporis* to the events in question, they having taken place in 2002 and 2003. Protocol No. 6 entered into force for Poland on 30 December 2000.

Further reading

A. Adinolfi, 'Premier instrument international sur l'abolition de la peine de mort', (1987) 58 *Revue internationale de droit pénal* 321.

Frowein/Peukert, *MenschenRechtsKonvention,* pp. 700–1.

Peter Leuprecht, 'The First International Instrument for the Abolition of the Death Penalty', (1983) 2 *Forum* 2.

---

[20] Report of the Independent Expert on the Protection of Human Rights and Fundamental Freedoms while Countering Terrorism to the UN Commission on Human Rights, UN Doc. E/CN.4/2005/103, 7 February 2005, para. 56.

[21] *Registe v. the Netherlands* (dec.), no. 28620/09, 23 March 2010.

[22] Ibid. News reports from the United States indicate that assurances were given: WTVM News, 24 July 2009.

[23] *Al-Saadoon and Mufdhi v. the United Kingdom*, no. 61498/08, § 115, ECHR 2010 (extracts).

[24] *Al Nashiri v. Poland*, no. 28761/11, § 579, 24 July 2014.

[25] Ibid., § 589.

Erik Harremoes, 'The Council of Europe and its Efforts to Promote the Abolition of the Death Penalty', (1986) 12–13 *Crime Prevention and Criminal Justice Newsletter* 62.

Gilbert Guillaume, 'Protocole No 6, Articles 1–4', in Pettiti et al., *La Convention européenne*, pp. 1067–72.

Hans-Christian Kruger, 'Protocol No. 6 to the European Convention on Human Rights', in *The Death Penalty: Abolition in Europe*, Strasbourg: Council of Europe Publishing, 1999, pp. 69–78.

Khadine L. Ritter, 'The Russian Death Penalty Dilemma: Square Pegs and Round Holes', (2000) 32 *Case Western Reserve Journal of International Law* 129.

William A. Schabas, *The Abolition of the Death Penalty in International Law*, 3rd edn, Cambridge: Cambridge University Press, 2003.

William A. Schabas, 'A Step to Universal Abolition of the Death Penalty: Protocol No. 6 to the European Convention', in Olivier Delas and Michaela Leuprecht, eds, *Liber Amicorum Peter Leuprecht*, Brussels: Bruylant, 2012, pp. 297–320.

Jeroen Schokkenbroek, 'Abolition of the Death Penalty (Article 1 of Protocol No. 6)', in Van Dijk et al., *Theory and Practice*, pp. 911–35.

Jon Yorke, 'The Right to Life and Abolition of the Death Penalty in the Council of Europe', (2009) 34 *European Law Review* 205 (2009).

Jon Yorke, 'Inhuman and Degrading Punishment and Abolition of the Death Penalty in the Council of Europe', (2010) 16 *European Public Law* 77.

Jon Yorke, 'The Right to Life and Abolition of the Death Penalty in the Council of Europe', in Jon Yorke, ed., *The Right to Life and the Value of Life; Orientations in Law, Politics and Ethics*, Farnham, UK: Ashgate, 2010, pp. 233–67.

Article 2. Death penalty in time of war/Peine de mort en temps de guerre

A State may make provision in its law for the death penalty in respect of acts committed in time of war or of imminent threat of war; such penalty shall be applied only in the instances laid down in the law and in accordance with its provisions. The State shall communicate to the Secretary General of the Council of Europe the relevant provisions of that law.

Un État peut prévoir dans sa législation la peine de mort pour des actes commis en temps de guerre ou de danger imminent de guerre; une telle peine ne sera appliquée que dans les cas prévus par cette législation et conformément à ses dispositions. Cet État communiquera au Secrétaire Général du Conseil de l'Europe les dispositions afférentes de la législation en cause.

Introductory comments

Article 2 sets out the sole exception to the principle of abolition stated in article 1 of Protocol No. 6. A State may make provision in its law for the death penalty in respect of acts committed in time of war or of imminent threat of war. According to the Explanatory Report, '[a] State can in fact become a Party to the Protocol even if its law (present or future) makes provision for the death penalty in respect of acts committed in time of war or of imminent threat of war'. Were it not for article 2 of Protocol No. 6, the adoption of Protocol No. 13 nearly two decades later would not have been necessary. The third recital to the Preamble of Protocol No. 13 states: 'Noting that Protocol No. 6 to the Convention, concerning the Abolition of the Death Penalty, signed at Strasbourg on 28 April 1983, does not exclude the death penalty in respect of acts committed in time of war or of imminent threat of war.'

When the United Nations began surveying domestic practice on capital punishment, in 1974, it distinguished between States that were 'abolitionist by law' and those that were 'abolitionist by law for ordinary crimes only', describing them as 'countries whose laws provide the death penalty only for exceptional crimes and/or under exceptional circumstances'.[1] At the time, eleven States were listed as fully abolitionist, while seventeen no longer imposed the death penalty for ordinary crimes. Several of the latter were members of the Council of Europe. Recognition that many States remove the death penalty in stages, initially removing it for 'ordinary crimes' but leaving it in force under certain conditions including time or war, provides a rationale for Protocol No. 6.

The corresponding protocols in the United Nations and the Inter-American systems are somewhat more robust. The Second Optional Protocol to the International Covenant on Civil and Political Rights proclaims full abolition of capital punishment but allows States, at the time of ratification or accession, to formulate a reservation providing for 'application of the death penalty in time of war pursuant to a conviction for a most serious

---

[1] Capital Punishment, Report of the Secretary General, UN Doc. E/5616, Annex I, pp. 2–3.

crime of a military nature committed during wartime'.[2] The Additional Protocol to the American Convention on Human Rights is similar.[3]

Drafting of the provision

The instructions from the Committee of Ministers to the Steering Committee on Human Rights were to draft a protocol providing for abolition of the death penalty 'in peacetime'. During the drafting, it was argued that the title should specify this point, but it was decided this was unnecessary. The intention of the drafters was apparently to avoid drawing attention to the wartime exception. They had considerable difficult agreeing upon the text of article 2. Some would have preferred a general declaration abolishing the death penalty but allowing reservations in wartime, the approach taken years later by the United Nations and the Organisation of American States. Another proposal was a text declaring the death penalty abolished 'in peacetime'. This would have necessitated some definition of the term 'peacetime'. The result is a compromise, a principle accompanied by an exception but with no possibility of reservation.[4]

During the drafting, there were suggestions that the terms 'time of war or of imminent threat of war' be replaced by 'international armed conflict', the expression used in Protocol Additional I to the 1949 Geneva Conventions.[5] However, the term 'time of war' was retained because the same expression is used in article 15 of the European Convention, where derogation is permitted 'in time of war or other public emergency threatening the life of the nation'.[6]

The heading of article 2 was added by Protocol No. 11.[7]

Analysis and interpretation

The Explanatory Report states that article 2:

clarifies the scope of the Protocol by limiting the obligation to abolish the death penalty to peacetime. A State can in fact become a Party to the Protocol even if its law (present or future) makes provision for the death penalty in respect of acts committed in time of war or of imminent threat of war. It is however specified that, where this is so, the death penalty shall be applied only in the instances laid down in the law and in accordance with its provisions. Furthermore, a state whose law makes provision for the death penalty in such cases must communicate the relevant provisions to the Secretary General of the Council of Europe. It is clear that any declaration made under this article may be withdrawn or modified by notification to the Secretary General.

---

[2] Second Optional Protocol to the International Covenant on Civil and Political Rights, (1991) 1642 UNTS 414, art. 2(1).

[3] Protocol to the American Convention on Human Rights to Abolish the Death Penalty, OASTS No. 73, art. 2(1).

[4] Gilbert Guillaume, 'Protocole No 6, Articles 1–4', in Pettiti et al., *La Convention européenne*, p. 1067–72, at p. 1069.

[5] Protocol Additional I to the 1949 Geneva Conventions and relating to the Protection of Victims of International Armed Conflicts, (1979) 1125 UNTS 3.

[6] Jacques Velu and Rusen Ergec, *La Convention européenne des droits de l'homme*, Brussels: Bruylant, 1990, at p. 185.

[7] Protocol No. 11 to the Convention for the Protection of Human Rights and Fundamental Freedoms, restructuring the control machinery established thereby, ETS 155, art. 2(6)(a).

However, the Protocol does not use the term 'peacetime'. The restriction authorized by article 2 is permitted 'in time of war or of imminent threat of war'. It is accompanied by conditions of substance and of form: the death penalty can only be imposed according to law, the provisions of such law being communicated to the Secretary General or the Council of Europe.

The only significant judicial application of article 2 of Protocol No. 6 is the work of the Human Rights Chamber of Bosnia and Herzegovina. Protocol No. 6 was directly incorporated in domestic law as a consequence of the 1995 Dayton Peace Agreement. The Chamber began by noting that exceptions to rights and freedoms guaranteed by the European Convention and its Protocols must be narrowly interpreted.[8] It said that article 2 of the Convention, guaranteeing the right to life, is 'one of the most fundamental provisions' that 'enshrined one of the basic values of the democratic societies making up the Council of Europe'.[9] Moreover, deprivations of life should be subject to 'the most careful scrutiny'.[10] The Chamber said these observations were equally applicable to article 2 of Protocol No. 6: 'The Chamber must therefore construe this provision strictly and scrutinise carefully the whole circumstances surrounding the threatened execution of the applicant, including the relevant laws, in order to determine whether the execution would be compatible with Protocol No. 6 or not.'[11]

Two judges of the Chamber issued a separate concurring opinion with their own interpretation of article 2 of Protocol No. 6:

As it is evident from the facts of the case, the applicant has committed the impugned acts in time of war, however, the sentence has not been executed so far, that is, during the wartime period. The main point at issue is the interpretation of Article 2 of the Protocol, namely: would it be possible for the respondent Party to execute the applicant in time of peace, provided that the requirements of Article 2 were met? In other words, how should the provisions of Article 2 be interpreted: do they imply that a state is entitled to apply the death penalty even in peace time for acts committed in time of war or imminent threat of war? Taking into account the primary aim of Protocol No. 6, which has been adopted by the contracting states with a clear intention to abolish capital punishment in peace time, and considering also the last developments in the penal policy of European democratic states (at this particular moment of development death penalty is regarded as an alien institution within the system of European democratic values), the answer should be a negative one.[12]

Specific issues discussed in the judgment, including the possible imposition of capital punishment during peacetime but for a wartime offence as well as the scope of the term 'prescribed by law' are discussed below.

Death penalty 'in time of war'

The expression 'in time of war' is used in article 15(1) of the European Convention and there is no good reason to interpret it differently in article 2 of Protocol No. 6. Indeed, there should be a strong presumption favouring the view that the Committee of Ministers intended the same meaning, absent indications to the contrary in the Explanatory Report.

---

[8] *Damjanović v. Federation of Bosnia and Herzegovina*, Human Rights Chamber CH/96/30, 5 September 1997, para. 29.

[9] Ibid.

[10] Ibid.

[11] Ibid.

[12] Ibid., Concurring opinion of Viktor Masenko-Mavi and Rona Aybay, para. 3.

The notion of 'imminent threat of war' may have been added in order to avoid debates about when war is formally declared, a practice that was once common and that is today essentially obsolete. The European Social Charter of the Council of Europe allows derogation 'in time of war or other public emergency', like the European Convention on Human Rights of which it is the companion in the area of economic, social, and cultural rights. The Charter provides specifically that '[t]he term "in time of war or other public emergency" shall be so understood as to cover also the threat of war'.[13] Unlike article 15(1) of the Convention, article 2 of Protocol No. 6 does not extend the permissibility of restrictions to 'other public emergency threatening the life of the nation'.

'Time of war' should not be confused with the military death penalty. Some States provide for capital punishment in their military code but not in their general criminal law.[14] The military death penalty is prohibited by Protocol No. 6 except, of course, in time of war. Unlike the Second Optional Protocol to the International Covenant on Civil and Political Rights, which only permits the death penalty for military crimes of a serious nature, Protocol No. 6 establishes no limit *ratione materiae* on use of the death penalty during wartime. During the drafting of the Protocol, suggestions to restrict the death penalty in wartime to the 'most serious crimes' were rejected.[15] In any case, the European Convention continues to apply, and an execution imposed in wartime for a crime that was not very serious could violate articles 2 and 3 of the Convention. Various provisions of the Geneva Conventions and their Optional Protocols concern capital punishment, and these could also be applicable to the use of the death penalty in time of war. For example, article 68 of the fourth Geneva Convention prohibits imposition of the death penalty on civilian non-combatants except for espionage, 'serious acts of sabotage against the military installations of the Occupying Power', or 'intentional offences which have caused the death of one or more persons'.[16]

There has been some academic debate as to whether the 'war' contemplated by article 2 could be a non-international armed conflict. Some have taken the view that the Protocol only applies to international armed conflict, noting that a more explicit intent to extend the scope to non-international armed conflict would need to be expressed.[17] This is probably an outdated view, given the tendency towards a blurring of distinctions between the law applicable to international and non-international armed conflict. In any case, in light of Protocol No. 13 the issue is entirely academic.

Although the Explanatory Report declares that the purpose of Protocol No. 6 is to abolish the death penalty in peacetime, in fact article 2 permits capital punishment for acts perpetrated in wartime, but it does not exclude the possibility of an execution for such acts taking place when the war is over.[18] This problem presented itself before the Human Rights Chamber of Bosnia and Herzegovina in the case mentioned above. The Chamber

---

[13] European Social Charter, (1965) 529 UNTS 89, art. 30.

[14] Christine van den Wyngaert, 'Military Offences, International Crimes and the Death Penalty', (1987) 58 *Revue internationale de droit pénal* 737.

[15] Gilbert Guillaume, 'Protocole No 6, Articles 1–4', in Pettiti et al., *La Convention européenne*, p. 1067–72, at p. 1069.

[16] Convention (IV) Relative to the Protection of Civilian Persons in Time of War, (1950) 75 UNTS 287.

[17] Jacques Velu and Rusen Ergec, *La Convention européenne des droits de l'homme*, Brussels: Bruylant, 1990, at p. 185.

[18] *Damjanović v. Federation of Bosnia and Herzegovina*, Human Rights Chamber CH/96/30, 5 September 1997, para. 37. See also *Maktouf and Damjanović v. Bosnia and Herzegovina* [GC], nos 2312/08 and 34179/08, § 27, ECHR 2013 (extracts).

did not seem to think that Protocol No. 6 automatically ruled out an execution during peacetime for an offence committed in wartime. However, the Chamber noted a reference in the Constitution to the Second Optional Protocol to the International Covenant on Civil and Political Rights, an instrument that more clearly excludes the death penalty in peacetime than Protocol No. 6. It held that compliance with Protocol No. 6 required the observance of the Second Optional Protocol and that consequently the death penalty could not be imposed in peacetime.[19]

Prescribed by law

The second clause of the first sentence of article 2 says that if the death penalty is used in time of war or imminent threat of war, it 'shall be applied only in the instances laid down in the law and in accordance with its provisions'. This requirement, which seems broadly similar to other formulations of the rule of law in provisions of the European Convention, should especially be considered in light of articles 2 and 15. Article 2(1) authorizes capital punishment as a restriction on the right to life pursuant to 'a sentence of a court following his conviction of a crime for which this penalty is provided by law'. Article 15(2) prohibits derogation from article 2 'except in respect of deaths resulting from lawful acts of war'. If the rule of law requirement in article 2 of Protocol No. 6 may seem somewhat superfluous, possibly it is there to reinforce the argument that when capital punishment is imposed in wartime the requirements of articles 6 and 7 of the Convention are themselves non-derogable.

The Human Rights Chamber of Bosnia and Herzegovina referred to case law concerning other provisions of the European Convention imposing a requirement that measures be 'lawful' or 'in accordance with law'. Necessarily, any such measures must also be compatible with domestic law. The law must also be accessible and foreseeable. Thus, '[b]earing in mind these principles', the Chamber said that '[a]rticle 2 requires that before it can apply the legislature should have considered and defined the circumstances in which, exceptionally in the context of a legal system where the death penalty has been abolished, such penalty may nevertheless be applied in respect of acts committed in time of war or imminent threat thereof'.[20] Noting that the applicant had been convicted of genocide on the basis of a law of general application, the Chamber said this was not 'a valid basis for the application of Article 2 of the Protocol'.[21] It held that another provision dealing with war crimes lacked the requisite specificity in that it did not make it possible to determine which crimes were subject to capital punishment and which were not.[22]

Communication of the law to the Secretary General

By contrast with the comparable instruments in the United Nations and Organisation of American States systems, where the use of capital punishment in wartime can only be permissible if a reservation is submitted at the time of accession or ratification, Protocol No. 6 requires only that '[t]he State shall communicate to the Secretary General of the Council of Europe the relevant provisions' of the legislation in question. The Explanatory

---

[19] Ibid.
[20] Ibid., para. 32.
[21] Ibid., para. 33.
[22] Ibid.

Report uses the word 'must'. It also indicates that 'any declaration made under this article may be withdrawn or modified by notification to the Secretary General'. Recognizing the possibility of 'modification' provides support for the position that a State could even introduce new legislation well after the Protocol had entered into force as long as it makes prompt communication to the Secretary General. It would seem that any applicable legislation in force at the time of ratification should be communicated to the Secretary General without delay.

There is no indication of the consequences of a failure to comply with the communication requirement. Obviously, it would be a violation of the second sentence of article 2. But it is not obvious that a death sentence pronounced or carried out in time of war in the absence of adequate communication to the Secretary General would also constitute a breach of article 1 of the Protocol. In this respect, it is important to recall the mandate given by the Committee of Ministers to draft an instrument to abolish the death penalty in peacetime, and the rejection of any possibility of reservation or derogation, with their own formalities of notification that are familiar enough in public international law.

Communications to the Secretary General have been made pursuant to article 2, by Switzerland, the Netherlands, Cyprus, and Ukraine. At the time of ratification of Protocol No. 6, these States had legislation allowing for the death penalty in time of war. Some States whose legislation allowed for the death penalty in wartime—Spain,[23] Italy,[24] and Malta[25]—ratified the Protocol without making any declaration under article 2.

In the case of Switzerland, the communication states that the Swiss legal system 'allows the death penalty to be reintroduced on grounds of necessity ("droit de nécessité")'. The example is provided of such a declaration, in 1940, at the outbreak of the Second World War.[26] Switzerland's communication was withdrawn in 1997.[27]

The communication by the Netherlands noted that 'bills for the abolition of capital punishment, insofar as it is still provided for under Dutch military law and Dutch regulations governing wartime offences, have been before Parliament since 1981. It should be noted, however, that under the provisions of the Constitution of the Netherlands, which came into force on 17 February 1983, capital punishment may not be imposed.' The Netherlands also pointed to legislation in force in the Netherlands Antilles and Aruba authorizing the death penalty for the crime of entering into an understanding with a foreign power with a view to inducing that power to engage in hostilities or war against the State, on the condition that the hostilities are carried out or the state of war occurs.[28]

---

[23] The death penalty in wartime in Spain was also discussed in the Human Rights Committee: Third Periodic Report of Spain, UN Doc. CCPR/C/58/Add. 1 and 3, UN Doc. CCPR/C/SR.1018–1021, UN Doc. A/46/40, pp. 35–45. Spain made a reservation to the Second Optional Protocol that was withdrawn on 13 January 1998.

[24] Italy was challenged about its maintenance of the death penalty in wartime by Sir Vincent Evans in the Human Rights Committee: UN Doc. CCPR/C/SR.257, § 37. In 1994, Italy abolished the death penalty in wartime as well as in peacetime.

[25] Malta ratified the Protocol on 26 March 1991. Malta made a reservation to the Second Optional Protocol that was withdrawn on 15 June 2000.

[26] (1987) 30 YB 5–6.

[27] (1997) 40 YB 53.

[28] (1986) 29 YB 4.

When Cyprus ratified the Protocol, in 1999, it informed the Secretary General of several provisions allowing for the death penalty. Some apply not only in wartime but also during a 'state of emergency'.[29]

The communication by Ukraine reads:

On 29 December 1999, the Constitutional Court of Ukraine ruled that the provisions of the Criminal Code of Ukraine which provided for death penalty were unconstitutional. According to the Law of Ukraine of 22 February 2000 'On the Introduction of Amendments to the Criminal, Criminal Procedure and Correctional Labour Codes of Ukraine', the Criminal Code of Ukraine has been brought into conformity with the above-mentioned ruling of the Constitutional Court of Ukraine. The death penalty was replaced by life imprisonment (Article 25 of the Criminal Code of Ukraine). The Law of Ukraine 'On the ratification of Protocol No. 6 to the Convention for the Protection of Human Rights and Fundamental Freedoms concerning the abolition of the Death Penalty, of 1983' envisages retaining of application of the death penalty for offences committed in time of war by means of introduction of appropriate amendments to the legislation in force. Pursuant to Article 2 of the Protocol No. 6 to the Convention for the Protection of Human Rights and Fundamental Freedoms, Ukraine will notify the Secretary General of the Council of Europe in case of introduction of these amendments.[30]

Of interest is the final sentence, which in effect reserves the right of Ukraine to introduce new legislation concerning the death penalty within the limits permitted by article 2.

Further reading

A. Adinolfi, 'Premier instrument international sur l'abolition de la peine de mort', (1987) 58 *Revue internationale de droit pénal* 321.

B. Dunér and H. Geurtsen, 'The Death Penalty and War', (2002) 6 *International Journal of Human Rights* 1.

Frowein/Peukert, *MenschenRechtsKonvention*, p. 702.

Gilbert Guillaume, 'Protocole No 6, Articles 1–4', in Pettiti et al., *La Convention européenne*, pp. 1067–72.

Erik Harremoes, 'The Council of Europe and Its Efforts to Promote the Abolition of the Death Penalty', (1986) 12–13 *Crime Prevention and Criminal Justice Newsletter* 62.

Peter Leuprecht, 'The First International Instrument for the Abolition of the Death Penalty', (1983) 2 *Forum* 2.

William A. Schabas, *The Abolition of the Death Penalty in International Law*, 3rd edn, Cambridge: Cambridge University Press, 2003.

Jon Yorke, 'The Right to Life and Abolition of the Death Penalty in the Council of Europe,' (2009) 34 *European Law Review* 205 (2009).

Jon Yorke, 'Inhuman and Degrading Punishment and Abolition of the Death Penalty in the Council of Europe', (2010) 16 *European Public Law* 77.

---

[29] (2000) 43 YB 15–18.
[30] (2000) 43 YB 18.

Article 3. Prohibition of derogations/Interdiction de dérogation

No derogation from the provisions of this Protocol shall be made under Article 15 of the Convention.

Aucune dérogation n'est autorisée aux dispositions du présent Protocole au titre de l'article 15 de la Convention.

Introductory comments

As the Explanatory Report on Protocol No. 6 observes, under article 15 of the European Convention States may take measures derogating from their obligations 'in time of war or other public emergency threatening the life of the nation'. Article 3 of Protocol No. 6 is 'more restrictive' in its exclusion of any possibility of derogation. Some provisions of the Convention are deemed non-derogable, however. With the logical exception of Protocol No. 13, and of the protection against double jeopardy found in article 4 of Protocol No. 7, none of the other Protocols to the Convention establishes any of the rights it sets out as being non-derogable.

Drafting of the provision

There is no information on the drafting of article 3 in the Explanatory Report. The heading for article 3 was added according to the provisions of Protocol No. 11.[1]

Analysis and interpretation

Although article 15(2) deems certain provisions of the European Convention to be not subject to derogation, the prohibition of capital punishment is the first norm contained in a protocol to the Convention to be placed in such a category. Subsequently, article 4(3) of Protocol No. 7 declared that the prohibition of multiple convictions for the same offence was non-derogable.

Like article 2 of Protocol No. 6, article 15(2) of the European Convention acknowledges the exceptional nature of wartime in that it allows exceptions to the right to life for 'lawful acts of war'. Allowing for derogation with respect to capital punishment would have weakened the largely symbolic message of Protocol No. 6. It would also have extended the possibility of capital punishment to acts committed in peacetime to the extent that they might occur during a 'public emergency threatening the life of the nation'.

Further reading

Gilbert Guillaume, 'Protocole No 6, Articles 1-4', in Pettiti et al., *La Convention européenne*, pp. 1067–72.

---

[1] Protocol No. 11 to the Convention for the Protection of Human Rights and Fundamental Freedoms, restructuring the control machinery established thereby, ETS 155, art. 2(6)(a).

Article 4. Prohibition of reservations/Interdiction de réserves

No reservation may be made under Article 57 of the Convention in respect of the provisions of this Protocol.

Aucune réserve n'est admise aux dispositions du présent Protocole au titre de l'article 57 de la Convention.

Introductory comments

Reservations to the European Convention are permitted, subject to the terms of article 57, just as they are allowed for all multilateral treaties providing that they are compatible with the object and purpose of the instrument[1] and that no special rule is set out.[2] Article 4 of Protocol No. 6 is just such a special rule. Article 4 of Protocol No. 6 and the corresponding provision in Protocol No. 13 are the only blanket prohibitions on reservations in the European Convention system.

One of the drawbacks of an absolute prohibition of reservations is that it removes any flexibility in the ratification process and thereby hinders broad adherence to the treaty. On the other hand, when they are permitted, the scope of reservations can be difficult to control. The result may be the undermining of the integrity of the principles set out in the treaty. Article 4, like article 3, enhances the role of Protocol No. 6 as a declaration of fundamental principle.

Drafting of the provision

There is no information on the drafting of article 4 in the Explanatory Report. The original version of article 4 of Protocol No. 6 referred to article 64. This was changed to article 57 by Protocol No. 11 in light of the renumbering of the provisions of the Convention. The heading for article 4, 'Reservations', was added according to the provisions of Protocol No. 11.[3]

Analysis and interpretation

When reservations to treaties are allowed subject to certain conditions, as is the case with article 57 of the European Convention, difficulties arise in determining whether or not they are acceptable and compatible with the legal framework. The exclusion of reservations altogether appears to solve this problem. However, problems persist to the extent that although reservations may be permitted, interpretative declarations are not.[4] If a State

---

[1] Vienna Convention on the Law of Treaties, (1980) 1155 UNTS 331, art. 19.

[2] For another example of an absolute prohibition of reservations, see Rome Statute of the International Criminal Court, (2002) 2187 UNTS 90, art. 120.

[3] Protocol No. 11 to the Convention for the Protection of Human Rights and Fundamental Freedoms, restructuring the control machinery established thereby, ETS 155, art. 2(6)(a).

[4] *Belilos* v. *Switzerland*, 29 April 1988, Series A no. 132. See the discussion in the chapter on article 57 in this Commentary.

formulates a declaration at the time of ratification, it remains to be determined whether or not this may be a disguised reservation and therefore impermissible.

Article 2 of Protocol No. 6 actually contemplates the possibility that States make declarations to the Secretary-General and in one sense such declarations, indicating the content of legislation applicable to the death penalty in wartime, amount to something comparable to a reservation. Some of the communications made under article 2 indicate the existence of provisions allowing for capital punishment for acts that are not perpetrated in wartime or imminent threat of war. Application of these provisions would therefore constitute a violation of Protocol No. 6, irrespective of the communication. The reason is that the communication contemplated by article 2 is not in fact a reservation at all. It should therefore be unnecessary to examine the communications in order to determine whether they are in fact prohibited reservations.

States are also entitled to make territorial declarations in accordance with article 5 of the Protocol. Like reservations, they must be made at the time of ratification or accession. They may subsequently be withdrawn, in whole or in part, but they cannot be extended by a declaration that withdraws a territory initially subject to the Protocol from its scope.

Otherwise, there has only been one declaration formulated with respect to Protocol No. 6. At the time of ratification, Germany made an interpretative declaration to the effect that its non-criminal legislation is not affected by the Protocol. The German declaration states that its government considers the Protocol to contain no other obligation than to abolish the death penalty in its domestic legislation, something it points out that Germany has already done.[5]

Further reading

Gilbert Guillaume, 'Protocole No 6, Articles 1–4', in Pettiti et al., *La Convention européenne*, pp. 1067–72.

---

[5] (1989) 32 YB 5.

Article 5. Territorial application/Application territoriale

1. Any State may at the time of signature or when depositing its instrument of ratification, acceptance or approval, specify the territory or territories to which this Protocol shall apply.

2. Any State may at any later date, by a declaration addressed to the Secretary General of the Council of Europe, extend the application of this Protocol to any other territory specified in the declaration. In respect of such territory the Protocol shall enter into force on the first day of the month following the date of receipt of such a declaration by the Secretary General.

3. Any declaration made under the two preceding paragraphs may, in respect of any territory specified in such declaration, be withdrawn by a notification addressed to the Secretary General. The withdrawal shall become effective on the first day of the month following the date of receipt of such notification by the Secretary General.

1. Tout Etat peut, au moment de la signature ou au moment du dépôt de son instrument de ratification, d'acceptation ou d'approbation, désigner le ou les territoires auxquels s'appliquera le présent Protocole.

2. Tout Etat peut, à tout autre moment par la suite, par une déclaration adressée au Secrétaire Général du Conseil de l'Europe, étendre l'application du présent Protocole à tout autre territoire désigné dans la déclaration. Le Protocole entrera en vigueur à l'égard de ce territoire le premier jour du mois qui suit la date de réception de la déclaration par le Secrétaire Général.

3. Toute déclaration faite en vertu des deux paragraphes précédents pourra être retirée, en ce qui concerne tout territoire désigné dans cette déclaration, par notification adressée au Secrétaire Général. Le retrait prendra effet le premier jour du mois qui suit la date de réception de la notification par le Secrétaire Général.

Introductory comments

Territorial application of the Convention itself is addressed in article 56 of the Convention. Clauses governing territorial application also appear in several of the Protocols. They are known as 'colonial clauses' and have actually been applicable to only the small number of European States with dependent territories. Such clauses constitute an exception to the general law of treaties, codified in article 29 of the Vienna Convention on the Law of Treaties, by which a convention applies to the entire territory of a State Party. They have been criticized for permitting double standards but, in theory at least, they also permit the European State to show some deference for local autonomy.

Drafting of the provision

In September 1962, the Committee of Ministers of the Council of Europe adopted several model final clauses for use by those involved in drafting treaties. These were subsequently revised in light of the work of the International Law Commission on the subject and the adoption of the Vienna Convention on the Law of Treaties. A revised set of model final clauses was adopted in February 1980. The Explanatory Report on Protocol No. 6 states that article 5 is based on the territorial application clause contained in the Model Final Clauses.[1] The heading, 'Territorial application', was added by Protocol No. 11.[2]

Analysis and interpretation

The territorial application provision of Protocol No. 6 is formulated on the basis of the relevant text in the Model Final Clauses. The wording is significantly different from the corresponding provision in Protocols Nos 1 and 4, which are very flexible, and seems closer to the text of article 56 of the European Convention. Article 5 of Protocol No. 6 seems to provide a State Party with the possibility of specifying any territory or territories, whereas the other territorial clauses in the Convention and the Protocols speak of 'territories for the international relations of which it is responsible'. They are more clearly premised on the presumption that a treaty applies to the entire territory, codified in article 29 of the Vienna Convention on the Law of Treaties. The general rule under the Convention is that it applies to the metropolitan territory as a consequence of ratification but that it only applies to a territory for whose international relations the State Party is responsible if a specific declaration to that effect has been deposited. That is the interpretation given to article 5 of Protocol No. 6 by the European Court of Human Rights in a case filed against Portugal by a Chinese national threatened with deportation from Macao. The European Court of Human Rights found it was without jurisdiction *ratione loci* because of the absence of such a declaration.[3]

The Netherlands ratified Protocol No. 6 on 25 April 1986. The instrument of ratification was accompanied by a declaration accepting the Protocol for the Kingdom of the Netherlands in Europe, the Netherlands Antilles, and Aruba.[4] A declaration by Germany dated 5 July 1989 extended the protection of the Protocol to Land Berlin,[5] something that became quickly obsolete with the reunification of Germany and the extension of the Protocol's scope to the entire German territory. With its instrument of ratification of Protocol No. 6, dated 20 May 1999, the United Kingdom accepted 'the said Convention [sic] for the United Kingdom of Great Britain and Northern Ireland, the Bailiwick of Guernsey, the Bailiwick of Jersey and the Isle of Man, being territories for whose international relations the United Kingdom is responsible'.[6]

A declaration formulated by Azerbaijan is not, strictly speaking, contemplated by article 5, although it certainly concerns the territorial scope of the Protocol. Azerbaijan declared 'that it is unable to guarantee the application of the provisions of the Protocol in the territories occupied by the Republic of Armenia until these territories are liberated from that occupation'.

Further reading

Michael Wood, 'Protocole No 6, Article 5', in Pettiti et al., *La Convention européenne*, p. 1073.

---

[1] Explanatory Report on Protocol No. 6.
[2] Protocol No. 11 to the Convention for the Protection of Human Rights and Fundamental Freedoms, restructuring the control machinery established thereby, ETS 155, art. 2(6)(a).
[3] *Yonghong* v. *Portugal* (dec.), no. 50887/99), ECHR 1999-IX.
[4] (1986) 29 YB 4.
[5] (1989) 32 YB 5.
[6] (1999) 42 YB 7.

Article 6. Relationship to the Convention/Relations avec la Convention

As between the State Parties the provisions of Articles 1 to 5 of this Protocol shall be regarded as additional articles to the Convention and all the provisions of the Convention shall apply accordingly.

Les Etats Parties considèrent les articles 1 à 5 du présent Protocole comme des articles additionnels à la Convention et toutes les dispositions de la Convention s'appliquent en conséquence.

Introductory comments

In *Soering v. The United Kingdom*, the plenary Court explained that 'Protocol No. 6, as a subsequent written agreement, shows that the intention of the Contracting Parties as recently as 1983 was to adopt the normal method of amendment of the text in order to introduce a new obligation to abolish capital punishment in time of peace and, what is more, to do so by an optional instrument allowing each State to choose the moment when to undertake such an engagement'. The Court added that '[i]n these conditions, notwithstanding the special character of the Convention, Article 3 [of the Convention] cannot be interpreted as generally prohibiting the death penalty'.[1]

In other words, Protocol No. 6 was invoked by the Court as if it were an obstacle to the progressive interpretation of the Convention rather than a development that would build momentum for the ultimate goal of total abolition. The view that the Convention cannot be taken as prohibiting the death penalty altogether has been affirmed on several occasions by the Court since *Soering*.[2] Nevertheless, as explained in more detail elsewhere in this Commentary,[3] the position has now changed.[4]

Drafting of the provision

There is no information on the drafting of article 6 in the Explanatory Report. The heading of article 6, 'Relationship to the Convention', was added according to the provisions of Protocol No. 11.[5]

Analysis and interpretation

Article 6 of the Protocol explains that its provisions shall be considered to be additional articles to the Convention. As a result, the protection machinery established by the

---

[1] *Soering v. the United Kingdom*, 7 July 1989, § 103, Series A no. 161.

[2] *Shamayev and Others v. Georgia and Russia*, no. 36378/02, § 333, ECHR 2005-III; *Öcalan v. Turkey* [GC], no. 46221/99, § 162, ECHR 2005-IV.

[3] See in particular the chapter in this Commentary on article 2 of the Convention.

[4] *Al Nashiri v. Poland*, no. 28761/11, § 579, 24 July 2014; *Al-Saadoon and Mufdhi v. the United Kingdom*, no. 61498/08, § 120, ECHR 2010 (extracts).

[5] Protocol No. 11 to the Convention for the Protection of Human Rights and Fundamental Freedoms, restructuring the control machinery established thereby, ETS 155, art. 2(6)(a).

Convention applies. Article 6 also clarifies the fact that article 2(1) of the Convention continues to apply in cases where the death penalty is imposed in time of war or imminent threat of war. According to Pierre-Henri Imbert, the fact that States parties to Protocol No. 6 are automatically subject to the jurisdiction of the Court is further evidence of the absolute character of abolition of the death penalty, which was the objective of the drafters of the Protocol.[6]

The Explanatory Report on Protocol No. 6 states that article 6 'corresponds to Article 5 of the first Protocol to the European Convention on Human Rights and to Article 6, paragraph 1, of Protocol No. 4'. Readers of this Commentary are referred to the chapters on those provisions.

The Protocol itself remains *lex specialis* with regard to provisions ordinarily governed by the Convention but for which it establishes a special scheme, notably the matter of reservations. Where the Protocol is silent, such as with respect to denunciations, the ordinary rule in the Convention itself applies. Thus, the Protocol can only be denounced pursuant to the conditions set out in article 59. During the drafting of the Protocol, it was proposed that the terms of denunciation be made less onerous, for example, by providing for a notice period of six months but no minimum period of application of the Protocol.[7] Some critics have noted that Protocol No. 6 does not prevent a State from reintroducing the death penalty, although this is obviously something that would involve denunciation of the relevant Protocol. The Rapporteur of the Parliamentary Assembly said that with respect to an obligation no to re-introduce the death penalty, 'one might argue that this is not necessary, since there is no withdrawal clause in the draft Protocol'.[8] This is a misconception, however, because the denunciation clause applies to Protocol No. 6 as a consequence of article 6.

Further reading

Pierre-Henri Imbert, 'Article 65', in Pettiti et al., *La Convention européenne*, pp. 943–56.
Pierre-Henri Imbert, 'Protocole No 6, Article 6', in Pettiti et al., *La Convention européenne*, p. 1075.

---

[6] Pierre-Henri Imbert, 'Protocole no 6, article 6', in L.E. Pettiti, E. Decaux, and P.-H. Imbert, eds, *La Convention européenne des droits de l'homme, commentaire article par article*, Paris; Economica, 1995, p. 1075.

[7] Gilbert Guillaume, 'Protocole No 6, Articles 1–4', in Pettiti et al., *La Convention européenne*, p. 1067–72.

[8] Draft Protocol to the European Convention on Human Rights concerning the Abolition of the Death Penalty in All Circumstances, Report, Doc. 9316, para. 8.

Article 7. Signature and ratification/Signature et ratification

This Protocol shall be open for signature by member States of the Council of Europe which have signed the Convention. It is subject to ratification, acceptance or approval. A member State of the Council of Europe may not ratify, accept or approve this Protocol without previously or simultaneously ratifying the Convention. Instruments of ratification, acceptance or approval shall be deposited with the Secretary General of the Council of Europe.

Le présent Protocole est ouvert à la signature des Etats membres du Conseil de l'Europe qui ont signé la Convention. Il sera soumis à ratification, acceptation ou approbation. Un Etat membre du Conseil de l'Europe ne peut ratifier, accepter ou approuver le présent Protocole sans avoir simultanément ou antérieurement ratifié la Convention. Les instruments de ratification, d'acceptation ou d'approbation seront déposés près le Secrétaire Général du Conseil de l'Europe.

Introductory comments

This article is closely related to article 59 of the Convention, also entitled 'Signature and ratification'.

Drafting of the provision

In September 1962, the Committee of Ministers of the Council of Europe adopted several Model Final Clauses for use by those involved in drafting treaties. These were subsequently revised in light of the work of the International Law Commission on the subject and the adoption of the Vienna Convention on the Law of Treaties. A revised set of Model Final Clauses was adopted in February 1980. With respect to signature and ratification, the Committee of Ministers proposed the following: 'This Convention shall be open for signature by the member States of the Council of Europe. It is subject to ratification, acceptance or approval. Instruments of ratification, acceptance or approval shall be deposited with the Secretary General of the Council of Europe.' This text of article 7 of Protocol No. 6 is based on this Model Clause, completed with the addition of a third sentence.[1]

The title 'Signature and ratification' was introduced by Protocol No. 11.[2]

Analysis and interpretation

The signature and ratification provision of Protocol No. 6 differs from those of the Convention and Protocols No. 1 and No. 4 in that it provides for ratification, acceptance, or approval of the treaty. The other instruments were subject only to ratification. The Vienna Convention on the Law of Treaties refers to 'ratification', 'acceptance', 'approval',

[1] Explanatory Report on Protocol No. 11.
[2] Protocol No. 11 to the Convention for the Protection of Human Rights and Fundamental Freedoms, restructuring the control machinery established thereby, ETS 155, art. 2(6)(a).

and 'accession' as a description of the international act whereby a State establishes on the international plane its consent to be bound by a treaty.[3] Article 7 of Protocol No. 6, which is based on the Model Final Clauses proposed by the Committee of Ministers, does not include 'accession', an act that is not preceded by signature. Many multilateral international treaties set a time limit for the signature of the instrument. States that do not sign the text within that time have no alternative but to accede to the treaty. Protocol No. 6 sets no time limit for the signature of the treaty, however.

The requirement in the text that a Member State of the Council of Europe may not ratify, accept, or approve the Protocol without previously or simultaneously ratifying the Convention clarifies an issue that can, in any event, hardly be in doubt. This also confirms the relationship between the Protocol and the Convention. Unlike the earlier additional Protocols, whose purpose was to add new rights to the Convention system, Protocol No. 6 is specifically directed at adjusting article 2(1) of the Convention. It would make no sense to ratify Protocol No. 6 without also ratifying the Convention itself.

Protocol No. 6 was opened for signature on 28 April 1983. On that day, twelve of the twenty-one States Parties to the Convention signed the instrument: Austria, Belgium, Denmark, France, Germany, Luxembourg, the Netherlands, Norway, Portugal, Spain, Sweden, and Switzerland. All Member States of the Council of Europe have now signed and ratified Protocol No. 6 with the exception of Russia, which signed the Protocol on 16 April 1997 but which has never ratified. In its 2013 report to the United Nations Human Rights Council within the context of the Universal Periodic Review, Russia said that a Constitutional Court ruling of 19 November 2009 'finalises the legal ban on such punishment in Russia'.[4]

In 1994, the Parliamentary Assembly of the Council of Europe adopted a resolution calling upon Member States that had not yet done so to ratify Protocol No. 6.[5] The resolution praised Greece, which in 1993 had abolished the death penalty for crimes committed in wartime as well as in peacetime. It stated: 'In view of the irrefutable arguments against the imposition of capital punishment, it calls on the parliaments of all member states of the Council of Europe, and of all states whose legislative assemblies enjoy special guest status at the Assembly, which retain capital punishment for crimes committed in peacetime and/or in wartime, to strike it from their statute books completely.' It also affirmed that willingness to ratify Protocol No. 6 be made a prerequisite for membership of the Council of Europe. It concluded by urging all heads of State and all parliaments in whose countries death sentences are passed to grant clemency to the convicted.

In France, ratification of Protocol No. 6 provoked a debate in the National Assembly on the grounds that it would impinge on its sovereignty and violate article 16 of the Constitution.[6] The matter was submitted to the Conseil constitutionnel, which noted

[3] Vienna Convention on the Law of Treaties, (1980) 1155 UNTS 331, art. 1(b).

[4] National report submitted in accordance with paragraph 5 of the annex to Human Rights Council resolution 16/21, Russian Federation, UN Doc. A/HRC/WG.6/16/RUS/1, para. 31.

[5] Resolution 1044 on the abolition of capital punishment, 4 October 1994. See also Doc. 7154.

[6] Journal officiel des débats parlementaires, Assemblée nationale, 4 July 1983, p. 2938; Journal officiel des débats parlementaires, Assemblée nationale, 21 June 1985, pp. 1867–89.

that it was constitutionally permissible to ratify the Protocol. It stressed the fact that the Protocol could always be denounced in accordance with article 57 of the Convention.[7]

Further reading

Louis Favoreu, 'La décision du conseil constitutionnel du 22 May 1985 relative au protocole no 6 additionnel à la Convention européenne des droits de l'homme', [1985] *Annuaire français de droit international* 868.

Pierre-Henri Imbert, 'Protocole No 6, Article 7', in Pettiti et al., *La Convention européenne*, p. 1077.

[7] Louis Favoreu, 'La décision du conseil constitutionnel du 22 May 1985 relative au protocole no 6 additionnel à la Convention européenne des droits de l'homme', [1985] *Annuaire français de droit international* 868.

Article 8. Entry into force/Entrée en vigueur

1. This Protocol shall enter into force on the first day of the month following the date on which five member States of the Council of Europe have expressed their consent to be bound by the Protocol in accordance with the provisions of Article 7.

2. In respect of any member State which subsequently expresses its consent to be bound by it, the Protocol shall enter into force on the first day of the month following the date of the deposit of the instrument of ratification, acceptance or approval.

1. Le présent Protocole entrera en vigueur le premier jour du mois qui suit la date à laquelle cinq Etats membres du Conseil de l'Europe auront exprimé leur consentement à être liés par le Protocole conformément aux dispositions de l'article 7.

2. Pour tout Etat membre qui exprimera ultérieurement son consentement à être lié par le Protocole, celui-ci entrera en vigueur le premier jour du mois qui suit la date du dépôt de l'instrument de ratification, d'acceptation ou d'approbation.

Introductory comments

In contrast with the Convention itself and Protocols No. 1 and No. 4, Protocol No. 6 has a distinct provision dealing with entry into force.

Drafting of the provision

The Explanatory Report does not provide information about the drafting of article 8. The heading of article 8, 'Entry into force', was added according to the provisions of Protocol No. 11.[1]

Analysis and interpretation

Protocol No. 6 entered into force on 1 March 1985 after obtaining the five ratifications required by article 8.[2] When it was being drafted, there were suggestions that this be increased to seven and even ten, but the drafters eventually returned to the original suggestion made by the Steering Committee on Human Rights in 1979.[3]

Further reading

Pierre-Henri Imbert, 'Protocole No 6, Article 8', in Pettiti et al., *La Convention européenne*, p. 1079.

---

[1] Protocol No. 11 to the Convention for the Protection of Human Rights and Fundamental Freedoms, restructuring the control machinery established thereby, ETS 155, art. 2(6)(a).

[2] Pierre-Henri Imbert, 'Protocole No 6, Article 6', in Pettiti et al., *La Convention européenne*, p. 1079.

[3] Gilbert Guillaume, 'Protocole No 6, Articles 1–4', in Pettiti et al., *La Convention européenne*, pp. 1067–72.

Article 9. Depositary functions/Fonctions du dépositaire

The Secretary General of the Council of Europe shall notify all the member States of the Council of:

(a) any signature;

(b) the deposit of any instrument of ratification, acceptance or approval;

(c) any date of entry into force of this Protocol in accordance with Articles 6 and 9;

(d) any other act, notification or declaration relating to this Protocol.

Le Secrétaire Général du Conseil de l'Europe notifiera à tous les Etats membres du Conseil de l'Europe:

(a) toute signature;

(b) le dépôt de tout instrument de ratification, d'acceptation ou d'approbation;

(c) toute date d'entrée en vigueur du présent Protocole conformément à ses articles 6 et 9;

(d) tout autre acte, notification ou déclaration ayant trait au présent Protocole.

Introductory comments

Most multilateral treaties identify the depositary of the instrument. This is a government or organization responsible for various functions, the role being codified in article 77 of the Vienna Convention on the Law of Treaties. The function of depositary is not set out explicitly in the European Convention on Human Rights. Nevertheless, the inexorable conclusion is that this responsibility devolves to the Secretary General of the Council of Europe. Beginning with Protocol No. 6, Protocols to the Convention contain a provision entitled 'Depositary functions'.

Drafting of the provision

The text of article 9 of Protocol No. 6 is based on the relevant provision of the Model Final Clauses adopted in 1980 by the Committee of Ministers.[1] The only significant change is the removal of the reference to accession, given that States Parties cannot accede to the Convention and its Protocols. The title 'Depositary functions' was introduced by Protocol No. 11.[2]

Analysis and interpretation

Article 9 lists only some of the functions of the depositary. It is confined to notifying States Parties of the performance and deposit of various legal instruments listed in the provision. Articles 77 to 80 of the Vienna Convention on the Law of Treaties provide a much more detailed list of the tasks of the depositary. Most, if not all of them, are in fact carried out by the Secretary General of the Council of Europe, even in the absence of a specific reference in article 9 of Protocol No. 6, the Convention itself, and the other

---

[1] Explanatory Report on Protocol No. 11.

[2] Protocol No. 11 to the Convention for the Protection of Human Rights and Fundamental Freedoms, restructuring the control machinery established thereby, ETS 155, art. 2(6)(a).

Protocols. These include keeping custody of the original text of the treaty and of any full powers delivered to the depositary, preparing certified copies of the original text, verifying the formalities of signature of various instruments, the correction of errors in texts or in certified copies of treaties, and the registration of treaties with the Secretariat of the United Nations.

Further reading

Pierre-Henri Imbert, 'Protocole No 6, Article 9', in Pettiti et al., *La Convention européenne*, p. 1081.

PART SIX

PROTOCOL NO. 7 TO THE CONVENTION FOR THE PROTECTION OF HUMAN RIGHTS AND FUNDAMENTAL FREEDOMS

Preamble/Préambule

The member States of the Council of Europe signatory hereto,

Being resolved to take further steps to ensure the collective enforcement of certain rights and freedoms by means of the Convention for the Protection of Human Rights and Fundamental Freedoms signed at Rome on 4 November 1950 (hereinafter referred to as 'The Convention');

Have agreed as follows:

Les Etats membres du Conseil de l'Europe, signataires du présent Protocole,

Résolus à prendre de nouvelles mesures propres à assurer la garantie collective de certains droits et libertés par la Convention de Sauvegarde des Droits de l'Homme et des Libertés fondamentales, signée à Rome le 4 November 1950 (ci-après dénommée «la Convention»),

Sont convenus de ce qui suit:

Introductory comments

Like the predecessor Protocols to the Convention, the Preamble of Protocol No. 7 is succinct and quite perfunctory. It might well have acknowledged that the impetus for its adoption was the entry into force of the International Covenant on Civil and Political Rights, as well as the fact that it still did not complete the work of incorporating all of the provisions of the Universal Declaration of Human Rights within the Convention system.

Drafting of the provision

The Preamble is similar to the corresponding text of Protocol No. 4. The drafters of Protocol No. 4 rejected a more elaborate proposal from the Consultative Assembly out of concern that problems of interpretation could result. This explanation is probably valid with respect to Protocol No. 7, although there is no comment whatsoever on the Preamble in the Explanatory Report.

The heading 'Preamble' was added by Protocol No. 11.[1]

Analysis and interpretation

The Preamble to Protocol No. 7 does not contribute in any significant way to its interpretation. It does not seem that it has ever been cited in case law of the Convention organs.

---

[1] Protocol No. 11 to the Convention for the Protection of Human Rights and Fundamental Freedoms, restructuring the control machinery established thereby, ETS 155, art. 2(7)(a).

Article 1. Procedural safeguards relating to expulsion of aliens/ Garanties procédurales en cas d'expulsion d'étranger

1. An alien lawfully resident in the territory of a State shall not be expelled therefrom except in pursuance of a decision reached in accordance with law and shall be allowed:

(a) to submit reasons against his expulsion,

(b) to have his case reviewed, and

(c) to be represented for these purposes before the competent authority or a person or persons designated by that authority.

2. An alien may be expelled before the exercise of his rights under paragraph 1(a), (b) and (c) of this Article, when such expulsion is necessary in the interests of public order or is grounded on reasons of national security.

1. Un étranger résidant régulièrement sur le territoire d'un Etat ne peut en être expulsé qu'en exécution d'une décision prise conformément à la loi et doit pouvoir:

(a) faire valoir les raisons qui militent contre son expulsion,

(b) faire examiner son cas, et

(c) se faire représenter à ces fins devant l'autorité compétente ou une ou plusieurs personnes désignées par cette autorité.

2. Un étranger peut être expulsé avant l'exercice des droits énumérés au paragraphe 1.a, b et c de cet article lorsque cette expulsion est nécessaire dans l'intérêt de l'ordre public ou est basée sur des motifs de sécurité nationale.

Introductory comments

Article 1 of Protocol No. 7 is a form of *lex specialis* with respect to article 13 of the Convention. The latter has been interpreted 'as guaranteeing an "effective remedy before a national authority" to everyone who claims that his rights and freedoms under the Convention have been violated'.[1] As noted in the Explanatory Report, 'an alien lawfully in the territory of a member State of the Council of Europe already benefits from certain guarantees when a measure of expulsion is taken against him', including those provided by articles 3 and 8 of the Convention, as well as other international instruments, notably article 3 of the European Convention on Establishment of 1955, article 19(8) of the European Social Charter of 1961, article 48 of the Treaty establishing the European Economic Community of 1957, articles 32 and 33 of the Geneva Convention relating to the Status of Refugees of 1951 and article 13 of the International Covenant on Civil and Political Rights.[2]

Although adopted in order to reconcile the Convention system with the rights guaranteed by the International Covenant on Civil and Political Rights, the Explanatory Report notes that article 1 of Protocol No. 7 'contains some important specifications'. Unlike article 13(2) of the Covenant, article 1 of Protocol No. 7 'determines the circumstances in which an alien may be expelled before exercising the rights laid down in paragraph 1'.[3]

---

[1] *Klass and Others v. Germany*, 6 September 1978, § 64, Series A no. 28.
[2] Explanatory Report on Protocol No. 7, para. 7.
[3] Ibid., para. 8.

Drafting of the provision

The ancestor of article 1 can be found in the November 1959 proposal of the Consultative Assembly for the addition to the Convention of a provision on arbitrary expulsion of aliens. The draft text of what was then designated as Protocol No. 2 but that became Protocol No. 4 when two other Protocols intervened read as follows: 'An alien lawfully residing in the territory of a High Contracting Party may be expelled only if he endangers national security or offends against *ordre public* or morality.'[4] This was a substantive guarantee, a right of residence for non-citizens, that was far ahead of its time and that did not prosper. Subsequent paragraphs dealt with the procedural guarantees, but even this proved too difficult for the negotiators. Finally, the Committee of Ministers satisfied itself with article 4 of Protocol No. 4, the guarantee against collective expulsion of aliens.

The issue returned two decades later when Protocol No. 7 was being prepared. The Explanatory Report provides a modest amount of information about the drafting of article 1. It states:

Account being taken of the rights which are thus recognised in favour of aliens, the present article has been added to the European Convention on Human Rights in order to afford minimum guarantees to such persons in the event of expulsion from the territory of a Contracting Party. The addition of this article enables protection to be granted in those cases which are not covered by other international instruments and allows such protection to be brought within the purview of the system of control provided for in the European Convention on Human Rights.[5]

The heading, 'Procedural safeguards relating to expulsion of aliens', was added pursuant to Protocol No. 11.[6]

Analysis and interpretation

Article 1 of Protocol No. 7, like article 13 of the Convention itself, provides for a procedural remedy but does not guarantee a favourable result.[7] In principle, under the Convention and its Protocols non-nationals do not have a right to remain on the territory of a State. When the right to remain on the territory of a State was affirmed in article 3(1) of Protocol No. 4, it was explicitly reserved to 'nationals'. The Convention organs have acknowledged that 'the High Contracting Parties have a discretionary power to decide whether to expel an alien present in their territory but this power must be exercised in such a way as not to infringe the rights under the Convention of the person concerned'.[8]

Non-nationals may, of course, be protected against expulsion by other legal norms, such as the guarantees against *non-refoulement* of the Convention on the Status of Refugees,[9] the

---

[4] Report on the Second Protocol to the Convention on Human Rights, M. Lannung, Rapporteur, Doc. 1057, 17 November 1959.
[5] Explanatory Report on Protocol No. 7, para. 7.
[6] Protocol No. 11 to the Convention for the Protection of Human Rights and Fundamental Freedoms, restructuring the control machinery established thereby, ETS 155, art. 2(7)(a).
[7] *Takush v. Greece*, no. 2853/09, § 50, 17 January 2012; *Aparicio Benito v. Spain* (dec.), no. 36150/03, 4 May 2004.
[8] *Nolan and K. v. Russia*, no. 2512/04, § 114, 12 February 2009; *Bolat v. Russia*, no. 14139/03, § 81, ECHR 2006-XI (extracts); *Agee v. the United Kingdom*, no. 7729/76, Commission decision of 17 December 1976, DR 7, p. 164.
[9] Convention relating to the Status of Refugees, (1954) 189 UNTS 150, art. 33.

Convention Against Torture and Other Cruel, Inhuman and Degrading Treatment or Punishment,[10] and the International Convention for the Protection of All Persons from Enforced Disappearance.[11] According to the case law of the European Court of Human Rights, States Parties may be responsible for violations in cases of expulsion, deportation, or *refoulement* of a person to a third State where there is a real risk of a violation of articles 2[12] or 3[13] of the Convention, or of article 1 of Protocol No. 6 and Protocol No. 13,[14] or of a 'flagrant denial' of fair trial rights.[15] These extend even further than article 1 of Protocol No. 7 because they do not require that the victim be 'lawfully resident'.

Lawfully resident

The guarantees provided by article 1 of Protocol No. 7 only apply to an alien who is 'lawfully resident' in the territory of the State in question.[16] Reference should be made to article 2 of Protocol No. 4, protecting the liberty of movement of a person who is 'lawfully within the territory' of a State Party. It is broader in scope to the term 'lawfully resident' in article 1. According to the Explanatory Report on Protocol No. 7, the word 'resident' is meant to exclude from the application of article 1 an 'alien who has arrived at a port or other point of entry but has not yet passed through the immigration control or who has been admitted to the territory for the purpose only of transit or for a limited period for a non-residential purpose'.[17] Such an individual would probably meet the terms of article 2 of Protocol No. 4.

According to the Court, '[t]he notion of "residence" is akin to the autonomous concept of "home" developed under Article 8 of the Convention, in that both are not limited to physical presence but depend on the existence of sufficient and continuous links with a specific place'.[18] In a case involving someone who had resided on the territory of the respondent State for many years, where he had enjoyed resident status, the Court said it did not 'appear plausible' that every time he took a trip abroad he would cease to be a resident, however short the absence.[19] According to the Explanatory Report, article 1 applies both to aliens who have entered lawfully and to aliens who have entered unlawfully

---

[10] Convention against Torture and Other Cruel, Inhuman or Degrading Treatment or Punishment, (1987) 1465 UNTS 85, art. 3.

[11] International Convention for the Protection of All Persons from Enforced Disappearance, UN Doc. A/61/448, annex, art. 16.

[12] *Kaboulov v. Ukraine*, no. 41015/04, § 99, 19 November 2009.

[13] *Soering v. the United Kingdom*, 7 July 1989, § 88, Series A no. 161; *Chahal v. the United Kingdom*, 15 November 1996, § 74, *Reports of Judgments and Decisions* 1996-V; *Saadi v. Italy* [GC], no. 37201/06, § 125, ECHR 2008.

[14] *Al Nashiri v. Poland*, no. 28761/11, § 579, 24 July 2014; *Al-Saadoon and Mufdhi v. the United Kingdom*, no. 61498/08, § 115, ECHR 2010 (extracts).

[15] *Othman (Abu Qatada) v. the United Kingdom*, no. 8139/09, § 258, ECHR 2012 (extracts); *Zarmayev v. Belgium* (dec.), no. 35/10, 27 February 2014.

[16] Explanatory Report on Protocol No. 7, para. 9; *Sultani v. France*, no. 45223/05, §§ 87–89, ECHR 2007-IV (extracts); *Sejdovic and Sulejmanovic v. Italy* (dec.), no. 57575/00, 14 March 2002; *Sulejmanovic and Sultanovic v. Italy* (dec.), no. 57574/00, 14 March 2002; *Nowak v. Ukraine*, no. 60846/10, § 82, 31 March 2011.

[17] Explanatory Report on Protocol No. 7, para. 9. Cited in *Nolan and K. v. Russia*, no. 2512/04, § 48, 12 February 2009.

[18] *Nolan and K. v. Russia*, no. 2512/04, § 110, 12 February 2009.

[19] Ibid.

but whose position has been subsequently regularized.[20] The notion of 'residence' is broader than that of 'physical presence' on the territory of that State.[21]

The word 'lawfully' is a reference to the domestic law of the State in question. Thus, a determination as to whether the residence is 'lawful' involves analysis of the application of national law.[22] If the alien's admission and stay is conditional on certain conditions, such as a fixed period of residence, the person is no longer 'lawfully' resident if those conditions no longer apply.[23] Similarly, if a visa or residence permit has expired, the individual is no longer 'lawfully resident'.[24] The Explanatory Report makes reference to use of the term 'lawful residence' in other international instruments.[25] In particular, it notes article 11 of the European Convention on Social and Medical Assistance:

a. Residence by an alien in the territory of any of the Contracting Parties shall be considered lawful within the meaning of this Convention so long as there is in force in his case a permit or such other permission as is required by the laws and regulations of the country concerned to reside therein...
b. Lawful residence shall become unlawful from the date of any deportation order made out against the person concerned, unless a stay of execution is granted.[26]

It also mentions section II of the Protocol to the European Convention on Establishment:

a. Regulations governing the admission, residence and movement of aliens and also their right to engage in gainful occupations shall be unaffected by this Convention insofar as they are not inconsistent with it;
b. Nationals of a Contracting Party shall be considered as lawfully residing in the territory of another Party if they have conformed to the said regulations.[27]

Although the domestic law remains the touchstone for the notion of 'lawfully', this has not prevented the Court from examining whether it has been applied in an arbitrary or unreasonable manner. The Court has applied the notion of 'legitimate expectation' to the issue of lawful residence.[28]

Expulsion

The Explanatory Note indicates that the term 'expulsion' is to be interpreted broadly. It is used 'in a generic sense as meaning any measure compelling the departure of an alien from the territory but does not include extradition'.[29] Thus, 'any measure compelling the alien's departure from the territory where he was lawfully resident constitutes "expulsion" for the purposes of Article 1 of Protocol No. 7'.[30] Expulsion, as the term is used in

[20] Explanatory Report on Protocol No. 7, para. 9.
[21] *Nolan and K. v. Russia*, no. 2512/04, § 110, 12 February 2009.
[22] Explanatory Report on Protocol No. 7, para. 9.
[23] *Nolan and K. v. Russia*, no. 2512/04, § 48, 12 February 2009.
[24] *Voulfovitch and Oulianova v. Sweden*, no. 19373/92, Commission decision of 13 January 1993.
[25] Explanatory Report on Protocol No. 7, para. 9, fn. 2. Cited in *Bolat v. Russia*, no. 14139/03, § 77, ECHR 2006-XI (extracts).
[26] European Convention on Social and Medical Assistance, ETS 14, art. 11.
[27] Protocol to the European Convention on Establishment, ETS 19, Section II.
[28] *Bolat v. Russia*, no. 14139/03, § 77, ECHR 2006-XI (extracts); *Nolan and K. v. Russia*, no. 2512/04, § 111, 12 February 2009.
[29] Explanatory Report on Protocol No. 7, para. 10.
[30] *Bolat v. Russia*, no. 14139/03, § 79, ECHR 2006-XI (extracts); *Nolan and K. v. Russia*, no. 2512/04, § 112, 12 February 2009.

article 1, is an autonomous concept to be understood independently of definitions found in domestic legislation. As explained above, the *refoulement* of aliens who have entered the territory unlawfully is not contemplated by the provision unless their position has been subsequently regularized.[31] They find a more limited amount of protection under article 4 of Protocol No. 4, prohibiting collective expulsion, where there is no requirement that aliens be lawfully on the territory. The Court has applied article 1 of Protocol No. 7 to a person who was prevented from re-entering the country where he had resided for many years, noting that 'the Russian authorities sought to prevent him from re-entering Russian territory and to compel his definitive departure from Russia. The applicant may therefore be considered to have been "expelled".'[32]

A decision in accordance with law

Article 1 does not create a right of asylum. As the title it was given by Protocol No. 11 indicates, it is concerned with 'procedural safeguards relating to expulsion of aliens'. A person who is lawfully resident in a State Party may only be expelled 'in pursuance of a decision reached in accordance with law'. The Explanatory Report notes that '[n]o exceptions may be made to this rule'.[33]

The term 'law' refers to the domestic law of the State Party in question. 'The decision must therefore be taken by the competent authority in accordance with the provisions of substantive law and with the relevant procedural rules', says the Explanatory Report.[34] Nevertheless, the appreciation of the term 'law' has a substantive sense. This substantive dimension is often described as referring to the quality of the law.[35] The meaning to be given to the notion is the same as that applying throughout the Convention.[36] The decision ordering expulsion must be taken by the competent authority in accordance with the substantive and procedural rules that apply.[37] The law must be foreseeable and accessible.[38] The requirement of foreseeability means that the person in question must receive from the government some indication of the reasons for the expulsion; absent this, the Court will conclude that article 1 of Protocol No. 7 has been violated.[39]

The Court will scrutinize the conduct of the national authorities to ensure that they respect the applicable legal provisions. In a case where the applicant was summarily expelled from the country without being able to introduce an effective challenge, the Court concluded that 'la manière dont l'expulsion a été exécutée en l'espèce se concilie mal avec la nécessité de prévenir les atteintes arbitraires de la puissance publique aux droits garantis par la Convention'.[40]

---

[31] Explanatory Report on Protocol No. 7, para. 10.

[32] *Nolan and K. v. Russia*, no. 2512/04, § 112, 12 February 2009.

[33] Explanatory Report on Protocol No. 7, para. 11.

[34] Ibid.

[35] *Ahmed v. Romania*, no. 34621/03, § 52, 13 July 2010.

[36] *C.G. and Others v. Bulgaria*, no. 1365/07, § 73, 24 April 2008; *Kaushal and Others v. Bulgaria*, no. 1537/08, § 48, 2 September 2010.

[37] *Takush v. Greece*, no. 2853/09, § 57, 17 January 2012; *Bolat v. Russia*, no. 14139/03, § 81, ECHR 2006-XI (extracts).

[38] *Baltaji v. Bulgaria*, no. 12919/04, § 56, 12 July 2011.

[39] *Kaya v. Romania*, no. 33970/05, §59, 12 October 2006; *Lupsa v. Romania*, no. 10337/04, § 59, 8 June 2006; *Ahmed v. Romania*, no. 34621/03, §§ 53–56, 13 July 2010.

[40] *Takush v. Greece*, no. 2853/09, § 59, 17 January 2012.

The guarantees (art. 1(1)(a), (b) and (c))

Sub-paragraphs (a), (b), and (c) of article 1(1) set out three guarantees. These have been clearly distinguished in three separate sub-paragraphs,[41] in contrast with article 13 of the International Covenant on Civil and Political Rights, where essentially the same notions are set out in a lengthy phrase: 'to submit the reasons against his expulsion and to have his case reviewed by, and be represented for the purpose before, the competent authority or a person or persons especially designated by the competent authority'.

The first guarantee is the right of the alien threatened with expulsion to submit reasons against his or her expulsion. The actual exercise of this right is governed by domestic legislation. By including this guarantee in a separate sub-paragraph, the Explanatory Report states that 'the intention is to indicate clearly that an alien can exercise it even before being able to have his case reviewed'.[42]

The second and third guarantees apply to the review of the threatened expulsion 'before the competent authority or a person or persons designated by that authority'. Paragraph (b) recognizes a right to have the case reviewed, while paragraph (c) guarantees the right to be represented during the proceedings. According to the Explanatory Report, a two-stage procedure before different authorities is not necessarily required. Nor is there a requirement of an oral hearing.[43] It says that the form of the review is a matter left to domestic law, noting that in some States, an alien threatened with expulsion may be entitled to appeal the decision following review of his or her case. The Explanatory Report says that article 1(1) of Protocol No. 7 'does not relate to that stage of proceedings and does not therefore require that the person concerned should be permitted to remain in the territory of the State pending the outcome of the appeal introduced against the decision taken following the review of his case'.[44]

The review of the case must not be simply perfunctory. Where 'the national courts refused to gather evidence to confirm or dispel the allegations serving as a basis for the decision to expel him and subjected this decision to a purely formal examination, with the result that the first applicant was not able to have his case genuinely heard and reviewed in the light of reasons militating against his expulsion', the provision was held to have been violated.[45] A decision by the European Commission of Human Rights holding that a decision to expel an alien is outside the scope of article 6 of the Convention does 'not involve a determination of his civil rights and obligations or of any criminal charge against him'[46] is left unaltered by the adoption of article 1 of Protocol No. 7, according to the Explanatory Report.[47]

The 'competent authority' charged with reviewing the expulsion order may be administrative or judicial. It 'need not be the authority with whom the final decision on the question of expulsion rests'. The Explanatory Report notes that the requirements of

---

[41] Explanatory Report on Protocol No. 7, para. 12.

[42] Ibid., para. 13.1.

[43] Ibid., para. 14.

[44] Ibid., para. 13.2.

[45] *C.G. and Others v. Bulgaria*, no. 1365/07, § 74, 24 April 2008.

[46] *Agee v. the United Kingdom*, no. 7729/76, Commission decision of 17 December 1976, DR 7, p. 164. See also *X v. the United Kingdom*, no. 7902/77, Commission decision of 18 May 1977, DR 9, p. 224; *Singh and Uppal v. the United Kingdom*, no. 8244/78, Commission decision of 2 May 1979, DR 17, p. 149; *X, Y, and Z v. The United Kingdom*, no. 9285/81, Commission decision of 6 July 1982, § 4, DR, Vol. 29, p. 205.

[47] Explanatory Report on Protocol No. 7, para. 16.

article 1(1) would be satisfied if a court reviewed the matter and then made a recommendation to an administrative authority with the responsibility for taking the final decision on expulsion. Also, it is open to States Parties 'to establish different procedures and designate different authorities for certain categories of cases, provided that the guarantees contained in the article are otherwise respected'. This would not constitute an infringement of article 14.[48]

Expulsion pending review of the decision (art. 1(2))

Exceptionally, paragraph 2 of article 1 authorizes the State to expel the alien before the three procedural rights set out in paragraph 1 have been exercised, providing certain conditions have been met. This does not mean that the individual is deprived of the procedural rights in the first paragraph, only that he or she may be removed from the territory pending their exercise.[49] Paragraph 2 makes the permissibility of such an exception conditional on it being necessary in the interests of public order or on reasons of national security. The Explanatory Report notes that the general rule should be exercise of the procedural rights before expulsion. The exceptions set out in paragraph 2 'are to be applied taking into account the principle of proportionality as defined in the case-law of the European Court of Human Rights'.[50] According to the Explanatory Report, 'the State relying on public order to expel an alien before the exercise of the aforementioned rights must be able to show that this exceptional measure was necessary in the particular case or category of cases'.[51] Where it does not provide such a justification, there may be an infringement of article 1(2).[52] On the other hand, if expulsion is grounded on reasons of national security, the Explanatory Report says 'this in itself should be accepted as sufficient justification'.[53]

Reservations and declarations

There has been one reservation to article 1 of Protocol No. 7. Upon ratification, on 24 February 1988, Switzerland made the following reservation: 'When expulsion takes place in pursuance of a decision of the Federal Council taken in accordance with Article 70 of the Constitution on the grounds of a threat to the internal or external security of Switzerland, the person concerned does not enjoy the rights listed in paragraph 1 even after the execution of the expulsion.'[54]

At the time of signature of Protocol No. 7, on 11 May 2005, Belgium made a declaration: 'Belgium understands the words "resident" and "lawfully" mentioned in Article 1 of this Protocol in the sense that is given to them in paragraph 9 of its Explanatory Report.'[55] Upon ratification of the Protocol, in 2012, Belgium deposited a letter indicating that the declaration was withdrawn.

[48] Ibid., para. 13.3.
[49] *Kaya v. Romania*, no. 33970/05, §53, 12 October 2006.
[50] Explanatory Report on Protocol No. 7, para. 15.
[51] Ibid.
[52] *Takush v. Greece*, no. 2853/09, § 62, 17 January 2012.
[53] Explanatory Report on Protocol No. 7, para. 15.
[54] (1988) 31 YB 7.
[55] (2005) 48 YB 13.

Sweden made a declaration at the time of deposit of its instrument of ratification, on 8 November 1985, concerning a legislative provision by which an alien with a right to appeal an expulsion order may renounce this right irrevocably.[56]

Further reading

C. Campiglio, 'Espulsione e diritti dell'uomo a proposito dell'art. 1 nel Protocollo n. 7 addizionale alla Convenzine europea dei diritti dell'uomo', (1985) 68 *Rivista di diritto internazionale* 64.

Juan Fernando Durán Alba, 'Guarantees against Expulsion of Aliens under Article 1 of Protocol No. 7', in Javier García Roca and Pablo Santolaya, eds, *Europe of Rights: A Compendium on the European Convention of Human Rights*, Leiden/Boston: Martinus Nijhoff, 2012, pp. 635–40.

Cees Flinterman, 'Expulsion of Aliens (Article 1 of Protocol No. 7)', in Van Dijk et al., *Theory and Practice*, pp. 965–9.

Frowein/Peukert, *MenschenRechtsKonvention,* pp. 703–6.

Grabenwarter, *European Convention*, pp. 424–7.

Harris et al., *Law of the European Convention*, p. 747.

Danièle Lochak, 'Protocole No 7, Article 1', in Pettiti et al., *La Convention européenne*, pp. 1083–5.

---

[56] (1985) 28 YB 9.

Article 2. Right of appeal in criminal matters/Droit à un double degré de juridiction en matière pénale

1. Everyone convicted of a criminal offence by a tribunal shall have the right to have conviction or sentence reviewed by a higher tribunal. The exercise of this right, including the grounds on which it may be exercised, shall be governed by law.

2. This right may be subject to exceptions in regard to offences of a minor character, as prescribed by law, or in cases in which the person concerned was tried in the first instance by the highest tribunal or was convicted following an appeal against acquittal.

1. Toute personne déclarée coupable d'une infraction pénale par un tribunal a le droit de faire examiner par une juridiction supérieure la déclaration de culpabilité ou la condamnation. L'exercice de ce droit, y compris les motifs pour lesquels il peut être exercé, sont régis par la loi.

2. Ce droit peut faire l'objet d'exceptions pour des infractions mineures telles qu'elles sont définies par la loi ou lorsque l'intéressé a été jugé en première instance par la plus haute juridiction ou a été déclaré coupable et condamné à la suite d'un recours contre son acquittement.

Introductory comments

The right of appeal in criminal matters is first set out in international human rights law in article 14(5) of the International Covenant on Civil and Political Rights. It only appeared rather late in the drafting of the Covenant, the result a proposal by Israel during the debates in the Third Committee of the General Assembly in 1959.[1] The Covenant provision reads: 'Everyone convicted of a crime shall have the right to his conviction and sentence being reviewed by a higher tribunal according to law.'

The somewhat belated recognition of the appeal as a fundamental right can be seen in international criminal justice. There was no appeal before the International Military Tribunals held at the conclusion of the Second World War. In the 1990s, when the modern generation of international criminal courts was being created, it was recognized that this was now a fundamental right.[2] The Rome Statute of the International Criminal Court goes beyond the right to appeal a conviction, with quite elaborate provisions for interlocutory appeal as well as an appeal of both conviction and sentence. It also allows the Prosecutor to undertake appeals of acquittals. Judge Fausto Pocar of the Appeals Chamber of the International Criminal Tribunal for the former Yugoslavia has suggested that the right of appeal is 'an imperative norm of international law'.[3]

Drafting of the provision

The Explanatory Report notes that the word 'tribunal' has been included in article 2(1) of Protocol No. 7 but that it is not found in the corresponding provision of the International

---

[1] UN Doc. A/C.3/L.795/Rev.3.

[2] Report of the Secretary General Pursuant to Paragraph 2 of Security Council Resolution 808 (1993), UN Doc. S/25704, para. 116.

[3] *Prosecutor v. Rutaganda*, ICTR-96-3-A, Dissenting opinion of Judge Pocar, 26 May 2003, citing *Prosecutor v. Tadić*, IT-94-1-A-AR77, Appeal Judgment on Allegations of Contempt against Prior Counsel, Milan Vujin, 27 Feb. 2001, p. 3.

Covenant on Civil and Political Rights. It has been added 'to show clearly that this provision does not concern offences which have been tried by bodies which are not tribunals within the meaning of Article 6 of the Convention'.[4]

The heading 'Right of appeal in criminal matters' was added in accordance with Protocol No. 11.[5]

Analysis and interpretation

Article 2 of Protocol No. 7 can be understood as an amendment that completes article 6 of the Convention. It 'mostly regulates institutional matters, such as accessibility of the court of appeal or scope of review in appellate proceedings'.[6] In other international human rights instruments, such as article 14 of the International Covenant on Civil and Political Rights, appeal of criminal conviction is part of a broader list of procedural guarantees associated with the fair trial. Many cases before the Court raise issues that concern both article 6 of the Convention and article 2 of Protocol No. 7. The nature of the appeal may be considered solely from the standpoint of article 6, something of particular importance for States that have not ratified Protocol No. 7. The Court has cautioned that 'Article 2 of Protocol No. 7 cannot be construed *a contrario* as limiting the scope of Article 6 guarantees in appellate proceedings with respect to those Contracting Parties for which Protocol No. 7 is not in force'.[7] Sometimes, the Court finds that there has been a violation of article 6 of the Convention and then declares that there is no need for it to make a separate ruling on article 2 of Protocol No. 7.[8]

The existence of an appropriate appeal mechanism may also be debated when a violation of article 6 is alleged and the State contests the admissibility by arguing that remedies have not been exhausted. Then the Court must assess whether there can be a proper appeal under the circumstances, making a very similar assessment to what it is required to do when a violation of article 2 of Protocol No. 7 is charged.[9] The Court has cautioned that 'Article 2 of Protocol No. 7 cannot be construed *a contrario* as limiting the scope of Article 6 guarantees in appellate proceedings with respect to those Contracting Parties for which Protocol No. 7 is not in force.'[10] There is authority for the view that article 13 of the Convention does not provide for a right of appeal.[11]

Article 2 of Protocol No. 7 consists of two paragraphs, the first stating the principle of the right to appeal conviction and sentence, and the second providing for three limitations

---

[4] Explanatory Report on Protocol No. 7, para. 17.

[5] Protocol No. 11 to the Convention for the Protection of Human Rights and Fundamental Freedoms, restructuring the control machinery established thereby, ETS 155, art. 2(7)(a).

[6] *Shvydka v. Ukraine*, no. 17888/12, § 46, 30 October 2014; *Pesti and Frodl v. Austria* (dec.), nos 27618/95 and 27619/95, ECHR 2000-I (extracts).

[7] *Lalmahomed v. the Netherlands*, no. 26036/08, § 38, 22 February 2011; *Ekbatani v. Sweden*, 26 May 1988, § 26, Series A no. 134.

[8] *Ay Ali v. Italy*, no. 24691/04, §§ 49–51, 14 December 2006; *R. R. v. Italy*, no. 42191/02, § 64, 9 June 2005; *Baucher v. France*, no. 53640/00, § 52, 24 July 2007; *Nedzela v. France*, no. 73695/01, § 62, 27 July 2006.

[9] *E.g.*, *Galstyan v. Armenia*, no. 26986/03, § 42, 15 November 2007.

[10] *Lalmahomed v. the Netherlands*, no. 26036/08, § 38, 22 February 2011; *Ekbatani v. Sweden*, 26 May 1988, § 26, Series A no. 134.

[11] *Gurepka v. Ukraine (no. 2)*, no. 38789/04, § 27, 8 April 2010; *Kopczynski v. Poland* (dec.), no. 28863/95, 1 July 1998; *Csepyová v. Slovakia* (dec.), no. 67199/01, 14 May 2002.

or exceptions to this right. Despite the absence of any more general provisions permitting limitations on the right similar to what can be found with respect to other substantive provisions of the Convention and its Protocols, the Court has taken the view that States enjoy a wide margin of appreciation in determining how to ensure that the right set out in article 2 of Protocol No. 7 is secured.[12] Nevertheless, the Court has cautioned that 'any restrictions contained in domestic legislation on the right to a review mentioned in that provision must, by analogy with the right of access to a court embodied in Article 6 § 1 of the Convention, pursue a legitimate aim and not infringe the very essence of that right'.[13] The effectiveness of a remedy is one of the requirements associated with the right of access and therefore with the right of appeal. Issues may arise where sentences of detention are enforced upon conviction and notwithstanding an appeal, where the consequence is that the term has been served before the appeal is determined.[14]

One common limitation is restricting appellate review to questions of law. According to the Explanatory Report:

Different rules govern review by a higher tribunal in the various member States of the Council of Europe. In some countries, such review is in certain cases limited to questions of law, such as the *recours en cassation*. In others, there is a right to appeal against findings of facts as well as on the questions of law. The article leaves the modalities for the exercise of the right and the grounds on which it may be exercised to be determined by domestic law.[15]

There is much authority in the case law of the Convention organs for the position that appeal limited to questions of law complies with the requirements of article 2(1) of Protocol No. 7.[16] At the time of ratification, France formulated a declaration stating that '... in accordance with the meaning of Article 2, paragraph 1, the review by a higher court may be limited to a control of the application of the law, such as an appeal to the Supreme Court'. Similarly, Germany noted in a declaration that it was 'possible to restrict review to errors in law'.

Another feature of legislation governing criminal appeals is a requirement that they be subject to some form of authorization. The Explanatory Report addresses this:

In some States, a person wishing to appeal to a higher tribunal must in certain cases apply for leave to appeal. The right to apply to a tribunal or an administrative authority for leave to appeal is itself to be regarded as a form of review within the meaning of this article.[17]

The Court has confirmed this in several judgments.[18] A right of appeal may also be denied if the accused has pleaded guilty. According to the Explanatory Report, '... if the person

---

[12] *Krombach v. France*, no. 29731/96, § 96, ECHR 2001-II; *Haser v. Switzerland* (dec.), no. 33050/96, 27 April 2000.

[13] *Krombach v. France*, no. 29731/96, § 96, ECHR 2001-II; *Haser v. Switzerland* (dec.), no. 33050/96, 27 April 2000; *Panou v. Greece*, no. 44058/05, § 32, 8 January 2009.

[14] *Shvydka v. Ukraine*, no. 17888/12, §§ 46–55, 30 October 2014.

[15] Explanatory Report on Protocol No. 7, para. 18.

[16] *Loewenguth v. France* (dec.), no. 53183/99, ECHR 2000-VI; *Pesti and Frodl v. Austria*, nos 27618/95 and 27619/95, ECHR 2000-I (extracts), *Reports of Judgments and Decisions* 2000-I; *Nielsen v. Denmark*, no. 19028/91, Commission decision of 9 September 1992, (1992) 35 YB 72, DR 73, p. 239; *N.W. v. Luxembourg*, no. 19715/92, Commission decision of 8 December 1992; *Altieri v. France*, no. 28140/95, Commission decision of 15 May 1996; *Saussier v. France*, no. 35884/97, Commission decision of 20 May 1998.

[17] Explanatory Report on Protocol No. 7, para. 19.

[18] *Weh and Weh v. Austria* (dec.), no. 38544/97, 4 July 2002; *Hauser-Sporn v. Austria*, no. 37301/03, § 52, 7 December 2006; *Hubner v. Austria* (dec.) no. 34311/96, 31 August 1999; *Hauser v. Austria*, no. 26808/95,

convicted has pleaded guilty to the offence charged, the right may be restricted to a review of his sentence'.[19]

A provision in the French Penal Code explicitly excluded the possibility of an appeal to the Cour de cassation where the trial proceedings were conducted *in absentia*. The Government unsuccessfully argued that the absence of an appeal from such a proceeding, which 'by its very essence was provisional and unenforceable', was simply a 'logical consequence of the nature of the judgment', and that other remedies were available to someone tried *in absentia* in order to challenge the conviction.[20]

In one of the leading cases under article 2, the Court examined a legislative scheme imposing administrative penalties that were final and not subject to appeal. The text provided that the decision 'can be quashed or modified by the judge himself upon a protest of the prosecutor and, whether or not such a protest is lodged, by the chairman of the superior court'. This mechanism, said the Court, did not comply with article 2 because it lacked any clearly defined procedure or time limits and consistent application in practice.[21]

Exercise of the right governed by law

The second sentence of article 2(1) of Protocol No 7, declaring that '[t]he exercise of this right, including the grounds on which it may be exercised, shall be governed by law', is a somewhat unusual formulation in the Convention system. It is not a limitation or restriction clause in the strict sense; that role is fulfilled by paragraph 2, as well as by the general possibility of limitation or restriction that the Court has found to be implied and has developed by interpretation. There is some authority for the proposition that, by analogy with the right to a court guaranteed by article 6, in limiting the right of appeal the State has 'a certain margin of appreciation but in addition to pursuing a legitimate aim the limitations applied shall not restrict or reduce the access left to the individual in such a way that the very essence of the right is impaired'.[22]

Invoking the second sentence to support the proposition that a requirement of leave or permission in order to proceed with an appeal was consistent with article 2(1), the Commission said that 'as a matter of comparison' the right of access to the courts secured by article 6(1) of the Convention was also 'subject to limitations in the form of regulation by the State'. However, this holding is not based on any specific language in article 6(1) of the Convention.[23] The Commission explained:

Commission decision of 16 January 1996, DR 84, p. 164; *Stempfer v. Austria*, no. 18294/03, § 80, 26 July 2007; *Vitzthum v. Austria*, no. 8140/04, § 35, 26 July 2007.

[19] Explanatory Report on Protocol No. 7, para. 17.

[20] *Krombach v. France*, no. 29731/96, §§ 99–100, ECHR 2001-II. Also *Mariani v. France*, no. 43640/98, §§ 35, 45–46, 31 March 2005; *Papon v. France*, no. 54210/00, § 106, ECHR 2002-VII.

[21] *Galstyan v. Armenia*, no. 26986/03, §§ 40–41, 132, 15 November 2007. Similarly *Gurepka v. Ukraine*, no. 61406/00, §§ 57–62, 6 September 2005; *Gurepka v. Ukraine (no. 2)*, no. 38789/04, § 32, 8 April 2010; *Kakabadze and Others v. Georgia*, no. 1484/07, § 97, 2 October 2012; *Ashughyan v. Armenia*, no. 33268/03, §§ 108–110, 17 July 2008; *Kirakosyan v. Armenia*, no. 31237/03, §§ 85–86, 2 December 2008; *Tadevosyan v. Armenia*, no. 41698/04, §§ 79–80, 2 December 2008; *Karapetyan v. Armenia*, no. 22387/05, §§ 73–74, 27 October 2009; *Gasparyan v. Armenia (no. 2)*, no. 22571/05, §§ 36–37, 16 June 2009; *Hakobyan and Others v. Armenia*, no. 34320/04, §§ 140–141, 10 April 2012.

[22] *E.M. v. Norway*, no. 20087/92, Commission decision of 26 October 1995, DR 83-B, p. 5. Also *Haser v. Switzerland* (dec.), no. 33050/96, 27 April 2000.

[23] *E.M. v. Norway*, no. 20087/92, Commission decision of 26 October 1995, DR 83-B, p. 5.

The second sentence of this provision requires that the exercise of the right to a review by a higher tribunal shall be governed by law but it does not otherwise specify its scope or actual implementation. However, as the reference to the grounds for the review being governed by law clearly shows the Contracting States have a discretion as to the modalities for the exercise of the right of review. Consequently, the Article gives the States the possibility to regulate the review in several ways.[24]

In similar cases, a Chamber of the Court noted that the right set out in article 2(1) of Protocol No. 7 may be limited 'by virtue of the reference in paragraph 1 of this Article to national law'.[25]

All of these cases involved the requirement that leave be obtained for an appeal. The Commission pointed out that 'a right to apply for leave to appeal to a higher court can in itself be regarded as a review' within the meaning of article 2(1).[26] If the procedure for granting leave to appeal is to be regarded as providing an appeal, then there is no need to rely upon the second sentence of paragraph 1. In other cases, the position that subjecting the right to appeal to an application for leave meets the requirements of article 2(1) has been upheld without reference to the second sentence.[27]

For the same reasons, the scope of the appeal may be restricted. Some jurisdictions will confine the appeal to questions of law. This too is compatible with article 2(1).[28]

Criminal offence

The expression 'criminal offence' in article 2(1) of Protocol No. 2 also appears in article 6(3) of the Convention and has the same meaning.[29] In the French versions, somewhat different formulations are used: 'infraction pénale' in the Protocol and 'accusation en matière pénale' in the Convention. If an offence is found to be of a criminal character attracting the full guarantees of Article 6 of the Convention, it consequently attracts also those of Article 2 of Protocol No. 7.[30] Article 2 of Protocol No. 7 does not apply when the tribunal awards damages ('dédommagement') and does not apply a penalty or equivalent sanction.[31]

The authoritative statement on the interpretation of 'criminal offence' appears in *Engel and Others*:

[I]t is first necessary to know whether the provision(s) defining the offence charged belong, according to the legal system of the respondent State, to criminal law, disciplinary law or both concurrently. This however provides no more than a starting point. The indications so afforded

[24] Ibid. Also *Hauser v. Austria*, no. 26808/95, 16 January 1996; *Nielsen v. Denmark*, no. 19028/91, Commission decision of 9 September 1992, (1992) 35 YB 72, DR 73, p. 239.

[25] *Hauser-Sporn v. Austria*, no. 37301/03, § 52, 7 December 2006; *Müller v. Austria*, no. 12555/03, § 25, 5 October 2006; *Pesti and Frodl v. Austria* (dec.), nos 27618/95 and 27619/95, ECHR 2000-I (extracts).

[26] *Hauser v. Austria*, no. 26808/95, Commission decision of 16 January 1996.

[27] *Näss v. Sweden*, no. 18066/91, Commission decision of 6 April 1994, DR 77, p. 37.

[28] *Deperrois v. France* (dec.), no. 48203/99, 22 June 2000; *Loewenguth v. France* (dec.), 53183/99, ECHR 2000-VI; *Pesti and Frodl v. Austria* (dec.), nos 27618/95 and 27619/95, ECHR 2000-I (extracts); *Nielsen v. Denmark*, no. 19028/91, Commission decision of 9 September 1992, (1992) 35 YB 72, DR 73, p. 239; *N.W. v. Luxembourg*, no. 19715/92, Commission decision of 8 December 1992; *Altieri v. France, Cyprus, and Switzerland*, no. 28140/95, Commission decision of 15 May 1996.

[29] *Kamburov v. Bulgaria (no. 2)*, no. 31001/02, § 22, 23 April 2009; *Gourepka v. Ukraine*, no. 61406/00, § 55, 6 September 2005; *Zaicevs v. Latvia*, no. 65022/01, § 53, 31 July 2007.

[30] *Gurepka v. Ukraine*, no. 61406/00, § 55, 6 September 2005; *Galstyan v. Armenia*, no. 26986/03, § 120, 15 November 2007.

[31] *Rigolio v. Italy* (dec.), no. 20148/09, § 46, 13 May 2014.

have only a formal and relative value and must be examined in the light of the common denominator of the respective legislation of the various Contracting States.

The very nature of the offence is a factor of greater import. When a serviceman finds himself accused of an act or omission allegedly contravening a legal rule governing the operation of the armed forces, the State may in principle employ against him disciplinary law rather than criminal law. In this respect, the Court expresses its agreement with the Government.

However, supervision by the Court does not stop there. Such supervision would generally prove to be illusory if it did not also take into consideration the degree of severity of the penalty that the person concerned risks incurring. In a society subscribing to the rule of law, there belong to the 'criminal' sphere deprivations of liberty liable to be imposed as a punishment, except those which by their nature, duration or manner of execution cannot be appreciably detrimental. The seriousness of what is at stake, the traditions of the Contracting States and the importance attached by the Convention to respect for the physical liberty of the person all require that this should be so.[32]

In most States, the national law provides its own definition of crimes or criminal offences, or distinguishes it in some way from other violations and infractions. France has formulated a reservation confining the scope of article 2 to criminal offences as defined in French law. Without making formal reservations, Germany, Italy, Liechtenstein, the Netherlands, and Portugal have formulated declarations indicating their view that the scope of the term 'criminal offence' corresponds to the notion within their domestic legislation.

Exceptions to the right of appeal

Article 2(2) of Protocol No. 7 recognizes that the right of appeal is subject to three exceptions: offences of a minor character, as prescribed by law; cases in which the person concerned was tried in the first instance by the highest tribunal; and cases of conviction following an appeal against acquittal.

In determining whether an offence is one of 'a minor character', the Explanatory Report on Protocol No. 7 states that 'an important criterion is the question of whether the offence is punishable by imprisonment or not'.[33] It notes that these words were added by the Committee of Ministers 'having regard to the importance of the explanatory report for the purpose of interpreting the Protocol'. The Court has relied upon this remark in the Explanatory Report, holding that where an infraction may be punished by imprisonment it does not quality for the minor offence exception.[34] It has held that '[h]aving regard to the aim of Article 2 and the nature of the guarantees for which it provides, . . . an offence for which the law prescribes a custodial sentence as the main punishment cannot be described as "minor" within the meaning of the second paragraph of that Article'.[35]

There is a distinction between offences that are not sufficiently serious, in terms of their objective gravity or the consequences of conviction, to be judged criminal offences at all, and therefore outside the scope of article 2(1) of Protocol No. 7, and offences that are genuinely criminal in nature but 'of a minor character'. A prosecution for petty theft that

---

[32] *Engel and Others v. the Netherlands,* 8 June 1976, § 82, Series A no. 22. Cited in *Kamburov v. Bulgaria (no. 2),* no. 31001/02, § 22, 23 April 2009.

[33] Explanatory Report on Protocol No. 7, para. 21.

[34] *Grecu v. Romania,* no. 75101/01, § 82, 30 November 2006; *Stanchev v. Bulgaria,* no. 8682/02, §§ 47–48, 1 October 2009; *Gurepka v. Ukraine (no. 2),* no. 38789/04, § 33, 8 April 2010; *Zhelyazkov v. Bulgaria,* no. 11332/04, § 43, 9 October 2012.

[35] *Zaicevs v. Latvia,* no. 65022/01, § 55, 31 July 2007.

was not punishable by imprisonment was held to fall into the 'minor character' exception of article 2(2) of Protocol No. 7.[36]

The Commission held that an infraction described as an 'offence against the order in court' where there was a maximum penalty of 10,000 Austrian shillings or imprisonment not to exceed eight days was of a 'minor character'.[37] But for a Chamber of the Court, where a similar offence was capable of attracting a sentence of 15 days in detention, the qualification 'minor character' could not apply.[38]

A right of appeal is not required by article 2(2) of Protocol No. 7 if the trial itself is held by the highest tribunal in the country. Under some national constitutions, senior officials may only be tried by the highest-level courts. In such circumstances, there may be no mechanism for appeal, and the Protocol does not require this. Where there has been an appeal against acquittal and the person is then convicted, article 2(2) of Protocol No. 7 specifies that there is no requirement of an appeal from conviction. It is, of course, possible to waive the right of appeal. For example, this may happen where there is a plea bargain involving the settlement of a criminal prosecution in a manner deemed acceptable to both the accused and the prosecution and then endorsed by the tribunal.[39]

Reservations and declarations

There have been two reservations to article 2.

Denmark's reservation reads as follows:

The Government of Denmark declares that Article 2, paragraph 1 does not bar the use of rules of the Administration of Justice Act ("*Lov om rettens pleje*") according to which the possibility of review by a higher court—in cases subject to prosecution by the lower instance of the prosecution ("*politisager*")—is denied.

a. when the prosecuted, having been duly notified, fails to appear in court;

b. when the court has repealed the punishment; or

c. in cases where only sentences of fines or confiscation of objects below the amount or value established by law are imposed.[40]

When Denmark extended Protocol No. 7 to the Faroe Islands, on 2 September 1994, in accordance with article 6, it specified that the reservation to article 2(1) applied.

France made the following reservation: 'The Government of the French Republic declares that only those offences which under French law fall within the jurisdiction of the French criminal courts may be regarded as offences within the meaning of Articles 2 to 4 of this Protocol.' It also formulated a declaration at the time of signature that it confirmed on ratification to the effect that 'review by a higher court may be limited to a control of the application of the law, such as an appeal to the Supreme Court'.[41]

---

[36] *Luchaninova v. Ukraine*, no. 16347/02, §§ 71–73, 9 June 2011.

[37] *Putz v. Austria*, no. 18892/91, Commission decision of 3 December 1993, DR 76-A, p. 51.

[38] *Galstyan v. Armenia*, no. 26986/03, § 124, 15 November 2007.

[39] *Natsvlishvili and Togonidze v. Georgia*, no. 9043/05, §§ 96–97, 29 April 2014.

[40] (1988) 31 YB 8. In a declaration dated 1 August 1994, Denmark states that the reservation also applies to the Faroe Islands.

[41] (1986) 29 YB 4–5.

Several States—Italy, Liechtenstein,[42] Monaco,[43] the Netherlands,[44] and Portugal[45]—have made declarations in order to associate the scope of article 2 with the distinctions made in their own legal system. Austria and Monaco formulated declarations concerning the meaning given to the term 'higher tribunal', referring to their own legal provisions.

At the time of signature, on 19 March 1985, Germany made the following declaration: 'By "criminal offence" and "offence" in Article 2 to 4 of the present Protocol, the Federal Republic of Germany understands only such acts as are criminal offences under its law.' Germany made a second declaration: 'The Federal Republic of Germany applies Article 2(1) to convictions or sentences in the first instance only, it being possible to restrict review to errors in law and to hold such reviews in camera; in addition it understands that the application of Article 2(1) is not dependent on the written judgment of the previous instance being translated into a language other than the language used in court.'[46] Germany has not ratified the Protocol.

Further reading

Cees Flinterman, 'The Right to a Review by a Higher Tribunal (Article 2 of Protocol No. 7)', in Van Dijk et al., *Theory and Practice*, pp. 971–4.

Frowein/Peukert, *MenschenRechtsKonvention,* pp. 707–8.

Grabenwarter, *European Convention*, pp. 428–31.

Harris et al., *Law of the European Convention*, pp. 748–9.

Renée Koering-Joulin, 'Protocole No 7, Article 2', in Pettiti et al., *La Convention européenne*, pp. 1087–9.

---

[42] (2005) 48 YB 13.
[43] (2005) 48 YB 13.
[44] (1986) 29 YB 4.
[45] (2004) 47 YB 24.
[46] (1985) 28 YB 7–8.

Article 3. Compensation for wrongful conviction/Droit d'indemnisation en cas d'erreur judiciaire

When a person has by a final decision been convicted of a criminal offence and when subsequently his conviction has been reversed, or he has been pardoned, on the ground that a new or newly discovered fact shows conclusively that there has been a miscarriage of justice, the person who has suffered punishment as a result of such conviction shall be compensated according to the law or the practice of that State concerned, unless it is proved that the non-disclosure of the unknown fact in time is wholly or partly attributable to him.

Lorsqu'une condamnation pénale définitive est ultérieurement annulée, ou lorsque la grâce est accordée, parce qu'un fait nouveau ou nouvellement révélé prouve qu'il s'est produit une erreur judiciaire, la personne qui a subi une peine en raison de cette condamnation est indemnisée, conformément à la loi ou à l'usage en vigueur dans l'Etat concerné, à moins qu'il ne soit prouvé que la non-révélation en temps utile du fait inconnu lui est imputable en tout ou en partie.

Introductory comments

This is a provision inspired by article 14(6) of the International Covenant on Civil and Political Rights. According to Manfred Nowak's commentary on the Covenant, '[t]he right to compensation in the event of a sentence based on a miscarriage of justice was, at the time of its drafting, the most controversial provision in Art. 14'.[1] Professor Nowak noted that a series of attempts to delete the right to compensation were unsuccessful, although the provision survived some close votes aimed at its removal. The text of article 3 of Protocol No. 7 is almost identical to that of article 14(6) of the Covenant. There are only two differences: the first set of commas in article 3 has been added, and the words 'according to the law or practice of the State concerned' replace 'according to law'.

Drafting of the provision

The Explanatory Report does not provide any information on the drafting history of the provision. The heading 'Right not to be tried or punished twice' was added according to the provisions of Protocol No. 11.[2]

Analysis and interpretation

There are relationships between article 3 of Protocol No. 7 and articles 5 and 13 of the Convention, as well as with article 6(2), which enshrines the presumption of innocence.

---

[1] Manfred Nowak, *UN Covenant on Civil and Political Rights, CCPR Commentary*, 2nd rev. edn, Kehl, Germany: N.P. Engel, 2005, p. 352.
[2] Protocol No. 11 to the Convention for the Protection of Human Rights and Fundamental Freedoms, restructuring the control machinery established thereby, ETS 155, art. 2(7)(a).

However, the right to compensation for miscarriages of justice (*erreur judiciaire* in French[3]) is quite distinct from the right to compensation for wrongful detention, something addressed by article 5(5) of the Convention. Although recognition that there has been a miscarriage of justice relating to a criminal conviction is not necessarily equivalent to a finding of innocence, the reversal of such a conviction has the consequence of restoring the convicted person to a situation where he or she benefits, once again, from the presumption of innocence which is set out in article 6(2) of the Convention. The question of the relationship between article 3 of Protocol No. 7 and article 6(2) of the Convention may arise, particularly if the State in question has not yet ratified the Protocol. The Court has said that article 3 of Protocol No. 7 should not be considered as a *lex specialis* of article 6(2) of the Convention and that it does not mean that the a right to compensation for wrongful conviction is necessarily excluded form the scope of article 3.[4] The right to compensation for a miscarriage of justice set out in article 3 of Protocol No. 7 only applies with respect to criminal proceedings.[5]

Final decision

For the right set out in article 3 of Protocol No. 7 to exist, there must first be a final conviction for a criminal offence. It is inapplicable to a person who has been arrested but never brought to trial[6] or to someone who has been tried and acquitted.[7] According to the Explanatory Report:

First, the person concerned has to have been convicted of a criminal offence by a final decision and to have suffered punishment as a result of such conviction. According to the definition contained in the explanatory report of the European Convention on the International Validity of Criminal Judgments, a decision is final 'if, according to the traditional expression, it has acquired the force of *res judicata*. This is the case when it is irrevocable, that is to say when no further ordinary remedies are available or when the parties have exhausted such remedies or have permitted the time-limit to expire without availing themselves of them'. It follows therefore that a judgment by default is not considered as final as long as the domestic law allows the proceedings to be taken up again. Likewise, this article does not apply in cases where the charge is dismissed or the accused person is acquitted either by the court of first instance or, on appeal, by a higher tribunal. If, however, in one of the States in which such a possibility is provided for, the person has been granted leave to appeal after the normal time of appealing has expired, and his conviction is then reversed on appeal, then subject to the other conditions of the article, in particular the conditions described in paragraph 24 below, the article may apply.[8]

Paragraph 24 explains that where the non-disclosure of an unknown fact is wholly or partly attributable to the convict person, there is no right to compensation. Article 3 does not apply where a person has been acquitted on appeal.[9] Where two incidents of corruption are prosecuted in two separate proceedings, article 3 of Protocol No. 7 is inapplicable.[10]

---

[3] See, e.g., *Jeronovičs v. Latvia* (dec.), no. 547/02, § 77, 10 February 2009.
[4] *Allen v. the United Kingdom* [GC], no. 25424/09, 12 July 2013.
[5] *Glender v. Sweden* (dec.), no. 28070/03, 6 September 2005.
[6] *Nakov v. the Former Yugoslav Republic of Macedonia* (dec.), no. 68286/01, 24 October 2003.
[7] *Y.M. v. France*, no. 24948/94, Commission decision of 28 June 1995.
[8] Explanatory Report on Protocol No. 7, para. 22 (reference omitted).
[9] *Georgiou v. Greece* (dec.), no. 45138/98, § 4, 13 January 2000.
[10] *Acampora v. Italy* (dec.), no. 2072/08, § 32, 8 January 2013.

Reversal of conviction or pardon

The second condition for the application of article 3 of Protocol No. 7 is that:

the conviction has been reversed or he has been pardoned, in either case on the ground that a new or newly discovered fact shows conclusively that there has been a miscarriage of justice—that is, some serious failure in the judicial process involving grave prejudice to the convicted person. Therefore, there is no requirement under the article to pay compensation if the conviction has been reversed or a pardon has been granted on some other ground. Nor does the article seek to lay down any rules as to the nature of the procedure to be applied to establish a miscarriage of justice. This is a matter for the domestic law or practice of the State concerned. The words 'or he has been pardoned' have been included because under some systems of law pardon, rather than legal proceedings leading to the reversal of a conviction, may in certain cases be the appropriate remedy after there has been a final decision.[11]

In a case where there was an arguable claim of a wrongful conviction, but where the appeal was discontinued for technical reasons, article 3 of Protocol No. 4 could not be invoked because no decision had been reversed.[12]

New or newly discovered fact showing a miscarriage of justice

The third condition for a right to compensation is that there is a new or newly discovered fact showing conclusively that there has been a miscarriage of justice. In fact, these amount to two conditions because even if there is a miscarriage of justice, it must be based upon a new or newly discovered fact, and not for some other reason. If the reversal of an earlier judgment is not 'on the basis of the omission or concealment of facts which could or should have been known to the court in 1959, or by the coming to light of new facts which occurred after that date and which would have been of such nature as to cast fundamental doubt on the soundness of the criminal conviction' but rather 'because the applicable substantive criminal law had been seriously distorted and misapplied in that case', article 3 does not apply.[13] If non-disclosure of the unknown fact in time was wholly or partly attributable to the person convicted, there is no right under article 3.[14]

The term 'new or newly discovered fact' is also employed in article 4 of Protocol No. 7. The Explanatory Report notes with respect to article 4 that the term 'includes new means of proof relating to previously existing facts'.[15] However, to satisfy the conditions of article 3, it is not enough for the reviewing court to reassess evidence that had previously been considered. The fact must either be 'new', or 'newly discovered' in the sense that it existed at the time of the original trial but was not then known.[16]

The Explanatory Report suggests a very high test for the scope of the term 'miscarriage of justice'. It states that '[t]he intention' behind article 3 of Protocol No. 7 was 'that States would be obliged to compensate persons only in clear cases of miscarriage of justice, in the sense that there would be acknowledgement that the person concerned was clearly

---

[11] Explanatory Report on Protocol No. 7, para. 23.
[12] *Stamoulakatos v. Greece* (dec.), no. 42155/98, 9 November 1999.
[13] *Bachowski v. Poland* (dec.), no. 32463/06, 2 November 2010.
[14] Explanatory Report on Protocol No. 7, para. 24.
[15] Ibid., para. 31.
[16] *Matveyev v. Russia*, no. 26601/02, § 43, 3 July 2008.

innocent'. This phrase in the Explanatory Report has been considered by the Grand Chamber to be rather too severe:

It is wholly understandable that when seeking to identify the meaning of an ambiguous legislative notion such as 'miscarriage of justice' that has its origins in provisions figuring in international instruments—in the event, Article 14(6) of the ICCPR and Article 3 of Protocol No. 7—national judges should refer to the international case-law on those provisions and to their drafting history setting out the understanding of their drafters. However, the Explanatory Report itself provides that, although intended to facilitate the understanding of the provisions contained in the Protocol, it does not constitute an authoritative interpretation of the text...Its references to the need to demonstrate innocence must now be considered to have been overtaken by the Court's intervening case-law on Article 6 § 2.[17]

The Grand Chamber has noted that there is 'very little evidence from the practice of Contracting States regarding compensation which is relevant to the interpretation of "miscarriage of justice"'.[18]

The grant of an amnesty subsequent to a conviction cannot be considered as an acknowledgement that there was a miscarriage of justice.[19]

According to law or practice of the State

The reference to 'law or practice of the State' is discussed in the Explanatory Report:

In all cases in which these preconditions are satisfied, compensation is payable "according to the law or the practice of the State concerned". This does not mean that no compensation is payable if the law or practice makes no provision for such compensation. It means that the law or practice of the State should provide for the payment of compensation in all cases to which the article applies. The intention is that States would be obliged to compensate persons only in clear cases of miscarriage of justice, in the sense that there would be acknowledgement that the person concerned was clearly innocent. The article is not intended to give a right of compensation where all the preconditions are not satisfied, for example, where an appellate, court had quashed a conviction because it had discovered some fact which introduced a reasonable doubt as to the guilt of the accused and which had been overlooked by the trial judge.[20]

In a case involving British legislation modelled on article 3 of Protocol No. 7, the Grand Chamber examined the law and practice within the Council of Europe. It said that there was 'no uniform approach in respect of the law and practice on compensation proceedings following discontinuation or acquittal' and that '[s]ome States have more than one scheme in place, covering different types of compensation'. In ten Member States, 'available compensation proceedings appear to be linked directly to the criminal proceedings, with the tribunal which disposed of the criminal complaint having jurisdiction to assess a compensation claim where there has been an acquittal in the original trial proceedings'. In another thirty, the available compensation proceedings are independent of the criminal proceedings. The Grand Chamber found that time limits were in place in almost all States, 'linking the making of a compensation claim to the conclusion of the criminal proceedings'. In many

---

[17] *Allen v. the United Kingdom* [GC], no. 25424/09, § 128, 13 July 2013.

[18] Ibid. On 'miscarriage of justice', see also *Adams v. The United Kingdom* (dec.), no. 70601/11, §§ 16–31, 12 November 2013.

[19] *Tarbuk v. Croatia*, no. 31360/10, § 48, 11 December 2012.

[20] Explanatory Report on Protocol No. 7, para. 25.

States, 'compensation is essentially automatic following a finding of not guilty, the quashing of a conviction or the discontinuation of proceedings'.[21]

The reference to law or practice does not mean that no compensation is payable if there is no provision for compensation in national law. The Court has said that the purpose of article 3 'is not merely to recover any pecuniary loss caused by a wrongful conviction but also to provide a person convicted as a result of a miscarriage of justice with compensation for any non-pecuniary damage such as distress, anxiety, inconvenience and loss of enjoyment of life'.[22] On the other hand, the right to compensation does not mean that the victim of a violation of article 3 is entitled to be put back in the position as if the conviction, and the events which followed it, had never happened.[23]

Reservations and declarations

France made the only reservation to article 3 of Protocol No. 7 that is described as such. It states that 'only those offences which under French law fall within the jurisdiction of the French criminal courts may be regarded as offences' within the meaning of article 3. Austria, Germany, and Italy made similar statements, but described them as declarations rather than reservations. Austria's reservation has been deemed to be an invalid reservation because there is no brief statement of the law as required by article 57 of the Convention.[24]

At the time of signature, on 19 March 1985, Germany made two declarations concerning article 3: 'By "criminal offence" and "offence" in Article 2 to 4 of the present Protocol, the Federal Republic of Germany understands only such acts as are criminal offences under its law.' It also said that it 'understands the words "according to the law or the practice of the State concerned" to mean that Article 3 refers only to the retrial provided for in sections 359 et seq. of the Code of Criminal Procedure. (cf. *Strafprozessordnung*)'.[25] Germany has not ratified the Protocol.

San Marino made a declaration stating that 'although the principle is applied in practice, it is not enshrined in any legislative provision. Therefore the Government of the Republic undertakes to embody the principle and its regulation into a relevant legislative provision to be adopted within two years from today.'[26]

Further reading

Cees Flinterman, 'Compensation for Miscarriage of Justice (Article 3 of Protocol No. 7)', in Van Dijk et al., *Theory and Practice*, pp. 975–8.
Frowein/Peukert, *MenschenRechtsKonvention,* pp. 709–10.
Grabenwarter, *European Convention,* pp. 432–4.
Harris et al., *Law of the European Convention,* p. 750.
Renée Koering-Joulin, 'Protocole No 7, Article 3', in Pettiti et al., *La Convention européenne,* pp. 1091–2.

---

[21] *Allen v. the United Kingdom* [GC], no. 25424/09, §§ 73–76, 13 July 2013.
[22] *Poghosyan and Baghdasaryan v. Armenia,* no. 22999/06, § 51, ECHR 2012.
[23] *Matveyev and Matveyeva v. Russia* (dec.), no. 26601/02, § 6, 14 December 2004.
[24] *Gradinger v. Austria,* 23 October 1995, § 51, Series A no. 328-C.
[25] (1985) 28 YB 7–9.
[26] (1989) 32 YB 6.

Article 4. Right not to be tried or punished twice/Droit à ne pas être jugé ou puni deux fois

1. No one shall be liable to be tried or punished again in criminal proceedings under the jurisdiction of the same State for an offence for which he has already been finally acquitted or convicted in accordance with the law and penal procedure of the State.

2. The provisions of the preceding paragraph shall not prevent the re-opening of the case in accordance with the law and penal procedure of the State concerned, if there is evidence of new or newly discovered facts, or if there has been a fundamental defect in the previous proceedings, which could affect the outcome of the case.

3. No derogation from this Article shall be made under Article 15 of the Convention.

1. Nul ne peut être poursuivi ou puni pénalement par les juridictions du même Etat en raison d'une infraction pour laquelle il a déjà été acquitté ou condamné par un jugement définitif conformément à la loi et à la procédure pénale de cet Etat.

2. Les dispositions du paragraphe précédent n'empêchent pas la réouverture du procès, conformément à la loi et à la procédure pénale de l'Etat concerné, si des faits nouveaux ou nouvellement révélés ou un vice fondamental dans la procédure précédente sont de nature à affecter le jugement intervenu.

3. Aucune dérogation n'est autorisée au présent article au titre de l'article 15 de la Convention.

Introductory comments

The fifth amendment to the Constitution of the United States declares that no person shall 'be subject for the same offence to be twice put in jeopardy of life or limb'. The prohibition of trial and punishment when a person has already been judged is also known by the Latin expression *ne bis in idem.* A range of other expressions in various legal systems addresses the same phenomenon, including *res judicata*, issue estoppel, *chose jugée*, and the plea of *autrefois convict.*

There is no reference to *ne bis in idem* in the Universal Declaration of Human Rights. An American proposal that it be included[1] did not attract any support. It had only been present in a handful of the national constitutions canvassed by the United Nations at the start of the work on the Universal Declaration.[2] Nor did it appear in the early drafts of the International Covenant on Civil and Political Rights. Only late in the discussions, during consideration by the Third Committee of the General Assembly, did Italy and Japan present a text[3] that, after various amendments, resulted in article 14(7) of the Covenant: 'No one shall be liable to be tried or punished again for an offence for which he has already been finally convicted or acquitted in accordance with the law and penal procedure of each country.'

Noting that in the law of many European states a new criminal trial was permitted under extraordinary circumstances, the Committee of Experts of the Council of Europe

---

[1] United States Suggestions for Redrafts of Certain Articles in the Draft Outline E/CN.4/AC.1/3, UN Doc. E/CN.4/AC.1/8, p. 4; UN Doc. E/CN.4/AC.1/SR.13, p. 1.

[2] Constitution of Liberia, art. 1, sec. 7; Constitution of the Philippines, art. 3, sec. 1(20).

[3] UN Doc. A/C.3/L.803/Rev.1.

recommended that reservations be made to the International Covenant on Civil and Political Rights provision. Austria, Denmark, Finland, Iceland, the Netherlands, Norway, and Sweden followed this advice.

The European Charter of Fundamental Rights contains an equivalent provision:

Article 50. Right not to be tried or punished twice in criminal proceedings for the same criminal offence

No one shall be liable to be tried or punished again in criminal proceedings for an offence for which he or she has already been finally acquitted or convicted within the Union in accordance with the law.

Article 50 is meant to have the same meaning and scope as article 4 of Protocol No. 7 but its scope is extended to the European Union level between the Courts of the Member States.[4]

The *ne bis in idem* principle has taken on greater significance in recent years as a component of the international criminal justice regime. Statutes of the international criminal tribunals contain provisions aimed at regulating their relationship with national courts[5] so as to ensure two objectives: avoiding unfairness by exposing individuals to a second trial for the same crime, but at the same time preventing sham national proceedings from obstructing genuine efforts at international prosecution.

Drafting of the provision

The Explanatory Report does not provide any information on the drafting history of the provision. The heading 'Right not to be tried or punished twice' was added according to the provisions of Protocol No. 11.[6]

Analysis and interpretation

For article 4 of Protocol No. 7 to apply, there must be two sets of proceedings, and both of them must be criminal in nature. The first proceedings must be completed and final, but it is sufficient that the second proceedings have only begun for there to be an infringement of article 4.

The Convention system does not prohibit parallel proceedings. This is the phenomenon known as *lis pendens*, where two prosecutions may be underway at the same time. Presumably one finishes before the other. At that point, the problem addressed in article 4 of Protocol No. 7 arises. Where there are simultaneous proceedings, if the second proceedings are terminated upon a final judgment in the first proceedings, this should be deemed an acknowledgement of the violation of article 4. To the extent that the authorities provide adequate redress, for example by terminating or annulling the second

---

[4] Explanation relating to the Charter of Fundamental Rights, Official Journal of the European Union, C 303/34, 14 December 2007.

[5] Statute of the International Criminal Tribunal for the former Yugoslavia, UN Doc. S/RES/827 (1993), annex, art. 10; Statute of the International Criminal Tribunal for Rwanda, UN Doc. S/RES/955 (1994), annex, art. 9; Statute of the Special Court for Sierra Leone, (2002) 2178 UNTS 145, annex, art. 9; Rome Statute of the International Criminal Court, (2002) 2187 UNTS 90.

[6] Protocol No. 11 to the Convention for the Protection of Human Rights and Fundamental Freedoms, restructuring the control machinery established thereby, ETS 155, art. 2(7)(a).

set of proceedings and effacing its effects, the Court will conclude that the applicant is no longer a 'victim' within the meaning of the Convention.[7]

One of the differences between the formulation of the *ne bis in idem* principle in Protocol No. 7 by contrast with article 14(7) of the International Covenant on Civil and Political Rights is the addition, in the former, of the words 'under the jurisdiction of the same State'. The Human Rights Committee has nevertheless deemed this to be an implied condition of the Covenant provision.[8] According to the Explanatory Report on Protocol No. 7, '[t]he words "under the jurisdiction of the same State" limit the application of the article to the national level'.[9] The Report points to other Council of Europe conventions that govern the application of the principle at the international level.[10]

Final conviction or acquittal in the first proceedings

The *non bis in idem* issue with respect to the second set of proceedings must be assessed with respect to the first trial, where a final conviction or acquittal is required. Absent such a definitive *res judicata*, it is not possible to argue that the rule against double jeopardy has been infringed. The Explanatory Report states: 'The principle established in this provision applies only after the person has been finally acquitted or convicted in accordance with the law and penal procedure of the State concerned. This means that there must have been a final decision as defined above.'[11] The Report then cross-references the comment on the meaning of a final decision with respect to article 3 of Protocol No. 4:

First, the person concerned has to have been convicted of a criminal offence by a final decision and to have suffered punishment as a result of such conviction. According to the definition contained in the explanatory report of the European Convention on the International Validity of Criminal Judgments, a decision is final 'if, according to the traditional expression, it has acquired the force of *res judicata*. This is the case when it is irrevocable, that is to say when no further ordinary remedies are available or when the parties have exhausted such remedies or have permitted the time-limit to expire without availing themselves of them'. It follows therefore that a judgment by default is not considered as final as long as the domestic law allows the proceedings to be taken up again. Likewise, this article does not apply in cases where the charge is dismissed or the accused person is acquitted either by the court of first instance or, on appeal, by a higher tribunal. If, however, in one of the States in which such a possibility is provided for, the person has been granted leave to appeal after the normal time of appealing has expired, and his conviction is then reversed on appeal, then subject to the other conditions of the article, in particular the conditions described in paragraph 24 below, the article may apply.[12]

---

[7] *Sergey Zolotukhin v. Russia* [GC], no. 14939/03, §§ 113, 115, ECHR 2009; *Zigarella v. Italy* (dec.), no. 48154/99, 3 October 2002; *Falkner v. Austria* (dec.), no. 6072/02, 30 September 2004.

[8] *A.P. v. Italy*, No. 204/1986, UN Doc. CCPR/C/OP/2, p. 67, para. 7.3.

[9] Explanatory Report on Protocol No. 7, para. 27. See *Trabelsi v. Belgium*, no. 140/10, § 164, 4 September 2014; *Gestra v. Italy* (dec.), no. 21072/92, 16 January 1995; *Amrollahi v. Denmark* (dec.), no. 56811/00, 28 June 2001; *Da Luz Domingues Ferreira v. Belgium* (dec.), no. 50049/99, 6 July 2006; *Sarria v. Poland* (dec.), no. 45618/09, 18 December 2012.

[10] European Convention on Extradition, ETS 24; European Convention on the International Validity of Criminal Judgments, ETS 70; European Convention on the Transfer of Proceedings in Criminal Matters, ETS 73.

[11] Explanatory Report on Protocol No. 7, para. 29. See *Sergey Zolotukhin v. Russia* [GC], no. 14939/03, § 80, ECHR 2009; *Nikitin v. Russia*, no. 50178/99, § 37, ECHR 2004-VIII; *Horciag v. Romania* (dec.), no. 70982/01, 15 March 2005.

[12] Explanatory Report on Protocol No. 7, para. 22.

Paragraph 24 of the Explanatory Report says that 'there is no right to compensation under this provision if it can be shown that the non-disclosure of the unknown fact in time was wholly or partly attributable to the person convicted'.

The case law has added further precision to the remarks in the Explanatory Report. Thus, '[d]ecisions against which an ordinary appeal lies are excluded from the scope of the guarantee contained in Article 4 of Protocol No. 7 as long as the time-limit for lodging such an appeal has not expired'.[13] If a successful appeal results in the quashing of a conviction so that a new trial may be held, there is no final acquittal or conviction within the meaning of article 4(1).[14] Extraordinary remedies, such as a request to reopen proceedings when time limits for an appeal have been exceeded or an application not to take into account the time limits for filing of an appeal are not taken into account in determining whether the first set of proceedings is 'final'.[15] As pointed out by the Grand Chamber, Article 4 of Protocol No. 7 'does not preclude the reopening of the proceedings, as stated clearly by the second paragraph of Article 4'.[16]

In a Croatian case dealing with wartime atrocities, where the first proceedings terminated because an amnesty was granted, the Court said that this 'did not presuppose any investigation into the charges brought against the applicant and did not amount to an assessment of the applicant's guilt. The Court considers that it is therefore open to question whether it can be regarded as a "final acquittal or conviction"' as this is meant in article 4 of Protocol No. 7.[17] It did not rule definitively on the issue, however. In a Russian case, the Court declared inadmissible a claim in which the initial proceedings were discontinued by the public prosecutor. It said that there had been no acquittal or conviction and that therefore article 4 of Protocol No. 7 was not applicable.[18]

Duplication of proceedings (the '*bis*')

The right enshrined in article 4 of Protocol No. 7 applies not only to a second conviction for the same offence but even to a second prosecution. Indeed, it is violated by the initiation of proceedings and not just by their completion. Otherwise, 'it would not have been necessary to add the word "punished" to the word "tried" since this would be mere duplication. Article 4 of Protocol No. 7 applies even where the individual has merely been prosecuted in proceedings that have not resulted in a conviction.'[19] It applies 'even where the individual has merely been prosecuted in proceedings that have not resulted in a conviction'.[20] The right applies to a person who is convicted in the first proceeding and acquitted in the second, because he or she has been prosecuted a second time.[21] In other words, it has three distinct guarantees, providing 'that no one shall be (i) liable to be tried, (ii) tried or (iii) punished for the same offence'.[22]

---

[13] *Sergey Zolotukhin v. Russia* [GC], no. 14939/03, § 108, ECHR 2009.

[14] *Ehrmann and SCI VHI v. France* (dec.), no. 2777/10, § 5, 7 June 2011.

[15] *Sergey Zolotukhin v. Russia* [GC], no. 14939/03, § 108, ECHR 2009; *Nikitin v. Russia*, no. 50178/99, § 39, ECHR 2004-VIII.

[16] *Sergey Zolotukhin v. Russia* [GC], no. 14939/03, § 108, ECHR 2009.

[17] *Marguš v. Croatia*, no. 4455/10, § 67, 13 November 2012.

[18] *Smirnova and Smirnova v. Russia* (dec.), nos 46133/99 and 48183/99, 3 October 2002.

[19] *Lucky Dev v. Sweden*, no. 7356/10, § 58, 27 November 2014; *Nykänen v. Finland*, no. 11828/11, § 47, 20 May 2014.

[20] *Sergey Zolotukhin v. Russia* [GC], no. 14939/03, § 110, ECHR 2009.

[21] Ibid., § 111.

[22] Ibid., § 108; *Nikitin v. Russia*, no. 50178/99, § 36, ECHR 2004-VIII.

Proceedings brought in error, where the court was not aware of the earlier prosecution, may not be a violation of article 4. The Court has observed a lack of any indication in the Explanatory Report and said 'that it cannot content itself with a literal construction of the term in question, but should favour a teleological interpretation'. Noting that '[t]he object and aim of the provision in question imply, in the absence of any damage proved by the applicant', it concluded that 'only new proceedings brought in the knowledge that the defendant has already been tried in previous proceedings contravene this provision'.[23]

Criminal proceedings

As the Explanatory Report notes, because article 4 of Protocol No. 7 only applies to trial and conviction of a person in criminal proceedings, it does not prevent a person 'being made subject, for the same act, to action of a different character (for example, disciplinary action in the case of an official) as well as to criminal proceedings'.[24] Article 4 does not require that the offence itself be qualified as 'criminal'. According to the Explanatory Report, this was deemed not to be necessary, given that 'Article 4 already contains the terms "in criminal proceedings" and "penal procedure", which render unnecessary any further specification in the text of the article itself'.[25]

Article 4(1) refers to 'criminal proceedings' and, later in the provision, to 'penal procedure'. In this respect, the Court applies the three elements of the '*Engel* criteria': the classification of the offence under domestic law; the nature of the offence; and the nature and severity of the penalty.[26] With respect to the first of the criteria, the Court has frequently insisted that although it is relevant, the legal characterization of the procedure under national law is not determinative. 'Otherwise', it has held, 'the application of this provision would be left to the discretion of the Contracting States to a degree that might lead to results incompatible with the object and purpose of the Convention.'[27] Frequently, States respond to complaints with the argument that the second proceedings are administrative in nature rather than criminal or penal. As the Court has explained, defining an act as 'administrative' may sometimes embrace 'certain offences that have a criminal connotation but are too trivial to be governed by criminal law and procedure'.[28] The terms are to be interpreted 'in the light of the general principles concerning the corresponding words "criminal charge" and "penalty" in Articles 6 and 7 of the Convention respectively'.[29] Although the second and third of the *Engel* criteria are proposed in

[23] *Zigarella v. Italy* (dec.), no. 48154/99, 3 October 2002.

[24] Explanatory Report on Protocol No. 7, para. 32.

[25] Ibid., para. 28.

[26] *Engel and Others v. the Netherlands*, 8 June 1976, § 82, Series A no. 22. Also *Öztürk v. Germany*, 21 February 1984, § 50, Series A no. 73; *Jussila v. Finland* [GC], no. 73053/01, § 38, ECHR 2006-XIV.

[27] *Sergey Zolotukhin v. Russia* [GC], no. 14939/03, § 52, ECHR 2009; *Asadbeyli and Others v. Azerbaijan*, nos 3653/05, 14729/05, 20908/05, 26242/05, 36083/05, and 16519/06, § 151, 11 December 2012; *Storbråten v. Norway* (dec.), no. 12277/04; *Öztürk v. Germany*, 21 February 1984, § 49, Series A no. 73; *Toth v. Croatia* (dec.), no. 49635/10, 6 November 2012.

[28] *Sergey Zolotukhin v. Russia* [GC], no. 14939/03, § 54, ECHR 2009; *Menesheva v. Russia*, no. 59261/00, § 96, ECHR 2006-III; *Galstyan v. Armenia*, no. 26986/03, § 57, 15 November 2007; *Ziliberberg v. Moldova*, no. 61821/00, §§ 32–35, 1 February 2005; *Palaoro v. Austria*, 23 October 1995, §§ 33–35, Series A no. 329-B; *Asadbeyli and Others v. Azerbaijan*, nos 3653/05, 14729/05, 20908/05, 26242/05, 36083/05, and 16519/06, § 152, 11 December 2012.

[29] *Sergey Zolotukhin v. Russia* [GC], no. 14939/03., § 52, ECHR 2009; *Haarvig v. Norway* (dec.), no. 11187/05, 11 December 2007; *Rosenquist v. Sweden* (dec.), no. 60619/00, 14 September 2004; *Manasson v. Sweden* (dec.), no. 41265/98, 8 April 2003; *Göktan v. France*, no. 33402/96, § 48, ECHR 2002-V; *Malige v. France*, 23 September 1998, § 35, *Reports of Judgments and Decisions* 1998-VII; *Nilsson v. Sweden* (dec.), no. 73661/01.

the alternative, and a cumulative analysis is not required, sometimes it will be desirable 'where separate analysis of each criterion does not make it possible to reach a clear conclusion as to the existence of a criminal charge'.[30]

Factors to be considered are whether the offence 'served to guarantee the protection of human dignity and public order, values and interests which normally fall within the sphere of protection of criminal law'.[31] Nevertheless, 'there is nothing in the Convention to suggest that the criminal nature of an offence, within the meaning of the *Engel* criteria, necessarily requires a certain degree of seriousness'.[32] The aim in establishing the offence in question is relevant to the determination. If it consists of punishment and deterrence, this suggests that characteristics of criminal or penal law.[33]

An important factor is the extent of the penalty. This requires reference to the maximum penalty that may be imposed. Although the actual penalty, which may be considerably less than the maximum available, should be taken into consideration, this 'cannot diminish the importance of what was initially at stake'.[34] If the penalty involves loss of liberty, there is a presumption that the offence is 'criminal' in nature, although it can 'be rebutted entirely exceptionally, and only if the deprivation of liberty cannot be considered "appreciably detrimental" given their nature, duration or manner of execution'.[35] Where prison disciplinary offences are concerned, determining whether or not they are criminal in nature usually involves assessing whether the penalty involves a lengthening of the term of imprisonment or rather some aggravation of conditions, such as a period of solitary confinement. Many decisions of the Convention organs support the view that if the term of the sentence is unchanged the matter is not criminal in nature.[36]

In a case involving a disqualification order prohibiting an offender, who had already been convicted of aggravated embezzlement and aggravated breach of confidence, from establishing or managing a new limited liability company for a period of two years, the Court noted that this was not a general prohibition against engaging in business activities. It admitted that the disqualification order 'was capable of having a considerable impact on a person's reputation and ability to practise his or her profession', but said that 'what was at stake for the applicant was sufficiently important to warrant classifying it as "criminal"'.[37]

---

[30] *Sergey Zolotukhin v. Russia* [GC], no. 14939/03, § 53, ECHR 2009; *Jussila v. Finland* [GC], no. 73053/01, §§ 30–31, ECHR 2006-XIV; *Ezeh and Connors v. the United Kingdom* [GC], nos 39665/98 and 40086/98, §§ 82–86, ECHR 2003-X.

[31] *Sergey Zolotukhin v. Russia* [GC], no. 14939/03, § 55, ECHR 2009.

[32] *Sergey Zolotukhin v. Russia* [GC], no. 14939/03, § 55, ECHR 2009.; *Ezeh and Connors v. the United Kingdom* [GC], nos 39665/98 and 40086/98, § 104, 104, ECHR 2003-X.

[33] *Sergey Zolotukhin v. Russia* [GC], no. 14939/03, § 55, ECHR 2009; *Ezeh and Connors v. the United Kingdom* [GC], nos 39665/98 and 40086/98, §§ 82–86, 102, 105, ECHR 2003-X; *Asadbeyli and Others v. Azerbaijan*, nos 3653/05, 14729/05, 20908/05, 26242/05, 36083/05, and 16519/06, § 153, 11 December 2012.

[34] *Sergey Zolotukhin v. Russia* [GC], no. 14939/03, § 56, ECHR 2009; *Ezeh and Connors v. the United Kingdom* [GC], nos 39665/98 and 40086/98, § 120, ECHR 2003-X.

[35] *Engel and Others v. the Netherlands*, 8 June 1976, § 82, Series A no. 22; *Ezeh and Connors v. the United Kingdom* [GC], nos 39665/98 and 40086/98, § 126, ECHR 2003-X; *Sergey Zolotukhin v. Russia* [GC], no. 14939/03, § 56, ECHR 2009; *Asadbeyli and Others v. Azerbaijan*, nos 3653/05, 14729/05, 20908/05, 26242/05, 36083/05, and 16519/06, § 154, 11 December 2012.

[36] *Eggs v. Switzerland*, no. 7341/76, Commission decision of 4 March 1978, (1977) 20 YB 412; *X v. Switzerland*, no. 8778/79, Commission decision of 8 July 1980, (1980) 23 YB 404; *P. v. France*, no. 11691/85, Commission decision of 10 October 1986; *J.U. v. France*, no. 20978/92, Commission decision of 21 October 1993; *Štitić v. Croatia*, no. 29660/03, §§ 55 and 56, 8 November 2007; *Toth v. Croatia* (dec.), no. 49635/10, § 38, 6 November 2012.

[37] *Mjelde v. Norway* (dec.), no. 11143/04, 1 February 2007.

Problems of double incrimination arise with motor vehicle offences. Withdrawal of a driving licence after a conviction for driving while intoxicated does not infringe article 4 of Protocol No. 7.[38] However, conviction by an administrative authority for drunken driving under the Road Traffic Act followed by a conviction of causing death by negligence based upon the driver's intoxication is a violation of the Protocol.[39]

Identity of offences (the '*idem*')

The *ne bis in idem* norm, as formulated in article 4 of Protocol No. 4, requires that no person be prosecuted twice for the same 'offence'. Until an important ruling of the Grand Chamber in 2009, in *Sergey Zolotukhin v. Russia*, the attitude of the Court to this requirement had not been entirely consistent. One approach focused on the 'same conduct'. In *Gradinger v. Austria*, the Court found a violation of article 4 of Protocol No. 4 in an impaired driving case where the applicant was prosecuted under the Criminal Code for homicide where intoxication was an aggravating factor and under the Road Traffic Act for driving while intoxicated.[40] Another approach, concerned more with content than with form, emphasized the 'essential elements' of the two offences in question.[41]

Some decisions had taken a more formalist view, predicated on the idea that the same conduct may give rise to several offences, and that these may be tried in separate proceedings.[42] According to the Grand Chamber, 'the approach which emphasises the legal characterisation of the two offences is too restrictive on the rights of the individual' and 'risks undermining the guarantee enshrined in Article 4 of Protocol No. 7 rather than rendering it practical and effective'.[43] Thus, said the Grand Chamber, 'Article 4 of Protocol No. 7 must be understood as prohibiting the prosecution or trial of a second "offence" in so far as it arises from identical facts or facts which are substantially the same.'[44]

The starting point for the application of article 4 of Protocol No. 7 is the final decision bringing the first prosecution to a close with a definitive conviction or an acquittal. These are to be compared with the new charges in light of all of the materials involved in both prosecutions. Consequently, the Court's inquiry should focus on 'those facts which constitute a set of concrete factual circumstances involving the same defendant and inextricably linked together in time and space, the existence of which must be demonstrated in order to secure a conviction or institute criminal proceedings'.[45] Whether the new charges are upheld or dismissed in the second set of proceedings is irrelevant to the

---

[38] *Ponsetti and Chesnel v. France* (dec.), nos 36855/97 and 41731/98, ECHR 1999-VI; *Horciag v. Romania* (dec.), no. 70982/01, 15 March 2005; *R.T. v. Switzerland* (dec.), no. 31982/96, 30 May 2000; *Nilsson v. Sweden (dec.), no.* 73661/01, 13 December 2005.

[39] *Franz Fischer v. Austria*, no. 37950/97, § 31, 29 May 2001.

[40] *Gradinger v. Austria*, 23 October 1995, § 55, Series A no. 328-C.

[41] *Franz Fischer v. Austria*, no. 37950/97, § 25, 29 May 2001; *Sailer v. Austria* (dec.), no. 38237/97, 6 June 2002; *Manasson v. Sweden* (dec.), no. 41265/98, 8 April 2003; *Bachmaier v. Austria* (dec.), no. 77413/01, 2 September 2004; *Hauser-Sporn v. Austria*, no. 37301/03, §§ 43–46, 7 December 2006; *Schutte v. Austria*, no. 18015/03, § 42, 26 July 2007; *Garretta v. France* (dec.), no. 2529/04, 4 March 2008.

[42] *Oliveira v. Switzerland*, 30 July 1998, §§ 25–29, *Reports of Judgments and Decisions* 1998-V; *Göktan v. France*, no. 33402/96, § 50, ECHR 2002-V; *Gauthier v. France* (dec.), no. 61178/00, 24 June 2003; *Ongun v. Turkey* (dec.), no. 15737/02, 10 October 2006.

[43] *Sergey Zolotukhin v. Russia* [GC], no. 14939/03, § 81, ECHR 2009.

[44] Ibid., § 82.

[45] Ibid., § 84.

debate about a breach of article 4 of Protocol No. 4. As the Grand Chamber explained, the provision constitutes 'a safeguard against being tried or being liable to be tried again in new proceedings rather than a prohibition on a second conviction or acquittal'.[46]

For example, in a case taken against Azerbaijan, the applicant was arrested for failing to respect police orders during a demonstration in Azadliq Square in Baku. He was charged under the Code of Administrative Offences and given a custodial sentence of several days. Upon his release, he was charged under the Criminal Code with respect to the demonstration. The European Court acknowledged that it was hypothetically possible to be tried first under the Code of Administrative Offences for an isolated incident of non-compliance with police orders and then subsequently prosecuted under the Criminal Code for violent conduct. The Court noted that nothing in the documents concerning the two sets of proceedings suggested that the applicant was prosecuted for two distinct acts or sets of factual circumstances. It concluded that in both sets of proceedings the applicant was prosecuted 'in the events of 16 October 2003, comprising the entirety of the allegedly unlawful actions he might have committed on that day in Azadliq Square'.[47]

The identity must apply not only to the offence but also to the convicted person. In a Norwegian case, the Court noted that the criminal prosecution concerned tax advantages benefiting a company, whereas tax surcharges were imposed with respect to the applicant's personal tax liability. The Court said that although there was a close nexus between the company's and the applicant's tax evasion, 'the sanctions concerned two different legal entities'.[48]

Reopening of the case (art. 4(2))

Paragraph 2 of article 4 allows for an exception to the general rule by allowing 'the reopening of the case in accordance with the law and penal procedure of the State concerned, if there is evidence of new or newly discovered facts, or if there has been a fundamental defect in the previous proceedings, which could affect the outcome of the case'. The provision seems to have been interpreted rather broadly.

Several applications have dealt with Russian legislation by which a criminal case that has been finally resolved could be reopened on grounds of a judicial error concerning points of law and procedure. Known as 'supervisory review', the subject-matter of the proceedings was the same criminal charge. If granted, the result was the annulment of previous decisions and a new determination based upon the original charge. The Court has described this as a 'special type of reopening' rather than a 'second trial', holding that it falls within the scope of article 4(2) of Protocol No. 7.[49]

According to the Explanatory Report, the term 'new or newly discovered facts' includes new means of proof relating to previously existing facts. Article 4(2) does not 'prevent a reopening of the proceedings in favour of the convicted person and any other changing of the judgment to the benefit of the convicted person'.[50] It also allows for a second

---

[46] Ibid., § 83.

[47] *Asadbeyli and Others v. Azerbaijan*, nos 3653/05, 14729/05, 20908/05, 26242/05, 36083/05, and 16519/06, §§ 161–162, 11 December 2012.

[48] *Isaksen v. Norway* (dec.), no. 13596/02, 2 October 2003.

[49] *Nikitin v. Russia*, no. 50178/99, ECHR 2004-VIII; *Bratyakin v. Russia* (dec.), no. 72776/01, 9 March 2006. Also *Savinskiy v. Ukraine* (dec.), no. 6965/02, 31 May 2005.

[50] Explanatory Report on Protocol No. 7, para. 31.

prosecution if there has been a 'fundamental defect in the proceedings'. The wording is vague and general, and the Explanatory Report provides no guidance on its interpretation.[51] In a case concerning the prosecution by Croatia of a suspected war criminal for atrocities perpetrated during the conflict, the Court held that the first set of proceedings suffered from a 'fundamental defect' because it had terminated with an amnesty. According to the Chamber, '[g]ranting amnesty in respect of "international crimes"—which include crimes against humanity, war crimes and genocide—is increasingly considered to be prohibited by international law'.[52] The Chamber stopped short of a clear ruling on this point, but held that the amnesty was a fundamental defect '[i]n view of the practices and recommendations of various international bodies with a view to preventing or prohibiting the granting of amnesty in respect of war crimes'.[53] The Grand Chamber reached a similar result in the same case.[54]

Derogation (art. 4(3))

Paragraph 3 of article 4 indicates that derogation pursuant to article 15 of the European Convention is not permitted. Thus, the principle *ne bis in idem* joins a very select group of non-derogable norms. It is sometimes suggested that non-derogable norms are in some way more sacred or important than rights that are subject to derogation and that they may therefore be suspended under the circumstances permitted by article 15. Care should be taken in reaching such a conclusion, however. Other human rights treaties, such as the International Covenant on Civil and Political Rights, do not include the norm in the list of non-derogable provisions. Moreover, the right itself does not find any recognition whatsoever in the Universal Declaration of Human Rights.

Relative importance may be an important criteria, as evidenced by the non-derogable nature of the right to life in peacetime and the prohibition of torture and slavery. But other norms seem to be included in the list because there is no logical relationship between their implementation and the circumstances that would justify derogation. For example, the International Covenant on Civil and Political Rights prohibits derogation from the norm governing imprisonment for debt. As the Human Rights Committee explained, 'not all rights of profound importance... have in fact been made non-derogable. One reason for certain rights being made non-derogable is because their suspension is irrelevant to the legitimate control of the state of national emergency.'[55]

Reservations and declarations

France formulated a reservation at the time of ratification: 'The Government of the French Republic declares that only those offences which under French law fall within the jurisdiction of the French criminal courts may be regarded as offences within the meaning of Articles 2 to 4 of this Protocol.'

---

[51] Ibid., para. 30.

[52] *Marguš v. Croatia*, no. 4455/10, § 74, 13 November 2012.

[53] Ibid., § 75.

[54] *Marguš v. Croatia* [GC], no. 4455/10, §§ 139–141, 27 May 2015.

[55] General comment on issues relating to reservations made upon ratification or accession to the Covenant or the Optional Protocols thereto, or in relation to declarations under article 41 of the Covenant, UN Doc. CCPR/C/21/Rev.1/Add.6, para. 10.

Austria, Italy, Liechtenstein, and Portugal[56] have made declarations along similar lines to that of the French reservation. The Austrian reservation has been deemed to be a reservation and found to be invalid under the terms of article 57 of the Convention because there is no brief statement of the law.[57] Italy made a similar declaration.

At the time of signature, on 19 March 1985, Germany made the following declaration: 'By "criminal offence" and "offence" in Article 2 to 4 of the present Protocol, the Federal Republic of Germany understands only such acts as are criminal offences under its law.'[58] Germany has not ratified the Protocol.

Further reading

Cees Flinterman, 'Ne bis in idem (Article 4 of Protocol No. 7)', in Van Dijk et al., *Theory and Practice*, pp. 979–83.

Frowein/Peukert, *MenschenRechtsKonvention,* pp. 711–18.

Grabenwarter, *European Convention*, pp. 435–40.

Harris et al., *Law of the European Convention*, pp. 751–3.

Renée Koering-Joulin, 'Protocole No 7, Article 4', in Pettiti et al., *La Convention européenne*, pp. 1093–4.

Christine van den Wyngaert and Guy Stessens, 'The International *Non Bis in Idem* Principle: Resolving Some of the Unanswered Questions', (1999) 48 *ICLQ* 779.

---

[56] (2004) 47 YB 24.

[57] *Gradinger v. Austria*, 23 October 1995, § 51, Series A no. 328-C.

[58] (1985) 28 YB 7–8.

Article 5. Equality between spouses/Egalité entre époux

Spouses shall enjoy equality of rights and responsibilities of a private law character between them, and in their relations with their children, as to marriage, during marriage and in the event of its dissolution. This Article shall not prevent States from taking such measures as are necessary in the interests of the children.

Les époux jouissent de l'égalité de droits et de responsabilités de caractère civil entre eux et dans leurs relations avec leurs enfants au regard du mariage, durant le mariage et lors de sa dissolution. Le présent article n'empêche pas les Etats de prendre les mesures nécessaires dans l'intérêt des enfants.

Introductory comments

The Universal Declaration of Human Rights contains a rather lengthy provision that recognizes the right to marry and to found a family, and the equal rights of the spouses. Insisting upon robust recognition of the equality of the spouses in marriage was one of the first accomplishments of the Commission on the Status of Women, a body that functioned in parallel with the Commission on Human Rights.

The drafters of the European Convention quite deliberately incorporated the Universal Declaration's provision only partially, in article 12, recognizing the right to marry and to found a family but not the equality of the partners to the marriage. In contrast, the International Covenant on Civil and Political Rights, at the insistence of the Commission on the Status of Women,[1] rather faithfully reproduces the content of article 16 of the Universal Declaration. Article 5 of Protocol No. 7 aligns the European Convention more closely with the International Covenant.

Drafting of the provision

The Explanatory Report does not provide any information about the drafting of the provision. The heading 'Equality between spouses' was added in accordance with Protocol No. 11.[2]

Analysis and interpretation

Article 5 of Protocol No. 7 brings the European Convention on Human Rights into harmony with the International Covenant on Civil and Political Rights as well as the Universal Declaration of Human Rights. It has been argued that article 5 of Protocol No. 7 constitutes a *lex specialis* with respect to article 8 of the Convention.[3] But such an

---

[1] UN Doc. E/2401, paras 29–30; UN Doc. E/CN.4/686.

[2] Protocol No. 11 to the Convention for the Protection of Human Rights and Fundamental Freedoms, restructuring the control machinery established thereby, ETS 155, art. 2(7)(a).

[3] *Burghartz and Schnyder Burghartz v. Switzerland*, no. 16213/90, Commission decision of 19 February 1992.

interpretation has been rejected by the Court. It has insisted that article 5 is 'additional' to the provisions of the Convention.[4] Nevertheless, the Court will frequently conclude that complaints based on article 5 of Protocol No. 7 are better examined under article 8 of the Convention.[5]

According to the Explanatory Report, '[u]nder the terms of this article, equality must be ensured solely in the relations between the spouses themselves, in regard to their person or their property and in their relations with their children'.[6] Rights and responsibilities contemplated by article 6 are of a private law character; the article does not apply to other fields of law, such as administrative, fiscal, criminal, social, ecclesiastical, or labour laws.[7]

The provision 'essentially imposes a positive obligation on States to provide a satisfactory legal framework under which spouses have equal rights and obligations concerning such matters as their relations with their children'.[8] However, according to the Explanatory Report the fact that spouses shall enjoy equality of rights and responsibilities in their relations with their children does not prevent States from taking such measures as are necessary in the interests of the children.[9] This is set out in the second sentence of article 5: 'This Article shall not prevent States from taking such measures as are necessary in the interests of the children.' Indeed, the Convention organs have insisted on the need to take account of the interests of the child.[10]

The 'necessity clause', that is, the second sentence of article 5, 'should be interpreted in the same way as the necessity clauses contained in other provisions of the Convention'.[11] Accordingly, an interference with the right must correspond to a pressing social need and be proportionate to the legitimate aim pursued by the State. The State is left a margin of appreciation, but it is not unlimited. In its supervision, the Court must determine whether the reasons used to justify interference with the right are 'relevant and sufficient'. For example, a legislative decision to exclude the possibility of joint custody after divorce, although allowing for access and information rights to the non-custodial parent, was within this margin of appreciation.[12]

Article 5 is concerned with 'spouses' (*les époux*). The implication is that the right applies only to two persons who are married. The article does not appear to have been applied by the Convention organs in the case of marriages of two persons of the same sex or cohabiting couples who have not undertaken any formal recognition of their relationship. The Explanatory Report says that article 5 does not apply to 'the period preceding marriage', nor does it address conditions of capacity to enter into marriage provided by national law.[13] The Report adds that 'the words "as to marriage" relate to the legal effects

---

[4] *Burghartz v. Switzerland*, 22 February 1994, § 23, Series A no. 280-B.

[5] E.g., *Dorca v. Romania* (dec.), no. 59651/13, § 28, 15 April 2014; *Kaplan v. Austria*, no. 45983/99, § 37, 18 January 2007.

[6] Explanatory Report on Protocol No. 7, para. 35.

[7] Ibid.

[8] *Iosub Caras v. Romania*, no. 7198/04, § 56, 27 July 2006; *Cernecki v. Austria* (dec.), no. 31061/96, 11 July 2000; *Negyeliczky v. Hungary* (dec.), no. 42622/14, 14 October 2014.

[9] Explanatory Report on Protocol No. 7, para. 36.

[10] *Cernecki v. Austria* (dec.), no. 31061/96, 11 July 2000; *Chepelev v. Russia*, no. 58077/00, § 36, 26 July 2007.

[11] *Cernecki v. Austria* (dec.), no. 31061/96, 11 July 2000.

[12] Ibid. Also *R.W and v. T.G.-W. v. Austria* (dec.), no. 36222/97, 22 November 2001.

[13] Explanatory Report on Protocol No. 7, para. 37.

connected with the conclusion of marriage'.[14] It adds two provisos about what is not contemplated by article 5: 'this article should not be understood as preventing the national authorities from taking due account of all relevant factors when reaching decisions with regard to the division of property in the event of dissolution of marriage'[15] and '[t]he words "in the event of its dissolution" do not imply any obligation on a State to provide for dissolution of marriage or to provide any special forms of dissolution'.[16]

Reservations and declarations

There have been several reservations to article 5 of Protocol No. 7. France formulated a reservation declaring 'that Article 5 may not impede the application of the rules of the French legal system concerning the transmission of the patronymic name'.[17] Luxembourg made a similar reservation.[18] A second reservation to article 5 by France shelters 'the application of provisions of local law in the territorial collectivity of Mayotte and the territories of New Caledonia and of the Wallis and Futuna Archipelago'.[19]

Switzerland formulated a reservation respecting provisions governing the family name, acquisition of the right of citizenship, and 'certain provisions of transitional law on marriage settlement'.[20]

Further reading

Cees Flinterman, 'Equality of Rights and Responsibilities between Spouses During and After Marriage (Article 5 of Protocol No. 7)', in Van Dijk et al., *Theory and Practice*, pp. 985–8.

Frowein/Peukert, *MenschenRechtsKonvention*, pp. 718–19.

Grabenwarter, *European Convention*, pp. 441–2.

Harris et al., *Law of the European Convention*, pp. 753–6.

---

[14] Ibid., para. 37.
[15] Ibid., para. 38.
[16] Ibid.
[17] (1986) 29 YB 5.
[18] (1989) 32 YB 6.
[19] (1986) 29 YB 5.
[20] (1988) 31 YB 7. The reservation was invoked by Switzerland in *Burghartz and Schnyder Burghartz v. Switzerland*, no. 16213/90, Commission decision of 19 February 1992.

Article 6. Territorial application/Application territoriale

1. Any State may at the time of signature or when depositing its instrument of ratification, acceptance or approval, specify the territory or territories to which this Protocol shall apply and state the extent to which it undertakes that the provisions of this Protocol shall apply to this or these territories.

2. Any State may at any later date, by a declaration addressed to the Secretary-General of the Council of Europe, extend the application of this Protocol to any other territory specified in the declaration. In respect of such territory the Protocol shall enter into force on the first day of the month following the expiration of a period of two months after the date of receipt by the Secretary General of such declaration.

3. Any declaration made under the two preceding paragraphs may, in respect of any territory specified in such declaration, be withdrawn or modified by a notification addressed to the Secretary General. The withdrawal or modification shall become effective on the first day of the month following the expiration of a period of two months after the date of receipt of such notification by the Secretary General.

4. A declaration made in accordance with this Article shall be deemed to have been made in accordance with paragraph 1 of Article 56 of the Convention.

5. The territory of any State to which this Protocol applies by virtue of ratification, acceptance or approval by that State, and each territory to which this Protocol is applied by virtue of a declaration by that State under this Article, may be treated as separate territories for the purpose of the reference in Article 1 to the territory of a State.

6. Any State which has made a declaration in accordance with paragraph 1 or 2 of this Article may at any time thereafter declare on behalf of one or more of the territories

1. Tout Etat peut, au moment de la signature ou au moment du dépôt de son instrument de ratification, d'acceptation ou d'approbation, désigner le ou les territoires auxquels s'appliquera le présent Protocole, en indiquant la mesure dans laquelle il s'engage à ce que les dispositions du présent Protocole s'appliquent à ce ou ces territoires.

2. Tout Etat peut, à tout autre moment par la suite, par une déclaration adressée au Secrétaire Général du Conseil de l'Europe, étendre l'application du présent Protocole à tout autre territoire désigné dans la déclaration. Le Protocole entrera en vigueur à l'égard de ce territoire le premier jour du mois qui suit l'expiration d'une période de deux mois après la date de réception de la déclaration par le Secrétaire Général.

3. Toute déclaration faite en vertu des deux paragraphes précédents pourra être retirée ou modifiée en ce qui concerne tout territoire désigné dans cette déclaration, par notification adressée au Secrétaire Général. Le retrait ou la modification prendra effet le premier jour du mois qui suit l'expiration d'une période de deux mois après la date de réception de la notification par le Secrétaire Général.

4. Une déclaration faite conformément au présent article sera considérée comme ayant été faite conformément au paragraphe 1 de l'article 56 de la Convention.

5. Le territoire de tout Etat auquel le présent Protocole s'applique en vertu de sa ratification, de son acceptation ou de son approbation par ledit Etat, et chacun des territoires auxquels le Protocole s'applique en vertu d'une déclaration souscrite par le dit Etat conformément au présent article, peuvent être considérés comme des territoires distincts aux fins de la référence au territoire d'un Etat faite par l'article 1.

6. Tout Etat ayant fait une déclaration conformément au paragraphe 1 ou 2 du présent article peut, à tout moment par la suite, déclarer relativement à un ou plusieurs des territoires visés

to which the declaration relates that it accepts the competence of the Court to receive applications from individuals, non-governmental organisations or groups of individuals as provided in Article 34 of the Convention in respect of Articles 1 to 5 of this Protocol.

dans cette déclaration qu'il accepte la compétence de la Cour pour connaître des requêtes de personnes physiques, d'organisations non gouvernementales ou de groupes de particuliers, comme le prévoit l'article 34 de la Convention, au titre des articles 1 à 5 du présent Protocole.

Introductory comments

Territorial application of the Convention itself is governed by article 56 of the Convention. Clauses on territorial application also appear in several of the Protocols. In the past, they were known as 'colonial clauses'. In reality, they have been applicable to only the small number of European States with dependent territories. Such clauses constitute an exception to the general law of treaties, codified in article 29 of the Vienna Convention on the Law of Treaties, by which a convention applies to the entire territory of a State Party. They have been criticized for permitting double standards but, in theory at least, they also permit the European State to show some deference for local autonomy.

Drafting of the provision

According to the Explanatory Report, article 6 'deals with the territorial application of the Protocol and corresponds, as to the principle it embodies, to Article 63 of the Convention, Article 4 of Protocol No. 1 and Article 5 of Protocol No. 4, but is formulated in terms which take account of the relevant provisions in the model final clauses adopted by the Committee of Ministers in February 1980'.[1] The Report provides an explanation for paragraph 5, which is not part of the Model Final Clauses: 'Paragraph 5 specifies that a State which has extended the Protocol to certain territories may treat each of them and the territory to which the Protocol applies by virtue of its ratification, acceptance or approval by that State as separate territories for the purpose of Article 1.'[2] The Report concludes by noting that the intent of the provision is not to allow a federal State to exclude the Protocol with respect to part of its territory.[3]

Paragraph 6 was added by Protocol No. 11. The Explanatory Report provides no information about the drafting of the text or the intent of its authors. Paragraph 4 was amended as a result of Protocol No. 11 in order to take into account the renumbering of the Convention articles.[4] The heading, 'Territorial application', was added by Protocol No. 11.[5]

Analysis and interpretation

The territorial application provision of Protocol No. 7 is formulated on the basis of the relevant text in the Model Final Clauses, although reference must also be made to article 56 of the Convention and the corresponding provisions in Protocol No. 1, Protocol No.

---

[1] Explanatory Report on Protocol No. 7, para. 40.
[2] Ibid., para. 41.
[3] Ibid., para. 42.
[4] Protocol No. 11 to the Convention for the Protection of Human Rights and Fundamental Freedoms, restructuring the control machinery established thereby, ETS 155 000, art. 7(b).
[5] Ibid., art. 2(7)(a).

4, and Protocol No. 6. In particular, readers of the Commentary are referred to the chapter dealing with article 5 of Protocol No. 6, bearing in mind the differences between that provision and article 6 of Protocol No. 7. In particular, unlike the text of Protocol No. 6, article 6(1) of Protocol No. 7 allows a State to specify in its declaration 'the extent to which it undertakes that the provisions of this Protocol shall apply to this or these territories'. Paragraph 3 permits a State not only to withdraw such a declaration but also to modify it, although that may not really be of great significance given that a State could also withdraw a declaration and then formulate a new one in different terms. The provision has never been invoked.

The relevant text in the Model Final Clauses, already employed in article 5 of Protocol No. 6, seems to provide a State Party with the possibility of specifying any territory or territories, whereas the other territorial clauses in the Convention and the Protocols speak of 'territories for the international relations of which it is responsible'. According to the Explanatory Report on Protocol No. 7, '[i]t is to be noted that this article is not intended to allow a federal State to exclude acceptance of the Protocol in respect of part of its territory'.[6]

The reference to article 56(1) in paragraph 4 seems to exclude, as a consequence, the notorious 'local requirements' clause of article 56(3). It is perhaps for that reason that France formulated what it called a 'reservation', rather than a 'declaration', at the time of ratification of Protocol No. 7, specifying the application of the 'local requirements' criterion. There has been no case law on this point.

Paragraph 5 of article 6 has no equivalent in the corresponding provision of Protocol No. 6 or, for that matter, in any of the other territorial application clauses of the Convention or the Protocols. Paragraph 6 corresponds very broadly to article 56(4) of the Convention. On the latter provision, the reader is referred to the relevant chapter in the Commentary.

Declarations

There have been several declarations pursuant to article 6. France accompanied its instrument of ratification with what it called a 'reservation' specifying that the Protocol 'shall apply to the whole territory of the Republic, due regard being had where the overseas territories and the territorial collectivity of Mayotte are concerned, to the local requirements referred to in Article [56] of the European Convention on Human Rights and Fundamental Freedoms'.[7] Upon ratification on 18 August 1988, Denmark made what it described as a 'territorial reservation' upon ratification of Protocol No. 7 excluding the Faroe Islands from the scope of the instrument.[8] Six years later it withdrew the declaration, although at the same time it specified that its reservation with respect to article 2(1) applied to the Faroe Islands.[9]

Two declarations submitted with respect to Protocol No. 7 are not contemplated by article 6. When Spain ratified the Protocol, on 16 September 2009, its instrument was accompanied by the following: 'If this Protocol were to be extended by the United

---

[6] Explanatory Report to Protocol No. 7, para. 42.
[7] (1986) 29 YB 5.
[8] (1988) 31 YB 8.
[9] (1994) 37 YB 6.

Kingdom to Gibraltar, Spain would like to make the following declaration...' The declaration went on to address issues of sovereignty unrelated to the application of the Convention or Protocol No. 7. Azerbaijan made a declaration stating that it was 'unable to guarantee the application of the provisions of the Protocol in the territories occupied by the Republic of Armenia until these territories are liberated from that occupation'.

Further reading

Michael Wood, 'Protocole No 7, Article 6', in Pettiti et al., *La Convention européenne*, p. 1097.

Article 7. Relationship to the Convention/Relations avec la Convention

As between the State Parties, the provisions of Articles 1 to 6 of this Protocol shall be regarded as additional Articles to the Convention, and all the provisions of the Convention shall apply accordingly.

Les Etats Parties considèrent les articles 1 à 6 du présent Protocole comme des articles additionnels à la Convention et toutes les dispositions de la Convention s'appliquent en conséquence.

Introductory comments

All of the additional Protocols to the Convention contain a clause governing the relationship. The provision confirms that the Convention organs may exercise jurisdiction with respect to rights in the Protocol. Furthermore, provisions relating to such matters as reservation and denunciation are also deemed to apply. In this regard, the Explanatory Report drew particular attention to article 53 of the Convention: 'Nothing in this Convention shall be construed as limiting or derogating from any of the human rights and fundamental freedoms which may be ensured under the laws of any High Contracting Party or under any other agreement to which it is a Party.'[1]

Drafting of the provision

The Explanatory Report discusses the objective of the second paragraph of article 7. It concerns the acceptance of the right of individual petition to the Commission and the Court.[2] Under the Protocol, as an exception to the general rule in paragraph 1, individual petition required a supplementary declaration by the State Party. In contrast with the equivalent text in Protocol No. 4, a State Party had no option but to accept jurisdiction for all of the rights in the Protocol. Paragraph 2 of article 7 was removed by Protocol No. 11.

The heading 'Relationship to the Convention' was added by Protocol No. 11.[3]

Analysis and interpretation

The Grand Chamber referred to article 7 of Protocol No. 7 when it considered an argument by the respondent State to the effect that a right to compensation for wrongful conviction, as set out in article 3 of Protocol No. 7, could not be derived from the presumption of innocence recognized in article 6(2) of the Convention. The State Party had not ratified Protocol No. 7. The Court noted that 'Article 7 of Protocol No. 7 clarifies that the provisions of the substantive Articles of the Protocol are to be regarded as additional Articles to the Convention, and that "all the provisions of the Convention

---

[1] Explanatory Report on Protocol No. 7, para. 43.
[2] Ibid., para. 44.
[3] Protocol No. 11 to the Convention for the Protection of Human Rights and Fundamental Freedoms, restructuring the control machinery established thereby, ETS 155, art. 2(7)(a).

shall apply accordingly".' For that reason, 'Article 3 of Protocol No. 7 cannot therefore be said to constitute a form of *lex specialis* excluding the application of Article 6 § 2.'[4] A similar *lex specialis* argument was rejected with respect to article 5 of Protocol No. 7. Switzerland had contended article 5, to which it had formulated a reservation, had displaced article 8 of the Convention with respect to names, but the Court ruled otherwise.[5]

Declaration

On 2 September 1994, Denmark made a declaration, 'in accordance with Article 7, paragraph 2, of the Protocol' recognizing that the right of individual petition and the compulsory jurisdiction of the Court with regard to article 1 to 5 of the Protocol was also applicable to the Faroe Islands.

Further reading

Pierre-Henri Imbert, 'Protocole No 7, Article 7', in Pettiti et al., *La Convention européenne*, p. 1099.

[4] *Allen v. the United Kingdom* [GC], no. 25424/09, § 105, 12 July 2013.
[5] *Burghartz v. Switzerland*, 22 February 1994, § 23, Series A no. 280-B.

Article 8. Signature and ratification/Signature et ratification

This Protocol shall be open for signature by member States of the Council of Europe which have signed the Convention. It is subject to ratification, acceptance or approval. A member State of the Council of Europe may not ratify, accept or approve this Protocol without previously or simultaneously ratifying the Convention. Instruments of ratification, acceptance or approval shall be deposited with the Secretary General of the Council of Europe.

Le présent Protocole est ouvert à la signature des Etats membres du Conseil de l'Europe qui ont signé la Convention. Il sera soumis à ratification, acceptation ou approbation. Un Etat membre du Conseil de l'Europe ne peut ratifier, accepter ou approuver le présent Protocole sans avoir simultanément ou antérieurement ratifié la Convention. Les instruments de ratification, d'acceptation ou d'approbation seront déposés près le Secrétaire Général du Conseil de l'Europe.

Introductory comments

This article is closely related to article 59 of the Convention, also entitled 'Signature and ratification'.

Drafting of the provision

The Explanatory Report on Protocol No. 7 explains that article 8 is 'formulated in terms which take account of the new model final clauses adopted by the Committee of Ministers'.[1] The title 'Signature and ratification' was introduced by Protocol No. 11.[2]

Analysis and interpretation

Article 8 of Protocol No. 7 is identical to the text of article 7 of Protocol No. 6. Readers are referred to the chapter in this Commentary on article 7 of Protocol No. 6.

Protocol No. 7 was opened for signature on 22 November 1984. On that day, ten of the twenty-one States Parties to the Convention signed the instrument: Denmark, France, Greece, Italy, Luxembourg, the Netherlands, Norway, Portugal, Spain, and Sweden. All but four Member States of the Council of Europe have now signed and ratified Protocol No. 7. The United Kingdom has not signed Protocol No. 7. The Netherlands, which signed the Protocol on 22 November 1984, Turkey, which signed on 14 March 1985, and Germany, which signed on 19 March 1985, have not ratified. When the Council of Europe was enlarged during the 1990s with the membership of many States from Central

---

[1] Explanatory Report on Protocol No. 7, para. 45.
[2] Protocol No. 11 to the Convention for the Protection of Human Rights and Fundamental Freedoms, restructuring the control machinery established thereby, ETS 155, art. 2(7)(a).

and Eastern Europe, ratification of Protocol No. 7 within a year of becoming a member of the organization was one of the undertakings that were made.[3]

Further reading

Pierre-Henri Imbert, 'Protocole No 7, Article 8', in Pettiti et al., *La Convention européenne*, p. 1101.

[3] E.g., Application by Ukraine for membership of the Council of Europe, Opinion 190 (1995), para. 12.1; Application by Russia for membership of the Council of Europe, Opinion 193 (1996), para. 10.1; Application by Croatia for membership of the Council of Europe, Opinion 195 (1996), para. 9.2.

Article 9. Entry into force/Entrée en vigueur

1 This Protocol shall enter into force on the first day of the month following the expiration of a period of two months after the date on which seven member States of the Council of Europe have expressed their consent to be bound by the Protocol in accordance with the provisions of Article 8.

2 In respect to any member State which subsequently expresses its consent to be bound by it, the Protocol shall enter into force on the first day of the month following the expiration of a period of two months after the date of the deposit of the instrument of ratification, acceptance or approval.

1 Le présent Protocole entrera en vigueur le premier jour du mois qui suit l'expiration d'une période de deux mois après la date à laquelle sept Etats membres du Conseil de l'Europe auront exprimé leur consentement à être liés par le Protocole conformément aux dispositions de l'article 8.

2 Pour tout Etat membre qui exprimera ultérieurement son consentement à être lié par le Protocole, celui-ci entrera en vigueur le premier jour du mois qui suit l'expiration d'une période de deux mois après la date du dépôt de l'instrument de ratification, d'acceptation ou d'approbation.

The Explanatory Report on Protocol No. 7 states that article 9 is 'formulated in terms which take account of the new model final clauses adopted by the Committee of Ministers'.[1] The original model final clauses adopted in September 1962 by the Committee of Ministers were subsequently revised in light of the work of the International Law Commission on the subject and the text of the Vienna Convention on the Law of Treaties. A revised set of model final clauses was adopted in February 1980. The model final clause with respect to entry into force was a departure from what had been previous adopted in the Convention and its Protocols, where the issue had been relegated to a mere sentence in the general provision on signature and ratification. Past practice had also been for the instrument to enter into force immediately upon attaining the threshold of ratifications and accessions or, for States becoming parties subsequently, upon deposit of the relevant instrument.

Under the model final clause, entry into force was delayed for a period of months and, moreover, until the first day of the month following. Such grace periods are a feature of many modern treaties where they are generally intended to allow a little time for the start-up of the international mechanisms and of the bodies associated with the instrument. But the rationale for such a measure is harder to understand when all that a treaty does is add new rights to an existing corpus. All that it means is that despite the agreement to be bound by a minimum of ten States Parties, individuals subject to their jurisdiction are deprived of the protection of the Convention and its organs for two more months.

Ratification or accession by seven States is required for entry into for of Protocol No. 7. The Convention itself and Protocol No. 1 require ten States, whereas Protocols Nos 4 and 6 require five. Perhaps seven was chosen as a compromise? In subsequent additional Protocols, the Council of Europe returned to ten. In accordance with the model clauses,

---

[1] Explanatory Report on Protocol No. 7, para. 45.

provision is made for a grace period of two months following the deposit of the seventh ratification or accession.

The title 'Entry into force' was introduced by Protocol No. 11.[2]

Protocol No. 7 entered into force on 1 November 1988 following its ratification by seven Member States of the Council of Europe. The initial seven Member States were: Austria, Denmark, France, Greece, Iceland, Sweden, and Switzerland. All Member States are now parties to the Protocol with the exception of Germany, the Netherlands, Turkey, and the United Kingdom.

---

[2] Protocol No. 11 to the Convention for the Protection of Human Rights and Fundamental Freedoms, restructuring the control machinery established thereby, ETS 155, art. 2(6)(a).

Article 10. Depositary functions/Fonctions du dépositaire

The Secretary General of the Council of Europe shall notify all the member States of the Council of:

(a) any signature;

(b) the deposit of any instrument of ratification, acceptance or approval;

(c) any date of entry into force of this Protocol in accordance with Articles 6 and 9;

(d) any other act, notification or declaration relating to this Protocol.

Le Secrétaire Général du Conseil de l'Europe notifiera à tous les Etats membres du Conseil de l'Europe:

(a) toute signature;

(b) le dépôt de tout instrument de ratification, d'acceptation ou d'approbation;

(c) toute date d'entrée en vigueur du présent Protocole conformément à ses articles 6 et 9;

(d) tout autre acte, notification ou déclaration ayant trait au présent Protocole.

The Explanatory Report on Protocol No. 7 notes that article 10 is 'formulated in terms which take account of the new model final clauses adopted by the Committee of Ministers'.[1] The original Model Final Clauses adopted in September 1962 by the Committee of Ministers were subsequently revised in light of the work of the International Law Commission on the subject and the text of the Vienna Convention on the Law of Treaties. A revised set of model final clauses was adopted in February 1980. Article 10 of Protocol No. 7 is identical to article 9 of Protocol No. 6. Readers of the Commentary are referred to the chapter dealing with that provision. The title 'Depositary functions' was introduced by Protocol No. 11.[2]

---

[1] Explanatory Report on Protocol No. 7, para. 45.

[2] Protocol No. 11 to the Convention for the Protection of Human Rights and Fundamental Freedoms, restructuring the control machinery established thereby, ETS 155, art. 7(a).

PART SEVEN

PROTOCOL NO. 12 TO THE CONVENTION FOR THE PROTECTION OF HUMAN RIGHTS AND FUNDAMENTAL FREEDOMS

Preamble/Préambule

The member States of the Council of Europe signatory hereto:

Having regard to the fundamental principle according to which all persons are equal before the law and are entitled to the equal protection of the law;

Being resolved to take further steps to promote the equality of all persons through the collective enforcement of a general prohibition of discrimination by means of the Convention for the Protection of Human Rights and Fundamental Freedoms signed at Rome on 4 November 1950 (hereinafter referred to as 'the Convention');

Reaffirming that the principle of non-discrimination does not prevent States Parties from taking measures in order to promote full and effective equality, provided that there is an objective and reasonable justification for those measures,

Have agreed as follows:

Les Etats membres du Conseil de l'Europe, signataires du présent Protocole,

Prenant en compte le principe fondamental selon lequel toutes les personnes sont égales devant la loi et ont droit à une égale protection de la loi;

Résolus à prendre de nouvelles mesures pour promouvoir l'égalité de tous par la garantie collective d'une interdiction générale de discrimination par la Convention de sauvegarde des Droits de l'Homme et des Libertés fondamentales, signée à Rome le 4 novembre 1950 (ci-après dénommée «la Convention»);

Réaffirmant que le principe de non-discrimination n'empêche pas les Etats parties de prendre des mesures afin de promouvoir une égalité pleine et effective, à la condition qu'elles répondent à une justification objective et raisonnable,

Sont convenus de ce qui suit:

Introductory comments

The preambles of the earlier additional Protocols, starting with Protocol No. 1, are all very perfunctory. They provide little in the way of interpretative guidance, something that is the special mission of preambles to treaties. With Protocol No. 12, the Council of Europe begins a practice of more substantive preambles.

Drafting of the provision

The text of the Preamble was prepared by the Steering Committee on Human Rights. It had considered whether there should be an equality clause in article 1 or whether a reference to the principle of equality in the Preamble would suffice.[1] The Committee opted, 'by way of compromise',[2] for the latter solution. The Rapporteur of the Parliamentary Assembly's Committee on Legal Affairs and Human Rights made several criticisms of the draft. He said that the first recital of the Preamble 'does not correspond

---

[1] Jeroen Schokkenbroek, 'A New European Standard against Discrimination: Negotiating Protocol No. 12 to the European Convention on Human Rights', in J. Niessen and Isabelle Chopin, eds, *European Anti-Discrimination Standards and National Legislation*, Leiden/Boston: Martinus Nijhoff, 2004, pp. 61–79, at pp. 70–1.

[2] Ibid., p. 72.

to to the content of the Protocol' as it 'does not enshrine the principle of equality but extends the principle of non-discrimination, already set forth in the initial Convention in 1950, to include other rights'.[3] He said that the drafters were aware of the distinction because of the reference to equality in the final recital of the Preamble.[4] However, the Parliamentary Assembly did not formally request any changes to the Preamble as drafted by the Steering Committee.

Analysis and interpretation

Equality before the law and equal protection of the law

The first recital of the Preamble acknowledges 'the fundamental principle according to which all persons are equal before the law and are entitled to the equal protection of the law'. The Explanatory Report describes this as 'a fundamental and well-established general principle, and an essential element of the protection of human rights, which has been recognised in constitutions of member states and in international human rights law'.[5] The principle appears in article 7 of the Universal Declaration of Human Rights.

The second recital sets out what the Explanatory Report describes as 'the equality principle'.[6] It says that although the equality principle is not explicit in either article 14 of the Convention or article 1 of Protocol No. 12,

the non-discrimination and equality principles are closely intertwined. For example, the principle of equality requires that equal situations are treated equally and unequal situations differently. Failure to do so will amount to discrimination unless an objective and reasonable justification exists (see paragraph 18 below). The Court, in its case-law under Article 14, has already made reference to the 'principle of equality of treatment' (see, for example, the Court's judgment of 23 July 1968 in the 'Belgian Linguistic' case, Series A, No. 6, paragraph 10) or to 'equality of the sexes' (see, for example, the judgment of 28 May 1985 in the case of Abdulaziz, Cabales and Balkandali v. the United Kingdom, Series A, No. 94, paragraph 78).[7]

Many decades earlier, in the 1960s, the Council of Europe institutions considered recognizing a right to equality before the law when Protocol No. 4 to the Convention was being drafted. However, the Committee of Experts did not recommend inclusion and the proposal, which had come from the Parliamentary Assembly, was dropped. According to the Explanatory Report, the Committee had felt that 'the notion of equality before the law was subject to a wide variety of judicial interpretations and, for this reason, was not suitable for inclusion in a text which would have the binding legal force of a multilateral convention'.[8] Consideration was given to restricting the provision to a right to equal treatment or to equality in the application of the law along the lines of article 7 of the Universal Declaration of Human Rights. 'The majority of the experts thought that, even with this restriction, the provision was unacceptable, for reasons similar to those which

---

[3] Opinion of the Assembly on Draft Protocol No. 12 to the European Convention on Human Rights, Report, Committee on Legal Affairs and Human Rights, Doc. 8614, para. 25.

[4] Ibid., para. 26.

[5] Explanatory Report on Protocol No. 12, para. 14.

[6] Ibid., para. 15.

[7] Ibid.

[8] Explanatory Report on Protocol No. 4, para. 36.

prompted them to reject Article 5 of the Assembly's draft', says the Explanatory Report.[9] Furthermore:

[I]f such a provision were adopted, the organs provided for in the Convention would run the risk of becoming a superior authority to which appeals could be made against alleged errors in the appreciation of the facts or of the law on the part of national authorities. The Commission would then be faced with a large number of appeals against judgments by national courts which, allegedly, had not ensured equality in the application of the law to the person concerned. In practice, the Commission would be obliged to check a multitude of facts in order to decide whether the national court had applied the law correctly from the point of view of equality of treatment.[10]

At the same time, the Committee also recommended against including a provision recognizing the right of everyone to recognition as a person before the law, a norm derived from article 6 of the Universal Declaration of Human Rights. The Committee of Experts considered that it was unnecessary, given that it was already implied in articles 4, 6, and 14 of the Convention, but also because 'its ambiguous wording might lay it open to dangerous legal interpretations' and, finally, that it more properly belonged in a preamble.[11]

Measures to promote equality

Measures to promote 'full and effective equality' are recognized in the third recital of the Preamble. It states that such measures shall not be prohibited by the principle of non-discrimination. The third recital appears to be directed at what is often referred to as affirmative action or positive discrimination, defined as follows in article 1(4) of the International Convention on the Elimination of All Forms of Racial Discrimination:

Special measures taken for the sole purpose of securing adequate advancement of certain racial or ethnic groups or individuals requiring such protection as may be necessary in order to ensure such groups or individuals equal enjoyment or exercise of human rights and fundamental freedoms shall not be deemed racial discrimination, provided, however, that such measures do not, as a consequence, lead to the maintenance of separate rights for different racial groups and that they shall not be continued after the objectives for which they were taken have been achieved.

Similar provisions can be found in other treaties that focus on the prohibition of forms of discrimination.[12] According to one commentator, the final recital in the Preamble 'makes it absolutely clear that "positive measures" to seek to promote equality will not be prohibited by the Protocol, provided they do not constitute discrimination towards persons or groups not covered by such measures'.[13]

The Explanatory Report also makes clear that the Protocol is not intended to impose any obligation upon States to enact such special measures.

---

[9] Ibid.
[10] Ibid.
[11] Ibid., para. 35.
[12] Convention on the Elimination of All Forms of Discrimination Against Women, (1980) 1249 UNTS 13, art. 4(1); Framework Convention for the Protection of National Minorities, ETS 157, art. 4(3); Convention on the Rights of Persons with Disabilities, UN Doc. A/RES/61/106, Annex I, art. 5(4).
[13] Jeroen Schokkenbroek, 'A New European Standard Against Discrimination: Negotiating Protocol No. 12 to the European Convention on Human Rights', in J. Niessen and Isabelle Chopin, eds, *European Anti-Discrimination Standards and National Legislation*, Leiden/Boston: Martinus Nijhoff, 2004, pp. 61–79, at pp. 70–2.

The fact that there are certain groups or categories of persons who are disadvantaged, or the existence of de facto inequalities, may constitute justifications for adopting measures providing for specific advantages in order to promote equality, provided that the proportionality principle is respected. Indeed, there are several international instruments obliging or encouraging states to adopt positive measures (see, for example, Article 2, paragraph 2, of the International Convention on the Elimination of All Forms of Racial Discrimination, Article 4, paragraph 2, of the Framework Convention for the Protection of National Minorities and Recommendation No. R (85) 2 of the Committee of Ministers to member states on legal protection against sex discrimination). However, the present Protocol does not impose any obligation to adopt such measures. Such a programmatic obligation would sit ill with the whole nature of the Convention and its control system which are based on the collective guarantee of individual rights which are formulated in terms sufficiently specific to be justiciable.

This passage in the Explanatory Report reflects the cautious approach of the drafters of the Protocol No. 12 with respect to positive obligations, something discussed further in this Commentary in the chapter on article 1 of the Protocol.

Further reading

Jeroen Schokkenbroek, 'A New European Standard against Discrimination: Negotiating Protocol No. 12 to the European Convention on Human Rights', in J. Niessen and Isabelle Chopin, eds, *European Anti-Discrimination Standards and National Legislation*, Leiden/Boston: Martinus Nijhoff, 2004, pp. 61–79.
Jeroen Schokkenbroek, 'Towards a Stronger European Protection against Discrimination: The Preparation of a New Additional Protocol to the European Convention on Human Rights', in Gay Moon, ed., *Race Discrimination: Developing and Using a New European Legal Framework*, Oxford: Hart, 2000, pp. 29–37.

Article 1. General prohibition of discrimination/Interdiction générale de la discrimination

1. The enjoyment of any right set forth by law shall be secured without discrimination on any ground such as sex, race, colour, language, religion, political or other opinion, national or social origin, association with a national minority, property, birth or other status.

2. No one shall be discriminated against by any public authority on any ground such as those mentioned in paragraph 1.

1. La jouissance de tout droit prévu par la loi doit être assurée, sans discrimination aucune, fondée notamment sur le sexe, la race, la couleur, la langue, la religion, les opinions politiques ou toutes autres opinions, l'origine nationale ou sociale, l'appartenance à une minorité nationale, la fortune, la naissance ou toute autre situation.

2. Nul ne peut faire l'objet d'une discrimination de la part d'une autorité publique quelle qu'elle soit fondée notamment sur les motifs mentionnés au paragraphe 1.

Introductory comments

Equality and protection against discrimination lie at the core of modern human rights law. The Charter of the United Nations recognizes the importance of human rights in its Preamble: 'to reaffirm faith in fundamental human rights, in the dignity and worth of the human person, in the equal rights of men and women'. In article 1, it declares the purposes of the organization to include respect for the principle of equal rights of peoples and promoting and encouraging respect for human rights and fundamental freedoms for all 'without distinction as to race, sex, language, or religion'.

The importance of equality is confirmed in the Universal Declaration of Human Rights. Article 1 declares: 'All human beings are born free and equal in dignity and rights.' Article 2 builds on this idea with a statement about non-discrimination: 'Everyone is entitled to all the rights and freedoms set forth in this Declaration, without distinction of any kind, such as race, colour, sex, language, religion, political or other opinion, national or social origin, property, birth or other status.' Article 7 enshrines equality before the law: 'All are equal before the law and are entitled without any discrimination to equal protection of the law. All are entitled to equal protection against any discrimination in violation of this Declaration and against any incitement to such discrimination.'

The drafters of the European Convention on Human Rights seem to have had a more modest assessment of the role equality plays in the overall scheme of human rights protection. They incorporated equality and non-discrimination in article 14. Very largely modelled on article 2 of the Universal Declaration, it is a subsidiary provision that contemplates the prohibition of discrimination with respect to rights protected elsewhere in the Convention. The more general right to equality before the law and to equal protection of the law without discrimination does not appear. Noting the absence of anything in the *travaux préparatoires* of the European Convention that would indicate why the drafters did not incorporate a provision similar in scope to article 7 of the Universal Declaration, Michael Head has said that '[p]robably there was some underlying ideological problem with the concept of equality'.[1] According to Head,

when the European Convention was adopted, thinking about the equality principle was only in its infancy, like international law on human rights. At the time it was widely held that equality meant absolutely identical treatment for all. Viewed in those terms, equality consisted in according everyone exactly the same legal status, a utopian notion that was totally unrealistic from the legal standpoint. So while the immaturity of the equality concept in international law did not prevent its featuring prominently in the Universal Declaration of Human Rights, it did keep it out of the European Convention, a treaty containing both a catalogue of rights and a collective enforcement machinery.[2]

This is being a bit too charitable to the drafters of the European Convention. Within the United Nations, the discussion about equality and non-discrimination could not properly be described as being 'in its infancy'. Some of the indications of the backwardness of the Council of Europe in this respect, at the time the Convention was adopted, include the omission of discrimination based on sex in the initial working draft[3] and the decision of the Committee of Ministers to override the views of the Consultative Assembly and include a 'colonial clause'.[4]

In applying article 14, the Court has very often found a violation of one of the other rights in the Convention and then deemed it unnecessary to address whether or not article 14 was also violated. At the same time, article 14 has a degree of autonomy because it may apply even when another right protected by the Convention has not been breached to the extent that equality issues arise with respect to the substance of that right. Other provisions of the Convention have also taken on a role in addressing equality issues, including article 8 when privacy issues may be involved and article 3, under which severe forms of discrimination may be deemed degrading treatment. As provisions of the Convention go, article 14 was a 'late bloomer'. From its beginnings in 1959 until 1990, the Court found violations of article 14 in only four cases.[5] Between 1990 and 2000 there were nine findings of a breach of article 14.[6] From 2000 until 2010 there were 125 judgments concluding that article 14 had been violated.

Within the United Nations, the process of transforming the norms in the Universal Declaration of Human Rights into treaty provisions went further than that undertaken by the Council of Europe. In addition to a provision analogous to article 14 of the

---

[1] Michael Head, 'The Genesis of Protocol No. 12', in *Non-Discrimination, A Human Right—Seminar to Mark the Entry into Force of Protocol No. 12*, Strasbourg: Council of Europe Publishing, 2006, pp. 35–45, at p. 36.

[2] Ibid., p. 37.

[3] This is discussed in the chapter on article 14 in this Commentary.

[4] This is discussed in the chapter on article 56 in this Commentary.

[5] *Case 'relating to certain aspects of the laws on the use of languages in education in Belgium'* (merits), 23 July 1968, Series A no. 6; *Marckx v. Belgium*, 13 June 1979, Series A no. 31; *Abdulaziz, Cabales, and Balkandali v. the United Kingdom*, 28 May 1985, Series A no. 94; *Inze v. Austria*, 28 October 1987, Series A no. 126.

[6] *Chassagnou and Others v. France* [GC], nos 25088/94, 28331/95, and 28443/95, ECHR 1999-III; *Larkos v. Cyprus* [GC], no. 29515/95, ECHR 1999-I; *Salgueiro da Silva Mouta v. Portugal*, no. 33290/96, ECHR 1999-IX; *Canea Catholic Church v. Greece*, 16 December 1997, *Reports of Judgments and Decisions* 1997-VIII; *Van Raalte v. the Netherlands*, 21 February 1997, *Reports of Judgments and Decisions* 1997-I; *Gaygusuz v. Austria*, 16 September 1996, *Reports of Judgments and Decisions* 1996-IV; *Karlheinz Schmidt v. Germany*, 18 July 1994, Series A no. 291-B; *Hoffmann v. Austria*, 23 June 1993, Series A no. 255-C; *Burghartz v. Switzerland*, 22 February 1994, Series A no. 280-B.

European Convention,[7] the drafters of the International Covenant on Civil and Political Rights also adopted a second text providing for a prohibition of discrimination in general and not just with respect to other rights protected by the Covenant. Inspired in part by article 7 of the Universal Declaration, article 26 of the International Covenant on Civil and Political Rights reads as follows:

All persons are equal before the law and are entitled without any discrimination to the equal protection of the law. In this respect, the law shall prohibit any discrimination and guarantee to all persons equal and effective protection against discrimination on any ground such as race, colour, sex, language, religion, political or other opinion, national or social origin, property, birth or other status.

Pursuant to this provision, the Human Rights Committee has developed a body of case law dealing with discrimination in marriage, sexual orientation, entitlement to economic and social benefits, language, and residency.[8]

Drafting of the provision

In October 1997, the Steering Committee on Human Rights discussed the possible adoption of an additional protocol whose purpose would be to broaden the scope of article 14 of the Convention. The Committee prepared a draft provision that is for all pratical purposes identical to the text of article 1 of Protocol No. 12. In its report to the Committee of Ministers, the Committee said that the wording could be improved. Moreover, it said that a decision should be taken as to whether it would be sufficient to refer to equality in the Preamble or whether a specific clause was required in article 1. Finally, the Steering Committee said that the addition of a clause expressly allowing for positive measures should be considered.[9]

Several alternatives for paragraph 2 were considered by the drafters. The first variant began: 'No one shall be discriminated on any ground such as ...' It was considered to allow for substantial positive obligations 'since its wording did not distinguish between public authorities and private actors as being the source of the discrimination'. The second proposal started with the words '[t]he enjoyment of any right set forth by law shall be secured without discrimination on any ground such as ...' It was considered to be very close to article 14 of the Convention. The formulation was conservative in approach as a result of the words 'any right set forth by law', as these had already been interpreted by the European Court. The third option, which ultimately prevailed, opened with the following: 'No one shall be discriminated against by a public authority on any ground such as ...'[10]

The draft of article 1 prepared by the Committee of Ministers is identical to the final version.[11] Comments about the intent of the Committee of Ministers were included in

---

[7] International Covenant on Civil and Political Rights, (1976) 999 UNTS 171, art. 2(1).

[8] Manfred Nowak, *UN Covenant on Civil and Political Rights, CCPR Commentary*, 2nd rev. edn, Kehl, Germany: N.P. Engel, 2005, pp. 597–634.

[9] Jeroen Schokkenbroek, 'A New European Standard against Discrimination: Negotiating Protocol No. 12 to the European Convention on Human Rights', in J. Niessen and Isabelle Chopin, eds, *European Anti-Discrimination Standards and National Legislation*, Leiden/Boston: Martinus Nijhoff, 2004, pp. 61–79, at pp. 69–71.

[10] Ibid., p. 76.

[11] Draft Protocol No. 12 to the European Convention on Human Rights and Draft Explanatory Report, Doc. 8490, art. 1.

the draft Explanatory Report. These are discussed below with regard to the various issues of interpretation, as are the objections by the Parliamentary Assembly.

Analysis and interpretation

Protocol No. 12 has only one substantive provision. Article 1 consists of two paragraphs. The first paragraph bears a close resemblance to article 14 of the Convention. It does no more than replace the words 'of the rights and freedoms set forth in this Convention' that appear in article 14 with 'of any right set forth by law'. The second paragraph adds a prohibition of discrimination 'by any public authority'. Thus, article 1 of Protocol No. 12 deals with legislation and its implementation and with the behaviour and policy of public bodies.

The Explanatory Report cautions against analysis based upon distinguishing the two paragraphs, which it describes as 'complementary'. Instead it proposes that the Protocol's scope has four components:

1. the enjoyment of any right specifically granted to an individual under national law;
2. the enjoyment of a right which may be inferred from a clear obligation of a public authority under national law, that is, where a public authority is under an obligation under national law to behave in a particular manner;
3. the exercise of discretionary power by a public authority (for example, granting of certain subsidies);
4. any other act or omission by a public authority (for example, the conduct of law enforcement authorities in controlling a riot).[12]

In applying article 1, the European Court has made reference to the four categories listed in the Explanatory Report.[13] The Explanatory Report cautiously states that the emphasis on acts and omissions should not be viewed as excluding the existence of positive obligations.

When Protocol No. 12 was being adopted, the European Court warned that its entry into force 'will lead to a substantial increase in the Court's case-load', but those fears were exaggerated.[14] There has been very limited judicial interpretation of Protocol No. 12. In the leading case, *Sejdić and Finci v. Bosnia and Herzegovina*, the Grand Chamber observed that article 1 of Protocol No. 12 is 'similar—although not identical' to article 26 of the International Covenant on Civil and Political Rights.[15] Unlike article 26, it does not include references to equality before the law and equal protection of the law, originally derived from article 7 of the Universal Declaration of Human Rights. For this reason, Manfred Nowak has explained that article 1 of Protocol No. 12 'is not equivalent to a right to equality'.[16] The Rapporteur of the Parliamentary Assembly's Committee on Legal

---

[12] Explanatory Report on Protocol No. 12, para. 29.

[13] *Savez crkava 'Riječ života' and Others v. Croatia*, no. 7798/08, § 104, 9 December 2010; *Merschdorf v. Romania* (dec.), no. 31918/08, § 24, 21 May 2013.

[14] Opinion of the European Court of Human Rights on draft Protocol 12 to the European Convention on Human Rights (adopted at the plenary administrative session of the Court on 6 December 1999), Doc. 8608, para. 6.

[15] *Sejdić and Finci v. Bosnia and Herzegovina* [GC], nos 27996/06 and 34836/06, § 54, ECHR 2009.

[16] Manfred Nowak, *UN Covenant on Civil and Political Rights, CCPR Commentary*, 2nd rev. edn, Kehl, Germany: N.P. Engel, 2005, p. 600.

Affairs and Human Rights objected to the absence of a right to equality in article 1, noting that the draft Explanatory Report 'continually confuses two distinct concepts: non-discrimination and equality'.[17] Nevertheless, there is a recognition of the 'the fundamental principle according to which all persons are equal before the law and are entitled to the equal protection of the law' in recital 1 of the Preamble of Protocol No. 12.

Enjoyment of any right set forth by law

The Explanatory Report states that the expression 'any right set forth by the law' is intended to define the scope of the guarantee and at the same time limit its possible indirect horizontal effects.[18] This is the difference between article 1 of Protocol No. 12 and article 14 of the Convention. The Rapporteur of the Committee on Legal Affairs and Human Rights of the Parliamentary Assembly conceded that article 1 'nevertheless broadens the scope of non-discrimination'.[19] He wrote: 'The wording covers the rights secured by the Convention as well as other rights secured at national level. It obviously leaves considerable scope for the case-law of the European Court of Human Rights, which will be able to interpret it in an exhaustive manner.'[20]

The word 'law' is not defined, but reference to its use elsewhere in the Convention is surely a relevant approach. The European Court of Human Rights has held that the term 'law' may apply not only to statute law but also to common law, customary law, and case law.[21] The Explanatory Report says that the term may also cover international law, although 'this does not mean that this provision entails jurisdiction for the European Court of Human Rights to examine compliance with rules of law in other international instruments'.[22] This intriguing comment probably reflects the fact that '[s]ome governments apparently fear that if the scope of Protocol Twelve is extended to [international law] then significant new commitments could be introduced into domestic law'.[23] A representative of the United Kingdom has suggested this is a problem for his government because it may be interpreted to include rights in treaties such as the International Covenants, including economic and social rights.[24]

In *Sejdić and Finci*, the Grand Chamber held that the right to stand for election for the presidency of the country was 'set forth by law', regardless of whether it was recognized by article 3 of Protocol No. 1 to the European Convention.[25] In a case concerning the refusal of Croatian authorities to recognize the right of Protestant evangelical churches to perform certain religious services and to obtain official recognition of marriages conducted by them, the Court noted that applicable national legislation guaranteed 'the right' to religious communities to provide such services, although exercise of the right was to be

[17] Opinion of the Assembly on Draft Protocol No. 12 to the European Convention on Human Rights, Report, Committee on Legal Affairs and Human Rights, Doc. 8614, para. 29.
[18] Explanatory Report on Protocol No. 12, para. 29.
[19] Opinion of the Assembly on Draft Protocol No. 12 to the European Convention on Human Rights, Report, Committee on Legal Affairs and Human Rights, Doc. 8614, para. 16.
[20] Ibid., para. 17.
[21] *S.W. v. the United Kingdom*, 22 November 1995, § 46, Series A no. 335-B.
[22] Explanatory Report on Protocol No. 12, para. 29.
[23] Harris et al., *Law of the European Convention*, p. 612.
[24] John Kissane, 'Protocol No. 12—UK Government's Position', in *Non-Discrimination, A Human Right—Seminar to Mark the Entry into Force of Protocol No. 12*, Strasbourg: Council of Europe Publishing, 2006, pp. 87–91, at p. 88.
[25] *Sejdić and Finci v. Bosnia and Herzegovina* [GC], nos 27996/06 and 34836/06, § 54, ECHR 2009.

governed by an agreement. The Chamber observed that the agreement was not a condition for the existence of the right, but merely a manner of regulating its implementation. Consequently, this was a 'right specifically granted under national law', as set out in the first condition of the Explanatory Report and therefore subject to article 1(1) of the Protocol.[26] In several Romanian cases, a Chamber declared applications based upon a claim that property confiscated by an earlier regime could not be returned to them to be manifestly unfounded. The Chamber said that in order to claim the property taken from their parents, 'les requérants devaient remplir certaines conditions imposées par la loi no 18/1991, et qu'il ne s'agissait pas d'un droit ex lege... Dans ces conditions, la Cour estime que la situation des requérants n'entre dans aucune des quatre catégories mentionnées par le Rapport explicatif...'[27]

Without discrimination

The concept of 'discrimination' in article 1(1) of Protocol No. 12 is set out in language that is clearly modelled upon that of article 14 of the European Convention, and there is no good reason why it should be interpreted any differently. The Explanatory Report states that '[t]he meaning of the term "discrimination" in Article 1 is intended to be identical to that in Article 14 of the Convention'.[28] This is confirmed in the case law.[29] Prior to the adoption of the Protocol, the plenary Court adopted an opinion on the text that includes a discussion of the concept of discrimination:

As regards the substantive content of the Protocol, it notes, in relation to Article 1, that the draft Explanatory Report (see paragraph 18) refers to the notion of discrimination as consistently interpreted in the case-law of the Court, namely that a difference of treatment is discriminatory if it has no objective and reasonable justification, that is if it does not pursue a legitimate aim or if there is not a reasonable relationship of proportionality between the means employed and the aim sought to be realised. As the Court put it in the Belgian Linguistic case, 'the competent national authorities are frequently confronted with situations and problems which, on account of differences inherent therein, call for different legal solutions' (judgment of 23.7.68, Series A no. 6, p. 34, § 10). This is further reflected, consistently with the subsidiary character of the Convention system, in the margin of appreciation accorded to the national authorities in assessing whether and to what extent differences in otherwise similar situations justify a difference of treatment in law (see, among other authorities, Rasmussen v. Denmark, judgment of 28.11.84, Series A no. 87, p. 15, § 40).[30]

6. Notwithstanding such 'limitations' on the prohibition of discrimination as derive from the Court's case-law, it is foreseeable that the entry into force of Protocol No. 12 will lead to a substantial increase in the Court's case-load. The Court draws the attention of the Committee of Ministers to the impact of such an increase on a mechanism that is already under great pressure. While the extent of this impact can only be assessed at a later stage and would in any event not be

---

[26] *Savez crkava 'Riječ života' and Others v. Croatia*, no. 7798/08, § 106, 9 December 2010.

[27] *Merschdorf v. Romania* (dec.), no. 31918/08, § 28, 21 May 2013.

[28] Explanatory Report on Protocol No. 12, para. 18.

[29] *Sejdić and Finci v. Bosnia and Herzegovina* [GC], nos 27996/06 and 34836/06, § 55, ECHR 2009; *Šimšić v. Bosnia and Herzegovina* (dec.), no. 51552/10, § 31, 10 April 2012; *Maktouf and Damjanović v. Bosnia and Herzegovina*, nos 2312/08 and 34179/08, § 81, ECHR 2012 (extracts); *Zornić v. Bosnia and Herzegovina*, no. 3681/06, §§ 26–27, 15 July 2014.

[30] Opinion of the European Court of Human Rights on Draft Protocol 12 to the European Convention on Human Rights (adopted at the plenary administrative session of the Court on 6 December 1999), Doc. 8608, para. 5.

immediate, it should be taken into account in mid- and long-term planning and provision for the Court and the Convention system.[31]

This has been confirmed by the Court in the first cases dealing with Protocol No. 12.[32]

A rich body of case law has been developed by the Court and the Commission concerning the notion of discrimination within the framework of article 14. As the Explanatory Report notes:

The notion of discrimination has been interpreted consistently by the European Court of Human Rights in its case-law concerning Article 14 of the Convention. In particular, this case-law has made clear that not every distinction or difference of treatment amounts to discrimination. As the Court has stated, for example, in the judgment in the case of Abdulaziz, Cabales and Balkandali v. the United Kingdom: 'a difference of treatment is discriminatory if it 'has no objective and reasonable justification', that is, if it does not pursue a 'legitimate aim' or if there is not a 'reasonable relationship of proportionality between the means employed and the aim sought to be realised' (judgment of 28 May 1985, Series A, No. 94, paragraph 72).[33]

In declaring inadmissible a claim against Romania by children of individuals whose land had been confiscated, and who claimed they had not received restitution because they had declined to adopt Romanian nationality, the Chamber took into account the large margin of appreciation given to States in repairing prejudice caused prior to entry into force of the Convention. It said the differential treatment based upon the lack of Romanian nationality had an objective and reasonable justification.[34]

Although the language used in the English versions of article 14 of the Convention and article 1 of the Protocol is identical, the same cannot be said of the other official language of the Council of Europe. The French text of article 1(1) speaks of '*sans discrimination aucune*' whereas article 14 uses the words '*sans distinction aucune*'. According to the Explanatory Report, '[n]o difference of meaning is intended; on the contrary, this is a terminological adaptation intended to reflect better the concept of discrimination within the meaning of Article 14 by bringing the French text into line with the English (see, on this precise point, the Court's judgment of 23 July 1968 in the "Belgian Linguistic" case, Series A, No. 6, paragraph 10)'.[35]

The Explanatory Report observes that 'it was not considered necessary or appropriate to include a restriction clause'.[36] It explains that most domestic legal provisions concerning non-discrimination allow for distinctions based on nationality with respect to certain rights and entitlements to benefits. The Report recalls that 'not every distinction or difference of treatment amounts to discrimination', and that 'situations where such distinctions are acceptable are sufficiently safeguarded by the very meaning of the notion "discrimination" . . . since distinctions for which an objective and reasonable justification exists do not constitute discrimination'.[37] The Explanatory Report also notes that the

---

[31] Ibid., paras 5–6.
[32] *Sejdić and Finci v. Bosnia and Herzegovina* [GC], nos 27996/06 and 34836/06, § 55, ECHR 2009; *Šimšić v. Bosnia and Herzegovina* (dec.), no. 51552/10, § 31, 10 April 2012; *Ramaer and Van Willigen v. The Netherlands* (dec.), no. 34880/12, § 89–90, 23 October 2012; *Mijailović v. Serbia* (dec.), no. 14366/08, § 57, 5 February 2013.
[33] Explanatory Report on Protocol No. 12, para. 18.
[34] *Merschdorf v. Romania* (dec.), no. 31918/08, § 30, 21 May 2013.
[35] Explanatory Report on Protocol No. 12, para. 18.
[36] Ibid., para. 19.
[37] Ibid.

European Court of Human Rights will acknowledge that 'a certain margin of appreciation is allowed to national authorities in assessing whether and to what extent differences in otherwise similar situations justify a different treatment in law'.[38] Examples are provided to show how the margin of appreciation has been applied by the Court in article 14 cases.[39]

Prohibited grounds

The list of prohibited grounds for discrimination in article 1(1) of Protocol No. 12 is identical to that of article 14 of the Convention. It is based upon article 2, paragraph 1 of the Universal Declaration of Human Rights, although there are some slight differences, notably the inclusion of 'association with a national minority' in the European Convention. The enumerations of prohibited grounds adopted more than half a century ago in the Universal Declaration and the European Convention were prefaced with the words 'such as', leaving room for enlargement of the scope of the protection not only in order to take account of analogous grounds that had simply been overlooked but also to enable evolution in accordance with changing social values. Adoption of Protocol No. 12 was an opportunity to formalize these changes, but the drafters opted for a more conservative approach. The Charter of Fundamental Rights of the European Union, also adopted in 2000, built upon the list in article 14 of the European Convention with the addition of age, disability, genetic features, and sexual orientation. It also made other changes, replacing national origin with origin and religion with religion or belief.[40]

According to the Explanatory Report, the decision to reproduce the list in article 14 was a solution

> considered preferable over others, such as expressly including certain additional non-discrimination grounds (for example, physical or mental disability, sexual orientation or age), not because of a lack of awareness that such grounds have become particularly important in today's societies as compared with the time of drafting of Article 14 of the Convention, but because such an inclusion was considered unnecessary from a legal point of view since the list of non-discrimination grounds is not exhaustive, and because inclusion of any particular additional ground might give rise to unwarranted a contrario interpretations as regards discrimination based on grounds not so included.[41]

By way of example, the Report cites a 1999 decision of the European Court applying article 14 to discrimination on the basis of sexual orientation.[42] This does not mean that discrimination in respect of any particular ground that is not enumerated will justify a finding that article 1(1) has been breached. In a complaint about the assignment of an accused person to a particular jurisdiction, the Court noted that this was not based on any personal characteristics such as origin or religion, and consequently there was 'no appearance' of discrimination prohibited by the Protocol.[43]

---

[38] Explanatory Report on Protocol No. 12, para. 19.

[39] *Rasmussen v. Denmark*, 28 November 1984, § 40, Series A no. 87; *National & Provincial Building Society, Leeds Permanent Building Society, and Yorkshire Building Society v. the United Kingdom*, 23 October 1997, § 80, *Reports of Judgments and Decisions* 1997-VII.

[40] Charter of Fundamental Rights of the European Union, 2010 OJ C 83/02, art. 21.

[41] Explanatory Report on Protocol No. 12, para. 20.

[42] *Salgueiro da Silva Mouta v. Portugal*, no. 33290/96, ECHR 1999-IX.

[43] *Šimšić v. Bosnia and Herzegovina* (dec.), no. 51552/10, § 32, 10 April 2012.

The Parliamentary Assembly of the Council of Europe was not satisfied with the approach taken in the final draft of Protocol No. 12. According to the Rapporteur of the Committee on Legal Affairs and Human Rights:

However, society has changed since the adoption of the Convention in 1950 and account should have been taken of the changes. Although in 1950 some legislation was apparent as to including sexual orientation in the list of grounds, now, half a century later, it has become generally accepted that this form of discrimination has led and leads to diverse forms of discrimination and even persecution. Article 14 was formulated, in 1950, to ban such forms of discrimination and persecution. The explanatory report states that this was envisaged by the CDDH, which discussed the possibility of including grounds such as disability, sexual orientation and age, but that it was considered unnecessary from a legal point of view since the list of grounds for discrimination was not exhaustive and the inclusion of any particular additional ground might give rise to unwarranted interpretations. It should, however, be noted that the Amsterdam Treaty of 2 October 1997, which amends the Treaty of the European Union, includes sexual orientation in its prohibited discrimination grounds.[44]

But the reasoning of the Rapporteur seems confused in that he also argued that '[i]t would surely have been simpler not to give a list of grounds and to establish a general right to equality as in Article 3 of the Covenant on Civil and Political Rights'.[45] This is a rather simplistic understanding of the Covenant's provisions on equality and non-discrimination. The Parliamentary Assembly unsuccessfully requested a distinct provision reading 'Men and women are equal before the law' and the inclusion of sexual orientation within the list of prohibited grounds.[46]

It has been observed that 'the drafters, in line with Article 14 ECHR but contrary to the views of the Parliamentary Assembly, did not want to establish any sort of hierarchy between grounds explicitly mentioned and those not so mentioned in the protocol'. Apparently some experts had even suggested that if the grounds of discrimination were to be updated vis-à-vis the list in the 1950 text of the Convention, they would want to remove 'race' from the enumeration because the term was no longer accepted as a legitimate scientific category.[47]

Discrimination by any public authority

Paragraph 2 of article 1 completes the protection against discrimination by ensuring that acts of public authorities do not escape scrutiny. It was included out of caution because, as the Explanatory Report states, there may be 'some doubt' as to whether paragraph 1 on its own covers all four of the categories contemplated by the Protocol, and more specifically the third and fourth categories. According to the Explanatory Report, 'the first and second paragraphs of Article 1 are complementary. The result is that those four elements are at all events covered by Article 1 as a whole.'[48]

---

[44] Report, Committee on Legal Affairs and Human Rights, Doc. 8614, para. 19.

[45] Ibid., para. 21.

[46] Opinion No. 216 (2000), Draft Protocol No. 12 to the European Convention on Human Rights.

[47] Jeroen Schokkenbroek, 'A New European Standard against Discrimination: Negotiating Protocol No. 12 to the European Convention on Human Rights', in J. Niessen and Isabelle Chopin, eds, *European Anti-Discrimination Standards and National Legislation*, Leiden/Boston: Martinus Nijhoff, 2004, pp. 61–79, at p. 74, fn. 18.

[48] Explanatory Report on Protocol No. 12, para. 29.

According to the Explanatory Report, the term 'public authority' in paragraph 2 has been borrowed from articles 8(2) and 10(1) of the Convention and is intended to have the same meaning as in those provisions. Use of the term 'clearly seeks to limit horizontal effects, without excluding them altogether'.[49] The concept of public authority covers courts and legislative bodies, as well as the public administration. Examples of issues that might arise include access to public places and to goods, employment, the provision of services, the grant of nationality, and the conduct of law enforcement officials.

In the Croatian case concerning certain rights of religious institutions, the Chamber noted that the applicable legislation did not confer authority to provide religious education in schools and nurseries or to obtain official recognition of marriages celebrated by them. This was granted on the basis of agreements with the authorities made on a discretionary basis rather than as the consequence of an entitlement established by legislation. The Chamber said that although the issue did not fall under the first of the four categories in the Explanatory Report, because it was not a 'right specifically granted under national law', it was nevertheless covered by the third category because it involved alleged discrimination 'by a public authority in the exercise of discretionary power'.[50]

Positive obligations

The European Court of Human Rights has developed a framework of analysis for all fundamental rights that looks to positive obligations upon the government, requiring it to take action in order to address violations and not simply to refrain from acting. This is especially important with respect to so-called horizontal effects of human rights, where an individual may be a victim of a violation of human rights attributable to another individual or by a corporate body. This is obviously of particular relevance in the area of discrimination, where so many violations are attributable to individuals and other non-State actors.

Nevertheless, and no doubt fully aware of the orientation of the Court, the drafters of Protocol No. 12 approached the issue of positive obligations with considerable caution. The Explanatory Report affirms that although the existence of positive obligations 'cannot be excluded altogether', the 'prime objective of Article 1 is to embody a negative obligation for the Parties: the obligation not to discriminate against individuals'.[51] It continues:

> 25. On the one hand, Article 1 protects against discrimination by public authorities. The Article is not intended to impose a general positive obligation on the Parties to take measures to prevent or remedy all instances of discrimination in relations between private persons. An additional protocol to the Convention, which typically contains justiciable individual rights formulated in concise provisions, would not be a suitable instrument for defining the various elements of such a wide-ranging obligation of a programmatic character. Detailed and tailor-made rules have already been laid down in separate conventions exclusively devoted to the elimination of discrimination on the specific grounds covered by them (see, for example, the Convention on Elimination of All Forms of Racial Discrimination and the Convention on the Elimination of All Forms of Discrimination

---

[49]   Jeroen Schokkenbroek, 'A New European Standard against Discrimination: Negotiating Protocol No. 12 to the European Convention on Human Rights', in J. Niessen and Isabelle Chopin, eds, *European Anti-Discrimination Standards and National Legislation*, Leiden/Boston: Martinus Nijhoff, 2004, pp. 61–79, at p. 76.

[50]   *Savez crkava 'Riječ života' and Others v. Croatia*, no. 7798/08, § 107, 9 December 2010.

[51]   Explanatory Report on Protocol No. 12, para. 24.

against Women, which were both elaborated within the United Nations). It is clear that the present Protocol may not be construed as limiting or derogating from domestic or treaty provisions which provide further protection from discrimination (see the comment on Article 3 in paragraph 32 below).

26. On the other hand, it cannot be totally excluded that the duty to 'secure' under the first paragraph of Article 1 might entail positive obligations. For example, this question could arise if there is a clear lacuna in domestic law protection from discrimination. Regarding more specifically relations between private persons, a failure to provide protection from discrimination in such relations might be so clear-cut and grave that it might engage clearly the responsibility of the State and then Article 1 of the Protocol could come into play (see, mutatis mutandis, the judgment of the Court of 26 March 1985 in the case of X and Y v. the Netherlands, Series A, No 91, paragraphs 23–24, 27 and 30).

27. Nonetheless, the extent of any positive obligations flowing from Article 1 is likely to be limited. It should be borne in mind that the first paragraph is circumscribed by the reference to the 'enjoyment of any right set forth by law' and that the second paragraph prohibits discrimination 'by any public authority'. It should be noted that, in addition, Article 1 of the Convention sets a general limit on state responsibility which is particularly relevant in cases of discrimination between private persons.

28. These considerations indicate that any positive obligation in the area of relations between private persons would concern, at the most, relations in the public sphere normally regulated by law, for which the state has a certain responsibility (for example, arbitrary denial of access to work, access to restaurants, or to services which private persons may make available to the public such as medical care or utilities such as water and electricity, etc). The precise form of the response which the state should take will vary according to the circumstances. It is understood that purely private matters would not be affected. Regulation of such matters would also be likely to interfere with the individual's right to respect for his private and family life, his home and his correspondence, as guaranteed by Article 8 of the Convention.

The Explanatory Report has been described as 'a compromise', intended to reassure States that they will not be ordered by the Court to set up affirmative action programmes or otherwise interfere in largely private matters.[52] Uncertainty about the scope of the Protocol in this area may help account for the chequered pattern of signature and ratification. According to one textbook, '[s]ome states have been reluctant to ratify the Protocol as they consider that it contains too many uncertainties and that its application is potentially too wide. The British government, for example, has stated that it will "wait and see" how the Court interprets and applies Protocol Twelve before ratifying it.'[53] Fifteen years after the Protocol's adoption, the United Kingdom is still waiting.

For the time being, the case law is very meagre and it is difficult to anticipate the extent to which the Court will develop positive obligations within article 1 of the Protocol. According to Olivier de Schutter, '[a] positive obligation may be imposed on State Parties to adopt measures in order to prohibit discrimination by private parties, in situations where the failure to adopt such measures would be clearly unreasonable and result in depriving persons from the enjoyment of rights set forth by law'.[54]

---

[52] Fried van Hoof, 'General Prohibition of Discrimination (Article 1 of Protocol No. 12)', in Van Dijk et al., *Theory and Practice*, pp. 989–92, at p. 991.

[53] Harris et al., *Law of the European* Convention, p. 612.

[54] Olivier de Schutter, *The Prohibition of Discrimination under European Human Rights Law Relevance for EU Racial and Employment Equality Directives*, Brussels: European Commission, 2005, p. 25.

Further reading

Robert Badinter, 'Du protocole no 11 au protocole no 12', in G. Flécheux, ed., *Mélanges en hommage à Louis Edmond Pettiti*, Brussels: Bruylant, 1998, pp. 103–12.

M. Bell, 'Combating Racism through European Law: A Comparison of the Racial Equality Directive and Protocol 12', in Isabelle Chopin and J. Niessen, eds, *Combating Racial and Ethnic Discrimination: Taking the European Legislative Agenda Further*, London: Migration Policy Group and Commission for Racial Equality, 2002, p. 7.

Lucy Claridge, 'Protocol 12 and Sejdić and Finci v Bosnia and Herzegovina: A Missed Opportunity?', [2011] *EHRLR* 82.

Frowein/Peukert, *MenschenRechtsKonvention,* pp. 720–2.

Grabenwarter, *European Convention*, pp. 443–5.

Michael Head, *Non-Discrimination, A Human Right—Seminar to Mark the Entry into Force of Protocol No. 12*, Strasbourg: Council of Europe Publishing, 2006.

Fried van Hoof, 'General Prohibition of Discrimination (Article 1 of Protocol No. 12)', in Van Dijk et al., *Theory and Practice*, pp. 989–92.

Urfan Khaliq, 'Protocol 12 to the European Convention on Human Rights, a Step Forward or a Step Too Far?', (2001) 3 *Public Law* 457.

Gay Moon, 'The Draft Discrimination Protocol to the European Convention on Human Rights: A Progess Report', [2000] *EHRLR* 49.

Jeroen Schokkenbroek, 'A New European Standard against Discrimination: Negotiating Protocol No. 12 to the European Convention on Human Rights', in J. Niessen and Isabelle Chopin, eds, *European Anti-Discrimination Standards and National Legislation*, Leiden/Boston: Martinus Nijhoff, 2004, pp. 61–79.

Jeroen Schokkenbroek, 'Towards a Stronger European Protection against Discrimination: The Preparation of a New Additional Protocol to the European Convention on Human Rights', in Gay Moon, ed., *Race Discrimination: Developing and Using a New European Legal Framework*, Oxford: Oxford University Press, pp. 29–37.

O. De Schutter, *The Prohibition of Discrimination under European Human Rights Law Relevance for EU Racial and Employment Equality Directives*, Brussels: European Commission, 2005.

Article 2. Territorial application/Application territoriale

1. Any State may, at the time of signature or when depositing its instrument of ratification, acceptance or approval, specify the territory or territories to which this Protocol shall apply.

2. Any State may at any later date, by a declaration addressed to the Secretary General of the Council of Europe, extend the application of this Protocol to any other territory specified in the declaration. In respect of such territory the Protocol shall enter into force on the first day of the month following the expiration of a period of three months after the date of receipt by the Secretary General of such declaration.

3. Any declaration made under the two preceding paragraphs may, in respect of any territory specified in such declaration, be withdrawn or modified by a notification addressed to the Secretary General of the Council of Europe. The withdrawal or modification shall become effective on the first day of the month following the expiration of a period of three months after the date of receipt of such notification by the Secretary General.

4. A declaration made in accordance with this article shall be deemed to have been made in accordance with paragraph 1 of Article 56 of the Convention.

5. Any State which has made a declaration in accordance with paragraph 1 or 2 of this article may at any time thereafter declare on behalf of one or more of the territories to which the declaration relates that it accepts the competence of the Court to receive applications from individuals, non-governmental organisations or groups of individuals as provided by Article 34 of the Convention in respect of Article 1 of this Protocol.

1. Tout Etat peut, au moment de la signature ou au moment du dépôt de son instrument de ratification, d'acceptation ou d'approbation, désigner le ou les territoires auxquels s'appliquera le présent Protocole.

2. Tout Etat peut, à tout autre moment par la suite, par une déclaration adressée au Secrétaire Général du Conseil de l'Europe, étendre l'application du présent Protocole à tout autre territoire désigné dans la déclaration. Le Protocole entrera en vigueur à l'égard de ce territoire le premier jour du mois qui suit l'expiration d'une période de trois mois après la date de réception de la déclaration par le Secrétaire Général.

3. Toute déclaration faite en vertu des deux paragraphes précédents pourra être retirée ou modifiée, en ce qui concerne tout territoire désigné dans cette déclaration, par notification adressée au Secrétaire Général du Conseil de l'Europe. Le retrait ou la modification prendra effet le premier jour du mois qui suit l'expiration d'une période de trois mois après la date de réception de la notification par le Secrétaire Général.

4. Une déclaration faite conformément au présent article sera considérée comme ayant été faite conformément au paragraphe 1 de l'article 56 de la Convention..

5. Tout Etat ayant fait une déclaration conformément au paragraphe 1 ou 2 du présent article peut, à tout moment par la suite, déclarer relativement à un ou plusieurs des territoires visés dans cette déclaration qu'il accepte la compétence de la Cour pour connaître des requêtes de personnes physiques, d'organisations non gouvernementales ou de groupes de particuliers, comme le prévoit l'article 34 de la Convention, au titre de l'article 1 du présent Protocole.

The first three paragraphs of article 2 are based upon the relevant text in the Model Final Clauses. Paragraph 4 is derived from article 6(4) of Protocol No. 7. Paragraph 5 is based on article 56(4) of the Convention.[1] The reader is referred to the relevant chapters of this Commentary.

There have been two declarations pursuant to article 2. In its instrument of ratification deposited on 15 June 2001, Georgia declared: 'Georgia declines its responsibility for the violations of the provisions of the Protocol on the territories of Abkhazia and Tskhinvali region until the full jurisdiction of Georgia is restored over these territories.'[2] In its instrument of acceptance deposited on 28 July 2004, the Netherlands stated that it 'accepts the Protocol for the Kingdom in Europe, the Netherlands Antilles and Aruba'.[3]

---

[1] Explanatory Report on Protocol No. 12, para. 31.
[2] (2001) 44 YB 21.
[3] (2004) 47 YB 25.

Article 3. Relationship to the Convention/Relations avec la Convention

As between the States Parties, the provisions of Articles 1 and 2 of this Protocol shall be regarded as additional articles to the Convention, and all the provisions of the Convention shall apply accordingly.	Les Etats parties considèrent les articles 1 et 2 du présent Protocole comme des articles additionnels à la Convention et toutes les dispositions de la Convention s'appliquent en conséquence.

The Explanatory Report devotes two paragraphs to article 3:

32. The purpose of this article is to clarify the relationship of this Protocol to the Convention by indicating that all the provisions of the latter shall apply in respect of Articles 1 and 2 of the Protocol. Among those provisions, attention is drawn in particular to Article 53, under the terms of which 'Nothing in this Convention shall be construed as limiting or derogating from any of the human rights and fundamental freedoms which may be ensured under the laws of any High Contracting Party or under any other agreement to which it is a Party'. It is clear that this article will apply in the relations between the present Protocol and the Convention itself. It was decided not to include a reference to Article 16 of the Convention in this Protocol.

33. As has already been mentioned in paragraph 21 above, Article 1 of the Protocol encompasses, but is wider in scope than the protection offered by Article 14 of the Convention. As an additional Protocol, it does not amend or abrogate Article 14 of the Convention, which will therefore continue to apply, also in respect of States Parties to the Protocol. There is thus an overlap between the two provisions. In accordance with Article 32 of the Convention, any further questions of interpretation concerning the precise relationship between these provisions fall within the jurisdiction of the Court.

If the European Court of Human Rights makes a finding that article 14 of the Convention has been breached, it will not then consider the matter from the perspective of Protocol No. 12. No useful purpose would be served by such duplication.[1]

---

[1] *Savez crkava 'Riječ života' and Others v. Croatia*, no. 7798/08, § 115, 9 December 2010.

Article 4. Signature and ratification/Signature et ratification

This Protocol shall be open for signature by member States of the Council of Europe which have signed the Convention. It is subject to ratification, acceptance or approval. A member State of the Council of Europe may not ratify, accept or approve this Protocol without previously or simultaneously ratifying the Convention. Instruments of ratification, acceptance or approval shall be deposited with the Secretary General of the Council of Europe.

Le présent Protocole est ouvert à la signature des Etats membres du Conseil de l'Europe qui ont signé la Convention. Il sera soumis à ratification, acceptation ou approbation. Un Etat membre du Conseil de l'Europe ne peut ratifier, accepter ou approuver le présent Protocole sans avoir simultanément ou antérieurement ratifié la Convention. Les instruments de ratification, d'acceptation ou d'approbation seront déposés près le Secrétaire Général du Conseil de l'Europe.

The Explanatory Report on Protocol No. 12 explains that the text of article 4 'correspond[s] to the wording of the Model Final Clauses adopted by the Committee of Ministers of the Council of Europe'.[1] Article 4 of Protocol No. 12 is identical to the text of article 7 of Protocol No. 6. Readers are referred to the chapter in this Commentary on article 7 of Protocol No. 6.

Protocol No. 12 was opened for signature on 4 November 2000, the fiftieth anniversary of the adoption of the European Convention. On that day, twenty-six Member States of the Council of Europe signed the instrument. Since that time, it has been signed by another twelve Member States, almost all of them deposited prior to entry into force on 1 April 2005.[2] But subsequently, the Protocol seems to have run out of steam, and only two States, Spain and Andorra, have signed it since 2005. Several States have neither signed nor ratified Protocol No. 12: Bulgaria, Denmark, France, Lithuania, Malta, Monaco, Poland, Sweden, Switzerland, and the United Kingdom. The Protocol has been ratified by the following States: Albania, Andorra, Armenia, Bosnia and Herzegovina, Croatia, Cyprus, Finland, Georgia, Luxembourg, Macedonia, Montenegro, the Netherlands, Romania, San Marino, Serbia, Slovenia, Spain, and Ukraine.

---

[1] Explanatory Report on Protocol No. 12, para. 34.
[2] For a complaint declared inadmissible because Slovakia has signed but not ratified Protocol No. 12, see *Fehér and Dolník v. Slovakia* (dec.), nos 14927/12 and 30415/12, §§ 53–55, 21 May 2013.

Article 5. Entry into force/Entrée en vigueur

1. This Protocol shall enter into force on the first day of the month following the expiration of a period of three months after the date on which ten member States of the Council of Europe have expressed their consent to be bound by the Protocol in accordance with the provisions of Article 4.

2. In respect of any member State which subsequently expresses its consent to be bound by it, the Protocol shall enter into force on the first day of the month following the expiration of a period of three months after the date of the deposit of the instrument of ratification, acceptance or approval.

1. Le présent Protocole entrera en vigueur le premier jour du mois qui suit l'expiration d'une période de trois mois après la date à laquelle dix Etats membres du Conseil de l'Europe auront exprimé leur consentement à être liés par le présent Protocole conformément aux dispositions de son article 4.

2. Pour tout Etat membre qui exprimera ultérieurement son consentement à être lié par le présent Protocole, celui-ci entrera en vigueur le premier jour du mois qui suit l'expiration d'une période de trois mois après la date du dépôt de l'instrument de ratification, d'acceptation ou d'approbation.

This provision is the entry into force clause adopted by the Committee of Ministers in February 1980 as one of the Model Final Clauses. Readers of this Commentary are referred to the chapter on article 8 of Protocol No. 7. Unlike article 8 of Protocol No. 7, article 5 of Protocol No. 12 gives States a three-month delay following signature prior to entry into force.

Protocol No. 12 entered into force on 1 April 2005, following the tenth ratification.

Article 6. Depositary functions/Fonctions du dépositaire

The Secretary General of the Council of Europe shall notify all the member States of the Council of Europe of:

(a) any signature;
(b) the deposit of any instrument of ratification, acceptance or approval;
(c) any date of entry into force of this Protocol in accordance with Articles 2 and 5;

(d) any other act, notification or communication relating to this Protocol.

Le Secrétaire Général du Conseil de l'Europe notifiera à tous les Etats membres du Conseil de l'Europe:

a) toute signature;
b) le dépôt de tout instrument de ratification, d'acceptation ou d'approbation;
c) toute date d'entrée en vigueur du présent Protocole conformément à ses articles 2 et 5;

d) tout autre acte, notification ou communication, ayant trait au présent Protocole.

The Explanatory Report on Protocol No. 12 explains that article 6 'correspond[s] to the wording of the Model Final Clauses adopted by the Committee of Ministers of the Council of Europe'.[1] The text is virtually identical to article 9 of Protocol No. 6. Readers of the Commentary are referred to the chapter dealing with that provision.

---

[1] Explanatory Report on Protocol No. 12, para. 34.

PART EIGHT

PROTOCOL NO. 13 TO THE CONVENTION FOR THE PROTECTION OF HUMAN RIGHTS AND FUNDAMENTAL FREEDOMS, CONCERNING THE ABOLITION OF THE DEATH PENALTY IN ALL CIRCUMSTANCES

Preamble/Préambule

The member States of the Council of Europe signatory hereto,

Convinced that everyone's right to life is a basic value in a democratic society and that the abolition of the death penalty is essential for the protection of this right and for the full recognition of the inherent dignity of all human beings;

Wishing to strengthen the protection of the right to life guaranteed by the Convention for the Protection of Human Rights and Fundamental Freedoms signed at Rome on 4 November 1950 (hereinafter referred to as 'the Convention');

Noting that Protocol No. 6 to the Convention, concerning the Abolition of the Death Penalty, signed at Strasbourg on 28 April 1983, does not exclude the death penalty in respect of acts committed in time of war or of imminent threat of war;

Being resolved to take the final step in order to abolish the death penalty in all circumstances,

Have agreed as follows:

Les Etats membres du Conseil de l'Europe, signataires du présent Protocole,

Convaincus que le droit de toute personne à la vie est une valeur fondamentale dans une société démocratique, et que l'abolition de la peine de mort est essentielle à la protection de ce droit et à la pleine reconnaissance de la dignité inhérente à tous les êtres humains;

Souhaitant renforcer la protection du droit à la vie garanti par la Convention de sauvegarde des Droits de l'Homme et des Libertés Fondamentales signée à Rome le 4 novembre 1950 (ci-après dénommée «la Convention»);

Notant que le Protocole n° 6 à la Convention concernant l'abolition de la peine de mort, signé à Strasbourg le 28 avril 1983, n'exclut pas la peine de mort pour des actes commis en temps de guerre ou de danger imminent de guerre;

Résolus à faire le pas ultime afin d'abolir la peine de mort en toutes circonstances,

Sont convenus de ce qui suit:

Introductory comments

There is an abolitionist bent to article 6 of the International Covenant on Civil and Political Rights, adopted by the United Nations General Assembly in 1966. Article 6(6) states: 'Nothing in this article shall be invoked to delay or to prevent the abolition of capital punishment by any State Party to the present Covenant.'[1] The American Convention on Human Rights, adopted by the Organisation of American States three years later, prevents a State that has already abolished the death penalty from re-instating it.[2] In that sense, it is an abolitionist treaty, although the retention of capital punishment is not an obstacle to a State wishing to ratify the American Convention. Protocol No. 6 to the European Convention on Human Rights, adopted by the Council of Europe in 1983, was the first international treaty dedicated exclusively to the abolition of the death penalty. It was nevertheless an imperfect instrument because it did not exclude the death penalty in respect of acts committee in time of war or of imminent threat of war. The compromise that this represented with a more principled and absolute approach was justified at the

---

[1] International Covenant on Civil and Political Rights, (1976) 999 UNTS 171, art. 6(6).
[2] American Convention on Human Rights, (1979) 1144 UNTS 123, art. 4(3).

time as being necessary to obtain support for the instrument. That was perhaps a miscalculation. Attitudes were evolving more quickly than the ponderous negotiators in Strasbourg. In the end, only a few States actually availed themselves of the wartime exception offered them by article 2 of Protocol No. 6. Just as Protocol No. 6 was adopted in order to amend what had become an anachronistic reference in article 2(1) of the European Convention, so Protocol No. 13 was required in order to bring Protocol No. 6 into the twenty-first century.

Drafting of the provision

The initiative for a Preamble that was more elaborate and substantive than that of Protocol No. 6 came from several members of the Committee of Experts. The Committee agreed to an explicit reference to the right to life and to the concept of human dignity. Members of the Committee also proposed including a brief reference to the abolitionist process under way for two decades as well as to refer to abolition of the death penalty in law as well as in practice.[3] A proposal to insert a general sentence to the effect that criminal justice policy should aim at rehabilitation of criminals 'was not retained because it was too wide-ranging and might lead to problems of interpretation'.[4] Suggestions that arguments favouring abolition be included were rejected as being 'counter-productive, whereas the aim of the protocol was unequivocal rejection of capital punishment'.[5] There were several proposals on the notion of 'final step', 'decisive step', 'further step', or 'definitive step' and about the idea of 'abolishing unconditionally'. There was concern about a reference in the draft to the 'significant legal and political evolution' because this might serve as an *a contrario* argument in respect of other regions.[6]

Analysis and interpretation

The Preamble to Protocol No. 13 is much more elaborate than the corresponding text in Protocol No. 6. The latter consists of only two recitals, one of them a perfunctory reference to the European Convention, the other stating 'that the evolution that has occurred in several member States of the Council of Europe expresses a general tendency in favour of abolition of the death penalty'. The lengthy Preamble to Protocol No. 13 provides the philosophical underpinning for the Protocol. Given that the substantive provisions of Protocol No. 13 do nothing more than reiterate those of Protocol No. 6 minus the reference to capital punishment in wartime found in article 2 of that instrument, the substantial Preamble is the most significant difference in the texts of the two instruments.

The right to life

The first recital of the Preamble affirms the relationship of the right to life—initially set out in article 2 of the European Convention on Human Rights—to the subject of capital

---

[3] Steering Committee for Human Rights, 27th meeting, 22 June 2001, DH-DEV (2001) 3, para. 20.
[4] Ibid., para. 21.
[5] Ibid.
[6] Ibid., para. 23.

punishment: 'Convinced that everyone's right to life is a basic value in a democratic society and that the abolition of the death penalty is essential for the protection of this right and for the full recognition of the inherent dignity of all human beings...'[7] The second recital notes that the Protocol is intended to strengthen the protection of the right to life' guaranteed by the European Convention. The reference is to article 2 of the Convention, entitled 'Right to life', declared by article 15 as a right that is not subject to derogation except in the case of lawful acts of war.

It is not without interest that the Preamble does not in any way suggest a relationship with the prohibition of torture or inhuman or degrading treatment or punishment, given that it is within the framework of article 3 of the Convention that the Court's case law has addressed the subject of the death penalty.[8]

The Explanatory Report describes the right to life as 'an inalienable attribute of human beings' and a 'supreme value in the international hierarchy of human rights' that is 'unanimously guaranteed in legally binding standards at universal and regional levels'. It goes on to explain that when international standards to guarantee the right to life were drawn up, exceptions were made for the death penalty. Nevertheless, the Report states that 'there has since been an evolution in domestic and international law towards abolition of the death penalty, both in general and, more specifically, for acts committed in time of war'.[9]

Readers of this Commentary are referred to the chapter on article 2 of the Convention for a detailed discussion of the right to life.

Relationship to Protocol No. 6

The third recital refers to Protocol No. 6 in the following terms: 'Noting that Protocol No. 6 to the Convention, concerning the Abolition of the Death Penalty, signed at Strasbourg on 28 April 1983, does not exclude the death penalty in respect of acts committed in time of war or of imminent threat of war...' The Committee of Ministers, in the Explanatory Report on Protocol No. 13, described Protocol No. 6 as a 'landmark stage' in the 'evolution in domestic and international law towards abolition of the death penalty'.[10] This rather positive assessment of Protocol No. 6 cannot easily be deduced from the third recital, however.

Although Protocol No. 13 presents itself as an additional protocol to the Convention itself, in reality it is very much an additional protocol to Protocol No. 6. That is because it 'corrects' the wartime exception to the abolition of the death penalty in Protocol No. 6 in the same way that Protocol No. 6 'corrects' the reference to capital punishment in article 2(1) of the Convention. It would be easy, with the benefit of hindsight, to claim that the Council of Europe misjudged the situation in 1983 when Protocol No. 6 was adopted. It might well have omitted article 2, where the wartime exception is set out, without significantly hindering ratification by a large majority of States Parties to the European Convention. It is probably more uncertain to say the same thing about the reference to

---

[7] Cited in *Al Nashiri v. Poland*, no. 28761/11, § 577, 24 July 2014; *Al-Saadoon and Mufdhi v. the United Kingdom*, no. 61498/08, § 115, ECHR 2010 (extracts); *Öcalan v. Turkey* [GC], no. 46221/99, § 58, ECHR 2005-IV; *Öcalan v. Turkey*, no. 46221/99, § 56, 12 March 2003.

[8] *Al Nashiri v. Poland*, no. 28761/11, § 120, 24 July 2014.

[9] Explanatory Report on Protocol No. 13, paras 1–3.

[10] Ibid., paras 3–4.

capital punishment in article 2(1) of the Convention. Most of the original signatories of the European Convention had already, in November 1950, abandoned the death penalty in law or in practice. However, it lingered on in a handful of countries—Ireland, the United Kingdom, and France—for several more years. These three States might well have found themselves unable to ratify the Convention had it imposed a prohibition on capital punishment.

That the drafters of Protocol No. 6 showed good judgment in limiting the scope of the instrument to peacetime is also reflected in the subsequent protocols dealing with the death penalty adopted in the systems of United Nations and the Organisation of American States.[11]

The 'final step'

The fourth recital expresses the resolve of the Member States of the Council of Europe to abolish the death penalty in all circumstances. There is an interesting distinction with the equivalent formulation in Protocol No. 6 where the Preamble refers to 'The Member States of the Council of Europe, signatory to this Protocol'. Protocol No. 13 is the result of a consensus reached by all Member States. Although an additional rather than an amending protocol, with the consequence that it does not require unanimous ratification for entry into force, the Preamble seems to indicate that this is more than an instrument applicable only to those States that have signed, or eventually ratified, the instrument.

The Protocol is described as 'the final step' in full abolition. It is the first legal instrument in any of the international human rights systems to comprise such a measure.

Further reading

Jon Yorke, 'The Right to Life and Abolition of the Death Penalty in the Council of Europe,' (2009) 34 *European Law Review* 205 (2009).
Jon Yorke, 'Inhuman and Degrading Punishment and Abolition of the Death Penalty in the Council of Europe', (2010) 16 *European Public Law* 77.

---

[11] Second Optional Protocol to the International Covenant on Civil and Political Rights, (1991) 1642 UNTS 414; Protocol to the American Convention on Human Rights to Abolish the Death Penalty, OASTS No. 73.

Article 1. Abolition of the death penalty/Abolition de la peine de mort

The death penalty shall be abolished. No one shall be condemned to such penalty or executed.	La peine de mort est abolie. Nul ne peut être condamné à une telle peine ni exécuté.

Introductory comments

The Explanatory Report on Protocol No. 13 points not only to Protocol No. 6 but to 'universal and regional standards', an apparent reference to the additional protocols adopted to the International Covenant on Civil and Political Rights and the American Convention on Human Rights. These three instruments provide for partial abolition of capital punishment while acknowledging the possibility, in one form or another, of exceptions relating to wartime and military justice. The Report says 'there has since been an evolution in domestic and international law towards abolition of the death penalty, both in general and, more specifically, for acts committed in time of war'.

Drafting of the provision

Article 1 is identical to the draft text in the Swedish proposal. During discussion in the Committee of Experts, various proposed amendments were considered. The insertion of '[n]o one within the jurisdiction of a State Party to the present Protocol may be...' was deemed to be superfluous, as the notion was implied in all additional protocols as a result of article 1 of the Convention. The words '(No one shall be) condemned (...) or executed' were retained by the Committee of Experts in order to prohibit both imposition of sentence and execution.[1]

Analysis and interpretation

According to the Explanatory Report, article 1 'must be read in conjunction with Article 2 of the Protocol'. It 'affirms the principle of the abolition of the death penalty. This entails the obligation to abolish this penalty in all circumstances, including for acts committed in time of war or of imminent threat of war. The second sentence of this article aims to underline the fact that the right guaranteed is a subjective right of the individual.'[2]

Readers of the Commentary are referred to the detailed discussion in the chapter on article 1 of Protocol No. 6, a text that is identical to that of article 1 of Protocol No. 13.

---

[1] Steering Committee for Human Rights, 27th meeting, 22 June 2001, DH-DEV (2001) 3, para. 13.
[2] Ibid., para. 14.

Further reading

Jon Yorke, 'The Right to Life and Abolition of the Death Penalty in the Council of Europe', (2009) 34 *European Law Review* 205 (2009).

Jon Yorke, 'Inhuman and Degrading Punishment and Abolition of the Death Penalty in the Council of Europe', (2010) 16 *European Public Law* 77.

Article 2. Prohibition of derogations/Interdiction de dérogations

No derogation from the provisions of this Protocol shall be made under Article 15 of the Convention.

Aucune dérogation n'est autorisée aux dispositions du présent Protocole au titre de l'article 15 de la Convention.

Because article 5 deems the provisions of the Protocol to be regarded as additional articles to the Convention, with the consequence that all the provisions of the Convention shall apply accordingly, article 2 is necessary in order to prevent the application of article 15 of the Convention. Article 15 allows measures of derogation from the Convention 'in time of war or other public emergency threatening the life of the nation'. Thus, because the 'object and purpose' of the Protocol is abolition of the death penalty in time of war or of imminent threat of war as well as in time of peace, it was deemed necessary to exclude the application of article 15.[1]

This provision is identical to article 3 of Protocol No. 6. Readers of the Commentary are referred to the chapter dealing with that provision.

[1] Explanatory Report on Protocol No. 13, para. 15.

Article 3. Prohibition of reservations/Interdiction de réserves

No reservation may be made under Article 57 of the Convention in respect of the provisions of this Protocol.

Aucune réserve n'est admise aux dispositions du présent Protocole au titre de l'article 57 de la Convention.

According to the Explanatory Report, article 3 is meant as an exception to article 57 of the Convention.[1] Because article 5 of Protocol No. 13 confirms that the provisions of the Convention apply, it is necessary to exclude article 57 in order to prohibit reservations. The text of article 3 is virtually identical to that of article 4 of Protocol No. 6. Readers of the Commentary are referred to the chapter dealing with that provision.

---

[1] Explanatory Report on Protocol No. 13, para. 16.

Article 4. Territorial application/Application territoriale

1. Any State may, at the time of signature or when depositing its instrument of ratification, acceptance or approval, specify the territory or territories to which this Protocol shall apply.

2. Any State may at any later date, by a declaration addressed to the Secretary General of the Council of Europe, extend the application of this Protocol to any other territory specified in the declaration. In respect of such territory the Protocol shall enter into force on the first day of the month following the expiration of a period of three months after the date of receipt of such declaration by the Secretary General.

3. Any declaration made under the two preceding paragraphs may, in respect of any territory specified in such declaration, be withdrawn or modified by a notification addressed to the Secretary General. The withdrawal or modification shall become effective on the first day of the month following the expiration of a period of three months after the date of receipt of such notification by the Secretary General.

1. Tout Etat peut, au moment de la signature ou au moment du dépôt de son instrument de ratification, d'acceptation ou d'approbation, désigner le ou les territoires auxquels s'appliquera le présent Protocole.

2. Tout Etat peut, à tout autre moment par la suite, par une déclaration adressée au Secrétaire Général du Conseil de l'Europe, étendre l'application du présent Protocole à tout autre territoire désigné dans la déclaration. Le Protocole entrera en vigueur à l'égard de ce territoire le premier jour du mois qui suit l'expiration d'une période de trois mois après la date de réception de la déclaration par le Secrétaire Général.

3. Toute déclaration faite en vertu des deux paragraphes précédents pourra être retirée ou modifiée, en ce qui concerne tout territoire désigné dans cette déclaration, par notification adressée au Secrétaire Général du Conseil de l'Europe. Le retrait ou la modification prendra effet le premier jour du mois qui suit l'expiration d'une période de trois mois après la date de réception de la notification par le Secrétaire Général.

Article 4 is largely based upon the territorial application provision found in the Model Final Clauses adopted by the Committee of Ministers in February 1980.[1] The wording is very similar to that of article 5 of Protocol No. 6. According to the Explanatory Report:

[t]his clause was included only to facilitate a rapid ratification, acceptance or approval by the States concerned. The purpose of paragraph 3 is merely to make allowance for formal withdrawal or modification in case the State Party ceases to be responsible for the international relations of a territory specified in such a declaration and not to allow in any way states to re-introduce the death penalty in such territory.[2]

Denmark formulated declarations with respect to Greenland and the Faroe Islands[3] that have since been withdrawn.[4] The Kingdom of the Netherlands has accepted the Protocol for the Netherlands Antilles and Aruba in addition to its metropolitan territory in Europe.[5] The United Kingdom's ratification was accompanied by a declaration indicating

---

[1] Explanatory Report on Protocol No. 13, para. 17.
[2] Ibid.
[3] (2002) 45 YB 21.
[4] For the Faroe Islands: (2003) 46 YB 13.
[5] (2006) 49 YB 10.

that the Protocol would initially apply to the metropolitan area of Great Britain and Northern Ireland.[6] Subsequently, it issued a series of declarations extending the application of Protocol No. 13 to the Isle of Man, the Bailiwick of Guernsey, the Bailiwick of Jersey, the Sovereign Base Areas of Akrotiri and Dhekelia in Cyprus, Anguilla, Bermuda, the Falkland Islands, Gibraltar, Montserrat, St Helena, Ascension and Tristan da Cunha, South Georgia and the South Sandwich Islands, and the Turks and Caicos Islands.[7]

Article 4 does not contemplate declarations by which a portion of the territory is excluded from the scope of the Protocol. Two States that do not exercise sovereignty over portions of their territory, Georgia and Moldova, have made declarations in this respect.[8]

---

[6] (2003) 46 YB 13.

[7] (2004) 47 YB 25.

[8] Ibid. This issue is discussed in more detail in the chapter on article 56 of the Convention in this Commentary.

Article 5. Relationship to the Convention/Relations avec la Convention

As between the States Parties the provisions of Articles 1 to 4 of this Protocol shall be regarded as additional articles to the Convention, and all the provisions of the Convention shall apply accordingly.

Les Etats parties considèrent les articles 1 et 2 du présent Protocole comme des articles additionnels à la Convention et toutes les dispositions de la Convention s'appliquent en conséquence.

The text of article 5 is virtually identical to that of article 6 of Protocol No. 6. Readers of the Commentary are referred to the chapter dealing with that provision.

The Explanatory Report points out that Protocol No. 13 is an additional protocol and that, as such, it does not 'supersede Article 2 of the Convention, since the first sentence of paragraph 1 and the whole of paragraph 2 of that article still remain valid'. However, the Report adds that it is 'no longer applicable in respect of the States Parties to this Protocol'. Another consequence is that States Parties to Protocol No. 6 that ratify Protocol No. 13 cannot avail themselves of the wartime exception provided by article 2 of the former instrument.[1]

When Protocol No. 13 was being drafted, the Rapporteur of the Parliamentary Assembly proposed that a second paragraph be added to article 5: 'When this Protocol has come into force in all States Parties to the Convention, the second sentence of Article 2 Paragraph 1 of the Convention shall be replaced with the text of Article 1 of this Protocol, and in the first sentence of Article 57 of the Convention, after the words "provision of the Convention" the words "except for Article 2 paragraph 1" shall be added.'[2]

---

[1] Explanatory Report on Protocol No. 13, para. 18.
[2] Opinion No. 233 (2002) on the Draft Protocol to the European Convention on Human Rights concerning the Abolition of the Death Penalty in All Circumstances, para. 6; Report, Committee on Legal Affairs and Human Rights, Doc. 9316, para. 11.

Article 6. Signature and ratification/Signature et ratification

This Protocol shall be open for signature by member States of the Council of Europe which have signed the Convention. It is subject to ratification, acceptance or approval. A member State of the Council of Europe may not ratify, accept or approve this Protocol without previously or simultaneously ratifying the Convention. Instruments of ratification, acceptance or approval shall be deposited with the Secretary General of the Council of Europe.

Le présent Protocole est ouvert à la signature des Etats membres du Conseil de l'Europe qui ont signé la Convention. Il sera soumis à ratification, acceptation ou approbation. Un Etat membre du Conseil de l'Europe ne peut ratifier, accepter ou approuver le présent Protocole sans avoir simultanément ou antérieurement ratifié la Convention. Les instruments de ratification, d'acceptation ou d'approbation seront déposés près le Secrétaire Général du Conseil de l'Europe.

The Explanatory Report on Protocol No. 13 explains that the text of article 6 'correspond[s] to the wording of the Model Final Clauses adopted by the Committee of Ministers of the Council of Europe'.[1] Article 6 of Protocol No. 13 is identical to the text of article 7 of Protocol No. 6. Readers are referred to the chapter in this Commentary on article 7 of Protocol No. 6. Protocol No. 13 was opened for signature on 3 May 2002. On that day, 36 Member States of the Council of Europe signed the instrument. Since that time, it has been signed by all but two Member States, Azerbaijan and Russia. Protocol No. 13 has been ratified by forty-four Member States. Armenia signed Protocol No. 13 on 19 May 2006, but has not ratified.

[1] Explanatory Report on Protocol No. 13, para. 20.

Article 7. Entry into force/Entrée en vigueur

1. This Protocol shall enter into force on the first day of the month following the expiration of a period of three months after the date on which ten member States of the Council of Europe have expressed their consent to be bound by the Protocol in accordance with the provisions of Article 4.

2. In respect of any member State which subsequently expresses its consent to be bound by it, the Protocol shall enter into force on the first day of the month following the expiration of a period of three months after the date of the deposit of the instrument of ratification, acceptance or approval.

1. Le présent Protocole entrera en vigueur le premier jour du mois qui suit l'expiration d'une période de trois mois après la date à laquelle dix Etats membres du Conseil de l'Europe auront exprimé leur consentement à être liés par le présent Protocole conformément aux dispositions de son article 4.

2. Pour tout Etat membre qui exprimera ultérieurement son consentement à être lié par le présent Protocole, celui-ci entrera en vigueur le premier jour du mois qui suit l'expiration d'une période de trois mois après la date du dépôt de l'instrument de ratification, d'acceptation ou d'approbation.

This provision is the entry into force clause adopted by the Committee of Ministers in February 1980 as one of the Model Final Clauses. Article 7 of Protocol No. 13 is virtually identical to the text of article 8 of Protocol No. 6. Readers are referred to the chapter in this Commentary on article 8 of Protocol No. 6. Protocol No. 13 entered into force on 1 July 2003.

Article 8. Depositary functions/Fonctions du dépositaire

The Secretary General of the Council of Europe shall notify all the member States of the Council of Europe of:

(a) any signature

(b) the deposit of any instrument of ratification, acceptance or approval;

(c) any date of entry into force of this Protocol in accordance with Articles 2 and 5;

(d) any other act, notification or communication relating to this Protocol.

Le Secrétaire Général du Conseil de l'Europe notifiera à tous les Etats membres du Conseil de l'Europe:

a) toute signature;

b) le dépôt de tout instrument de ratification, d'acceptation ou d'approbation;

c) toute date d'entrée en vigueur du présent Protocole conformément à ses articles 2 et 5;

d) tout autre acte, notification ou communication, ayant trait au présent Protocole.

The Explanatory Report on Protocol No. 13 explains that article 8 'correspond[s] to the wording of the Model Final Clauses adopted by the Committee of Ministers of the Council of Europe'.[1] The text is virtually identical to article 9 of Protocol No. 6. Readers of the Commentary are referred to the chapter dealing with that provision.

---

[1] Explanatory Report on Protocol No. 13, para. 20.

PART NINE

PROTOCOL NO. 16 TO THE
CONVENTION FOR THE PROTECTION
OF HUMAN RIGHTS AND
FUNDAMENTAL FREEDOMS

Preamble/Préambule

The member States of the Council of Europe and other High Contracting Parties to the Convention for the Protection of Human Rights and Fundamental Freedoms, signed at Rome on 4 November 1950 (hereinafter referred to as 'the Convention'), signatories hereto,

Having regard to the provisions of the Convention and, in particular, Article 19 establishing the European Court of Human Rights (hereinafter referred to as 'the Court');

Considering that the extension of the Court's competence to give advisory opinions will further enhance the interaction between the Court and national authorities and thereby reinforce implementation of the Convention, in accordance with the principle of subsidiarity;

Having regard to Opinion No. 285 (2013) adopted by the Parliamentary Assembly of the Council of Europe on 28 June 2013,

Have agreed as follows:

Les Etats membres du Conseil de l'Europe et les autres Hautes Parties contractantes à la Convention de sauvegarde des droits de l'homme et des libertés fondamentales, signée à Rome le 4 November 1950 (ci-après dénommée « la Convention »), signataires du présent Protocole,

Vu les dispositions de la Convention, notamment l'article 19 établissant la Cour européenne des droits de l'homme (ci-après dénommée « la Cour »);

Considérant que l'extension de la compétence de la Cour pour donner des avis consultatifs renforcera l'interaction entre la Cour et les autorités nationales, et consolidera ainsi la mise en œuvre de la Convention, conformément au principe de subsidiarité;

Vu l'Avis n° 285 (2013), adopté par l'Assemblée parlementaire du Conseil de l'Europe le 28 juin 2013,

Sont convenus de ce qui suit:

Protocol No. 16 to the Convention, adopted in October 2013, enables the 'highest courts and tribunals' of a State Party to ask the Court for 'advisory opinions on questions of principle relating to the interpretation or application of the rights and freedoms defined in the Convention or the Protocols thereto'.[1] Dean Spielmann, the President of the European Court, has called it 'the Protocol of the dialogue'. According to the Preamble of the Protocol, 'the extension of the Court's competence to give advisory opinions will further enhance the interaction between the Court and national authorities and thereby reinforce implementation of the Convention, in accordance with the principle of subsidiarity'.[2]

The first recital in the Preamble begins with the words 'The member States of the Council of Europe and other High Contracting Parties to the Convention for the Protection of Human Rights and Fundamental Freedoms...' Although this unusual formulation is not discussed in the Explanatory Report, it would appear to be an acknowledgement of the future accession to the Convention by the European Union.[3]

The final recital in the Preamble to Protocol No. 16 refers to Opinion No. 285 (2013) adopted by the Parliamentary Assembly of the Council of Europe on 28 June 2013. The

---

[1] Protocol No. 16 to the Convention on the Protection of Human Rights and Fundamental Freedoms, ETS 214, art. 1(1).

[2] On the drafting of Protocol No. 16, see Explanatory Report on Protocol No. 16.

[3] Report, Committee on Legal Affairs and Human Rights, AS/Jur (2013) 21, Doc. 13220, para. 8.

Opinion expresses the wish of the Parliamentary Assembly that the Committee of Ministers adopt the Protocol. It includes the following statement:

2. This additional protocol to the Convention, which must be ratified by 10 High Contracting Parties to the Convention before it enters into force, is likely to:

    2.1. strengthen the link between the Court and States' highest courts by creating a platform for judicial dialogue, thereby facilitating the application of the Court's case law by national courts;

    2.2. help shift, from ex post to ex ante, the resolution of a number of questions of interpretation of the Convention's provisions in the domestic forum, saving—in the long run—the valuable resources of the Court; the speedier resolution of similar cases on the domestic plane will also reinforce the principle of subsidiarity.[4]

For general observations about the role of the preamble of a treaty, see the chapter in this Commentary on the Preamble to the European Convention on Human Rights.

---

[4] Draft Protocol No. 16 to the Convention for the Protection of Human Rights and Fundamental Freedoms, Opinion 285 (2013).

Article 1. [Requests for an advisory opinion]

1. Highest courts and tribunals of a High Contracting Party, as specified in accordance with Article 10, may request the Court to give advisory opinions on questions of principle relating to the interpretation or application of the rights and freedoms defined in the Convention or the protocols thereto.

2. The requesting court or tribunal may seek an advisory opinion only in the context of a case pending before it.

3. The requesting court or tribunal shall give reasons for its request and shall provide the relevant legal and factual background of the pending case.

1. Les plus hautes juridictions d'une Haute Partie contractante, telles que désignées conformément à l'article 10, peuvent adresser à la Cour des demandes d'avis consultatifs sur des questions de principe relatives à l'interprétation ou à l'application des droits et libertés définis par la Convention ou ses protocoles.

2. La juridiction qui procède à la demande ne peut solliciter un avis consultatif que dans le cadre d'une affaire pendante devant elle.

3. La juridiction qui procède à la demande motive sa demande d'avis et produit les éléments pertinents du contexte juridique et factuel de l'affaire pendante.

Formulation of the request (art. 1(1))

The word 'may' in the first sentence of article 1(1) of Protocol No. 16 indicates that States are in no way obliged to seek an advisory opinion. The procedure is optional. Moreover, although not spelled out in paragraph 1, the Explanatory Report declares that the requesting court or tribunal may withdraw its request.[1]

The domestic authority entitled to request an advisory opinion from the Court is described as the 'highest courts or tribunals', identified in accordance with article 10 of Protocol No. 16. Article 10 provides that a State Party is to designate the appropriate high court or tribunal by a declaration formulated at the time of ratification, although it may change the designated body subsequently. The Explanatory Report states that this is 'intended to avoid potential complications by allowing a certain freedom of choice'.[2] The Protocol does not indicate whether there is any control by the European Court over the choice by a State. Hypothetically, a State might designate a body that is not one of its 'highest courts or tribunals'. Could the European Court decline to issue an opinion because this condition is not fulfilled?

It seems clear enough from the Explanatory Report that a high degree of flexibility is sought, given the rather large variation in the structure and hierarchies of the judicial structures within the Member States of the Council of Europe. Although 'highest court or tribunal' is intended to refer to institutions 'at the summit of the national judicial system', the '[u]se of the term "highest", as opposed to "the highest", permits the potential inclusion of those courts or tribunals that, although inferior to the constitutional or supreme court, are nevertheless of especial relevance on account of being the "highest" for a particular category of case'.[3]

---

[1] Explanatory Report on Protocol No. 16, para. 7.
[2] Ibid., para. 8.
[3] Ibid.

The alternative terms 'court' and 'tribunal' also contribute to the desired flexibility. Clearly, they are used so as to avoid disputes about form rather than substance, as there is no real difference between a 'court' and a 'tribunal'. The Convention itself uses both terms in a manner that suggests there is no distinction: 'a sentence of a court' (art. 2(1)); 'a competent court' (art. 5(1)(a)); 'the lawful order of a court' (art. 5(1)(b)); 'by a court' (art. 5(4)); 'the opinion of the court' (art. 6(1)); 'the language used in court' (art. 6(3)(e)); 'an independent and impartial tribunal' (art. 6(1)); 'duly considered by a domestic tribunal' (art. 35(3)(b)). Article 2 of Protocol No. 7 speaks of a 'higher tribunal' and of the 'highest tribunal'.

The importance of limiting the choice to the 'highest' courts or tribunals is related to the idea of exhaustion of domestic remedies, 'although a "highest" court need not be one to which recourse must have been made in order to satisfy the requirement of exhaustion of domestic remedies' under article 35(1) of the European Convention. According to the Explanatory Report, this should 'avoid a proliferation of requests and would reflect the appropriate level at which the dialogue should take place'.[4]

The application of Protocol No. 16 raises issues concerning territories governed by article 56 of the Convention. States may have some territories to which the Convention applies and others where it is not applicable. In order to accommodate this situation, a State Party may specify the exclusion of application of Protocol No. 16 to certain territories when it makes its declaration under article 10.[5]

An advisory opinion may be sought with respect to 'questions of principle relating to the interpretation or application of the rights and freedoms defined in the Convention or the protocols thereto'. This language is inspired by the wording of article 43(2) of the Convention, governing referral to the Grand Chamber, although that provision refers to 'a serious question' rather than 'questions of principle'. The drafters of Protocol No. 16 'felt that there were certain parallels' between the request for an advisory opinion and referral to the Grand Chamber, 'not limited to the fact that advisory opinions would themselves be delivered by the Grand Chamber'. However, 'when applying the criteria, the different purposes of the procedure under this Protocol and that under Article 43, paragraph 2 of the Convention will have to be taken into account'.[6]

Context of a pending case (art. 1(2))

The request for an advisory opinion must be made in the context of a case pending before the requesting court or tribunal. Article 1(2) does not provide any guidance as to the scope of the term 'case'. However, the Explanatory Report indicates that the advisory opinion procedure 'is not intended, for example, to allow for abstract review of legislation which is not to be applied in that pending case'.[7]

The approach to be taken when national legislation itself provides for an advisory opinion to be delivered about draft legislation requires clarification. Whether the relevant court or tribunal in a State Party asks the European Court to deliver what would amount to an advisory opinion within an advisory opinion is a matter that may eventually have to be

---

[4] Ibid.
[5] Ibid.
[6] Ibid., para. 9.
[7] Ibid., para. 10.

decided. The requirement in article 1(3) that a request be accompanied by the 'factual background' would seem to argue against such a possibility.

Procedural requirements (art. 1(3))

The requirements of paragraph 3 'reflect the aim of the procedure, which is not to transfer the dispute to the Court but rather to give the requesting court or tribunal guidance on Convention issues when determining the case before it'.[8] Two purposes are served by the provision, according to the Explanatory Report. First, 'the requesting court or tribunal must have reflected upon the necessity and utility of requesting an advisory opinion of the Court, so as to be able to explain its reasons for doing so'. Second, it is expected that the requesting court or tribunal will be in a position to provide the relevant legal and factual background, 'thereby allowing the Court to focus on the question(s) of principle relating to the interpretation or application of the Convention or the Protocols'.[9]

In its opinion on the draft Protocol, the European Court of Human Rights noted that 'it should not be for the Strasbourg Court to have to work out for itself in which respect the national court requires its opinion. For the procedure to function properly, the relevant issues of Convention law should be adequately identified and discussed at the national level.'[10] Referring to paragraph 11 of the draft Explanatory Report, the Court said it agreed with emphasizing the need to allow the Court to focus on the question of principle brought before it. 'The Court should not be called upon to review the facts or the national law in the context of this procedure', it said. 'Nor is it for the Court to decide the case pending before the requesting court.'[11]

The Explanatory Report indicates the materials that should be provided with a request:

– The subject matter of the domestic case and relevant findings of fact made during the domestic proceedings, or at least a summary of the relevant factual issues;
– The relevant domestic legal provisions;
– The relevant Convention issues, in particular the rights or freedoms at stake;
– If relevant, a summary of the arguments of the parties to the domestic proceedings on the question;
– If possible and appropriate, a statement of its own views on the question, including any analysis it may itself have made of the question.[12]

The Explanatory Report also confirms that requests for an advisory opinion may be submitted in the national official language used in the domestic proceedings.[13] The Court expressed reservations about this obligation, out of concern for the burden of work and the cost that might be involved.[14]

---

[8] Ibid., para. 11.
[9] Ibid.
[10] Opinion of the European Court of Human Rights on Draft Protocol No. 16 to the European Convention on Human Rights extending its competence to give advisory opinions on the interpretation of the Convention, 6 May 2013, para. 8.
[11] Ibid.
[12] Explanatory Report on Protocol No. 16, para. 13.
[13] Ibid., para. 12.
[14] Opinion of the European Court of Human Rights on Draft Protocol No. 16 to the European Convention on Human Rights extending its competence to give advisory opinions on the interpretation of the Convention, 6 May 2013, para. 14.

Further reading

David Milner, 'Protocols no. 15 and 16 to the European Convention on Human Rights in the Context of the Perennial Process of Reform: A Long and Winding Road', [2014] *Zeitschrift für europarechtliche Studien* 19.

Linos-Alexandre Sicilianos, 'L'élargissement de la compétence consultative de la Cour européenne des droits de l'homme—A propos du Protocole n° 16 à la Convention européenne des droits de l'homme', [2014] *RTDH* 9.

Article 2. [Acceptance of requests]

1. A panel of five judges of the Grand Chamber shall decide whether to accept the request for an advisory opinion, having regard to Article 1. The panel shall give reasons for any refusal to accept the request.

2. If the panel accepts the request, the Grand Chamber shall deliver the advisory opinion.

3. The panel and the Grand Chamber, as referred to in the preceding paragraphs, shall include *ex officio* the judge elected in respect of the High Contracting Party to which the requesting court or tribunal pertains. If there is none or if that judge is unable to sit, a person chosen by the President of the Court from a list submitted in advance by that Party shall sit in the capacity of judge.

1. Un collège de cinq juges de la Grande Chambre se prononce sur l'acceptation de la demande d'avis consultatif au regard de l'article 1. Tout refus du collège d'accepter la demande est motivé.

2. Lorsque le collège accepte la demande, la Grande Chambre rend un avis consultatif.

3. Le collège et la Grande Chambre, visés aux paragraphes précédents, comprennent de plein droit le juge élu au titre de la Haute Partie contractante dont relève la juridiction qui a procédé à la demande. En cas d'absence de ce juge, ou lorsqu'il n'est pas en mesure de siéger, une personne choisie par le Président de la Cour sur une liste soumise au préalable par cette Partie siège en qualité de juge.

Acceptance of the request (art. 2(1))

Like the advisory opinion that the Court may issue pursuant to article 47 of the Convention, there is a degree of discretion and there is no obligation to comply with the request. Nevertheless, the Explanatory Report states that 'it is to be expected that the Court would hesitate to refuse a request that satisfies the relevant criteria by (i) relating to a question as defined in paragraph 1 of Article 1 and (ii) the requesting court or tribunal having fulfilled the procedural requirements as set out in paragraphs 2 and 3 of Article 1'.[1] But in contrast with the advisory opinion procedure set out in article 47, there is no preliminary stage by which leave or authorization is granted. To that extent, the advisory opinion mechanism established by Protocol No. 16 resembles the application to the Grand Chamber in accordance with article 43 of the Convention, whereby a five-judge panel must grant leave.

There is one important difference, however. Whereas the five-judge panel of the Grand Chamber does not provide reasons for its decision on leave under article 43, Protocol No. 16 requires the panel to give reasons for any refusal to accept the request for an advisory opinion from a domestic court or tribunal. The Explanatory Report says that the intention of this measure is 'to reinforce dialogue between the Court and national judicial systems, including through clarification of the Court's interpretation of what is meant by "questions of principle relating to the interpretation or application of the rights and freedoms defined in the Convention or the Protocols thereto", which would provide

---

[1] Explanatory Report on Protocol No. 16, para. 14.

guidance to domestic courts and tribunals when considering whether to make a request and thereby help to deter inappropriate requests'.[2]

In its opinion on the draft Protocol, the European Court of Human Rights said it welcomed the fact that the Grand Chamber would have discretion as to whether to accept a request but that it had not favoured the requirement that it give reasons if it refuses. But it said it accepted the utility of giving reasons, although it said they would not normally be extensive. It said this would 'enhance the aim of creating a constructive dialogue with the national courts'.[3]

Although there is no explicit requirement in the Protocol, the Explanatory Report says that the Court should inform the State Party concerned of the acceptance of any requests made by its courts or tribunals.[4]

Delivery of the advisory opinion (art. 2(2))

Article 2(2) specifies that the Grand Chamber deliver the advisory opinion. The Grand Chamber is defined in article 26 of the European Convention. According to the Explanatory Report, it is appropriate that the advisory opinion be delivered by a seventeen-judge Grand Chamber, 'given the nature of the questions on which an advisory opinion may be requested and the fact that only the highest domestic courts or tribunals may request it, along with the recognised similarities between the present procedure and that of referral to the Grand Chamber under Article 43 of the Convention'.[5]

The Explanatory Report says that the prioritization to be given to advisory opinion proceedings under Protocol No. 16 is a matter for the Court but that 'the nature of the question on which it would be appropriate for the Court to give its advisory opinion suggests that such proceedings would have high priority'.[6] It adds that the 'high priority' of advisory opinions applies at all stages of the procedure and to all concerned, including those who formulate the request, the participants in the proceedings, and the Court itself. 'Undue delay in the advisory opinion proceedings before the Court would also cause delay in proceedings in the case pending before the requesting court or tribunal and should therefore be avoided', the Explanatory Report notes.[7]

Ex officio national judge (art. 2(3))

Both the five-judge panel that considers leave to appeal and the plenary Grand Chamber are to include the national judge of the State Party concerned by the advisory opinion, according to article 2(3) of Protocol No. 16. The Explanatory Report points out that this is also the case for the Grand Chamber when it sits in its full composition on a case pursuant to articles 33 and 34 of the Convention. Where there is no such judge, or if the

---

[2] Ibid., para. 15.

[3] Opinion of the European Court of Human Rights on Draft Protocol No. 16 to the European Convention on Human Rights extending its competence to give advisory opinions on the Interpretation of the Convention, 6 May 2013, para. 9.

[4] Explanatory Report on Protocol No. 16, para 15.

[5] Ibid., para. 16.

[6] Ibid., para. 17.

[7] Ibid., para. 17.

judge cannot sit, article 2(3) provides that the President of the Court designate a replacement judge from a list submitted in advance by the State Party. The intent of the drafters was that the procedure be identical to what already exists under article 26(4) of the Convention, and that the list of candidates be the same.[8]

[8] Ibid., para. 18.

Article 3. [Participation in proceedings]

The Council of Europe Commissioner for Human Rights and the High Contracting Party to which the requesting court or tribunal pertains shall have the right to submit written comments and take part in any hearing. The President of the Court may, in the interest of the proper administration of justice, invite any other High Contracting Party or person also to submit written comments or take part in any hearing.	Le Commissaire aux droits de l'homme du Conseil de l'Europe et la Haute Partie contractante dont relève la juridiction qui a procédé à la demande ont le droit de présenter des observations écrites et de prendre part aux audiences. Le Président de la Cour peut, dans l'intérêt d'une bonne administration de la justice, inviter toute autre Haute Partie contractante ou personne à présenter également des observations écrites ou à prendre part aux audiences.

The right to participate in the proceedings is recognized to the Council of Europe Commissioner for Human Rights and to the State Party whose domestic court or tribunal has requested the advisory opinion. This consists of a right to submit written comments and to take part in any hearing. Whether or not a hearing is held remains within the discretion of the Grand Chamber.[1]

According to the Explanatory Report, the drafters intended that 'the Commissioner have an equivalent right under the Protocol to participate in advisory opinion proceedings as s/he does under Article 36, paragraph 3) of the Convention to make a third party intervention in proceedings before a Chamber or the Grand Chamber'.[2] The Report notes that the wording of article 3 of Protocol No. 16 is slightly different from what is used in article 36(3) of the Convention but that the same effect is intended. It goes on to note that because advisory opinion proceedings are not adversarial in nature, participation by the State Party is not obligatory, 'although it would always retain the right to do so, in the same way as does a High Contracting Party in proceedings brought by one of its nationals against another High Contracting Party' as provided for in article 36(1) of the Convention.[3]

Any other State Party and any other person may be authorized to submit written comments and to participate in any hearing where this would be in the interest of the proper administration of justice. The expression 'proper administration of justice' is also used in article 36(2) as the criterion for granting of leave to participate to third parties. The Explanatory Report says that '[i]t is expected that the parties to the case in the context of which the advisory opinion had been requested would be invited to take part in the proceedings'.[4]

This may lead to difficulties in terms of implementation of Protocol No. 16 at the domestic level. National law may entitle litigants to be present at all stages of the proceedings. The issue is especially important in criminal matters, where the accused may have a right to be present. The European Court can address this issue in part by

---

[1] Explanatory Report on Protocol No. 16, para. 19.
[2] Ibid., para. 21.
[3] Ibid., para. 19.
[4] Ibid., para. 20.

granting leave to participate systematically, as proposed by the Explanatory Report. But there may also be linguistic difficulties because it is likely that the national proceedings will take place in a language other than the two official languages of the European Court of Human Rights. The Rules of Court entitle participants in proceedings to interpretation in another language but this is at their own expense. Yet the implementation of Protocol No. 16 brings a dimension to national judicial proceedings that is not held in the national language that may, in practice, make genuine participation by one or more of the parties quite unrealistic. The 'sensitivity' of the language issue is considered in the Explanatory Report, but only in the context of article 4,[5] dealing with issuance of the advisory opinion itself, not article 3, although it also seems relevant to the written and oral proceedings.

---

[5] Ibid., para. 23.

Article 4. [Content and issuance of advisory opinions]

1. Reasons shall be given for advisory opinions.

2. If the advisory opinion does not represent, in whole or in part, the unanimous opinion of the judges, any judge shall be entitled to deliver a separate opinion.

3. Advisory opinions shall be communicated to the requesting court or tribunal and to the High Contracting Party to which that court or tribunal pertains.

4. Advisory opinions shall be published.

1. Les avis consultatifs sont motivés.

2. Si l'avis consultatif n'exprime pas, en tout ou en partie, l'opinion unanime des juges, tout juge a le droit d'y joindre l'exposé de son opinion séparée.

3. Les avis consultatifs sont transmis à la juridiction qui a procédé à la demande et à la Haute Partie contractante dont cette juridiction relève.

4. Les avis consultatifs sont publiés.

The Grand Chamber is required to give reasons for advisory opinions delivered pursuant to Protocol No. 16. Separate, dissenting, and concurring opinions may be issued by individual judges, or groups of them, as is the case with other proceedings on the merits before the Grand Chamber.

Article 4(3) requires the Court to communicate the advisory opinion to both the requesting court or tribunal and the relevant State Party. According to the Explanatory Report, '[i]t is expected that the advisory opinion would also be communicated to any other parties that have taken part in the proceedings in accordance with Article 3'.[1]

Protocol No. 16 does not specify the language of the advisory opinion. The general rule applies, then, by which it is delivered in one of the two official languages, English or French, and generally in both of them. The Explanatory Report notes 'the sensitivity of the issue of the language of advisory opinions', and that in most cases advisory opinions will be subsequently admitted as part of proceedings that take place in an official language of the State Party that is neither English nor French. It observes that it may not be possible for the domestic court or tribunal to resume proceedings that have been suspended pending the advisory opinion until the opinion is translated into the language of the requesting court or tribunal. In the event of concerns that the time taken for translation into the language of the requesting court or tribunal of an advisory opinion may delay the resumption of suspended domestic proceedings, it may be possible for the Court to co-operate with national authorities in the timely preparation of such translations.[2]

Publication of the advisory opinion is required by article 4(4) of Protocol No. 16. According to the Explanatory Report, '[i]t is expected that this will be done by the Court in accordance with its practice in similar matters and with due respect to applicable confidentiality rules'.[3]

---

[1] Explanatory Report on Protocol No. 16, para. 23.
[2] Ibid., para. 23.
[3] Ibid., para. 24.

Article 5. [Non-binding nature of advisory opinions]

Advisory opinions shall not be binding.   **Les avis consultatifs ne sont pas contraignants.**

Advisory opinions issued in accordance with Protocol No. 16 'shall not be binding'. The term 'binding' is used only once in the European Convention itself, in the title to article 46: 'Binding force and execution of judgments'. Article 46(1) states: 'The High Contracting Parties undertake to abide by the final judgment of the Court in any case to which they are parties.' That notion does not apply to an advisory opinion requested by a domestic court or tribunal because the State Party concerned may not even be a participant in the proceedings from which the advisory opinion has been generated. The non-binding nature of an 'advisory opinion' seems apparent from the name of the proceeding itself. Instead, as the Explanatory Report notes, advisory opinions 'take place in the context of the judicial dialogue between the Court and domestic courts and tribunals. Accordingly, the requesting court decides on the effects of the advisory opinion in the domestic proceedings.'[1] In its opinion on the draft Protocol, the European Court of Human Rights concurred, stating that 'it is in the nature of a dialogue that it should be for the requesting court to decide on the effects of the advisory opinion in the domestic proceedings'.[2]

Because the advisory opinion is not binding, the individual litigant's rights are also reserved. The fact that the European Court has issued an advisory opinion on a question that arises in a case pending before a domestic court or tribunal does not prevent a party in those proceedings from subsequently raising the issue in an individual application before the European Court pursuant to article 34 of the Convention. Nevertheless, according to the Explanatory Report, 'where an application is made subsequent to proceedings in which an advisory opinion of the Court has effectively been followed, it is expected that such elements of the application that relate to the issues addressed in the advisory opinion would be declared inadmissible or struck out'.[3]

In that sense, the affirmation in article 5 of Protocol No. 16 that an advisory opinion is not binding may require some qualification. The Explanatory Report acknowledges that an individual judge, a Committee, or a Chamber will consider itself 'bound' by an advisory opinion that has already been issued concerning the same subject-matter. However, in its opinion on the draft Protocol, the Court said that a good reason for the non-binding nature of advisory opinions is to leave open the possibility of a dissatisfied party bringing an application to Strasbourg once a final decision has been delivered by the national courts.[4]

---

[1] Explanatory Report on Protocol No. 16, para. 25.

[2] Opinion of the European Court of Human Rights on Draft Protocol No. 16 to the European Convention on Human Rights extending its competence to give advisory opinions on the interpretation of the Convention, 6 May 2013, para. 12.

[3] Explanatory Report on Protocol No. 16, para. 26.

[4] Opinion of the European Court of Human Rights on Draft Protocol No. 16 to the European Convention on Human Rights extending its competence to give advisory opinions on the interpretation of the Convention, 6 May 2013, para. 9.

Similarly, although advisory opinions have no direct effect on subsequent applications, they do make up part of the case law of the Court. In other words, '[t]he interpretation of the Convention and the Protocols thereto contained in such advisory opinions would be analogous in its effect to the interpretative elements set out by the Court in judgments and decisions'.[5] With regard to paragraph 27 of the Explanatory Report, the Rapporteur of the Parliamentary Assembly's Committee on Legal Affairs and Human Rights, in his Report on Protocol No. 16, wrote that 'although advisory opinions will not have the binding character of Grand Chamber judgments in contentious cases, they would nevertheless have "undeniable legal effects"'.[6]

---

[5] Explanatory Report on Protocol No. 16, para. 27.
[6] Report, Committee on Legal Affairs and Human Rights, AS/Jur (2013) 21, Doc. 13220, para. 11.

Article 6. [Relationship to the Convention]

As between the High Contracting Parties the provisions of Articles 1 to 5 of this Protocol shall be regarded as additional articles to the Convention, and all the provisions of the Convention shall apply accordingly.

Les Hautes Parties contractantes considèrent les articles 1 à 5 du présent Protocole comme des articles additionnels à la Convention, et toutes les dispositions de la Convention s'appliquent en conséquence.

The advisory opinion mechanism provided by Protocol No. 16 does not amend the text of the Convention itself. It is an additional protocol in the sense that Member States of the Council of Europe are in no way required to sign and ratify the Protocol. It is for this reason that article 6 of Protocol No. 16 specifies that the provisions of articles 1 to 5 apply to those States that have accepted the Protocol (and only them).[1] Amongst them, the provisions of the first five articles of the Protocol are deemed to be additional articles to the Convention.

According to the Explanatory Report, '[i]t is understood that this, in conjunction with Article 58 of the Convention, would allow a High Contracting Party to denounce the Protocol without denouncing the Convention'.[2]

Article 6 of Protocol No. 16 is essentially identical to provisions on the same subject in Protocols Nos 1, 4, 6, 7, 12, and 13.

---

[1] Explanatory Report on Protocol No. 16, para. 28.
[2] Ibid.

Article 7. [Signature and ratification]

1. This Protocol shall be open for signature by the High Contracting Parties to the Convention, which may express their consent to be bound by:

(a) signature without reservation as to ratification, acceptance or approval; or

(b) signature subject to ratification, acceptance or approval, followed by ratification, acceptance or approval.

2. The instruments of ratification, acceptance or approval shall be deposited with the Secretary General of the Council of Europe.

1. Le présent Protocole est ouvert à la signature des Hautes Parties contractantes à la Convention, qui peuvent exprimer leur consentement à être liées par:

(a) la signature sans réserve de ratification, d'acceptation ou d'approbation; ou

(b) la signature sous réserve de ratification, d'acceptation ou d'approbation, suivie de ratification, d'acceptation ou d'approbation.

2. Les instruments de ratification, d'acceptation ou d'approbation seront déposés près le Secrétaire Général du Conseil de l'Europe.

The Explanatory Report on Protocol No. 16 states that the text of article 7 'is based on one of the model final clauses approved by the Committee of Ministers and contains the provisions under which a High Contracting Party to the Convention may become bound by the Protocol'. When the Committee of Ministers of the Council of Europe adopted several model final clauses for use by those involved in drafting treaties, in February 1980, it proposed two alternatives with respect to signature and ratification. The first was for 'agreements', while the second was for 'conventions'. Although the signature and ratification clauses in Protocols Nos 6, 7, and 12 are based on the text proposed for conventions, the text of article 7 of Protocol No. 16 uses the alternative formulation, designed for agreements.

Unlike signature and ratification clauses in earlier protocols to the Convention, which specified expressly that a Member State of the Council of Europe could not ratify, accept, or approve the Protocol without previously or simultaneously ratifying the Convention, the formulation does not appear in article 7 of Protocol No. 16. Instead, the provision itself begins by declaring that the Protocol is 'open for signature by the High Contracting Parties to the Convention'.

Protocol No. 16 was opened for signature on 2 October 2013. On that date it was signed by Armenia, Finland, France, Italy, San Marino, Slovakia, and Slovenia. Subsequently, nine other States have signed the Protocol. There are no ratifications or definitive signatures.

Article 8. [Entry into force]

1. This Protocol shall enter into force on the first day of the month following the expiration of a period of three months after the date on which ten High Contracting Parties to the Convention have expressed their consent to be bound by the Protocol in accordance with the provisions of Article 7.

2. In respect of any High Contracting Party to the Convention which subsequently expresses its consent to be bound by it, the Protocol shall enter into force on the first day of the month following the expiration of a period of three months after the date of the expression of its consent to be bound by the Protocol in accordance with the provisions of Article 7.

1. Le présent Protocole entrera en vigueur le premier jour du mois qui suit l'expiration d'une période de trois mois après la date à laquelle dix Hautes Parties contractantes à la Convention auront exprimé leur consentement à être liées par le Protocole conformément aux dispositions de l'article 7.

2. Pour toute Haute Partie contractante à la Convention qui exprimera ultérieurement son consentement à être liée par le présent Protocole, celui-ci entrera en vigueur le premier jour du mois qui suit l'expiration d'une période de trois mois après la date de l'expression de son consentement à être liée par le Protocole conformément aux dispositions de l'article 7.

Article 8 is taken from Article 7 of Protocol No. 9 to the Convention and is based on the model final clauses approved by the Committee of Ministers.[1] The number of States Parties required for the Protocol to enter into force is set at ten, the same number that is required by Protocols Nos 1, 12, and 13.

---

[1] Explanatory Report on Protocol No. 16, para. 30.

Article 9. [Reservations]

No reservation may be made under Article 57 of the Convention in respect of the provisions of this Protocol.

Aucune réserve n'est admise aux dispositions du présent Protocole au titre de l'article 57 de la Convention.

Pursuant to article 6, the provisions of Protocol No. 16 are deemed to be additional articles to the Convention, with the result that all the provisions of the Convention shall apply accordingly. The drafters of Protocol No. 16 chose to exclude the possibility of reservations, something authorized by article 57 of the Convention. Consequently, article 9 of Protocol No. 16 is necessary in order to neutralize article 57 of the Convention.[1]

---

[1] Explanatory Report on Protocol No. 16, para. 31.

Article 10. [Designation of courts or tribunals]

Each High Contracting Party to the Convention shall, at the time of signature or when depositing its instrument of ratification, acceptance or approval, by means of a declaration addressed to the Secretary General of the Council of Europe, indicate the courts or tribunals that it designates for the purposes of Article 1, paragraph 1, of this Protocol. This declaration may be modified at any later date and in the same manner.

Chaque Haute Partie contractante à la Convention indique, au moment de la signature ou du dépôt de son instrument de ratification, d'acceptation ou d'approbation, au moyen d'une déclaration adressée au Secrétaire Général du Conseil de l'Europe, quelles juridictions elle désigne aux fins de l'article 1, paragraphe 1, du présent Protocole. Cette déclaration peut être modifiée à tout moment de la même manière.

Article 10 is based on a standard clause used in Council of Europe treaties.[1] It provides States Parties to the Convention a mechanism by which they may specify the courts or tribunals that will be able to request advisory opinions from the Court. They may make subsequent changes, also by means of a declaration. Declarations pursuant to article 10 are addressed to the Secretary General of the Council of Europe, as depository of multilateral agreements made within the organization.

There has been only one declaration. At the time of signature, Romania formulated a *note verbale* designating national courts for the purposes of article 1(1) of the Protocol. It said that its declaration would enter into force at the time of ratification of the Protocol.

---

[1] Explanatory Report on Protocol No. 16, para. 32.

Article 11. [Depositary functions]

The Secretary General of the Council of Europe shall notify the member States of the Council of Europe and the other High Contracting Parties to the Convention of:

(a) any signature;

(b) the deposit of any instrument of ratification, acceptance or approval;

(c) any date of entry into force of this Protocol in accordance with Article 8;

(d) any declaration made in accordance with Article 10; and

(e) any other act, notification or communication relating to this Protocol.

Le Secrétaire Général du Conseil de l'Europe notifiera aux Etats membres du Conseil de l'Europe et aux autres Hautes Parties contractantes à la Convention:

a) toute signature;

b) le dépôt de tout instrument de ratification, d'acceptation ou d'approbation;

c) toute date d'entrée en vigueur du présent Protocole, conformément à l'article 8;

d) toute déclaration faite en vertu de l'article 10; et

e) tout autre acte, notification ou communication ayant trait au présent Protocole.

The Explanatory Report on Protocol No. 16 states that article 11 'is one of the usual final clauses included in treaties prepared within the Council of Europe'.[1] The text is similar to article 9 of Protocol No. 6 and readers of the Commentary are referred to the chapter dealing with that provision. There are two small differences between the two texts. The *chapeau* requires that notification be given to 'member States of the Council of Europe and the other High Contracting Parties', presumably contemplating the accession of the European Union. Paragraph (d), referring to the procedure established under article 10 of the Protocol for specifying which of a High Contacting Party's highest courts or tribunals may request advisory opinions from the Court, is not part of the Model Final Clauses and does not appear in the equivalent provisions of Protocols Nos 6, 7, and 12.

---

[1] Explanatory Report on Protocol No. 16, para. 33.

Index

Note: please see under entries for individual countries for specific topics relating to that country.

Aarhus Convention 24
Abkhazia 914, 938, 1190
abortion
  chilling effect 373
  confidentiality 383, 404–5
  demonstrations, protection of 493
  forced abortion 543
  legitimate aim/purpose, restrictions for a 405
  life, right to 117, 124–5
  margin of appreciation 81–2, 383
  marry and found a family, right to 543
  positive obligations 373
  private life 373, 383, 404–6
  procedures to determine availability, access to 373
  religion or belief, freedom to manifest 431
  women as prevailing over men, rights of 543
absence/presence of accused at trial 81, 316–17, 1137, 1222–3
abuse of rights, prohibition of 611–22, 625
  access to court, right of 620–1
  admissibility, Article 17 as exception to 614–16
  Charter of Fundamental Rights of the EU 611–12
  Committee of Experts 613–14
  Committee of Ministers 613–14
  Conference of Senior Officials 614
  Consultative Assembly 613–14
  Council of Europe, aims and principles of 612
  de minimis principle 781–2
  declarations 622
  democracy 612–13, 616, 618
  destruction of Convention rights 616–20
  discrimination 618
  extraterritoriality 616
  freedom of assembly and association 615, 617, 620
  freedom of expression 615, 617–20
  individual applications 780–1
  International Covenant on Civil and Political Rights 611, 616
  interpretation 614–22
  liberty and security, right to 621
  limitation/restriction clauses 616, 618, 620
  limitation to a greater extent, meaning of 620–2
  margin of appreciation 615
  necessary in a democratic society, restrictions which are 615, 621
  political parties
    anti-democratic views, dissolution of parties with 618
    Islam, advocating ban on parties not based on 619

pressing social need, restrictions due to 621
private and family life, right to respect for 617, 620
proportionality 621
racial discrimination 616, 618–19
restrictions/limitations 616, 618–22
sex discrimination, advocacy of 619
summary execution, justification of 619
torture, justification of 619
totalitarianism 611–12, 616–19
Universal Declaration of Human Rights 611, 613
war crimes, justification of 619
access to court, right of 100, 284–7, 322, 324, 551, 620–1, 1136
access to documents 825–9
accessibility and foreseeability of law
  criminal law 385
  education 998–9
  expropriation 976
  expulsions 1130
  freedom of assembly and association 510–11, 523
  freedom of expression 469–71
  freedom of movement and migration 1063–4
  manifest religion or belief, freedom to 435
  margin of appreciation 340–2
  no punishment without law 336–42, 345, 353
  private and family life, right to respect for 403
  time limits 342–3
acquittals 304–6, 744, 1134, 1139–40
ad hoc judges 687, 689, 691, 892
Adam, HT 58
addition of new rights *see* protocols
administrative trials 265, 270–1
admissibility *see* admissibility criteria; Chambers on admissibility and merits, decisions by
admissibility criteria 753–86 *see also under* individual main entries
  6-month rule 757–8, 763, 770–3
    date of knowledge 772
    date of running of time 772
    prejudice 772
    self-represented litigants 772
    time of the essence 770–1
    waiver, prohibition of 770
    weekends and holidays 772
additional written observations, requests for 763
anonymous applications 773–4
another international body, submission to another 776–8
assignment of cases to Sections 763
caseload 761

admissibility criteria (*cont.*)
  Chambers 763
  Committee of Experts 755–7
  Committee of Ministers 755, 758–9
  Committees 689, 698, 699–703, 763, 779, 851
  Conference of Senior Officials 757
  consolidating the institutions and further
      reform 705–7, 759–60, 762, 785
  Consultative Assembly 754–5, 758–60
  de minimis rule 762, 781–5
  declarations 786
  discrimination 563
  drafting 754–62
  ECommHR 632, 754–9, 779
  ECtHR 759
  estoppel 764
  exhaustion of domestic remedies 754–5, 757,
      763, 764–9
  filtering and processing applications 760–2
  formalism 754
  frivolous or mischievous petitions 754
  general principles of international law 754, 756
  Grand Chamber 763–4
  grounds 759–62, 778–9
  hearings 763
  incompatibility with provisions of ECHR 778–9
  individual applications 707, 746–7, 762, 776, 780–1
  interpretation 762–86
  inter-State applications 706–7, 726–9, 757,
      762–3, 776
  irregular petitions, rejection of 756–7
  jurisdiction 778–9
  manifestly ill-founded applications, rejection
      of 705, 711, 727, 755–9, 778, 779–81, 1071
  merits
      grounds 778
      joint rulings on 763–4
  notification of Respondent State 763
  objections 786
  Parliamentary Assembly 760
  President of the Section 763
  procedure 762–4
  protocols, incorporation into domestic law of 760
  ratione loci jurisdiction 778
  ratione materiae jurisdiction 778–9
  ratione personae jurisdiction 778
  ratione temporis jurisdiction 772, 778
  re-activation of elements of claims 763–4
  reply, written observations in 806
  Rules of Court 762, 764
  significant damage criteria 760, 762
  single-judge formation 697–8, 699, 763
  stage of proceedings, rejection of applications at
      any 785–6
  statements of compliance 763
  substantially the same, matters which are 774–5
  time limits 757–8, 763, 770–3
adoption of children 367, 407–8, 543, 573, 584, 826–7

adoption of ECHR 3–10, 27–8, 55 *see also* Alternative
      A and A/2 (Enumeration of Human Rights);
      Alternative B (Definition of Human Rights)
  commission, proposal for a 4, 6–10
  Committee of Experts 5–7, 8
  Committee of Ministers 4, 5–9, 167
  Conference of Senior Officials 7, 167–8
  Congress of Europe 1948 3, 6, 27
  Consultative Assembly 4, 5–8, 61
  contents of rights 4, 6, 8
  Council of Europe 3–10
  court, proposals for a 3, 4, 6–8, 10
  draft text 4–8
  economic, social, and cultural rights 4, 6
  education of children, right of parents to
      determine 4, 8
  elections, right to free 8
  enforcement 3, 4, 6–9
  entry into force 8–10
  final stages 8
  implementation of rights 6–7
  interpretation 8
  property, right to 4, 8
  signing ceremony 8–9
  substantive rights, definition of 8
  Universal Declaration of Human Rights 4, 7, 61,
      84, 167
adversarial proceedings 310
adverse inferences, drawing 811–14
adverse possession 969, 974
advisory opinions 633, 874–83, 884–5
  acceptance of requests 1219–21
  admissibility 882, 1225
  binding, opinions as 877
  caseload 876, 882
  Charter of UN 874, 878
  Committee of Experts 26, 875–6, 883–5
  Committee of Ministers 26, 31–2, 874–82, 1214
  Commonwealth of Independent States (CIS)
      Convention on Human Rights, relationship
      with 876, 878, 881–2, 885
  concurring opinions 1224
  Consultative Assembly 26, 875, 878
  contents 878–80, 1224
  criminal law 1222–3
  declarations 1215, 1231
  delay 1220, 1224
  delivery of opinions 1220–1
  denunciations 1227
  depositary functions 1232
  designation of court or tribunal 1215, 1231
  discretion 877, 882
  dissenting or separate opinions 859, 887, 1224
  drafting 875–6, 884, 887
  ECommHR 26–7, 875–6
  entry into force 26–7, 1229
  ex officio national judges 1220–1
  exhaustion of domestic remedies 1216

formulation of request (Article 1) 1215–17
Grand Chamber 691–2, 713, 876, 878–85, 1216, 1219–22
Group of Wise Persons report 31–2
highest courts or tribunals 1215–16, 1220
institutions, consolidating the 876, 877, 882
interpretation 31–2, 876–85, 1213, 1216, 1219–20, 1223, 1226
issuance of opinions 1224
judgeship, list of candidates for 877, 885
judicial dialogue 26, 31–2, 1213, 1220, 1225
jurisdiction 884–5
language 1217, 1223, 1224
legal question, meaning of 878
national courts and tribunals, requests of 875, 877
non-binding nature 1225–6
oral hearings 882
Parliamentary Assembly 32, 876–7, 879–80, 1225–6
participation in proceedings 1222–3
pending case, context of a 1216–17
Permanent Court of International Justice 731, 874
Plenary Court 876, 883
preambles to protocols 1213–14
principle, questions of 1216, 1217, 1219
prioritization 1220
procedure 882–3, 1217
ratification 26–7
reasons 887
reform 876, 877, 882
Registrar 882
relationship of protocols to ECHR 1227
reservations 1230
restrictions/limitations 880–2
Rules of Court 882
separate opinions 1224
signature and ratification 1228
striking out 1225
subsidiarity 1213
territorial application 924, 1216
third party interventions 1222
travaux préparatoires 878, 880
written comments, right to submit 1222
advocacy organizations or associations, victim status of 741–2
affirmative action/positive discrimination 566–8, 1175–6, 1187
African Commission on Human and Peoples' Rights (ACHPR) 959
African Court on Human and Peoples' Rights (AfCHPR) 643
African slave trade, litigation over 201
age
  adoptive parents 573, 584
  criminal responsibility, age of 318–19
    Beijing Rules 318
    fitness to stand trial 310
  discrimination 556, 573, 575, 583–4, 1184
  Employment Equality Directive 583

judges 31, 583–4, 650, 654–5, 670–4
liberty and security, right to 240–1, 251
majority, age of 240
marry and found a family, right to 537
retirement age 31, 567, 584
vote, right to 1026
aggression, crime of 602
AIDS/HIV 126, 160, 172, 827
airports, security control at 1059
Albania 908, 1031
Algeria 588
aliens *see also* collective expulsion of aliens; expulsion of aliens, procedural safeguards relating to; political activity of aliens, restrictions on
  discrimination 560
  obligation to respect human rights 85
Alternative A and A/2 (Enumeration of Human Rights) 6–8, 121
  derogations 590
  effective remedy, right to an 549
  fair trial, right to a 267–8
  freedom of assembly and association 488
  freedom of expression 449
  life, right to 121
  no punishment without law 333
  obligation to respect human rights 86
  political activity of aliens, restrictions on 607
  private and family life, right to respect for 364
  slavery and forced labour 204
  thought, conscience and religion, freedom of 418
  torture 167–8
Alternative B and B/2 (Definition of Human Rights) 6–8, 121, 167–8, 204
  derogations 590
  effective remedy, right to an 549
  fair trial, right to a 267–8
  freedom of assembly and association 488
  freedom of expression 449
  life, right to 121
  no punishment without law 333
  obligation to respect human rights 86
  political activity of aliens, restrictions on 607–8
  private and family life, right to respect for 364
  slavery and forced labour 204–5
  thought, conscience and religion, freedom of 418
alternative dispute resolution *see* exclusion of other means of dispute resolution
amendment of ECHR and reform of machinery 26–32, 49, 639, 649–51 *see also* consolidating the institutions and further reform; protocols
American Convention on Human Rights (ACHR)
  abortion 124
  death penalty 15, 1197, 1200, 1201
    abolitionist treaty, ACHR as 1197
    life, right to 140–1
    military justice 1201
    wartime 1104

American Convention on Human Rights (ACHR) (*cont.*)
  derogations 587, 592, 594
  ex officio or national judges 693
  freedom of expression 452, 459
  Inter-American Court of Human Rights 139, 643, 655, 693, 874
  lex mitior principle 350
  life, right to 140–1
  prior restraint 452
  sources of international law 39
  vote, right to 1026
amicus curiae briefs 788, 793, 807
amnesties 67, 128–9, 1145, 1150, 1155
Ancel, Marc 14–15
Andorra 262, 604, 820, 937, 1009
anonymity 313, 746, 773–4
anti-communism 612
anti-Semitism 479, 619
Apollinaire, Guillaume 464, 472
apostasy, advocating death penalty for 619
appeal in criminal matters, right of 1134–41
  absence of accused, proceedings in 1137
  access to court, right of 1136
  acquittals 1134, 1139–40
  admissibility 1135
  Committee of Ministers 1139
  convictions 1135–6, 1139–41
  criminal offences, restricted to 1138–9
  damages 1138
  declarations 1140–1
  detention/deprivation of liberty 1136
  drafting 1134–5
  effective remedy, right to an 1136
  exceptions 1139–40
  exhaustion of domestic remedies 1135
  fair trial, right to a 1135
  governed by law, exercise of right 1137–8
  guilty pleas 1136–7
  highest tribunal, exception where offence tried at first instance by 1139–40
  interpretation 1135–40
  leave 1138
  legitimate aim/purpose, restrictions for a 1136
  margin of appreciation 1136
  minor character, offences of 1139–40
  plea bargaining 1140
  prescribed by law, restrictions which are 1139
  procedural safeguards 1135
  questions of law, restricted to 1136, 1138
  reservations 1139, 1140
  rule of law 1139
  sentences 1135–6, 1141
  time limits 1137
  waiver 1140
applicable law 719–20
arbitration 43, 766, 907, 910–11
armed conflict *see* armed conflicts and right to life; death penalty in time of war; war/armed conflicts

armed conflict and right to life
  civilians 155–8
  derogations 153–6
  ECtHR 154–6
  illegal wars 157
  inhuman or degrading treatment 157
  international humanitarian law 154–8
  legitimate aim 156–8
  Martens Clause 158
  occupation 154
  procedural/investigative obligation 153–4
  proportionality 156–8
  St Petersburg Declaration 158
  use of lethal force 155–7
  war crimes 155
armed forces *see* military service
Armenia
  Azerbaijan, territory occupied in 938, 1114, 1163
  death penalty 1114
  genocide, denial of 479–80
  International Covenant on Civil and Political Rights 588
  Jehovah's Witnesses 434
  Mountainous Karabakh 938
  prisoners 1028
  territorial application 1114, 1163
arrest
  compensation 224, 257–8
  extradition 245–6
  liberty and security, right to 221–4, 227, 234, 237–9, 243–6, 254
  use of lethal force 146, 150–2
artificial insemination 389, 539–40
Aruba 1036, 1084, 1190, 1108, 1114, 1205
assembly, freedom of *see* freedom of assembly and association
association, freedom of *see* freedom of assembly and association
asylum seekers *see* refugees and asylum seekers
atheism and agnosticism 423–4
Austria
  abortion 493
  adoption 408
  candidate for election, right to stand as a 1030
  death penalty 1095
  declarations 1141, 1156
  demonstrations 493
  discrimination 217
  expulsion 1073
  freedom of expression 472–3
  inter-State applications 725–6
  Italy 913
  ne bis in idem 1156
  no punishment without law 349
  peaceful enjoyment of possessions 983
  political activity of aliens, restrictions on 609
  public hearings 323
  reasons 936

regional assemblies 1020
religious discrimination 579
reservations 323, 609, 936–7, 983, 1073, 1146
same sex partners 800
succession to tenancies 407
Süd Tirol/Alto Adige, dispute between Austria and
    Italy over 913
autonomy
    freedom of assembly and association 490–1, 500,
        503–4, 513
    private life 370, 371, 375–80
autrefois convict see ne bis in idem
Azara, Antonio 832
Azerbaijan
    Armenia, territory occupied by 938, 1114, 1163
    death penalty 17, 349–50, 1114
    declarations 1009
    freedom of assembly and association 510
    liberty and security, right to 627
    mass media ownership 481
    military discipline 324–5
    ne bis in idem 1154
    police orders, non-compliance with 1154
    reservations 938
    territorial application 938, 1114, 1163
Azkoul, Karim 583

Bacon, Alice 576 n.147
bail 250–1, 253, 1058
Ballodore Pallieri, Giorgio 682
Begtrup, Bodil 5
Belém do Pará Convention (OAS) 576
belief *see* religion and belief *see also* Islam; manifest
        religion or belief, freedom to; thought,
        conscience and religion, freedom of
Belgium
    Belgian Congo 925
    children, detention of 170
    Constitution 358, 903
    death penalty and right to life 140
    declarations 786, 1132
    education 579
    expulsion 1132
    extradition of terrorist suspects to United
        States 750, 837
    fair trial, right to a 288
    language 579
    no punishment without law 330
    political activity of aliens, restrictions on 609
    private and family life, right to respect for 358
    race discrimination 618
    regional assemblies 1021
    reservations 609
    safeguards for existing human rights 903
    Slovakian Roma, expulsion of 1078
    universal suffrage 1011
    vagrants, detention of 243
Bensouda, Fatou 723 n.1

Benvenuti, Lodovico 613
Berlin Wall 1052
Bernardino, Minerva 5
Bernhardt, Rudolf 682
bias *see* independence and impartiality
Bill of Rights 1688 444
binding force and execution of judgments 861–72
    administrative changes 861–2
    advisory opinions 866
    civil society, pressure from 871
    condemnation and disapproval 871
    Committee of Experts 863
    Committee of Ministers, supervision by 797–8,
        821–2, 864–7, 871, 872, 905
    compensation 868, 970
    consolidating the institutions and further
        reform 864, 866
    Consultative Assembly 862–3, 871
    criminal proceedings 869
    declarations 866, 870–1
    disappearances 870
    drafting 862–6
    failure to fulfil an obligation 872
    fair trial, right to a 276, 869–70
    final judgments, interpretation of 865
    freedom to determine means of discharging
        obligations 867–9
    friendly settlements 871
    general measures 868–71
    individual measures 868–9
    infringement proceedings 865–6
    interpretation 865, 866–72
    inter-State applications 867–70
    just satisfaction 867, 871
    legislative changes 861–2
    moral pressure 862
    new issues 869
    no punishment without law 870
    non-execution 862–3
    Plenary Court 680
    pilot-judgment procedure 870–1
    political pressure 871
    precedent 866
    reparations 867–8
    res judicata 866
    restitutio in integrum principle 868
    retrials 869
    role of the Court 869–71
    sanctions 862
    State responsibility 868–9
    structural or system problems 870
    subsidiarity 870
    supervision of execution 797–8, 821–2, 864–7,
        871, 872, 905
    Vienna Convention on the Law of Treaties 866
Bindschedler-Robert, Denise 664
Bingham, Tom 72
Bîrsan, Corneliu 893

birth or other status, discrimination on grounds
        of 558–61, 574, 582–4
Blackstone, William 457
boat, *refoulement* of migrants arriving by 1079–80,
        1083
Bonello, Giovanni 62, 67, 91–2, 159
Bosnia and Herzegovina
    admissibility criteria 777
    Constitution 1031
    Dayton Agreement 565–6, 768, 1105
    death penalty in time of war 1105, 1106–7
    discrimination 565–6
    elections, right to free 1031, 1181
    exhaustion of domestic remedies 768
    fair trial in criminal proceedings, right to 295
    military service 215
    presidential election candidates and
            discrimination 565–6, 871
    sentencing 573
Brandeis, Louis 358
Bratza, Nicolas 296, 342–3, 682, 696, 795
Brighton High Level Conference 2012 31–2, 58,
        650–1
Broda, Christian 15
Bulgaria
    Constitution 984
    declarations 1009
    education, fees for 1005–6
    expulsion 435
    family life 435
    freedom of assembly and association 497, 512
        Jehovah's Witnesses 435
    leave a country, freedom to 1062, 1064–5
    medication without regulatory approval 372
    prisoners' right to vote 1028
    racial discrimination 160, 553
    reservations 984
    Roma 553
    sexual assault 192
burden of proof
    beyond reasonable doubt 810
    examination of the case 810–12
    exhaustion of domestic remedies 766, 768
    fugitives 317
    general principles of international law 810
    inter-State applications 811
    life, right to 123
    presumption of innocence 298–300
    release from detention 252
    reversal 299–300, 811
    standard of proof 300
Bureau 683–4

Caflish, Lucius 646
Caldarera, Ugo 13
Camus, Albert 1091
Canada, death penalty in 1093
Canary Islands, regional assembly in 1020–1

Cançado Trindade, Antônio Augusto 179
candidate in elections, right to stand as a 1012, 1018,
        1025, 1029–30
    conditions 1022–3
    diplomats 1030
    discrimination 524–5
    dual nationality, persons with 1030
    executive, members of 1030
    freedom of assembly and association 512, 517,
            524–5
    grounds for disqualification 1029–30
    independence and impartiality 1030
    independent candidates 1023
    judicial office, holders of 511, 1030
    margin of appreciation 1023
    Masons 511, 512, 517, 524–5
    military, members of 1030
    police officers 1030
    proportionality 1029
    residency requirements 1030
    restrictions/limitations 1029
    separation of powers 1029–30
    signature of electors threshold 1022, 1030
capital punishment *see* death penalty; death penalty
        and right to life
Cardozo, Benjamin 423
Casadevall, Josep 682
case management 686
caseload 28–30
    admissibility criteria 27, 761
    Chambers 27, 782
    Committee of Ministers 28
    Committees 702
    de minimis principle 782
    delay 30–1
    direct access, right of individual 27–8
    discrimination 1180
    ECommHR 27–9, 633
    ECtHR, establishment of 633
    filtering and processing applications 27, 30–1
    friendly settlements 816
    individual applications 27–8
    judicial formations 686
    Plenary Court 680
    single-judge formation 696–7
Cassese, Antonio 345
Cassin, René 1, 5, 61, 412, 645, 655, 682
cellular samples 384
Central and Eastern Europe *see also* individual countries
    Berlin Wall 1052
    Cold War 1052–3
    communist parties 521
    freedom of movement and migration 1052–3, 1088
    judges 655
    lustration 1026
    military service 215
    national and ethnic minorities, protection of 631
    national security 1062

Nuremberg Military Tribunal 344–5
peaceful enjoyment of possessions 970
signatories and ratification 1166–7
time limits 342
vote, right to 1026
Chagos Islands 104
Chambers *see also* Chambers on admissibility and
    merits, decisions by
2 or more judges 687
5 judges 687
7 judge benches 805, 687–9, 691
9 judge benches 688–9
authorization to set up Chambers 27
enlargement 688
ex officio participation 687–8, 690, 692
examination of the case 806–8
interim measures 749
investigations 807–8
judicial formations 686–9, 690–1
nationality 687, 691
opinions or reports, requests for 807
Plenary Court 678–9, 682–3
Presidents/Vice-Presidents 683, 691, 746, 748,
    827–8, 843, 859
reduced size 687, 689
Sections, members drawn from 691
session periods 690
single court, creation of 29
size 686–9
striking out 797
substitute judges 691
third-party intervention 792
urgent cases 690
witnesses 806
Chambers on admissibility and merits, decisions
    by 705–8
7 judge benches 707, 763
caseload, reduction of 782
Committees 707
distinction between admissibility and applications
    on merits 705–6
drafting 706
exhaustion of domestic remedies 707
final decisions 708
friendly settlements, proposal for 707
Grand Chamber 707
hearings 763
individual applications 707
inhuman or degrading treatment 707
interpretation 707–8
inter-State applications 707
judicial formations 691
jurisdiction 707
just satisfaction, proposals for 707
life, right to 707
manifestly ill-founded applications 705
procedural/investigative obligation 707
Rules of Court 707

single-judge formation 707
Charter of Fundamental Rights of the EU
abuse of rights, prohibition of 611–12
age 573, 583
candidate, right to stand as a 1012
collective expulsion of aliens 1075
data protection 382
death penalty 165, 1093, 1097
detention 183
disabilities, persons with 573, 583
discrimination 556, 573, 583, 1184
education, right to 988
effective remedy, right to an 547
elections, right to free 1012
European Parliament, elections to 1012
expulsion 165
fair trial, right to a 265–6, 272
freedom of assembly and association 484
freedom of expression 445
freedom of movement and migration 1053
genetic features 573
human dignity 66
lex mitior principle 350
liberty and security, right to 220–1
life, right to 119
limitation on use of restrictions 623
marital status 583
marry and found a family, right to 529, 536–7
ne bis in idem 1148
no punishment without law 330
peaceful enjoyment of possessions 960
political activity of aliens, restrictions on 606,
    609–10
private and family life, right to respect for 359
religion or belief, freedom to manifest 433
sexual orientation 537, 573
sources of international law 39
thought, conscience and religion, freedom of 414
torture 165
transgender persons 536, 583
Vienna Convention on the Law of Treaties 39
Charter of UN
advisory opinions 874, 878
common understanding and observance of human
    rights 69
discrimination 555–7, 575–6, 1177
exclusion of other means of dispute resolution 913
International Court of Justice 874
ratione personae jurisdiction 106–7
sex discrimination 555, 557, 575–6
war/armed conflict 602
chattel slavery 202
Chaumont, Charles 803–4, 818, 863, 909
Chechnya 155–7, 197, 899–900, 1065
children *see also* Convention on the Rights of the Child
    1989; education, right to
abduction 392–3, 1063
access 292–3

children (*cont.*)
  adoption 367, 407–8, 543, 573, 584, 826–7
  adoptive parents, age of 573, 584
  age of criminal responsibility 318–19
  age of majority 240
  American Convention on Human Rights 592
  best interests of the child 392–3
  biological parents, right to know identity of 376
  care, children in 392, 899
  circumcision 430
  criminal prosecutions 240–1
  custody disputes 392–3, 826–7, 1072
  detention 170, 584
  discrimination in education 569
  equality between spouses 1158
  freedom of assembly and association 496
  freedom of movement and migration 745,
    1060, 1063
  illegitimate children, discrimination against 390,
    538, 583, 820
  in camera hearings 827
  immigration legislation 392
  liberty and security, right to 240–1, 251
  lone parents 389
  margin of appreciation 393
  parents, relationship with 391–4
  paternity 390–1
  pre-trial detention 251
  prison, parents in 398
  privileges and immunities of children of judges 892
  religious discrimination in custody disputes 579–80
  removal of parental rights 394
  reunion 391
  sexual orientation and parental rights 584
  totalitarian states 370
  wishes and views of the child 392
chilling effects 373, 476, 500, 517, 747–8, 812–13
Church of England, ordination of women in 577
Churchill, Winston 862, 1011
Cingolani, Mario 360, 557
circumcision 430
citizenship 379, 404–5, 1057, 1072, 1082
civic obligations 216, 217, 218
civil and political rights *see also* International Covenant
    on Civil and Political Rights
  derogations 587
  elections, right to free 986
  freedom of assembly and association 483–5
  minorities 22
  peaceful enjoyment of possessions 986
civil rights and obligations 265–6, 270–6, 287–9, 345
civil servants *see* public sector/officials
Clemenceau, Georges 413
closed shops 64, 493–4, 506–8, 788–9
clothing and dress
  face coverings 376–7, 402, 405–6, 437, 439
  Islamic veil 173, 402, 405–6, 437, 439
  jewellery, wearing 439

nudity in public 377, 455
prison inmates, shaving heads of 376
private and family life, right to respect for 376–7,
    402, 405–6, 439
religion or belief, freedom to manifest 437, 439
turbans, wearing 439
Cocks, Seymour 166
cohabitees 538, 544, 1158–9
Cold War 1052–3
collective agreements 493, 524
collective bargaining 484, 494, 506–7, 524
collective enforcement
  aims and ideals of Council of Europe 73
  ECommHR 73
  ECtHR, establishment of 640
  education 957
  elections, right to free 957
  freedom of movement and migration 1046–7
  individual applications 735
  inter-State applications 725, 727
  peaceful enjoyment of possessions 957
  Preamble to ECHR 62, 64, 73–4
  subsidiarity 73–4
  Universal Declaration of Human Rights 73
collective expulsion of aliens 1068, 1070–1, 1075–80
  asylum seekers 1077–8
  boat, *refoulement* of migrants arriving by 1079–80,
    1083
  Charter of Fundamental Rights of the EU 1075
  collective expulsion, definition of 1077
  Committee of Experts 1076–9
  Consultative Assembly 1075–6
  declarations 1080
  drafting 1075–7
  effective remedy, right to an 1075
  European Convention on Establishment 1076
  extraterritorial jurisdiction 1079
  fair trial, right to a 1075
  Grand Chamber 1078–9
  High Commissioner for Refugees (UN) 1079
  interpretation 1075, 1077–80
  liberty and security, right to 1075
  limitation on use of restrictions 625
  national security 1076–7
  nationality 1076
  non-nationals 1075
  procedural guarantees 1076–8, 1130
  reservations 1080
  travaux préparatoires 1078–9
colonial clause *see* territorial application
colonies and overseas territories *see also* territorial
    application
  corporal punishment 1007
  Denmark 917
  derogations 596
  discrimination 562
  France 916, 921–2, 926–7, 1036, 1162
  Italy 920–1

Netherlands 324, 917, 1036, 1073–4, 1084, 1190, 1108, 1114, 1205
  obligation to respect human rights 84–5
  Preamble to ECHR 62
  succession to treaties 946
  United Kingdom
    corporal punishment 188–9, 1007
    Cyprus 9, 188, 596, 725, 917–18, 924
    derogations 596
    territorial application 916–28, 1036
colour, discrimination on grounds of 556, 558–61, 577, 580, 583
comity 100, 286, 891
Commission on Human Rights (UN) *see also under* individual main entries
Committee of Experts (CoE) *see also under* individual main entries
  adoption of ECHR 5–7, 8
  Committee of Ministers 5–6
  women, lack of participation of 5
Committee of Ministers (CoE) *see also under* individual main entries
  adoption of ECHR 4, 5–9, 167
  binding force and execution of judgments 864–8
  composition of Committee 905–6
  Conference of Senior Officials 905
  Council of Europe, Statute of 905–6
  execution of judgments, supervision of 797–8, 821–2, 864–7, 871, 872, 905
  Foreign Affairs Ministers of each State 906
  interpretation 852, 905–6
  powers 905–6
  suspension of States 906
Committees (three judge formation) *see also* competence of Committees
  admissibility criteria 689, 698, 699–703, 763, 779, 851
  Chambers on admissibility and merits, decisions by 707
  conduct of the examination 805
  full-time, sitting 690
  gender balance 665
  interpretation 844
  introduction of Committees 690
  President of the Section 690
  Sections 690
  single court, creation of 29
  single judges, competence of 698
  term of office 690
common heritage 69–70, 71
Commonwealth of Independent States (CIS) Convention on Human Rights 876, 878, 881–2, 885
communism 503–4, 612, 619, 958, 1052–3
compensation/reparations *see also* compensation for wrongful conviction; damages
  acquittals 306
  arrest 224, 257–8

  assessment 817–18, 821, 836–7
  binding force and execution of judgments 868, 970
  causal link 836
  effective remedy, right to an 552
  friendly settlements 817–18, 821
  HIV, contamination with 160
  hunting rights 973
  inquiries by the Secretary General 899
  interest 837
  just satisfaction 830, 832–9
  liberty and security, right to 224–6, 257–9
  moral damages 838
  ne bis in idem 1150
  non-pecuniary damages 838
  peaceful enjoyment of possessions 963–4
  pecuniary damages 837–8
  psychological harm 838
  Rules of Court 836
  terrorism 836–7
compensation for wrongful conviction 306, 1142–6
  amnesties 1145
  appeals discontinued for technical reasons, where 1144
  declarations 1146
  drafting 1142
  final decisions 1143
  Grand Chamber 1145
  International Covenant on Civil and Political Rights 1142, 1145
  interpretation 1142–6, 1164
  law and practice of state, according to 1145–6
  liberty and security, right to 110, 1143
  new or newly discovered facts showing miscarriage of justice 1144–5
  presumption of innocence 1142, 1164
  reservations 1146
  reversal of convictions or pardons 1144
  wrongful detention, damages for 1143
competence *see* competence of Committees; competence of single judges
competence of Committees 699–704
  3-judge committees 699, 700–2
  accelerated procedure 703
  admissibility 699–703
  caseload 699–700, 702
  consolidating the institutions and further reform 699–700, 701
  Consultative Assembly 700
  declarations 703–4
  drafting 700–1
  ECommHR 699, 700, 702
  exhaustion of domestic remedies 703
  filtering and processing applications 699
  Grand Chamber 702
  interpretation 701–3
  judicial function 700
  merits, ruling on the 700–3
  national judges 703

competence of Committees (*cont.*)
  new Court 700, 701
  Parliamentary Assembly 701
  plenary Commission, proposal for 700
  repetitive cases 700–2
  replacement of members 703
  Rules of Court 700
  simplified procedure 703
  single-judges, transfer of filtering role to 699, 700–2
  striking out 702
  Sub-Commission, proposal for 7-member 700
  well-established case law 702–3
competence of single judges 696–8
  admissibility 697–8, 699
  caseload 696–7
  Committees 698
  declarations 698
  drafting 697
  examination of the case 805
  filtering and processing applications 696
  final judgments 851
  function of single judge 697
  interpretation 697–8
  nationality 698
  pilot judgments 696–7
  repetitive cases 696
  statistics 696
  striking out 697
  success of single-judge procedure 696
conciliation 817–18
condemnation and disapproval 871
Condorelli, Luigi 978–9
Conference of Senior Officials (CoE) *see also under*
    individual main entries
  adoption of ECHR 7, 167–8
  Committee of Ministers 905
confidentiality
  abortion 383, 404–5
  access to documents 828–9
  data protection 383
  examination of the case 814
  freedom of expression 467, 471, 473
  friendly settlements 781, 820, 822–3
  journalists' sources, confidentiality of 459, 470
  legal representatives 748
  private life 383–4, 404–5
  professional secrecy 386
  terrorism 239
  without prejudice 822
confiscation 304, 378 *see also* expropriation;
    forfeiture
conflicts of jurisdiction 907–9
Conforti, Benedetto 646
Congress of Europe 1948 3, 6, 27
conscientious objections
  military service 204–5, 214–16, 433–4, 569, 848
  religious symbols 424
  tax, payment of 422

thought, conscience and religion, freedom of 414,
    422, 424, 433–4, 848
consolidating the institutions and further
    reforms 28–31
  admissibility 705–7, 759–60, 762, 785
  advisory opinions 876, 877, 882
  binding force and execution of judgments 864, 866
  caseload 28–30
  Chambers 690–1, 707
  Committees 690, 699–700, 701
  control mechanisms 29
  ECommHR 735
  ECtHR, establishment of 639
  entry into force 30
  ex officio or national judges 692–3
  examination of the case 804–5
  exhaustion of domestic remedies 759
  existing human rights, safeguards for 902
  expansion of Council of Europe 29
  expenditure on ECtHR 889
  expulsion of aliens, procedural safeguards relating
    to 1130
  final judgments 850–1
  freedom of movement and migration 1085–6
  friendly settlements 819–20
  Grand Chamber 688–9, 691–2, 710–12, 841,
    843–4, 846–7
  individual applications 723, 735
  inter-State applications 723, 725, 729
  judges
    criteria for office 649–51, 654–6
    dismissal 672
    election 660, 663
    ex officio or national 692–3
    formations 688–9
    number 644–6
    privileges and immunities 891–2
    terms of office 670–1
  jurisdiction 719, 720
  judgments 841
  jurisdiction 719, 720
  just satisfaction 833
  margin of appreciation 78–9
  merger of ECtHR and ECommHR 28–30
  merits, decisions on the 706
  Plenary Court 680, 682, 684–5
  Preamble to ECHR 58, 955, 1045
  privileges and immunities 891–2
  public hearings 825–6
  ratification 29
  ratione temporis jurisdiction 109
  reasons for judgments and decisions 858
  registry of ECtHR 675, 677
  Secretary-General, inquiries by 898
  single court, creation of 29–30
  striking out 797
  territorial application 917, 921, 928, 937–8
  third-party intervention 791

consular immunity 102
Consultative Assembly (CoE) *see also under* individual
    main entries
  adoption of ECHR 4, 5–8, 61
  Committees, competence of 700
  Parliamentary Assembly, change of name to 660
  political blocs 4
contents of rights 4, 6, 8
contractual obligations, failure to fulfil 1048–51
Convention on the Rights of the Child 1989
  adoption 394
  age of criminal responsibility 318
  child soldiers 941
  discrimination 556
  education, right to 987, 996–7
  freedom of movement and migration 1060
  pornography 941
  Vienna Convention on the Law of Treaties 38
convictions *see* compensation for wrongful conviction
cooperate, obligation to 812–14
copyright 480, 971
corporal punishment
  common heritage 70
  education 1007
  inhuman or degrading treatment 170, 180,
    188–9, 191
  private and family life, right to respect for 189
  reasonable chastisement 189
  religious and philosophical convictions of
    parents 189, 1002–4
  striking out 800
  territorial application 927–8
  whipping 188
corporations
  freedom of expression 741
  individual applications 736–7
  inhuman or degrading treatment 741
  legal personality 736
  lifting the corporate veil 736
  locus standi 736
  peaceful enjoyment of possessions 741, 969
  public corporations 737
  shareholders, interests of 741
  tax 1154
  victim status 741, 742
correspondence 400–1, 404
corruption 893, 1022, 1031–2
Costa, Jean-Paul 66, 682, 927
Council of Europe (CoE)
  adoption of ECHR 3–10
  aims and principles 65–6, 73, 416, 486, 576, 612
  cultural homogeneity 413
  discrimination 440, 556
  ECtHR distinguished from organs of CoE 641
  expansion 29
  expenditure on ECtHR 889, 890
  foundation 3, 59
  founding States 59

  Preparatory Commission 3–4
  Secretary General 897
  Statute 3, 69, 905–6
  treaty system 912
  Universal Declaration of Human Rights 3–4
Cremona, Jean 682
crime and family, extension of ECHR to
  adoption of International Covenant on Civil and
    Political Rights 18
  collective expulsion of aliens 1079
  Committee of Experts 18
  Consultative Assembly 1125
  declarations 1165
  denunciation 1164
  depositary functions 1170
  differences between ECHR and International
    Covenant on Civil and Political Rights 18
  drafting 1125
  entry into force of International Covenant on Civil
    and Political Rights 18, 1125
  entry into force 1168–9
  equality and non-discrimination 19
  exclusions 19
  Explanatory Report 19
  extension of rights in ECHR 18
  fair trial, right to a 265, 1165
  freedom of expression 468
  Grand Chamber 1164
  hate propaganda, prohibition of 19
  International Covenant on Civil and Political Rights,
    concordance with 18–19, 1125
  interpretation 1125, 1164–5
  jurisdiction 1164
  minorities, protection of 19
  'no one' formulation 169
  Parliamentary Assembly 18–19
  Preamble 1125
  private and family life, right to respect for 402
  public service, equal access to 19
  relationship to ECHR 1164–5
  reservations 1164–5
  restrictions/limitations 1164
  self-determination, right to 19
  Steering Committee for Human Rights 18–19
  Universal Declaration of Human Rights 1125
  victim status 745
  war propaganda, prohibition of 19
  wrongful convictions, right to compensation
    for 110
crimes against humanity 136, 202, 343–5,
  354–5, 1095
criminal offences *see also* appeal in criminal matters,
  right of; compensation for wrongful
  conviction; fair trial in criminal proceedings,
  right to; crime and family, extension of ECHR
  to; *ne bis in idem*; sexual assault; war crimes
  absence/presence of accused at trial 81, 316–17,
    1137, 1222–3

criminal offences (*cont.*)
advisory opinions 1222–3
arrest 221–4, 227, 234, 237–9, 243–6, 254, 257–9
attribution 128
bail 250–1, 253, 1058
binding force and execution of judgments 869
child pornography 941
corruption 893, 1022, 1031–2
crimes against humanity 136, 202, 343–5,
354–5, 1095
de minimis principle 784
defamation 476
discrimination 569–71
domestic violence 129
economic crimes 293
effective remedy, right to an 550–1
fair trial, right to a 869
former regimes, crimes committed under 128
freedom of assembly and association 496
freedom of expression 454, 470–1, 474–6
freedom of movement and migration 1057–9,
1061–2, 1063
general principles of international law 332, 336,
350, 351–5
grave breaches 128
homicide 127–9, 136, 342–3
homosexual activity 381, 408–9
honour and reputation, attacks on 385
independent and impartial tribunal 128
inhuman or degrading treatment 185, 192–4
investigations
effective 550–1
investigative duty 134–6
Islamic veil 173
juvenile offenders, exclusion of media from trial
of 480
legal representatives, proceedings against 747–8
liberty and security, right to 221–7, 235–40,
245–53, 261
life, right to 127–9, 134–6
medical malpractice 111, 128
metal cages, accused in 185
no punishment without law 336–7, 339–41, 343–5
organised crime 125, 209–10, 230, 239, 281,
398, 1058
preventive measures 129
private life 385
public hearings 289
reasons for judgments 857
reporting restrictions 460, 480
self-defence 148–9
sophisticated crimes 293
standard of proof 569–70
subsidiarity 78
surveillance 386–7
transnational crimes 344
victim status 743
criteria for judicial office 647–56

advertising 652, 654
age limits 584, 650, 654–5
caseload 648–9
Committee of Experts 648
Committee of Ministers 651–4
consolidating the institutions and further
reform 649–51, 654–5
Consultative Assembly 648
drafting 648–50
ECommHR 648–9
election 648, 650–1, 653, 655
experience in field of human rights 654
high moral character 647–8, 651–2
incompatible offices, holding 648, 656
independence and impartiality 647–9, 656
individual capacity, sitting in 656
International Court of Justice 648, 651, 655
interpretation 651–6
inter-State applications 647
jurisconsults 647–8, 651–2
languages, fluency in official 652–4
legal expertise/knowledge 647–8, 651–2
nationality 647–8
oaths of office 656
Parliamentary Assembly 649, 651, 653–5
Permanent Court of Arbitration 647
Permanent Court of International Justice, Statute
of 647
political figures 647
qualifications 647–8, 651–2
revision of ECHR 649–51
term of office 650
United Kingdom 652, 654
Croatia
obscene speech 456
peaceful enjoyment of possessions 973
public hearings 323
religious institutions to provide marriage services,
right of 1181–2, 1186
rent control 980
reservations 323
Roma, discrimination against 1004
war crimes 1150, 1155
culture
adoption 394
discrimination 562, 566, 575
diversity 582, 1025
education, right to 998
elections, right to free 1025
expropriation 976–7
freedom of assembly and association 500, 503
freedom of expression 451, 472
heritage 500, 472
homogeneity 413
identity 503
information, public exchange of 451
marry and found a family, right to 542–4
minorities 12–13, 22

custodial sentences *see* imprisonment for debt,
    prohibition of
customary international law
    derogations 593
    erga omnes obligations 65, 725–6
    expropriation 977–8
    jus cogens 44, 164, 179–80, 328, 593
    languages 46
    law, definition of 337
    no punishment without law 344
    ratione materiae jurisdiction 94
    source of international law, as 38, 40–3, 352
    territorial application 924
    torture 164
    truth, right to 139
    universal jurisdiction 102
    Vienna Convention on the Law of Treaties 38,
        40–4, 46
    war/armed conflict 602
Cyprus *see also* Cyprus, Turkish occupation of
        Northern
    age of criminal responsibility 318
    buffer zone 103–4
    corporal punishment 188
    death penalty and right to life 140
    exclusion of other means of dispute resolution 914
    expulsion 1072
    freedom of assembly and association 496, 510
    friendly settlements 820
    independent and impartial tribunals 295, 696
    individual applications 775
    language 999
    military service 215
    no punishment without law 336–7, 347
    on-site visits 808–9
    peaceful enjoyment of possessions 867, 973
    prostitution 207
    reservations 1078
    revision of judgments 854
    Sovereign Base Areas 924, 928
    state of emergency 1108
    territorial application 924
    trafficking 207
    United Kingdom
        colonies and overseas territories 9, 188, 596,
            725, 917–18, 924
        death penalty 140
        derogations 596
        emergency powers 188, 596
        independence 9, 725
        Sovereign Base Areas 924, 928
    Universal Periodic Review 915
    use of lethal force 150–1, 153
Cyprus, Turkish occupation of Northern
    compensation 68, 834
    curfews 808
    declarations 1080
    derogations 602–3

disappearances 229, 775, 867, 871
    education 999
    effective control 104
    examination of the case 808
    exhaustion of domestic remedies 769
    freedom of assembly and association 510
    freedom of movement and migration 496
    judges, recusal of 695
    Karpas Greek-Cypriot population 564, 835, 838
    life, right to 150–1, 153, 1072
    marital status 820
    mass expulsions 400, 1072
    other means of dispute resolution, exclusion
        of 914–15
    property, access to 727, 854, 867, 973
    Security Council (UN), mechanisms under 914
    State agents, use of lethal force by 150–1, 153
    territorial application 938
Czech Republic
    Czechoslovakia, break up of 672, 950
    judges, term of office of 672
    military service 215, 324–5
    Roma, discrimination against 1004
    succession to treaties 950

damages 68, 276, 839, 1139 *see also* compensation/
        reparations
data protection 374, 382–4
De Gaetano, Vincent A 424
de la Vallée-Poussin, Etienne 918
De Meyer, Jan 143, 541, 544
de minimis rule 762, 781–5
de Schutter, Olivier 1187
de Visscher, Charles 5
de Visscher, Fernand 1068
death and dying *see also* death penalty; life, right to
    burial 382
    homicide 127–9, 136, 342–3
    next-of-kin applications 738–40, 798
    private life 382, 406
    striking out 798
    suicide 132–3, 172, 382
    use of lethal force 117, 122–3, 125, 127, 135,
        146–57
    victims, dead persons as 738–9, 742
death penalty 1098–101 *see also* death penalty and
        right to life; death penalty in time of war
    abolition in all circumstances 14–17, 1091–2, 1094,
        1097–101, 1101, 1110, 1115, 1197–210
    accession 1118
    American Convention on Human Rights 15,
        1197, 1200
    apostasy, advocating death penalty for 619
    Charter of Fundamental Rights of the EU 1093,
        1097
    Committee of Experts 17, 1198, 1201
    Committee of Ministers 15–17, 1093–4, 1113,
        1117–18, 1121, 1198, 1199

death penalty (*cont.*)
  Consultative Assembly 15
  continuing violations 110
  crimes against humanity 1095
  custom, States which are abolitionist by 1095
  death row phenomenon 190–1
  declarations 1111–12, 1205–6
  denunciations 1116, 1119
  depositary functions 1121–2, 1210
  derogations 592, 594, 1100, 1203
  drafting 1093–4, 1098, 1110–15, 1117, 1120–1,
    1198, 1201
  ECommHR 1099
  entry into force 16, 17, 1099, 1120, 1209
  EU law 1092
  European Committee on Crime Problems 1093
  evolution that has occurred 1094–5
  expulsion 165, 1093, 1099–101, 1128
  extraterritoriality 1099
  fully abolitionist States, list of 1095
  inhuman or degrading treatment 11, 15, 16, 186–7,
    190–1, 1094, 1199
  International Covenant on Civil and Political
    Rights 1092, 1094, 1097, 1197
  interpretation 47, 49, 1094–101, 1110–22,
    1198–200, 1201
  life imprisonment, replacement with 349–50
  Model Final Clauses 1113–14, 1117–18, 1121,
    1206, 1208, 1210
  ne bis in idem 1110
  'no one' formulation 169
  Parliamentary Assembly 15–16, 1116, 1118
  peacetime, abolition in 1093–4
  Plenary Court 1091–2
  preamble to protocols 1197–200
  procedural safeguards 1128
  ratione loci jurisdiction 1114
  ratione temporis jurisdiction 110
  relationship of protocols to ECHR 1115–16, 1207
  reservations 1111–12, 1204
  restrictions 1197, 1198, 1100–22, 1199–200
  retentionist States 1095–6
  right not to be subjected to death penalty 1099–101
  Secretary-General 1112, 1121
  signatories and ratification 16–17, 1094, 1099,
    1101, 1117–20, 1208
  summary execution, justification of 619
  tendency in favour of abolition, general 1097
  territorial application 1113–14, 1205–6
  terrorism 1095–6
  third-party intervention 794
  torture 16
  Universal Periodic Review 1118
  Vienna Convention on the Law of Treaties 1113,
    1117–18, 1121
  war crimes 1094–5
death penalty and right to life 11, 14–17
  American Convention on Human Rights 140–1

Committee of Experts 120, 140, 145–6
Council of Europe 140–1, 144–6
court, sentence pronounced by the 141
death row phenomenon 142–3
derogations 592, 594
diplomatic assurances 145–6
ECommHR 141–2
ECtHR 142–6
extradition, deportation, or expulsion and
  refoulement 127, 140–6
extraterritoriality 140
fair trial, right to a 141, 144
human dignity 1198–9
independent and impartial tribunal 141
inhuman or degrading treatment 47, 142–5,
  186–7, 190–1, 434
International Covenant on Civil and Political
  Rights 140–1, 145
interpretation 117, 122, 143
limitation on use of restrictions 625
Preamble 1091–2, 1094
pre-emption, doctrine of 144
provided for by law, sentence must be 141, 143
retrospectivity 49
sham trials 337
Soering case 141–6
State practice 37, 144
Vienna Convention on the Law of Treaties 37
wartime exception 1105, 1199
death penalty in time of war 16–17, 1098, 1103–9
  abolitionist by law States 1103
  abolitionist by law for ordinary crimes only
    States 1103
  American Convention on Human Rights 1104, 1201
  armed conflict, use of term international 1104
  Committee of Ministers 1104, 1105
  derogations 594, 601, 1100, 1104, 1106, 1108
  drafting 1104
  formal declarations of war 1106
  fully abolitionist States 1103
  Geneva Conventions 1104, 1106
  in time of war, meaning of 1105–6
  International Covenant on Civil and Political
    Rights 1103–4, 1106–7, 1201
  interpretation 1104–9
  life, right to 1105, 1199
  military death penalty 1106, 1108, 1201
  non-international armed conflict 1106
  Organization of American States 1104
  prescribed by law, restrictions which are 1105, 1107
  ratione materiae jurisdiction 1106
  relationship of protocols to ECHR 1116, 1207
  reservations 1108–9, 1112
  rule of law 1107
  Secretary-General, notification of 897, 1107–8
  summary executions against non-combatants 354
  threat of war 17, 1099, 1103–7, 1112, 1116, 1197,
    1199, 1201, 1203

debts *see also* imprisonment for debt, prohibition of
  debt bondage 202
  freedom of movement and migration 1063–4
  judgment debts 971
  travel bans to enforce private debts 1063–4
Decaux, Emmanuel 609, 904, 913
declarations *see also under* individual main entries
  admissibility criteria 698, 786
  Committees, competence of 703–4
  de facto reservations 1009
  de minimis principle 785
  exhaustion of domestic remedies 769
  filtering and processing applications 703–4
  freedom of movement and migration 1057, 1065–6
  interpretive declarations 109, 933, 937, 1111–12
  reservations 932–4, 936–9, 1009
  striking out 799–800
  territorial application 943
  unilateral declarations 799–800, 822, 823
  withdrawal 943
Dedov, Dmitry 45
defamation 472, 476–8, 479
defence, adequate time and facilities for 46,
    308–10, 311
Dehousse, Fernand 55, 84, 119, 165, 331, 445,
    484–5, 557, 960
delay
  administrative practices 766
  advisory opinions 1220, 1224
  evidence 813–14
  fair trial, right to a 109
  inter-State applications 766
  languages 46
  liberty and security, right to 234
  ratione temporis jurisdiction 109
  reasonable time, right to trial within a 287,
    291–3, 551
democracy *see also* European Commission for
    Democracy through Law (Venice
    Commission)
  abuse of rights, prohibition of 612–13, 616, 618
  education, right to 993
  elections, right to free 1011–18, 1021, 1023, 1026
  freedom of assembly and association 483, 490–1,
    495, 497, 499–500, 503–4, 513–15
  freedom of expression 445–6, 451–2, 458, 460,
    463, 465
  limitation on use of restrictions 627
  militant democracy 445, 519–21
  political democracy 68–9
  pressing social needs, restrictions for 515
  reservations 1031
  subsidiarity 78
  threats to democracy 515
  totalitarian movements 519–20
  trade unions 515
demonstrations/protests 492–8
  abortion 493

  authorization 492, 495–7
  chilling effect 517
  counter-demonstrations 494–5
  freedom of assembly and association 492–8,
    514–18, 742
  freedom of movement and migration 1058–9
  incitement to violence 495–6, 518
  location 497–8, 517
  margin of appreciation 517–18
  necessary in a democratic society, restrictions
    which are 514
  peaceful assembly 495–6
  police, obstruction of 1058–9
  positive obligations 494, 498
  prior notification 497–8
  proportionality 516–17
  punishment for presence 514
  sentencing 475–6
  suicide 132
  tolerance 514
  victim status 742
denaturalization 1069–70
denialism 479–80, 615, 619
Denmark
  colonies 917
  Constitution 358
  death penalty 1205–6
  declarations 1165, 1205
  expulsion 397
  Faroe Islands 1140, 1162, 1165, 1205–6
  Greenland 1205
  individual applications 1165
  police officers in Turkey, training of 820
  private and family life, right to respect for 358
  reservations 1140
  South Schleswig 558
  territorial application 1162, 1205–6
denunciations 941–3
  advisory opinions 1227
  Child Soldiers Protocol to Convention on Rights
    of the Child 941
  colonial clause 942
  Committee of Ministers 942–3
  derogations 942
  Disabilities Convention 941
  drafting 942
  International Covenant on Civil and Political
    Rights 941
  interpretation 942–3
  Pornography Protocol to Convention on Rights of
    the Child 941
  restrictions/limitations 942
  Secretary-General, notification of 897
  territorial application, withdrawal of declarations
    of 943
  time limits 942
deportation
  Charter of Fundamental Rights of the EU 165

deportation (*cont.*)
  criminal activity, due to 395–6
  death penalty and right to life 127, 140–6
  education, right to 999
  fair trial, right to a 275, 282
  family life 394–8, 405
  liberty and security, right to 233–4,
    243–5, 259–60
  life, right to 127, 140–6
  religion or belief, freedom to manifest 434–5
  torture 179
  victim status 740–1, 743, 744–5
depositary
  accession, instruments of 85
  advisory opinions 1232
  declarations 85, 603, 1114, 1132–3
  functions 1121–2, 1170, 1194, 1210, 1232
  Model Final Clauses 1210
  public hearings 825–7
  reservations 931–4, 1007, 1065, 1073
  Secretary-General 897, 950
  signature and ratification 944–51, 1039–41,
    1087–8, 1117–19, 1166–7, 1192, 1208, 1228
deprivation of liberty *see* detention/deprivation of
  liberty
derogation in time of emergency 587–604
  Alternative A and A/2 590
  Alternative B and B/2 590
  American Convention on Human Rights 587,
    592, 594
  civil and political rights, treaties on 587
  Committee of Experts 589–90
  Committee of Ministers 589–91
  Conference of Senior Officials 590
  Consultative Assembly 588–91
  customary international law 593
  death penalty 592, 594, 1104, 1106, 1108, 1203
  declarations 604
  denunciations 942
  detention 588
  discrimination 598, 600
  domestic scrutiny, requirement for 593–4
  drafting 588–92, 595
  European Social Charter 587–8, 594, 1106
  executive 594
  freedom of assembly 599
  freedom of movement and migration 591–2, 599
  future risks 595
  general limitation clauses 589
  hierarchy of rights 592–3
  High Contracting Party 591
  inhuman or degrading treatment 592
  International Covenant on Civil and Political
    Rights 587, 592–6, 599–601, 603–4,
    1051, 1155
  international humanitarian law 588, 601
  international law, consistency with other obligations
    under 600–1

  interpretation 592–604
  jus cogens 593
  liberty and security, right to 588, 600
  life, right to 153–6, 592
  limitation on use of restrictions 625
  margin of appreciation 596, 599
  ne bis in idem 952
  no punishment without law 592–3, 600
  non-derogable rights 592–3, 598–9
  notification 596–8, 602–4
  Parliamentary Assembly 588
  parliamentary scrutiny 593–4
  practice 596–8
  proclamations 600–1, 603
  proportionality 594, 599, 602
  public safety, health, and order 595, 603
  reservations 593, 604
  restrictions/limitations 598–602
  rule of law 600
  safeguards for existing human rights 902
  Secretary General, notification of 602–4
  Security Council (UN) 601
  slavery and forced labour 592
  strictly required by the exigencies of the situation,
    meaning of 599–600
  subsidiarity 77
  terrorism 588, 595, 597
  thought, conscience and religion, freedom of 593
  time of war or other emergency, meaning of 594–6
  torture 592–3
  Universal Declaration of Human Rights 588–90
  war/armed conflict 153–6, 588–9, 592,
    594–6, 601–2
detention/deprivation of liberty 11, 24–5 *see also* life
    imprisonment; prisoners
  appeal in criminal matters, right of 1136
  Charter of Fundamental Rights of the EU 183
  children 170
  conditions 173, 180–2, 184–6
  damages for wrongful detention 1143
  derogations 588
  discrimination 197, 584
  educational purposes, for 584
  extradition 829
  extraordinary rendition 96, 145, 793, 809–10, 827,
    836–7, 899–901
  freedom of movement and migration 1056–7
  imprisonment for debt, prohibition of 1049–51
  inquiries by the Secretary General 899–900
  inhuman or degrading treatment 169–70, 173–4,
    180–6, 197
  international criminal tribunals 98
  life, right to 123, 133–4, 136
  medical care 133–4, 174, 183, 185–6
  precautions 133
  preventive detention 348
  proportionality 182–3
  racial discrimination 197

rape 175–6
restraints 185
slavery and forced labour 205, 213–14
social and sensory isolation 173–4, 186
terrorists 598, 836–7
torture 175–6
visits 165
war/armed conflict 154
Dickins, Charles 1048
Diderot, Denis 444
diplomatic assurances 145–6, 195–6, 1100
diplomats
    candidate in elections, right to stand as a 1030
    diplomatic protection 105, 725–6, 731,
        792, 834–5
    extraterritoriality 105
    immunity 100, 102, 478
    life, right to 100
disabilities, persons with
    denunciations 941
    Disabilities Convention 556, 583, 941
    discrimination 573, 575, 583, 941, 1184
    military service 380
    Parliamentary Assembly 583
    third-party intervention 794–5
disappearances
    accountability 137, 870
    crimes against humanity 136
    death, presumption of 811
    effective investigations 870
    Enforced Disappearances Convention 136–7, 1128
    evidence 811
    expulsion of aliens, procedural safeguards for 1128
    extra-judicial execution 136
    inhuman or degrading treatment 137, 171, 193
    just satisfaction 871
    liberty and security, right to 229
    life, right to 123, 126, 136–7
    ratione temporis jurisdiction 109–10
    victim status 739–40
    Working Group on Enforced and Involuntary
        Disappearances 778
disciplinary measures
    education, right to 998, 1003–4
    fair trial, right to 278–9, 282–3
    legal representatives, proceedings against 747–8
    liberty and security, right to 228, 235, 260–1
    military 260–1, 278, 324–5
    presumption of innocence 305
    prisoners 228, 1152
    religion 1003–4
    same criminal charge, arising out of 305
disclosure
    fair trial in criminal proceedings, right to 310
    medical records 383
discontinuance 281, 286, 292, 299, 303, 305–7,
        797–8, 819
discretionary life sentences 256

discrimination 19–21, 555–85 *see also* racial
        discrimination; sex discrimination/gender
        equality
    abuse of rights, prohibition of 618
    admissibility 563
    adoption 408
    affirmative action 566–8, 1175–6, 1187
    age 556, 573, 575, 583–4, 1184
    aliens 560
    arrest 259
    autonomous nature 563
    balancing exercise 565
    birth or other status 558–61, 574, 582–4
    candidate in elections, right to stand for 1181
    caseload 1180
    Charter of Fundamental Rights of the EU 165, 556,
        573, 583, 1184
    Charter of UN 555–7, 1177
    civic obligations 217
    colonies 562, 921
    colour 556, 558–61, 577, 583
    Committee of Experts 20, 559–60, 1174–5
    Committee of Ministers 20–1, 559, 562, 1177,
        1179–80
    Consultative Assembly 19, 558–9, 575
    Convention on the Rights of the Child 556
    crime and family, extension of ECHR to 19
    culture 562, 566, 575
    customs 562
    declarations 1190
    definition 564–8
    derogations 598, 600
    detention 259–60, 584
    disability 556, 575, 583, 1184
    drafting 557–62, 575–6, 582–3, 1173–4, 1177,
        1179–80
    ECommHR 1182
    education, right to 1004–6
    effective remedy, right to an 546, 552–3
    ejusdem generis interpretation 572
    elections, right to free 1031
    employment 20
    enjoyment of any right set forth by law 1181–2
    entry into force 21, 1193
    equal pay 555
    equal protection of the law 1174–5, 1180–1
    equality before the law 19–21, 555, 558, 1174–5,
        1177, 1180–1
    ethnic groups 565–6, 574–5
    European Social Charter 556
    evidence 811
    expropriation 1182–3
    extreme forms 563–4
    fair trial, right to a 269, 321–3
    freedom of assembly and association 511, 512,
        517, 523–5
    freedom of expression 466, 467, 478, 479–81
    freedom of movement and migration 1065

discrimination (*cont.*)
  general prohibition 1177–87
  genetic features 1184
  grounds 572–84
  hierarchy between grounds 574, 1185
  hunting rights 982
  identity 381
  illegitimate children 390, 538, 583, 820
  incitement 555
  indirect discrimination 439–40, 568–9, 572
  inhuman or degrading treatment 177, 192–3,
      196–8, 563–4, 1178
  intention 566
  International Covenant on Civil and Political
      Rights 21, 556, 600, 1179–80, 1185
  international law 1181
  interpretation 556, 562–84, 1173–6, 1180–7
  intolerance, declaration on 20
  judges, election of 661
  jus cogens 44
  justification 564–6
  language 555–6, 558–61, 579, 583, 600
  legitimate aim/purpose, restrictions for a 564, 575
  less favourable treatment 565–6
  liberty and security, right to 259–60
  life, right to 159–60
  margin of appreciation 480, 567
  marriage ceremonies 562–3
  marry and found a family, right to 528, 531–2,
      537, 543–4
  media 480–1
  minorities 525, 556, 558–62, 572–3, 577, 580–2,
      1184
  Model Final Clauses 1189–90, 1192–3
  national origins 555–6, 558–62, 573, 580–3
  national security 525
  nationality 407, 556, 574, 581, 600
  natural rights 557
  'no one' formulation 169
  no punishment without law 355–6
  non-discrimination and equality clauses in treaties
      and conventions 556
  objectivity 564–6
  Parliamentary Assembly 20–1, 1180–7
  peaceful enjoyment of possessions 981–2
  pensions 982
  personal features 565, 572–3
  pluralism 575, 580
  political or other opinions 555–61, 580, 583
  political parties 525
  positive discrimination 566–8, 1175–6, 1187
  positive obligations 1176, 1180, 1186–7
  preamble to protocols 1173–6
  private and family life, right to respect for 375–6,
      407–8, 556, 1178
  procedural/investigative obligation 160
  prohibited grounds, definition of 1184–5
  proof of discrimination 569–72
  property 555–6, 558–60, 573–4, 582–3
  proportionality 565–6, 574–5, 600, 1176
  public authorities 1180, 1185–6
  ratification 21, 1190
  reasonable accommodation 440
  recognition before the law 1175
  relationship of protocols to ECHR 1191
  religion 428, 555–63, 579–80, 583, 600,
      1181–2, 1186
    identity cards 428
    inhuman or degrading treatment 196–7
    marriage services, right of institutions to
        provide 1181–2, 1186
    thought, conscience and religion, freedom
        of 440–1
  reservations 584–5, 933–4
  sentencing 573
  sexual orientation 381, 408, 438–9, 525, 556,
      573–4, 584, 1179, 1184–5
  signature and ratification 1192
  slavery and forced labour 217
  social origins 555–6, 559–61, 580–1, 583, 600
  social security 981–2
  special measures 566–8, 1175–6
  statistics on breach 1178
  subsidiary provision, as 563
  substantive provisions, no requirement for
      breach of 563
  tax 982
  territorial application 921, 1177, 1189–90
  torture 177
  trade unions 508, 524–5
  transgender persons 535–7, 544, 583
  travaux préparatoires 1177–8
  Universal Declaration of Human Rights 555–8,
      562, 572, 1174–5, 1177–9, 1184
  victims 743
  without discrimination, definition of 1182–4
  witnesses, compellability of spouses as 538, 544
diseases, detention of persons with infectious 241
dismissal of judges 668, 670, 672
disqualification orders 1152
dissenting opinions 781–2, 857–9, 887, 1224
documents
  access to documents 825–9
  evidence 807, 812–14
domestic courts *see* national courts
domestic laws *see* national laws
domestic remedies *see* exhaustion of domestic remedies
domestic violence 129, 160, 192, 198, 385, 576–7
Dominedo, Francesco 862
double jeopardy *see* ne bis in idem
Downing, HJ 532–3, 591, 614, 669
Dowson, Oscar 416, 487, 548, 613, 1048–9
drafting 4–8 *see also under* individual main entries
  Committee of Ministers 905
  Committees, competence of 700–1
  contents of rights 6

women, lack of participation of 5, 576
dress *see* clothing and dress
driving offences 283, 299–300, 783, 1153
drugs 299, 344
drunks/alcoholics, detention of 222–3, 241–2
due diligence 771
Dugard, John 179

Eastern Europe *see* Central and Eastern Europe
ECommHR
   admissibility 632
   authorization of access to ECtHR 732
   Committee of Ministers 632
   establishment 631
   individual applications 636
   investigatory function 634
   merger, proposal for 28–30, 632, 639
   organs of the Council of Europe, distinguishing
      Commission from 641
   petition, right to 634
   referrals 706
   merger, proposal for 632, 649
   referrals to 706
   single Court, replacement by 632–3
   workload 633
economic crimes 293
economic, social, and cultural rights *see also*
      International Covenant on Economic, Social,
      and Cultural Rights
   adoption of ECHR 4, 6
   education 23, 986–7, 995
   exclusion 1, 4, 23, 63, 499
   free employment services, access to 23
   freedom of assembly and association 499
   individual applications 23
   paid activity, right to freely choose or to
      accept a 23
   Preamble to ECHR 63
   Social Charter, transfer of rights from 23
   social security scheme, right to be affiliated to a 23
   standard of living in event of involuntary
      unemployment 23
   trade union rights 23
   vocational guidance or training 23
ECtHR *see* European Court of Human Rights
Edberg, Rolf 557
education
   absolute, as not being 996
   access to educational institutions, right of 997
   adoption of ECHR 4, 8
   bullying 370
   Charter of Fundamental Rights of the EU 988
   civil and political rights 986
   collective enforcement 957
   Committee of Experts 12, 955–6, 989–92, 994,
      1037–40
   Committee of Ministers 12, 986, 989–90, 993–4,
      998, 1038, 1040

Consultative Assembly 986, 989–94, 1038, 1040
content of education 987
continuing training, access to 988
Convention on the Elimination of All Forms of
      Discrimination against Women 987
corporal punishment 1002, 1003–4
Convention on the Rights of the Child 987, 996–7
crucifixes in classrooms 433, 1003
culture 998
declarations 1006–9, 1037
democracy 993
denunciations 1037, 1038
deportation 999
disciplinary measures 998, 1003–4
discrimination 1004–6
drafting 11–12, 955–6, 986, 988–95, 1037–40
economic, social and cultural rights 23, 986–7, 995
elementary education 996–7
entry into force 12
exceptions 996
expulsion 998
family rights 988–9
fees 1005–6
foreseeability 998–9
gender roles and stereotypes, elimination of 987
general principles of international law 45
General Assembly (UN) 987
grants 994
headscarf bans 437
home schooling 1002, 1006
indoctrination 1003
International Convention on the Elimination of All
      Forms of Racial Discrimination 987
International Covenant on Economic, Social and
      Cultural Rights 987, 997
interpretation 955–7, 995–1006, 1038, 1040–1
language 579, 992, 998–1000
margin of appreciation 1003, 1005
minorities 13, 998, 999
negative formulation 992–3, 996
organization by government 991
parents, rights of 23, 988–91
political formulation 992
positive statements of rights 992–3
Preamble to ECHR 955
Preamble to Protocol 955–7
primary education 997
prisoners, rights of 998–9
private education 986, 992, 994, 1002
private life 379–80
professional accreditation 997–8
proportionality 998–9, 1005
quotas 998
racial discrimination 1004
religion or belief, freedom to manifest 428, 433
religious and philosophical convictions of parents,
      respect for 23, 380, 419, 433, 986, 989–95,
      1000–9

education (*cont.*)
    religious education, opting out of 580
    reservations 1006–9, 1037
    restrictions/limitations 986, 995, 998–9
    resources 998, 1005–6
    right to education 11–12, 986–1009
    secondary education 997–8
    sex education 1003
    signature and ratification 1039–41
    subsidies from government 991
    suspension 998, 1004
    tertiary education 997–8
    textbooks and school programmes, revision of
        stereotyping in 987
    thought, conscience and religion,
        freedom of 1001
    totalitarian regimes 989, 991, 993
    travaux préparatoires 997
    UNESCO Convention against Discrimination in
        Education 987
    Universal Declaration of Human Rights 4, 956–7,
        986–8, 995–7
    universal public education 986
    universities 437, 997–8, 1005
    vocational training, access to 988, 998
effective remedy, right to an 546–54
    access to a court 551
    Alternative A and A/2 549
    Alternative B and B/2 549
    appeal in criminal matters, right of 1136
    arguable claim standard 551–2
    Charter of Fundamental Rights of the EU 547
    collective expulsion of aliens 1075
    Committee of Experts 547–9
    Committee of Ministers 550
    compensation 552
    Conference of Senior Officials 550
    Consultative Assembly 547, 550
    core obligation, as 546
    criminal investigations 550–1
    discrimination 546, 552–3
    drafting 547–50
    European Movement, International Council of
        the 547
    exhaustion of domestic remedies 551, 765–6
    expulsion 740–1, 1126, 1128
    individual applications 731
    international bill of rights 546
    International Covenant on Civil and Political
        Rights 546
    interpretation 550–2
    national courts 550
    Preamble 551
    racial discrimination 571
    reasonable time, right to trial within a 551
    reservations 554
    subsidiarity 76
    Universal Declaration of Human Rights 546–9

effectiveness, principle of
    Committee of Ministers 50
    ECommHR 49–50
    liberal interpretation 49–50
Eissen, Marc-André 20
election of judges 658–66
    absolute majorities 663
    accountability 661
    Advisory Panel of Experts 664
    balance and division of powers 660
    campaigning and bartering 658
    casual vacancies 659–60
    Committee of Legal Experts 659
    Committee of Ministers 658–9, 663–5
    Conference of Senior Officials 659
    Consultative Assembly 658–60
    criteria for office 648, 650–1, 653, 655
    discrimination 661
    drafting 658–60
    ECommHR 648
    gender balance 660, 662–6
    General Assembly (UN) 658
    high moral character 662
    independence and impartiality 658
    interpretation 660–6
    interviews 663
    nationality 659
    new court 661
    nomination of candidates 659–65
    Parliamentary Assembly 660–6
    Plenary Court 680
    politicised processes 662
    procedure 660–4
    publication of results 663
    qualifications 662, 664–5
    quality 658
    ranking of candidates 662
    re-election 669–72
    rejection of lists 661, 665
    relative majorities 663
    rule of law 661
    Security Council (UN) resolutions 658
    State Parties, one judge for each of the 658
    Sub-Committee on the Election of Judges to the
        ECHR 663
    suitability 664
    transparency 661
    withdrawal of candidates 663
elections *see* election of judges; elections, right to free
elections, right to free 11–12, 1011–31 *see also*
        candidate in elections, right to stand as a
    active aspects 1026, 1029
    adoption of ECHR 8
    Charter of Fundamental Rights of the EU 1012
    civil and political rights 986
    collective enforcement 957
    Committee of Experts 12, 955–7, 1014–17, 1037–40
    Committee of Ministers 12, 1014–18, 1038–40

Conference of Senior Officials 1015
conditions 1012, 1015–18, 1025
constitutional structure of States 1020
Consultative Assembly 11, 1013–18, 1038, 1040
cultural diversity 1025
democracy 68, 1011–18, 1021, 1023, 1026
denunciations 1037, 1038
discrimination 1031, 1181
drafting 11–12, 955–6, 1012–18, 1037–40
ECommHR 1019–20, 1023
electoral machinery 1014, 1018
entry into force 12, 1039–40
European Parliament 1012, 1021
fair trial, right to a 274
financing campaigns 1022
freedom of assembly and association 499, 515, 518,
    1011, 1017
freedom of expression 1011, 1016–20, 1025, 1030
funding of parties 1022
general principles of international law 45
Grand Chamber 1012, 1023, 1025, 1038
implied limitations 1023–6
independence and impartiality 1020
independent candidates 1023
indirect elections 1020
individual applications 1018
institutional approach 1014–15, 1019
International Covenant on Civil and Political
    Rights 1012, 1019
interpretation 955–7, 1016–31, 1038, 1040–1
jurisdiction, declarations on 1037
lawfulness of restrictions 1024
legitimate aim/purpose, restrictions for a 1023–4
linguistic minorities 1023–4
loyalty to State, principle of 1023
margin of appreciation 1023–5
media, access to the 1022, 1023
necessity 1024
no punishment without law 1025
non-elected chambers, parliaments with 1017–18,
    1020
organization of elections 1014, 1018, 1019–23
passive aspects 1026, 1029
pluralism 1018–20, 1022
political activity of aliens, restrictions on 606,
    608, 609–10
political parties
    corruption 1022
    freedom of assembly and association 499,
        515, 518
    funding 1022
    media, access to 1023
    membership of 1018
    national minorities 515, 518
    proportionality 1024
positive obligations 1026
Preamble to ECHR 63, 955
Preamble to Protocol No. 1 955–7

presidential/head of state elections 1021–2
pressing social need 1024
prisoners 915, 1023, 1028–9
procedural fairness 1025
proportional representation 1016–17, 1022, 1025
proportionality 1024
ratifications 12, 1040–1
reasonable intervals, at 1014–15, 1020
referendums 1021
regional assemblies 1020–1
regulation of elections 1022–3
relationship of protocols to ECHR 1037–8
reservations 1031–2, 1037
restrictions/limitations 1014, 1018, 1023–6
rule of law 956, 1011–12, 1023–4
secret ballots 1012–20
signature and ratification 1039–41
simple majority systems 1025
subjective rights 1018–19, 1023
systems of elections 1025
transparency 1020
travaux préparatoires 956, 1018
Universal Declaration of Human Rights 11, 956–7,
    1012, 1014
universal suffrage 1011–15, 1019, 1021, 1026
victims 1018
vote, right to 915, 1026–9
electronic communications 400, 457, 684, 855
electronic publication of judgments 855
emergencies *see also* derogation in time of emergency
    emergency services 132–4, 216, 217
    firearms by State agents, use of 130–1
    medical care and right to life 133–4
    rescue operations 102
    slavery and forced labour, compulsory work
        as 216, 217
employment *see also* slavery and forced labour
    conscientious objections 433
    discrimination 20, 322, 558, 584–5
    dismissal 432–3
    email, Internet and telephone use, monitoring 387
    Employment Equality Directive 583
    European Social Charter 432
    free employment services, access to 23
    freedom of expression 464–5
    loyalty, duty of 465
    Migrant Workers Convention 1060
    nationality discrimination 584–5
    paid activity, right to freely choose or to accept a 23
    political activities 375
    private life 374–5, 377, 387
    public employees 274, 501, 522–3
    public holidays 432
    religion or belief, freedom to manifest 432–4, 438–9
    religious discrimination 558
    rest days 432
    sex discrimination 322
    sexual orientation 438–9

employment (*cont.*)
  slavery and forced labour 433–4
  standard of living in event of involuntary
      unemployment 23
  video surveillance 377
  whistleblowing 25, 465, 469, 475
enforced disappearances *see* disappearances
enforcement *see also* binding force and execution of
      judgments
  adoption of ECHR 3, 4, 6–9
  collective enforcement 73
  subsidiarity 76–7
Engels, Friedrich 958
entry into force
  adoption of ECHR 8–19
  advisory opinions 1229
  crime and family, extension of ECHR to 1168–9
  death penalty 16, 17, 1099, 1209
  discrimination 21, 1193
  drafting 1169
  filtering and processing applications 14, 699,
      702, 707
  freedom of movement and migration 12, 1087–8
  International Covenant on Civil and Political
      Rights 18, 1125
  Model Final Clauses 1168, 1193
  protocols 30, 735, 1039, 1087, 1120, 1168, 1193,
      1209, 1229
  ratione temporis jurisdiction 108
  signature and ratification 108, 944–5, 949–50
environment 11, 23–4, 172, 387–8
equal protection of the law 1174–5, 1180–1
equality before the law 12, 13, 19–21, 555, 558,
      1174–5, 1177, 1180–1
equality between spouses 1157–9
  children, interests of 1158
  cohabitees 1158–9
  Commission on the Status of Women 1157
  declarations 1159
  dissolution 1158–9
  drafting 1157
  International Covenant on Civil and Political
      Rights 1157
  interpretation 1157–9
  legitimate aim/purpose, restrictions for a 1158
  margin of appreciation 1158
  marry and found a family, right to 1157
  necessity clause 1158
  positive obligations 1158
  pressing social needs 1158
  private and family life, right to respect for 1157–8
  reservations 1159
  same sex couples 1158–9
  Universal Declaration of Human Rights 1157
equality of arms 28, 288
Ergec, Rusen 594
erga omnes obligations 65, 725–6
Estonia 323, 984, 1028

estoppel *see also ne bis in idem*
  admissibility criteria 764
  examination of the case 814–15
  exhaustion of domestic remedies 814–15
ethnic cleansing 344, 914, 1067
EU law *see also* Charter of Fundamental Rights
      of the EU
  accession to ECHR 948–9
  Committee of Ministers, representation at 949
  Court of Justice 948–9
  death penalty 1092
  Employment Equality Directive 583
  expulsion 1071, 1126
  leave a country, freedom to 1064
  legislation by ECtHR, consideration of 948
  Lisbon Treaty 948
  Racial Equality Directive 568
  ratification 948
  Schengen zone 1053
  Vienna Convention on the Law of Treaties 948
eugenics 373
European Commission for Democracy through Law
      (Venice Commission)
  customary international law 41
  freedom of assembly and association 484
  funding of parties 505 n.171, 807
  opinions, provision of 807
  political parties 484, 505 n.171, 807
  rule of law 72
  succession to treaties 951
  third-party intervention 793
European Commission of Human Rights
      (ECommHR) *see also under* individual main
      entries
  abolition 27, 30, 699, 735, 809
  access to ECtHR, authorization of 732
  admissibility criteria 699, 700, 702, 706,
      754–9, 779
  appointments, procedure for 645
  case law 54
  caseload 27–9, 633
  collective enforcement 73
  Committees, competence of 699, 700, 702
  declaration, acceptance by 8, 9
  ECtHR
    admissibility 632
    Committee of Ministers 632
    establishment 631
    individual applications 636
    investigatory function 634
    merger, proposal for 28–30, 632, 639, 649
    organs of the Council of Europe, distinguishing
        Commission from 641
    petition, right to 634
    referrals 706
    single Court, replacement by 28–9, 632–3
  elections 9
  examination of the case 803, 808–9

filtering and processing applications 699, 700, 702, 706, 754, 779

first inter-State complaint 9

individual applications 8, 9–10, 636, 732–3, 735

inter-State applications 9

investigations 634, 808–9

manifestly ill-founded applications, rejection of 779

merger, proposal for 632, 639

merits, decisions on the 706

premises, move into new 29–30

proposal for a commission 4, 6–10

reservations 939

rotation of terms of members of ECtHR and ECommHR 26

Sub-Commission, abolition of 26

European Committee on Crime Problems 14, 15, 1093

European Convention for the Peaceful Settlement of Disputes (CoE) 912

European Convention on Establishment 1071, 1076, 1126, 1129

European Court of Human Rights (ECtHR) *see also* Chambers; Grand Chamber; jurisdiction of ECtHR; Plenary Court; Rules of Court

advisory opinions 633

appeals 632

application of ECHR 633, 641–2

budget, amount of 890

case law 54–5, 366–7

caseload 28–9, 633

collective enforcement 640

Committee of Experts 632, 636–7

Committee of Legal Experts 638–9

Committee of Ministers 632–4, 636–9

Conference of Senior Officials 637–9

consolidating the institutions and further reform 639

Consultative Assembly 635–8, 641

corporate persons 634

declarations 638–9

Draft Statute 635

drafting 631, 634–9

establishment of court 631–42

European Agreement relating to Persons Participating in Proceedings of ECtHR 747

European Ministerial Conference on Human Rights 1985 632

examination of the case 803–15

expenditure 889–90

final judgments 849–55

Geneva Conventions 641

individual applications, right to 632, 636

International Court of Justice 632, 635, 637

International Covenant on Civil and Political Rights 631

interpretation 633, 639–42

inter-State applications 633

jurisdiction 632–5, 639, 641–2, 644

natural persons 634

new Court 632–3, 639, 661, 670, 700, 701, 889

opposition to ECtHR 631–2

Optional Court, proposal for 637

organs of the Council of Europe, distinguishing ECtHR from 641

Parliamentary Assembly 632

permanent Court, ECtHR as 639

Permanent Court of International Justice 631, 635

pilot-judgment procedure 640

Preamble 640

precedent 46–7, 711, 866

premises, move into new 29–30

Presidents/Vice-Presidents 27, 673, 681–4, 688–92, 694–5, 709, 843, 846

proposals for a court 3, 4, 6–8, 10

protocol, proposal for a

    drafting 632–3

    Steering Committee for Human Rights 632

public order (*ordre public*) 640

public policy 640

publication of judgments 851, 855

rapporteurs 677

rationale for Court, commentary on 634

rectification of judgments 849, 852–5

reform 632–3, 639

revision of judgments 849, 852–4

rotation of terms of members of ECtHR and ECommHR 26

seat 639, 641

specificity of tasks 641

Steering Committee for Human Rights 632

Strasbourg, seat in 30, 639, 641

supervisory role 451, 474–5, 521

travel to and from seat 747

Universal Declaration of Human Rights 631

Vienna Convention on the Law of Treaties 642

European Parliament, elections to 1012, 1021

European Social Charter (ESC)

death penalty 1106

derogations 587–8, 594, 1106

discrimination 556

economic, social and cultural rights 23

expulsion of aliens, procedural safeguards relating to 1126

freedom of assembly and association 484, 499, 506, 515–16, 522

marry and found a family, right to 529

reporting procedures 898

rest days 432

trade unions 506, 515–16

Vienna Convention on the Law of Treaties 38

European Torture Convention 912

euthanasia 117, 128, 132–3

Everett, James 360, 558

evidence

admissibility 312, 320–1, 810, 813, 815

adverse inferences, drawing 811–14

beyond reasonable doubt 810

evidence *(cont.)*
  burden of proof 810–12
  confidentiality 814
  cooperate, obligation to 812–14
  delay 813–14
  disappearances 811
  discrimination 811
  documentary evidence 807, 812–14
  examination of the case 803, 805–15
  fair trial in criminal proceedings, right to 310–13,
    320–1
  general principles of international law 810
  government sources 812
  hearsay 239, 312
  international human rights organizations, reports
    of 812
  life, right to 810
  national laws 320
  national security 814
  new evidence 1154–5
  private and family life, right to respect for 320
  probative value 810
  State responsibility 810
  telephone tapping 320
  torture 320–1, 810
  unlawfully, improperly or unfairly evidence,
    exclusion of 320–1
ex officio or national judges 687–8, 690–4, 1220–1
examination of the case 803–15
  additional submissions 806
  admissibility 806
  amicus curiae briefs 807
  Chambers 806–8
  Committee of Experts 803–4
  Committee of Ministers 803–4
  Committees, assignment to 3 judge 805
  conduct of the examination 805–7
  Conference of Senior Officials 804
  consolidating the institutions and further
    reform 804–5
  Consultative Assembly 803–4
  cooperate, obligation to 812–14
  delegation, investigations by 807–8
  documentary evidence 807, 812–14
  drafting 803–5
  ECommHR 803, 808–9
  electronic filing 806
  estoppel 814–15
  evidence 803, 805–15
  exhaustion of domestic remedies 807
  expert witnesses 806–7, 809
  factual information, documents and other materials,
    requests for 805–7
  filing 806
  filtering and processing applications 805–6
  friendly settlements 805
  hearings 808
  in camera hearings 806, 808, 814

  individual applications 805–6, 809, 811–12
  inquiries, conducting 807
  interim measures 808
  interpretation 805–15
  inter-State applications 806, 811, 814
  investigations and fact-finding 805, 807–10
  jura novit curiae 815
  national laws, application of 807
  notice of applications 806
  on-site visits 807, 808–10
  oral hearings 806
  preliminary reviews 805
  procedural/investigative obligation 812–13
  public hearings 806
  record of hearings 806
  reply, written observations in 806
  rule of law 814
  Rules of Court 803, 805–8
  single judge, assignment to 805
  time limits 806
  witnesses 806–10
  written submissions 806
exclusion of other means of dispute resolution 907–15
  admissibility criteria 911
  application of ECHR 907, 911
  arbitration tribunals 907, 910–11
  aspects of disputes addressed in other for a 913–14
  Charter of UN 913
  Committee of Experts 909–10
  Committee of Ministers 909–13
  Conference of Senior Officials 910
  conflicts of jurisdiction 907–9
  Consultative Assembly 907–9
  Council of Europe treaty system 912
  drafting 907–10
  ECommHR 914
  establishment of ECtHR, discussions over 907–11
  European Convention for the Peaceful Settlement of
    Disputes (CoE) 912
  European Torture Convention 912
  fragmentation 907–8
  International Court of Justice, demarcation of
    jurisdiction with 907–10, 912–14
  International Covenant on Civil and Political
    Rights 912
  interpretation 907, 911, 912–15
  inter-State applications 907, 912–15
  non-European judges, political or philosophical
    leanings of 907
  special agreements 914
  Süd Tirol/Alto Adige, dispute between Austria and
    Italy over 913
  Universal Periodic Review 915
execution of judgments *see* binding force and execution
  of judgments
exhaustion of domestic remedies
  6-month rule 754, 757, 763
  actio popularis 766

administrative practices consisting of repetitive
   acts 766
admissibility 764–9
advisory opinions 1216
appeal in criminal matters, right of 1135
arbitral tribunals 768
burden of proof 766, 768
Committees, competence of 703
consolidation of institutions and reform 31
constitutions 768–9
de minimis principle 785
declarations 769
delays 766
discretionary or extraordinary remedies 769
drafting 755–8
ECommHR 765, 767
effective remedy, right to an 551, 765–6
estoppel 814–15
examination of the case 807
expulsion 1071
flexibility 764
formalism 764
friendly settlements 816
general principles of international law 757, 767
Grand Chamber 764–5, 769
individual applications 754
International Court of Justice 767
international remedies 768
inter-State applications 728–9, 763, 766
jurisdiction 717
just satisfaction 835–6
legislative practices 766
life, right to 728
Permanent Court of International Justice 767–8
purpose of rule 764–5
ratione materiae jurisdiction 94
ratione temporis jurisdiction 108–9
subsidiarity 75–6, 765, 807
time limits 771–2
existing human rights, safeguards for 902–4
expedited procedure 293, 542
expenditure on ECtHR 889–90
   budget, amount of 890
   Committee of Experts 889
   Committee of Ministers 889–90
   Consultative Assembly 889
   Council of Europe, responsibility of 889, 890
   drafting 889
   interpretation 890
   jurisdiction, optional declarations on acceptance
      of 889
   new court 889
   ratified ECHR, responsibility of States that have 889
   salaries and social security contributions of
      judges 889, 890
   staff and equipment 889
expert witnesses 806–7, 809
expression, freedom of *see* freedom of expression

expropriation *see also* expropriation, compensation for
   abuse of rights, prohibition of 621–2
   conditions provided by law 974–7
   continuing violations 109
   cultural property 976–7
   customary international law 977–8
   de facto/constructive expropriation 848, 974–5
   discrimination 1182–3
   due process 978
   general principles of international law 974–5, 977–9
   margin of appreciation 1183
   nationality 1183
   peaceful enjoyment of possessions 621–2, 958, 960,
      964–7, 970–9
   proportionality 976–7
   public interest 965, 967, 974–8
   restitution 1183
   statelessness 109
expropriation, compensation for
   amount 978
   full market value, reimbursement of 976–7
   general principles of international law 939, 965–7
   just satisfaction 837–8
   peaceful enjoyment of possessions 964–7, 974,
      976–7
   reservations 939
expulsion 1067–74 *see also* collective expulsion of
      aliens; deportation; expulsion of aliens,
      procedural safeguards relating to; extradition
   activists 608–9
   admissibility 1071–2
   arbitrary exile 12, 1068–9, 1071–2
   child custody disputes 1072
   citizenship 1072
   collective expulsion 1068, 1070–1
   Committee of Experts 1069–71, 1073
   Consultative Assembly 1068–9
   death penalty 127, 140–6, 1093
   declarations 97, 1072, 1073–4
   denaturalization 1069–70
   dependence 397–8
   diplomatic assurances 145–6
   drafting 1068–71
   ECommHR 1072, 1073
   education, right to 998
   effective remedy, right to an 740–1
   entry, freedom of 1069–71
   ethnic cleansing 1067
   EU law 1071
   European Convention on Establishment 1071
   exhaustion of domestic remedies 1071
   fair trial, right to a 275, 282
   family life 394–8, 405, 435
   freedom of movement and migration 1060, 1082
   General Assembly (UN) 1068
   Genocide Convention 1067
   immigration status 396
   inhuman or degrading treatment 168–9, 740–1

expulsion *(cont.)*
  interim measures 244
  International Covenant on Civil and Political
       Rights 1068–71
  interpretation 12, 1069, 1071–3
  liberty and security, right to 243–5, 259–60
  life, right to 127, 740–1
  long-term migrants, right to citizenship of 395, 297
  manifestly ill-founded applications 1071
  military service 1070
  nationality 1069–70, 1072
  nationals 1068–70, 1072
  no punishment without law 347, 349
  non-nationals 1068
  political activity of aliens, restrictions on 608–9
  population transfers 1067–8
  potential victims 743
  private life 396–7
  proportionality 396
  ratification 1073
  ratione loci jurisdiction 95–7
  ratione temporis jurisdiction 1071
  religion or belief, freedom to manifest 434–5
  reservations 1069, 1072, 1073–4
  return to country, right to 1068
  statelessness 1071
  terrorism 168
  torture 179
  Universal Declaration of Human Rights 1068–9
  victim status 740–1, 743, 744–5
expulsion of aliens, procedural safeguards relating
     to 1126–33
  accessibility of law 1130
  collective expulsion 1130
  Committee of Ministers 1127
  death penalty 1128
  declarations 1132–3
  disappearances 1128
  drafting 1127
  effective remedy, right to an 1126, 1128
  EU law 1126
  European Social Charter 1126
  expulsion, definition of 1129–30
  foreseeability of law 1130
  guarantees 1131–2
  in accordance with law, decisions 1130
  inhuman or degrading treatment 395, 1126, 1128
  International Covenant on Civil and Political
       Rights 1126, 1131
  interpretation 1127–33
  lawfully resident, meaning of 1128–9
  life, right to 1128
  national security 1132
  nationals 1127
  pending review, expulsions 1132
  private and family life, right to respect
       for 1126, 1128
  proportionality 1132

public order 1132
reasons against expulsion, right to submit 1131
Refugee Convention 1126, 1127
representation, right to 1131
reservations 1132
reviews by competent authorities 1131–2
Russia 1130
torture 395, 1128
extradition 1069, 1071–2, 1073
  arrest 245–6
  Charter of Fundamental Rights of the EU 165
  death penalty 127, 140–6, 165, 1093, 1099–101
  detention/deprivation of liberty 829
  diplomatic assurances 145–6, 1100–1
  disguised extradition 228
  fair trial, right to 274–5, 282
  inhuman or degrading treatment 1100–1
  liberty and security, right to 232, 243–6
  life, right to 127, 140–6
  ratione loci jurisdiction 95–7
  terrorist suspects 750, 837
  torture 179, 1100–1
  victim status 745
extraordinary rendition 96, 145, 793, 809–10, 827,
     836–7, 899–901
extraterritoriality
  abuse of rights, prohibition of 616
  collective expulsion of aliens 1079
  death penalty 140, 1099
  diplomatic protection 105
  effective control over an area 102–3
  expulsion 95–6, 1079
  inhuman or degrading treatment 101, 194–6
  legal space 104
  life, right to 140
  ratione loci jurisdiction 95–6, 100–5
  state agent authority and control 101–2
  State responsibility 100–1
extremism *see also* totalitarianism
  fascism 372, 445, 519, 525, 726, 942–3, 1095
  freedom of expression 445, 447–8, 463–4
  militant democracy 445, 519–21

fact-finding *see* investigations and fact-finding
fair trial in criminal proceedings, right to 265–72,
     298–321, 1165 *see also* presumption of
     innocence
  acquittals 744
  adversarial procedure 310
  age of criminal responsibility 318–19
  appeals 286, 1135
  binding force and execution of judgments 869
  Charter of Fundamental Rights of the EU 266, 272
  classification of offence 277–8
  collective expulsion of aliens 1075
  collective guilt 280
  Committee of Legal Experts 270
  criminal charges, determination of 276–84, 869

death penalty and right to life 141, 144
defence, adequate time and facilities for 308–10, 311
defence in person 310–11
disciplinary offences 278–9, 282–3
disclosure 310
discontinuance 281, 286, 292, 299, 303, 305–7
discrimination 323
enforcement of judgments 276
Engel criteria 277–9
equality of arms 288
evidence 310–13, 320–1
expulsion, deportation and extradition 282
forfeiture measures 281–2
hearsay 312
independent and impartial tribunal 271, 294
information about nature and cause of
        charge 307–8
International Covenant on Civil and Political
        Rights 265, 316, 318
interpreters 314–16
investigation stage, evidence gathered at 310–11, 312
jura novit curiae 815
legal aid 269, 282, 310–11
legal assistance 309, 310–11
military discipline 278
minimum guarantees 265, 271, 307–21
miscarriages of justice 267, 319
nature of offence 277
oral hearings 289
plea bargaining 271
positive obligations 313
presence at trial 316–17
prisoners 275
procedural stages 280–2
public hearings 270, 287–9
public interest 309–10
ratione temporis jurisdiction 110
reasonable time, within a 291–3
reasoned decisions 297–8
reclassification of offences 310
regulatory offences 283–4
rule of law 265
self-incrimination 287, 300–2, 310, 319
severity of penalty 277–8
silence, right to 319
substantive criminal law 279–80
Universal Declaration of Human Rights 265
vulnerable persons 311, 313
waiver 309, 317
witnesses, examination of 312–13
fair trial, right to a 264–325 *see also* fair trial in criminal
        proceedings, right to
access to a court 284–7, 322, 324
administrative trials 265, 270–1
arbitrariness 271
Belgium 288
Charter of Fundamental Rights of the
        EU 265–6, 272

civil rights and obligations 265–6, 270–6, 287–8
Committee of Experts 267
Committee of Legal Experts 270
Committee of Ministers 266–70
competent authority 276
Conference of Senior Officials 268
constitutional proceedings 274
Consultative Assembly 266–7, 270
damages 276
delay 109
disciplinary offences 278–9, 282–3
discrimination 269, 321–3
drafting 266–70
ECtHR 265–6
elections 274
entry, right of 275
equality of arms 288
errors of law and fact 271
execution of judgments 276
expulsion and deportation 275
extradition 274–5
fourth instance doctrine 271
freedom of expression 460, 473–4
good faith 271
government employees 274
independent and impartial tribunal established by
        law 287, 294–6, 321
individual applications 731
injunctions 275–6
inquiries by the Secretary General 899
interim measures 272, 275–6
International Covenant on Civil and Political
        Rights 267
legal aid 267, 269, 322
legal representatives 284, 309, 310–11, 317
liberty and security, right to 275
limitation on use of restrictions 625
military discipline 324–5
minimum guarantees 265, 271, 307–21
national court decisions, review of 266, 271
oral hearings 324
preliminary proceedings 272, 275
presumption of innocence 271, 298–307, 325
pre-trial publicity 287
procedural safeguards 276
public hearings 287–98, 323, 825–6
public law proceedings 274
racist or discriminatory attitudes 321–2
ratione temporis jurisdiction 108–10
reasonable time, within a 287, 291–3
reasoned decisions/judgments 297–8, 857, 936
regulatory offences 283–4
remain, right to 275
reporting restrictions 460
reservations and declarations 323–6
rule of law 72, 265, 285–6, 294
sex discrimination 322–3
social security benefits and contributions 274

fair trial, right to a (*cont.*)
    sovereign immunity 286–7
    speedy determination 276
    State sovereignty 274
    tax assessments 274
    Universal Declaration of Human Rights 265–6
    waiver 271
    witnesses 269–70, 325
Falkland Islands 928, 1206
families *see* crime and family, extension of ECHR to;
        family life; marry and found a family, right to
family life 388–98 *see also* private and family life, right
    to respect for
    adoption 394, 407
    American Convention on Human Rights 592
    artificial insemination 389
    biological family, right to know identity of 367
    children
        parents, relationship with 391–4
        totalitarian states 370
    close family ties 389–91
    close relationships falling short of family life 391
    Consultative Assembly 360–1
    de facto family ties 389–90
    diversity in family life 389
    drafting 359–61
    expulsion and deportation 394–8, 405, 435
    families, types of 389
    grandparents 389
    illegitimate children 390
    interpretation 367, 375–6, 370, 379, 388–98
    lifestyles 379
    lone parents 389
    marriage
        gender equality 407
        names 375–6, 407
        racial restrictions 360
        right to marry and found a family 375, 388, 534
        totalitarian states 360
    migrants 366–7
    minorities 379
    modernization of family law 820
    names 375–6, 407
    natural and fundamental unit of society, family
        as 361, 388
    natural rights 360
    negative obligations 388
    paternity 390–1
    positive obligations 388
    prisoners 390, 398
    private life, dividing line with 366–7
    ratione materiae 389
    reservations 409
    same sex couples 390, 407–8
    siblings 389
    totalitarian states 360–1, 393
    Universal Declaration of Human Rights 388
fascism 372, 445, 519, 525, 726, 942–3, 1095

fasting 430 *see also* hunger strikes
Fayat, Henri 266, 862
Ferrari Bravo, Luigi 646
fertility and fertility treatment
    artificial insemination 389, 739–40
    private life 372–4
    sterilization 183–4, 372, 543
filtering and processing applications
    ad hoc judges 689
    admissibility criteria 706–7, 760–2
    binding force and execution of
        judgments 864–5, 872
    caseload 30–1
    Chambers 683, 707
    Committees, competence of 599, 699–704
    de minimis principle 782, 785
    declarations 703–4, 786
    ECommHR 699, 700, 702, 706, 754, 779
    entry into force 14, 30–1, 699, 702, 707
    examination of the case 805–6
    Explanatory Report 14–15, 74–5, 701–3, 680, 683
    friendly settlements 819–22
    Grand Chamber 714
    individual applications 805–6
    interpretation 79
    inter-State applications 806
    judges
        election of 660, 664
        formations 689–90
        gender balance 664
        number 645
        single judges 689–90, 696–8, 699, 700–2
        term of office 670–1
    jurisdiction 720
    margin of appreciation 79
    merits, decisions on the 706–7
    Plenary Court 680, 683
    Preamble 680, 683, 697
    ratification 14, 30
    registry 675–6
    repetitive applications, expedited procedure for 30
    routine applications 30
    signature and ratification 948, 698
    single-judge formation 689–90, 696–8, 699, 700–2
    third-party intervention 793–4
    travaux préparatoires 79
final judgments 849–55
    Chambers 841–2, 851
    Committee of Experts 850
    Committees 851
    Conference of Senior Officials 850
    Consultative Assembly 850
    decisions, application to 851
    dissemination of judgments 851, 855
    documents related to proceedings, publication
        of 851
    drafting 850–1
    general principles of international law 849

Grand Chamber 847, 851
International Court of Justice, Statute of 849
interpretation 841, 849–55
national courts 109
ne bis in idem 849
no punishment without law 849
publication of judgments 851, 855
rectification of errors in decisions and
    judgments 854–5
res judicata 842, 849
revision of judgments after ECtHR has made
    error 849, 852–4
rule of law 849
Rules of Court 851
single-judge formation 851
striking out 851
fingerprints 384
Finland 14, 324, 1095, 1148, 1192, 1228
firearms by State officials, use of 129–31, 148–51
First World War 118, 413
fitness to stand trial 318
Fitzmaurice, Gerald 41, 48, 172, 924
force, use of *see* use of force
forced labour *see* slavery and forced labour
foreign nationals *see* collective expulsion of aliens;
    expulsion of aliens, procedural safeguards
    relating to; political activity of aliens,
    restrictions on
foreseeability of law *see* accessibility and foreseeability of
    law
forfeiture 281–2, 974 *see also* confiscation
formalism 745, 754, 764, 859
former Yugoslavia *see* International Criminal Tribunal
    for the former Yugoslavia (ICTY)
Former Yugoslav Republic of Macedonia *see* Macedonia
Foster, John 557
France
    abortion 125
    broadcasting 481, 737
    Cambodia, ships flagged on 102
    colonies and overseas territories 916, 921–2, 926–7,
        1036, 1162
    death penalty 140, 1095, 1118–19
    Declaration of the Rights of Man and
        Citizen 328, 958
    declarations 481
    discrimination 480–1
    drug enforcement officials 102
    equality between spouses 1159
    expulsion 1083
    freedom of expression 470, 480–1, 618, 926–7
    habeas corpus 220, 254
    Holocaust denial 615
    hunting rights 973
    International Covenant on Civil and Political
        Rights 588
    leave a country, freedom to 1061
    Mayotte 1159, 1162

military discipline 324–5
ne bis in idem 1155
New Caledonia 608, 927, 1159
no punishment without law 330, 342
overseas territories 608–9
paternity 390
patronymic names 1159
political activity of aliens, restrictions on 608–9
political parties, funding of 505
recidivism 350
religious discrimination 579
reservations 324–5, 605, 1139, 1140, 1146,
    1155, 1159
sex offenders register, placement on 346, 348
slavery and forced labour 201
territorial application 1083, 1162
terrorism 617
torture 176
universal suffrage 1011
veils, ban on Islamic 402, 405–6, 437, 743
Franklin, Benjamin 423
freedom of assembly and association 483–525
    abuse of a dominant position 491, 514
    abuse of rights, prohibition of 615, 617, 620
    accessibility 510, 523
    administration of State 490
    assembly, definition of 494–5
    autonomous role of Article 11 491–2
    balancing exercise 491, 494, 513, 516
    Charter of Fundamental Rights of the EU 484
    children 496
    chilling effect 500
    civil society 499
    collective bargaining 484
    Committee of Experts 486–8
    Committee of Legal Experts 490
    Committee of Ministers 486, 490, 501
    Conference of Senior Officials 489
    Consultative Assembly 485–6
    Council of Europe, aims and principles of 486
    criminal prosecutions 496
    culture 500, 503
    democracy 68, 483, 490–1, 495, 497, 499–500,
        503–4, 513–15, 519–21
    demonstrations/protests 492–8, 514–18, 742
    derogations 599
    discrimination 511, 512, 517, 523–5
    dispersal by police 496–7, 516
    dissolution 501
    drafting 484–90
    economic, social, and cultural rights 499
    ECtHR, supervisory role of 521
    elections 515, 518, 1017, 1011
    ethnic identity 500, 503
    European Social Charter 484, 499, 506,
        515–16, 522
    foreseeability 510–11, 523
    freedom of association, definition of 499–508

freedom of assembly and association (*cont.*)
 freedom of expression 452, 464, 483, 491–2,
  502, 517
 freedom of peaceable assembly, definition of 494–8
 general principles of international law 485
 International Covenant on Civil and Political
  Rights 509
 International Covenant on Economic, Social and
  Cultural Rights 508, 510
 International Labour Organization 484, 508–9,
  515, 522
 interpretation 490–525
 judges 673
 labour relations 483–5, 487, 489–90
 legitimate aim, restrictions for a 495, 509, 511–13,
  516–17
 limitation on use of restrictions 625
 margin of appreciation 515, 517–18
 militant democracy 519–21
 military service 490, 509
 minorities 491, 494, 514–15, 518, 525
 national security 511–13, 525
 necessary in a democratic society, restrictions which
  are 509, 512, 513–21
 negative aspects 493, 502
 non-governmental organizations (NGOs),
  dissolution of 501
 not to join, right 487, 502
 Parliamentary Assembly 484
 peaceful assembly, meaning of 495–6
 peaceful enjoyment of possessions 491
 personal autonomy 502
 pluralism 490–1, 500, 503–4, 513
 police 490, 509, 516, 522
 political activity of aliens, restrictions on 607–8
 political parties 484, 499, 503–5, 511–12, 515,
  520–1, 525
 political rights 483–5
 positive obligation or interference 492–4, 502, 516,
  519, 521
 prescribed by law, restrictions which are 509,
  510–11, 523
 pressing social need, restrictions for 514–16
 prevention of disorder or crime 509, 512
 prior notification 497–8
 private and family life, right to respect for 364, 491
 proportionality 498, 510, 513, 516–17, 523
 protection of legal rights of others 485
 public employees, lawful restrictions on 522–3
 public morality, public order and public
  safety 485–6, 489, 509, 511–13
 public office 490, 509, 512, 516–17, 522, 524–5
 racist or xenophobic ideas 525
 recognition of associations 500–1
 registration 500, 511
 religion or belief, freedom to manifest 429
 religious organizations 499, 501, 511
 reservations 525

 restrictions/limitations 485–6, 490–1, 496–502,
  509–23
 riot or insurrection, quelling 152
 rule of law 503, 510
 sanctions, nature and severity of 517
 secret associations 511
 security measures 497
 sexual orientation discrimination 525
 territorial integrity 512
 thought, conscience and religion, freedom of 440,
  483, 491, 499, 502, 512
 tolerance, exercise of 498, 513
 trade unions 483–9, 493–4, 499–502, 505–9,
  514–16, 522–5
 traffic, disruption of 498
 travaux préparatoires 64
 types of organization 499
 Universal Declaration of Human Rights 483–5,
  487–9, 509
 victims 500, 742
freedom of expression 444–81
 abuse of rights, prohibition of 615, 617–20
 accessibility 469–70
 American Convention on Human Rights 452, 459
 apologies 470
 artistic expression 39, 451, 463–4, 472, 477
 balancing exercise 380, 384–5, 453–4, 480
 Bill of Rights 1688 444
 broadcasting, television, or cinema enterprises,
  licensing of 466–7
 Charter of Fundamental Rights of the EU 445
 civil or public servants 464–5, 476–8
 Committee of Experts 446–9
 Committee of Ministers 446, 450, 460, 462,
  466, 478–9
 Conference of Senior Officials 449
 confidentiality 467, 471, 473
 Consultative Assembly 446–8, 450
 copyright 480
 corporate bodies 741
 criminal offences 454, 470–1, 474–6
 criticism and insult, distinction between 473
 cultural heritage, protection of 472
 cultural information, public exchange of 451
 declarations 457, 481
 defamation 472, 476–8, 479
 democracy 68, 445–6, 451–2, 458, 460, 463, 465
 derogations 457
 diplomatic immunity 478
 discretion, exercise of 451, 469
 discrimination 466, 467, 478, 479–81
 drafting 445–50, 466, 473
 duties and responsibilities, notion of 468–9
 ECtHR, supervisory function of 451, 474–5
 elections, right to free 1011, 1016–20, 1025, 1030
 employment 464–5, 469
 expression, definition of 456
 extremist ideas 445, 447–8, 463–4

fair trial, right to a 460, 473–4
fiction, defamation in 477
foreseeability 469–71
formalities 467–80
freedom of assembly and association 452, 464, 483,
    491–2, 502, 517
Freedom of Information Convention (UN) 447
freedom of movement and migration 468
frontiers, regardless of 466
general principles of international law 445
gravity of interference 475–6
hate speech 445, 478–80
injunctions 475
International Covenant on Civil and Political
    Rights 463, 468, 478
Internet 462–3, 466
interpretation 450–81
journalists 454, 458–9, 461–2, 468–70, 473, 477–8
judges 467–8, 473–4, 673
juries, publication of deliberations of 461
legal advice, taking 470
legal persons 455
legitimate aim/purpose, restrictions for a 451, 467,
    471–5
lewd ideas 456
licensing 445, 466–7
limitation on use of restrictions 625
literary and artistic expression 463–4
margin of appreciation 454, 474, 476
media 453–4, 457–62, 466–8, 474–7, 480–1
military service 465
minorities 450
national courts 458, 474–5
national security 448, 467, 471–2
natural persons 455
necessary in a democratic society, restrictions which
    are 474–80
negative obligations 454, 456–7
novels, defamation in 477
nudity in public 455
obscene speech 456
offends, shocks or disturbs, speech that 451, 456
opinions, freedom to hold 445–8, 451–3,
    455–7, 491
overlap with other rights 452–3
peaceful enjoyment of possessions 468, 480
penalties 467–80
photographs 377–8, 461
pluralism 451, 453, 467, 491
political activities 375, 607–8
political expression 455–6, 458, 461–4, 474,
    476–8, 580
political parties 491, 503
positive obligation or interference 453–4, 460, 464
prescribed by law, restrictions which are 469–71, 474
press 457–62, 474–5
pressing social needs 474
presumption of innocence 460

prevention of disorder or crime 447–9, 463, 467–8,
    471–2
prior restraint 452
private and family life, right to respect for 368, 375,
    377–8, 380, 452, 460, 468
propaganda 448
proportionality 451, 465, 475–7
protection of legal rights of others 445
public figures 478
public interest 454, 458–62, 474
public morality, order and security 445–7, 467–8,
    471–3, 476–7
reasons for interference, relative and sufficient 451
receive and impart information, freedom to 445,
    451, 457, 467
religion 412, 423, 440, 467
reputation 458, 465, 469, 471–3, 476
reservations 481
restrictions/limitations 445–7, 451, 467–80
rule of law 445, 460, 470
safeguards for existing human rights 903
scope 455–65
sentencing 454, 475–6
sexual orientation 915
style of communication 456
territorial integrity 448, 450, 467–8, 471–2
thought, conscience and religion, freedom of 452,
    457, 468, 472–3
tolerance 451, 479
trade unions 464–5, 469, 471, 473
travaux préparatoires 450
Universal Declaration of Human Rights 444–8,
    451, 464, 466, 468, 478–9
value judgments and statements of fact 477
whistleblowing 465, 469, 475
freedom of information 364, 447
freedom of movement and migration 1052–66
accessibility of law 1063
administrative action 1055, 1063
bail
    change residence, requirement not to 1058
    conditions 1058
Charter of Fundamental Rights of the EU 1053
checkpoints 1059
children 745, 1060, 1063
citizenship 1057
Cold War 1052–3
collective enforcement 1046–7
Commissioner on Human Rights (UN) 1052
Committee of Experts 13–14, 1046, 1054–6, 1082,
    1085, 1087
Committee of Ministers 14, 1046
Communist regimes 1052–3
Consultative Assembly 12–13, 1054–6, 1082,
    1085, 1087
Convention on the Rights of the Child 1060
criminal sanctions 1057–9, 1061–2, 1063
cultural life, right of minorities to their own 12

freedom of movement and migration (*cont.*)
  debts, travel bans to enforce private 1063–4
  declarations 1057, 1065–6, 1082–6
  demonstrations, obstructing police at 1058–9
  deprivation of liberty 1056–7
  derogations 591–2
  discrimination 1065
  drafting 13, 1046, 1054–6, 1082–3, 1085–7
  emigrate, freedom to 12
  enter one's own country, right to 12, 1054
  entry into force 12, 1087–8
  equality before the law 12, 13
  exile, prohibition of arbitrary 12
  Explanatory Report 14, 45
  expulsion 12, 1060
  extraterritoriality 101
  family life 366–7
  foreseeability of law 1063–4
  freedom of assembly and association 496
  freedom of expression 468
  freedom of movement, definition of 1057–9
  general principles of international law 1055
  Grand Chamber 1058
  high seas, interception on the 1083–4
  human trafficking 207
  identity checks 1059
  identity documents, dispossession of 1058, 1061
  imprisonment for debt 591–2
  in accordance with the law, restrictions which
      are 1056, 1059, 1063
  inhuman or degrading treatment 101
  internal travel, restrictions on 1057–9, 1063, 1065
  International Covenant on Civil and Political
      Rights 12–13, 18–19, 1046, 1053–6, 1060
  interpretation 1045–7, 1056–65, 1086–8
  lawfully resident, persons who are 1057
  lawfully within the territory, definition of 1057
  leave a country, freedom to 1055, 1060–5
  legitimate aim/purpose, restrictions for a 1063
  liberty and security, right to 233–4, 243
  marriages of convenience 540
  Migrant Workers Convention 1060
  minority rights 12–13
  national minorities 13
  national security 1062, 1063
  nationality 1060
  necessary in a democratic society, restrictions which
      are 1056, 1058, 1063–5
  'no one' formulation 169
  non-citizens 1057
  object and purpose of ECHR 1045–6
  Parliamentary Assembly 1087
  police, requirements to report to 1059
  Preamble 1045–7
  prescribed by law, restrictions which are 1063
  pressing social needs 1064
  prevention of entry 243–4
  private life 366–7

proportionality 1058–9, 1060–1, 1063–5
public interest 1056, 1062, 1064
public order (*ordre public*) 1055–6, 1063
public service, removal of right of equal access
    to 12–13
ratione materiae jurisdiction 94
ratione temporis jurisdiction 1086
recognition as a person before the law, right to 12, 13
relationship of protocol to ECHR 1085–6
religion or belief, freedom to manifest 434
reservations 1065
residence, freedom to choose one's own 12, 1060
restrictions/limitations 1054–65
Schengen zone 1053
signature and ratification 14, 1057, 1065, 1084–8
stateless persons 1057
subsidiarity 76
technology 1052
territorial application 1081–4
terrorism 1052
Universal Declaration of Human Rights 13, 1046,
    1053, 1060
victim status 745
freedom to manifest religion or belief *see* manifest
    religion or belief, freedom to
friendly settlements 816–23
  admissibility 706–7, 820–3
  caseload 816
  Chambers 707, 819, 821–2
  Committee of Experts 817–18
  Committee of Ministers 818
  compensation, assessment of 817–18, 821
  conciliation, use of term 817–18
  Conference of Senior Officials 818
  confidentiality 781, 820, 822–3
  Consultative Assembly 817
  decision, striking out by means of a 821–2
  discontinuance 819
  drafting 816–20
  examination of the case 805
  exceptional circumstances 823
  exhaustion of domestic remedies 816
  Grand Chamber, approval by 846
  interpretation 820–3
  inter-State applications 817–18, 820
  judgment, striking out by means of a 821–2
  just satisfaction 821
  legitimacy 816
  media 822
  merits, decisions on the 706–7
  notice of applications 821
  Parliamentary Assembly 816
  pilot-judgment procedure 871
  protocols 822
  Registry, assistance of 819, 821
  repetitive cases 820
  reports 817
  role of ECtHR 821–2

Rules of Court 819, 821–2
statistics 821
striking out 797–8, 801, 819–23
subsidiarity 816
terms 871
unilateral declarations 822, 823
frivolous, vexatious or mischievous proceedings 6, 272, 754
Fuerst, Irmgard 946

Ganshof van der Meersch, Walter-Jean 682
Garlicki, Lech 144
Gaza flotilla, obstruction of 723 n.1
gender *see also* sex discrimination/gender equality
marry and found a family, right to 535–7
transgender persons 173, 380–1, 535–7, 544, 583
General Assembly (UN)
aggression, crime of 602
education, right to 987
expropriation 978
expulsion 1068
genocide 343
International Court of Justice, requests for opinions from 874, 877
judges, election of 658
torture 175, 177
women, participation of 5
general principles of international law
admissibility criteria 754, 756
burden of proof 810
Committee of Experts 352–3
criminal law 332, 336, 350, 351–5
exhaustion of domestic remedies 764–5, 769
expropriation 939, 965–7, 974–5, 977–9
final judgments 849
freedom of assembly and association 485
freedom of expression 445
freedom of movement and migration 1055
Genocide Convention 352
interim measures 749
International Covenant on Civil and Political Rights 353
International Military Tribunal 352–3
jurisdiction 719
just satisfaction 834
lex mitior principle 350
limitation on use of restrictions 623
no punishment without law 332, 336, 350, 351–5
political activity of aliens, restrictions on 607
private and family life, right to respect for 359–60
public hearings 825
source of international law, as 35, 38, 41–2, 352–3
summary executions 354
thought, conscience and religion, freedom of 415
travaux préparatoires 352–4
Vienna Convention on the Law of Treaties 35, 38, 41–2, 45

genetic features, discrimination on grounds of 573, 1184
Geneva Conventions 37–8, 158, 345, 601–2, 641, 1104, 1106
genocide
Armenian genocide, denial of 479–80
crimes against humanity 343–4
crimes against peace 343–4
definition 1099 n.3
denialism 479–80, 615, 619
discrimination 579
ethnic cleansing 344, 914, 1067
expulsion 1067
forced transfers of minority groups 1067
freedom of expression 479–80
general principles of international law 352
Genocide Convention 1, 39, 352, 1067
hate speech 479–80
Holocaust 479–80, 579, 615, 619
Holocaust denial 479–80, 615, 619
life, right to 121–2
no punishment without law 343–4
war crimes 343–4
Georgia
Abkhazia 914, 938, 1190
collective expulsion of aliens 1078
cooperate, obligation to 814
death penalty 1206
declarations 1009
ethnic cleansing in South Ossetia and Abkhazia 914
International Covenant on Civil and Political Rights 588
migration control 627
no punishment without law 341
peaceful enjoyment of possessions 984
prisoners' right to vote 1028
reservations 938, 984
Russia 627, 814, 914
territorial application 1190, 1206
Tskhinvali 938, 1190
witnesses 809
Germany
Basic Law 611
Berlin Wall 1052
border guard cases 355
death penalty 1095, 1112, 1114
declarations 1008–9, 1141, 1146, 1156
hijacked aircraft, shooting down 148
Holocaust denial 479
International Covenant on Civil and Political Rights 356
Land Berlin 1083, 1114
liberty and security, right to 259–60
life imprisonment 187
Nazi regime 202, 329, 342, 353, 479, 619, 1095
ne bis in idem 1156
political activity of aliens, restrictions on 609
prisoners 259–60

Germany (*cont.*)
  regional assemblies 1020
  religion 428, 437, 1008–9
  reservations 356, 609, 1112, 1139, 1146
  Saarland 946–7, 949, 1040
  social therapy treatments 259–60
  territorial application 917, 1083, 1114
  terrorism 148
  thought, conscience and religion, freedom of 424, 425–6
Gibraltar 928, 1007, 1036, 1084, 1162–3, 1206
Gloerfelt-Tarp, Kirsten 576 n.147
Grand Chamber *see also* Grand Chamber,
    relinquishment of jurisdiction to the; *under*
    individual main entries; referral to the Grand
    Chamber
  ad hoc judges 691
  admissibility criteria 707, 763–4
  admissibility decisions of Chamber, Grand Chamber
    as bound by 714
  advisory opinions 691–2, 713, 876, 878–85, 1216,
    1219–22
  balanced representation from each Chamber 714
  Committee of Ministers 691–2, 713–14
  Committees, competence of 702
  composition 688–9, 691–2
  de minimis principle 782
  ex officio, sitting 690, 691–3
  finality 841
  former Court 689
  full-time, sitting 690
  inconsistent judgments 691
  individual applications 713
  interpretation 691–2, 714
  inter-State applications 713
  judicial formations 688–9, 690–2
  jurisdiction, confirmation of 713–14
  just satisfaction 834
  lots, drawing 691–2
  manifestly ill-founded applications, rejection of 779
  meetings 682
  merits, decisions on 707
  nationality 691
  non-compliance, referral of situations of 691
  on-site visits 809–10
  Plenary Court 692, 713
  powers 713–14
  President of the Court 688, 691–2
  reasons for judgments 857–8
  refusal to comply 714
  refusal of referral 851
  Rules of Court 692, 713
  serious questions affecting interpretation 691, 1216
  session periods 690
  stage of proceedings, rejection of applications at
    any 785
  striking out 799
  substitute judges 691
  time limits 773, 849
  urgent cases 690
Grand Chamber, relinquishment of jurisdiction
    to the 709–12, 713
  accelerated procedures 710
  additional judges 709
  admissibility 711, 712
  Chambers which have relinquished jurisdiction,
    judges of 709
  composition of Grand Chamber 709–10
  consolidation of institutions and reform 710, 712
  drafting 709–10
  inadmissible aspects, rejection of 711
  inconsistent judgments, risk of 710–11
  interpretation 709–12
  judicial formations 688, 691
  mandatory relinquishment 710–11
  manifestly ill-founded applications 711
  merits and admissibility at same time, consideration
    of 712
  objections, duly reasoned 712
  own initiative, submission on own 709
  plenary Court 710
  precedent, prohibition on reversing 711
  President of the Court 709
  reasons for relinquishment, no requirement for 710,
    712
  referrals 709, 711
  re-hearings 844–5
  Rules of Court 709–10, 712
  serious questions of interpretation 709–11
  settled case law, departure from 710–11
  Vice-President of the Court 709
grandparents 534
Greece
  bank deposits 974
  boat, *refoulement* of migrants arriving by 1079–80
  civil partnerships 407–8
  courts martial, maintenance of extraordinary 599
  death penalty 16, 140, 1095, 1118
  denunciations 598, 599, 603, 942–3
  detention/deprivation of liberty 599
  education 934–5, 1006–7
  employment 374
  exhaustion of domestic remedies 769
  fascist junta 599, 726, 942–3
  Holy Monasteries 737
  identity cards showing religion 428
  inter-State applications 725–6
  liberty and security, right to 599
  national security 599
  oaths 428
  Palestine, property rights in 731
  population transfers 1067
  reservations 939, 1006–7
  Roma, discrimination against 1004–5
  signatories 9
  United Kingdom 725

universal suffrage 1011
vote, right to 1028
Greenland 338, 1205
Grotius, Hugo 201
guardian, duty to act as a 217
Guernsey 597, 925, 928, 1007, 1036, 1114, 1206
guilty pleas 1136–7
Gypsies 582

habeas corpus 220, 253–4
Hague Convention 1907 602
Hague Convention on the Peaceful Settlement of
    International Disputes 1899 647
Hague Regulations 102
hate speech 19, 445, 478–80
Head, Michael 1178
heads of state 100, 478, 617, 784, 1021–2
health *see* medical treatment and health
health and safety 131–2, 138, 439
hearings *see also* oral hearings; public hearings
    admissibility criteria 763
    examination of the case 806, 808
    in camera 290, 806, 808, 814, 826–7
    records 806
    re-hearings 844, 846
    Rules of Court 808
hearsay 239, 312
Hess, Rudolf 98
Hettier de Boislambert, Claude 966
hierarchy of rights 119, 164, 592–3, 1199
High Contracting Parties 88–90, 591, 645
high seas, vessels on the 102, 1079–80, 1083
Hitler, Adolf 136, 329
HIV/AIDS 126, 160, 172, 827
Hoare, Samuel 364, 818, 910, 931–2
Holocaust 479–80, 579, 615, 619
home, respect for the
    drafting 359–60
    illegal communities 400
    interpretation 379, 399–400
    legitimate expectations 400
    lifestyles 379
    margin of appreciation 400
    nuisance 399–400
    offices and business premises 399
    peaceful enjoyment of possessions 399–400, 402
    private life 399
    proportionality 400
    raiding of homes 360
    sanctity of the home 359–60
    social policy 400
    war/armed conflict 400
holidays 432, 437
homicide 127–9, 136, 342–3
homosexuals *see* sexual orientation
Hong Kong 922
honour and reputation, attacks on 358–9, 361–3,
    384–5

housing 20, 63, 81, 304, 400, 407, 544, 959, 979–80
    see also rent control; tenancies
Huber, Max 1068
Humphrey, John 358
human dignity, right to
    Charter of Fundamental Rights of the EU 66
    inhuman or degrading treatment 181, 184,
        196, 898
    Islamic veil 437
    life imprisonment 187
    life, right to 1198–9
    no punishment without law 330
    racial discrimination 571
human trafficking 63, 202–3, 207, 209–10, 229
Hungary
    access to a court 324
    communist and socialist movements, symbols of 619
    freedom of assembly and association 496
    freedom of expression 455
    military service 215
    prisoners' right to vote 1028
    reservations 324
    Roma, discrimination against 1004
hunger strikes 132
hunting rights 973
husband and wife *see* equality between spouses

Iceland 478, 682, 947, 949, 1040, 1088, 1095, 1148
identification of perpetrators 387
identity
    checks 1059
    discrimination 381
    documents
        dispossession 1058, 1061
        passports 8, 376, 378, 1058, 1061
        religious denomination, indicating 428
    driving licences 378
    face coverings 405
    fraud 405
    passports 8, 376, 378, 1058, 1061
    private life 374, 375–6, 378–81
    stereotyping 380
    thought, conscience and religion, freedom of 420
    transgender persons 380–1
    victims 827
illegitimate children, discrimination against 390, 538,
    583, 820
image 377
Imbert, Pierre-Henri 1116
immigration/migrants *see* freedom of movement and
    migration
immunities
    consular immunity 102
    diplomatic immunity 100, 102, 478
    fair trial, right to a 286–7
    General Agreement on Privileges and Immunities of
        CofE 680, 892–3
    heads of State 100

immunities (*cont.*)
  international organizations, functionaries of 100
  judges 891–3
  no punishment without law 331
  parliamentary immunities 79, 286, 287
  Plenary Court 680–1
  ratione loci jurisdiction 95, 100, 102–3
  sovereign immunity 44, 100, 286–7, 478, 554
  suit, from 747
  waiver 680
impartiality *see* independence and impartiality
impeachment 617
imprisonment for debt, prohibition 591–2, 1048–51
  Committee of Experts 1048–50
  Committee of Ministers 1048
  Consultative Assembly 1049–50
  contractual obligations, failure to fulfil 1048–51
  deprivation of liberty 1049–51
  drafting 1048–50
  ECommHR 1050–1
  International Covenant on Civil and Political
      Rights 12, 592, 1048, 1051
  interpretation 1050–1
  negligence 1050
  Preamble 1046
  travaux préparatoires 1049
  Universal Declaration of Human Rights 1048–9
  victim status 745
impunity 139, 192–4, 322, 773
in accordance with law, decisions which are
  expulsion of aliens, procedural safeguards relating
      to 1130
  freedom of movement and migration 1056, 1059,
      1063
  private and family life, right to respect for 402–4
in camera hearings 290, 806, 808, 814, 826–7
incest 82, 381
inconsistent judgments, risk of 679, 691, 710–11,
      844–5
independence and impartiality
  candidate for election, right to stand as a 1030
  criminal proceedings 128, 271, 294
  death penalty and right to life 141
  elections, right to free 1020
  independent and impartial tribunal established by
      law 287, 294–6, 321
  judges
    criteria for judicial office 647–9, 656
    election 658
    ex officio or national judges 693
    formations 694–5
    term of office 668, 671, 673
  liberty and security, right to 249
  privileges and immunities of judges 891–2
  rule of law 71
indigenous people 926, 959
individual applications 731–51 *see also under*
      individual main entries

abuse of right, prohibition of 780–1
admissibility 707, 746–7, 762, 776, 780–1
anonymity 746
application, use of term 735
caseload 27–8, 735
chilling effect 747
collective enforcement 735
Committee of Experts 732
Committee of Ministers 732–4, 747
communication freely with organs, ability to 747
Conference of Senior Officials 732–3
Consultative Assembly 732–4
content of the application 745–6
corporations 736–7
decentralized authorities 737
declarations 723, 734–5, 751
diplomatic protection 731
drafting 731–5
ECommHR 8, 9–10, 636, 732–3, 735
effective exercise of right of application 746–8
effective remedy, right to an 731
equality of arms 28
European Agreement relating to Persons
      Participating in Proceedings of ECtHR 747
examination of applications 748
exclusions 734
exhaustion of domestic remedies 728
fair trial, right to a 731
forms 746
frivolous and vexatious applications 780–1
governmental bodies 737
Grand Chamber 735
groups of individuals 734–7
inhuman or degrading treatment 734
interim measures 732, 749–51
inter-State applications 723, 724–8, 757
languages 746
League of Nations 731
legal aid 748
legal representatives 745–8
life, right to 734
locus standi 736–7
mandatory, as 725
merits, decisions on the 707
no punishment without law 734
non-governmental organizations 734–7, 745, 748
optional clause 632, 734
opt-out clause 734
peaceful enjoyment of possessions 731
Permanent Court of International Justice 731
petition, use of term 735
political interests 781
post, application must be submitted by 745
powers of attorney 745
Preamble 735
press or television interviews 781
pressure to withdraw or modify complaints 747
prisoners 747–8

protocols 735
public corporations 737
publicity or propaganda motive 781
ratification 735
reservations 939
slavery and forced labour 734
state monopolies 737
statements of violations 746
victim status 737–45
vulnerable applicants 747–8
written applications 745
Ingushetia 1065
inhuman or degrading treatment, prohibition of
absolute right, as 164, 168–9
admissibility 707, 773
age of criminal responsibility 318
assisting in suicide, prosecution of person 172
burqas or veils, criminal sanctions for wearing 173
common heritage 70
corporal punishment 170, 180, 188–9, 191
corporate bodies 741
courtroom, incarceration in metal cages in 185
criminal justice 185, 192–4
cruel, use of term 164, 167–8, 180
death penalty 11, 15, 16, 47, 142–5, 186–7,
190–1, 434, 1094
definition 180–1
deprivation of liberty 182
derogations 168–9, 592
detention/deprivation of liberty 169–70, 173–4,
180–6, 197
deterrence 183
disappearances 137, 171, 193
discrimination 177, 192–3, 196–8, 563–4, 1178
domestic violence 192, 198
drafting 180
environment 172
expulsion or *refoulement* 95–6, 168–9, 395, 740–1,
1126, 1128
extraterritoriality 194–6
extreme punishments 186–91
free movement and migration 101
gender reassignment surgery, difficulty in
obtaining 173
human dignity 66–7, 181, 184, 196
impunity 192–4
individual applications 734
inhuman or degrading, definition of 180–1
intention 180–1, 191
interim measures 750
journalists 461
jus cogens 180
life imprisonment 187–8
life, right to 47, 118, 137–8, 142–5, 157, 164,
169, 434
margin of appreciation 182
medical treatment 174, 183–6
merits, decisions on the 707

military, expulsion of homosexual persons from
the 172–3
no punishment without law 110, 349
private and family life, right to respect for 171–3
positive obligations 191–4, 197
procedural/investigative obligation 191–4, 773
proportionality 182–3, 194
public protection 183
punishment 182–3, 186–91, 194
racial discrimination 192–3, 197–8
rape 175–6, 576
rehabilitation 183
reservations 198
severity threshold 169, 171–6, 196, 563–4
sexual orientation 584
standard of proof 169
State agents 172, 191–2
sterilization of Roma women 372
third-party intervention 792
threshold of application 169, 171–6, 196
torture 101, 169, 174–80
treatment or punishment, definition of 182–4
Universal Declaration of Human Rights 180
victims 169–71
war/armed conflict 157
injunctions 275–6, 475
innocence, presumption of *see* presumption of
innocence
inquiries by the Secretary General 897–901
all State party, request directed to 898
care, children and young persons in 899
Committee of Experts 897–8
Committee of Senior Officials 898
compensation, right to 899
Consultative Assembly 897–8
detention sites relating to CIA activities,
secret 899–900
discretion 898
drafting 897–8
fair trial procedures 899
implementation of ECHR, requests for States to
furnish explanation of effective 897–901
interpretation 898–901
reporting procedures 898
scope 899
single State party, request directed to 898
time limits 900
institutions, consolidating the *see* consolidating the
institutions and further reforms
intellectual property 480, 959–60, 971
Inter-American Court of Human Rights
(IACtHR) 139, 643, 655, 693, 874
interception of communications *see* surveillance
interest 837
interim measures
binding upon States, as 749–50
Chambers 749
ECommHR 749

interim measures (*cont.*)
  examination of the case 808
  expulsion 244
  fair trial, right to a 272, 275–6
  general principles of international law 749
  individual applications 732, 749–51
  inhuman or degrading treatment 750
  International Court of Justice 749, 914
  liberty and security, right to 244
  life, right to 750
  objective impediments with compliance, onus to
      show 751
  private and family life, right to respect for 750
  Rules of Court 749
  single-judge formation 690
Interlaken Conference 31, 652, 658, 782
internal travel, restrictions on 1057–9, 1063, 1065
international bill of rights 1–2, 5–6, 61, 546, 776
International Convention on the Elimination of All
      Forms of Racial Discrimination 413, 556,
      566–7, 577, 914, 987, 1060, 1175–6
International Court of Justice
  admissibility 705, 776
  advisory opinions 874, 877–8
  Charter of UN 874
  declarations 913
  dissenting opinions 887
  ECtHR
    competition with 635
    establishment 632, 635, 637
  ex officio or national judges 693
  exclusion of other means of dispute
      resolution 907–10, 912–14
  exhaustion of domestic remedies 767
  final judgments 849
  gender balance 664
  general principles of international law 352–3, 719
  genocide 344
  interim measures 749
  inter-State applications 723–5, 912–13
  judges
    criteria for office 655
    dismissal 670
    election 658
    gender balance 664
    number 643
    privileges and immunities 891
    term of office 668
  jurisdiction 716, 719, 720
  merits, decisions on the 705
  optional clause 632
  overlapping jurisdiction 623
  pacta sunt servanda 866
  ratification 913
  ratione loci jurisdiction 937
  reasons for judgments 857
  referrals 724
  revision of judgments 852

Rules of Court 684
source of international law, Statute as 39
Statute of the International Court of Justice *see*
      Statute of the International Court of Justice
torture 164, 179
victim status 741
Vienna Convention on the Law of Treaties 40–4
war/armed conflict 154, 156
International Covenant on Civil and Political Rights *see*
      also under individual main entries
  concordance with ECHR 18–19, 1125
  derogations 587, 592–6, 599–601, 603–4, 1051,
      1155
  entry into force 18, 1125
  hate speech 463, 468, 478
  hierarchy of rights 593
  individual applications 21
  language 1179
  marriage 1179
  minorities 581
  no punishment without law 330, 343, 351–2, 356
  Optional Protocol in individual petitions 61
  person, right to recognition as a 592
  political activity of aliens, restrictions on 609
  Preamble 59, 61
  residence 1179
  safeguards for existing human rights 902
  social benefits, entitlement to 1179
  Universal Declaration of Human Rights 59, 61
  war/armed conflict 601
International Covenant on Economic, Social, and
      Cultural Rights
  education, right to 995–1006
  Optional Protocol in individual petitions 61
  peaceful enjoyment of possessions 959
  Preamble 59, 61
  thought, conscience and religion, freedom of 412
  trade unions 508
  Universal Declaration of Human Rights 59, 61
International Criminal Court (ICC) and
      Rome Statute
  access to documents 828
  age limits of judges 655
  aggression, definition of 602
  appeals 1134
  disappearances 136
  gender balance 664
  interpreters 315
  inter-State applications 723
  judges
    election 664
    gender balance 664
    term of office 668
  lex mitior principle 350
  standard of proof 123
  State responsibility 98–9
  superior orders defence 341–2
  thought, conscience and religion, freedom of 424

UN Security Council, triggering of prosecutions
    to 723
war/armed conflict 345, 602
International Criminal Tribunal for Rwanda 98, 658
International Criminal Tribunal for the former
    Yugoslavia
  age limits 655
  appeals 1134
  armed conflict, definition of 594–5
  completion strategy 99
  Dayton Agreement 99
  genocide 344
  judges
    dismissal 668
    election 658
    term of office 668
  jus cogens 179
  life, right to 157–8
  parole 260
  superior orders defence 342
  war crimes 99
international humanitarian law 37–8, 158, 345, 588,
    601–2, 641, 1104, 1106
International Labour Organization
  Committee on Freedom of Association 777
  Forced Labour Convention No 29 1930 202,
    213–16
  freedom of assembly and association 484, 508–9,
    515, 522
  freedom of expression 464, 473
  Indigenous and Tribal Peoples Convention 959
  League of Nations 464
  Social Security (Minimum Standards) Convention
    982
  trade unions 508, 515
International Law Commission Draft Articles on State
    Responsibility 101, 837, 868
International Military Tribunal
  Charter 202
  Control Council Law No 10 202
  crimes against humanity 343–4, 354
  death penalty 140, 1094–5
  derogations 602
  detention facilities 98
  general principles of international law 352–3
  judges, election of 658
  no punishment without law 329–30, 331, 352–4
  peace, crimes against 329, 343–4
  Charter 354
  superior orders defence 341
  war crimes 343–4
International Military Tribunal for the Far East
    (the Tokyo Tribunal) 353
international organisations *see also* particular
    organisations
  immunity 100
  ratione personae jurisdiction 105–6
  State responsibility 97–9

Internet
  defamation 387
  employees, use of email and Internet by 387
  freedom of expression 462–3, 466
  hyperlinks 463
  identification of perpetrators 387
  private and family life, right to respect for 463
  social media 359
interpretation 8, 33–50 *see also under* individual main
    entries; Vienna Convention on the Law of
    Treaties
  amendment mechanisms 49
  Committee of Ministers 905–6
  Committees, competence of 701–3
  consistency and harmony 47
  constitutional interpretation 48, 70
  death penalty 47, 49
  declarations 1009
  dynamic and evolutive interpretation 47–9
  ECtHR 33–48
  effectiveness, principle of 49–50
  ejusdem generis interpretation 572
  judicial law-making 48–9
  literal, historical interpretation 33
  living instrument principle 48
  maintenance and further realisation, meaning of 66
  Permanent Court of International Justice 33
  personal prejudices 33
  policy orientations 33
  Preamble 47–8
  precedent 46–7
  principle of interpretation, as 614–15
  protocols 49
  purposive/teleological interpretation 34
  restrictive interpretation 48
  rules and principles 33–4
  safeguards for existing human rights 903–4
  strict interpretation 34
  travaux préparatoires 34
  Universal Declaration of Human Rights 47–8
  whole, reading as a 47
interpreters 314–16
inter-State applications 723–9 *see also under* individual
    main entries
  acceptance of mechanism, no requirement
    for 724–5
  administrative practices 727–9
  admissibility 706–7, 726–9, 757, 762–3, 776
  collective enforcement 725, 727
  Committee of Experts 724
  compromis 724
  Conference of Senior Officials 724
  Consultative Assembly 724
  declarations, no requirement for 724
  delays 766
  diplomatic protection 725–6
  drafting 723–5
  ECommHR 9, 723–5, 727–8

inter-State applications (*cont.*)
  ECtHR, establishment of 633
  erga omnes obligations 725–6
  ex officio or national judges 693
  exhaustion of domestic remedies 728–9
  individual applications 723, 724–8, 757
  interim measures 729
  interpretation 725–9
  investigations and fact-finding 807–9
  just satisfaction 726
  life, right to 728
  manifestly ill-founded applications 727
  merits, decisions on the 706–7
  Permanent Court of International Justice 725
  public order, enforcement of 725–6
  ratification 723
  Rules of Court 729
  special agreement, cases brought by 724
  substantially the same, matters which are 775
  Universal Periodic Review 915
investigations and fact-finding
  ECommHR 634, 808–9
  examination of the case 805, 807–10
  fair trial in criminal proceedings, right
    to 310–11, 312
  individual applications 809
  interpreters 314–15
  inter-State applications 807–9
  national courts, deference to 807
  Rules of Court, Annex to 807–8
investigative duty *see* procedural/investigative obligation
Iraq
  death penalty 190–1, 1101
  life, right to 144, 190, 750
  state agent authority and control 101–2
  territorial application 923
Ireland
  abortion 81, 125, 373
  age of criminal responsibility 318
  broadcasting interviews with Sinn Fein, restrictions
    on 617
  Constitution 540–2
  death penalty 140, 1095
  declarations 1006, 1073
  derogations 598, 599, 603
  detention without trial 599
  ECommHR 808–9
  expulsion 1073
  extradition 1073
  family law, modernization of 820
  friendly settlements 820
  home schooling 1006
  illegitimate children 820
  legal aid 324
  liberty and security, right to 621
  marriage, dissolution of 541
  on-site visits 809
  reservations 324

terrorist suspects 598
torture 175, 177
Islam
  adoption (*kefala*) 394
  circumcision 430
  education 1003
  headscarf/veil 402, 437, 439, 743, 848
  Islamophobia 619
  political parties not based in Islam, call for ban
    on 619
  thought, conscience and religion, freedom of 413
  victim status 742
Isle of Man, corporal punishment in 70, 188–9,
    926–7, 1007
Israel
  abuse of rights, prohibition of 619
  derogations 588
  exist, right to 619
  Gaza flotilla, obstruction of 723 n.1, 899 n.1
  Geneva Conventions 158
  international humanitarian law 158
  life, right to 158
  Palestine 158, 731
  Red Cross 158
issue estoppel *see ne bis in idem*
Italy
  assisted pregnancies 373
  Austria 913
  boat, *refoulement* of migrants arriving by 1079–80
  child abduction 393
  colonies 920–1
  Constitution 769, 1073
  crucifixes in classrooms 433, 1003
  death penalty 1095
  declarations 1973, 1141, 1156
  discrimination 524–5
  expulsion 1071–3, 1073
  flag, violations on vessels carrying 102
  freedom of assembly and association 501, 511–12,
    517, 524–5
  freedom of expression 470
  HIV, contamination with 160
  inter-State applications 725–6
  Masons 512, 517, 524–5
  military service 215
  monarch, expulsion of 1071–2, 1073
  ne bis in idem 1156
  prisoners 398, 404
  quotas for professional accreditation 998
  regulatory offences 284
  rescue operations 102
  reservations 933–4, 1139
  secret associations 511
  Somaliland 920–1
  Süd Tirol/Alto Adige, dispute between Austria and
    Italy over 913
  vagrants, detention of 243
İzmir High Level Conference 2011 31, 750, 847

Jacobs, Francis 623
Jaquet, Gérard 557
Jehovah's Witnesses
  custody disputes 579–80
  education 1004
  employment 374–5
  inhuman or degrading treatment 196–7
  profession, freedom of 568–9
  religion or belief, freedom to manifest 430, 434, 435, 436
  thought, conscience and religion, freedom of 425, 426, 440–1
Jersey 597, 925, 928, 1036, 1114, 1206
jewellery, wearing 439
Jews
  anti-Semitism 479, 619
  circumcision 430
  elections, right to free 1031
  freedom of assembly and association 519
  Holocaust 479–80, 579, 615, 619
  marriage 544
  thought, conscience and religion, freedom of 413, 432, 437
journalists, freedom of expression of
  criticism, extent of acceptable 477–8
  defamation 478
  due diligence 458
  duties and responsibilities, notion of 468–9
  ethics 458
  exaggeration and provocation 458
  harassment 461
  inhuman or degrading treatment 461
  privilege 459
  public interest 459, 461–2
  punishment 454, 473
  sources, confidentiality of 459, 470
judges see also competence of single judges; election of
    judges; judges of ECtHR, number of; judicial
    formations
  ad hoc judges 687, 689, 691, 892
  age 31, 583–4, 650, 654–5, 670–4
  appointment by the executive or legislature 295
  Basic Principles on the Independence of the
    Judiciary (UN) 294
  candidate for election, right to stand as a 1030
  career prospects after office, maintenance of 673
  casual vacancies 671
  definition 474
  dialogue 26, 31–2, 1213, 1220, 1225
  dismissal 294, 668, 670, 672, 681
  executive, independence from the 294–5
  freedom of assembly and association 511
  freedom of expression 467–8, 473–4
  independent and impartiality 287, 294–6, 321, 467–8, 473–4
  investigations 807–8
  judicial law-making 48–9
  list of candidates 877, 885

Masons, as 511
  national judges 703
  nationality 644–8, 659, 686–8, 691, 698
  non-European judges, political or philosophical
    leanings of 907
  personal convictions 295
  precedence 673–4
  privileges and immunities 891–3
  resignation 672
  retirement 31, 672
  rotation 670
  salaries and social security contributions of
    judges 294, 673, 889, 890
  secret associations 511
  security of tenure 294
  separation of powers 294–5
  terms of office 294, 668–74
  withdrawal of judges, existence of rules for 296
  working conditions 672–3
judges, number of 643–6
  African Court on Human and Peoples' Rights 643
  Committee of Experts 643–4
  Committee of Ministers 644–5
  Conference of Senior Officials 644
  drafting 643–5
  ECommHR, procedure for appointments to 645
  Grand Chamber 709–10
  High Contracting Parties, use of term 645
  Inter-American Court of Human Rights 643
  International Court of Justice 643
  interpretation 645–6
  nationality, more than one judge with 644–6
  number of States Parties, equivalent to 643–5
  Parliamentary Assembly 645
  routine processing 643
judgments and decisions *see also* binding force and
    execution of judgments; final judgments
  appeals 841
  Chambers 841–2
  contents, guidance on 859
  definition 842
  dissenting opinions 781–2, 857–9, 887, 1224
  drafting 841
  finality 841–2
  Grand Chamber, referrals to 841
  inconsistent judgments, risk of 679, 691, 710–11, 844–5
  interpretation 841–2
  pronouncement/publication 288–9, 290–1, 825
  reasons 857–9
  res judicata 842
  revisions 841, 842, 847, 849, 852–4
  striking out 797–8, 821–2
judicial formations 686–95
  ad hoc judges 687, 689, 694–5
  case management 686
  caseload 686, 688
  Chambers 686–9, 690–1

judicial formations (*cont.*)
  Committee of Experts 687
  Committee of Ministers 688
  Committees
    filtering and processing applications 30
    full-time, sitting 690
    interpretation 690
    President of the Section 690
    Sections 690
    term of office 690
  composition 686
  Conference of Senior Officials 687
  Consultative Assembly 687
  Draft Statute 687
  drafting 687–9
  enlargement 688
  ex officio or national judges 687–8, 690, 692–4
  excusal 695
  filtering and processing applications 30
  Grand Chamber
    ad hoc judges 691
    advisory opinions, requests for 691–2
    authorization of referrals 692
    Committee of Ministers, referrals by 691–2
    composition 688–9, 691–2
    former Court 689
    full-time, sitting 690
    ex officio, sitting 690, 691–2
    inconsistent judgments, risk of 691
    interpretation 691–2
    judges of Chamber that relinquished
      jurisdiction 688
    lots, drawing 691–2
    nationality 691
    non-compliance, referral of situations of 691
    Plenary Court 692
    President of the Court 688, 691–2
    referrals following judgments by
      Chambers 691–2
    relinquishment of jurisdiction to 688, 691
    Rules of Court 692
    serious questions affecting interpretation 691
    session periods 690
    size 688–9
    substitute judges 691
    urgent cases 690
    Vice-President of the Court 688, 691–2
  incompatible professional activities 695
  independent and impartial tribunal 694–5
  interpretation 689–95
  nationality 687
  number of judges 686–8
  Parliamentary Assembly 689
  Plenary Court, relinquishment of jurisdiction
    to 688
  rapporteurs, assistance from 690
  recusal 695
  reserve list 689
routine applications 30
Rules of Court 688, 690, 694
session periods 690
single-judge formation 28–30, 689–90, 694–702,
    707, 763, 779, 805, 851
size of chambers 686–9
substitute judges 691
travaux préparatoires 688
urgent cases 690
Jungwiert, Karel 627
jura novit curiae 721, 815
juries
  directions 298
  publication of deliberations 461
  reasoned decisions 297–8
  self-incrimination 301
  sex discrimination 217, 566
  slavery and forced labour 216, 217
jurisconsults 647–8, 651–2
jurisdiction of ECtHR 715–22 *see also* Grand
      Chamber, relinquishment of jurisdiction to the
  admissibility 93, 705, 707, 721–2, 778–9
  advisory opinions 884–5
  applicable law 719–20
  Committee of Experts 717–18
  Committee of Ministers 715, 717, 720
  Consultative Assembly 716–17
  Conference of Senior Officials 718
  consent to jurisdiction 721
  consolidating the institutions and further
      reform 719, 720
  Consultative Assembly 719
  declarations of acceptance 692
  definition of jurisdiction 715
  denial of justice, notion of 716–17
  disputes about jurisdiction 721–2
  dissolution of States 93
  drafting 715–19
  ECommHR 718–22
  ECtHR, establishment of 632–5
  estoppel 93
  executive acts 715
  exhaustion of domestic remedies 717
  general principles of international law 719
  Grand Chamber 713–14
  individual applications 639
  International Court of Justice, Statute of 716,
      719, 720
  interpretation 633, 641–2, 718–22
  jura novit curiae doctrine 721
  juridical acts 715
  legislative acts 715
  merits, decisions on the 705, 707
  more than one State, violations by 93
  obligation to respect human rights 84, 92–112
  optional clause 632, 637, 644
  optional declarations 889
  personal jurisdiction 720

Plenary Court 688, 719–20
protocols, interpretation of 721
ratione loci jurisdiction 84, 93, 95–105, 720, 937–8
ratione materiae jurisdiction 84, 93–5, 107, 389,
    720–1, 778–9, 934, 1106
ratione personae jurisdiction 84, 93, 105–7,
    720, 778
ratione temporis jurisdiction 93, 107–12, 720, 772,
    778, 935
succession to ECHR 720
supervisory jurisdiction 639
universal jurisdiction 102
victims 93
Vienna Convention on the Law of Treaties 719
voting on decisions 859
jus ad bellum 156, 601
jus cogens 44, 164, 179–80, 328, 593
jus in bello 156, 602
just satisfaction 830–9
    administrative action 830
    binding force and execution of judgments 867, 871
    causal link 836
    Chambers on admissibility and merits, decisions
        by 707
    Committee of Experts 831, 834–5
    Committee of Ministers 832–3
    compensation 830, 832–9
    Conference of Senior Officials 832
    Consultative Assembly 830–3, 835
    death of applicants 853
    definition 830
    diplomatic protection 834–5
    drafting 830–3
    exhaustion of domestic remedies 835–6
    friendly settlements 821
    general principles of international law 834
    Grand Chamber 834
    internal law of High Contracting Party involved,
        meaning of 835–6
    interpretation 833–9
    inter-State applications 726, 834
    invalid, substitution for declarations that national
        law is 830
    just satisfaction, definition of 836–9
    national laws 835–6
    national sovereignty 835
    penal action 830
    punitive damages 839
    protocols 839
    reparations 830, 832–9
    repeal, cancellation or amendment of acts 830
    restitutio in integrum principle 837–8
    systemic violations 830
    travaux préparatoires 834
    Universal Declaration of Human Rights 830
    victim status 738
justice and peace 66–8
Justinian, Digest of 220

Kabardino-Balkaria 1065
Karpas peninsula in northern Cyprus 835, 838
Katyn massacre in Soviet Union 139, 171
Kazakhstan 146, 1100
Keller, Helen 439, 646
Kelsen, Hans 329–30
Kleffner, Jann 55
Koestler, Arthur 1091
kompetenz-kompetenz 884
Kosovo, peacekeeping in 106
Kraft, Ole Bjorn 558
Kurds 157, 401, 453, 464, 471–2, 598, 739, 998

Lagergren, Gunnar 69
languages
    advisory opinions 1217, 1223, 1224
    Copenhagen Document of CSCE 1023
    Council of Europe Declaration 1023
    customary international law 46
    defence, adequate time and facilities for
        preparation of 46
    delay 46
    discrimination 555–6, 558–61, 579, 583, 600
    education 579, 992, 998–1000
    elections, right to free 1023–4
    European Charter for Minority or Regional
        Languages 581, 1024
    Framework Convention for the Protection of
        National Minorities 1024
    fluency in official languages 652–3
    individual applications 746
    interpreters 314–16
    judicial office, criteria for 652–4
    minorities 13, 22, 998, 999, 1023–4
    official languages 746, 851, 855
    prisoners, correspondence of 401
    private and family life, right to respect for 1000
    publication of judgments 851, 855
    Roma 1005
    translations 401
    Vienna Convention on the Law of
        Treaties 35, 45–6
Lannung, Hermod 13, 22, 558–9, 562, 576 n.147,
    920, 1049, 1069, 1082
Latvia 140, 215, 375–6, 434, 584, 984
Lauterpacht, Hersch 5, 49, 158, 528
law, definition of 336–8
Layton, Walter (Lord Layton) 56, 360–1, 530–1,
    636, 960
League of Nations 329, 464, 731, 874
Lebanon 98, 222, 328, 658, 668
left alone, right to be 358
legal aid 249, 267, 269, 282, 310–11, 322, 748
legal certainty *see* no punishment without law
legal personality 106, 379, 440, 501, 736
legal representatives/profession
    disbarment 976
    disciplinary measures 283

legal representatives/profession (*cont.*)
    fair trial, right to a 284, 309, 310–11, 317
    individual applications 745–8
    legal aid appointed counsel 311
    right to legal assistance 25
    slavery and forced labour 217
    special advocates 257
legal secretaries (law clerks) 675
legality, principle of *see* no punishment without law
legitimate aim/purpose, restrictions for a *see also under*
    individual main entries
legitimate expectations 340, 400, 969, 1129
Leuprecht, Peter 906
lex mitior principle 330, 350–1, 904
liberty and security, right to 219–63
    abuse of rights, prohibition of 621
    administrative detention 242, 262
    appeals 236, 255–7
    arbitrariness 220–1, 223, 226, 231–6, 239
    arrest 221, 223–4, 227, 234, 237–9, 243–6,
        254, 257–9
    asylum seekers 243
    bail 250–1, 253
    burden of proof for release 252
    cell, confinement to 228
    Charter of Fundamental Rights of the EU 220–1
    coercion 226–7
    collective expulsion of aliens 1075
    Committee of Experts 221–6, 242
    Committee of Legal Experts 226
    Committee of Ministers 221, 224–6
    compensation, right to 110, 224–6, 257–9, 1143
    competent legal authority 238, 240–1, 248–50
    conditional release 245
    conditions of detention 232
    Conference of Senior Officials 225
    Consultative Assembly 221–2
    conviction, detention after 236
    criminal justice 221–7, 235–40, 245–53, 261
    deception 232–3
    derogations 37, 588, 600
    delay 234
    deportation 233–4, 243–5, 259–60
    deprivation of liberty, what amounts to 226–7
    disappearances 229
    disciplinary measures 228, 235, 260–1
    discretionary life sentences 256
    discrimination 259–60
    drafting 221–6, 245
    drunks/alcoholics 222–3, 241–2
    due diligence 234
    duration of deprivation of liberty 227, 230–1, 234,
        237, 262
    entry, prevention of 243–4
    exceptions 226
    exile and other measures 220–1, 223
    expulsion 96, 243–5, 259–60
    extension of time in detention 230

    extradition 96, 228, 232, 243–6
    fair trial, right to a 275
    foreign courts, orders imposed by 235
    Geneva Conventions 37, 641
    good faith 232–3, 243
    grounds for detention 234–44
    guarantees to appear for trial 253
    habeas corpus 220, 253–4
    human trafficking 229
    immigration 233–4, 243
    indefinite detention 231, 239
    independence and impartiality 249
    indeterminate sentences 259
    infectious diseases 241
    International Covenant on Civil and Political
        Rights 244, 250
    internment 235, 260
    interpretation 226–61
    judicial review 254, 262
    lawfulness 229–33, 239, 244, 254–6
    legal aid 249
    life sentences 256
    limitation on use of restrictions 625–7
    mandatory life sentences 256
    medical reasons, detention for 220, 227–8, 234,
        241–3, 245
    mental disabilities 220, 227–8, 234, 241–3
    military discipline, reservations on 260–1
    minors 240–1, 251, 261
    national laws 229–33
    national security 234, 257
    no punishment without law 231–2, 258
    non-compliance with a court order or legal
        obligation 236–8
    objective factors 227
    organized crime 239
    parole, right to automatic 259–60
    physical liberty 226–8
    place of detention 232
    political motivations 626
    positive obligations 228–9
    post-conviction detention 235–6
    presumption of innocence 250, 257
    pre-trial detention 251
    preventive detention 235
    prisoners 228, 259–60, 275
    procedural fairness 254–5
    procedural/investigative obligation 229
    procedure prescribed by law 234
    prompt appearance before judicial
        authorities 246–50
    proportionality 238–9, 260
    provisional measures 244
    provisional release 250
    public interest 233
    punitiveness 237–8
    reasonable suspicion 238–9, 249, 252, 254
    reasonableness 238–9

reasons, duty to give 224, 233, 244–6
release pending trial 250–3
remedies 257
reservations 260–2
restrictions on freedom of movement 226
reviews 230, 248–50, 254–7, 262
rule of law 247, 254
scope of application 226–8
security of person, definition of 228–9
slavery and forced labour 205
social reasons, for 220, 227–8, 234, 241–3
stop and search 226–7
terrorism 239, 588
travaux préparatoires 245
trial within a reasonable time or release pending
    trial 250–3
Universal Declaration of Human Rights 220–5, 228
unsound mind, persons of 220, 227–8,
    234, 241–3
vagrants 220, 222–3, 243
Vienna Convention on the Law of Treaties 36–7
vulnerable persons 229
wartime 36–7, 235
wrongful convictions, compensation for 110, 1143
licensing
business activities, to 973
freedom of expression 445, 466–7
peaceful enjoyment of possessions 973
Liechtenstein
age of criminal responsibility 318
death penalty 1095–6
declarations 1141, 1156
family life 409
homosexuality, criminalization of 408–9
illegitimate children, status of 409
ne bis in idem 1156
private and family life, right to respect for 408–9
public hearings 323
reservations 161, 323, 408–9, 934, 1139
self-defence 161
women, status of 409
life imprisonment
death penalty, replacement of 349–50
discretionary life sentences 256
human dignity 187
inhuman or degrading treatment 187–8
liberty and security, right to 256
mandatory life sentences 256
no punishment without law 336–7
preventive detention 188
reviews 187
life, right to 117–61 *see also* armed conflict and right to
    life; death penalty and right to life
abortion 81–2, 117, 124–5
absolute right, as 118
accountability 135, 137
beneficiaries of right 124–6
burden of proof 123

Chambers on admissibility and merits, decisions
    by 707
Charter of Fundamental Rights of the EU 119
Committee of Experts 120–1
Committee of Ministers 121
Conference of Senior Officials 121
constitutions 118
Consultative Assembly 119–20
Council of Europe 124
criminal justice 111, 127–9, 134–6
death penalty 117, 120, 122, 127, 140–6, 1091–2,
    1094, 1197–202
derogations 592, 1155
detainees 123, 133–4, 136
diplomatic immunity 100
disappearances, enforced 123, 126, 136–7
discrimination 159–60
drafting 119–22, 139–40
ECommHR 117, 128, 139–40
ECtHR 117, 119, 122–31, 137, 159–60
emergency medical care 133–4
euthanasia 117, 128, 132–3
everyone, definition of 124–6
evidence 810
exceptions 118, 122–3
expulsion 740–1, 1128
extradition, deportation or expulsion 96, 127
firearms by State officials, use of 129–31
genocide 121–2
Grand Chamber, referral to 848
health and safety 131–2
homicide 127–9
hunger strikes of prisoners 132
impunity 139
indirect victims 742
individual applications 734
inhuman or degrading treatment 118, 137–8,
    164, 169
intention 139–40
interim measures 750
International Covenant on Civil and Political
    Rights 592, 118–19
interpretation 117, 124–6, 135
inter-State applications 728
law enforcement 118
legal and administrative framework, putting into
    place a 126–7
margin of appreciation 81–2, 124–5
medical treatment 131, 133–4, 138
mercy, prerogative of 117
military, medical care for 134
missing persons 123, 126, 136–7
national security 121
negative dimensions 126
negligent acts 118, 128, 131–2, 136, 138–9
next-of-kin applications 740
no punishment without law 110
nuclear arms 117

life, right to (*cont.*)
  omissions 128
  police 815
  positive obligations 126–39
  post-First World War treaties 118
  presumption of death 123, 126
  preventive measures 129–30, 133, 139–40
  private and family life, right to respect for 125–7
  procedural/investigative obligation 111–12, 122,
    134–9, 160, 578–9, 773, 848
  proportionality 122, 127
  protected by law, meaning of 126–39
  protest, suicide as a 132
  quality of life 127
  racial violence 578–9
  ratione temporis jurisdiction 111–12, 134, 139
  reservations 160–1
  rule of law 128, 139
  self-defence 118, 160–1
  self-harm 132
  standard of proof 123
  State agents 133, 815
  suicide 132–3
  third-party intervention 792
  time limits 773
  torture 118, 164, 169
  truth, right to 138–9
  Universal Declaration of Human Rights 118–21
  use of lethal force by State agents 117, 122–3, 125,
    127, 135, 146–53, 815
  war/armed conflict 153–8, 592
limitation on use of restrictions on rights 623–7
  absorption approach 621
  abuse of rights 625
  Charter of Fundamental Rights of the EU 623
  Committee of Experts 623
  Committee of Ministers 624
  Conference of Senior Officials 623–4
  democracy 627
  derogations 625
  drafting 623–4
  expulsion of aliens 625
  fair trial, right to a 625
  freedom of assembly and association 625
  freedom of expression 625
  general principles of international law 623
  good faith 626
  interpretation 623, 624–7
  liberty and security, right to 625–7
  life, right to 625
  political activities of aliens 625
  private and family life, right to respect for 625
  protocols 627
  restrictions/limitations clause 625
  specialized limitations clause 623
  standard of proof 625–6
  subsidiary, Article 18 as 624–5
  thought, conscience and religion, freedom of 625

  Universal Declaration of Human Rights 623
limitation periods *see* time limits
limitations *see* limitation on use of restrictions on rights;
  under individual main entries; legitimate aim/
  purpose, restrictions for a; necessary in a
  democratic society, restrictions which are;
  prescribed by law, restrictions which are
lis pendens 355, 1148–9
Lithuania
  civil partnerships 408
  impeachment of head of state 617
  liberty and security, right to 232, 935
  regulatory offences 284
  reservations 935
living instrument principle 48, 176, 211
Locke, John 444
locus standi 736–45, 795
Loewenstein, Karl 519
Loucaides, Loukis 423
Luxembourg
  hunting rights 973
  no punishment without law 330
  patronymic names 1159
  peaceful enjoyment of possessions 983
  ratification 9
  reservations 983

MacBride, Seán 733, 962–3, 990, 1016
Maccas, Leon 612
MacDonald, Ronald St John 646
Macedonia
  Constitution 511, 1008
  education 1008
  ethnic identity 511
  extraordinary rendition 900–1
  freedom of assembly and association 511, 513
  reservations 1008
MacEntee, Sean 266, 360, 361–2, 531, 558
McNair, Arnold 682
Macao 922, 1114
Magna Carta 220
Mahoney, Paul 348
Malawi 946
Malik, Charles 611
Malinverni, Giorgio 646
Malta
  declarations 1009
  jury service 217, 566
  no punishment without law 340
  Parliamentary Assembly, dispute with 876–7
  paternity 390–1
  political activities 481, 609
  presumption of innocence 325
  rent control 980
  reservations 160–1, 325, 609, 1009
  self-defence 160–1
  territorial application 924
  women candidates for judgeship 876–7

manifest religion or belief, freedom to 427–40
  abortion 383, 431
  accessibility 435
  alone or in a community 429–30
  balancing exercise 429, 437–9
  buildings, tax status of 429
  Charter of Fundamental Rights of the EU 433
  circumcision 430
  clothing 437, 439
  collective dimension 429
  conscientious objection 433–4
  discrimination 428
  education 428, 433
  employment 432–4, 438–9
  expulsion and deportation 434–5, 1071
  face coverings, ban on 437, 439
  fasting 430
  foreseeability 435
  freedom of assembly and association 429
  Grand Chamber, relinquishment of jurisdiction to
      the 711
  harmful activities 429–30
  headscarf ban in universities 437
  holidays 432, 437
  identity cards indicating religious domination 428
  immigration 434
  interference with freedom 432–5
  International Covenant on Civil and Political
      Rights 435
  Jehovah's Witnesses 430, 434, 435, 436
  legitimate purpose, restrictions for a 420, 436–7, 440
  link between act and underlying belief 427
  margin of appreciation 429, 436, 438
  marriage 438
  necessary in a democratic society, restrictions which
      are 420, 437–40
  negative aspect 428
  non-believers, requirement for people to reveal
      they are 428
  oaths 428
  observance 427, 431–2
  pluralism 429, 432, 437
  positive obligation 428–9, 438
  practice 427, 431–2
  prescribed by law, restrictions which have
      been 420, 435–6
  prisoners 435, 440
  proportionality 438–9
  proselytizing 426–7, 1002
  protection of rights and freedom of others 435
  public or private, in 430–1
  public order, health or morals 435, 437
  public safety 435, 437
  reasonable accommodation 439–40
  restrictions/limitations 420, 435–40
  reveal faith, requirement to 428
  rule of law 436
  sects 437
  sexual orientation 438–9
  tax 429
  teaching 427, 431–2
  terrorism 436
  tolerance 438
  travaux préparatoires 434
  turbans, wearing 439
  Universal Declaration of Human Rights 435
  vegetarian diet 435, 440
  worship 427, 431–2
manifestly ill-founded applications, rejection of
  admissibility criteria 705, 711, 727, 755–9, 778,
      779–81, 1071
  discrimination 217, 565, 568
  enjoyment of any right set forth by law 1182
  thought, conscience and religion, freedom
      of 439, 1059
margin of appreciation *see also under* individual main
    entries
  abortion 81–2
  academic literature 79–80
  accessibility 340–2
  accused at trial, presence of 81
  collective enforcement 79
  competing rights 82
  consolidation of institutions and reform 78–9
  derogations 79, 82–3
  ECommHR 79–80
  economic or social strategy, measures of 81
  ECtHR, case law of 79
  emergencies, derogations in 82–3
  filtering and processing applications 79
  housing 81
  inter-State applications 727
  life, right to 81–2
  limitations on rights 82
  margin of discretion, use of term 80
  Parliamentary Assembly 79
  parliamentary immunities 79
  planning 81
  punishment, just and proportionate 81
  Steering Committee for Human Rights 79
  university admission 1005
Maridakis, Georges 672, 684
marital rape 339
marriage *see also* marry and found a family, right to
  dissolution 1158–9
  equality between spouses 1157–9
  International Covenant on Civil and Political
      Rights 1179
  marriage ceremonies 562–3, 1181–2, 1186
  polygamy 438, 538–9
  religion
    ceremonies, freedom to provide wedding 562–3,
        1181–2, 1186
    manifest religion or belief, freedom to 438
  underage marriage 438
marry and found a family, right to 528–45

marry and found a family, right to (*cont.*)
  abortion 543
  absolute, right as being 533
  age 537
  balancing exercise 540
  blood, relatives by 539
  capacity 534
  Charter of Fundamental Rights of the EU 529,
      536–7, 583
  cohabitation 538, 544
  Commission on the Status of Women 528, 540
  Committee of Experts 532
  Committee of Ministers 531–2
  Conference of Senior Officials 532
  consent 534
  constitutions 528
  Consultative Assembly 530–2
  convenience, marriages of 540, 544
  culture 542–4
  de facto marriage 538
  discrimination 528, 531–2, 537, 543–4
  dissolution of marriage 540–2, 544
  drafting 528, 529–33, 541
  equality between spouses 1157
  European Social Charter 529
  family life 360, 375–6, 388, 407, 534
  found a family, right to 542–3
  gender 407, 535–7
  grandparents 534
  illegitimate children 538
  International Covenant on Civil and Political
      Rights 529
  interpretation 533–43
  legitimate aim/purpose, restrictions
      for a 539, 542
  margin of appreciation 533–4, 536, 539–40
  marriage, relatives by 539
  married women, discrimination against 528
  men and women, definition of 535–7
  motives 538
  names 375–6, 407, 544
  natural rights 529
  natural unit of society, family as 531
  not to marry, freedom 538
  parental consent 537
  paternity rights 530
  pensions, access to 544
  polygamy 538–9
  prisoners 539–40
  private and family life, right to respect for 542
  procreate, no right to 534
  proportionality 533
  public interest 542
  religious rites 544
  reservations 545
  restrictions/limitations 533–4
  right to marry, definition of 539–42
  same sex marriage 535

  sexual life and activity 406
  signing ceremonies 532
  social benefits, eligibility for 544
  social changes 535–6
  sterilization 543
  thought, conscience and religion, freedom of 541
  totalitarian states 360
  traditional marriage 535–6
  transgender persons 535–7, 544
  travaux préparatoires 64, 541
  Universal Declaration of Human Rights 528–30,
      532, 535, 540–1
  witnesses, compellability of spouses as 538, 544
Martens Clause 158
Marx, Karl 958
Masons 511, 512, 517, 524–5
Mauritania 202
Maxwell Fyfe, David 8–9, 55, 57, 84, 119, 168, 331,
      445, 484–5, 557, 591, 612, 719, 733, 754,
      921, 960
Mayotte 1159, 1162
media *see also* journalists, freedom of expression of
  access 453
  audiovisual 457–8, 467, 480–1
  broadcasting interviews with Sinn Fein, restrictions
      on 617
  chilling effects 476
  criminal justice 185
  democracy 460
  discrimination 480–1
  dissemination, extent of 477
  duties and responsibilities, notion of 468
  elections, right to free 1022, 1023
  electronic media 457
  freedom of expression 453–4, 457–62, 466–8,
      474–7, 480–1
  freedom of the press 384–5
  friendly settlements 821
  head of state, insulting the 784
  honour and reputation, attacks on 384–5
  individual applications 781
  juvenile offenders, exclusion of media from trial
      of 480
  licensing of broadcasting, television, or cinema
      enterprises 466–7
  margin of appreciation 462
  necessary in a democratic society, restrictions which
      are 474
  political expression 458, 461–2
  political parties 1023
  press 457–62, 474–5
  presumption of innocence 299, 302–3
  private and family life, right to respect for 359, 368,
      385, 461–2
  public interest 368
  replies and rectification 459–60
  reporting restrictions 460, 480
  sanctions, severity of 475

medical treatment and health 131, 133–4, 138, 371–4
   see also abortion
  access to information 374, 383
  data protection 374, 383
  detention for medical reasons 220, 227–8, 234,
    241–3, 245
  emergencies 133–4
  environment 388
  European Social and Medical Assistance
    Convention 1129
  health professionals, standards of 131, 138
  HIV/AIDS 126, 160, 172, 827
  inhuman or degrading treatment 174, 183–6, 372
  life, right to 133
  medical or scientific experimentation, consent
    to 164, 166–7
  medical malpractice 111, 128, 131, 138
  medication
    access 131
    without regulatory approval 371–2
  military service 134
  necessity 183
  parent, right to be a 372–3
  patient information 290
  prisoners/detainees
    correspondence 401
    medical care 133–4, 174, 183, 185–6
    release of 186
  public hearings 290, 827
  public safety, public health, and public order 435,
    437, 595, 603
  records, disclosure of 374, 383
  reproductive health 372–4
  sterilization of Roma women 183–4, 372
  torture 164, 166–7
  vaccinations 371
Mehta, Hansa 5
mental disabilities 220, 227–8, 234, 241–3
mercy, prerogative of 117
Meron, Theodor 655
migration *see* freedom of movement and migration
Milanovic, Marko 917
militant democracy 445, 519–21
military service
  candidate in elections, right to stand as a 1030
  civilian service, provision of an alternative 215
  compulsory service 205, 214–16
  conscientious objection 204–5, 214–16, 433–4,
    569, 848
  death penalty 1095
  disabilities, persons with 380
  discipline 260–1, 278, 324–5
  exemption 569
  expulsion 1070
  freedom of assembly and association 490, 509, 522
  freedom of expression 470
  homosexuals, expulsion of 172–3, 198, 381
  medical care 134

  private life 381
  slavery and forced labour 214–16
  thought, conscience and religion, freedom of 215
Milton, John 444
minorities
  Committee of Ministers 22
  crime and family, extension of ECHR to 19
  culture 12–13, 22, 582
  discrimination 525, 556, 558–62, 572–3, 577,
    580–2, 1184
  education 13
  elections 515, 518
  European Charter for Minority or Regional
    Languages 581
  family life 379
  First World War 413
  forced transfers 1067
  Framework Convention for the Protection of
    National Minorities 38, 491, 581–2
  freedom of assembly and association 491, 494,
    514–15, 518, 525
  freedom of expression 450
  freedom of movement and migration 13
  Gypsies 582
  homes, raiding 363
  International Covenant on Civil and Political
    Rights 22, 581
  interpreters 316
  language 13, 22, 998, 999
  national minorities 11, 21–3, 556, 558–62,
    573, 581–2
    association with a 561, 572–3, 577, 580–2
    definition 582
    discrimination 1184
    elections 515, 518
    freedom of assembly and association 491,
      515, 518
    freedom of expression 450
    freedom of movement and migration 13
    private and family life, right to respect for 363
    thought, conscience and religion, freedom of 418
    Vienna Convention on the Law of Treaties 38
  Parliamentary Assembly 22, 581–2
  political rights 22
  private and family life, right to respect for 360, 363
  religion 13, 22, 1002
  Roma 582
  sexual minorities 518
  Sinti 582
  thought, conscience and religion, freedom of 413
  Travellers 582
  Universal Declaration of Human Rights 11, 21–2
minors *see* children
miscarriages of justice 267, 306, 319 *see also*
    compensation for wrongful conviction
missing persons *see* disappearances
mistake or ignorance of the law 341
Mitchison, Gilbert 56–8, 562

Modinos, Poly 20
Moldova
  candidate for election, right to stand as a 1030
  death penalty 1206
  declarations 1009
  domestic violence 198
  dual nationality 1030
  freedom of assembly and association 498
  identity 404
  inquiries by the Secretary General 899
  ratione loci jurisdiction 938
  reservations 218, 937
  slavery and forced labour 218
  territorial application 1206
  Transdniestria 99, 809–10, 937, 999–1000
Monaco
  Constitution 584–5
  death penalty 14
  declarations 751, 1141
  expulsion 1065
  fair trial, right to a 324–5
  individual applications 751
  professional activity, authorization to exercise a 409
  radio and TV broadcasting, State monopoly of 481
  reservations 324–5, 409, 554, 937, 1065
  sovereign immunity 554
Mosler, Hermann 682
motoring offences 283, 299–300, 783, 1153
Muslims *see* Islam

names
  American Convention on Human Rights 592
  family life 375–6, 407
  legitimate aim/purpose, restrictions for a 544
  married names 375–6, 407
  marry and found a family, right to 544
  patronymic names 1159
  private life 375–6
  proportionality 544
  sex discrimination 407
national courts *see also* exhaustion of domestic remedies
  African slave trade, litigation over 202
  effective remedy, right to an 550
  final judgments 109
  freedom of expression 458, 474–5
  investigations and fact-finding, defence to national
    courts with regard to 807
  law, definition of 337–8
  review of decisions 266, 271
  sentencing 454
  sources of international law, decisions as 43–4
  subsidiarity 77–8
  war crimes 99
national laws
  advisory opinions 1222–3
  evidence 320
  examination of the case 807
  just satisfaction 835–6

liberty and security, right to 229–33
no punishment without law 336, 355
polygamy 539
private and family life, right to respect for 403–4
replies and rectifications in media 460
safeguards for existing human rights 904
national origins, discrimination on grounds of 555–6,
    580–1, 583
national security
  collective expulsion of aliens 1076–7
  discrimination 525
  evidence 814
  expulsion of aliens, procedural safeguards relating
    to 1132
  freedom of assembly and association 511–13, 525
  freedom of expression 448, 467, 471–2
  freedom of movement and migration 1062, 1063
  in camera hearings 827
  liberty and security, right to 234, 257
  life, right to 121
  private and family life, right to respect for 404–5
  public hearings 290–1
  refugee claims 828
  special advocates 257
nationality
  ad hoc judges 686–8
  American Convention on Human Rights 592
  Chambers 687, 691
  change of nationality 581
  discrimination 407, 556, 574, 581, 600
  expropriation 1183
  expulsion 1069–70, 1072, 1076
  freedom of movement and migration 1060
  Grand Chamber 691
  judges 644–8, 659, 686–8, 691, 698
  national origins distinguished 581
  private and family life, right to respect
    for 378–9, 1072
  right to a nationality 1072
  statelessness 581
  suspect grounds 574
  terrorist organizations, withdrawal for citizens
    joining 1072
  third-party intervention 788–9, 792
  Universal Declaration of Human Rights 581, 1072
NATO (North Atlantic Treaty Organization)
  Belgrade, bombing of 97, 103–4
  Status of Forces Agreement 98, 1100
natural rights 359–60, 529, 557
Nazi regime 202, 329, 342, 353, 479, 619, 1095
ne bis in idem 1147–56
  amnesties 1150, 1155
  appeals, time limits for 1149–50
  Charter of Fundamental Rights of the EU 1148
  Committee of Experts 1147–8
  compensation 1150
  criminal proceedings, definition of 1151–3
  death penalty 1110

declarations 1156
derogations 592, 1155
disqualification orders 1152
drafting 1148
duplication of proceedings (*bis*) 1150–3
Engel procedure 1151–2
error, proceedings brought in 1151
final conviction or acquittal in first
proceedings 1149–50
final judgments 849
Grand Chamber 1153–4
identity of offences (*idem*) 1153–4
International Covenant on Civil and Political
Rights 1147–9, 1155
interpretation 1148–55
motor vehicle offences 1153
newly discovered facts, reopening case with evidence
of 1154–5
parallel proceedings 1148–9
penal procedure 1151–2
penalties, extent of 1152
prison discipline 1152
reopening of the case 1154–5
reservations 1155
Universal Declaration of Human Rights 1147,
1155
necessary in a democratic society, restrictions which are
see also under individual main entries
negative obligations
education 992–3, 996, 1001
family life 388
freedom of assembly and association 493, 502,
507–8
freedom of expression 454, 456–7
individual applications 748
life, right to 126
manifest a religion, right to 428
obligation to respect human rights 90–1
private and family life, right to respect for 367–9
ratione loci jurisdiction 103
'shall secure . . . negative and positive
obligations' 90–1
vulnerable applicants 748
negligence 118, 128, 131–2, 136, 138–9, 1050
Netherlands
Aruba 1036, 1084, 1190, 1108, 1114, 1205
colonies 324, 917, 1036, 1073–4, 1084, 1190,
1108, 1114, 1205
Constitution 358
death penalty 1099–100, 1101, 1108, 1114
declarations 1006, 1065–6, 1073–4, 1141
DNA sampling 346
expulsion 1073–4
freedom of movement and migration 1059,
1065–6, 1084
journalists' sources, confidentiality of 470
legal aid 324
military discipline 876

Netherlands Antilles 324, 1036, 1073–4, 1084,
1190, 1108, 1114, 1205
no punishment without law 330
private and family life, right to respect for 358
reservations 324, 1139
Surinam 324, 946, 1036
territorial application 324, 1036, 1073–4, 1084,
1190, 1114, 1205
torture, diplomatic assurances on 1100–1
Netherlands Antilles 324, 1036, 1073–4, 1084, 1190,
1108, 1114, 1205
New Caledonia 608, 927, 1159
next-of-kin applications 738–40, 798
NGOs *see* non-governmental organizations
no punishment without law 328–56
accessibility 336–7, 342, 345, 353
analogy, definition of crimes by 334–5
binding force and execution of judgments 870
Charter of Fundamental Rights of the EU 330
collaboration with the enemy 353, 355
Committee of Experts 332–3
Committee of Ministers 331, 333–4
Conference of Senior Officials 333
Consultative Assembly 331–2
crimes against humanity 344–5, 355
criminal law 336–7, 339–41, 343–4
death penalty and right to life 49
derogations 328, 335, 592–3, 600
discrimination 355–6
drafting 331–4, 355
ECtHR, case law of 330
elections, right to free 1025
final judgments 849
foreseeability 335–42, 345, 353
general principles of international law 332, 336,
350, 351–5
Geneva Conventions 345
genocide 343–4
heavier penalties 336–7, 339, 345–50
human dignity 330
immunity 331
individual applications 734
inhuman or degrading treatment 110
International Covenant on Civil and Political
Rights 330, 343, 351–2, 356, 592
international law 336, 343–5
International Military Tribunal 329–30, 331, 352–4
interpretation 334–50
judicial interpretation and case law, role of 338–40
jus cogens 328
law, definition of 336–8
legitimate expectations 340
lex mitior principle (imposition of lighter
penalties) 330, 350–1
liberty and security, right to 231–2, 258
life imprisonment 336–7
life, right to 110
limitation periods 356

no punishment without law (*cont.*)
  lis pendens 355
  marital rape 339
  mistake or ignorance of the law 341
  national laws 336, 355
  Paris Peace Conference of 1919 328
  peace, crimes against 329–30
  peaceful enjoyment of possessions 974
  penalties/punishment 328–30, 333–5
  Permanent Court of International Justice 329
  Preamble 335
  proportionality 330
  ratione temporis jurisdiction 107–10
  res judicata 355
  reservations 356, 936
  rule of law 335–6, 342, 351
  Second World War 329–30, 331, 333, 352–5
  sentencing 339
  strict interpretation 335
  superior orders, defence of 341–2
  time limits 342–3
  treason 355
  Universal Declaration of Human Rights 328,
      330–3, 343, 355
  Versailles, Treaty of 328–9
  Vienna Convention on the Law of Treaties 786
  war crimes 345, 355
noise 388
non-discrimination *see* discrimination
non-governmental organizations
  applications by authorized representatives, signing
      of 745
  freedom of assembly and association 501
  individual applications 734–7, 745, 748
  next-of-kin applications 739
  third-party intervention 793–5
  victim status 737, 741
non-self-governing territories 916–17
Northern Ireland
  derogations 596–7, 600–1
  detention/deprivation of liberty 154, 235, 237,
      260, 597, 600, 854
  discrimination 472, 475, 480, 558, 579
  employment, access to 558
  housing, access to 558
  inhuman or degrading treatment 181
  internment 154, 235, 237
  Maze Prison 809
  on-site visits 809
  political opinions 558
  prison, ban on sectarian symbols in 472,
      475, 480
  religious discrimination 558, 579
  sectarianism 472, 475, 480, 579
  terrorism 260
  torture 175
  truth, right to 139
Norton, William 862

Norway
  Constitution 358
  education 1003
  expulsion 398
  no punishment without law 330
  private and family life, right to respect for 358
  religion 1003
  rent control 980
  tax liability 1154
Nowak, Manfred 614, 1142, 1180
nuclear weapons 117
nudity in public 377, 455
nuisance 388, 399–400
nullum crimen nulla poena sine lege see no punishment
      without law
Nuremberg Military Tribunal *see* International Military
      Tribunal
Nußberger, Angelika 627

oaths 428, 656, 677, 810
obligation to respect human rights 84–112
  aliens 85
  binding character of ECHR 88
  colonies and overseas territories 84–5
  Committee of Experts 85–6
  Committee of Ministers 87
  Conference of Senior Officials 86–7
  Consultative Assembly 85
  diplomatic protection 105
  drafting 84–7
  Explanatory Report 86
  guarantees 85–6
  High Contracting Parties, use of term 88–90
  International Covenant on Civil and Political
      Rights 84–5
  interpretation 88–112
  jurisdiction 84, 92–1012
  limitations 88
  protocols, application to 88, 92
  ratione loci jurisdiction 84, 93, 95–104
  ratione materiae jurisdiction 84, 93, 94–5
  ratione personae jurisdiction 84, 93, 105–7
  ratione temporis jurisdiction 93, 107–12
  'shall secure...negative and positive obligations' 90–1
  'to everyone' 91–2
  travaux préparatoires 87
  universality 91–2
  'within their jurisdiction' 92–3
obscene speech 456
occupation, situations of 95, 102–4, 154
on-site visits 807, 808–10
opinions *see* advisory opinions
oral hearings
  admissibility 806
  advisory opinions 882
  examination of the case 806
  fair trial, right to 324, 289
  third-party intervention 788–9, 792, 794

Organization of American States (OAS) 576, 1093, 1104
Organisation for Security and Cooperation in Europe (OSCE) 484
organised crime 125, 209–10, 230, 239, 281, 398, 1058
Osho movement 425–6
overseas territories *see* colonies and overseas territories

pacifism 1004
pacta sunt servanda 89, 814, 866
Paderewski, Ignacy Jan 413
paid activity, right to freely choose or to accept a 23
Palestine 158, 723 n.1, 731
Pallieri, Giorgio Balladore 1068
Palm, Elizabeth 664, 682
parallel proceedings 1148–9
pardons 128
parents and children, relationship between 391–3
Paris Peace Conference 1919 328
Paris Peace Conference 1946 631
Parliamentary Assembly (CoE) *see also under* individual main entries
    ad hoc judges, approval of 689
    Committees, competence of 701
    Consultative Assembly, change of name from 660
    Social Charter, transfer of rights from 23
parole 99, 256, 259–60, 281, 347, 539
participation in proceedings 1222–3
partners see equality between spouses; marriage
passports 8, 376, 378, 1058, 1061
paternity
    fair trial, right to a 273, 322
    marry and found a family, right to 529–30
    private and family life, right to respect for 359–60, 376, 390–1
    rights 530
peace, crimes against 329–30, 343–4
peaceful enjoyment of possessions 11–12, 906, 958–84
    abuse of rights, prohibition of 621–2
    adoption of ECHR 4, 8
    adverse possession 969, 974
    arbitrary deprivation of property 958, 960
    Charter of Fundamental Rights of the EU 960
    civil and political rights 986
    collective enforcement 957
    Committee of Experts 12, 955–6, 961–5
    Committee of Ministers 12, 961, 963–7
    compensation 963–4
    Conference of Senior Officials 961
    Consultative Assembly 11, 960–6
    control of use of property 958, 979–81
    declarations 983–4
    deprivation of property/expropriation 958, 960, 964–7, 970–9
    discrimination 981–2
    drafting 11–12, 960–7
    entry into force 12

expropriation, compensation for 621–2, 964–7, 974, 976–8
freedom of assembly and association 491
freedom of expression 468, 480
future income 971
gender equality 959
general principles of international law 45
Grand Chamber 968–70, 974
home, respect for the 399–400, 402
housing 959
hunting rights 973
indigenous people 959
individual applications 731
inquiries by the Secretary General 899
intellectual property 959
interference with possessions 967–8
International Covenant on Civil and Political Rights 959
International Covenant on Economic, Social and Cultural Rights 959
interpretation 955–7, 967–82
inter-State applications 867
judgment debts 971
legitimate expectations 969
licence to conduct business activities, withdrawal of 973
natural or legal persons, definition of 969
no punishment without law 974
non-physical assets 971
peaceful enjoyment of possessions, definition of 972–4
pensions 972
positive obligations 968
possessions, definition of 969–72
poverty 959
Preamble to ECHR 63, 955
Preamble to Protocol No. 1 955–7
proportionality 967, 972
ratifications 12
relationship to ECHR 1037–8
rent control 958, 973–4
reservations 983–4
restitution 970, 984
Roman law 972
rule of law 956
signature and ratification 1039–41
social policy 958
social security payments 971–2
tax liability, forfeiture and seizure for 974
temporal jurisdiction 970
time limits 974
totalitarian regimes 961
travaux préparatoires 956
Universal Declaration of Human Rights 4, 11, 956–60
Pellonpää, Matti 296
pensions
    access 544

pensions (*cont.*)
  discrimination 982
  judges 673
  peaceful enjoyment of possessions 972
  pensionable age 567
  prisoners 214
Perassi, Tomasso 831, 835, 863, 910
Permanent Court of Arbitration 647
Permanent Court of International Justice
  advisory opinions 731, 874
  Central and Eastern Europe, protection of national
    and ethnic minorities in 631
  education, right to 999
  ECtHR, establishment of 631, 635
  exhaustion of domestic remedies 767–8
  individual applications 731
  interpretation 33
  inter-State applications 725
  judicial office, criteria for 647
  language 631, 999
  minorities 731
  no punishment without law 329
  schools, access to 631
  sources of international law, decisions as 39
  Statute 647
Persico, Giovanni 121–2, 221, 920
person, right to recognition as a 592, 1175
persons, jurisdiction over *see ratione personae* (persons)
  jurisdiction
petition, right of *see* individual applications
photographs 377–8, 461
Pictet, Jean 158
pilot-judgment procedure 640, 696–7, 870–1
Pinheiro Farinha, João de Deus 541
Pinto de Albuquerque, Paulo 63, 68, 424, 726, 743,
  839, 998
piracy 344
planning 81
plea bargaining 271, 1140
Plenary Court 678–85 *see also under* individual main
  entries
  adjudicative role 679
  annual sessions 679, 681
  Bureau 683–4
  caseload, reduction of 680
  Chambers 678–9, 682–3
  Committee of Experts 678
  Committee of Ministers 680
  common interest, dispute about existence of 679
  composition 678
  consolidating the institutions and further
    reform 680, 682
  Consultative Assembly 678
  death penalty 1091–2
  dismissal of judges 681
  doubt or disputes as to whether Party has right to
    bring case 679
  drafting 678–80

  execution of judgments 680
  filtering and processing applications 680, 683
  functions 678–80
  gender balance 683
  Grand Chamber 682, 692, 710, 713, 844
  immunity, waiver of 680–1
  inconsistent judgments 679
  interpretation 679, 680–5
  judges
    dismissal 681
    election 680
    formations 688
    judicial function, ceasing to have a 844
  jurisdiction 688, 719–20
  President of the Court 678–84
  Presidents of the Chambers 683
  procedure, determination of 679
  protocols, opinions on adoption of 680
  quorum 679, 681
  Registrar/Deputy-Registrars 680, 681
  Rules of Court 678–9, 681–5, 688
  serious questions affecting interpretation 679
  Steering Committee on Human Rights 680
  Vice-Presidents 678–84
Pocar, Fausto 1134
Poland
  abortion 81–2, 373, 383, 404–5
  death penalty 1101
  declarations 786
  elections 515, 518
  extraordinary rendition 145, 793, 809–10, 827,
    836–7, 899–900
  imprisonment for debt, prohibition of 1050–1
  independent and impartial tribunals 295
  liberty and security, right to 234
  national minorities as political parties, organizations
    of 515, 518
  prisoners 435, 440
  racist organizations 519–20
  reasonable accommodation 440
  rent control 973–4
  sexual orientation 525
police
  candidate for election, right to stand as a 1030
  demonstrations, dispersal of 496–7, 516
  European Code of Police Ethics 522
  freedom of assembly and association 490, 509,
    516, 522
  life, right to 815
  political parties 522
  racist motives for killing 570–1
  report to police, requirements for migrants to 1059
  trade unions 500
  training 820–1
political activities *see also* political activity of aliens,
    restrictions on
  employees 375
  public officials 481

strike, right to 522
political activity of aliens, restrictions on 606–10, 625
  Alternative A and A/2 607
  Alternative B and B/2 607–8
  Charter of Fundamental Rights of the EU 606,
      609–10
  Committee of Experts 606–7
  Committee of Ministers 606, 608
  Conference of Senior Officials 608
  Consultative Assembly 606, 608
  drafting 606–8
  elections, participation in 606, 608, 609–10
  expulsion of activists 608–9
  freedom of assembly and association 607–8
  freedom of expression 607–8
  general principles of international law 607
  International Covenant on Civil and Political
      Rights 609
  interpretation 608–10
  non-discrimination clause 608
  Parliamentary Assembly 609
  political activity, definition of 608
  reservations 609
  slavery and forced labour 607
  trade unions, right to form and join 607
  Universal Declaration of Human Rights 606–7
political democracy
  effectiveness 68–9
  electoral rights 68
  European public order 68
  freedom of assembly and association 68
  freedom of expression 68
political or other opinions
  discrimination 555–61, 580, 583
  freedom of expression 455–6, 458, 461–4, 474,
      476–8
political parties
  abuse of rights, prohibition of 618–19
  anti-democratic views, dissolution of parties
      with 618
  corruption 1022
  democracy 503–4
  discrimination 525
  dissolution 484, 512, 521
  elections, right to free 1022
  extreme political parties 502, 519–21
  foreign parties, funding by 505
  freedom of assembly and association 484, 499,
      503–5, 511–12, 520–1
  freedom of expression 491, 503
  funding 484, 504–5, 1022
  Islam, advocating ban on parties not based on 619
  margin of appreciation 521
  media, access to 1023
  membership 1018
  militant democracy 519–21
  necessary in a democratic society, restrictions which
      are 503, 521

number of members, minimum requirements
    for 503
  pluralism 503–4
  police 522
  pressing social needs 515
  proportionality 520–1
  regional parties 504–5
  registration 515
  religion 520–1
  restrictions/limitations 521
  Venice Commission 484, 505 n.171, 807
political rights *see* civil and political rights; International
      Covenant on Civil and Political Rights
polygamy 438, 538–9
Popović, Dragoljub 439
population transfers 1067–8
pornography 941
Portugal
  civic obligations 218
  Constitution 939, 1008
  death penalty 14, 1114
  declarations 1141, 1156
  education, right to 1008
  lock-outs 525
  Macao 922, 1114
  military service 215
  ne bis in idem 1156
  peaceful enjoyment of possessions 983
  police 356
  reservations 356, 983, 1008, 1139
  slavery and forced labour 218
  television ownership 481
  territorial application 1114
positive discrimination/affirmative action 566–8,
    1175–6, 1187
positive obligations
  abortion 373
  data protection 383
  discrimination 1173–6
  education 1001
  elections, right to free 1026
  environment 388
  equality between spouses 1158
  family life 388
  freedom of assembly and association 492–4, 502,
      516, 519, 521
  inhuman or degrading treatment 191–4, 197
  jura novit curiae 815
  liberty and security, right to 228–9
  life, right to 126–39
  peaceful enjoyment of possessions 968
  private and family life, right to respect for 365,
      366–9, 373, 375
  racial discrimination 578
  ratione loci jurisdiction 95, 103
  ratione personae jurisdiction 105–6
  religion or belief, freedom to manifest 428–9, 438
  sex discrimination 576

positive obligations (*cont.*)
'shall secure . . . negative and positive
obligations' 90–1
slavery and forced labour 206
thought, conscience and religion,
freedom of 421–2
torture 191
trade unions 507
use of lethal force 127
vulnerable applicants 745
witnesses 313
Potocki, André 627
poverty 203, 959
Power-Forde, Ann 187
powers of attorney 745
Preamble to ECHR 53–83
accession 59
aims of Council of Europe 65–6, 73
amendment 955, 1045
collective enforcement 62, 64, 73–4
colonies and territories, application to 62
commencement of legal order 59
Committee of Legal Experts 58
Committee of Ministers 54, 56–9
common heritage 69–70, 71
common understanding and observance of human
rights 69
consolidation of institutions and reform 955, 1045
Consultative Assembly 56, 58, 63
date of signature 59
de minimis principle 782
drafting 55–8
ECommHR, case law of 54
economic, social, and cultural rights 63
ECtHR 54–5, 640
effective remedy, right to an 551
erga omnes obligations 65
founding States of Council of Europe 59
'the governments signatory hereto . . .' 59
historical context 54
importance 54
individual applications 735
interpretation 47–8, 54–5, 59–69
justice and peace 66–8
margin of appreciation 58, 78–83
no punishment without law 335
political democracy, effective 68
ratification 59
ratione materiae jurisdiction 94
recitals 58–83
rule of law 53, 65, 69, 70–3
signature 59
signing ceremony 59
subsidiarity 58, 74–8
text 55–8
travaux préparatoires 64
treaties, ECtHR's references to preambles in
other 54–5

Universal Declaration of Human Rights 56, 59–65,
69
Vienna Convention on the Law of Treaties 36, 54
website of ECtHR, absence from 54
preambles *see* Preamble to ECHR; preambles to
protocols
preambles to protocols
advisory opinions 1213–14
consolidation of institutions and reform 31
death penalty 1091, 1197
discrimination 1173–6
freedom of movement and migration 1045–7
Universal Declaration of Human Rights 11
precedent
binding force and execution of judgments 866
dynamic and evolutive interpretation 47
ECtHR 46–7, 711
interpretation 46–7
stare decisis 711
Preparatory Commission 3–4
presence/absence of accused at trial 81, 316–17, 1137,
1222–3
Presidents/Vice-Presidents
Bureau 683–4
Chamber, of the 683, 691, 746, 748, 827–8, 843,
859
Court, of the 27, 673, 681–4, 688–92, 694–5, 709,
843, 846
election 678–9, 680–2
gender balance 681–2
list of presidents 682
nationality 682
Plenary Court 681–4
salaries 673
Section, of the 673, 690–1, 763, 846
term of office 681–2
third-party intervention 792
prescribed by law, restrictions which are *see also under*
individual main entries
pressing social needs, restrictions due to *see also under*
individual main entries
presumption of innocence 271, 281, 298–307, 319
acquittals 304–6
burden of proof 298–300
civil proceedings after acquittal 305
compensation 304–7, 1142
concluded proceedings, link with 305
confiscation of assets 304
costs 304
disciplinary proceedings arising out of same
charge 305
drug prosecutions 299
fair trial in criminal proceedings, right to 271, 281,
298–307, 319, 325
freedom of expression 460
government officials 299
identity of drivers 299–300
liberty and security, right to 250, 257

media 299, 302–3
miscarriages of justice 306, 319, 1142
negative comments and publicity 302–3
related proceedings 303–5
reservations 325
self-incrimination, protection against 300–2
standard of proof 300
strict/absolute liability 300
tax 299
Universal Declaration of Human Rights 298
pre-trial publicity 287
prisoners *see also* detention/deprivation of liberty; life
      imprisonment
artificial insemination 389, 739–40
cells, confinement to 228
children 398
close family ties 398
conditional release 205, 214
correspondence 401, 404
disciplinary measures 228, 1152
discrimination 259–60
documents, access to 748
education, right to 998–9
European Prison Rules 998
fair trial in criminal proceedings, right to 275
family life 390, 398
hunger strikes 132
ill-health, release on grounds of 186
individual applications 747–8
liberty and security, right to 228, 259–60, 275
literacy and numeracy needs 998
margin of appreciation 539–40
marry and found a family, right to 539–40
obstruction of communications 747
parole 99, 256, 259–60, 281, 347, 539
prisoners of war 155, 235, 576 n.147
private and family life, right to respect for 376, 747
proportionality 1029
religion or belief, freedom to manifest 435, 440
remuneration 213–14
riot or insurrection, quelling 153
shaving heads 376
slavery and forced labour 213–14
state pensions, entitlement to 214
translations 401
vegetarian diet 435, 440
visits, limits on 398
vocational training 998
vote, right to 915, 1023, 1028–9
private and family life, right to respect for 358–409
      see also family life; home, respect for the
abortion 125
abuse of rights, prohibition of 617, 620
accessibility 403
adoption 367
Charter of Fundamental Rights of the EU 359
children 827
clothing 439

Committee of Experts 362–5, 402
Committee of Ministers 363–4, 366
competing interests 368
Conference of Senior Officials 364–5
constitutions 358
Consultative Assembly 360–3, 366
corporal punishment 189
correspondence 400–1
discrimination 407–8, 556, 1178
drafting 359–66, 402
economic well-being of country 404–5
ECtHR, case law of 366–7
education 1001
environment 172
equality between spouses 1157–8
evidence 320
expulsion of aliens, procedural safeguards relating
      to 1126, 1128
foreseeability 403
freedom of assembly and association 364, 491
freedom of expression 368, 452, 460, 468
freedom of movement and migration 402
freedom of information 364
general principles of international law 359–60
identity of victims 827
in accordance with the law 402–4
in camera hearings 827
incest 82
inhuman or degrading treatment 171–3
interim measures 750
International Covenant on Civil and Political
      Rights 402
Internet 463
interpretation 366–408
jura novit curiae 815
language 1000
legitimate purpose 404–6
life, right to 126–7
limitation on use of restrictions 625
margin of appreciation 82, 368
marry and found a family, right to 542
media 461–2
minimum guarantees 361
minorities 360, 363
national laws 403–4
national security 404
nationality 1072
natural rights 359–60
necessary in a democratic society 406
negative obligations 367–9
paternity 359–60, 376, 390–1
positive obligations 365, 366–9
prisoners 747
private law 366
proportionality 367
public authorities 364–8
public order 404
public safety 404–5

private and family life, right to respect for (*cont.*)
  religion 1001
  reservations 408–9
  respect 367–9
  restrictions/limitations 359–60, 363–4, 367, 401–6
  rule of law 367–8, 384, 403
  same sex partnerships 82
  sexual assault 827
  statelessness 109
  telephone tapping 320
  thought, conscience and religion, freedom of 440
  totalitarian regimes 360, 361
  United States Constitution 358
  Universal Declaration of Human Rights 358–64, 367
private life 369–88 *see also* private and family life, right
    to respect for
  abortion 373, 383, 404–6
  assisted pregnancies 373
  autonomy 370, 371, 375–80
  balancing exercise 368, 377, 380, 384–5
  biological parents, right to know identity of 376
  bullying in schools 370
  cellular samples 384
  citizenship 379, 404–5
  confidentiality 383–4, 404–5
  covert filming 377
  criminal law 369–70, 381, 384–7
  data protection 382–4
  death and dying 382, 406
  definition 369
  deterrence 369
  disabilities, persons with 380
  discrimination 375–6
  DNA 384
  drafting 358–9, 365
  dress 376–7, 402, 405–6
  driving licences 378
  education 379–80
  employment and professional activities 374–5, 377,
    386–7
  environment 387–8
  ethnicity 379, 404
  expulsion 396–7
  family life, dividing line with 366–7
  fingerprints 384
  freedom of expression 375, 377–8, 380
  freedom of the press 384–5
  gender discrimination 375–6
  general interest, areas of 377–8
  health and medical care 371–4
  home, respect for the 399
  homosexual activity, criminalization of 381
  honour and reputation, attacks on 358–9, 361–3,
    384–5
  identification of perpetrators 387
  identity 374, 375–6, 378–81
  image 377
  incest 381

  International Covenant on Civil and Political
    Rights 369
  interpretation 366–88
  intimate aspects of private life 368, 380–1
  legal personality 379
  left alone, right to be 358
  legitimate purpose 404
  margin of appreciation 368, 372, 381 406
  media 359, 368, 385
  migrants 366–7
  military, expulsion of homosexuals from the 381
  monitoring outside the home 387
  moral integrity 370
  names 375–6
  national security 404–5
  nationality, right to 378–9
  negative obligations 368
  negative stereotyping 380
  others, interference by 368
  passports 378
  paternity, determination of 376, 391
  personal autonomy 370, 371, 375–80
  personality, development of 369–70
  philosophical convictions 379–80
  photographs 377–8
  physical integrity 370, 371, 377
  positive obligations 365, 368, 373, 375
  procedural aspects 388
  psychological integrity 370
  public interest 368, 377–8
  quality of life 370
  relationships with other people 369–70, 374
  religious convictions 379–80
  restrictions/limitations 365, 402
  sado-masochism 381, 385
  same sex couples 407
  search and seizure 385–7
  sexual life and activity 380–1, 406
  sexual offences notification requirements 384
  sexual orientation 381, 406–7
  social identity 374, 375–6
  social media 359
  stereotyping 380
  surveillance 383, 386–7, 403
  technology 358–9, 377, 387
  Universal Declaration of Human Rights 360, 369,
    378–9, 402
  zone of interaction 370
privileges and immunities of judges 891–3
  ad hoc judges 892
  children 892
  Committee of Experts 891
  Committee of Ministers 892
  Consultative Assembly 891
  corruption 893
  drafting 891–2
  General Agreement on Privileges and Immunities of
    Council of Europe 892–3

independence and impartiality 891–2
International Court of Justice, Statute of 891
interpretation 892
spouses 892–3
waiver 893
procedural adjustments 26–7, 31
procedural/investigative obligation
Chambers on admissibility and merits, decisions
by 707
chilling effect 812–13
cooperate, obligation to 812–13
criminal proceedings 134–6, 369, 370
discrimination 160
domestic violence 192
examination of the case 812–13
inhuman or degrading treatment 191–4, 707, 773
liberty and security, right to 229
life, right to 111–12, 122, 134–9, 160, 848
Chambers on admissibility and merits, decisions
by 707
racial violence 578–9
time limits 773
war/armed conflict 153–4
racial violence 578–9
ratione temporis jurisdiction 110–11
slavery and forced labour 206–7
time limits 773
torture 170–1, 191, 193
use of lethal force 135
war/armed conflict 153–4
professions *see also* legal representatives/profession
private life 386–7
professional secrecy 386
quotas 998
right to freedom of profession 568–9
search and seizure 386
prohibition of abuse of rights *see* abuse of rights,
prohibition of
propaganda 19, 448
property *see also* peaceful enjoyment of possessions
discrimination 555–6, 558–60, 573–4, 582–3
Universal Declaration of Human Rights 582–3
proportional representation 1016–17, 1022, 1025
proportionality
abuse of rights, prohibition of 621
adoptive parents, age of 584
adverse possession 974
candidate for election, right to stand as a 1029
derogations 594, 599, 602
detention/deprivation of liberty 182–3
discrimination 556, 564–5, 573, 600, 1176
education, right to 998–9
elections, right to free 1024
expropriation 976–7
expulsion 396, 1132
freedom of assembly and association 498, 510, 513,
516–17, 523
freedom of expression 451, 465, 475–7

freedom of movement and migration 1058–9,
1060–1, 1063–5
home, respect for the 400
inhuman or degrading treatment 182–3, 194
lex mitior principle 351
liberty and security, right to 238–9, 260
life, right to 122, 127, 156–8
marry and found a family, right to 533, 544
no punishment without law 330
peaceful enjoyment of possessions 967, 972
political parties 520–1, 1022, 1024
private and family life, right to respect for 367
racial discrimination 578
reasonable accommodation 569
religion or belief, freedom to manifest 438–9
sentencing 330, 475–6
slavery and forced labour 206
university admission 1005
use of lethal force 147–8, 150
war/armed conflict 156–8
proselytizing 426–7, 440
prostitution 202, 207, 209
protests *see* demonstrations/protests
protocols 11–25
additional protocols 877, 955, 1037, 1085, 1200,
1227
admissibility criteria 760
advisory opinions 880
amending protocols 26, 877, 1037, 1085, 1200,
1227
Committee of Experts 25
Committee of Ministers 22–5
consent 26
Council of Europe 11
death penalty 11, 1091, 1197
deprivation of freedom 11, 24–5
discrimination 1173
economic, social, and cultural rights 23
ECtHR, establishment of 632–3
environment 11, 23–4
friendly settlements 822
gender equality 11, 24
Grand Chamber, referral to 843, 845–6
individual applications 735
interpretation 49, 721, 880
jurisdiction 94, 721
just satisfaction 839
legal assistance, right to 25
limitation on use of restrictions 625
national minorities 11, 21–3
obligation to respect human rights 88, 92
Parliamentary Assembly 22–5
ratifications 11
ratione personae jurisdiction 93
slavery and forced labour 205, 217
Steering Committee for Human Rights 632
unanimous consent 26
unfinished business 21–5

protocols (*cont.*)
  Universal Declaration of Human Rights 11, 21–2
  victim status 737, 745
  whistle-blowers, protection of 25
Proudhon, Pierre-Joseph 958
provisional measures *see* interim measures
psychological harm, compensation for 838
psychological integrity 370
public authorities *see* public sector/officials
public hearings 288–91
  access must be genuine 289–90
  access to documents 825–9
  civil rights and obligations 288–9
  Committee of Ministers 826
  consolidating the institutions and further
    reform 825–6
  Consultative Assembly 825
  criminal charges 289
  derogations 826
  drafting 825–6
  ECommHR 826
  examination of the case 806
  fair trial, right to 270, 287–98, 825–6
  general principles of international law 825
  in camera hearings 290, 826–7
  interpretation 826–9
  judgments, pronouncement/publication of 288–9,
    290–1, 825
  national security 290–1
  patient information 290
  presence of parties 826
  public character of hearings 826–7
  reservations 291, 323
  Rules of Court 825
  travaux préparatoires 291
  Universal Declaration of Human Rights 825
  waiver 290
public interest
  discrimination 568
  expropriation 965, 967, 974–8
  fair trial in criminal proceedings, right to 309–10
  freedom of expression 454, 458–62, 474
  freedom of movement and migration 1056,
    1062, 1064
  liberty and security, right to 233
  margin of appreciation 975
  marry and found a family, right to 542
  media 368
  necessity tests 975
  private life 368, 377–8
  whistleblowing 465, 475
public law proceedings 274
public opinion 302, 452, 476, 525, 634, 862, 927,
  1020, 1028
public order (*ordre public*)
  ECtHR, establishment of 640
  expulsion of aliens, procedural safeguards relating
    to 1132

freedom of movement and migration 1055–6, 1063
  inter-State applications 725–6
  private and family life, right to respect for 404
  religion or belief, freedom to manifest 435, 437
  victim status 738
public policy 309, 640, 800
public sector/officials *see also* candidate in elections,
    right to stand as a; police; State agents
  data protection 383
  discrimination 1180, 1185–6
  extraterritoriality 101–2
  firearms by State officials, use of 129–31
  freedom of assembly and association 522–3
  freedom of expression 464–5, 476–8
  individual applications by public corporations 737
  lawful restrictions on employees 522–3
  life, right to 133
  medical treatment 133
  presumption of innocence 299
  private and family life, right to respect for 364–8
  ratione loci jurisdiction 101–2
  state monopolies 737
  suicide, prevention of 133
  trade unions 509, 515–16, 522
  whistleblowing 465
public services, equal access to 12–13, 19
publication of judgments 851, 855
  electronic publication 855
  languages, official 851, 855
  official reports of ECtHR 855

qualifications for judgeship 647–8, 651–2, 662, 664–5
quotas 998

Raimondi, Guido 682
racial discrimination *see also* Roma, discrimination against
  abuse of rights, prohibition of 616, 618–19
  affirmative action 566, 1175–6
  anti-Semitism 479, 619
  citizenship 379
  colour 556, 558–61, 577, 580, 583, 600
  Committee for the Elimination of Racial
    Discrimination (UN) 379, 566
  derogations 600
  detention/deprivation of liberty 197
  discrimination 21, 1185
  dissolution of racist organizations 618
  drafting 557–8, 583
  education, right to 987
  effective remedy, right to an 553, 571
  elections, right to free 1031
  ethnic cleansing 344, 914, 1067
  ethnic groups 379, 404, 491, 500, 503, 565–6,
    574–5, 1031
  ethnic origins 577–9
  European Centre on Racism and Intolerance 160
  European Commission against Racism and
    Intolerance 379, 577–8, 1004

fair trial, right to a 321–2
freedom of assembly and association 500, 503, 525
human dignity, right to 66 n.73, 571
indirect discrimination 568
inhuman or degrading treatment 192–3, 197–8
International Convention on the Elimination of All
    Forms of Racial Discrimination 413, 556,
    566–7, 577, 914, 987, 1060, 1175–6
justification, objective and reasonable 578
killing, racist motive for 570–1
life, right to 159–60
militant democracy 519–20
minorities 491
police 570–1
positive discrimination/affirmative action 566,
    1175–6
positive obligations 578–9
proportionality 578
racial discrimination, definition of 577–8
Racial Equality Directive 568
re-hearings 844, 846
religious discrimination 579
scientific category, race as not being a
    legitimate 1185
special measures 566–7
suspect grounds 574–5, 578
violence 570–1, 578–9
rape 175–6, 339, 576
rapporteurs of ECtHR 675, 677
ratification *see* signature and ratification
ratione loci (territorial) jurisdiction 84, 93, 95–105,
    720 *see also* territorial application
admissibility criteria 778
attribution 95
declarations 104
diplomatic protection 105
effective control over an area 95, 102–4
extradition, expulsion, and *refoulement* 95–7
extraterritorial jurisdiction 95–6, 100–5
full control of territory, states without 938
immunity 95, 100, 102–3
International Court of Justice 937
international organizations, State responsibility
    for 97–9
international relations, territory over which State
    exercises responsibility for 100
negative dimensions of rights 103
objections 938–9
obligation to respect human rights 84, 93, 95–104
positive obligations 95, 103
Preamble to ECHR 62
reservations 937–8
state agent authority and control 101–2
State responsibility 95, 99, 101–3
territory not controlled by the State 99
Vienna Convention on the Law of Treaties 937
ratione materiae (subject matter) jurisdiction 84, 93,
    94–5, 720–1

admissibility criteria 778–9
asylum, right to political 94
customary international law 94
death penalty in time of war 1106
enter and reside, right of foreign nationals to 94
exhaustion of domestic remedies 94
family life 389
obligation to respect human rights 84, 93, 94–5
Preamble 94
protocols 94
reservations 93, 94, 934
Security Council (UN) 107
self-determination 94
Universal Declaration of Human Rights 94
Universal Periodic Review 94
ratione personae (persons) jurisdiction 84, 93,
    105–7, 720
admissibility criteria 778
attribution 105, 107
Charter of UN 106–7
individuals 105
international organizations 105–6
obligation to respect human rights 84, 93, 105–7
positive obligations 105–6
protocols 93
Security Council (UN) resolutions 106–7
third States 105
United Nations (UN) 106–7
ratione temporis (temporal) jurisdiction 93, 107–12, 720
accessions 108
accountability 110
admissibility criteria 772, 778
consolidating the institutions and further reform 108
continuing violations 109–10
critical date 107–11
death penalty 110
declarations 108
delay 109
disappearances 109–10
ECommHR 108
ECtHR 108–11
entry into force 108, 949–50
exhaustion of domestic remedies 108–9
expulsion 1071
fair trial, right to a 108–10
final judgments of national courts 109
freedom of movement and migration 1086
humanitarian clause, scope of 111–12
life, right to 111–12, 134, 139
obligation to respect human rights 93, 107–12
peaceful enjoyment of possessions 974
procedural/investigative obligation 110–11
ratifications 108
reciprocity 108
res judicata 109
reservations 935
retroactivity 107–10
reasonable accommodation 439–40, 569

reasonable time, right to trial within a 287, 291–3, 551
reasons
    advisory opinions 887
    arrest 224, 244–6
    decisions and judgments, distinction between 859
    dissenting or separate opinions 857–8, 859
    drafting 857–8
    ECommHR 857
    fair trial, right to a 297–9, 857, 936
    formalism 859
    Grand Chamber 857–8
    International Court of Justice, Statute of 857
    interpretation 858–9
    judgments and decisions 857–9
    juries 297–8
    liberty and security, right to 224, 233, 244–6
    reservations 936
    Rules of Court 859
recidivism 350
reciprocity, principle of 693
recognition before the law, right to 592, 1175
rectification of errors in decisions and
    judgments 849, 852–5
    clerical errors 853
    costs 855
    Court of its own motion, by 854–5
    obvious mistakes 854–5
    request of parties, at 854
    revision, distinction between rectification and 855
    time limits 854–5
Red Cross, International Committee of the 139, 158
referendums 1021
referral to the Grand Chamber 691–2, 841, 843–8
    admissibility 845–6
    authorization of referral 846–7
    case, meaning of 845
    caseload 844
    Committee of Ministers 844
    conscientious objections 848
    drafting 843–4
    enlarged composition 843
    exceptional cases 846
    exclusions from panel 846
    expropriation 848
    final judgments 847
    friendly settlement, approval of 846
    inconsistent judgments, risk of 844–5
    interpretation 843–8
    life, right to 848
    new issues, list of 848
    plenary Court ceasing to have judicial function 844
    President of the Court 843, 846
    Presidents of Sections 846
    Presidents of the Chamber 843
    protocols 843, 845–6
    quality and consistency of case law 844
    re-hearings 844, 846
    relinquishment of jurisdiction 844–5

requests
    5 judge panels 846
    exceptional cases 846
    reasons for refusal 846
    statistics for successful referrals 845
    time limits 846
    res judicata 844
    revision, requests for 847
    Rules of Court 844
    serious issues 847–8
    serious questions affecting interpretation or
        application 691, 709–12, 843–5, 847–8
    striking out 846
    time limits 846
    Vice-Presidents of the Court 843
refugees and asylum seekers
    collective expulsion of aliens 1077–8
    expulsion 395, 1126, 1127
    family life 395
    freedom of movement and migration 1053
    High Commissioner for Refugees (UN) 794, 1079
    International Covenant on Civil and Political
        Rights 1053
    jus cogens 44
    liberty and security, right to 243
    national security 828
    non-refoulement 44, 395
    ratione materiae jurisdiction 94
    Refugee Convention 76, 395, 947, 1053
    subsidiarity 76
    third-party intervention 795
regional assemblies 1020–1
registry of ECtHR 675–7
    access to documents 827
    advisory opinions 882
    archives 676–7
    case-processing divisions 676
    consolidating the institutions and further
        reform 675, 677
    Deputy Registrars 680
    drafting 675–6
    Explanatory Report 677
    filtering and processing applications 675–6
    friendly settlements 819, 821
    General Instructions 676
    interpretation 676–7
    legal secretaries (law clerks) 675
    publication of judgments 851, 855
    Registrar 676–7, 797, 882
    removal 680, 681
    Rules of Court 684
    Section Registries 676
    striking out 797
    third-party intervention 794
regulatory offences 283–4
religion and belief *see also* Islam; Jehovah's Witnesses;
        manifest religion or belief, freedom to;
        thought, conscience and religion, freedom of

apostasy, advocating death penalty for 619
Christianity 577, 579
Church of England
   marriages of convenience 544
   ordination of women in 577
convictions, definition of 1001
corporal punishment 1002, 1003–4
crucifixes in classrooms 1003
derogations 600
   discipline 1003–4
   discrimination 428, 555–63, 579–80, 583, 600,
      1181–2, 1186
   identity cards 428
   inhuman or degrading treatment 196–7
drafting 557–8, 583
education 23, 380, 580, 986, 989–91, 1000–4
freedom of assembly and association 499, 501, 511
Holocaust 579
home schooling 1002
identity cards 428
indoctrination 1003
inhuman or degrading treatment 196–7
margin of appreciation 1003
marriage ceremonies 562–3, 1181–2, 1186
marry and found a family, right to 544
minorities 13, 22, 1002
negative obligations 1001
neutrality and impartiality of States 1001
pacifism 1004
philosophical convictions 379–80
pluralism 100, 1002–3
political parties 520–1
positive obligations 1001
private and family life, right to respect for 379–80,
   1001
private or separate schooling 1002
profession, freedom of 568–9
proselytism 1002
race and ethnicity 579
religious organisations 499, 501, 511
   legal status 501
   marriage ceremonies 562–3, 1181–2, 1186
   registration 501, 511
   victim status 742
religious studies in schools, opting out 580
Second World War 579
secularism 1002
sex education 1003
stigmatization 580
status of religious organizations 563
symbols in classroom 1003
totalitarian regimes 989, 991, 993
trade unions 499, 516
remedies *see* compensation/reparations; effective
      remedy, right to an; exhaustion of domestic
      remedies; interim measures
   damages 68, 276, 839, 1139
   injunctions 275–6, 475

rent control 958, 973–4, 980
reparations *see* compensation/reparations
repetitive cases 696, 700–2
Repik, Bohumil 672
reporting procedures 898
reporting restrictions 460, 480
representation, right to 1131
reproductive health *see* fertility and fertility treatment
reputation
   freedom of expression 458, 465, 469, 471–3, 476
   honour and reputation, attacks on 358–9, 361–3,
      384–5
   private life 358–9, 361–3, 384–5
res judicata see also ne bis in idem
   admissibility 842
   binding force and execution of judgments 866
   final judgments 849
   Grand Chamber, referral to 844
   no punishment without law 355
   ratione temporis jurisdiction 109
reservations 930–9 *see also under* individual main
      entries
   brief statement of law, need for 931, 933, 936–7
   broad reservations within UN system 930–1
   Committee of Experts 931
   Committee of Ministers 931–2
   Conference of Senior Officials 931–2
   Consultative Assembly 932
   de facto reservations 1009
   declarations 932–4, 936–9, 1009
   definition 933
   depositary 931–4, 1007, 1065, 1073
   disguised reservations 937, 1112
   drafting 931–3
   ECommHR 935–6
   formal requirements 930
   freedom of movement and migration 933–4
   general character, prohibition of reservations of
      a 931, 932–3, 935–6
   individual applications 939
   International Law Commission 936, 939
   interpretation 933–9
   interpretative declarations 933, 937, 1111–12
   law then in force 935
   modification 934
   no punishment without law 936
   object and purpose, consistency with 930, 933
   objections 934, 938–9
   Parliamentary Assembly 931
   provisions, restricted to certain 930
   ratione materiae 934
   reasons, requirement to give 936
   signature or ratification, formulation at time
      of 934–5
   slavery and forced labour 218
   substance, of 930, 936
   temporal scope 935
   territorial reservations 937–8

reservations (*cont.*)
    thought, conscience and religion, freedom of 932
    time limits for withdrawal 931
    transitional provisions 931–2
    treaties and conventions, reservations with respect
        to 937
    Universal Periodic Review 931
    validity 934, 936
    Vienna Convention on the Law of Treaties 930,
        933–4, 939
    withdrawal 931, 934–5
residence
    discrimination 1175
    enter and reside, right of foreign nationals to 94
    freedom to choose 12, 1060
respect for human rights *see* obligation to respect
    human rights
Ress, George 36
restitutio in integrum principle 837–8, 868
restraints 185
restrictions *see* limitation on use of restrictions on
    rights; *under* individual main entries
retrospectivity *see* no punishment without law
return to country, right to 1068
revision of judgments 841, 842, 847, 849, 852–4
right to an effective remedy *see* effective remedy,
    right to an
right to education *see* education, right to
right to free elections *see* elections, right to free
right to liberty and security *see* liberty and security,
    right to
right to life *see* life, right to
right to marry and found a family *see* marry and found a
    family, right to
right to petition *see* individual applications
right to respect for private and family life *see* private and
    family life, right to respect for
riot or insurrection, quelling 146, 152–3
Roberts, Emrys 562
Robertson, AH 532, 591, 614, 660, 670, 994
Rogers, Richard 29
Rolin, Henri 62, 446, 591, 635, 682, 908, 921,
    961, 989
Roma, discrimination against
    children to special schools, assignment of 569, 1004
    culture 543–4
    effective remedy, right to an 553, 571
    European Commission against Racism and
        Intolerance 1004
    expulsion 1078
    fair trial, right to a 321–2
    language 1005
    legitimate aim/purpose, restrictions for a 1005
    marry and found a family, right to 543–4
    minorities 582
    racist motives for killing 570–1
    segregation 1004–5
    special protection 578

stereotyping 380
sterilization 183–4, 372
Roman law 972
Romania
    children to leave country, right of 745
    declarations 1009
    detention/deprivation of liberty 181
    expropriation 1182–3
    immunities 681
    liberty and security, right to 258
    military service 215
    privileges and immunities of judges 893
    religious organizations, freedom of association
        of 499, 516
    Roma, sterilization of 183–4
    stray dogs, problem of 370
    truth, right to 138
Roosevelt, Eleanor 5, 576
Roosevelt, Franklin D 69, 412, 444, 483
Rousseau, Charles 55
Rousseau, Jean-Jacques 201
Rules of Court *see under* individual main entries
    breach 685
    development 678
    drafting 684
    Plenary Court 678–9, 681–5
    Practice Directions 684
    publication of judgments 855
    records of hearings 806
    Registry 684
Russia
    access to documents 828–9
    anonymous applications 773
    Chechnya 155–7, 197, 899–900, 1065
    civilians 155–7
    cooperate, obligation to 814
    corporal punishment 189
    death penalty 17, 146, 1092, 1118
    demonstrations 496–8
    derogations 588
    detention/deprivation of liberty 173, 197
    diplomatic assurances 146
    discrimination 1065
    ethnic cleansing in South Ossetia and Abkhazia 914
    expulsion 434, 1130
    extradition 829
    filtering and processing applications 703–4
    freedom of assembly and association 501, 511
    freedom of movement and migration 1057,
        1059, 1065
    Georgia 627, 814, 1078
    Ingushetia 1065
    inhuman or degrading treatment 185
    interim measures 750
    Jehovah's Witnesses 430
    Kabardino-Balkaria 1065
    liberty and security, right to 232, 253, 626
    life, right to 155–7

migration control 627
Moscow theatre siege in 147–8
national security 1062
ne bis in idem 1154
non-retroactivity of treaties 786
political parties 503–5
prisoners' right to vote 1028
religious organizations, freedom of association
  of 501
residence, freedom to choose 1060
serfdom 202
sexual orientation 518, 915
stateless persons 1057
torture 177–8
use of lethal force 147–9
Uzbekistan 1100
war/armed conflict 155–7
witnesses 809
Ryssdal, Rolv 611, 682

Saarland 946–7, 949, 1040
sado-masochism 381, 385
safeguards for existing human rights 902–4
  Committee of Experts 902–3
  Convention on the Elimination of All Forms of
    Discrimination against Women 902
  derogation of rights from other sources, no 902
  drafting 902–3
  freedom of expression 903
  International Covenant on Civil and Political
    Rights 902
  interpretation 903–4
  lex mitior principle 904
  national law as a source 904
  restrictions/limitations on other sources, no 902–3
  savings clause, as 902
  sources of law 902–4
  Torture Convention (UN) 902
  treaties and conventions as source 904
Saint-Just, Louis Antoine de 611
St Lot, Emile 917
St Petersburg Declaration 158
Salén, Torsten 448, 863
samples 384
San Marino 14, 525, 937, 983, 1146
sanctions
  access to documents 828
  binding force and execution of judgments 862
  freedom of assembly and association 517
  freedom of expression 465, 475
  no punishment without law 328–30, 333–5
Scelle, Georges 1068
Schengen zone 1053
Schuman, Robert 59, 734
Scientology 425
Scotland
  corporal punishment 1003–4
  voting age 1026

screening *see* filtering and processing applications
search and seizure 385–7
Second World War *see also* International Military
    Tribunal
  abuse of rights, prohibition of 611, 615, 618–19
  collaboration with the enemy 333, 355
  Holocaust denial 479–80, 615, 619
  Nazi regime 202, 329, 342, 353, 479, 619, 1095
  no punishment without law 329–30, 331, 333,
    352–5
  population transfers 1067
  religious discrimination 579
  totalitarian regimes 611
  treason 333, 355
  war crimes 333, 353–4
  Weimar Germany 611
secret associations 511
secret ballots 1012–20
sectarianism 579
Sections
  assignment of cases 763
  Chambers 691
  Committees 690
  Presidents/Vice-Presidents 673, 690–1, 763, 846
  Registries 676
Secretary General (CoE) *see also* inquiries by the
    Secretary General
  administrative functions 897
  death penalty in time of war, notification of 897
  depositary, as 897, 950
  establishment of position 897
  notifications 897, 950
  role 897
secularism 413, 1002
security *see* national security
Security Council (UN)
  attribution 107
  Chapter VII initiatives 107
  Cyprus, Turkish occupation of 914
  derogations 601–2
  International Court of Justice, requests for opinions
    from 874, 877
  judges, election of 658
  maintenance of international peace and security 107
  peacekeeping 106
  ratione materiae jurisdiction 107
  ratione personae jurisdiction 106–7
  resolutions 106–7
  terrorism 1052
  travel bans 1052
security, right to *see* liberty and security, right to
segregation 1004–5
Selden, John 292
self-defence 118, 128, 130, 146–51, 160–1, 602
self-determination 19, 94
self-harm 132
self-incrimination 287, 300–2, 310, 319
Senghor, Léopold 62, 562, 921

sentencing 293, 573, 1135–6, 1141 *see also* death
    penalty; imprisonment for debt, prohibition
    of; life imprisonment
  custodial sentences, conversion of fines into 347
  freedom of expression 454, 475–6
  indeterminate sentences 259
  just and proportionate punishment 81
  national courts 454
  no punishment without law 339
  political protests 475–6
  proportionality 330, 475–6
  remission 347
  severity 475–6
  slavery and forced labour 218
separation of powers 1029–30
Serbia and Montenegro
  effective remedy, right to an 554
  fair trial, right to a 323–4, 325
  peaceful enjoyment of possessions 906
  public hearings 323
  reservations 323–4, 325, 554
  secession of Montenegro 719, 950–1
servitude *see* slavery and forced labour
sessions
  judicial formations 690
  periods 690
  Plenary Court 679, 681
settlements *see* friendly settlements
sex discrimination/gender equality 555–62, 575–7,
    1177
  abortion 543
  access to courts 322
  advocacy of discrimination 619
  Charter of UN 555, 557, 575–6
  Church of England, ordination of women in 577
  Committee for the Elimination of Discrimination
    against Women (UN) 576
  Committee of Experts, absence of women on 5
  Committee of Ministers 24, 576
  Commission on the Status of Women 5, 528,
    540, 1157
  Consultative Assembly 24, 575
  Convention on the Elimination of All Forms of
    Discrimination against Women 192, 556,
    567, 902, 987
  Council of Europe 575–6
  culture 566
  de facto equality 567
  derogations 600
  domestic violence 129, 160, 192, 198, 385, 576–7
  drafting 11, 21, 557–8, 575–6, 583
  education, right to 987
  emergency services, service in 217
  employment 322
  equal pay 555
  fair trial, right to a 322–3
  gender roles and stereotypes 322–3, 566–7,
    982, 987

General Assembly (UN), participation of
    women in 5
inhuman or degrading treatment 198
Inter-American Convention on the Prevention,
    Punishment, and Eradication of Violence
    against Women 192
Islamic veil 402, 437
judges
  ad hoc 694
  gender balance 660, 662–6, 683, 694
jury service 217, 566
married women 528
names 407
objective justification 567
Parliamentary Assembly 24
participation of women 5, 576 n.147
peaceful enjoyment of possessions 959
pensionable age 567
positive obligations 576
private life 375–6
private sphere 576
rape 576
slavery and forced labour 217
special measures 567
spouses, equality between 1157
suspect grounds 574–5
titles, inheriting 375
travaux préparatoires t, 575, 576 n.147
Universal Declaration of Human Rights 557–8,
    576
universal suffrage 1011
violence 576
sexual assault
  impunity 192
  notification requirements 346, 348, 384
  rape 175–6, 339, 576
  sex offenders register, placement on 346, 348
  witnesses 313
sexual life and activity 380–1, 406
sexual orientation
  Charter of Fundamental Rights of the EU 537, 573
  civil partnerships 407–8
  criminalisation of homosexual activity 381, 408–9
  discrimination 381, 408, 438–9, 525, 556, 573–4,
    584, 1179, 1184–5
  employment 438–9
  family life 390, 407–8
  freedom of assembly and association 525
  freedom of expression 915
  inhuman or degrading treatment 584
  marry and found a family, right to 535
  military, expulsion from the 172–3, 198, 381
  minorities 518
  parental rights 584
  religion or belief, freedom to manifest 438–9
  same sex couples 82, 390, 407–8, 424, 535, 741–2,
    800, 1158–9
  succession to tenancies 800

suspect grounds/categories 574, 584
Shahabuddeen, Mohamed 655
sham trials 337
signature and ratification 9, 944–51 *see also under
    individual main entries*
  accession 944–6
  associate membership 946
  colonies 946–7
  Committee of Experts 944, 947
  Committee of Ministers 945, 947, 1166
  Conference of Senior Officials 945
  Consultative Assembly 944
  Council of Europe, Statute of 946
  date of opening for signature 947
  date of signature 59
  death penalty 950
  depositary 944–51, 1039–41, 1087–8, 1117–19,
      1166–7, 1192, 1208, 1228
  drafting 944–6, 1166
  entry into force 108, 944–5, 949–50
  European Union, accession of 948–9
  expulsion 1073
  filtering and processing application 648, 698
  interpretation 946–51, 1166–7
  legal obligations of signature 947
  list of signatories 947, 1166–7
  methods of expressing intention to be bound 947
  Model Final Clauses 1166
  non-European States, exclusion of 946
  non-member States, accession of 947
  notification by Secretary-General 950
  number of accessions and ratifications 944
  original signatories, list of 947
  Parliamentary Assembly 947
  rule of law 946
  Secretary-General, notification of 897
  signature clause 945–6, 951
  signing ceremony 8–9, 59
  succession 946, 950–1
  technical adjustments 945
  United Kingdom as first State to ratify 947
  Vienna Convention on the Law of Treaties 947, 950
Sikhs 439
silence, right to 319
simplified procedure 703
Simpson, Brian 140, 917
single-judge formation 28–30, 689–90, 694–702,
      707, 763, 779, 805, 851
Sinti 582
slavery and forced labour 201–18
  African slave trade, litigation over 201
  Alternative A and A/2 204
  Alternative B and B/2 204–5
  chattel slavery 202
  civic obligations 216, 217, 218
  Committee of Experts 204
  Committee of Ministers 204–5
  Conference of Senior Officials 204–5

conscientious objection 205, 214–15, 433–4
Consultative Assembly 203–4
Council of Europe 214–15
cooperation with other States 207
court, lawful orders of a 205
crimes against humanity 202
criminal sentences, enforcement of 218
debt bondage 202
derogations 205–6, 592, 1155
detention, work associated with 205, 213–14
discrimination 217
domestic slavery/servitude 202–3, 208–9, 210
drafting 203–5
ECommHR 207
emergency service 216, 217
families 206
forced or compulsory labour, definition of 210–12
forced prostitution 202
gender equality 217
guardian, duty to act as a 217
human trafficking 202–3, 207, 209–10
ILO Forced Labour Convention No 29 1930 202,
    213–16
individual applications 734
International Covenant on Civil and Political
    Rights 592
interpretation 205–17
jury duty 216, 217
lawyers, special obligations imposed on 217
legislative and administrative framework, existence
    of 207
liberty and security, right to 205
military service 205, 214–16
national courts over African slave trade, litigation
    in 202
operational measures 206
Parliamentary Assembly 202–3
positive obligations 206
prisoners 205, 213–14
procedural/investigative obligation 206–7
prohibition of slave trade 201–2
proportionality 206
protective measures 206
protocols 205, 217
punishment 206–7
reservations 218
servitude, definition of 207–9, 213
Slavery Convention 1926 202
slavery, definition of 207
transnational dimension 207
travaux préparatoires 213–15
Universal Declaration of Human Rights 202–5,
    209, 213
Slovakia
  domestic violence 385
  military service 215, 324–5
  rent control 980
  reservations 324–5

Slovakia (*cont.*)
  Roma
    expulsion of 1078
    sterilization 372
  trade unions 500
Slovenia
  citizenship 379, 404–5, 407
  erased persons 404–5, 581, 870
  national security 405
  nationality discrimination 407
  private life 404–5, 407
social identity 374, 375–6
social media 359
social origins, discrimination on grounds of 555–6,
    559–61, 580–1, 583, 600
social security benefits and contributions 23, 274, 544,
    971–2, 981–2, 1179
source of international law 38–44, 352–3, 902–4
South Africa, death penalty in 1093
South Ossetia 914
sovereign immunity 44, 100, 286–7, 478, 554
Soviet Union *see also* Russia
  Constitution 580
  dissolution 505
  Katyn massacre in Soviet Union 139, 171
  social origins, discrimination on grounds of 580
Spaak, Paul-Henri 9
Spain
  access to a court 322
  broadcasting 481
  Canary Island, regional assembly for 1020–1
  Constitution 622, 984
  death penalty 14
  declarations 481, 604, 622
  derogations 604
  expropriation, compensation for 984
  expulsion 349
  Gibraltar 1084, 1162–3
  lèse majesté 478
  military service 215, 324–5
  no punishment without law 348
  private life 375
  public interest 984
  reservations 324–5, 525
  Roma 543–4
  sentencing 339
  sex discrimination 322
  territorial application 1162–3
  trade unions, public officials in 525
Special Court for Sierra Leone 658, 668
Special Tribunal for Lebanon 98, 328, 658, 668
speech, freedom of *see* freedom of expression
Spielmann, Dean 682, 1213
Spiropoulos, Jean 1068
spouses *see also* equality between spouses; marriage
  married names 375–6, 407
  privileges and immunities of judges 892–3
  testimonial privilege 544

standard of proof 123, 169, 300, 625–6
standing 736–45, 795
State agents *see also* police; public sector/officials
  authority and control 101–2
  inhuman or degrading treatment 172, 191–2
  life, right to 133
  torture 191
  use of force 101–2, 117, 122–3, 125, 127, 135,
    146–53
State immunity 44, 100, 286–7, 478, 554
State monopolies 737
State responsibility
  binding force and execution of judgments 868–9
  evidence 810
  expulsion 95–7
  Draft Articles on State Responsibility 101,
    837, 868
  ratione loci jurisdiction 95, 99, 101–3
  state agent authority and control 101–2
  Vienna Convention on the Law of Treaties 42
State security *see* national security
State sovereignty 274, 835
statelessness 109, 379, 581, 1057, 1071
Statute of the International Court of Justice 38, 40,
    41, 42, 44, 352, 632, 635, 637, 641, 648, 651,
    658, 672, 693, 716, 719, 720, 724, 849, 852,
    857, 877, 878, 891, 911
stereotyping 192, 380, 576, 987
sterilization 183–4, 372, 543
stigmatization 580
stop and search 226–7
Street, Jessie 5
strict/absolute liability 300
strike, right to 508, 522
striking out applications 796–802
  admissibility 706, 800
  advisory opinions 1225
  caseload 796–7, 799–801
  Chamber 797
  Committee of Minsters 797–8, 802
  Committees, competence of 702
  corporal punishment 800
  costs 802
  de minimis rule 800
  death of applicants 798
  decision, by means of a 797, 821–2
  discontinuance 797–8
  drafting 796–7
  failure to pursue and application 798–802
  friendly settlements 797–8, 801, 819–23
  Grand Chamber 799, 846
  interpretation 797–8
  inter-State applications 797
  judgment, by means of a 797–8, 821–2
  matter resolved, where matter is 798
  merits, decisions on the 706
  moral dimension 800
  no longer justified, where action 799–800

notification of Registrar of intention not to
    proceed 797
offers of settlement 799
public policy 800
respect for human rights requires striking out,
    where 800–1
restoration to the list 801
same sex partners, succession to tenancies of 800
single judges, competence of 697
unilateral declarations 799–800
victim, loss of status of 797, 798
subject matter jurisdiction *see ratione materiae* (subject
    matter) jurisdiction
subsidiarity
    advisory opinions 1213
    binding force and execution of judgments 870
    collective enforcement 73–4
    consolidation of institutions and reform 75
    criminal law 78
    de minimis principle 784–5
    democratic ideals 78
    derogations 77
    domestic courts, deference to 77–8
    effective remedy, right to an 76
    enforcement 76–7
    exhaustion of local remedies 75–6, 765, 807
    Explanatory Report 74
    first-instance court, court as not being a 77–8
    fourth-instance court, court as not being a 77
    friendly settlements 816
    immigration cases 76
    incorporation into national law 76
    Parliamentary Assembly 75
    Preamble to ECHR 58, 74–8
    Refugee Convention 76
    United Kingdom 75, 77
substantive rights, definition of 8
succession to treaties 720, 946, 950–1
Süd Tirol/Alto Adige, dispute between Austria and Italy
    over 913
suicide
    assisted suicide 133, 172, 382
    life, right to 132–3
    protest, as 132
summary executions against non-combatants 354
Sundt, Arthur 863
superior orders, defence of 341–2
Surinam 324, 946, 1036
surveillance
    covert filming 377
    employees, use of email, Internet and telephone use
        by 387
    GPS 383, 387
    home, outside the 387
    private life 386–7, 403
    satellite navigation devices attached to cars 383
    telephone tapping 320, 386–7, 403
    video surveillance 377

suspension of States 906
Sweden
    death penalty 17, 1092
    declarations 1133
    education, right to 1007–8
    expulsion 1133
    no punishment without law 330
    reservations 1007–8
    signatories 9
    trade unions 524
Switzerland
    age of criminal responsibility 318
    assisted suicide 133
    children, detention of 261
    Constitution 1132
    crime and family, extension to 1164–5
    expulsion 1132
    fair trial, right to a 324–5
    freedom of assembly and association 513
    freedom of expression 467, 472–3, 479–80
    genocide, denial of 479–80
    legal aid 324
    marriage, dissolution of 542
    military service 215
    minarets 742
    names 544
    national security 1132
    oral hearings 324
    patronymic names 1159
    reasons 936
    reservations 324–5, 936, 1165

tax
    discrimination 982
    fair trial, right to a 274
    forfeiture 974
    military service, exemption from 569
    ne bis in idem 1154
    peaceful enjoyment of possessions 979, 980–1
    presumption of innocence 299
    religion 429
Teitgen, Pierre-Henri 4, 8, 12, 55, 61, 84, 119,
    165–6, 203, 221, 270, 331, 360–2, 415–16,
    423, 445–6, 484–5, 530, 547, 557–9, 589,
    612–13, 635, 717, 754–5, 832–3, 835, 863,
    908, 960, 962, 966, 988, 990, 1013, 1016,
    1035
telephone tapping 320, 386–7, 403
temporal jurisdiction *see ratione temporis* (temporal)
    jurisdiction
tenancies 400, 407, 800, 979
terms of office of judges 668–74
    ad hoc institutions 668
    age
        career prospects after office, maintenance of 673
        limits 670–1, 672
        maximum 670–1, 672
        precedence 673–4

terms of office of judges (*cont.*)
  career prospects after office, maintenance of 673
  casual vacancies 671
  Committee of Legal Experts 669–70
  Committee of Ministers 672–3
  Conference of Senior Officials 669
  Consultative Assembly 672
  drafting 669–71
  ECommHR 669
  filtering and processing applications 670–1
  former court 670
  freedom of assembly and association 673
  freedom of expression 673
  independence and impartiality 668, 671, 673
  International Court of Justice 668
  International Criminal Court 668
  International Criminal Tribunal for Rwanda 668
  International Criminal Tribunal for the former
    Yugoslavia 668
  interpretation 671–2
  new court 670
  new Member States 670
  Parliamentary Assembly 671, 673
  pensions 673
  precedence 673–4
  President of the Court 673
  Presidents of the Sections 673
  re-election 669–72
  resignation, notification of 671
  retirement 672
  rotation 670
  safety and security 673
  salaries 673
  status 672–3
  transitional provisions 670
  Vice-Presidents of the Court 673
  withdrawal of State from Council of Europe 672
  working conditions 672–3
territorial application 916–28
  advisory opinions 924, 1216
  Committee of Experts 918–19, 1033–4, 1082
  Committee of Ministers 918–21, 1033, 1035, 1161
  Conference of Senior Officials 919
  consent 919–20
  Consultative Assembly 917, 918–21, 1035, 1082
  customary international law 924
  declarations 921–8, 943, 1162–3, 1082–4, 1190
  denunciations 942–3
  discrimination 921, 1177, 1189–90
  Draft Colonial Application Clause 919
  drafting 918–22, 1033–4, 1161, 1082–3
  due regard for local requirements, meaning
    of 926–7
  effective control principle 95, 102–4, 923–4
  European Commission for Human Rights 926
  freedom of movement and migration 922, 1081–4
  Genocide Convention 924
  high seas, interception of people on 1083

  independence, colonies' acquisition of 924
  individual applications 922, 927–8
  international relations, responsibility for 100,
    924–5
  interpretation 922–8, 1036, 1161–2, 1083–4
  local requirements 918–19, 922, 926–7, 1033
  metropolitan and dependent territories,
    distinguishing between 924–5
  Model Final Clauses 1161–2, 1189–90
  negative colonial clause 922
  non-self-governing territories 916–17
  overseas territories, use of term 921–4
  protocols 922–3
  Secretary-General, notification of 897
  signatories and ratification 1036, 1084, 1190
  territories for whose international relations it is
    responsible, meaning of 924–5
  Universal Declaration of Human Rights 916–17,
    920–1
  universal jurisdiction 916–17, 926
  Vienna Convention on the Law of Treaties 922,
    924–5, 1033, 1161, 1082
territorial jurisdiction *see ratione loci* (territorial)
    jurisdiction; territorial application
terrorism
  abuse of rights, prohibition of 616, 617
  arrest, detention, and transport by foreign
    agencies 900 n.10
  confidentiality 239
  death penalty 1095–6
  derogations 588, 595, 597
  detention/deprivation of liberty 836–7
  expulsion 168
  extradition 750, 837
  freedom of movement and migration 1052
  Independent Expert on Protection of Human Rights
    while Countering Terrorism (UN) 1100–1
  just satisfaction 836–7
  liberty and security, right to 239, 588
  no punishment without law 344
  religion or belief, freedom to manifest 436
  Security Council travel bans 1052
  September 11, 2001 terrorist attacks 595, 597, 617
  use of lethal force 148
third-party intervention 788–95
  admissibility 788
  advisory opinions 1222
  amicus curiae briefs 788, 793
  Chambers 792
  closed shop case 788–9
  Commissioner for Human Rights (CoE) 794–5
  death penalty 794
  diplomatic protection 792
  drafting 789–91
  ECommHR 788
  filtering and processing applications 793–4
  governmental organizations 793
  High Commissioner for Human Rights (UN) 794

High Commissioner for Refugees (UN) 794
individuals 793
intergovernmental organizations 793
inter-State applications 788
leave, with 792–4
nationality 788–9, 792
non-governmental organizations 793–5
oral hearings 788–9, 792
President of the Court 792
return to State of nationality, risks of violation of
    rights on 792
right to intervene 792
Rules of Court 788–9, 792–3
time limits 792–3
Venice Commission 793
written submissions 788
thought, conscience and religion, freedom of 412–41
    see also manifest religion or belief, freedom to
absolute nature of freedom 420, 426
abuse of rights, prohibition of 617, 620
administration and justice, smooth working of 418
advantages, offering social and material 426–7
atheism and agnosticism 423–4
balancing exercise 422
benefits, claims for recognition as religion to
    claim 425
change religion or belief, freedom to 413, 420,
    426–7
Charter of Fundamental Rights of the EU 414
Committee of Experts 416–18
Conference of Senior Officials 419
conscientious objection 414, 422, 424, 433–4, 848
Consultative Assembly 415–16
corporal punishment 189
Council of Europe
    aims and principles 416
    cultural homogeneity of 413
    discrimination 440
cultural homogeneity 413
dangerous religious practices or activities,
    government warnings on 422
Declaration on the Elimination of All Forms of
    Intolerance and of Discrimination Based on
    Religion or Belief (UN) 413–14
declarations 441
derogations 416–18, 420, 593
discrimination 440–1, 568–9, 579–80
drafting 414–19
education 419, 1001
freedom of assembly and association 440, 483, 491,
    499, 502, 512
freedom of conscience, definition of 423–4
freedom of expression 412, 423, 440, 452, 457,
    468, 472–3
freedom of religion and belief, definition of 425–6
freedom of thought, definition of 423
general principles of international law 415
identity 420

institutions, foundations and confessions, national
    rules on 416–18
International Convention on the Elimination of All
    Forms of Racial Discrimination 413
International Covenant on Civil and Political
    Rights 412, 423, 592
International Covenant on Economic, Social, and
    Cultural Rights 412
International Criminal Court, Rome Statute of 424
interpretation 419–41
Islam 413
legal rights of others, protection of 415
legitimacy of beliefs 425
legitimate purpose 420
limitation on use of restrictions 625
margin of appreciation 424, 426
marry and found a family, right to 541
military service 215
minorities 413
moral or ethical dimension 424
morality, public order and general welfare 415
natural persons 421
necessary in a democratic society 420
pluralism 421
positive obligation or interference 421–2
prescribed by law 420
private and family life, right to respect for 440
proselytization 426–7
reasonable accommodation 569
reservations 441, 932
restrictions/limitations 414–18, 420–1
rule of law 436
same sex partnerships 424
sects and schisms 425
secularism 413
State, interference by the 421–2
territorial integrity 418
thought and conscience 420
Universal Declaration of Human Rights 412–16
Utrecht, Treaty of (1713) 413
time limits
    admissibility criteria 757–8, 763, 770–3
    appeals in criminal matters, right to 1137
    crimes against humanity 354
    date of knowledge 772
    date of running of time 772
    denunciations 942
    examination of the case 806
    Grand Chamber, referral to 846, 851
    homicide 128
    inquiries by the Secretary General 900
    no punishment without law 342–3, 356
    prejudice 772
    ratione temporis 770
    rectification of judgments 854–5
    reservations, withdrawal of 931
    revision of judgments 852
    rule of law 72

time limits (*cont.*)
  third-party intervention 792–4
  time of the essence 770–1
  waiver 770
  War Crimes, Convention on Non-Applicability of
    Statutory Limitations to 39
  weekends and holidays 772
  written submissions 806
Tokyo Military Tribunal (TMT) 353
torture, prohibition of 164–98
  absolute right, as 164, 168–9
  abuse of rights, prohibition of 619
  Charter of Fundamental Rights of the EU 165
  Committee for the Prevention of Torture
    (CPT) 165, 379, 820
  Committee of Experts 167
  Committee of Ministers 167–8, 173
  common heritage 70
  Consultative Assembly 165–7
  Council of Europe 165, 174
  customary international law 164
  death penalty 16
  definition 174–7
  deliberate and purposive dimension 174, 176–8
  derogations 168–9, 592–3, 1155
  detention/deprivation of liberty 175–8
  discrimination 177
  drafting 165–8
  European Torture Convention 174, 912
  evidence 321, 810
  expulsion 395
  extradition, deportation or expulsion 95–6, 179,
    1128
  General Assembly (UN) Declaration 175, 177
  information or confessions, purpose of
    obtaining 174, 178
  inhuman or degrading treatment distinguished 169,
    174–9
  International Court of Justice 164, 179
  International Covenant on Civil and Political
    Rights 164, 592
  interpretation 165, 168–98
  jus cogens 44, 164, 179–80
  life, right to 118, 164, 169
  living instrument principle 176
  medical or scientific experimentation, consent
    to 164, 166–7
  'no one' formulation 169
  no punishment without law 342
  positive obligations 191
  procedural/investigative obligation 170–1, 191, 193
  rape in detention 175–6
  safeguards for existing human rights 902
  severity threshold 171–2, 175–9
  Special Rapporteur on Torture (UN) 177
  standard of proof 169
  State agents 191
  threshold of application 171–2, 175–9

Torture Convention (UN) 39, 164, 169, 176–7,
    321, 902, 1128
  travaux préparatoires 167–8
  Universal Declaration of Human Rights 164–8
  victims 169–71
  Vienna Convention on the Law of Treaties 39
  visits to places of detention 165
totalitarianism
  abuse of rights, prohibition of 611–12, 616–19
  education, right to 989, 991, 993
  family life 360–1, 393
  freedom of expression 445
  militant democracy 519–20
  private and family life, right to respect for 360, 361
  Second World War 611
trade unions
  closed shop 64, 493–4, 506–8, 788–9
  collective agreements 493, 524
  collective bargaining 494, 506–7, 524
  compulsion to join 502
  democracy, threats to 515
  de-recognition 494
  discrimination 508, 524–5
  economic, social and cultural rights 23
  European Social Charter 506, 515–16
  expulsion 502
  extreme political parties, exclusion of members of 502
  financial contributions, compulsory 508
  freedom of assembly and association 483–9, 493–4,
    499–502, 505–9, 514–16, 522–5
  freedom of expression 464–5, 469, 471, 473
  International Covenant on Economic, Social and
    Cultural Rights 508
  International Labour Organization 508, 515
  join, right to 505, 508, 607
  necessary in a democratic society, restrictions
    which are 514
  negative aspects 507–8
  not to join, right 487
  police 487
  political activity of aliens, restrictions on 607
  political neutrality 522
  pressing social needs, restrictions for 514
  private sector 509, 515
  public sector 509, 515–16, 522
  registration 516, 525
  religious organisations 499, 516
  right to form unions 505, 516, 607
  strike, right to 508, 522
  travaux préparatoires 507
  Universal Declaration of Human Rights 507
  work, right to 499
trafficking 63, 202–3, 207, 209–10, 229, 344
Transdniestria 99, 809–10, 937, 999–1000
transgender persons 173, 380–1, 535–7, 544, 583
travaux préparatoires see also under individual main entries
  interpretation 34
  women, participation of 5, 575, 576 n.147

travel bans 1052, 1063–4
Travellers 582
treason 333, 355
Trechsel, Stefan 142
truth, right to 138–9
Tsotsoria, Nona 627
Tulkens, Françoise 66, 439, 682
turbans, wearing 439
Turkey *see also* Cyprus, Turkish occupation of
    Northern
  abuse of rights, prohibition of 613–14, 618, 620
  Bologna Process 1005
  Copenhagen Process 1005
  death penalty 143–4, 1095–6
  democracy 515
  denigrating Turkishness, offence of 470–1
  derogations 588, 598, 600, 603–4
  detention/deprivation of liberty 600, 775
  disappearances 229, 871
  domestic violence 160, 198, 577
  education, right to 998, 1003, 1008
  exhaustion of domestic remedies 769
  expropriation, compensation for 977
  extremism 447–8, 620
  freedom of assembly and association 501–2, 507,
      512, 515
  freedom of expression 447–8, 464, 470–2
  headscarves/veil 437, 848
  independence and impartiality 695
  Internet 466
  Islam 437, 1003
  Kurds 157, 401, 453, 464, 471–2, 598,
      739, 998
  language 401, 998
  liberty and security, right to 246, 259
  life, right to 118, 157, 160
  margin of appreciation 600
  on-site visits 809
  peaceful enjoyment of possessions 867, 973
  police training 820–1
  political parties
    dissolution of 512, 618
    funding 1022
  population transfers 1067
  prisoners' right to vote 1028
  proportionality 618
  ratifications 12
  reservations 604, 939, 1008, 1078
  revision of judgments 854
  Roma, stereotyping of 380
  terrorism 436, 600
  torture 175–6, 179, 600, 820–1
  trade unions 507, 515
  Universal Periodic Review 915
  universities 437, 998, 1005
  use of force by State agents 101–2
  vote, right to 1027
  war/armed conflict 157

Turks and Caicos Islands, corruption in local
    government in 1031–2
Tymoshenko, Yulia 456, 626–7

Ukraine
  death penalty 1092, 1100
  detention/deprivation of liberty 239
  election of judges 661
  freedom of expression 455–6, 470
  liberty and security, right to 626–7
  pensions 982
  Refugee Convention 947
  reservations 325
  Roma 160
  witnesses 325
Ungoed-Thomas, Lynn 636
United Kingdom *see also* Northern Ireland
  adverse possession 974
  age of criminal responsibility 318
  Chagos Islands 104
  child custody 826–7
  citizenship 1082
  colonies
    corporal punishment 188–9, 1007
    Cyprus 9, 188, 596, 725, 917–18, 924
    derogations 596
    territorial application 916–28, 1036
  corporal punishment 70, 188–9, 927–8, 1007
  Cyprus
    colonies and overseas territories 9, 188, 596,
        725, 917–18, 924
    death penalty 140
    derogations 596
    emergency powers 188, 596
    independence 9, 725
    Sovereign Base Areas 924, 928
  death penalty 120, 140–6, 190–1, 750, 1093,
      1095, 1114, 1205–6
  declarations 596, 800
  derogations 587–8, 596–7, 600–1
  ECommHR 809
  education, right to 1006, 1007
  emergency powers 188, 596
  estoppel 815
  expulsion 169–70, 405, 1082
  Falkland Islands 928, 1206
  freedom of movement and migration 1082, 1083
  Gibraltar 928, 1007, 1036, 1084, 1162–3, 1206
  Greece 725
  Guernsey 597, 925, 928, 1007, 1036, 1114, 1206
  Hong Kong 922
  in camera hearings 827
  individual applications 928
  interim measures 750
  International Court of Justice 908
  Iraq
    death row phenomenon 190–1
    transfer of detainees to 750

United Kingdom (*cont.*)
Isle of Man, corporal punishment in 70, 188–9, 926–7, 1007
Jersey 597, 925, 928, 1036, 1114, 1206
judicial office, criteria for 652, 654
liberty and security, right to 222–3, 225, 240, 253–4, 259–60, 621
life imprisonment 187
life, right to 120–1
London terrorist attacks, July, 2005 595
marriage
  de facto 538
  marriages of convenience 540
Military Manual 602
national security 597, 600
nationality for citizens joining terrorist organizations, withdrawal of 1072
no punishment without law 330
peaceful enjoyment of possessions 983
pensionable age 567
prisoners' right to vote 915, 1028
racial discrimination 575
ratification 9, 947
refugees and asylum seekers 800
religious discrimination 467
reservations
  education, right to 1006, 1007
  peaceful enjoyment of possessions 983
rule of law 71–2
Scotland 1003–4, 1026
sex discrimination 575
slavery and forced labour 201, 204
subsidiarity 75, 77
territorial application 916–28, 942, 1036, 1162–3
  death penalty 1114, 1205–6
  freedom of movement and migration 1082, 1083
terrorism 597, 1072
torture 167, 177
trade unions 506–7
vote, right to 1026, 1028
United Nations *see also* General Assembly (UN)
activities of UN and subordinate bodies, distinction between 106–7
Commission on the Status of Women 5
developing countries 4
political blocs 4
ratione personae jurisdiction 106–7
Sub-Commission on Freedom of Information (UN) 466
women, participation of 5
United States
Belgium, extradition of terrorist suspects from 750, 837
Constitution 220, 254, 358, 385–6, 483, 1147
death penalty
  death row phenomenon in 142–3
  life, right to 142–3, 146
diplomatic assurances 146

expulsion 169–70
extraordinary rendition 96, 145, 793, 809–10, 827, 836–7, 899–901
freedom of assembly and association 483
freedom of expression 444–5
habeas corpus 220, 254
homosexual activity, criminalization of 381
ne bis in idem 1147
private and family life, right to respect for 358
search and seizure 385–6
September 11, 2001 terrorist attacks 595, 597, 617
slavery and forced labour 202
Supreme Court 381, 423
Universal Declaration of Human Rights *see also under* individual main entries
abuse of rights, prohibition of 611, 613
adoption 1–2
adoption of ECHR 4, 7, 61, 84, 167
collective enforcement 73
Commission on Human Rights 2, 5, 576
common heritage 69–70
common understanding and observance of human rights 69
constitutions contained retroactivity conditions 330
Council of Europe 3–4
court, proposal for a 6
Documented Outline 330
drafting 55
experts 5
human trafficking 63, 209
implementation 62–3
importance 64–5
International Bill of Rights, as part of 1–2, 6, 61
International Covenant on Civil and Political Rights 59, 61
interpretation 47–8
justice and peace 66
non-binding, as 62, 64–5
regional instruments, preamble of 59–60
rule of law 71
universal, definition of 1
Universal Periodic Review 65
women, participation of 5, 576
universal jurisdiction 91–2, 102
Universal Periodic Review
exclusion of other means of dispute resolution 915
freedom of expression 915
inter-State applications 915
prisoners' right to vote in UK 915
ratione materiae jurisdiction 94
reservations 931
universal suffrage 1011–15, 1019, 1021, 1026
universities 997–8, 1005
urgent cases 690
use of force 146–53
arbitrariness 147, 151
arrest, effecting a lawful 146, 150–2
civilians in conflict zones 146–7

defence from unlawful violence 146–7, 148–50
ECommHR 149, 152–3
ECtHR 152–3
escape, preventing an 146, 150–2
exceptions 146–7
firearms 125, 129–31, 148–51
injuries to law enforcement officials 153
interpretation 117, 122–3, 149
law enforcement operations 147
lethal force 117, 122–3, 125, 127, 135, 146–57
life, right to 117, 122–3, 125, 127, 135, 146–57
means of force 148
mines, location and deactivation of 148
mistake 147
necessity 123, 147, 149–51
permitted force 122–3, 146–53
positive obligations 127
procedural/investigative obligation 135
proportionality 147–8, 150
riot or insurrection, quelling 146, 152–3
self-defence 146–7, 148–51
State agents 101–2, 117, 122–3, 125, 127, 135,
     146–53
war/armed conflict 146–7, 155–7
warning shots 129–30
Uzbekistan 1100

vaccinations 371
vagrants, detention of 220, 222–3, 243
vegetarian diet 435, 440
Vehabović, Faris 348
Venice Commission *see* European Commission for
     Democracy through Law (Venice Commission)
Verdross, Aldred 45
Versailles, Treaty of 328–9
Vice-Presidents *see* Presidents/Vice-Presidents
victims
   acquittals 744
   actio popularis 738
   advocacy organizations or associations 741–2
   appropriate and sufficient redress 744
   corporate bodies 741, 742
   dead persons 738–9, 742
   direct victims 742
   disappearances 739–40
   elections, right to free 1018
   expulsion 740–1, 743, 744–5
   extradition 745
   families 170–1
   freedom of assembly and association 500, 742
   groups of individuals 737
   hierarchy of victims 742
   in camera hearings 827
   indirect victims 742
   individual applications 737–45
   inhuman or degrading treatment 169–71
   International Court of Justice 741
   just satisfaction 738

locus standi 737–45
loss of status 797, 798
next-of-kin applications 738–40
non-governmental organizations 737, 741
potential victims 743–4
public order 738
stage of proceedings, rejection of applications at
     any 785–6
torture 169–71
Universal Declaration of Human Rights 740
Victor Emmanuel of Savoy, Prince of Naples 1073
Vienna Convention on the Law of Treaties 34–46
binding force and execution of judgments 866
Charter of Fundamental Rights of the EU 39
Committee of Ministers, recommendations and
     resolutions of 41, 45
Convention on the Rights of the Child 38
customary international law 38, 40–4, 46
death penalty 37
declarations 37
dynamic or evolutive interpretation 37
ECommHR 37
ECtHR 35–42, 642
European Social Charter 38
Explanatory Reports 45
external context 36
Framework Convention for the Protection of
     National Minorities 38
general means 34, 36
general principles of international law 35, 38,
     41–2, 45
Geneva Conventions 38
Genocide Convention 39
good faith 36
ILC draft articles on immunities 41
internal context 36
International Court of Justice, Statute of 40–4
International Covenant on Civil and Political
     Rights 39
international humanitarian law instruments 39
jurisdiction 719
jus cogens 44, 180, 593
languages 35, 45–6
liberty and security, right to 36–7
life, right to 154
literal, historical interpretation 45
no punishment without law 786
pacta sunt servanda 814
Preamble to ECHR 36, 54
reservations 42, 930, 933–4, 939
rule of law 36
sources of international law 35, 38–44
state responsibility 42
subsequent practice 36–7
supplementary means 35, 45
Torture Convention (UN) 39
travaux préparatoires 45
Universal Declaration of Human Rights 36, 45

Vienna Convention on the Law of Treaties (*cont.*)
   war/armed conflict 39, 154
   War Crimes, Convention on Non-Applicability of
      Statutory Limitations to 39
Vilhjálmsson, Thór 682
Villiger, Mark 646
vocational guidance or training 23
Voltaire (Arouet, François-Marie) 444
vote, right to 1026–9
   age 1026
   American Convention on Human Rights 1026
   eligibility 1026
   Grand Chamber 1027
   non-residents 1027–8
   Parliamentary Assembly 1027
   prisoners/convicted persons 915, 1023, 1028–9
   residence requirements 1027–8
Vučinić, Nebojša 424
vulnerable persons
   fair trial in criminal proceedings, right to 311, 313
   individual applications 747–8
   liberty and security, right to 229
   negative obligations 748
   positive obligations 748
   witnesses 313

Wagner, Richard 136
waiver
   appeals in criminal trials, right to 1140
   fair trial, right to 271, 309, 317
   interpreters 314
   public hearings 290
   time limits 770
Waldock, Humphrey 682
war/armed conflict *see also* armed conflict and right to
      life; Second World War; war crimes
   aggression 602
   armed conflict, definition of 594–5
   Charter of UN 602
   civilians in conflict zones 146–7
   customary international law 602
   deaths 589, 592, 602
   derogations 594–5, 601–2
   Geneva Conventions 37–8, 158, 345, 601–2, 641,
      1104, 1106
   Hague Convention 1907 602
   Hague Regulations 102
   home, respect for the 400
   internal displacement 400
   International Covenant on Civil and Political
      Rights 592, 601
   International Criminal Court, Rome Statute of 602
   international humanitarian law 37–8, 158, 345,
      588, 601–2, 641, 1104, 1106
   jus ad bellum 156, 601
   jus in bello 156, 602
   lawful acts of war 601–2
   liberty and security, right to 36–7, 235
   life, right to 153–8

mass expulsions 400
Military Manual of 1958 (UK) 602
prisoners of war 155, 235, 576 n.147
propaganda 19
summary executions against non-combatants 354
use of lethal force 146–7
war crimes
   abuse of rights, prohibition of 619
   amnesties 1150
   death penalty 1094–5
   international law 333 n.27
   life, right to 155
   national courts, chambers of 99
   no punishment without law 343–5, 355
   Second World War, tribunals after the 333 n.27
   superior orders defence 341–2
   time limits 343
   War Crimes, Convention on Non-Applicability of
      Statutory Limitations to 39
Weber, Helene 576 n.147
Weimar Germany 611
Wells, HG 528
whipping 188
whistleblowing 25, 465, 469, 475
Wiarda, Gérard 682
Wildhaber, Luzius 646, 682
Wilson, Woodrow 555
witnesses
   anonymity 313
   Chambers 806
   discrimination 544
   equality 269–70
   examination of the case 806–10
   expert witnesses 806–7, 809
   failure to appear 808
   fair trial, right to 269–70, 312–13
   non-attendance 312–13
   oaths or solemn declarations 810
   reservations 325
   Rules of Court 808
   sexual assault 313
   spouses, compellability of 538, 544
   summons 808
   vulnerable witnesses 313
Wojtyczek, Krzysztof 65–6, 68–70, 903
work, right to 499
World War One *see* First World War
World War Two *see* Second World War
written submissions 794, 806
wrongful convictions *see* compensation for wrongful
      conviction

Yugoslavia *see* International Criminal Tribunal for the
      former Yugoslavia (ICTY)

Zekia, Mehmed 620
Ziemele, Ineta 36, 773
Zimbabwe, death penalty in 1093
Zupančič, Boštjan 835